McDougal Littell

CLASSZONE

Visit classzone.com and get connected.

ClassZone resources provide instruction, practice and learning support for students and parents.

Help with the Math

- @Home Tutor enables students to focus on the math and be more prepared for class, using animated examples and instruction.
- Extra examples similar to those in the book provide additional support.
- Hints and Homework Help offers assistance solving select homework exercises.

Practice, Practice, Practice

- eWorkbook includes interactive worksheets with additional practice problems.
- Problem of the Week features a new problem to solve every week.

Games and Activities

- Crossword puzzles, memory games, and other activities help students connect to essential math concepts.
- Math Vocabulary Flipcards are a fun way to learn math terminology.

Math

- Engaging activities with animated problem-solving graphics support each lesson.

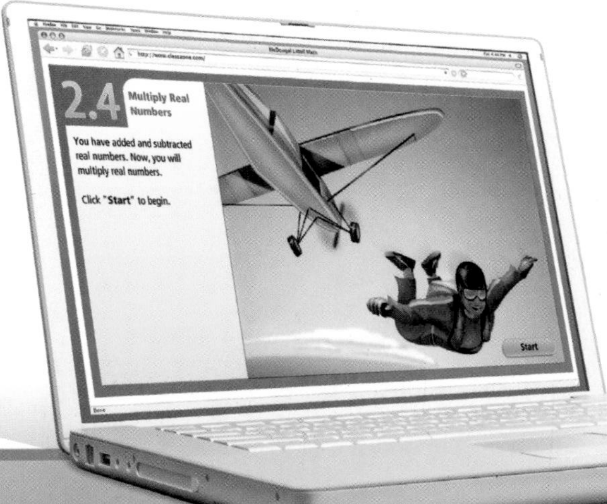

Access the online version of your textbook at classzone.com

Your complete text is available for immediate use!

McDougal Littell

Where Great Lessons Begin

NEW YORK

ALGEBRA 2

Ron Larson
Laurie Boswell
Timothy D. Kanold
Lee Stiff

McDougal Littell
A DIVISION OF HOUGHTON MIFFLIN COMPANY
Evanston, Illinois • Boston • Dallas

About *Algebra 2*

The content of *Algebra 2* is organized around families of functions, including linear, quadratic, exponential, logarithmic, radical, and rational functions. As you study each family of functions, you will learn to represent them in multiple ways—as verbal descriptions, equations, tables, and graphs. You will also learn to model real-world situations using functions in order to solve problems arising from those situations.

In addition to its algebra content, *Algebra 2* includes lessons on probability and data analysis as well as numerous examples and exercises involving geometry and trigonometry. These math topics often appear on standardized tests, so maintaining your familiarity with them is important. To help you prepare for standardized tests, *Algebra 2* provides instruction and practice on standardized test questions in a variety of formats—multiple choice, short response, extended response, and so on. Technology support for both learning algebra and preparing for standardized tests is available at classzone.com.

ISBN-13: 978-0-618-91240-7
ISBN-10: 0-618-91240-1   45678 0914 13 12 11 10 09

Internet Web Site: http://www.mcdougallittell.com

About the Authors

Ron Larson is a professor of mathematics at Penn State University at Erie, where he has taught since receiving his Ph.D. in mathematics from the University of Colorado. Dr. Larson is well known as the author of a comprehensive program for mathematics that spans middle school, high school, and college courses. Dr. Larson's numerous professional activities keep him in constant touch with the needs of teachers and supervisors. He closely follows developments in mathematics standards and assessment.

Laurie Boswell is a mathematics teacher at The Riverside School in Lyndonville, Vermont, and has taught mathematics at all levels, elementary through college. A recipient of the Presidential Award for Excellence in Mathematics Teaching, she was also a Tandy Technology Scholar. She served on the NCTM Board of Directors (2002–2005), and she speaks frequently at regional and national conferences on topics related to instructional strategies and course content.

Timothy D. Kanold is the superintendent of Adlai E. Stevenson High School District 125 in Lincolnshire, Illinois. Dr. Kanold served as a teacher and director of mathematics for 17 years prior to becoming superintendent. He is the recipient of the Presidential Award for Excellence in Mathematics and Science Teaching, and a past president of the Council for Presidential Awardees in Mathematics. Dr. Kanold is a frequent speaker at national and international mathematics meetings.

Lee Stiff is a professor of mathematics education in the College of Education and Psychology of North Carolina State University at Raleigh and has taught mathematics at the high school and middle school levels. He served on the NCTM Board of Directors and was elected President of NCTM for the years 2000–2002. He is a recipient of the W. W. Rankin Award for Excellence in Mathematics Education presented by the North Carolina Council of Teachers of Mathematics.

Advisers and Reviewers

New York Advisers and Reviewers

Marie Bobb
Mathematics Department Chair
Webster Thomas High School
Webster, NY

Heidi Christman
Mathematics Administrator K-12
Mohonassen CSD
Schenectady, NY

Sharon Cichocki
Secondary Mathematics Coordinator
Hamburg Central Schools
Hamburg, NY

Ron Labrocca
Mathematics Chairperson
Stimson Middle School
Huntington Station, NY

Douglas Lohnas, Ed.D.
Director of Mathematics
Niskayuna School District
Niskayuna, NY

Joe Mahoney
Mathematics Teacher and K-12 Mathematics Coordinator
Putnam Valley High School
Putnam Valley, NY

Regina Newman
Curriculum Associate Mathematics K-12
North Shore High School
Glen Head, NY

Steve Weiss
Mathematics Department Chair
Roslyn High School
Roslyn, NY

Nancy Zarach
Coordinator for Mathematics, Science, and Technology
Syracuse City Schools, NY

Curriculum Advisers and Reviewers

Craig Edward Auten
Mathematics Teacher
Walled Lake Central High School
Walled Lake, MI

Cindy L. Blair
Curriculum Instructional Coordinator
Thomas Jefferson High School
San Antonio, TX

Michael Bolling
Instructional Specialist for Mathematics
Chesterfield County Public Schools
Chesterfield, VA

Barbara J. Brooks
Mathematics Teacher
Mumford High School
Detroit, MI

Ronnee Sue Carpenter
Mathematics Teacher
Flint Southwestern Academy High School
Flint, MI

Brian Croston
Mathematics Teacher
Frisco Centennial High School
Frisco, TX

Randy Daniels
Mathematics Teacher
Ankeny High School
Ankeny, IA

Bonnie Davis
Mathematics Consultant (retired)
Gilmer Independent School District
Gilmer, TX

Brett Duffney
Mathematics Teacher
Preble High School
Green Bay, WI

Robert W. Ewing
Mathematics Teacher
Austin High School
El Paso, TX

Diana Faoro
Mathematics Teacher
Romeo Engineering and Technology Center
Washington, MI

Nancy L. Fisher
Mathematics Teacher
Hilliard Davidson High School
Hilliard, OH

Curriculum Advisers and Reviewers

Kristen Karbon
Mathematics Teacher
Troy High School
Troy, MI

Kathryn Laster
Mathematics Teacher
Lake Highlands High School
Dallas, TX

Kelly Leal
Mathematics Teacher
The Colony High School
The Colony, TX

Jamie K. Lipsey
Mathematics Teacher
Skyline High School
Dallas, TX

Lois M. McCarty
Mathematics Chair and Teacher
Midland Independent School District
Midland, TX

Mohammad Moshfeghian
Mathematics Department Chair
Homer Hanna High School
Brownsville, TX

Susan B. Nelson
Team Leader
Spring High School
Spring, TX

Anne Papakonstantinou
Director, School Mathematics Project
Rice University
Houston, TX

Richard Parr
Director of Educational Technology, School Mathematics Project
Rice University
Houston, TX

Joseph F. Pawloski
Mathematics Teacher
Brighton High School
Brighton, MI

Donald J. Pratt
Mathematics Teacher
Huron High School
Ann Arbor, MI

Wayne Rumple
Mathematics Teacher
Monroe Senior High School
Monroe, MI

Michael Schulte
Mathematics Consultant
Warren Mott High School
Warren, MI

Shirley K. Ward
Mathematics Teacher
Westside High School
Houston, TX

Denise Weatherford
Mathematics Teacher
Central High School
Beaumont, TX

Peggy S. Winfree White
Mathematics Teacher
Caprock High School
Amarillo, TX

Dianne Young
Mathematics Department Chair
Robert E. Lee Freshman High School
Midland, TX

New York

Overview
New York Student Edition

Liberty Island, New York © Christopher Hill/Alamy

NEW YORK TABLE OF CONTENTS

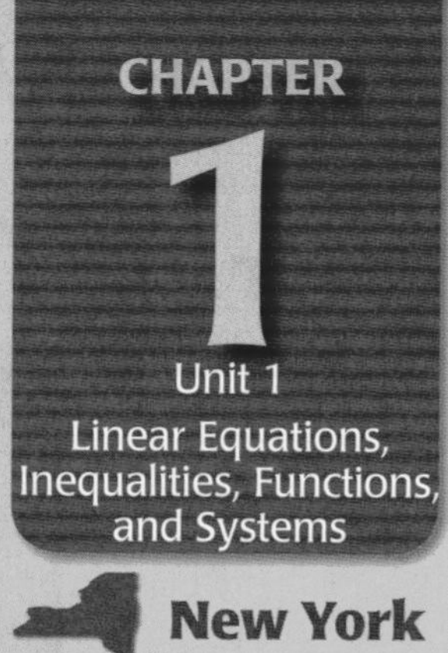

Work Rates, p. 20

$\frac{1}{8}t + \frac{1}{6}t = 7$

Equations and Inequalities

New York

ASSESSMENT

- New York Practice Examples, 3, 19, 36
- New York Daily Practice, 9, 16, 24, 32, 40, 47, 58
- New York Preparation and Practice, 6, 8, 9, 14, 15, 21, 23, 24, 29, 30, 31, 32, 33, 37, 38, 45, 46, 47, 55, 56, 59, 66
- Writing, 6, 13, 21, 30, 37, 44, 55

PROBLEM SOLVING

- New York Mixed Review, 33, 59
- Multiple Representations, 15, 24, 35, 39, 48, 57
- Multi-Step Problems, 8, 23, 32, 33, 39, 47, 57, 59
- Using Alternative Methods, 48
- Real-World Problem Solving Examples, 3, 5, 11, 13, 19, 20, 29, 35, 36, 42, 44, 54

TECHNOLOGY

At classzone.com:

- Animated Algebra, 1, 5, 11, 20, 27, 34, 42, 53
- @Home Tutor, NY 64, 8, 15, 17, 23, 25, 31, 38, 46, 57, 61
- Online Quiz, 9, 16, 24, 32, 40, 47, 58
- State Test Practice, 33, 59, 69

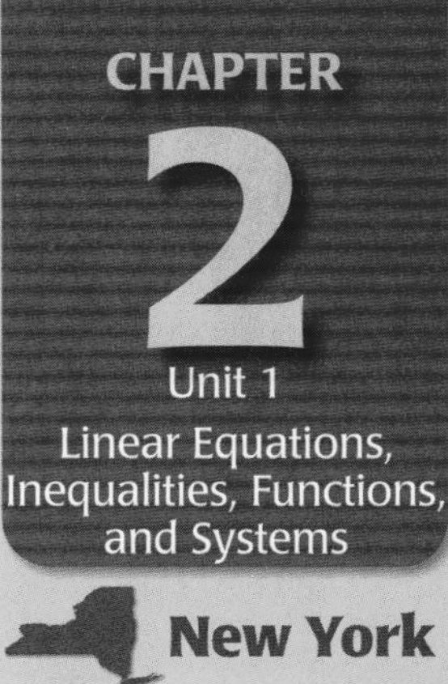

Linear Functions, p. 76
$P(d) = 1 + 0.03d$

Linear Equations and Functions

New York

ASSESSMENT

- New York Practice Examples, 82, 132
- New York Daily Practice, 79, 88, 96, 104, 111, 120, 129, 138
- New York Preparation and Practice, 77, 78, 79, 85, 86, 87, 88, 91, 93, 94, 95, 102, 103, 106, 109, 110, 111, 118, 119, 127, 128, 129, 134, 136, 137, 139, 146
- Writing, 76, 86, 93, 101, 109, 117, 127, 128, 135, 136

PROBLEM SOLVING

- New York Mixed Review, 106, 139
- Multiple Representations, 95, 104, 105, 119, 129
- Multi-Step Problems, 78, 88, 95, 103, 106, 137, 139
- Using Alternative Methods, 105
- Real-World Problem Solving Examples, 74, 76, 85, 91, 100, 108, 115, 125, 134

TECHNOLOGY

At classzone.com:

- Animated Algebra, 71, 73, 86, 90, 95, 98, 102, 107, 115, 133
- @Home Tutor, 70, 78, 87, 94, 97, 103, 110, 119, 121, 128, 137, 141
- Online Quiz, 79, 88, 96, 104, 111, 120, 129, 138
- Electronic Function Library, 140
- State Test Practice, 106, 139, 149

Linear Systems, p. 155
$y = x + 30; y = 2.5x$

Linear Systems and Matrices

New York

ASSESSMENT
- New York Practice Examples, 155, 162
- New York Daily Practice, 158, 167, 173, 185, 193, 202, 209, 217
- New York Preparation and Practice, 156, 157, 158, 165, 166, 170, 171, 172, 173, 183, 184, 185, 186, 189, 191, 192, 199, 200, 201, 202, 206, 207, 208, 209, 213, 214, 215, 216, 220, 228
- Writing, 156, 164, 171, 182, 190, 199, 207, 214, 222

PROBLEM SOLVING
- New York Mixed Review, 186, 220
- Multiple Representations, 157, 173, 216, 218
- Multi-Step Problems, 184, 186, 200, 201, 209, 216, 220
- Using Alternative Methods, 218
- Real-World Problem Solving Examples, 155, 162, 170, 181, 189, 198, 206, 213

TECHNOLOGY
At classzone.com:
- Animated Algebra, 151, 161, 168, 196, 211
- @Home Tutor, 150, 157, 159, 165, 172, 184, 192, 194, 200, 208, 215, 222
- Online Quiz, 158, 167, 173, 185, 193, 202, 209, 217
- State Test Practice, 186, 220, 231

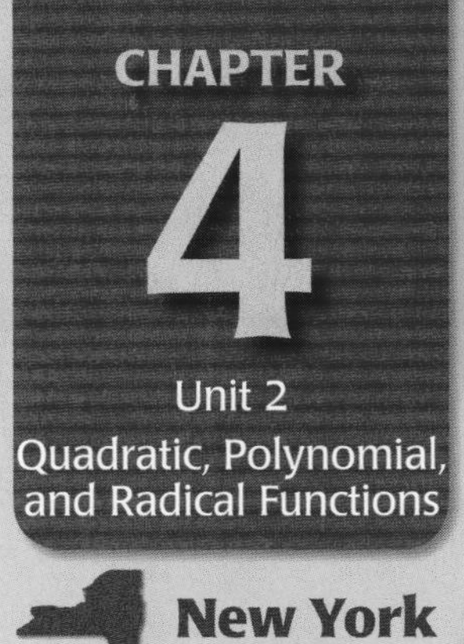

Complex Numbers, p. 281
$f(z) = z^2 + c$

Quadratic Functions and Factoring

New York

ASSESSMENT

- New York Practice Examples, 254, 268, 286
- New York Daily Practice, 243, 251, 258, 265, 271, 282, 291, 299, 307, 315
- New York Preparation and Practice, 239, 241, 242, 249, 250, 251, 256, 257, 258, 262, 263, 264, 270, 271, 274, 280, 281, 282, 288, 289, 290, 296, 297, 298, 299, 305, 306, 311, 312, 313, 315, 316, 324
- Writing, 240, 255, 263, 269, 279, 296, 304, 312

PROBLEM SOLVING

- New York Mixed Review, 274, 316
- Multiple Representations, 242, 258, 272, 290, 306, 314
- Multi-Step Problems, 250, 257, 274, 298, 307, 314, 316
- Using Alternative Methods, 272
- Real-World Problem Solving Examples, 239, 246, 254, 262, 277, 287, 295, 303, 311

TECHNOLOGY

At classzone.com:

- Animated Algebra, 235, 238, 247, 269, 279, 287, 300
- @Home Tutor, 234, 242, 244, 250, 257, 264, 270, 281, 290, 298, 306, 308, 314, 318,
- Online Quiz, 243, 251, 258, 265, 271, 282, 291, 299, 307, 315
- Electronic Function Library, 317
- State Test Practice, 274, 316, 327

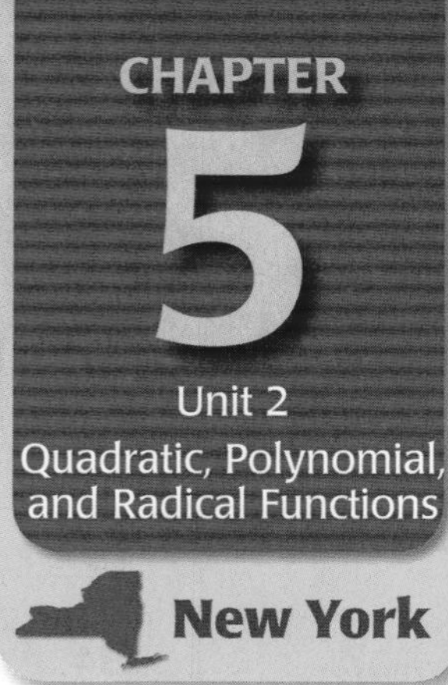

Polynomial Functions, p. 340
$E = 0.0029s^4$

Polynomials and Polynomial Functions

New York

ASSESSMENT

- New York Practice Examples, 332, 339, 355, 365
- New York Daily Practice, 335, 344, 352, 359, 368, 377, 386, 392, 399
- New York Preparation and Practice, 333, 334, 335, 340, 342, 344, 349, 350, 356, 357, 359, 367, 368, 369, 373, 375, 376, 383, 384, 386, 391, 392, 396, 397, 398, 400, 408, 409
- Writing, 333, 341, 349, 356, 366, 374, 383, 390, 397

PROBLEM SOLVING

- New York Mixed Review, 369, 400
- Multiple Representations, 343, 367, 392
- Multi-Step Problems, 335, 344, 351, 358, 369, 376, 398, 400
- Using Alternative Methods, 360
- Real-World Problem Solving Examples, 331, 333, 340, 348, 356, 365, 373, 383, 389, 396

TECHNOLOGY

At classzone.com:

- Animated Algebra, 329, 331, 340, 371, 388, 396
- @Home Tutor, 328, 334, 343, 345, 351, 358, 367, 376, 378, 385, 391, 398, 402
- Online Quiz, 335, 344, 352, 359, 368, 377, 386, 392, 399
- Electronic Function Library, 401
- State Test Practice, 369, 400, 411

Square Root Functions, p. 451

$v_t = 33.7\sqrt{\frac{W}{A}}$

Rational Exponents and Radical Functions

New York

ASSESSMENT

- New York Practice Examples, 430, 453
- New York Daily Practice, 419, 427, 434, 445, 451, 459
- New York Preparation and Practice, 417, 419, 424, 425, 426, 427, 429, 431, 432, 433, 436, 439, 443, 444, 447, 449, 450, 456, 457, 458, 464
- Writing, 417, 424, 432, 442, 449, 456

PROBLEM SOLVING

- New York Mixed Review, 436, 464
- Multiple Representations, 434, 451, 460
- Multi-Step Problems, 418, 433, 436, 444, 458, 464
- Using Alternative Methods, 460
- Real-World Problem Solving Examples, 416, 421, 429, 441, 447, 453

TECHNOLOGY

At classzone.com:

- Animated Algebra, 413, 431, 444, 448, 458
- @Home Tutor, 412, 418, 426, 433, 435, 444, 457, 458, 466
- Online Quiz, 419, 427, 434, 445, 451
- Electronic Function Library, 465
- State Test Practice, 436, 464, 473

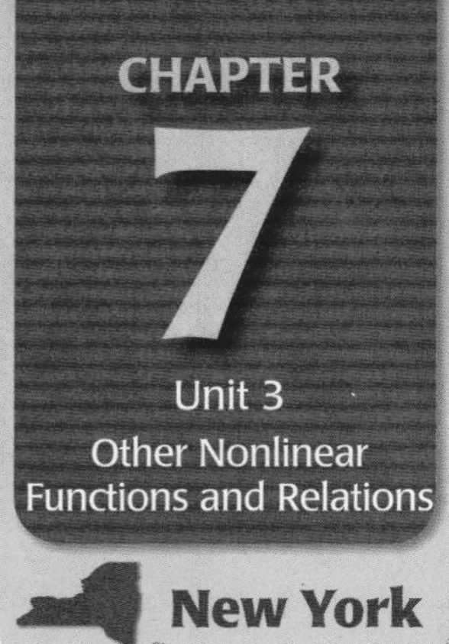

Power Functions, p. 532
$y = 0.0784x^{2.5}$

Exponential and Logarithmic Functions

New York

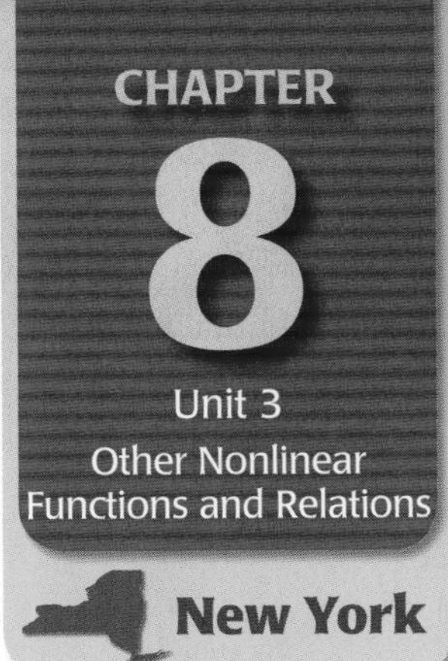

Rational Equations, p. 562

$$t = \frac{1000}{0.6T + 331}$$

Rational Functions

New York

ASSESSMENT

- New York Practice Examples, 575, 590
- New York Daily Practice, 557, 563, 571, 580, 588, 595
- New York Preparation and Practice, 555, 556, 557, 560, 561, 562, 563, 567, 568, 569, 570, 572, 574, 578, 579, 580, 587, 588, 593, 594, 601, 608
- Writing, 555, 561, 568, 577, 586, 592

PROBLEM SOLVING

- New York Mixed Review, 572, 601
- Multiple Representations, 562, 570
- Multi-Step Problems, 556, 570, 572, 580, 601
- Using Alternative Methods, 596
- Real-World Problem Solving Examples, 552, 560, 567, 574, 585, 592

TECHNOLOGY

At classzone.com:

- Animated Algebra, 549, 554, 559, 568, 587
- @Home Tutor, 548, 556, 562, 564, 569, 570, 579, 581, 587, 594, 603
- Online Quiz, 557, 563, 571, 580, 588, 595
- Electronic Function Library, 602
- State Test Practice, 572, 601, 611

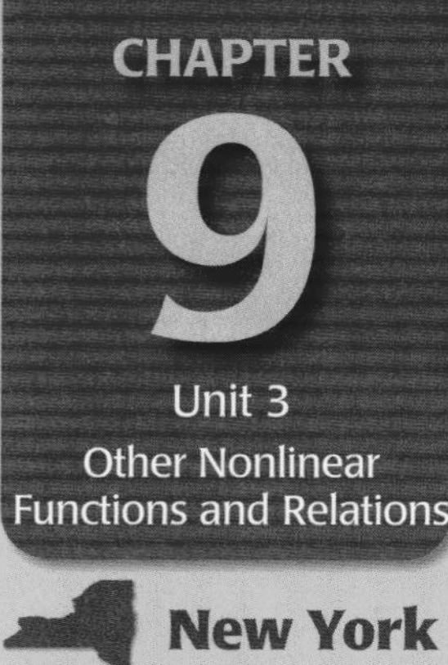

Classify Conic Sections, p. 656
$21y^2 - 210y - 4x^2 = -441$

Quadratic Relations and Conic Sections

New York

ASSESSMENT

PROBLEM SOLVING

TECHNOLOGY

At classzone.com:

New York

Counting Methods and Probability

New York

ASSESSMENT

- New York Practice Examples, 708, 717
- New York Daily Practice, 689, 697, 704, 713, 723, 730
- New York Preparation and Practice, 687, 688, 691, 695, 696, 702, 704, 705, 710, 711, 712, 720, 721, 722, 723, 728, 730, 732, 738, 739
- Writing, 686, 694, 701, 710, 721, 727

PROBLEM SOLVING

- New York Mixed Review, 705, 732
- Multiple Representations, 703, 714, 729
- Multi-Step Problems, 688, 696, 705, 712, 732
- Using Alternative Methods, 714
- Real-World Problem Solving Examples, 683, 685, 691, 699, 700, 708, 709, 719, 720, 726

TECHNOLOGY

At classzone.com:

- Animated Algebra, 681, 701, 711, 716, 722, 726
- @Home Tutor, 680, 688, 696, 703, 711, 722, 729, 731, 734
- Online Quiz, 689, 697, 704, 713, 723, 730
- State Test Practice, 705, 732, 741

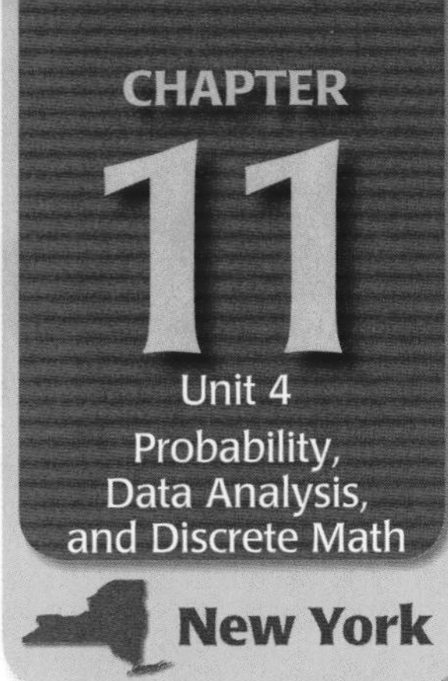

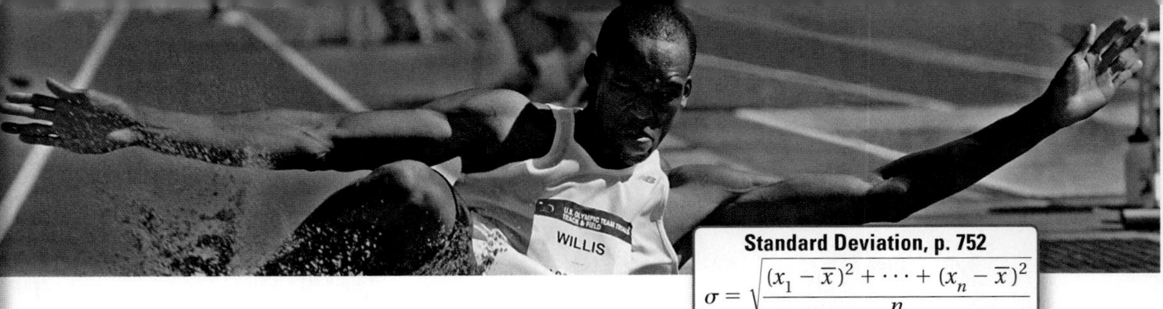

Standard Deviation, p. 752

$$\sigma = \sqrt{\frac{(x_1 - \bar{x})^2 + \cdots + (x_n - \bar{x})^2}{n}}$$

New York

Data Analysis and Statistics

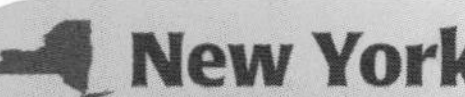

New York

ASSESSMENT
- New York Practice Examples, 745, 769
- New York Daily Practice, 749, 755, 762, 771, 780
- New York Preparation and Practice, 747, 748, 749, 753, 754, 756, 760, 761, 762, 770, 771, 778, 779, 782, 788
- Writing, 747, 753, 760, 769, 778, 784

PROBLEM SOLVING
- New York Mixed Review, 756, 782
- Multiple Representations, 754, 779, 781
- Multi-Step Problems, 748, 756, 761, 771, 782
- Using Alternative Methods, 781
- Real-World Problem Solving Examples, 746, 752, 759, 767, 776

TECHNOLOGY
At classzone.com:
- Animated Algebra, 743, 744, 754, 757, 776
- @Home Tutor, 742, 748, 750, 753, 761, 770, 774, 779, 784
- Online Quiz, 749, 755, 762, 771, 780
- State Test Practice, 756, 782, 791

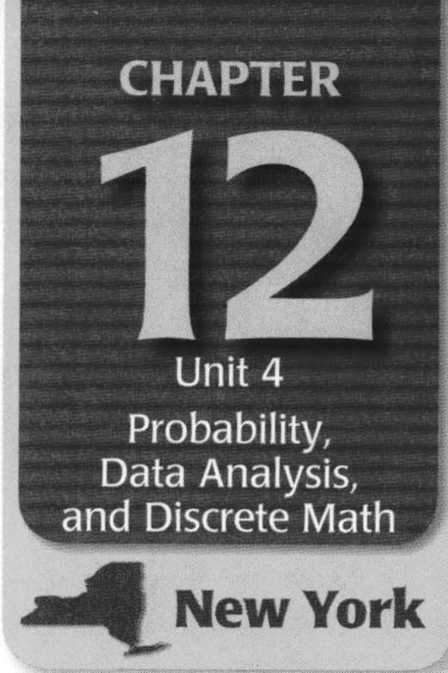

Infinite Series, p. 825

$$8 + \sum_{n=1}^{\infty} 16(0.75)^n$$

Sequences and Series

New York

ASSESSMENT

- New York Daily Practice, 805, 821
- New York Preparation and Practice, 795, 798, 799, 800, 806, 807, 809, 814, 815, 816, 818, 823, 824, 825, 829, 830, 831, 832, 844
- Writing, 798, 806, 807, 814, 823, 830

PROBLEM SOLVING

- New York Mixed Review, 818, 838
- Multiple Representations, 808, 816
- Multi-Step Problems, 800, 818, 838
- Using Alternative Methods, 834
- Real-World Problem Solving Examples, 795, 805, 813, 822, 829

TECHNOLOGY

At classzone.com:

- Animated Algebra, 793, 805, 811, 820, 832
- @Home Tutor, 792, 799, 801, 808, 815, 824, 826, 832, 840
- Online Quiz, 800, 809, 817, 825, 833
- State Test Practice, 756, 838, 847

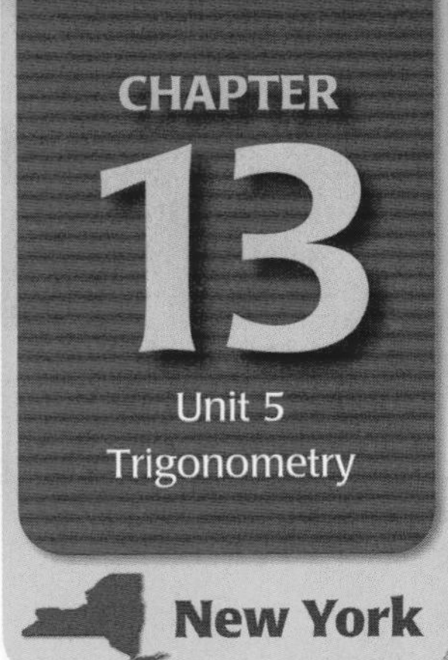

Law of Cosines, p. 893
$a^2 = b^2 + c^2 - 2bc \cos A$

Trigonometric Ratios and Functions

New York

ASSESSMENT

- New York Practice Examples, 853, 877
- New York Daily Practice, 858, 865, 872, 880, 888, 894
- New York Preparation and Practice, 856, 857, 858, 862, 863, 864, 870, 871, 872, 873, 878, 879, 886, 887, 888, 891, 892, 893, 894, 896, 902
- Writing, 856, 862, 870, 878, 886, 892

PROBLEM SOLVING

- New York Mixed Review, 873, 896
- Multiple Representations, 857, 887, 895
- Multi-Step Problems, 864, 872, 873, 888, 893, 896
- Using Alternative Methods, 895
- Real-World Problem Solving Examples, 855, 862, 869, 877, 885, 890

TECHNOLOGY

At classzone.com:

- Animated Algebra, 851, 854, 867, 884
- @Home Tutor, 850, 857, 864, 871, 879, 881, 887, 893, 898
- Online Quiz, 858, 865, 872, 880, 888, 894
- Electronic Function Library, 897
- State Test Practice, 873, 896, 905

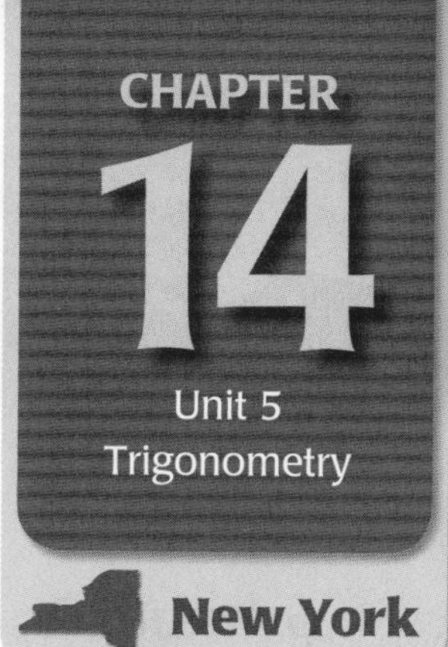

New York

Difference Formulas, p. 954

$\tan(a - b) = \dfrac{\tan a - \tan b}{1 + \tan a \tan b}$

Trigonometric Graphs, Identities, and Equations

New York

ASSESSMENT

- New York Practice Examples, 933, 956
- New York Daily Practice, 914, 922, 930, 937, 947, 954, 962
- New York Preparation and Practice, 913, 914, 920, 921, 922, 928, 929, 930, 935, 936, 940, 944, 945, 946, 951, 952, 954, 959, 960, 961, 962, 963
- Writing, 912, 919, 927, 935, 944, 945, 952, 959

PROBLEM SOLVING

- New York Mixed Review, 940, 963
- Multiple Representations, 914, 929, 937
- Multi-Step Problems, 921, 940, 946, 954, 961, 963
- Using Alternative Methods, 938
- Real-World Problem Solving Examples, 910, 916, 927, 932, 942, 951, 957

TECHNOLOGY

At classzone.com:

- Animated Algebra, 907, 912, 917, 961
- @Home Tutor, 906, 913, 921, 923, 929, 936, 945, 953, 961
- Online Quiz, 914, 922, 930, 937, 947, 954, 962
- Electronic Function Library, 964
- State Test Practice, 940, 963, 973

Contents of Student Resources

NEW YORK

Student Guide to the Standards

The New York Mathematics Core Curriculum

- The New York Mathematics Core Curriculum are goals set by the state to ensure that you are being taught a thoughtful, complete curriculum.
- Teachers and other educators use the performance indicators when developing courses and tests.
- Lessons in your book connect to a performance indicator, which is listed next to the lesson in the table of contents beginning on NY 8. These indicators are also shown on the first page of each lesson throughout the book.

Liberty Island, New York © Christopher Hill/Alamy

NEW YORK STUDENT GUIDE

Guide to the New York Mathematics Core Curriculum

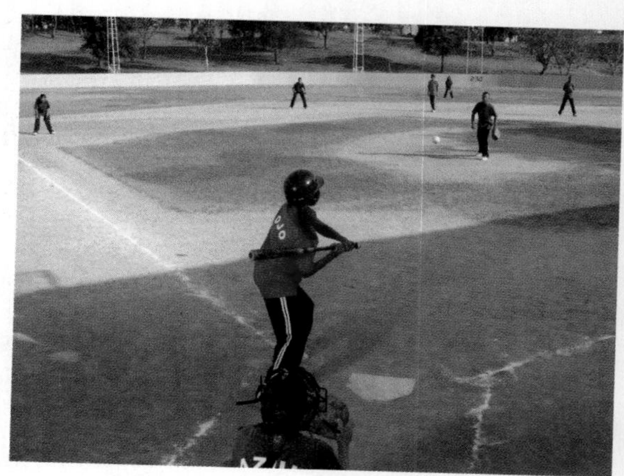

Learning the New York Mathematics Core Curriculum will help you hit a homerun!

© Jorge Albán/McDougal Littell/Houghton Mifflin Co.

Did you know . . .

. . . that baseball and math standards have some things in common?

. . . and, that your math standards have been written as a commitment to you, the New York student?

So . . .

. . . "What are Math Standards and what do they have in common with baseball?"

Compare the standards to a set of rules that must be followed in a sport event. For example, in a baseball game, the batter must move from first base to second base and then third base before proceeding to the home plate to score a run. Learning this rule enables the team to win the game.

Without the knowledge of how a baseball game is played, the team will not have the fundamental concepts to compete.

Math standards, like the rules in baseball, help you focus on a common foundation of mathematical concepts that you will use in everyday life and later in the workplace.

And . . .

. . . How will learning the New York Mathematics Core Curriculum make a difference for you, the student?

It is important to learn material that is closely aligned to the math standards because they are what you will be tested on when it comes time to take your state test.

The New York state standards have been written as a commitment to you, the student, to help you focus on the proper content to achieve both depth and understanding of mathematical knowledge.

New York Mathematics Core Curriculum Decoder

Part 1 **The math standards for New York are organized under the following content strands:**

N. Number Sense and Operations
A. Algebra
M. Measurement
S. Statistics and Probability

Part 2 **Each level is divided into strands.**

Part 3 **Each strand is broken down into performance indicators. The information from the 3 parts will help you break the standard code!**

Here is an example:

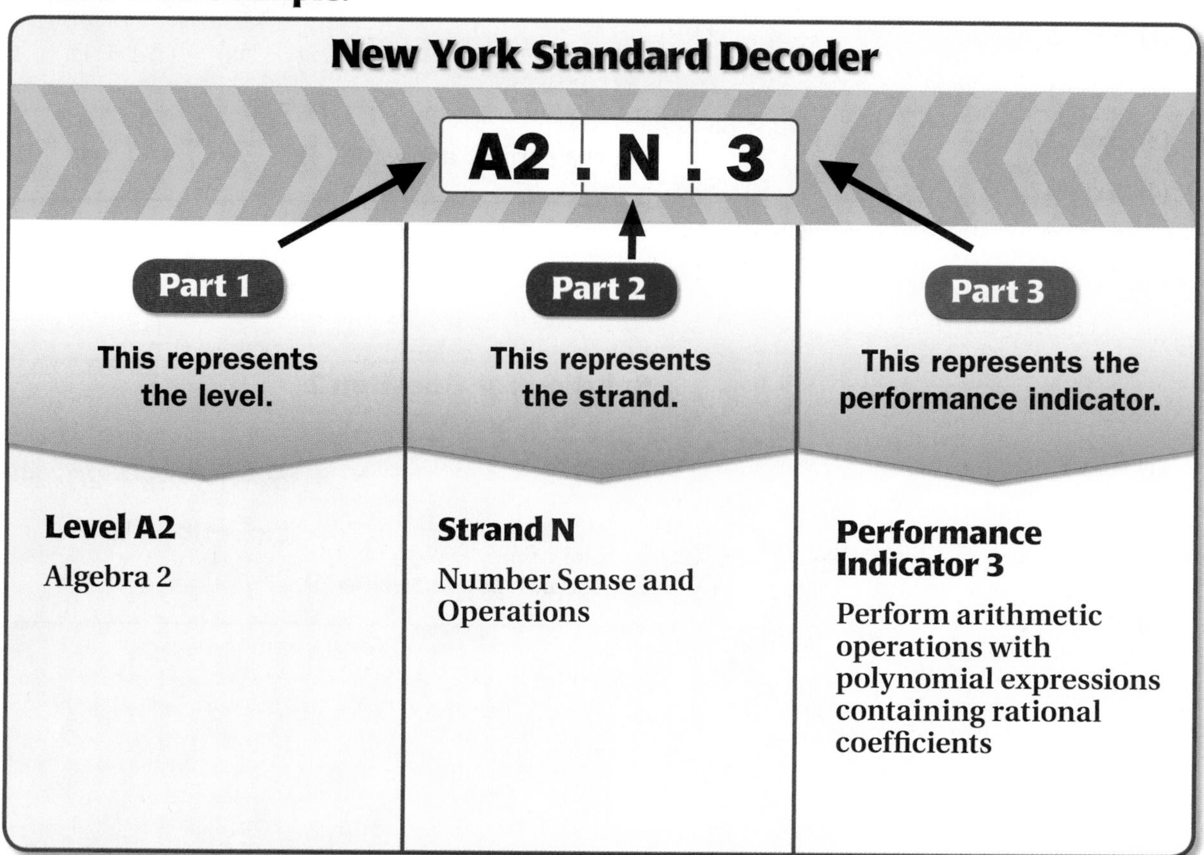

New York Mathematics Core Curriculum

N. Number Sense and Operations Strand

Bands

Operations Students will understand meanings of operations and procedures, and how they relate to one another.

What It Means To You

All students studying math should develop an understanding of the properties of, and the relationships among, numbers. Numbers are the cornerstone of any mathematics curriculum and permeate all areas of life.

Here is what questions might look like on the Regents Exam:

A2.N.3 Perform arithmetic operations with polynomial expressions containing rational coefficients

Simplify the expression $4(2x - 8) - 3(x + 5)$.

(1) $5x - 3$

(2) $5x - 17$

(3) $5x - 27$

(4) $5x - 47$

Solution for Question 1

$$4(2x - 8) - 3(x + 5) = 8x - 32 - 3x - 15$$
$$= (8x - 3x) - (32 + 15)$$
$$= 5x - 47$$

So, the correct answer is (4).

Which expression is equivalent to $-2(x - 6) + 5x(3x + 4)$.

(1) $15x^2 + 18x + 12$

(2) $15x^2 + 18x - 12$

(3) $15x^2 - 2x + 32$

(4) $15x^2 - 2x + 8$

Solution for Question 2

$$-2(x - 6) + 5x(3x + 4) = -2x + 12 + 15x^2 + 20x$$
$$= 15x^2 + (-2x + 20x) + 12$$
$$= 15x^2 + 18 + 12$$

So, the correct answer is (1).

A. Algebra Strand

Bands

Equations and Inequalities Students will perform algebraic procedures accurately.

Variables and Expressions Students will represent and analyze algebraically a wide variety of problem solving situations.

Patterns, Relations, and Functions Students will recognize, use, and represent algebraically patterns, relations, and functions.

What It Means To You

Algebra is the branch of mathematics in which symbols are used to represent numbers and quantities. Thinking algebraically includes recognizing and analyzing patterns, studying and representing relationships, making generalizations, and analyzing how things change. Algebra emphasizes learning about functions, which helps develop the ability to form generalizations that will lay the foundation for studying other areas of math, such as geometry and data analysis.

Here is what questions might look like on the Regents Exam:

A2.A.23 Solve rational equations and inequalities

Alicia is making flower arrangements. Vases cost \$3.75 each and flowers cost \$3.50 per bundle. Alicia has a budget of \$40. Which inequality describes the possible number of vases, v, and bundles of flowers, b, that she can buy on her budget?

(1) $40 \geq 3.75v + 3.5b$

(2) $40 \geq 3.5v + 3.75b$

(3) $40 \leq 3.75v + 3.5b$

(4) $40 \leq 3.5v + 3.75b$

Solution for Question 1

Write a verbal model to write an inequality.

Total cost	$\geq$	Cost per vase	•	Number of vases	+	Cost per bundle	•	Bundles of flowers
40	$\geq$	3.75	•	v	+	3.5	•	b

The correct answer is (1).

Thomas earns \$5.25 per hour waiting tables at a cafe plus an average tip of \$2.50 for each customer he serves. Which equation describes his total earnings, e, for h hours worked and c customers served?

(1) $e = 2.5h + 5.25c$

(2) $e = 2.5h - 5.25c$

(3) $e = 5.25h + 2.5c$

(4) $e = 5.25h - 2.5c$

Solution for Question 2

Write a verbal model to write an inequality.

Total earnings	=	Hourly rate	•	Number of hours	+	Tip per customer	•	Customers served
e	=	5.25	•	h	+	2.5	•	c

The correct answer is (3).

M. Measurement Strand

Bands	What It Means To You
Units of Measurement Students will determine what can be measured and how, using appropriate methods and formulas.	Measurement is the assignment of a numerical value to a characteristic of an object, such as length. The study of measurement is important in the mathematics curriculum because of its practicality and occurrence in so many aspects of everyday life.

Here is what a question might look like on the Regents Exam:

A2.M.2 Convert between radian and degree measures

On a recent test, 6 students received A's. 13 students received B's, 5 students C's, and 1 student received a D. Which circle graph best represents that data?

(1)

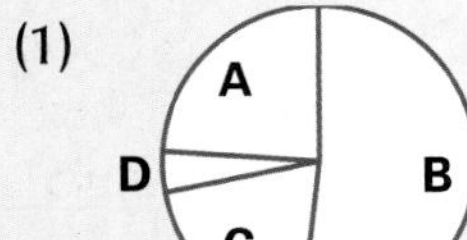

(2)

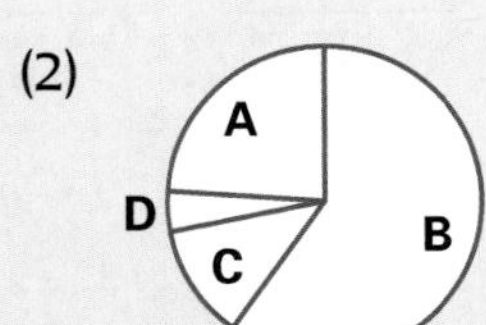

(3)

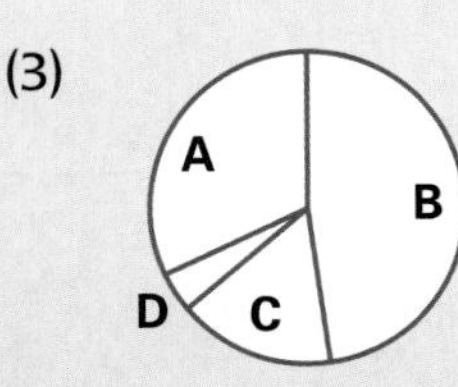

(4)

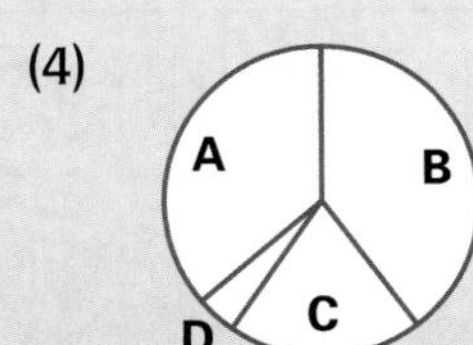

Solution

A total of 25 students received grades on the test. So, the percent of students receiving each grade is:

A: $\frac{6}{25} = 24\%$

B: $\frac{13}{25} = 52\%$

C: $\frac{5}{25} = 20\%$

D: $\frac{1}{25} = 4\%$

The correct answer is (1).

S. Statistics and Probability Strand

Bands

Collection of Data Students will collect, organize, display, and analyze data.

Organization and Display Data

What It Means To You

Data analysis involves using data and statistics to solve problems that come up in work and in life. Probability is the study of the likelihood that a given event will occur. These topics are important to know about in order to reason statistically.

Here is what a question might look like on the Regents Exam:

A2.S.10 Calculate the number of possible permutations ($_nP_r$) of *n* items taken *r* at a time

Five runners are entered in a race. Which expression gives the number of possible arrangements in which the runners can come in first, second, and third place?

(1) $3 \times 2 \times 1$

(2) $5 + 4 + 3$

(3) $5 \times 4 \times 3$

(4) 5^3

Solution

There are 5 runners who could come in first. Once the first-place runner is decided, there are 4 runners who can come in second, then 3 runners who can come in third. Calculate $5 \times 4 \times 3$ to find the number of possible arrangements

The correct answer is (3).

STANDARDS

NEW YORK

Countdown to the Regents Examination

What is the the Regents Examination?

- The New York Regents Examination is given in the spring to students as a high school exit exam.
- The test has multiple-choice and open-ended questions that evaluate your knowledge of the New York Mathematics Core Curriculum.

Getting Ready

You can use the questions on the following pages to practice for the New York Regents Examination. Each question addresses a performance indicator.

The questions are in the same format as those on the New York Regents Examination, and are organized by content strands. (For example, Strand N is Number Sense and Operations.)

If you need practice with a particular performance indicator, use the chart on the next page to find which questions address that strand and performance indicator. If you need additional preparation, the chart lists lessons you can review.

You will have more opportunities to practice for the New York Regents Examination in every lesson and chapter throughout the book.

Liberty Island, New York © Christopher Hill/Alamy

Countdown Reference Chart

This chart lists what performance indicator is being addressed for each question. Lesson support is referenced and the full text of the strands is available on S1.

NY Standard Code	Practice Questions for the Regents Exam	Lesson-by-Lesson Regents Exam Support
Strand N: Number Sense and Operations		
A2.N.1	1, 2, 3, 4, 5	Lesson 5.1
A2.N.2	6, 7	Lesson 6.2
A2.N.3	8, 9	Lesson 5.3
A2.N.4	98	Lesson 6.2
A2.N.5	10, 11	Lessons 4.5, 6.2
A2.N.6	12	Lesson 4.6
A2.N.7	13	Lesson 4.6
A2.N.8	14	Lesson 4.6
A2.N.9	15	Lesson 4.6
A2.N.10	16, 17	Lesson 12.1
Strand A: Algebra		
A2.A.1	18, 19, 99	Lessons 1.6, 1.7
A2.A.2	20	Lesson 4.8
A2.A.3	100	Lesson 9.7
A2.A.4	21, 22	Lesson 4.9
A2.A.5	23, 24	Lessons 2.5, 8.1
A2.A.6	25	Lesson 7.6
A2.A.7	101	Lesson 5.4
A2.A.8	26	Lesson 5.1
A2.A.9	27	Lesson 6.1
A2.A.11	28	Lesson 6.1
A2.A.12	102	Lesson 1.2
A2.A.13	29, 30, 31, 32	Lessons 4.5, 6.2
A2.A.14	33	Lesson 6.2
A2.A.16	34, 35	Lessons 8.4, 8.5
A2.A.17	103	Lesson 8.5
A2.A.18	36	Lesson 7.4
A2.A.19	37, 104	Lesson 7.5
A2.A.22	113	Lesson 6.6
A2.A.23	114	Lesson 8.6
A2.A.24	38	Lesson 4.7
A2.A.25	105	Lesson 4.8
A2.A.26	106	Lesson 5.7
A2.A.27	39	Lesson 7.6
A2.A.28	40	Lesson 7.6
A2.A.29	41, 42	Lesson 12.1
A2.A.30	43	Lesson 12.2
A2.A.31	44	Lesson 12.3
A2.A.32	45	Lesson 12.3
A2.A.33	46	Lesson 12.5
A2.A.34	107	Lesson 12.1
A2.A.35	47	Lesson 12.2
A2.A.36	48	Lesson 10.2
A2.A.37	49, 50, 51	Lesson 2.1
A2.A.38	52	Lesson 2.1

NY Standard Code	Practice Questions for the Regents Exam	Lesson-by-Lesson Regents Exam Support
A2.A.39	53	Lesson 8.2
A2.A.41	54	Lesson 5.2
A2.A.42	55, 56	Lesson 6.3
A2.A.44	108	Lesson 6.4
A2.A.45	120	Lesson 6.4
A2.A.46	57	Lesson 2.7
A2.A.48	58	Lesson 9.3
A2.A.49	59	Lesson 9.3
A2.A.50	109	Lesson 5.8
A2.A.51	60, 61, 110	Lessons 6.5, 7.2, 8.2
A2.A.52	62	Lesson 2.1
A2.A.53	121	Lesson 7.1
A2.A.54	63	Lesson 7.4
A2.A.55	64, 65	Lesson 13.1
A2.A.56	66, 67	Lesson 13.3
A2.A.57	68	Lesson 13.3
A2.A.58	69	Lesson 14.3
A2.A.59	70	Lesson 14.3
A2.A.60	122	Lesson 13.2
A.2.A.61	71	Lesson 13.2
A.2.A.62	115	Lesson 13.3
A2.A.63	72	Lesson 13.4
A2.A.64	73	Lesson 13.4
A2.A.66	74	Lesson 13.1
A2.A.68	75	Lesson 14.4
A2.A.69	116	Lesson 14.1
A2.A.70	76, 123	Lesson 14.1
A2.A.71	77	Lesson 14.1
A2.A.72	111	Lesson 14.5
A2.A.73	78, 79	Lesson 13.5
A2.A.74	117	Lesson 13.5
A2.A.75	124	Lesson 13.5
A2.A.77	80	Lesson 14.7
Strand M: Measurement		
A2.M.2	81	Lesson 13.2
Strand S: Statistics and Probability		
A2.S.2	112	Lesson 11.4
A2.S.4	125	Lesson 11.1
A2.S.5	118	Lesson 11.3
A2.S.6	82	Lesson 11.5
A2.S.7	119	Lesson 11.5
A2.S.8	83, 84, 85	Lesson 2.6
A2.S.9	86	Lesson 10.2
A2.S.10	87, 88, 89	Lesson 10.1
A2.S.11	90	Lesson 10.2
A2.S.12	91	Lesson 10.1
A2.S.13	92, 93	Lesson 10.3
A2.S.14	94, 95	Lesson 10.3
A2.S.15	96	Lesson 10.6
A2.S.16	97	Lesson 11.3

A2.N.1 Evaluate numerical expressions with negative and or fractional exponents, without the aid of a calculator (when the answers are rational numbers)

1. What is the product of (2×10^{-3}) and (1.25×10^{8})? *(p. 333, prob. 15–23)*

(1) 2.5×10^{-24}

(2) 3.25×10^{-24}

(3) 2.5×10^{5}

(4) 3.25×10^{5}

2. Which of the following is the simplified form of $\frac{y^{-10}}{y^{10}}$? *(p. 333, prob. 24–35)*

(1) 0

(2) 1

(3) $\frac{1}{y^{20}}$

(4) y^{20}

3. Which exponent property is NOT used when simplifying $(p^5q)^{-1}$? *(p. 333, prob. 24–35)*

(1) Quotient of Powers

(2) Product of Powers

(3) Negative Exponent

(4) Power of a Power

4. What is the simplified form of $(m^{-8}n)(m^3n^{-4})$? *(p. 333, prob. 24–35)*

(1) $\frac{1}{m^5n^3}$

(2) $\frac{1}{m^5n^4}$

(3) $\frac{m^5}{n^4}$

(4) $\frac{1}{m^{24}n^4}$

5. What is the simplified form of $\frac{x^{-1}y}{x^{-4}y^2}$? *(p. 333, prob. 24–35)*

(1) x^3y

(2) x^5y^2

(3) $\frac{x^3}{y}$

(4) $\frac{x^3}{y^2}$

Go On

Strand N Number Sense and Operations

A2.N.2 Perform arithmetic operations (addition, subtraction, multiplication, division) with expressions containing irrational numbers in radical form

6. What is the simplified form of $6\sqrt[3]{7} + 2\sqrt[3]{7}$? *(p. 424, prob. 32–40)*

(1) $8\sqrt[3]{7}$

(2) $8\sqrt[3]{18}$

(3) 24

(4) $24\sqrt[3]{3}$

7. What is the simplified form of $9\sqrt[4]{80} - 3\sqrt[4]{5}$? *(p. 424, prob. 32–40)*

(1) $6\sqrt[4]{75}$

(2) 15

(3) $15\sqrt[4]{5}$

(4) $33\sqrt[4]{5}$

A2.N.3 Perform arithmetic operations with polynomial expressions containing rational coefficients

8. What is the result when $5x^5 + 3x^2 + 4$ is added to $7x^5 + 4x^4 - 3x^2 - x$? *(p. 349, prob. 3–14)*

(1) $12x^5 + 4x^4 - x + 4$

(2) $12x^{10} + 4x^4 - x + 4$

(3) $12x^5 + 4x^4 + 6x^2 - x + 4$

(4) $12x^5 + 4x^4 - 6x^2 - x + 4$

9. The length of a rectangle is $w^2 + 6w - 4$ and the width is $w + 5$. Which of the following represents the area of this rectangle? *(p. 349, prob. 16–25)*

(1) $w^3 + 6w^2 - 20$

(2) $w^3 + 11w^2 - 26w - 20$

(3) $w^3 + 11w^2 + 26w - 20$

(4) $w^3 + 11w^2 + 30w - 24$

Go On 

A2.N.5 Rationalize a denominator containing a radical expression

10. What is the simplest form of $\frac{3}{7 - \sqrt{5}}$? *(p. 269, prob. 3–18)*

(1) $\frac{21 + 3\sqrt{5}}{44}$

(2) $\frac{21 - 3\sqrt{5}}{44}$

(3) $\frac{21 + 3\sqrt{5}}{54}$

(4) $\frac{21 - 3\sqrt{5}}{54}$

11. What is the simplest form of the expression $\sqrt[3]{\frac{1}{5}}$? *(p. 424, prob. 24–31)*

(1) $\frac{\sqrt[3]{5}}{5}$

(2) $\frac{\sqrt[3]{25}}{5}$

(3) $\sqrt[3]{5}$

(4) $\sqrt[3]{25}$

A2.N.6 Write square roots of negative numbers in terms of *i*

12. What is the simplified form of $\sqrt{-96}$? *(p. 279, prob. 3–11)*

(1) $4i\sqrt{6}$

(2) $-4i\sqrt{6}$

(3) $4i\sqrt{-6}$

(4) $-4i\sqrt{-6}$

A2.N.7 Simplify powers of *i*

13. What is the value of i^{16}? *(p. 281, prob. 69)*

(1) $-i$

(2) -1

(3) i

(4) 1

A2.N.8 Determine the conjugate of a complex number

14. What is the complex conjugate of $6 + 3i$? *(p. 279, prob. 1)*

(1) $-6 + 3i$

(2) $-6 - 3i$

(3) $6 - 3i$

(4) $6 + 3i$

A2.N.9 Perform arithmetic operations on complex numbers and write the answer in the form *a* + *bi* Note: This includes simplifying expressions with complex denominators.

15. What is the simplified form of the expression $\frac{4 + 2i}{3 - i}$? *(p. 280, prob. 28–33)*

(1) $1 + i$

(2) $1 - i$

(3) $\frac{7}{5} + i$

(4) $\frac{7}{5} - i$

Go On 

Strand N Number Sense and Operations

A2.N.10 Know and apply sigma notation

16. Which of the following represents the series $8 + 11 + 14 + 17 + \ldots$?
(p. 798, prob. 37–44)

(1) $\sum_{i=1}^{\infty} 3i - 5$

(2) $\sum_{i=1}^{\infty} 3i + 5$

(3) $\sum_{i=1}^{\infty} 5i - 3$

(4) $\sum_{i=1}^{\infty} 5i + 3$

17. What is the sum of $\sum_{n=1}^{7} 4n^2$?
(p. 799, prob. 45–56)

(1) 196

(2) 364

(3) 560

(4) 816

Strand A Algebra

A2.A.1 Solve absolute value equations and inequalities involving linear expressions in one variable

18. Which of the following graphs shows solutions for $3x + 6 \geq 7x - 2$?
(p. 45, prob. 28–33)

(1) 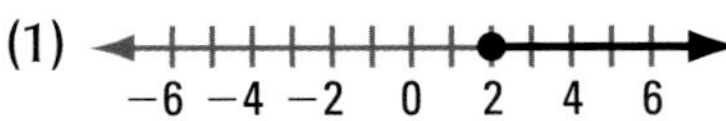

(2) 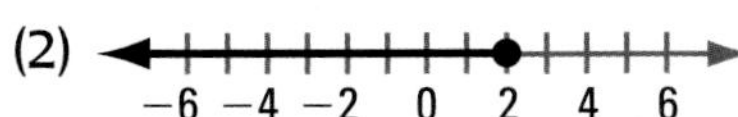

(3) −6 −4 −2 0 2 4 6

(4) −6 −4 −2 0 2 4 6

19. What is the solution of $|4x + 6| = 10$?
(p. 55, prob. 21–32)

(1) $-4, 1$

(2) $-4, -1$

(3) $1, 4$

(4) $4, -1$

A2.A.2 Use the discriminant to determine the nature of the roots of a quadratic equation

20. Which of the following describes the solutions of $3x^2 + 8x + 7$?
(p. 296, prob. 31–39)

(1) one real solution

(2) two real solutions

(3) one imaginary solution

(4) two imaginary solutions

Go On 

A2.A.4 Solve quadratic inequalities in one and two variables, algebraically and graphically

21. What is the solution of $x^2 - 2x - 35 > 0$? *(p. 305, prob. 44–45)*

(1) $-5 < x < 7$

(2) $-7 < x < 5$

(3) $x > 5$ or $x < -7$

(4) $x > 7$ or $x < -5$

22. Which of the following inequalities is represented by the graph shown? *(p. 304, prob. 3–5)*

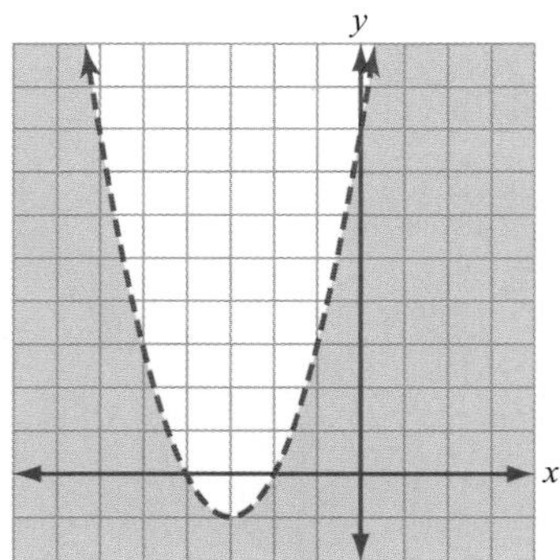

(1) $y < x^2 - 6x + 8$

(2) $y > x^2 - 6x + 8$

(3) $y < x^2 + 6x + 8$

(4) $y > x^2 + 6x + 8$

A2.A.5 Use direct and inverse variation to solve for unknown values

23. The Gray-cheeked Thrush migrates from Louisiana to Alaska each year. If the bird travels 1040 miles in 8 days, which equation relates the distance traveled m and the number of days traveled d? *(p. 110, prob. 38–40)*

(1) $d = 8m$

(2) $d = 130m$

(3) $m = 8d$

(4) $m = 130d$

24. The time it takes to get to school varies inversely with the speed at which a student travels. A student travels 3.5 miles per hour and arrives at school in 15 minutes. If the student travels at 4.2 miles per hour, how long will it take the student to reach school? *(p. 555, prob. 12–19)*

(1) 12 minutes

(2) 12.5 minutes

(3) 13 minutes

(4) 13.5 minutes

A2.A.6 Solve an application which results in an exponential function

25. You deposit a sum of $500 in your savings account. The account pays 4% annual interest compounded quarterly. After what year will the balance exceed $800? *(p. 521, prob. 56)*

(1) the 10th year

(2) the 11th year

(3) the 12th year

(4) the 13th year

Go On 

Strand A Algebra

A2.A.8 Apply the rules of exponents to simplify expressions involving negative and/or fractional exponents

26. Which of the following is equivalent to $\frac{x^3y^{-2}z^{-4}}{x^{-3}y^5z^{-1}}$? *(p. 333, prob. 24–35)*

(1) $\frac{z^5}{y^3}$

(2) $\frac{1}{y^2z^3}$

(3) $\frac{x^6y^3}{z^3}$

(4) $\frac{x^6}{y^7z^3}$

A2.A.9 Rewrite algebraic expressions that contain negative exponents using only positive exponents

27. Which of the following is equivalent to $8^{-2/3}$? *(p. 417, prob.38)*

(1) $\frac{1}{16}$

(2) $\frac{1}{4}$

(3) $\frac{16}{3}$

(4) 4

A2.A.11 Rewrite algebraic expressions in radical form as expressions with fractional exponents

28. Which of the following is equivalent to $\sqrt[4]{8^3}$? *(p. 417, prob. 7–10)*

(1) $4^{3/8}$

(2) $4^{8/3}$

(3) $8^{3/4}$

(4) $8^{4/3}$

A2.A.13 Simplify radical expressions

29. What is the product of $\sqrt{27}$ and $\sqrt{12}$? *(p. 269, prob. 3–14)*

(1) $\sqrt{15}$

(2) $\sqrt{39}$

(3) 18

(4) 39

30. What is $\sqrt{\frac{1}{16}}$ in simplest form? *(p. 269, prob. 3–14)*

(1) $\frac{1}{8}$

(2) $\frac{1}{4}$

(3) 4

(4) 8

Go On 

A2.A.13 Simplify radical expressions

Use the following information for questions 31 and 32.

The figure below is a rectangle with measurements as shown.

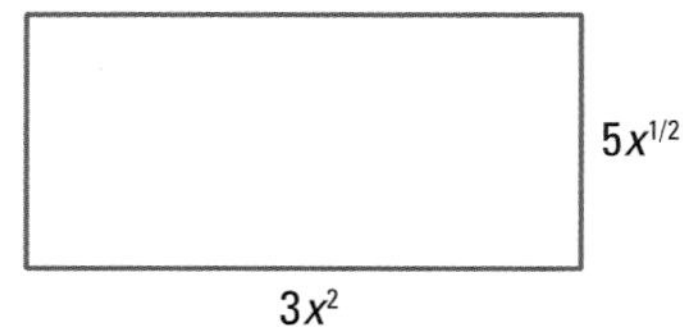

31. Which expression represents the area of the rectangle? *(p. 425, prob. 66–68)*

(1) $8x$
(2) $8x^{5/2}$
(3) $15x$
(4) $15x^{5/2}$

32. Which expression represents the perimeter of the rectangle? *(p. 425, prob. 66–68)*

(1) $16x$
(2) $16x^{3/2}$
(3) $6x^2 + 10x^{1/2}$
(4) $6x^4 + 10x$

A2.A.14 Perform addition, subtraction, multiplication and division of radical expressions

33. What is the simplest form of $4\sqrt[3]{54} \cdot \left(8\sqrt[3]{6}\right)$? *(p. 424, prob. 23)*

(1) $\sqrt[3]{12}$
(2) $32\sqrt[3]{12}$
(3) $96\sqrt[3]{12}$
(4) $288\sqrt[3]{12}$

A2.A.16 Perform arithmetic operations with rational expressions and rename to lowest terms

34. What is the simplified form of $\dfrac{x^2 + x - 12}{x^2 - 9}$? *(p. 577, prob. 6–17)*

(1) $-\dfrac{4}{3}$
(2) $x + 4$
(3) $\dfrac{x + 4}{x + 3}$
(4) $\dfrac{x - 12}{-9}$

35. Which of the following is equivalent to $\dfrac{3}{4x} + \dfrac{7}{5x}$? *(p. 586, prob. 16–24)*

(1) $\dfrac{10}{9x}$
(2) $\dfrac{10}{9x^2}$
(3) $\dfrac{43}{9x}$
(4) $\dfrac{43}{20x}$

A2.A.18 Evaluate logarithmic expressions in any base

36. What is $\log_5 \dfrac{1}{25}$? *(p. 503, prob. 8–19)*

(1) -5
(2) -2
(3) 2
(4) 5

Go On

Strand A Algebra

A2.A.19 Apply the properties of logarithms to rewrite logarithmic expressions in equivalent forms

37. Which of the following is equivalent to $5 \log_3 x - 7 \log_3 y$? *(p. 510, prob. 35–42)*

(1) $\log_3 \frac{x^5}{y^7}$

(2) $\log_3 \frac{y^7}{x^5}$

(3) $\log_3 \frac{5^x}{7^y}$

(4) $\log_3 \frac{7^y}{5^x}$

A2.A.24 Know and apply the technique of completing the square

38. What value of c will make $x^2 + 12x + c$ a perfect square trinomial?
(p. 288, prob. 13–21)

(1) 6

(2) 12

(3) 36

(4) 144

A2.A.27 Solve exponential equations with and without common bases

39. What is the solution of $81^{4x+1} = \left(\frac{1}{3}\right)^{2x-2}$? *(p. 519, prob. 3–11)*

(1) $-\frac{1}{9}$

(2) $-\frac{1}{3}$

(3) $\frac{1}{3}$

(4) $\frac{1}{9}$

A2.A.28 Solve a logarithmic equation by rewriting as an exponential equation

40. Which of the following is closest to the solution of $5 \log_6 (3x - 1) = 8$?
(p. 520, prob. 32–44)

(1) 0.69

(2) 1.35

(3) 5.53

(4) 6.19

A2.A.29 Identify an arithmetic or geometric sequence and find the formula for its *n*th term

41. Which rule can be used to find the nth term of the sequence 3, 5, 7, 9, . . .?
(p. 798, prob. 15–27)

(1) $a_n = 2n - 1$

(2) $a_n = 2n + 1$

(3) $a_n = 4n - 1$

(4) $a_n = 4n + 1$

42. Which rule can be used to find the nth term of the sequence $\frac{1}{2}, \frac{2}{3}, \frac{3}{4}, \frac{4}{5}, \ldots$?
(p. 798, prob. 15–27)

(1) $a_n = \frac{n}{n+1}$

(2) $a_n = \frac{1}{n}$

(3) $a_n = \frac{n-1}{n}$

(4) $a_n = \frac{n+1}{n+2}$

Go On

A2.A.30 Determine the common difference in an arithmetic sequence

43. Look at the sequence below:

1.25, 0.75, 0.25, −0.25, . . .

Which of the following is true? *(p. 806, prob. 3–11)*

(1) The sequence is arithmetic with a common difference of −0.5.

(2) The sequence is arithmetic with a common difference of −0.25.

(3) The sequence is arithmetic with a common difference of 0.5.

(4) The sequence is not arithmetic.

A2.A.31 Determine the common ratio in a geometric sequence

44. Look at the sequence below:

$\frac{1}{2}, \frac{1}{4}, \frac{1}{6}, \frac{1}{8}, \ldots$

Which of the following is true? *(p. 814, prob. 3–14)*

(1) The sequence is geometric with a common ratio of $\frac{1}{4}$.

(2) The sequence is geometric with a common ratio of $\frac{1}{2}$.

(3) The sequence is geometric with a common ratio of 2.

(4) The sequence is not geometric.

A2.A.32 Determine a specified term of an arithmetic or geometric sequence

45. The second term of a geometric sequence is 8 and the first term is 2. What is the fifth term? *(p. 814, prob. 28–36)*

(1) 26

(2) 32

(3) 128

(4) 512

A2.A.33 Specify terms of a sequence, given its recursive definition

46. If $a_1 = 3$ is the first term of a sequence and $a_n = 5 - a_{n-1}$, what are the next 3 terms of the sequence? *(p. 833, prob. 7–9)*

(1) 2, −1, −4

(2) 2, 3, 2

(3) −2, −7, −13

(4) 2, 1, 0

Go On 

Strand A Algebra

A2.A.35 Determine the sum of the first n terms of an arithmetic or geometric series

47. What is the sum of the series $\sum_{i=1}^{10}(4 - 3i)$? (p. 807, prob. 40–45)

(1) -126

(2) -125

(3) -99

(4) -26

A2.A.36 Apply the binomial theorem to expand a binomial and determine a specific term of a binomial expansion

48. What is the coefficient of x^3 in the expansion of $(x + 6)^8$? (p. 695, prob. 32–34)

(1) 7,776

(2) 12,096

(3) 435,456

(4) 1,679,616

A2.A.37 Define a relation and function

49. The relation given by the ordered pairs $(-2, 3)$, $(6, 1)$, $(4, -8)$, and $(0, 3)$ is a function. Which ordered pair could be included in this relation so that it is still a function? (p. 77, prob. 16–20)

(1) (0, 4)

(2) (6, 3)

(3) (3, 0)

(4) $(-2, 8)$

50. What is the domain of the relation $(-5, 2)$, $(-3, 7)$, $(-1, 1)$, and $(5, 8)$? (p. 76, prob. 3–8)

(1) $-3, 4, 0, 13$

(2) $-5, -3, -1, 5$

(3) 1, 2, 7, 8

(4) $-3, 1, 7, 6$

51. What is the range of the relation (5, 10), (15, 25), (30, 40), and (45, 80)? (p. 76, prob. 3–8)

(1) 5, 15, 30, 45

(2) 10, 25, 40, 80

(3) 5, 10, 15, 25

(4) 30, 40, 45, 80

Go On

A2.A.38 Determine when a relation is a function

52. Which table represents a relation that is a function? *(p. 77, prob. 16–20)*

(1)

x	−7	2	3	6
y	6	2	2	6

(2)

x	−2	3	2	−2
y	5	5	5	5

(3)

x	1	1	2	2
y	7	8	9	−1

(4)

x	−3	4	−3	2
y	0	1	10	9

A2.A.41 Use functional notation to evaluate functions for given values in the domain

54. A population of rabbits in a certain park increased rapidly from 1950 to 1960 due to an absence of predators. For a short period of time, the population of rabbits could be approximated by $f(x) = -0.1x^5 + 2.1x^4 + 1200$, where x is the number of years after 1950. What was the population of rabbits in this park in 1956? *(p. 343, prob. 54)*

(1) 2200

(2) 3144

(3) 4561

(4) 6525

A2.A.39 Determine the domain and range of a function from its equation

53. Which of the following describes the domain and range of the equation $y = \frac{8}{x-3}$? *(p. 561, prob. 11–22)*

(1) The domain is all real numbers except −3. The range is all real numbers except 0.

(2) The domain is all real numbers except −3. The range is all real numbers except −8.

(3) The domain is all real numbers except 3. The range is all real numbers except −3.

(4) The domain is all real numbers except 3. The range is all real numbers except 0.

A2.A.42 Find the composition of functions

Use the following information for questions 55 and 56.

$f(x) = 4x + 1 \quad g(x) = x - 3 \quad h(x) = \frac{x^2}{x-3}$

55. What is $f(g(2))$? *(p. 432, prob. 20–27)*

(1) −5

(2) −3

(3) −1

(4) 3

56. What is $h(g(-3))$? *(p. 432, prob. 20–27)*

(1) −12

(2) −4

(3) 0

(4) 4

Go On 

Strand A Algebra

A2.A.46 Perform transformations with functions and relations: $f(x + a)$, $f(x) + a$, $f(-x)$, $-f(x)$, $af(x)$

57. The highest point on the graph of $y = f(x)$ is $(-2, 5)$. What is the highest point on the graph of $y = f(x + 2) + 4$? *(p. 127, prob. 28)*

(1) $(0, 1)$

(2) $(0, 9)$

(3) $(-4, 1)$

(4) $(-4, 9)$

A2.A.48 Write the equation of a circle, given its center and a point on the circle

58. What is the equation in standard form of the circle that passes through $(4, -8)$ and is centered at the origin? *(p. 630, prob. 31–42)*

(1) $x^2 + y^2 = 80$

(2) $x^2 + y^2 = \sqrt{80}$

(3) $x^2 + y^2 = 32$

(4) $x^2 + y^2 = \sqrt{32}$

A2.A.49 Write the equation of a circle from its graph

59. Which equation represents the graph of the circle below? *(p. 629, prob. 3–8)*

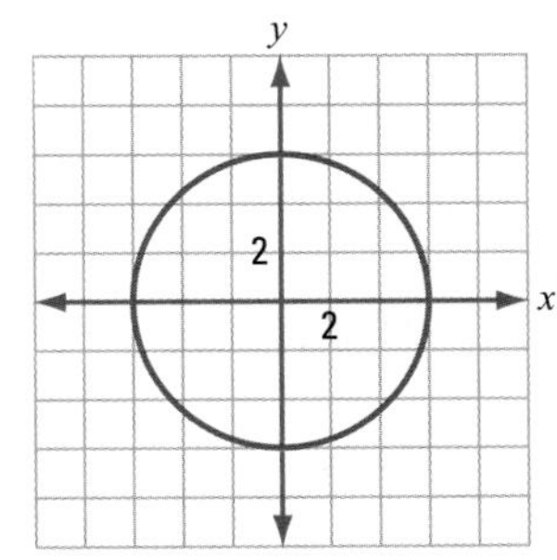

(1) $x^2 + y^2 = 3$

(2) $x^2 + y^2 = 6$

(3) $x^2 + y^2 = 9$

(4) $x^2 + y^2 = 36$

A2.A.51 Determine the domain and range of a function from its graph

60. What are the domain and range of the function $y = -3\sqrt{x}$? *(p. 449, prob. 3–8)*

(1) domain: $x \geq 0$; range: $y \geq 0$

(2) domain: $x \geq 0$; range: $y \leq 0$

(3) domain: $x \leq 0$; range: $y \geq 0$

(4) domain: $x \leq 0$; range: $y \leq 0$

61. Which of the following functions has a domain of all real numbers and a range of $y > -3$? *(p. 489, prob. 16–24)*

(1) $y = -3^x$

(2) $y = \left(\frac{1}{4}\right)^x$

(3) $y = \left(\frac{1}{4}\right)^x - 3$

(4) $y = \left(\frac{1}{4}\right)^x + 3$

Go On 

A2.A.52 Identify relations and functions, using graphs

62. Which graph represents a relation that is not a function? *(p. 77, prob. 21–23)*

(1)
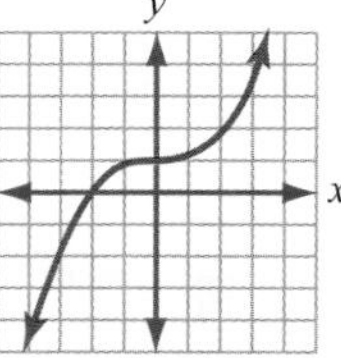

(2)
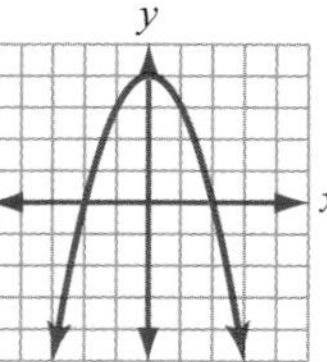

(3)
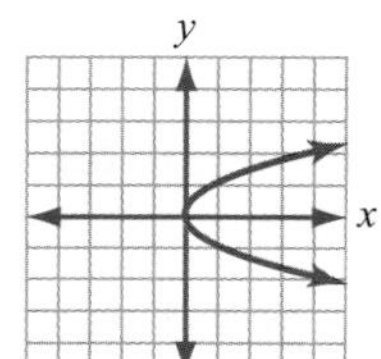

(4)
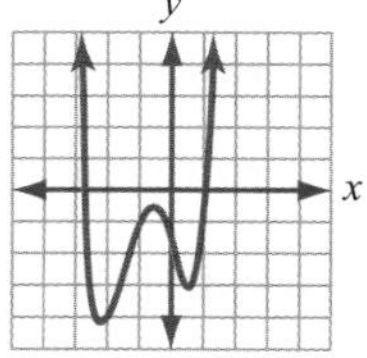

A2.A.54 Graph logarithmic functions, using the inverse of the related exponential function

63. The graph below shows the function $y = 3^x$.

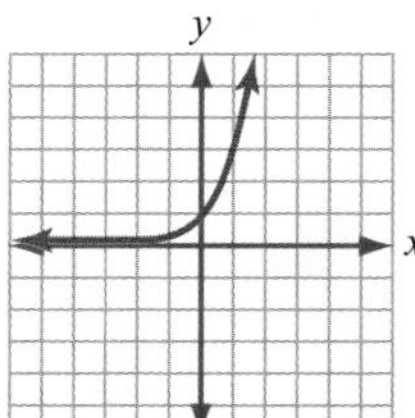

Which of the following graphs shows the inverse of $y = 3^x$? *(p. 504, prob. 37–44)*

(1)
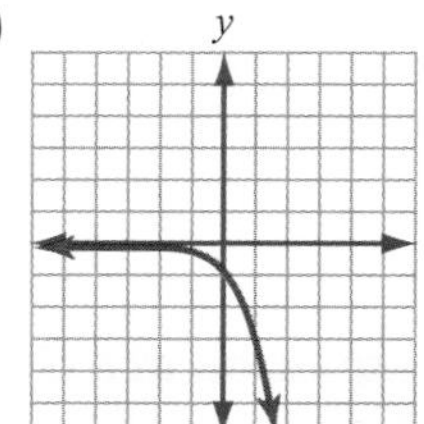

(2)
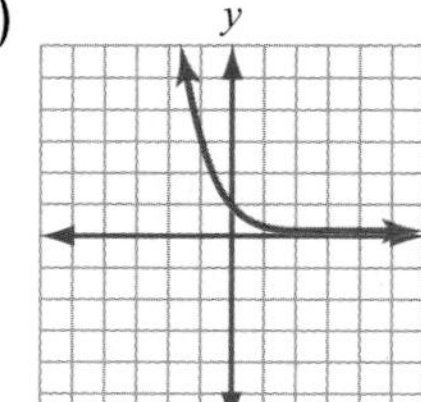

(3)
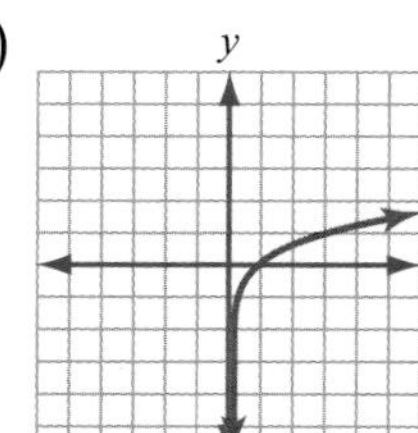

(4)
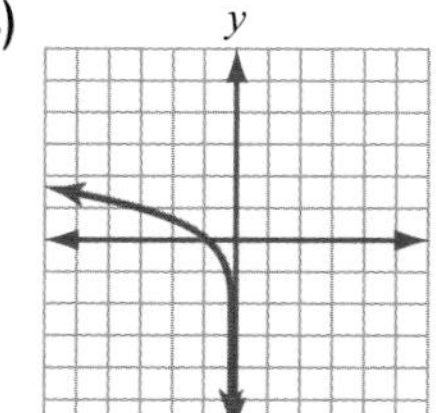

Go On 

A2.A.55 Express and apply the six trigonometric functions as ratios of the sides of a right triangle

Use the following information for questions 64 and 65.

Let θ be the acute angle of a right triangle and cos θ be $\frac{15}{17}$.

64. What is the tangent of θ? *(p. 856, prob. 9–14)*

(1) $\frac{8}{17}$

(2) $\frac{8}{15}$

(3) $\frac{15}{8}$

(4) $\frac{17}{15}$

65. What is the cosecant of θ? *(p. 856, prob. 9–14)*

(1) $\frac{8}{17}$

(2) $\frac{17}{15}$

(3) $\frac{15}{8}$

(4) $\frac{17}{8}$

A2.A.56 Know the exact and approximate values of the sine, cosine, and tangent of 0°, 30°, 45°, 60°, 90°, 180°, and 270° angles

66. What is tangent of 30? *(p. 871, prob. 24–31)*

(1) $\frac{1}{2}$

(2) $\frac{\sqrt{3}}{3}$

(3) $\frac{\sqrt{2}}{2}$

(4) $\frac{\sqrt{3}}{2}$

67. What is cos $(-150°)$? *(p. 871, prob. 12–15)*

(1) $-\frac{\sqrt{3}}{2}$

(2) $-\frac{1}{2}$

(3) $\frac{1}{2}$

(4) $\frac{\sqrt{3}}{2}$

COUNTDOWN *to* REGENTS EXAM

Go On 

A2.A.57 Sketch and use the reference angle for angles in standard position

68. What is the reference angle for an angle measuring 225°? *(p. 871, prob. 16–23)*

(1) $-135°$

(2) $-45°$

(3) $45°$

(4) $135°$

A2.A.58 Know and apply the co-function and reciprocal relationships between trigonometric ratios

69. If $\sin \theta = \frac{2}{3}$ and $0 < \theta < \frac{\pi}{2}$, what is the value of $\cos \theta$? *(p. 927, prob. 3–8)*

(1) $\frac{\sqrt{5}}{9}$

(2) $\frac{2}{3}$

(3) $\frac{\sqrt{5}}{3}$

(4) $\frac{3}{2}$

A2.A.59 Use the reciprocal and co-function relationships to find the value of the secant, cosecant, and cotangent of 0°, 30°, 45°, 60°, 90°, 180°, and 270° angles

70. If sin 30° is $\frac{1}{2}$, what is the cosecant of 30°? *(p. 928, prob. 9)*

(1) $\frac{1}{2}$

(2) $\frac{\sqrt{3}}{2}$

(3) 1

(4) 2

A2.A.61 Determine the length of an arc of a circle, given its radius and the measure of its central angle

71. A sector has a radius of 5 m with a central angle of 90°. What is the length of the arc of the circle? *(p. 863, prob. 32–37)*

(1) 1.3 m

(2) 5.9 m

(3) 7.9 m

(4) 15.7 m

Go On 

Strand A Algebra

A2.A.63 Restrict the domain of the sine, cosine, and tangent functions to ensure the existence of an inverse function

72. Which of the following is undefined? *(p. 878, prob. 2)*

(1) $\sin^{-1} 1$

(2) $\cos^{-1} -1$

(3) $\tan^{-1} 2$

(4) $\sin^{-1} 2$

A2.A.64 Use inverse functions to find the measure of an angle, given its sine, cosine, or tangent

73. What is the measure of θ in the triangle below? *(p. 878, prob. 27–29)*

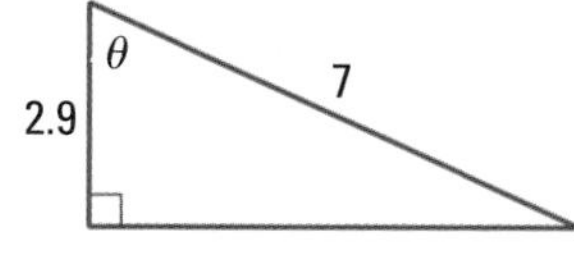

(1) 22.5°

(2) 24.5°

(3) 62.5°

(4) 65.5°

A2.A.66 Determine the trigonometric functions of any angle, using technology

74. A flagpole casts the shadow shown. What is the height of the flagpole rounded to the nearest whole number? *(p. 857, prob. 30)*

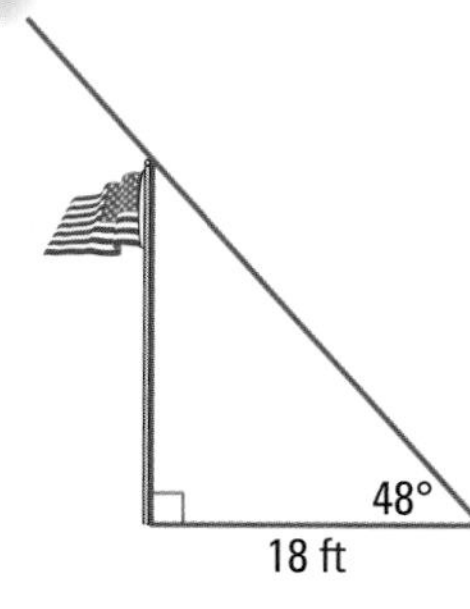

(1) 20 ft

(2) 22 ft

(3) 24 ft

(4) 26 ft

A2.A.68 Solve trigonometric equations for all values of the variable from 0° to 360°

75. Which of the following is a solution for the equation $4 + 3 \cos x - 1 = 0$? *(p. 935, prob. 3–8)*

(1) $\frac{\pi}{4}$

(2) $\frac{\pi}{2}$

(3) π

(4) 2π

Go On

COUNTDOWN *to* REGENTS EXAM

A2.A.70 Sketch and recognize one cycle of a function of the form $y = A \sin Bx$ or $y = A \cos Bx$

76. The graph below shows which of the following functions? *(p. 913, prob. 6–13)*

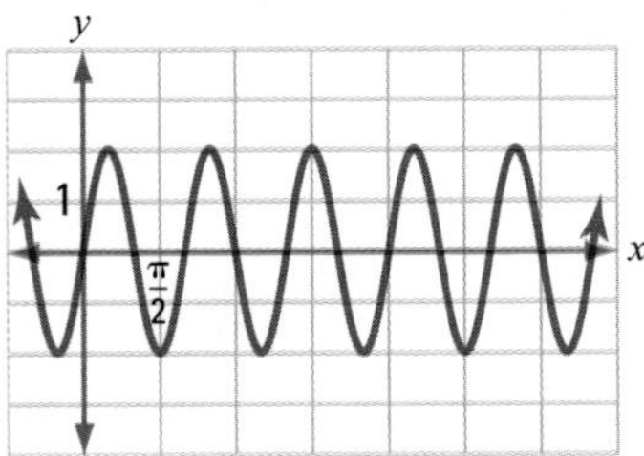

(1) 2 sin 3x

(2) 3 sin 2x

(3) 2 cos 3x

(4) 3 cos 2x

A2.A.71 Sketch and recognize the graphs of the functions $y = \sec(x)$, $y = \csc(x)$, $y = \tan(x)$, and $y = \cot(x)$

77. The graph below shows which of the following functions? *(p. 913, prob. 26–28)*

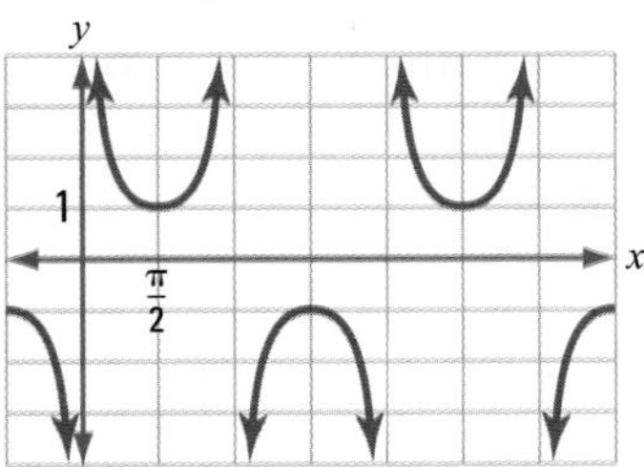

(1) sec x

(2) csc x

(3) tan x

(4) cot x

A2.A.73 Solve for an unknown side or angle, using the Law of Sines or the Law of Cosines

Use the following information to answer questions 78 and 79.

Look at the triangle below.

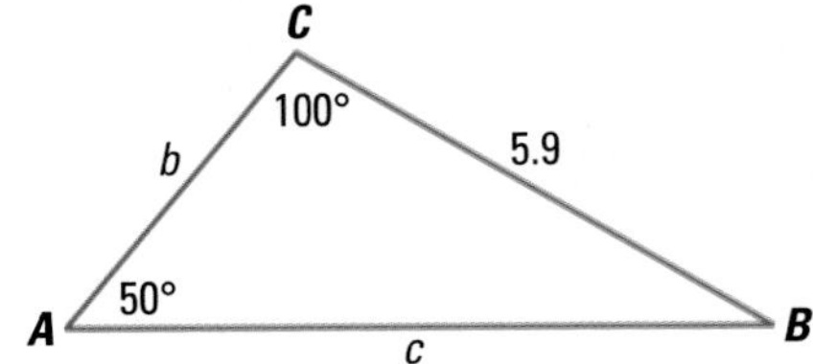

78. What is the value of c to the nearest tenth? *(p. 886, prob. 18–26)*

(1) 4.5

(2) 4.6

(3) 5.8

(4) 7.6

79. What is the value of b to the nearest tenth? *(p. 886, prob. 18–26)*

(1) 2.7

(2) 3.9

(3) 4.6

(4) 7.9

Go On 

Strand A Algebra

A2.A.77 Apply the double-angle and half-angle formulas for trigonometric functions

80. Which of the following is the exact value of $\cos \frac{5\pi}{12}$? *(p. 959, prob. 3–10)*

(1) $-\frac{\sqrt{2-\sqrt{3}}}{2}$

(2) $-\frac{\sqrt{2+\sqrt{3}}}{2}$

(3) $\frac{\sqrt{2-\sqrt{3}}}{2}$

(4) $\frac{\sqrt{2+\sqrt{3}}}{2}$

Strand M Measurement

A2.M.2 Convert between radian and degree measures

81. Which of the following is the equivalent degree measure for $\frac{7\pi}{3}$? *(p. 863, prob. 23–30)*

(1) 120°

(2) 300°

(3) 420°

(4) 450°

COUNTDOWN *to* REGENTS EXAM

Go On 

A2.S.6 Determine from a scatter plot whether a linear, logarithmic, exponential, or power regression model is most appropriate

82. Which type of function best models the data points shown? *(p. 778, prob. 5)*

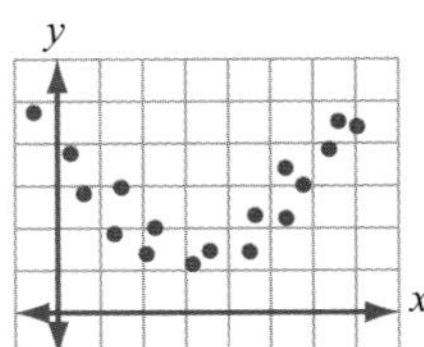

(1) Linear

(2) Quadratic

(3) Cubic

(4) Exponential

A2.S.8 Interpret within the linear regression model the value of the correlation coefficient as a measure of the strength of the relationship

83. The graph shows a line of best fit drawn for the data in the scatter plot. What is the best prediction of the value of y when $x = 14$? *(p. 119, prob. 26–28)*

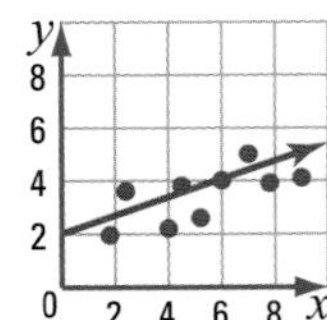

(1) 6

(2) 10

(3) 14

(4) 20

84. The graph shows a line of best fit drawn for the data in the scatter plot. What is the best prediction of the value of y when $x = 30$? *(p. 119, prob. 26–28)*

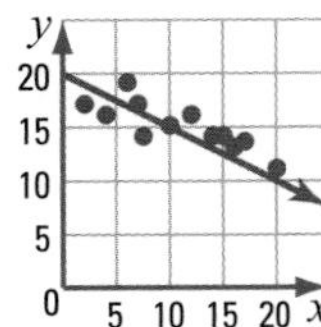

(1) 5

(2) 9

(3) 15

(4) 25

Go On

Strand S Statistics and Probability

A2.S.8 Interpret within the linear regression model the value of the correlation coefficient as a measure of the strength of the relationship

85. Which scatter plot shows data with a positive correlation? *(p. 117, prob. 3–5)*

(1)
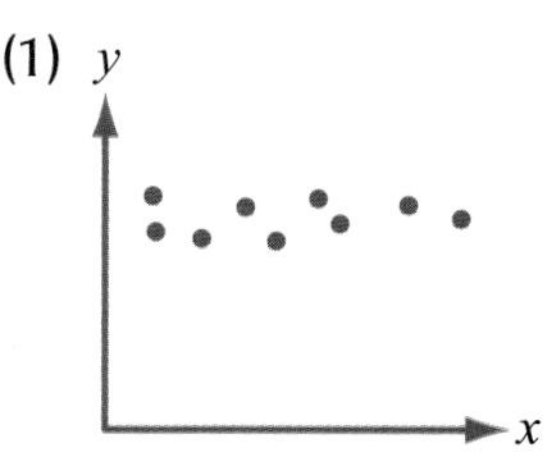

(2)
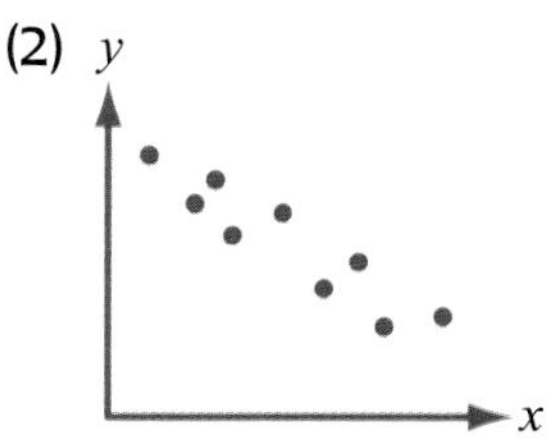

(3)
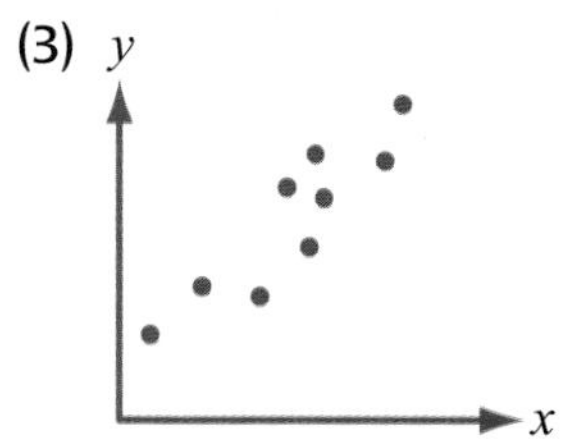

(4)
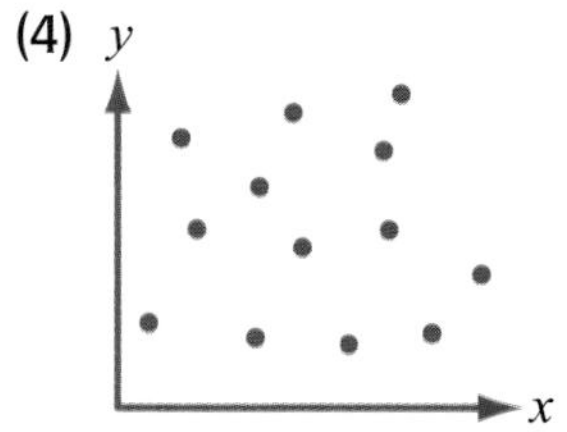

A2.S.9 Differentiate between situations requiring permutations and those requiring combinations

86. A race is run with 10 people. You are required to find how many different ways the race can be won. Which of the following requires combinations to find the answer? *(p. 695, prob. 38–39)*

(1) The top 3 runners win a blue ribbon.

(2) Different prizes are awarded for 1st, 2nd and 3rd place.

(3) Blue ribbons are awarded for first place. Red ribbons are awarded for second place.

(4) A medal is awarded for 1st place and a ribbon is awarded for second place.

Go On

A2.S.10 Calculate the number of possible permutations ($_nP_r$) of n items taken r at a time

87. What is $_8P_2$? *(p. 687, prob. 30–41)*

(1) 16

(2) 28

(3) 56

(4) 64

88. Which of the following is used to find $_5P_4$? *(p. 687, prob. 30–41)*

(1) $\frac{4!}{(5-4)!}$

(2) $\frac{4!}{5!-4!}$

(3) $\frac{5!}{5!-4!}$

(4) $\frac{5!}{(5-4)!}$

89. What is the number of distinguishable permutations of the letters in the word GREEN? *(p. 687, prob. 43–55)*

(1) 20

(2) 60

(3) 120

(4) 240

A2.S.11 Calculate the number of possible combinations ($_nC_r$) of n items taken r at a time

90. An ice cream shop has 45 flavors of ice cream. A customer would like to order 3 scoops of different kinds of ice cream. How many different ways can the customer order the 3 scoops? *(p. 695, prob. 39)*

(1) 11,480

(2) 14,190

(3) 85,140

(4) 91,125

A2.S.12 Use permutations, combinations, and the Fundamental Principle of Counting to determine the number of elements in a sample space and a specific subset (event)

91. A furniture store sells a piece of furniture that comes in 4 different types of wood and 3 different sizes. How many possible different pieces of furniture are there? *(p. 686, prob.3–8)*

(1) 6

(2) 7

(3) 12

(4) 16

Go On

Strand S Statistics and Probability

A2.S.13 Calculate theoretical probabilities, including geometric applications

92. What is the probability that an object thrown at the target will hit the shaded region? *(p. 703, prob. 35–37)*

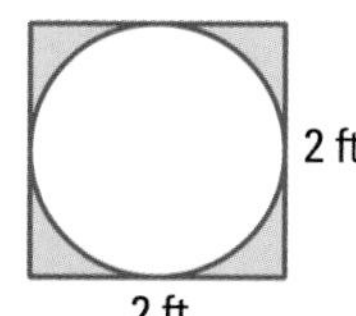

(1) 0.21

(2) 0.43

(3) 0.57

(4) 0.80

93. What is the probability that an object thrown at the target will hit the shaded region? *(p. 703, prob. 35–37)*

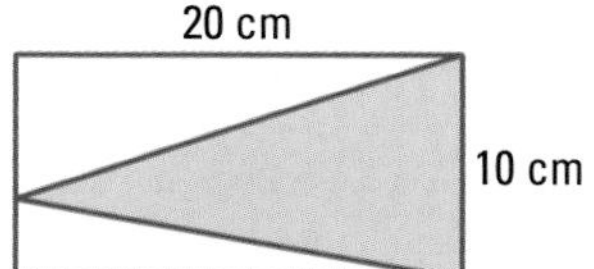

(1) $\frac{1}{4}$

(2) $\frac{1}{3}$

(3) $\frac{1}{2}$

(4) $\frac{3}{4}$

A2.S.14 Calculate empirical probabilities

94. The results of spinning a spinner 120 times are shown. From the table, what is the experimental probability of spinning an even number? (Assume the outcomes are equally likely.) *(p. 702, prob. 28–32)*

Spin	1	2	3	4	5	6	7	8
Number of Occurences	14	16	5	12	11	25	10	27

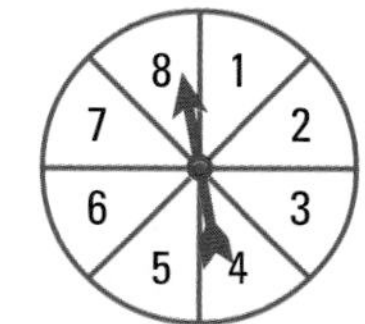

(1) $\frac{1}{2}$ (3) $\frac{3}{4}$

(2) $\frac{2}{3}$ (4) $\frac{5}{6}$

95. A survey was conducted to find out how 10th graders at Oliver School get to school. The results are shown in the bar graph. What is the experimental probability that a randomly selected 10th grader gets to school by public transportation? *(p. 700, Example 4)*

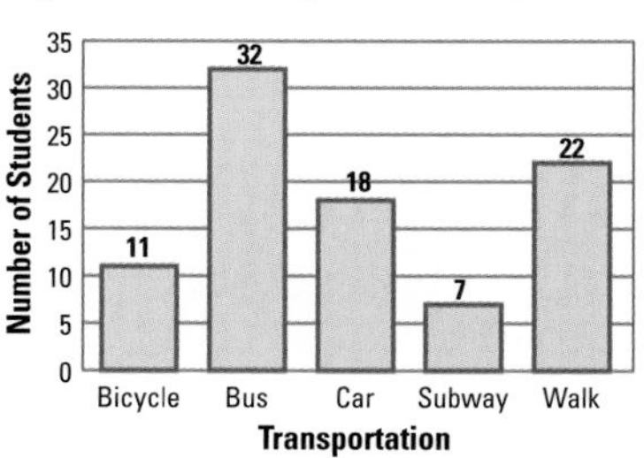

(1) about 0.2 (3) about 0.433

(2) about 0.356 (4) about 0.756

Go On 

COUNTDOWN *to* REGENTS EXAM

Strand S Statistics and Probability

A2.S.15 Know and apply the binomial probability formula to events involving the terms exactly, at least, and at most

96. Your school is having a raffle. The probability of winning is 3%. What is the probability that exactly 1 person in your class of 30 will win the raffle? *(p. 729, prob. 43)*

(1) 0.363

(2) 0.372

(3) 0.480

(4) 0.900

A2.S.16 Use the normal distribution as an approximation for binomial probabilities

97. One study has shown that about 8% of drivers own yellow cars. A local town has 500 drivers. Using a normal approximation, what is the probability that at most 31 drivers will own yellow cars? *(p. 765, prob. 19–22)*

(1) 0.06

(2) 0.07

(3) 0.89

(4) 0.93

Strand N Number Sense and Operations

A2.N.4 Perform arithmetic operations on irrational expressions

98. **(OE)** What is the simplified form of $\frac{6}{7}\sqrt[4]{9} - \frac{2}{7}\sqrt[4]{9}$? *(p. 424, prob. 32–40)*

Go On

Strand A Algebra

A2.A.1 Solve absolute value equations and inequalities involving linear expressions in one variable

99. (OE) A restaurant was serving coffee at a temperature between 180°F and 190°F. What is the absolute value inequality for this temperature range? *(p. 57, prob. 79)*

A2.A.3 Solve systems of equations involving one linear equation and one quadratic equation algebraically Note: This includes rational equations that result in linear equations with extraneous roots.

100. (OE) What are the solutions of the functions $y = 6x^2 + 3x$ and $y = -3x + 7$? Round answers to the nearest hundredth. *(p. 661, prob. 9–20)*

A2.A.7 Factor polynomial expressions completely, using any combination of the following techniques: common factor extraction, difference of two perfect squares, quadratic trinomials

101. (OE) What is the complete factorization of $24x^3 - 30x^2 - 9x$? *(p. 357, prob. 42–50)*

A2.A.12 Evaluate exponential expressions, including those with base *e*

102. (OE) What is the value of $3x - (2x - 1)^2$ when $x = 4$? *(p. 14, prob. 16–23)*

A2.A.17 Simplify complex fractional expressions

103. (OE) What is the simplified form of

$$\frac{\frac{8}{x+3}}{\frac{2}{x+3}+\frac{5}{x}}?$$

(p. 587, prob. 31–36)

A2.A.19 Apply the properties of logarithms to rewrite logarithmic expressions in equivalent forms

104. (OE) What is the simplified form of $\log 5 + 2 \log 3 - \log 9$? *(p. 510, prob. 33–42)*

Go On

A2.A.25 Solve quadratic equations, using the quadratic formula

105. (OE) What are the solutions of the equation $4x^2 + 16x + 15 = 0$?
(p. 296, prob. 22–30)

A2.A.26 Find the solution to polynomial equations of higher degree that can be solved using factoring and/or the quadratic formula

106. (OE) What are all the solutions of $x^3 - x^2 - 9x + 9 = 0$? *(p. 384, prob. 10–19)*

A2.A.34 Represent the sum of a series, using sigma notation

107. (OE) Write the summation notation for the series $9 + 13 + 17 + 21 + \ldots$
(p. 798, prob. 37–44)

A2.A.44 Define the inverse of a function

108. (OE) Find the inverse of $y = 5x + 2$. Explain. *(p. 442, prob. 3–11)*

A2.A.50 Approximate the solution to polynomial equations of higher degree by inspecting the graph

109. (OE) What are the approximate solutions of the graph shown?
(p. 390, prob. 15–20)

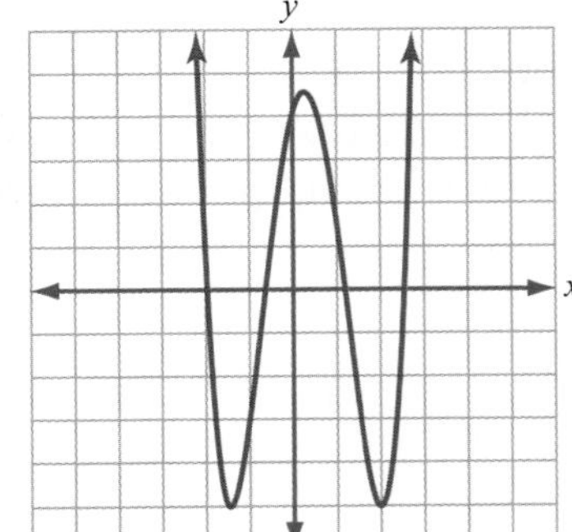

Go On

Strand A Algebra

Strand S Statistics and Probability

A2.A.51 Determine the domain and range of a function from its graph

110. (OE) What are the domain and range of the function $h(x) = \frac{4}{x-3} + 5$? *(p. 561, prob. 11–22)*

A2.A.72 Write the trigonometric function that is represented by a given periodic graph

111. (OE) What is the function for the sinusoid shown below? *(p. 944, prob. 3–6)*

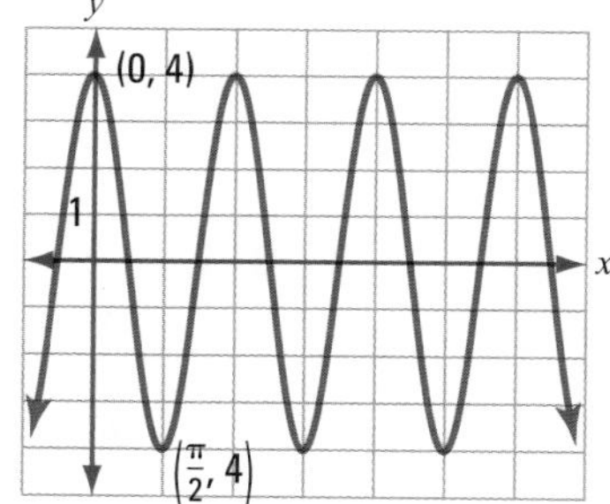

A2.S.2 Determine factors which may affect the outcome of a survey

112. (OE) National park rangers would like to know if more bike paths are needed in the park. Rangers survey people driving into the park. What is a factor that might affect the outcome of this survey? *(p. 769, prob. 3–5)*

Go On

A2.A.22 Solve radical equations

113. **(OE)** Solve the equation $x + 3 = \sqrt{7x + 29}$. Show how to check for extraneous roots. *(p. 457, prob. 34–42)*

A2.A.23 Solve rational equations and inequalities

114. **(OE)** You own a catering business and it takes you 3 hours to do the prep work for an event. It takes your friend 5 hours to complete the prep work for the same event. The equation $\frac{1}{3} + \frac{1}{5} = \frac{1}{t}$ is used to find the amount of time it will take to do the prep work if you and your friend work together. How long will it take you and your friend to complete the prep work? Show your work. *(p. 594, prob. 36)*

A2.A.62 Find the value of trigonometric functions, if given a point on the terminal side of angle θ

115. **(OE)** Let $(-5, 12)$ be a point on the terminal side of an angle θ in standard position. Evaluate the six trigonometric functions of θ. *(p. 870, prob. 3–10)*

A2.A.69 Determine amplitude, period, frequency, and phase shift, given the graph or equation of a periodic function

116. **(OE)** A graph is given by $y = \sin 6x$.

What is the amplitude of the function?

What is the period of the function?

(p. 913, prob. 15)

A2.A.74 Determine the area of a triangle or a parallelogram, given the measure of two sides and the included angle

117. **(OE)** What is the area of $\triangle ABC$? Show your work. *(p. 887, prob. 29–37)*

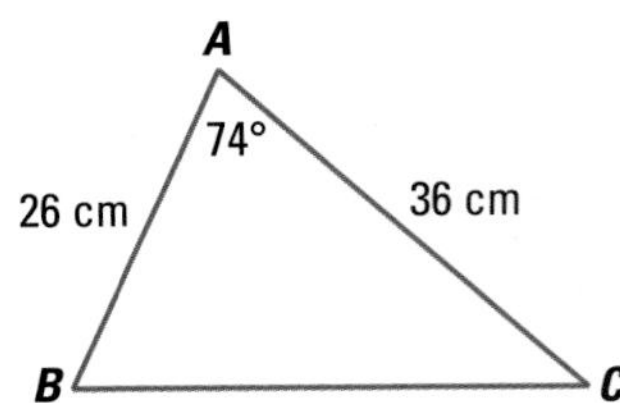

Go On

Strand S Statistics and Probability

A2.S.5 Know and apply the characteristics of the normal distribution

118. (OE) A normal distribution has a mean of 85 and a standard deviation of 2. Using the Standard Normal Table, what is the probability that a randomly selected x-value is at least 88? Show your work. *(p. 760, prob. 11–16)*

Standard Normal Table

z	.0	.1	.2	.3	.4	.5	.6	.7	.8	.9
−3	.0013	.0010	.0007	.0005	.0003	.0002	.0002	.0001	.0001	.0000+
−2	.0228	.0179	.0139	.0107	.0082	.0062	.0548	.0035	.0026	.0019
−1	.1587	.1357	.1151	.0968	.0808	.0668	.0548	.0446	.0359	.0287
−0	.5000	.4602	.4207	.3821	.3446	.3085	.2743	.2420	.2119	.1841
0	.5000	.5398	.5793	.6179	.6554	.6915	.7257	.7580	.7881	.8159
1	.8413	.8643	.8849	.9032	.9192	.9332	.9452	.9554	.9641	.9713
2	.9772	.9821	.9861	.9893	.9918	.9938	.9953	.9965	.9974	.9981
3	.9987	.9990	.9993	.9995	.9997	.9998	.9998	.9999	.9999	1.000−

A2.S.7. Determine the function for the regression model, using appropriate technology, and use the regression function to interpolate and extrapolate from the data

119. (OE) A restaurant kept track of the number of desserts y it sold depending on the price of the dessert.

x	\$.50	\$1.00	\$2.00	\$3.50	\$4.00	\$4.50	\$6.00
y	25	24	23	19	17	15	7

Using your calculator, what is the quadratic function that best models this data?

About how many desserts will be sold if the price is \$3.25 per dessert? Show your work. *(p. 779, prob. 13)*

Go On 

A2.A.45 Determine the inverse of a function and use composition to justify the result

120. **(OE)** Consider the function $f(x) = \frac{1}{3}x^2$.

What is the inverse of this function?

Show that the given function and your answer are inverse functions. Explain. *(p. 443, prob. 15–20)*

A2.A.53 Graph exponential functions of the form $y = b^x$ for positive values of b, including $b = e$

121. **(OE)** In 1998, the number of students with cell phones in a certain state was 1094. During the next 4 years, the number of students with cell phones increased by 58% each year.

Write an exponential growth model giving the number n of cell phones t years after 1998. About how many cell phones were there in 2002?

Graph the model.

Use the graph to estimate the year when there were 40,000 students with cell phones. *(p. 484, prob. 39)*

A2.A.60 Sketch the unit circle and represent angles in standard position

122. **(OE)** Sketch a circle with radius 1.

Mark angles at 0°, 30°, 45°, 60°, 90°, 180°, 270°, and 360°.

Indicate measures in radian and degrees for each angle. *(p. 863, prob. 6–13)*

A2.A.70 Sketch and recognize one cycle of a function of the form $y = A \sin Bx$ or $y = A \cos Bx$

123. **(OE)** A graph is given by $y = 3 \cos (2\pi x)$.

What is the amplitude and period of this graph?

What are the intercepts, maximums and minimums of this graph over the interval $0 \leq x \leq 1$?

Sketch the graph of this function on the interval $0 \leq x \leq 2$. *(p. 913, prob. 16–23)*

Go On

Strand A Algebra

A2.A.75 Determine the solution(s) from the SSA situation (ambiguous case)

124. (OE) $\triangle ABC$ has the measures shown.

$$A = 85°, a = 8, b = 5$$

Show whether the measurements determine one triangle, two triangles, or no triangle. Sketch the possible triangle(s). Explain. *(p. 886, prob. 3–11)*

Strand S Statistics and Probability

A2.S.4 Calculate measures of dispersion (range, quartiles, interquartile range, standard deviation, variance) for both samples and populations

125. (OE) The data set below gives the number of cars sold at a car dealership over 6 months.

5, 6, 4, 6, 23, 4

Calculate the mean, median, and mode.

Use the formula

$$\sigma = \sqrt{\frac{(x_1 - \bar{x})^2 + (x_2 - \bar{x})^2 + \ldots + (x_n - \bar{x})^2}{n}}$$

to calculate the standard deviation. Show your work.

It is suspected that 23 is an outlier. Calculate the new standard deviation without the data value of 23. Describe what happened to the standard deviation and why. *(p. 748, prob. 26)*

1 Equations and Inequalities

Before

In previous courses, you learned the following skills, which you'll use in Chapter 1: simplifying numerical expressions, using formulas, and writing algebraic expressions.

Prerequisite Skills

VOCABULARY CHECK

Copy and complete the statement.

1. The **area** of the rectangle is _?_.
2. The **perimeter** of the rectangle is _?_.
3. The **opposite** of any number a is _?_.

SKILLS CHECK

Perform the indicated operation. *(Review p. 975 for 1.1, 1.2.)*

4. $5 \cdot (-3)$
5. $3 + (-4)$
6. $-28 \div (-7)$
7. $8 - (-15)$

Find the area of the figure. *(Review pp. 991–992 for 1.4.)*

8. A square with side length 7 ft
9. A circle with radius 3 m

Write an expression to answer the question. *(Review p. 984 for 1.5.)*

10. How much is a 15% tip on a restaurant bill of x dollars?
11. You have \$15 and buy r raffle tickets for \$.50 each. How much money do you have left?

Now

In Chapter 1, you will apply the big ideas listed below and reviewed in the Chapter Summary on page 60. You will also use the key vocabulary listed below.

Big Ideas

1. **Using properties to evaluate and simplify expressions**
2. **Using problem solving strategies and verbal models**
3. **Solving linear and absolute value equations and inequalities**

KEY VOCABULARY

- reciprocal, *p. 4*
- power, *p. 10*
- exponent, *p. 10*
- base, *p. 10*
- variable, *p. 11*
- coefficient, *p. 12*
- like terms, *p. 12*
- equivalent expressions, *p. 12*
- linear equation, *p. 18*
- equivalent equations, *p. 18*
- solve for a variable, *p. 26*
- linear inequality, *p. 41*
- compound inequality, *p. 41*
- absolute value, *p. 51*
- extraneous solution, *p. 52*

Why?

You can use equations to solve problems about work rates. For example, if two people complete a job at different rates, you can find how long it will take them if they work together.

Animated Algebra

The animation illustrated below for Exercise 76 on page 24 helps you answer this question: If two people paint a community mural at different rates, how long will it take them to complete the mural if they work together?

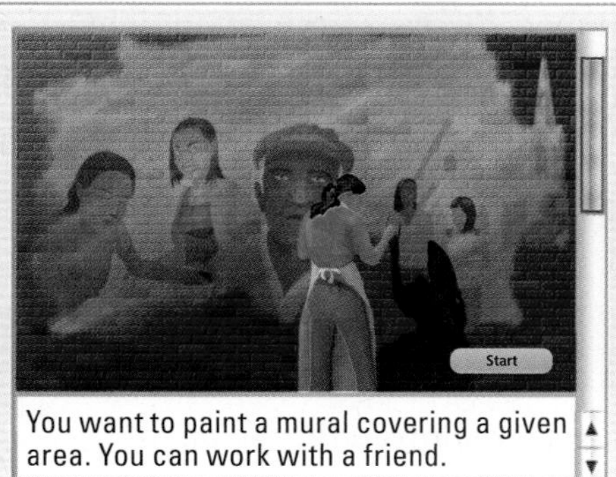

You want to paint a mural covering a given area. You can work with a friend.

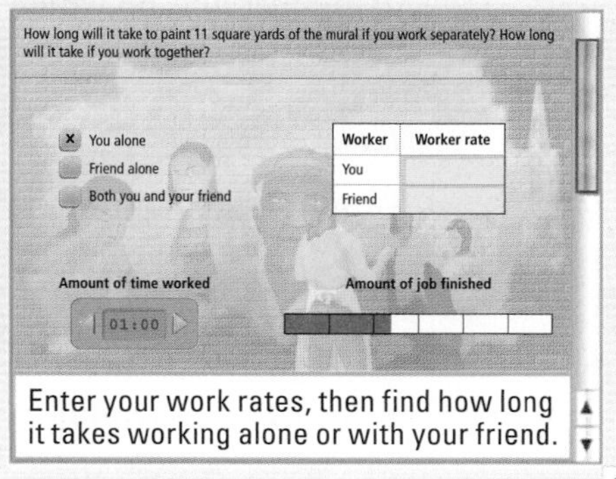

Enter your work rates, then find how long it takes working alone or with your friend.

Animated Algebra at classzone.com

Other animations for Chapter 1: pages 5, 11, 20, 27, 34, 42, and 53

1.1 Apply Properties of Real Numbers

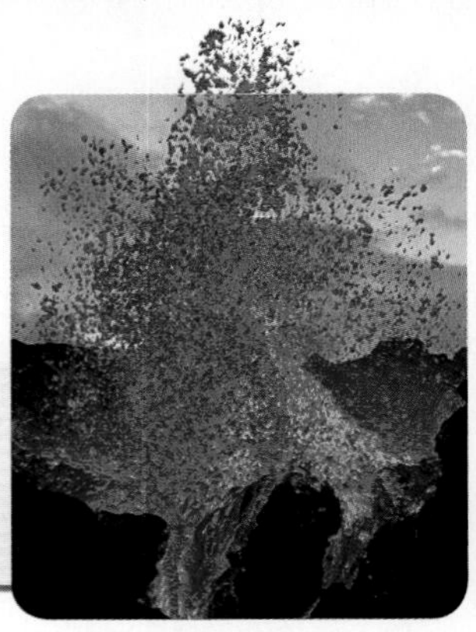

Before You performed operations with real numbers.
Now You will study properties of real numbers.
Why? So you can order elevations, as in Ex. 58.

Key Vocabulary
- opposite
- reciprocal

KEY CONCEPT — *For Your Notebook*

Subsets of the Real Numbers

The *real numbers* consist of the *rational numbers* and the *irrational numbers.* Two subsets of the rational numbers are the *whole numbers* (0, 1, 2, 3, . . .) and the *integers* (. . . , −3, −2, −1, 0, 1, 2, 3, . . .).

REAL NUMBERS

Rational Numbers	Irrational Numbers
$\frac{3}{4} = 0.75$, $-\frac{1}{3} = -0.333...$	$\sqrt{2} = 1.414213...$
Integers: −4, −1, −27	$-\sqrt{14} = -3.74165...$
Whole Numbers: 0, 5, 16	$\pi = 3.14159...$

Rational Numbers
- can be written as quotients of integers
- can be written as decimals that terminate or repeat

Irrational Numbers
- cannot be written as quotients of integers
- cannot be written as decimals that terminate or repeat

NUMBER LINE Real numbers can be graphed as points on a line called a *real number line,* on which numbers increase from left to right.

EXAMPLE 1 Graph real numbers on a number line

Graph the real numbers $-\frac{5}{4}$ and $\sqrt{3}$ on a number line.

Solution

Note that $-\frac{5}{4} = -1.25$. Use a calculator to approximate $\sqrt{3}$ to the nearest tenth: $\sqrt{3} \approx 1.7$. (The symbol $\approx$ means *is approximately equal to.*)

So, graph $-\frac{5}{4}$ between −2 and −1, and graph $\sqrt{3}$ between 1 and 2, as shown on the number line below.

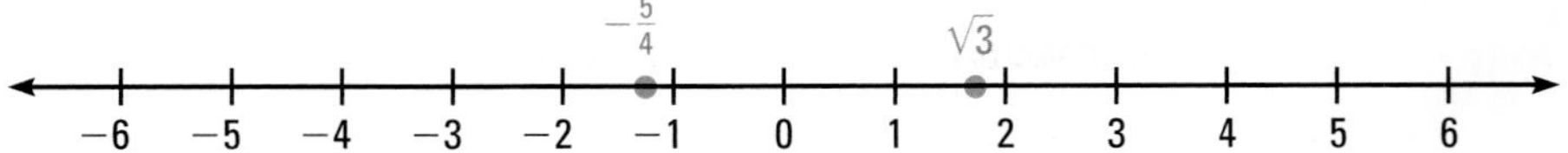

★ EXAMPLE 2 Standardized Test Practice

The table shows the lowest elevations of six continents. Which list shows the elevations from lowest to highest?

Continent	Africa	Asia	Australia	Europe	North America	South America
Lowest elevation	−156 m	−408 m	−16 m	−28 m	−86 m	−40 m

Ⓐ −408, −156, −86, −28, −40, −16 Ⓑ −408, −156, −28, −86, −40, −16

Ⓒ −16, −28, −40, −86, −156, −408 Ⓓ −408, −156, −86, −40, −28, −16

ELIMINATE CHOICES
The problem asks for the elevations from lowest to highest, not from highest to lowest. So, you can eliminate choice C.

Solution

From lowest to highest, the elevations are −408, −156, −86, −40, −28, and −16.

▶ The correct answer is D. Ⓐ Ⓑ Ⓒ Ⓓ

GUIDED PRACTICE for Examples 1 and 2

1. Graph the numbers $-0.2, \frac{7}{10}, -1, \sqrt{2}$, and -4 on a number line.

2. Which list shows the numbers in increasing order?

   Ⓐ $-0.5, 1.5, -2, -0.75, \sqrt{7}$ Ⓑ $-0.5, -2, -0.75, 1.5, \sqrt{7}$

   Ⓒ $-2, -0.75, -0.5, 1.5, \sqrt{7}$ Ⓓ $\sqrt{7}, 1.5, -0.5, -0.75, -2$

PROPERTIES OF REAL NUMBERS You learned in previous courses that when you add or multiply real numbers, there are several properties you can use.

KEY CONCEPT *For Your Notebook*

Properties of Addition and Multiplication

Let a, b, and c be real numbers.

Property	Addition	Multiplication
Closure	$a + b$ is a real number.	ab is a real number.
Commutative	$a + b = b + a$	$ab = ba$
Associative	$(a + b) + c = a + (b + c)$	$(ab)c = a(bc)$
Identity	$a + 0 = a, 0 + a = a$	$a \cdot 1 = a, 1 \cdot a = a$
Inverse	$a + (-a) = 0$	$a \cdot \frac{1}{a} = 1, a \neq 0$

The following property involves both addition and multiplication.

Distributive $a(b + c) = ab + ac$

EXAMPLE 3 Identify properties of real numbers

Identify the property that the statement illustrates.

a. $7 + 4 = 4 + 7$

b. $13 \cdot \frac{1}{13} = 1$

Solution

a. Commutative property of addition

b. Inverse property of multiplication

KEY CONCEPT *For Your Notebook*

Defining Subtraction and Division

Subtraction is defined as *adding the opposite.* The **opposite**, or *additive inverse,* of any number b is $-b$. If b is positive, then $-b$ is negative. If b is negative, then $-b$ is positive.

$a - b = a + (-b)$ Definition of subtraction

Division is defined as *multiplying by the reciprocal.* The **reciprocal**, or *multiplicative inverse,* of any nonzero number b is $\frac{1}{b}$.

$a \div b = a \cdot \frac{1}{b}, b \neq 0$ Definition of division

EXAMPLE 4 Use properties and definitions of operations

Use properties and definitions of operations to show that $a + (2 - a) = 2$. Justify each step.

Solution

$a + (2 - a) = a + [2 + (-a)]$	Definition of subtraction
$= a + [(-a) + 2]$	Commutative property of addition
$= [a + (-a)] + 2$	Associative property of addition
$= 0 + 2$	Inverse property of addition
$= 2$	Identity property of addition

GUIDED PRACTICE for Examples 3 and 4

Identify the property that the statement illustrates.

3. $(2 \cdot 3) \cdot 9 = 2 \cdot (3 \cdot 9)$

4. $15 + 0 = 15$

5. $4(5 + 25) = 4(5) + 4(25)$

6. $1 \cdot 500 = 500$

Use properties and definitions of operations to show that the statement is true. *Justify* each step.

7. $b \cdot (4 \div b) = 4$ when $b \neq 0$

8. $3x + (6 + 4x) = 7x + 6$

UNIT ANALYSIS When you use operations in real-life problems, you should use *unit analysis* to check that the units in your calculations make sense.

EXAMPLE 5 Use unit analysis with operations

a. You work 4 hours and earn \$36. What is your earning rate?

b. You travel for 2.5 hours at 50 miles per hour. How far do you go?

c. You drive 45 miles per hour. What is your speed in feet per second?

Solution

a. $\frac{36 \text{ dollars}}{4 \text{ hours}} = 9$ dollars per hour

b. $(2.5 \text{ hours})\left(\frac{50 \text{ miles}}{1 \text{ hour}}\right) = 125$ miles

c. $\left(\frac{45 \text{ miles}}{1 \text{ hour}}\right)\left(\frac{1 \text{ hour}}{60 \text{ minutes}}\right)\left(\frac{1 \text{ minute}}{60 \text{ seconds}}\right)\left(\frac{5280 \text{ feet}}{1 \text{ mile}}\right) = 66$ feet per second

Animated Algebra at classzone.com

EXAMPLE 6 Use unit analysis with conversions

DRIVING DISTANCE The distance from Montpelier, Vermont, to Montreal, Canada, is about 132 miles. The distance from Montreal to Quebec City is about 253 kilometers.

a. Convert the distance from Montpelier to Montreal to kilometers.

b. Convert the distance from Montreal to Quebec City to miles.

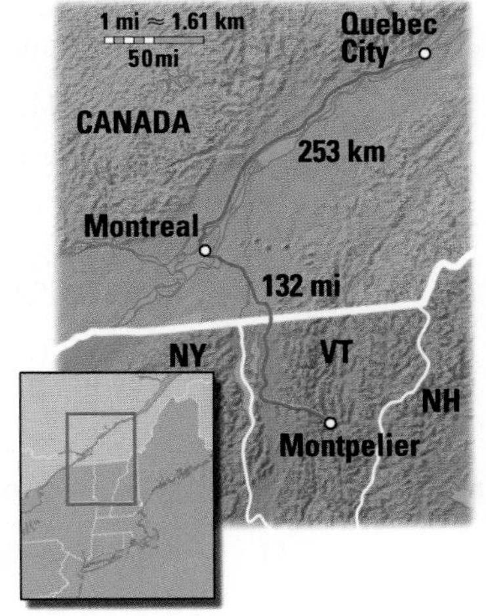

Solution

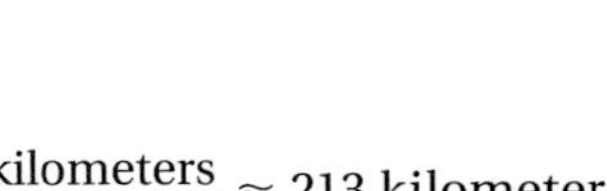

a. $132 \text{ miles} \cdot \frac{1.61 \text{ kilometers}}{1 \text{ mile}} \approx 213$ kilometers

b. $253 \text{ kilometers} \cdot \frac{1 \text{ mile}}{1.61 \text{ kilometers}} \approx 157$ miles

✓ GUIDED PRACTICE for Examples 5 and 6

Solve the problem. Use unit analysis to check your work.

9. You work 6 hours and earn \$69. What is your earning rate?

10. How long does it take to travel 180 miles at 40 miles per hour?

11. You drive 60 kilometers per hour. What is your speed in miles per hour?

Perform the indicated conversion.

12. 150 yards to feet **13.** 4 gallons to pints **14.** 16 years to seconds

REVIEW MEASURES
For help with converting units, see the Table of Measures on p. 1025.

1.1 EXERCISES

HOMEWORK KEY

○ = **WORKED-OUT SOLUTIONS** on p. WS1 for Exs. 21, 31, and 59

★ = **STANDARDIZED TEST PRACTICE** Exs. 2, 9, 10, 23, 24, 60, and 61

SKILL PRACTICE

1. **VOCABULARY** Copy and complete: The __?__ of any nonzero number b is $\frac{1}{b}$.

2. ★ **WRITING** Express the associative property of addition in words.

EXAMPLE 1 on p. 2 for Exs. 3–8

GRAPHING NUMBERS Graph the numbers on a number line.

3. $-\frac{3}{4}, 5, \frac{9}{2}, -2, -1$

4. $-3, \frac{5}{2}, 2, -\frac{9}{4}, 4$

5. $1, \sqrt{3}, -\frac{2}{3}, -\frac{5}{4}, 2$

6. $6, -\sqrt{5}, 2.7, -2, \frac{7}{3}$

7. $-0.4, \frac{3}{2}, 0, \sqrt{10}, -1$

8. $-1.7, 5, \frac{9}{2}, -\sqrt{8}, -3$

EXAMPLE 2 on p. 3 for Exs. 9–10

ORDERING NUMBERS In Exercises 9 and 10, use the table of elevations below.

State	Alabama	California	Kentucky	Louisiana	Tennessee
Highest elevation	2407 ft	14,494 ft	4145 ft	535 ft	6643 ft
Lowest elevation	0 ft	−282 ft	257 ft	−8 ft	178 ft

Louisiana bayou

9. ★ **MULTIPLE CHOICE** Which list shows the highest elevations in order from least to greatest?

   Ⓐ 2407; 14,494; 4145; 535; 6643
   Ⓑ 535; 2407; 4145; 6643; 14,494
   Ⓒ 14,494; 2407; 4145; 535; 6643
   Ⓓ 14,494; 6643; 4145; 2407; 535

10. ★ **MULTIPLE CHOICE** Which list shows the lowest elevations in order from greatest to least?

   Ⓐ 0, −8, 178, 257, −282
   Ⓑ −282, −8, 0, 178, 257
   Ⓒ −282, 257, 178, −8, 0
   Ⓓ 257, 178, 0, −8, −282

EXAMPLE 3 on p. 4 for Exs. 11–16

IDENTIFYING PROPERTIES Identify the property that the statement illustrates.

11. $(4 + 9) + 3 = 4 + (9 + 3)$

12. $15 \cdot 1 = 15$

13. $6 \cdot 4 = 4 \cdot 6$

14. $5 + (-5) = 0$

15. $7(2 + 8) = 7(2) + 7(8)$

16. $(6 \cdot 5) \cdot 7 = 6 \cdot (5 \cdot 7)$

EXAMPLE 4 on p. 4 for Exs. 17–22

USING PROPERTIES Use properties and definitions of operations to show that the statement is true. *Justify* each step.

17. $6 \cdot (a \div 3) = 2a$

18. $15 \cdot (3 \div b) = 45 \div b$

19. $(c - 3) + 3 = c$

20. $(a + b) - c = a + (b - c)$

21. $7a + (4 + 5a) = 12a + 4$

22. $(12b + 15) - 3b = 15 + 9b$

23. ★ **OPEN-ENDED MATH** Find values of a and b such that a is a whole number, b is a rational number but not an integer, and $a \div b = -8$.

24. ★ **OPEN-ENDED MATH** Write three equations using integers to illustrate the distributive property.

EXAMPLE 5
on p. 5
for Exs. 25–30

OPERATIONS AND UNIT ANALYSIS **Solve the problem. Use unit analysis to check your work.**

25. You work 10 hours and earn \$85. What is your earning rate?

26. You travel 60 kilometers in 1.5 hours. What is your average speed?

27. You work for 5 hours at \$7.25 per hour. How much do you earn?

28. You buy 6 gallons of juice at \$1.25 per gallon. What is your total cost?

29. You drive for 3 hours at 65 miles per hour. How far do you go?

30. You ride in a train for 175 miles at an average speed of 50 miles per hour. How many hours does the trip take?

EXAMPLE 6
on p. 5
for Exs. 31–40

CONVERSION OF MEASUREMENTS **Perform the indicated conversion.**

31. 350 feet to yards

32. 15 meters to millimeters

33. 2.2 kilograms to grams

34. 5 hours to minutes

35. 7 quarts to gallons

36. 3.5 tons to pounds

37. 56 ounces to tons

38. 6800 seconds to hours

Animated Algebra at classzone.com

ERROR ANALYSIS ***Describe*** **and correct the error in the conversion.**

39. $25 \text{ dollars} \cdot \frac{1 \text{ dollar}}{0.82 \text{ euro}} \approx 30.5 \text{ euros}$ ✗

40. $5 \text{ pints} \cdot \frac{1 \text{ cup}}{2 \text{ pints}} = 2.5 \text{ cups}$ ✗

CONVERSION OF RATES **Convert the rate into the given units.**

41. 20 mi/h to feet per second

42. 6 ft/sec to miles per hour

43. 50 km/h to miles per hour

44. 40 mi/h to kilometers per hour

45. 1 gal/h to ounces per second

46. 6 oz/sec to gallons per hour

47. **ROCKET SLED** On a track at an Air Force base in New Mexico, a rocket sled travels 3 miles in 6 seconds. What is the average speed in miles per hour?

48. **ELEVATOR SPEED** The elevator in the Washington Monument takes 60 seconds to rise 500 feet. What is the average speed in miles per hour?

REASONING **Tell whether the statement is *always, sometimes,* or *never* true for real numbers *a, b,* and *c*. *Explain* your answer.**

49. $(a + b) + c = a + (b + c)$

50. $(a \cdot b) \cdot c = a \cdot (b \cdot c)$

51. $(a - b) - c = a - (b - c)$

52. $(a \div b) \div c = a \div (b \div c)$

53. $a(b - c) = ab - ac$

54. $a(b \div c) = ab \div ac$

55. **REASONING** Show that $\frac{a}{b} \div \frac{c}{d} = \frac{a}{c} \div \frac{b}{d}$ for nonzero real numbers $a, b, c,$ and d. *Justify* each step in your reasoning.

56. **CHALLENGE** Let $\frac{a}{b}$ and $\frac{c}{d}$ be two distinct rational numbers. Find the rational number that lies exactly halfway between $\frac{a}{b}$ and $\frac{c}{d}$ on a number line.

PROBLEM SOLVING

EXAMPLE 2 on p. 3 for Exs. 57–59

57. **MINIATURE GOLF** The table shows the scores of people playing 9 holes of miniature golf.

Lance	+2	+1	0	0	−1	+1	+3	0	0
Darcy	−1	+3	0	−1	+1	0	0	+1	−1
Javier	+1	0	+1	0	0	−1	+1	0	+1
Sandra	−1	−1	0	0	+1	−1	0	0	0

a. Find the sum of the scores for each player.

b. List the players from best (lowest) to worst (highest) total score.

@HomeTutor for problem solving help at classzone.com

58. **VOLCANOES** The following list shows the elevations (in feet) of several volcano summits above or below sea level.

641, 3976, 610, −59, 1718, 1733, −137

Order the elevations from lowest to highest.

@HomeTutor for problem solving help at classzone.com

(59.) **MULTI-STEP PROBLEM** The chart shows the average daytime surface temperatures on the planets in our solar system.

a. **Sort by Temperature** List the planets in order from least to greatest daytime surface temperature.

b. **Sort by Distance** List the planets in order from least to greatest distance from the sun.

c. **Find Patterns** What pattern do you notice between surface temperature and distance from the sun?

d. **Analyze** Which planet does not follow the general pattern you found in part (c)?

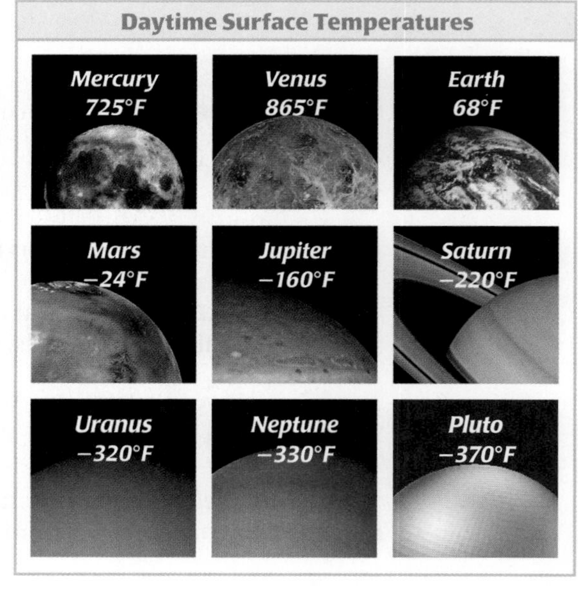

EXAMPLES 5 and 6 on p. 5 for Exs. 60–61

60. ★ **EXTENDED RESPONSE** The average weight of the blue whale (the largest mammal) is 120 tons, and the average weight of the bumblebee bat (the smallest mammal) is 0.07 ounce.

a. **Convert** Convert the weight of the blue whale from tons to pounds. Convert the weight of the bumblebee bat from ounces to pounds.

b. **Compare** About how many times as heavy as the bat is the blue whale?

c. **Find a Method** Besides converting the weights to pounds, what is another method for comparing the weights of the mammals?

○ = WORKED-OUT SOLUTIONS on p. WS1 ★ = STANDARDIZED TEST PRACTICE

61. ★ **SHORT RESPONSE** The table shows the maximum speeds of various animals in miles per hour or feet per second.

Animal	Speed (mi/h)	Speed (ft/s)
Cheetah	70	?
Three-toed sloth	?	0.22
Squirrel	12	?
Grizzly bear	?	44

Three-toed sloth

a. Copy and complete the table.

b. *Compare* the speeds of the fastest and slowest animals in the table.

62. **CHALLENGE** A newspaper gives the exchange rates of some currencies with the U.S. dollar, as shown below. Copy and complete the statements.

	1 USD	in USD
Australian dollar	1.31234	0.761998
Canadian dollar	1.1981	0.834655
Hong Kong dollar	7.7718	0.12867
New Zealand dollar	1.43926	0.694801
Singapore dollar	1.6534	0.604814

This row indicates that $1 U.S. ≈ $1.31 Australian and $1 Australian ≈ $.76 U.S.

a. 1 Singapore dollar ≈ ? Canadian dollar(s)

b. 1 Hong Kong dollar ≈ ? New Zealand dollar(s)

NEW YORK MIXED REVIEW

TEST PRACTICE at classzone.com

63. Susan purchased a television on sale for \$315. The original price of the television was \$370. Which expression can be used to determine the percent of the original price that Susan saved on the purchase of this television?

Ⓐ $\frac{315}{370} \times 100$

Ⓑ $\frac{370}{315} \times 100$

Ⓒ $\frac{370 - 315}{315 \times 100}$

Ⓓ $\frac{370 - 315}{370} \times 100$

64. In the figure, what is the length of $\overline{QR}$ in inches?

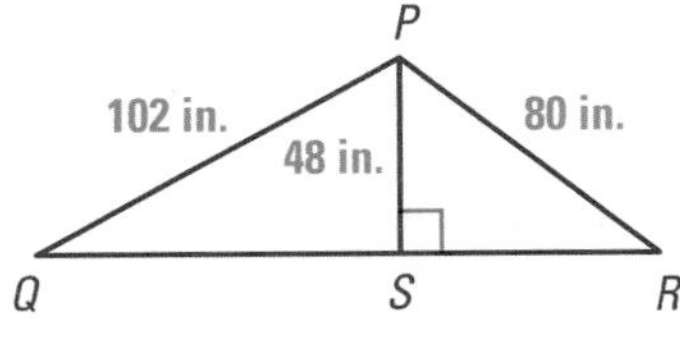

Ⓐ 86 in. Ⓑ 90 in. Ⓒ 122 in. Ⓓ 154 in.

1.2 Evaluate and Simplify Algebraic Expressions

 **A2.A.12** Evaluate exponential expressions, including those with base *e*

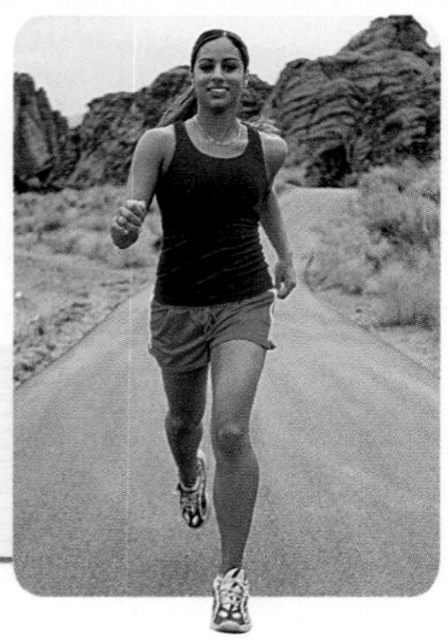

Before You studied properties of real numbers.

Now You will evaluate and simplify expressions involving real numbers.

Why? So you can estimate calorie use, as in Ex. 60.

Key Vocabulary
- **power**
- **variable**
- **term**
- **coefficient**
- **identity**

A **numerical expression** consists of numbers, operations, and grouping symbols. An expression formed by repeated multiplication of the same factor is a **power**.

A power has two parts: an *exponent* and a *base*. The **exponent** represents the number of times the **base** is used as a factor. In the power shown below, the base 7 is used as a factor 3 times.

exponent

base → $7^3 = 7 \cdot 7 \cdot 7$

power

You do not usually write the exponent when it is 1. For instance, you can write 8^1 simply as 8.

EXAMPLE 1 Evaluate powers

a. $(-5)^4 = (-5) \cdot (-5) \cdot (-5) \cdot (-5) = 625$

b. $-5^4 = -(5 \cdot 5 \cdot 5 \cdot 5) = -625$

In Example 1, notice how parentheses are used in part (a) to indicate that the base is −5. In part (b), the base of the power is 5, not −5. An *order of operations* helps avoid confusion when evaluating expressions.

KEY CONCEPT — For Your Notebook

Order of Operations

	Steps	Example
STEP 1	**First**, do operations that occur within grouping symbols.	$1 + 7^2 \cdot (5 - 3)$
STEP 2	**Next**, evaluate powers.	$= 1 + 7^2 \cdot 2$
STEP 3	**Then**, do multiplications and divisions from left to right.	$= 1 + 49 \cdot 2$
STEP 4	**Finally**, do additions and subtractions from left to right.	$= 1 + 98$ $= 99$

VARIABLES A **variable** is a letter that is used to represent one or more numbers. An expression involving variables is called an **algebraic expression**. When you substitute a number for each variable in an algebraic expression and simplify, you are *evaluating* the algebraic expression.

EXAMPLE 2 Evaluate an algebraic expression

Evaluate $-4x^2 - 6x + 11$ when $x = -3$.

$-4x^2 - 6x + 11 = -4(-3)^2 - 6(-3) + 11$	**Substitute −3 for *x*.**
$= -4(9) - 6(-3) + 11$	**Evaluate power.**
$= -36 + 18 + 11$	**Multiply.**
$= -7$	**Add.**

Animated Algebra at classzone.com

EXAMPLE 3 Use a verbal model to solve a problem

CRAFT FAIR You are selling homemade candles at a craft fair for \$3 each. You spend \$120 to rent the booth and buy materials for the candles.

- Write an expression that shows your profit from selling c candles.
- Find your profit if you sell 75 candles.

Solution

STEP 1 **Write** a verbal model. Then write an algebraic expression. Use the fact that profit is the difference between income and expenses.

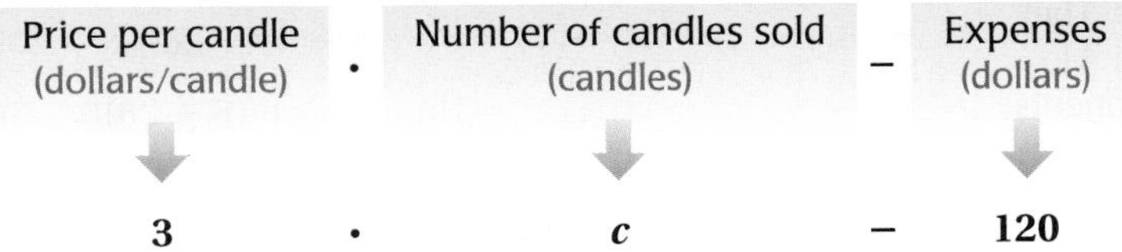

An expression that shows your profit is $3c - 120$.

STEP 2 **Evaluate** the expression in Step 1 when $c = 75$.

$3c - 120 = 3(75) - 120$	**Substitute 75 for *c*.**
$= 225 - 120$	**Multiply.**
$= 105$	**Subtract.**

▶ Your profit is \$105.

✓ GUIDED PRACTICE for Examples 1, 2, and 3

Evaluate the expression.

1. 6^3

2. -2^6

3. $(-2)^6$

4. $5x(x - 2)$ when $x = 6$

5. $3y^2 - 4y$ when $y = -2$

6. $(z + 3)^3$ when $z = 1$

7. **WHAT IF?** In Example 3, find your profit if you sell 135 candles.

KEY CONCEPT — For Your Notebook

Terms and Coefficients

In an expression that can be written as a sum, the parts added together are called **terms**.

A term that has a variable part is called a **variable term**. A term that has no variable part is called a **constant term**.

When a term is a product of a number and a power of a variable, the number is called the **coefficient** of the power.

variable terms — constant term

$3x^2 + 5x + (-7)$

coefficients

SIMPLIFYING An expression is simplified if it contains no grouping symbols and all *like terms* are combined. **Like terms** are terms that have the same variable parts. (Constant terms are also considered like terms.) The distributive property allows you to *combine like terms* by adding coefficients.

EXAMPLE 4 Simplify by combining like terms

a. $8x + 3x = (8 + 3)x$ Distributive property

$= 11x$ Add coefficients.

b. $5p^2 + p - 2p^2 = (5p^2 - 2p^2) + p$ Group like terms.

$= 3p^2 + p$ Combine like terms.

AVOID ERRORS
The terms $3p^2$ and p are not like terms. They use the same variable but different exponents, so the terms cannot be combined.

c. $3(y + 2) - 4(y - 7) = 3y + 6 - 4y + 28$ Distributive property

$= (3y - 4y) + (6 + 28)$ Group like terms.

$= -y + 34$ Combine like terms.

d. $2x - 3y - 9x + y = (2x - 9x) + (-3y + y)$ Group like terms.

$= -7x - 2y$ Combine like terms.

IDENTITIES Two algebraic expressions are **equivalent expressions** if they have the same value for all values of their variable(s). For instance, in part (a) of Example 4, the expressions $8x + 3x$ and $11x$ are equivalent. A statement such as $8x + 3x = 11x$ that equates two equivalent expressions is called an **identity**.

✓ GUIDED PRACTICE for Example 4

8. Identify the terms, coefficients, like terms, and constant terms in the expression $2 + 5x - 6x^2 + 7x - 3$. Then simplify the expression.

Simplify the expression.

9. $15m - 9m$ **10.** $2n - 1 + 6n + 5$ **11.** $3p^3 + 5p^2 - p^3$

12. $2q^2 + q - 7q - 5q^2$ **13.** $8(x - 3) - 2(x + 6)$ **14.** $-4y - x + 10x + y$

EXAMPLE 5 Simplify a mathematical model

DIGITAL PHOTO PRINTING You send 15 digital images to a printing service that charges \$.80 per print in large format and \$.20 per print in small format. Write and simplify an expression that represents the total cost if n of the 15 prints are in large format. Then find the total cost if 5 of the 15 prints are in large format.

Solution

Write a verbal model. Then write an algebraic expression.

Price of large print (dollars/print)	·	Number of large prints (prints)	+	Price of small print (dollars/print)	·	Number of small prints (prints)
0.8	·	n	+	**0.2**	·	**(15 − n)**

INTERPRET EXPRESSIONS

The total number of prints is 15, so if n are in large format, then $15 - n$ are in small format.

An expression for the total cost is $0.8n + 0.2(15 - n)$.

$0.8n + 0.2(15 - n) = 0.8n + 3 - 0.2n$ **Distributive property**

$= (0.8n - 0.2n) + 3$ **Group like terms.**

$= 0.6n + 3$ **Combine like terms.**

▶ When $n = 5$, the total cost is $0.6(5) + 3 = 3 + 3 = \$6$.

✓ GUIDED PRACTICE for Example 5

15. **WHAT IF?** In Example 5, write and simplify an expression for the total cost if the price of a large print is \$.75 and the price of a small print is \$.25.

1.2 EXERCISES

HOMEWORK KEY

○ = **WORKED-OUT SOLUTIONS** on p. WS1 for Exs. 21, 29, and 59

★ = **STANDARDIZED TEST PRACTICE** Exs. 2, 24, 33, 51, and 59

◆ = **MULTIPLE REPRESENTATIONS** Ex. 61

SKILL PRACTICE

1. **VOCABULARY** Copy 12^7 and label the base and the exponent.

2. ★ **WRITING** *Explain* what it means for terms to be like terms.

3. **ERROR ANALYSIS** *Describe* and correct the error in evaluating the power shown at the right.

$-3^4 = 81$ ✗

EXAMPLE 1 on p. 10 for Exs. 4–15

EVALUATING POWERS **Evaluate the power.**

4. 2^3
5. 3^4
6. 4^3
7. 7^2
8. -5^2
9. -2^5
10. -8^3
11. -10^4
12. $(-3)^2$
13. $(-4)^3$
14. $(-2)^8$
15. $(-8)^2$

EXAMPLE 2
on p. 11
for Exs. 16–24

ORDER OF OPERATIONS Evaluate the expression for the given value of the variable.

16. $5d - 6$ when $d = 7$

17. $-10f + 15$ when $f = 2$

18. $6h \div 2 + h$ when $h = 4$

19. $5j - 3j \cdot 5$ when $j = 10$

20. $(k + 2)^2 - 6k$ when $k = 5$

21. $8m + (2m - 9)^3$ when $m = 6$

22. $n^3 - 4n + 10$ when $n = -3$

23. $2x^4 - 4x^3$ when $x = -1$

Animated Algebra at classzone.com

24. ★ **MULTIPLE CHOICE** What is the value of $2x^2 - 6x + 15$ when $x = -2$?

(A) 11 (B) 19 (C) 35 (D) 43

EXAMPLE 4
on p. 12
for Exs. 25–33

SIMPLIFYING EXPRESSIONS Simplify the expression.

25. $9x - 4x + 5$

26. $y^2 + 2y + 3y^2$

27. $5z^2 - 2z + 8z^2 + 10$

28. $10w^2 - 4w + 3w^2 + 18w$

29. $7(m - 3) + 4(m + 5)$

30. $10(n^2 + n) - 6(n^2 - 2)$

31. $4p^2 - 12p - 9p^2 + 3(4p + 7)$

32. $6(q - 2) - 2(q^2 + 6q)$

33. ★ **MULTIPLE CHOICE** Which terms are like terms?

(A) $2x, 2y$ (B) $3x^2, 4x$ (C) x^2, y^2 (D) $10x^3, 2x^3$

GEOMETRY Write a simplified expression for the perimeter of the figure. Then evaluate the expression for the given value(s) of the variable(s).

34. $a = 3, b = 10$

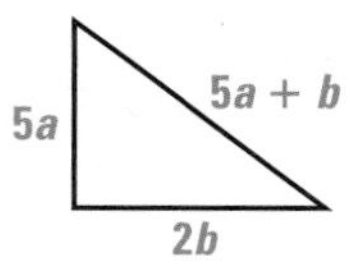

35. $n = 2$

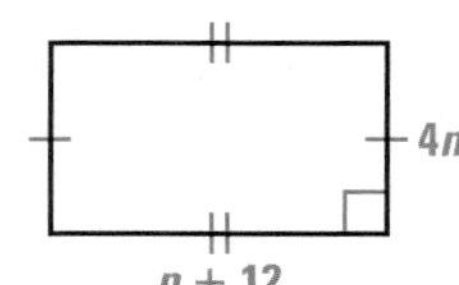

36. $g = 5, h = 4$

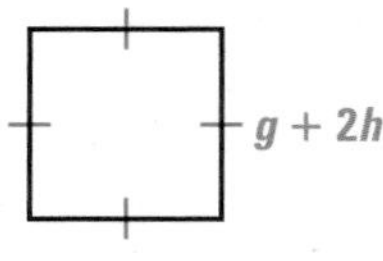

EVALUATING EXPRESSIONS Evaluate the expression for the given values of *x* and *y*.

37. $5x + 6y$ when $x = 16$ and $y = -9$

38. $16x + 11y$ when $x = -2$ and $y = -3$

39. $x^3 + 5y$ when $x = 4$ and $y = -3$

40. $(3x)^2 - y^3$ when $x = 4$ and $y = 5$

41. $\frac{x - y}{x + y}$ when $x = 10$ and $y = 8$

42. $\frac{x + 2y}{4x - y}$ when $x = -3$ and $y = 4$

HINT
Fraction bars are grouping symbols.

SIMPLIFYING EXPRESSIONS Simplify the expression.

43. $16c - 10d + 3d - 5c$

44. $9j + 4k - 2j - 7k$

45. $2m^2 - 5n^2 + 6n^2 - 8m$

46. $p^3 + 3q^2 - q + 3p^3$

47. $10m^2 + 3n - 8 + 3m^2 - 3n + 3$

48. $3y^2 + 5x - 12x + 9y^2 - 5$

49. $8(s - t) + 16(t - s)$

50. $3(x^2 - y) + 9(x^2 + 2y)$

51. ★ **OPEN-ENDED MATH** Write an algebraic expression that includes three coefficients, two like terms, and one constant term. Then simplify the expression.

GROUPING SYMBOLS Add parentheses to make a true statement.

52. $9 + 12 \div 3 - 1 = 15$

53. $4 + 3 \cdot 5 - 2 = 21$

54. $8 + 5^2 - 6 \div 3 = 9$

55. $3 \cdot 4^2 - 2^3 + 3^2 = 23$

56. **CHALLENGE** Under what conditions are the expressions $(x + y)^2$ and $x^2 + y^2$ equal? Are the expressions equivalent? *Explain.*

PROBLEM SOLVING

EXAMPLE 3 on p. 11 for Exs. 57–59

57. **MOVIE COSTS** In the United States, the average movie ticket price (in dollars) since 1974 can be modeled by $0.131x + 1.89$ where x is the number of years since 1974. What values of x should you use to find the ticket prices in 1974, 1984, 1994, and 2004? Find the ticket prices for those years.

@HomeTutor for problem solving help at classzone.com

58. **MILEAGE** You start driving a used car when the odometer reads 96,882. After a typical month of driving, the reading is 97,057. Write an expression for the reading on the odometer after m months, assuming the amount you drive each month is the same. Predict the reading after 12 months.

@HomeTutor for problem solving help at classzone.com

59. ★ **SHORT RESPONSE** A student has a debit card with a prepaid amount of \$270 to use for school lunches. The cafeteria charges \$4.50 per lunch. Write an expression for the balance on the card after buying x lunches. Does your expression make sense for all positive integer values of x? *Explain.*

EXAMPLE 5 on p. 13 for Exs. 60–62

60. **CROSS-TRAINING** You exercise for 60 minutes, spending w minutes walking and the rest of the time running. Use the information in the diagram below to write and simplify an expression for the number of calories burned. Find the calories burned if you spend 20 minutes walking.

61. ◆ **MULTIPLE REPRESENTATIONS** A theater has 30 rows of seats with 20 seats in each row. Tickets for the seats in the n rows closest to the stage cost \$45 and tickets for the other rows cost \$35.

a. **Visual Thinking** Make a sketch of the theater seating.

b. **Modeling** Write a verbal model for the income if all seats are sold.

c. **Simplifying** Write and simplify an expression for the income.

d. **Making a Table** Make a table for the income when $n = 5$, 10, and 15.

62. **COMPUTERS** A company offers each of its 80 workers either a desktop computer that costs \$900 or a laptop that costs \$1550. Write and simplify an expression for the cost of all the computers when n workers choose desktop computers. Find the cost if 65 workers choose desktop computers.

63. **CHALLENGE** You want to buy 25 fish for an aquarium. You decide to buy danios, tetras, and rainbowfish.

Write and simplify an expression for the total cost of x danios, y tetras, and the rest rainbowfish. You buy 8 danios, 10 tetras, and the rest rainbowfish. What is the total cost?

NEW YORK MIXED REVIEW

TEST PRACTICE at classzone.com

64. A roadside fruit stand sells three apples for a total of $0.79. The total cost, c, of purchasing n apples can be found by—

Ⓐ multiplying n by c
Ⓑ multiplying n by the cost of 1 apple
Ⓒ dividing n by c
Ⓓ dividing c by the cost of 1 apple

65. A rectangle has a length of 6 feet and a perimeter of 22 feet. What is the perimeter of a similar rectangle with a width of 20 feet?

Ⓐ 52 ft Ⓑ 82 ft Ⓒ 88 ft Ⓓ 100 ft

QUIZ for Lessons 1.1–1.2

Graph the numbers on a number line. *(p. 2)*

1. $-5, \frac{7}{2}, 1, -\frac{4}{3}$
2. $-6.2, 5.4, \sqrt{5}, -2.5$
3. $0, -7.3, -\frac{2}{5}, 2\sqrt{3}$

Identify the property that the statement illustrates. *(p. 2)*

4. $6(4 + 9) = 6(4) + 6(9)$
5. $-5 \cdot 8 = 8 \cdot (-5)$
6. $17 + (-17) = 0$

Evaluate the expression for the given value of the variable. *(p. 10)*

7. $10m + 32$ when $m = -5$
8. $12 + (8 - n)^3$ when $n = 5$
9. $p^3 - 3p^2$ when $p = -2$

Simplify the expression. *(p. 10)*

10. $8x + 6x^2 - 9x^2 - 4x$
11. $5(x + 9) - 2(4 - x)$
12. $24x - 6y + 15y - 18x$

13. **CD COSTS** CDs are on sale for $8 each and you have a gift card worth $100. Write an expression for the amount of money left on the gift card after purchasing n CDs. Evaluate the expression to find the amount of money left after purchasing 6 CDs. *(p. 10)*

Graphing Calculator **ACTIVITY** *Use after Lesson 1.2*

@HomeTutor
classzone.com
Keystrokes

1.2 Evaluate Expressions

QUESTION How can you use a calculator to evaluate expressions?

You can use a scientific calculator or a graphing calculator to evaluate expressions. Keystrokes for evaluating several expressions are shown below.

Note that to enter a negative number, you use the [+/−] key on a scientific calculator or the [(−)] key (not the [−] key) on a graphing calculator.

EXAMPLE Evaluate expressions

	EXPRESSION	CALCULATOR	KEYSTROKES	RESULT
a.	$-4^2 + 6$	Scientific	4 [x²] [+/−] [+] 6 [=]	**−10**
	$-4^2 + 6$	Graphing	[(−)] 4 [x²] [+] 6 [ENTER]	**−10**
b.	$(-4)^2 + 6$	Scientific	4 [+/−] [x²] [+] 6 [=]	**22**
	$(-4)^2 + 6$	Graphing	[(] [(−)] 4 [)] [x²] [+] 6 [ENTER]	**22**
c.	$(39 \div 3)^3$	Scientific	[(] 39 [÷] 3 [)] [yˣ] 3 [=]	**2197**
	$(39 \div 3)^3$	Graphing	[(] 39 [÷] 3 [)] [^] 3 [ENTER]	**2197**
d.	$\frac{64 - 5 \cdot 8}{4}$	Scientific	[(] 64 [−] 5 [×] 8 [)] [÷] 4 [=]	**6**
	$\frac{64 - 5 \cdot 8}{4}$	Graphing	[(] 64 [−] 5 [×] 8 [)] [÷] 4 [ENTER]	**6**

PRACTICE

Use a calculator to evaluate the expression.

1. $50.2 - 15 \div 3$

2. $-11(20) - 66$

3. $21(-8) + 51$

4. $(-4)^4$

5. $7(44.5 - 8^2)$

6. $\frac{9.2 - 15.9}{-19 + 14}$

Use a calculator to evaluate the expression when $x = -3$, $y = 5$, and $z = -6$.

7. $7z + y$

8. x^6

9. $6y - z^3$

10. $\frac{10x}{2z - 3}$

11. $(x + y)^2 + 3z$

12. $(-4x + 9) \div (y + 2)$

13. ERROR ANALYSIS A student evaluated the expression $7 + (-4)^3$ on a graphing calculator by pressing 7 [+] [(] [−] 4 [)] [^] 3 [ENTER]. The calculator displayed an error message. *Describe* and correct the error.

1.3 Solve Linear Equations

Before You simplified algebraic expressions.
Now You will solve linear equations.
Why? So you can solve problems about earnings, as in Example 2.

Key Vocabulary
- **equation**
- **linear equation**
- **solution**
- **equivalent equations**

An **equation** is a statement that two expressions are equal. A **linear equation** in one variable is an equation that can be written in the form $ax + b = 0$ where a and b are constants and $a \neq 0$.

A number is a **solution** of an equation in one variable if substituting the number for the variable results in a true statement. Two equations are **equivalent equations** if they have the same solution(s).

KEY CONCEPT *For Your Notebook*

Transformations That Produce Equivalent Equations

Addition Property of Equality	*Add* the same number to each side.	If $a = b$, then $a + c = b + c$.
Subtraction Property of Equality	*Subtract* the same number from each side.	If $a = b$, then $a - c = b - c$.
Multiplication Property of Equality	*Multiply* each side by the same nonzero number.	If $a = b$ and $c \neq 0$, then $a \cdot c = b \cdot c$.
Division Property of Equality	*Divide* each side by the same nonzero number.	If $a = b$ and $c \neq 0$, then $a \div c = b \div c$.

EXAMPLE 1 Solve an equation with a variable on one side

ANOTHER WAY
You can also solve the equation in Example 1 by multiplying each side by 5 first.

$$5\left(\frac{4}{5}x + 8\right) = 5(20)$$
$$4x + 40 = 100$$
$$4x = 60$$
$$x = 15$$

Solve $\frac{4}{5}x + 8 = 20$.

$\frac{4}{5}x + 8 = 20$ **Write original equation.**

$\frac{4}{5}x = 12$ **Subtract 8 from each side.**

$x = \frac{5}{4}(12)$ **Multiply each side by $\frac{5}{4}$, the reciprocal of $\frac{4}{5}$.**

$x = 15$ **Simplify.**

▸ The solution is 15.

CHECK Check $x = 15$ in the original equation.

$$\frac{4}{5}x + 8 = \frac{4}{5}(15) + 8 = 12 + 8 = 20 \checkmark$$

EXAMPLE 2 Write and use a linear equation

RESTAURANT During one shift, a waiter earns wages of \$30 and gets an additional 15% in tips on customers' food bills. The waiter earns \$105. What is the total of the customers' food bills?

Solution

Write a verbal model. Then write an equation. Write 15% as a decimal.

Income (dollars)	=	Wages (dollars)	+	Percent for tips	·	Food bills (dollars)
105	=	**30**	+	**0.15**	·	x

$105 = 30 + 0.15x$ **Write equation.**

$75 = 0.15x$ **Subtract 30 from each side.**

$500 = x$ **Divide each side by 0.15.**

▶ The total of the customers' food bills is \$500.

GUIDED PRACTICE for Examples 1 and 2

Solve the equation. Check your solution.

1. $4x + 9 = 21$
2. $7x - 41 = -13$
3. $-\frac{3}{5}x + 1 = 4$
4. **REAL ESTATE** A real estate agent's base salary is \$22,000 per year. The agent earns a 4% commission on total sales. How much must the agent sell to earn \$60,000 in one year?

EXAMPLE 3 Standardized Test Practice

What is the solution of $7p + 13 = 9p - 5$?

Ⓐ −9 Ⓑ −4 Ⓒ 4 Ⓓ 9

Solution

$7p + 13 = 9p - 5$ **Write original equation.**

$13 = 2p - 5$ **Subtract $7p$ from each side.**

$18 = 2p$ **Add 5 to each side.**

$9 = p$ **Divide each side by 2.**

▶ The correct answer is D. Ⓐ Ⓑ Ⓒ Ⓓ

CHECK $7p + 13 = 9p - 5$ **Write original equation.**

$7(9) + 13 \stackrel{?}{=} 9(9) - 5$ **Substitute 9 for p.**

$63 + 13 \stackrel{?}{=} 81 - 5$ **Multiply.**

$76 = 76$ ✓ **Solution checks.**

EXAMPLE 4 Solve an equation using the distributive property

Solve $3(5x - 8) = -2(-x + 7) - 12x$.

$3(5x - 8) = -2(-x + 7) - 12x$	**Write original equation.**
$15x - 24 = 2x - 14 - 12x$	**Distributive property**
$15x - 24 = -10x - 14$	**Combine like terms.**
$25x - 24 = -14$	**Add 10*x* to each side.**
$25x = 10$	**Add 24 to each side.**
$x = \frac{2}{5}$	**Divide each side by 25 and simplify.**

▶ The solution is $\frac{2}{5}$.

CHECK

$3\left(5 \cdot \frac{2}{5} - 8\right) \stackrel{?}{=} -2\left(-\frac{2}{5} + 7\right) - 12 \cdot \frac{2}{5}$	**Substitute $\frac{2}{5}$ for *x*.**
$3(-6) \stackrel{?}{=} \frac{4}{5} - 14 - \frac{24}{5}$	**Simplify.**
$-18 = -18$ ✓	**Solution checks.**

EXAMPLE 5 Solve a work problem

CAR WASH It takes you 8 minutes to wash a car and it takes a friend 6 minutes to wash a car. How long does it take the two of you to wash 7 cars if you work together?

Solution

STEP 1 **Write** a verbal model. Then write an equation.

Your rate (cars/minute)	·	Time (minutes)	+	Friend's rate (cars/minute)	·	Time (minutes)	=	Cars washed (cars)
$\frac{1 \text{ car}}{8 \text{ min}}$	·	t min	+	$\frac{1 \text{ car}}{6 \text{ min}}$	·	t min	=	7 cars

STEP 2 **Solve** the equation for *t*.

$\frac{1}{8}t + \frac{1}{6}t = 7$	**Write equation.**
$24\left(\frac{1}{8}t + \frac{1}{6}t\right) = 24(7)$	**Multiply each side by the LCD, 24.**
$3t + 4t = 168$	**Distributive property**
$7t = 168$	**Combine like terms.**
$t = 24$	**Divide each side by 7.**

AVOID ERRORS
Be sure to multiply *both* sides of the equation by the LCD, not just one side.

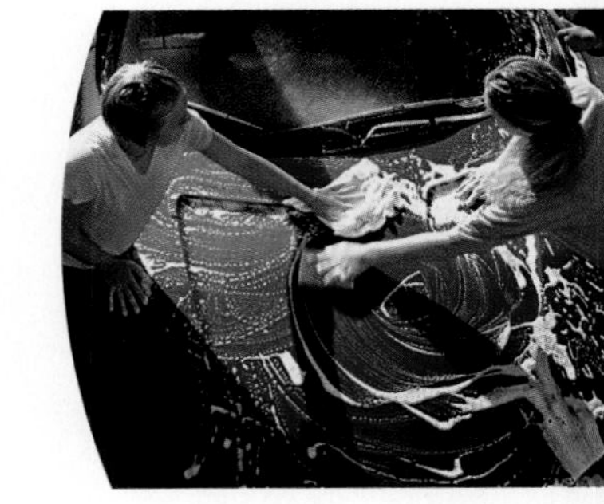

▶ It will take 24 minutes to wash 7 cars if you work together.

CHECK You wash $\frac{1}{8} \cdot 24 = 3$ cars and your friend washes $\frac{1}{6} \cdot 24 = 4$ cars in 24 minutes. Together, you wash 7 cars. ✓

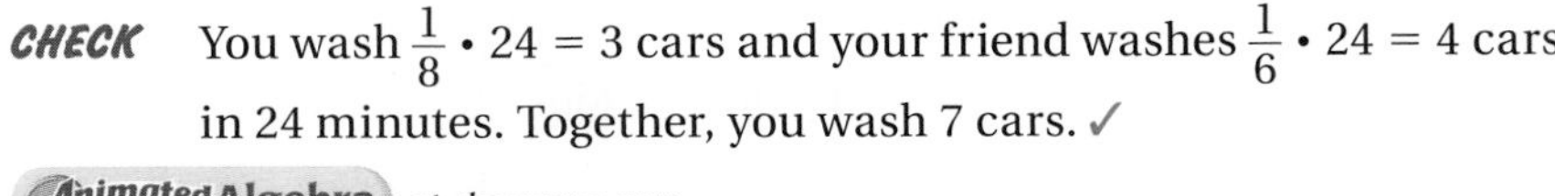

at classzone.com

✓ **GUIDED PRACTICE** for Examples 3, 4, and 5

Solve the equation. Check your solution.

5. $-2x + 9 = 2x - 7$

6. $10 - x = -6x + 15$

7. $3(x + 2) = 5(x + 4)$

8. $-4(2x + 5) = 2(-x - 9) - 4x$

9. $\frac{1}{4}x + \frac{2}{5}x = 39$

10. $\frac{2}{3}x + \frac{5}{6} = x - \frac{1}{2}$

11. **WHAT IF?** In Example 5, suppose it takes you 9 minutes to wash a car and it takes your friend 12 minutes to wash a car. How long does it take the two of you to wash 7 cars if you work together?

1.3 EXERCISES

HOMEWORK KEY

○ = **WORKED-OUT SOLUTIONS** on p. WS1 for Exs. 23, 43, and 71

★ = **STANDARDIZED TEST PRACTICE** Exs. 2, 19, 32, 72, and 77

◆ = **MULTIPLE REPRESENTATIONS** Ex. 74

SKILL PRACTICE

1. **VOCABULARY** Copy and complete: If a number is substituted for a variable in an equation and the resulting statement is true, the number is called a(n) __?__ of the equation.

2. ★ **WRITING** Give an example of two equivalent equations. How do you know they are equivalent?

EXAMPLE 1 on p. 18 for Exs. 3–19

VARIABLE ON ONE SIDE **Solve the equation. Check your solution.**

3. $x + 8 = 11$ **4.** $y - 4 = 7$ **5.** $z - 13 = -1$ **6.** $-3 = w + 5$

7. $5d = 30$ **8.** $4 = \frac{2}{5}g$ **9.** $\frac{9}{2}h = -1$ **10.** $-16k = -8$

11. $6m - 3 = 21$ **12.** $4n - 10 = 12$ **13.** $3 = 2p + 5$ **14.** $-3q + 4 = 13$

15. $1 = \frac{1}{3}a - 5$ **16.** $\frac{3}{11}b + 5 = 5$ **17.** $7 - \frac{5}{3}c = 22$ **18.** $3 + \frac{8}{7}d = -1$

19. ★ **MULTIPLE CHOICE** What is the solution of $4x - 7 = -15$?

(A) -12 (B) -2 (C) 2 (D) $\frac{11}{2}$

EXAMPLE 3 on p. 19 for Exs. 20–32

VARIABLE ON BOTH SIDES **Solve the equation. Check your solution.**

20. $3a + 4 = 2a + 15$ **21.** $5w + 2 = 2w + 5$ **22.** $6x + 7 = 2x + 59$

23. $5b - 4 = 2b + 8$ **24.** $3y + 7 = y - 3$ **25.** $2z - 3 = 6z + 25$

26. $4n - 7 = 5 - 2n$ **27.** $2c + 14 = 6 - 4c$ **28.** $5m - 2 = -m - 2$

29. $p + 5 = 25 - 4p$ **30.** $6 - 5q = q + 9$ **31.** $17 - 6r = 25 - 3r$

32. ★ **MULTIPLE CHOICE** What is the solution of $7t - 5 = 3t + 11$?

(A) $-\frac{3}{2}$ (B) $\frac{3}{2}$ (C) $\frac{8}{5}$ (D) 4

EXAMPLE 4 on p. 20 for Exs. 33–40

THE DISTRIBUTIVE PROPERTY **Solve the equation. Check your solution.**

33. $2(b + 3) = 4b - 2$

34. $5d + 17 = 4(d + 3)$

35. $3(m - 5) = 6(m + 1)$

36. $-4(n + 2) = 3(n - 4)$

37. $12(r + 3) = 2(r + 5) - 3r$

38. $7(t - 3) = 2(t - 9) + 2t$

39. $10(w - 4) = 4(w + 4) + 4w$

40. $3(2x - 5) - x = -7(x + 3)$

ERROR ANALYSIS ***Describe*** **and correct the error in solving the equation.**

41.

$$\frac{3}{7}x + 2 = 17$$
$$\frac{3}{7}x = 15$$
$$x = 15 - \frac{3}{7}$$
$$x = 14\frac{4}{7}$$

42.

$$\frac{1}{5}x + \frac{1}{2} = 1$$
$$10\left(\frac{1}{5}x + \frac{1}{2}\right) = 1$$
$$2x + 5 = 1$$
$$x = -2$$

EXAMPLE 5 on p. 20 for Exs. 43–50

EQUATIONS WITH FRACTIONS **Solve the equation. Check your solution.**

43. $\frac{1}{2}t + \frac{1}{3}t = 10$

44. $\frac{1}{5}d + \frac{1}{8}d = 2$

45. $\frac{2}{3}m - \frac{3}{5}m = 4$

46. $\frac{4}{7}z + \frac{2}{3}z = 13$

47. $\frac{3}{7}w - \frac{2}{9} = \frac{4}{9}w + \frac{1}{7}$

48. $\frac{1}{2}x + 4 = -\frac{2}{3}x + \frac{1}{2}$

49. $\frac{2}{5}k + \frac{1}{6} = \frac{3}{10}k + \frac{1}{3}$

50. $\frac{2}{3}q - \frac{1}{12} = q + \frac{1}{8}$

Animated Algebra at classzone.com

GEOMETRY **Solve for x. Then find the length of each side of the figure.**

51. Perimeter = 46

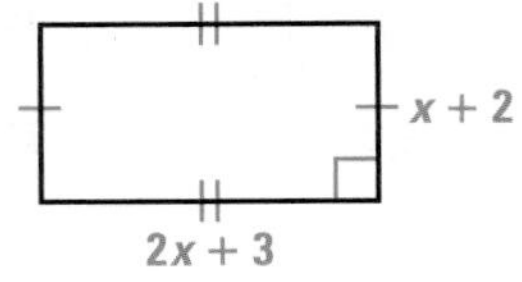

52. Perimeter = 26

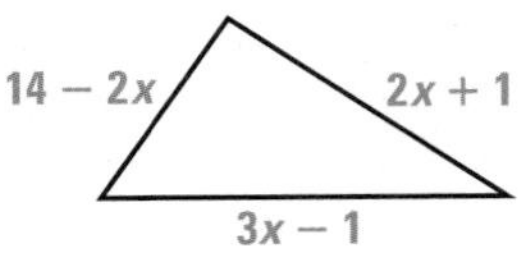

53. Perimeter = 15

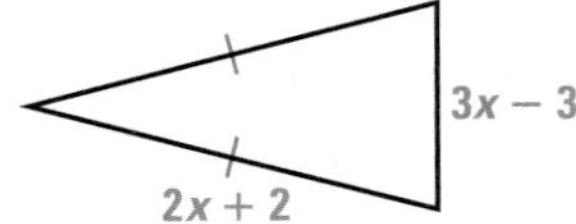

54. Perimeter = 26

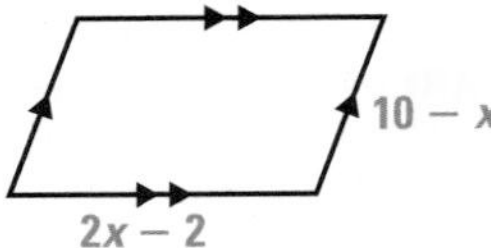

EQUATIONS WITH DECIMALS **Solve the equation. Check your solution.**

55. $0.6g + 0.5 = 2.9$

56. $1.1h + 1.3 = 6.8$

57. $0.4k - 0.6 = 1.3k + 1.2$

58. $6.5m + 1.5 = 4.3m - 0.7$

59. $3.8w + 3.2 = 2.3(w + 4)$

60. $1.7(x + 5) = 2.1x + 9.7$

61. $2.25b + 3.81 = 1.75b + 5.26$

62. $18.13 - 5.18c = 6.32c - 8.32$

◯ = WORKED-OUT SOLUTIONS on p. WS1

★ = STANDARDIZED TEST PRACTICE

SPECIAL EQUATIONS Solve the equation. If there is no solution, write *no solution*. If the equation is always true, write *all real numbers*.

63. $5(x - 4) = 5x + 12$

64. $3(x + 5) = 3x + 15$

65. $5(2 - x) = 3 - 2x + 7 - 3x$

66. $-2(4 - 3x) + 7 = 6(x + 1)$

67. **CHALLENGE** Solve the equation $ax + b = cx + d$ for x in terms of a, b, c, and d. Under what conditions is there no solution? Under what conditions are all real numbers solutions?

PROBLEM SOLVING

EXAMPLE 2 on p. 19 for Exs. 68–71

68. **CATALOG PURCHASE** You are ordering T-shirts from a catalog. Each T-shirt costs $15. The cost of shipping is $6 no matter how many you order. The total cost is $111. How many T-shirts did you order?

@HomeTutor for problem solving help at classzone.com

69. **BICYCLE REPAIR** The bill for the repair of your bicycle was $180. The cost of parts was $105. The cost of labor was $25 per hour. How many hours did the repair work take?

@HomeTutor for problem solving help at classzone.com

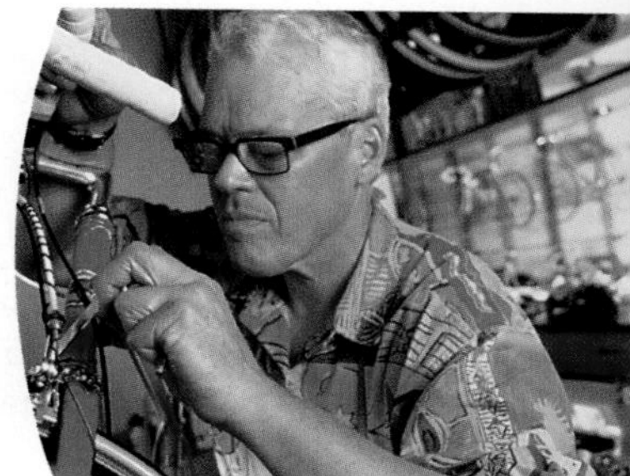

70. **CAR SALES** A salesperson at a car dealership has a base salary of $25,000 per year and earns a 5% commission on total sales. How much must the salesperson sell to earn $50,000 in one year?

71. **SUMMER JOBS** You have two summer jobs. In the first job, you work 25 hours per week and earn $7.75 per hour. In the second job, you earn $6.25 per hour and can work as many hours as you want. You want to earn $250 per week. How many hours must you work at the second job?

72. ★ **SHORT RESPONSE** Your friend bought a total of 10 CDs and DVDs as gifts for $199. The price per CD was $15 and the price per DVD was $22. Write and solve an equation to find how many CDs and how many DVDs your friend bought. How would your answer change if the total cost of the CDs and DVDs was $185? *Explain.*

73. **MULTI-STEP PROBLEM** You are working on the layout of a yearbook. The page is 9 inches wide, has $\frac{1}{2}$ inch margins, and has three columns of equal width.

a. Write and simplify an equation that relates the column width c and the gap g between columns to the total width of the page.

b. Copy and complete the table by substituting the given value into your equation from part (a) and solving to find the unknown value.

Gap, g (in.)	$\frac{5}{8}$	?	$\frac{3}{8}$	?
Column width, c (in.)	?	$2\frac{1}{3}$	?	$2\frac{1}{2}$

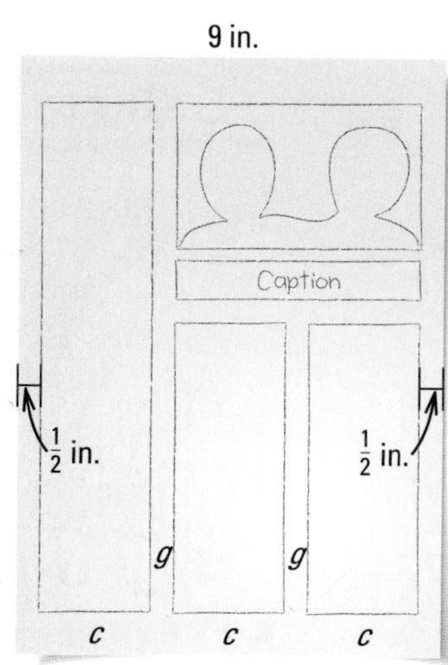

74. **MULTIPLE REPRESENTATIONS** You want to enlarge a 4 inch by 5 inch photo to fit into a 1 inch wide frame that has an outer perimeter of 53 inches.

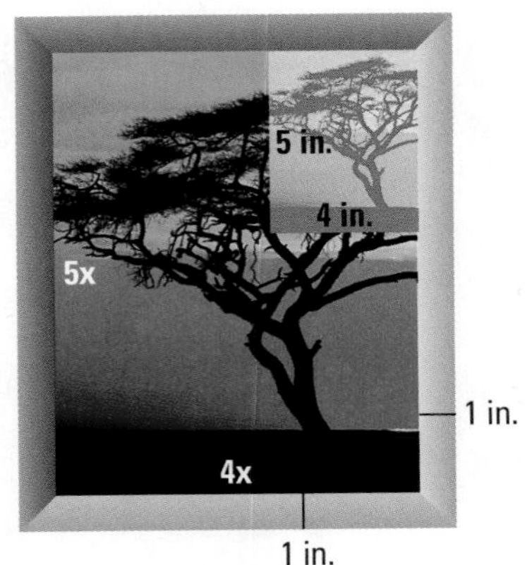

a. **Using a Diagram** Write an expression for the outer perimeter of the picture frame.

b. **Making a Table** Evaluate the perimeter expression when $x = 1.5, 2, 2.5, 3$, and 3.5. Make a table of your results. For what value of x is the perimeter 53 inches?

c. **Using an Equation** Write and solve an equation to find x. *Explain* what the value of x tells you about how much you should enlarge the original photo.

EXAMPLE 5
on p. 20
for Exs. 75–77

75. **RAKING LEAVES** It takes you 30 minutes to rake the leaves in your yard and it takes your brother 45 minutes. How long does it take the two of you to rake the leaves when working together?

76. **MURAL PAINTING** You paint 2 square yards of a community mural in 3 hours and a friend paints 4 square yards in 5 hours. How long does it take the two of you to paint 11 square yards when working together?

Animated Algebra at classzone.com

77. ★ **MULTIPLE CHOICE** Three students use calligraphy pens to write the names of graduating seniors on their diplomas. One writes 7 names in 6 minutes, another writes 17 names in 10 minutes, and the third writes 23 names in 15 minutes. How long, to the nearest minute, will the students take to write names on 440 diplomas if they work together?

Ⓐ 97 minutes Ⓑ 100 minutes Ⓒ 103 minutes Ⓓ 290 minutes

78. **CHALLENGE** A cylindrical thermos with an inside diameter of $2\frac{1}{2}$ inches is filled with liquid to a height of 9 inches. If the liquid is poured into a cylindrical travel mug with an inside diameter of $3\frac{1}{2}$ inches, what will be the height h of the liquid?

NEW YORK MIXED REVIEW

TEST PRACTICE at classzone.com

79. Andy is saving money for a digital music player that costs \$350. He makes \$7 per hour as a lifeguard. How many hours must he work to earn enough money to buy the digital music player if he uses a coupon for 20% off?

Ⓐ 10 h Ⓑ 25 h Ⓒ 40 h Ⓓ 43 h

80. Two runners are running at constant speeds in the same direction around a track. The faster runner travels 8 miles per hour and completes 4 laps each time the slower runner completes 3 laps. What is the slower runner's speed?

Ⓐ 2 mph Ⓑ 4 mph Ⓒ 6 mph Ⓓ 7 mph

@HomeTutor
classzone.com
Keystrokes

1.3 Use Tables to Solve Equations

QUESTION How can you use tables to solve linear equations?

You can use the *table* feature of a graphing calculator to solve linear equations.

EXAMPLE Solve a linear equation

Use the *table* feature of a graphing calculator to solve the equation $3x + 8 = 9x - 16$.

STEP 1 *Enter expressions*

Press [Y=]. Enter the left side of the equation as $y_1 = 3x + 8$. Enter the right side of the equation as $y_2 = 9x - 16$.

STEP 2 *Make a table*

Press [2nd] [TBLSET]. Set the starting x-value TblStart to 0 and the step value ΔTbl (the value by which the x-values increase) to 1.

STEP 3 *Identify solution*

Press [2nd] [TABLE] to display the table. Scroll through the table until you find an x-value for which both sides of the equation have the same value.

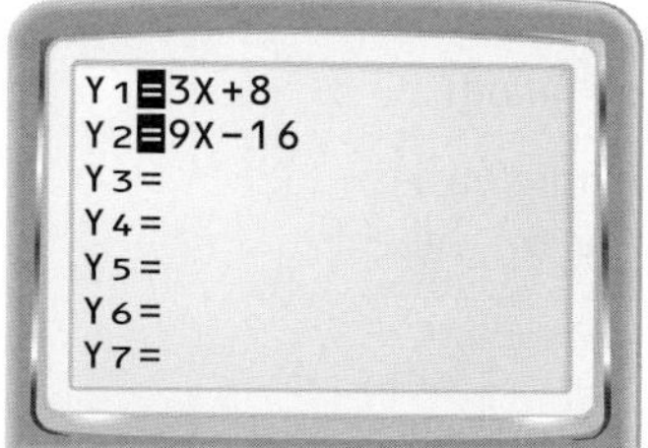

X	Y1	Y2
0	8	-16
1	11	-7
2	14	2
3	17	11
4	20	20
5	23	29

X=4

Both sides of the equation have a value of 20 when $x = 4$. So, the solution of $3x + 8 = 9x - 16$ is 4.

PRACTICE

Use the *table* feature of a graphing calculator to solve the equation.

1. $7x - 3 = -x + 13$
2. $-6x + 8 = 12 - 5x$
3. $-2x - 13 = -3x - 5$
4. $22 + 15x = -9x - 2$
5. $4x + 27 = -8 + 11x$
6. $7 - 8x = -9 - 10x$

7. **REASONING** Consider the equation $4x + 18 = 9x - 9$.
   a. Attempt to solve the equation using the *table* feature of a graphing calculator with step value ΔTbl = 1. Between what two integers does the solution lie? How do you know?
   b. Use a smaller value of ΔTbl to find the exact solution.

8. **WRITING** Solve the equation $3x + 8 = 9x - 16$ by writing it in the form $ax + b = 0$, entering $y_1 = ax + b$ on a graphing calculator, and using a table to find the x-value for which $y_1 = 0$. What are the advantages and disadvantages of this method compared to the method shown above?

1.4 Rewrite Formulas and Equations

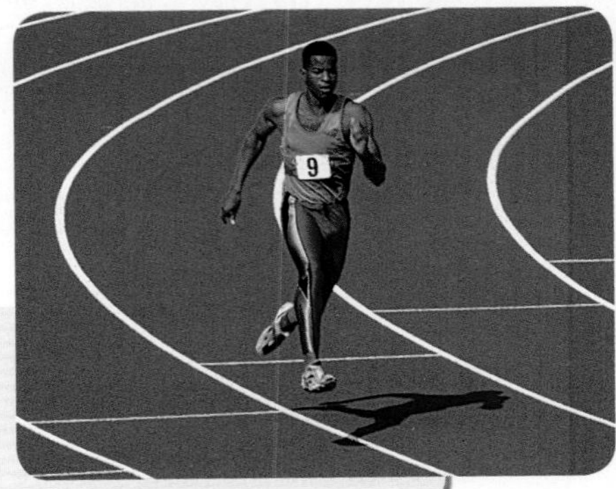

Before You solved equations.

Now You will rewrite and evaluate formulas and equations.

Why? So you can apply geometric formulas, as in Ex. 36.

Key Vocabulary
- **formula**
- **solve for a variable**

A **formula** is an equation that relates two or more quantities, usually represented by variables. Some common formulas are shown below.

Quantity	Formula	Meaning of variables
Distance	$d = rt$	d = distance, r = rate, t = time
Temperature	$F = \frac{9}{5}C + 32$	F = degrees Fahrenheit, C = degrees Celsius
Area of a triangle	$A = \frac{1}{2}bh$	A = area, b = base, h = height
Area of a rectangle	$A = \ell w$	A = area, ℓ = length, w = width
Perimeter of a rectangle	$P = 2\ell + 2w$	P = perimeter, ℓ = length, w = width
Area of a trapezoid	$A = \frac{1}{2}(b_1 + b_2)h$	A = area, b_1 = one base, b_2 = other base, h = height
Area of a circle	$A = \pi r^2$	A = area, r = radius
Circumference of a circle	$C = 2\pi r$	C = circumference, r = radius

READING
The variables b_1 and b_2 are read as "b sub one" and "b sub two." The small lowered numbers are called *subscripts*.

To **solve for a variable** means to rewrite an equation as an equivalent equation in which the variable is on one side and does not appear on the other side.

EXAMPLE 1 Rewrite a formula with two variables

Solve the formula $C = 2\pi r$ for r. Then find the radius of a circle with a circumference of 44 inches.

Solution

STEP 1 **Solve** the formula for r.

$C = 2\pi r$ **Write circumference formula.**

$\frac{C}{2\pi} = r$ **Divide each side by 2π.**

STEP 2 **Substitute** the given value into the rewritten formula.

$r = \frac{C}{2\pi} = \frac{44}{2\pi} \approx 7$ **Substitute 44 for C and simplify.**

▶ The radius of the circle is about 7 inches.

GUIDED PRACTICE for Example 1

1. Find the radius of a circle with a circumference of 25 feet.
2. The formula for the distance d between opposite vertices of a regular hexagon is $d = \frac{2a}{\sqrt{3}}$ where a is the distance between opposite sides. Solve the formula for a. Then find a when $d = 10$ centimeters.

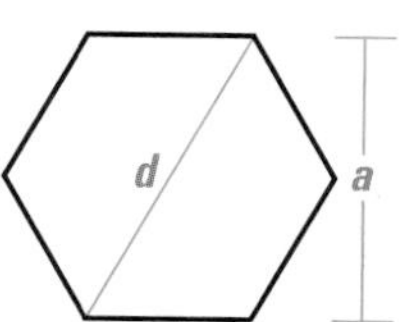

EXAMPLE 2 Rewrite a formula with three variables

Solve the formula $P = 2\ell + 2w$ for w. Then find the width of a rectangle with a length of 12 meters and a perimeter of 41 meters.

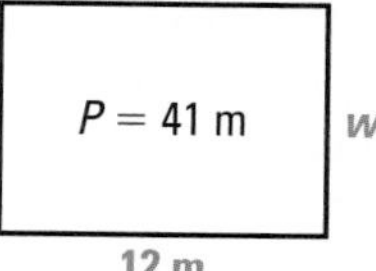

Solution

STEP 1 **Solve** the formula for w.

$P = 2\ell + 2w$	Write perimeter formula.
$P - 2\ell = 2w$	Subtract 2ℓ from each side.
$\frac{P - 2\ell}{2} = w$	Divide each side by 2.

STEP 2 **Substitute** the given values into the rewritten formula.

$w = \frac{41 - 2(12)}{2}$	Substitute 41 for P and 12 for ℓ.
$w = 8.5$	Simplify.

▶ The width of the rectangle is 8.5 meters.

GUIDED PRACTICE for Example 2

3. Solve the formula $P = 2\ell + 2w$ for ℓ. Then find the length of a rectangle with a width of 7 inches and a perimeter of 30 inches.
4. Solve the formula $A = \ell w$ for w. Then find the width of a rectangle with a length of 16 meters and an area of 40 square meters.

Solve the formula for the variable in red. Then use the given information to find the value of the variable.

5. $A = \frac{1}{2}bh$

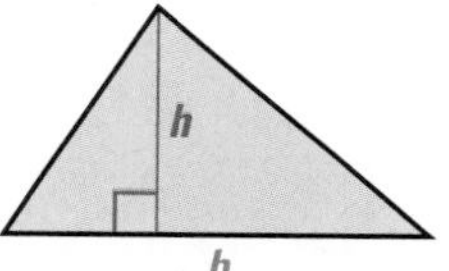

Find h if $b = 12$ m and $A = 84$ m^2.

6. $A = \frac{1}{2}bh$

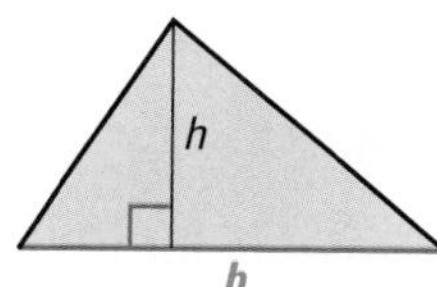

Find b if $h = 3$ cm and $A = 9$ cm^2.

7. $A = \frac{1}{2}(b_1 + b_2)h$

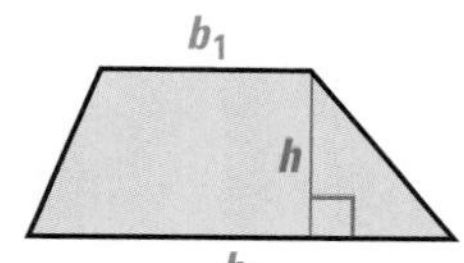

Find h if $b_1 = 6$ in., $b_2 = 8$ in., and $A = 70$ in.^{2}

REWRITING EQUATIONS The approach you use to solve a formula for a variable can be applied to other algebraic equations.

EXAMPLE 3 Rewrite a linear equation

Solve $9x - 4y = 7$ for y. Then find the value of y when $x = -5$.

Solution

STEP 1 **Solve** the equation for y.

$9x - 4y = 7$ Write original equation.

$-4y = 7 - 9x$ Subtract $9x$ from each side.

$y = -\frac{7}{4} + \frac{9}{4}x$ Divide each side by -4.

AVOID ERRORS
When dividing each side of an equation by the same number, remember to divide every term by the number.

STEP 2 **Substitute** the given value into the rewritten equation.

$y = -\frac{7}{4} + \frac{9}{4}(-5)$ Substitute -5 for x.

$y = -\frac{7}{4} - \frac{45}{4}$ Multiply.

$y = -13$ Simplify.

CHECK $9x - 4y = 7$ Write original equation.

$9(-5) - 4(-13) \stackrel{?}{=} 7$ Substitute -5 for x and -13 for y.

$7 = 7$ ✓ Solution checks.

EXAMPLE 4 Rewrite a nonlinear equation

Solve $2y + xy = 6$ for y. Then find the value of y when $x = -3$.

Solution

STEP 1 **Solve** the equation for y.

$2y + xy = 6$ Write original equation.

$(2 + x)y = 6$ Distributive property

$y = \frac{6}{2 + x}$ Divide each side by $(2 + x)$.

AVOID ERRORS
If you rewrite the equation as $y = \frac{6 - 2y}{x}$, then you have not solved for y because y still appears on both sides of the equation.

STEP 2 **Substitute** the given value into the rewritten equation.

$y = \frac{6}{2 + (-3)}$ Substitute -3 for x.

$y = -6$ Simplify.

✓ GUIDED PRACTICE for Examples 3 and 4

Solve the equation for y. Then find the value of y when $x = 2$.

8. $y - 6x = 7$ **9.** $5y - x = 13$ **10.** $3x + 2y = 12$

11. $2x + 5y = -1$ **12.** $3 = 2xy - x$ **13.** $4y - xy = 28$

EXAMPLE 5 Solve a multi-step problem

MOVIE RENTAL A video store rents new movies for one price and older movies for a lower price, as shown at the right.

- Write an equation that represents the store's monthly revenue.
- Solve the revenue equation for the variable representing the number of new movies rented.
- The owner wants $12,000 in revenue per month. How many new movies must be rented if the number of older movies rented is 500? 1000?

Solution

STEP 1 **Write** a verbal model. Then write an equation.

Monthly revenue (dollars)	=	Price of new movies (dollars/movie)	·	Number of new movies (movies)	+	Price of older movies (dollars/movie)	·	Number of older movies (movies)
R	=	5	·	n_1	+	3	·	n_2

An equation is $R = 5n_1 + 3n_2$.

STEP 2 **Solve** the equation for n_1.

$R = 5n_1 + 3n_2$ **Write equation.**

$R - 3n_2 = 5n_1$ **Subtract $3n_2$ from each side.**

$\frac{R - 3n_2}{5} = n_1$ **Divide each side by 5.**

STEP 3 **Calculate** n_1 for the given values of R and n_2.

If $n_2 = 500$, then $n_1 = \frac{12{,}000 - 3 \cdot 500}{5} = 2100$.

If $n_2 = 1000$, then $n_1 = \frac{12{,}000 - 3 \cdot 1000}{5} = 1800$.

▸ If 500 older movies are rented, then 2100 new movies must be rented. If 1000 older movies are rented, then 1800 new movies must be rented.

✓ GUIDED PRACTICE for Example 5

14. **WHAT IF?** In Example 5, how many new movies must be rented if the number of older movies rented is 1500?

15. **WHAT IF?** In Example 5, how many new movies must be rented if customers rent *no* older movies at all?

16. Solve the equation in Step 1 of Example 5 for n_2.

1.4 EXERCISES

HOMEWORK KEY

○ = **WORKED-OUT SOLUTIONS** on p. WS1 for Exs. 3, 9, and 35

★ = **STANDARDIZED TEST PRACTICE** Exs. 2, 6, 15, 27, 36, and 38

SKILL PRACTICE

1. **VOCABULARY** Copy and complete: A(n) __?__ is an equation that relates two or more quantities.

2. ★ **WRITING** What does it mean to solve for a variable in an equation?

EXAMPLES 1 and 2 on pp. 26–27 for Exs. 3–6

REWRITING FORMULAS Solve the formula for the indicated variable. Then use the given information to find the value of the variable.

3. Solve $A = \ell w$ for ℓ. Then find the length of a rectangle with a width of 50 millimeters and an area of 250 square millimeters.

4. Solve $A = \frac{1}{2}bh$ for b. Then find the base of a triangle with a height of 6 inches and an area of 24 square inches.

5. Solve $A = \frac{1}{2}(b_1 + b_2)h$ for h. Then find the height of a trapezoid with bases of lengths 10 centimeters and 15 centimeters and an area of 75 square centimeters.

6. ★ **MULTIPLE CHOICE** What equation do you obtain when you solve the formula $A = \frac{1}{2}(b_1 + b_2)h$ for b_1?

   (A) $b_1 = \frac{2A}{h} - b_2$ (B) $b_1 = \frac{A}{2h} - b_2$

   (C) $b_1 = 2A - b_2h$ (D) $b_1 = \frac{2A}{h - b_2}$

EXAMPLE 3 on p. 28 for Exs. 7–17

REWRITING EQUATIONS Solve the equation for *y*. Then find the value of *y* for the given value of *x*.

7. $3x + y = 26;\ x = 7$
8. $4y + x = 24;\ x = 8$
9. $6x + 5y = 31;\ x = -4$
10. $15x + 4y = 9;\ x = -3$
11. $9x - 6y = 63;\ x = 5$
12. $10x - 18y = 84;\ x = 6$
13. $8y - 14x = -22;\ x = 5$
14. $9y - 4x = -30;\ x = 8$

15. ★ **MULTIPLE CHOICE** What equation do you obtain when you solve the equation $4x - 5y = 20$ for y?

   (A) $x = \frac{5}{4}y + 5$ (B) $y = -\frac{4}{5}x + 4$ (C) $y = \frac{4}{5}x - 4$ (D) $y = \frac{4}{5}x - 20$

ERROR ANALYSIS *Describe* and correct the error in solving the equation for *y*.

16.
$$-7x + 5y = 2$$
$$5y = 7x + 2$$
$$y = \frac{7}{5}x + 2$$

17.
$$4y - xy = 9$$
$$4y = 9 + xy$$
$$y = \frac{9 + xy}{4}$$

GEOMETRY **Solve the formula for the variable in red. Then use the given information to find the value of the variable. Round to the nearest tenth.**

18. Area of a circular ring

$A = 2\pi rw$

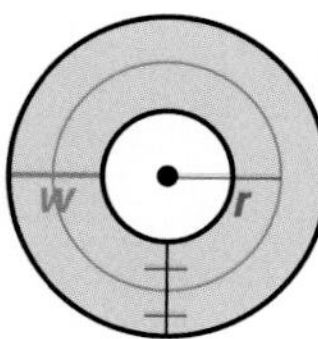

Find r if $w = 4$ ft and $A = 120$ ft^2.

19. Lateral surface area of a truncated cylinder

$S = \pi r(h + k)$

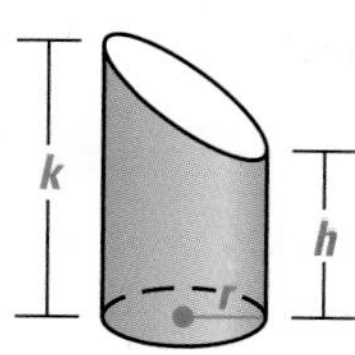

Find h if $r = 2$ cm, $k = 3$ cm, and $S = 50$ cm^2.

20. Volume of an ellipsoid

$V = \frac{4}{3}\pi abc$

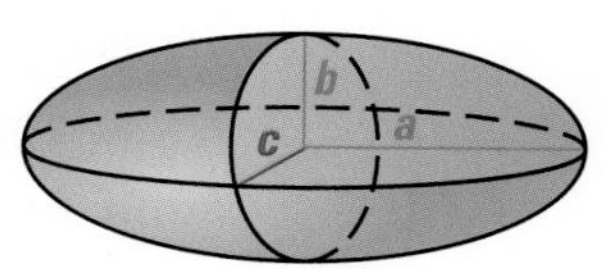

Find c if $a = 4$ in., $b = 3$ in., and $V = 60$ in.^{3}

EXAMPLE 4 on p. 28 for Exs. 21–26

REWRITING EQUATIONS **Solve the equation for y. Then find the value of y for the given value of x.**

21. $xy - 3x = 40; x = 5$

22. $7x - xy = -18; x = -4$

23. $3xy - 28 = 16x; x = 4$

24. $9y + 6xy = 30; x = -6$

25. $y - 2xy = 15; x = -1$

26. $4x + 7y + 5xy = 0; x = 1$

27. ★ **SHORT RESPONSE** Consider the equation $15x - 9y = 27$. To find the value of y when $x = 2$, you can use two methods.

Method 1 *Solve the original equation for y and then substitute 2 for x.*

Method 2 *Substitute 2 for x and then solve the resulting equation for y.*

Show the steps of the two methods. Which method is more efficient if you need to find the value of y for several values of x? *Explain.*

REASONING **Solve for the indicated variable.**

28. Solve $xy = x + y$ for y.

29. Solve $xyz = x + y + z$ for z.

30. Solve $\frac{1}{x} + \frac{1}{y} = 1$ for y.

31. Solve $\frac{1}{x} + \frac{1}{y} + \frac{1}{z} = 1$ for z.

32. **CHALLENGE** Write a formula giving the area of a circle in terms of its circumference.

PROBLEM SOLVING

EXAMPLE 5 on p. 29 for Exs. 33–38

33. **TREE DIAMETER** You can estimate the diameter of a tree without boring through it by measuring its circumference. Solve the formula $C = \pi d$ for d. Then find the diameter of an oak that has a circumference of 113 inches.

@HomeTutor for problem solving help at classzone.com

34. **DESIGN** The fabric panels on a kite are rhombuses. For the panel shown, a formula for the length of the long diagonal d is $d = s\sqrt{3}$ where s is the length of a side. Solve the formula for s. Then find the value of s when $d = 15$ inches.

@HomeTutor for problem solving help at classzone.com

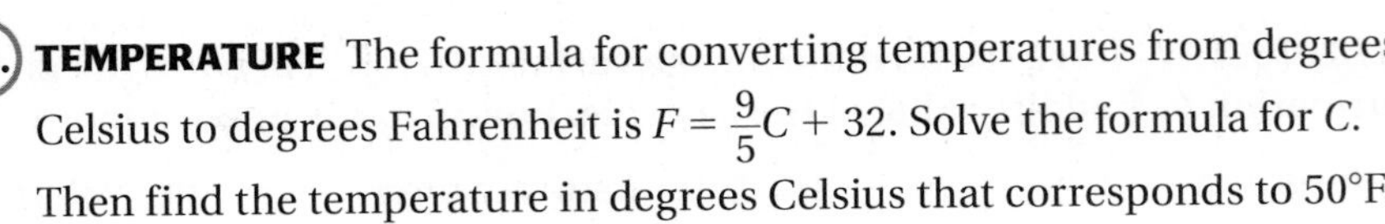

35. **TEMPERATURE** The formula for converting temperatures from degrees Celsius to degrees Fahrenheit is $F = \frac{9}{5}C + 32$. Solve the formula for C. Then find the temperature in degrees Celsius that corresponds to 50°F.

36. ★ **EXTENDED RESPONSE** A quarter mile running track is shaped as shown. The formula for the inside perimeter is $P = 2\pi r + 2x$.

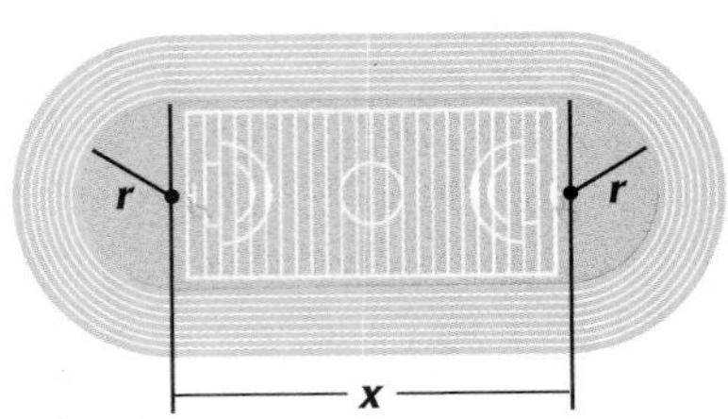

   a. Solve the perimeter formula for r.

   b. For a quarter mile track, $P = 440$ yards. Find r when $x = 75$ yards, 100 yards, 120 yards, and 150 yards.

   c. What are the greatest and least possible values of r if $P = 440$ yards? *Explain* how you found the values, and sketch the track corresponding to each extreme value.

37. **MULTI-STEP PROBLEM** A tuxedo shop rents classic tuxedos for \$80 and designer tuxedos for \$150. Write an equation that represents the shop's revenue. Solve the equation for the variable representing the number of designer tuxedos rented. The shop owner wants \$60,000 in revenue during prom season. How many designer tuxedos must be rented if the number of classic tuxedos rented is 600? 450? 300?

38. ★ **OPEN-ENDED MATH** The volume of a donut-like shape called a *torus* is given by the formula $V = 2\pi^2 r^2 R$ where r and R are the radii shown and $r \le R$.

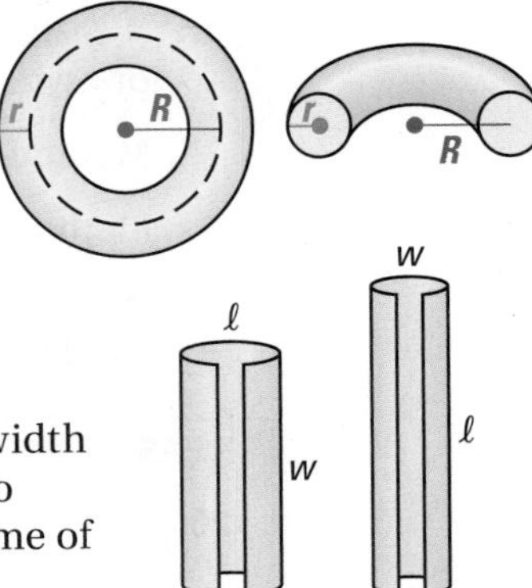

   a. Solve the formula for R.

   b. A metal ring in the shape of a torus has a volume of 100 cubic centimeters. Choose three possible values of r, and find the corresponding values of R.

39. **CHALLENGE** A rectangular piece of paper with length ℓ and width w can be rolled to form the lateral surface of a cylinder in two ways, assuming no overlapping. Write a formula for the volume of each cylinder in terms of ℓ and w.

New York Mixed Review

40. Jill is mailing a gift in a rectangular box that is 14 inches by 10 inches by 8 inches. She wants to mail this box in a larger box that is 18 inches by 15 inches by 10 inches. How many cubic inches of packing material does she need to surround the gift?

   (A) 1120 in.^{3} (B) 1580 in.^{3} (C) 2700 in.^{3} (D) 3820 in.^{3}

41. If $\angle A$ and $\angle B$ are supplementary angles and $m\angle A$ is 56°, what is $m\angle B$?

   (A) 34° (B) 112° (C) 124° (D) 306°

42. What is the solution of the equation $3(r - 1) = -2(r + 7) + 1$?

   (A) −3 (B) −2 (C) 2 (D) 3

EXTRA PRACTICE for Lesson 1.4, p. 1010 **ONLINE QUIZ** at classzone.com

Lessons 1.1–1.4

1. **CAR RENTALS** There is a $50 fee to join an urban car rental service. Using the car costs $8.50 per hour. What is the cost to join and drive for 20 hours?

   (1) $119

   (2) $135

   (3) $170

   (4) $220

2. **MUSEUM COSTS** You visit a museum. You have $50 to spend. Admission to the museum is $15. Admission to each special exhibit inside the museum is $10. What is the number of special exhibits you can include in your visit?

   (1) 2 (3) 6

   (2) 3 (4) 7

3. **HOCKEY STATISTICS** In hockey, each player has a statistic called plus/minus, which is the difference between the number of goals scored by the player's team and the number of goals scored by the other team when the player is on the ice. Which list shows the players in order from least to greatest plus/minus?

Player	Plus/Minus
Vincent Lecavalier	23
Dave Andreychuk	−9
Ruslan Fedotenko	14
Martin St. Louis	35
Cory Sarich	5
Tim Taylor	−5

   (1) Andreychuk, Taylor, Sarich, Fedotenko, Lecavalier, St. Louis

   (2) St. Louis, Lecavalier, Fedotenko, Andreychuk, Sarich, Taylor

   (3) Taylor, Andreychuk, Sarich, Fedotenko, Lecavalier, St. Louis

   (4) St. Louis, Lecavalier, Fedotenko, Sarich, Taylor, Andreychuk

4. **SCHOOL PICNIC SUPPLIES** You are in charge of buying food for a school picnic. You have $45 to spend on ground beef and chicken. Ground beef costs $1.80 per pound and chicken costs $1.00 per pound. You want to buy equal amounts of ground beef and chicken. About how many pounds of meat you can buy?

   (1) 16.07 pounds

   (2) 25 pounds

   (3) 32.14 pounds

   (4) 112.5 pounds

5. **OPEN-ENDED** Erin is driving from Chicago to St. Louis, a distance of 290 miles. Her average speed is 60 miles per hour.

   About how many hours does the trip take? Round you answer to the nearest tenth of an hour.

   On the way back to Chicago, Erin completes the drive in 4.2 hours. What was her average speed on this trip?

6. **OPEN-ENDED** In one year, the Bureau of Engraving and Printing printed $10 and $20 bills with a total value of $66,368,000. The total number of $10 and $20 bills was 3,577,600.

	Number	Value
$10 bills	x	$10x$
$20 bills	?	?
Total	3,577,600	66,368,000

   Copy and complete the table.

   Write and solve an equation to find how many $10 bills and how many $20 bills were printed.

   Compare the total value of the $10 bills printed with the total value of the $20 bills printed.

1.5 Use Problem Solving Strategies and Models

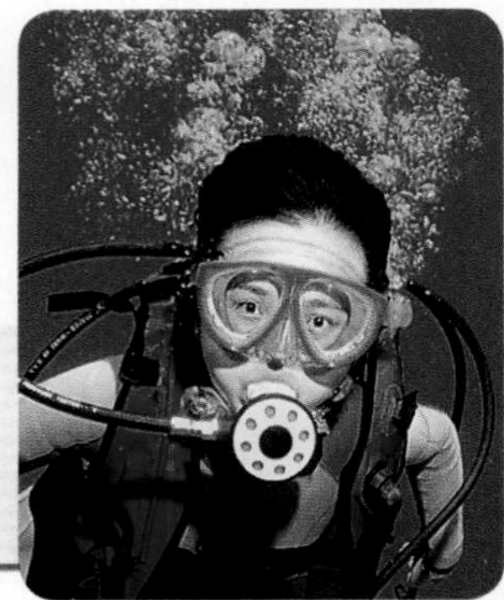

Before You wrote and solved equations.
Now You will solve problems using verbal models.
Why? So you can solve constant rate problems, as in Ex. 26.

Key Vocabulary
- **verbal model**

As you have seen in this chapter, it is helpful when solving real-life problems to write an equation in words *before* you write it in mathematical symbols. This word equation is called a **verbal model.**

Sometimes problem solving strategies can be used to write a verbal or algebraic model. Examples of such strategies are *use a formula, look for a pattern,* and *draw a diagram.*

EXAMPLE 1 Use a formula

HIGH-SPEED TRAIN The Acela train travels between Boston and Washington, a distance of 457 miles. The trip takes 6.5 hours. What is the average speed?

Solution

You can use the formula for distance traveled as a verbal model.

Distance (miles)	=	Rate (miles/hour)	•	Time (hours)
↓		↓		↓
457	=	***r***	•	**6.5**

An equation for this situation is $457 = 6.5r$. Solve for r.

$457 = 6.5r$ **Write equation.**

$70.3 \approx r$ **Divide each side by 6.5.**

▶ The average speed of the train is about 70.3 miles per hour.

CHECK You can use unit analysis to check your answer.

$$457 \text{ miles} \approx \frac{70.3 \text{ miles}}{1 \text{ hour}} \cdot 6.5 \text{ hours}$$

 at classzone.com

 **GUIDED PRACTICE** for Example 1

1. **AVIATION** A jet flies at an average speed of 540 miles per hour. How long will it take to fly from New York to Tokyo, a distance of 6760 miles?

EXAMPLE 2 Look for a pattern

PARAMOTORING A paramotor is a parachute propelled by a fan-like motor. The table shows the height h of a paramotorist t minutes after beginning a descent. Find the height of the paramotorist after 7 minutes.

Time (min), t	0	1	2	3	4
Height (ft), h	2000	1750	1500	1250	1000

Solution

The height decreases by 250 feet per minute.

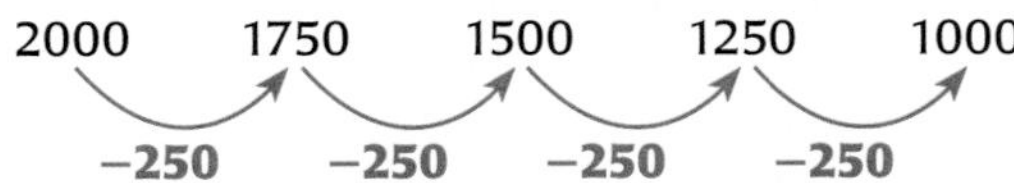

You can use this pattern to write a verbal model for the height.

Height (feet)	=	Initial height (feet)	−	Rate of descent (feet/minute)	·	Time (minutes)
h	=	2000	−	250	·	t

An equation for the height is $h = 2000 - 250t$.

▶ So, the height after 7 minutes is $h = 2000 - 250(7) = 250$ feet.

EXAMPLE 3 Draw a diagram

BANNERS You are hanging four championship banners on a wall in your school's gym. The banners are 8 feet wide. The wall is 62 feet long. There should be an equal amount of space between the ends of the wall and the banners, and between each pair of banners. How far apart should the banners be placed?

Solution

Begin by drawing and labeling a diagram, as shown below.

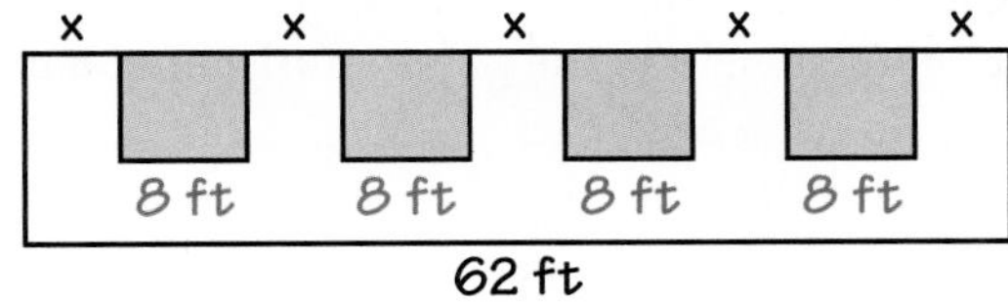

From the diagram, you can write and solve an equation to find x.

$x + 8 + x + 8 + x + 8 + x + 8 + x = 62$	**Write equation.**
$5x + 32 = 62$	**Combine like terms.**
$5x = 30$	**Subtract 32 from each side.**
$x = 6$	**Divide each side by 5.**

▶ The banners should be placed 6 feet apart.

REVIEW STRATEGIES
For help with other problem solving strategies, see p. 998.

EXAMPLE 4 Standardized Test Practice

A car used 16 gallons of gasoline and traveled a total distance of 460 miles. The car's fuel efficiency is 30 miles per gallon on the highway and 25 miles per gallon in the city. How many gallons of gasoline were used on the highway?

Ⓐ 8 gallons Ⓑ 12 gallons Ⓒ $15\frac{1}{3}$ gallons Ⓓ 16 gallons

Solution

STEP 1 **Write** a verbal model. Then write an equation.

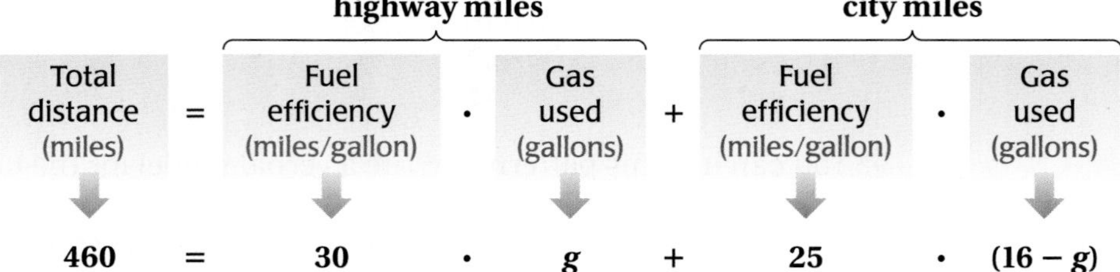

$460 = 30 \cdot g + 25 \cdot (16 - g)$

An equation for the situation is $460 = 30g + 25(16 - g)$.

STEP 2 **Solve** for g to find the number of gallons used on the highway.

$460 = 30g + 25(16 - g)$	**Write equation.**
$460 = 30g + 400 - 25g$	**Distributive property**
$460 = 5g + 400$	**Combine like terms.**
$60 = 5g$	**Subtract 400 from each side.**
$12 = g$	**Divide each side by 5.**

The car used 12 gallons on the highway.

▶ The correct answer is B. Ⓐ Ⓑ Ⓒ Ⓓ

CHECK $30 \cdot 12 + 25(16 - 12) = 360 + 100 = 460$ ✓

✓ GUIDED PRACTICE for Examples 2, 3, and 4

2. **PARAMOTORING** The table shows the height h of a paramotorist after t minutes. Find the height of the paramotorist after 8 minutes.

Time (min), t	0	1	2	3	4
Height (ft), h	2400	2190	1980	1770	1560

3. **WHAT IF?** In Example 3, how would your answer change if there were only three championship banners?

4. **FUEL EFFICIENCY** A truck used 28 gallons of gasoline and traveled a total distance of 428 miles. The truck's fuel efficiency is 16 miles per gallon on the highway and 12 miles per gallon in the city. How many gallons of gasoline were used in the city?

1.5 EXERCISES

HOMEWORK KEY

○ = **WORKED-OUT SOLUTIONS** on p. WS2 for Exs. 3, 11, and 27

★ = **STANDARDIZED TEST PRACTICE** Exs. 2, 15, 16, 21, and 27

◆ = **MULTIPLE REPRESENTATIONS** Ex. 28

SKILL PRACTICE

1. **VOCABULARY** Copy and complete: A word equation that represents a real-life problem is called a(n) __?__.

2. ★ **WRITING** Give an example of how a problem solving strategy can help you write an equation that models a real-life problem.

EXAMPLE 1 on p. 34 for Exs. 3–10

USING A FORMULA Use the formula $d = rt$ for distance traveled to solve for the missing variable.

3. $d = 20$ mi, $r = 40$ mi/h, $t =$ __?__
4. $d = 300$ mi, $r =$ __?__, $t = 4$ h
5. $d =$ __?__, $r = 30$ mi/h, $t = 3$ h
6. $d = 250$ mi, $r = 50$ mi/h, $t =$ __?__

GEOMETRY Use the formula $P = 2\ell + 2w$ for the perimeter of a rectangle to solve for the missing variable.

7. $P =$ __?__, $\ell = 15$ ft, $w = 12$ ft
8. $P = 46$ in., $\ell =$ __?__, $w = 4$ in.
9. $P = 100$ m, $\ell = 30$ m, $w =$ __?__
10. $P = 25$ cm, $w = 5$ cm, $\ell =$ __?__

EXAMPLE 2 on p. 35 for Exs. 11–15

USING PATTERNS Look for a pattern in the table. Then write an equation that represents the table.

11.

x	0	1	2	3
y	11	15	19	23

12.

x	0	1	2	3
y	60	45	30	15

13.

x	0	1	2	3
y	46	36	26	16

14.

x	0	1	2	3
y	57	107	157	207

15. ★ **MULTIPLE CHOICE** Which equation represents the table at the right?

Ⓐ $y = 5x + 7$ Ⓑ $y = 7x + 5$

Ⓒ $y = 12x - 5$ Ⓓ $y = 7x + 12$

x	0	1	2	3
y	12	19	26	33

16. ★ **SHORT RESPONSE** The first story of a building is 24 feet high, and each additional story is 18 feet high. Write an expression for the height to the top of the nth story. *Explain* the meaning of each term in the expression.

EXAMPLE 3 on p. 35 for Exs. 17–18

USING DIAGRAMS Write and solve an equation to find x.

17.

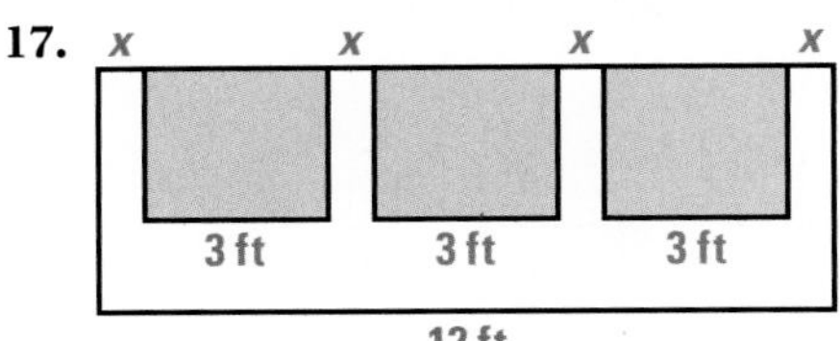

18.

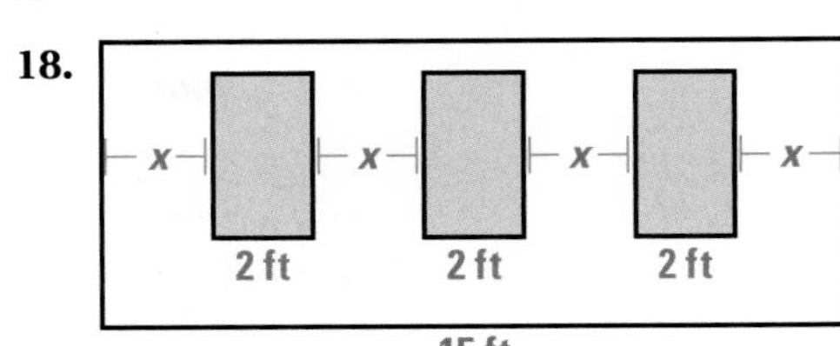

ERROR ANALYSIS ***Describe*** **and correct the error in writing the equation.**

19.

x	0	1	2	3
y	75	65	55	45

An equation that represents the table is $y = 75x - 10$.

20.

x	0	5	10	15
y	7	17	27	37

An equation that represents the table is $y = 7 + 10x$.

21. ★ **MULTIPLE CHOICE** A car used 15 gallons of gasoline and traveled a total distance of 350 miles. The car's fuel efficiency is 25 miles per gallon on the highway and 20 miles per gallon in the city. Which equation can you solve to find h, the number of gallons that were used on the highway?

Ⓐ $350 = 25(15 - h) + 20h$

Ⓑ $25h + 20(15 - h) = 350$

Ⓒ $350 = \left(\frac{25 + 20}{2}\right)h$

Ⓓ $15 = \frac{350}{25h} + \frac{350}{20h}$

CHALLENGE **Write an equation that represents the table.**

22.

x	0	3	6	9
y	12	30	48	66

23.

x	4	5	6	7
y	12	19	26	33

PROBLEM SOLVING

EXAMPLE 1 on p. 34 for Exs. 24–26

24. DAYTONA 500 A recent Daytona 500 race was won by Dale Earnhardt, Jr. He completed the 500 mile race in 3.2 hours. What was his average racing speed?

@HomeTutor for problem solving help at classzone.com

25. MAGLEV TRAIN A magnetic levitation (maglev) train travels between the city center of Shanghai, China, and Pudong International Airport. The trip covers 30 kilometers in just 8 minutes. What is the average speed of the train?

@HomeTutor for problem solving help at classzone.com

26. SCUBA DIVING A scuba diver is returning to the surface from a depth of 165 feet. The safe ascent rate for a diver is 30 feet per minute. How many minutes will it take for the diver to return to the surface?

EXAMPLE 2 on p. 35 for Exs. 27–28

27. ★ **SHORT RESPONSE** The table shows the height of a bamboo shoot during a period of fast growth. Use the table to write an equation modeling the growth. Do you think it is reasonable to assume the pattern in the table continues indefinitely? *Explain.*

Day	0	1	2	3	4
Bamboo height (ft)	15	16.5	18	19.5	21

28. **MULTIPLE REPRESENTATIONS** Your cell phone plan costs $40 per month plus $.10 per text message. You receive a bill for $53.80.

a. **Making a Table** Copy and complete the table below. Use the table to estimate how many text messages you sent.

Text messages	0	50	100	150	200
Monthly bill	$40	?	?	?	?

b. **Writing a Model** Write an equation for the situation. Solve it to find exactly how many text messages you sent.

c. **Comparing Answers** Is your estimate from part (a) compatible with the exact answer from part (b)? *Explain.*

EXAMPLE 3 on p. 35 for Exs. 29–30

29. **WOOD SHOP** You have a piece of wood that is 72 inches long. You cut the wood into three pieces. The second piece is 6 inches longer than the first piece. The third piece is 6 inches longer than the second piece. Draw a diagram and then write and solve an equation to find the lengths of the three pieces.

30. **POSTERS** You want to tape five posters on a wall so that the spaces between posters are the same. You also want the spaces at the left and right of the group of posters to be three times the space between any two adjacent posters. The wall is 15 feet wide and the posters are 1.5 feet wide. Draw a diagram and then write and solve an equation to find how to position the posters.

EXAMPLE 4 on p. 36 for Exs. 31–32

31. **PACKING WEIGHT** A moving company weighs 20 boxes you have packed that contain either books or clothes and says the total weight is 404 pounds. You know that a box of books weighs 40 pounds and a box of clothes weighs 7 pounds. Write and solve an equation to find how many boxes of books and how many boxes of clothes you packed.

32. **MULTI-STEP PROBLEM** A duathlon consists of a run, a bike ride, and a second run. Use the information below about the average rates of one participant who completed a 55 kilometer duathlon in 2 hours 35 minutes.

a. **Model** Write a verbal model that shows the race distance as the sum of the total running distance and the biking distance.

b. **Translate** Write an equation based on the verbal model.

c. **Solve** Solve the equation to find how much time the participant spent running and how much time the participant spent biking.

d. **Check** Find the total running distance and the biking distance, and verify that their sum is 55 kilometers.

33. **CHALLENGE** You are hanging fliers around a cylindrical kiosk that has a diameter of 5 feet. You want to hang 15 fliers that are 8.5 inches wide so they are evenly spaced. How far apart should the fliers be placed?

NEW YORK MIXED REVIEW

TEST PRACTICE at classzone.com

34. Curtis takes a bag of trail mix on a camping trip. On the first day, he eats one fourth of the trail mix. On the second day, he eats half of the remaining trail mix. On the third day, he eats one third of the remaining trail mix. When Curtis goes home, he has one-half pound of trail mix. How many pounds of trail mix did Curtis take on the camping trip?

(A) 2 lb (B) 4 lb (C) 8 lb (D) 12 lb

35. The number of students participating in extracurricular activities at Alexander High School this year is 25% higher than the previous year's participation of 740 students. What percent of this year's participation is last year's participation?

(A) 20% (B) 57% (C) 75% (D) 80%

36. How many yards of rope are needed to rope off a rectangular region having a width of 9 yards and a diagonal of 15 yards?

(A) 24 yd (B) 33 yd (C) 36 yd (D) 42 yd

QUIZ *for Lessons 1.3–1.5*

Solve the equation. Check your solution. *(p. 18)*

1. $5b - 2 = 8$

2. $2d - 3 = 8d + 15$

3. $2(m - 4) = m + 2$

4. $\frac{2}{3}k + \frac{2}{7} = \frac{3}{7}k + \frac{1}{2}$

Solve the equation for *y*. Then find the value of *y* for the given value of *x*. *(p. 26)*

5. $4x + y = 12; x = 4$

6. $3x - 2y = 14; x = 6$

7. $3xy - 4x = 19; x = 2$

8. $11y + 2xy = 9; x = -5$

Look for a pattern in the table. Then write an equation that represents the table. *(p. 34)*

9.

x	0	1	2	3
y	0	13	26	39

10.

x	0	1	2	3
y	−5	−2	1	4

11. TUTORING FEE A chess tutor charges a fee for the first lesson that is 1.5 times the fee for later lessons. You spend \$315 for 10 lessons. How much does the first lesson cost? How much does a later lesson cost? *(p. 34)*

12. FLOWER PRICES You buy some calla lilies and peonies at a flower store. Calla lilies cost \$3.50 each and peonies cost \$5.50 each. The total cost of 12 flowers is \$52. How many calla lilies and how many peonies did you buy? *(p. 34)*

1.6 Solve Linear Inequalities

A2.A.1 Solve absolute value equations and inequalities involving linear expressions in one variable

Before You solved linear equations.

Now You will solve linear inequalities.

Why? So you can describe temperature ranges, as in Ex. 54.

Key Vocabulary
- **linear inequality**
- **compound inequality**
- **equivalent inequalities**

A **linear inequality** in one variable can be written in one of the following forms, where a and b are real numbers and $a \neq 0$:

$$ax + b < 0 \qquad ax + b > 0 \qquad ax + b \leq 0 \qquad ax + b \geq 0$$

A **solution** of an inequality in one variable is a value that, when substituted for the variable, results in a true statement. The **graph** of an inequality in one variable consists of all points on a number line that represent solutions.

EXAMPLE 1 Graph simple inequalities

a. Graph $x < 2$.

The solutions are all real numbers less than 2.

An open dot is used in the graph to indicate 2 is *not* a solution.

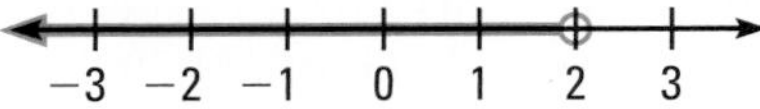

b. Graph $x \geq -1$.

The solutions are all real numbers greater than or equal to -1.

A solid dot is used in the graph to indicate -1 *is* a solution.

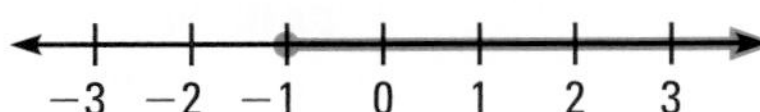

COMPOUND INEQUALITIES A **compound inequality** consists of two simple inequalities joined by "and" or "or."

EXAMPLE 2 Graph compound inequalities

READ INEQUALITIES
The compound inequality $-1 < x < 2$ is another way of writing "$x > -1$ **and** $x < 2$."

a. Graph $-1 < x < 2$.

The solutions are all real numbers that are greater than -1 **and** less than 2.

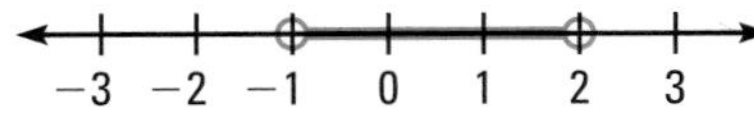

b. Graph $x \leq -2$ or $x > 1$.

The solutions are all real numbers that are less than or equal to -2 **or** greater than 1.

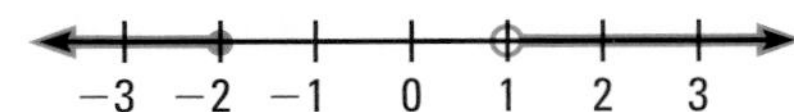

GUIDED PRACTICE for Examples 1 and 2

Graph the inequality.

1. $x > -5$ **2.** $x \leq 3$ **3.** $-3 \leq x < 1$ **4.** $x < 1$ or $x \geq 2$

SOLVING INEQUALITIES To solve a linear inequality in one variable, you isolate the variable using transformations that produce **equivalent inequalities**, which are inequalities that have the same solutions as the original inequality.

KEY CONCEPT *For Your Notebook*

Transformations That Produce Equivalent Inequalities

Transformation applied to inequality	Original inequality	Equivalent inequality
Add the same number to each side.	$x - 7 < 4$	$x < 11$
Subtract the same number from each side.	$x + 3 \geq -1$	$x \geq -4$
Multiply each side by the same *positive* number.	$\frac{1}{2}x > 10$	$x > 20$
Divide each side by the same *positive* number.	$5x \leq 15$	$x \leq 3$
Multiply each side by the same *negative* number and *reverse* the inequality.	$-x < 17$	$x > -17$
Divide each side by the same *negative* number and *reverse* the inequality.	$-9x \geq 45$	$x \leq -5$

EXAMPLE 3 Solve an inequality with a variable on one side

FAIR You have \$50 to spend at a county fair. You spend \$20 for admission. You want to play a game that costs \$1.50. Describe the possible numbers of times you can play the game.

ANOTHER WAY
For alternative methods for solving the problem in Example 3, turn to page 48 for the **Problem Solving Workshop**.

Solution

STEP 1 **Write** a verbal model. Then write an inequality.

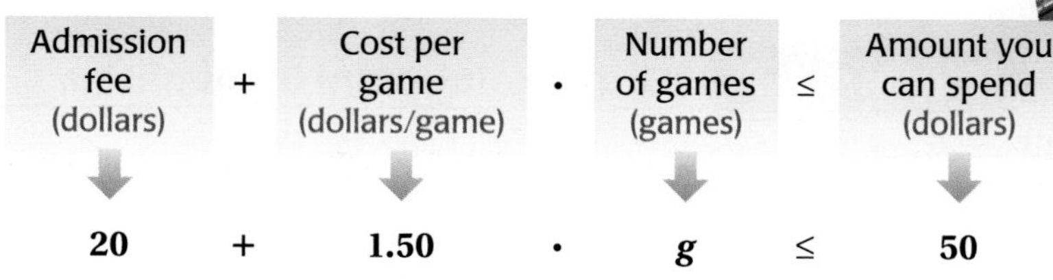

An inequality is $20 + 1.5g \leq 50$.

STEP 2 **Solve** the inequality.

$20 + 1.5g \leq 50$ **Write inequality.**

$1.5g \leq 30$ **Subtract 20 from each side.**

$g \leq 20$ **Divide each side by 1.5.**

▶ You can play the game 20 times or fewer.

Animated Algebra at classzone.com

EXAMPLE 4 Solve an inequality with a variable on both sides

Solve $5x + 2 > 7x - 4$. Then graph the solution.

$5x + 2 > 7x - 4$	**Write original inequality.**
$-2x + 2 > -4$	**Subtract 7*x* from each side.**
$-2x > -6$	**Subtract 2 from each side.**
$x < 3$	**Divide each side by −2 and reverse the inequality.**

▸ The solutions are all real numbers less than 3. The graph is shown below.

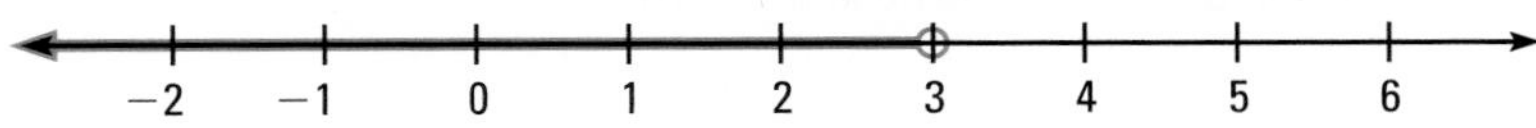

AVOID ERRORS

Don't forget to reverse the inequality symbol if you multiply or divide each side of an inequality by a negative number.

GUIDED PRACTICE for Examples 3 and 4

Solve the inequality. Then graph the solution.

5. $4x + 9 < 25$ **6.** $1 - 3x \geq -14$ **7.** $5x - 7 \leq 6x$ **8.** $3 - x > x - 9$

EXAMPLE 5 Solve an "and" compound inequality

Solve $-4 < 6x - 10 \leq 14$. Then graph the solution.

$-4 < 6x - 10 \leq 14$	**Write original inequality.**
$-4 + 10 < 6x - 10 + 10 \leq 14 + 10$	**Add 10 to each expression.**
$6 < 6x \leq 24$	**Simplify.**
$1 < x \leq 4$	**Divide each expression by 6.**

▸ The solutions are all real numbers greater than 1 and less than or equal to 4. The graph is shown below.

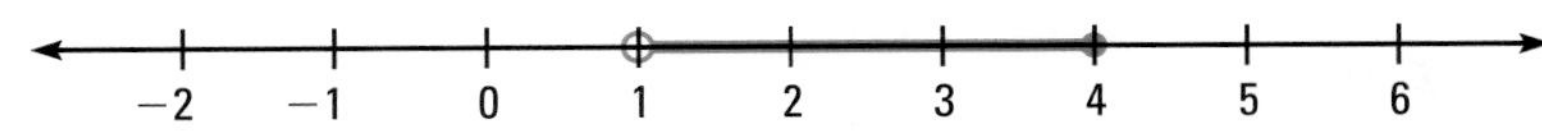

EXAMPLE 6 Solve an "or" compound inequality

Solve $3x + 5 \leq 11$ or $5x - 7 \geq 23$. Then graph the solution.

Solution

A solution of this compound inequality is a solution of *either* of its parts.

First Inequality		**Second Inequality**	
$3x + 5 \leq 11$	**Write first inequality.**	$5x - 7 \geq 23$	**Write second inequality.**
$3x \leq 6$	**Subtract 5 from each side.**	$5x \geq 30$	**Add 7 to each side.**
$x \leq 2$	**Divide each side by 3.**	$x \geq 6$	**Divide each side by 5.**

▸ The graph is shown below. The solutions are all real numbers **less than or equal to 2** or **greater than or equal to 6**.

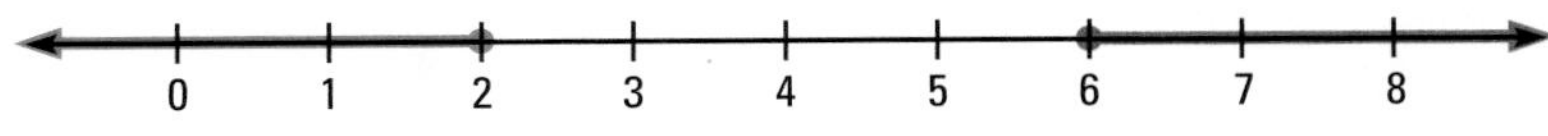

EXAMPLE 7 Write and use a compound inequality

BIOLOGY A monitor lizard has a temperature that ranges from 18°C to 34°C. Write the range of temperatures as a compound inequality. Then write an inequality giving the temperature range in degrees Fahrenheit.

Monitor lizard

Solution

The range of temperatures C can be represented by the inequality $18 \le C \le 34$. Let F represent the temperature in degrees Fahrenheit.

$18 \le C \le 34$	**Write inequality.**
$18 \le \frac{5}{9}(F - 32) \le 34$	**Substitute $\frac{5}{9}(F - 32)$ for C.**
$32.4 \le F - 32 \le 61.2$	**Multiply each expression by $\frac{9}{5}$, the reciprocal of $\frac{5}{9}$.**
$64.4 \le F \le 93.2$	**Add 32 to each expression.**

USE A FORMULA
In Example 7, use the temperature formula $C = \frac{5}{9}(F - 32)$.

▶ The temperature of the monitor lizard ranges from 64.4°F to 93.2°F.

GUIDED PRACTICE for Examples 5, 6, and 7

Solve the inequality. Then graph the solution.

9. $-1 < 2x + 7 < 19$

10. $-8 \le -x - 5 \le 6$

11. $x + 4 \le 9$ or $x - 3 \ge 7$

12. $3x - 1 < -1$ or $2x + 5 \ge 11$

13. **WHAT IF?** In Example 7, write a compound inequality for a lizard whose temperature ranges from 15°C to 30°C. Then write an inequality giving the temperature range in degrees Fahrenheit.

1.6 EXERCISES

HOMEWORK KEY
○ = **WORKED-OUT SOLUTIONS on p. WS2 for Exs. 13, 25, and 55**
★ = **STANDARDIZED TEST PRACTICE Exs. 2, 15, 36, 56, and 59**

SKILL PRACTICE

1. **VOCABULARY** Copy and complete: The set of all points on a number line that represent solutions of an inequality is called the __?__ of the inequality.

2. ★ **WRITING** The first transformation on page 42 can be written as follows:

If a, b, and c are real numbers and $a > b$, then $a + c > b + c$.

Write similar statements for the other transformations listed on page 42.

EXAMPLE 1 on p. 41 for Exs. 3–10

GRAPHING INEQUALITIES **Graph the inequality.**

3. $x > 4$

4. $x < -1$

5. $x \le -5$

6. $x \ge 3$

7. $6 \ge x$

8. $-2 < x$

9. $x \ge -3.5$

10. $x < 2.5$

EXAMPLE 2
on p. 41
for Exs. 11–21

WRITING COMPOUND INEQUALITIES **Write the compound inequality that is represented by the graph.**

11. 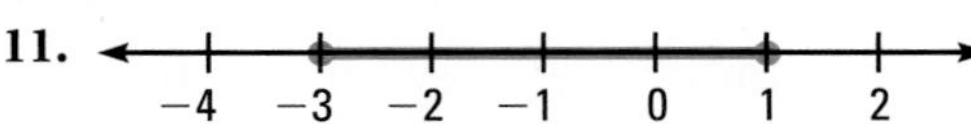

12. 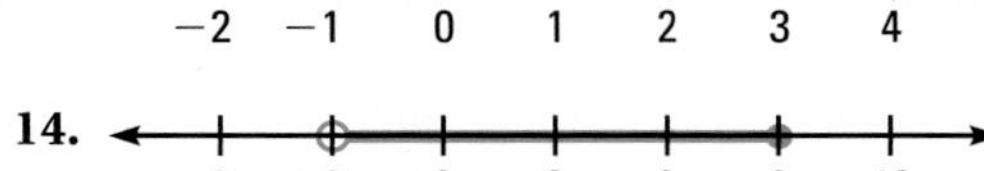

13. −6 −4 −2 0 2 4 6

14. −6 −3 0 3 6 9 12

15. ★ **MULTIPLE CHOICE** What compound inequality is graphed below?

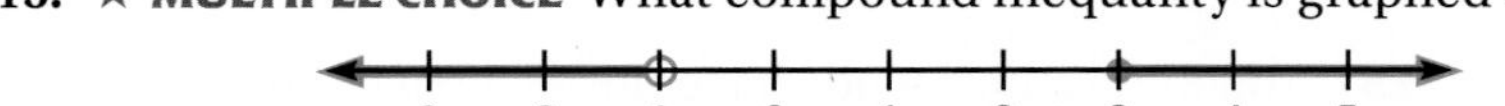

Ⓐ $-1 < x < 3$
Ⓑ $x \le -1$ or $x > 3$
Ⓒ $x < -1$ or $x \ge 3$
Ⓓ $x > -1$ or $x \le 3$

GRAPHING COMPOUND INEQUALITIES **Graph the compound inequality.**

16. $2 \le x \le 5$
17. $-3 < x < 4$
18. $5 \le x < 10$
19. $x < 0$ or $x > 2$
20. $x \le -1$ or $x > 1$
21. $x > -2$ or $x < -5$

EXAMPLES 3 and 4
on pp. 42–43
for Exs. 22–35

SOLVING INEQUALITIES **Solve the inequality. Then graph the solution.**

22. $x + 4 > 10$
23. $x - 3 \le -5$
24. $4x - 8 \ge -4$
25. $15 - 3x > 3$
26. $11 + 8x \ge 7$
27. $4 + \frac{3}{2}x \le 13$
28. $2x - 6 > 3 - x$
29. $4x + 14 < 3x + 6$
30. $5 - 8x \le 19 - 10x$
31. $21x + 7 < 3x + 16$
32. $18 + 2x \le 9x + 4$
33. $2(x - 4) > 4x + 6$

ERROR ANALYSIS ***Describe*** **and correct the error in solving the inequality.**

34.
$2x + 8 \le 6x - 4$
$-4x \le -12$
$x \le 3$

35.
$10 + 3x > 5x$
$10 < 2x$
$5 < x$

36. ★ **OPEN-ENDED MATH** Write two different inequalities of the form $ax + b > c$ that have a solution of $x > 5$.

EXAMPLE 5
on p. 43
for Exs. 37–42

"AND" COMPOUND INEQUALITIES **Solve the inequality. Then graph the solution.**

37. $-5 < x + 1 < 4$
38. $2 \le x - 3 \le 6$
39. $-3 < 4 - x \le 3$
40. $2 < 3x - 1 \le 6$
41. $-4 \le 2 + 4x < 0$
42. $0 \le \frac{3}{4}x + 3 \le 4$

EXAMPLE 6
on p. 43
for Exs. 43–48

"OR" COMPOUND INEQUALITIES **Solve the inequality. Then graph the solution.**

43. $x + 1 < -3$ or $x - 2 > 0$
44. $x - 4 \le -6$ or $x + 2 > 5$
45. $2x - 3 \le -4$ or $3x + 1 \ge 4$
46. $2 + 3x < -13$ or $4 + 2x > 7$
47. $0.3x - 0.5 < -1.7$ or $0.4x \ge 2.4$
48. $-x - 4 \ge 1$ or $2 - 5x \le -8$

CHALLENGE **Solve the inequality. If there is no solution, write *no solution*. If the inequality is always true, write *all real numbers*.**

49. $2(x - 4) > 2x + 1$
50. $4x - 5 \le 4(x + 2)$
51. $2(3x - 1) > 3(2x + 3)$

PROBLEM SOLVING

EXAMPLE 3 on p. 42 for Exs. 52–53

52. **SWIMMING** You have budgeted \$100 to improve your swimming over the summer. At your local pool, it costs \$50 to join the swim association and \$5 for each swim class. Write and solve an inequality to find the possible numbers of swim classes you can attend within your budget.

@HomeTutor for problem solving help at classzone.com

53. **VIDEO CONTEST** You and some friends have raised \$250 to help make a video for a contest. You need \$35 to buy videotapes. It costs \$45 per day to rent the video camera. Write and solve an inequality to find the possible numbers of days you can rent the video camera.

@HomeTutor for problem solving help at classzone.com

54. **WAKEBOARDING** What you wear when you wakeboard depends on the air temperature. Copy and complete the table by writing an inequality for each temperature range. Assume each range includes the lower temperature but not the higher temperature. (The first inequality has been written for you.)

Temperature	Gear	Inequality
60°F to 65°F	Full wetsuit	$60 \le T < 65$
65°F to 72°F	Full leg wetsuit	?
72°F to 80°F	Wetsuit trunks	?
80°F or warmer	No special gear	?

55. **BOTANY** In Olympic National Park in Washington, different plants grow depending on the elevation, as shown in the diagram. Assume each range includes the lower elevation but not the higher elevation.

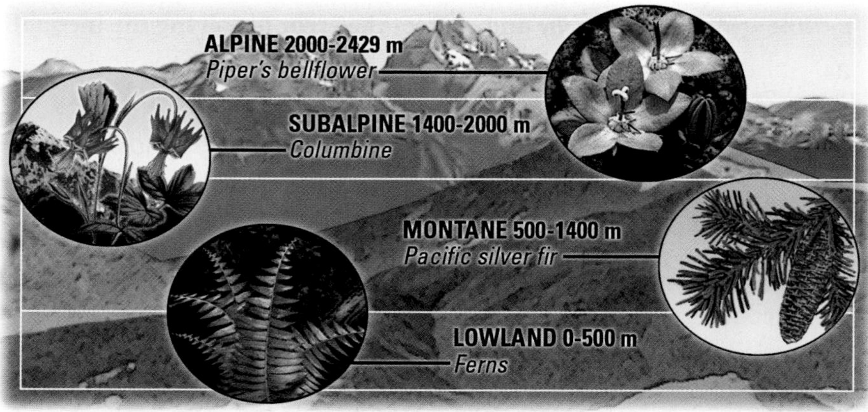

a. Write an inequality for elevations in the lowland zone.

b. Write an inequality for elevations in the alpine and subalpine zones combined.

c. Write an inequality for elevations *not* in the montane zone.

56. ★ **MULTIPLE CHOICE** Canoe rental costs \$18 for the first two hours and \$3 per hour after that. You want to canoe for more than 2 hours but can spend no more than \$30. Which inequality represents the situation, where t is the total number of hours you can canoe?

Ⓐ $18 + t \le 30$ Ⓑ $18 + 3t \le 30$

Ⓒ $18 + 3(t + 2) \le 30$ Ⓓ $18 + 3(t - 2) \le 30$

EXAMPLE 7
on p. 44
for Exs. 57–58

57. LAPTOP COMPUTERS A computer manufacturer states that its laptop computer can operate within a temperature range of 50°F to 95°F. Write a compound inequality for the temperature range. Then rewrite the inequality in degrees Celsius.

58. MULTI-STEP PROBLEM On a certain highway, there is a minimum speed of 45 miles per hour and a maximum speed of 70 miles per hour.

a. Write a compound inequality for the legal speeds on the highway.

b. Write a compound inequality for the illegal speeds on the highway.

c. Write each compound inequality from parts (a) and (b) so that it expresses the speeds in kilometers per hour. (1 mi $\approx$ 1.61 km)

59. ★ EXTENDED RESPONSE A math teacher announces that grades will be calculated by adding 65% of a student's homework score, 15% of the student's quiz score, and 20% of the student's final exam score. All scores range from 0 to 100 points.

a. Write Inequalities Write an inequality for each student that can be used to find the possible final exam scores that result in a grade of 85 or better.

b. Solve Solve the inequalities from part (a).

c. Interpret For which students is a grade of 85 or better possible? *Explain.*

Name	Homework	Quiz	Exam
Amy	84	80	w
Brian	80	100	x
Clara	75	95	y
Dan	80	90	z

60. CHALLENGE You are shopping for single-use cameras to hand out at a party. The daylight cameras cost \$2.75 and the flash cameras cost \$4.25. You must buy exactly 20 cameras and you want to spend between \$65 and \$75, inclusive. Write and solve a compound inequality for this situation. Then list all the solutions that involve whole numbers of cameras.

NEW YORK MIXED REVIEW

TEST PRACTICE at classzone.com

61. Steve has 6 fewer trading cards than Kevin. Thomas has twice as many trading cards as Steve. The three students have a total of 22 trading cards. Which equation can be used to find the number of trading cards that Kevin has?

Ⓐ $x - 6x + \frac{1}{2}x = 22$

Ⓑ $x + (x - 6) + 2x = 22$

Ⓒ $x + (x - 6) + 2(x - 6) = 22$

Ⓓ $2x + (x - 6) + (x - 6) = 22$

62. The radius and height of a cylindrical can are doubled. How does the surface area of the new cylindrical can compare with the surface area of the original cylindrical can?

Ⓐ The new surface area is two times the original surface area.

Ⓑ The new surface area is four times the original surface area.

Ⓒ The new surface area is six times the original surface area.

Ⓓ The new surface area is eight times the original surface area.

PROBLEM SOLVING WORKSHOP
LESSON 1.6

Using ALTERNATIVE METHODS

Another Way to Solve Example 3, page 42

MULTIPLE REPRESENTATIONS Example 3 of Lesson 1.6 involved solving an inequality using algebra. You can also solve an inequality using a table or a graphing calculator's *test* feature, which tells when an inequality is true or false.

PROBLEM

FAIR You have \$50 to spend at a county fair. You spend \$20 for admission. You want to play a game that costs \$1.50. Describe the possible numbers of times you can play the game.

METHOD 1

Using a Table One alternative approach is to make a table of values.

STEP 1 **Write** an expression for the total cost of admission and playing x games.

Admission fee + Cost per game · Number of games

$20 + 1.50 \cdot x$

STEP 2 **Enter** the equation $y = 20 + 1.5x$ into a graphing calculator.

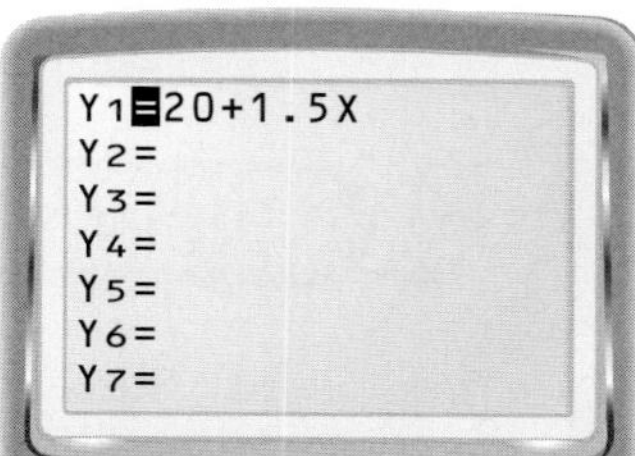

STEP 3 **Make** a table of values for the equation.

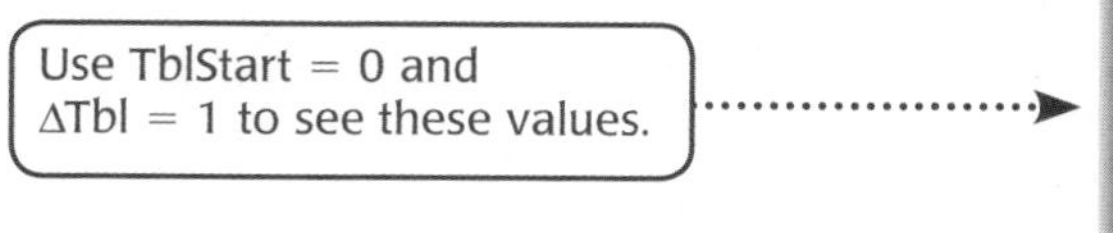

X	Y1
0	20
1	21.5
2	23
3	24.5
4	26

X=0

STEP 4 **Scroll** through the table of values to find when the total cost is \$50. You can see that $y = 50$ when $x = 20$.

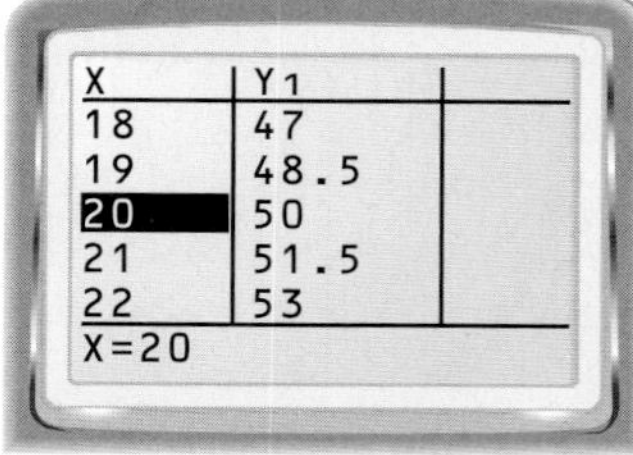

▶ The table suggests that $20 + 1.5x \leq 50$ when $x \leq 20$. So, you can play the game at the fair 20 times or fewer.

METHOD 2 **Using a Graph** Another approach is to use a graph.

If your graphing calculator has a *test* feature, you can enter the inequality and evaluate its truth for various values of x.

- When the inequality is *true*, the calculator returns a 1.
- When the inequality is *false*, the calculator returns a 0.

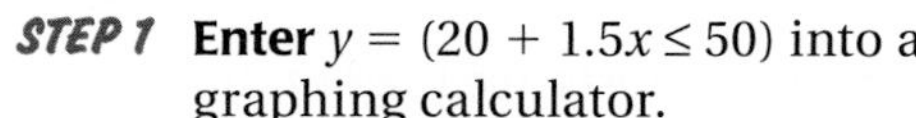

STEP 1 **Enter** $y = (20 + 1.5x \leq 50)$ into a graphing calculator.

Press 2nd [TEST] 6 to enter the ≤ symbol.

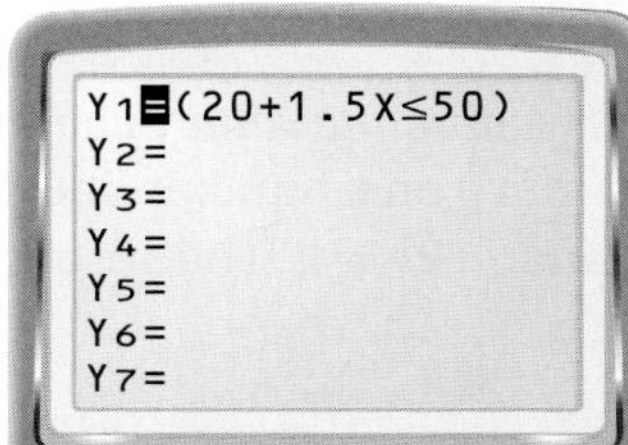

STEP 2 **Graph** the result.

The y-value is 1 for all x-values that make the inequality true.

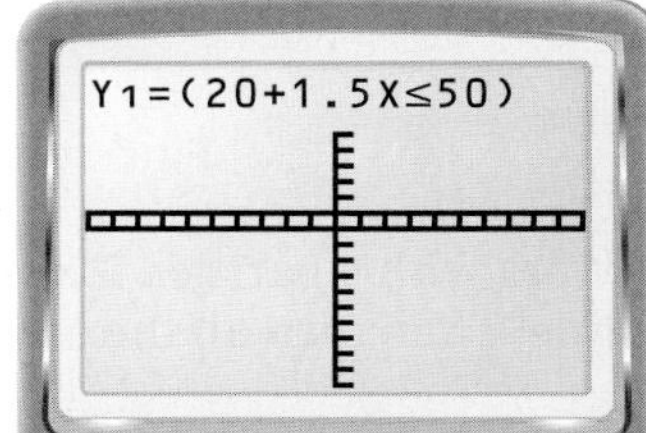

STEP 3 **Find** the point where the inequality changes from true to false by using the *trace* feature.

▶ The graph suggests that the inequality is true when $x \leq 20$. So, you can play the game at the fair 20 times or fewer.

PRACTICE

1. **REASONING** Determine the equation that gives the table below. For what x-values is $y < -500$?

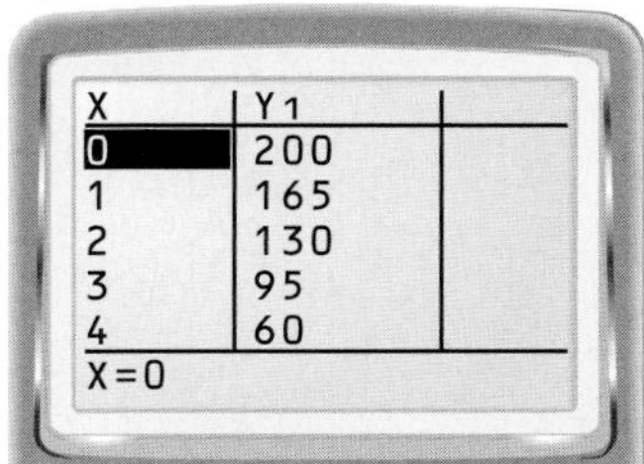

X	Y1	
0	200	
1	165	
2	130	
3	95	
4	60	
X=0		

2. **GIFT** You have \$16.50 to spend for a friend's birthday. You spend \$3 on a card and want to buy some chocolates that cost \$.75 each. What are the numbers of chocolates you can buy? Solve using a table and using a graph.

3. **SALESPERSON** A salesperson has a weekly salary of \$1550 and gets a 5% commission on sales. What are the amounts the salesperson can sell to earn at least \$1900 per week? Solve using a table and using a graph.

4. **WRITING** *Explain* how to use a table like the one below to solve $0.5x - 1.5 \leq 3 - 0.4x$.

X	Y1	Y2
0	-1.5	3
1	-1	2.6
2	-.5	2.2
3	0	1.8
4	.5	1.4
X=0		

1.7 Absolute Value Equations and Inequalities

MATERIALS • 13 index cards numbered with the integers from −6 to 6

QUESTION **What does the solution of an absolute value equation or inequality look like on a number line?**

The *absolute value* of a number x, written $|x|$, is the distance the number is from 0 on a number line. Because 2 and −2 are both 2 units from 0, $|2| = 2$ and $|-2| = 2$. The absolute value of a number is never negative.

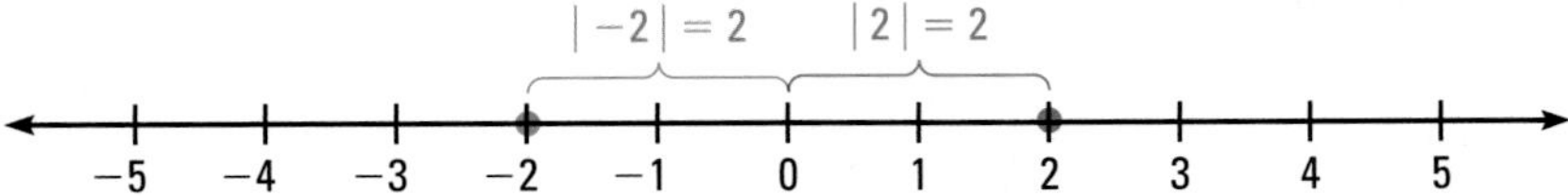

EXPLORE **Find solutions of absolute value equations and inequalities**

Work with a partner. Place the numbered index cards in a row to form a number line. Then turn all the cards face down.

STEP 1

Solve equations
Turn over cards to reveal numbers that are solutions of the equations below.

a. $|x| = 2$

b. $|x - 2| = 1$

c. $|x + 1| = 3$

STEP 2

Solve inequalities with $\leq$
Turn over cards to reveal numbers that are solutions of the inequalities below.

d. $|x| \leq 2$

e. $|x - 2| \leq 1$

f. $|x + 1| \leq 3$

STEP 3

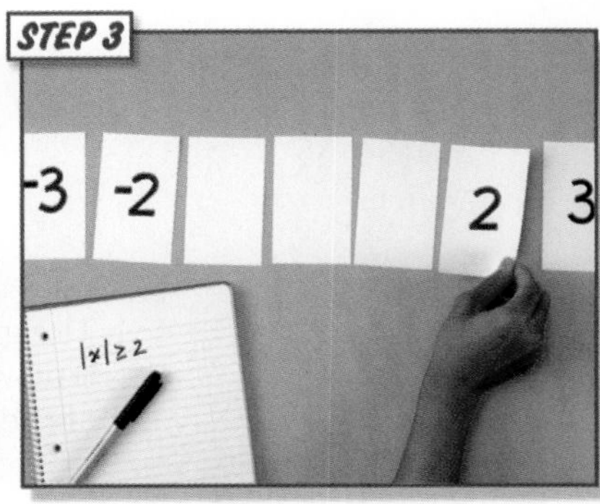

Solve inequalities with $\geq$
Turn over cards to reveal numbers that are solutions of the inequalities below.

g. $|x| \geq 2$

h. $|x - 2| \geq 1$

i. $|x + 1| \geq 3$

DRAW CONCLUSIONS **Use your observations to complete these exercises**

1. *Describe* the solutions of the absolute value equations in Step 1. Will all absolute value equations have the same number of solutions? *Explain.*

2. *Compare* the solutions of the absolute value inequalities in Steps 2 and 3. How does the inequality symbol ($\leq$ or $\geq$) affect the pattern of the solutions?

1.7 Solve Absolute Value Equations and Inequalities

A2.A.1 Solve absolute value equations and inequalities involving linear expressions in one variable

Before You solved linear equations and inequalities.

Now You will solve absolute value equations and inequalities.

Why? So you can describe hearing ranges of animals, as in Ex. 81.

Key Vocabulary
- **absolute value**
- **extraneous solution**

Recall that the **absolute value** of a number x, written $|x|$, is the distance the number is from 0 on a number line. This understanding of absolute value can be extended to apply to simple absolute value equations.

$$|x| = \begin{cases} x, & \text{if } x \text{ is positive} \\ 0, & \text{if } x = 0 \\ -x, & \text{if } x \text{ is negative} \end{cases}$$

KEY CONCEPT — *For Your Notebook*

Interpreting Absolute Value Equations

Equation	$\lvert x\rvert = \lvert x - 0\rvert = k$	$\lvert x - b\rvert = k$
Meaning	The distance between x and 0 is k.	The distance between x and b is k.
Graph	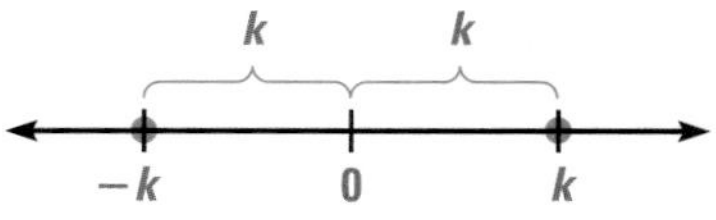	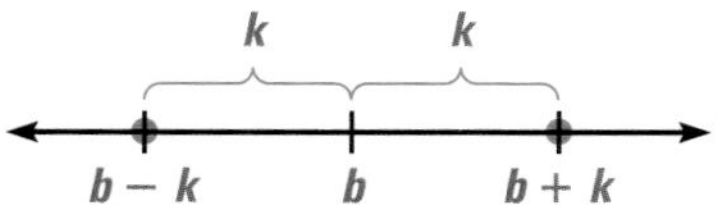
Solutions	$x - 0 = -k$ or $x - 0 = k$	$x - b = -k$ or $x - b = k$
	$x = -k$ or $x = k$	$x = b - k$ or $x = b + k$

EXAMPLE 1 Solve a simple absolute value equation

Solve $|x - 5| = 7$. Graph the solution.

Solution

$\lvert x - 5\rvert = 7$			**Write original equation.**
$x - 5 = -7$	or	$x - 5 = 7$	**Write equivalent equations.**
$x = 5 - 7$	or	$x = 5 + 7$	**Solve for x.**
$x = -2$	or	$x = 12$	**Simplify.**

▶ The solutions are -2 and 12. These are the values of x that are 7 units away from 5 on a number line. The graph is shown below.

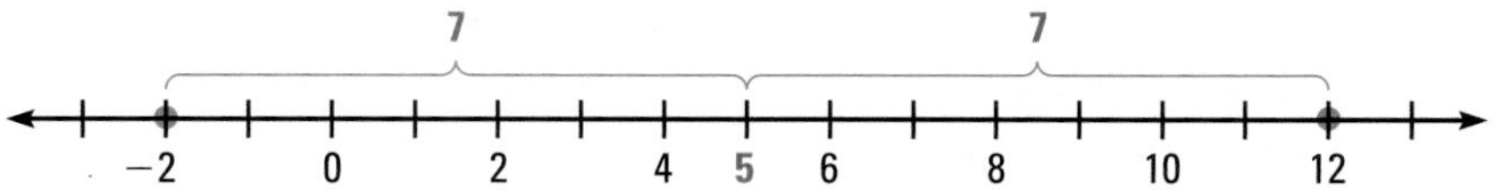

KEY CONCEPT — For Your Notebook

Solving an Absolute Value Equation

Use these steps to solve an absolute value equation $|ax + b| = c$ where $c > 0$.

STEP 1 **Write** two equations: $ax + b = c$ or $ax + b = -c$.

STEP 2 **Solve** each equation.

STEP 3 **Check** each solution in the original absolute value equation.

EXAMPLE 2 Solve an absolute value equation

Solve $|5x - 10| = 45$.

$|5x - 10| = 45$			**Write original equation.**
$5x - 10 = 45$	or	$5x - 10 = -45$	**Expression can equal 45 or −45.**
$5x = 55$	or	$5x = -35$	**Add 10 to each side.**
$x = 11$	or	$x = -7$	**Divide each side by 5.**

▶ The solutions are 11 and −7. Check these in the original equation.

CHECK

$|5x - 10| = 45$	$|5x - 10| = 45$
$|5(11) - 10| \stackrel{?}{=} 45$	$|5(-7) - 10| \stackrel{?}{=} 45$
$|45| \stackrel{?}{=} 45$	$|-45| \stackrel{?}{=} 45$
$45 = 45$ ✓	$45 = 45$ ✓

EXTRANEOUS SOLUTIONS When you solve an absolute value equation, it is possible for a solution to be *extraneous*. An **extraneous solution** is an apparent solution that must be rejected because it does not satisfy the original equation.

EXAMPLE 3 Check for extraneous solutions

Solve $|2x + 12| = 4x$. Check for extraneous solutions.

$|2x + 12| = 4x$			**Write original equation.**
$2x + 12 = 4x$	or	$2x + 12 = -4x$	**Expression can equal $4x$ or $-4x$.**
$12 = 2x$	or	$12 = -6x$	**Subtract $2x$ from each side.**
$6 = x$	or	$-2 = x$	**Solve for x.**

AVOID ERRORS
Always check your solutions in the original equation to make sure that they are not extraneous.

Check the apparent solutions to see if either is extraneous.

CHECK

$|2x + 12| = 4x$	$|2x + 12| = 4x$
$|2(6) + 12| \stackrel{?}{=} 4(6)$	$|2(-2) + 12| \stackrel{?}{=} 4(-2)$
$|24| \stackrel{?}{=} 24$	$|8| \stackrel{?}{=} -8$
$24 = 24$ ✓	$8 \neq -8$

▶ The solution is 6. Reject −2 because it is an extraneous solution.

GUIDED PRACTICE for Examples 1, 2, and 3

Solve the equation. Check for extraneous solutions.

1. $|x| = 5$
2. $|x - 3| = 10$
3. $|x + 2| = 7$
4. $|3x - 2| = 13$
5. $|2x + 5| = 3x$
6. $|4x - 1| = 2x + 9$

INEQUALITIES You can solve an absolute value inequality by rewriting it as a compound inequality and then solving each part.

KEY CONCEPT *For Your Notebook*

Absolute Value Inequalities

Inequality	Equivalent form	Graph of solution
$\lvert ax + b \rvert < c$	$-c < ax + b < c$	
$\lvert ax + b \rvert \le c$	$-c \le ax + b \le c$	
$\lvert ax + b \rvert > c$	$ax + b < -c$ or $ax + b > c$	
$\lvert ax + b \rvert \ge c$	$ax + b \le -c$ or $ax + b \ge c$	

EXAMPLE 4 Solve an inequality of the form $|ax + b| > c$

Solve $|4x + 5| > 13$. Then graph the solution.

Solution

The absolute value inequality is equivalent to $4x + 5 < -13$ or $4x + 5 > 13$.

First Inequality		Second Inequality
$4x + 5 < -13$	Write inequalities.	$4x + 5 > 13$
$4x < -18$	Subtract 5 from each side.	$4x > 8$
$x < -\frac{9}{2}$	Divide each side by 4.	$x > 2$

▶ The solutions are all real numbers less than $-\frac{9}{2}$ or greater than 2. The graph is shown below.

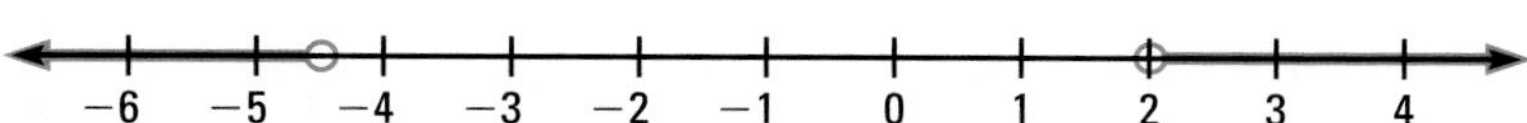

at classzone.com

GUIDED PRACTICE for Example 4

Solve the inequality. Then graph the solution.

7. $|x + 4| \ge 6$
8. $|2x - 7| > 1$
9. $|3x + 5| \ge 10$

EXAMPLE 5 Solve an inequality of the form $|ax + b| \le c$

READING
Tolerance is the maximum acceptable deviation of an item from some ideal or mean measurement.

BASEBALL A professional baseball should weigh 5.125 ounces, with a *tolerance* of 0.125 ounce. Write and solve an absolute value inequality that describes the acceptable weights for a baseball.

Solution

STEP 1 **Write** a verbal model. Then write an inequality.

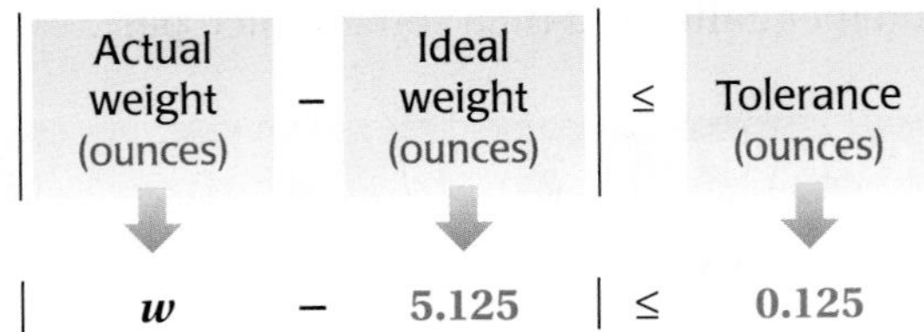

STEP 2 **Solve** the inequality.

$|w - 5.125| \le 0.125$ **Write inequality.**

$-0.125 \le w - 5.125 \le 0.125$ **Write equivalent compound inequality.**

$5 \le w \le 5.25$ **Add 5.125 to each expression.**

▶ So, a baseball should weigh between 5 ounces and 5.25 ounces, inclusive. The graph is shown below.

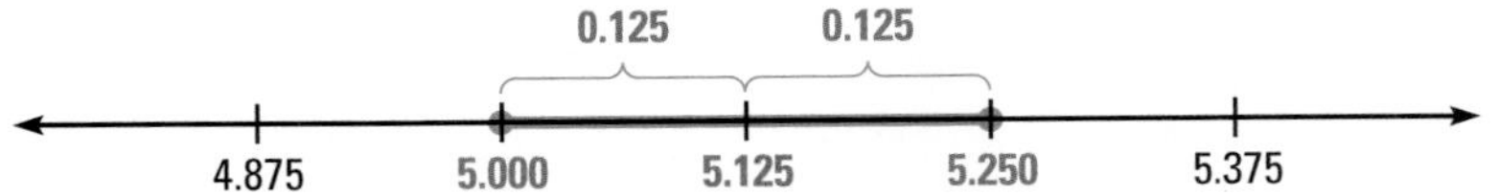

EXAMPLE 6 Write a range as an absolute value inequality

GYMNASTICS The thickness of the mats used in the rings, parallel bars, and vault events must be between 7.5 inches and 8.25 inches, inclusive. Write an absolute value inequality describing the acceptable mat thicknesses.

Solution

REVIEW MEAN
For help with finding a mean, see p. 1005.

STEP 1 **Calculate** the mean of the extreme mat thicknesses.

$$\text{Mean of extremes} = \frac{7.5 + 8.25}{2} = 7.875$$

STEP 2 **Find** the tolerance by subtracting the mean from the upper extreme.

$$\text{Tolerance} = 8.25 - 7.875 = 0.375$$

STEP 3 **Write** a verbal model. Then write an inequality.

| Actual thickness (inches) | – | Mean of extremes (inches) | ≤ | Tolerance (inches) |

$$|\, t \quad - \quad 7.875 \,| \le 0.375$$

▶ A mat is acceptable if its thickness t satisfies $|t - 7.875| \le 0.375$.

✓ **GUIDED PRACTICE** for Examples 5 and 6

Solve the inequality. Then graph the solution.

10. $|x + 2| < 6$

11. $|2x + 1| \leq 9$

12. $|7 - x| \leq 4$

13. GYMNASTICS For Example 6, write an absolute value inequality describing the *unacceptable* mat thicknesses.

1.7 EXERCISES

HOMEWORK KEY

○ = **WORKED-OUT SOLUTIONS** on p. WS2 for Exs. 21, 47, and 77

★ = **STANDARDIZED TEST PRACTICE** Exs. 2, 33, 40, 63, and 64

◆ = **MULTIPLE REPRESENTATIONS** Ex. 78

SKILL PRACTICE

1. VOCABULARY What is an extraneous solution of an equation?

2. ★ WRITING The absolute value of a number cannot be negative. How, then, can the absolute value of x be $-x$ for certain values of x?

CHECKING SOLUTIONS **Decide whether the given number is a solution of the equation.**

3. $|b - 1| = 14; -13$

4. $|d + 6| = 10; -4$

5. $|32 - 6f| = 20; -2$

6. $|2m + 6| = 10; -8$

7. $|3n - 7| = 4; 1$

8. $|17 - 8r| = 15; 4$

EXAMPLE 1 on p. 51 for Exs. 9–20

SOLVING EQUATIONS **Solve the equation. Graph the solution.**

9. $|x| = 9$

10. $|y| = -5$

11. $|z| = 0$

12. $|f - 5| = 3$

13. $|g - 2| = 7$

14. $|h - 4| = 4$

15. $|k + 3| = 6$

16. $|m + 5| = 1$

17. $|n + 9| = 10$

18. $|6 - p| = 4$

19. $|5 - q| = 7$

20. $|-4 - r| = 4$

EXAMPLE 2 on p. 52 for Exs. 21–32

SOLVING EQUATIONS **Solve the equation.**

(21.) $|2d - 5| = 13$

22. $|3g + 14| = 7$

23. $|7h - 10| = 4$

24. $|3p - 6| = 21$

25. $|2q + 3| = 11$

26. $|4r + 7| = 43$

27. $|5 + 2j| = 9$

28. $|6 - 3k| = 21$

29. $|20 - 9m| = 7$

30. $\left|\frac{1}{4}x - 3\right| = 10$

31. $\left|\frac{1}{2}y + 4\right| = 6$

32. $\left|\frac{2}{3}z - 6\right| = 12$

33. ★ SHORT RESPONSE The equation $|5x - 10| = 45$ in Example 2 has two solutions. Does the equation $|5x - 10| = -45$ also have two solutions? *Explain.*

EXAMPLE 3 on p. 52 for Exs. 34–42

EXTRANEOUS SOLUTIONS **Solve the equation. Check for extraneous solutions.**

34. $|3x - 4| = x$

35. $|x + 24| = -7x$

36. $|8x - 1| = 6x$

37. $|4x + 5| = 2x + 4$

38. $|9 - 2x| = 10 + 3x$

39. $|8 + 5x| = 7 - x$

40. ★ **MULTIPLE CHOICE** What is (are) the solution(s) of $|3x + 7| = 5x$?

Ⓐ $-4, -\frac{2}{3}$ Ⓑ $-\frac{7}{8}, \frac{7}{2}$ Ⓒ $\frac{7}{8}, \frac{7}{2}$ Ⓓ $\frac{7}{2}$

ERROR ANALYSIS ***Describe*** **and correct the error in solving the equation.**

41.

$|5x - 9| = x + 3$

$5x - 9 = x + 3$ or $5x - 9 = -x + 3$

$4x - 9 = 3$ or $6x - 9 = 3$

$4x = 12$ or $6x = 12$

$x = 3$ or $x = 2$

The solutions are 3 and 2.

42.

$|n - 7| = 3n - 1$

$n - 7 = 3n - 1$ or $n - 7 = -3n + 1$

$-7 = 2n - 1$ or $4n - 7 = 1$

$-6 = 2n$ or $4n = 8$

$-3 = n$ or $n = 2$

The solutions are −3 and 2.

EXAMPLES 4 and 5 on pp. 53–54 for Exs. 43–63

SOLVING INEQUALITIES **Solve the inequality. Then graph the solution.**

43. $|j| \le 5$ 44. $|k| > 4$ 45. $|m - 2| < 7$ 46. $|n - 11| \ge 1$

47. $|d + 4| \ge 3$ 48. $|f + 6| < 2$ 49. $|g - 1| > 0$ 50. $|h + 10| \le 10$

51. $|3w - 15| < 30$ 52. $|2x + 6| \ge 10$ 53. $|4y - 9| \le 7$ 54. $|5z + 1| > 14$

55. $|16 - p| > 3$ 56. $|24 - q| \le 11$ 57. $|7 - 2r| < 19$ 58. $|19 - 5t| > 7$

59. $\left|\frac{1}{2}x - 10\right| \le 4$ 60. $\left|\frac{1}{3}m - 15\right| < 6$ 61. $\left|\frac{1}{7}y + 2\right| - 5 > 3$ 62. $\left|\frac{2}{5}n - 8\right| + 4 \ge 12$

Animated Algebra at classzone.com

63. ★ **MULTIPLE CHOICE** What is the solution of $|6x - 9| \ge 33$?

Ⓐ $-4 \le x \le 7$ Ⓑ $-7 \le x \le 4$

Ⓒ $x \le -4$ or $x \ge 7$ Ⓓ $x \le -7$ or $x \ge 4$

64. ★ **MULTIPLE CHOICE** Which absolute value inequality represents the graph shown below?

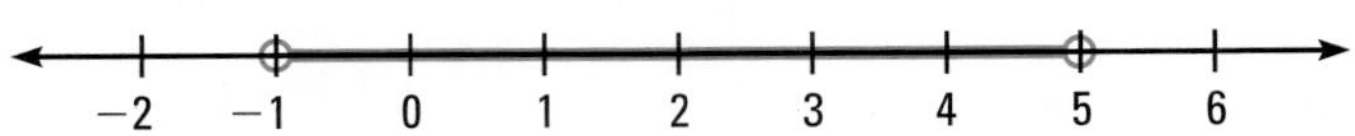

Ⓐ $-1 < |x| < 5$ Ⓑ $|x + 2| < 3$ Ⓒ $|x - 2| < 3$ Ⓓ $|x - 2| < 5$

65. **REASONING** For the equation $|ax + b| = c$ (where a, b, and c are real numbers and $a \ne 0$), describe the value(s) of c that yield two solutions, one solution, and no solution.

SOLVING INEQUALITIES **Solve the inequality. Then graph the solution.**

66. $|x + 1| \ge -16$ 67. $|2x - 1| < -25$ 68. $|7x + 3| \le 0$ 69. $|x - 9| > 0$

CHALLENGE **Solve the inequality for x in terms of a, b, and c. Assume a, b, and c are real numbers and $c > 0$.**

70. $|ax + b| < c$ where $a > 0$ 71. $|ax + b| \ge c$ where $a > 0$

72. $|ax + b| \le c$ where $a < 0$ 73. $|ax + b| > c$ where $a < 0$

○ = WORKED-OUT SOLUTIONS on p. WS1 ★ = STANDARDIZED TEST PRACTICE ◆ = MULTIPLE REPRESENTATIONS

PROBLEM SOLVING

EXAMPLE 5
on p. 54
for Exs. 74–78

74. GYMNASTICS The horizontal bar used in gymnastics events should be placed 110.25 inches above the ground, with a tolerance of 0.4 inch. Write an absolute value inequality for the acceptable bar heights.

@HomeTutor for problem solving help at classzone.com

75. SOIL PH LEVELS Cucumbers grow in soil having a pH level of 6.5, with a tolerance of 1 point on the pH scale. Write an absolute value inequality that describes the pH levels of soil in which cucumbers can grow.

@HomeTutor for problem solving help at classzone.com

76. MULTI-STEP PROBLEM A baseball has a cushioned cork center called the *pill*. The pill must weigh 0.85 ounce, with a tolerance of 0.05 ounce.

a. Write an absolute value inequality that describes the acceptable weights for the pill of a baseball.

b. Solve the inequality to find the acceptable weights for the pill.

c. Look back at Example 5 on page 54. Find the minimum and maximum percentages of a baseball's total weight that the pill can make up.

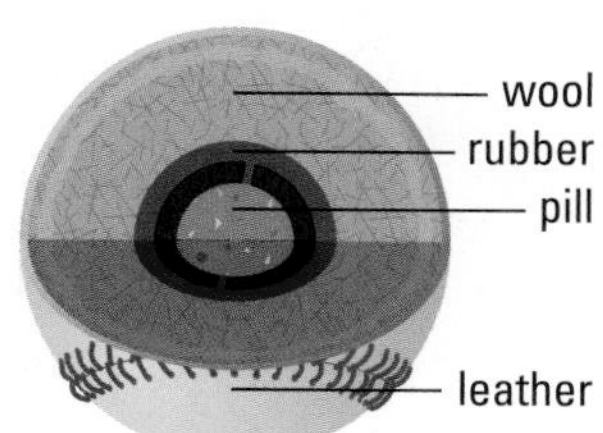

77. MANUFACTURING A regulation basketball should weigh 21 ounces, with a tolerance of 1 ounce. Write an absolute value inequality describing the weights of basketballs that should be *rejected*.

78. MULTIPLE REPRESENTATIONS The strength of eyeglass lenses is measured in units called *diopters*. The diopter number x is negative for nearsighted vision and positive for farsighted vision.

Nearsightedness (focus is in front of retina)	
Mild	$\|x + 1.5\| < 1.5$
Moderate	$\|x + 4.5\| < 1.5$
Severe	$\|x + 7.5\| < 1.5$

Retina
Focus

Retina
Focus

Farsightedness (focus is behind retina)	
Mild	$\|x - 1\| < 1$
Moderate	$\|x - 3\| < 1$
Severe	$\|x - 5\| < 1$

a. **Writing Inequalities** Write an equivalent compound inequality for each vision category shown above. Solve the inequalities.

b. **Making a Graph** Illustrate the six vision categories by graphing their ranges of diopter numbers on the same number line. Label each range with the corresponding category name.

EXAMPLE 6
on p. 54
for Exs. 79–81

79. SLEEPING BAGS A manufacturer of sleeping bags suggests that one model is best suited for temperatures between 30°F and 60°F, inclusive. Write an absolute value inequality for this temperature range.

80. TEMPERATURE The recommended oven setting for cooking a pizza in a professional brick-lined oven is between 550°F and 650°F, inclusive. Write an absolute value inequality for this temperature range.

81. **AUDIBLE FREQUENCIES** An elephant can hear sounds with frequencies from 16 hertz to 12,000 hertz. A mouse can hear sounds with frequencies from 1000 hertz to 91,000 hertz. Write an absolute value inequality for the hearing range of each animal.

82. **CHALLENGE** The depth finder on a fishing boat gives readings that are within 5% of the actual water depth. When the depth finder reading is 250 feet, the actual water depth x lies within a range given by the following inequality:

$$|x - 250| \leq 0.05x$$

a. Write the absolute value inequality as a compound inequality.

b. Solve each part of the compound inequality for x. What are the possible actual water depths if the depth finder's reading is 250 feet?

NEW YORK MIXED REVIEW

TEST PRACTICE at classzone.com

83. A car dealership hires Anne to wash cars. She is paid \$28 per day plus \$6 for every car she washes. Anne shares the money equally with a friend who assists her. After five days, Anne's share of the pay is \$130. How many cars did Anne and her friend wash?

Ⓐ 17 Ⓑ 20 Ⓒ 32 Ⓓ 39

84. Pentagon $ABCDE$ is the outline of the front of a cabin. The measure of $\angle ABC$ is 115°. What is the measure of $\angle BCD$?

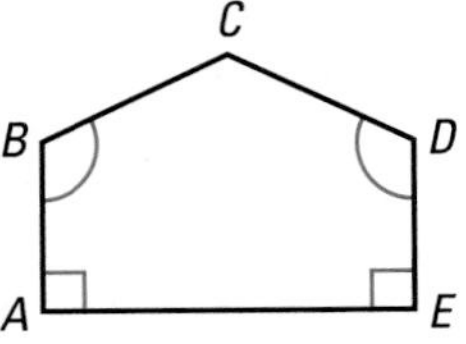

Ⓐ 90° Ⓑ 115°

Ⓒ 130° Ⓓ 155°

QUIZ *for Lessons 1.6–1.7*

Solve the inequality. Then graph the solution. *(p. 41)*

1. $4k - 17 < 27$
2. $14n - 8 \geq 90$
3. $-9p + 15 \leq 96$
4. $-8r - 11 > 45$
5. $3(x - 7) < 6(10 - x)$
6. $-25 - 4z > 66 - 17z$

Solve the equation or inequality. *(p. 51)*

7. $|x - 6| = 9$
8. $|3y + 3| = 12$
9. $|2z + 5| = -9z$
10. $|p + 7| > 2$
11. $|2q - 3| \leq 3$
12. $|5 - r| \geq 4$

13. **TEST SCORES** Your final grade in a course is 80% of your current grade, plus 20% of your final exam score. Your current grade is 83 and your goal is to get a final grade of 85 or better. Write and solve an inequality to find the final exam scores that will meet your goal. *(p. 41)*

14. **GROCERY WEIGHTS** A container of potato salad from your grocer's deli is supposed to weigh 1.5 pounds, with a tolerance of 0.025 pound. Write and solve an absolute value inequality that describes the acceptable weights for the container of potato salad. *(p. 51)*

Lessons 1.5–1.7

1. **HYBRID CAR** A hybrid car gets about 60 miles per gallon of gas in the city and about 51 miles per gallon on the highway. During one week, the hybrid uses 12 gallons of gas and travels 675 miles. How much gas was used on the highway?

   (1) 4 gallons

   (2) 5 gallons

   (3) 7 gallons

   (4) 8 gallons

2. **POPCORN** A popcorn manufacturer's ideal weight for a bag of microwave popcorn is 3.5 ounces, with a tolerance of 0.25 ounce. What is the range of acceptable weights w (in ounces) of a bag of popcorn?

   (1) $w \geq 3.75$

   (2) $w \leq 3.25$

   (3) $-0.25 \leq w \leq 0.25$

   (4) $3.25 \leq w \leq 3.75$

3. **LIQUID OXYGEN** Oxygen exists as a liquid between −369°F and −297°F, inclusive. Which compound inequality gives the range of temperatures T for liquid oxygen?

   (1) $-369 \leq T \leq -297$

   (2) $-369 < T < -297$

   (3) $-297 \leq T \leq -369$

   (4) $-297 < T < -369$

4. **FOOTBALL** A football kicker scores 1 point for each extra point and 3 points for each field goal. One season, a kicker made 34 extra points and scored a total of 112 points. How many field goals did the kicker make?

   (1) 13

   (2) 26

   (3) 48

   (4) 78

5. **SWIMMING POOL** You are draining a swimming pool. The table shows the depth of the water at different times. How long will it take the pool to empty?

Time (h)	0	1	2	3
Depth (ft)	12	10.5	9	7.5

   (1) 4.8 hours (3) 8 hours

   (2) 6.7 hours (4) 24 hours

6. **TRIANGLE INEQUALITY** The triangle inequality relationship from geometry states that the sum of the lengths of any two sides of a triangle is greater than the length of the third side. If the lengths of the three sides of a triangle are x, $2x$, and 9, which of the following is a possible value of x?

   (1) 2 (2) 3 (3) 5 (4) 10

7. **OPEN-ENDED** A video store rents movies for \$2.95 each. Recently, the store has added a special deal that allows you to rent an unlimited number of movies for \$15.95 per month. *Explain* when the special deal is less expensive than renting movies at the usual price. Write and solve an inequality to justify your answer.

8. **OPEN-ENDED** For a rope trick, a magician cuts a 72 inch piece of rope into three pieces of different lengths. The length of one piece must be the mean of the lengths of the other two pieces, as shown below.

short | long | medium

a | b | $\frac{1}{2}(a + b)$

72 in.

Find the length of the second-longest piece.

Write an equation that relates a and b. Explain what this equation expresses about the short and long lengths of the ropes.

Give a pair of possible lengths for the shortest and longest pieces of rope.

1 CHAPTER SUMMARY

BIG IDEAS

For Your Notebook

Big Idea 1

Using Properties to Evaluate and Simplify Expressions

	Example	Answer
To **evaluate a numerical expression**, use order of operations and properties of real numbers.	$3 + (-3)^2$	$3 + 9 = 12$
To **evaluate an algebraic expression**, substitute the value(s) of the variable(s) into the expression, and then evaluate the resulting numerical expression.	$4x - 5$ when $x = 1$	$4(1) - 5 = -1$
To **simplify an algebraic expression**, combine like terms.	$3y - 4 + 2y - 6$	$5y - 10$

Big Idea 2

Using Problem Solving Strategies and Verbal Models

You may be able to write a **verbal model** that describes a real-world problem and use it to write an equation or inequality you can solve. To write the verbal model, analyze the information you are given and use a problem solving strategy if appropriate.

If this is what you know...	...try this strategy.
A formula can be applied to the situation.	Use a Formula
Numerical information is given in a table or a list.	Look for a Pattern
There is a geometric or physical context.	Draw a Diagram

Big Idea 3

Solving Linear and Absolute Value Equations and Inequalities

Use the following guidelines when solving equations and inequalities.

Linear Equation

$$ax + b = 0$$

Use properties of equality to isolate x.

Add or **subtract** the same number from each side of the equation, or **multiply** or **divide** each side by the same nonzero number.

Linear Inequality

$$ax + b \leq 0$$

Use properties similar to those used in solving equations.

Remember to **reverse the inequality** when multiplying or dividing by a **negative** number.

Absolute Value Equation

$$|ax + b| = c$$

Rewrite as follows and solve:

$$ax + b = c \quad \text{or} \quad ax + b = -c$$

Check for **extraneous** solutions.

Absolute Value Inequality

$|ax + b| > c$ → Solve $ax + b < -c$ or $ax + b > c$.

$|ax + b| < c$ → Solve $-c < ax + b < c$.

1 CHAPTER REVIEW

@HomeTutor
classzone.com
- Multi-Language Glossary
- Vocabulary practice

REVIEW KEY VOCABULARY

- opposite, *p. 4*
- reciprocal, *p. 4*
- numerical expression, *p. 10*
- power, *p. 10*
- exponent, *p. 10*
- base, *p. 10*
- variable, *p. 11*
- algebraic expression, *p. 11*
- term, *p. 12*
- variable term, *p. 12*
- constant term, *p. 12*
- coefficient, *p. 12*
- like terms, *p. 12*
- equivalent expressions, *p. 12*
- identity, *p. 12*
- equation, *p. 18*
- linear equation, *p. 18*
- solution of an equation, *p. 18*
- equivalent equations, *p. 18*
- formula, *p. 26*
- solve for a variable, *p. 26*
- verbal model, *p. 34*
- linear inequality, *p. 41*
- solution of an inequality, *p. 41*
- graph of an inequality, *p. 41*
- compound inequality, *p. 41*
- equivalent inequalities, *p. 42*
- absolute value, *p. 51*
- extraneous solution, *p. 52*

VOCABULARY EXERCISES

1. Copy and complete: In a power, the ___?___ represents the number of times the ___?___ is used as a factor.
2. Copy and complete: If substituting a number for a variable in an equation results in a true statement, then the number is a(n) ___?___ of the equation.
3. Copy and complete: A(n) ___?___ is an apparent solution that must be rejected because it does not satisfy the original equation.
4. Identify the like terms in the expression $40 + 3x^3 + 3x^2 - 7 - x^2$.
5. Give an example of two equivalent algebraic expressions.
6. **WRITING** *Compare* the procedures for solving a linear equation and a linear inequality. How are they similar? How are they different?

REVIEW EXAMPLES AND EXERCISES

Use the review examples and exercises below to check your understanding of the concepts you have learned in each lesson of Chapter 1.

1.1 Apply Properties of Real Numbers *pp. 2–9*

EXAMPLE

Identify the property that the statement illustrates.

a. $2(w + \ell) = 2w + 2\ell$

Distributive property

b. $6 + (2 + 4) = 6 + (4 + 2)$

Commutative property of addition

EXERCISES

EXAMPLE 3 on p. 4 for Exs. 7–9

Identify the property that the statement illustrates.

7. $17 \cdot \frac{1}{17} = 1$ **8.** $60 + 0 = 60$ **9.** $3a + 7a = (3 + 7)a$

1 CHAPTER REVIEW

1.2 Evaluate and Simplify Algebraic Expressions

pp. 10–16

EXAMPLE

Simplify the expression.

$5(y-4)-3(2y-9) = 5y-20-6y+27$ **Distributive property**

$= (5y-6y)+(-20+27)$ **Group like terms.**

$= -y+7$ **Combine like terms.**

EXERCISES

EXAMPLES 3 and 4 on pp. 11–12 for Exs. 10–16

Simplify the expression.

10. $25x+14-17-6x$

11. $6y+12x-12y-9x$

12. $6(n-2)-8n+40$

13. $5(2b+3)+8(b-6)$

14. $3g+9g^2-12g^2+g$

15. $7t^4+7t^2-2t^2-9t^4$

16. TAXI RATES A New York City taxi charges \$2.50, plus \$.40 for each fifth of a mile if it is not delayed by traffic. Write an expression for the cost of the ride if you travel x miles in the taxi with no traffic delays.

1.3 Solve Linear Equations

pp. 18–24

EXAMPLE

Solve $-4(3x+5) = -2(5-x)$.

$-4(3x+5) = -2(5-x)$ **Write original equation.**

$-12x-20 = -10+2x$ **Distributive property**

$-20 = -10+14x$ **Add $12x$ to each side.**

$-10 = 14x$ **Add 10 to each side.**

$-\frac{5}{7} = x$ **Divide each side by 14 and simplify.**

EXERCISES

EXAMPLES 1, 2, 3, and 4 on pp. 18–20 for Exs. 17–24

Solve the equation. Check your solution.

17. $24x+16=12$

18. $-6y+15=-9$

19. $4(q-5)=16$

20. $7m+38=-5m-16$

21. $48j+25=12j-11$

22. $8(2n-5)=3(6n-2)$

23. SALES TAX You buy a jacket, and the sales tax is 6%. The total cost is \$79.49. Find the cost of the jacket before the tax.

24. FOOD SHOPPING At a vegetable stand, you bought 3 pounds of peppers for \$4.50. Green peppers cost \$1 per pound and orange peppers cost \$4 per pound. Find how many pounds of each kind of pepper you bought.

@HomeTutor
classzone.com
Chapter Review Practice

1.4 Rewrite Formulas and Equations

pp. 26–32

EXAMPLE

Solve $5x - 11y = 7$ for y. Then find the value of y when $x = 4$.

STEP 1 $5x - 11y = 7$ **Write original equation.**

$-11y = 7 - 5x$ **Subtract 5x from each side.**

$y = -\frac{7}{11} + \frac{5}{11}x$ **Divide each side by −11.**

STEP 2 $y = -\frac{7}{11} + \frac{5}{11}(4)$ **Substitute 4 for x.**

$y = \frac{13}{11}$ **Simplify.**

EXERCISES

EXAMPLES 2, 3, and 4 on pp. 27–28 for Exs. 25–31

Solve the equation for y. Then find the value of y for the given value of x.

25. $10x + y = 7; x = 3$
26. $8y - 3x = 18; x = 2$
27. $xy - 6y = -15; x = 5$
28. $4x = 6y + 9; x = 9$
29. $5x - 2y = 10; x = -6$
30. $x - 3xy = 1; x = -5$

31. **GEOMETRY** The formula $S = 2\pi rh + 2\pi r^2$ gives the surface area S of a cylinder with height h and radius r. Solve the formula for h. Find h if $r = 5$ centimeters and $S = 400$ square centimeters.

1.5 Use Problem Solving Strategies and Models

pp. 34–40

EXAMPLE

Find the time it takes to drive 525 miles at 50 miles per hour.

Distance (miles)	=	Rate (miles/hour)	•	Time (hours)
↓		↓		↓
525	=	**50**	•	***t***

$525 = 50t$ **Write equation.**

$10.5 = t$ **Divide each side by 50.**

▶ It takes 10.5 hours to drive 525 miles at 50 miles per hour.

EXERCISES

EXAMPLES 1 and 4 on pp. 34–36 for Exs. 32–33

32. **AVERAGE SPEED** It takes 3 hours for a train to travel 175 miles. What is the average speed of the train?

33. **CAR RENTAL** While on vacation, your family rented a car for \$293. The car rental cost \$180, plus \$.25 for every mile driven over 150 miles. How many miles did you drive while on vacation?

1 CHAPTER REVIEW

1.6 Solve Linear Inequalities

pp. 41–47

EXAMPLE

Solve $25 - 3x \le 10$. Then graph the solution.

$25 - 3x \le 10$ — Write original inequality.

$-3x \le -15$ — Subtract 25 from each side.

$x \ge 5$ — Divide each side by -3 and reverse the inequality.

Graph the solution.

EXERCISES

EXAMPLES 1, 2, 3, and 4 on pp. 41–43 for Exs. 34–40

Solve the inequality. Then graph the solution.

34. $2x - 3 < -1$
35. $7 - 3x \ge -11$
36. $15x + 8 > 9x - 22$
37. $13x + 24 \le 16 - 3x$
38. $-5 < 10 - x < 5$
39. $-8 \le 3x + 1 \le 10$

40. **GEOMETRY** A triangle has sides of lengths 10, $2x$, and $3x$. The sum of the lengths of any two sides is greater than the length of the third side. Write and solve three inequalities to find the possible values of x.

1.7 Solve Absolute Value Equations and Inequalities

pp. 51–58

EXAMPLE

Solve $|3x - 7| > 2$. Then graph the solution.

$|3x - 7| > 2$ — Write original inequality.

$3x - 7 < -2$ or $3x - 7 > 2$ — Write equivalent compound inequality.

$3x < 5$ or $3x > 9$ — Add 7 to each side.

$x < \frac{5}{3}$ or $x > 3$ — Divide each side by 3.

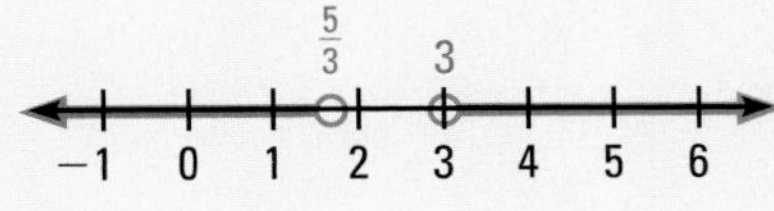

Graph the solution.

EXERCISES

EXAMPLES 2, 3, 4, and 5 on pp. 52–54 for Exs. 41–47

Solve the equation. Check for extraneous solutions.

41. $|3p + 2| = 7$
42. $|9q - 5| = 2q$
43. $|8r + 1| = 3r$

Solve the inequality. Then graph the solution.

44. $|x - 5| \ge 1$
45. $|5 - 2y| > 7$
46. $|6z + 5| \le 25$

47. **VOLLEYBALL** The circumference of a volleyball should be 26 inches, with a tolerance of 0.5 inch. Write and solve an absolute value inequality that describes the acceptable circumferences of a volleyball.

1 CHAPTER TEST

Graph the numbers on a number line.

1. $-2, -\frac{7}{4}, 6.5, \sqrt{30}, \frac{1}{3}$

2. $\frac{9}{2}, 0.8, -5.5, -\sqrt{10}, -\frac{3}{4}$

Use properties and definitions of operations to show that the statement is true. *Justify* each step.

3. $5 + (x - 5) = x$

4. $(3d + 7) - d + 5 = 2d + 12$

Evaluate the expression for the given values of *x* and *y*.

5. $4x - 6y$ when $x = 5$ and $y = -3$

6. $3x^2 - 9y$ when $x = 2$ and $y = 4$

Simplify the expression.

7. $5n + 10 - 8n + 6$

8. $10m - 4(3m + 7) + 6m$

9. $11 + q - 3q^2 + 18q^2 - 2$

10. $9t^2 + 14 - 17t + 6t - 8t^2$

11. $5(x - 3y) + 2(4y - x)$

12. $5(2u + 3w) - 2(5u - 7w)$

Solve the equation. Check your solution.

13. $5n + 11 = -9$

14. $6k + 7 = 4 + 12k$

15. $-t - 2 = 9(t - 8)$

Solve the equation for *y*. Then find the value of *y* for the given value of *x*.

16. $12x - 28y = 40; x = 6$

17. $x + 4y = 12; x = 2$

18. $15y + 2xy = -30; x = 5$

Solve the inequality. Then graph the solution.

19. $-5x - 6 < 19$

20. $x + 22 \geq -3x - 10$

21. $5 < 2x + 3 \leq 11$

Solve the equation. Check for extraneous solutions.

22. $|3d - 4| = 14$

23. $|f + 3| = 2f + 4$

24. $|10 - 7g| = 2g$

Solve the inequality. Then graph the solution.

25. $|x - 5| \leq 30$

26. $|3y + 4| > 2$

27. $\left|\frac{2}{3}z - 5\right| < 5$

28. **WIRELESS NETWORK** To set up a wireless network for Internet access at home, you buy a network router for \$75. The fee for DSL service is \$18 per month. Write an expression for the amount of money you spend in *n* months. How much money do you spend in 12 months?

29. **CAR REPAIR** The bill for the repair of a car was \$420. The cost of parts was \$240. The cost of labor was \$45 per hour. How many hours did the repair take?

30. **HOUSEHOLD CHORES** You can wash one window in 15 minutes and your sister can wash one window in 20 minutes. How many minutes will it take to wash 12 windows if you work together?

31. **GEOMETRY** The formula $V = \frac{1}{3}\pi r^2 h$ gives the volume V of a cone with height h and base radius r. Solve the formula for h. Then find h when $r = 2$ inches and $V = 45$ cubic inches.

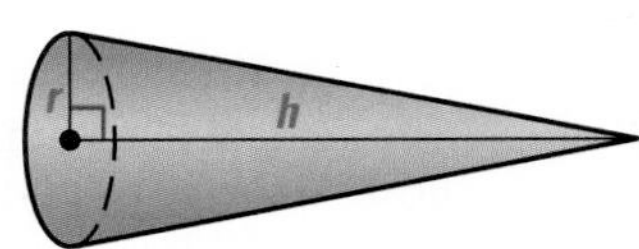

Scoring Rubric

Full Credit
- solution is complete and correct

Partial Credit
- solution is complete but has errors,
  or
- solution is without error but incomplete

No Credit
- no solution is given,
  or
- solution makes no sense

OPEN-ENDED QUESTIONS

PROBLEM

A national bank offers a checking account for a fee of \$3.90 per month. The first 10 transactions per month are free, but every additional transaction costs \$.15. A local bank offers a checking account with no monthly fee, but every transaction costs \$.36. When is it less expensive to use the national bank?

Below are sample solutions to the problem. Read each solution and the comments on the left to see why the sample represents full credit, partial credit, or no credit.

SAMPLE 1: Full credit solution

If you make 10 transactions or fewer per month, the local bank is less expensive because it costs \$3.60 or less, compared to \$3.90 for the national bank. If the number of transactions is more than 10, you can use the following model, where x is the number of transactions per month.

The verbal model explains how the inequality is obtained.

National bank						Local bank		
Cost per transaction over 10	•	Number of transactions over 10	+	Fee	<	Cost per transaction	•	Number of transactions
0.15	•	$(x - 10)$	+	3.90	<	0.36	•	x

The inequality is solved correctly, step by step.

Solve the inequality to find when it is less expensive to use the national bank.

$$0.15(x - 10) + 3.90 < 0.36x$$
$$0.15x - 1.5 + 3.90 < 0.36x$$
$$2.4 < 0.21x$$
$$11.4 < x$$

The answer is correct. An integer makes sense in this context.

A noninteger answer does not make sense, so round up. The national bank is less expensive if you make 12 or more transactions per month.

SAMPLE 2: Partial credit solution

The inequality is correct when $x > 10$. The case when $x \le 10$ is not considered.

$$0.15(x - 10) + 3.90 < 0.36x$$
$$0.15x - 1.5 + 3.90 < 0.36x$$
$$2.4 < 0.21x$$
$$2.19 < x$$

The student made an error in the last step. The answer is incorrect.

The national bank is less expensive if you make 3 or more transactions.

TEST PREPARATION

SAMPLE 3: Partial credit solution

Calculations are shown for 12 transactions only.

Find the cost for each bank when there are 12 transactions.

National bank: \$3.90 + 2(\$.15) = \$4.20 **Local bank:** 12(\$.36) = \$4.32

The answer is correct, but it is not justified.

The national bank is less expensive when you make 12 or more transactions.

SAMPLE 4: No credit solution

The inequality is incorrect. The national bank does not charge \$.15 for every transaction.

$0.15x + 3.90 < 0.36x$

$3.9 < 0.21x$

$18.6 < x$

The answer is incorrect.

The national bank is less expensive when you make 19 or more transactions.

PRACTICE Apply the Scoring Rubric

Use the rubric on page 66 to score the solution to the problem below as *full credit, partial credit,* or *no credit. Explain* your reasoning.

PROBLEM You plant a 1.5 foot tall sawtooth oak that grows 3.5 feet per year and a 5 foot tall chestnut oak that grows 2 feet per year. When will the sawtooth oak be taller than the chestnut oak?

1. The sawtooth oak will be taller than the chestnut oak in about 2.33 years.

2. Let x be the number of years.

Sawtooth initial height	+	Sawtooth growth	>	Chestnut initial height	+	Chestnut growth
1.5	+	3.5x	>	5	+	2x

Solve the inequality for x.

$1.5 + 3.5x > 5 + 2x$

$1.5x > 3.5$

$x > 2.33$

The sawtooth oak will be taller than the chestnut oak after about 2.33 years.

3. $1.5x + 3.5 > 5x + 2$

$1.5 > 3.5x$

$0.43 > x$, so after 0.43 year, the sawtooth oak will be taller.

TEST PREPARATION

TEST PREPARATION

OPEN-ENDED

1. A teacher is buying rulers. At an online site, rulers cost \$.89 each plus \$5 for shipping for the entire order. At a store, each ruler costs \$.95. Under what conditions is the store less expensive? If there is free shipping for online orders over \$50, how does your answer change?

2. Jessica goes on a vacation to Mexico. She exchanges \$150 into pesos. The exchange rate is 11.377 pesos per dollar. She spends 1250 pesos. When she exchanges her remaining pesos back into dollars, how much does she get, to the nearest dollar? *Justify* all of your steps.

3. Consider the equation $|x + h| = a$. For what values of h and a are the solutions of the equation 8 and -12? *Describe* the method you used to solve the problem.

4. Write and solve an equation to find x. Then find the area of the shaded region. *Explain* your reasoning.

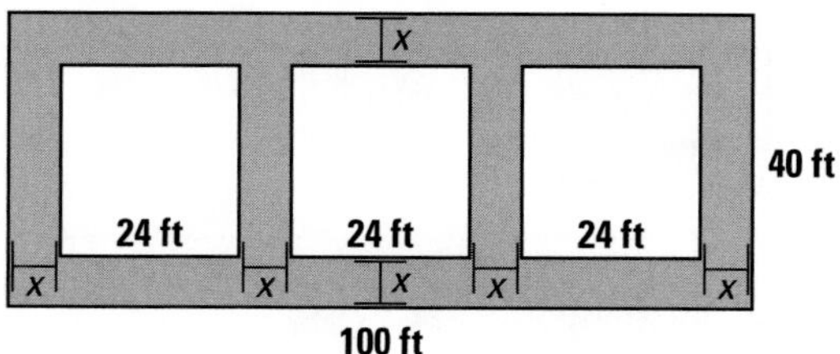

5. The table shows the number of goals g and assists a for four players on a girls' varsity soccer team. Each player is assigned a point total given by $p = 2g + a$.

Player	Goals, *g*	Assists, *a*
Sandra	2	6
Kim	3	5
Jen	4	1
Melanie	5	2

Which player earned the most points?

Is it possible for two players to earn the same number of points but have different numbers of goals and assists? *Justify* your answer.

6. A community is having a Taste of the Town event featuring the area's best restaurants. The admission is \$25 in advance and \$35 at the door. If 220 people pay in advance and the total amount collected is \$7495, how many people pay at the door? How much more money is collected in advance than at the door? *Explain* your solution.

7. Jared and 7 of his friends have a bowling party. Jared's parents pay for bowling, shoe rental, and snacks for all 8 children. The prices of these items are shown in the table. Jared's parents want the total cost to be at most \$80.

Bowling	\$2.70 per person, per game
Shoe rental	\$1.25 per pair
Snacks	\$2.80 per person

If each person bowls the same number of games, what are the possible numbers of games each can bowl? How does your answer change if Jared's parents decide to pay at most \$100? *Explain.*

8. At a used book sale, each hardcover costs \$2 and each paperback costs \$1. Carol bought 15 books as gifts for \$21. How many more paperbacks than hardcovers did she buy? *Justify* each step of your solution.

9. A *pica* is a unit of measure that equals one sixth of an inch. What is the area, in square inches, of a rectangle that is 9 picas long and 8 picas wide? *Describe* the method you used to find the answer.

10. The volume V of a rectangular prism with a square base is given by $V = s^2h$ where h is the height and s is the length of one side of the base.

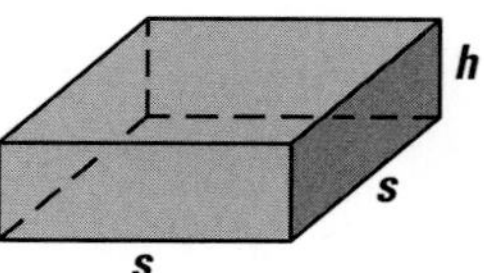

Suppose such a prism has a volume of 1000 cubic centimeters. Choose three possible values of s and find the corresponding values of h. Is there a maximum value that s can have? *Explain.*

OPEN-ENDED

11. The melting points and boiling points of lithium, carbon, nitrogen, oxygen, and magnesium are shown, to the nearest degree.

	Li	C	N	O	Mg
Melting point (°C)	?	3500	?	−218	?
Melting point (°F)	357	?	−346	?	1202
Boiling point (°C)	1347	?	−196	?	1107
Boiling point (°F)	?	8721	?	−297	?

Copy the table. Use the formula $F = \frac{9}{5}C + 32$ to convert the Celsius temperatures in the table to Fahrenheit temperatures. Record the results.

Rewrite the formula so that it gives the Celsius temperature in terms of the Fahrenheit temperature. *Justify* each step.

Use the rewritten formula to convert the Fahrenheit temperatures in the table to Celsius temperatures. Record the results.

12. A baseball pitcher's earned run average (ERA) can be calculated using this formula: ERA = 9 • earned runs ÷ innings pitched.

During one season, Johan Santana gave up 66 earned runs in 228 innings pitched. To the nearest hundredth, what was his ERA?

After pitching 2296 innings, Pedro Martinez had a career ERA of 2.71. Write and solve an equation to find the number of earned runs he allowed in those innings. *Explain* why there are two possible answers.

A pitcher who expects to pitch 200 innings in a season wants his ERA to be less than 4.00. Write and solve an inequality to find the possible numbers of earned runs he can allow. *Explain* how you need to round your answer.

TEST PREPARATION

MULTIPLE CHOICE

13. Which graph represents the solution of the inequality $2x - 7 < 11$?

(1) 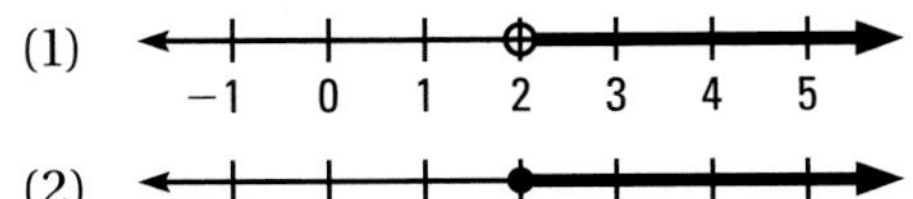

(2) 

(3) 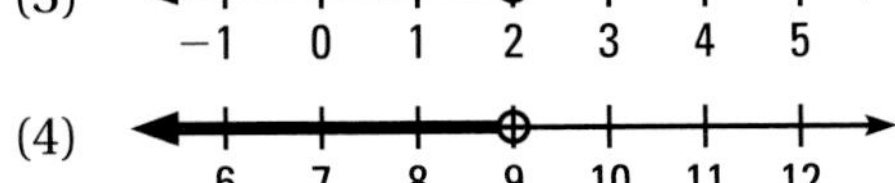

(4) 6 7 8 9 10 11 12

14. Which equation has −5 as a solution?

(1) $-3x - 6 = 10$ (3) $5 - x = 10$

(2) $1.5 + 3x = -14.5$ (4) $-9x = -45$

15. What is the solution of the equation $-t + 12 = 5t + 3$?

(1) $\frac{4}{9}$ (3) $\frac{3}{2}$

(2) $\frac{2}{3}$ (4) $\frac{9}{4}$

16. What is a solution of the absolute value equation $|x + 5| = 15 - 3x$?

(1) 2.5 (3) both 10 and 2.5

(2) 10 (4) neither 10 nor 2.5

17. What is the greatest value of x for which $|2x - 5| \leq 7$?

(1) −6 (3) 1

(2) −1 (4) 6

2 Linear Equations and Functions

Before

In Chapter 1, you learned the following skills, which you'll use in Chapter 2: evaluating algebraic expressions, solving linear equations, and rewriting equations.

Prerequisite Skills

VOCABULARY CHECK

Copy and complete the statement.

1. A **linear equation** in one variable is an equation that can be written in the form __?__ where a and b are constants and $a \neq 0$.
2. The **absolute value** of a real number is the distance the number is from __?__ on a number line.

SKILLS CHECK

Evaluate the expression for the given value of x. *(Review p. 10 for 2.1.)*

3. $-2(x + 1)$ when $x = -5$
4. $11x - 14$ when $x = -3$
5. $x^2 + x + 1$ when $x = 4$
6. $-x^2 - 3x + 7$ when $x = 1$

Solve the equation. Check your solution. *(Review p. 18 for 2.3.)*

7. $5x - 2 = 8$
8. $-6x - 10 = 20$
9. $-x + 9 = 2x - 27$

Solve the equation for y. *(Review p. 26 for 2.4.)*

10. $2x + 3y = 6$
11. $-x - y = 10$
12. $x + 4y = -5$

Now

In Chapter 2, you will apply the big ideas listed below and reviewed in the Chapter Summary on page 140. You will also use the key vocabulary listed below.

Big Ideas

1. **Representing relations and functions**
2. **Graphing linear equations and inequalities in two variables**
3. **Writing linear equations and inequalities in two variables**

KEY VOCABULARY

- domain, range, *p. 72*
- function, *p. 73*
- linear function, *p. 75*
- slope, *p. 82*
- rate of change, *p. 85*
- parent function, *p. 89*
- *y*-intercept, *p. 89*
- slope-intercept form, *p. 90*
- *x*-intercept, *p. 91*
- point-slope form, *p. 98*
- direct variation, *p. 107*
- correlation coefficient, *p. 114*
- best-fitting line, *p. 114*
- absolute value function, *p. 123*
- transformation, *p. 123*
- linear inequality in two variables, *p. 132*

Why?

You can use rates of change to find linear models. For example, you can use an average rate of change to model distance traveled as a function of time.

Animated Algebra

The animation illustrated below for Exercise 44 on page 111 helps you answer this question: If a whale migrates at a given rate, how far will it travel in different periods of time?

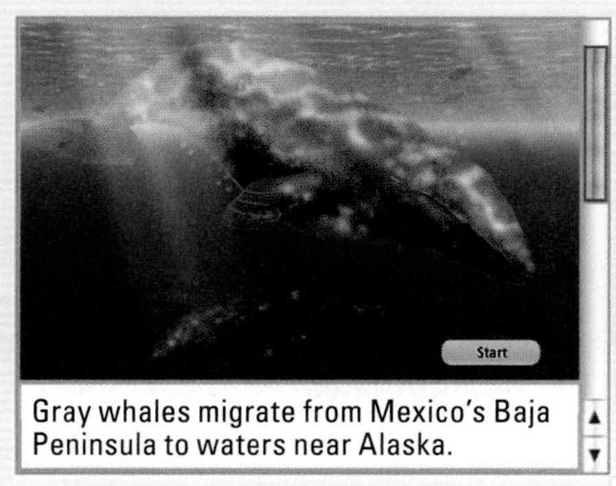

Gray whales migrate from Mexico's Baja Peninsula to waters near Alaska.

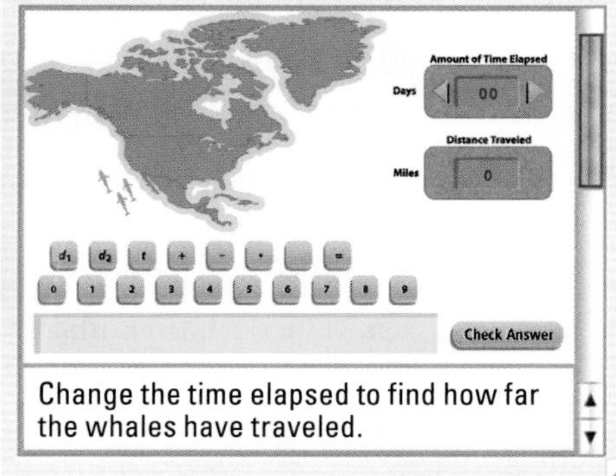

Change the time elapsed to find how far the whales have traveled.

Animated Algebra at classzone.com

Other animations for Chapter 2: pages 73, 86, 90, 95, 98, 102, 107, 115, 133, and 140

2.1 Represent Relations and Functions

A2.A.38 Determine when a relation is a function

Before You solved linear equations.

Now You will represent relations and graph linear functions.

Why? So you can model changes in elevation, as in Ex. 48.

Key Vocabulary
- relation
- domain
- range
- function
- equation in two variables
- linear function

A **relation** is a *mapping*, or pairing, of input values with output values. The set of input values is the **domain**, and the set of output values is the **range**.

KEY CONCEPT *For Your Notebook*

Representing Relations

A relation can be represented in the following ways.

Ordered Pairs

$(-2, 2)$

$(-2, -2)$

$(0, 1)$

$(3, 1)$

Table

x	y
−2	2
−2	−2
0	1
3	1

Graph

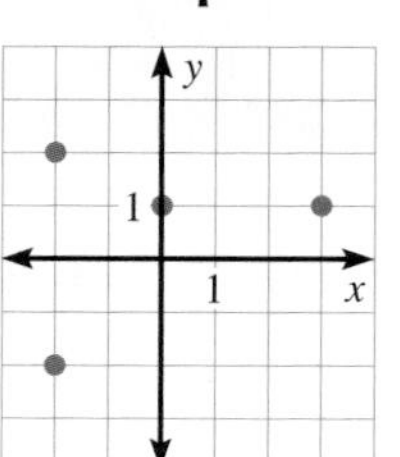

Mapping Diagram

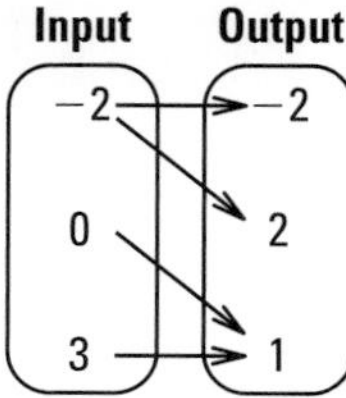

EXAMPLE 1 Represent relations

Consider the relation given by the ordered pairs $(-2, -3)$, $(-1, 1)$, $(1, 3)$, $(2, -2)$, and $(3, 1)$.

a. Identify the domain and range.

b. Represent the relation using a graph and a mapping diagram.

Solution

a. The domain consists of all the x-coordinates: -2, -1, 1, 2, and 3.
The range consists of all the y-coordinates: -3, -2, 1, and 3.

REVIEW GRAPHING
For help with plotting points in a coordinate plane, see p. 987.

b. Graph

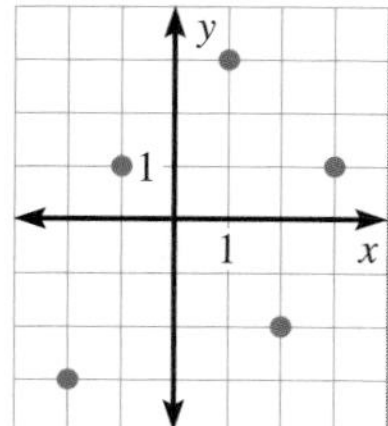

Mapping Diagram

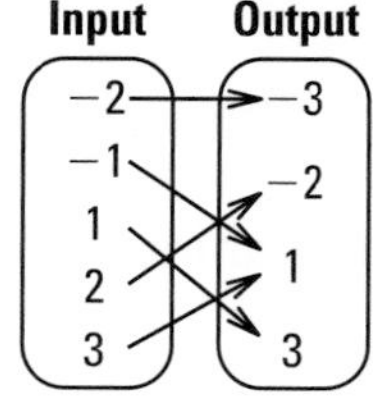

FUNCTIONS A **function** is a relation for which each input has exactly one output. If any input of a relation has more than one output, the relation is *not* a function.

EXAMPLE 2 Identify functions

AVOID ERRORS
A relation can map more than one input onto the same output and still be a function.

Tell whether the relation is a function. Explain.

a. 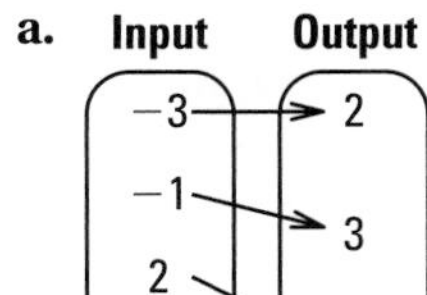

b. 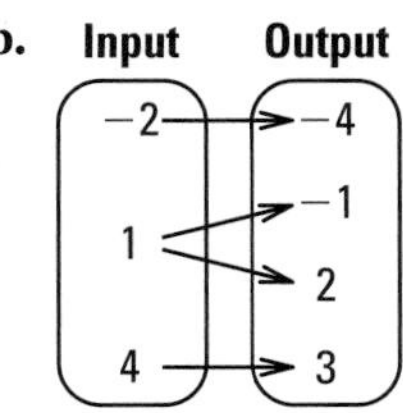

Solution

a. The relation *is* a function because each input is mapped onto exactly one output.

b. The relation *is not* a function because the input 1 is mapped onto both −1 and 2.

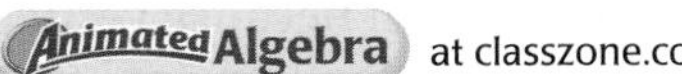

at classzone.com

✓ GUIDED PRACTICE for Examples 1 and 2

1. Consider the relation given by the ordered pairs (−4, 3), (−2, 1), (0, 3), (1, −2), and (−2, −4).
   a. Identify the domain and range.
   b. Represent the relation using a table and a mapping diagram.

2. Tell whether the relation is a function. *Explain.*

x	−2	−1	0	1	3
y	−4	−4	−4	−4	−4

VERTICAL LINE TEST You can use the graph of a relation to determine whether it is a function by applying the *vertical line test.*

REVIEW LOGICAL STATEMENTS
For help with "if and only if" statements, see p. 1002.

KEY CONCEPT *For Your Notebook*

Vertical Line Test

A relation is a function if and only if no vertical line intersects the graph of the relation at more than one point.

Function

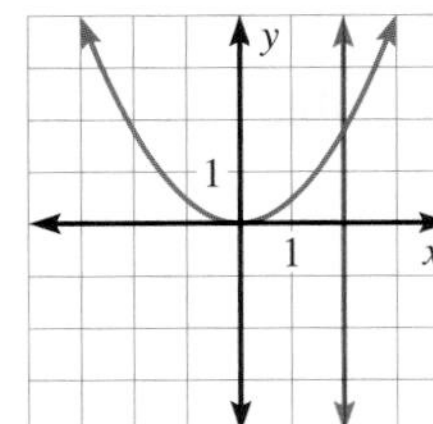

Not a function

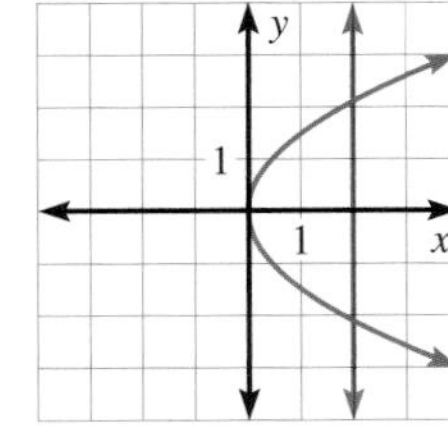

EXAMPLE 3 Use the vertical line test

BASKETBALL The first graph below plots average points per game versus age at the end of the 2003–2004 NBA regular season for the 8 members of the Minnesota Timberwolves with the highest averages. The second graph plots average points per game versus age for one team member, Kevin Garnett, over his first 9 seasons. Are the relations shown by the graphs functions? Explain.

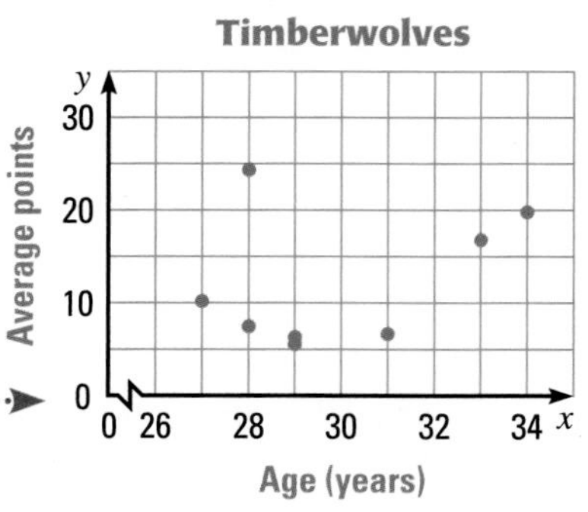

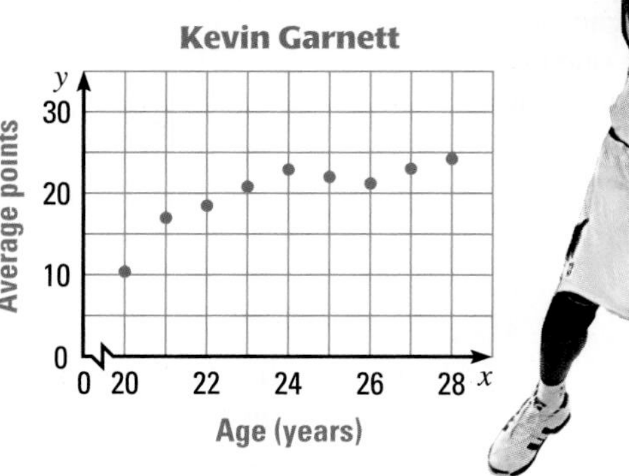

READING GRAPHS
The zigzag symbol on the horizontal axis of each graph indicates that values of x were skipped.

Solution

The team graph *does not* represent a function because vertical lines at $x = 28$ and $x = 29$ each intersect the graph at more than one point. The graph for Kevin Garnett *does* represent a function because no vertical line intersects the graph at more than one point.

GUIDED PRACTICE for Example 3

3. **WHAT IF?** In Example 3, suppose that Kevin Garnett averages 24.2 points per game in his tenth season as he did in his ninth. If the relation given by the second graph is revised to include the tenth season, is the relation still a function? *Explain.*

EQUATIONS IN TWO VARIABLES Many functions can be described by an **equation in two variables**, such as $y = 3x - 5$. The input variable (in this case, x) is called the **independent variable**. The output variable (in this case, y) is called the **dependent variable** because its value *depends* on the value of the input variable.

An ordered pair (x, y) is a **solution** of an equation in two variables if substituting x and y in the equation produces a true statement. For example, $(2, 1)$ is a solution of $y = 3x - 5$ because $1 = 3(2) - 5$ is true. The **graph** of an equation in two variables is the set of all points (x, y) that represent solutions of the equation.

KEY CONCEPT *For Your Notebook*

Graphing Equations in Two Variables

To graph an equation in two variables, follow these steps:

STEP 1 **Construct** a table of values.

STEP 2 **Plot** enough points from the table to recognize a pattern.

STEP 3 **Connect** the points with a line or a curve.

EXAMPLE 4 Graph an equation in two variables

Graph the equation $y = -2x - 1$.

Solution

STEP 1 **Construct** a table of values.

x	−2	−1	0	1	2
y	3	1	−1	−3	−5

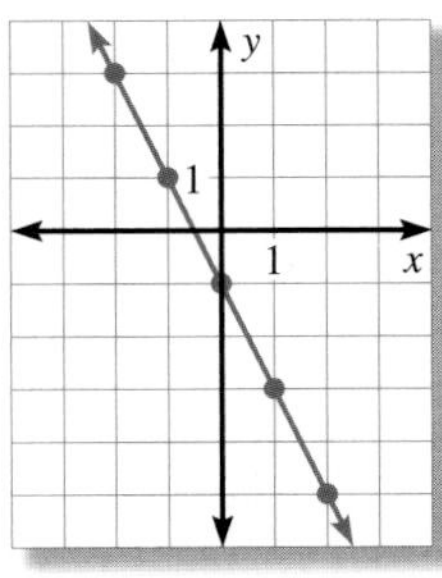

STEP 2 **Plot** the points. Notice that they all lie on a line.

STEP 3 **Connect** the points with a line.

READING The parentheses in $f(x)$ do not indicate multiplication. The symbol $f(x)$ does not mean "f times x."

LINEAR FUNCTIONS The function $y = -2x - 1$ in Example 4 is a **linear function** because it can be written in the form $y = mx + b$ where m and b are constants. The graph of a linear function is a line. By renaming y as $f(x)$, you can write $y = mx + b$ using **function notation**.

$y = mx + b$ **Linear function in *x*-*y* notation**

$f(x) = mx + b$ **Linear function in function notation**

The notation $f(x)$ is read "the value of f at x," or simply "f of x," and identifies x as the independent variable. The domain consists of all values of x for which $f(x)$ is defined. The range consists of all values of $f(x)$ where x is in the domain of f.

EXAMPLE 5 Classify and evaluate functions

Tell whether the function is linear. Then evaluate the function when $x = -4$.

a. $f(x) = -x^2 - 2x + 7$

b. $g(x) = 5x + 8$

Solution

a. The function f is not linear because it has an x^2-term.

$f(x) = -x^2 - 2x + 7$ **Write function.**

$f(-4) = -(-4)^2 - 2(-4) + 7$ **Substitute −4 for *x*.**

$= -1$ **Simplify.**

REPRESENT FUNCTIONS Letters other than f, such as g or h, can also name functions.

b. The function g is linear because it has the form $g(x) = mx + b$.

$g(x) = 5x + 8$ **Write function.**

$g(-4) = 5(-4) + 8$ **Substitute −4 for *x*.**

$= -12$ **Simplify.**

✓ GUIDED PRACTICE for Examples 4 and 5

4. Graph the equation $y = 3x - 2$.

Tell whether the function is linear. Then evaluate the function when $x = -2$.

5. $f(x) = x - 1 - x^3$

6. $g(x) = -4 - 2x$

DOMAINS IN REAL LIFE In Example 5, the domain of each function is all real numbers because there is an output for every real number x. In real life, you may need to restrict the domain so that it is reasonable in the given situation.

EXAMPLE 6 Use a function in real life

DIVING A diver using a Diver Propulsion Vehicle (DPV) descends to a depth of 130 feet. The pressure P (in atmospheres) on the diver is given by $P(d) = 1 + 0.03d$ where d is the depth (in feet). Graph the function, and determine a reasonable domain and range. What is the pressure on the diver at a depth of 33 feet?

Solution

The graph of $P(d)$ is shown. Because the depth varies from 0 feet to 130 feet, a reasonable domain is $0 \le d \le 130$.

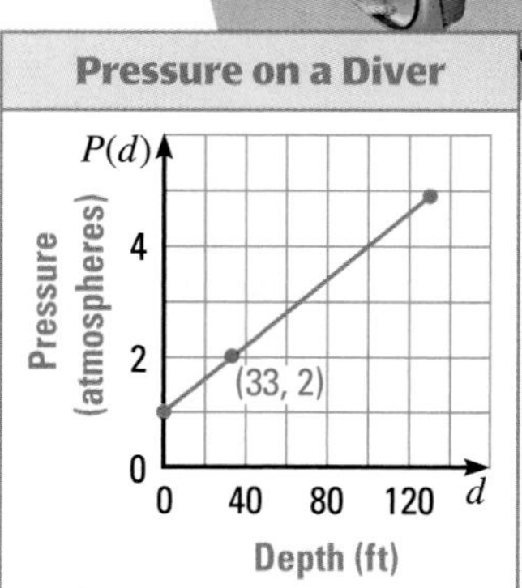

The minimum value of $P(d)$ is $P(0) = 1$, and the maximum value of $P(d)$ is $P(130) = 4.9$. So, a reasonable range is $1 \le P(d) \le 4.9$.

▶ At a depth of 33 feet, the pressure on the diver is $P(33) = 1 + 0.03(33) \approx 2$ atmospheres, which you can verify from the graph.

GUIDED PRACTICE for Example 6

7. **OCEAN EXPLORATION** In 1960, the deep-sea vessel *Trieste* descended to an estimated depth of 35,800 feet. Determine a reasonable domain and range of the function $P(d)$ in Example 6 for this trip.

2.1 EXERCISES

HOMEWORK KEY

○ = **WORKED-OUT SOLUTIONS** on p. WS2 for Exs. 7, 17, and 45

★ = **STANDARDIZED TEST PRACTICE** Exs. 2, 9, 20, 24, 40, 46, and 49

SKILL PRACTICE

1. **VOCABULARY** Copy and complete: In the equation $y = x + 5$, x is the __?__ variable and y is the __?__ variable.

2. ★ **WRITING** *Describe* how to find the domain and range of a relation given by a set of ordered pairs.

EXAMPLE 1 on p. 72 for Exs. 3–9

REPRESENTING RELATIONS Identify the domain and range of the given relation. Then represent the relation using a graph and a mapping diagram.

3. $(-2, 3), (1, 2), (3, -1), (-4, -3)$
4. $(5, -2), (-3, -2), (3, 3), (-1, -1)$
5. $(6, -1), (-2, -3), (1, 8), (-2, 5)$
6. $(-7, 4), (2, -5), (1, -2), (-3, 6)$
7. $(5, 20), (10, 20), (15, 30), (20, 30)$
8. $(4, -2), (4, 2), (16, -4), (16, 4)$

9. ★ **MULTIPLE CHOICE** What is the domain of the relation given by the ordered pairs $(-4, 2)$, $(-1, -3)$, $(1, 4)$, $(1, -3)$, and $(2, 1)$?

(A) $-3, 1, 2,$ and 4 (B) $-4, -1, 1,$ and 2

(C) $-4, -3, -1,$ and 2 (D) $-4, -3, -1, 1, 2,$ and 4

EXAMPLE 2 on p. 73 for Exs. 10–20

IDENTIFYING FUNCTIONS **Tell whether the relation is a function. *Explain.***

10.

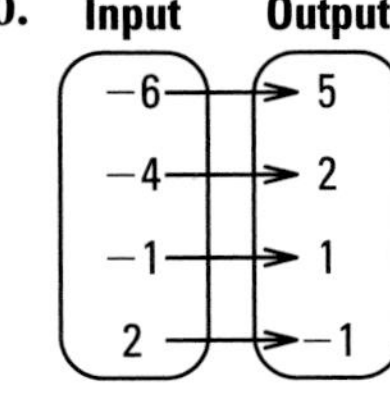

11. Input Output

−5, −3, 1, 2 | −2, 1, 4

12.

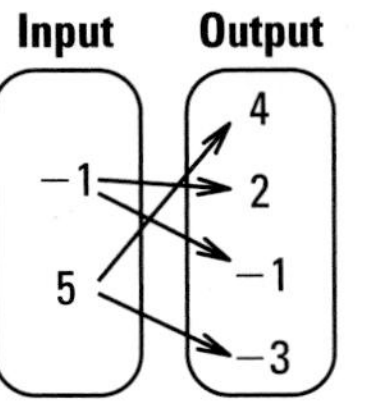

13.

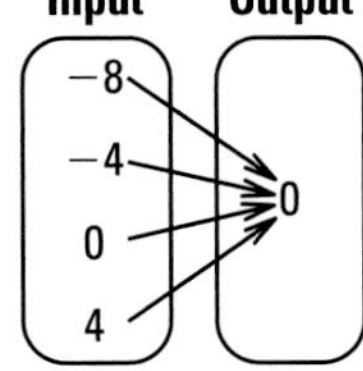

ERROR ANALYSIS ***Describe*** **and correct the error in the student's work.**

14. The relation given by the ordered pairs (−4, 2), (−1, 5), (3, 6), and (7, 2) is not a function because the inputs −4 and 7 are both mapped to the output 2.

15.

x	0	1	2	1	0
y	5	6	7	8	9

The relation given by the table is a function because there is only one value of x for each value of y.

IDENTIFYING FUNCTIONS **Tell whether the relation is a function. *Explain.***

16. $(3, -2)$, $(0, 1)$, $(1, 0)$, $(-2, -1)$, $(2, -1)$

17. $(2, -5)$, $(-2, 5)$, $(-1, 4)$, $(-2, 0)$, $(3, -4)$

18. $(0, 1)$, $(1, 0)$, $(2, 3)$, $(3, 2)$, $(4, 4)$

19. $(-1, -1)$, $(2, 5)$, $(4, 8)$, $(-5, -9)$, $(-1, -5)$

20. ★ **MULTIPLE CHOICE** The relation given by the ordered pairs $(-6, 3)$, $(-2, 4)$, $(1, 5)$, and $(4, 0)$ is a function. Which ordered pair can be included with this relation to form a new relation that is also a function?

(A) $(1, -5)$ (B) $(6, 3)$ (C) $(-2, 19)$ (D) $(4, 4)$

EXAMPLE 3 on p. 74 for Exs. 21–23

VERTICAL LINE TEST **Use the vertical line test to tell whether the relation is a function.**

21.

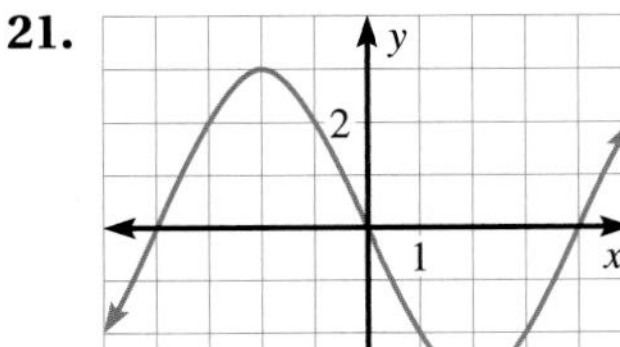

22.

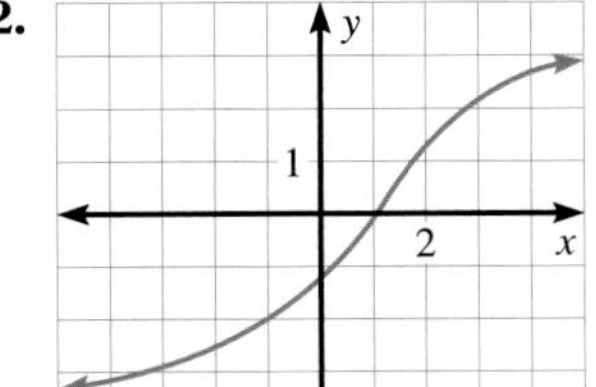

23.

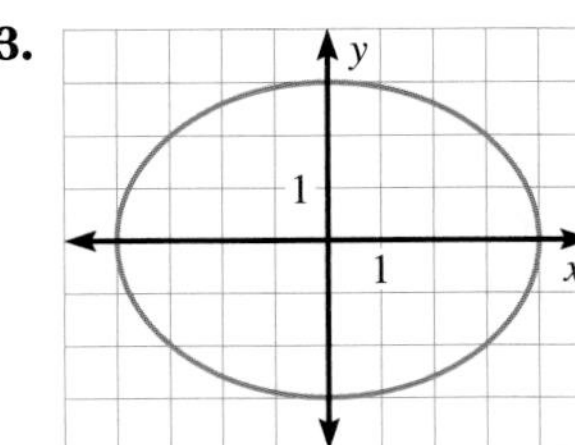

24. ★ **SHORT RESPONSE** *Explain* why a relation is not a function if a vertical line intersects the graph of the relation more than once.

EXAMPLE 4 on p. 75 for Exs. 25–33

GRAPHING EQUATIONS **Graph the equation.**

25. $y = x + 2$ **26.** $y = -x + 5$ **27.** $y = 3x + 1$

28. $y = 5x - 3$ **29.** $y = 2x - 7$ **30.** $y = -3x + 2$

31. $y = -2x$ **32.** $y = \frac{1}{2}x + 2$ **33.** $y = -\frac{3}{4}x - 1$

EXAMPLE 5
on p. 75
for Exs. 34–39

EVALUATING FUNCTIONS Tell whether the function is linear. Then evaluate the function for the given value of x.

34. $f(x) = x + 15; f(8)$

35. $f(x) = x^2 + 1; f(-3)$

36. $f(x) = |x| + 10; f(-4)$

37. $f(x) = 6; f(2)$

38. $g(x) = x^3 - 2x^2 + 5x - 8; g(-5)$

39. $h(x) = 7 - \frac{2}{3}x; h(15)$

40. ★ **SHORT RESPONSE** Which, if any, of the relations described by the equations $y = |x|$, $x = |y|$, and $|y| = |x|$ represent functions? *Explain.*

41. **CHALLENGE** Let f be a function such that $f(a + b) = f(a) + f(b)$ for all real numbers a and b. Show that $f(2a) = 2 \cdot f(a)$ and that $f(0) = 0$.

PROBLEM SOLVING

EXAMPLE 3
on p. 74
for Exs. 42–43

42. **BICYCLING** The graph shows the ages of the top three finishers in the Mt. Washington Auto Road Bicycle Hillclimb each year from 2002 through 2004. Do the ordered pairs (age, finishing place) represent a function? *Explain.*

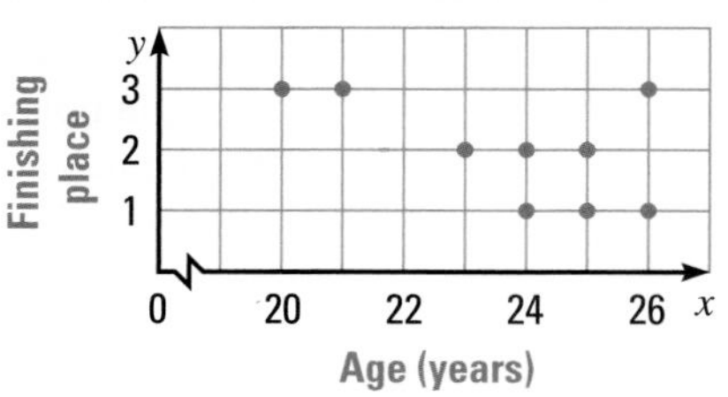

@HomeTutor for problem solving help at classzone.com

43. **BASEBALL** The graph shows the number of games started and the number of wins for each starting pitcher on a baseball team during a regular season. Do the ordered pairs (starts, wins) represent a function? *Explain.*

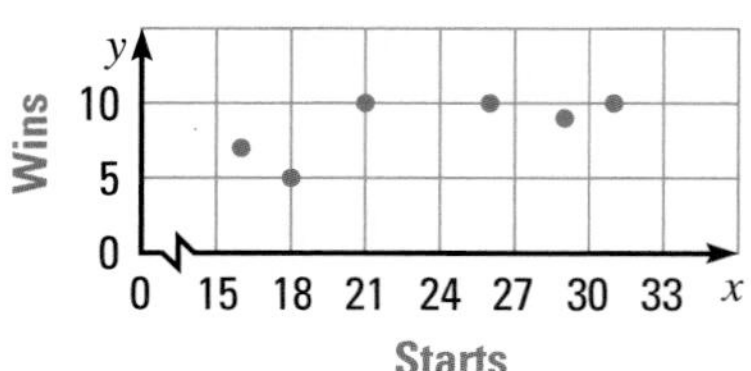

@HomeTutor for problem solving help at classzone.com

44. **GEOMETRY** The volume V of a cube with edge length s is given by the function $V(s) = s^3$. Find $V(4)$. *Explain* what $V(4)$ represents.

45. **GEOMETRY** The volume V of a sphere with radius r is given by the function $V(r) = \frac{4}{3}\pi r^3$. Find $V(6)$. *Explain* what $V(6)$ represents.

EXAMPLE 6
on p. 76
for Exs. 46–48

46. ★ **SHORT RESPONSE** For the period 1999–2004, the average number of acres w (in thousands), used to grow watermelons in the United States can be modeled by the function $w(t) = -6.26t + 172$ where t is the number of years since 1999. Determine a reasonable domain and range for $w(t)$. *Explain* the meaning of the range.

47. **MULTI-STEP PROBLEM** Anthropologists can estimate a person's height from the length of certain bones. The height h (in inches) of an adult human female can be modeled by the function $h(\ell) = 1.95\ell + 28.7$ where ℓ is the length (in inches) of the femur, or thigh bone. The function is valid for femur lengths between 15 inches and 24 inches, inclusive.

a. Graph the function, and determine a reasonable domain and range.

b. Suppose a female's femur is 15.5 inches long. About how tall was she?

c. If an anthropologist estimates a female's height as 5 feet 11 inches, about how long is her femur?

○ = WORKED-OUT SOLUTIONS on p. WS1

★ = STANDARDIZED TEST PRACTICE

48. **MOUNTAIN CLIMBING** A climber on Mount Rainier in Washington hikes from an elevation of 5400 feet above sea level to Camp Muir, which has an elevation of 10,100 feet. The elevation h (in feet) as the climber ascends can be modeled by $h(t) = 1000t + 5400$ where t is the time (in hours). Graph the function, and determine a reasonable domain and range. What is the climber's elevation after hiking 3.5 hours?

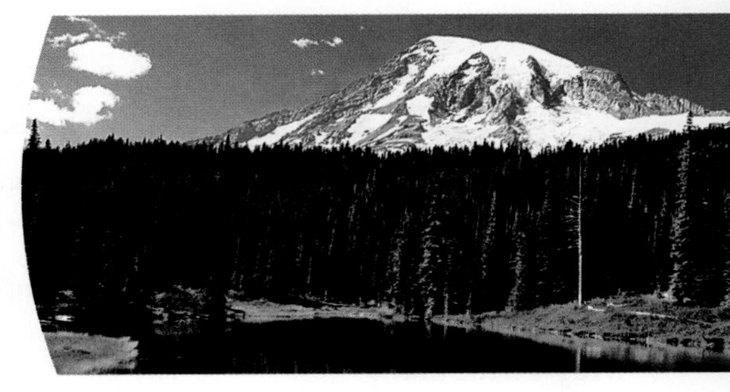

49. ★ **EXTENDED RESPONSE** The table shows the populations of several states and their electoral votes in the 2004 and 2008 U.S. presidential elections. The figures are based on U.S. census data for the year 2000.

 a. Identify the domain and range of the relation given by the ordered pairs (p, v).

 b. Is the relation from part (a) a function? *Explain.*

 c. Is the relation given by the ordered pairs (v, p) a function? *Explain.*

State	Population (millions), p	Electoral votes, v
California	33.87	55
Florida	15.98	27
Illinois	12.42	21
New York	18.98	31
Ohio	11.35	20
Pennsylvania	12.28	21
Texas	20.85	34

50. **CHALLENGE** The table shows ground shipping charges for an online retail store.

 a. Is the shipping cost a function of the merchandise cost? *Explain.*

 b. Is the merchandise cost a function of the shipping cost? *Explain.*

Merchandise cost	Shipping cost
\$.01–\$30.00	\$4.50
\$30.01–\$60.00	\$7.25
\$60.01–\$100.00	\$9.50
Over \$100.00	\$12.50

NEW YORK MIXED REVIEW

TEST PRACTICE at classzone.com

51. Kate is studying a bacteria culture in biology class. The table shows the number of bacteria, b, in the culture after t hours. How many bacteria are there after 10 hours?

Time (hours), t	0	1	2	3	4	5
Bacteria (billions), b	1	2	4	8	16	32

Ⓐ 64 billion Ⓑ 128 billion Ⓒ 256 billion Ⓓ 1024 billion

52. What is the area of the composite figure?

Ⓐ 138 cm^2 Ⓑ 141 cm^2

Ⓒ 162 cm^2 Ⓓ 210 cm^2

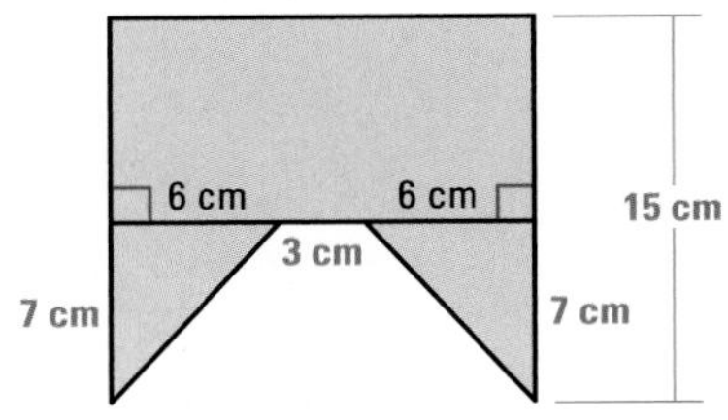

Extension

Use after Lesson 2.1

Use Discrete and Continuous Functions

GOAL Graph and classify discrete and continuous functions.

Key Vocabulary
- **discrete function**
- **continuous function**

The graph of a function may consist of *discrete,* or separate and unconnected, points in a plane. The graph of a function may also be a *continuous,* or unbroken, line or curve or part of a line or curve.

KEY CONCEPT *For Your Notebook*

Discrete and Continuous Functions

The graph of a **discrete function** consists of separate points.

The graph of a **continuous function** is unbroken.

EXAMPLE 1 Graph and classify functions

Graph the function $f(x) = 0.5x + 1$ for the given domain. Classify the function as *discrete* or *continuous* for the domain. Then identify the range.

a. Domain: $x = -2, 0, 2, 4$

b. Domain: $x \geq -3$

Solution

a. Make a table using the x-values in the domain.

x	−2	0	2	4
y	0	1	2	3

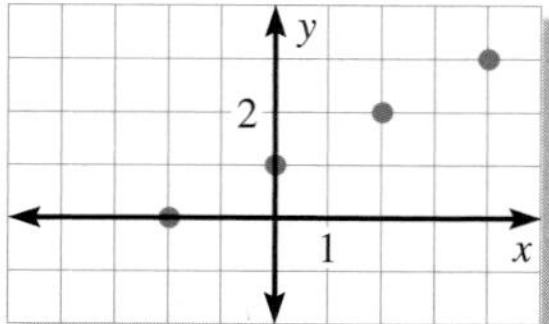

The graph consists of separate points, so the function is discrete. Its range is 0, 1, 2, 3.

b. Note that $f(x)$ is a linear function defined for $x \geq -3$, and that $f(-3) = -0.5$. So, the graph is the ray with endpoint $(-3, -0.5)$ that passes through all the points from the table in part (a).

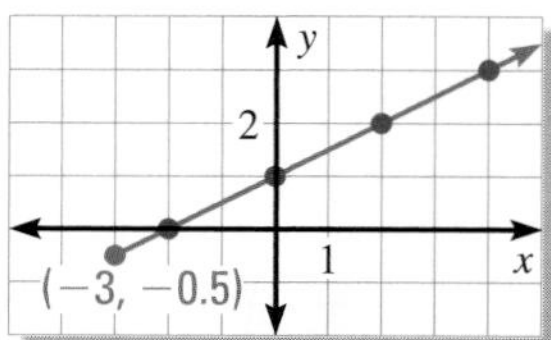

The graph is unbroken, so the function is continuous. Its range is $y \geq -0.5$.

EXAMPLE 2 Graph and classify real-world functions

Write and graph the function described. Determine the domain and range. Then tell whether the function is *discrete* or *continuous*.

a. A student group is selling chocolate bars for \$2 each. The function $f(x)$ gives the amount of money collected after selling x chocolate bars.

b. A low-flow shower head releases 1.8 gallons of water per minute. The function $V(x)$ gives the volume of water released after x minutes.

Solution

a. The function is $f(x) = 2x$. The first four points of the graph of $f(x)$ are shown. Only whole chocolate bars can be sold, so the domain is the set of whole numbers 0, 1, 2, 3, ... From the graph, you can see that the range is 0, 2, 4, 6, ... The graph consists of separate points, so the function is discrete.

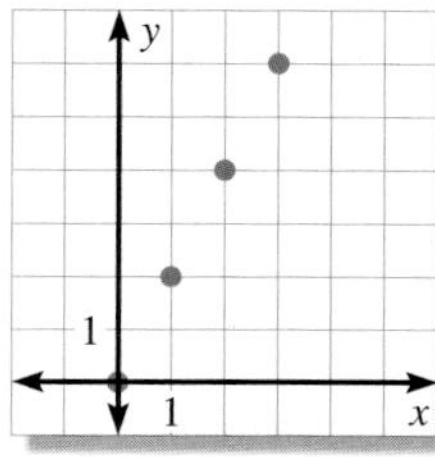

b. The function is $V(x) = 1.8x$. You can run the shower any nonnegative amount of time, so the domain is $x \geq 0$. From the graph, you can see that the range is $y \geq 0$. The graph is unbroken, so the function is continuous.

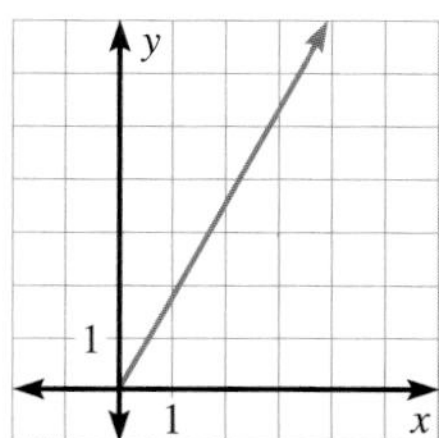

PRACTICE

EXAMPLE 1 on p. 80 for Exs. 1–4

Graph the function for the given domain. Classify the function as *discrete* or *continuous*. Then identify the range of the function.

1. $y = 2x + 3$; domain: $-2, -1, 0, 1, 2$
2. $f(x) = 0.5x - 4$; domain: $-4, -2, 0, 2, 4$
3. $y = -3x + 9$; domain: $x < 5$
4. $f(x) = \frac{1}{3}x + 6$; domain: $x \geq -6$

EXAMPLE 2 on p. 81 for Exs. 5–8

Write and graph the function described. Determine the domain and range. Then tell whether the function is *discrete* or *continuous*.

5. Amanda walks at an average speed of 3.5 miles per hour. The function $d(x)$ gives the distance (in miles) Amanda walks in x hours.
6. A token to ride a subway costs \$1.25. The function $s(x)$ gives the cost of riding the subway x times.
7. A family has 3 gallons of milk delivered every Thursday. The function $m(x)$ gives the total amount of milk that is delivered to the family after x weeks.
8. Steel cable that is $\frac{3}{8}$ inch in diameter weighs 0.24 pound per foot. The function $w(x)$ gives the weight of x feet of steel cable.
9. On a number line, the *signed distance* from a number a to a number b is given by $b - a$. The function $d(x)$ gives the signed distance from 3 to any number x.

2.2 Find Slope and Rate of Change

Before You graphed linear functions.

Now You will find slopes of lines and rates of change.

Why? So you can model growth rates, as in Ex. 46.

Key Vocabulary
- **slope**
- **parallel**
- **perpendicular**
- **rate of change**
- **reciprocal,** *p. 4*

KEY CONCEPT *For Your Notebook*

Slope of a Line

Words

The **slope** m of a nonvertical line is the ratio of vertical change (the *rise*) to horizontal change (the *run*).

Algebra

$$m = \frac{y_2 - y_1}{x_2 - x_1} = \frac{\text{rise}}{\text{run}}$$

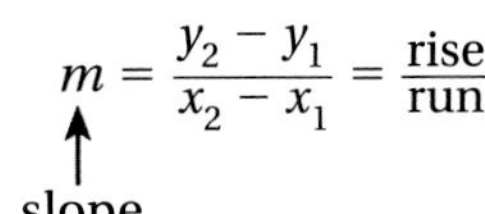

Graph

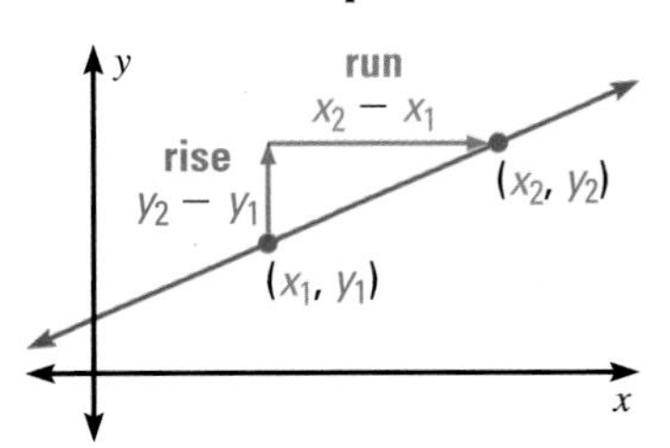

EXAMPLE 1 Find slope in real life

SKATEBOARDING A skateboard ramp has a rise of 15 inches and a run of 54 inches. What is its slope?

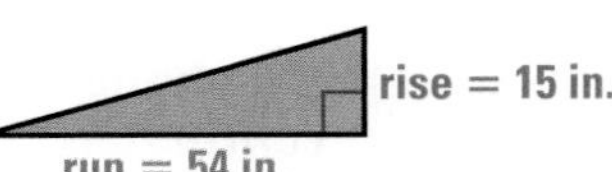

Solution

$$\text{slope} = \frac{\text{rise}}{\text{run}} = \frac{15}{54} = \frac{5}{18}$$

▶ The slope of the ramp is $\frac{5}{18}$.

★ EXAMPLE 2 Standardized Test Practice

What is the slope of the line passing through the points (−1, 3) and (2, −1)?

Ⓐ $-\frac{4}{3}$ Ⓑ $-\frac{3}{4}$ Ⓒ $\frac{3}{4}$ Ⓓ $\frac{4}{3}$

Solution

Let $(x_1, y_1) = (-1, 3)$ and $(x_2, y_2) = (2, -1)$.

$$m = \frac{y_2 - y_1}{x_2 - x_1} = \frac{-1 - 3}{2 - (-1)} = -\frac{4}{3}$$

▶ The correct answer is A. Ⓐ Ⓑ Ⓒ Ⓓ

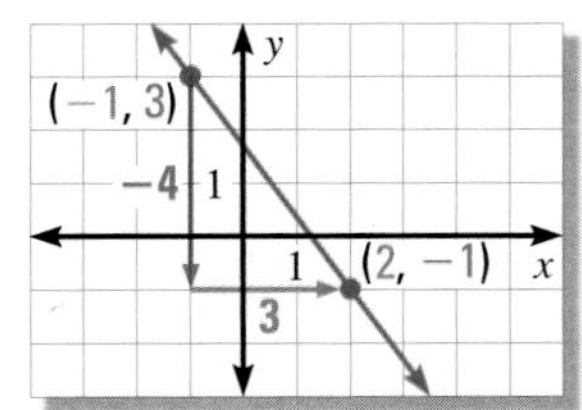

AVOID ERRORS

When calculating slope, be sure to subtract the *x*- and *y*-coordinates in a consistent order.

GUIDED PRACTICE for Examples 1 and 2

1. **WHAT IF?** In Example 1, suppose that the rise of the ramp is changed to 12 inches without changing the run. What is the slope of the ramp?

2. What is the slope of the line passing through the points $(-4, 9)$ and $(-8, 3)$?

   Ⓐ $-\frac{2}{3}$ Ⓑ $-\frac{1}{2}$ Ⓒ $\frac{2}{3}$ Ⓓ $\frac{3}{2}$

Find the slope of the line passing through the given points.

3. $(0, 3), (4, 8)$
4. $(-5, 1), (5, -4)$
5. $(-3, -2), (6, 1)$
6. $(7, 3), (-1, 7)$

KEY CONCEPT *For Your Notebook*

Classification of Lines by Slope

The slope of a line indicates whether the line rises from left to right, falls from left to right, is horizontal, or is vertical.

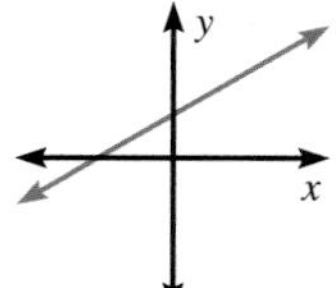

Positive slope
Rises from left to right

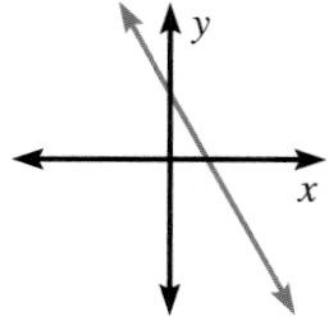

Negative slope
Falls from left to right

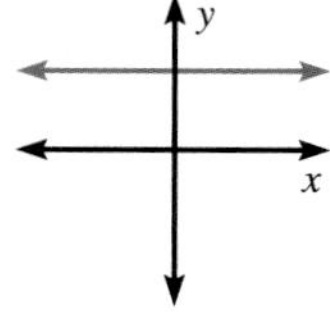

Zero slope
Horizontal

Undefined slope
Vertical

READING
A vertical line has "undefined slope" because for any two points, the slope formula's denominator becomes 0, and division by 0 is undefined.

EXAMPLE 3 Classify lines using slope

Without graphing, tell whether the line through the given points *rises, falls, is horizontal,* or *is vertical.*

a. $(-5, 1), (3, 1)$ **b.** $(-6, 0), (2, -4)$ **c.** $(-1, 3), (5, 8)$ **d.** $(4, 6), (4, -1)$

Solution

a. $m = \frac{1 - 1}{3 - (-5)} = \frac{0}{8} = 0$ Because $m = 0$, the line is horizontal.

b. $m = \frac{-4 - 0}{2 - (-6)} = \frac{-4}{8} = -\frac{1}{2}$ Because $m < 0$, the line falls.

c. $m = \frac{8 - 3}{5 - (-1)} = \frac{5}{6}$ Because $m > 0$, the line rises.

d. $m = \frac{-1 - 6}{4 - 4} = \frac{-7}{0}$ Because m is undefined, the line is vertical.

GUIDED PRACTICE for Example 3

Without graphing, tell whether the line through the given points *rises, falls, is horizontal,* or *is vertical.*

7. $(-4, 3), (2, -6)$
8. $(7, 1), (7, -1)$
9. $(3, -2), (5, -2)$
10. $(5, 6), (1, -4)$

PARALLEL AND PERPENDICULAR LINES Recall that two lines in a plane are **parallel** if they do not intersect. Two lines in a plane are **perpendicular** if they intersect to form a right angle.

Slope can be used to determine whether two different nonvertical lines are parallel or perpendicular.

KEY CONCEPT *For Your Notebook*

Slopes of Parallel and Perpendicular Lines

Consider two different nonvertical lines ℓ_1 and ℓ_2 with slopes m_1 and m_2.

Parallel Lines The lines are parallel if and only if they have the same slope.

$$m_1 = m_2$$

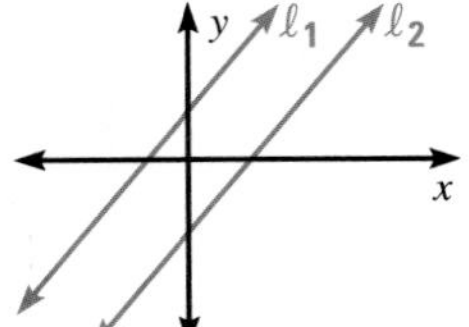

Perpendicular Lines The lines are perpendicular if and only if their slopes are negative reciprocals of each other.

$$m_1 = -\frac{1}{m_2}, \text{ or } m_1m_2 = -1$$

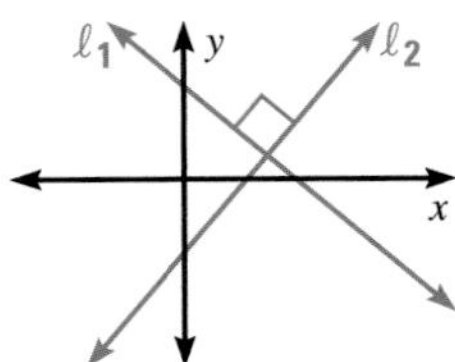

EXAMPLE 4 Classify parallel and perpendicular lines

Tell whether the lines are *parallel, perpendicular,* or *neither.*

a. Line 1: through (−2, 2) and (0, −1)
Line 2: through (−4, −1) and (2, 3)

b. Line 1: through (1, 2) and (4, −3)
Line 2: through (−4, 3) and (−1, −2)

Solution

a. Find the slopes of the two lines.

$$m_1 = \frac{-1 - 2}{0 - (-2)} = \frac{-3}{2} = -\frac{3}{2}$$

$$m_2 = \frac{3 - (-1)}{2 - (-4)} = \frac{4}{6} = \frac{2}{3}$$

▶ Because $m_1m_2 = -\frac{3}{2} \cdot \frac{2}{3} = -1$, m_1 and m_2 are negative reciprocals of each other. So, the lines are perpendicular.

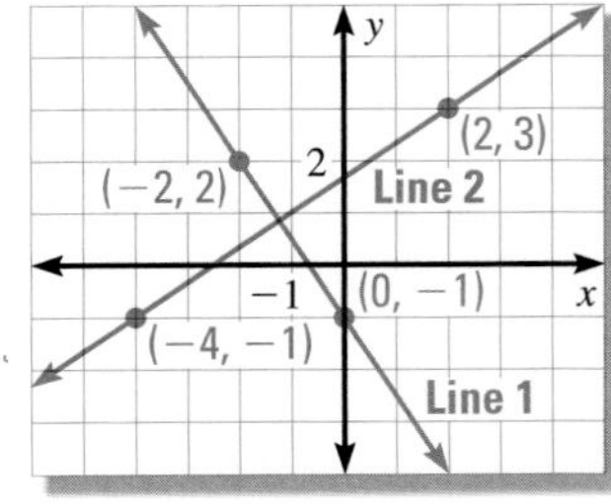

b. Find the slopes of the two lines.

$$m_1 = \frac{-3 - 2}{4 - 1} = \frac{-5}{3} = -\frac{5}{3}$$

$$m_2 = \frac{-2 - 3}{-1 - (-4)} = \frac{-5}{3} = -\frac{5}{3}$$

▶ Because $m_1 = m_2$ (and the lines are different), you can conclude that the lines are parallel.

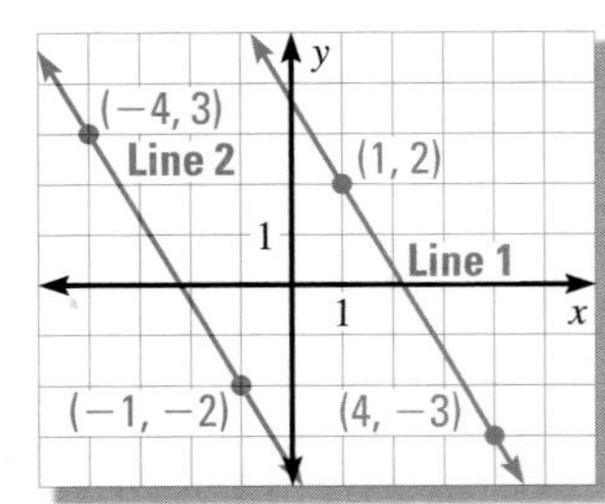

GUIDED PRACTICE for Example 4

Tell whether the lines are *parallel, perpendicular,* or *neither.*

11. Line 1: through $(-2, 8)$ and $(2, -4)$
Line 2: through $(-5, 1)$ and $(-2, 2)$

12. Line 1: through $(-4, -2)$ and $(1, 7)$
Line 2: through $(-1, -4)$ and $(3, 5)$

REVIEW RATES
Remember that a *rate* is a ratio of two quantities that have *different* units.

RATE OF CHANGE Slope can be used to represent an average **rate of change**, or how much one quantity changes, on average, relative to the change in another quantity. A slope that is a real-life rate of change involves units of measure such as miles per hour or degrees per day.

EXAMPLE 5 Solve a multi-step problem

FORESTRY Use the diagram, which illustrates the growth of a giant sequoia, to find the average rate of change in the diameter of the sequoia over time. Then predict the sequoia's diameter in 2065.

1965

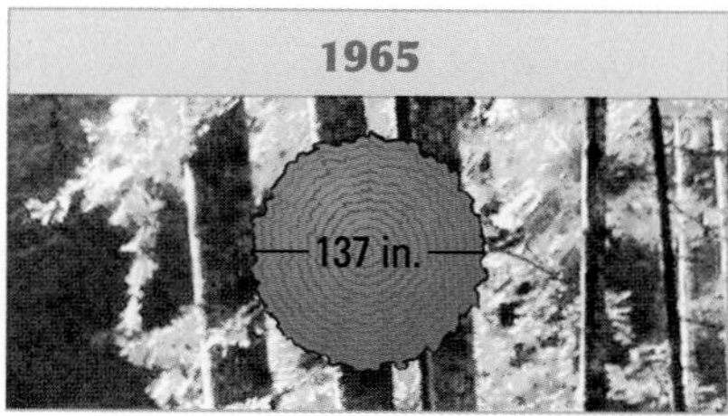

2005

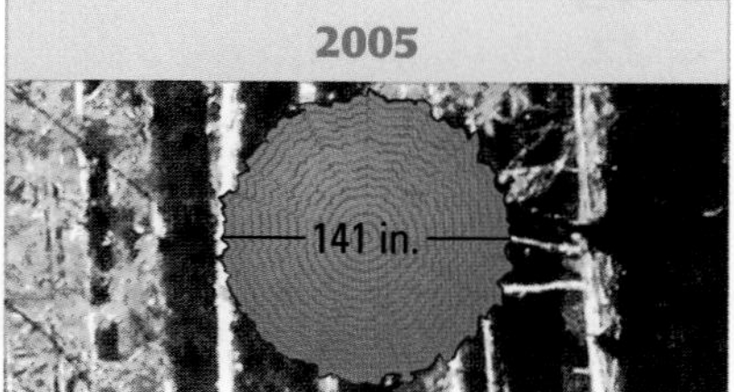

Solution

STEP 1 **Find** the average rate of change.

$$\text{Average rate of change} = \frac{\text{Change in diameter}}{\text{Change in time}}$$
$$= \frac{141 \text{ in.} - 137 \text{ in.}}{2005 - 1965}$$
$$= \frac{4 \text{ in.}}{40 \text{ years}}$$
$$= 0.1 \text{ inch per year}$$

STEP 2 **Predict** the diameter of the sequoia in 2065.

Find the number of years from 2005 to 2065. Multiply this number by the average rate of change to find the total increase in diameter during the period 2005–2065.

Number of years $= 2065 - 2005 = 60$
Increase in diameter $= (60 \text{ years})(0.1 \text{ inch/year}) = 6$ inches

▶ In 2065, the diameter of the sequoia will be about $141 + 6 = 147$ inches.

GUIDED PRACTICE for Example 5

13. WHAT IF? In Example 5, suppose that the diameter of the sequoia is 248 inches in 1965 and 251 inches in 2005. Find the average rate of change in the diameter, and use it to predict the diameter in 2105.

2.2 EXERCISES

HOMEWORK KEY

○ = **WORKED-OUT SOLUTIONS** on p. WS2 for Exs. 9, 19, and 45

★ = **STANDARDIZED TEST PRACTICE** Exs. 2, 17, 35, 36, 44, 45, and 48

SKILL PRACTICE

1. **VOCABULARY** Copy and complete: The __?__ of a nonvertical line is the ratio of vertical change to horizontal change.

2. ★ **WRITING** How can you use slope to decide whether two nonvertical lines are parallel? whether two nonvertical lines are perpendicular?

EXAMPLES 2 and 3 on pp. 82–83 for Exs. 3–17

FINDING SLOPE **Find the slope of the line passing through the given points. Then tell whether the line *rises, falls, is horizontal,* or *is vertical.***

3. (2, −4), (4, −1)
4. (8, 9), (−4, 3)
5. (5, 1), (8, −4)
6. (−3, −2), (3, −2)
7. (−1, 4), (1, −4)
8. (−6, 5), (−6, −5)
9. (−5, −4), (−1, 3)
10. (−3, 6), (−7, 3)
11. (4, 4), (4, 9)
12. (5, 5), (7, 3)
13. (0, −3), (4, −3)
14. (1, −1), (−1, −4)

Animated Algebra at classzone.com

ERROR ANALYSIS ***Describe*** **and correct the error in finding the slope of the line passing through the given points.**

15. (−4, −3), (2, −1)

$$m = \frac{-1-(-3)}{-4-2} = -\frac{1}{3}$$

16. (−1, 4), (5, 1)

$$m = \frac{5-(-1)}{1-4} = -2$$

17. ★ **MULTIPLE CHOICE** What is true about the line through (2, −4) and (5, 1)?

Ⓐ It rises from left to right.
Ⓑ It falls from left to right.
Ⓒ It is horizontal.
Ⓓ It is vertical.

EXAMPLE 4 on p. 84 for Exs. 18–23

CLASSIFYING LINES **Tell whether the lines are *parallel, perpendicular,* or *neither.***

18. Line 1: through (3, −1) and (6, −4)
Line 2: through (−4, 5) and (−2, 7)

19. Line 1: through (1, 5) and (3, −2)
Line 2: through (−3, 2) and (4, 0)

20. Line 1: through (−1, 4) and (2, 5)
Line 2: through (−6, 2) and (0, 4)

21. Line 1: through (5, 8) and (7, 2)
Line 2: through (−7, −2) and (−4, −1)

22. Line 1: through (−3, 2) and (5, 0)
Line 2: through (−1, −4) and (3, −3)

23. Line 1: through (1, −4) and (4, −2)
Line 2: through (8, 1) and (14, 5)

EXAMPLE 5 on p. 85 for Exs. 24–27

AVERAGE RATE OF CHANGE **Find the average rate of change in y relative to x for the ordered pairs. Include units of measure in your answer.**

24. (2, 12), (5, 30) x is measured in hours and y is measured in dollars
25. (0, 11), (3, 50) x is measured in gallons and y is measured in miles
26. (3, 10), (5, 18) x is measured in seconds and y is measured in feet
27. (1, 8), (7, 20) x is measured in seconds and y is measured in meters

28. **REASONING** The Key Concept box on page 84 states that lines ℓ_1 and ℓ_2 must be nonvertical. *Explain* why this condition is necessary.

FINDING SLOPE Find the slope of the line passing through the given points.

29. $\left(-1, \frac{3}{2}\right), \left(0, \frac{7}{2}\right)$

30. $\left(-\frac{3}{4}, -2\right), \left(\frac{5}{4}, -3\right)$

31. $\left(-\frac{1}{2}, \frac{5}{2}\right), \left(\frac{5}{2}, 3\right)$

32. $(-4.2, 0.1), (-3.2, 0.1)$

33. $(-0.3, 2.2), (1.7, -0.8)$

34. $(3.5, -2), (4.5, 0.5)$

35. ★ **SHORT RESPONSE** Does it make a difference which two points on a line you choose when finding the slope? Does it make a difference which point is (x_1, y_1) and which point is (x_2, y_2) in the formula for slope? Support your answers using three different pairs of points on the line shown.

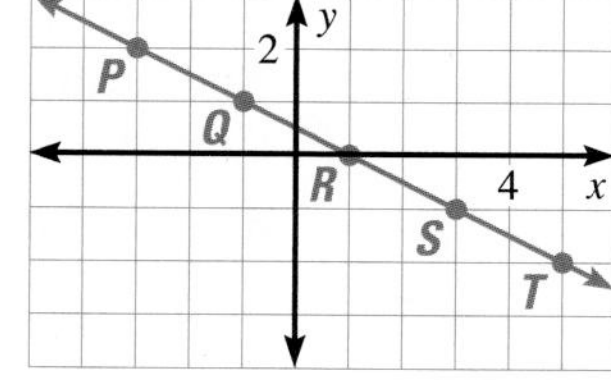

36. ★ **OPEN-ENDED MATH** Find two additional points on the line that passes through (0, 3) and has a slope of −4.

CHALLENGE Find the value of k so that the line through the given points has the given slope. Check your solution.

37. $(2, -3)$ and $(k, 7)$; $m = -2$

38. $(0, k)$ and $(3, 4)$; $m = 1$

39. $(-4, 2k)$ and $(k, -5)$; $m = -1$

40. $(-2, k)$ and $(2k, 2)$; $m = -0.25$

PROBLEM SOLVING

EXAMPLE 1 on p. 82 for Exs. 41–44

41. **ESCALATORS** An escalator in an airport rises 28 feet over a horizontal distance of 48 feet. What is the slope of the escalator?

@HomeTutor for problem solving help at classzone.com

42. **INCLINE RAILWAY** The Duquesne Incline, a cable car railway, rises 400 feet over a horizontal distance of 685 feet on its ascent to an overlook of Pittsburgh, Pennsylvania. What is the slope of the incline?

@HomeTutor for problem solving help at classzone.com

43. **ROAD GRADE** A road's *grade* is its slope expressed as a percent. A road rises 195 feet over a horizontal distance of 3000 feet. What is the grade of the road?

44. ★ **SHORT RESPONSE** The diagram shows a three-section ramp to a bridge. For a person walking up the ramp, each section has the same positive slope. *Compare* this slope with the slope that a single-section ramp would have if it rose directly to the bridge from the same starting point. *Explain* the benefits of a three-section ramp in this situation.

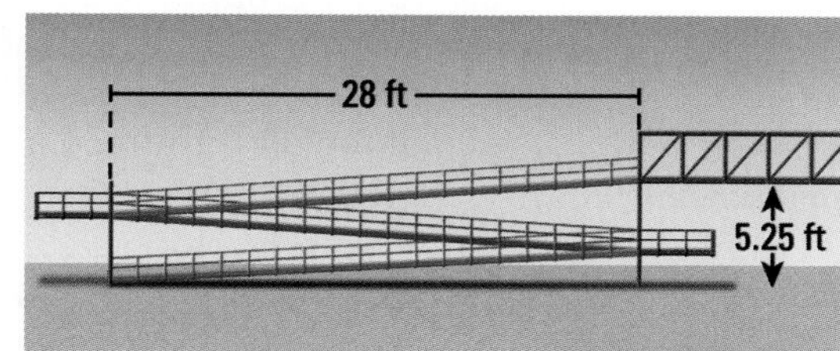

EXAMPLE 5 on p. 85 for Exs. 45–46

45. ★ **MULTIPLE CHOICE** Over a 30 day period, the amount of propane in a tank that stores propane for heating a home decreases from 400 gallons to 214 gallons. What is the average rate of change in the amount of propane?

Ⓐ −6.2 gallons per day
Ⓑ −6 gallons per day
Ⓒ −0.16 gallon per day
Ⓓ 6 gallons per day

46. **BIOLOGY** A red sea urchin grows its entire life, which can last 200 years. The diagram gives information about the growth in the diameter d of one red sea urchin. What is the average growth rate of this urchin over the given period?

47. **MULTI-STEP PROBLEM** A building code requires the minimum slope, or *pitch*, of an asphalt-shingle roof to be a rise of 3 feet for each 12 feet of run. The asphalt-shingle roof of an apartment building has the dimensions shown.

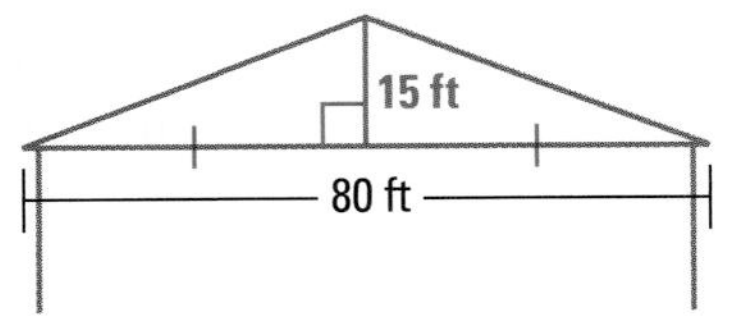

a. **Calculate** What is the slope of the roof?

b. **Interpret** Does the roof satisfy the building code?

c. **Reasoning** If you answered "no" to part (b), by how much must the rise be increased to satisfy the code? If you answered "yes," by how much does the rise exceed the code minimum?

48. ★ **EXTENDED RESPONSE** Plans for a new water slide in an amusement park call for the slide to descend from a platform 80 feet tall. The slide will drop 1 foot for every 3 feet of horizontal distance.

a. What horizontal distance do you cover when descending the slide?

b. Use the Pythagorean theorem to find the length of the slide.

c. Engineers decide to shorten the slide horizontally by 5 feet to allow for a wider walkway at the slide's base. The plans for the platform remain unchanged. How will this affect the slope of the slide? *Explain.*

49. **CHALLENGE** A car travels 36 miles per gallon of gasoline in highway driving and 24 miles per gallon in city driving. If you drive the car equal distances on the highway and in the city, how many miles per gallon can you expect to average? (*Hint:* The average fuel efficiency for all the driving is the total distance traveled divided by the total amount of gasoline used.)

NEW YORK MIXED REVIEW

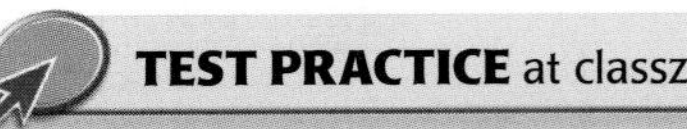

TEST PRACTICE at classzone.com

50. A city is building a rectangular playground in a community park. The city has 560 feet of fencing to enclose the playground. The length of the playground should be 40 feet longer than the width. What is the length of the playground if all of the fencing is used?

Ⓐ 120 ft Ⓑ 160 ft

Ⓒ 200 ft Ⓓ 300 ft

51. A computer technician charges $185 for parts needed to fix a computer and $45 for each hour that he works on the computer. Which equation best represents the relationship between the number of hours, h, the technician works on the computer and the total charges, c?

Ⓐ $c = 45 - 185h$ Ⓑ $c = 45 + 185h$

Ⓒ $c = 185 - 45h$ Ⓓ $c = 185 + 45h$

2.3 Graph Equations of Lines

Before You graphed linear equations by making tables of values.

Now You will graph linear equations in slope-intercept or standard form.

Why? So you can model motion, as in Ex. 64.

Key Vocabulary
- **parent function**
- ***y*-intercept**
- **slope-intercept form**
- **standard form of a linear equation**
- ***x*-intercept**

A *family* of functions is a group of functions with shared characteristics. The **parent function** is the most basic function in a family.

KEY CONCEPT *For Your Notebook*

Parent Function for Linear Functions

The parent function for the family of all linear functions is $f(x) = x$. The graph of $f(x) = x$ is shown.

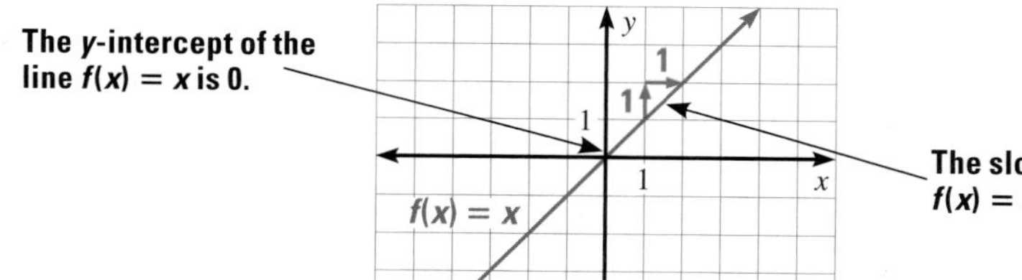

In general, a ***y*-intercept** of a graph is the y-coordinate of a point where the graph intersects the y-axis.

DEFINE Y-INTERCEPT

A y-intercept is sometimes defined as a *point* where a graph intersects the y-axis. Using this definition, the y-intercept of the line $f(x) = x$ is (0, 0), not 0.

EXAMPLE 1 Graph linear functions

Graph the equation. Compare the graph with the graph of $y = x$.

a. $y = 2x$ **b.** $y = x + 3$

Solution

a.

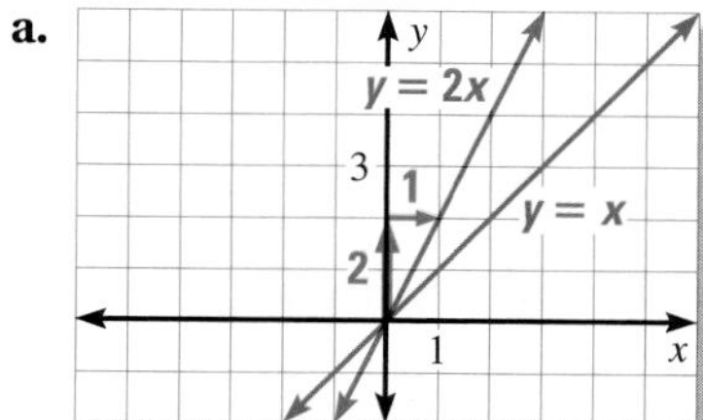

The graphs of $y = 2x$ and $y = x$ both have a y-intercept of 0, but the graph of $y = 2x$ has a slope of 2 instead of 1.

b.

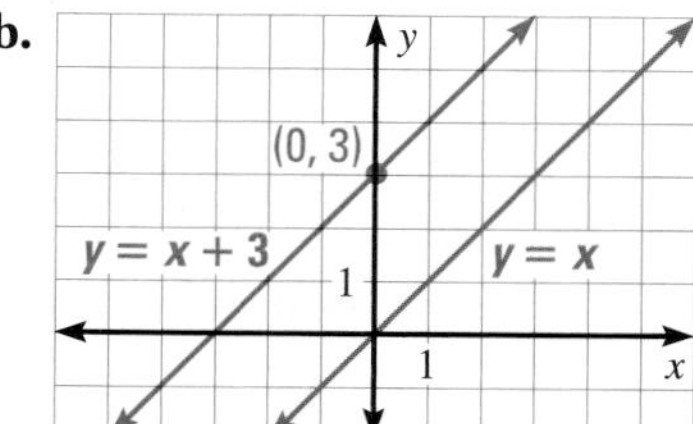

The graphs of $y = x + 3$ and $y = x$ both have a slope of 1, but the graph of $y = x + 3$ has a y-intercept of 3 instead of 0.

SLOPE-INTERCEPT FORM If you write the equations in Example 1 as $y = 2x + 0$ and $y = 1x + 3$, you can see that the x-coefficients, 2 and 1, are the slopes of the lines, while the constant terms, 0 and 3, are the y-intercepts. In general, a line with equation $y = mx + b$ has slope m and y-intercept b. The equation $y = mx + b$ is said to be in **slope-intercept form**.

KEY CONCEPT *For Your Notebook*

Using Slope-Intercept Form to Graph an Equation

STEP 1 **Write** the equation in slope-intercept form by solving for y.

STEP 2 **Identify** the y-intercept b and use it to plot the point $(0, b)$ where the line crosses the y-axis.

STEP 3 **Identify** the slope m and use it to plot a second point on the line.

STEP 4 **Draw** a line through the two points.

EXAMPLE 2 Graph an equation in slope-intercept form

Graph $y = -\frac{2}{3}x - 1$.

Solution

STEP 1 The equation is already in slope-intercept form.

STEP 2 **Identify** the y-intercept. The y-intercept is -1, so plot the point $(0, -1)$ where the line crosses the y-axis.

STEP 3 **Identify** the slope. The slope is $-\frac{2}{3}$, or $\frac{-2}{3}$, so plot a second point on the line by starting at $(0, -1)$ and then moving down 2 units and right 3 units. The second point is $(3, -3)$.

ANOTHER WAY

Because $-\frac{2}{3} = \frac{2}{-3}$, you could also plot a second point by moving up 2 units and left 3 units.

STEP 4 **Draw** a line through the two points.

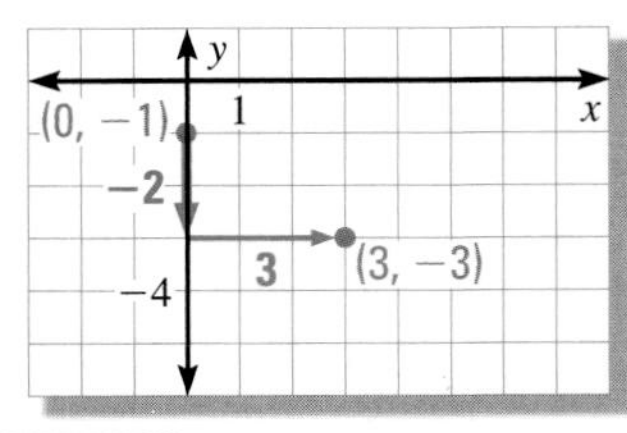

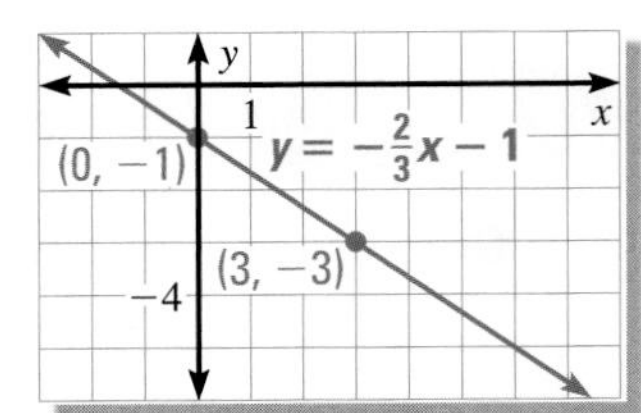

Animated **Algebra** at classzone.com

✓ **GUIDED PRACTICE** for Examples 1 and 2

Graph the equation. *Compare* the graph with the graph of $y = x$.

1. $y = -2x$
2. $y = x - 2$
3. $y = 4x$

Graph the equation.

4. $y = -x + 2$
5. $y = \frac{2}{5}x + 4$
6. $y = \frac{1}{2}x - 3$
7. $y = 5 + x$
8. $f(x) = 1 - 3x$
9. $f(x) = 10 - x$

REAL-LIFE PROBLEMS In a real-life context, a line's slope can represent an average rate of change. The y-intercept in a real-life context is often an initial value.

EXAMPLE 3 Solve a multi-step problem

BIOLOGY The body length y (in inches) of a walrus calf can be modeled by $y = 5x + 42$ where x is the calf's age (in months).

- Graph the equation.
- Describe what the slope and y-intercept represent in this situation.
- Use the graph to estimate the body length of a calf that is 10 months old.

Solution

STEP 1 **Graph** the equation.

STEP 2 **Interpret** the slope and y-intercept. The slope, 5, represents the calf's rate of growth in inches per month. The y-intercept, 42, represents a newborn calf's body length in inches.

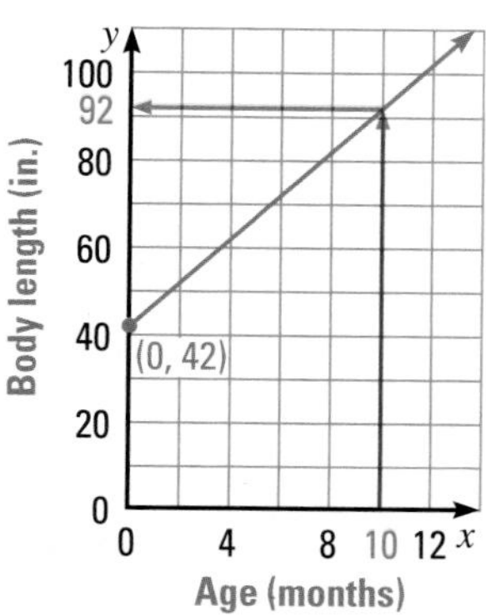

STEP 3 **Estimate** the body length of the calf at age 10 months by starting at 10 on the x-axis and moving up until you reach the graph. Then move left to the y-axis. At age 10 months, the body length of the calf is about 92 inches.

ANOTHER WAY
You can check the result you obtained from the graph by substituting 10 for x in $y = 5x + 42$ and simplifying.

✓ GUIDED PRACTICE for Example 3

10. **WHAT IF?** In Example 3, suppose that the body length of a fast-growing calf is modeled by $y = 6x + 48$. Repeat the steps of the example for the new model.

STANDARD FORM The **standard form** of a linear equation is $Ax + By = C$ where A and B are not both zero. You can graph an equation in standard form by identifying and plotting the x- and y-intercepts. An **x-intercept** is the x-coordinate of a point where a graph intersects the x-axis.

DEFINE X-INTERCEPT
An x-intercept is sometimes defined as a *point* where a graph intersects the x-axis, not the x-coordinate of such a point.

KEY CONCEPT *For Your Notebook*

Using Standard Form to Graph an Equation

STEP 1 **Write** the equation in standard form.

STEP 2 **Identify** the x-intercept by letting $y = 0$ and solving for x. Use the x-intercept to plot the point where the line crosses the x-axis.

STEP 3 **Identify** the y-intercept by letting $x = 0$ and solving for y. Use the y-intercept to plot the point where the line crosses the y-axis.

STEP 4 **Draw** a line through the two points.

EXAMPLE 4 Graph an equation in standard form

Graph $5x + 2y = 10$.

ANOTHER WAY

You can also graph $5x + 2y = 10$ by first solving for y to obtain $y = -\frac{5}{2}x + 5$ and then using the procedure for graphing an equation in slope-intercept form.

Solution

STEP 1 The equation is already in standard form.

STEP 2 **Identify** the x-intercept.

$5x + 2(0) = 10$ **Let $y = 0$.**

$x = 2$ **Solve for x.**

The x-intercept is 2. So, plot the point $(2, 0)$.

STEP 3 **Identify** the y-intercept.

$5(0) + 2y = 10$ **Let $x = 0$.**

$y = 5$ **Solve for y.**

The y-intercept is 5. So, plot the point $(0, 5)$.

STEP 4 **Draw** a line through the two points.

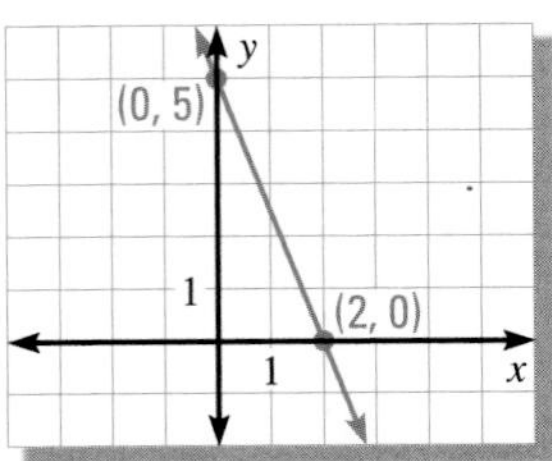

HORIZONTAL AND VERTICAL LINES The equation of a vertical line cannot be written in slope-intercept form because the slope is not defined. However, every linear equation—even that of a vertical line—can be written in standard form.

KEY CONCEPT *For Your Notebook*

Horizontal and Vertical Lines

Horizontal Lines The graph of $y = c$ is the horizontal line through $(0, c)$.

Vertical Lines The graph of $x = c$ is the vertical line through $(c, 0)$.

EXAMPLE 5 Graph horizontal and vertical lines

Graph (a) $y = 2$ and (b) $x = -3$.

Solution

a. The graph of $y = 2$ is the horizontal line that passes through the point $(0, 2)$. Notice that every point on the line has a y-coordinate of 2.

b. The graph of $x = -3$ is the vertical line that passes through the point $(-3, 0)$. Notice that every point on the line has an x-coordinate of -3.

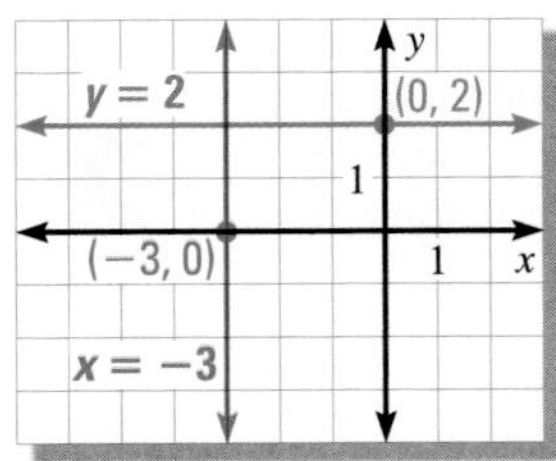

GUIDED PRACTICE for Examples 4 and 5

Graph the equation.

11. $2x + 5y = 10$ **12.** $3x - 2y = 12$ **13.** $x = 1$ **14.** $y = -4$

2.3 EXERCISES

HOMEWORK KEY

○ = **WORKED-OUT SOLUTIONS** on p. WS3 for Exs. 15, 37, and 61

★ = **STANDARDIZED TEST PRACTICE** Exs. 2, 23, 30, 55, 56, 63, and 68

◆ = **MULTIPLE REPRESENTATIONS** Ex. 67

SKILL PRACTICE

1. **VOCABULARY** Copy and complete: The linear equation $y = 2x + 5$ is written in _?_ form.

2. ★ **WRITING** *Describe* how to graph an equation of the form $Ax + By = C$.

EXAMPLE 1 on p. 89 for Exs. 3–8

GRAPHING LINEAR FUNCTIONS **Graph the equation. *Compare* the graph with the graph of $y = x$.**

3. $y = 3x$
4. $y = -x$
5. $y = x + 5$
6. $y = x - 2$
7. $y = 2x - 1$
8. $y = -3x + 2$

EXAMPLE 2 on p. 90 for Exs. 9–22

SLOPE-INTERCEPT FORM **Graph the equation.**

9. $y = -x - 3$
10. $y = x - 6$
11. $y = 2x + 6$
12. $y = 3x - 4$
13. $y = 4x - 1$
14. $y = \frac{2}{3}x - 2$
15. $f(x) = -\frac{1}{2}x - 1$
16. $f(x) = -\frac{5}{4}x + 1$
17. $f(x) = \frac{3}{2}x - 3$
18. $f(x) = \frac{5}{3}x + 4$
19. $f(x) = -1.5x + 2$
20. $f(x) = 3x - 1.5$

ERROR ANALYSIS ***Describe*** **and correct the error in graphing the equation.**

21. $y = 2x + 3$

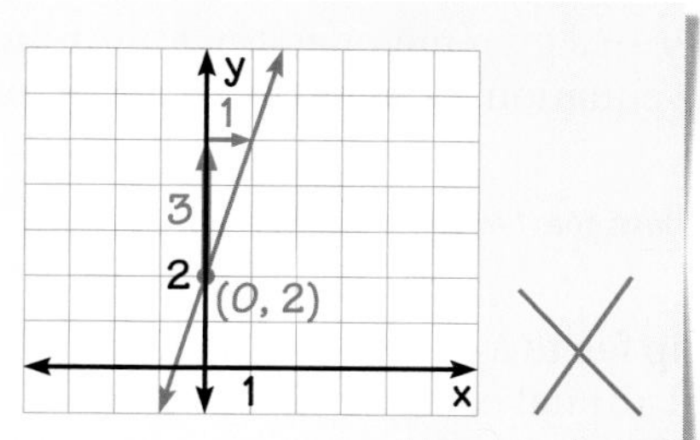

22. $y = 4x - 2$

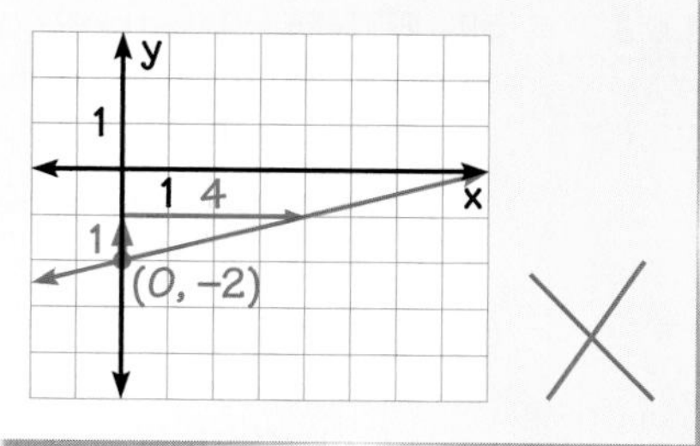

23. ★ **MULTIPLE CHOICE** What is the slope-intercept form of $4x - 3y = 18$?

Ⓐ $y = \frac{3}{4}x - 6$ Ⓑ $y = -\frac{3}{4}x - 6$ Ⓒ $y = \frac{4}{3}x - 6$ Ⓓ $y = -\frac{4}{3}x + 6$

EXAMPLES 4 and 5 on p. 92 for Exs. 24–42

FINDING INTERCEPTS **Find the x- and y-intercepts of the line with the given equation.**

24. $x - y = 4$
25. $x + 5y = -15$
26. $3x - 4y = -12$
27. $2x - y = 10$
28. $4x - 5y = 20$
29. $-6x + 8y = -36$

30. ★ **MULTIPLE CHOICE** What is the x-intercept of the graph of $5x - 6y = 30$?

Ⓐ -5 Ⓑ $\frac{5}{6}$ Ⓒ 6 Ⓓ 30

STANDARD FORM **Graph the equation. Label any intercepts.**

31. $x + 4y = 8$
32. $2x - 6y = -12$
33. $x = 4$
34. $y = -2$
35. $5x - y = 3$
36. $3x + 4y = 12$
37. $-5x + 10y = 20$
38. $-x - y = 6$
39. $y = 1.5$
40. $2.5x - 5y = -15$
41. $x = -\frac{5}{2}$
42. $\frac{1}{2}x + 2y = -2$

CHOOSING A METHOD **Graph the equation using any method.**

43. $6y = 3x + 6$
44. $-3 + x = 0$
45. $y + 7 = -2x$
46. $4y = 16$
47. $8y = -2x + 20$
48. $4x = -\frac{1}{2}y - 1$
49. $-4x = 8y + 12$
50. $3.5x = 10.5$
51. $y - 5.5x = 6$
52. $14 - 3x = 7y$
53. $2y - 5 = 0$
54. $5y = 7.5 - 2.5x$

55. ★ **OPEN-ENDED MATH** Write equations of two lines, one with an x-intercept but no y-intercept and one with a y-intercept but no x-intercept.

56. ★ **SHORT RESPONSE** Sketch $y = mx$ for several values of m, both positive and negative. *Describe* the relationship between m and the steepness of the line.

57. **REASONING** Consider the graph of $Ax + By = C$ where $B \neq 0$. What are the slope and y-intercept in terms of A, B, and C?

58. **CHALLENGE** Prove that the slope of the line $y = mx + b$ is m. (*Hint:* First find two points on the line by choosing convenient values of x.)

PROBLEM SOLVING

EXAMPLE 3 on p. 91 for Exs. 59–62

59. **FITNESS** The total cost y (in dollars) of a gym membership after x months is given by $y = 45x + 75$. Graph the equation. What is the total cost of the membership after 9 months?

@HomeTutor for problem solving help at classzone.com

60. **CAMPING** Your annual membership fee to a nature society lets you camp at several campgrounds. Your total annual cost y (in dollars) to use the campgrounds is given by $y = 5x + 35$ where x is the number of nights you camp. Graph the equation. What do the slope and y-intercept represent?

@HomeTutor for problem solving help at classzone.com

61. **SPORTS** Bowling alleys often charge a fixed fee to rent shoes and then charge for each game you bowl. The function $C(g) = 3g + 1.5$ gives the total cost C (in dollars) to bowl g games. Graph the function. What is the cost to rent shoes? What is the cost per game?

62. **PHONE CARDS** You purchase a 300 minute phone card. The function $M(w) = -30w + 300$ models the number M of minutes that remain on the card after w weeks. *Describe* how to determine a reasonable domain and range. Graph the function. How many minutes per week do you use the card?

63. ★ **SHORT RESPONSE** You receive a \$30 gift card to a shop that sells fruit smoothies for \$3. If you graph an equation of the line that represents the money y remaining on the card after you buy x smoothies, what will the y-intercept be? Will the line rise or fall from left to right? *Explain.*

64. **MULTI-STEP PROBLEM** You and a friend kayak 1800 yards down a river. You drift with the current partway at 30 yards per minute and paddle partway at 90 yards per minute. The trip is modeled by $30x + 90y = 1800$ where x is the drifting time and y is the paddling time (both in minutes).

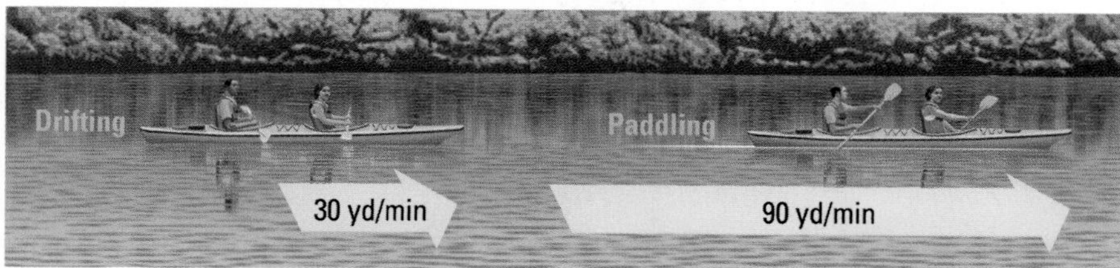

   a. Graph the equation, and determine a reasonable domain and range. What do the x- and y-intercepts represent?

   b. If you paddle for 5 minutes, what is the total trip time?

   c. If you paddle and drift equal amounts of time, what is the total trip time?

65. **VOLUNTEERING** You participate in a 14 mile run/walk for charity. You run partway at 6 miles per hour and walk partway at 3.5 miles per hour. A model for this situation is $6r + 3.5w = 14$ where r is the time you run and w is the time you walk (both in hours). Graph the equation. Give three possible combinations of running and walking times.

66. **TICKETS** An honor society has \$150 to buy science museum and art museum tickets for student awards. The numbers of tickets that can be bought are given by $5s + 7a = 150$ where s is the number of science museum tickets (at \$5 each) and a is the number of art museum tickets (at \$7 each). Graph the equation. Give two possible combinations of tickets that use all \$150.

67. **MULTIPLE REPRESENTATIONS** A hot air balloon is initially 200 feet above the ground. The burners are then turned on, causing the balloon to ascend at a rate of 150 feet per minute.

   a. **Making a Table** Make a table showing the height h (in feet) of the balloon t minutes after the burners are turned on where $0 \le t \le 5$.

   b. **Drawing a Graph** Plot the points from the table in part (a). Draw a line through the points for the domain $0 \le t \le 5$.

   c. **Writing an Equation** The balloon's height is its initial height plus the product of the ascent rate and time. Write an equation representing this.

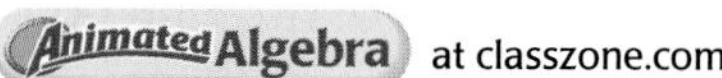

at classzone.com

68. ★ **EXTENDED RESPONSE** You and a friend are each typing your research papers on computers. The function $y = 1400 - 50x$ models the number y of words you have left to type after x minutes. For your friend, $y = 1200 - 50x$ models the number y of words left to type after x minutes.

   a. Graph the two equations in the same coordinate plane. *Describe* how the graphs are related geometrically.

   b. What do the x-intercepts, y-intercepts, and slopes represent?

   c. Who will finish first? *Explain.*

69. CHALLENGE You want to cover a five-by-five grid completely with x three-by-one rectangles and y four-by-one rectangles that do not overlap or extend beyond the grid.

3 by 1 4 by 1 5 by 5

a. *Explain* why x and y must be whole numbers that satisfy the equation $3x + 4y = 25$.

b. Find all solutions (x, y) of the equation in part (a) such that x and y are whole numbers.

c. Do all the solutions from part (b) represent combinations of rectangles that can actually cover the grid? Use diagrams to support your answer.

NEW YORK MIXED REVIEW

TEST PRACTICE at classzone.com

70. In isosceles triangle ABC, the interior angle A measures 110°. The measures of all three interior angles of triangle ABC are—

Ⓐ 110°, 110°, and 140° Ⓑ 110°, 110°, and 110°

Ⓒ 110°, 40°, and 30° Ⓓ 110°, 35°, and 35°

71. A paper cup is shaped like the cone shown. What is the approximate volume of this paper cup?

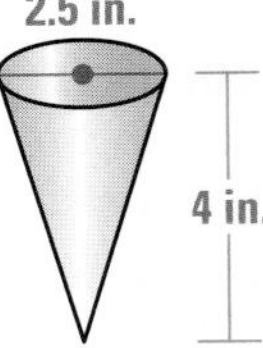

Ⓐ 6.5 in.^{3} Ⓑ 10.5 in.^{3}

Ⓒ 26.2 in.^{3} Ⓓ 41.9 in.^{3}

QUIZ *for Lessons 2.1–2.3*

Tell whether the relation is a function. *Explain.* *(p. 72)*

1.

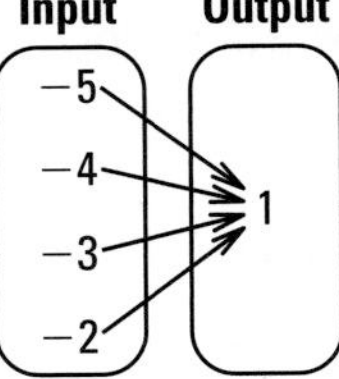

2.

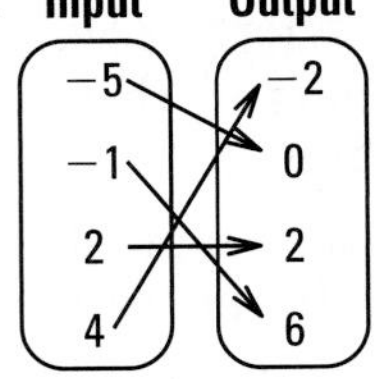

3.

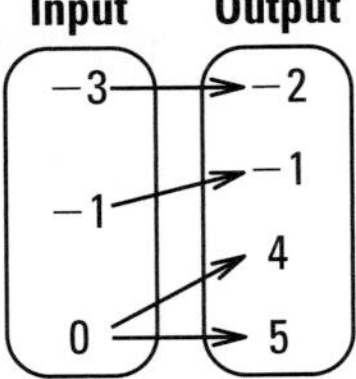

Tell whether the lines are *parallel, perpendicular,* or *neither.* *(p. 82)*

4. Line 1: through (−3, −7) and (1, 9)
Line 2: through (−1, −4) and (0, −2)

5. Line 1: through (2, 7) and (−1, −2)
Line 2: through (3, −6) and (−6, −3)

Graph the equation. *(p. 89)*

6. $y = -5x + 3$ **7.** $x = 10$ **8.** $4x + 3y = -24$

9. ROWING SPEED In 1999, Tori Murden became the first woman to row across the Atlantic Ocean. She rowed a total of 3333 miles during her crossing. The distance d rowed (in miles) can be modeled by $d = 41t$ where t represents the time rowed (in days) at an average rate of 41 miles per day. Graph the function, and determine a reasonable domain and range. Then estimate how long it took Tori Murden to row 1000 miles. *(p. 72)*

@HomeTutor classzone.com Keystrokes

2.3 Graph Equations

QUESTION How can you use a graphing calculator to graph an equation?

You can use a graphing calculator to graph equations in two variables. On most calculators, you must first write the equation in the form $y = f(x)$.

EXAMPLE Graph a linear equation

Graph the equation $x + 4y = 8$.

STEP 1 *Solve for y*

First, solve the equation for y so that it can be entered into the calculator.

$$x + 4y = 8$$
$$4y = -x + 8$$
$$y = -\frac{1}{4}x + 2$$

STEP 2 *Enter equation*

For fractional coefficients, use parentheses. So, enter the equation as $y = -(1/4)x + 2$.

STEP 3 *Set viewing window and graph*

Enter minimum and maximum x- and y-values and x- and y-scales. The viewing window should show the intercepts. The *standard viewing window* settings and the corresponding graph are shown below.

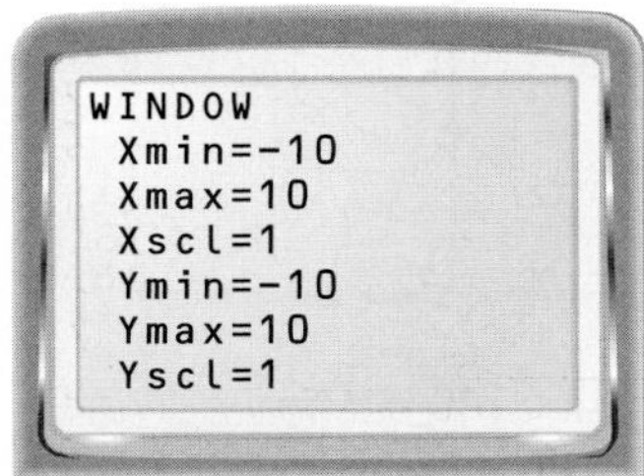

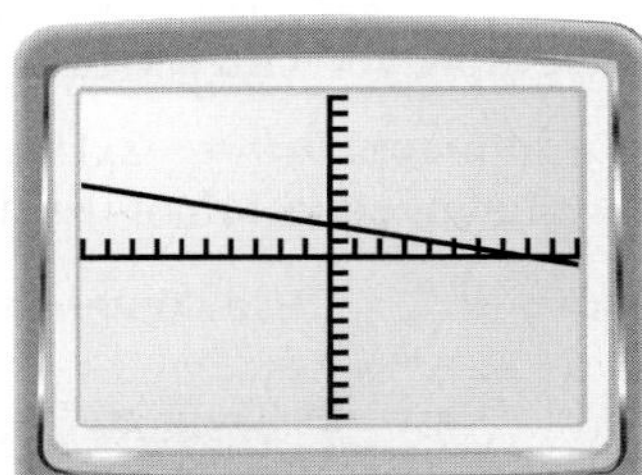

PRACTICE

Graph the equation in a graphing calculator's standard viewing window.

1. $y + 14 = 17 - 2x$ **2.** $3x - y = 4$ **3.** $3x - 6y = -18$

Graph the equation using a graphing calculator. Use a viewing window that shows the x- and y-intercepts.

4. $8x = 5y + 16$ **5.** $4x = 25y - 240$ **6.** $1.25x + 4.2y = 28.7$

2.4 Write Equations of Lines

Before You graphed linear equations.
Now You will write linear equations.
Why? So you can model a steady increase or decrease, as in Ex. 51.

Key Vocabulary
- point-slope form

KEY CONCEPT *For Your Notebook*

Writing an Equation of a Line

Given slope m and y-intercept b	Use slope-intercept form: $y = mx + b$
Given slope m and a point (x_1, y_1)	Use **point-slope form**: $y - y_1 = m(x - x_1)$
Given points (x_1, y_1) and (x_2, y_2)	First use the slope formula to find m. Then use point-slope form with either given point.

EXAMPLE 1 **Write an equation given the slope and y-intercept**

Write an equation of the line shown.

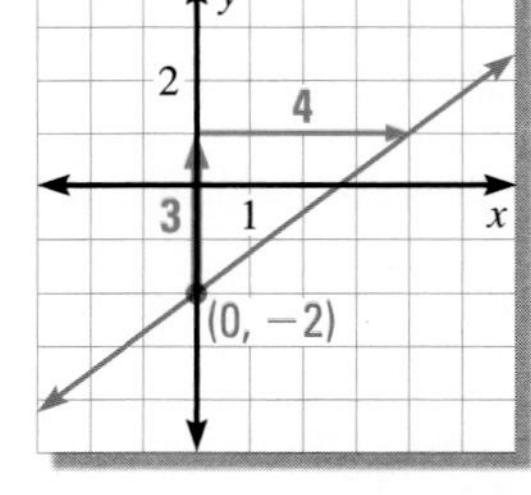

Solution

From the graph, you can see that the slope is $m = \frac{3}{4}$ and the y-intercept is $b = -2$. Use slope-intercept form to write an equation of the line.

$y = mx + b$ Use slope-intercept form.

$y = \frac{3}{4}x + (-2)$ Substitute $\frac{3}{4}$ for m and -2 for b.

$y = \frac{3}{4}x - 2$ Simplify.

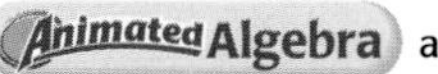
Animated Algebra at classzone.com

✓ **GUIDED PRACTICE** for Example 1

Write an equation of the line that has the given slope and y-intercept.

1. $m = 3, b = 1$ **2.** $m = -2, b = -4$ **3.** $m = -\frac{3}{4}, b = \frac{7}{2}$

EXAMPLE 2 Write an equation given the slope and a point

Write an equation of the line that passes through (5, 4) and has a slope of −3.

Solution

Because you know the slope and a point on the line, use point-slope form to write an equation of the line. Let $(x_1, y_1) = (5, 4)$ and $m = -3$.

SIMPLIFY EQUATIONS

In this book, equations written in point-slope form will be simplified to slope-intercept form.

$y - y_1 = m(x - x_1)$	**Use point-slope form.**
$y - \mathbf{4} = \mathbf{-3}(x - \mathbf{5})$	**Substitute for m, x_1, and y_1.**
$y - 4 = -3x + 15$	**Distributive property**
$y = -3x + 19$	**Write in slope-intercept form.**

EXAMPLE 3 Write equations of parallel or perpendicular lines

Write an equation of the line that passes through (−2, 3) and is (a) parallel to, and (b) perpendicular to, the line $y = -4x + 1$.

Solution

a. The given line has a slope of $m_1 = -4$. So, a line parallel to it has a slope of $m_2 = m_1 = -4$. You know the slope and a point on the line, so use the point-slope form with $(x_1, y_1) = (-2, 3)$ to write an equation of the line.

$y - y_1 = m_2(x - x_1)$	**Use point-slope form.**
$y - \mathbf{3} = \mathbf{-4}(x - (\mathbf{-2}))$	**Substitute for m_2, x_1, and y_1.**
$y - 3 = -4(x + 2)$	**Simplify.**
$y - 3 = -4x - 8$	**Distributive property**
$y = -4x - 5$	**Write in slope-intercept form.**

b. A line perpendicular to a line with slope $m_1 = -4$ has a slope of $m_2 = -\frac{1}{m_1} = \frac{1}{4}$. Use point-slope form with $(x_1, y_1) = (-2, 3)$.

$y - y_1 = m_2(x - x_1)$	**Use point-slope form.**
$y - \mathbf{3} = \frac{\mathbf{1}}{\mathbf{4}}(x - (\mathbf{-2}))$	**Substitute for m_2, x_1, and y_1.**
$y - 3 = \frac{1}{4}(x + 2)$	**Simplify.**
$y - 3 = \frac{1}{4}x + \frac{1}{2}$	**Distributive property**
$y = \frac{1}{4}x + \frac{7}{2}$	**Write in slope-intercept form.**

✓ GUIDED PRACTICE for Examples 2 and 3

4. Write an equation of the line that passes through (−1, 6) and has a slope of 4.

5. Write an equation of the line that passes through (4, −2) and is **(a)** parallel to, and **(b)** perpendicular to, the line $y = 3x - 1$.

EXAMPLE 4 Write an equation given two points

Write an equation of the line that passes through (5, −2) and (2, 10).

ANOTHER WAY

For an alternative method for solving the problem in Example 4, turn to page 105 for the **Problem Solving Workshop**.

Solution

The line passes through $(x_1, y_1) = (5, -2)$ and $(x_2, y_2) = (2, 10)$. Find its slope.

$$m = \frac{y_2 - y_1}{x_2 - x_1} = \frac{10 - (-2)}{2 - 5} = \frac{12}{-3} = -4$$

You know the slope and a point on the line, so use point-slope form with either given point to write an equation of the line. Choose $(x_1, y_1) = (2, 10)$.

$y - y_1 = m(x - x_1)$ **Use point-slope form.**

$y - 10 = -4(x - 2)$ **Substitute for m, x_1, and y_1.**

$y - 10 = -4x + 8$ **Distributive property**

$y = -4x + 18$ **Write in slope-intercept form.**

EXAMPLE 5 Write a model using slope-intercept form

SPORTS In the school year ending in 1993, 2.00 million females participated in U.S. high school sports. By 2003, the number had increased to 2.86 million. Write a linear equation that models female sports participation.

Solution

STEP 1 **Define** the variables. Let x represent the time (in years) since 1993 and let y represent the number of participants (in millions).

STEP 2 **Identify** the initial value and rate of change. The initial value is 2.00. The rate of change is the slope m.

AVOID ERRORS

Because time is defined in years since 1993 in Step 1, 1993 corresponds to $x_1 = 0$ and 2003 corresponds to $x_2 = 10$.

$$m = \frac{y_2 - y_1}{x_2 - x_1} = \frac{2.86 - 2.00}{10 - 0} = \frac{0.86}{10} = 0.086$$

Use $(x_1, y_1) = (0, 2.00)$ and $(x_2, y_2) = (10, 2.86)$.

STEP 3 **Write** a verbal model. Then write a linear equation.

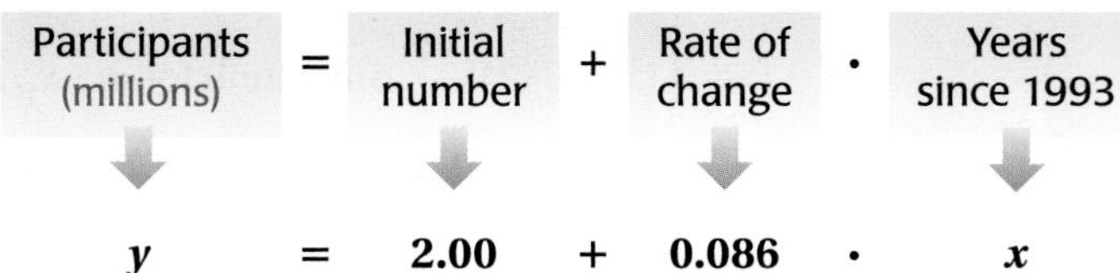

$y = 2.00 + 0.086 \cdot x$

▶ In slope-intercept form, a linear model is $y = 0.086x + 2.00$.

✓ GUIDED PRACTICE for Examples 4 and 5

Write an equation of the line that passes through the given points.

6. (−2, 5), (4, −7) **7.** (6, 1), (−3, −8) **8.** (−1, 2), (10, 0)

9. SPORTS In Example 5, the corresponding data for males are 3.42 million participants in 1993 and 3.99 million participants in 2003. Write a linear equation that models male participation in U.S. high school sports.

EXAMPLE 6 Write a model using standard form

ONLINE MUSIC You have $30 to spend on downloading songs for your digital music player. Company A charges $.79 per song, and company B charges $.99 per song. Write an equation that models this situation.

Solution

Write a verbal model. Then write an equation.

Company A song price (dollars/song)	·	Songs from company A (songs)	+	Company B song price (dollars/song)	·	Songs from company B (songs)	=	Your budget (dollars)
↓		↓		↓		↓		↓
0.79	·	x	+	**0.99**	·	y	=	**30**

▶ An equation for this situation is $0.79x + 0.99y = 30$.

GUIDED PRACTICE for Example 6

10. **WHAT IF?** In Example 6, suppose that company A charges $.69 per song and company B charges $.89 per song. Write an equation that models this situation.

2.4 EXERCISES

HOMEWORK KEY

○ = **WORKED-OUT SOLUTIONS** on p. WS3 for Exs. 15, 35, and 53

★ = **STANDARDIZED TEST PRACTICE** Exs. 2, 26, 39, 47, and 53

◆ = **MULTIPLE REPRESENTATIONS** Ex. 57

SKILL PRACTICE

1. **VOCABULARY** Copy and complete: The linear equation $6x + 8y = 72$ is written in _?_ form.

2. ★ **WRITING** Given two points on a line, explain how you can use point-slope form to write an equation of the line.

EXAMPLE 1 on p. 98 for Exs. 3–8

SLOPE-INTERCEPT FORM **Write an equation of the line that has the given slope and y-intercept.**

3. $m = 0, b = 2$
4. $m = 3, b = -4$
5. $m = 6, b = 0$
6. $m = \frac{2}{3}, b = 4$
7. $m = -\frac{5}{4}, b = 7$
8. $m = -5, b = -1$

EXAMPLE 2 on p. 99 for Exs. 9–19

POINT-SLOPE FORM **Write an equation of the line that passes through the given point and has the given slope.**

9. $(0, -2), m = 4$
10. $(3, -1), m = -3$
11. $(-4, 3), m = 2$
12. $(-5, -6), m = 0$
13. $(8, 13), m = -9$
14. $(12, 0), m = \frac{3}{4}$
15. $(7, -3), m = -\frac{4}{7}$
16. $(-4, 2), m = \frac{3}{2}$
17. $(9, -5), m = -\frac{1}{3}$

ERROR ANALYSIS *Describe* **and correct the error in writing an equation of the line that passes through the given point and has the given slope.**

18. $(-4, 2)$, $m = 3$

$y - y_1 = m(x - x_1)$

$y - 2 = 3(x - 4)$

$y - 2 = 3x - 12$

$y = 3x - 10$ ✗

19. $(5, 1)$, $m = -2$

$y - y_1 = m(x - x_1)$

$y - 5 = -2(x - 1)$

$y - 5 = -2x + 2$

$y = -2x + 7$ ✗

EXAMPLE 3
on p. 99
for Exs. 20–26

PARALLEL AND PERPENDICULAR LINES **Write an equation of the line that passes through the given point and satisfies the given condition.**

20. $(-3, -5)$; parallel to $y = -4x + 1$

21. $(7, 1)$; parallel to $y = -x + 3$

22. $(2, 8)$; parallel to $y = 3x - 2$

23. $(4, 1)$; perpendicular to $y = \frac{1}{3}x + 3$

24. $(-6, 2)$; perpendicular to $y = -2$

25. $(3, -1)$; perpendicular to $y = 4x + 1$

26. ★ **MULTIPLE CHOICE** What is an equation of the line that passes through $(1, 4)$ and is perpendicular to the line $y = 2x - 3$?

Ⓐ $y = 2x + 2$ Ⓑ $y = \frac{1}{2}x + \frac{7}{2}$ Ⓒ $y = -\frac{1}{2}x + \frac{9}{2}$ Ⓓ $y = -\frac{1}{2}x + 4$

EXAMPLE 4
on p. 100
for Exs. 27–38

VISUAL THINKING **Write an equation of the line.**

27.

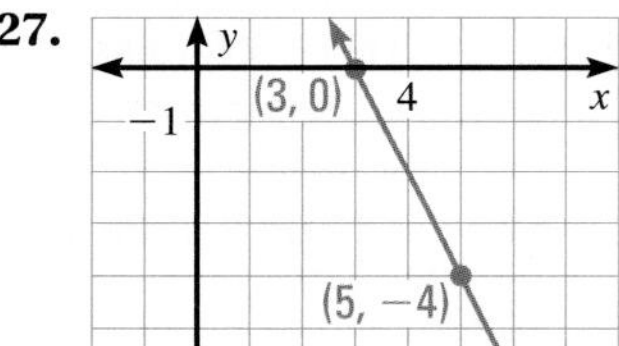

28.

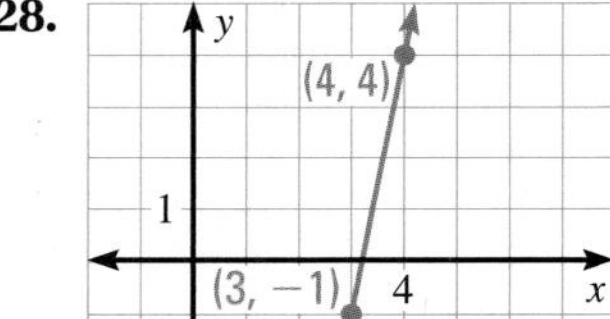

29.

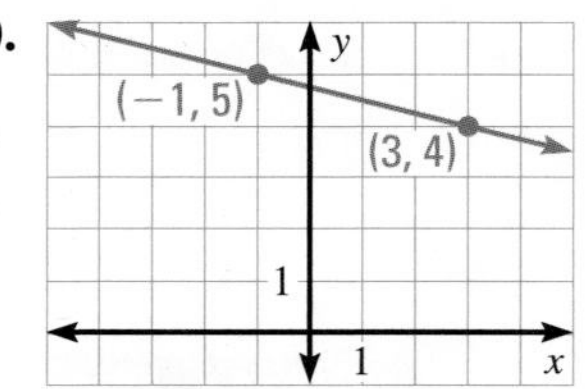

WRITING EQUATIONS **Write an equation of the line that passes through the given points.**

30. $(-1, 3)$, $(2, 9)$

31. $(4, -1)$, $(6, -7)$

32. $(-2, -3)$, $(2, -1)$

33. $(0, 7)$, $(3, 5)$

34. $(-1, 2)$, $(3, -4)$

35. $(-5, -2)$, $(-3, 8)$

36. $(15, 20)$, $(-12, 29)$

37. $(3.5, 7)$, $(-1, 20.5)$

38. $(0.6, 0.9)$, $(3.4, -2.6)$

39. ★ **MULTIPLE CHOICE** Which point lies on the line that passes through the point $(9, -5)$ and has a slope of -6?

Ⓐ $(6, 10)$ Ⓑ $(6, 6)$ Ⓒ $(7, 7)$ Ⓓ $(6, -4)$

STANDARD FORM **Write an equation in standard form $Ax + By = C$ of the line that satisfies the given conditions. Use integer values for A, B, and C.**

40. $m = -3$, $b = 5$

41. $m = 4$, $b = -3$

42. $m = -\frac{3}{2}$, passes through $(4, -7)$

43. $m = \frac{4}{5}$, passes through $(2, 3)$

44. passes through $(-1, 3)$ and $(-6, -7)$

45. passes through $(2, 8)$ and $(-4, 16)$

Animated **Algebra** at classzone.com

46. **REASONING** Write an equation of the line that passes through (3, 4) and satisfies the given condition.

a. Parallel to $y = -2$

b. Perpendicular to $y = -2$

c. Parallel to $x = -2$

d. Perpendicular to $x = -2$

47. ★ **OPEN-ENDED MATH** Write an equation of a line ℓ such that ℓ and the lines $y = -3x + 5$ and $y = 2x + 1$ form a right triangle.

48. **REASONING** Consider two distinct nonvertical lines $A_1x + B_1y = C_1$ and $A_2x + B_2y = C_2$. Show that the following statements are true.

a. If the lines are parallel, then $A_1B_2 = A_2B_1$.

b. If the lines are perpendicular, then $A_1A_2 + B_1B_2 = 0$.

49. **CHALLENGE** Show that an equation of the line with x-intercept a and y-intercept b is $\frac{x}{a} + \frac{y}{b} = 1$. This is the *intercept form* of a linear equation.

PROBLEM SOLVING

EXAMPLE 5 on p. 100 for Exs. 50–51

50. **CAR EXPENSES** You buy a used car for $6500. The monthly cost of owning the car (including insurance, fuel, maintenance, and taxes) averages $350. Write an equation that models the total cost of buying and owning the car.

@HomeTutor for problem solving help at classzone.com

51. **HOUSING** Since its founding, a volunteer group has restored 50 houses. It plans to restore 15 houses per year in the future. Write an equation that models the total number n of restored houses t years from now.

@HomeTutor for problem solving help at classzone.com

EXAMPLE 6 on p. 101 for Exs. 52–54

52. **GARDENING** You have a rectangular plot measuring 16 feet by 25 feet in a community garden. You want to grow tomato plants that each need 8 square feet of space and pepper plants that each need 5 square feet. Write an equation that models how many tomato plants and how many pepper plants you can grow. How many pepper plants can you grow if you grow 15 tomato plants?

53. ★ **SHORT RESPONSE** Concert tickets cost $15 for general admission, but only $9 with a student ID. Ticket sales total $4500. Write and graph an equation that models this situation. *Explain* how to use your graph to find how many student tickets were sold if 200 general admission tickets were sold.

54. **MULTI-STEP PROBLEM** A company will lease office space in two buildings. The annual cost is $21.75 per square foot in the first building and $17 per square foot in the second. The company has $86,000 budgeted for rent.

a. Write an equation that models the possible amounts of space rented in the buildings.

b. How many square feet of space can be rented in the first building if 2500 square feet are rented in the second?

c. If the company wants to rent equal amounts of space in the buildings, what is the total number of square feet that can be rented?

55. CABLE TELEVISION In 1994, the average monthly cost for expanded basic cable television service was \$21.62. In 2004, this cost had increased to \$38.23. Write a linear equation that models the monthly cost as a function of the number of years since 1994. Predict the average monthly cost of expanded basic cable television service in 2010.

56. TIRE PRESSURE Automobile tire pressure increases about 1 psi (pound per square inch) for each 10°F increase in air temperature. At an air temperature of 55°F, a tire's pressure is 30 psi. Write an equation that models the tire's pressure as a function of air temperature.

57. MULTIPLE REPRESENTATIONS Your class wants to make a rectangular spirit display, and has 24 feet of decorative border to enclose the display

GO BEARS! (w, ℓ)

a. **Writing an Equation** Write an equation in standard form relating the possible lengths ℓ and widths w of the display.

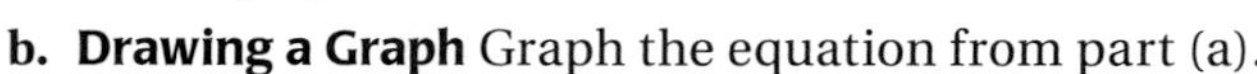

b. **Drawing a Graph** Graph the equation from part (a).

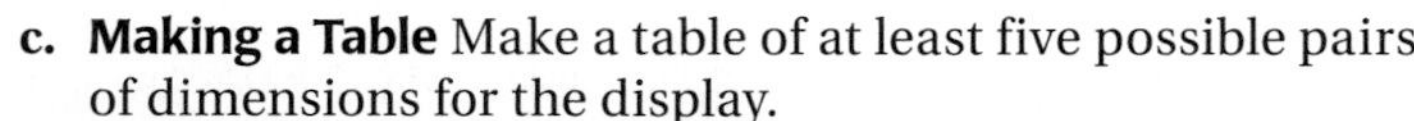

c. **Making a Table** Make a table of at least five possible pairs of dimensions for the display.

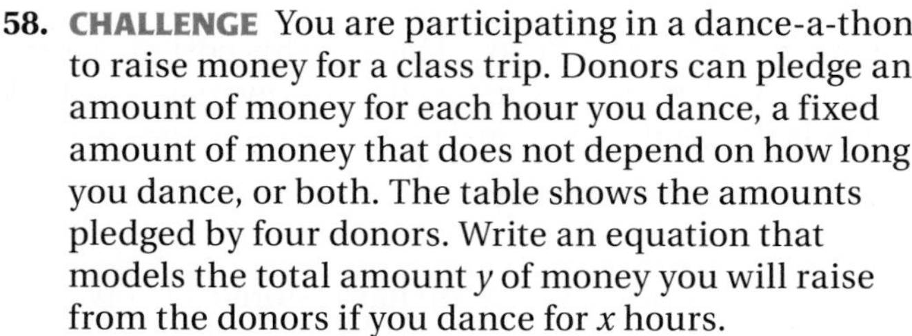

58. CHALLENGE You are participating in a dance-a-thon to raise money for a class trip. Donors can pledge an amount of money for each hour you dance, a fixed amount of money that does not depend on how long you dance, or both. The table shows the amounts pledged by four donors. Write an equation that models the total amount y of money you will raise from the donors if you dance for x hours.

Donor	Hourly amount	Fixed amount
Clare	\$4	\$15
Emilia	\$8	None
Julio	None	\$35
Max	\$3	\$20

NEW YORK MIXED REVIEW

TEST PRACTICE at classzone.com

59. At the end of the week, John has \$180 in his bank account. During the week he withdrew \$30 for lunches, deposited a \$125 paycheck, and withdrew \$22 to buy a shirt. How much money did John have in his account at the beginning of the week?

Ⓐ \$95 Ⓑ \$100 Ⓒ \$107 Ⓓ \$117

60. Use the table to determine the expression that best represents the total measure of the interior angles of any convex polygon having n sides.

Number of sides, n	3	4	5	6	7
Total measure of interior angles (in degrees)	180	360	540	720	900

Ⓐ $90(n-1)$ Ⓑ $180(n-2)$

Ⓒ $360(n-3)$ Ⓓ $\frac{360}{n-1}$

PROBLEM SOLVING WORKSHOP
LESSON 2.4

Using ALTERNATIVE METHODS

Another Way to Solve Example 4, page 100

MULTIPLE REPRESENTATIONS In Example 4 on page 100, you wrote an equation of a line through two given points by first writing the equation in point-slope form and then rewriting it in slope-intercept form. You can also write an equation of a line through two points by using the slope-intercept form to solve for the y-intercept.

PROBLEM

Write an equation of the line that passes through $(5, -2)$ and $(2, 10)$.

METHOD

Solving for the y-Intercept To write an equation of a line through two points, you can substitute the slope and the coordinates of one of the points into $y = mx + b$ and solve for the y-intercept b.

STEP 1 **Find** the slope of the line.

$$m = \frac{10 - (-2)}{2 - 5} = \frac{12}{-3} = -4$$

STEP 2 **Substitute** the slope and the coordinates of one point into the slope-intercept form. Use the point $(5, -2)$.

$$y = mx + b$$
$$-2 = -4(5) + b$$

STEP 3 **Solve** for b.

$$-2 = -20 + b$$
$$18 = b$$

STEP 4 **Substitute** m and b into the slope-intercept form.

$$y = -4x + 18$$

PRACTICE

1. **WRITE AN EQUATION** Use the method above to write an equation of the line that passes through $(2, 15)$ and $(7, 35)$.

2. **FITNESS** At a speed of 45 yards per minute, a 120 pound swimmer burns 420 calories per hour and a 172 pound swimmer burns 600 calories per hour. Use two different methods to write a linear equation that models the number of calories burned per hour as a function of a swimmer's weight.

3. **SAFETY** A motorist lights an emergency flare after having a flat tire. After burning for 6 minutes, the flare is 13 inches long. After burning for 20 minutes, it is 6 inches long. Use two different methods to write a linear equation that models the flare's length as a function of time.

4. **SNOWFALL** After 4 hours of snowfall, the snow depth is 8 inches. After 6 hours of snowfall, the snow depth is 9.5 inches. Use two different methods to write a linear equation that models the snow depth as a function of time.

5. **ARCHAEOLOGY** Ancient cities often rose in elevation through time as citizens built on top of accumulating rubble and debris. An archaeologist at a site dates artifacts from a depth of 54 feet as 3500 years old and artifacts from a depth of 26 feet as 2600 years old. Use two different methods to write a linear equation that models an artifact's age as a function of depth.

6. **REASONING** Suppose a line has slope m and passes through (x_1, y_1). Write an expression for the y-intercept b in terms of m, x_1, and y_1.

Lessons 2.1–2.4

1. **WEBSITES** From January through June, the number of visitors to a news website increased by about 1200 per month. In January, there were 50,000 visitors to the website. Which equation shows the number of visitors v as a function of the number of months t since January?

   (1) $v = 50{,}000 - 1200t$

   (2) $v = 50{,}000 + 1200t$

   (3) $v = 1200 - 50{,}000t$

   (4) $v = 1200 + 50{,}000t$

2. **SLOPE** What is the slope of a line parallel to the line $\frac{1}{4}y - 3x = 5$?

   (1) -3

   (2) $-\frac{3}{4}$

   (3) $\frac{1}{4}$

   (4) 12

3. **PARALLEL LINES** Which equation represents a line that is parallel to the line $x + 3y = 12$ and contains no points in Quadrant I?

   (1) $y = -\frac{1}{3}x - 4$

   (2) $y = -\frac{1}{3}x + 8$

   (3) $y = -3x - 4$

   (4) $y = 3x + 4$

4. **POPULATION** The official population of Baton Rouge, Louisiana, was 219,478 in 1990 and 227,818 in 2000. What is the average rate of change in the population from 1990 to 2000?

   (1) -8340 people per year

   (2) -834 people per year

   (3) 834 people per year

   (4) 8340 people per year

5. **FOOTBALL** The costs of general admission and student tickets to a high school football game cost \$7, while student tickets cost \$4. Ticket sales for one game totaled \$11,200. Which equation gives the possible numbers of general admission tickets g and student tickets s that were sold?

   (1) $11{,}200 = 4g - 7s$

   (2) $11{,}200 = 4g + 7s$

   (3) $11{,}200 = 7g - 4s$

   (4) $11{,}200 = 7g + 4s$

6. **OPEN-ENDED** Your digital camera has a 512 megabyte memory card. You take low resolution pictures requiring 4 megabytes of memory each and high resolution pictures requiring 8 megabytes of memory each.

   Write and graph an equation for the possible numbers of low and high resolution pictures you can take.

   Describe the meaning of the slope and intercepts in the context of the problem.

7. **OPEN-ENDED** Refer to the graph below.

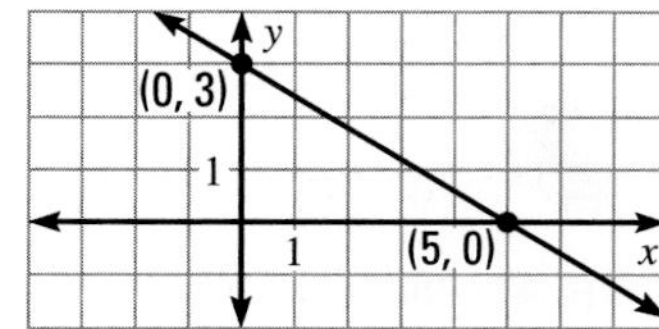

   What is the equation of the graphed line?

   What is the equation of the vertical line through the x-intercept of the graphed line?

   What is the equation of any line that is perpendicular to the graphed line?

2.5 Model Direct Variation

A2.A.5 Use direct and inverse variation to solve for unknown values

Before You wrote and graphed linear equations.

Now You will write and graph direct variation equations.

Why? So you can model animal migration, as in Ex. 44.

Key Vocabulary
- **direct variation**
- **constant of variation**

KEY CONCEPT — *For Your Notebook*

Direct Variation

Equation The equation $y = ax$ represents **direct variation** between x and y, and y is said to *vary directly* with x. The nonzero constant a is called the **constant of variation**.

Graph The graph of a direct variation equation $y = ax$ is a line with slope a and y-intercept 0.

The family of direct variation graphs consists of lines through the origin, such as those shown.

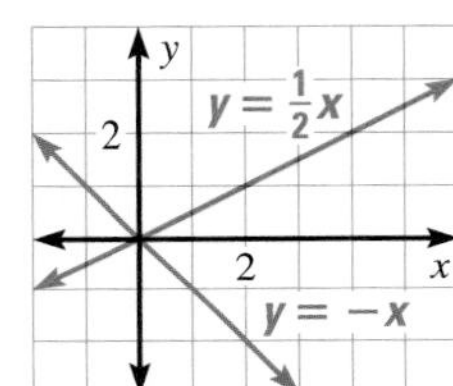

EXAMPLE 1 Write and graph a direct variation equation

Write and graph a direct variation equation that has $(-4, 8)$ as a solution.

Solution

Use the given values of x and y to find the constant of variation.

$y = ax$	**Write direct variation equation.**
$8 = a(-4)$	**Substitute 8 for y and -4 for x.**
$-2 = a$	**Solve for a.**

▶ Substituting -2 for a in $y = ax$ gives the direct variation equation $y = -2x$. Its graph is shown.

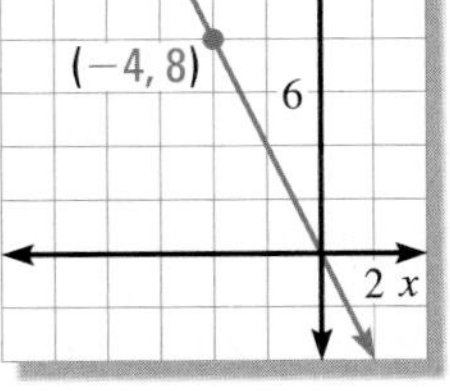

Animated Algebra at classzone.com

✓ GUIDED PRACTICE for Example 1

Write and graph a direct variation equation that has the given ordered pair as a solution.

1. $(3, -9)$ **2.** $(-7, 4)$ **3.** $(5, 3)$ **4.** $(6, -2)$

EXAMPLE 2 Write and apply a model for direct variation

METEOROLOGY Hailstones form when strong updrafts support ice particles high in clouds, where water droplets freeze onto the particles. The diagram shows a hailstone at two different times during its formation.

a. Write an equation that gives the hailstone's diameter d (in inches) after t minutes if you assume the diameter varies directly with the time the hailstone takes to form.

b. Using your equation from part (a), predict the diameter of the hailstone after 20 minutes.

Solution

a. Use the given values of t and d to find the constant of variation.

$d = at$ Write direct variation equation.

$0.75 = a(12)$ Substitute 0.75 for d and 12 for t.

$0.0625 = a$ Solve for a.

An equation that relates t and d is $d = 0.0625t$.

b. After $t = 20$ minutes, the predicted diameter of the hailstone is $d = 0.0625(20) = 1.25$ inches.

RATIOS AND DIRECT VARIATION Because the direct variation equation $y = ax$ can be written as $\frac{y}{x} = a$, a set of data pairs (x, y) shows direct variation if the ratio of y to x is constant.

EXAMPLE 3 Use ratios to identify direct variation

SHARKS Great white sharks have triangular teeth. The table below gives the length of a side of a tooth and the body length for each of six great white sharks. Tell whether tooth length and body length show direct variation. If so, write an equation that relates the quantities.

Tooth length, t (cm)	1.8	2.4	2.9	3.6	4.7	5.8
Body length, b (cm)	215	290	350	430	565	695

Solution

Find the ratio of the body length b to the tooth length t for each shark.

AVOID ERRORS
For real-world data, the ratios do not have to be *exactly* the same to show that direct variation is a plausible model.

$\frac{215}{1.8} \approx 119$ $\frac{290}{2.4} \approx 121$ $\frac{350}{2.9} = 121$

$\frac{430}{3.6} \approx 119$ $\frac{565}{4.7} \approx 120$ $\frac{695}{5.8} \approx 120$

▶ Because the ratios are approximately equal, the data show direct variation. An equation relating tooth length and body length is $\frac{b}{t} = 120$, or $b = 120t$.

✓ **GUIDED PRACTICE** for Examples 2 and 3

5. **WHAT IF?** In Example 2, suppose that a hailstone forming in a cloud has a radius of 0.6 inch. Predict how long it has been forming.

6. **SHARKS** In Example 3, the respective body masses m (in kilograms) of the great white sharks are 80, 220, 375, 730, 1690, and 3195. Tell whether tooth length and body mass show direct variation. If so, write an equation that relates the quantities.

2.5 EXERCISES

HOMEWORK KEY

○ = **WORKED-OUT SOLUTIONS** on p. WS3 for Exs. 5, 15, and 41

★ = **STANDARDIZED TEST PRACTICE** Exs. 2, 17, 30, 40, and 44

SKILL PRACTICE

1. **VOCABULARY** Define the constant of variation for two variables x and y that vary directly.

2. ★ **WRITING** Given a table of ordered pairs (x, y), describe how to determine whether x and y show direct variation.

EXAMPLE 1 on p. 107 for Exs. 3–10

WRITING AND GRAPHING Write and graph a direct variation equation that has the given ordered pair as a solution.

3. $(2, 6)$
4. $(-3, 12)$
5. $(6, -21)$
6. $(4, 10)$
7. $(-5, -1)$
8. $(24, -8)$
9. $\left(\frac{4}{3}, -4\right)$
10. $(12.5, 5)$

EXAMPLE 2 on p. 108 for Exs. 11–17

WRITING AND EVALUATING The variables x and y vary directly. Write an equation that relates x and y. Then find y when $x = 12$.

11. $x = 4, y = 8$
12. $x = -3, y = -5$
13. $x = 35, y = -7$
14. $x = -18, y = 4$
15. $x = -4.8, y = -1.6$
16. $x = \frac{2}{3}, y = -10$

17. ★ **MULTIPLE CHOICE** Which equation is a direct variation equation that has (3, 18) as a solution?

Ⓐ $y = 2x^2$　Ⓑ $y = \frac{1}{6}x$　Ⓒ $y = 6x$　Ⓓ $y = 4x + 6$

IDENTIFYING DIRECT VARIATION Tell whether the equation represents direct variation. If so, give the constant of variation.

18. $y = -8x$
19. $y - 4 = 3x$
20. $3y - 7 = 10x$
21. $2y - 5x = 0$
22. $5y = -4x$
23. $6y = x$

WRITING AND SOLVING The variables x and y vary directly. Write an equation that relates x and y. Then find x when $y = -4$.

24. $x = 5, y = -15$
25. $x = -6, y = 8$
26. $x = -18, y = -2$
27. $x = -12, y = 84$
28. $x = -\frac{20}{3}, y = -\frac{15}{8}$
29. $x = -0.5, y = 3.6$

30. ★ **OPEN-ENDED MATH** Give an example of two real-life quantities that show direct variation. *Explain* your reasoning.

EXAMPLE 3 on p. 108 for Exs. 31–34

IDENTIFYING DIRECT VARIATION **Tell whether the data in the table show direct variation. If so, write an equation relating *x* and *y*.**

31.

x	3	6	9	12	15
y	−1	−2	−3	−4	−5

32.

x	1	2	3	4	5
y	7	9	11	13	15

33.

x	−5	−4	−3	−2	−1
y	20	16	12	8	4

34.

x	−8	−4	4	8	12
y	8	4	−4	−8	−12

35. **ERROR ANALYSIS** A student tried to determine whether the data pairs (1, 24), (2, 12), (3, 8), and (4, 6) show direct variation. *Describe* and correct the error in the student's work.

$1 \cdot 24 = 24$ $2 \cdot 12 = 24$
$3 \cdot 8 = 24$ $4 \cdot 6 = 24$

Because the products xy are constant, y varies directly with x.

36. **REASONING** Let (x_1, y_1) be a solution, other than (0, 0), of a direct variation equation. Write a second direct variation equation whose graph is perpendicular to the graph of the first equation.

37. **CHALLENGE** Let (x_1, y_1) and (x_2, y_2) be any two distinct solutions of a direct variation equation. Show that $\frac{x_2}{x_1} = \frac{y_2}{y_1}$.

PROBLEM SOLVING

EXAMPLE 2 on p. 108 for Exs. 38–40

38. **SCUBA DIVING** The time *t* it takes a diver to ascend safely to the surface varies directly with the depth *d*. It takes a minimum of 0.75 minute for a safe ascent from a depth of 45 feet. Write an equation that relates *d* and *t*. Then predict the minimum time for a safe ascent from a depth of 100 feet.

@HomeTutor for problem solving help at classzone.com

39. **WEATHER** Hail 0.5 inch deep and weighing 1800 pounds covers a roof. The hail's weight *w* varies directly with its depth *d*. Write an equation that relates *d* and *w*. Then predict the weight on the roof of hail that is 1.75 inches deep.

@HomeTutor for problem solving help at classzone.com

40. ★ **MULTIPLE CHOICE** Your weight *M* on Mars varies directly with your weight *E* on Earth. If you weigh 116 pounds on Earth, you would weigh 44 pounds on Mars. Which equation relates *E* and *M*?

(A) $M = E - 72$ (B) $44M = 116E$ (C) $M = \frac{29}{11}E$ (D) $M = \frac{11}{29}E$

EXAMPLE 3 on p. 108 for Exs. 41–43

41. **INTERNET DOWNLOADS** The ordered pairs (4.5, 23), (7.8, 40), and (16.0, 82) are in the form (*s*, *t*) where *t* represents the time (in seconds) needed to download an Internet file of size *s* (in megabytes). Tell whether the data show direct variation. If so, write an equation that relates *s* and *t*.

○ = WORKED-OUT SOLUTIONS on p. WS1 ★ = STANDARDIZED TEST PRACTICE

GEOMETRY In Exercises 42 and 43, consider squares with side lengths of 1, 2, 3, and 4 centimeters.

42. Copy and complete the table.

Side length, s (cm)	1	2	3	4
Perimeter, P (cm)	?	?	?	?
Area, A (cm^2)	?	?	?	?

43. Tell whether the given variables show direct variation. If so, write an equation relating the variables. If not, explain why not.

a. s and P **b.** s and A **c.** P and A

44. ★ **EXTENDED RESPONSE** Each year, gray whales migrate from Mexico's Baja Peninsula to feeding grounds near Alaska. A whale may travel 6000 miles at an average rate of 75 miles per day.

a. Write an equation that gives the distance d_1 traveled in t days of migration.

b. Write an equation that gives the distance d_2 that remains to be traveled after t days of migration.

c. Tell whether the equations from parts (a) and (b) represent direct variation. *Explain* your answers.

Animated Algebra at classzone.com

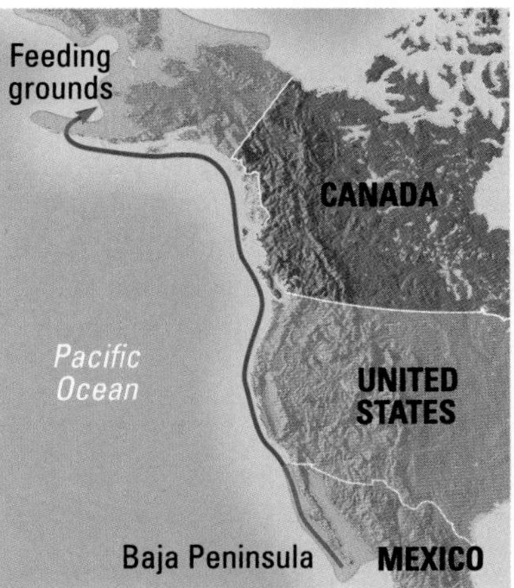

45. **CHALLENGE** At a jewelry store, the price p of a gold necklace varies directly with its length ℓ. Also, the weight w of a necklace varies directly with its length. Show that the price of a necklace varies directly with its weight.

NEW YORK MIXED REVIEW

TEST PRACTICE at classzone.com

46. An Internet service provider has a 15% off sale on a 6 month subscription. Which statement best represents the functional relationship between the sale price of the subscription and the original price?

Ⓐ The original price is dependent on the sale price.

Ⓑ The sale price is dependent on the original price.

Ⓒ The sale price and the original price are independent of each other.

Ⓓ The relationship cannot be determined.

47. Rose works as a salesperson at a car stereo store. She earns an 8% commission on every sale. She wants to earn $300 from commissions in the next 5 days. What is the average amount of car stereo sales Rose must make per day to reach her goal?

Ⓐ $480 Ⓑ $750 Ⓒ $1000 Ⓓ $3750

2.6 Fitting a Line to Data

MATERIALS • overhead projector • overhead transparency • metric ruler • meter stick • graph paper

QUESTION How can you approximate the *best-fitting line* for a set of data?

EXPLORE Collect and record data

STEP 1 Set up

Position an overhead projector a convenient distance from a projection screen. Draw a line segment 15 centimeters long on a transparency, and place the transparency on the projector.

STEP 2 Collect data

Measure the distance, in centimeters, from the projector to the screen and the length of the line segment as it appears on the screen. Reposition the projector several times, each time taking these measurements.

STEP 3 Record data

Record your measurements from Step 2 in a table like the one shown below.

Distance from projector to screen (cm), x	Length of line segment on screen (cm), y
200	?
210	?
220	?
230	?
240	?
250	?
260	?
270	?
280	?
290	?

DRAW CONCLUSIONS Use your observations to complete these exercises

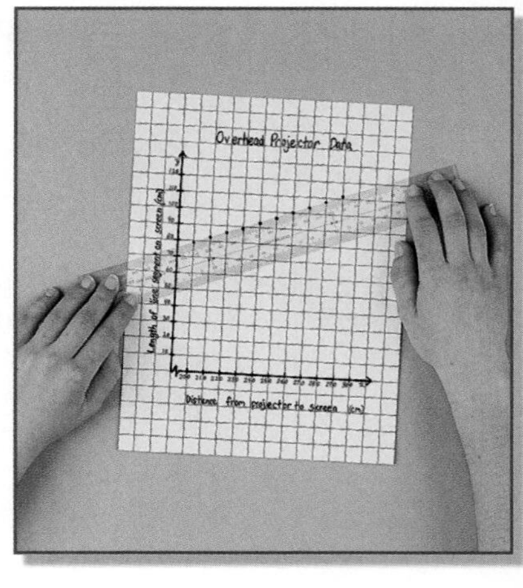

1. Graph the data pairs (x, y). What pattern do you observe?
2. Use a ruler to draw a line that lies as close as possible to all of the points on the graph, as shown at the right. The line does not have to pass through any of the points. There should be about as many points above the line as below it.
3. Estimate the coordinates of two points on your line. Use your points to write an equation of the line.
4. Using your equation from Exercise 3, predict the length of the line segment on the screen for a particular projector-to-screen distance less than those in your table and for a particular projector-to-screen distance greater than those in your table.
5. Test your predictions from Exercise 4. How accurate were they?

2.6 Draw Scatter Plots and Best-Fitting Lines

A2.S.7 Determine the function for the regression model, using appropriate technology, and use the regression function to interpolate. . .

Before You wrote equations of lines.

Now You will fit lines to data in scatter plots.

Why? So you can model sports trends, as in Ex. 27.

Key Vocabulary
- scatter plot
- positive correlation
- negative correlation
- correlation coefficient
- best-fitting line

A **scatter plot** is a graph of a set of data pairs (x, y). If y tends to increase as x increases, then the data have a **positive correlation**. If y tends to decrease as x increases, then the data have a **negative correlation**. If the points show no obvious pattern, then the data have *approximately no correlation.*

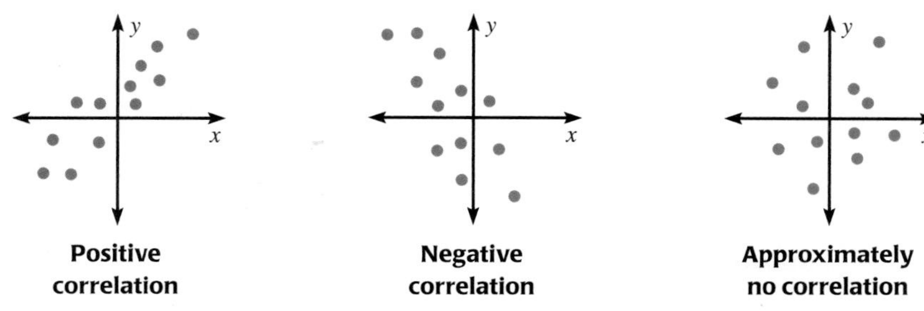

EXAMPLE 1 Describe correlation

TELEPHONES Describe the correlation shown by each scatter plot.

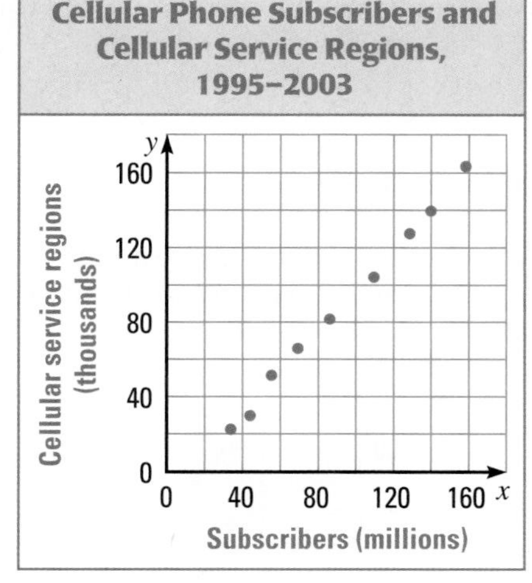

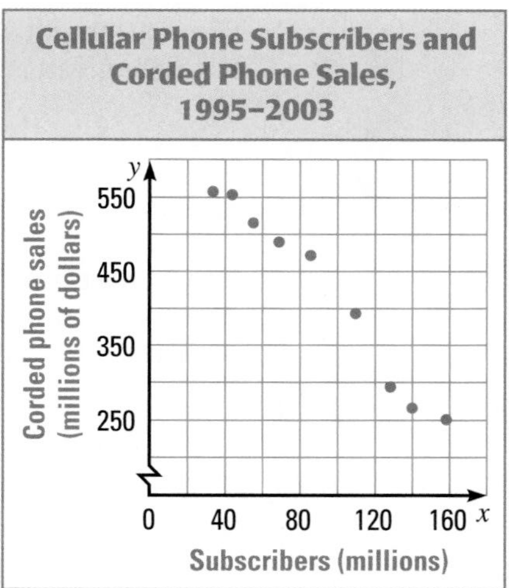

Solution

The first scatter plot shows a positive correlation, because as the number of cellular phone subscribers increased, the number of cellular service regions tended to increase.

The second scatter plot shows a negative correlation, because as the number of cellular phone subscribers increased, corded phone sales tended to decrease.

CORRELATION COEFFICIENTS A **correlation coefficient**, denoted by r, is a number from -1 to 1 that measures how well a line fits a set of data pairs (x, y). If r is near 1, the points lie close to a line with positive slope. If r is near -1, the points lie close to a line with negative slope. If r is near 0, the points do not lie close to any line.

$r = -1$	$r = 0$	$r = 1$
Points lie near line with a negative slope.	**Points do not lie near any line.**	**Points lie near line with positive slope.**

EXAMPLE 2 Estimate correlation coefficients

Tell whether the correlation coefficient for the data is closest to -1, -0.5, 0, 0.5, or 1.

a. 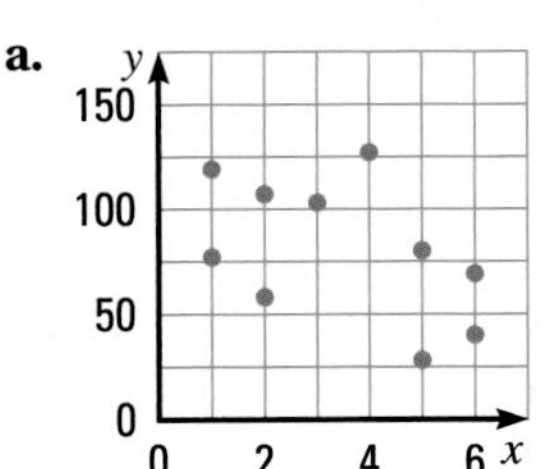

b. 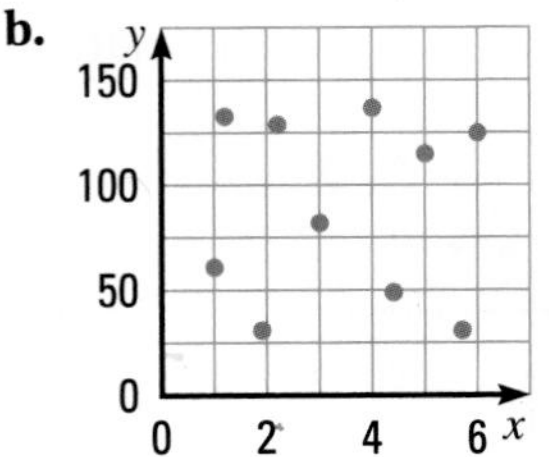

c. 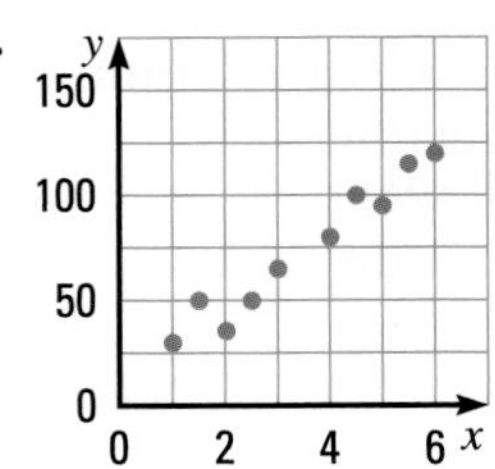

Solution

a. The scatter plot shows a clear but fairly weak negative correlation. So, r is between 0 and -1, but not too close to either one. The best estimate given is $r = -0.5$. (The actual value is $r \approx -0.46$.)

b. The scatter plot shows approximately no correlation. So, the best estimate given is $r = 0$. (The actual value is $r \approx -0.02$.)

c. The scatter plot shows a strong positive correlation. So, the best estimate given is $r = 1$. (The actual value is $r \approx 0.98$.)

✓ GUIDED PRACTICE for Examples 1 and 2

For each scatter plot, (a) tell whether the data have a *positive correlation*, a *negative correlation*, or *approximately no correlation*, and (b) tell whether the correlation coefficient is closest to -1, -0.5, 0, 0.5, or 1.

1. 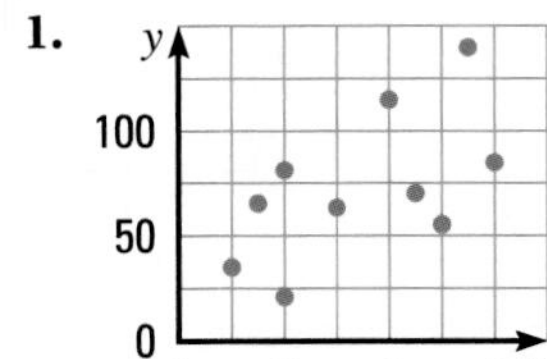

2. 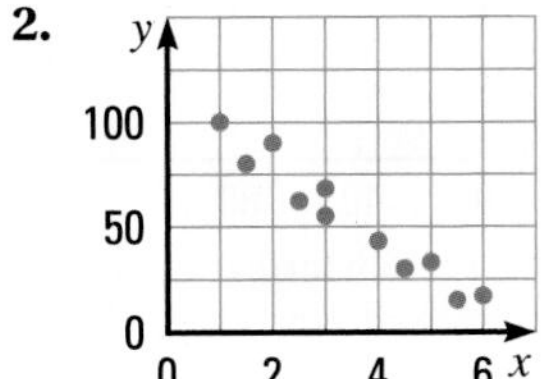

3. 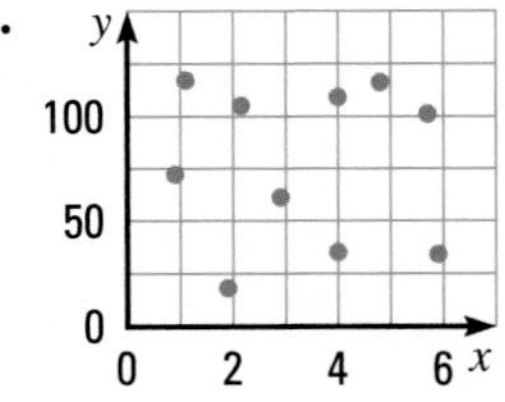

BEST-FITTING LINES If the correlation coefficient for a set of data is near ±1, the data can be reasonably modeled by a line. The **best-fitting line** is the line that lies as close as possible to all the data points. You can approximate a best-fitting line by graphing.

KEY CONCEPT — For Your Notebook

Approximating a Best-Fitting Line

STEP 1 **Draw** a scatter plot of the data.

STEP 2 **Sketch** the line that appears to follow most closely the trend given by the data points. There should be about as many points above the line as below it.

STEP 3 **Choose** two points on the line, and estimate the coordinates of each point. These points do not have to be original data points.

STEP 4 **Write** an equation of the line that passes through the two points from Step 3. This equation is a model for the data.

EXAMPLE 3 Approximate a best-fitting line

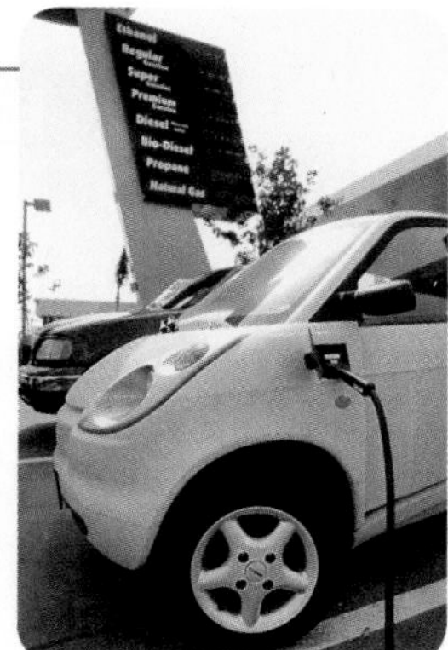

ALTERNATIVE-FUELED VEHICLES The table shows the number y (in thousands) of alternative-fueled vehicles in use in the United States x years after 1997. Approximate the best-fitting line for the data.

x	0	1	2	3	4	5	6	7
y	280	295	322	395	425	471	511	548

Solution

STEP 1 **Draw** a scatter plot of the data.

STEP 2 **Sketch** the line that appears to best fit the data. One possibility is shown.

STEP 3 **Choose** two points that appear to lie on the line. For the line shown, you might choose (1, 300), which is not an original data point, and (7, 548), which is an original data point.

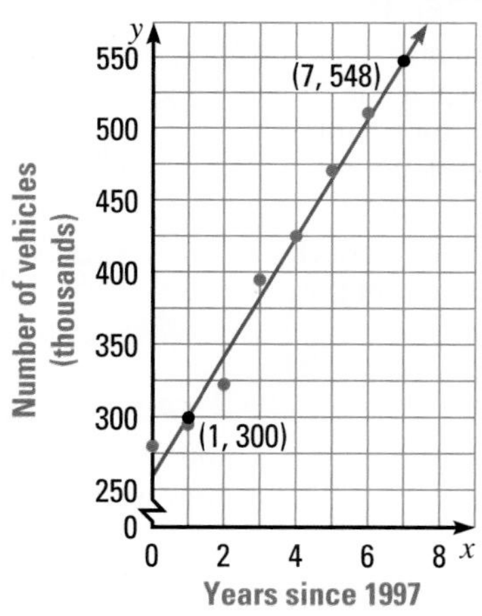

STEP 4 **Write** an equation of the line. First find the slope using the points (1, 300) and (7, 548).

$$m = \frac{548 - 300}{7 - 1} = \frac{248}{6} \approx 41.3$$

Use point-slope form to write the equation. Choose $(x_1, y_1) = (1, 300)$.

$y - y_1 = m(x - x_1)$ **Point-slope form**

$y - \mathbf{300} = \mathbf{41.3}(x - \mathbf{1})$ **Substitute for m, x_1, and y_1.**

$y \approx 41.3x + 259$ **Simplify.**

▶ An approximation of the best-fitting line is $y = 41.3x + 259$.

Animated **Algebra** at classzone.com

EXAMPLE 4 Use a line of fit to make a prediction

Use the equation of the line of fit from Example 3 to predict the number of alternative-fueled vehicles in use in the United States in 2010.

Solution

Because 2010 is 13 years after 1997, substitute 13 for x in the equation from Example 3.

$$y = 41.3x + 259 = 41.3(13) + 259 \approx 796$$

▶ You can predict that there will be about 796,000 alternative-fueled vehicles in use in the United States in 2010.

LINEAR REGRESSION Many graphing calculators have a *linear regression* feature that can be used to find the best-fitting line for a set of data.

EXAMPLE 5 Use a graphing calculator to find a best-fitting line

Use the *linear regression* feature on a graphing calculator to find an equation of the best-fitting line for the data in Example 3.

Solution

STEP 1 **Enter** the data into two *lists*. Press STAT and then select Edit. Enter years since 1997 in L_1 and number of alternative-fueled vehicles in L_2.

L1	L2	L3
0	280	
1	295	
2	322	
3	395	
4	425	

L1(2)=1

FIND CORRELATION
If your calculator does not display the correlation coefficient r when it displays the regression equation, you may need to select DiagnosticOn from the CATALOG menu.

STEP 2 **Find** an equation of the best-fitting (linear regression) line. Press STAT, choose the CALC menu, and select LinReg(ax+b). The equation can be rounded to $y = 40.9x + 263$.

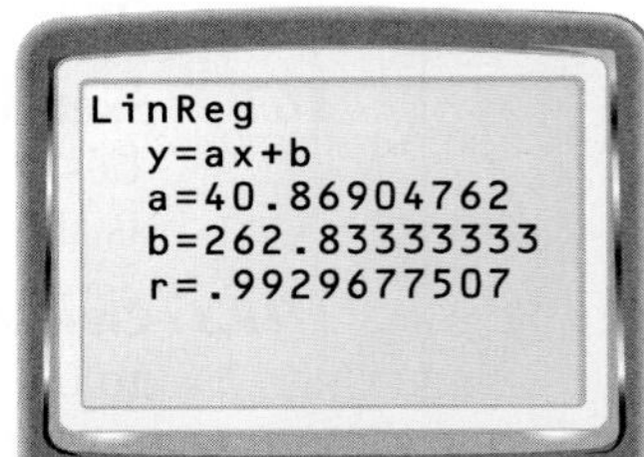

STEP 3 **Make** a scatter plot of the data pairs to see how well the regression equation models the data. Press 2nd [STAT PLOT] to set up your plot. Then select an appropriate window for the graph.

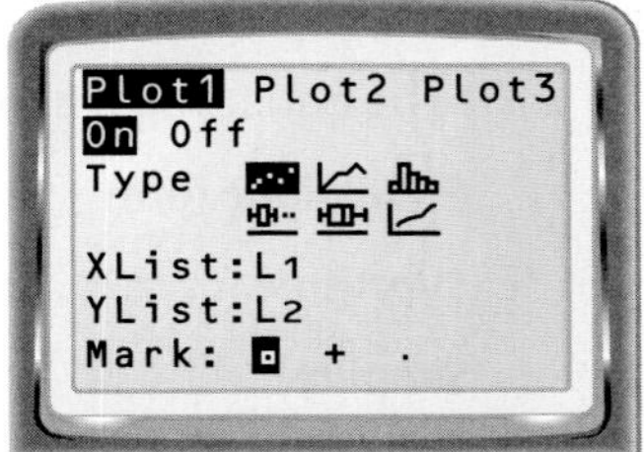

STEP 4 **Graph** the regression equation with the scatter plot by entering the equation $y = 40.9x + 263$. The graph (displayed in the window $0 \le x \le 8$ and $200 \le y \le 600$) shows that the line fits the data well.

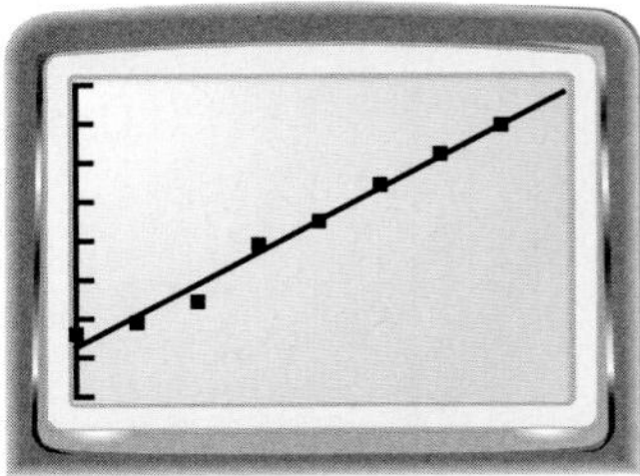

▶ An equation of the best-fitting line is $y = 40.9x + 263$.

✓ GUIDED PRACTICE for Examples 3, 4, and 5

4. **OIL PRODUCTION** The table shows the U.S. daily oil production y (in thousands of barrels) x years after 1994.

x	0	1	2	3	4	5	6	7	8
y	6660	6560	6470	6450	6250	5880	5820	5800	5750

a. Approximate the best-fitting line for the data.

b. Use your equation from part (a) to predict the daily oil production in 2009.

c. Use a graphing calculator to find and graph an equation of the best-fitting line. Repeat the prediction from part (b) using this equation.

2.6 EXERCISES

HOMEWORK KEY

◯ = **WORKED-OUT SOLUTIONS** on p. WS3 for Exs. 9, 11, and 25

★ = **STANDARDIZED TEST PRACTICE** Exs. 2, 16, 18, 21, and 28

◆ = **MULTIPLE REPRESENTATIONS** Ex. 27

SKILL PRACTICE

1. **VOCABULARY** Copy and complete: A line that lies as close as possible to a set of data points (x, y) is called the _?_ for the data points.

2. ★ **WRITING** *Describe* how to tell whether a set of data points shows a positive correlation, a negative correlation, or approximately no correlation.

EXAMPLE 1 on p. 113 for Exs. 3–5

DESCRIBING CORRELATIONS Tell whether the data have a *positive correlation*, a *negative correlation*, or *approximately no correlation*.

3. 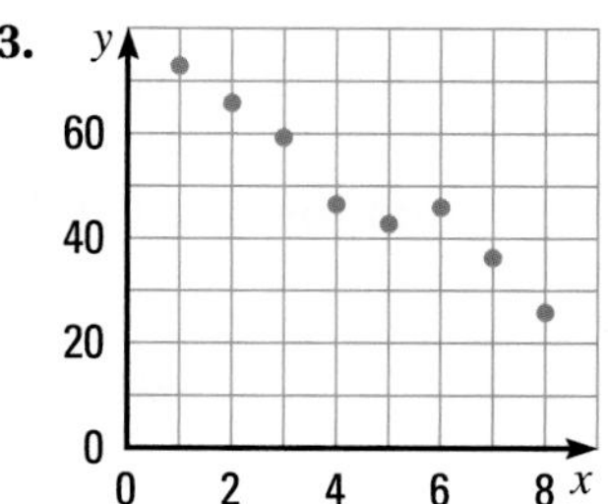

4. 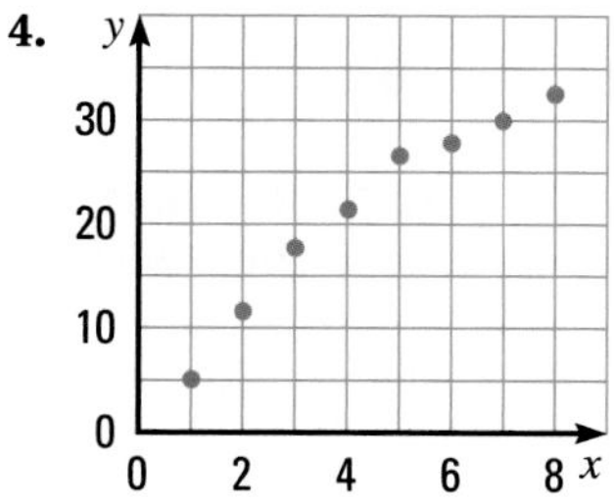

5. 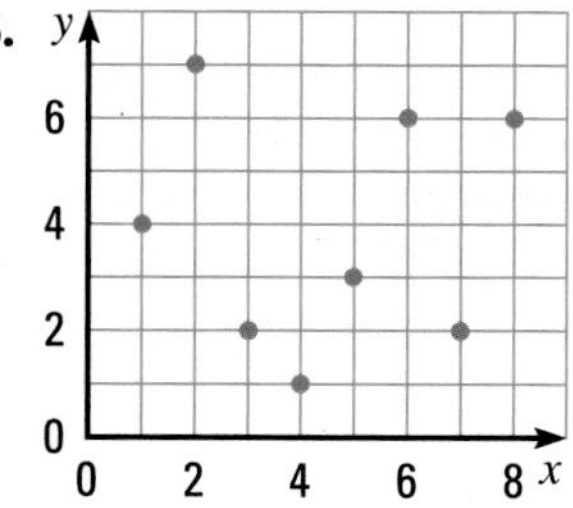

6. **REASONING** *Explain* how you can determine the type of correlation for a set of data pairs by examining the data in a table without drawing a scatter plot.

EXAMPLE 2 on p. 114 for Exs. 7–9

CORRELATION COEFFICIENTS Tell whether the correlation coefficient for the data is closest to −1, −0.5, 0, 0.5, or 1.

7. 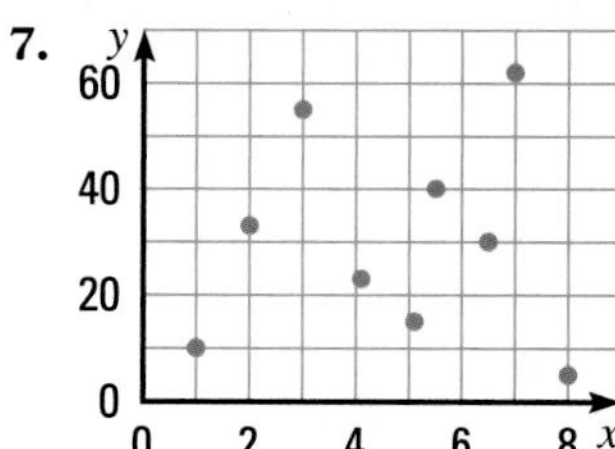

8. 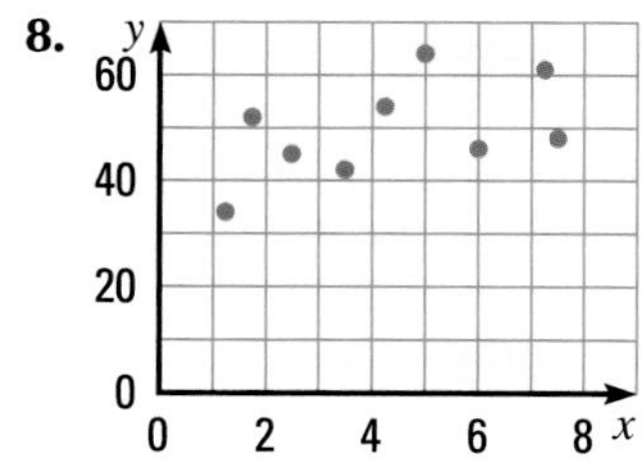

9. 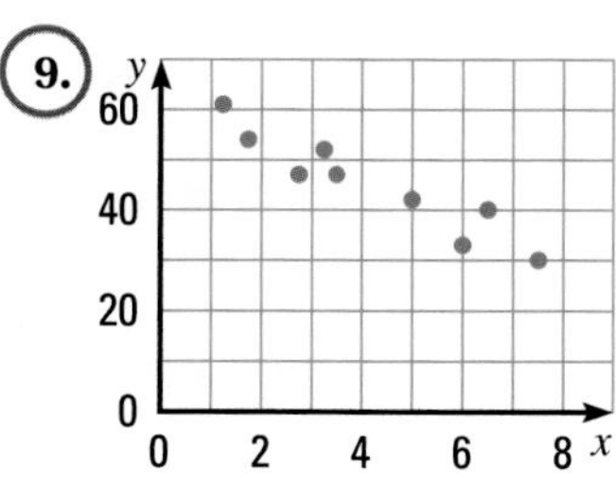

EXAMPLES 3 and 4
on pp. 115–116
for Exs. 10–15

BEST-FITTING LINES **In Exercises 10–15, (a) draw a scatter plot of the data, (b) approximate the best-fitting line, and (c) estimate y when $x = 20$.**

10.

x	1	2	3	4	5
y	10	22	35	49	62

11.

x	1	2	3	4	5
y	120	101	87	57	42

12.

x	12	25	36	50	64
y	100	75	52	26	9

13.

x	3	7	10	15	18
y	16	45	82	102	116

14.

x	5.6	6.2	7	7.3	8.4
y	120	130	141	156	167

15.

x	16	24	39	55	68
y	3.9	3.7	3.4	2.9	2.6

16. ★ **MULTIPLE CHOICE** Which equation best models the data in the scatter plot?

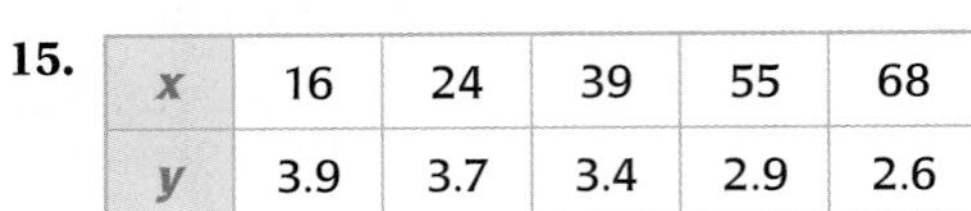

Ⓐ $y = 15$ Ⓑ $y = -\frac{1}{2}x + 26$

Ⓒ $y = -\frac{2}{5}x + 19$ Ⓓ $y = -\frac{4}{5}x + 33$

17. **ERROR ANALYSIS** The graph shows one student's approximation of the best-fitting line for the data in the scatter plot. *Describe* and correct the error in the student's work.

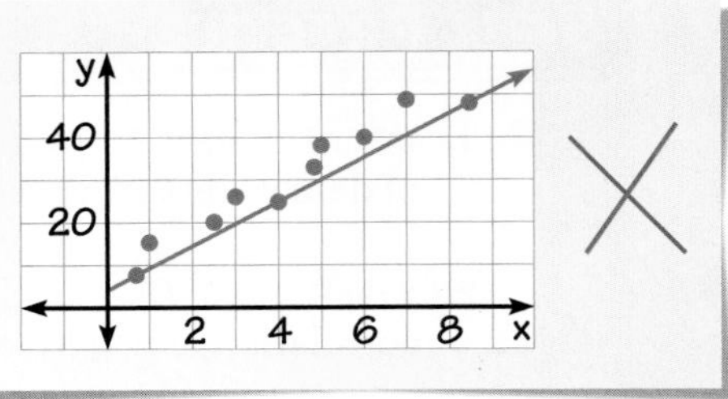

18. ★ **MULTIPLE CHOICE** A set of data has correlation coefficient r. For which value of r would the data points lie closest to a line?

Ⓐ $r = -0.96$ Ⓑ $r = 0$ Ⓒ $r = 0.38$ Ⓓ $r = 0.5$

EXAMPLE 5
on p. 116
for Exs. 19–20

GRAPHING CALCULATOR **In Exercises 19 and 20, use a graphing calculator to find and graph an equation of the best-fitting line.**

19.

x	78	74	68	76	80	84	50	76	55	93
y	5.1	5.0	4.6	4.9	5.3	5.5	3.7	5.0	3.9	5.8

20.

x	7000	7400	7800	8100	8500	8800	9200	9500	9800
y	56.0	54.5	51.9	50.0	47.3	45.6	43.1	41.6	39.9

21. ★ **OPEN-ENDED MATH** Give two real-life quantities that have **(a)** a positive correlation, **(b)** a negative correlation, and **(c)** approximately no correlation.

22. **REASONING** A set of data pairs has correlation coefficient $r = 0.1$. Is it logical to use the best-fitting line to make predictions from the data? *Explain.*

23. **CHALLENGE** If x and y have a positive correlation and y and z have a negative correlation, what can you say about the correlation between x and z? *Explain.*

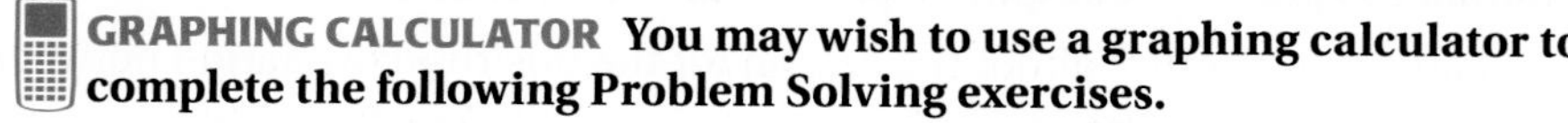

PROBLEM SOLVING

EXAMPLES 3, 4, and 5 on pp. 115–116 for Exs. 24–28

GRAPHING CALCULATOR **You may wish to use a graphing calculator to complete the following Problem Solving exercises.**

24. **POPULATION** The data pairs (x, y) give the population y (in millions) of Texas x years after 1997. Approximate the best-fitting line for the data.

    (0, 19.7), (1, 20.2), (2, 20.6), (3, 20.9), (4, 21.3), (5, 21.7), (6, 22.1), (7, 22.5)

    @HomeTutor for problem solving help at classzone.com

25. **TUITION** The data pairs (x, y) give U.S. average annual public college tuition y (in dollars) x years after 1997. Approximate the best-fitting line for the data.

    (0, 2271), (1, 2360), (2, 2430), (3, 2506), (4, 2562), (5, 2727), (6, 2928)

    @HomeTutor for problem solving help at classzone.com

26. **PHYSICAL SCIENCE** The diagram shows the boiling point of water at various elevations. Approximate the best-fitting line for the data pairs (x, y) where x represents the elevation (in feet) and y represents the boiling point (in degrees Fahrenheit). Then use this line to estimate the boiling point at an elevation of 14,000 feet.

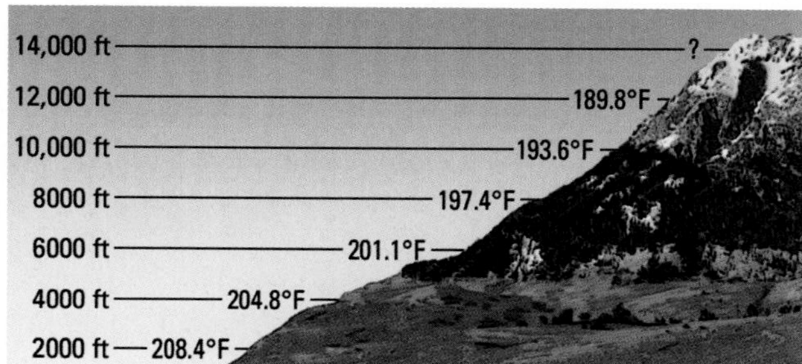

27. **MULTIPLE REPRESENTATIONS** The table shows the numbers of countries that participated in the Winter Olympics from 1980 to 2002.

Year	1980	1984	1988	1992	1994	1998	2002
Countries	37	49	57	64	67	72	77

    a. **Making a List** Use the table to make a list of data pairs (x, y) where x represents years since 1980 and y represents the number of countries.
    b. **Drawing a Graph** Draw a scatter plot of the data pairs from part (a).
    c. **Writing an Equation** Write an equation that approximates the best-fitting line, and use it to predict the number of participating countries in 2014.

28. ★ **EXTENDED RESPONSE** The table shows manufacturers' shipments (in millions) of cassettes and CDs in the United States from 1988 to 2002.

Year	1988	1990	1992	1994	1996	1998	2000	2002
Cassettes	450.1	442.2	336.4	345.4	225.3	158.5	76.0	31.1
CDs	149.7	286.5	407.5	662.1	778.9	847.0	942.5	803.3

    a. Draw a scatter plot of the data pairs (year, shipments of cassettes). *Describe* the correlation shown by the scatter plot.
    b. Draw a scatter plot of the data pairs (year, shipments of CDs). *Describe* the correlation shown by the scatter plot.
    c. *Describe* the correlation between cassette shipments and CD shipments. What real-world factors might account for this?

29. **CHALLENGE** Data from some countries in North America show a positive correlation between the average life expectancy in a country and the number of personal computers per capita in that country.

a. Make a conjecture about the reason for the positive correlation between life expectancy and number of personal computers per capita.

b. Is it reasonable to conclude from the data that giving residents of a country more personal computers will lengthen their lives? *Explain.*

NEW YORK MIXED REVIEW

TEST PRACTICE at classzone.com

30. Ted is planting flowers in a rectangular garden. The length of the garden is 55 feet and the perimeter is 150 feet. What is the area of the garden?

Ⓐ 900 ft^2 Ⓑ 1100 ft^2 Ⓒ 1800 ft^2 Ⓓ 2025 ft^2

31. What is the y-intercept of the line shown?

Ⓐ $-\frac{2}{3}$ Ⓑ $\frac{2}{3}$

Ⓒ 2 Ⓓ 3

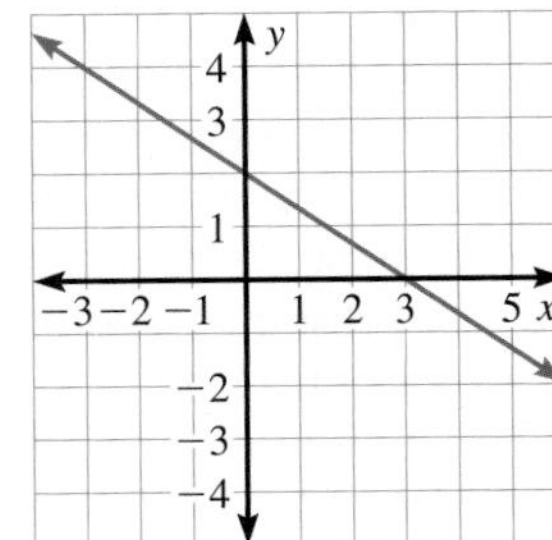

QUIZ *for Lessons 2.4–2.6*

Write an equation of the line that satisfies the given conditions. *(p. 98)*

1. $m = -5, b = 3$
2. $m = 2, b = 12$
3. $m = 4$, passes through $(-3, 6)$
4. $m = -7$, passes through $(1, -4)$
5. passes through $(0, 7)$ and $(-3, -2)$
6. passes through $(-9, 9)$ and $(-9, 0)$

Write and graph a direct variation equation that has the given ordered pair as a solution. *(p. 107)*

7. $(1, 2)$
8. $(-2, 8)$
9. $(5, -16)$
10. $(12, 4)$

The variables x and y vary directly. Write an equation that relates x and y. Then find y when $x = 8$. *(p. 107)*

11. $x = 4, y = 12$
12. $x = -3, y = -8$
13. $x = 40, y = -5$
14. $x = 12, y = 2$

15. **CONCERT TICKETS** The table shows the average price of a concert ticket to one of the top 50 musical touring acts for the years 1999–2004. Write an equation that approximates the best-fitting line for the data pairs (x, y). Use the equation to predict the average price of a ticket in 2010. *(p. 113)*

Years since 1999, x	0	1	2	3	4	5
Ticket price (dollars), y	38.56	44.80	46.69	50.81	51.81	58.71

@HomeTutor
classzone.com
Keystrokes

2.7 Exploring Transformations

MATERIALS • graphing calculator

QUESTION **How are the equation and the graph of an absolute value function related?**

You can investigate families of *absolute value functions* with equations of the form $y = a|x - h| + k$ by varying the values of a, h, and k and then graphing. The resulting graphs are *transformations* of the graph of the parent function $y = |x|$.

EXAMPLE 1 Graph $y = |x| + k$

Graph and describe the family of absolute value functions of the form $y = |x| + k$.

STEP 1 ***Vary the value of k***

Enter $y = |x|$, $y = |x| + 2$, $y = |x| + 5$, and $y = |x| - 3$.

Y1=abs(X)
Y2=abs(X)+2
Y3=abs(X)+5
Y4=abs(X)−3
Y5=
Y6=
Y7=

STEP 2 ***Display graphs***

Graph the equations in the standard viewing window by pressing ZOOM 6.

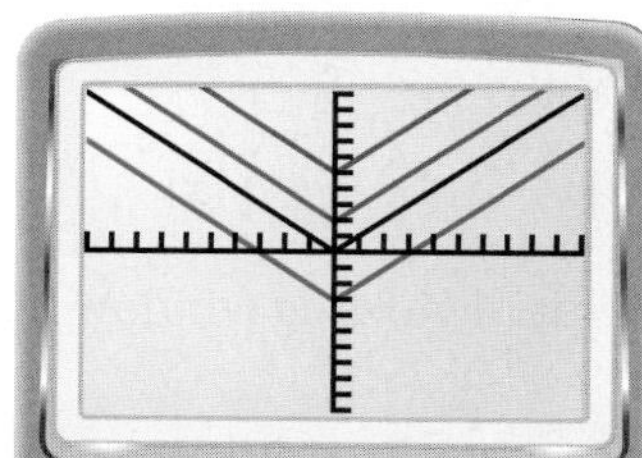

STEP 3 ***Compare graphs***

Describe how the family of graphs of $y = |x| + k$ is related to the graph of $y = |x|$.

The graphs of absolute value functions of the form $y = |x| + k$ have the same shape as the graph of $y = |x|$, but are shifted k units vertically.

EXAMPLE 2 Graph $y = |x - h|$

Graph and describe the family of absolute value functions of the form $y = |x - h|$.

STEP 1 ***Vary the value of h***

Enter $y = |x|$, $y = |x - 2|$, $y = |x - 4|$, and $y = |x + 5|$.

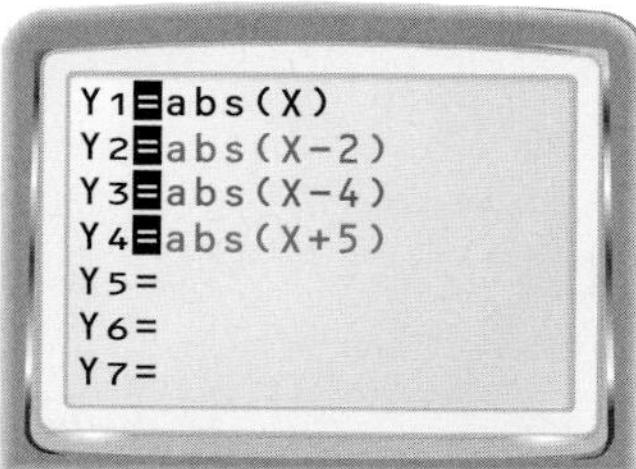

STEP 2 ***Display graphs***

Graph the equations in the standard viewing window by pressing ZOOM 6.

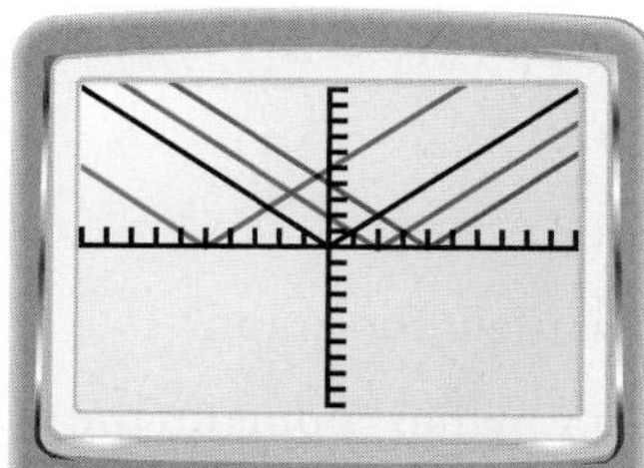

STEP 3 ***Compare graphs***

Describe how the family of graphs of $y = |x - h|$ is related to the graph of $y = |x|$.

The graphs of absolute value functions of the form $y = |x - h|$ have the same shape as the graph of $y = |x|$, but are shifted h units horizontally.

EXAMPLE 3 Graph $y = a|x|$ where a is a positive number

Graph and describe the family of absolute value functions of the form $y = a|x|$ where $a > 0$.

STEP 1 *Vary the value of a*

Enter $y = |x|$, $y = 2|x|$, $y = 5|x|$, and $y = \frac{1}{2}|x|$.

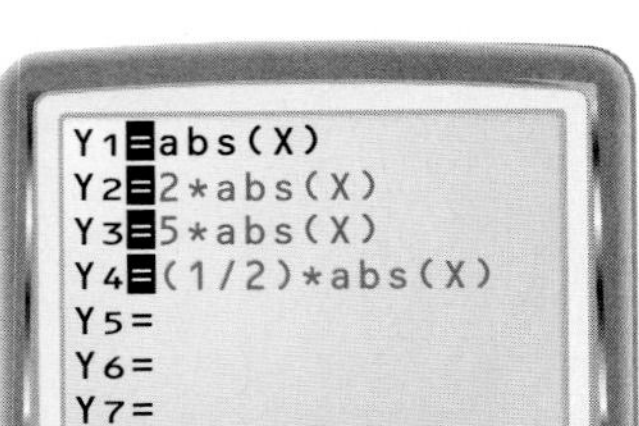

STEP 2 *Display graphs*

Graph the equations in the standard viewing window by pressing ZOOM 6.

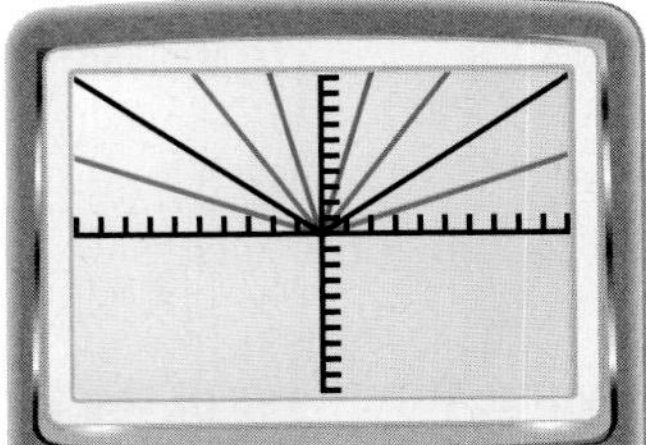

STEP 3 *Compare graphs*

Describe how the family of graphs of $y = a|x|$ where $a > 0$ is related to the graph of $y = |x|$.

As with $y = |x|$, the graph of $y = a|x|$ ($a > 0$) has its lowest point at the origin. If $a > 1$, the graph is narrower than that of $y = |x|$. If $0 < a < 1$, the graph is wider than that of $y = |x|$.

PRACTICE

1. Graph and describe the family of absolute value functions of the form $y = a|x|$ where $a < 0$. Follow these steps:

   STEP 1 Enter $y = |x|$, $y = -|x|$, $y = -3|x|$, and $y = -\frac{1}{2}|x|$.

   STEP 2 Graph the equations in the standard viewing window by pressing ZOOM 6.

   STEP 3 Describe how the family of graphs of $y = a|x|$ where $a < 0$ is related to the graph of $y = |x|$.

Describe **how the graph of the given equation is related to the graph of $y = |x|$. Then graph the given equation along with $y = |x|$ to confirm your answer.**

2. $y = |x| + 6$
3. $y = |x| - 4$
4. $y = |x - 3|$
5. $y = |x + 2|$
6. $y = \frac{2}{3}|x|$
7. $y = -6|x|$
8. $y = |x - 1| + 2$
9. $y = 3|x + 2|$
10. $y = -0.5|x + 1| + 7$

DRAW CONCLUSIONS

Answer the following questions about the graph of $y = a|x - h| + k$.

11. How does the value of k affect the graph?
12. How does the value of h affect the graph?
13. How do the sign and absolute value of a affect the graph?
14. What are the coordinates of the lowest or highest point on the graph? How can you tell whether this point is the lowest point or the highest point?

2.7 Use Absolute Value Functions and Transformations

A2.A.46 Perform transformations with functions and relations: $f(x + a), f(x) + a, f(-x), -f(x), af(x)$

Before You graphed and wrote linear functions.

Now You will graph and write absolute value functions.

Why? So you can model structures, as in Ex. 39.

Key Vocabulary
- **absolute value function**
- **vertex of an absolute value graph**
- **transformation**
- **translation**
- **reflection**

In Lesson 1.7, you learned that the absolute value of a real number x is defined as follows.

$$|x| = \begin{cases} x, & \text{if } x \text{ is positive} \\ 0, & \text{if } x = 0 \\ -x, & \text{if } x \text{ is negative} \end{cases}$$

You can also define an **absolute value function** $f(x) = |x|$.

KEY CONCEPT *For Your Notebook*

Parent Function for Absolute Value Functions

The parent function for the family of all absolute value functions is $f(x) = |x|$. The graph of $f(x) = |x|$ is V-shaped and is symmetric about the y-axis. So, for every point (x, y) on the graph, the point $(-x, y)$ is also on the graph.

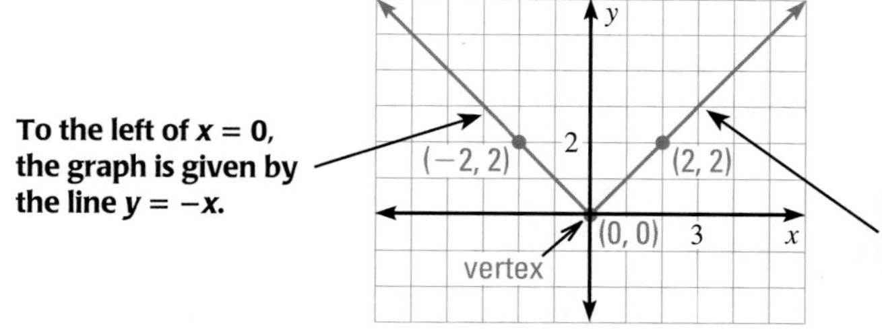

The highest or lowest point on the graph of an absolute value function is called the **vertex**. The vertex of the graph of $f(x) = |x|$ is $(0, 0)$.

REVIEW GEOMETRY
For help with transformations, see p. 988.

TRANSLATIONS You can derive new absolute value functions from the parent function through *transformations* of the parent graph.

A **transformation** changes a graph's size, shape, position, or orientation. A **translation** is a transformation that shifts a graph horizontally and/or vertically, but does not change its size, shape, or orientation.

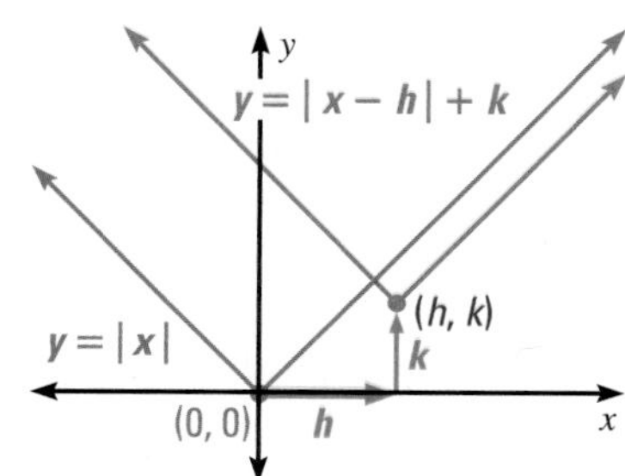

The graph of $y = |x - h| + k$ is the graph of $y = |x|$ translated h units horizontally and k units vertically, as shown in the diagram. The vertex of $y = |x - h| + k$ is (h, k).

EXAMPLE 1 Graph a function of the form $y = |x - h| + k$

Graph $y = |x + 4| - 2$. Compare the graph with the graph of $y = |x|$.

INTERPRET FUNCTIONS
To identify the vertex, rewrite the given function as $y = |x - (-4)| + (-2)$. So, $h = -4$ and $k = -2$. The vertex is $(-4, -2)$.

Solution

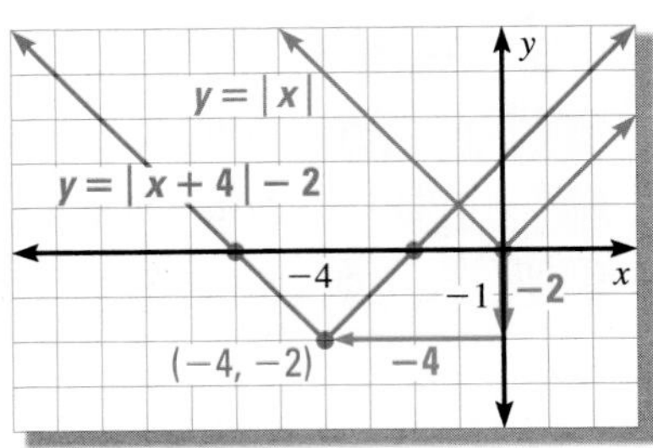

STEP 1 **Identify** and plot the vertex, $(h, k) = (-4, -2)$.

STEP 2 **Plot** another point on the graph, such as $(-2, 0)$. Use symmetry to plot a third point, $(-6, 0)$.

STEP 3 **Connect** the points with a V-shaped graph.

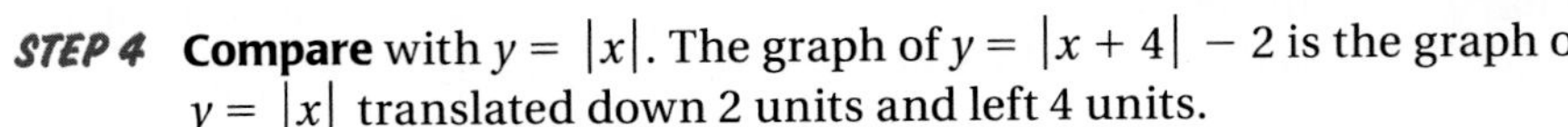

STEP 4 **Compare** with $y = |x|$. The graph of $y = |x + 4| - 2$ is the graph of $y = |x|$ translated down 2 units and left 4 units.

STRETCHES, SHRINKS, AND REFLECTIONS When $|a| \neq 1$, the graph of $y = a|x|$ is a vertical *stretch* or a vertical *shrink* of the graph of $y = |x|$, depending on whether $|a|$ is less than or greater than 1.

For $\|a\| > 1$	For $\|a\| < 1$
• The graph is vertically *stretched*, or elongated. • The graph of $y = a\|x\|$ is *narrower* than the graph of $y = \|x\|$.	• The graph is vertically *shrunk*, or compressed. • The graph of $y = a\|x\|$ is *wider* than the graph of $y = \|x\|$.

When $a = -1$, the graph of $y = a|x|$ is a **reflection** in the x-axis of the graph of $y = |x|$. When $a < 0$ but $a \neq -1$, the graph of $y = a|x|$ is a vertical stretch or shrink with a reflection in the x-axis of the graph of $y = |x|$.

EXAMPLE 2 Graph functions of the form $y = a|x|$

Graph (a) $y = \frac{1}{2}|x|$ and (b) $y = -3|x|$. Compare each graph with the graph of $y = |x|$.

Solution

a. The graph of $y = \frac{1}{2}|x|$ is the graph of $y = |x|$ vertically shrunk by a factor of $\frac{1}{2}$. The graph has vertex $(0, 0)$ and passes through $(-4, 2)$ and $(4, 2)$.

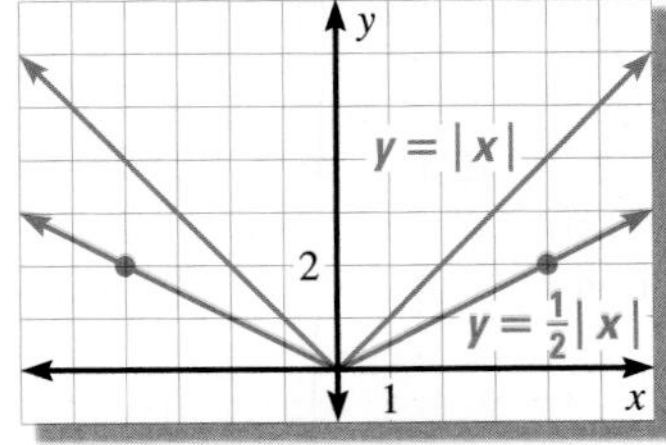

b. The graph of $y = -3|x|$ is the graph of $y = |x|$ vertically stretched by a factor of 3 and then reflected in the x-axis. The graph has vertex $(0, 0)$ and passes through $(-1, -3)$ and $(1, -3)$.

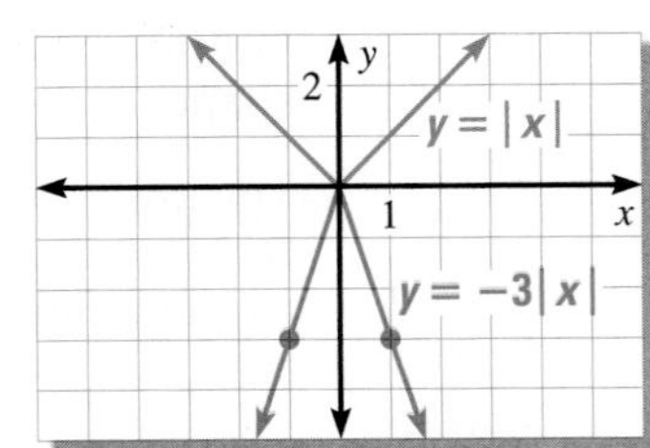

MULTIPLE TRANSFORMATIONS In part (b) of Example 2, graphing $y = -3|x|$ involves both vertically stretching and reflecting the graph of $y = |x|$. A graph may be related to a parent graph by even more than two transformations. For example, the graph of $y = a|x - h| + k$ can involve a vertical stretch or shrink, a reflection, and a translation of the graph of $y = |x|$.

EXAMPLE 3 Graph a function of the form $y = a|x - h| + k$

Graph $y = -2|x - 1| + 3$. Compare the graph with the graph of $y = |x|$.

Solution

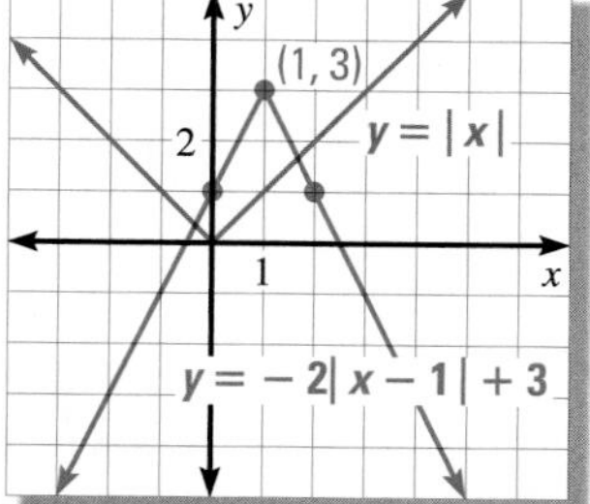

STEP 1 **Identify** and plot the vertex, $(h, k) = (1, 3)$.

STEP 2 **Plot** another point on the graph, such as $(0, 1)$. Use symmetry to plot a third point, $(2, 1)$.

STEP 3 **Connect** the points with a V-shaped graph.

STEP 4 **Compare** with $y = |x|$. The graph of $y = -2|x - 1| + 3$ is the graph of $y = |x|$ stretched vertically by a factor of 2, then reflected in the x-axis, and finally translated right 1 unit and up 3 units.

✓ **GUIDED PRACTICE** for Examples 1, 2, and 3

Graph the function. *Compare* the graph with the graph of $y = |x|$.

1. $y = |x - 2| + 5$ **2.** $y = \frac{1}{4}|x|$ **3.** $f(x) = -3|x + 1| - 2$

EXAMPLE 4 Write an absolute value function

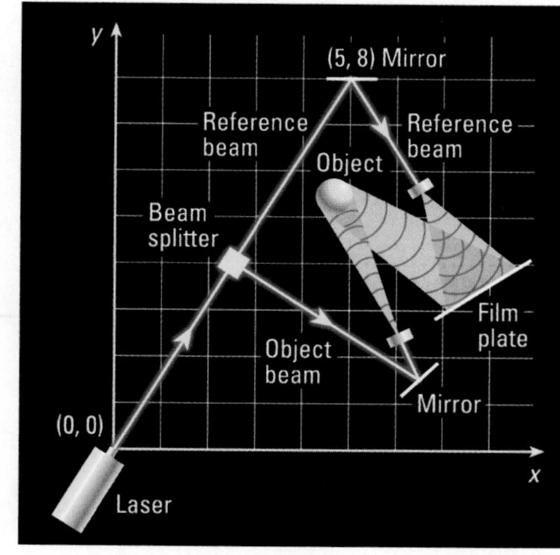

HOLOGRAMS In holography, light from a laser beam is split into two beams, a reference beam and an object beam. Light from the object beam reflects off an object and is recombined with the reference beam to form images on film that can be used to create three-dimensional images. Write an equation for the path of the reference beam.

Solution

The vertex of the path of the reference beam is $(5, 8)$. So, the equation has the form $y = a|x - 5| + 8$. Substitute the coordinates of the point $(0, 0)$ into the equation and solve for a.

$0 = a|0 - 5| + 8$ **Substitute 0 for *y* and 0 for *x*.**

$-1.6 = a$ **Solve for *a*.**

▶ An equation for the path of the reference beam is $y = -1.6|x - 5| + 8$.

TRANSFORMATIONS OF ANY GRAPH You can perform transformations on the graph of *any* function f in the same way as for absolute value graphs.

KEY CONCEPT — *For Your Notebook*

Transformations of General Graphs

The graph of $y = a \cdot f(x - h) + k$ can be obtained from the graph of any function $y = f(x)$ by performing these steps:

STEP 1 **Stretch or shrink** the graph of $y = f(x)$ vertically by a factor of $|a|$ if $|a| \neq 1$. If $|a| > 1$, stretch the graph. If $|a| < 1$, shrink the graph.

STEP 2 **Reflect** the resulting graph from Step 1 in the x-axis if $a < 0$.

STEP 3 **Translate** the resulting graph from Step 2 horizontally h units and vertically k units.

EXAMPLE 5 Apply transformations to a graph

The graph of a function $y = f(x)$ is shown. Sketch the graph of the given function.

a. $y = 2 \cdot f(x)$

b. $y = -f(x + 2) + 1$

Solution

AVOID ERRORS
In Example 5, part (b), the value of h is -2 because $-f(x + 2) + 1 = -f(x - (-2)) + 1$. Because $-2 < 0$, the horizontal translation is to the left.

a. The graph of $y = 2 \cdot f(x)$ is the graph of $y = f(x)$ stretched vertically by a factor of 2. (There is no reflection or translation.) To draw the graph, multiply the y-coordinate of each labeled point on the graph of $y = f(x)$ by 2 and connect their images.

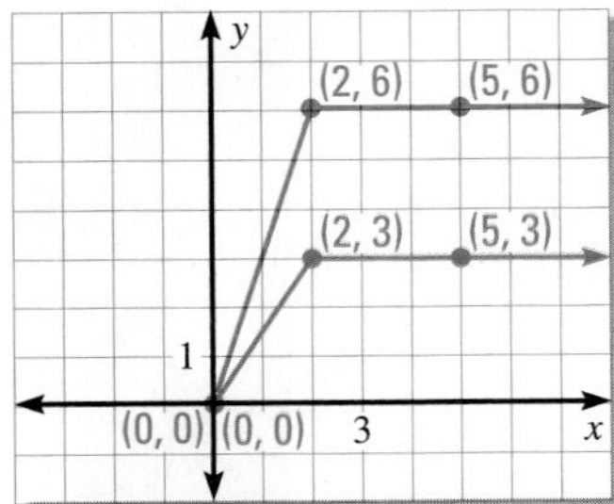

b. The graph of $y = -f(x + 2) + 1$ is the graph of $y = f(x)$ reflected in the x-axis, then translated left 2 units and up 1 unit. To draw the graph, first reflect the labeled points and connect their images. Then translate and connect these points to form the final image.

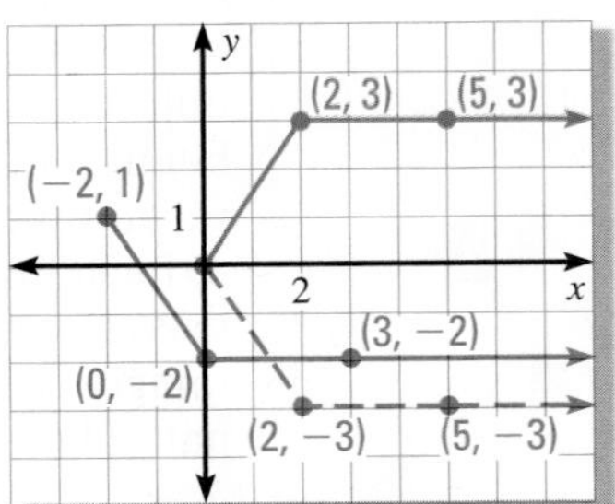

✓ GUIDED PRACTICE for Examples 4 and 5

4. WHAT IF? In Example 4, suppose the reference beam originates at (3, 0) and reflects off a mirror at (5, 4). Write an equation for the path of the beam.

Use the graph of $y = f(x)$ from Example 5 to graph the given function.

5. $y = 0.5 \cdot f(x)$ **6.** $y = -f(x - 2) - 5$ **7.** $y = 2 \cdot f(x + 3) - 1$

2.7 EXERCISES

HOMEWORK KEY

◯ = **WORKED-OUT SOLUTIONS** on p. WS4 for Exs. 13, 19, and 39

★ = **STANDARDIZED TEST PRACTICE** Exs. 2, 27, 28, 31, 32, 33, 38, and 40

◆ = **MULTIPLE REPRESENTATIONS** Ex. 41

SKILL PRACTICE

1. **VOCABULARY** The point (h, k) is the __?__ of the graph of $y = a|x - h| + k$.

2. ★ **WRITING** *Describe* three different types of transformations.

EXAMPLES 1, 2, and 3 on pp. 124–125 for Exs. 3–14

GRAPHING FUNCTIONS **Graph the function. *Compare* the graph with the graph of $y = |x|$.**

3. $y = |x| - 7$
4. $y = |x + 2|$
5. $y = |x + 4| - 2$
6. $f(x) = |x - 1| + 4$
7. $f(x) = 2|x|$
8. $f(x) = -3|x|$
9. $y = -\frac{1}{3}|x|$
10. $y = \frac{3}{4}|x|$
11. $y = 2|x + 1| - 6$
12. $f(x) = -4|x + 2| - 3$
13. $f(x) = -\frac{1}{2}|x - 1| + 5$
14. $f(x) = \frac{1}{4}|x - 4| + 3$

EXAMPLE 4 on p. 125 for Exs. 15–20

WRITING EQUATIONS **Write an equation of the graph.**

15.

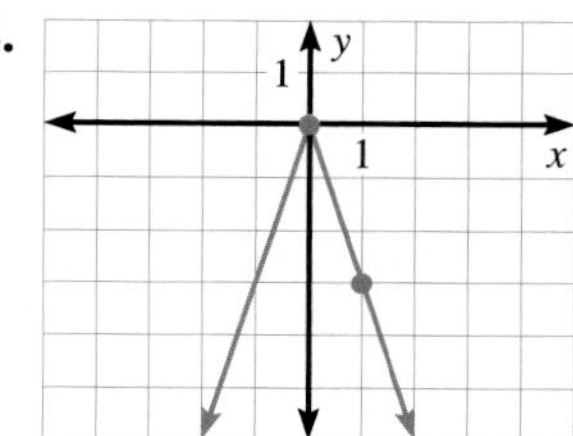

16.

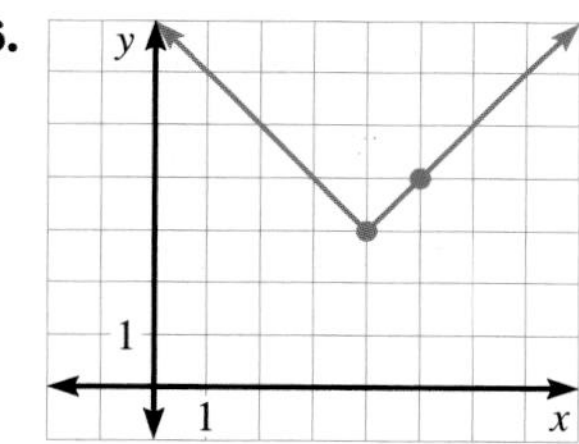

17.

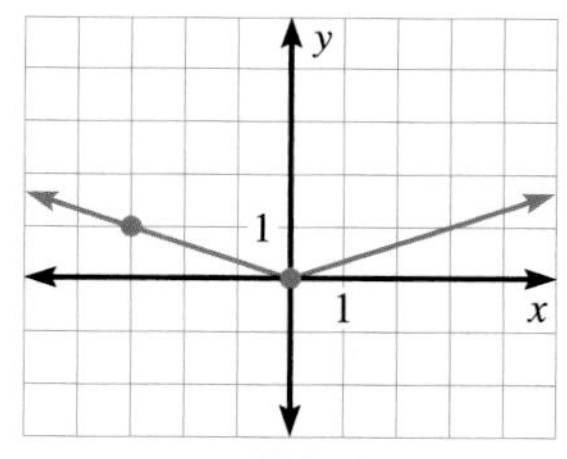

18.

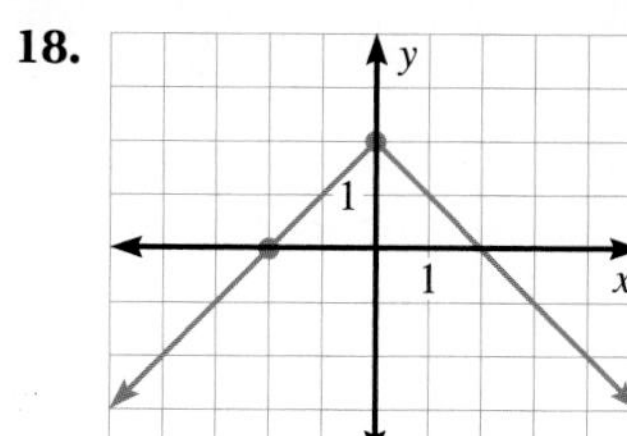

19.

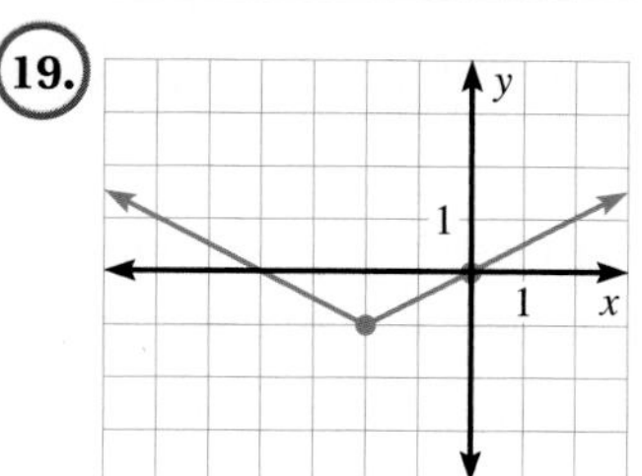

20.

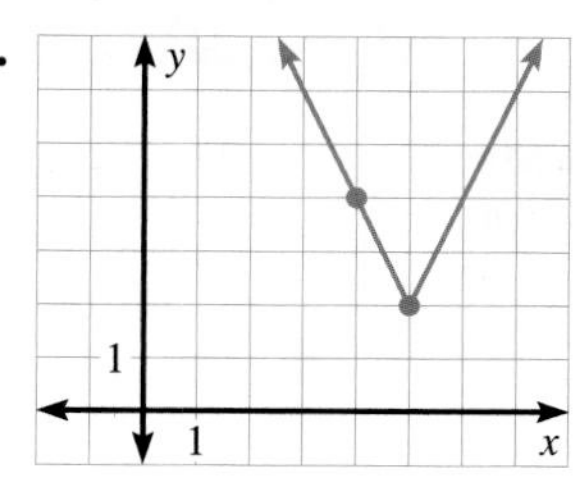

EXAMPLE 5 on p. 126 for Exs. 21–28

TRANSFORMATIONS **Use the graph of $y = f(x)$ shown to sketch the graph of the given function.**

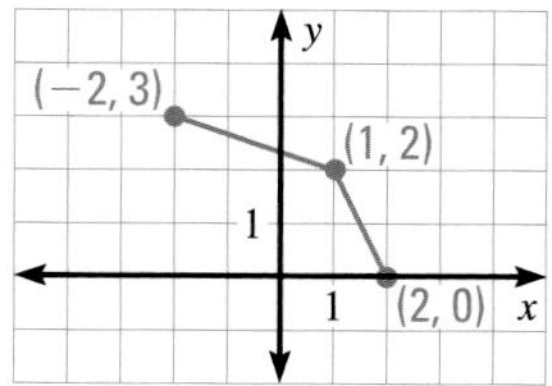

21. $y = f(x + 2) - 3$
22. $y = f(x - 4) + 1$
23. $y = \frac{1}{2} \cdot f(x)$
24. $y = -3 \cdot f(x)$
25. $y = -f(x - 1) + 4$
26. $y = 2 \cdot f(x + 3) - 1$

27. ★ **OPEN-ENDED MATH** Create a graph of a function $y = f(x)$. Then sketch the graphs of **(a)** $y = f(x + 3) - 4$, **(b)** $y = 2 \cdot f(x)$, and **(c)** $y = -f(x)$.

28. ★ **MULTIPLE CHOICE** The highest point on the graph of $y = f(x)$ is $(-1, 6)$. What is the highest point on the graph of $y = 4 \cdot f(x - 3) + 5$?

Ⓐ $(-11, 6)$ Ⓑ $(8, 11)$ Ⓒ $(-4, 29)$ Ⓓ $(2, 29)$

ERROR ANALYSIS *Describe* **and correct the error in graphing** $y = |x + 3|$.

29.

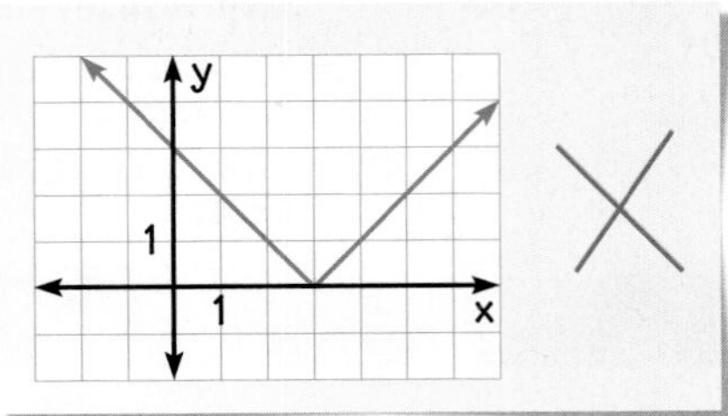

30.

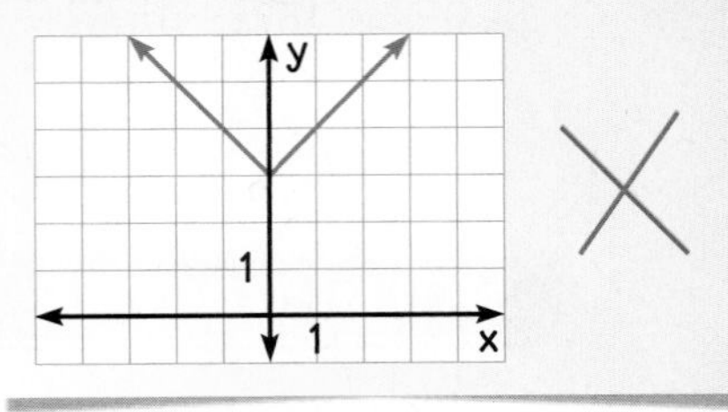

31. ★ **MULTIPLE CHOICE** Which equation has the graph shown?

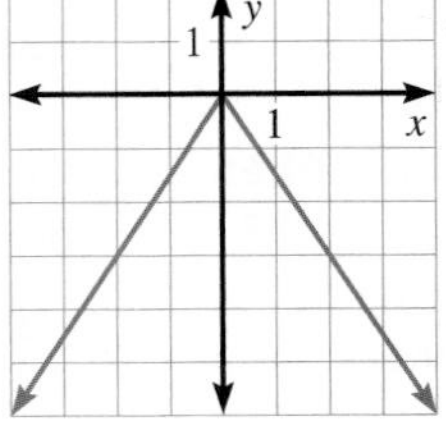

Ⓐ $y = \frac{3}{2}|x|$ Ⓑ $y = \frac{2}{3}|x|$

Ⓒ $y = -\frac{2}{3}|x|$ Ⓓ $y = -\frac{3}{2}|x|$

32. ★ **WRITING** *Describe* how the signs of h and k affect how to obtain the graph of $y = f(x - h) + k$ from the graph of $y = f(x)$.

33. ★ **SHORT RESPONSE** The graph of the relation $x = |y|$ is shown at the right. Is the relation a function? *Explain.*

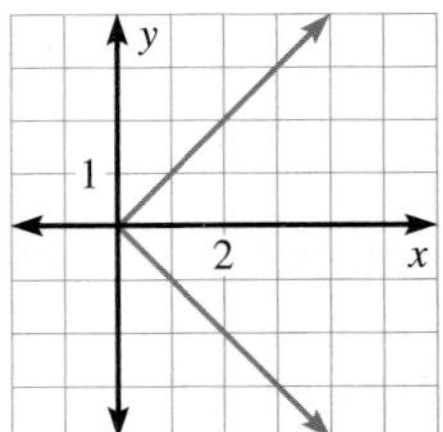

34. REASONING Is it true in general that $|x + h| = |x| + |h|$? *Justify* your answer by considering how the graphs of $y = |x + h|$ and $y = |x| + |h|$ are related to the graph of $y = |x|$.

35. CHALLENGE The graph of $y = a|x - h| + k$ passes through $(-2, 4)$ and $(4, 4)$. *Describe* the possible values of h and k for $a \neq 0$.

PROBLEM SOLVING

EXAMPLE 1 on p. 124 for Ex. 36

36. SPEEDOMETER A car's speedometer reads 60 miles per hour. The error E in this measurement is $E = |a - 60|$ where a is the actual speed. Graph the function. For what value(s) of a will E be 2.5 miles per hour?

@HomeTutor for problem solving help at classzone.com

EXAMPLE 3 on p. 125 for Ex. 37

37. SALES Weekly sales s (in thousands) of a new basketball shoe increase steadily for a while and then decrease as described by the function $s = -2|t - 15| + 50$ where t is the time (in weeks). Graph the function. What is the greatest number of pairs of shoes sold in one week?

@HomeTutor for problem solving help at classzone.com

EXAMPLE 4 on p. 125 for Exs. 38–39

38. ★ **SHORT RESPONSE** On the pool table shown, you bank the five ball off the side at $(-1.25, 5)$. You want the ball to go in the pocket at $(-5, 0)$.

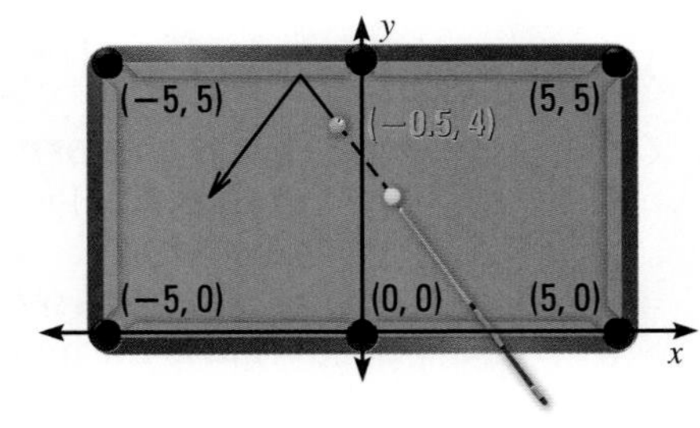

a. Write an equation for the path of the ball.

b. Do you make the shot? *Explain* how you found your answer.

39. **ENGINEERING** The Leonard P. Zakim Bunker Hill Bridge spans the Charles River in Boston. The bridge is suspended from two towers. Each tower has the dimensions shown. Write an absolute value function that represents the inverted V-shaped portion of a tower.

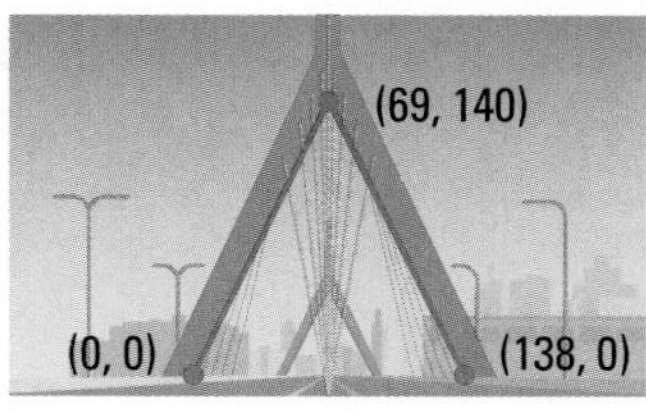

40. ★ **EXTENDED RESPONSE** A snowstorm begins with light snow that increases to very heavy snow before decreasing again. The snowfall rate r (in inches per hour) is given by $r(t) = -0.5|t - 4| + 2$ where t is the time (in hours).
    a. **Graph** Graph the function.
    b. **Interpret** When is the snowfall heaviest? What is the maximum snowfall rate? How are your answers related to the function's graph?
    c. **Extend** The total snowfall is given by the area of the triangle formed by the graph of $r(t)$ and the t-axis. What is the total snowfall?

41. **MULTIPLE REPRESENTATIONS** The diagram shows a truck driving toward a radio station transmitter that has a broadcasting range of 50 miles.

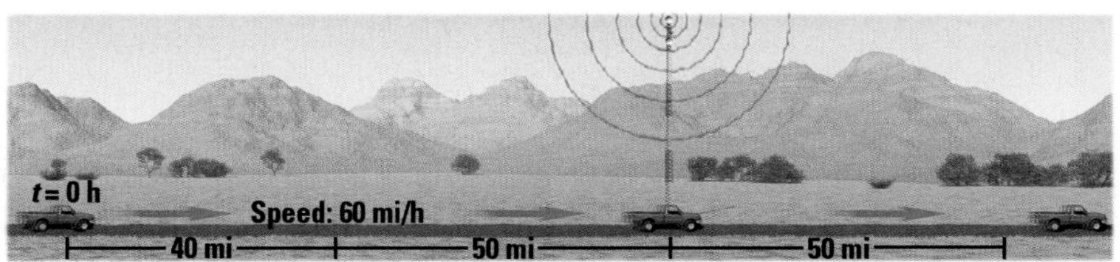

    a. **Making a Table** Make a table that shows the truck's distance d (in miles) from the transmitter after $t = 0, 0.5, 1, 1.5, 2, 2.5,$ and 3 hours.
    b. **Drawing a Graph** Use your table from part (a) to draw a graph that shows d as a function of t.
    c. **Writing an Equation** Write an equation that gives d as a function of t. During what driving times is the truck within range of the transmitter?

42. **CHALLENGE** A hiker walks up and down a hill. The hill has a cross section that can be modeled by $y = -\frac{4}{3}|x - 300| + 400$ where x and y are measured in feet and $0 \le x \le 600$. How far does the hiker walk?

NEW YORK MIXED REVIEW

43. Which expression is equivalent to $12(n^2 + n) - 5(n^2 + 3n - 2)$?

    (A) $-7n^2 + 3n - 10$
    (B) $7n^2 - 3n + 10$
    (C) $17n^2 + 27n - 10$
    (D) $17n^2 - 13n + 10$

44. In the figure shown, what is the length of $\overline{YX}$ in inches?

    (A) 20 in.
    (B) 36 in.
    (C) 56 in.
    (D) 3136 in.

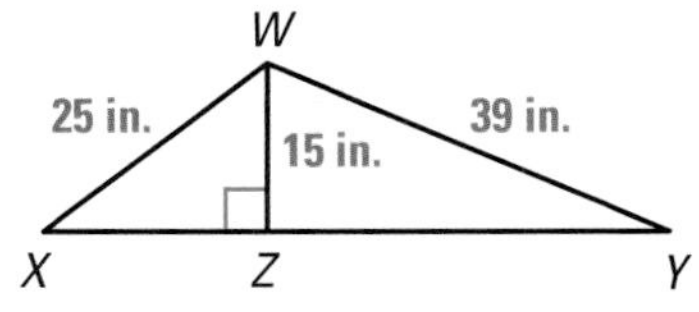

Extension Use Piecewise Functions

Use after Lesson 2.7

GOAL Evaluate, graph, and write piecewise functions.

Key Vocabulary
- **piecewise function**
- **step function**

A **piecewise function** is defined by at least two equations, each of which applies to a different part of the function's domain. One example of a piecewise function is the absolute value function $f(x) = |x|$, which can be defined by the equations $y = -x$ for $x < 0$ and $y = x$ for $x \geq 0$. Another example is given below.

$$g(x) = \begin{cases} 2x - 1, & \text{if } x \leq 1 \\ 3x + 1, & \text{if } x > 1 \end{cases}$$

The equation $y = 2x - 1$ gives the value of $g(x)$ when x is less than or equal to 1, and the equation $y = 3x + 1$ gives the value of $g(x)$ when x is greater than 1.

EXAMPLE 1 Evaluate a piecewise function

Evaluate the function $g(x)$ above when (a) $x = 1$ and (b) $x = 5$.

Solution

a. $g(x) = 2x - 1$ — Because $1 \leq 1$, use first equation.

$g(1) = 2(1) - 1 = 1$ — Substitute 1 for x and simplify.

b. $g(x) = 3x + 1$ — Because $5 > 1$, use second equation.

$g(5) = 3(5) + 1 = 16$ — Substitute 5 for x and simplify.

EXAMPLE 2 Graph a piecewise function

Graph the function $f(x) = \begin{cases} -\frac{3}{2}x - 1, & \text{if } x < -2 \\ x + 1, & \text{if } -2 \leq x \leq 1 \\ 3, & \text{if } x > 1 \end{cases}$

Solution

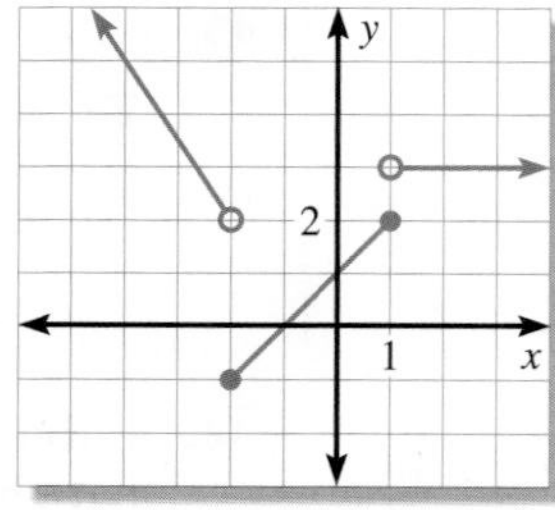

STEP 1 To the left of $x = -2$, graph $y = -\frac{3}{2}x - 1$. Use an open dot at $(-2, 2)$ because the equation $y = -\frac{3}{2}x - 1$ does not apply when $x = -2$.

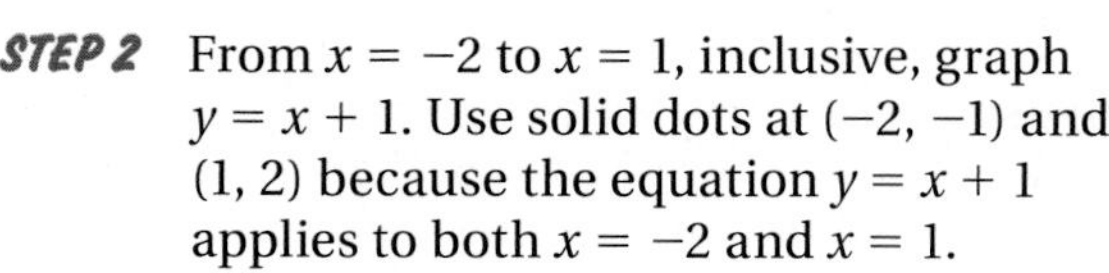

STEP 2 From $x = -2$ to $x = 1$, inclusive, graph $y = x + 1$. Use solid dots at $(-2, -1)$ and $(1, 2)$ because the equation $y = x + 1$ applies to both $x = -2$ and $x = 1$.

STEP 3 To the right of $x = 1$, graph $y = 3$. Use an open dot at $(1, 3)$ because the equation $y = 3$ does not apply when $x = 1$.

EXAMPLE 3 Write a piecewise function

Write a piecewise function for the graph shown.

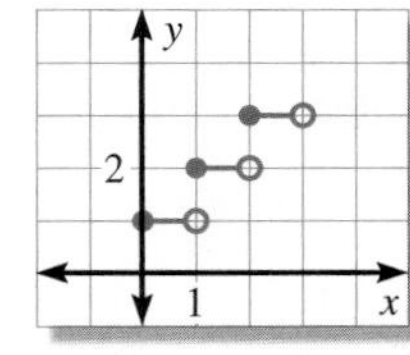

Solution

For x between 0 and 1, including $x = 0$, the graph is the line segment given by $y = 1$.

For x between 1 and 2, including $x = 1$, the graph is the line segment given by $y = 2$.

For x between 2 and 3, including $x = 2$, the graph is the line segment given by $y = 3$. So, a piecewise function for the graph is as follows:

$$f(x) = \begin{cases} 1, & \text{if } 0 \le x < 1 \\ 2, & \text{if } 1 \le x < 2 \\ 3, & \text{if } 2 \le x < 3 \end{cases}$$

STEP FUNCTIONS The piecewise function in Example 3 is called a **step function** because its graph resembles a set of stairs. A step function is defined by a constant value over each part of its domain. The constant values can increase with each "step" as in Example 3, or they can decrease with each step.

PRACTICE

EXAMPLE 1 on p. 130 for Exs. 1–4

EVALUATING FUNCTIONS **Evaluate the function below for the given value of x.**

$$f(x) = \begin{cases} 9x - 4, & \text{if } x > 3 \\ \frac{1}{2}x + 1, & \text{if } x \le 3 \end{cases}$$

1. $f(-4)$
2. $f(2)$
3. $f(3)$
4. $f(5)$

EXAMPLE 2 on p. 130 for Exs. 5–8

GRAPHING FUNCTIONS **Graph the function.**

5. $f(x) = \begin{cases} 2x + 1, & \text{if } x \ge 0 \\ -x + 1, & \text{if } x < 0 \end{cases}$

6. $g(x) = \begin{cases} -\frac{1}{2}x - 1, & \text{if } x < 2 \\ 3x - 7, & \text{if } x \ge 2 \end{cases}$

7. $h(x) = \begin{cases} 3, & \text{if } 0 < x \le 2 \\ 1, & \text{if } 2 < x \le 4 \\ 5, & \text{if } 4 < x \le 6 \end{cases}$

8. **POSTAL RATES** In 2005, the cost C (in dollars) to send U.S. Postal Service Express Mail up to 5 pounds depended on the weight w (in ounces) according to the function at the right.

$$C(w) = \begin{cases} 13.65, & \text{if } 0 < w \le 8 \\ 17.85, & \text{if } 8 < w \le 32 \\ 21.05, & \text{if } 32 < w \le 48 \\ 24.20, & \text{if } 48 < w \le 64 \\ 27.30, & \text{if } 64 < w \le 80 \end{cases}$$

   a. Graph the function.

   b. What is the cost to send a parcel weighing 2 pounds 9 ounces?

EXAMPLE 3 on p. 131 for Exs. 9–10

SPECIAL STEP FUNCTIONS **Write and graph the piecewise function described using the domain $-3 \le x \le 3$.**

9. **Rounding Function** The output $f(x)$ is the input x rounded to the nearest integer. (If the decimal part of x is 0.5, then x is rounded up when x is positive and x is rounded down when x is negative.)

10. **Greatest Integer Function** The output $f(x)$ is the greatest integer less than or equal to the input x.

2.8 Graph Linear Inequalities in Two Variables

Before	You solved linear inequalities in one variable.
Now	You will graph linear inequalities in two variables.
Why?	So you can model data encoding, as in Example 4.

Key Vocabulary
- **linear inequality in two variables**
- **solution of a linear inequality**
- **graph of a linear inequality**
- **half-plane**

A **linear inequality in two variables** can be written in one of these forms:

$Ax + By < C \qquad Ax + By \leq C \qquad Ax + By > C \qquad Ax + By \geq C$

An ordered pair (x, y) is a **solution** of a linear inequality in two variables if the inequality is true when the values of x and y are substituted into the inequality.

EXAMPLE 1  Standardized Test Practice

Which ordered pair is a solution of $3x + 4y > 8$?

Ⓐ $(6, -3)$ Ⓑ $(0, 2)$ Ⓒ $(-2, -1)$ Ⓓ $(-3, 5)$

Solution

Ordered Pair	Substitute	Conclusion
$(6, -3)$	$3(6) + 4(-3) = 6 \ngtr 8$	$(6, -3)$ is not a solution.
$(0, 2)$	$3(0) + 4(2) = 8 \ngtr 8$	$(0, 2)$ is not a solution.
$(-2, -1)$	$3(-2) + 4(-1) = -10 \ngtr 8$	$(-2, -1)$ is not a solution.
$(-3, 5)$	$3(-3) + 4(5) = 11 > 8$	$(-3, 5)$ is a solution.

▶ The correct answer is D. Ⓐ Ⓑ Ⓒ Ⓓ

 **GUIDED PRACTICE** for Example 1

Tell whether the given ordered pair is a solution of $5x - 2y \leq 6$.

1. $(0, -4)$
2. $(2, 2)$
3. $(-3, 8)$
4. $(-1, -7)$

GRAPHING INEQUALITIES The **graph** of a linear inequality in two variables is the set of all points in a coordinate plane that represent solutions of the inequality.

INTERPRET GRAPHS
A dashed boundary line means that points on the line are *not* solutions. A solid boundary line means that points on the line *are* solutions.

All solutions of $3x - 2y > 2$ lie on one side of the *boundary line* $3x - 2y = 2$.

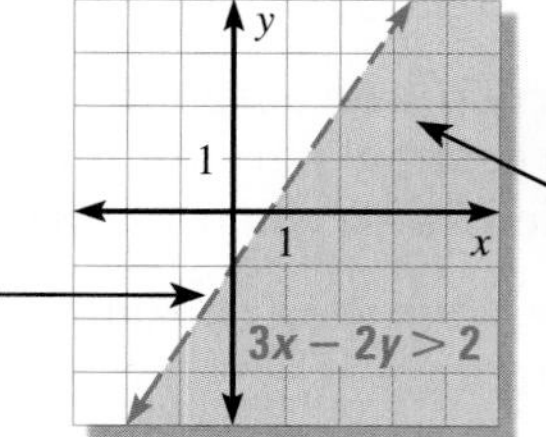

The boundary line divides the plane into two half-planes. The shaded half-plane is the graph of $3x - 2y > 2$.

KEY CONCEPT *For Your Notebook*

Graphing a Linear Inequality

To graph a linear inequality in two variables, follow these steps:

STEP 1 **Graph** the boundary line for the inequality. Use a dashed line for $<$ or $>$ and a solid line for $\le$ or $\ge$.

STEP 2 **Test** a point *not* on the boundary line to determine whether it is a solution of the inequality. If it is a solution, shade the half-plane containing the point. If it is not a solution, shade the other half-plane.

EXAMPLE 2 Graph linear inequalities with one variable

Graph (a) $y \le -3$ and (b) $x < 2$ in a coordinate plane.

a. Graph the boundary line $y = -3$. Use a solid line because the inequality symbol is $\le$.

Test the point (0, 0). Because (0, 0) is *not* a solution of the inequality, shade the half-plane that does not contain (0, 0).

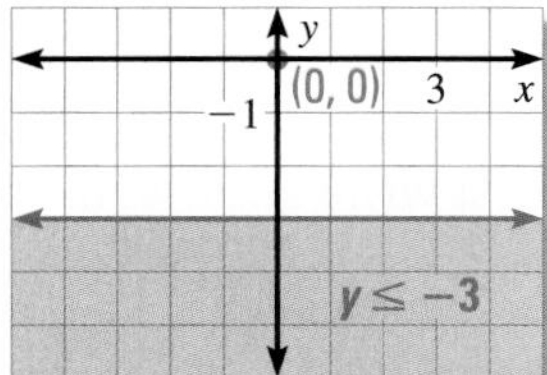

b. Graph the boundary line $x = 2$. Use a dashed line because the inequality symbol is $<$.

Test the point (0, 0). Because (0, 0) *is* a solution of the inequality, shade the half-plane that contains (0, 0).

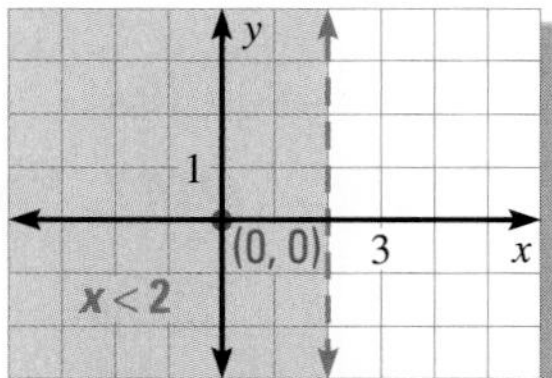

EXAMPLE 3 Graph linear inequalities with two variables

Graph (a) $y > -2x$ and (b) $5x - 2y \le -4$ in a coordinate plane.

a. Graph the boundary line $y = -2x$. Use a dashed line because the inequality symbol is $>$.

Test the point (1, 1). Because (1, 1) *is* a solution of the inequality, shade the half-plane that contains (1, 1).

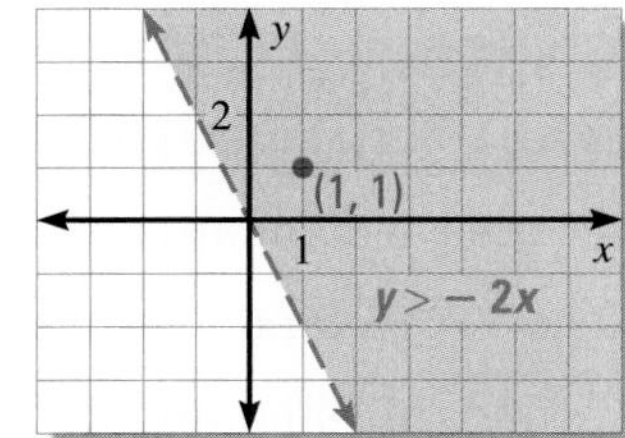

b. Graph the boundary line $5x - 2y = -4$. Use a solid line because the inequality symbol is $\le$.

Test the point (0, 0). Because (0, 0) is *not* a solution of the inequality, shade the half-plane that does not contain (0, 0).

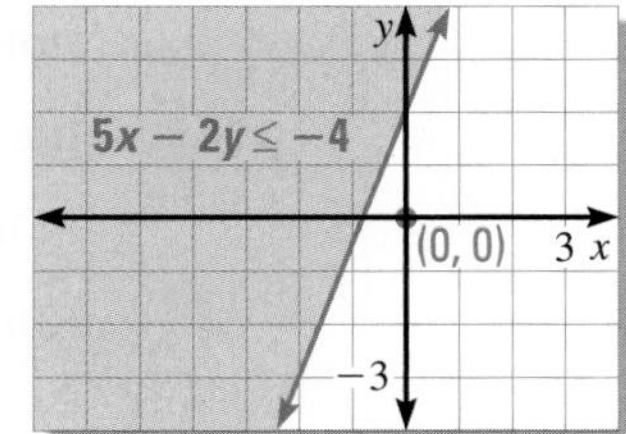

AVOID ERRORS
It is often convenient to use (0, 0) as a test point. However, if (0, 0) lies on the boundary line, you must choose a different test point.

Animated Algebra at classzone.com

GUIDED PRACTICE for Examples 2 and 3

Graph the inequality in a coordinate plane.

5. $y > -1$ **6.** $x \ge -4$ **7.** $y \ge -3x$

8. $y < 2x + 3$ **9.** $x + 3y < 9$ **10.** $2x - 6y > 12$

EXAMPLE 4 Solve a multi-step problem

MOVIE RECORDING A film class is recording a DVD of student-made short films. Each student group is allotted up to 300 megabytes (MB) of video space. The films are encoded on the DVD at two different rates: a standard rate of 0.4 MB/sec for normal scenes and a high-quality rate of 1.2 MB/sec for complex scenes.

- Write an inequality describing the possible amounts of time available for standard and high-quality video.
- Graph the inequality.
- Identify three possible solutions of the inequality.

Solution

STEP 1 **Write** an inequality. First write a verbal model.

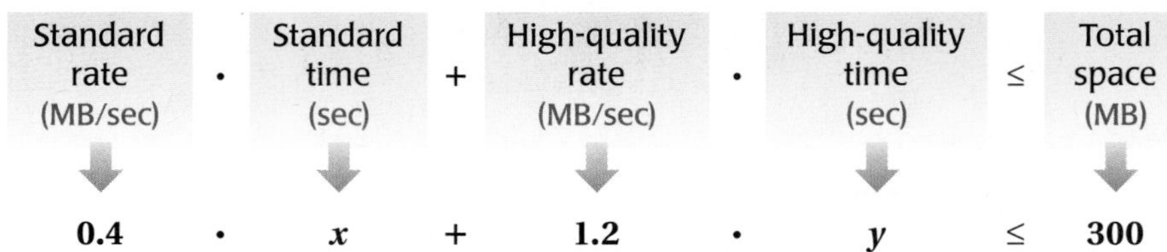

An inequality is $0.4x + 1.2y \le 300$.

STEP 2 **Graph** the inequality. First graph the boundary line $0.4x + 1.2y = 300$. Use a solid line because the inequality symbol is $\le$.

Test the point (0, 0). Because (0, 0) *is* a solution of the inequality, shade the half-plane that contains (0, 0). Because x and y cannot be negative, shade only points in the first quadrant.

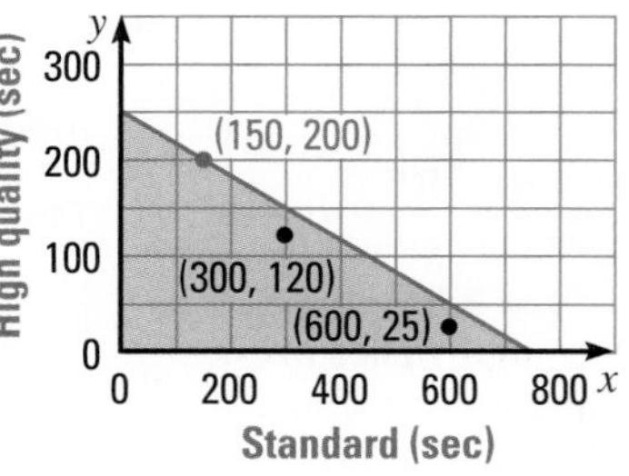

STEP 3 **Identify** solutions. Three solutions are given below and on the graph.

(150, 200) ← 150 seconds of standard and 200 seconds of high quality

(300, 120) ← 300 seconds of standard and 120 seconds of high quality

(600, 25) ← 600 seconds of standard and 25 seconds of high quality

For the first solution, $0.4(150) + 1.2(200) = 300$, so all of the available space is used. For the other two solutions, not all of the space is used.

ABSOLUTE VALUE INEQUALITIES Graphing an absolute value inequality is similar to graphing a linear inequality, but the boundary is an absolute value graph.

EXAMPLE 5 Graph an absolute value inequality

Graph $y > -2|x - 3| + 4$ in a coordinate plane.

Solution

STEP 1 **Graph** the equation of the boundary, $y = -2|x - 3| + 4$. Use a dashed line because the inequality symbol is >.

STEP 2 **Test** the point (0, 0). Because (0, 0) *is* a solution of the inequality, shade the portion of the coordinate plane outside the absolute value graph.

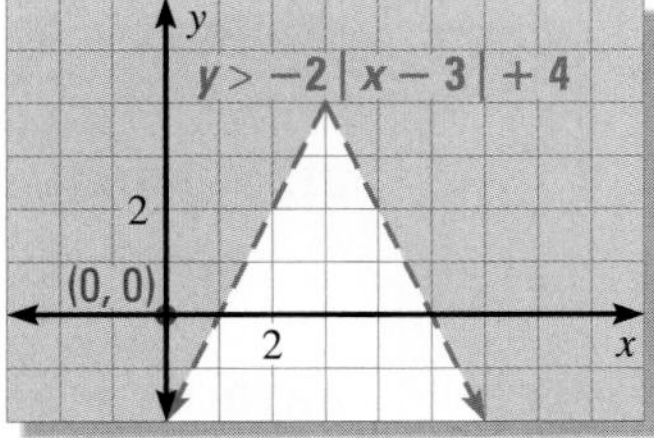

✓ GUIDED PRACTICE for Examples 4 and 5

11. **WHAT IF?** Repeat the steps of Example 4 if each student group is allotted up to 420 MB of video space.

Graph the inequality in a coordinate plane.

12. $y \le |x - 2| + 1$
13. $y \ge -|x + 3| - 2$
14. $y < 3|x - 1| - 3$

2.8 EXERCISES

HOMEWORK KEY

○ = **WORKED-OUT SOLUTIONS** on p. WS4 for Exs. 15, 25, and 45

★ = **STANDARDIZED TEST PRACTICE** Exs. 2, 21, 28, 39, 40, 41, 46, and 48

SKILL PRACTICE

1. **VOCABULARY** Copy and complete: The graph of a linear inequality in two variables is a(n) __?__.

2. ★ **WRITING** *Compare* the graph of a linear inequality in two variables with the graph of a linear equation in two variables.

EXAMPLE 1 on p. 132 for Exs. 3–6

CHECKING SOLUTIONS Tell whether the given ordered pairs are solutions of the inequality.

3. $x > -7$; (0, 10), (−8, −5)
4. $y \le -5x$; (3, 2), (−2, 1)
5. $y \ge -2x + 4$; (0, 4), (−1, 8)
6. $2x - y < 3$; (0, 0), (2, −2)

EXAMPLES 2 and 3 on p. 133 for Exs. 7–20

GRAPHING INEQUALITIES Graph the inequality in a coordinate plane.

7. $x < 3$
8. $x \ge 6$
9. $y > -2$
10. $-2y \le 8$
11. $y \le -2x - 1$
12. $y < 3x + 3$
13. $y > \frac{3}{4}x + 1$
14. $y \ge -\frac{2}{3}x - 2$
15. (circled) $2x + y < 6$
16. $x + 4y > -12$
17. $3x - y \ge 1$
18. $2x + 5y \le -10$

ERROR ANALYSIS *Describe* and correct the error in graphing the inequality.

19. $y < 2x + 3$

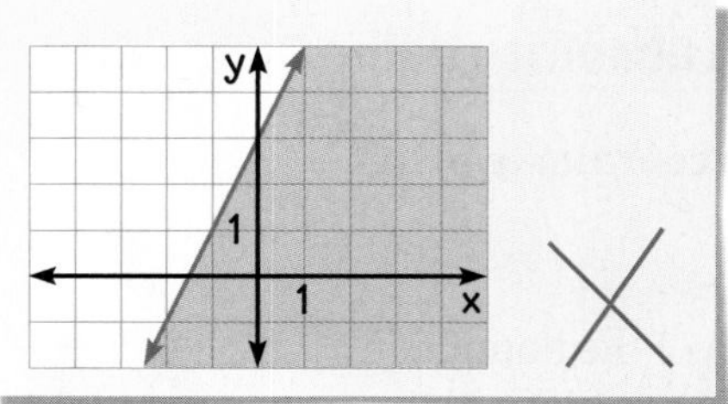

20. $y \geq -3x - 2$

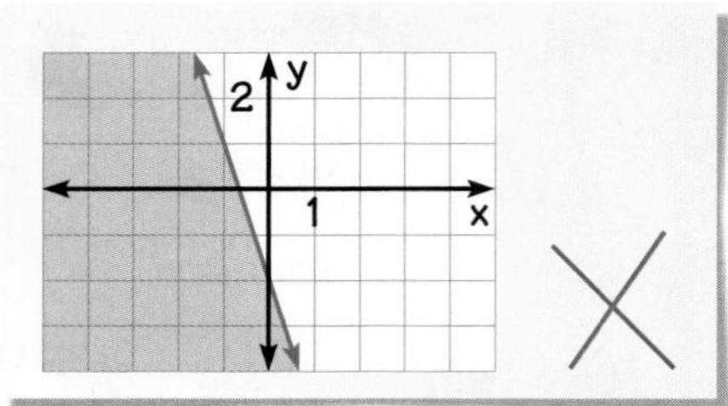

21. ★ **MULTIPLE CHOICE** Which ordered pair is *not* a solution of $3x - 5y < 30$?

Ⓐ (0, 0) Ⓑ (−1, 7) Ⓒ (1, −7) Ⓓ (−5, −5)

EXAMPLE 5 on p. 135 for Exs. 22–28

ABSOLUTE VALUE INEQUALITIES Graph the inequality in a coordinate plane.

22. $y > |x - 1|$

23. $y < |x| + 5$

24. $y > |x + 4| - 3$

25. $y \leq -\frac{1}{2}|x - 2| + 1$

26. $y < 3|x| + 2$

27. $y \geq 2|x - 1| - 4$

28. ★ **MULTIPLE CHOICE** The graph of which inequality is shown?

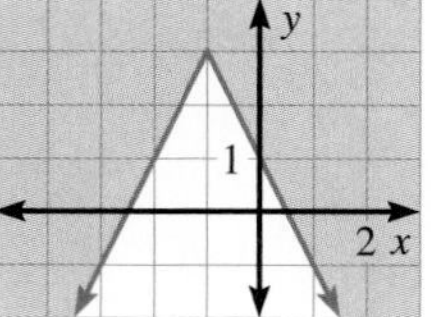

Ⓐ $y \leq -2|x + 1| + 3$ Ⓑ $y \geq -2|x - 1| + 3$

Ⓒ $y > -2|x + 1| + 3$ Ⓓ $y \geq -2|x + 1| + 3$

CHECKING SOLUTIONS Tell whether the given ordered pairs are solutions of the inequality.

29. $y \geq -\frac{2}{3}x + \frac{1}{2}$; (−6, 8), (−3, −3)

30. $4.5 + y < 1.6x$; (0.5, 1), (3.8, 0)

31. $0.2x + 0.7y > -1$; (0.5, −1), (−3, −1.5)

32. $\frac{1}{4}x - y > 1$; $\left(\frac{4}{3}, 0\right), \left(\frac{2}{3}, -4\right)$

GRAPHING INEQUALITIES Graph the inequality in a coordinate plane.

33. $3y < 4.5x + 15$

34. $-1.5y - 2x > 3$

35. $-y - 0.2 > -0.6x$

36. $\frac{2}{3}x + \frac{1}{2}y > 2$

37. $y \geq -\frac{5}{2}|x - 3| - \frac{3}{2}$

38. $2y - 4 \leq -3|x + 2|$

39. ★ **OPEN-ENDED MATH** Write a linear inequality in two variables that has (−1, 3) and (1, 6) as solutions, but does not have (4, 0) as a solution.

40. ★ **WRITING** *Explain* why it is not helpful when graphing a linear inequality in two variables to choose a test point that lies on the boundary line.

41. ★ **SHORT RESPONSE** Write an inequality for the graph shown. *Explain* how you came up with the inequality. Then describe a real-life situation that the first-quadrant portion of the graph could represent.

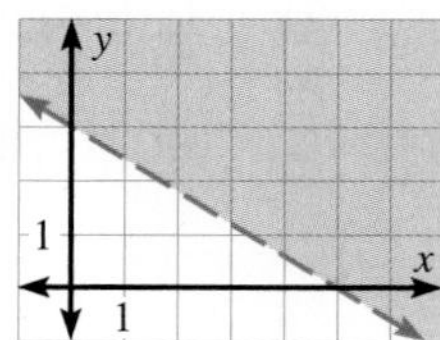

42. **CHALLENGE** Write an absolute value inequality that has exactly one solution in common with $y \geq 2|x - 3| + 5$. The common solution should not be the vertex (3, 5) of the boundary. *Explain* how you found your inequality.

PROBLEM SOLVING

EXAMPLE 4 on p. 134 for Exs. 43–48

43. **CALLING CARDS** You have a $20 phone card. Calls made using the card cost $.03 per minute to destinations within the United States and $.06 per minute to destinations in Brazil. Write an inequality describing the numbers of minutes you can use for calls to U.S. destinations and to Brazil.

@HomeTutor for problem solving help at classzone.com

44. **RESTAURANT MANAGEMENT** A pizza shop has 300 pounds (4800 ounces) of dough. A small pizza uses 12 ounces of dough and a large pizza uses 18 ounces of dough. Write and graph an inequality describing the possible numbers of small and large pizzas that can be made. Then give three possible solutions.

@HomeTutor for problem solving help at classzone.com

45. **CRAFTS** Cotton lace costs $1.50 per yard and linen lace costs $2.50 per yard. You plan to order at most $75 of lace for crafts. Write and graph an inequality describing how much of each type of lace you can order. If you buy 24 yards of cotton lace, what are the amounts of linen lace you can buy?

46. ★ **SHORT RESPONSE** You sell T-shirts for $15 each and caps for $10 each. Write and graph an inequality describing how many shirts and caps you must sell to exceed $1800 in sales. *Explain* how you can modify this inequality to describe how many shirts and caps you must sell to exceed $600 in *profit* if you make a 40% profit on shirts and a 30% profit on caps.

47. **MULTI-STEP PROBLEM** On a two week vacation, you and your brother can rent one canoe for $11 per day or rent two mountain bikes for $13 each per day. Together, you have $120 to spend.

    a. Write and graph an inequality describing the possible numbers of days you and your brother can canoe or bicycle together.

    b. Give three possible solutions of the inequality from part (a).

    c. You decide that on one day you will canoe alone and your brother will bicycle alone. Repeat parts (a) and (b) using this new condition.

48. ★ **EXTENDED RESPONSE** While camping, you and a friend filter river water into two cylindrical containers with the radii and heights shown. You then use these containers to fill the water cooler shown.

    a. Find the volumes of the containers and the cooler in cubic inches.

    b. Using your results from part (a), write and graph an inequality describing how many times the containers can be filled and emptied into the water cooler without the cooler overflowing.

    c. Convert the volumes from part (a) to gallons ($1 \text{ in.}^3 \approx 0.00433$ gal). Then rewrite the inequality from part (b) in terms of these converted volumes.

    d. Graph the inequality from part (c). *Compare* the graph with your graph from part (b), and explain why the results make sense.

49. CHALLENGE A widescreen television image has a width w and a height h that satisfy the inequality $\frac{w}{h} > \frac{4}{3}$.

a. Does the television screen shown at the right meet the requirements of a widescreen image?

b. Let d be the length of a diagonal of a television image. Write an inequality describing the possible values of d and h for a widescreen image.

NEW YORK MIXED REVIEW

TEST PRACTICE at classzone.com

50. Which equation represents the line that passes through the points (1, 4) and (5, −2)?

Ⓐ $y = -\frac{2}{3}x + \frac{14}{3}$ Ⓑ $y = \frac{2}{3}x + \frac{10}{3}$

Ⓒ $y = -\frac{3}{2}x + \frac{11}{2}$ Ⓓ $y = \frac{3}{2}x + \frac{5}{2}$

51. The map shows two different paths from the library to the cafeteria. How many meters shorter is the walk along the sidewalk than the walk on the covered walkway?

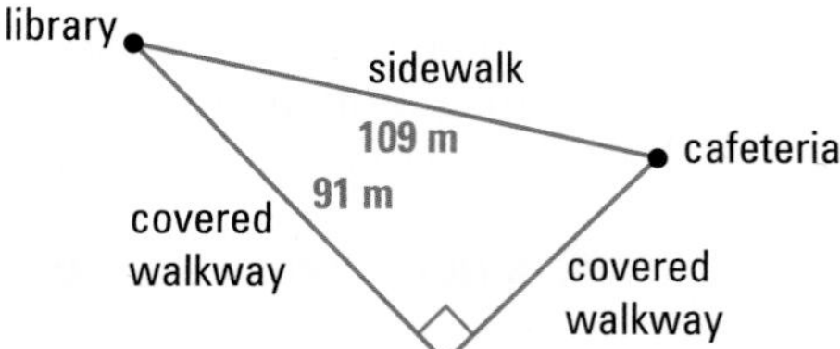

Ⓐ 18 m Ⓑ 42 m

Ⓒ 50 m Ⓓ 60 m

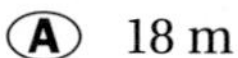

QUIZ for Lessons 2.7–2.8

Graph the function. *Compare* the graph with the graph of $y = |x|$. *(p. 123)*

1. $y = |x + 7| + 4$ **2.** $y = -2|x + 10| - 1$ **3.** $f(x) = \frac{1}{2}|x - 1| - 5$

Write an equation of the graph. *(p. 123)*

4.

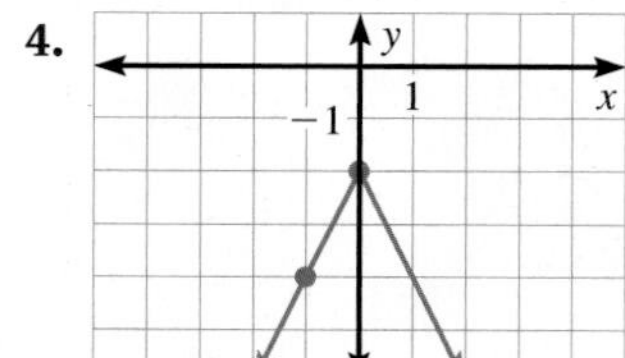

5.

6.

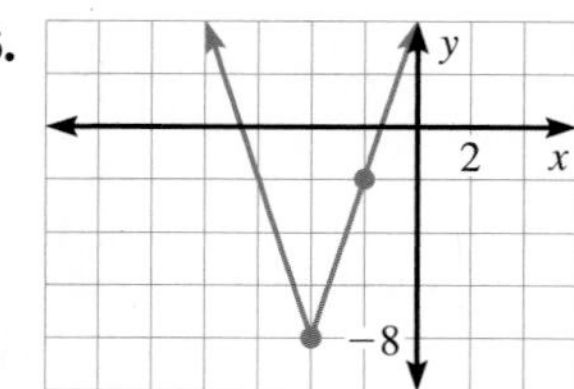

Graph the inequality in a coordinate plane. *(p. 132)*

7. $y > -2$ **8.** $y \le 3x + 1$ **9.** $2x - 5y \ge 10$

10. MINI-CARS You have a 20 credit gift pass to a mini-car raceway. It takes 2 credits to drive the cars on the Rally track and 3 credits to drive the cars on the Grand Prix track. Write and graph an inequality describing how many times you can race on the two tracks using your gift pass. Then give three possible solutions. *(p. 132)*

EXTRA PRACTICE for Lesson 2.8, p. 1011 **ONLINE QUIZ** at classzone.com

Lessons 2.5–2.8

1. **ARCHITECTURE** An "A-frame" house is shown below. The coordinates x and y are both measured in feet. Which absolute value function models the front of the house?

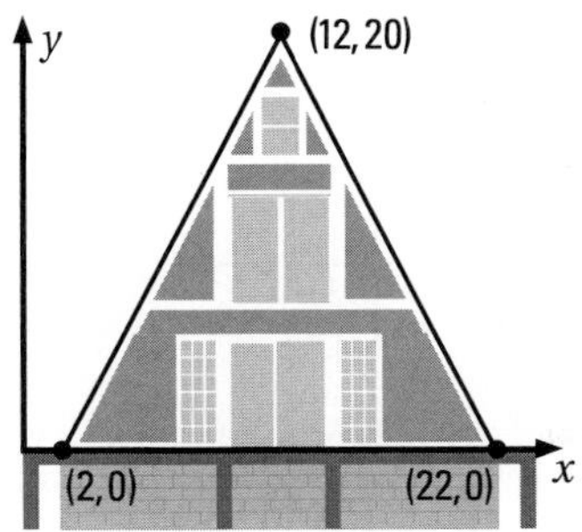

(1) $y = -2|x - 12|$

(2) $y = 2|x| + 20$

(3) $y = -2|x - 12| + 20$

(4) $y = 2|x - 12| - 20$

2. **LINEAR INEQUALITIES** The graph of which inequality is shown?

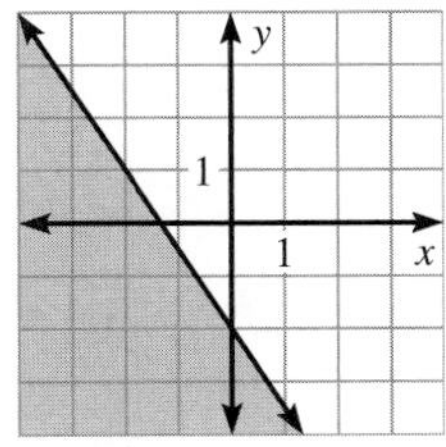

(1) $-x + y \geq 2$

(2) $3x + 2y \leq -4$

(3) $4x + 3y \geq -10$

(4) $9x + 4y \leq -24$

3. **INTERNET COST** The cost of an Internet service subscription varies directly with the length of the subscription. A 3 month subscription costs \$32.85. How much does a 12 month subscription cost?

(1) \$32.85 (3) \$131.40

(2) \$36 (4) \$133.33

4. **SUNSPOTS** Based on the data in the graph, which conclusion is most accurate?

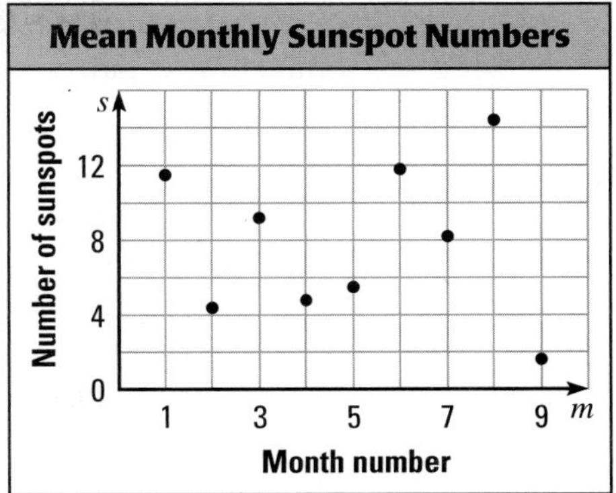

(1) The sunspot data show a positive correlation.

(2) The sunspot data show a negative correlation.

(3) The sunspot data show approximately no correlation.

(4) The sunspot data show a strong correlation.

5. **OPEN-ENDED** A greenhouse sells marigolds for \$2 each and dahlias for \$3 each. You have a total of \$30 to spend. Write an inequality describing the numbers of marigolds and dahlias you can buy.

6. **OPEN-ENDED** The table below shows the number of readers of daily newspapers in the U.S. from 1900 to 1960 in intervals of 20 years.

Year	1900	1920	1940	1960
Readers (millions)	15.1	27.8	41.1	58.9

Draw a scatter plot of all (x, y) pairs of the form (years since 1900, readers).

Find the equation of the best-fitting line.

Use the equation to predict the number of readers in 1980.

In 1980, the actual number of readers was 62.2 million. Compare this value to your prediction. What does this indicate about the yearly rate of change of circulation?

2 CHAPTER SUMMARY

Animated Algebra
classzone.com
Electronic Function Library

BIG IDEAS

For Your Notebook

Big Idea 1

Representing Relations and Functions

A relation pairs input values with output values. A relation is a function if each input value is paired with exactly one output value.

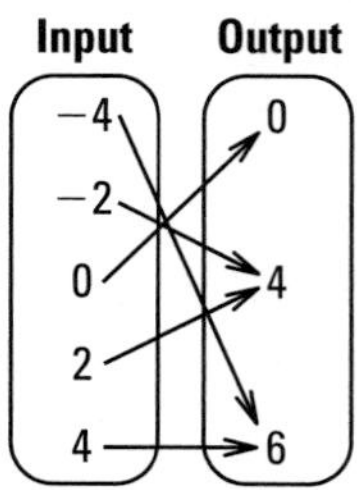

This relation is a function because each input has exactly one output.

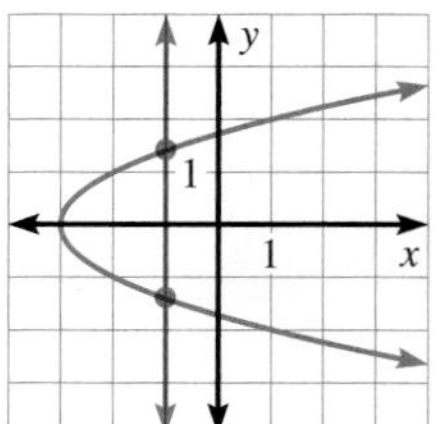

This relation is not a function because a vertical line intersects the graph at more than one point.

Big Idea 2

Graphing Linear Equations and Inequalities in Two Variables

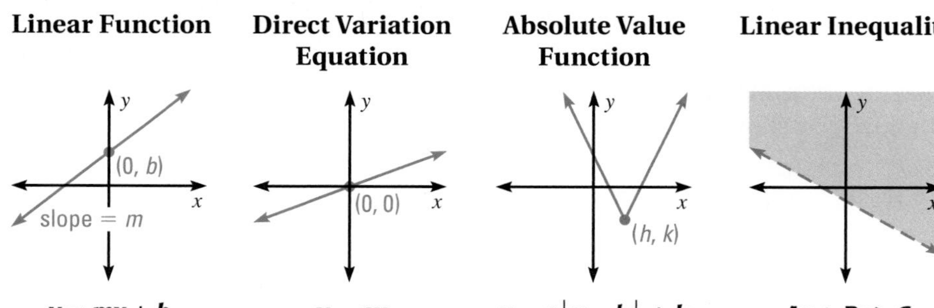

$y = mx + b$ $\quad$ $y = ax$ $\quad$ $y = a|x - h| + k$ $\quad$ $Ax + By > C$

Big Idea 3

Writing Linear Equations and Inequalities in Two Variables

Form	Equation	Key Facts
Slope-intercept form	$y = mx + b$	The graph is a line with slope m and y-intercept b.
Standard form	$Ax + By = C$	The graph is a line with intercepts $x = \frac{C}{A}$ and $y = \frac{C}{B}$.
Point-slope form	$y - y_1 = m(x - x_1)$	The graph is a line that has slope m and passes through (x_1, y_1).
Direct variation	$y = ax, a \neq 0$	The graph is a line that passes through the origin and has slope a (the constant of variation).
Linear inequality	$Ax + By > C$	The graph is a half-plane with boundary line $Ax + By = C$.

29. ★ **MULTIPLE CHOICE** How would you classify the system?

$$-12x + 16y = 10$$
$$3x + 4y = -6$$

(A) Consistent and independent
(B) Consistent and dependent
(C) Inconsistent
(D) None of these

30. ★ **OPEN-ENDED MATH** Write a system of two linear equations that has the given number of solutions.

a. One solution **b.** No solution **c.** Infinitely many solutions

GRAPH AND CHECK Graph the system and estimate the solution(s). Then check the solution(s) algebraically.

31. $y = |x + 2|$
$y = x$

32. $y = |x - 1|$
$y = -x + 4$

33. $y = |x| - 2$
$y = 2$

34. **CHALLENGE** State the conditions on the constants a, b, c, and d for which the system below is **(a)** consistent and independent, **(b)** consistent and dependent, and **(c)** inconsistent.

$$y = ax + b$$
$$y = cx + d$$

PROBLEM SOLVING

EXAMPLE 4
on p. 155
for Exs. 35–39

35. **WORK SCHEDULE** You worked 14 hours last week and earned a total of \$96 before taxes. Your job as a lifeguard pays \$8 per hour, and your job as a cashier pays \$6 per hour. How many hours did you work at each job?

@HomeTutor for problem solving help at classzone.com

36. **LAW ENFORCEMENT** During one calendar year, a state trooper issued a total of 375 citations for warnings and speeding tickets. Of these, there were 37 more warnings than speeding tickets. How many warnings and how many speeding tickets were issued?

@HomeTutor for problem solving help at classzone.com

37. ★ **SHORT RESPONSE** A gym offers two options for membership plans. Option A includes an initiation fee of \$121 and costs \$1 per day. Option B has no initiation fee but costs \$12 per day. After how many days will the total costs of the gym membership plans be equal? How does your answer change if the daily cost of Option B increases? *Explain.*

38. **MULTIPLE REPRESENTATIONS** The price of refrigerator A is \$600, and the price of refrigerator B is \$1200. The cost of electricity needed to operate the refrigerators is \$50 per year for refrigerator A and \$40 per year for refrigerator B.

a. Writing Equations Write an equation for the cost of owning refrigerator A and an equation for the cost of owning refrigerator B.

b. Graphing Equations Graph the equations from part (a). After how many years are the total costs of owning the refrigerators equal?

c. Checking Reasonableness Is your solution from part (b) reasonable in this situation? *Explain.*

39. ★ **EXTENDED RESPONSE** The table below gives the winning times (in seconds) in the Olympic 100 meter freestyle swimming event for the period 1972–2000.

Years since 1972, x	0	4	8	12	16	20	24	28
Men's time, m	51.2	50.0	50.4	49.8	48.6	49.0	48.7	48.3
Women's time, w	58.6	55.7	54.8	55.9	54.9	54.6	54.4	53.8

a. Use a graphing calculator to fit a line to the data pairs (x, m).

b. Use a graphing calculator to fit a line to the data pairs (x, w).

c. Graph the lines and predict when the women's performance will catch up to the men's performance.

d. Do you think your prediction from part (c) is reasonable? *Explain.*

40. **CHALLENGE** Your house and your friend's house are both on a street that passes by a park, as shown below.

At 1:00 P.M., you and your friend leave your houses on bicycles and head toward the park. You travel at a speed of 25 feet per second, and your friend also travels at a constant speed. You both reach the park at the same time.

a. Write and graph an equation giving your distance d (in feet) from the park after t seconds.

b. At what speed does your friend travel to the park? *Explain* how you found your answer.

c. Write an equation giving your friend's distance d (in feet) from the park after t seconds. Graph the equation in the same coordinate plane you used for part (a).

NEW YORK MIXED REVIEW

TEST PRACTICE at classzone.com

41. A realtor earns a base salary of \$31,000 plus 2.5% of the value of any real estate sold. Which equation best represents the realtor's total salary, s, in terms of the value, x, of the real estate sold?

Ⓐ $s = 31{,}000 - 0.025x$
Ⓑ $s = 31{,}000x + 0.025$
Ⓒ $s = 31{,}000 + 0.025x$
Ⓓ $s = 31{,}000 + 2.5x$

42. In $\triangle MNP$, the measure of $\angle M$ is 40°. The measure of $\angle N$ is four times the measure of $\angle P$. What is $m\angle P$?

Ⓐ 28° Ⓑ 35° Ⓒ 45° Ⓓ 112°

Graphing Calculator **ACTIVITY** *Use after Lesson 3.1*

@HomeTutor
classzone.com
Keystrokes

3.1 Graph Systems of Equations

QUESTION **How can you solve a system of linear equations using a graphing calculator?**

In Lesson 3.1, you learned to *estimate* the solution of a linear system by graphing. You can use the *intersect* feature of a graphing calculator to get an answer that is very close to, and sometimes *exactly* equal to, the actual solution.

EXAMPLE **Solve a system**

Use a graphing calculator to solve the system.

$6x - 9y = -20$ **Equation 1**
$2x + 4y = -52$ **Equation 2**

STEP 1 ***Enter equations***

Solve each equation for y. Then enter the revised equations into a graphing calculator.

```
Y1=(2/3)X+(20/9)
Y2=-(1/2)X-13
Y3=
Y4=
Y5=
Y6=
Y7=
```

STEP 2 ***Graph equations***

Graph the equations in the standard viewing window.

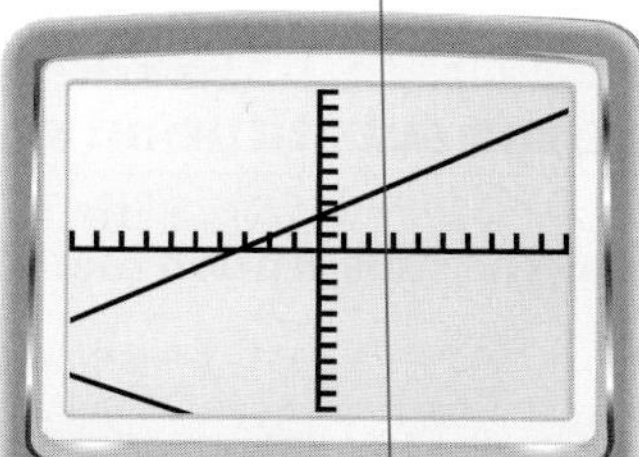

STEP 3 ***Find the solution***

Adjust the viewing window, and use the *intersect* feature to find the intersection point.

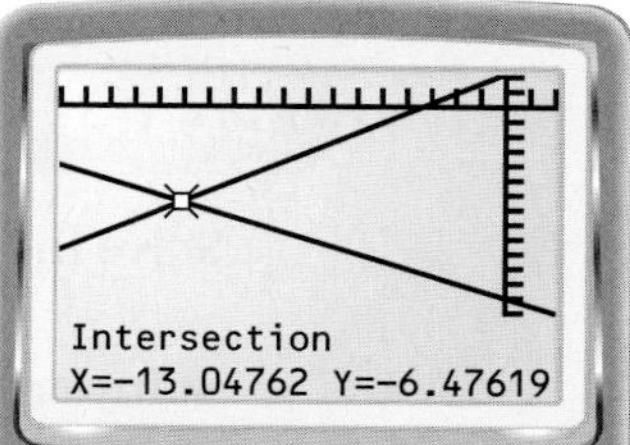

▶ The solution is about (−13.05, −6.48).

PRACTICE

Solve the linear system using a graphing calculator.

1. $y = -x + 2$
$y = 2x - 5$

2. $y = -2x + 15$
$y = 5x - 4$

3. $-9x + 7y = 14$
$-3x + y = -17$

4. $-11x - 6y = -6$
$4x + 2y = 10$

5. $5x + 8y = -48$
$x + 3y = 27$

6. $-2x + 16y = 56$
$4x + 7y = -35$

7. **VACATION** Your family is planning a 7 day trip to Texas. You estimate that it will cost \$275 per day in San Antonio and \$400 per day in Dallas. Your budget for the 7 days is \$2300. How many days should you spend in each city?

8. **MOVIE TICKETS** In one day, a movie theater collected \$4600 from 800 people. The price of admission is \$7 for an adult and \$5 for a child. How many adults and how many children were admitted to the movie theater that day?

3.2 Solve Linear Systems Algebraically

Before You solved linear systems graphically.

Now You will solve linear systems algebraically.

Why? So you can model guitar sales, as in Ex. 55.

Key Vocabulary
- **substitution method**
- **elimination method**

In this lesson, you will study two algebraic methods for solving linear systems. The first method is called the **substitution method**.

KEY CONCEPT — *For Your Notebook*

The Substitution Method

STEP 1 **Solve** one of the equations for one of its variables.

STEP 2 **Substitute** the expression from Step 1 into the other equation and solve for the other variable.

STEP 3 **Substitute** the value from Step 2 into the revised equation from Step 1 and solve.

EXAMPLE 1 Use the substitution method

Solve the system using the substitution method.

$2x + 5y = -5$ **Equation 1**

$x + 3y = 3$ **Equation 2**

Solution

STEP 1 **Solve** Equation 2 for x.

$x = -3y + 3$ **Revised Equation 2**

STEP 2 **Substitute** the expression for x into Equation 1 and solve for y.

$2x + 5y = -5$ **Write Equation 1.**

$2(-3y + 3) + 5y = -5$ **Substitute $-3y + 3$ for x.**

$y = 11$ **Solve for y.**

STEP 3 **Substitute** the value of y into revised Equation 2 and solve for x.

$x = -3y + 3$ **Write revised Equation 2.**

$x = -3(11) + 3$ **Substitute 11 for y.**

$x = -30$ **Simplify.**

▶ The solution is $(-30, 11)$.

CHECK Check the solution by substituting into the original equations.

$2(-30) + 5(11) \stackrel{?}{=} -5$ **Substitute for x and y.** $-30 + 3(11) \stackrel{?}{=} 3$

$-5 = -5$ ✓ **Solution checks.** $3 = 3$ ✓

ELIMINATION METHOD Another algebraic method that you can use to solve a system of equations is the **elimination method**. The goal of this method is to eliminate one of the variables by adding equations.

KEY CONCEPT — *For Your Notebook*

The Elimination Method

STEP 1 **Multiply** one or both of the equations by a constant to obtain coefficients that differ only in sign for one of the variables.

STEP 2 **Add** the revised equations from Step 1. Combining like terms will eliminate one of the variables. Solve for the remaining variable.

STEP 3 **Substitute** the value obtained in Step 2 into either of the original equations and solve for the other variable.

EXAMPLE 2 Use the elimination method

Solve the system using the elimination method.

$3x - 7y = 10$ **Equation 1**
$6x - 8y = 8$ **Equation 2**

Solution

STEP 1 **Multiply** Equation 1 by **−2** so that the coefficients of x differ only in sign.

$3x - 7y = 10$ → × −2 → $-6x + 14y = -20$
$6x - 8y = 8$ → $6x - 8y = 8$

STEP 2 **Add** the revised equations and solve for y.

$6y = -12$
$y = -2$

STEP 3 **Substitute** the value of y into one of the original equations. Solve for x.

$3x - 7y = 10$ **Write Equation 1.**

$3x - 7(-2) = 10$ **Substitute −2 for *y*.**

$3x + 14 = 10$ **Simplify.**

$x = -\frac{4}{3}$ **Solve for *x*.**

▸ The solution is $\left(-\frac{4}{3}, -2\right)$.

SOLVE SYSTEMS In Example 2, one coefficient of x is a multiple of the other. In this case, it is easier to eliminate the x-terms because you need to multiply only one equation by a constant.

CHECK You can check the solution algebraically using the method shown in Example 1. You can also use a graphing calculator to check the solution.

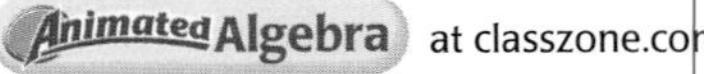

at classzone.com

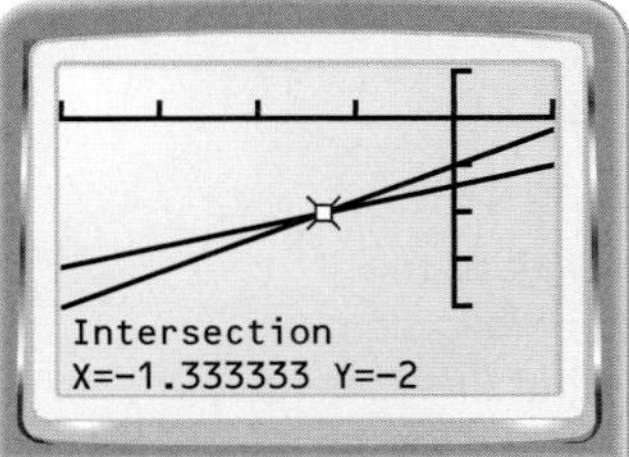

GUIDED PRACTICE for Examples 1 and 2

Solve the system using the substitution or the elimination method.

1. $4x + 3y = -2$
   $x + 5y = -9$

2. $3x + 3y = -15$
   $5x - 9y = 3$

3. $3x - 6y = 9$
   $-4x + 7y = -16$

EXAMPLE 3 Standardized Test Practice

To raise money for new football uniforms, your school sells silk-screened T-shirts. Short sleeve T-shirts cost the school \$5 each and are sold for \$8 each. Long sleeve T-shirts cost the school \$7 each and are sold for \$12 each. The school spends a total of \$2500 on T-shirts and sells all of them for \$4200. How many of the short sleeve T-shirts are sold?

Ⓐ 50 Ⓑ 100 Ⓒ 150 Ⓓ 250

Solution

STEP 1 **Write** verbal models for this situation.

Equation 1

Short sleeve cost (dollars/shirt)	•	Short sleeve shirts (shirts)	+	Long sleeve cost (dollars/shirt)	•	Long sleeve shirts (shirts)	=	Total cost (dollars)
5	•	x	+	**7**	•	y	=	**2500**

Equation 2

STEP 2 **Write** a system of equations.

Equation 1	$5x + 7y = 2500$	**Total cost for all T-shirts**
Equation 2	$8x + 12y = 4200$	**Total revenue from all T-shirts sold**

STEP 3 **Solve** the system using the elimination method.

Multiply Equation 1 by **−8** and Equation 2 by **5** so that the coefficients of x differ only in sign.

$5x + 7y = 2500$ → **× −8** → $-40x - 56y = -20{,}000$

$8x + 12y = 4200$ → **× 5** → $40x + 60y = 21{,}000$

Add the revised equations and solve for y.

$$4y = 1000$$
$$y = 250$$

Substitute the value of y into one of the original equations and solve for x.

$5x + 7y = 2500$	**Write Equation 1.**
$5x + 7(250) = 2500$	**Substitute 250 for *y*.**
$5x + 1750 = 2500$	**Simplify.**
$x = 150$	**Solve for *x*.**

The school sold 150 short sleeve T-shirts and 250 long sleeve T-shirts.

▸ The correct answer is C. Ⓐ Ⓑ Ⓒ Ⓓ

AVOID ERRORS

Choice D gives the number of *long* sleeve T-shirts, but the question asks for the number of *short* sleeve T-shirts. So you still need to solve for x in Step 3.

✓ GUIDED PRACTICE for Example 3

4. **WHAT IF?** In Example 3, suppose the school spends a total of \$3715 on T-shirts and sells all of them for \$6160. How many of each type of T-shirt are sold?

CHOOSING A METHOD In general, the substitution method is convenient when one of the variables in a system of equations has a coefficient of 1 or −1, as in Example 1. If neither variable in a system has a coefficient of 1 or −1, it is usually easier to use the elimination method, as in Examples 2 and 3.

EXAMPLE 4 Solve linear systems with many or no solutions

Solve the linear system.

a. $x - 2y = 4$
$3x - 6y = 8$

b. $4x - 10y = 8$
$-14x + 35y = -28$

Solution

a. Because the coefficient of x in the first equation is 1, use the substitution method.

Solve the first equation for x.

$x - 2y = 4$ **Write first equation.**

$x = 2y + 4$ **Solve for x.**

Substitute the expression for x into the second equation.

$3x - 6y = 8$ **Write second equation.**

$3(2y + 4) - 6y = 8$ **Substitute $2y + 4$ for x.**

$12 = 8$ **Simplify.**

▶ Because the statement $12 = 8$ is never true, there is *no solution*.

b. Because no coefficient is 1 or −1, use the elimination method.

AVOID ERRORS
When multiplying an equation by a constant, make sure you multiply each term of the equation by the constant.

Multiply the first equation by **7** and the second equation by **2**.

$4x - 10y = 8$ → × 7 → $28x - 70y = 56$

$-14x + 35y = -28$ → × 2 → $-28x + 70y = -56$

Add the revised equations. $0 = 0$

▶ Because the equation $0 = 0$ is always true, there are *infinitely many solutions*.

✓ GUIDED PRACTICE for Example 4

Solve the linear system using any algebraic method.

5. $12x - 3y = -9$
$-4x + y = 3$

6. $6x + 15y = -12$
$-2x - 5y = 9$

7. $5x + 3y = 20$
$-x - \frac{3}{5}y = -4$

8. $12x - 2y = 21$
$3x + 12y = -4$

9. $8x + 9y = 15$
$5x - 2y = 17$

10. $5x + 5y = 5$
$5x + 3y = 4.2$

3.2 EXERCISES

HOMEWORK KEY

○ = **WORKED-OUT SOLUTIONS** on p. WS5 for Exs. 5, 29, and 59

★ = **STANDARDIZED TEST PRACTICE** Exs. 2, 40, 50, 57, 58, and 60

SKILL PRACTICE

1. **VOCABULARY** Copy and complete: To solve a linear system where one of the coefficients is 1 or -1, it is usually easiest to use the _?_ method.

2. ★ **WRITING** *Explain* how to use the elimination method to solve a linear system.

EXAMPLES 1 and 4 on pp. 160–163 for Exs. 3–14

SUBSTITUTION METHOD **Solve the system using the substitution method.**

3. $2x + 5y = 7$; $x + 4y = 2$
4. $3x + y = 16$; $2x - 3y = -4$
5. $6x - 2y = 5$; $-3x + y = 7$
6. $x + 4y = 1$; $3x + 2y = -12$
7. $3x - y = 2$; $6x + 3y = 14$
8. $3x - 4y = -5$; $-x + 3y = -5$
9. $3x + 2y = 6$; $x - 4y = -12$
10. $6x - 3y = 15$; $-2x + y = -5$
11. $3x + y = -1$; $2x + 3y = 18$
12. $2x - y = 1$; $8x + 4y = 6$
13. $3x + 7y = 13$; $x + 3y = -7$
14. $2x + 5y = 10$; $-3x + y = 36$

EXAMPLES 2 and 4 on pp. 161–163 for Exs. 15–27

ELIMINATION METHOD **Solve the system using the elimination method.**

15. $2x + 6y = 17$; $2x - 10y = 9$
16. $4x - 2y = -16$; $-3x + 4y = 12$
17. $3x - 4y = -10$; $6x + 3y = -42$
18. $4x - 3y = 10$; $8x - 6y = 20$
19. $5x - 3y = -3$; $2x + 6y = 0$
20. $10x - 2y = 16$; $5x + 3y = -12$
21. $2x + 5y = 14$; $3x - 2y = -36$
22. $7x + 2y = 11$; $-2x + 3y = 29$
23. $3x + 4y = 18$; $6x + 8y = 18$
24. $2x + 5y = 13$; $6x + 2y = -13$
25. $4x - 5y = 13$; $6x + 2y = 48$
26. $6x - 4y = 14$; $2x + 8y = 21$

27. **ERROR ANALYSIS** *Describe* and correct the error in the first step of solving the system.

$$3x + 2y = 7$$
$$5x + 4y = 15$$

$$-6x - 4y = 7$$
$$5x + 4y = 15$$
$$-x = 22$$
$$x = -22$$

CHOOSING A METHOD **Solve the system using any algebraic method.**

28. $3x + 2y = 11$; $4x + y = -2$
29. $2x - 3y = 8$; $-4x + 5y = -10$
30. $3x + 7y = -1$; $2x + 3y = 6$
31. $4x - 10y = 18$; $-2x + 5y = -9$
32. $3x - y = -2$; $5x + 2y = 15$
33. $x + 2y = -8$; $3x - 4y = -24$
34. $2x + 3y = -6$; $3x - 4y = 25$
35. $3x + y = 15$; $-x + 2y = -19$
36. $4x - 3y = 8$; $-8x + 6y = 16$
37. $4x - y = -10$; $6x + 2y = -1$
38. $7x + 5y = -12$; $3x - 4y = 1$
39. $2x + y = -1$; $-4x + 6y = 6$

40. ★ **MULTIPLE CHOICE** What is the solution of the linear system?

$$3x + 2y = 4$$
$$6x - 3y = -27$$

Ⓐ $(-2, -5)$ Ⓑ $(-2, 5)$ Ⓒ $(2, -5)$ Ⓓ $(2, 5)$

GEOMETRY Find the coordinates of the point where the diagonals of the quadrilateral intersect.

41. 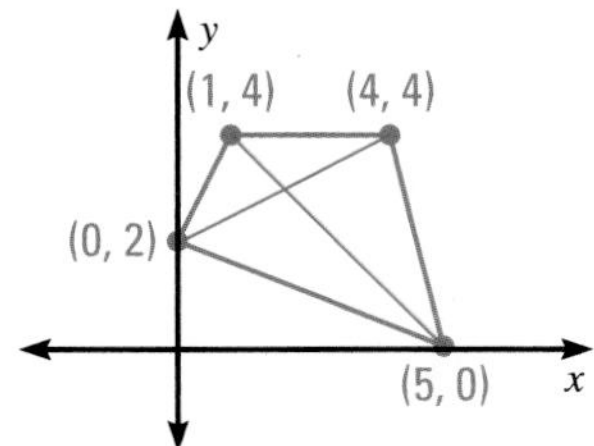

42. 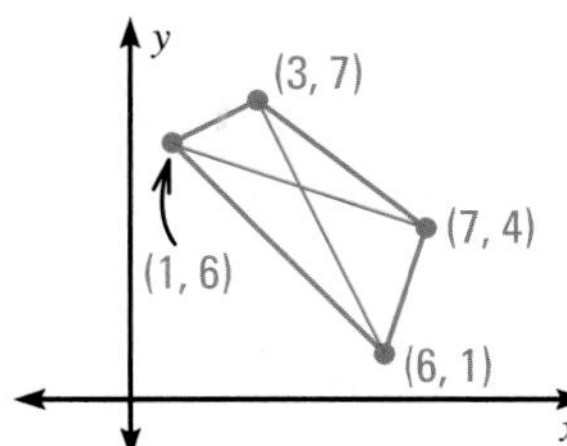

43. 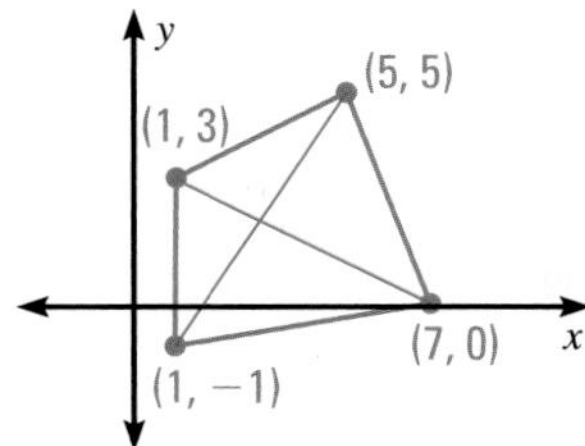

SOLVING LINEAR SYSTEMS Solve the system using any algebraic method.

44. $0.02x - 0.05y = -0.38$
$0.03x + 0.04y = 1.04$

45. $0.05x - 0.03y = 0.21$
$0.07x + 0.02y = 0.16$

46. $\frac{2}{3}x + 3y = -34$
$x - \frac{1}{2}y = -1$

47. $\frac{1}{2}x + \frac{2}{3}y = \frac{5}{6}$
$\frac{5}{12}x + \frac{7}{12}y = \frac{3}{4}$

48. $\frac{x+3}{4} + \frac{y-1}{3} = 1$
$2x - y = 12$

49. $\frac{x-1}{2} + \frac{y+2}{3} = 4$
$x - 2y = 5$

50. ★ **OPEN-ENDED MATH** Write a system of linear equations that has $(-1, 4)$ as its only solution. Verify that $(-1, 4)$ is a solution using either the substitution method or the elimination method.

SOLVING NONLINEAR SYSTEMS Use the elimination method to solve the system.

51. $7y + 18xy = 30$
$13y - 18xy = 90$

52. $xy - x = 14$
$5 - xy = 2x$

53. $2xy + y = 44$
$32 - xy = 3y$

54. **CHALLENGE** Find values of r, s, and t that produce the indicated solution(s).

$$-3x - 5y = 9$$
$$rx + sy = t$$

a. No solution **b.** Infinitely many solutions **c.** A solution of $(2, -3)$

PROBLEM SOLVING

EXAMPLE 3 on p. 162 for Exs. 55–59

55. **GUITAR SALES** In one week, a music store sold 9 guitars for a total of \$3611. Electric guitars sold for \$479 each and acoustic guitars sold for \$339 each. How many of each type of guitar were sold?

@HomeTutor for problem solving help at classzone.com

56. **COUNTY FAIR** An adult pass for a county fair costs \$2 more than a children's pass. When 378 adult and 214 children's passes were sold, the total revenue was \$2384. Find the cost of an adult pass.

@HomeTutor for problem solving help at classzone.com

57. ★ **SHORT RESPONSE** A company produces gas mowers and electric mowers at two factories. The company has orders for 2200 gas mowers and 1400 electric mowers. The production capacity of each factory (in mowers per week) is shown in the table.

	Factory A	Factory B
Gas mowers	200	400
Electric mowers	100	300

Describe how the company can fill its orders by operating the factories simultaneously at full capacity. Write and solve a linear system to support your answer.

58. ★ **MULTIPLE CHOICE** The cost of 11 gallons of regular gasoline and 16 gallons of premium gasoline is $58.55. Premium costs $.20 more per gallon than regular. What is the cost of a gallon of premium gasoline?

Ⓐ $2.05 Ⓑ $2.25 Ⓒ $2.29 Ⓓ $2.55

59. **TABLE TENNIS** One evening, 76 people gathered to play doubles and singles table tennis. There were 26 games in progress at one time. A doubles game requires 4 players and a singles game requires 2 players. How many games of each kind were in progress at one time if all 76 people were playing?

60. ★ **EXTENDED RESPONSE** A local hospital is holding a two day marathon walk to raise funds for a new research facility. The total distance of the marathon is 26.2 miles. On the first day, Martha starts walking at 10:00 A.M. She walks 4 miles per hour. Carol starts two hours later than Martha but decides to run to catch up to Martha. Carol runs at a speed of 6 miles per hour.

a. Write an equation to represent the distance Martha travels.

b. Write an equation to represent the distance Carol travels.

c. Solve the system of equations to find when Carol will catch up to Martha.

d. Carol wants to reduce the time she takes to catch up to Martha by 1 hour. How can she do this by changing her starting time? How can she do this by changing her speed? *Explain* whether your answers are reasonable.

61. **BUSINESS** A nut wholesaler sells a mix of peanuts and cashews. The wholesaler charges $2.80 per pound for peanuts and $5.30 per pound for cashews. The mix is to sell for $3.30 per pound. How many pounds of peanuts and how many pounds of cashews should be used to make 100 pounds of the mix?

62. **AVIATION** Flying with the wind, a plane flew 1000 miles in 5 hours. Flying against the wind, the plane could fly only 500 miles in the same amount of time. Find the speed of the plane in calm air and the speed of the wind.

63. **CHALLENGE** For a recent job, an electrician earned $50 per hour, and the electrician's apprentice earned $20 per hour. The electrician worked 4 hours more than the apprentice, and together they earned a total of $550. How much money did each person earn?

EXAMPLE 2 Graph a system with no solution

Graph the system of inequalities.

$2x + 3y < 6$ **Inequality 1**

$y \geq -\frac{2}{3}x + 4$ **Inequality 2**

Solution

STEP 1 **Graph** each inequality in the system. Use red for $2x + 3y < 6$ and blue for $y \geq -\frac{2}{3}x + 4$.

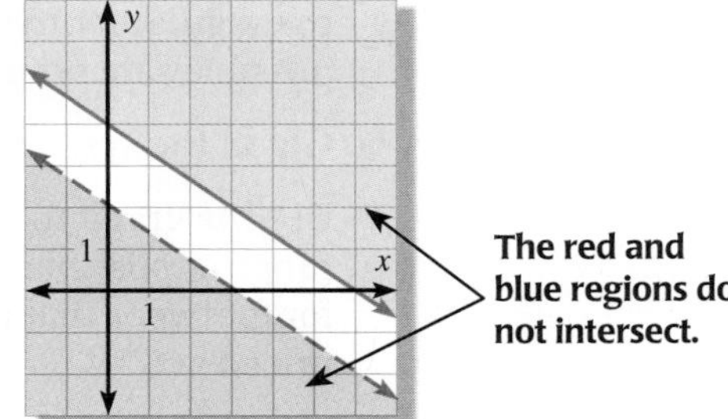

STEP 2 **Identify** the region that is common to both graphs. There is no region shaded both red and blue. So, the system has no solution.

EXAMPLE 3 Graph a system with an absolute value inequality

Graph the system of inequalities.

$y \leq 3$ **Inequality 1**

$y > |x + 4|$ **Inequality 2**

REVIEW ABSOLUTE VALUE
For help with graphing absolute value inequalities, see p. 132.

Solution

STEP 1 **Graph** each inequality in the system. Use red for $y \leq 3$ and blue for $y > |x + 4|$.

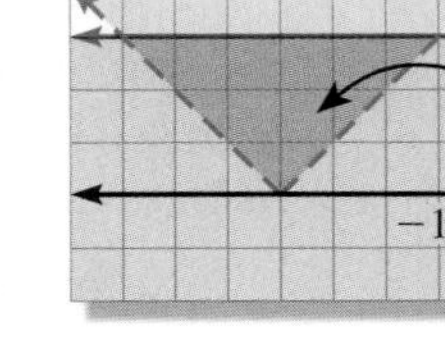

STEP 2 **Identify** the region that is common to both graphs. It is the region that is shaded **purple**.

✓ GUIDED PRACTICE for Examples 1, 2, and 3

Graph the system of inequalities.

1. $y \leq 3x - 2$
   $y > -x + 4$
2. $2x - \frac{1}{2}y \geq 4$
   $4x - y \leq 5$
3. $x + y > -3$
   $-6x + y < 1$
4. $y \leq 4$
   $y \geq |x - 5|$
5. $y > -2$
   $y \leq -|x + 2|$
6. $y \geq 2|x + 1|$
   $y < x + 1$

SYSTEMS OF THREE OR MORE INEQUALITIES You can also graph a system of three or more linear inequalities, as shown in Example 4.

EXAMPLE 4 Solve a multi-step problem

SHOPPING A discount shoe store is having a sale, as described in the advertisement shown.

- Use the information in the ad to write a system of inequalities for the regular footwear prices and possible sale prices.
- Graph the system of inequalities.
- Use the graph to estimate the range of possible sale prices for footwear that is regularly priced at $70.

Solution

STEP 1 **Write** a system of inequalities. Let x be the regular footwear price and let y be the sale price. From the information in the ad, you can write the following four inequalities.

$x \geq 20$ **Regular price must be at least $20.**

$x \leq 80$ **Regular price can be at most $80.**

$y \geq 0.4x$ **Sale price is at least (100 − 60)% = 40% of regular price.**

$y \leq 0.9x$ **Sale price is at most (100 − 10)% = 90% of regular price.**

STEP 2 **Graph** each inequality in the system. Then identify the region that is common to all the graphs. It is the region that is shaded.

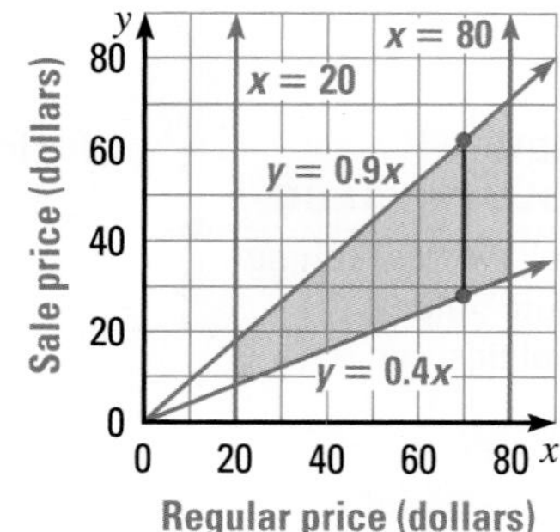

STEP 3 **Identify** the range of possible sale prices for $70 footwear. From the graph you can see that when $x = 70$, the value of y is between these values:

$$0.4(70) = 28 \text{ and } 0.9(70) = 63$$

So, the value of y satisfies $28 \leq y \leq 63$.

▸ Therefore, footwear regularly priced at $70 sells for between $28 and $63, inclusive, during the sale.

✓ GUIDED PRACTICE for Example 4

7. **WHAT IF?** In Example 4, suppose the advertisement showed a range of discounts of 20%–50% and a range of regular prices of $40–$100.
   a. Write and graph a system of inequalities for the regular footwear prices and possible sale prices.
   b. Use the graph to estimate the range of possible sale prices for footwear that is regularly priced at $60.

3.3 EXERCISES

HOMEWORK KEY

○ = **WORKED-OUT SOLUTIONS** on p. WS5 for Exs. 9, 19, and 37

★ = **STANDARDIZED TEST PRACTICE** Exs. 2, 3, 26, 27, 36, and 39

◆ = **MULTIPLE REPRESENTATIONS** Ex. 37

SKILL PRACTICE

1. **VOCABULARY** What must be true in order for an ordered pair to be a solution of a system of linear inequalities?

2. ★ **WRITING** *Describe* how to graph a system of linear inequalities.

EXAMPLES 1, 2, and 3 on pp. 168–169 for Exs. 3–16

3. ★ **MULTIPLE CHOICE** Which system of inequalities is represented by the graph?

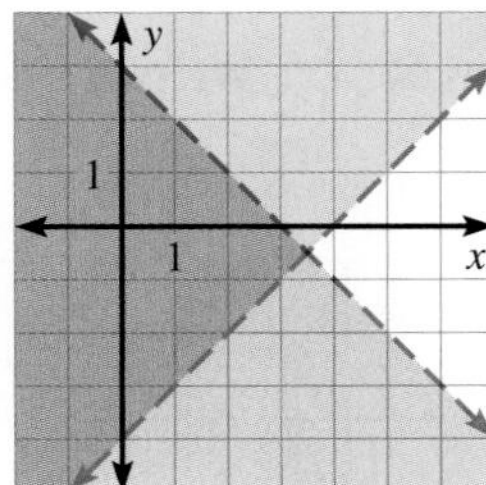

Ⓐ $x + y > 3$
$-x + y < -4$

Ⓑ $-x + y \geq -4$
$x + y \leq 3$

Ⓒ $-2x + y > -4$
$2x + y < 3$

Ⓓ $-x + y > -4$
$x + y < 3$

SYSTEMS OF TWO INEQUALITIES **Graph the system of inequalities.**

4. $x > -1$
$x < 3$

5. $x \leq 2$
$y \leq 5$

6. $y \geq 5$
$y \leq 1$

7. $-x + y < -3$
$-x + y > 4$

8. $y < 10$
$y > |x|$

9. $4x - 4y \geq -16$
$-x + 2y \geq -4$

10. $-x \geq y$
$-x + y \geq -5$

11. $y > |x| - 4$
$3y < -2x + 9$

12. $x + y \geq -3$
$-6x + 4y < 14$

13. $2y < -5x - 10$
$5x + 2y > -2$

14. $3x - y > 12$
$-x + 8y > -4$

15. $x - 4y \leq -10$
$y \leq 3|x - 1|$

16. **ERROR ANALYSIS** *Describe* and correct the error in graphing the system of inequalities.

$y \geq -3$
$y \leq 2x - 2$

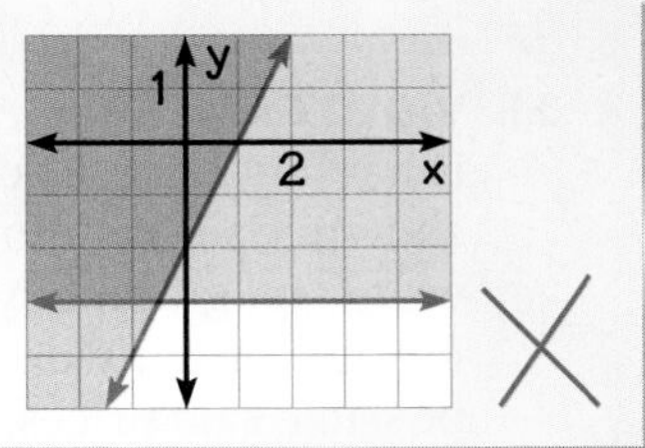

EXAMPLE 4 on p. 170 for Exs. 17–25

SYSTEMS OF THREE OR MORE INEQUALITIES **Graph the system of inequalities.**

17. $x < 6$
$y > -1$
$y < x$

18. $x \geq -8$
$y \leq -1$
$y < -2x - 4$

19. $3x + 2y > -6$
$-5x + 2y > -2$
$y < 5$

20. $x + y < 5$
$2x - y > 0$
$-x + 5y > -20$

21. $x \geq 2$
$-3x + y < -1$
$4x + 3y < 12$

22. $y \geq x$
$x + 3y < 5$
$2x + y \geq -3$

23. $y \geq 0$
$x > 3$
$x + y \geq -2$
$y < 4x$

24. $x + y < 5$
$x + y > -5$
$x - y < 4$
$x - y > -2$

25. $x \leq 10$
$x \geq -2$
$3x + 2y < 6$
$6x + 4y > -12$

26. ★ **MULTIPLE CHOICE** Which quadrant of the coordinate plane contains no solutions of the system of inequalities?

$$y \le -|x - 3| + 2$$
$$4x - 5y \le 20$$

Ⓐ Quadrant I Ⓑ Quadrant II Ⓒ Quadrant III Ⓓ Quadrant IV

27. ★ **OPEN-ENDED MATH** Write a system of two linear inequalities that has (2, −1) as a solution.

ABSOLUTE VALUE SYSTEMS **Graph the system of inequalities.**

28. $y < |x|$
$y > -|x|$

29. $y \le |x - 2|$
$y \ge |x| - 2$

30. $y \le -|x - 3| + 2$
$y > |x - 3| - 1$

CHALLENGE **Write a system of linear inequalities for the shaded region.**

31. 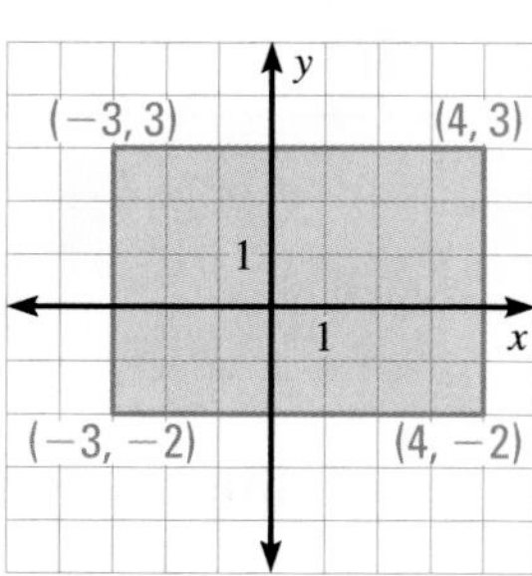

32. 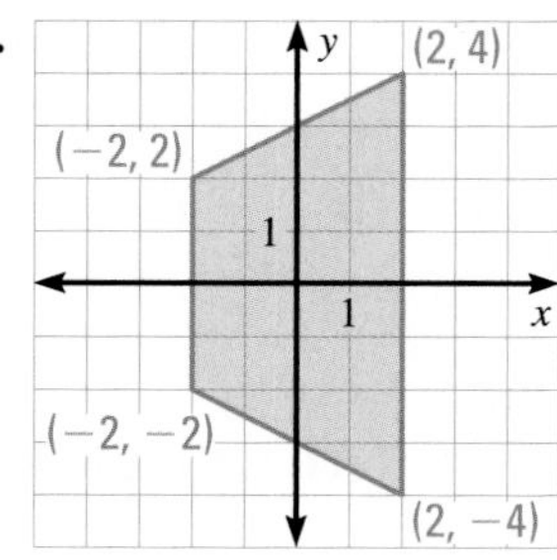

33. 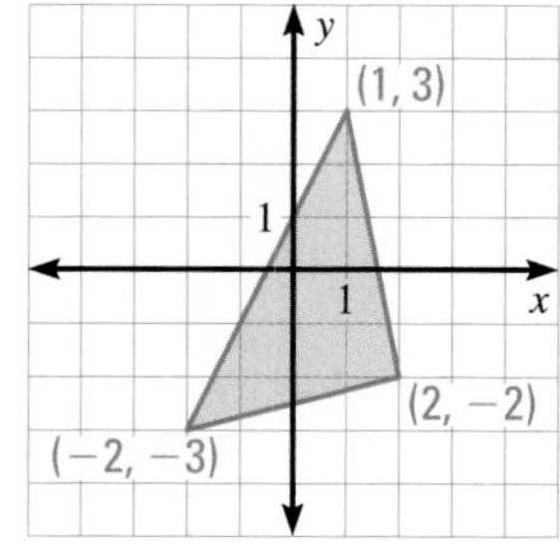

PROBLEM SOLVING

EXAMPLE 4
on p. 170
for Exs. 34–39

34. **SUMMER JOBS** You can work at most 20 hours next week. You need to earn at least \$92 to cover your weekly expenses. Your dog-walking job pays \$7.50 per hour and your job as a car wash attendant pays \$6 per hour. Write a system of linear inequalities to model the situation.

@HomeTutor for problem solving help at classzone.com

35. **VIDEO GAME SALE** An online media store is having a sale, as described in the ad shown. Use the information in the ad to write and graph a system of inequalities for the regular video game prices and possible sale prices. Then use the graph to estimate the range of possible sale prices for games that are regularly priced at \$20.

@HomeTutor for problem solving help at classzone.com

36. ★ **SHORT RESPONSE** A book on the care of tropical fish states that the pH level of the water should be between 8.0 and 8.3 pH units and the temperature of the water should be between 76°F and 80°F. Let x be the pH level and y be the temperature. Write and graph a system of inequalities that describes the proper pH level and temperature of the water. *Compare* this graph to the graph you would obtain if the temperatures were given in degrees Celsius.

37. **MULTIPLE REPRESENTATIONS** The Junior-Senior Prom Committee must consist of 5 to 8 representatives from the junior and senior classes. The committee must include at least 2 juniors and at least 2 seniors. Let x be the number of juniors and y be the number of seniors.

a. **Writing a System** Write a system of inequalities to describe the situation.

b. **Graphing a System** Graph the system you wrote in part (a).

c. **Finding Solutions** Give two possible solutions for the numbers of juniors and seniors on the prom committee.

38. **BASEBALL** In baseball, the strike zone is a rectangle the width of home plate that extends from the batter's knees to a point halfway between the shoulders S and the top T of the uniform pants. The width of home plate is 17 inches. Suppose a batter's knees are 20 inches above the ground and the point halfway between his shoulders and the top of his pants is 42 inches above the ground. Write and graph a system of inequalities that represents the strike zone.

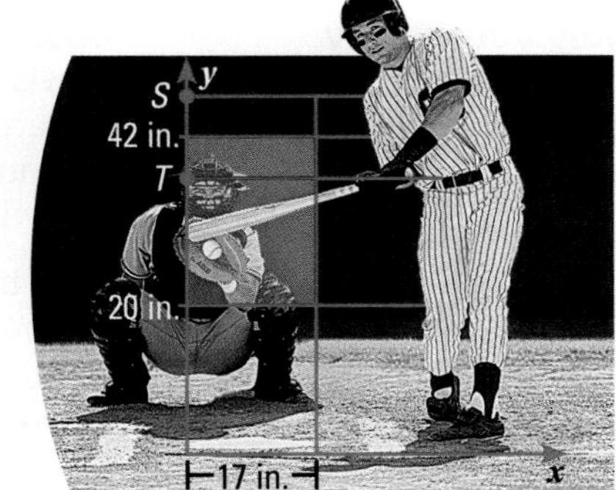

39. ★ **EXTENDED RESPONSE** A person's theoretical maximum heart rate (in heartbeats per minute) is $220 - x$ where x is the person's age in years $(20 \le x \le 65)$. When a person exercises, it is recommended that the person strive for a heart rate that is at least 50% of the maximum and at most 75% of the maximum.

a. Write a system of linear inequalities that describes the given information.

b. Graph the system you wrote in part (a).

c. A 40-year-old person has a heart rate of 158 heartbeats per minute when exercising. Is the person's heart rate in the target zone? *Explain.*

40. **CHALLENGE** You and a friend are trying to guess the number of pennies in a jar. You both agree that the jar contains at least 500 pennies. You guess that there are x pennies, and your friend guesses that there are y pennies. The actual number of pennies in the jar is 1000. Write and graph a system of inequalities describing the values of x and y for which your guess is closer than your friend's guess to the actual number of pennies.

NEW YORK MIXED REVIEW

TEST PRACTICE at classzone.com

41. What is the value of x in the equation $-6(-2x + 1) = -12(x - 3) - 6x$?

Ⓐ -7 Ⓑ $-\frac{7}{5}$ Ⓒ $\frac{7}{5}$ Ⓓ 7

42. Rick enlarges a 4 inch by 6 inch digital photo using his computer. The dimensions of the resulting photo are 175% of the dimensions of the original photo. What are the dimensions of the enlarged photo?

Ⓐ 4.1 in. by 6.15 in. Ⓑ 5.3 in. by 8 in.

Ⓒ 7 in. by 10.5 in. Ⓓ 11 in. by 16.5 in.

Extension

Use after Lesson 3.3

Use Linear Programming

GOAL Solve linear programming problems.

Key Vocabulary
- **constraints**
- **objective function**
- **linear programming**
- **feasible region**

BUSINESS A potter wants to make and sell serving bowls and plates. A bowl uses 5 pounds of clay. A plate uses 4 pounds of clay. The potter has 40 pounds of clay and wants to make at least 4 bowls.

Let x be the number of bowls made and let y be the number of plates made. You can represent the information above using linear inequalities called **constraints**.

$x \geq 4$	Make at least 4 bowls.
$y \geq 0$	Number of plates cannot be negative.
$5x + 4y \leq 40$	Can use up to 40 pounds of clay.

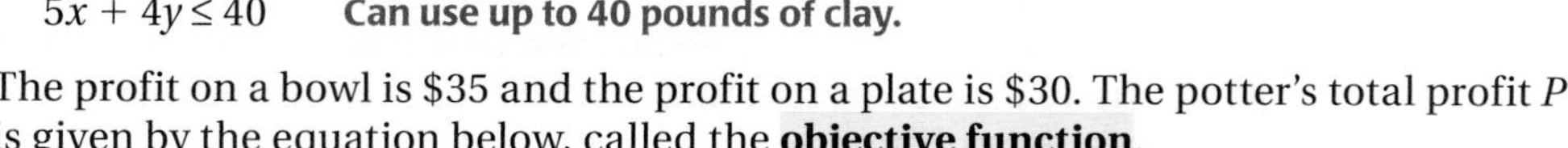

The profit on a bowl is \$35 and the profit on a plate is \$30. The potter's total profit P is given by the equation below, called the **objective function**.

$$P = 35x + 30y$$

It is reasonable for the potter to want to maximize profit subject to the given constraints. The process of maximizing or minimizing a linear objective function subject to constraints that are linear inequalities is called **linear programming**.

If the constraints are graphed, all of the points in the intersection are the combinations of bowls and plates that the potter can make. The intersection of the graphs is called the **feasible region**.

The following result tells you how to determine the optimal solution of a linear programming problem.

READING
A feasible region is *bounded* if it is completely enclosed by line segments.

KEY CONCEPT *For Your Notebook*

Optimal Solution of a Linear Programming Problem

If the feasible region for a linear programming problem is bounded, then the objective function has both a maximum value and a minimum value on the region. Moreover, the maximum and minimum values each occur at a vertex of the feasible region.

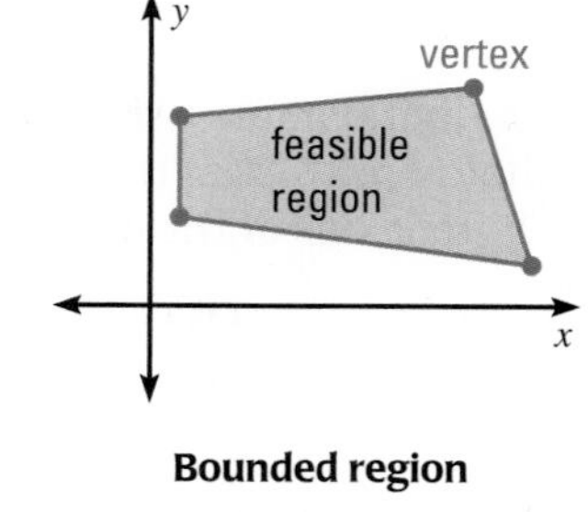

Bounded region

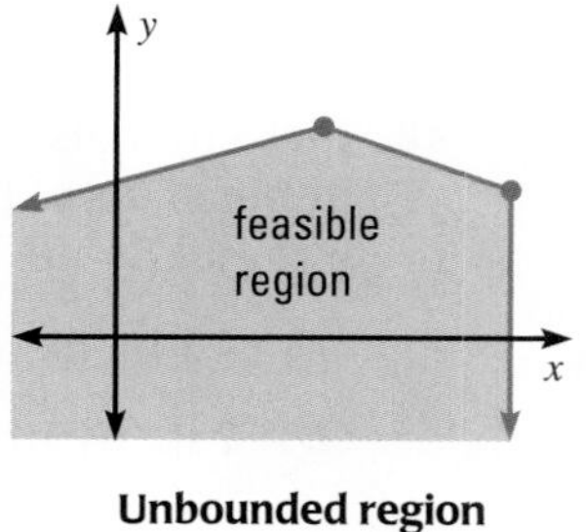

Unbounded region

EXAMPLE 1 Use linear programming to maximize profit

BUSINESS How many bowls and how many plates should the potter described on page 174 make in order to maximize profit?

Solution

STEP 1 **Graph** the system of constraints:

$x \geq 4$	**Make at least 4 bowls.**
$y \geq 0$	**Number of plates cannot be negative.**
$5x + 4y \leq 40$	**Can use up to 40 pounds of clay.**

y
(4, 5)
1
1 (4, 0) (8, 0) x

STEP 2 **Evaluate** the profit function $P = 35x + 30y$ at each vertex of the feasible region.

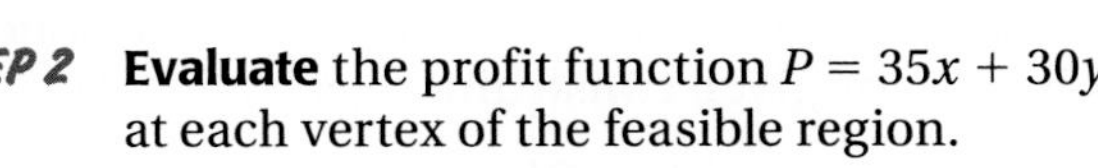

At (4, 0): $P = 35(4) + 30(0) = 140$
At (8, 0): $P = 35(8) + 30(0) = 280$
At (4, 5): $P = 35(4) + 30(5) = 290$ ⟵ **Maximum**

▶ The potter can maximize profit by making 4 bowls and 5 plates.

EXAMPLE 2 Solve a linear programming problem

Find the minimum value and the maximum value of the objective function $C = 4x + 5y$ subject to the following constraints.

$x \geq 0$

$y \geq 0$

$x + 2y \leq 16$

$5x + y \leq 35$

Solution

STEP 1 **Graph** the system of constraints. Find the coordinates of the vertices of the feasible region by solving systems of two linear equations. For example, the solution of the system

$$x + 2y = 16$$
$$5x + y = 35$$

gives the vertex (6, 5). The other three vertices are (0, 0), (7, 0), and (0, 8).

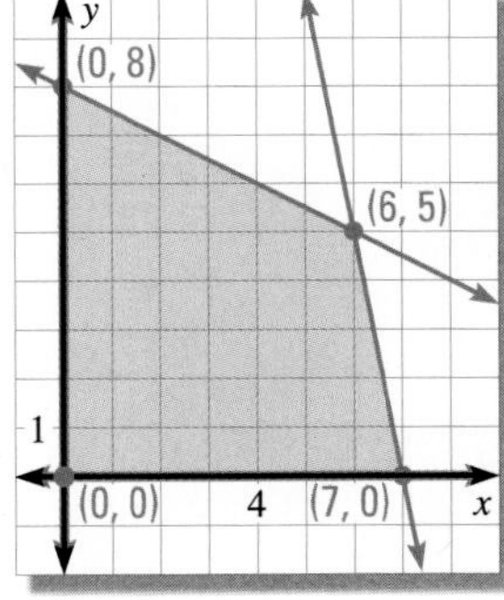

STEP 2 **Evaluate** the function $C = 4x + 5y$ at each of the vertices.

At (0, 0): $C = 4(0) + 5(0) = 0$ ⟵ **Minimum**
At (7, 0): $C = 4(7) + 5(0) = 28$
At (6, 5): $C = 4(6) + 5(5) = 49$ ⟵ **Maximum**
At (0, 8): $C = 4(0) + 5(8) = 40$

▶ The minimum value of C is 0. It occurs when $x = 0$ and $y = 0$.
The maximum value of C is 49. It occurs when $x = 6$ and $y = 5$.

PRACTICE

EXAMPLES 1 and 2 on p. 175 for Exs. 1–9

CHECKING VERTICES **Find the minimum and maximum values of the objective function for the given feasible region.**

1. $C = x + 2y$

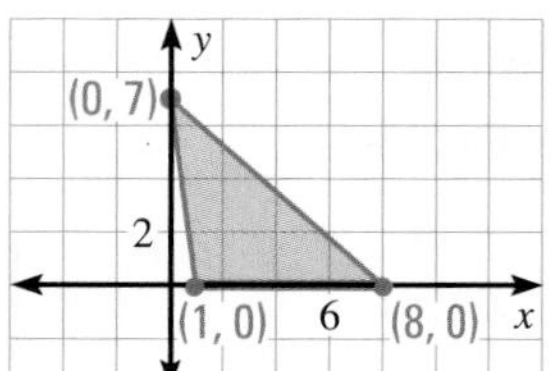

2. $C = 4x - 2y$

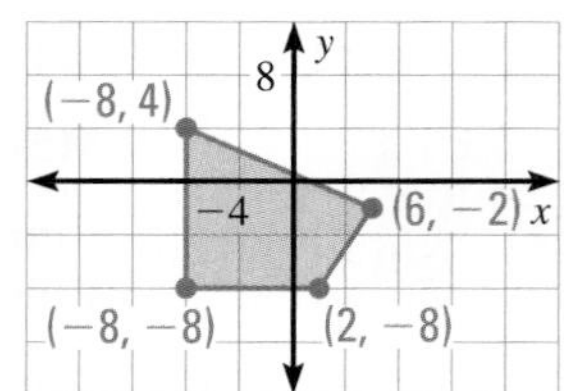

3. $C = 3x + 5y$

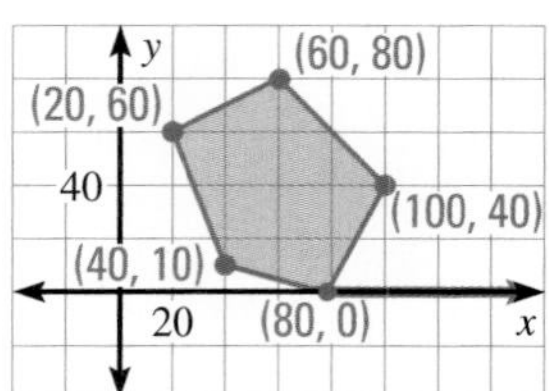

FINDING VALUES **Find the minimum and maximum values of the objective function subject to the given constraints.**

4. **Objective function:**
   $C = 3x + 4y$

   Constraints:
   $x \ge 0$
   $y \ge 0$
   $x + y \le 5$

5. **Objective function:**
   $C = 2x + 5y$

   Constraints:
   $x \le 5$
   $y \ge 3$
   $-3x + 5y \le 30$

6. **Objective function:**
   $C = 3x + y$

   Constraints:
   $x \ge 0$
   $y \ge -2$
   $y \ge -x$
   $x - 4y \ge -16$

7. **CRAFT FAIR** Piñatas are made to sell at a craft fair. It takes 2 hours to make a mini piñata and 3 hours to make a regular-sized piñata. The owner of the craft booth will make a profit of $12 for each mini piñata sold and $24 for each regular-sized piñata sold. If the craft booth owner has no more than 30 hours available to make piñatas and wants to have at least 12 piñatas to sell, how many of each size piñata should be made to maximize profit?

8. **MANUFACTURING** A company manufactures two types of printers, an inkjet printer and a laser printer. The company can make a total of 60 printers per day, and it has 120 labor-hours per day available. It takes 1 labor-hour to make an inkjet printer and 3 labor-hours to make a laser printer. The profit is $40 per inkjet printer and $60 per laser printer. How many of each type of printer should the company make to maximize its daily profit?

9. **FARM STAND SALES** You have 140 tomatoes and 13 onions left over from your garden. You want to use these to make jars of tomato sauce and jars of salsa to sell at a farm stand. A jar of tomato sauce requires 10 tomatoes and 1 onion, and a jar of salsa requires 5 tomatoes and $\frac{1}{4}$ onion. You will make a profit of $2 on every jar of tomato sauce sold and a profit of $1.50 on every jar of salsa sold. The owner of the farm stand wants at least three times as many jars of tomato sauce as jars of salsa. How many jars of each should you make to maximize profit?

10. **CHALLENGE** Consider the objective function $C = 2x + 3y$. Draw a feasible region that satisfies the given condition.

    a. C has a maximum value but no minimum value on the region.

    b. C has a minimum value but no maximum value on the region.

3.4 Graphing Linear Equations in Three Variables

MATERIALS • graph paper • ruler

QUESTION What is the graph of a linear equation in three variables?

A *linear equation in three variables* has the form $ax + by + cz = d$. You can graph this type of equation in a three-dimensional coordinate system formed by three axes that divide space into eight *octants*. Each point in space is represented by an *ordered triple* (x, y, z).

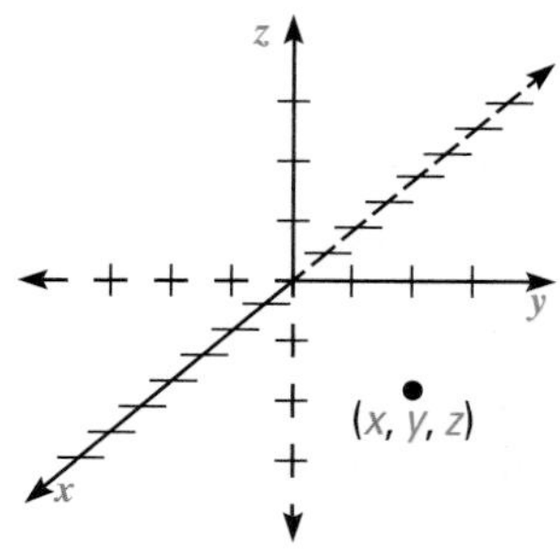

The graph of any equation in three variables is the set of all points (x, y, z) whose coordinates make the equation true. For a linear equation in three variables, the graph is a plane.

EXPLORE Graph $3x + 4y + 6z = 12$

STEP 1 ***Find x-intercept***
Find the x-intercept by setting y and z equal to 0 and solving the resulting equation, $3x = 12$. The x-intercept is 4, so plot $(4, 0, 0)$.

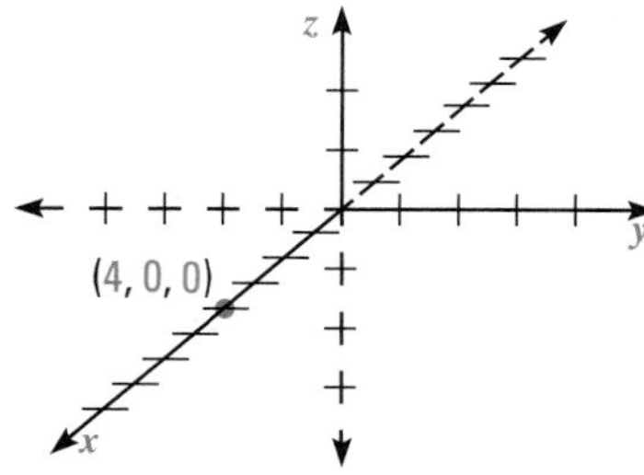

STEP 2 ***Find y-intercept***
Find the y-intercept by setting x and z equal to 0 and solving the resulting equation, $4y = 12$. The y-intercept is 3, so plot $(0, 3, 0)$.

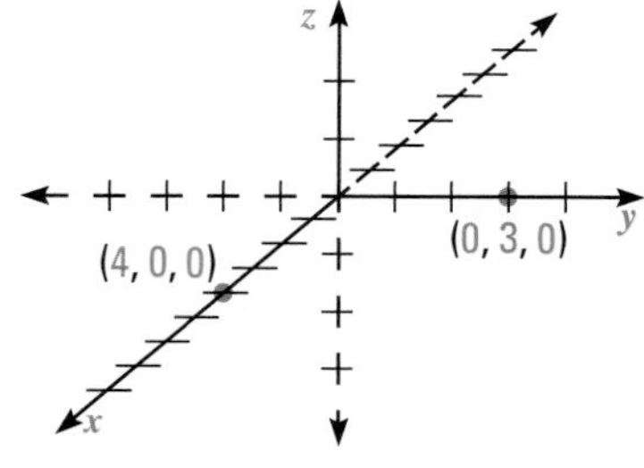

STEP 3 ***Find z-intercept***
Find the z-intercept by setting x and y equal to 0 and solving the resulting equation, $6z = 12$. The z-intercept is 2, so plot $(0, 0, 2)$. Then connect the points.

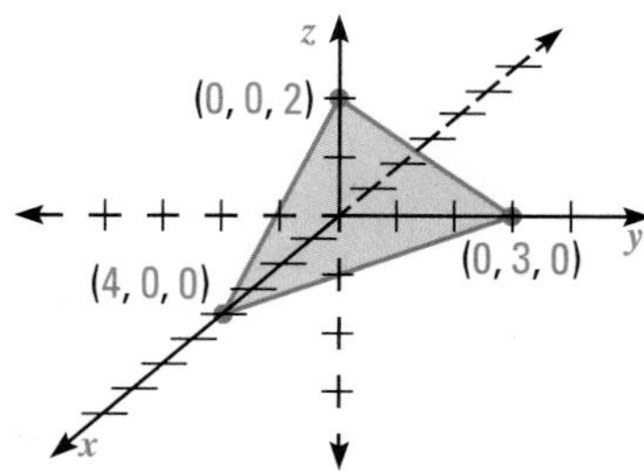

The triangular region shown in Step 3 is the portion of the graph of $3x + 4y + 6z = 12$ that lies in the first octant.

DRAW CONCLUSIONS Use your observations to complete these exercises

Sketch the graph of the equation.

1. $4x + 3y + 2z = 12$
2. $2x + 2y + 3z = 6$
3. $x + 5y + 3z = 15$
4. $5x - y - 2z = 10$
5. $-7x + 7y + 2z = 14$
6. $2x + 9y - 3z = -18$
7. Suppose three linear equations in three variables are graphed in the same coordinate system. In how many different ways can the planes intersect? *Explain* your reasoning.

3.4 Solve Systems of Linear Equations in Three Variables

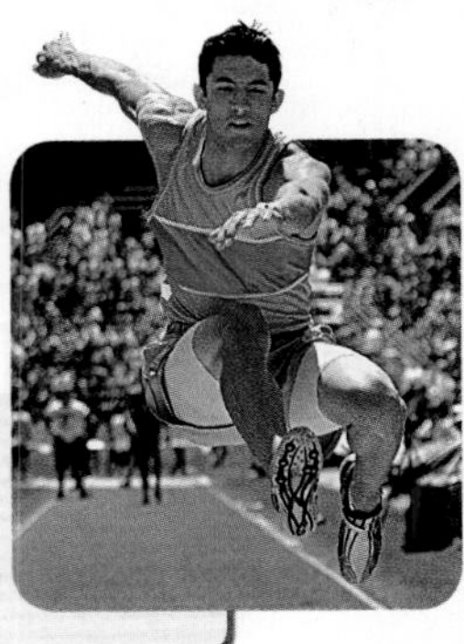

Before You solved systems of equations in two variables.

Now You will solve systems of equations in three variables.

Why? So you can model the results of a sporting event, as in Ex. 45.

Key Vocabulary
- **linear equation in three variables**
- **system of three linear equations**
- **solution of a system of three linear equations**
- **ordered triple**

A **linear equation in three variables** x, y, and z is an equation of the form $ax + by + cz = d$ where a, b, and c are not all zero.

The following is an example of a **system of three linear equations** in three variables.

$$2x + y - z = 5 \quad \text{Equation 1}$$
$$3x - 2y + z = 16 \quad \text{Equation 2}$$
$$4x + 3y - 5z = 3 \quad \text{Equation 3}$$

A **solution** of such a system is an **ordered triple** (x, y, z) whose coordinates make each equation true.

The graph of a linear equation in three variables is a plane in three-dimensional space. The graphs of three such equations that form a system are three planes whose intersection determines the number of solutions of the system, as shown in the diagrams below.

Exactly one solution

The planes intersect in a single point.

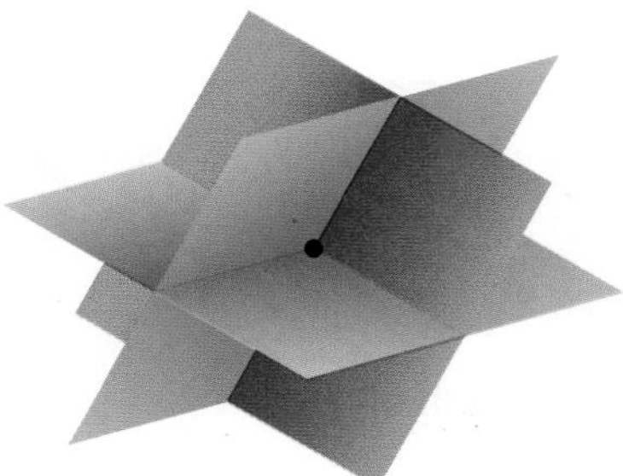

Infinitely many solutions

The planes intersect in a line or are the same plane.

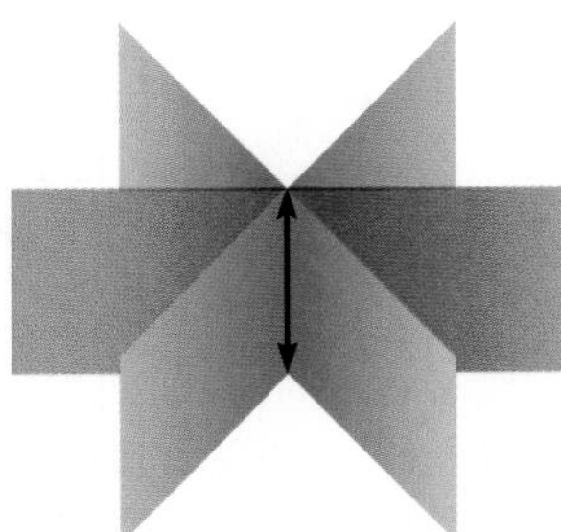

No solution

The planes have no common point of intersection.

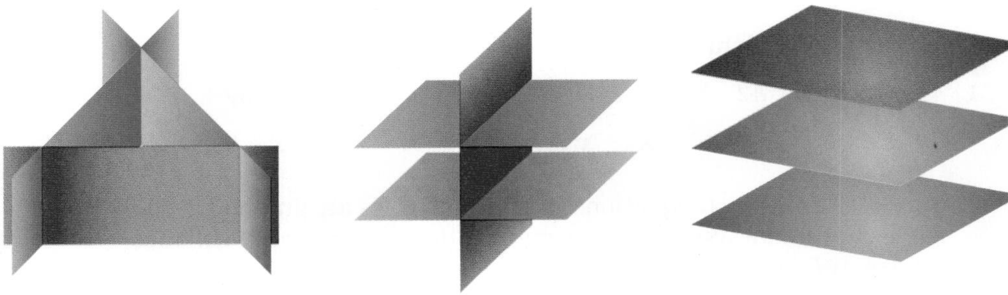

ELIMINATION METHOD The elimination method you studied in Lesson 3.2 can be extended to solve a system of linear equations in three variables.

KEY CONCEPT *For Your Notebook*

The Elimination Method for a Three-Variable System

STEP 1 **Rewrite** the linear system in three variables as a linear system in two variables by using the elimination method.

STEP 2 **Solve** the new linear system for both of its variables.

STEP 3 **Substitute** the values found in Step 2 into one of the original equations and solve for the remaining variable.

If you obtain a false equation, such as $0 = 1$, in any of the steps, then the system has no solution.

If you do not obtain a false equation, but obtain an identity such as $0 = 0$, then the system has infinitely many solutions.

EXAMPLE 1 Use the elimination method

Solve the system.

$4x + 2y + 3z = 1$ **Equation 1**

$2x - 3y + 5z = -14$ **Equation 2**

$6x - y + 4z = -1$ **Equation 3**

Solution

ANOTHER WAY In Step 1, you could also eliminate x to get two equations in y and z, or you could eliminate z to get two equations in x and y.

STEP 1 **Rewrite** the system as a linear system in *two* variables.

$4x + 2y + 3z = 1$
$12x - 2y + 8z = -2$ **Add 2 times Equation 3 to Equation 1.**

$16x + 11z = -1$ **New Equation 1**

$2x - 3y + 5z = -14$
$-18x + 3y - 12z = 3$ **Add −3 times Equation 3 to Equation 2.**

$-16x - 7z = -11$ **New Equation 2**

STEP 2 **Solve** the new linear system for both of its variables.

$16x + 11z = -1$
$-16x - 7z = -11$ **Add new Equation 1 and new Equation 2.**

$4z = -12$

$z = -3$ **Solve for z.**

$x = 2$ **Substitute into new Equation 1 or 2 to find x.**

STEP 3 **Substitute** $x = 2$ and $z = -3$ into an original equation and solve for y.

$6x - y + 4z = -1$ **Write original Equation 3.**

$6(2) - y + 4(-3) = -1$ **Substitute 2 for x and −3 for z.**

$y = 1$ **Solve for y.**

▶ The solution is $x = 2$, $y = 1$, and $z = -3$, or the ordered triple $(2, 1, -3)$. Check this solution in each of the original equations.

EXAMPLE 2 Solve a three-variable system with no solution

Solve the system.

$x + y + z = 3$ Equation 1
$4x + 4y + 4z = 7$ Equation 2
$3x - y + 2z = 5$ Equation 3

REVIEW SYSTEMS
For help with solving linear systems with many solutions or no solution, see p. 160.

Solution

When you multiply Equation 1 by −4 and add the result to Equation 2, you obtain a false equation.

$$\begin{aligned} -4x - 4y - 4z &= -12 \\ 4x + 4y + 4z &= 7 \\ \hline 0 &= -5 \end{aligned}$$

Add −4 times Equation 1 to Equation 2.

New Equation 1

▶ Because you obtain a false equation, you can conclude that the original system has no solution.

EXAMPLE 3 Solve a three-variable system with many solutions

Solve the system.

$x + y + z = 4$ Equation 1
$x + y - z = 4$ Equation 2
$3x + 3y + z = 12$ Equation 3

Solution

STEP 1 **Rewrite** the system as a linear system in *two* variables.

$$\begin{aligned} x + y + z &= 4 \\ x + y - z &= 4 \\ \hline 2x + 2y &= 8 \end{aligned}$$

Add Equation 1 to Equation 2.

New Equation 1

$$\begin{aligned} x + y - z &= 4 \\ 3x + 3y + z &= 12 \\ \hline 4x + 4y &= 16 \end{aligned}$$

Add Equation 2 to Equation 3.

New Equation 2

STEP 2 **Solve** the new linear system for both of its variables.

$$\begin{aligned} -4x - 4y &= -16 \\ 4x + 4y &= 16 \\ \hline 0 &= 0 \end{aligned}$$

Add −2 times new Equation 1 to new Equation 2.

Because you obtain the identity $0 = 0$, the system has infinitely many solutions.

STEP 3 **Describe** the solutions of the system. One way to do this is to divide new Equation 1 by 2 to get $x + y = 4$, or $y = -x + 4$. Substituting this into original Equation 1 produces $z = 0$. So, any ordered triple of the form $(x, -x + 4, 0)$ is a solution of the system.

GUIDED PRACTICE for Examples 1, 2, and 3

Solve the system.

1. $3x + y - 2z = 10$
$6x - 2y + z = -2$
$x + 4y + 3z = 7$

2. $x + y - z = 2$
$2x + 2y - 2z = 6$
$5x + y - 3z = 8$

3. $x + y + z = 3$
$x + y - z = 3$
$2x + 2y + z = 6$

EXAMPLE 4 Solve a system using substitution

MARKETING The marketing department of a company has a budget of \$30,000 for advertising. A television ad costs \$1000, a radio ad costs \$200, and a newspaper ad costs \$500. The department wants to run 60 ads per month and have as many radio ads as television and newspaper ads combined. How many of each type of ad should the department run each month?

Solution

STEP 1 **Write** verbal models for the situation.

TV ads	+	Radio ads	+	Newspaper ads	=	Total ads	Equation 1

1000 ·	TV ads	+ 200 ·	Radio ads	+ 500 ·	Newspaper ads	=	Monthly budget	Equation 2

Radio ads	=	TV ads	+	Newspaper ads	Equation 3

STEP 2 **Write** a system of equations. Let x be the number of TV ads, y be the number of radio ads, and z be the number of newspaper ads.

$$x + y + z = 60 \quad \text{Equation 1}$$
$$1000x + 200y + 500z = 30{,}000 \quad \text{Equation 2}$$
$$y = x + z \quad \text{Equation 3}$$

STEP 3 **Rewrite** the system in Step 2 as a linear system in *two* variables by substituting $x + z$ for y in Equations 1 and 2.

$$x + y + z = 60 \quad \text{Write Equation 1.}$$
$$x + (x + z) + z = 60 \quad \text{Substitute } x + z \text{ for } y.$$
$$2x + 2z = 60 \quad \text{New Equation 1}$$

$$1000x + 200y + 500z = 30{,}000 \quad \text{Write Equation 2.}$$
$$1000x + 200(x + z) + 500z = 30{,}000 \quad \text{Substitute } x + z \text{ for } y.$$
$$1200x + 700z = 30{,}000 \quad \text{New Equation 2}$$

STEP 4 **Solve** the linear system in two variables from Step 3.

$$-1200x - 1200z = -36{,}000 \quad \text{Add } -600 \text{ times new Equation 1}$$
$$1200x + 700z = 30{,}000 \quad \text{to new Equation 2.}$$
$$-500z = -6000$$
$$z = 12 \quad \text{Solve for } z.$$
$$x = 18 \quad \text{Substitute into new Equation 1 or 2 to find } x.$$
$$y = 30 \quad \text{Substitute into an original equation to find } y.$$

▶ The solution is $x = 18$, $y = 30$, and $z = 12$, or (18, 30, 12). So, the department should run 18 TV ads, 30 radio ads, and 12 newspaper ads each month.

AVOID ERRORS

In Example 4, be careful not to write the ordered triple in the order in which you solved for the variables.

(12, 18, 30) ✗

(18, 30, 12) ✓

✓ GUIDED PRACTICE for Example 4

4. **WHAT IF?** In Example 4, suppose the monthly budget is \$25,000. How many of each type of ad should the marketing department run each month?

3.4 EXERCISES

HOMEWORK KEY

○ = **WORKED-OUT SOLUTIONS** on p. WS5 for Exs. 11, 25, and 45

★ = **STANDARDIZED TEST PRACTICE** Exs. 2, 23, 24, 34, 45, and 47

SKILL PRACTICE

1. **VOCABULARY** Write a linear equation in three variables. What is the graph of such an equation?

2. ★ **WRITING** *Explain* how to use the substitution method to solve a system of three linear equations in three variables.

EXAMPLES 1, 2, and 3 on pp. 179–180 for Exs. 3–14

CHECKING SOLUTIONS **Tell whether the given ordered triple is a solution of the system.**

3. $(1, 4, -3)$
$2x - y + z = -5$
$5x + 2y - 2z = 19$
$x - 3y + z = -5$

4. $(-1, -2, 5)$
$4x - y + 3z = 13$
$x + y + z = 2$
$x + 3y - 2z = -17$

5. $(6, 0, -3)$
$x + 4y - 2z = 12$
$3x - y + 4z = 6$
$-x + 3y + z = -9$

6. $(-5, 1, 0)$
$3x + 4y - 2z = -11$
$2x + y - z = 11$
$x + 4y + 3z = -1$

7. $(2, 8, 4)$
$3x - y + 5z = 34$
$x + 3y - 6z = 2$
$-3x + y - 2z = -6$

8. $(0, -4, 7)$
$2x + 4y - z = -23$
$x - 5y - 3z = -1$
$-x + y + 4z = 24$

ELIMINATION METHOD **Solve the system using the elimination method.**

9. $3x + y + z = 14$
$-x + 2y - 3z = -9$
$5x - y + 5z = 30$

10. $2x - y + 2z = -7$
$-x + 2y - 4z = 5$
$x + 4y - 6z = -1$

11. $3x - y + 2z = 4$
$6x - 2y + 4z = -8$
$2x - y + 3z = 10$

12. $4x - y + 2z = -18$
$-x + 2y + z = 11$
$3x + 3y - 4z = 44$

13. $5x + y - z = 6$
$x + y + z = 2$
$3x + y = 4$

14. $2x + y - z = 9$
$-x + 6y + 2z = -17$
$5x + 7y + z = 4$

EXAMPLE 4 on p. 181 for Exs. 15–20

SUBSTITUTION METHOD **Solve the system using the substitution method.**

15. $x + y - z = 4$
$3x + 2y + 4z = 17$
$-x + 5y + z = 8$

16. $2x - y - z = 15$
$4x + 5y + 2z = 10$
$-x - 4y + 3z = -20$

17. $4x + y + 5z = -40$
$-3x + 2y + 4z = 10$
$x - y - 2z = -2$

18. $x + 3y - z = 12$
$2x + 4y - 2z = 6$
$-x - 2y + z = -6$

19. $2x - y + z = -2$
$6x + 3y - 4z = 8$
$-3x + 2y + 3z = -6$

20. $3x + 5y - z = 12$
$x + y + z = 0$
$-x + 2y + 2z = -27$

ERROR ANALYSIS ***Describe*** **and correct the error in the first step of solving the system.**

$2x + y - 2z = 23$
$3x + 2y + z = 11$
$x - y + z = -2$

21.
$2x + y - 2z = 23$
$6x + 2y + 2z = 22$
$8x + 3y = 45$
✗

22.
$z = 11 + 3x + 2y$
$2x + y - 2(11 + 3x + 2y) = 23$
$-4x - 3y = 45$
✗

23. ★ **MULTIPLE CHOICE** Which ordered triple is a solution of the system?

$$2x + 5y + 3z = 10$$
$$3x - y + 4z = 8$$
$$5x - 2y + 7z = 12$$

Ⓐ (7, 1, −3) Ⓑ (7, −1, −3) Ⓒ (7, 1, 3) Ⓓ (−7, 1, −3)

24. ★ **MULTIPLE CHOICE** Which ordered triple describes all of the solutions of the system?

$$2x - 2y - z = 6$$
$$-x + y + 3z = -3$$
$$3x - 3y + 2z = 9$$

Ⓐ $(-x, x + 2, 0)$ Ⓑ $(x, x - 3, 0)$ Ⓒ $(x + 2, x, 0)$ Ⓓ $(0, y, y + 4)$

CHOOSING A METHOD Solve the system using any algebraic method.

25. $x + 5y - 2z = -1$, $-x - 2y + z = 6$, $-2x - 7y + 3z = 7$

26. $4x + 5y + 3z = 15$, $x - 3y + 2z = -6$, $-x + 2y - z = 3$

27. $6x + y - z = -2$, $x + 6y + 3z = 23$, $-x + y + 2z = 5$

28. $x + 2y = -1$, $3x - y + 4z = 17$, $-4x + 2y - 3z = -30$

29. $2x - y + 2z = -21$, $x + 5y - z = 25$, $-3x + 2y + 4z = 6$

30. $4x - 8y + 2z = 10$, $-3x + y - 2z = 6$, $2x - 4y + z = 8$

31. $-x + 5y - z = -16$, $2x + 3y + 4z = 18$, $x + y - z = -8$

32. $2x - y + 4z = 19$, $-x + 3y - 2z = -7$, $4x + 2y + 3z = 37$

33. $x + y + z = 3$, $3x - 4y + 2z = -28$, $-x + 5y + z = 23$

34. ★ **OPEN-ENDED MATH** Write a system of three linear equations in three variables that has the given number of solutions.

a. One solution **b.** No solution **c.** Infinitely many solutions

SYSTEMS WITH FRACTIONS Solve the system using any algebraic method.

35. $x + \frac{1}{2}y + \frac{1}{2}z = \frac{5}{2}$, $\frac{3}{4}x + \frac{1}{4}y + \frac{3}{2}z = \frac{7}{4}$, $\frac{1}{3}x + \frac{3}{2}y + \frac{2}{3}z = \frac{13}{6}$

36. $\frac{1}{3}x + \frac{5}{6}y + \frac{2}{3}z = \frac{4}{3}$, $\frac{1}{6}x + \frac{2}{3}y + \frac{1}{4}z = \frac{5}{6}$, $\frac{2}{3}x + \frac{1}{6}y + \frac{3}{2}z = \frac{4}{3}$

37. **REASONING** For what values of a, b, and c does the linear system shown have $(-1, 2, -3)$ as its only solution? *Explain* your reasoning.

$$x + 2y - 3z = a$$
$$-x - y + z = b$$
$$2x + 3y - 2z = c$$

CHALLENGE Solve the system of equations. *Describe* each step of your solution.

38. $w + x + y + z = 2$, $2w - x + 2y - z = 1$, $-w + 2x - y + 2z = -2$, $3w + x + y - z = -5$

39. $2w + x - 3y + z = 4$, $w - 3x + y + z = 32$, $-w + 2x + 2y - z = -10$, $w + x - y + 3z = 14$

40. $w + 2x + 5y = 11$, $-2w + x + 4y + 2z = -7$, $w + 2x - 2y + 5z = 3$, $-3w + x = -1$

41. $2w + 7x - 3y = 41$, $-w - 2x + y = -13$, $-2w + 4x + z = 12$, $-w - x + y = -8$

PROBLEM SOLVING

EXAMPLE 4 on p. 181 for Exs. 42–47

42. **PIZZA SPECIALS** At a pizza shop, two small pizzas, a liter of soda, and a salad cost \$14; one small pizza, a liter of soda, and three salads cost \$15; and three small pizzas and a liter of soda cost \$16. What is the cost of one small pizza? of one liter of soda? of one salad?

   @HomeTutor for problem solving help at classzone.com

43. **HEALTH CLUB** The juice bar at a health club receives a delivery of juice at the beginning of each month. Over a three month period, the health club received 1200 gallons of orange juice, 900 gallons of pineapple juice, and 1000 gallons of grapefruit juice. The table shows the composition of each juice delivery. How many gallons of juice did the health club receive in each delivery?

   @HomeTutor for problem solving help at classzone.com

Juice	1st delivery	2nd delivery	3rd delivery
Orange	70%	50%	30%
Pineapple	20%	30%	30%
Grapefruit	10%	20%	40%

44. **MULTI-STEP PROBLEM** You make a tape of your friend's three favorite TV shows: a comedy, a drama, and a reality show. An episode of the comedy lasts 30 minutes, while an episode of the drama or the reality show lasts 60 minutes. The tape can hold 360 minutes of programming. You completely fill the tape with 7 episodes and include twice as many episodes of the drama as the comedy.

   a. Write a system of equations to represent this situation.

   b. Solve the system from part (a). How many episodes of each show are on the tape?

   c. How would your answer to part (b) change if you completely filled the tape with only 5 episodes but still included twice as many episodes of the drama as the comedy?

45. ★ **SHORT RESPONSE** The following Internet announcement describes the results of a high school track meet.

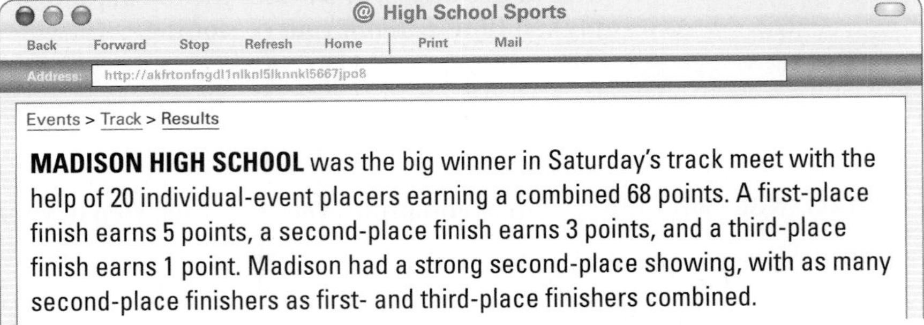

MADISON HIGH SCHOOL was the big winner in Saturday's track meet with the help of 20 individual-event placers earning a combined 68 points. A first-place finish earns 5 points, a second-place finish earns 3 points, and a third-place finish earns 1 point. Madison had a strong second-place showing, with as many second-place finishers as first- and third-place finishers combined.

   a. Write and solve a system of equations to find the number of athletes who finished in first place, in second place, and in third place.

   b. Suppose the announcement had claimed that the Madison athletes scored a total of 70 points instead of 68 points. Show that this claim must be false because the solution of the resulting linear system is not reasonable.

46. **FIELD TRIP** You and two friends buy snacks for a field trip. You spend a total of \$8, Jeff spends \$9, and Curtis spends \$9. The table shows the amounts of mixed nuts, granola, and dried fruit that each person purchased. What is the price per pound of each type of snack?

	Mixed nuts	Granola	Dried fruit
You	1 lb	0.5 lb	1 lb
Jeff	2 lb	0.5 lb	0.5 lb
Curtis	1 lb	2 lb	0.5 lb

47. ★ **EXTENDED RESPONSE** A florist must make 5 identical bridesmaid bouquets for a wedding. She has a budget of \$160 and wants 12 flowers for each bouquet. Roses cost \$2.50 each, lilies cost \$4 each, and irises cost \$2 each. She wants twice as many roses as the other two types of flowers combined.

   a. **Write** Write a system of equations to represent this situation.

   b. **Solve** Solve the system of equations. How many of each type of flower should be in each bouquet?

   c. **Analyze** Suppose there is no limitation on the total cost of the bouquets. Does the problem still have a unique solution? If so, state the unique solution. If not, give three possible solutions.

48. **CHALLENGE** Write a system of equations to represent the first three pictures below. Use the system to determine how many tangerines will balance the apple in the final picture. *Note:* The first picture shows that one tangerine and one apple balance one grapefruit.

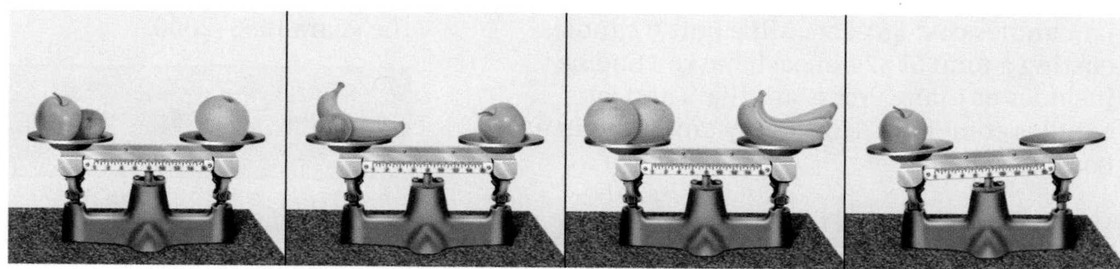

NEW YORK MIXED REVIEW

49. What are the vertices of a triangle congruent to $\triangle PQR$ shown at the right?

   Ⓐ (3, 1), (1, −2), (4, −5) Ⓑ (2, 3), (−1, 1), (2, −2)

   Ⓒ (0, 2), (−2, −1), (−3, −4) Ⓓ (−2, −3), (−4, 1), (−1, 4)

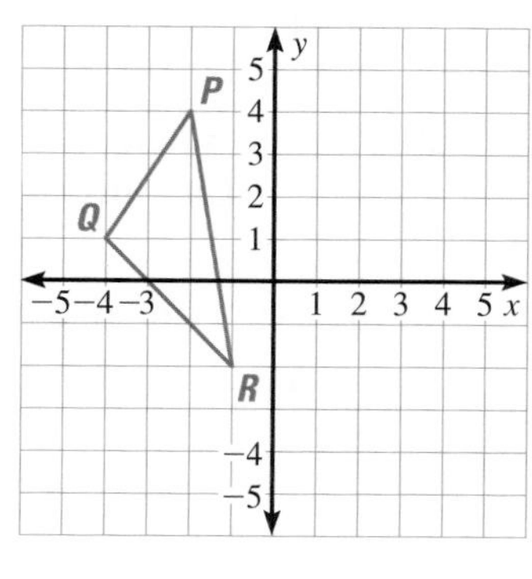

50. What special type of quadrilateral has the vertices $K(-4, 3)$, $L(-7, 3)$, $M(-9, -1)$, and $N(-2, -1)$?

   Ⓐ Square Ⓑ Trapezoid

   Ⓒ Kite Ⓓ Parallelogram

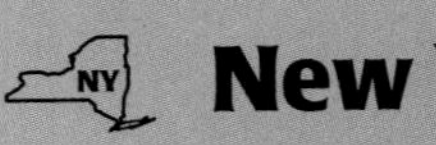

New York *Mixed Review*

TEST PRACTICE classzone.com

Lessons 3.1–3.4

1. **JEWELRY** Melinda is making jewelry to sell at a craft fair. The cost of materials is \$3.50 to make one necklace and \$2.50 to make one bracelet. She sells the necklaces for \$9.00 each and the bracelets for \$7.50 each. She spends a total of \$121 on materials and sells all of the jewelry for a total of \$324. Which system of equations represents the situation, where x is the number of necklaces and y is the number of bracelets?

   (1) $2.5x - 3.5y = 121$
   $7.5x - 9y = 324$

   (2) $2.5x + 3.5y = 324$
   $9x + 7.5y = 121$

   (3) $3.5x - 2.5y = 324$
   $7.5x + 9y = 121$

   (4) $3.5x + 2.5y = 121$
   $9x + 7.5y = 324$

2. **GIFT BASKETS** Mike is making gift baskets. Each basket will contain three different kinds of candles: tapers, pillars, and jar candles. Tapers cost \$1 each, pillars cost \$4 each, and jar candles cost \$6 each. Mike puts 8 candles costing a total of \$24 in each basket, and he includes as many tapers as pillars and jar candles combined. How many tapers are in a basket?

   (1) 1 taper

   (2) 2 tapers

   (3) 4 tapers

   (4) 5 tapers

3. **BASEBALL** From 1999 through 2002, the average annual salary s (in thousands of dollars) of players on two Major League Baseball teams can be modeled by the equations below, where t is the number of years since 1990.

   Florida Marlins: $s = 320t - 2300$
   Kansas City Royals: $s = 440t - 3500$

   In what year were the average annual salaries of the two baseball teams equal?

   (1) 1999 (3) 2001

   (2) 2000 (4) 2002

4. **RESTAURANT SEATING** A restaurant has 20 tables. Each table can seat either 4 people or 6 people. The restaurant can seat a total of 90 people. How many 6 seat tables does the restaurant have?

   (1) 1 table

   (2) 5 tables

   (3) 7 tables

   (4) 15 tables

5. **OPEN-ENDED** A store orders rocking chairs, hand paints them, and sells the chairs for a profit. A small chair costs the store \$51 and sells for \$80. A large chair costs the store \$70 and sells for \$110. The store wants to pay no more than \$2000 for its next order of chairs and wants to sell them all for at least \$2750. Identify three possible combinations of small and large rocking chairs that the store can buy and sell.

6. **OPEN-ENDED** The table below shows the expected life spans for men and women born in the years 1996–2000.

Years since 1996 (x)	Men's Life Span (years) (m)	Women's Life Span (years) (w)
0	73.0	79.0
1	73.6	79.4
2	73.8	79.5
3	73.9	79.4
4	74.3	79.7

   Write an equation for the best-fitting line for the data pairs (x, m).

   Write an equation for the best-fitting line for the data pairs (x, w).

   Assuming that the trend continues, what is the point of intersection of these two lines? *Explain* what both coordinates of this point represent.

3.5 Perform Basic Matrix Operations

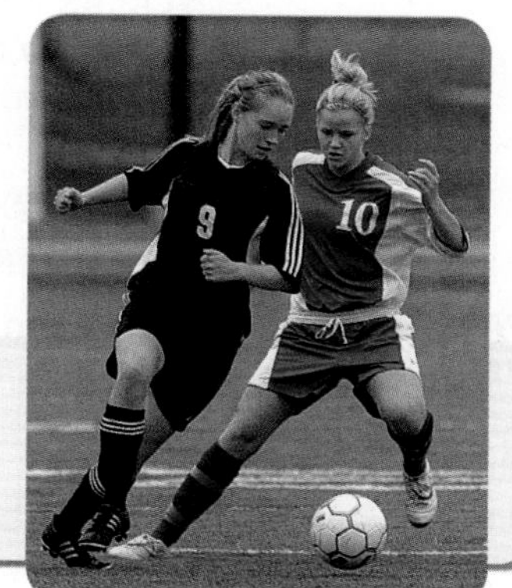

Before You performed operations with real numbers.

Now You will perform operations with matrices.

Why? So you can organize sports data, as in Ex. 34.

Key Vocabulary
- **matrix**
- **dimensions**
- **elements**
- **equal matrices**
- **scalar**
- **scalar multiplication**

A **matrix** is a rectangular arrangement of numbers in rows and columns. For example, matrix A below has two rows and three columns. The **dimensions** of a matrix with m rows and n columns are $m \times n$ (read "m by n"). So, the dimensions of matrix A are 2×3. The numbers in a matrix are its **elements**.

$$A = \begin{bmatrix} 4 & -1 & 5 \\ 0 & 6 & 3 \end{bmatrix}$$

2 rows

3 columns

The element in the first row and third column is 5.

Two matrices are **equal** if their dimensions are the same and the elements in corresponding positions are equal.

KEY CONCEPT — *For Your Notebook*

Adding and Subtracting Matrices

To add or subtract two matrices, simply add or subtract elements in corresponding positions. You can add or subtract matrices only if they have the same dimensions.

Adding Matrices $\begin{bmatrix} a & b \\ c & d \end{bmatrix} + \begin{bmatrix} e & f \\ g & h \end{bmatrix} = \begin{bmatrix} a+e & b+f \\ c+g & d+h \end{bmatrix}$

Subtracting Matrices $\begin{bmatrix} a & b \\ c & d \end{bmatrix} - \begin{bmatrix} e & f \\ g & h \end{bmatrix} = \begin{bmatrix} a-e & b-f \\ c-g & d-h \end{bmatrix}$

EXAMPLE 1 Add and subtract matrices

AVOID ERRORS
Be sure to verify that the dimensions of two matrices are equal before adding or subtracting them.

Perform the indicated operation, if possible.

a. $\begin{bmatrix} 3 & 0 \\ -5 & -1 \end{bmatrix} + \begin{bmatrix} -1 & 4 \\ 2 & 0 \end{bmatrix} = \begin{bmatrix} 3+(-1) & 0+4 \\ -5+2 & -1+0 \end{bmatrix} = \begin{bmatrix} 2 & 4 \\ -3 & -1 \end{bmatrix}$

b. $\begin{bmatrix} 7 & 4 \\ 0 & -2 \\ -1 & 6 \end{bmatrix} - \begin{bmatrix} -2 & 5 \\ 3 & -10 \\ -3 & 1 \end{bmatrix} = \begin{bmatrix} 7-(-2) & 4-5 \\ 0-3 & -2-(-10) \\ -1-(-3) & 6-1 \end{bmatrix} = \begin{bmatrix} 9 & -1 \\ -3 & 8 \\ 2 & 5 \end{bmatrix}$

SCALAR MULTIPLICATION In matrix algebra, a real number is often called a **scalar**. To multiply a matrix by a scalar, you multiply each element in the matrix by the scalar. This process is called **scalar multiplication**.

EXAMPLE 2 Multiply a matrix by a scalar

COMPARE ORDER OF OPERATIONS

The order of operations for matrix expressions is similar to that for real numbers. In particular, you perform scalar multiplication before matrix addition and subtraction.

Perform the indicated operation, if possible.

a. $-2\begin{bmatrix} 4 & -1 \\ 1 & 0 \\ 2 & 7 \end{bmatrix} = \begin{bmatrix} -2(4) & -2(-1) \\ -2(1) & -2(0) \\ -2(2) & -2(7) \end{bmatrix} = \begin{bmatrix} -8 & 2 \\ -2 & 0 \\ -4 & -14 \end{bmatrix}$

b. $4\begin{bmatrix} -2 & -8 \\ 5 & 0 \end{bmatrix} + \begin{bmatrix} -3 & 8 \\ 6 & -5 \end{bmatrix} = \begin{bmatrix} 4(-2) & 4(-8) \\ 4(5) & 4(0) \end{bmatrix} + \begin{bmatrix} -3 & 8 \\ 6 & -5 \end{bmatrix}$

$= \begin{bmatrix} -8 & -32 \\ 20 & 0 \end{bmatrix} + \begin{bmatrix} -3 & 8 \\ 6 & -5 \end{bmatrix}$

$= \begin{bmatrix} -8 + (-3) & -32 + 8 \\ 20 + 6 & 0 + (-5) \end{bmatrix}$

$= \begin{bmatrix} -11 & -24 \\ 26 & -5 \end{bmatrix}$

✓ GUIDED PRACTICE for Examples 1 and 2

Perform the indicated operation, if possible.

1. $\begin{bmatrix} -2 & 5 & 11 \\ 4 & -6 & 8 \end{bmatrix} + \begin{bmatrix} -3 & 1 & -5 \\ -2 & -8 & 4 \end{bmatrix}$

2. $\begin{bmatrix} -4 & 0 \\ 7 & -2 \\ -3 & 1 \end{bmatrix} - \begin{bmatrix} 2 & 2 \\ -3 & 0 \\ 5 & -14 \end{bmatrix}$

3. $-4\begin{bmatrix} 2 & -1 & -3 \\ -7 & 6 & 1 \\ -2 & 0 & -5 \end{bmatrix}$

4. $3\begin{bmatrix} 4 & -1 \\ -3 & -5 \end{bmatrix} + \begin{bmatrix} -2 & -2 \\ 0 & 6 \end{bmatrix}$

MATRIX PROPERTIES Many of the properties you have used with real numbers can be applied to matrices as well.

CONCEPT SUMMARY *For Your Notebook*

Properties of Matrix Operations

Let A, B, and C be matrices with the same dimensions, and let k be a scalar.

Associative Property of Addition	$(A + B) + C = A + (B + C)$
Commutative Property of Addition	$A + B = B + A$
Distributive Property of Addition	$k(A + B) = kA + kB$
Distributive Property of Subtraction	$k(A - B) = kA - kB$

ORGANIZING DATA Matrices are useful for organizing data and for performing the same operations on large numbers of data values.

EXAMPLE 3 Solve a multi-step problem

MANUFACTURING A company manufactures small and large steel DVD racks with wooden bases. Each size of rack is available in three types of wood: walnut, pine, and cherry. Sales of the racks for last month and this month are shown below.

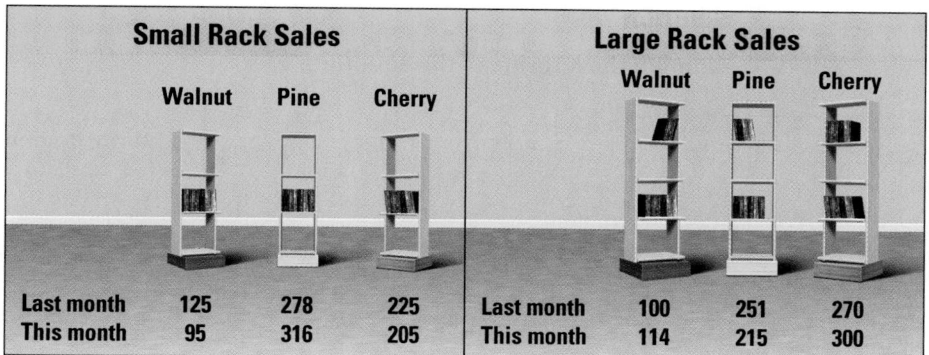

Organize the data using two matrices, one for last month's sales and one for this month's sales. Then write and interpret a matrix giving the average monthly sales for the two month period.

Solution

STEP 1 **Organize** the data using two 3×2 matrices, as shown.

	Last Month (A)		This Month (B)	
	Small	Large	Small	Large
Walnut	125	100	95	114
Pine	278	251	316	215
Cherry	225	270	205	300

STEP 2 **Write** a matrix for the average monthly sales by first adding A and B to find the total sales and then multipling the result by $\frac{1}{2}$.

$$\frac{1}{2}(A + B) = \frac{1}{2}\left(\begin{bmatrix} 125 & 100 \\ 278 & 251 \\ 225 & 270 \end{bmatrix} + \begin{bmatrix} 95 & 114 \\ 316 & 215 \\ 205 & 300 \end{bmatrix}\right)$$

$$= \frac{1}{2}\begin{bmatrix} 220 & 214 \\ 594 & 466 \\ 430 & 570 \end{bmatrix}$$

$$= \begin{bmatrix} 110 & 107 \\ 297 & 233 \\ 215 & 285 \end{bmatrix}$$

ANOTHER WAY
You can also evaluate $\frac{1}{2}(A + B)$ by first using the distributive property to rewrite the expression as $\frac{1}{2}A + \frac{1}{2}B$.

STEP 3 **Interpret** the matrix from Step 2. The company sold an average of 110 small walnut racks, 107 large walnut racks, 297 small pine racks, 233 large pine racks, 215 small cherry racks, and 285 large cherry racks.

SOLVING MATRIX EQUATIONS You can use what you know about matrix operations and matrix equality to solve an equation involving matrices.

EXAMPLE 4 Solve a matrix equation

Solve the matrix equation for *x* and *y*.

$$3\left(\begin{bmatrix} 5x & -2 \\ 6 & -4 \end{bmatrix} + \begin{bmatrix} 3 & 7 \\ -5 & -y \end{bmatrix}\right) = \begin{bmatrix} -21 & 15 \\ 3 & -24 \end{bmatrix}$$

Solution

Simplify the left side of the equation.

$$3\left(\begin{bmatrix} 5x & -2 \\ 6 & -4 \end{bmatrix} + \begin{bmatrix} 3 & 7 \\ -5 & -y \end{bmatrix}\right) = \begin{bmatrix} -21 & 15 \\ 3 & -24 \end{bmatrix}$$ **Write original equation.**

$$3\begin{bmatrix} 5x + 3 & 5 \\ 1 & -4 - y \end{bmatrix} = \begin{bmatrix} -21 & 15 \\ 3 & -24 \end{bmatrix}$$ **Add matrices inside parentheses.**

$$\begin{bmatrix} 15x + 9 & 15 \\ 3 & -12 - 3y \end{bmatrix} = \begin{bmatrix} -21 & 15 \\ 3 & -24 \end{bmatrix}$$ **Perform scalar multiplication.**

Equate corresponding elements and solve the two resulting equations.

$$15x + 9 = -21 \qquad -12 - 3y = -24$$
$$x = -2 \qquad y = 4$$

▶ The solution is $x = -2$ and $y = 4$.

✓ GUIDED PRACTICE for Examples 3 and 4

5. In Example 3, find $B - A$ and explain what information this matrix gives.

6. Solve $-2\left(\begin{bmatrix} -3x & -1 \\ 4 & y \end{bmatrix} + \begin{bmatrix} 9 & -4 \\ -5 & 3 \end{bmatrix}\right) = \begin{bmatrix} 12 & 10 \\ 2 & -18 \end{bmatrix}$ for *x* and *y*.

3.5 EXERCISES

HOMEWORK KEY

○ = **WORKED-OUT SOLUTIONS** on p. WS6 for Exs. 5, 21, and 33

★ = **STANDARDIZED TEST PRACTICE** Exs. 2, 28, 29, 33, and 34

SKILL PRACTICE

1. **VOCABULARY** Copy and complete: The __?__ of a matrix with 3 rows and 4 columns are 3×4.

2. ★ **WRITING** *Describe* how to determine whether two matrices are equal.

EXAMPLE 1 on p. 187 for Exs. 3–9

3. **ERROR ANALYSIS** *Describe* and correct the error in adding the matrices.

$$\begin{bmatrix} 9 \\ -5 \end{bmatrix} + \begin{bmatrix} 4.1 \\ 3.8 \end{bmatrix} = \begin{bmatrix} 9 & 4.1 \\ -5 & 3.8 \end{bmatrix}$$ ✗

ADDING AND SUBTRACTING MATRICES **Perform the indicated operation, if possible. If not possible, state the reason.**

4. $\begin{bmatrix} 5 & 2 \\ -1 & 8 \end{bmatrix} + \begin{bmatrix} -8 & 10 \\ -6 & 3 \end{bmatrix}$

(5.) $\begin{bmatrix} 10 & -8 \\ 5 & -3 \end{bmatrix} - \begin{bmatrix} 12 & -3 \\ 3 & -4 \end{bmatrix}$

6. $\begin{bmatrix} 4 & -5 \\ 8 & 1 \end{bmatrix} - \begin{bmatrix} 2 \\ -1 \end{bmatrix}$

7. $\begin{bmatrix} 1.2 & 5.3 \\ 0.1 & 4.4 \\ 6.2 & 0.7 \end{bmatrix} + \begin{bmatrix} 2.4 & -0.6 \\ 6.1 & 3.1 \\ 8.1 & -1.9 \end{bmatrix}$

8. $\begin{bmatrix} 8 & 3 \\ 9 & -1 \\ 4 & 5 \end{bmatrix} + \begin{bmatrix} 5 & -1 & 0 \\ 6 & 2 & -3 \\ 8 & -1 & 2 \end{bmatrix}$

9. $\begin{bmatrix} 7 & -3 \\ 12 & 5 \\ -4 & 11 \end{bmatrix} - \begin{bmatrix} 9 & 2 \\ -2 & 6 \\ 6 & 5 \end{bmatrix}$

EXAMPLE 2
on p. 188
for Exs. 10–15

MULTIPLYING BY A SCALAR **Perform the indicated operation.**

10. $2\begin{bmatrix} -1 & 4 \\ 3 & -6 \end{bmatrix}$

11. $-3\begin{bmatrix} 2 & 0 & -5 \\ 4 & 7 & -3 \end{bmatrix}$

12. $-4\begin{bmatrix} 2 & -3 & -2 \\ -\frac{5}{8} & \frac{11}{2} & \frac{7}{4} \end{bmatrix}$

13. $1.5\begin{bmatrix} -2 & 3.4 & 1.6 \\ 5.4 & 0 & -3 \end{bmatrix}$

14. $\frac{1}{2}\begin{bmatrix} -2 & 8 & 12 \\ 20 & -1 & 0 \\ -8 & 10 & 2 \end{bmatrix}$

15. $-2.2\begin{bmatrix} 6 & 3.1 & 4.5 \\ -1 & 0 & 2.5 \\ 5.5 & -1.8 & 6.4 \end{bmatrix}$

MATRIX OPERATIONS **Use matrices A, B, C, and D to evaluate the matrix expression.**

$A = \begin{bmatrix} 5 & -4 \\ 3 & -1 \end{bmatrix}$ $B = \begin{bmatrix} 18 & -12 \\ -6 & 0 \end{bmatrix}$ $C = \begin{bmatrix} 1.8 & -1.5 & 10.6 \\ -8.8 & 3.4 & 0 \end{bmatrix}$ $D = \begin{bmatrix} 7.2 & 0 & -5.4 \\ 2.1 & -1.9 & 3.3 \end{bmatrix}$

16. $A + B$ **17.** $B - A$ **18.** $4A - B$ **19.** $\frac{2}{3}B$

20. $C + D$ **(21.)** $C + 3D$ **22.** $D - 2C$ **23.** $0.5C - D$

EXAMPLE 4
on p. 190
for Exs. 24–27

SOLVING MATRIX EQUATIONS **Solve the matrix equation for x and y.**

24. $\begin{bmatrix} -1 & 3x \\ -4 & 5 \end{bmatrix} = \begin{bmatrix} -1 & -18 \\ 2y & 5 \end{bmatrix}$

25. $\begin{bmatrix} -2x & 6 \\ 1 & -8 \end{bmatrix} + 2\begin{bmatrix} 5 & -1 \\ -7 & 6 \end{bmatrix} = \begin{bmatrix} -9 & 4 \\ -13 & y \end{bmatrix}$

26. $2\begin{bmatrix} 8 & -x \\ 5 & 6 \end{bmatrix} - \begin{bmatrix} 3 & -9 \\ 10 & -4y \end{bmatrix} = \begin{bmatrix} 13 & 4 \\ 0 & 16 \end{bmatrix}$

27. $4x\begin{bmatrix} -1 & 2 \\ 3 & 6 \end{bmatrix} = \begin{bmatrix} 8 & -16 \\ -24 & 3y \end{bmatrix}$

28. ★ **MULTIPLE CHOICE** Based on the equation below, what is the value of the expression $3x - 2y$?

$$\begin{bmatrix} 2x & 0 \\ 0.5 & -0.75 \end{bmatrix} = \begin{bmatrix} 6.4 & 0 \\ 0.5 & 3y \end{bmatrix}$$

Ⓐ 7.15 Ⓑ 9.1 Ⓒ 10.1 Ⓓ 20.7

29. ★ **OPEN-ENDED MATH** Find two matrices A and B such that $2A - 3B = \begin{bmatrix} 5 & 0 \\ -1 & 2 \end{bmatrix}$.

30. **CHALLENGE** Find the matrix X that makes the equation true.

a. $X + \begin{bmatrix} -5 & 0 \\ 4 & -3 \end{bmatrix} = \begin{bmatrix} 7 & -8 \\ -3 & 5 \end{bmatrix}$

b. $X - \begin{bmatrix} 2 & 3 \\ 5 & 0 \end{bmatrix} = \begin{bmatrix} 8 & 6 \\ -1 & 3 \end{bmatrix}$

c. $-X + \begin{bmatrix} -3 & 1 \\ 4 & 7 \end{bmatrix} = \begin{bmatrix} 8 & -9 \\ 0 & 10 \end{bmatrix}$

d. $3X - \begin{bmatrix} 11 & -6 \\ 2 & 1 \end{bmatrix} = \begin{bmatrix} -13 & 15 \\ -19 & 2 \end{bmatrix}$

PROBLEM SOLVING

EXAMPLE 3 on p. 189 for Exs. 31–34

31. SNOWBOARD SALES A sporting goods store sells snowboards in several different styles and lengths. The matrices below show the number of each type of snowboard sold in 2003 and 2004. Write a matrix giving the change in sales for each type of snowboard from 2003 to 2004.

Sales for 2003

	150 cm	155 cm	160 cm	165 cm
Freeride	32	42	29	20
Alpine	12	17	25	16
Freestyle	28	40	32	21

Sales for 2004

	150 cm	155 cm	160 cm	165 cm
Freeride	32	47	30	19
Alpine	5	16	20	14
Freestyle	29	39	36	31

@HomeTutor for problem solving help at classzone.com

32. FUEL ECONOMY A car dealership sells four different models of cars. The fuel economy (in miles per gallon) is shown below for each model. Organize the data using a matrix. Then write a new matrix giving the fuel economy figures for next year's models if each measure of fuel economy increases by 8%.

Economy car: 32 mpg in city driving, 40 mpg in highway driving

Mid-size car: 24 mpg in city driving, 34 mpg in highway driving

Mini-van: 18 mpg in city driving, 25 mpg in highway driving

SUV: 19 mpg in city driving, 22 mpg in highway driving

@HomeTutor for problem solving help at classzone.com

33. ★ **EXTENDED RESPONSE** In a certain city, an electronics chain has a downtown store and a store in the mall. Each store carries three models of digital camera. Sales of the cameras for May and June are shown.

May Downtown sales: 31 of model A, 42 of model B, 18 of model C
Mall sales: 22 of model A, 25 of model B, 11 of model C

June Downtown sales: 25 of model A, 36 of model B, 12 of model C
Mall sales: 38 of model A, 32 of model B, 15 of model C

a. Organize the information using two matrices M and J that represent the sales for May and June, respectively.

b. Find $M + J$ and describe what this matrix sum represents.

c. Write a matrix giving the average monthly sales for the two month period.

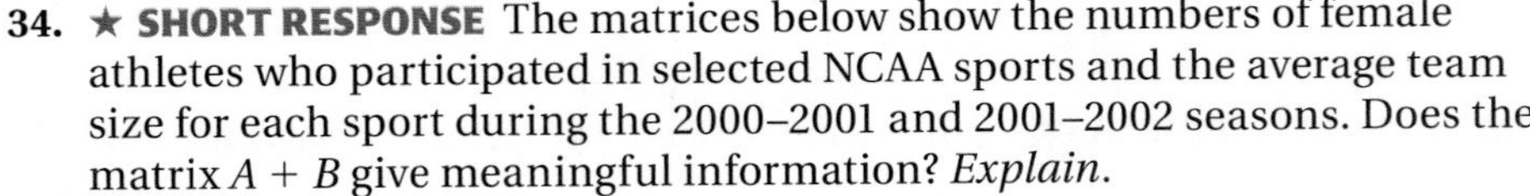

34. ★ **SHORT RESPONSE** The matrices below show the numbers of female athletes who participated in selected NCAA sports and the average team size for each sport during the 2000–2001 and 2001–2002 seasons. Does the matrix $A + B$ give meaningful information? *Explain.*

2000–2001 (*A*)

	Athletes	Team size
Basketball	14,439	14.5
Gymnastics	1,397	15.7
Skiing	526	11.9
Soccer	18,548	22.5

2001–2002 (*B*)

	Athletes	Team size
Basketball	14,524	14.3
Gymnastics	1,440	16.2
Skiing	496	11.0
Soccer	19,467	22.4

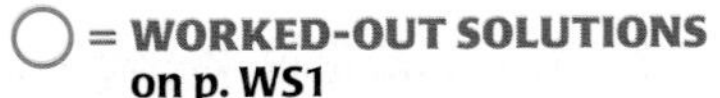

○ = **WORKED-OUT SOLUTIONS** on p. WS1

★ = **STANDARDIZED TEST PRACTICE**

35. **CHALLENGE** A rectangle has vertices (1, 1), (1, 4), (5, 1), and (5, 4). Write a 2×4 matrix A whose columns are the vertices of the rectangle. Multiply matrix A by 3. In the same coordinate plane, draw the rectangles represented by the matrices A and $3A$. How are the rectangles related?

NEW YORK MIXED REVIEW

TEST PRACTICE at classzone.com

36. A health teacher surveyed 100 students to determine their favorite exercise activity or combination of exercise activities. The results are shown at the right. How many of the students surveyed chose only running as their favorite exercise activity?

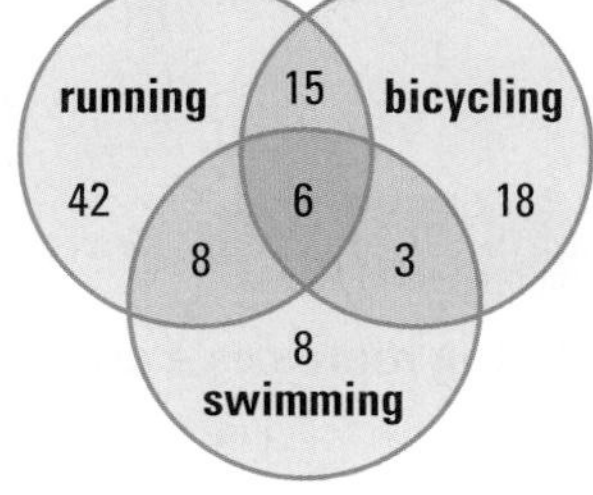

Ⓐ 13 Ⓑ 29

Ⓒ 42 Ⓓ 71

37. Which statement best describes the effect on the graph shown when the y-intercept is decreased by 4?

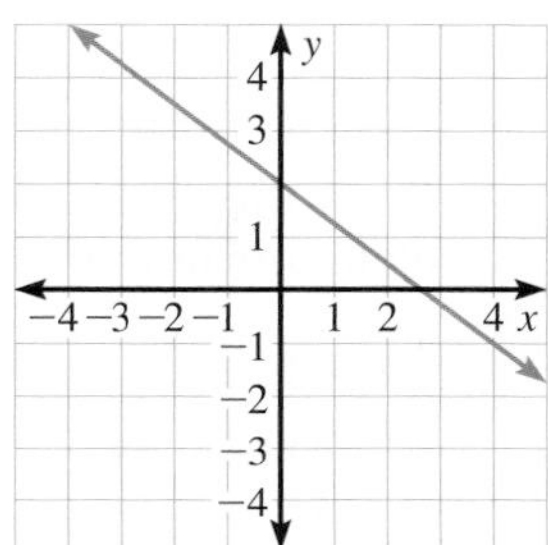

Ⓐ The x-intercept decreases.

Ⓑ The slope decreases.

Ⓒ The x-intercept increases.

Ⓓ The slope increases.

QUIZ for Lessons 3.3–3.5

Graph the system of inequalities. *(p. 168)*

1. $y < 6$
$x + y > -2$

2. $x \ge -1$
$-2x + y \le 5$

3. $x + 3y > 3$
$x + 3y < -9$

4. $x - y \ge 4$
$2x + 4y \ge -10$

5. $x + 2y \le 10$
$y \ge |x + 2|$

6. $-y < x$
$2y < 5x + 9$

Solve the system using any algebraic method. *(p. 178)*

7. $2x - y - 3z = 5$
$x + 2y - 5z = -11$
$-x - 3y = 10$

8. $x + y + z = -3$
$2x - 3y + z = 9$
$4x - 5y + 2z = 16$

9. $2x - 4y + 3z = 1$
$6x + 2y + 10z = 19$
$-2x + 5y - 2z = 2$

Use matrices *A*, *B*, and *C* to evaluate the matrix expression, if possible. If not possible, state the reason. *(p. 187)*

$$A = \begin{bmatrix} 2 & -5 \\ 3 & -1 \end{bmatrix} \qquad B = \begin{bmatrix} -4 & 3 \\ 8 & 10 \end{bmatrix} \qquad C = \begin{bmatrix} -6 & -2 & 9 \\ 1 & -4 & -1 \end{bmatrix}$$

10. $A + B$

11. $B - 2A$

12. $3A + C$

13. $\frac{2}{3}C$

14. **APPLES** You have \$25 to spend on 21 pounds of three types of apples. Empire apples cost \$1.40 per pound, Red Delicious apples cost \$1.10 per pound, and Golden Delicious apples cost \$1.30 per pound. You want twice as many Red Delicious apples as the other two kinds combined. Use a system of equations to find how many pounds of each type you should buy. *(p. 178)*

Graphing Calculator **ACTIVITY** *Use after Lesson 3.5*

@HomeTutor
classzone.com
Keystrokes

3.5 Use Matrix Operations

QUESTION **How can you use a graphing calculator to perform matrix operations?**

EXAMPLE **Perform operations with matrices**

Using matrices A and B below, find $A + B$ and $3A - 2B$.

$$A = \begin{bmatrix} 8 & -1 & 2 \\ 3 & -7 & 9 \end{bmatrix} \qquad B = \begin{bmatrix} 1 & 0 & -5 \\ -4 & 6 & 10 \end{bmatrix}$$

***STEP 1* Enter matrix A**

Enter the dimensions and elements of matrix A.

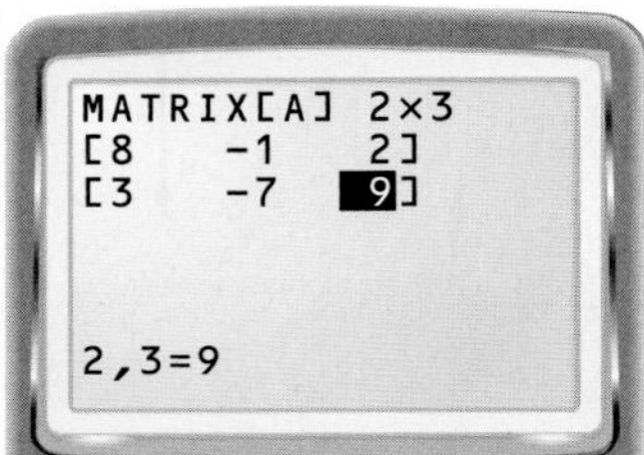

***STEP 2* Enter matrix B**

Enter the dimensions and elements of matrix B.

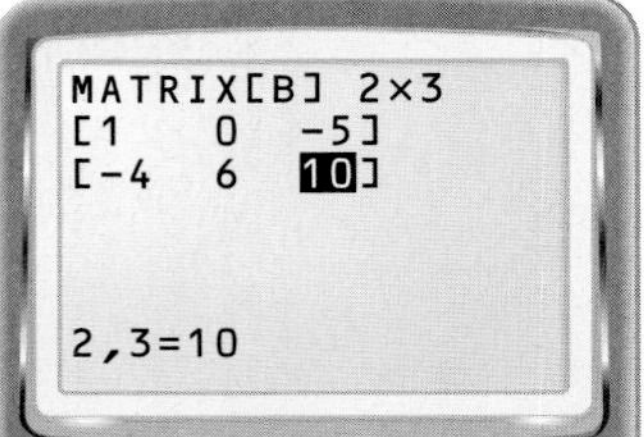

***STEP 3* Perform calculations**

From the home screen, calculate $A + B$ and $3A - 2B$.

```
[A]+[B]
  [[9    -1    -3]
   [-1   -1    19]]
3[A]-2[B]
  [[22   -3    16]
   [17   -33   7 ]]
```

PRACTICE

Use a graphing calculator to perform the indicated operation(s).

1. $\begin{bmatrix} 7 & 3 \\ 5 & -2 \end{bmatrix} + \begin{bmatrix} 12 & -8 \\ 3 & -6 \end{bmatrix}$

2. $2.6\begin{bmatrix} 12.4 & 6.8 & -1.2 \\ -0.8 & 5.6 & -3.2 \end{bmatrix}$

3. $\begin{bmatrix} 3 & 1 & -2 \\ -1 & 5 & 6 \\ 4 & 13 & 0 \end{bmatrix} + \begin{bmatrix} -9 & 10 & -3 \\ 0 & 6 & 1 \\ 14 & 7 & -8 \end{bmatrix}$

4. $3\begin{bmatrix} 4 & -3 \\ 8 & -7 \\ -1 & 2 \end{bmatrix} - 2\begin{bmatrix} -5 & 8 \\ -7 & 9 \\ 4 & -3 \end{bmatrix}$

5. BOOK SALES The matrices below show book sales (in thousands of dollars) at a chain of bookstores for July and August. The book formats are hardcover and paperback. The categories of books are romance (R), mystery (M), science fiction (S), and children's (C). Find the total sales of each format and category for July and August.

	July				August			
	R	**M**	**S**	**C**	**R**	**M**	**S**	**C**
Hardcover	18	16	21	13	26	20	17	8
Paperback	36	20	14	30	40	24	8	20

3.6 Multiply Matrices

Before You added and subtracted matrices.

Now You will multiply matrices.

Why? So you can calculate the cost of sports equipment, as in Example 4.

Key Vocabulary
- **matrix,** *p. 187*
- **dimensions,** *p. 187*
- **elements,** *p. 187*

The product of two matrices A and B is defined provided the number of columns in A is equal to the number of rows in B.

If A is an $m \times n$ matrix and B is an $n \times p$ matrix, then the product AB is an $m \times p$ matrix.

$$\underset{m \times n}{A} \cdot \underset{n \times p}{B} = \underset{m \times p}{AB}$$

equal

dimensions of ***AB***

EXAMPLE 1 Describe matrix products

State whether the product AB is defined. If so, give the dimensions of AB.

a. A: 4×3, B: 3×2

b. A: 3×4, B: 3×2

Solution

a. Because A is a 4×3 matrix and B is a 3×2 matrix, the product AB is defined and is a 4×2 matrix.

b. Because the number of columns in A (four) does not equal the number of rows in B (three), the product AB is not defined.

GUIDED PRACTICE for Example 1

State whether the product AB is defined. If so, give the dimensions of AB.

1. A: 5×2, B: 2×2

2. A: 3×2, B: 3×2

KEY CONCEPT *For Your Notebook*

Multiplying Matrices

Words To find the element in the ith row and jth column of the product matrix AB, multiply each element in the ith row of A by the corresponding element in the jth column of B, then add the products.

Algebra

$$\underset{A}{\begin{bmatrix} a & b \\ c & d \end{bmatrix}} \cdot \underset{B}{\begin{bmatrix} e & f \\ g & h \end{bmatrix}} = \underset{AB}{\begin{bmatrix} ae + bg & af + bh \\ ce + dg & cf + dh \end{bmatrix}}$$

EXAMPLE 2 Find the product of two matrices

Find AB if $A = \begin{bmatrix} 1 & 4 \\ 3 & -2 \end{bmatrix}$ and $B = \begin{bmatrix} 5 & -7 \\ 9 & 6 \end{bmatrix}$.

AVOID ERRORS
Order is important when multiplying matrices. To find *AB*, write matrix *A* on the left and matrix *B* on the right.

Solution

Because A is a 2×2 matrix and B is a 2×2 matrix, the product AB is defined and is a 2×2 matrix.

STEP 1 **Multiply** the numbers in the first row of A by the numbers in the first column of B, add the products, and put the result in the first row, first column of AB.

$$\begin{bmatrix} 1 & 4 \\ 3 & -2 \end{bmatrix}\begin{bmatrix} 5 & -7 \\ 9 & 6 \end{bmatrix} = \begin{bmatrix} 1(5) + 4(9) & \\ & \end{bmatrix}$$

STEP 2 **Multiply** the numbers in the first row of A by the numbers in the second column of B, add the products, and put the result in the first row, second column of AB.

$$\begin{bmatrix} 1 & 4 \\ 3 & -2 \end{bmatrix}\begin{bmatrix} 5 & -7 \\ 9 & 6 \end{bmatrix} = \begin{bmatrix} 1(5) + 4(9) & 1(-7) + 4(6) \\ & \end{bmatrix}$$

STEP 3 **Multiply** the numbers in the second row of A by the numbers in the first column of B, add the products, and put the result in the second row, first column of AB.

$$\begin{bmatrix} 1 & 4 \\ 3 & -2 \end{bmatrix}\begin{bmatrix} 5 & -7 \\ 9 & 6 \end{bmatrix} = \begin{bmatrix} 1(5) + 4(9) & 1(-7) + 4(6) \\ 3(5) + (-2)(9) & \end{bmatrix}$$

STEP 4 **Multiply** the numbers in the second row of A by the numbers in the second column of B, add the products, and put the result in the second row, second column of AB.

$$\begin{bmatrix} 1 & 4 \\ 3 & -2 \end{bmatrix}\begin{bmatrix} 5 & -7 \\ 9 & 6 \end{bmatrix} = \begin{bmatrix} 1(5) + 4(9) & 1(-7) + 4(6) \\ 3(5) + (-2)(9) & 3(-7) + (-2)(6) \end{bmatrix}$$

STEP 5 **Simplify** the product matrix.

$$\begin{bmatrix} 1(5) + 4(9) & 1(-7) + 4(6) \\ 3(5) + (-2)(9) & 3(-7) + (-2)(6) \end{bmatrix} = \begin{bmatrix} 41 & 17 \\ -3 & -33 \end{bmatrix}$$

Animated Algebra at classzone.com

For the matrices A and B in Example 2, notice that the product BA is not the same as the product AB.

$$BA = \begin{bmatrix} 5 & -7 \\ 9 & 6 \end{bmatrix}\begin{bmatrix} 1 & 4 \\ 3 & -2 \end{bmatrix} = \begin{bmatrix} -16 & 34 \\ 27 & 24 \end{bmatrix} \neq AB$$

In general, matrix multiplication is *not* commutative.

✓ GUIDED PRACTICE for Example 2

3. Find AB if $A = \begin{bmatrix} -3 & 3 \\ 1 & -2 \end{bmatrix}$ and $B = \begin{bmatrix} 1 & 5 \\ -3 & -2 \end{bmatrix}$.

EXAMPLE 3 Use matrix operations

Using the given matrices, evaluate the expression.

$$A = \begin{bmatrix} 4 & 3 \\ -1 & -2 \\ 2 & 0 \end{bmatrix}, B = \begin{bmatrix} -3 & 0 \\ 1 & -2 \end{bmatrix}, C = \begin{bmatrix} 1 & 4 \\ -3 & -1 \end{bmatrix}$$

a. $A(B + C)$ **b.** $AB + AC$

Solution

a. $$A(B + C) = \begin{bmatrix} 4 & 3 \\ -1 & -2 \\ 2 & 0 \end{bmatrix}\left(\begin{bmatrix} -3 & 0 \\ 1 & -2 \end{bmatrix} + \begin{bmatrix} 1 & 4 \\ -3 & -1 \end{bmatrix}\right)$$

$$= \begin{bmatrix} 4 & 3 \\ -1 & -2 \\ 2 & 0 \end{bmatrix}\begin{bmatrix} -2 & 4 \\ -2 & -3 \end{bmatrix} = \begin{bmatrix} -14 & 7 \\ 6 & 2 \\ -4 & 8 \end{bmatrix}$$

b. $$AB + AC = \begin{bmatrix} 4 & 3 \\ -1 & -2 \\ 2 & 0 \end{bmatrix}\begin{bmatrix} -3 & 0 \\ 1 & -2 \end{bmatrix} + \begin{bmatrix} 4 & 3 \\ -1 & -2 \\ 2 & 0 \end{bmatrix}\begin{bmatrix} 1 & 4 \\ -3 & -1 \end{bmatrix}$$

$$= \begin{bmatrix} -9 & -6 \\ 1 & 4 \\ -6 & 0 \end{bmatrix} + \begin{bmatrix} -5 & 13 \\ 5 & -2 \\ 2 & 8 \end{bmatrix} = \begin{bmatrix} -14 & 7 \\ 6 & 2 \\ -4 & 8 \end{bmatrix}$$

MULTIPLICATION PROPERTIES Notice in Example 3 that $A(B + C) = AB + AC$, which is true in general. This and other properties of matrix multiplication are summarized below.

REVIEW PROPERTIES
For help with properties of real numbers, see p. 2.

CONCEPT SUMMARY *For Your Notebook*

Properties of Matrix Multiplication

Let *A*, *B*, and *C* be matrices and let *k* be a scalar.

Associative Property of Matrix Multiplication	$A(BC) = (AB)C$
Left Distributive Property	$A(B + C) = AB + AC$
Right Distributive Property	$(A + B)C = AC + BC$
Associative Property of Scalar Multiplication	$k(AB) = (kA)B = A(kB)$

✓ GUIDED PRACTICE for Example 3

Using the given matrices, evaluate the expression.

$$A = \begin{bmatrix} -1 & 2 \\ -3 & 0 \\ 4 & 1 \end{bmatrix}, B = \begin{bmatrix} 3 & 2 \\ -2 & -1 \end{bmatrix}, C = \begin{bmatrix} -4 & 5 \\ 1 & 0 \end{bmatrix}$$

4. $A(B - C)$ **5.** $AB - AC$ **6.** $-\frac{1}{2}(AB)$

COST MATRICES Matrix multiplication is useful in business applications because an *inventory* matrix, when multiplied by a *cost per item* matrix, results in a *total cost* matrix.

$$\begin{bmatrix}\text{Inventory}\\ \text{matrix}\end{bmatrix} \cdot \begin{bmatrix}\text{Cost per item}\\ \text{matrix}\end{bmatrix} = \begin{bmatrix}\text{Total cost}\\ \text{matrix}\end{bmatrix}$$

$$m \times n \qquad\qquad n \times p \qquad\qquad m \times p$$

For the total cost matrix to be meaningful, the column labels for the inventory matrix must match the row labels for the cost per item matrix.

EXAMPLE 4 Use matrices to calculate total cost

SPORTS Two hockey teams submit equipment lists for the season as shown.

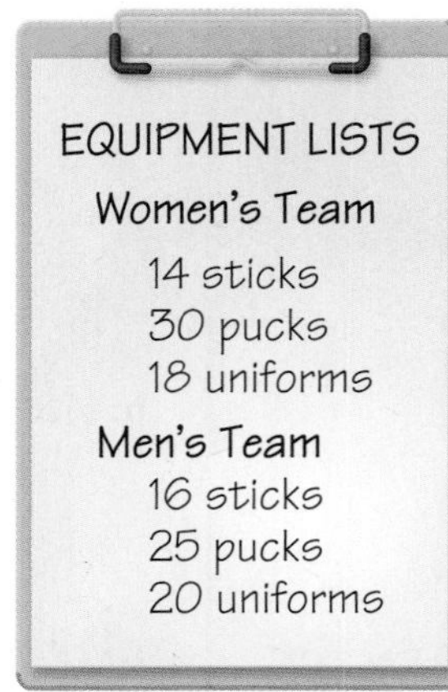

Each stick costs \$60, each puck costs \$2, and each uniform costs \$35. Use matrix multiplication to find the total cost of equipment for each team.

Solution

To begin, write the equipment lists and the costs per item in matrix form. In order to use matrix multiplication, set up the matrices so that the columns of the equipment matrix match the rows of the cost matrix.

Equipment

	Sticks	Pucks	Uniforms
Women's team	14	30	18
Men's team	16	25	20

Cost

	Dollars
Sticks	60
Pucks	2
Uniforms	35

The total cost of equipment for each team can be found by multiplying the equipment matrix by the cost matrix. The equipment matrix is 2×3 and the cost matrix is 3×1. So, their product is a 2×1 matrix.

$$\begin{bmatrix} 14 & 30 & 18 \\ 16 & 25 & 20 \end{bmatrix}\begin{bmatrix} 60 \\ 2 \\ 35 \end{bmatrix} = \begin{bmatrix} 14(60) + 30(2) + 18(35) \\ 16(60) + 25(2) + 20(35) \end{bmatrix} = \begin{bmatrix} 1530 \\ 1710 \end{bmatrix}$$

The labels for the product matrix are shown below.

Total Cost

	Dollars
Women's team	1530
Men's team	1710

▶ The total cost of equipment for the women's team is \$1530, and the total cost for the men's team is \$1710.

✓ **GUIDED PRACTICE** for Example 4

7. **WHAT IF?** In Example 4, suppose a stick costs \$75, a puck costs \$1, and a uniform costs \$45. Find the total cost of equipment for each team.

3.6 EXERCISES

HOMEWORK KEY
○ = **WORKED-OUT SOLUTIONS** on p. WS6 for Exs. 13, 23, and 41
★ = **STANDARDIZED TEST PRACTICE** Exs. 2, 9, 21, 35, 41, and 44

SKILL PRACTICE

1. **VOCABULARY** Copy and complete: The product of matrices A and B is defined provided the number of _?_ in A is equal to the number of _?_ in B.

2. ★ **WRITING** Suppose A and B are two matrices and AB is defined. *Explain* how to find the element in the first row and first column of AB.

EXAMPLE 1 on p. 195 for Exs. 3–9

MATRIX PRODUCTS State whether the product AB is defined. If so, give the dimensions of AB.

3. A: 2×2, B: 2×2
4. A: 3×4, B: 4×2
5. A: 2×1, B: 2×2
6. A: 1×2, B: 2×3
7. A: 4×3, B: 2×3
8. A: 2×1, B: 1×5

9. ★ **MULTIPLE CHOICE** If A is a 2×3 matrix and B is a 3×2 matrix, what are the dimensions of AB?

Ⓐ 2×2 Ⓑ 3×3 Ⓒ 3×2 Ⓓ 2×3

EXAMPLE 2 on p. 196 for Exs. 10–21

MULTIPLYING MATRICES Find the product. If the product is not defined, state the reason.

10. $\begin{bmatrix} 3 & -1 \end{bmatrix}\begin{bmatrix} 5 \\ 7 \end{bmatrix}$

11. $\begin{bmatrix} 1 \\ 4 \end{bmatrix}\begin{bmatrix} -2 & 1 \end{bmatrix}$

12. $\begin{bmatrix} -1 & 0 \\ 5 & 4 \end{bmatrix}\begin{bmatrix} 4 & -6 \end{bmatrix}$

13. $\begin{bmatrix} 9 & -3 \\ 0 & 2 \end{bmatrix}\begin{bmatrix} 0 & 1 \\ 4 & -2 \end{bmatrix}$

14. $\begin{bmatrix} 5 & 0 \\ -4 & 1 \end{bmatrix}\begin{bmatrix} -3 & 2 \\ 6 & 2 \end{bmatrix}$

15. $\begin{bmatrix} 5 & 2 \\ 0 & -4 \\ 1 & 6 \end{bmatrix}\begin{bmatrix} 3 & 7 \\ -2 & 0 \end{bmatrix}$

16. $\begin{bmatrix} 0 & -4 \\ 2 & 5 \\ 4 & 0 \end{bmatrix}\begin{bmatrix} 2 & 8 \\ 3 & 0 \\ -5 & -2 \end{bmatrix}$

17. $\begin{bmatrix} 1 & 3 & 0 \\ 2 & 12 & -4 \end{bmatrix}\begin{bmatrix} 9 & 1 \\ 4 & -3 \\ -2 & 4 \end{bmatrix}$

18. $\begin{bmatrix} 2 & 5 \\ -1 & 4 \\ 3 & -7 \end{bmatrix}\begin{bmatrix} 0 & 1 & 5 \\ -3 & 10 & -4 \end{bmatrix}$

ERROR ANALYSIS *Describe* and correct the error in finding the element in the first row and first column of the matrix product.

19.
$$\begin{bmatrix} 3 & -1 \\ 6 & 2 \end{bmatrix}\begin{bmatrix} 7 & 0 \\ 1 & -6 \end{bmatrix} =$$
$$\begin{bmatrix} 3(7) + (-1)(0) & \\ & \end{bmatrix} = \begin{bmatrix} 21 & \\ & \end{bmatrix}$$

20.
$$\begin{bmatrix} 2 & 5 \\ 1 & 7 \end{bmatrix}\begin{bmatrix} 4 & -8 \\ 3 & -1 \end{bmatrix} =$$
$$\begin{bmatrix} 2(4) + 1(-8) & \\ & \end{bmatrix} = \begin{bmatrix} 0 & \\ & \end{bmatrix}$$

21. ★ **MULTIPLE CHOICE** What is the product of $\begin{bmatrix} 1 & -4 \\ 3 & -2 \end{bmatrix}$ and $\begin{bmatrix} 4 & -1 \\ 0 & -3 \end{bmatrix}$?

Ⓐ $\begin{bmatrix} -4 & 12 \\ 3 & -3 \end{bmatrix}$ Ⓑ $\begin{bmatrix} 4 & 11 \\ 12 & 3 \end{bmatrix}$ Ⓒ $\begin{bmatrix} -4 & 11 \\ 12 & -3 \end{bmatrix}$ Ⓓ $\begin{bmatrix} 4 & -11 \\ 0 & 3 \end{bmatrix}$

EXAMPLE 3
on p. 197
for Exs. 22–29

EVALUATING EXPRESSIONS **Using the given matrices, evaluate the expression.**

$$A = \begin{bmatrix} 5 & -3 \\ -2 & 4 \end{bmatrix},\ B = \begin{bmatrix} 0 & 1 \\ 4 & -2 \end{bmatrix},\ C = \begin{bmatrix} -6 & 3 \\ 4 & 1 \end{bmatrix},\ D = \begin{bmatrix} 1 & 3 & 2 \\ -3 & 1 & 4 \\ 2 & 1 & -2 \end{bmatrix},\ E = \begin{bmatrix} -3 & 1 & 4 \\ 7 & 0 & -2 \\ 3 & 4 & -1 \end{bmatrix}$$

22. $3AB$ | **23.** $-\frac{1}{2}AC$ | **24.** $AB + AC$ | **25.** $AB - BA$

26. $E(D + E)$ | **27.** $(D + E)D$ | **28.** $-2(BC)$ | **29.** $4AC + 3AB$

SOLVING MATRIX EQUATIONS **Solve for *x* and *y*.**

30. $\begin{bmatrix} -2 & 1 & 2 \\ 3 & 2 & 4 \\ 0 & -2 & 4 \end{bmatrix}\begin{bmatrix} 1 \\ x \\ 3 \end{bmatrix} = \begin{bmatrix} 6 \\ 19 \\ y \end{bmatrix}$

31. $\begin{bmatrix} 4 & 1 & 3 \\ -2 & x & 1 \end{bmatrix}\begin{bmatrix} 9 & -2 \\ 2 & 1 \\ -1 & 1 \end{bmatrix} = \begin{bmatrix} y & -4 \\ -13 & 8 \end{bmatrix}$

FINDING POWERS **Using the given matrix, find $A^2 = AA$ and $A^3 = AAA$.**

32. $A = \begin{bmatrix} 1 & -1 \\ 0 & 2 \end{bmatrix}$

33. $A = \begin{bmatrix} -4 & 1 \\ 2 & -1 \end{bmatrix}$

34. $A = \begin{bmatrix} 2 & 0 & -1 \\ 1 & 3 & 2 \\ -2 & -1 & 0 \end{bmatrix}$

35. ★ **OPEN-ENDED MATH** Find two matrices *A* and *B* such that $A \neq B$ and $AB = BA$.

36. **CHALLENGE** Let $A = \begin{bmatrix} a & b \\ c & d \end{bmatrix}$ and $B = \begin{bmatrix} e & f \\ g & h \end{bmatrix}$, and let *k* be a scalar. Prove the associative property of scalar multiplication for 2×2 matrices by showing that $k(AB) = (kA)B = A(kB)$.

PROBLEM SOLVING

EXAMPLE 4
on p. 198
for Exs. 37–42

In Exercises 37 and 38, write an inventory matrix and a cost per item matrix. Then use matrix multiplication to write a total cost matrix.

37. SOFTBALL A softball team needs to buy 12 bats, 45 balls, and 15 uniforms. Each bat costs \$21, each ball costs \$4, and each uniform costs \$30.

@HomeTutor for problem solving help at classzone.com

38. ART SUPPLIES A teacher is buying supplies for two art classes. For class 1, the teacher buys 24 tubes of paint, 12 brushes, and 17 canvases. For class 2, the teacher buys 20 tubes of paint, 14 brushes, and 15 canvases. Each tube of paint costs \$3.35, each brush costs \$1.75, and each canvas costs \$4.50.

@HomeTutor for problem solving help at classzone.com

39. MULTI-STEP PROBLEM Tickets to the senior class play cost \$2 for students, \$5 for adults, and \$4 for senior citizens. At Friday night's performance, there were 120 students, 150 adults, and 40 senior citizens in attendance. At Saturday night's performance, there were 192 students, 215 adults, and 54 senior citizens in attendance. Organize the information using matrices. Then use matrix multiplication to find the income from ticket sales for Friday and Saturday nights' performances.

○ = WORKED-OUT SOLUTIONS on p. WS1

★ = STANDARDIZED TEST PRACTICE

40. SUMMER OLYMPICS The top three countries in the final medal standings for the 2004 Summer Olympics were the United States, China, and Russia. Each gold medal is worth 3 points, each silver medal is worth 2 points, and each bronze medal is worth 1 point. Organize the information using matrices. How many points did each country score?

Medals Won

	Gold	Silver	Bronze
USA	35	39	29
China	32	17	14
Russia	27	27	38

41. ★ **SHORT RESPONSE** Matrix S gives the numbers of three types of cars sold in February by two car dealers, dealer A and dealer B. Matrix P gives the profit for each type of car sold. Which matrix is defined, SP or PS? Find this matrix and explain what its elements represent.

Matrix S

	A	B
Compact	21	16
Mid-size	40	33
Full-size	15	19

Matrix P

	Compact	Mid-size	Full-size
Profit	\$650	\$825	\$1050

42. GRADING Your overall grade in math class is a weighted average of three components: homework, quizzes, and tests. Homework counts for 20% of your grade, quizzes count for 30%, and tests count for 50%. The spreadsheet below shows the grades on homework, quizzes, and tests for five students. Organize the information using a matrix, then multiply the matrix by a matrix of weights to find each student's overall grade.

	A	B	C	D
1	Name	Homework	Quizzes	Test
2	Jean	82	88	86
3	Ted	92	88	90
4	Pat	82	73	81
5	Al	74	75	78
6	Matt	88	92	90

43. MULTI-STEP PROBLEM Residents of a certain suburb commute to a nearby city either by driving or by using public transportation. Each year, 20% of those who drive switch to public transportation, and 5% of those who use public transportation switch to driving.

a. The information above can be represented by the *transition matrix*

$$T = \begin{bmatrix} 1 - p & q \\ p & 1 - q \end{bmatrix}$$

where p is the percent of commuters who switch from driving to public transportation and q is the percent of commuters who switch from public transportation to driving. (Both p and q are expressed as decimals.) Write a transition matrix for the given situation.

b. Suppose 5000 commuters drive and 8000 commuters take public transportation. Let M_0 be the following matrix:

$$M_0 = \begin{bmatrix} 5000 \\ 8000 \end{bmatrix}$$

Find $M_1 = TM_0$. What does this matrix represent?

c. Find $M_2 = TM_1$, $M_3 = TM_2$, and $M_4 = TM_3$. What do these matrices represent?

44. ★ **EXTENDED RESPONSE** Two students have a business selling handmade scarves. The scarves come in four different styles: plain, with the class year, with the school name, and with the school mascot. The costs of making each style of scarf are \$10, \$15, \$20, and \$20, respectively. The prices of each style of scarf are \$15, \$20, \$25, and \$30, respectively.

   a. Write a 4×1 matrix C that gives the cost of making each style of scarf and a 4×1 matrix P that gives the price of each style of scarf.

   b. The sales for the first three years of the business are shown below.

   Year 1: *0 plain, 20 class year, 100 school name, 0 school mascot*

   Year 2: *10 plain, 100 class year, 50 school name, 30 school mascot*

   Year 3: *20 plain, 300 class year, 100 school name, 50 school mascot*

   Write a 3×4 matrix S that gives the sales for the first three years.

   c. Find SC and SP. What do these matrices represent?

   d. Find $SP - SC$. What does this matrix represent?

45. **CHALLENGE** Matrix A is a 90° rotational matrix. Matrix B contains the coordinates of the vertices of the triangle shown in the graph.

$$A = \begin{bmatrix} 0 & -1 \\ 1 & 0 \end{bmatrix} \qquad B = \begin{bmatrix} -7 & -4 & -4 \\ 4 & 8 & 2 \end{bmatrix}$$

   a. Find AB. Draw the triangle whose vertices are given by AB.

   b. Find the 180° and 270° rotations of the original triangle by using repeated multiplication of the 90° rotational matrix. What are the coordinates of the vertices of the rotated triangles?

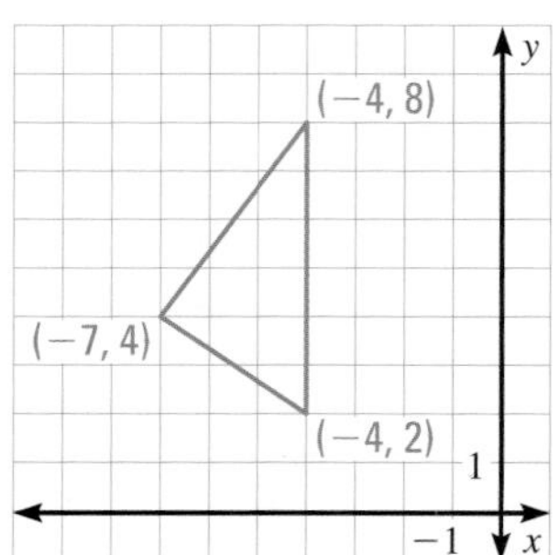

NEW YORK MIXED REVIEW

46. The graph shows the value of a comic book over a period of 9 years. What is a reasonable conclusion about the value of the comic book during the time shown on the graph?

   (A) It appreciated \$2 every year.

   (B) It appreciated \$3 every 2 years.

   (C) Its value at 5 years was twice its value at 2 years.

   (D) Its value at 7 years was half its value at 3 years.

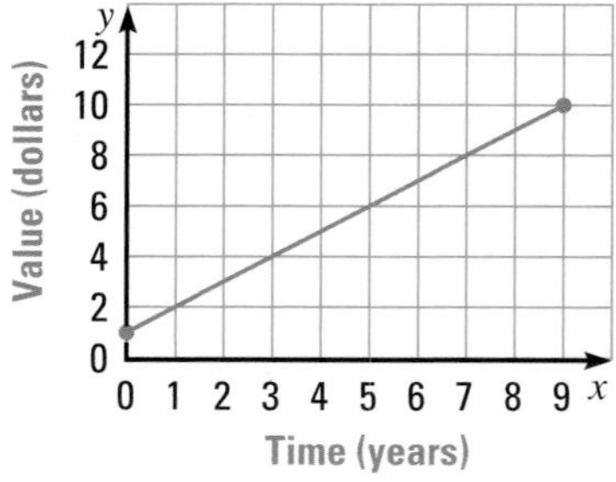

47. Use the information in the diagram. What is the distance x across the river?

   (A) 10 m   (B) 12 m

   (C) 22 m   (D) 30 m

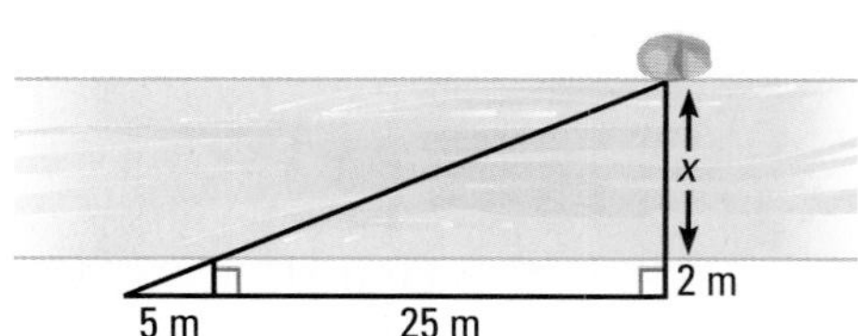

3.7 Evaluate Determinants and Apply Cramer's Rule

Before You added, subtracted, and multiplied matrices.

Now You will evaluate determinants of matrices.

Why? So you can find areas of habitats, as in Example 2.

Key Vocabulary
- **determinant**
- **Cramer's rule**
- **coefficient matrix**

Associated with each square ($n \times n$) matrix is a real number called its **determinant**. The determinant of a matrix A is denoted by det A or by $|A|$.

KEY CONCEPT *For Your Notebook*

The Determinant of a Matrix

Determinant of a 2 × 2 Matrix

$$\det\begin{bmatrix} a & b \\ c & d \end{bmatrix} = \begin{vmatrix} a & b \\ c & d \end{vmatrix} = ad - cb$$

The determinant of a 2 × 2 matrix is the difference of the products of the elements on the diagonals.

Determinant of a 3 × 3 Matrix

STEP 1 **Repeat** the first two columns to the right of the determinant.

STEP 2 **Subtract** the sum of the red products from the sum of the blue products.

$$\det\begin{bmatrix} a & b & c \\ d & e & f \\ g & h & i \end{bmatrix} = \begin{vmatrix} a & b & c \\ d & e & f \\ g & h & i \end{vmatrix}\begin{matrix} a & b \\ d & e \\ g & h \end{matrix} = (aei + bfg + cdh) - (gec + hfa + idb)$$

EXAMPLE 1 Evaluate determinants

Evaluate the determinant of the matrix.

a. $\begin{bmatrix} 5 & 4 \\ 3 & 1 \end{bmatrix}$ **b.** $\begin{bmatrix} 2 & -1 & -3 \\ 4 & 1 & 0 \\ 3 & -4 & -2 \end{bmatrix}$

Solution

a. $\begin{vmatrix} 5 & 4 \\ 3 & 1 \end{vmatrix} = 5(1) - 3(4) = 5 - 12 = -7$

b. $\begin{vmatrix} 2 & -1 & -3 \\ 4 & 1 & 0 \\ 3 & -4 & -2 \end{vmatrix}\begin{matrix} 2 & -1 \\ 4 & 1 \\ 3 & -4 \end{matrix} = (-4 + 0 + 48) - (-9 + 0 + 8) = 44 - (-1) = 45$

AREA OF A TRIANGLE You can use a determinant to find the area of a triangle whose vertices are points in a coordinate plane.

KEY CONCEPT *For Your Notebook*

Area of a Triangle

The area of a triangle with vertices (x_1, y_1), (x_2, y_2), and (x_3, y_3) is given by

$$\text{Area} = \pm\frac{1}{2}\begin{vmatrix} x_1 & y_1 & 1 \\ x_2 & y_2 & 1 \\ x_3 & y_3 & 1 \end{vmatrix}$$

where the symbol $\pm$ indicates that the appropriate sign should be chosen to yield a positive value.

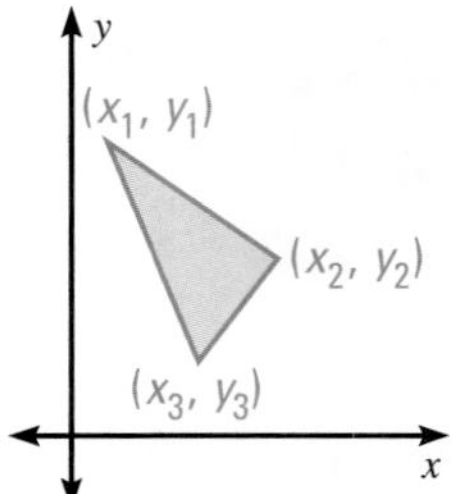

EXAMPLE 2 Find the area of a triangular region

SEA LIONS Off the coast of California lies a triangular region of the Pacific Ocean where huge populations of sea lions and seals live. The triangle is formed by imaginary lines connecting Bodega Bay, the Farallon Islands, and Año Nuevo Island, as shown. (In the map, the coordinates are measured in miles.) Use a determinant to estimate the area of the region.

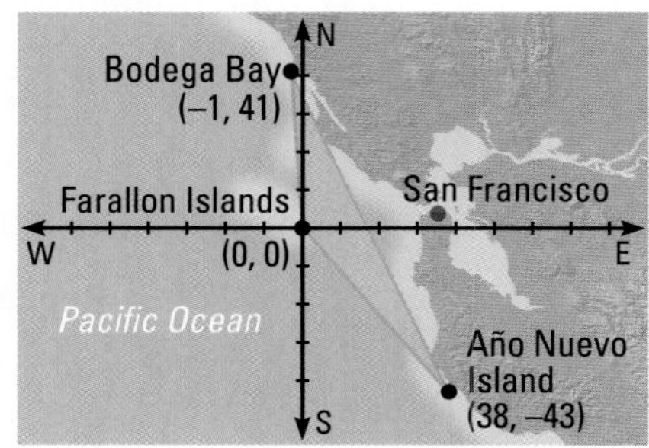

Solution

The approximate coordinates of the vertices of the triangular region are $(-1, 41)$, $(38, -43)$, and $(0, 0)$. So, the area of the region is:

$$\text{Area} = \pm\frac{1}{2}\begin{vmatrix} -1 & 41 & 1 \\ 38 & -43 & 1 \\ 0 & 0 & 1 \end{vmatrix} = \pm\frac{1}{2}\begin{vmatrix} -1 & 41 & 1 \\ 38 & -43 & 1 \\ 0 & 0 & 1 \end{vmatrix}\begin{matrix} -1 & 41 \\ 38 & -43 \\ 0 & 0 \end{matrix}$$

$$= \pm\frac{1}{2}[(43 + 0 + 0) - (0 + 0 + 1558)]$$

$$= 757.5$$

▶ The area of the region is about 758 square miles.

✓ **GUIDED PRACTICE** for Examples 1 and 2

Evaluate the determinant of the matrix.

1. $\begin{bmatrix} 3 & -2 \\ 6 & 1 \end{bmatrix}$

2. $\begin{bmatrix} 4 & -1 & 2 \\ -3 & -2 & -1 \\ 0 & 5 & 1 \end{bmatrix}$

3. $\begin{bmatrix} 10 & -2 & 3 \\ 2 & -12 & 4 \\ 0 & -7 & -2 \end{bmatrix}$

4. Find the area of the triangle with vertices $A(5, 11)$, $B(9, 2)$, and $C(1, 3)$.

43. **MULTI-STEP PROBLEM** An ice cream shop sells the following sizes of ice cream cones: single scoop for \$.90, double scoop for \$1.20, and triple scoop for \$1.60. One day, a total of 120 cones are sold for \$134, as many single-scoop cones are sold as double-scoop and triple-scoop cones combined.

a. Use a linear system and Cramer's rule to find how many of each size of cone are sold.

b. The next day, the shop raises prices by 10%. As a result, the number of each size of cone sold falls by 5%. What is the revenue from cone sales?

44. **SCIENCE** The atomic weights of three compounds are shown in the table. Use a linear system and Cramer's rule to find the atomic weights of fluorine (F), sodium (Na), and chlorine (Cl).

Compound	Formula	Atomic weight
Sodium fluoride	FNa	42
Sodium chloride	NaCl	58.5
Chlorine pentafluoride	ClF_5	130.5

45. ★ **EXTENDED RESPONSE** In Utah and Colorado, an area called the Dinosaur Diamond is known for containing many dinosaur fossils. The map at the right shows the towns at the four vertices of the diamond. The coordinates given are measured in miles.

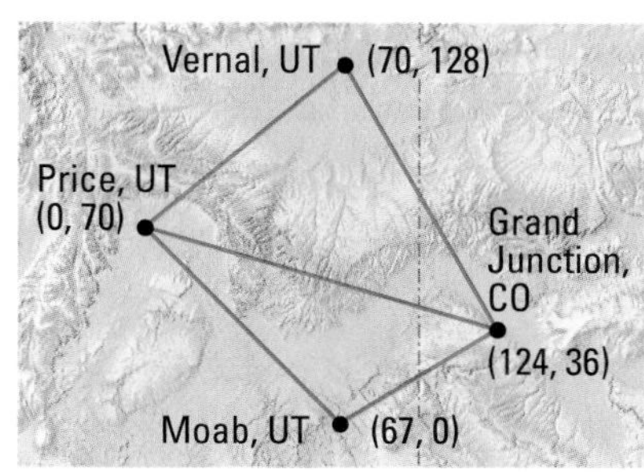

a. Find the area of the top triangular region.

b. Find the area of the bottom triangular region.

c. What is the total area of the Dinosaur Diamond?

d. *Describe* another way in which you can divide the Dinosaur Diamond into two triangles in order to find its area.

46. **CHALLENGE** A farmer is fencing off a triangular region of a pasture, as shown. The area of the region should be 5000 square feet. The farmer has planted the first two fence posts at (0, 0) and (100, 50). He wants to plant the final post along his neighbor's fence, which lies on the horizontal line $y = 120$. At which *two* points could the farmer plant the final post so that the triangular region has the desired area?

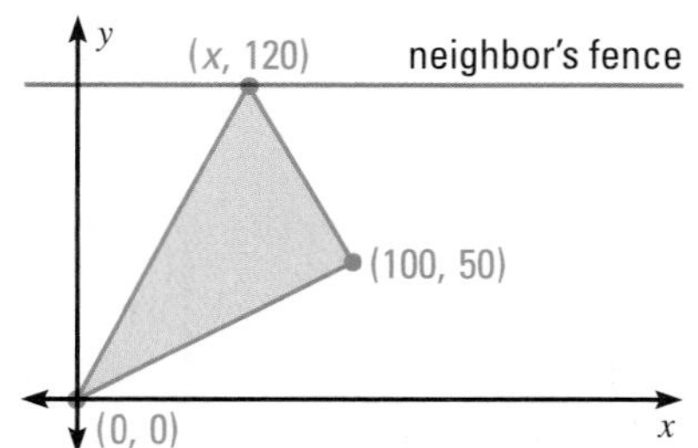

NEW YORK MIXED REVIEW

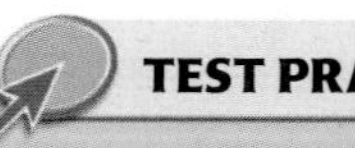

TEST PRACTICE at classzone.com

47. Nadia's weekly salary is \$390, and she receives a \$5 bonus for each new customer she brings in. Which inequality represents the number of new customers, c, she needs to bring in per week to earn at least \$450 per week?

Ⓐ $c < 60$　Ⓑ $c < 12$　Ⓒ $c \geq 12$　Ⓓ $c \geq 60$

48. How many edges does the pentagonal prism have?

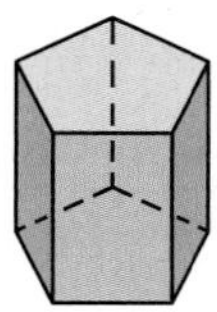

Ⓐ 7　Ⓑ 10

Ⓒ 15　Ⓓ 17

3.8 Use Inverse Matrices to Solve Linear Systems

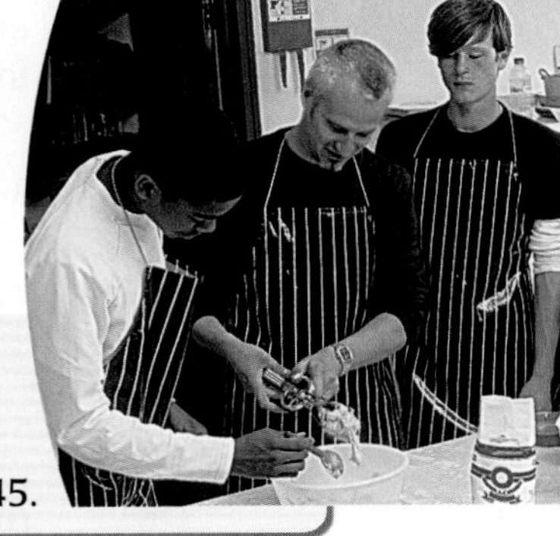

Before You solved linear systems using Cramer's rule.

Now You will solve linear systems using inverse matrices.

Why? So you can find how many batches of a recipe to make, as in Ex. 45.

Key Vocabulary
- **identity matrix**
- **inverse matrices**
- **matrix of variables**
- **matrix of constants**

The $n \times n$ **identity matrix** is a matrix with 1's on the main diagonal and 0's elsewhere. If A is any $n \times n$ matrix and I is the $n \times n$ identity matrix, then $AI = A$ and $IA = A$.

2 × 2 Identity Matrix

$$I = \begin{bmatrix} 1 & 0 \\ 0 & 1 \end{bmatrix}$$

3 × 3 Identity Matrix

$$I = \begin{bmatrix} 1 & 0 & 0 \\ 0 & 1 & 0 \\ 0 & 0 & 1 \end{bmatrix}$$

Two $n \times n$ matrices A and B are **inverses** of each other if their product (in both orders) is the $n \times n$ identity matrix. That is, $AB = I$ and $BA = I$. An $n \times n$ matrix A has an inverse if and only if $\det A \neq 0$. The symbol for the inverse of A is A^{-1}.

KEY CONCEPT *For Your Notebook*

The Inverse of a 2 × 2 Matrix

The inverse of the matrix $A = \begin{bmatrix} a & b \\ c & d \end{bmatrix}$ is

$$A^{-1} = \frac{1}{|A|}\begin{bmatrix} d & -b \\ -c & a \end{bmatrix} = \frac{1}{ad - cb}\begin{bmatrix} d & -b \\ -c & a \end{bmatrix} \text{ provided } ad - cb \neq 0.$$

EXAMPLE 1 Find the inverse of a 2 × 2 matrix

CHECK INVERSES
In Example 1, you can check the inverse by showing that $AA^{-1} = I = A^{-1}A$.

Find the inverse of $A = \begin{bmatrix} 3 & 8 \\ 2 & 5 \end{bmatrix}$.

$$A^{-1} = \frac{1}{15 - 16}\begin{bmatrix} 5 & -8 \\ -2 & 3 \end{bmatrix} = -1\begin{bmatrix} 5 & -8 \\ -2 & 3 \end{bmatrix} = \begin{bmatrix} -5 & 8 \\ 2 & -3 \end{bmatrix}$$

GUIDED PRACTICE for Example 1

Find the inverse of the matrix.

1. $\begin{bmatrix} 6 & 1 \\ 2 & 4 \end{bmatrix}$

2. $\begin{bmatrix} -1 & 5 \\ -4 & 8 \end{bmatrix}$

3. $\begin{bmatrix} -3 & -4 \\ -1 & -2 \end{bmatrix}$

EXAMPLE 2 Solve a matrix equation

Solve the matrix equation $AX = B$ for the 2×2 matrix X.

$$\overbrace{\begin{bmatrix} 2 & -7 \\ -1 & 4 \end{bmatrix}}^{A} X = \overbrace{\begin{bmatrix} -21 & 3 \\ 12 & -2 \end{bmatrix}}^{B}$$

Solution

Begin by finding the inverse of A.

$$A^{-1} = \frac{1}{8-7}\begin{bmatrix} 4 & 7 \\ 1 & 2 \end{bmatrix} = \begin{bmatrix} 4 & 7 \\ 1 & 2 \end{bmatrix}$$

To solve the equation for X, multiply both sides of the equation by A^{-1} *on the left*.

$$\begin{bmatrix} 4 & 7 \\ 1 & 2 \end{bmatrix}\begin{bmatrix} 2 & -7 \\ -1 & 4 \end{bmatrix} X = \begin{bmatrix} 4 & 7 \\ 1 & 2 \end{bmatrix}\begin{bmatrix} -21 & 3 \\ 12 & -2 \end{bmatrix} \qquad A^{-1}AX = A^{-1}B$$

$$\begin{bmatrix} 1 & 0 \\ 0 & 1 \end{bmatrix} X = \begin{bmatrix} 0 & -2 \\ 3 & -1 \end{bmatrix} \qquad IX = A^{-1}B$$

$$X = \begin{bmatrix} 0 & -2 \\ 3 & -1 \end{bmatrix} \qquad X = A^{-1}B$$

Animated Algebra at classzone.com

✓ GUIDED PRACTICE for Example 2

4. Solve the matrix equation $\begin{bmatrix} -4 & 1 \\ 0 & 6 \end{bmatrix} X = \begin{bmatrix} 8 & 9 \\ 24 & 6 \end{bmatrix}$.

INVERSE OF A 3×3 MATRIX The inverse of a 3×3 matrix is difficult to compute by hand. A calculator that will compute inverse matrices is useful in this case.

EXAMPLE 3 Find the inverse of a 3×3 matrix

Use a graphing calculator to find the inverse of A. Then use the calculator to verify your result.

$$A = \begin{bmatrix} 2 & 1 & -2 \\ 5 & 3 & 0 \\ 4 & 3 & 8 \end{bmatrix}$$

Solution

Enter matrix A into a graphing calculator and calculate A^{-1}. Then compute AA^{-1} and $A^{-1}A$ to verify that you obtain the 3×3 identity matrix.

```
[A]-1
  [[12   -7   3 ]
   [-20  12   -5]
   [1.5  -1   .5]]
```

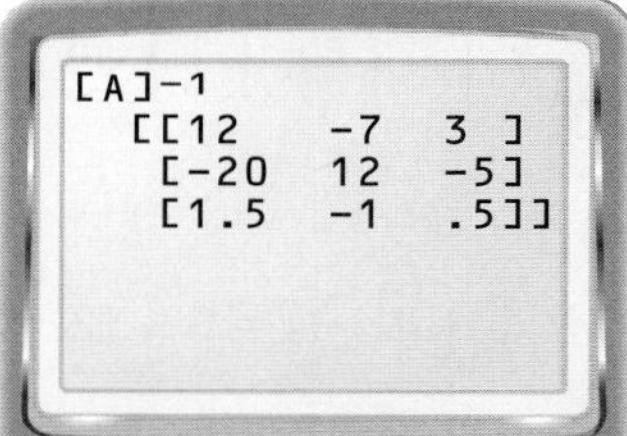

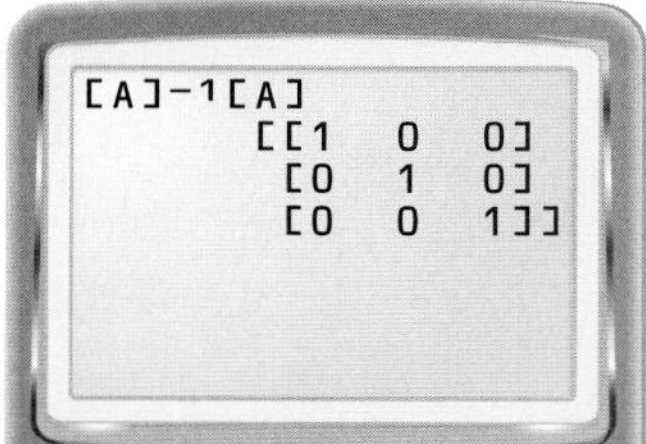

GUIDED PRACTICE for Example 3

Use a graphing calculator to find the inverse of the matrix A. Check the result by showing that $AA^{-1} = I$ and $A^{-1}A = I$.

5. $A = \begin{bmatrix} 2 & -2 & 0 \\ 2 & 0 & -2 \\ 12 & -4 & -6 \end{bmatrix}$

6. $A = \begin{bmatrix} -3 & 4 & 5 \\ 1 & 5 & 0 \\ 5 & 2 & 2 \end{bmatrix}$

7. $A = \begin{bmatrix} 2 & 1 & -2 \\ 5 & 3 & 0 \\ 4 & 3 & 8 \end{bmatrix}$

KEY CONCEPT *For Your Notebook*

Using an Inverse Matrix to Solve a Linear System

STEP 1 **Write** the system as a matrix equation $AX = B$. The matrix A is the coefficient matrix, X is the **matrix of variables**, and B is the **matrix of constants**.

STEP 2 **Find** the inverse of matrix A.

STEP 3 **Multiply** each side of $AX = B$ by A^{-1} *on the left* to find the solution $X = A^{-1}B$.

EXAMPLE 4 Solve a linear system

Use an inverse matrix to solve the linear system.

$2x - 3y = 19$ Equation 1

$x + 4y = -7$ Equation 2

SOLVE SYSTEMS

You can use the method shown in Example 4 if A has an inverse. If A does not have an inverse, then the system has either no solution or infinitely many solutions.

Solution

STEP 1 **Write** the linear system as a matrix equation $AX = B$.

coefficient matrix (A) · matrix of variables (X) = matrix of constants (B)

$$\begin{bmatrix} 2 & -3 \\ 1 & 4 \end{bmatrix} \cdot \begin{bmatrix} x \\ y \end{bmatrix} = \begin{bmatrix} 19 \\ -7 \end{bmatrix}$$

STEP 2 **Find** the inverse of matrix A.

$$A^{-1} = \frac{1}{8 - (-3)}\begin{bmatrix} 4 & 3 \\ -1 & 2 \end{bmatrix} = \begin{bmatrix} \frac{4}{11} & \frac{3}{11} \\ -\frac{1}{11} & \frac{2}{11} \end{bmatrix}$$

STEP 3 **Multiply** the matrix of constants by A^{-1} on the left.

$$X = A^{-1}B = \begin{bmatrix} \frac{4}{11} & \frac{3}{11} \\ -\frac{1}{11} & \frac{2}{11} \end{bmatrix}\begin{bmatrix} 19 \\ -7 \end{bmatrix} = \begin{bmatrix} 5 \\ -3 \end{bmatrix} = \begin{bmatrix} x \\ y \end{bmatrix}$$

▶ The solution of the system is (5, −3).

CHECK $2(5) - 3(-3) = 10 + 9 = 19$ ✓ $5 + 4(-3) = 5 - 12 = -7$ ✓

Animated Algebra at classzone.com

EXAMPLE 5 Solve a multi-step problem

GIFTS A company sells three types of movie gift baskets. A basic basket with 2 movie passes and 1 package of microwave popcorn costs \$15.50. A medium basket with 2 movie passes, 2 packages of popcorn, and 1 DVD costs \$37. A super basket with 4 movie passes, 3 packages of popcorn, and 2 DVDs costs \$72.50. Find the cost of each item in the gift baskets.

ANOTHER WAY
For an alternative method for solving the problem in Example 5, turn to page 218 for the **Problem Solving Workshop**.

Solution

STEP 1 **Write** verbal models for the situation.

2 · [Cost of movie pass] + [Cost of popcorn] = [Cost of basic basket] — **Equation 1**

2 · [Cost of movie pass] + 2 · [Cost of popcorn] + [Cost of DVD] = [Cost of medium basket] — **Equation 2**

4 · [Cost of movie pass] + 3 · [Cost of popcorn] + 2 · [Cost of DVD] = [Cost of super basket] — **Equation 3**

STEP 2 **Write** a system of equations. Let m be the cost of a movie pass, p be the cost of a package of popcorn, and d be the cost of a DVD.

$2m + p = 15.50$ **Equation 1**
$2m + 2p + d = 37.00$ **Equation 2**
$4m + 3p + 2d = 72.50$ **Equation 3**

STEP 3 **Rewrite** the system as a matrix equation.

$$\begin{bmatrix} 2 & 1 & 0 \\ 2 & 2 & 1 \\ 4 & 3 & 2 \end{bmatrix}\begin{bmatrix} m \\ p \\ d \end{bmatrix} = \begin{bmatrix} 15.50 \\ 37.00 \\ 72.50 \end{bmatrix}$$

STEP 4 **Enter** the coefficient matrix A and the matrix of constants B into a graphing calculator. Then find the solution $X = A^{-1}B$.

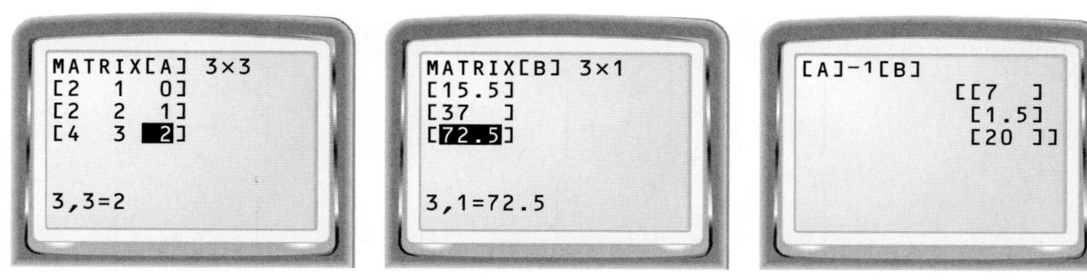

▶ A movie pass costs \$7, a package of popcorn costs \$1.50, and a DVD costs \$20.

✓ GUIDED PRACTICE for Examples 4 and 5

Use an inverse matrix to solve the linear system.

8. $4x + y = 10$
$3x + 5y = -1$

9. $2x - y = -6$
$6x - 3y = -18$

10. $3x - y = -5$
$-4x + 2y = 8$

11. WHAT IF In Example 5, how does the answer change if a basic basket costs \$17, a medium basket costs \$35, and a super basket costs \$69?

3.8 EXERCISES

HOMEWORK KEY

○ = **WORKED-OUT SOLUTIONS** on p. WS7 for Exs. 3, 25, and 47

★ = **STANDARDIZED TEST PRACTICE** Exs. 2, 12, 34, 41, and 46

◆ = **MULTIPLE REPRESENTATIONS** Ex. 45

SKILL PRACTICE

1. **VOCABULARY** Identify the matrix of variables and the matrix of constants in the matrix equation. $\begin{bmatrix} -1 & 2 \\ 3 & 4 \end{bmatrix}\begin{bmatrix} x \\ y \end{bmatrix} = \begin{bmatrix} 4 \\ -2 \end{bmatrix}$

2. ★ **WRITING** *Explain* how to find the inverse of a 2×2 matrix A where $\det A \neq 0$.

EXAMPLE 1 on p. 210 for Exs. 3–12

FINDING INVERSES **Find the inverse of the matrix.**

3. $\begin{bmatrix} 1 & -5 \\ -1 & 4 \end{bmatrix}$
4. $\begin{bmatrix} -2 & 3 \\ -3 & 4 \end{bmatrix}$
5. $\begin{bmatrix} 6 & 2 \\ 5 & 2 \end{bmatrix}$
6. $\begin{bmatrix} -7 & -9 \\ 2 & 3 \end{bmatrix}$
7. $\begin{bmatrix} -4 & -6 \\ 4 & 7 \end{bmatrix}$
8. $\begin{bmatrix} 6 & -22 \\ -12 & 20 \end{bmatrix}$
9. $\begin{bmatrix} -24 & 60 \\ -6 & 30 \end{bmatrix}$
10. $\begin{bmatrix} \frac{4}{3} & \frac{5}{6} \\ -4 & -1 \end{bmatrix}$

11. **ERROR ANALYSIS** *Describe* and correct the error in finding the inverse of the matrix $\begin{bmatrix} 2 & 4 \\ 1 & 5 \end{bmatrix}$.

$$\begin{bmatrix} 2 & 4 \\ 1 & 5 \end{bmatrix}^{-1} = 6\begin{bmatrix} 5 & -4 \\ -1 & 2 \end{bmatrix} = \begin{bmatrix} 30 & -24 \\ -6 & 12 \end{bmatrix} \times$$

12. ★ **MULTIPLE CHOICE** What is the inverse of the matrix $\begin{bmatrix} 10 & -3 \\ 3 & -1 \end{bmatrix}$?

(A) $\begin{bmatrix} -10 & 3 \\ -3 & 1 \end{bmatrix}$ (B) $\begin{bmatrix} -1 & 3 \\ -3 & 10 \end{bmatrix}$ (C) $\begin{bmatrix} 1 & -3 \\ 3 & -10 \end{bmatrix}$ (D) $\begin{bmatrix} 10 & -3 \\ 3 & -1 \end{bmatrix}$

EXAMPLE 2 on p. 211 for Exs. 13–18

SOLVING EQUATIONS **Solve the matrix equation.**

13. $\begin{bmatrix} 1 & 1 \\ 4 & 5 \end{bmatrix}X = \begin{bmatrix} 2 & 3 \\ -1 & 6 \end{bmatrix}$
14. $\begin{bmatrix} 6 & 8 \\ 2 & 3 \end{bmatrix}X = \begin{bmatrix} 4 & 3 \\ 0 & -2 \end{bmatrix}$
15. $\begin{bmatrix} -1 & 0 \\ 6 & 4 \end{bmatrix}X = \begin{bmatrix} 3 & -1 \\ 4 & 5 \end{bmatrix}$
16. $\begin{bmatrix} -3 & 6 \\ 1 & 2 \end{bmatrix}X = \begin{bmatrix} 5 & -1 \\ 8 & 2 \end{bmatrix}$
17. $\begin{bmatrix} 1 & 5 \\ 0 & -2 \end{bmatrix}X = \begin{bmatrix} 3 & -1 & 0 \\ 6 & 8 & 4 \end{bmatrix}$
18. $\begin{bmatrix} -5 & 2 \\ -9 & 3 \end{bmatrix}X = \begin{bmatrix} 4 & 5 & 0 \\ 3 & 1 & 6 \end{bmatrix}$

EXAMPLE 3 on p. 211 for Exs. 19–24

FINDING INVERSES **Use a graphing calculator to find the inverse of matrix A. Check the result by showing that $AA^{-1} = I$ and $A^{-1}A = I$.**

19. $A = \begin{bmatrix} 1 & 1 & -2 \\ -2 & 0 & 3 \\ 3 & 1 & 0 \end{bmatrix}$
20. $A = \begin{bmatrix} 1 & 0 & 2 \\ 2 & 1 & 3 \\ 1 & 4 & 4 \end{bmatrix}$
21. $A = \begin{bmatrix} 1 & -1 & 2 \\ -2 & 3 & 10 \\ 3 & -1 & 2 \end{bmatrix}$
22. $A = \begin{bmatrix} -2 & 5 & -1 \\ 0 & 8 & 1 \\ 12 & -5 & 0 \end{bmatrix}$
23. $A = \begin{bmatrix} 3 & -8 & 0 \\ 2 & 4 & 1 \\ -1 & 0 & -6 \end{bmatrix}$
24. $A = \begin{bmatrix} 4 & 1 & 5 \\ -2 & 2 & 1 \\ 3 & -1 & 6 \end{bmatrix}$

EXAMPLE 4 on p. 212 for Exs. 25–34

SYSTEMS OF TWO EQUATIONS **Use an inverse matrix to solve the linear system.**

25. $4x - y = 10$
$-7x - 2y = -25$

26. $4x + 7y = -16$
$2x + 3y = -4$

27. $3x - 2y = 5$
$6x - 5y = 14$

28. $x - y = 4$
$9x - 10y = 45$

29. $-2x - 9y = -2$
$4x + 16y = 8$

30. $2x - 7y = -6$
$-x + 5y = 3$

31. $6x + y = -2$
$-x + 3y = -25$

32. $2x + y = -2$
$2x + 5y = 38$

33. $5x + 7y = 20$
$3x + 5y = 16$

34. ★ **MULTIPLE CHOICE** What is the solution of the system shown?

$3x - 5y = -26$
$-x + 2y = 10$

Ⓐ (3, 7) Ⓑ (7, −1) Ⓒ (−2, 4) Ⓓ (68, 110)

EXAMPLE 5 on p. 213 for Exs. 35–40

SYSTEMS OF THREE EQUATIONS **Use an inverse matrix and a graphing calculator to solve the linear system.**

35. $x - y - 3z = 2$
$5x + 2y + z = -17$
$-3x - y = 8$

36. $-3x + y - 8z = 18$
$x - 2y + z = -11$
$2x - 2y + 5z = -17$

37. $2x + 4y + 5z = 5$
$x + 2y + 3z = 4$
$5x - 4y - 2z = -3$

38. $4x - y - z = -20$
$6x - z = -27$
$-x + 4y + 5z = 23$

39. $3x + 2y - z = 14$
$-x - 5y + 4z = -48$
$4x + y + z = 2$

40. $6x + y + 2z = 11$
$x - y + z = -5$
$-x + 4y - z = 14$

41. ★ **OPEN-ENDED MATH** Write a 2×2 matrix that has no inverse.

42. **CHALLENGE** Solve the linear system using the given inverse of the coefficient matrix.

$2w + 5x - 4y + 6z = 0$
$2x + y - 7z = 52$
$4w + 8x - 7y + 14z = -25$
$3w + 6x - 5y + 10z = -16$

$$A^{-1} = \begin{bmatrix} -10 & 4 & 27 & -29 \\ 5 & -2 & -16 & 18 \\ 4 & -2 & -17 & 20 \\ 2 & -1 & -7 & 8 \end{bmatrix}$$

PROBLEM SOLVING

EXAMPLES 4 and 5 on pp. 212–213 for Exs. 43–48

43. **AVIATION** A pilot has 200 hours of flight time in single-engine airplanes and twin-engine airplanes. Renting a single-engine airplane costs \$60 per hour, and renting a twin-engine airplane costs \$240 per hour. The pilot has spent \$21,000 on airplane rentals. Use an inverse matrix to find how many hours the pilot has flown each type of airplane.

@HomeTutor for problem solving help at classzone.com

44. **BASKETBALL** During the 2003–2004 NBA season, Dirk Nowitzki of the Dallas Mavericks made a total of 976 shots and scored 1680 points. His shots consisted of 3-point field goals, 2-point field goals, and 1-point free throws. He made 135 more 2-point field goals than free throws. Use an inverse matrix to find how many of each type of shot he made.

@HomeTutor for problem solving help at classzone.com

45. **MULTIPLE REPRESENTATIONS** A cooking class wants to use up 8 cups of buttermilk and 11 eggs by baking rolls and muffins to freeze. A batch of rolls uses 2 cups of buttermilk and 3 eggs. A batch of muffins uses 1 cup of buttermilk and 1 egg.

a. **Writing a System** Write a system of equations for this situation.

b. **Writing a Matrix Equation** Write the system of equations from part (a) as a matrix equation $AX = B$.

c. **Solving a System** Use an inverse matrix to solve the system of equations. How many batches of each recipe should the class make?

46. ★ **EXTENDED RESPONSE** A company sells party platters with varying assortments of meats and cheeses. A basic platter with 2 cheeses and 3 meats costs \$18, a medium platter with 3 cheeses and 5 meats costs \$28, and a super platter with 7 cheeses and 10 meats costs \$60.

a. Write and solve a system of equations using the information about the basic platter and the medium platter.

b. Write and solve a system of equations using the information about the medium platter and the super platter.

c. *Compare* the results from parts (a) and (b) and make a conjecture about why there is a discrepancy.

47. **NUTRITION** The table shows the calories, fat, and carbohydrates per ounce for three brands of cereal. How many ounces of each brand should be combined to get 500 calories, 3 grams of fat, and 100 grams of carbohydrates? Round your answers to the nearest tenth of an ounce.

Cereal	Calories	Fat	Carbohydrates
Bran Crunchies	78	1 g	22 g
Toasted Oats	104	0 g	25.5 g
Whole Wheat Flakes	198	0.6 g	23.8 g

48. **MULTI-STEP PROBLEM** You need 9 square feet of glass mosaic tiles to decorate a wall of your kitchen. You want the area of the red tiles to equal the combined area of the yellow and blue tiles. The cost of a sheet of glass tiles having an area of 0.75 square foot is \$6.50 for red, \$4.50 for yellow, and \$8.50 for blue. You have \$80 to spend.

a. Write a system of equations to represent this situation.

b. Rewrite the system as a matrix equation.

c. Use an inverse matrix to find how many sheets of each color tile you should buy.

Mosaic tiles

49. **GEOMETRY** The columns of matrix T below give the coordinates of the vertices of a triangle. Matrix A is a transformation matrix.

$$A = \begin{bmatrix} 0 & 1 \\ -1 & 0 \end{bmatrix} \qquad T = \begin{bmatrix} 1 & 3 & 5 \\ 1 & 4 & 2 \end{bmatrix}$$

a. Find AT and AAT. Then draw the original triangle and the two transformed triangles. What transformation does A represent?

b. *Describe* how to use matrices to obtain the original triangle represented by T from the transformed triangle represented by AAT.

○ = **WORKED-OUT SOLUTIONS** on p. WS1   ★ = **STANDARDIZED TEST PRACTICE**   = **MULTIPLE REPRESENTATIONS**

50. **CHALLENGE** Verify the formula on page 210 for the inverse of a 2×2 matrix by showing that $AB = I$ and $BA = I$ for the matrices A and B given below.

$$A = \begin{bmatrix} a & b \\ c & d \end{bmatrix} \qquad B = \frac{1}{ad - cb}\begin{bmatrix} d & -b \\ -c & a \end{bmatrix}$$

NEW YORK MIXED REVIEW

TEST PRACTICE at classzone.com

51. A grocer wants to mix peanuts worth \$2.50 per pound with 12 pounds of cashews worth \$4.75 per pound. To obtain a nut mixture worth \$4 per pound, how many pounds of peanuts are needed?

Ⓐ 3.6 lb Ⓑ 6 lb Ⓒ 12 lb Ⓓ 18 lb

52. The sum of three numbers is 141. The second number is 5 less than three times the first number. The third number is 2 more than four times the first number. Which equation represents the relationship between the three numbers where n is the first number?

Ⓐ $141 = n - (3n - 5) - (4n + 2)$ Ⓑ $141 = n + (4n - 5) + (3n + 2)$

Ⓒ $141 = n + (3n - 5) + (4n + 2)$ Ⓓ $141 = n + (5 - 3n) + (2 + 4n)$

53. Which ordered pair is the solution of this system of linear equations?

$$5x + y = -17$$
$$2x - 7y = 8$$

Ⓐ $(-3, -2)$ Ⓑ $(-3, 2)$ Ⓒ $\left(3, -\frac{2}{7}\right)$ Ⓓ $(11, 2)$

QUIZ *for Lessons 3.6–3.8*

Using the given matrices, evaluate the expression. *(p. 195)*

$$A = \begin{bmatrix} 1 & -4 \\ 5 & 2 \end{bmatrix}, B = \begin{bmatrix} 2 & -3 \\ 0 & 1 \end{bmatrix}, C = \begin{bmatrix} -6 & -1 \\ 2 & 4 \end{bmatrix}$$

1. $2AB$
2. $AB + AC$
3. $A(B + C)$
4. $(B - A)C$

Evaluate the determinant of the matrix. *(p. 203)*

5. $\begin{bmatrix} 5 & 4 \\ -2 & -3 \end{bmatrix}$

6. $\begin{bmatrix} 1 & 0 & -2 \\ -3 & 1 & 4 \\ 2 & 3 & -1 \end{bmatrix}$

7. $\begin{bmatrix} 2 & -1 & 5 \\ -3 & 6 & 9 \\ -2 & 3 & 1 \end{bmatrix}$

Use an inverse matrix to solve the linear system. *(p. 210)*

8. $x + 3y = -2$
   $2x + 7y = -6$

9. $3x - 4y = 5$
   $2x - 3y = 3$

10. $-3x + 2y = -13$
    $6x - 5y = 24$

11. $3x - y = -4$
    $2x - 2y = -8$

12. $7x + 4y = 6$
    $5x + 3y = -25$

13. $4x + y = -2$
    $-6x + y = 18$

14. **BOATING** You are making a triangular sail for a sailboat. The vertices of the sail are $(0, 2)$, $(12, 2)$, and $(12, 26)$ where the coordinates are measured in feet. Find the area of the sail. *(p. 203)*

PROBLEM SOLVING WORKSHOP
LESSON 3.8

Using ALTERNATIVE METHODS

Another Way to Solve Example 5, page 213

MULTIPLE REPRESENTATIONS In Example 5 on page 213, you solved a linear system using an inverse matrix. You can also solve systems using *augmented matrices*. An **augmented matrix** for a system contains the system's coefficient matrix and matrix of constants.

Linear System		Augmented Matrix
$x - 4y = 9$ $-6x + 7y = -2$	→	$\left[\begin{array}{rr\|r} 1 & -4 & 9 \\ -6 & 7 & -2 \end{array}\right]$

Recall from Lesson 3.2 that an equation in a system can be multiplied by a constant, or a multiple of one equation can be added to another equation. Similar operations can be performed on the rows of an augmented matrix to solve the corresponding system.

KEY CONCEPT *For Your Notebook*

Elementary Row Operations for Augmented Matrices

Two augmented matrices are *row-equivalent* if their corresponding systems have the same solution(s). Any of these row operations performed on an augmented matrix will produce a matrix that is row-equivalent to the original:

- Interchange two rows.
- Multiply a row by a nonzero constant.
- Add a multiple of one row to another row.

PROBLEM

GIFTS A company sells three types of movie gift baskets. A basic basket with 2 movie passes and 1 package of microwave popcorn costs $15.50. A medium basket with 2 movie passes, 2 packages of popcorn, and 1 DVD costs $37. A super basket with 4 movie passes, 3 packages of popcorn, and 2 DVDs costs $72.50. Find the cost of each item in the gift baskets.

METHOD

Using an Augmented Matrix You need to write a linear system, write the corresponding augmented matrix, and use row operations to transform the augmented matrix into a matrix with 1's along the main diagonal and 0's below the main diagonal. Such a matrix is in *triangular form* and can be used to solve for the variables in the system.

Let m be the cost of a movie pass, p be the cost of a package of popcorn, and d be the cost of a DVD.

STEP 1 **Write** a linear system and then write an augmented matrix.

$$2m + p = 15.5 \qquad \left[\begin{array}{ccc|c} 2 & 1 & 0 & 15.5 \\ 2 & 2 & 1 & 37 \\ 4 & 3 & 2 & 72.5 \end{array}\right]$$
$$2m + 2p + d = 37$$
$$4m + 3p + 2d = 72.5$$

STEP 2 **Add** −2 times the first row to the third row.

$$(-2)R_1 + R_3 \longrightarrow \left[\begin{array}{ccc|c} 2 & 1 & 0 & 15.5 \\ 2 & 2 & 1 & 37 \\ 0 & 1 & 2 & 41.5 \end{array}\right]$$

STEP 3 **Add** −1 times the first row to the second row.

$$(-1)R_1 + R_2 \longrightarrow \left[\begin{array}{ccc|c} 2 & 1 & 0 & 15.5 \\ 0 & 1 & 1 & 21.5 \\ 0 & 1 & 2 & 41.5 \end{array}\right]$$

STEP 4 **Add** −1 times the second row to the third row.

$$(-1)R_2 + R_3 \longrightarrow \left[\begin{array}{ccc|c} 2 & 1 & 0 & 15.5 \\ 0 & 1 & 1 & 21.5 \\ 0 & 0 & 1 & 20 \end{array}\right]$$

STEP 5 **Multiply** the first row by 0.5.

$$0.5R_1 \longrightarrow \left[\begin{array}{ccc|c} 1 & 0.5 & 0 & 7.75 \\ 0 & 1 & 1 & 21.5 \\ 0 & 0 & 1 & 20 \end{array}\right]$$

The third row of the matrix tells you that $d = 20$. Substitute 20 for d in the equation for the second row, $p + d = 21.5$, to obtain $p + 20 = 21.5$, or $p = 1.5$. Then substitute 1.5 for p in the equation for the first row, $m + 0.5p = 7.75$, to obtain $m + 0.5(1.5) = 7.75$, or $m = 7$.

▶ A movie pass costs \$7, a package of popcorn costs \$1.50, and a DVD costs \$20.

PRACTICE

1. **WHAT IF?** In the problem on page 218, suppose a basic basket costs \$17.75, a medium basket costs \$34.50, and a super basket costs \$67.25. Use an augmented matrix to find the cost of each item.

2. **FINANCE** You have \$18,000 to invest. You want an overall annual return of 8%. The expected annual returns are 10% for a stock fund, 7% for a bond fund, and 5% for a money market fund. You want to invest as much in stocks as in bonds and the money market combined. Use an augmented matrix to find how much to invest in each fund.

3. **BIRDSEED** A pet store sells 20 pounds of birdseed for \$10.85. The birdseed is made from two kinds of seeds, sunflower seeds and thistle seeds. Sunflower seeds cost \$.34 per pound and thistle seeds cost \$.79 per pound. Use an augmented matrix to find how many pounds of each variety are in the mixture.

4. **REASONING** Solve the given system using an augmented matrix. What can you say about the system's solution(s)?

$$x - 2y + 4z = -10$$
$$5x + y - z = 24$$
$$3x - 6y + 12z = -30$$

Lessons 3.5–3.8

1. **TV COMMERCIALS** The cost (in thousands of dollars) of a 30 second commercial on two cable TV networks is shown below for two cities. The cost varies based on when the commercial airs: daytime (D), prime time (P), and late night (L).

Costs in City A

	D	P	L
Network 1	4.5	6	2.5
Network 2	5.5	8	2.5

Costs in City B

	D	P	L
Network 1	4	6.5	3.25
Network 2	5	8.5	3.25

Organize this information using two matrices *A* and *B* that give the costs for city A and city B, respectively. What is $B - A$?

(1) $\begin{bmatrix} 0.5 & -0.5 & -0.75 \\ 0.5 & -0.5 & -0.75 \end{bmatrix}$

(2) $\begin{bmatrix} -0.5 & 0.5 & 0.75 \\ -0.5 & 0.5 & 0.75 \end{bmatrix}$

(3) $\begin{bmatrix} -0.5 & -0.5 & 0.75 \\ -0.5 & -0.5 & 0.75 \end{bmatrix}$

(4) $\begin{bmatrix} 9.5 & 12.5 & 5.75 \\ 10.5 & 16.5 & 5.75 \end{bmatrix}$

2. **COINS** A person has 85 coins, of which n are nickels, d are dimes, and q are quarters. The value of the coins is \$13.25. There are twice as many quarters as dimes. The situation can be modeled using the matrix equation below. How many quarters does the person have?

$$\begin{bmatrix} 1 & 1 & 1 \\ 0.05 & 0.1 & 0.25 \\ 0 & -2 & 1 \end{bmatrix}\begin{bmatrix} n \\ d \\ q \end{bmatrix} = \begin{bmatrix} 85 \\ 13.25 \\ 0 \end{bmatrix}$$

(1) 20 (2) 25 (3) 40 (4) 45

3. **ATOMIC WEIGHTS** The atomic weights of three compounds are shown in the table.

Compound	Formula	Atomic weight
Nitric acid	HNO_3	63
Nitrous oxide	N_2O	44
Water	H_2O	18

Let *H*, *N*, and *O* represent the atomic weights of hydrogen, nitrogen, and oxygen, respectively. What is the atomic weight of nitrogen? Use Cramer's rule.

(1) 1 (2) 2 (3) 14 (4) 16

4. **OPEN-ENDED** A farmer harvests his crops and receives \$2.35 per bushel of corn, \$5.40 per bushel of soybeans, and \$3.60 per bushel of wheat. The farmer harvests a total of 1700 bushels of crops and receives a total of \$4837. The amount of corn harvested is 3.25 times the combined amount of soybeans and wheat harvested. How many bushels of wheat were harvested?

5. **OPEN-ENDED** A store has three departments: clothing (C), housewares (H), and electronics (E). Matrix *A* shows the total sales (in dollars) for two salespeople, Mary and Mark, in each department. Matrix *B* shows the commission on sales in each department. Which matrix is defined, *AB* or *BA*? Find this matrix and explain what its elements represent.

Matrix *A* (rows C, H, E; columns Mary, Mark)

$$\begin{bmatrix} 175 & 270 \\ 370 & 225 \\ 200 & 255 \end{bmatrix}$$

Matrix *B* (columns C, H, E)

$$\begin{bmatrix} 3\% & 5\% & 8\% \end{bmatrix}$$

3 CHAPTER SUMMARY

BIG IDEAS

For Your Notebook

Big Idea 1

Solving Systems of Equations Using a Variety of Methods

Method	When to use
Graphing: Graph each equation in the system. A point where the graphs intersect is a solution.	The equations have only two variables and are given in a form that is easy to graph.
Substitution: Solve one equation for one of the variables and substitute into the other equation(s).	One of the variables in the system has a coefficient of 1 or -1.
Elimination: Multiply equations by constants, then add the revised equations to eliminate a variable.	None of the variables in the system have a coefficient of 1 or -1.
Cramer's rule: Use determinants to find the solution.	The determinant of the coefficient matrix is not zero.
Inverse matrices: Write the system as a matrix equation $AX = B$. Multiply each side by A^{-1} on the left to obtain the solution $X = A^{-1}B$.	The determinant of the coefficient matrix is not zero.

Big Idea 2

Graphing Systems of Equations and Inequalities

System of equations with 1 solution

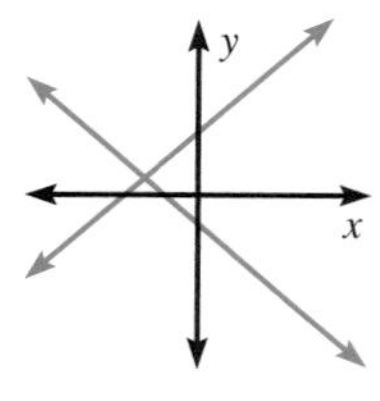

Intersecting lines

System of equations with many solutions

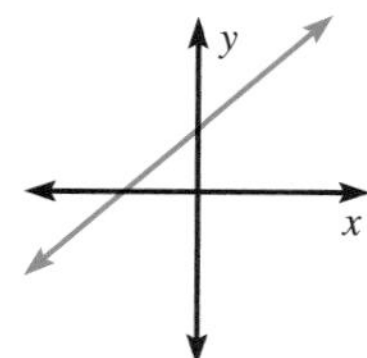

Coinciding lines

System of equations with no solution

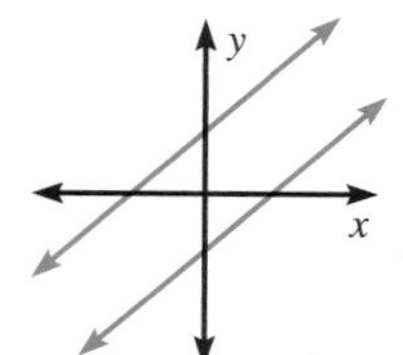

Parallel lines

System of inequalities

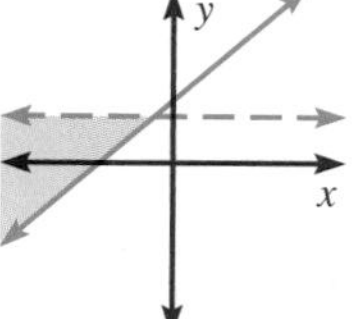

Shaded region

Big Idea 3

Using Matrices

Addition, subtraction, and scalar multiplication	Matrix multiplication	Inverse matrices
$\begin{bmatrix} a & b \\ c & d \end{bmatrix} + \begin{bmatrix} e & f \\ g & h \end{bmatrix} = \begin{bmatrix} a+e & b+f \\ c+g & d+h \end{bmatrix}$ $\begin{bmatrix} a & b \\ c & d \end{bmatrix} - \begin{bmatrix} e & f \\ g & h \end{bmatrix} = \begin{bmatrix} a-e & b-f \\ c-g & d-h \end{bmatrix}$ $k\begin{bmatrix} a & b \\ c & d \end{bmatrix} = \begin{bmatrix} ka & kb \\ kc & kd \end{bmatrix}$	$\begin{bmatrix} a & b \\ c & d \end{bmatrix}\begin{bmatrix} e & f \\ g & h \end{bmatrix} =$ $\begin{bmatrix} ae+bg & af+bh \\ ce+dg & cf+dh \end{bmatrix}$	If $A = \begin{bmatrix} a & b \\ c & d \end{bmatrix}$, then $A^{-1} = \frac{1}{\lvert A \rvert}\begin{bmatrix} d & -b \\ -c & a \end{bmatrix}$ or $A^{-1} = \frac{1}{ad-cb}\begin{bmatrix} d & -b \\ -c & a \end{bmatrix}$.

3 CHAPTER REVIEW

@HomeTutor
classzone.com
• Multi-Language Glossary
• Vocabulary practice

REVIEW KEY VOCABULARY

- system of two linear equations in two variables, *p. 153*
- solution of a system of linear equations, *p. 153*
- consistent, inconsistent, independent, dependent, *p. 154*
- substitution method, *p. 160*
- elimination method, *p. 161*
- system of linear inequalities in two variables, *p. 168*
- solution, graph of a system of inequalities, *p. 168*
- linear equation in three variables, *p. 178*
- system of three linear equations in three variables, *p. 178*
- solution of a system of three linear equations, *p. 178*
- ordered triple, *p. 178*
- matrix, *p. 187*
- dimensions, elements of a matrix, *p. 187*
- equal matrices, *p. 187*
- scalar, *p. 188*
- scalar multiplication, *p. 188*
- determinant, *p. 203*
- Cramer's rule, *p. 205*
- coefficient matrix, *p. 205*
- identity matrix, inverse matrices, *p. 210*
- matrix of variables, *p. 212*
- matrix of constants, *p. 212*

VOCABULARY EXERCISES

1. Copy and complete: A system of linear equations with at least one solution is __?__, while a system with no solution is __?__.
2. Copy and complete: A solution (x, y, z) of a system of linear equations in three variables is called a(n) __?__.
3. **WRITING** *Explain* when the product of two matrices is defined.

REVIEW EXAMPLES AND EXERCISES

Use the review examples and exercises below to check your understanding of the concepts you have learned in each lesson of Chapter 3.

3.1 Solve Linear Systems by Graphing — *pp. 153–158*

EXAMPLE

Graph the system and estimate the solution. Check the solution algebraically.

$3x + y = 3$ **Equation 1**
$4x + 3y = -1$ **Equation 2**

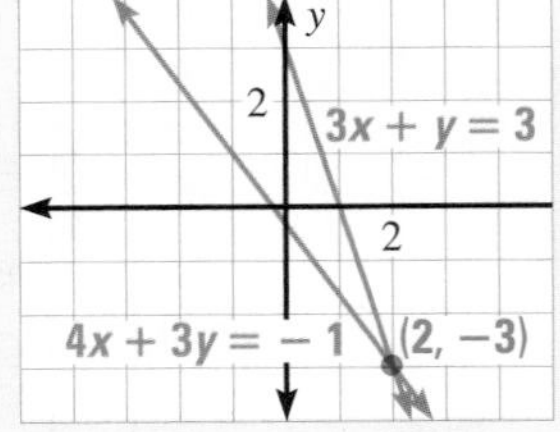

Graph both equations. From the graph, the lines appear to intersect at $(2, -3)$. You can check this algebraically.

$3(2) + (-3) = 3$ ✓ **Equation 1 checks.**

$4(2) + 3(-3) = -1$ ✓ **Equation 2 checks.**

EXERCISES

EXAMPLE 1 on p. 153 for Exs. 4–6

Graph the system and estimate the solution. Check the solution algebraically.

4. $2x - y = 9$
   $x + 3y = 8$

5. $2x - 3y = -2$
   $x + y = -6$

6. $3x + y = 6$
   $-x + 2y = 12$

@HomeTutor
classzone.com
Chapter Review Practice

3.2 Solve Linear Systems Algebraically

pp. 160–167

EXAMPLE

Solve the system using the elimination method.

$2x + 5y = 8$ Equation 1
$4x + 3y = -12$ Equation 2

Multiply Equation 1 by -2 so that the coefficients of x differ only in sign.

$2x + 5y = 8$ × −2 → $-4x - 10y = -16$

$4x + 3y = -12$ → $4x + 3y = -12$

Add the revised equations and solve for y. $-7y = -28$

$y = 4$

Substitute the value of y into one of the original equations and solve for x.

$2x + 5(4) = 8$ **Substitute 4 for y in Equation 1.**

$2x = -12$ **Subtract 5(4) = 20 from each side.**

$x = -6$ **Divide each side by 2.**

▶ The solution is $(-6, 4)$.

EXERCISES

EXAMPLES 2 and 3 on pp. 161–162 for Exs. 7–10

Solve the system using the elimination method.

7. $3x + 2y = 5$
$-2x + 3y = 27$

8. $3x + 5y = 5$
$2x - 3y = 16$

9. $2x + 3y = 9$
$-3x + y = 25$

10. **FUEL COSTS** The cost of 14 gallons of regular gasoline and 10 gallons of premium gasoline is \$46.68. Premium costs \$.30 more per gallon than regular. What is the cost per gallon of each type of gasoline?

3.3 Graph Systems of Linear Inequalities

pp. 168–173

EXAMPLE

Graph the system of linear inequalities.

$3x - y \leq 4$ Inequality 1
$x + y > 1$ Inequality 2

Graph each inequality in the system. Use a different color for each half-plane. Then identify the region that is common to both graphs. It is the region that is shaded purple.

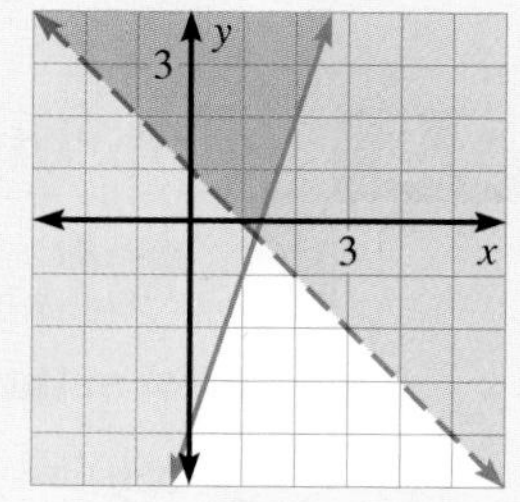

EXERCISES

EXAMPLE 1 on p. 168 for Exs. 11–13

Graph the system of linear inequalities.

11. $4x + y < 1$
$-x + 2y \leq 5$

12. $2x + 3y > 6$
$2x - y \leq 8$

13. $x + 3y \geq 5$
$-x + 2y < 4$

3 CHAPTER REVIEW

3.4 Solve Systems of Linear Equations in Three Variables *pp. 178–185*

EXAMPLE

Solve the system.

$$\begin{aligned} 2x + y + 3z &= 5 && \text{Equation 1} \\ -x + 3y + z &= -14 && \text{Equation 2} \\ 3x - y - 2z &= 11 && \text{Equation 3} \end{aligned}$$

Rewrite the system as a linear system in two variables. Add −3 times Equation 1 to Equation 2. Then add Equation 1 and Equation 3.

$$\begin{array}{rl} -6x - 3y - 9z &= -15 \\ -x + 3y + z &= -14 \\ \hline -7x - 8z &= -29 \end{array} \qquad \begin{array}{rl} 2x + y + 3z &= 5 \\ 3x - y - 2z &= 11 \\ \hline 5x + z &= 16 \end{array}$$

Solve the new linear system for both of its variables.

$$\begin{array}{rll} -7x - 8z &= -29 & \text{Add new Equation 1 to} \\ 40x + 8z &= 128 & \text{8 times new Equation 2.} \\ \hline 33x &= 99 & \\ x &= 3 & \text{Solve for } x. \\ z &= 1 & \text{Substitute into new Equation 1 or 2 to find } z. \end{array}$$

Substituting $x = 3$ and $z = 1$ into one of the original equations and solving for y gives $y = -4$. The solution is $(3, -4, 1)$.

EXERCISES

EXAMPLES 1 and 4 on pp. 179–181 for Exs. 14–17

Solve the system.

14. $x - y + z = 10$
$4x + y - 2z = 15$
$-3x + 5y - z = -18$

15. $6x - y + 4z = 6$
$-x - 3y + z = 31$
$2x + 2y - 5z = -42$

16. $5x + y - z = 40$
$x + 7y + 4z = 44$
$-x + 3y + z = 16$

17. MUSIC Fifteen band members from a school were selected to play in the state orchestra. Twice as many students who play a wind instrument were selected as students who play a string or percussion instrument combined. Of the students selected, one fifth play a string instrument. How many of the students selected play each type of instrument?

3.5 Perform Basic Matrix Operations *pp. 187–193*

EXAMPLE

Perform the indicated operation.

a. $\begin{bmatrix} 4 & -1 \\ 2 & 5 \end{bmatrix} + \begin{bmatrix} -5 & 2 \\ -3 & 1 \end{bmatrix} = \begin{bmatrix} 4 + (-5) & -1 + 2 \\ 2 + (-3) & 5 + 1 \end{bmatrix} = \begin{bmatrix} -1 & 1 \\ -1 & 6 \end{bmatrix}$

b. $4\begin{bmatrix} -2 & 0 \\ 3 & 5 \end{bmatrix} = \begin{bmatrix} 4(-2) & 4(0) \\ 4(3) & 4(5) \end{bmatrix} = \begin{bmatrix} -8 & 0 \\ 12 & 20 \end{bmatrix}$

@HomeTutor
classzone.com
Chapter Review Practice

EXAMPLES 2 and 3
on pp. 188–189 for Exs. 18–23

EXERCISES

Perform the indicated operation.

18. $\begin{bmatrix} 4 & -5 \\ 2 & 3 \end{bmatrix} + \begin{bmatrix} -1 & 3 \\ -7 & 4 \end{bmatrix}$

19. $\begin{bmatrix} -1 & 8 \\ 2 & -3 \end{bmatrix} + \begin{bmatrix} 7 & -4 \\ 6 & -1 \end{bmatrix}$

20. $\begin{bmatrix} 10 & -4 \\ 5 & 1 \end{bmatrix} - \begin{bmatrix} 0 & 9 \\ 2 & 7 \end{bmatrix}$

21. $\begin{bmatrix} -2 & 3 & 5 \\ -1 & 6 & -2 \end{bmatrix} - \begin{bmatrix} -4 & 7 & 5 \\ -8 & 0 & -9 \end{bmatrix}$

22. $-3\begin{bmatrix} 5 & -2 \\ 3 & 6 \end{bmatrix}$

23. $8\begin{bmatrix} 8 & 4 & 5 \\ -1 & 6 & -2 \end{bmatrix}$

3.6 Multiply Matrices

pp. 195–202

EXAMPLE

Find AB if $A = \begin{bmatrix} 2 & -3 \\ -1 & 0 \\ 4 & 5 \end{bmatrix}$ and $B = \begin{bmatrix} -2 & 3 \\ 3 & 1 \end{bmatrix}$.

$$AB = \begin{bmatrix} 2 & -3 \\ -1 & 0 \\ 4 & 5 \end{bmatrix}\begin{bmatrix} -2 & 3 \\ 3 & 1 \end{bmatrix} = \begin{bmatrix} 2(-2) + (-3)(3) & 2(3) + (-3)(1) \\ -1(-2) + 0(3) & -1(3) + 0(1) \\ 4(-2) + 5(3) & 4(3) + 5(1) \end{bmatrix}$$

$$= \begin{bmatrix} -13 & 3 \\ 2 & -3 \\ 7 & 17 \end{bmatrix}$$

EXAMPLES 2 and 4
on pp. 196–198 for Exs. 24–28

EXERCISES

Find the product.

24. $\begin{bmatrix} -1 & -1 \end{bmatrix}\begin{bmatrix} 8 & 2 \\ -6 & -9 \end{bmatrix}$

25. $\begin{bmatrix} 11 & 7 \\ 1 & -5 \end{bmatrix}\begin{bmatrix} 0 & -5 \\ 4 & -3 \end{bmatrix}$

26. $\begin{bmatrix} 4 & -1 \\ 1 & 7 \end{bmatrix}\begin{bmatrix} 5 & -2 & 4 \\ 3 & 12 & 6 \end{bmatrix}$

27. $\begin{bmatrix} -2 & 5 \\ 0 & 3 \end{bmatrix}\begin{bmatrix} 6 & -3 & 5 \\ 2 & 0 & -1 \end{bmatrix}$

28. **MANUFACTURING** A company manufactures three models of flat-screen color TVs: a 19 inch model, a 27 inch model, and a 32 inch model. The TVs are shipped to two warehouses. The numbers of units shipped to each warehouse are given in matrix A, and the prices of the models are given in matrix B. Write a matrix that gives the total value of the TVs in each warehouse.

Matrix *A*

	19 in.	27 in.	32 in.
Warehouse 1	5,000	6,000	8,000
Warehouse 2	4,000	10,000	5,000

Matrix *B*

	Price
19 inch	$109.99
27 inch	$319.99
32 inch	$549.99

3 CHAPTER REVIEW

3.7 Evaluate Determinants and Apply Cramer's Rule *pp. 203–209*

EXAMPLE

Evaluate the determinant of $\begin{bmatrix} 2 & 1 \\ 5 & 7 \end{bmatrix}$.

$$\begin{vmatrix} 2 & 1 \\ 5 & 7 \end{vmatrix} = 2(7) - 5(1) = 14 - 5 = 9$$

EXERCISES

EXAMPLES 1 and 2 on pp. 203–204 for Exs. 29–32

Evaluate the determinant of the matrix.

29. $\begin{bmatrix} -4 & 2 \\ 5 & 8 \end{bmatrix}$

30. $\begin{bmatrix} 3 & -5 \\ 2 & 6 \end{bmatrix}$

31. $\begin{bmatrix} 3 & 0 \\ 1 & 6 \end{bmatrix}$

32. SCHOOL SPIRIT You are making a large triangular pennant for your school football team. The vertices of the triangle are (0, 0), (0, 50), and (70, 20) where the coordinates are measured in inches. How many square *feet* of material will you need to make the pennant?

3.8 Use Inverse Matrices to Solve Linear Systems *pp. 210–217*

EXAMPLE

Use an inverse matrix to solve the linear system at the right.

$$x - 2y = 14$$
$$2x + y = 8$$

Write the linear system as a matrix equation $AX = B$.

$$\begin{bmatrix} 1 & -2 \\ 2 & 1 \end{bmatrix}\begin{bmatrix} x \\ y \end{bmatrix} = \begin{bmatrix} 14 \\ 8 \end{bmatrix}$$

Find the inverse of the coefficient matrix A.

$$A^{-1} = \frac{1}{1 - (-4)}\begin{bmatrix} 1 & 2 \\ -2 & 1 \end{bmatrix} = \begin{bmatrix} 0.2 & 0.4 \\ -0.4 & 0.2 \end{bmatrix}$$

Then multiply the matrix of constants by A^{-1} on the left.

$$X = A^{-1}B = \begin{bmatrix} 0.2 & 0.4 \\ -0.4 & 0.2 \end{bmatrix}\begin{bmatrix} 14 \\ 8 \end{bmatrix} = \begin{bmatrix} 6 \\ -4 \end{bmatrix} = \begin{bmatrix} x \\ y \end{bmatrix}$$

▶ The solution of the system is (6, −4).

EXERCISES

EXAMPLE 4 on p. 212 for Exs. 33–35

Use an inverse matrix to solve the linear system.

33. $x + 4y = 11$
$2x - 5y = 9$

34. $3x + y = -1$
$-x + 2y = 12$

35. $3x + 2y = -11$
$4x - 3y = 8$

3 CHAPTER TEST

Graph the linear system and estimate the solution. Then check the solution algebraically.

1. $4x + y = 5$
$3x - y = 2$

2. $x + 2y = -6$
$-6x - 2y = -14$

3. $2x - 3y = 15$
$x - \frac{3}{2}y = -3$

4. $3x - y = 12$
$-x + 8y = -4$

Graph the system of linear inequalities.

5. $2x + y < 6$
$y > -2$

6. $x - 3y \geq 9$
$\frac{1}{3}x - y \leq 3$

7. $x - 2y \leq -14$
$y \geq |x|$

8. $-3x + 4y > -12$
$y < -2|x| + 5$

Solve the system using any algebraic method.

9. $3x + y = -9$
$x - 2y = -10$

10. $2x + 3y = -2$
$4x + 7y = -6$

11. $x + 4y = -26$
$-5x - 2y = -14$

12. $x - y + z = -3$
$2x - y + 5z = 4$
$4x + 2y - z = 2$

13. $x + y + z = 3$
$-x + 3y + 2z = -8$
$5y + z = 2$

14. $2x - 5y - z = 17$
$x + y + 3z = 19$
$-4x + 6y + z = -20$

Use the given matrices to evaluate the expression, if possible. If not possible, state the reason.

$$A = \begin{bmatrix} 1 & -2 \\ 4 & -3 \end{bmatrix}, B = \begin{bmatrix} 3 & 5 \\ -1 & 0 \end{bmatrix}, C = \begin{bmatrix} -6 & 8 \\ 10 & 15 \end{bmatrix}, D = \begin{bmatrix} -1 & 3 & -2 \\ 2 & 0 & -1 \end{bmatrix}, E = \begin{bmatrix} 4 & -1 & 3 \\ 6 & -2 & 1 \end{bmatrix}$$

15. $2A + B$

16. $C - 3B$

17. $A - 2D$

18. $4D + E$

19. AC

20. DE

21. $(A + B)D$

22. $A(C - B)$

Evaluate the determinant of the matrix.

23. $\begin{bmatrix} 3 & -2 \\ 4 & 1 \end{bmatrix}$

24. $\begin{bmatrix} -4 & 5 \\ 2 & -1 \end{bmatrix}$

25. $\begin{bmatrix} -1 & 3 & 1 \\ 0 & 2 & -3 \\ 5 & 1 & -2 \end{bmatrix}$

26. $\begin{bmatrix} 2 & 0 & -1 \\ 5 & -3 & 2 \\ 1 & 4 & 6 \end{bmatrix}$

Use an inverse matrix to solve the linear system.

27. $3x + 4y = 6$
$4x + 5y = 7$

28. $2x - 7y = -36$
$x - 3y = -16$

29. $5x + 3y = -5$
$-9x - 6y = 12$

30. $3x + 2y = 15$
$-x + 4y = -33$

31. FINANCE A total of \$15,000 is invested in two corporate bonds that pay 5% and 7% simple annual interest. The investor wants to earn \$880 in interest per year from the bonds. How much should be invested in each bond?

32. TICKET SALES For the opening day of a carnival, 800 admission tickets were sold. The receipts totaled \$3775. Tickets for children cost \$3 each, tickets for adults cost \$8 each, and tickets for senior citizens cost \$5 each. There were twice as many children's tickets sold as adult tickets. How many of each type of ticket were sold?

33. BOATING On a certain river, a motorboat can travel 34 miles per hour with the current and 28 miles per hour against the current. Find the speed of the motorboat in still water and the speed of the current.

MULTIPLE CHOICE QUESTIONS

If you have difficulty solving a multiple choice problem directly, you may be able to use another approach to eliminate incorrect answer choices and obtain the correct answer.

PROBLEM 1

On a treadmill, you jog at 6 miles per hour and sprint at 8 miles per hour. You cover $3\frac{1}{3}$ miles in $\frac{1}{2}$ hour. How long did you spend at each activity?

(1) 25 minutes jogging, 5 minutes sprinting

(2) 20 minutes jogging, 10 minutes sprinting

(3) 10 minutes jogging, 20 minutes sprinting

(4) 5 minutes jogging, 25 minutes sprinting

METHOD 1

SOLVE DIRECTLY Write and solve a linear system.

STEP 1 **Write** a system of equations. Let x be the jogging time and y be the sprinting time.

$$6x + 8y = 3\frac{1}{3} \quad \text{Equation 1}$$

$$x + y = \frac{1}{2} \quad \text{Equation 2}$$

STEP 2 **Solve** Equation 2 for y to get $y = \frac{1}{2} - x$.

STEP 3 **Substitute** $\frac{1}{2} - x$ for y in Equation 1 and solve for x.

$$6x + 8\left(\frac{1}{2} - x\right) = 3\frac{1}{3}$$

$$-2x + 4 = 3\frac{1}{3}$$

$$x = \frac{1}{3}$$

STEP 4 **Substitute** the value of x into revised Equation 2 and solve for y.

$$y = \frac{1}{2} - x = \frac{1}{2} - \frac{1}{3} = \frac{1}{6}$$

You jog for $\frac{1}{3}$ hour, or 20 minutes.

You sprint for $\frac{1}{6}$ hour, or 10 minutes.

▸ The correct answer is (2).

METHOD 2

ELIMINATE CHOICES Another method is to eliminate incorrect answer choices by considering what happens if you jog the entire time or sprint the entire time.

STEP 1 **Find** the distance you cover if you spend the entire time jogging or the entire time sprinting.

If you jog the entire time, then you cover $6 \cdot \frac{1}{2} = 3$ miles.

If you sprint the entire time, then you cover $8 \cdot \frac{1}{2} = 4$ miles.

Because $3\frac{1}{3}$ is closer to 3 than to 4, you must spend more time jogging than sprinting. So, you can eliminate choices (3) and (4).

STEP 2 **Calculate** the distances for the remaining choices. Use the fact that 5 min $= \frac{1}{12}$ h.

Choice (1): $6 \cdot \frac{5}{12} + 8 \cdot \frac{1}{12} = \frac{38}{12} = 3\frac{1}{6}$ miles

Choice (2): $6 \cdot \frac{4}{12} + 8 \cdot \frac{2}{12} = \frac{40}{12} = 3\frac{1}{3}$ miles

▸ The correct answer is (2).

PROBLEM 2

What is the inverse of $A = \begin{bmatrix} 3 & -3 \\ -7 & 6 \end{bmatrix}$?

(1) $\begin{bmatrix} 1 & 0 \\ 0 & 1 \end{bmatrix}$ (2) $\begin{bmatrix} 2 & 1 \\ \frac{7}{3} & 1 \end{bmatrix}$ (3) $\begin{bmatrix} 1 & -1 \\ -\frac{7}{3} & 2 \end{bmatrix}$ (4) $\begin{bmatrix} -2 & -1 \\ -\frac{7}{3} & -1 \end{bmatrix}$

METHOD 1

SOLVE DIRECTLY Find the inverse of matrix A by using the formula below.

$$A^{-1} = \frac{1}{|A|}\begin{bmatrix} d & -b \\ -c & a \end{bmatrix}$$

The inverse of $A = \begin{bmatrix} 3 & -3 \\ -7 & 6 \end{bmatrix}$ is:

$$A^{-1} = \frac{1}{3(6) - (-7)(-3)}\begin{bmatrix} 6 & 3 \\ 7 & 3 \end{bmatrix}$$

$$= \frac{1}{18 - 21}\begin{bmatrix} 6 & 3 \\ 7 & 3 \end{bmatrix}$$

$$= -\frac{1}{3}\begin{bmatrix} 6 & 3 \\ 7 & 3 \end{bmatrix}$$

$$= \begin{bmatrix} -2 & -1 \\ -\frac{7}{3} & -1 \end{bmatrix}$$

▶ The correct answer is (4).

METHOD 2

ELIMINATE CHOICES Use the fact that $A^{-1}A = I$ to eliminate incorrect answer choices.

Multiply the matrix in each answer choice by matrix A. You can stop as soon as you realize that the product $A^{-1}A$ is not the identity matrix.

Choice (1): $\begin{bmatrix} 1 & 0 \\ 0 & 1 \end{bmatrix}\begin{bmatrix} 3 & -3 \\ -7 & 6 \end{bmatrix} = \begin{bmatrix} 3 & \\ & \end{bmatrix}$ ✗

Choice (2): $\begin{bmatrix} 2 & 1 \\ \frac{7}{3} & 1 \end{bmatrix}\begin{bmatrix} 3 & -3 \\ -7 & 6 \end{bmatrix} = \begin{bmatrix} -1 & \\ & \end{bmatrix}$ ✗

Choice (3): $\begin{bmatrix} 1 & -1 \\ -\frac{7}{3} & 2 \end{bmatrix}\begin{bmatrix} 3 & -3 \\ -7 & 6 \end{bmatrix} = \begin{bmatrix} 10 & \\ & \end{bmatrix}$ ✗

Choice (4): $\begin{bmatrix} -2 & -1 \\ -\frac{7}{3} & -1 \end{bmatrix}\begin{bmatrix} 3 & -3 \\ -7 & 6 \end{bmatrix} = \begin{bmatrix} 1 & 0 \\ 0 & 1 \end{bmatrix}$ ✓

▶ The correct answer is (4).

TEST PREPARATION

PRACTICE

Explain why you can eliminate the highlighted answer choice.

1. What is the solution of the system?

$$x + y + z = 2$$
$$2x - 3y + z = 11$$
$$x + 2y - 3z = -12$$

(1) (1, −2, 3) ✗(2) (−1, 2, −3) (3) (3, −2, 1) (4) (1, 3, −2)

2. What is the solution of the matrix equation? $\begin{bmatrix} 3 & 4 \\ 2 & 3 \end{bmatrix}X = \begin{bmatrix} 4 & -10 \\ 1 & -6 \end{bmatrix}$

(1) $\begin{bmatrix} 8 & -6 \\ -5 & 2 \end{bmatrix}$ (2) $\begin{bmatrix} 4 & 6 \\ 0 & -1 \end{bmatrix}$ (3) $\begin{bmatrix} 3 & -4 \\ -2 & 3 \end{bmatrix}$ ✗(4) $\begin{bmatrix} 1 & 0 \\ 0 & 1 \end{bmatrix}$

New York **Test Practice**

MULTIPLE CHOICE

1. The two top-selling DVDs of 2003 grossed a combined total of $600.9 million. The top-selling DVD grossed $39.9 million more than the DVD ranked second. How much did the top-selling DVD gross?

(1) $240.6 million

(2) $280.5 million

(3) $320.4 million

(4) $561 million

2. Which system has (0, 4) as a solution?

(1) $x + y = 4$, $x - y = 4$

(2) $2x + y = -4$, $x - 2y = 8$

(3) $3x + 2y = 8$, $x - 4y = -16$

(4) $-x + y = 4$, $3x - 2y = 12$

3. Which system of inequalities is graphed below?

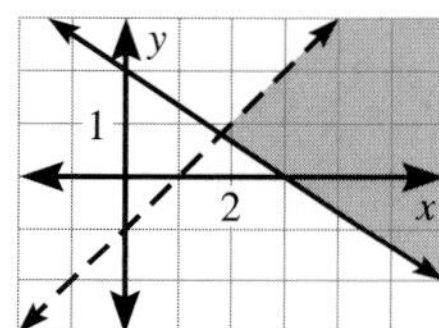

(1) $y > x - 1$, $2x + 3y \leq 6$

(2) $y < x - 1$, $2x + 3y \geq 6$

(3) $y < x - 1$, $3x + 2y \geq 6$

(4) $y \geq x - 1$, $3x + 2y < 6$

4. Julia bought scarves and gloves as gifts for family members. Each scarf costs $3 less than each pair of gloves. A pair of gloves costs $9. Julia bought 8 items for $66. How many scarves did she buy?

(1) 2

(2) 4

(3) 5

(4) 6

5. What is the solution of the matrix equation?

$$\begin{bmatrix} 2 & -3 \\ -5 & 7 \end{bmatrix} X = \begin{bmatrix} 4 & 6 \\ 0 & -1 \end{bmatrix}$$

(1) $\begin{bmatrix} 2 & -2 \\ 0 & -\frac{7}{2} \end{bmatrix}$

(2) $\begin{bmatrix} -7 & -3 \\ -5 & -2 \end{bmatrix}$

(3) $\begin{bmatrix} 8 & 15 \\ 20 & 37 \end{bmatrix}$

(4) $\begin{bmatrix} -28 & -39 \\ -20 & -28 \end{bmatrix}$

6. A driver's education program consists of a total of 46 hours of classroom instruction, driving, and observation. You must spend 3 times as much time in the classroom as driving, and 4 hours longer driving than observing. How much time do you spend driving?

(1) 6 hours

(2) 10 hours

(3) 14 hours

(4) 30 hours

7. What is the solution of the linear system?

$$2x - 3y = 9$$
$$y = \frac{2}{3}x + 2$$

(1) (6, 6)

(2) (9, 3)

(3) No solution

(4) Infinitely many solutions

8. Which set of vertices forms a triangle having the same area as the triangle with vertices (1, −5), (2, 3), and (12, 2)?

(1) (−1, 5), (2, 3), (−12, 2)

(2) (0, 0), (6, 6), (8, 6)

(3) (1, 1), (8, 1), (−2, −8)

(4) (−1, 0), (5, 9), (8, 0)

9. Madeline paid $19.43 for 6 packages of bulbs for her flower garden. The cost of 1 package of each type of bulb is shown. She bought twice as many packages of phlox bulbs as lily bulbs. How many packages of lily bulbs did she buy?

Peony bulbs	Phlox bulbs	Lily bulbs
$3.99	$2.61	$2.24

(1) None

(2) 1 package

(3) 2 packages

(4) 3 packages

10. Which matrix has *no* inverse?

(1) $\begin{bmatrix} 6 & 0 \\ 0 & 5 \end{bmatrix}$

(2) $\begin{bmatrix} 4 & 6 \\ -6 & -9 \end{bmatrix}$

(3) $\begin{bmatrix} -2 & 4 \\ 3 & 6 \end{bmatrix}$

(4) $\begin{bmatrix} 1 & 1 \\ 0 & 1 \end{bmatrix}$

TEST PREPARATION

MULTIPLE CHOICE

11. What is the y-coordinate of the solution of the linear system below?

$$\begin{aligned} 2x - 5y &= -10 \\ x + 4y &= 21 \end{aligned}$$

(1) -5　　(3) 4

(2) -4　　(4) 5

12. For the matrix equation below, what is the value of $x + 4y$?

$$2\begin{bmatrix} 5x & 0 \\ -2 & 3 \end{bmatrix} - \begin{bmatrix} 3 & -1 \\ 4y & -2 \end{bmatrix} = \begin{bmatrix} 17 & 1 \\ -10 & 8 \end{bmatrix}$$

(1) $1\frac{1}{2}$　　(3) 8

(2) 2　　(4) $9\frac{1}{2}$

13. The solution of the linear system below is $(-1, -2, z)$. What is the value of z?

$$\begin{aligned} x + 2y + 2z &= 7 \\ 2x - 3y - z &= -2 \\ -4x + y - 3z &= -16 \end{aligned}$$

(1) -6　　(3) -1

(2) -2　　(4) 6

14. A second-run movie theater sells matinee tickets for \$4 and regular tickets for \$6. During one week, the theater earned \$6000. The theater sold 890 more regular tickets than matinee tickets. How many matinee tickets were sold?

(1) 66　　(3) 824

(2) 84　　(4) 956

OPEN-ENDED

15. The table shows U.S. consumer spending on video games and at the box office (in dollars per person per year) for the years 1996 to 2002.

	1996	1997	1998	1999	2000	2001	2002
Video games	11.5	16.5	18.5	24.5	24.7	26.9	30.5
Box office	27.1	28.9	31.2	33.1	32.5	35.5	39.7

Approximate the best-fitting line for the video game data.

Approximate the best-fitting line for the box office data.

Use the best-fitting lines to estimate the year when consumer spending on video games will catch up to consumer spending at the box office. *Explain* how you found your answer.

16. A triangle has an area of 100 square units. Its vertices are (0, 0), (20, 0), and (x, y).

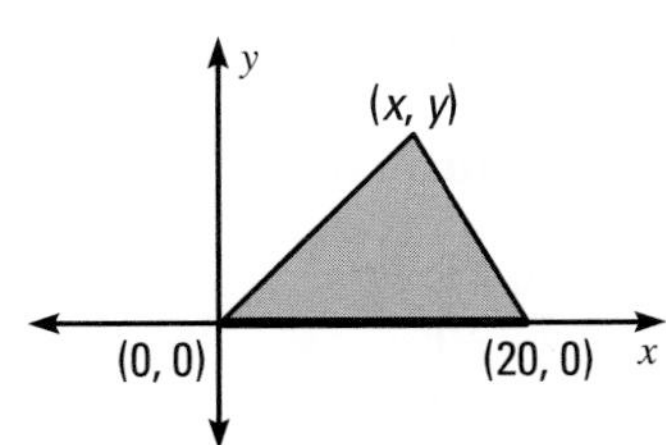

Write an equation involving a determinant that you can use to find the coordinates of the unknown vertex.

Solve the equation. Show all of your steps.

What does your answer tell you about the coordinates of the unknown vertex?

TEST PREPARATION

3 CUMULATIVE REVIEW Chapters 1–3

Simplify the expression. *(p. 10)*

1. $3x^2 - 8x + 12x - 5x^2 + 3x$ **2.** $15x - 6x + 10y - 3y + 4x$ **3.** $3(x + 2) - 4x^2 + 3x + 9$

Solve the equation. Check your solution.

4. $6x - 7 = -2x + 9$ *(p. 18)* **5.** $4(x - 3) = 16x + 18$ *(p. 18)* **6.** $\frac{1}{3}x + 3 = -\frac{7}{2}x - \frac{3}{2}$ *(p. 18)*

7. $|x + 3| = 5$ *(p. 51)* **8.** $|4x - 1| = 27$ *(p. 51)* **9.** $|9 - 2x| = 41$ *(p. 51)*

Solve the inequality. Then graph the solution.

10. $6(x - 4) > 2x + 8$ *(p. 41)* **11.** $3 \le x - 2 \le 8$ *(p. 41)* **12.** $2x < -6$ or $x + 2 > 5$ *(p. 41)*

13. $|x - 4| < 5$ *(p. 51)* **14.** $|x + 3| \ge 15$ *(p. 51)* **15.** $|6x + 1| < 23$ *(p. 51)*

Find the slope of the line passing through the given points. Then tell whether the line *rises, falls, is horizontal,* or *is vertical.* *(p. 82)*

16. $(3, 2), (-1, -5)$ **17.** $(-7, 4), (5, -3)$ **18.** $(-4, -6), (-4, 4)$ **19.** $\left(-\frac{5}{4}, 3\right), \left(\frac{2}{3}, 3\right)$

Graph the equation or inequality.

20. $y = 3x + 5$ *(p. 89)* **21.** $x = -6$ *(p. 89)* **22.** $-x + 4y = 16$ *(p. 89)*

23. $y = 2|x|$ *(p. 123)* **24.** $y = |x - 3|$ *(p. 123)* **25.** $y = -4|x| + 5$ *(p. 123)*

26. $y \le x - 7$ *(p. 132)* **27.** $2x + y > 1$ *(p. 132)* **28.** $2x - 5y \ge -15$ *(p. 132)*

Graph the relation. Then tell whether the relation is a function. *(p. 72)*

29.

x	−4	−2	0	2	4
y	−1	0	1	2	3

30.

x	4	−2	1	1	−3
y	−2	0	1	4	3

Solve the system using any algebraic method.

31. $4x - 3y = 32$
$-2x + y = -14$ *(p. 160)*

32. $5x - 2y = -4$
$3x + 6y = 36$ *(p. 160)*

33. $x - y + 2z = -4$
$3x + y - 4z = -6$
$2x + 3y + z = 9$ *(p. 178)*

Use the given matrices to evaluate the expression. *(p. 195)*

$$A = \begin{bmatrix} -2 & 6 \\ 1 & 4 \end{bmatrix}, B = \begin{bmatrix} 3 & -1 \\ 5 & 2 \end{bmatrix}, C = \begin{bmatrix} -4 & 8 \\ -7 & 12 \end{bmatrix}, D = \begin{bmatrix} 1 & 0 & -4 \\ -2 & 3 & -1 \end{bmatrix}$$

34. $B - 3A$ **35.** $2(A + B) - C$ **36.** $(C - A)B$ **37.** $(B + C)D$

Find the inverse of the matrix. *(p. 210)*

38. $\begin{bmatrix} 5 & 4 \\ 4 & 3 \end{bmatrix}$ **39.** $\begin{bmatrix} 6 & 9 \\ -3 & -4 \end{bmatrix}$ **40.** $\begin{bmatrix} -2 & 2 \\ 4 & 1 \end{bmatrix}$ **41.** $\begin{bmatrix} -5 & 8 \\ 2 & -8 \end{bmatrix}$

42. **CITY PARK** A triangular section of a city park is being turned into a playground. The triangle's vertices are (0, 0), (15, 10), and (8, 25) where the coordinates are measured in yards. Find the area of the playground. *(p. 203)*

43. **BASEBALL** The Pythagorean Theorem of Baseball is a formula for approximating a team's ratio of wins to games played. Let R be the number of runs the team scores during the season, A be the number of runs allowed to opponents, W be the number of wins, and T be the total number of games played. Then the formula below approximates the team's ratio of wins to games played. *(p. 26)*

$$\frac{W}{T} = \frac{R^2}{R^2 + A^2}$$

  a. Solve the formula for W.

  b. In 2004 the Boston Red Sox scored 949 runs and allowed 768 runs. How many of its 162 games would you estimate the team won? *Compare* your answer to the team's actual number of wins, which was 98.

44. **HIGHWAY DRIVING** A sport utility vehicle has a 21 gallon gas tank. On a long highway trip, gas is used at a rate of approximately 4 gallons per hour. Assume the gas tank is full at the start of the trip. *(p. 72)*

  a. Write a function giving the number of gallons g of gasoline in the tank after traveling for t hours.

  b. Graph the function from part (a).

  c. Identify the domain and range of the function from part (a).

45. **COMMISSION** A real estate agent's commission c varies directly with the selling price p of a house. An agent made \$3900 in commission after selling a \$78,000 house. Write an equation that gives c as a function of p. Predict the agent's commission if the selling price of a house is \$125,000. *(p. 107)*

46. **WASTE RECOVERY** The table shows the amount of material (in millions of tons) recovered from solid waste in the United States from 1994 to 2001. Make a scatter plot of the data and approximate the best-fitting line. Predict the amount of material that will be recovered from solid waste in 2010. *(p. 113)*

Years since 1994, t	0	1	2	3	4	5	6	7
Recovered material, m	50.6	54.9	57.3	59.4	61.1	64.8	67.7	68.0

47. **WEIGHTLIFTING RECORDS** The men's world weightlifting records for the 105-kg-and-over weight category are shown in the table. The combined lift is the sum of the snatch lift and the clean and jerk lift. Let s be the weight lifted in the snatch and let j be the weight lifted in the clean and jerk. Write and graph a system of inequalities to describe the weights an athlete could lift to break the records for both the snatch and combined lifts, but *not* the clean and jerk lift. *(p. 168)*

Men's 105+ kg World Weightlifting Records		
Snatch	**Clean and Jerk**	**Combined**
213.0	263.0	472.5

4 Quadratic Functions and Factoring

Before

In previous chapters, you learned the following skills, which you'll use in Chapter 4: evaluating expressions, graphing functions, and solving equations.

Prerequisite Skills

VOCABULARY CHECK

Copy and complete the statement.

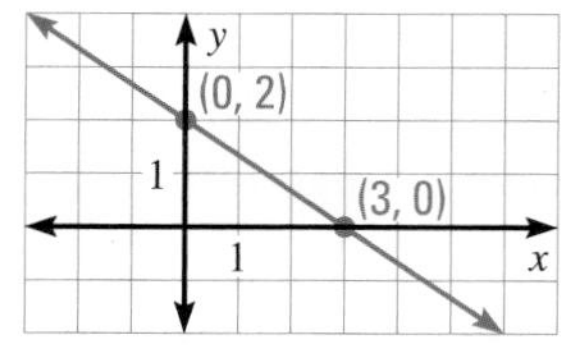

1. The **x-intercept** of the line shown is __?__.
2. The **y-intercept** of the line shown is __?__.

SKILLS CHECK

Evaluate the expression when $x = -3$. *(Review p. 10 for 4.1, 4.7.)*

3. $-5x^2 + 1$
4. $x^2 - x - 8$
5. $(x + 4)^2$
6. $-3(x - 7)^2 + 2$

Graph the function and label the vertex. *(Review p. 123 for 4.2.)*

7. $y = |x| + 2$
8. $y = |x - 3|$
9. $y = -2|x|$
10. $y = |x - 5| + 4$

Solve the equation. *(Review p. 18 for 4.3, 4.4.)*

11. $x + 8 = 0$
12. $3x - 5 = 0$
13. $2x + 1 = x$
14. $4(x - 3) = x + 9$

Now

In Chapter 4, you will apply the big ideas listed below and reviewed in the Chapter Summary on page 317. You will also use the key vocabulary listed below.

Big Ideas

1. **Graphing and writing quadratic functions in several forms**
2. **Solving quadratic equations using a variety of methods**
3. **Performing operations with square roots and complex numbers**

KEY VOCABULARY

- standard form of a quadratic function, *p. 236*
- parabola, *p. 236*
- vertex form, *p. 245*
- intercept form, *p. 246*
- quadratic equation, *p. 253*
- root of an equation, *p. 253*
- zero of a function, *p. 254*
- square root, *p. 266*
- complex number, *p. 276*
- imaginary number, *p. 276*
- completing the square, *p. 284*
- quadratic formula, *p. 292*
- discriminant, *p. 294*
- best-fitting quadratic model, *p. 311*

Why?

You can use quadratic functions to model the heights of projectiles. For example, the height of a baseball hit by a batter can be modeled by a quadratic function.

Animated Algebra

The animation illustrated below for Example 7 on page 287 helps you answer this question: How does changing the ball speed and hitting angle affect the maximum height of a baseball?

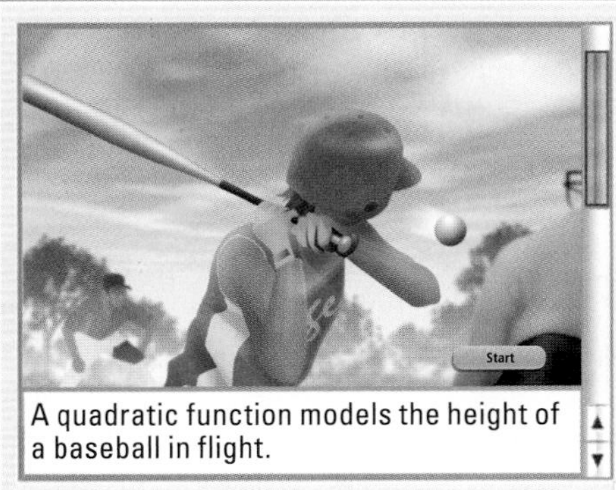

A quadratic function models the height of a baseball in flight.

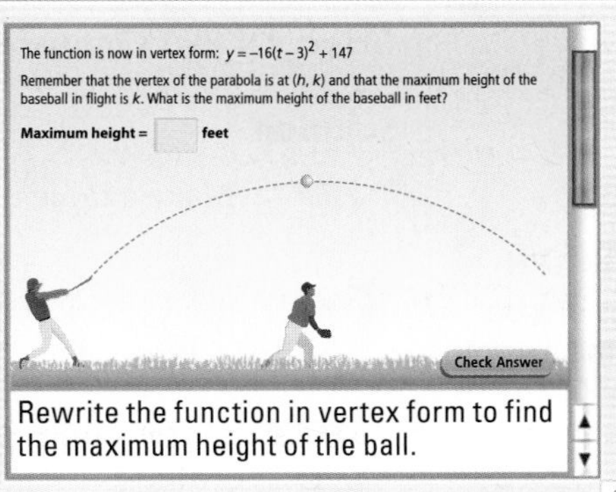

Rewrite the function in vertex form to find the maximum height of the ball.

Animated Algebra at classzone.com

Other animations for Chapter 4: pages 238, 247, 269, 279, 300, and 317

4.1 Graph Quadratic Functions in Standard Form

 **A2.A.40** Write functions in functional notation

Before You graphed linear functions.

Now You will graph quadratic functions.

Why? So you can model sports revenue, as in Example 5.

Key Vocabulary
- **quadratic function**
- **parabola**
- **vertex**
- **axis of symmetry**
- **minimum value**
- **maximum value**

A **quadratic function** is a function that can be written in the **standard form** $y = ax^2 + bx + c$ where $a \neq 0$. The graph of a quadratic function is a **parabola**.

KEY CONCEPT *For Your Notebook*

Parent Function for Quadratic Functions

The parent function for the family of all quadratic functions is $f(x) = x^2$. The graph of $f(x) = x^2$ is the parabola shown below.

The lowest or highest point on a parabola is the vertex. The vertex for $f(x) = x^2$ is (0, 0).

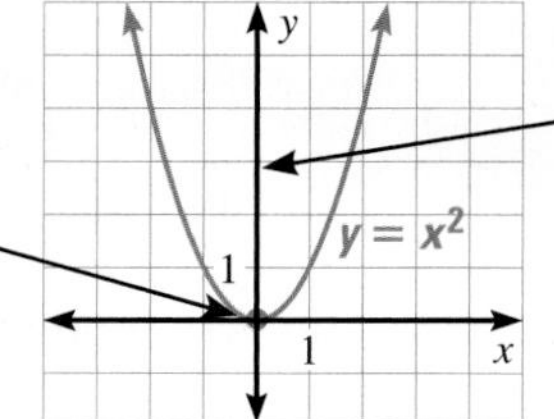

The axis of symmetry divides the parabola into mirror images and passes through the vertex.

For $f(x) = x^2$, and for any quadratic function $g(x) = ax^2 + bx + c$ where $b = 0$, the vertex lies on the y-axis and the axis of symmetry is $x = 0$.

EXAMPLE 1 Graph a function of the form $y = ax^2$

Graph $y = 2x^2$. Compare the graph with the graph of $y = x^2$.

Solution

STEP 1 **Make** a table of values for $y = 2x^2$.

SKETCH A GRAPH
Choose values of x on *both* sides of the axis of symmetry $x = 0$.

x	−2	−1	0	1	2
y	8	2	0	2	8

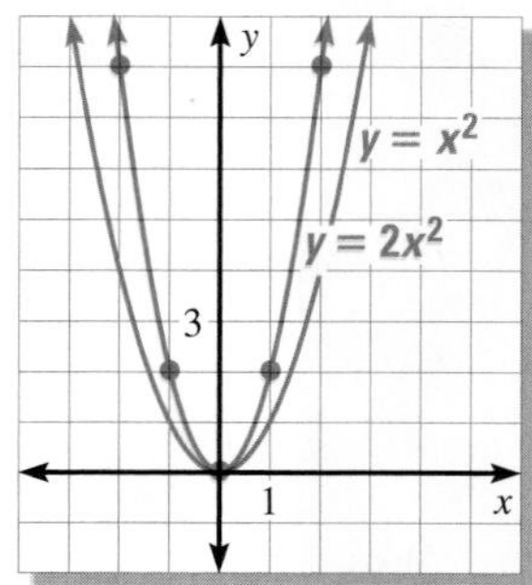

STEP 2 **Plot** the points from the table.

STEP 3 **Draw** a smooth curve through the points.

STEP 4 **Compare** the graphs of $y = 2x^2$ and $y = x^2$. Both open up and have the same vertex and axis of symmetry. The graph of $y = 2x^2$ is narrower than the graph of $y = x^2$.

EXAMPLE 2 Graph a function of the form $y = ax^2 + c$

Graph $y = -\frac{1}{2}x^2 + 3$. Compare the graph with the graph of $y = x^2$.

Solution

STEP 1 **Make** a table of values for $y = -\frac{1}{2}x^2 + 3$.

SKETCH A GRAPH
Choose values of x that are multiples of 2 so that the values of y will be integers.

x	−4	−2	0	2	4
y	−5	1	3	1	−5

STEP 2 **Plot** the points from the table.

STEP 3 **Draw** a smooth curve through the points.

STEP 4 **Compare** the graphs of $y = -\frac{1}{2}x^2 + 3$ and $y = x^2$. Both graphs have the same axis of symmetry. However, the graph of $y = -\frac{1}{2}x^2 + 3$ opens down and is wider than the graph of $y = x^2$. Also, its vertex is 3 units higher.

✓ GUIDED PRACTICE for Examples 1 and 2

Graph the function. Compare the graph with the graph of $y = x^2$.

1. $y = -4x^2$

2. $y = -x^2 - 5$

3. $f(x) = \frac{1}{4}x^2 + 2$

GRAPHING ANY QUADRATIC FUNCTION You can use the following properties to graph *any* quadratic function $y = ax^2 + bx + c$, including a function where $b \neq 0$.

KEY CONCEPT *For Your Notebook*

Properties of the Graph of $y = ax^2 + bx + c$

$y = ax^2 + bx + c, a > 0$

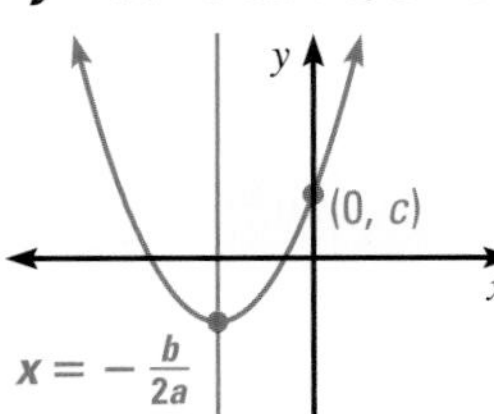

$y = ax^2 + bx + c, a < 0$

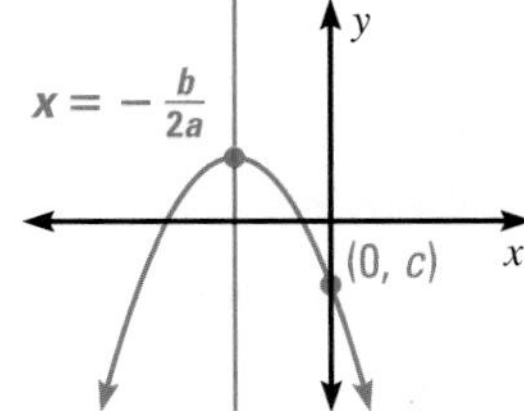

Characteristics of the graph of $y = ax^2 + bx + c$:

- The graph opens up if $a > 0$ and opens down if $a < 0$.
- The graph is narrower than the graph of $y = x^2$ if $|a| > 1$ and wider if $|a| < 1$.
- The axis of symmetry is $x = -\frac{b}{2a}$ and the vertex has x-coordinate $-\frac{b}{2a}$.
- The y-intercept is c. So, the point $(0, c)$ is on the parabola.

EXAMPLE 3 Graph a function of the form $y = ax^2 + bx + c$

Graph $y = 2x^2 - 8x + 6$.

Solution

STEP 1 **Identify** the coefficients of the function. The coefficients are $a = 2$, $b = -8$, and $c = 6$. Because $a > 0$, the parabola opens up.

STEP 2 **Find** the vertex. Calculate the x-coordinate.

AVOID ERRORS
Be sure to include the negative sign before the fraction when calculating the x-coordinate of the vertex.

$$x = -\frac{b}{2a} = -\frac{(-8)}{2(2)} = 2$$

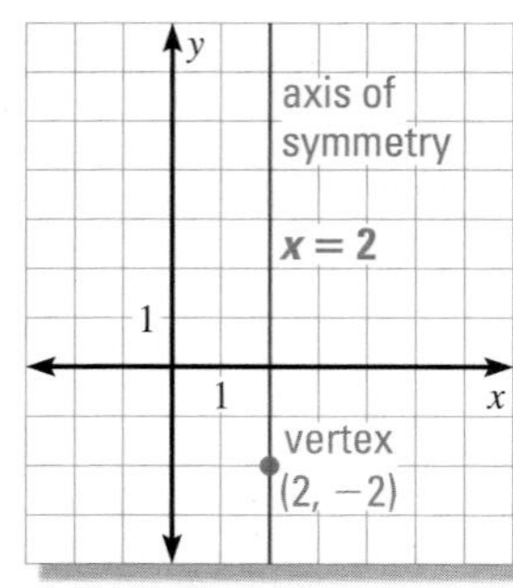

Then find the y-coordinate of the vertex.

$$y = 2(2)^2 - 8(2) + 6 = -2$$

So, the vertex is $(2, -2)$. Plot this point.

STEP 3 **Draw** the axis of symmetry $x = 2$.

STEP 4 **Identify** the y-intercept c, which is 6. Plot the point $(0, 6)$. Then reflect this point in the axis of symmetry to plot another point, $(4, 6)$.

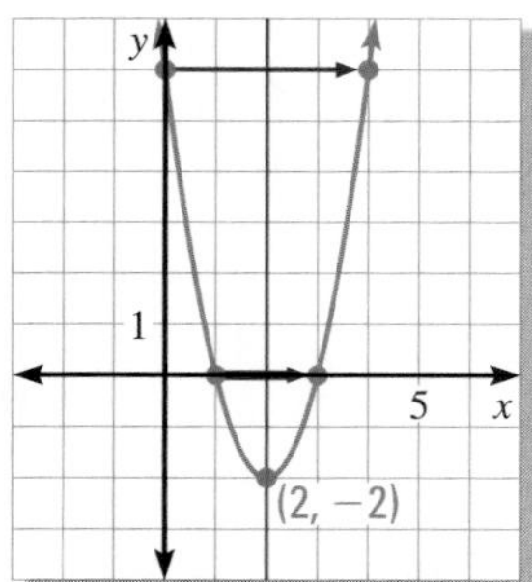

STEP 5 **Evaluate** the function for another value of x, such as $x = 1$.

$$y = 2(1)^2 - 8(1) + 6 = 0$$

Plot the point $(1, 0)$ and its reflection $(3, 0)$ in the axis of symmetry.

STEP 6 **Draw** a parabola through the plotted points.

Animated Algebra at classzone.com

✓ GUIDED PRACTICE for Example 3

Graph the function. Label the vertex and axis of symmetry.

4. $y = x^2 - 2x - 1$

5. $y = 2x^2 + 6x + 3$

6. $f(x) = -\frac{1}{3}x^2 - 5x + 2$

KEY CONCEPT *For Your Notebook*

Minimum and Maximum Values

Words For $y = ax^2 + bx + c$, the vertex's y-coordinate is the **minimum value** of the function if $a > 0$ and the **maximum value** if $a < 0$.

Graphs

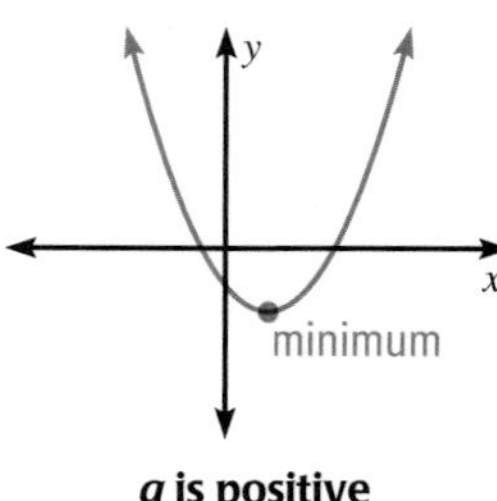

***a* is positive**

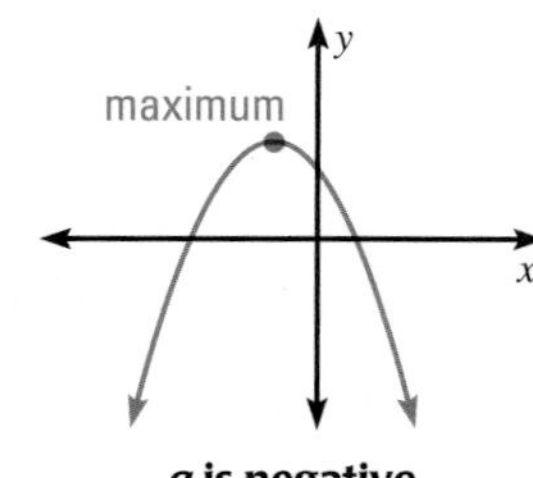

***a* is negative**

EXAMPLE 4 Find the minimum or maximum value

Tell whether the function $y = 3x^2 - 18x + 20$ has a *minimum value* or a *maximum value*. Then find the minimum or maximum value.

Solution

Because $a > 0$, the function has a minimum value. To find it, calculate the coordinates of the vertex.

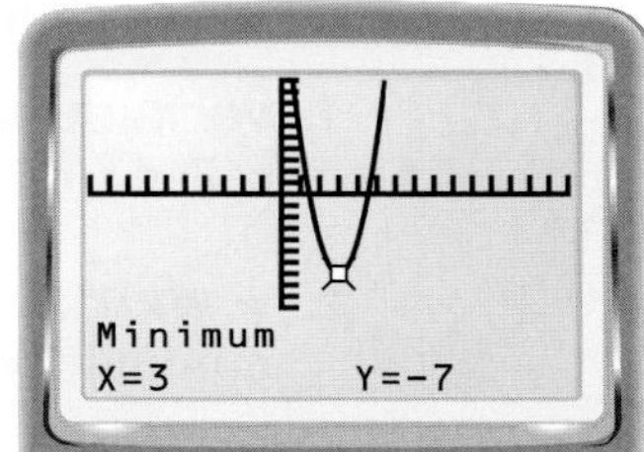

$$x = -\frac{b}{2a} = -\frac{(-18)}{2(3)} = 3$$

$$y = 3(3)^2 - 18(3) + 20 = -7$$

▶ The minimum value is $y = -7$. You can check the answer on a graphing calculator.

EXAMPLE 5 Solve a multi-step problem

GO-CARTS A go-cart track has about 380 racers per week and charges each racer \$35 to race. The owner estimates that there will be 20 more racers per week for every \$1 reduction in the price per racer. How can the owner of the go-cart track maximize weekly revenue?

Solution

STEP 1 **Define** the variables. Let x represent the price reduction and $R(x)$ represent the weekly revenue.

STEP 2 **Write** a verbal model. Then write and simplify a quadratic function.

Revenue (dollars)	=	Price (dollars/racer)	•	Attendance (racers)
$\mathbf{R(x)}$	=	$\mathbf{(35 - x)}$	•	$\mathbf{(380 + 20x)}$
$R(x)$	=	$13{,}300 + 700x - 380x - 20x^2$		
$R(x)$	=	$-20x^2 + 320x + 13{,}300$		

INTERPRET FUNCTIONS
Notice that $a = -20 < 0$, so the revenue function has a maximum value.

STEP 3 **Find** the coordinates $(x, R(x))$ of the vertex.

$$x = -\frac{b}{2a} = -\frac{320}{2(-20)} = 8$$ **Find x-coordinate.**

$$R(8) = -20(8)^2 + 320(8) + 13{,}300 = 14{,}580$$ **Evaluate $R(8)$.**

▶ The vertex is (8, 14,580), which means the owner should reduce the price per racer by \$8 to increase the weekly revenue to \$14,580.

✓ GUIDED PRACTICE for Examples 4 and 5

7. Find the minimum value of $y = 4x^2 + 16x - 3$.

8. **WHAT IF?** In Example 5, suppose each \$1 reduction in the price per racer brings in 40 more racers per week. How can weekly revenue be maximized?

4.1 EXERCISES

HOMEWORK KEY

○ = **WORKED-OUT SOLUTIONS** on p. WS7 for Exs. 15, 37, and 57

★ = **STANDARDIZED TEST PRACTICE** Exs. 2, 39, 40, 43, 53, 58, and 60

◆ = **MULTIPLE REPRESENTATIONS** Ex. 59

SKILL PRACTICE

1. VOCABULARY Copy and complete: The graph of a quadratic function is called a(n) _?_.

2. ★ WRITING *Describe* how to determine whether a quadratic function has a minimum value or a maximum value.

EXAMPLE 1 on p. 236 for Exs. 3–12

USING A TABLE Copy and complete the table of values for the function.

3. $y = 4x^2$

x	−2	−1	0	1	2
y	?	?	?	?	?

4. $y = -3x^2$

x	−2	−1	0	1	2
y	?	?	?	?	?

5. $y = \frac{1}{2}x^2$

x	−4	−2	0	2	4
y	?	?	?	?	?

6. $y = -\frac{1}{3}x^2$

x	−6	−3	0	3	6
y	?	?	?	?	?

MAKING A GRAPH Graph the function. *Compare* the graph with the graph of $y = x^2$.

7. $y = 3x^2$ **8.** $y = 5x^2$ **9.** $y = -2x^2$

10. $y = -x^2$ **11.** $f(x) = \frac{1}{3}x^2$ **12.** $g(x) = -\frac{1}{4}x^2$

EXAMPLE 2 on p. 237 for Exs. 13–18

13. $y = 5x^2 + 1$ **14.** $y = 4x^2 + 1$ **15.** $f(x) = -x^2 + 2$

16. $g(x) = -2x^2 - 5$ **17.** $f(x) = \frac{3}{4}x^2 - 5$ **18.** $g(x) = -\frac{1}{5}x^2 - 2$

ERROR ANALYSIS *Describe* and correct the error in analyzing the graph of $y = 4x^2 + 24x - 7$.

19.

The x-coordinate of the vertex is:

$x = \frac{b}{2a} = \frac{24}{2(4)} = 3$

20.

The y-intercept of the graph is the value of c, which is 7.

EXAMPLE 3 on p. 238 for Exs. 21–32

MAKING A GRAPH Graph the function. Label the vertex and axis of symmetry.

21. $y = x^2 + 2x + 1$ **22.** $y = 3x^2 - 6x + 4$ **23.** $y = -4x^2 + 8x + 2$

24. $y = -2x^2 - 6x + 3$ **25.** $g(x) = -x^2 - 2x - 1$ **26.** $f(x) = -6x^2 - 4x - 5$

27. $y = \frac{2}{3}x^2 - 3x + 6$ **28.** $y = -\frac{3}{4}x^2 - 4x - 1$ **29.** $g(x) = -\frac{3}{5}x^2 + 2x + 2$

30. $f(x) = \frac{1}{2}x^2 + x - 3$ **31.** $y = \frac{8}{5}x^2 - 4x + 5$ **32.** $y = -\frac{5}{3}x^2 - x - 4$

EXAMPLE 4
on p. 239 for Exs. 33–38

MINIMUMS OR MAXIMUMS Tell whether the function has a *minimum value* or a *maximum value*. Then find the minimum or maximum value.

33. $y = -6x^2 - 1$
34. $y = 9x^2 + 7$
35. $f(x) = 2x^2 + 8x + 7$
36. $g(x) = -3x^2 + 18x - 5$
37. $f(x) = \frac{3}{2}x^2 + 6x + 4$
38. $y = -\frac{1}{4}x^2 - 7x + 2$

39. ★ **MULTIPLE CHOICE** What is the effect on the graph of the function $y = x^2 + 2$ when it is changed to $y = x^2 - 3$?

    Ⓐ The graph widens.
    Ⓑ The graph narrows.
    Ⓒ The graph opens down.
    Ⓓ The vertex moves down the y-axis.

40. ★ **MULTIPLE CHOICE** Which function has the widest graph?

    Ⓐ $y = 2x^2$
    Ⓑ $y = x^2$
    Ⓒ $y = 0.5x^2$
    Ⓓ $y = -x^2$

IDENTIFYING COEFFICIENTS In Exercises 41 and 42, identify the values of *a*, *b*, and *c* for the quadratic function.

41. The path of a basketball thrown at an angle of 45° can be modeled by $y = -0.02x^2 + x + 6$.

42. The path of a shot put released at an angle of 35° can be modeled by $y = -0.01x^2 + 0.7x + 6$.

43. ★ **OPEN-ENDED MATH** Write three different quadratic functions whose graphs have the line $x = 4$ as an axis of symmetry but have different y-intercepts.

MATCHING In Exercises 44–46, match the equation with its graph.

44. $y = 0.5x^2 - 2x$
45. $y = 0.5x^2 + 3$
46. $y = 0.5x^2 - 2x + 3$

A. 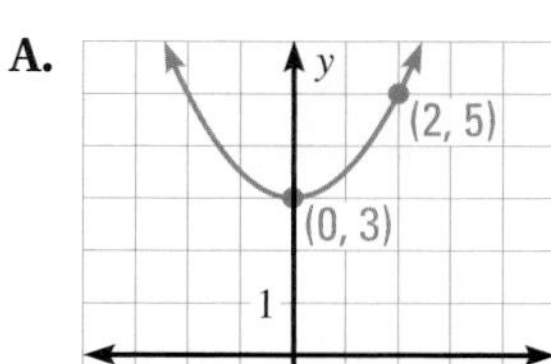

B. 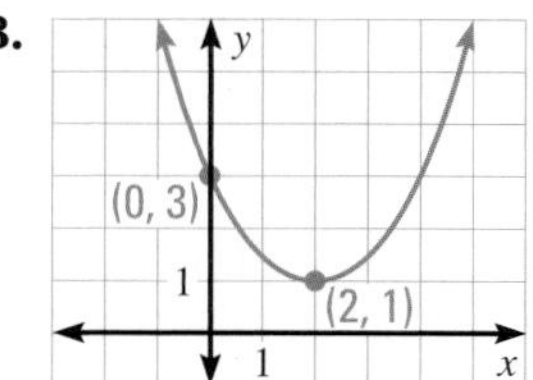

C. 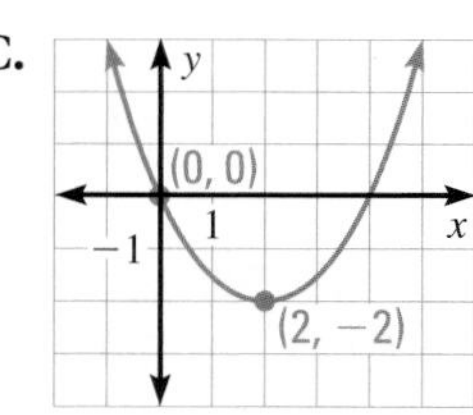

MAKING A GRAPH Graph the function. Label the vertex and axis of symmetry.

47. $f(x) = 0.1x^2 + 2$
48. $g(x) = -0.5x^2 - 5$
49. $y = 0.3x^2 + 3x - 1$
50. $y = 0.25x^2 - 1.5x + 3$
51. $f(x) = 4.2x^2 + 6x - 1$
52. $g(x) = 1.75x^2 - 2.5$

53. ★ **SHORT RESPONSE** The points (2, 3) and (−4, 3) lie on the graph of a quadratic function. *Explain* how these points can be used to find an equation of the axis of symmetry. Then write an equation of the axis of symmetry.

54. **CHALLENGE** For the graph of $y = ax^2 + bx + c$, show that the y-coordinate of the vertex is $-\frac{b^2}{4a} + c$.

PROBLEM SOLVING

EXAMPLE 5 on p. 239 for Exs. 55–58

55. **ONLINE MUSIC** An online music store sells about 4000 songs each day when it charges \$1 per song. For each \$.05 increase in price, about 80 fewer songs per day are sold. Use the verbal model and quadratic function to find how the store can maximize daily revenue.

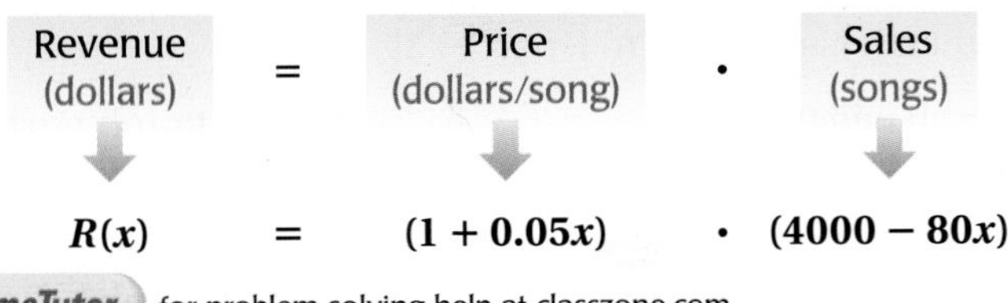

$$R(x) = (1 + 0.05x) \cdot (4000 - 80x)$$

@HomeTutor for problem solving help at classzone.com

56. **DIGITAL CAMERAS** An electronics store sells about 70 of a new model of digital camera per month at a price of \$320 each. For each \$20 decrease in price, about 5 more cameras per month are sold. Write a function that models the situation. Then tell how the store can maximize monthly revenue from sales of the camera.

@HomeTutor for problem solving help at classzone.com

57. **GOLDEN GATE BRIDGE** Each cable joining the two towers on the Golden Gate Bridge can be modeled by the function

$$y = \frac{1}{9000}x^2 - \frac{7}{15}x + 500$$

where x and y are measured in feet. What is the height h above the road of a cable at its lowest point?

58. ★ **SHORT RESPONSE** A woodland jumping mouse hops along a parabolic path given by $y = -0.2x^2 + 1.3x$ where x is the mouse's horizontal position (in feet) and y is the corresponding height (in feet). Can the mouse jump over a fence that is 3 feet high? *Explain.*

59. ◆ **MULTIPLE REPRESENTATIONS** A community theater sells about 150 tickets to a play each week when it charges \$20 per ticket. For each \$1 decrease in price, about 10 more tickets per week are sold. The theater has fixed expenses of \$1500 per week.

    a. **Writing a Model** Write a verbal model and a quadratic function to represent the theater's weekly profit.

    b. **Making a Table** Make a table of values for the quadratic function.

    c. **Drawing a Graph** Use the table to graph the quadratic function. Then use the graph to find how the theater can maximize weekly profit.

60. ★ **EXTENDED RESPONSE** In 1971, astronaut Alan Shepard hit a golf ball on the moon. The path of a golf ball hit at an angle of 45° and with a speed of 100 feet per second can be modeled by

$$y = -\frac{g}{10,000}x^2 + x$$

where x is the ball's horizontal position (in feet), y is the corresponding height (in feet), and g is the acceleration due to gravity (in feet per second squared).

a. **Model** Use the information in the diagram to write functions for the paths of a golf ball hit on Earth and a golf ball hit on the moon.

GRAPHING CALCULATOR
In part (b), use the calculator's *zero* feature to answer the questions.

b. **Graphing Calculator** Graph the functions from part (a) on a graphing calculator. How far does the golf ball travel on Earth? on the moon?

c. **Interpret** *Compare* the distances traveled by a golf ball on Earth and on the moon. Your answer should include the following:

- a calculation of the ratio of the distances traveled
- a discussion of how the distances and values of g are related

61. **CHALLENGE** Lifeguards at a beach want to rope off a rectangular swimming section. They have P feet of rope with buoys. In terms of P, what is the maximum area that the swimming section can have?

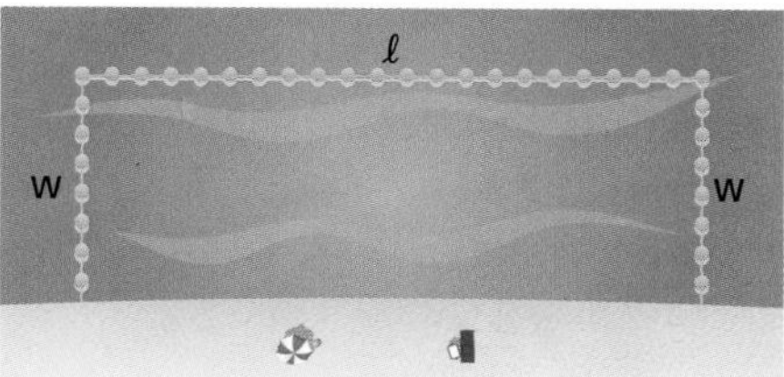

NEW YORK MIXED REVIEW

62. Liz's high score in a video game is 1200 points less than three times her friend's high score. Let x represent her friend's high score. Which expression can be used to determine Liz's high score?

Ⓐ $1200 - 3x$ Ⓑ $\frac{x - 1200}{3}$ Ⓒ $\frac{x}{3} - 1200$ Ⓓ $3x - 1200$

63. The total cost, c, of a school banquet is given by $c = 25n + 1400$, where n is the total number of students attending the banquet. The total cost of the banquet was \$9900. How many students attended the banquet?

Ⓐ 177 Ⓑ 340 Ⓒ 396 Ⓓ 452

@HomeTutor
classzone.com
Keystrokes

4.1 Find Maximum and Minimum Values

QUESTION How can you use a graphing calculator to find the maximum or minimum value of a function?

EXAMPLE Find the maximum value of a function

Find the maximum value of $y = -2x^2 - 10x - 5$ and the value of x where it occurs.

***STEP 1* Graph function**

Graph the given function and select the *maximum* feature.

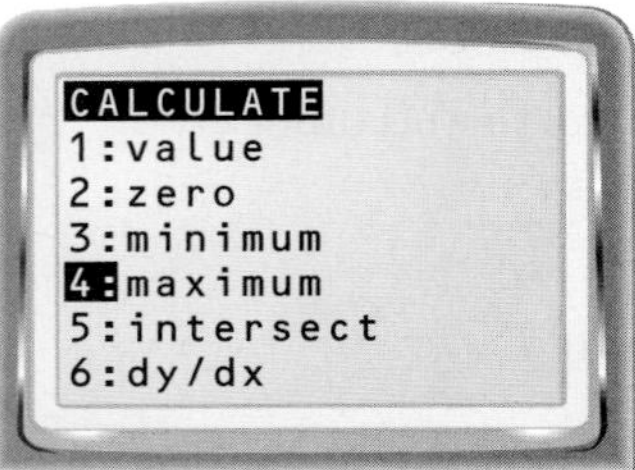

***STEP 2* Choose left bound**

Move the cursor to the left of the maximum point. Press ENTER.

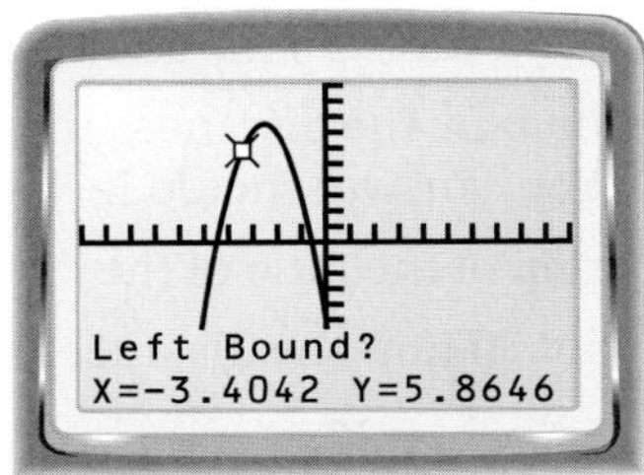

***STEP 3* Choose right bound**

Move the cursor to the right of the maximum point. Press ENTER.

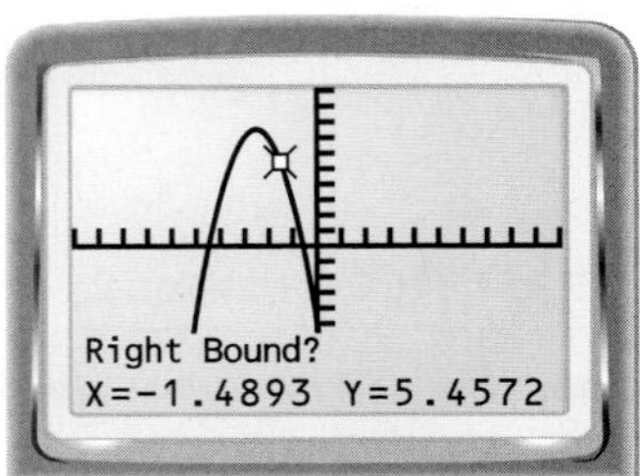

***STEP 4* Find maximum**

Put the cursor approximately on the maximum point. Press ENTER.

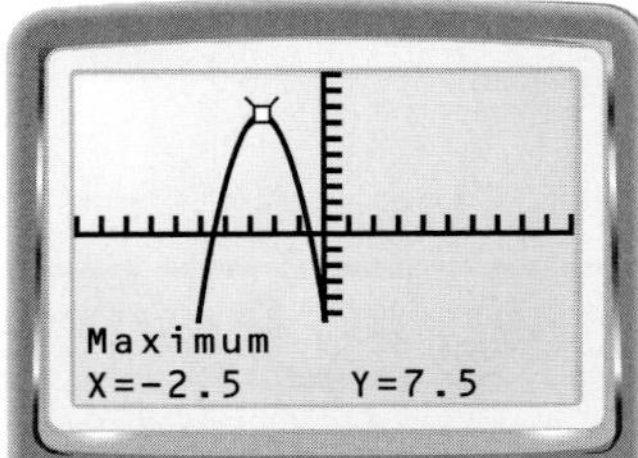

▶ The maximum value of the function is $y = 7.5$ and occurs at $x = -2.5$.

PRACTICE

Tell whether the function has a *maximum value* or a *minimum value*. Then find the maximum or minimum value and the value of x where it occurs.

1. $y = x^2 - 6x + 4$

2. $f(x) = x^2 - 3x + 3$

3. $y = -3x^2 + 9x + 2$

4. $y = 0.5x^2 + 0.8x - 2$

5. $h(x) = \frac{1}{2}x^2 - 3x + 2$

6. $y = -\frac{3}{8}x^2 + 6x - 5$

4.2 Graph Quadratic Functions in Vertex or Intercept Form

A2.N.3 Perform arithmetic operations with polynomial expressions containing rational coefficients

Before You graphed quadratic functions in standard form.

Now You will graph quadratic functions in vertex form or intercept form.

Why? So you can find the height of a jump, as in Ex. 51.

Key Vocabulary
- vertex form
- intercept form

In Lesson 4.1, you learned that the standard form of a quadratic function is $y = ax^2 + bx + c$ where $a \neq 0$. Another useful form of a quadratic function is the **vertex form**, $y = a(x - h)^2 + k$.

KEY CONCEPT *For Your Notebook*

Graph of Vertex Form $y = a(x - h)^2 + k$

The graph of $y = a(x - h)^2 + k$ is the parabola $y = ax^2$ translated horizontally h units and vertically k units.

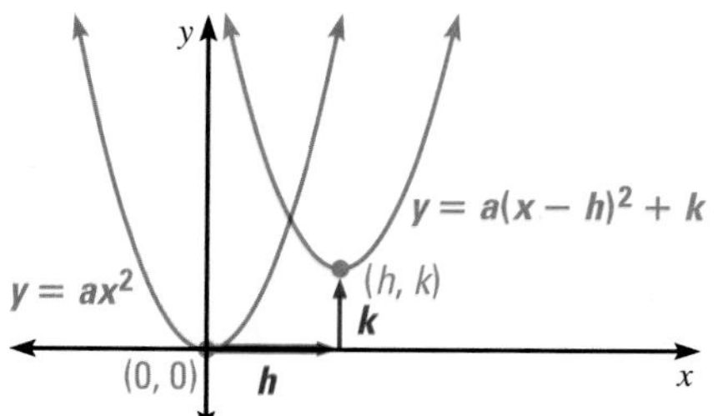

Characteristics of the graph of $y = a(x - h)^2 + k$:
- The vertex is (h, k).
- The axis of symmetry is $x = h$.
- The graph opens up if $a > 0$ and down if $a < 0$.

EXAMPLE 1 Graph a quadratic function in vertex form

Graph $y = -\frac{1}{4}(x + 2)^2 + 5$.

Solution

STEP 1 **Identify** the constants $a = -\frac{1}{4}$, $h = -2$, and $k = 5$. Because $a < 0$, the parabola opens down.

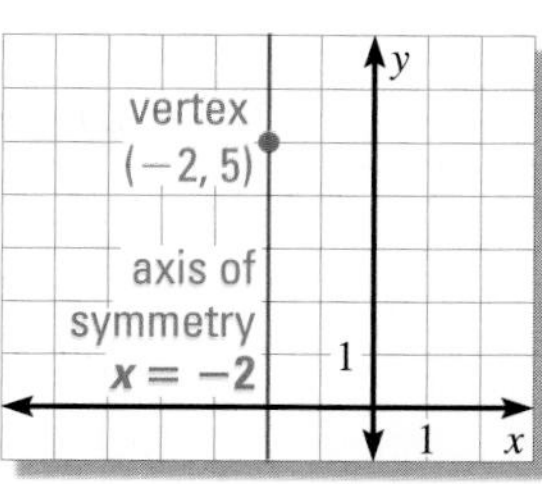

STEP 2 **Plot** the vertex $(h, k) = (-2, 5)$ and draw the axis of symmetry $x = -2$.

STEP 3 **Evaluate** the function for two values of x.

$$x = 0:\ y = -\frac{1}{4}(0 + 2)^2 + 5 = 4$$

$$x = 2:\ y = -\frac{1}{4}(2 + 2)^2 + 5 = 1$$

Plot the points (0, 4) and (2, 1) and their reflections in the axis of symmetry.

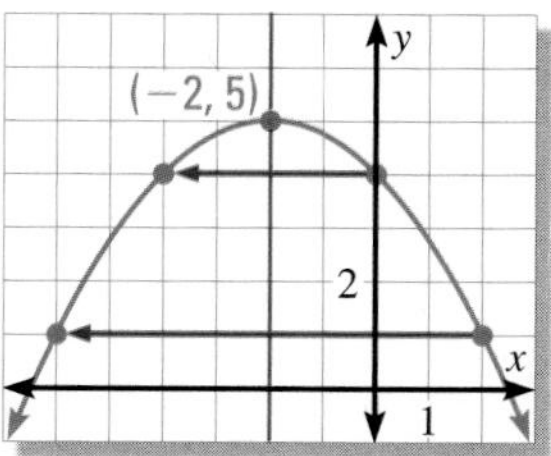

STEP 4 **Draw** a parabola through the plotted points.

EXAMPLE 2 Use a quadratic model in vertex form

CIVIL ENGINEERING The Tacoma Narrows Bridge in Washington has two towers that each rise 307 feet above the roadway and are connected by suspension cables as shown. Each cable can be modeled by the function

$$y = \frac{1}{7000}(x - 1400)^2 + 27$$

where x and y are measured in feet. What is the distance d between the two towers?

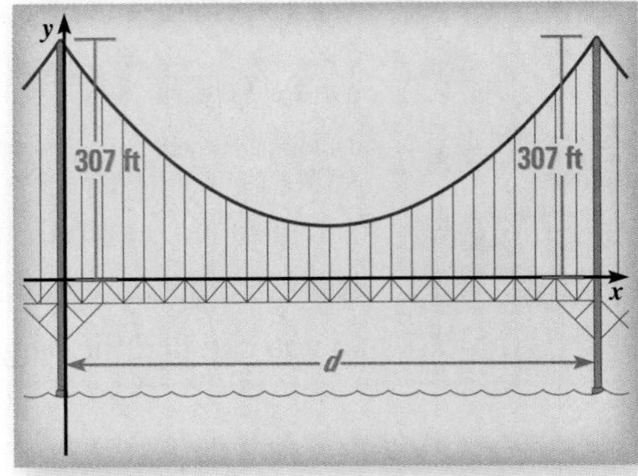

Not drawn to scale

Solution

The vertex of the parabola is (1400, 27). So, a cable's lowest point is 1400 feet from the left tower shown above. Because the heights of the two towers are the same, the symmetry of the parabola implies that the vertex is also 1400 feet from the right tower. So, the distance between the two towers is $d = 2(1400) = 2800$ feet.

GUIDED PRACTICE for Examples 1 and 2

Graph the function. Label the vertex and axis of symmetry.

1. $y = (x + 2)^2 - 3$
2. $y = -(x - 1)^2 + 5$
3. $f(x) = \frac{1}{2}(x - 3)^2 - 4$
4. **WHAT IF?** Suppose an architect designs a bridge with cables that can be modeled by $y = \frac{1}{6500}(x - 1400)^2 + 27$ where x and y are measured in feet. Compare this function's graph to the graph of the function in Example 2.

INTERCEPT FORM If the graph of a quadratic function has at least one x-intercept, then the function can be represented in **intercept form**, $y = a(x - p)(x - q)$.

KEY CONCEPT *For Your Notebook*

Graph of Intercept Form $y = a(x - p)(x - q)$

Characteristics of the graph of $y = a(x - p)(x - q)$:

- The x-intercepts are p and q.
- The axis of symmetry is halfway between $(p, 0)$ and $(q, 0)$. It has equation $x = \frac{p + q}{2}$.
- The graph opens up if $a > 0$ and opens down if $a < 0$.

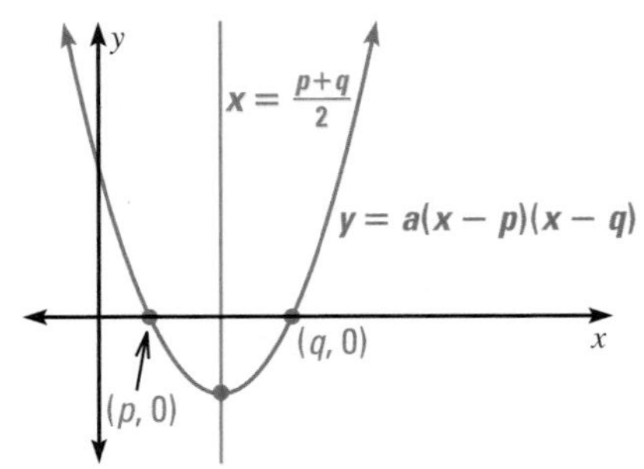

EXAMPLE 3 Graph a quadratic function in intercept form

Graph $y = 2(x + 3)(x - 1)$.

Solution

AVOID ERRORS
Remember that the x-intercepts for a quadratic function written in the form $y = a(x - p)(x - q)$ are p and q, not $-p$ and $-q$.

STEP 1 **Identify** the x-intercepts. Because $p = -3$ and $q = 1$, the x-intercepts occur at the points $(-3, 0)$ and $(1, 0)$.

STEP 2 **Find** the coordinates of the vertex.

$$x = \frac{p + q}{2} = \frac{-3 + 1}{2} = -1$$

$$y = 2(-1 + 3)(-1 - 1) = -8$$

So, the vertex is $(-1, -8)$.

STEP 3 **Draw** a parabola through the vertex and the points where the x-intercepts occur.

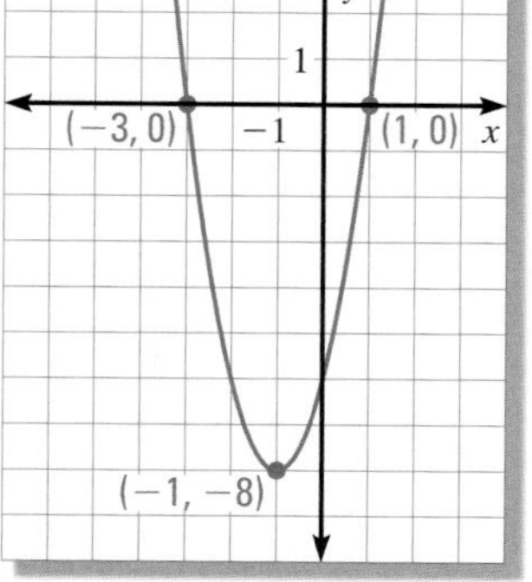

Animated Algebra at classzone.com

EXAMPLE 4 Use a quadratic function in intercept form

FOOTBALL The path of a placekicked football can be modeled by the function $y = -0.026x(x - 46)$ where x is the horizontal distance (in yards) and y is the corresponding height (in yards).

a. How far is the football kicked?

b. What is the football's maximum height?

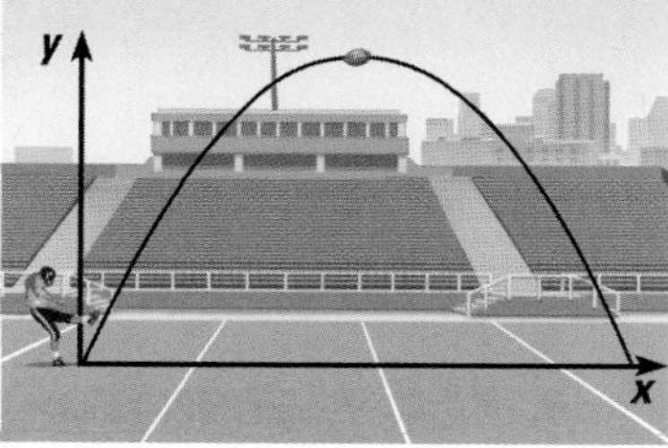

Solution

a. Rewrite the function as $y = -0.026(x - 0)(x - 46)$. Because $p = 0$ and $q = 46$, you know the x-intercepts are 0 and 46. So, you can conclude that the football is kicked a distance of 46 yards.

b. To find the football's maximum height, calculate the coordinates of the vertex.

$$x = \frac{p + q}{2} = \frac{0 + 46}{2} = 23$$

$$y = -0.026(23)(23 - 46) \approx 13.8$$

The maximum height is the y-coordinate of the vertex, or about 13.8 yards.

GUIDED PRACTICE for Examples 3 and 4

Graph the function. Label the vertex, axis of symmetry, and x-intercepts.

5. $y = (x - 3)(x - 7)$ **6.** $f(x) = 2(x - 4)(x + 1)$ **7.** $y = -(x + 1)(x - 5)$

8. WHAT IF? In Example 4, what is the maximum height of the football if the football's path can be modeled by the function $y = -0.025x(x - 50)$?

FOIL METHOD You can change quadratic functions from intercept form or vertex form to standard form by multiplying algebraic expressions. One method for multiplying two expressions each containing two terms is *FOIL*.

KEY CONCEPT — *For Your Notebook*

FOIL Method

Words To multiply two expressions that each contain two terms, add the products of the **F**irst terms, the **O**uter terms, the **I**nner terms, and the **L**ast terms.

Example

F O I L

$(x + 4)(x + 7) = x^2 + 7x + 4x + \mathbf{28} = x^2 + 11x + 28$

EXAMPLE 5 Change from intercept form to standard form

REVIEW FOIL
For help with using the FOIL method, see p. 985.

Write $y = -2(x + 5)(x - 8)$ in standard form.

$y = -2(x + 5)(x - 8)$	**Write original function.**
$= -2(x^2 - 8x + 5x - 40)$	**Multiply using FOIL.**
$= -2(x^2 - 3x - 40)$	**Combine like terms.**
$= -2x^2 + 6x + 80$	**Distributive property**

EXAMPLE 6 Change from vertex form to standard form

Write $f(x) = 4(x - 1)^2 + 9$ in standard form.

$f(x) = 4(x - 1)^2 + 9$	**Write original function.**
$= 4(x - 1)(x - 1) + 9$	**Rewrite $(x - 1)^2$.**
$= 4(x^2 - x - x + 1) + 9$	**Multiply using FOIL.**
$= 4(x^2 - 2x + 1) + 9$	**Combine like terms.**
$= 4x^2 - 8x + 4 + 9$	**Distributive property**
$= 4x^2 - 8x + 13$	**Combine like terms.**

GUIDED PRACTICE for Examples 5 and 6

Write the quadratic function in standard form.

9. $y = -(x - 2)(x - 7)$

10. $y = -4(x - 1)(x + 3)$

11. $f(x) = 2(x + 5)(x + 4)$

12. $y = -7(x - 6)(x + 1)$

13. $y = -3(x + 5)^2 - 1$

14. $g(x) = 6(x - 4)^2 - 10$

15. $f(x) = -(x + 2)^2 + 4$

16. $y = 2(x - 3)^2 + 9$

4.2 EXERCISES

HOMEWORK KEY

○ = **WORKED-OUT SOLUTIONS** on p. WS8 for Exs. 19, 29, and 53

★ = **STANDARDIZED TEST PRACTICE** Exs. 2, 12, 22, 49, 54, and 55

SKILL PRACTICE

1. **VOCABULARY** Copy and complete: A quadratic function in the form $y = a(x - h)^2 + k$ is in __?__ form.

2. ★ **WRITING** *Explain* how to find a quadratic function's maximum value or minimum value when the function is given in intercept form.

EXAMPLE 1 on p. 245 for Exs. 3–12

GRAPHING WITH VERTEX FORM Graph the function. Label the vertex and axis of symmetry.

3. $y = (x - 3)^2$
4. $y = (x + 4)^2$
5. $f(x) = -(x + 3)^2 + 5$
6. $y = 3(x - 7)^2 - 1$
7. $g(x) = -4(x - 2)^2 + 4$
8. $y = 2(x + 1)^2 - 3$
9. $f(x) = -2(x - 1)^2 - 5$
10. $y = -\frac{1}{4}(x + 2)^2 + 1$
11. $y = \frac{1}{2}(x - 3)^2 + 2$

12. ★ **MULTIPLE CHOICE** What is the vertex of the graph of the function $y = 3(x + 2)^2 - 5$?

Ⓐ (2, −5) Ⓑ (−2, −5) Ⓒ (−5, 2) Ⓓ (5, −2)

EXAMPLE 3 on p. 247 for Exs. 13–23

GRAPHING WITH INTERCEPT FORM Graph the function. Label the vertex, axis of symmetry, and x-intercepts.

13. $y = (x + 3)(x - 3)$
14. $y = (x + 1)(x - 3)$
15. $y = 3(x + 2)(x + 6)$
16. $f(x) = 2(x - 5)(x - 1)$
17. $y = -(x - 4)(x + 6)$
18. $g(x) = -4(x + 3)(x + 7)$
19. $y = (x + 1)(x + 2)$
20. $f(x) = -2(x - 3)(x + 4)$
21. $y = 4(x - 7)(x + 2)$

22. ★ **MULTIPLE CHOICE** What is the vertex of the graph of the function $y = -(x - 6)(x + 4)$?

Ⓐ (1, 25) Ⓑ (−1, 21) Ⓒ (−6, 4) Ⓓ (6, −4)

23. **ERROR ANALYSIS** *Describe* and correct the error in analyzing the graph of the function $y = 5(x - 2)(x + 3)$.

The x-intercepts of the graph are −2 and 3.

EXAMPLES 5 and 6 on p. 248 for Exs. 24–32

WRITING IN STANDARD FORM Write the quadratic function in standard form.

24. $y = (x + 4)(x + 3)$
25. $y = (x - 5)(x + 3)$
26. $h(x) = 4(x + 1)(x - 6)$
27. $y = -3(x - 2)(x - 4)$
28. $f(x) = (x + 5)^2 - 2$
29. $y = (x - 3)^2 + 6$
30. $g(x) = -(x + 6)^2 + 10$
31. $y = 5(x + 3)^2 - 4$
32. $f(x) = 12(x - 1)^2 + 4$

MINIMUM OR MAXIMUM VALUES Find the minimum value or the maximum value of the function.

33. $y = 3(x - 3)^2 - 4$
34. $g(x) = -4(x + 6)^2 - 12$
35. $y = 15(x - 25)^2 + 130$
36. $f(x) = 3(x + 10)(x - 8)$
37. $y = -(x - 36)(x + 18)$
38. $y = -12x(x - 9)$
39. $y = 8x(x + 15)$
40. $y = 2(x - 3)(x - 6)$
41. $g(x) = -5(x + 9)(x - 4)$

42. **GRAPHING CALCULATOR** Consider the function $y = a(x - h)^2 + k$ where $a = 1$, $h = 3$, and $k = -2$. Predict the effect of each change in a, h, or k described in parts (a)–(c). Use a graphing calculator to check your prediction by graphing the original and revised functions in the same coordinate plane.

a. a changes to -3 **b.** h changes to -1 **c.** k changes to 2

MAKING A GRAPH **Graph the function. Label the vertex and axis of symmetry.**

43. $y = 5(x - 2.25)^2 - 2.75$

44. $g(x) = -8(x + 3.2)^2 + 6.4$

45. $y = -0.25(x - 5.2)^2 + 8.5$

46. $y = -\frac{2}{3}\left(x - \frac{1}{2}\right)^2 + \frac{4}{5}$

47. $f(x) = -\frac{3}{4}(x + 5)(x + 8)$

48. $g(x) = \frac{5}{2}\left(x - \frac{4}{3}\right)\left(x - \frac{2}{5}\right)$

49. ★ **OPEN-ENDED MATH** Write two different quadratic functions in intercept form whose graphs have axis of symmetry $x = 3$.

50. **CHALLENGE** Write $y = a(x - h)^2 + k$ and $y = a(x - p)(x - q)$ in standard form. Knowing the vertex of the graph of $y = ax^2 + bx + c$ occurs at $x = -\frac{b}{2a}$, show that the vertex of the graph of $y = a(x - h)^2 + k$ occurs at $x = h$ and that the vertex of the graph of $y = a(x - p)(x - q)$ occurs at $x = \frac{p + q}{2}$.

PROBLEM SOLVING

EXAMPLES 2 and 4 on pp. 246–247 for Exs. 51–54

51. **BIOLOGY** The function $y = -0.03(x - 14)^2 + 6$ models the jump of a red kangaroo where x is the horizontal distance (in feet) and y is the corresponding height (in feet). What is the kangaroo's maximum height? How long is the kangaroo's jump?

@HomeTutor for problem solving help at classzone.com

52. **CIVIL ENGINEERING** The arch of the Gateshead Millennium Bridge forms a parabola with equation $y = -0.016(x - 52.5)^2 + 45$ where x is the horizontal distance (in meters) from the arch's left end and y is the distance (in meters) from the base of the arch. What is the width of the arch?

@HomeTutor for problem solving help at classzone.com

(53.) **MULTI-STEP PROBLEM** Although a football field appears to be flat, its surface is actually shaped like a parabola so that rain runs off to both sides. The cross section of a field with synthetic turf can be modeled by

$$y = -0.000234x(x - 160)$$

where x and y are measured in feet.

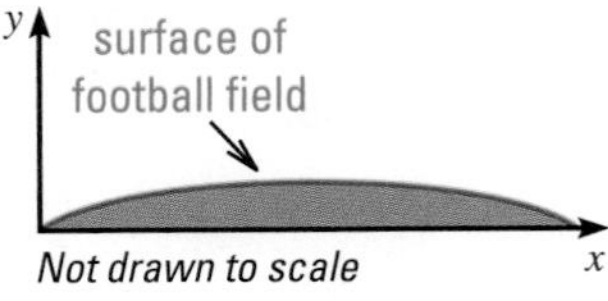

a. What is the field's width?

b. What is the maximum height of the field's surface?

◯ = **WORKED-OUT SOLUTIONS** on p. WS1 ★ = **STANDARDIZED TEST PRACTICE**

54. ★ **SHORT RESPONSE** A jump on a pogo stick with a conventional spring can be modeled by $y = -0.5(x - 6)^2 + 18$, and a jump on a pogo stick with a bow spring can be modeled by $y = -1.17(x - 6)^2 + 42$, where x and y are measured in inches. *Compare* the maximum heights of the jumps on the two pogo sticks. Which constants in the functions affect the maximum heights of the jumps? Which do not?

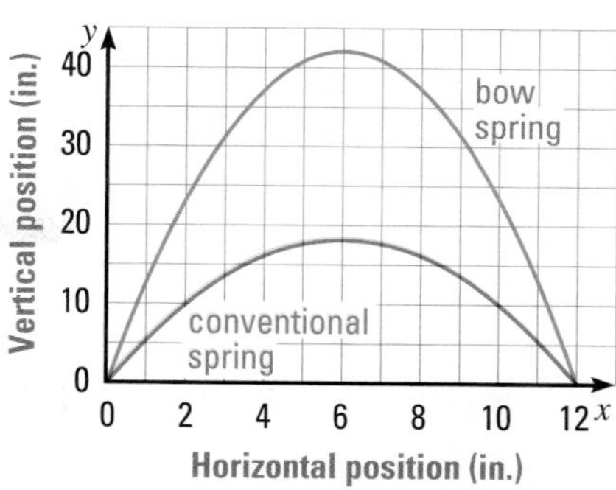

55. ★ **EXTENDED RESPONSE** A kernel of popcorn contains water that expands when the kernel is heated, causing it to pop. The equations below give the "popping volume" y (in cubic centimeters per gram) of popcorn with moisture content x (as a percent of the popcorn's weight).

Hot-air popping: $y = -0.761(x - 5.52)(x - 22.6)$

Hot-oil popping: $y = -0.652(x - 5.35)(x - 21.8)$

a. **Interpret** For hot-air popping, what moisture content maximizes popping volume? What is the maximum volume?

b. **Interpret** For hot-oil popping, what moisture content maximizes popping volume? What is the maximum volume?

c. **Graphing Calculator** Graph the functions in the same coordinate plane. What are the domain and range of each function in this situation? *Explain* how you determined the domain and range.

56. **CHALLENGE** Flying fish use their pectoral fins like airplane wings to glide through the air. Suppose a flying fish reaches a maximum height of 5 feet after flying a horizontal distance of 33 feet. Write a quadratic function $y = a(x - h)^2 + k$ that models the flight path, assuming the fish leaves the water at (0, 0). *Describe* how changing the value of a, h, or k affects the flight path.

NEW YORK MIXED REVIEW

TEST PRACTICE at classzone.com

57. A salesperson wants to analyze the time he spends driving to visit clients. In a typical week, the salesperson drives 870 miles during a period of 22 hours. His average speed is 65 miles per hour on the highway and 30 miles per hour in the city. About how many hours a week does the salesperson spend driving in the city?

Ⓐ 6 h Ⓑ 8.2 h Ⓒ 13.9 h Ⓓ 16 h

58. What is the approximate area of the shaded region?

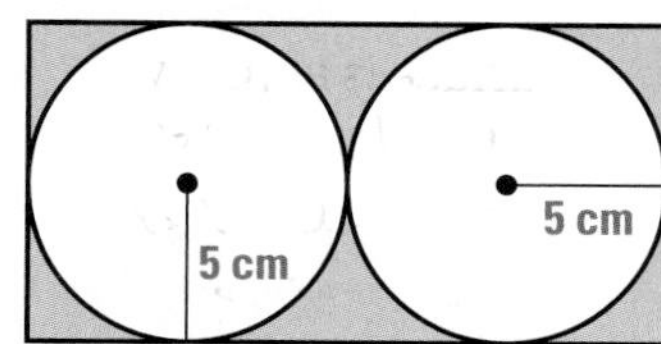

Ⓐ 21.5 cm^2

Ⓑ 42.9 cm^2

Ⓒ 121.4 cm^2

Ⓓ 150 cm^2

4.3 Solve $x^2 + bx + c = 0$ by Factoring

Before	You graphed quadratic functions.
Now	You will solve quadratic equations.
Why?	So you can double the area of a picnic site, as in Ex. 42.

Key Vocabulary
- monomial
- binomial
- trinomial
- quadratic equation
- root of an equation
- zero of a function

A **monomial** is an expression that is either a number, a variable, or the product of a number and one or more variables. A **binomial**, such as $x + 4$, is the sum of two monomials. A **trinomial**, such as $x^2 + 11x + 28$, is the sum of three monomials.

You know how to use FOIL to write $(x + 4)(x + 7)$ as $x^2 + 11x + 28$. You can use factoring to write a trinomial as a product of binomials. To factor $x^2 + bx + c$, find integers m and n such that:

$$x^2 + bx + c = (x + m)(x + n)$$
$$= x^2 + (m + n)x + mn$$

So, the *sum* of m and n must equal b and the *product* of m and n must equal c.

EXAMPLE 1 Factor trinomials of the form $x^2 + bx + c$

Factor the expression.

a. $x^2 - 9x + 20$ **b.** $x^2 + 3x - 12$

Solution

a. You want $x^2 - 9x + 20 = (x + m)(x + n)$ where $mn = 20$ and $m + n = -9$.

AVOID ERRORS
When factoring $x^2 + bx + c$ where $c > 0$, you must choose factors $x + m$ and $x + n$ such that m and n have the same sign.

Factors of 20: m, n	1, 20	−1, −20	2, 10	−2, −10	4, 5	**−4, −5**
Sum of factors: $m + n$	21	−21	12	−12	9	**−9**

▶ Notice that $m = -4$ and $n = -5$. So, $x^2 - 9x + 20 = (x - 4)(x - 5)$.

b. You want $x^2 + 3x - 12 = (x + m)(x + n)$ where $mn = -12$ and $m + n = 3$.

Factors of −12: m, n	−1, 12	1, −12	−2, 6	2, −6	−3, 4	3, −4
Sum of factors: $m + n$	11	−11	4	−4	1	−1

▶ Notice that there are no factors m and n such that $m + n = 3$. So, $x^2 + 3x - 12$ cannot be factored.

GUIDED PRACTICE for Example 1

Factor the expression. If the expression cannot be factored, say so.

1. $x^2 - 3x - 18$ **2.** $n^2 - 3n + 9$ **3.** $r^2 + 2r - 63$

FACTORING SPECIAL PRODUCTS Factoring quadratic expressions often involves trial and error. However, some expressions are easy to factor because they follow special patterns.

KEY CONCEPT — *For Your Notebook*

Special Factoring Patterns

Pattern Name	Pattern	Example
Difference of Two Squares	$a^2 - b^2 = (a + b)(a - b)$	$x^2 - 4 = (x + 2)(x - 2)$
Perfect Square Trinomial	$a^2 + 2ab + b^2 = (a + b)^2$	$x^2 + 6x + 9 = (x + 3)^2$
	$a^2 - 2ab + b^2 = (a - b)^2$	$x^2 - 4x + 4 = (x - 2)^2$

EXAMPLE 2 Factor with special patterns

Factor the expression.

a. $x^2 - 49 = x^2 - 7^2$ Difference of two squares

$= (x + 7)(x - 7)$

b. $d^2 + 12d + 36 = d^2 + 2(d)(6) + 6^2$ Perfect square trinomial

$= (d + 6)^2$

c. $z^2 - 26z + 169 = z^2 - 2(z)(13) + 13^2$ Perfect square trinomial

$= (z - 13)^2$

✓ GUIDED PRACTICE for Example 2

Factor the expression.

4. $x^2 - 9$ **5.** $q^2 - 100$ **6.** $y^2 + 16y + 64$ **7.** $w^2 - 18w + 81$

SOLVING QUADRATIC EQUATIONS You can use factoring to solve certain *quadratic equations*. A **quadratic equation** in one variable can be written in the form $ax^2 + bx + c = 0$ where $a \neq 0$. This is called the **standard form** of the equation. The solutions of a quadratic equation are called the **roots** of the equation. If the left side of $ax^2 + bx + c = 0$ can be factored, then the equation can be solved using the *zero product property.*

KEY CONCEPT — *For Your Notebook*

Zero Product Property

Words If the product of two expressions is zero, then one or both of the expressions equal zero.

Algebra If A and B are expressions and $AB = 0$, then $A = 0$ or $B = 0$.

Example If $(x + 5)(x + 2) = 0$, then $x + 5 = 0$ or $x + 2 = 0$. That is, $x = -5$ or $x = -2$.

EXAMPLE 3 Standardized Test Practice

UNDERSTAND ANSWER CHOICES

Sometimes a standardized test question may ask for the *solution set* of an equation. The answer choices will be given in the format $\{a, b\}$.

What are the roots of the equation $x^2 - 5x - 36 = 0$?

Ⓐ $-4, -9$ Ⓑ $4, -9$ Ⓒ $-4, 9$ Ⓓ $4, 9$

Solution

$x^2 - 5x - 36 = 0$	**Write original equation.**
$(x - 9)(x + 4) = 0$	**Factor.**
$x - 9 = 0$ or $x + 4 = 0$	**Zero product property**
$x = 9$ or $x = -4$	**Solve for *x*.**

▶ The correct answer is C. Ⓐ Ⓑ Ⓒ Ⓓ

EXAMPLE 4 Use a quadratic equation as a model

NATURE PRESERVE A town has a nature preserve with a rectangular field that measures 600 meters by 400 meters. The town wants to double the area of the field by adding land as shown. Find the new dimensions of the field.

Solution

New area (square meters) = New length (meters) • New width (meters)

$$2(600)(400) = (600 + x) \cdot (400 + x)$$

$480{,}000 = 240{,}000 + 1000x + x^2$	**Multiply using FOIL.**
$0 = x^2 + 1000x - 240{,}000$	**Write in standard form.**
$0 = (x - 200)(x + 1200)$	**Factor.**
$x - 200 = 0$ or $x + 1200 = 0$	**Zero product property**
$x = 200$ or $x = -1200$	**Solve for *x*.**

▶ Reject the negative value, -1200. The field's length and width should each be increased by 200 meters. The new dimensions are 800 meters by 600 meters.

✓ GUIDED PRACTICE for Examples 3 and 4

8. Solve the equation $x^2 - x - 42 = 0$.

9. WHAT IF? In Example 4, suppose the field initially measures 1000 meters by 300 meters. Find the new dimensions of the field.

ZEROS OF A FUNCTION In Lesson 4.2, you learned that the x-intercepts of the graph of $y = a(x - p)(x - q)$ are p and q. Because the function's value is zero when $x = p$ and when $x = q$, the numbers p and q are also called **zeros** of the function.

EXAMPLE 5 Find the zeros of quadratic functions

UNDERSTAND REPRESENTATIONS

If a real number k is a zero of the function $y = ax^2 + bx + c$, then k is an x-intercept of this function's graph and k is also a root of the equation $ax^2 + bx + c = 0$.

Find the zeros of the function by rewriting the function in intercept form.

a. $y = x^2 - x - 12$

b. $y = x^2 + 12x + 36$

Solution

a. $y = x^2 - x - 12$ **Write original function.**

$= (x + 3)(x - 4)$ **Factor.**

The zeros of the function are -3 and 4.

CHECK Graph $y = x^2 - x - 12$. The graph passes through $(-3, 0)$ and $(4, 0)$.

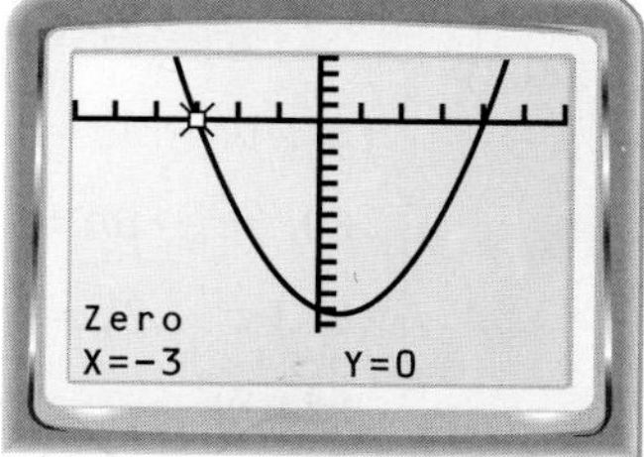

b. $y = x^2 + 12x + 36$ **Write original function.**

$= (x + 6)(x + 6)$ **Factor.**

The zero of the function is -6.

CHECK Graph $y = x^2 + 12x + 36$. The graph passes through $(-6, 0)$.

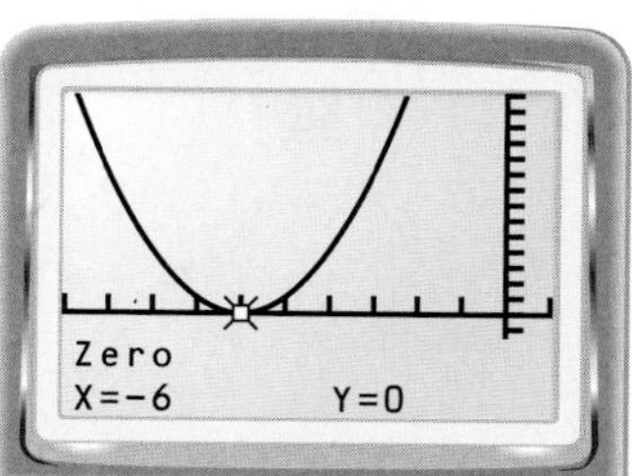

✓ GUIDED PRACTICE for Example 5

Find the zeros of the function by rewriting the function in intercept form.

10. $y = x^2 + 5x - 14$

11. $y = x^2 - 7x - 30$

12. $f(x) = x^2 - 10x + 25$

4.3 EXERCISES

HOMEWORK KEY

○ = **WORKED-OUT SOLUTIONS** on p. WS8 for Exs. 33, 47, and 67

★ = **STANDARDIZED TEST PRACTICE** Exs. 2, 41, 56, 58, 63, and 71

◆ = **MULTIPLE REPRESENTATIONS** Ex. 68

SKILL PRACTICE

1. VOCABULARY What is a zero of a function $y = f(x)$?

2. ★ WRITING *Explain* the difference between a monomial, a binomial, and a trinomial. Give an example of each type of expression.

EXAMPLE 1 on p. 252 for Exs. 3–14

FACTORING **Factor the expression. If the expression cannot be factored, say so.**

3. $x^2 + 6x + 5$

4. $x^2 - 7x + 10$

5. $a^2 - 13a + 22$

6. $r^2 + 15r + 56$

7. $p^2 + 2p + 4$

8. $q^2 - 11q + 28$

9. $b^2 + 3b - 40$

10. $x^2 - 4x - 12$

11. $x^2 - 7x - 18$

12. $c^2 - 9c - 18$

13. $x^2 + 9x - 36$

14. $m^2 + 8m - 65$

EXAMPLE 2
on p. 253
for Exs. 15–23

FACTORING WITH SPECIAL PATTERNS **Factor the expression.**

15. $x^2 - 36$ **16.** $b^2 - 81$ **17.** $x^2 - 24x + 144$

18. $t^2 - 16t + 64$ **19.** $x^2 + 8x + 16$ **20.** $c^2 + 28c + 196$

21. $n^2 + 14n + 49$ **22.** $s^2 - 26s + 169$ **23.** $z^2 - 121$

EXAMPLE 3
on p. 254
for Exs. 24–41

SOLVING EQUATIONS **Solve the equation.**

24. $x^2 - 8x + 12 = 0$ **25.** $x^2 - 11x + 30 = 0$ **26.** $x^2 + 2x - 35 = 0$

27. $a^2 - 49 = 0$ **28.** $b^2 - 6b + 9 = 0$ **29.** $c^2 + 5c + 4 = 0$

30. $n^2 - 6n = 0$ **31.** $t^2 + 10t + 25 = 0$ **32.** $w^2 - 16w + 48 = 0$

33. $z^2 - 3z = 54$ **34.** $r^2 + 2r = 80$ **35.** $u^2 = -9u$

36. $m^2 = 7m$ **37.** $14x - 49 = x^2$ **38.** $-3y + 28 = y^2$

ERROR ANALYSIS ***Describe*** **and correct the error in solving the equation.**

39.

$x^2 - x - 6 = 0$

$(x - 2)(x + 3) = 0$

$x - 2 = 0$ or $x + 3 = 0$

$x = 2$ or $x = -3$

40.

$x^2 + 7x + 6 = 14$

$(x + 6)(x + 1) = 14$

$x + 6 = 14$ or $x + 1 = 14$

$x = 8$ or $x = 13$

41. ★ **MULTIPLE CHOICE** What are the roots of the equation $x^2 + 2x - 63 = 0$?

Ⓐ 7, −9 Ⓑ −7, −9 Ⓒ −7, 9 Ⓓ 7, 9

EXAMPLE 4
on p. 254
for Exs. 42–43

WRITING EQUATIONS **Write an equation that you can solve to find the value of x.**

42. A rectangular picnic site measures 24 feet by 10 feet. You want to double the site's area by adding the same distance x to the length and the width.

43. A rectangular performing platform in a park measures 10 feet by 12 feet. You want to triple the platform's area by adding the same distance x to the length and the width.

EXAMPLE 5
on p. 255
for Exs. 44–55

FINDING ZEROS **Find the zeros of the function by rewriting the function in intercept form.**

44. $y = x^2 + 6x + 8$ **45.** $y = x^2 - 8x + 16$ **46.** $y = x^2 - 4x - 32$

47. $y = x^2 + 7x - 30$ **48.** $f(x) = x^2 + 11x$ **49.** $g(x) = x^2 - 8x$

50. $y = x^2 - 64$ **51.** $y = x^2 - 25$ **52.** $f(x) = x^2 - 12x - 45$

53. $g(x) = x^2 + 19x + 84$ **54.** $y = x^2 + 22x + 121$ **55.** $y = x^2 + 2x + 1$

56. ★ **MULTIPLE CHOICE** What are the zeros of $f(x) = x^2 + 6x - 55$?

Ⓐ −11, −5 Ⓑ −11, 5 Ⓒ −5, 11 Ⓓ 5, 11

57. **REASONING** Write a quadratic equation of the form $x^2 + bx + c = 0$ that has roots 8 and 11.

58. ★ **SHORT RESPONSE** For what integers b can the expression $x^2 + bx + 7$ be factored? *Explain.*

○ = **WORKED-OUT SOLUTIONS on p. WS1** ★ = **STANDARDIZED TEST PRACTICE**

GEOMETRY Find the value of x.

59. Area of rectangle = 36

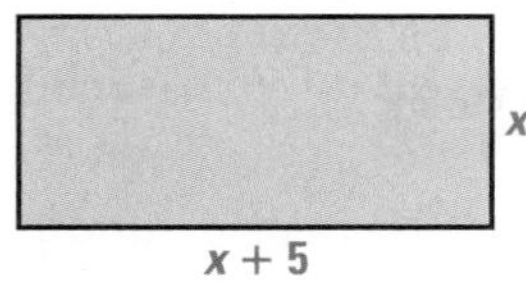

60. Area of rectangle = 84

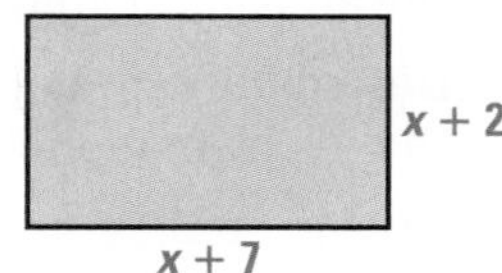

61. Area of triangle = 42

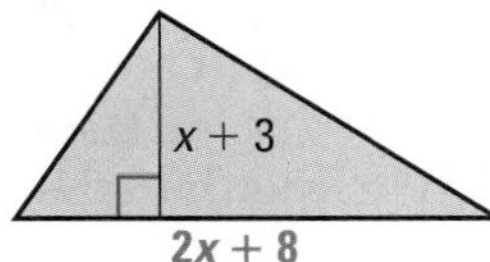

62. Area of trapezoid = 32

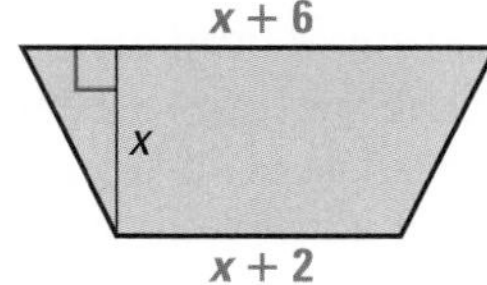

63. ★ **OPEN-ENDED MATH** Write a quadratic function with zeros that are equidistant from 10 on a number line.

64. CHALLENGE Is there a formula for factoring the *sum* of two squares? You will investigate this question in parts (a) and (b).

a. Consider the sum of two squares $x^2 + 16$. If this sum can be factored, then there are integers m and n such that $x^2 + 16 = (x + m)(x + n)$. Write two equations that m and n must satisfy.

b. Show that there are no integers m and n that satisfy both equations you wrote in part (a). What can you conclude?

PROBLEM SOLVING

EXAMPLE 4 on p. 254 for Exs. 65–67

65. SKATE PARK A city's skate park is a rectangle 100 feet long by 50 feet wide. The city wants to triple the area of the skate park by adding the same distance x to the length and the width. Write and solve an equation to find the value of x. What are the new dimensions of the skate park?

@HomeTutor for problem solving help at classzone.com

66. ZOO A rectangular enclosure at a zoo is 35 feet long by 18 feet wide. The zoo wants to double the area of the enclosure by adding the same distance x to the length and the width. Write and solve an equation to find the value of x. What are the new dimensions of the enclosure?

@HomeTutor for problem solving help at classzone.com

67. MULTI-STEP PROBLEM A museum has a café with a rectangular patio. The museum wants to add 464 square feet to the area of the patio by expanding the existing patio as shown.

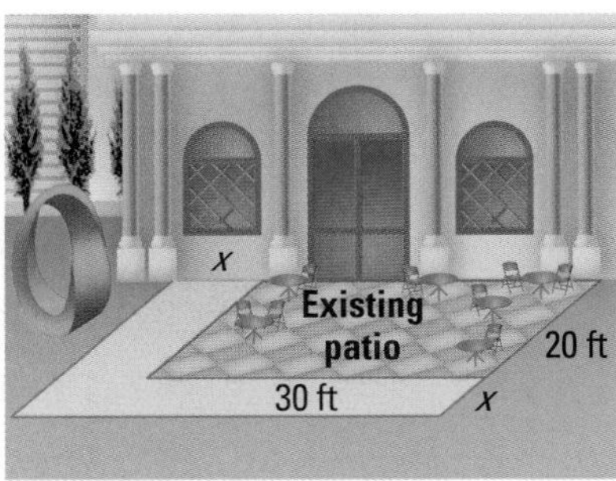

a. Find the area of the existing patio.

b. Write a verbal model and an equation that you can use to find the value of x.

c. Solve your equation. By what distance x should the length and the width of the patio be expanded?

68. ◆ **MULTIPLE REPRESENTATIONS** Use the diagram shown.

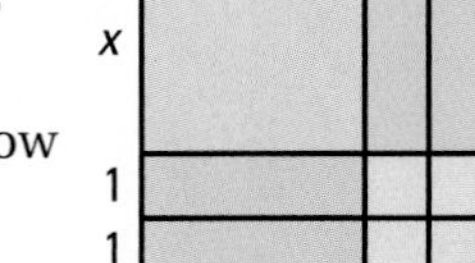

a. Writing an Expression Write a quadratic trinomial that represents the area of the diagram.

b. Describing a Model Factor the expression from part (a). *Explain* how the diagram models the factorization.

c. Drawing a Diagram Draw a diagram that models the factorization $x^2 + 8x + 15 = (x + 5)(x + 3)$.

69. SCHOOL FAIR At last year's school fair, an 18 foot by 15 foot rectangular section of land was roped off for a dunking booth. The length and width of the section will each be increased by x feet for this year's fair in order to triple the original area. Write and solve an equation to find the value of x. What is the length of rope needed to enclose the new section?

70. RECREATION CENTER A rectangular deck for a recreation center is 21 feet long by 20 feet wide. Its area is to be halved by subtracting the same distance x from the length and the width. Write and solve an equation to find the value of x. What are the deck's new dimensions?

71. ★ **SHORT RESPONSE** A square garden has sides that are 10 feet long. A gardener wants to double the area of the garden by adding the same distance x to the length and the width. Write an equation that x must satisfy. Can you solve the equation you wrote by factoring? *Explain* why or why not.

72. CHALLENGE A grocery store wants to double the area of its parking lot by expanding the existing lot as shown. By what distance x should the lot be expanded?

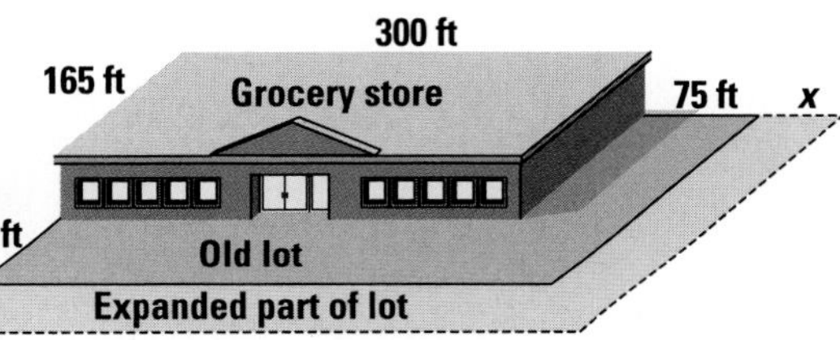

NEW YORK MIXED REVIEW

73. What is the slope of the line shown?

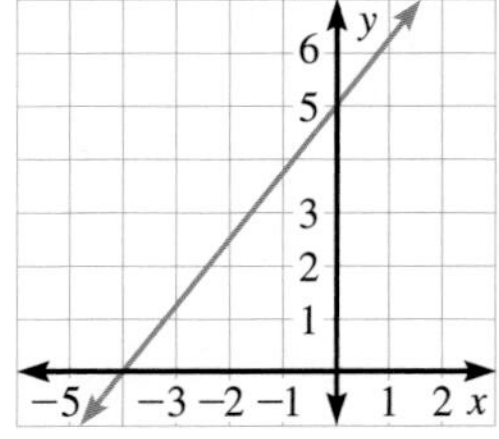

Ⓐ $-\frac{5}{4}$ Ⓑ $-\frac{4}{5}$

Ⓒ $\frac{4}{5}$ Ⓓ $\frac{5}{4}$

74. Which of the following best describes the graphs of the equations below?

$$y = 3x - 2$$

$$-4y = x + 8$$

Ⓐ The lines have the same x-intercept.

Ⓑ The lines have the same y-intercept.

Ⓒ The lines are perpendicular to each other.

Ⓓ The lines are parallel to each other.

4.4 Solve $ax^2 + bx + c = 0$ by Factoring

Before	You used factoring to solve equations of the form $x^2 + bx + c = 0$.
Now	You will use factoring to solve equations of the form $ax^2 + bx + c = 0$.
Why?	So you can maximize a shop's revenue, as in Ex. 64.

Key Vocabulary
- **monomial,** *p. 252*

To factor $ax^2 + bx + c$ when $a \neq 1$, find integers k, l, m, and n such that:

$$ax^2 + bx + c = (kx + m)(lx + n) = klx^2 + (kn + lm)x + mn$$

So, k and l must be factors of a, and m and n must be factors of c.

EXAMPLE 1 Factor $ax^2 + bx + c$ where $c > 0$

Factor $5x^2 - 17x + 6$.

FACTOR EXPRESSIONS

When factoring $ax^2 + bx + c$ where $a > 0$, it is customary to choose factors $kx + m$ and $lx + n$ such that k and l are positive.

Solution

You want $5x^2 - 17x + 6 = (kx + m)(lx + n)$ where k and l are factors of 5 and m and n are factors of 6. You can assume that k and l are positive and $k \geq l$. Because $mn > 0$, m and n have the same sign. So, m and n must both be negative because the coefficient of x, -17, is negative.

k, l	5, 1	5, 1	5, 1	5, 1
m, n	−6, −1	−1, −6	−3, −2	−2, −3
$(kx + m)(lx + n)$	$(5x - 6)(x - 1)$	$(5x - 1)(x - 6)$	$(5x - 3)(x - 2)$	$(5x - 2)(x - 3)$
$ax^2 + bx + c$	$5x^2 - 11x + 6$	$5x^2 - 31x + 6$	$5x^2 - 13x + 6$	$5x^2 - 17x + 6$

▶ The correct factorization is $5x^2 - 17x + 6 = (5x - 2)(x - 3)$.

EXAMPLE 2 Factor $ax^2 + bx + c$ where $c < 0$

Factor $3x^2 + 20x - 7$.

Solution

You want $3x^2 + 20x - 7 = (kx + m)(lx + n)$ where k and l are factors of 3 and m and n are factors of -7. Because $mn < 0$, m and n have opposite signs.

k, l	3, 1	3, 1	3, 1	3, 1
m, n	7, −1	−1, 7	−7, 1	1, −7
$(kx + m)(lx + n)$	$(3x + 7)(x - 1)$	$(3x - 1)(x + 7)$	$(3x - 7)(x + 1)$	$(3x + 1)(x - 7)$
$ax^2 + bx + c$	$3x^2 + 4x - 7$	$3x^2 + 20x - 7$	$3x^2 - 4x - 7$	$3x^2 - 20x - 7$

▶ The correct factorization is $3x^2 + 20x - 7 = (3x - 1)(x + 7)$.

✓ GUIDED PRACTICE for Examples 1 and 2

Factor the expression. If the expression cannot be factored, say so.

1. $7x^2 - 20x - 3$ **2.** $5z^2 + 16z + 3$ **3.** $2w^2 + w + 3$

4. $3x^2 + 5x - 12$ **5.** $4u^2 + 12u + 5$ **6.** $4x^2 - 9x + 2$

FACTORING SPECIAL PRODUCTS If the values of a and c in $ax^2 + bx + c$ are perfect squares, check to see whether you can use one of the special factoring patterns from Lesson 4.3 to factor the expression.

EXAMPLE 3 Factor with special patterns

Factor the expression.

a. $9x^2 - 64 = (3x)^2 - 8^2$ **Difference of two squares**

$= (3x + 8)(3x - 8)$

b. $4y^2 + 20y + 25 = (2y)^2 + 2(2y)(5) + 5^2$ **Perfect square trinomial**

$= (2y + 5)^2$

c. $36w^2 - 12w + 1 = (6w)^2 - 2(6w)(1) + 1^2$ **Perfect square trinomial**

$= (6w - 1)^2$

✓ GUIDED PRACTICE for Example 3

Factor the expression.

7. $16x^2 - 1$ **8.** $9y^2 + 12y + 4$ **9.** $4r^2 - 28r + 49$

10. $25s^2 - 80s + 64$ **11.** $49z^2 + 42z + 9$ **12.** $36n^2 - 9$

FACTORING OUT MONOMIALS When factoring an expression, first check to see whether the terms have a common monomial factor.

EXAMPLE 4 Factor out monomials first

AVOID ERRORS
Be sure to factor out the common monomial from all of the terms of the expression, not just the first term.

Factor the expression.

a. $5x^2 - 45 = 5(x^2 - 9)$

$= 5(x + 3)(x - 3)$

b. $6q^2 - 14q + 8 = 2(3q^2 - 7q + 4)$

$= 2(3q - 4)(q - 1)$

c. $-5z^2 + 20z = -5z(z - 4)$

d. $12p^2 - 21p + 3 = 3(4p^2 - 7p + 1)$

✓ GUIDED PRACTICE for Example 4

Factor the expression.

13. $3s^2 - 24$ **14.** $8t^2 + 38t - 10$ **15.** $6x^2 + 24x + 15$

16. $12x^2 - 28x - 24$ **17.** $-16n^2 + 12n$ **18.** $6z^2 + 33z + 36$

SOLVING QUADRATIC EQUATIONS As you saw in Lesson 4.3, if the left side of the quadratic equation $ax^2 + bx + c = 0$ can be factored, then the equation can be solved using the zero product property.

EXAMPLE 5 Solve quadratic equations

Solve (a) $3x^2 + 10x - 8 = 0$ and (b) $5p^2 - 16p + 15 = 4p - 5$.

a. $3x^2 + 10x - 8 = 0$ — **Write original equation.**

$(3x - 2)(x + 4) = 0$ — **Factor.**

$3x - 2 = 0$ or $x + 4 = 0$ — **Zero product property**

$x = \frac{2}{3}$ or $x = -4$ — **Solve for x.**

b. $5p^2 - 16p + 15 = 4p - 5$ — **Write original equation.**

$5p^2 - 20p + 20 = 0$ — **Write in standard form.**

$p^2 - 4p + 4 = 0$ — **Divide each side by 5.**

$(p - 2)^2 = 0$ — **Factor.**

$p - 2 = 0$ — **Zero product property**

$p = 2$ — **Solve for p.**

INTERPRET EQUATIONS
If the square of an expression is zero, then the expression itself must be zero.

EXAMPLE 6 Use a quadratic equation as a model

QUILTS You have made a rectangular quilt that is 5 feet by 4 feet. You want to use the remaining 10 square feet of fabric to add a decorative border of uniform width to the quilt. What should the width of the quilt's border be?

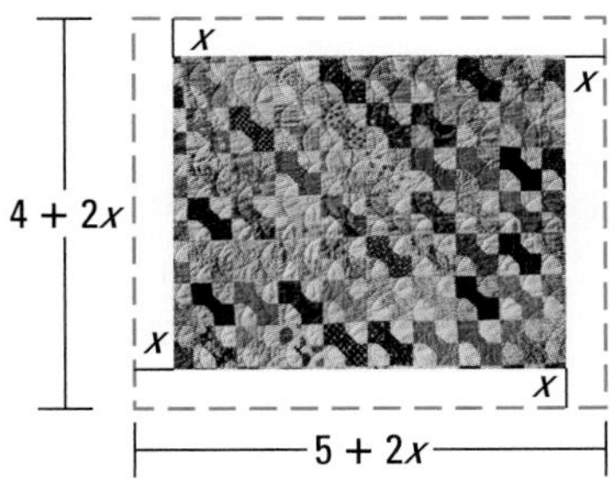

Solution

Write a verbal model. Then write an equation.

Area of border (square feet)	=	Area of quilt and border (square feet)	−	Area of quilt (square feet)
10	**=**	**$(5 + 2x)(4 + 2x)$**	**−**	**$(5)(4)$**

$10 = 20 + 18x + 4x^2 - 20$ — **Multiply using FOIL.**

$0 = 4x^2 + 18x - 10$ — **Write in standard form.**

$0 = 2x^2 + 9x - 5$ — **Divide each side by 2.**

$0 = (2x - 1)(x + 5)$ — **Factor.**

$2x - 1 = 0$ or $x + 5 = 0$ — **Zero product property**

$x = \frac{1}{2}$ or $x = -5$ — **Solve for x.**

▶ Reject the negative value, -5. The border's width should be $\frac{1}{2}$ ft, or 6 in.

FACTORING AND ZEROS To find the maximum or minimum value of a quadratic function, you can first use factoring to write the function in intercept form $y = a(x - p)(x - q)$. Because the function's vertex lies on the axis of symmetry $x = \frac{p + q}{2}$, the maximum or minimum occurs at the *average* of the zeros p and q.

EXAMPLE 7 Solve a multi-step problem

MAGAZINES A monthly teen magazine has 28,000 subscribers when it charges $10 per annual subscription. For each $1 increase in price, the magazine loses about 2000 subscribers. How much should the magazine charge to maximize annual revenue? What is the maximum annual revenue?

Solution

STEP 1 **Define** the variables. Let x represent the price increase and $R(x)$ represent the annual revenue.

STEP 2 **Write** a verbal model. Then write and simplify a quadratic function.

Annual revenue (dollars)	=	Number of subscribers (people)	•	Subscription price (dollars/person)
$R(x)$	=	$(28{,}000 - 2000x)$	•	$(10 + x)$

$$R(x) = (-2000x + 28{,}000)(x + 10)$$

$$R(x) = -2000(x - 14)(x + 10)$$

STEP 3 **Identify** the zeros and find their average. Find how much each subscription should cost to maximize annual revenue.

The zeros of the revenue function are 14 and −10. The average of the zeros is $\frac{14 + (-10)}{2} = 2$. To maximize revenue, each subscription should cost $\$10 + \$2 = \$12$.

STEP 4 **Find** the maximum annual revenue.

$R(2) = -2000(2 - 14)(2 + 10) = \$288{,}000$

▶ The magazine should charge $12 per subscription to maximize annual revenue. The maximum annual revenue is $288,000.

✓ GUIDED PRACTICE for Examples 5, 6, and 7

Solve the equation.

19. $6x^2 - 3x - 63 = 0$ **20.** $12x^2 + 7x + 2 = x + 8$ **21.** $7x^2 + 70x + 175 = 0$

22. **WHAT IF?** In Example 7, suppose the magazine initially charges $11 per annual subscription. How much should the magazine charge to maximize annual revenue? What is the maximum annual revenue?

4.4 EXERCISES

HOMEWORK KEY

○ = **WORKED-OUT SOLUTIONS** on p. WS8 for Exs. 27, 39, and 63

★ = **STANDARDIZED TEST PRACTICE** Exs. 2, 12, 64, 65, and 67

SKILL PRACTICE

1. **VOCABULARY** What is the greatest common monomial factor of the terms of the expression $12x^2 + 8x + 20$?

2. ★ **WRITING** *Explain* how the values of a and c in $ax^2 + bx + c$ help you determine whether you can use a perfect square trinomial factoring pattern.

EXAMPLES 1 and 2 on p. 259 for Exs. 3–12

FACTORING Factor the expression. If the expression cannot be factored, say so.

3. $2x^2 + 5x + 3$
4. $3n^2 + 7n + 4$
5. $4r^2 + 5r + 1$
6. $6p^2 + 5p + 1$
7. $11z^2 + 2z - 9$
8. $15x^2 - 2x - 8$
9. $4y^2 - 5y - 4$
10. $14m^2 + m - 3$
11. $9d^2 - 13d - 10$

12. ★ **MULTIPLE CHOICE** Which factorization of $5x^2 + 14x - 3$ is correct?

(A) $(5x - 3)(x + 1)$ (B) $(5x + 1)(x - 3)$

(C) $5(x - 1)(x + 3)$ (D) $(5x - 1)(x + 3)$

EXAMPLE 3 on p. 260 for Exs. 13–21

FACTORING WITH SPECIAL PATTERNS Factor the expression.

13. $9x^2 - 1$
14. $4r^2 - 25$
15. $49n^2 - 16$
16. $16s^2 + 8s + 1$
17. $49x^2 + 70x + 25$
18. $64w^2 + 144w + 81$
19. $9p^2 - 12p + 4$
20. $25t^2 - 30t + 9$
21. $36x^2 - 84x + 49$

EXAMPLE 4 on p. 260 for Exs. 22–31

FACTORING MONOMIALS FIRST Factor the expression.

22. $12x^2 - 4x - 40$
23. $18z^2 + 36z + 16$
24. $32v^2 - 2$
25. $6u^2 - 24u$
26. $12m^2 - 36m + 27$
27. $20x^2 + 124x + 24$
28. $21x^2 - 77x - 28$
29. $-36n^2 + 48n - 15$
30. $-8y^2 + 28y - 60$

31. **ERROR ANALYSIS** *Describe* and correct the error in factoring the expression.

$$4x^2 - 36 = 4(x^2 - 36)$$
$$= 4(x + 6)(x - 6)$$

EXAMPLE 5 on p. 261 for Exs. 32–40

SOLVING EQUATIONS Solve the equation.

32. $16x^2 - 1 = 0$
33. $11q^2 - 44 = 0$
34. $14s^2 - 21s = 0$
35. $45n^2 + 10n = 0$
36. $4x^2 - 20x + 25 = 0$
37. $4p^2 + 12p + 9 = 0$
38. $15x^2 + 7x - 2 = 0$
39. $6r^2 - 7r - 5 = 0$
40. $36z^2 + 96z + 15 = 0$

EXAMPLE 7 on p. 262 for Exs. 41–49

FINDING ZEROS Find the zeros of the function by rewriting the function in intercept form.

41. $y = 4x^2 - 19x - 5$
42. $g(x) = 3x^2 - 8x + 5$
43. $y = 5x^2 - 27x - 18$
44. $f(x) = 3x^2 - 3x$
45. $y = 11x^2 - 19x - 6$
46. $y = 16x^2 - 2x - 5$
47. $y = 15x^2 - 5x - 20$
48. $y = 18x^2 - 6x - 4$
49. $g(x) = 12x^2 + 5x - 7$

GEOMETRY **Find the value of x.**

50. Area of square = 36

51. Area of rectangle = 30

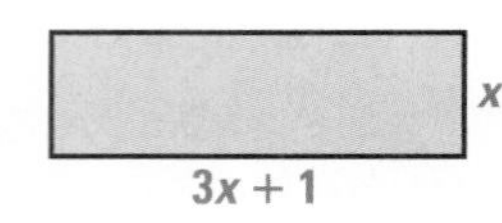

52. Area of triangle = 115

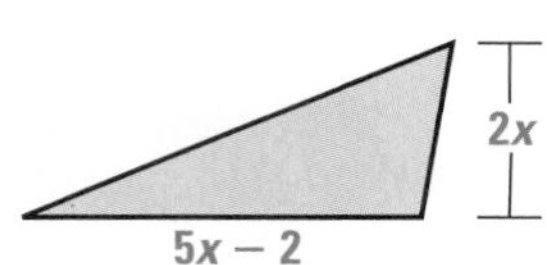

SOLVING EQUATIONS **Solve the equation.**

53. $2x^2 - 4x - 8 = -x^2 + x$

54. $24x^2 + 8x + 2 = 5 - 6x$

55. $18x^2 - 22x = 28$

56. $13x^2 + 21x = -5x^2 + 22$

57. $x = 4x^2 - 15x$

58. $(x + 8)^2 = 16 - x^2 + 9x$

CHALLENGE **Factor the expression.**

59. $2x^3 - 5x^2 + 3x$

60. $8x^4 - 8x^3 - 6x^2$

61. $9x^3 - 4x$

PROBLEM SOLVING

EXAMPLE 6 on p. 261 for Exs. 62–63

62. ARTS AND CRAFTS You have a rectangular stained glass window that measures 2 feet by 1 foot. You have 4 square feet of glass with which to make a border of uniform width around the window. What should the width of the border be?

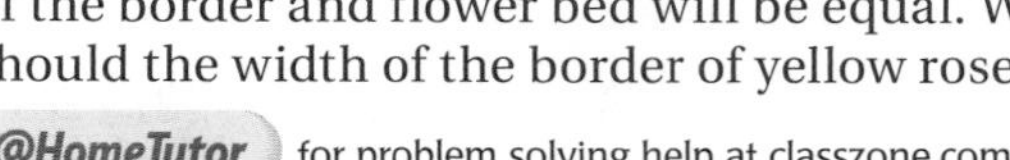

63. URBAN PLANNING You have just planted a rectangular flower bed of red roses in a city park. You want to plant a border of yellow roses around the flower bed as shown. Because you bought the same number of red and yellow roses, the areas of the border and flower bed will be equal. What should the width of the border of yellow roses be?

@HomeTutor for problem solving help at classzone.com

EXAMPLE 7 on p. 262 for Exs. 64–65

64. ★ MULTIPLE CHOICE A surfboard shop sells 45 surfboards per month when it charges \$500 per surfboard. For each \$20 decrease in price, the store sells 5 more surfboards per month. How much should the shop charge per surfboard in order to maximize monthly revenue?

Ⓐ \$340 Ⓑ \$492 Ⓒ \$508 Ⓓ \$660

65. ★ SHORT RESPONSE A restaurant sells about 330 sandwiches each day at a price of \$6 each. For each \$.25 decrease in price, 15 more sandwiches are sold per day. How much should the restaurant charge to maximize daily revenue? *Explain* each step of your solution. What is the maximum daily revenue?

66. PAINTINGS You place a mat around a 25 inch by 21 inch painting as shown. The mat is twice as wide at the left and right of the painting as it is at the top and bottom of the painting. The area of the mat is 714 square inches. How wide is the mat at the left and right of the painting? at the top and bottom of the painting?

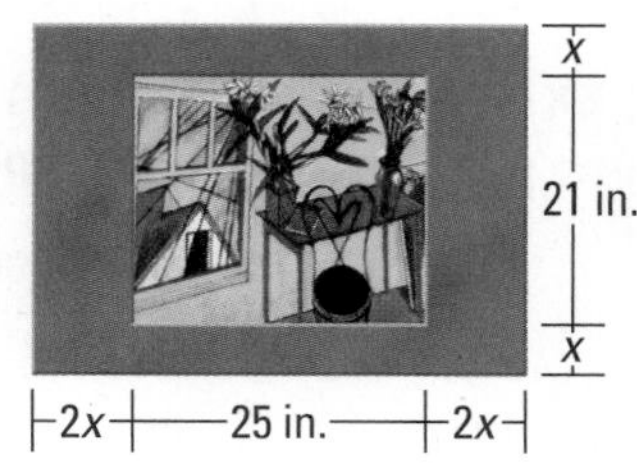

○ = **WORKED-OUT SOLUTIONS on p. WS1**

★ = **STANDARDIZED TEST PRACTICE**

67. ★ **EXTENDED RESPONSE** A U.S. Postal Service guideline states that for a rectangular package like the one shown, the sum of the length and the girth cannot exceed 108 inches. Suppose that for one such package, the length is 36 inches and the girth is as large as possible.

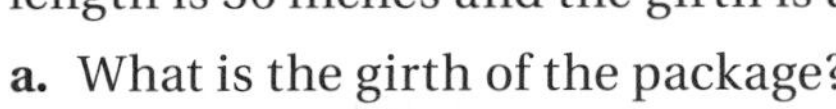

a. What is the girth of the package?

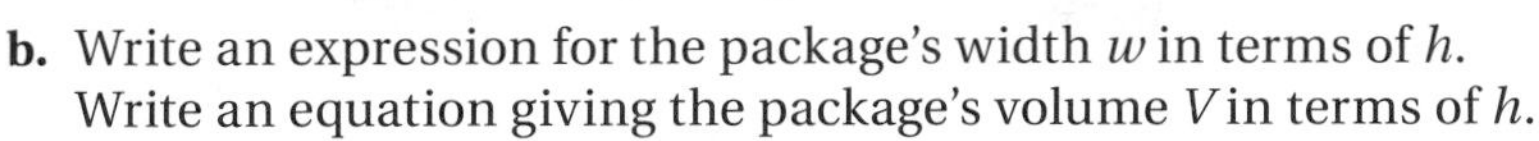

b. Write an expression for the package's width w in terms of h. Write an equation giving the package's volume V in terms of h.

c. What height and width maximize the volume of the package? What is the maximum volume? *Explain* how you found it.

68. **CHALLENGE** Recall from geometry the theorem about the products of the lengths of segments of two chords that intersect in the interior of a circle. Use this theorem to find the value of x in the diagram.

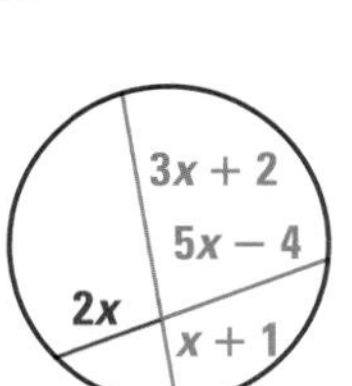

NEW YORK MIXED REVIEW

69. A pizza is divided into 12 equal slices as shown. The diameter of the pizza is 16 inches. What is the approximate area of one slice of pizza?

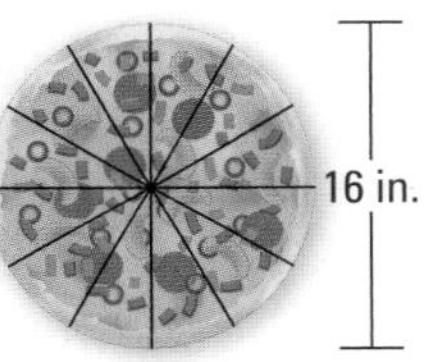

Ⓐ 15.47 in.^{2} Ⓑ 16.76 in.^{2}

Ⓒ 21.21 in.^{2} Ⓓ 67.02 in.^{2}

70. While shopping at Store A, Sam finds a television on sale for \$210. His friend tells him that the same television at Store B is on sale for \$161. About what percent of the cost of the television at Store A does Sam save by buying the television at Store B?

Ⓐ 20% Ⓑ 23% Ⓒ 30% Ⓓ 77%

QUIZ *for Lessons 4.1–4.4*

Graph the function. Label the vertex and axis of symmetry. *(p. 236)*

1. $y = x^2 - 6x + 14$
2. $y = 2x^2 + 8x + 15$
3. $f(x) = -3x^2 + 6x - 5$

Write the quadratic function in standard form. *(p. 245)*

4. $y = (x - 4)(x - 8)$
5. $g(x) = -2(x + 3)(x - 7)$
6. $y = 5(x + 6)^2 - 2$

Solve the equation.

7. $x^2 + 9x + 20 = 0$ *(p. 252)*
8. $n^2 - 11n + 24 = 0$ *(p. 252)*
9. $z^2 - 3z - 40 = 0$ *(p. 252)*
10. $5s^2 - 14s - 3 = 0$ *(p. 259)*
11. $7a^2 - 30a + 8 = 0$ *(p. 259)*
12. $4x^2 + 20x + 25 = 0$ *(p. 259)*

13. **DVD PLAYERS** A store sells about 50 of a new model of DVD player per month at a price of \$140 each. For each \$10 decrease in price, about 5 more DVD players per month are sold. How much should the store charge in order to maximize monthly revenue? What is the maximum monthly revenue? *(p. 259)*

4.5 Solve Quadratic Equations by Finding Square Roots

 **A2.N.5** Rationalize a denominator containing a radical expression

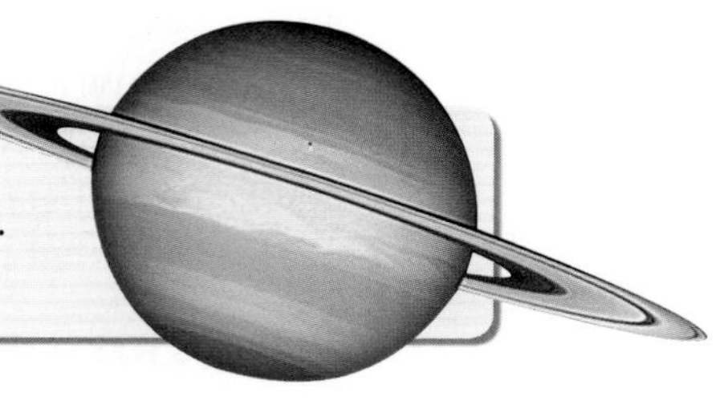

Before You solved quadratic equations by factoring.

Now You will solve quadratic equations by finding square roots.

Why? So you can solve problems about astronomy, as in Ex. 39.

Key Vocabulary
- **square root**
- **radical**
- **radicand**
- **rationalizing the denominator**
- **conjugates**

A number r is a **square root** of a number s if $r^2 = s$. A positive number s has two square roots, written as $\sqrt{s}$ and $-\sqrt{s}$. For example, because $3^2 = 9$ and $(-3)^2 = 9$, the two square roots of 9 are $\sqrt{9} = 3$ and $-\sqrt{9} = -3$. The positive square root of a number is also called the *principal* square root.

The expression $\sqrt{s}$ is called a **radical**. The symbol $\sqrt{\ }$ is a *radical sign*, and the number s beneath the radical sign is the **radicand** of the expression.

KEY CONCEPT *For Your Notebook*

Properties of Square Roots ($a > 0, b > 0$)

Product Property $\sqrt{ab} = \sqrt{a} \cdot \sqrt{b}$ **Example** $\sqrt{18} = \sqrt{9} \cdot \sqrt{2} = 3\sqrt{2}$

Quotient Property $\sqrt{\frac{a}{b}} = \frac{\sqrt{a}}{\sqrt{b}}$ **Example** $\sqrt{\frac{2}{25}} = \frac{\sqrt{2}}{\sqrt{25}} = \frac{\sqrt{2}}{5}$

SIMPLIFYING SQUARE ROOTS You can use the properties above to simplify expressions containing square roots. A square-root expression is simplified if:

- no radicand has a perfect-square factor other than 1, and
- there is no radical in a denominator

EXAMPLE 1 Use properties of square roots

USE A CALCULATOR
You can use a calculator to approximate $\sqrt{s}$ when s is not a perfect square. For example, $\sqrt{80} \approx 8.944$.

Simplify the expression.

a. $\sqrt{80} = \sqrt{16} \cdot \sqrt{5} = 4\sqrt{5}$

b. $\sqrt{6} \cdot \sqrt{21} = \sqrt{126} = \sqrt{9} \cdot \sqrt{14} = 3\sqrt{14}$

c. $\sqrt{\frac{4}{81}} = \frac{\sqrt{4}}{\sqrt{81}} = \frac{2}{9}$

d. $\sqrt{\frac{7}{16}} = \frac{\sqrt{7}}{\sqrt{16}} = \frac{\sqrt{7}}{4}$

 **GUIDED PRACTICE** for Example 1

Simplify the expression.

1. $\sqrt{27}$ **2.** $\sqrt{98}$ **3.** $\sqrt{10} \cdot \sqrt{15}$ **4.** $\sqrt{8} \cdot \sqrt{28}$

5. $\sqrt{\frac{9}{64}}$ **6.** $\sqrt{\frac{15}{4}}$ **7.** $\sqrt{\frac{11}{25}}$ **8.** $\sqrt{\frac{36}{49}}$

RATIONALIZING THE DENOMINATOR Suppose the denominator of a fraction has the form $\sqrt{b}$, $a + \sqrt{b}$, or $a - \sqrt{b}$ where a and b are rational numbers. The table shows how to eliminate the radical from the denominator. This is called **rationalizing the denominator**.

The expressions $a + \sqrt{b}$ and $a - \sqrt{b}$ are called **conjugates** of each other. Their product is always a rational number.

Form of the denominator	Multiply numerator and denominator by:
$\sqrt{b}$	$\sqrt{b}$
$a + \sqrt{b}$	$a - \sqrt{b}$
$a - \sqrt{b}$	$a + \sqrt{b}$

EXAMPLE 2 Rationalize denominators of fractions

Simplify (a) $\sqrt{\frac{5}{2}}$ and (b) $\frac{3}{7 + \sqrt{2}}$.

Solution

a. $\sqrt{\frac{5}{2}} = \frac{\sqrt{5}}{\sqrt{2}}$

$= \frac{\sqrt{5}}{\sqrt{2}} \cdot \frac{\sqrt{2}}{\sqrt{2}}$

$= \frac{\sqrt{10}}{2}$

b. $\frac{3}{7 + \sqrt{2}} = \frac{3}{7 + \sqrt{2}} \cdot \frac{7 - \sqrt{2}}{7 - \sqrt{2}}$

$= \frac{21 - 3\sqrt{2}}{49 - 7\sqrt{2} + 7\sqrt{2} - 2}$

$= \frac{21 - 3\sqrt{2}}{47}$

SOLVING QUADRATIC EQUATIONS You can use square roots to solve some types of quadratic equations. For example, if $s > 0$, then the equation $x^2 = s$ has two real-number solutions: $x = \sqrt{s}$ and $x = -\sqrt{s}$. These solutions are often written in condensed form as $x = \pm\sqrt{s}$ (read as "plus or minus the square root of s").

EXAMPLE 3 Solve a quadratic equation

Solve $3x^2 + 5 = 41$.

$3x^2 + 5 = 41$	**Write original equation.**
$3x^2 = 36$	**Subtract 5 from each side.**
$x^2 = 12$	**Divide each side by 3.**
$x = \pm\sqrt{12}$	**Take square roots of each side.**
$x = \pm\sqrt{4} \cdot \sqrt{3}$	**Product property**
$x = \pm 2\sqrt{3}$	**Simplify.**

AVOID ERRORS
When solving an equation of the form $x^2 = s$ where $s > 0$, make sure to find both the positive and negative solutions.

▸ The solutions are $2\sqrt{3}$ and $-2\sqrt{3}$.

CHECK Check the solutions by substituting them into the original equation.

$3x^2 + 5 = 41$ | $3x^2 + 5 = 41$

$3(2\sqrt{3})^2 + 5 \stackrel{?}{=} 41$ | $3(-2\sqrt{3})^2 + 5 \stackrel{?}{=} 41$

$3(12) + 5 \stackrel{?}{=} 41$ | $3(12) + 5 \stackrel{?}{=} 41$

$41 = 41$ ✓ | $41 = 41$ ✓

EXAMPLE 4 Standardized Test Practice

What are the solutions of the equation $\frac{1}{5}(z + 3)^2 = 7$?

Ⓐ $-38, 32$ Ⓑ $-3 - 5\sqrt{7}, -3 + 5\sqrt{7}$

Ⓒ $-3 - \sqrt{35}, -3 + \sqrt{35}$ Ⓓ $-3 - \frac{\sqrt{35}}{5}, -3 + \frac{\sqrt{35}}{5}$

Solution

$\frac{1}{5}(z + 3)^2 = 7$ Write original equation.

$(z + 3)^2 = 35$ Multiply each side by 5.

$z + 3 = \pm\sqrt{35}$ Take square roots of each side.

$z = -3 \pm \sqrt{35}$ Subtract 3 from each side.

The solutions are $-3 + \sqrt{35}$ and $-3 - \sqrt{35}$.

▶ The correct answer is C. Ⓐ Ⓑ Ⓒ Ⓓ

GUIDED PRACTICE for Examples 2, 3, and 4

Simplify the expression.

9. $\sqrt{\frac{6}{5}}$ **10.** $\sqrt{\frac{9}{8}}$ **11.** $\sqrt{\frac{17}{12}}$ **12.** $\sqrt{\frac{19}{21}}$

13. $\frac{-6}{7 - \sqrt{5}}$ **14.** $\frac{2}{4 + \sqrt{11}}$ **15.** $\frac{-1}{9 + \sqrt{7}}$ **16.** $\frac{4}{8 - \sqrt{3}}$

Solve the equation.

17. $5x^2 = 80$ **18.** $z^2 - 7 = 29$ **19.** $3(x - 2)^2 = 40$

MODELING DROPPED OBJECTS When an object is dropped, its height h (in feet) above the ground after t seconds can be modeled by the function

$$h = -16t^2 + h_0$$

where h_0 is the object's initial height (in feet). The graph of $h = -16t^2 + 200$, representing the height of an object dropped from an initial height of 200 feet, is shown at the right.

The model $h = -16t^2 + h_0$ assumes that the force of air resistance on the object is negligible. Also, this model works only on Earth. For planets with stronger or weaker gravity, different models are used (see Exercise 39).

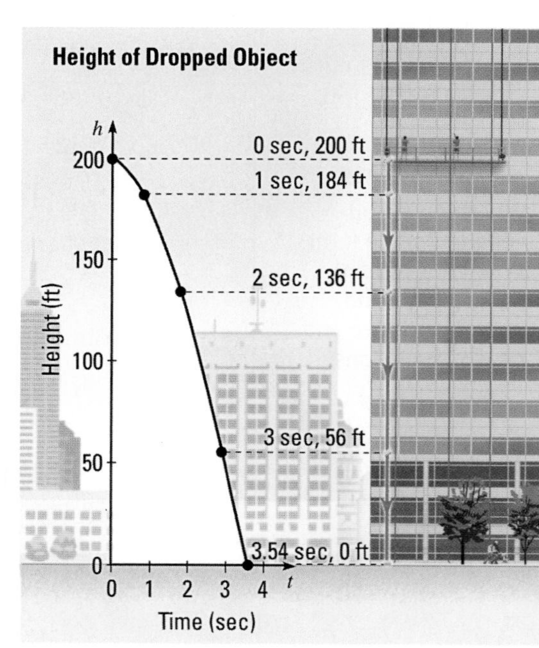

EXAMPLE 5 Model a dropped object with a quadratic function

SCIENCE COMPETITION For a science competition, students must design a container that prevents an egg from breaking when dropped from a height of 50 feet. How long does the container take to hit the ground?

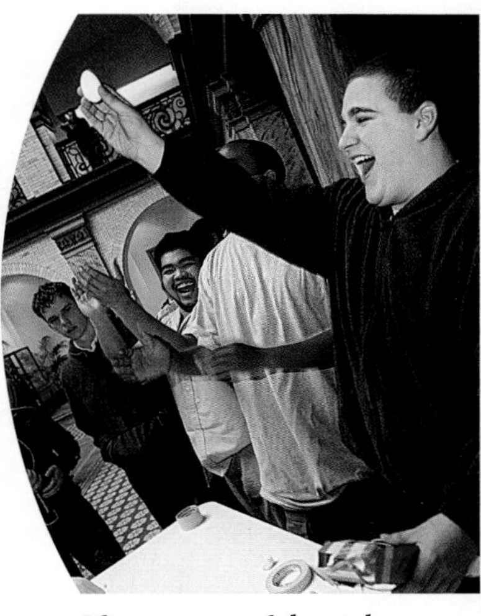

After a successful egg drop

ANOTHER WAY
For alternative methods for solving the problem in Example 5, turn to page 272 for the **Problem Solving Workshop**.

Solution

$h = -16t^2 + h_0$	**Write height function.**
$0 = -16t^2 + 50$	**Substitute 0 for h and 50 for h_0.**
$-50 = -16t^2$	**Subtract 50 from each side.**
$\frac{50}{16} = t^2$	**Divide each side by −16.**
$\pm\sqrt{\frac{50}{16}} = t$	**Take square roots of each side.**
$\pm 1.8 \approx t$	**Use a calculator.**

▶ Reject the negative solution, −1.8, because time must be positive. The container will fall for about 1.8 seconds before it hits the ground.

Animated Algebra at classzone.com

GUIDED PRACTICE for Example 5

20. **WHAT IF?** In Example 5, suppose the egg container is dropped from a height of 30 feet. How long does the container take to hit the ground?

4.5 EXERCISES

HOMEWORK KEY
○ = **WORKED-OUT SOLUTIONS on p. WS8 for Exs. 17, 27, and 41**
★ = **STANDARDIZED TEST PRACTICE Exs. 2, 19, 34, 35, 36, 40, and 41**

SKILL PRACTICE

1. **VOCABULARY** In the expression $\sqrt{72}$, what is 72 called?

2. ★ **WRITING** *Explain* what it means to "rationalize the denominator" of a quotient containing square roots.

EXAMPLES 1 and 2
on pp. 266–267 for Exs. 3–20

SIMPLIFYING RADICAL EXPRESSIONS **Simplify the expression.**

3. $\sqrt{28}$
4. $\sqrt{192}$
5. $\sqrt{150}$
6. $\sqrt{3} \cdot \sqrt{27}$
7. $4\sqrt{6} \cdot \sqrt{6}$
8. $5\sqrt{24} \cdot 3\sqrt{10}$
9. $\sqrt{\frac{5}{16}}$
10. $\sqrt{\frac{35}{36}}$
11. $\frac{8}{\sqrt{3}}$
12. $\frac{7}{\sqrt{12}}$
13. $\sqrt{\frac{18}{11}}$
14. $\sqrt{\frac{13}{28}}$
15. $\frac{2}{1-\sqrt{3}}$
16. $\frac{1}{5+\sqrt{6}}$
17. $\frac{\sqrt{2}}{4+\sqrt{5}}$
18. $\frac{3+\sqrt{7}}{2-\sqrt{10}}$

19. ★ **MULTIPLE CHOICE** What is a completely simplified expression for $\sqrt{108}$?

(A) $2\sqrt{27}$ (B) $3\sqrt{12}$ (C) $6\sqrt{3}$ (D) $10\sqrt{8}$

ERROR ANALYSIS ***Describe*** **and correct the error in simplifying the expression or solving the equation.**

20.
$$\sqrt{96} = \sqrt{4} \cdot \sqrt{24}$$
$$= 2\sqrt{24}$$

21.
$$5x^2 = 405$$
$$x^2 = 81$$
$$x = 9$$

EXAMPLES 3 and 4 on pp. 267–268 for Exs. 21–34

SOLVING QUADRATIC EQUATIONS **Solve the equation.**

22. $s^2 = 169$
23. $a^2 = 50$
24. $x^2 = 84$
25. $6z^2 = 150$
26. $4p^2 = 448$
27. $-3w^2 = -213$
28. $7r^2 - 10 = 25$
29. $\frac{x^2}{25} - 6 = -2$
30. $\frac{t^2}{20} + 8 = 15$
31. $4(x - 1)^2 = 8$
32. $7(x - 4)^2 - 18 = 10$
33. $2(x + 2)^2 - 5 = 8$

34. ★ **MULTIPLE CHOICE** What are the solutions of $3(x + 2)^2 + 4 = 13$?

(A) $-5, 1$ (B) $-1, 5$ (C) $-2 \pm \sqrt{3}$ (D) $2 \pm \sqrt{3}$

35. ★ **SHORT RESPONSE** *Describe* two different methods for solving the equation $x^2 - 4 = 0$. Include the steps for each method.

36. ★ **OPEN-ENDED MATH** Write an equation of the form $x^2 = s$ that has **(a)** two real solutions, **(b)** exactly one real solution, and **(c)** no real solutions.

37. **CHALLENGE** Solve the equation $a(x + b)^2 = c$ in terms of a, b, and c.

PROBLEM SOLVING

EXAMPLE 5 on p. 269 for Exs. 38–39

38. **CLIFF DIVING** A cliff diver dives off a cliff 40 feet above water. Write an equation giving the diver's height h (in feet) above the water after t seconds. How long is the diver in the air?

for problem solving help at classzone.com

39. **ASTRONOMY** On any planet, the height h (in feet) of a falling object t seconds after it is dropped can be modeled by $h = -\frac{g}{2}t^2 + h_0$ where h_0 is the object's initial height (in feet) and g is the acceleration (in feet per second squared) due to the planet's gravity. For each planet in the table, find the time it takes for a rock dropped from a height of 150 feet to hit the surface.

Planet	Earth	Mars	Jupiter	Saturn	Pluto
g (ft/sec^2)	32	12	76	30	2

@HomeTutor for problem solving help at classzone.com

40. ★ **SHORT RESPONSE** The equation $h = 0.019s^2$ gives the height h (in feet) of the largest ocean waves when the wind speed is s knots. *Compare* the wind speeds required to generate 5 foot waves and 20 foot waves.

41. ★ **EXTENDED RESPONSE** You want to transform a square gravel parking lot with 10 foot sides into a circular lot. You want the circle to have the same area as the square so that you do not have to buy any additional gravel.

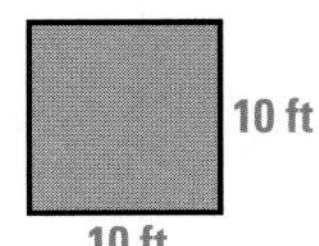

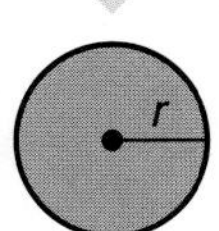

a. **Model** Write an equation you can use to find the radius r of the circular lot.

b. **Solve** What should the radius of the circular lot be?

c. **Generalize** In general, if a square has sides of length s, what is the radius r of a circle with the same area? *Justify* your answer algebraically.

42. BICYCLING The air resistance R (in pounds) on a racing cyclist is given by the equation $R = 0.00829s^2$ where s is the bicycle's speed (in miles per hour).

a. What is the speed of a racing cyclist who experiences 5 pounds of air resistance?

b. What happens to the air resistance if the cyclist's speed doubles? *Justify* your answer algebraically.

43. CHALLENGE For a swimming pool with a rectangular base, Torricelli's law implies that the height h of water in the pool t seconds after it begins draining is given by $h = \left(\sqrt{h_0} - \frac{2\pi d^2\sqrt{3}}{lw}t\right)^2$ where l and w are the pool's length and width, d is the diameter of the drain, and h_0 is the water's initial height. (All measurements are in inches.) In terms of l, w, d, and h_0, what is the time required to drain the pool when it is completely filled?

New York Mixed Review

TEST PRACTICE at classzone.com

44. The graph of which inequality is shown?

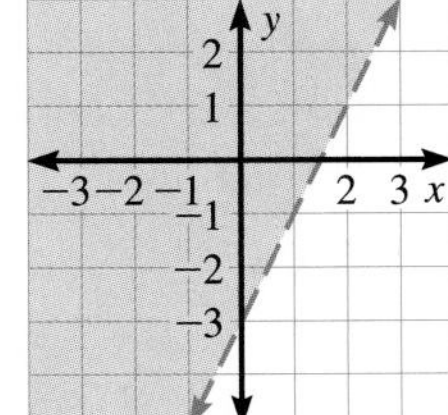

Ⓐ $y < 2x - 3$

Ⓑ $y > 2x - 3$

Ⓒ $y \leq 2x - 3$

Ⓓ $y \geq 2x - 3$

45. Which two lines are perpendicular?

Ⓐ $3x + y = -1$ and $x + 3y = -24$

Ⓑ $3x - y = 12$ and $3x + y = 15$

Ⓒ $3x + y = -1$ and $-x + 3y = 6$

Ⓓ $3x - y = 12$ and $x - 3y = 9$

PROBLEM SOLVING WORKSHOP LESSON 4.5

Using ALTERNATIVE METHODS

Another Way to Solve Example 5, page 269

MULTIPLE REPRESENTATIONS In Example 5 on page 269, you solved a quadratic equation by finding square roots. You can also solve a quadratic equation using a table or a graph.

PROBLEM

SCIENCE COMPETITION For a science competition, students must design a container that prevents an egg from breaking when dropped from a height of 50 feet. How long does the container take to hit the ground?

METHOD 1

Using a Table One alternative approach is to write a quadratic equation and then use a table of values to solve the equation. You can use a graphing calculator to make the table.

STEP 1 **Write** an equation that models the situation using the height function $h = -16t^2 + h_0$.

$h = -16t^2 + h_0$ **Write height function.**

$0 = -16t^2 + 50$ **Substitute 0 for h and 50 for h_0.**

STEP 2 **Enter** the function $y = -16x^2 + 50$ into a graphing calculator. Note that time is now represented by x and height is now represented by y.

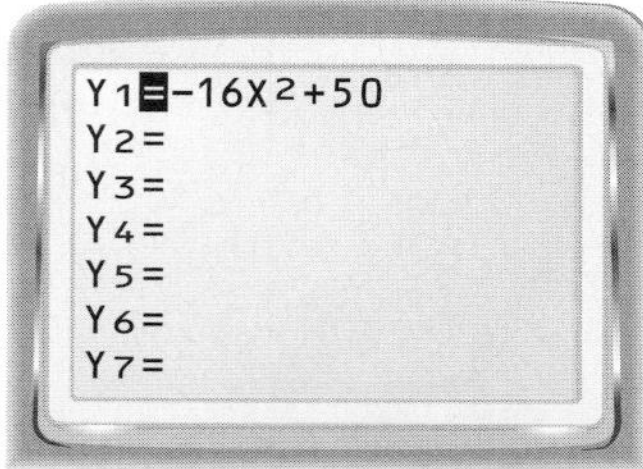

STEP 3 **Make** a table of values for the function. Set the table so that the x-values start at 0 and increase in increments of 0.1.

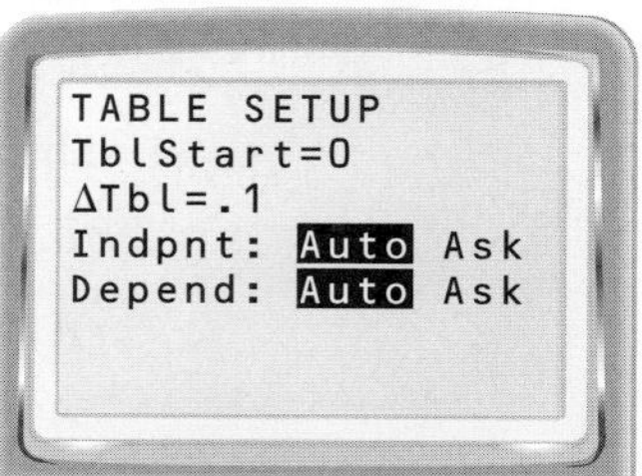

STEP 4 **Scroll** through the table to find the time x at which the height y of the container is 0 feet.

The table shows that $y = 0$ between $x = 1.7$ and $x = 1.8$ because y has a change of sign.

X	Y1	
1.5	14	
1.6	9.04	
1.7	3.76	
1.8	-1.84	
1.9	-7.76	

X=1.8

▸ The container hits the ground between 1.7 and 1.8 seconds after it is dropped.

METHOD 2

Using a Graph Another approach is to write a quadratic equation and then use a graph to solve the equation. You can use a graphing calculator to make the graph.

STEP 1 **Write** an equation that models the situation using the height function $h = -16t^2 + h_0$.

$h = -16t^2 + h_0$ **Write height function.**

$0 = -16t^2 + 50$ **Substitute 0 for h and 50 for h_0.**

STEP 2 **Enter** the function $y = -16x^2 + 50$ into a graphing calculator. Note that time is now represented by x and height is now represented by y.

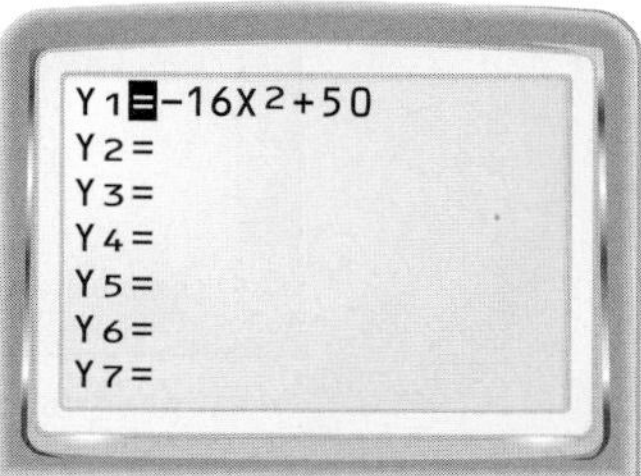

STEP 3 **Graph** the height function. Adjust the viewing window so that you can see the point where the graph crosses the positive x-axis. Find the positive x-value for which $y = 0$ using the *zero* feature. The graph shows that $y = 0$ when $x \approx 1.8$.

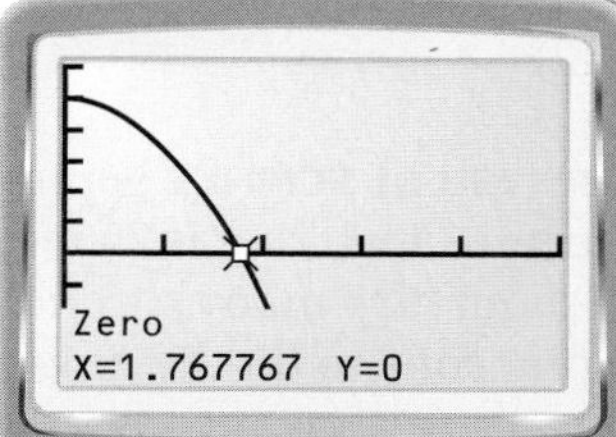

▶ The container hits the ground about 1.8 seconds after it is dropped.

PRACTICE

SOLVING EQUATIONS Solve the quadratic equation using a table and using a graph.

1. $2x^2 - 12x + 10 = 0$
2. $x^2 + 7x + 12 = 0$
3. $9x^2 - 30x + 25 = 0$
4. $7x^2 - 3 = 0$
5. $x^2 + 3x - 6 = 0$
6. **WHAT IF?** How long does it take for an egg container to hit the ground when dropped from a height of 100 feet? Find the answer using a table and using a graph.
7. **WIND PRESSURE** The pressure P (in pounds per square foot) from wind blowing at s miles per hour is given by $P = 0.00256s^2$. What wind speed produces a pressure of 30 lb/ft^2? Solve this problem using a table and using a graph.
8. **BIRDS** A bird flying at a height of 30 feet carries a shellfish. The bird drops the shellfish to break it and get the food inside. How long does it take for the shellfish to hit the ground? Find the answer using a table and using a graph.
9. **DROPPED OBJECT** You are dropping a ball from a window 29 feet above the ground to your friend who will catch it 4 feet above the ground. How long is the ball in the air before your friend catches it? Solve this problem using a table and using a graph.
10. **REASONING** *Explain* how to use the *table* feature of a graphing calculator to approximate the solution of the problem on page 272 to the nearest hundredth of a second. Use this procedure to find the approximate solution.

Lessons 4.1–4.5

1. **CRAFTS** You are creating a metal border of uniform width for a rectangular wall mirror that is 20 inches by 24 inches. You have 416 square inches of metal to use. What is the greatest possible width x of the border?

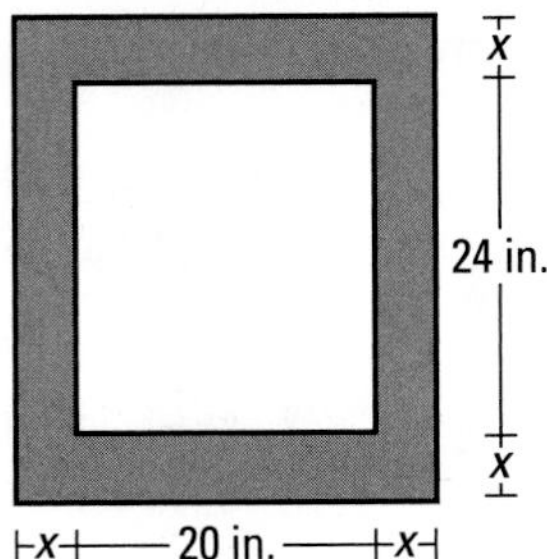

(1) 2 inches (3) 16 inches
(2) 4 inches (4) 26 inches

2. **PHYSICAL SCIENCE** A pinecone falls from a tree branch that is 20 feet above the ground. About how many seconds does it take for the pinecone to hit the ground?

(1) 0.80 second
(2) 0.89 second
(3) 1.12 seconds
(4) 1.25 seconds

3. **FIREFIGHTING** Some harbor police departments have firefighting boats with water cannons. The boats are used to fight fires that occur within the harbor. The function $y = -0.0035x(x - 143.9)$ models the path of water shot by a water cannon where x is the horizontal distance (in feet) and y is the corresponding height (in feet). How far does the water cannon shoot?

(1) 12.0 feet
(2) 71.9 feet
(3) 143.9 feet
(4) 287.8 feet

4. **COMPUTERS** The diagonal of the screen on a laptop computer measures 15 inches. The ratio of the screen's width w to its height h is 4 : 3. What is the height of the laptop screen?

(1) 3 inches (3) 12 inches
(2) 9 inches (4) 81 inches

5. **QUADRATIC FUNCTION** Which function's graph has a vertex of $(-3, 2)$?

(1) $y = -3x^2 - 18x - 25$

(2) $y = -\frac{1}{2}x^2 + 2x + 5$

(3) $y = x^2 + x - 6$

(4) $y = x^2 - 4x - 25$

6. **OPEN-ENDED** You have a rectangular vegetable garden that measures 42 feet by 8 feet. You want to double the area of the garden by expanding the length and width as shown. What is the value of x?

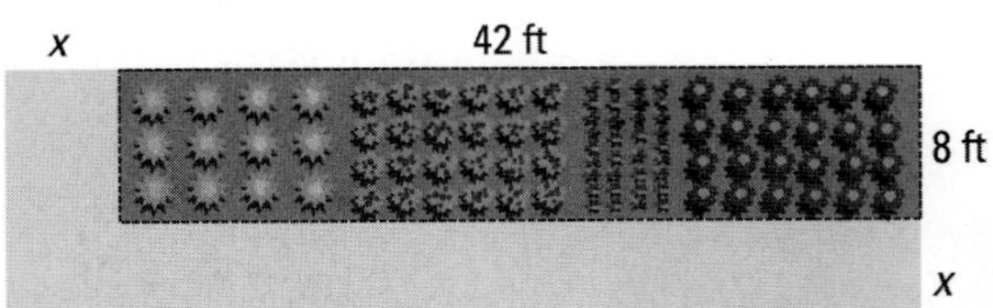

7. **OPEN-ENDED** When Lou's Pizza Shop charges \$2 per slice, it sells about 80 slices of pizza each day. Each time it increases the price by \$.25, the shop sells 5 fewer slices each day.

Identify the number of slices and the price per slice in terms of x, the number of price increases.

Write a function for the shop's total revenue, R, if there are x price increases.

What value of x maximizes R? Explain the meaning of your answer in this situation.

4.6 Perform Operations with Complex Numbers

 **A2.N.9** Perform arithmetic operations on complex numbers and write the answer in the form $a + bi$. . .

Before You performed operations with real numbers.

Now You will perform operations with complex numbers.

Why? So you can solve problems involving fractals, as in Exs. 70–73.

Key Vocabulary
- **imaginary unit *i***
- **complex number**
- **imaginary number**
- **complex conjugates**
- **complex plane**
- **absolute value of a complex number**

Not all quadratic equations have real-number solutions. For example, $x^2 = -1$ has no real-number solutions because the square of any real number x is never a negative number.

To overcome this problem, mathematicians created an expanded system of numbers using the **imaginary unit *i***, defined as $i = \sqrt{-1}$. Note that $i^2 = -1$. The imaginary unit i can be used to write the square root of *any* negative number.

KEY CONCEPT *For Your Notebook*

The Square Root of a Negative Number

Property	Example
1. If r is a positive real number, then $\sqrt{-r} = i\sqrt{r}$.	$\sqrt{-3} = i\sqrt{3}$
2. By Property (1), it follows that $(i\sqrt{r})^2 = -r$.	$(i\sqrt{3})^2 = i^2 \cdot 3 = -3$

EXAMPLE 1 Solve a quadratic equation

Solve $2x^2 + 11 = -37$.

$2x^2 + 11 = -37$ **Write original equation.**

$2x^2 = -48$ **Subtract 11 from each side.**

$x^2 = -24$ **Divide each side by 2.**

$x = \pm\sqrt{-24}$ **Take square roots of each side.**

$x = \pm i\sqrt{24}$ **Write in terms of *i*.**

$x = \pm 2i\sqrt{6}$ **Simplify radical.**

▶ The solutions are $2i\sqrt{6}$ and $-2i\sqrt{6}$.

 **GUIDED PRACTICE** for Example 1

Solve the equation.

1. $x^2 = -13$ **2.** $x^2 = -38$ **3.** $x^2 + 11 = 3$

4. $x^2 - 8 = -36$ **5.** $3x^2 - 7 = -31$ **6.** $5x^2 + 33 = 3$

COMPLEX NUMBERS A **complex number** written in **standard form** is a number $a + bi$ where a and b are real numbers. The number a is the *real part* of the complex number, and the number bi is the *imaginary part*.

If $b \neq 0$, then $a + bi$ is an **imaginary number**. If $a = 0$ and $b \neq 0$, then $a + bi$ is a **pure imaginary number**. The diagram shows how different types of complex numbers are related.

Two complex numbers $a + bi$ and $c + di$ are equal if and only if $a = c$ and $b = d$. For example, if $x + yi = 5 - 3i$, then $x = 5$ and $y = -3$.

Complex Numbers ($a + bi$)

KEY CONCEPT — *For Your Notebook*

Sums and Differences of Complex Numbers

To add (or subtract) two complex numbers, add (or subtract) their real parts and their imaginary parts separately.

Sum of complex numbers: $(a + bi) + (c + di) = (a + c) + (b + d)i$

Difference of complex numbers: $(a + bi) - (c + di) = (a - c) + (b - d)i$

EXAMPLE 2 Add and subtract complex numbers

Write the expression as a complex number in standard form.

a. $(8 - i) + (5 + 4i)$ **b.** $(7 - 6i) - (3 - 6i)$ **c.** $10 - (6 + 7i) + 4i$

Solution

a. $(8 - i) + (5 + 4i) = (8 + 5) + (-1 + 4)i$ Definition of complex addition

$= 13 + 3i$ Write in standard form.

b. $(7 - 6i) - (3 - 6i) = (7 - 3) + (-6 + 6)i$ Definition of complex subtraction

$= 4 + 0i$ Simplify.

$= 4$ Write in standard form.

c. $10 - (6 + 7i) + 4i = [(10 - 6) - 7i] + 4i$ Definition of complex subtraction

$= (4 - 7i) + 4i$ Simplify.

$= 4 + (-7 + 4)i$ Definition of complex addition

$= 4 - 3i$ Write in standard form.

✓ GUIDED PRACTICE for Example 2

Write the expression as a complex number in standard form.

7. $(9 - i) + (-6 + 7i)$ **8.** $(3 + 7i) - (8 - 2i)$ **9.** $-4 - (1 + i) - (5 + 9i)$

EXAMPLE 3 Use addition of complex numbers in real life

ELECTRICITY Circuit components such as resistors, inductors, and capacitors all oppose the flow of current. This opposition is called *resistance* for resistors and *reactance* for inductors and capacitors. A circuit's total opposition to current flow is *impedance.* All of these quantities are measured in ohms (Ω).

READING
Note that while a component's resistance or reactance is a real number, its impedance is a complex number.

Component and symbol	Resistor	Inductor	Capacitor
Resistance or reactance	R	L	C
Impedance	R	Li	$-Ci$

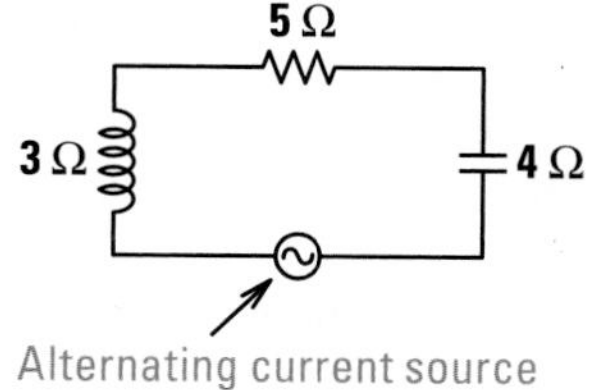

The table shows the relationship between a component's resistance or reactance and its contribution to impedance. A *series circuit* is also shown with the resistance or reactance of each component labeled.

The impedance for a series circuit is the sum of the impedances for the individual components. Find the impedance of the circuit shown above.

Solution

The resistor has a resistance of 5 ohms, so its impedance is 5 ohms. The inductor has a reactance of 3 ohms, so its impedance is $3i$ ohms. The capacitor has a reactance of 4 ohms, so its impedance is $-4i$ ohms.

Impedance of circuit $= 5 + 3i + (-4i)$ **Add the individual impedances.**

$= 5 - i$ **Simplify.**

▶ The impedance of the circuit is $5 - i$ ohms.

MULTIPLYING COMPLEX NUMBERS To multiply two complex numbers, use the distributive property or the FOIL method just as you do when multiplying real numbers or algebraic expressions.

EXAMPLE 4 Multiply complex numbers

Write the expression as a complex number in standard form.

a. $4i(-6 + i)$

b. $(9 - 2i)(-4 + 7i)$

Solution

a. $4i(-6 + i) = -24i + 4i^2$ **Distributive property**

$= -24i + 4(-1)$ **Use $i^2 = -1$.**

$= -24i - 4$ **Simplify.**

$= -4 - 24i$ **Write in standard form.**

AVOID ERRORS
When simplifying an expression that involves complex numbers, be sure to simplify i^2 to -1.

b. $(9 - 2i)(-4 + 7i) = -36 + 63i + 8i - 14i^2$ **Multiply using FOIL.**

$= -36 + 71i - 14(-1)$ **Simplify and use $i^2 = -1$.**

$= -36 + 71i + 14$ **Simplify.**

$= -22 + 71i$ **Write in standard form.**

COMPLEX CONJUGATES Two complex numbers of the form $a + bi$ and $a - bi$ are called **complex conjugates**. The product of complex conjugates is always a real number. For example, $(2 + 4i)(2 - 4i) = 4 - 8i + 8i + 16 = 20$. You can use this fact to write the quotient of two complex numbers in standard form.

EXAMPLE 5 Divide complex numbers

Write the quotient $\frac{7 + 5i}{1 - 4i}$ in standard form.

REWRITE QUOTIENTS
When a quotient has an imaginary number in the denominator, rewrite the denominator as a real number so you can express the quotient in standard form.

$\frac{7 + 5i}{1 - 4i} = \frac{7 + 5i}{1 - 4i} \cdot \frac{1 + 4i}{1 + 4i}$ **Multiply numerator and denominator by $1 + 4i$, the complex conjugate of $1 - 4i$.**

$= \frac{7 + 28i + 5i + 20i^2}{1 + 4i - 4i - 16i^2}$ **Multiply using FOIL.**

$= \frac{7 + 33i + 20(-1)}{1 - 16(-1)}$ **Simplify and use $i^2 = 1$.**

$= \frac{-13 + 33i}{17}$ **Simplify.**

$= -\frac{13}{17} + \frac{33}{17}i$ **Write in standard form.**

✓ GUIDED PRACTICE for Examples 3, 4, and 5

10. **WHAT IF?** In Example 3, what is the impedance of the circuit if the given capacitor is replaced with one having a reactance of 7 ohms?

Write the expression as a complex number in standard form.

11. $i(9 - i)$
12. $(3 + i)(5 - i)$
13. $\frac{5}{1 + i}$
14. $\frac{5 + 2i}{3 - 2i}$

COMPLEX PLANE Just as every real number corresponds to a point on the real number line, every complex number corresponds to a point in the **complex plane**. As shown in the next example, the complex plane has a horizontal axis called the *real axis* and a vertical axis called the *imaginary axis*.

EXAMPLE 6 Plot complex numbers

Plot the complex numbers in the same complex plane.

a. $3 - 2i$ **b.** $-2 + 4i$ **c.** $3i$ **d.** $-4 - 3i$

Solution

a. To plot $3 - 2i$, start at the origin, move 3 units to the right, and then move 2 units down.

b. To plot $-2 + 4i$, start at the origin, move 2 units to the left, and then move 4 units up.

c. To plot $3i$, start at the origin and move 3 units up.

d. To plot $-4 - 3i$, start at the origin, move 4 units to the left, and then move 3 units down.

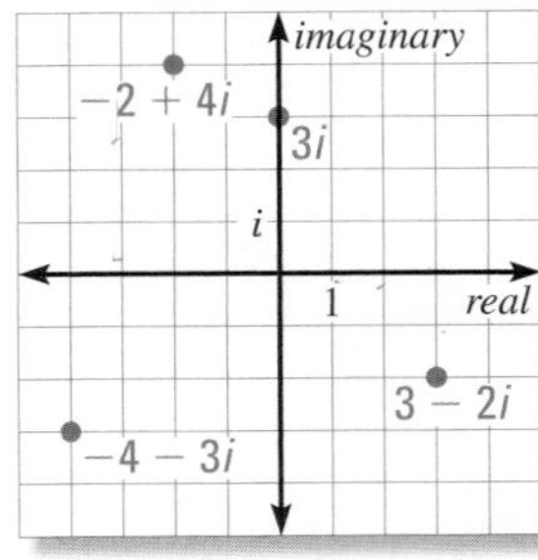

KEY CONCEPT *For Your Notebook*

Absolute Value of a Complex Number

The **absolute value** of a complex number $z = a + bi$, denoted $|z|$, is a nonnegative real number defined as $|z| = \sqrt{a^2 + b^2}$. This is the distance between z and the the origin in the complex plane.

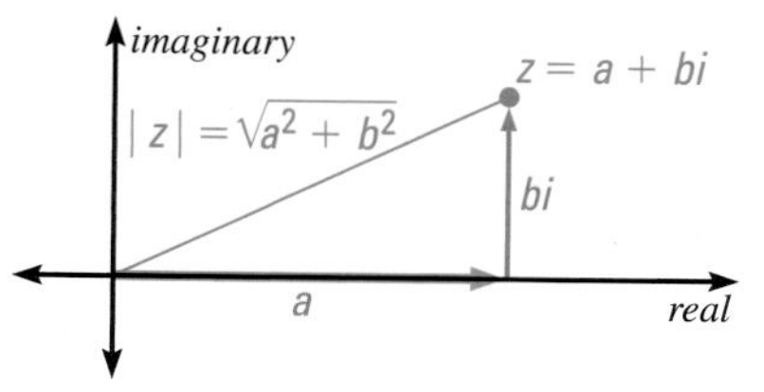

EXAMPLE 7 Find absolute values of complex numbers

Find the absolute value of (a) $-4 + 3i$ and (b) $-3i$.

a. $|-4 + 3i| = \sqrt{(-4)^2 + 3^2} = \sqrt{25} = 5$

b. $|-3i| = |0 + (-3i)| = \sqrt{0^2 + (-3)^2} = \sqrt{9} = 3$

Animated Algebra at classzone.com

✓ **GUIDED PRACTICE** for Examples 6 and 7

Plot the complex numbers in the same complex plane. Then find the absolute value of each complex number.

15. $4 - i$ **16.** $-3 - 4i$ **17.** $2 + 5i$ **18.** $-4i$

4.6 EXERCISES

HOMEWORK KEY

○ = **WORKED-OUT SOLUTIONS** on p. WS8 for Exs. 11, 29, and 67

★ = **STANDARDIZED TEST PRACTICE** Exs. 2, 21, 50, 60, 69, and 74

SKILL PRACTICE

1. VOCABULARY What is the complex conjugate of $a - bi$?

2. ★ WRITING Is every complex number an imaginary number? *Explain.*

EXAMPLE 1 on p. 275 for Exs. 3–11

SOLVING QUADRATIC EQUATIONS **Solve the equation.**

3. $x^2 = -28$ **4.** $r^2 = -624$ **5.** $z^2 + 8 = 4$

6. $s^2 - 22 = -112$ **7.** $2x^2 + 31 = 9$ **8.** $9 - 4y^2 = 57$

9. $6t^2 + 5 = 2t^2 + 1$ **10.** $3p^2 + 7 = -9p^2 + 4$ **(11.)** $-5(n - 3)^2 = 10$

EXAMPLE 2 on p. 276 for Exs. 12–21

ADDING AND SUBTRACTING **Write the expression as a complex number in standard form.**

12. $(6 - 3i) + (5 + 4i)$ **13.** $(9 + 8i) + (8 - 9i)$ **14.** $(-2 - 6i) - (4 - 6i)$

15. $(-1 + i) - (7 - 5i)$ **16.** $(8 + 20i) - (-8 + 12i)$ **17.** $(8 - 5i) - (-11 + 4i)$

18. $(10 - 2i) + (-11 - 7i)$ **19.** $(14 + 3i) + (7 + 6i)$ **20.** $(-1 + 4i) + (-9 - 2i)$

21. ★ **MULTIPLE CHOICE** What is the standard form of the expression $(2 + 3i) - (7 + 4i)$?

Ⓐ -4 Ⓑ $-5 + 7i$ Ⓒ $-5 - i$ Ⓓ $5 + i$

EXAMPLES 4 and 5 on pp. 277–278 for Exs. 22–33

MULTIPLYING AND DIVIDING Write the expression as a complex number in standard form.

22. $6i(3 + 2i)$
23. $-i(4 - 8i)$
24. $(5 - 7i)(-4 - 3i)$
25. $(-2 + 5i)(-1 + 4i)$
26. $(-1 - 5i)(-1 + 5i)$
27. $(8 - 3i)(8 + 3i)$
28. $\frac{7i}{8 + i}$
29. $\frac{6i}{3 - i}$
30. $\frac{-2 - 5i}{3i}$
31. $\frac{4 + 9i}{12i}$
32. $\frac{7 + 4i}{2 - 3i}$
33. $\frac{-1 - 6i}{5 + 9i}$

EXAMPLE 6 on p. 278 for Exs. 34–41

PLOTTING COMPLEX NUMBERS Plot the numbers in the same complex plane.

34. $1 + 2i$
35. $-5 + 3i$
36. $-6i$
37. $4i$
38. $-7 - i$
39. $5 - 5i$
40. 7
41. -2

EXAMPLE 7 on p. 279 for Exs. 42–50

FINDING ABSOLUTE VALUE Find the absolute value of the complex number.

42. $4 + 3i$
43. $-3 + 10i$
44. $10 - 7i$
45. $-1 - 6i$
46. $-8i$
47. $4i$
48. $-4 + i$
49. $7 + 7i$

50. ★ **MULTIPLE CHOICE** What is the absolute value of $9 + 12i$?

Ⓐ 7 Ⓑ 15 Ⓒ 108 Ⓓ 225

STANDARD FORM Write the expression as a complex number in standard form.

51. $-8 - (3 + 2i) - (9 - 4i)$
52. $(3 + 2i) + (5 - i) + 6i$
53. $5i(3 + 2i)(8 + 3i)$
54. $(1 - 9i)(1 - 4i)(4 - 3i)$
55. $\frac{(5 - 2i) + (5 + 3i)}{(1 + i) - (2 - 4i)}$
56. $\frac{(10 + 4i) - (3 - 2i)}{(6 - 7i)(1 - 2i)}$

ERROR ANALYSIS ***Describe*** **and correct the error in simplifying the expression.**

57.
$(1 + 2i)(4 - i)$
$= 4 - i + 8i - 2i^2$
$= -2i^2 + 7i + 4$

58.
$|2 - 3i| = \sqrt{2^2 - 3^2}$
$= \sqrt{-5}$
$= i\sqrt{5}$

59. **ADDITIVE AND MULTIPLICATIVE INVERSES** The additive inverse of a complex number z is a complex number z_a such that $z + z_a = 0$. The multiplicative inverse of z is a complex number z_m such that $z \cdot z_m = 1$. Find the additive and multiplicative inverses of each complex number.

a. $z = 2 + i$
b. $z = 5 - i$
c. $z = -1 + 3i$

60. ★ **OPEN-ENDED MATH** Find two imaginary numbers whose sum is a real number. How are the imaginary numbers related?

CHALLENGE Write the expression as a complex number in standard form.

61. $\frac{a + bi}{c + di}$
62. $\frac{a - bi}{c - di}$
63. $\frac{a + bi}{c - di}$
64. $\frac{a - bi}{c + di}$

PROBLEM SOLVING

EXAMPLE 3 on p. 277 for Exs. 65–67

CIRCUITS **In Exercises 65–67, each component of the circuit has been labeled with its resistance or reactance. Find the impedance of the circuit.**

65.

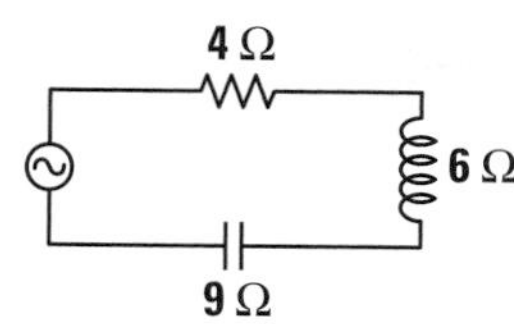

66.

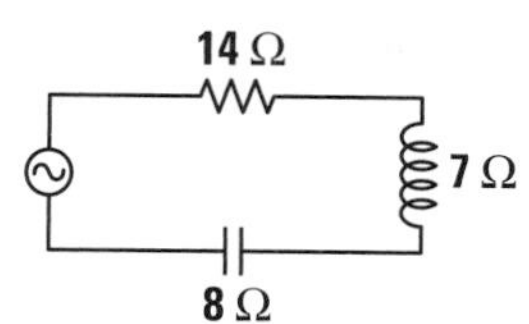

67.

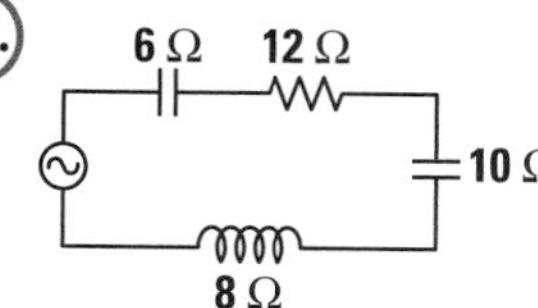

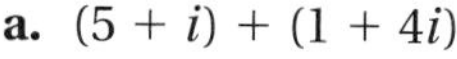

for problem solving help at classzone.com

68. **VISUAL THINKING** The graph shows how you can geometrically add two complex numbers (in this case, $4 + i$ and $2 + 5i$) to find their sum (in this case, $6 + 6i$). Find each of the following sums by drawing a graph.

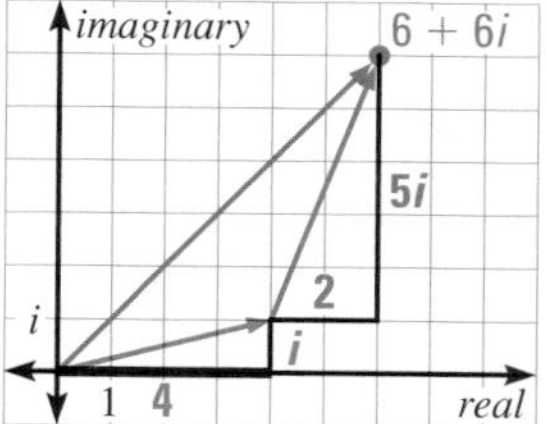

a. $(5 + i) + (1 + 4i)$ **b.** $(-7 + 3i) + (2 - 2i)$

c. $(3 - 2i) + (-1 - i)$ **d.** $(4 + 2i) + (-5 - 3i)$

69. ★ **SHORT RESPONSE** Make a table that shows the powers of i from i^1 to i^8 in the first row and the simplified forms of these powers in the second row. *Describe* the pattern you observe in the table. Verify that the pattern continues by evaluating the next four powers of i.

In Exercises 70–73, use the example below to determine whether the complex number c belongs to the Mandelbrot set. *Justify* your answer.

EXAMPLE Investigate the Mandelbrot set

Consider the function $f(z) = z^2 + c$ and this infinite list of complex numbers: $z_0 = 0$, $z_1 = f(z_0)$, $z_2 = f(z_1)$, $z_3 = f(z_2)$, ... If the absolute values of $z_0, z_1, z_2, z_3, \ldots$ are all less than some fixed number N, then c belongs to the *Mandelbrot set*. If the absolute values become infinitely large, then c does not belong to the Mandelbrot set.

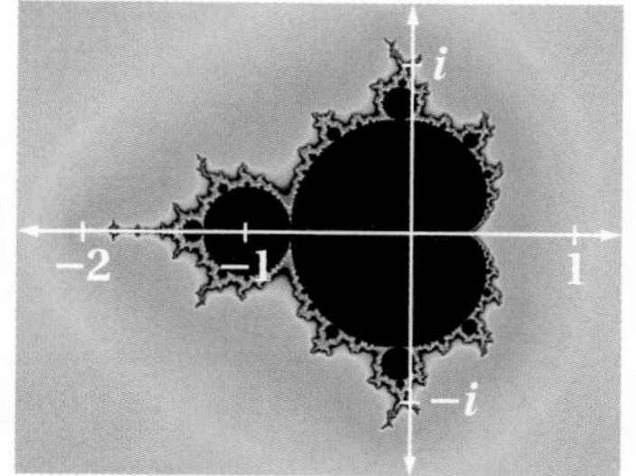

The Mandelbrot set is the black region in the complex plane above.

Tell whether $c = 1 + i$ belongs to the Mandelbrot set.

Solution

Let $f(z) = z^2 + (1 + i)$.

$z_0 = 0$ $|z_0| = 0$

$z_1 = f(0) = 0^2 + (1 + i) = 1 + i$ $|z_1| \approx 1.41$

$z_2 = f(1 + i) = (1 + i)^2 + (1 + i) = 1 + 3i$ $|z_2| \approx 3.16$

$z_3 = f(1 + 3i) = (1 + 3i)^2 + (1 + i) = -7 + 7i$ $|z_3| \approx 9.90$

$z_4 = f(-7 + 7i) = (-7 + 7i)^2 + (1 + i) = 1 - 97i$ $|z_4| \approx 97.0$

▶ Because the absolute values are becoming infinitely large, $c = 1 + i$ does not belong to the Mandelbrot set.

70. $c = i$ **71.** $c = -1 + i$ **72.** $c = -1$ **73.** $c = -0.5i$

74. ★ **SHORT RESPONSE** Evaluate $\sqrt{-4} \cdot \sqrt{-25}$ and $\sqrt{100}$. Does the rule $\sqrt{a} \cdot \sqrt{b} = \sqrt{ab}$ on page 266 hold when a and b are negative numbers?

75. **PARALLEL CIRCUITS** In a *parallel circuit*, there is more than one pathway through which current can flow. To find the impedance Z of a parallel circuit with two pathways, first calculate the impedances Z_1 and Z_2 of the pathways separately by treating each pathway as a series circuit. Then apply this formula:

$$Z = \frac{Z_1 Z_2}{Z_1 + Z_2}$$

What is the impedance of each parallel circuit shown below?

a. 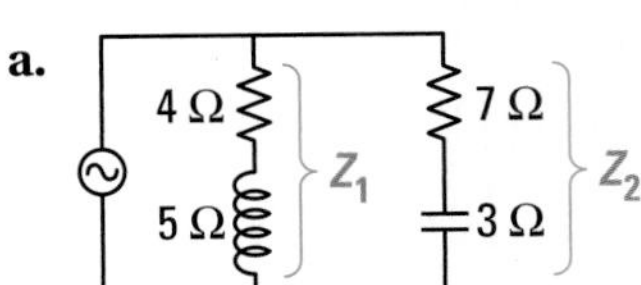

b. 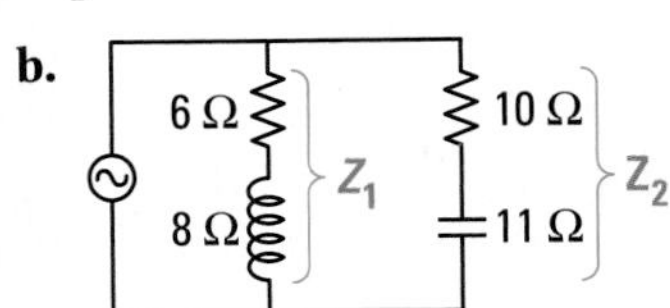

c. 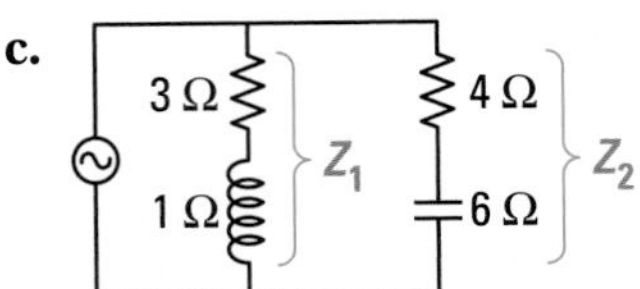

76. **CHALLENGE** *Julia sets*, like the Mandelbrot set shown on page 281, are fractals defined on the complex plane. For every complex number c, there is an associated Julia set determined by the function $f(z) = z^2 + c$.

For example, the Julia set corresponding to $c = 1 + i$ is determined by the function $f(z) = z^2 + 1 + i$. A number z_0 is a member of this Julia set if the absolute values of the numbers $z_1 = f(z_0)$, $z_2 = f(z_1)$, $z_3 = f(z_2)$, . . . are all less than some fixed number N, and z_0 is not a member if these absolute values grow infinitely large.

A Julia set

Tell whether the given number z_0 belongs to the Julia set associated with the function $f(z) = z^2 + 1 + i$.

a. $z_0 = i$ **b.** $z_0 = 1$ **c.** $z_0 = 2i$ **d.** $z_0 = 2 + 3i$

NEW YORK MIXED REVIEW

TEST PRACTICE at classzone.com

77. There are 185 students in this year's freshman class. What additional information is needed to predict the number of students in next year's freshman class?

Ⓐ The rate of change in the number of students in the freshman class

Ⓑ The number of females in this year's freshman class

Ⓒ The number of students in this year's senior class

Ⓓ The maximum number of students in the school

78. What are the slope m and y-intercept b of the line that contains the point $(-4, 1)$ and has the same y-intercept as $3x - 2y = 10$?

Ⓐ $m = -\frac{3}{2}, b = -5$ Ⓑ $m = 1, b = 5$

Ⓒ $m = \frac{3}{2}, b = 7$ Ⓓ $m = \frac{9}{4}, b = 10$

4.7 Using Algebra Tiles to Complete the Square

MATERIALS • algebra tiles

QUESTION **How can you use algebra tiles to complete the square for a quadratic expression?**

If you are given an expression of the form $x^2 + bx$, you can add a constant c to the expression so that the result $x^2 + bx + c$ is a perfect square trinomial. This process is called *completing the square.*

EXPLORE **Complete the square for the expression $x^2 + 6x$**

STEP 1

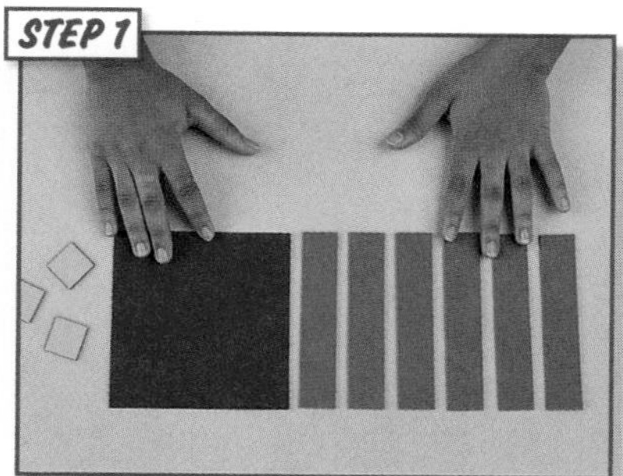

Model the expression

Use algebra tiles to model the expression $x^2 + 6x$. You will need to use one x^2-tile and six x-tiles for this expression.

STEP 2

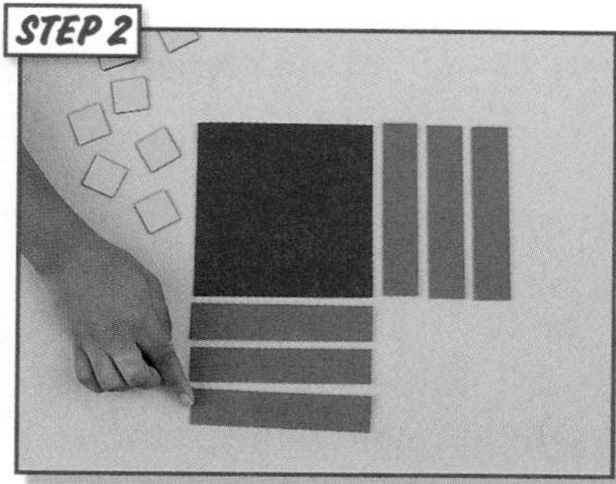

Make a square

Arrange the tiles in a square. You want the length and width of the square to be equal. Your arrangement will be incomplete in one of the corners.

STEP 3

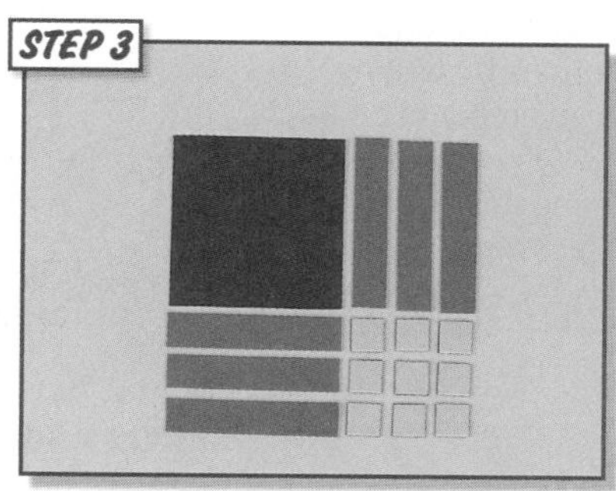

Complete the square

Find the number of 1-tiles needed to complete the square. By adding nine 1-tiles, you can see that $x^2 + 6x + 9$ is equal to $(x + 3)^2$.

DRAW CONCLUSIONS **Use your observations to complete these exercises**

1. Copy and complete the table at the right by following the steps above.

2. Look for patterns in the last column of your table. Consider the general statement $x^2 + bx + c = (x + d)^2$.

   a. How is d related to b in each case?

   b. How is c related to d in each case?

   c. How can you obtain the numbers in the table's second column directly from the coefficients of x in the expressions from the first column?

Completing the Square

Expression	Number of 1-tiles needed to complete the square	Expression written as a square
$x^2 + 2x +$?	?	?
$x^2 + 4x +$?	?	?
$x^2 + 6x +$?	9	$x^2 + 6x + 9 = (x + 3)^2$
$x^2 + 8x +$?	?	?
$x^2 + 10x +$?	?	?

4.7 Complete the Square

A2.A.24 Know and apply the technique of completing the square

Before You solved quadratic equations by finding square roots.

Now You will solve quadratic equations by completing the square.

Why? So you can find a baseball's maximum height, as in Example 7.

Key Vocabulary
- **completing the square**

In Lesson 4.5, you solved equations of the form $x^2 = k$ by finding square roots. This method also works if one side of an equation is a perfect square trinomial.

EXAMPLE 1 Solve a quadratic equation by finding square roots

Solve $x^2 - 8x + 16 = 25$.

$x^2 - 8x + 16 = 25$ **Write original equation.**

$(x - 4)^2 = 25$ **Write left side as a binomial squared.**

$x - 4 = \pm 5$ **Take square roots of each side.**

$x = 4 \pm 5$ **Solve for x.**

▶ The solutions are $4 + 5 = 9$ and $4 - 5 = -1$.

ANOTHER WAY
You can also find the solutions by writing the given equation as $x^2 - 8x - 9 = 0$ and solving this equation by factoring.

PERFECT SQUARES In Example 1, the trinomial $x^2 - 8x + 16$ is a perfect square because it equals $(x - 4)^2$. Sometimes you need to add a term to an expression $x^2 + bx$ to make it a square. This process is called **completing the square**.

KEY CONCEPT *For Your Notebook*

Completing the Square

Words To complete the square for the expression $x^2 + bx$, add $\left(\frac{b}{2}\right)^2$.

Diagrams In each diagram, the combined area of the shaded regions is $x^2 + bx$. Adding $\left(\frac{b}{2}\right)^2$ completes the square in the second diagram.

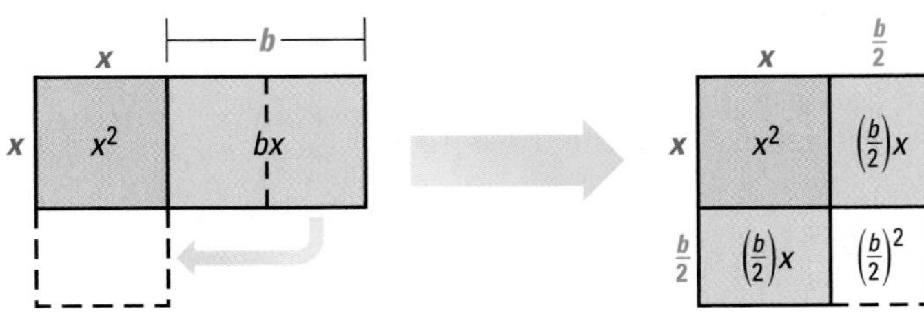

Algebra $x^2 + bx + \left(\frac{b}{2}\right)^2 = \left(x + \frac{b}{2}\right)\left(x + \frac{b}{2}\right) = \left(x + \frac{b}{2}\right)^2$

EXAMPLE 2 Make a perfect square trinomial

Find the value of c that makes $x^2 + 16x + c$ a perfect square trinomial. Then write the expression as the square of a binomial.

Solution

STEP 1 **Find** half the coefficient of x. $\frac{16}{2} = 8$

STEP 2 **Square** the result of Step 1. $8^2 = 64$

STEP 3 **Replace** c with the result of Step 2. $x^2 + 16x + 64$

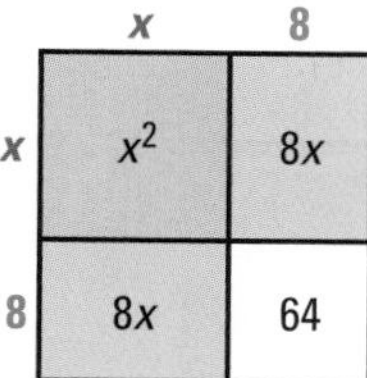

▶ The trinomial $x^2 + 16x + c$ is a perfect square when $c = 64$. Then $x^2 + 16x + 64 = (x + 8)(x + 8) = (x + 8)^2$.

✓ GUIDED PRACTICE for Examples 1 and 2

Solve the equation by finding square roots.

1. $x^2 + 6x + 9 = 36$ **2.** $x^2 - 10x + 25 = 1$ **3.** $x^2 - 24x + 144 = 100$

Find the value of c that makes the expression a perfect square trinomial. Then write the expression as the square of a binomial.

4. $x^2 + 14x + c$ **5.** $x^2 + 22x + c$ **6.** $x^2 - 9x + c$

SOLVING EQUATIONS The method of completing the square can be used to solve *any* quadratic equation. When you complete a square as part of solving an equation, you must add the same number to *both* sides of the equation.

EXAMPLE 3 Solve $ax^2 + bx + c = 0$ when $a = 1$

Solve $x^2 - 12x + 4 = 0$ by completing the square.

$x^2 - 12x + 4 = 0$ Write original equation.

$x^2 - 12x = -4$ Write left side in the form $x^2 + bx$.

$x^2 - 12x + 36 = -4 + 36$ Add $\left(\frac{-12}{2}\right)^2 = (-6)^2 = 36$ to each side.

$(x - 6)^2 = 32$ Write left side as a binomial squared.

$x - 6 = \pm\sqrt{32}$ Take square roots of each side.

$x = 6 \pm \sqrt{32}$ Solve for x.

$x = 6 \pm 4\sqrt{2}$ Simplify: $\sqrt{32} = \sqrt{16} \cdot \sqrt{2} = 4\sqrt{2}$

REVIEW RADICALS
For help with simplifying square roots, see p. 266.

▶ The solutions are $6 + 4\sqrt{2}$ and $6 - 4\sqrt{2}$.

CHECK You can use algebra or a graph.

Algebra Substitute each solution in the original equation to verify that it is correct.

Graph Use a graphing calculator to graph $y = x^2 - 12x + 4$. The x-intercepts are about $0.34 \approx 6 - 4\sqrt{2}$ and $11.66 \approx 6 + 4\sqrt{2}$.

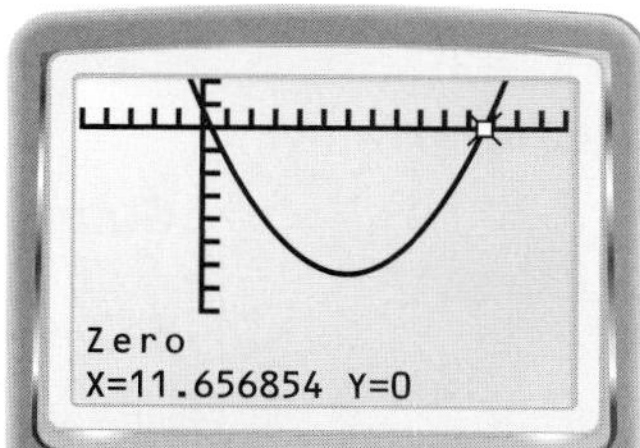

EXAMPLE 4 Solve $ax^2 + bx + c = 0$ when $a \neq 1$

Solve $2x^2 + 8x + 14 = 0$ by completing the square.

$2x^2 + 8x + 14 = 0$	Write original equation.
$x^2 + 4x + 7 = 0$	Divide each side by the coefficient of x^2.
$x^2 + 4x = -7$	Write left side in the form $x^2 + bx$.
$x^2 + 4x + 4 = -7 + 4$	Add $\left(\frac{4}{2}\right)^2 = 2^2 = 4$ to each side.
$(x + 2)^2 = -3$	Write left side as a binomial squared.
$x + 2 = \pm\sqrt{-3}$	Take square roots of each side.
$x = -2 \pm \sqrt{-3}$	Solve for x.
$x = -2 \pm i\sqrt{3}$	Write in terms of the imaginary unit i.

▶ The solutions are $-2 + i\sqrt{3}$ and $-2 - i\sqrt{3}$.

EXAMPLE 5 Standardized Test Practice

The area of the rectangle shown is 72 square units. What is the value of x?

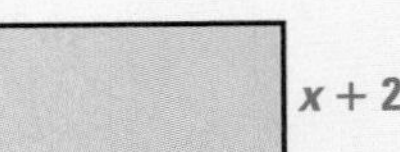

Ⓐ -6 Ⓑ 4

Ⓒ 8.48 Ⓓ -6 or 4

ELIMINATE CHOICES

You can eliminate choices A and D because the side lengths are negative when $x = -6$.

Solution

Use the formula for the area of a rectangle to write an equation.

$3x(x + 2) = 72$	Length × Width = Area
$3x^2 + 6x = 72$	Distributive property
$x^2 + 2x = 24$	Divide each side by the coefficient of x^2.
$x^2 + 2x + 1 = 24 + 1$	Add $\left(\frac{2}{2}\right)^2 = 1^2 = 1$ to each side.
$(x + 1)^2 = 25$	Write left side as a binomial squared.
$x + 1 = \pm 5$	Take square roots of each side.
$x = -1 \pm 5$	Solve for x.

So, $x = -1 + 5 = 4$ or $x = -1 - 5 = -6$. You can reject $x = -6$ because the side lengths would be -18 and -4, and side lengths cannot be negative.

▶ The value of x is 4. The correct answer is B. Ⓐ Ⓑ Ⓒ Ⓓ

✓ GUIDED PRACTICE for Examples 3, 4, and 5

Solve the equation by completing the square.

7. $x^2 + 6x + 4 = 0$
8. $x^2 - 10x + 8 = 0$
9. $2n^2 - 4n - 14 = 0$
10. $3x^2 + 12x - 18 = 0$
11. $6x(x + 8) = 12$
12. $4p(p - 2) = 100$

VERTEX FORM Recall from Lesson 4.2 that the vertex form of a quadratic function is $y = a(x - h)^2 + k$ where (h, k) is the vertex of the function's graph. To write a quadratic function in vertex form, use completing the square.

EXAMPLE 6 Write a quadratic function in vertex form

Write $y = x^2 - 10x + 22$ in vertex form. Then identify the vertex.

$y = x^2 - 10x + 22$	Write original function.
$y + \boxed{?} = (x^2 - 10x + \boxed{?}) + 22$	Prepare to complete the square.
$y + 25 = (x^2 - 10x + 25) + 22$	Add $\left(\frac{-10}{2}\right)^2 = (-5)^2 = 25$ to each side.
$y + 25 = (x - 5)^2 + 22$	Write $x^2 - 10x + 25$ as a binomial squared.
$y = (x - 5)^2 - 3$	Solve for y.

▶ The vertex form of the function is $y = (x - 5)^2 - 3$. The vertex is $(5, -3)$.

EXAMPLE 7 Find the maximum value of a quadratic function

BASEBALL The height y (in feet) of a baseball t seconds after it is hit is given by this function:

$$y = -16t^2 + 96t + 3$$

Find the maximum height of the baseball.

Solution

The maximum height of the baseball is the y-coordinate of the vertex of the parabola with the given equation.

$y = -16t^2 + 96t + 3$	Write original function.
$y = -16(t^2 - 6t) + 3$	Factor -16 from first two terms.
$y + (-16)(\boxed{?}) = -16(t^2 - 6t + \boxed{?}) + 3$	Prepare to complete the square.
$y + (-16)(9) = -16(t^2 - 6t + 9) + 3$	Add $(-16)(9)$ to each side.
$y - 144 = -16(t - 3)^2 + 3$	Write $t^2 - 6t + 9$ as a binomial squared.
$y = -16(t - 3)^2 + 147$	Solve for y.

AVOID ERRORS
When you complete the square, be sure to add $(-16)(9) = -144$ to each side, not just 9.

▶ The vertex is $(3, 147)$, so the maximum height of the baseball is 147 feet.

Animated Algebra at classzone.com

✓ GUIDED PRACTICE for Examples 6 and 7

Write the quadratic function in vertex form. Then identify the vertex.

13. $y = x^2 - 8x + 17$ **14.** $y = x^2 + 6x + 3$ **15.** $f(x) = x^2 - 4x - 4$

16. **WHAT IF?** In Example 7, suppose the height of the baseball is given by $y = -16t^2 + 80t + 2$. Find the maximum height of the baseball.

4.7 EXERCISES

HOMEWORK KEY

○ = **WORKED-OUT SOLUTIONS** on p. WS8 for Exs. 27, 45, and 65

★ = **STANDARDIZED TEST PRACTICE** Exs. 2, 12, 34, 58, 59, and 67

◆ = **MULTIPLE REPRESENTATIONS** Ex. 66

SKILL PRACTICE

1. **VOCABULARY** What is the difference between a binomial and a trinomial?

2. ★ **WRITING** *Describe* what completing the square means for an expression of the form $x^2 + bx$.

EXAMPLE 1 on p. 284 for Exs. 3–12

SOLVING BY SQUARE ROOTS **Solve the equation by finding square roots.**

3. $x^2 + 4x + 4 = 9$
4. $x^2 + 10x + 25 = 64$
5. $n^2 + 16n + 64 = 36$
6. $m^2 - 2m + 1 = 144$
7. $x^2 - 22x + 121 = 13$
8. $x^2 - 18x + 81 = 5$
9. $t^2 + 8t + 16 = 45$
10. $4u^2 + 4u + 1 = 75$
11. $9x^2 - 12x + 4 = -3$

12. ★ **MULTIPLE CHOICE** What are the solutions of $x^2 - 4x + 4 = -1$?

(A) $2 \pm i$ (B) $-2 \pm i$ (C) $-3, -1$ (D) $1, 3$

EXAMPLE 2 on p. 285 for Exs. 13–21

FINDING C **Find the value of *c* that makes the expression a perfect square trinomial. Then write the expression as the square of a binomial.**

13. $x^2 + 6x + c$
14. $x^2 + 12x + c$
15. $x^2 - 24x + c$
16. $x^2 - 30x + c$
17. $x^2 - 2x + c$
18. $x^2 + 50x + c$
19. $x^2 + 7x + c$
20. $x^2 - 13x + c$
21. $x^2 - x + c$

EXAMPLES 3 and 4 on pp. 285–286 for Exs. 22–34

COMPLETING THE SQUARE **Solve the equation by completing the square.**

22. $x^2 + 4x = 10$
23. $x^2 + 8x = -1$
24. $x^2 + 6x - 3 = 0$
25. $x^2 + 12x + 18 = 0$
26. $x^2 - 18x + 86 = 0$
27. $x^2 - 2x + 25 = 0$
28. $2k^2 + 16k = -12$
29. $3x^2 + 42x = -24$
30. $4x^2 - 40x - 12 = 0$
31. $3s^2 + 6s + 9 = 0$
32. $7t^2 + 28t + 56 = 0$
33. $6r^2 + 6r + 12 = 0$

34. ★ **MULTIPLE CHOICE** What are the solutions of $x^2 + 10x + 8 = -5$?

(A) $5 \pm 2\sqrt{3}$ (B) $5 \pm 4\sqrt{3}$ (C) $-5 \pm 2\sqrt{3}$ (D) $-5 \pm 4\sqrt{3}$

EXAMPLE 5 on p. 286 for Exs. 35–38

GEOMETRY **Find the value of *x*.**

35. Area of rectangle = 50

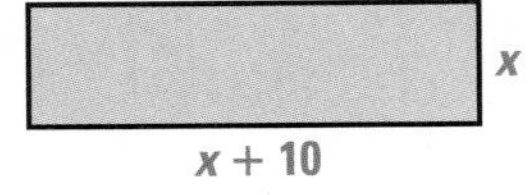

36. Area of parallelogram = 48

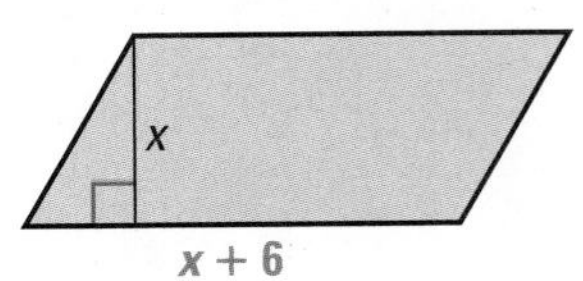

37. Area of triangle = 40

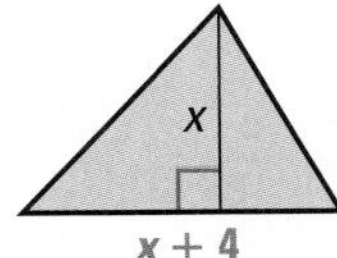

38. Area of trapezoid = 20

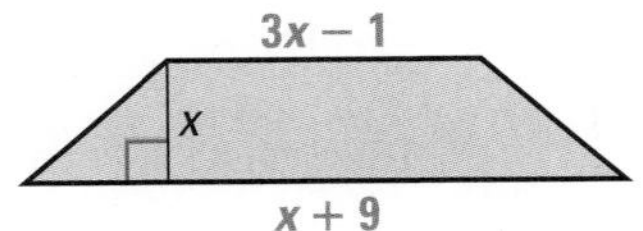

FINDING THE VERTEX **In Exercises 39 and 40, use completing the square to find the vertex of the given function's graph. Then tell what the vertex represents.**

Buckingham Fountain

39. At Buckingham Fountain in Chicago, the water's height h (in feet) above the main nozzle can be modeled by $h = -16t^2 + 89.6t$ where t is the time (in seconds) since the water has left the nozzle.

40. When you walk x meters per minute, your rate y of energy use (in calories per minute) can be modeled by $y = 0.0085x^2 - 1.5x + 120$.

EXAMPLES 6 and 7 on p. 287 for Exs. 41–49

WRITING IN VERTEX FORM **Write the quadratic function in vertex form. Then identify the vertex.**

41. $y = x^2 - 8x + 19$

42. $y = x^2 - 4x - 1$

43. $y = x^2 + 12x + 37$

44. $y = x^2 + 20x + 90$

45. $f(x) = x^2 - 3x + 4$

46. $g(x) = x^2 + 7x + 2$

47. $y = 2x^2 + 24x + 25$

48. $y = 5x^2 + 10x + 7$

49. $y = 2x^2 - 28x + 99$

ERROR ANALYSIS ***Describe*** **and correct the error in solving the equation.**

50.

$$x^2 + 10x + 13 = 0$$
$$x^2 + 10x = -13$$
$$x^2 + 10x + 25 = -13 + 25$$
$$(x + 5)^2 = 12$$
$$x + 5 = \pm\sqrt{12}$$
$$x = -5 \pm \sqrt{12}$$
$$x = -5 \pm 4\sqrt{3}$$

51.

$$4x^2 + 24x - 11 = 0$$
$$4(x^2 + 6x) = 11$$
$$4(x^2 + 6x + 9) = 11 + 9$$
$$4(x + 3)^2 = 20$$
$$(x + 3)^2 = 5$$
$$x + 3 = \pm\sqrt{5}$$
$$x = -3 \pm \sqrt{5}$$

COMPLETING THE SQUARE **Solve the equation by completing the square.**

52. $x^2 + 9x + 20 = 0$

53. $x^2 + 3x + 14 = 0$

54. $7q^2 + 10q = 2q^2 + 155$

55. $3x^2 + x = 2x - 6$

56. $0.1x^2 - x + 9 = 0.2x$

57. $0.4v^2 + 0.7v = 0.3v - 2$

58. ★ **OPEN-ENDED MATH** Write a quadratic equation with real-number solutions that can be solved by completing the square but not by factoring.

59. ★ **SHORT RESPONSE** In this exercise, you will investigate the graphical effect of completing the square.

a. Graph each pair of functions in the same coordinate plane.

$y = x^2 + 2x$	$y = x^2 + 4x$	$y = x^2 - 6x$
$y = (x + 1)^2$	$y = (x + 2)^2$	$y = (x - 3)^2$

b. *Compare* the graphs of $y = x^2 + bx$ and $y = \left(x + \frac{b}{2}\right)^2$. What happens to the graph of $y = x^2 + bx$ when you complete the square?

60. **REASONING** For what value(s) of k does $x^2 + bx + \left(\frac{b}{2}\right)^2 = k$ have exactly 1 real solution? 2 real solutions? 2 imaginary solutions?

61. **CHALLENGE** Solve $x^2 + bx + c = 0$ by completing the square. Your answer will be an expression for x in terms of b and c.

PROBLEM SOLVING

EXAMPLE 7 on p. 287 for Exs. 62–65

62. **DRUM MAJOR** While marching, a drum major tosses a baton into the air and catches it. The height h (in feet) of the baton after t seconds can be modeled by $h = -16t^2 + 32t + 6$. Find the maximum height of the baton.

@HomeTutor for problem solving help at classzone.com

63. **VOLLEYBALL** The height h (in feet) of a volleyball t seconds after it is hit can be modeled by $h = -16t^2 + 48t + 4$. Find the volleyball's maximum height.

@HomeTutor for problem solving help at classzone.com

64. **SKATEBOARD REVENUE** A skateboard shop sells about 50 skateboards per week for the price advertised. For each $1 decrease in price, about 1 more skateboard per week is sold. The shop's revenue can be modeled by $y = (70 - x)(50 + x)$. Use vertex form to find how the shop can maximize weekly revenue.

65. **VIDEO GAME REVENUE** A store sells about 40 video game systems each month when it charges $200 per system. For each $10 increase in price, about 1 less system per month is sold. The store's revenue can be modeled by $y = (200 + 10x)(40 - x)$. Use vertex form to find how the store can maximize monthly revenue.

66. **MULTIPLE REPRESENTATIONS** The path of a ball thrown by a softball player can be modeled by the function

$$y = -0.0110x^2 + 1.23x + 5.50$$

where x is the softball's horizontal position (in feet) and y is the corresponding height (in feet).

a. **Rewriting a Function** Write the given function in vertex form.

b. **Making a Table** Make a table of values for the function. Include values of x from 0 to 120 in increments of 10.

c. **Drawing a Graph** Use your table to graph the function. What is the maximum height of the softball? How far does it travel?

67. ★ **EXTENDED RESPONSE** Your school is adding a rectangular outdoor eating section along part of a 70 foot side of the school. The eating section will be enclosed by a fence along its three open sides. The school has 120 feet of fencing and plans to use 1500 square feet of land for the eating section.

a. Write an equation for the area of the eating section.

b. Solve the equation. *Explain* why you must reject one of the solutions.

c. What are the dimensions of the eating section?

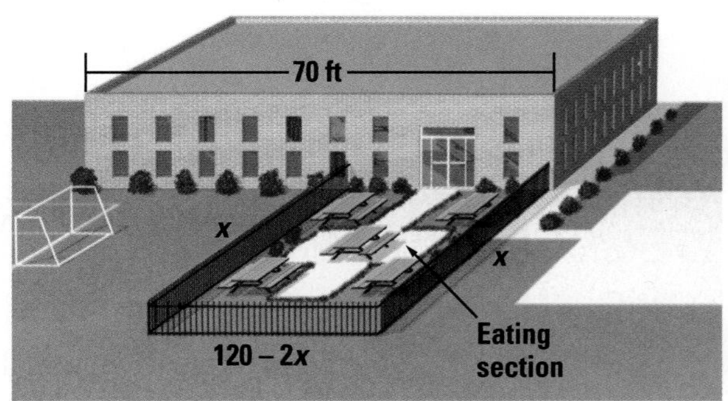

GEOMETRY REVIEW

The volume of clay equals the difference of the volumes of two cylinders.

68. **CHALLENGE** In your pottery class, you are given a lump of clay with a volume of 200 cubic centimeters and are asked to make a cylindrical pencil holder. The pencil holder should be 9 centimeters high and have an inner radius of 3 centimeters. What thickness x should your pencil holder have if you want to use all of the clay?

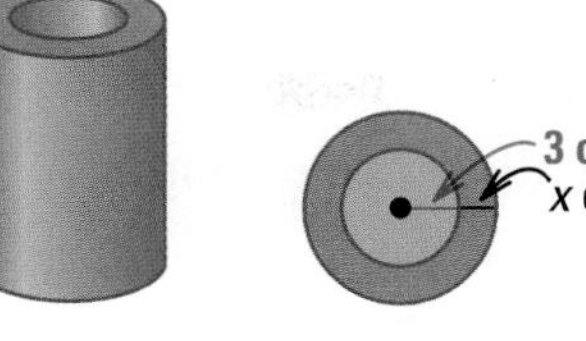

Top view

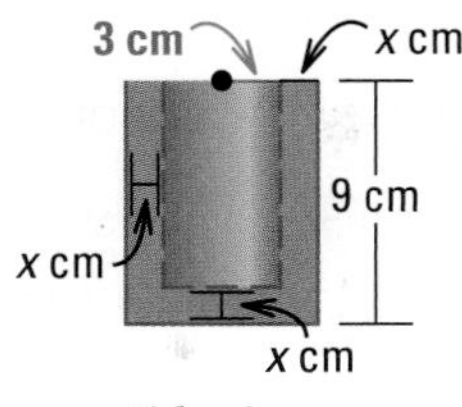

Side view

NEW YORK MIXED REVIEW

69. If quadrilateral $MNPQ$ is reflected in the line $y = 3$, in which quadrant will the image of point N appear?

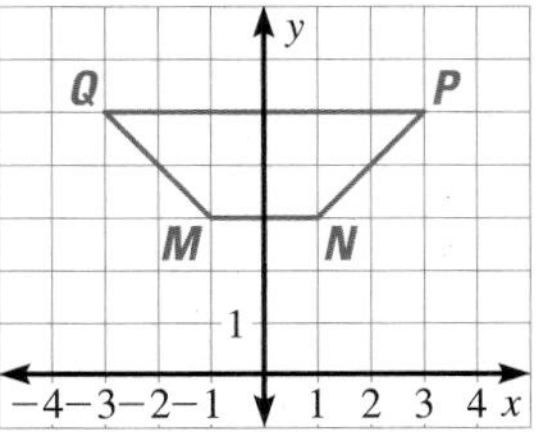

Ⓐ Quadrant I   Ⓑ Quadrant II

Ⓒ Quadrant III   Ⓓ Quadrant IV

70. A hose adds 120 gallons of water to a swimming pool in 1.5 hours. How many hours will it take for the hose to fill a different swimming pool that holds 600 gallons of water?

Ⓐ 5 h   Ⓑ 6.25 h   Ⓒ 7.5 h   Ⓓ 8 h

QUIZ for Lessons 4.5–4.7

Solve the equation.

1. $4x^2 = 64$ *(p. 266)*
2. $3(p - 1)^2 = 15$ *(p. 266)*
3. $16(m + 5)^2 = 8$ *(p. 266)*
4. $-2z^2 = 424$ *(p. 275)*
5. $s^2 + 12 = 9$ *(p. 275)*
6. $7x^2 - 4 = -6$ *(p. 275)*

Write the expression as a complex number in standard form. *(p. 275)*

7. $(5 - 3i) + (-2 + 5i)$
8. $(-2 + 9i) - (7 + 8i)$
9. $3i(7 - 9i)$
10. $(8 - 3i)(-6 - 10i)$
11. $\dfrac{4i}{-6 - 11i}$
12. $\dfrac{3 - 2i}{-8 + 5i}$

Write the quadratic function in vertex form. Then identify the vertex. *(p. 284)*

13. $y = x^2 - 4x + 9$
14. $y = x^2 + 14x + 45$
15. $f(x) = x^2 - 10x + 17$
16. $g(x) = x^2 - 2x - 7$
17. $y = x^2 + x + 1$
18. $y = x^2 + 9x + 19$

19. **FALLING OBJECT** A student drops a ball from a school roof 45 feet above ground. How long is the ball in the air? *(p. 266)*

4.8 Use the Quadratic Formula and the Discriminant

 **A2.A.25** Solve quadratic equations, using the quadratic formula

Before You solved quadratic equations by completing the square.

Now You will solve quadratic equations using the quadratic formula.

Why? So you can model the heights of thrown objects, as in Example 5.

Key Vocabulary
- **quadratic formula**
- **discriminant**

In Lesson 4.7, you solved quadratic equations by completing the square for *each equation separately.* By completing the square *once* for the general equation $ax^2 + bx + c = 0$, you can develop a formula that gives the solutions of *any* quadratic equation. (See Exercise 67.) The formula for the solutions is called the **quadratic formula**.

KEY CONCEPT *For Your Notebook*

The Quadratic Formula

Let a, b, and c be real numbers such that $a \neq 0$. The solutions of the quadratic equation $ax^2 + bx + c = 0$ are $x = \frac{-b \pm \sqrt{b^2 - 4ac}}{2a}$.

EXAMPLE 1 Solve an equation with two real solutions

Solve $x^2 + 3x = 2$.

$x^2 + 3x = 2$ — **Write original equation.**

$x^2 + 3x - 2 = 0$ — **Write in standard form.**

$x = \frac{-b \pm \sqrt{b^2 - 4ac}}{2a}$ — **Quadratic formula**

$x = \frac{-3 \pm \sqrt{3^2 - 4(1)(-2)}}{2(1)}$ — $a = 1, b = 3, c = -2$

$x = \frac{-3 \pm \sqrt{17}}{2}$ — **Simplify.**

AVOID ERRORS
Remember to write the quadratic equation in standard form before applying the quadratic formula.

▶ The solutions are $x = \frac{-3 + \sqrt{17}}{2} \approx 0.56$ and $x = \frac{-3 - \sqrt{17}}{2} \approx -3.56$.

CHECK Graph $y = x^2 + 3x - 2$ and note that the x-intercepts are about 0.56 and about -3.56. ✓

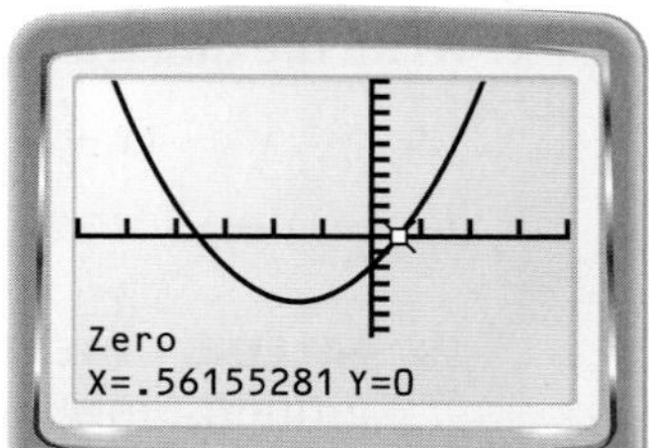

EXAMPLE 2 Solve an equation with one real solution

Solve $25x^2 - 18x = 12x - 9$.

> **ANOTHER WAY**
> You can also use factoring to solve this equation because the left side factors as $(5x - 3)^2$.

$25x^2 - 18x = 12x - 9$	**Write original equation.**
$25x^2 - 30x + 9 = 0$	**Write in standard form.**
$x = \frac{30 \pm \sqrt{(-30)^2 - 4(25)(9)}}{2(25)}$	**$a = 25$, $b = -30$, $c = 9$**
$x = \frac{30 \pm \sqrt{0}}{50}$	**Simplify.**
$x = \frac{3}{5}$	**Simplify.**

▶ The solution is $\frac{3}{5}$.

CHECK Graph $y = 25x^2 - 30x + 9$ and note that the only x-intercept is $0.6 = \frac{3}{5}$. ✓

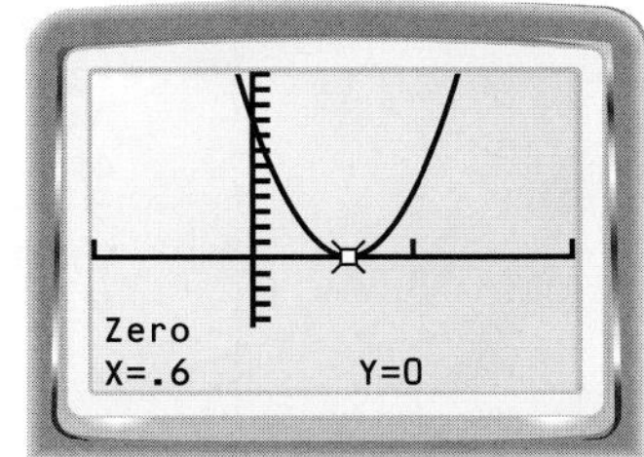

EXAMPLE 3 Solve an equation with imaginary solutions

Solve $-x^2 + 4x = 5$.

$-x^2 + 4x = 5$	**Write original equation.**
$-x^2 + 4x - 5 = 0$	**Write in standard form.**
$x = \frac{-4 \pm \sqrt{4^2 - 4(-1)(-5)}}{2(-1)}$	**$a = -1$, $b = 4$, $c = -5$**
$x = \frac{-4 \pm \sqrt{-4}}{-2}$	**Simplify.**
$x = \frac{-4 \pm 2i}{-2}$	**Rewrite using the imaginary unit *i*.**
$x = 2 \pm i$	**Simplify.**

▶ The solutions are $2 + i$ and $2 - i$.

CHECK Graph $y = -x^2 + 4x - 5$. There are no x-intercepts. So, the original equation has no real solutions. The algebraic check for the imaginary solution $2 + i$ is shown.

$$-(2 + i)^2 + 4(2 + i) \stackrel{?}{=} 5$$

$$-3 - 4i + 8 + 4i \stackrel{?}{=} 5$$

$$5 = 5 \checkmark$$

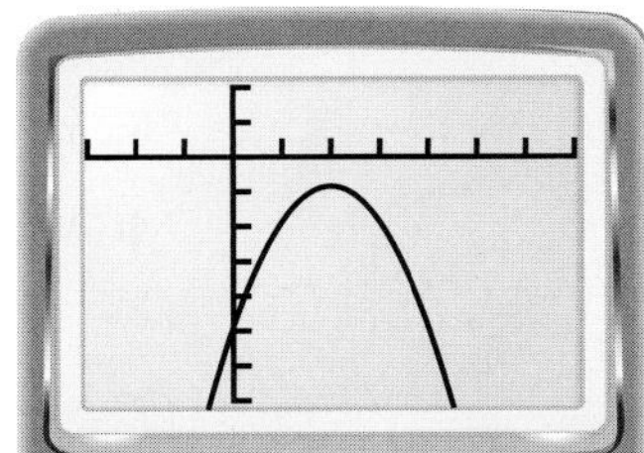

✓ GUIDED PRACTICE for Examples 1, 2, and 3

Use the quadratic formula to solve the equation.

1. $x^2 = 6x - 4$
2. $4x^2 - 10x = 2x - 9$
3. $7x - 5x^2 - 4 = 2x + 3$

DISCRIMINANT In the quadratic formula, the expression $b^2 - 4ac$ is called the **discriminant** of the associated equation $ax^2 + bx + c = 0$.

$$x = \frac{-b \pm \sqrt{b^2 - 4ac}}{2a}$$ ← discriminant

You can use the discriminant of a quadratic equation to determine the equation's number and type of solutions.

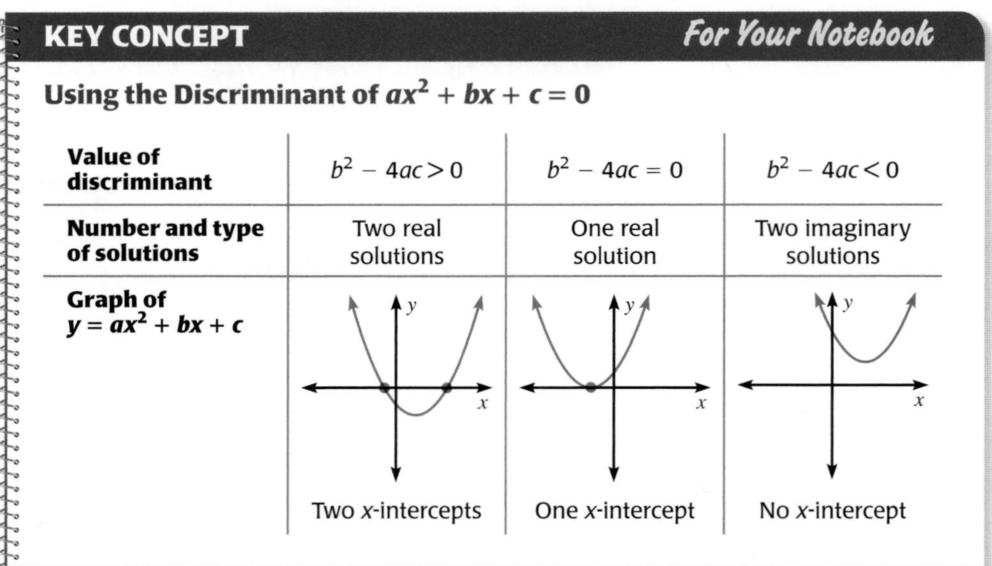

KEY CONCEPT *For Your Notebook*

Using the Discriminant of $ax^2 + bx + c = 0$

Value of discriminant	$b^2 - 4ac > 0$	$b^2 - 4ac = 0$	$b^2 - 4ac < 0$
Number and type of solutions	Two real solutions	One real solution	Two imaginary solutions
Graph of $y = ax^2 + bx + c$	Two x-intercepts	One x-intercept	No x-intercept

EXAMPLE 4 Use the discriminant

Find the discriminant of the quadratic equation and give the number and type of solutions of the equation.

a. $x^2 - 8x + 17 = 0$ **b.** $x^2 - 8x + 16 = 0$ **c.** $x^2 - 8x + 15 = 0$

Solution

Equation	**Discriminant**	**Solution(s)**
$ax^2 + bx + c = 0$	$b^2 - 4ac$	$x = \frac{-b \pm \sqrt{b^2 - 4ac}}{2a}$
a. $x^2 - 8x + 17 = 0$	$(-8)^2 - 4(1)(17) = -4$	Two imaginary: $4 \pm i$
b. $x^2 - 8x + 16 = 0$	$(-8)^2 - 4(1)(16) = 0$	One real: 4
c. $x^2 - 8x + 15 = 0$	$(-8)^2 - 4(1)(15) = 4$	Two real: 3, 5

✓ GUIDED PRACTICE for Example 4

Find the discriminant of the quadratic equation and give the number and type of solutions of the equation.

4. $2x^2 + 4x - 4 = 0$ **5.** $3x^2 + 12x + 12 = 0$ **6.** $8x^2 = 9x - 11$

7. $7x^2 - 2x = 5$ **8.** $4x^2 + 3x + 12 = 3 - 3x$ **9.** $3x - 5x^2 + 1 = 6 - 7x$

MODELING LAUNCHED OBJECTS In Lesson 4.5, the function $h = -16t^2 + h_0$ was used to model the height of a *dropped* object. For an object that is *launched or thrown*, an extra term v_0t must be added to the model to account for the object's initial vertical velocity v_0 (in feet per second). Recall that h is the height (in feet), t is the time in motion (in seconds), and h_0 is the initial height (in feet).

$h = -16t^2 + h_0$ **Object is dropped.**

$h = -16t^2 + v_0t + h_0$ **Object is launched or thrown.**

As shown below, the value of v_0 can be positive, negative, or zero depending on whether the object is launched upward, downward, or parallel to the ground.

$v_0 > 0$ $v_0 < 0$ $v_0 = 0$

EXAMPLE 5 Solve a vertical motion problem

JUGGLING A juggler tosses a ball into the air. The ball leaves the juggler's hand 4 feet above the ground and has an initial vertical velocity of 40 feet per second. The juggler catches the ball when it falls back to a height of 3 feet. How long is the ball in the air?

Solution

Because the ball is thrown, use the model $h = -16t^2 + v_0t + h_0$. To find how long the ball is in the air, solve for t when $h = 3$.

$h = -16t^2 + v_0t + h_0$ **Write height model.**

$3 = -16t^2 + 40t + 4$ **Substitute 3 for *h*, 40 for v_0, and 4 for h_0.**

$0 = -16t^2 + 40t + 1$ **Write in standard form.**

$t = \frac{-40 \pm \sqrt{40^2 - 4(-16)(1)}}{2(-16)}$ **Quadratic formula**

$t = \frac{-40 \pm \sqrt{1664}}{-32}$ **Simplify.**

$t \approx -0.025$ or $t \approx 2.5$ **Use a calculator.**

▶ Reject the solution -0.025 because the ball's time in the air cannot be negative. So, the ball is in the air for about 2.5 seconds.

GUIDED PRACTICE for Example 5

10. WHAT IF? In Example 5, suppose the ball leaves the juggler's hand with an initial vertical velocity of 50 feet per second. How long is the ball in the air?

4.8 EXERCISES

HOMEWORK KEY

○ = **WORKED-OUT SOLUTIONS** on p. WS9 for Exs. 19, 39, and 71

★ = **STANDARDIZED TEST PRACTICE** Exs. 2, 12, 51, 55, 62, 69, 72, and 73

SKILL PRACTICE

1. **VOCABULARY** Copy and complete: You can use the __?__ of a quadratic equation to determine the equation's number and type of solutions.

2. ★ **WRITING** *Describe* a real-life situation in which you can use the model $h = -16t^2 + v_0t + h_0$ but not the model $h = -16t^2 + h_0$.

EXAMPLES 1, 2, and 3 on pp. 292–293 for Exs. 3–30

EQUATIONS IN STANDARD FORM **Use the quadratic formula to solve the equation.**

3. $x^2 - 4x - 5 = 0$
4. $x^2 - 6x + 7 = 0$
5. $t^2 + 8t + 19 = 0$
6. $x^2 - 16x + 7 = 0$
7. $8w^2 - 8w + 2 = 0$
8. $5p^2 - 10p + 24 = 0$
9. $4x^2 - 8x + 1 = 0$
10. $6u^2 + 4u + 11 = 0$
11. $3r^2 - 8r - 9 = 0$

12. ★ **MULTIPLE CHOICE** What are the complex solutions of the equation $2x^2 - 16x + 50 = 0$?

Ⓐ $4 + 3i, 4 - 3i$ Ⓑ $4 + 12i, 4 - 12i$

Ⓒ $16 + 3i, 16 - 3i$ Ⓓ $16 + 12i, 16 - 12i$

EQUATIONS NOT IN STANDARD FORM **Use the quadratic formula to solve the equation.**

13. $3w^2 - 12w = -12$
14. $x^2 + 6x = -15$
15. $s^2 = -14 - 3s$
16. $-3y^2 = 6y - 10$
17. $3 - 8v - 5v^2 = 2v$
18. $7x - 5 + 12x^2 = -3x$
19. $4x^2 + 3 = x^2 - 7x$
20. $6 - 2t^2 = 9t + 15$
21. $4 + 9n - 3n^2 = 2 - n$

SOLVING USING TWO METHODS **Solve the equation using the quadratic formula. Then solve the equation by factoring to check your solution(s).**

22. $z^2 + 15z + 24 = -32$
23. $x^2 - 5x + 10 = 4$
24. $m^2 + 5m - 99 = 3m$
25. $s^2 - s - 3 = s$
26. $r^2 - 4r + 8 = 5r$
27. $3x^2 + 7x - 24 = 13x$
28. $45x^2 + 57x + 1 = 5$
29. $5p^2 + 40p + 100 = 25$
30. $9n^2 - 42n - 162 = 21n$

EXAMPLE 4 on p. 294 for Exs. 31–39

USING THE DISCRIMINANT **Find the discriminant of the quadratic equation and give the number and type of solutions of the equation.**

31. $x^2 - 8x + 16 = 0$
32. $s^2 + 7s + 11 = 0$
33. $8p^2 + 8p + 3 = 0$
34. $-4w^2 + w - 14 = 0$
35. $5x^2 + 20x + 21 = 0$
36. $8z - 10 = z^2 - 7z + 3$
37. $8n^2 - 4n + 2 = 5n - 11$
38. $5x^2 + 16x = 11x - 3x^2$
39. $7r^2 - 5 = 2r + 9r^2$

SOLVING QUADRATIC EQUATIONS **Solve the equation using any method.**

40. $16t^2 - 7t = 17t - 9$
41. $7x - 3x^2 = 85 + 2x^2 + 2x$
42. $4(x - 1)^2 = 6x + 2$
43. $25 - 16v^2 = 12v(v + 5)$
44. $\frac{3}{2}y^2 - 6y = \frac{3}{4}y - 9$
45. $3x^2 + \frac{9}{2}x - 4 = 5x + \frac{3}{4}$
46. $1.1(3.4x - 2.3)^2 = 15.5$
47. $19.25 = -8.5(2r - 1.75)^2$
48. $4.5 = 1.5(3.25 - s)^2$

ERROR ANALYSIS ***Describe* and correct the error in solving the equation.**

49.

$$3x^2 + 6x + 15 = 0$$
$$x = \frac{-6 \pm \sqrt{6^2 - 4(3)(15)}}{2(3)}$$
$$= \frac{-6 \pm \sqrt{-144}}{6}$$
$$= \frac{-6 \pm 12}{6}$$
$$= 1 \text{ or } -3$$

50.

$$x^2 + 6x + 8 = 2$$
$$x = \frac{-6 \pm \sqrt{6^2 - 4(1)(8)}}{2(1)}$$
$$= \frac{-6 \pm \sqrt{4}}{2}$$
$$= \frac{-6 \pm 2}{2}$$
$$= -2 \text{ or } -4$$

51. ★ **SHORT RESPONSE** For a quadratic equation $ax^2 + bx + c = 0$ with two real solutions, show that the mean of the solutions is $-\frac{b}{2a}$. How is this fact related to the symmetry of the graph of $y = ax^2 + bx + c$?

VISUAL THINKING **In Exercises 52–54, the graph of a quadratic function $y = ax^2 + bx + c$ is shown. Tell whether the discriminant of $ax^2 + bx + c = 0$ is *positive, negative,* or *zero.***

52.

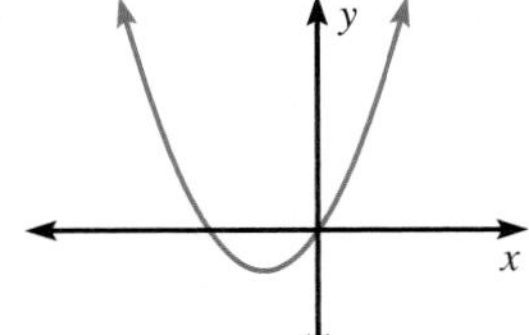

53.

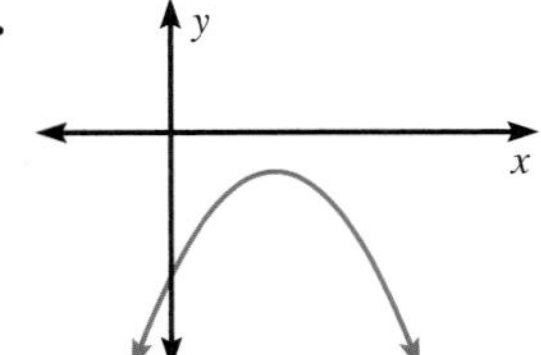

54.

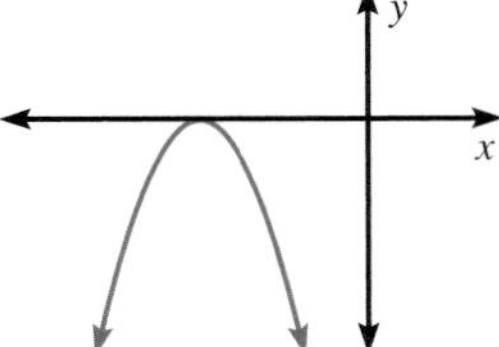

55. ★ **MULTIPLE CHOICE** What is the value of c if the discriminant of $2x^2 + 5x + c = 0$ is -23?

Ⓐ -23　　Ⓑ -6　　Ⓒ 6　　Ⓓ 14

THE CONSTANT TERM **Use the discriminant to find all values of c for which the equation has (a) two real solutions, (b) one real solution, and (c) two imaginary solutions.**

56. $x^2 - 4x + c = 0$

57. $x^2 + 8x + c = 0$

58. $-x^2 + 16x + c = 0$

59. $3x^2 + 24x + c = 0$

60. $-4x^2 - 10x + c = 0$

61. $x^2 - x + c = 0$

62. ★ **OPEN-ENDED MATH** Write a quadratic equation in standard form that has a discriminant of -10.

WRITING EQUATIONS **Write a quadratic equation in the form $ax^2 + bx + c = 0$ such that $c = 4$ and the equation has the given solutions.**

63. -4 and 3

64. $-\frac{4}{3}$ and -1

65. $-1 + i$ and $-1 - i$

66. **REASONING** Show that there is no quadratic equation $ax^2 + bx + c = 0$ such that a, b, and c are real numbers and $3i$ and $-2i$ are solutions.

67. **CHALLENGE** Derive the quadratic formula by completing the square to solve the general quadratic equation $ax^2 + bx + c = 0$.

PROBLEM SOLVING

EXAMPLE 5 on p. 295 for Exs. 68–69

68. FOOTBALL In a football game, a defensive player jumps up to block a pass by the opposing team's quarterback. The player bats the ball downward with his hand at an initial vertical velocity of -50 feet per second when the ball is 7 feet above the ground. How long do the defensive player's teammates have to intercept the ball before it hits the ground?

@HomeTutor for problem solving help at classzone.com

69. ★ **MULTIPLE CHOICE** For the period 1990–2002, the number S (in thousands) of cellular telephone subscribers in the United States can be modeled by $S = 858t^2 + 1412t + 4982$ where t is the number of years since 1990. In what year did the number of subscribers reach 50 million?

(A) 1991 (B) 1992 (C) 1996 (D) 2000

@HomeTutor for problem solving help at classzone.com

70. MULTI-STEP PROBLEM A stunt motorcyclist makes a jump from one ramp 20 feet off the ground to another ramp 20 feet off the ground. The jump between the ramps can be modeled by $y = -\frac{1}{640}x^2 + \frac{1}{4}x + 20$ where x is the horizontal distance (in feet) and y is the height above the ground (in feet).

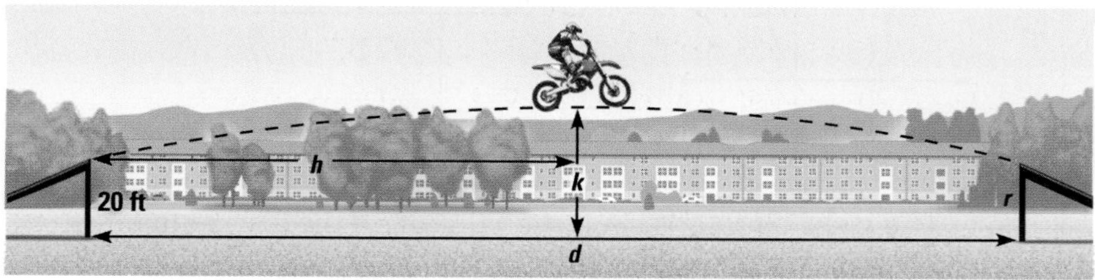

a. What is the motorcycle's height r when it lands on the ramp?

b. What is the distance d between the ramps?

c. What is the horizontal distance h the motorcycle has traveled when it reaches its maximum height?

d. What is the motorcycle's maximum height k above the ground?

71. BIOLOGY The number S of ant species in Kyle Canyon, Nevada, can be modeled by the function $S = -0.000013E^2 + 0.042E - 21$ where E is the elevation (in meters). Predict the elevation(s) at which you would expect to find 10 species of ants.

72. ★ **SHORT RESPONSE** A city planner wants to create adjacent sections for athletics and picnics in the yard of a youth center. The sections will be rectangular and will be surrounded by fencing as shown. There is 900 feet of fencing available. Each section should have an area of 12,000 square feet.

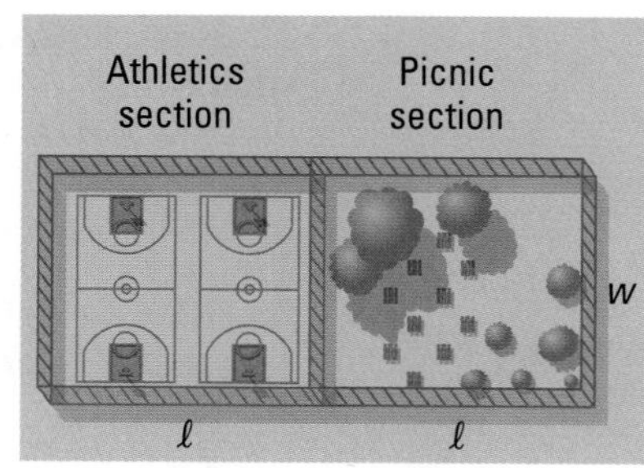

a. Show that $w = 300 - \frac{4}{3}\ell$.

b. Find the possible dimensions of each section.

○ = WORKED-OUT SOLUTIONS on p. WS1

★ = STANDARDIZED TEST PRACTICE

73. ★ **EXTENDED RESPONSE** You can model the position (x, y) of a moving object using a pair of *parametric equations*. Such equations give x and y in terms of a third variable t that represents time. For example, suppose that when a basketball player attempts a free throw, the path of the basketball can be modeled by the parametric equations

$$x = 20t$$

$$y = -16t^2 + 21t + 6$$

where x and y are measured in feet, t is measured in seconds, and the player's feet are at (0, 0).

a. Evaluate Make a table of values giving the position (x, y) of the basketball after 0, 0.25, 0.5, 0.75, and 1 second.

b. Graph Use your table from part (a) to graph the parametric equations.

c. Solve The position of the basketball rim is (15, 10). The top of the backboard is (15, 12). Does the player make the free throw? *Explain.*

74. CHALLENGE The Stratosphere Tower in Las Vegas is 921 feet tall and has a "needle" at its top that extends even higher into the air. A thrill ride called the Big Shot catapults riders 160 feet up the needle and then lets them fall back to the launching pad.

a. The height h (in feet) of a rider on the Big Shot can be modeled by $h = -16t^2 + v_0t + 921$ where t is the elapsed time (in seconds) after launch and v_0 is the initial vertical velocity (in feet per second). Find v_0 using the fact that the maximum value of h is $921 + 160 = 1081$ feet.

b. A brochure for the Big Shot states that the ride up the needle takes two seconds. *Compare* this time with the time given by the model $h = -16t^2 + v_0t + 921$ where v_0 is the value you found in part (a). Discuss the model's accuracy.

New York Mixed Review

TEST PRACTICE at classzone.com

75. In the figure shown, $\overline{AB}$ is parallel to $\overline{ED}$. Which equation can be used to find the value of x?

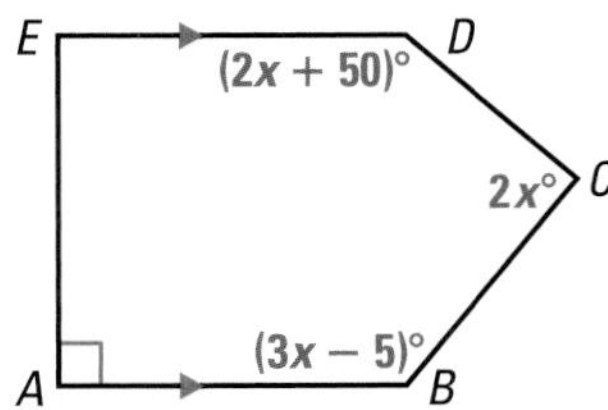

(A) $5x + 225 = 360$ (B) $5x + 235 = 540$

(C) $7x + 235 = 360$ (D) $7x + 225 = 540$

76. Music recital tickets are \$4 for students and \$6 for adults. A total of 725 tickets are sold and \$3650 is collected. Which pair of equations can be used to determine the number of students, s, and the number of adults, a, who attended the music recital?

(A) $s + a = 725$
$4s + 6a = 3650$

(B) $s + a = 725$
$6s + 4a = 3650$

(C) $s - a = 725$
$4s - 6a = 3650$

(D) $4s + 6a = 725$
$s + a = 3650$

4.9 Graph and Solve Quadratic Inequalities

A2.A.4 Solve quadratic inequalities in one and two variables, algebraically and graphically

Before You graphed and solved linear inequalities.

Now You will graph and solve quadratic inequalities.

Why? So you can model the strength of a rope, as in Example 2.

Key Vocabulary
- **quadratic inequality in two variables**
- **quadratic inequality in one variable**

A **quadratic inequality in two variables** can be written in one of the following forms:

$y < ax^2 + bx + c$ $\quad$ $y \leq ax^2 + bx + c$ $\quad$ $y > ax^2 + bx + c$ $\quad$ $y \geq ax^2 + bx + c$

The graph of any such inequality consists of all solutions (x, y) of the inequality.

KEY CONCEPT *For Your Notebook*

Graphing a Quadratic Inequality in Two Variables

To graph a quadratic inequality in one of the forms above, follow these steps:

STEP 1 **Graph** the parabola with equation $y = ax^2 + bx + c$. Make the parabola *dashed* for inequalities with < or > and *solid* for inequalities with ≤ or ≥.

STEP 2 **Test** a point (x, y) inside the parabola to determine whether the point is a solution of the inequality.

STEP 3 **Shade** the region inside the parabola if the point from Step 2 is a solution. Shade the region outside the parabola if it is not a solution.

EXAMPLE 1 Graph a quadratic inequality

Graph $y > x^2 + 3x - 4$.

Solution

AVOID ERRORS
Be sure to use a dashed parabola if the symbol is > or < and a solid parabola if the symbol is ≥ or ≤.

STEP 1 **Graph** $y = x^2 + 3x - 4$. Because the inequality symbol is >, make the parabola dashed.

STEP 2 **Test** a point inside the parabola, such as (0, 0).

$$y > x^2 + 3x - 4$$
$$0 \overset{?}{>} 0^2 + 3(0) - 4$$
$$0 > -4 \checkmark$$

So, (0, 0) is a solution of the inequality.

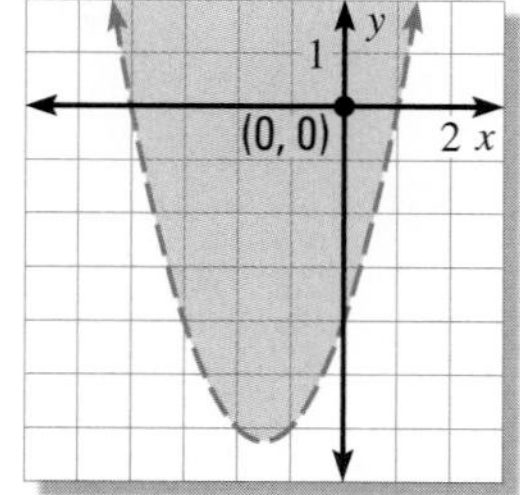

STEP 3 **Shade** the region inside the parabola.

at classzone.com

EXAMPLE 2 Use a quadratic inequality in real life

RAPPELLING A manila rope used for rappelling down a cliff can safely support a weight W (in pounds) provided

$$W \leq 1480d^2$$

where d is the rope's diameter (in inches). Graph the inequality.

Solution

Graph $W = 1480d^2$ for nonnegative values of d. Because the inequality symbol is $\leq$, make the parabola solid. Test a point inside the parabola, such as (1, 2000).

$$W \leq 1480d^2$$

$$2000 \stackrel{?}{\leq} 1480(1)^2$$

$$2000 \leq 1480 \text{ ✗}$$

Because (1, 2000) is not a solution, shade the region below the parabola.

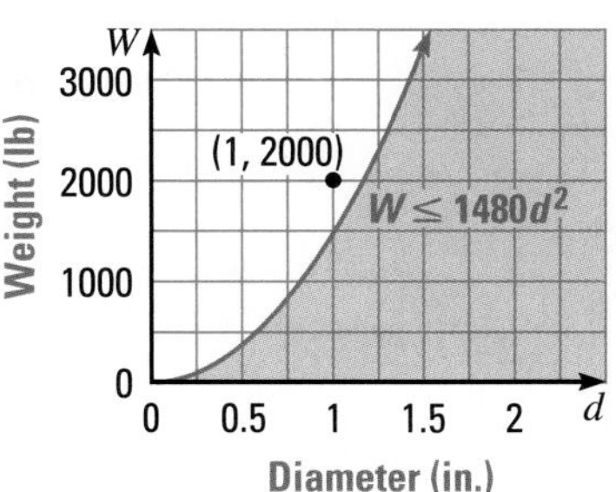

SYSTEMS OF QUADRATIC INEQUALITIES Graphing a *system* of quadratic inequalities is similar to graphing a system of linear inequalities. First graph each inequality in the system. Then identify the region in the coordinate plane common to all of the graphs. This region is called the *graph of the system.*

EXAMPLE 3 Graph a system of quadratic inequalities

Graph the system of quadratic inequalities.

$y \leq -x^2 + 4$ **Inequality 1**
$y > x^2 - 2x - 3$ **Inequality 2**

Solution

STEP 1 **Graph** $y \leq -x^2 + 4$. The graph is the red region inside and including the parabola $y = -x^2 + 4$.

STEP 2 **Graph** $y > x^2 - 2x - 3$. The graph is the blue region inside (but not including) the parabola $y = x^2 - 2x - 3$.

STEP 3 **Identify** the **purple region** where the two graphs overlap. This region is the graph of the system.

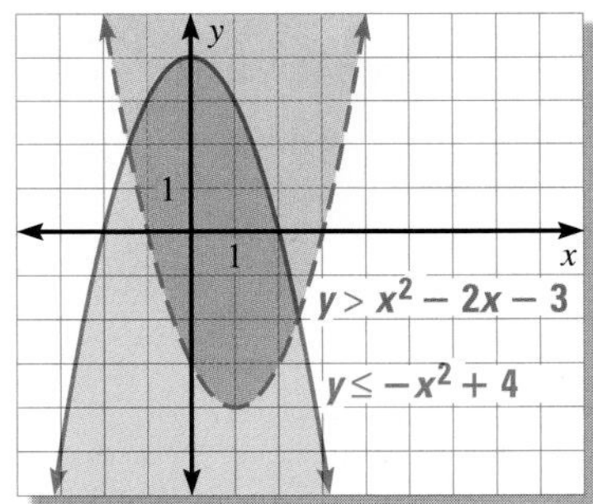

GUIDED PRACTICE for Examples 1, 2, and 3

Graph the inequality.

1. $y > x^2 + 2x - 8$
2. $y \leq 2x^2 - 3x + 1$
3. $y < -x^2 + 4x + 2$
4. Graph the system of inequalities consisting of $y \geq x^2$ and $y < -x^2 + 5$.

ONE-VARIABLE INEQUALITIES A **quadratic inequality in one variable** can be written in one of the following forms:

$ax^2 + bx + c < 0 \qquad ax^2 + bx + c \le 0 \qquad ax^2 + bx + c > 0 \qquad ax^2 + bx + c \ge 0$

You can solve quadratic inequalities using tables, graphs, or algebraic methods.

EXAMPLE 4 Solve a quadratic inequality using a table

Solve $x^2 + x \le 6$ using a table.

Solution

Rewrite the inequality as $x^2 + x - 6 \le 0$. Then make a table of values.

MAKE A TABLE
To give the exact solution, your table needs to include the *x*-values for which the value of the quadratic expression is 0.

x	−5	−4	−3	−2	−1	0	1	2	3	4
$x^2 + x - 6$	14	6	0	−4	−6	−6	−4	0	6	14

Notice that $x^2 + x - 6 \le 0$ when the values of x are between −3 and 2, inclusive.

▶ The solution of the inequality is $-3 \le x \le 2$.

GRAPHING TO SOLVE INEQUALITIES Another way to solve $ax^2 + bx + c < 0$ is to first graph the related function $y = ax^2 + bx + c$. Then, because the inequality symbol is <, identify the *x*-values for which the graph lies *below* the *x*-axis. You can use a similar procedure to solve quadratic inequalities that involve ≤, >, or ≥.

EXAMPLE 5 Solve a quadratic inequality by graphing

Solve $2x^2 + x - 4 \ge 0$ by graphing.

Solution

The solution consists of the *x*-values for which the graph of $y = 2x^2 + x - 4$ lies on or above the *x*-axis. Find the graph's *x*-intercepts by letting $y = 0$ and using the quadratic formula to solve for x.

$0 = 2x^2 + x - 4$

$x = \dfrac{-1 \pm \sqrt{1^2 - 4(2)(-4)}}{2(2)}$

$x = \dfrac{-1 \pm \sqrt{33}}{4}$

$x \approx 1.19$ or $x \approx -1.69$

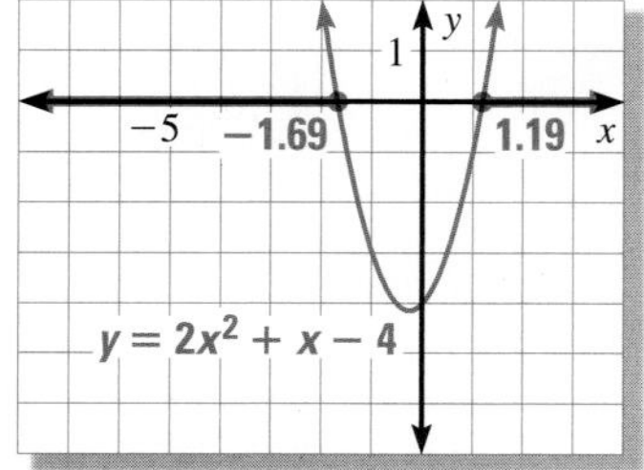

Sketch a parabola that opens up and has 1.19 and −1.69 as *x*-intercepts. The graph lies on or above the *x*-axis to the left of (and including) $x = -1.69$ and to the right of (and including) $x = 1.19$.

▶ The solution of the inequality is approximately $x \le -1.69$ or $x \ge 1.19$.

✓ **GUIDED PRACTICE** for Examples 4 and 5

5. Solve the inequality $2x^2 + 2x \le 3$ using a table and using a graph.

EXAMPLE 6 Use a quadratic inequality as a model

ROBOTICS The number T of teams that have participated in a robot-building competition for high school students can be modeled by

$$T(x) = 7.51x^2 - 16.4x + 35.0,\ 0 \le x \le 9$$

where x is the number of years since 1992. For what years was the number of teams greater than 100?

Solution

You want to find the values of x for which:

$$T(x) > 100$$

$$7.51x^2 - 16.4x + 35.0 > 100$$

$$7.51x^2 - 16.4x - 65 > 0$$

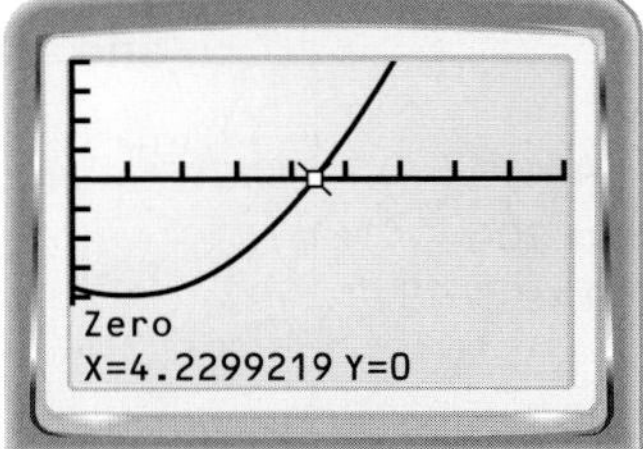

Graph $y = 7.51x^2 - 16.4x - 65$ on the domain $0 \le x \le 9$. The graph's x-intercept is about 4.2. The graph lies above the x-axis when $4.2 < x \le 9$.

▶ There were more than 100 teams participating in the years 1997–2001.

EXAMPLE 7 Solve a quadratic inequality algebraically

Solve $x^2 - 2x > 15$ algebraically.

Solution

First, write and solve the equation obtained by replacing $>$ with $=$.

$x^2 - 2x = 15$	**Write equation that corresponds to original inequality.**
$x^2 - 2x - 15 = 0$	**Write in standard form.**
$(x + 3)(x - 5) = 0$	**Factor.**
$x = -3$ or $x = 5$	**Zero product property**

The numbers -3 and 5 are the *critical x-values* of the inequality $x^2 - 2x > 15$. Plot -3 and 5 on a number line, using open dots because the values do not satisfy the inequality. The critical x-values partition the number line into three intervals. Test an x-value in each interval to see if it satisfies the inequality.

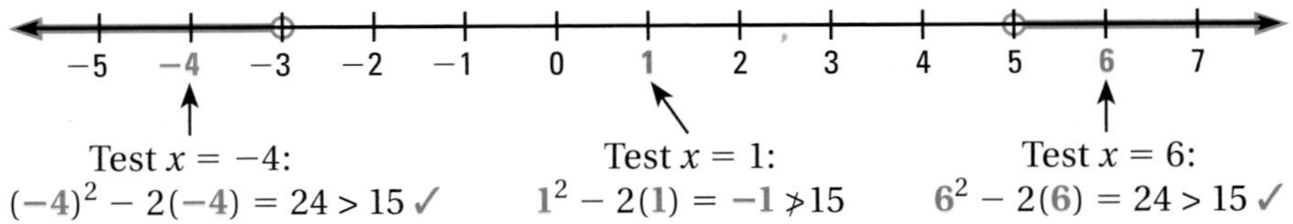

Test $x = -4$: $(-4)^2 - 2(-4) = 24 > 15$ ✓

Test $x = 1$: $1^2 - 2(1) = -1 \not> 15$

Test $x = 6$: $6^2 - 2(6) = 24 > 15$ ✓

▶ The solution is $x < -3$ or $x > 5$.

✓ GUIDED PRACTICE for Examples 6 and 7

6. **ROBOTICS** Use the information in Example 6 to determine in what years at least 200 teams participated in the robot-building competition.
7. Solve the inequality $2x^2 - 7x > 4$ algebraically.

4.9 EXERCISES

HOMEWORK KEY

○ = **WORKED-OUT SOLUTIONS** on p. WS9 for Exs. 17, 39, and 73

★ = **STANDARDIZED TEST PRACTICE** Exs. 2, 44, 45, 68, and 73

◆ = **MULTIPLE REPRESENTATIONS** Ex. 74

SKILL PRACTICE

1. **VOCABULARY** Give an example of a quadratic inequality in one variable and an example of a quadratic inequality in two variables.

2. ★ **WRITING** *Explain* how to solve $x^2 + 6x - 8 < 0$ using a table, by graphing, and algebraically.

EXAMPLE 1 on p. 300 for Exs. 3–19

MATCHING INEQUALITIES WITH GRAPHS **Match the inequality with its graph.**

3. $y \le x^2 + 4x + 3$

4. $y > -x^2 + 4x - 3$

5. $y < x^2 - 4x + 3$

A. 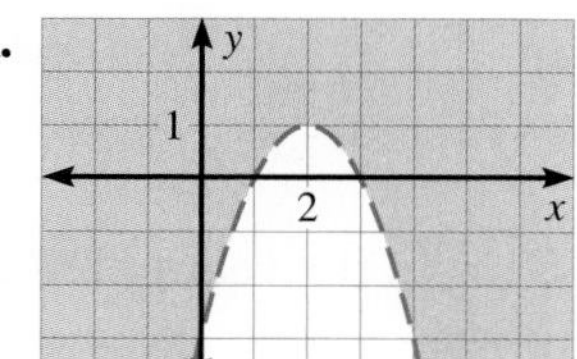

B. 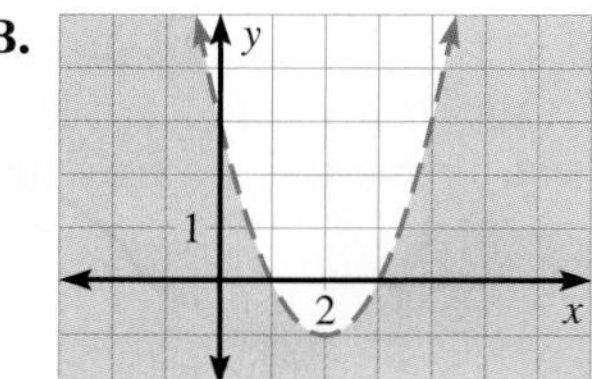

C. 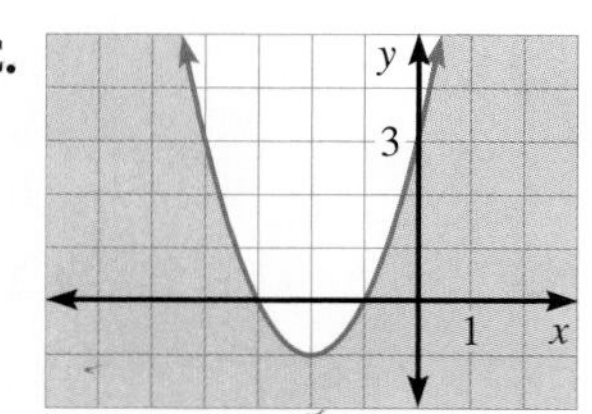

GRAPHING QUADRATIC INEQUALITIES **Graph the inequality.**

6. $y < -x^2$

7. $y \ge 4x^2$

8. $y > x^2 - 9$

9. $y \le x^2 + 5x$

10. $y < x^2 + 4x - 5$

11. $y > x^2 + 7x + 12$

12. $y \le -x^2 + 3x + 10$

13. $y \ge 2x^2 + 5x - 7$

14. $y \ge -2x^2 + 9x - 4$

15. $y < 4x^2 - 3x - 5$

16. $y > 0.1x^2 - x + 1.2$

17. $y \le -\frac{2}{3}x^2 + 3x + 1$

ERROR ANALYSIS **Describe and correct the error in graphing $y \ge x^2 + 2$.**

18. 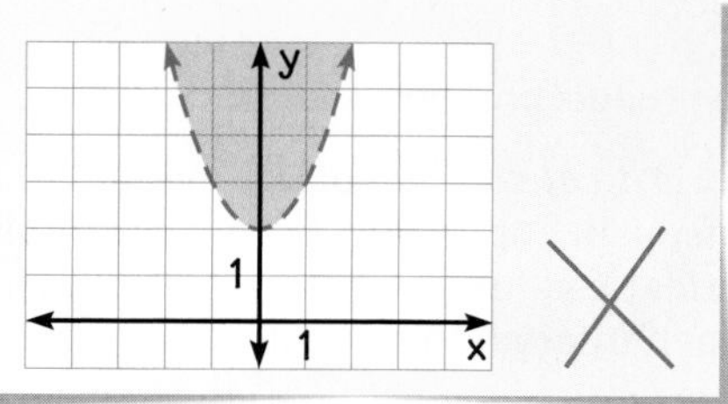

19. 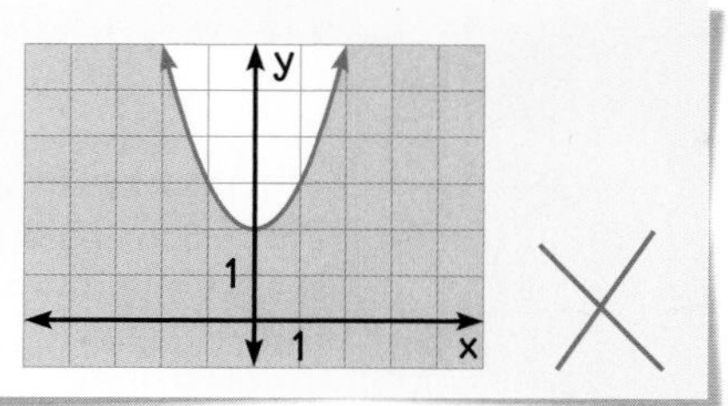

EXAMPLE 3 on p. 301 for Exs. 20–25

GRAPHING SYSTEMS **Graph the system of inequalities.**

20. $y \ge 2x^2$
    $y < -x^2 + 1$

21. $y > -5x^2$
    $y > 3x^2 - 2$

22. $y \ge x^2 - 4$
    $y \le -2x^2 + 7x + 4$

23. $y \le -x^2 + 4x - 4$
    $y < 2x^2 + x - 8$

24. $y > 3x^2 + 3x - 5$
    $y < -x^2 + 5x + 10$

25. $y \ge x^2 - 3x - 6$
    $y \ge 2x^2 + 7x + 6$

EXAMPLE 4 on p. 302 for Exs. 26–34

SOLVING USING A TABLE **Solve the inequality using a table.**

26. $x^2 - 5x < 0$

27. $x^2 + 2x - 3 > 0$

28. $x^2 + 3x \le 10$

29. $x^2 - 2x \ge 8$

30. $-x^2 + 15x - 50 > 0$

31. $x^2 - 10x < -16$

32. $x^2 - 4x > 12$

33. $3x^2 - 6x - 2 \le 7$

34. $2x^2 - 6x - 9 \ge 11$

EXAMPLE 5 on p. 302 for Exs. 35–43

SOLVING BY GRAPHING **Solve the inequality by graphing.**

35. $x^2 - 6x < 0$

36. $x^2 + 8x \leq -7$

37. $x^2 - 4x + 2 > 0$

38. $x^2 + 6x + 3 > 0$

39. $3x^2 + 2x - 8 \leq 0$

40. $3x^2 + 5x - 3 < 1$

41. $-6x^2 + 19x \geq 10$

42. $-\frac{1}{2}x^2 + 4x \geq 1$

43. $4x^2 - 10x - 7 < 10$

44. ★ **MULTIPLE CHOICE** What is the solution of $3x^2 - x - 4 > 0$?

(A) $x < -1$ or $x > \frac{4}{3}$

(B) $-1 < x < \frac{4}{3}$

(C) $x < -\frac{4}{3}$ or $x > 1$

(D) $1 < x < \frac{4}{3}$

45. ★ **MULTIPLE CHOICE** What is the solution of $2x^2 + 9x \leq 56$?

(A) $x \leq -8$ or $x \geq 3.5$

(B) $-8 \leq x \leq 3.5$

(C) $x \leq 0$ or $x \geq 4.5$

(D) $0 \leq x \leq 4.5$

EXAMPLE 7 on p. 303 for Exs. 46–57

SOLVING ALGEBRAICALLY **Solve the inequality algebraically.**

46. $4x^2 < 25$

47. $x^2 + 10x + 9 < 0$

48. $x^2 - 11x \geq -28$

49. $3x^2 - 13x > 10$

50. $2x^2 - 5x - 3 \leq 0$

51. $4x^2 + 8x - 21 \geq 0$

52. $-4x^2 - x + 3 \leq 0$

53. $5x^2 - 6x - 2 \leq 0$

54. $-3x^2 + 10x > -2$

55. $-2x^2 - 7x \geq 4$

56. $3x^2 + 1 < 15x$

57. $6x^2 - 5 > 8x$

58. **GRAPHING CALCULATOR** In this exercise, you will use a different graphical method to solve Example 6 on page 303.

a. Enter the equations $y = 7.51x^2 - 16.4x + 35.0$ and $y = 100$ into a graphing calculator.

b. Graph the equations from part (a) for $0 \leq x \leq 9$ and $0 \leq y \leq 300$.

c. Use the *intersect* feature to find the point where the graphs intersect.

d. During what years was the number of participating teams greater than 100? *Explain* your reasoning.

CHOOSING A METHOD **Solve the inequality using any method.**

59. $8x^2 - 3x + 1 < 10$

60. $4x^2 + 11x + 3 \geq -3$

61. $-x^2 - 2x - 1 > 2$

62. $-3x^2 + 4x - 5 \leq 2$

63. $x^2 - 7x + 4 > 5x - 2$

64. $2x^2 + 9x - 1 \geq -3x + 1$

65. $3x^2 - 2x + 1 \leq -x^2 + 1$

66. $5x^2 + x - 7 < 3x^2 - 4x$

67. $6x^2 - 5x + 2 < -3x^2 + x$

68. ★ **OPEN-ENDED MATH** Write a quadratic inequality in one variable that has a solution of $x < -2$ or $x > 5$.

69. **CHALLENGE** The area A of the region bounded by a parabola and a horizontal line is given by $A = \frac{2}{3}bh$ where b and h are as defined in the diagram. Find the area of the region determined by each pair of inequalities.

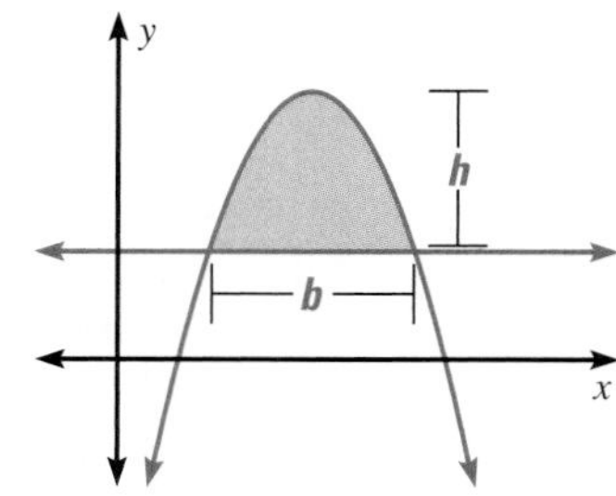

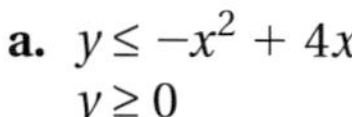

a. $y \leq -x^2 + 4x$
$y \geq 0$

b. $y \geq x^2 - 4x - 5$
$y \leq 3$

PROBLEM SOLVING

EXAMPLE 2 on p. 301 for Exs. 70–71

70. **ENGINEERING** A wire rope can safely support a weight W (in pounds) provided $W \le 8000d^2$ where d is the rope's diameter (in inches). Graph the inequality.

    @HomeTutor for problem solving help at classzone.com

71. **WOODWORKING** A hardwood shelf in a wooden bookcase can safely support a weight W (in pounds) provided $W \le 115x^2$ where x is the shelf's thickness (in inches). Graph the inequality.

    @HomeTutor for problem solving help at classzone.com

EXAMPLE 6 on p. 303 for Exs. 72–74

72. **ARCHITECTURE** The arch of the Sydney Harbor Bridge in Sydney, Australia, can be modeled by $y = -0.00211x^2 + 1.06x$ where x is the distance (in meters) from the left pylons and y is the height (in meters) of the arch above the water. For what distances x is the arch above the road?

73. ★ **SHORT RESPONSE** The length L (in millimeters) of the larvae of the black porgy fish can be modeled by

$$L(x) = 0.00170x^2 + 0.145x + 2.35,\ 0 \le x \le 40$$

where x is the age (in days) of the larvae. Write and solve an inequality to find at what ages a larvae's length tends to be greater than 10 millimeters. *Explain* how the given domain affects the solution.

74. **MULTIPLE REPRESENTATIONS** A study found that a driver's reaction time $A(x)$ to audio stimuli and his or her reaction time $V(x)$ to visual stimuli (both in milliseconds) can be modeled by

$$A(x) = 0.0051x^2 - 0.319x + 15,\ 16 \le x \le 70$$

$$V(x) = 0.005x^2 - 0.23x + 22,\ 16 \le x \le 70$$

where x is the driver's age (in years).

a. **Writing an Inequality** Write an inequality that you can use to find the x-values for which $A(x)$ is less than $V(x)$.

b. **Making a Table** Use a table to find the solution of the inequality from part (a). Your table should contain x-values from 16 to 70 in increments of 6.

c. **Drawing a Graph** Check the solution you found in part (b) by using a graphing calculator to solve the inequality $A(x) < V(x)$ graphically. *Describe* how you used the domain $16 \le x \le 70$ to determine a reasonable solution.

d. **Interpret** Based on your results from parts (b) and (c), do you think a driver would react more quickly to a traffic light changing from green to yellow or to the siren of an approaching ambulance? *Explain.*

75. SOCCER The path of a soccer ball kicked from the ground can be modeled by

$$y = -0.0540x^2 + 1.43x$$

where x is the horizontal distance (in feet) from where the ball was kicked and y is the corresponding height (in feet).

a. A soccer goal is 8 feet high. Write and solve an inequality to find at what values of x the ball is low enough to go into the goal.

b. A soccer player kicks the ball toward the goal from a distance of 15 feet away. No one is blocking the goal. Will the player score a goal? *Explain* your reasoning.

76. MULTI-STEP PROBLEM A truck that is 11 feet tall and 7 feet wide is traveling under an arch. The arch can be modeled by

$$y = -0.0625x^2 + 1.25x + 5.75$$

where x and y are measured in feet.

a. Will the truck fit under the arch? *Explain* your reasoning.

b. What is the maximum width that a truck 11 feet tall can have and still make it under the arch?

c. What is the maximum height that a truck 7 feet wide can have and still make it under the arch?

77. CHALLENGE For clear blue ice on lakes and ponds, the maximum weight w (in tons) that the ice can support is given by

$$w(x) = 0.1x^2 - 0.5x - 5$$

where x is the thickness of the ice (in inches).

a. Calculate What thicknesses of ice can support a weight of 20 tons?

b. Interpret *Explain* how you can use the graph of $w(x)$ to determine the minimum x-value in the domain for which the function gives meaningful results.

NEW YORK MIXED REVIEW

TEST PRACTICE at classzone.com

78. Rachel is a cross-country runner. Her coach recorded the data shown at the right during a timed practice run. If Rachel continues to run at the same rate, what is the approximate distance she will run in 25 minutes?

Time (minutes)	Distance (kilometers)
6	1.2
12	2.4
15	3

Ⓐ 4.2 km   Ⓑ 5 km

Ⓒ 6 km   Ⓓ 10 km

79. Which set of dimensions corresponds to a pyramid similar to the one shown?

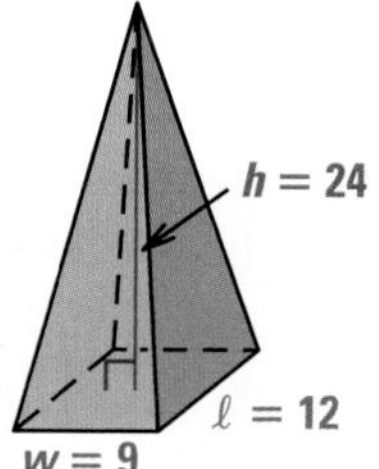

Ⓐ $w = 1$ unit, $\ell = 2$ units, $h = 4$ units

Ⓑ $w = 2$ units, $\ell = 3$ units, $h = 6$ units

Ⓒ $w = 3$ units, $\ell = 4$ units, $h = 8$ units

Ⓓ $w = 4$ units, $\ell = 6$ units, $h = 12$ units

Investigating Algebra ACTIVITY *Use before Lesson 4.10*

@HomeTutor classzone.com Keystrokes

4.10 Modeling Data with a Quadratic Function

MATERIALS • compass • 50 pennies • graphing calculator

QUESTION **How can you fit a quadratic function to a set of data?**

EXPLORE **Collect and model quadratic data**

STEP 1 ***Collect data***

Draw five circles using a compass. Use diameters of 1 inch, 2 inches, 3 inches, 4 inches, and 5 inches. Place as many pennies as you can in each circle, making sure that each penny is completely within the circle.

STEP 2 ***Record data***

Record your results from Step 1 in a table like the one shown at the right. Also, record the number of pennies that would fit in a circle with a diameter of 0 inch.

Diameter of circle (in.), x	Number of pennies, y
0	?
1	?
2	?
3	?
4	?
5	?

STEP 3 ***Enter data***

Enter the data you collected into two lists of a graphing calculator.

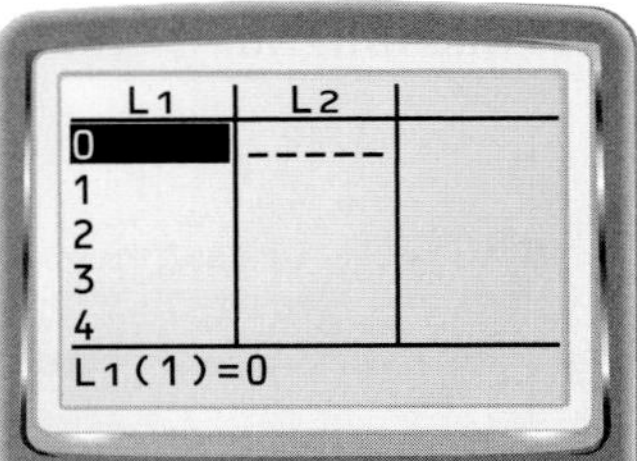

STEP 4 ***Display data***

Display the data in a scatter plot. Notice that the points appear to lie on a parabola.

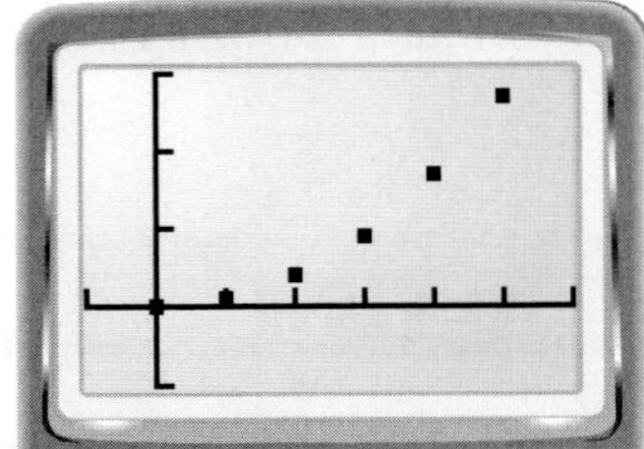

STEP 5 ***Find model***

Use the *quadratic regression* feature to find a quadratic model for the data.

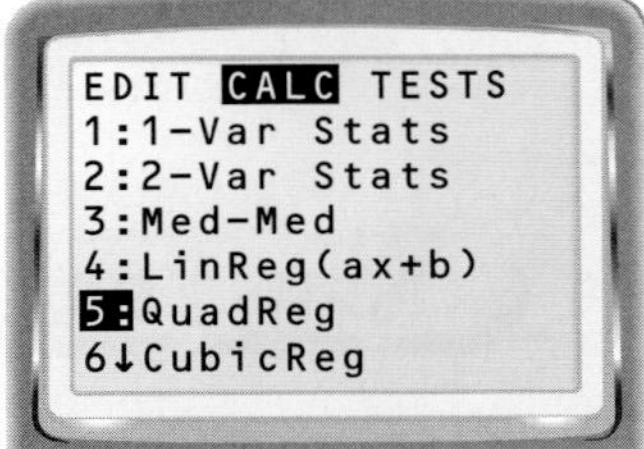

DRAW CONCLUSIONS **Use your observations to complete these exercises**

1. Graph your model from Step 5 on the same screen as the scatter plot. *Describe* how well the model fits the data.
2. Use your model from Step 5 to predict the number of pennies that will fit in a circle with a diameter of 6 inches. Check your prediction by drawing a circle with a diameter of 6 inches and filling it with pennies.
3. *Explain* why you would expect the number of pennies that fit inside a circle to be a quadratic function of the circle's diameter.
4. The diameter of a penny is 0.75 inch. Use this fact to write a quadratic function giving an upper limit L on the number of pennies that can fit inside a circle with diameter x inches.

4.10 Write Quadratic Functions and Models

 **A2.A.40** Write functions in functional notation

Before You wrote linear functions and models.

Now You will write quadratic functions and models.

Why? So you can model the cross section of parabolic dishes, as in Ex. 46.

Key Vocabulary
- **best-fitting quadratic model**

In Lessons 4.1 and 4.2, you learned how to graph quadratic functions. In this lesson, you will write quadratic functions given information about their graphs.

EXAMPLE 1 Write a quadratic function in vertex form

Write a quadratic function for the parabola shown.

Solution

Use vertex form because the vertex is given.

$y = a(x - h)^2 + k$ **Vertex form**

$y = a(x - 1)^2 - 2$ **Substitute 1 for *h* and −2 for *k*.**

Use the other given point, (3, 2), to find a.

$2 = a(3 - 1)^2 - 2$ **Substitute 3 for *x* and 2 for *y*.**

$2 = 4a - 2$ **Simplify coefficient of *a*.**

$1 = a$ **Solve for *a*.**

▸ A quadratic function for the parabola is $y = (x - 1)^2 - 2$.

EXAMPLE 2 Write a quadratic function in intercept form

Write a quadratic function for the parabola shown.

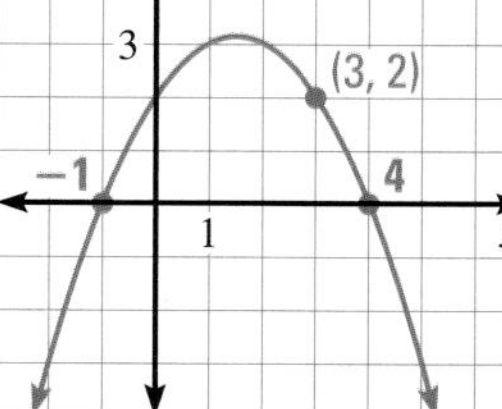

Solution

Use intercept form because the x-intercepts are given.

$y = a(x - p)(x - q)$ **Intercept form**

$y = a(x + 1)(x - 4)$ **Substitute −1 for *p* and 4 for *q*.**

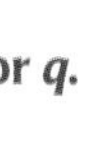

Use the other given point, (3, 2), to find a.

$2 = a(3 + 1)(3 - 4)$ **Substitute 3 for *x* and 2 for *y*.**

$2 = -4a$ **Simplify coefficient of *a*.**

$-\frac{1}{2} = a$ **Solve for *a*.**

▸ A quadratic function for the parabola is $y = -\frac{1}{2}(x + 1)(x - 4)$.

AVOID ERRORS
Be sure to substitute the x-intercepts and the coordinates of the given point for the correct letters in $y = a(x - p)(x - q)$.

EXAMPLE 3 Write a quadratic function in standard form

Write a quadratic function in standard form for the parabola that passes through the points (−1, −3), (0, −4), and (2, 6).

Solution

STEP 1 **Substitute** the coordinates of each point into $y = ax^2 + bx + c$ to obtain the system of three linear equations shown below.

$-3 = a(-1)^2 + b(-1) + c$ — Substitute −1 for *x* and −3 for *y*.

$-3 = a - b + c$ — Equation 1

$-4 = a(0)^2 + b(0) + c$ — Substitute 0 for *x* and −4 for *y*.

$-4 = c$ — Equation 2

$6 = a(2)^2 + b(2) + c$ — Substitute 2 for *x* and 6 for *y*.

$6 = 4a + 2b + c$ — Equation 3

REVIEW SYSTEMS OF EQUATIONS

For help with solving systems of linear equations in three variables, see p. 178.

STEP 2 **Rewrite** the system of three equations in Step 1 as a system of two equations by substituting −4 for *c* in Equations 1 and 3.

$a - b + c = -3$ — Equation 1

$a - b - 4 = -3$ — Substitute −4 for *c*.

$a - b = 1$ — Revised Equation 1

$4a + 2b + c = 6$ — Equation 3

$4a + 2b - 4 = 6$ — Substitute −4 for *c*.

$4a + 2b = 10$ — Revised Equation 3

STEP 3 **Solve** the system consisting of revised Equations 1 and 3. Use the elimination method.

$a - b = 1$ **× 2** → $2a - 2b = 2$

$4a + 2b = 10$ → $4a + 2b = 10$

$6a = 12$

$a = 2$

So $2 - b = 1$, which means $b = 1$.

The solution is $a = 2$, $b = 1$, and $c = -4$.

▶ A quadratic function for the parabola is $y = 2x^2 + x - 4$.

✓ GUIDED PRACTICE for Examples 1, 2, and 3

Write a quadratic function whose graph has the given characteristics.

1. vertex: (4, −5)
passes through: (2, −1)

2. vertex: (−3, 1)
passes through: (0, −8)

3. *x*-intercepts: −2, 5
passes through: (6, 2)

Write a quadratic function in standard form for the parabola that passes through the given points.

4. (−1, 5), (0, −1), (2, 11)

5. (−2, −1), (0, 3), (4, 1)

6. (−1, 0), (1, −2), (2, −15)

QUADRATIC REGRESSION In Chapter 2, you used a graphing calculator to perform linear regression on a data set in order to find a linear model for the data. A graphing calculator can also be used to perform *quadratic regression*. The model given by quadratic regression is called the **best-fitting quadratic model**.

EXAMPLE 4 Solve a multi-step problem

PUMPKIN TOSSING A pumpkin tossing contest is held each year in Morton, Illinois, where people compete to see whose catapult will send pumpkins the farthest. One catapult launches pumpkins from 25 feet above the ground at a speed of 125 feet per second. The table shows the horizontal distances (in feet) the pumpkins travel when launched at different angles. Use a graphing calculator to find the best-fitting quadratic model for the data.

Angle (degrees)	20	30	40	50	60	70
Distance (feet)	372	462	509	501	437	323

Solution

STEP 1 **Enter** the data into two lists of a graphing calculator.

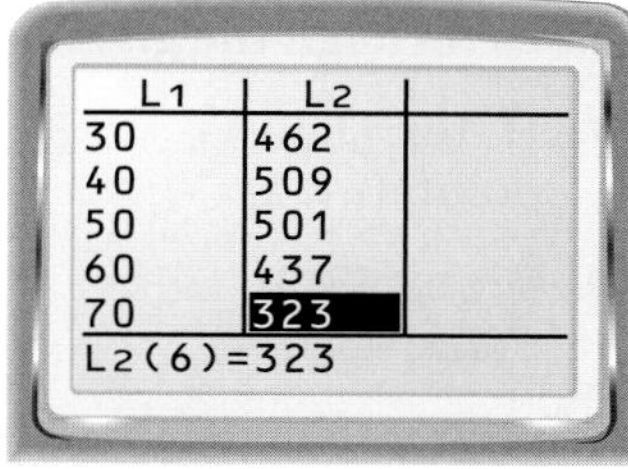

STEP 2 **Make** a scatter plot of the data. Note that the points show a parabolic trend.

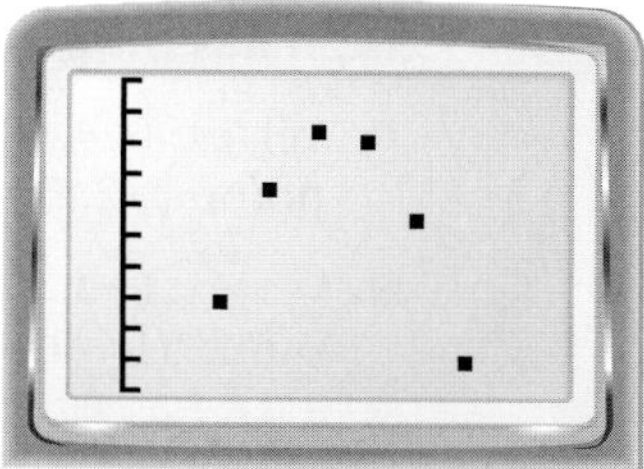

STEP 3 **Use** the quadratic regression feature to find the best-fitting quadratic model for the data.

STEP 4 **Check** how well the model fits the data by graphing the model and the data in the same viewing window.

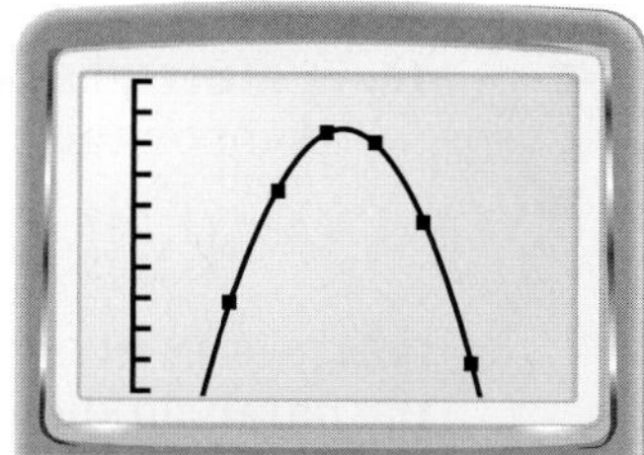

▶ The best-fitting quadratic model is $y = -0.261x^2 + 22.6x + 23.0$.

✓ GUIDED PRACTICE for Example 4

7. **PUMPKIN TOSSING** In Example 4, at what angle does the pumpkin travel the farthest? *Explain* how you found your answer.

4.10 EXERCISES

HOMEWORK KEY

○ = **WORKED-OUT SOLUTIONS** on p. WS9 for Exs. 19, 35, and 49

★ = **STANDARDIZED TEST PRACTICE** Exs. 2, 15, 16, 43, 44, and 51

◆ = **MULTIPLE REPRESENTATIONS** Ex. 50

SKILL PRACTICE

1. **VOCABULARY** Copy and complete: When you perform quadratic regression on a set of data, the quadratic model obtained is called the _?_.

2. ★ **WRITING** *Describe* how to write an equation of a parabola if you know three points on the parabola that are not the vertex or x-intercepts.

EXAMPLE 1 on p. 309 for Exs. 3–15

WRITING IN VERTEX FORM **Write a quadratic function in vertex form for the parabola shown.**

3. 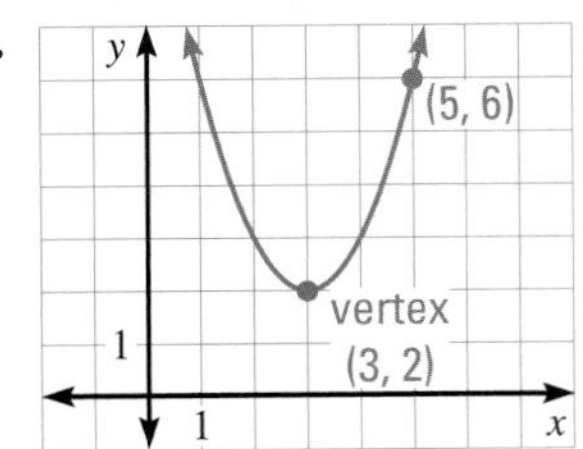

4. 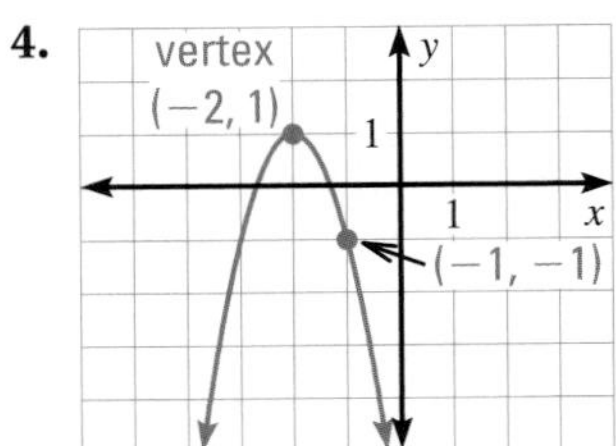

5. 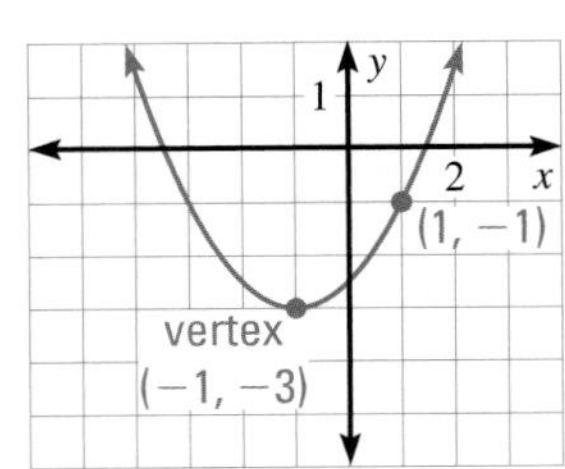

WRITING IN VERTEX FORM **Write a quadratic function in vertex form whose graph has the given vertex and passes through the given point.**

6. vertex: (−4, 1)
point: (−2, 5)

7. vertex: (1, 6)
point: (−1, 2)

8. vertex: (5, −4)
point: (1, 20)

9. vertex: (−3, 3)
point: (1, −1)

10. vertex: (5, 0)
point: (2, −27)

11. vertex: (−4, −2)
point: (0, 30)

12. vertex: (2, 1)
point: (4, −2)

13. vertex: (−1, −4)
point: (2, −1)

14. vertex: (3, 5)
point: (7, −3)

15. ★ **MULTIPLE CHOICE** The vertex of a parabola is (5, −3) and another point on the parabola is (1, 5). Which point is also on the parabola?

Ⓐ (0, 3) Ⓑ (−1, 9) Ⓒ (−1, 15) Ⓓ (7, 7)

EXAMPLE 2 on p. 309 for Exs. 16–26

16. ★ **MULTIPLE CHOICE** The x-intercepts of a parabola are 4 and 7 and another point on the parabola is (2, −20). Which point is also on the parabola?

Ⓐ (1, 21) Ⓑ (8, −4) Ⓒ (5, −40) Ⓓ (5, 4)

WRITING IN INTERCEPT FORM **Write a quadratic function in intercept form for the parabola shown.**

17. 

18. 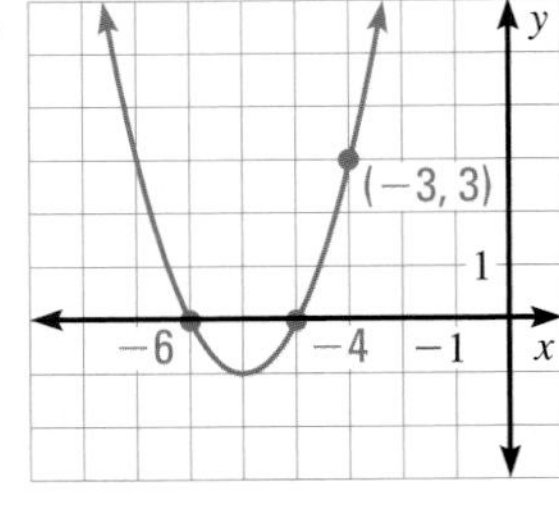

19. 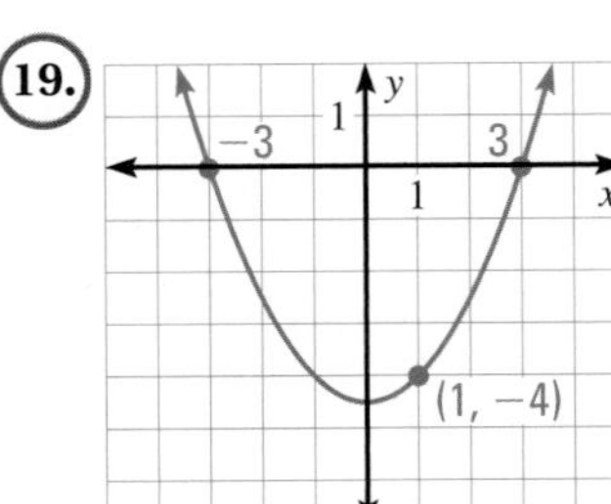

WRITING IN INTERCEPT FORM Write a quadratic function in intercept form whose graph has the given x-intercepts and passes through the given point.

20. x-intercepts: 2, 5
point: (4, −2)

21. x-intercepts: −3, 0
point: (2, 10)

22. x-intercepts: −1, 4
point: (2, 4)

23. x-intercepts: 3, 7
point: (6, −9)

24. x-intercepts: −5, −1
point: (−7, −24)

25. x-intercepts: −6, 3
point: (0, −9)

ERROR ANALYSIS *Describe* and correct the error in writing a quadratic function whose graph has the given x-intercepts or vertex and passes through the given point.

26. x-intercepts: 4, −3; point: (5, −5)

$$y = a(x - 5)(x + 5)$$
$$-3 = a(4 - 5)(4 + 5)$$
$$-3 = -9a$$
$$\frac{1}{3} = a, \text{ so } y = \frac{1}{3}(x - 5)(x + 5)$$

27. vertex: (2, 3); point: (1, 5)

$$y = a(x - 2)(x - 3)$$
$$5 = a(1 - 2)(1 - 3)$$
$$5 = 2a$$
$$\frac{5}{2} = a, \text{ so } y = \frac{5}{2}(x - 2)(x - 3)$$

EXAMPLE 3 on p. 310 for Exs. 28–39

WRITING IN STANDARD FORM Write a quadratic function in standard form for the parabola shown.

28.

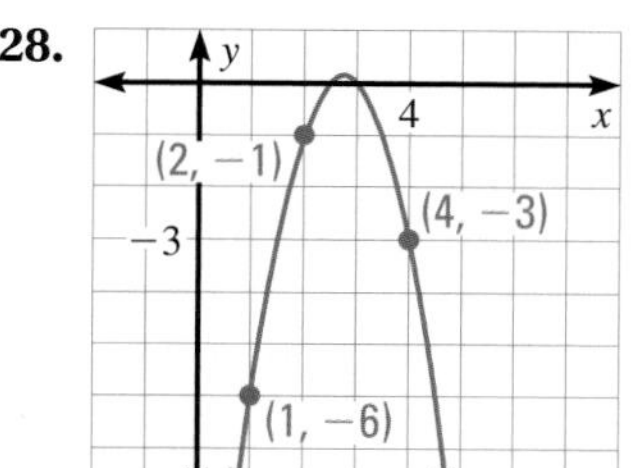

29.

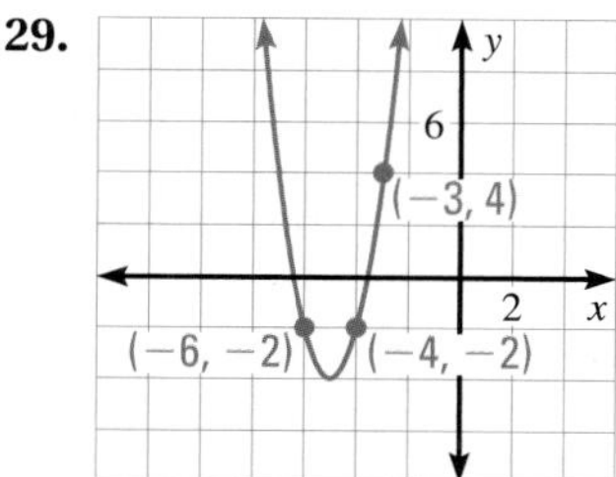

30.

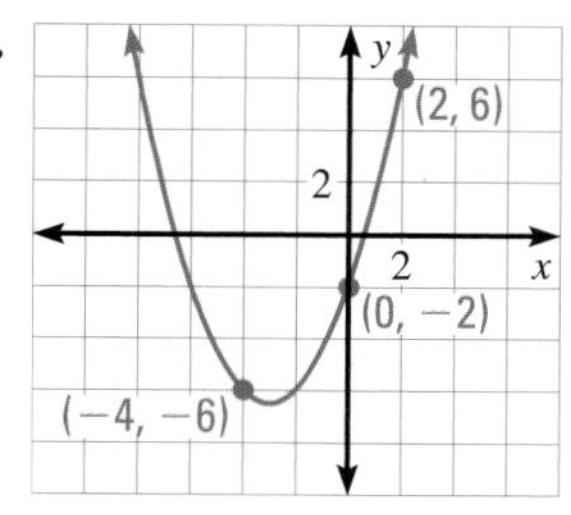

WRITING IN STANDARD FORM Write a quadratic function in standard form for the parabola that passes through the given points.

31. (−4, −3), (0, −2), (1, 7)

32. (−2, −4), (0, −10), (3, −7)

33. (−2, 4), (0, 5), (1, −11)

34. (−1, −1), (1, 11), (3, 7)

35. (−1, 9), (1, 1), (3, 17)

36. (−6, −1), (−3, −4), (3, 8)

37. (−2, −13), (2, 3), (4, 5)

38. (−6, 29), (−4, 12), (2, −3)

39. (−3, −2), (3, 10), (6, −2)

WRITING QUADRATIC FUNCTIONS Write a quadratic function whose graph has the given characteristics.

40. passes through:
(−0.5, −1), (2, 8), (11, 25)

41. x-intercepts: −11, 3
passes through: (1, −192)

42. vertex: (4.5, 7.25)
passes through: (7, −3)

43. ★ **OPEN-ENDED MATH** Draw a parabola that passes through (−2, 3). Write a function for the parabola in standard form, intercept form, and vertex form.

44. ★ **SHORT RESPONSE** Suppose you are given a set of data pairs (x, y). *Describe* how you can use ratios to determine whether the data can be modeled by a quadratic function of the form $y = ax^2$.

45. **CHALLENGE** Find a function of the form $y = ax^2 + bx + c$ whose graph passes through (1, −4), (−3, −16), and (7, 14). *Explain* what the model tells you about the points.

PROBLEM SOLVING

EXAMPLES 1 and 3 on pp. 309–310 for Exs. 46–47

46. **ANTENNA DISH** Three points on the parabola formed by the cross section of an antenna dish are (0, 4), (2, 3.25), and (5, 3.0625). Write a quadratic function that models the cross section.

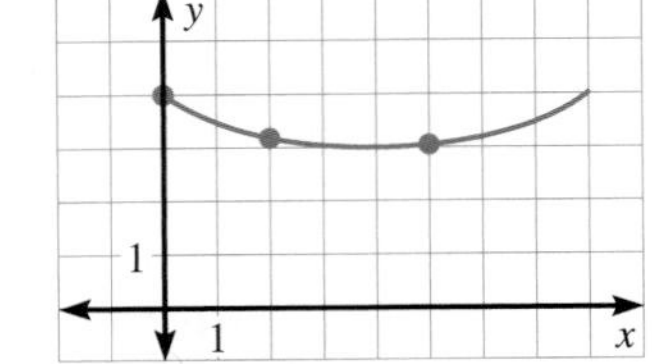

@HomeTutor for problem solving help at classzone.com

47. **FOOTBALL** Two points on the parabolic path of a kicked football are (0, 0) and the vertex (20, 15). Write a quadratic function that models the path.

@HomeTutor for problem solving help at classzone.com

EXAMPLE 4 on p. 311 for Exs. 48–50

48. **MULTI-STEP PROBLEM** The bar graph shows the average number of hours per person per year spent on the Internet in the United States for the years 1997–2001.

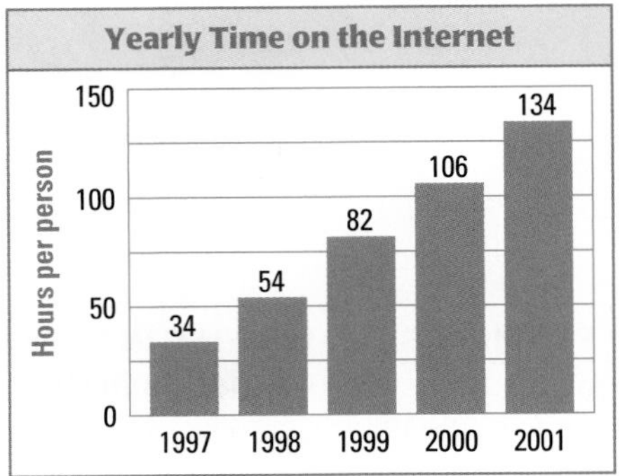

a. Use a graphing calculator to create a scatter plot.

b. Use the quadratic regression feature of the calculator to find the best-fitting quadratic model for the data.

c. Use your model from part (b) to predict the average number of hours a person will spend on the Internet in 2010.

(49.) **RUNNING** The table shows how wind affects a runner's performance in the 200 meter dash. Positive wind speeds correspond to tailwinds, and negative wind speeds correspond to headwinds. The change t in finishing time is the difference beween the runner's time when the wind speed is s and the runner's time when there is no wind.

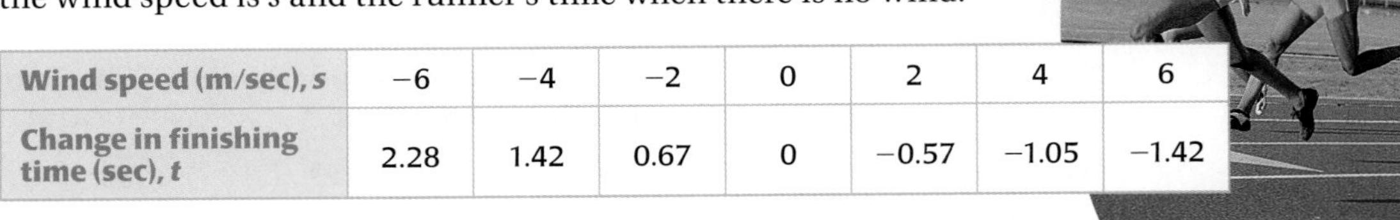

Wind speed (m/sec), s	−6	−4	−2	0	2	4	6
Change in finishing time (sec), t	2.28	1.42	0.67	0	−0.57	−1.05	−1.42

a. Use a graphing calculator to find the best-fitting quadratic model.

b. Predict the change in finishing time when the wind speed is 10 m/sec.

50. ◆ **MULTIPLE REPRESENTATIONS** The table shows the number of U.S. households (in millions) with color televisions from 1970 through 2000.

Years since 1970	0	5	10	15	20	25	30
Households with color TVs (millions)	21	47	63	78	90	94	101

a. **Drawing a Graph** Make a scatter plot of the data. Draw the parabola that you think best fits the data.

b. **Writing a Function** Estimate the coordinates of three points on the parabola. Use the points to write a quadratic function for the data.

c. **Making a Table** Use your function from part (b) to make a table of data for the years listed in the original table above. *Compare* the numbers of households given by your function with the numbers in the original table.

51. ★ **MULTIPLE CHOICE** The Garabit Viaduct in France has a parabolic arch as part of its support. Three points on the parabola that models the arch are (0, 0), (40, 38.2), and (165, 0) where x and y are measured in meters. Which point is also on the parabola?

Ⓐ (10, −11.84) Ⓑ (26.74, 25) Ⓒ (80, 51.95) Ⓓ (125, 45)

52. **CHALLENGE** Let R be the maximum number of regions into which a circle can be divided using n chords. For example, the diagram shows that $R = 4$ when $n = 2$. Copy and complete the table. Then write a quadratic model giving R as a function of n.

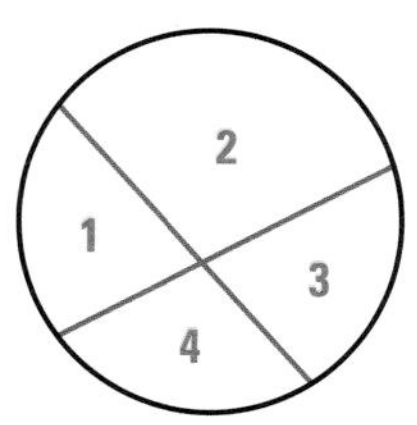

n	0	1	2	3	4	5	6
R	?	?	4	?	?	?	?

NEW YORK MIXED REVIEW

TEST PRACTICE at classzone.com

53. Charlie receives some money for his birthday. He deposits one third of the money in the bank. He purchases a concert ticket for \$45. Then he spends half of the remaining money on dinner. Charlie has \$8.50 left. How much money did he receive for his birthday?

Ⓐ \$80 Ⓑ \$93 Ⓒ \$118 Ⓓ \$124

54. Which equation represents a line that is parallel to the line that passes through (−4, 9) and (5, −3)?

Ⓐ $-4x + 3y = 29$ Ⓑ $2x + 3y = 9$

Ⓒ $4x + 3y = -12$ Ⓓ $2x - 3y = 11$

QUIZ *for Lessons 4.8–4.10*

Use the quadratic formula to solve the equation. *(p. 292)*

1. $x^2 - 4x + 5 = 0$
2. $2x^2 - 8x + 1 = 0$
3. $3x^2 + 5x + 4 = 0$

Graph the inequality. *(p. 300)*

4. $y < -3x^2$
5. $y > -x^2 + 2x$
6. $y \geq -x^2 + 2x + 3$

Solve the inequality. *(p. 300)*

7. $0 \geq x^2 + 5$
8. $12 \leq x^2 - 7x$
9. $2x^2 + 2 > -5x$

Write a quadratic function whose graph has the given characteristics. *(p. 309)*

10. vertex: (5, 7)
passes through: (3, 11)
11. x-intercepts: −3, 5
passes through: (7, −40)
12. passes through:
(−1, 2), (4, −23), (2, −7)

13. **SPORTS** A person throws a baseball into the air with an initial vertical velocity of 30 feet per second and then lets the ball hit the ground. The ball is released 5 feet above the ground. How long is the ball in the air? *(p. 292)*

Lessons 4.6–4.10

1. **GAMES** You are playing a lawn version of tic-tac-toe in which you toss bean bags onto a large board. One of your tosses can be modeled by the function $y = -0.12x^2 + 1.2x + 2$ where x is the bean bag's horizontal position (in feet) and y is the corresponding height (in feet). What is the bean bag's maximum height?

   (1) 2.5 feet

   (2) 5 feet

   (3) 6 feet

   (4) 10 feet

2. **MUSICAL INSTRUMENTS** A music store sells about 50 of a new model of drum per month at a price of $120 each. For each $5 decrease in price, about 4 more drums per month are sold. Which inequality can you use to find the prices that result in monthly revenues over $6500?

   (1) $(50 + 5x)(120 - 4x) > 6500$

   (2) $(50 - 5x)(120 + 4x) > 6500$

   (3) $(50 - 4x)(120 + 5x) > 6500$

   (4) $(50 + 4x)(120 - 5x) > 6500$

3. **SPORTS** You throw a ball to your friend. The ball leaves your hand 5 feet above the ground and has an initial vertical velocity of 50 feet per second. Your friend catches the ball when it falls to a height of 3 feet. About how long is the ball in the air?

   (1) 0.04 second

   (2) 0.1 second

   (3) 3.16 seconds

   (4) 3.22 seconds

4. **ABSOLUTE VALUE** What is the absolute value of $-4 + 5i$?

   (1) 3

   (2) $2\sqrt{10}$

   (3) $\sqrt{41}$

   (4) $3\sqrt{5}$

5. **OPEN-ENDED** The diagram shows a design for a hanging glass lamp. Write a quadratic function that models the parabolic cross section of the lamp. *Explain* how you can verify that your model is correct.

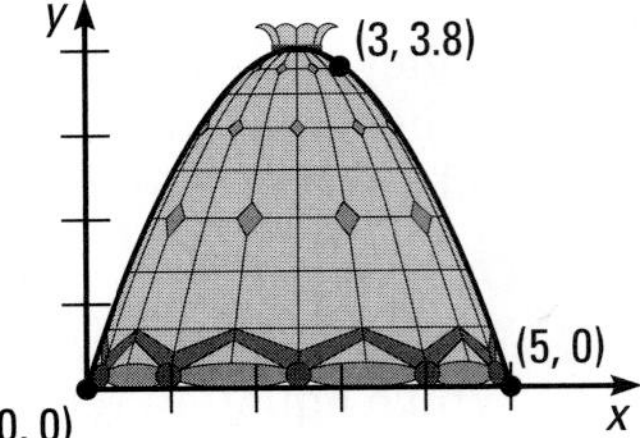

6. **OPEN-ENDED** You are designing notepaper with solid stripes along the paper's top and left sides as shown. The stripes will take up one third of the area of the paper. The paper measures 5 inches by 8 inches.

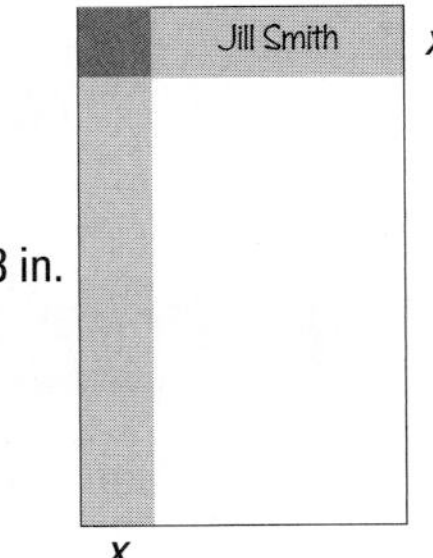

   Write an equation that you can use to solve for x.

   Find all values of x that are solutions to the equation.

   What is the width of the stripes? Why must you reject one of the solutions?

CHAPTER SUMMARY

BIG IDEAS

For Your Notebook

Big Idea 1

Graphing and Writing Quadratic Functions in Several Forms

You can graph or write a quadratic function in standard form, vertex form, or intercept form.

Form	Equation	Information about quadratic function
Standard form	$y = ax^2 + bx + c$	• The x-coordinate of the vertex is $-\frac{b}{2a}$. • The axis of symmetry is $x = -\frac{b}{2a}$.
Vertex form	$y = a(x - h)^2 + k$	• The vertex is (h, k). • The axis of symmetry is $x = h$.
Intercept form	$y = a(x - p)(x - q)$	• The x-intercepts are p and q. • The axis of the symmetry is $x = \frac{p + q}{2}$.

Big Idea 2

Solving Quadratic Equations Using a Variety of Methods

There are several different methods you can use to solve a quadratic equation.

Equation contains:	Example	Method
Binomial without x-term	$5x^2 - 45 = 0$	Isolate the x^2-term. Then take square roots of each side.
Factorable trinomial	$x^2 - 5x + 6 = 0$	Factor the trinomial. Then use the zero product property.
Unfactorable trinomial	$x^2 - 8x + 35 = 0$	Complete the square, *or* use the quadratic formula.

Big Idea 3

Performing Operations with Square Roots and Complex Numbers

You can use the following properties to simplify expressions involving square roots or complex numbers.

Square roots	If $a > 0$ and $b > 0$, then $\sqrt{ab} = \sqrt{a} \cdot \sqrt{b}$ and $\sqrt{\frac{a}{b}} = \frac{\sqrt{a}}{\sqrt{b}}$.
Complex numbers	• The imaginary unit i is defined as $i = \sqrt{-1}$, so that $i^2 = -1$. • If r is a positive real number, then $\sqrt{-r} = i\sqrt{r}$ and $(i\sqrt{r})^2 = -r$. • $(a + bi) + (c + di) = (a + c) + (b + d)i$ • $(a + bi) - (c + di) = (a - c) + (b - d)i$ • $\lvert a + bi \rvert = \sqrt{a^2 + b^2}$

4 CHAPTER REVIEW

@HomeTutor
classzone.com
- Multi-Language Glossary
- Vocabulary practice

REVIEW KEY VOCABULARY

- quadratic function, *p. 236*
- standard form of a quadratic function, *p. 236*
- parabola, *p. 236*
- vertex, *p. 236*
- axis of symmetry, *p. 236*
- minimum, maximum value, *p. 238*
- vertex form, *p. 245*
- intercept form, *p. 246*
- monomial, binomial, trinomial, *p. 252*
- quadratic equation, *p. 253*
- standard form of a quadratic equation, *p. 253*
- root of an equation, *p. 253*
- zero of a function, *p. 254*
- square root, *p. 266*
- radical, radicand, *p. 266*
- rationalizing the denominator, *p. 267*
- conjugates, *p. 267*
- imaginary unit *i*, *p. 275*
- complex number, *p. 276*
- standard form of a complex number, *p. 276*
- imaginary number, *p. 276*
- pure imaginary number, *p. 276*
- complex conjugates, *p. 278*
- complex plane, *p. 278*
- absolute value of a complex number, *p. 279*
- completing the square, *p. 284*
- quadratic formula, *p. 292*
- discriminant, *p. 294*
- quadratic inequality in two variables, *p. 300*
- quadratic inequality in one variable, *p. 302*
- best-fitting quadratic model, *p. 311*

VOCABULARY EXERCISES

1. **WRITING** Given a quadratic function in standard form, explain how to determine whether the function has a maximum value or a minimum value.
2. Copy and complete: A(n) __?__ is a complex number $a + bi$ where $a = 0$ and $b \neq 0$.
3. Copy and complete: A function of the form $y = a(x - h)^2 + k$ is written in __?__.
4. Give an example of a quadratic equation that has a negative discriminant.

REVIEW EXAMPLES AND EXERCISES

Use the review examples and exercises below to check your understanding of the concepts you have learned in each lesson of Chapter 4.

4.1 Graph Quadratic Functions in Standard Form *pp. 236–243*

EXAMPLE

Graph $y = -x^2 - 4x - 5$.

Because $a < 0$, the parabola opens down. Find and plot the vertex $(-2, -1)$. Draw the axis of symmetry $x = -2$. Plot the y-intercept at $(0, -5)$, and plot its reflection $(-4, -5)$ in the axis of symmetry. Plot two other points: $(-1, -2)$ and its reflection $(-3, -2)$ in the axis of symmetry. Draw a parabola through the plotted points.

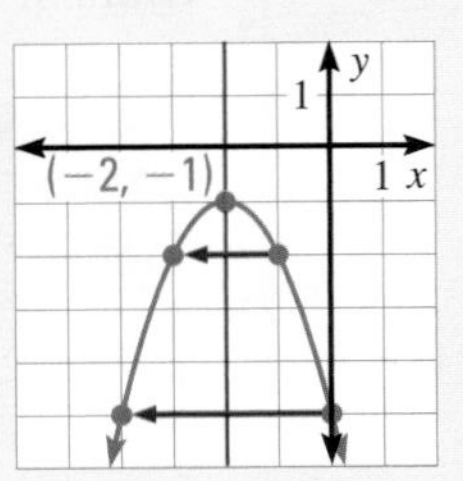

EXAMPLE 3 on p. 238 for Exs. 5–7

EXERCISES

Graph the function. Label the vertex and axis of symmetry.

5. $y = x^2 + 2x - 3$
6. $y = -3x^2 + 12x - 7$
7. $f(x) = -x^2 - 2x - 6$

@HomeTutor
classzone.com
Chapter Review Practice

4.2 Graph Quadratic Functions in Vertex or Intercept Form *pp. 245–251*

EXAMPLE

Graph $y = (x - 4)(x + 2)$.

Identify the x-intercepts. The quadratic function is in intercept form $y = a(x - p)(x - q)$ where $a = 1$, $p = 4$, and $q = -2$. Plot the x-intercepts at (4, 0) and (−2, 0).

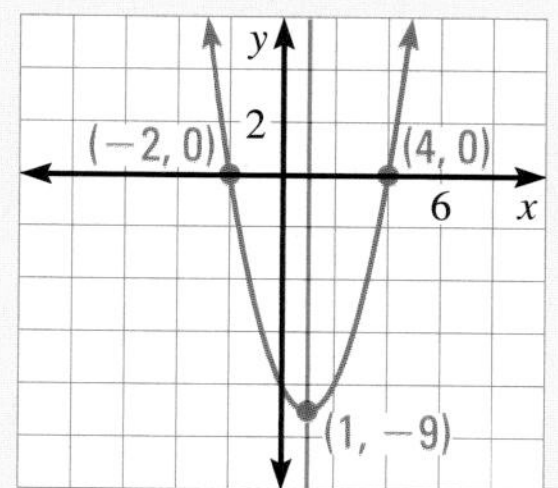

Find the coordinates of the vertex.

$$x = \frac{p + q}{2} = \frac{4 + (-2)}{2} = 1$$

$$y = (1 - 4)(1 + 2) = -9$$

Plot the vertex at (1, −9). Draw a parabola through the plotted points as shown.

EXERCISES

EXAMPLES 1, 3, and 4 on pp. 245–247 for Exs. 8–14

Graph the function. Label the vertex and axis of symmetry.

8. $y = (x - 1)(x + 5)$ **9.** $g(x) = (x + 3)(x - 2)$ **10.** $y = -3(x + 1)(x - 6)$

11. $y = (x - 2)^2 + 3$ **12.** $f(x) = (x + 6)^2 + 8$ **13.** $y = -2(x + 8)^2 - 3$

14. BIOLOGY A flea's jump can be modeled by the function $y = -0.073x(x - 33)$ where x is the horizontal distance (in centimeters) and y is the corresponding height (in centimeters). How far did the flea jump? What was the flea's maximum height?

4.3 Solve $x^2 + bx + c = 0$ by Factoring *pp. 252–258*

EXAMPLE

Solve $x^2 - 13x - 48 = 0$.

Use factoring to solve for x.

$x^2 - 13x - 48 = 0$	**Write original equation.**
$(x - 16)(x + 3) = 0$	**Factor.**
$x - 16 = 0$ or $x + 3 = 0$	**Zero product property**
$x = 16$ or $x = -3$	**Solve for *x*.**

EXERCISES

EXAMPLE 3 on p. 254 for Exs. 15–21

Solve the equation.

15. $x^2 + 5x = 0$ **16.** $z^2 = 63z$ **17.** $s^2 - 6s - 27 = 0$

18. $k^2 + 12k - 45 = 0$ **19.** $x^2 + 18x = -81$ **20.** $n^2 + 5n = 24$

21. URBAN PLANNING A city wants to double the area of a rectangular playground that is 72 feet by 48 feet by adding the same distance x to the length and the width. Write and solve an equation to find the value of x.

4 CHAPTER REVIEW

4.4 Solve $ax^2 + bx + c = 0$ by Factoring

pp. 259–264

EXAMPLE

Solve $-30x^2 + 9x + 12 = 0$.

$-30x^2 + 9x + 12 = 0$	Write original equation.
$10x^2 - 3x - 4 = 0$	Divide each side by -3.
$(5x - 4)(2x + 1) = 0$	Factor.
$5x - 4 = 0$ or $2x + 1 = 0$	Zero product property
$x = \frac{4}{5}$ or $x = -\frac{1}{2}$	Solve for x.

EXERCISES

EXAMPLE 5 on p. 261 for Exs. 22–24

Solve the equation.

22. $16 = 38r - 12r^2$

23. $3x^2 - 24x - 48 = 0$

24. $20a^2 - 13a - 21 = 0$

4.5 Solve Quadratic Equations by Finding Square Roots

pp. 266–271

EXAMPLE

Solve $4(x - 7)^2 = 80$.

$4(x - 7)^2 = 80$	Write original equation.
$(x - 7)^2 = 20$	Divide each side by 4.
$x - 7 = \pm\sqrt{20}$	Take square roots of each side.
$x = 7 \pm 2\sqrt{5}$	Add 7 to each side and simplify.

EXERCISES

EXAMPLES 3 and 4 on pp. 267–268 for Exs. 25–28

Solve the equation.

25. $3x^2 = 108$

26. $5y^2 + 4 = 14$

27. $3(p + 1)^2 = 81$

28. GEOGRAPHY The total surface area of Earth is 510,000,000 square kilometers. Use the formula $S = 4\pi r^2$, which gives the surface area of a sphere with radius r, to find the radius of Earth.

4.6 Perform Operations with Complex Numbers

pp. 275–282

EXAMPLE

Write $(6 - 4i)(1 - 3i)$ as a complex number in standard form.

$(6 - 4i)(1 - 3i) = 6 - 18i - 4i + 12i^2$	Multiply using FOIL.
$= 6 - 22i + 12(-1)$	Simplify and use $i^2 = -1$.
$= -6 - 22i$	Write in standard form.

@HomeTutor
classzone.com
Chapter Review Practice

EXAMPLES 2, 4, and 5 on pp. 276–278 for Exs. 29–34

EXERCISES

Write the expression as a complex number in standard form.

29. $-9i(2 - i)$

30. $(5 + i)(4 - 2i)$

31. $(2 - 5i)(2 + 5i)$

32. $(8 - 6i) + (7 + 4i)$

33. $(2 - 3i) - (6 - 5i)$

34. $\dfrac{4i}{-3 + 6i}$

4.7 Complete the Square

pp. 284–291

EXAMPLE

Solve $x^2 - 8x + 13 = 0$ by completing the square.

$x^2 - 8x + 13 = 0$ — Write original equation.

$x^2 - 8x = -13$ — Write left side in the form $x^2 + bx$.

$x^2 - 8x + 16 = -13 + 16$ — Add $\left(\frac{-8}{2}\right)^2 = (-4)^2 = 16$ to each side.

$(x - 4)^2 = 3$ — Write left side as a binomial squared.

$x - 4 = \pm\sqrt{3}$ — Take square roots of each side.

$x = 4 \pm \sqrt{3}$ — Solve for x.

EXAMPLES 3 and 4 on pp. 285–286 for Exs. 35–37

EXERCISES

Solve the equation by completing the square.

35. $x^2 - 6x - 15 = 0$

36. $3x^2 - 12x + 1 = 0$

37. $x^2 + 3x - 1 = 0$

4.8 Use the Quadratic Formula and the Discriminant

pp. 292–299

EXAMPLE

Solve $3x^2 + 6x = -2$.

$3x^2 + 6x = -2$ — Write original equation.

$3x^2 + 6x + 2 = 0$ — Write in standard form.

$x = \dfrac{-6 \pm \sqrt{6^2 - 4(3)(2)}}{2(3)}$ — Use $a = 3$, $b = 6$, and $c = 2$ in quadratic formula.

$x = \dfrac{-3 \pm \sqrt{3}}{3}$ — Simplify.

EXAMPLES 1, 2, 3, and 5 on pp. 292–295 for Exs. 38–41

EXERCISES

Use the quadratic formula to solve the equation.

38. $x^2 + 4x - 3 = 0$

39. $9x^2 = -6x - 1$

40. $6x^2 - 8x = -3$

41. **VOLLEYBALL** A person spikes a volleyball over a net when the ball is 9 feet above the ground. The volleyball has an initial vertical velocity of -40 feet per second. The volleyball is allowed to fall to the ground. How long is the ball in the air after it is spiked?

4.9 Graph and Solve Quadratic Inequalities
pp. 300–307

EXAMPLE

Solve $-2x^2 + 2x + 5 \le 0$.

The solution consists of the x-values for which the graph of $y = -2x^2 + 2x + 5$ lies on or below the x-axis. Find the graph's x-intercepts by letting $y = 0$ and using the quadratic formula to solve for x.

$$x = \frac{-2 \pm \sqrt{2^2 - 4(-2)(5)}}{2(-2)}$$

$$= \frac{-2 \pm \sqrt{44}}{-4} = \frac{-1 \pm \sqrt{11}}{-2}$$

$$x \approx -1.16 \text{ or } x \approx 2.16$$

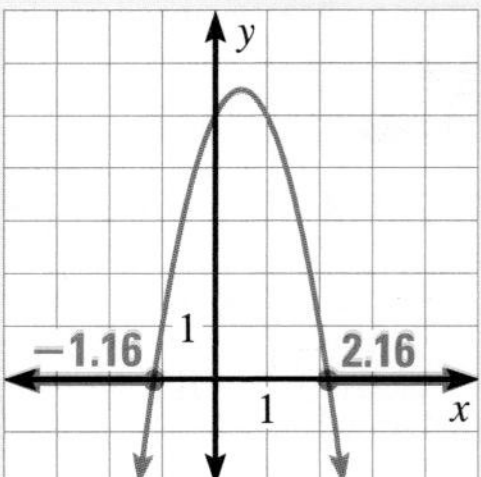

Sketch a parabola that opens down and has -1.16 and 2.16 as x-intercepts. The solution of the inequality is approximately $x \le -1.16$ or $x \ge 2.16$.

EXERCISES

EXAMPLE 5 on p. 302 for Exs. 42–44

Solve the inequality by graphing.

42. $2x^2 - 11x + 5 < 0$

43. $-x^2 + 4x + 3 \ge 0$

44. $\frac{1}{2}x^2 + 3x - 6 > 0$

4.10 Write Quadratic Functions and Models
pp. 309–315

EXAMPLE

Write a quadratic function for the parabola shown.

Because you are given the x-intercepts $p = -3$ and $q = 2$, use the intercept form $y = a(x - p)(x - q) = a(x + 3)(x - 2)$.

Use the other given point, $(1, -2)$, to find a.

$-2 = a(1 + 3)(1 - 2)$ **Substitute 1 for x and −2 for y.**

$-2 = -4a$ **Simplify coefficient of a.**

$\frac{1}{2} = a$ **Solve for a.**

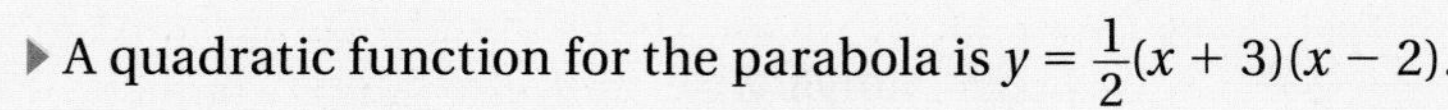

▶ A quadratic function for the parabola is $y = \frac{1}{2}(x + 3)(x - 2)$.

EXERCISES

EXAMPLES 1 and 2 on p. 309 for Exs. 45–48

Write a quadratic function whose graph has the given characteristics.

45. x-intercepts: $-3, 2$
passes through: $(3, 12)$

46. passes through:
$(5, 2)$, $(0, 2)$, $(8, -6)$

47. vertex: $(2, 7)$
passes through: $(4, 2)$

48. SOCCER The parabolic path of a soccer ball that is kicked from the ground passes through the point $(0, 0)$ and has vertex $(12, 7)$ where the coordinates are in feet. Write a quadratic function that models the soccer ball's path.

4 CHAPTER TEST

Graph the function. Label the vertex and axis of symmetry.

1. $y = x^2 - 8x - 20$

2. $y = -(x + 3)^2 + 5$

3. $f(x) = 2(x + 4)(x - 2)$

Factor the expression.

4. $x^2 - 11x + 30$

5. $z^2 + 2z - 15$

6. $n^2 - 64$

7. $2s^2 + 7s - 15$

8. $9x^2 + 30x + 25$

9. $6t^2 + 23t + 20$

Solve the equation.

10. $x^2 - 3x - 40 = 0$

11. $r^2 - 13r + 42 = 0$

12. $2w^2 + 13w - 7 = 0$

13. $10y^2 + 11y - 6 = 0$

14. $2(m - 7)^2 = 16$

15. $(x + 2)^2 - 12 = 36$

Write the expression as a complex number in standard form.

16. $(3 + 4i) - (2 - 5i)$

17. $(2 - 7i)(1 + 2i)$

18. $\frac{3 + i}{2 - 3i}$

Solve the equation by completing the square.

19. $x^2 + 4x - 14 = 0$

20. $x^2 - 10x - 7 = 0$

21. $4x^2 + 8x + 3 = 0$

Use the quadratic formula to solve the equation.

22. $3x^2 + 10x - 5 = 0$

23. $2x^2 - x + 6 = 0$

24. $5x^2 + 2x + 5 = 0$

Graph the inequality.

25. $y \geq x^2 - 8$

26. $y < x^2 + 4x - 21$

27. $y > -x^2 + 5x + 50$

Write a quadratic function whose graph has the given characteristics.

28. x-intercepts: $-7, -3$
passes through: $(-1, 12)$

29. vertex: $(-3, -2)$
passes through: $(1, -10)$

30. passes through:
$(4, 8), (7, -4), (8, 0)$

31. ASPECT RATIO The *aspect ratio* of a widescreen TV is the ratio of the screen's width to its height, or 16 : 9. What are the width and the height of a 32 inch widescreen TV? (*Hint:* Use the Pythagorean theorem and the fact that TV sizes such as 32 inches refer to the length of the screen's diagonal.)

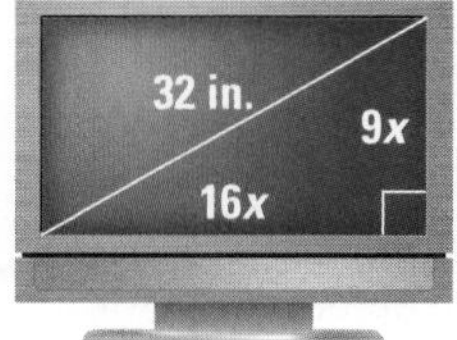

32. WOOD STRENGTH The data show how the strength of Douglas fir wood is related to the percent moisture in the wood. The strength value for wood with 2% moisture is defined to be 1. All other strength values are relative to this value. (For example, wood with 4% moisture is 97.9% as strong as wood with 2% moisture.) Use the quadratic regression feature of a graphing calculator to find the best-fitting quadratic model for the data.

Percent moisture, m	2	4	6	8	10
Strength, s	1	0.979	0.850	0.774	0.714
Percent moisture, m	12	14	16	18	20
Strength, s	0.643	0.589	0.535	0.494	0.458

MULTIPLE CHOICE QUESTIONS

Some of the information you need to solve a multiple choice question may appear in a table, a diagram, or a graph.

PROBLEM 1

The area of the shaded region is 56 square meters. What is the height of the trapezoid?

(1) 3 meters (3) 6 meters

(2) 4 meters (4) 7.5 meters

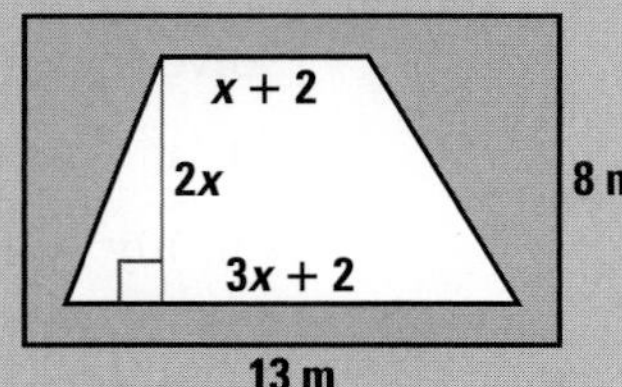

Plan

INTERPRET THE DIAGRAM You know the area of the shaded region. Use the diagram to find the area of the rectangle, and write an expression for the area of the trapezoid. The difference of these two areas is the area of the shaded region.

Solution

STEP 1 Find expressions for the two areas.

Area of rectangle:

$A = \ell w$

$= 13(8)$

$= 104\ \text{m}^2$

Area of trapezoid:

$A = \frac{1}{2}(b_1 + b_2)h$

$= \frac{1}{2}[(x + 2) + (3x + 2)](2x)$

$= \frac{1}{2}(2x)(4x + 4)$

$= x(4x + 4)$

$= 4x^2 + 4x$

STEP 2 Write an equation for the area of the shaded region and solve by factoring.

Area of shaded region = Area of rectangle − Area of trapezoid

$56 = 104 - (4x^2 + 4x)$ **Substitute.**

$-48 = -4x^2 - 4x$ **Subtract 104 from each side.**

$4x^2 + 4x - 48 = 0$ **Write in standard form.**

$x^2 + x - 12 = 0$ **Divide each side by 4.**

$(x - 3)(x + 4) = 0$ **Factor.**

$x = 3$ or $x = -4$ **Zero product property**

STEP 3 Find the possible heights.

The height of the trapezoid is given by the expression $2x$. Therefore, the possible heights are $2(3) = 6$ meters and $2(-4) = -8$ meters.

STEP 4 Reject the negative height.

Because height cannot be negative, the height of the trapezoid is 6 meters.

▶ The correct answer is (3).

TEST PRACTICE
classzone.com

PROBLEM 2

The height h (in feet) of a lobbed tennis ball after t seconds is shown by the graph. What is the initial vertical velocity of the tennis ball?

(1) 3 feet/second (3) 37.5 feet/second

(2) 16 feet/second (4) 47 feet/second

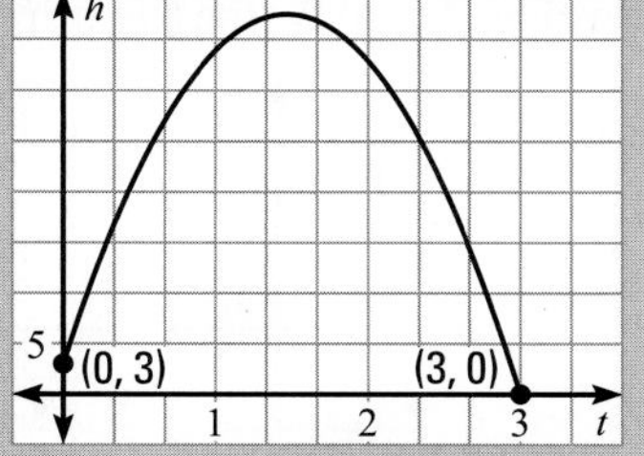

Plan

INTERPRET THE GRAPH The graph is a parabola passing through the points (0, 3) and (3, 0). In order to find the initial vertical velocity of the tennis ball, you must write an equation of the parabola.

Solution

STEP 1 Write the model for an object that is launched.

Because the tennis ball is launched, the parabola has an equation of the form $h = -16t^2 + v_0t + h_0$ where v_0 is the initial vertical velocity and h_0 is the initial height of the tennis ball.

STEP 2 Use the initial height in your model.

The graph passes through (0, 3), so the initial height of the tennis ball is 3 feet. When you substitute 3 for h_0 in the model, you obtain $h = -16t^2 + v_0t + 3$.

STEP 3 Find the initial vertical velocity by substituting a point on the parabola.

Use the fact that the graph of $h = -16t^2 + v_0t + 3$ passes through (3, 0) to find the initial vertical velocity v_0.

$\mathbf{0} = -16(\mathbf{3})^2 + v_0(\mathbf{3}) + 3$ **Substitute 0 for *h* and 3 for *t*.**

$0 = -141 + 3v_0$ **Simplify.**

$47 = v_0$ **Solve for v_0.**

The initial vertical velocity is 47 feet per second.

▶ The correct answer is (4).

PRACTICE

In Exercises 1 and 2, use the graph in Problem 2.

1. What is the maximum height of the tennis ball to the nearest tenth of a foot?

(1) 36.3 feet (2) 36.8 feet (3) 37.5 feet (4) 38.0 feet

2. What does the x-coordinate of the vertex of the graph represent?

(1) The maximum height of the tennis ball

(2) The number of seconds the ball is in the air

(3) The number of seconds it takes the ball to reach its maximum height

(4) The initial height of the tennis ball

TEST PREPARATION

New York **Test Practice**

TEST PREPARATION

MULTIPLE CHOICE

In Exercises 1 and 2, use the parabola below.

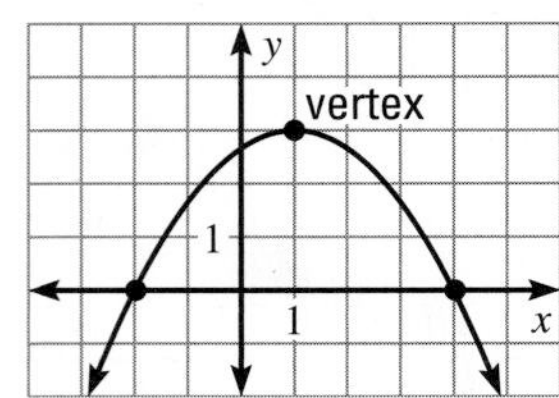

1. Which statement is *not* true about the parabola?

(1) The x-intercepts are -2 and 4.

(2) The y-intercept is -2.

(3) The maximum value is 3.

(4) The axis of symmetry is $x = 1$.

2. What is an equation of the parabola?

(1) $y = (x - 2)(x + 4)$

(2) $y = -\frac{1}{3}(x + 2)(x - 4)$

(3) $y = -(x + 2)(x - 4)$

(4) $y = -3(x + 2)(x - 4)$

3. You are using glass tiles to make a picture frame for a square photograph with sides 10 inches long. You want the frame to form a uniform border around the photograph. You have enough tiles to cover 300 square inches. What is the largest possible frame width x?

(1) 3.6 inches

(2) 5 inches

(3) 7.3 inches

(4) 15 inches

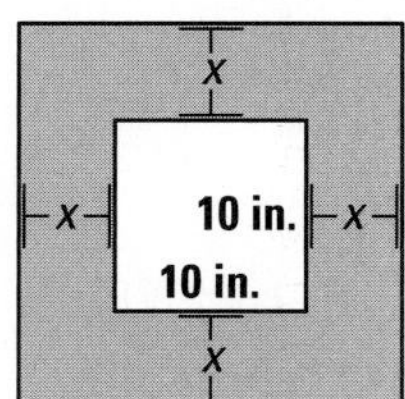

4. At a flea market held each weekend, an artist sells handmade earrings. The table below shows the average number of pairs of earrings sold for several prices. Given the pattern in the table, how much should the artist charge to maximize revenue?

Price	\$15	\$14	\$13	\$12
Pairs sold	50	60	70	80

(1) \$5 (2) \$7.50 (3) \$10 (4) \$15

5. The graph of which inequality is shown?

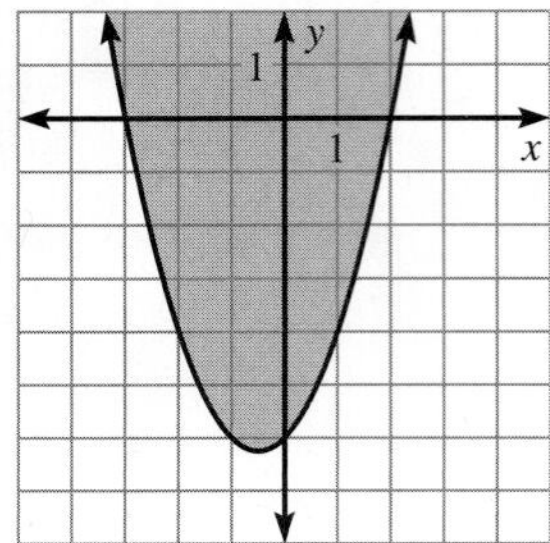

(1) $y \geq -x^2 - x + 6$

(2) $y \geq x^2 + x - 6$

(3) $y > 2x^2 + 2x - 12$

(4) $y \geq -2x^2 - 2x + 12$

In Exercises 6 and 7, use the information below.

The graph shows the height h (in feet) after t seconds of a horseshoe tossed during a game of horseshoes. The initial vertical velocity of the horseshoe is 30 feet per second.

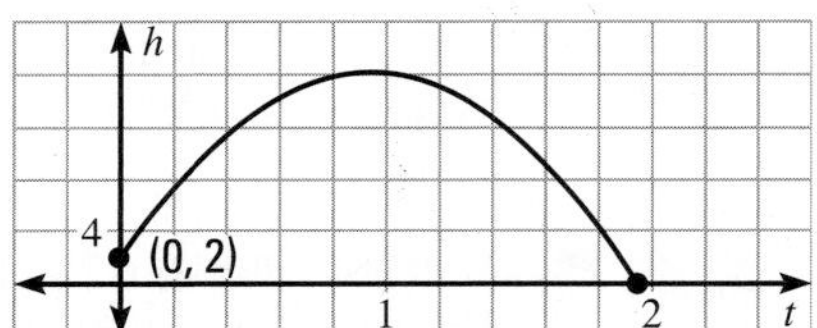

6. To the nearest tenth of a second, how long is the horseshoe in the air?

(1) 0.1 seconds

(2) 1.9 seconds

(3) 2.1 seconds

(4) 3.9 seconds

7. To the nearest tenth of a foot, what is the maximum height of the horseshoe?

(1) 51.9 feet

(2) 16.1 feet

(3) 29.2 feet

(4) 32.2 feet

8. The diagram shows a circle inscribed in a square. The area of the shaded region is 21.5 square inches. To the nearest tenth of an inch, how long is a side of the square?

(1) 4.6 inches

(2) 8.7 inches

(3) 9.7 inches

(4) 10.0 inches

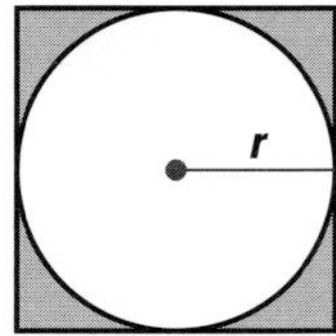

MULTIPLE CHOICE

9. What is the value of k in the equation $6x^2 - 11x - 10 = (3x + 2)(2x - k)$?

(1) -8

(2) -5

(3) 5

(4) 8

10. What is the real part of the standard form of the expression $(5 + i)(10 - i)$?

(1) 49 (3) 51

(2) 50 (4) 54

11. For what value of c is $x^2 - 7x + c$ a perfect square trinomial?

(1) $\frac{7}{2}$ (3) $\frac{49}{2}$

(2) $\frac{49}{4}$ (4) 49

12. What is the maximum value of the function $f(x) = -3(x - 2)^2 + 6$?

(1) -6

(2) 2

(3) 6

(4) There is no maximum value.

13. What is the greatest zero of the function $y = x^2 - 25x + 66$?

(1) -22 (3) 3

(2) -3 (4) 22

14. What is the absolute value of $-5 + 12i$?

(1) 5 (3) 13

(2) 7 (4) 17

OPEN-ENDED

15. What is the x-coordinate of the vertex of the parabola that passes through the points $(0, -22)$, $(2, -6)$, and $(5, -12)$?

16. What is the minimum value of the function $f(x) = 4x^2 + 24x + 39$?

17. The surface area y of a cube is given by the function $y = 6x^2$ where x is an edge length. Graph the function. *Compare* this graph to the graph of $y = x^2$.

18. At what two points do the graphs of $y = 2x^2 - 5x - 12$ and $y = \frac{1}{2}x^2 - 3x + 4$ intersect? *Explain* your reasoning.

19. A volleyball is hit upward by a player in a game. The height h (in feet) of the volleyball after t seconds is given by the function $h = -16t^2 + 30t + 6$.

What is the maximum height of the volleyball? *Explain* your reasoning.

After how many seconds does the volleyball reach its maximum height?

After how many seconds does the volleyball hit the ground?

TEST PREPARATION

5 Polynomials and Polynomial Functions

Before

In previous chapters, you learned the following skills, which you'll use in Chapter 5: graphing functions, factoring, and solving equations.

Prerequisite Skills

VOCABULARY CHECK

Copy and complete the statement.

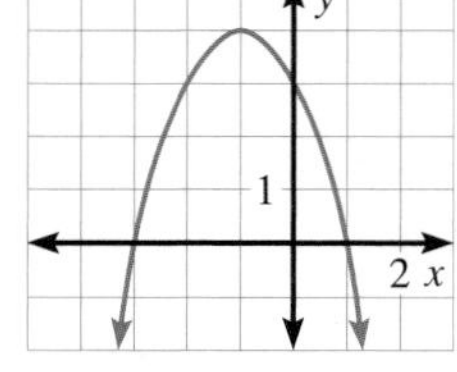

1. The **zeros** of the function graphed are _?_.
2. The **maximum value** of the function graphed is _?_.
3. The **standard form** of a quadratic equation in one variable is _?_ where $a \neq 0$.

SKILLS CHECK

Graph the function. Label the vertex and the axis of symmetry. *(Review pp. 236, 245 for 5.2.)*

4. $y = -2(x - 1)^2 + 4$
5. $y = 3(x - 2)(x + 3)$
6. $y = -x^2 - 4x + 4$

Factor the expression. *(Review pp. 252, 259 for 5.4.)*

7. $x^2 + 9x + 20$
8. $2x^2 + 5x - 3$
9. $9x^2 - 64$

Solve the equation. *(Review pp. 252, 259 for 5.4–5.7.)*

10. $2x^2 + x + 6 = 0$
11. $10x^2 + 13x = 3$
12. $x^2 + 6x + 2 = 20$

@HomeTutor Prerequisite skills practice at classzone.com

Now

In Chapter 5, you will apply the big ideas listed below and reviewed in the Chapter Summary on page 401. You will also use the key vocabulary listed below.

Big Ideas

1. **Graphing polynomial functions**
2. **Performing operations with polynomials**
3. **Solving polynomial equations and finding zeros**

KEY VOCABULARY

- polynomial, *p. 337*
- polynomial function, *p. 337*
- synthetic substitution, *p. 338*
- end behavior, *p. 339*
- factored completely, *p. 353*
- factor by grouping, *p. 354*
- quadratic form, *p. 355*
- polynomial long division, *p. 362*
- synthetic division, *p. 363*
- repeated solution, *p. 379*
- local maximum, *p. 388*
- local minimum, *p. 388*
- finite differences, *p. 393*

Why?

You can use polynomial functions to model real-life situations. For example, you can use a polynomial function to model the relationship between the speed of an object and the power needed to maintain that speed.

Animated Algebra

The animation illustrated below for Exercise 61 on page 351 helps you answer this question: How does the power needed to keep a bicycle moving at a constant speed change as the conditions change?

The power exerted by a bicyclist depends on speed and resistance.

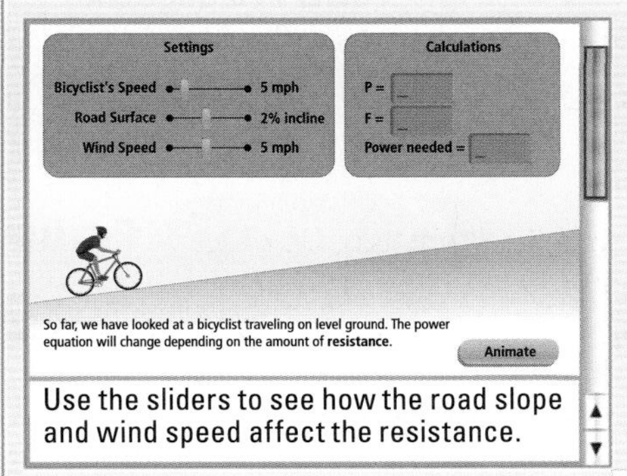

Use the sliders to see how the road slope and wind speed affect the resistance.

Animated Algebra at classzone.com

Other animations for Chapter 5: pages 331, 340, 371, 388, 396, and 401

5.1 Use Properties of Exponents

A2.A.8 Apply the rules of exponents to simplify expressions involving negative and/or fractional exponents

Before You evaluated powers.

Now You will simplify expressions involving powers.

Why? So you can compare the volumes of two stars, as in Example 5.

Key Vocabulary
- **scientific notation**

Consider what happens when you multiply two powers that have the same base:

$$2^3 \cdot 2^5 = (2 \cdot 2 \cdot 2) \cdot (2 \cdot 2 \cdot 2 \cdot 2 \cdot 2) = 2^8$$

Note that the exponent 8 in the product is the sum of the exponents 3 and 5 in the factors. This property is one of several properties of exponents shown below.

AVOID ERRORS
When you multiply powers, do not multiply the bases. For example, $3^2 \cdot 3^5 \neq 9^7$.

KEY CONCEPT *For Your Notebook*

Properties of Exponents

Let a and b be real numbers and let m and n be integers.

Property Name	Definition	Example
Product of Powers	$a^m \cdot a^n = a^{m+n}$	$5^3 \cdot 5^{-1} = 5^{3+(-1)} = 5^2 = 25$
Power of a Power	$(a^m)^n = a^{mn}$	$(3^3)^2 = 3^{3 \cdot 2} = 3^6 = 729$
Power of a Product	$(ab)^m = a^m b^m$	$(2 \cdot 3)^4 = 2^4 \cdot 3^4 = 1296$
Negative Exponent	$a^{-m} = \frac{1}{a^m}, a \neq 0$	$7^{-2} = \frac{1}{7^2} = \frac{1}{49}$
Zero Exponent	$a^0 = 1, a \neq 0$	$(-89)^0 = 1$
Quotient of Powers	$\frac{a^m}{a^n} = a^{m-n}, a \neq 0$	$\frac{6^{-3}}{6^{-6}} = 6^{-3-(-6)} = 6^3 = 216$
Power of a Quotient	$\left(\frac{a}{b}\right)^m = \frac{a^m}{b^m}, b \neq 0$	$\left(\frac{4}{7}\right)^2 = \frac{4^2}{7^2} = \frac{16}{49}$

EXAMPLE 1 Evaluate numerical expressions

a. $(-4 \cdot 2^5)^2 = (-4)^2 \cdot (2^5)^2$ — **Power of a product property**

$= 16 \cdot 2^{5 \cdot 2}$ — **Power of a power property**

$= 16 \cdot 2^{10} = 16{,}384$ — **Simplify and evaluate power.**

b. $\left(\frac{11^5}{11^8}\right)^{-1} = \frac{11^8}{11^5}$ — **Negative exponent property**

$= 11^{8-5}$ — **Quotient of powers property**

$= 11^3 = 1331$ — **Simplify and evaluate power.**

SCIENTIFIC NOTATION A number is expressed in **scientific notation** if it is in the form $c \times 10^n$ where $1 \le c < 10$ and n is an integer. When you work with numbers in scientific notation, the properties of exponents can make calculations easier.

EXAMPLE 2 Use scientific notation in real life

LOCUSTS A swarm of locusts may contain as many as 85 million locusts per square kilometer and cover an area of 1200 square kilometers. About how many locusts are in such a swarm?

Solution

Number of locusts = Locusts per square kilometer × Number of square kilometers

	$= 85{,}000{,}000 \times 1200$	**Substitute values.**
	$= (8.5 \times 10^7)(1.2 \times 10^3)$	**Write in scientific notation.**
	$= (8.5 \times 1.2)(10^7 \times 10^3)$	**Use multiplication properties.**
	$= 10.2 \times 10^{10}$	**Product of powers property**
	$= 1.02 \times 10^1 \times 10^{10}$	**Write 10.2 in scientific notation.**
	$= 1.02 \times 10^{11}$	**Product of powers property**

▶ The number of locusts is about 1.02×10^{11}, or about 102,000,000,000.

REVIEW SCIENTIFIC NOTATION
For help with scientific notation, see p. 982.

GUIDED PRACTICE for Examples 1 and 2

Evaluate the expression. Tell which properties of exponents you used.

1. $(4^2)^3$ **2.** $(-8)(-8)^3$ **3.** $\left(\frac{2}{9}\right)^3$ **4.** $\frac{6 \cdot 10^{-4}}{9 \cdot 10^7}$

SIMPLIFYING EXPRESSIONS You can use the properties of exponents to simplify algebraic expressions. A simplified expression contains only positive exponents.

EXAMPLE 3 Simplify expressions

a. $b^{-4}b^6b^7 = b^{-4+6+7} = b^9$ **Product of powers property**

b. $\left(\frac{r^{-2}}{s^3}\right)^{-3} = \frac{(r^{-2})^{-3}}{(s^3)^{-3}}$ **Power of a quotient property**

$= \frac{r^6}{s^{-9}}$ **Power of a power property**

$= r^6s^9$ **Negative exponent property**

c. $\frac{16m^4n^{-5}}{2n^{-5}} = 8m^4n^{-5-(-5)}$ **Quotient of powers property**

$= 8m^4n^0 = 8m^4$ **Zero exponent property**

Animated Algebra at classzone.com

INTERPRET BASES
In this book, it is assumed that any base with a zero or negative exponent is nonzero.

EXAMPLE 4 Standardized Test Practice

What is the simplified form of $\frac{(x^{-3}y^3)^2}{x^5y^6}$?

Ⓐ x^{11} Ⓑ $\frac{1}{x^{11}}$ Ⓒ $\frac{1}{x^6y}$ Ⓓ $\frac{1}{x^{11}y}$

Solution

$$\frac{(x^{-3}y^3)^2}{x^5y^6} = \frac{(x^{-3})^2(y^3)^2}{x^5y^6}$$ Power of a product property

$$= \frac{x^{-6}y^6}{x^5y^6}$$ Power of a power property

$$= x^{-6-5}y^{6-6}$$ Quotient of powers property

$$= x^{-11}y^0$$ Simplify exponents.

$$= x^{-11} \cdot 1$$ Zero exponent property

$$= \frac{1}{x^{11}}$$ Negative exponent property

▶ The correct answer is B. Ⓐ Ⓑ Ⓒ Ⓓ

EXAMPLE 5 Compare real-life volumes

ASTRONOMY Betelgeuse is one of the stars found in the constellation Orion. Its radius is about 1500 times the radius of the sun. How many times as great as the sun's volume is Betelgeuse's volume?

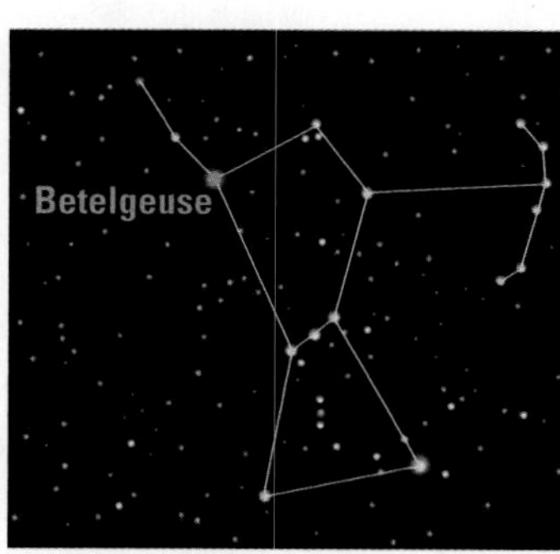

Solution

Let r represent the sun's radius. Then $1500r$ represents Betelgeuse's radius.

$$\frac{\text{Betelgeuse's volume}}{\text{Sun's volume}} = \frac{\frac{4}{3}\pi(1500r)^3}{\frac{4}{3}\pi r^3}$$ The volume of a sphere is $\frac{4}{3}\pi r^3$.

$$= \frac{\frac{4}{3}\pi 1500^3 r^3}{\frac{4}{3}\pi r^3}$$ Power of a product property

$$= 1500^3 r^0$$ Quotient of powers property

$$= 1500^3 \cdot 1$$ Zero exponent property

$$= 3{,}375{,}000{,}000$$ Evaluate power.

▶ Betelgeuse's volume is about 3.4 billion times as great as the sun's volume.

GUIDED PRACTICE for Examples 3, 4, and 5

Simplify the expression. Tell which properties of exponents you used.

5. $x^{-6}x^5x^3$ 6. $(7y^2z^5)(y^{-4}z^{-1})$ 7. $\left(\frac{s^3}{t^{-4}}\right)^2$ 8. $\left(\frac{x^4y^{-2}}{x^3y^6}\right)^3$

5.1 EXERCISES

HOMEWORK KEY

○ = **WORKED-OUT SOLUTIONS** on p. WS9 for Exs. 17, 31, and 51

★ = **STANDARDIZED TEST PRACTICE** Exs. 2, 36, 46, 51, and 53

SKILL PRACTICE

1. **VOCABULARY** State the name of the property illustrated.

a. $a^m \cdot a^n = a^{m+n}$ b. $a^{-m} = \frac{1}{a^m}, a \neq 0$ c. $(ab)^m = a^m b^m$

2. ★ **WRITING** Is the number 25.2×10^{-3} in scientific notation? *Explain.*

EXAMPLE 1 on p. 330 for Exs. 3–14

EVALUATING NUMERICAL EXPRESSIONS Evaluate the expression. Tell which properties of exponents you used.

3. $3^3 \cdot 3^2$ 4. $(4^{-2})^3$ 5. $(-5)(-5)^4$ 6. $(2^4)^2$

7. $\frac{5^2}{5^5}$ 8. $\left(\frac{3}{5}\right)^4$ 9. $\left(\frac{2}{7}\right)^{-3}$ 10. $9^3 \cdot 9^{-1}$

11. $\frac{3^4}{3^{-2}}$ 12. $\left(\frac{2}{3}\right)^{-5}\left(\frac{2}{3}\right)^4$ 13. $6^3 \cdot 6^0 \cdot 6^{-5}$ 14. $\left(\left(\frac{1}{2}\right)^{-5}\right)^2$

EXAMPLE 2 on p. 331 for Exs. 15–23

SCIENTIFIC NOTATION Write the answer in scientific notation.

15. $(4.2 \times 10^3)(1.5 \times 10^6)$ 16. $(1.2 \times 10^{-3})(6.7 \times 10^{-7})$ 17. $(6.3 \times 10^5)(8.9 \times 10^{-12})$

18. $(7.2 \times 10^9)(9.4 \times 10^8)$ 19. $(2.1 \times 10^{-4})^3$ 20. $(4.0 \times 10^3)^4$

21. $\frac{8.1 \times 10^{12}}{5.4 \times 10^9}$ 22. $\frac{1.1 \times 10^{-3}}{5.5 \times 10^{-8}}$ 23. $\frac{(7.5 \times 10^8)(4.5 \times 10^{-4})}{1.5 \times 10^7}$

EXAMPLES 3 and 4 on pp. 331–332 for Exs. 24–39

SIMPLIFYING ALGEBRAIC EXPRESSIONS Simplify the expression. Tell which properties of exponents you used.

24. $\frac{w^{-2}}{w^6}$ 25. $(2^2y^3)^5$ 26. $(p^3q^2)^{-1}$ 27. $(w^3x^{-2})(w^6x^{-1})$

28. $(5s^{-2}t^4)^{-3}$ 29. $(3a^3b^5)^{-3}$ 30. $\frac{x^{-1}y^2}{x^2y^{-1}}$ 31. $\frac{3c^3d}{9cd^{-1}}$

32. $\frac{4r^4s^5}{24r^4s^{-5}}$ 33. $\frac{2a^3b^{-4}}{3a^5b^{-2}}$ 34. $\frac{y^{11}}{4z^3} \cdot \frac{8z^7}{y^7}$ 35. $\frac{x^2y^{-3}}{3y^2} \cdot \frac{y^2}{x^{-4}}$

36. ★ **MULTIPLE CHOICE** What is the simplified form of $\frac{2x^2y}{6xy^{-1}}$?

Ⓐ $\frac{y^2}{3}$ Ⓑ $\frac{xy^2}{3}$ Ⓒ $\frac{x}{3}$ Ⓓ $\frac{1}{3}$

ERROR ANALYSIS ***Describe*** **and correct the error in simplifying the expression.**

37. $\frac{x^{10}}{x^2} = x^5$ ✗

38. $x^5 \cdot x^3 = x^{15}$ ✗

39. $(-3)^2(-3)^4 = 9^6$ ✗

GEOMETRY **Write an expression for the figure's area or volume in terms of *x*.**

40. $A = \frac{\sqrt{3}}{4}s^2$

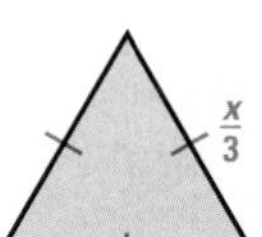

41. $V = \pi r^2 h$

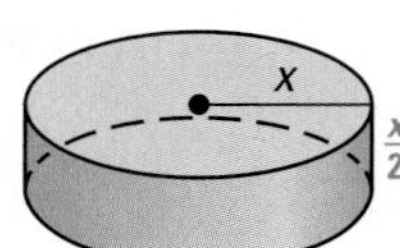

42. $V = \ell wh$

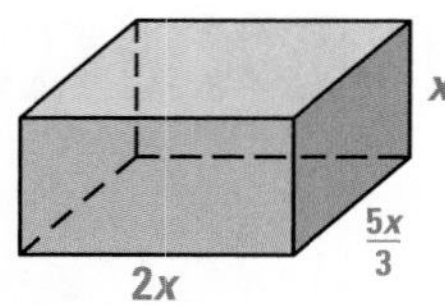

REASONING **Write an expression that makes the statement true.**

43. $x^{15}y^{12}z^8 = x^4y^7z^{11} \cdot ?$

44. $3x^3y^2 = \frac{12x^2y^5}{?}$

45. $(a^5b^4)^2 = a^{14}b^{-1} \cdot ?$

46. ★ **OPEN-ENDED MATH** Find three different ways to complete the following statement so that it is true: $x^{12}y^{16} = (x^?y^?)(x^?y^?)$.

CHALLENGE **Refer to the properties of exponents on page 330.**

47. Show how the negative exponent property can be derived from the quotient of powers property and the zero exponent property.

48. Show how the quotient of powers property can be derived from the product of powers property and the negative exponent property.

PROBLEM SOLVING

EXAMPLE 2
on p. 331
for Exs. 49–50

49. OCEAN VOLUME The table shows the surface areas and average depths of four oceans. Calculate the volume of each ocean by multiplying the surface area of each ocean by its average depth. Write your answers in scientific notation.

Ocean	Surface area (square meters)	Average depth (meters)
Pacific	1.56×10^{14}	4.03×10^3
Atlantic	7.68×10^{13}	3.93×10^3
Indian	6.86×10^{13}	3.96×10^3
Arctic	1.41×10^{13}	1.21×10^3

@HomeTutor for problem solving help at classzone.com

50. EARTH SCIENCE The continents of Earth move at a very slow rate. The South American continent has been moving about 0.000022 mile per year for the past 125,000,000 years. How far has the continent moved in that time? Write your answer in scientific notation.

@HomeTutor for problem solving help at classzone.com

EXAMPLE 5
on p. 332
for Exs. 51–52

51. ★ **SHORT RESPONSE** A typical cultured black pearl is made by placing a bead with a diameter of 6 millimeters inside an oyster. The resulting pearl has a diameter of about 9 millimeters. *Compare* the volume of the resulting pearl with the volume of the bead.

52. **MULTI-STEP PROBLEM** A can of tennis balls consists of three spheres of radius r stacked vertically inside a cylinder of radius r and height h.

a. Write an expression for the total volume of the three tennis balls in terms of r.

b. Write an expression for the volume of the cylinder in terms of r and h.

c. Write an expression for h in terms of r using the fact that the height of the cylinder is the sum of the diameters of the three tennis balls.

d. What fraction of the can's volume is taken up by the tennis balls?

53. ★ **EXTENDED RESPONSE** You can think of a penny as a cylinder with a radius of about 9.53 millimeters and a height of about 1.55 millimeters.

a. **Calculate** Approximate the volume of a penny. Give your answer in cubic meters.

b. **Estimate** Approximate the volume of your classroom in cubic meters. *Explain* how you obtained your answer.

c. **Interpret** Use your results from parts (a) and (b) to estimate how many pennies it would take to fill your classroom. Do you think your answer is an overestimate or an underestimate? *Explain*.

54. **CHALLENGE** Earth's core is approximately spherical in shape and is divided into a solid inner core (the yellow region in the diagram shown) and a liquid outer core (the dark orange region in the diagram).

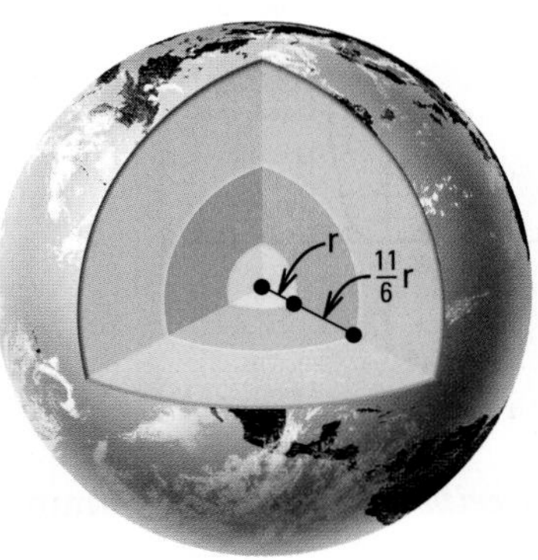

a. Earth's radius is about 5 times as great as the radius of Earth's inner core. Find the ratio of Earth's total volume to the volume of Earth's inner core.

b. Find the ratio of the volume of Earth's outer core to the volume of Earth's inner core.

NEW YORK MIXED REVIEW

TEST PRACTICE at classzone.com

55. What are the zeros of the function $y = 2x^2 + 5x - 12$?

Ⓐ $-\frac{3}{2}, -4$ Ⓑ $-\frac{3}{2}, 4$ Ⓒ $\frac{3}{2}, -4$ Ⓓ $\frac{3}{2}, 4$

56. In the diagram, $\overrightarrow{NP}$ bisects $\angle MNQ$ and $m\angle MNP$ is $x°$. Which equation can be used to find y, which represents $m\angle MNQ$?

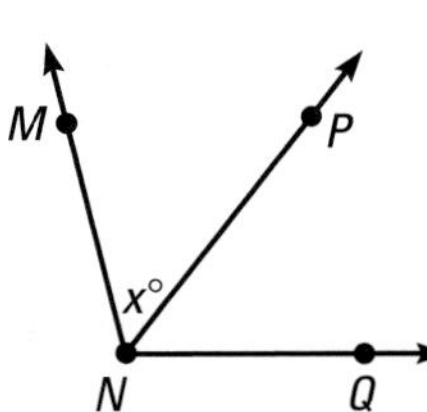

Ⓐ $y = \frac{x}{2}$ Ⓑ $y = x$

Ⓒ $y = 2x$ Ⓓ $y = 180 - x$

@HomeTutor
classzone.com
Keystrokes

5.2 End Behavior of Polynomial Functions

MATERIALS • graphing calculator

QUESTION **How is the end behavior of a polynomial function related to the function's equation?**

Functions of the form $f(x) = \pm x^n$, where n is a positive integer, are examples of *polynomial functions*. The *end behavior* of a polynomial function's graph is its behavior as x approaches positive infinity $(+\infty)$ or as x approaches negative infinity $(-\infty)$.

EXPLORE **Investigate the end behavior of $f(x) = \pm x^n$ where n is even**

Graph the function. Describe the end behavior of the graph.

a. $f(x) = x^4$ **b.** $f(x) = -x^4$

STEP 1 ***Graph functions*** Graph each function on a graphing calculator.

a.

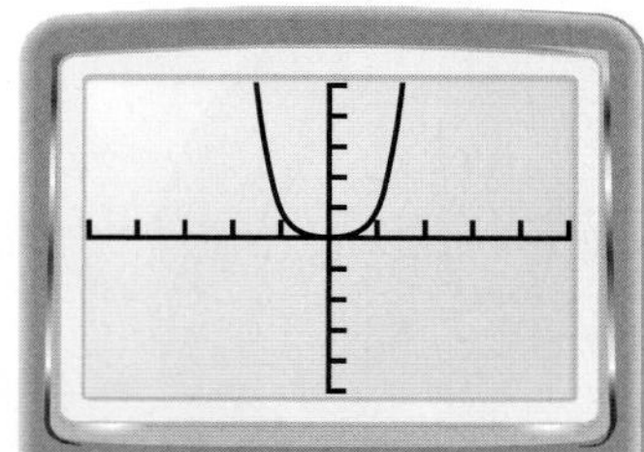

b.

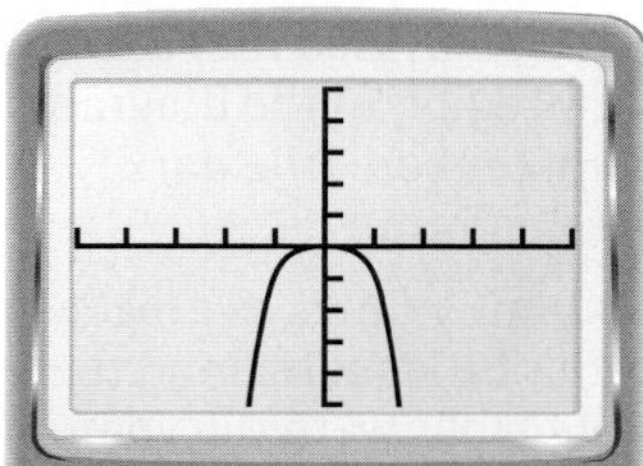

STEP 2 ***Describe end behavior*** Summarize the end behavior of each function.

Function	As x approaches $-\infty$	As x approaches $+\infty$
a. $f(x) = x^4$	$f(x)$ approaches $+\infty$	$f(x)$ approaches $+\infty$
b. $f(x) = -x^4$	$f(x)$ approaches $-\infty$	$f(x)$ approaches $-\infty$

DRAW CONCLUSIONS **Use your observations to complete these exercises**

Graph the function. Then describe its end behavior as shown above.

1. $f(x) = x^5$ **2.** $f(x) = -x^5$ **3.** $f(x) = x^6$ **4.** $f(x) = -x^6$

5. Make a conjecture about the end behavior of each family of functions.

a. $f(x) = x^n$ where n is odd **b.** $f(x) = -x^n$ where n is odd

c. $f(x) = x^n$ where n is even **d.** $f(x) = -x^n$ where n is even

6. Make a conjecture about the end behavior of the function $f(x) = x^6 - x$. *Explain* your reasoning.

5.2 Evaluate and Graph Polynomial Functions

A2.A.41 Use functional notation to evaluate functions for given values in the domain

Before You evaluated and graphed linear and quadratic functions.

Now You will evaluate and graph other polynomial functions.

Why? So you can model skateboarding participation, as in Ex. 55.

Key Vocabulary
- polynomial
- polynomial function
- synthetic substitution
- end behavior

Recall that a monomial is a number, a variable, or a product of numbers and variables. A **polynomial** is a monomial or a sum of monomials. A **polynomial function** is a function of the form

$$f(x) = a_n x^n + a_{n-1} x^{n-1} + \cdots + a_1 x + a_0$$

where $a_n \neq 0$, the exponents are all whole numbers, and the coefficients are all real numbers. For this function, a_n is the **leading coefficient**, n is the **degree**, and a_0 is the **constant term**. A polynomial function is in **standard form** if its terms are written in descending order of exponents from left to right.

Common Polynomial Functions			
Degree	**Type**	**Standard form**	**Example**
0	Constant	$f(x) = a_0$	$f(x) = -14$
1	Linear	$f(x) = a_1x + a_0$	$f(x) = 5x - 7$
2	Quadratic	$f(x) = a_2x^2 + a_1x + a_0$	$f(x) = 2x^2 + x - 9$
3	Cubic	$f(x) = a_3x^3 + a_2x^2 + a_1x + a_0$	$f(x) = x^3 - x^2 + 3x$
4	Quartic	$f(x) = a_4x^4 + a_3x^3 + a_2x^2 + a_1x + a_0$	$f(x) = x^4 + 2x - 1$

EXAMPLE 1 Identify polynomial functions

Decide whether the function is a polynomial function. If so, write it in standard form and state its degree, type, and leading coefficient.

a. $h(x) = x^4 - \frac{1}{4}x^2 + 3$

b. $g(x) = 7x - \sqrt{3} + \pi x^2$

c. $f(x) = 5x^2 + 3x^{-1} - x$

d. $k(x) = x + 2^x - 0.6x^5$

Solution

a. The function is a polynomial function that is already written in standard form. It has degree 4 (quartic) and a leading coefficient of 1.

b. The function is a polynomial function written as $g(x) = \pi x^2 + 7x - \sqrt{3}$ in standard form. It has degree 2 (quadratic) and a leading coefficient of π.

c. The function is not a polynomial function because the term $3x^{-1}$ has an exponent that is not a whole number.

d. The function is not a polynomial function because the term 2^x does not have a variable base and an exponent that is a whole number.

EXAMPLE 2 Evaluate by direct substitution

Use direct substitution to evaluate $f(x) = 2x^4 - 5x^3 - 4x + 8$ when $x = 3$.

$f(x) = 2x^4 - 5x^3 - 4x + 8$ **Write original function.**

$f(3) = 2(3)^4 - 5(3)^3 - 4(3) + 8$ **Substitute 3 for x.**

$= 162 - 135 - 12 + 8$ **Evaluate powers and multiply.**

$= 23$ **Simplify.**

✓ GUIDED PRACTICE for Examples 1 and 2

Decide whether the function is a polynomial function. If so, write it in standard form and state its degree, type, and leading coefficient.

1. $f(x) = 13 - 2x$
2. $p(x) = 9x^4 - 5x^{-2} + 4$
3. $h(x) = 6x^2 + \pi - 3x$

Use direct substitution to evaluate the polynomial function for the given value of x.

4. $f(x) = x^4 + 2x^3 + 3x^2 - 7;\ x = -2$
5. $g(x) = x^3 - 5x^2 + 6x + 1;\ x = 4$

SYNTHETIC SUBSTITUTION Another way to evaluate a polynomial function is to use **synthetic substitution**. This method, shown in the next example, involves fewer operations than direct substitution.

EXAMPLE 3 Evaluate by synthetic substitution

Use synthetic substitution to evaluate $f(x)$ from Example 2 when $x = 3$.

Solution

AVOID ERRORS
The row of coefficients for $f(x)$ must include a coefficient of 0 for the "missing" x^2-term.

STEP 1 **Write** the coefficients of $f(x)$ in order of descending exponents. Write the value at which $f(x)$ is being evaluated to the left.

x-value → 3 | 2 −5 0 −4 8 ← **coefficients**

STEP 2 **Bring down** the leading coefficient. **Multiply** the leading coefficient by the x-value. Write the product under the second coefficient. **Add.**

3 | 2 −5 0 −4 8
6
2 1

STEP 3 **Multiply** the previous sum by the x-value. Write the product under the third coefficient. **Add.** Repeat for all of the remaining coefficients. The final sum is the value of $f(x)$ at the given x-value.

3 | 2 −5 0 −4 8

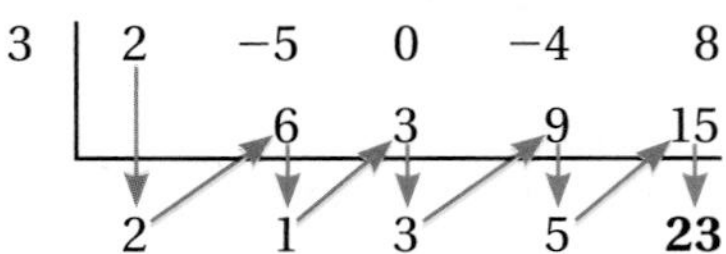

▶ Synthetic substitution gives $f(3) = 23$, which matches the result in Example 2.

END BEHAVIOR The **end behavior** of a function's graph is the behavior of the graph as x approaches positive infinity ($+\infty$) or negative infinity ($-\infty$). For the graph of a polynomial function, the end behavior is determined by the function's degree and the sign of its leading coefficient.

READING
The expression "$x \to +\infty$" is read as "x approaches positive infinity."

KEY CONCEPT — *For Your Notebook*

End Behavior of Polynomial Functions

Degree: odd
Leading coefficient: positive

$f(x) \to +\infty$ as $x \to +\infty$

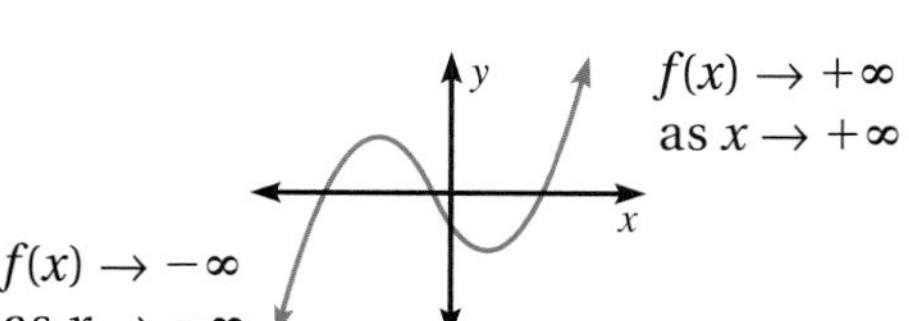

$f(x) \to -\infty$ as $x \to -\infty$

Degree: odd
Leading coefficient: negative

$f(x) \to +\infty$ as $x \to -\infty$

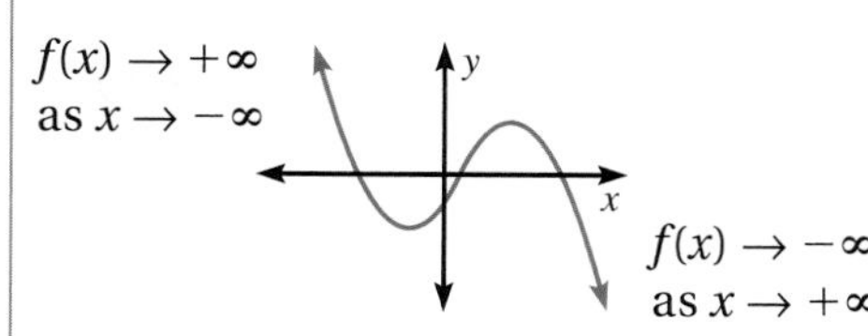

$f(x) \to -\infty$ as $x \to +\infty$

Degree: even
Leading coefficient: positive

$f(x) \to +\infty$ as $x \to -\infty$

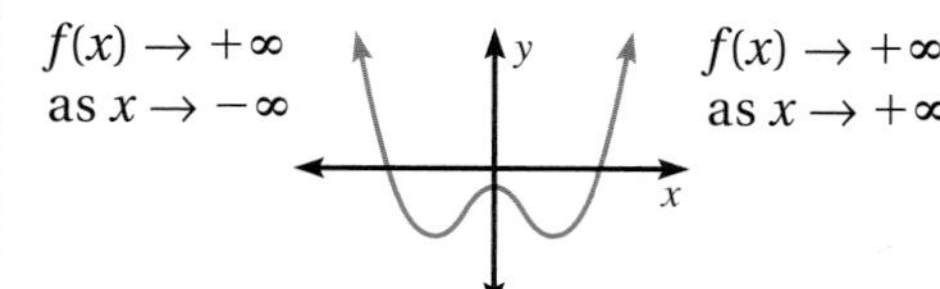

$f(x) \to +\infty$ as $x \to +\infty$

Degree: even
Leading coefficient: negative

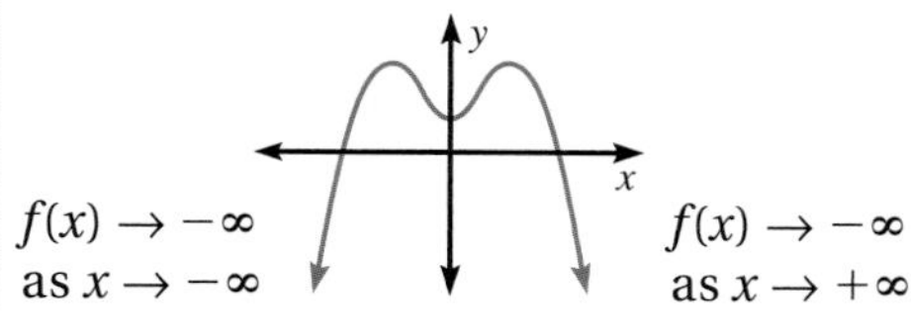

$f(x) \to -\infty$ as $x \to -\infty$

$f(x) \to -\infty$ as $x \to +\infty$

EXAMPLE 4 Standardized Test Practice

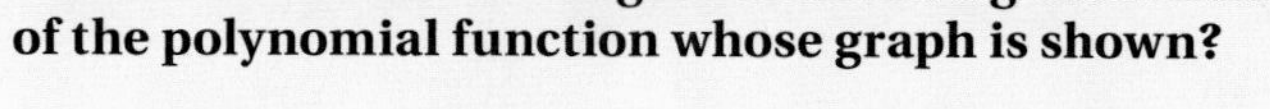

What is true about the degree and leading coefficient of the polynomial function whose graph is shown?

Ⓐ Degree is odd; leading coefficient is positive

Ⓑ Degree is odd; leading coefficient is negative

Ⓒ Degree is even; leading coefficient is positive

Ⓓ Degree is even; leading coefficient is negative

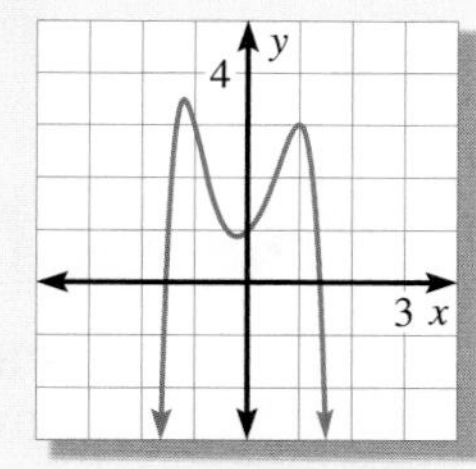

From the graph, $f(x) \to -\infty$ as $x \to -\infty$ and $f(x) \to -\infty$ as $x \to +\infty$. So, the degree is even and the leading coefficient is negative.

▶ The correct answer is D. Ⓐ Ⓑ Ⓒ Ⓓ

GUIDED PRACTICE for Examples 3 and 4

Use synthetic substitution to evaluate the polynomial function for the given value of x.

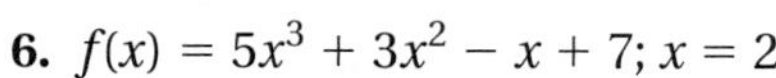

6. $f(x) = 5x^3 + 3x^2 - x + 7; x = 2$

7. $g(x) = -2x^4 - x^3 + 4x - 5; x = -1$

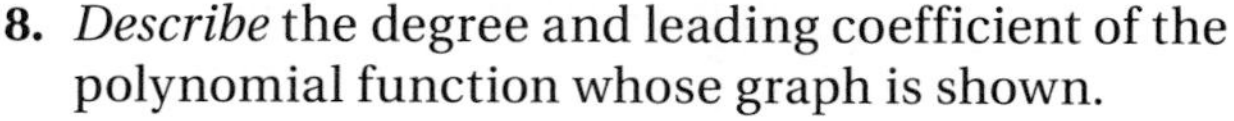

8. *Describe* the degree and leading coefficient of the polynomial function whose graph is shown.

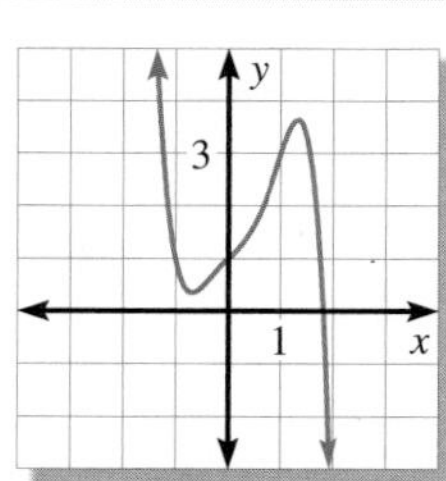

GRAPHING POLYNOMIAL FUNCTIONS To graph a polynomial function, first plot points to determine the shape of the graph's middle portion. Then use what you know about end behavior to sketch the ends of the graph.

EXAMPLE 5 Graph polynomial functions

Graph (a) $f(x) = -x^3 + x^2 + 3x - 3$ and (b) $f(x) = x^4 - x^3 - 4x^2 + 4$.

Solution

a. To graph the function, make a table of values and plot the corresponding points. Connect the points with a smooth curve and check the end behavior.

x	−3	−2	−1	0	1	2	3
y	24	3	−4	−3	0	−1	−12

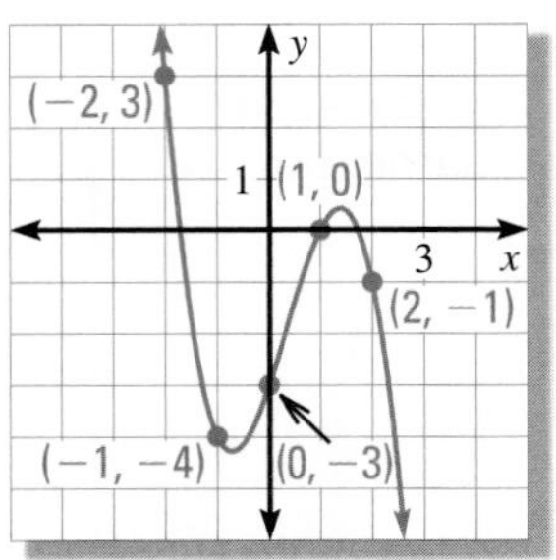

The degree is odd and leading coefficient is negative. So, $f(x) \to +\infty$ as $x \to -\infty$ and $f(x) \to -\infty$ as $x \to +\infty$.

b. To graph the function, make a table of values and plot the corresponding points. Connect the points with a smooth curve and check the end behavior.

x	−3	−2	−1	0	1	2	3
y	76	12	2	4	0	−4	22

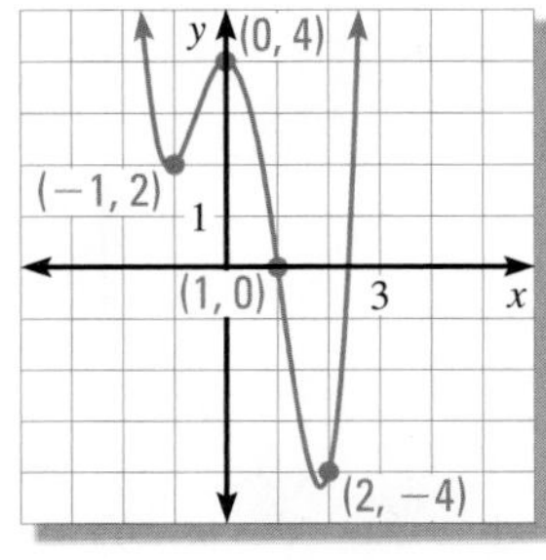

The degree is even and leading coefficient is positive. So, $f(x) \to +\infty$ as $x \to -\infty$ and $f(x) \to +\infty$ as $x \to +\infty$.

Animated Algebra at classzone.com

EXAMPLE 6 Solve a multi-step problem

PHYSICAL SCIENCE The energy E (in foot-pounds) in each square foot of a wave is given by the model $E = 0.0029s^4$ where s is the wind speed (in knots). Graph the model. Use the graph to estimate the wind speed needed to generate a wave with 1000 foot-pounds of energy per square foot.

Solution

STEP 1 **Make** a table of values. The model only deals with positive values of s.

s	0	10	20	30	40
E	0	29	464	2349	7424

STEP 2 **Plot** the points and connect them with a smooth curve. Because the leading coefficient is positive and the degree is even, the graph rises to the right.

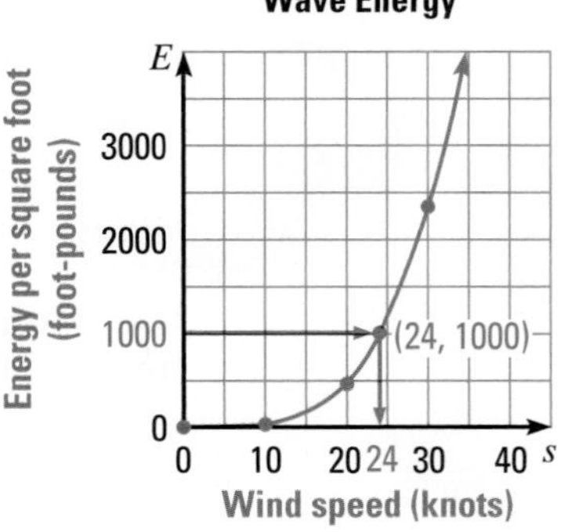

STEP 3 **Examine** the graph to see that $s \approx 24$ when $E = 1000$.

▶ The wind speed needed to generate the wave is about 24 knots.

✓ **GUIDED PRACTICE** for Examples 5 and 6

Graph the polynomial function.

9. $f(x) = x^4 + 6x^2 - 3$
10. $f(x) = -x^3 + x^2 + x - 1$
11. $f(x) = 4 - 2x^3$

12. **WHAT IF?** If wind speed is measured in miles per hour, the model in Example 6 becomes $E = 0.0051s^4$. Graph this model. What wind speed is needed to generate a wave with 2000 foot-pounds of energy per square foot?

5.2 EXERCISES

HOMEWORK KEY

○ = **WORKED-OUT SOLUTIONS** on p. WS10 for Exs. 21, 27, and 57

★ = **STANDARDIZED TEST PRACTICE** Exs. 2, 24, 37, 50, 52, and 59

◆ = **MULTIPLE REPRESENTATIONS** Ex. 56

SKILL PRACTICE

1. **VOCABULARY** Identify the degree, type, leading coefficient, and constant term of the polynomial function $f(x) = 6 + 2x^2 - 5x^4$.

2. ★ **WRITING** *Explain* what is meant by the end behavior of a polynomial function.

EXAMPLE 1 on p. 337 for Exs. 3–8

POLYNOMIAL FUNCTIONS Decide whether the function is a polynomial function. If so, write it in standard form and state its degree, type, and leading coefficient.

3. $f(x) = 8 - x^2$
4. $f(x) = 6x + 8x^4 - 3$
5. $g(x) = \pi x^4 + \sqrt{6}$
6. $h(x) = x^3\sqrt{10} + 5x^{-2} + 1$
7. $h(x) = -\frac{5}{2}x^3 + 3x - 10$
8. $g(x) = 8x^3 - 4x^2 + \frac{2}{x}$

EXAMPLE 2 on p. 338 for Exs. 9–14

DIRECT SUBSTITUTION Use direct substitution to evaluate the polynomial function for the given value of *x*.

9. $f(x) = 5x^3 - 2x^2 + 10x - 15;\ x = -1$
10. $f(x) = 8x + 5x^4 - 3x^2 - x^3;\ x = 2$
11. $g(x) = 4x^3 - 2x^5;\ x = -3$
12. $h(x) = 6x^3 - 25x + 20;\ x = 5$
13. $h(x) = x + \frac{1}{2}x^4 - \frac{3}{4}x^3 + 10;\ x = -4$
14. $g(x) = 4x^5 + 6x^3 + x^2 - 10x + 5;\ x = -2$

EXAMPLE 3 on p. 338 for Exs. 15–23

SYNTHETIC SUBSTITUTION Use synthetic substitution to evaluate the polynomial function for the given value of *x*.

15. $f(x) = 5x^3 - 2x^2 - 8x + 16;\ x = 3$
16. $f(x) = 8x^4 + 12x^3 + 6x^2 - 5x + 9;\ x = -2$
17. $g(x) = x^3 + 8x^2 - 7x + 35;\ x = -6$
18. $h(x) = -8x^3 + 14x - 35;\ x = 4$
19. $f(x) = -2x^4 + 3x^3 - 8x + 13;\ x = 2$
20. $g(x) = 6x^5 + 10x^3 - 27;\ x = -3$
21. $h(x) = -7x^3 + 11x^2 + 4x;\ x = 3$
22. $f(x) = x^4 + 3x - 20;\ x = 4$

23. **ERROR ANALYSIS** *Describe* and correct the error in evaluating the polynomial function $f(x) = -4x^4 + 9x^2 - 21x + 7$ when $x = -2$.

−2	−4	9	−21	7
		8	−34	110
	−4	17	−55	117

EXAMPLE 4
on p. 339
for Exs. 24–27

24. ★ **MULTIPLE CHOICE** The graph of a polynomial function is shown. What is true about the function's degree and leading coefficient?

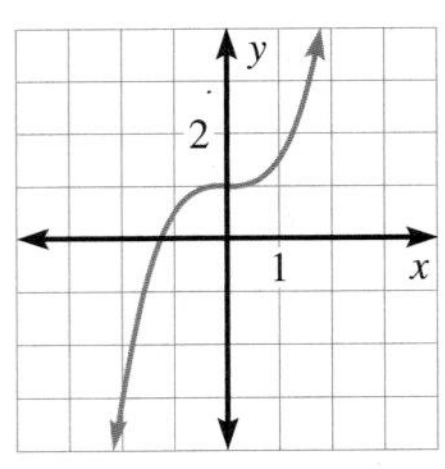

Ⓐ The degree is odd and the leading coefficient is positive.

Ⓑ The degree is odd and the leading coefficient is negative.

Ⓒ The degree is even and the leading coefficient is positive.

Ⓓ The degree is even and the leading coefficient is negative.

USING END BEHAVIOR ***Describe*** **the degree and leading coefficient of the polynomial function whose graph is shown.**

25. 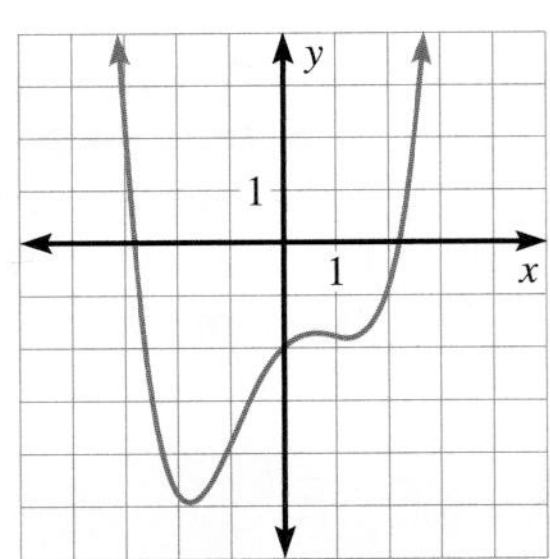

26. 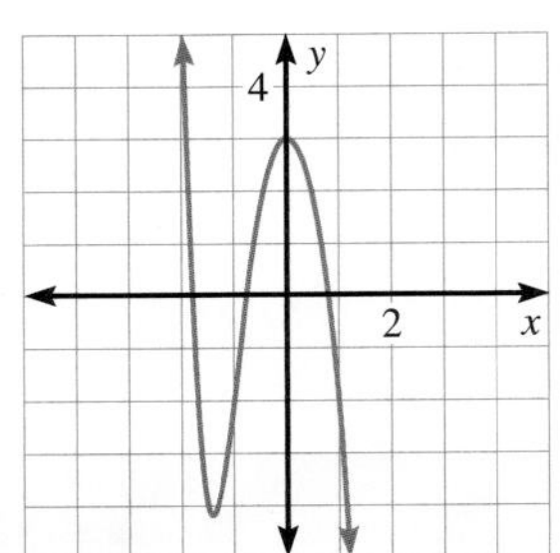

27. 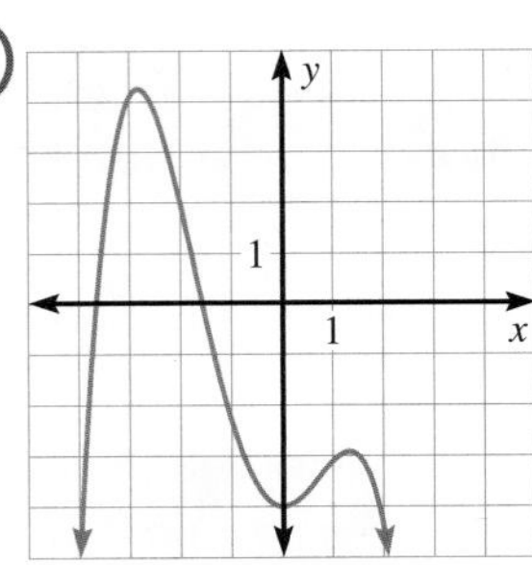

DESCRIBING END BEHAVIOR ***Describe*** **the end behavior of the graph of the polynomial function by completing these statements:** $f(x) \to$ **_?_ as** $x \to -\infty$ **and** $f(x) \to$ **_?_ as** $x \to +\infty$.

28. $f(x) = 10x^4$

29. $f(x) = -x^6 + 4x^3 - 3x$

30. $f(x) = -2x^3 + 7x - 4$

31. $f(x) = x^7 + 3x^4 - x^2$

32. $f(x) = 3x^{10} - 16x$

33. $f(x) = -6x^5 + 14x^2 + 20$

34. $f(x) = 0.2x^3 - x + 45$

35. $f(x) = 5x^8 + 8x^7$

36. $f(x) = -x^{273} + 500x^{271}$

37. ★ **OPEN-ENDED MATH** Write a polynomial function f of degree 5 such that the end behavior of the graph of f is given by $f(x) \to +\infty$ as $x \to -\infty$ and $f(x) \to -\infty$ as $x \to +\infty$. Then graph the function to verify your answer.

EXAMPLE 5
on p. 340
for Exs. 38–50

GRAPHING POLYNOMIALS **Graph the polynomial function.**

38. $f(x) = x^3$

39. $f(x) = -x^4$

40. $f(x) = x^5 + 3$

41. $f(x) = x^4 - 2$

42. $f(x) = -x^3 + 5$

43. $f(x) = x^3 - 5x$

44. $f(x) = -x^4 + 8x$

45. $f(x) = x^5 + x$

46. $f(x) = -x^3 + 3x^2 - 2x + 5$

47. $f(x) = x^5 + x^2 - 4$

48. $f(x) = x^4 - 5x^2 + 6$

49. $f(x) = -x^4 + 3x^3 - x + 1$

50. ★ **MULTIPLE CHOICE** Which function is represented by the graph shown?

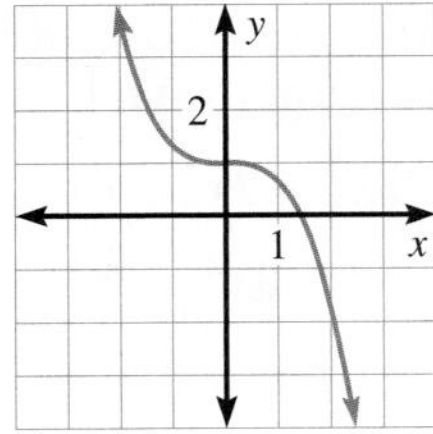

Ⓐ $f(x) = \frac{1}{3}x^3 + 1$ Ⓑ $f(x) = -\frac{1}{3}x^3 + 1$

Ⓒ $f(x) = \frac{1}{3}x^3 - 1$ Ⓓ $f(x) = -\frac{1}{3}x^3 - 1$

51. **VISUAL THINKING** Suppose $f(x) \to +\infty$ as $x \to -\infty$ and $f(x) \to -\infty$ as $x \to +\infty$. *Describe* the end behavior of $g(x) = -f(x)$.

52. ★ **SHORT RESPONSE** A cubic polynomial function f has leading coefficient 2 and constant term -5. If $f(1) = 0$ and $f(2) = 3$, what is $f(-5)$? *Explain* how you found your answer.

53. CHALLENGE Let $f(x) = x^3$ and $g(x) = x^3 - 2x^2 + 4x$.

a. Copy and complete the table.

b. Use the numbers in the table to complete this statement: As $x \to +\infty$, $\frac{f(x)}{g(x)} \to$ __?__.

c. *Explain* how the result from part (b) shows that the functions f and g have the same end behavior as $x \to +\infty$.

x	$f(x)$	$g(x)$	$\frac{f(x)}{g(x)}$
10	?	?	?
20	?	?	?
50	?	?	?
100	?	?	?
200	?	?	?

PROBLEM SOLVING

EXAMPLE 6 on p. 340 for Exs. 54–59

54. DIAMONDS The weight of an ideal round-cut diamond can be modeled by

$$w = 0.0071d^3 - 0.090d^2 + 0.48d$$

where w is the diamond's weight (in carats) and d is its diameter (in millimeters). According to the model, what is the weight of a diamond with a diameter of 15 millimeters?

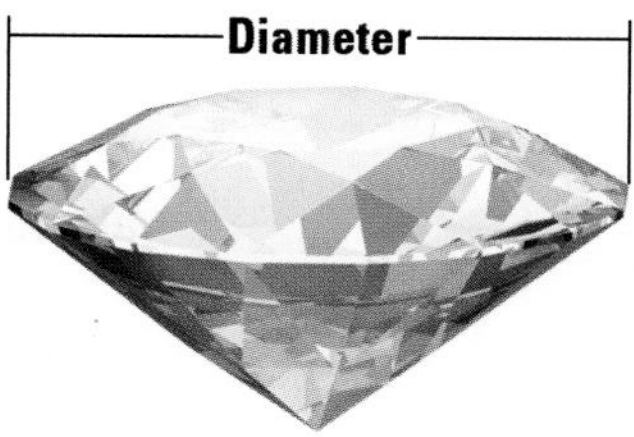

for problem solving help at classzone.com

55. SKATEBOARDING From 1992 to 2003, the number of people in the United States who participated in skateboarding can be modeled by

$$S = -0.0076t^4 + 0.14t^3 - 0.62t^2 + 0.52t + 5.5$$

where S is the number of participants (in millions) and t is the number of years since 1992. Graph the model. Then use the graph to estimate the first year that the number of skateboarding participants was greater than 8 million.

@HomeTutor for problem solving help at classzone.com

56. MULTIPLE REPRESENTATIONS From 1987 to 2003, the number of indoor movie screens M in the United States can be modeled by

$$M = -11.0t^3 + 267t^2 - 592t + 21{,}600$$

where t is the number of years since 1987.

a. **Classifying a Function** State the degree and type of the function.

b. **Making a Table** Make a table of values for the function.

c. **Sketching a Graph** Use your table to graph the function.

57. SNOWBOARDING From 1992 to 2003, the number of people in the United States who participated in snowboarding can be modeled by

$$S = 0.0013t^4 - 0.021t^3 + 0.084t^2 + 0.037t + 1.2$$

where S is the number of participants (in millions) and t is the number of years since 1992. Graph the model. Use the graph to estimate the first year that the number of snowboarding participants was greater than 2 million.

58. MULTI-STEP PROBLEM From 1980 to 2002, the number of quarterly periodicals P published in the United States can be modeled by

$$P = 0.138t^4 - 6.24t^3 + 86.8t^2 - 239t + 1450$$

where t is the number of years since 1980.

a. *Describe* the end behavior of the graph of the model.

b. Graph the model on the domain $0 \le t \le 22$.

c. Use the model to predict the number of quarterly periodicals in the year 2010. Is it appropriate to use the model to make this prediction? *Explain.*

59. ★ EXTENDED RESPONSE The weight of Sarus crane chicks S and hooded crane chicks H (both in grams) during the 10 days following hatching can be modeled by the functions

$$S = -0.122t^3 + 3.49t^2 - 14.6t + 136$$

$$H = -0.115t^3 + 3.71t^2 - 20.6t + 124$$

where t is the number of days after hatching.

a. Calculate According to the models, what is the difference in weight between 5-day-old Sarus crane chicks and hooded crane chicks?

b. Graph Sketch the graphs of the two models.

c. Apply A biologist finds that the weight of a crane chick after 3 days is 130 grams. What species of crane is the chick more likely to be? *Explain* how you found your answer.

60. CHALLENGE The weight y (in pounds) of a rainbow trout can be modeled by $y = 0.000304x^3$ where x is the length of the trout (in inches).

a. Write a function that relates the weight y and length x of a rainbow trout if y is measured in kilograms and x is measured in centimeters. Use the fact that 1 kilogram $\approx$ 2.20 pounds and 1 centimeter $\approx$ 0.394 inch.

b. Graph the original function and the function from part (a) in the same coordinate plane. What type of transformation can you apply to the graph of $y = 0.000304x^3$ to produce the graph from part (a)?

NEW YORK MIXED REVIEW

TEST PRACTICE at classzone.com

61. Amanda starts a business that sells silk-screened shirts. Her overhead costs are \$500, and then she pays an additional \$4.25 per shirt in material costs. If Amanda sells the silk-screened shirts for \$10.50 each, how many shirts must she sell before she can make a profit?

Ⓐ 34 Ⓑ 48

Ⓒ 80 Ⓓ 118

62. Which equation best represents the line that passes through the point $(-4, -3)$ and is perpendicular to the line shown?

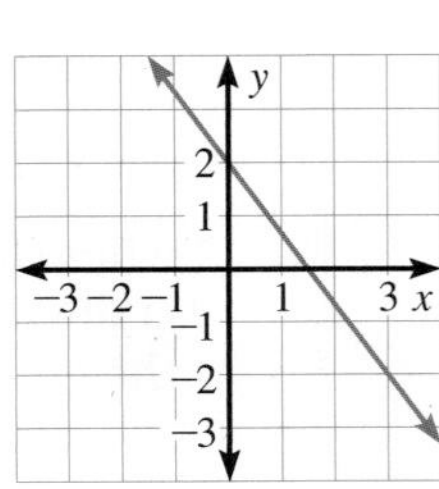

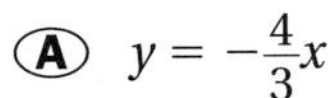

Ⓐ $y = -\frac{4}{3}x$ Ⓑ $y = \frac{3}{4}x$

Ⓒ $y = -\frac{4}{3}x - \frac{25}{3}$ Ⓓ $y = \frac{3}{4}x + 1$

Graphing Calculator **ACTIVITY** *Use after Lesson 5.2*

@HomeTutor
classzone.com
Keystrokes

5.2 Set a Good Viewing Window

QUESTION **What is a good viewing window for a polynomial function?**

When you graph a function with a graphing calculator, you should choose a viewing window that displays the important characteristics of the graph.

EXAMPLE **Graph a polynomial function**

Graph $f(x) = 0.2x^3 - 5x^2 + 38x - 97$.

STEP 1 ***Graph the function***

Graph the function in the standard viewing window.

STEP 2 ***Adjust horizontally***

Adjust the horizontal scale so that the end behavior of the graph as $x \to +\infty$ is visible.

STEP 3 ***Adjust vertically***

Adjust the vertical scale so that the turning points and end behavior of the graph as $x \to -\infty$ are visible.

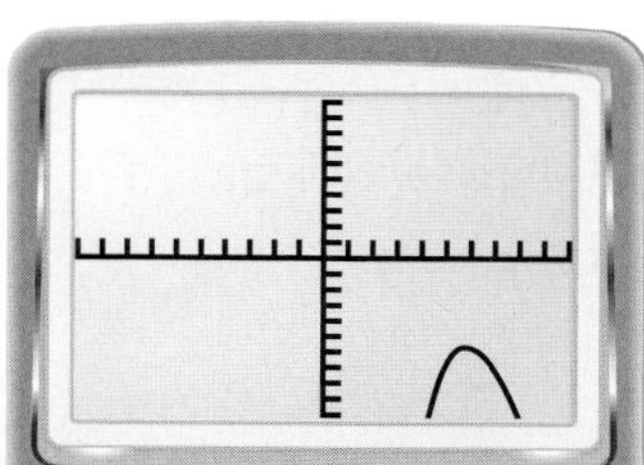

$-10 \le x \le 10,\ -10 \le y \le 10$

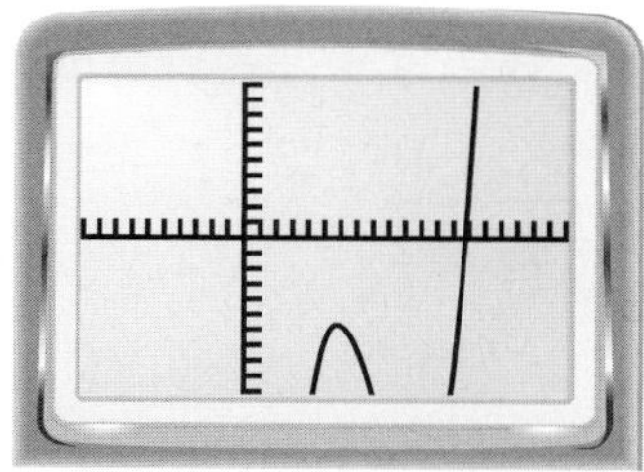

$-10 \le x \le 20,\ -10 \le y \le 10$

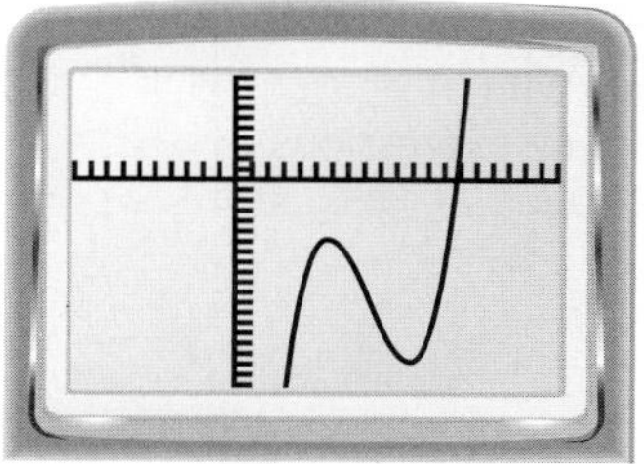

$-10 \le x \le 20,\ -20 \le y \le 10$

PRACTICE

Find intervals for x and y that describe a good viewing window for the graph of the polynomial function.

1. $f(x) = x^3 + 4x^2 - 8x + 11$
2. $f(x) = -x^3 + 36x^2 - 10$
3. $f(x) = x^4 - 4x^2 + 2$
4. $f(x) = -x^4 - 2x^3 + 3x^2 - 4x + 5$
5. $f(x) = -x^4 + 3x^3 + 15x$
6. $f(x) = 2x^4 - 7x^3 + x - 8$
7. $f(x) = -x^5 + 9x^3 - 12x + 18$
8. $f(x) = x^5 - 7x^4 + 25x^3 - 40x^2 + 13x$
9. **REASONING** Let $g(x) = f(x) + c$ where $f(x)$ and $g(x)$ are polynomial functions and c is a positive constant. How is a good viewing window for the graph of $f(x)$ related to a good viewing window for the graph of $g(x)$?
10. **BASEBALL** From 1994 to 2003, the average salary S (in thousands of dollars) for major league baseball players can be modeled by

$$S(x) = -4.10x^3 + 67.4x^2 - 121x + 1170$$

where x is the number of years since 1994. Find intervals for the horizontal and vertical axes that describe a good viewing window for the graph of S.

5.3 Add, Subtract, and Multiply Polynomials

 **A2.N.3** Perform arithmetic operations with polynomial expressions containing rational coefficients

Before You evaluated and graphed polynomial functions.

Now You will add, subtract, and multiply polynomials.

Why? So you can model collegiate sports participation, as in Ex. 63.

Key Vocabulary
- **like terms,** *p. 12*

To add or subtract polynomials, add or subtract the coefficients of like terms. You can use a vertical or horizontal format.

EXAMPLE 1 Add polynomials vertically and horizontally

a. Add $2x^3 - 5x^2 + 3x - 9$ and $x^3 + 6x^2 + 11$ in a vertical format.

b. Add $3y^3 - 2y^2 - 7y$ and $-4y^2 + 2y - 5$ in a horizontal format.

REVIEW SIMPLIFYING
For help with simplifying expressions, see p. 10.

Solution

a.
$$\begin{array}{rrrrr} & 2x^3 & - 5x^2 & + 3x & - 9 \\ + & x^3 & + 6x^2 & & + 11 \\ \hline & 3x^3 & + x^2 & + 3x & + 2 \end{array}$$

b. $(3y^3 - 2y^2 - 7y) + (-4y^2 + 2y - 5)$
$= 3y^3 - 2y^2 - 4y^2 - 7y + 2y - 5$
$= 3y^3 - 6y^2 - 5y - 5$

EXAMPLE 2 Subtract polynomials vertically and horizontally

a. Subtract $3x^3 + 2x^2 - x + 7$ from $8x^3 - x^2 - 5x + 1$ in a vertical format.

b. Subtract $5z^2 - z + 3$ from $4z^2 + 9z - 12$ in a horizontal format.

Solution

a. Align like terms, then add the opposite of the subtracted polynomial.

$$\begin{array}{rrrrr} & 8x^3 & - x^2 & - 5x & + 1 \\ - & (3x^3 & + 2x^2 & - x & + 7) \\ \hline \end{array} \quad \longrightarrow \quad \begin{array}{rrrrr} & 8x^3 & - x^2 & - 5x & + 1 \\ + & -3x^3 & - 2x^2 & + x & - 7 \\ \hline & 5x^3 & - 3x^2 & - 4x & - 6 \end{array}$$

b. Write the opposite of the subtracted polynomial, then add like terms.

$(4z^2 + 9z - 12) - (5z^2 - z + 3) = 4z^2 + 9z - 12 - 5z^2 + z - 3$
$= 4z^2 - 5z^2 + 9z + z - 12 - 3$
$= -z^2 + 10z - 15$

 **GUIDED PRACTICE** for Examples 1 and 2

Find the sum or difference.

1. $(t^2 - 6t + 2) + (5t^2 - t - 8)$
2. $(8d - 3 + 9d^3) - (d^3 - 13d^2 - 4)$

MULTIPLYING POLYNOMIALS To multiply two polynomials, you multiply each term of the first polynomial by each term of the second polynomial.

EXAMPLE 3 Multiply polynomials vertically and horizontally

a. Multiply $-2y^2 + 3y - 6$ and $y - 2$ in a vertical format.

b. Multiply $x + 3$ and $3x^2 - 2x + 4$ in a horizontal format.

Solution

a.

$$\begin{array}{r} -2y^2 + 3y - 6 \\ \times \qquad\quad y - 2 \\ \hline 4y^2 - 6y + 12 \\ -2y^3 + 3y^2 - 6y \qquad \\ \hline -2y^3 + 7y^2 - 12y + 12 \end{array}$$

Multiply $-2y^2 + 3y - 6$ by -2.

Multiply $-2y^2 + 3y - 6$ by y.

Combine like terms.

b. $(x + 3)(3x^2 - 2x + 4) = (x + 3)3x^2 - (x + 3)2x + (x + 3)4$

$= 3x^3 + 9x^2 - 2x^2 - 6x + 4x + 12$

$= 3x^3 + 7x^2 - 2x + 12$

EXAMPLE 4 Multiply three binomials

Multiply $x - 5$, $x + 1$, and $x + 3$ in a horizontal format.

$(x - 5)(x + 1)(x + 3) = (x^2 - 4x - 5)(x + 3)$

$= (x^2 - 4x - 5)x + (x^2 - 4x - 5)3$

$= x^3 - 4x^2 - 5x + 3x^2 - 12x - 15$

$= x^3 - x^2 - 17x - 15$

PRODUCT PATTERNS Some binomial products occur so frequently that it is worth memorizing their patterns. You can verify these product patterns by multiplying.

AVOID ERRORS
In general, $(a \pm b)^2 \neq a^2 \pm b^2$ and $(a \pm b)^3 \neq a^3 \pm b^3$.

KEY CONCEPT *For Your Notebook*

Special Product Patterns

Sum and Difference	**Example**
$(a + b)(a - b) = a^2 - b^2$	$(x + 4)(x - 4) = x^2 - 16$

Square of a Binomial	**Example**
$(a + b)^2 = a^2 + 2ab + b^2$	$(y + 3)^2 = y^2 + 6y + 9$
$(a - b)^2 = a^2 - 2ab + b^2$	$(3z^2 - 5)^2 = 9z^4 - 30z^2 + 25$

Cube of a Binomial	**Example**
$(a + b)^3 = a^3 + 3a^2b + 3ab^2 + b^3$	$(x + 2)^3 = x^3 + 6x^2 + 12x + 8$
$(a - b)^3 = a^3 - 3a^2b + 3ab^2 - b^3$	$(p - 3)^3 = p^3 - 9p^2 + 27p - 27$

EXAMPLE 5 Use special product patterns

a. $(3t + 4)(3t - 4) = (3t)^2 - 4^2$ **Sum and difference**

$= 9t^2 - 16$

b. $(8x - 3)^2 = (8x)^2 - 2(8x)(3) + 3^2$ **Square of a binomial**

$= 64x^2 - 48x + 9$

c. $(pq + 5)^3 = (pq)^3 + 3(pq)^2(5) + 3(pq)(5)^2 + 5^3$ **Cube of a binomial**

$= p^3q^3 + 15p^2q^2 + 75pq + 125$

✓ GUIDED PRACTICE for Examples 3, 4, and 5

Find the product.

3. $(x + 2)(3x^2 - x - 5)$ **4.** $(a - 5)(a + 2)(a + 6)$ **5.** $(xy - 4)^3$

EXAMPLE 6 Use polynomial models

PETROLEUM Since 1980, the number W (in thousands) of United States wells producing crude oil and the average daily oil output per well O (in barrels) can be modeled by

$$W = -0.575t^2 + 10.9t + 548 \quad \text{and} \quad O = -0.249t + 15.4$$

where t is the number of years since 1980. Write a model for the average *total* amount T of crude oil produced per day. What was the average total amount of crude oil produced per day in 2000?

Oil refinery in Long Beach, California

DETERMINE SIGNIFICANT DIGITS
When multiplying models, round your result so that its terms have the same number of significant digits as the model with the fewest number of significant digits.

Solution

To find a model for T, multiply the two given models.

$$\begin{array}{rrrr} & -0.575t^2 + & 10.9t + & 548 \\ \times & & -\ 0.249t + & 15.4 \\ \hline & -\ 8.855t^2 + & 167.86t + & 8439.2 \\ 0.143175t^3 - & 2.7141t^2 - & 136.452t & \\ \hline 0.143175t^3 - & 11.5691t^2 + & 31.408t + & 8439.2 \end{array}$$

▶ Total daily oil output can be modeled by $T = 0.143t^3 - 11.6t^2 + 31.4t + 8440$ where T is measured in thousands of barrels. By substituting $t = 20$ into the model, you can estimate that the average total amount of crude oil produced per day in 2000 was about 5570 thousand barrels, or 5,570,000 barrels.

GUIDED PRACTICE for Example 6

6. INDUSTRY The models below give the average depth D (in feet) of new wells drilled and the average cost per foot C (in dollars) of drilling a new well. In both models, t represents the number of years since 1980. Write a model for the average *total* cost T of drilling a new well.

$$D = 109t + 4010 \quad \text{and} \quad C = 0.542t^2 - 7.16t + 79.4$$

5.3 EXERCISES

HOMEWORK KEY

◯ = **WORKED-OUT SOLUTIONS on p. WS10 for Exs. 11, 21, and 61**

★ = **STANDARDIZED TEST PRACTICE Exs. 2, 15, 47, 56, and 63**

SKILL PRACTICE

1. **VOCABULARY** When you add or subtract polynomials, you add or subtract the coefficients of __?__.

2. ★ **WRITING** *Explain* how a polynomial subtraction problem is equivalent to a polynomial addition problem.

EXAMPLES 1 and 2 on p. 346 for Exs. 3–15

ADDING AND SUBTRACTING POLYNOMIALS **Find the sum or difference.**

3. $(3x^2 - 5) + (7x^2 - 3)$
4. $(x^2 - 3x + 5) - (-4x^2 + 8x + 9)$
5. $(4y^2 + 9y - 5) - (4y^2 - 5y + 3)$
6. $(z^2 + 5z - 7) + (5z^2 - 11z - 6)$
7. $(3s^3 + s) + (4s^3 - 2s^2 + 7s + 10)$
8. $(2a^2 - 8) - (a^3 + 4a^2 - 12a + 4)$
9. $(5c^2 + 7c + 1) + (2c^3 - 6c + 8)$
10. $(4t^3 - 11t^2 + 4t) - (-7t^2 - 5t + 8)$
11. $(5b - 6b^3 + 2b^4) - (9b^3 + 4b^4 - 7)$
12. $(3y^2 - 6y^4 + 5 - 6y) + (5y^4 - 6y^3 + 4y)$
13. $(x^4 - x^3 + x^2 - x + 1) + (x + x^4 - 1 - x^2)$
14. $(8v^4 - 2v^2 + v - 4) - (3v^3 - 12v^2 + 8v)$

15. ★ **MULTIPLE CHOICE** What is the result when $2x^4 - 8x^2 - x + 10$ is subtracted from $8x^4 - 4x^3 - x + 2$?

Ⓐ $-6x^4 + 4x^3 - 8x^2 + 8$
Ⓑ $6x^4 - 4x^3 + 8x^2 - 8$
Ⓒ $10x^4 - 8x^3 - 4x^2 + 12$
Ⓓ $6x^4 + 4x^3 - 2x - 8$

EXAMPLE 3 on p. 347 for Exs. 16–25

MULTIPLYING POLYNOMIALS **Find the product of the polynomials.**

16. $x(2x^2 - 5x + 7)$
17. $5x^2(6x + 2)$
18. $(y - 7)(y + 6)$
19. $(3z + 1)(z - 3)$
20. $(w + 4)(w^2 + 6w - 11)$
21. $(2a - 3)(a^2 - 10a - 2)$
22. $(5c^2 - 4)(2c^2 + c - 3)$
23. $(-x^2 + 4x + 1)(x^2 - 8x + 3)$
24. $(-d^2 + 4d + 3)(3d^2 - 7d + 6)$
25. $(3y^2 + 6y - 1)(4y^2 - 11y - 5)$

ERROR ANALYSIS ***Describe*** **and correct the error in simplifying the expression.**

26.
$$(x^2 - 3x + 4) - (x^3 + 7x - 2)$$
$$= x^2 - 3x + 4 - x^3 + 7x - 2$$
$$= -x^3 + x^2 + 4x + 2$$

27.
$$(2x - 7)^3 = (2x)^3 - 7^3$$
$$= 8x^3 - 343$$

EXAMPLE 4 on p. 347 for Exs. 28–37

MULTIPLYING THREE BINOMIALS **Find the product of the binomials.**

28. $(x + 4)(x - 6)(x - 5)$
29. $(x + 1)(x - 7)(x + 3)$
30. $(z - 4)(-z + 2)(z + 8)$
31. $(a - 6)(2a + 5)(a + 1)$
32. $(3p + 1)(p + 3)(p + 1)$
33. $(b - 2)(2b - 1)(-b + 1)$
34. $(2s + 1)(3s - 2)(4s - 3)$
35. $(w - 6)(4w - 1)(-3w + 5)$
36. $(4x - 1)(-2x - 7)(-5x - 4)$
37. $(3q - 8)(-9q + 2)(q - 2)$

EXAMPLE 5
on p. 348
for Exs. 38–47

SPECIAL PRODUCTS **Find the product.**

38. $(x + 5)(x - 5)$
39. $(w - 9)^2$
40. $(y + 4)^3$
41. $(2c + 5)^2$
42. $(3t - 4)^3$
43. $(5p - 3)(5p + 3)$
44. $(7x - y)^3$
45. $(2a + 9b)(2a - 9b)$
46. $(3z + 7y)^3$

47. ★ **MULTIPLE CHOICE** Which expression is equivalent to $(3x - 2y)^2$?

(A) $9x^2 - 4y^2$
(B) $9x^2 + 4y^2$
(C) $9x^2 + 12xy + 4y^2$
(D) $9x^2 - 12xy + 4y^2$

GEOMETRY **Write the figure's volume as a polynomial in standard form.**

48. $V = \ell wh$

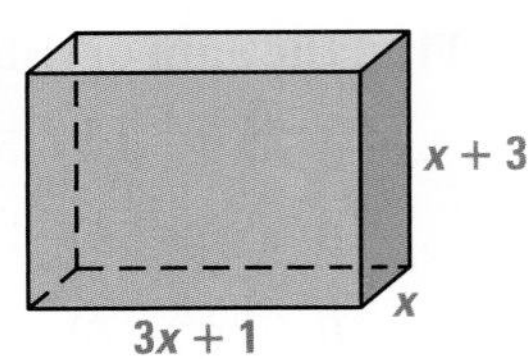

49. $V = \pi r^2 h$

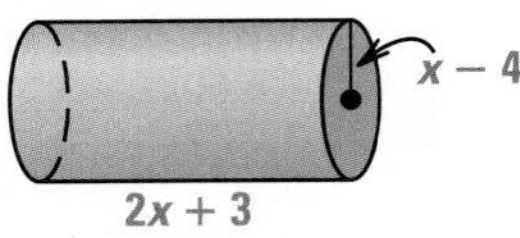

50. $V = s^3$

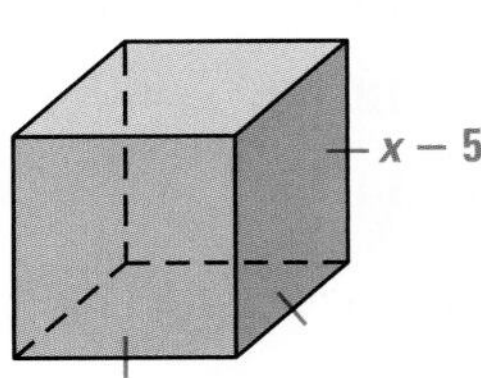

51. $V = \frac{1}{3}Bh$

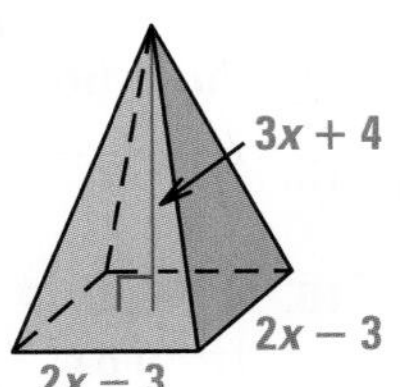

SPECIAL PRODUCTS **Verify the special product pattern by multiplying.**

52. $(a + b)(a - b) = a^2 - b^2$
53. $(a + b)^2 = a^2 + 2ab + b^2$
54. $(a + b)^3 = a^3 + 3a^2b + 3ab^2 + b^3$
55. $(a - b)^3 = a^3 - 3a^2b + 3ab^2 - b^3$

56. ★ **EXTENDED RESPONSE** Let $p(x) = x^4 - 7x + 14$ and $q(x) = x^2 - 5$.

a. What is the degree of the polynomial $p(x) + q(x)$?

b. What is the degree of the polynomial $p(x) - q(x)$?

c. What is the degree of the polynomial $p(x) \cdot q(x)$?

d. In general, if $p(x)$ and $q(x)$ are polynomials such that $p(x)$ has degree m, $q(x)$ has degree n, and $m > n$, what are the degrees of $p(x) + q(x)$, $p(x) - q(x)$, and $p(x) \cdot q(x)$?

57. **FINDING A PATTERN** Look at the following polynomial factorizations.

$x^2 - 1 = (x - 1)(x + 1)$

$x^3 - 1 = (x - 1)(x^2 + x + 1)$

$x^4 - 1 = (x - 1)(x^3 + x^2 + x + 1)$

a. Factor $x^5 - 1$ and $x^6 - 1$ into the product of $x - 1$ and another polynomial. Check your answers by multiplying.

b. In general, how can $x^n - 1$ be factored? Show that this factorization works by multiplying the factors.

58. **CHALLENGE** Suppose $f(x) = (x + a)(x + b)(x + c)(x + d)$. If $f(x)$ is written in standard form, show that the coefficient of x^3 is the sum of a, b, c, and d, and the constant term is the product of a, b, c, and d.

○ = WORKED-OUT SOLUTIONS on p. WS1

★ = STANDARDIZED TEST PRACTICE

PROBLEM SOLVING

EXAMPLE 6
on p. 348
for Exs. 59–61

59. **HIGHER EDUCATION** Since 1970, the number (in thousands) of males M and females F attending institutes of higher education can be modeled by

$$M = 0.091t^3 - 4.8t^2 + 110t + 5000 \quad \text{and} \quad F = 0.19t^3 - 12t^2 + 350t + 3600$$

where t is the number of years since 1970. Write a model for the total number of people attending institutes of higher education.

@HomeTutor for problem solving help at classzone.com

60. **ELECTRONICS** From 1999 to 2004, the number of DVD players D (in millions) sold in the United States and the average price per DVD player P (in dollars) can be modeled by

$$D = 4.11t + 4.44 \quad \text{and} \quad P = 6.82t^2 - 61.7t + 265$$

where t is the number of years since 1999. Write a model for the total revenue R from DVD sales. According to the model, what was the total revenue in 2002?

@HomeTutor for problem solving help at classzone.com

61. **BICYCLING** The equation $P = 0.00267sF$ gives the power P (in horsepower) needed to keep a certain bicycle moving at speed s (in miles per hour), where F is the force (in pounds) of road and air resistance. On level ground, the equation

$$F = 0.0116s^2 + 0.789$$

models the force F. Write a model (in terms of s only) for the power needed to keep the bicycle moving at speed s on level ground. How much power is needed to keep the bicycle moving at 10 miles per hour?

Animated Algebra at classzone.com

62. **MULTI-STEP PROBLEM** A dessert is made by taking a hemispherical mound of marshmallow on a 0.5 centimeter thick cookie and covering it with a chocolate shell 1 centimeter thick. Use the diagrams to write two polynomial functions in standard form: $M(r)$ for the combined volume of the marshmallow plus cookie, and $D(r)$ for the volume of the entire dessert. Then use $M(r)$ and $D(r)$ to write a function $C(r)$ for the volume of the chocolate.

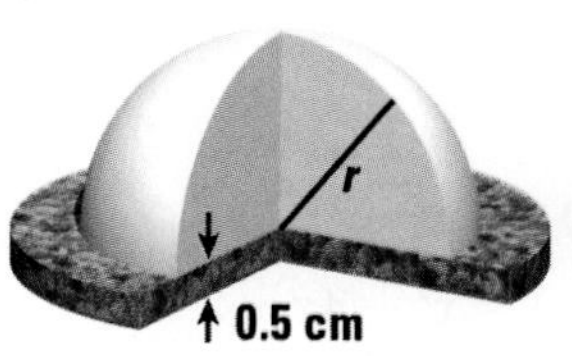

Marshmallow on cookie

Chocolate layer added

63. ★ **SHORT RESPONSE** From 1997 to 2002, the number of NCAA lacrosse teams for men L_m and women L_w, as well as the average size of a men's team S_m and a women's team S_w, can be modeled by

$$L_m = 5.57t + 182 \quad \text{and} \quad S_m = -0.127t^3 + 0.822t^2 - 1.02t + 31.5$$

$$L_w = 12.2t + 185 \quad \text{and} \quad S_w = -0.0662t^3 + 0.437t^2 - 0.725t + 22.3$$

where t is the number of years since 1997. Write a model for the *total* number of people N on NCAA lacrosse teams. *Explain* how you obtained your model.

64. **CHALLENGE** From 1970 to 2002, the circulation C (in millions) of Sunday newspapers in the United States can be modeled by

$$C = -0.00105t^3 + 0.0281t^2 + 0.465t + 48.8$$

where t is the number of years since 1970. Rewrite C as a function of s, where s is the number of years since 1975.

NY NEW YORK MIXED REVIEW

TEST PRACTICE at classzone.com

65. The table shows the total cost y of heating oil. Which equation best represents the total cost of the heating oil as a function of the number of gallons x?

Number of gallons (x)	Total cost (y)
50	$75
200	$300
500	$750

Ⓐ $x = 0.67y$ Ⓑ $y = 0.67x$

Ⓒ $x = 1.5y$ Ⓓ $y = 1.5x$

66. A student is making a circle graph of the results of a survey that asked what people's favorite sport is. What central angle should be used for the section representing basketball?

Activity	Number of people
Basketball	350
Soccer	210
Softball or Baseball	200
Other	240

Ⓐ 35° Ⓑ 105°

Ⓒ 126° Ⓓ 234°

QUIZ for Lessons 5.1–5.3

Evaluate the expression. *(p. 330)*

1. $3^5 \cdot 3^{-1}$
2. $(2^4)^2$
3. $\left(\frac{2}{3^{-2}}\right)^2$
4. $\left(\frac{3}{5}\right)^{-2}$

Simplify the expression. *(p. 330)*

5. $(x^4y^{-2})(x^{-3}y^8)$
6. $(a^2b^{-5})^{-3}$
7. $\frac{x^3y^7}{x^{-4}y^0}$
8. $\frac{c^3d^{-2}}{c^5d^{-1}}$

Graph the polynomial function. *(p. 337)*

9. $g(x) = 2x^3 - 3x + 1$
10. $h(x) = x^4 - 4x + 2$
11. $f(x) = -2x^3 + x^2 - 5$

Perform the indicated operation. *(p. 346)*

12. $(x^3 + x^2 - 6) - (2x^2 + 4x - 8)$
13. $(-3x^2 + 4x - 10) + (x^2 - 9x + 15)$
14. $(x - 5)(x^2 - 5x + 7)$
15. $(x + 3)(x - 6)(3x - 1)$

16. **NATIONAL DEBT** On July 21, 2004, the national debt of the United States was about $7,282,000,000,000. The population of the United States at that time was about 294,000,000. Suppose the national debt was divided evenly among everyone in the United States. How much would each person owe? *(p. 330)*

5.4 Factor and Solve Polynomial Equations

A2.N.3 Perform arithmetic operations with polynomial expressions containing rational coefficients

Before You factored and solved quadratic equations.

Now You will factor and solve other polynomial equations.

Why? So you can find dimensions of archaeological ruins, as in Ex. 58.

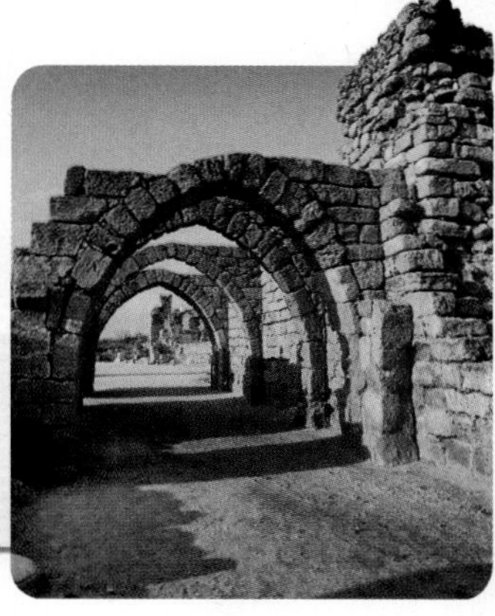

Key Vocabulary
- **factored completely**
- **factor by grouping**
- **quadratic form**

In Chapter 4, you learned how to factor the following types of quadratic expressions.

Type	Example
General trinomial	$2x^2 - 3x - 20 = (2x + 5)(x - 4)$
Perfect square trinomial	$x^2 + 8x + 16 = (x + 4)^2$
Difference of two squares	$9x^2 - 1 = (3x + 1)(3x - 1)$
Common monomial factor	$8x^2 + 20x = 4x(2x + 5)$

You can also factor polynomials with degree greater than 2. Some of these polynomials can be *factored completely* using techniques learned in Chapter 4.

KEY CONCEPT *For Your Notebook*

Factoring Polynomials

Definition

A factorable polynomial with integer coefficients is **factored completely** if it is written as a product of unfactorable polynomials with integer coefficients.

Examples

$2(x + 1)(x - 4)$ and $5x^2(x^2 - 3)$ are factored completely.

$3x(x^2 - 4)$ is *not* factored completely because $x^2 - 4$ can be factored as $(x + 2)(x - 2)$.

EXAMPLE 1 Find a common monomial factor

Factor the polynomial completely.

a. $x^3 + 2x^2 - 15x = x(x^2 + 2x - 15)$ **Factor common monomial.**

$= x(x + 5)(x - 3)$ **Factor trinomial.**

b. $2y^5 - 18y^3 = 2y^3(y^2 - 9)$ **Factor common monomial.**

$= 2y^3(y + 3)(y - 3)$ **Difference of two squares**

c. $4z^4 - 16z^3 + 16z^2 = 4z^2(z^2 - 4z + 4)$ **Factor common monomial.**

$= 4z^2(z - 2)^2$ **Perfect square trinomial**

FACTORING PATTERNS In part (b) of Example 1, the special factoring pattern for the difference of two squares is used to factor the expression completely. There are also factoring patterns that you can use to factor the sum or difference of two *cubes*.

KEY CONCEPT *For Your Notebook*

Special Factoring Patterns

Sum of Two Cubes	**Example**
$a^3 + b^3 = (a + b)(a^2 - ab + b^2)$	$8x^3 + 27 = (2x)^3 + 3^3$
	$= (2x + 3)(4x^2 - 6x + 9)$
Difference of Two Cubes	**Example**
$a^3 - b^3 = (a - b)(a^2 + ab + b^2)$	$64x^3 - 1 = (4x)^3 - 1^3$
	$= (4x - 1)(16x^2 + 4x + 1)$

EXAMPLE 2 Factor the sum or difference of two cubes

Factor the polynomial completely.

a. $x^3 + 64 = x^3 + 4^3$ — Sum of two cubes

$= (x + 4)(x^2 - 4x + 16)$

b. $16z^5 - 250z^2 = 2z^2(8z^3 - 125)$ — Factor common monomial.

$= 2z^2\left[(2z)^3 - 5^3\right]$ — Difference of two cubes

$= 2z^2(2z - 5)(4z^2 + 10z + 25)$

GUIDED PRACTICE for Examples 1 and 2

Factor the polynomial completely.

1. $x^3 - 7x^2 + 10x$ **2.** $3y^5 - 75y^3$ **3.** $16b^5 + 686b^2$ **4.** $w^3 - 27$

FACTORING BY GROUPING For some polynomials, you can **factor by grouping** pairs of terms that have a common monomial factor. The pattern for factoring by grouping is shown below.

$$ra + rb + sa + sb = r(a + b) + s(a + b)$$
$$= (r + s)(a + b)$$

EXAMPLE 3 Factor by grouping

AVOID ERRORS
An expression is not factored completely until *all* factors, such as $x^2 - 16$, cannot be factored further.

Factor the polynomial $x^3 - 3x^2 - 16x + 48$ completely.

$x^3 - 3x^2 - 16x + 48 = x^2(x - 3) - 16(x - 3)$ — Factor by grouping.

$= (x^2 - 16)(x - 3)$ — Distributive property

$= (x + 4)(x - 4)(x - 3)$ — Difference of two squares

QUADRATIC FORM An expression of the form $au^2 + bu + c$, where u is any expression in x, is said to be in **quadratic form**. The factoring techniques you studied in Chapter 4 can sometimes be used to factor such expressions.

EXAMPLE 4 Factor polynomials in quadratic form

IDENTIFY QUADRATIC FORM
The expression $16x^4 - 81$ is in quadratic form because it can be written as $u^2 - 81$ where $u = 4x^2$.

Factor completely: (a) $16x^4 - 81$ and (b) $2p^8 + 10p^5 + 12p^2$.

a. $16x^4 - 81 = (4x^2)^2 - 9^2$ — **Write as difference of two squares.**

$= (4x^2 + 9)(4x^2 - 9)$ — **Difference of two squares**

$= (4x^2 + 9)(2x + 3)(2x - 3)$ — **Difference of two squares**

b. $2p^8 + 10p^5 + 12p^2 = 2p^2(p^6 + 5p^3 + 6)$ — **Factor common monomial.**

$= 2p^2(p^3 + 3)(p^3 + 2)$ — **Factor trinomial in quadratic form.**

GUIDED PRACTICE for Examples 3 and 4

Factor the polynomial completely.

5. $x^3 + 7x^2 - 9x - 63$ **6.** $16g^4 - 625$ **7.** $4t^6 - 20t^4 + 24t^2$

SOLVING POLYNOMIAL EQUATIONS In Chapter 4, you learned how to use the zero product property to solve factorable quadratic equations. You can extend this technique to solve some higher-degree polynomial equations.

★ EXAMPLE 5 Standardized Test Practice

What are the real-number solutions of the equation $3x^5 + 15x = 18x^3$?

Ⓐ 0, 1, 3, 5 Ⓑ −1, 0, 1

Ⓒ 0, 1, $\sqrt{5}$ Ⓓ $-\sqrt{5}$, −1, 0, 1, $\sqrt{5}$

Solution

$3x^5 + 15x = 18x^3$ — **Write original equation.**

$3x^5 - 18x^3 + 15x = 0$ — **Write in standard form.**

$3x(x^4 - 6x^2 + 5) = 0$ — **Factor common monomial.**

$3x(x^2 - 1)(x^2 - 5) = 0$ — **Factor trinomial.**

$3x(x + 1)(x - 1)(x^2 - 5) = 0$ — **Difference of two squares**

$x = 0, x = -1, x = 1, x = \sqrt{5}$, or $x = -\sqrt{5}$ — **Zero product property**

▶ The correct answer is D. Ⓐ Ⓑ Ⓒ Ⓓ

AVOID ERRORS
Do not divide each side of an equation by a variable or a variable expression, such as $3x$. Doing so will result in the loss of solutions.

GUIDED PRACTICE for Example 5

Find the real-number solutions of the equation.

8. $4x^5 - 40x^3 + 36x = 0$ **9.** $2x^5 + 24x = 14x^3$ **10.** $-27x^3 + 15x^2 = -6x^4$

EXAMPLE 6 Solve a polynomial equation

CITY PARK You are designing a marble basin that will hold a fountain for a city park. The basin's sides and bottom should be 1 foot thick. Its outer length should be twice its outer width and outer height.

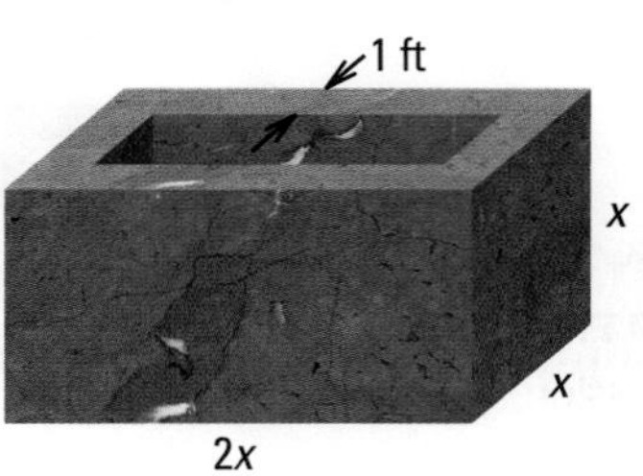

What should the outer dimensions of the basin be if it is to hold 36 cubic feet of water?

ANOTHER WAY
For alternative methods to solving the problem in Example 6, turn to page 360 for the **Problem Solving Workshop**.

Solution

Volume (cubic feet)	=	Interior length (feet)	·	Interior width (feet)	·	Interior height (feet)
36	=	$(2x - 2)$	·	$(x - 2)$	·	$(x - 1)$

$36 = (2x - 2)(x - 2)(x - 1)$ **Write equation.**

$0 = 2x^3 - 8x^2 + 10x - 40$ **Write in standard form.**

$0 = 2x^2(x - 4) + 10(x - 4)$ **Factor by grouping.**

$0 = (2x^2 + 10)(x - 4)$ **Distributive property**

▶ The only real solution is $x = 4$. The basin is 8 ft long, 4 ft wide, and 4 ft high.

✓ GUIDED PRACTICE for Example 6

11. **WHAT IF?** In Example 6, what should the basin's dimensions be if it is to hold 40 cubic feet of water and have outer length $6x$, width $3x$, and height x?

5.4 EXERCISES

HOMEWORK KEY

◯ = **WORKED-OUT SOLUTIONS** on p. WS10 for Exs. 7, 23, and 61

★ = **STANDARDIZED TEST PRACTICE** Exs. 2, 9, 41, 63, and 64

SKILL PRACTICE

1. **VOCABULARY** The expression $8x^6 + 10x^3 - 3$ is in __?__ form because it can be written as $2u^2 + 5u - 3$ where $u = 2x^3$.

2. ★ **WRITING** What condition must the factorization of a polynomial satisfy in order for the polynomial to be factored completely?

EXAMPLE 1 on p. 353 for Exs. 3–9

MONOMIAL FACTORS Factor the polynomial completely.

3. $14x^2 - 21x$
4. $30b^3 - 54b^2$
5. $c^3 + 9c^2 + 18c$
6. $z^3 - 6z^2 - 72z$
7. $3y^5 - 48y^3$
8. $54m^5 + 18m^4 + 9m^3$

9. ★ **MULTIPLE CHOICE** What is the complete factorization of $2x^7 - 32x^3$?

Ⓐ $2x^3(x + 2)(x - 2)(x^2 + 4)$
Ⓑ $2x^3(x^2 + 2)(x^2 - 2)$
Ⓒ $2x^3(x^2 + 4)^2$
Ⓓ $2x^3(x + 2)^2(x - 2)^2$

EXAMPLE 2 on p. 354 for Exs. 10–17

SUM OR DIFFERENCE OF CUBES **Factor the polynomial completely.**

10. $x^3 + 8$ **11.** $y^3 - 64$ **12.** $27m^3 + 1$ **13.** $125n^3 + 216$

14. $27a^3 - 1000$ **15.** $8c^3 + 343$ **16.** $192w^3 - 3$ **17.** $-5z^3 + 320$

EXAMPLE 3 on p. 354 for Exs. 18–23

FACTORING BY GROUPING **Factor the polynomial completely.**

18. $x^3 + x^2 + x + 1$ **19.** $y^3 - 7y^2 + 4y - 28$ **20.** $n^3 + 5n^2 - 9n - 45$

21. $3m^3 - m^2 + 9m - 3$ **22.** $25s^3 - 100s^2 - s + 4$ **23.** $4c^3 + 8c^2 - 9c - 18$

EXAMPLE 4 on p. 355 for Exs. 24–29

QUADRATIC FORM **Factor the polynomial completely.**

24. $x^4 - 25$ **25.** $a^4 + 7a^2 + 6$ **26.** $3s^4 - s^2 - 24$

27. $32z^5 - 2z$ **28.** $36m^6 + 12m^4 + m^2$ **29.** $15x^5 - 72x^3 - 108x$

EXAMPLE 5 on p. 355 for Exs. 30–41

ERROR ANALYSIS ***Describe*** **and correct the error in finding all real-number solutions.**

30.

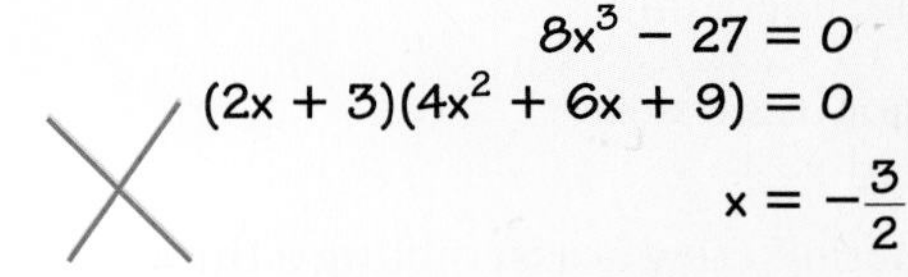

31.

$$3x^3 - 48x = 0$$
$$3x(x^2 - 16) = 0$$
$$x^2 - 16 = 0$$
$$x = -4 \text{ or } x = 4$$

SOLVING EQUATIONS **Find the real-number solutions of the equation.**

32. $y^3 - 5y^2 = 0$ **33.** $18s^3 = 50s$ **34.** $g^3 + 3g^2 - g - 3 = 0$

35. $m^3 + 6m^2 - 4m - 24 = 0$ **36.** $4w^4 + 40w^2 - 44 = 0$ **37.** $4z^5 = 84z^3$

38. $5b^3 + 15b^2 + 12b = -36$ **39.** $x^6 - 4x^4 - 9x^2 + 36 = 0$ **40.** $48p^5 = 27p^3$

41. ★ **MULTIPLE CHOICE** What are the real-number solutions of the equation $3x^4 - 27x^2 + 9x = x^3$?

Ⓐ $-1, 0, 3$ Ⓑ $-3, 0, 3$ Ⓒ $-3, 0, \frac{1}{3}, 3$ Ⓓ $-3, -\frac{1}{3}, 0, 3$

CHOOSING A METHOD **Factor the polynomial completely using any method.**

42. $16x^3 - 44x^2 - 42x$ **43.** $n^4 - 4n^2 - 60$ **44.** $-4b^4 - 500b$

45. $36a^3 - 15a^2 + 84a - 35$ **46.** $18c^4 + 57c^3 - 10c^2$ **47.** $2d^4 - 13d^2 - 45$

48. $32x^5 - 108x^2$ **49.** $8y^6 - 38y^4 - 10y^2$ **50.** $z^5 - 3z^4 - 16z + 48$

GEOMETRY **Find the possible value(s) of x.**

51. Area = 48

$x + 4$

$3x + 2$

52. Volume = 40

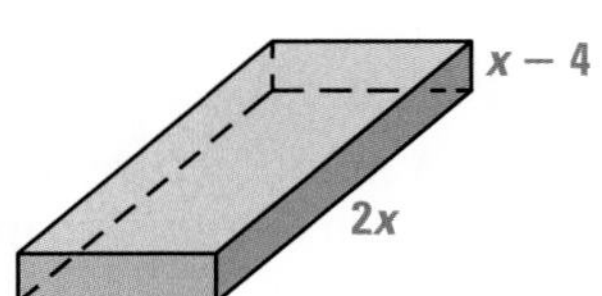

53. Volume = 125π

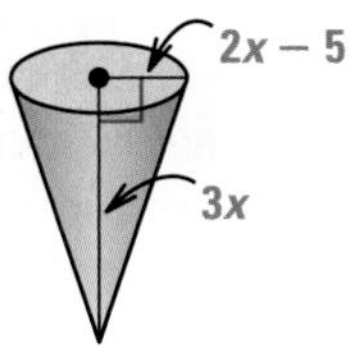

CHOOSING A METHOD **Factor the polynomial completely using any method.**

54. $x^3y^6 - 27$ **55.** $7ac^2 + bc^2 - 7ad^2 - bd^2$ **56.** $x^{2n} - 2x^n + 1$

57. **CHALLENGE** Factor $a^5b^2 - a^2b^4 + 2a^4b - 2ab^3 + a^3 - b^2$ completely.

PROBLEM SOLVING

EXAMPLE 6 on p. 356 for Exs. 58–63

58. **ARCHAEOLOGY** At the ruins of Caesarea, archaeologists discovered a huge hydraulic concrete block with a volume of 945 cubic meters. The block's dimensions are x meters high by $12x - 15$ meters long by $12x - 21$ meters wide. What is the height of the block?

@HomeTutor for problem solving help at classzone.com

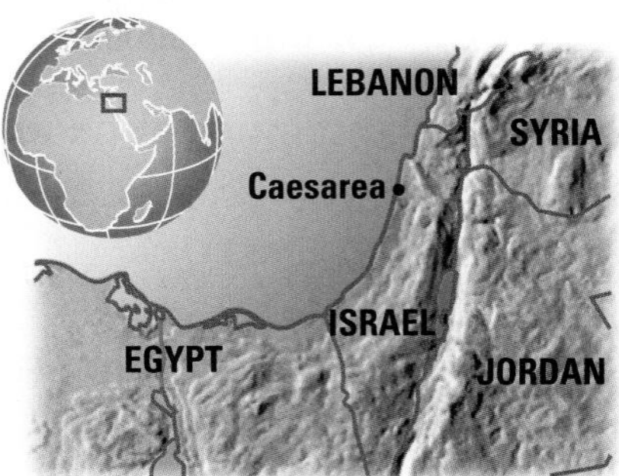

59. **CHOCOLATE MOLD** You are designing a chocolate mold shaped like a hollow rectangular prism for a candy manufacturer. The mold must have a thickness of 1 centimeter in all dimensions. The mold's outer dimensions should also be in the ratio 1 : 3 : 6. What should the outer dimensions of the mold be if it is to hold 112 cubic centimeters of chocolate?

@HomeTutor for problem solving help at classzone.com

60. **MULTI-STEP PROBLEM** A production crew is assembling a three-level platform inside a stadium for a performance. The platform has the dimensions shown in the diagrams, and has a total volume of 1250 cubic feet.

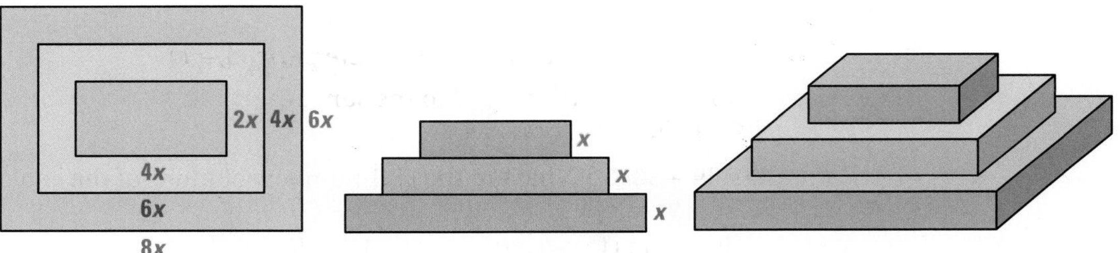

a. **Write Expressions** What is the volume, in terms of x, of each of the three levels of the platform?

b. **Write an Equation** Use what you know about the total volume to write an equation involving x.

c. **Solve** Solve the equation from part (b). Use your solution to calculate the dimensions of each of the three levels of the platform.

61. **SCULPTURE** Suppose you have 250 cubic inches of clay with which to make a sculpture shaped as a rectangular prism. You want the height and width each to be 5 inches less than the length. What should the dimensions of the prism be?

62. **MANUFACTURING** A manufacturer wants to build a rectangular stainless steel tank with a holding capacity of 670 gallons, or about 89.58 cubic feet. The tank's walls will be one half inch thick, and about 6.42 cubic feet of steel will be used for the tank. The manufacturer wants the outer dimensions of the tank to be related as follows:

- The width should be 2 feet less than the length.
- The height should be 8 feet more than the length.

What should the outer dimensions of the tank be?

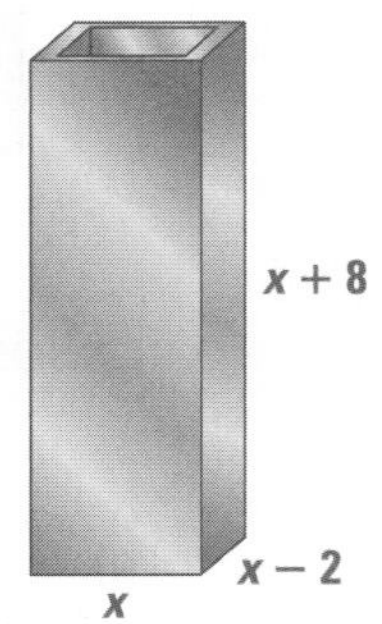

63. ★ **SHORT RESPONSE** A platform shaped like a rectangular prism has dimensions $x - 2$ feet by $3 - 2x$ feet by $3x + 4$ feet. *Explain* why the volume of the platform cannot be $\frac{7}{3}$ cubic feet.

64. ★ **EXTENDED RESPONSE** In 2000 B.C., the Babylonians solved polynomial equations using tables of values. One such table gave values of $y^3 + y^2$. To be able to use this table, the Babylonians sometimes had to manipulate the equation, as shown below.

$ax^3 + bx^2 = c$	**Original equation**
$\frac{a^3x^3}{b^3} + \frac{a^2x^2}{b^2} = \frac{a^2c}{b^3}$	**Multiply each side by $\frac{a^2}{b^3}$.**
$\left(\frac{ax}{b}\right)^3 + \left(\frac{ax}{b}\right)^2 = \frac{a^2c}{b^3}$	**Rewrite cubes and squares.**

They then found $\frac{a^2c}{b^3}$ in the $y^3 + y^2$ column of the table. Because the corresponding y-value was $y = \frac{ax}{b}$, they could conclude that $x = \frac{by}{a}$.

a. Calculate $y^3 + y^2$ for $y = 1, 2, 3, \ldots, 10$. Record the values in a table.

b. Use your table and the method described above to solve $x^3 + 2x^2 = 96$.

c. Use your table and the method described above to solve $3x^3 + 2x^2 = 512$.

d. How can you modify the method described above for equations of the form $ax^4 + bx^3 = c$?

65. **CHALLENGE** Use the diagram to complete parts (a)–(c).

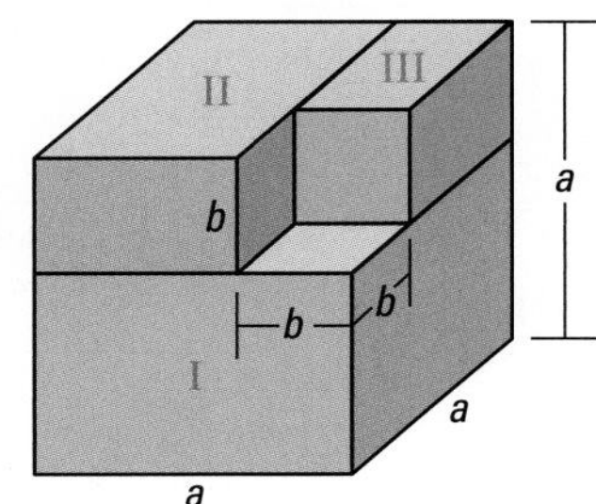

a. *Explain* why $a^3 - b^3$ is equal to the sum of the volumes of solid I, solid II, and solid III.

b. Write an algebraic expression for the volume of each of the three solids. Leave your expressions in factored form.

c. Use the results from parts (a) and (b) to derive the factoring pattern for $a^3 - b^3$ given on page 354.

NEW YORK MIXED REVIEW

TEST PRACTICE at classzone.com

66. Which inequality best describes the range of the function represented by the graph shown?

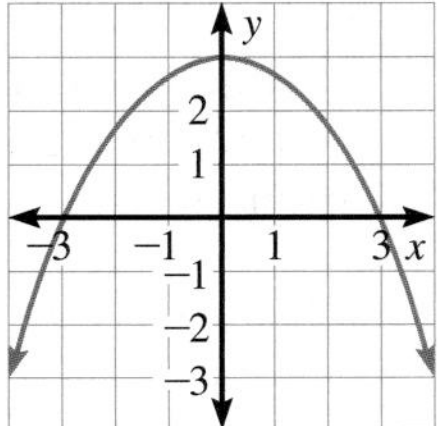

Ⓐ $y \leq 3$ Ⓑ $y \geq 3$

Ⓒ $-3 \leq y \leq 3$ Ⓓ $-4 \leq y \leq 4$

67. A poster is shaped like an equilateral triangle with a side length of 30 inches. What is the approximate area of the poster?

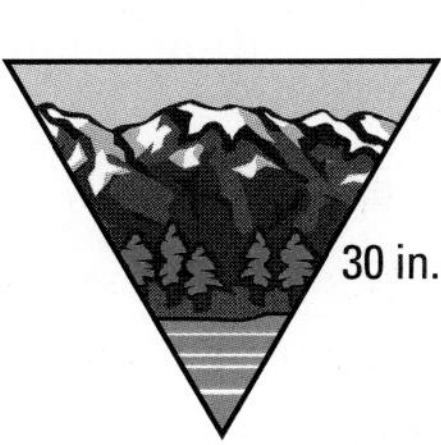

Ⓐ 195 in.^{2} Ⓑ 318 in.^{2}

Ⓒ 390 in.^{2} Ⓓ 780 in.^{2}

PROBLEM SOLVING WORKSHOP
LESSON 5.4

Using ALTERNATIVE METHODS

Another Way to Solve Example 6, page 356

MULTIPLE REPRESENTATIONS In Example 6 on page 356, you solved a polynomial equation by factoring. You can also solve a polynomial equation using a table or a graph.

PROBLEM

CITY PARK You are designing a marble basin that will hold a fountain for a city park. The basin's sides and bottom should be 1 foot thick. Its outer length should be twice its outer width and outer height.

What should the outer dimensions of the basin be if it is to hold 36 cubic feet of water?

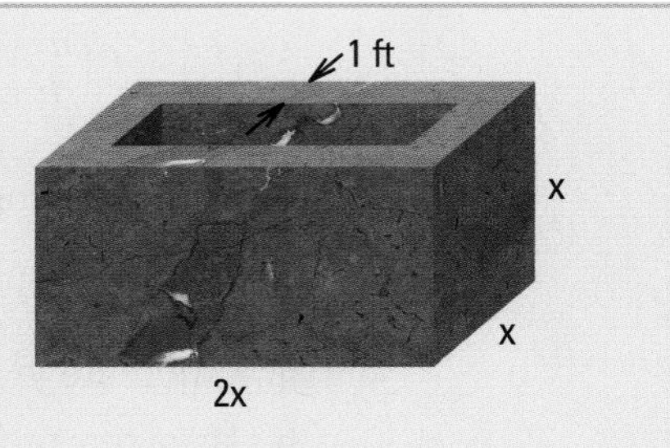

METHOD 1

Using a Table One alternative approach is to write a function for the volume of the basin and make a table of values for the function. Using the table, you can find the value of x that makes the volume of the basin 36 cubic feet.

STEP 1 **Write** the function. From the diagram, you can see that the volume y of water the basin can hold is given by this function:

$$y = (2x - 2)(x - 2)(x - 1)$$

STEP 2 **Make** a table of values for the function. Use only positive values of x because the basin's dimensions must be positive.

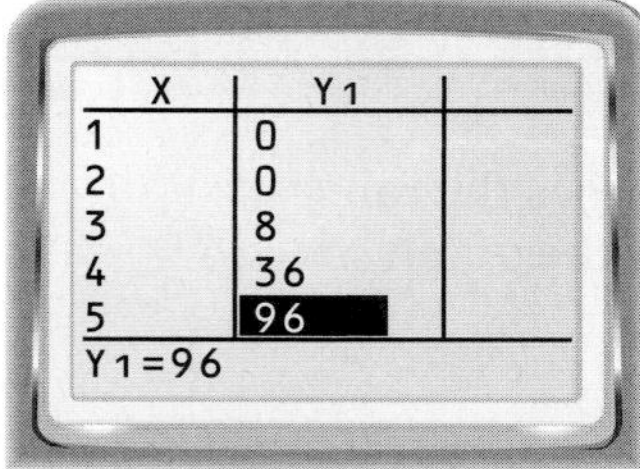

X	Y1
1	0
2	0
3	8
4	36
5	96

Y1=96

STEP 3 **Identify** the value of x for which $y = 36$. The table shows that $y = 36$ when $x = 4$.

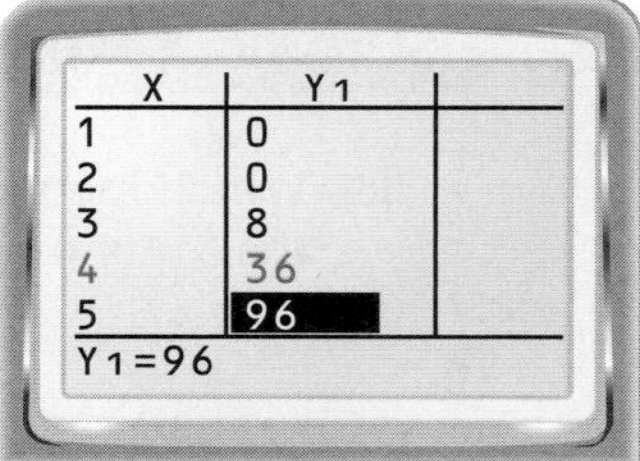

X	Y1
1	0
2	0
3	8
4	36
5	96

Y1=96

▸ The volume of the basin is 36 cubic feet when x is 4 feet. So, the outer dimensions of the basin should be as follows:

Length $= 2x = 8$ feet

Width $= x = 4$ feet

Height $= x = 4$ feet

METHOD 2

Using a Graph Another approach is to make a graph. You can use the graph to find the value of x that makes the volume of the basin 36 cubic feet.

STEP 1 **Write** the function. From the diagram, you can see that the volume y of water the basin can hold is given by this function:

$$y = (2x - 2)(x - 2)(x - 1)$$

STEP 2 **Graph** the equations $y = 36$ and $y = (x - 1)(2x - 2)(x - 2)$. Choose a viewing window that shows the intersection of the graphs.

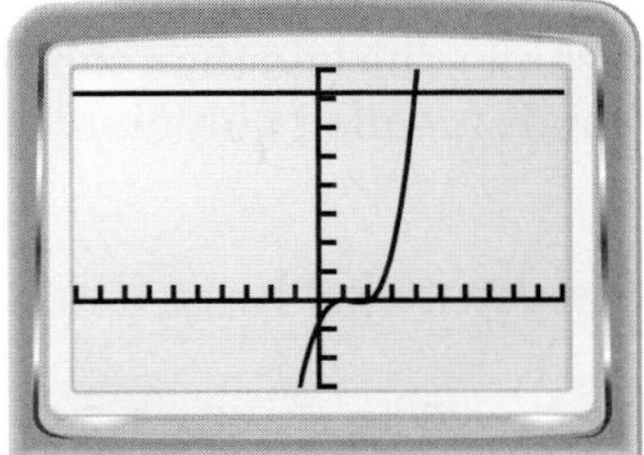

STEP 3 **Identify** the coordinates of the intersection point. On a graphing calculator, you can use the *intersect* feature. The intersection point is (4, 36).

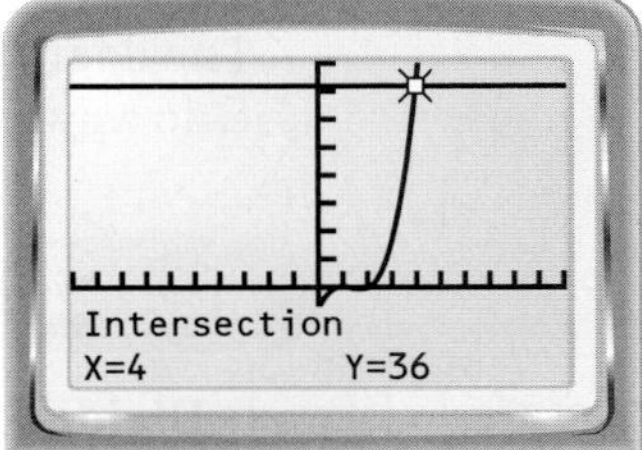

▶ The volume of the basin is 36 cubic feet when x is 4 feet. So, the outer dimensions of the basin should be as follows:

Length $= 2x = 8$ feet

Width $= x = 4$ feet

Height $= x = 4$ feet

PRACTICE

SOLVING EQUATIONS Solve the polynomial equation using a table or using a graph.

1. $x^3 + 4x^2 - 8x = 96$
2. $x^3 - 9x^2 - 14x + 7 = -33$
3. $2x^3 - 11x^2 + 3x + 5 = 59$
4. $x^4 + x^3 - 15x^2 - 8x + 6 = -45$
5. $-x^4 + 2x^3 + 6x^2 + 17x - 4 = 32$
6. $-3x^4 + 4x^3 + 8x^2 + 4x - 11 = 13$
7. $4x^4 - 16x^3 + 29x^2 - 95x = -150$
8. **WHAT IF?** In the problem on page 360, suppose the basin is to hold 200 cubic feet of water. Find the outer dimensions of the basin using a table and using a graph.
9. **PACKAGING** A factory needs a box that has a volume of 1728 cubic inches. The width should be 4 inches less than the height, and the length should be 6 inches greater than the height. Find the dimensions of the box using a table and using a graph.
10. **AGRICULTURE** From 1970 to 2002, the average yearly pineapple consumption P (in pounds) per person in the United States can be modeled by the function

    $$P(x) = 0.0000984x^4 - 0.00712x^3 + 0.162x^2 - 1.11x + 12.3$$

    where x is the number of years since 1970. In what year was the pineapple consumption about 9.97 pounds per person? Solve the problem using a table and a graph.

5.5 Apply the Remainder and Factor Theorems

A2.N.3 Perform arithmetic operations with polynomial expressions containing rational coefficients

Before You used special patterns to factor polynomials.

Now You will use theorems to factor polynomials.

Why? So you can determine attendance at sports games, as in Ex. 43.

Key Vocabulary
- **polynomial long division**
- **synthetic division**

When you divide a polynomial $f(x)$ by a divisor $d(x)$, you get a quotient polynomial $q(x)$ and a remainder polynomial $r(x)$.

$$\frac{f(x)}{d(x)} = q(x) + \frac{r(x)}{d(x)}$$

The degree of the remainder must be less than the degree of the divisor. One way to divide polynomials is called **polynomial long division**.

EXAMPLE 1 Use polynomial long division

Divide $f(x) = 3x^4 - 5x^3 + 4x - 6$ by $x^2 - 3x + 5$.

Solution

Write polynomial division in the same format you use when dividing numbers. Include a "0" as the coefficient of x^2 in the dividend. At each stage, divide the term with the highest power in what is left of the dividend by the first term of the divisor. This gives the next term of the quotient.

$$\begin{array}{rrrrrrl}
 & & & 3x^2 + & 4x - & 3 & \leftarrow \text{quotient} \\
x^2 - 3x + 5 \,) & 3x^4 - & 5x^3 + & 0x^2 + & 4x - & 6 & \\
 & 3x^4 - & 9x^3 + & 15x^2 & & & \text{Multiply divisor by } 3x^4/x^2 = 3x^2. \\
 & & 4x^3 - & 15x^2 + & 4x & & \text{Subtract. Bring down next term.} \\
 & & 4x^3 - & 12x^2 + & 20x & & \text{Multiply divisor by } 4x^3/x^2 = 4x. \\
 & & & -3x^2 - & 16x - & 6 & \text{Subtract. Bring down next term.} \\
 & & & -3x^2 + & 9x - & 15 & \text{Multiply divisor by } -3x^2/x^2 = -3. \\
 & & & & -25x + & 9 & \leftarrow \text{remainder}
\end{array}$$

▶ $$\frac{3x^4 - 5x^3 + 4x - 6}{x^2 - 3x + 5} = 3x^2 + 4x - 3 + \frac{-25x + 9}{x^2 - 3x + 5}$$

AVOID ERRORS
The expression added to the quotient in the result of the long division problem is $\frac{r(x)}{d(x)}$, not $r(x)$.

CHECK You can check the result of a division problem by multiplying the quotient by the divisor and adding the remainder. The result should be the dividend.

$(3x^2 + 4x - 3)(x^2 - 3x + 5) + (-25x + 9)$

$= 3x^2(x^2 - 3x + 5) + 4x(x^2 - 3x + 5) - 3(x^2 - 3x + 5) - 25x + 9$

$= 3x^4 - 9x^3 + 15x^2 + 4x^3 - 12x^2 + 20x - 3x^2 + 9x - 15 - 25x + 9$

$= 3x^4 - 5x^3 + 4x - 6$ ✓

EXAMPLE 2 Use polynomial long division with a linear divisor

Divide $f(x) = x^3 + 5x^2 - 7x + 2$ by $x - 2$.

$$\begin{array}{rrrrl}
 & x^2 + & 7x + & 7 & \leftarrow \textbf{quotient} \\
x - 2 \,\big)\, x^3 + & 5x^2 - & 7x + & 2 & \\
x^3 - & 2x^2 & & & \text{Multiply divisor by } x^3/x = x^2. \\
 & 7x^2 - & 7x & & \text{Subtract.} \\
 & 7x^2 - & 14x & & \text{Multiply divisor by } 7x^2/x = 7x. \\
 & & 7x + & 2 & \text{Subtract.} \\
 & & 7x - & 14 & \text{Multiply divisor by } 7x/x = 7. \\
 & & & 16 & \leftarrow \textbf{remainder}
\end{array}$$

▶ $\frac{x^3 + 5x^2 - 7x + 2}{x - 2} = x^2 + 7x + 7 + \frac{16}{x - 2}$

GUIDED PRACTICE for Examples 1 and 2

Divide using polynomial long division.

1. $(2x^4 + x^3 + x - 1) \div (x^2 + 2x - 1)$

2. $(x^3 - x^2 + 4x - 10) \div (x + 2)$

SYNTHETIC DIVISION If you use synthetic substitution to evaluate $f(x)$ in Example 2 when $x = 2$, as shown below, you can see that $f(2)$ equals the remainder when $f(x)$ is divided by $x - 2$. Also, the other values below the line match the coefficients of the quotient. For this reason, synthetic substitution is sometimes called **synthetic division**. Synthetic division can be used to divide any polynomial by a divisor of the form $x - k$.

$$\begin{array}{r|rrrr}
2 & 1 & 5 & -7 & 2 \\
 & & 2 & 14 & 14 \\
\hline
 & 1 & 7 & 7 & 16
\end{array}$$

coefficients of quotient → 1 7 7 | 16 ← remainder

KEY CONCEPT — *For Your Notebook*

Remainder Theorem

If a polynomial $f(x)$ is divided by $x - k$, then the remainder is $r = f(k)$.

EXAMPLE 3 Use synthetic division

Divide $f(x) = 2x^3 + x^2 - 8x + 5$ by $x + 3$ using synthetic division.

DIVIDE POLYNOMIALS
Because the divisor is $x + 3 = x - (-3)$, evaluate the dividend when $x = -3$.

$$\begin{array}{r|rrrr}
-3 & 2 & 1 & -8 & 5 \\
 & & -6 & 15 & -21 \\
\hline
 & 2 & -5 & 7 & -16
\end{array}$$

▶ $\frac{2x^3 + x^2 - 8x + 5}{x + 3} = 2x^2 - 5x + 7 - \frac{16}{x + 3}$

FACTOR THEOREM Suppose the remainder is 0 when a polynomial $f(x)$ is divided by $x - k$. Then

$$\frac{f(x)}{x-k} = q(x) + \frac{0}{x-k} = q(x)$$

where $q(x)$ is the quotient polynomial. Therefore, $f(x) = (x - k) \cdot q(x)$, so that $x - k$ is a factor of $f(x)$. This result is summarized by the *factor theorem.*

KEY CONCEPT *For Your Notebook*

Factor Theorem

A polynomial $f(x)$ has a factor $x - k$ if and only if $f(k) = 0$.

The factor theorem can be used to solve a variety of problems.

Problem	Example
Given one *factor* of a polynomial, find the other *factors.*	See Example 4 below.
Given one *zero* of a polynomial function, find the other *zeros.*	See Example 5 on page 365.
Given one *solution* of a polynomial equation, find the other *solutions.*	See Example 6 on page 365.

EXAMPLE 4 Factor a polynomial

Factor $f(x) = 3x^3 - 4x^2 - 28x - 16$ completely given that $x + 2$ is a factor.

Solution

AVOID ERRORS
The remainder after using synthetic division should always be zero when you are dividing a polynomial by one of its factors.

Because $x + 2$ is a factor of $f(x)$, you know that $f(-2) = 0$. Use synthetic division to find the other factors.

$$\begin{array}{r|rrrr} -2 & 3 & -4 & -28 & -16 \\ & & -6 & 20 & 16 \\ \hline & 3 & -10 & -8 & 0 \end{array}$$

Use the result to write $f(x)$ as a product of two factors and then factor completely.

$f(x) = 3x^3 - 4x^2 - 28x - 16$ **Write original polynomial.**

$= (x + 2)(3x^2 - 10x - 8)$ **Write as a product of two factors.**

$= (x + 2)(3x + 2)(x - 4)$ **Factor trinomial.**

✓ **GUIDED PRACTICE** for Examples 3 and 4

Divide using synthetic division.

3. $(x^3 + 4x^2 - x - 1) \div (x + 3)$

4. $(4x^3 + x^2 - 3x + 7) \div (x - 1)$

Factor the polynomial completely given that $x - 4$ is a factor.

5. $f(x) = x^3 - 6x^2 + 5x + 12$

6. $f(x) = x^3 - x^2 - 22x + 40$

EXAMPLE 5 Standardized Test Practice

One zero of $f(x) = x^3 - 2x^2 - 23x + 60$ is $x = 3$. What is another zero of f?

Ⓐ -5 Ⓑ -4 Ⓒ 2 Ⓓ 5

Solution

Because $f(3) = 0$, $x - 3$ is a factor of $f(x)$. Use synthetic division.

$$\begin{array}{r|rrrr} 3 & 1 & -2 & -23 & 60 \\ & & 3 & 3 & -60 \\ \hline & 1 & 1 & -20 & 0 \end{array}$$

Use the result to write $f(x)$ as a product of two factors. Then factor completely.

$$f(x) = x^3 - 2x^2 - 23x + 60 = (x - 3)(x^2 + x - 20) = (x - 3)(x + 5)(x - 4)$$

The zeros are 3, -5, and 4.

▶ The correct answer is A. Ⓐ Ⓑ Ⓒ Ⓓ

EXAMPLE 6 Use a polynomial model

BUSINESS The profit P (in millions of dollars) for a shoe manufacturer can be modeled by $P = -21x^3 + 46x$ where x is the number of shoes produced (in millions). The company now produces 1 million shoes and makes a profit of $25,000,000, but would like to cut back production. What lesser number of shoes could the company produce and still make the same profit?

Solution

$25 = -21x^3 + 46x$ **Substitute 25 for P in $P = -21x^3 + 46x$.**

$0 = 21x^3 - 46x + 25$ **Write in standard form.**

You know that $x = 1$ is one solution of the equation. This implies that $x - 1$ is a factor of $21x^3 - 46x + 25$. Use synthetic division to find the other factors.

$$\begin{array}{r|rrrr} 1 & 21 & 0 & -46 & 25 \\ & & 21 & 21 & -25 \\ \hline & 21 & 21 & -25 & 0 \end{array}$$

So, $(x - 1)(21x^2 + 21x - 25) = 0$. Use the quadratic formula to find that $x \approx 0.7$ is the other positive solution.

▶ The company could still make the same profit producing about 700,000 shoes.

GUIDED PRACTICE for Examples 5 and 6

Find the other zeros of f given that $f(-2) = 0$.

7. $f(x) = x^3 + 2x^2 - 9x - 18$

8. $f(x) = x^3 + 8x^2 + 5x - 14$

9. **WHAT IF?** In Example 6, how does the answer change if the profit for the shoe manufacturer is modeled by $P = -15x^3 + 40x$?

5.5 EXERCISES

HOMEWORK KEY

○ = **WORKED-OUT SOLUTIONS** on p. WS10 for Exs. 17, 25, and 43

★ = **STANDARDIZED TEST PRACTICE** Exs. 2, 35, 39, 44, and 45

◆ = **MULTIPLE REPRESENTATIONS** Ex. 38

SKILL PRACTICE

1. **VOCABULARY** State the remainder theorem.

2. ★ **WRITING** Synthetic division has been used to divide $f(x) = x^4 - 5x^2 + 8x - 2$ by $x + 3$. *Explain* what the colored numbers represent in the division problem.

−3	1	0	−5	8	−2
		−3	9	−12	12
	1	−3	4	−4	10

EXAMPLES 1 and 2 on pp. 362–363 for Exs. 3–10

USING LONG DIVISION **Divide using polynomial long division.**

3. $(x^2 + x - 17) \div (x - 4)$
4. $(3x^2 - 11x - 26) \div (x - 5)$
5. $(x^3 + 3x^2 + 3x + 2) \div (x - 1)$
6. $(8x^2 + 34x - 1) \div (4x - 1)$
7. $(3x^3 + 11x^2 + 4x + 1) \div (x^2 + x)$
8. $(7x^3 + 11x^2 + 7x + 5) \div (x^2 + 1)$
9. $(5x^4 - 2x^3 - 7x^2 - 39) \div (x^2 + 2x - 4)$
10. $(4x^4 + 5x - 4) \div (x^2 - 3x - 2)$

EXAMPLE 3 on p. 363 for Exs. 11–20

USING SYNTHETIC DIVISION **Divide using synthetic division.**

11. $(2x^2 - 7x + 10) \div (x - 5)$
12. $(4x^2 - 13x - 5) \div (x - 2)$
13. $(x^2 + 8x + 1) \div (x + 4)$
14. $(x^2 + 9) \div (x - 3)$
15. $(x^3 - 5x^2 - 2) \div (x - 4)$
16. $(x^3 - 4x + 6) \div (x + 3)$
17. $(x^4 - 5x^3 - 8x^2 + 13x - 12) \div (x - 6)$
18. $(x^4 + 4x^3 + 16x - 35) \div (x + 5)$

ERROR ANALYSIS ***Describe*** **and correct the error in using synthetic division to divide $x^3 - 5x + 3$ by $x - 2$.**

19.

2	1	0	−5	3
		2	4	−2
	1	2	−1	1

$$\frac{x^3 - 5x + 3}{x - 2} = x^3 + 2x^2 - x + 1$$

20.

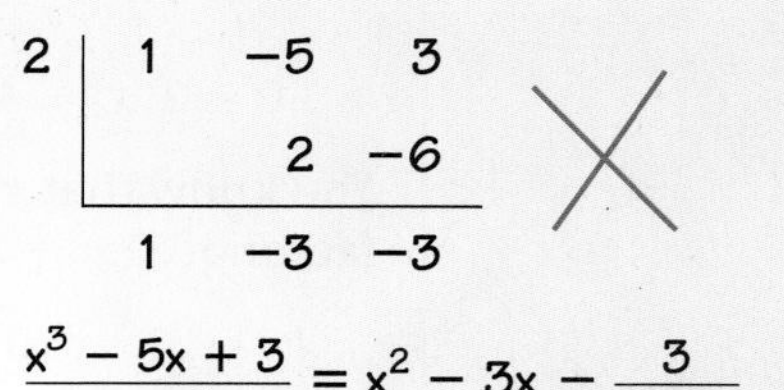

EXAMPLE 4 on p. 364 for Exs. 21–28

FACTOR **Given polynomial $f(x)$ and a factor of $f(x)$, factor $f(x)$ completely.**

21. $f(x) = x^3 - 10x^2 + 19x + 30;\ x - 6$
22. $f(x) = x^3 + 6x^2 + 5x - 12;\ x + 4$
23. $f(x) = x^3 - 2x^2 - 40x - 64;\ x - 8$
24. $f(x) = x^3 + 18x^2 + 95x + 150;\ x + 10$
25. $f(x) = x^3 + 2x^2 - 51x + 108;\ x + 9$
26. $f(x) = x^3 - 9x^2 + 8x + 60;\ x + 2$
27. $f(x) = 2x^3 - 15x^2 + 34x - 21;\ x - 1$
28. $f(x) = 3x^3 - 2x^2 - 61x - 20;\ x - 5$

EXAMPLE 5 on p. 365 for Exs. 29–35

FIND ZEROS **Given polynomial function f and a zero of f, find the other zeros.**

29. $f(x) = x^3 - 2x^2 - 21x - 18;\ -3$
30. $f(x) = 4x^3 - 25x^2 - 154x + 40;\ 10$
31. $f(x) = 10x^3 - 81x^2 + 71x + 42;\ 7$
32. $f(x) = 3x^3 + 34x^2 + 72x - 64;\ -4$
33. $f(x) = 2x^3 - 10x^2 - 71x - 9;\ 9$
34. $f(x) = 5x^3 - x^2 - 18x + 8;\ -2$

35. ★ **MULTIPLE CHOICE** One zero of $f(x) = 4x^3 + 15x^2 - 63x - 54$ is $x = -6$. What is another zero of f?

(A) -9 (B) -3 (C) -1 (D) 3

GEOMETRY You are given an expression for the volume of the rectangular prism. Find an expression for the missing dimension.

36. $V = 2x^3 + 17x^2 + 46x + 40$

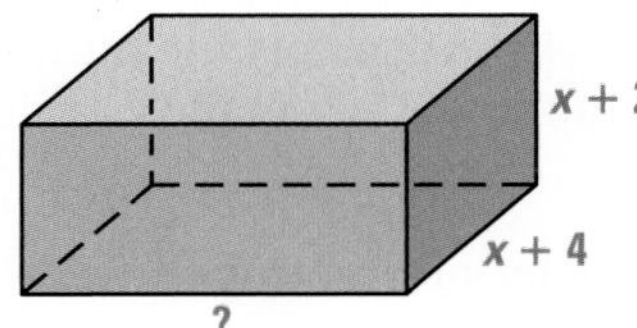

37. $V = x^3 + 13x^2 + 34x - 48$

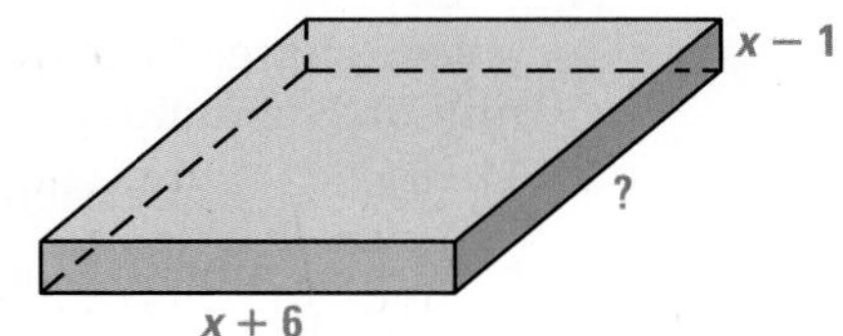

38. **MULTIPLE REPRESENTATIONS** Consider the polynomial function $f(x) = x^3 - 5x^2 - 12x + 36$.

a. **Zeros of a Function** Given that $f(2) = 0$, find the other zeros of f.

b. **Factors of an Expression** Based on your results from part (a), what are the factors of the polynomial $x^3 - 5x^2 - 12x + 36$?

c. **Solutions of an Equation** What are the solutions of the polynomial equation $x^3 - 5x^2 - 12x + 36 = 0$?

39. ★ **MULTIPLE CHOICE** What is the value of k such that $x - 5$ is a factor of $x^3 - x^2 + kx - 30$?

(A) -14 (B) -2 (C) 26 (D) 32

40. **CHALLENGE** It can be shown that $2x - 1$ is a factor of the polynomial function $f(x) = 30x^3 + 7x^2 - 39x + 14$.

a. What can you conclude is a zero of f?

b. Use synthetic division to write $f(x)$ in the form $(x - k) \cdot q(x)$.

c. Write $f(x)$ as the product of linear factors with integer coefficients.

PROBLEM SOLVING

EXAMPLE 6 on p. 365 for Exs. 41–43

41. **CLOTHING** The profit P (in millions of dollars) for a T-shirt manufacturer can be modeled by $P = -x^3 + 4x^2 + x$ where x is the number of T-shirts produced (in millions). Currently, the company produces 4 million T-shirts and makes a profit of $4,000,000. What lesser number of T-shirts could the company produce and still make the same profit?

@HomeTutor for problem solving help at classzone.com

42. **MP3 PLAYERS** The profit P (in millions of dollars) for a manufacturer of MP3 players can be modeled by $P = -4x^3 + 12x^2 + 16x$ where x is the number of MP3 players produced (in millions). Currently, the company produces 3 million MP3 players and makes a profit of $48,000,000. What lesser number of MP3 players could the company produce and still make the same profit?

@HomeTutor for problem solving help at classzone.com

43. **WOMEN'S BASKETBALL** From 1985 to 2003, the total attendance A (in thousands) at NCAA women's basketball games and the number T of NCAA women's basketball teams can be modeled by

$$A = -1.95x^3 + 70.1x^2 - 188x + 2150 \quad \text{and} \quad T = 14.8x + 725$$

where x is the number of years since 1985. Write a function for the average attendance per team from 1985 to 2003.

44. ★ **EXTENDED RESPONSE** The price p (in dollars) that a radio manufacturer is able to charge for a radio is given by $p = 40 - 4x^2$ where x is the number (in millions) of radios produced. It costs the company \$15 to make a radio.

a. Write an expression for the company's total revenue in terms of x.

b. Write a function for the company's profit P by subtracting the total cost to make x radios from the expression in part (a).

c. Currently, the company produces 1.5 million radios and makes a profit of \$24,000,000. Write and solve an equation to find a lesser number of radios that the company could produce and still make the same profit.

d. Do all the solutions in part (c) make sense in this situation? *Explain.*

45. ★ **SHORT RESPONSE** Since 1990, overnight stays S and total visits V (both in millions) to national parks can be modeled by

$$S = -0.00722x^4 + 0.176x^3 - 1.40x^2 + 3.39x + 17.6$$

$$V = 3.10x + 256$$

where x is the number of years since 1990. Write a function for the percent of visits to national parks that were overnight stays. *Explain* how you constructed your function.

Joshua Tree National Park, California

46. **CHALLENGE** The profit P (in millions of dollars) for a DVD manufacturer can be modeled by $P = -6x^3 + 72x$ where x is the number of DVDs produced (in millions). Show that 2 million DVDs is the only production level for the company that yields a profit of \$96,000,000.

NEW YORK MIXED REVIEW

TEST PRACTICE at classzone.com

47. James leaves his home to walk to school. Four minutes later, his friend leaves her home to ride her bike to school. James averages 3 miles per hour and his friend averages 10 miles per hour. James and his friend travel a combined total of 8 miles and arrive at school at the same time. How long did it take James to walk to school?

Ⓐ 34 min   Ⓑ 38 min

Ⓒ 40 min   Ⓓ 44 min

48. What are the coordinates of the x-intercept of the graph of $2x + 3y = 15$?

Ⓐ $\left(-\frac{15}{2}, 0\right)$ Ⓑ $\left(\frac{15}{2}, 0\right)$

Ⓒ $(0, 5)$ Ⓓ $(13, 0)$

Lessons 5.1–5.5

1. **ASTRONOMY** The average distance between Earth and the sun is 1.64×10^{11} yards. The length of a football field, including the end zones, is 1.20×10^2 yards. About how many football fields stretched end-to-end would it take to reach from Earth to the sun?

(1) 1.37×10^7

(2) 1.37×10^9

(3) 1.37×10^{10}

(4) 1.37×10^{13}

2. **PRODUCT DESIGN** You are designing a rectangular picnic cooler with length 4 times its width and height 2 times its width. The cooler has insulation that is 1 inch thick on each of the four sides and 2 inches thick on the top and bottom. Let x represent the width of the cooler. What is a polynomial function $C(x)$ in standard form for the volume of the inside of the cooler?

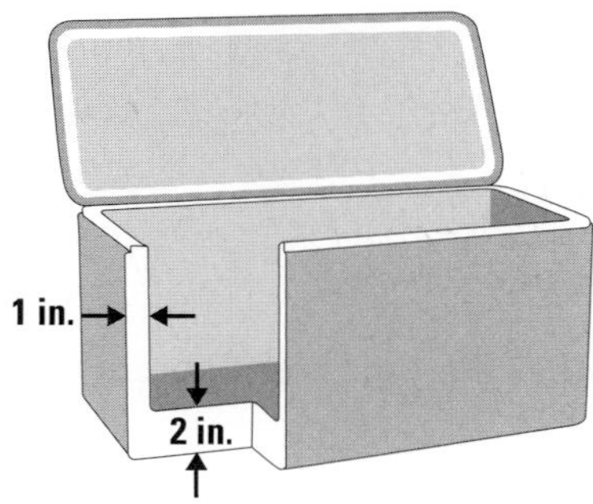

(1) $C(x) = 8x^3 - 18x^2 + 12x - 2$

(2) $C(x) = 8x^3 - 28x^2 + 28x - 8$

(3) $C(x) = 8x^3 - 36x^2 + 48x - 16$

(4) $C(x) = 8x^3 + 36x^2 + 48x + 16$

3. **END BEHAVIOR** Which polynomial function has degree 4 and end behavior given by $f(x) \to -\infty$ as $x \to -\infty$ and $f(x) \to -\infty$ as $x \to +\infty$?

(1) $f(x) = 4x^3 - 4x^2 + x + 5$

(2) $f(x) = x^4 - x^3 + 2x^2 - 5x + 2$

(3) $f(x) = -x^4 + 5x^2 - x + 20$

(4) $f(x) = -4x^6 + x^4 + 4$

4. **PACKAGING DESIGN** A floral shop has a rectangular gift box with a volume of 540 cubic inches. The width of the gift box is 3 inches less than the height, and the length is 15 inches greater than the height. What is the height of the gift box to the nearest tenth of an inch?

(1) 3.7 inches

(2) 6.7 inches

(3) 12.0 inches

(4) 21.7 inches

5. **OPEN-ENDED** The price p (in dollars) that a camera manufacturer is able to charge for a camera is given by $p = 100 - 10x^2$ where x is the number (in millions) of cameras produced. It costs the company $30 to make a camera. Currently, the company produces 2 million cameras and makes a profit of $60,000,000.

Write a function that gives the total revenue R in terms of x.

Write a function that gives the company's profit P in terms of x.

Write and solve an equation to find other values of x that yield a profit of $60,000,000.

Do all the solutions in the previous part make sense in this situation? *Explain.*

6. **OPEN-ENDED** From 1995 to 2003, the average monthly cell phone bill C (in dollars) for subscribers in the United States can be modeled by the function

$$C = -0.027t^4 + 0.32t^3 - 0.25t^2 - 4.9t + 51$$

where t is the number of years since 1995.

According to this model, what was the average monthly cell phone bill in 2001?

Do you think the model will accurately predict cell phone bills for years beyond 2006? *Explain* your answer.

5.6 Find Rational Zeros

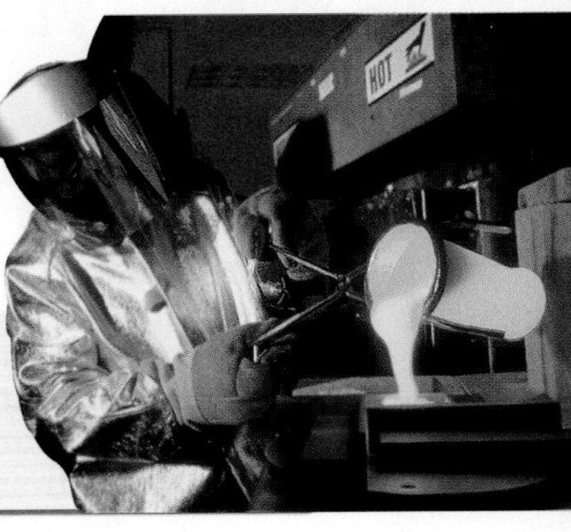

 **A2.A.50** Approximate the solution to polynomial equations of higher degree by inspecting the graph

Before You found the zeros of a polynomial function given one zero.

Now You will find all real zeros of a polynomial function.

Why? So you can model manufacturing processes, as in Ex. 45.

Key Vocabulary
- **zero of a function,** *p. 254*
- **constant term,** *p. 337*
- **leading coefficient,** *p. 337*

The polynomial function $f(x) = 64x^3 + 152x^2 - 62x - 105$ has $-\frac{5}{2}$, $-\frac{3}{4}$, and $\frac{7}{8}$ as its zeros. Notice that the numerators of these zeros (-5, -3, and 7) are factors of the constant term, -105. Also notice that the denominators (2, 4, and 8) are factors of the leading coefficient, 64. These observations are generalized by the *rational zero theorem.*

KEY CONCEPT *For Your Notebook*

The Rational Zero Theorem

If $f(x) = a_nx^n + \cdots + a_1x + a_0$ has *integer* coefficients, then every rational zero of f has the following form:

$$\frac{p}{q} = \frac{\text{factor of constant term } a_0}{\text{factor of leading coefficient } a_n}$$

EXAMPLE 1 List possible rational zeros

List the possible rational zeros of f using the rational zero theorem.

a. $f(x) = x^3 + 2x^2 - 11x + 12$

Factors of the constant term: $\pm1, \pm2, \pm3, \pm4, \pm6, \pm12$

Factors of the leading coefficient: ±1

Possible rational zeros: $\pm\frac{1}{1}, \pm\frac{2}{1}, \pm\frac{3}{1}, \pm\frac{4}{1}, \pm\frac{6}{1}, \pm\frac{12}{1}$

Simplified list of possible zeros: $\pm1, \pm2, \pm3, \pm4, \pm6, \pm12$

AVOID ERRORS
Be sure your lists include both the positive and negative factors of the constant term and the leading coefficient.

b. $f(x) = 4x^4 - x^3 - 3x^2 + 9x - 10$

Factors of the constant term: $\pm1, \pm2, \pm5, \pm10$

Factors of the leading coefficient: $\pm1, \pm2, \pm4$

Possible rational zeros:

$\pm\frac{1}{1}, \pm\frac{2}{1}, \pm\frac{5}{1}, \pm\frac{10}{1}, \pm\frac{1}{2}, \pm\frac{2}{2}, \pm\frac{5}{2}, \pm\frac{10}{2}, \pm\frac{1}{4}, \pm\frac{2}{4}, \pm\frac{5}{4}, \pm\frac{10}{4}$

Simplified list of possible zeros: $\pm1, \pm2, \pm5, \pm10, \pm\frac{1}{2}, \pm\frac{5}{2}, \pm\frac{1}{4}, \pm\frac{5}{4}$

✓ GUIDED PRACTICE for Example 1

List the possible rational zeros of f using the rational zero theorem.

1. $f(x) = x^3 + 9x^2 + 23x + 15$
2. $f(x) = 2x^3 + 3x^2 - 11x - 6$

VERIFYING ZEROS In Lesson 5.5, you found zeros of polynomial functions when one zero was known. The rational zero theorem is a starting point for finding zeros when no zeros are known.

However, the rational zero theorem lists only *possible* zeros. In order to find the *actual* zeros of a polynomial function f, you must test values from the list of possible zeros. You can test a value by evaluating $f(x)$ using the test value as x.

EXAMPLE 2 Find zeros when the leading coefficient is 1

Find all real zeros of $f(x) = x^3 - 8x^2 + 11x + 20$.

Solution

STEP 1 **List** the possible rational zeros. The leading coefficient is 1 and the constant term is 20. So, the possible rational zeros are:

$$x = \pm\frac{1}{1}, \pm\frac{2}{1}, \pm\frac{4}{1}, \pm\frac{5}{1}, \pm\frac{10}{1}, \pm\frac{20}{1}$$

AVOID ERRORS

Notice that not every *possible* zero generated by the rational zero theorem is an *actual* zero of *f*.

STEP 2 **Test** these zeros using synthetic division.

Test $x = 1$:

$$\begin{array}{r|rrrr} 1 & 1 & -8 & 11 & 20 \\ & & 1 & -7 & 4 \\ \hline & 1 & -7 & 4 & 24 \end{array}$$

1 is not a zero.

Test $x = -1$:

$$\begin{array}{r|rrrr} -1 & 1 & -8 & 11 & 20 \\ & & -1 & 9 & -20 \\ \hline & 1 & -9 & 20 & 0 \end{array}$$

−1 is a zero.

Because −1 is a zero of f, you can write $f(x) = (x + 1)(x^2 - 9x + 20)$.

STEP 3 **Factor** the trinomial in $f(x)$ and use the factor theorem.

$$f(x) = (x + 1)(x^2 - 9x + 20) = (x + 1)(x - 4)(x - 5)$$

▶ The zeros of f are −1, 4, and 5.

Animated Algebra at classzone.com

✓ GUIDED PRACTICE for Example 2

Find all real zeros of the function.

3. $f(x) = x^3 - 4x^2 - 15x + 18$
4. $f(x) = x^3 - 8x^2 + 5x + 14$

LIMITING THE SEARCH FOR ZEROS In Example 2, the leading coefficient of the polynomial function is 1. When the leading coefficient is not 1, the list of possible rational zeros can increase dramatically. In such cases, the search can be shortened by sketching the function's graph.

EXAMPLE 3 Find zeros when the leading coefficient is not 1

Find all real zeros of $f(x) = 10x^4 - 11x^3 - 42x^2 + 7x + 12$.

Solution

STEP 1 **List** the possible rational zeros of f: $\pm\frac{1}{1}, \pm\frac{2}{1}, \pm\frac{3}{1}, \pm\frac{4}{1}, \pm\frac{6}{1}, \pm\frac{12}{1},$

$\pm\frac{1}{2}, \pm\frac{3}{2}, \pm\frac{1}{5}, \pm\frac{2}{5}, \pm\frac{3}{5}, \pm\frac{4}{5}, \pm\frac{6}{5}, \pm\frac{12}{5}, \pm\frac{1}{10}, \pm\frac{3}{10}$

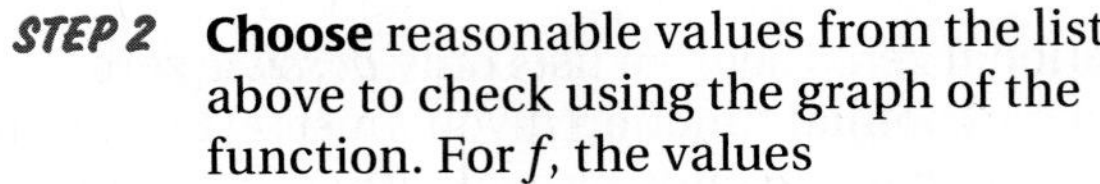

STEP 2 **Choose** reasonable values from the list above to check using the graph of the function. For f, the values

$$x = -\frac{3}{2}, x = -\frac{1}{2}, x = \frac{3}{5}, \text{ and } x = \frac{12}{5}$$

are reasonable based on the graph shown at the right.

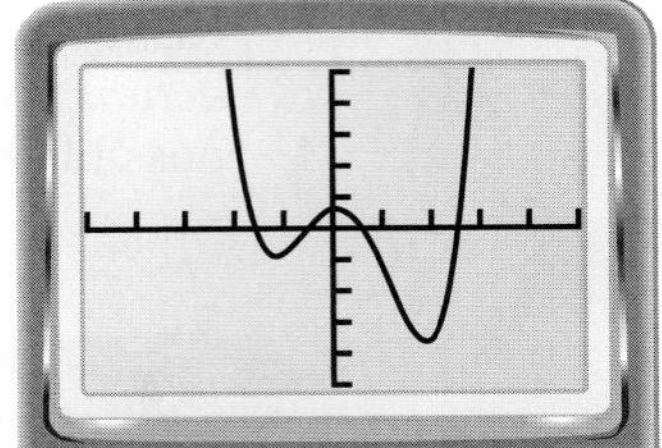

STEP 3 **Check** the values using synthetic division until a zero is found.

$$\begin{array}{r|rrrrr} -\frac{3}{2} & 10 & -11 & -42 & 7 & 12 \\ & & -15 & 39 & \frac{9}{2} & -\frac{69}{4} \\ \hline & 10 & -26 & -3 & \frac{23}{2} & -\frac{21}{4} \end{array}$$

$$\begin{array}{r|rrrrr} -\frac{1}{2} & 10 & -11 & -42 & 7 & 12 \\ & & -5 & 8 & 17 & -12 \\ \hline & 10 & -16 & -34 & 24 & 0 \end{array}$$

$-\frac{1}{2}$ **is a zero.**

STEP 4 **Factor** out a binomial using the result of the synthetic division.

$f(x) = \left(x + \frac{1}{2}\right)(10x^3 - 16x^2 - 34x + 24)$ **Write as a product of factors.**

$= \left(x + \frac{1}{2}\right)(2)(5x^3 - 8x^2 - 17x + 12)$ **Factor 2 out of the second factor.**

$= (2x + 1)(5x^3 - 8x^2 - 17x + 12)$ **Multiply the first factor by 2.**

STEP 5 **Repeat** the steps above for $g(x) = 5x^3 - 8x^2 - 17x + 12$. Any zero of g will also be a zero of f. The possible rational zeros of g are:

$$x = \pm 1, \pm 2, \pm 3, \pm 4, \pm 6, \pm 12, \pm\frac{1}{5}, \pm\frac{2}{5}, \pm\frac{3}{5}, \pm\frac{4}{5}, \pm\frac{6}{5}, \pm\frac{12}{5}$$

The graph of g shows that $\frac{3}{5}$ may be a zero. Synthetic division shows that $\frac{3}{5}$ *is* a zero and $g(x) = \left(x - \frac{3}{5}\right)(5x^2 - 5x - 20) = (5x - 3)(x^2 - x - 4)$. It follows that:

$$f(x) = (2x + 1) \cdot g(x) = (2x + 1)(5x - 3)(x^2 - x - 4)$$

STEP 6 **Find** the remaining zeros of f by solving $x^2 - x - 4 = 0$.

$x = \frac{-(-1) \pm \sqrt{(-1)^2 - 4(1)(-4)}}{2(1)}$ **Substitute 1 for *a*, −1 for *b*, and −4 for *c* in the quadratic formula.**

$x = \frac{1 \pm \sqrt{17}}{2}$ **Simplify.**

▶ The real zeros of f are $-\frac{1}{2}, \frac{3}{5}, \frac{1 + \sqrt{17}}{2}$, and $\frac{1 - \sqrt{17}}{2}$.

GUIDED PRACTICE for Example 3

Find all real zeros of the function.

5. $f(x) = 48x^3 + 4x^2 - 20x + 3$

6. $f(x) = 2x^4 + 5x^3 - 18x^2 - 19x + 42$

EXAMPLE 4 Solve a multi-step problem

ICE SCULPTURES Some ice sculptures are made by filling a mold with water and then freezing it. You are making such an ice sculpture for a school dance. It is to be shaped like a pyramid with a height that is 1 foot greater than the length of each side of its square base. The volume of the ice sculpture is 4 cubic feet. What are the dimensions of the mold?

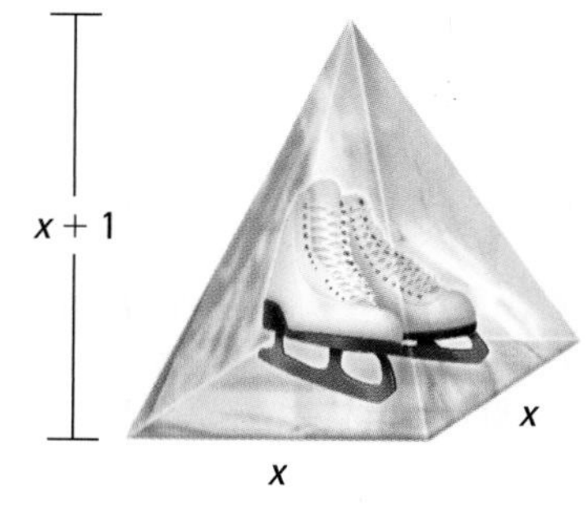

Solution

STEP 1 **Write** an equation for the volume of the ice sculpture.

Volume (cubic feet)	= $\frac{1}{3}$ ·	Area of base (square feet)	·	Height (feet)
4	= $\frac{1}{3}$ ·	x^2	·	$(x + 1)$

$4 = \frac{1}{3}x^2(x + 1)$ **Write equation.**

$12 = x^3 + x^2$ **Multiply each side by 3 and simplify.**

$0 = x^3 + x^2 - 12$ **Subtract 12 from each side.**

STEP 2 **List** the possible rational solutions: $\pm\frac{1}{1}, \pm\frac{2}{1}, \pm\frac{3}{1}, \pm\frac{4}{1}, \pm\frac{6}{1}, \pm\frac{12}{1}$

STEP 3 **Test** possible solutions. Only positive x-values make sense.

$$\begin{array}{r|rrrr} 1 & 1 & 1 & 0 & -12 \\ & & 1 & 2 & 2 \\ \hline & 1 & 2 & 2 & -10 \end{array} \qquad \begin{array}{r|rrrr} 2 & 1 & 1 & 0 & -12 \\ & & 2 & 6 & 12 \\ \hline & 1 & 3 & 6 & 0 \end{array}$$

2 is a solution.

STEP 4 **Check** for other solutions. The other two solutions, which satisfy $x^2 + 3x + 6 = 0$, are $x = \frac{-3 \pm i\sqrt{15}}{2}$ and can be discarded because they are imaginary numbers.

▶ The only reasonable solution is $x = 2$. The base of the mold is 2 feet by 2 feet. The height of the mold is $2 + 1 = 3$ feet.

GUIDED PRACTICE for Example 4

7. **WHAT IF?** In Example 4, suppose the base of the ice sculpture has sides that are 1 foot longer than the height. The volume of the ice sculpture is 6 cubic feet. What are the dimensions of the mold?

5.6 EXERCISES

HOMEWORK KEY
○ = **WORKED-OUT SOLUTIONS** on p. WS11 for Exs. 7, 21, and 47
★ = **STANDARDIZED TEST PRACTICE** Exs. 2, 23, 38, 39, 40, and 50

SKILL PRACTICE

1. **VOCABULARY** Copy and complete: If a polynomial function has integer coefficients, then every rational zero of the function has the form $\frac{p}{q}$, where p is a factor of the __?__ and q is a factor of the __?__.

2. ★ **WRITING** *Describe* a method you can use to shorten the list of possible rational zeros when using the rational zero theorem.

EXAMPLE 1 on p. 370 for Exs. 3–10

LISTING RATIONAL ZEROS List the possible rational zeros of the function using the rational zero theorem.

3. $f(x) = x^3 - 3x + 28$
4. $g(x) = x^3 - 4x^2 + x - 10$
5. $f(x) = 2x^4 + 6x^3 - 7x + 9$
6. $h(x) = 2x^3 + x^2 - x - 18$
7. $g(x) = 4x^5 + 3x^3 - 2x - 14$
8. $f(x) = 3x^4 + 5x^3 - 3x + 42$
9. $h(x) = 8x^4 + 4x^3 - 10x + 15$
10. $h(x) = 6x^3 - 3x^2 + 12$

EXAMPLE 2 on p. 371 for Exs. 11–18

FINDING REAL ZEROS Find all real zeros of the function.

11. $f(x) = x^3 - 12x^2 + 35x - 24$
12. $f(x) = x^3 - 5x^2 - 22x + 56$
13. $g(x) = x^3 - 31x - 30$
14. $h(x) = x^3 + 8x^2 - 9x - 72$
15. $h(x) = x^4 + 7x^3 + 26x^2 + 44x + 24$
16. $f(x) = x^4 - 2x^3 - 9x^2 + 10x - 24$
17. $f(x) = x^4 + 2x^3 - 9x^2 - 2x + 8$
18. $g(x) = x^4 - 16x^2 - 40x - 25$

EXAMPLE 3 on p. 372 for Exs. 19–35

ELIMINATING POSSIBLE ZEROS Use the graph to shorten the list of possible rational zeros of the function. Then find all real zeros of the function.

19. $f(x) = 4x^3 - 20x + 16$

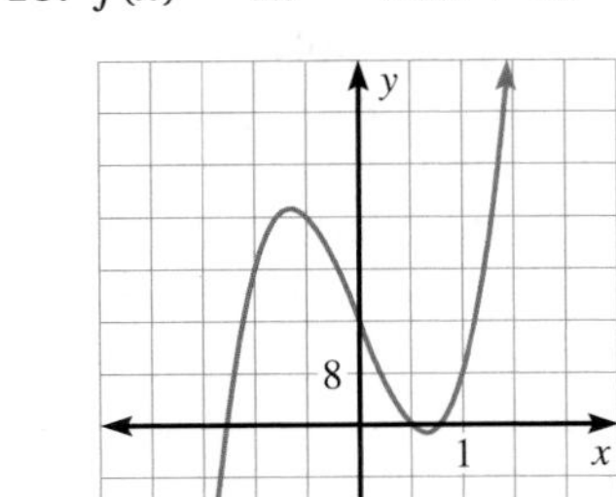

20. $f(x) = 4x^3 - 12x^2 - x + 15$

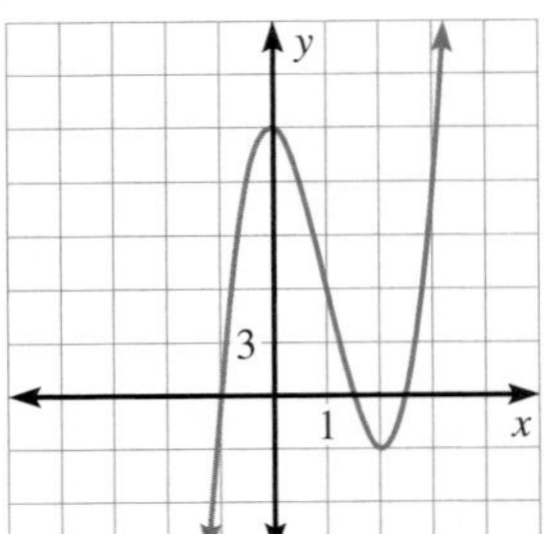

21. $f(x) = 6x^3 + 25x^2 + 16x - 15$

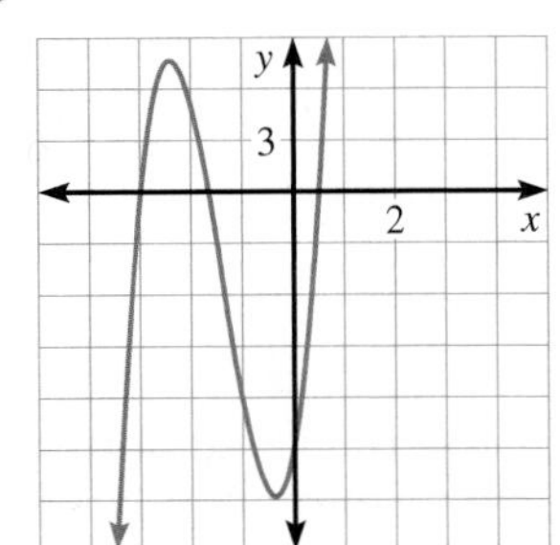

22. $f(x) = -3x^3 + 20x^2 - 36x + 16$

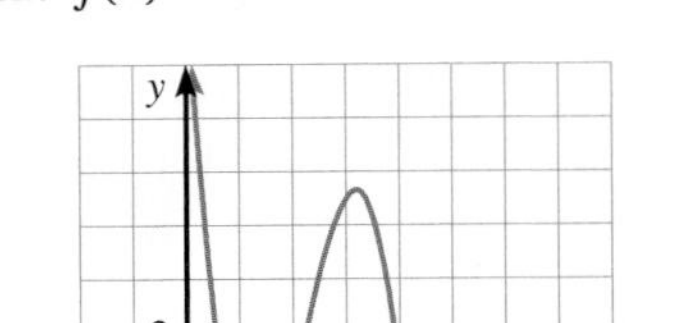

23. ★ **MULTIPLE CHOICE** According to the rational zero theorem, which is *not* a possible zero of the function $f(x) = 2x^4 - 5x^3 + 10x^2 - 9$?

Ⓐ -9 Ⓑ $-\frac{1}{2}$ Ⓒ $\frac{5}{2}$ Ⓓ 3

FINDING REAL ZEROS Find all real zeros of the function.

24. $f(x) = 2x^3 + 2x^2 - 8x - 8$
25. $g(x) = 2x^3 - 7x^2 + 9$
26. $h(x) = 2x^3 - 3x^2 - 14x + 15$
27. $f(x) = 3x^3 + 4x^2 - 35x - 12$
28. $f(x) = 3x^3 + 19x^2 + 4x - 12$
29. $g(x) = 2x^3 + 5x^2 - 11x - 14$
30. $g(x) = 2x^4 + 9x^3 + 5x^2 + 3x - 4$
31. $h(x) = 2x^4 - x^3 - 7x^2 + 4x - 4$
32. $h(x) = 3x^4 - 6x^3 - 32x^2 + 35x - 12$
33. $f(x) = 2x^4 - 9x^3 + 37x - 30$
34. $f(x) = x^5 - 3x^4 - 5x^3 + 15x^2 + 4x - 12$
35. $h(x) = 2x^5 + 5x^4 - 3x^3 - 2x^2 - 5x + 3$

ERROR ANALYSIS ***Describe*** **and correct the error in listing the possible rational zeros of the function.**

36.

$f(x) = x^3 + 7x^2 + 2x + 14$

Possible zeros:

1, 2, 7, 14 ✗

37.

$f(x) = 6x^3 - 3x^2 + 12x + 5$

Possible zeros:

$\pm 1, \pm 2, \pm 3, \pm 6, \pm \frac{1}{5}, \pm \frac{2}{5}, \pm \frac{3}{5}, \pm \frac{6}{5}$ ✗

38. ★ **OPEN-ENDED MATH** Write a polynomial function f that has a leading coefficient of 4 and has 12 possible rational zeros according to the rational zero theorem.

39. ★ **MULTIPLE CHOICE** Which of the following is *not* a zero of the function $f(x) = 40x^5 - 42x^4 - 107x^3 + 107x^2 + 33x - 36$?

Ⓐ $-\frac{3}{2}$ Ⓑ $-\frac{3}{8}$ Ⓒ $\frac{3}{4}$ Ⓓ $\frac{4}{5}$

40. ★ **SHORT RESPONSE** Let a_n be the leading coefficient of a polynomial function f and a_0 be the constant term. If a_n has r factors and a_0 has s factors, what is the largest number of possible rational zeros of f that can be generated by the rational zero theorem? *Explain* your reasoning.

MATCHING Find all real zeros of the function. Then match each function with its graph.

41. $f(x) = x^3 - 2x^2 - x + 2$
42. $g(x) = x^3 - 3x^2 + 2$
43. $h(x) = x^3 + x^2 - x + 2$

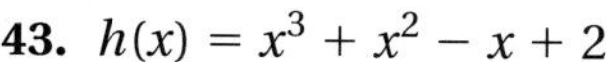

A.

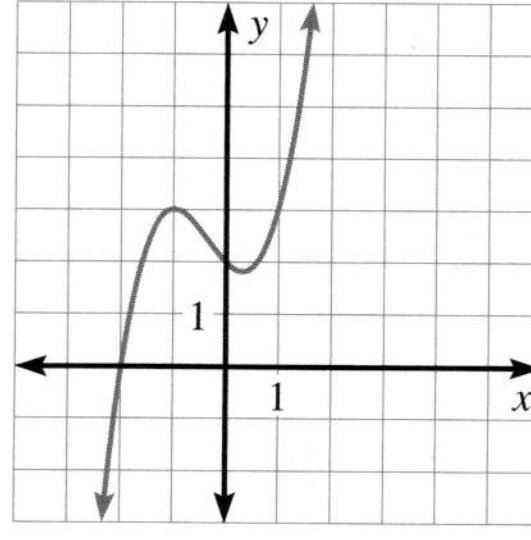

B.

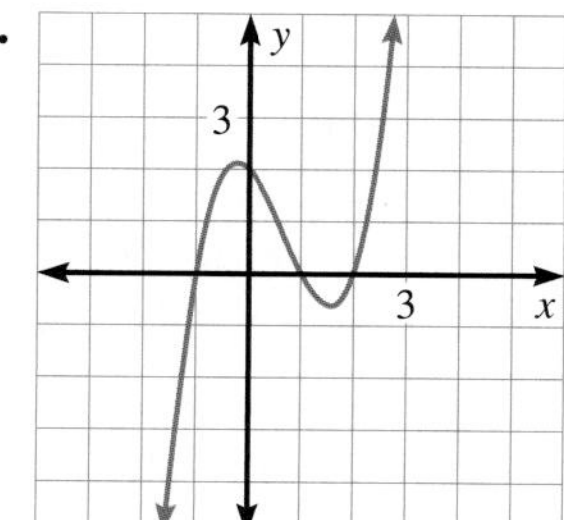

C.

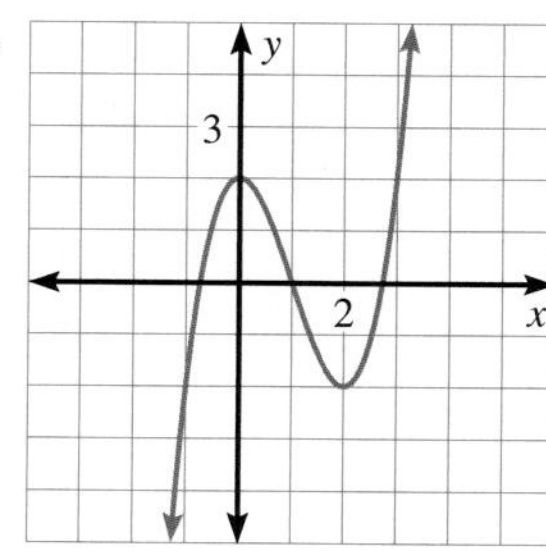

44. **CHALLENGE** Is it possible for a cubic function to have more than three real zeros? Is it possible for a cubic function to have no real zeros? *Explain.*

PROBLEM SOLVING

EXAMPLE 4 on p. 373 for Exs. 45–48

45. MANUFACTURING At a factory, molten glass is poured into molds to make paperweights. Each mold is a rectangular prism with a height 4 inches greater than the length of each side of its square base. Each mold holds 63 cubic inches of molten glass. What are the dimensions of the mold?

@HomeTutor for problem solving help at classzone.com

46. SWIMMING POOL You are designing a rectangular swimming pool that is to be set into the ground. The width of the pool is 5 feet more than the depth, and the length is 35 feet more than the depth. The pool holds 2000 cubic feet of water. What are the dimensions of the pool?

@HomeTutor for problem solving help at classzone.com

GEOMETRY In Exercises 47 and 48, write a polynomial equation to model the situation. Then list the possible rational solutions of the equation.

47. A rectangular prism has edges of lengths x, $x - 1$, and $x - 2$ and a volume of 24.

48. A pyramid has a square base with sides of length x, a height of $2x - 5$, and a volume of 3.

49. MULTI-STEP PROBLEM From 1994 to 2003, the amount of athletic equipment E (in millions of dollars) sold domestically can be modeled by

$$E(t) = -10t^3 + 140t^2 - 20t + 18{,}150$$

where t is the number of years since 1994. Use the following steps to find the year when about \$20,300,000,000 of athletic equipment was sold.

a. Write a polynomial equation that can be used to find the answer.

b. List the possible whole-number solutions of the equation in part (a) that are less than 10.

c. Use synthetic division to determine which of the possible solutions in part (b) is an actual solution. Then calculate the year which corresponds to the solution.

50. ★ EXTENDED RESPONSE Since 1990, the number of U.S. travelers to foreign countries F (in thousands) can be modeled by

$$F(t) = 12t^4 - 264t^3 + 2028t^2 - 3924t + 43{,}916$$

where t is the number of years since 1990. Use the following steps to find the year when there were about 56,300,000 travelers.

a. Write a polynomial equation that can be used to find the answer.

b. List the possible whole-number solutions of the equation in part (a) that are less than or equal to 10.

c. Use synthetic division to determine which of the possible solutions in part (b) is an actual solution.

d. Graph the function $F(t)$ and explain why there are no other reasonable solutions. Then calculate the year which corresponds to the solution.

51. **CHALLENGE** You are building a pair of ramps for a loading platform. The left ramp is twice as long as the right ramp. If 150 cubic feet of concrete are used to build the two ramps, what are the dimensions of each ramp?

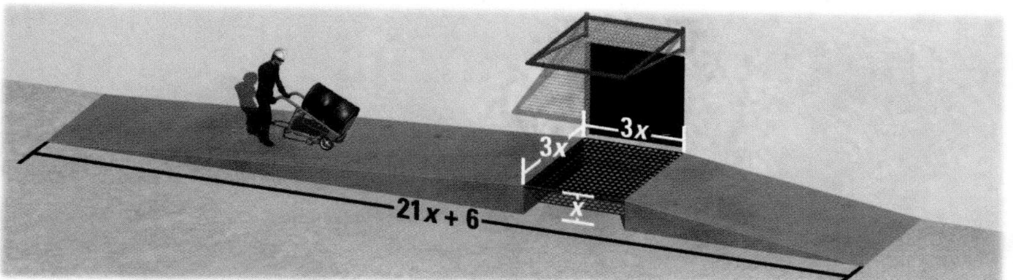

NY NEW YORK MIXED REVIEW

TEST PRACTICE at classzone.com

52. An electronics store has a 30%-off sale on all DVD players. Which statement best represents the functional relationship between the sale price of a DVD player and the original price?

   (A) The original price is dependent on the sale price.

   (B) The sale price is dependent on the original price.

   (C) The sale price and the original price are independent of each other.

   (D) The relationship cannot be determined.

53. The area of a rectangle is $132s^8t^{17}$ square units. The length of the rectangle is $12s^5t^9$ units. What is the width of the rectangle?

   (A) $11s^3t^8$ units   (B) $120s^3t^8$ units

   (C) $144s^{13}t^{26}$ units   (D) $1584s^{13}t^{26}$ units

QUIZ *for Lessons 5.4–5.6*

Factor the polynomial completely. *(p. 353)*

1. $2x^3 - 54$
2. $x^3 - 3x^2 + 2x - 6$
3. $x^3 + x^2 + x + 1$
4. $6x^5 - 150x$
5. $3x^4 - 24x^2 + 48$
6. $2x^3 - 3x^2 - 12x + 18$

Divide using polynomial long division or synthetic division. *(p. 362)*

7. $(x^4 + x^3 - 8x^2 + 5x + 5) \div (x^2 + 5x - 2)$
8. $(4x^3 + 27x^2 + 3x + 64) \div (x + 7)$

Find all real zeros of the function. *(p. 370)*

9. $f(x) = 2x^3 - 19x^2 + 50x + 30$
10. $f(x) = x^3 - 4x^2 - 25x - 56$
11. $f(x) = x^4 + 4x^3 - 13x^2 - 4x + 12$
12. $f(x) = 4x^4 - 5x^2 + 42x - 20$

13. **LANDSCAPING** You are a landscape artist designing a square patio that is to be made from 128 cubic feet of concrete. The thickness of the patio is 15.5 feet less than each side length. What are the dimensions of the patio? *(p. 370)*

Spreadsheet **ACTIVITY** *Use after Lesson 5.6*

@HomeTutor
classzone.com
Keystrokes

5.6 Use the Location Principle

QUESTION **How can you use the Location Principle to identify zeros of a polynomial function?**

You can use the following result, called the *Location Principle*, to help you find zeros of polynomial functions:

> If f is a polynomial function and a and b are two numbers such that $f(a) < 0$ and $f(b) > 0$, then f has at least one real zero between a and b.

EXAMPLE **Find zeros of a polynomial function**

Find all real zeros of $f(x) = 6x^3 + 5x^2 - 17x - 6$.

STEP 1 ***Enter values for x***

Enter "x" into cell A1. Enter "0" into cell A2. Type "=A2+1" into cell A3. Select cells A3 through A7, and use the *fill down* command to fill in values of x.

	A	B
1	x	
2	0	
3	1	
4	2	
5	3	
6	4	
7	5	

STEP 2 ***Enter values for f(x)***

Enter "$f(x)$" into cell B1. Enter "=6*A2^3+5*A2^2−17*A2−6" into cell B2. Select cells B2 through B7, and use the *fill down* command to fill in the values of $f(x)$.

	A	B
1	x	f(x)
2	0	−6
3	1	−12
4	2	28
5	3	150
6	4	390
7	5	784

STEP 3 ***Use Location Principle***

The spreadsheet in Step 2 shows that $f(1) < 0$ and $f(2) > 0$. So, by the Location Principle, f has a zero between 1 and 2. The rational zero theorem shows that the only possible *rational* zero between 1 and 2 is $\frac{3}{2}$. Synthetic division confirms that $\frac{3}{2}$ is a zero and that f can be factored as:

$$f(x) = \left(x - \frac{3}{2}\right)(6x^2 + 14x + 4) = (2x - 3)(3x^2 + 7x + 2) = (2x - 3)(3x + 1)(x + 2)$$

▶ The zeros of f are $\frac{3}{2}$, $-\frac{1}{3}$, and -2.

PRACTICE

Find all real zeros of the function.

1. $f(x) = 6x^3 - 10x^2 - 6x + 10$
2. $f(x) = 24x^4 - 38x^3 - 191x^2 - 157x - 28$
3. $f(x) = 36x^3 + 109x^2 - 341x + 70$
4. $f(x) = 12x^4 + 25x^3 - 160x^2 - 305x - 132$

5.7 Apply the Fundamental Theorem of Algebra

A2.A.26 Find the solution to polynomial equations of higher degree that can be solved using factoring and/or the quadratic formula

Before You found zeros using the rational zero theorem.

Now You will classify the zeros of polynomial functions.

Why? So you can determine boat speed, as in Example 6.

Key Vocabulary
- **repeated solution**
- **irrational conjugates,** *p. 267*
- **complex conjugates,** *p. 278*

The equation $x^3 - 5x^2 - 8x + 48 = 0$, which becomes $(x + 3)(x - 4)^2 = 0$ when factored, has only two distinct solutions: -3 and 4. Because the factor $x - 4$ appears twice, however, you can count the solution 4 twice. So, with 4 counted as a **repeated solution**, this *third*-degree equation has *three* solutions: -3, 4, and 4.

The previous result is generalized by the *fundamental theorem of algebra*, first proved by the German mathematician Karl Friedrich Gauss (1777–1855).

KEY CONCEPT *For Your Notebook*

The Fundamental Theorem of Algebra

Theorem: If $f(x)$ is a polynomial of degree n where $n > 0$, then the equation $f(x) = 0$ has at least one solution in the set of complex numbers.

Corollary: If $f(x)$ is a polynomial of degree n where $n > 0$, then the equation $f(x) = 0$ has exactly n solutions provided each solution repeated twice is counted as 2 solutions, each solution repeated three times is counted as 3 solutions, and so on.

The corollary to the fundamental theorem of algebra also implies that an nth-degree polynomial function f has exactly n zeros.

EXAMPLE 1 Find the number of solutions or zeros

a. How many solutions does the equation $x^3 + 5x^2 + 4x + 20 = 0$ have?

b. How many zeros does the function $f(x) = x^4 - 8x^3 + 18x^2 - 27$ have?

Solution

a. Because $x^3 + 5x^2 + 4x + 20 = 0$ is a polynomial equation of degree 3, it has three solutions. (The solutions are -5, $-2i$, and $2i$.)

b. Because $f(x) = x^4 - 8x^3 + 18x^2 - 27$ is a polynomial function of degree 4, it has four zeros. (The zeros are -1, 3, 3, and 3.)

✓ **GUIDED PRACTICE** for Example 1

1. How many solutions does the equation $x^4 + 5x^2 - 36 = 0$ have?
2. How many zeros does the function $f(x) = x^3 + 7x^2 + 8x - 16$ have?

EXAMPLE 2 Find the zeros of a polynomial function

Find all zeros of $f(x) = x^5 - 4x^4 + 4x^3 + 10x^2 - 13x - 14$.

Solution

STEP 1 **Find** the rational zeros of f. Because f is a polynomial function of degree 5, it has 5 zeros. The possible rational zeros are ±1, ±2, ±7, and ±14. Using synthetic division, you can determine that -1 is a zero repeated twice and 2 is also a zero.

STEP 2 **Write** $f(x)$ in factored form. Dividing $f(x)$ by its known factors $x + 1$, $x + 1$, and $x - 2$ gives a quotient of $x^2 - 4x + 7$. Therefore:

$$f(x) = (x + 1)^2(x - 2)(x^2 - 4x + 7)$$

STEP 3 **Find** the complex zeros of f. Use the quadratic formula to factor the trinomial into linear factors.

$$f(x) = (x + 1)^2(x - 2)\left[x - (2 + i\sqrt{3})\right]\left[x - (2 - i\sqrt{3})\right]$$

▶ The zeros of f are -1, -1, 2, $2 + i\sqrt{3}$, and $2 - i\sqrt{3}$.

BEHAVIOR NEAR ZEROS The graph of f in Example 2 is shown at the right. Note that only the *real* zeros appear as x-intercepts. Also note that the graph is tangent to the x-axis at the repeated zero $x = -1$, but crosses the x-axis at the zero $x = 2$. This concept can be generalized as follows:

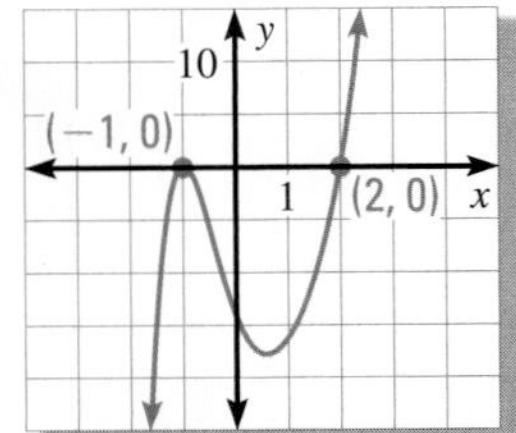

- When a factor $x - k$ of a function f is raised to an odd power, the graph of f crosses the x-axis at $x = k$.
- When a factor $x - k$ of a function f is raised to an even power, the graph of f is tangent to the x-axis at $x = k$.

✓ GUIDED PRACTICE for Example 2

Find all zeros of the polynomial function.

3. $f(x) = x^3 + 7x^2 + 15x + 9$

4. $f(x) = x^5 - 2x^4 + 8x^2 - 13x + 6$

REVIEW COMPLEX NUMBERS
For help with complex conjugates, see p. 278.

COMPLEX CONJUGATES Also in Example 2, notice that the zeros $2 + i\sqrt{3}$ and $2 - i\sqrt{3}$ are complex conjugates. This illustrates the first theorem given below. A similar result applies to irrational zeros of polynomial functions, as shown in the second theorem below.

KEY CONCEPT *For Your Notebook*

Complex Conjugates Theorem

If f is a polynomial function with real coefficients, and $a + bi$ is an imaginary zero of f, then $a - bi$ is also a zero of f.

Irrational Conjugates Theorem

Suppose f is a polynomial function with rational coefficients, and a and b are rational numbers such that $\sqrt{b}$ is irrational. If $a + \sqrt{b}$ is a zero of f, then $a - \sqrt{b}$ is also a zero of f.

EXAMPLE 3 Use zeros to write a polynomial function

Write a polynomial function f of least degree that has rational coefficients, a leading coefficient of 1, and 3 and $2 + \sqrt{5}$ as zeros.

Solution

Because the coefficients are rational and $2 + \sqrt{5}$ is a zero, $2 - \sqrt{5}$ must also be a zero by the irrational conjugates theorem. Use the three zeros and the factor theorem to write $f(x)$ as a product of three factors.

$f(x) = (x - 3)[x - (2 + \sqrt{5})][x - (2 - \sqrt{5})]$	Write $f(x)$ in factored form.
$= (x - 3)[(x - 2) - \sqrt{5}][(x - 2) + \sqrt{5}]$	Regroup terms.
$= (x - 3)[(x - 2)^2 - 5]$	Multiply.
$= (x - 3)[(x^2 - 4x + 4) - 5]$	Expand binomial.
$= (x - 3)(x^2 - 4x - 1)$	Simplify.
$= x^3 - 4x^2 - x - 3x^2 + 12x + 3$	Multiply.
$= x^3 - 7x^2 + 11x + 3$	Combine like terms.

CHECK You can check this result by evaluating $f(x)$ at each of its three zeros.

$$f(3) = 3^3 - 7(3)^2 + 11(3) + 3 = 27 - 63 + 33 + 3 = 0 \checkmark$$

$$f(2 + \sqrt{5}) = (2 + \sqrt{5})^3 - 7(2 + \sqrt{5})^2 + 11(2 + \sqrt{5}) + 3$$

$$= 38 + 17\sqrt{5} - 63 - 28\sqrt{5} + 22 + 11\sqrt{5} + 3$$

$$= 0 \checkmark$$

Since $f(2 + \sqrt{5}) = 0$, by the irrational conjugates theorem $f(2 - \sqrt{5}) = 0$. ✓

GUIDED PRACTICE for Example 3

Write a polynomial function f of least degree that has rational coefficients, a leading coefficient of 1, and the given zeros.

5. $-1, 2, 4$

6. $4, 1 + \sqrt{5}$

7. $2, 2i, 4 - \sqrt{6}$

8. $3, 3 - i$

DESCARTES' RULE OF SIGNS French mathematician René Descartes (1596–1650) found the following relationship between the coefficients of a polynomial function and the number of positive and negative zeros of the function.

KEY CONCEPT *For Your Notebook*

Descartes' Rule of Signs

Let $f(x) = a_nx^n + a_{n-1}x^{n-1} + \cdots + a_2x^2 + a_1x + a_0$ be a polynomial function with real coefficients.

- The number of *positive real zeros* of f is equal to the number of changes in sign of the coefficients of $f(x)$ or is less than this by an even number.
- The number of *negative real zeros* of f is equal to the number of changes in sign of the coefficients of $f(-x)$ or is less than this by an even number.

EXAMPLE 4 Use Descartes' rule of signs

Determine the possible numbers of positive real zeros, negative real zeros, and imaginary zeros for $f(x) = x^6 - 2x^5 + 3x^4 - 10x^3 - 6x^2 - 8x - 8$.

Solution

$$f(x) = x^6 - 2x^5 + 3x^4 - 10x^3 - 6x^2 - 8x - 8$$

The coefficients in $f(x)$ have **3 sign changes**, so f has 3 or 1 positive real zero(s).

$$f(-x) = (-x)^6 - 2(-x)^5 + 3(-x)^4 - 10(-x)^3 - 6(-x)^2 - 8(-x) - 8$$
$$= x^6 + 2x^5 + 3x^4 + 10x^3 - 6x^2 + 8x - 8$$

The coefficients in $f(-x)$ have **3 sign changes**, so f has 3 or 1 negative real zero(s).

The possible numbers of zeros for f are summarized in the table below.

Positive real zeros	Negative real zeros	Imaginary zeros	Total zeros
3	3	0	6
3	1	2	6
1	3	2	6
1	1	4	6

✓ GUIDED PRACTICE for Example 4

Determine the possible numbers of positive real zeros, negative real zeros, and imaginary zeros for the function.

9. $f(x) = x^3 + 2x - 11$

10. $g(x) = 2x^4 - 8x^3 + 6x^2 - 3x + 1$

APPROXIMATING ZEROS All of the zeros of the function in Example 4 are irrational or imaginary. Irrational zeros can be approximated using technology.

EXAMPLE 5 Approximate real zeros

Approximate the real zeros of $f(x) = x^6 - 2x^5 + 3x^4 - 10x^3 - 6x^2 - 8x - 8$.

Solution

ANOTHER WAY
In Example 5, you can also approximate the zeros of f using the calculator's *trace* feature. However, this generally gives less precise results than the *zero* (or *root*) feature.

Use the *zero* (or *root*) feature of a graphing calculator, as shown below.

Zero
X=-.7320508 Y=0

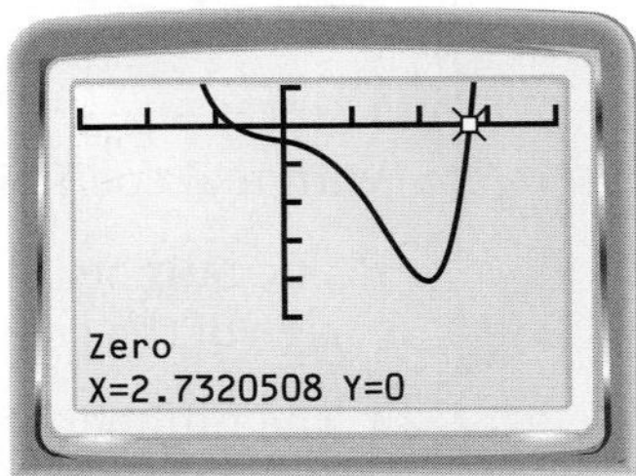

▸ From these screens, you can see that the zeros are $x \approx -0.73$ and $x \approx 2.73$.

EXAMPLE 6 Approximate real zeros of a polynomial model

TACHOMETER A tachometer measures the speed (in revolutions per minute, or RPMs) at which an engine shaft rotates. For a certain boat, the speed x of the engine shaft (in 100s of RPMs) and the speed s of the boat (in miles per hour) are modeled by

$$s(x) = 0.00547x^3 - 0.225x^2 + 3.62x - 11.0$$

What is the tachometer reading when the boat travels 15 miles per hour?

Solution

Substitute 15 for $s(x)$ in the given function. You can rewrite the resulting equation as:

$$0 = 0.00547x^3 - 0.225x^2 + 3.62x - 26.0$$

Then, use a graphing calculator to approximate the real zeros of $f(x) = 0.00547x^3 - 0.225x^2 + 3.62x - 26.0$.

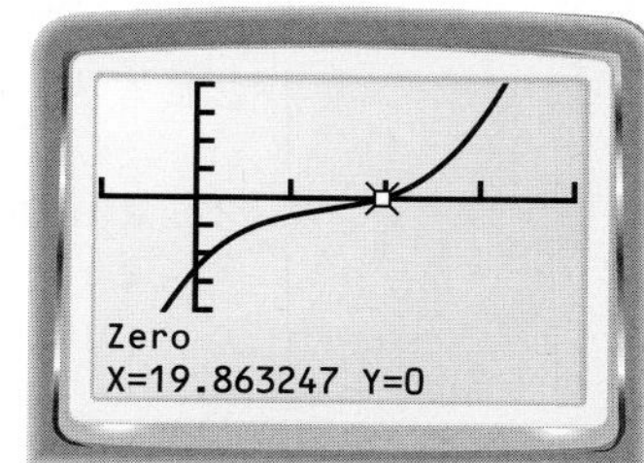

From the graph, there is one real zero: $x \approx 19.9$.

▶ The tachometer reading is about 1990 RPMs.

✓ GUIDED PRACTICE for Examples 5 and 6

11. Approximate the real zeros of $f(x) = 3x^5 + 2x^4 - 8x^3 + 4x^2 - x - 1$.

12. WHAT IF? In Example 6, what is the tachometer reading when the boat travels 20 miles per hour?

5.7 EXERCISES

HOMEWORK KEY

○ = **WORKED-OUT SOLUTIONS** on p. WS11 for Exs. 15, 37, and 61

★ = **STANDARDIZED TEST PRACTICE** Exs. 2, 9, 33, 51, 52, 63, and 64

SKILL PRACTICE

1. VOCABULARY Copy and complete: For the equation $(x - 1)^2(x + 2) = 0$, a(n) _?_ solution is 1 because the factor $x - 1$ appears twice.

2. ★ WRITING *Explain* the difference between complex conjugates and irrational conjugates.

EXAMPLE 1 on p. 379 for Exs. 3–9

NUMBER OF SOLUTIONS OR ZEROS **Identify the number of solutions or zeros.**

3. $x^4 + 2x^3 - 4x^2 + x - 10 = 0$

4. $5y^3 - 3y^2 + 8y = 0$

5. $9t^6 - 14t^3 + 4t - 1 = 0$

6. $f(z) = -7z^4 + z^2 - 25$

7. $g(s) = 12s^7 - 9s^6 + 4s^5 - s^3 - 20s + 50$

8. $h(x) = -x^{12} + 7x^8 + 5x^4 - 8x + 6$

9. ★ MULTIPLE CHOICE How many zeros does the function $f(x) = 16x - 22x^3 + 6x^6 + 19x^5 - 3$ have?

Ⓐ 1 Ⓑ 3 Ⓒ 5 Ⓓ 6

EXAMPLE 2 on p. 380 for Exs. 10–19

FINDING ZEROS Find all zeros of the polynomial function.

10. $f(x) = x^4 - 6x^3 + 7x^2 + 6x - 8$
11. $f(x) = x^4 + 5x^3 - 7x^2 - 29x + 30$
12. $g(x) = x^4 - 9x^2 - 4x + 12$
13. $h(x) = x^3 + 5x^2 - 4x - 20$
14. $f(x) = x^4 + 15x^2 - 16$
15. $f(x) = x^4 + x^3 + 2x^2 + 4x - 8$
16. $h(x) = x^4 + 4x^3 + 7x^2 + 16x + 12$
17. $g(x) = x^4 - 2x^3 - 3x^2 + 2x + 2$
18. $g(x) = 4x^4 + 4x^3 - 11x^2 - 12x - 3$
19. $h(x) = 2x^4 + 13x^3 + 19x^2 - 10x - 24$

EXAMPLE 3 on p. 381 for Exs. 20–32

WRITING POLYNOMIAL FUNCTIONS Write a polynomial function *f* of least degree that has rational coefficients, a leading coefficient of 1, and the given zeros.

20. 1, 2, 3
21. $-2, 1, 3$
22. $-5, -1, 2$
23. $-3, 1, 6$
24. $2, -i, i$
25. $3i, 2 - i$
26. $-1, 2, -3i$
27. $5, 5, 4 + i$
28. $4, -\sqrt{5}, \sqrt{5}$
29. $-4, 1, 2 - \sqrt{6}$
30. $-2, -1, 2, 3, \sqrt{11}$
31. $3, 4 + 2i, 1 + \sqrt{7}$

32. **ERROR ANALYSIS** *Describe* and correct the error in writing a polynomial function with rational coefficients and zeros 2 and $1 + i$.

$$\begin{aligned} f(x) &= (x - 2)[x - (1 + i)] \\ &= x(x - 1 - i) - 2(x - 1 - i) \\ &= x^2 - x - ix - 2x + 2 + 2i \\ &= x^2 - (3 + i)x + (2 + 2i) \end{aligned}$$

33. ★ **OPEN-ENDED MATH** Write a polynomial function of degree 5 with zeros 1, 2, and $-i$.

EXAMPLE 4 on p. 382 for Exs. 34–41

CLASSIFYING ZEROS Determine the possible numbers of positive real zeros, negative real zeros, and imaginary zeros for the function.

34. $f(x) = x^4 - x^2 - 6$
35. $g(x) = -x^3 + 5x^2 + 12$
36. $g(x) = x^3 - 4x^2 + 8x + 7$
37. $h(x) = x^5 - 2x^3 - x^2 + 6x + 5$
38. $h(x) = x^5 - 3x^3 + 8x - 10$
39. $f(x) = x^5 + 7x^4 - 4x^3 - 3x^2 + 9x - 15$
40. $g(x) = x^6 + x^5 - 3x^4 + x^3 + 5x^2 + 9x - 18$
41. $f(x) = x^7 + 4x^4 - 10x + 25$

EXAMPLE 5 on p. 382 for Exs. 42–49

APPROXIMATING ZEROS Use a graphing calculator to graph the function. Then use the *zero* (or *root*) feature to approximate the real zeros of the function.

42. $f(x) = x^3 - x^2 - 8x + 5$
43. $f(x) = -x^4 - 4x^2 + x + 8$
44. $g(x) = x^3 - 3x^2 + x + 6$
45. $h(x) = x^4 - 5x - 3$
46. $h(x) = 3x^3 - x^2 - 5x + 3$
47. $g(x) = x^4 - x^3 + 2x^2 - 6x - 3$
48. $f(x) = 2x^6 + x^4 + 31x^2 - 35$
49. $g(x) = x^5 - 16x^3 - 3x^2 + 42x + 30$

50. **REASONING** Two zeros of $f(x) = x^3 - 6x^2 - 16x + 96$ are 4 and -4. *Explain* why the third zero must also be a real number.

51. ★ **SHORT RESPONSE** *Describe* the possible numbers of positive real, negative real, and imaginary zeros for a cubic function with rational coefficients.

52. ★ **MULTIPLE CHOICE** Which is *not* a possible classification of the zeros of $f(x) = x^5 - 4x^3 + 6x^2 + 12x - 6$ according to Descartes' rule of signs?

Ⓐ 3 positive real zeros, 2 negative real zeros, and 0 imaginary zeros

Ⓑ 3 positive real zeros, 0 negative real zeros, and 2 imaginary zeros

Ⓒ 1 positive real zero, 4 negative real zeros, and 0 imaginary zeros

Ⓓ 1 positive real zero, 2 negative real zeros, and 2 imaginary zeros

○ = WORKED-OUT SOLUTIONS on p. WS1

★ = STANDARDIZED TEST PRACTICE

CLASSIFYING ZEROS Determine the numbers of positive real zeros, negative real zeros, and imaginary zeros for the function with the given degree and graph. *Explain* your reasoning.

53. Degree: 3

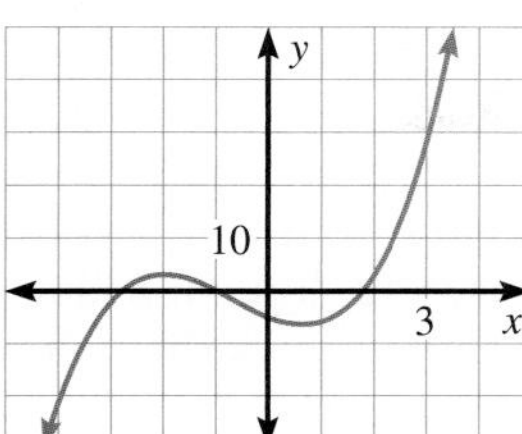

54. Degree: 4

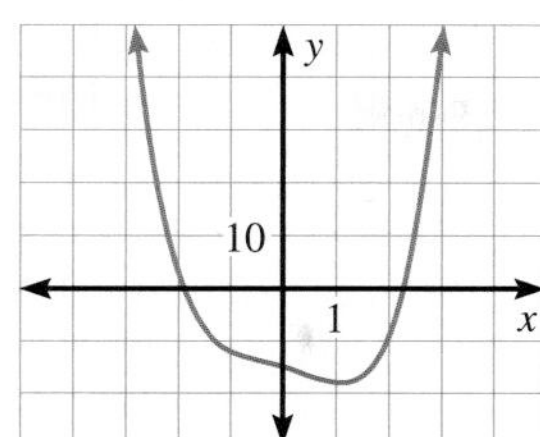

55. Degree: 5

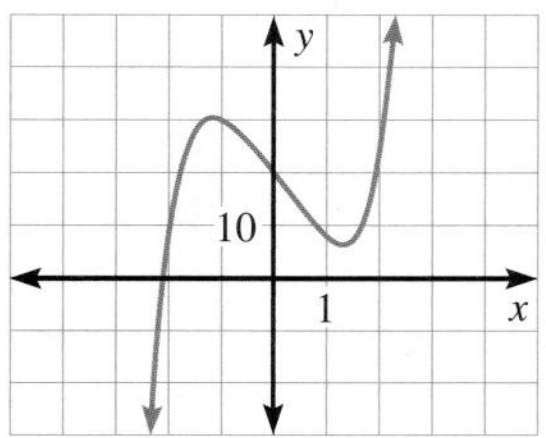

CHALLENGE Show that the given number is a zero of the given function but that the conjugate of the number is *not* a zero.

56. $f(x) = x^3 - 2x^2 + 2x + 5i; 2 - i$

57. $g(x) = x^3 + 2x^2 + 2i - 2; -1 + i$

58. *Explain* why the results of Exercises 56 and 57 do not contradict the complex conjugate theorem on page 380.

PROBLEM SOLVING

EXAMPLE 6 on p. 383 for Exs. 59–62

59. BUSINESS For the 12 years that a grocery store has been open, its annual revenue R (in millions of dollars) can be modeled by the function

$$R = 0.0001(-t^4 + 12t^3 - 77t^2 + 600t + 13{,}650)$$

where t is the number of years since the store opened. In which year(s) was the revenue \$1.5 million?

@HomeTutor for problem solving help at classzone.com

60. ENVIRONMENT From 1990 to 2003, the number N of inland lakes in Michigan infested with zebra mussels can be modeled by the function

$$N = -0.028t^4 + 0.59t^3 - 2.5t^2 + 8.3t - 2.5$$

where t is the number of years since 1990. In which year did the number of infested inland lakes first reach 120?

@HomeTutor for problem solving help at classzone.com

Pipe clogged with zebra mussels

61. PHYSIOLOGY A study group found that a person's score S on a step-climbing exercise test was related to his or her amount of hemoglobin x (in grams per 100 milliliters of blood) by this function:

$$S = -0.015x^3 + 0.6x^2 - 2.4x + 19$$

Given that the normal range of hemoglobin is 12–18 grams per 100 milliliters of blood, what is the most likely amount of hemoglobin for a person who scores 75?

62. POPULATION From 1890 to 2000, the American Indian, Eskimo, and Aleut population P (in thousands) can be modeled by the function

$$P = 0.0035t^3 - 0.235t^2 + 4.87t + 243$$

where t is the number of years since 1890. In which year did the population first reach 722,000?

63. ★ **SHORT RESPONSE** A 60-inch-long bookshelf is warped under 180 pounds of books. The deflection d of the bookshelf (in inches) is given by

$$d = (2.724 \times 10^{-7})x^4 - (3.269 \times 10^{-5})x^3 + (9.806 \times 10^{-4})x^2$$

where x is the distance (in inches) from the bookshelf's left end. Approximate the real zeros of the function on the domain $0 \le x \le 60$. *Explain* why all your answers make sense in this situation.

64. ★ **EXTENDED RESPONSE** You plan to save \$1000 each year towards buying a used car in four years. At the end of each summer, you deposit \$1000 earned from summer jobs into your bank account. The table shows the value of your deposits over the four year period. In the table, g is the growth factor $1 + r$ where r is the annual interest rate expressed as a decimal.

	Year 1	Year 2	Year 3	Year 4
Value of 1st deposit	1000	$1000g$	$1000g^2$	$1000g^3$
Value of 2nd deposit	–	1000	?	?
Value of 3rd deposit	–	–	1000	?
Value of 4th deposit	–	–	–	1000

a. **Apply** Copy and complete the table.

b. **Model** Write a polynomial function that gives the value v of your account at the end of the fourth summer in terms of g.

c. **Reasoning** You want to buy a car that costs about \$4300. What growth factor do you need to obtain this amount? What annual interest rate do you need? *Explain* how you found your answers.

65. **CHALLENGE** A monument with the dimensions shown is to be built using 1000 cubic feet of marble. What is the value of x?

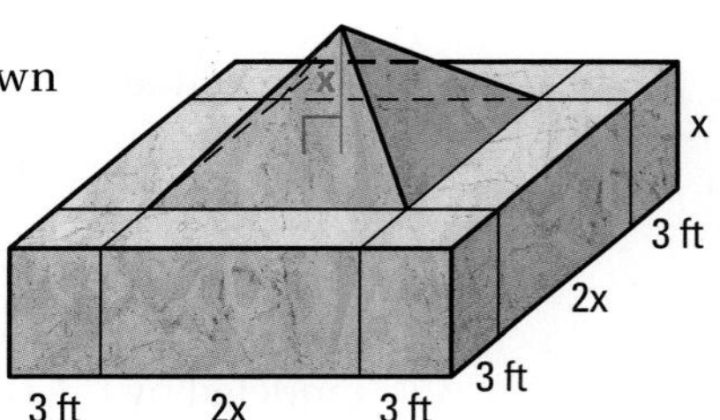

NY NEW YORK MIXED REVIEW

66. Which of the following is the solution of this system of linear equations?

$$-2x + 3y = 20$$
$$4x + 4y = -15$$

Ⓐ $\left(-\frac{25}{4}, \frac{5}{2}\right)$ Ⓑ $\left(\frac{5}{2}, -\frac{25}{4}\right)$ Ⓒ $\left(\frac{25}{2}, \frac{35}{4}\right)$ Ⓓ No solution

67. What is the approximate volume of the bird feeder shown?

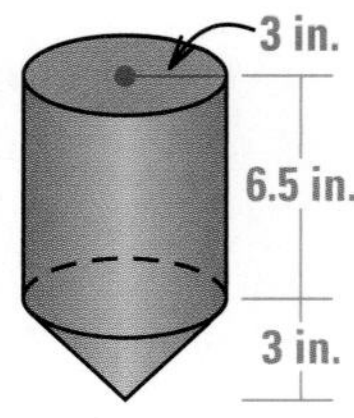

Ⓐ 156 in.^{3} Ⓑ 184 in.^{3}

Ⓒ 212 in.^{3} Ⓓ 269 in.^{3}

5.8 Analyze Graphs of Polynomial Functions

A2.A.50 Approximate the solution to polynomial equations of higher degree by inspecting the graph

Before You graphed polynomial functions by making tables.

Now You will use intercepts to graph polynomial functions.

Why? So you can maximize the volume of structures, as in Ex. 42.

Key Vocabulary
- **local maximum**
- **local minimum**

In this chapter you have learned that zeros, factors, solutions, and x-intercepts are closely related concepts. The relationships are summarized below.

CONCEPT SUMMARY *For Your Notebook*

Zeros, Factors, Solutions, and Intercepts

Let $f(x) = a_nx^n + a_{n-1}x^{n-1} + \cdots + a_1x + a_0$ be a polynomial function. The following statements are equivalent.

Zero: k is a zero of the polynomial function f.

Factor: $x - k$ is a factor of the polynomial $f(x)$.

Solution: k is a solution of the polynomial equation $f(x) = 0$.

x-intercept: If k is a real number, k is an x-intercept of the graph of the polynomial function f. The graph of f passes through $(k, 0)$.

EXAMPLE 1 Use x-intercepts to graph a polynomial function

Graph the function $f(x) = \frac{1}{6}(x + 3)(x - 2)^2$.

Solution

STEP 1 **Plot** the intercepts. Because -3 and 2 are zeros of f, plot $(-3, 0)$ and $(2, 0)$.

STEP 2 **Plot** points between and beyond the x-intercepts.

x	-2	-1	0	1	3
y	$\frac{8}{3}$	3	2	$\frac{2}{3}$	1

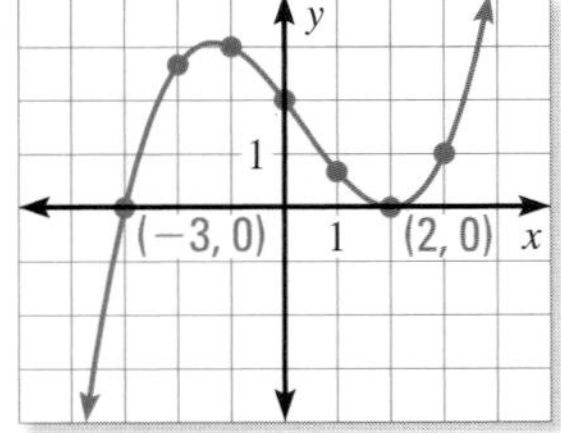

STEP 3 **Determine** end behavior. Because f has three factors of the form $x - k$ and a constant factor of $\frac{1}{6}$, it is a cubic function with a positive leading coefficient. So, $f(x) \to -\infty$ as $x \to -\infty$ and $f(x) \to +\infty$ as $x \to +\infty$.

STEP 4 **Draw** the graph so that it passes through the plotted points and has the appropriate end behavior.

TURNING POINTS Another important characteristic of graphs of polynomial functions is that they have *turning points* corresponding to local maximum and minimum values.

- The y-coordinate of a turning point is a **local maximum** of the function if the point is higher than all nearby points.
- The y-coordinate of a turning point is a **local minimum** of the function if the point is lower than all nearby points.

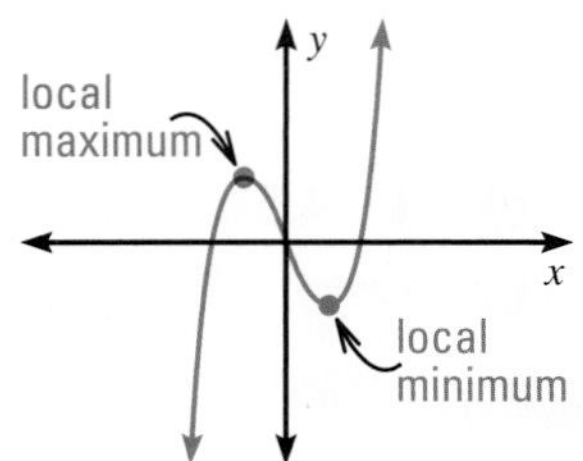

KEY CONCEPT *For Your Notebook*

Turning Points of Polynomial Functions

1. The graph of every polynomial function of degree n has *at most* $n - 1$ turning points.
2. If a polynomial function has n distinct real zeros, then its graph has *exactly* $n - 1$ turning points.

EXAMPLE 2 Find turning points

Graph the function. Identify the x-intercepts and the points where the local maximums and local minimums occur.

a. $f(x) = x^3 - 3x^2 + 6$ **b.** $g(x) = x^4 - 6x^3 + 3x^2 + 10x - 3$

Solution

a. Use a graphing calculator to graph the function.

Notice that the graph of f has one x-intercept and two turning points.

You can use the graphing calculator's *zero, maximum,* and *minimum* features to approximate the coordinates of the points.

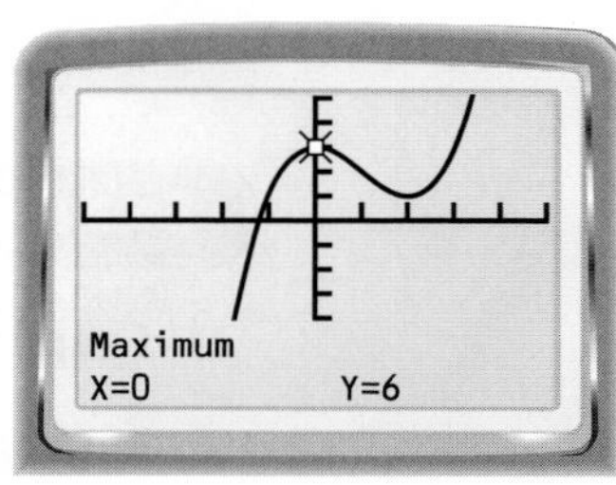

▶ The x-intercept of the graph is $x \approx -1.20$. The function has a local maximum at **(0, 6)** and a local minimum at **(2, 2)**.

b. Use a graphing calculator to graph the function.

Notice that the graph of g has four x-intercepts and three turning points.

You can use the graphing calculator's *zero, maximum,* and *minimum* features to approximate the coordinates of the points.

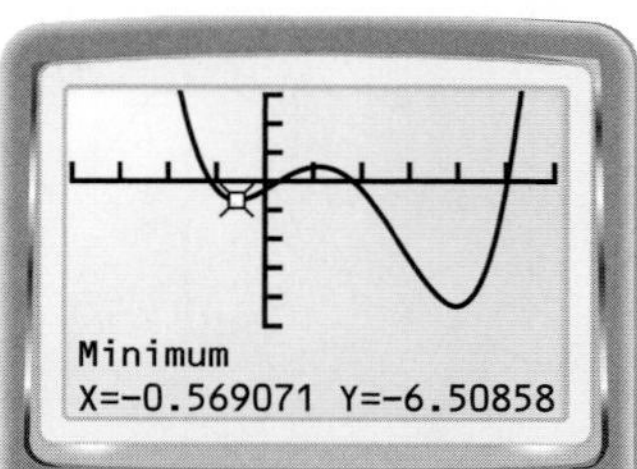

▶ The x-intercepts of the graph are $x \approx -1.14$, $x \approx 0.29$, $x \approx 1.82$, and $x \approx 5.03$. The function has a local maximum at **(1.11, 5.11)** and local minimums at **(−0.57, −6.51)** and **(3.96, −43.04)**.

Animated **Algebra** at classzone.com

FIND MAXIMUMS AND MINIMUMS
For help with using the *maximum* and *minimum* features of a graphing calculator, see p. 244.

EXAMPLE 3 Maximize a polynomial model

ARTS AND CRAFTS You are making a rectangular box out of a 16-inch-by-20-inch piece of cardboard. The box will be formed by making the cuts shown in the diagram and folding up the sides. You want the box to have the greatest volume possible.

- How long should you make the cuts?
- What is the maximum volume?
- What will the dimensions of the finished box be?

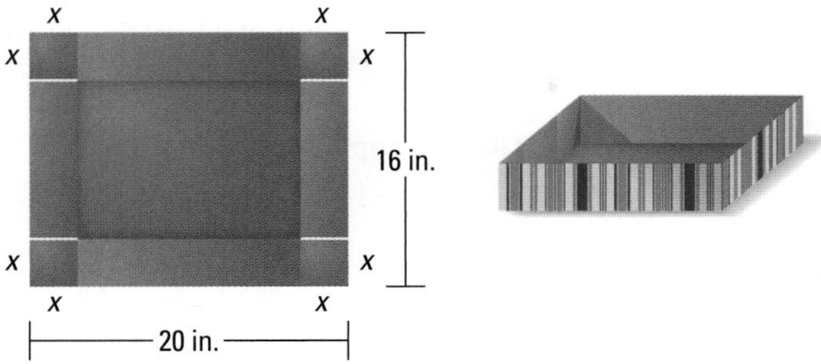

Solution

Write a verbal model for the volume. Then write a function.

Volume (cubic inches)	=	Length (inches)	·	Width (inches)	·	Height (inches)
V	=	$(20 - 2x)$	·	$(16 - 2x)$	·	x

$= (320 - 72x + 4x^2)x$ **Multiply binomials.**

$= 4x^3 - 72x^2 + 320x$ **Write in standard form.**

To find the maximum volume, graph the volume function on a graphing calculator, as shown at the right. Consider only the interval $0 < x < 8$ because this describes the physical restrictions on the size of the flaps.

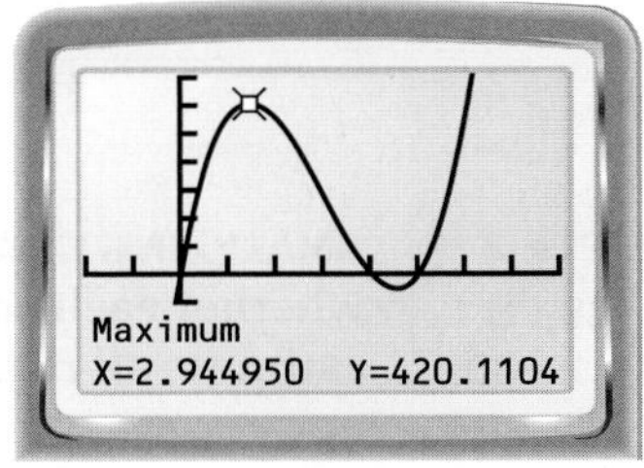

From the graph, you can see that the maximum volume is about 420 and occurs when $x \approx 2.94$.

▶ You should make the cuts about 3 inches long. The maximum volume is about 420 cubic inches. The dimensions of the box with this volume will be about 3 inches by 10 inches by 14 inches.

✓ GUIDED PRACTICE for Examples 1, 2, and 3

Graph the function. Identify the x-intercepts and the points where the local maximums and local minimums occur.

1. $f(x) = 0.25(x + 2)(x - 1)(x - 3)$
2. $g(x) = 2(x - 1)^2(x - 4)$
3. $h(x) = 0.5x^3 + x^2 - x + 2$
4. $f(x) = x^4 + 3x^3 - x^2 - 4x - 5$
5. **WHAT IF?** In Example 3, how do the answers change if the piece of cardboard is 10 inches by 15 inches?

5.8 EXERCISES

HOMEWORK KEY

○ = **WORKED-OUT SOLUTIONS** on p. WS11 for Exs. 3, 19, and 41

★ = **STANDARDIZED TEST PRACTICE** Exs. 2, 21, 30, 32, 33, and 43

◆ = **MULTIPLE REPRESENTATIONS** Ex. 42

SKILL PRACTICE

1. **VOCABULARY** Copy and complete: A local maximum or local minimum of a polynomial function occurs at a __?__ point of the function's graph.

2. ★ **WRITING** *Explain* what a local maximum of a function is and how it may be different from the maximum value of the function.

EXAMPLE 1 on p. 387 for Exs. 3–14

GRAPHING POLYNOMIAL FUNCTIONS **Graph the function.**

3. $f(x) = (x - 2)^2(x + 1)$
4. $f(x) = (x + 1)^2(x - 1)(x - 3)$
5. $g(x) = \frac{1}{3}(x - 5)(x + 2)(x - 3)$
6. $h(x) = \frac{1}{12}(x + 4)(x + 8)(x - 1)$
7. $h(x) = 4(x + 1)(x + 2)(x - 1)$
8. $f(x) = 0.2(x - 4)^2(x + 1)^2$
9. $f(x) = 2(x + 2)^2(x + 4)^2$
10. $h(x) = 5(x - 1)(x - 2)(x - 3)$
11. $g(x) = (x - 3)(x^2 + x + 1)$
12. $h(x) = (x - 4)(2x^2 - 2x + 1)$

ERROR ANALYSIS ***Describe*** **and correct the error in graphing *f*.**

13. $f(x) = (x + 2)(x - 1)^2$

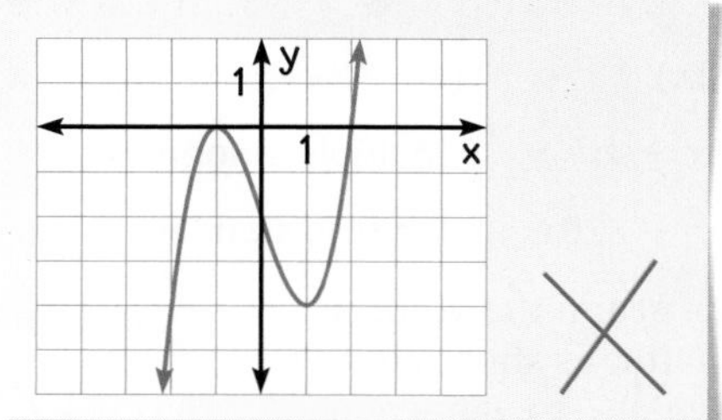

14. $f(x) = x(x - 3)^3$

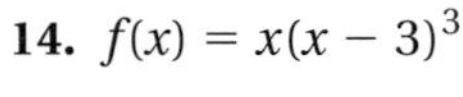

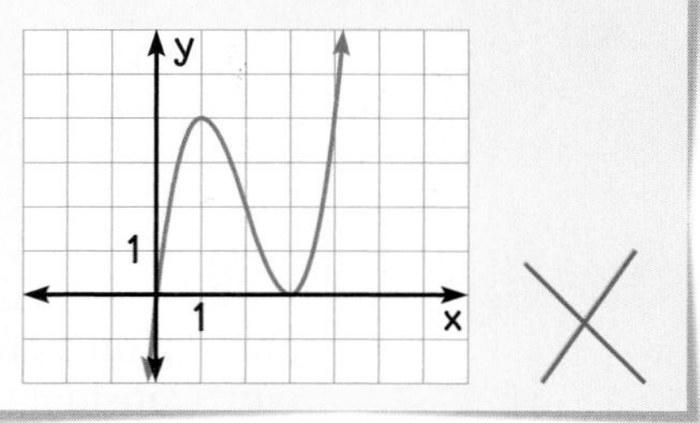

EXAMPLE 2 on p. 388 for Exs. 15–30

ANALYZING GRAPHS **Estimate the coordinates of each turning point and state whether each corresponds to a local maximum or a local minimum. Then estimate all real zeros and determine the least degree the function can have.**

15.

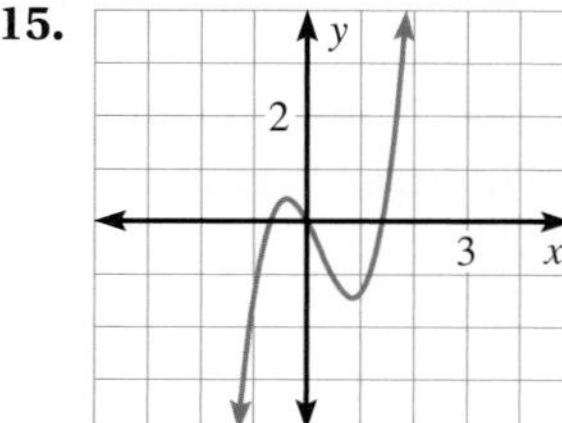

16.

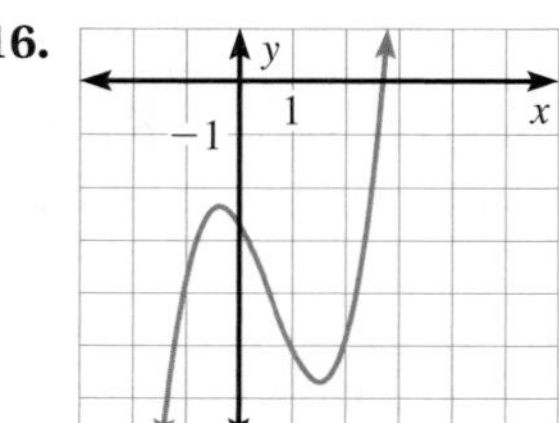

17.

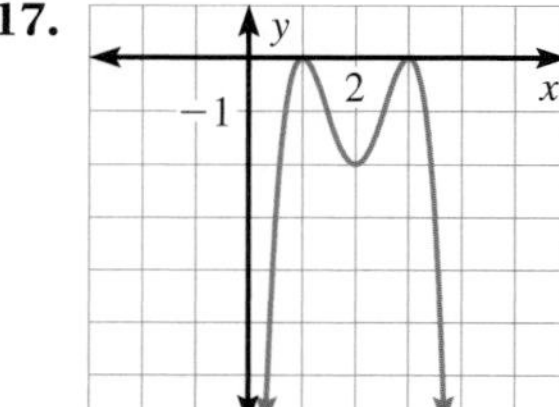

18.

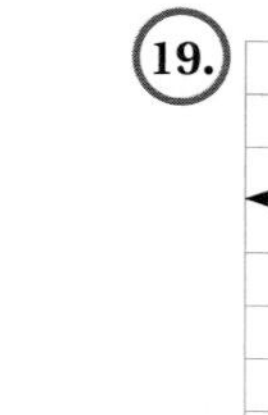

19.

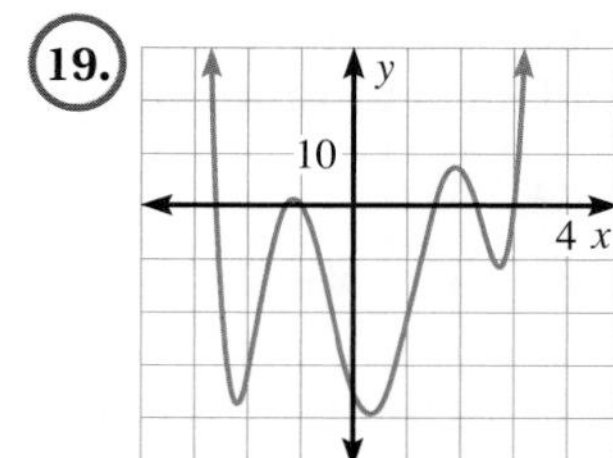

20.

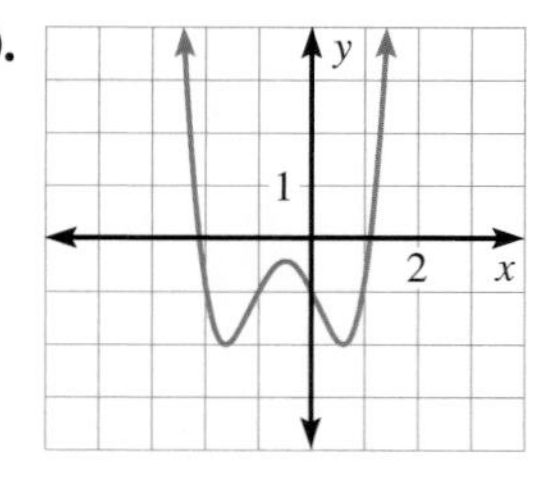

21. ★ **MULTIPLE CHOICE** Which point is a local maximum of the function $f(x) = 0.25(x + 2)(x - 1)^2$?

Ⓐ $(-2, 0)$ Ⓑ $(-1, 1)$ Ⓒ $(1, 0)$ Ⓓ $(2, 1)$

GRAPHING CALCULATOR Use a graphing calculator to graph the polynomial function. Identify the x-intercepts and the points where the local maximums and local minimums occur.

22. $f(x) = 2x^3 + 8x^2 - 3$

23. $g(x) = 0.5x^3 - 2x + 2.5$

24. $h(x) = -x^4 + 3x$

25. $f(x) = x^5 - 4x^3 + x^2 + 2$

26. $g(x) = x^4 - 3x^2 + x$

27. $h(x) = x^4 - 5x^3 + 2x^2 + x - 3$

28. $h(x) = x^5 + 2x^2 - 17x - 4$

29. $g(x) = 0.7x^4 - 8x^3 + 5x$

30. ★ **MULTIPLE CHOICE** What is a turning point of the graph of the function $g(x) = x^4 - 9x^2 + 4x + 12$?

Ⓐ $(-3, 0)$ Ⓑ $(-1, 0)$ Ⓒ $(0, 12)$ Ⓓ $(2, 0)$

31. **REASONING** Why is the adjective *local* used to describe the maximums and minimums of cubic functions but not quadratic functions?

32. ★ **SHORT RESPONSE** Does a cubic function *always, sometimes,* or *never* have a turning point? *Justify* your answer.

33. ★ **OPEN-ENDED MATH** Write a cubic function, a quartic function, and a fifth-degree function whose graphs have x-intercepts only at $x = -2$, 0, and 4.

DOMAIN AND RANGE Graph the function. Then identify its domain and range.

34. $f(x) = x(x - 3)^2$

35. $f(x) = x^2(x - 2)(x - 4)(x - 5)$

36. $f(x) = (x + 1)^3(x - 1)$

37. $f(x) = (x + 2)(x + 1)(x - 1)^2(x - 2)^2$

38. **CHALLENGE** In general, what can you say about the domain and range of odd-degree polynomial functions? What can you say about the domain and range of even-degree polynomial functions?

PROBLEM SOLVING

EXAMPLE 3 on p. 389 for Exs. 39–40

In Exercises 39 and 40, assume that the box is constructed using the method illustrated in Example 3 on page 389.

39. **POSTCARDS** Marcie wants to make a box to hold her postcard collection from a piece of cardboard that is 10 inches by 18 inches. What are the dimensions of the box with the maximum volume? What is the maximum volume of the box?

@HomeTutor for problem solving help at classzone.com

40. **COIN COLLECTION** Jorge is making a box for his coin collection from a piece of cardboard that is 30 centimeters by 40 centimeters. What are the dimensions of the box with the maximum volume? What is the maximum volume of the box?

@HomeTutor for problem solving help at classzone.com

41. **SWIMMING** For a swimmer doing the breaststroke, the function

$$S = -241t^7 + 1060t^6 - 1870t^5 + 1650t^4 - 737t^3 + 144t^2 - 2.43t$$

models the swimmer's speed S (in meters per second) during one complete stroke, where t is the number of seconds since the start of the stroke. Graph the function. According to the model, at what time during the stroke is the swimmer going the fastest?

42. **MULTIPLE REPRESENTATIONS** You have 600 square feet of material for building a greenhouse that is shaped like half a cylinder.

a. **Writing an Expression** The surface area S of the greenhouse is given by $S = \pi r^2 + \pi r\ell$. Substitute 600 for S and then write an expression for ℓ in terms of r.

b. **Writing a Function** The volume V of the greenhouse is given by $V = \frac{1}{2}\pi r^2\ell$. Write an equation that gives V as a polynomial function of r alone.

c. **Graphing a Function** Graph the volume function from part (b). What are the dimensions r and ℓ that maximize the volume of the greenhouse? What is the maximum volume?

43. ★ **EXTENDED RESPONSE** From 1960 to 2001, the number of students S (in thousands) enrolled in public schools in the United States can be modeled by $S = 1.64x^3 - 102x^2 + 1710x + 36{,}300$ where x is the number of years since 1960.

a. Graph the function.

b. Identify any turning points on the domain $0 \le x \le 41$. What real-life meaning do these points have?

c. What is the range of the function?

44. **CHALLENGE** A cylinder is inscribed in a sphere of radius 8. Write an equation for the volume of the cylinder as a function of h. Find the value of h that maximizes the volume of the inscribed cylinder. What is the maximum volume of the cylinder?

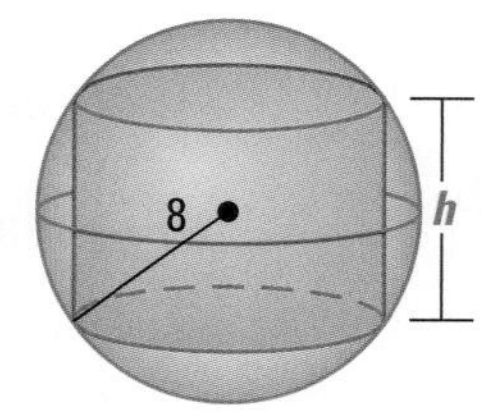

NEW YORK MIXED REVIEW

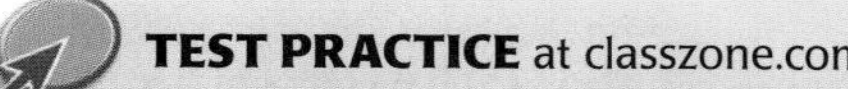

45. A painter is repainting a spherical section of a sculpture. Which measure would be most useful in determining the amount of paint the painter needs to buy?

Ⓐ Radius
Ⓑ Circumference
Ⓒ Volume
Ⓓ Surface area

46. Which equation is the parent function of the graph represented?

Ⓐ $y = x$
Ⓑ $y = |x|$
Ⓒ $y = x^2$
Ⓓ $y = x^3$

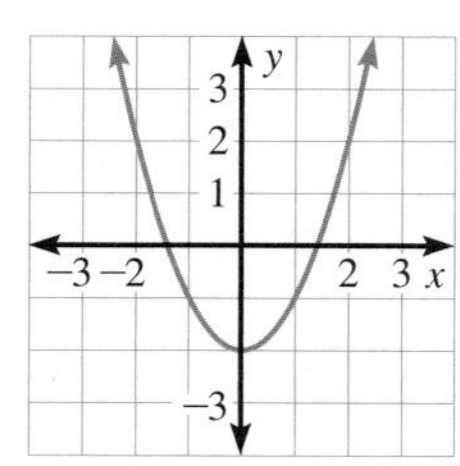

EXAMPLE 3 Model with finite differences

The first seven triangular pyramidal numbers are shown below. Find a polynomial function that gives the *n*th triangular pyramidal number.

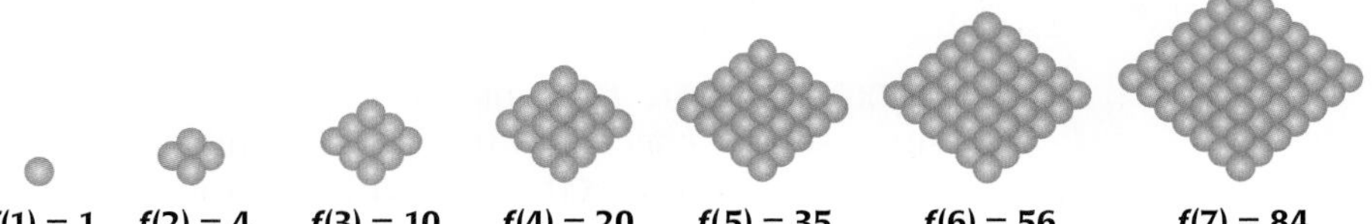

$f(1) = 1$ $f(2) = 4$ $f(3) = 10$ $f(4) = 20$ $f(5) = 35$ $f(6) = 56$ $f(7) = 84$

Solution

Begin by finding the finite differences.

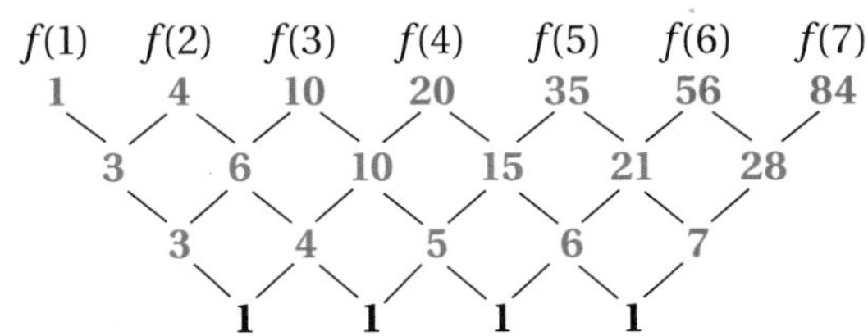

Write function values for equally-spaced *n*-values.

First-order differences

Second-order differences

Third-order differences

Because the third-order differences are constant, you know that the numbers can be represented by a cubic function of the form $f(n) = an^3 + bn^2 + cn + d$.

By substituting the first four triangular pyramidal numbers into the function, you obtain a system of four linear equations in four variables.

$$a(1)^3 + b(1)^2 + c(1) + d = 1 \quad \longrightarrow \quad a + b + c + d = 1$$

$$a(2)^3 + b(2)^2 + c(2) + d = 4 \quad \longrightarrow \quad 8a + 4b + 2c + d = 4$$

$$a(3)^3 + b(3)^2 + c(3) + d = 10 \quad \longrightarrow \quad 27a + 9b + 3c + d = 10$$

$$a(4)^3 + b(4)^2 + c(4) + d = 20 \quad \longrightarrow \quad 64a + 16b + 4c + d = 20$$

REVIEW SYSTEMS
For help with using matrices to solve linear systems, see p. 210.

Write the linear system as a matrix equation $AX = B$. Enter the matrices A and B into a graphing calculator, and then calculate the solution $X = A^{-1}B$.

$$\underset{A}{\begin{bmatrix} 1 & 1 & 1 & 1 \\ 8 & 4 & 2 & 1 \\ 27 & 9 & 3 & 1 \\ 64 & 16 & 4 & 1 \end{bmatrix}} \underset{X}{\begin{bmatrix} a \\ b \\ c \\ d \end{bmatrix}} = \underset{B}{\begin{bmatrix} 1 \\ 4 \\ 10 \\ 20 \end{bmatrix}}$$

```
[A]-1[B]
 [[.1666666667]
  [.5         ]
  [.3333333333]
  [0          ]]
```

Calculate $X = A^{-1}B$.

▶ The solution is $a = \frac{1}{6}$, $b = \frac{1}{2}$, $c = \frac{1}{3}$, and $d = 0$. So, the nth triangular pyramidal number is given by $f(n) = \frac{1}{6}n^3 + \frac{1}{2}n^2 + \frac{1}{3}n$.

✓ GUIDED PRACTICE for Example 3

4. Use finite differences to find a polynomial function that fits the data in the table.

x	1	2	3	4	5	6
$f(x)$	6	15	22	21	6	−29

CUBIC REGRESSION In Examples 1 and 3, you found a cubic model that *exactly* fits a set of data points. In many real-life situations, you cannot find a simple model to fit data points exactly. Instead, you can use the *regression* feature of a graphing calculator to find an nth-degree polynomial model that best fits the data.

EXAMPLE 4 Solve a multi-step problem

SPACE EXPLORATION The table shows the typical speed y (in feet per second) of a space shuttle x seconds after launch. Find a polynomial model for the data. Use the model to predict the time when the shuttle's speed reaches 4400 feet per second, at which point its booster rockets detach.

x	10	20	30	40	50	60	70	80
y	202.4	463.3	748.2	979.3	1186.3	1421.3	1795.4	2283.5

Solution

STEP 1 **Enter** the data into a graphing calculator and make a scatter plot. The points suggest a cubic model.

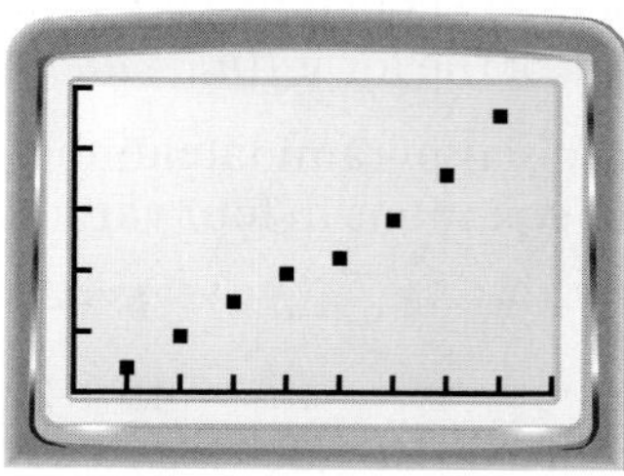

STEP 2 **Use** cubic regression to obtain this polynomial model:

$y = 0.00650x^3 - 0.739x^2 + 49.0x - 236$

```
CubicReg
 y=ax³+bx²+cx+d
 a=.0065012626
 b=-.7393668831
 c=48.95620491
 d=-235.8857143
```

STEP 3 **Check** the model by graphing it and the data in the same viewing window.

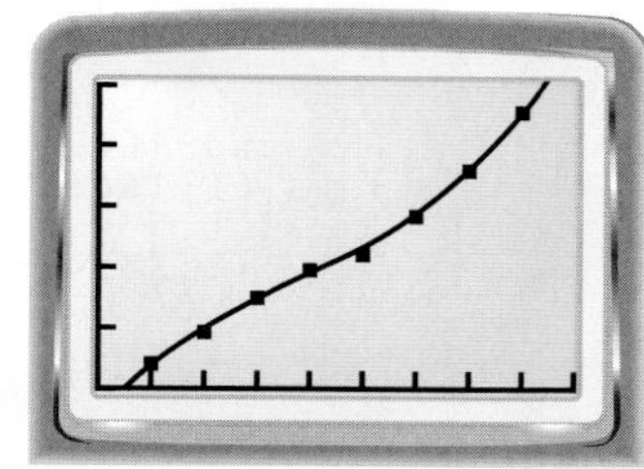

STEP 4 **Graph** the model and $y = 4400$ in the same viewing window. Use the *intersect* feature.

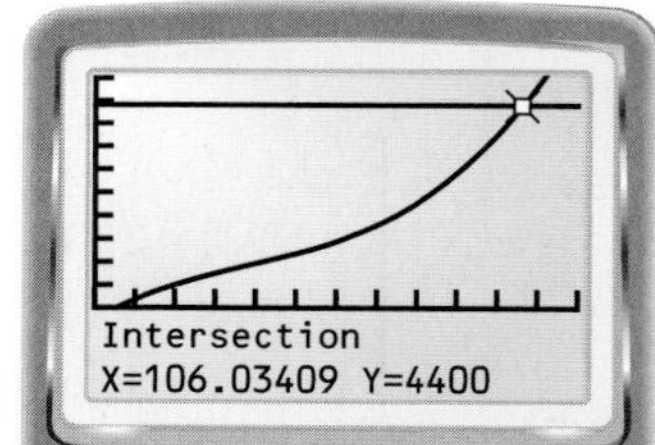

▶ The booster rockets detach about 106 seconds after launch.

Animated **Algebra** at classzone.com

ANOTHER WAY

You can also find the value of x for which $y = 4400$ by subtracting 4400 from the right side of the cubic model, graphing the resulting function, and using the *zero* feature to find the graph's x-intercept.

✓ **GUIDED PRACTICE** for Example 4

Use a graphing calculator to find a polynomial function that fits the data.

5.

x	1	2	3	4	5	6
$f(x)$	5	13	17	11	11	56

6.

x	0	2	4	6	8	10
$f(x)$	8	0	15	69	98	87

5.9 EXERCISES

HOMEWORK KEY
○ = **WORKED-OUT SOLUTIONS** on p. WS11 for Exs. 9, 15, and 27
★ = **STANDARDIZED TEST PRACTICE** Exs. 2, 10, 22, 23, and 28

SKILL PRACTICE

1. **VOCABULARY** Copy and complete: When the x-values in a data set are equally spaced, the differences of consecutive y-values are called _?_.

2. ★ **WRITING** *Describe* first-order differences and second-order differences.

EXAMPLE 1 on p. 393 for Exs. 3–11

WRITING CUBIC FUNCTIONS **Write the cubic function whose graph is shown.**

3. 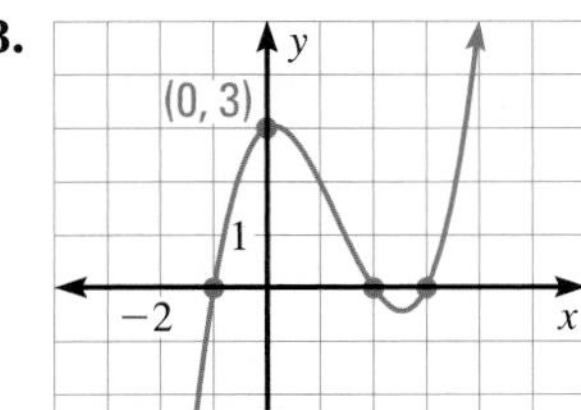

4. 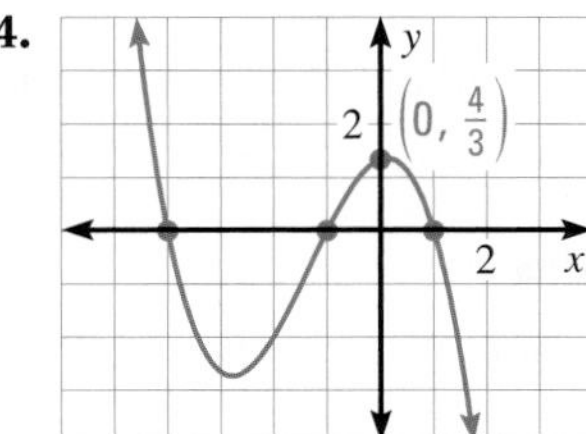

5. 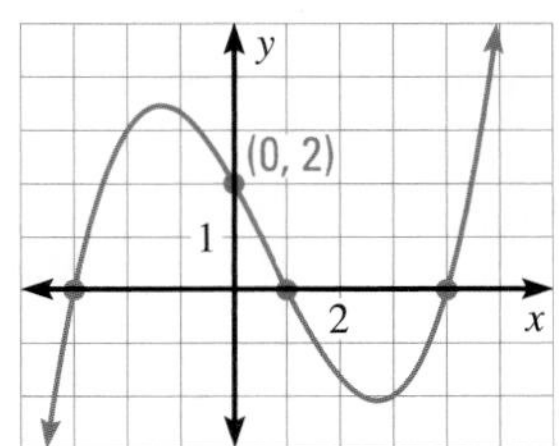

CUBIC MODELS **Write a cubic function whose graph passes through the points.**

6. $(-3, 0), (-1, 10), (0, 0), (4, 0)$

7. $(-2, 0), (-1, 0), (0, -8), (2, 0)$

8. $(-3, 0), (1, 0), (3, 2), (4, 0)$

9. $(-5, 0), (0, 0), (1, -12), (6, 0)$

10. ★ **MULTIPLE CHOICE** Which cubic function's graph passes through the points $(-3, 0), (-1, 0), (3, 0)$, and $(0, 3)$?

Ⓐ $f(x) = (x - 3)(x + 3)(x - 1)$

Ⓑ $f(x) = -\frac{1}{3}(x - 3)(x + 3)(x + 1)$

Ⓒ $f(x) = -2(x - 3)(x + 3)(x - 1)$

Ⓓ $f(x) = (x - 3)(x + 3)(x + 1)$

11. **ERROR ANALYSIS** A student tried to write a cubic function whose graph has x-intercepts -1, 2, and 5, and passes through $(1, 3)$. *Describe* and correct the error in the student's calculation of the leading coefficient a.

$$1 = a(3 + 1)(3 - 2)(3 - 5)$$
$$1 = -8a$$
$$-\frac{1}{8} = a$$

EXAMPLE 2 on p. 394 for Exs. 12–17

FINDING FINITE DIFFERENCES **Show that the *n*th-order differences for the given function of degree *n* are nonzero and constant.**

12. $f(x) = 5x^3 - 10$

13. $f(x) = -2x^2 + 5x$

14. $f(x) = x^4 - 3x^2 + 2$

15. $f(x) = 4x^2 - 9x + 2$

16. $f(x) = x^3 - 4x^2 - x + 1$

17. $f(x) = 2x^5 - 3x^2 + x$

EXAMPLE 3 on p. 395 for Exs. 18–21

FINDING A MODEL **Use finite differences and a system of equations to find a polynomial function that fits the data in the table.**

18.

x	1	2	3	4	5	6
$f(x)$	0	−3	−8	−15	−24	−35

19.

x	1	2	3	4	5	6
$f(x)$	11	14	9	−4	−25	−54

20.

x	1	2	3	4	5	6
$f(x)$	−12	−14	−10	6	40	98

21.

x	1	2	3	4	5	6
$f(x)$	5	14	27	41	53	60

22. ★ **OPEN-ENDED MATH** Write two different cubic functions whose graphs pass through the points $(-3, 0)$, $(-1, 0)$, and $(2, 6)$.

23. ★ **SHORT RESPONSE** How many points do you need to determine a quartic function? a quintic (fifth-degree) function? *Justify* your answers.

24. **CHALLENGE** Substitute the expressions $k, k + 1, k + 2, \ldots, k + 5$ for x in the function $f(x) = ax^3 + bx^2 + cx + d$ to generate six equally-spaced ordered pairs. Then show that third-order differences are constant.

PROBLEM SOLVING

EXAMPLE 3 on p. 395 for Ex. 25

25. **GEOMETRY** Find a polynomial function that gives the number of diagonals d of a polygon with n sides.

Number of sides, *n*	3	4	5	6	7	8
Number of diagonals, *d*	0	2	5	9	14	20

@HomeTutor for problem solving help at classzone.com

EXAMPLE 4 on p. 396 for Exs. 26–28

26. **AVIATION** The table shows the number of active pilots (in thousands) with airline transport licenses in the United States for the years 1997 to 2004. Use a graphing calculator to find a polynomial model for the data.

Years since 1997, *t*	0	1	2	3	4	5	6	7
Transport pilots, *p*	131	135	138	142	145	145	144	145

@HomeTutor for problem solving help at classzone.com

27. **MULTI-STEP PROBLEM** The table shows the average U.S. movie ticket price (in dollars) for various years from 1983 to 2003.

Years since 1983, *t*	0	4	8	12	16	20
Movie ticket price, *m*	3.15	3.91	4.21	4.35	5.08	6.03

a. Use a graphing calculator to find a polynomial model for the data.

b. Estimate the average U.S. movie ticket price in 2010.

c. In which year was the average U.S. movie ticket price about $4.50?

28. ★ **SHORT RESPONSE** Based on data collected from friends, you estimate the cumulative profits (in dollars) after each of six months for two potential businesses. Find a polynomial function that models the profit for each business. Which business will yield the greatest long-term profit? Why?

Yard work	Month, t	1	2	3	4	5	6
	Profit, p	30	210	410	680	1070	1630
Pet care	Month, t	1	2	3	4	5	6
	Profit, p	30	50	220	540	1010	1630

29. **GEOMETRY** The maximum number of regions R into which space can be divided by n intersecting spheres is given by $R(n) = \frac{1}{3}n^3 - n^2 + \frac{8}{3}n$. Show that this function has constant third-order differences.

30. **CHALLENGE** A cylindrical cake is divided into the maximum number of pieces p by c planes. When $c = 1, 2, 3, 4, 5,$ and 6 the values of $p(c)$ are 2, 4, 8, 15, 26, and 42 respectively. What is the maximum number of pieces into which the cake can be divided when it is cut by 8 planes?

NEW YORK MIXED REVIEW

TEST PRACTICE at classzone.com

31. Graph the linear system. What is the solution of the system?

$$-3x - 2y = -8$$
$$2x - y = 10$$

Ⓐ $(-4, -18)$ Ⓑ $(4, -2)$ Ⓒ $(12, 14)$ Ⓓ No solution

32. The height h above the ground (in feet) of a stuntman falling from a window is given by $h = -16t^2 + 90$ where t is the time (in seconds). An air cushion that is 9 feet high is positioned on the ground below the window. About how many seconds will the stuntman fall before he hits the air cushion?

Ⓐ 2.25 sec Ⓑ 2.37 sec Ⓒ 8.66 sec Ⓓ 9.48 sec

QUIZ for Lessons 5.7–5.9

Find all zeros of the polynomial function. *(p. 379)*

1. $f(x) = x^3 - 4x^2 - 11x + 30$
2. $f(x) = 2x^4 - 2x^3 - 49x^2 + 9x + 180$

Write a polynomial function f of least degree that has rational coefficients, a leading coefficient of 1, and the given zeros. *(p. 379)*

3. $-4, -1, 2$
4. $4, 1 + i$
5. $-3, 5, 7 + \sqrt{2}$
6. $1, -2i, 3 - \sqrt{6}$

Graph the function. *(p. 387)*

7. $f(x) = -(x - 3)(x - 2)(x + 2)$
8. $f(x) = 3(x - 1)(x + 1)(x - 4)$
9. $f(x) = x(x - 4)(x - 1)(x + 2)$
10. $f(x) = (x - 3)(x + 2)^2(x + 3)^2$

Write a cubic function whose graph passes through the given points. *(p. 393)*

11. $(-5, 0), (-2, 0), (1, 9), (2, 0)$
12. $(-1, 0), (0, 16), (2, 0), (4, 0)$

13. **DRIVE-INS** The table shows the number of U.S. drive-in movie theaters for the years 1995 to 2002. Find a polynomial model that fits the data. *(p. 393)*

Years since 1995, *t*	0	1	2	3	4	5	6	7
Drive-in movie theaters, *D*	848	826	815	750	737	667	663	634

New York Mixed Review

Lessons 5.6–5.9

1. **POLYNOMIAL FUNCTIONS** Which polynomial function has zeros −2, 1, and $4 - i$?

   (1) $f(x) = x^4 - 7x^3 + 2x^2 + 28x - 24$

   (2) $f(x) = x^4 - 7x^3 + 7x^2 + 33x - 34$

   (3) $f(x) = x^4 - 9x^3 + 18x^2 + 4x - 24$

   (4) $f(x) = x^4 - 9x^3 + 23x^2 - x - 34$

2. **GEOMETRY** The volume of the rectangular prism shown is 180 cubic inches. What is the height of the rectangular prism?

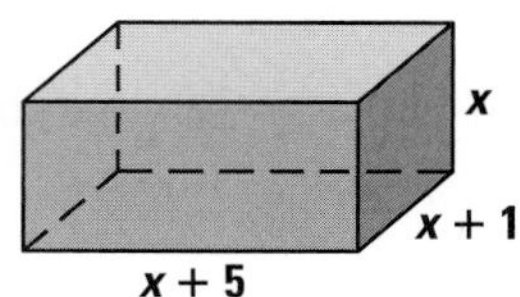

   (1) 3 inches

   (2) 4 inches

   (3) 5 inches

   (4) 8 inches

3. **MAXIMUM VOLUME** You want to make an open box (four sides and a bottom) from a rectangular piece of cardboard that is 20 inches by 30 inches. You will cut an x-by-x square from each corner. What value of x will maximize the volume of the box?

   (1) 3.9 inches

   (2) 7.8 inches

   (3) 10 inches

   (4) 12.2 inches

4. **DESCARTES' RULE OF SIGNS** How many positive real zeros does the following function have?

   $$f(x) = 2x^5 + 5x^4 + 5x^3 + 25x^2 + 7x - 10$$

   (1) 1

   (2) 2

   (3) 4

   (4) 5

5. **SCULPTURE** You are making a sculpture that is a pyramid with a square base. You want the height of the pyramid to be 4 inches less than the length of a side of the base. You want the volume of the sculpture to be 200 cubic inches. What is the approximate length of a side of the sculpture's base?

   (1) 6.3 inches

   (2) 7.5 inches

   (3) 10 inches

   (4) 11.3 inches

6. **OPEN-ENDED** Your friend has started a golf caddying business. The table shows the profit p (in dollars) of the business in the first 5 months. Use finite differences to find a polynomial model for the data. Then use the model to predict the profit when $t = 7$.

Month, t	1	2	3	4	5
Profit, p	4	2	6	22	56

7. **OPEN-ENDED** The table below shows the average relationship between length (in inches) and weight (in pounds) for an alligator as it grows.

Length	Weight
12	0.2
24	0.7
36	8.6
48	17.7
54	28.0
60	39.6
66	45.4
72	49.6

Use a calculator to find a 3rd-degree polynomial model for this data.

Use your model to find the average weight of alligators 75 inches long.

5 CHAPTER SUMMARY

Animated Algebra
classzone.com
Electronic Function Library

BIG IDEAS

For Your Notebook

Big Idea 1

Graphing Polynomial Functions

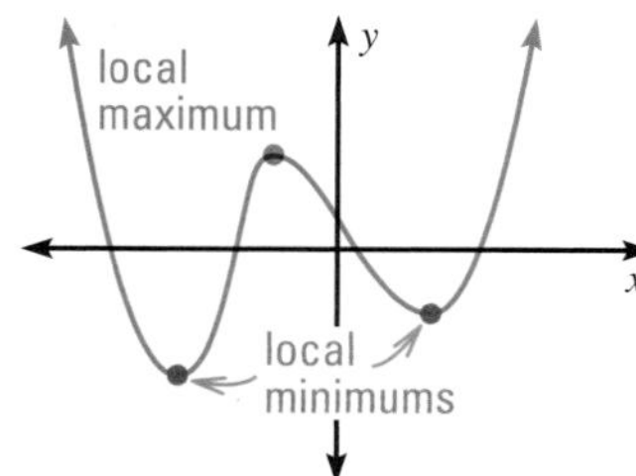

The end behavior of the graph of $f(x)$ is

$f(x) \to +\infty$ as $x \to -\infty$ and $f(x) \to +\infty$ as $x \to +\infty$

so $f(x)$ is of even degree and has a positive leading coefficient.

The graph has 3 turning points, so the degree of $f(x)$ is *at least* 4 and $f(x)$ has *at least* 4 zeros.

Big Idea 2

Performing Operations with Polynomials

You can add, subtract, multiply, and divide polynomials. You can also factor polynomials using any combination of the methods below.

Factoring method	Example
General trinomial	$6x^2 - 7x - 3 = (3x + 1)(2x - 3)$
Perfect square trinomial	$x^2 + 10x + 25 = (x + 5)^2$
Difference of two squares	$x^2 - 49 = (x + 7)(x - 7)$
Common monomial factor	$15x^3 + 9x^2 = 3x^2(5x + 3)$
Sum or difference of two cubes	$8x^3 - 27 = (2x - 3)(4x^2 + 6x + 9)$
Factor by grouping	$x^3 - 5x^2 + 9x - 45 = x^2(x - 5) + 9(x - 5) = (x^2 + 9)(x - 5)$

Big Idea 3

Solving Polynomial Equations and Finding Zeros

The terms *zero, factor, solution,* and *x-intercept* are closely related. Consider the function $f(x) = 2x^3 - x^2 - 13x - 6$.

-2 is a **zero** of f.	$f(-2) = 2(-2)^3 - (-2)^2 - 13(-2) - 6 = 0$
$x + 2$ is a **factor** of $f(x)$.	$2x^3 - x^2 - 13x - 6 = (x + 2)(x - 3)(2x + 1)$
$x = -2$ is a **solution** of the equation $f(x) = 0$.	$2(-2)^3 - (-2)^2 - 13(-2) - 6 = 0$
-2 is an ***x*-intercept** of the graph of f.	y, 5, −2, 1, x

CHAPTER REVIEW

@HomeTutor
classzone.com
- Multi-Language Glossary
- Vocabulary practice

REVIEW KEY VOCABULARY

- scientific notation, *p. 331*
- polynomial, *p. 337*
- polynomial function, *p. 337*
- leading coefficient, *p. 337*
- degree, *p. 337*
- constant term, *p. 337*
- standard form of a polynomial function, *p. 337*
- synthetic substitution, *p. 338*
- end behavior, *p. 339*
- factored completely, *p. 353*
- factor by grouping, *p. 354*
- quadratic form, *p. 355*
- polynomial long division, *p. 362*
- synthetic division, *p. 363*
- repeated solution, *p. 379*
- local maximum, *p. 388*
- local minimum, *p. 388*
- finite differences, *p. 393*

VOCABULARY EXERCISES

1. Copy and complete: At each of its turning points, the graph of a polynomial function has a(n) __?__ or a(n) __?__.

2. **WRITING** *Explain* how you can tell whether a solution of a polynomial equation is a repeated solution when the equation is written in factored form.

3. **WRITING** *Explain* how you can tell whether a number is expressed in scientific notation.

4. Let f be a fourth-degree polynomial function with four distinct real zeros. How many turning points does the graph of f have?

REVIEW EXAMPLES AND EXERCISES

Use the review examples and exercises below to check your understanding of the concepts you have learned in each lesson of Chapter 5.

5.1 Use Properties of Exponents *pp. 330–335*

EXAMPLE

Simplify the expression.

$(x^2y^3)^3x^4 = (x^2)^3(y^3)^3x^4$	**Power of a product property**
$= x^6y^9x^4$	**Power of a power property**
$= x^{6+4}y^9$	**Product of powers property**
$= x^{10}y^9$	**Simplify exponent.**

EXERCISES

EXAMPLES 1, 2, 3, and 4 on pp. 330–332 for Exs. 5–12

Evaluate or simplify the expression. Tell which properties of exponents you used.

5. $2^2 \cdot 2^5$
6. $(3^2)^{-3}(3^3)$
7. $(x^{-2}y^5)^2$
8. $(3x^4y^{-2})^{-3}$
9. $\left(\frac{3}{4}\right)^{-2}$
10. $\frac{8 \times 10^7}{2 \times 10^3}$
11. $\left(\frac{x^2}{y^{-2}}\right)^{-4}$
12. $\frac{2x^{-6}y^5}{16x^3y^{-2}}$

@HomeTutor
classzone.com
Chapter Review Practice

5.2 Evaluate and Graph Polynomial Functions

pp. 337–344

EXAMPLE

Graph the polynomial function $f(x) = x^3 - 2x^2 + 3$.

Make a table of values.

x	−2	−1	0	1	2	3
$f(x)$	−13	0	3	2	3	12

Plot the points, connect the points with a smooth curve, and check the end behavior.

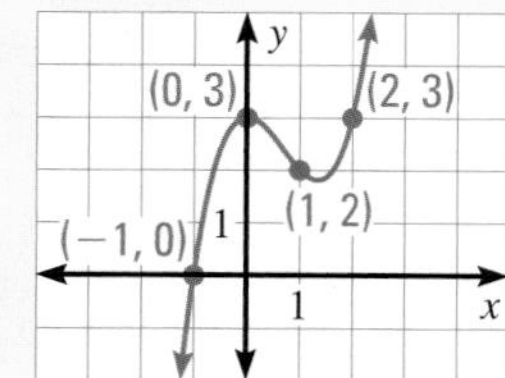

The degree is odd and the leading coefficient is positive, so $f(x) \to -\infty$ as $x \to -\infty$ and $f(x) \to +\infty$ as $x \to +\infty$.

EXERCISES

EXAMPLES 5 and 6 on p. 340 for Exs. 13–16

Graph the polynomial function.

13. $f(x) = -x^4$

14. $f(x) = x^3 - 4$

15. $f(x) = x^3 + 2x + 3$

16. **FISH CONSUMPTION** From 1990 to 2002, the amount of fish F (in millions of pounds) caught for human consumption in the United States can be modeled by

$$F = -0.907t^4 + 28.0t^3 - 258t^2 + 902t + 12{,}700$$

where t is the number of years since 1990. Graph the function. Use the graph to estimate the year when the amount of fish caught first was greater than 14.5 *billion* pounds.

5.3 Add, Subtract, and Multiply Polynomials

pp. 346–352

EXAMPLE

Perform the indicated operation.

a. $(3x^3 - 6x^2 - 7x + 5) + (x^3 + 8x + 3) = 3x^3 + x^3 - 6x^2 - 7x + 8x + 5 + 3$

$= 4x^3 - 6x^2 + x + 8$

b. $(x - 4)(2x^2 - 7x + 5) = (x - 4)2x^2 - (x - 4)7x + (x - 4)5$

$= 2x^3 - 8x^2 - 7x^2 + 28x + 5x - 20$

$= 2x^3 - 15x^2 + 33x - 20$

EXERCISES

EXAMPLES 1, 2, 4, and 5 on pp. 346–348 for Exs. 17–20

Perform the indicated operation.

17. $(5x^3 - x + 3) + (x^3 - 9x^2 + 4x)$

18. $(x^3 + 4x^2 - 5x) - (4x^3 + x^2 - 7)$

19. $(x - 6)(5x^2 + x - 8)$

20. $(x - 4)(x + 7)(5x - 1)$

5 CHAPTER REVIEW

5.4 Factor and Solve Polynomial Equations

pp. 353–359

EXAMPLE

Factor the polynomial completely.

a.	$x^3 + 125 = x^3 + 5^3 = (x + 5)(x^2 - 5x + 25)$	**Sum of two cubes**
b.	$x^3 + 5x^2 - 9x - 45 = x^2(x + 5) - 9(x + 5)$	**Factor by grouping.**
	$= (x^2 - 9)(x + 5)$	**Distributive property**
	$= (x + 3)(x - 3)(x + 5)$	**Difference of two squares**
c.	$3x^6 + 12x^4 - 96x^2 = 3x^2(x^4 + 4x^2 - 32)$	**Factor common monomial.**
	$= 3x^2(x^2 - 4)(x^2 + 8)$	**Factor trinomial in quadratic form.**
	$= 3x^2(x + 2)(x - 2)(x^2 + 8)$	**Difference of two squares**

EXERCISES

EXAMPLES 2, 3, 4, and 6 on pp. 354–356 for Exs. 21–24

Factor the polynomial completely.

21. $64x^3 - 8$ **22.** $2x^5 - 12x^3 + 10x$ **23.** $2x^3 - 7x^2 - 8x + 28$

24. SCULPTURE You have 240 cubic inches of clay with which to make a sculpture shaped as a rectangular prism. You want the width to be 4 inches less than the length and the height to be 2 inches more than 3 times the length. What should the dimensions of the sculpture be?

5.5 Apply the Remainder and Factor Theorems

pp. 362–368

EXAMPLE

Divide $f(x) = 4x^4 + 29x^3 + 4x^2 - 14x + 37$ by $x + 7$.

Rewrite the divisor in the form $x - k$. Because $x + 7 = x - (-7)$, $k = -7$.

−7	4	29	4	−14	37
		−28	−7	21	−49
	4	1	−3	7	−12

So, $\dfrac{4x^4 + 29x^3 + 4x^2 - 14x + 37}{x + 7} = 4x^3 + x^2 - 3x + 7 - \dfrac{12}{x + 7}$.

EXERCISES

EXAMPLES 1, 3, and 4 on pp. 362–364 for Exs. 25–32

Divide.

25. $(x^3 - 3x^2 - x - 10) \div (x^2 + 3x - 1)$ **26.** $(4x^4 - 17x^2 + 9x - 18) \div (2x^2 - 2)$

27. $(2x^3 - 11x^2 + 13x - 44) \div (x - 5)$ **28.** $(5x^4 + 2x^2 - 15x + 10) \div (x + 2)$

Given polynomial $f(x)$ and a factor of $f(x)$, factor $f(x)$ completely.

29. $f(x) = x^3 - 5x^2 - 2x + 24;\ x + 2$ **30.** $f(x) = x^3 - 11x^2 + 14x + 80;\ x - 8$

31. $f(x) = 9x^3 - 9x^2 - 4x + 4;\ x - 1$ **32.** $f(x) = 2x^3 + 7x^2 - 33x - 18;\ x + 6$

@HomeTutor
classzone.com
Chapter Review Practice

5.6 Find Rational Zeros

pp. 370–377

EXAMPLE

Find all real zeros of $f(x) = x^3 + 6x^2 + 5x - 12$.

The leading coefficient is 1 and the constant term is -12.

Possible rational zeros: $x = \pm\frac{1}{1}, \pm\frac{2}{1}, \pm\frac{3}{1}, \pm\frac{4}{1}, \pm\frac{6}{1}, \pm\frac{12}{1}$

Test these zeros using synthetic division. Test $x = 1$:

$$\begin{array}{r|rrrr} 1 & 1 & 6 & 5 & -12 \\ & & 1 & 7 & 12 \\ \hline & 1 & 7 & 12 & 0 \end{array} \leftarrow \textbf{1 is a zero.}$$

You can write $f(x) = (x - 1)(x^2 + 7x + 12)$. Factor the trinomial.

$$f(x) = (x - 1)(x^2 + 7x + 12) = (x - 1)(x + 3)(x + 4)$$

The zeros of f are 1, -3, and -4.

EXAMPLES 2 and 3 on pp. 371–372 for Exs. 33–34

EXERCISES

Find all real zeros of the function.

33. $f(x) = x^3 - 4x^2 - 11x + 30$

34. $f(x) = 2x^4 - x^3 - 42x^2 + 16x + 160$

5.7 Apply the Fundamental Theorem of Algebra

pp. 379–386

EXAMPLE

Write a polynomial function f of least degree that has rational coefficients, a leading coefficient of 1, and -4 and $5 + \sqrt{2}$ as zeros.

Because $5 + \sqrt{2}$ is a zero, $5 - \sqrt{2}$ must also be a zero.

$f(x) = (x + 4)\left[x - (5 + \sqrt{2})\right]\left[x - (5 - \sqrt{2})\right]$ **Write $f(x)$ in factored form.**

$= (x + 4)\left[(x - 5) - \sqrt{2}\right]\left[(x - 5) + \sqrt{2}\right]$ **Regroup terms.**

$= (x + 4)[(x - 5)^2 - 2]$ **Multiply.**

$= x^3 - 6x^2 - 17x + 92$ **Multiply.**

EXAMPLES 3 and 6 on pp. 381–383 for Exs. 35–38

EXERCISES

Write a polynomial function f of least degree that has rational coefficients, a leading coefficient of 1, and the given zeros.

35. $-4, 1, 5$

36. $-1, -1, 6, 3i$

37. $2, 7, 3 - \sqrt{5}$

38. ECONOMICS For the 15 years that a computer store has been open, its annual revenue R (in millions of dollars) can be modeled by

$$R = -0.0040t^4 + 0.088t^3 - 0.36t^2 - 0.55t + 5.8$$

where t is the number of years since the store opened. In what year was the revenue first greater than \$7 million?

5 CHAPTER REVIEW

5.8 Analyze Graphs of Polynomial Functions

pp. 387–392

EXAMPLE

Graph the function $f(x) = x^3 - 4x + 2$. Identify the x-intercepts and the points where the local maximums and local minimums occur.

Use a graphing calculator to graph the function.

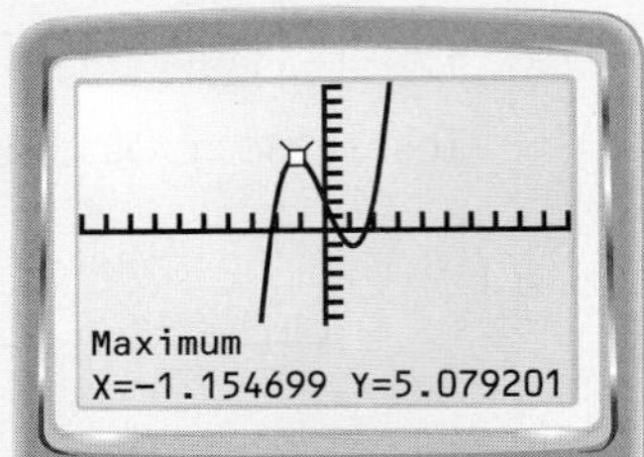

Notice that the graph has three x-intercepts and two turning points. You can use the graphing calculator's *zero, maximum,* and *minimum* features to approximate the coordinates of the points.

The x-intercepts of the graph are about -2.21, 0.54, and 1.68. The function has a local maximum at $(-1.15, 5.08)$ and a local minimum at $(1.15, -1.08)$.

EXERCISES

EXAMPLE 2 on p. 388 for Exs. 39–40

Use a graphing calculator to graph the function. Identify the x-intercepts and the points where the local maximums and local minimums occur.

39. $f(x) = -2x^3 - 3x^2 - 1$

40. $f(x) = x^4 + 3x^3 - x^2 - 8x + 2$

5.9 Write Polynomial Functions and Models

pp. 393–399

EXAMPLE

Use finite differences and a system of equations to find a polynomial function that fits the data.

x	1	2	3	4	5	6
$f(x)$	1	9	23	43	69	101

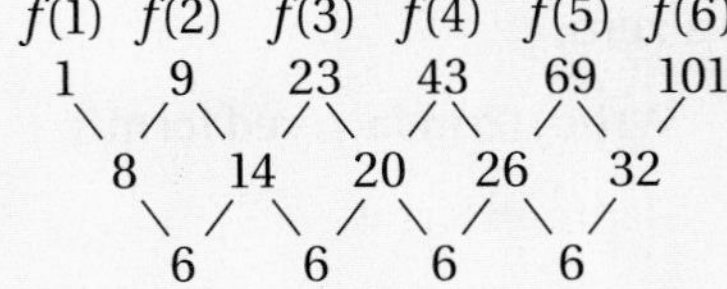

Write function values for equally-spaced x-values.

First-order differences

Second-order differences

Because the second-order differences are constant, the data can be represented by a function of the form $f(x) = ax^2 + bx + c$. By substituting the first 3 data points into the function, you obtain a system of 3 linear equations in 3 variables.

$a(1)^2 + b(1) + c = 1 \quad \rightarrow \quad a + b + c = 1$

$a(2)^2 + b(2) + c = 9 \quad \rightarrow \quad 4a + 2b + c = 9$

$a(3)^2 + b(3) + c = 23 \quad \rightarrow \quad 9a + 3b + c = 23$

Solve the system. The solution is $(3, -1, -1)$, so $f(x) = 3x^2 - x - 1$.

EXERCISES

EXAMPLE 3 on p. 395 for Ex. 41

41. Use finite differences to find a polynomial function that fits the data.

x	1	2	3	4	5	6
$f(x)$	−6	−21	−40	−57	−66	−61

5 CHAPTER TEST

Simplify the expression. Tell which properties of exponents you used.

1. $x^3 \cdot x^2 \cdot x^{-4}$
2. $(2x^{-2}y^3)^{-5}$
3. $\left(\frac{x^{-4}}{y^2}\right)^{-2}$
4. $\frac{3(xy)^3}{27x - 5y^3}$

Graph the polynomial function.

5. $f(x) = -x^3$
6. $f(x) = x^4 - 2x^2 - 5x + 1$
7. $f(x) = x^5 - x^4 - 9$

Perform the indicated operation.

8. $(2x^3 + 5x^2 - 7x + 4) + (x^3 - 3x^2 - 4x)$
9. $(3x^3 - 4x^2 + 3x - 5) - (x^2 + 4x - 8)$
10. $(3x - 2)(x^2 + 4x - 7)$
11. $(3x - 5)^3$
12. $(3x^3 - 14x^2 + 16x - 22) \div (x - 4)$
13. $(6x^4 + 7x^2 + 4x - 17) \div (3x^2 - 3x + 2)$

Factor the polynomial completely.

14. $8x^3 + 27$
15. $x^4 + 5x^2 - 6$
16. $x^3 - 3x^2 - 4x + 12$

Find all real zeros of the function.

17. $f(x) = x^3 + x^2 - 22x - 40$
18. $f(x) = 4x^4 - 8x^3 - 19x^2 + 23x - 6$

Write a polynomial function *f* of least degree that has rational coefficients, a leading coefficient of 1, and the given zeros.

19. $-1, 3, 4$
20. $6, 2i$
21. $-3, -1, 1 - \sqrt{5}$
22. $1 + 3i, 4 + \sqrt{10}$

Use a graphing calculator to graph the function. Identify the *x*-intercepts and the points where the local maximums and local minimums occur.

23. $f(x) = x^3 - 5x^2 + 3x + 4$
24. $f(x) = x^4 + 3x^3 - x^2 - 6x + 2$

Use finite differences and a system of equations to find a polynomial function that fits the data in the table.

25.

x	1	2	3	4	5	6
$f(x)$	3	1	1	3	7	13

26.

x	1	2	3	4	5	6
$f(x)$	0	−7	−4	21	80	185

27. **GROSS DOMESTIC PRODUCT** In 2003, the gross domestic product (GDP) of the United States was about 1.099×10^{13} dollars. The population of the U.S. in 2003 was about 2.91×10^8. What was the per capita GDP in 2003?

28. **TELEVISION** From 1980 to 2002, the number T (in millions) of households in the United States with televisions and the percent P of those households with VCRs can be modeled by

$$T = 1.22x + 76.9 \quad \text{and} \quad P = -0.205x^2 + 8.36x + 1.98$$

where x is the number of years since 1980. Write a polynomial model for the total number of U.S. households with both televisions and VCRs.

29. **GEOMETRY** A rectangular prism has edges of lengths x, $x + 2$, and $2x - 3$ inches. The volume of the prism is 1040 cubic inches. Write a polynomial equation that models the prism's volume. What are the prism's dimensions?

OPEN-ENDED QUESTIONS

Scoring Rubric

Full Credit
- solution is complete and correct

Partial Credit
- solution is complete but has errors,

or
- solution is without error but incomplete

No Credit
- no solution is given,

or
- solution makes no sense

PROBLEM

The width of a rectangular prism is 2 meters less than its length, and the height is 1 meter less than its width. The volume of the prism is 30 cubic meters. Find the dimensions of the prism. *Explain* your reasoning.

Below are sample solutions to the problem. Read each solution and the comments on the left to see why the sample represents full credit, partial credit, or no credit.

SAMPLE 1: Full credit solution

The expressions for the dimensions are clearly explained.

Let the length of the prism be x.
The width is 2 meters less than the length, so width $= x - 2$.
The height is 1 meter less than the width, so height $= (x - 2) - 1 = x - 3$.

The volume of a rectangular prism is the product of its length, width, and height.

The equation is correct and all steps are clearly shown.

$30 = x(x - 2)(x - 3)$ **Write equation.**

$30 = x(x^2 - 5x + 6)$ **Multiply binomials.**

$0 = x^3 - 5x^2 + 6x - 30$ **Write in standard form.**

$0 = x^2(x - 5) + 6(x - 5)$ **Factor by grouping.**

$0 = (x^2 + 6)(x - 5)$ **Distributive property**

The solution of the equation is correct.

The only real solution is $x = 5$. The factor $x^2 + 6$ does not produce any real solutions.

Use substitution to find the dimensions: length $= \boldsymbol{x} = \mathbf{5}$ meters

width $= \boldsymbol{x} - 2 = \mathbf{5} - 2 = 3$ meters

height $= \boldsymbol{x} - 3 = \mathbf{5} - 3 = 2$ meters

The dimensions are correct.

The prism is 5 meters long, 3 meters wide, and 2 meters high.

SAMPLE 2: Partial credit solution

Let length $= x$, width $= x - 2$, and height $= x - 3$.

The equation is correct.

$30 = x(x - 2)(x - 3)$

$0 = x^3 - 5x^2 + 6x - 30$

$0 = (x^2 + 6)(x - 5)$

$x = \pm i\sqrt{6}$ or $x = 5$

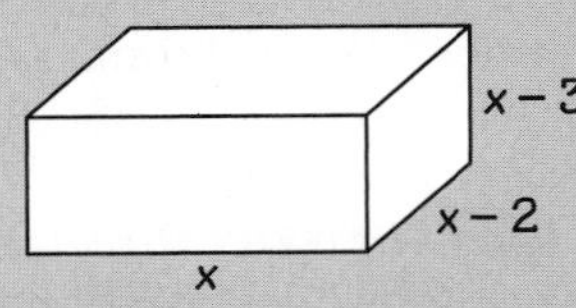

Imaginary solutions should be discarded. Dimensions are not given.

SAMPLE 3: No credit solution

The volume of a prism is the length cubed.

$x^3 = 30$ — The equation is incorrect.

$x \approx 3.11$

The length of the prism is 3.11 meters. — The answer is incorrect.

PRACTICE Apply the Scoring Rubric

Use the rubric on page 408 to score the solution to the problem below as *full credit, partial credit,* or *no credit. Explain* your reasoning.

PROBLEM The volume of a sphere with radius r is given by the function $V = \frac{4}{3}\pi r^3$. Graph the function. Then use the graph to estimate the radius of a sphere with a volume of 750 cubic feet.

1. The table shows the volumes of spheres with radii from 0 to 7 feet. Only positive r-values make sense.

r	0	1	2	3	4	5	6	7
V	0	4.189	33.51	113.1	268.1	523.6	904.8	1437

From the graph, you can see that the r-coordinate that corresponds to a V-coordinate of 750 is about 5.6.

A sphere with a volume of 750 cubic feet has a radius of about 5.6 feet.

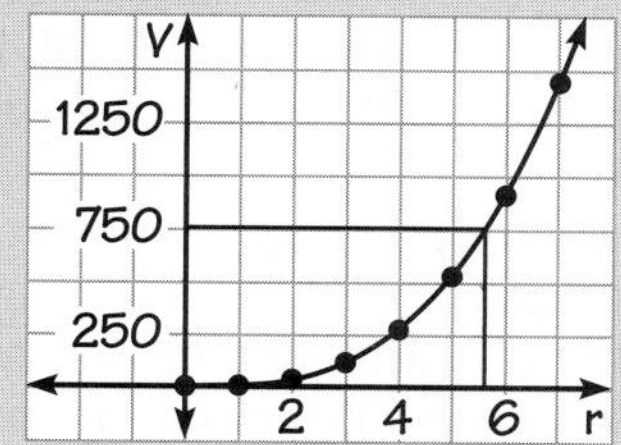

2. The table shows the volume V of a sphere with radius r.

r	0	2	4	6	8	10
V	0	10.67	85.33	288.0	682.7	1333

The r-coordinate that corresponds to a V-coordinate of 750 is 8.2, so the radius of a sphere with a volume of 750 cubic feet is about 8.2 feet.

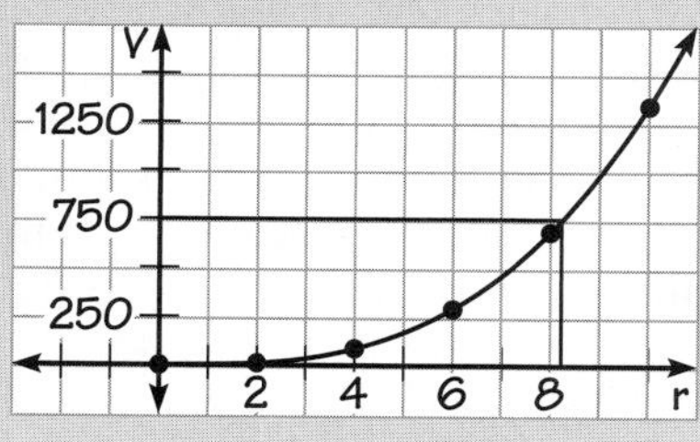

New York Test Practice

OPEN-ENDED

1. Since 1960, the number of voters y (in millions) in United States federal elections can be modeled by the function

$y = -0.0006x^3 + 0.0383x^2 + 0.383x + 68.6$

where x is the number of years since 1960. According to the model, how many more people voted in 1980 than in 1960? *Explain* your reasoning.

2. Show two different ways to evaluate the polynomial $-3x^4 - 2x^3 + 7x^2 - 9$ when $x = -4$.

3. What does the graph of the polynomial function tell you about the sign of the leading coefficient, the degree of the function, and the number of real zeros? *Explain* your reasoning.

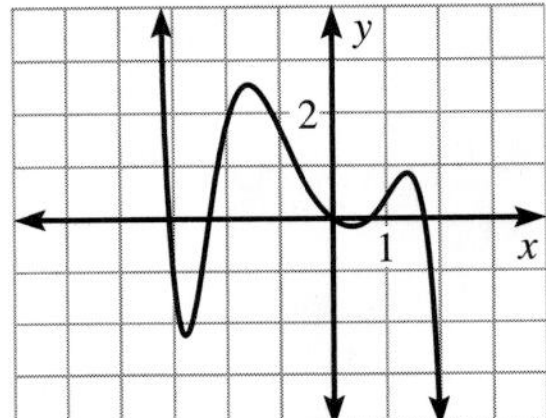

4. Since 1970, the average fuel efficiency E (in miles per gallon) for all vehicles in the United States can be modeled by the function $E = -0.0007t^3 + 0.0278t^2 - 0.0843t + 12.0$ where t is the number of years since 1970. Use a graphing calculator to graph the function, and identify any turning points on the interval $0 \le t \le 30$. What real-life meaning does a turning point have in this situation?

5. Find all roots of the function $f(x) = x^4 + 4x^2 - 5$. *Explain* your reasoning.

6. The profit P (in millions of dollars) for a manufacturer of winter coats can be modeled by $P = -x^3 + 3x^2 + 15x$ where x is the number of winter coats produced (in millions). Currently, the company produces 5 million winter coats and makes a profit of $25,000,000. *Explain* how the company can make the same profit by producing a lesser number of coats.

7. The volume of the rectangular prism shown below is given by the expression $2x^3 + 5x^2 - 19x - 42$.

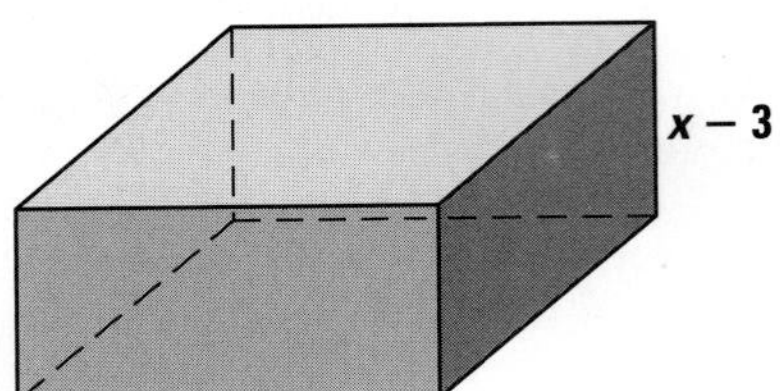

Write a polynomial in standard form that represents the area of the base of the prism. Show all of your steps.

8. From 1990 to 2003, the number of CD singles (in millions) sold in the United States can be modeled by the polynomial function

$y = 0.014x^5 - 0.40x^4 + 3.8x^3 - 13x^2 + 15x + 1.2$

where x is the number of years since 1990.

Use a graphing calculator to graph the function on the domain $0 \le x \le 13$. According to the model, in which year were the most CD singles sold?

Do you think that sales will continue to follow the model indefinitely? *Explain* your reasoning.

9. Use finite differences and a system of equations to find a polynomial function that fits the data in each table. Then find $f(x) + g(x)$. *Explain* all of your steps.

x	1	2	3	4	5	6
f(x)	4	9	26	57	104	169

x	1	2	3	4	5	6
g(x)	−2	−2	12	52	130	258

10. The population of the United States in 1800 was 5.308×10^6, and the land area was 8.647×10^5 square miles. By 2000, the population had increased to 2.814×10^8, and the land area was 3.537×10^6 square miles. By how many people per square mile of land did the population density increase from 1800 to 2000? *Explain* your reasoning.

TEST PREPARATION

TEST PRACTICE
classzone.com

OPEN-ENDED

11. You are making an open box to hold paper clips out of a piece of cardboard that is 5 inches by 8 inches. The box will be formed by making the cuts shown in the diagram and folding up the sides. You want the box to have the greatest volume possible.

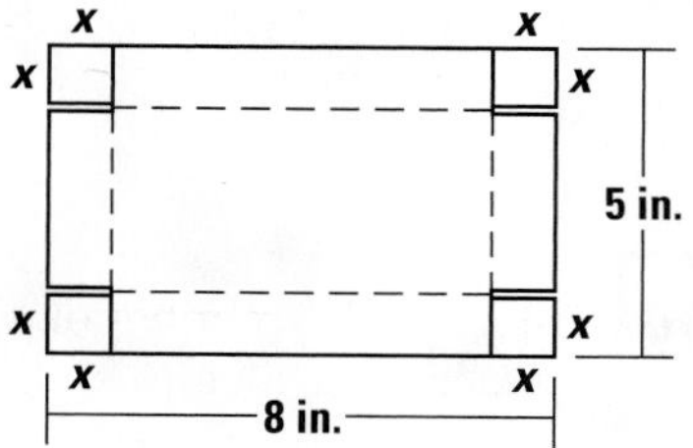

Use a graphing calculator to find how long you should make the cuts. *Explain* your reasoning.

What is the maximum volume of the box?

What will the dimensions of the finished box be?

12. From 1980 to 2002, the number of hospitals H in the United States and the average number of hospital beds B in each hospital can be modeled by

$$H = -58.7t + 7070 \quad \text{and} \quad B = 0.0066t^3 - 0.192t^2 - 0.174t + 196$$

where t is the number of years since 1980.

Write a model for the total number of hospital beds in U.S. hospitals.

According to the model, how many beds were in U.S. hospitals in 1995?

How does the model change if you want to find the number of hospital beds *in thousands*? *Explain* your reasoning.

MULTIPLE CHOICE

13. Which expression is equivalent to $\frac{x^2y}{z^4}$?

(1) $\frac{z^{-4}y^0}{x^{-2}}$

(2) $xyz \cdot \frac{x}{z^{-3}}$

(3) $(x^{-1}y^2z^2)^2(x^{-1}y^1z^2)^{-4}$

(4) $\frac{(x^2yz)^3}{x^4y^2z^7}$

14. What are all the real solutions of the equation $x^4 = 125x$?

(1) 0 (3) 0, 5

(2) 0, 5, −5 (4) $0, 5i, -5i$

15. Which polynomial function has −1, 3, and $-4i$ as zeros?

(1) $f(x) = x^4 - 2x^3 + 13x^2 - 32x - 48$

(2) $f(x) = x^4 + 2x^3 + 13x^2 + 32x - 48$

(3) $f(x) = x^4 - 2x^3 - 19x^2 + 32x + 48$

(4) $f(x) = x^4 + 2x^3 + 19x^2 - 32x + 48$

16. How many *real* zeros does the function $f(x) = 2x^4 + 3x^2 - 1$ have?

(1) 0 real zeros (3) 2 real zeros

(2) 1 real zero (4) 4 real zeros

17. Evaluate the expression $\left(\frac{3}{2}\right)^{-2}$.

(1) $\frac{4}{9}$ (3) $\sqrt{\frac{2}{3}}$

(2) $\frac{9}{4}$ (4) $\sqrt{\frac{3}{2}}$

18. The graph of a quartic function is shown. How many imaginary zeros does the function have?

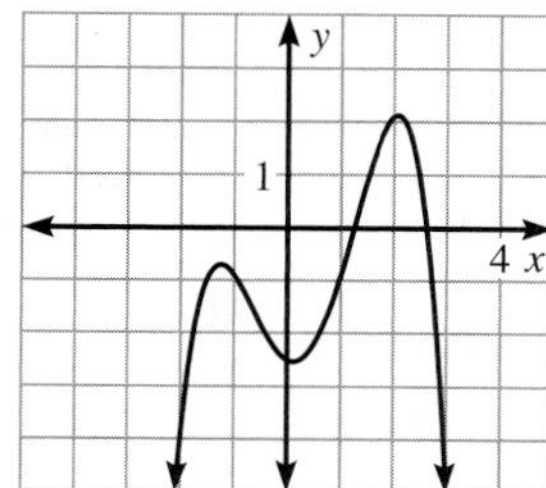

(1) 0 imaginary zeros (3) 2 imaginary zeros

(2) 1 imaginary zero (4) 4 imaginary zeros

TEST PREPARATION

6 Rational Exponents and Radical Functions

Before

In previous chapters, you learned the following skills, which you'll use in Chapter 6: simplifying expressions involving exponents, rewriting equations, and graphing polynomial functions.

Prerequisite Skills

VOCABULARY CHECK

Copy and complete the statement.

1. The **square roots** of 81 are _?_ and _?_.
2. In the expression 2^5, the **exponent** is _?_.
3. For the polynomial function whose graph is shown, the sign of the **leading coefficient** is _?_.

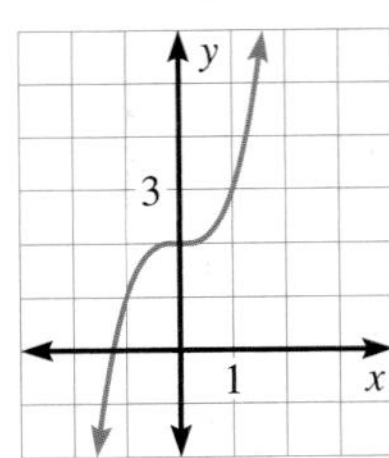

SKILLS CHECK

Simplify the expression. *(Review p. 330 for 6.2.)*

4. $\dfrac{5x^2y}{15x^3y^{-1}}$
5. $\dfrac{32x^{-3}y^4}{24x^{-3}y^{-2}} \cdot \dfrac{3x}{9y}$
6. $(2x^5y^{-3})^{-3}$

Solve the equation for *y*. *(Review p. 26 for 6.4.)*

7. $-2x - 5y = 10$
8. $x - \frac{1}{3}y = -1$
9. $8x - 4xy = 3$

Graph the polynomial function. *(Review p. 337 for 6.5.)*

10. $f(x) = x^3 - 4x + 6$
11. $f(x) = -x^5 + 7x^2 + 2$
12. $f(x) = x^4 - 4x^2 + x$

Now

In Chapter 6, you will apply the big ideas listed below and reviewed in the Chapter Summary on page 465. You will also use the key vocabulary listed below.

Big Ideas

1. **Using rational exponents**
2. **Performing function operations and finding inverse functions**
3. **Graphing radical functions and solving radical equations**

KEY VOCABULARY

- nth root of a, *p. 414*
- index of a radical, *p. 414*
- simplest form of a radical, *p. 422*
- like radicals, *p. 422*
- power function, *p. 428*
- composition, *p. 430*
- inverse relation, *p. 438*
- inverse function, *p. 438*
- radical function, *p. 446*
- radical equation, *p. 452*

Why?

You can use a radical function to model the time you are suspended in the air during a jump. For example, the hang time of a basketball player can be modeled by a radical function.

Animated Algebra

The animation illustrated below for Exercise 60 on page 458 helps you answer this question: What is the relationship between the height of a jump and the time the jumper is suspended in air?

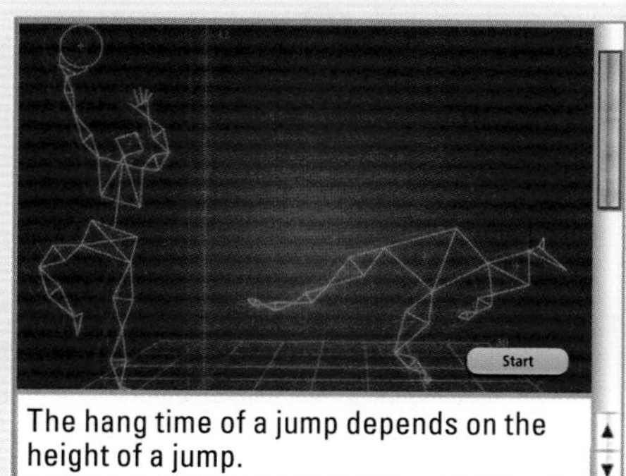

The hang time of a jump depends on the height of a jump.

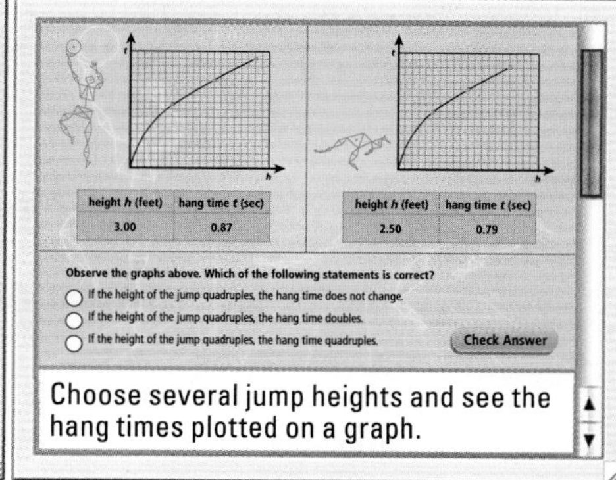

Choose several jump heights and see the hang times plotted on a graph.

Animated Algebra at classzone.com

Other animations for Chapter 6: pages 431, 444, 448, and 465

6.1 Evaluate *n*th Roots and Use Rational Exponents

 **A2.A.8** Apply the rules of exponents to simplify expressions involving negative and/or fractional exponents

Before	You evaluated square roots and used properties of exponents.
Now	You will evaluate *n*th roots and study rational exponents.
Why?	So you can find the radius of a spherical object, as in Ex. 60.

Key Vocabulary
- ***n*th root of *a***
- **index of a radical**

You can extend the concept of a square root to other types of roots. For example, 2 is a cube root of 8 because $2^3 = 8$. In general, for an integer n greater than 1, if $b^n = a$, then b is an ***n*th root of *a***. An nth root of a is written as $\sqrt[n]{a}$ where n is the **index** of the radical.

You can also write an nth root of a as a power of a. If you assume the power of a power property applies to rational exponents, then the following is true:

$$(a^{1/2})^2 = a^{(1/2) \cdot 2} = a^1 = a$$

$$(a^{1/3})^3 = a^{(1/3) \cdot 3} = a^1 = a$$

$$(a^{1/4})^4 = a^{(1/4) \cdot 4} = a^1 = a$$

Because $a^{1/2}$ is a number whose square is a, you can write $\sqrt{a} = a^{1/2}$. Similarly, $\sqrt[3]{a} = a^{1/3}$ and $\sqrt[4]{a} = a^{1/4}$. In general, $\sqrt[n]{a} = a^{1/n}$ for any integer n greater than 1.

KEY CONCEPT *For Your Notebook*

Real *n*th Roots of *a*

Let n be an integer ($n > 1$) and let a be a real number.

***n* is an even integer.**	***n* is an odd integer.**
$a<0$ No real nth roots.	$a<0$ One real nth root: $\sqrt[n]{a} = a^{1/n}$
$a=0$ One real nth root: $\sqrt[n]{0} = 0$	$a=0$ One real nth root: $\sqrt[n]{0} = 0$
$a>0$ Two real nth roots: $\pm\sqrt[n]{a} = \pm a^{1/n}$	$a>0$ One real nth root: $\sqrt[n]{a} = a^{1/n}$

EXAMPLE 1 **Find *n*th roots**

Find the indicated real *n*th root(s) of *a*.

a. $n = 3, a = -216$ **b.** $n = 4, a = 81$

Solution

a. Because $n = 3$ is odd and $a = -216 < 0$, -216 has one real cube root. Because $(-6)^3 = -216$, you can write $\sqrt[3]{-216} = -6$ or $(-216)^{1/3} = -6$.

b. Because $n = 4$ is even and $a = 81 > 0$, 81 has two real fourth roots. Because $3^4 = 81$ and $(-3)^4 = 81$, you can write $\pm\sqrt[4]{81} = \pm 3$ or $\pm 81^{1/4} = \pm 3$.

RATIONAL EXPONENTS A rational exponent does not have to be of the form $\frac{1}{n}$. Other rational numbers such as $\frac{3}{2}$ and $-\frac{1}{2}$ can also be used as exponents. Two properties of rational exponents are shown below.

KEY CONCEPT *For Your Notebook*

Rational Exponents

Let $a^{1/n}$ be an nth root of a, and let m be a positive integer.

$$a^{m/n} = (a^{1/n})^m = (\sqrt[n]{a})^m$$

$$a^{-m/n} = \frac{1}{a^{m/n}} = \frac{1}{(a^{1/n})^m} = \frac{1}{(\sqrt[n]{a})^m},\ a \neq 0$$

EXAMPLE 2 Evaluate expressions with rational exponents

Evaluate (a) $16^{3/2}$ and (b) $32^{-3/5}$.

Solution

	Rational Exponent Form	Radical Form
a.	$16^{3/2} = (16^{1/2})^3 = 4^3 = 64$	$16^{3/2} = (\sqrt{16})^3 = 4^3 = 64$
b.	$32^{-3/5} = \frac{1}{32^{3/5}} = \frac{1}{(32^{1/5})^3} = \frac{1}{2^3} = \frac{1}{8}$	$32^{-3/5} = \frac{1}{32^{3/5}} = \frac{1}{(\sqrt[5]{32})^3} = \frac{1}{2^3} = \frac{1}{8}$

AVOID ERRORS
Be sure to use parentheses to enclose a rational exponent: 9^(1/5) ≈ 1.552. Without them, the calculator evaluates a power and then divides: 9^1/5 = 1.8.

EXAMPLE 3 Approximate roots with a calculator

	Expression	Keystrokes	Display
a.	$9^{1/5}$	9 [^] [(] 1 [÷] 5 [)] [ENTER]	1.551845574
b.	$12^{3/8}$	12 [^] [(] 3 [÷] 8 [)] [ENTER]	2.539176951
c.	$(\sqrt[4]{7})^3 = 7^{3/4}$	7 [^] [(] 3 [÷] 4 [)] [ENTER]	4.303517071

✓ **GUIDED PRACTICE** for Examples 1, 2, and 3

Find the indicated real nth root(s) of a.

1. $n = 4, a = 625$
2. $n = 6, a = 64$
3. $n = 3, a = -64$
4. $n = 5, a = 243$

Evaluate the expression without using a calculator.

5. $4^{5/2}$
6. $9^{-1/2}$
7. $81^{3/4}$
8. $1^{7/8}$

Evaluate the expression using a calculator. Round the result to two decimal places when appropriate.

9. $4^{2/5}$
10. $64^{-2/3}$
11. $(\sqrt[4]{16})^5$
12. $(\sqrt[3]{-30})^2$

EXAMPLE 4 Solve equations using *n*th roots

Solve the equation.

a. $4x^5 = 128$

$x^5 = 32$ **Divide each side by 4.**

$x = \sqrt[5]{32}$ **Take fifth root of each side.**

$x = 2$ **Simplify.**

b. $(x - 3)^4 = 21$

$x - 3 = \pm\sqrt[4]{21}$ **Take fourth roots of each side.**

$x = \pm\sqrt[4]{21} + 3$ **Add 3 to each side.**

$x = \sqrt[4]{21} + 3$ or $x = -\sqrt[4]{21} + 3$ **Write solutions separately.**

$x \approx 5.14$ or $x \approx 0.86$ **Use a calculator.**

AVOID ERRORS
When n is even and $a > 0$, be sure to consider both the positive and negative nth roots of a.

EXAMPLE 5 Use *n*th roots in problem solving

BIOLOGY A study determined that the weight w (in grams) of coral cod near Palawan Island, Philippines, can be approximated using the model

$$w = 0.0167\ell^3$$

where ℓ is the coral cod's length (in centimeters). Estimate the length of a coral cod that weighs 200 grams.

Solution

$w = 0.0167\ell^3$ **Write model for weight.**

$200 = 0.0167\ell^3$ **Substitute 200 for *w*.**

$11{,}976 \approx \ell^3$ **Divide each side by 0.0167.**

$\sqrt[3]{11{,}976} \approx \ell$ **Take cube root of each side.**

$22.9 \approx \ell$ **Use a calculator.**

▸ A coral cod that weighs 200 grams is about 23 centimeters long.

GUIDED PRACTICE for Examples 4 and 5

Solve the equation. Round the result to two decimal places when appropriate.

13. $x^3 = 64$ **14.** $\frac{1}{2}x^5 = 512$ **15.** $3x^2 = 108$

16. $\frac{1}{4}x^3 = 2$ **17.** $(x - 2)^3 = -14$ **18.** $(x + 5)^4 = 16$

19. WHAT IF? Use the information from Example 5 to estimate the length of a coral cod that has the given weight.

a. 275 grams **b.** 340 grams **c.** 450 grams

6.1 EXERCISES

HOMEWORK KEY

○ = **WORKED-OUT SOLUTIONS** on p. WS12 for Exs. 9, 25, and 63

★ = **STANDARDIZED TEST PRACTICE** Exs. 2, 33, 46, 47, and 65

SKILL PRACTICE

1. **VOCABULARY** Copy and complete: In the expression $\sqrt[4]{10{,}000}$, the number 4 is called the _?_.

2. ★ **WRITING** *Explain* how the sign of a determines the number of real fourth roots of a and the number of real fifth roots of a.

EXAMPLE 1 on p. 414 for Exs. 3–20

MATCHING EXPRESSIONS Match the expression in rational exponent notation with the equivalent expression in radical notation.

3. $2^{1/3}$ 4. $2^{3/2}$ 5. $2^{2/3}$ 6. $2^{1/2}$

A. $(\sqrt{2})^3$ B. $\sqrt{2}$ C. $\sqrt[3]{2}$ D. $(\sqrt[3]{2})^2$

USING RATIONAL EXPONENT NOTATION Rewrite the expression using rational exponent notation.

7. $\sqrt[3]{12}$ 8. $\sqrt[5]{8}$ (9.) $(\sqrt[3]{10})^7$ 10. $(\sqrt[8]{15})^3$

USING RADICAL NOTATION Rewrite the expression using radical notation.

11. $5^{1/4}$ 12. $7^{1/3}$ 13. $14^{2/5}$ 14. $21^{9/4}$

FINDING *N*TH ROOTS Find the indicated real *n*th root(s) of *a*.

15. $n = 2, a = 64$ 16. $n = 3, a = -27$ 17. $n = 4, a = 0$

18. $n = 3, a = 343$ 19. $n = 4, a = -16$ 20. $n = 5, a = -32$

EXAMPLE 2 on p. 415 for Exs. 21–33

EVALUATING EXPRESSIONS Evaluate the expression without using a calculator.

21. $\sqrt[6]{64}$ 22. $8^{1/3}$ 23. $16^{3/2}$ 24. $\sqrt[3]{-125}$

(25.) $27^{2/3}$ 26. $(-243)^{1/5}$ 27. $(\sqrt[3]{8})^{-2}$ 28. $(\sqrt[3]{-64})^4$

29. $(\sqrt[4]{16})^{-7}$ 30. $25^{3/2}$ 31. $64^{-2/3}$ 32. $\frac{1}{81^{-3/4}}$

33. ★ **MULTIPLE CHOICE** What is the value of $128^{5/7}$?

(A) 8 (B) 16 (C) 32 (D) 64

EXAMPLE 3 on p. 415 for Exs. 34–46

APPROXIMATING ROOTS Evaluate the expression using a calculator. Round the result to two decimals places when appropriate.

34. $\sqrt[5]{32{,}768}$ 35. $\sqrt[7]{1695}$ 36. $\sqrt[9]{-230}$ 37. $85^{1/6}$

38. $25^{-1/3}$ 39. $20{,}736^{1/4}$ 40. $(\sqrt[4]{187})^3$ 41. $(\sqrt{6})^{-5}$

42. $(\sqrt[5]{-8})^8$ 43. $86^{-5/6}$ 44. $1974^{2/7}$ 45. $\frac{1}{(-17)^{3/5}}$

46. ★ **MULTIPLE CHOICE** Which expression has the greatest value?

(A) $27^{3/5}$ (B) $5^{3/2}$ (C) $\sqrt[3]{81}$ (D) $(\sqrt[3]{2})^8$

47. ★ **OPEN-ENDED MATH** Write two different expressions of the form $a^{1/n}$ that equal 3, where a is a real number and n is an integer greater than 1.

EXAMPLE 4
on p. 416
for Exs. 48–58

ERROR ANALYSIS ***Describe*** **and correct the error in solving the equation.**

48.

$x^3 = 27$

$x = \sqrt[3]{27}$

$x = 9$

49.

$x^4 = 81$

$x = \sqrt[4]{81}$

$x = 3$

SOLVING EQUATIONS **Solve the equation. Round the result to two decimal places when appropriate.**

50. $x^3 = 125$ **51.** $5x^3 = 1080$ **52.** $x^6 + 36 = 100$

53. $(x - 5)^4 = 256$ **54.** $x^5 = -48$ **55.** $7x^4 = 56$

56. $x^3 + 40 = 25$ **57.** $(x + 10)^5 = 70$ **58.** $x^6 - 34 = 181$

59. CHALLENGE The general shape of the graph of $y = x^n$, where n is a positive *even* integer, is shown in red.

a. *Explain* how the graph justifies the results in the Key Concept box on page 414 when n is a positive *even* integer.

b. Draw a similar graph that justifies the results in the Key Concept box when n is a positive *odd* integer.

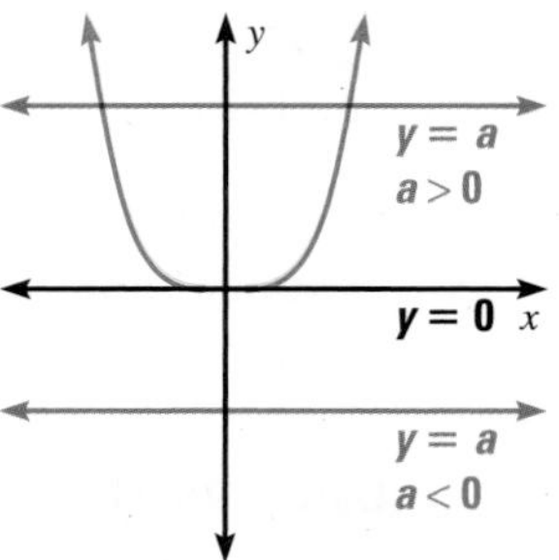

PROBLEM SOLVING

EXAMPLE 5
on p. 416
for Exs. 60–65

60. SHOT PUT The shot used in men's shot put has a volume of about 905 cubic centimeters. Find the radius of the shot. (*Hint:* Use the formula $V = \frac{4}{3}\pi r^3$ for the volume of a sphere.)

@HomeTutor for problem solving help at classzone.com

61. BOWLING A bowling ball has a surface area of about 232 square inches. Find the radius of the bowling ball. (*Hint:* Use the formula $S = 4\pi r^2$ for the surface area of a sphere.)

@HomeTutor for problem solving help at classzone.com

62. INFLATION If the average price of an item increases from p_1 to p_2 over a period of n years, the annual rate of inflation r (expressed as a decimal) is given by $r = \left(\frac{p_2}{p_1}\right)^{1/n} - 1$. Find the rate of inflation for each item in the table. Write each answer as a percent rounded to the nearest tenth.

Item	Price in 1950	Price in 1990
Butter (lb)	\$.7420	\$2.195
Chicken (lb)	\$.4430	\$1.087
Eggs (dozen)	\$.6710	\$1.356
Sugar (lb)	\$.0936	\$.4560

63. MULTI-STEP PROBLEM The power p (in horsepower) used by a fan with rotational speed s (in revolutions per minute) can be modeled by the formula $p = ks^3$ for some constant k. A certain fan uses 1.2 horsepower when its speed is 1700 revolutions per minute. First find the value of k for this fan. Then find the speed of the fan if it uses 1.5 horsepower.

○ = WORKED-OUT SOLUTIONS on p. WS1 ★ = STANDARDIZED TEST PRACTICE

64. **WATER RATE** A *weir* is a dam that is built across a river to regulate the flow of water. The flow rate Q (in cubic feet per second) can be calculated using the formula $Q = 3.367\ell h^{3/2}$ where ℓ is the length (in feet) of the bottom of the spillway and h is the depth (in feet) of the water on the spillway. Determine the flow rate of a weir with a spillway that is 20 feet long and has a water depth of 5 feet.

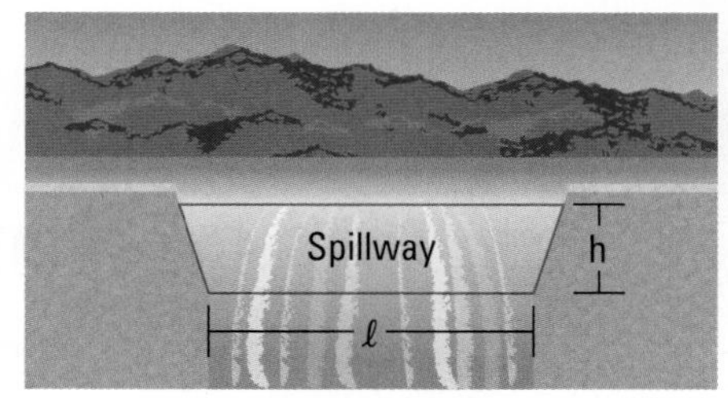

65. ★ **EXTENDED RESPONSE** Some games use dice in the shape of regular polyhedra. You are designing dice and want them all to have the same volume as a cube with an edge length of 16 millimeters.

Name	Tetrahedron	Octahedron	Dodecahedron	Icosahedron
Number of faces	4	8	12	20
Volume formula	$V = 0.118x^3$	$V = 0.471x^3$	$V = 7.663x^3$	$V = 2.182x^3$

a. Find the volume of a cube with an edge length of 16 millimeters.

b. Find the edge length x for each of the polyhedra shown in the table.

c. Does the polyhedron with the greatest number of faces have the smallest edge length? *Explain.*

66. **CHALLENGE** The mass of the particles that a river can transport is proportional to the sixth power of the speed of the river. A certain river normally flows at a speed of 1 meter per second. What must its speed be in order to transport particles that are twice as massive as usual? 10 times as massive? 100 times as massive?

NEW YORK MIXED REVIEW

67. Which expression is equivalent to $2x(4x + 1) - (7x + 3)(x - 4)$?

Ⓐ $x^2 - 23x - 12$ Ⓑ $15x^2 - 23x - 12$

Ⓒ $-x^2 + 27x + 12$ Ⓓ $x^2 + 27x + 12$

68. Frank digs a trench around the triangular garden shown. What is the approximate length of the trench that he digs?

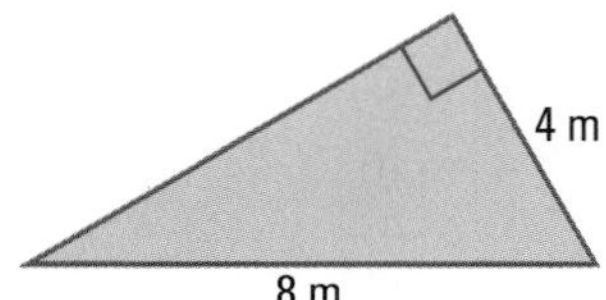

Ⓐ 18.9 m

Ⓑ 19.3 m

Ⓒ 25.9 m

Ⓓ 37.9 m

6.2 Apply Properties of Rational Exponents

A2.N.5 Rationalize a denominator containing a radical expression

Before You simplified expressions involving integer exponents.

Now You will simplify expressions involving rational exponents.

Why? So you can find velocities, as in Ex. 84.

Key Vocabulary
- **simplest form of a radical**
- **like radicals**

The properties of integer exponents you learned in Lesson 5.1 can also be applied to rational exponents.

KEY CONCEPT — *For Your Notebook*

Properties of Rational Exponents

Let a and b be real numbers and let m and n be rational numbers. The following properties have the same names as those listed on page 330, but now apply to rational exponents as illustrated.

Property	Example
1. $a^m \cdot a^n = a^{m+n}$	$5^{1/2} \cdot 5^{3/2} = 5^{(1/2+3/2)} = 5^2 = 25$
2. $(a^m)^n = a^{mn}$	$(3^{5/2})^2 = 3^{(5/2 \cdot 2)} = 3^5 = 243$
3. $(ab)^m = a^m b^m$	$(16 \cdot 9)^{1/2} = 16^{1/2} \cdot 9^{1/2} = 4 \cdot 3 = 12$
4. $a^{-m} = \frac{1}{a^m}, a \neq 0$	$36^{-1/2} = \frac{1}{36^{1/2}} = \frac{1}{6}$
5. $\frac{a^m}{a^n} = a^{m-n}, a \neq 0$	$\frac{4^{5/2}}{4^{1/2}} = 4^{(5/2-1/2)} = 4^2 = 16$
6. $\left(\frac{a}{b}\right)^m = \frac{a^m}{b^m}, b \neq 0$	$\left(\frac{27}{64}\right)^{1/3} = \frac{27^{1/3}}{64^{1/3}} = \frac{3}{4}$

EXAMPLE 1 Use properties of exponents

Use the properties of rational exponents to simplify the expression.

a. $7^{1/4} \cdot 7^{1/2} = 7^{(1/4+1/2)} = 7^{3/4}$

b. $(6^{1/2} \cdot 4^{1/3})^2 = (6^{1/2})^2 \cdot (4^{1/3})^2 = 6^{(1/2 \cdot 2)} \cdot 4^{(1/3 \cdot 2)} = 6^1 \cdot 4^{2/3} = 6 \cdot 4^{2/3}$

c. $(4^5 \cdot 3^5)^{-1/5} = [(4 \cdot 3)^5]^{-1/5} = (12^5)^{-1/5} = 12^{[5 \cdot (-1/5)]} = 12^{-1} = \frac{1}{12}$

d. $\frac{5}{5^{1/3}} = \frac{5^1}{5^{1/3}} = 5^{(1-1/3)} = 5^{2/3}$

e. $\left(\frac{42^{1/3}}{6^{1/3}}\right)^2 = \left[\left(\frac{42}{6}\right)^{1/3}\right]^2 = (7^{1/3})^2 = 7^{(1/3 \cdot 2)} = 7^{2/3}$

EXAMPLE 2 Apply properties of exponents

BIOLOGY A mammal's surface area S (in square centimeters) can be approximated by the model $S = km^{2/3}$ where m is the mass (in grams) of the mammal and k is a constant. The values of k for some mammals are shown below. Approximate the surface area of a rabbit that has a mass of 3.4 kilograms (3.4×10^3 grams).

Mammal	Sheep	Rabbit	Horse	Human	Monkey	Bat
k	8.4	9.75	10.0	11.0	11.8	57.5

Solution

$S = km^{2/3}$ **Write model.**

$= 9.75(3.4 \times 10^3)^{2/3}$ **Substitute 9.75 for k and 3.4×10^3 for m.**

$= 9.75(3.4)^{2/3}(10^3)^{2/3}$ **Power of a product property**

$\approx 9.75(2.26)(10^2)$ **Power of a power property**

≈ 2200 **Simplify.**

▸ The rabbit's surface area is about 2200 square centimeters.

GUIDED PRACTICE for Examples 1 and 2

Simplify the expression.

1. $(5^{1/3} \cdot 7^{1/4})^3$ **2.** $2^{3/4} \cdot 2^{1/2}$ **3.** $\frac{3}{3^{1/4}}$ **4.** $\left(\frac{20^{1/2}}{5^{1/2}}\right)^3$

5. BIOLOGY Use the information in Example 2 to approximate the surface area of a sheep that has a mass of 95 kilograms (9.5×10^4 grams).

PROPERTIES OF RADICALS The third and sixth properties on page 420 can be expressed using radical notation when $m = \frac{1}{n}$ for some integer n greater than 1.

KEY CONCEPT *For Your Notebook*

Properties of Radicals

Product property of radicals

$$\sqrt[n]{a \cdot b} = \sqrt[n]{a} \cdot \sqrt[n]{b}$$

Quotient property of radicals

$$\sqrt[n]{\frac{a}{b}} = \frac{\sqrt[n]{a}}{\sqrt[n]{b}},\ b \neq 0$$

EXAMPLE 3 Use properties of radicals

Use the properties of radicals to simplify the expression.

a. $\sqrt[3]{12} \cdot \sqrt[3]{18} = \sqrt[3]{12 \cdot 18} = \sqrt[3]{216} = 6$ **Product property**

b. $\frac{\sqrt[4]{80}}{\sqrt[4]{5}} = \sqrt[4]{\frac{80}{5}} = \sqrt[4]{16} = 2$ **Quotient property**

SIMPLEST FORM A radical with index n is in **simplest form** if the radicand has no perfect nth powers as factors and any denominator has been rationalized.

EXAMPLE 4 Write radicals in simplest form

Write the expression in simplest form.

a. $\sqrt[3]{135} = \sqrt[3]{27 \cdot 5}$ **Factor out perfect cube.**

$= \sqrt[3]{27} \cdot \sqrt[3]{5}$ **Product property**

$= 3\sqrt[3]{5}$ **Simplify.**

REVIEW RADICALS
For help with rationalizing denominators of radical expressions, see p. 266.

b. $\frac{\sqrt[5]{7}}{\sqrt[5]{8}} = \frac{\sqrt[5]{7}}{\sqrt[5]{8}} \cdot \frac{\sqrt[5]{4}}{\sqrt[5]{4}}$ **Make denominator a perfect fifth power.**

$= \frac{\sqrt[5]{28}}{\sqrt[5]{32}}$ **Product property**

$= \frac{\sqrt[5]{28}}{2}$ **Simplify.**

LIKE RADICALS Radical expressions with the same index and radicand are **like radicals**. To add or subtract like radicals, use the distributive property.

EXAMPLE 5 Add and subtract like radicals and roots

Simplify the expression.

a. $\sqrt[4]{10} + 7\sqrt[4]{10} = (1 + 7)\sqrt[4]{10} = 8\sqrt[4]{10}$

b. $2(8^{1/5}) + 10(8^{1/5}) = (2 + 10)(8^{1/5}) = 12(8^{1/5})$

c. $\sqrt[3]{54} - \sqrt[3]{2} = \sqrt[3]{27} \cdot \sqrt[3]{2} - \sqrt[3]{2} = 3\sqrt[3]{2} - \sqrt[3]{2} = (3 - 1)\sqrt[3]{2} = 2\sqrt[3]{2}$

✓ GUIDED PRACTICE for Examples 3, 4, and 5

Simplify the expression.

6. $\sqrt[4]{27} \cdot \sqrt[4]{3}$ **7.** $\frac{\sqrt[3]{250}}{\sqrt[3]{2}}$ **8.** $\sqrt[5]{\frac{3}{4}}$ **9.** $\sqrt[3]{5} + \sqrt[3]{40}$

VARIABLE EXPRESSIONS The properties of rational exponents and radicals can also be applied to expressions involving variables. Because a variable can be positive, negative, or zero, sometimes absolute value is needed when simplifying a variable expression.

	Rule	Example
When n is odd	$\sqrt[n]{x^n} = x$	$\sqrt[7]{5^7} = 5$ and $\sqrt[7]{(-5)^7} = -5$
When n is even	$\sqrt[n]{x^n} = \lvert x \rvert$	$\sqrt[4]{3^4} = 3$ and $\sqrt[4]{(-3)^4} = 3$

Absolute value is not needed when all variables are assumed to be positive.

EXAMPLE 6 Simplify expressions involving variables

Simplify the expression. Assume all variables are positive.

a. $\sqrt[3]{64y^6} = \sqrt[3]{4^3(y^2)^3} = \sqrt[3]{4^3} \cdot \sqrt[3]{(y^2)^3} = 4y^2$

b. $(27p^3q^{12})^{1/3} = 27^{1/3}(p^3)^{1/3}(q^{12})^{1/3} = 3p^{(3 \cdot 1/3)}q^{(12 \cdot 1/3)} = 3pq^4$

c. $\sqrt[4]{\frac{m^4}{n^8}} = \frac{\sqrt[4]{m^4}}{\sqrt[4]{n^8}} = \frac{\sqrt[4]{m^4}}{\sqrt[4]{(n^2)^4}} = \frac{m}{n^2}$

d. $\frac{14xy^{1/3}}{2x^{3/4}z^{-6}} = 7x^{(1 - 3/4)}y^{1/3}z^{-(-6)} = 7x^{1/4}y^{1/3}z^6$

EXAMPLE 7 Write variable expressions in simplest form

Write the expression in simplest form. Assume all variables are positive.

a. $\sqrt[5]{4a^8b^{14}c^5} = \sqrt[5]{4a^5a^3b^{10}b^4c^5}$ — Factor out perfect fifth powers.

$= \sqrt[5]{a^5b^{10}c^5} \cdot \sqrt[5]{4a^3b^4}$ — Product property

$= ab^2c\sqrt[5]{4a^3b^4}$ — Simplify.

AVOID ERRORS
You must multiply both the numerator *and* denominator of the fraction by y so that the value of the fraction does not change.

b. $\sqrt[3]{\frac{x}{y^8}} = \sqrt[3]{\frac{x \cdot y}{y^8 \cdot y}}$ — Make denominator a perfect cube.

$= \sqrt[3]{\frac{xy}{y^9}}$ — Simplify.

$= \frac{\sqrt[3]{xy}}{\sqrt[3]{y^9}}$ — Quotient property

$= \frac{\sqrt[3]{xy}}{y^3}$ — Simplify.

EXAMPLE 8 Add and subtract expressions involving variables

Perform the indicated operation. Assume all variables are positive.

a. $\frac{1}{5}\sqrt{w} + \frac{3}{5}\sqrt{w} = \left(\frac{1}{5} + \frac{3}{5}\right)\sqrt{w} = \frac{4}{5}\sqrt{w}$

b. $3xy^{1/4} - 8xy^{1/4} = (3 - 8)xy^{1/4} = -5xy^{1/4}$

c. $12\sqrt[3]{2z^5} - z\sqrt[3]{54z^2} = 12z\sqrt[3]{2z^2} - 3z\sqrt[3]{2z^2} = (12z - 3z)\sqrt[3]{2z^2} = 9z\sqrt[3]{2z^2}$

✓ GUIDED PRACTICE for Examples 6, 7, and 8

Simplify the expression. Assume all variables are positive.

10. $\sqrt[3]{27q^9}$ **11.** $\sqrt[5]{\frac{x^{10}}{y^5}}$ **12.** $\frac{6xy^{3/4}}{3x^{1/2}y^{1/2}}$ **13.** $\sqrt{9w^5} - w\sqrt{w^3}$

6.2 EXERCISES

HOMEWORK KEY

○ = **WORKED-OUT SOLUTIONS** on p. WS12 for Exs. 5, 27, and 85

★ = **STANDARDIZED TEST PRACTICE** Exs. 2, 23, 51, 69, 86, and 89

SKILL PRACTICE

1. **VOCABULARY** Are $2\sqrt{5}$ and $2\sqrt[3]{5}$ like radicals? *Explain* why or why not.

2. ★ **WRITING** Under what conditions is a radical expression in simplest form?

EXAMPLE 1 on p. 420 for Exs. 3–14

PROPERTIES OF RATIONAL EXPONENTS Simplify the expression.

3. $5^{3/2} \cdot 5^{1/2}$
4. $(6^{2/3})^{1/2}$
5. $3^{1/4} \cdot 27^{1/4}$
6. $\frac{9}{9^{-4/5}}$
7. $\frac{80^{1/4}}{5^{-1/4}}$
8. $\left(\frac{7^3}{4^3}\right)^{-1/3}$
9. $\frac{11^{2/5}}{11^{4/5}}$
10. $(12^{3/5} \cdot 8^{3/5})^5$
11. $\frac{120^{-2/5} \cdot 120^{2/5}}{7^{-3/4}}$
12. $\frac{64^{5/9} \cdot 64^{2/9}}{4^{3/4}}$
13. $(16^{5/9} \cdot 5^{7/9})^{-3}$
14. $\frac{13^{3/7}}{13^{5/7}}$

EXAMPLE 3 on p. 421 for Exs. 15–22

PROPERTIES OF RADICALS Simplify the expression.

15. $\sqrt{20} \cdot \sqrt{5}$
16. $\sqrt[3]{16} \cdot \sqrt[3]{4}$
17. $\sqrt[4]{8} \cdot \sqrt[4]{8}$
18. $(\sqrt[3]{3} \cdot \sqrt[4]{3})^{12}$
19. $\frac{\sqrt[5]{64}}{\sqrt[5]{2}}$
20. $\frac{\sqrt{3}}{\sqrt{75}}$
21. $\frac{\sqrt[4]{36} \cdot \sqrt[4]{9}}{\sqrt[4]{4}}$
22. $\frac{\sqrt[4]{8} \cdot \sqrt[4]{16}}{\sqrt[8]{2} \cdot \sqrt[8]{3}}$

EXAMPLE 4 on p. 422 for Exs. 23–31

23. ★ **MULTIPLE CHOICE** What is the simplest form of the expression $3\sqrt[4]{32} \cdot (-6\sqrt[4]{5})$?

Ⓐ $\sqrt[4]{10}$ Ⓑ $-18\sqrt[4]{10}$ Ⓒ $-36\sqrt[4]{10}$ Ⓓ $36\sqrt[8]{10}$

SIMPLEST FORM Write the expression in simplest form.

24. $\sqrt{72}$
25. $\sqrt[6]{256}$
26. $\sqrt[3]{108} \cdot \sqrt[3]{4}$
27. $5\sqrt[4]{64} \cdot 2\sqrt[4]{8}$
28. $\sqrt[3]{\frac{1}{6}}$
29. $\frac{3}{\sqrt[4]{144}}$
30. $\sqrt[6]{\frac{81}{4}}$
31. $\frac{\sqrt[3]{9}}{\sqrt[5]{27}}$

EXAMPLE 5 on p. 422 for Exs. 32–41

COMBINING RADICALS AND ROOTS Simplify the expression.

32. $2\sqrt[6]{3} + 7\sqrt[6]{3}$
33. $\frac{3}{5}\sqrt[3]{5} - \frac{1}{5}\sqrt[3]{5}$
34. $25\sqrt[5]{2} - 15\sqrt[5]{2}$
35. $\frac{1}{8}\sqrt[4]{7} + \frac{3}{8}\sqrt[4]{7}$
36. $6\sqrt[3]{5} + 4\sqrt[3]{625}$
37. $-6\sqrt[7]{2} + 2\sqrt[7]{256}$
38. $12\sqrt[4]{2} - 7\sqrt[4]{512}$
39. $2\sqrt[4]{1250} - 8\sqrt[4]{32}$
40. $5\sqrt[3]{48} - \sqrt[3]{750}$

ERROR ANALYSIS ***Describe*** **and correct the error in simplifying the expression.**

41.
$$2\sqrt[3]{10} + 6\sqrt[3]{5} = (2 + 6)\sqrt[3]{15} = 8\sqrt[3]{15}$$

42.
$$\sqrt[3]{\frac{x}{y^2}} = \sqrt[3]{\frac{x}{y^2 \cdot y}} = \sqrt[3]{\frac{x}{y^3}} = \frac{\sqrt[3]{x}}{y}$$

EXAMPLE 6
on p. 423
for Exs. 43–51

VARIABLE EXPRESSIONS **Simplify the expression. Assume all variables are positive.**

43. $x^{1/4} \cdot x^{1/3}$

44. $(y^4)^{1/6}$

45. $\sqrt[4]{81x^4}$

46. $\dfrac{2}{x^{-3/2}}$

47. $\dfrac{x^{2/5}y}{xy^{-1/3}}$

48. $\sqrt[3]{\dfrac{x^{15}}{y^6}}$

49. $\left(\sqrt[3]{x^2} \cdot \sqrt[6]{x^4}\right)^{-3}$

50. $\dfrac{\sqrt[3]{x} \cdot \sqrt{x^5}}{\sqrt{25x^{16}}}$

51. ★ **OPEN-ENDED MATH** Write two variable expressions with noninteger exponents whose quotient is $x^{3/4}$.

EXAMPLE 7
on p. 423
for Exs. 52–59

SIMPLEST FORM **Write the expression in simplest form. Assume all variables are positive.**

52. $\sqrt{49x^5}$

53. $\sqrt[4]{12x^2y^6z^{12}}$

54. $\sqrt[3]{4x^3y^5} \cdot \sqrt[3]{12y^2}$

55. $\sqrt{x^2yz^3} \cdot \sqrt{x^3z^5}$

56. $\dfrac{-3}{\sqrt[5]{x^6}}$

57. $\sqrt[3]{\dfrac{x^3}{y^4}}$

58. $\sqrt{\dfrac{20x^3y^2}{9xz^3}}$

59. $\dfrac{\sqrt[4]{x^6}}{\sqrt[7]{x^5}}$

EXAMPLE 8
on p. 423
for Exs. 60–65

COMBINING VARIABLE EXPRESSIONS **Perform the indicated operation. Assume all variables are positive.**

60. $3\sqrt[5]{x} + 9\sqrt[5]{x}$

61. $\frac{3}{4}y^{3/2} - \frac{1}{4}y^{3/2}$

62. $-7\sqrt[3]{y} + 16\sqrt[3]{y}$

63. $(x^4y)^{1/2} + (xy^{1/4})^2$

64. $x\sqrt{9x^3} - 2\sqrt{x^5}$

65. $y\sqrt[4]{32x^6} + \sqrt[4]{162x^2y^4}$

GEOMETRY **Find simplified expressions for the perimeter and area of the given figure.**

66.

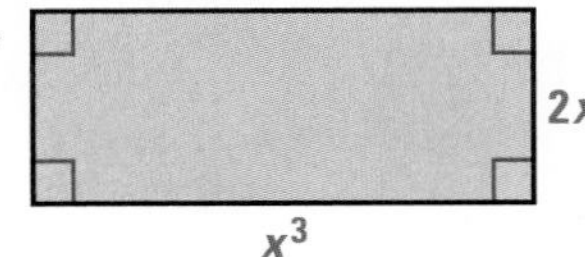

67.

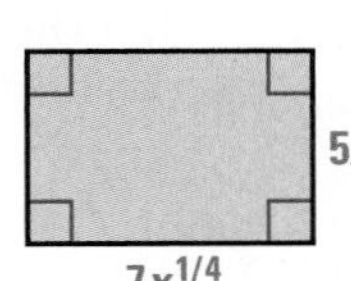

68.

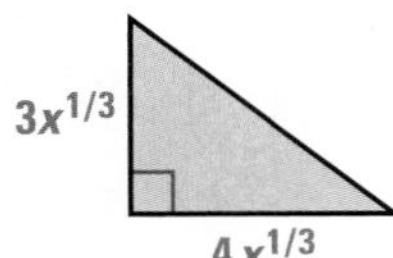

69. ★ **MULTIPLE CHOICE** What is the simplified form of $-\frac{1}{6}\sqrt{4x} - \frac{1}{6}\sqrt{9x}$?

Ⓐ $-\frac{1}{3}\sqrt{x}$ Ⓑ $-\frac{1}{3}\sqrt{36x}$ Ⓒ $-\frac{5}{6}\sqrt{x}$ Ⓓ $-\frac{5}{6}\sqrt{36x}$

DECIMAL EXPONENTS **Simplify the expression. Assume all variables are positive.**

70. $x^{0.5} \cdot x^2$

71. $y^{-0.6} \cdot y^{-6}$

72. $(x^6y^2)^{-0.75}$

73. $\dfrac{x^{0.3}}{x^{1.5}}$

74. $(x^5y^{-3})^{-0.25}$

75. $\dfrac{y^{-0.5}}{y^{0.8}}$

76. $10x^{0.6} + (4x^{0.3})^2$

77. $15z^{0.3} - (2z^{0.1})^3$

IRRATIONAL EXPONENTS **The properties in this lesson can also be applied to irrational exponents. Simplify the expression. Assume all variables are positive.**

78. $\dfrac{x^{5\sqrt{3}}}{x^{2\sqrt{3}}}$

79. $(x^{\sqrt{2}})^{\sqrt{3}}$

80. $\left(\dfrac{x^{\pi}}{x^{\pi/3}}\right)^2$

81. $x^2y^{\sqrt{2}} + 3x^2y^{\sqrt{2}}$

82. **CHALLENGE** Solve the equation using the properties of rational exponents.

a. $\dfrac{3}{9^x} = 243$ **b.** $2^x \cdot 2^{x+1} = \dfrac{1}{16}$ **c.** $(4^x)^{x+2} = 64$

Problem Solving

EXAMPLE 2 on p. 421 for Exs. 83–84

83. BIOLOGY Look back at Example 2 on page 421. Use the model $S = km^{2/3}$ to approximate the surface area of the mammal given its mass.

a. Bat: 32 grams

b. Human: 59 kilograms

@HomeTutor for problem solving help at classzone.com

84. AIRPLANE VELOCITY The velocity v (in feet per second) of a jet can be approximated by the model

$$v = 8.8\sqrt{\frac{L}{A}}$$

where A is the area of the wings (in square feet) and L is the lift (in Newtons). Find the velocity of a jet with a wing area of 5.5×10^3 square feet and a lift of 1.4×10^7 Newtons.

@HomeTutor for problem solving help at classzone.com

85. PINHOLE CAMERA The optimum diameter d (in millimeters) of the pinhole in a pinhole camera can be modeled by

$$d = 1.9\left[(5.5 \times 10^{-4})\ell\right]^{1/2}$$

where ℓ is the length of the camera box (in millimeters). Find the optimum pinhole diameter for a camera box with a length of 10 centimeters.

86. ★ SHORT RESPONSE Show that the hypotenuse of an isosceles right triangle with legs of length x is $x\sqrt{2}$.

87. STAR MAGNITUDE The *apparent magnitude* of a star is a number that indicates how faint the star is in relation to other stars. The expression $\frac{2.512^{m_1}}{2.512^{m_2}}$ tells how many times fainter a star with magnitude m_1 is than a star with magnitude m_2.

a. How many times fainter is Altair than Vega?

b. How many times fainter is Deneb than Altair?

c. How many times fainter is Deneb than Vega?

Star	Apparent magnitude	Constellation
Vega	0.03	Lyra
Altair	0.77	Aquila
Deneb	1.25	Cygnus

88. PHYSICAL SCIENCE The maximum horizontal distance d that an object can travel when launched at an optimum angle of projection is given by

$$d = \frac{v_0\sqrt{(v_0)^2 + 2gh_0}}{g}$$

where h_0 is the object's initial height, v_0 is its initial speed, and g is the acceleration due to gravity. Simplify the model when $h_0 = 0$.

89. ★ **EXTENDED RESPONSE** You have filled two round balloons with water. One balloon contains twice as much water as the other balloon.

a. Solve the formula for the volume of a sphere, $V = \frac{4}{3}\pi r^3$, for r.

b. Substitute the expression for r from part (a) into the formula for the surface area of a sphere, $S = 4\pi r^2$. Simplify to show that $S = (4\pi)^{1/3}(3V)^{2/3}$.

c. *Compare* the surface areas of the two water balloons using the formula from part (b).

90. **CHALLENGE** Substitute different combinations of odd and even positive integers for m and n in the expression $\sqrt[n]{x^m}$. If x is not always positive, when is absolute value needed in simplifying the expression?

NEW YORK MIXED REVIEW

TEST PRACTICE at classzone.com

91. Which equation best represents a line parallel to the line shown?

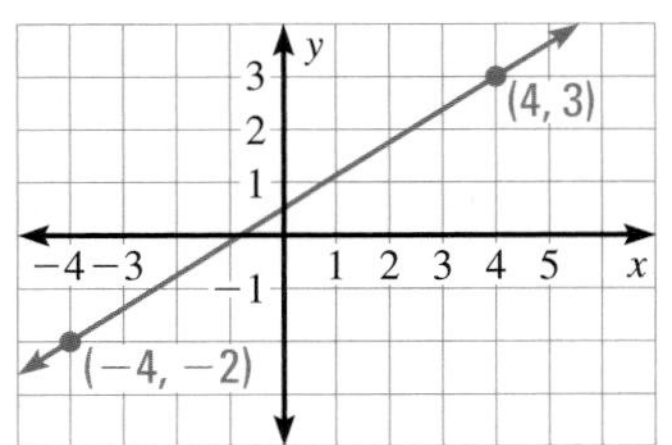

Ⓐ $-5x + 8y = 14$ Ⓑ $-2x + 4y = -3$

Ⓒ $-x - 4y = 14$ Ⓓ $8x + 5y = 20$

92. What is the solution of the inequality $-5 \le -6x + 3 \le 15$?

Ⓐ $-3 \le x \le \frac{1}{3}$ Ⓑ $-2 \le x \le \frac{4}{3}$ Ⓒ $\frac{1}{3} \le x \le -3$ Ⓓ $\frac{4}{3} \le x \le -2$

QUIZ for Lessons 6.1–6.2

Evaluate the expression without using a calculator. *(p. 414)*

1. $36^{3/2}$ 2. $64^{-2/3}$ 3. $-(625^{3/4})$ 4. $(-32)^{2/5}$

Solve the equation. Round your answer to two decimal places when appropriate. *(p. 414)*

5. $x^4 = 20$ 6. $x^5 = -10$ 7. $x^6 + 5 = 26$ 8. $(x + 3)^3 = -16$

Simplify the expression. Assume all variables are positive. *(p. 420)*

9. $\sqrt[4]{32} \cdot \sqrt[4]{8}$ 10. $(\sqrt{10} \cdot \sqrt[3]{10})^8$ 11. $(x^6y^4)^{1/8} + 2(x^{1/3}y^{1/4})^2$

12. $\dfrac{3\sqrt{7^3} + 4\sqrt{7^3}}{\sqrt{7^5}}$ 13. $\dfrac{2\sqrt{x} \cdot \sqrt{x^3}}{\sqrt{64x^{15}}}$ 14. $y^2\sqrt[5]{64x^6} - 6\sqrt[5]{2x^6y^{10}}$

15. 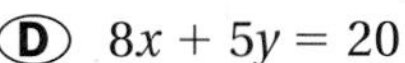 **GEOMETRY** Find a radical expression for the perimeter of the red triangle inscribed in the square shown to the right. Simplify the expression. *(p. 420)*

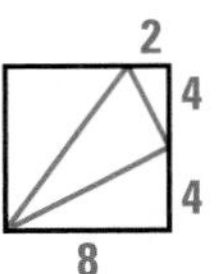

6.3 Perform Function Operations and Composition

A2.A.39 Determine the domain and range of a function from its equation

Before You performed operations with algebraic expressions.

Now You will perform operations with functions.

Why? So you can model biological processes, as in Example 3.

Key Vocabulary
- **power function**
- **composition**

In Chapter 5 you learned how to add, subtract, multiply, and divide polynomial functions. These operations can be defined for any number of functions.

KEY CONCEPT *For Your Notebook*

Operations on Functions

Let f and g be any two functions. A new function h can be defined by performing any of the four basic operations on f and g.

Operation	Definition	Example: $f(x) = 5x$, $g(x) = x + 2$
Addition	$h(x) = f(x) + g(x)$	$h(x) = 5x + (x + 2) = 6x + 2$
Subtraction	$h(x) = f(x) - g(x)$	$h(x) = 5x - (x + 2) = 4x - 2$
Multiplication	$h(x) = f(x) \cdot g(x)$	$h(x) = 5x(x + 2) = 5x^2 + 10x$
Division	$h(x) = \frac{f(x)}{g(x)}$	$h(x) = \frac{5x}{x + 2}$

The domain of h consists of the x-values that are in the domains of both f and g. Additionally, the domain of the quotient does not include x-values for which $g(x) = 0$.

POWER FUNCTIONS So far you have studied several types of functions, including linear functions, quadratic functions, and polynomial functions of higher degree. Another common type of function is a **power function**, which has the form $y = ax^b$ where a is a real number and b is a rational number.

EXAMPLE 1 Add and subtract functions

Let $f(x) = 4x^{1/2}$ and $g(x) = -9x^{1/2}$. Find the following.

a. $f(x) + g(x)$ **b.** $f(x) - g(x)$ **c.** the domains of $f + g$ and $f - g$

Solution

a. $f(x) + g(x) = 4x^{1/2} + (-9x^{1/2}) = [4 + (-9)]x^{1/2} = -5x^{1/2}$

b. $f(x) - g(x) = 4x^{1/2} - (-9x^{1/2}) = [4 - (-9)]x^{1/2} = 13x^{1/2}$

c. The functions f and g each have the same domain: all nonnegative real numbers. So, the domains of $f + g$ and $f - g$ also consist of all nonnegative real numbers.

REVIEW DOMAIN
For help with domains of functions, see p. 72.

EXAMPLE 2 Multiply and divide functions

Let $f(x) = 6x$ and $g(x) = x^{3/4}$. Find the following.

a. $f(x) \cdot g(x)$ **b.** $\frac{f(x)}{g(x)}$ **c.** the domains of $f \cdot g$ and $\frac{f}{g}$

Solution

a. $f(x) \cdot g(x) = (6x)(x^{3/4}) = 6x^{(1 + 3/4)} = 6x^{7/4}$

b. $\frac{f(x)}{g(x)} = \frac{6x}{x^{3/4}} = 6x^{(1 - 3/4)} = 6x^{1/4}$

c. The domain of f consists of all real numbers, and the domain of g consists of all nonnegative real numbers. So, the domain of $f \cdot g$ consists of all nonnegative real numbers. Because $g(0) = 0$, the domain of $\frac{f}{g}$ is restricted to all *positive* real numbers.

EXAMPLE 3 Solve a multi-step problem

RHINOS For a white rhino, heart rate r (in beats per minute) and life span s (in minutes) are related to body mass m (in kilograms) by these functions:

$$r(m) = 241m^{-0.25} \qquad s(m) = (6 \times 10^6)m^{0.2}$$

- Find $r(m) \cdot s(m)$.
- Explain what this product represents.

Solution

STEP 1 **Find** and simplify $r(m) \cdot s(m)$.

$r(m) \cdot s(m) = 241m^{-0.25}[(6 \times 10^6)m^{0.2}]$	Write product of $r(m)$ and $s(m)$.
$= 241(6 \times 10^6)m^{(-0.25 + 0.2)}$	Product of powers property
$= (1446 \times 10^6)m^{-0.05}$	Simplify.
$= (1.446 \times 10^9)m^{-0.05}$	Use scientific notation.

STEP 2 **Interpret** $r(m) \cdot s(m)$.

Multiplying heart rate by life span gives the total number of heartbeats for a white rhino over its entire lifetime.

✓ GUIDED PRACTICE for Examples 1, 2, and 3

Let $f(x) = -2x^{2/3}$ and $g(x) = 7x^{2/3}$. Find the following.

1. $f(x) + g(x)$ **2.** $f(x) - g(x)$ **3.** the domains of $f + g$ and $f - g$

Let $f(x) = 3x$ and $g(x) = x^{1/5}$. Find the following.

4. $f(x) \cdot g(x)$ **5.** $\frac{f(x)}{g(x)}$ **6.** the domains of $f \cdot g$ and $\frac{f}{g}$

7. RHINOS Use the result of Example 3 to find a white rhino's number of heartbeats over its lifetime if its body mass is 1.7×10^5 kilograms.

COMPOSITION OF FUNCTIONS Another operation that can be performed with two functions is *composition*.

READING
As with subtraction and division of functions, you need to be alert to the order of functions when they are composed. In general, $f(g(x))$ is not equal to $g(f(x))$.

KEY CONCEPT — *For Your Notebook*

Composition of Functions

The **composition** of a function g with a function f is:

$$h(x) = g(f(x))$$

The domain of h is the set of all x-values such that x is in the domain of f and $f(x)$ is in the domain of g.

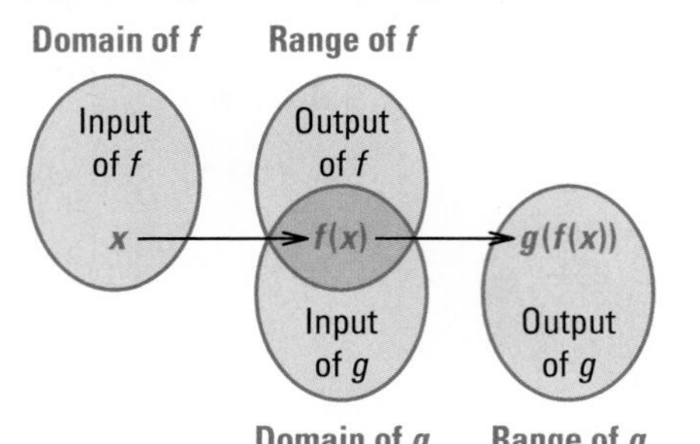

EXAMPLE 4 Standardized Test Practice

Let $f(x) = 2x - 7$ and $g(x) = x^2 + 4$. What is the value of $g(f(3))$?

Ⓐ -5 Ⓑ -3 Ⓒ 3 Ⓓ 5

Solution

To evaluate $g(f(3))$, you first must find $f(3)$.

$$f(3) = 2(3) - 7 = -1$$

Then $g(f(3)) = g(-1) = (-1)^2 + 4 = 1 + 4 = 5$.

So, the value of $g(f(3))$ is 5.

▶ The correct answer is D. Ⓐ Ⓑ Ⓒ Ⓓ

EXAMPLE 5 Find compositions of functions

Let $f(x) = 4x^{-1}$ and $g(x) = 5x - 2$. Find the following.

a. $f(g(x))$ **b.** $g(f(x))$

c. $f(f(x))$ **d.** the domain of each composition

Solution

a. $f(g(x)) = f(5x - 2) = 4(5x - 2)^{-1} = \dfrac{4}{5x - 2}$

b. $g(f(x)) = g(4x^{-1}) = 5(4x^{-1}) - 2 = 20x^{-1} - 2 = \dfrac{20}{x} - 2$

c. $f(f(x)) = f(4x^{-1}) = 4(4x^{-1})^{-1} = 4(4^{-1}x) = 4^0x = x$

d. The domain of $f(g(x))$ consists of all real numbers except $x = \dfrac{2}{5}$ because $g\left(\dfrac{2}{5}\right) = 0$ is not in the domain of f. (Note that $f(0) = \dfrac{4}{0}$, which is undefined.) The domains of $g(f(x))$ and $f(f(x))$ consist of all real numbers except $x = 0$, again because 0 is not in the domain of f.

AVOID ERRORS
You cannot always determine the domain of a composition from its equation. For instance, the domain of $f(f(x)) = x$ appears to be all real numbers, but it is actually all real numbers except zero.

EXAMPLE 6 Solve a multi-step problem

PAINT STORE You have a $10 gift certificate to a paint store. The store is offering 15% off your entire purchase of any paints and painting supplies. You decide to purchase a $30 can of paint and $25 worth of painting supplies.

Use composition of functions to do the following:

- Find the sale price of your purchase when the $10 gift certificate is applied before the 15% discount.
- Find the sale price of your purchase when the 15% discount is applied before the $10 gift certificate.

Solution

STEP 1 **Find** the total amount of your purchase. The total amount for the paint and painting supplies is $\$30 + \$25 = \$55$.

STEP 2 **Write** functions for the discounts. Let x be the regular price, $f(x)$ be the price after the $10 gift certificate is applied, and $g(x)$ be the price after the 15% discount is applied.

Function for $10 gift certificate: $f(x) = x - 10$

Function for 15% discount: $g(x) = x - 0.15x = 0.85x$

STEP 3 **Compose** the functions.

The composition $g(f(x))$ represents the sale price when the $10 gift certificate is applied before the 15% discount.

$g(f(x)) = g(x - 10) = 0.85(x - 10)$

The composition $f(g(x))$ represents the sale price when the 15% discount is applied before the $10 gift certificate.

$f(g(x)) = f(0.85x) = 0.85x - 10$

STEP 4 **Evaluate** the functions $g(f(x))$ and $f(g(x))$ when $x = 55$.

$g(f(55)) = 0.85(55 - 10) = 0.85(45) = \$38.25$

$f(g(55)) = 0.85(55) - 10 = 46.75 - 10 = \$36.75$

▶ The sale price is $38.25 when the $10 gift certificate is applied before the 15% discount. The sale price is $36.75 when the 15% discount is applied before the $10 gift certificate.

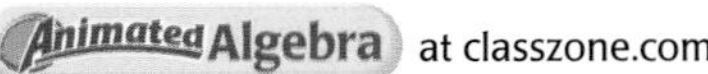

✓ GUIDED PRACTICE for Examples 4, 5, and 6

Let $f(x) = 3x - 8$ and $g(x) = 2x^2$. Find the following.

8. $g(f(5))$ **9.** $f(g(5))$ **10.** $f(f(5))$ **11.** $g(g(5))$

12. Let $f(x) = 2x^{-1}$ and $g(x) = 2x + 7$. Find $f(g(x))$, $g(f(x))$, and $f(f(x))$. Then state the domain of each composition.

13. WHAT IF? In Example 6, how do your answers change if the gift certificate to the paint store is $15 and the store discount is 20%?

6.3 EXERCISES

HOMEWORK KEY

○ = **WORKED-OUT SOLUTIONS** on p. WS12 for Exs. 3, 13, and 45

★ = **STANDARDIZED TEST PRACTICE** Exs. 2, 11, 38, 39, and 44

◆ = **MULTIPLE REPRESENTATIONS** Ex. 46

SKILL PRACTICE

1. **VOCABULARY** Copy and complete: The function $h(x) = g(f(x))$ is called the _?_ of the function g with the function f.

2. ★ **WRITING** Tell whether the sum of two power functions is *sometimes*, *always*, or *never* a power function. *Explain* your reasoning.

EXAMPLE 1 on p. 428 for Exs. 3–11

ADD AND SUBTRACT FUNCTIONS **Let $f(x) = -3x^{1/3} + 4x^{1/2}$ and $g(x) = 5x^{1/3} + 4x^{1/2}$. Perform the indicated operation and state the domain.**

3. $f(x) + g(x)$
4. $g(x) + f(x)$
5. $f(x) + f(x)$
6. $g(x) + g(x)$
7. $f(x) - g(x)$
8. $g(x) - f(x)$
9. $f(x) - f(x)$
10. $g(x) - g(x)$

11. ★ **MULTIPLE CHOICE** What is $f(x) + g(x)$ if $f(x) = -7x^{2/3} - 1$ and $g(x) = 2x^{2/3} + 6$?

(A) $5x^{2/3} - 5$ (B) $-5x^{2/3} + 5$ (C) $9x^{2/3} + 7$ (D) $-9x^{2/3} - 7$

EXAMPLE 2 on p. 429 for Exs. 12–19

MULTIPLY AND DIVIDE FUNCTIONS **Let $f(x) = 4x^{2/3}$ and $g(x) = 5x^{1/2}$. Perform the indicated operation and state the domain.**

12. $f(x) \cdot g(x)$
13. $g(x) \cdot f(x)$
14. $f(x) \cdot f(x)$
15. $g(x) \cdot g(x)$
16. $\frac{f(x)}{g(x)}$
17. $\frac{g(x)}{f(x)}$
18. $\frac{f(x)}{f(x)}$
19. $\frac{g(x)}{g(x)}$

EXAMPLE 4 on p. 430 for Exs. 20–27

EVALUATE COMPOSITIONS OF FUNCTIONS **Let $f(x) = 3x + 2$, $g(x) = -x^2$, and $h(x) = \frac{x-2}{5}$. Find the indicated value.**

20. $f(g(-3))$
21. $g(f(2))$
22. $h(f(-9))$
23. $g(h(8))$
24. $h(g(5))$
25. $f(f(7))$
26. $h(h(-4))$
27. $g(g(-5))$

EXAMPLE 5 on p. 430 for Exs. 28–38

FIND COMPOSITIONS OF FUNCTIONS **Let $f(x) = 3x^{-1}$, $g(x) = 2x - 7$, and $h(x) = \frac{x+4}{3}$. Perform the indicated operation and state the domain.**

28. $f(g(x))$
29. $g(f(x))$
30. $h(f(x))$
31. $g(h(x))$
32. $h(g(x))$
33. $f(f(x))$
34. $h(h(x))$
35. $g(g(x))$

ERROR ANALYSIS **Let $f(x) = x^2 - 3$ and $g(x) = 4x$. *Describe* and correct the error in the composition.**

36.
$f(g(x)) = f(4x)$
$= (x^2 - 3)(4x)$
$= 4x^3 - 12x$

37.
$g(f(x)) = g(x^2 - 3)$
$= 4x^2 - 3$

38. ★ **MULTIPLE CHOICE** What is $g(f(x))$ if $f(x) = 7x^2$ and $g(x) = 3x^{-2}$?

Ⓐ $\frac{3}{49x^4}$ Ⓑ 21 Ⓒ $21x^4$ Ⓓ $\frac{7}{9x^4}$

39. ★ **OPEN-ENDED MATH** Find two different functions f and g such that $f(g(x)) = g(f(x))$.

CHALLENGE **Find functions f and g such that $f(g(x)) = h(x)$, $g(x) \neq x$, and $f(x) \neq x$.**

40. $h(x) = \sqrt[3]{x + 2}$

41. $h(x) = \frac{4}{3x^2 + 7}$

42. $h(x) = |2x + 9|$

PROBLEM SOLVING

EXAMPLE 3 on p. 429 for Exs. 43, 46

43. **BIOLOGY** For a mammal that weighs w grams, the volume b (in milliliters) of air breathed in and the volume d (in milliliters) of "dead space" (the portion of the lungs not filled with air) can be modeled by:

$$b(w) = 0.007w \qquad d(w) = 0.002w$$

The breathing rate r (in breaths per minute) of a mammal that weighs w grams can be modeled by:

$$r(w) = \frac{1.1w^{0.734}}{b(w) - d(w)}$$

Simplify $r(w)$ and calculate the breathing rate for body weights of 6.5 grams, 300 grams, and 70,000 grams.

@HomeTutor for problem solving help at classzone.com

EXAMPLE 6 on p. 431 for Exs. 44–45

44. ★ **SHORT RESPONSE** The cost (in dollars) of producing x sneakers in a factory is given by $C(x) = 60x + 750$. The number of sneakers produced in t hours is given by $x(t) = 50t$. Find $C(x(t))$. Evaluate $C(x(5))$ and explain what this number represents.

@HomeTutor for problem solving help at classzone.com

45. **MULTI-STEP PROBLEM** An online movie store is having a sale. You decide to open a charge account and buy four DVDs.

a. Use composition of functions to find the sale price of $85 worth of DVDs when the $15 discount is applied before the 10% discount.

b. Use composition of functions to find the sale price of $85 worth of DVDs when the 10% discount is applied before the $15 discount.

c. Which order of discounts gives you a better deal? *Explain.*

46. **MULTIPLE REPRESENTATIONS** A mathematician at a lake throws a tennis ball from point A along the water's edge to point B in the water, as shown. His dog, Elvis, first runs along the beach from point A to point D and then swims to fetch the ball at point B.

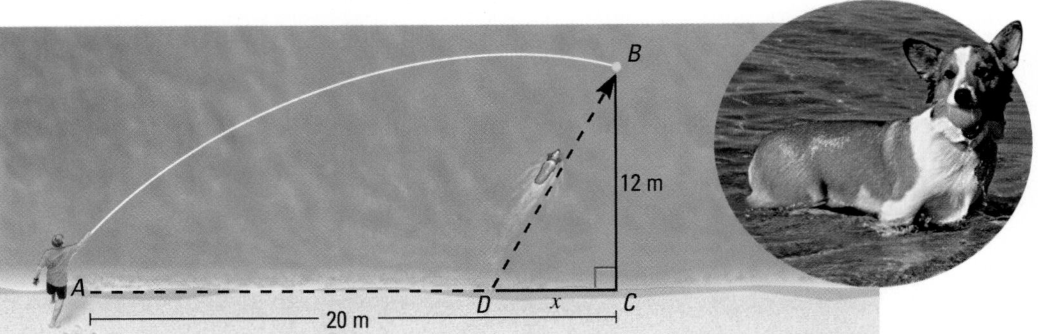

a. **Using a Diagram** Elvis's running speed is about 6.4 meters per second. Write a function $r(x)$ for the time he spends running from point A to point D. Elvis's swimming speed is about 0.9 meter per second. Write a function $s(x)$ for the time he spends swimming from point D to point B.

b. **Writing a Function** Write a function $t(x)$ that represents the total time Elvis spends traveling from point A to point D to point B.

c. **Using a Graph** Use a graphing calculator to graph $t(x)$. Find the value of x that minimizes $t(x)$. *Explain* the meaning of this value.

47. **CHALLENGE** To approximate the square root of a number n, the Babylonians used a method that involves starting with an initial guess x and calculating a sequence of values that approaches the exact answer. Their method was based on the function shown at the right.

$$f(x) = \frac{x + \frac{n}{x}}{2}$$

a. Let $n = 2$, and choose $x = 1$ as an initial guess for $\sqrt{n} = \sqrt{2}$. Calculate $f(x)$, $f(f(x))$, $f(f(f(x)))$, and $f(f(f(f(x))))$.

b. How many times do you need to compose the function in order for the result to approximate $\sqrt{2}$ to three decimal places? six decimal places?

NEW YORK MIXED REVIEW

TEST PRACTICE at classzone.com

48. Which expression is equivalent to $(6x^3y^5z^{-1})(-3x^{-4}y^2)$?

Ⓐ $-\frac{18y^{10}}{x^{12}z}$ Ⓑ $-\frac{18z}{x^7y^3}$ Ⓒ $-\frac{18y^7}{xz}$ Ⓓ $-\frac{y^7}{18xz}$

49. In a high school marching band, 68% of the members are underclassmen. The rest of the members of the marching band are seniors. Which equation best represents the number of seniors, s, in the band in terms of the total number of students, t, in the band?

Ⓐ $s = \frac{8}{17}t$ Ⓑ $s = \frac{8}{25}t$

Ⓒ $s = \frac{17}{8}t$ Ⓓ $s = \frac{25}{8}t$

Graphing Calculator **ACTIVITY** *Use after Lesson 6.3*

@HomeTutor
classzone.com
Keystrokes

6.3 Use Operations with Functions

QUESTION How can you use a graphing calculator to perform operations with functions?

EXAMPLE Perform function operations

Let $f(x) = x^2 - 3x + 6$ and $g(x) = x - 4$. Find $f(4) + g(4)$ and $f(g(-2))$.

STEP 1 *Form sum*

Enter $y_1 = x^2 - 3x + 6$ and $y_2 = x - 4$. The sum can be entered as $y_3 = y_1 + y_2$. To do so, press VARS, choose the Y-Vars menu, and select Function.

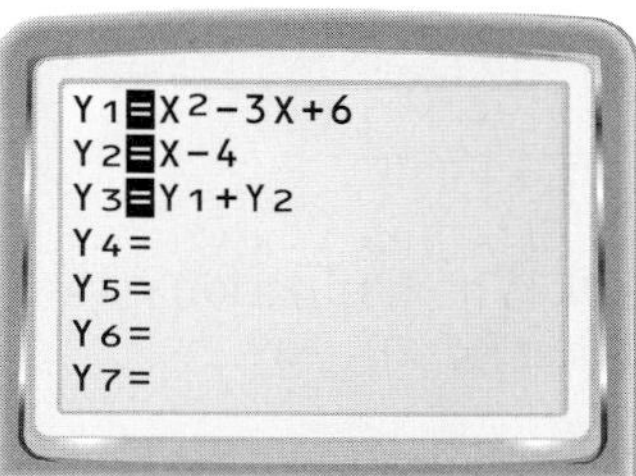

STEP 2 *Evaluate sum*

On the home screen, enter $y_3(4)$ and press ENTER. The screen shows that $y_3(4) = 10$, so $f(4) + g(4) = 10$.

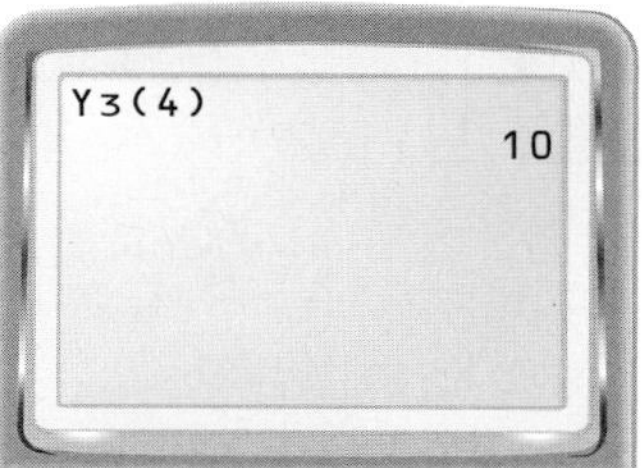

STEP 3 *Form composition*

The composition $f(g(x))$ can be entered as $y_3 = y_1(y_2)$.

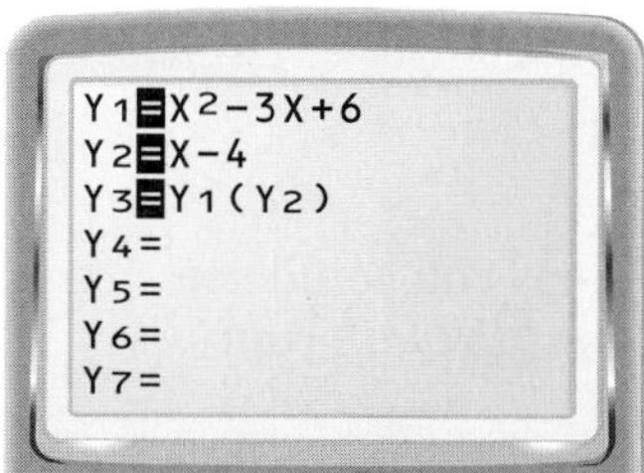

STEP 4 *Evaluate composition*

On the home screen, enter $y_3(-2)$ and press ENTER. The screen shows that $y_3(-2) = 60$, so $f(g(-2)) = 60$.

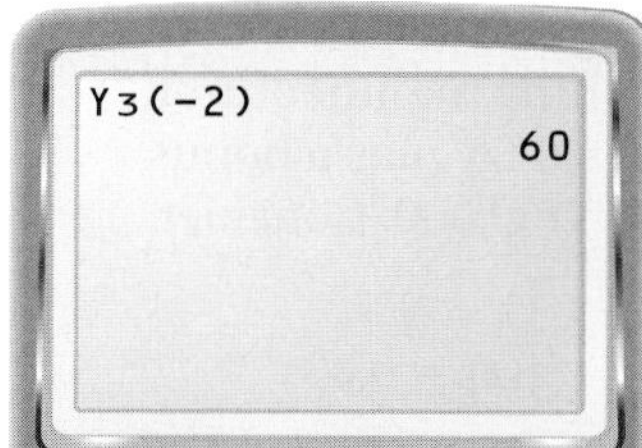

PRACTICE

Use a graphing calculator and the functions f and g to find the indicated value.

1. $f(x) = x^3 + 5x - 3$, $g(x) = -3x^2 - x$: $g(7) + f(7)$

2. $f(x) = x^{1/3}$, $g(x) = 9x$: $\frac{f(-8)}{g(-8)}$

3. $f(x) = 5x^3 - 3x^2$, $g(x) = -2x^2 - 5$: $g(2) - f(2)$

4. $f(x) = 2x^2 + 7x - 2$, $g(x) = x - 6$: $f(g(5))$

Lessons 6.1–6.3

1. **BOWLING** The formula for the volume V of a sphere in terms of its surface area S is $V = 3^{-1}(4\pi)^{-1/2}(S^3)^{1/2}$. A candlepin bowling ball has a surface area of about 79 square inches. What is its volume to the nearest cubic inch?

   (1) 66 in.^{3} (3) 368 in.^{3}

   (2) 184 in.^{3} (4) 594 in.^{3}

2. **AREA OF SHADED REGION** A triangle is inscribed in a square, as shown. Which function $r(x)$ represents the area of the shaded region?

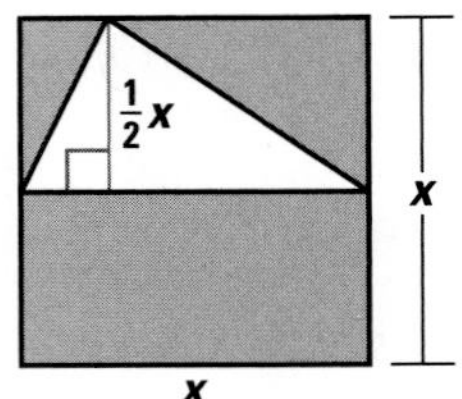

   (1) $r(x) = \frac{3}{4}x$

   (2) $r(x) = \frac{1}{4}x^2$

   (3) $r(x) = \frac{3}{4}x^2$

   (4) $r(x) = \frac{1}{2}x^4$

3. **SALARY** You are working as a sales representative for a clothing manufacturer. You are paid an annual salary plus a bonus of 3% of your sales over \$100,000. Consider these two functions:

   $f(x) = x - 100{,}000 \qquad g(x) = 0.03x$

   Which expression represents your bonus when $x > 100{,}000$?

   (1) $f(x) \cdot g(x)$

   (2) $\frac{f(x)}{g(x)}$

   (3) $f(g(x))$

   (4) $g(f(x))$

4. **SWIMMING POOL** A cylindrical above-ground pool has a height of 5 feet and a radius of x feet. You use a hose to fill the pool with water. Water flows from the hose at a rate of 128 cubic feet per hour. After 8.8 hours, the pool is half full. What is the radius of the pool to the nearest foot? Use 3.14 for π.

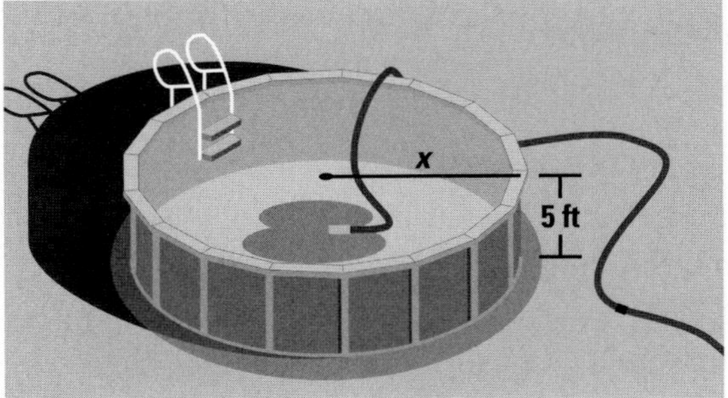

   (1) 6 feet (3) 12 feet

   (2) 7 feet (4) 24 feet

5. **FUNCTION COMPOSITION** Which function $f(x)$ satisfies the condition that $f(f(x)) = x$?

   (1) $f(x) = 3x^{-2}$

   (2) $f(x) = x + 3$

   (3) $f(x) = 5 - x$

   (4) $f(x) = x^{1/2}$

6. **OPEN-ENDED** *Describe* the steps you would use to simplify this expression:

   $$\left(\frac{16^{1/2}}{4^{1/2}}\right)^5?$$

   Is there another set of steps you could use to simplify the expression? *Explain* your reasoning.

7. **OPEN-ENDED** The volume of a sphere is 900 cubic inches. Use the formula for the volume of a sphere, $V = \frac{4}{3}\pi r^3$, to find the radius r of the sphere to the nearest hundredth of an inch. Use 3.14 for π.

   What happens to the volume when the radius is doubled?

6.4 Exploring Inverse Functions

MATERIALS • graph paper • straightedge

QUESTION How are a function and its *inverse* related?

EXPLORE Find the inverse of $f(x) = \frac{x-3}{2}$

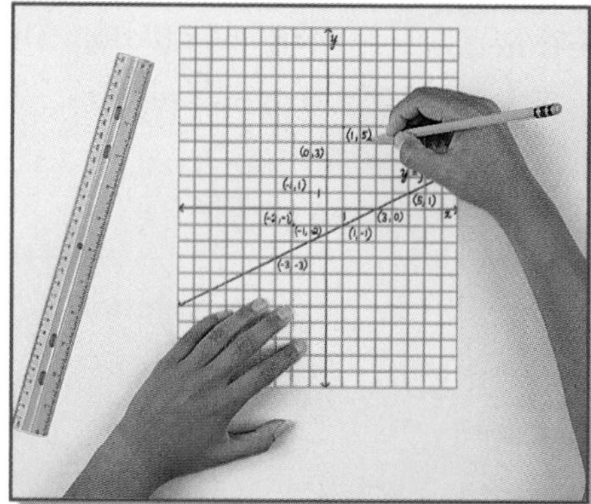

STEP 1 ***Graph function*** Choose values of x and find the corresponding values of $y = f(x)$. Plot the points and draw the line that passes through them.

STEP 2 ***Interchange coordinates*** Interchange the x- and y-coordinates of the ordered pairs found in Step 1. Plot the new points and draw the line that passes through them.

STEP 3 ***Write equation*** Write an equation of the line from Step 2. Call this function g.

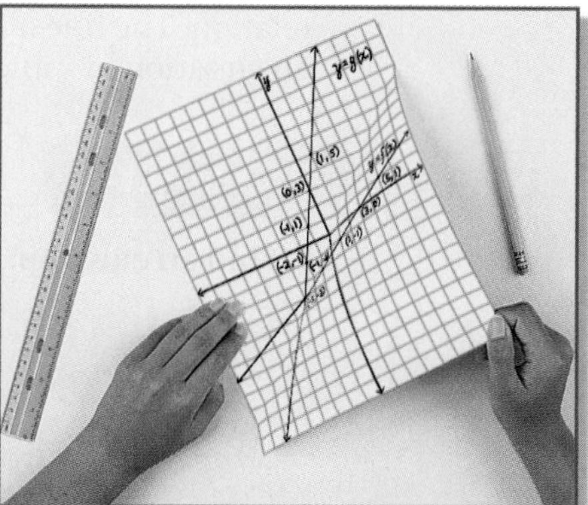

STEP 4 ***Compare graphs*** Fold your graph paper so that the graphs of f and g coincide. How are the graphs geometrically related?

STEP 5 ***Describe functions*** In words, f is the function that subtracts 3 from x and then divides the result by 2. Describe the function g in words.

STEP 6 ***Find compositions*** Predict what the compositions $f(g(x))$ and $g(f(x))$ will be. Confirm your predictions by finding $f(g(x))$ and $g(f(x))$.

The functions f and g are called *inverses* of each other.

DRAW CONCLUSIONS Use your observations to complete these exercises

Complete Exercises 1–3 for each function below.

$f(x) = 3x + 2$ $\qquad$ $f(x) = \frac{x-1}{6}$ $\qquad$ $f(x) = 4 - \frac{3}{2}x$

1. Complete Steps 1–3 above to find the inverse of the function.
2. Complete Step 4. How can you graph the inverse of a function without first finding ordered pairs (x, y)?
3. Complete Steps 5 and 6. How can you test to see if the function you found in Exercise 1 is indeed the inverse of the original function?

6.4 Use Inverse Functions

 **A2.A.44** Define the inverse of a function

Before You performed operations with functions.

Now You will find inverse functions.

Why? So you can convert temperatures, as in Ex. 48.

Key Vocabulary
- **inverse relation**
- **inverse function**

In Lesson 2.1, you learned that a relation is a pairing of input values with output values. An **inverse relation** interchanges the input and output values of the original relation. This means that the domain and range are also interchanged.

Original relation

x	0	1	2	3	4
y	6	4	2	0	−2

Inverse relation

x	6	4	2	0	−2
y	0	1	2	3	4

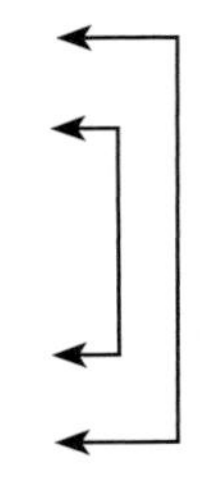

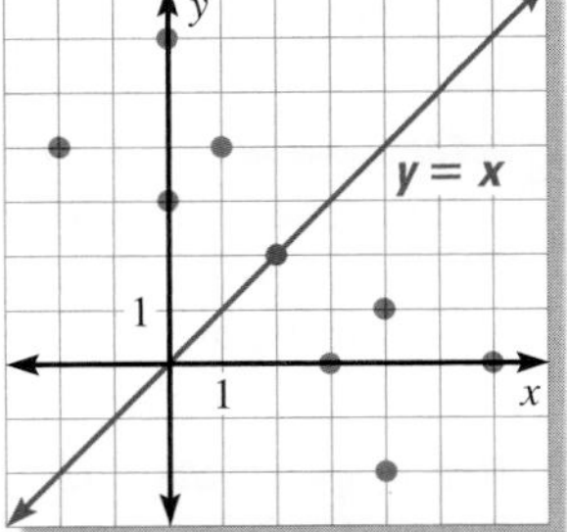

The graph of an inverse relation is a *reflection* of the graph of the original relation. The line of reflection is $y = x$. To find the inverse of a relation given by an equation in x and y, switch the roles of x and y and solve for y.

EXAMPLE 1 Find an inverse relation

Find an equation for the inverse of the relation $y = 3x - 5$.

$y = 3x - 5$	**Write original relation.**
$x = 3y - 5$	**Switch x and y.**
$x + 5 = 3y$	**Add 5 to each side.**
$\frac{1}{3}x + \frac{5}{3} = y$	**Solve for y. This is the inverse relation.**

In Example 1, both the original relation and the inverse relation happen to be functions. In such cases, the two functions are called **inverse functions**.

READING
The symbol −1 in f^{-1} is not to be interpreted as an exponent. In other words, $f^{-1}(x) \neq \frac{1}{f(x)}$.

KEY CONCEPT *For Your Notebook*

Inverse Functions

Functions f and g are inverses of each other provided:

$$f(g(x)) = x \quad \text{and} \quad g(f(x)) = x$$

The function g is denoted by f^{-1}, read as "f inverse."

EXAMPLE 2 Verify that functions are inverses

Verify that $f(x) = 3x - 5$ and $f^{-1}(x) = \frac{1}{3}x + \frac{5}{3}$ are inverse functions.

Solution

STEP 1 **Show** that $f(f^{-1}(x)) = x$.

$$f(f^{-1}(x)) = f\left(\frac{1}{3}x + \frac{5}{3}\right)$$
$$= 3\left(\frac{1}{3}x + \frac{5}{3}\right) - 5$$
$$= x + 5 - 5$$
$$= x \checkmark$$

STEP 2 **Show** that $f^{-1}(f(x)) = x$.

$$f^{-1}(f(x)) = f^{-1}(3x - 5)$$
$$= \frac{1}{3}(3x - 5) + \frac{5}{3}$$
$$= x - \frac{5}{3} + \frac{5}{3}$$
$$= x \checkmark$$

EXAMPLE 3 Solve a multi-step problem

FITNESS Elastic bands can be used in exercising to provide a range of resistance. A band's resistance R (in pounds) can be modeled by $R = \frac{3}{8}L - 5$ where L is the total length of the stretched band (in inches).

- Find the inverse of the model.
- Use the inverse function to find the length at which the band provides 19 pounds of resistance.

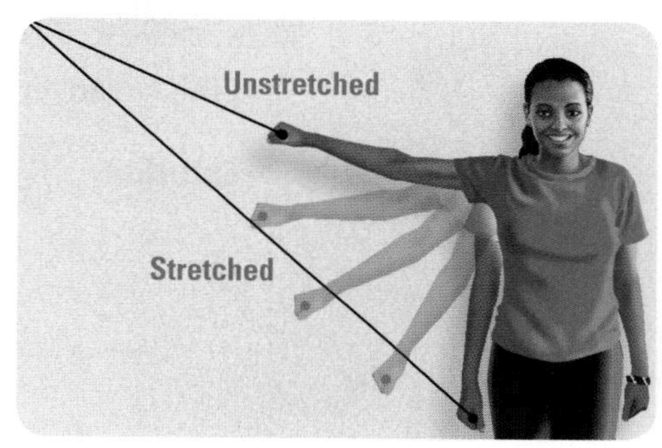

Solution

FIND INVERSES
Notice that you do not switch the variables when you are finding inverses of models. This would be confusing because the letters are chosen to remind you of the real-life quantities they represent.

STEP 1 **Find** the inverse function.

$$R = \frac{3}{8}L - 5 \quad \text{Write original model.}$$
$$R + 5 = \frac{3}{8}L \quad \text{Add 5 to each side.}$$
$$\frac{8}{3}R + \frac{40}{3} = L \quad \text{Multiply each side by } \frac{8}{3}.$$

STEP 2 **Evaluate** the inverse function when $R = 19$.

$$L = \frac{8}{3}R + \frac{40}{3} = \frac{8}{3}(19) + \frac{40}{3} = \frac{152}{3} + \frac{40}{3} = \frac{192}{3} = 64$$

▶ The band provides 19 pounds of resistance when it is stretched to 64 inches.

✓ GUIDED PRACTICE for Examples 1, 2, and 3

Find the inverse of the given function. Then verify that your result and the original function are inverses.

1. $f(x) = x + 4$
2. $f(x) = 2x - 1$
3. $f(x) = -3x + 1$
4. **FITNESS** Use the inverse function in Example 3 to find the length at which the band provides 13 pounds of resistance.

INVERSES OF NONLINEAR FUNCTIONS The graphs of the power functions $f(x) = x^2$ and $g(x) = x^3$ are shown below along with their reflections in the line $y = x$. Notice that the inverse of $g(x) = x^3$ is a function, but that the inverse of $f(x) = x^2$ is *not* a function.

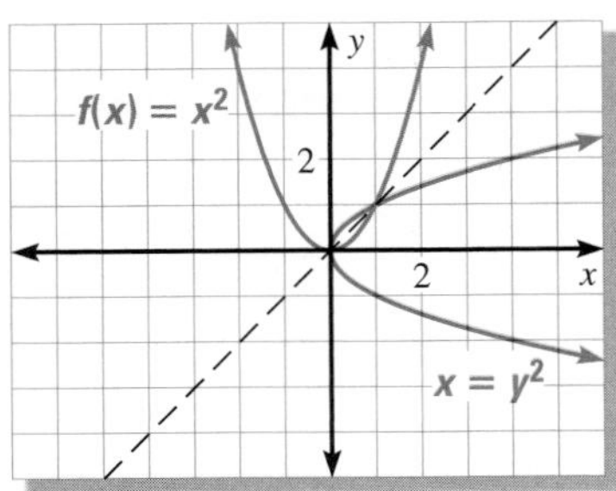

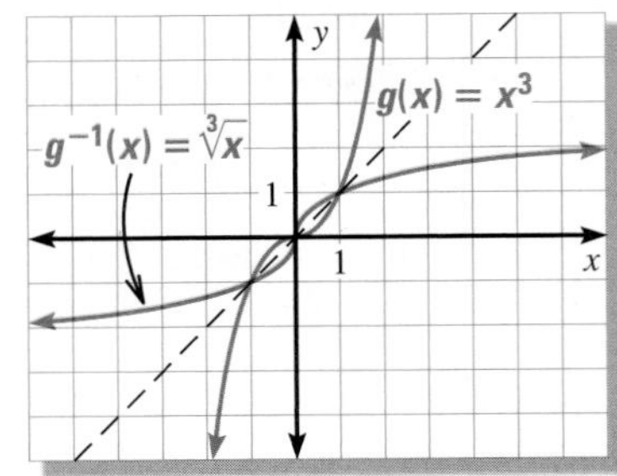

If the domain of $f(x) = x^2$ is *restricted* to only nonnegative real numbers, then the inverse of f *is* a function.

EXAMPLE 4 Find the inverse of a power function

Find the inverse of $f(x) = x^2, x \geq 0$. Then graph f and f^{-1}.

Solution

$f(x) = x^2$	**Write original function.**
$y = x^2$	**Replace $f(x)$ with y.**
$x = y^2$	**Switch x and y.**
$\pm\sqrt{x} = y$	**Take square roots of each side.**

The domain of f is restricted to nonnegative values of x. So, the range of f^{-1} must also be restricted to nonnegative values, and therefore the inverse is $f^{-1}(x) = \sqrt{x}$. (If the domain was restricted to $x \leq 0$, you would choose $f^{-1}(x) = -\sqrt{x}$.)

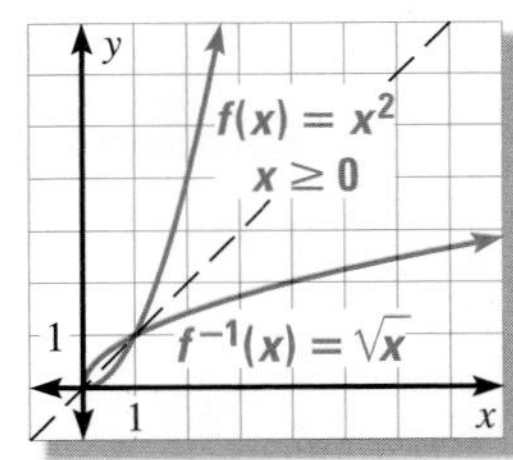

CHECK SOLUTION
You can check the solution of Example 4 by noting that the graph of $f^{-1}(x) = \sqrt{x}$ is the reflection of the graph of $f(x) = x^2, x \geq 0$, in the line $y = x$.

HORIZONTAL LINE TEST You can use the graph of a function f to determine whether the inverse of f is a function by applying the *horizontal line test*.

KEY CONCEPT — *For Your Notebook*

Horizontal Line Test

The inverse of a function f is also a function if and only if no horizontal line intersects the graph of f more than once.

Inverse is a function

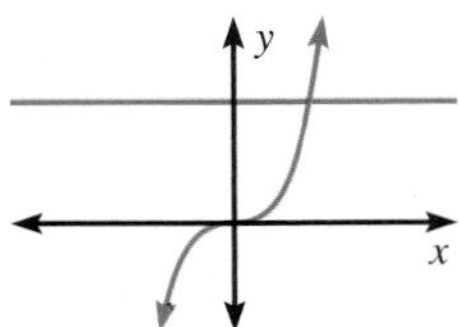

Inverse is not a function

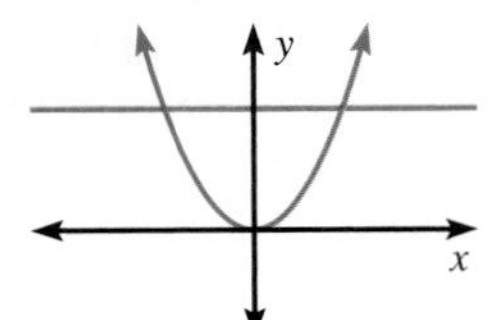

EXAMPLE 5 Find the inverse of a cubic function

Consider the function $f(x) = 2x^3 + 1$. Determine whether the inverse of f is a function. Then find the inverse.

Solution

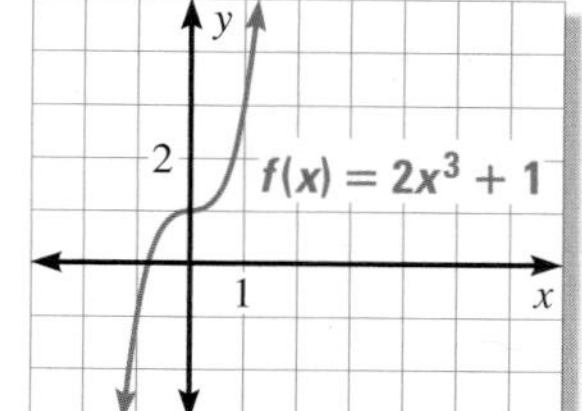

Graph the function f. Notice that no horizontal line intersects the graph more than once. So, the inverse of f is itself a function. To find an equation for f^{-1}, complete the following steps:

$f(x) = 2x^3 + 1$	**Write original function.**
$y = 2x^3 + 1$	**Replace $f(x)$ with y.**
$x = 2y^3 + 1$	**Switch x and y.**
$x - 1 = 2y^3$	**Subtract 1 from each side.**
$\frac{x-1}{2} = y^3$	**Divide each side by 2.**
$\sqrt[3]{\frac{x-1}{2}} = y$	**Take cube root of each side.**

▸ The inverse of f is $f^{-1}(x) = \sqrt[3]{\frac{x-1}{2}}$.

✓ GUIDED PRACTICE for Examples 4 and 5

Find the inverse of the function. Then graph the function and its inverse.

5. $f(x) = x^6, x \geq 0$
6. $g(x) = \frac{1}{27}x^3$
7. $f(x) = -\frac{64}{125}x^3$
8. $f(x) = -x^3 + 4$
9. $f(x) = 2x^5 + 3$
10. $g(x) = -7x^5 + 7$

EXAMPLE 6 Find the inverse of a power model

TICKET PRICES The average price P (in dollars) for a National Football League ticket can be modeled by

$$P = 35t^{0.192}$$

where t is the number of years since 1995. Find the inverse model that gives time as a function of the average ticket price.

Solution

$P = 35t^{0.192}$	**Write original model.**
$\frac{P}{35} = t^{0.192}$	**Divide each side by 35.**
$\left(\frac{P}{35}\right)^{1/0.192} = \left(t^{0.192}\right)^{1/0.192}$	**Raise each side to the power $\frac{1}{0.192}$.**
$\left(\frac{P}{35}\right)^{5.2} \approx t$	**Simplify. This is the inverse model.**

EXAMPLE 7 Use an inverse power model to make a prediction

Use the inverse power model from Example 6 to predict the year when the average ticket price will reach \$58.

Solution

$t = \left(\frac{P}{35}\right)^{5.2}$ **Write inverse power model.**

$= \left(\frac{58}{35}\right)^{5.2}$ **Substitute 58 for *P*.**

≈ 14 **Use a calculator.**

▶ You can predict that the average ticket price will reach \$58 about 14 years after 1995, or in 2009.

GUIDED PRACTICE for Examples 6 and 7

11. **TICKET PRICES** The average price P (in dollars) for a Major League Baseball ticket can be modeled by $P = 10.7t^{0.272}$ where t is the number of years since 1995. Write the inverse model. Then use the inverse to predict the year when the average ticket price will reach \$25.

6.4 EXERCISES

HOMEWORK KEY

○ = **WORKED-OUT SOLUTIONS** on p. WS12 for Exs. 7, 15, and 49

★ = **STANDARDIZED TEST PRACTICE** Exs. 2, 14, 21, 28, and 48

SKILL PRACTICE

1. **VOCABULARY** State the definition of an inverse relation.

2. ★ **WRITING** *Explain* how to determine whether a function g is an inverse of f.

EXAMPLE 1 on p. 438 for Exs. 3–13

INVERSE RELATIONS Find an equation for the inverse relation.

3. $y = 4x - 1$
4. $y = -2x + 5$
5. $y = 7x - 6$
6. $y = 10x - 28$
7. $y = 12x + 7$
8. $y = -18x - 5$
9. $y = 5x + \frac{1}{3}$
10. $y = -\frac{2}{3}x + 2$
11. $y = -\frac{3}{5}x + \frac{7}{5}$

ERROR ANALYSIS *Describe* and correct the error in finding the inverse of the relation.

12.

$y = 6x - 11$

$x = 6y - 11$

$x + 11 = 6y$

$\frac{x}{6} + 11 = y$

13.

$y = -x + 3$

$-x = y + 3$

$-x - 3 = y$

14. ★ **OPEN-ENDED MATH** Write a function f such that the graph of f^{-1} is a line with a slope of 3.

EXAMPLE 2 on p. 439 for Exs. 15–21

VERIFYING INVERSE FUNCTIONS **Verify that f and g are inverse functions.**

15. $f(x) = x + 4, g(x) = x - 4$

16. $f(x) = 2x + 3, g(x) = \frac{1}{2}x - \frac{3}{2}$

17. $f(x) = \frac{1}{4}x^3, g(x) = (4x)^{1/3}$

18. $f(x) = \frac{1}{5}x - 1, g(x) = 5x + 5$

19. $f(x) = 4x + 9, g(x) = \frac{1}{4}x - \frac{9}{4}$

20. $f(x) = 5x^2 - 2, x \geq 0; g(x) = \left(\frac{x+2}{5}\right)^{1/2}$

21. ★ **MULTIPLE CHOICE** What is the inverse of the function whose graph is shown?

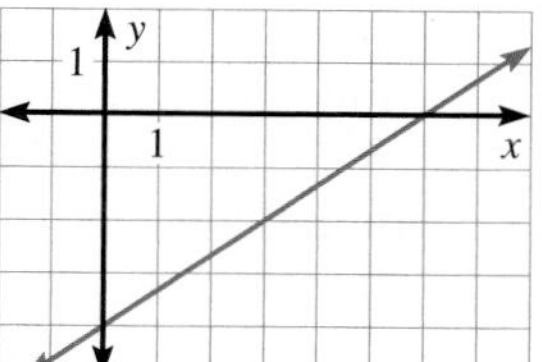

Ⓐ $g(x) = \frac{3}{2}x - 6$ Ⓑ $g(x) = \frac{3}{2}x + 6$

Ⓒ $g(x) = \frac{2}{3}x - 6$ Ⓓ $g(x) = \frac{3}{2}x + 12$

EXAMPLE 4 on p. 440 for Exs. 22–28

INVERSES OF POWER FUNCTIONS **Find the inverse of the power function.**

22. $f(x) = x^7$

23. $f(x) = 4x^4, x \geq 0$

24. $f(x) = -10x^6, x \leq 0$

25. $f(x) = 32x^5$

26. $f(x) = -\frac{2}{5}x^3$

27. $f(x) = \frac{16}{25}x^2, x \leq 0$

28. ★ **MULTIPLE CHOICE** What is the inverse of $f(x) = -\frac{1}{64}x^3$?

Ⓐ $g(x) = -4x^3$ Ⓑ $g(x) = 4\sqrt[3]{x}$ Ⓒ $g(x) = -4\sqrt[3]{x}$ Ⓓ $g(x) = \sqrt[3]{-4x}$

EXAMPLE 5 on p. 441 for Exs. 29–43

HORIZONTAL LINE TEST **Graph the function f. Then use the graph to determine whether the inverse of f is a function.**

29. $f(x) = 3x + 1$

30. $f(x) = -x - 5$

31. $f(x) = \frac{1}{4}x^2 - 1$

32. $f(x) = -6x^2, x \geq 0$

33. $f(x) = \frac{1}{3}x^3$

34. $f(x) = x^3 - 2$

35. $f(x) = (x - 4)(x + 1)$

36. $f(x) = |x| + 4$

37. $f(x) = 4x^4 - 5x^2 - 6$

INVERSES OF NONLINEAR FUNCTIONS **Find the inverse of the function.**

38. $f(x) = \frac{3}{2}x^4, x \geq 0$

39. $f(x) = x^3 - 2$

40. $f(x) = \frac{3}{4}x^5 + 5$

41. $f(x) = -\frac{2}{5}x^6 + 8, x \leq 0$

42. $f(x) = \frac{2x^3 - 6}{9}$

43. $f(x) = x^4 - 9, x \geq 0$

44. **REASONING** Determine whether the statement is *true* or *false*. *Explain* your reasoning.

   a. If $f(x) = x^n$ where n is a positive even integer, then the inverse of f is a function.

   b. If $f(x) = x^n$ where n is a positive odd integer, then the inverse of f is a function.

45. **CHALLENGE** Show that the inverse of any linear function $f(x) = mx + b$, where $m \neq 0$, is also a linear function. Give the slope and y-intercept of the graph of f^{-1} in terms of m and b.

PROBLEM SOLVING

EXAMPLE 3 on p. 439 for Exs. 46–48

46. EXCHANGE RATES The *euro* is the unit of currency for the European Union. On a certain day, the number E of euros that could be obtained for D dollars was given by this function:

$$E = 0.81419D$$

Find the inverse of the function. Then use the inverse to find the number of dollars that could be obtained for 250 euros on that day.

@HomeTutor for problem solving help at classzone.com

47. MULTI-STEP PROBLEM When calibrating a spring scale, you need to know how far the spring stretches for various weights. Hooke's law states that the length a spring stretches is proportional to the weight attached to it. A model for one scale is $\ell = 0.5w + 3$ where ℓ is the total length (in inches) of the stretched spring and w is the weight (in pounds) of the object.

a. Find the inverse of the given model.

b. If you place a weight on the scale and the spring stretches to a total length of 6.5 inches, how heavy is the weight?

@HomeTutor for problem solving help at classzone.com

48. ★ EXTENDED RESPONSE At the start of a dog sled race in Anchorage, Alaska, the temperature was 5°C. By the end of the race, the temperature was −10°C. The formula for converting temperatures from degrees Fahrenheit F to degrees Celsius C is $C = \frac{5}{9}(F - 32)$.

a. Find the inverse of the given model. *Describe* what information you can obtain from the inverse.

b. Find the Fahrenheit temperatures at the start and end of the race.

c. Use a graphing calculator to graph the original function and its inverse. Find the temperature that is the same on both temperature scales.

EXAMPLES 6 and 7 on pp. 441–442 for Exs. 49–50

49. BOAT SPEED The maximum hull speed v (in knots) of a boat with a displacement hull can be approximated by

$$v = 1.34\sqrt{\ell}$$

where ℓ is the length (in feet) of the boat's waterline. Find the inverse of the model. Then find the waterline length needed to achieve a maximum speed of 7.5 knots.

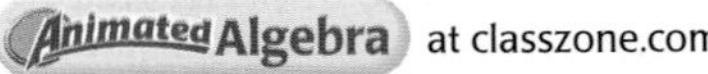

at classzone.com

50. BIOLOGY The body surface area A (in square meters) of a person with a mass of 60 kilograms can be approximated by the model

$$A = 0.2195h^{0.3964}$$

where h is the person's height (in centimeters). Find the inverse of the model. Then estimate the height of a 60 kilogram person who has a body surface area of 1.6 square meters.

51. CHALLENGE Consider the function $g(x) = -x$.

a. Graph $g(x) = -x$ and explain why it is its own inverse. Also verify that $g(x) = g^{-1}(x)$ algebraically.

b. Graph other linear functions that are their own inverses. Write equations of the lines you graphed.

c. Use your results from part (b) to write a general equation describing the family of linear functions that are their own inverses.

NEW YORK MIXED REVIEW

TEST PRACTICE at classzone.com

52. What is the value of $f(x) = -5x^4 + 3x^3 + 10x^2 - x - 8$ when $x = -1$?

Ⓐ -5 Ⓑ -1 Ⓒ 1 Ⓓ 3

53. At a school's annual choir competition, there are a total of 750 adults and students in the audience. The number of students, s, is 30 more than three times the number of adults, a. Which system of linear equations could be used to determine the numbers of students and adults in the audience?

Ⓐ $s + a = 30$, $s = 750 - 3a$

Ⓑ $s + a = 750$, $s = 30 + 3a$

Ⓒ $s + a = 750$, $a = 30 + 3s$

Ⓓ $s + a = 30$, $a = 750 - 3s$

QUIZ for Lessons 6.3–6.4

Let $f(x) = 4x^2 - x$ and $g(x) = 2x^2$. Perform the indicated operation and state the domain. *(p. 428)*

1. $f(x) + g(x)$ **2.** $g(x) - f(x)$ **3.** $f(x) \cdot g(x)$ **4.** $\frac{f(x)}{g(x)}$

5. $f(g(x))$ **6.** $g(f(x))$ **7.** $f(f(x))$ **8.** $g(g(x))$

Verify that f and g are inverse functions. *(p. 438)*

9. $f(x) = x - 9$, $g(x) = x + 9$

10. $f(x) = 5x^3$, $g(x) = \sqrt[3]{\frac{x}{5}}$

11. $f(x) = -\frac{3}{2}x + \frac{1}{4}$, $g(x) = -\frac{2}{3}x + \frac{1}{6}$

12. $f(x) = 6x^2 + 1, x \geq 0$; $g(x) = \left(\frac{x-1}{6}\right)^{1/2}$

Find the inverse of the function. *(p. 438)*

13. $f(x) = -\frac{1}{3}x + 5$ **14.** $f(x) = x^2 - 16, x \geq 0$ **15.** $f(x) = -\frac{2}{9}x^5$

16. $f(x) = 5x + 12$ **17.** $f(x) = -3x^3 - 4$ **18.** $f(x) = 9x^4 - 49, x \leq 0$

19. GASOLINE COSTS The cost (in dollars) of g gallons of gasoline can be modeled by $C(g) = 2.15g$. The amount of gasoline used by a car can be modeled by $g(d) = 0.02d$ where d is the distance (in miles) that the car has been driven. Find $C(g(d))$ and $C(g(400))$. What does $C(g(400))$ represent? *(p. 428)*

6.5 Graph Square Root and Cube Root Functions

A2.A.51 Determine the domain and range of a function from its graph

Before You graphed polynomial functions.

Now You will graph square root and cube root functions.

Why? So you can graph the speed of a racing car, as in Ex. 38.

Key Vocabulary
- **radical function**
- **parent function,** *p. 89*

In Lesson 6.4, you saw the graphs of $y = \sqrt{x}$ and $y = \sqrt[3]{x}$. These are examples of **radical functions**. In this lesson, you will learn to graph functions of the form $y = a\sqrt{x-h} + k$ and $y = a\sqrt[3]{x-h} + k$.

KEY CONCEPT *For Your Notebook*

Parent Functions for Square Root and Cube Root Functions

The parent function for the family of square root functions is $f(x) = \sqrt{x}$.

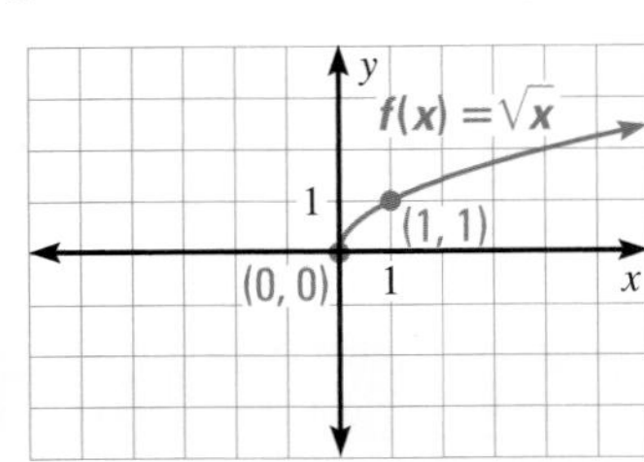

Domain: $x \geq 0$, **Range:** $y \geq 0$

The parent function for the family of cube root functions is $g(x) = \sqrt[3]{x}$.

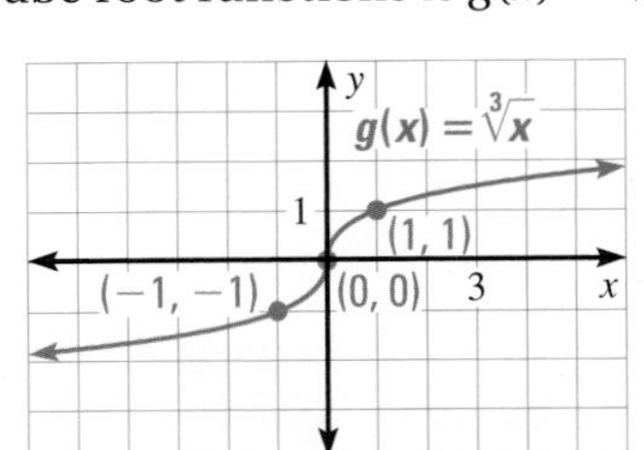

Domain and range: all real numbers

EXAMPLE 1 Graph a square root function

Graph $y = \frac{1}{2}\sqrt{x}$, and state the domain and range. Compare the graph with the graph of $y = \sqrt{x}$.

Solution

Make a table of values and sketch the graph.

x	0	1	2	3	4
y	0	0.5	0.71	0.87	1

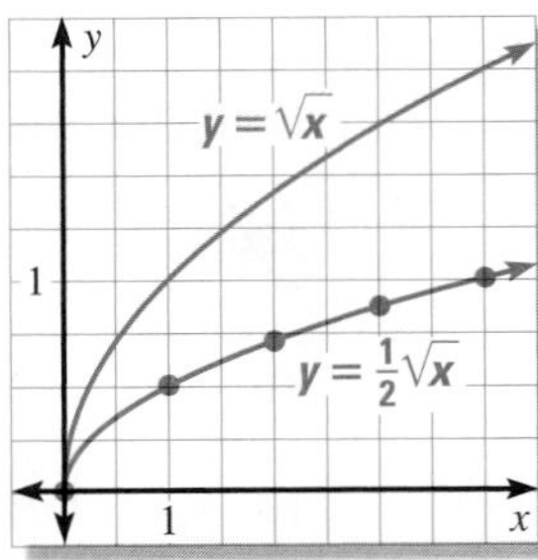

REVIEW DOMAIN AND RANGE
For help with the domain and range of a function, see p. 72.

The radicand of a square root must be nonnegative. So, the domain is $x \geq 0$. The range is $y \geq 0$.

The graph of $y = \frac{1}{2}\sqrt{x}$ is a vertical shrink of the graph of $y = \sqrt{x}$ by a factor of $\frac{1}{2}$.

EXAMPLE 2 Graph a cube root function

Graph $y = -3\sqrt[3]{x}$, and state the domain and range. Compare the graph with the graph of $y = \sqrt[3]{x}$.

Solution

Make a table of values and sketch the graph.

x	−2	−1	0	1	2
y	3.78	3	0	−3	−3.78

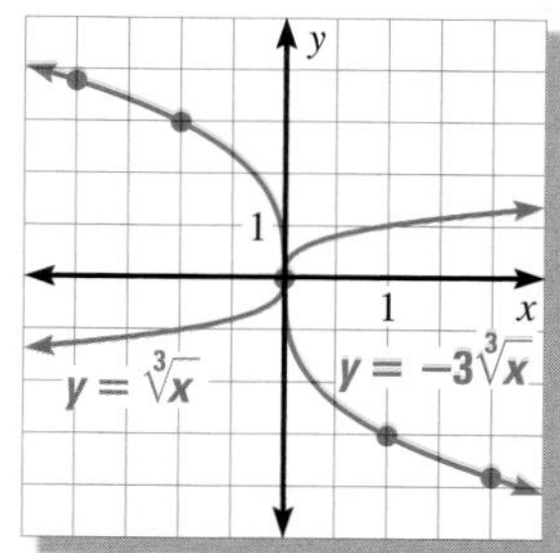

REVIEW STRETCHES AND SHRINKS

For help with vertical stretches and shrinks, see p. 123.

The domain and range are all real numbers.

The graph of $y = -3\sqrt[3]{x}$ is a vertical stretch of the graph of $y = \sqrt[3]{x}$ by a factor of 3 followed by a reflection in the x-axis.

EXAMPLE 3 Solve a multi-step problem

PENDULUMS The *period* of a pendulum is the time the pendulum takes to complete one back-and-forth swing. The period T (in seconds) can be modeled by $T = 1.11\sqrt{\ell}$ where ℓ is the pendulum's length (in feet).

- Use a graphing calculator to graph the model.
- How long is a pendulum with a period of 3 seconds?

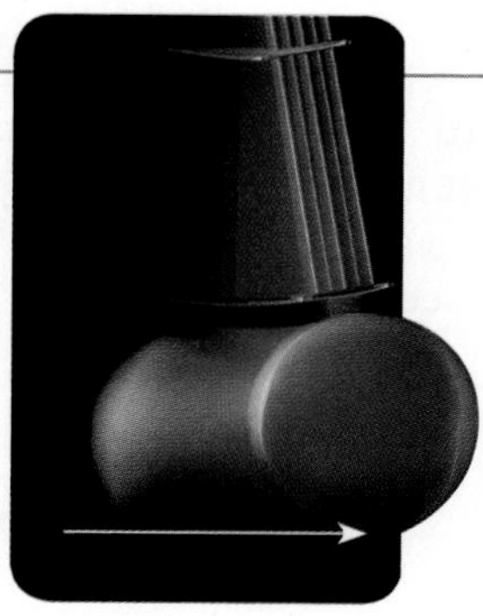

Solution

STEP 1 **Graph** the model. Enter the equation $y = 1.11\sqrt{x}$. The graph is shown below.

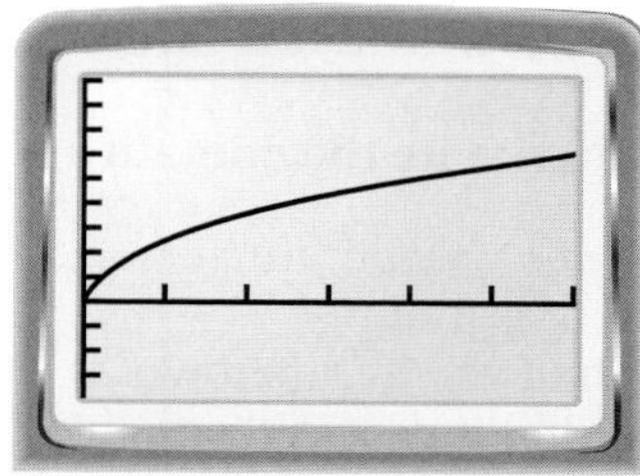

STEP 2 **Use** the *trace* feature to find the value of x when $y = 3$. The graph shows $x \approx 7.3$.

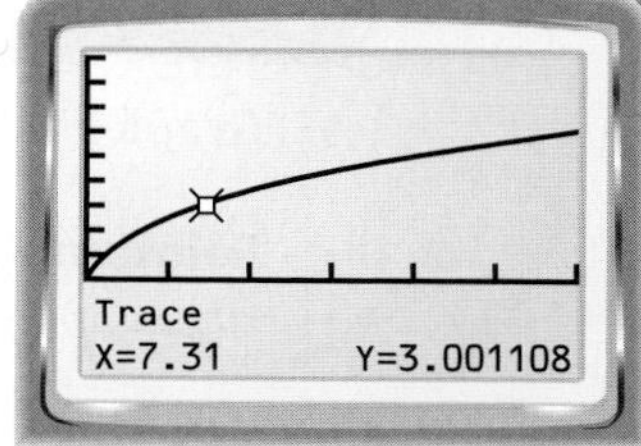

▶ A pendulum with a period of 3 seconds is about 7.3 feet long.

✓ GUIDED PRACTICE for Examples 1, 2, and 3

Graph the function. Then state the domain and range.

1. $y = -3\sqrt{x}$
2. $f(x) = \frac{1}{4}\sqrt{x}$
3. $y = -\frac{1}{2}\sqrt[3]{x}$
4. $g(x) = 4\sqrt[3]{x}$

5. **WHAT IF?** Use the model in Example 3 to find the length of a pendulum with a period of 1 second.

TRANSLATIONS OF RADICAL FUNCTIONS The procedure for graphing functions of the form $y = a\sqrt{x - h} + k$ and $y = a\sqrt[3]{x - h} + k$ is described below.

KEY CONCEPT *For Your Notebook*

Graphs of Radical Functions

To graph $y = a\sqrt{x - h} + k$ or $y = a\sqrt[3]{x - h} + k$, follow these steps:

STEP 1 **Sketch** the graph of $y = a\sqrt{x}$ or $y = a\sqrt[3]{x}$.

STEP 2 **Translate** the graph horizontally h units and vertically k units.

EXAMPLE 4 Graph a translated square root function

Graph $y = -2\sqrt{x - 3} + 2$. Then state the domain and range.

Solution

STEP 1 **Sketch** the graph of $y = -2\sqrt{x}$ (shown in blue). Notice that it begins at the origin and passes through the point $(1, -2)$.

REVIEW TRANSLATIONS
For help with translating graphs, see p. 123.

STEP 2 **Translate** the graph. For $y = -2\sqrt{x - 3} + 2$, $h = 3$ and $k = 2$. So, shift the graph of $y = -2\sqrt{x}$ right 3 units and up 2 units. The resulting graph starts at $(3, 2)$ and passes through $(4, 0)$.

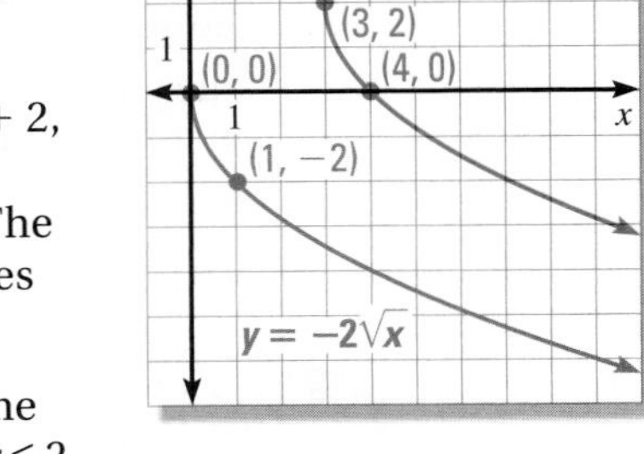

From the graph, you can see that the domain of the function is $x \geq 3$ and the range of the function is $y \leq 2$.

Animated Algebra at classzone.com

EXAMPLE 5 Graph a translated cube root function

Graph $y = 3\sqrt[3]{x + 4} - 1$. Then state the domain and range.

Solution

STEP 1 **Sketch** the graph of $y = 3\sqrt[3]{x}$ (shown in blue). Notice that it passes through the origin and the points $(-1, -3)$ and $(1, 3)$.

STEP 2 **Translate** the graph. Note that for $y = 3\sqrt[3]{x + 4} - 1$, $h = -4$ and $k = -1$. So, shift the graph of $y = 3\sqrt[3]{x}$ left 4 units and down 1 unit. The resulting graph passes through the points $(-5, -4)$, $(-4, -1)$, and $(-3, 2)$.

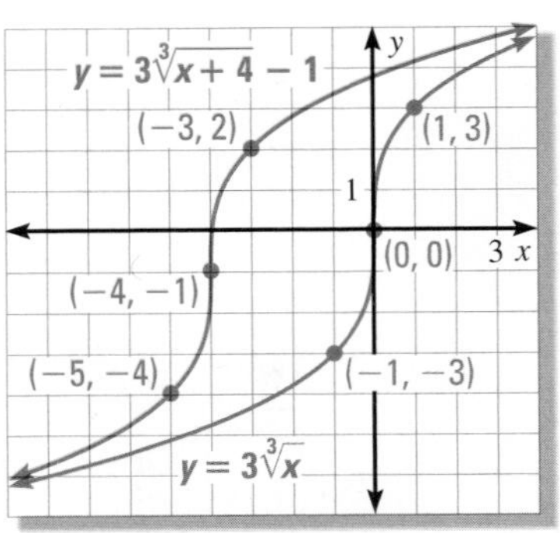

From the graph, you can see that the domain and range of the function are both all real numbers.

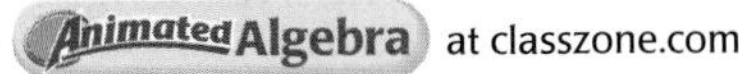 at classzone.com

GUIDED PRACTICE for Examples 4 and 5

Graph the function. Then state the domain and range.

6. $y = -4\sqrt{x} + 2$
7. $y = 2\sqrt{x + 1}$
8. $f(x) = \frac{1}{2}\sqrt{x - 3} - 1$
9. $y = 2\sqrt[3]{x - 4}$
10. $y = \sqrt[3]{x} - 5$
11. $g(x) = -\sqrt[3]{x + 2} - 3$

6.5 EXERCISES

HOMEWORK KEY
○ = **WORKED-OUT SOLUTIONS** on p. WS12 for Exs. 11, 17, and 37
★ = **STANDARDIZED TEST PRACTICE** Exs. 2, 9, 25, 27, and 37
◆ = **MULTIPLE REPRESENTATIONS** Ex. 39

SKILL PRACTICE

1. **VOCABULARY** Copy and complete: Square root functions and cube root functions are examples of _?_ functions.

2. ★ **WRITING** The graph of $y = \sqrt{x}$ is the graph of $y = a\sqrt{x - h} + k$ with $a = 1$, $h = 0$, and $k = 0$. Predict how the graph of $y = \sqrt{x}$ will change if:
   a. $a = -3$ b. $h = 2$ c. $k = 4$

EXAMPLE 1 on p. 446 for Exs. 3–9

SQUARE ROOT FUNCTIONS Graph the function. Then state the domain and range.

3. $y = -4\sqrt{x}$
4. $f(x) = \frac{1}{2}\sqrt{x}$
5. $y = -\frac{4}{5}\sqrt{x}$
6. $y = -6\sqrt{x}$
7. $y = 5\sqrt{x}$
8. $g(x) = 9\sqrt{x}$

9. ★ **MULTIPLE CHOICE** The graph of which function is shown?

   Ⓐ $y = \frac{3}{4}\sqrt{x}$ Ⓑ $y = -\frac{3}{4}\sqrt{x}$

   Ⓒ $y = \frac{3}{2}\sqrt{x}$ Ⓓ $y = -\frac{3}{2}\sqrt{x}$

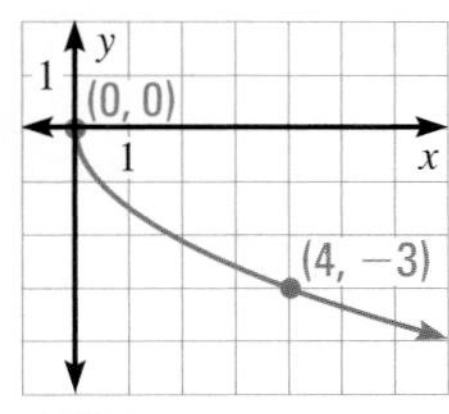

EXAMPLE 2 on p. 447 for Exs. 10–15

CUBE ROOT FUNCTIONS Graph the function. Then state the domain and range.

10. $y = \frac{1}{4}\sqrt[3]{x}$
11. $y = 2\sqrt[3]{x}$
12. $f(x) = -5\sqrt[3]{x}$
13. $h(x) = -\frac{1}{7}\sqrt[3]{x}$
14. $g(x) = 6\sqrt[3]{x}$
15. $y = \frac{7}{9}\sqrt[3]{x}$

EXAMPLES 4 and 5 on p. 448 for Exs. 16–24

RADICAL FUNCTIONS Graph the function. Then state the domain and range.

16. $f(x) = 2\sqrt{x - 1} + 3$
17. $y = (x + 1)^{1/2} + 8$
18. $y = -4\sqrt{x - 5} + 1$
19. $y = \frac{3}{4}x^{1/3} - 1$
20. $y = -2\sqrt[3]{x + 5} + 5$
21. $h(x) = -3\sqrt[3]{x + 7} - 6$
22. $y = -\sqrt{x - 4} - 7$
23. $g(x) = -\frac{1}{3}\sqrt[3]{x} - 6$
24. $y = 4\sqrt[3]{x - 4} + 5$

25. ★ **SHORT RESPONSE** *Explain* why there are limitations on the domain and range of the function $y = \sqrt{x - 5} + 4$.

26. **ERROR ANALYSIS** A student tried to explain how the graphs of $y = -2\sqrt[3]{x}$ and $y = -2\sqrt[3]{x+1} - 3$ are related. *Describe* and correct the error.

> The graph of $y = -2\sqrt[3]{x+1} - 3$ is the graph of $y = -2\sqrt[3]{x}$ translated right 1 unit and down 3 units.

27. ★ **MULTIPLE CHOICE** If the graph of $y = 3\sqrt[3]{x}$ is shifted left 2 units, what is the equation of the translated graph?

Ⓐ $y = 3\sqrt[3]{x-2}$ Ⓑ $y = 3\sqrt[3]{x} - 2$ Ⓒ $y = 3\sqrt[3]{x+2}$ Ⓓ $y = 3\sqrt[3]{x} + 2$

REASONING Find the domain and range of the function without graphing. *Explain* how you found your answers.

28. $y = \sqrt{x+5}$
29. $y = \sqrt{x-12}$
30. $y = \frac{1}{3}\sqrt{x} - 4$
31. $y = \frac{1}{2}\sqrt[3]{x} + 7$
32. $g(x) = \sqrt[3]{x+7}$
33. $f(x) = \frac{1}{4}\sqrt{x-3} + 6$

34. **CHALLENGE** Graph $y = \sqrt[4]{x}$, $y = \sqrt[5]{x}$, $y = \sqrt[6]{x}$, and $y = \sqrt[7]{x}$ on a graphing calculator. Make generalizations about the graph of $y = \sqrt[n]{x}$ when n is even and when n is odd.

PROBLEM SOLVING

EXAMPLE 3 on p. 447 for Exs. 35–36

35. **INDIRECT MEASUREMENT** The distance d (in miles) that a pilot can see to the horizon can be modeled by $d = 1.22\sqrt{a}$ where a is the plane's altitude (in feet above sea level). Graph the model on a graphing calculator. Then determine at what altitude the pilot can see 8 miles.

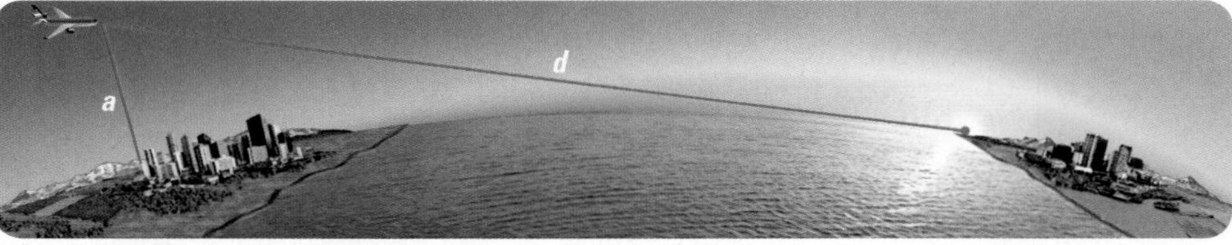

@HomeTutor for problem solving help at classzone.com

36. **PENDULUMS** Use the model $T = 1.11\sqrt{\ell}$ for the period of a pendulum from Example 3 on page 447.

a. Find the period of a pendulum with a length of 2 feet.

b. Find the length of a pendulum with a period of 2 seconds.

@HomeTutor for problem solving help at classzone.com

37. ★ **SHORT RESPONSE** The speed v (in meters per second) of sound waves in air depends on the temperature K (in kelvins) and can be modeled by:

$$v = 331.5\sqrt{\frac{K}{273.15}},\ K \geq 0$$

a. Kelvin temperature K is related to Celsius temperature C by the formula $K = 273.15 + C$. Write an equation that gives the speed v of sound waves in air as a function of the temperature C in degrees Celsius.

b. What are a reasonable domain and range for the function from part (a)?

◯ = WORKED-OUT SOLUTIONS on p. WS1 ★ = STANDARDIZED TEST PRACTICE ◆ = MULTIPLE REPRESENTATIONS

38. **DRAG RACING** For a given total weight, the speed of a car at the end of a drag race is a function of the car's power. For a car with a total weight of 3500 pounds, the speed s (in miles per hour) can be modeled by $s = 14.8\sqrt[3]{p}$ where p is the power (in horsepower). Graph the model. Then determine the power of a 3500 pound car that reaches a speed of 200 miles per hour.

39. **MULTIPLE REPRESENTATIONS** Under certain conditions, a skydiver's terminal velocity v_t (in feet per second) is given by

$$v_t = 33.7\sqrt{\frac{W}{A}}$$

where W is the weight of the skydiver (in pounds) and A is the skydiver's cross-sectional surface area (in square feet). Note that skydivers can vary their cross-sectional surface area by changing positions as they fall.

a. **Writing an Equation** Write an equation that gives v_t as a function of A for a skydiver who weighs 165 pounds.

b. **Making a Table** Make a table of values for the equation from part (a).

c. **Drawing a Graph** Use your table to graph the equation.

40. **CHALLENGE** The surface area S of a right circular cone with a slant height of 1 unit is given by $S = \pi r + \pi r^2$ where r is the cone's radius.

a. Use completing the square to show the following:

$$r = \frac{1}{\sqrt{\pi}}\sqrt{S + \frac{\pi}{4}} - \frac{1}{2}$$

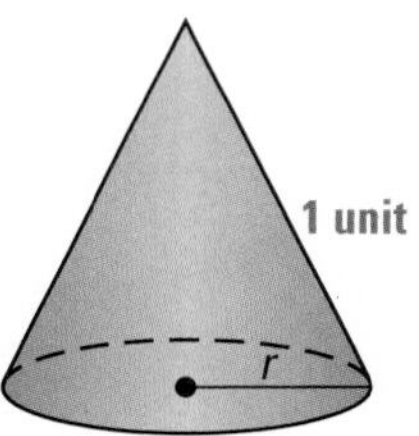

b. Graph the equation from part (a) using a graphing calculator.

c. Find the radius of a right circular cone with a slant height of 1 unit and a surface area of $\frac{3\pi}{4}$ square units.

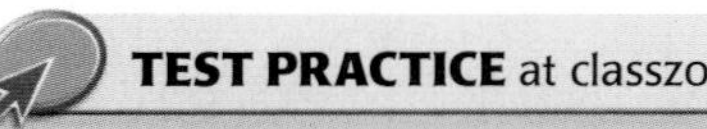

TEST PRACTICE at classzone.com

NEW YORK MIXED REVIEW

41. Which equation best represents the relationship between x and y shown in the table?

x	y
0	0
1	37
2	58
3	63

Ⓐ $y = 25x + 12$

Ⓑ $y = 45x - 8x^2$

Ⓒ $y = 8x^2 - 45x$

Ⓓ $y = 70 - 33x^3$

42. The two polygons are similar. What is the value of y?

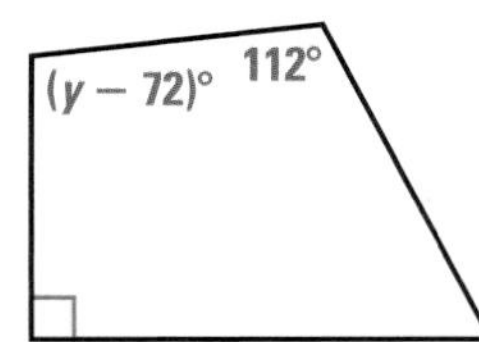

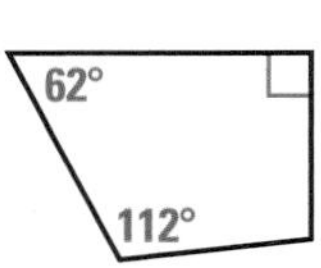

Ⓐ 24 Ⓑ 134

Ⓒ 168 Ⓓ 204

6.6 Solve Radical Equations

 **A2.A.22** Solve radical equations

Before You solved polynomial equations.

Now You will solve radical equations.

Why? So you can calculate hang time, as in Ex. 60.

Key Vocabulary
- **radical equation**
- **extraneous solution,** *p. 52*

Equations with radicals that have variables in their radicands are called **radical equations**. An example of a radical equation is $\sqrt[3]{2x+7}=3$.

KEY CONCEPT *For Your Notebook*

Solving Radical Equations

To solve a radical equation, follow these steps:

STEP 1 **Isolate** the radical on one side of the equation, if necessary.

STEP 2 **Raise** each side of the equation to the same power to eliminate the radical and obtain a linear, quadratic, or other polynomial equation.

STEP 3 **Solve** the polynomial equation using techniques you learned in previous chapters. Check your solution.

EXAMPLE 1 Solve a radical equation

Solve $\sqrt[3]{2x+7}=3$.

$\sqrt[3]{2x+7}=3$ Write original equation.

$(\sqrt[3]{2x+7})^3=3^3$ Cube each side to eliminate the radical.

$2x+7=27$ Simplify.

$2x=20$ Subtract 7 from each side.

$x=10$ Divide each side by 2.

CHECK Check $x=10$ in the original equation.

$\sqrt[3]{2(10)+7}\stackrel{?}{=}3$ Substitute 10 for *x*.

$\sqrt[3]{27}\stackrel{?}{=}3$ Simplify.

$3=3$ ✓ Solution checks.

 **GUIDED PRACTICE** for Example 1

Solve the equation. Check your solution.

1. $\sqrt[3]{x}-9=-1$
2. $\sqrt{x+25}=4$
3. $2\sqrt[3]{x-3}=4$

EXAMPLE 2 Solve a radical equation given a function

WIND VELOCITY In a hurricane, the mean sustained wind velocity v (in meters per second) is given by

$$v(p) = 6.3\sqrt{1013 - p}$$

where p is the air pressure (in millibars) at the center of the hurricane. Estimate the air pressure at the center of a hurricane when the mean sustained wind velocity is 54.5 meters per second.

ANOTHER WAY
For alternative methods for solving the problem in Example 2, turn to page 460 for the **Problem Solving Workshop**.

Solution

$v(p) = 6.3\sqrt{1013 - p}$	Write given function.
$54.5 = 6.3\sqrt{1013 - p}$	Substitute 54.5 for $v(p)$.
$8.65 \approx \sqrt{1013 - p}$	Divide each side by 6.3.
$(8.65)^2 \approx (\sqrt{1013 - p})^2$	Square each side.
$74.8 \approx 1013 - p$	Simplify.
$-938.2 \approx -p$	Subtract 1013 from each side.
$938.2 \approx p$	Divide each side by -1.

 The air pressure at the center of the hurricane is about 938 millibars.

✓ GUIDED PRACTICE for Example 2

4. **WHAT IF?** Use the function in Example 2 to estimate the air pressure at the center of a hurricane when the mean sustained wind velocity is 48.3 meters per second.

RATIONAL EXPONENTS When an equation contains a power with a rational exponent, you can solve the equation using a procedure similar to the one for solving radical equations. In this case, you first isolate the power and then raise each side of the equation to the reciprocal of the rational exponent.

EXAMPLE 3 Standardized Test Practice

What is the solution of the equation $4x^{3/2} = 108$?

Ⓐ 3 Ⓑ 6 Ⓒ 9 Ⓓ 27

Solution

$4x^{3/2} = 108$	Write original equation.
$x^{3/2} = 27$	Divide each side by 4.
$(x^{3/2})^{2/3} = 27^{2/3}$	Raise each side to the power $\frac{2}{3}$.
$x = 9$	Simplify.

▶ The correct answer is C. Ⓐ Ⓑ Ⓒ Ⓓ

EXAMPLE 4 Solve an equation with a rational exponent

Solve $(x + 2)^{3/4} - 1 = 7$.

$(x + 2)^{3/4} - 1 = 7$	Write original equation.
$(x + 2)^{3/4} = 8$	Add 1 to each side.
$\left[(x + 2)^{3/4}\right]^{4/3} = 8^{4/3}$	Raise each side to the power $\frac{4}{3}$.
$x + 2 = (8^{1/3})^4$	Apply properties of exponents.
$x + 2 = 2^4$	Simplify.
$x + 2 = 16$	Simplify.
$x = 14$	Subtract 2 from each side.

▶ The solution is 14. Check this in the original equation.

✓ GUIDED PRACTICE for Examples 3 and 4

Solve the equation. Check your solution.

5. $3x^{3/2} = 375$
6. $-2x^{3/4} = -16$
7. $-\frac{2}{3}x^{1/5} = -2$
8. $(x + 3)^{5/2} = 32$
9. $(x - 5)^{5/3} = 243$
10. $(x + 2)^{1/3} + 3 = 7$

EXTRANEOUS SOLUTIONS Raising each side of an equation to the same power may introduce extraneous solutions. When you use this procedure, you should always check each apparent solution in the *original* equation.

EXAMPLE 5 Solve an equation with an extraneous solution

Solve $x + 1 = \sqrt{7x + 15}$.

$x + 1 = \sqrt{7x + 15}$	Write original equation.
$(x + 1)^2 = (\sqrt{7x + 15})^2$	Square each side.
$x^2 + 2x + 1 = 7x + 15$	Expand left side and simplify right side.
$x^2 - 5x - 14 = 0$	Write in standard form.
$(x - 7)(x + 2) = 0$	Factor.
$x - 7 = 0$ or $x + 2 = 0$	Zero-product property
$x = 7$ or $x = -2$	Solve for x.

REVIEW FACTORING
For help with factoring, see p. 252.

CHECK

Check $x = 7$ in the original equation.

$$x + 1 = \sqrt{7x + 15}$$
$$7 + 1 \stackrel{?}{=} \sqrt{7(7) + 15}$$
$$8 \stackrel{?}{=} \sqrt{64}$$
$$8 = 8 \checkmark$$

Check $x = -2$ in the original equation.

$$x + 1 = \sqrt{7x + 15}$$
$$-2 + 1 \stackrel{?}{=} \sqrt{7(-2) + 15}$$
$$-1 \stackrel{?}{=} \sqrt{1}$$
$$-1 \neq 1$$

▶ The only solution is 7. (The apparent solution −2 is extraneous.)

SQUARING TWICE When an equation contains two radicals, you may need to square each side twice in order to eliminate both radicals.

EXAMPLE 6 Solve an equation with two radicals

Solve $\sqrt{x+2}+1=\sqrt{3-x}$.

Solution

METHOD 1 **Solve** using algebra.

$\sqrt{x+2}+1=\sqrt{3-x}$	Write original equation.
$(\sqrt{x+2}+1)^2=(\sqrt{3-x})^2$	Square each side.
$x+2+2\sqrt{x+2}+1=3-x$	Expand left side and simplify right side.
$2\sqrt{x+2}=-2x$	Isolate radical expression.
$\sqrt{x+2}=-x$	Divide each side by 2.
$(\sqrt{x+2})^2=(-x)^2$	Square each side again.
$x+2=x^2$	Simplify.
$0=x^2-x-2$	Write in standard form.
$0=(x-2)(x+1)$	Factor.
$x-2=0$ or $x+1=0$	Zero-product property
$x=2$ or $x=-1$	Solve for x.

REVIEW FOIL METHOD
For help with multiplying algebraic expressions using the FOIL method, see p. 245.

Check $x=2$ in the original equation.

$$\sqrt{x+2}+1=\sqrt{3-x}$$
$$\sqrt{2+2}+1\stackrel{?}{=}\sqrt{3-2}$$
$$\sqrt{4}+1\stackrel{?}{=}\sqrt{1}$$
$$3\neq 1$$

Check $x=-1$ in the original equation.

$$\sqrt{x+2}+1=\sqrt{3-x}$$
$$\sqrt{-1+2}+1\stackrel{?}{=}\sqrt{3-(-1)}$$
$$\sqrt{1}+1\stackrel{?}{=}\sqrt{4}$$
$$2=2\ \checkmark$$

▶ The only solution is -1. (The apparent solution 2 is extraneous.)

METHOD 2 **Use** a graph to solve the equation.

Use a graphing calculator to graph $y_1=\sqrt{x+2}+1$ and $y_2=\sqrt{3-x}$. Then find the intersection points of the two graphs by using the *intersect* feature. You will find that the only point of intersection is $(-1, 2)$. Therefore, -1 is the only solution of the equation $\sqrt{x+2}+1=\sqrt{3-x}$.

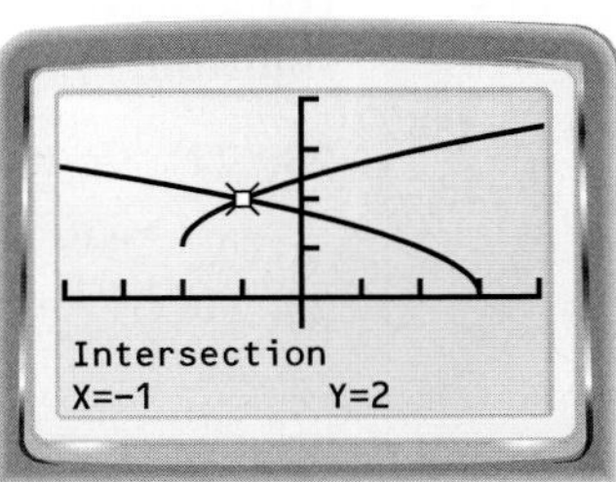

GUIDED PRACTICE for Examples 5 and 6

Solve the equation. Check for extraneous solutions.

11. $x-\frac{1}{2}=\sqrt{\frac{1}{4}x}$

12. $\sqrt{10x+9}=x+3$

13. $\sqrt{2x+5}=\sqrt{x+7}$

14. $\sqrt{x+6}-2=\sqrt{x-2}$

6.6 EXERCISES

HOMEWORK KEY

○ = **WORKED-OUT SOLUTIONS** on p. WS12 for Exs. 5, 13, and 59

★ = **STANDARDIZED TEST PRACTICE** Exs. 2, 12, 22, 43, 44, 59, and 60

SKILL PRACTICE

1. **VOCABULARY** Copy and complete: When you solve an equation algebraically, an apparent solution that must be rejected because it does not satisfy the original equation is called a(n) __?__ solution.

2. ★ **WRITING** A student was asked to solve $\sqrt{3x-1} - \sqrt{9x-5} = 0$. His first step was to square each side. While trying to isolate x, he gave up in frustration. What could the student have done to avoid this situation?

EXAMPLE 1 on p. 452 for Exs. 3–21

EQUATIONS WITH SQUARE ROOTS **Solve the equation. Check your solution.**

3. $\sqrt{5x+1} = 6$
4. $\sqrt{3x+10} = 8$
5. $\sqrt{9x} + 11 = 14$
6. $\sqrt{2x} - \frac{2}{3} = 0$
7. $-2\sqrt{24x} + 13 = -11$
8. $8\sqrt{10x} - 7 = 9$
9. $\sqrt{x-25} + 3 = 5$
10. $-4\sqrt{x} - 6 = -20$
11. $\sqrt{-2x+3} - 2 = 10$

12. ★ **MULTIPLE CHOICE** What is the solution of $\sqrt{8x+3} = 3$?

Ⓐ $-\frac{3}{4}$ Ⓑ 0 Ⓒ $\frac{3}{4}$ Ⓓ $\frac{9}{8}$

EQUATIONS WITH CUBE ROOTS **Solve the equation. Check your solution.**

13. $\sqrt[3]{x} - 10 = -3$
14. $\sqrt[3]{x-16} = 2$
15. $\sqrt[3]{12x} - 13 = -7$
16. $3\sqrt[3]{16x} - 7 = 17$
17. $-5\sqrt[3]{8x} + 12 = -8$
18. $\sqrt[3]{4x+5} = \frac{1}{2}$
19. $\sqrt[3]{x-3} + 2 = 4$
20. $\sqrt[3]{4x+2} - 6 = -10$
21. $-4\sqrt[3]{x+10} + 3 = 15$

22. ★ **OPEN-ENDED MATH** Write a radical equation of the form $\sqrt[3]{ax+b} = c$ that has -3 as a solution. *Explain* the method you used to find your equation.

EXAMPLES 3 and 4 on pp. 453–454 for Exs. 23–33

EQUATIONS WITH RATIONAL EXPONENTS **Solve the equation. Check your solution.**

23. $2x^{3/2} = 16$
24. $\frac{1}{2}x^{5/2} = 16$
25. $9x^{3/5} = 72$
26. $(16x)^{3/4} + 44 = 556$
27. $\frac{1}{7}(x+9)^{3/2} = 49$
28. $(x-5)^{5/3} - 73 = 170$
29. $\left(\frac{1}{3}x - 11\right)^{1/2} = 5$
30. $(5x-19)^{5/6} = 32$
31. $(3x+5)^{7/3} + 22 = 150$

ERROR ANALYSIS ***Describe*** **and correct the error in solving the equation.**

32.
$$\sqrt[3]{x} + 2 = 4$$
$$(\sqrt[3]{x} + 2)^3 = 4^3$$
$$x + 8 = 64$$
$$x = 56$$

33.
$$(x+7)^{1/2} = 5$$
$$[(x+7)^{1/2}]^2 = 5$$
$$x + 7 = 5$$
$$x = -2$$

EXAMPLE 5
on p. 454
for Exs. 34–44

SOLVING RADICAL EQUATIONS **Solve the equation. Check for extraneous solutions.**

34. $x - 6 = \sqrt{3x}$

35. $x - 10 = \sqrt{9x}$

36. $x = \sqrt{16x + 225}$

37. $\sqrt{21x + 1} = x + 5$

38. $\sqrt{44 - 2x} = x - 10$

39. $\sqrt{x^2 + 4} = x + 5$

40. $x - 2 = \sqrt{\frac{3}{2}x - 2}$

41. $\sqrt[4]{3 - 8x^2} = 2x$

42. $\sqrt[3]{8x^3 - 1} = 2x - 1$

43. ★ **MULTIPLE CHOICE** What is (are) the solution(s) of $\sqrt{32x - 64} = 2x$?

Ⓐ 4 Ⓑ −16 Ⓒ 4, −16 Ⓓ 1, 3

44. ★ **SHORT RESPONSE** *Explain* how you can tell that $\sqrt{x + 4} = -5$ has no solution without solving it.

EXAMPLE 6
on p. 455
for Exs. 45–52

EQUATIONS WITH TWO RADICALS **Solve the equation. Check for extraneous solutions.**

45. $\sqrt{4x + 1} = \sqrt{x + 10}$

46. $\sqrt[3]{12x - 5} - \sqrt[3]{8x + 15} = 0$

47. $\sqrt{3x - 8} + 1 = \sqrt{x + 5}$

48. $\sqrt{\frac{2}{3}x - 4} = \sqrt{\frac{2}{5}x - 7}$

49. $\sqrt{x + 2} = 2 - \sqrt{x}$

50. $\sqrt{2x + 3} + 2 = \sqrt{6x + 7}$

51. $\sqrt{2x + 5} = \sqrt{x + 2} + 1$

52. $\sqrt{5x + 6} + 3 = \sqrt{3x + 3} + 4$

SOLVING SYSTEMS **Solve the system of equations.**

53. $3\sqrt{x} + 5\sqrt{y} = 31$
$5\sqrt{x} - 5\sqrt{y} = -15$

54. $5\sqrt{x} - 2\sqrt{y} = 4\sqrt{2}$
$2\sqrt{x} + 3\sqrt{y} = 13\sqrt{2}$

55. CHALLENGE Give an example of a radical equation that has two extraneous solutions.

PROBLEM SOLVING

EXAMPLE 2
on p. 453
for Exs. 56–57

56. MAXIMUM SPEED In an amusement park ride called the Sky Flyer, a rider suspended by a cable swings back and forth like a pendulum from a tall tower. A rider's maximum speed v (in meters per second) occurs at the bottom of each swing and can be approximated by $v = \sqrt{2gh}$ where h is the height (in meters) at the top of each swing and g is the acceleration due to gravity ($g \approx 9.8$ m/sec^2). If a rider's maximum speed was 15 meters per second, what was the rider's height at the top of the swing?

@HomeTutor for problem solving help at classzone.com

57. **BURNING RATE** A burning candle has a radius of r inches and was initially h_0 inches tall. After t minutes, the height of the candle has been reduced to h inches. These quantities are related by the formula

$$r = \sqrt{\frac{kt}{\pi(h_0 - h)}}$$

where k is a constant. How long will it take for the entire candle to burn if its radius is 0.875 inch, its initial height is 6.5 inches, and $k = 0.04$?

@HomeTutor for problem solving help at classzone.com

58. **CONSTRUCTION** The length ℓ (in inches) of a standard nail can be modeled by $\ell = 54d^{3/2}$ where d is the diameter (in inches) of the nail. What is the diameter of a standard nail that is 3 inches long?

59. ★ **SHORT RESPONSE** Biologists have discovered that the shoulder height h (in centimeters) of a male African elephant can be modeled by

$$h = 62.5\sqrt[3]{t} + 75.8$$

where t is the age (in years) of the elephant. *Compare* the ages of two elephants, one with a shoulder height of 150 centimeters and the other with a shoulder height of 250 centimeters.

60. ★ **EXTENDED RESPONSE** "Hang time" is the time you are suspended in the air during a jump. Your hang time t (in seconds) is given by the function $t = 0.5\sqrt{h}$ where h is the height of the jump (in feet). A basketball player jumps and has a hang time of 0.81 second. A kangaroo jumps and has a hang time of 1.12 seconds.

  a. **Solve** Find the heights that the basketball player and the kangaroo jumped.

  b. **Calculate** Double the hang times of the basketball player and the kangaroo and calculate the corresponding heights of each jump.

  c. **Interpret** If the hang time doubles, does the height of the jump double? *Explain.*

Animated Algebra at classzone.com

61. **MULTI-STEP PROBLEM** The Beaufort wind scale was devised to measure wind speed. The Beaufort numbers B, which range from 0 to 12, can be modeled by

$$B = 1.69\sqrt{s + 4.25} - 3.55$$

where s is the speed (in miles per hour) of the wind.

  a. Find the wind speed that corresponds to the Beaufort number $B = 0$.

  b. Find the wind speed that corresponds to the Beaufort number $B = 12$.

  c. Write an inequality that describes the range of wind speeds represented by the Beaufort model.

Beaufort Wind Scale

Beaufort number	Force of wind
0	Calm
3	Gentle breeze
6	Strong breeze
9	Strong gale
12	Hurricane

62. CHALLENGE You are trying to determine a truncated pyramid's height, which cannot be measured directly. The height h and slant height ℓ of the truncated pyramid are related by the formula shown below.

$$\ell = \sqrt{h^2 + \frac{1}{4}(b_2 - b_1)^2}$$

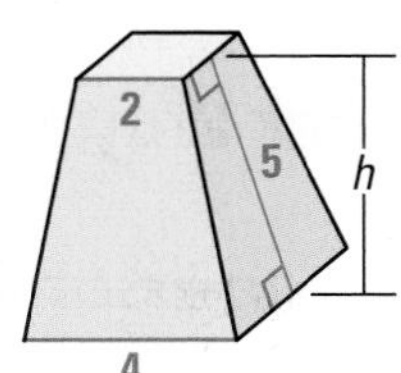

In the given formula, b_1 and b_2 are the side lengths of the upper and lower bases of the pyramid, respectively. If $\ell = 5$, $b_1 = 2$, and $b_2 = 4$, what is the height of the pyramid?

NEW YORK MIXED REVIEW

TEST PRACTICE at classzone.com

63. What are the zeros of the function $y = 12x^2 + 11x - 15$?

Ⓐ $-\frac{5}{3}, \frac{3}{4}$ Ⓑ $\frac{5}{3}, -\frac{3}{4}$ Ⓒ $-1, \frac{5}{4}$ Ⓓ $2, \frac{5}{2}$

64. Which equation represents the line that contains the point $(-4, 2)$ and has slope $-\frac{5}{2}$?

Ⓐ $-5x - 2y = 1$ Ⓑ $-2x + 5y = 18$

Ⓒ $2x - 5y = -16$ Ⓓ $5x + 2y = -16$

QUIZ *for Lessons 6.5–6.6*

Graph the function. Then state the domain and range. *(p. 446)*

1. $y = 4\sqrt{x}$ **2.** $y = \sqrt{x} + 3$ **3.** $g(x) = \sqrt{x + 2} - 5$

4. $y = -\frac{1}{2}\sqrt[3]{x}$ **5.** $f(x) = \sqrt[3]{x} - 4$ **6.** $y = \sqrt[3]{x - 3} + 2$

Solve the equation. Check for extraneous solutions. *(p. 452)*

7. $\sqrt{6x + 15} = 9$ **8.** $\frac{1}{4}(7x + 8)^{3/2} = 54$ **9.** $\sqrt[3]{3x + 5} + 2 = 5$

10. $x - 3 = \sqrt{10x - 54}$ **11.** $\sqrt{4x - 4} = \sqrt{5x - 1} - 1$ **12.** $\sqrt[3]{\frac{4}{5}x - 9} = \sqrt[3]{x - 6}$

13. ASTRONOMY According to Kepler's third law of planetary motion, the function $P = 0.199a^{3/2}$ relates a planet's orbital period P (in days) to the length a (in millions of kilometers) of the orbit's minor axis. The orbital period of Mars is about 1.88 years. What is the length of the orbit's minor axis? *(p. 452)*

PROBLEM SOLVING WORKSHOP LESSON 6.6

Using ALTERNATIVE METHODS

Another Way to Solve Example 2, page 453

MULTIPLE REPRESENTATIONS In Example 2 on page 453, you solved a radical equation algebraically. You can also solve a radical equation using a table or a graph.

PROBLEM

WIND VELOCITY In a hurricane, the mean sustained wind velocity v (in meters per second) is given by

$$v(p) = 6.3\sqrt{1013 - p}$$

where p is the air pressure (in millibars) at the center of the hurricane. Estimate the air pressure at the center of a hurricane when the mean sustained wind velocity is 54.5 meters per second.

METHOD 1

Using a Table The problem requires solving the radical equation $6.3\sqrt{1013 - p} = 54.5$. One way to solve this equation is to make a table of values. You can use a graphing calculator to make the table.

STEP 1 **Enter** the function $y = 6.3\sqrt{1013 - x}$ into a graphing calculator. Note that x represents air pressure and y represents wind velocity. Set up a table to display x-values starting at 900 and increasing in increments of 10.

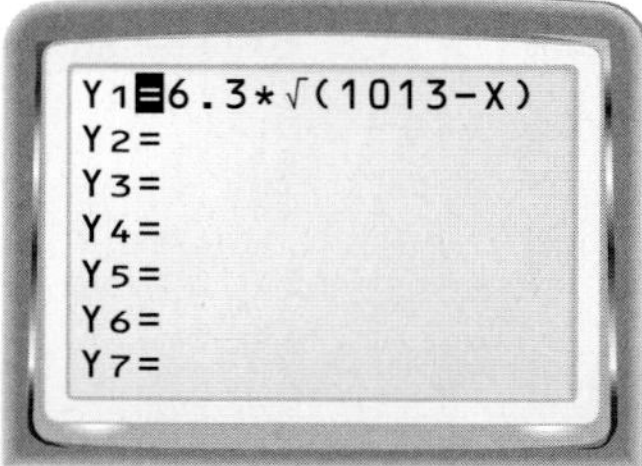

TABLE SETUP
TblStart=900
ΔTbl=10
Indpnt: Auto Ask
Depend: Auto Ask

STEP 2 **Make** a table of values for the function. The first table below shows that $y = 54.5$ between $x = 930$ and $x = 940$. To approximate x more precisely, set up the table to display x-values starting at 930 and increasing in increments of 1. The second table below shows that $y = 54.5$ between $x = 938$ and $x = 939$.

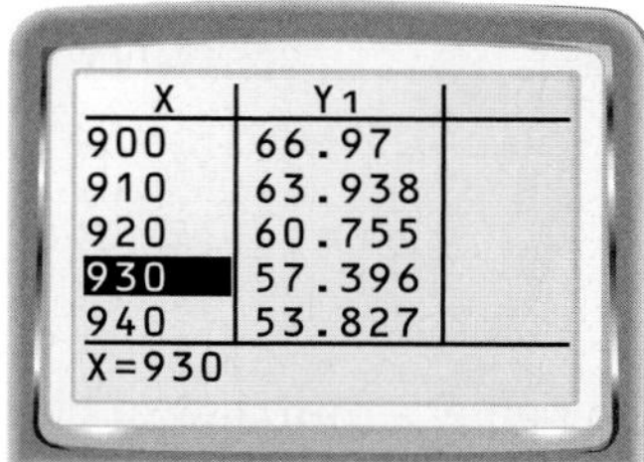

X	Y1
900	66.97
910	63.938
920	60.755
930	57.396
940	53.827

X=930

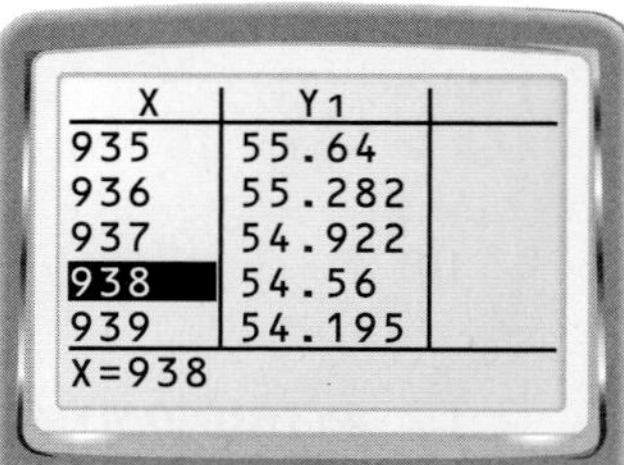

X	Y1
935	55.64
936	55.282
937	54.922
938	54.56
939	54.195

X=938

▶ The mean sustained wind velocity is 54.5 meters per second when the air pressure is between 938 and 939 millibars.

METHOD 2

Using a Graph You can also use a graph to solve the equation $6.3\sqrt{1013 - p} = 54.5$.

STEP 1 **Enter** the functions $y = 6.3\sqrt{1013 - x}$ and $y = 54.5$ into a graphing calculator.

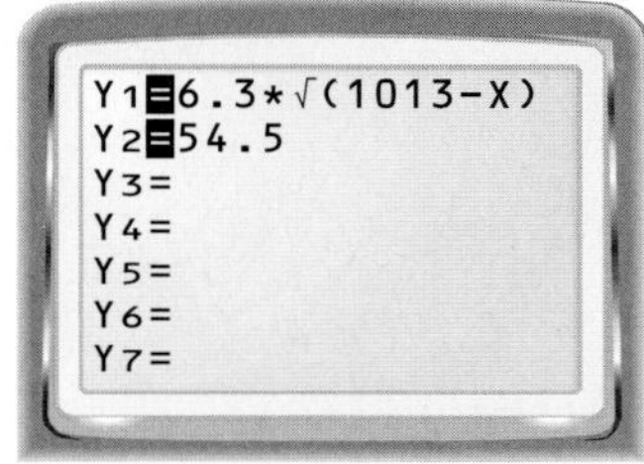

STEP 2 **Graph** the functions from Step 1. Adjust the viewing window so that it shows the interval $800 \le x \le 1100$ with a scale of 50 and the interval $25 \le y \le 75$ with a scale of 5.

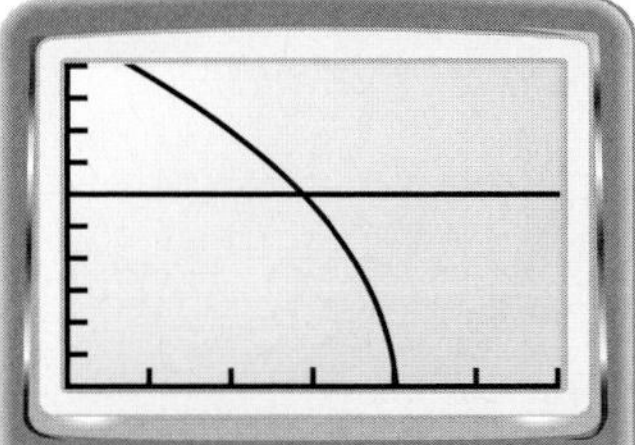

STEP 3 **Find** the intersection point of the two graphs using the *intersect* feature. The graphs intersect at about (938, 54.5).

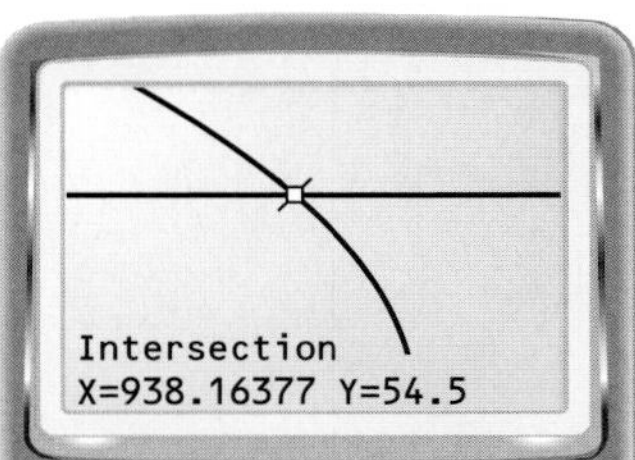

▶ The mean sustained wind velocity is 54.5 meters per second when the air pressure is about 938 millibars.

PRACTICE

SOLVING EQUATIONS Solve the radical equation using a table and using a graph.

1. $\sqrt{25 - x} = 8$

2. $2.3\sqrt{x - 1} = 11.5$

3. $4.3\sqrt{x - 7} = 30$

4. $6\sqrt{2 - 7x} - 1.2 = 22.8$

5. **ROCKETS** A model rocket is launched 25 feet from you. When the rocket is at height h, the distance d between you and the rocket is given by $d = \sqrt{625 + h^2}$ where h and d are measured in feet. What is the rocket's height when the distance between you and the rocket is 100 feet?

6. **WHAT IF?** In the problem on page 460, what is the air pressure at the center of a hurricane when the mean sustained wind velocity is 25 meters per second?

7. **GEOMETRY** The lateral surface area L of a right circular cone is given by

$$L = \pi r\sqrt{r^2 + h^2}$$

where r is the radius and h is the height. Find the height of a right circular cone with a radius of 7.5 centimeters and a lateral surface area of 900 square centimeters.

Extension
Use after Lesson 6.6

Solve Radical Inequalities

GOAL Solve radical inequalities by using tables and graphs.

In Chapter 4, you learned how to use tables and graphs to solve quadratic inequalities. You can also use tables and graphs to solve radical inequalities.

EXAMPLE 1 Solve a radical inequality using a table

Use a table to solve $3\sqrt{x} - 1 \le 11$.

Solution

STEP 1 **Enter** the function $y = 3\sqrt{x} - 1$ into a graphing calculator.

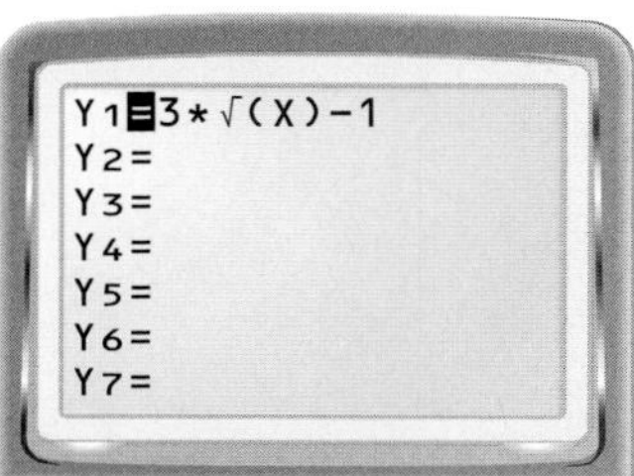

STEP 2 **Set up** the table to display x-values starting at 0 and increasing in increments of 1.

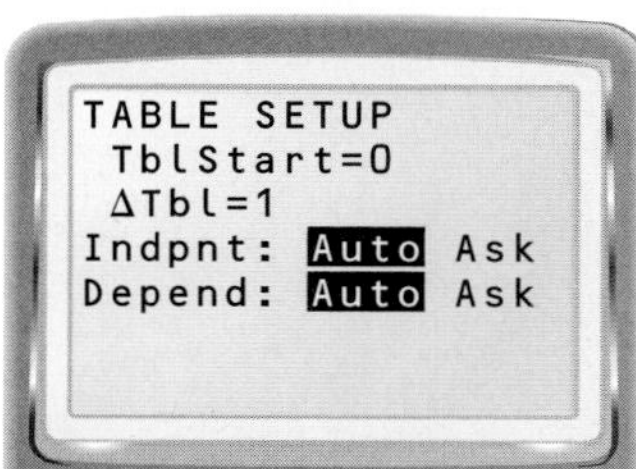

STEP 3 **Make** the table of values for $y = 3\sqrt{x} - 1$. Scroll through the table to find the x-value for which $y = 11$. This x-value is 16. It appears that $3\sqrt{x} - 1 \le 11$ when $x \le 16$.

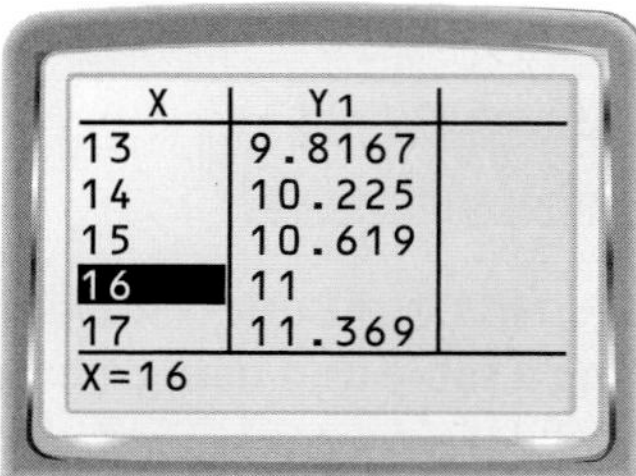

STEP 4 **Check** the domain of $y = 3\sqrt{x} - 1$. The domain is $x \ge 0$, so the solutions of $3\sqrt{x} - 1 \le 11$ cannot be negative. (This is indicated by the word ERROR next to the negative x-values.)

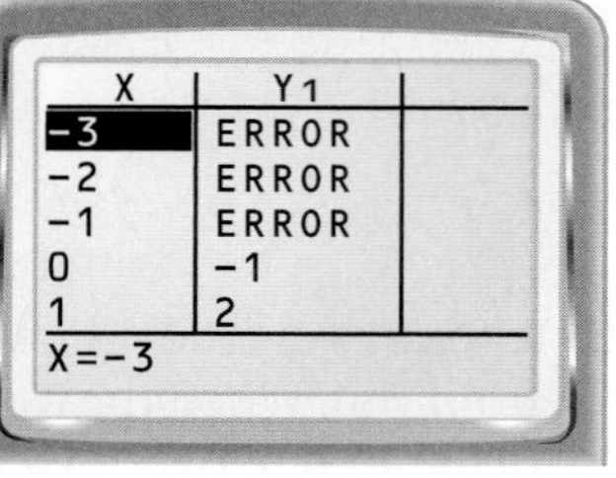

▶ The solution of the inequality is $x \le 16$ *and* $x \ge 0$, which you can write as $0 \le x \le 16$.

EXAMPLE 2 Solve a radical inequality using a graph

Use a graph to solve $\sqrt{x-5} > 3$.

Solution

STEP 1 **Enter** the functions $y = \sqrt{x-5}$ and $y = 3$ into a graphing calculator.

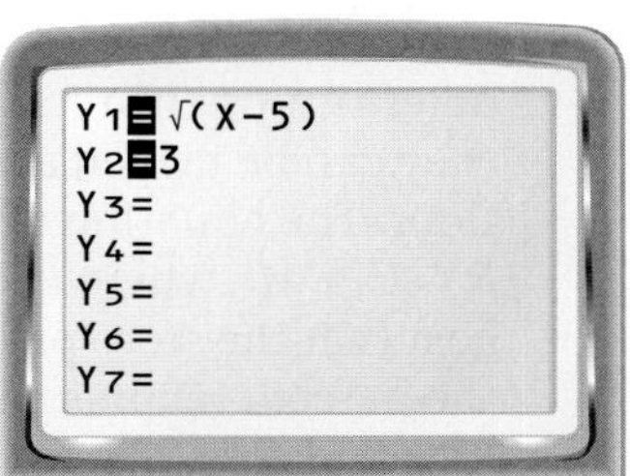

STEP 2 **Graph** the functions from Step 1. Adjust the viewing window so that the x-axis shows $0 \le x \le 30$ with a scale of 5 and the y-axis shows $-3 \le y \le 8$ with a scale of 1.

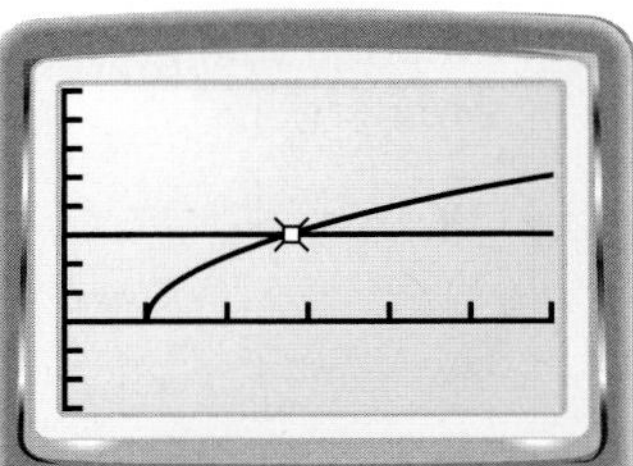

STEP 3 **Identity** the x-values for which the graph of $y = \sqrt{x-5}$ lies above the graph of $y = 3$. You can use the *intersect* feature to show that the graphs intersect when $x = 14$. The graph of $y = \sqrt{x-5}$ lies above the graph of $y = 3$ when $x > 14$.

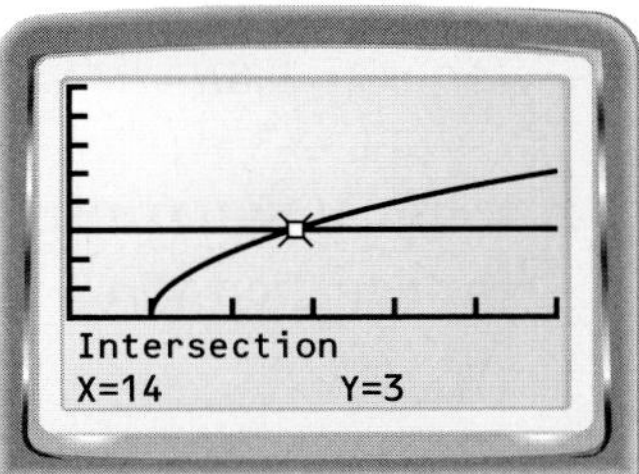

INTERPRET DOMAIN
In Example 2, note that the domain of $y = \sqrt{x-5}$ is $x \ge 5$. Therefore, the domain does not affect the solution.

▶ The solution of the inequality is $x > 14$.

PRACTICE

EXAMPLE 1 on p. 462 for Exs. 1–6

Use a table to solve the inequality.

1. $2\sqrt{x} - 5 \ge 3$

2. $\sqrt{x-4} \le 5$

3. $4\sqrt{x} + 1 \le 9$

4. $\sqrt{x+7} \ge 3$

5. $\sqrt{x} + \sqrt{x+3} \ge 3$

6. $\sqrt{x} + \sqrt{x-5} \le 5$

EXAMPLE 2 on p. 463 for Exs. 7–12

Use a graph to solve the inequality.

7. $2\sqrt{x} + 3 \le 8$

8. $\sqrt{x+3} \ge 2.6$

9. $7\sqrt{x} + 1 < 9$

10. $4\sqrt{3x-7} > 7.8$

11. $\sqrt{x} - \sqrt{x+5} < -1$

12. $\sqrt{x+2} + \sqrt{x-1} \le 9$

13. SAILBOAT RACE In order to compete in the America's Cup sailboat race, a boat must satisfy the rule

$$\ell + 1.25\sqrt{s} - 9.8\sqrt[3]{d} \le 16$$

where ℓ is the length (in meters) of the boat, s is the area (in square meters) of the sails, and d is the volume (in cubic meters) of water displaced by the boat. A boat has a length of 20 meters and displaces 27 cubic meters of water. What is the maximum allowable value for s?

Lessons 6.4–6.6

1. **BUSINESS** A manager at a clothing store is determining the retail prices of items so that they can be tagged and placed on the sales floor. The equation that the manager uses is $R = C + MC$ where R is the retail price, C is the cost that the store pays for the item, and M is the percent (expressed as a decimal) that the item is marked up. The markup for women's sweaters is 40%. What is the inverse of the function that gives the retail price of women's sweaters?

   (1) $C = \frac{R}{1.4}$

   (2) $C = \frac{R}{0.6}$

   (3) $C = 1.4R$

   (4) $C = 0.6R$

2. **RADICAL EQUATIONS** What is the solution of the equation $\sqrt{3x - 5} = 4$?

   (1) 4 (3) 7

   (2) 5 (4) 10

3. **MONETARY EXCHANGE** On a certain day, the function that gives Swedish kronor in terms of U.S. dollars is $k = 0.134d$ where k represents kronor and d represents U.S. dollars. How many dollars do you receive for 25 kronor?

   (1) \$3.35 (3) \$28.35

   (2) \$21.65 (4) \$186.57

4. **RADICAL FUNCTIONS** Which radical function has a domain of $x \geq 4$?

   (1) $y = -5\sqrt{x + 4}$

   (2) $y = -\sqrt{x} - 4$

   (3) $y = 4\sqrt{x}$

   (4) $y = 2\sqrt{x - 4} + 8$

5. **VERTICAL MOTION** An object is launched upward from ground level and reaches a maximum height of h feet. The initial velocity v (in feet per second) of the object is given by the function $v = 8\sqrt{h}$. What is the approximate maximum height of an object that is launched upward with an initial velocity of 110 feet per second?

   (1) 83.9 feet (3) 189.1 feet

   (2) 156.3 feet (4) 311.1 feet

6. **OPEN-ENDED** Your friend releases a weather balloon 50 feet from you. When the balloon is at height h, the distance d between you and the balloon is given by

$$d = \sqrt{2500 + h^2}$$

where h and d are measured in feet, as shown in the diagram below.

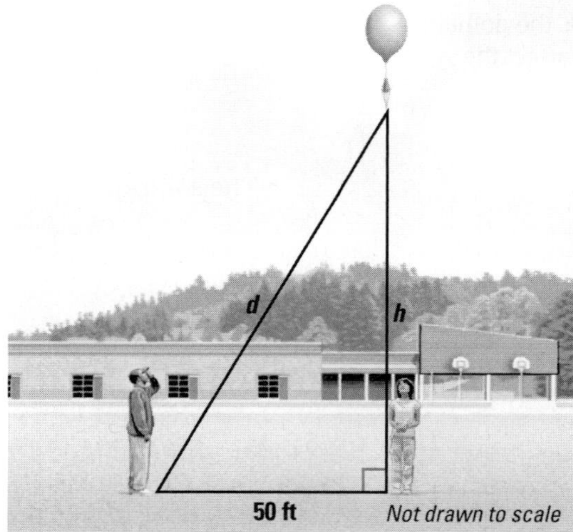

Explain why this equation is correct.

To the nearest foot, what is the height of the balloon when the distance between you and the balloon is 100 feet?

The distance will never be less than 50 feet, which is the horizontal distance along the ground. *Explain* how the equation models this fact.

6 CHAPTER SUMMARY

Animated Algebra
classzone.com
Electronic Function Library

BIG IDEAS For Your Notebook

Big Idea 1

Using Rational Exponents

The following are properties of rational exponents. Let a and b be real numbers and let m and n be rational numbers.

Property	Example
$a^m \cdot a^n = a^{m+n}$	$4^{5/2} \cdot 4^{1/2} = 4^3 = 64$
$(a^m)^n = a^{mn}$	$(2^8)^{1/4} = 2^2 = 4$
$(ab)^m = a^m b^m$	$(25 \cdot 4)^{1/2} = 25^{1/2} \cdot 4^{1/2} = 5 \cdot 2 = 10$
$a^{-m} = \frac{1}{a^m}, a \neq 0$	$8^{-1/3} = \frac{1}{8^{1/3}} = \frac{1}{2}$
$\frac{a^m}{a^n} = a^{m-n}, a \neq 0$	$\frac{9^{5/8}}{9^{1/8}} = 9^{4/8} = 9^{1/2} = 3$
$\left(\frac{a}{b}\right)^m = \frac{a^m}{b^m}, b \neq 0$	$\left(\frac{16}{81}\right)^{1/4} = \frac{16^{1/4}}{81^{1/4}} = \frac{2}{3}$

Big Idea 2

Performing Function Operations and Finding Inverse Functions

Operation	Definition	Example: $f(x) = 2x, g(x) = x - 5$
Addition	$h(x) = f(x) + g(x)$	$h(x) = 2x + (x - 5) = 3x - 5$
Subtraction	$h(x) = f(x) - g(x)$	$h(x) = 2x - (x - 5) = x + 5$
Multiplication	$h(x) = f(x) \cdot g(x)$	$h(x) = 2x(x - 5) = 2x^2 - 10x$
Division	$h(x) = \frac{f(x)}{g(x)}$	$h(x) = \frac{2x}{x - 5}$
Composition	$h(x) = g(f(x))$	$h(x) = 2x - 5$
Inverse	$h(x) = g^{-1}(x)$	$h(x) = x + 5$

Big Idea 3

Graphing Radical Functions and Solving Radical Equations

To **graph** radical functions, use the graph of the parent functions. For example, to graph $y = \sqrt{x+1} - 2$, translate the graph of $y = \sqrt{x}$ left 1 unit and down 2 units.

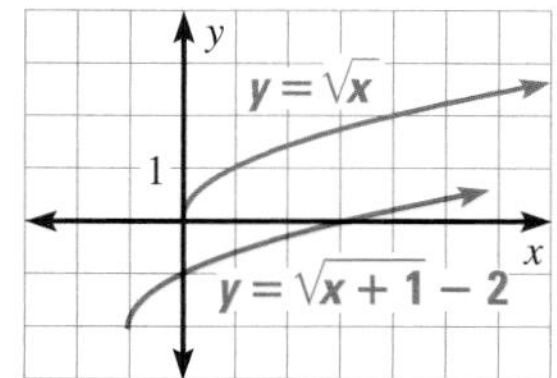

To **solve** a radical equation, first isolate the radical. Then raise each side of the equation to the same power and solve the polynomial equation.

$\sqrt{2x - 5} - 3 = 2$ **Write equation.**

$\sqrt{2x - 5} = 5$ **Isolate radical.**

$(\sqrt{2x - 5})^2 = 5^2$ **Square each side.**

$2x - 5 = 25$ **Simplify.**

$x = 15$ **Solve.**

6 CHAPTER REVIEW

@HomeTutor
classzone.com
- Multi-Language Glossary
- Vocabulary practice

REVIEW KEY VOCABULARY

- *n*th root of *a*, *p. 414*
- index of a radical, *p. 414*
- simplest form of a radical, *p. 422*
- like radicals, *p. 422*
- power function, *p. 428*
- composition, *p. 430*
- inverse relation, *p. 438*
- inverse function, *p. 438*
- radical function, *p. 446*
- radical equation, *p. 452*

VOCABULARY EXERCISES

1. Copy and complete: The index of the radical $\sqrt[4]{7}$ is _?_.

2. List two different pairs of like radicals.

3. Copy and complete: A(n) _?_ function has the form $y = ax^b$ where a is a real number and b is a rational number.

4. **WRITING** *Explain* how the graph of a function and the graph of its inverse are related.

5. **WRITING** *Explain* how to use the horizontal line test to determine whether the inverse of a function f is also a function.

6. **WRITING** *Describe* how the graph of $y = \sqrt[3]{x-4} + 5$ is related to the graph of the parent function $y = \sqrt[3]{x}$.

7. **REASONING** A student began solving the equation $x^{2/3} = 5$ by cubing each side. What will the student have to do next? What could the student have done to solve the equation in just one step?

REVIEW EXAMPLES AND EXERCISES

Use the review examples and exercises below to check your understanding of the concepts you have learned in each lesson of Chapter 6.

6.1 Evaluate *n*th Roots and Use Rational Exponents *pp. 414–419*

EXAMPLE

Evaluate the expression.

a. $(\sqrt[4]{16})^5 = 2^5 = 32$

b. $27^{-4/3} = \frac{1}{27^{4/3}} = \frac{1}{(27^{1/3})^4} = \frac{1}{3^4} = \frac{1}{81}$

EXERCISES

EXAMPLE 2 on p. 415 for Exs. 8–15

Evaluate the expression without using a calculator.

8. $81^{1/4}$ **9.** $0^{1/3}$ **10.** $\sqrt[3]{-64}$ **11.** $\sqrt[3]{125}$

12. $256^{3/4}$ **13.** $27^{-2/3}$ **14.** $(\sqrt[3]{8})^7$ **15.** $\frac{1}{(\sqrt[5]{-32})^{-3}}$

@HomeTutor
classzone.com
Chapter Review Practice

6.2 Apply Properties of Rational Exponents

pp. 420–427

EXAMPLE

Write the expression in simplest form. Assume all variables are positive.

a. $\sqrt[3]{48} = \sqrt[3]{8 \cdot 6} = \sqrt[3]{8} \cdot \sqrt[3]{6} = 2\sqrt[3]{6}$

b. $\left(\frac{x^4}{y^8}\right)^{1/2} = \frac{(x^4)^{1/2}}{(y^8)^{1/2}} = \frac{x^{4 \cdot 1/2}}{y^{8 \cdot 1/2}} = \frac{x^2}{y^4}$

EXERCISES

EXAMPLES 4, 6, and 7 on pp. 422–423 for Exs. 16–19

Write the expression in simplest form. Assume all variables are positive.

16. $\sqrt[3]{80}$ **17.** $(3^4 \cdot 5^4)^{-1/4}$ **18.** $(25a^{10}b^{16})^{1/2}$ **19.** $\sqrt{\frac{18x^5y^4}{49xz^3}}$

6.3 Perform Function Operations and Composition

pp. 428–434

EXAMPLE

Let $f(x) = 3x^2 + 1$ and $g(x) = x + 4$. Perform the indicated operation.

a. $f(x) + g(x) = (3x^2 + 1) + (x + 4) = 3x^2 + x + 5$

b. $f(x) \cdot g(x) = (3x^2 + 1)(x + 4) = 3x^3 + 12x^2 + x + 4$

c. $f(g(x)) = f(x + 4) = 3(x + 4)^2 + 1 = 3(x^2 + 8x + 16) + 1 = 3x^2 + 24x + 49$

EXERCISES

EXAMPLES 1, 2, and 5 on pp. 428–430 for Exs. 20–23

Let $f(x) = 4x - 6$ and $g(x) = x + 8$. Perform the indicated operation.

20. $f(x) + g(x)$ **21.** $f(x) - g(x)$ **22.** $f(x) \cdot g(x)$ **23.** $f(g(x))$

6.4 Use Inverse Functions

pp. 438–445

EXAMPLE

Find the inverse of the function $y = 3x + 7$.

$y = 3x + 7$	**Write original function.**
$x = 3y + 7$	**Switch x and y.**
$x - 7 = 3y$	**Subtract 7 from each side.**
$\frac{1}{3}x - \frac{7}{3} = y$	**Divide each side by 3.**

EXERCISES

EXAMPLES 1, 4, and 5 on pp. 438–441 for Exs. 24–26

Find the inverse of the function.

24. $y = \frac{1}{3}x + 4$ **25.** $y = 4x^2 + 9, x \geq 0$ **26.** $f(x) = x^3 - 4$

6 CHAPTER REVIEW

6.5 Graph Square Root and Cube Root Functions *pp. 446–451*

EXAMPLE

Graph $y = -\sqrt{x-3} + 2$.

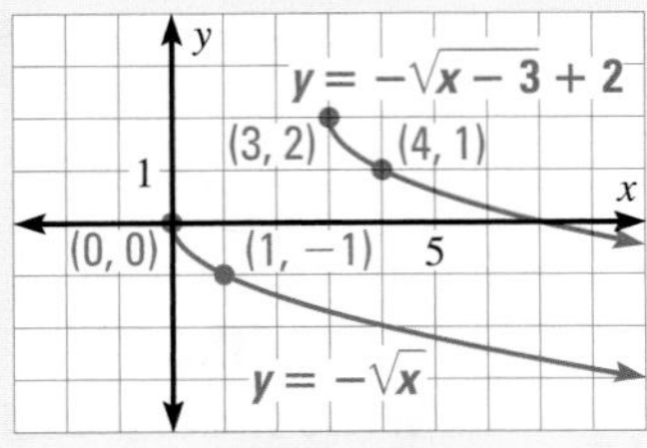

Sketch the graph of $y = -\sqrt{x}$. Notice that it begins at the origin and passes through the point $(1, -1)$.

For $y = -\sqrt{x-3} + 2$, $h = 3$, and $k = 2$. So, shift the graph of $y = -\sqrt{x}$ right 3 units and up 2 units. The resulting graph begins at the point $(3, 2)$ and passes through the point $(4, 1)$.

EXAMPLE

Graph $y = \sqrt[3]{x+2} - 4$.

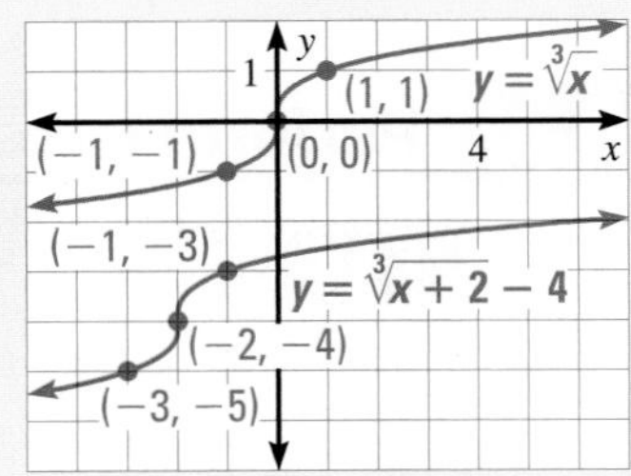

Sketch the graph of $y = \sqrt[3]{x}$. Notice that it passes through the points $(-1, -1)$, $(0, 0)$, and $(1, 1)$.

For $y = \sqrt[3]{x+2} - 4$, $h = -2$ and $k = -4$. So, shift the graph of $y = \sqrt[3]{x}$ left 2 units and down 4 units. The resulting graph passes through the points $(-3, -5)$, $(-2, -4)$, and $(-1, -3)$.

EXAMPLES 4 and 5 on p. 448 for Exs. 27–29

EXERCISES

Graph the function. Then state the domain and range.

27. $y = \sqrt{x+3} + 5$ **28.** $y = 3\sqrt{x+1} - 4$ **29.** $y = \sqrt[3]{x-4} - 5$

6.6 Solve Radical Equations *pp. 452–459*

EXAMPLE

Solve $\sqrt{4x+9} = 5$.

$\sqrt{4x+9} = 5$	**Write original equation.**
$(\sqrt{4x+9})^2 = 5^2$	**Square each side to eliminate the radical.**
$4x + 9 = 25$	**Simplify.**
$4x = 16$	**Subtract 9 from each side.**
$x = 4$	**Divide each side by 4.**

CHECK Check $x = 4$ in the original equation.

$\sqrt{4x+9} = \sqrt{4(4)+9} = \sqrt{25} = 5$ ✓

EXAMPLES 1, 3, and 5 on pp. 452–454 for Exs. 30–32

EXERCISES

Solve the equation. Check for extraneous solutions.

30. $\sqrt[3]{5x-4} = 2$ **31.** $3x^{3/4} = 24$ **32.** $\sqrt{x^2 - 10} = \sqrt{3x}$

6 CHAPTER TEST

Evaluate the expression without using a calculator.

1. $-125^{1/3}$
2. $32^{1/5}$
3. $\sqrt[4]{81}$
4. $\sqrt[3]{27}$
5. $8^{5/3}$
6. $16^{-3/2}$
7. $(\sqrt[3]{-27})^2$
8. $(\sqrt[3]{64})^{-4}$

Write the expression in simplest form. Assume all variables are positive.

9. $\sqrt[3]{88}$
10. $\sqrt[5]{16} \cdot \sqrt[5]{8}$
11. $\sqrt{\frac{12}{49}}$
12. $\frac{\sqrt[3]{24}}{\sqrt[3]{9}}$
13. $\sqrt[3]{64x^4y^2}$
14. $\sqrt[4]{2x^6y^8z}$
15. $\sqrt[5]{\frac{x^6}{y^4}}$
16. $\sqrt{\frac{75x^5y^6}{36xz^5}}$

Let $f(x) = 2x + 9$ and $g(x) = 3x - 1$. Perform the indicated operation and state the domain.

17. $f(x) + g(x)$
18. $f(x) - g(x)$
19. $f(x) \cdot g(x)$
20. $\frac{f(x)}{g(x)}$
21. $f(g(x))$
22. $g(f(x))$
23. $f(f(x))$
24. $g(g(x))$

Find the inverse of the function.

25. $y = -2x + 5$
26. $y = \frac{1}{3}x + 4$
27. $f(x) = 5x - 12$
28. $y = \frac{1}{2}x^4, x \geq 0$
29. $f(x) = x^3 + 5$
30. $f(x) = -2x^3 + 1$

Graph the function. Then state the domain and range.

31. $y = -6\sqrt[3]{x}$
32. $y = \sqrt{x - 4} - 2$
33. $f(x) = -\sqrt[3]{x + 3} + 4$

Solve the equation. Check for extraneous solutions.

34. $\sqrt{3x + 7} = 4$
35. $\sqrt{3x} - \sqrt{x + 6} = 0$
36. $x - 3 = \sqrt{x - 1}$

37. **KINETIC ENERGY** The kinetic energy E (in joules) of a 1250 kilogram compact car is given by the equation $E = 625s^2$ where s is the speed of the car (in meters per second).
    a. Write an inverse model that gives the speed of the car as a function of its kinetic energy.
    b. Use the inverse model to find the speed of the car if its kinetic energy is 120,000 joules. Give the speed in kilometers per hour.
    c. If the kinetic energy doubles, will the speed double? *Explain* why or why not.

38. **BOWLING SCORES** In bowling, a *handicap* is a change in score to adjust for differences in players' abilities. You belong to a bowling league in which each bowler's handicap h is determined by his or her average a using this formula:

$$h = 0.9(200 - a)$$

If a bowler's average is over 200, the handicap is 0. Find the inverse of the model. Then find your average if your handicap is 36.

MULTIPLE CHOICE QUESTIONS

If you have difficulty solving a multiple choice problem directly, you may be able to use another approach to eliminate incorrect answer choices and obtain the correct answer.

PROBLEM 1

The volume of a sphere is given by $V = \frac{4}{3}\pi r^3$. The surface area of a sphere is given by $S = 4\pi r^2$. Which choice correctly expresses S as a function of V?

(1) $4\pi V^2$ (2) $\sqrt[3]{\frac{9V^2}{4\pi}}$ (3) $\sqrt[3]{36\pi V^2}$ (4) $\sqrt[3]{\frac{3V^2}{4\pi}}$

METHOD 1

SOLVE DIRECTLY Solve for r in terms of V and substitute this expression in the formula for S.

STEP 1 **Solve** for r in terms of V.

$$V = \frac{4}{3}\pi r^3$$

$$\frac{3}{4\pi}V = r^3$$

$$r = \sqrt[3]{\frac{3}{4\pi}V}$$

STEP 2 **Substitute** the above expression for r in the formula for S.

$$S = 4\pi r^2$$

$$= 4\pi\left(\sqrt[3]{\frac{3}{4\pi}V}\right)^2$$

STEP 3 **Simplify** the expression into a form similar to the answer choices.

$$S = 4\pi\left(\sqrt[3]{\frac{3}{4\pi}V}\right)^2 = 4\pi\sqrt[3]{\frac{9V^2}{4^2\pi^2}}$$

$$= \sqrt[3]{\frac{4^3\pi^3 9V^2}{4^2\pi^2}} = \sqrt[3]{36\pi V^2}$$

▸ The correct answer is (3).

METHOD 2

ELIMINATE CHOICES Choose a value of r that will produce associated values of V and S. Then check the answer choices.

STEP 1 **Compute** the volume and surface area for a single value of r, such as $r = 2$.

Volume: $V = \frac{4}{3}\pi r^3 = \frac{4}{3}\pi(2)^3 \approx 33.51$

Surface Area: $S = 4\pi r^2 = 4\pi(2)^2 \approx 50.27$

STEP 2 **Substitute** $V \approx 33.51$ into the answer choices. The correct choice will yield a surface area of 50.27.

Choice (1): $4\pi V^2 = 4\pi(33.51)^2 \approx 14{,}111 \neq 50.27$ ✗

Choice (2): $\sqrt[3]{\frac{9V^2}{4\pi}} = \sqrt[3]{\frac{9(33.51)^2}{4\pi}} \approx 9.30 \neq 50.27$ ✗

Choice (3): $\sqrt[3]{36\pi V^2} = \sqrt[3]{36\pi(50.27)} \approx 50.27$ ✓

Choice (4): $\sqrt[3]{\frac{3V^2}{4\pi}} = \sqrt[3]{\frac{3(33.51)^2}{4\pi}} \approx 6.45 \neq 50.27$ ✗

▸ The correct answer is (3).

PROBLEM 2

Find all solutions of the equation $\sqrt{2x-1}+3=6$.

(1) 1 (2) 2 (3) 4 (4) 5

METHOD 1

SOLVE DIRECTLY

STEP 1 **Solve** the equation for x.

$$\sqrt{2x-1}+3=6$$
$$\sqrt{2x-1}=3$$
$$2x-1=9$$
$$2x=10$$
$$x=5$$

STEP 2 **Check** to avoid including an extraneous root.

$$\sqrt{2x-1}+3=\sqrt{2(5)-1}+3$$
$$=\sqrt{9}+3$$
$$=3+3$$
$$=6$$

▸ The correct answer is (4).

METHOD 2

ELIMINATE CHOICES Another method is to test which value of x in the answer choices satisfies the equation.

Choice (1): $\sqrt{2x-1}+3=\sqrt{2(1)-1}+3$
$=\sqrt{1}+3$
$=1+3$
$4\neq 6$ ✗

Choice (2): $\sqrt{2x-1}+3=\sqrt{2(2)-1}+3$
$=\sqrt{3}+3$
$\sqrt{3}+3\neq 6$ ✗

Choice (3): $\sqrt{2x-1}+3=\sqrt{2(4)-1}+3$
$=\sqrt{7}+3$
$\sqrt{7}+3\neq 6$ ✗

Choice (4): $\sqrt{2x-1}+3=\sqrt{2(5)-1}+3$
$=\sqrt{9}+3$
$=3+3$
$6=6$ ✓

▸ The correct answer is (4).

TEST PREPARATION

PRACTICE

Explain why you can eliminate the highlighted answer choice.

1. What is the solution of the equation $\sqrt{2x-3}-3=6$?

(1) 0 ✗(2) 6 (3) 39 (4) 42

2. Which expression is equivalent to $(9x^{3/2})^{-1/2}$?

(1) $\frac{9}{x^{3/4}}$ (2) $\frac{1}{3x^{3/4}}$ ✗(3) $9x^3$ (4) $3x^{3/4}$

New York **Test Practice**

MULTIPLE CHOICE

1. Simplify the expression $4^{1/2} \cdot 2^4$.

(1) 16 (3) 32

(2) $8^{4^{1/2}}$ (4) 64

2. If $f(x) = 2x^{-3/2}$, then $f(0.25)$ equals:

(1) -8 (3) -0.25

(2) -4 (4) 16

3. What is the solution of the equation $(8x)^{3/5} = 8$?

(1) $8^{-2/5}$ (3) 1

(2) $8^{2/5}$ (4) 4

4. Most carnivorous dinosaurs, called theropods, walked on 2 legs. The height at the hip of a theropod can be modeled by the function $h(\ell) = 3.49\ell^{1.14}$, where ℓ is the length (in centimeters) of the dinosaur's instep. The length of the instep can be modeled by $\ell(p) = 1.2p$, where p is the footprint length (in centimeters). Which expression represents h in terms of p?

(1) $4.188p$ (3) $4.30p$

(2) $4.188p^{1.14}$ (4) $4.30p^{1.14}$

5. In the equation $\sqrt[4]{16x^3y^4z} = 2x^a yz^b$, what is the sum of a and b? Assume all variables are positive.

(1) $\frac{1}{2}$ (3) $\frac{7}{4}$

(2) 1 (4) 4

6. The expression $\frac{5y^2 - 15y}{3y^2 - y^3}$ is equivalent to:

(1) $-\frac{5}{y}$ (3) $-\frac{10}{3}$

(2) $\frac{5}{y}$ (4) $\frac{5}{3} - \frac{15}{y^2}$

7. What is the value of $\frac{1}{(\sqrt[4]{625})^{-2}}$?

(1) $\frac{1}{25}$ (3) 25

(2) $\frac{1}{5}$ (4) 78,125

8. Let $f(x) = \frac{2}{5}x^{-0.25}$ and $g(x) = 5x^{3.25}$. Approximated to three decimal places, what is the value of $f(x) \cdot g(x)$ when $x = 3$?

(1) 0.054 (3) 54.000

(2) 0.110 (4) 93.531

9. What is the y-intercept of the graph of the function $y = \sqrt[3]{x - 8}$?

(1) -8 (3) 2

(2) -2 (4) 8

10. Let $f(x) = \sqrt{x - 2} + 3$ and $g(x) = \sqrt{x + 13}$. For what value of x does $f(x) = g(x)$?

(1) -4 (3) 3

(2) -3 (4) 9

11. Consider the function $y = 3x + 9$. What is the slope of the graph of the inverse function?

(1) -3 (3) $\frac{1}{3}$

(2) $-\frac{1}{3}$ (4) 3

12. The expression $(k^{-1/2})\sqrt[3]{k^4}$ is equivalent to:

(1) $k^{-2/3}$

(2) k^3

(3) $k^{3/5}$

(4) $k^{5/6}$

13. Simplify $(-4x^3)(5x^4)$.

(1) $-20x^{12}$

(2) $-20x^7$

(3) $-2x^{12}$

(4) $-2x^7$

TEST PREPARATION

MULTIPLE CHOICE

14. What is the solution of the equation $\sqrt{2x + 3} = 5$?

(1) -14 (3) 1
(2) -4 (4) 11

15. The graph of which function is shown?

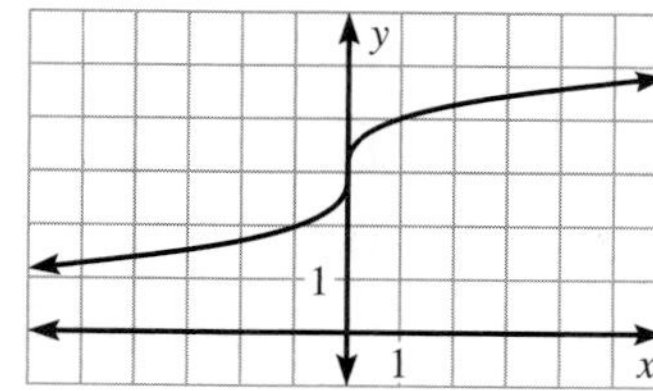

(1) $y = \sqrt[3]{x + 3}$ (3) $y = \sqrt[3]{x} + 3$
(2) $y = \sqrt[3]{x - 3}$ (4) $y = \sqrt[3]{x} - 3$

16. What is the inverse of $y = -2x^5 + 10$?

(1) $y = \sqrt[5]{5 - \frac{1}{2}x}$ (3) $y = \sqrt[5]{2x} - 20$
(2) $y = 20 - \sqrt[5]{2x}$ (4) $y = \sqrt[5]{\frac{1}{2}x - 5}$

17. Let $f(x) = 2x^{1/2}$ and $g(x) = 4x^2$. What is the value of $g(f(-9))$?

(1) -36 (3) 192
(2) 36 (4) undefined

18. What is the value of $\left(\frac{5^5}{2^5}\right)^{-1/5}$?

(1) $\frac{1}{160}$ (3) $\frac{2}{5}$
(2) $\frac{1}{10}$ (4) $\frac{5}{2}$

19. Which expression is equivalent to $\sqrt{9x^2y^3}$ for *all* real numbers x and y?

(1) $3xy^{3/2}$
(2) $3x|y|^{3/2}$
(3) $3|x|(|y|)^{3/2}$
(4) all of the above

OPEN-ENDED

20. Solve the equation $-\sqrt{x + 4} = \sqrt{x - 1} + 1$ algebraically. Then solve the equation by graphing. Are the results the same? *Explain* why or why not.

21. A function for converting x millimeters to y inches is $y = 0.03937x$. Find the inverse of the function. What information can you obtain from the inverse function? Use the inverse function to find the area (in square millimeters) of a 3 inch by 5 inch index card.

22. You have a \$10 gift card to spend at a local toy store. The store has a sale offering 15% off all board games. Use composition of functions to find the final price of a board game that originally costs \$27 when the \$10 is subtracted before the 15% discount is applied. Then use composition of functions to find the final price of the board game when the 15% discount is applied before the \$10 is subtracted. How much more money can you save if the store applies the 15% discount first?

23. The graphs of two functions f and g are shown at the right. Are f and g inverse functions? *Explain* why or why not.

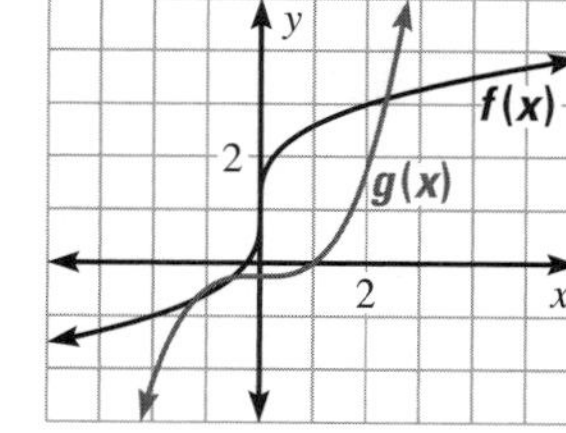

CUMULATIVE REVIEW Chapters 1–6

Write an equation of the line that passes through the given point and has the given slope. *(p. 98)*

1. $(3, 1), m = 4$
2. $(4, 6), m = 7$
3. $(-3, 2), m = -8$
4. $(1, -5), m = 9$
5. $(-5, 8), m = \frac{4}{5}$
6. $(2, -10), m = -\frac{3}{4}$

Solve the equation. Check your solution(s).

7. $-2x + 7 = 15$ *(p. 18)*
8. $|4x - 6| = 14$ *(p. 51)*
9. $x^2 - 9x + 14 = 0$ *(p. 252)*
10. $4x^2 - 6x + 9 = 0$ *(p. 292)*
11. $x^3 + 3x^2 - 10x = 0$ *(p. 353)*
12. $\sqrt{8x + 1} = 7$ *(p. 452)*

Graph the equation or inequality in a coordinate plane.

13. $y = 3x - 5$ *(p. 89)*
14. $y = -|x + 4| + 3$ *(p. 123)*
15. $y < -2x + 5$ *(p. 132)*
16. $y = x^2 - 2x - 4$ *(p. 236)*
17. $y = 2(x - 6)^2 - 5$ *(p. 245)*
18. $y > x^2 + 2x + 1$ *(p. 300)*
19. $y = x^3 - 2$ *(p. 337)*
20. $y = 3(x + 2)(x - 1)^2$ *(p. 387)*
21. $y = -\sqrt{x - 2} + 4$ *(p. 446)*

Solve the system of linear equations using any method.

22. $2x + 5y = 1$ *(p. 160)*
    $3x - 2y = 30$
23. $3x - y = -9$ *(p. 160)*
    $4x + 3y = 14$
24. $2x + 3y = 47$ *(p. 178)*
    $7x - 8y = -2$
    $2x - y + 3z = -19$

Write the expression as a complex number in standard form. *(p. 275)*

25. $(4 - 2i) + (5 + i)$
26. $(3 + 4i) - (7 + 2i)$
27. $(4 - 2i)(6 + 5i)$

Write the quadratic function in vertex form by completing the square. *(p. 284)*

28. $y = x^2 + 6x + 16$
29. $y = -x^2 + 12x - 46$
30. $y = 2x^2 - 4x + 7$

Simplify the expression. Assume all variables are positive.

31. $(2x^3y^2)^3$ *(p. 330)*
32. $(x^8)^{-3/4}$ *(p. 420)*
33. $\frac{x^3y^{-4}}{x^{-4}y^{-5}}$ *(p. 330)*
34. $\left(\frac{x^2y^{1/3}}{x^{1/4}y}\right)^2$ *(p. 420)*

Perform the indicated operation.

35. $(x^2 + 11x - 9) + (4x^2 - 5x - 7)$ *(p. 346)*
36. $(x^3 + 3x - 10) - (2x^3 + 3x^2 + 8x)$ *(p. 346)*
37. $(2x - 5)(x^2 + 4x - 7)$ *(p. 346)*
38. $(x^3 - 10x^2 + 33x - 28) \div (x - 5)$ *(p. 362)*

Factor the polynomial completely. *(p. 353)*

39. $x^4 - 3x^2 - 40$
40. $x^3 - 125$
41. $x^3 - 6x^2 - 9x + 54$

Let $f(x) = 2x - 6$ and $g(x) = 5x + 1$. Perform the indicated operation and state the domain. *(p. 428)*

42. $f(x) + g(x)$
43. $f(x) \cdot g(x)$
44. $f(g(x))$
45. $g(f(x))$

Find the inverse of the function. *(p. 438)*

46. $f(x) = 4x + 6$
47. $f(x) = \frac{3}{7}x + 7$
48. $f(x) = \frac{1}{3}x - \frac{2}{3}$
49. $f(x) = \frac{x^3 - 5}{6}$
50. $f(x) = \sqrt[3]{\frac{2x + 7}{3}}$
51. $f(x) = -\frac{8}{9}x^5 + 2$

52. **BICYCLE COSTS** You want to buy a bicycle that costs \$360. In order to pay for the bicycle, you save \$30 per week. How many weeks will it take to save enough money to buy the bicycle? *(p. 34)*

53. **CHARITABLE DONATIONS** The table below shows the amounts of money (in millions of dollars) received by a charitable organization during the first 6 years of its existence. Approximate the best-fitting line for the data. Then use the best-fitting line to predict the amount of money the organization will receive in the eighth year of its existence. *(p. 113)*

Year	1	2	3	4	5	6
Donations (millions of dollars)	1.71	2.3	2.78	3.22	3.69	4.28

54. **ICE SHOW** The attendance at an ice show was 9800 people. The tickets for the ice show were \$35 for lower-level seats and \$25 for upper-level seats. The total income from ticket sales was \$280,000. Use a linear system to find the numbers of lower-level and upper-level tickets sold for the ice show. *(p. 160)*

55. **CONCERT TICKETS** Tickets to a school's band concert are \$4 for students, \$8 for adults, and \$6 for senior citizens. At Friday night's concert, there were 140 students, 170 adults, and 55 senior citizens in attendance. At Saturday night's concert, there were 126 students, 188 adults, and 64 senior citizens in attendance. Organize this information using matrices. Then use matrix multiplication to find the income from ticket sales for Friday and Saturday nights' concerts. *(p. 195)*

56. **PHYSICAL SCIENCE** While standing at the edge of a cliff, you drop a rock from a height of 85 feet above the ground. Write an equation giving the height h (in feet) of the rock above the ground after t seconds. How long does it take for the rock to hit the ground? *(p. 266)*

57. **BASEBALL** Three points on the parabola formed by throwing a baseball are (0, 6), (20, 56), and (36, 24). Write a quadratic function that models the baseball's path. *(p. 309)*

58. **MANUFACTURING** At a factory, molten plastic is poured into molds to make toy blocks. Each mold is a rectangular prism with a height that is 3 inches greater than the length of each side of the square base. A machine pours 200 cubic inches of liquid plastic into each mold. What are the dimensions of a mold? *(p. 370)*

59. **PROFIT** Your friend starts a housekeeping business. The table below shows the profit (in dollars) of the business during the first 6 months of its existence. Use a graphing calculator to find a polynomial model for the data. Predict the profit in the ninth month. *(p. 393)*

Month	1	2	3	4	5	6
Profit (dollars)	2	4	18	50	106	192

60. **GEOMETRY** You have a beach ball that has a volume of approximately 7240 cubic inches. Find the radius of the beach ball. (*Hint:* Use the formula $V = \frac{4}{3}\pi r^3$ for the volume of a sphere.) *(p. 414)*

7

Exponential and Logarithmic Functions

Before

In previous chapters, you learned the following skills, which you'll use in Chapter 7: graphing functions, finding inverse functions, and writing functions.

Prerequisite Skills

VOCABULARY CHECK

Copy and complete the statement using the graph at the right.

1. The **domain** of the function is __?__.

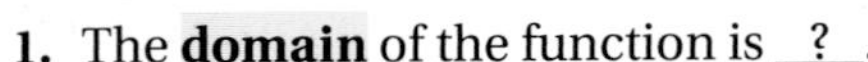

2. The **range** of the function is __?__.
3. The **inverse** of the function is __?__.

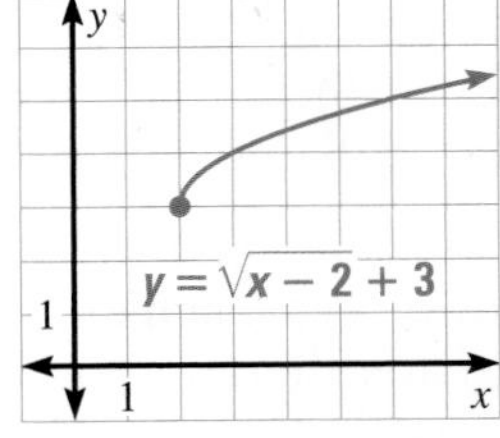

SKILLS CHECK

Graph the function. State the domain and range. *(Review p. 446 for 7.1–7.3.)*

4. $y = -2\sqrt{x} - 1$ **5.** $y = \sqrt{x+3}$ **6.** $y = \sqrt[3]{x-2} + 5$

Find the inverse of the function. *(Review p. 438 for 7.4.)*

7. $y = 3x + 5$ **8.** $y = -2x^3 + 1$ **9.** $y = \frac{1}{2}x^2, x \geq 0$

Write a quadratic function in standard form for the parabola that passes through the given points. *(Review p. 309 for 7.7.)*

10. $(0, -1), (1, 2), (3, 14)$ **11.** $(3, 8), (4, 17), (7, 56)$ **12.** $(-3, 9), (1, -7), (5, -55)$

Now

In Chapter 7, you will apply the big ideas listed below and reviewed in the Chapter Summary on page 538. You will also use the key vocabulary listed below.

Big Ideas

1. **Graphing exponential and logarithmic functions**
2. **Solving exponential and logarithmic equations**
3. **Writing and applying exponential and power functions**

KEY VOCABULARY

- exponential function, *p. 478*
- exponential growth function, *p. 478*
- growth factor, *p. 478*
- asymptote, *p. 478*
- exponential decay function, *p. 486*
- decay factor, *p. 486*
- natural base *e*, *p. 492*
- logarithm of *y* with base *b*, *p. 499*
- common logarithm, *p. 500*
- natural logarithm, *p. 500*
- exponential equation, *p. 515*
- logarithmic equation, *p. 517*

Why?

You can use exponential and logarithmic functions to model many scientific relationships. For example, you can use a logarithmic function to relate the size of a telescope lens and the ability of the telescope to see certain stars.

Animated Algebra

The animation illustrated below for Example 7 on page 519 helps you answer this question: How is the diameter of a telescope's objective lens related to the apparent magnitude of the dimmest star that can be seen with the telescope?

The magnitude of stars is a measure of their brightness as viewed from Earth.

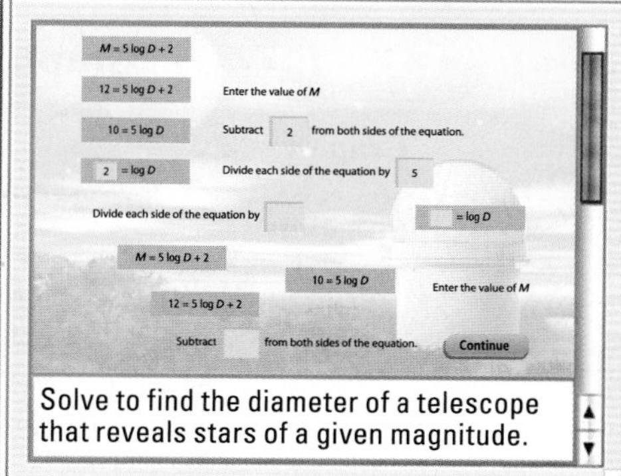

Solve to find the diameter of a telescope that reveals stars of a given magnitude.

Animated Algebra at classzone.com

Other animations for Chapter 7: pages 480, 487, 502, and 538

7.1 Graph Exponential Growth Functions

A2.A.53 Graph exponential functions of the form $y = bx$ for positive values of b, including $b = e$

Before You graphed polynomial and radical functions.

Now You will graph and use exponential growth functions.

Why? So you can model sports equipment costs, as in Ex. 40.

Key Vocabulary
- **exponential function**
- **exponential growth function**
- **growth factor**
- **asymptote**

An **exponential function** has the form $y = ab^x$ where $a \neq 0$ and the base b is a positive number other than 1. If $a > 0$ and $b > 1$, then the function $y = ab^x$ is an **exponential growth function**, and b is called the **growth factor**. The simplest type of exponential growth function has the form $y = b^x$.

KEY CONCEPT *For Your Notebook*

Parent Function for Exponential Growth Functions

The function $f(x) = b^x$, where $b > 1$, is the parent function for the family of exponential growth functions with base b. The general shape of the graph of $f(x) = b^x$ is shown below.

The x-axis is an **asymptote** of the graph. An asymptote is a line that a graph approaches more and more closely.

$f(x) = b^x$ $(b > 1)$; points $(0, 1)$, $(1, b)$

The graph rises from left to right, passing through the points (0, 1) and (1, b).

The domain of $f(x) = b^x$ is all real numbers. The range is $y > 0$.

EXAMPLE 1 Graph $y = b^x$ for $b > 1$

Graph $y = 2^x$.

Solution

STEP 1 **Make** a table of values.

x	−2	−1	0	1	2	3
y	$\frac{1}{4}$	$\frac{1}{2}$	1	2	4	8

STEP 2 **Plot** the points from the table.

STEP 3 **Draw,** from *left* to *right*, a smooth curve that begins just above the x-axis, passes through the plotted points, and moves up to the right.

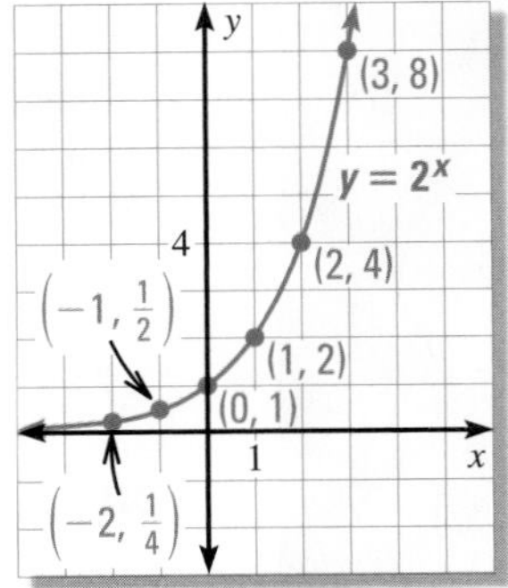

The graph of a function $y = ab^x$ is a vertical stretch or shrink of the graph of $y = b^x$. The y-intercept of the graph of $y = ab^x$ occurs at $(0, a)$ rather than $(0, 1)$.

EXAMPLE 2 Graph $y = ab^x$ for $b > 1$

Graph the function.

a. $y = \frac{1}{2} \cdot 4^x$

b. $y = -\left(\frac{5}{2}\right)^x$

Solution

a. Plot $\left(0, \frac{1}{2}\right)$ and $(1, 2)$. Then, from *left* to *right*, draw a curve that begins just above the x-axis, passes through the two points, and moves up to the right.

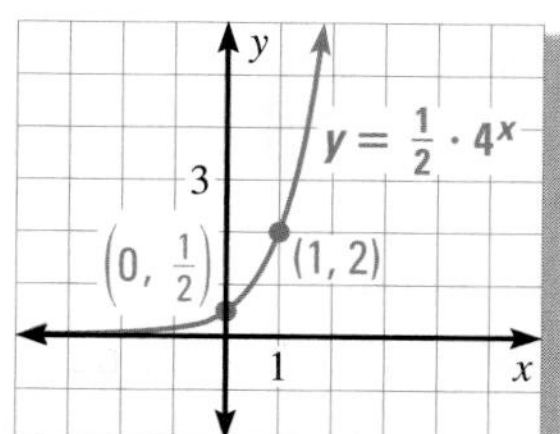

b. Plot $(0, -1)$ and $\left(1, -\frac{5}{2}\right)$. Then, from *left* to *right*, draw a curve that begins just below the x-axis, passes through the two points, and moves down to the right.

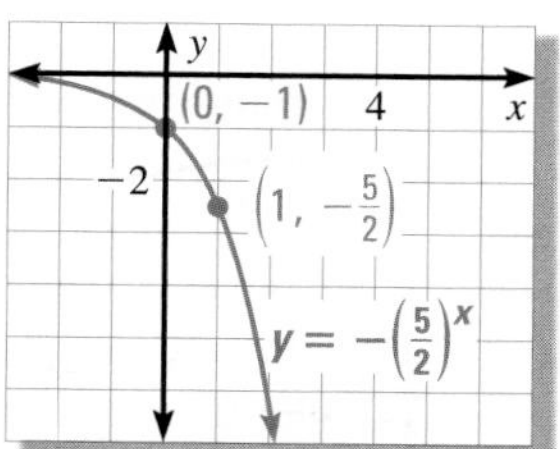

CLASSIFY FUNCTIONS

Note that the function in part (b) of Example 2 is not an exponential growth function because $a = -1 < 0$.

TRANSLATIONS To graph a function of the form $y = ab^{x-h} + k$, begin by sketching the graph of $y = ab^x$. Then translate the graph horizontally by h units and vertically by k units.

EXAMPLE 3 Graph $y = ab^{x-h} + k$ for $b > 1$

Graph $y = 4 \cdot 2^{x-1} - 3$. State the domain and range.

Solution

Begin by sketching the graph of $y = 4 \cdot 2^x$, which passes through $(0, 4)$ and $(1, 8)$. Then translate the graph right 1 unit and down 3 units to obtain the graph of $y = 4 \cdot 2^{x-1} - 3$.

The graph's asymptote is the line $y = -3$. The domain is all real numbers, and the range is $y > -3$.

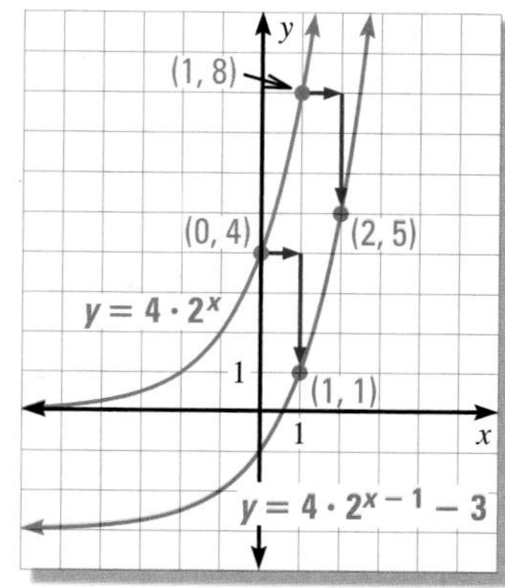

✓ GUIDED PRACTICE for Examples 1, 2, and 3

Graph the function. State the domain and range.

1. $y = 4^x$

2. $y = \frac{1}{2} \cdot 3^x$

3. $f(x) = 3^{x+1} + 2$

EXPONENTIAL GROWTH MODELS When a real-life quantity increases by a fixed percent each year (or other time period), the amount y of the quantity after t years can be modeled by the equation

$$y = a(1 + r)^t$$

where a is the initial amount and r is the percent increase expressed as a decimal. Note that the quantity $1 + r$ is the growth factor.

EXAMPLE 4 Solve a multi-step problem

COMPUTERS In 1996, there were 2573 computer viruses and other computer security incidents. During the next 7 years, the number of incidents increased by about 92% each year.

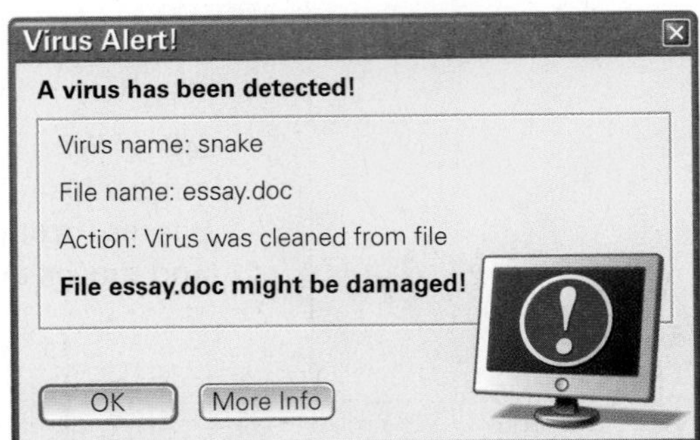

- Write an exponential growth model giving the number n of incidents t years after 1996. About how many incidents were there in 2003?
- Graph the model.
- Use the graph to estimate the year when there were about 125,000 computer security incidents.

Solution

STEP 1 The initial amount is $a = 2573$ and the percent increase is $r = 0.92$. So, the exponential growth model is:

$n = a(1 + r)^t$ — **Write exponential growth model.**

$= 2573(1 + 0.92)^t$ — **Substitute 2573 for *a* and 0.92 for *r*.**

$= 2573(1.92)^t$ — **Simplify.**

AVOID ERRORS
Notice that the percent increase and the growth factor are two different values. An increase of 92% corresponds to a growth factor of 1.92.

Using this model, you can estimate the number of incidents in 2003 ($t = 7$) to be $n = 2573(1.92)^7 \approx 247,485$.

STEP 2 The graph passes through the points (0, 2573) and (1, 4940.16). Plot a few other points. Then draw a smooth curve through the points.

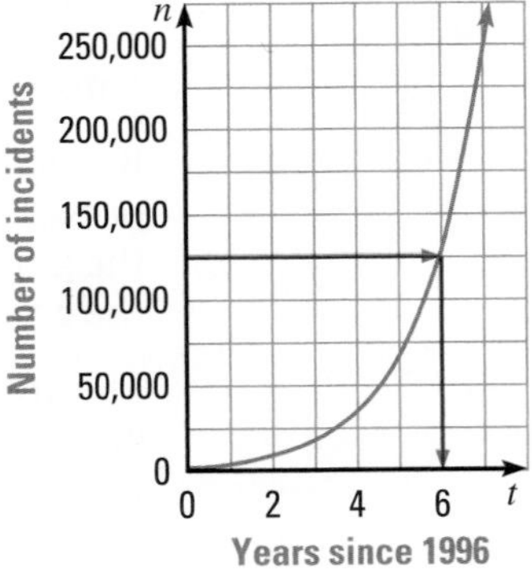

STEP 3 Using the graph, you can estimate that the number of incidents was about 125,000 during 2002 ($t \approx 6$).

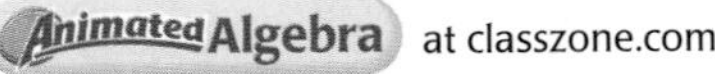

at classzone.com

GUIDED PRACTICE for Example 4

4. **WHAT IF?** In Example 4, estimate the year in which there were about 250,000 computer security incidents.

5. In the exponential growth model $y = 527(1.39)^x$, identify the initial amount, the growth factor, and the percent increase.

COMPOUND INTEREST Exponential growth functions are used in real-life situations involving *compound interest.* Compound interest is interest paid on the initial investment, called the *principal,* and on previously earned interest. Interest paid only on the principal is called *simple interest.*

KEY CONCEPT *For Your Notebook*

Compound Interest

Consider an initial principal P deposited in an account that pays interest at an annual rate r (expressed as a decimal), compounded n times per year. The amount A in the account after t years is given by this equation:

$$A = P\left(1 + \frac{r}{n}\right)^{nt}$$

EXAMPLE 5 Find the balance in an account

FINANCE You deposit \$4000 in an account that pays 2.92% annual interest. Find the balance after 1 year if the interest is compounded with the given frequency.

a. Quarterly

b. Daily

Solution

a. With interest compounded quarterly, the balance after 1 year is:

$A = P\left(1 + \frac{r}{n}\right)^{nt}$	**Write compound interest formula.**
$= 4000\left(1 + \frac{0.0292}{4}\right)^{4 \cdot 1}$	$P = 4000, r = 0.0292, n = 4, t = 1$
$= 4000(1.0073)^4$	**Simplify.**
≈ 4118.09	**Use a calculator.**

▶ The balance at the end of 1 year is \$4118.09.

b. With interest compounded daily, the balance after 1 year is:

$A = P\left(1 + \frac{r}{n}\right)^{nt}$	**Write compound interest formula.**
$= 4000\left(1 + \frac{0.0292}{365}\right)^{365 \cdot 1}$	$P = 4000, r = 0.0292, n = 365, t = 1$
$= 4000(1.00008)^{365}$	**Simplify.**
≈ 4118.52	**Use a calculator.**

▶ The balance at the end of 1 year is \$4118.52.

✓ **GUIDED PRACTICE** for Example 5

6. **FINANCE** You deposit \$2000 in an account that pays 4% annual interest. Find the balance after 3 years if the interest is compounded daily.

7.1 EXERCISES

HOMEWORK KEY

○ = **WORKED-OUT SOLUTIONS** on p. WS13 for Exs. 17, 29, and 37

★ = **STANDARDIZED TEST PRACTICE** Exs. 2, 24, 25, 32, 40, and 41

◆ = **MULTIPLE REPRESENTATIONS** Ex. 42

SKILL PRACTICE

1. **VOCABULARY** In the exponential growth model $y = 2.4(1.5)^x$, identify the initial amount, the growth factor, and the percent increase.

2. ★ **WRITING** What is an asymptote?

EXAMPLES 1 and 2 on pp. 478–479 for Exs. 3–14

MATCHING GRAPHS **Match the function with its graph.**

3. $y = 3 \cdot 2^x$
4. $y = -3 \cdot 2^x$
5. $y = 2 \cdot 3^x$

A.
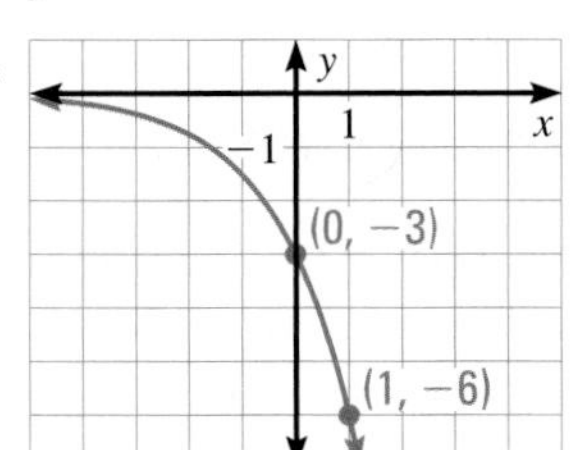

B.
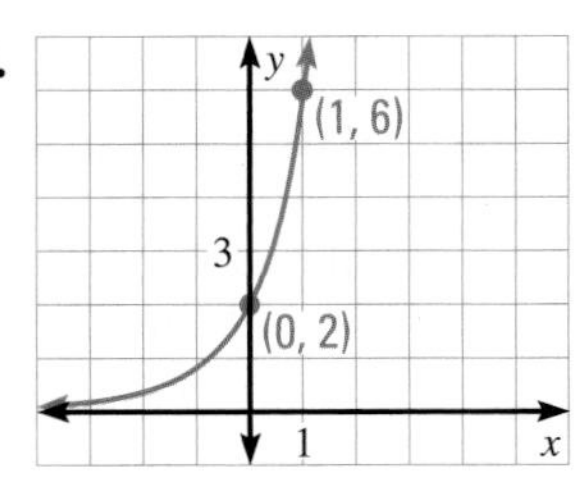

C.
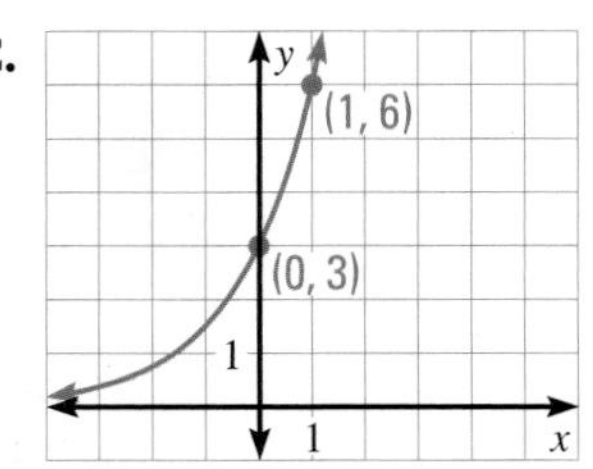

GRAPHING FUNCTIONS **Graph the function.**

6. $y = 3^x$
7. $y = -2^x$
8. $f(x) = 5 \cdot 2^x$
9. $y = 5^x$
10. $y = 2 \cdot 4^x$
11. $g(x) = -(1.5)^x$
12. $y = 3\left(\frac{4}{3}\right)^x$
13. $y = \frac{1}{2} \cdot 3^x$
14. $h(x) = -2(2.5)^x$

EXAMPLE 3 on p. 479 for Exs. 15–24

TRANSLATING GRAPHS **Graph the function. State the domain and range.**

15. $y = -3 \cdot 2^{x+2}$
16. $y = 5 \cdot 4^x + 2$
17. $y = 2^{x+1} + 3$
18. $y = 3^{x-2} - 1$
19. $y = 2 \cdot 3^{x-2} - 1$
20. $y = -3 \cdot 4^{x-1} - 2$
21. $f(x) = 6 \cdot 2^{x-3} + 3$
22. $g(x) = 5 \cdot 3^{x+2} - 4$
23. $h(x) = -2 \cdot 5^{x-1} + 1$

24. ★ **MULTIPLE CHOICE** The graph of which function is shown?

Ⓐ $f(x) = 2(1.5)^x - 1$

Ⓑ $f(x) = 2(1.5)^x + 1$

Ⓒ $f(x) = 3(1.5)^x - 1$

Ⓓ $f(x) = 3(1.5)^x + 1$

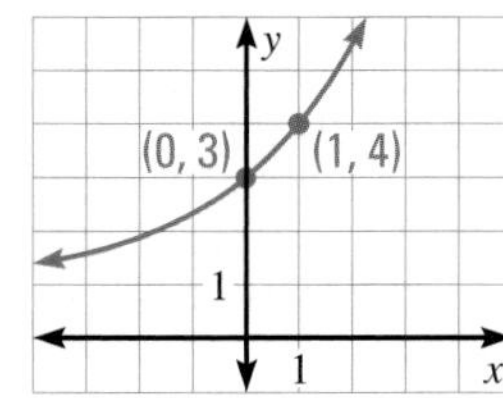

25. ★ **MULTIPLE CHOICE** The student enrollment E of a high school was 1310 in 1998 and has increased by 10% per year since then. Which exponential growth model gives the school's student enrollment in terms of t, where t is the number of years since 1998?

Ⓐ $E = 0.1(1310)^t$

Ⓑ $E = 1310(0.1)^t$

Ⓒ $E = 1.1(1310)^t$

Ⓓ $E = 1310(1.1)^t$

ERROR ANALYSIS ***Describe*** **and correct the error in graphing the function.**

26. $y = 2 \cdot 4^x$

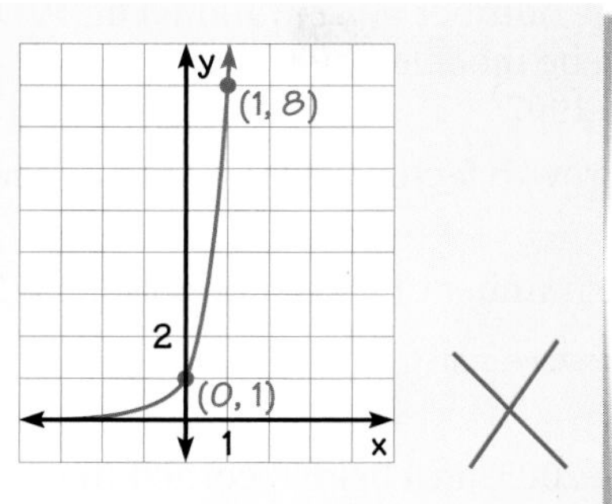

27. $y = 2^{x-3} + 3$

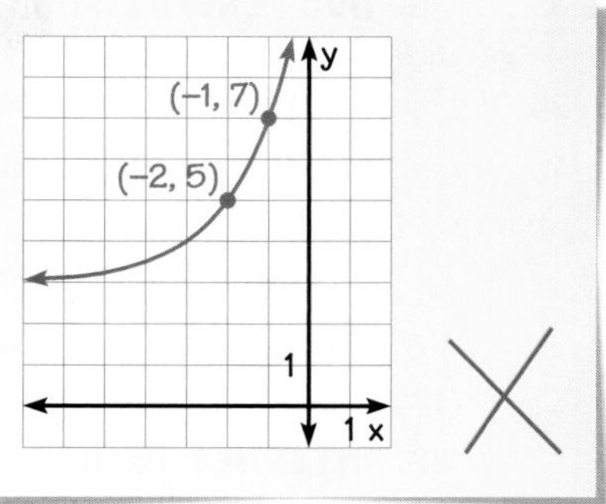

WRITING MODELS In Exercises 28–30, write an exponential growth model that describes the situation.

28. In 1992, 1219 monk parakeets were observed in the United States. For the next 11 years, about 12% more parakeets were observed each year.

29. You deposit \$800 in an account that pays 2% annual interest compounded daily.

30. You purchase an antique table for \$450. The value of the table increases by 6% per year.

31. GRAPHING CALCULATOR You deposit \$1500 in a bank account that pays 3% annual interest compounded yearly.

a. Type 1500 into a graphing calculator and press ENTER. Then enter the formula ANS * 1.03, as shown at the right. Press ENTER seven times to find your balance after 7 years.

```
1500
                1500
Ans*1.03
                1545
             1591.35
           1639.0905
         1688.263215
```

b. Find the number of years it takes for your balance to exceed \$2500.

32. ★ **OPEN-ENDED MATH** Write an exponential function of the form $y = ab^{x-h} + k$ whose graph has a y-intercept of 5 and an asymptote of $y = 2$.

33. GRAPHING CALCULATOR Consider the exponential growth function $y = ab^{x-h} + k$ where $a = 2$, $b = 5$, $h = -4$, and $k = 3$. Predict the effect on the function's graph of each change in a, b, h, or k described in parts (a)–(d). Use a graphing calculator to check your prediction.

a. a changes to 1 **b.** b changes to 4 **c.** h changes to 3 **d.** k changes to -1

34. CHALLENGE Consider the exponential function $f(x) = ab^x$.

a. Show that $\dfrac{f(x+1)}{f(x)} = b$.

b. Use the result from part (a) to explain why there is no exponential function of the form $f(x) = ab^x$ whose graph passes through the points in the table below.

x	0	1	2	3	4
y	4	4	8	24	72

PROBLEM SOLVING

EXAMPLE 4
on p. 480
for Exs. 35–36

35. DVD PLAYERS From 1997 to 2002, the number n (in millions) of DVD players sold in the United States can be modeled by $n = 0.42(2.47)^t$ where t is the number of years since 1997.

a. Identify the initial amount, the growth factor, and the annual percent increase.

b. Graph the function. Estimate the number of DVD players sold in 2001.

@HomeTutor for problem solving help at classzone.com

36. INTERNET Each March from 1998 to 2003, a website recorded the number y of referrals it received from Internet search engines. The results can be modeled by $y = 2500(1.50)^t$ where t is the number of years since 1998.

a. Identify the initial amount, the growth factor, and the annual percent increase.

b. Graph the function and state the domain and range. Estimate the number of referrals the website received from Internet search engines in March of 2002.

@HomeTutor for problem solving help at classzone.com

EXAMPLE 5
on p. 481
for Exs. 37–38

37. ACCOUNT BALANCE You deposit \$2200 in a bank account. Find the balance after 4 years for each of the situations described below.

a. The account pays 3% annual interest compounded quarterly.

b. The account pays 2.25% annual interest compounded monthly.

c. The account pays 2% annual interest compounded daily.

38. DEPOSITING FUNDS You want to have \$3000 in your savings account after 3 years. Find the amount you should deposit for each of the situations described below.

a. The account pays 2.25% annual interest compounded quarterly.

b. The account pays 3.5% annual interest compounded monthly.

c. The account pays 4% annual interest compounded yearly.

39. MULTI-STEP PROBLEM In 1990, the population of Austin, Texas, was 494,290. During the next 10 years, the population increased by about 3% each year.

a. Write a model giving the population P (in thousands) of Austin t years after 1990. What was the population in 2000?

b. Graph the model and state the domain and range.

c. Estimate the year when the population was about 590,000.

Austin, Texas

40. ★ SHORT RESPONSE At an online auction, the opening bid for a pair of in-line skates is \$50. The price of the skates increases by 10.5% per bid during the next 6 bids.

a. Write a model giving the price p (in dollars) of the skates after n bids.

b. What was the price after 5 bids? According to the model, what will the price be after 100 bids? Is this predicted price reasonable? *Explain.*

○ = WORKED-OUT SOLUTIONS on p. WS1 ★ = STANDARDIZED TEST PRACTICE ◆ = MULTIPLE REPRESENTATIONS

41. ★ **EXTENDED RESPONSE** In 2000, the average price of a football ticket for a Minnesota Viking's game was \$48.28. During the next 4 years, the price increased an average of 6% each year.

   a. Write a model giving the average price p (in dollars) of a ticket t years after 2000.

   b. Graph the model. Estimate the year when the average price of a ticket was about \$60.

   c. *Explain* how you can use the graph of $p(t)$ to determine the minimum and maximum t-values in the domain for which the function gives meaningful results.

42. ◆ **MULTIPLE REPRESENTATIONS** In 1977, there were 41 breeding pairs of bald eagles in Maryland. Over the next 24 years, the number of breeding pairs increased by about 8.9% each year.

   a. **Writing an Equation** Write a model giving the number n of breeding pairs of bald eagles in Maryland t years after 1977.

   b. **Making a Table** Make a table of values for the model.

   c. **Drawing a Graph** Graph the model.

   d. **Using a Graph** About how many breeding pairs of bald eagles were in Maryland in 2001?

43. **REASONING** Is investing \$3000 at 6% annual interest and \$3000 at 8% annual interest equivalent to investing \$6000 (the total of the two principals) at 7% annual interest (the average of the two interest rates)? *Explain.*

44. **CHALLENGE** The yearly cost for residents to attend a state university has increased from \$5200 to \$9000 in the last 5 years.

   a. To the nearest tenth of a percent, what has been the average annual growth rate in cost?

   b. If this growth rate continues, what will the cost be in 5 more years?

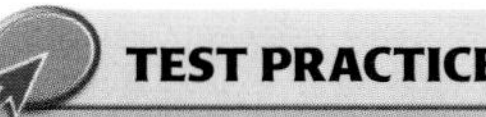

TEST PRACTICE at classzone.com

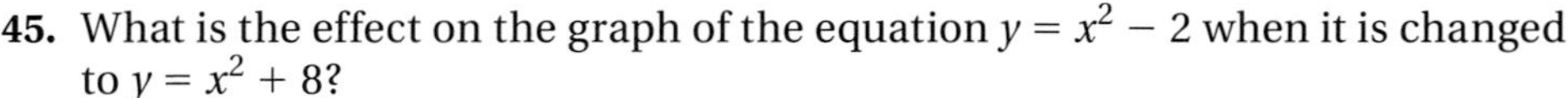

NEW YORK MIXED REVIEW

45. What is the effect on the graph of the equation $y = x^2 - 2$ when it is changed to $y = x^2 + 8$?

   Ⓐ The graph is translated 10 units up.

   Ⓑ The graph is translated 10 units down.

   Ⓒ The graph is translated 10 units to the right.

   Ⓓ The graph is translated 10 units to the left.

46. What is the approximate length of arc AB?

   Ⓐ 5.3 cm   Ⓑ 8.4 cm

   Ⓒ 16.8 cm   Ⓓ 33.5 cm

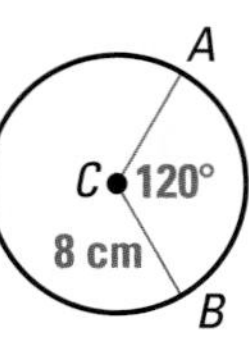

7.2 Graph Exponential Decay Functions

A2.A.53 Graph exponential functions of the form $y = bx$ for positive values of b, including $b = e$

Before You graphed and used exponential growth functions.

Now You will graph and use exponential decay functions.

Why? So you can model depreciation, as in Ex. 31.

Key Vocabulary
- **exponential decay function**
- **decay factor**

In Lesson 7.1 you studied exponential growth functions. In this lesson, you will study **exponential decay functions**, which have the form $y = ab^x$ where $a > 0$ and $0 < b < 1$. The base b of an exponential decay function is called the **decay factor**.

KEY CONCEPT *For Your Notebook*

Parent Function for Exponential Decay Functions

The function $f(x) = b^x$, where $0 < b < 1$, is the parent function for the family of exponential decay functions with base b. The general shape of the graph of $f(x) = b^x$ is shown below.

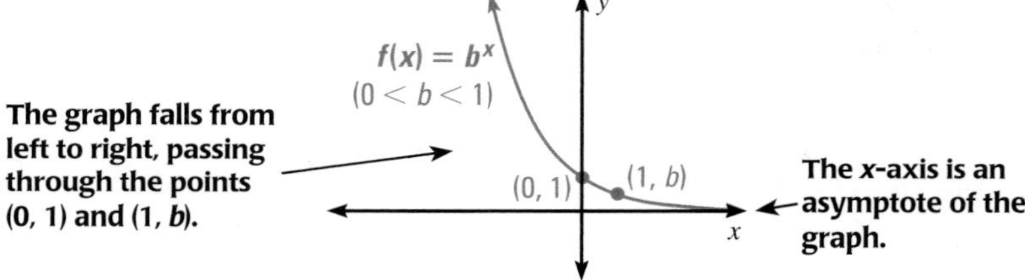

The domain of $f(x) = b^x$ is all real numbers. The range is $y > 0$.

EXAMPLE 1 Graph $y = b^x$ for $0 < b < 1$

Graph $y = \left(\frac{1}{2}\right)^x$.

Solution

STEP 1 **Make** a table of values.

x	−3	−2	−1	0	1	2
y	8	4	2	1	$\frac{1}{2}$	$\frac{1}{4}$

STEP 2 **Plot** the points from the table.

STEP 3 **Draw,** from *right* to *left*, a smooth curve that begins just above the x-axis, passes through the plotted points, and moves up to the left.

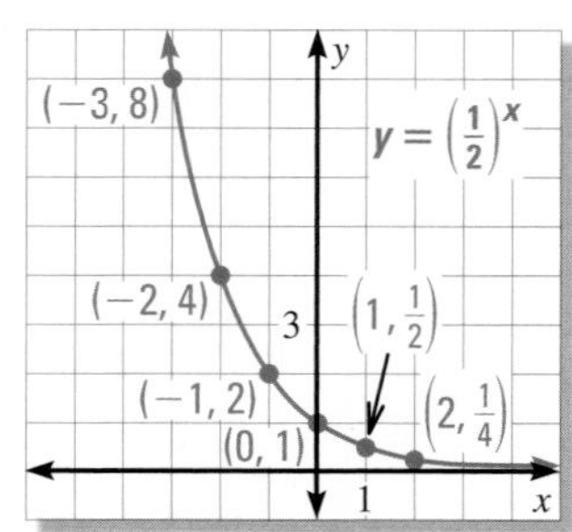

TRANSFORMATIONS Recall from Lesson 7.1 that the graph of a function $y = ab^x$ is a vertical stretch or shrink of the graph of $y = b^x$, and the graph of $y = ab^{x-h} + k$ is a translation of the graph of $y = ab^x$.

EXAMPLE 2 Graph $y = ab^x$ for $0 < b < 1$

CLASSIFY FUNCTIONS
Note that the function in part (b) of Example 2 is not an exponential decay function because $a = -3 < 0$.

Graph the function.

a. $y = 2\left(\frac{1}{4}\right)^x$

b. $y = -3\left(\frac{2}{5}\right)^x$

Solution

a. Plot (0, 2) and $\left(1, \frac{1}{2}\right)$. Then, from *right* to *left*, draw a curve that begins just above the *x*-axis, passes through the two points, and moves up to the left.

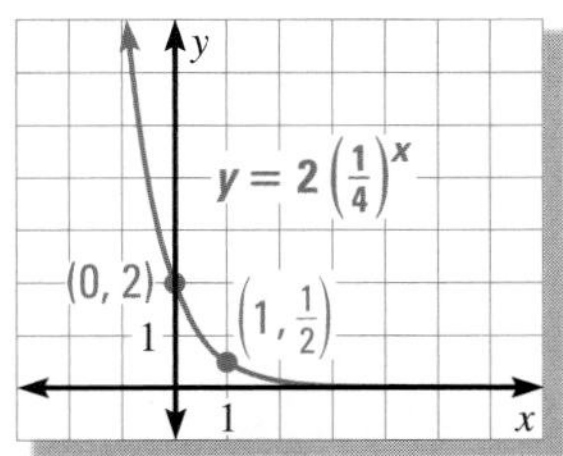

b. Plot (0, −3) and $\left(1, -\frac{6}{5}\right)$. Then, from *right* to *left*, draw a curve that begins just below the *x*-axis, passes through the two points, and moves down to the left.

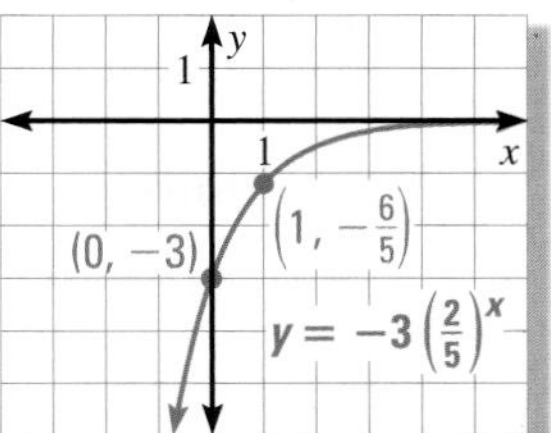

Animated Algebra at classzone.com

GUIDED PRACTICE for Examples 1 and 2

Graph the function.

1. $y = \left(\frac{2}{3}\right)^x$

2. $y = -2\left(\frac{3}{4}\right)^x$

3. $f(x) = 4\left(\frac{1}{5}\right)^x$

EXAMPLE 3 Graph $y = ab^{x-h} + k$ for $0 < b < 1$

Graph $y = 3\left(\frac{1}{2}\right)^{x+1} - 2$. State the domain and range.

Solution

Begin by sketching the graph of $y = 3\left(\frac{1}{2}\right)^x$, which passes through (0, 3) and $\left(1, \frac{3}{2}\right)$.

Then translate the graph left 1 unit and down 2 units. Notice that the translated graph passes through (−1, 1) and $\left(0, -\frac{1}{2}\right)$.

The graph's asymptote is the line $y = -2$. The domain is all real numbers, and the range is $y > -2$.

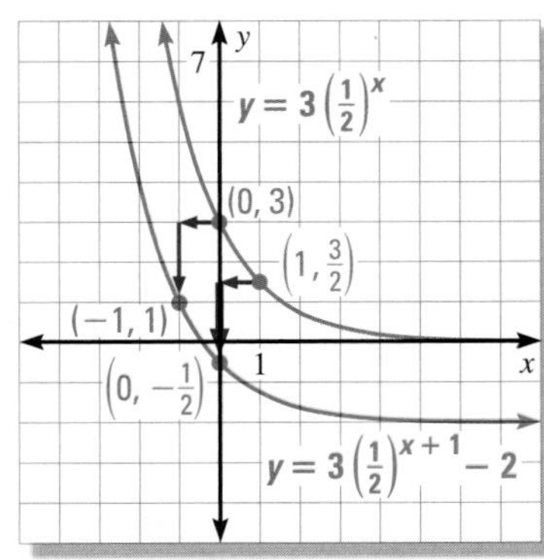

EXPONENTIAL DECAY MODELS When a real-life quantity decreases by a fixed percent each year (or other time period), the amount y of the quantity after t years can be modeled by the equation

$$y = a(1 - r)^t$$

where a is the initial amount and r is the percent decrease expressed as a decimal. Note that the quantity $1 - r$ is the decay factor.

EXAMPLE 4 Solve a multi-step problem

SNOWMOBILES A new snowmobile costs \$4200. The value of the snowmobile decreases by 10% each year.

- Write an exponential decay model giving the snowmobile's value y (in dollars) after t years. Estimate the value after 3 years.
- Graph the model.
- Use the graph to estimate when the value of the snowmobile will be \$2500.

Solution

STEP 1 The initial amount is $a = 4200$ and the percent decrease is $r = 0.10$. So, the exponential decay model is:

$y = a(1 - r)^t$	**Write exponential decay model.**
$= 4200(1 - 0.10)^t$	**Substitute 4200 for *a* and 0.10 for *r*.**
$= 4200(0.90)^t$	**Simplify.**

When $t = 3$, the snowmobile's value is $y = 4200(0.90)^3 = \$3061.80$.

AVOID ERRORS

Notice that the percent decrease, 10%, tells you how much value the snowmobile *loses* each year. The decay factor, 0.90, tells you what fraction of the snowmobile's value *remains* each year.

STEP 2 The graph passes through the points (0, 4200) and (1, 3780). It has the t-axis as an asymptote. Plot a few other points. Then draw a smooth curve through the points.

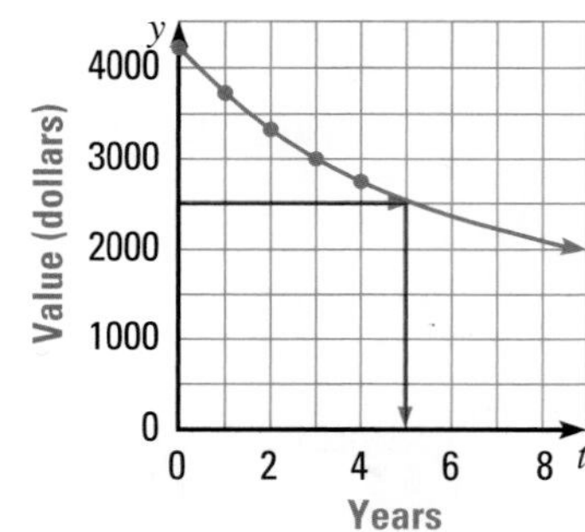

STEP 3 Using the graph, you can estimate that the value of the snowmobile will be \$2500 after about 5 years.

GUIDED PRACTICE for Examples 3 and 4

Graph the function. State the domain and range.

4. $y = \left(\frac{1}{4}\right)^{x-1} + 1$ **5.** $y = 5\left(\frac{2}{3}\right)^{x+1} - 2$ **6.** $g(x) = -3\left(\frac{3}{4}\right)^{x-5} + 4$

7. WHAT IF? In Example 4, suppose the value of the snowmobile decreases by 20% each year. Write and graph an equation to model this situation. Use the graph to estimate when the value of the snowmobile will be \$2500.

8. SNOWMOBILE The value of a snowmobile has been decreasing by 7% each year since it was new. After 3 years, the value is \$3000. Find the original cost of the snowmobile.

7.2 EXERCISES

HOMEWORK KEY

○ = **WORKED-OUT SOLUTIONS** on p. WS13 for Exs. 9, 19, and 33

★ = **STANDARDIZED TEST PRACTICE** Exs. 2, 15, 27, 28, 33, and 35

SKILL PRACTICE

1. **VOCABULARY** In the exponential decay model $y = 1250(0.85)^t$, identify the initial amount, the decay factor, and the percent decrease.

2. ★ **WRITING** *Explain* how to tell whether the function $y = b^x$ represents exponential growth or exponential decay.

CLASSIFYING FUNCTIONS **Tell whether the function represents *exponential growth* or *exponential decay.***

3. $f(x) = 3\left(\frac{3}{4}\right)^x$
4. $f(x) = 4\left(\frac{5}{2}\right)^x$
5. $f(x) = \frac{2}{7} \cdot 4^x$
6. $f(x) = 25(0.25)^x$

EXAMPLES 1 and 2 on pp. 486–487 for Exs. 7–15

GRAPHING FUNCTIONS **Graph the function.**

7. $y = \left(\frac{1}{4}\right)^x$
8. $y = \left(\frac{1}{3}\right)^x$
9. $f(x) = 2\left(\frac{1}{5}\right)^x$
10. $y = -(0.2)^x$
11. $y = -4\left(\frac{1}{3}\right)^x$
12. $g(x) = 2(0.75)^x$
13. $y = \left(\frac{3}{5}\right)^x$
14. $h(x) = -3\left(\frac{3}{8}\right)^x$

15. ★ **MULTIPLE CHOICE** The graph of which function is shown?

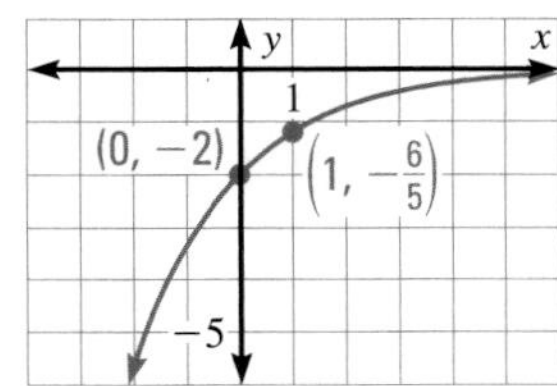

Ⓐ $y = 2\left(-\frac{3}{5}\right)^x$ Ⓑ $y = -2\left(\frac{3}{5}\right)^x$

Ⓒ $y = -2\left(\frac{2}{5}\right)^x$ Ⓓ $y = 2\left(-\frac{2}{5}\right)^x$

EXAMPLE 3 on p. 487 for Exs. 16–25

TRANSLATING GRAPHS **Graph the function. State the domain and range.**

16. $y = \left(\frac{1}{3}\right)^x + 1$
17. $y = -\left(\frac{1}{2}\right)^{x-1}$
18. $y = 2\left(\frac{1}{3}\right)^{x+1} - 3$
19. $y = \left(\frac{2}{3}\right)^{x-4} - 1$
20. $y = 3(0.25)^x + 3$
21. $y = \left(\frac{1}{3}\right)^{x-2} + 2$
22. $f(x) = -3\left(\frac{1}{4}\right)^{x-1}$
23. $g(x) = 6\left(\frac{1}{2}\right)^{x+5} - 2$
24. $h(x) = 4\left(\frac{1}{2}\right)^{x+1}$

25. **GRAPHING CALCULATOR** Consider the exponential decay function $y = ab^{x-h} + k$ where $a = 3$, $b = 0.4$, $h = 2$, and $k = -1$. Predict the effect on the function's graph of each change in a, b, h, or k described in parts (a)–(d). Use a graphing calculator to check your prediction.

    a. a changes to 4
    b. b changes to 0.2
    c. h changes to 5
    d. k changes to 3

26. **ERROR ANALYSIS** You invest $500 in the stock of a company. The value of the stock decreases 2% each year. *Describe* and correct the error in writing a model for the value of the stock after t years.

$y = \left(\text{Initial amount}\right)\left(\text{Decay factor}\right)^t$

$y = 500(0.02)^t$ ✗

27. ★ **MULTIPLE CHOICE** What is the asymptote of the graph of $y = \left(\frac{1}{2}\right)^{x-2} + 3$?

Ⓐ $y = -3$ Ⓑ $y = -2$ Ⓒ $y = 2$ Ⓓ $y = 3$

28. ★ **OPEN-ENDED MATH** Write an exponential function whose graph lies between the graphs of $y = (0.5)^x$ and $y = (0.25)^x + 3$.

29. **CHALLENGE** Do $f(x) = 5(4)^{-x}$ and $g(x) = 5(0.25)^x$ represent the same function? *Justify* your answer.

PROBLEM SOLVING

EXAMPLE 4 on p. 488 for Exs. 30–31

30. **MEDICINE** When a person takes a dosage of I milligrams of ibuprofen, the amount A (in milligrams) of medication remaining in the person's bloodstream after t hours can be modeled by the equation $A = I(0.71)^t$.

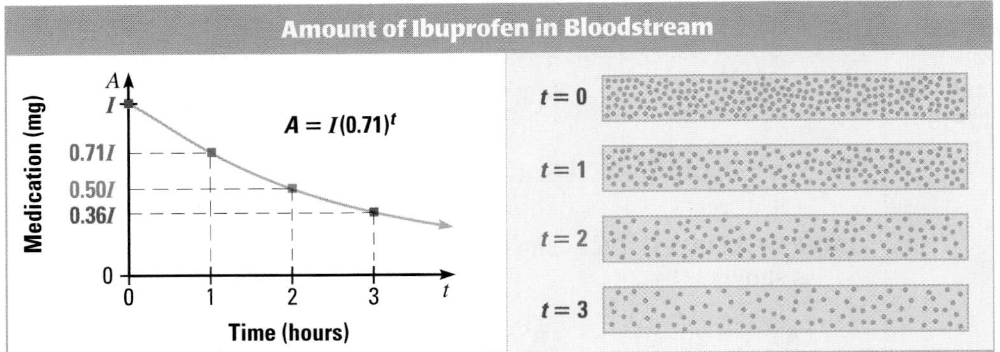

Find the amount of ibuprofen remaining in a person's bloodstream for the given dosage and elapsed time since the medication was taken.

a. Dosage: 200 mg
Time: 1.5 hours

b. Dosage: 325 mg
Time: 3.5 hours

c. Dosage: 400 mg
Time: 5 hours

@HomeTutor for problem solving help at classzone.com

31. **BIKE COSTS** You buy a new mountain bike for \$200. The value of the bike decreases by 25% each year.

a. Write a model giving the mountain bike's value y (in dollars) after t years. Use the model to estimate the value of the bike after 3 years.

b. Graph the model.

c. Estimate when the value of the bike will be \$100.

@HomeTutor for problem solving help at classzone.com

32. **DEPRECIATION** The table shows the amount d that a boat depreciates during each year t since it was new. Show that the ratio of depreciation amounts for consecutive years is constant. Then write an equation that gives d as a function of t.

Year, t	1	2	3	4	5
Depreciation, d	\$1906	\$1832	\$1762	\$1692	\$1627

○ = WORKED-OUT SOLUTIONS on p. WS1

★ = STANDARDIZED TEST PRACTICE

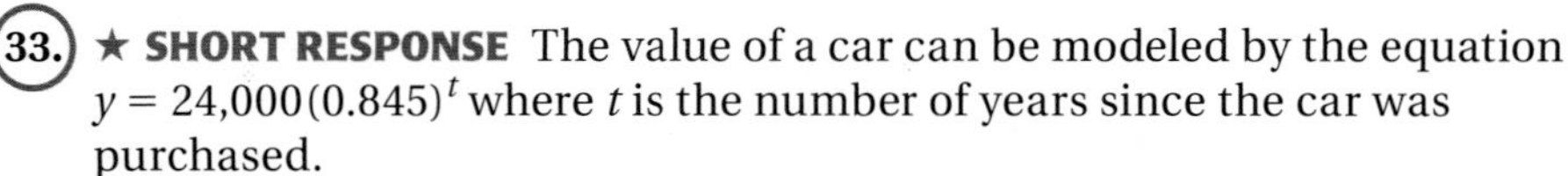

33. ★ **SHORT RESPONSE** The value of a car can be modeled by the equation $y = 24{,}000(0.845)^t$ where t is the number of years since the car was purchased.

   a. Graph the model. Estimate when the value of the car will be \$10,000.

   b. Use the model to predict the value of the car after 50 years. Is this a reasonable value? *Explain.*

34. **MULTI-STEP PROBLEM** When a plant or animal dies, it stops acquiring carbon-14 from the atmosphere. Carbon-14 decays over time with a half-life of about 5730 years. The percent P of the original amount of carbon-14 that remains in a sample after t years is given by this equation:

$$P = 100\left(\frac{1}{2}\right)^{t/5730}$$

   a. What percent of the original carbon-14 remains in a sample after 2500 years? 5000 years? 10,000 years?

   b. Graph the model.

   c. An archaeologist found a bison bone that contained about 37% of the carbon-14 present when the bison died. Use the graph to estimate the age of the bone when it was found.

35. ★ **EXTENDED RESPONSE** The number E of eggs a Leghorn chicken produces per year can be modeled by the equation $E = 179.2(0.89)^{w/52}$ where w is the age (in weeks) of the chicken and $w \geq 22$.

   a. **Interpret** Identify the decay factor and the percent decrease.

   b. **Graph** Graph the model.

   c. **Estimate** Estimate the egg production of a chicken that is 2.5 years old.

   d. **Reasoning** *Explain* how you can rewrite the given equation so that time is measured in years rather than in weeks.

36. **CHALLENGE** You buy a new stereo for \$1300 and are able to sell it 4 years later for \$275. Assume that the resale value of the stereo decays exponentially with time. Write an equation giving the stereo's resale value V (in dollars) as a function of the time t (in years) since you bought it.

NEW YORK MIXED REVIEW

TEST PRACTICE at classzone.com

37. If $\triangle PQR$ is translated to the left 3 units and down 2 units, in which quadrant will the image of point Q appear?

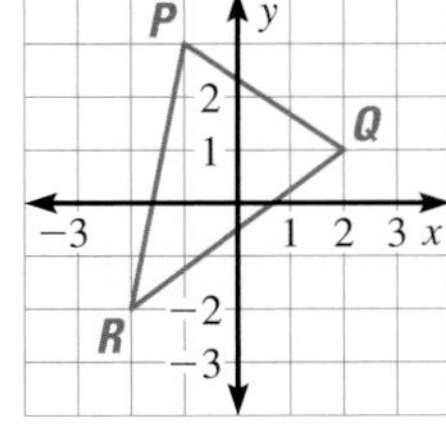

   Ⓐ Quadrant I Ⓑ Quadrant II

   Ⓒ Quadrant III Ⓓ Quadrant IV

38. This year's price for a certain laptop computer is 16.7% lower than last year's price of \$960. Approximately what percent of this year's price for the computer is last year's price?

   Ⓐ 83.3% Ⓑ 85.0% Ⓒ 116.7% Ⓓ 120.0%

7.3 Use Functions Involving e

A2.A.53 Graph exponential functions of the form $y = bx$ for positive values of b, including $b = e$

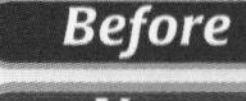

Before You studied exponential growth and decay functions.

Now You will study functions involving the natural base e.

Why? So you can model visibility underwater, as in Ex. 59.

Key Vocabulary
- **natural base e**

The history of mathematics is marked by the discovery of special numbers such as π and i. Another special number is denoted by the letter e. The number is called the **natural base e** or the *Euler number* after its discoverer, Leonhard Euler (1707–1783). The expression $\left(1 + \frac{1}{n}\right)^n$ approaches e as n increases.

n	10^1	10^2	10^3	10^4	10^5	10^6
$\left(1 + \frac{1}{n}\right)^n$	2.59374	2.70481	2.71692	2.71815	2.71827	2.71828

KEY CONCEPT *For Your Notebook*

The Natural Base e

The natural base e is irrational. It is defined as follows:

As n approaches $+\infty$, $\left(1 + \frac{1}{n}\right)^n$ approaches $e \approx 2.718281828$.

EXAMPLE 1 Simplify natural base expressions

REVIEW EXPONENTS
For help with properties of exponents, see p. 330.

Simplify the expression.

a. $e^2 \cdot e^5 = e^{2+5}$
$= e^7$

b. $\frac{12e^4}{3e^3} = 4e^{4-3}$
$= 4e$

c. $(5e^{-3x})^2 = 5^2(e^{-3x})^2$
$= 25e^{-6x} = \frac{25}{e^{6x}}$

EXAMPLE 2 Evaluate natural base expressions

Use a calculator to evaluate the expression.

	Expression	Keystrokes	Display
a.	e^4	2nd [e^x] 4) ENTER	54.59815003
b.	$e^{-0.09}$	2nd [e^x] (–) .09) ENTER	0.9139311853

✓ **GUIDED PRACTICE** for Examples 1 and 2

Simplify the expression.

1. $e^7 \cdot e^4$
2. $2e^{-3} \cdot 6e^5$
3. $\frac{24e^8}{4e^5}$
4. $(10e^{-4x})^3$
5. Use a calculator to evaluate $e^{3/4}$.

KEY CONCEPT *For Your Notebook*

Natural Base Functions

A function of the form $y = ae^{rx}$ is called a *natural base exponential function.*

- If $a > 0$ and $r > 0$, the function is an exponential growth function.
- If $a > 0$ and $r < 0$, the function is an exponential decay function.

The graphs of the basic functions $y = e^x$ and $y = e^{-x}$ are shown below.

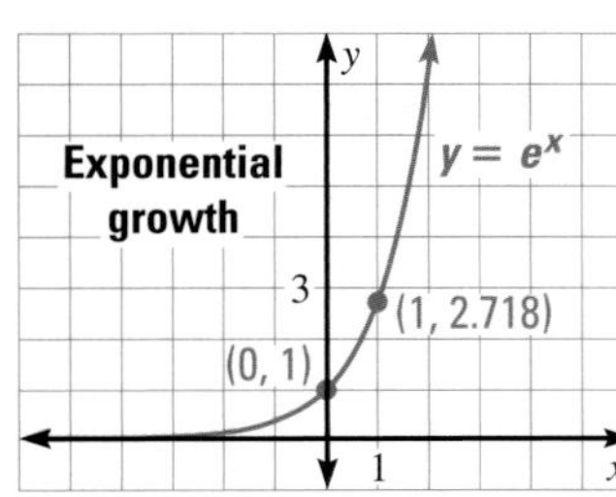

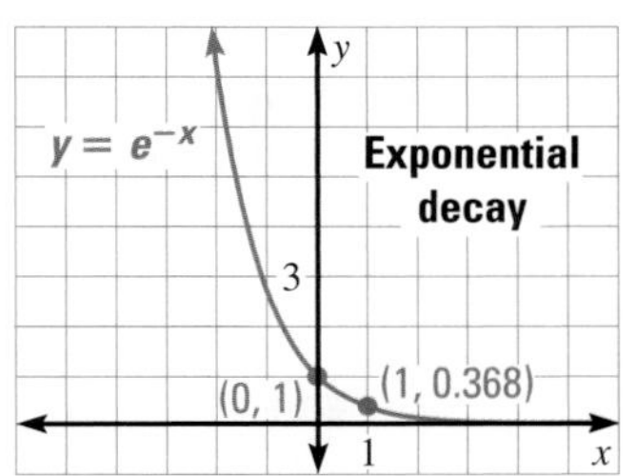

EXAMPLE 3 Graph natural base functions

Graph the function. State the domain and range.

a. $y = 3e^{0.25x}$

b. $y = e^{-0.75(x-2)} + 1$

Solution

ANOTHER WAY
You can also write the function from part (a) in the form $y = ab^x$ in order to graph it:

$y = 3e^{0.25x}$

$y = 3(e^{0.25})^x$

$y \approx 3(1.28)^x$

a. Because $a = 3$ is positive and $r = 0.25$ is positive, the function is an exponential growth function. Plot the points (0, 3) and (1, 3.85) and draw the curve.

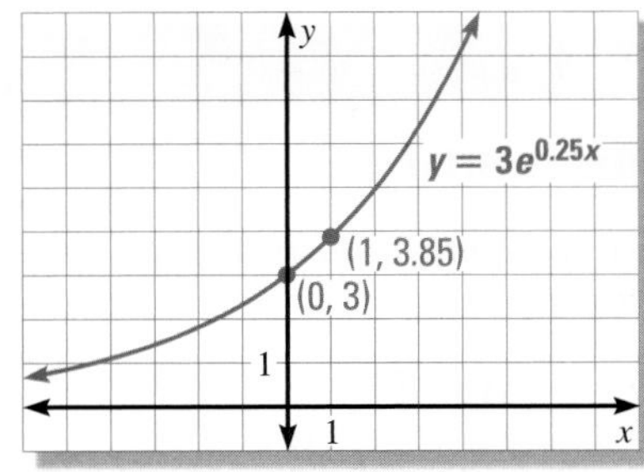

The domain is all real numbers, and the range is $y > 0$.

b. $a = 1$ is positive and $r = -0.75$ is negative, so the function is an exponential decay function. Translate the graph of $y = e^{-0.75x}$ right 2 units and up 1 unit.

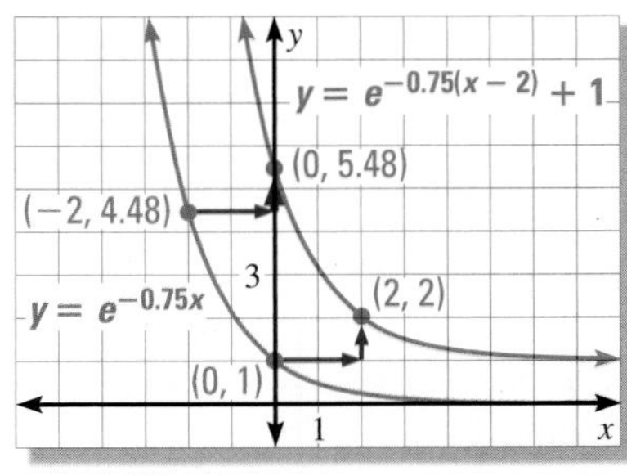

The domain is all real numbers, and the range is $y > 1$.

EXAMPLE 4 Solve a multi-step problem

BIOLOGY The length ℓ (in centimeters) of a tiger shark can be modeled by the function

$$\ell = 337 - 276e^{-0.178t}$$

where t is the shark's age (in years).

- Graph the model.
- Use the graph to estimate the length of a tiger shark that is 3 years old.

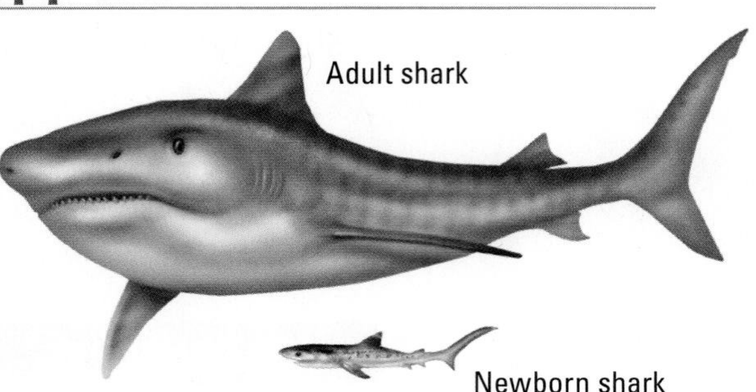

INTERPRET VARIABLES
On a graphing calculator, enter the function $\ell = 337 - 276e^{-0.178t}$ using the variables x and y, as shown below: $y = 337 - 276e^{-0.178x}$

Solution

STEP 1 **Graph** the model, as shown.

STEP 2 **Use** the *trace* feature to determine that $\ell \approx 175$ when $t = 3$.

▶ The length of a 3-year-old tiger shark is about 175 centimeters.

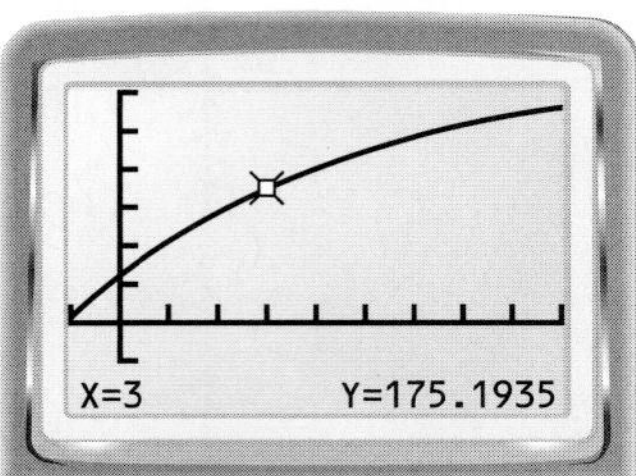

✓ GUIDED PRACTICE for Examples 3 and 4

Graph the function. State the domain and range.

6. $y = 2e^{0.5x}$

7. $f(x) = \frac{1}{2}e^{-x} + 1$

8. $y = 1.5e^{0.25(x - 1)} - 2$

9. **WHAT IF?** In Example 4, use the given function to estimate the length of a tiger shark that is 5 years old.

CONTINUOUSLY COMPOUNDED INTEREST In Lesson 7.1, you learned that the balance of an account earning compound interest is given by this formula:

$$A = P\left(1 + \frac{r}{n}\right)^{nt}$$

As the frequency n of compounding approaches positive infinity, the compound interest formula approximates the following formula.

KEY CONCEPT *For Your Notebook*

Continuously Compounded Interest

When interest is compounded *continuously*, the amount A in an account after t years is given by the formula

$$A = Pe^{rt}$$

where P is the principal and r is the annual interest rate expressed as a decimal.

EXAMPLE 5 Model continuously compounded interest

FINANCE You deposit \$4000 in an account that pays 6% annual interest compounded continuously. What is the balance after 1 year?

Solution

Use the formula for continuously compounded interest.

$A = Pe^{rt}$ **Write formula.**

$= 4000e^{0.06(1)}$ **Substitute 4000 for P, 0.06 for r, and 1 for t.**

≈ 4247.35 **Use a calculator.**

▶ The balance at the end of 1 year is \$4247.35.

GUIDED PRACTICE for Example 5

10. **FINANCE** You deposit \$2500 in an account that pays 5% annual interest compounded continuously. Find the balance after each amount of time.

    a. 2 years   b. 5 years   c. 7.5 years

11. **FINANCE** Find the amount of interest earned in parts (a)–(c) of Exercise 10.

7.3 EXERCISES

HOMEWORK KEY

○ = **WORKED-OUT SOLUTIONS on p. WS13 for Exs. 5, 35, and 57**

★ = **STANDARDIZED TEST PRACTICE Exs. 2, 15, 16, 52, 53, and 60**

SKILL PRACTICE

1. **VOCABULARY** Copy and complete: The number _?_ is an irrational number approximately equal to 2.71828.

2. ★ **WRITING** Tell whether the function $f(x) = \frac{1}{3}e^{4x}$ is an example of *exponential growth* or *exponential decay. Explain.*

EXAMPLE 1 on p. 492 for Exs. 3–18

SIMPLIFYING EXPRESSIONS Simplify the expression.

3. $e^3 \cdot e^4$
4. $e^{-2} \cdot e^6$
5. $(2e^{3x})^3$
6. $(2e^{-2})^{-4}$
7. $(3e^{5x})^{-1}$
8. $e^x \cdot e^{-3x} \cdot e^4$
9. $\sqrt{9e^6}$
10. $e^x \cdot 5e^{x+3}$
11. $\frac{3e}{e^x}$
12. $\frac{4e^x}{e^{4x}}$
13. $\sqrt[3]{8e^{9x}}$
14. $\frac{6e^{4x}}{8e}$

15. ★ **MULTIPLE CHOICE** What is the simplified form of $(4e^{2x})^3$?

    Ⓐ $4e^{6x}$ Ⓑ $4e^{8x}$ Ⓒ $64e^{6x}$ Ⓓ $64e^{8x}$

16. ★ **MULTIPLE CHOICE** What is the simplified form of $\sqrt{\frac{4(27e^{13}x)}{3e^7x^{-3}}}$?

    Ⓐ $6e^{10}x$ Ⓑ $6e^6x^4$ Ⓒ $\frac{6e^3}{x^2}$ Ⓓ $6e^3x^2$

ERROR ANALYSIS *Describe* and correct the error in simplifying the expression.

17. $(3e^{5x})^2 = 3e^{(5x)(2)}$
$= 3e^{10x}$ ✗

18. $\frac{e^{6x}}{e^{-2x}} = e^{6x-2x}$
$= e^{4x}$ ✗

EXAMPLE 2 on p. 492 for Exs. 19–30

EVALUATING EXPRESSIONS Use a calculator to evaluate the expression.

19. e^3 **20.** $e^{-3/4}$ **21.** $e^{2.2}$ **22.** $e^{1/2}$

23. $e^{-2/5}$ **24.** $e^{4.3}$ **25.** e^7 **26.** e^{-4}

27. $2e^{-0.3}$ **28.** $5e^{2/3}$ **29.** $-6e^{2.4}$ **30.** $0.4e^{4.1}$

GROWTH OR DECAY Tell whether the function is an example of *exponential growth* or *exponential decay.*

31. $f(x) = 3e^{-x}$ **32.** $f(x) = \frac{1}{3}e^{4x}$ **33.** $f(x) = e^{-4x}$ **34.** $f(x) = \frac{3}{5}e^{x}$

35. $f(x) = \frac{1}{4}e^{-5x}$ **36.** $f(x) = e^{3x}$ **37.** $f(x) = 2e^{4x}$ **38.** $f(x) = 4e^{-2x}$

EXAMPLE 3 on p. 493 for Exs. 39–50

MATCHING GRAPHS Match the function with its graph.

39. $y = 0.5e^{0.5x}$ **40.** $y = 2e^{0.5x}$ **41.** $y = e^{0.5x} + 2$

A.

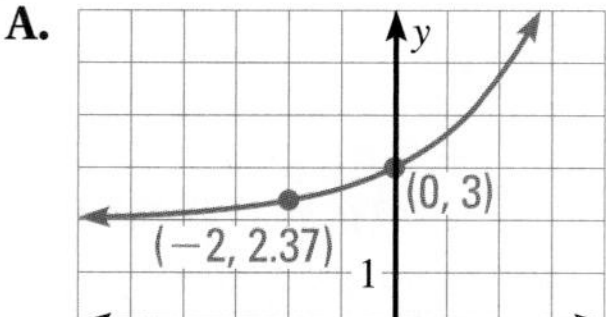

B.

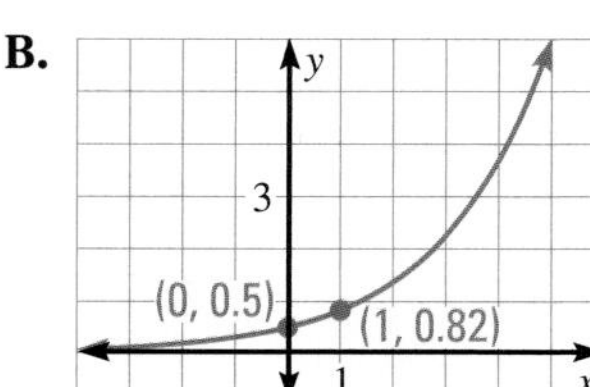

C.

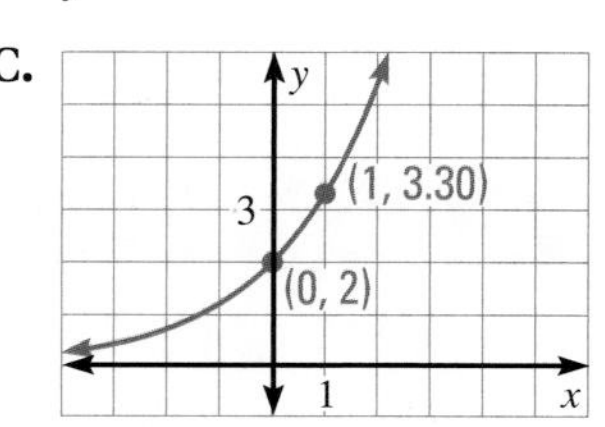

GRAPHING FUNCTIONS Graph the function. State the domain and range.

42. $y = e^{-2x}$ **43.** $y = 3e^{x}$ **44.** $y = 0.5e^{x}$

45. $y = 2e^{-3x} - 1$ **46.** $y = 2.5e^{-0.5x} + 2$ **47.** $y = 0.6e^{x-2}$

48. $f(x) = \frac{1}{2}e^{x+3} - 2$ **49.** $g(x) = \frac{4}{3}e^{x-1} + 1$ **50.** $h(x) = e^{-2(x+1)} - 3$

51. GRAPHING CALCULATOR Use the *table* feature of a graphing calculator to find the value of n for which $\left(1 + \frac{1}{n}\right)^n$ gives the value of e correct to 9 decimal places. *Explain* the process you used to find your answer.

52. ★ SHORT RESPONSE Can e be expressed as a ratio of two integers? *Explain* your reasoning.

53. ★ OPEN-ENDED MATH Find values of a, b, r, and q such that $f(x) = ae^{rx}$ and $g(x) = be^{qx}$ are exponential *decay* functions and $\frac{f(x)}{g(x)}$ is an exponential *growth* function.

54. CHALLENGE *Explain* why $A = P\left(1 + \frac{r}{n}\right)^{nt}$ approximates $A = Pe^{rt}$ as n approaches positive infinity. $\left(\textit{Hint:} \text{ Let } m = \frac{n}{r}.\right)$

Problem Solving

EXAMPLE 4 on p. 494 for Exs. 55–56

55. **CAMERA PHONES** The number of camera phones shipped globally can be modeled by the function $y = 1.28e^{1.31x}$ where x is the number of years since 1997 and y is the number of camera phones shipped (in millions). How many camera phones were shipped in 2002?

@HomeTutor for problem solving help at classzone.com

56. **BIOLOGY** Scientists used traps to study the Formosan subterranean termite population in New Orleans. The mean number y of termites collected annually can be modeled by $y = 738e^{0.345t}$ where t is the number of years since 1989. What was the mean number of termites collected in 1999?

@HomeTutor for problem solving help at classzone.com

EXAMPLE 5 on p. 495 for Exs. 57–58

57. **FINANCE** You deposit $2000 in an account that pays 4% annual interest compounded continuously. What is the balance after 5 years?

58. **FINANCE** You deposit $800 in an account that pays 2.65% annual interest compounded continuously. What is the balance after 12.5 years?

59. **MULTI-STEP PROBLEM** The percent L of surface light that filters down through bodies of water can be modeled by the exponential function $L(x) = 100e^{kx}$ where k is a measure of the murkiness of the water and x is the depth below the surface (in meters).

    a. A recreational submersible is traveling in clear water with a k-value of about -0.02. Write and graph an equation giving the percent of surface light that filters down through clear water as a function of depth.

    b. Use your graph to estimate the percent of surface light available at a depth of 40 meters.

    c. Use your graph to estimate how deep the submersible can descend in clear water before only 50% of surface light is available.

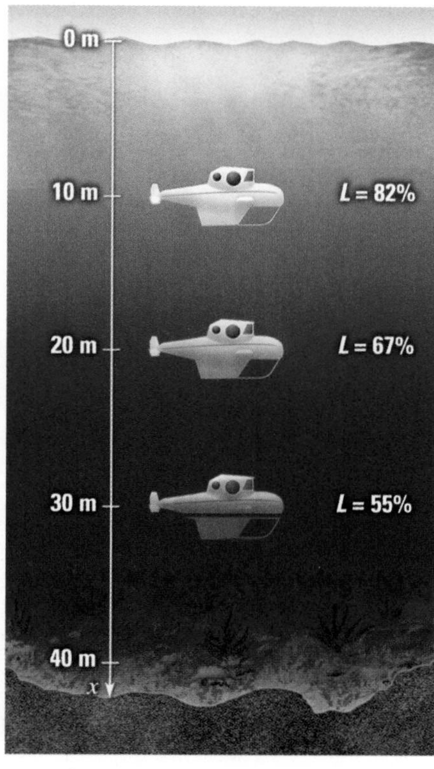

60. ★ **EXTENDED RESPONSE** The growth of the bacteria *mycobacterium tuberculosis* can be modeled by the function $P(t) = P_0e^{0.116t}$ where $P(t)$ is the population after t hours and P_0 is the population when $t = 0$.

    a. **Model** At 1:00 P.M., there are 30 *mycobacterium tuberculosis* bacteria in a sample. Write a function for the number of bacteria after 1:00 P.M.

    b. **Graph** Graph the function from part (a).

    c. **Estimate** What is the population at 5:00 P.M.?

    d. **Reasoning** *Describe* how to find the population at 3:45 P.M.

61. **RATE OF HEALING** The area of a wound decreases exponentially with time. The area A of a wound after t days can be modeled by $A = A_0e^{-0.05t}$ where A_0 is the initial wound area. If the initial wound area is 4 square centimeters, what is the area after 14 days?

62. **CHALLENGE** The height y (in feet) of the Gateway Arch in St. Louis, Missouri, can be modeled by the function $y = 757.7 - 63.85(e^{x/127.7} + e^{-x/127.7})$ where x is the horizontal distance (in feet) from the center of the arch.

    a. Use a graphing calculator to graph the function. How tall is the arch at its highest point?

    b. About how far apart are the ends of the arch?

NEW YORK MIXED REVIEW

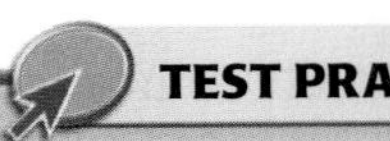

TEST PRACTICE at classzone.com

63. Which of the following shows that the conjecture is false? "The square root of a number x is always less than x."

    Ⓐ $x = \frac{1}{4}$ Ⓑ $x = 4$ Ⓒ $x = 48$ Ⓓ $x = 900$

64. Quadrilateral $MNPQ$ is a rhombus. $\angle P$ measures 55°. What are the measures of $\angle M$, $\angle N$, and $\angle Q$?

    Ⓐ 55°, 35°, and 35° Ⓑ 55°, 55°, and 55°

    Ⓒ 55°, 110°, and 110° Ⓓ 55°, 125°, and 125°

QUIZ for Lessons 7.1–7.3

Graph the function. State the domain and range.

1. $y = 2 \cdot 3^{x-2}$ *(p. 478)* 2. $y = \left(\frac{2}{5}\right)^x$ *(p. 486)* 3. $f(x) = \left(\frac{3}{8}\right)^x + 2$ *(p. 486)*

Simplify the expression. *(p. 492)*

4. $3e^4 \cdot e^3$ 5. $(-5e^{3x})^3$ 6. $\frac{e^{4x}}{5e}$ 7. $\frac{8e^{5x}}{6e^{2x}}$

Graph the function. State the domain and range. *(p. 492)*

8. $y = 2e^x$ 9. $y = 3e^{-2x}$ 10. $y = e^{x+1} - 2$ 11. $g(x) = 4e^{-3x} + 1$

12. **TV SALES** From 1997 to 2001, the number n (in millions) of black-and-white TVs sold in the United States can be modeled by $n = 26.8(0.85)^t$ where t is the number of years since 1997. Identify the decay factor and the percent decrease. Graph the model and state the domain and range. Estimate the number of black-and-white TVs sold in 1999. *(p. 478)*

13. **FINANCE** You deposit \$1200 in an account that pays 4.5% annual interest compounded continuously. What is the balance after 5 years? *(p. 492)*

EXTRA PRACTICE for Lesson 7.3, p. 1016 **ONLINE QUIZ** at classzone.com

7.4 Evaluate Logarithms and Graph Logarithmic Functions

 **A2.A.18** Evaluate logarithmic expressions in any base

Before You evaluated and graphed exponential functions.

Now You will evaluate logarithms and graph logarithmic functions.

Why? So you can model the wind speed of a tornado, as in Example 4.

Key Vocabulary
- **logarithm of y with base b**
- **common logarithm**
- **natural logarithm**

You know that $2^2 = 4$ and $2^3 = 8$. However, for what value of x does $2^x = 6$? Mathematicians define this x-value using a *logarithm* and write $x = \log_2 6$. The definition of a logarithm can be generalized as follows.

KEY CONCEPT *For Your Notebook*

Definition of Logarithm with Base b

Let b and y be positive numbers with $b \neq 1$. The **logarithm of y with base b** is denoted by $\log_b y$ and is defined as follows:

$$\log_b y = x \quad \text{if and only if} \quad b^x = y$$

The expression $\log_b y$ is read as "log base b of y."

This definition tells you that the equations $\log_b y = x$ and $b^x = y$ are equivalent. The first is in *logarithmic form* and the second is in *exponential form*.

EXAMPLE 1 **Rewrite logarithmic equations**

	Logarithmic Form	Exponential Form
a.	$\log_2 8 = 3$	$2^3 = 8$
b.	$\log_4 1 = 0$	$4^0 = 1$
c.	$\log_{12} 12 = 1$	$12^1 = 12$
d.	$\log_{1/4} 4 = -1$	$\left(\frac{1}{4}\right)^{-1} = 4$

Parts (b) and (c) of Example 1 illustrate two special logarithm values that you should learn to recognize. Let b be a positive real number such that $b \neq 1$.

Logarithm of 1

$\log_b 1 = 0$ because $b^0 = 1$.

Logarithm of b with Base b

$\log_b b = 1$ because $b^1 = b$.

 **GUIDED PRACTICE** for Example 1

Rewrite the equation in exponential form.

1. $\log_3 81 = 4$ **2.** $\log_7 7 = 1$ **3.** $\log_{14} 1 = 0$ **4.** $\log_{1/2} 32 = -5$

EXAMPLE 2 Evaluate logarithms

Evaluate the logarithm.

a. $\log_4 64$ **b.** $\log_5 0.2$ **c.** $\log_{1/5} 125$ **d.** $\log_{36} 6$

Solution

To help you find the value of $\log_b y$, ask yourself what power of b gives you y.

a. 4 to what power gives 64? $4^3 = 64$, so $\log_4 64 = 3$.

b. 5 to what power gives 0.2? $5^{-1} = 0.2$, so $\log_5 0.2 = -1$.

c. $\frac{1}{5}$ to what power gives 125? $\left(\frac{1}{5}\right)^{-3} = 125$, so $\log_{1/5} 125 = -3$.

d. 36 to what power gives 6? $36^{1/2} = 6$, so $\log_{36} 6 = \frac{1}{2}$.

SPECIAL LOGARITHMS A **common logarithm** is a logarithm with base 10. It is denoted by $\log_{10}$ or simply by log. A **natural logarithm** is a logarithm with base e. It can be denoted by $\log_e$, but is more often denoted by ln.

Common Logarithm	Natural Logarithm
$\log_{10} x = \log x$	$\log_e x = \ln x$

Most calculators have keys for evaluating common and natural logarithms.

EXAMPLE 3 Evaluate common and natural logarithms

Expression	Keystrokes	Display	Check
a. log 8	LOG 8) ENTER	0.903089987	$10^{0.903} \approx 8$ ✓
b. ln 0.3	LN .3) ENTER	−1.203972804	$e^{-1.204} \approx 0.3$ ✓

EXAMPLE 4 Evaluate a logarithmic model

TORNADOES The wind speed s (in miles per hour) near the center of a tornado can be modeled by

$$s = 93 \log d + 65$$

where d is the distance (in miles) that the tornado travels. In 1925, a tornado traveled 220 miles through three states. Estimate the wind speed near the tornado's center.

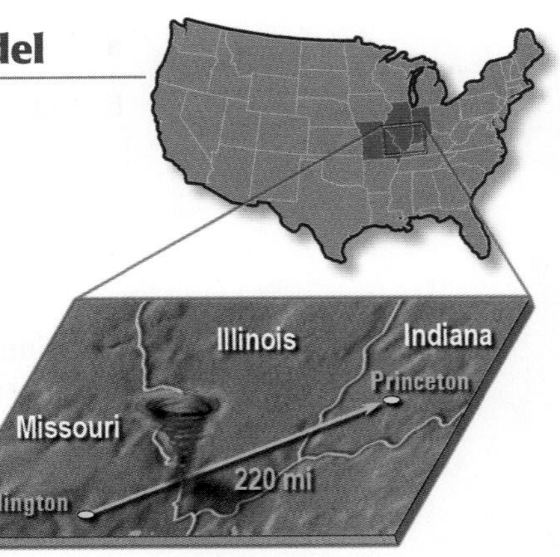

Not drawn to scale

Solution

$s = 93 \log d + 65$ **Write function.**

$= 93 \log 220 + 65$ **Substitute 220 for d.**

$\approx 93(2.342) + 65$ **Use a calculator.**

$= 282.806$ **Simplify.**

▶ The wind speed near the tornado's center was about 283 miles per hour.

✓ **GUIDED PRACTICE** for Examples 2, 3, and 4

Evaluate the logarithm. Use a calculator if necessary.

5. $\log_2 32$ **6.** $\log_{27} 3$ **7.** $\log 12$ **8.** $\ln 0.75$

9. **WHAT IF?** Use the function in Example 4 to estimate the wind speed near a tornado's center if its path is 150 miles long.

INVERSE FUNCTIONS By the definition of a logarithm, it follows that the logarithmic function $g(x) = \log_b x$ is the inverse of the exponential function $f(x) = b^x$. This means that:

$$g(f(x)) = \log_b b^x = x \quad \text{and} \quad f(g(x)) = b^{\log_b x} = x$$

EXAMPLE 5 Use inverse properties

Simplify the expression.

a. $10^{\log 4}$ **b.** $\log_5 25^x$

Solution

a. $10^{\log 4} = 4$ $\quad b^{\log_b x} = x$

b. $\log_5 25^x = \log_5 (5^2)^x$ $\quad$ **Express 25 as a power with base 5.**

$= \log_5 5^{2x}$ $\quad$ **Power of a power property**

$= 2x$ $\quad$ $\log_b b^x = x$

EXAMPLE 6 Find inverse functions

Find the inverse of the function.

a. $y = 6^x$ **b.** $y = \ln(x + 3)$

REVIEW INVERSES

For help with finding inverses of functions, see p. 437.

Solution

a. From the definition of logarithm, the inverse of $y = 6^x$ is $y = \log_6 x$.

b.

$y = \ln(x + 3)$ $\quad$ **Write original function.**

$x = \ln(y + 3)$ $\quad$ **Switch *x* and *y*.**

$e^x = y + 3$ $\quad$ **Write in exponential form.**

$e^x - 3 = y$ $\quad$ **Solve for *y*.**

▶ The inverse of $y = \ln(x + 3)$ is $y = e^x - 3$.

✓ **GUIDED PRACTICE** for Examples 5 and 6

Simplify the expression.

10. $8^{\log_8 x}$ **11.** $\log_7 7^{-3x}$ **12.** $\log_2 64^x$ **13.** $e^{\ln 20}$

14. Find the inverse of $y = 4^x$.

15. Find the inverse of $y = \ln(x - 5)$.

GRAPHING LOGARITHMIC FUNCTIONS You can use the inverse relationship between exponential and logarithmic functions to graph logarithmic functions.

KEY CONCEPT *For Your Notebook*

Parent Graphs for Logarithmic Functions

The graph of $f(x) = \log_b x$ is shown below for $b > 1$ and for $0 < b < 1$. Because $f(x) = \log_b x$ and $g(x) = b^x$ are inverse functions, the graph of $f(x) = \log_b x$ is the reflection of the graph of $g(x) = b^x$ in the line $y = x$.

Graph of $f(x) = \log_b x$ for $b > 1$

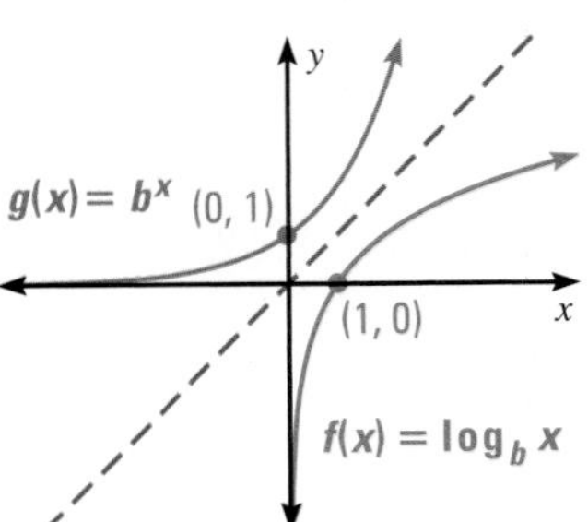

Graph of $f(x) = \log_b x$ for $0 < b < 1$

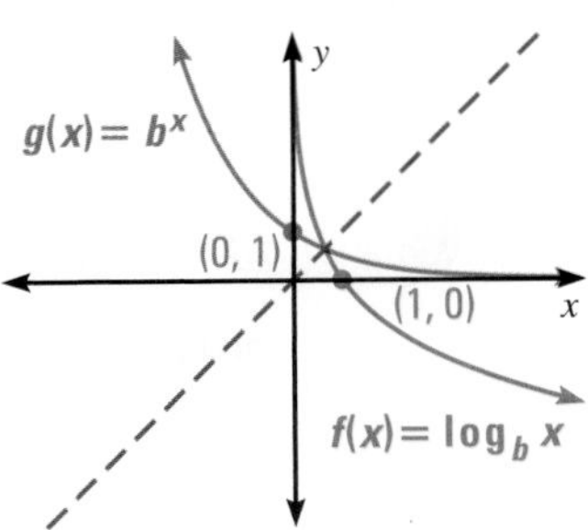

Note that the y-axis is a vertical asymptote of the graph of $f(x) = \log_b x$. The domain of $f(x) = \log_b x$ is $x > 0$, and the range is all real numbers.

EXAMPLE 7 Graph logarithmic functions

Graph the function.

a. $y = \log_3 x$

b. $y = \log_{1/2} x$

Solution

a. Plot several convenient points, such as (1, 0), (3, 1), and (9, 2). The y-axis is a vertical asymptote.

From *left* to *right*, draw a curve that starts just to the right of the y-axis and moves up through the plotted points, as shown below.

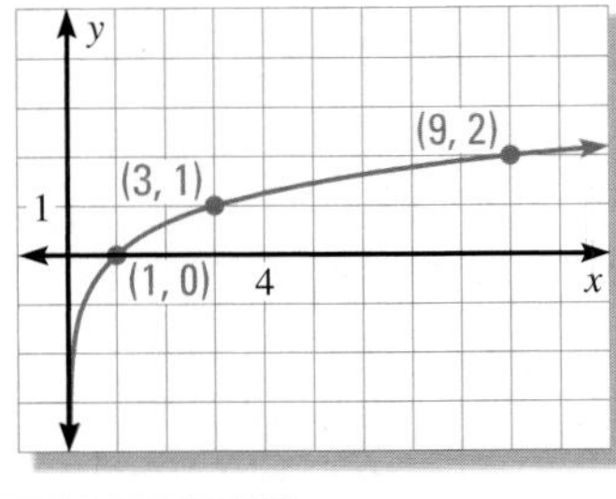

b. Plot several convenient points, such as (1, 0), (2, −1), (4, −2), and (8, −3). The y-axis is a vertical asymptote.

From *left* to *right*, draw a curve that starts just to the right of the y-axis and moves down through the plotted points, as shown below.

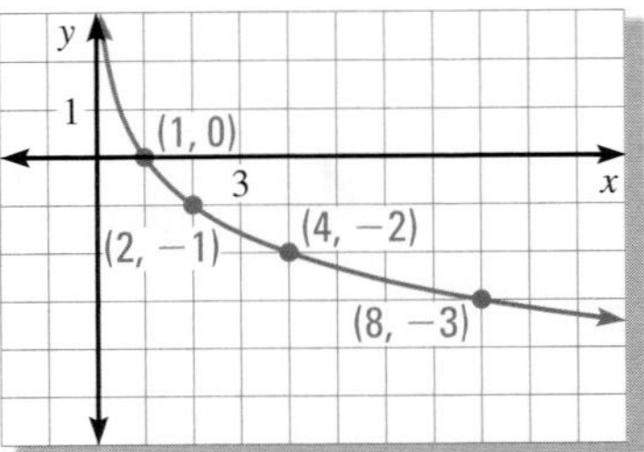

Animated Algebra at classzone.com

TRANSLATIONS You can graph a logarithmic function of the form $y = \log_b (x - h) + k$ by translating the graph of the parent function $y = \log_b x$.

EXAMPLE 8 Translate a logarithmic graph

Graph $y = \log_2 (x + 3) + 1$. State the domain and range.

Solution

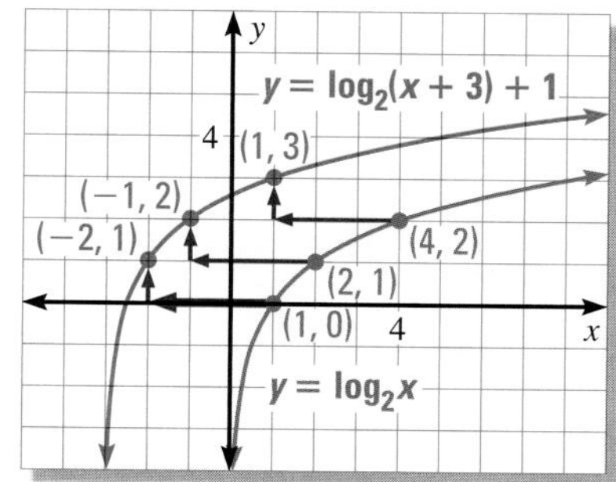

STEP 1 **Sketch** the graph of the parent function $y = \log_2 x$, which passes through (1, 0), (2, 1), and (4, 2).

STEP 2 **Translate** the parent graph left 3 units and up 1 unit. The translated graph passes through (−2, 1), (−1, 2), and (1, 3). The graph's asymptote is $x = -3$. The domain is $x > -3$, and the range is all real numbers.

✓ **GUIDED PRACTICE** for Examples 7 and 8

Graph the function. State the domain and range.

16. $y = \log_5 x$ **17.** $y = \log_{1/3} (x - 3)$ **18.** $f(x) = \log_4 (x + 1) - 2$

7.4 EXERCISES

HOMEWORK KEY
○ = **WORKED-OUT SOLUTIONS on p. WS13 for Exs. 13, 33, and 61**
★ = **STANDARDIZED TEST PRACTICE Exs. 2, 36, 61, and 62**

SKILL PRACTICE

1. VOCABULARY Copy and complete: A logarithm with base 10 is called a(n) _?_ logarithm.

2. ★ **WRITING** *Describe* the relationship between $y = 5^x$ and $y = \log_5 x$.

EXAMPLE 1 on p. 499 for Exs. 3–7

EXPONENTIAL FORM Rewrite the equation in exponential form.

3. $\log_4 16 = 2$ **4.** $\log_7 343 = 3$ **5.** $\log_6 \frac{1}{36} = -2$ **6.** $\log_{64} 1 = 0$

7. ERROR ANALYSIS *Describe* and correct the error in rewriting the equation $2^{-3} = \frac{1}{8}$ in logarithmic form.

$\log_2 -3 = \frac{1}{8}$ ✗

EXAMPLE 2 on p. 500 for Exs. 8–19

EVALUATING LOGARITHMS Evaluate the logarithm without using a calculator.

8. $\log_{15} 15$ **9.** $\log_7 49$ **10.** $\log_6 216$ **11.** $\log_2 64$

12. $\log_9 1$ **(13.)** $\log_{1/2} 8$ **14.** $\log_3 \frac{1}{27}$ **15.** $\log_{16} \frac{1}{4}$

16. $\log_{1/4} 16$ **17.** $\log_8 512$ **18.** $\log_5 625$ **19.** $\log_{11} 121$

EXAMPLE 3
on p. 500
for Exs. 20–27

CALCULATING LOGARITHMS Use a calculator to evaluate the logarithm.

20. $\log 14$ **21.** $\ln 6$ **22.** $\ln 0.43$ **23.** $\log 6.213$

24. $\log 27$ **25.** $\ln 5.38$ **26.** $\log 0.746$ **27.** $\ln 110$

EXAMPLE 5
on p. 501
for Exs. 28–36

USING INVERSE PROPERTIES Simplify the expression.

28. $7^{\log_7 x}$ **29.** $\log_5 5^x$ **30.** $30^{\log_{30} 4}$ **31.** $10^{\log 8}$

32. $\log_6 36^x$ **33.** $\log_3 81^x$ **34.** $\log_5 125^x$ **35.** $\log_2 32^x$

36. ★ **MULTIPLE CHOICE** Which expression is equivalent to $\log 100^x$?

Ⓐ x Ⓑ $2x$ Ⓒ $10x$ Ⓓ $100x$

EXAMPLE 6
on p. 501
for Exs. 37–44

FINDING INVERSES Find the inverse of the function.

37. $y = \log_8 x$ **38.** $y = 7^x$ **39.** $y = (0.4)^x$ **40.** $y = \log_{1/2} x$

41. $y = e^{x+2}$ **42.** $y = 2^x - 3$ **43.** $y = \ln (x + 1)$ **44.** $y = 6 + \log x$

EXAMPLES 7 and 8
on pp. 502–503
for Exs. 45–53

GRAPHING FUNCTIONS Graph the function. State the domain and range.

45. $y = \log_4 x$ **46.** $y = \log_6 x$ **47.** $y = \log_{1/3} x$

48. $y = \log_{1/5} x$ **49.** $y = \log_2 (x - 3)$ **50.** $y = \log_3 x + 4$

51. $f(x) = \log_4 (x + 2) - 1$ **52.** $g(x) = \log_6 (x - 4) + 2$ **53.** $h(x) = \log_5 (x + 1) - 3$

CHALLENGE Evaluate the logarithm. (*Hint:* For each logarithm $\log_b x$, rewrite b and x as powers of the same number.)

54. $\log_{27} 9$ **55.** $\log_8 32$ **56.** $\log_{125} 625$ **57.** $\log_4 128$

PROBLEM SOLVING

EXAMPLE 4
on p. 500
for Exs. 58–59

58. ALTIMETER Skydivers use an instrument called an altimeter to track their altitude as they fall. The altimeter determines altitude by measuring air pressure. The altitude h (in meters) above sea level is related to the air pressure P (in pascals) by the function in the diagram below.

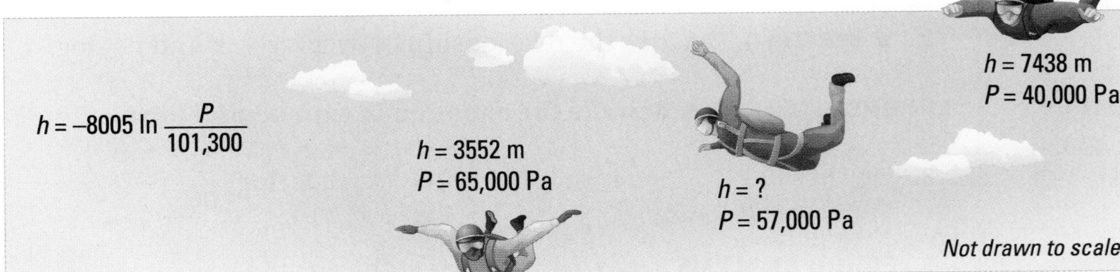

What is the altitude above sea level when the air pressure is 57,000 pascals?

@HomeTutor for problem solving help at classzone.com

59. CHEMISTRY The pH value for a substance measures how acidic or alkaline the substance is. It is given by the formula $\text{pH} = -\log [H^+]$ where H^+ is the hydrogen ion concentration (in moles per liter). Lemon juice has a hydrogen ion concentration of $10^{-2.3}$ moles per liter. What is its pH value?

@HomeTutor for problem solving help at classzone.com

60. **MULTI-STEP PROBLEM** Biologists have found that an alligator's length ℓ (in inches) and weight w (in pounds) are related by the function $\ell = 27.1 \ln w - 32.8$. Graph the function. Use your graph to estimate the weight of an alligator that is 10 feet long.

61. ★ **SHORT RESPONSE** The energy magnitude M of an earthquake can be modeled by

$$M = 0.29(\ln E) - 9.9$$

where E is the amount of energy released (in ergs).

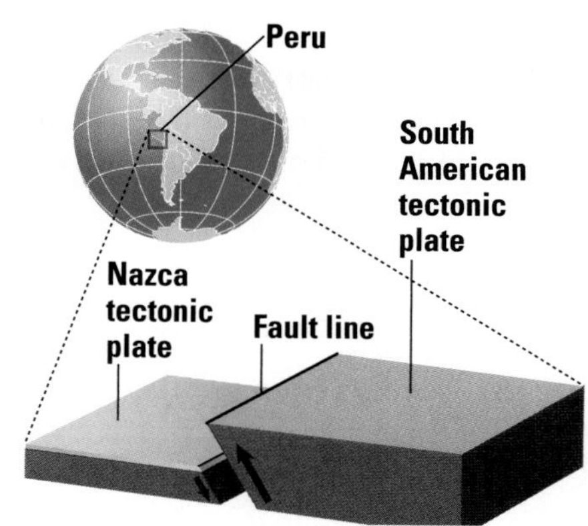

a. In 2001, a powerful earthquake in Peru, caused by the slippage of two tectonic plates along a fault, released 2.5×10^{24} ergs. What was the energy magnitude of the earthquake?

b. Find the inverse of the given function. *Describe* what it represents.

62. ★ **EXTENDED RESPONSE** A study in Florida found that the number of fish species s in a pool or lake can be modeled by the function

$$s = 30.6 - 20.5(\log A) + 3.8(\log A)^2$$

where A is the area (in square meters) of the pool or lake.

a. Graph Use a graphing calculator to graph the function on the domain $200 \le A \le 35{,}000$.

b. Estimate Use your graph to estimate the number of fish species in a lake with an area of 30,000 square meters.

c. Estimate Use your graph to estimate the area of a lake that contains 6 species of fish.

d. Reasoning *Describe* what happens to the number of fish species as the area of a pool or lake increases. *Explain* why your answer makes sense.

63. **CHALLENGE** The function $s = 0.159 + 0.118(\log d)$ gives the slope s of a beach in terms of the average diameter d (in millimeters) of sand particles on the beach. Find the inverse of this function. Then use the inverse to estimate the average diameter of the sand particles on a beach with a slope of 0.2.

NEW YORK MIXED REVIEW

64. Which statement best describes the graph of a person's distance traveled over time?

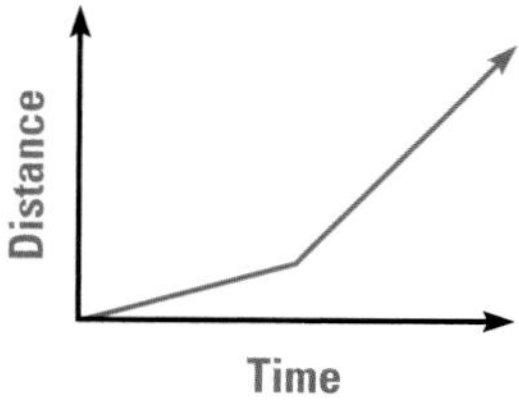

Ⓐ The person first runs, then walks.

Ⓑ The person travels at a constant speed.

Ⓒ The person first walks, then runs.

Ⓓ The person's speed decreases over time.

65. A window is a regular hexagon. Its perimeter is 60 inches. What is the approximate area of the window?

Ⓐ 155.9 in.^{2} Ⓑ 259.8 in.^{2} Ⓒ 300.0 in.^{2} Ⓓ 519.6 in.^{2}

New York Mixed Review

Lessons 7.1–7.4

1. **COMPOUND INTEREST** You deposit \$2000 in an account that pays 5.6% annual interest compounded continuously. When will your savings first reach \$2,500?

   (1) 2 years from today

   (2) 3 years from today

   (3) 4 years from today

   (4) 5 years from today

2. **GEOMETRIC PATTERNS** When a piece of paper is folded in half, the paper is divided into two regions, each of which has half the area of the paper. If this process is repeated, the number of regions increases while the area of each region decreases. The table below shows the number of regions and the fractional area of each region after each successive fold. Which function can be used to find the fractional area $A(n)$ of each region after n folds?

Fold number	0	1	2	3	4
Number of regions	1	2	4	8	16
Fractional area of each region	1	$\frac{1}{2}$	$\frac{1}{4}$	$\frac{1}{8}$	$\frac{1}{16}$

   (1) $A(n) = \frac{1}{2^n}$

   (2) $A(n) = \frac{1}{(n+1)^n}$

   (3) $A(n) = \frac{1}{n+1}$

   (4) $A(n) = 2^n$

3. **CERTIFICATES OF DEPOSIT** A local bank offers certificate of deposit (CD) accounts that you can use to save money and earn interest. You deposit \$1500 into a three year CD that pays 2% annual interest. The interest for the CD is compounded monthly. How much interest will the CD earn by the end of its term?

   (1) \$87.42 (3) \$92.68

   (2) \$90.83 (4) \$124.50

4. **PETROLEUM** The amount y (in billions of barrels) of oil collected by a petroleum company drilling on the U.S. continental shelf can be modeled by $y = 12.263 \ln x - 45.381$ where x is the number of wells drilled. About how many barrels of oil would you expect to be collected if 1000 wells are drilled?

   (1) 11.1 billion

   (2) 30.5 billion

   (3) 39.3 billion

   (4) 84.7 billion

5. **OPEN-ENDED** The graph shown below is a translation of the graph of $y = \log_3 x$.

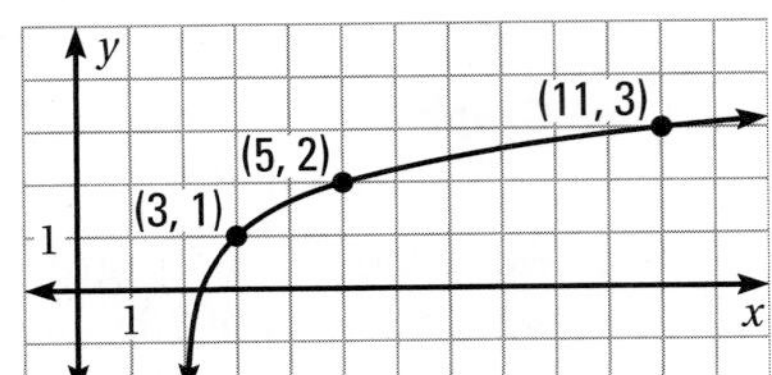

   Write an equation of the graph.

   Graph the inverse of the function whose graph is shown above.

6. **OPEN-ENDED** Tritium is a radioactive substance used to illuminate exit signs. The amount of tritium disappears over time, a process called radioactive decay. If you start with a 10 milligram sample of tritium, the number y of milligrams left after t years is given by $y = 10e^{-0.0564t}$.

   How many milligrams of tritium are left after 10 years? Round your answer to the nearest hundredth of a milligram.

   After how long will the amount be exactly 5 milligrams? Round your answer to the nearest number of months.

7.5 Apply Properties of Logarithms

A2.A.19 Apply the properties of logarithms to rewrite logarithmic expressions in equivalent forms

Before You evaluated logarithms.

Now You will rewrite logarithmic expressions.

Why? So you can model the loudness of sounds, as in Ex. 63.

Key Vocabulary
- **base,** *p. 10*

KEY CONCEPT *For Your Notebook*

Properties of Logarithms

Let b, m, and n be positive numbers such that $b \neq 1$.

Product Property $\log_b mn = \log_b m + \log_b n$

Quotient Property $\log_b \frac{m}{n} = \log_b m - \log_b n$

Power Property $\log_b m^n = n \log_b m$

EXAMPLE 1 Use properties of logarithms

Use $\log_4 3 \approx 0.792$ and $\log_4 7 \approx 1.404$ to evaluate the logarithm.

AVOID ERRORS
Note that in general $\log_b \frac{m}{n} \neq \frac{\log_b m}{\log_b n}$ and $\log_b mn \neq (\log_b m)(\log_b n)$.

a. $\log_4 \frac{3}{7} = \log_4 3 - \log_4 7$ **Quotient property**

$\approx 0.792 - 1.404$ **Use the given values of $\log_4 3$ and $\log_4 7$.**

$= -0.612$ **Simplify.**

b. $\log_4 21 = \log_4 (3 \cdot 7)$ **Write 21 as $3 \cdot 7$.**

$= \log_4 3 + \log_4 7$ **Product property**

$\approx 0.792 + 1.404$ **Use the given values of $\log_4 3$ and $\log_4 7$.**

$= 2.196$ **Simplify.**

c. $\log_4 49 = \log_4 7^2$ **Write 49 as 7^2.**

$= 2 \log_4 7$ **Power property**

$\approx 2(1.404)$ **Use the given value of $\log_4 7$.**

$= 2.808$ **Simplify.**

GUIDED PRACTICE for Example 1

Use $\log_6 5 \approx 0.898$ and $\log_6 8 \approx 1.161$ to evaluate the logarithm.

1. $\log_6 \frac{5}{8}$ **2.** $\log_6 40$ **3.** $\log_6 64$ **4.** $\log_6 125$

REWRITING EXPRESSIONS You can use the properties of logarithms to expand and condense logarithmic expressions.

EXAMPLE 2 Expand a logarithmic expression

REWRITE EXPRESSIONS
When you are expanding or condensing an expression involving logarithms, you may assume any variables are positive.

Expand $\log_6 \frac{5x^3}{y}$.

$\log_6 \frac{5x^3}{y} = \log_6 5x^3 - \log_6 y$ **Quotient property**

$= \log_6 5 + \log_6 x^3 - \log_6 y$ **Product property**

$= \log_6 5 + 3\log_6 x - \log_6 y$ **Power property**

EXAMPLE 3 Standardized Test Practice

Which of the following is equivalent to log 9 + 3 log 2 − log 3?

Ⓐ log 8 Ⓑ log 14 Ⓒ log 18 Ⓓ log 24

Solution

$\log 9 + 3\log 2 - \log 3 = \log 9 + \log 2^3 - \log 3$ **Power property**

$= \log (9 \cdot 2^3) - \log 3$ **Product property**

$= \log \frac{9 \cdot 2^3}{3}$ **Quotient property**

$= \log 24$ **Simplify.**

▶ The correct answer is D. Ⓐ Ⓑ Ⓒ Ⓓ

✓ GUIDED PRACTICE for Examples 2 and 3

5. Expand $\log 3x^4$.

6. Condense $\ln 4 + 3\ln 3 - \ln 12$.

CHANGE-OF-BASE FORMULA Logarithms with any base other than 10 or *e* can be written in terms of common or natural logarithms using the *change-of-base formula.* This allows you to evaluate any logarithm using a calculator.

KEY CONCEPT *For Your Notebook*

Change-of-Base Formula

If *a*, *b*, and *c* are positive numbers with $b \neq 1$ and $c \neq 1$, then:

$$\log_c a = \frac{\log_b a}{\log_b c}$$

In particular, $\log_c a = \frac{\log a}{\log c}$ and $\log_c a = \frac{\ln a}{\ln c}$.

EXAMPLE 4 Use the change-of-base formula

Evaluate $\log_3 8$ using common logarithms and natural logarithms.

Solution

Using common logarithms: $\log_3 8 = \frac{\log 8}{\log 3} \approx \frac{0.9031}{0.4771} \approx 1.893$

Using natural logarithms: $\log_3 8 = \frac{\ln 8}{\ln 3} \approx \frac{2.0794}{1.0986} \approx 1.893$

EXAMPLE 5 Use properties of logarithms in real life

SOUND INTENSITY For a sound with intensity I (in watts per square meter), the loudness $L(I)$ of the sound (in decibels) is given by the function

$$L(I) = 10 \log \frac{I}{I_0}$$

where I_0 is the intensity of a barely audible sound (about 10^{-12} watts per square meter). An artist in a recording studio turns up the volume of a track so that the sound's intensity doubles. By how many decibels does the loudness increase?

Solution

Let I be the original intensity, so that $2I$ is the doubled intensity.

Increase in loudness $= L(2I) - L(I)$	**Write an expression.**
$= 10 \log \frac{2I}{I_0} - 10 \log \frac{I}{I_0}$	**Substitute.**
$= 10\left(\log \frac{2I}{I_0} - \log \frac{I}{I_0}\right)$	**Distributive property**
$= 10\left(\log 2 + \log \frac{I}{I_0} - \log \frac{I}{I_0}\right)$	**Product property**
$= 10 \log 2$	**Simplify.**
≈ 3.01	**Use a calculator.**

▸ The loudness increases by about 3 decibels.

GUIDED PRACTICE for Examples 4 and 5

Use the change-of-base formula to evaluate the logarithm.

7. $\log_5 8$ **8.** $\log_8 14$ **9.** $\log_{26} 9$ **10.** $\log_{12} 30$

11. WHAT IF? In Example 5, suppose the artist turns up the volume so that the sound's intensity triples. By how many decibels does the loudness increase?

7.5 EXERCISES

HOMEWORK KEY

○ = **WORKED-OUT SOLUTIONS** on p. WS13 for Exs. 11, 17, and 71

★ = **STANDARDIZED TEST PRACTICE** Exs. 2, 43, 44, 64, 71, and 73

SKILL PRACTICE

1. **VOCABULARY** Copy and complete: To condense the expression $\log_3 2x + \log_3 y$, you need to use the _?_ property of logarithms.

2. ★ **WRITING** *Describe* two ways to evaluate $\log_7 12$ using a calculator.

EXAMPLE 1 on p. 507 for Exs. 3–14

MATCHING EXPRESSIONS **Match the expression with the logarithm that has the same value.**

3. $\ln 6 - \ln 2$
4. $2 \ln 6$
5. $6 \ln 2$
6. $\ln 6 + \ln 2$

A. $\ln 64$ B. $\ln 3$ C. $\ln 12$ D. $\ln 36$

APPROXIMATING EXPRESSIONS **Use $\log 4 \approx 0.602$ and $\log 12 \approx 1.079$ to evaluate the logarithm.**

7. $\log 3$
8. $\log 48$
9. $\log 16$
10. $\log 64$
11. $\log 144$
12. $\log \frac{1}{3}$
13. $\log \frac{1}{4}$
14. $\log \frac{1}{12}$

EXAMPLE 2 on p. 508 for Exs. 15–32

EXPANDING EXPRESSIONS **Expand the expression.**

15. $\log_3 4x$
16. $\ln 15x$
17. $\log 3x^4$
18. $\log_5 x^5$
19. $\log_2 \frac{2}{5}$
20. $\ln \frac{12}{5}$
21. $\log_4 \frac{x}{3y}$
22. $\ln 4x^2y$
23. $\log_7 5x^3yz^2$
24. $\log_6 36x^2$
25. $\ln x^2y^{1/3}$
26. $\log 10x^3$
27. $\log_2 \sqrt{x}$
28. $\ln \frac{6x^2}{y^4}$
29. $\ln \sqrt[4]{x^3}$
30. $\log_3 \sqrt{9x}$

ERROR ANALYSIS ***Describe*** **and correct the error in expanding the logarithmic expression.**

31. $\log_2 5x = (\log_2 5)(\log_2 x)$ ✗

32.

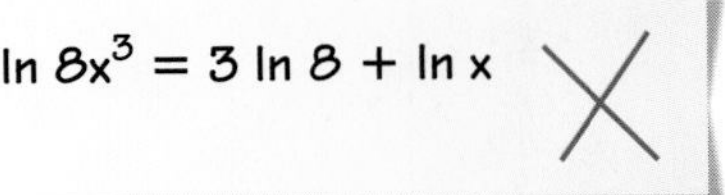

EXAMPLE 3 on p. 508 for Exs. 33–43

CONDENSING EXPRESSIONS **Condense the expression.**

33. $\log_4 7 - \log_4 10$
34. $\ln 12 - \ln 4$
35. $2 \log x + \log 11$
36. $6 \ln x + 4 \ln y$
37. $5 \log x - 4 \log y$
38. $5 \log_4 2 + 7 \log_4 x + 4 \log_4 y$
39. $\ln 40 + 2 \ln \frac{1}{2} + \ln x$
40. $\log_5 4 + \frac{1}{3} \log_5 x$
41. $6 \ln 2 - 4 \ln y$
42. $2(\log_3 20 - \log_3 4) + 0.5 \log_3 4$

43. ★ **MULTIPLE CHOICE** Which of the following is equivalent to $3 \log_4 6$?

Ⓐ $\log_4 18$ Ⓑ $\log_4 72$ Ⓒ $\log_4 216$ Ⓓ $\log_4 256$

44. ★ **MULTIPLE CHOICE** Which of the following statements is *not* correct?

Ⓐ $\log_3 48 = \log_3 16 + \log_3 3$ Ⓑ $\log_3 48 = 3\log_3 2 + \log_3 6$

Ⓒ $\log_3 48 = 2\log_3 4 + \log_3 3$ Ⓓ $\log_3 48 = \log_3 8 + 2\log_3 3$

EXAMPLE 4 on p. 509 for Exs. 45–61

CHANGE-OF-BASE FORMULA Use the change-of-base formula to evaluate the logarithm.

45. $\log_4 7$ 46. $\log_5 13$ 47. $\log_3 15$ 48. $\log_8 22$

49. $\log_3 6$ 50. $\log_5 14$ 51. $\log_6 17$ 52. $\log_2 28$

53. $\log_7 19$ 54. $\log_4 48$ 55. $\log_9 27$ 56. $\log_8 32$

57. $\log_6 \frac{24}{5}$ 58. $\log_2 \frac{15}{7}$ 59. $\log_3 \frac{9}{40}$ 60. $\log_7 \frac{3}{16}$

61. **ERROR ANALYSIS** *Describe* and correct the error in using the change-of-base formula.

$$\log_3 7 = \frac{\log 3}{\log 7}$$ ✗

EXAMPLE 5 on p. 509 for Exs. 62–63

SOUND INTENSITY In Exercises 62 and 63, use the function in Example 5.

62. Find the decibel level of the sound made by each object shown below.

a.

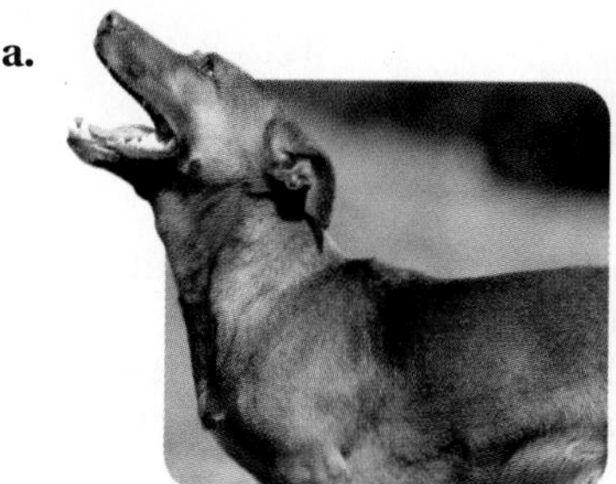

Barking dog: $I = 10^{-4}$ W/m²

b.

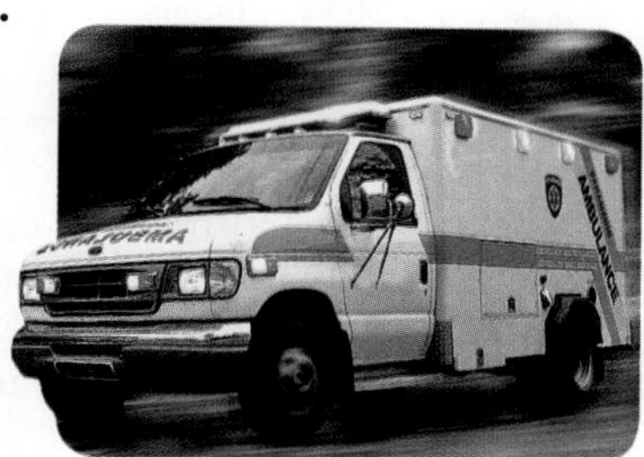

Ambulance siren: $I = 10^0$ W/m²

c.

Bee: $I = 10^{-6.5}$ W/m²

63. The intensity of the sound of a trumpet is 10^3 watts per square meter. Find the decibel level of a trumpet.

64. ★ **OPEN-ENDED MATH** For each statement, find positive numbers M, N, and b (with $b \neq 1$) that show the statement is false in general.

a. $\log_b (M + N) = \log_b M + \log_b N$ **b.** $\log_b (M - N) = \log_b M - \log_b N$

CHALLENGE In Exercises 65–68, use the given hint and properties of exponents to prove the property of logarithms.

65. **Product property** $\log_b mn = \log_b m + \log_b n$
(*Hint:* Let $x = \log_b m$ and let $y = \log_b n$. Then $m = b^x$ and $n = b^y$.)

66. **Quotient property** $\log_b \frac{m}{n} = \log_b m - \log_b n$
(*Hint:* Let $x = \log_b m$ and let $y = \log_b n$. Then $m = b^x$ and $n = b^y$.)

67. **Power property** $\log_b m^n = n \log_b m$
(*Hint:* Let $x = \log_b m$. Then $m = b^x$ and $m^n = b^{nx}$.)

68. **Change-of-base formula** $\log_c a = \frac{\log_b a}{\log_b c}$
(*Hint:* Let $x = \log_b a$, $y = \log_b c$, and $z = \log_c a$. Then $a = b^x$, $c = b^y$, and $a = c^z$, so that $b^x = c^z$.)

PROBLEM SOLVING

EXAMPLE 5 on p. 509 for Exs. 69–72

69. CONVERSATION Three groups of people are having separate conversations in a room. The sound of each conversation has an intensity of 1.4×10^{-5} watts per square meter. What is the decibel level of the combined conversations in the room?

@HomeTutor for problem solving help at classzone.com

70. PARKING GARAGE The sound made by each of five cars in a parking garage has an intensity of 3.2×10^{-4} watts per square meter. What is the decibel level of the sound made by all five cars in the parking garage?

@HomeTutor for problem solving help at classzone.com

71. ★ **SHORT RESPONSE** The intensity of the sound TV ads make is ten times as great as the intensity for an average TV show. How many decibels louder is a TV ad? *Justify* your answer using properties of logarithms.

Intensity of Television Sound

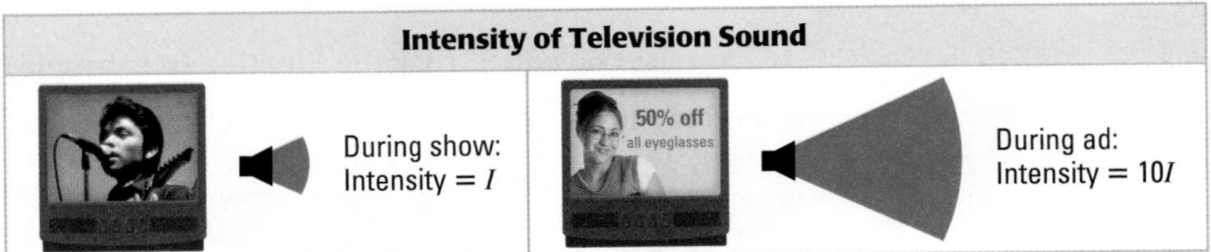

72. BIOLOGY The loudest animal on Earth is the blue whale. It can produce a sound with an intensity of $10^{6.8}$ watts per square meter. The loudest sound a human can make has an intensity of $10^{0.8}$ watts per square meter. *Compare* the decibel levels of the sounds made by a blue whale and a human.

73. ★ **EXTENDED RESPONSE** The f-stops on a 35 millimeter camera control the amount of light that enters the camera. Let s be a measure of the amount of light that strikes the film and let f be the f-stop. Then s and f are related by the equation:

$$s = \log_2 f^2$$

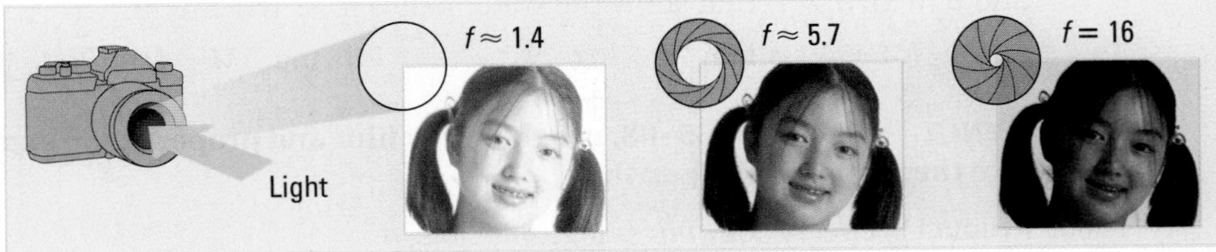

a. **Use Properties** Expand the expression for s.

b. **Calculate** The table shows the first eight f-stops on a 35 millimeter camera. Copy and complete the table. *Describe* the pattern you observe.

f	1.414	2.000	2.828	4.000	5.657	8.000	11.314	16.000
s	?	?	?	?	?	?	?	?

c. **Reasoning** Many 35 millimeter cameras have nine f-stops. What do you think the ninth f-stop is? *Explain* your reasoning.

○ = **WORKED-OUT SOLUTIONS** on p. WS1 ★ = **STANDARDIZED TEST PRACTICE**

74. **CHALLENGE** Under certain conditions, the wind speed s (in knots) at an altitude of h meters above a grassy plain can be modeled by this function:

$$s(h) = 2 \ln (100h)$$

a. By what factor does the wind speed increase when the altitude doubles?

b. Show that the given function can be written in terms of common logarithms as $s(h) = \frac{2}{\log e}(\log h + 2)$.

NEW YORK MIXED REVIEW

TEST PRACTICE at classzone.com

75. Which of the following is *not* an example of a Pythagorean triple?

Ⓐ 8, 15, 17 Ⓑ 48, 64, 80 Ⓒ 7, 23, 25 Ⓓ 11, 60, 61

76. Which inequality best describes the range of the function whose graph is shown?

Ⓐ $y \leq -1$ Ⓑ $y \leq 3$

Ⓒ $y \geq -1$ Ⓓ $y \geq 3$

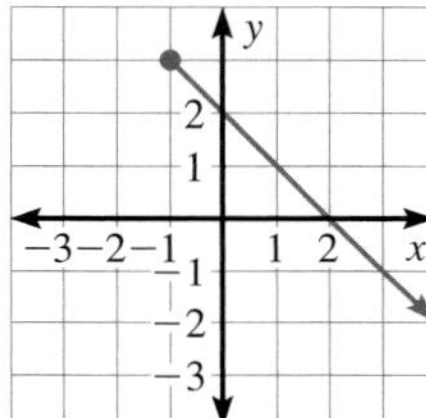

QUIZ *for Lessons 7.4–7.5*

Evaluate the logarithm without using a calculator. *(p. 499)*

1. $\log_4 16$ 2. $\log_5 1$ 3. $\log_8 8$ 4. $\log_{1/2} 32$

Graph the function. State the domain and range. *(p. 499)*

5. $y = \log_2 x$ 6. $y = \ln x + 2$ 7. $y = \log_3 (x + 4) - 1$

Expand the expression. *(p. 507)*

8. $\log_2 5x$ 9. $\log_5 x^7$ 10. $\ln 5xy^3$ 11. $\log_3 \frac{6y^4}{x^8}$

Condense the expression. *(p. 507)*

12. $\log_3 5 - \log_3 20$ 13. $\ln 6 + \ln 4x$ 14. $\log_6 5 + 3 \log_6 2$ 15. $4 \ln x - 5 \ln x$

Use the change-of-base formula to evaluate the logarithm. *(p. 507)*

16. $\log_3 10$ 17. $\log_7 14$ 18. $\log_5 24$ 19. $\log_8 40$

20. **SOUND INTENSITY** The sound of an alarm clock has an intensity of $I = 10^{-4}$ watts per square meter. Use the model $L(I) = 10 \log \frac{I}{I_0}$, where $I_0 = 10^{-12}$ watts per square meter, to find the alarm clock's loudness $L(I)$. *(p. 507)*

Graphing Calculator **ACTIVITY** *Use after Lesson 7.5*

@HomeTutor
classzone.com
Keystrokes

7.5 Graph Logarithmic Functions

QUESTION **How can you graph logarithmic functions on a graphing calculator?**

You can use a graphing calculator to graph logarithmic functions simply by using the LOG or LN key. To graph a logarithmic function having a base other than 10 or *e*, you need to use the change-of-base formula to rewrite the function in terms of common or natural logarithms.

EXAMPLE **Graph logarithmic functions**

Use a graphing calculator to graph $y = \log_2 x$ and $y = \log_2 (x - 3) + 1$.

***STEP 1* Rewrite functions** Use the change-of-base formula to rewrite each function in terms of common logarithms.

$$y = \log_2 x = \frac{\log x}{\log 2} \qquad y = \log_2 (x - 3) + 1 = \frac{\log (x - 3)}{\log 2} + 1$$

***STEP 2* Enter functions**
Enter each function into a graphing calculator.

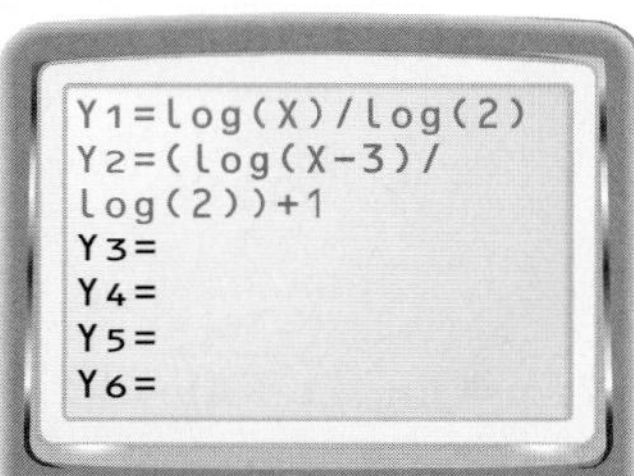

***STEP 3* Graph functions**
Graph the functions.

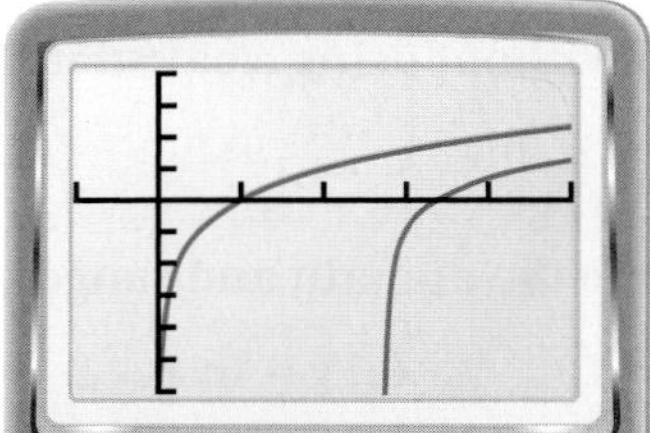

PRACTICE

Use a graphing calculator to graph the function.

1. $y = \log_4 x$
2. $y = \log_8 x$
3. $f(x) = \log_3 x$
4. $y = \log_5 x$
5. $y = \log_{12} x$
6. $g(x) = \log_9 x$
7. $y = \log_3 (x + 2)$
8. $y = \log_5 x - 1$
9. $f(x) = \log_4 (x - 5) - 2$
10. $y = \log_2 (x + 4) - 7$
11. $y = \log_7 (x - 5) + 3$
12. $g(x) = \log_3 (x + 6) - 6$
13. **REASONING** Graph $y = \ln x$. If your calculator did not have a natural logarithm key, explain how you could graph $y = \ln x$ using the LOG key.

7.6 Solve Exponential and Logarithmic Equations

A2.A.27 Solve exponential equations with and without common bases

Before You studied exponential and logarithmic functions.

Now You will solve exponential and logarithmic equations.

Why? So you can solve problems about astronomy, as in Example 7.

Key Vocabulary
- **exponential equation**
- **logarithmic equation**
- **extraneous solution,** *p. 52*

Exponential equations are equations in which variable expressions occur as exponents. The result below is useful for solving certain exponential equations.

KEY CONCEPT *For Your Notebook*

Property of Equality for Exponential Equations

Algebra If b is a positive number other than 1, then $b^x = b^y$ if and only if $x = y$.

Example If $3^x = 3^5$, then $x = 5$. If $x = 5$, then $3^x = 3^5$.

EXAMPLE 1 Solve by equating exponents

Solve $4^x = \left(\frac{1}{2}\right)^{x-3}$.

$4^x = \left(\frac{1}{2}\right)^{x-3}$ — **Write original equation.**

$(2^2)^x = (2^{-1})^{x-3}$ — **Rewrite 4 and $\frac{1}{2}$ as powers with base 2.**

$2^{2x} = 2^{-x+3}$ — **Power of a power property**

$2x = -x + 3$ — **Property of equality for exponential equations**

$x = 1$ — **Solve for x.**

▶ The solution is 1.

CHECK Check the solution by substituting it into the original equation.

$4^1 \stackrel{?}{=} \left(\frac{1}{2}\right)^{1-3}$ — **Substitute 1 for x.**

$4 \stackrel{?}{=} \left(\frac{1}{2}\right)^{-2}$ — **Simplify.**

$4 = 4$ ✓ — **Solution checks.**

GUIDED PRACTICE for Example 1

Solve the equation.

1. $9^{2x} = 27^{x-1}$

2. $100^{7x+1} = 1000^{3x-2}$

3. $81^{3-x} = \left(\frac{1}{3}\right)^{5x-6}$

When it is not convenient to write each side of an exponential equation using the same base, you can solve the equation by taking a logarithm of each side.

EXAMPLE 2 Take a logarithm of each side

ANOTHER WAY

For an alternative method for solving the problem in Example 2, turn to page 523 for the **Problem Solving Workshop**.

Solve $4^x = 11$.

$4^x = 11$	**Write original equation.**
$\log_4 4^x = \log_4 11$	**Take $\log_4$ of each side.**
$x = \log_4 11$	**$\log_b b^x = x$**
$x = \frac{\log 11}{\log 4}$	**Change-of-base formula**
$x \approx 1.73$	**Use a calculator.**

▶ The solution is about 1.73. Check this in the original equation.

NEWTON'S LAW OF COOLING An important application of exponential equations is *Newton's law of cooling*. This law states that for a cooling substance with initial temperature T_0, the temperature T after t minutes can be modeled by

$$T = (T_0 - T_R)e^{-rt} + T_R$$

where T_R is the surrounding temperature and r is the substance's cooling rate.

EXAMPLE 3 Use an exponential model

CARS You are driving on a hot day when your car overheats and stops running. It overheats at 280°F and can be driven again at 230°F. If $r = 0.0048$ and it is 80°F outside, how long (in minutes) do you have to wait until you can continue driving?

Solution

$T = (T_0 - T_R)e^{-rt} + T_R$	**Newton's law of cooling**
$230 = (280 - 80)e^{-0.0048t} + 80$	**Substitute for T, T_0, T_R, and r.**
$150 = 200e^{-0.0048t}$	**Subtract 80 from each side.**
$0.75 = e^{-0.0048t}$	**Divide each side by 200.**
$\ln 0.75 = \ln e^{-0.0048t}$	**Take natural log of each side.**
$-0.2877 \approx -0.0048t$	**$\ln e^x = \log_e e^x = x$**
$60 \approx t$	**Divide each side by −0.0048.**

▶ You have to wait about 60 minutes until you can continue driving.

GUIDED PRACTICE for Examples 2 and 3

Solve the equation.

4. $2^x = 5$ **5.** $7^{9x} = 15$ **6.** $4e^{-0.3x} - 7 = 13$

SOLVING LOGARITHMIC EQUATIONS **Logarithmic equations** are equations that involve logarithms of variable expressions. You can use the following property to solve some types of logarithmic equations.

KEY CONCEPT *For Your Notebook*

Property of Equality for Logarithmic Equations

Algebra If b, x, and y are positive numbers with $b \neq 1$, then $\log_b x = \log_b y$ if and only if $x = y$.

Example If $\log_2 x = \log_2 7$, then $x = 7$. If $x = 7$, then $\log_2 x = \log_2 7$.

EXAMPLE 4 Solve a logarithmic equation

Solve $\log_5 (4x - 7) = \log_5 (x + 5)$.

$\log_5 (4x - 7) = \log_5 (x + 5)$ — **Write original equation.**

$4x - 7 = x + 5$ — **Property of equality for logarithmic equations**

$3x - 7 = 5$ — **Subtract x from each side.**

$3x = 12$ — **Add 7 to each side.**

$x = 4$ — **Divide each side by 3.**

▶ The solution is 4.

CHECK Check the solution by substituting it into the original equation.

$\log_5 (4x - 7) = \log_5 (x + 5)$ — **Write original equation.**

$\log_5 (4 \cdot 4 - 7) \stackrel{?}{=} \log_5 (4 + 5)$ — **Substitute 4 for x.**

$\log_5 9 = \log_5 9$ ✓ — **Solution checks.**

EXPONENTIATING TO SOLVE EQUATIONS The property of equality for exponential equations on page 515 implies that if you are given an equation $x = y$, then you can *exponentiate* each side to obtain an equation of the form $b^x = b^y$. This technique is useful for solving some logarithmic equations.

EXAMPLE 5 Exponentiate each side of an equation

Solve $\log_4 (5x - 1) = 3$.

$\log_4 (5x - 1) = 3$ — **Write original equation.**

$4^{\log_4 (5x - 1)} = 4^3$ — **Exponentiate each side using base 4.**

$5x - 1 = 64$ — $b^{\log_b x} = x$

$5x = 65$ — **Add 1 to each side.**

$x = 13$ — **Divide each side by 5.**

▶ The solution is 13.

CHECK $\log_4 (5x - 1) = \log_4 (5 \cdot 13 - 1) = \log_4 64$

Because $4^3 = 64$, $\log_4 64 = 3$. ✓

EXTRANEOUS SOLUTIONS Because the domain of a logarithmic function generally does not include all real numbers, be sure to check for extraneous solutions of logarithmic equations. You can do this algebraically or graphically.

EXAMPLE 6 Standardized Test Practice

ELIMINATE CHOICES
Instead of solving the equation in Example 6 directly, you can substitute each possible answer into the equation to see whether it is a solution.

What is (are) the solution(s) of $\log 2x + \log (x - 5) = 2$?

Ⓐ −5, 10 Ⓑ 5 Ⓒ 10 Ⓓ 5, 10

Solution

$\log 2x + \log (x - 5) = 2$	**Write original equation.**
$\log [2x(x - 5)] = 2$	**Product property of logarithms**
$10^{\log [2x(x-5)]} = 10^2$	**Exponentiate each side using base 10.**
$2x(x - 5) = 100$	$b^{\log_b x} = x$
$2x^2 - 10x = 100$	**Distributive property**
$2x^2 - 10x - 100 = 0$	**Write in standard form.**
$x^2 - 5x - 50 = 0$	**Divide each side by 2.**
$(x - 10)(x + 5) = 0$	**Factor.**
$x = 10$ or $x = -5$	**Zero product property**

CHECK Check the apparent solutions 10 and −5 using algebra or a graph.

Algebra Substitute 10 and −5 for x in the original equation.

$$\log 2x + \log (x - 5) = 2$$
$$\log (2 \cdot 10) + \log (10 - 5) \stackrel{?}{=} 2$$
$$\log 20 + \log 5 \stackrel{?}{=} 2$$
$$\log 100 \stackrel{?}{=} 2$$
$$2 = 2 \checkmark$$

So, 10 is a solution.

$$\log 2x + \log (x - 5) = 2$$
$$\log [2(-5)] + \log (-5 - 5) \stackrel{?}{=} 2$$
$$\log (-10) + \log (-10) \stackrel{?}{=} 2$$

Because $\log (-10)$ is not defined, −5 is *not* a solution.

Graph Graph $y = \log 2x + \log (x - 5)$ and $y = 2$ in the same coordinate plane. The graphs intersect only once, when $x = 10$. So, 10 is the only solution.

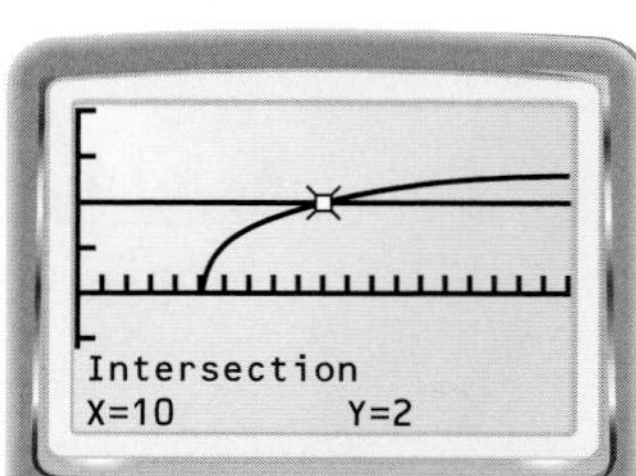

▶ The correct answer is C. Ⓐ Ⓑ Ⓒ Ⓓ

GUIDED PRACTICE for Examples 4, 5, and 6

Solve the equation. Check for extraneous solutions.

7. $\ln (7x - 4) = \ln (2x + 11)$

8. $\log_2 (x - 6) = 5$

9. $\log 5x + \log (x - 1) = 2$

10. $\log_4 (x + 12) + \log_4 x = 3$

EXAMPLE 7 Use a logarithmic model

ASTRONOMY The *apparent magnitude* of a star is a measure of the brightness of the star as it appears to observers on Earth. The apparent magnitude M of the dimmest star that can be seen with a telescope is given by the function

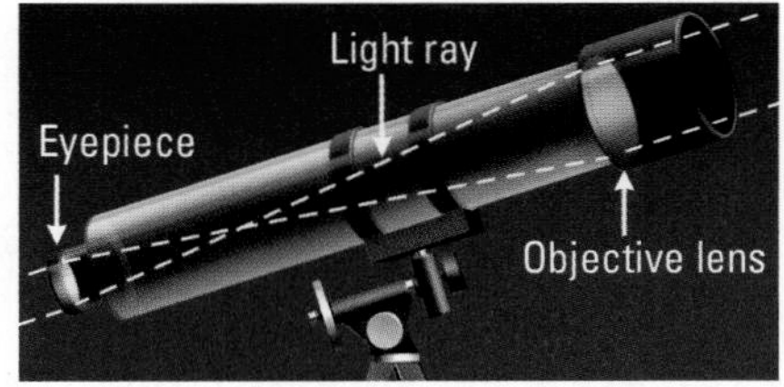

$$M = 5 \log D + 2$$

where D is the diameter (in millimeters) of the telescope's objective lens. If a telescope can reveal stars with a magnitude of 12, what is the diameter of its objective lens?

ANOTHER WAY
For an alternative method for solving the problem in Example 7, turn to page 523 for the **Problem Solving Workshop**.

Solution

$M = 5 \log D + 2$	**Write original equation.**
$12 = 5 \log D + 2$	**Substitute 12 for *M*.**
$10 = 5 \log D$	**Subtract 2 from each side.**
$2 = \log D$	**Divide each side by 5.**
$10^2 = 10^{\log D}$	**Exponentiate each side using base 10.**
$100 = D$	**Simplify.**

▶ The diameter is 100 millimeters.

Animated Algebra at classzone.com

✓ **GUIDED PRACTICE** for Example 7

11. **WHAT IF?** Use the information from Example 7 to find the diameter of the objective lens of a telescope that can reveal stars with a magnitude of 7.

7.6 EXERCISES

HOMEWORK KEY
○ = **WORKED-OUT SOLUTIONS** on p. WS14 for Exs. 15, 35, and 57
★ = **STANDARDIZED TEST PRACTICE** Exs. 2, 44, 47, 58, and 60
◆ = **MULTIPLE REPRESENTATIONS** Ex. 59

SKILL PRACTICE

1. **VOCABULARY** Copy and complete: The equation $5^x = 8$ is an example of a(n) _?_ equation.

2. ★ **WRITING** When do logarithmic equations have extraneous solutions?

EXAMPLE 1
on p. 515
for Exs. 3–11

SOLVING EXPONENTIAL EQUATIONS **Solve the equation.**

3. $5^{x-4} = 25^{x-6}$
4. $7^{3x+4} = 49^{2x+1}$
5. $8^{x-1} = 32^{3x-2}$
6. $27^{4x-1} = 9^{3x+8}$
7. $4^{2x-5} = 64^{3x}$
8. $3^{3x-7} = 81^{12-3x}$
9. $36^{5x+2} = \left(\frac{1}{6}\right)^{11-x}$
10. $10^{3x-10} = \left(\frac{1}{100}\right)^{6x-1}$
11. $25^{10x+8} = \left(\frac{1}{125}\right)^{4-2x}$

EXAMPLE 2
on p. 516
for Exs. 12–23

SOLVING EXPONENTIAL EQUATIONS **Solve the equation.**

12. $8^x = 20$
13. $e^{-x} = 5$
14. $7^{3x} = 18$
15. $11^{5x} = 33$
16. $7^{6x} = 12$
17. $4e^{-2x} = 17$
18. $10^{3x} + 4 = 9$
19. $-3e^{2x} + 16 = 5$
20. $0.5^x - 0.25 = 4$
21. $\frac{1}{3}(6)^{-4x} + 1 = 6$
22. $2^{0.1x} - 5 = 7$
23. $\frac{3}{4}e^{2x} + \frac{7}{2} = 4$

EXAMPLE 4
on p. 517
for Exs. 24–31

SOLVING LOGARITHMIC EQUATIONS **Solve the equation. Check for extraneous solutions.**

24. $\log_5 (5x + 9) = \log_5 6x$
25. $\ln (4x - 7) = \ln (x + 11)$
26. $\ln (x + 19) = \ln (7x - 8)$
27. $\log_5 (2x - 7) = \log_5 (3x - 9)$
28. $\log (12x - 11) = \log (3x + 13)$
29. $\log_3 (18x + 7) = \log_3 (3x + 38)$
30. $\log_6 (3x - 10) = \log_6 (14 - 5x)$
31. $\log_8 (5 - 12x) = \log_8 (6x - 1)$

EXAMPLES 5 and 6
on pp. 517–518
for Exs. 32–44

EXPONENTIATING TO SOLVE EQUATIONS **Solve the equation. Check for extraneous solutions.**

32. $\log_4 x = -1$
33. $5 \ln x = 35$
34. $\frac{1}{3} \log_5 12x = 2$
35. $5.2 \log_4 2x = 16$
36. $\log_2 (x - 4) = 6$
37. $\log_2 x + \log_2 (x - 2) = 3$
38. $\log_4 (-x) + \log_4 (x + 10) = 2$
39. $\ln (x + 3) + \ln x = 1$
40. $4 \ln (-x) + 3 = 21$
41. $\log_5 (x + 4) + \log_5 (x + 1) = 2$
42. $\log_6 3x + \log_6 (x - 1) = 3$
43. $\log_3 (x - 9) + \log_3 (x - 3) = 2$

44. ★ **MULTIPLE CHOICE** What is the solution of $3 \log_8 (2x + 7) + 8 = 10$?

(A) -1.5 (B) -1.179 (C) 4 (D) 4.642

ERROR ANALYSIS ***Describe*** **and correct the error in solving the equation.**

45.

$3^{x+1} = 6^x$

$\log_3 3^{x+1} = \log_3 6^x$

$x + 1 = x \log_3 6$

$x + 1 = 2x$

$1 = x$

46.

$\log_3 10x = 5$

$e^{\log_3 10x} = e^5$

$10x = e^5$

$x = \frac{e^5}{10}$

47. ★ **OPEN-ENDED MATH** Give an example of an exponential equation whose only solution is 4 and an example of a logarithmic equation whose only solution is -3.

CHALLENGE **Solve the equation.**

48. $3^{x+4} = 6^{2x-5}$
49. $10^{3x-8} = 2^{5-x}$
50. $\log_2 (x + 1) = \log_8 3x$
51. $\log_3 x = \log_9 6x$
52. $2^{2x} - 12 \cdot 2^x + 32 = 0$
53. $5^{2x} + 20 \cdot 5^x - 125 = 0$

○ = WORKED-OUT SOLUTIONS on p. WS1 ★ = STANDARDIZED TEST PRACTICE ◆ = MULTIPLE REPRESENTATIONS

PROBLEM SOLVING

EXAMPLE 3 on p. 516 for Exs. 54–58

54. **COOKING** You are cooking beef stew. When you take the beef stew off the stove, it has a temperature of 200°F. The room temperature is 75°F and the cooling rate of the beef stew is $r = 0.054$. How long (in minutes) will it take to cool the beef stew to a serving temperature of 100°F?

@HomeTutor for problem solving help at classzone.com

55. **THERMOMETER** As you are hanging an outdoor thermometer, its reading drops from the indoor temperature of 75°F to 37°F in one minute. If the cooling rate is $r = 1.37$, what is the outdoor temperature?

@HomeTutor for problem solving help at classzone.com

56. **COMPOUND INTEREST** You deposit $100 in an account that pays 6% annual interest. How long will it take for the balance to reach $1000 for each given frequency of compounding?

a. Annual **b.** Quarterly **c.** Daily

57. **RADIOACTIVE DECAY** One hundred grams of radium are stored in a container. The amount R (in grams) of radium present after t years can be modeled by $R = 100e^{-0.00043t}$. After how many years will only 5 grams of radium be present?

58. ★ **MULTIPLE CHOICE** You deposit $800 in an account that pays 2.25% annual interest compounded continuously. About how long will it take for the balance to triple?

Ⓐ 24 years Ⓑ 36 years

Ⓒ 48.8 years Ⓓ 52.6 years

EXAMPLE 7 on p. 519 for Ex. 59

59. **MULTIPLE REPRESENTATIONS** The Richter scale is used for measuring the magnitude of an earthquake. The Richter magnitude R is given by the function

$$R = 0.67 \log (0.37E) + 1.46$$

where E is the energy (in kilowatt-hours) released by the earthquake.

a. Making a Graph Graph the function using a graphing calculator. Use your graph to approximate the amount of energy released by each earthquake indicated in the diagram above.

b. Solving Equations Write and solve a logarithmic equation to find the amount of energy released by each earthquake in the diagram.

60. ★ **EXTENDED RESPONSE** If X-rays of a fixed wavelength strike a material x centimeters thick, then the intensity $I(x)$ of the X-rays transmitted through the material is given by $I(x) = I_0e^{-\mu x}$, where I_0 is the initial intensity and μ is a number that depends on the type of material and the wavelength of the X-rays. The table shows the values of μ for various materials. These μ-values apply to X-rays of medium wavelength.

Material	Aluminum	Copper	Lead
Value of μ	0.43	3.2	43

a. Find the thickness of aluminum shielding that reduces the intensity of X-rays to 30% of their initial intensity. (*Hint:* Find the value of x for which $I(x) = 0.3I_0$.)

b. Repeat part (a) for copper shielding.

c. Repeat part (a) for lead shielding.

d. **Reasoning** Your dentist puts a lead apron on you before taking X-rays of your teeth to protect you from harmful radiation. Based on your results from parts (a)–(c), explain why lead is a better material to use than aluminum or copper.

61. **CHALLENGE** You plant a sunflower seedling in your garden. The seedling's height h (in centimeters) after t weeks can be modeled by the function below, which is called a *logistic function*.

$$h(t) = \frac{256}{1 + 13e^{-0.65t}}$$

Find the time it takes the sunflower seedling to reach a height of 200 centimeters.

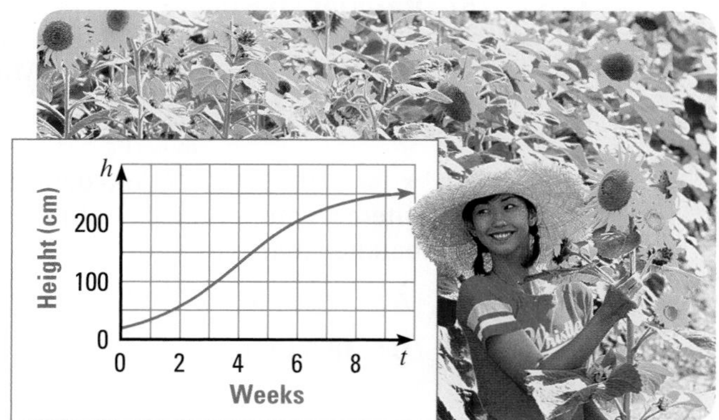

NEW YORK MIXED REVIEW

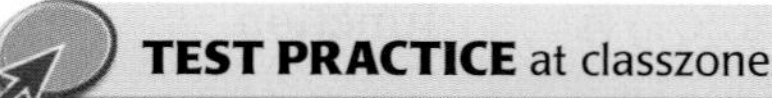

62. Which list shows the functions in order from the widest graph to the narrowest graph?

Ⓐ $y = -5x^2, y = -\frac{2}{3}x^2, y = \frac{5}{6}x^2, y = 8x^2$

Ⓑ $y = -\frac{2}{3}x^2, y = \frac{5}{6}x^2, y = -5x^2, y = 8x^2$

Ⓒ $y = \frac{5}{6}x^2, y = -\frac{2}{3}x^2, y = 8x^2, y = -5x^2$

Ⓓ $y = 8x^2, y = \frac{5}{6}x^2, y = -\frac{2}{3}x^2, y = -5x^2$

63. In the diagram, $m\angle 2 = m\angle 3$. What is $m\angle 1$?

Ⓐ 136°　　Ⓑ 164°

Ⓒ 174°　　Ⓓ 194°

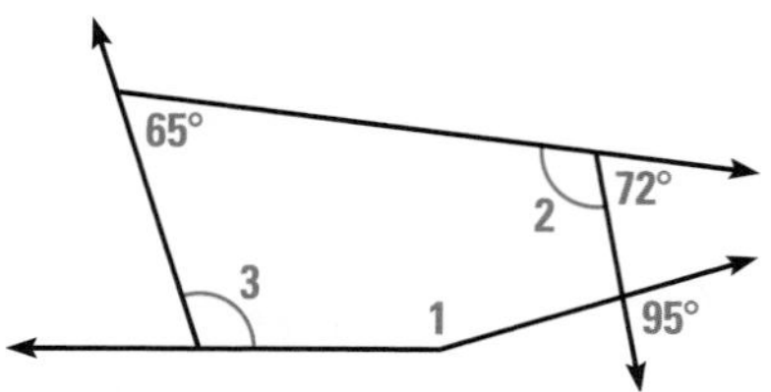

PROBLEM SOLVING WORKSHOP
LESSON 7.6

Using ALTERNATIVE METHODS

Another Way to Solve Examples 2 and 7, pp. 516 and 519

MULTIPLE REPRESENTATIONS In Examples 2 and 7 on pages 516 and 519, respectively, you solved exponential and logarithmic equations algebraically. You can also solve such equations using tables and graphs.

PROBLEM 1

Solve the following exponential equation: $4^x = 11$.

METHOD 1

Using a Table One way to solve the equation is to make a table of values.

STEP 1 **Enter** the function $y = 4^x$ into a graphing calculator.

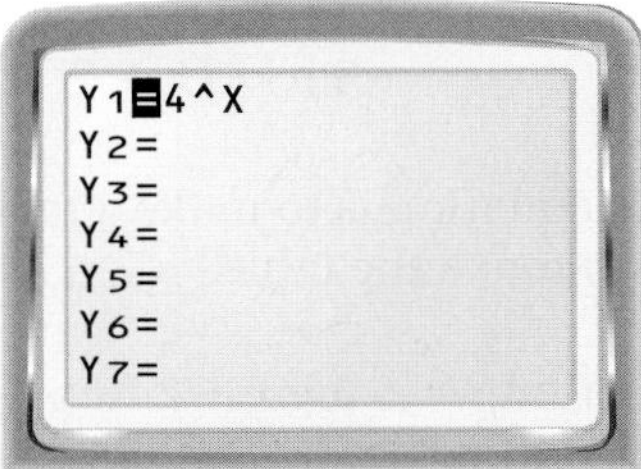

STEP 2 **Create** a table of values for the function.

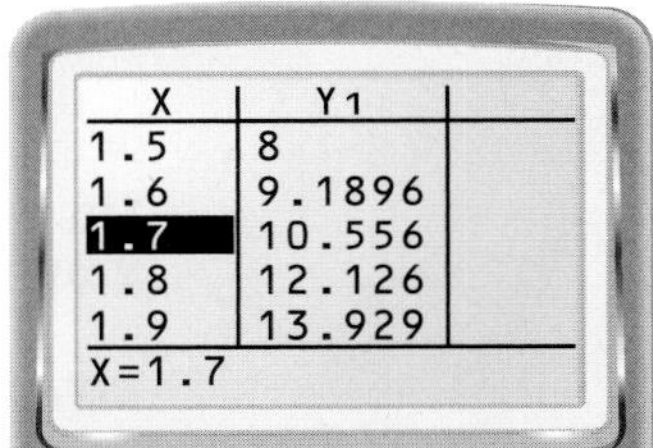

STEP 3 **Scroll** through the table to find when $y = 11$. The table in Step 2 shows that $y = 11$ between $x = 1.7$ and $x = 1.8$.

▸ The solution of $4^x = 11$ is between 1.7 and 1.8.

METHOD 2

Using a Graph You can also use a graph to solve the equation.

STEP 1 **Enter** the functions $y = 4^x$ and $y = 11$ into a graphing calculator.

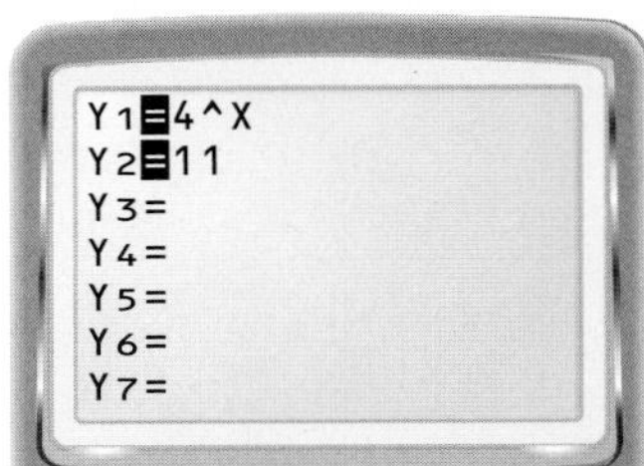

STEP 2 **Graph** the functions. Use the *intersect* feature to find the intersection point of the graphs. The graphs intersect at about (1.73, 11).

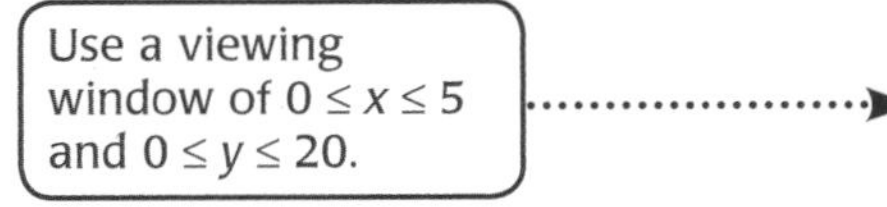

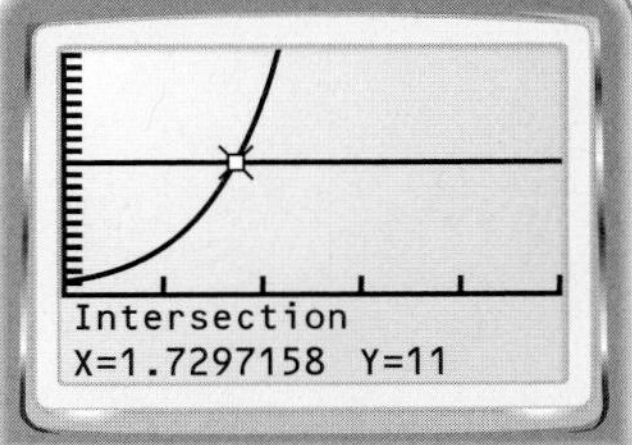

▸ The solution of $4^x = 11$ is about 1.73.

PROBLEM 2

ASTRONOMY The *apparent magnitude* of a star is a measure of the brightness of the star as it appears to observers on Earth. The apparent magnitude M of the dimmest star that can be seen with a telescope is given by the function

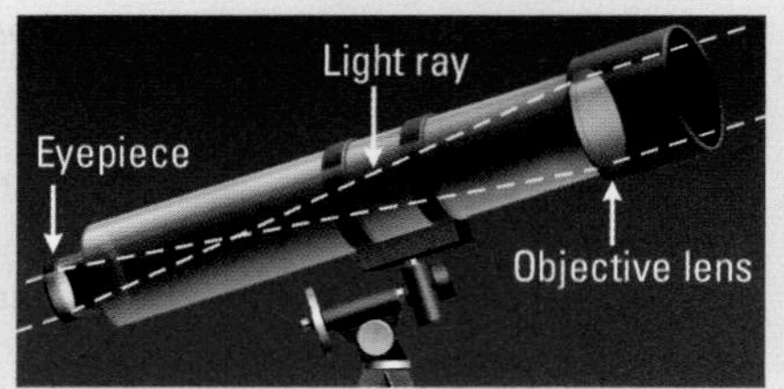

$$M = 5 \log D + 2$$

where D is the diameter (in millimeters) of the telescope's objective lens. If a telescope can reveal stars with a magnitude of 12, what is the diameter of its objective lens?

METHOD 1

Using a Table Notice that the problem requires solving the following logarithmic equation:

$$5 \log D + 2 = 12$$

One way to solve this equation is to make a table of values. You can use a graphing calculator to make the table.

STEP 1 **Enter** the function $y = 5 \log x + 2$ into a graphing calculator.

STEP 2 **Create** a table of values for the function. Make sure that the x-values are in the domain of the function ($x > 0$).

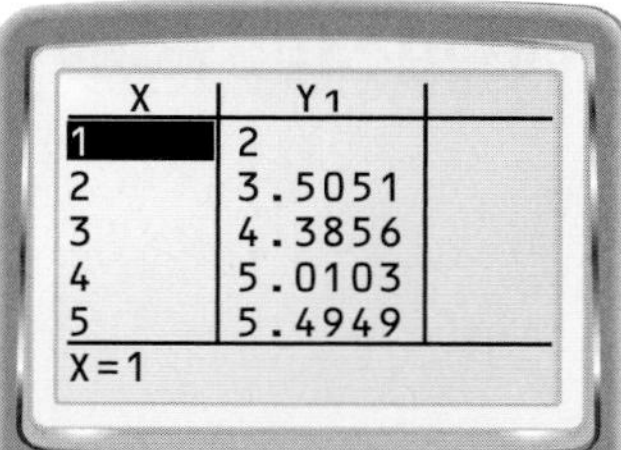

X	Y1
1	2
2	3.5051
3	4.3856
4	5.0103
5	5.4949

X=1

STEP 3 **Scroll** through the table of values to find when $y = 12$.

The table shows that $y = 12$ when $x = 100$.

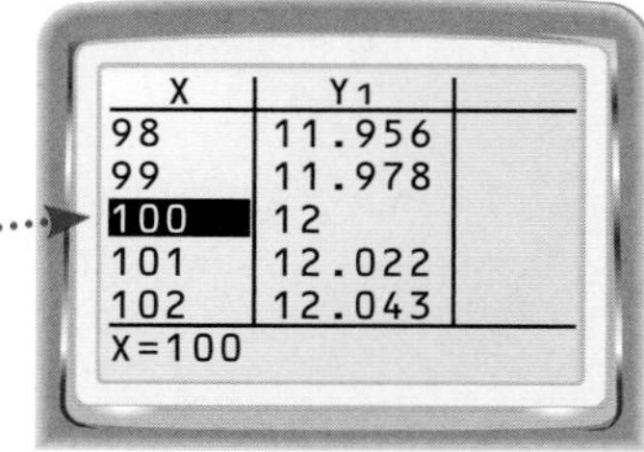

X	Y1
98	11.956
99	11.978
100	12
101	12.022
102	12.043

X=100

▶ To reveal stars with a magnitude of 12, a telescope must have an objective lens with a diameter of 100 millimeters.

METHOD 2 **Using a Graph** You can also use a graph to solve the equation $5 \log D + 2 = 12$.

STEP 1 **Enter** the functions $y = 5 \log x + 2$ and $y = 12$ into a graphing calculator.

STEP 2 **Graph** the functions. Use the *intersect* feature to find the intersection point of the graphs. The graphs intersect at (100, 12).

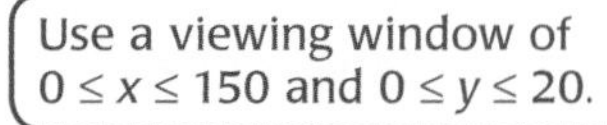

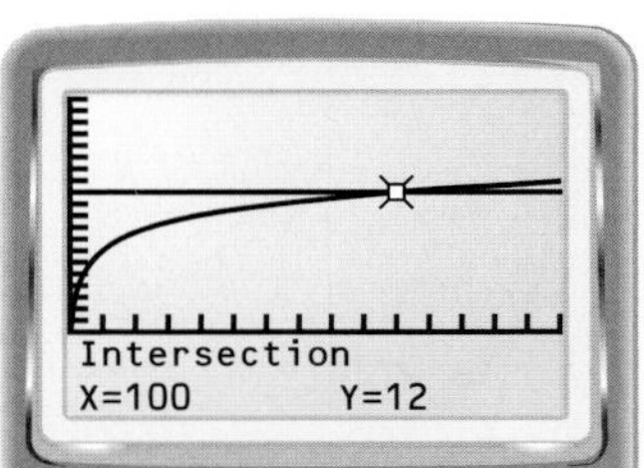

▶ To reveal stars with a magnitude of 12, a telescope must have an objective lens with a diameter of 100 millimeters.

PRACTICE

EXPONENTIAL EQUATIONS Solve the equation using a table and using a graph.

1. $8 - 2e^{3x} = -14$
2. $7 - 10^{5-x} = -9$
3. $e^{5x-8} + 3 = 15$
4. $1.6(3)^{-4x} + 5.6 = 6$

LOGARITHMIC EQUATIONS Solve the equation using a table and using a graph.

5. $\log_2 5x = 2$
6. $\log(-3x + 7) = 1$
7. $4 \ln x + 6 = 12$
8. $11 \log(x + 9) - 5 = 8$
9. **ECONOMICS** From 1998 to 2003, the United States gross national product y (in billions of dollars) can be modeled by $y = 8882(1.04)^x$ where x is the number of years since 1998. Use a table and a graph to find the year when the gross national product was \$10 trillion.
10. **WRITING** In Method 1 of Problem 1 on page 523, explain how you could use a table to find the solution of $4^x = 11$ more precisely.
11. **WHAT IF?** In Problem 2 on page 524, suppose the telescope can reveal stars of magnitude 14. Find the diameter of the telescope's objective lens using a table and using a graph.
12. **FINANCE** You deposit \$5000 in an account that pays 3% annual interest compounded quarterly. How long will it take for the balance to reach \$6000? Solve the problem using a table and using a graph.
13. **OCEANOGRAPHY** The density d (in grams per cubic centimeter) of seawater with a salinity of 30 parts per thousand is related to the water temperature T (in degrees Celsius) by the following equation:

$$d = 1.0245 - e^{0.1226T - 7.828}$$

For deep water in the South Atlantic Ocean off Antarctica, $d = 1.0241$ g/cm^3. Use a table and a graph to find the water's temperature.

Solve Exponential and Logarithmic Inequalities

GOAL Solve exponential and logarithmic inequalities using tables and graphs.

In the Problem Solving Workshop on pages 523–525, you learned how to solve exponential and logarithmic equations using tables and graphs. You can use these same methods to solve exponential and logarithmic inequalities.

EXAMPLE 1 Solve an exponential inequality

CARS Your family purchases a new car for \$20,000. Its value decreases by 15% each year. During what interval of time does the car's value exceed \$10,000?

Solution

Let y represent the value of the car (in dollars) x years after it is purchased. A function relating x and y is $y = 20{,}000(1 - 0.15)^x$, or $y = 20{,}000(0.85)^x$. To find the values of x for which $y > 10{,}000$, solve the inequality $20{,}000(0.85)^x > 10{,}000$.

METHOD 1 Use a table

STEP 1 **Enter** the function $y = 20{,}000(0.85)^x$ into a graphing calculator. Set the starting x-value of the table to 0 and the step value to 0.1.

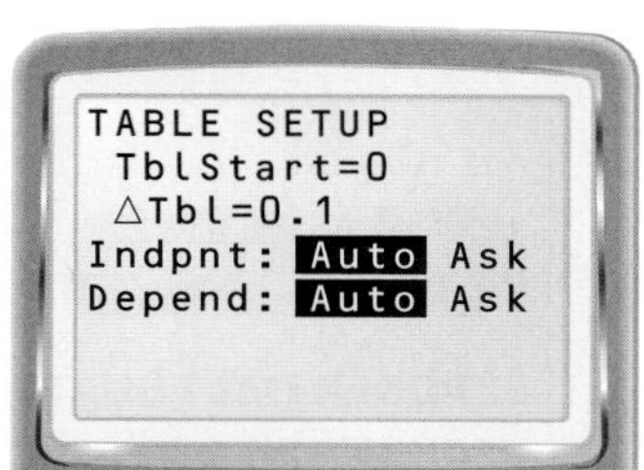

STEP 2 **Use** the *table* feature to create a table of values. Scrolling through the table shows that $y > 10{,}000$ when $0 \le x \le 4.2$.

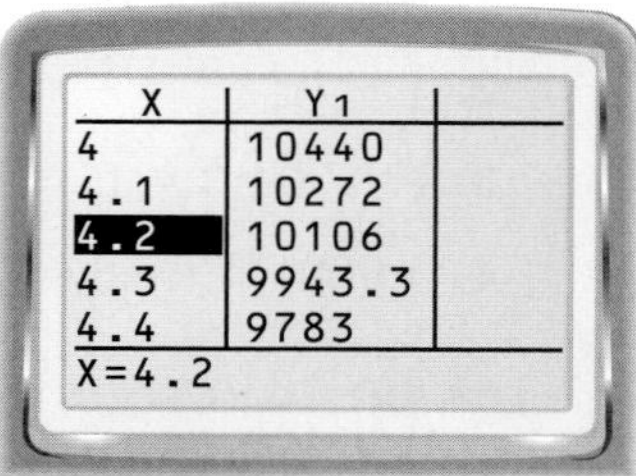

▶ The car value exceeds \$10,000 for about the first 4.2 years after it is purchased.

To check the solution's reasonableness, note that $y \approx 10{,}440$ when $x = 4$ and $y \approx 8874$ when $x = 5$. So, $4 < x < 5$, which agrees with the solution obtained above.

METHOD 2 Use a graph

Graph $y = 20{,}000(0.85)^x$ and $y = 10{,}000$ in the same viewing window. Set the viewing window to show $0 \le x \le 8$ and $0 \le y \le 25{,}000$. Using the *intersect* feature, you can determine that the graphs intersect when $x \approx 4.27$.

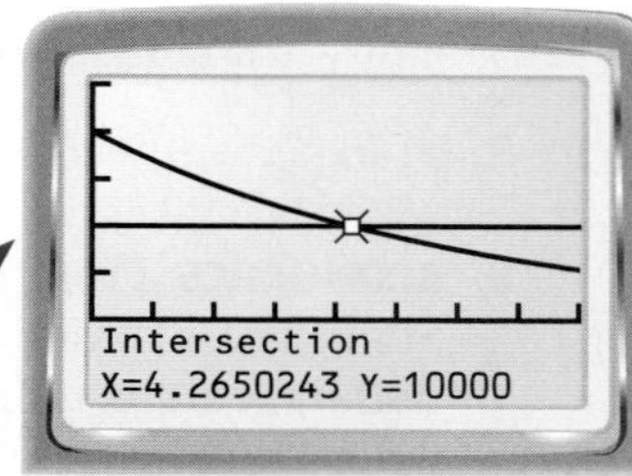

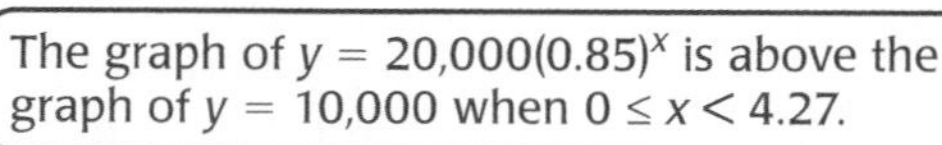
The graph of $y = 20{,}000(0.85)^x$ is above the graph of $y = 10{,}000$ when $0 \le x < 4.27$.

▶ The car value exceeds \$10,000 for about the first 4.27 years after it is purchased.

EXAMPLE 2 Solve a logarithmic inequality

Solve $\log_2 x \le 2$.

Solution

METHOD 1 Use a table

STEP 1 **Enter** the function $y = \log_2 x$ into a graphing calculator as $y = \frac{\log x}{\log 2}$.

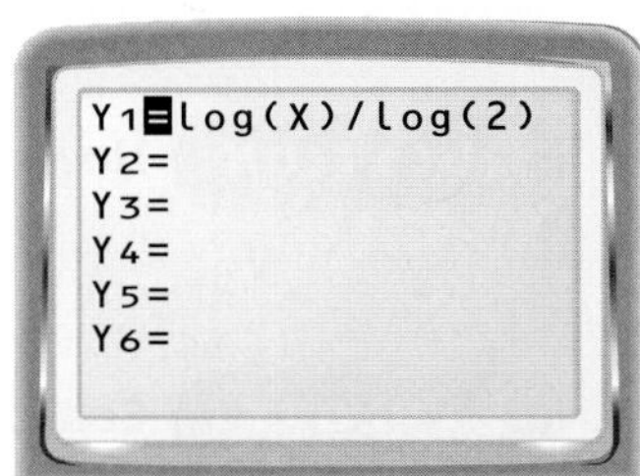

STEP 2 **Use** the *table* feature to create a table of values. Identify the x-values for which $y \le 2$. These x-values are given by $0 < x \le 4$.

Make sure that the x-values are reasonable and in the domain of the function ($x > 0$).

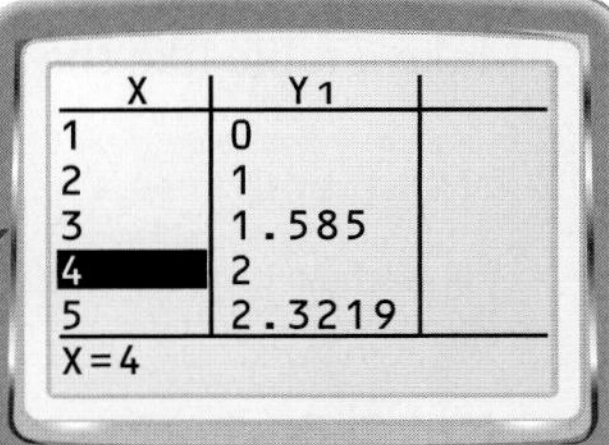

▸ The solution is $0 < x \le 4$.

METHOD 2 Use a graph

Graph $y = \log_2 x$ and $y = 2$ in the same viewing window. Using the *intersect* feature, you can determine that the graphs intersect when $x = 4$.

The graph of $y = \log_2 x$ is on or below the graph of $y = 2$ when $0 < x \le 4$.

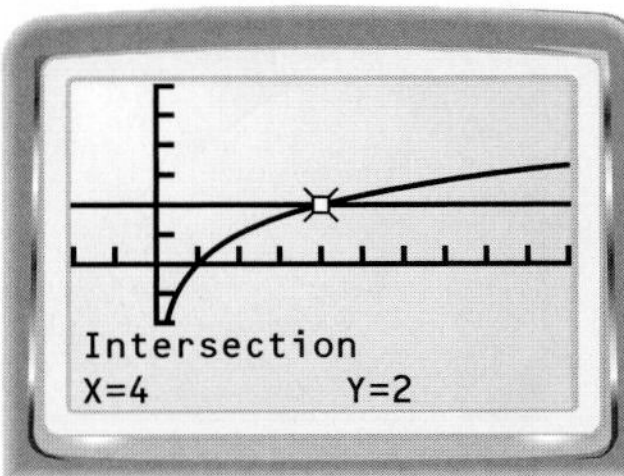

▸ The solution is $0 < x \le 4$.

PRACTICE

EXAMPLE 1 on p. 526 for Exs. 1–6

Solve the exponential inequality using a table and using a graph.

1. $3^x \le 20$

2. $28\left(\frac{2}{3}\right)^x > 9$

3. $244(0.35)^x \ge 50$

4. $-63(0.96)^x < -27$

5. $95(1.6)^x \le 1620$

6. $-284\left(\frac{9}{7}\right)^x > -135$

EXAMPLE 2 on p. 527 for Exs. 7–12

Solve the logarithmic inequality using a table and using a graph.

7. $\log_3 x \ge 3$

8. $\log_5 x < 2$

9. $\log_6 x + 9 \le 11$

10. $2 \log_4 x - 1 > 4$

11. $-4 \log_2 x > -20$

12. $0 \le \log_7 x \le 1$

13. FINANCE You deposit \$1000 in an account that pays 3.5% annual interest compounded monthly. When is your balance at least \$1200?

14. RATES OF RETURN An investment that earns a rate of return r doubles in value in t years, where $t = \frac{\ln 2}{\ln (1 + r)}$ and r is expressed as a decimal. What rates of return will double the value of an investment in less than 10 years?

Investigating Algebra ACTIVITY *Use before Lesson 7.7*

@HomeTutor
classzone.com
Keystrokes

7.7 Model Data with an Exponential Function

MATERIALS • 100 pennies • cup • graphing calculator

QUESTION **How can you model data with an exponential function?**

EXPLORE **Collect and record data**

STEP 1 ***Make a table***

Make a table like the one shown to record your results.

Number of toss, x	0	1	2	3	4	5	6	7
Number of pennies remaining, y	?	?	?	?	?	?	?	?

STEP 2 ***Perform an experiment***

Record the initial number of pennies in the table, and place the pennies in a cup. Shake the pennies, and then spill them onto a flat surface.

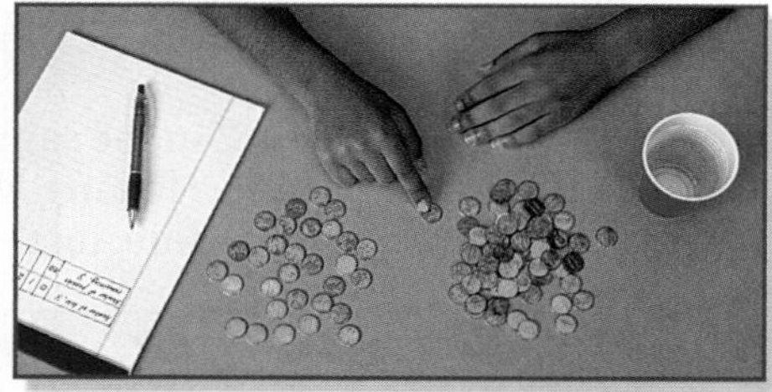

Remove all of the pennies showing "heads." Count the number of pennies remaining, and record this number in the table.

STEP 3 ***Continue collecting data***

Repeat Step 2 with the remaining pennies until there are no pennies left to return to the cup.

DRAW CONCLUSIONS **Use your observations to complete these exercises**

1. What is the initial number of pennies? By what percent would you expect the number of pennies remaining to decrease after each toss?
2. Use your answers from Exercise 1 to write an exponential function that should model the data in the table.
3. Use a graphing calculator to make a scatter plot of the data pairs (x, y). In the same viewing window, graph your function from Exercise 2. Is the function a good model for the data? *Explain.*
4. Use the calculator's *exponential regression* feature to find an exponential function that models the data. *Compare* this function with the function you wrote in Exercise 2.

7.7 Write and Apply Exponential and Power Functions

 **A2.A.6** Solve an application which results in an exponential function

Before You wrote linear, quadratic, and other polynomial functions.

Now You will write exponential and power functions.

Why? So you can model biology problems, as in Example 5.

Key Vocabulary
- **power function,** *p. 428*
- **exponential function,** *p. 478*

In Chapter 2, you learned that two points determine a line. Similarly, two points determine an exponential curve.

EXAMPLE 1 Write an exponential function

Write an exponential function $y = ab^x$ whose graph passes through (1, 12) and (3, 108).

Solution

STEP 1 **Substitute** the coordinates of the two given points into $y = ab^x$.

$12 = ab^1$ **Substitute 12 for *y* and 1 for *x*.**

$108 = ab^3$ **Substitute 108 for *y* and 3 for *x*.**

STEP 2 **Solve** for a in the first equation to obtain $a = \frac{12}{b}$, and substitute this expression for a in the second equation.

$108 = \left(\frac{12}{b}\right)b^3$ **Substitute $\frac{12}{b}$ for *a* in second equation.**

$108 = 12b^2$ **Simplify.**

$9 = b^2$ **Divide each side by 12.**

$3 = b$ **Take the positive square root because $b > 0$.**

STEP 3 **Determine** that $a = \frac{12}{b} = \frac{12}{3} = 4$. So, $y = 4 \cdot 3^x$.

TRANSFORMING EXPONENTIAL DATA A set of more than two points (x, y) fits an exponential pattern if and only if the set of transformed points $(x, \ln y)$ fits a linear pattern.

Graph of points (*x*, *y*)

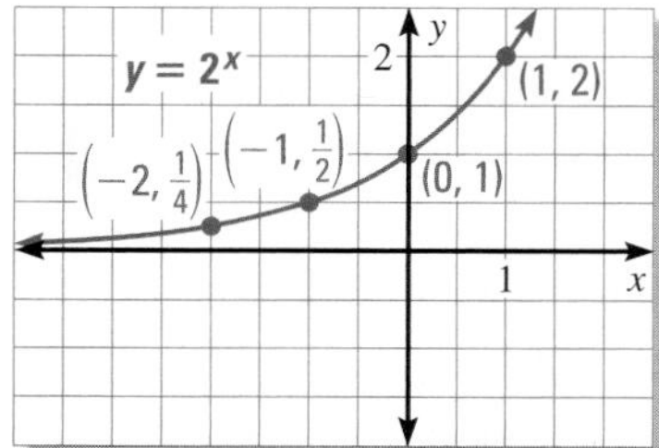

The graph is an exponential curve.

Graph of points (*x*, ln *y*)

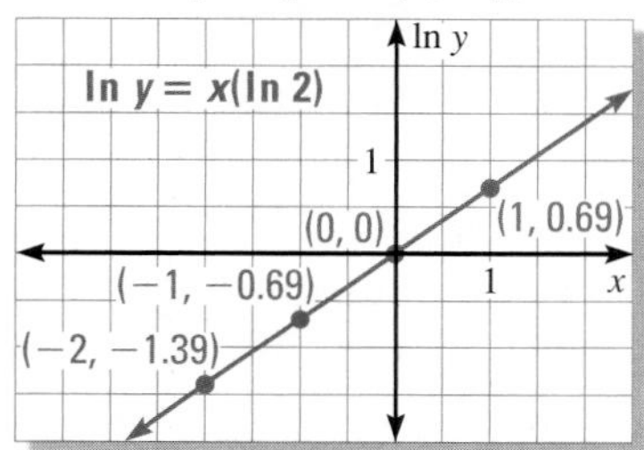

The graph is a line.

EXAMPLE 2 Find an exponential model

SCOOTERS A store sells motor scooters. The table shows the number y of scooters sold during the xth year that the store has been open.

Year, x	1	2	3	4	5	6	7
Number of scooters sold, y	12	16	25	36	50	67	96

- Draw a scatter plot of the data pairs $(x, \ln y)$. Is an exponential model a good fit for the original data pairs (x, y)?
- Find an exponential model for the original data.

Solution

STEP 1 **Use** a calculator to create a table of data pairs $(x, \ln y)$.

x	1	2	3	4	5	6	7
$\ln y$	2.48	2.77	3.22	3.58	3.91	4.20	4.56

STEP 2 **Plot** the new points as shown. The points lie close to a line, so an exponential model should be a good fit for the original data.

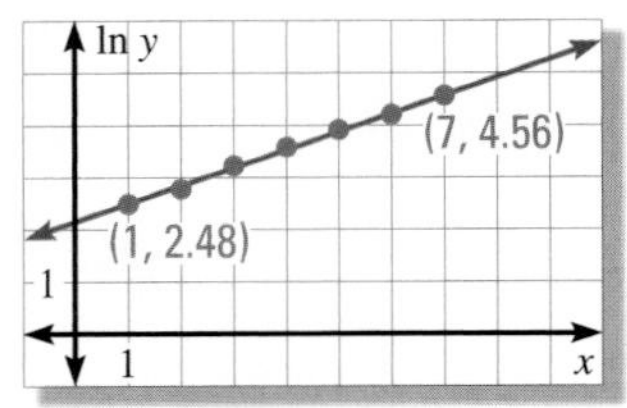

STEP 3 **Find** an exponential model $y = ab^x$ by choosing two points on the line, such as (1, 2.48) and (7, 4.56). Use these points to write an equation of the line. Then solve for y.

$\ln y - 2.48 = 0.35(x - 1)$ — **Equation of line**

$\ln y = 0.35x + 2.13$ — **Simplify.**

$y = e^{0.35x + 2.13}$ — **Exponentiate each side using base *e*.**

$y = e^{2.13}(e^{0.35})^x$ — **Use properties of exponents.**

$y = 8.41(1.42)^x$ — **Exponential model**

USE POINT-SLOPE FORM

Because the axes are x and $\ln y$, the point-slope form is rewritten as $\ln y - y_1 = m(x - x_1)$. The slope of the line through (1, 2.48) and (7, 4.56) is:

$$\frac{4.56 - 2.48}{7 - 1} \approx 0.35$$

EXPONENTIAL REGRESSION A graphing calculator that performs exponential regression uses all of the original data to find the best-fitting model.

EXAMPLE 3 Use exponential regression

SCOOTERS Use a graphing calculator to find an exponential model for the data in Example 2. Predict the number of scooters sold in the eighth year.

Solution

Enter the original data into a graphing calculator and perform an exponential regression. The model is $y = 8.46(1.42)^x$.

Substituting $x = 8$ (for year 8) into the model gives $y = 8.46(1.42)^8 \approx 140$ scooters sold.

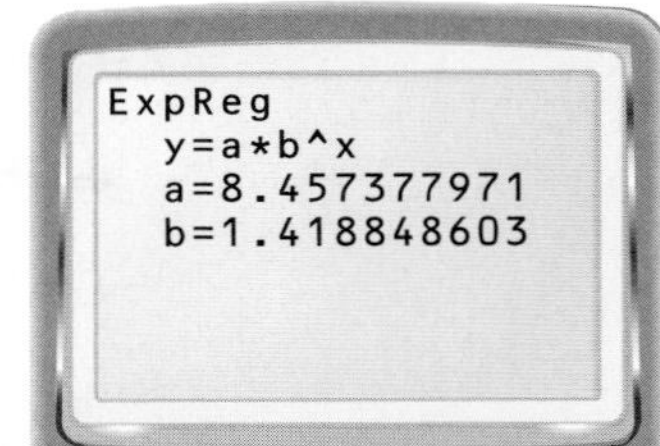

GUIDED PRACTICE for Examples 1, 2, and 3

Write an exponential function $y = ab^x$ whose graph passes through the given points.

1. (1, 6), (3, 24)
2. (2, 8), (3, 32)
3. (3, 8), (6, 64)

4. **WHAT IF?** In Examples 2 and 3, how would the exponential models change if the scooter sales were as shown in the table below?

Year, x	1	2	3	4	5	6	7
Number of scooters sold, y	15	23	40	52	80	105	140

WRITING POWER FUNCTIONS Recall from Lesson 6.3 that a power function has the form $y = ax^b$. Because there are only two constants (a and b), only two points are needed to determine a power curve through the points.

EXAMPLE 4 Write a power function

Write a power function $y = ax^b$ whose graph passes through (3, 2) and (6, 9).

Solution

STEP 1 **Substitute** the coordinates of the two given points into $y = ax^b$.

$2 = a \cdot 3^b$ Substitute 2 for y and 3 for x.

$9 = a \cdot 6^b$ Substitute 9 for y and 6 for x.

STEP 2 **Solve** for a in the first equation to obtain $a = \frac{2}{3^b}$, and substitute this expression for a in the second equation.

$9 = \left(\frac{2}{3^b}\right)6^b$ Substitute $\frac{2}{3^b}$ for a in second equation.

$9 = 2 \cdot 2^b$ Simplify.

$4.5 = 2^b$ Divide each side by 2.

$\log_2 4.5 = b$ Take $\log_2$ of each side.

$\frac{\log 4.5}{\log 2} = b$ Change-of-base formula

$2.17 \approx b$ Use a calculator.

STEP 3 **Determine** that $a = \frac{2}{3^{2.17}} \approx 0.184$. So, $y = 0.184x^{2.17}$.

GUIDED PRACTICE for Example 4

Write a power function $y = ax^b$ whose graph passes through the given points.

5. (2, 1), (7, 6)
6. (3, 4), (6, 15)
7. (5, 8), (10, 34)

8. **REASONING** Try using the method of Example 4 to find a power function whose graph passes through (3, 5) and (3, 7). What can you conclude?

TRANSFORMING POWER DATA A set of more than two points (x, y) fits a power pattern if and only if the set of transformed points $(\ln x, \ln y)$ fits a linear pattern.

Graph of points (x, y)

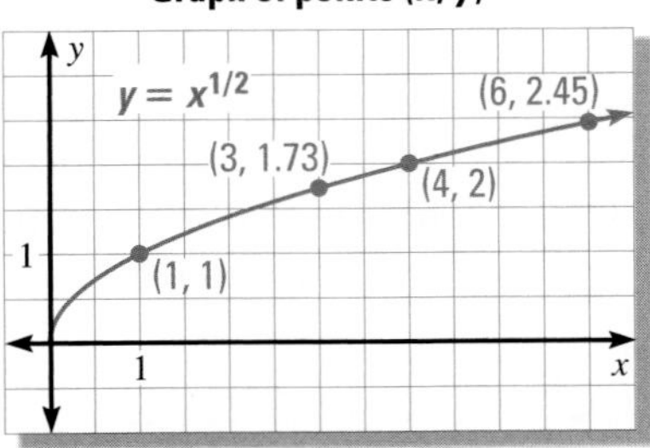

The graph is a power curve.

Graph of points $(\ln x, \ln y)$

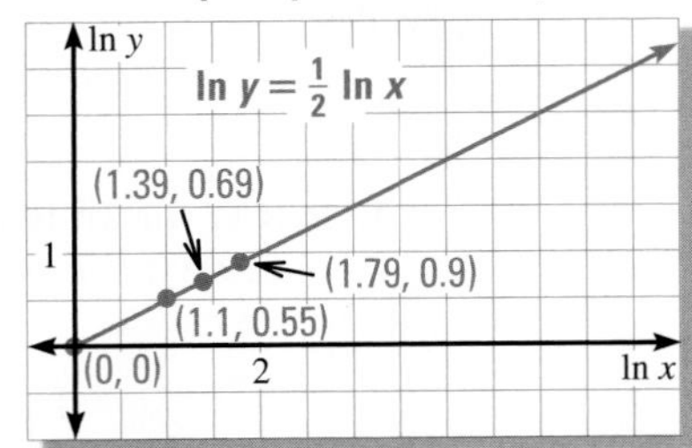

The graph is a line.

EXAMPLE 5 Find a power model

BIOLOGY The table at the right shows the typical wingspans x (in feet) and the typical weights y (in pounds) for several types of birds.

- Draw a scatter plot of the data pairs $(\ln x, \ln y)$. Is a power model a good fit for the original data pairs (x, y)?
- Find a power model for the original data.

Bird	Wingspan (ft), x	Weight (lb), y
Cuckoo	1.90	0.23
Crow	2.92	1.04
Curlew	3.41	1.69
Goose	5.35	6.76
Vulture	8.40	16.03

Solution

STEP 1 **Use** a calculator to create a table of data pairs $(\ln x, \ln y)$.

$\ln x$	0.642	1.072	1.227	1.677	2.128
$\ln y$	−1.470	0.039	0.525	1.911	2.774

STEP 2 **Plot** the new points as shown. The points lie close to a line, so a power model should be a good fit for the original data.

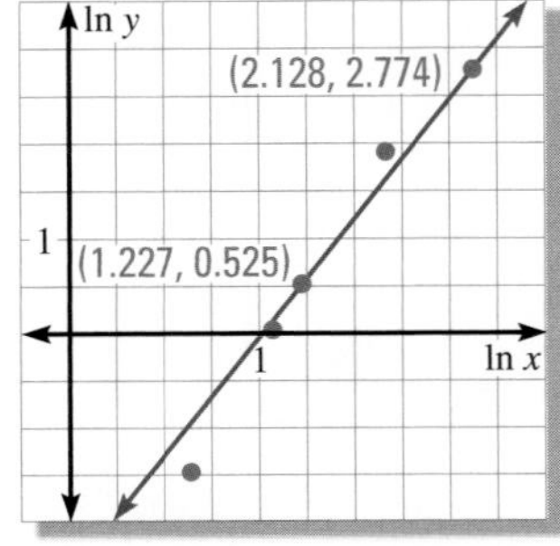

STEP 3 **Find** a power model $y = ax^b$ by choosing two points on the line, such as (1.227, 0.525) and (2.128, 2.774). Use these points to write an equation of the line. Then solve for y.

$\ln y - y_1 = m(\ln x - x_1)$ **Equation when axes are ln x and ln y**

$\ln y - 2.774 = 2.5(\ln x - 2.128)$ **Substitute.**

$\ln y = 2.5 \ln x - 2.546$ **Simplify.**

$\ln y = \ln x^{2.5} - 2.546$ **Power property of logarithms**

$y = e^{\ln x^{2.5} - 2.546}$ **Exponentiate each side using base e.**

$y = e^{-2.546} \cdot e^{\ln x^{2.5}}$ **Product of powers property**

$y = 0.0784x^{2.5}$ **Simplify.**

USE POINT-SLOPE FORM

The slope of the line is $\frac{2.774 - 0.525}{2.128 - 1.227} \approx 2.50$.

POWER REGRESSION A graphing calculator that performs power regression uses all of the original data to find the best-fitting model.

EXAMPLE 6 Use power regression

BIOLOGY Use a graphing calculator to find a power model for the data in Example 5. Estimate the weight of a bird with a wingspan of 4.5 feet.

Solution

Enter the original data into a graphing calculator and perform a power regression. The model is $y = 0.0442x^{2.87}$.

Substituting $x = 4.5$ into the model gives $y = 0.0442(4.5)^{2.87} \approx 3.31$ pounds.

GUIDED PRACTICE for Examples 5 and 6

9. The table below shows the atomic number x and the melting point y (in degrees Celsius) for the alkali metals. Find a power model for the data.

Alkali metal	Lithium	Sodium	Potassium	Rubidium	Cesium
Atomic number, x	3	11	19	37	55
Melting point, y	180.5	97.8	63.7	38.9	28.5

7.7 EXERCISES

HOMEWORK KEY
○ = **WORKED-OUT SOLUTIONS** on p. WS14 for Exs. 11, 23, and 33
★ = **STANDARDIZED TEST PRACTICE** Exs. 2, 27, 33, and 35

SKILL PRACTICE

1. **VOCABULARY** Copy and complete: Given a set of more than two data pairs (x, y), you can decide whether a(n) _?_ function fits the data well by making a scatter plot of the points $(x, \ln y)$.

2. ★ **WRITING** *Explain* how you can determine whether a power function is a good model for a set of data pairs (x, y).

EXAMPLE 1 on p. 529 for Exs. 3–10

WRITING EXPONENTIAL FUNCTIONS **Write an exponential function $y = ab^x$ whose graph passes through the given points.**

3. (1, 3), (2, 12)
4. (2, 24), (3, 144)
5. (3, 1), (5, 4)
6. (3, 27), (5, 243)
7. (1, 2), (3, 50)
8. (1, 40), (3, 640)
9. (−1, 10), (4, 0.31)
10. (2, 6.4), (5, 409.6)

EXAMPLE 2 on p. 530 for Exs. 11–14

FINDING EXPONENTIAL MODELS **Use the points (x, y) to draw a scatter plot of the points $(x, \ln y)$. Then find an exponential model for the data.**

11. (1, 18), (2, 36), (3, 72), (4, 144), (5, 288)
12. (1, 3.3), (2, 10.1), (3, 30.6), (4, 92.7), (5, 280.9)
13. (1, 9.8), (2, 12.2), (3, 15.2), (4, 19), (5, 23.8)
14. (1, 1.4), (2, 6.7), (3, 32.9), (4, 161.4), (5, 790.9)

EXAMPLE 4
on p. 531
for Exs. 15–22

WRITING POWER FUNCTIONS **Write a power function $y = ax^b$ whose graph passes through the given points.**

15. (4, 3), (8, 15)
16. (5, 9), (8, 34)
17. (2, 3), (6, 12)
18. (3, 14), (9, 44)
19. (4, 8), (8, 30)
20. (5, 10), (12, 81)
21. (4, 6.2), (7, 23)
22. (3.1, 5), (6.8, 9.7)

EXAMPLE 5
on p. 532
for Exs. 23–26

FINDING POWER MODELS **Use the given points (x, y) to draw a scatter plot of the points $(\ln x, \ln y)$. Then find a power model for the data.**

23. (1, 0.6), (2, 4.1), (3, 12.4), (4, 27), (5, 49.5)
24. (1, 1.5), (2, 4.8), (3, 9.5), (4, 15.4), (5, 22.3)
25. (1, 2.5), (2, 3.7), (3, 4.7), (4, 5.5), (5, 6.2)
26. (1, 0.81), (2, 0.99), (3, 1.11), (4, 1.21), (5, 1.29)

27. ★ **MULTIPLE CHOICE** Which equation is equivalent to $\log y = 2x + 1$?

Ⓐ $y = 10(100)^x$ Ⓑ $y = 10^x$ Ⓒ $y = e^{2x+1}$ Ⓓ $y = e^2$

ERROR ANALYSIS ***Describe*** **and correct the error in writing y as a function of x.**

28.

$\ln y = 2x + 1$
$y = e^{2x+1}$
$y = e^{2x} + e^1$
$y = (e^2)^x + e$
$y = 7.39^x + 2.72$

29.

$\ln y = 3 \ln x - 2$
$\ln y = \ln 3x - 2$
$y = e^{\ln 3x - 2}$
$y = e^{\ln 3x} \cdot e^{-2}$
$y = (3x)(0.135) = 0.405x$

30. **CHALLENGE** Take the natural logarithm of both sides of the equations $y = ab^x$ and $y = ax^b$. What are the slope and y-intercept of the line relating x and $\ln y$ for $y = ab^x$? of the line relating $\ln x$ and $\ln y$ for $y = ax^b$?

PROBLEM SOLVING

GRAPHING CALCULATOR **You may wish to use a graphing calculator to complete the following Problem Solving exercises.**

EXAMPLES 2, 3, 5, and 6
on pp. 530–533
for Exs. 31–35

31. **BIOLOGY** Scientists use the circumference of an animal's femur to estimate the animal's weight. The table shows the femur circumference C (in millimeters) and the weight W (in kilograms) for several animals.

Animal	Giraffe	Polar bear	Lion	Squirrel	Otter
C (mm)	173	135	93.5	13	28
W (kg)	710	448	143	0.399	9.68

a. Draw a scatter plot of the data pairs $(\ln C, \ln W)$.

b. Find a power model for the original data.

c. Predict the weight of a cheetah if the circumference of its femur is 68.7 millimeters.

@HomeTutor for problem solving help at classzone.com

32. **ASTRONOMY** The table shows the mean distance x from the sun (in astronomical units) and the period y (in years) of six planets. Draw a scatter plot of the data pairs $(\ln x, \ln y)$. Find a power model for the original data.

Planet	Mercury	Venus	Earth	Mars	Jupiter	Saturn
x	0.387	0.723	1.000	1.524	5.203	9.539
y	0.241	0.615	1.000	1.881	11.862	29.458

@HomeTutor for problem solving help at classzone.com

33. ★ **SHORT RESPONSE** The table shows the numbers of business and non-business users of instant messaging for the years 1998–2004.

Years since 1997	1	2	3	4	5	6	7
Business users (in millions)	1	2	5	7	20	40	80
Non-business users (in millions)	55	97	140	160	195	235	260

a. Find an exponential model for the number of business users over time.

b. *Explain* how to tell whether a linear, exponential, or power function best models the number of non-business users over time. Then find the best-fitting model.

34. **MULTI-STEP PROBLEM** The boiling point of water increases with atmospheric pressure. At sea level, where the atmospheric pressure is about 760 millimeters of mercury, water boils at 100°C. The table shows the boiling point T of water (in degrees Celsius) for several different values of atmospheric pressure P (in millimeters of mercury).

P	T
149	60
234	70
355	80
526	90
760	100
1075	110

a. **Graph** Draw a scatter plot of the data pairs $(\ln P, \ln T)$.

b. **Model** Find a power model for the original data.

c. **Predict** When the atmospheric pressure is 620 millimeters of mercury, at what temperature does water boil?

35. ★ **EXTENDED RESPONSE** Your visual *near point* is the closest point at which your eyes can see an object distinctly. Your near point moves farther away from you as you grow older. The diagram shows the near point y (in centimeters) at age x (in years).

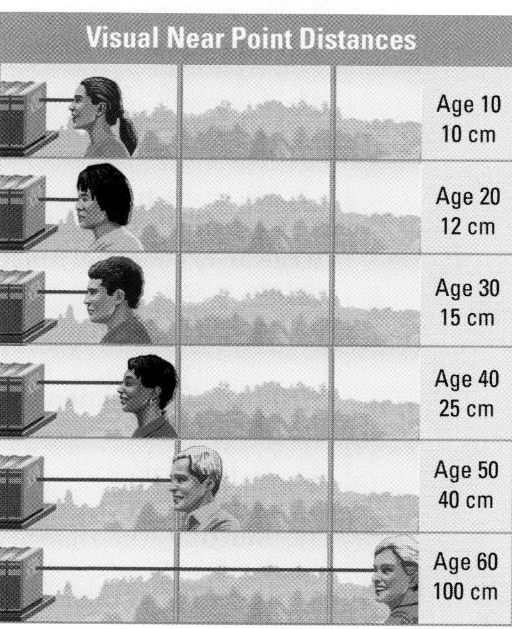

a. **Graph** Draw a scatter plot of the data pairs $(x, \ln y)$.

b. **Graph** Draw a scatter plot of the data pairs $(\ln x, \ln y)$.

c. **Interpret** Based on your scatter plots, does an exponential function or a power function best fit the original data? *Explain* your reasoning.

d. **Model** Based on your answer for part (c), write a model for the original data. Use your model to predict the near point for an 80-year-old person.

36. **CHALLENGE** A doctor measures an astronaut's pulse rate y (in beats per minute) at various times x (in minutes) after the astronaut has finished exercising. The results are shown in the table. The astronaut's resting pulse rate is 70 beats per minute. Write an exponential model for the data.

x	0	2	4	6	8	10	12	14
y	172	132	110	92	84	78	75	72

TEST PRACTICE at classzone.com

NEW YORK MIXED REVIEW

37. A poster is 8 inches taller than it is wide. The area of the poster is 384 square inches. Which equation can be used to find the width of the poster?

Ⓐ $x + 8 = 384$ Ⓑ $x(x + 8) = 384$

Ⓒ $x^2 + (x + 8)^2 = 384^2$ Ⓓ $x + (x + 8) = 384$

38. Use the graph of $y = -\frac{3}{4}x + 1$ to solve the equation for x when $y = -2$.

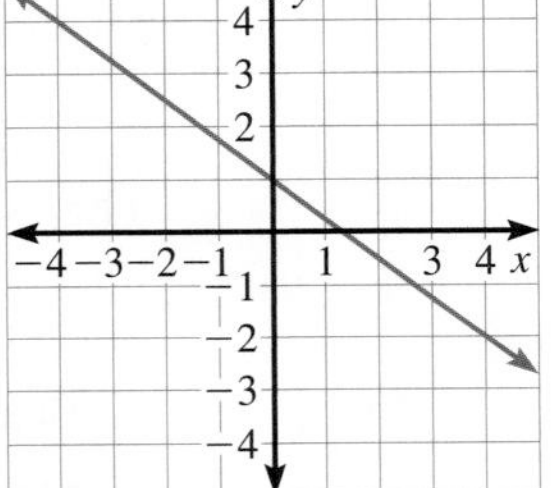

Ⓐ $x = 3$ Ⓑ $x = 4$

Ⓒ $x = 8$ Ⓓ $x = 11$

QUIZ *for Lessons 7.6–7.7*

Solve the equation. Check for extraneous solutions. *(p. 515)*

1. $2^{x+1} = 16^{x+2}$
2. $e^{-x} = 4$
3. $3^{2x} + 5 = 13$
4. $3^{x+1} - 5 = 10$
5. $\log_4 (4x + 7) = \log_4 11x$
6. $\ln (3x - 2) = \ln 6x$
7. $\log_3 x = -1$
8. $6 \ln x = 30$
9. $\log_2 (x + 4) = 5$

Write an exponential function $y = ab^x$ whose graph passes through the given points. *(p. 529)*

10. $(1, 5), (2, 30)$
11. $(1, 4), (2, 32)$
12. $(2, 15), (3, 45)$

Write a power function $y = ax^b$ whose graph passes through the given points. *(p. 529)*

13. $(4, 8), (9, 23)$
14. $(3, 12), (10, 36)$
15. $(5, 4), (11, 51)$

16. **BIOLOGY** The average weight y (in kilograms) of an Atlantic cod from the Gulf of Maine can be modeled by $y = 0.51(1.46)^x$ where x is the age of the cod (in years). Estimate the age of a cod that weighs 15 kilograms. *(p. 515)*

Lessons 7.5–7.7

1. **MUSIC** In music, a *cent* is a unit that is used to express a small step up or down in pitch. The number c of cents by which two notes differ in pitch is given by

$$c = 1200 \log_2 \frac{a}{b}$$

where a and b are the frequencies of the notes a and b.

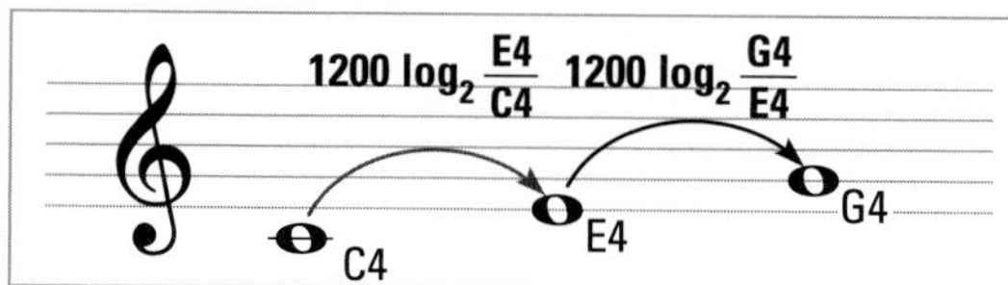

Three notes on the standard scale are C4, E4, and G4. You can compare the difference in the number of cents from C4 to E4 with the difference in the number of cents from E4 to G4 by evaluating this expression:

$$1200 \log_2 \frac{\text{E4}}{\text{C4}} - 1200 \log_2 \frac{\text{G4}}{\text{E4}}$$

Which of the following is the expression written as a single logarithm?

(1) $1200 \log_2 \frac{\text{C4}}{\text{G4}}$

(2) $1200 \log_2 \frac{\text{G4}}{\text{C4}}$

(3) $1200 \log_2 \frac{\text{E4}}{\text{C4} \cdot \text{G4}}$

(4) $1200 \log_2 \frac{(\text{E4})^2}{\text{C4} \cdot \text{G4}}$

2. **EXPONENTIAL FUNCTIONS** Which exponential function of the form $y = ab^x$ has a graph that passes through the points (2, 7) and (5, 56)?

(1) $y = 0.28(5)^x$

(2) $y = 1.75(2)^x$

(3) $y = 2(1.75)^x$

(4) $y = 18.35(1.25)^x$

3. **INTEREST RATES** The *effective interest rate* is a rate associated with the formula for continuously compounded interest. The effective interest rate takes into account the effects of compounding on the *nominal interest rate* (the interest rate in the formula for continuous compounding). The relationship between the effective interest rate E and the nominal interest rate N is given by the equation $N = \ln(E + 1)$ where E and N are expressed as decimals. Which of the following is the approximate effective interest rate for an account that has a nominal interest rate of 10%?

(1) 1.0% (3) 10.5%

(2) 9.5% (4) 11.5%

4. **OPEN-ENDED** The total number of miles traveled by motor vehicles in the United States is shown below for various years. Does an exponential model or a power model best fit the data? *Explain* your reasoning.

Years since 1990, x	Miles (billions), y
7	2562
8	2632
9	2691
10	2747
11	2782

5. **OPEN-ENDED** The total expenditures y (in billions of dollars) for U.S. elementary and secondary schools can be modeled by $y = 385(1.04)^x$ where x is the number of years since 1996.

Explain the real-world meaning of the values 385 and 1.04 in this model.

During which year did the total expenditures first surpass $550 billion? *Explain* how you found your answer.

7 CHAPTER SUMMARY

Animated Algebra
classzone.com
Electronic Function Library

BIG IDEAS *For Your Notebook*

Big Idea 1

Graphing Exponential and Logarithmic Functions

Parent functions for exponential functions have the form $y = b^x$. Parent functions for logarithmic functions have the form $y = \log_b x$.

Exponential Growth

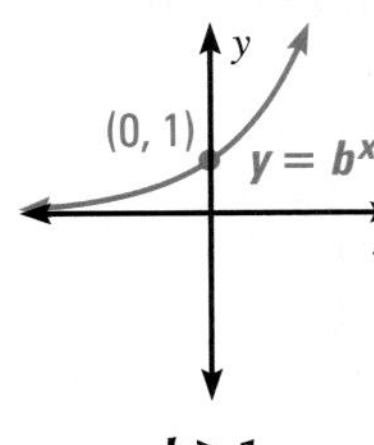

$b > 1$

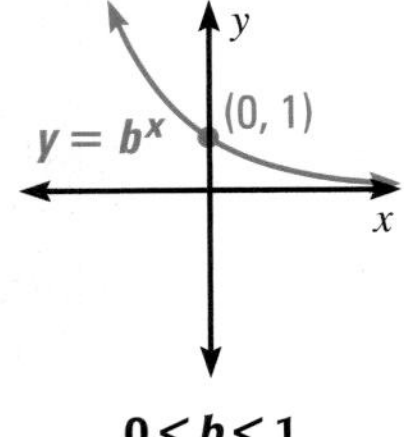

$0 < b < 1$

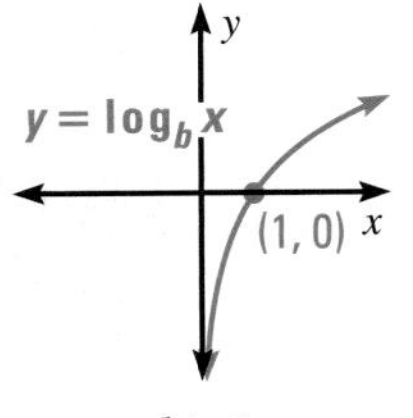

$b > 1$

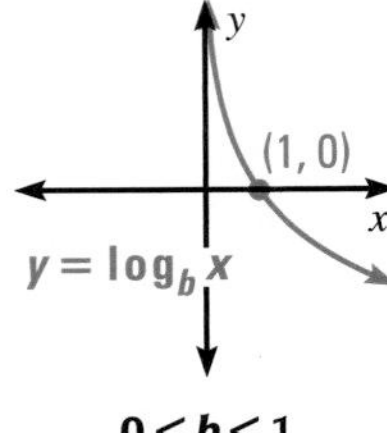

$0 < b < 1$

Big Idea 2

Solving Exponential and Logarithmic Equations

Solving an Exponential Equation	Solving a Logarithmic Equation
If each side can be written using the same base, equate exponents. $3^{x+1} = 9^x$ $3^{x+1} = (3^2)^x$ $x + 1 = 2x$ $1 = x$	If the equation has the form $\log_b x = \log_b y$, use the fact that $x = y$. $\log_2 (4x - 2) = \log_2 3x$ $4x - 2 = 3x$ $x = 2$
If each side cannot be written using the same base, take a logarithm of each side. $6^x = 15$ $\log_6 6^x = \log_6 15$ $x = \frac{\log 15}{\log 6} \approx 1.511$	If a logarithm is set equal to a constant, exponentiate each side. $\log_5 (x + 1) = 2$ $x + 1 = 5^2$ $x = 24$

Big Idea 3

Writing and Applying Exponential and Power Functions

Write an Exponential Model	Write a Power Model
An exponential model fits a set of data pairs (x, y) if a linear model fits the set of data pairs $(x, \ln y)$. $y = b^x$; $\ln y = x \ln b$	A power model fits a set of data pairs (x, y) if a linear model fits the set of data pairs $(\ln x, \ln y)$. $y = x^b$; $\ln y = b \ln x$

7 CHAPTER REVIEW

@HomeTutor
classzone.com
- Multi-Language Glossary
- Vocabulary practice

REVIEW KEY VOCABULARY

- exponential function, *p. 478*
- exponential growth function, *p. 478*
- growth factor, *p. 478*
- asymptote, *p. 478*
- exponential decay function, *p. 486*
- decay factor, *p. 486*
- natural base *e*, *p. 492*
- logarithm of *y* with base *b*, *p. 499*
- common logarithm, *p. 500*
- natural logarithm, *p. 500*
- exponential equation, *p. 515*
- logarithmic equation, *p. 517*

VOCABULARY EXERCISES

1. What is the asymptote of the graph of the function $y = -2\left(\frac{1}{4}\right)^{x+1} + 5$?
2. Identify the decay factor in the model $y = 7.2(0.89)^x$.
3. **WRITING** *Explain* the meaning of $\log_b y$.
4. Copy and complete: A logarithm with base *e* is called a(n) __?__ logarithm.
5. Is $y = (1.4)^x$ an *exponential function* or a *power function*? *Explain.*

REVIEW EXAMPLES AND EXERCISES

Use the review examples and exercises below to check your understanding of the concepts you have learned in each lesson of Chapter 7.

7.1 Graph Exponential Growth Functions

pp. 478–485

EXAMPLE

Graph $y = 2 \cdot 3^{x-2} + 3$. State the domain and range.

Begin by sketching the graph of $y = 2 \cdot 3^x$, which passes through (0, 2) and (1, 6). Then translate the graph right 2 units and up 3 units. Notice that the translated graph passes through (2, 5) and (3, 9).

The graph's asymptote is the line $y = 3$. The domain is all real numbers, and the range is $y > 3$.

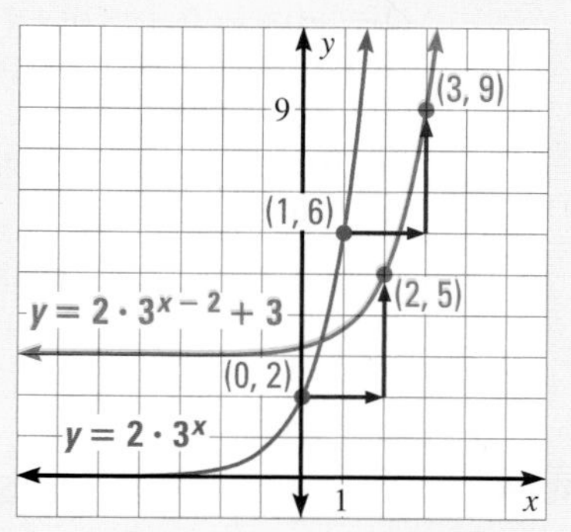

EXERCISES

EXAMPLES 1, 2, 3, and 5 on pp. 478–481 for Exs. 6–9

Graph the function. State the domain and range.

6. $y = 5^x$
7. $y = 3(2.5)^x$
8. $f(x) = -3 \cdot 4^{x+1} - 2$
9. **FINANCE** You deposit $1500 in an account that pays 7% annual interest compounded daily. Find the balance after 2 years.

7 CHAPTER REVIEW

7.2 Graph Exponential Decay Functions

pp. 486–491

EXAMPLE

Graph $y = 2\left(\frac{1}{4}\right)^{x+2} - 2$. State the domain and range.

Begin by sketching the graph of $y = 2\left(\frac{1}{4}\right)^{x}$, which passes through (0, 2) and $\left(1, \frac{1}{2}\right)$. Then translate the graph left 2 units and down 2 units. Notice that the translated graph passes through (−2, 0) and $\left(-1, -\frac{3}{2}\right)$.

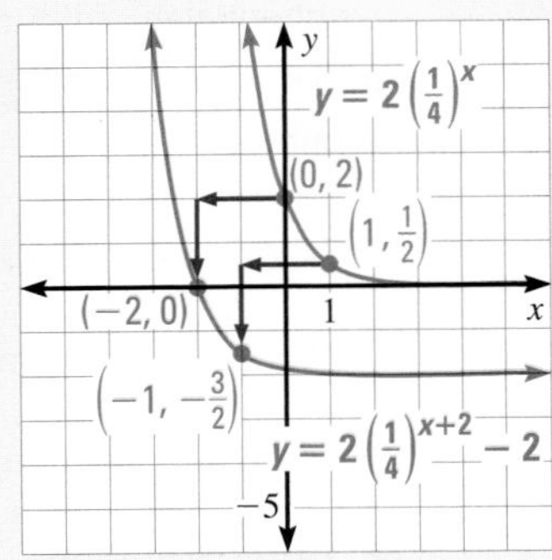

The graph's asymptote is the line $y = -2$. The domain is all real numbers, and the range is $y > -2$.

EXERCISES

EXAMPLES 1, 2, and 3 on pp. 486–487 for Exs. 10–12

Graph the function. State the domain and range.

10. $y = \left(\frac{1}{8}\right)^x$

11. $y = \left(\frac{1}{3}\right)^x - 4$

12. $f(x) = 2(0.8)^{x-1} + 3$

7.3 Use Functions Involving *e*

pp. 492–498

EXAMPLE

Graph $y = e^{0.25(x-1)} - 5$. State the domain and range.

Because $a = 1$ is positive and $r = 0.25$ is positive, the function is an exponential growth function. Begin by sketching the graph of $y = e^{0.25x}$. Translate the graph right 1 unit and down 5 units.

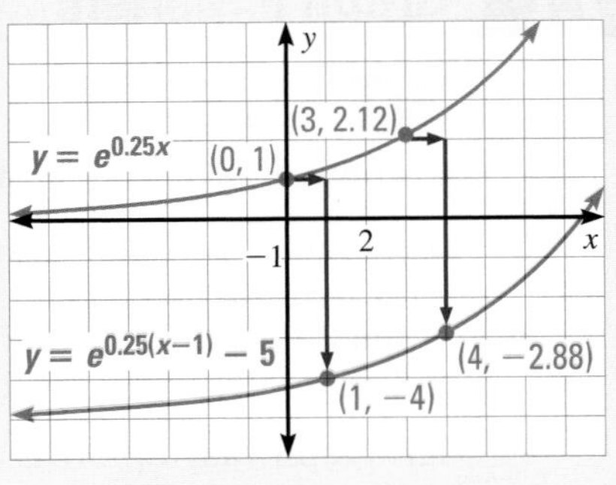

The domain is all real numbers, and the range is $y > -5$.

EXERCISES

EXAMPLES 3 and 5 on pp. 493–495 for Exs. 13–16

Graph the function. State the domain and range.

13. $y = 2e^{-x}$

14. $y = e^{x-2}$

15. $f(x) = e^{-0.4(x+2)} + 6$

16. **PHYSIOLOGY** Nitrogen-13 is a radioactive isotope of nitrogen used in a physiological test called positron emission tomograph (PET). A typical PET scan begins with 6.9 picograms of nitrogen-13 (1 picogram $= 10^{-12}$ grams). The number N of picograms of nitrogen-13 remaining after t minutes can be modeled by $N = 6.9e^{-0.0695t}$. How many picograms of nitrogen-13 remain after 10 minutes?

@HomeTutor
classzone.com
Chapter Review Practice

7.4 Find Logarithms and Graph Logarithmic Functions *pp. 499–505*

EXAMPLE

Evaluate the logarithm.

a. $\log_5 625$ **b.** $\log 0.001$ **c.** $\log_{125} 5$ **d.** $\log_2 \frac{1}{64}$

To help you find the value of $\log_b y$, ask yourself what power of b gives you y.

a. 5 to what power gives 625?
$5^4 = 625$, so $\log_5 625 = 4$.

b. 10 to what power gives 0.001?
$10^{-3} = 0.001$, so $\log 0.001 = -3$.

c. 125 to what power gives 5?
$125^{1/3} = 5$, so $\log_{125} 5 = \frac{1}{3}$.

d. 2 to what power gives $\frac{1}{64}$?
$2^{-6} = \frac{1}{64}$, so $\log_2 \frac{1}{64} = -6$.

EXERCISES

EXAMPLES 2, 4, 7, and 8 on pp. 500–503 for Exs. 17–24

Evaluate the logarithm without using a calculator.

17. $\log_3 243$ **18.** $\log_7 1$ **19.** $\log_{1/6} 216$ **20.** $\log_{125} \frac{1}{5}$

Graph the function. State the domain and range.

21. $y = \log_{1/6} x$ **22.** $y = \log_3 x - 4$ **23.** $f(x) = \ln(x - 1) + 3$

24. BIOLOGY Researchers have found that after 25 years of age, the average size of the pupil in a person's eye decreases. The relationship between pupil diameter d (in millimeters) and age a (in years) can be modeled by $d = -2.1158 \ln a + 13.669$. What is the average diameter of a pupil for a person 25 years old? 50 years old?

7.5 Apply Properties of Logarithms *pp. 507–513*

EXAMPLES

Expand the expression.

$$\log_5 \frac{6x}{y^3} = \log_5 6x - \log_5 y^3$$
$$= \log_5 6 + \log_5 x - \log_5 y^3$$
$$= \log_5 6 + \log_5 x - 3\log_5 y$$

Condense the expression.

$$3\log_3 8 - \log_3 16 = \log_3 8^3 - \log_3 16$$
$$= \log_3 \frac{8^3}{16}$$
$$= \log_3 32$$

EXERCISES

EXAMPLES 2 and 3 on p. 508 for Exs. 25–31

Expand the expression.

25. $\log_8 3xy$ **26.** $\ln 10x^3y$ **27.** $\log \frac{8}{y^4}$ **28.** $\ln \frac{3y}{x^5}$

Condense the expression.

29. $3\log_7 4 + \log_7 6$ **30.** $\ln 12 - 2\ln x$ **31.** $2\ln 3 + 5\ln 2 - \ln 8$

7 CHAPTER REVIEW

7.6 Solve Exponential and Logarithmic Equations

pp. 515–522

EXAMPLE

Solve the equation.

a. $7^x = 12$

$\log_7 7^x = \log_7 12$

$x = \log_7 12$

$x = \frac{\log 12}{\log 7} \approx 1.277$

b. $\log_2 (3x - 7) = 5$

$2^{\log_2 (3x - 7)} = 2^5$

$3x - 7 = 32$

$x = 13$

EXAMPLES 2, 5, and 6 on pp. 516–518 for Exs. 32–34

EXERCISES

Solve the equation. Check for extraneous solutions.

32. $5^x = 32$

33. $\log_3 (2x - 5) = 2$

34. $\ln x + \ln (x + 2) = 3$

7.7 Write and Apply Exponential and Power Functions

pp. 529–536

EXAMPLE

Write an exponential function $y = ab^x$ whose graph passes through (−1, 2) and (3, 32).

Substitute the coordinates of the two given points into $y = ab^x$.

$2 = ab^{-1}$ **Substitute 2 for *y* and −1 for *x*.**

$32 = ab^3$ **Substitute 32 for *y* and 3 for *x*.**

Solve for a in the first equation to obtain $a = 2b$, and substitute this expression for a in the second equation.

$32 = (2b)b^3$ **Substitute 2*b* for *a* in second equation.**

$32 = 2b^4$ **Product of powers property**

$16 = b^4$ **Divide each side by 2.**

$2 = b$ **Take the positive fourth root because $b > 0$.**

Because $b = 2$, it follows that $a = 2(2) = 4$. So, $y = 4 \cdot 2^x$.

EXAMPLES 1 and 5 on pp. 529–532 for Exs. 35–38

EXERCISES

Write an exponential function $y = ab^x$ whose graph passes through the points.

35. (3, 8), (5, 2)

36. (−2, 2), (1, 0.25)

37. (2, 9), (4, 324)

38. SPORTING GOODS A store begins selling a new type of basketball shoe. The table shows sales of the shoe over time. Find a power model for the data.

Week, *x*	1	2	3	4	5	6
Pairs sold, *y*	28	47	64	79	94	107

7 CHAPTER TEST

Graph the function. State the domain and range.

1. $y = 3^x$
2. $y = 2 \cdot 4^{x-2}$
3. $f(x) = -5 \cdot 2^{x+3} + 3$
4. $y = 4(0.25)^x$
5. $y = 2\left(\frac{1}{3}\right)^{x+2}$
6. $g(x) = \left(\frac{2}{3}\right)^x + 2$
7. $y = \frac{1}{2}e^{-x}$
8. $y = 2.5e^{-0.5x} + 1$
9. $h(x) = \frac{1}{3}e^{x-1} - 2$

Evaluate the logarithm without using a calculator.

10. $\log_5 25$
11. $\log_2 \frac{1}{32}$
12. $\log_6 1$

Graph the function. State the domain and range.

13. $y = \log_2 x$
14. $y = \ln x - 3$
15. $f(x) = \log(x + 3) + 2$

Condense the expression.

16. $2 \ln 7 - 3 \ln 4$
17. $\log_4 3 + 5 \log_4 2$
18. $\log 5 + \log x - 2 \log 3$

Use the change-of-base formula to evaluate the logarithm.

19. $\log_5 50$
20. $\log_6 23$
21. $\log_9 45$

Solve the equation. Check for extraneous solutions.

22. $7^{2x} = 30$
23. $3 \log(x - 4) = 6$
24. $\log_4 x + \log_4 (x + 6) = 2$

25. Write an exponential function $y = ab^x$ whose graph passes through $(-1, 48)$ and $(2, 6)$.

26. Write a power function $y = ax^b$ whose graph passes through $(3, 8)$ and $(6, 15)$.

27. **LANDSCAPING** From 1996 to 2001, the number of households that purchased lawn and garden products at home gardening centers increased by about 4.85% per year. In 1996, about 62 million households purchased lawn and garden products. Write a function giving the number of households H (in millions) that purchased lawn and garden products t years after 1996.

28. **FINANCE** You deposit \$2500 in an account that pays 3.5% annual interest compounded continuously. What is the balance after 8 years?

29. **EARTH SCIENCE** Rivers and streams carry small particles of sediment downstream. The table shows the diameter x (in millimeters) of several particles of sediment and the speed y (in meters per second) of the current needed to carry each particle downstream.

    a. Draw a scatter plot of the data pairs $(\ln x, \ln y)$.

    b. Find a power model for the original data. Estimate the speed of the current needed to carry a particle with a diameter of 120 millimeters downstream.

Type of sediment	x	y
Mud	0.2	0.10
Gravel	5	0.50
Coarse gravel	11	0.75
Pebbles	20	1.00
Small stones	45	1.50

MULTIPLE CHOICE QUESTIONS

If you have difficulty solving a multiple choice problem directly, you may be able to use another approach to eliminate incorrect answer choices and obtain the correct answer.

PROBLEM 1

Which exponential function has a graph that passes through the points (2, −12) and (4, −48)?

(1) $y = 3 \cdot 2^x$ (2) $y = -\sqrt{3} \cdot 2^x$ (3) $y = -\frac{4}{3} \cdot 3^x$ (4) $y = -3 \cdot 2^x$

METHOD 1

SOLVE DIRECTLY Substitute the coordinates of the two points into $y = ab^x$ and solve the resulting system.

STEP 1 **Substitute** the coordinates of the points into $y = ab^x$.

$-12 = ab^2$ **Substitute (2, −12).**

$-48 = ab^4$ **Substitute (4, −48).**

STEP 2 **Solve** the first equation for a.

$\frac{-12}{b^2} = a$ **Divide each side by b^2.**

STEP 3 **Substitute** $\frac{-12}{b^2}$ for a in the second equation and solve for b.

$-48 = \left(\frac{-12}{b^2}\right)b^4$ **Substitute.**

$-48 = -12b^2$ **Simplify.**

$4 = b^2$ **Divide each side by −12.**

$2 = b$ **Take the positive square root because $b > 0$.**

STEP 4 **Substitute** the value of b into $a = \frac{-12}{b^2}$ to find the value of a.

$$a = \frac{-12}{b^2} = \frac{-12}{2^2} = \frac{-12}{4} = -3$$

The equation is $y = -3 \cdot 2^x$.

▸ The correct answer is (4).

METHOD 2

ELIMINATE CHOICES Another method is to check whether both of the points are solutions of the equations given in the answer choices.

Substitute the coordinates of the points into the equation in each answer choice. You can stop as soon as you realize that one of the points is not a solution.

Choice (1): $y = 3 \cdot 2^x$

$-12 \stackrel{?}{=} 3 \cdot 2^2$

$-12 \neq 12$

Choice (2): $y = -\sqrt{3} \cdot 2^x$

$-12 \stackrel{?}{=} -\sqrt{3} \cdot 2^2$

$-12 \neq -4\sqrt{3}$

Choice (3): $y = -\frac{4}{3} \cdot 3^x$ $y = -\frac{4}{3} \cdot 3^x$

$-12 \stackrel{?}{=} -\frac{4}{3} \cdot 3^2$ $-48 \stackrel{?}{=} -\frac{4}{3} \cdot 3^4$

$-12 = -12$ ✓ $-48 \neq -108$

Choice (4): $y = -3 \cdot 2^x$ $y = -3 \cdot 2^x$

$-12 \stackrel{?}{=} -3 \cdot 2^2$ $-48 \stackrel{?}{=} -3 \cdot 2^4$

$-12 = -12$ ✓ $-48 = -48$ ✓

▸ The correct answer is (4).

PROBLEM 2

You buy a new personal computer for \$1600. It is estimated that the computer's value will decrease by 50% each year. After about how many years will the computer be worth \$250?

(1) $1\frac{1}{3}$ years (2) 2 years (3) $2\frac{2}{3}$ years (4) 3 years

METHOD 1

SOLVE DIRECTLY Write and solve an equation to find the time it takes for the computer to depreciate to \$250.

Let y be the value (in dollars) of the computer t years after the purchase. An exponential decay model for the value is:

$$y = a(1 - r)^t$$

$$250 = 1600(1 - 0.5)^t$$

$$0.156 \approx (0.5)^t$$

$$\log_{0.5} 0.156 = \log_{0.5} (0.5)^t$$

$$\frac{\log 0.156}{\log 0.5} \approx 2.68 \approx t$$

The computer will be worth \$250 after about $2.68 \approx 2\frac{2}{3}$ years.

▶ The correct answer is (3).

METHOD 2

ELIMINATE CHOICES Use estimation to find how long it will take for the computer to depreciate to \$250.

The computer depreciates by 50% each year.

After 0 years, it is worth \$1600.

After 1 year, it will be worth 0.5(\$1600) = \$800.

After 2 years, it will be worth 0.5(\$800) = \$400.

After 3 years, it will be worth 0.5(\$400) = \$200.

The computer will be worth \$250 at some time strictly between 2 and 3 years after purchase. So, you can eliminate choices (1), (2), and (4).

▶ The correct answer is (3).

TEST PREPARATION

PRACTICE

Explain why you can eliminate the highlighted answer choice.

1. Which power function has a graph that passes through the points $(-2, -16)$ and $(1, 2)$?

   (1) $y = \frac{1}{2}x^5$ (2) $y = 2x^5$ ╳(3) $y = 2x^{1/2}$ (4) $y = 2x^3$

2. For which equation is 4 a solution?

   ╳(1) $e^{2x} + 1 = 17$ (3) $3^{x-2} + 1 = 10$

   (2) $\log_2 (x + 2) = \log_2 2x$ (4) $\ln (x + 2) + \ln x = 1$

3. What is the domain of the function $y = -5 \cdot 2^{x+2}$?

   (1) All real numbers (3) All real numbers less than 0

   ╳(2) All real numbers except -2 (4) All real numbers greater than -5

New York **Test Practice**

MULTIPLE CHOICE

1. In 1999, the tuition for one year at Harvard University was \$22,054. During the next 4 years, the tuition increased by 4.25% each year. Which model represents the situation?

(1) $y = 22{,}054(0.0425)^t$

(2) $y = 22{,}054(0.425)^t$

(3) $y = 22{,}054(1.0425)^t$

(4) $y = 22{,}054(1.425)^t$

2. You deposit \$1000 in an account that pays 3% annual interest. How much more interest is earned after 2 years if the interest is compounded daily than if the interest is compounded monthly?

(1) \$.07 (3) \$61.76

(2) \$1.27 (4) \$1061.76

3. The graph of which function is shown?

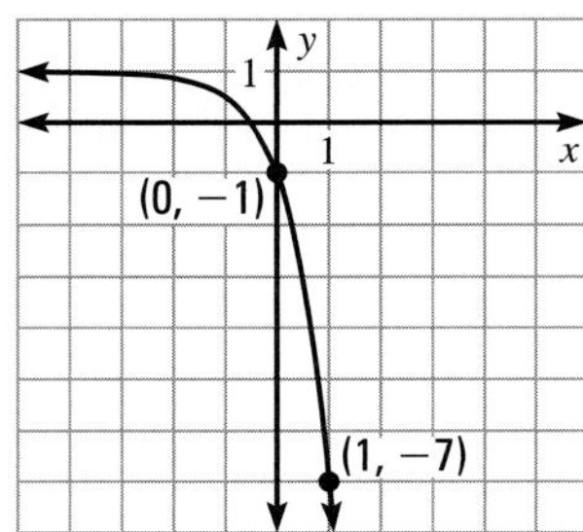

(1) $y = 2 \cdot 4^x + 1$ (3) $y = 2 \cdot 4^x - 1$

(2) $y = -2 \cdot 4^x + 1$ (4) $y = -2 \cdot 4^x - 1$

4. Which function can be obtained by translating the graph of $y = \log_3 (x + 2) - 4$ left 1 unit?

(1) $y = \log_3 (x + 2) - 5$

(2) $y = \log_3 (x + 2) - 3$

(3) $y = \log_3 (x + 1) - 4$

(4) $y = \log_3 (x + 3) - 4$

5. Which expression is equivalent to $3 \log x + \log 3$?

(1) $\log 9x$ (3) $\log 3x^3$

(2) $4 \log 3x$ (4) $\log (x^3 + 3)$

6. The population of the United States is expected to increase by 0.9% each year from 2003 to 2014. The U.S. population was about 290 million in 2003. To the nearest million, what is the projected population for 2010?

(1) 295 million

(2) 309 million

(3) 574 million

(4) 4891 million

7. Which expression is equivalent to $\sqrt{100e^{6x}}$?

(1) $10e^{3x}$ (3) $(2e^x)^3$

(2) $7e^x + 3e^{2x}$ (4) $10e^{\sqrt{6x}}$

8. Which function is an exponential decay function?

(1) $y = 2 \cdot 5^x$ (3) $y = 2e^x$

(2) $y = -2 \cdot 5^x$ (4) $y = 2(0.5)^x$

9. Which function is the inverse of $y = e^{2x} - 3$?

(1) $y = 2 \ln (x + 3)$ (3) $y = \dfrac{\ln (x + 3)}{2}$

(2) $y = 2 \ln (x - 3)$ (4) $y = \dfrac{\ln (x - 3)}{2}$

10. What is (are) the solution(s) of the equation $\log (x + 3) + \log x = 1$?

(1) 2, −5 (3) 5

(2) 2 (4) 2, 5

11. The graph of which function is shown?

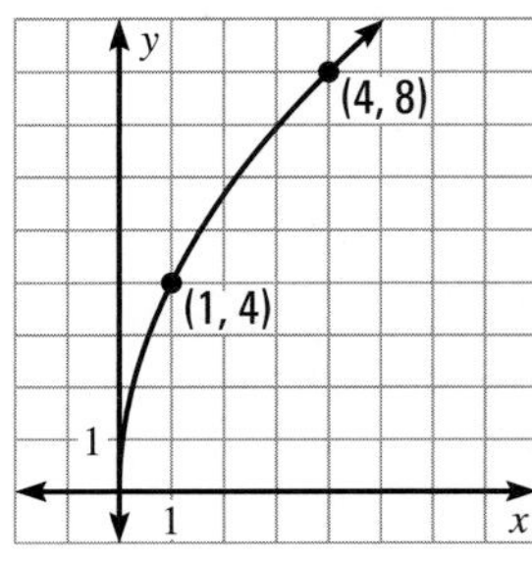

(1) $y = 4x^{0.25}$ (3) $y = \frac{1}{2}x^2$

(2) $y = 4x^{0.5}$ (4) $y = 2x^{1/3}$

TEST PREPARATION

MULTIPLE CHOICE

12. What is the solution of the equation $\log_3 (5x + 3) = 5$?

(1) $\frac{2}{5}$ (2) 415 (3) $\frac{12}{5}$ (4) 48

13. The graph of $f(x) = ab^x$ passes through the point (0, 8) and (2, 2). What is the value of $f(5)$?

(1) $\frac{1}{4}$ (3) 8

(2) 2 (4) 40

14. The model $y = 7.7e^{0.14x}$ gives the number y (in thousands per cubic centimeter) of bacteria in a liquid culture after x hours. To the nearest tenth of an hour, after how many hours will there be 50,000 bacteria per cubic centimeter?

(1) 1.87 hr (3) 46.4 hr

(2) 13.4 hr (4) 62.7 hr

15. What is the solution to the equation $9^{2x+1} = 3^{5x-1}$?

(1) $\frac{3}{8}$ (2) $\frac{2}{3}$ (3) 2 (4) 3

16. The diagram below shows the first three stages of a sequence. What fraction of the circle is shaded in the nth stage?

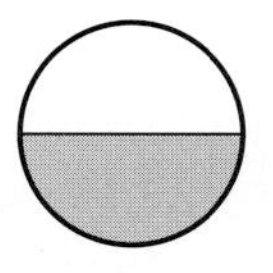
Stage 1

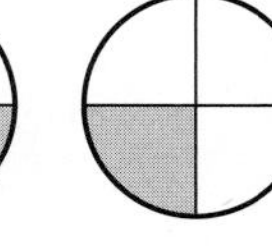
Stage 2

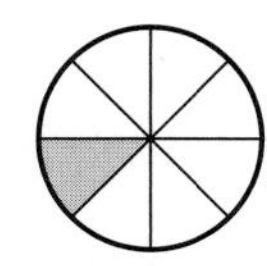
Stage 3

(1) $\frac{1}{2n}$ (2) $2n$ (3) 2^n (4) 2^{-n}

OPEN-ENDED

17. A movie grosses \$37 million in its first week of release. The weekly gross y decreases by 30% each week. Write an exponential decay model for the weekly gross in week x. What is a reasonable domain for this situation? *Explain* your reasoning.

18. The table shows the number of transistors per integrated circuit for computers introduced in various years.

Let x be the number of years since 1974, and let y be the number of transistors. Draw a scatter plot of the data pairs $(x, \ln y)$.

Find an exponential model for the original data.

Use your model to predict the number of transistors per integrated circuit in 2008.

In 1965, Gordon Moore made an observation that became known as Moore's law. Moore's law states that the number of transistors per integrated circuit would double about every 18 months. According to your model, does Moore's law hold? *Explain* your reasoning.

Year	Transistors
1974	6,000
1979	29,000
1982	134,000
1985	275,000
1989	1,200,000
1993	3,100,000
1997	7,500,000
1999	9,500,000
2000	42,000,000
2004	125,000,000

19. For a temperature of 60°F and a height of h feet above sea level, the air pressure P (in pounds per square inch) can be modeled by the equation $P = 14.7e^{-0.0004h}$, and the air density D (in pounds per cubic foot) can be modeled by the equation $D = 0.0761e^{-0.0004h}$.

What is the air density at 10,000 feet above sea level?

To the nearest foot, at what height is the air pressure 12 pounds per square inch?

What is the relationship between air pressure and air density at 60°F? *Explain* your reasoning.

One rule of thumb states that air pressure decreases by about 1% for every 80 meter increase in altitude. Do you agree with this? *Explain.*

TEST PREPARATION

8 Rational Functions

Before

In previous chapters, you learned the following skills, which you'll use in Chapter 8: writing direct variation equations, factoring polynomials, and performing polynomial operations.

Prerequisite Skills

VOCABULARY CHECK

1. The **asymptote** of the graph at the right is ___?___.
2. Two variables x and y show **direct variation** provided ___?___ where a is a nonzero constant.
3. An **extraneous solution** of a transformed equation is not an actual ___?___ of the original equation.

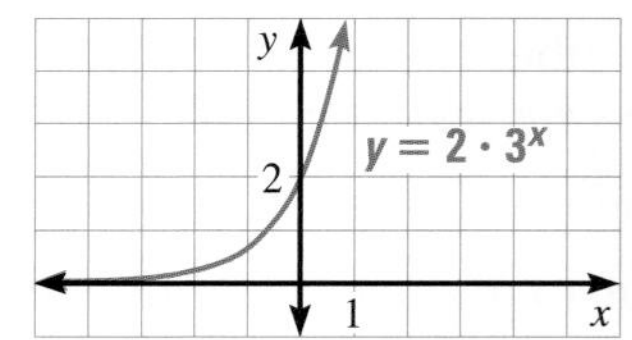

SKILLS CHECK

The variables x and y vary directly. Write an equation that relates x and y. Then find the value of y when $x = -2$. *(Review p. 107 for 8.1.)*

4. $x = 2, y = 8$
5. $x = -1, y = 4$
6. $x = 12, y = 2$

Factor the polynomial completely. *(Review pp. 252, 353 for 8.4, 8.5.)*

7. $x^2 - 11x - 26$
8. $2x^3 - 4x^2 + 2x$
9. $6x^4 - 4x^3 - 24x + 16$

Perform the indicated operation. *(Review p. 346 for 8.4, 8.5.)*

10. $(3x^2 - 6) + (7x^2 - x)$
11. $(-2x^2 + 6) - (x^2 - x)$
12. $(x + 2)(x - 9)^2$

Now

In Chapter 8, you will apply the big ideas listed below and reviewed in the Chapter Summary on page 602. You will also use the key vocabulary listed below.

Big Ideas

1. **Graphing rational functions**
2. **Performing operations with rational expressions**
3. **Solving rational equations**

KEY VOCABULARY

- inverse variation, *p. 551*
- constant of variation, *p. 551*
- joint variation, *p. 553*
- rational function, *p. 558*
- simplified form of a rational expression, *p. 573*
- complex fraction, *p. 584*
- cross multiplying, *p. 589*

Why?

You can use rational functions to model real-life situations. For example, you can model the time it takes to travel across the United States and back in an airplane.

Animated Algebra

The animation illustrated below for Exercise 41 on page 587 helps you answer this question: How does the time required to fly from New York to Los Angeles and back depend on the speeds of the airplane and the jet stream?

The winds of the jet stream affect the overall speed of an airplane.

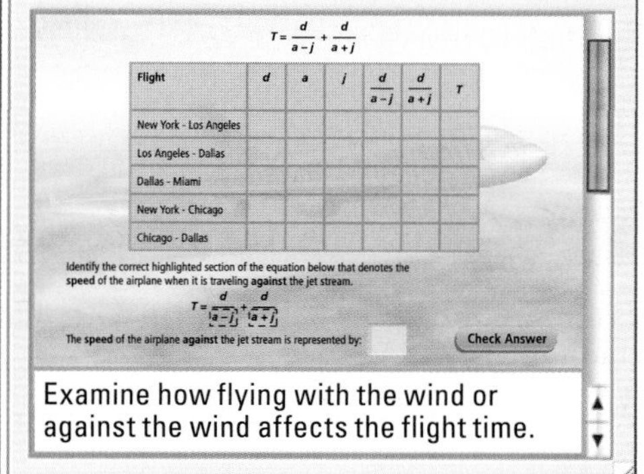

Examine how flying with the wind or against the wind affects the flight time.

Animated Algebra at classzone.com

Other animations for Chapter 8: pages 554, 559, 568, and 602

8.1 Investigating Inverse Variation

MATERIALS • tape measure or meter stick • centimeter ruler • masking tape

QUESTION How can you model data that show inverse variation?

EXPLORE Collect and record data

STEP 1 *Mark distances*
Work with a partner. Have your partner stand against a wall. Place the end of the tape measure against the wall between your partner's feet. Use tape to mark off distances from 3 meters to 9 meters away from the wall.

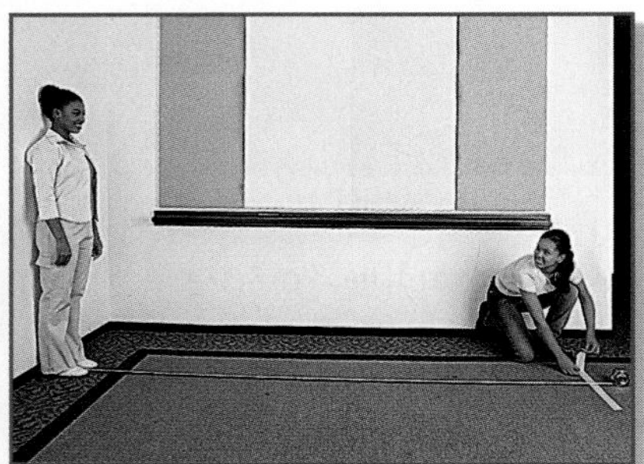

STEP 2 *Measure apparent height*
Face your partner, with your toes touching the 3 meter mark. Hold a centimeter ruler at arm's length and line up the "0" end of the ruler with the top of your partner's head. Measure the apparent height of your partner to the nearest centimeter.

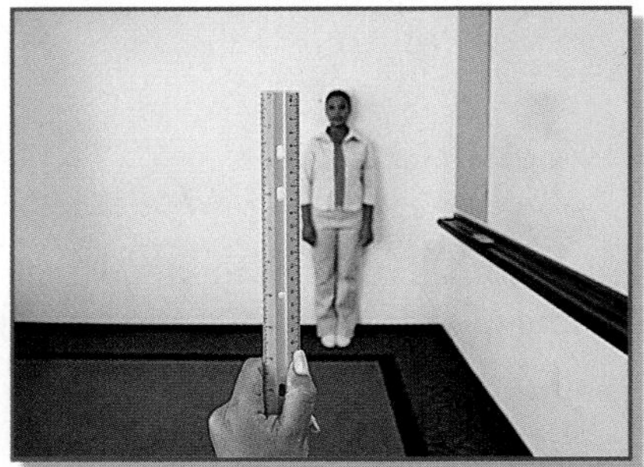

STEP 3 *Repeat for other distances*
Repeat Step 2 for each marked distance and record your results in a table like the one shown.

Distance (m), x	3	4	5	6	7	8	9
Apparent height (cm), y	?	?	?	?	?	?	?

DRAW CONCLUSIONS Use your observations to complete these exercises

1. Does apparent height vary directly with distance? *Justify* your answer mathematically.
2. Find the product $x \cdot y$ for each ordered pair in the table. What do you notice?
3. Based on your results from Exercise 2, write an equation relating distance and apparent height.
4. Use your equation to predict your partner's apparent height at an unmeasured distance. Then test your prediction by measuring your partner's apparent height at that distance. How close was your prediction?

8.1 Model Inverse and Joint Variation

A2.A.5 Use direct and inverse variation to solve for unknown values

Before You wrote and used direct variation models.

Now You will use inverse variation and joint variation models.

Why? So you can model music frequencies, as in Ex. 40.

Key Vocabulary
- **inverse variation**
- **constant of variation**
- **joint variation**

You have learned that two variables x and y show direct variation if $y = ax$ for some nonzero constant a. Another type of variation is called *inverse variation*.

KEY CONCEPT *For Your Notebook*

Inverse Variation

Two variables x and y show **inverse variation** if they are related as follows:

$$y = \frac{a}{x}, a \neq 0$$

The constant a is the **constant of variation**, and y is said to *vary inversely* with x.

EXAMPLE 1 Classify direct and inverse variation

Tell whether x and y show *direct variation*, *inverse variation*, or *neither*.

	Given Equation	Rewritten Equation	Type of Variation
a.	$xy = 7$	$y = \frac{7}{x}$	Inverse
b.	$y = x + 3$		Neither
c.	$\frac{y}{4} = x$	$y = 4x$	Direct

REVIEW DIRECT VARIATION
The equation in part (b) does not show direct variation because $y = x + 3$ is not of the form $y = ax$.

EXAMPLE 2 Write an inverse variation equation

The variables x and y vary inversely, and $y = 7$ when $x = 4$. Write an equation that relates x and y. Then find y when $x = -2$.

$y = \frac{a}{x}$ **Write general equation for inverse variation.**

$7 = \frac{a}{4}$ **Substitute 7 for y and 4 for x.**

$28 = a$ **Solve for a.**

▶ The inverse variation equation is $y = \frac{28}{x}$. When $x = -2$, $y = \frac{28}{-2} = -14$.

EXAMPLE 3 Write an inverse variation model

MP3 PLAYERS The number of songs that can be stored on an MP3 player varies inversely with the average size of a song. A certain MP3 player can store 2500 songs when the average size of a song is 4 megabytes (MB).

- Write a model that gives the number n of songs that will fit on the MP3 player as a function of the average song size s (in megabytes).
- Make a table showing the number of songs that will fit on the MP3 player if the average size of a song is 2 MB, 2.5 MB, 3 MB, and 5 MB as shown below. What happens to the number of songs as the average song size increases?

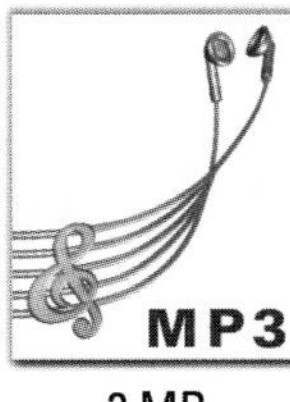

2 MB

MP3

2.5 MB

3 MB

5 MB

Solution

STEP 1 **Write** an inverse variation model.

$n = \frac{a}{s}$ **Write general equation for inverse variation.**

$2500 = \frac{a}{4}$ **Substitute 2500 for *n* and 4 for *s*.**

$10{,}000 = a$ **Solve for *a*.**

▶ A model is $n = \frac{10{,}000}{s}$.

STEP 2 **Make** a table of values.

Average size of song (MB), *s*	2	2.5	3	5
Number of songs, *n*	5000	4000	3333	2000

▶ From the table, you can see that the number of songs that will fit on the MP3 player decreases as the average song size increases.

GUIDED PRACTICE for Examples 1, 2, and 3

Tell whether x and y show *direct variation*, *inverse variation*, or *neither*.

1. $3x = y$ **2.** $xy = 0.75$ **3.** $y = x - 5$

The variables x and y vary inversely. Use the given values to write an equation relating x and y. Then find y when $x = 2$.

4. $x = 4, y = 3$ **5.** $x = 8, y = -1$ **6.** $x = \frac{1}{2}, y = 12$

7. **WHAT IF?** In Example 3, what is a model for the MP3 player if it stores 3000 songs when the average song size is 5 MB?

CHECKING FOR INVERSE VARIATION The general equation $y = \frac{a}{x}$ for inverse variation can be rewritten as $xy = a$. This tells you that a set of data pairs (x, y) shows inverse variation if the products xy are constant or approximately constant.

EXAMPLE 4 Check data for inverse variation

COMPUTER CHIPS The table compares the area A (in square millimeters) of a computer chip with the number c of chips that can be obtained from a silicon wafer.

- Write a model that gives c as a function of A.
- Predict the number of chips per wafer when the area of a chip is 81 square millimeters.

Area (mm^2), A	58	62	66	70
Number of chips, c	448	424	392	376

Solution

AVOID ERRORS
To check data pairs (x, y) for *direct* variation, you find the *quotients* $\frac{y}{x}$. However, to check data pairs for *inverse* variation, you find the *products xy*.

STEP 1 **Calculate** the product $A \cdot c$ for each data pair in the table.

$58(448) = 25{,}984$

$62(424) = 26{,}288$

$66(392) = 25{,}872$

$70(376) = 26{,}320$

Each product is approximately equal to 26,000. So, the data show inverse variation. A model relating A and c is:

$$A \cdot c = 26{,}000, \text{ or } c = \frac{26{,}000}{A}$$

STEP 2 **Make** a prediction. The number of chips per wafer for a chip with an area of 81 square millimeters is $c = \frac{26{,}000}{81} \approx 321$.

✓ GUIDED PRACTICE for Example 4

8. **WHAT IF?** In Example 4, predict the number of chips per wafer when the area of each chip is 79 square millimeters.

KEY CONCEPT *For Your Notebook*

Joint Variation

Joint variation occurs when a quantity varies directly with *the product of two or more* other quantities. In the equations below, a is a nonzero constant.

$z = axy$ **z varies jointly with x and y.**

$p = aqrs$ **p varies jointly with q, r, and s.**

EXAMPLE 5 Write a joint variation equation

The variable z varies jointly with x and y. Also, $z = -75$ when $x = 3$ and $y = -5$. Write an equation that relates x, y, and z. Then find z when $x = 2$ and $y = 6$.

Solution

STEP 1 **Write** a general joint variation equation.

$z = axy$

STEP 2 **Use** the given values of z, x, and y to find the constant of variation a.

$-75 = a(3)(-5)$ Substitute -75 for z, 3 for x, and -5 for y.

$-75 = -15a$ Simplify.

$5 = a$ Solve for a.

STEP 3 **Rewrite** the joint variation equation with the value of a from Step 2.

$z = 5xy$

STEP 4 **Calculate** z when $x = 2$ and $y = 6$ using substitution.

$z = 5xy = 5(2)(6) = 60$

EXAMPLE 6 Compare different types of variation

Write an equation for the given relationship.

	Relationship	Equation
a.	y varies inversely with x.	$y = \frac{a}{x}$
b.	z varies jointly with x, y, and r.	$z = axyr$
c.	y varies inversely with the square of x.	$y = \frac{a}{x^2}$
d.	z varies directly with y and inversely with x.	$z = \frac{ay}{x}$
e.	x varies jointly with t and r and inversely with s.	$x = \frac{atr}{s}$

Animated Algebra at classzone.com

✓ GUIDED PRACTICE for Examples 5 and 6

The variable z varies jointly with x and y. Use the given values to write an equation relating x, y, and z. Then find z when $x = -2$ and $y = 5$.

9. $x = 1, y = 2, z = 7$

10. $x = 4, y = -3, z = 24$

11. $x = -2, y = 6, z = 18$

12. $x = -6, y = -4, z = 56$

Write an equation for the given relationship.

13. x varies inversely with y and directly with w.

14. p varies jointly with q and r and inversely with s.

8.1 EXERCISES

HOMEWORK KEY
○ = **WORKED-OUT SOLUTIONS** on p. WS14 for Exs. 15, 21, and 39
★ = **STANDARDIZED TEST PRACTICE** Exs. 2, 11, 30, 35, and 41

SKILL PRACTICE

1. **VOCABULARY** Copy and complete: If z varies directly with the product of x and y, then z is said to vary _?_ with x and y.

2. ★ **WRITING** *Describe* how to tell whether a set of data pairs (x, y) shows inverse variation.

EXAMPLE 1 on p. 551 for Exs. 3–11

DETERMINING VARIATION Tell whether x and y show *direct variation, inverse variation,* or *neither.*

3. $xy = \frac{1}{5}$
4. $y = x + 4$
5. $\frac{y}{x} = 8$
6. $4x = y$
7. $y = \frac{2}{x}$
8. $x + y = 6$
9. $8y = x$
10. $xy = 12$

11. ★ **MULTIPLE CHOICE** Which equation represents inverse variation?

Ⓐ $y = 4x$ Ⓑ $y = x - 1$ Ⓒ $xy = 5$ Ⓓ $\frac{y}{7} = x$

EXAMPLE 2 on p. 551 for Exs. 12–19

USING INVERSE VARIATION The variables x and y vary inversely. Use the given values to write an equation relating x and y. Then find y when $x = 3$.

12. $x = 5, y = -4$
13. $x = 1, y = 9$
14. $x = -3, y = 8$
15. $x = 7, y = 2$
16. $x = \frac{3}{4}, y = 28$
17. $x = -4, y = -\frac{5}{4}$
18. $x = -12, y = -\frac{1}{6}$
19. $x = \frac{5}{3}, y = -7$

EXAMPLE 4 on p. 553 for Exs. 20–23

INTERPRETING DATA Determine whether x and y show *direct variation, inverse variation,* or *neither.*

20.

x	y
1.5	40
2.5	24
4	15
7.5	8
10	6

21.

x	y
12	132
18	198
23	253
29	319
34	374

22.

x	y
4	16
5	11
6.2	10
7	9
11	6

23.

x	y
4	21
6	14
8	10.5
8.4	10
12	7

EXAMPLE 5 on p. 554 for Exs. 24–30

USING JOINT VARIATION Write an equation relating x, y, and z given that z varies jointly with x and y. Then find z when $x = -4$ and $y = 5$.

24. $x = 2, y = -6, z = 24$
25. $x = 8, y = 6, z = 12$
26. $x = -\frac{1}{4}, y = -3, z = 15$
27. $x = 6, y = -7, z = -3$
28. $x = 9, y = -2, z = 6$
29. $x = 5, y = -3, z = 75$

30. ★ **MULTIPLE CHOICE** Suppose z varies jointly with x and y, and $z = -36$ when $x = -3$ and $y = -4$. What is the constant of variation?

Ⓐ -3 Ⓑ -2 Ⓒ 3 Ⓓ 12

EXAMPLE 6 on p. 554 for Exs. 31–33

WRITING EQUATIONS **Write an equation for the given relationship.**

31. x varies directly with y and inversely with z.

32. y varies jointly with x and the square of z.

33. w varies inversely with y and jointly with x and z.

34. **ERROR ANALYSIS** A variable z varies jointly with x and the cube of y and inversely with the square root of w. *Describe* and correct the error in writing an equation relating the variables.

$$z = \frac{a\sqrt{w}}{xy^3}$$ ✗

35. ★ **OPEN-ENDED MATH** Let $f(x)$ represent a direct variation function, $g(x)$ represent an inverse variation function, and $h(x)$ be the sum of $f(x)$ and $g(x)$. Write possible functions $f(x)$ and $g(x)$ so that $h(2) = 5$.

36. **CHALLENGE** Suppose x varies inversely with y and y varies inversely with z. How does x vary with z? *Justify* your answer algebraically.

PROBLEM SOLVING

EXAMPLES 3 and 4 on pp. 552–553 for Exs. 37–39

37. **DIGITAL CAMERAS** The number n of photos your digital camera can store varies inversely with the average size s (in megapixels) of the photos. Your digital camera can store 54 photos when the average photo size is 1.92 megapixels. Write a model that gives n as a function of s. How many photos can your camera store when the average photo size is 3.87 megapixels?

@HomeTutor for problem solving help at classzone.com

38. **ELECTRONICS** The table below compares the current I (in milliamps) with the resistance R (in ohms) for several electrical circuits. Write a model that gives R as a function of I. Then predict R when $I = 34$ milliamps.

Current (milliamps), I	7.4	8.9	12.1	17.9
Resistance (ohms), R	1200	1000	750	500

@HomeTutor for problem solving help at classzone.com

39. **SNOWSHOES** When you stand on snow, the average pressure P (in pounds per square inch) that you exert on the snow varies inversely with the total area A (in square inches) of the soles of your footwear. Suppose the pressure is 0.43 pound per square inch when you wear the snowshoes shown. Write an equation that gives P as a function of A. Then find the pressure if you wear the boots shown.

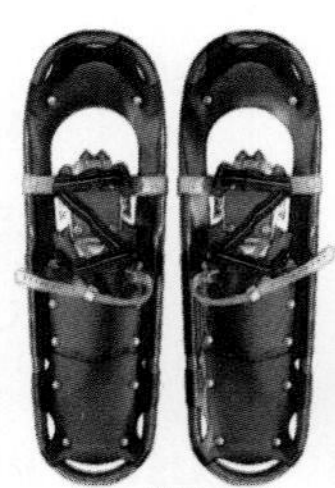

$A = 400$ in.² $A = 60$ in.²

40. **MULTI-STEP PROBLEM** A piano string's frequency f (in hertz) varies directly with the square root of the string's tension T (in Newtons) and inversely with both the string's length L and diameter d (each in centimeters).

a. The middle C note has a frequency of 262 Hz. The string producing this note has a tension of 670 N, a length of 62 cm, and a diameter of 0.1025 cm. Write an equation relating f, T, L, and d.

b. Find the frequency of the note produced by a string with a tension of 1629 N, a length of 201.6 cm, and a diameter of 0.49 cm.

○ = WORKED-OUT SOLUTIONS on p. WS1 ★ = STANDARDIZED TEST PRACTICE

41. ★ **EXTENDED RESPONSE** The *law of universal gravitation* states that the gravitational force F (in Newtons) between two objects varies jointly with their masses m_1 and m_2 (in kilograms) and inversely with the square of the distance d (in meters) between the two objects. The constant of variation is denoted by G and is called the *universal gravitational constant.*

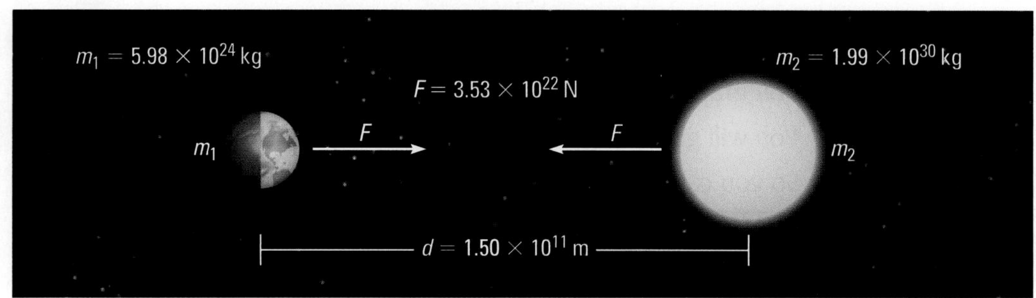

a. **Model** Write an equation that gives F in terms of m_1, m_2, d and G.

b. **Approximate** Use the information above about Earth and the Sun to approximate the universal gravitational constant G.

c. **Reasoning** *Explain* what happens to the gravitational force as the masses of the two objects increase and the distance between them is held constant. *Explain* what happens to the gravitational force as the masses of the two objects are held constant and the distance between them increases.

42. **CHALLENGE** The load P (in pounds) that can be safely supported by a horizontal beam varies jointly with the beam's width W and the square of its depth D, and inversely with its unsupported length L.

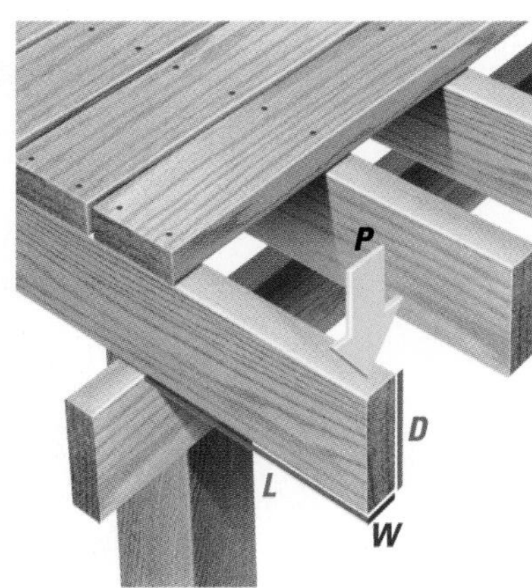

a. How does P change when the width and length of the beam are doubled?

b. How does P change when the width and depth of the beam are doubled?

c. How does P change when all three dimensions are doubled?

d. *Describe* several ways a beam can be modified if the safe load it is required to support is increased by a factor of 4.

NEW YORK MIXED REVIEW

TEST PRACTICE at classzone.com

43. What is the approximate area of $\triangle MNP$?

(A) 40.5 cm^2 (B) 57.3 cm^2
(C) 70.1 cm^2 (D) 114.6 cm^2

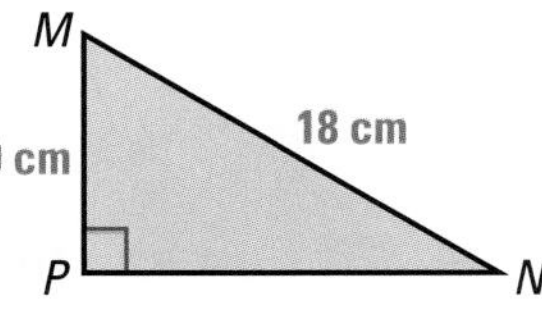
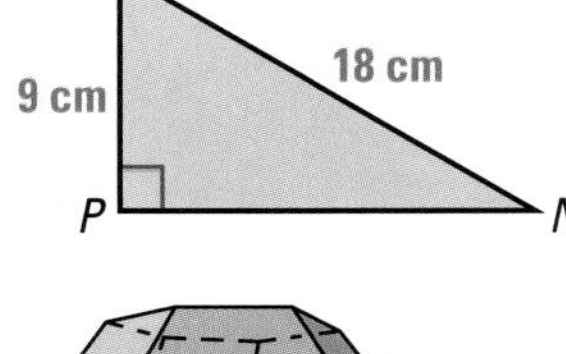

44. The solid at the right has 14 faces: 8 hexagons and 6 squares. How many vertices does the solid have?

(A) 24 (B) 32
(C) 44 (D) 88

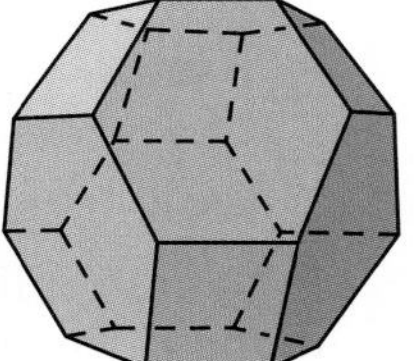

8.2 Graph Simple Rational Functions

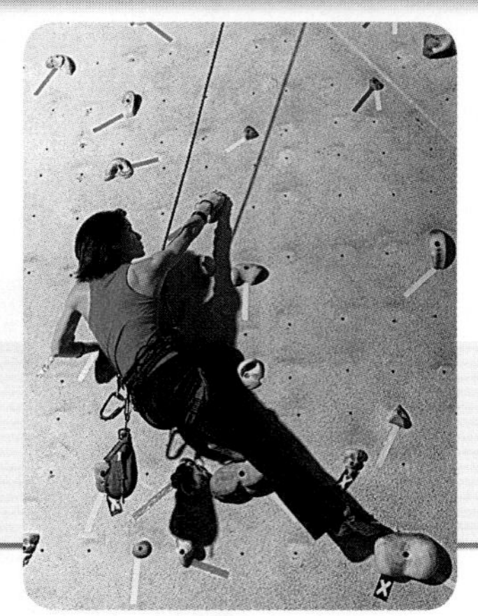

A2.A.51 Determine the domain and range of a function from its graph

Before You graphed polynomial functions.

Now You will graph rational functions.

Why? So you can find average monthly costs, as in Ex. 38.

Key Vocabulary
- **rational function**
- **domain,** *p. 72*
- **range,** *p. 72*
- **asymptote,** *p. 478*

A **rational function** has the form $f(x) = \frac{p(x)}{q(x)}$ where $p(x)$ and $q(x)$ are polynomials and $q(x) \neq 0$. The inverse variation function $f(x) = \frac{a}{x}$ is a rational function. The graph of this function when $a = 1$ is shown below.

KEY CONCEPT — *For Your Notebook*

Parent Function for Simple Rational Functions

The graph of the parent function $f(x) = \frac{1}{x}$ is a *hyperbola,* which consists of two symmetrical parts called *branches*. The domain and range are all nonzero real numbers.

Any function of the form $g(x) = \frac{a}{x}$ $(a \neq 0)$ has the same asymptotes, domain, and range as the function $f(x) = \frac{1}{x}$.

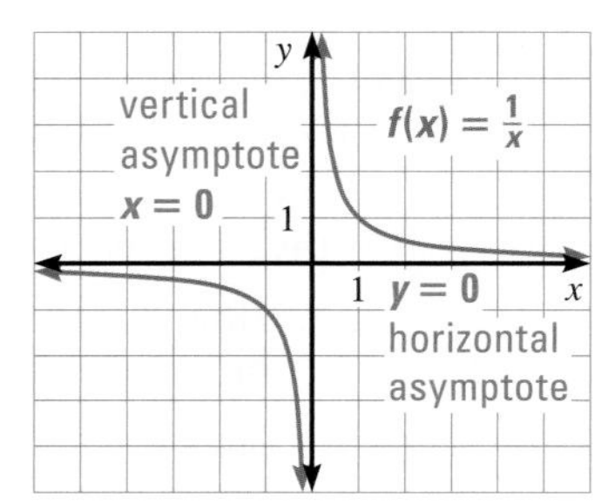

EXAMPLE 1 Graph a rational function of the form $y = \frac{a}{x}$

Graph the function $y = \frac{6}{x}$. Compare the graph with the graph of $y = \frac{1}{x}$.

Solution

INTERPRET TRANSFORMATIONS
The graph of $y = \frac{6}{x}$ is a vertical stretch of the graph of $y = \frac{1}{x}$ by a factor of 6.

STEP 1 **Draw** the asymptotes $x = 0$ and $y = 0$.

STEP 2 **Plot** points to the left and to the right of the vertical asymptote, such as $(-3, -2)$, $(-2, -3)$, $(2, 3)$, and $(3, 2)$.

STEP 3 **Draw** the branches of the hyperbola so that they pass through the plotted points and approach the asymptotes.

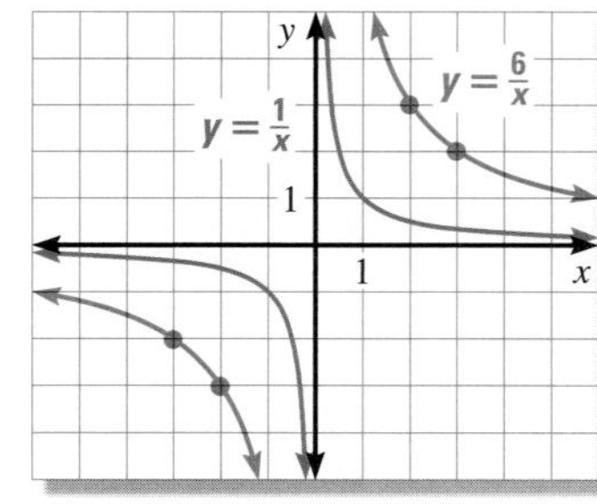

The graph of $y = \frac{6}{x}$ lies farther from the axes than the graph of $y = \frac{1}{x}$. Both graphs lie in the first and third quadrants and have the same asymptotes, domain, and range.

KEY CONCEPT *For Your Notebook*

Graphing Translations of Simple Rational Functions

To graph a rational function of the form $y = \frac{a}{x - h} + k$, follow these steps:

STEP 1 **Draw** the asymptotes $x = h$ and $y = k$.

STEP 2 **Plot** points to the left and to the right of the vertical asymptote.

STEP 3 **Draw** the two branches of the hyperbola so that they pass through the plotted points and approach the asymptotes.

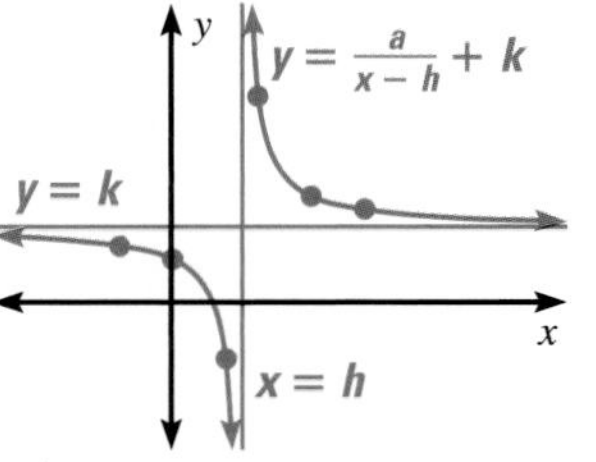

EXAMPLE 2 Graph a rational function of the form $y = \frac{a}{x - h} + k$

Graph $y = \frac{-4}{x + 2} - 1$. State the domain and range.

Solution

STEP 1 **Draw** the asymptotes $x = -2$ and $y = -1$.

STEP 2 **Plot** points to the left of the vertical asymptote, such as $(-3, 3)$ and $(-4, 1)$, and points to the right, such as $(-1, -5)$ and $(0, -3)$.

STEP 3 **Draw** the two branches of the hyperbola so that they pass through the plotted points and approach the asymptotes.

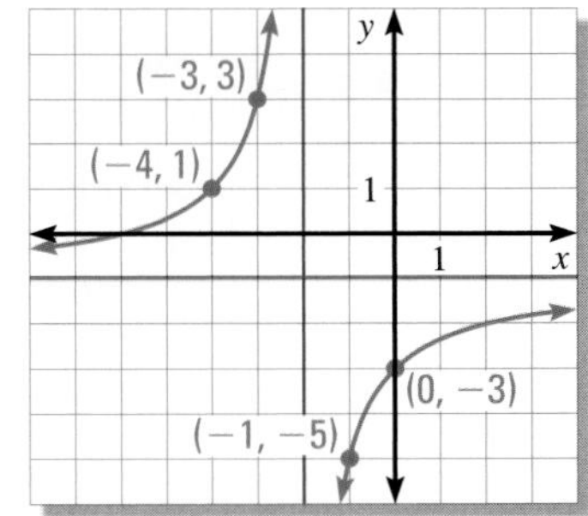

The domain is all real numbers except -2, and the range is all real numbers except -1.

Animated Algebra at classzone.com

INTERPRET TRANSFORMATIONS

The graph of $y = \frac{-4}{x + 2} - 1$ is the graph of $y = \frac{-4}{x}$ translated left 2 units and down 1 unit.

✓ **GUIDED PRACTICE** for Examples 1 and 2

Graph the function. State the domain and range.

1. $f(x) = \frac{-4}{x}$

2. $y = \frac{8}{x} - 5$

3. $y = \frac{1}{x - 3} + 2$

OTHER RATIONAL FUNCTIONS All rational functions of the form $y = \frac{ax + b}{cx + d}$ also have graphs that are hyperbolas.

- The vertical asymptote of the graph is the line $x = -\frac{d}{c}$, because the function is undefined when the denominator $cx + d$ is zero.
- The horizontal asymptote is the line $y = \frac{a}{c}$.

EXAMPLE 3 Graph a rational function of the form $y = \frac{ax + b}{cx + d}$

Graph $y = \frac{2x + 1}{x - 3}$. State the domain and range.

Solution

STEP 1 **Draw** the asymptotes. Solve $x - 3 = 0$ for x to find the vertical asymptote $x = 3$. The horizontal asymptote is the line $y = \frac{a}{c} = \frac{2}{1} = 2$.

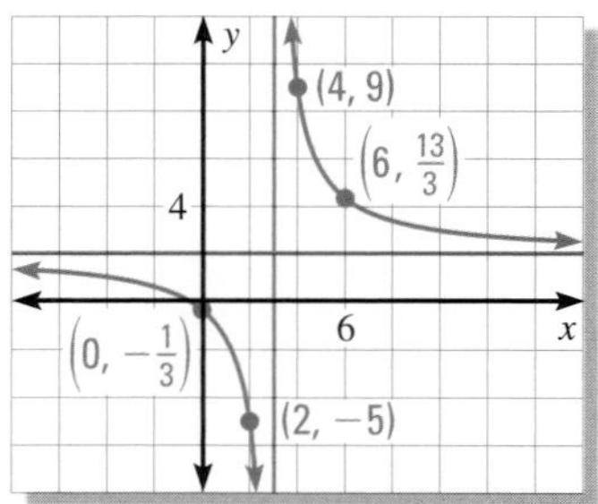

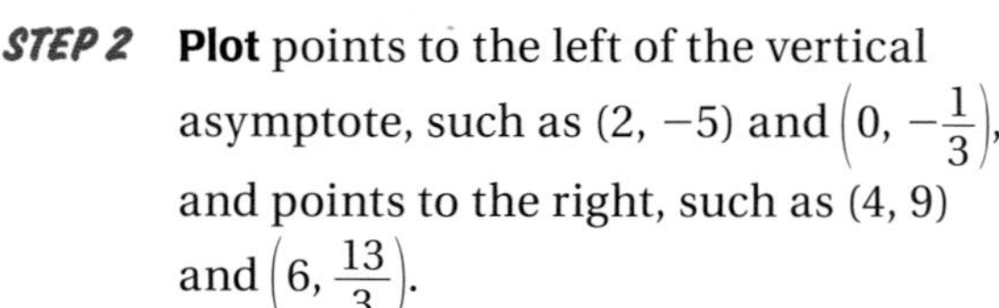

STEP 2 **Plot** points to the left of the vertical asymptote, such as $(2, -5)$ and $\left(0, -\frac{1}{3}\right)$, and points to the right, such as $(4, 9)$ and $\left(6, \frac{13}{3}\right)$.

STEP 3 **Draw** the two branches of the hyperbola so that they pass through the plotted points and approach the asymptotes.

▸ The domain is all real numbers except 3.
The range is all real numbers except 2.

EXAMPLE 4 Solve a multi-step problem

3-D MODELING A 3-D printer builds up layers of material to make three-dimensional models. Each deposited layer bonds to the layer below it. A company decides to make small display models of engine components using a 3-D printer. The printer costs \$24,000. The material for each model costs \$300.

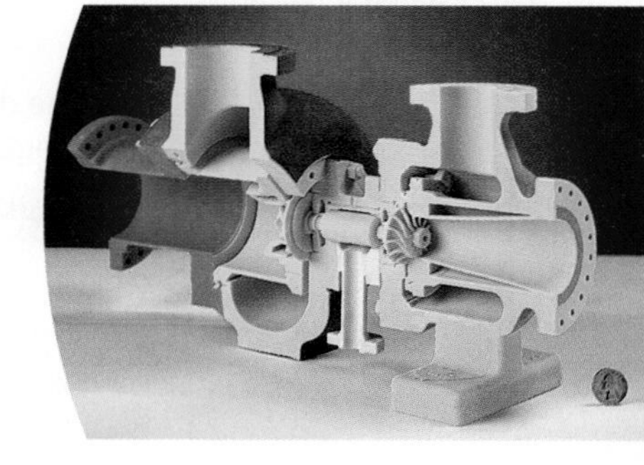

- Write an equation that gives the average cost per model as a function of the number of models printed.
- Graph the function. Use the graph to estimate how many models must be printed for the average cost per model to fall to \$700.
- What happens to the average cost as more models are printed?

Solution

STEP 1 **Write** a function. Let c be the average cost and m be the number of models printed.

$$c = \frac{\text{Unit cost} \cdot \text{Number printed} + \text{Cost of printer}}{\text{Number printed}} = \frac{300m + 24{,}000}{m}$$

DRAW GRAPHS
Because the number of models and average cost cannot be negative, graph only the branch of the hyperbola that lies in the first quadrant.

STEP 2 **Graph** the function. The asymptotes are the lines $m = 0$ and $c = 300$. The average cost falls to \$700 per model after 60 models are printed.

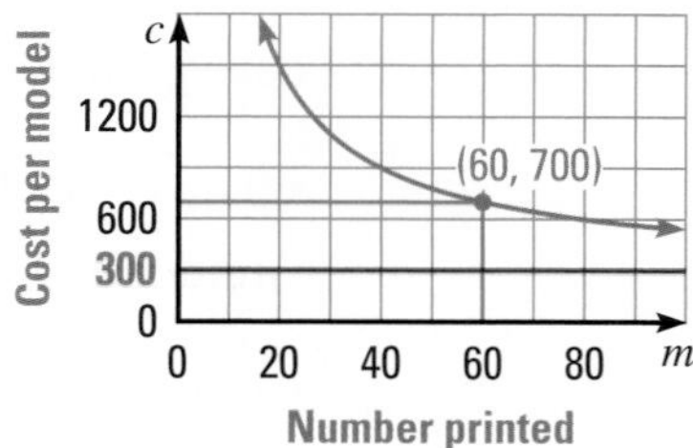

STEP 3 **Interpret** the graph. As more models are printed, the average cost per model approaches \$300.

✓ **GUIDED PRACTICE** for Examples 3 and 4

Graph the function. State the domain and range.

4. $y = \frac{x - 1}{x + 3}$

5. $y = \frac{2x + 1}{4x - 2}$

6. $f(x) = \frac{-3x + 2}{-x - 1}$

7. **WHAT IF?** In Example 4, how do the function and graph change if the cost of the 3-D printer is $21,000?

8.2 EXERCISES

HOMEWORK KEY

○ = **WORKED-OUT SOLUTIONS** on p. WS14 for Exs. 5, 21, and 39

★ = **STANDARDIZED TEST PRACTICE** Exs. 2, 23, 35, 40, and 41

◆ = **MULTIPLE REPRESENTATIONS** Ex. 39

SKILL PRACTICE

1. **VOCABULARY** Copy and complete: The function $y = \frac{7}{x + 4} + 3$ has a(n) _?_ of all real numbers except 3 and a(n) _?_ of all real numbers except −4.

2. ★ **WRITING** Is $f(x) = \frac{-3x + 5}{2^x + 1}$ a rational function? *Explain* your answer.

EXAMPLE 1 on p. 558 for Exs. 3–10

GRAPHING FUNCTIONS **Graph the function. Compare the graph with the graph of $y = \frac{1}{x}$.**

3. $y = \frac{3}{x}$

4. $y = \frac{10}{x}$

5. $y = \frac{-5}{x}$

6. $y = \frac{-0.5}{x}$

7. $y = \frac{0.1}{x}$

8. $f(x) = \frac{15}{x}$

9. $g(x) = \frac{-6}{x}$

10. $h(x) = \frac{-3}{x}$

EXAMPLE 2 on p. 559 for Exs. 11–23

GRAPHING FUNCTIONS **Graph the function. State the domain and range.**

11. $y = \frac{4}{x} + 3$

12. $y = \frac{3}{x} - 2$

13. $y = \frac{6}{x - 1}$

14. $f(x) = \frac{1}{x + 2}$

15. $y = \frac{-5}{x} - 7$

16. $y = \frac{-6}{x} + 4$

17. $y = \frac{-3}{x + 2}$

18. $g(x) = \frac{-2}{x - 7}$

19. $y = \frac{-4}{x + 4} + 3$

20. $y = \frac{10}{x + 7} - 5$

21. $y = \frac{-3}{x - 4} - 1$

22. $h(x) = \frac{11}{x - 9} + 9$

23. ★ **MULTIPLE CHOICE** What are the asymptotes of the graph of $y = \frac{3}{x + 8} - 3$?

Ⓐ $x = 8, y = 3$ Ⓑ $x = 8, y = -3$ Ⓒ $x = -8, y = 3$ Ⓓ $x = -8, y = -3$

24. **GRAPHING CALCULATOR** Consider the function $y = \frac{a}{x - h} + k$ where $a = 1$, $h = 3$, and $k = -2$. Predict the effect on the functions graph of each change in a, h, or k described in parts (a)–(c). Use a graphing calculator to check your prediction by graphing the original and revised functions in the same coordinate plane.

a. a changes to −3 **b.** h changes to −1 **c.** k changes to 2

ERROR ANALYSIS *Describe* and correct the error in the graph.

25. $y = \frac{-8}{x}$

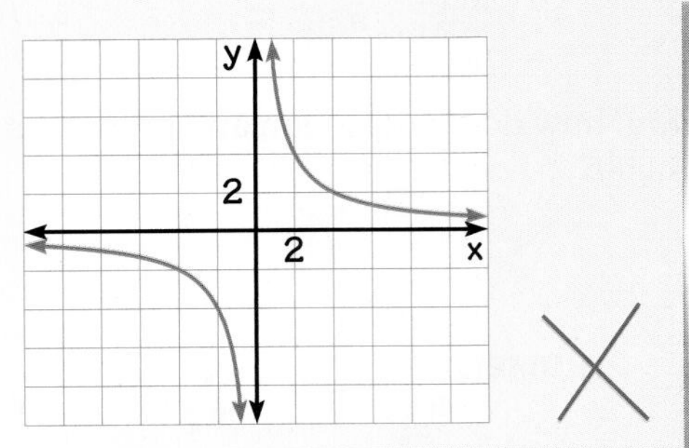

26. $y = \frac{2}{x-1} - 2$

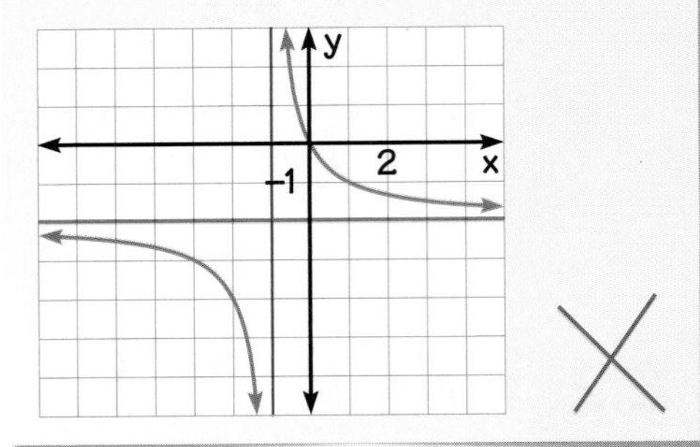

EXAMPLE 3
on p. 560
for Exs. 27–34

GRAPHING FUNCTIONS Graph the function. State the domain and range.

27. $y = \frac{x+4}{x-3}$

28. $y = \frac{x-1}{x+5}$

29. $y = \frac{x+6}{4x-8}$

30. $y = \frac{8x+3}{2x-6}$

31. $y = \frac{-5x+2}{4x+5}$

32. $f(x) = \frac{6x-1}{3x-1}$

33. $g(x) = \frac{5x}{2x+3}$

34. $h(x) = \frac{5x+3}{-x+10}$

35. ★ **OPEN-ENDED MATH** Write a rational function such that the domain is all real numbers except −8 and the range is all real numbers except 3.

36. **CHALLENGE** Show that the equation $f(x) = \frac{a}{x-h} + k$ represents a rational function by writing the right side as a quotient of polynomials.

PROBLEM SOLVING

EXAMPLE 4
on p. 560
for Exs. 37–38

37. **INTERNET SERVICE** An Internet service provider charges a \$50 installation fee and a monthly fee of \$43. Write and graph an equation that gives the average cost per month as a function of the number of months of service. After how many months will the average cost be \$53?

@HomeTutor for problem solving help at classzone.com

38. **ROCK CLIMBING GYM** To join a rock climbing gym, you must pay an initial fee of \$100 and a monthly fee of \$59. Write and graph an equation that gives the average cost per month as a function of the number of months of membership. After how many months will the average cost be \$69?

@HomeTutor for problem solving help at classzone.com

39. ◆ **MULTIPLE REPRESENTATIONS** The time t (in seconds) it takes for sound to travel 1 kilometer can be modeled by $t = \frac{1000}{0.6T + 331}$ where T is the air temperature (in degrees Celsius).

   a. **Evaluating a Function** How long does it take for sound to travel 5 kilometers when the air temperature is 25°C? *Explain.*

   b. **Drawing a Graph** Suppose you are 1 kilometer from a lightning strike, and it takes 3 seconds to hear the thunder. Graph the given function, and use the graph to estimate the air temperature.

40. ★ **SHORT RESPONSE** A business is studying the cost to remove a pollutant from the ground at its site. The function $y = \frac{15x}{1.1 - x}$ models the estimated cost y (in thousands of dollars) to remove x percent (expressed as a decimal) of the pollutant.

a. Graph the function. *Describe* a reasonable domain and range.

b. How much does it cost to remove 20% of the pollutant? 40% of the pollutant? 80% of the pollutant? Does doubling the percent of the pollutant removed double the cost? *Explain.*

41. ★ **EXTENDED RESPONSE** The *Doppler effect* occurs when the source of a sound is moving relative to a listener, so that the frequency f_l (in hertz) heard by the listener is different from the frequency f_s (in hertz) at the source. The frequency heard depends on whether the sound source is approaching or moving away from the listener. In both equations below, r is the speed (in miles per hour) of the sound source.

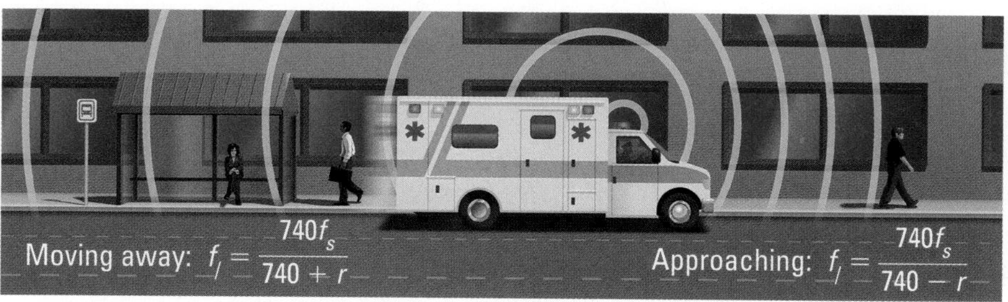

a. An ambulance siren has a frequency of 2000 hertz. Write two equations modeling the frequencies you hear when the ambulance is approaching and when the ambulance is moving away.

b. Graph the equations from part (a) using the domain $0 \le r \le 60$.

c. For any speed r, how does the frequency heard for an approaching sound source compare with the frequency heard when the source moves away?

42. **CHALLENGE** A sailboat travels at a speed of 10 knots for 3 hours. It then uses a motor for power, which increases its speed to 15 knots. Write and graph an equation giving the boat's average speed s (in knots) for the entire trip as a function of the time t (in hours) that it uses the motor for power.

New York Mixed Review

TEST PRACTICE at classzone.com

43. On Monday, Anna reads one quarter of a novel. On Tuesday, she reads one third of the remaining pages. On Wednesday, she reads one quarter of the remaining pages. On Thursday, she reads the remaining 105 pages. How many pages does the novel have?

Ⓐ 219 Ⓑ 280 Ⓒ 340 Ⓓ 420

44. Which equation best describes the relationship between x and y shown in the table?

x	0.2	0.5	0.8	1.1
y	0.16	1	2.56	4.84

Ⓐ $y = 4x$ Ⓑ $x = 4y$ Ⓒ $x = 4y^2$ Ⓓ $y = 4x^2$

Graphing Calculator ACTIVITY Use after Lesson 8.2

@HomeTutor classzone.com Keystrokes

8.2 Graph Rational Functions

QUESTION **How can you use a graphing calculator to graph rational functions?**

Most graphing calculators have two graphing modes: *connected* mode and *dot* mode. *Connected* mode displays the graph of a rational function as a smooth curve, while *dot* mode displays the graph as a series of dots.

EXAMPLE **Graph a rational function**

Graph $y = \frac{x+3}{x-3}$.

STEP 1 ***Enter function***

Enter the rational function, using parentheses.

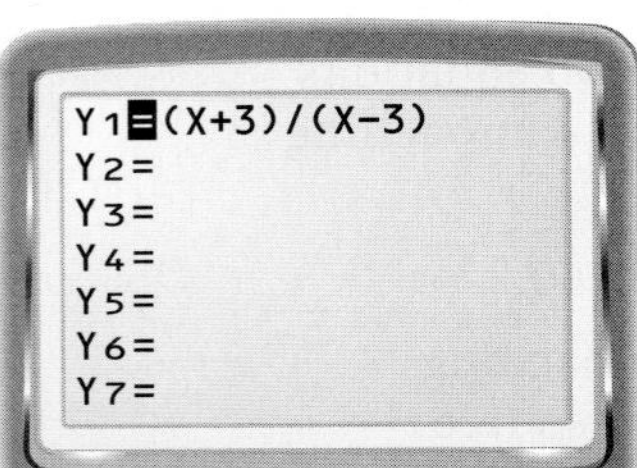

STEP 2 ***Use connected mode***

Graph the function in *connected* mode.

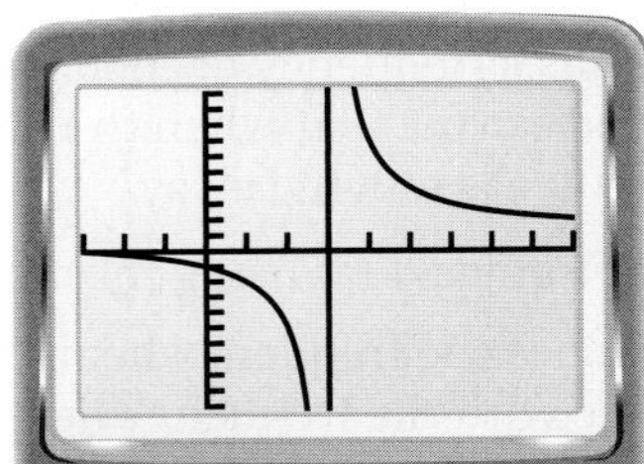

STEP 3 ***Use dot mode***

Graph the function in *dot* mode.

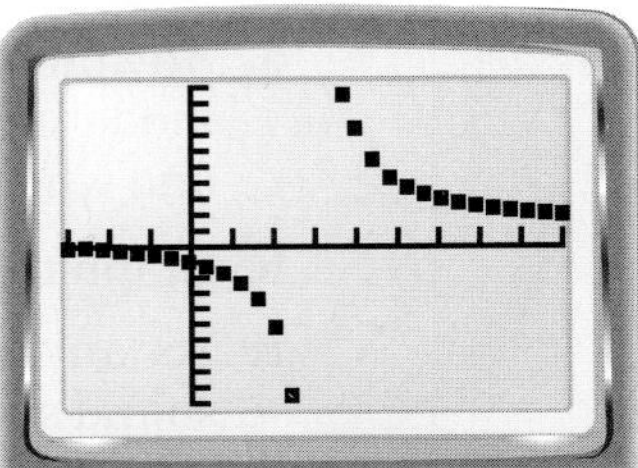

The graph in Step 2 includes a vertical line at approximately $x = 3$. This line is *not* part of the graph. It is simply the graphing calculator's attempt at connecting the two branches of the graph.

PRACTICE

Use a graphing calculator to graph the rational function. Choose a viewing window that displays the important characteristics of the graph.

1. $y = \frac{5}{x} + 2$

2. $y = 7 - \frac{3}{x}$

3. $y = 4 + \frac{2}{x-5}$

4. $y = \frac{6}{x+1} + 2$

5. $y = \frac{7}{2x+8}$

6. $y = \frac{9-2x}{x-3}$

7. $f(x) = \frac{x-4}{x+2}$

8. $g(x) = \frac{5x-2}{3x+9}$

9. SKATEBOARDING You are trying to decide whether it is worth joining a skate park. It costs $100 to join and then $4 for each visit. Write a function that gives the average cost y per visit after x visits. Graph the function. What happens to the average cost as the number of visits increases? What are a reasonable domain and range for the function?

8.3 Graph General Rational Functions

A2.A.51 Determine the domain and range of a function from its graph

Before You graphed rational functions involving linear polynomials.

Now You will graph rational functions with higher-degree polynomials.

Why? So you can solve problems about altitude, as in Ex. 35.

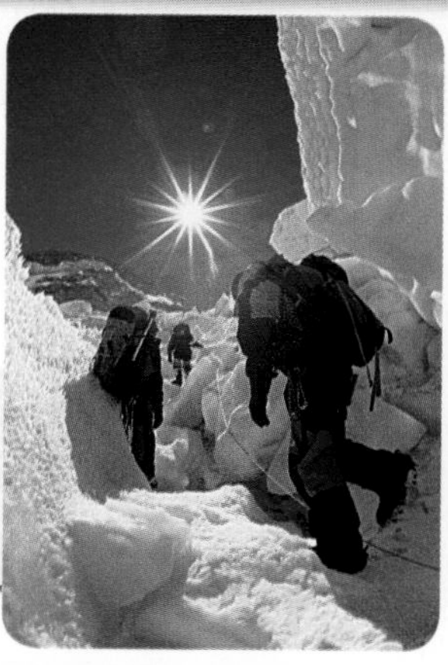

Key Vocabulary
- **end behavior,** *p. 339*
- **asymptote,** *p. 478*
- **rational function,** *p. 558*

KEY CONCEPT *For Your Notebook*

Graphs of Rational Functions

Let $p(x)$ and $q(x)$ be polynomials with no common factors other than ± 1. The graph of the following rational function has the characteristics listed below.

$$f(x) = \frac{p(x)}{q(x)} = \frac{a_m x^m + a_{m-1}x^{m-1} + \cdots + a_1 x + a_0}{b_n x^n + b_{n-1}x^{n-1} + \cdots + b_1 x + b_0}$$

1. The x-intercepts of the graph of f are the real zeros of $p(x)$.
2. The graph of f has a vertical asymptote at each real zero of $q(x)$.
3. The graph of f has at most one horizontal asymptote, which is determined by the degrees m and n of $p(x)$ and $q(x)$.

$m < n$	The line $y = 0$ is a horizontal asymptote.
$m = n$	The line $y = \frac{a_m}{b_n}$ is a horizontal asymptote.
$m > n$	The graph has no horizontal asymptote. The graph's end behavior is the same as the graph of $y = \frac{a_m}{b_n}x^{m-n}$.

EXAMPLE 1 Graph a rational function ($m < n$)

Graph $y = \frac{6}{x^2 + 1}$. State the domain and range.

Solution

The numerator has no zeros, so there is no x-intercept. The denominator has no real zeros, so there is no vertical asymptote.

The degree of the numerator, 0, is less than the degree of the denominator, 2. So, the line $y = 0$ (the x-axis) is a horizontal asymptote.

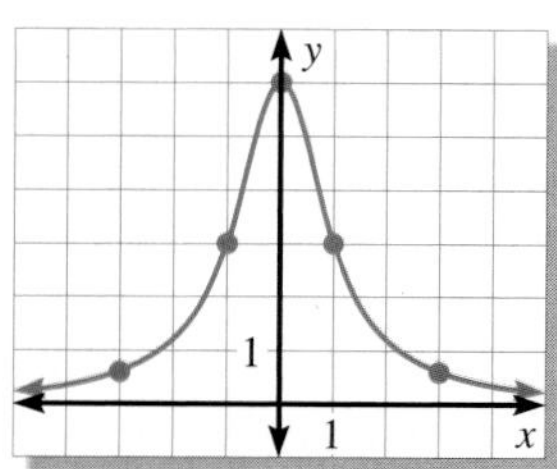

The graph passes through the points $(-3, 0.6)$, $(-1, 3)$, $(0, 6)$, $(1, 3)$, and $(3, 0.6)$. The domain is all real numbers, and the range is $0 < y \le 6$.

EXAMPLE 2 Graph a rational function ($m = n$)

Graph $y = \dfrac{2x^2}{x^2 - 9}$.

REVIEW ZEROS OF FUNCTIONS
For help with finding zeros of functions, see p. 252.

Solution

The zero of the numerator $2x^2$ is 0, so 0 is an x-intercept. The zeros of the denominator $x^2 - 9$ are ± 3, so $x = 3$ and $x = -3$ are vertical asymptotes.

The numerator and denominator have the same degree, so the horizontal asymptote is $y = \dfrac{a_m}{b_n} = \dfrac{2}{1} = 2$.

Plot points between and beyond the vertical asymptotes.

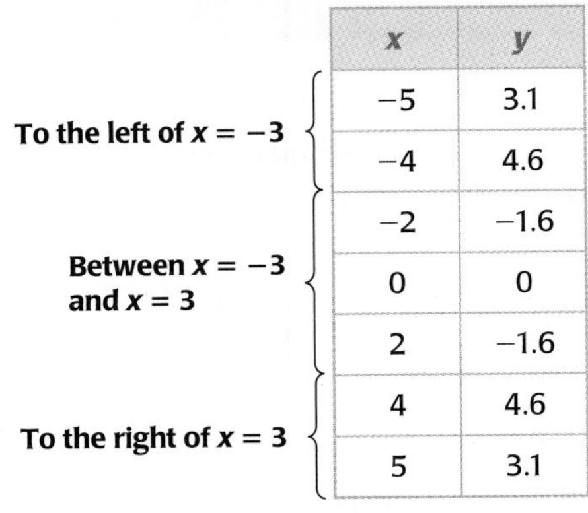

	x	y
To the left of $x = -3$	−5	3.1
	−4	4.6
Between $x = -3$ and $x = 3$	−2	−1.6
	0	0
	2	−1.6
To the right of $x = 3$	4	4.6
	5	3.1

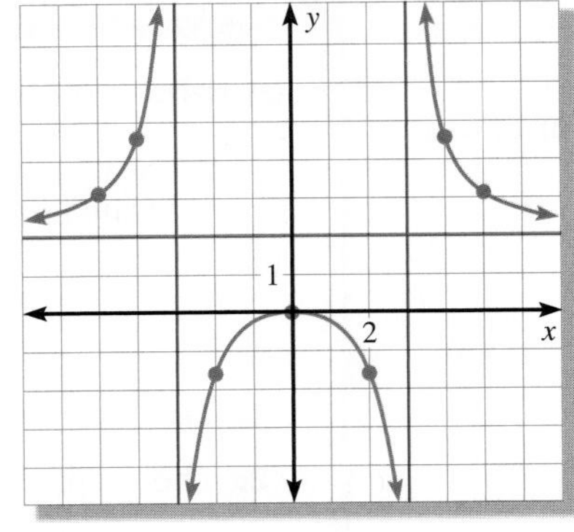

EXAMPLE 3 Graph a rational function ($m > n$)

Graph $y = \dfrac{x^2 + 3x - 4}{x - 2}$.

Solution

The numerator factors as $(x + 4)(x - 1)$, so the x-intercepts are -4 and 1. The zero of the denominator $x - 2$ is 2, so $x = 2$ is a vertical asymptote.

The degree of the numerator, 2, is greater than the degree of the denominator, 1, so the graph has no horizontal asymptote. The graph has the same end behavior as the graph of $y = x^{2-1} = x$. Plot points on each side of the vertical asymptote.

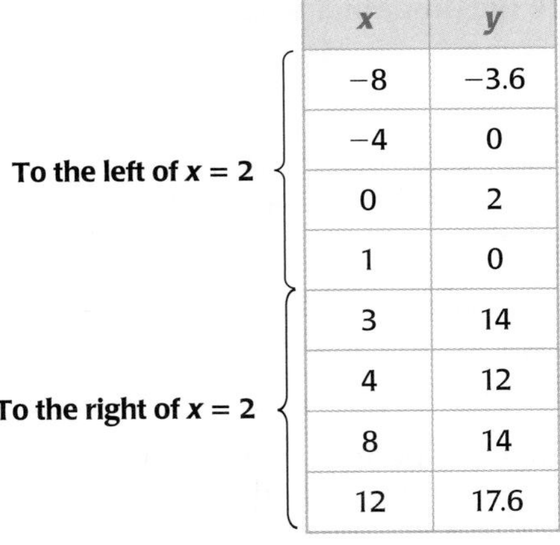

	x	y
To the left of $x = 2$	−8	−3.6
	−4	0
	0	2
	1	0
To the right of $x = 2$	3	14
	4	12
	8	14
	12	17.6

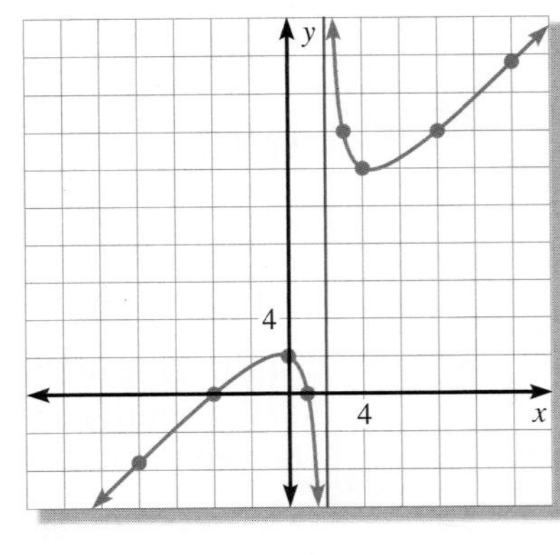

✓ GUIDED PRACTICE for Examples 1, 2, and 3

Graph the function.

1. $y = \dfrac{4}{x^2 + 2}$ **2.** $y = \dfrac{3x^2}{x^2 - 1}$ **3.** $f(x) = \dfrac{x^2 - 5}{x^2 + 1}$ **4.** $y = \dfrac{x^2 - 2x - 3}{x - 4}$

EXAMPLE 4 Solve a multi-step problem

MANUFACTURING A food manufacturer wants to find the most efficient packaging for a can of soup with a volume of 342 cubic centimeters. Find the dimensions of the can that has this volume and uses the least amount of material possible.

Solution

STEP 1 **Write** an equation that gives the height h of the soup can in terms of its radius r. Use the formula for the volume of a cylinder and the fact that the soup can's volume is 342 cubic centimeters.

$V = \pi r^2 h$	**Formula for volume of cylinder**
$342 = \pi r^2 h$	**Substitute 342 for *V*.**
$\dfrac{342}{\pi r^2} = h$	**Solve for *h*.**

STEP 2 **Write** a function that gives the surface area S of the soup can in terms of only its radius r.

$S = 2\pi r^2 + 2\pi rh$	**Formula for surface area of cylinder**
$= 2\pi r^2 + 2\pi r\left(\dfrac{342}{\pi r^2}\right)$	**Substitute $\dfrac{342}{\pi r^2}$ for *h*.**
$= 2\pi r^2 + \dfrac{684}{r}$	**Simplify.**

INTERPRET FUNCTIONS
The function for the surface area is a rational function because it can be written as a quotient of polynomials:

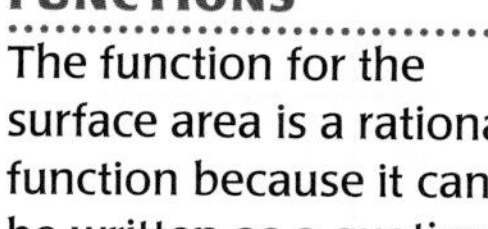

$S = \dfrac{2\pi r^3 + 684}{r}$

STEP 3 **Graph** the function for the surface area S using a graphing calculator. Then use the *minimum* feature to find the minimum value of S.

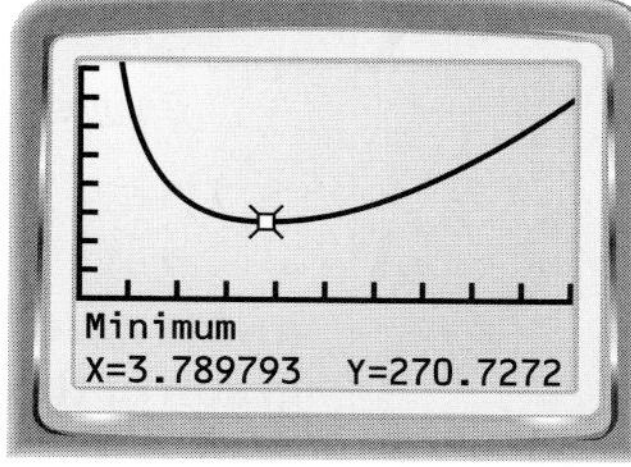

You get a minimum value of about 271, which occurs when $r \approx 3.79$ and

$h \approx \dfrac{342}{\pi(3.79)^2} \approx 7.58.$

▸ So, the soup can using the least amount of material has a radius of about 3.79 centimeters and a height of about 7.58 centimeters. Notice that the height and the diameter are equal for this can.

GUIDED PRACTICE for Example 4

5. WHAT IF? In Example 4, suppose the manufacturer wants to find the most efficient packaging for a soup can with a volume of 544 cubic centimeters. Find the dimensions of this can.

8.3 EXERCISES

HOMEWORK KEY

○ = **WORKED-OUT SOLUTIONS** on p. WS15 for Exs. 7, 15, and 33

★ = **STANDARDIZED TEST PRACTICE** Exs. 2, 6, 14, 24, and 35

◆ = **MULTIPLE REPRESENTATIONS** Ex. 33

SKILL PRACTICE

1. **VOCABULARY** Copy and complete: The graph of a rational function f has no _?_ when the degree of the function's numerator is greater than the degree of its denominator.

2. ★ **WRITING** Let $f(x) = \frac{p(x)}{q(x)}$ where $p(x)$ and $q(x)$ are polynomials with no common factors other than ± 1. *Describe* how to find the x-intercepts and the vertical asymptotes of the graph of f.

EXAMPLES 1, 2, and 3 on pp. 565–566 for Exs. 3–23

MATCHING GRAPHS **Match the function with its graph.**

3. $y = \frac{-10}{x^2 - 9}$

4. $y = \frac{x^2 - 10}{x^2 + 3}$

5. $y = \frac{x^3}{x^2 - 4}$

A. 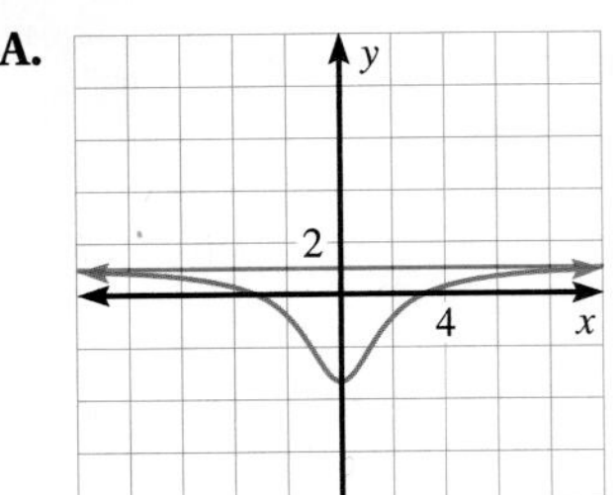

B. 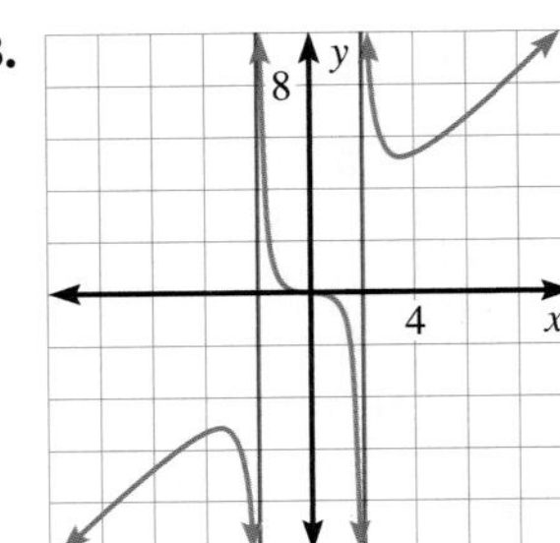

C. 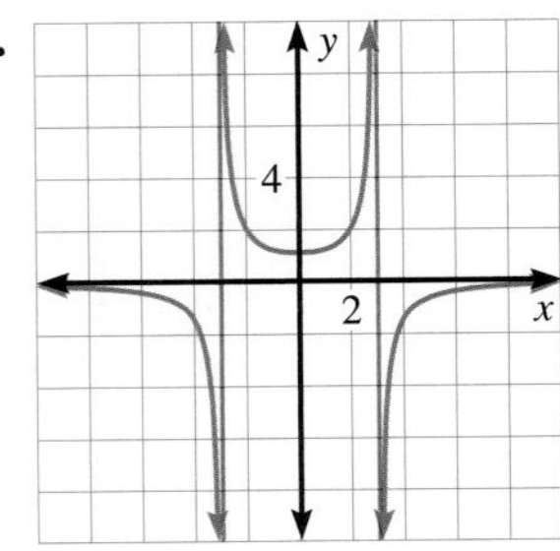

6. ★ **MULTIPLE CHOICE** The graph of which function is shown?

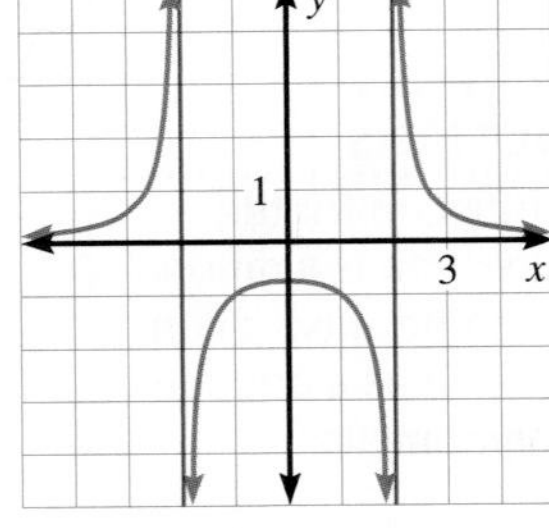

Ⓐ $y = \frac{3}{x^2 - 4}$

Ⓑ $y = \frac{3x^2}{x^2 - 4}$

Ⓒ $y = \frac{x^2 - 4}{3x^2}$

Ⓓ $y = \frac{x^3}{x^2 - 4}$

Animated Algebra at classzone.com

ANALYZING GRAPHS **Identify the x-intercept(s) and vertical asymptote(s) of the graph of the function.**

7. $y = \frac{5}{x^2 - 1}$

8. $y = \frac{x + 1}{x^2 + 5}$

9. $f(x) = \frac{x^2 + 9}{x^2 - 2x - 15}$

10. $y = \frac{x^2 - 7x - 60}{x + 3}$

11. $y = \frac{x^3 + 27}{3x^2 + x}$

12. $g(x) = \frac{2x^2 - 3x - 20}{x^2 + 1}$

13. **ERROR ANALYSIS** *Describe* and correct the error in finding the vertical asymptote(s) of $f(x) = \frac{x - 2}{x^2 - 8x + 7}$.

The vertical asymptote occurs at the zero of the numerator $x - 2$. So, the vertical asymptote is $x = 2$.

14. ★ **MULTIPLE CHOICE** What is the horizontal asymptote of the graph of the function $y = \frac{4x^2 - 21x + 5}{x^2 - 12}$?

Ⓐ $y = 0$ Ⓑ $y = \frac{1}{4}$ Ⓒ $y = 4$ Ⓓ $y = 4x$

GRAPHING FUNCTIONS Graph the function.

15. $y = \frac{2x}{x^2 - 1}$

16. $y = \frac{8}{x^2 - x - 6}$

17. $f(x) = \frac{x^2 - 9}{2x^2 + 1}$

18. $y = \frac{x - 4}{x^2 - 3x}$

19. $y = \frac{x^2 + 11x + 18}{2x + 1}$

20. $g(x) = \frac{x^3 - 8}{6 - x^2}$

21. $y = \frac{x^2 + 3}{2x^3}$

22. $y = \frac{x^2 - 5x - 36}{3x}$

23. $h(x) = \frac{3x^2 + 10x - 8}{x^2 + 4}$

24. ★ **OPEN-ENDED MATH** Write two different rational functions whose graphs have the same end behavior as the graph of $y = 3x^2$.

GRAPHING CALCULATOR Use a graphing calculator to find the range of the rational function.

25. $y = \frac{15}{x^2 + 2}$

26. $y = \frac{3x^2}{x^2 - 9}$

27. $y = \frac{x^2 - 2x}{2x + 3}$

CHALLENGE The graph of a function of the form $f(x) = \frac{a}{x^2 + b}$ is shown. Find the values of a and b.

28.

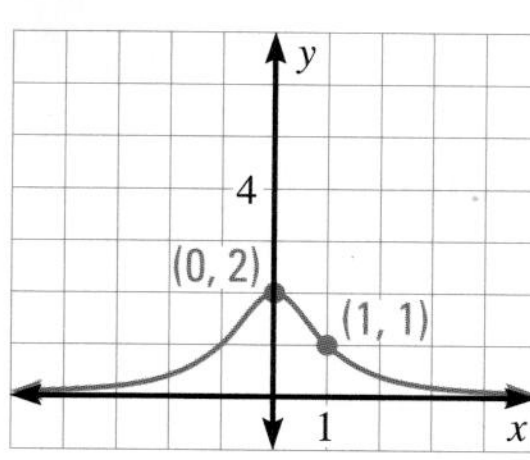

29.

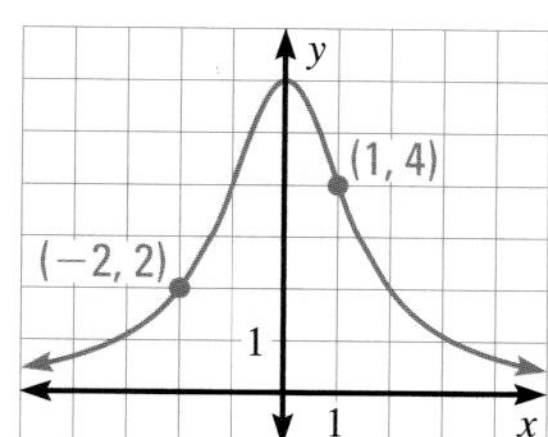

30.

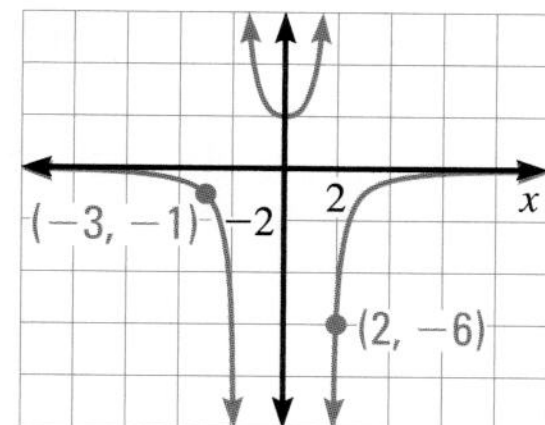

PROBLEM SOLVING

EXAMPLE 4
on p. 567
for Exs. 31–32

GRAPHING CALCULATOR You may wish to use a graphing calculator to complete the following Problem Solving exercises.

31. **AGRICULTURE** A farmer makes cylindrical bales of hay that have a volume of 100 cubic feet. Each bale is to be wrapped in plastic to keep the hay dry.

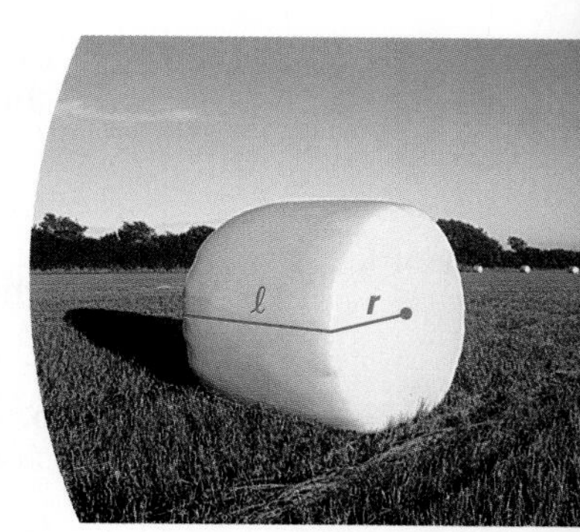

a. Using the formula for the volume of a cylinder, write an equation that gives the length ℓ of a bale in terms of the radius r.

b. Write a function that gives the surface area of a bale in terms of only the radius r.

c. Find the dimensions of a bale that has the given volume and uses the least amount of plastic possible when the bale is wrapped.

@HomeTutor for problem solving help at classzone.com

32. **AQUARIUM DESIGN** A manufacturer is designing an aquarium whose base is a regular hexagon. The aquarium should have a volume of 24 cubic feet and use the least amount of material possible. Let s be the length (in feet) of a side of the base, and let h be the height (in feet).

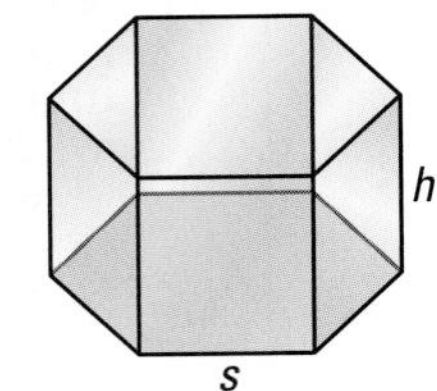

a. Write an equation that gives h in terms of s. (*Hint:* The volume of the aquarium is given by $V = \frac{3\sqrt{3}}{2}s^2h$.)

b. Find the dimensions s and h that minimize the amount of material used. (*Hint:* The surface area of the aquarium is given by $S = \frac{3\sqrt{3}}{2}s^2 + 6sh$.)

@HomeTutor for problem solving help at classzone.com

33. ◆ **MULTIPLE REPRESENTATIONS** The mean temperature T (in degrees Celsius) of the Atlantic Ocean between latitudes 40°N and 40°S can be modeled by

$$T = \frac{17{,}800d + 20{,}000}{3d^2 + 740d + 1000}$$

where d is the depth (in meters).

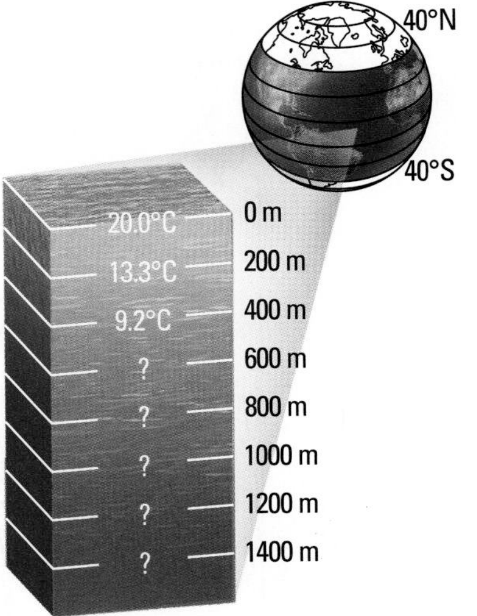

a. **Making a Table** Make a table of values showing the mean temperature for depths from 1000 meters to 1300 meters in 50 meter intervals.

b. **Using a Graph** Graph the model. Use your graph to estimate the depth at which the mean temperature is 4°C.

34. **MULTI-STEP PROBLEM** From 1993 to 2002, the number n (in billions) of shares of stock sold on the New York Stock Exchange can be modeled by

$$n = \frac{1054t + 6204}{-6.62t + 100}$$

where t is the number of years since 1993.

a. Graph the model.

b. *Describe* the general trends shown by the graph.

c. Estimate the year when the number of shares of stock sold was first greater than 100 billion.

35. ★ **EXTENDED RESPONSE** The acceleration due to gravity g (in meters per second squared) changes as altitude changes and is given by the function

$$g = \frac{3.99 \times 10^{14}}{h^2 + (1.28 \times 10^7)h + (4.07 \times 10^{13})}$$

where h is the altitude (in meters) above sea level.

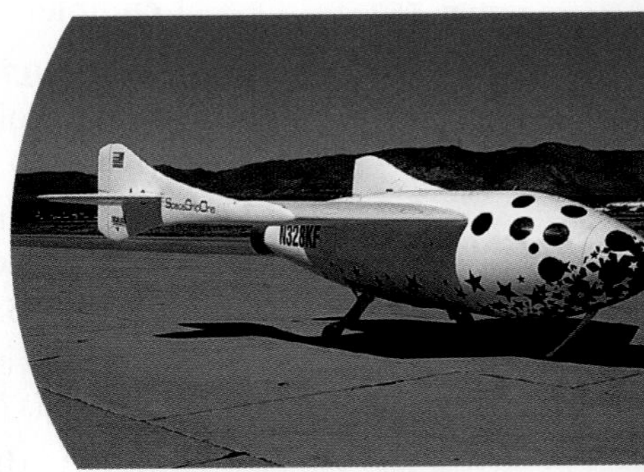

This spacecraft reached an altitude of 112 km in 2004.

a. **Graph** Graph the function.

b. **Apply** A mountaineer is climbing to a height of 8000 meters. What is the value of g at this altitude?

c. **Apply** A spacecraft reaches an altitude of 112 kilometers above Earth. What is the value of g at this altitude?

d. **Explain** *Describe* what happens to the value of g as altitude increases.

36. CHALLENGE You need to build a cylindrical water tank using 100 cubic feet of concrete. The sides and the base of the tank must be 1 foot thick.

a. Write an equation that gives the tank's inner height h in terms of its inner radius r.

b. Write an equation that gives the volume V of water that the tank can hold as a function of r.

c. Graph the equation from part (b). What values of r and h maximize the tank's capacity?

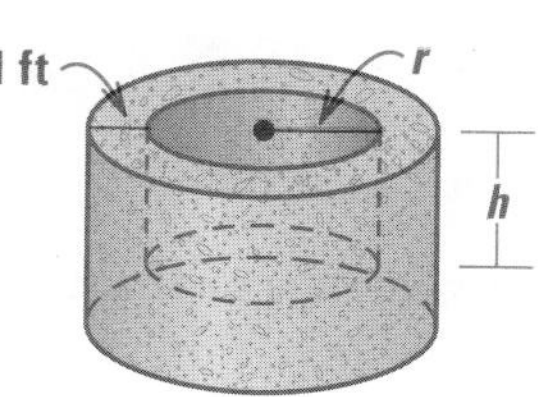

NEW YORK MIXED REVIEW

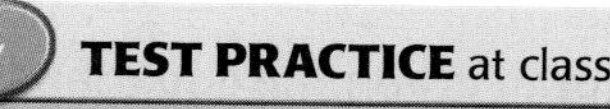

37. Doris plants a 75 square foot rectangular garden. She uses 36 feet of fencing to enclose the garden. What are the approximate dimensions of the garden?

Ⓐ 5.6 ft by 13.4 ft Ⓑ 5.7 ft by 12.3 ft Ⓒ 6.0 ft by 12.0 ft Ⓓ 6.6 ft by 11.4 ft

38. The circle graph represents 840 students. The red section of the circle graph represents the number of students who ride a bus to school everyday. How many students ride a bus to school everyday?

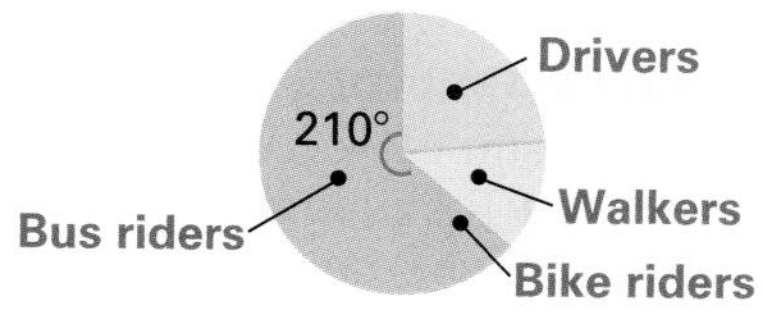

Ⓐ 176 Ⓑ 350

Ⓒ 490 Ⓓ 513

QUIZ for Lessons 8.1–8.3

The variables x and y vary inversely. Use the given values to write an equation relating x and y. Then find y when $x = -4$. *(p. 551)*

1. $x = 8, y = 3$ **2.** $x = 2, y = -9$ **3.** $x = -5, y = \frac{8}{3}$ **4.** $x = -\frac{1}{4}, y = -32$

Graph the function.

5. $y = \frac{3}{2x}$ *(p. 558)* **6.** $y = \frac{4}{x-2} + 1$ *(p. 558)* **7.** $f(x) = \frac{-2x}{3x-6}$ *(p. 558)*

8. $y = \frac{-8}{x^2-1}$ *(p. 565)* **9.** $y = \frac{x^2-6}{x^2+2}$ *(p. 565)* **10.** $g(x) = \frac{x^3-8}{2x^2}$ *(p. 565)*

11. SOFTBALL A pitcher throws 16 strikes in her first 38 pitches. The table shows how the pitcher's strike percentage changes if she throws x consecutive strikes after the first 38 pitches. Write a rational function for the strike percentage in terms of x. Graph the function. How many consecutive strikes must the pitcher throw to reach a strike percentage of 0.60? *(p. 558)*

x	Total strikes	Total pitches	Strike percentage
0	16	38	0.42
5	21	43	0.49
10	26	48	0.54
x	$x + 16$	$x + 38$	?

New York Mixed Review

TEST PRACTICE
classzone.com

Lessons 8.1–8.3

1. **EFFICIENT PACKAGING** A food manufacturer wants to find the most efficient packaging for a cylindrical canister of oatmeal with a volume of 1663 cubic centimeters. An equation that gives the canister's surface area S in terms of its radius r is $S = 2\pi r^2 + \frac{3326}{r}$. Use a graphing calculator to graph the equation. What is the approximate radius r of the canister that uses the least material possible?

   (1) 5.1 inches

   (2) 6.4 inches

   (3) 6.6 inches

   (4) 8.1 inches

2. **BODY MASS INDEX** The body mass index b of a person varies directly with the person's weight w (in kilograms) and inversely with the square of the person's height h (in meters). A person who is 1.6 meters tall and weighs 51.2 kilograms has a body mass index of 20. What is the approximate height of a person who weighs 45 kilograms and has a body mass index of 20?

   (1) 1.2 meters

   (2) 1.4 meters

   (3) 1.5 meters

   (4) 2.3 meters

3. **CANDY SALES** The number y of boxes of candy a manufacturer sells each month varies inversely with the price x (in dollars). In one month, the manufacturer sells 800 boxes of candy at a price of \$5 per box. About how many boxes of candy will the manufacturer sell at a price of \$7 per box?

   (1) 457 boxes (3) 643 boxes

   (2) 571 boxes (4) 686 boxes

4. **INVERSE VARIATION** Which equation represents inverse variation?

   (1) $y = x + 3$ (3) $y = \frac{x}{3}$

   (2) $y = 2x$ (4) $xy = 11$

5. **PLAYGROUND AREA** You are designing a rectangular playground that has an area of 200 square yards. A building borders the length of the playground. You use fencing for the other three sides. Which length ℓ and width w minimize the amount of fencing needed?

   (1) $\ell = 14$ yards; $w = 14$ yards

   (2) $\ell = 20$ yards; $w = 10$ yards

   (3) $\ell = 25$ yards; $w = 8$ yards

   (4) $\ell = 28$ yards; $w = 7$ yards

6. **PHOTO PRINTING** Your family buys a photo printer. The printer costs \$200. The ink and paper cost about \$.60 for each photo you print. Which equation gives the average cost C of a printed photo as a function of the number x of photos printed?

   (1) $C = \frac{200 - 0.6x}{x}$

   (2) $C = \frac{200 + 0.6x}{x}$

   (3) $C = 200 + 0.6x$

   (4) $C = 200.6x$

7. **OPEN-ENDED** The intensity I of a sound (in watts per square meter) varies inversely with the square of the distance d (in meters) from the source of the sound. At a distance of 1 meter from the stage, the intensity of the sound of a rock concert is about 10 watts per square meter. What is the intensity in watts per square meter of the sound you hear if you are 15 meters from the stage? Write your answer as a decimal rounded to the nearest hundredth.

8. **OPEN-ENDED** The value M (in dollars) of a motorcycle t years after it was purchased new can be estimated using the function $M(t) = \frac{3500}{t} + 500$, where $t \geq 1$.

   Estimate the motorcycle's value 5 years after it was purchased.

   What does the value of the motorcycle approach as time passes? *Explain.*

   Can you use this particular model to determine the initial price of the motorcycle? *Explain.*

8.4 Multiply and Divide Rational Expressions

 **A2.A.16** Perform arithmetic operations with rational expressions and rename to lowest terms

Before You graphed rational functions.

Now You will multiply and divide rational expressions.

Why? So you can compare the efficiencies of two designs, as in Ex. 51.

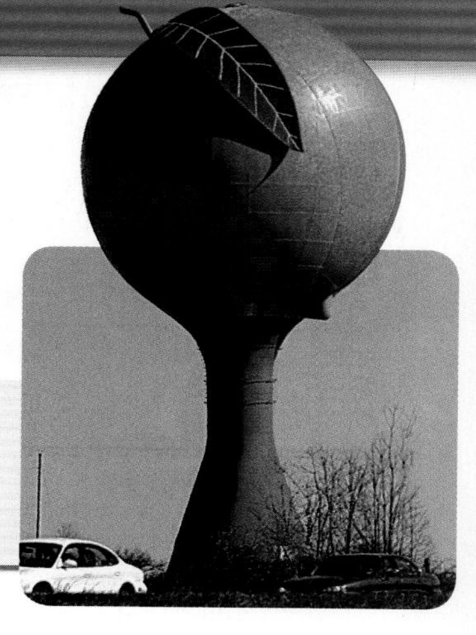

Key Vocabulary
- **simplified form of a rational expression**
- **reciprocal,** *p. 4*

A rational expression is in **simplified form** if its numerator and denominator have no common factors (other than ± 1). To simplify a rational expression, apply the following property.

KEY CONCEPT *For Your Notebook*

Simplifying Rational Expressions

Let a, b, and c be expressions with $b \neq 0$ and $c \neq 0$. Then the following property applies.

Property $\frac{a\cancel{c}}{b\cancel{c}} = \frac{a}{b}$ — Divide out the common factor c.

Examples $\frac{15}{65} = \frac{3 \cdot \cancel{5}}{13 \cdot \cancel{5}} = \frac{3}{13}$ — Divide out the common factor 5.

$\frac{4\cancel{(x+3)}}{(x-5)\cancel{(x+3)}} = \frac{4}{x-5}$ — Divide out the common factor $x + 3$.

Simplifying a rational expression usually requires two steps. First, factor the numerator and denominator. Then, divide out any factors that are common to both the numerator and denominator. Here is an example:

$$\frac{x^2 + 7x}{x^2} = \frac{\cancel{x}(x+7)}{\cancel{x} \cdot x} = \frac{x+7}{x}$$

Notice that you can divide out common factors in the second expression above. However, you cannot divide out like terms in the third expression.

EXAMPLE 1 Simplify a rational expression

Simplify: $\frac{x^2 - 2x - 15}{x^2 - 9}$

$\frac{x^2 - 2x - 15}{x^2 - 9} = \frac{(x+3)(x-5)}{(x+3)(x-3)}$ — Factor numerator and denominator.

$= \frac{\cancel{(x+3)}(x-5)}{\cancel{(x+3)}(x-3)}$ — Divide out common factor.

$= \frac{x-5}{x-3}$ — Simplified form

AVOID ERRORS
Do not divide out variable terms that are not factors.

$\frac{x-5}{x-3} \neq \frac{-5}{-3}$

EFFICIENCY Manufacturers often package their products in a way that uses the least amount of packaging material. One measure of the efficiency of a package is the ratio of its surface area to its volume. The smaller the ratio, the more efficient the packaging.

EXAMPLE 2 Solve a multi-step problem

PACKAGING A company makes a tin to hold flavored popcorn. The tin is a rectangular prism with a square base. The company is designing a new tin with the same base and twice the height of the old tin.

- Find the surface area and volume of each tin.
- Calculate the ratio of surface area to volume for each tin.
- What do the ratios tell you about the efficiencies of the two tins?

Solution

	Old tin	**New tin**	
STEP 1	$S = 2s^2 + 4sh$	$S = 2s^2 + 4s(2h)$	**Find surface area, *S*.**
		$= 2s^2 + 8sh$	
	$V = s^2h$	$V = s^2(2h)$	**Find volume, *V*.**
		$= 2s^2h$	
STEP 2	$\frac{S}{V} = \frac{2s^2 + 4sh}{s^2h}$	$\frac{S}{V} = \frac{2s^2 + 8sh}{2s^2h}$	**Write ratio of *S* to *V*.**
	$= \frac{\cancel{s}(2s + 4h)}{\cancel{s}(sh)}$	$= \frac{\cancel{2s}(s + 4h)}{\cancel{2s}(sh)}$	**Divide out common factor.**
	$= \frac{2s + 4h}{sh}$	$= \frac{s + 4h}{sh}$	**Simplified form**

STEP 3 $\frac{2s + 4h}{sh} > \frac{s + 4h}{sh}$ because the left side of the inequality has a greater numerator than the right side and both have the same (positive) denominator. The ratio of surface area to volume is *greater* for the old tin than for the new tin. So, the old tin is *less* efficient than the new tin.

✓ GUIDED PRACTICE for Examples 1 and 2

Simplify the expression, if possible.

1. $\frac{2(x + 1)}{(x + 1)(x + 3)}$

2. $\frac{40x + 20}{10x + 30}$

3. $\frac{4}{x(x + 2)}$

4. $\frac{x + 4}{x^2 - 16}$

5. $\frac{x^2 - 2x - 3}{x^2 - x - 6}$

6. $\frac{2x^2 + 10x}{3x^2 + 16x + 5}$

7. **WHAT IF?** In Example 2, suppose the new popcorn tin is the same height as the old tin but has a base with sides twice as long. What is the ratio of surface area to volume for this tin?

KEY CONCEPT *For Your Notebook*

Multiplying Rational Expressions

The rule for multiplying rational expressions is the same as the rule for multiplying numerical fractions: multiply numerators, multiply denominators, and write the new fraction in simplified form.

Let a, b, c, and d be expressions with $b \neq 0$ and $d \neq 0$.

Property $\frac{a}{b} \cdot \frac{c}{d} = \frac{ac}{bd}$ **Simplify $\frac{ac}{bd}$ if possible.**

Example $\frac{5x^2}{2xy^2} \cdot \frac{6xy^3}{10y} = \frac{30x^3y^3}{20xy^3} = \frac{\cancel{10} \cdot 3 \cdot \cancel{x} \cdot x^2 \cdot \cancel{y^3}}{\cancel{10} \cdot 2 \cdot \cancel{x} \cdot \cancel{y^3}} = \frac{3x^2}{2}$

EXAMPLE 3 Standardized Test Practice

What is a simplified form of $\frac{8x^3y}{2xy^2} \cdot \frac{7x^4y^3}{4y}$?

Ⓐ $\frac{5}{2}x^6y$ Ⓑ $7x^6y$ Ⓒ $7x^{11}y$ Ⓓ $7x^7y^{4/3}$

ANOTHER WAY

In Example 3, you can also first simplify each fraction, then multiply, and finally simplify the result:

$$\frac{8x^3y}{2xy^2} \cdot \frac{7x^4y^3}{4y} = \frac{4x^2}{y} \cdot \frac{7x^4y^2}{4} = \frac{\cancel{4} \cdot 7 \cdot x^6 \cdot \cancel{y} \cdot y}{\cancel{4} \cdot \cancel{y}} = 7x^6y$$

Solution

$\frac{8x^3y}{2xy^2} \cdot \frac{7x^4y^3}{4y} = \frac{56x^7y^4}{8xy^3}$ **Multiply numerators and denominators.**

$= \frac{\cancel{8} \cdot 7 \cdot \cancel{x} \cdot x^6 \cdot \cancel{y^3} \cdot y}{\cancel{8} \cdot \cancel{x} \cdot \cancel{y^3}}$ **Factor and divide out common factors.**

$= 7x^6y$ **Simplified form**

▶ The correct answer is B. Ⓐ Ⓑ Ⓒ Ⓓ

EXAMPLE 4 Multiply rational expressions

Multiply: $\frac{3x - 3x^2}{x^2 + 4x - 5} \cdot \frac{x^2 + x - 20}{3x}$

$\frac{3x - 3x^2}{x^2 + 4x - 5} \cdot \frac{x^2 + x - 20}{3x} = \frac{3x(1 - x)}{(x - 1)(x + 5)} \cdot \frac{(x + 5)(x - 4)}{3x}$ **Factor numerators and denominators.**

$= \frac{3x(1 - x)(x + 5)(x - 4)}{(x - 1)(x + 5)(3x)}$ **Multiply numerators and denominators.**

$= \frac{3x(-1)(x - 1)(x + 5)(x - 4)}{(x - 1)(x + 5)(3x)}$ **Rewrite $1 - x$ as $(-1)(x - 1)$.**

$= \frac{\cancel{3x}(-1)\cancel{(x - 1)}\cancel{(x + 5)}(x - 4)}{\cancel{(x - 1)}\cancel{(x + 5)}\cancel{(3x)}}$ **Divide out common factors.**

$= (-1)(x - 4)$ **Simplify.**

$= -x + 4$ **Multiply.**

EXAMPLE 5 Multiply a rational expression by a polynomial

Multiply: $\frac{x+2}{x^3-27} \cdot (x^2+3x+9)$

$$\frac{x+2}{x^3-27} \cdot (x^2+3x+9) = \frac{x+2}{x^3-27} \cdot \frac{x^2+3x+9}{1}$$ Write polynomial as a rational expression.

$$= \frac{(x+2)(x^2+3x+9)}{(x-3)(x^2+3x+9)}$$ Factor denominator.

$$= \frac{(x+2)\cancel{(x^2+3x+9)}}{(x-3)\cancel{(x^2+3x+9)}}$$ Divide out common factors.

$$= \frac{x+2}{x-3}$$ Simplified form

GUIDED PRACTICE for Examples 3, 4, and 5

Multiply the expressions. Simplify the result.

8. $\frac{3x^5y^2}{8xy} \cdot \frac{6xy^2}{9x^3y}$

9. $\frac{2x^2-10x}{x^2-25} \cdot \frac{x+3}{2x^2}$

10. $\frac{x+5}{x^3-1} \cdot (x^2+x+1)$

KEY CONCEPT *For Your Notebook*

Dividing Rational Expressions

To divide one rational expression by another, multiply the first rational expression by the reciprocal of the second rational expression.

Let a, b, c, and d be expressions with $b \neq 0$, $c \neq 0$ and $d \neq 0$.

Property $\frac{a}{b} \div \frac{c}{d} = \frac{a}{b} \cdot \frac{d}{c} = \frac{ad}{bc}$ Simplify $\frac{ad}{bc}$ if possible.

Examples $\frac{2}{5} \div \frac{7}{3} = \frac{2}{5} \cdot \frac{3}{7} = \frac{6}{35}$

$\frac{7}{x+1} \div \frac{x+2}{2x-3} = \frac{7}{x+1} \cdot \frac{2x-3}{x+2} = \frac{7(2x-3)}{(x+1)(x+2)}$

EXAMPLE 6 Divide rational expressions

Divide: $\frac{7x}{2x-10} \div \frac{x^2-6x}{x^2-11x+30}$

$$\frac{7x}{2x-10} \div \frac{x^2-6x}{x^2-11x+30} = \frac{7x}{2x-10} \cdot \frac{x^2-11x+30}{x^2-6x}$$ Multiply by reciprocal.

$$= \frac{7x}{2(x-5)} \cdot \frac{(x-5)(x-6)}{x(x-6)}$$ Factor.

$$= \frac{7\cancel{x}\cancel{(x-5)}\cancel{(x-6)}}{2\cancel{(x-5)}\cancel{(x)}\cancel{(x-6)}}$$ Divide out common factors.

$$= \frac{7}{2}$$ Simplified form

EXAMPLE 7 Divide a rational expression by a polynomial

Divide: $\frac{6x^2 + x - 15}{4x^2} \div (3x^2 + 5x)$

$$\frac{6x^2 + x - 15}{4x^2} \div (3x^2 + 5x) = \frac{6x^2 + x - 15}{4x^2} \cdot \frac{1}{3x^2 + 5x}$$ Multiply by reciprocal.

$$= \frac{(3x + 5)(2x - 3)}{4x^2} \cdot \frac{1}{x(3x + 5)}$$ Factor.

$$= \frac{\cancel{(3x + 5)}(2x - 3)}{4x^2(x)\cancel{(3x + 5)}}$$ Divide out common factors.

$$= \frac{2x - 3}{4x^3}$$ Simplified form

✓ GUIDED PRACTICE for Examples 6 and 7

Divide the expressions. Simplify the result.

11. $\frac{4x}{5x - 20} \div \frac{x^2 - 2x}{x^2 - 6x + 8}$

12. $\frac{2x^2 + 3x - 5}{6x} \div (2x^2 + 5x)$

8.4 EXERCISES

HOMEWORK KEY
○ = **WORKED-OUT SOLUTIONS** on p. WS15 for Exs. 7, 25, and 49
★ = **STANDARDIZED TEST PRACTICE** Exs. 2, 20, 23, 50, and 52

SKILL PRACTICE

1. **VOCABULARY** Copy and complete: To divide one rational expression by another, multiply the first rational expression by the _?_ of the second rational expression.

2. ★ **WRITING** How do you know when a rational expression is simplified?

EXAMPLE 1 on p. 573 for Exs. 3–20

REASONING **Match the rational expression with its simplified form.**

3. $\frac{x^2 - 9x + 14}{x^2 - 5x - 14}$

4. $\frac{x^2 - 4}{x^2 + 9x + 14}$

5. $\frac{x^2 + 5x - 14}{x^2 - 4x + 4}$

A. $\frac{x - 2}{x + 7}$

B. $\frac{x - 2}{x + 2}$

C. $\frac{x + 7}{x - 2}$

SIMPLIFYING **Simplify the rational expression, if possible.**

6. $\frac{4x^2}{20x^2 - 12x}$

7. $\frac{x^2 - x - 20}{x^2 + 2x - 15}$

8. $\frac{x^2 + 2x - 24}{x^2 + 7x + 6}$

9. $\frac{x^2 - 11x + 24}{x^2 - 3x - 40}$

10. $\frac{x^2 + 4x + 4}{x^2 - 5x + 4}$

11. $\frac{2x^2 + 2x - 4}{x^2 - 5x - 14}$

12. $\frac{x - 4}{x^3 - 64}$

13. $\frac{x^2 - 36}{x^2 + 12x + 36}$

14. $\frac{3x^3 + 6x^2 + 12x}{x^3 - 8}$

15. $\frac{8x^2 + 10x - 3}{6x^2 + 13x + 6}$

16. $\frac{5x^2 + 18x - 8}{10x^2 - x - 2}$

17. $\frac{x^3 - 5x^2 - 3x + 15}{x^2 - 8x + 15}$

ERROR ANALYSIS ***Describe*** **and correct the error in simplifying the rational expression.**

18. $\dfrac{\cancel{x^2} + 16x - 80}{\cancel{x^2} - 16} = \dfrac{16x - 80}{-16} = -x + 5$ ✗

19. $\dfrac{x^2 + \cancel{16}x + \cancel{48}}{x^2 + \cancel{8}x + \cancel{16}} = \dfrac{x^2 + 2x + 3}{x^2 + x + 1}$ ✗

20. ★ **MULTIPLE CHOICE** Which rational expression is in simplified form?

Ⓐ $\dfrac{x^2 - x - 6}{x^2 + 3x + 2}$ Ⓑ $\dfrac{x^2 + 6x + 8}{x^2 + 2x - 3}$ Ⓒ $\dfrac{x^2 - 6x + 9}{x^2 - 2x - 3}$ Ⓓ $\dfrac{x^2 + 3x - 4}{x^2 + x - 2}$

EXAMPLE 2 on p. 574 for Exs. 21–23

GEOMETRY **A farmer wants to fence in the field shown. Write a simplified rational expression for the ratio of the field's perimeter to its area.**

21.

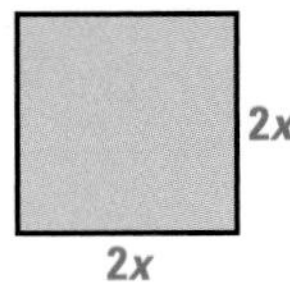

22.

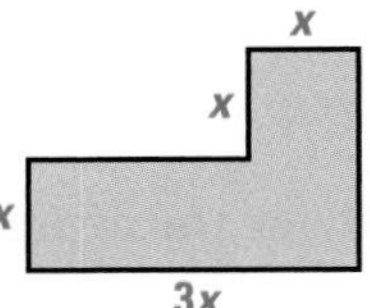

23. ★ **SHORT RESPONSE** Which of the fields in Exercises 21 and 22 has the lower fencing cost per unit of area? *Explain.*

EXAMPLES 3, 4, and 5 on pp. 575–576 for Exs. 24–33

MULTIPLYING **Multiply the expressions. Simplify the result.**

24. $\dfrac{5x^3y}{x^2y^2} \cdot \dfrac{y^3}{15x^2}$

25. $\dfrac{48x^5y^3}{y^4} \cdot \dfrac{x^2y}{6x^3y^2}$

26. $\dfrac{x(x-3)}{x-2} \cdot \dfrac{(x+3)(x-2)}{x}$

27. $\dfrac{4(x+5)}{x^2} \cdot \dfrac{x(x+1)}{2(x+5)}$

28. $\dfrac{3x-12}{x+5} \cdot \dfrac{x+6}{2x-8}$

29. $\dfrac{x+5}{4x-16} \cdot \dfrac{2x^2-32}{x^2-25}$

30. $\dfrac{x^2+3x-4}{x^2+4x+4} \cdot \dfrac{2x^2+4x}{x^2-4x+3}$

31. $\dfrac{x^2-3x-10}{x^2-2x-15} \cdot (x^2+10x+21)$

32. $\dfrac{x^2+5x-36}{x^2-49} \cdot (x^2-11x+28)$

33. $\dfrac{4x^2+20x}{x^3+4x^2} \cdot (x^2+8x+16)$

EXAMPLES 6 and 7 on pp. 576–577 for Exs. 34–43

DIVIDING **Divide the expressions. Simplify the result.**

34. $\dfrac{5x^2y^3}{x^7} \div \dfrac{30xy^4}{y^3}$

35. $\dfrac{8x^2y^2z}{xz^3} \div \dfrac{10xy}{x^4z}$

36. $\dfrac{(x+3)(x-2)}{x(x+1)} \div \dfrac{x+3}{x}$

37. $\dfrac{8x^2}{x+4} \div \dfrac{x}{2(x-4)}$

38. $\dfrac{x^2-6x-27}{2x^2+2x} \div \dfrac{x^2-14x+45}{x^2}$

39. $\dfrac{x^2-4x-5}{x+5} \div (x^2+6x+5)$

40. $\dfrac{3x^2+13x+4}{x^2-4} \div \dfrac{4x+16}{x+2}$

41. $\dfrac{x^2-x-2}{x^2+4x-5} \div \dfrac{x-2}{5x+25}$

42. $\dfrac{x^2-8x+15}{x^2+4x} \div (x^2-x-20)$

43. $\dfrac{x^2+12x+32}{6x+42} \div \dfrac{x^2+4x}{x^2-49}$

○ = WORKED-OUT SOLUTIONS on p. WS1 ★ = STANDARDIZED TEST PRACTICE

POINT DISCONTINUITY In Exercises 44–46, use the following information.

The graph of a rational function can have a hole in it, called a *point discontinuity,* where the function is undefined. An example is shown below.

$$y = \frac{x^2 - 16}{x + 4} = \frac{(x + 4)(x - 4)}{x + 4} = x - 4$$

The graph of $y = \frac{x^2 - 16}{x + 4}$ is the same as the graph of $y = x - 4$ except that there is a hole at $(-4, -8)$ because the rational function is not defined when $x = -4$.

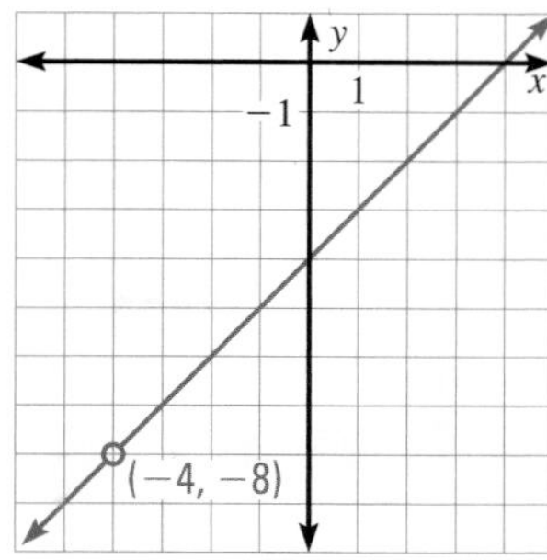

Graph the rational function. Use an open circle for a point discontinuity.

44. $y = \frac{x^2 + 10x + 21}{x + 3}$

45. $y = \frac{x^2 - 36}{x - 6}$

46. $y = \frac{2x^2 - x - 10}{x + 2}$

47. CHALLENGE Find the ratio of the perimeter to the area of the triangle shown at the right.

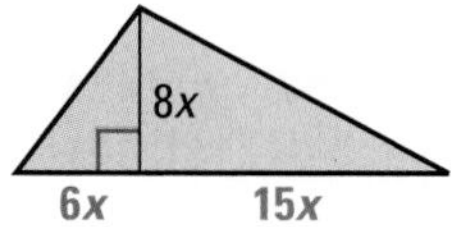

PROBLEM SOLVING

EXAMPLE 2 on p. 574 for Exs. 48, 50–52

48. GEOMETRY Find the ratio of the volume of the square pyramid to the volume of the inscribed cone. Write your answer in simplified form.

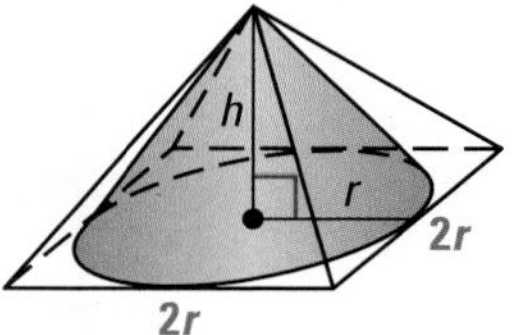

@HomeTutor for problem solving help at classzone.com

49. ENTERTAINMENT From 1992 to 2002, the gross ticket sales S (in millions of dollars) to Broadway shows and the total attendance A (in millions) at the shows can be modeled by

$$S = \frac{-6420t + 292{,}000}{6.02t^2 - 125t + 1000} \quad \text{and} \quad A = \frac{-407t + 7220}{5.92t^2 - 131t + 1000}$$

where t is the number of years since 1992. Write a model for the *average* dollar amount a person paid per ticket as a function of the year. What was the average amount a person paid per ticket in 1999?

@HomeTutor for problem solving help at classzone.com

50. ★ SHORT RESPONSE Almost all of the energy generated by a long-distance runner is released in the form of heat. For a runner with height H and speed V, the rate h_g of heat generated and the rate h_r of heat released can be modeled by $h_g = k_1H^3V^2$ and $h_r = k_2H^2$ where k_1 and k_2 are constants.

a. Write the ratio of heat generated to heat released. Simplify the expression.

b. When the ratio of heat generated to heat released equals 1, how is speed related to height? Does a taller or shorter runner have the advantage? *Explain.*

Thermogram of runner

51. **MULTI-STEP PROBLEM** A manufacturer is comparing two designs for a water tower: a sphere and a cylinder. Both designs have the same volume and the same radius.

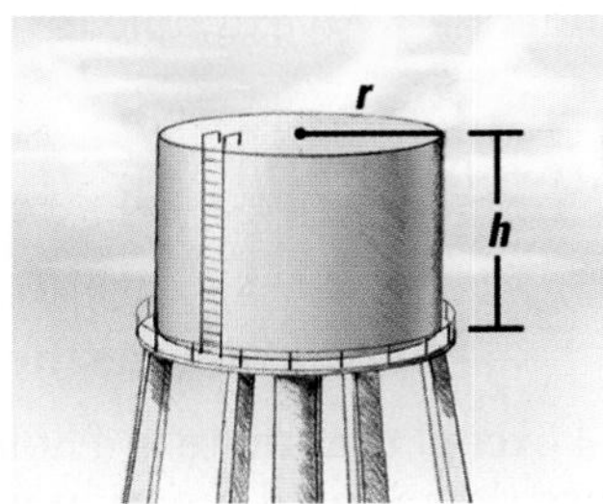

a. Show that the height h of the cylindrical tank is $\frac{4}{3}r$.

b. Write an expression for the surface area of each tank in terms of r.

c. Find the ratio of the surface area of the spherical tank to the surface area of the cylindrical tank. *Explain* what the ratio tells you about which water tower would take less material to build.

52. ★ **EXTENDED RESPONSE** The surface area S and the volume V of a cylindrical can are given by $S = 2\pi r^2 + 2\pi rh$ and $V = \pi r^2 h$ where r is the radius and h is the height.

a. **Model** Write and simplify an expression for the efficiency ratio $\frac{S}{V}$.

b. **Calculate** Find the efficiency ratio for each can listed in the table.

	Soup can	Coffee can	Paint can
Height, h	10.2 cm	15.9 cm	19.4 cm
Radius, r	3.4 cm	7.8 cm	8.4 cm

c. **Compare** Rank the three cans in part (b) according to efficiency. *Explain* your ranking.

53. **CHALLENGE** A fuel storage container is shaped like a cylinder with a hemisphere on each end, as shown. The length of the cylinder is ℓ and the radius of each hemisphere is r. Show that the ratio of the surface area to the volume of the container is $\frac{6(2r + \ell)}{r(4r + 3\ell)}$.

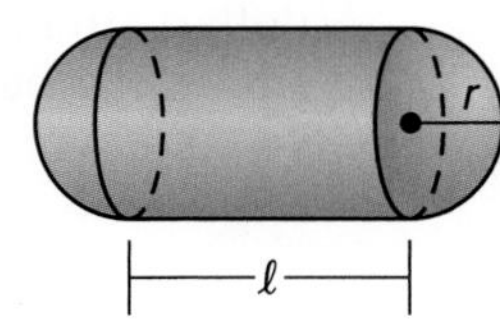

NEW YORK MIXED REVIEW

TEST PRACTICE at classzone.com

54. Which expression is equivalent to $3y[4 - (y + 2)] + 5y(y - 3)$?

Ⓐ $2y^2 - 9y$ Ⓑ $2y^2 - 3y$ Ⓒ $2y - 9$ Ⓓ $2y^2 - 6y + 15$

55. Each year about 6800 freshmen attend the University of Texas. This is about 16% of the total enrollment. About how many students attend the University of Texas?

Ⓐ 17,700 Ⓑ 41,300 Ⓒ 42,500 Ⓓ 46,000

@HomeTutor
classzone.com
Keystrokes

8.4 Verify Operations with Rational Expressions

QUESTION How can you use a graphing calculator to verify the results of operations on rational expressions?

EXAMPLE Check a simplified rational expression in two ways

Simplify $\frac{x^2 - x - 12}{x^2 - 9x + 20}$. Then verify the result numerically and graphically.

STEP 1 *Simplify expression*

Simplify the rational expression by factoring the numerator and denominator, then dividing out common factors.

$$\frac{x^2 - x - 12}{x^2 - 9x + 20} = \frac{\cancel{(x-4)}(x+3)}{\cancel{(x-4)}(x-5)} = \frac{x+3}{x-5}$$

STEP 2 *Enter expressions*

Enter the original expression as y_1 and the simplified result as y_2. Use the *thick* graph style for y_2.

```
\Y1=(X2-X-12)/
  (X2-9X+20)
\Y2=(X+3)/(X-5)
\Y3=
\Y4=
\Y5=
\Y6=
```

Remember to use parentheses correctly.

STEP 3 *Display table*

Use the *table* feature to examine corresponding values of the two expressions.

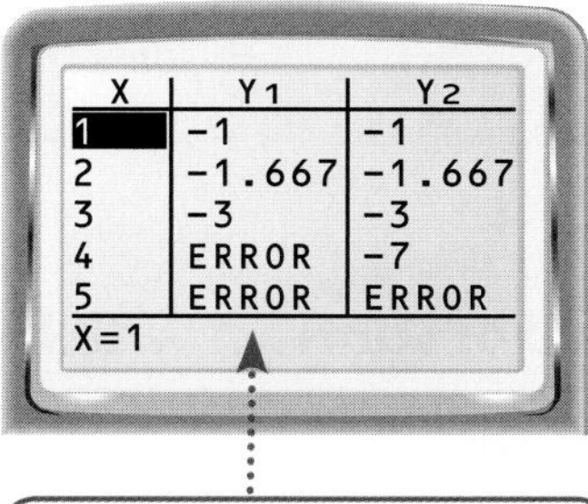

X	Y1	Y2
1	-1	-1
2	-1.667	-1.667
3	-3	-3
4	ERROR	-7
5	ERROR	ERROR
X=1		

The values of y_1 and y_2 are the same, except that y_1 is undefined when $x = 4$ and $x = 5$, and y_2 is undefined only when $x = 5$.

STEP 4 *Display graphs*

Put your calculator in *connected* mode. Display the graphs in an appropriate viewing window.

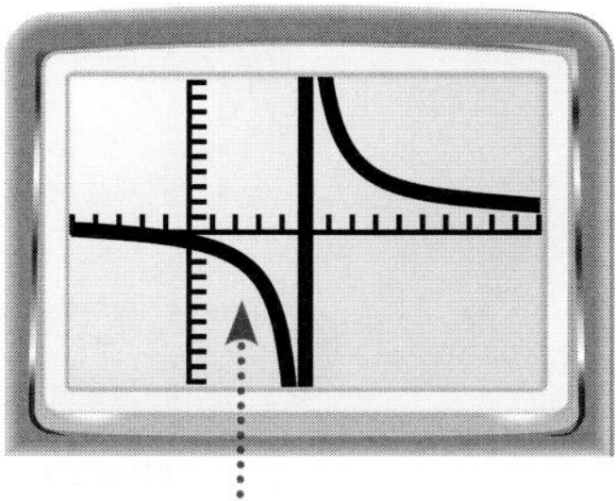

By using the *thick* graph style for y_2, you can see the graph of y_2 being drawn over the graph of y_1. So, the graphs coincide.

PRACTICE

Simplify the expression. Verify your result numerically and graphically.

1. $\frac{x^2 - 5x}{x^2 - 7x + 10}$
2. $\frac{3x^2 + 6x}{x^2 - 2x - 8}$
3. $\frac{x^2 + 5x + 4}{x^2 + x - 12}$

Perform the indicated operation and simplify. Verify your result numerically and graphically.

4. $\frac{x + 3}{5x^2} \cdot \frac{x - 1}{x + 3}$
5. $\frac{4x^2 - 8x}{5x + 15} \div \frac{x - 2}{x + 3}$
6. $\frac{x^2 - 3x - 10}{x^2 + 3x + 3} \cdot \frac{x^2 + 2x - 3}{x^2 + x - 2}$

8.5 Add and Subtract Rational Expressions

A2.A.16 Perform arithmetic operations with rational expressions and rename to lowest terms

Before You multiplied and divided rational expressions.

Now You will add and subtract rational expressions.

Why? So you can determine monthly car loan payments, as in Ex. 43.

Key Vocabulary
- **complex fraction**

As with numerical fractions, the procedure used to add (or subtract) two rational expressions depends upon whether the expressions have *like* or *unlike* denominators.

KEY CONCEPT *For Your Notebook*

Adding or Subtracting with Like Denominators

To add (or subtract) rational expressions with *like* denominators, simply add (or subtract) their numerators. Then place the result over the common denominator.

Let a, b, and c be expressions with $c \neq 0$.

	Addition	**Subtraction**
Properties	$\frac{a}{c} + \frac{b}{c} = \frac{a+b}{c}$	$\frac{a}{c} - \frac{b}{c} = \frac{a-b}{c}$
Examples	$\frac{3x}{5x^2} + \frac{7}{5x^2} = \frac{3x+7}{5x^2}$	$\frac{9x^3}{x+1} - \frac{x^2}{x+1} = \frac{9x^3 - x^2}{x+1}$

EXAMPLE 1 Add or subtract with like denominators

Perform the indicated operation.

a. $\frac{7}{4x} + \frac{3}{4x}$ **b.** $\frac{2x}{x+6} - \frac{5}{x+6}$

Solution

a. $\frac{7}{4x} + \frac{3}{4x} = \frac{7+3}{4x} = \frac{10}{4x} = \frac{5}{2x}$ **Add numerators and simplify result.**

b. $\frac{2x}{x+6} - \frac{5}{x+6} = \frac{2x-5}{x+6}$ **Subtract numerators.**

GUIDED PRACTICE for Example 1

Perform the indicated operation and simplify.

1. $\frac{7}{12x} - \frac{5}{12x}$ **2.** $\frac{2}{3x^2} + \frac{1}{3x^2}$ **3.** $\frac{4x}{x-2} - \frac{x}{x-2}$ **4.** $\frac{2x^2}{x^2+1} + \frac{2}{x^2+1}$

KEY CONCEPT — *For Your Notebook*

Adding or Subtracting with Unlike Denominators

To add (or subtract) two rational expressions with *unlike* denominators, find a common denominator. Rewrite each rational expression using the common denominator. Then add (or subtract).

Let a, b, c, and d be expressions with $c \neq 0$ and $d \neq 0$.

Addition

$$\frac{a}{c} + \frac{b}{d} = \frac{ad}{cd} + \frac{bc}{cd} = \frac{ad + bc}{cd}$$

Subtraction

$$\frac{a}{c} - \frac{b}{d} = \frac{ad}{cd} - \frac{bc}{cd} = \frac{ad - bc}{cd}$$

You can always find a common denominator of two rational expressions by multiplying their denominators, as shown above. However, if you use the least common denominator (LCD), which is the least common multiple (LCM) of the denominators, you may have less simplifying to do.

EXAMPLE 2 Find a least common multiple (LCM)

Find the least common multiple of $4x^2 - 16$ and $6x^2 - 24x + 24$.

Solution

STEP 1 **Factor** each polynomial. Write numerical factors as products of primes.

$$4x^2 - 16 = 4(x^2 - 4) = (2^2)(x + 2)(x - 2)$$

$$6x^2 - 24x + 24 = 6(x^2 - 4x + 4) = (2)(3)(x - 2)^2$$

STEP 2 **Form** the LCM by writing each factor to the highest power it occurs in either polynomial.

$$\text{LCM} = (2^2)(3)(x + 2)(x - 2)^2 = 12(x + 2)(x - 2)^2$$

EXAMPLE 3 Add with unlike denominators

Add: $\frac{7}{9x^2} + \frac{x}{3x^2 + 3x}$

REVIEW LCDS

For help with finding least common denominators, see p. 986.

Solution

To find the LCD, factor each denominator and write each factor to the highest power it occurs. Note that $9x^2 = 3^2x^2$ and $3x^2 + 3x = 3x(x + 1)$, so the LCD is $3^2x^2(x + 1) = 9x^2(x + 1)$.

$$\frac{7}{9x^2} + \frac{x}{3x^2 + 3x} = \frac{7}{9x^2} + \frac{x}{3x(x + 1)}$$ **Factor second denominator.**

$$= \frac{7}{9x^2} \cdot \frac{x + 1}{x + 1} + \frac{x}{3x(x + 1)} \cdot \frac{3x}{3x}$$ **LCD is $9x^2(x + 1)$.**

$$= \frac{7x + 7}{9x^2(x + 1)} + \frac{3x^2}{9x^2(x + 1)}$$ **Multiply.**

$$= \frac{3x^2 + 7x + 7}{9x^2(x + 1)}$$ **Add numerators.**

EXAMPLE 4 Subtract with unlike denominators

Subtract: $\frac{x+2}{2x-2} - \frac{-2x-1}{x^2-4x+3}$

Solution

$$\frac{x+2}{2x-2} - \frac{-2x-1}{x^2-4x+3}$$

$$= \frac{x+2}{2(x-1)} - \frac{-2x-1}{(x-1)(x-3)}$$ **Factor denominators.**

$$= \frac{x+2}{2(x-1)} \cdot \frac{x-3}{x-3} - \frac{-2x-1}{(x-1)(x-3)} \cdot \frac{2}{2}$$ **LCD is $2(x-1)(x-3)$.**

$$= \frac{x^2-x-6}{2(x-1)(x-3)} - \frac{-4x-2}{2(x-1)(x-3)}$$ **Multiply.**

$$= \frac{x^2-x-6-(-4x-2)}{2(x-1)(x-3)}$$ **Subtract numerators.**

$$= \frac{x^2+3x-4}{2(x-1)(x-3)}$$ **Simplify numerator.**

$$= \frac{\cancel{(x-1)}(x+4)}{2\cancel{(x-1)}(x-3)}$$ **Factor numerator. Divide out common factor.**

$$= \frac{x+4}{2(x-3)}$$ **Simplify.**

AVOID ERRORS
After you simplify the numerator, check to see if the numerator has a factor in common with the denominator. If so, the expression can be simplified further.

✓ GUIDED PRACTICE for Examples 2, 3, and 4

Find the least common multiple of the polynomials.

5. $5x^3$ and $10x^2 - 15x$

6. $8x - 16$ and $12x^2 + 12x - 72$

Perform the indicated operation and simplify.

7. $\frac{3}{4x} - \frac{1}{7}$

8. $\frac{1}{3x^2} + \frac{x}{9x^2-12x}$

9. $\frac{x}{x^2-x-12} + \frac{5}{12x-48}$

10. $\frac{x+1}{x^2+4x+4} - \frac{6}{x^2-4}$

KEY CONCEPT *For Your Notebook*

Simplifying Complex Fractions

A **complex fraction** is a fraction that contains a fraction in its numerator or denominator. A complex fraction can be simplified using either of the methods below.

Method 1: If necessary, simplify the numerator and denominator by writing each as a single fraction. Then divide the numerator by the denominator.

Method 2: Multiply the numerator and the denominator by the least common denominator (LCD) of *every* fraction in the numerator and denominator. Then simplify.

EXAMPLE 5 Simplify a complex fraction (Method 1)

PHYSICS Let f be the focal length of a thin camera lens, p be the distance between an object being photographed and the lens, and q be the distance between the lens and the film. For the photograph to be in focus, the variables should satisfy the *lens equation* below. Simplify the complex fraction.

Lens equation: $f = \dfrac{1}{\frac{1}{p} + \frac{1}{q}}$

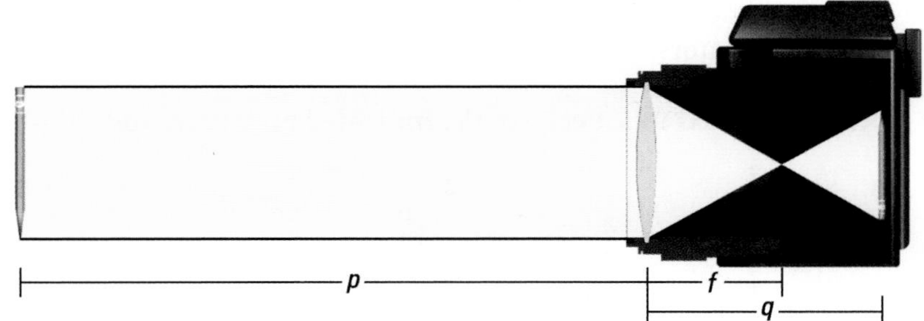

Solution

$$f = \frac{1}{\frac{1}{p} + \frac{1}{q}} = \frac{1}{\frac{q}{pq} + \frac{p}{pq}} = \frac{1}{\frac{q+p}{pq}}$$ **Write denominator as a single fraction.**

$$= \frac{pq}{q+p}$$ **Divide numerator by denominator.**

EXAMPLE 6 Simplify a complex fraction (Method 2)

Simplify: $\dfrac{\frac{5}{x+4}}{\frac{1}{x+4} + \frac{2}{x}}$

Solution

The LCD of all the fractions in the numerator and denominator is $x(x + 4)$.

$$\frac{\frac{5}{x+4}}{\frac{1}{x+4} + \frac{2}{x}} = \frac{\frac{5}{x+4}}{\frac{1}{x+4} + \frac{2}{x}} \cdot \frac{x(x+4)}{x(x+4)}$$ **Multiply numerator and denominator by the LCD.**

$$= \frac{5x}{x + 2(x+4)}$$ **Simplify.**

$$= \frac{5x}{3x+8}$$ **Simplify.**

✓ **GUIDED PRACTICE** for Examples 5 and 6

Simplify the complex fraction.

11. $\dfrac{\frac{x}{6} - \frac{x}{3}}{\frac{x}{5} - \frac{7}{10}}$

12. $\dfrac{\frac{2}{x} - 4}{\frac{2}{x} + 3}$

13. $\dfrac{\frac{3}{x+5}}{\frac{2}{x-3} + \frac{1}{x+5}}$

8.5 EXERCISES

HOMEWORK KEY

○ = **WORKED-OUT SOLUTIONS** on p. WS15 for Exs. 5, 17, and 43

★ = **STANDARDIZED TEST PRACTICE** Exs. 2, 15, 26, 37, and 44

SKILL PRACTICE

1. **VOCABULARY** Copy and complete: A fraction that contains a fraction in its numerator or denominator is called a(n) __?__.

2. ★ **WRITING** *Explain* how to add rational expressions with unlike denominators.

EXAMPLE 1 on p. 582 for Exs. 3–8

LIKE DENOMINATORS **Perform the indicated operation and simplify.**

3. $\frac{15}{4x} + \frac{5}{4x}$
4. $\frac{x}{16x^2} - \frac{4}{16x^2}$
5. $\frac{9}{x+1} - \frac{2x}{x+1}$
6. $\frac{3x^2}{x-8} + \frac{6x}{x-8}$
7. $\frac{5x}{x+3} + \frac{15}{x+3}$
8. $\frac{4x^2}{2x-1} - \frac{1}{2x-1}$

EXAMPLE 2 on p. 583 for Exs. 9–15

FINDING LCMS **Find the least common multiple of the polynomials.**

9. $3x$ and $3(x-2)$
10. $2x^2$ and $4x + 12$
11. $2x$ and $2x(x-5)$
12. $24x^2$ and $8x^2 - 16x$
13. $x^2 - 25$, x, and $x - 5$
14. $9x^2 - 16$ and $3x^2 - 2x - 8$

15. ★ **MULTIPLE CHOICE** What is the least common multiple of the polynomials $3x^2 - 9x$ and $6x^2$?

Ⓐ $3x(x-3)$ Ⓑ $6x^2$ Ⓒ $6x(x-3)$ Ⓓ $6x^2(x-3)$

EXAMPLES 3 and 4 on pp. 583–584 for Exs. 16–26

UNLIKE DENOMINATORS **Perform the indicated operation and simplify.**

16. $\frac{12}{5x} + \frac{7}{6x}$
17. $\frac{8}{3x^2} - \frac{5}{4x}$
18. $\frac{x-4}{5x} - \frac{12}{5(x-4)}$
19. $\frac{12}{x^2+5x-24} + \frac{3}{x-3}$
20. $\frac{3}{x+4} - \frac{1}{x+6}$
21. $\frac{9}{x-3} + \frac{2x}{x+1}$
22. $\frac{x+4}{x^2-4} - \frac{15}{x-2}$
23. $\frac{-15x}{x^2-8x+16} + \frac{12}{x-4}$
24. $\frac{x^2-5}{x^2+5x-14} - \frac{x+3}{x+7}$

25. **ERROR ANALYSIS** *Describe* and correct the error in adding the rational expressions.

$$\frac{x}{x+2} + \frac{4}{x-5} = \frac{x+4}{(x+2)(x-5)} \quad ✗$$

26. ★ **MULTIPLE CHOICE** Which expression is equivalent to $\frac{2x}{x+4} - \frac{x^2+4}{x^2-16}$?

Ⓐ $\frac{1}{x+4}$ Ⓑ $\frac{(x+2)(x-2)}{(x+4)(x-4)}$ Ⓒ $\frac{x^2-8x-4}{(x+4)(x-4)}$ Ⓓ $\frac{3x^2-8x+4}{(x+4)(x-4)}$

UNLIKE DENOMINATORS **Perform the indicated operation(s) and simplify.**

27. $\frac{x}{x^2-9} + \frac{x+1}{x^2+6x+9}$
28. $\frac{x+3}{x^2-2x-8} - \frac{x-5}{x^2-12x+32}$
29. $\frac{x+2}{x-4} + \frac{2}{x} + \frac{5x}{3x-1}$
30. $\frac{x+3}{x^2-25} - \frac{x-1}{x-5} + \frac{3}{x+3}$

EXAMPLES 5 and 6
on p. 585 for Exs. 31–36

SIMPLIFYING COMPLEX FRACTIONS **Simplify the complex fraction.**

31. $\dfrac{\frac{x}{3} - 6}{10 + \frac{4}{x}}$

32. $\dfrac{15 - \frac{2}{x}}{\frac{x}{5} + 4}$

33. $\dfrac{\frac{16}{x-2}}{\frac{4}{x+1} + \frac{6}{x}}$

34. $\dfrac{\frac{1}{2x-5} - \frac{7}{8x-20}}{\frac{x}{2x-5}}$

35. $\dfrac{\frac{3}{x-2} - \frac{6}{x^2-4}}{\frac{3}{x+2} + \frac{1}{x-2}}$

36. $\dfrac{\frac{1}{3x^2-3}}{\frac{5}{x+1} - \frac{x+4}{x^2-3x-4}}$

37. ★ **OPEN-ENDED MATH** Write two different complex fractions that each simplify to $\frac{x-3}{x+4}$.

CHALLENGE **Simplify the complex fraction.**

38. $\dfrac{\frac{1}{x} - \frac{x}{x^{-1}+1}}{\frac{5}{x}}$

39. $\dfrac{\frac{3-2x}{x^3}}{\frac{2}{x^2} - \frac{1}{x^3+x^2}}$

40. $\dfrac{3x^{-2} + (2x-1)^{-1}}{\frac{6}{x^{-1}+2} + 3x^{-1}}$

PROBLEM SOLVING

EXAMPLE 3
on p. 583 for Ex. 41

41. **JET STREAM** The total time T (in hours) needed to fly from New York to Los Angeles and back (ignoring layovers) can be modeled by the equation in the diagram, where d is the distance each way (in miles), a is the average airplane speed (in miles per hour), and j is the average speed of the jet stream (in miles per hour).

$$T = \frac{d}{a-j} + \frac{d}{a+j}$$

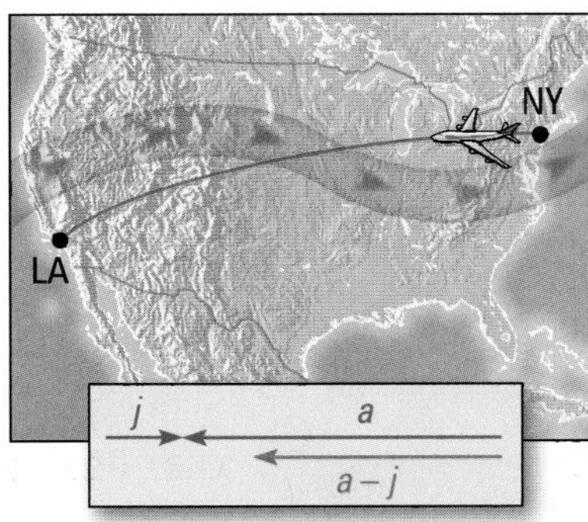

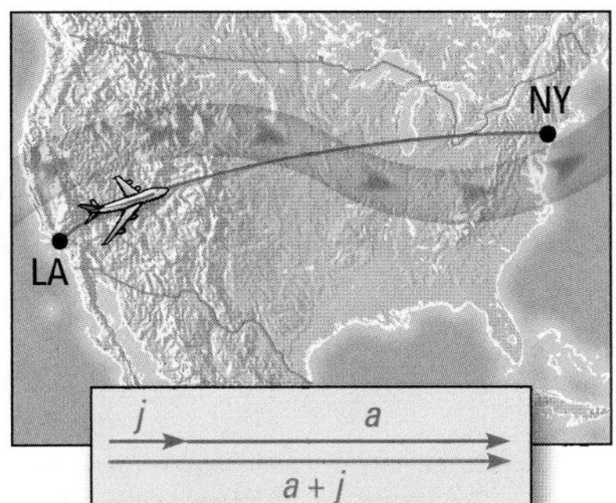

Rewrite the equation so that the right side is simplified. Then find the total time if $d = 2468$ miles, $a = 510$ mi/h, and $j = 115$ mi/h.

Animated Algebra at classzone.com

EXAMPLES 5 and 6
on p. 585 for Exs. 42–43

42. **ELECTRONICS** If two resistors in a parallel circuit have resistances R_1 and R_2 (both in ohms), then the total resistance R_t (in ohms) is given by the equation shown. Simplify the complex fraction. Then find the total resistance if $R_1 = 2000$ ohms and $R_2 = 5600$ ohms.

R_t = [R_1 and R_2 in parallel]

$$R_t = \frac{1}{\frac{1}{R_1} + \frac{1}{R_2}}$$

@HomeTutor for problem solving help at classzone.com

43. **CAR LOANS** If you borrow P dollars to buy a car and agree to repay the loan over t years at a monthly interest rate of i (expressed as a decimal), then your monthly payment M is given by either formula below.

Formula 1: $M = \dfrac{Pi}{1 - \left(\dfrac{1}{1+i}\right)^{12t}}$ **Formula 2:** $M = \dfrac{Pi(1+i)^{12t}}{(1+i)^{12t} - 1}$

a. Show that the formulas are equivalent by simplifying the first formula.

b. Find your monthly payment if you borrow \$15,500 at a monthly interest rate of 0.5% and repay the loan over 4 years.

44. ★ **EXTENDED RESPONSE** The amount A (in milligrams) of aspirin in a person's bloodstream can be modeled by

$$A = \frac{391t^2 + 0.112}{0.218t^4 + 0.991t^2 + 1}$$

where t is the time (in hours) after one dose is taken.

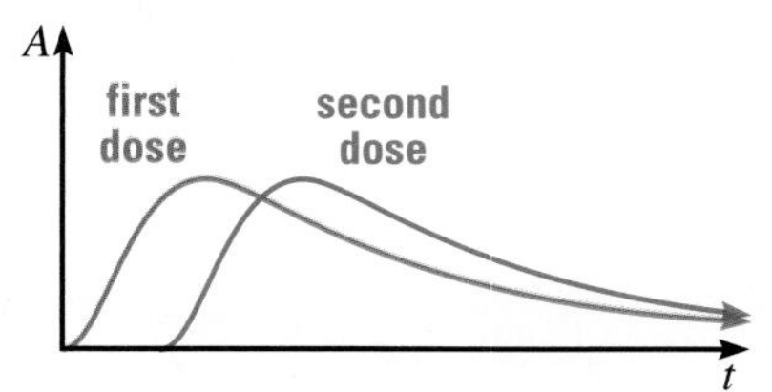

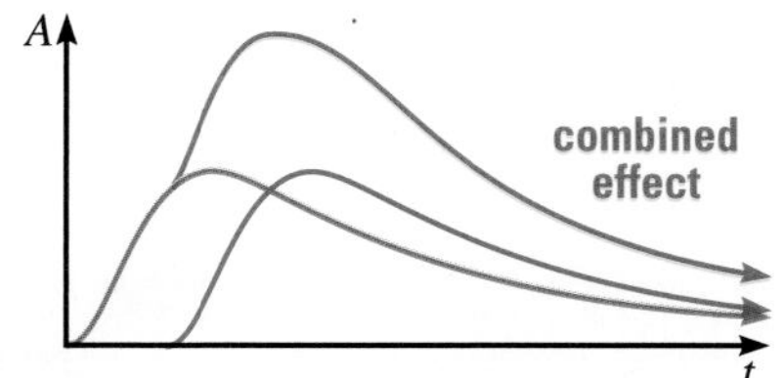

a. Graph the equation using a graphing calculator.

b. A second dose of the drug is taken 1 hour after the first dose. Write an equation to model the amount of the second dose in the bloodstream.

c. Write and graph a model for the *total* amount of aspirin in the bloodstream after the second dose is taken.

d. About how long after the second dose has been taken is the greatest amount of aspirin in the bloodstream?

45. **CHALLENGE** Find the next two expressions in the pattern shown. Then simplify all five expressions. What value do the expressions approach?

$$1 + \cfrac{1}{2 + \cfrac{1}{2}},\ 1 + \cfrac{1}{2 + \cfrac{1}{2 + \cfrac{1}{2}}},\ 1 + \cfrac{1}{2 + \cfrac{1}{2 + \cfrac{1}{2 + \cfrac{1}{2}}}},\ \ldots$$

NEW YORK MIXED REVIEW

TEST PRACTICE at classzone.com

46. One leg of a right triangle is 4 centimeters longer than the other leg. The hypotenuse is 20 centimeters. About how long is the shorter leg?

Ⓐ 10.4 cm Ⓑ 12.0 cm Ⓒ 12.6 cm Ⓓ 16.0 cm

47. Which of the following is the solution of this system of linear equations?

$$3x - 4y = -18$$
$$5x + 2y = -4$$

Ⓐ (−2, −3) Ⓑ (−2, 3) Ⓒ (2, −3) Ⓓ (3, −2)

8.6 Solve Rational Equations

A2.A.23 Solve rational equations and inequalities

Before	You solved polynomial equations.
Now	You will solve rational equations.
Why?	So you can model mobile phone costs, as in Ex. 38.

Key Vocabulary
- **cross multiplying**
- **extraneous solution,** *p. 52*

You can use **cross multiplying** to solve a rational equation when each side of the equation is a single rational expression.

EXAMPLE 1 Solve a rational equation by cross multiplying

Solve: $\frac{3}{x+1} = \frac{9}{4x+5}$

$\frac{3}{x+1} = \frac{9}{4x+5}$	**Write original equation.**
$3(4x+5) = 9(x+1)$	**Cross multiply.**
$12x + 15 = 9x + 9$	**Distributive property**
$3x + 15 = 9$	**Subtract 9*x* from each side.**
$3x = -6$	**Subtract 15 from each side.**
$x = -2$	**Divide each side by 3.**

▸ The solution is −2. Check this in the original equation.

EXAMPLE 2 Write and use a rational model

ALLOYS An *alloy* is formed by mixing two or more metals. Sterling silver is an alloy composed of 92.5% silver and 7.5% copper by weight. Jewelry silver is composed of 80% silver and 20% copper by weight. How much pure silver should you mix with 15 ounces of jewelry silver to make sterling silver?

Solution

$$\text{Percent of copper in mixture} = \frac{\text{Weight of copper in mixture}}{\text{Total weight of mixture}}$$

$\frac{7.5}{100} = \frac{0.2(15)}{15+x}$	***x* is the amount of silver added.**
$7.5(15+x) = 100(0.2)(15)$	**Cross multiply.**
$112.5 + 7.5x = 300$	**Simplify.**
$7.5x = 187.5$	**Subtract 112.5 from each side.**
$x = 25$	**Divide each side by 7.5.**

▸ You should mix 25 ounces of pure silver with the jewelry silver.

✓ GUIDED PRACTICE for Examples 1 and 2

Solve the equation by cross multiplying. Check your solution(s).

1. $\frac{3}{5x} = \frac{2}{x-7}$

2. $\frac{-4}{x+3} = \frac{5}{x-3}$

3. $\frac{1}{2x+5} = \frac{x}{11x+8}$

4. **WHAT IF?** In Example 2, suppose you have 10 ounces of jewelry silver. How much pure silver must be mixed with the jewelry silver to make sterling silver?

USING LCDS When a rational equation is not expressed as a proportion, you can solve it by multiplying each side of the equation by the least common denominator of each rational expression.

EXAMPLE 3 Standardized Test Practice

What is the solution of $\frac{5}{x} + \frac{7}{4} = -\frac{9}{x}$?

Ⓐ −10 Ⓑ −8 Ⓒ −4 Ⓓ 6

ELIMINATE CHOICES
You can eliminate choice D because it yields a positive value on the left side of the equation and a negative value on the right side.

Solution

$\frac{5}{x} + \frac{7}{4} = -\frac{9}{x}$	Write original equation.
$4x\left(\frac{5}{x} + \frac{7}{4}\right) = 4x\left(-\frac{9}{x}\right)$	Multiply each side by the LCD, $4x$.
$20 + 7x = -36$	Simplify.
$7x = -56$	Subtract 20 from each side.
$x = -8$	Divide each side by 7.

▸ The correct answer is B. Ⓐ Ⓑ Ⓒ Ⓓ

EXAMPLE 4 Solve a rational equation with two solutions

Solve: $1 - \frac{8}{x-5} = \frac{3}{x}$

$1 - \frac{8}{x-5} = \frac{3}{x}$	Write original equation.
$x(x-5)\left(1 - \frac{8}{x-5}\right) = x(x-5) \cdot \frac{3}{x}$	Multiply each side by the LCD, $x(x-5)$.
$x(x-5) - 8x = 3(x-5)$	Simplify.
$x^2 - 5x - 8x = 3x - 15$	Simplify.
$x^2 - 16x + 15 = 0$	Write in standard form.
$(x-1)(x-15) = 0$	Factor.
$x = 1$ or $x = 15$	Zero product property

▸ The solutions are 1 and 15. Check these in the original equation.

EXTRANEOUS SOLUTIONS When solving a rational equation, you may obtain solutions that are extraneous. Be sure to check for extraneous solutions by substituting back into the original equation.

EXAMPLE 5 Check for extraneous solutions

Solve: $\frac{6}{x-3} = \frac{8x^2}{x^2-9} - \frac{4x}{x+3}$

Solution

Write each denominator in factored form. The LCD is $(x+3)(x-3)$.

$$\frac{6}{x-3} = \frac{8x^2}{(x+3)(x-3)} - \frac{4x}{x+3}$$

$$(x+3)(x-3) \cdot \frac{6}{x-3} = (x+3)(x-3) \cdot \frac{8x^2}{(x+3)(x-3)} - (x+3)(x-3) \cdot \frac{4x}{x+3}$$

$$6(x+3) = 8x^2 - 4x(x-3)$$

$$6x + 18 = 8x^2 - 4x^2 + 12x$$

$$0 = 4x^2 + 6x - 18$$

$$0 = 2x^2 + 3x - 9$$

$$0 = (2x-3)(x+3)$$

$$2x - 3 = 0 \quad \text{or} \quad x + 3 = 0$$

$$x = \frac{3}{2} \quad \text{or} \quad x = -3$$

REVIEW EXTRANEOUS SOLUTIONS
For help with extraneous solutions, see p. 51.

You can use algebra or a graph to check whether either of the two solutions is extraneous.

Algebra The solution $\frac{3}{2}$ checks, but the apparent solution -3 is extraneous, because substituting it in the equation results in division by zero, which is undefined.

$$\frac{6}{-3-3} \neq \frac{8(-3)^2}{(-3)^2-9} - \frac{4(-3)}{-3+3}$$

Division by zero is undefined

Graph Graph $y = \frac{6}{x-3}$ and $y = \frac{8x^2}{x^2-9} - \frac{4x}{x+3}$.

The graphs intersect when $x = \frac{3}{2}$, but not when $x = -3$.

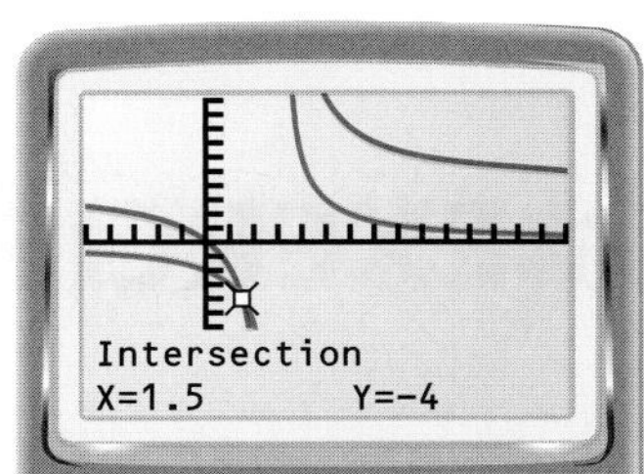

▶ The solution is $\frac{3}{2}$.

✓ GUIDED PRACTICE for Examples 3, 4, and 5

Solve the equation by using the LCD. Check for extraneous solutions.

5. $\frac{7}{2} + \frac{3}{x} = 3$

6. $\frac{2}{x} + \frac{4}{3} = 2$

7. $\frac{3}{7} + \frac{8}{x} = 1$

8. $\frac{3}{2} + \frac{4}{x-1} = \frac{x+1}{x-1}$

9. $\frac{3x}{x+1} - \frac{5}{2x} = \frac{3}{2x}$

10. $\frac{5x}{x-2} = 7 + \frac{10}{x-2}$

EXAMPLE 6 Solve a rational equation given a function

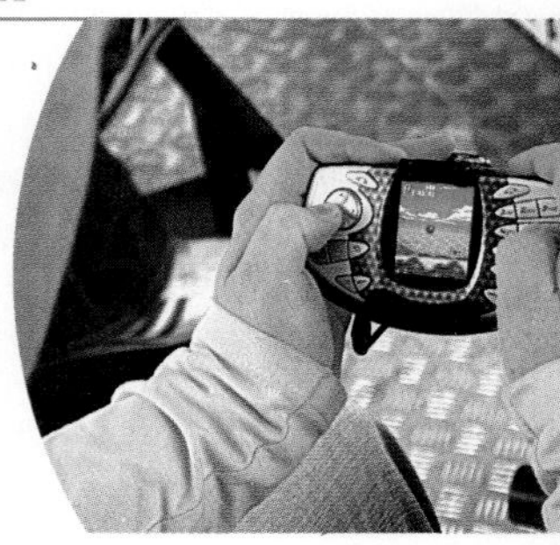

VIDEO GAME SALES From 1995 through 2003, the annual sales S (in billions of dollars) of entertainment software can be modeled by

$$S(t) = \frac{848t^2 + 3220}{115t^2 + 1000}, \quad 0 \le t \le 8$$

where t is the number of years since 1995. For which year were the total sales of entertainment software about \$5.3 billion?

ANOTHER WAY

For alternative methods for solving the problem in Example 6, turn to page 596 for the **Problem Solving Workshop**.

Solution

$S(t) = \frac{848t^2 + 3220}{115t^2 + 1000}$	**Write given function.**
$5.3 = \frac{848t^2 + 3220}{115t^2 + 1000}$	**Substitute 5.3 for $S(t)$.**
$5.3(115t^2 + 1000) = 848t^2 + 3220$	**Multiply each side by $115t^2 + 1000$.**
$609.5t^2 + 5300 = 848t^2 + 3220$	**Simplify.**
$5300 = 238.5t^2 + 3220$	**Subtract $609.5t^2$ from each side.**
$2080 = 238.5t^2$	**Subtract 3220 from each side.**
$8.72 \approx t^2$	**Divide each side by 238.5.**
$\pm 2.95 \approx t$	**Take square roots of each side.**

Because -2.95 is not in the domain $(0 \le t \le 8)$, the only solution is 2.95.

▶ So, the total sales of entertainment software were about \$5.3 billion about 3 years after 1995, or in 1998.

GUIDED PRACTICE for Example 6

11. WHAT IF? Use the information in Example 6 to determine in which year the total sales of entertainment software were about \$4.5 billion.

8.6 EXERCISES

HOMEWORK KEY

◯ = **WORKED-OUT SOLUTIONS** on p. WS15 for Exs. 5, 15, and 35

★ = **STANDARDIZED TEST PRACTICE** Exs. 2, 13, 28, 29, 34, and 36

SKILL PRACTICE

1. **VOCABULARY** Copy and complete: When you write $\frac{x}{3} = \frac{x+2}{5}$ as $5x = 3(x + 2)$, you are __?__.

2. ★ **WRITING** A student solved the equation $\frac{5}{x-4} = \frac{x}{x-4}$ and got the solutions 4 and 5. Which, if either, of these is extraneous? *Explain.*

3. **REASONING** *Describe* how you can use a graph to determine if an apparent solution of a rational equation is extraneous.

EXAMPLE 1
on p. 589
for Exs. 4–13

CROSS MULTIPLYING Solve the equation by cross multiplying. Check for extraneous solutions.

4. $\frac{4}{2x} = \frac{5}{x+6}$
5. $\frac{9}{3x} = \frac{4}{x+2}$
6. $\frac{6}{x-1} = \frac{9}{x+1}$
7. $\frac{8}{3x-2} = \frac{2}{x-1}$
8. $\frac{x}{x+1} = \frac{3}{x+1}$
9. $\frac{x-3}{x+5} = \frac{x}{x+2}$
10. $\frac{x}{x^2-2} = \frac{-1}{x}$
11. $\frac{4(x-4)}{x^2+2x-8} = \frac{4}{x+4}$
12. $\frac{9}{x^2-6x+9} = \frac{3x}{x^2-3x}$

13. ★ **MULTIPLE CHOICE** What is the solution of $\frac{3}{x+2} = \frac{6}{x-1}$?

Ⓐ -5 Ⓑ -4 Ⓒ -1 Ⓓ 4

EXAMPLES 3, 4, and 5
on pp. 590–591
for Exs. 14–27

LEAST COMMON DENOMINATOR Solve the equation by using the LCD. Check for extraneous solutions.

14. $\frac{4}{x} + x = 5$
15. $\frac{2}{3x} + \frac{1}{6} = \frac{4}{3x}$
16. $\frac{5}{x} - 2 = \frac{2}{x+3}$
17. $\frac{1}{2x} + \frac{3}{x+7} = \frac{-1}{x}$
18. $\frac{1}{x-2} + 2 = \frac{3x}{x+2}$
19. $\frac{5}{x^2+x-6} = 2 + \frac{x-3}{x-2}$
20. $\frac{x+1}{x+6} + \frac{1}{x} = \frac{2x+1}{x+6}$
21. $\frac{2}{x-3} + \frac{1}{x} = \frac{x-1}{x-3}$
22. $\frac{6x}{x+4} + 4 = \frac{2x+2}{x-1}$
23. $\frac{10}{x} + 3 = \frac{x+9}{x-4}$
24. $\frac{18}{x^2-3x} - \frac{6}{x-3} = \frac{5}{x}$
25. $\frac{x+3}{x-3} + \frac{x}{x-5} = \frac{x+5}{x-5}$

ERROR ANALYSIS *Describe* and correct the error in the first step of solving the equation.

26.
$$\frac{3}{2x} + \frac{4}{x^2} = 1$$
$$3x^2 + 8x = 1$$

27.
$$\frac{5}{x} + \frac{23}{6} = \frac{45}{x}$$
$$\frac{28}{x+6} = \frac{45}{x}$$

28. ★ **MULTIPLE CHOICE** What is (are) the solution(s) of $\frac{2}{x-3} = \frac{1}{x^2-2x-3}$?

Ⓐ $-3, -\frac{1}{2}$ Ⓑ $-\frac{1}{2}, 3$ Ⓒ $-\frac{1}{2}$ Ⓓ 3

29. ★ **OPEN-ENDED MATH** Give an example of a rational equation that you would solve using cross multiplication. Then give an example of a rational equation that you would solve by multiplying each side by the LCD of the fractions.

CHALLENGE In Exercises 30–32, *a* is a nonzero real number. Tell whether the algebraic statement is *always true, sometimes true,* or *never true. Explain* your answer.

30. For the equation $\frac{1}{x-a} = \frac{x}{x-a}$, $x = a$ is an extraneous solution.

31. The equation $\frac{3}{x-a} = \frac{x}{x-a}$ has exactly one solution.

32. The equation $\frac{1}{x-a} = \frac{2}{x+a} + \frac{2a}{x^2-a^2}$ has no solution.

PROBLEM SOLVING

EXAMPLE 2 on p. 589 for Exs. 33–34

33. VOLLEYBALL So far in your volleyball match, you have put into play 37 of the 44 serves you have attempted. Solve the equation $\frac{90}{100} = \frac{37 + x}{44 + x}$ to find the number of consecutive serves you need to put into play in order to raise your service percentage to 90%.

@HomeTutor for problem solving help at classzone.com

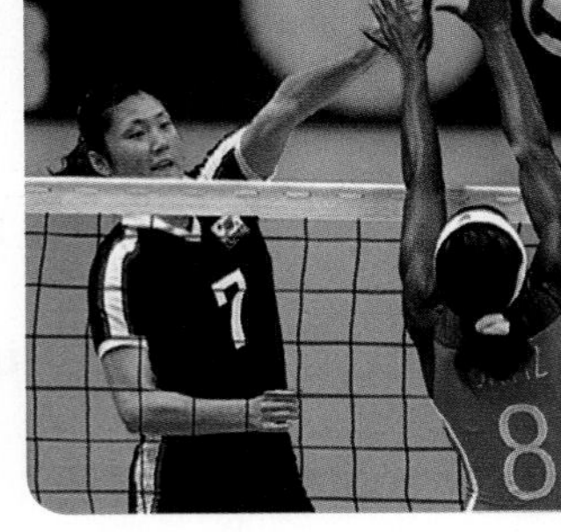

34. ★ EXTENDED RESPONSE A speed skater travels 9 kilometers in the same amount of time that it takes a second skater to travel 8 kilometers. The first skater travels 4.38 kilometers per hour faster than the second skater.

a. Use the verbal model below to write an equation that relates the skating times of the skaters.

$$\frac{\text{Distance for skater 1}}{\text{Skater 1 speed}} = \frac{\text{Distance for skater 2}}{\text{Skater 2 speed}}$$

b. Solve the equation in part (a) to find the speeds of both skaters.

c. How long did the skaters skate? *Explain* your answer.

@HomeTutor for problem solving help at classzone.com

EXAMPLE 6 on p. 592 for Ex. 35

35. MUSIC INDUSTRY From 1994 through 2003, the number n (in millions) of CDs shipped can be modeled by

$$n = \frac{635t^2 - 7350t + 27{,}200}{t^2 - 11.5t + 39.4}, \quad 0 \le t \le 9$$

where t is the number of years since 1994. During which year was the total number of CDs shipped about 720 million?

36. ★ EXTENDED RESPONSE You can paint a room in 8 hours. Working together, you and your friend can paint the room in just 5 hours.

a. Let t be the time (in hours) your friend would take to paint the room when working alone. Copy and complete the table.

	Work Rate •	Time =	Work Done
You	$\frac{1 \text{ room}}{8 \text{ hours}}$	5 hours	?
Friend	?	5 hours	?

b. What is the sum of the expressions in the table's last column? *Explain.*

c. Write and solve an equation to find how long your friend would take to paint the room when working alone. *Explain* your answer.

37. GEOMETRY *Golden rectangles* are rectangles for which the ratio of the width w to the length ℓ is equal to the ratio of ℓ to $\ell + w$. The ratio of the length to the width for these rectangles is called the *golden ratio*. Find the value of the golden ratio using a rectangle with a width of 1 unit.

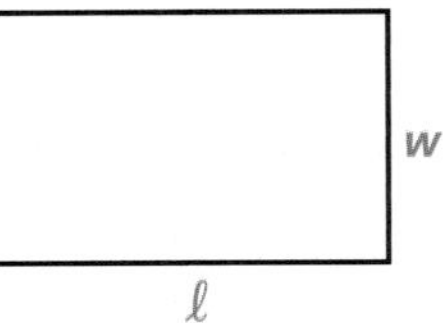

○ = WORKED-OUT SOLUTIONS on p. WS1 ★ = STANDARDIZED TEST PRACTICE

38. CHALLENGE Let x be the number of years since 1998, let $g(x)$ be the average monthly bill (in dollars) for mobile phone users in the United States, and let $h(x)$ be the average number of minutes used by U.S. mobile phone users. Then $g(x)$ and $h(x)$ are as given below.

$$g(x) = -0.27x^3 + 1.40x^2 + 1.05x + 39.4$$
$$h(x) = -8.25x^3 + 53.1x^2 - 7.82x + 138$$

a. Write a rational function $f(x)$ that gives the average price per minute x years after 1998.

b. Find the average price per minute in 1998.

c. In what year did the average price per minute fall to 11 cents?

NEW YORK MIXED REVIEW

TEST PRACTICE at classzone.com

39. What are the coordinates of the y-intercept of the line $-2x - \frac{1}{3}y = 12$?

(A) $(-6, 0)$ (B) $(0, -36)$ (C) $(0, 4)$ (D) $(12, 0)$

40. What is the value of x?

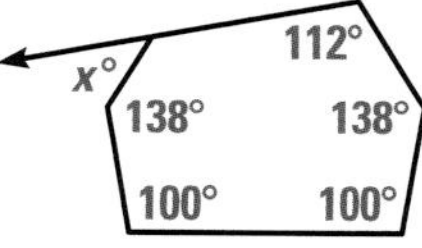

(A) 38 (B) 48

(C) 58 (D) 68

QUIZ *for Lessons 8.4–8.6*

Perform the indicated operation and simplify. *(p. 573)*

1. $\frac{x^2 - 2x - 24}{x^2 + 3x - 10} \cdot \frac{3x^2 - 6x}{x^3 + 4x^2}$

2. $\frac{x^2 - 10x + 16}{x^2 - 1} \cdot (x - 1)$

3. $\frac{x^2 + 9x + 20}{x^2 - 11x + 28} \div \frac{x^2 + 8x + 15}{x^2 - 3x - 4}$

4. $\frac{x^2 + 12x + 36}{x^2 - 8x + 12} \div (x^2 - 36)$

Perform the indicated operation and simplify. *(p. 582)*

5. $\frac{1}{x + 4} + \frac{1}{x - 4}$

6. $\frac{4x + 3}{x^2 - 16} + \frac{2}{x - 4}$

7. $\frac{4}{x + 5} - \frac{6x - 1}{x^2 + 10x + 25}$

Solve the equation. Check for extraneous solutions. *(p. 589)*

8. $\frac{x - 4}{x - 1} = \frac{10}{x + 7}$

9. $\frac{x - 4}{x - 2} - \frac{2x - 1}{x - 2} = 2$

10. $\frac{3x + 6}{x^2 - 4} = \frac{x + 1}{x - 2}$

11. $\frac{5}{x} + \frac{x + 1}{x + 2} = \frac{2x + 9}{x + 2}$

12. $\frac{x - 3}{x + 2} = \frac{x - 1}{3x - 1}$

13. $\frac{x - 1}{x} + \frac{2x - 1}{x + 3} = \frac{x + 6}{x + 3}$

14. BATTING AVERAGE So far this baseball season, you have gotten a hit 12 times out of 60 at-bats. Solve the equation $0.360 = \frac{12 + x}{60 + x}$ to find the number of consecutive hits you have to get to raise your batting average to 0.360. *(p. 589)*

PROBLEM SOLVING WORKSHOP
LESSON 8.6

Using ALTERNATIVE METHODS

Another Way to Solve Example 6, page 592

MULTIPLE REPRESENTATIONS In Example 6 on page 592, you solved a rational equation algebraically. You can also solve rational equations using tables and graphs.

PROBLEM

VIDEO GAME SALES From 1995 through 2003, the annual sales S (in billions of dollars) of entertainment software can be modeled by

$$S(t) = \frac{848t^2 + 3220}{115t^2 + 1000}, \quad 0 \le t \le 8$$

where t is the number of years since 1995. For which year were the total sales of entertainment software about \$5.3 billion?

METHOD 1

Using a Table The problem requires solving the following rational equation:

$$5.3 = \frac{848t^2 + 3220}{115t^2 + 1000}$$

One way to solve this equation is to make a table of values. You can use a graphing calculator to make the table.

STEP 1 **Enter** the function $y = \frac{848x^2 + 3220}{115x^2 + 1000}$ into a graphing calculator.

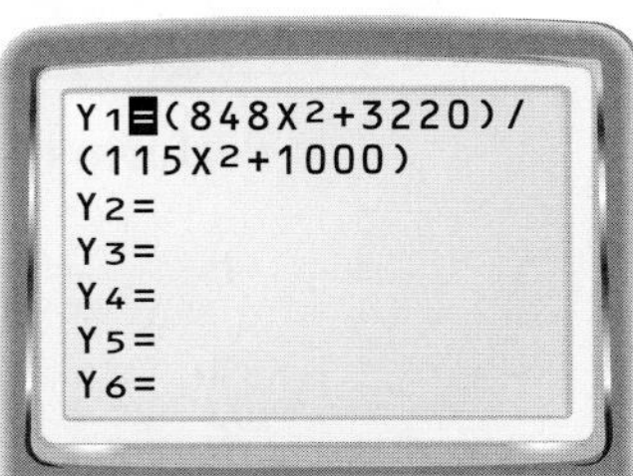

STEP 2 **Set up** a table of values for the function. Start the table at zero so that the first several x-values in the table are in the domain of the function. The step value ($\triangle$Tbl) should represent one entire year.

STEP 3 **Create** the table of values. You can see that $y \approx 5.3$ when $x = 3$.

X	Y1
0	3.22
1	3.6484
2	4.5288
3	5.3327
4	5.9113

X=3

▶ Because $x = 3$ represents the number of years after 1995, total sales of entertainment software were about \$5.3 billion in 1998.

METHOD 2

Using a Graph You can also use a graph to solve $5.3 = \frac{848t^2 + 3220}{115t^2 + 1000}$.

STEP 1 **Enter** the functions $y = \frac{848x^2 + 3220}{115x^2 + 1000}$ and $y = 5.3$ into a graphing calculator.

STEP 2 **Graph** the functions. Adjust the viewing window so that it shows the point in the first quadrant where the graphs intersect.

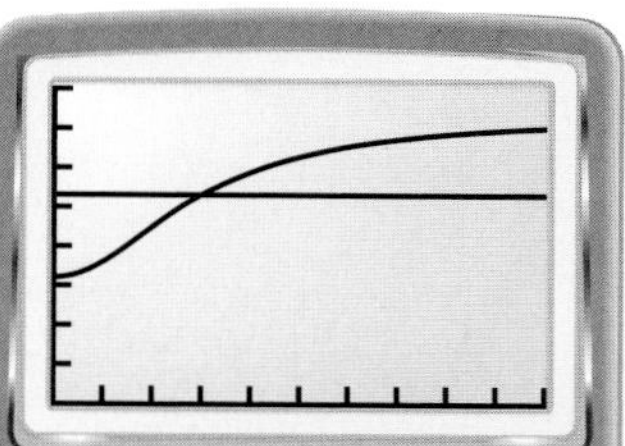

STEP 3 **Find** the intersection point of the graphs using the calculator's *intersect* feature. The graphs intersect at about (3.0, 5.3).

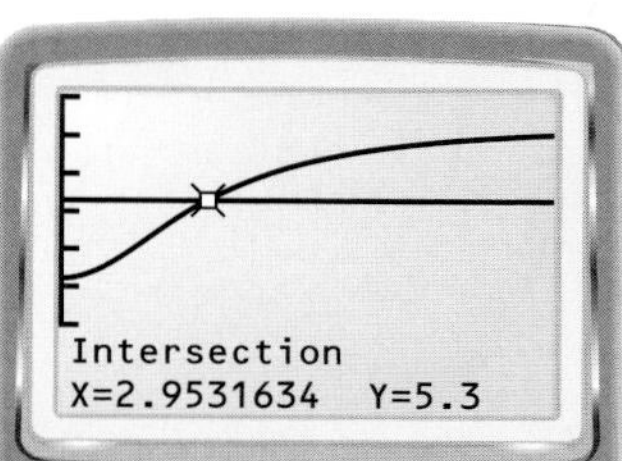

▸ Total sales of entertainment software were about \$5.3 billion 3 years after 1995, or in the year 1998.

PRACTICE

RATIONAL EQUATIONS Solve the equation using a table and using a graph.

1. $\frac{80x^2 + 300}{15x^2 + 200} = 4.2$

2. $\frac{5x + 5}{x^2 + 4} = 2$

3. $\frac{9x + 2}{x - 5} = 20.75$

4. $\frac{6x^2}{2x - 3} = 18$

5. $\frac{14x^2 + 60}{5x^2 + 7} = 3.5$

6. **WHAT IF?** In the problem on page 596, suppose you want to find the year when total sales of entertainment software were \$4.5 billion. Find this year using a table and using a graph.

7. **DIVING** The recommended percent p of oxygen (by volume) in the air that a diver breathes is given by $p = \frac{660}{d + 33}$ where d is the depth (in feet) of the diver.

   a. At what depth is air containing 5% oxygen recommended? Use a table to find the answer.

   b. At what depth is air containing 10% oxygen recommended? Use a graph to find the answer.

Solve Rational Inequalities

GOAL Find solutions of rational inequalities.

In Lesson 8.6, you solved rational equations. You can also solve rational inequalities using tables, graphs, or algebraic methods.

EXAMPLE 1 Solve a rational inequality using a table

Use a table to solve $\frac{x^2 - 2x + 1}{x - 2} > x$.

Solution

Subtract x from each side of the inequality so that 0 is on one side.

$$\frac{x^2 - 2x + 1}{x - 2} - x > 0 \quad \textbf{Subtract } x \textbf{ from each side.}$$

Enter $y = \frac{x^2 - 2x + 1}{x - 2} - x$ into a graphing calculator.

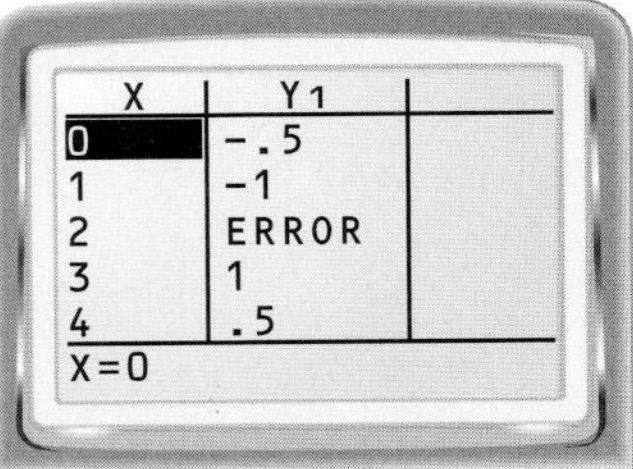

Use the *table* feature to find values of x for which y is positive.

The value of y is undefined when $x = 2$ and appears to be positive when $x > 2$. Use a smaller step value for x to convince yourself of this.

▶ The solution is $x > 2$.

EXAMPLE 2 Solve a rational inequality by graphing

From 1990 to 2001, the number d (in thousands) of doctors in the United States can be modeled by the function $d = \frac{966t^2 + 50{,}300}{t^2 + 79.7}$ where t is the number of years since 1990. When were there fewer than 800,000 doctors?

Solution

The problem requires solving this inequality:

$$\frac{966t^2 + 50{,}300}{t^2 + 79.7} < 800$$

Enter $y_1 = \frac{966x^2 + 50{,}300}{x^2 + 79.7}$ and $y_2 = 800$ into a graphing calculator.

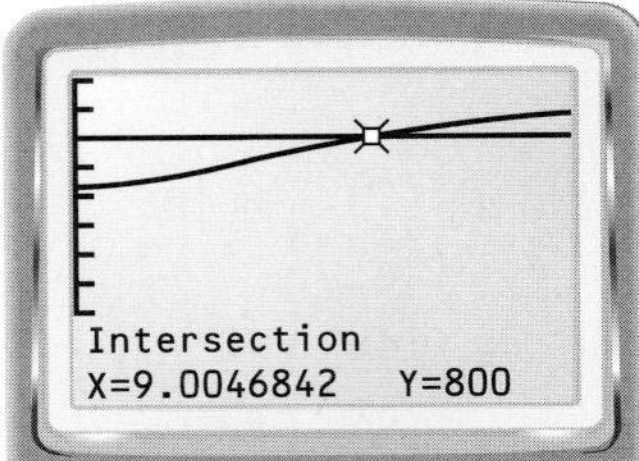

Graph the functions and use the *intersect* feature. The graph of y_1 lies below the graph of y_2 when $0 \le x \le 9$.

▶ In the years 1990–1999, there were fewer than 800,000 doctors.

EXAMPLE 3 Solve a rational inequality algebraically

Solve $\frac{6}{x-2} \geq -4$ algebraically.

Solution

STEP 1 **Rewrite** the inequality so that one side is 0. Then write the other side as a simplified rational expression.

> **AVOID ERRORS**
> Do not multiply each side of an inequality by an expression involving *x* if the expression can take on both positive and negative values.

$\frac{6}{x-2} \geq -4$ **Write original inequality.**

$\frac{6}{x-2} + 4 \geq 0$ **Add 4 to each side.**

$\frac{6 + 4(x-2)}{x-2} \geq 0$ **Write left side as a single fraction.**

$\frac{4x-2}{x-2} \geq 0$ **Simplify.**

STEP 2 **Identify** the *critical x-values*, which are the *x*-values that make the numerator or denominator equal to 0.

Numerator equal to 0:	**Denominator equal to 0:**
$4x - 2 = 0$	$x - 2 = 0$
$x = \frac{1}{2}$	$x = 2$

So, the critical *x*-values are $x = \frac{1}{2}$ and $x = 2$.

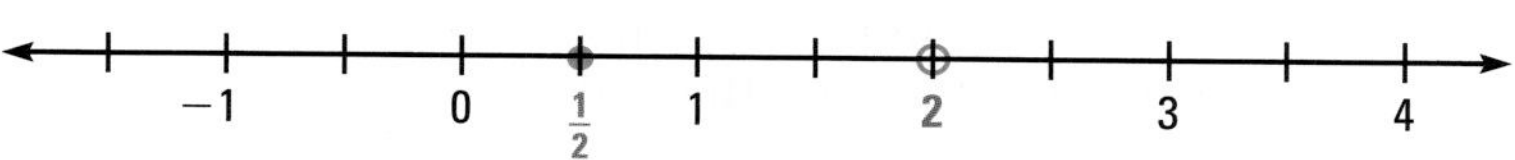

The critical *x*-values divide the number line into three intervals. Note that $x = \frac{1}{2}$ will be included in the solution, but $x = 2$ will not because it results in division by zero.

STEP 3 **Test** an *x*-value in each interval to see if it satisfies the original inequality. If it does, *every* *x*-value in the interval will satisfy the inequality. If it does not, *no* *x*-value in the interval will satisfy the inequality.

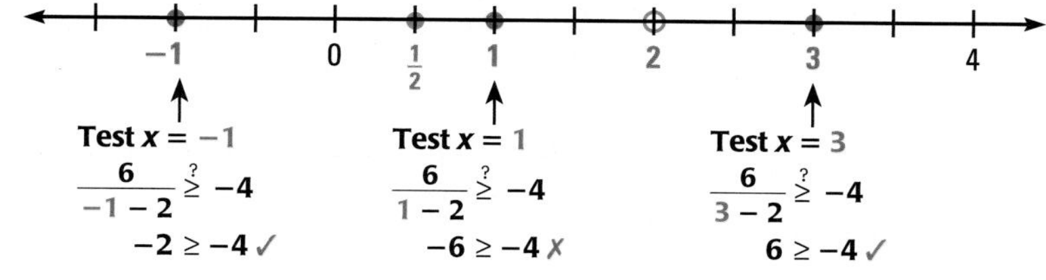

STEP 4 **Graph** the intervals where the tested *x*-values produce true statements.

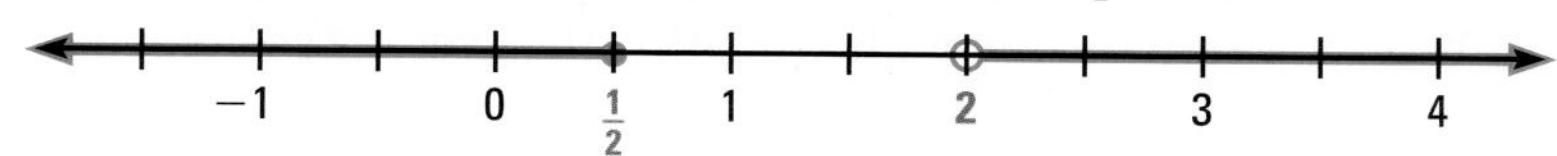

STEP 5 **Write** inequalities to describe the solution.

▶ The solution is $x \leq \frac{1}{2}$ or $x > 2$.

PRACTICE

EXAMPLE 1
on p. 598
for Exs. 1–6

Use a table to solve the inequality.

1. $\frac{5}{x-2} < 0$
2. $\frac{x-5}{x+3} > 1$
3. $\frac{x^2-3x+2}{x-3} < x$
4. $\frac{10}{x+2} > 0$
5. $\frac{-2x-3}{x-4} > 0$
6. $\frac{x^2-4x+8}{x-1} < x$

EXAMPLE 2
on p. 598
for Exs. 7–12

Use a graph to solve the inequality.

7. $-\frac{4}{x+5} < 0$
8. $\frac{4}{x-3} < 0$
9. $\frac{8}{x^2+1} \geq 4$
10. $\frac{20}{x^2+1} < 2$
11. $\frac{3x+2}{x-1} < -2$
12. $\frac{3x+2}{x-1} > x$

EXAMPLE 3
on p. 599
for Exs. 13–18

Solve the inequality algebraically.

13. $\frac{3}{x+2} > 0$
14. $-\frac{1}{x+5} \leq -2$
15. $\frac{2}{x+2} > \frac{1}{x+3}$
16. $\frac{5}{x-4} < \frac{1}{x+4}$
17. $\frac{5}{x+3} \geq \frac{4}{x+2}$
18. $\frac{2}{x+6} > \frac{-3}{x-3}$

19. **EGG PRODUCTION** From 1994 to 2002, the total number E (in billions) of eggs produced in the United States can be modeled by

$$E = \frac{-3680}{t-50}, \quad 0 \leq t \leq 8$$

where t is the number of years since 1994. For what years was the number of eggs produced greater than 80 billion?

20. **PHONE COSTS** One phone company advertises a flat rate of \$.07 per minute for long-distance calls. Your long-distance plan charges \$5.00 per month plus a rate of \$.05 per minute. How many minutes do you have to talk each month so that your average cost is less than \$.07 per minute?

21. **SATELLITE TV** You subscribe to a satellite television service. The monthly cost for programming is \$43, and there is a one-time installation fee of \$50. The average monthly cost c of the service is given by $c = \frac{43t+50}{t}$ where t is the time (in months) that you have subscribed to the service. For what subscription times is the average monthly cost at most \$47? Solve the problem using a table and using a graph.

22. **FUNDRAISER** Your school is publishing a wildlife calendar to raise money for a local charity. The total cost of using the photos in the calendar is \$710. In addition to this one-time charge, the unit cost of printing each calendar is \$4.50.
    a. The school wants the average cost per calendar to be below \$10. Write a rational inequality relating the average cost per calendar to the desired cost per calendar.
    b. Solve the inequality from part (a) by graphing. How many calendars need to be printed to bring the average cost per calendar below \$10?
    c. Suppose the school wanted to have the average cost per calendar be below \$6. How many calendars would then need to be printed?

Lessons 8.4–8.6

1. **TRAVEL** A car travels 120 miles in the same amount of time that it takes a truck to travel 100 miles. The car travels 10 miles per hour faster than the truck. Use the verbal model to find the speed of the truck.

$$\frac{\text{Distance for car}}{\text{Speed of car}} = \frac{\text{Distance for truck}}{\text{Speed of truck}}$$

(1) 40 miles/hour
(2) 50 miles/hour
(3) 55 miles/hour
(4) 60 miles/hour

2. **RIVER CURRENT** The speed of a river's current is 3 miles per hour. You travel 2 miles with the current and then return to where you started in a total time of 1.25 hours. What is your approximate speed in still water?

(1) 3.0 miles/hour
(2) 3.9 miles/hour
(3) 5.0 miles/hour
(4) 5.5 miles/hour

3. **CYCLING** A cyclist travels 50 miles from her home to a state park at a speed of s miles per hour. On the return trip, she increases her speed by 5 miles per hour. Which expression represents the *total* time of the cyclist's round trip?

(1) $100s + 250$
(2) $\frac{2s + 5}{50}$
(3) $\frac{250}{s^2 - 5s}$
(4) $\frac{100s + 250}{s^2 + 5s}$

4. **ALLOYS** Brass is an alloy composed of 55% copper and 45% zinc by weight. You have 25 ounces of copper. About how many ounces of zinc do you need to make brass?

(1) 20.45 ounces
(2) 22.73 ounces
(3) 25.45 ounces
(4) 30.56 ounces

5. **OPEN-ENDED** Find the ratio of the volume of the sphere to the volume of the cube.

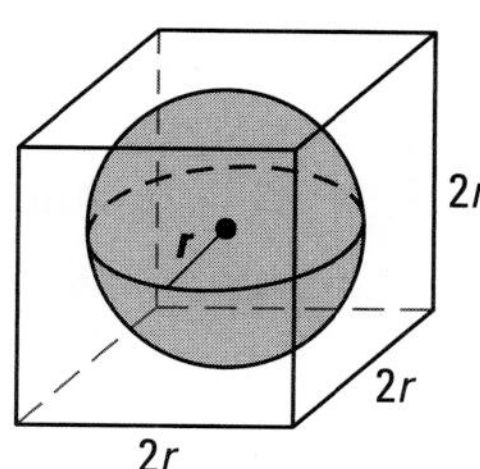

Use the formula $V = \frac{4}{3}\pi r^3$ for the volume of a sphere and the formula $V = s^3$ for the volume of a cube where r is the radius of the sphere and s is the side length of the cube. Write your answer as a decimal rounded to the nearest hundredth.

6. **OPEN-ENDED** A manufacturer of instant rice is considering two different styles of packaging. One is a rectangular container with a square base. The other is a cylinder.

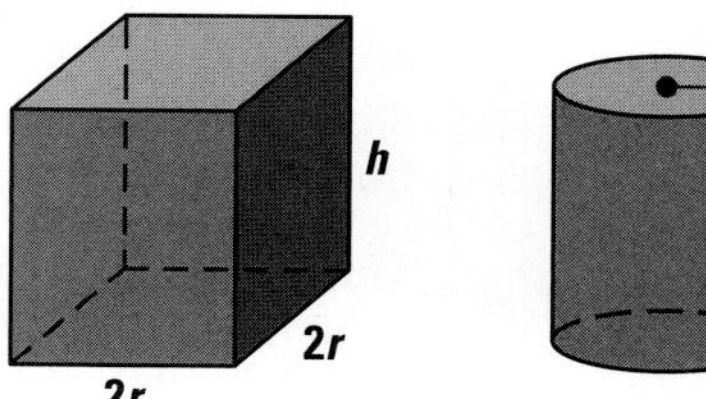

Find the ratio of surface area to volume for each container.

Using the ratios, what can you determine about the efficiencies of the containers?

8 CHAPTER SUMMARY

Animated Algebra
classzone.com
Electronic Function Library

BIG IDEAS

For Your Notebook

Big Idea 1

Graphing Rational Functions

Use the following steps to graph $f(x) = \frac{p(x)}{q(x)} = \frac{a_m x^m + a_{m-1}x^{m-1} + \cdots + a_1 x + a_0}{b_n x^n + b_{n-1}x^{n-1} + \cdots + b_1 x + b_0}$

where $p(x)$ and $q(x)$ have no common factors other than ± 1.

STEP 1 **Plot** the x-intercepts. The x-intercepts are the real zeros of $p(x)$.

STEP 2 **Draw** the vertical asymptote(s). A vertical asymptote occurs at each real zero of $q(x)$.

STEP 3 **Draw** the horizontal asymptote, if it exists.

If $m < n$, $y = 0$ is a horizontal asymptote.

If $m = n$, $y = \frac{a_m}{b_n}$ is a horizontal asymptote.

If $m > n$, there is no horizontal asymptote.

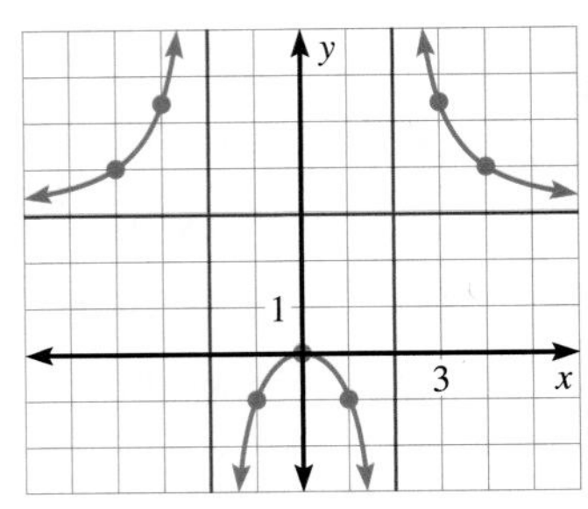

$y = \frac{3x^2}{x^2 - 4}$

STEP 4 **Plot** several points on both sides of each vertical asymptote.

Big Idea 2

Performing Operations with Rational Expressions

Operation	Example
Simplify Divide out common factors from the numerator and denominator.	$\frac{x^2 + 3x}{x^2 + 8x + 15} = \frac{x\cancel{(x+3)}}{(x+5)\cancel{(x+3)}} = \frac{x}{x+5}$
Multiply Multiply numerators and denominators. Then simplify.	$\frac{x}{15} \cdot \frac{3}{x^2 + 7x} = \frac{3x}{15x(x+7)} = \frac{1}{5(x+7)}$
Divide Multiply the first expression by the reciprocal of the second expression. Then simplify.	$\frac{x^2}{3x+1} \div \frac{1}{6x+2} = \frac{x^2}{3x+1} \cdot \frac{2(3x+1)}{1} = 2x^2$
Add or Subtract Write the expressions with like denominators. Then add or subtract the numerators over the common denominator. Lastly, simplify.	$\frac{5}{x} + \frac{x}{x+2} = \frac{5(x+2)}{x(x+2)} + \frac{x^2}{x(x+2)} = \frac{x^2 + 5x + 10}{x(x+2)}$

Big Idea 3

Solving Rational Equations

Solve $\frac{x}{x+1} + \frac{2}{x+4} = 1$.

STEP 1 **Find** the LCD. LCD is $(x + 1)(x + 4)$.

STEP 2 **Multiply** each side of the equation by the LCD. $x(x + 4) + 2(x + 1) = (x + 1)(x + 4)$

STEP 3 **Solve** the resulting equation.

$$x^2 + 4x + 2x + 2 = x^2 + 5x + 4$$
$$6x + 2 = 5x + 4$$
$$x = 2$$

8 CHAPTER REVIEW

@HomeTutor
classzone.com
- Multi-Language Glossary
- Vocabulary practice

REVIEW KEY VOCABULARY

- inverse variation, *p. 551*
- constant of variation, *p. 551*
- joint variation, *p. 553*
- rational function, *p. 558*
- simplified form of a rational expression, *p. 573*
- complex fraction, *p. 584*
- cross multiplying, *p. 589*

VOCABULARY EXERCISES

1. Copy and complete: If two variables x and y are related by an equation of the form $y = \frac{a}{x}$ where $a \neq 0$, then x and y show __?__.
2. Suppose z varies jointly with x and y. What can you say about $\frac{z}{xy}$?
3. Copy and complete: A function of the form $f(x) = \frac{p(x)}{q(x)}$ where $p(x)$ and $q(x)$ are polynomials and $q(x) \neq 0$ is called a(n) __?__.
4. Give two examples of a complex fraction.
5. Copy and complete: When you rewrite the equation $\frac{3}{x} = \frac{2}{x-1}$ as $3(x-1) = 2x$, you are __?__.

REVIEW EXAMPLES AND EXERCISES

Use the review examples and exercises below to check your understanding of the concepts you have learned in each lesson of Chapter 8.

8.1 Model Inverse and Joint Variation

pp. 551–557

EXAMPLE

The variables x and y vary inversely, and $y = 12$ when $x = 3$. Write an equation that relates x and y. Then find y when $x = -4$.

$y = \frac{a}{x}$ **Write general equation for inverse variation.**

$12 = \frac{a}{3}$ **Substitute 12 for y and 3 for x.**

$36 = a$ **Solve for a.**

▶ The inverse variation equation is $y = \frac{36}{x}$. When $x = -4$, $y = \frac{36}{-4} = -9$.

EXERCISES

EXAMPLE 2 on p. 551 for Exs. 6–9

The variables x and y vary inversely. Use the given values to write an equation relating x and y. Then find y when $x = -3$.

6. $x = 1, y = 5$
7. $x = -4, y = -6$
8. $x = \frac{5}{2}, y = 18$
9. $x = -12, y = \frac{2}{3}$

8 CHAPTER REVIEW

8.2 Graph Simple Rational Functions

pp. 558–563

EXAMPLE

Graph $y = \frac{2x + 5}{x - 1}$. State the domain and range.

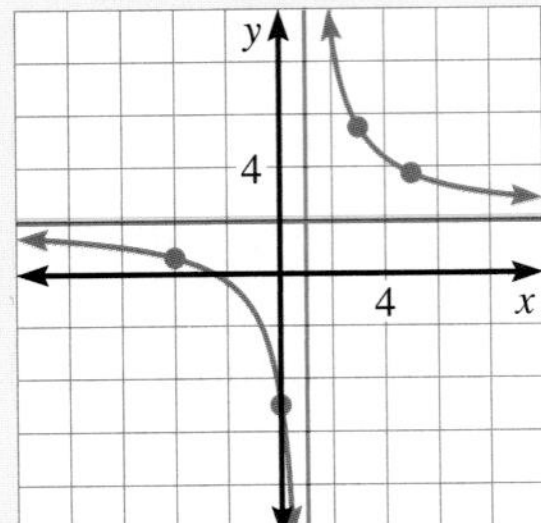

STEP 1 **Draw** the asymptotes. Solve $x - 1 = 0$ for x to find the vertical asymptote $x = 1$. The horizontal asymptote is the line $y = \frac{2}{1} = 2$.

STEP 2 **Plot** points to the left and to the right of the vertical asymptote.

STEP 3 **Draw** the two branches of the hyperbola so that they pass through the plotted points and approach the asymptotes.

▶ The domain is all real numbers except 1. The range is all real numbers except 2.

EXERCISES

EXAMPLES 2 and 3 on pp. 559–560 for Exs. 10–12

Graph the function. State the domain and range.

10. $y = \frac{4}{x - 3}$

11. $y = \frac{1}{x + 5} + 2$

12. $f(x) = \frac{3x - 2}{x - 4}$

8.3 Graph General Rational Functions

pp. 565–571

EXAMPLE

Graph $y = \frac{2x^2}{x + 2}$.

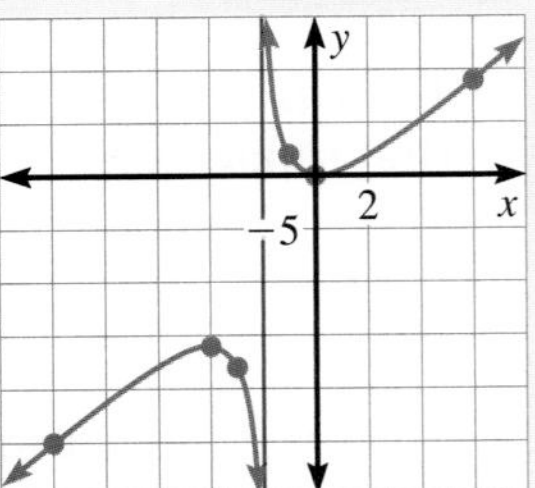

- The numerator has 0 as its only zero, so the graph has an x-intercept at (0, 0).
- The denominator has −2 as its only zero, so the graph has a vertical asymptote at $x = -2$.
- The degree of the numerator (2) is greater than the degree of the denominator (1). So, there is no horizontal asymptote. The graph has the same end behavior as the graph of $y = \frac{2}{1}x^{2-1} = 2x$.

EXERCISES

EXAMPLES 1, 2, and 3 on pp. 565–566 for Exs. 13–18

Graph the function.

13. $y = \frac{5}{x^2 + 1}$

14. $y = \frac{4x^2}{x - 1}$

15. $h(x) = \frac{6x^2}{x - 2}$

16. $y = \frac{-8}{x^2 + 3}$

17. $y = \frac{x^2 + 6}{x^2 - 3x - 40}$

18. $g(x) = \frac{x^2 - 1}{x + 4}$

@HomeTutor
classzone.com
Chapter Review Practice

8.4 Multiply and Divide Rational Expressions *pp. 573–580*

EXAMPLE

Divide: $\frac{3x+27}{6x-48} \div \frac{x^2+9x}{x^2-4x-32}$

$$\frac{3x+27}{6x-48} \div \frac{x^2+9x}{x^2-4x-32} = \frac{3x+27}{6x-48} \cdot \frac{x^2-4x-32}{x^2+9x}$$ **Multiply by reciprocal.**

$$= \frac{3(x+9)}{6(x-8)} \cdot \frac{(x+4)(x-8)}{x(x+9)}$$ **Factor.**

$$= \frac{\cancel{3}\cancel{(x+9)}(x+4)\cancel{(x-8)}}{2\cancel{(3)}\cancel{(x-8)}(x)\cancel{(x+9)}}$$ **Divide out common factors.**

$$= \frac{x+4}{2x}$$ **Simplified form**

EXERCISES

EXAMPLES 3, 4, 6, and 7 on pp. 575–577 for Exs. 19–22

Perform the indicated operation. Simplify the result.

19. $\frac{80x^4}{y^3} \cdot \frac{xy}{5x^2}$

20. $\frac{x-3}{2x-8} \cdot \frac{6x^2-96}{x^2-9}$

21. $\frac{16x^2-8x+1}{x^3-7x^2+12x} \div \frac{20x^2-5x}{15x^3}$

22. $\frac{x^2-13x+40}{x^2-2x-15} \div (x^2-5x-24)$

8.5 Add and Subtract Rational Expressions *pp. 582–588*

EXAMPLE

Add: $\frac{x}{6x+24} + \frac{x+2}{x^2+9x+20}$

The denominators factor as $6(x+4)$ and $(x+4)(x+5)$, so the LCD is $6(x+4)(x+5)$. Use this result to rewrite each expression with a common denominator, and then add.

$$\frac{x}{6x+24} + \frac{x+2}{x^2+9x+20} = \frac{x}{6(x+4)} + \frac{x+2}{(x+4)(x+5)}$$

$$= \frac{x}{6(x+4)} \cdot \frac{x+5}{x+5} + \frac{x+2}{(x+4)(x+5)} \cdot \frac{6}{6}$$

$$= \frac{x^2+5x}{6(x+4)(x+5)} + \frac{6x+12}{6(x+4)(x+5)}$$

$$= \frac{x^2+11x+12}{6(x+4)(x+5)}$$

EXERCISES

EXAMPLES 3 and 4 on pp. 583–584 for Exs. 23–25

Perform the indicated operation and simplify.

23. $\frac{5}{6(x+3)} + \frac{x+4}{2x}$

24. $\frac{5x}{x+8} + \frac{4x-9}{x^2+5x-24}$

25. $\frac{x+2}{x^2+4x+3} - \frac{5x}{x^2-9}$

8 CHAPTER REVIEW

8.6 Solve Rational Equations

pp. 589–595

EXAMPLE

Solve: $\frac{3x}{x+1} + \frac{6}{2x} = \frac{7}{x}$

The least common denominator is $2x(x + 1)$.

$\frac{3x}{x+1} + \frac{6}{2x} = \frac{7}{x}$	**Write original equation.**
$2x(x+1)\left(\frac{3x}{x+1} + \frac{6}{2x}\right) = 2x(x+1) \cdot \frac{7}{x}$	**Multiply each side by the LCD, $2x(x + 1)$.**
$2x(3x) + 6(x + 1) = 2(x + 1)(7)$	**Simplify.**
$6x^2 + 6x + 6 = 14x + 14$	**Simplify.**
$6x^2 - 8x - 8 = 0$	**Write in standard form.**
$3x^2 - 4x - 4 = 0$	**Divide each side by 2.**
$(3x + 2)(x - 2) = 0$	**Factor.**
$3x + 2 = 0$ or $x - 2 = 0$	**Zero product property**
$x = -\frac{2}{3}$ or $x = 2$	**Solve for x.**

▶ The solutions are $-\frac{2}{3}$ and 2. Check these in the original equation to make sure neither solution is extraneous.

EXERCISES

EXAMPLES 1, 4, and 5 on pp. 589–591 for Exs. 26–36

Solve the equation by cross multiplying. Check your solution(s).

26. $\frac{2x}{9} = \frac{2}{x}$

27. $\frac{5}{x} = \frac{7}{x+2}$

28. $\frac{x-1}{4} = \frac{3x}{9}$

29. $\frac{2}{x+2} = \frac{6}{2x+5}$

30. $\frac{x+12}{3} = \frac{2x+3}{x+2}$

31. $\frac{2x}{x+4} = \frac{-3x}{4x-3}$

Solve the equation by using the LCD. Check for extraneous solutions.

32. $\frac{5}{2} + \frac{3}{x} = 3$

33. $\frac{8(x-1)}{x^2-4} = \frac{4}{x+2}$

34. $\frac{3x}{x+1} = \frac{12}{x^2-1} + 2$

35. $\frac{2(x+7)}{x+4} - 2 = \frac{2x+20}{2x+8}$

36. BASKETBALL So far this season, a basketball player has made 60 of 75 free-throw attempts.

a. Write a rational expression that represents the player's free-throw percentage (expressed as a decimal) if she makes her next x free throws.

b. How many consecutive free throws must the player make in order to raise her free-throw percentage to at least 82%?

8 CHAPTER TEST

The variables x and y vary inversely. Use the given values to write an equation relating x and y. Then find y when $x = 4$.

1. $x = 5, y = 2$

2. $x = -2, y = 8$

3. $x = \frac{3}{2}, y = 10$

4. $x = 3, y = 6$

5. $x = -4, y = \frac{7}{2}$

6. $x = \frac{3}{4}, y = \frac{5}{8}$

Graph the function. State the domain and range.

7. $y = \frac{2}{x + 5} - 3$

8. $y = \frac{-1}{x - 4} - 1$

9. $f(x) = \frac{6 - x}{2x + 1}$

Graph the function.

10. $y = \frac{4}{x^2 + 2}$

11. $y = \frac{x^2 - 4}{x^2 + 8x + 15}$

12. $g(x) = \frac{x^2 + 3}{2x - 1}$

Find the least common multiple of the polynomials.

13. $(x - 3)(x + 5)$ and $x(x + 5)$

14. $4x^2(x - 2)$ and $8x(x + 2)$

15. $x^2 - 4x$ and $x^2 - 2x - 8$

16. $2x + 6$ and $x^3 + 10x^2 + 21x$

Perform the indicated operation and simplify.

17. $\frac{3x^2y}{4x^3y^5} \div \frac{6y^2}{2xy^3}$

18. $\frac{x^2 - 3x - 4}{x^2 - 3x - 18} \cdot \frac{x - 6}{x + 1}$

19. $\frac{x^2 - 8x + 15}{x^2 + 12x + 32} \cdot \frac{x + 4}{x^2 - 25}$

20. $\frac{x^2 - 11x + 28}{x^2 + 5x + 4} \div (x^2 - 16)$

21. $\frac{3x}{x + 5} - \frac{4x + 1}{x + 5}$

22. $\frac{4}{x - 3} + \frac{2}{x + 6}$

23. $\frac{3x}{x^2 + x - 12} - \frac{6}{x + 4}$

24. $\frac{4}{x + 5} + \frac{2x}{x^2 - 25}$

Solve the equation. Check for extraneous solutions.

25. $\frac{3}{x + 2} = \frac{x - 3}{2x + 4}$

26. $\frac{1}{x + 6} + \frac{x + 1}{x} = \frac{13}{x + 6}$

27. $\frac{x - 2}{x - 1} = \frac{x + 2}{x + 4}$

28. SOUND INTENSITY The intensity I of a sound varies inversely with the square of the distance r from the source of the sound. Write an equation relating I, r, and a constant a.

29. CABLE TV You have subscribed to a cable television service. The cable company charges you a one-time installation fee of \$30 and a monthly fee of \$50. Write and graph a model that gives the average cost per month as a function of the number of months you have subscribed to the service. After how many months will the average cost be \$56?

30. WEB HOSTING You are building a new website for your school. A company that hosts websites offers a dedicated server for a \$50 setup fee plus a monthly fee of \$99. How many months would you need to use this service in order for your average monthly cost to fall to \$100?

MULTIPLE CHOICE QUESTIONS

Some of the information you need to solve a multiple choice question may appear in a table, a diagram, or a graph.

PROBLEM 1

Which rational expression represents the ratio of the perimeter to the area of the playground shown in the diagram?

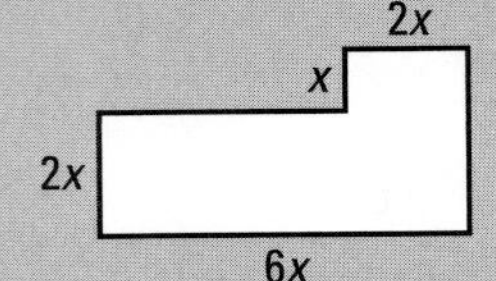

(1) $\frac{9}{7x}$ (3) $\frac{11}{14x}$

(2) $\frac{1}{x}$ (4) $\frac{1}{2x}$

Plan

INTERPRET THE DIAGRAM Determine the missing dimensions on the diagram. Then use them to write expressions for the perimeter and area of the playground.

Solution

STEP 1 Find the missing dimensions and write an expression for the perimeter.

Copy the diagram. Then find and label the missing dimensions.

Use subtraction and addition to find the dimensions that are not labeled on the diagram. The missing dimensions are $\mathbf{4x}$ and $\mathbf{3x}$.

$6x - 2x = 4x$; $x + 2x = 3x$

$$\text{Perimeter} = \mathbf{4x} + x + 2x + \mathbf{3x} + 6x + 2x$$
$$= 18x$$

STEP 2 Write an expression for the area.

The playground consists of two rectangles, one with dimensions $\boldsymbol{x}$ **by** $\mathbf{2x}$ and the other with dimensions $\mathbf{2x}$ **by** $\mathbf{6x}$.

To find the area of the playground, add the areas of the two rectangles.

$$\text{Area} = \mathbf{x(2x)} + \mathbf{2x(6x)}$$
$$= 2x^2 + 12x^2$$
$$= 14x^2$$

STEP 3 Find the ratio of the perimeter to the area.

The ratio of the perimeter to the area is:

$$\frac{\text{Perimeter}}{\text{Area}} = \frac{18x}{14x^2} = \frac{\cancel{2x}(9)}{\cancel{2x}(7x)} = \frac{9}{7x}$$

▸ The correct answer is (1).

PROBLEM 2

The table shows how the force F (in pounds) needed to loosen a certain bolt with a wrench depends on the length ℓ (in inches) of the wrench's handle. Which equation relates ℓ and F?

ℓ (in.)	F (lb)
4	375
6	250
10	150
12	125

(1) $F = 1500\ell$ (3) $F = \dfrac{1500}{\ell}$

(2) $F = 93.75\ell$ (4) $F = \dfrac{93.75}{\ell}$

Plan

INTERPRET THE TABLE The table shows four data pairs (ℓ, F). To write an equation relating ℓ and F, you need to find a pattern in the data.

Solution

STEP 1 Identify a pattern in the data pairs (ℓ, F).

Find the product $\ell \cdot F$ for each data pair.

$4(375) = 1500$ $6(250) = 1500$

$10(150) = 1500$ $12(125) = 1500$

Each product equals 1500, so the data show inverse variation.

STEP 2 Write an equation that relates ℓ and F.

An equation relating ℓ and F is the following:

$\ell \cdot F = 1500$ **Use the result from Step 1.**

$F = \dfrac{1500}{\ell}$ **Solve for F.**

▶ The correct answer is (3).

PRACTICE

1. Which rational expression represents the ratio of the perimeter to the area of the figure shown?

(1) $\dfrac{29}{67x}$ (3) $\dfrac{11x}{18x^2}$

(2) $\dfrac{3}{10x^2}$ (4) $\dfrac{9}{23x}$

2. Which equation represents the ordered pairs in the table?

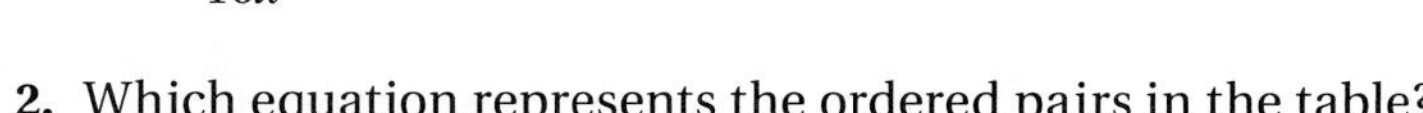

x	2	4	6	8	10
y	180	90	60	45	36

(1) $y = \dfrac{360}{x}$ (2) $y = \dfrac{x}{360}$ (3) $y = \dfrac{90}{x}$ (4) $y = \dfrac{x}{90}$

New York *Test Practice*

TEST PREPARATION

MULTIPLE CHOICE

In Exercises 1 and 2, use the given graph of a rational function.

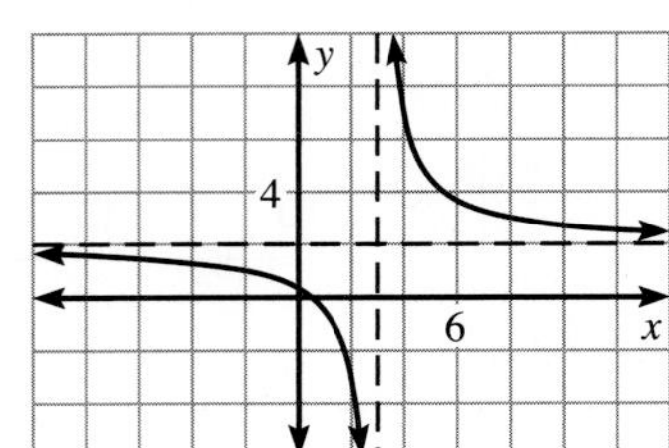

1. What is the range of the function?
   (1) All real numbers
   (2) All real numbers except 2
   (3) All real numbers except 3
   (4) All real numbers except 5

2. Which statement is false?
   (1) The line $x = 3$ is an asymptote.
   (2) The line $y = 2$ is an asymptote.
   (3) The function is undefined for $x = 2$.
   (4) The point $(-2, 1)$ lies on the graph.

In Exercises 3 and 4, use the given table.

p	−12	3	30	−1.5
q	2	1	−5	−0.5
r	−2	1	−2	1

3. What is the relationship among the variables?
   (1) The variable *p* varies jointly with *q* and *r*.
   (2) The variable *p* varies jointly with *q* and the square of *r*.
   (3) The variable *r* varies inversely with the sum of *p* and *q*.
   (4) The variable *q* varies inversely with the sum of *p* and *r*.

4. What is the value of *r* when $p = 20$ and $q = -4$?
   (1) -5 (3) $-\frac{5}{3}$
   (2) $-\frac{10}{3}$ (4) $-\frac{1}{5}$

In Exercises 5 and 6, use the given graph of a rational function.

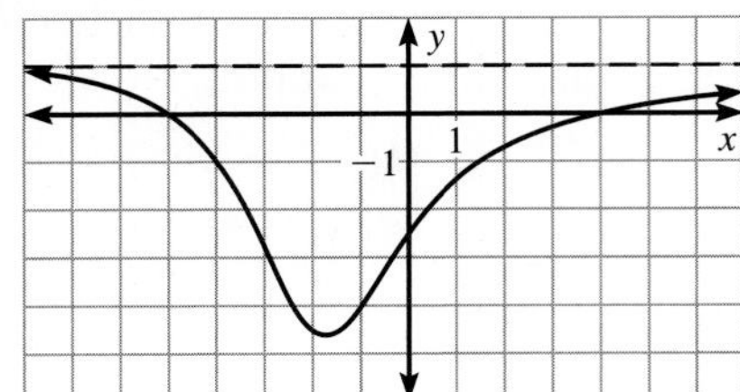

5. What are the *x*-intercepts of the graph?
   (1) −5 and −2.5 (3) −4 and 5
   (2) −2.5 and 4 (4) −5 and 4

6. What is the horizontal asymptote of the graph?
   (1) $x = -2$ (3) $x = 1$
   (2) $y = 0$ (4) $y = 1$

7. Consider a rectangle whose dimensions change but whose area remains constant. The rectangle's length ℓ varies inversely with its width w. The diagram below shows the rectangle at one moment in time. Which equation relates ℓ and w?

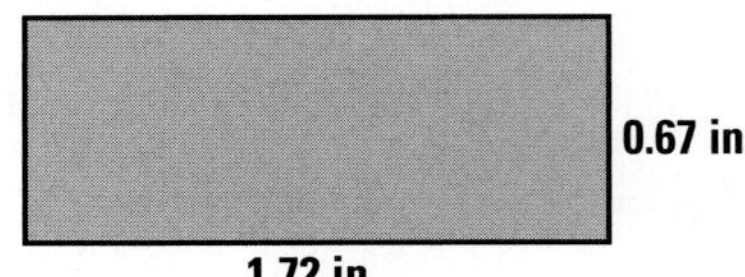

   (1) $w = 0.67\ell$ (3) $w = 1.72\ell$
   (2) $\ell w = 1.1524$ (4) $\ell = 1.1524w$

8. What is the approximate radius of a cylinder that has the same volume as the rectangular prism below and has the least surface area possible?

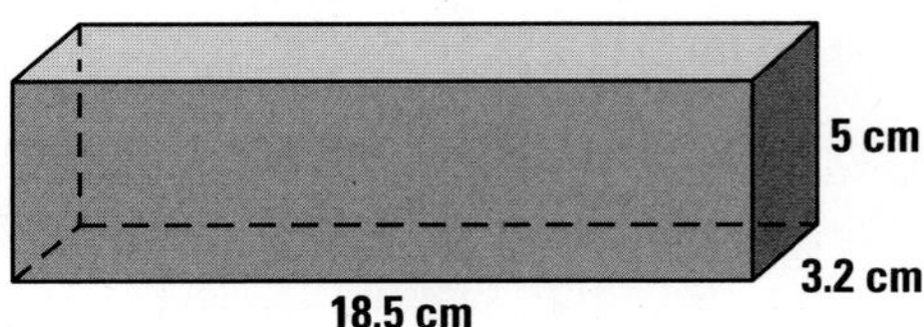

   (1) 3.61 cm (3) 6.00 cm
   (2) 3.84 cm (4) 7.66 cm

MULTIPLE CHOICE

9. What is the solution to the equation below?

$$\frac{4}{x+1} - \frac{1}{x} = 1$$

(1) -1

(2) 0

(3) $\frac{2}{3}$

(4) 1

10. What is the domain of the function below?

$$f(x) = \frac{x-3}{2x^2 - 4x + 2}$$

(1) all real numbers except 3

(2) all real numbers except 1

(3) all real numbers except 1 and 3

(4) all real numbers

11. The variables m and n vary inversely, and $m = -2$ when $n = -8$. What is the value of n when $m = 5$?

(1) -4

(2) -3.2

(3) 3.2

(4) 4

12. So far, Luis has turned in 15 of 17 homework assignments. However, Luis plans to do every future assignment. What is the *least* number of assignments that Luis must do in order to have a homework percentage of exactly 95%? Find out by solving the equation $\frac{15+x}{17+x} = 0.95$.

(1) 3 assignments

(2) 23 assignments

(3) 38 assignments

(4) Luis cannot raise his percentage to 95.

OPEN-ENDED

13. Lisa steps onto an escalator and begins descending. After riding for 12 feet, she realizes that she dropped her keys on the upper floor and walks back up the escalator to retrieve them. The total time T of her trip down and up the escalator is given by the equation

$$T = \frac{12}{s} + \frac{12}{w-s}$$

where s is the speed of the escalator and w is Lisa's walking speed. The trip took 9 seconds and Lisa walked at a speed of 6 feet per second. Find the speed of the escalator.

14. From 1960 to 1995 in the United States, the daily water consumption C (in billions of gallons) and the population P (in thousands) can be modeled by

$$C = \frac{2.89x^2 + 61.0}{0.0293x^2 + 1} \text{ and } P = 2460x + 180{,}000$$

where x represents the number of years since 1960. Write a model for the daily *per capita* water consumption (in gallons per person) as a function of the year. *Explain* all of your steps.

15. A digital video recorder costs \$99.99, and a programming service for the digital video recorder costs \$12.95 per month.

Write a model that gives the average cost per month C as a function of the number of months m you have subscribed to the service.

Graph the model. Use the graph to estimate the number of months that you need to subscribe before the average cost drops to \$14 per month.

What is the equation of the horizontal asymptote? What does the asymptote represent?

TEST PREPARATION

9 Quadratic Relations and Conic Sections

Before

In previous chapters, you learned the following skills, which you'll use in Chapter 9: graphing quadratic functions, completing the square, and solving linear systems.

Prerequisite Skills

VOCABULARY CHECK

Copy and complete the statement.

1. The graph of a(n) __?__ function is a **parabola**.
2. The graph of the **rational function** $y = \frac{2}{x}$, shown at the right, is a __?__.
3. Two equations of the form $Ax + By = C$ and $Dx + Ey = F$ form a __?__ **system of equations**.

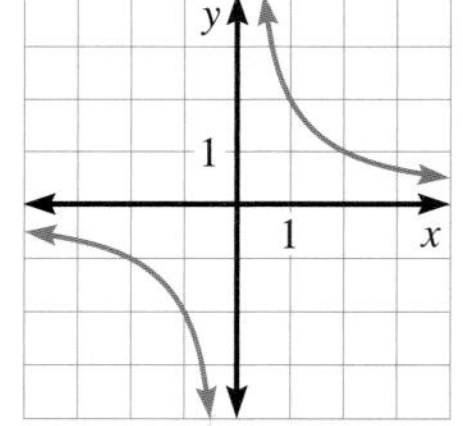

SKILLS CHECK

Graph. Label the vertex and axis of symmetry. *(Review pp. 236, 245 for 9.2.)*

4. $y = x^2 - 3$
5. $y = -0.25x^2$
6. $y = 3(x + 1)^2$
7. $y = 0.5(x - 2)^2 + 4$

Solve the equation by completing the square. *(Review p. 284 for 9.6.)*

8. $x^2 - 4x + 7 = 0$
9. $x^2 - 8x - 15 = 0$
10. $3x^2 + 9x - 12 = 0$

Solve the system using any algebraic method. *(Review p. 160 for 9.7.)*

11. $2x - y = 11$
 $-x - 2y = -3$
12. $x + 5y = -17$
 $-2x - 3y = 13$
13. $-4x + 7y = -14$
 $2x - 6y = 12$

@HomeTutor Prerequisite skills practice at classzone.com

In Chapter 9, you will apply the big ideas listed below and reviewed in the Chapter Summary on page 668. You will also use the key vocabulary listed below.

Big Ideas

1. **Writing equations of conic sections**
2. **Graphing equations of conic sections**
3. **Solving quadratic systems**

KEY VOCABULARY

- distance formula, *p. 614*
- focus, foci, *pp. 620, 634, 642*
- directrix, *p. 620*
- circle, *p. 626*
- ellipse, *p. 634*
- vertices, *pp. 634, 642*
- major axis, *p. 634*
- co-vertices, *p. 634*
- minor axis, *p. 634*
- hyperbola, *p. 642*
- transverse axis, *p. 642*
- conic sections, *p. 650*
- general second-degree equation, *p. 653*
- quadratic system, *p. 658*

You can use conic sections to describe the shapes of real-world objects. For example, you can use a parabola to model the cross section of a radio telescope.

Animated Algebra

The animation illustrated below for Exercise 58 on page 625 helps you answer this question: How do the dimensions of a radio telescope determine the equation that models its cross section?

Radio telescopes have a parabolic cross section that concentrates radio waves.

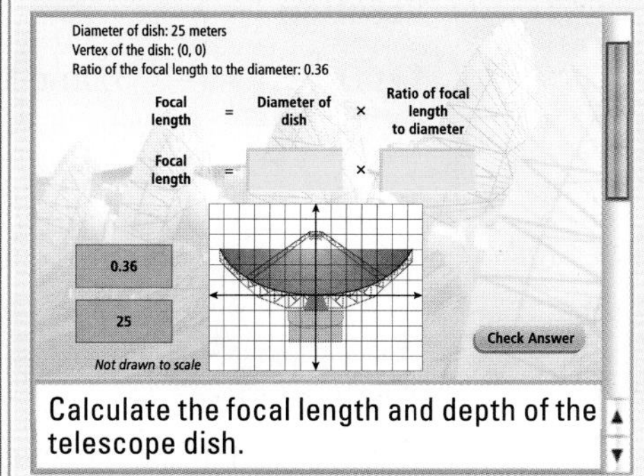

Calculate the focal length and depth of the telescope dish.

Animated Algebra at classzone.com

Other animations for Chapter 9: pages 615, 621, 635, 643, 649, and 651

9.1 Apply the Distance and Midpoint Formulas

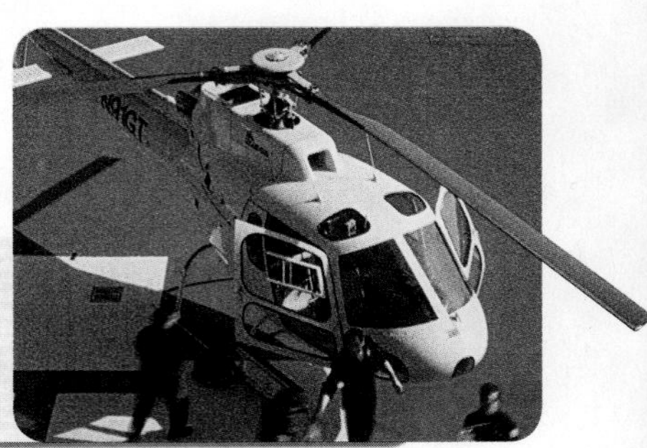

Before You found the slope of a line passing through two points.

Now You will find the length and midpoint of a line segment.

Why? So you can find real-world distances, as in Exs. 48–51.

Key Vocabulary
- **distance formula**
- **midpoint formula**

To find the distance d between $A(x_1, y_1)$ and $B(x_2, y_2)$, apply the Pythagorean theorem to right triangle ABC.

$$(AB)^2 = (AC)^2 + (BC)^2$$

$$d^2 = (x_2 - x_1)^2 + (y_2 - y_1)^2$$

$$d = \sqrt{(x_2 - x_1)^2 + (y_2 - y_1)^2}$$

The final equation is the **distance formula**.

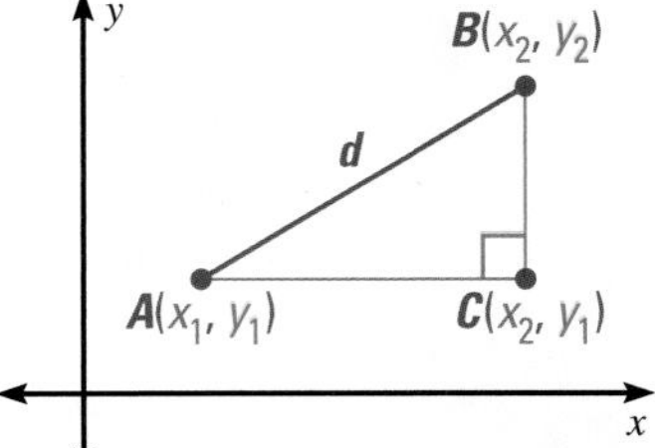

KEY CONCEPT — *For Your Notebook*

The Distance Formula

The distance d between (x_1, y_1) and (x_2, y_2) is $d = \sqrt{(x_2 - x_1)^2 + (y_2 - y_1)^2}$.

★ EXAMPLE 1 Standardized Test Practice

What is the distance between (−3, 5) and (4, −1)?

Ⓐ $\sqrt{13}$ Ⓑ $\sqrt{65}$ Ⓒ $\sqrt{85}$ Ⓓ 13

Solution

Let $(x_1, y_1) = (-3, 5)$ and $(x_2, y_2) = (4, -1)$.

$$d = \sqrt{(x_2 - x_1)^2 + (y_2 - y_1)^2} = \sqrt{(4 - (-3))^2 + (-1 - 5)^2} = \sqrt{49 + 36} = \sqrt{85}$$

▶ The correct answer is C. Ⓐ Ⓑ Ⓒ Ⓓ

EXAMPLE 2 Classify a triangle using the distance formula

Classify $\triangle ABC$ as *scalene*, *isosceles*, or *equilateral*.

$$AB = \sqrt{(7 - 4)^2 + (3 - 6)^2} = \sqrt{18} = 3\sqrt{2}$$

$$BC = \sqrt{(2 - 7)^2 + (1 - 3)^2} = \sqrt{29}$$

$$AC = \sqrt{(2 - 4)^2 + (1 - 6)^2} = \sqrt{29}$$

▶ Because $BC = AC$, $\triangle ABC$ is isosceles.

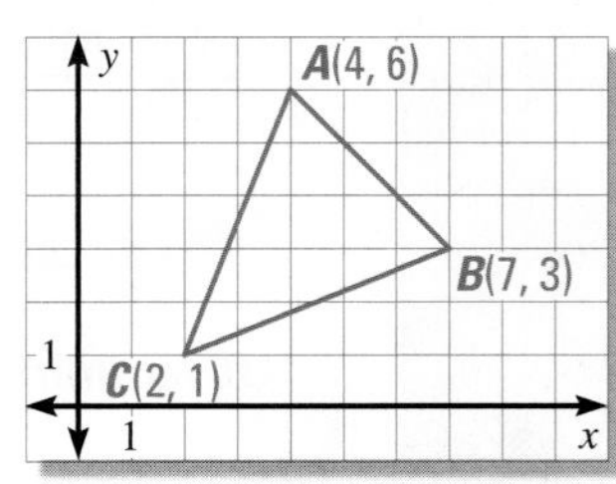

✓ GUIDED PRACTICE for Examples 1 and 2

1. What is the distance between $(3, -3)$ and $(-1, 5)$?

2. The vertices of a triangle are $R(-1, 3)$, $S(5, 2)$, and $T(3, 6)$. Classify $\triangle RST$ as *scalene, isosceles,* or *equilateral.*

KEY CONCEPT — *For Your Notebook*

The Midpoint Formula

A line segment's *midpoint* is equidistant from the segment's endpoints. The **midpoint formula**, shown below, gives the midpoint of the line segment joining $A(x_1, y_1)$ and $B(x_2, y_2)$.

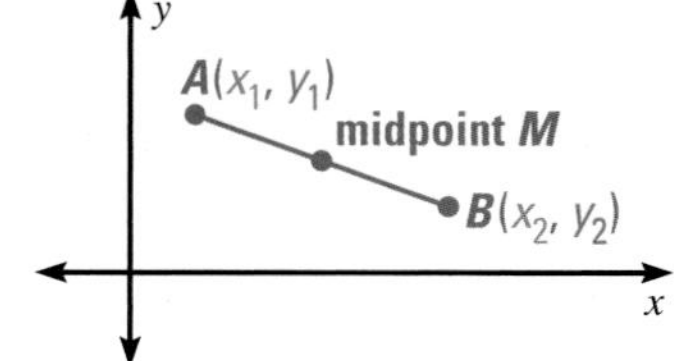

$$M\left(\frac{x_1 + x_2}{2}, \frac{y_1 + y_2}{2}\right)$$

In words, each coordinate of M is the mean of the corresponding coordinates of A and B.

EXAMPLE 3 Find the midpoint of a line segment

Find the midpoint of the line segment joining $(-5, 1)$ and $(-1, 6)$.

Solution

Let $(x_1, y_1) = (-5, 1)$ and $(x_2, y_2) = (-1, 6)$.

$$\left(\frac{x_1 + x_2}{2}, \frac{y_1 + y_2}{2}\right) = \left(\frac{-5 + (-1)}{2}, \frac{1 + 6}{2}\right) = \left(-3, \frac{7}{2}\right)$$

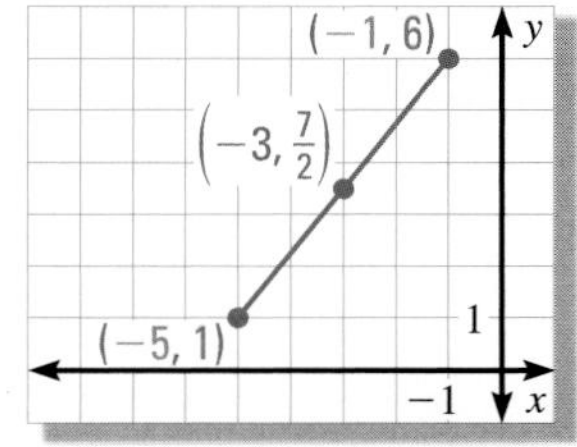

Animated Algebra at classzone.com

EXAMPLE 4 Find a perpendicular bisector

REVIEW EQUATIONS
For help with writing equations of perpendicular lines, see p. 98.

Write an equation for the perpendicular bisector of the line segment joining $A(-3, 4)$ and $B(5, 6)$.

Solution

STEP 1 **Find** the midpoint of the line segment.

$$\left(\frac{x_1 + x_2}{2}, \frac{y_1 + y_2}{2}\right) = \left(\frac{-3 + 5}{2}, \frac{4 + 6}{2}\right) = (1, 5)$$

STEP 2 **Calculate** the slope of $\overline{AB}$.

$$m = \frac{y_2 - y_1}{x_2 - x_1} = \frac{6 - 4}{5 - (-3)} = \frac{2}{8} = \frac{1}{4}$$

STEP 3 **Find** the slope of the perpendicular bisector: $-\frac{1}{m} = -\frac{1}{1/4} = -4$.

STEP 4 **Use** point-slope form: $y - 5 = -4(x - 1)$, or $y = -4x + 9$.

▸ An equation for the perpendicular bisector of $\overline{AB}$ is $y = -4x + 9$.

FINDING A CIRCLE'S CENTER Recall from geometry that the perpendicular bisector of any chord of a circle passes through the circle's center. You can use this theorem to find the center of a circle given three points on the circle.

EXAMPLE 5 Solve a multi-step problem

ASTEROID CRATER Many scientists believe that an asteroid slammed into Earth about 65 million years ago on what is now Mexico's Yucatan peninsula, creating an enormous crater that is now deeply buried by sediment. Use the labeled points on the outline of the circular crater to estimate its diameter. (Each unit in the coordinate plane represents 1 mile.)

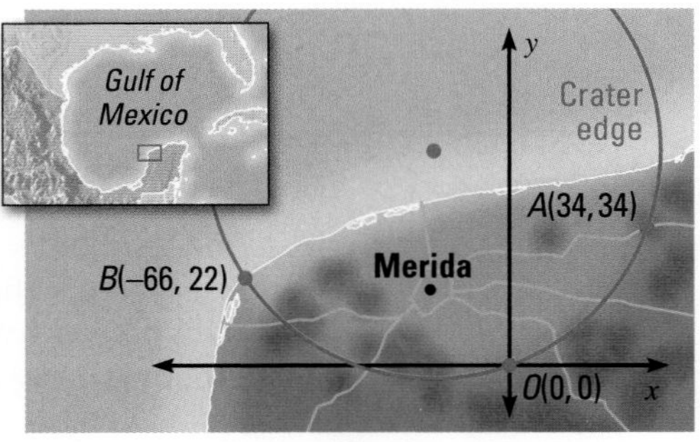

Solution

STEP 1 **Write** equations for the perpendicular bisectors of $\overline{AO}$ and $\overline{OB}$ using the method of Example 4.

$y = -x + 34$ **Perpendicular bisector of $\overline{AO}$**

$y = 3x + 110$ **Perpendicular bisector of $\overline{OB}$**

STEP 2 **Find** the coordinates of the center of the circle, where $\overline{AO}$ and $\overline{OB}$ intersect, by solving the system formed by the two equations in Step 1.

REVIEW SYSTEMS
For help with solving systems of equations, see p. 160.

$y = -x + 34$	**Write first equation.**
$3x + 110 = -x + 34$	**Substitute for *y*.**
$4x = -76$	**Simplify.**
$x = -19$	**Solve for *x*.**
$y = -(-19) + 34$	**Substitute the *x*-value into the first equation.**
$y = 53$	**Solve for *y*.**

The center of the circle is $C(-19, 53)$.

STEP 3 **Calculate** the radius of the circle using the distance formula. The radius is the distance between C and any of the three given points.

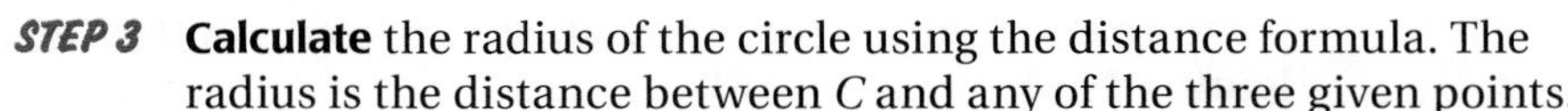

$$OC = \sqrt{(-19 - 0)^2 + (53 - 0)^2} = \sqrt{3170} \approx 56.3$$ **Use $(x_1, y_1) = (0, 0)$ and $(x_2, y_2) = (-19, 53)$.**

▶ The crater has a diameter of about $2(56.3) = 112.6$ miles.

GUIDED PRACTICE for Examples 3, 4, and 5

For the line segment joining the two given points, (a) find the midpoint and (b) write an equation for the perpendicular bisector.

3. (0, 0), (−4, 12) **4.** (−2, 1), (4, −7) **5.** (3, 8), (−5, −10)

6. The points (0, 0), (6, −2), and (16, 8) lie on a circle. Use the method given in Example 5 to find the diameter of the circle.

9.1 EXERCISES

HOMEWORK KEY ◯ = **WORKED-OUT SOLUTIONS** on p. WS15 for Exs. 7, 27, and 53
★ = **STANDARDIZED TEST PRACTICE** Exs. 2, 18, 19, 37, and 56

SKILL PRACTICE

1. **VOCABULARY** State the distance and midpoint formulas.

2. ★ **WRITING** When finding the midpoint of a line segment joining two points, does it matter which point you choose as (x_1, y_1)? *Explain.*

EXAMPLES 1 and 3 on pp. 614–615 for Exs. 3–21

USING THE FORMULAS Find the distance between the two points. Then find the midpoint of the line segment joining the two points.

3. (0, 0), (8, 15)
4. (0, 0), (4, 2)
5. (0, 6), (5, −4)
6. (−7, 0), (5, 3)
7. (2, −1), (6, −5)
8. (−1, −2), (8, 4)
9. (−4, 8), (8, −4)
10. (6, −3), (10, −9)
11. (−4, 4), (5, −4)
12. (11, −12), (18, 12)
13. (−5, 1), (15, 8)
14. (9, 9), (−16, −16)
15. (−3.8, 15), (6.2, −11)
16. (1.5, 4), (2.3, 9)
17. (−2.4, −6.7), (3.1, −5.3)

18. ★ **MULTIPLE CHOICE** What is the distance between (−4, 3) and (6, 6)?

Ⓐ $\sqrt{13}$ Ⓑ $\sqrt{85}$ Ⓒ $\sqrt{109}$ Ⓓ $\sqrt{181}$

19. ★ **MULTIPLE CHOICE** What is the midpoint of the line segment joining (−3, 7) and (5, −2)?

Ⓐ $\left(1, \frac{5}{2}\right)$ Ⓑ $\left(-4, \frac{5}{2}\right)$ Ⓒ $\left(1, \frac{9}{2}\right)$ Ⓓ $\left(-4, \frac{9}{2}\right)$

ERROR ANALYSIS *Describe* and correct the error in finding the distance between the two points.

20. (5, −1), (2, 6)

$$d = \sqrt{(2-5)^2 + (6-1)^2} = \sqrt{9 + 25} = \sqrt{34}$$

21. (−4, 3), (2, 8)

$$d = \sqrt{(2-(-4))^2 - (8-3)^2} = \sqrt{36 - 25} = \sqrt{11}$$

EXAMPLE 2 on p. 614 for Exs. 22–30

CLASSIFYING TRIANGLES The vertices of a triangle are given. Classify the triangle as *scalene, isosceles,* or *equilateral.*

22. (−5, 0), (0, 6), (5, 0)
23. (0, −3), (0, 3), (3, 0)
24. (3, 5), (5, −3), (7, −3)
25. (−2, 5), (1, −1), (4, 6)
26. (1, 4), (4, 1), (7, 4)
27. (−4, 1), (−2, 6), (0, −1)
28. (−1, −6), (1, 1), (4, −5)
29. (−4, 3), (2, −1), (8, −1)
30. (3, 5), (6, 9), (11, 9)

EXAMPLE 4 on p. 615 for Exs. 31–36

WRITING EQUATIONS Write an equation for the perpendicular bisector of the line segment joining the two points.

31. (3, 8), (7, 14)
32. (−5, 6), (1, 8)
33. (−3, −6), (−1, 2)
34. (1, 4), (6, −6)
35. (−3, −5), (9, −2)
36. (5, 10), (10, 7)

37. ★ **OPEN-ENDED MATH** Find two points not on the lines $x = 4$ or $y = 2$ such that the midpoint of the line segment joining the points is (4, 2).

GEOMETRY A *median* of a triangle is a line segment joining a vertex and the midpoint of the opposite side. The ordered pairs represent vertices of a triangle. Write an equation of the line containing the median that joins the first vertex to the side opposite it.

38. (8, 4), (0, 0), (10, 0) **39.** (3, 10), (4, 2), (10, 8) **40.** (2, 6), (3, 1), (7, 5)

FINDING A COORDINATE Use the given distance d between the two points to find the value of x or y.

41. $(0, 3), (x, 5); d = 2\sqrt{10}$

42. $(-3, -1), (2, y); d = \sqrt{41}$

43. $(x, 7), (-4, 1); d = 6\sqrt{2}$

44. $(1, y), (8, 13); d = \sqrt{74}$

45. REASONING Let (x, y) be any point on the line $y = 2x$. Write and simplify an equation that gives the distance d between (x, y) and $(2, 3)$ as a function of x alone. Then find the coordinates of two points on the line $y = 2x$ that are each $\sqrt{10}$ units from $(2, 3)$.

46. CHALLENGE Show that $M\left(\frac{x_1 + x_2}{2}, \frac{y_1 + y_2}{2}\right)$ is the midpoint of the line segment with endpoints (x_1, y_1) and (x_2, y_2). To do this, show that M is equidistant from each endpoint and that M lies on the line containing (x_1, y_1) and (x_2, y_2).

PROBLEM SOLVING

EXAMPLE 1 on p. 614 for Exs. 47–52

47. ROBOTS A remote-controlled robot can be instructed to move by entering coordinates on a control panel. If the robot is instructed to move from (6, 11) straight to (−2, 26), how far does the robot move? Assume the coordinates are in meters.

@HomeTutor for problem solving help at classzone.com

HELICOPTER RESCUE In Exercises 48–51, use the information given to find the distance a medical evacuation ("medevac") helicopter would have to fly to Memorial Medical Center from each location.

The Highway Department in Sangamon County, Illinois, uses a map that has its origin in central Springfield. Each unit on the map represents 1 mile, and the letters N, S, E, and W indicate direction. For example, 4W 5.6N is 4 miles west and 5.6 miles north of the origin. On a coordinate plane, 4W 5.6N corresponds to the point (−4, 5.6). Memorial Medical is at 0 0.5N, or (0, 0.5).

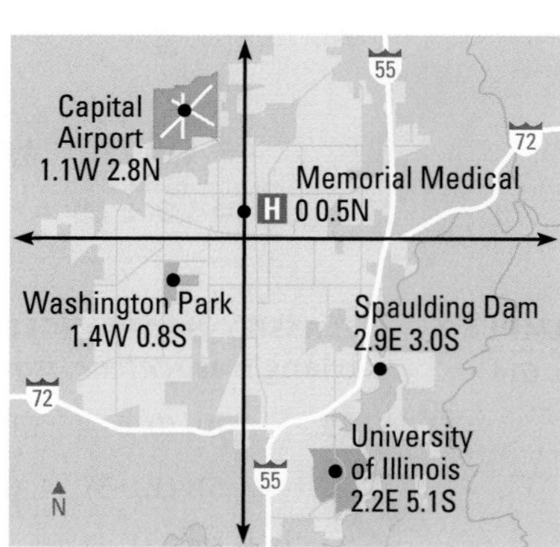

48. Capital Airport **49.** University of Illinois

50. Washington Park **51.** Spaulding Dam

@HomeTutor for problem solving help at classzone.com

52. COMMUTING To get from her home to her office, Li must drive around a lake. If she drives 2 miles north, then 5 miles east, and then 4 miles south, what is the straight-line distance between Li's home and her office?

○ = **WORKED-OUT SOLUTIONS on p. WS1**

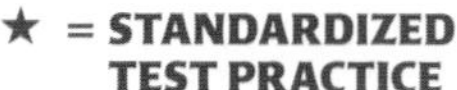
★ = **STANDARDIZED TEST PRACTICE**

EXAMPLE 3
on p. 615
for Ex. 53

53. **MULTI-STEP PROBLEM** The diagram shows part of a trail system at a nature preserve. Each unit represents 0.1 mile. Suppose that you go from the visitor center V to the observation stand S, and then take a break at M, halfway between the observation stand and the picnic area P.

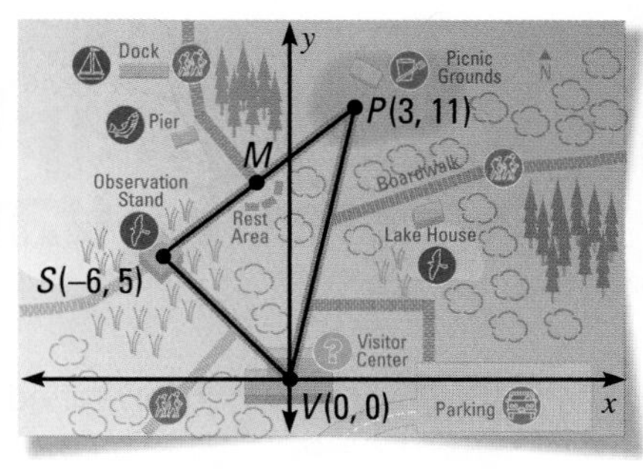

a. What are the coordinates of M?

b. What is the total distance traveled from V to M?

c. What is the distance from M back to V through P?

EXAMPLE 5
on p. 616
for Exs. 54–55

54. **ARCHAEOLOGY** While on an archaeological dig, you uncover a piece of a circular dish. You lay the piece on a coordinate plane and mark three points on the dish's edge at $(-4, 2)$, $(0, 0)$, and $(6, 4)$ where each unit represents 1 inch. What was the original diameter of the dish?

55. **METEOR CRATERS** Five meteor craters are clustered together near Odessa, Texas. Three points on the edge of the circular main crater can be represented by $(-220, 220)$, $(0, 0)$, and $(200, 40)$ where each unit represents 1 foot. What is the diameter of the crater to the nearest 10 feet?

56. ★ **EXTENDED RESPONSE** You are ordering a triangular sail for your sailboat. When you get the sail, you plan to sew a thin decorative strip connecting the midpoints M_1 and M_2 of two sides of the sail, as shown in the diagram.

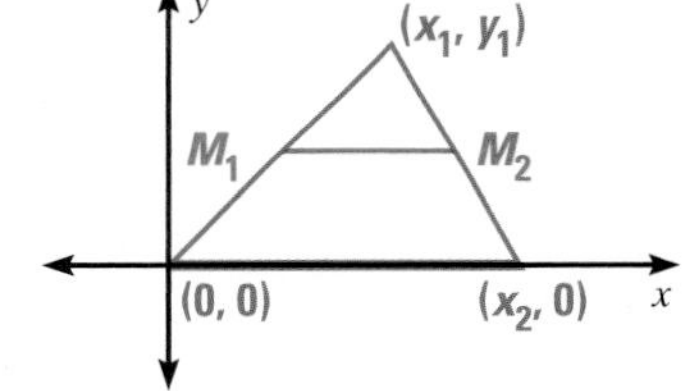

a. Write expressions for the coordinates of M_1 and M_2.

b. Write a simplified expression for the length of the strip. *Compare* this length with the length of the sail's base.

c. Do your results from part (b) depend upon the shape of the triangular sail? *Explain.*

57. **CHALLENGE** At time $t = 0$, a car begins traveling east at 60 miles per hour from a point 100 miles west and 40 miles north of a radio tower. The tower has a transmission range of 50 miles. Use the distance formula to find the times t during which the car is in range of the tower.

NEW YORK MIXED REVIEW

TEST PRACTICE at classzone.com

58. What are the x-intercepts of the graph of the function $y = 3x^2 - 12x - 15$?

Ⓐ $x = -1, x = 5$ Ⓑ $x = -5, x = 1$

Ⓒ $x = -5, x = \frac{1}{3}$ Ⓓ $x = -1, x = \frac{5}{3}$

59. What is the approximate surface area of the three-dimensional figure represented by the net shown?

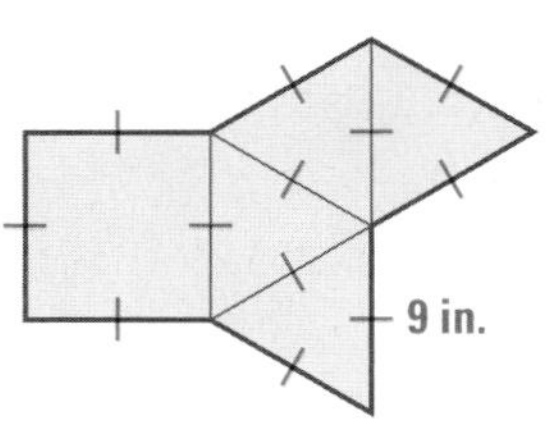

Ⓐ 221 in.^{2} Ⓑ 243 in.^{2}

Ⓒ 324 in.^{2} Ⓓ 405 in.^{2}

9.2 Graph and Write Equations of Parabolas

Before You graphed and wrote equations of parabolas that open up or down.

Now You will graph and write equations of parabolas that open left or right.

Why? So you can model sound projection, as in Ex. 56.

Key Vocabulary
- **focus**
- **directrix**
- **parabola,** *p. 236*
- **vertex,** *p. 236*

You know that the graph of $y = ax^2$ is a parabola that opens up or down with vertex (0, 0) and axis of symmetry $x = 0$. On any parabola, each point is equidistant from a point called the **focus** and a line called the **directrix**.

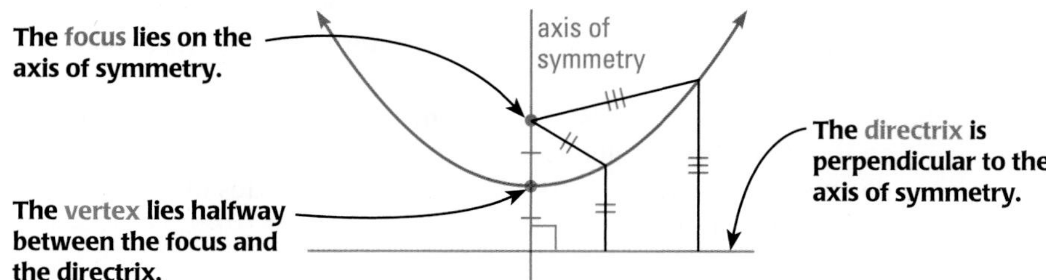

The equation of a parabola that opens up or down and has vertex (0, 0) can also be written in the form $x^2 = 4py$. Parabolas can open left or right as well, in which case the equation has the form $y^2 = 4px$ when the vertex is (0, 0). Note below that for any parabola, the focus and directrix each lie $|p|$ units from the vertex.

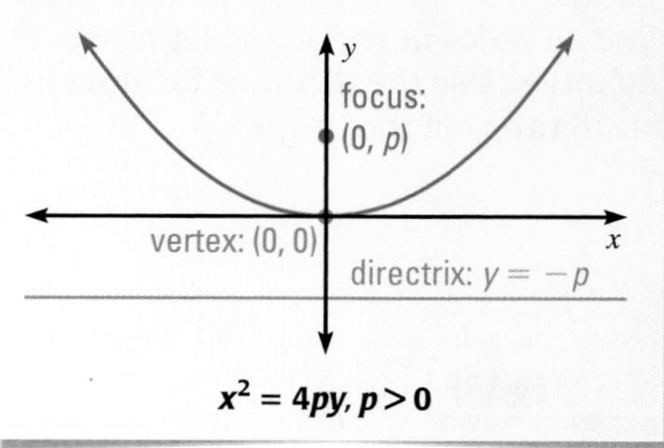

$x^2 = 4py, p > 0$

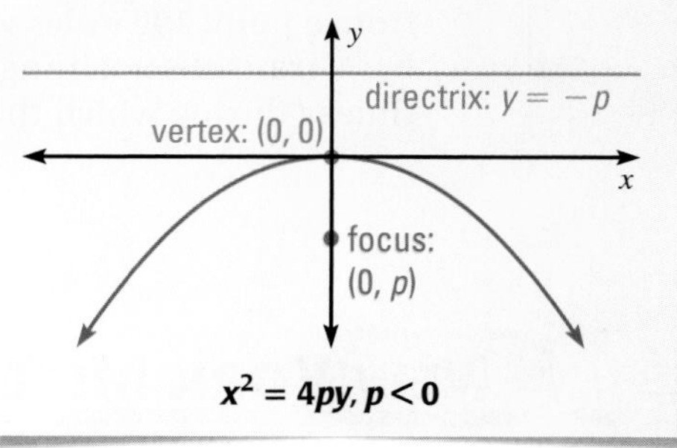

$x^2 = 4py, p < 0$

IDENTIFY FUNCTIONS
Notice that parabolas that open left or right do *not* represent functions.

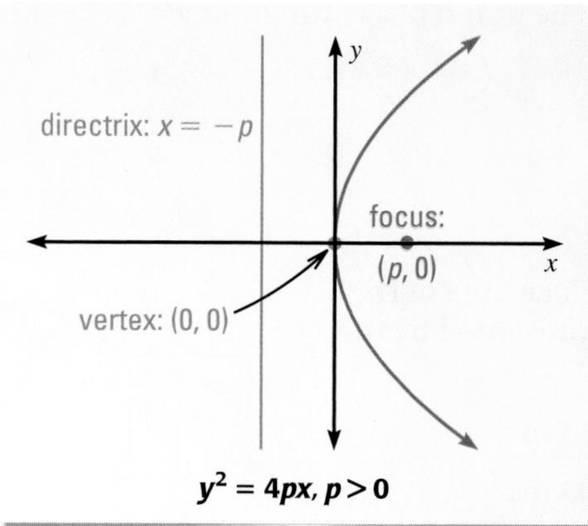

$y^2 = 4px, p > 0$

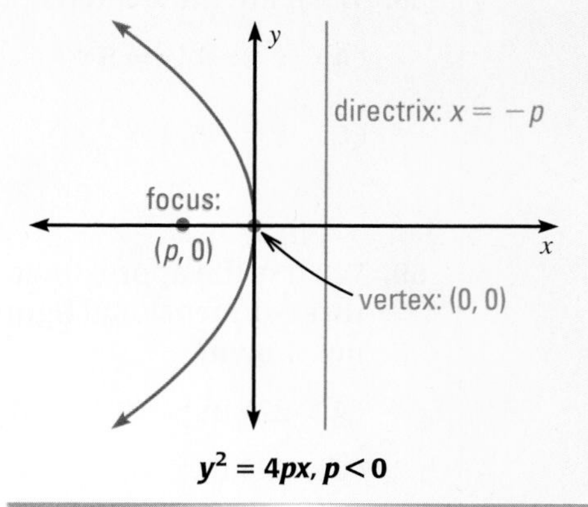

$y^2 = 4px, p < 0$

KEY CONCEPT *For Your Notebook*

Standard Equation of a Parabola with Vertex at the Origin

The standard form of the equation of a parabola with vertex at (0, 0) is as follows:

Equation	Focus	Directrix	Axis of Symmetry
$x^2 = 4py$	$(0, p)$	$y = -p$	Vertical ($x = 0$)
$y^2 = 4px$	$(p, 0)$	$x = -p$	Horizontal ($y = 0$)

EXAMPLE 1 Graph an equation of a parabola

Graph $x = -\frac{1}{8}y^2$. Identify the focus, directrix, and axis of symmetry.

Solution

STEP 1 **Rewrite** the equation in standard form.

$$x = -\frac{1}{8}y^2 \quad \text{Write original equation.}$$

$$-8x = y^2 \quad \text{Multiply each side by } -8.$$

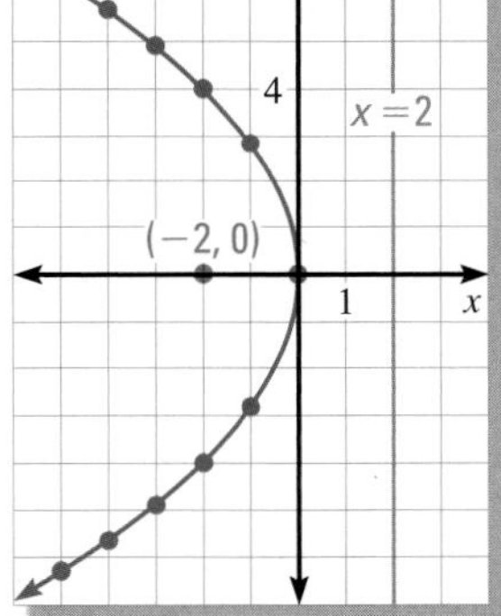

STEP 2 **Identify** the focus, directrix, and axis of symmetry. The equation has the form $y^2 = 4px$ where $p = -2$. The focus is $(p, 0)$, or $(-2, 0)$. The directrix is $x = -p$, or $x = 2$. Because y is squared, the axis of symmetry is the x-axis.

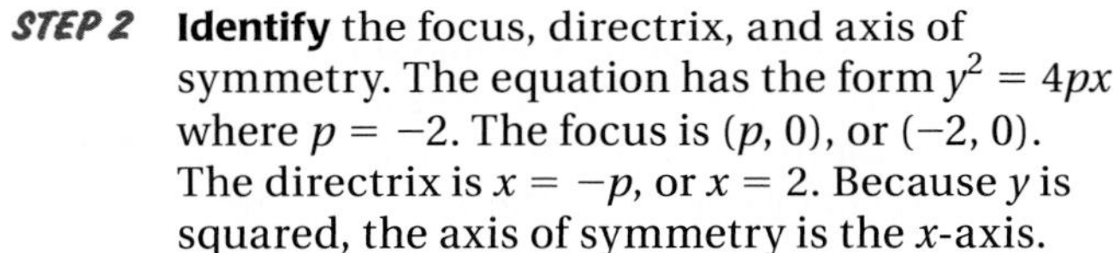

STEP 3 **Draw** the parabola by making a table of values and plotting points. Because $p < 0$, the parabola opens to the left. So, use only negative x-values.

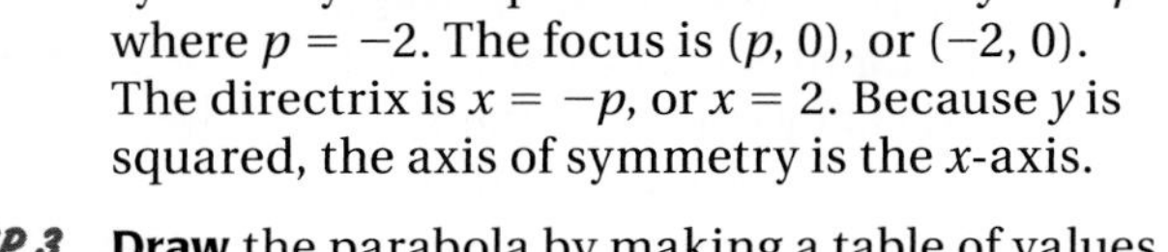

x	−1	−2	−3	−4	−5
y	±2.83	±4	±4.90	±5.66	±6.32

SOLVE FOR Y
To fill in the table, note that because $-8x = y^2$, $y = \pm\sqrt{-8x}$. The value of y will be a real number only when $x \le 0$.

Animated Algebra at classzone.com

EXAMPLE 2 Write an equation of a parabola

Write an equation of the parabola shown.

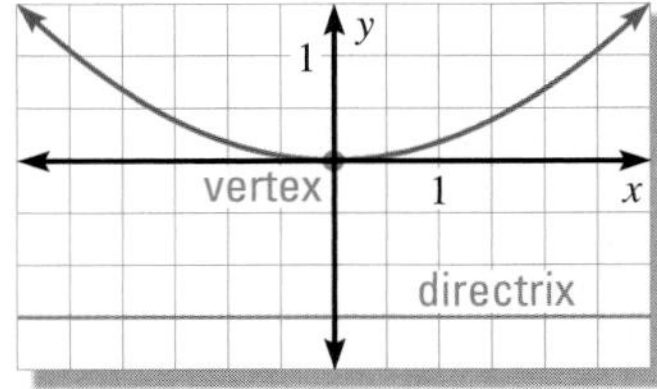

Solution

The graph shows that the vertex is (0, 0) and the directrix is $y = -p = -\frac{3}{2}$. Substitute $\frac{3}{2}$ for p in the standard form of the equation of a parabola.

$$x^2 = 4py \quad \text{Standard form, vertical axis of symmetry}$$

$$x^2 = 4\left(\frac{3}{2}\right)y \quad \text{Substitute } \frac{3}{2} \text{ for } p.$$

$$x^2 = 6y \quad \text{Simplify.}$$

✓ GUIDED PRACTICE for Examples 1 and 2

Graph the equation. Identify the focus, directrix, and axis of symmetry of the parabola.

1. $y^2 = -6x$ **2.** $x^2 = 2y$ **3.** $y = -\frac{1}{4}x^2$ **4.** $x = \frac{1}{3}y^2$

Write the standard form of the equation of the parabola with vertex at (0, 0) and the given directrix or focus.

5. Directrix: $y = 2$ **6.** Directrix: $x = 4$ **7.** Focus: $(-2, 0)$ **8.** Focus: $(0, 3)$

PARABOLIC REFLECTORS *Parabolic reflectors* have cross sections that are parabolas. Incoming sound, light, or other energy that arrives at a parabolic reflector parallel to the axis of symmetry is directed to the focus (Diagram 1). Similarly, energy that is emitted from the focus of a parabolic reflector and then strikes the reflector is directed parallel to the axis of symmetry (Diagram 2).

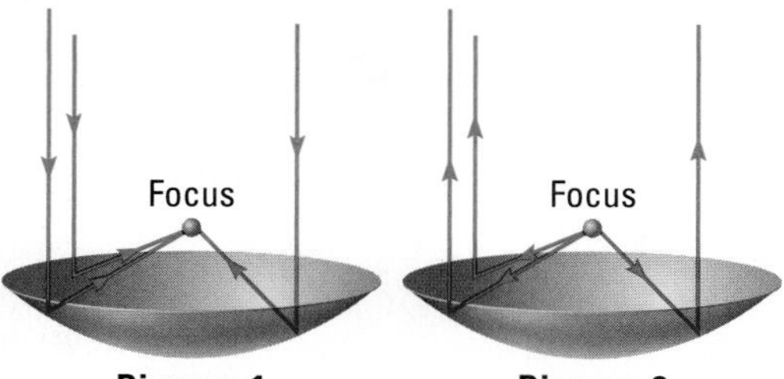

EXAMPLE 3 Solve a multi-step problem

SOLAR ENERGY The EuroDish, developed to provide electricity in remote areas, uses a parabolic reflector to concentrate sunlight onto a high-efficiency engine located at the reflector's focus. The sunlight heats helium to 650°C to power the engine.

- Write an equation for the EuroDish's cross section with its vertex at (0, 0).
- How deep is the dish?

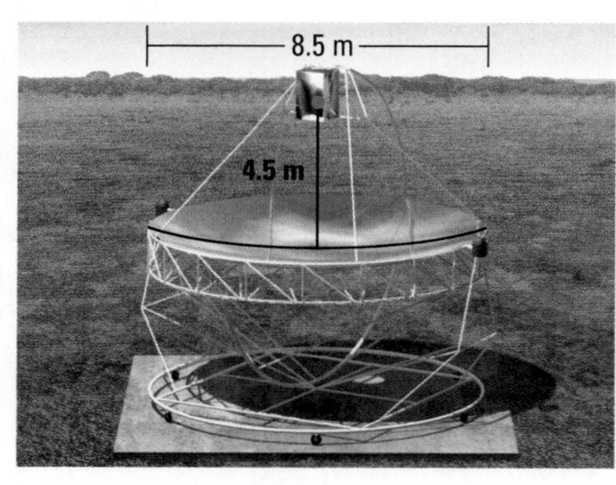

Solution

STEP 1 **Write** an equation for the cross section. The engine is at the focus, which is $|p| = 4.5$ meters from the vertex. Because the focus is above the vertex, p is positive, so $p = 4.5$. An equation for the cross section of the EuroDish with its vertex at the origin is as follows:

$x^2 = 4py$ **Standard form, vertical axis of symmetry**

$x^2 = 4(4.5)y$ **Substitute 4.5 for *p*.**

$x^2 = 18y$ **Simplify.**

STEP 2 **Find** the depth of the EuroDish. The depth is the y-value at the dish's outside edge. The dish extends $\frac{8.5}{2} = 4.25$ meters to either side of the vertex (0, 0), so substitute 4.25 for x in the equation from Step 1.

$x^2 = 18y$ **Equation for the cross section**

$(4.25)^2 = 18y$ **Substitute 4.25 for *x*.**

$1.0 \approx y$ **Solve for *y*.**

▸ The dish is about 1 meter deep.

 **GUIDED PRACTICE** for Example 3

9. **MICROWAVES** A parabolic microwave antenna is 16 feet in diameter. Find an equation for the cross section of the antenna with its vertex at the origin and its focus 10 feet to the right of its vertex. Then find the antenna's depth.

9.2 EXERCISES

HOMEWORK KEY

○ = **WORKED-OUT SOLUTIONS on p. WS16 for Exs. 15, 27, and 57**

★ = **STANDARDIZED TEST PRACTICE Exs. 2, 25, 38, 51, 52, and 59**

SKILL PRACTICE

1. **VOCABULARY** Copy and complete: A parabola is the set of all points in a plane equidistant from a point called the _?_ and a line called the _?_.

2. ★ **WRITING** *Compare* the graphs of $x^2 = 4py$ and $y^2 = 4px$.

EXAMPLE 1 on p. 621 for Exs. 3–25

GRAPHING **Graph the equation. Identify the focus, directrix, and axis of symmetry of the parabola.**

3. $y^2 = 16x$
4. $x^2 = -6y$
5. $x^2 = 20y$
6. $y^2 = 28x$
7. $y^2 = -10x$
8. $x^2 = 30y$
9. $y^2 = -2x$
10. $x^2 = -36y$
11. $x^2 = 12y$
12. $-2y = x^2$
13. $x = 4y^2$
14. $-x^2 = 48y$
15. $5x^2 = -15y$
16. $-y^2 = 18x$
17. $-24x = 3y^2$
18. $14x = 6y^2$
19. $\frac{1}{8}x^2 - y = 0$
20. $4x - 11y^2 = 0$
21. $5x^2 + 12y = 0$
22. $-5x + \frac{1}{3}y^2 = 0$

ERROR ANALYSIS ***Describe*** **and correct the error in graphing the parabola.**

23.

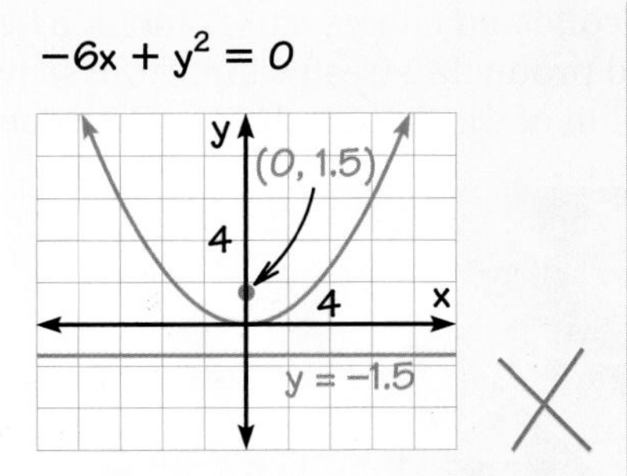

24.

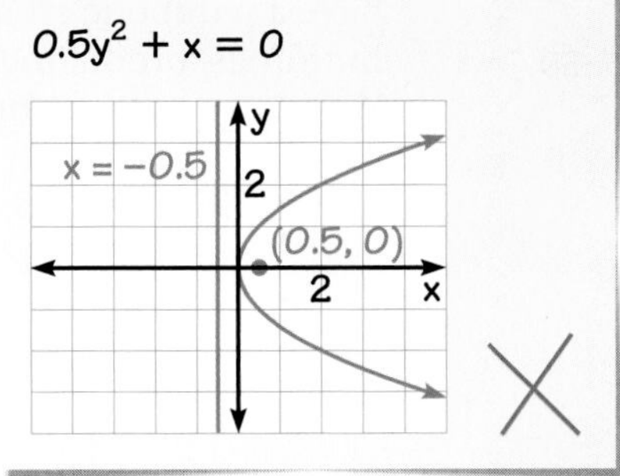

25. ★ **MULTIPLE CHOICE** What is the directrix of the parabola $15y + 3x^2 = 0$?

Ⓐ $x = -5$ Ⓑ $x = -1.25$ Ⓒ $y = -1.25$ Ⓓ $y = 1.25$

EXAMPLE 2 on p. 621 for Exs. 26–50

WRITING EQUATIONS **Write the standard form of the equation of the parabola with the given focus and vertex at (0, 0).**

26. $(2, 0)$
27. $(-5, 0)$
28. $(3, 0)$
29. $(0, -4)$
30. $(0, 8)$
31. $(0, -10)$
32. $(0, -6)$
33. $(-9, 0)$
34. $\left(0, \frac{7}{4}\right)$
35. $\left(0, -\frac{3}{8}\right)$
36. $\left(\frac{5}{2}, 0\right)$
37. $\left(-\frac{9}{16}, 0\right)$

38. ★ **MULTIPLE CHOICE** What is an equation of the parabola with focus at $(-8, 0)$ and vertex at $(0, 0)$?

Ⓐ $y^2 = -32x$ Ⓑ $y^2 = -0.5x$ Ⓒ $x^2 = -8y$ Ⓓ $x^2 = -32y$

WRITING EQUATIONS Write the standard form of the equation of the parabola with the given directrix and vertex at (0, 0).

39. $x = 3$	**40.** $y = -7$	**41.** $x = -5$	**42.** $y = 12$
43. $y = -4$	**44.** $x = -2$	**45.** $y = 6$	**46.** $x = 11$
47. $x = -\frac{3}{2}$	**48.** $y = \frac{5}{12}$	**49.** $y = -\frac{11}{6}$	**50.** $x = -\frac{1}{18}$

51. ★ **SHORT RESPONSE** Predict how the indicated change in a will affect the focus, directrix, and shape of the given equation's graph. Then graph both the original and revised equations in the same coordinate plane.

a. $x^2 = ay$; a changes from 1 to 4 **b.** $y^2 = ax$; a changes from 6 to $-\frac{1}{2}$

52. ★ **WRITING** Suppose that $x^2 = 4py$ and $y = ax^2$ represent the same parabola. *Explain* how a and p are related.

53. **VISUAL THINKING** As $|p|$ increases, how does the width of the graph of $x^2 = 4py$ change? *Explain.*

54. **CHALLENGE** Consider the parabola with focus $(0, p)$ and directrix $y = -p$. Let (x, y) be any point on the parabola. Use the fact that (x, y) is equidistant from the focus and directrix to show that $x^2 = 4py$.

PROBLEM SOLVING

EXAMPLE 3 on p. 622 for Exs. 55–59

55. **SOLAR ENERGY** Solar energy can be concentrated using long troughs that have a parabolic cross section. The collected energy's uses include heating buildings, producing electricity, and producing fresh water from seawater. Write an equation for the cross section of the trough shown. How deep is it?

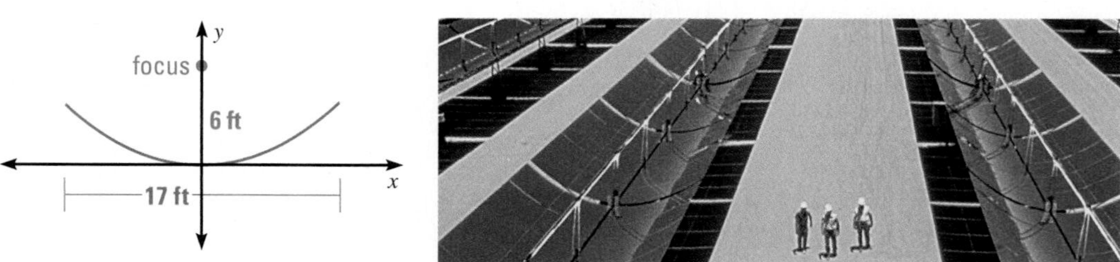

@HomeTutor for problem solving help at classzone.com

56. **BIOLOGY** Scientists studying dolphin *echolocation* can simulate the projection of a dolphin's clicking sounds using computer models. The models originate the sounds at the focus of a parabolic reflector. The parabola in the graph models the cross section (with units in inches) of the reflector used to simulate sound projection for a bottlenose dolphin. What is the *focal length* (the distance from the vertex to the focus)?

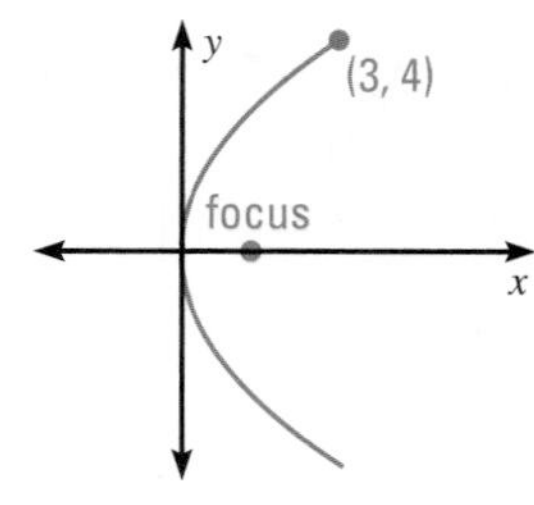

@HomeTutor for problem solving help at classzone.com

○ = **WORKED-OUT SOLUTIONS on p. WS1** ★ = **STANDARDIZED TEST PRACTICE**

57. **MULTI-STEP PROBLEM** The parabolic antenna used by a television station to transmit is 146 inches in diameter. Its focus is 48 inches from the vertex.

a. Sketch the antenna twice: once opening upward and once opening left.

b. Use your sketches from part (a) to write two equations for the antenna's cross section: one of the form $x^2 = 4py$ and one of the form $y^2 = 4px$.

c. How deep is the antenna's dish? Does it matter which equation from part (b) you use to find your answer? *Explain.*

58. **RADIO TELESCOPES** The Very Large Array in New Mexico consists of 27 radio telescopes. For each parabolic telescope dish, the diameter is 25 meters and the distance between the vertex and focus is 0.36 times the diameter. Write an equation for the cross section of a dish opening upward with its vertex at the origin. How deep is each dish?

Animated Algebra at classzone.com

59. ★ **EXTENDED RESPONSE** Searchlights use parabolic reflectors to project their beams. The cross section of a 9.5-inch-deep searchlight reflector has equation $x^2 = 10.5y$.

a. How wide is the beam of light projected from the searchlight's reflector?

b. Write an equation for the cross section of a reflector that has the same depth as the original reflector, but which projects a wider beam. *Explain* how you found your answer. How wide is the new reflector's beam?

c. Repeat part (b) for a beam narrower than the original.

60. **CHALLENGE** The *latus rectum* of a parabola is the line segment that is parallel to the directrix, passes through the focus, and has endpoints that lie on the parabola. Find the length in terms of p of the latus rectum of a parabola with equation $x^2 = 4py$.

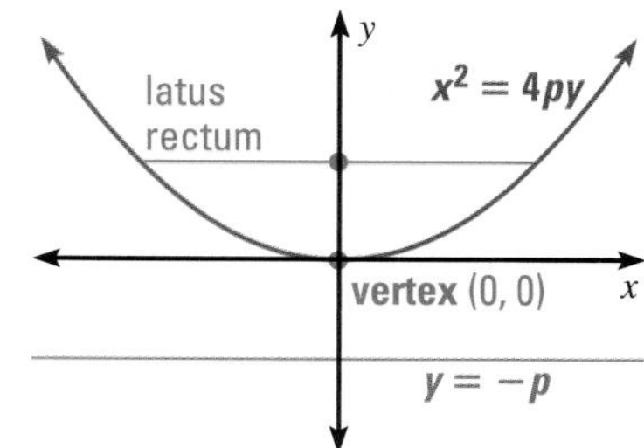

NEW YORK MIXED REVIEW

TEST PRACTICE at classzone.com

61. The figure shows a triangular city park. What is the perimeter of the park?

Ⓐ 170 yd　Ⓑ 190 yd
Ⓒ 200 yd　Ⓓ 273 yd

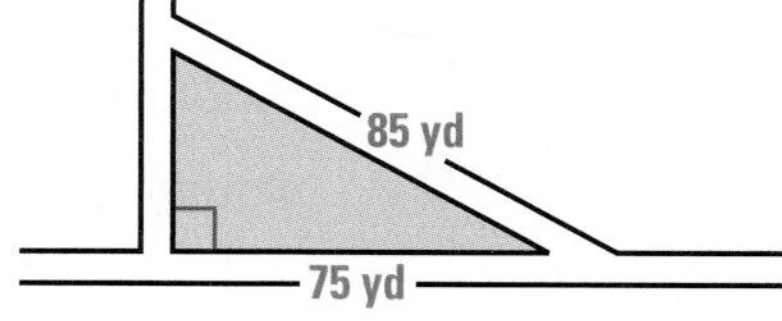

62. Sarah has 9 points less than she needs to make a grade of A in her mathematics course. Her point total for the course is 423 points. How many points are possible in the course? (Assume she needs 90% of the total possible points for an A.)

Ⓐ 460　Ⓑ 470　Ⓒ 480　Ⓓ 490

9.3 Graph and Write Equations of Circles

A2.A.49 Write the equation of a circle from its graph

Before You graphed and wrote equations of parabolas.

Now You will graph and write equations of circles.

Why? So you can model transmission ranges, as in Ex. 62.

Key Vocabulary
- circle
- center
- radius

A **circle** is the set of all points (x, y) in a plane that are equidistant from a fixed point, called the **center** of the circle. The distance r between the center and any point (x, y) on the circle is the **radius**.

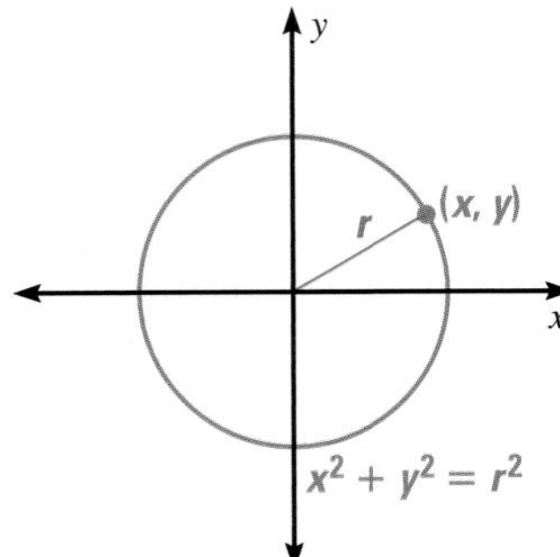

For a circle with center at the origin and radius r, the distance between any point (x, y) on the circle and the center $(0, 0)$ is r, so the following is true:

$$\sqrt{(x-0)^2 + (y-0)^2} = r \quad \text{Distance formula}$$

$$(x-0)^2 + (y-0)^2 = r^2 \quad \text{Square each side.}$$

$$x^2 + y^2 = r^2 \quad \text{Simplify.}$$

KEY CONCEPT *For Your Notebook*

Standard Equation of a Circle with Center at the Origin

The standard form of the equation of a circle with center at $(0, 0)$ and radius r is as follows:

$$x^2 + y^2 = r^2$$

EXAMPLE 1 Graph an equation of a circle

Graph $y^2 = -x^2 + 36$. Identify the radius of the circle.

Solution

STEP 1 **Rewrite** the equation $y^2 = -x^2 + 36$ in standard form as $x^2 + y^2 = 36$.

STEP 2 **Identify** the center and radius. From the equation, the graph is a circle centered at the origin with radius $r = \sqrt{36} = 6$.

STEP 3 **Draw** the circle. First plot several convenient points that are 6 units from the origin, such as $(0, 6)$, $(6, 0)$, $(0, -6)$, and $(-6, 0)$. Then draw the circle that passes through the points.

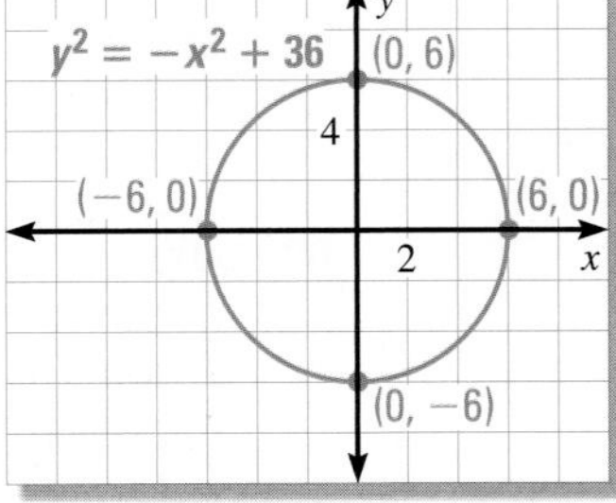

Animated Algebra at classzone.com

EXAMPLE 2 Write an equation of a circle

The point (2, −5) lies on a circle whose center is the origin. Write the standard form of the equation of the circle.

Solution

Because the point (2, −5) lies on the circle, the circle's radius r must be the distance between the center (0, 0) and (2, −5). Use the distance formula.

$r = \sqrt{(2-0)^2 + (-5-0)^2} = \sqrt{4+25} = \sqrt{29}$ **The radius is $\sqrt{29}$.**

Use the standard form with $r = \sqrt{29}$ to write an equation of the circle.

$x^2 + y^2 = r^2$ **Standard form**

$x^2 + y^2 = (\sqrt{29})^2$ **Substitute $\sqrt{29}$ for r.**

$x^2 + y^2 = 29$ **Simplify.**

EXAMPLE 3 Standardized Test Practice

What is an equation of the line tangent to the circle $x^2 + y^2 = 13$ at (−3, 2)?

Ⓐ $y = \frac{2}{3}x + 4$ Ⓑ $y = \frac{3}{2}x - \frac{5}{2}$ Ⓒ $y = \frac{3}{2}x + \frac{13}{2}$ Ⓓ $y = -\frac{3}{2}x + \frac{13}{3}$

ELIMINATE CHOICES
In Example 3, you can eliminate choice D because a quick sketch of the circle shows that the slope of the tangent line at (−3, 2) must be positive.

Solution

A line tangent to a circle is perpendicular to the radius at the point of tangency. Because the radius to the point (−3, 2) has slope $m = \frac{2-0}{-3-0} = -\frac{2}{3}$, the slope of the tangent line at (−3, 2) is the negative reciprocal of $-\frac{2}{3}$, or $\frac{3}{2}$. An equation of the tangent line is as follows:

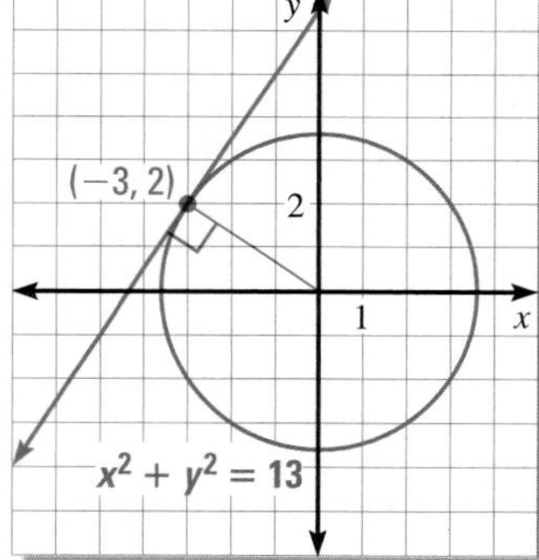

$y - 2 = \frac{3}{2}(x - (-3))$ **Point-slope form**

$y - 2 = \frac{3}{2}x + \frac{9}{2}$ **Distributive property**

$y = \frac{3}{2}x + \frac{13}{2}$ **Solve for y.**

▶ The correct answer is C. Ⓐ Ⓑ Ⓒ Ⓓ

✓ GUIDED PRACTICE for Examples 1, 2, and 3

Graph the equation. Identify the radius of the circle.

1. $x^2 + y^2 = 9$ **2.** $y^2 = -x^2 + 49$ **3.** $x^2 - 18 = -y^2$

4. Write the standard form of the equation of the circle that passes through (5, −1) and whose center is the origin.

5. Write an equation of the line tangent to the circle $x^2 + y^2 = 37$ at (6, 1).

CIRCLES AND INEQUALITIES The regions inside and outside the circle $x^2 + y^2 = r^2$ can be described by inequalities, with $x^2 + y^2 < r^2$ representing the region inside the circle and $x^2 + y^2 > r^2$ representing the region outside the circle.

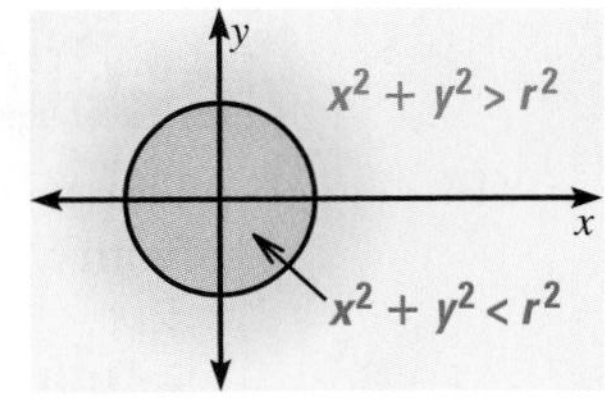

EXAMPLE 4 Write a circular model

CELL PHONES A cellular phone tower services a 10 mile radius. You get a flat tire 4 miles east and 9 miles north of the tower. Are you in the tower's range?

Solution

STEP 1 **Write** an inequality for the region covered by the tower. From the diagram, this region is all points that satisfy the following inequality:

$$x^2 + y^2 < 10^2$$

STEP 2 **Substitute** the coordinates (4, 9) into the inequality from Step 1.

$x^2 + y^2 < 10^2$	**Inequality from Step 1**
$4^2 + 9^2 \stackrel{?}{<} 10^2$	**Substitute for *x* and *y*.**
$97 < 100$ ✓	**The inequality is true.**

▶ So, you are in the tower's range.

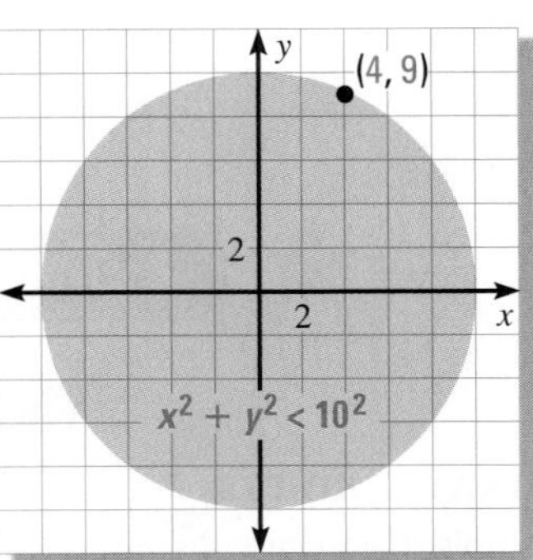

In the diagram above, the origin represents the tower and the positive *y*-axis represents north.

EXAMPLE 5 Apply a circular model

CELL PHONES In Example 4, suppose that you fix your tire and then drive south. For how many more miles will you be in range of the tower?

Solution

When you leave the tower's range, you will be at a point on the circle $x^2 + y^2 = 10^2$ whose x-coordinate is 4 and whose y-coordinate is negative. Find the point $(4, y)$ where $y < 0$ on the circle $x^2 + y^2 = 10^2$.

$x^2 + y^2 = 10^2$	**Equation of the circle**
$4^2 + y^2 = 10^2$	**Substitute 4 for *x*.**
$y = \pm\sqrt{84}$	**Solve for *y*.**
$y \approx \pm 9.2$	**Use a calculator.**

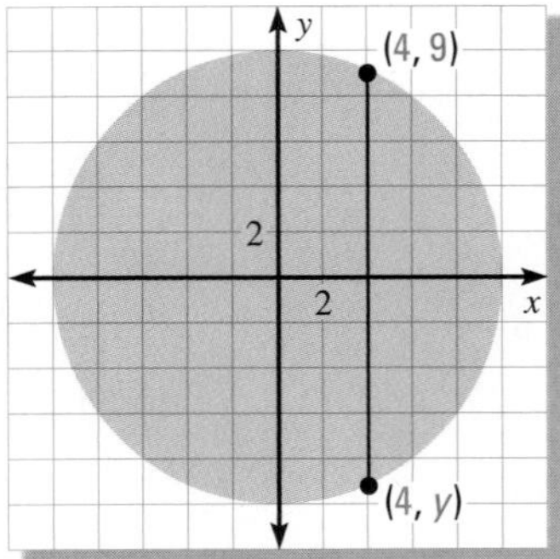

▶ Because $y < 0$, $y \approx -9.2$. You will be in the tower's range from (4, 9) to (4, −9.2), a distance of $|9 - (-9.2)| = 18.2$ miles.

✓ GUIDED PRACTICE for Examples 4 and 5

6. **WHAT IF?** In Examples 4 and 5, suppose you drive west after fixing your tire. For how many more miles will you be in range of the tower?

9.3 EXERCISES

HOMEWORK KEY

○ = **WORKED-OUT SOLUTIONS** on p. WS16 for Exs. 17, 39, and 65

★ = **STANDARDIZED TEST PRACTICE** Exs. 2, 21, 43, 59, 64, and 66

◆ = **MULTIPLE REPRESENTATIONS** Ex. 68

SKILL PRACTICE

1. **VOCABULARY** The radius of a circle is the distance from any point on the circle to a fixed point called the circle's ___?___.

2. ★ **WRITING** How are the slope of a line tangent to a circle and the slope of the radius at the point of tangency related?

EXAMPLE 1 on p. 626 for Exs. 3–21

MATCHING GRAPHS Match the equation with its graph.

3. $x^2 + y^2 = 9$
4. $x^2 + y^2 = 36$
5. $x^2 + y^2 = 4$
6. $x^2 + y^2 = 6$
7. $x^2 + y^2 = 16$
8. $x^2 + y^2 = 3$

A.

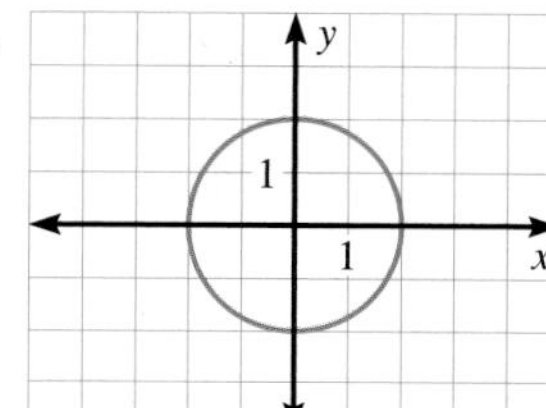

B.

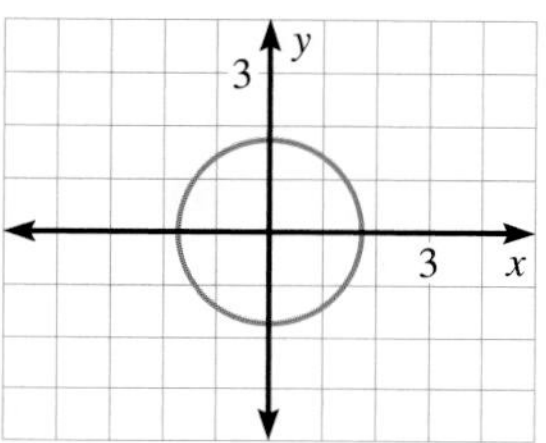

C.

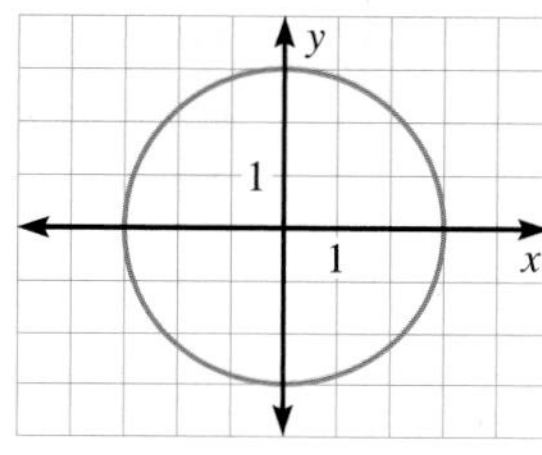

D.

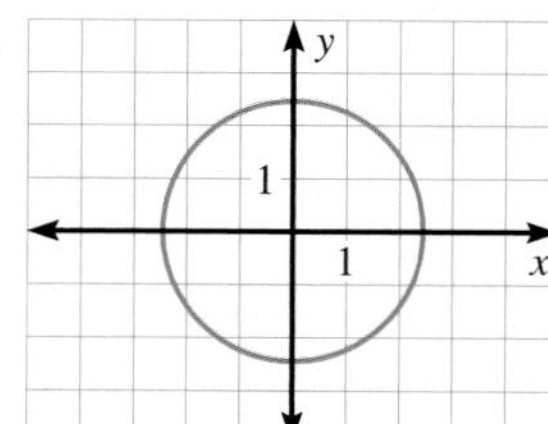

E.

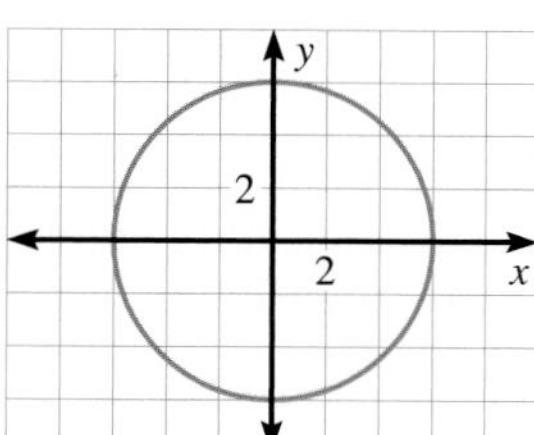

F.

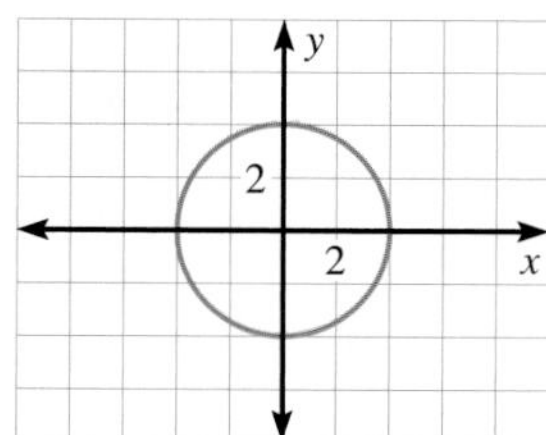

GRAPHING Graph the equation. Identify the radius of the circle.

9. $x^2 + y^2 = 1$
10. $x^2 + y^2 = 81$
11. $x^2 + y^2 = 25$
12. $x^2 + y^2 = 12$
13. $y^2 = 27 - x^2$
14. $x^2 = -y^2 + 40$
15. $x^2 = 15 - y^2$
16. $y^2 = -x^2 + 9$
17. $15x^2 + 15y^2 = 60$
18. $7x^2 + 7y^2 = 112$
19. $4x^2 + 4y^2 = 128$
20. $8x^2 + 8y^2 = 192$

21. ★ **MULTIPLE CHOICE** What is the radius of the circle $3x^2 + 3y^2 = 54$?

(A) $3\sqrt{2}$ (B) $3\sqrt{6}$ (C) 18 (D) 54

EXAMPLE 2 on p. 627 for Exs. 22–43

WRITING EQUATIONS Write the standard form of the equation of the circle with the given radius and whose center is the origin.

22. 12
23. 8
24. 2
25. 16
26. $\sqrt{2}$
27. $\sqrt{15}$
28. $5\sqrt{2}$
29. $4\sqrt{6}$

30. **ERROR ANALYSIS** *Describe* and correct the error in writing an equation of the circle with the given center and radius.

> Center: (0, 0); Radius: 12
> Equation: $x^2 + y^2 = 12$ ✗

WRITING EQUATIONS Write the standard form of the equation of the circle that passes through the given point and whose center is the origin.

31. $(-6, 0)$ **32.** $(0, 5)$ **33.** $(-4, 3)$ **34.** $(2, -4)$

35. $(-6, 8)$ **36.** $(-9, 2)$ **37.** $(4, -10)$ **38.** $(-8, -5)$

39. $(-8, 14)$ **40.** $(5, -12)$ **41.** $(-11, -11)$ **42.** $(9, 40)$

43. ★ **MULTIPLE CHOICE** What is the equation in standard form of the circle that passes through the point $(4, -6)$ and whose center is the origin?

(A) $x^2 + y^2 = 5$ (B) $x^2 + y^2 = 10$ (C) $x^2 + y^2 = 52$ (D) $x^2 + y^2 = 2\sqrt{13}$

GRAPHING In Exercises 44–52, equations of both circles and parabolas are given. Graph the equation.

44. $y^2 + x^2 = 49$ **45.** $4x^2 + y = 0$ **46.** $7x^2 + 7y^2 = 63$

47. $y^2 - 121 = -x^2$ **48.** $x^2 + 16y = 0$ **49.** $3x = -y^2$

50. $12x^2 + 12y^2 = 192$ **51.** $2x^2 + 2y^2 = 16$ **52.** $6x + 6y^2 = 0$

EXAMPLE 3 on p. 627 for Exs. 53–58

TANGENT LINES Write an equation of the line tangent to the given circle at the given point.

53. $x^2 + y^2 = 17$; $(1, 4)$ **54.** $x^2 + y^2 = 13$; $(2, -3)$ **55.** $x^2 + y^2 = 34$; $(-5, 3)$

56. $x^2 + y^2 = 40$; $(-6, -2)$ **57.** $x^2 + y^2 = 106$; $(-5, 9)$ **58.** $x^2 + y^2 = 250$; $(15, 5)$

59. ★ **OPEN-ENDED MATH** Write equations in standard form for three circles centered at the origin so that each circle passes between $(-3, 5)$ and $(-6, 2)$.

60. REASONING Use the diagram to show that an angle inscribed in a semicircle is a right angle. (*Hint:* Show that the segments meeting at (x, y) have slopes that are negative reciprocals.)

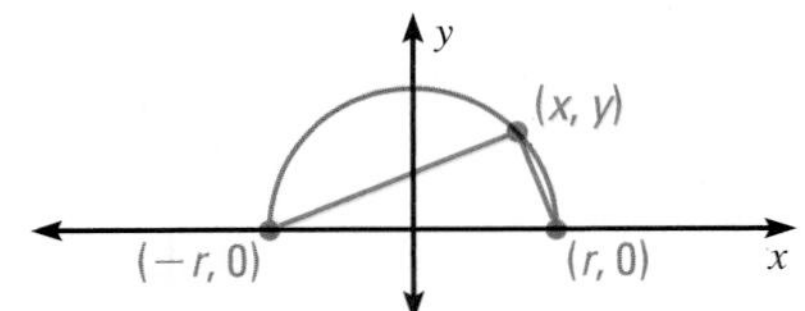

61. CHALLENGE Suppose two congruent circles intersect so that each passes through the other's center, as shown. Write an equation that gives the length ℓ of the chord formed by joining the intersection points in terms of the radius r of each circle.

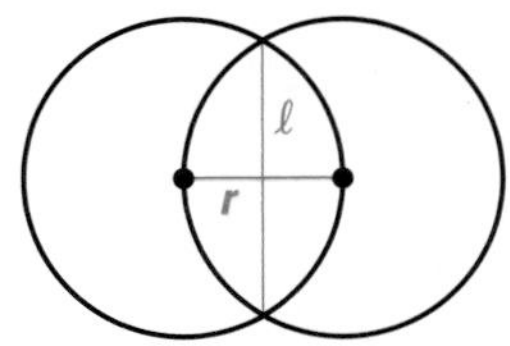

PROBLEM SOLVING

EXAMPLE 4 on p. 628 for Exs. 62–64

62. CELL PHONES A cellular phone tower services a 15 mile radius. On a hiking trip, you are 9 miles east and 11 miles north of the cell tower. Are you in the region served by the tower?

@HomeTutor for problem solving help at classzone.com

63. BATS During the warmer months, more than 1 million Mexican free-tailed bats live under the Congress Avenue Bridge in Austin, Texas. The bats have an estimated feeding range of 50 miles. Is a location 40 miles north and 25 miles west of the bridge located within this range?

@HomeTutor for problem solving help at classzone.com

◯ = WORKED-OUT SOLUTIONS on p. WS1 ★ = STANDARDIZED TEST PRACTICE

64. ★ **MULTIPLE CHOICE** An appliance store claims to provide free delivery up to 100 miles from the store. The following points represent the locations of houses, with the origin representing the store. (All coordinates are in miles.) Which house is located outside the free delivery area?

Ⓐ (95, 30) Ⓑ (90, 35) Ⓒ (80, 55) Ⓓ (75, 70)

EXAMPLE 5 on p. 628 for Exs. 65–67

65. **MULTI-STEP PROBLEM** "Class B" airspace sometimes consists of a stack of cylindrical layers as shown. Seen from above, the airspace forms circles whose origin is the control tower. A plane in straight and level flight flies through the top layer along the line $y = -4$, as shown.

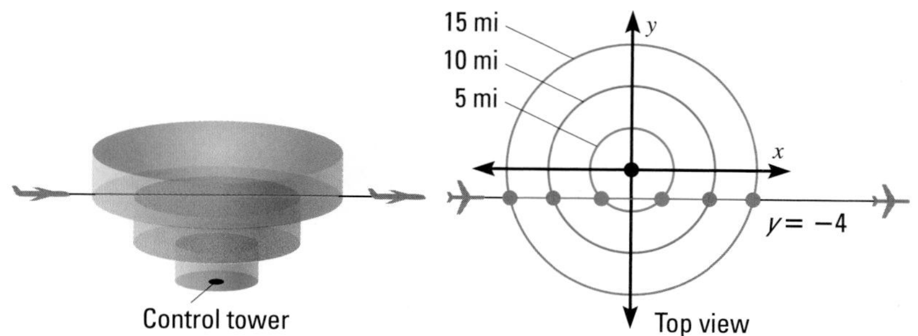

a. For how many miles will the plane be in the top-most layer of Class B airspace?

b. For how many miles will the plane be above the middle layer of Class B airspace?

c. For how many miles will the plane be above the lowest layer of Class B airspace?

66. ★ **SHORT RESPONSE** A circular utility tunnel 8 feet in diameter has a 6-foot-wide walkway across its bottom. Could a worker who is 6 feet 2 inches tall walk down the center of the walkway without ducking? *Explain.* (*Hint:* Write an equation of the tunnel's cross section. Find the x-coordinate of an endpoint of the walkway and substitute to find the y-coordinate.)

67. **GROUNDSKEEPING** A row of sprinklers is to be installed parallel to and 4.5 feet away from the back edge of a flower bed. Each sprinkler waters a region with a 6 foot radius. How far apart should the sprinklers be placed to water the entire flower bed with the least possible overlap in coverage, as shown?

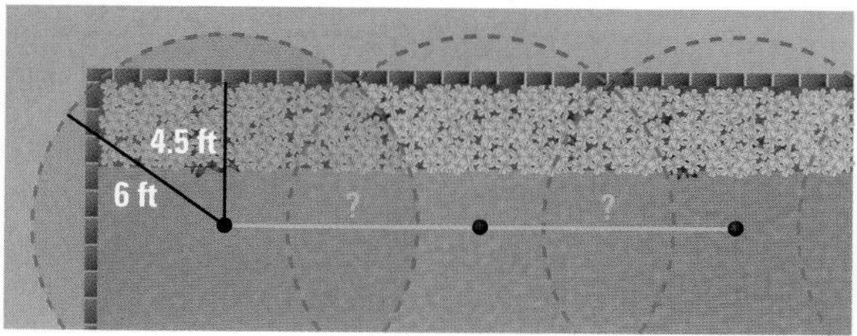

68. ◆ **MULTIPLE REPRESENTATIONS** The Modified Mercalli Intensity Scale rates an earthquake's "shaking strength." In general, the rating decreases as distance from the earthquake's epicenter increases. Suppose an earthquake has a Mercalli rating of 6.0 at its epicenter, a 5.7 rating 15 miles away from the epicenter, a 5.4 rating 25 miles away, and a 5.1 rating 35 miles away.

a. **Drawing Graphs** Represent the situation described above using circles in a coordinate plane.

b. **Writing Inequalities** For each circle from part (a), write an inequality describing the coordinates of locations with a Mercalli rating *at least* as great as the Mercalli rating represented by the circle.

c. **Making a Prediction** What can you predict about the Mercalli rating 12 miles west and 16 miles south of the epicenter? *Explain.*

69. **CHALLENGE** Two radio transmitters, one with a 40 mile range and one with a 60 mile range, stand 80 miles apart. You are driving 60 miles per hour on a highway parallel to the line segment connecting the two towers. How long will you be within range of *both* transmitters simultaneously?

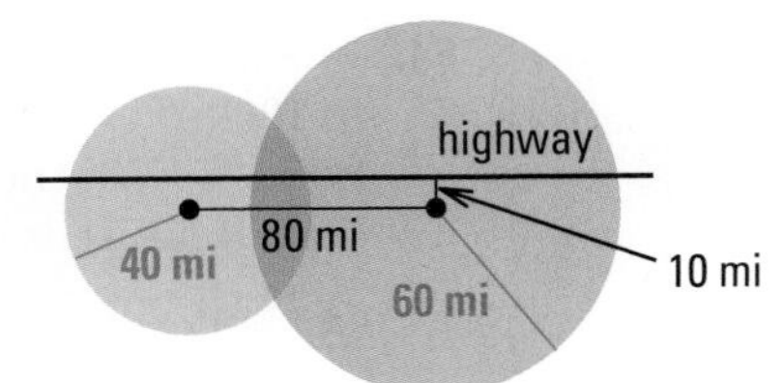

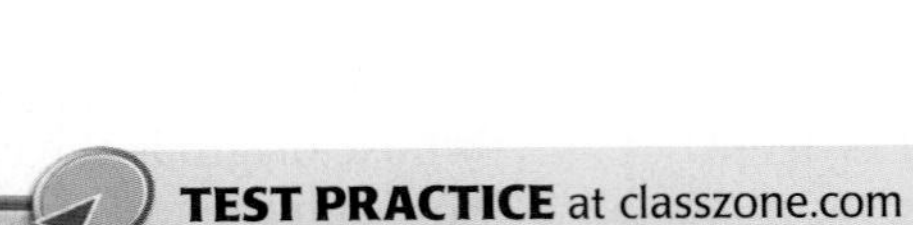

70. How many solutions does the system of equations below have?

$$-12x + 3y = -27$$
$$8x - 2y = 18$$

(A) None (B) One (C) Two (D) Infinitely many

71. What is the approximate perimeter of quadrilateral $PQRS$?

(A) 11.7 units

(B) 16.4 units

(C) 20.8 units

(D) 21.5 units

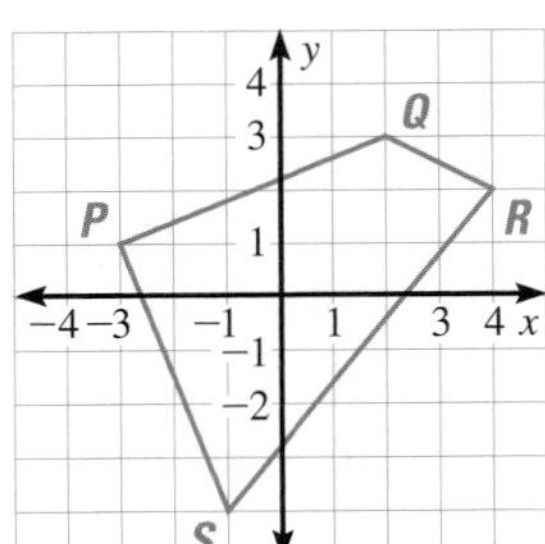

QUIZ *for Lessons 9.1–9.3*

Find the distance between the two points. Then find the midpoint of the line segment joining the two points. *(p. 614)*

1. (4, −3), (8, −7)
2. (−2, 5), (4, 9)
3. (−5, 1), (−4, 8)
4. (1, 2), (7, 1)
5. (−6, −5), (−1, 8)
6. (3, −2), (6, 5)

Write the standard form of the equation of the parabola with the given focus and vertex at (0, 0). *(p. 620)*

7. (0, 3)
8. (−2, 0)
9. (6, 0)
10. (0, −4)
11. (0, 5)
12. (−1, 0)

Graph the equation. Identify the radius of the circle. *(p. 626)*

13. $x^2 + y^2 = 4$
14. $x^2 + y^2 = 64$
15. $x^2 + y^2 = 20$
16. $x^2 + y^2 = 75$
17. $3x^2 + 3y^2 = 48$
18. $6x^2 + 6y^2 = 108$

19. **ASTRONOMY** If the plane in which Jupiter orbits the sun is a coordinate plane with its origin at the sun and coordinates in millions of miles, then a circle through the point (350, 370) just encloses Jupiter's orbit. Imagine replacing the sun with the star KY Cygni, whose radius is about 650 million miles. Would KY Cygni contain Jupiter's orbit? *Explain.* *(p. 626)*

Graphing Calculator **ACTIVITY** *Use after Lesson 9.3*

@HomeTutor
classzone.com
Keystrokes

9.3 Graph Equations of Circles

QUESTION How can you use a graphing calculator to graph a circle?

To graph a circle on most graphing calculators, you must first rewrite the circle's equation as two functions that taken together represent the circle.

EXAMPLE Graph a circle

Use a graphing calculator to graph $x^2 + y^2 = 25$.

STEP 1 *Solve for y*

Begin by solving the equation for y.

$$x^2 + y^2 = 25$$
$$y^2 = 25 - x^2$$
$$y = \pm\sqrt{25 - x^2}$$

Together, the functions $y = \sqrt{25 - x^2}$ and $y = -\sqrt{25 - x^2}$ represent the circle.

STEP 2 *Enter functions*

Enter the two functions as y_1 and y_2. You can enter y_2 as $-y_1$.

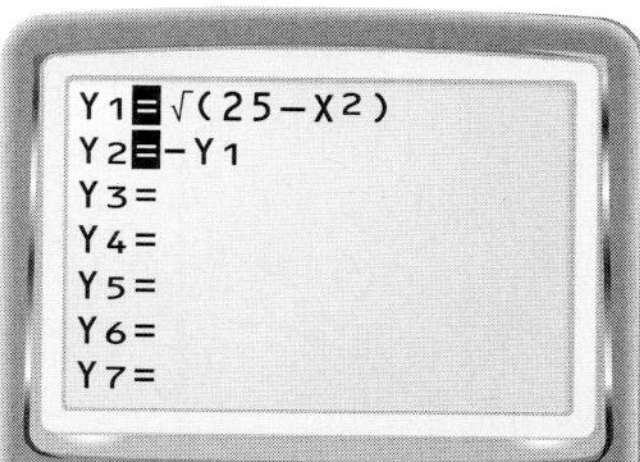

STEP 3 *Graph functions*

The graphs are shown in the standard window ($-10 \leq x \leq 10$ and $-10 \leq y \leq 10$). Because the calculator screen is not square, a horizontal distance of 1 unit is longer than a vertical distance of 1 unit, and the circle is stretched into an oval.

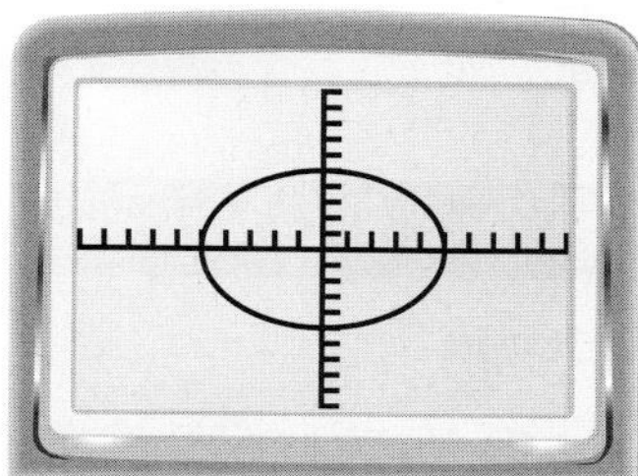

STEP 4 *Adjust graph*

To show the circle in true proportion, set a window so that the ratio of (Xmax − Xmin) to (Ymax − Ymin) is 3:2. Such a "square window" can also be obtained by pressing ZOOM and selecting ZSquare.

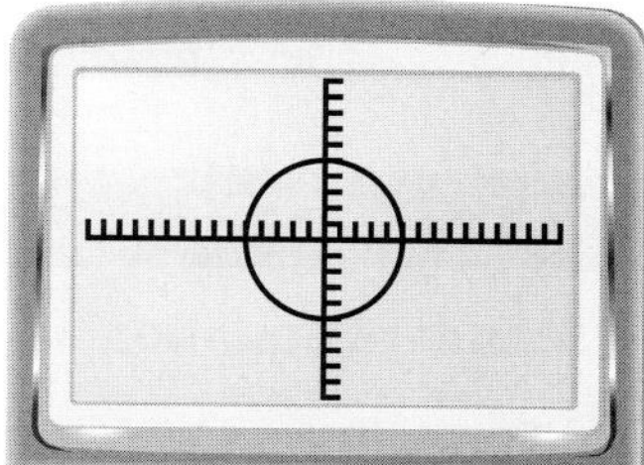

PRACTICE

Use a graphing calculator to graph the equation. Give the viewing window that you used and verify that it is a "square window."

1. $x^2 + y^2 = 144$
2. $x^2 + y^2 = 80$
3. $x^2 + y^2 = 576$
4. $0.5x^2 + 0.5y^2 = 12$
5. $7x^2 + 7y^2 = 105$
6. $16x^2 + 16y^2 = 9$

9.4 Graph and Write Equations of Ellipses

Before You graphed and wrote equations of parabolas and circles.

Now You will graph and write equations of ellipses.

Why? So you can model an elliptical region, as in Example 3.

Key Vocabulary
- ellipse
- foci
- vertices
- major axis
- center
- co-vertices
- minor axis

An **ellipse** is the set of all points P in a plane such that the sum of the distances between P and two fixed points, called the **foci**, is a constant.

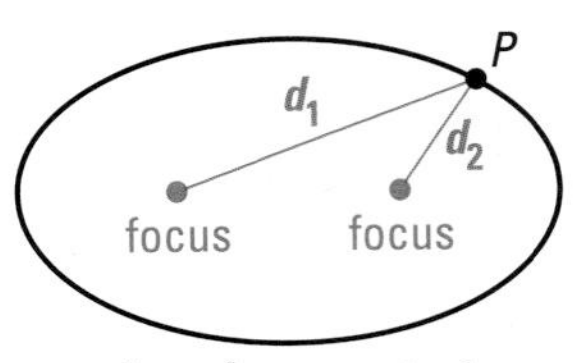

$d_1 + d_2 = \text{constant}$

The line through the foci intersects the ellipse at the two **vertices**. The **major axis** joins the vertices. Its midpoint is the ellipse's **center**. The line perpendicular to the major axis at the center intersects the ellipse at the two **co-vertices**, which are joined by the **minor axis**. In this chapter, ellipses have a horizontal or a vertical major axis.

IDENTIFY AXES

Observe that the major axis of an ellipse contains the foci and is always longer than the minor axis.

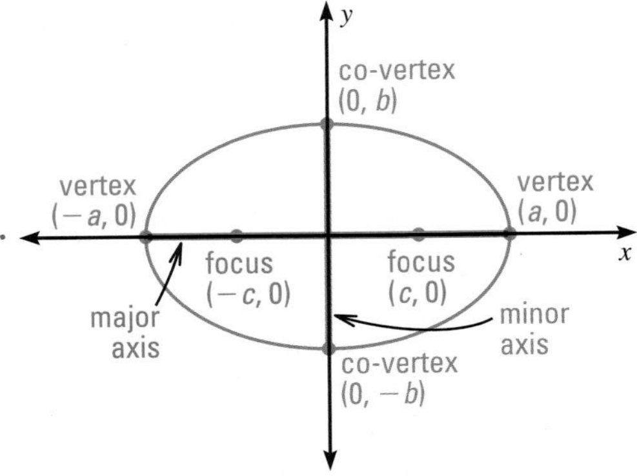

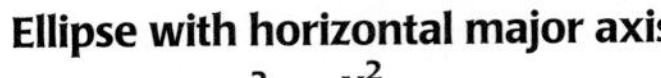

Ellipse with horizontal major axis

$$\frac{x^2}{a^2} + \frac{y^2}{b^2} = 1$$

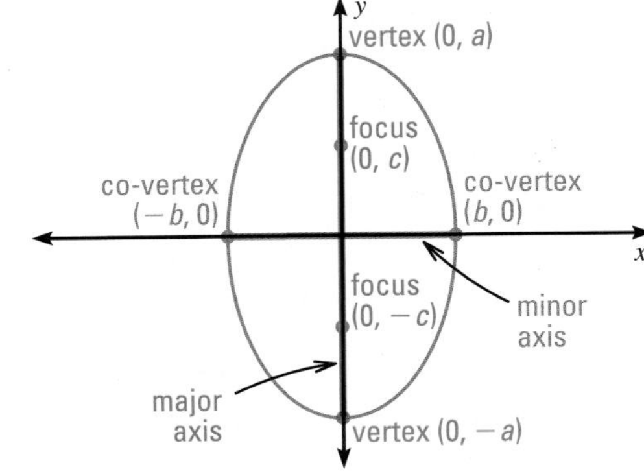

Ellipse with vertical major axis

$$\frac{x^2}{b^2} + \frac{y^2}{a^2} = 1$$

KEY CONCEPT — *For Your Notebook*

Standard Equation of an Ellipse with Center at the Origin

Equation	Major Axis	Vertices	Co-Vertices
$\frac{x^2}{a^2} + \frac{y^2}{b^2} = 1$	Horizontal	$(\pm a, 0)$	$(0, \pm b)$
$\frac{x^2}{b^2} + \frac{y^2}{a^2} = 1$	Vertical	$(0, \pm a)$	$(\pm b, 0)$

The major and minor axes are of lengths $2a$ and $2b$, respectively, where $a > b > 0$. The foci of the ellipse lie on the major axis at a distance of c units from the center, where $c^2 = a^2 - b^2$.

EXAMPLE 1 Graph an equation of an ellipse

Graph the equation $4x^2 + 25y^2 = 100$. Identify the vertices, co-vertices, and foci of the ellipse.

Solution

STEP 1 **Rewrite** the equation in standard form.

$$4x^2 + 25y^2 = 100 \qquad \text{Write original equation.}$$

$$\frac{4x^2}{100} + \frac{25y^2}{100} = \frac{100}{100} \qquad \text{Divide each side by 100.}$$

$$\frac{x^2}{25} + \frac{y^2}{4} = 1 \qquad \text{Simplify.}$$

STEP 2 **Identify** the vertices, co-vertices, and foci. Note that $a^2 = 25$ and $b^2 = 4$, so $a = 5$ and $b = 2$. The denominator of the x^2-term is greater than that of the y^2-term, so the major axis is horizontal.

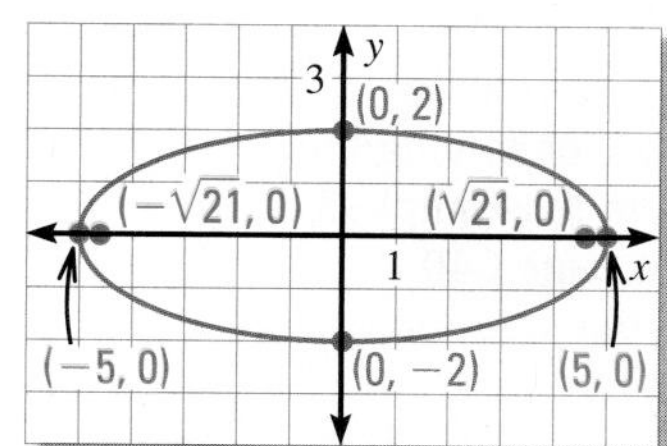

The vertices of the ellipse are at $(\pm a, 0) = (\pm 5, 0)$. The co-vertices are at $(0, \pm b) = (0, \pm 2)$. Find the foci.

$$c^2 = a^2 - b^2 = 5^2 - 2^2 = 21, \text{ so } c = \sqrt{21}$$

The foci are at $(\pm\sqrt{21}, 0)$, or about $(\pm 4.6, 0)$.

STEP 3 **Draw** the ellipse that passes through each vertex and co-vertex.

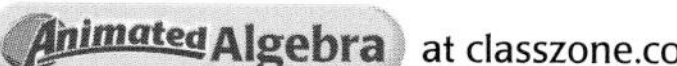

at classzone.com

ANOTHER WAY

You can graph the ellipse using a graphing calculator by solving for y to obtain

$$y = \pm 2\sqrt{1 - \frac{x^2}{25}}$$

and then entering this equation as two separate functions.

✓ GUIDED PRACTICE for Example 1

Graph the equation. Identify the vertices, co-vertices, and foci of the ellipse.

1. $\frac{x^2}{16} + \frac{y^2}{9} = 1$
2. $\frac{x^2}{36} + \frac{y^2}{49} = 1$
3. $25x^2 + 9y^2 = 225$

EXAMPLE 2 Write an equation given a vertex and a co-vertex

Write an equation of the ellipse that has a vertex at (0, 4), a co-vertex at (−3, 0), and center at (0, 0).

Solution

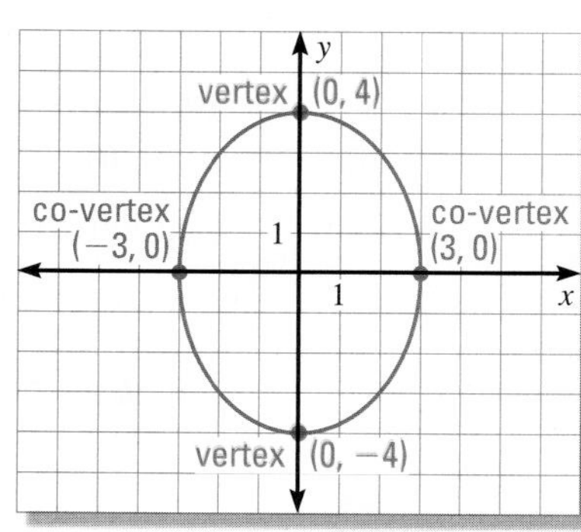

Sketch the ellipse as a check for your final equation. By symmetry, the ellipse must also have a vertex at (0, −4) and a co-vertex at (3, 0).

Because the vertex is on the y-axis and the co-vertex is on the x-axis, the major axis is vertical with $a = 4$, and the minor axis is horizontal with $b = 3$.

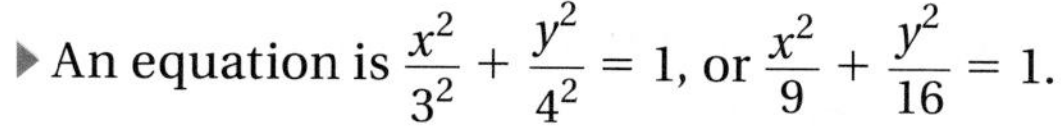

▶ An equation is $\frac{x^2}{3^2} + \frac{y^2}{4^2} = 1$, or $\frac{x^2}{9} + \frac{y^2}{16} = 1$.

EXAMPLE 3 Solve a multi-step problem

LIGHTNING When lightning strikes, an elliptical region where the strike most likely hit can often be identified. Suppose it is determined that there is a 50% chance that a lightning strike hit within the elliptical region shown in the diagram.

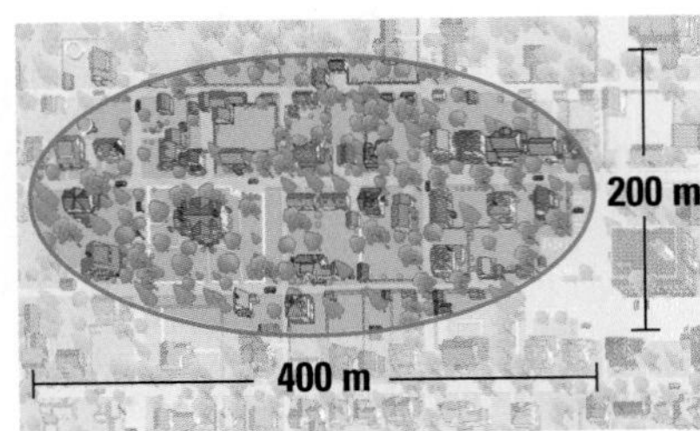

- Write an equation of the ellipse.
- The area A of an ellipse is $A = \pi ab$. Find the area of the elliptical region.

ANOTHER WAY
For an alternative method for solving the problem in Example 3, turn to page 640 for the **Problem Solving Workshop**.

Solution

STEP 1 The major axis is horizontal, with $a = \frac{400}{2} = 200$ and $b = \frac{200}{2} = 100$.

An equation is $\frac{x^2}{200^2} + \frac{y^2}{100^2} = 1$, or $\frac{x^2}{40{,}000} + \frac{y^2}{10{,}000} = 1$.

STEP 2 The area is $A = \pi(200)(100) \approx 62{,}800$ square meters.

EXAMPLE 4 Write an equation given a vertex and a focus

Write an equation of the ellipse that has a vertex at (−8, 0), a focus at (4, 0), and center at (0, 0).

Solution

Make a sketch of the ellipse. Because the given vertex and focus lie on the x-axis, the major axis is horizontal, with $a = 8$ and $c = 4$. To find b, use the equation $c^2 = a^2 - b^2$.

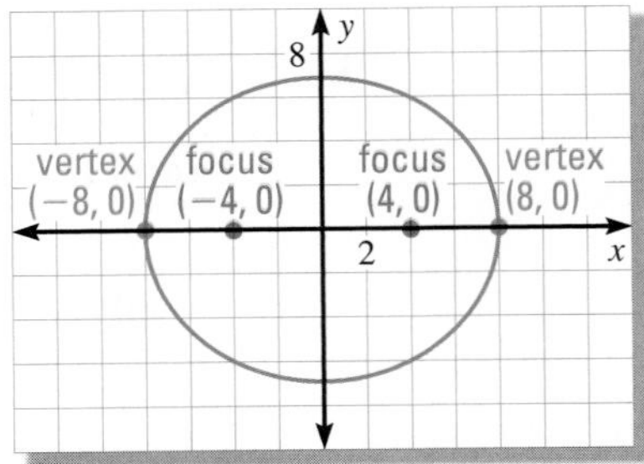

$$4^2 = 8^2 - b^2$$

$$b^2 = 8^2 - 4^2 = 48$$

$$b = \sqrt{48}, \text{ or } 4\sqrt{3}$$

▶ An equation is $\frac{x^2}{8^2} + \frac{y^2}{(4\sqrt{3})^2} = 1$, or $\frac{x^2}{64} + \frac{y^2}{48} = 1$.

✓ GUIDED PRACTICE for Examples 2, 3, and 4

Write an equation of the ellipse with the given characteristics and center at (0, 0).

4. Vertex: (7, 0); co-vertex: (0, 2)
5. Vertex: (0, 6); co-vertex: (−5, 0)
6. Vertex: (0, 8); focus: (0, −3)
7. Vertex: (−5, 0); focus: (3, 0)
8. **WHAT IF?** In Example 3, suppose that the elliptical region is 250 meters from east to west and 350 meters from north to south. Write an equation of the elliptical boundary and find the area of the region.

9.4 EXERCISES

HOMEWORK KEY

○ = **WORKED-OUT SOLUTIONS** on p. WS16 for Exs. 11, 29, and 49

★ = **STANDARDIZED TEST PRACTICE** Exs. 2, 35, 45, 46, 51, and 52

SKILL PRACTICE

1. **VOCABULARY** Copy and complete: An ellipse is the set of all points P such that the sum of the distances between P and two fixed points, called the _?_, is a constant.

2. ★ **WRITING** *Describe* how to find the foci of an ellipse given the coordinates of its vertices and co-vertices.

EXAMPLE 1 on p. 635 for Exs. 3–16

GRAPHING Graph the equation. Identify the vertices, co-vertices, and foci of the ellipse.

3. $\frac{x^2}{16} + \frac{y^2}{4} = 1$
4. $\frac{x^2}{4} + y^2 = 25$
5. $\frac{x^2}{9} + \frac{y^2}{49} = 1$
6. $\frac{x^2}{144} + \frac{y^2}{64} = 1$
7. $\frac{x^2}{400} + \frac{y^2}{81} = 1$
8. $\frac{x^2}{36} + \frac{y^2}{225} = 1$
9. $4x^2 + y^2 = 36$
10. $9x^2 + y^2 = 9$
11. $16x^2 + 9y^2 = 144$
12. $25x^2 + 49y^2 = 1225$
13. $16x^2 + 25y^2 = 1600$
14. $72x^2 + 8y^2 = 648$

ERROR ANALYSIS *Describe* and correct the error in graphing the ellipse.

15.

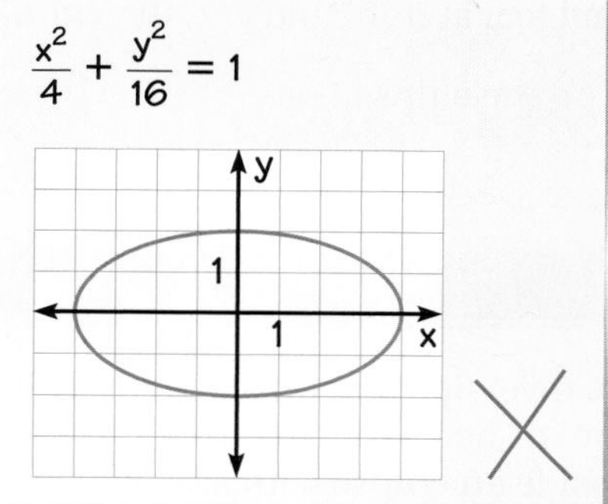

16.

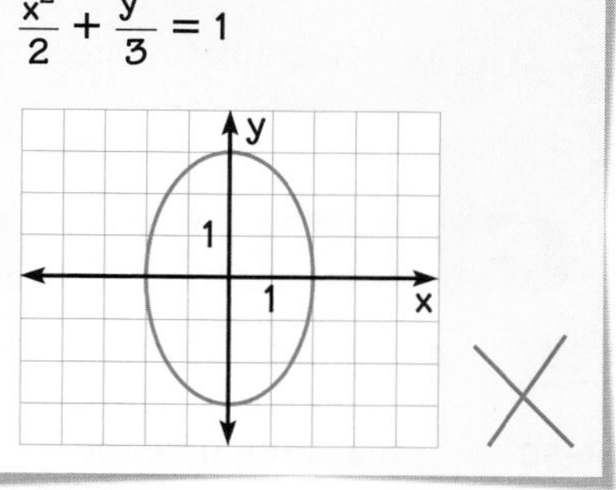

EXAMPLES 2 and 4 on pp. 635–636 for Exs. 17–35

WRITING EQUATIONS Write an equation of the ellipse with the given characteristics and center at (0, 0).

17. Vertex: (5, 0)
Co-vertex: (0, −3)
18. Vertex: (0, −10)
Co-vertex: (6, 0)
19. Vertex: (14, 0)
Co-vertex: (0, −9)
20. Vertex: (0, −6)
Co-vertex: (4, 0)
21. Vertex: (0, 12)
Co-vertex: (11, 0)
22. Vertex: (20, 0)
Co-vertex: (0, −16)
23. Vertex: (0, 8)
Focus: (0, 6)
24. Vertex: (4, 0)
Focus: $(\sqrt{7}, 0)$
25. Vertex: (0, 9)
Focus: $(0, -4\sqrt{2})$
26. Vertex: (−5, 0)
Focus: (3, 0)
27. Vertex: (0, −4)
Focus: $(0, -2\sqrt{3})$
28. Vertex: (13, 0)
Focus: $(-4\sqrt{3}, 0)$
29. Co-vertex: $(0, \sqrt{7})$
Focus: (−3, 0)
30. Co-vertex: $(-3\sqrt{5}, 0)$
Focus: (0, 6)
31. Co-vertex: $(0, -5\sqrt{7})$
Focus: (−15, 0)
32. Co-vertex: (0, 15)
Focus: (−8, 0)
33. Co-vertex: $(2\sqrt{15}, 0)$
Focus: (0, 14)
34. Co-vertex: (−32, 0)
Focus: (0, 24)

35. ★ **MULTIPLE CHOICE** What is an equation of the ellipse with center at the origin, a vertex at (0, −12), and a co-vertex at (−8, 0)?

Ⓐ $\frac{x^2}{144} + \frac{y^2}{64} = 1$ Ⓑ $\frac{x^2}{64} + \frac{y^2}{144} = 1$ Ⓒ $\frac{x^2}{12} + \frac{y^2}{8} = 1$ Ⓓ $\frac{x^2}{8} + \frac{y^2}{12} = 1$

GRAPHING In Exercises 36–44, the equations of parabolas, circles, and ellipses are given. Graph the equation.

36. $x^2 + y^2 = 64$
37. $25x^2 + 81y^2 = 2025$
38. $36y + x^2 = 0$
39. $65y^2 = 130x$
40. $30x^2 + 30y^2 = 480$
41. $\frac{x^2}{75} + \frac{4y}{25} = 0$
42. $\frac{3x^2}{48} + \frac{4y^2}{400} = 1$
43. $\frac{x^2}{64} + \frac{y^2}{64} = 4$
44. $16x^2 + 10y^2 = 160$

45. ★ **SHORT RESPONSE** Consider the graph of $\frac{x^2}{9} + \frac{y^2}{25} = 1$. *Describe* the effects on the graph of changing the denominator of the y^2-term first from 25 to 9 and then from 9 to 4. Graph the original equation and the two revised equations in the same coordinate plane.

46. ★ **OPEN-ENDED MATH** Write an equation of an ellipse in standard form. Graph the equation on a graphing calculator by rewriting it as two functions. Give a viewing window that does not distort the shape of the ellipse, and explain how you found your viewing window.

47. **CHALLENGE** Use the definition of an ellipse to show that $c^2 = a^2 - b^2$ for any ellipse with equation $\frac{x^2}{a^2} + \frac{y^2}{b^2} = 1$ and foci at $(c, 0)$ and $(-c, 0)$. (*Hint:* Draw a diagram. Consider the point $P(a, 0)$ on the ellipse.)

PROBLEM SOLVING

EXAMPLE 3 on p. 636 for Exs. 48–50

48. **MARS** On January 3, 2004, the Mars rover Spirit bounced on its airbags to a landing within Gusev crater. Scientists had estimated that there was a 99% chance the rover would land inside an ellipse with a major axis 81 kilometers long and a minor axis 12 kilometers long. Write an equation of the ellipse. Then find its area.

Artist's rendering of landing

@HomeTutor for problem solving help at classzone.com

49. **AUSTRALIAN FOOTBALL** The playing field for Australian football is an ellipse that is between 135 and 185 meters long and between 110 and 155 meters wide. Write equations of ellipses with vertical major axes that model the largest and smallest fields described. Then write an inequality that describes the possible areas of these fields.

@HomeTutor for problem solving help at classzone.com

○ = WORKED-OUT SOLUTIONS on p. WS1   ★ = STANDARDIZED TEST PRACTICE

50. **HEALTH CARE** A *lithotripter* uses shock waves to break apart kidney stones or gallstones inside the body. Shock waves generated at one focus of an *ellipsoid* (a three-dimensional shape with an elliptical cross section) reflect to the stone positioned at the second focus. Write an equation for the cross section of the ellipsoid with the dimensions shown. How far apart are the foci?

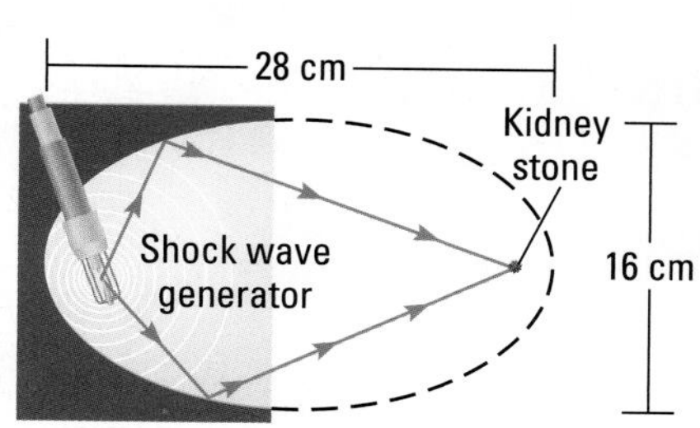

51. ★ **SHORT RESPONSE** Halley's comet ranges from 0.59 to 35.3 astronomical units from the sun, which is at one focus of the comet's elliptical orbit. (An *astronomical unit* is Earth's mean distance from the sun.) *Explain* using a sketch how to find a and c. Then write an equation for the orbit.

52. ★ **EXTENDED RESPONSE** A small airplane with enough fuel to fly 600 miles safely will take off from airport A and land at airport B, 450 miles away.

    a. **Reason** The region in which the airplane can fly is bounded by an ellipse. *Explain* why this is so.

    b. **Calculate** Let (0, 0) represent the center of the ellipse. Find the coordinates of each airport.

    c. **Apply** Suppose the plane flies from airport A straight past airport B to a vertex of the ellipse and then straight back to airport B. How far does the plane fly? Use your answer to find the coordinates of the vertex.

    d. **Model** Write an equation of the ellipse.

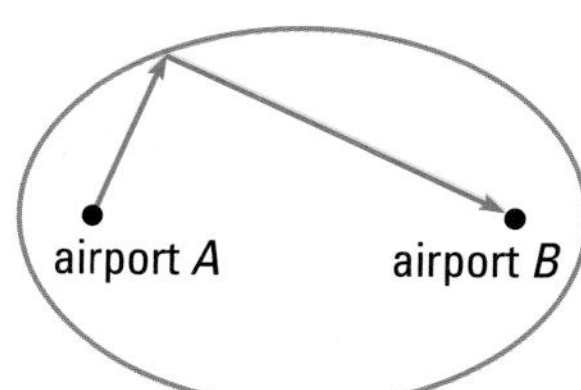

53. **CHALLENGE** An art museum worker leaves an 8-foot-tall painting leaning against a wall. Later, the top of the painting slides down the wall, and the painting falls to the floor. Use the diagram to find an equation of the path of the point (x, y) as the painting falls.

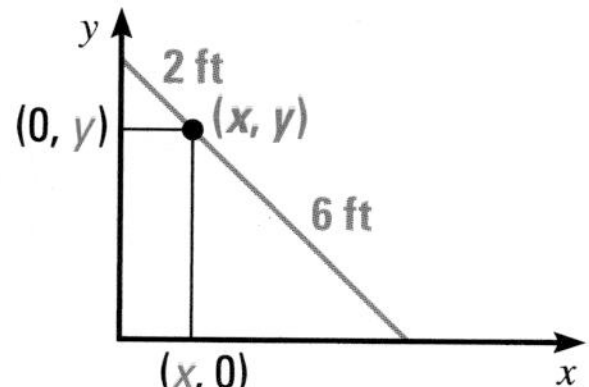

NEW YORK MIXED REVIEW

54. Iris wants to make candles shaped like rectangular prisms that measure 3 inches long, 2 inches wide, and 5 inches high. To make the candles, she melts the cylindrical block of wax shown. How many candles can she make?

    Ⓐ 113 Ⓑ 126

    Ⓒ 136 Ⓓ 288

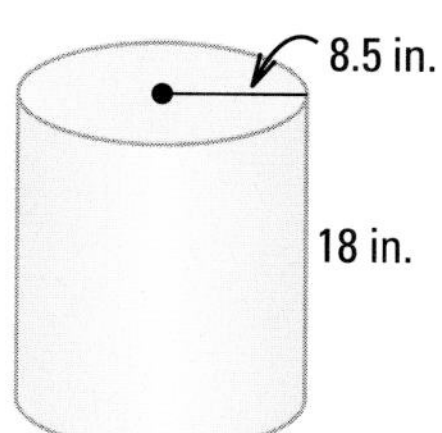

55. The area of a triangle is $45m^7n^{13}$ square units and its height is $15m^{10}n^9$ units. What is the length of the triangle's base?

    Ⓐ $\frac{3m^3}{n^4}$ units Ⓑ $\frac{6n^4}{m^3}$ units

    Ⓒ $3m^3n^4$ units Ⓓ $6m^{17}n^{22}$ units

PROBLEM SOLVING WORKSHOP
LESSON 9.4

Using ALTERNATIVE METHODS

Another Way to Solve Example 3, page 636

MULTIPLE REPRESENTATIONS In the second part of Example 3 on page 636, you found the area of an ellipse using a formula. You can also approximate the area of an ellipse by summing the areas of rectangles.

PROBLEM

LIGHTNING When lightning strikes, an elliptical region where the strike most likely hit can often be identified. Suppose it is determined that there is a 50% chance that a lightning strike hit within the elliptical region shown in the diagram.

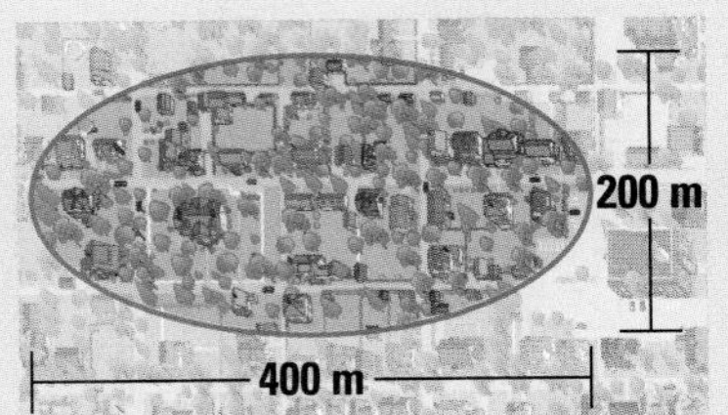

- Write an equation of the ellipse.
- Find the area of the elliptical region.

METHOD

Summing Rectangles As you saw on page 636, the ellipse has the equation $\frac{x^2}{200^2} + \frac{y^2}{100^2} = 1$. Approximate the area of the ellipse as follows.

STEP 1 **Graph** the first-quadrant portion of the ellipse. Then draw rectangles of width 40 and height equal to the y-value of the ellipse at the rectangle's left edge. The first rectangle's height is $y_1 = 100$. To find the other y-values, solve for y to obtain $y = \sqrt{100^2 - \frac{x^2}{4}}$. Use a calculator to get $y_2 \approx 98.0$, $y_3 \approx 91.7$, $y_4 = 80$, and $y_5 = 60$.

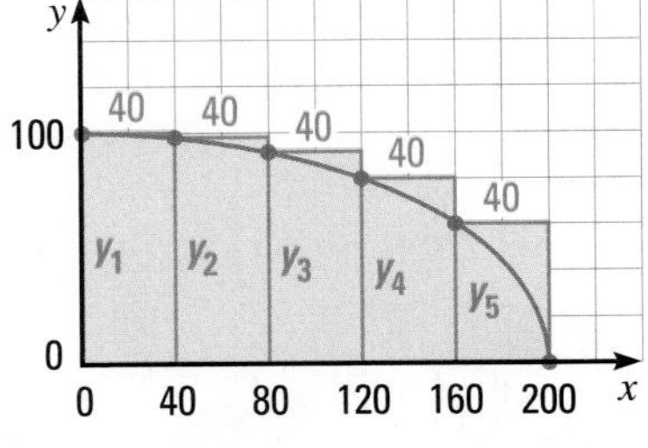

STEP 2 **Calculate** the total area A of the rectangles.

$$A \approx 40(100) + 40(98.0) + 40(91.7) + 40(80) + 40(60) = 17{,}188 \text{ m}^2$$

STEP 3 **Multiply** the total area of the rectangles by 4 to obtain an estimate of $4(17{,}188) \approx 68{,}800$ square meters for the area of the ellipse.

PRACTICE

1. Solve the problem above using rectangles of width 20. Is this estimate better or worse than the estimate above? *Explain.*

2. **REASONING** *Explain* using your results from Exercise 1 how to obtain a closer and closer approximation of the ellipse's area.

3. **WHAT IF?** Suppose that the ellipse in the problem had a horizontal major axis of 250 meters and a minor axis of 200 meters.
   a. Write an equation of the ellipse.
   b. Use the method above to approximate the area of the ellipse.

Lessons 9.1–9.4

1. **PARABOLIC REFLECTORS** Parabolic reflectors with a microphone at the focus allow the operator to listen to sounds from far away. A certain parabolic microphone has a reflector that is 22.4 inches in diameter and 6 inches deep. Approximately how far is the focus from the vertex?

   (1) 5.2 inches (3) 11.2 inches

   (2) 6 inches (4) 24.8 inches

2. **RADAR** An anchored fishing boat's radar has a range of 16 miles. A second boat 6 miles north and 4 miles east of the fishing boat begins moving westward. For approximately what distance will the second boat be in radar range of the first boat?

   (1) 14.8 miles

   (2) 18.8 miles

   (3) 21.5 miles

   (4) 29.6 miles

3. **PLANETARY ORBIT** In its elliptical orbit, Mercury ranges from 29 million miles to 44 million miles from the sun. The sun is at one focus of the orbit. Which equation could represent Mercury's orbit?

   (1) $\frac{x^2}{(36.5)^2} + \frac{y^2}{(7.5)^2} = 1$

   (2) $\frac{x^2}{(44)^2} + \frac{y^2}{(29)^2} = 1$

   (3) $\frac{x^2}{(36.5)^2} + \frac{y^2}{(29)^2} = 1$

   (4) $\frac{x^2}{(36.5)^2} + \frac{y^2}{(35.7)^2} = 1$

4. **DRIVING DISTANCE** To get from your home to the beach, you drive 8 miles south, then 16 miles east, and then 4 miles south. What is the straight-line distance from your home to the beach?

   (1) 16.5 miles (3) 21.5 miles

   (2) 20 miles (4) 28 miles

5. **TANGENT LINES** Two lines are tangent to the circle $x^2 + y^2 = 13$, one at $(-2, -3)$ and one at $(3, -2)$. What is the relationship between the two lines?

   (1) The two lines are parallel.

   (2) The two lines are perpendicular.

   (3) The two lines intersect at the origin.

   (4) The two lines intersect at $\left(0, \frac{13}{2}\right)$.

6. **OPEN-ENDED** You can make a solar hot dog cooker by shaping foil-lined cardboard into a parabolic trough and passing a wire through the focus of each end piece. For the trough shown, how far from the bottom, to the nearest tenth of an inch, should you place the wire?

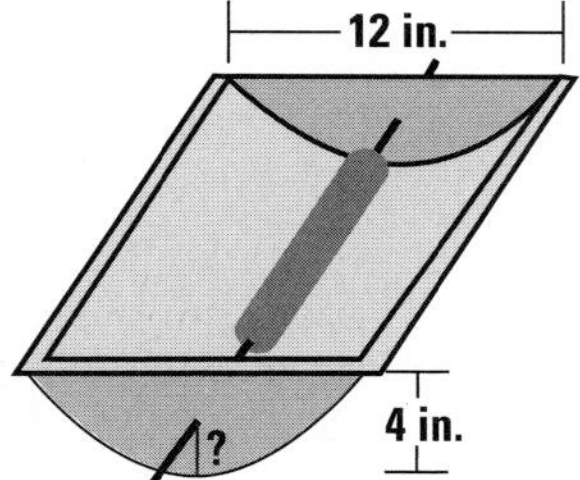

7. **OPEN-ENDED** A car skids while turning to avoid an accident. The car's speed v (in meters per second) can be estimated using $v = \sqrt{9.8\mu r}$ where r is the radius (in meters) of the circular skid mark and μ is a constant that depends on the road surface and weather conditions ($0 \le \mu \le 1$).

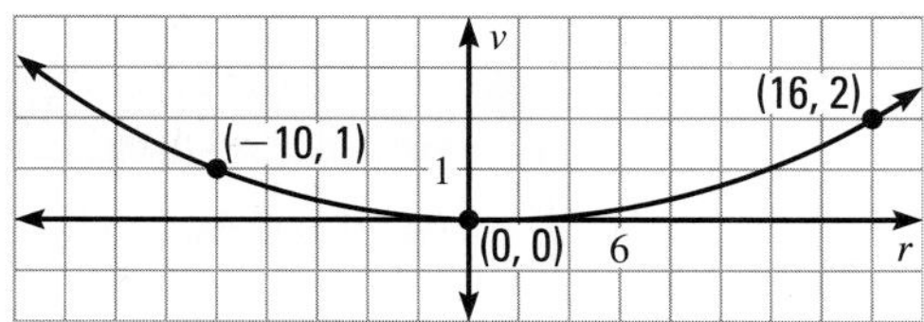

Find the radius of the skid mark shown.

Estimate how fast the car was traveling if it is determined that $\mu = 0.7$.

How does the car's speed while skidding affect the radius of the circle? *Explain.*

9.5 Graph and Write Equations of Hyperbolas

Before You graphed and wrote equations of parabolas, circles, and ellipses.

Now You will graph and write equations of hyperbolas.

Why? So you can model curved mirrors, as in Example 3.

Key Vocabulary
- **hyperbola**
- **foci**
- **vertices**
- **transverse axis**
- **center**

Recall that an ellipse is the set of all points P in a plane such that the *sum* of the distances between P and two fixed points (the foci) is a constant.

A **hyperbola** is the set of all points P such that the *difference* of the distances between P and two fixed points, again called the **foci**, is a constant.

The line through the foci intersects the hyperbola at the two **vertices**. The **transverse axis** joins the vertices. Its midpoint is the hyperbola's **center**. A hyperbola has two *branches*, and has two asymptotes that contain the diagonals of a rectangle centered at the hyperbola's center, as shown.

IDENTIFY AXES
If the x^2-term in the equation of a hyperbola is positive, the transverse axis lies on the x-axis. If the y^2-term is positive, the transverse axis lies on the y-axis.

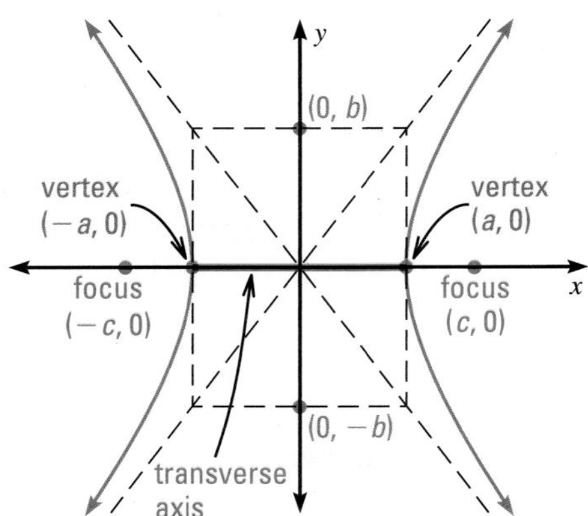

Hyperbola with horizontal transverse axis

$$\frac{x^2}{a^2} - \frac{y^2}{b^2} = 1$$

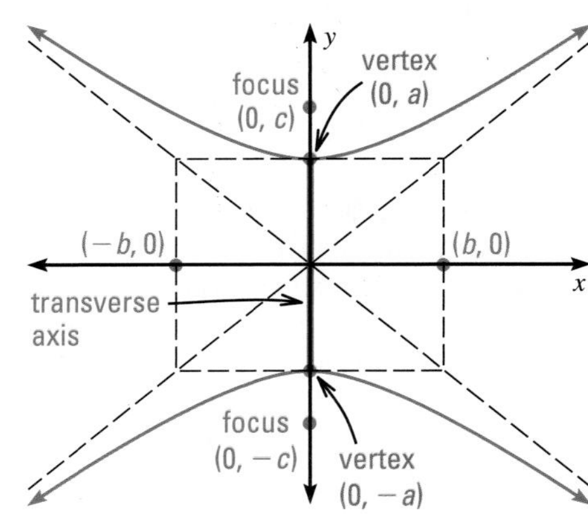

Hyperbola with vertical transverse axis

$$\frac{y^2}{a^2} - \frac{x^2}{b^2} = 1$$

KEY CONCEPT *For Your Notebook*

Standard Equation of a Hyperbola with Center at the Origin

Equation	Transverse Axis	Asymptotes	Vertices
$\frac{x^2}{a^2} - \frac{y^2}{b^2} = 1$	Horizontal	$y = \pm\frac{b}{a}x$	$(\pm a, 0)$
$\frac{y^2}{a^2} - \frac{x^2}{b^2} = 1$	Vertical	$y = \pm\frac{a}{b}x$	$(0, \pm a)$

The foci lie on the transverse axis, c units from the center, where $c^2 = a^2 + b^2$.

EXAMPLE 1 Graph an equation of a hyperbola

Graph $25y^2 - 4x^2 = 100$. Identify the vertices, foci, and asymptotes of the hyperbola.

Solution

STEP 1 **Rewrite** the equation in standard form.

$$25y^2 - 4x^2 = 100 \qquad \textbf{Write original equation.}$$

$$\frac{25y^2}{100} - \frac{4x^2}{100} = \frac{100}{100} \qquad \textbf{Divide each side by 100.}$$

$$\frac{y^2}{4} - \frac{x^2}{25} = 1 \qquad \textbf{Simplify.}$$

STEP 2 **Identify** the vertices, foci, and asymptotes. Note that $a^2 = 4$ and $b^2 = 25$, so $a = 2$ and $b = 5$. The y^2-term is positive, so the transverse axis is vertical and the vertices are at $(0, \pm 2)$. Find the foci.

$$c^2 = a^2 + b^2 = 2^2 + 5^2 = 29, \text{ so } c = \sqrt{29}$$

The foci are at $(0, \pm\sqrt{29}) \approx (0, \pm 5.4)$.

The asymptotes are $y = \pm\frac{a}{b}x$, or $y = \pm\frac{2}{5}x$.

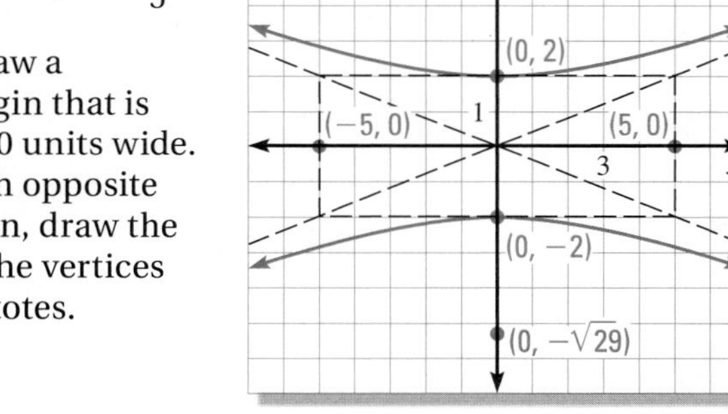

STEP 3 **Draw** the hyperbola. First draw a rectangle centered at the origin that is $2a = 4$ units high and $2b = 10$ units wide. The asymptotes pass through opposite corners of the rectangle. Then, draw the hyperbola passing through the vertices and approaching the asymptotes.

SOLVE FOR Y

To plot points on the hyperbola, solve its equation for y to obtain $y = \pm 2\sqrt{1 + \frac{x^2}{25}}$. Then make a table of values.

Animated Algebra at classzone.com

EXAMPLE 2 Write an equation of a hyperbola

Write an equation of the hyperbola with foci at $(-4, 0)$ and $(4, 0)$ and vertices at $(-3, 0)$ and $(3, 0)$.

Solution

The foci and vertices lie on the x-axis equidistant from the origin, so the transverse axis is horizontal and the center is the origin. The foci are each 4 units from the center, so $c = 4$. The vertices are each 3 units from the center, so $a = 3$.

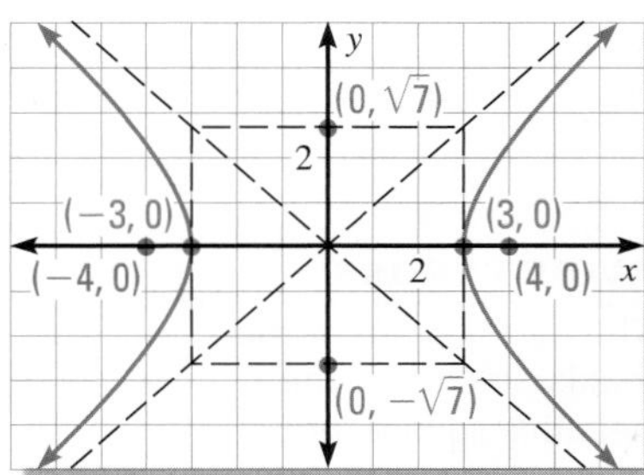

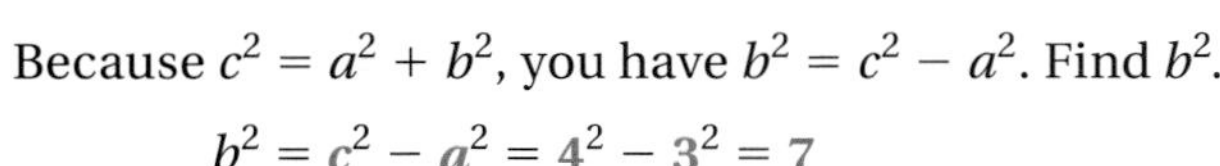

Because $c^2 = a^2 + b^2$, you have $b^2 = c^2 - a^2$. Find b^2.

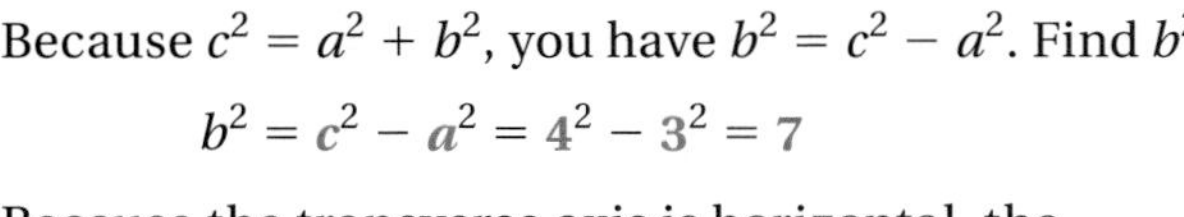

$$b^2 = c^2 - a^2 = 4^2 - 3^2 = 7$$

Because the transverse axis is horizontal, the standard form of the equation is as follows:

$$\frac{x^2}{3^2} - \frac{y^2}{7} = 1 \qquad \textbf{Substitute 3 for } a \textbf{ and 7 for } b^2.$$

$$\frac{x^2}{9} - \frac{y^2}{7} = 1 \qquad \textbf{Simplify.}$$

✓ GUIDED PRACTICE for Examples 1 and 2

Graph the equation. Identify the vertices, foci, and asymptotes of the hyperbola.

1. $\frac{x^2}{16} - \frac{y^2}{49} = 1$

2. $\frac{y^2}{36} - x^2 = 1$

3. $4y^2 - 9x^2 = 36$

Write an equation of the hyperbola with the given foci and vertices.

4. Foci: $(-3, 0), (3, 0)$
Vertices: $(-1, 0), (1, 0)$

5. Foci: $(0, -10), (0, 10)$
Vertices: $(0, -6), (0, 6)$

EXAMPLE 3 Solve a multi-step problem

PHOTOGRAPHY You can take panoramic photographs using a hyperbolic mirror. Light rays heading toward the focus behind the mirror are reflected to a camera positioned at the other focus as shown. After a photograph is taken, computers can "unwarp" the distorted image into a 360° view.

- Write an equation for the cross section of the mirror.
- The mirror is 6 centimeters wide. How tall is it?

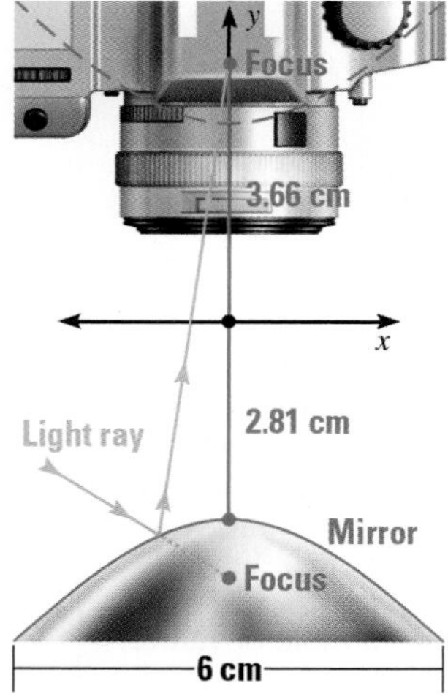

Solution

STEP 1 From the diagram, $a = 2.81$ and $c = 3.66$.

To write an equation, find b^2.

$$b^2 = c^2 - a^2 = 3.66^2 - 2.81^2 \approx 5.50$$

▶ Because the transverse axis is vertical, the standard form of the equation for the cross section of the mirror is as follows:

$$\frac{y^2}{2.81^2} - \frac{x^2}{5.50} = 1, \quad \text{or} \quad \frac{y^2}{7.90} - \frac{x^2}{5.50} = 1$$

STEP 2 Find the y-coordinate at the mirror's bottom edge. Because the mirror is 6 centimeters wide, substitute $x = 3$ into the equation and solve.

$$\frac{y^2}{7.90} - \frac{3^2}{5.50} = 1$$ **Substitute 3 for *x*.**

$$y^2 \approx 20.83$$ **Solve for y^2.**

$$y \approx -4.56$$ **Solve for *y*.**

▶ So, the mirror has a height of $-2.81 - (-4.56) = 1.75$ centimeters.

AVOID ERRORS
The mirror is below the x-axis, so choose the negative square root.

✓ GUIDED PRACTICE for Example 3

6. **WHAT IF?** In Example 3, suppose that the mirror remains 6 centimeters wide, but that $a = 3$ centimeters and $c = 5$ centimeters. How tall is the mirror?

9.5 EXERCISES

HOMEWORK KEY

○ = **WORKED-OUT SOLUTIONS** on p. WS17 for Exs. 13, 23, and 41

★ = **STANDARDIZED TEST PRACTICE** Exs. 2, 15, 26, 33, 35, and 43

◆ = **MULTIPLE REPRESENTATIONS** Ex. 42

SKILL PRACTICE

1. **VOCABULARY** Copy and complete: The points (−2, 0) and (2, 0) in the graph at the right are the _?_ of the hyperbola. The line segment joining these two points is the _?_.

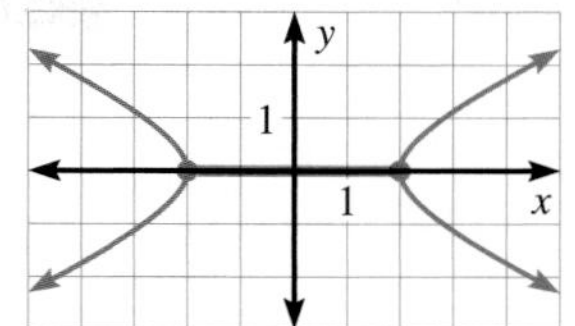

2. ★ **WRITING** *Compare* the definitions of an ellipse and a hyperbola.

EXAMPLE 1 on p. 643 for Exs. 3–17

GRAPHING **Graph the equation. Identify the vertices, foci, and asymptotes of the hyperbola.**

3. $\frac{x^2}{25} - \frac{y^2}{4} = 1$
4. $\frac{x^2}{9} - \frac{y^2}{36} = 1$
5. $\frac{y^2}{81} - \frac{x^2}{25} = 1$
6. $\frac{x^2}{144} - \frac{y^2}{36} = 1$
7. $\frac{y^2}{196} - \frac{x^2}{100} = 1$
8. $\frac{y^2}{49} - \frac{x^2}{121} = 1$
9. $4x^2 - y^2 = 256$
10. $49x^2 - 4y^2 = 196$
11. $9y^2 - 25x^2 = 225$
12. $25y^2 - 64x^2 = 1600$
13. $81x^2 - 16y^2 = 1296$
14. $49y^2 - 100x^2 = 4900$

15. ★ **MULTIPLE CHOICE** What are the foci of the hyperbola with equation $45y^2 - 200x^2 = 1800$?

(A) $(\pm 2\sqrt{10}, 0)$ (B) $(0, \pm 2\sqrt{10})$ (C) $(\pm 7, 0)$ (D) $(0, \pm 7)$

ERROR ANALYSIS *Describe* **and correct the error in graphing the equation.**

16.

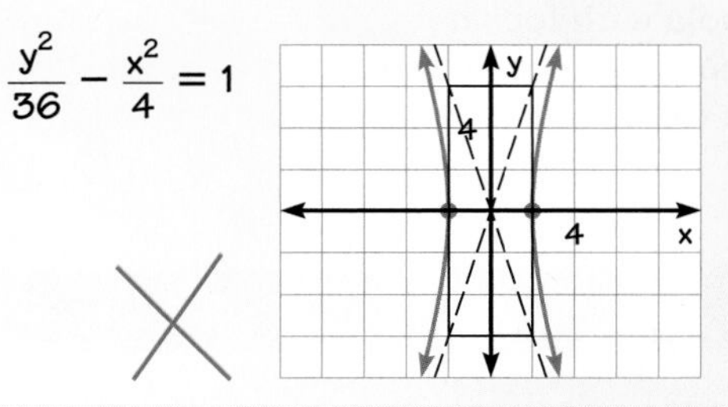

17.

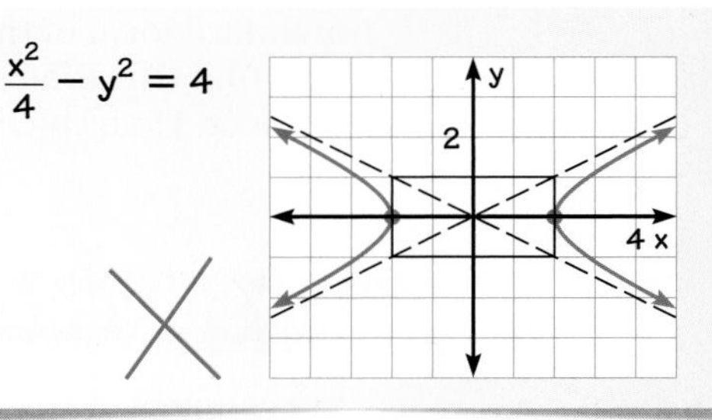

EXAMPLE 2 on p. 643 for Exs. 18–26

WRITING EQUATIONS **Write an equation of the hyperbola with the given foci and vertices.**

18. Foci: (0, −4), (0, 4)
Vertices: (0, −2), (0, 2)

19. Foci: (−6, 0), (6, 0)
Vertices: (−2, 0), (2, 0)

20. Foci: (−5, 0), (5, 0)
Vertices: (−1, 0), (1, 0)

21. Foci: (0, −12), (0, 12)
Vertices: (0, −7), (0, 7)

22. Foci: (−10, 0), (10, 0)
Vertices: $(-5\sqrt{3}, 0)$, $(5\sqrt{3}, 0)$

23. Foci: $(0, -4\sqrt{5})$, $(0, 4\sqrt{5})$
Vertices: (0, −4), (0, 4)

24. Foci: (0, −3), (0, 3)
Vertices: $(0, -2\sqrt{2})$, $(0, 2\sqrt{2})$

25. Foci: $(-3\sqrt{6}, 0)$, $(3\sqrt{6}, 0)$
Vertices: (−2, 0), (2, 0)

26. ★ **MULTIPLE CHOICE** What is an equation of the hyperbola with foci at $(0, -6\sqrt{3})$ and $(0, 6\sqrt{3})$ and with vertices at $(0, -8)$ and $(0, 8)$?

Ⓐ $\frac{x^2}{64} - \frac{y^2}{108} = 1$ Ⓑ $\frac{x^2}{44} - \frac{y^2}{68} = 1$ Ⓒ $\frac{y^2}{64} - \frac{x^2}{44} = 1$ Ⓓ $\frac{y^2}{108} - \frac{x^2}{64} = 1$

GRAPHING In Exercises 27–32, the equations of parabolas, circles, ellipses, and hyperbolas are given. Graph the equation.

27. $\frac{x^2}{25} - \frac{y^2}{49} = 1$
28. $y^2 = 18x$
29. $48x^2 + 12y^2 = 48$
30. $\frac{x^2}{144} + \frac{y^2}{256} = 1$
31. $\frac{y^2}{25} - \frac{x^2}{121} = 1$
32. $18x^2 + 18y^2 = 288$

33. ★ **SHORT RESPONSE** *Describe* the effects of the indicated change on the shape of the hyperbola and on the locations of the vertices and foci.

a. $\frac{x^2}{9} - \frac{y^2}{36} = 1$; change 36 to 4
b. $\frac{y^2}{16} - \frac{x^2}{4} = 1$; change 4 to 25

34. **GRAPHING CALCULATOR** Graph each hyperbola using a graphing calculator. Tell what two functions you entered into the calculator.

a. $\frac{y^2}{15} - \frac{x^2}{30} = 1$
b. $\frac{x^2}{8.4} - \frac{y^2}{5.5} = 1$
c. $5x^2 - 7.5y^2 = 12$

35. ★ **OPEN-ENDED MATH** Give equations of three hyperbolas with horizontal transverse axes and asymptotes $y = \pm 2x$. *Compare* the hyperbolas.

36. **REASONING** Use the diagram at the right to show that $|d_2 - d_1| = 2a$. (*Hint:* $|d_2 - d_1|$ is constant, so choose a convenient location for (x, y).)

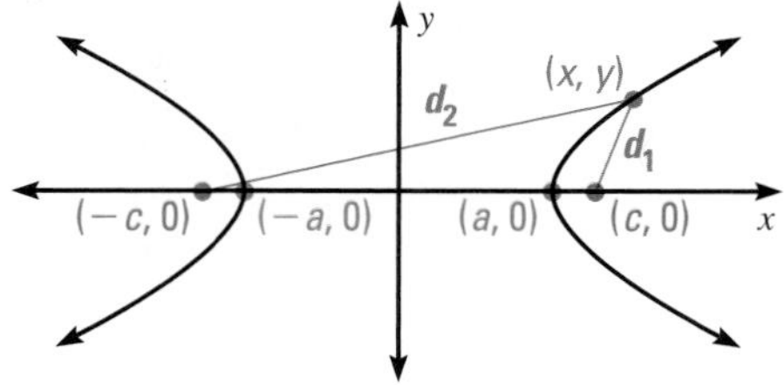

37. **CHALLENGE** Using the distance formula and the definition of a hyperbola, write an equation in standard form of the hyperbola with foci at $(\pm 2, 0)$ if the difference in the distances from a point (x, y) on the hyperbola to the foci is 2.

PROBLEM SOLVING

EXAMPLE 3 on p. 644 for Exs. 38–40

38. **TELESCOPES** A satellite is carrying a telescope that has a hyperbolic mirror for which $a = 33$ and $c = 56$ (in centimeters). Write an equation for the cross section of the mirror if the transverse axis is horizontal.

@HomeTutor for problem solving help at classzone.com

39. **SPINNING CUBE** The outline of a cube spinning around an axis through a pair of opposite corners contains a portion of a hyperbola, as shown. The coordinates given represent a vertex and a focus of the hyperbola for a cube that measures 1 unit on each edge. Write an equation that models this hyperbola.

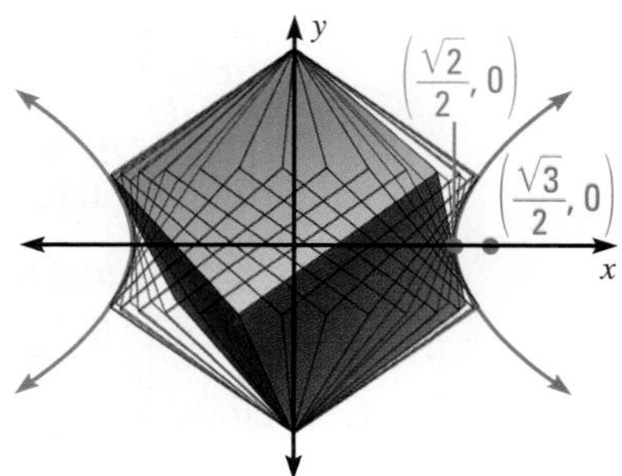

@HomeTutor for problem solving help at classzone.com

○ = WORKED-OUT SOLUTIONS on p. WS1 ★ = STANDARDIZED TEST PRACTICE ◆ = MULTIPLE REPRESENTATIONS

40. **SUN'S SHADOW** Each day, except at the fall and spring equinoxes, the tip of the shadow of a vertical pole traces a branch of a hyperbola across the ground. The diagram shows shadow paths for a 20 meter tall flagpole in Dallas, Texas.

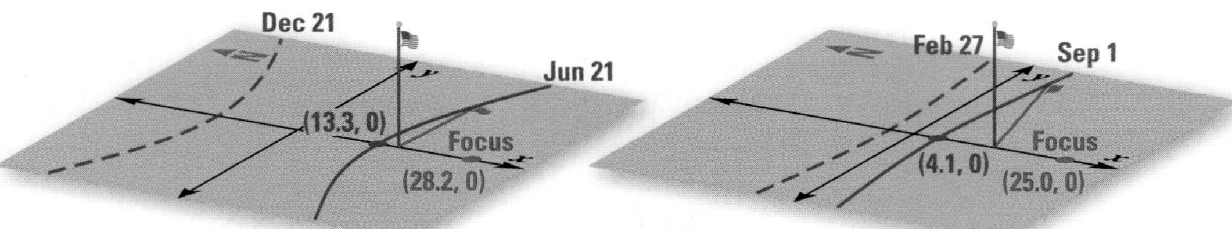

a. Write an equation of the hyperbola with center at the origin that models the June 21 path, given that $a = 13.3$ meters and $c = 28.2$ meters.

b. Write an equation of the hyperbola with center at the origin that models the September 1 path, given that $a = 4.1$ meters and $c = 25.0$ meters.

41. **MULTI-STEP PROBLEM** The roof of the St. Louis Science Center has a hyperbolic cross section with the dimensions shown.

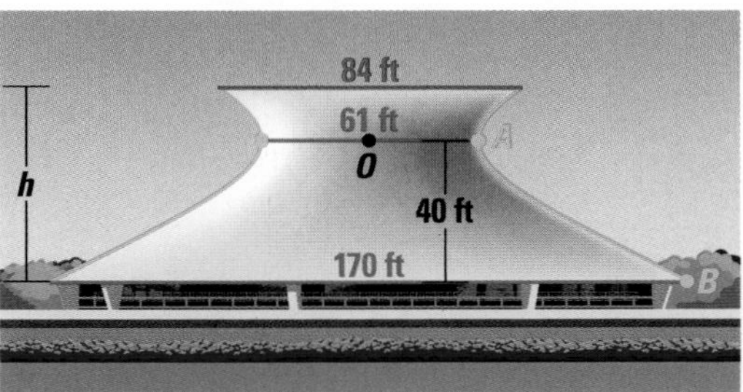

a. Suppose a coordinate grid is overlaid on the diagram with its origin at *O*, the center of the narrowest part of the roof. What are the coordinates of the points at *A* and *B*?

b. Use your answers from part (a) to write an equation that models the cross section.

c. Find the total height *h* of the roof.

42. **MULTIPLE REPRESENTATIONS** A circular walkway is to be built around a statue in a park. There is enough concrete available for the walkway to have an area of 600 square feet.

a. **Writing an Equation** Let the inside and outside radii of the walkway be *x* feet and *y* feet, respectively. Draw a diagram of the situation. Then write an equation relating *x* and *y*.

b. **Making a Table** Give four possible pairs of dimensions *x* and *y* that satisfy the equation from part (a).

c. **Drawing a Graph** Graph the equation from part (a). What portion of the graph represents solutions that make sense in this situation?

d. **Reasoning** How does the width of the walkway, $y - x$, change as both *x* and *y* increase? *Explain* why this makes sense.

43. ★ **SHORT RESPONSE** Two stones dropped at the same time into still water produce circular ripples whose intersection points form hyperbolas with foci where the stones hit the water. The graph shows one hyperbola formed by stones dropped 12 feet apart with ripples at 1 foot intervals.

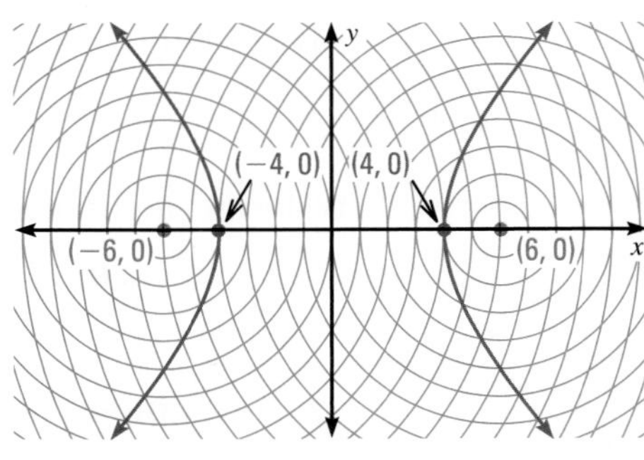

a. Write an equation of this hyperbola.

b. Use the definition of a hyperbola to explain why the graph shown is a hyperbola. (*Hint:* Examine the distances from each intersection point to the foci.)

44. **CHALLENGE** Two microphones placed 1 mile apart record the bugling of a bull elk. Microphone A receives the sound 2 seconds after microphone B. Sound travels at 1100 feet per second. Is this enough information to determine where the elk is located? If so, give the location. If not, explain why not.

NEW YORK MIXED REVIEW

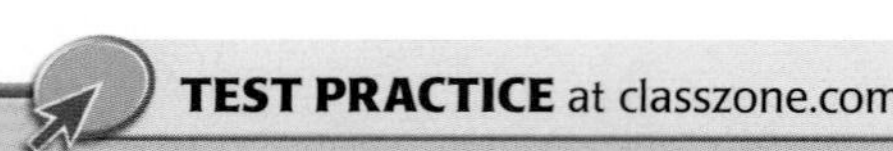

45. Which equation does the graph represent?

(A) $-3x + 2y = 14$

(B) $-2x + 3y = 6$

(C) $2x + 3y = -18$

(D) $3x + 2y = 1$

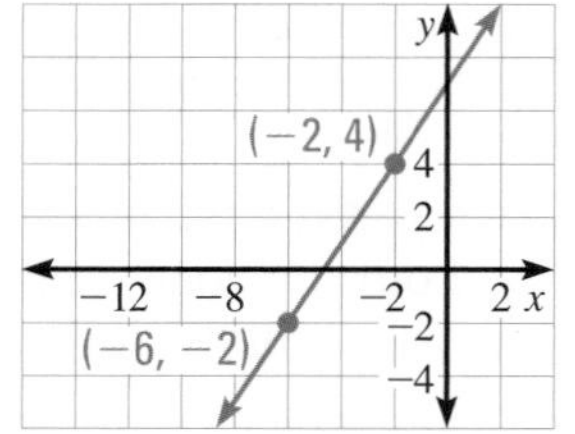

46. The endpoints of a diameter of a circle are $(-5, 8)$ and $(9, -3)$. What is the center of the circle?

(A) $\left(-8, \frac{17}{2}\right)$ (B) $(2, 3)$ (C) $\left(2, \frac{5}{2}\right)$ (D) $\left(7, -\frac{11}{2}\right)$

QUIZ for Lessons 9.4–9.5

Graph the equation. Identify the vertices, co-vertices, and foci of the ellipse. *(p. 634)*

1. $\frac{x^2}{25} + \frac{y^2}{4} = 1$

2. $\frac{x^2}{16} + \frac{y^2}{49} = 1$

3. $36x^2 + 9y^2 = 324$

Write an equation of the ellipse with the given characteristics and center at (0, 0). *(p. 634)*

4. Vertex: $(0, 5)$
Co-vertex: $(-4, 0)$

5. Vertex: $(10, 0)$
Focus: $(-8, 0)$

6. Co-vertex: $(-\sqrt{15}, 0)$
Focus: $(0, -5)$

Graph the equation. Identify the vertices, foci, and asymptotes of the hyperbola. *(p. 642)*

7. $\frac{y^2}{25} - \frac{x^2}{64} = 1$

8. $4x^2 - 16y^2 = 64$

9. $12y^2 - 20x^2 = 240$

Write an equation of the hyperbola with the given foci and vertices. *(p. 642)*

10. Foci: $(-5, 0), (5, 0)$
Vertices: $(-2, 0), (2, 0)$

11. Foci: $(0, -3), (0, 3)$
Vertices: $(0, -1), (0, 1)$

12. Foci: $(-3\sqrt{6}, 0), (3\sqrt{6}, 0)$
Vertices: $(-3, 0), (3, 0)$

13. **ASTEROIDS** The largest asteroid, 1 Ceres, ranges from 2.55 astronomical units to 2.98 astronomical units from the sun, which is located at one focus of the asteroid's elliptical orbit. Find a and c. Then write an equation of the orbit of 1 Ceres. *(p. 634)*

Animated Algebra
classzone.com

9.6 Exploring Intersections of Planes and Cones

MATERIALS • flashlight • graph paper

QUESTION **How do a plane and a double-napped cone intersect to form different conic sections?**

The reason that parabolas, circles, ellipses, and hyperbolas are called *conics* or *conic sections* is that each can be formed by the intersection of a plane and a double-napped cone, as shown below.

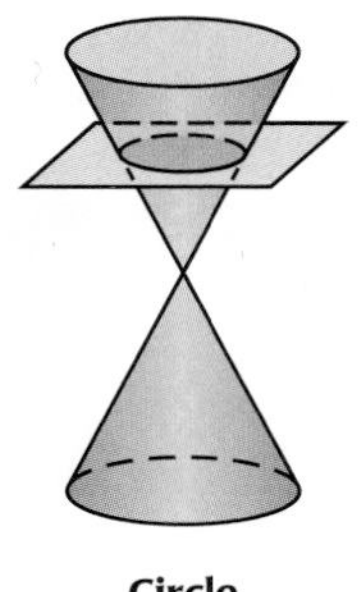
Circle

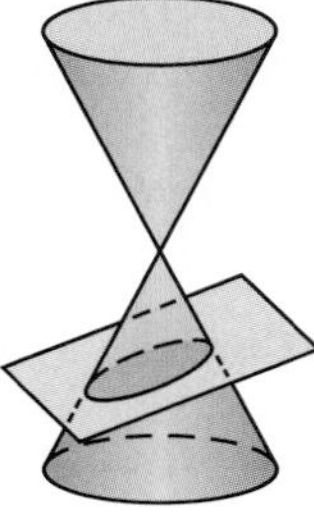
Ellipse

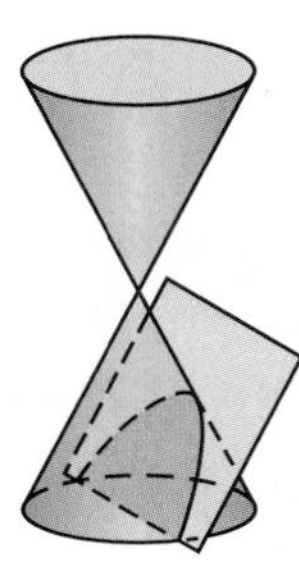
Parabola

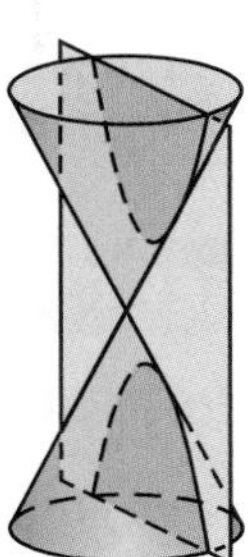
Hyperbola

EXPLORE **Find an equation of a conic**

STEP 1 ***Draw axes***

Work in a group. On a piece of graph paper, draw x- and y-axes to make a coordinate plane. Then tape the paper to a wall.

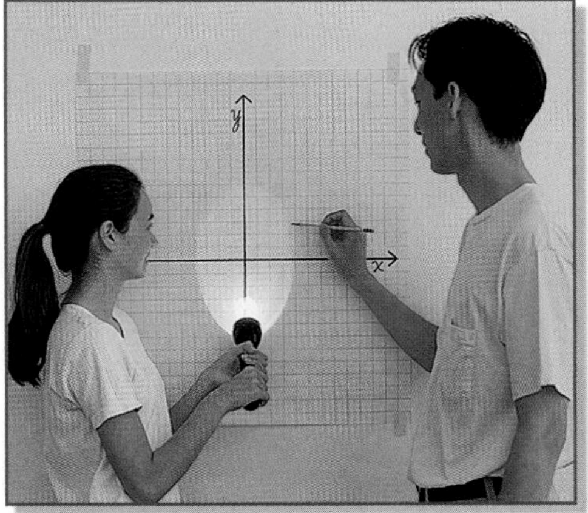

STEP 2 ***Model a circle***

Aim a flashlight perpendicular to the paper so that the light forms a circle centered on the origin of the coordinate plane. Trace the circle on the graph paper. Find the circle's radius, and use it to write the standard form of the circle's equation.

STEP 3 ***Model an ellipse***

Tilt the flashlight, and aim it at the paper to form an ellipse with a vertical major axis and center at the origin. Trace the ellipse and write the standard form of its equation.

DRAW CONCLUSIONS **Use your observations to complete these exercises**

1. *Compare* the equations for your circle and for your ellipse with the equations of other groups. Are your equations all the same? Why or why not?
2. Refer to the diagram of a hyperbola to explain how you can orient the flashlight beam to form a branch of a hyperbola on the wall.

9.6 Translate and Classify Conic Sections

 **A2.A.24** Know and apply the technique of completing the square

Before You graphed and wrote equations of conic sections.

Now You will translate conic sections.

Why? So you can model motion, as in Ex. 49.

Key Vocabulary
- **conic sections (conics)**
- **general second-degree equation**
- **discriminant**

Because parabolas, circles, ellipses, and hyperbolas are formed when a plane intersects a double-napped cone, they are called **conic sections** or **conics**.

Previously, you studied equations of parabolas with vertices at the origin and equations of circles, ellipses, and hyperbolas with centers at the origin. Now you will study how translating conics in the coordinate plane affects their equations.

KEY CONCEPT *For Your Notebook*

Standard Form of Equations of Translated Conics

In the following equations, the point (h, k) is the *vertex* of the parabola and the *center* of the other conics.

Circle $(x - h)^2 + (y - k)^2 = r^2$

	Horizontal axis	Vertical axis
Parabola	$(y - k)^2 = 4p(x - h)$	$(x - h)^2 = 4p(y - k)$
Ellipse	$\frac{(x - h)^2}{a^2} + \frac{(y - k)^2}{b^2} = 1$	$\frac{(x - h)^2}{b^2} + \frac{(y - k)^2}{a^2} = 1$
Hyperbola	$\frac{(x - h)^2}{a^2} - \frac{(y - k)^2}{b^2} = 1$	$\frac{(y - k)^2}{a^2} - \frac{(x - h)^2}{b^2} = 1$

EXAMPLE 1 Graph the equation of a translated circle

Graph $(x - 2)^2 + (y + 3)^2 = 9$.

Solution

STEP 1 **Compare** the given equation to the standard form of an equation of a circle. You can see that the graph is a circle with center at $(h, k) = (2, -3)$ and radius $r = \sqrt{9} = 3$.

STEP 2 **Plot** the center. Then plot several points that are each 3 units from the center:

$(2 + 3, -3) = (5, -3)$ $(2 - 3, -3) = (-1, -3)$

$(2, -3 + 3) = (2, 0)$ $(2, -3 - 3) = (2, -6)$

STEP 3 **Draw** a circle through the points.

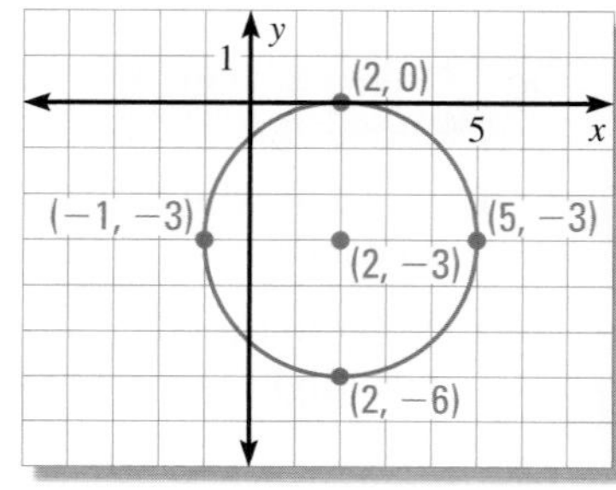

EXAMPLE 2 Graph the equation of a translated hyperbola

Graph $\frac{(y-3)^2}{4} - \frac{(x+1)^2}{9} = 1$.

Solution

STEP 1 **Compare** the given equation to the standard forms of equations of hyperbolas. The equation's form tells you that the graph is a hyperbola with a vertical transverse axis. The center is at $(h, k) = (-1, 3)$. Because $a^2 = 4$ and $b^2 = 9$, you know that $a = 2$ and $b = 3$.

STEP 2 **Plot** the center, vertices, and foci. The vertices lie $a = 2$ units above and below the center, at $(-1, 5)$ and $(-1, 1)$. Because $c^2 = a^2 + b^2 = 13$, the foci lie $c = \sqrt{13} \approx 3.6$ units above and below the center, at $(-1, 6.6)$ and $(-1, -0.6)$.

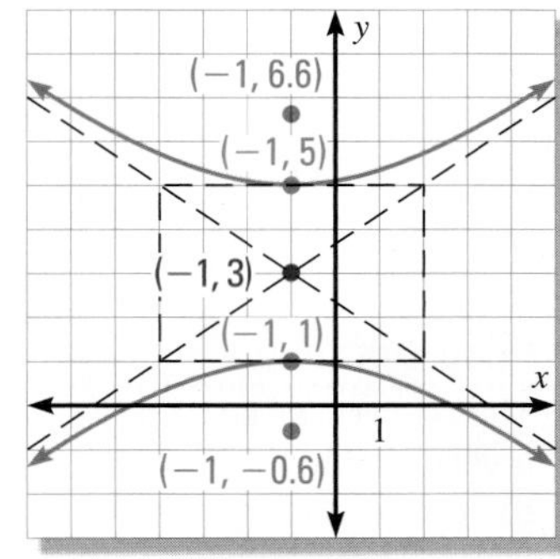

STEP 3 **Draw** the hyperbola. Draw a rectangle centered at $(-1, 3)$ that is $2a = 4$ units high and $2b = 6$ units wide. Draw the asymptotes through the opposite corners of the rectangle. Then draw the hyperbola passing through the vertices and approaching the asymptotes.

SOLVE FOR Y
To plot additional points on the hyperbola, solve for y to obtain
$y = 3 \pm 2\sqrt{1 + \frac{(x+1)^2}{9}}$.
Then make a table of values.

Animated Algebra at classzone.com

✓ GUIDED PRACTICE for Examples 1 and 2

Graph the equation. Identify the important characteristics of the graph.

1. $(x+1)^2 + (y-3)^2 = 4$
2. $(x-2)^2 = 8(y+3)$
3. $(x+3)^2 - \frac{(y-4)^2}{4} = 1$
4. $\frac{(x-2)^2}{16} + \frac{(y-1)^2}{9} = 1$

EXAMPLE 3 Write an equation of a translated parabola

Write an equation of the parabola whose vertex is at $(-2, 3)$ and whose focus is at $(-4, 3)$.

Solution

STEP 1 **Determine** the form of the equation. Begin by making a rough sketch of the parabola. Because the focus is to the left of the vertex, the parabola opens to the left, and its equation has the form $(y-k)^2 = 4p(x-h)$ where $p < 0$.

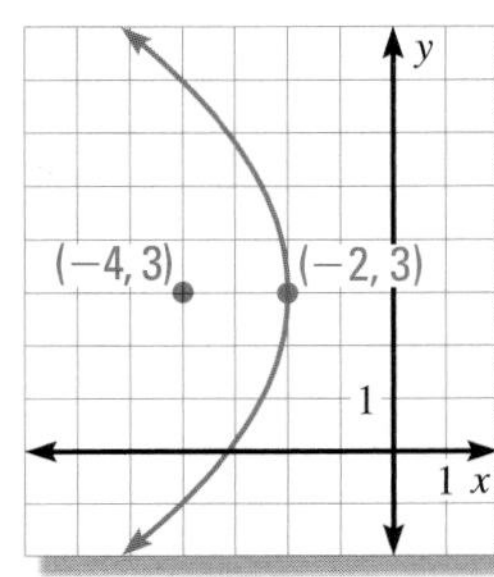

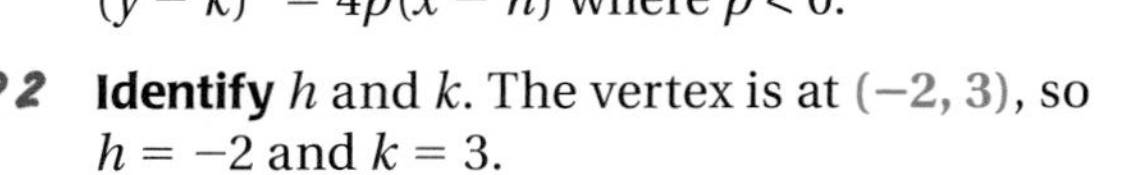

STEP 2 **Identify** h and k. The vertex is at $(-2, 3)$, so $h = -2$ and $k = 3$.

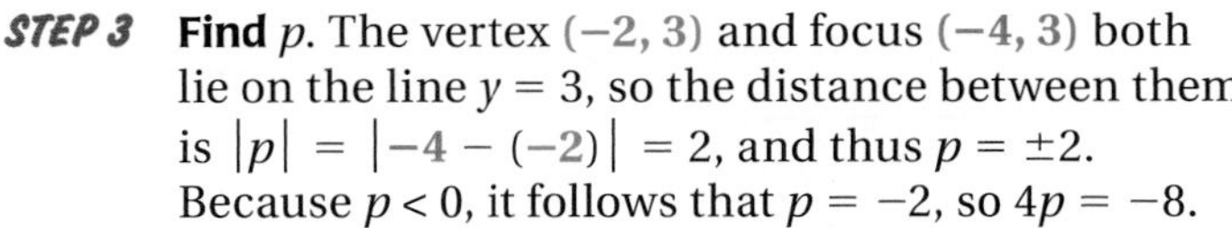

STEP 3 **Find** p. The vertex $(-2, 3)$ and focus $(-4, 3)$ both lie on the line $y = 3$, so the distance between them is $|p| = |-4 - (-2)| = 2$, and thus $p = \pm 2$. Because $p < 0$, it follows that $p = -2$, so $4p = -8$.

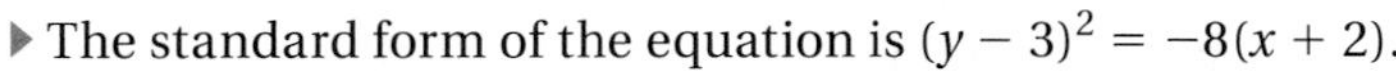

▶ The standard form of the equation is $(y-3)^2 = -8(x+2)$.

EXAMPLE 4 Write an equation of a translated ellipse

Write an equation of the ellipse with foci at (1, 2) and (7, 2) and co-vertices at (4, 0) and (4, 4).

Solution

STEP 1 **Determine** the form of the equation. First sketch the ellipse. The foci lie on the major axis, so the axis is horizontal. The equation has this form:

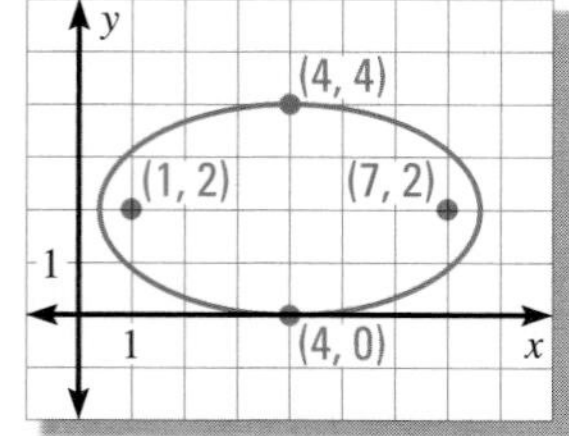

$$\frac{(x-h)^2}{a^2} + \frac{(y-k)^2}{b^2} = 1$$

STEP 2 **Identify** h and k by finding the center, which is halfway between the foci (or the co-vertices).

$$(h, k) = \left(\frac{1+7}{2}, \frac{2+2}{2}\right) = (4, 2)$$

FIND DISTANCE
The co-vertices lie on a vertical line through the center and the foci lie on a horizontal line through the center, so you do not have to use the distance formula.

STEP 3 **Find** b, the distance between a co-vertex and the center (4, 2), and c, the distance between a focus and the center. Choose the co-vertex (4, 4) and the focus (1, 2): $b = |4 - 2| = 2$ and $c = |1 - 4| = 3$.

STEP 4 **Find** a. For an ellipse, $a^2 = b^2 + c^2 = 2^2 + 3^2 = 13$, so $a = \sqrt{13}$.

▶ The standard form of the equation is $\frac{(x-4)^2}{13} + \frac{(y-2)^2}{4} = 1$.

EXAMPLE 5 Identify symmetries of conic sections

Identify the line(s) of symmetry for each conic section in Examples 1–4.

Solution

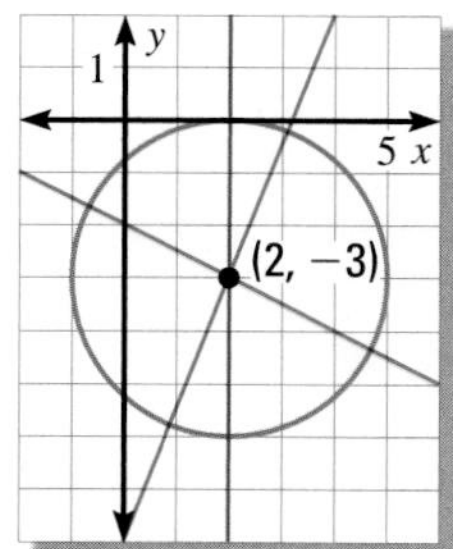

For the circle in Example 1, any line through the center (2, −3) is a line of symmetry.

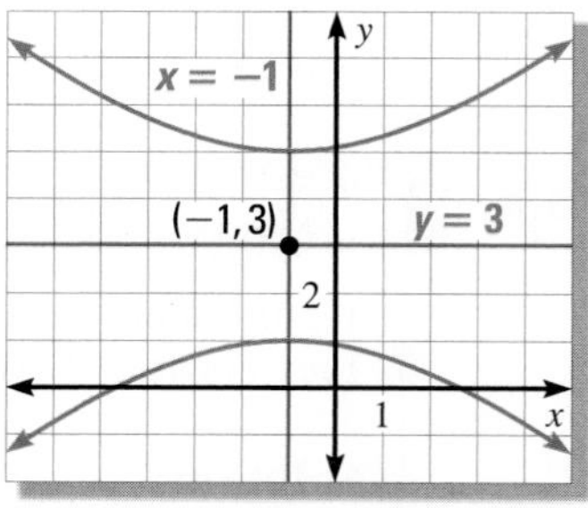

For the hyperbola in Example 2, $x = -1$ and $y = 3$ are lines of symmetry.

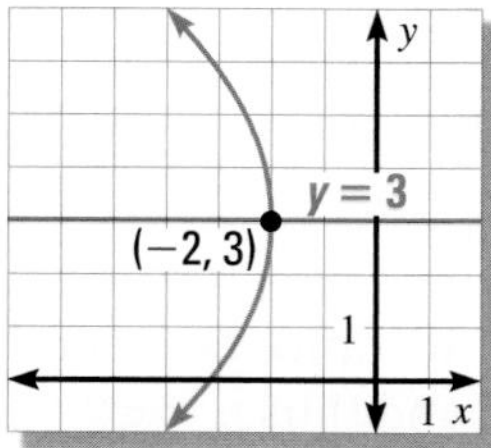

For the parabola in Example 3, $y = 3$ is a line of symmetry.

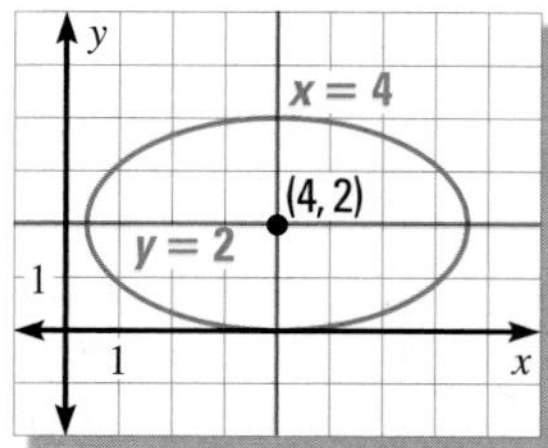

For the ellipse in Example 4, $x = 4$ and $y = 2$ are lines of symmetry.

GUIDED PRACTICE for Examples 3, 4, and 5

Write an equation of the conic section.

5. Parabola with vertex at (3, −1) and focus at (3, 2)
6. Hyperbola with vertices at (−7, 3) and (−1, 3) and foci at (−9, 3) and (1, 3)

Identify the line(s) of symmetry for the conic section.

7. $\frac{(x-5)^2}{64} + \frac{y^2}{16} = 1$
8. $(x+5)^2 = 8(y-2)$
9. $\frac{(x-1)^2}{49} - \frac{(y-2)^2}{121} = 1$

KEY CONCEPT — For Your Notebook

Classifying Conics Using Their Equations

Any conic can be described by a **general second-degree equation** in x and y: $Ax^2 + Bxy + Cy^2 + Dx + Ey + F = 0$. The expression $B^2 - 4AC$ is the **discriminant** of the equation and can be used to identify the type of conic.

Discriminant	Type of Conic
$B^2 - 4AC < 0$, $B = 0$, and $A = C$	Circle
$B^2 - 4AC < 0$ and either $B \neq 0$ or $A \neq C$	Ellipse
$B^2 - 4AC = 0$	Parabola
$B^2 - 4AC > 0$	Hyperbola

If $B = 0$, each axis of the conic is horizontal or vertical.

EXAMPLE 6 Classify a conic

Classify the conic given by $4x^2 + y^2 - 8x - 8 = 0$. Then graph the equation.

Solution

Note that $A = 4$, $B = 0$, and $C = 1$, so the value of the discriminant is:

$$B^2 - 4AC = 0^2 - 4(4)(1) = -16$$

Because $B^2 - 4AC < 0$ and $A \neq C$, the conic is an ellipse.

COMPLETE THE SQUARE
For help with completing the square, see p. 284.

To graph the ellipse, first complete the square in x.

$$4x^2 + y^2 - 8x - 8 = 0$$
$$(4x^2 - 8x) + y^2 = 8$$
$$4(x^2 - 2x) + y^2 = 8$$
$$4(x^2 - 2x + ?) + y^2 = 8 + 4(?)$$
$$4(x^2 - 2x + 1) + y^2 = 8 + 4(1)$$
$$4(x-1)^2 + y^2 = 12$$
$$\frac{(x-1)^2}{3} + \frac{y^2}{12} = 1$$

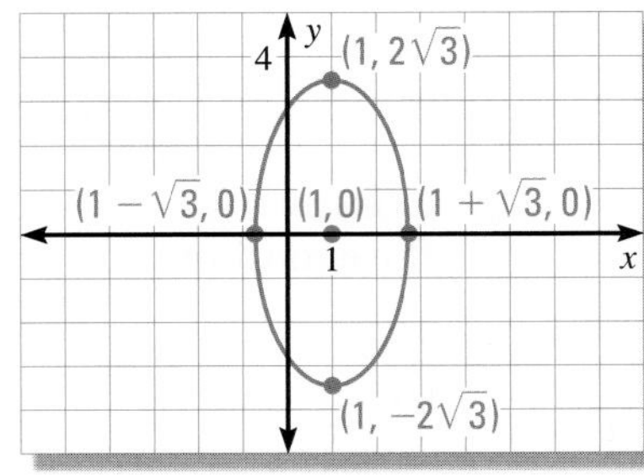

From the equation, you can see that $(h, k) = (1, 0)$, $a = \sqrt{12} = 2\sqrt{3}$, and $b = \sqrt{3}$. Use these facts to draw the ellipse.

EXAMPLE 7 Solve a multi-step problem

PHYSICAL SCIENCE In a lab experiment, you record images of a steel ball rolling past a magnet. The equation $16x^2 - 9y^2 - 96x + 36y - 36 = 0$ models the ball's path.

- What is the shape of the path?
- Write an equation for the path in standard form.
- Graph the equation of the path.

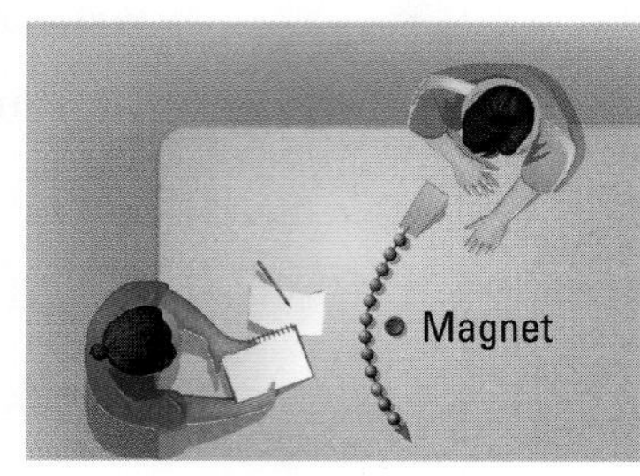

Solution

STEP 1 **Identify** the shape. The equation is a general second-degree equation with $A = 16$, $B = 0$, and $C = -9$. Find the value of the discriminant.

$$B^2 - 4AC = 0^2 - 4(16)(-9) = 576$$

Because $B^2 - 4AC > 0$, the shape of the path is a hyperbola.

STEP 2 **Write** an equation. To write an equation of the hyperbola, complete the square in both x and y simultaneously.

AVOID ERRORS
To complete the square in two variables, you must add a quantity to or subtract a quantity from each side for *each* variable.

$$16x^2 - 9y^2 - 96x + 36y - 36 = 0$$

$$(16x^2 - 96x) - (9y^2 - 36y) = 36$$

$$16(x^2 - 6x + ?) - 9(y^2 - 4y + ?) = 36 + 16(?) - 9(?)$$

$$16(x^2 - 6x + 9) - 9(y^2 - 4y + 4) = 36 + 16(9) - 9(4)$$

$$16(x - 3)^2 - 9(y - 2)^2 = 144$$

$$\frac{(x-3)^2}{9} - \frac{(y-2)^2}{16} = 1$$

STEP 3 **Graph** the equation. From the equation, the transverse axis is horizontal, $(h, k) = (3, 2)$, $a = \sqrt{9} = 3$, and $b = \sqrt{16} = 4$. The vertices are at $(3 \pm a, 2)$, or $(6, 2)$ and $(0, 2)$.

Plot the center and vertices. Then draw a rectangle $2a = 6$ units wide and $2b = 8$ units high centered at $(3, 2)$, draw the asymptotes, and draw the hyperbola.

Notice that the path of the ball is modeled by just the right-hand branch of the hyperbola.

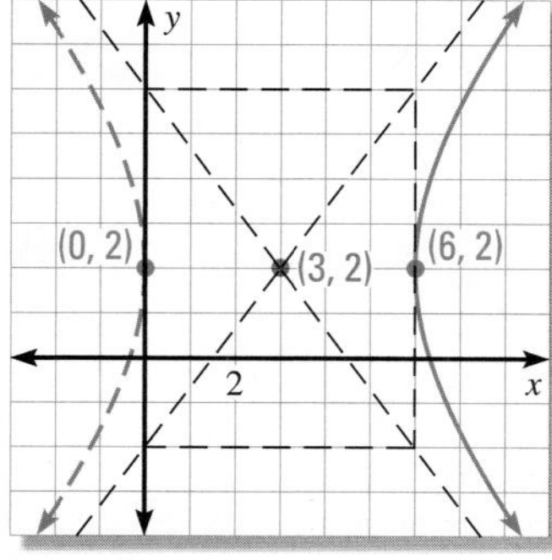

✓ GUIDED PRACTICE for Examples 6 and 7

Classify the conic section and write its equation in standard form. Then graph the equation.

10. $x^2 + y^2 - 2x + 4y + 1 = 0$

11. $2x^2 + y^2 - 4x - 4 = 0$

12. $y^2 - 4y - 2x + 6 = 0$

13. $4x^2 - y^2 - 16x - 4y - 4 = 0$

14. **ASTRONOMY** An asteroid's path is modeled by $4x^2 + 6.25y^2 - 12x - 16 = 0$ where x and y are in astronomical units from the sun. Classify the path and write its equation in standard form. Then graph the equation.

9.6 EXERCISES

HOMEWORK KEY
○ = **WORKED-OUT SOLUTIONS** on p. WS17 for Exs. 3, 19, and 49
★ = **STANDARDIZED TEST PRACTICE** Exs. 2, 12, 36, 45, 51, and 52

SKILL PRACTICE

1. **VOCABULARY** *Explain* why circles, ellipses, parabolas, and hyperbolas are called conic sections.

2. ★ **WRITING** *Explain* how the discriminant of a general second-degree equation can be used to identify what conic the equation represents.

EXAMPLES 1 and 2 on pp. 650–651 for Exs. 3–12

GRAPHING Graph the equation. Identify the important characteristics of the graph.

3. $(x+4)^2 = -8(y-2)$
4. $(x-2)^2 + (y-7)^2 = 9$
5. $\frac{(x-6)^2}{25} - (y+1)^2 = 1$
6. $\frac{(y+4)^2}{49} - \frac{(x+8)^2}{9} = 1$
7. $\frac{(x+2)^2}{16} + \frac{(y-2)^2}{36} = 1$
8. $(x-5)^2 + (y+1)^2 = 64$
9. $(y-1)^2 = 4(x+6)$
10. $\frac{x^2}{25} + \frac{(y-2)^2}{4} = 1$
11. $\frac{(x+3)^2}{9} - \frac{(y-4)^2}{16} = 1$

12. ★ **MULTIPLE CHOICE** What are the coordinates of the co-vertices of the ellipse with equation $\frac{(x-4)^2}{16} + \frac{(y-1)^2}{4} = 1$?

   (A) (0, 1), (8, 1) (B) (−8, 1), (0, 1) (C) (4, 3), (4, −1) (D) (−4, 3), (−4, −1)

EXAMPLES 3 and 4 on pp. 651–652 for Exs. 13–21

WRITING EQUATIONS Write an equation of the conic section.

13. Circle with center at (−5, 1) and radius 6
14. Circle with center at (9, −1) and radius 2
15. Parabola with vertex at (−4, −3) and focus at (1, −3)
16. Parabola with vertex at (5, 3) and directrix $y = 6$
17. Ellipse with vertices at (−3, 4) and (5, 4) and foci at (−1, 4) and (3, 4)
18. Ellipse with vertices at (−2, 1) and (−2, 9) and co-vertices at (−4, 5) and (0, 5)
19. Hyperbola with vertices at (6, −3) and (6, 1) and foci at (6, −6) and (6, 4)
20. Hyperbola with vertices at (1, 7) and (7, 7) and foci at (−1, 7) and (9, 7)

21. **ERROR ANALYSIS** *Describe* and correct the error in writing an equation of the ellipse with vertices at (−7, 3) and (3, 3) and co-vertices at (−2, 6) and (−2, 0).

   Axis is horizontal; (h, k) = (−2, 3);
   $a = |-7-(-2)| = 5$; $b = |6-3| = 3$;
   Equation: $\frac{(x-2)^2}{25} + \frac{(y+3)^2}{9} = 1$ ✗

EXAMPLE 5 on p. 652 for Exs. 22–27

LINES OF SYMMETRY Identify the line(s) of symmetry for the conic section.

22. $\frac{(x+5)^2}{49} + \frac{(y-2)^2}{16} = 1$
23. $(y-4)^2 = 6(x+6)$
24. $\frac{(x-1)^2}{36} - \frac{(y-2)^2}{9} = 1$
25. $(y-5)^2 - \frac{(x-3)^2}{9} = 1$
26. $(x+3)^2 = 10(y-1)$
27. $(x+2)^2 + (y+1)^2 = 121$

EXAMPLE 6
on p. 653
for Exs. 28–36

CLASSIFYING CONICS **Use the discriminant to classify the conic section.**

28. $6x^2 - 2y^2 + 24x + 2y - 1 = 0$

29. $x^2 + y^2 - 10x - 6y + 18 = 0$

30. $y^2 - 10y - 5x + 57 = 0$

31. $4x^2 + y^2 - 48x - 14y + 189 = 0$

32. $9x^2 + 4y^2 + 8y + 18x - 41 = 0$

33. $x^2 - 18x + 6y + 99 = 0$

34. $x^2 + y^2 - 6x + 8y - 24 = 0$

35. $8x^2 - 9y^2 - 40x + 4y + 145 = 0$

36. ★ **MULTIPLE CHOICE** The equation $4x^2 + y^2 + 32x - 10y + 85 = 0$ represents what conic section?

Ⓐ Circle Ⓑ Ellipse Ⓒ Hyperbola Ⓓ Parabola

EXAMPLES 6 and 7
on pp. 653–654
for Exs. 37–44

CLASSIFYING AND GRAPHING **Classify the conic section and write its equation in standard form. Then graph the equation.**

37. $x^2 + y^2 - 14x + 4y - 11 = 0$

38. $x^2 + 4y^2 - 10x + 16y + 37 = 0$

39. $x^2 - 16x - 8y + 80 = 0$

40. $9y^2 - x^2 - 54y + 8x + 56 = 0$

41. $9x^2 + 4y^2 - 36x - 24y + 36 = 0$

42. $y^2 + 14y + 16x + 33 = 0$

43. $x^2 + y^2 + 16x - 8y + 16 = 0$

44. $x^2 - 4y^2 + 8x - 24y - 24 = 0$

45. ★ **SHORT RESPONSE** Consider a general second-degree equation where $B = 0$. *Explain* how you can classify the equation's graph without graphing or using the discriminant.

46. **REASONING** In Chapter 8, you graphed hyperbolas with equations of the form $y = \frac{a}{x}$. Write $y = \frac{a}{x}$ as a general second-degree equation, and use the discriminant to show that the graph is a hyperbola.

47. **CHALLENGE** Find expressions in terms of c, h, and k for the coordinates of the foci of a hyperbola with a vertical transverse axis and center (h, k). Then find equations of the asymptotes in terms of a, b, h, and k.

PROBLEM SOLVING

EXAMPLES 3 and 4
on pp. 651–652
for Ex. 48

48. **ICE SKATING** A figure skater practices skating figure eights, which are formed by etching two externally tangent circles in the ice. Write equations for the circles in a figure eight if each is 8 feet in diameter, the circles intersect at the origin, and the centers of the circles are on the y-axis.

@HomeTutor for problem solving help at classzone.com

EXAMPLES 6 and 7
on pp. 653–654
for Exs. 49–50

49. **JUMPING STILTS** The leap of a person wearing "jumping stilts" is modeled by $x^2 - 10x + 4y = 0$ where x and y are in feet and the origin marks the start of the leap. Write an equation in standard form for the path of the leap. How high and how far does the person jump?

@HomeTutor for problem solving help at classzone.com

50. **SPACECRAFT** A spacecraft uses Saturn's gravitational force to "slingshot" around the planet on the path $21y^2 - 210y - 4x^2 = -441$, where the origin represents Saturn's center and x and y are in hundreds of thousands of kilometers. What is the shape of the path? Write an equation in standard form for the path. Then graph the equation.

○ = WORKED-OUT SOLUTIONS on p. WS1

★ = STANDARDIZED TEST PRACTICE

51. ★ **EXTENDED RESPONSE** You are in a park surfing the Internet on a wireless connection. A hotel's wireless transmitter is located 100 yards east and 60 yards south of you. It has a range of 150 yards. A café's transmitter is located 80 yards west and 70 yards south of you. It has a range of 100 yards.

   a. With your location as the origin, write inequalities for circular regions around the hotel and café in which you can get wireless Internet access.

   b. Graph the inequalities. Are you in only one region or in both? *Explain.*

   c. *Explain* how to determine whether the regions overlap without graphing.

52. ★ **SHORT RESPONSE** Tell what conic section is formed in the situation described. *Explain* your reasoning.

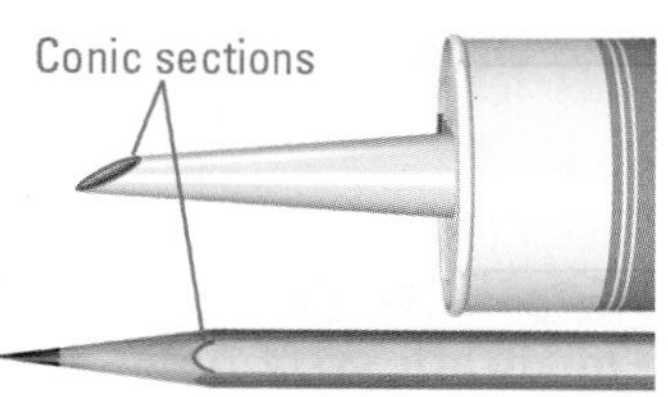

   a. To use a new tube of caulk for the first time, you cut the cone-shaped tip diagonally as shown.

   b. When you sharpen a pencil with flat sides, each side intersects the cone-shaped tip as shown.

53. **CHALLENGE** A *degenerate* conic results when the intersection of a plane with a double-napped cone is not a parabola, circle, ellipse, or hyperbola.

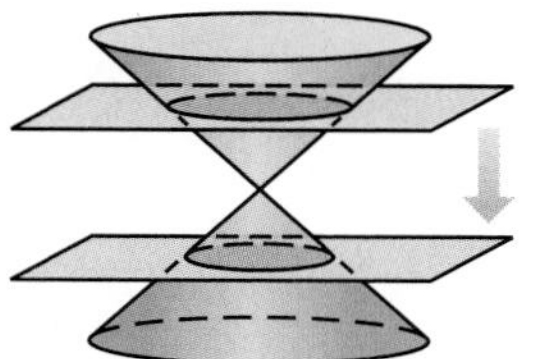

Diagram 1

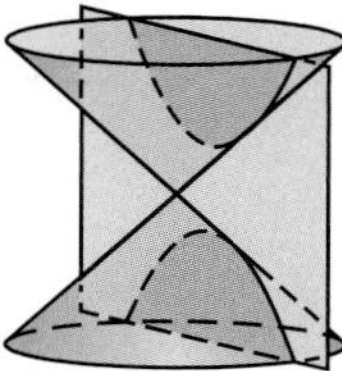

Diagram 2

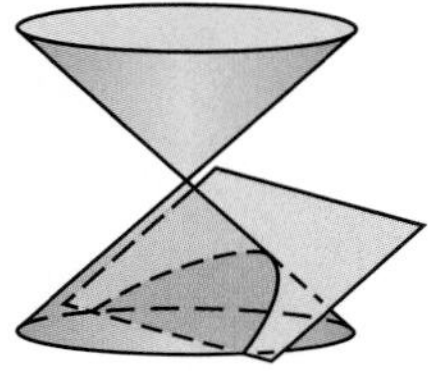

Diagram 3

   a. In Diagram 1, a plane perpendicular to the cone's axis passes through the cone, intersecting it in a circle whose radius decreases and then increases. When is the intersection not a circle? What is it?

   b. In Diagram 2, a plane parallel to the cone's axis passes through the cone, intersecting it in a hyperbola whose vertices get closer together and then farther apart. When is the intersection not a hyperbola? What is it?

   c. In Diagram 3, a plane parallel to the cone's nappe passes through the cone, intersecting it in a parabola that first gets narrower, then flips and gets wider. When is the intersection not a parabola? What is it?

NEW YORK MIXED REVIEW

TEST PRACTICE at classzone.com

54. In 2003, the population of Texas was about 39,000 less than 3 times the population of Virginia. Let x represent the population of Virginia. Which expression represents the population of Texas?

   Ⓐ $39{,}000 - 3x$ Ⓑ $\frac{x - 39{,}000}{3}$

   Ⓒ $\frac{x}{3} - 39{,}000$ Ⓓ $3x - 39{,}000$

55. The measure of each interior angle of a regular polygon is 135°. How many sides does the polygon have?

   Ⓐ 6   Ⓑ 7   Ⓒ 8   Ⓓ 9

9.7 Solve Quadratic Systems

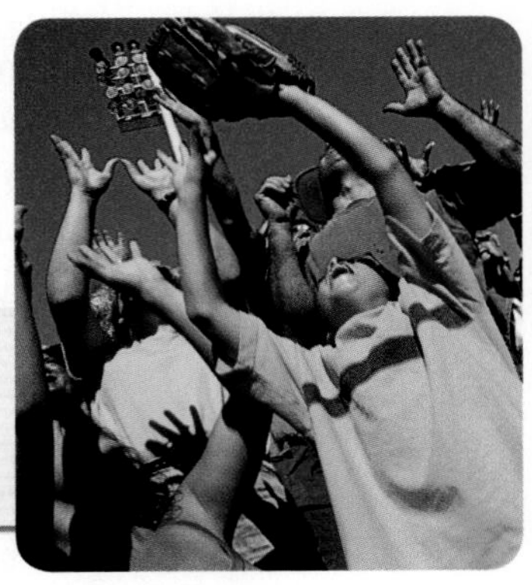

A2.A.3 Solve systems of equations involving one linear equation and one quadratic equation algebraically. . .

Before You solved linear systems.

Now You will solve quadratic systems.

Why? So you can find intersections involving conics, as in Ex. 40.

Key Vocabulary
- **quadratic system**

In Chapter 3, you solved systems of linear equations by graphing, substitution, and elimination. You can use the same techniques to solve systems that include one or more equations of conics. These systems are called **quadratic systems**.

If the graphs of the equations in a system are a line and a conic section, the graphs can intersect in zero, one, or two points, and so the system can have zero, one, or two solutions. Three possible scenarios are shown below.

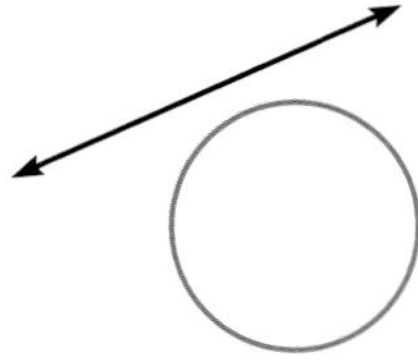

No solution

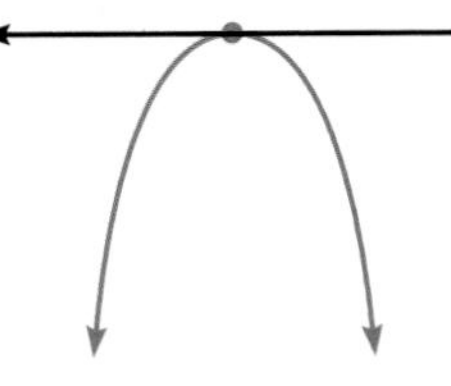

One solution

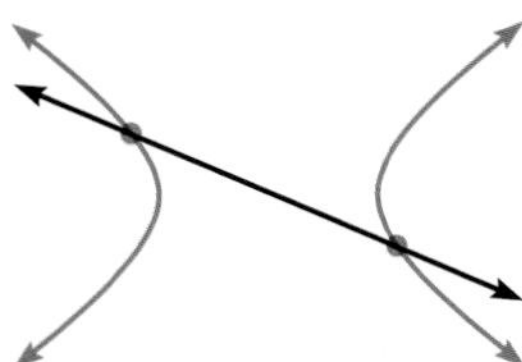

Two solutions

EXAMPLE 1 Solve a linear-quadratic system by graphing

Solve the system using a graphing calculator.

$y^2 - 7x + 3 = 0$ Equation 1

$2x - y = 3$ Equation 2

Solution

STEP 1 **Solve** each equation for y.

$y^2 - 7x + 3 = 0$

$y^2 = 7x - 3$

$y = \pm\sqrt{7x - 3}$ Equation 1

$2x - y = 3$

$-y = -2x + 3$

$y = 2x - 3$ Equation 2

AVOID ERRORS
To graph Equation 1, be sure to enter both $y = \sqrt{7x - 3}$ and $y = -\sqrt{7x - 3}$ into the graphing calculator.

STEP 2 **Graph** the equations $y = \sqrt{7x - 3}$, $y = -\sqrt{7x - 3}$, and $y = 2x - 3$.

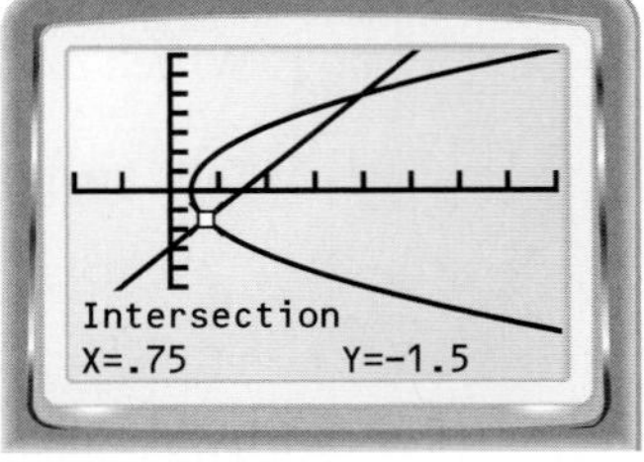

Use the calculator's *intersect* feature to find the coordinates of the intersection points. The graphs of $y = -\sqrt{7x - 3}$ and $y = 2x - 3$ intersect at (0.75, −1.5). The graphs of $y = \sqrt{7x - 3}$ and $y = 2x - 3$ intersect at (4, 5).

▶ The solutions are (0.75, −1.5) and (4, 5). Check the solutions by substituting the coordinates of the points into each of the original equations.

EXAMPLE 2 Solve a linear-quadratic system by substitution

Solve the system using substitution.

$x^2 + y^2 = 10$ Equation 1
$y = -3x + 10$ Equation 2

Solution

Substitute $-3x + 10$ for y in Equation 1 and solve for x.

$x^2 + y^2 = 10$ Equation 1

$x^2 + (-3x + 10)^2 = 10$ Substitute for *y*.

$x^2 + 9x^2 - 60x + 100 = 10$ Expand the power.

$10x^2 - 60x + 90 = 0$ Combine like terms.

$x^2 - 6x + 9 = 0$ Divide each side by 10.

$(x - 3)^2 = 0$ Perfect square trinomial

$x = 3$ Zero product property

AVOID ERRORS

You can also substitute $x = 3$ in Equation 1 to find *y*. This yields *two* apparent solutions, (3, 1) and (3, −1). However, (3, −1) is extraneous because it does not satisfy Equation 2.

To find the *y*-coordinate of the solution, substitute $x = 3$ in Equation 2.

$y = -3(3) + 10 = 1$

▸ The solution is (3, 1).

CHECK You can check the solution by graphing the equations in the system. You can see from the graph shown that the line and the circle intersect only at the point (3, 1).

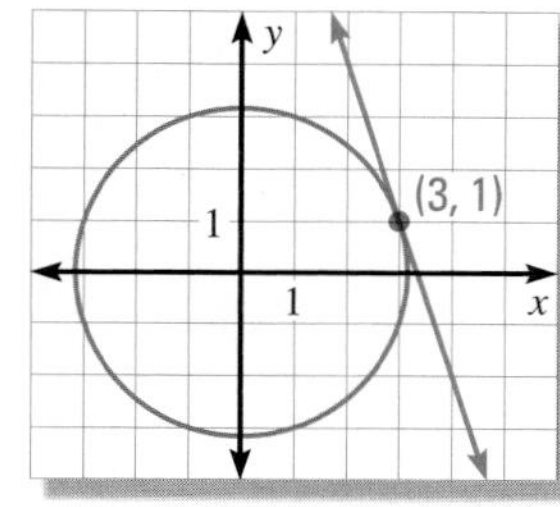

✓ GUIDED PRACTICE for Examples 1 and 2

Solve the system using a graphing calculator.

1. $x^2 + y^2 = 13$
   $y = x - 1$

2. $x^2 + 8y^2 - 4 = 0$
   $y = 2x + 7$

3. $y^2 + 6x - 1 = 0$
   $y = -0.4x + 2.6$

Solve the system using substitution.

4. $y = 0.5x - 3$
   $x^2 + 4y^2 - 4 = 0$

5. $y^2 - 2x - 10 = 0$
   $y = -x - 1$

6. $y = 4x - 8$
   $9x^2 - y^2 - 36 = 0$

QUADRATIC SYSTEMS Two distinct conic sections can have from zero to four points of intersection. Several possible scenarios are shown below.

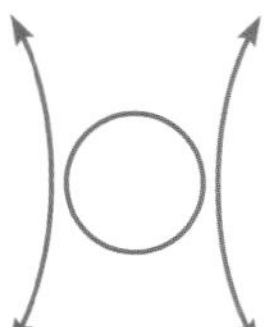
No solution

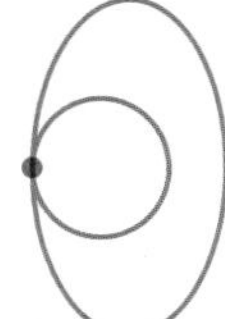
One solution

Two solutions

Three solutions

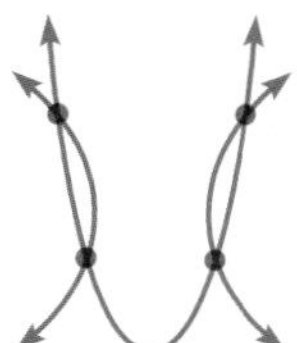
Four solutions

In the examples on the next page, you will use elimination to solve systems of two second-degree equations.

EXAMPLE 3 Solve a quadratic system by elimination

Solve the system by elimination. $9x^2 + y^2 - 90x + 216 = 0$ **Equation 1**
$x^2 - y^2 - 16 = 0$ **Equation 2**

Solution

ANOTHER WAY
You can also solve by substitution: Solve Equation 2 for y^2, then substitute the result in Equation 1.

Add the equations to eliminate the y^2-term and obtain a quadratic equation in x.

$$\begin{array}{r} 9x^2 + y^2 - 90x + 216 = 0 \\ x^2 - y^2 \qquad\quad - 16 = 0 \\ \hline 10x^2 \qquad - 90x + 200 = 0 \end{array} \quad \textbf{Add.}$$

$x^2 - 9x + 20 = 0$ **Divide each side by 10.**

$(x - 4)(x - 5) = 0$ **Factor.**

$x = 4$ or $x = 5$ **Zero product property**

When $x = 4$, $y = 0$. When $x = 5$, $y = \pm 3$.

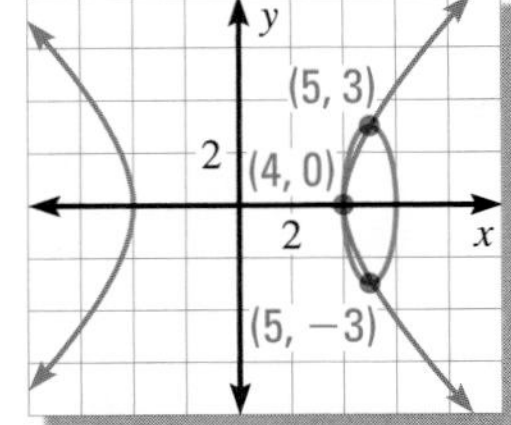

▶ The solutions are (4, 0), (5, 3), and (5, −3), as shown.

EXAMPLE 4 Solve a real-life quadratic system

NAVIGATION A ship uses LORAN (long-distance radio navigation) to find its position. Radio signals from stations A and B locate the ship on the blue hyperbola, and signals from stations B and C locate the ship on the red hyperbola. The equations of the hyperbolas are given below. Find the ship's position if it is east of the y-axis.

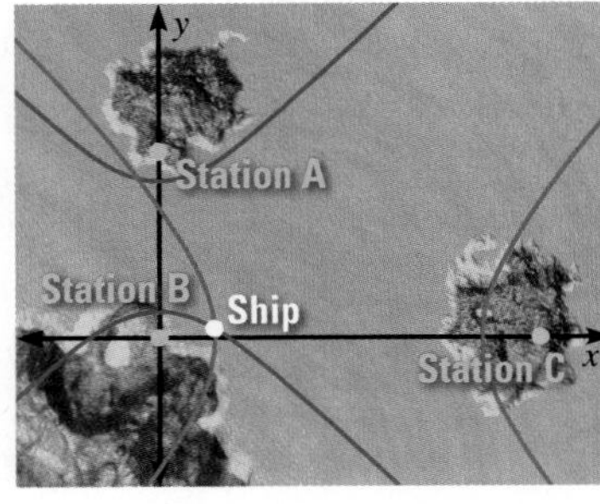

$x^2 - y^2 - 16x + 32 = 0$ **Equation 1**
$-x^2 + y^2 - 8y + 8 = 0$ **Equation 2**

Solution

STEP 1 **Add** the equations to eliminate the x^2- and y^2-terms.

$$\begin{array}{r} x^2 - y^2 - 16x \qquad + 32 = 0 \\ -x^2 + y^2 \qquad - 8y + 8 = 0 \\ \hline -16x - 8y + 40 = 0 \end{array} \quad \textbf{Add.}$$

$y = -2x + 5$ **Solve for y.**

STEP 2 **Substitute** $-2x + 5$ for y in Equation 1 and solve for x.

$x^2 - y^2 - 16x + 32 = 0$ **Equation 1**

$x^2 - (-2x + 5)^2 - 16x + 32 = 0$ **Substitute for y.**

$3x^2 - 4x - 7 = 0$ **Simplify.**

$(x + 1)(3x - 7) = 0$ **Factor.**

$x = -1$ or $x = \frac{7}{3}$ **Zero product property**

STEP 3 **Substitute** for x in $y = -2x + 5$ to find the solutions $(-1, 7)$ and $\left(\frac{7}{3}, \frac{1}{3}\right)$.

▶ Because the ship is east of the y-axis, it is at $\left(\frac{7}{3}, \frac{1}{3}\right)$.

✓ GUIDED PRACTICE for Examples 3 and 4

Solve the system.

7. $-2y^2 + x + 2 = 0$
$x^2 + y^2 - 1 = 0$

8. $x^2 + y^2 - 16x + 39 = 0$
$x^2 - y^2 - 9 = 0$

9. $x^2 + 4y^2 + 4x + 8y = 8$
$y^2 - x + 2y = 5$

10. **WHAT IF?** In Example 4, suppose that a ship's LORAN system locates the ship on the two hyperbolas whose equations are given below. Find the ship's location if it is south of the x-axis.

$x^2 - y^2 - 12x + 18 = 0$ Equation 1
$y^2 - x^2 - 4y + 2 = 0$ Equation 2

9.7 EXERCISES

HOMEWORK KEY
◯ = **WORKED-OUT SOLUTIONS** on p. WS17 for Exs. 5, 15, and 41
★ = **STANDARDIZED TEST PRACTICE** Exs. 2, 21, 34, 42, and 44

SKILL PRACTICE

1. **VOCABULARY** Copy and complete: The equations $x^2 + 5x + 3y^2 = 9$ and $4x^2 - 12y + 16 = 0$ form a(n) __?__ system of equations.

2. ★ **WRITING** *Explain* what method you would use to solve the following system. Do not solve the system.

$3x^2 + y^2 - 5x = 0$ Equation 1
$2x^2 + y^2 - 15 = 0$ Equation 2

EXAMPLE 1 on p. 658 for Exs. 3–8

SOLVING BY GRAPHING **Solve the system using a graphing calculator.**

3. $x^2 + y^2 - 32 = 0$
$y - x = 0$

4. $y + 2x^2 - 9 = 0$
$y + 4x + 1 = 0$

5. $y - 3x + 4 = 0$
$-3x^2 + y^2 - 6 = 0$

6. $y + 2x = 6$
$3x^2 + y^2 = 12$

7. $x^2 + y^2 = 16$
$y - 2x = 1$

8. $3(y + 3)^2 + 4x = 0$
$y - 2x = 11$

EXAMPLE 2 on p. 659 for Exs. 9–21

SOLVING BY SUBSTITUTION **Solve the system using substitution.**

9. $y^2 - x - 6 = 0$
$y + x = 0$

10. $x^2 + y^2 - 25 = 0$
$y = 2x - 10$

11. $-2x + y - 8 = 0$
$x^2 + 4y^2 - 40 = 0$

12. $-x^2 + 2y^2 = 8$
$-x + y = -2$

13. $6x^2 + 3y^2 = 12$
$y = -x + 2$

14. $-3x + y = 6$
$8x + y^2 + 24 = 0$

15. $4x^2 - 5y^2 = -76$
$2x + y = -6$

16. $x^2 + y^2 = 20$
$y = x - 4$

17. $9x^2 + 4y^2 = 36$
$-x + y = -4$

18. $x^2 + 6x + 4y - 3 = 0$
$y + 3x + 1 = 0$

19. $4x^2 + 2y^2 - x - y = 6$
$3x - y = 2$

20. $4x^2 - y^2 - 32x - 2y = -59$
$2x + y - 7 = 0$

21. ★ **MULTIPLE CHOICE** Which ordered pair is a solution of the linear-quadratic system below?

$6x^2 - 5x + 8y^2 + y = 23$
$-x + y = -1$

Ⓐ $(-1, -2)$ Ⓑ $(2, 1)$ Ⓒ $(3, 2)$ Ⓓ $(-2, -3)$

EXAMPLES 3 and 4
on p. 660 for Exs. 22–35

SOLVING QUADRATIC SYSTEMS **Solve the system.**

22. $6x^2 - y^2 - 15 = 0$
$x^2 + y^2 - 13 = 0$

23. $5x^2 + 25y^2 - 125 = 0$
$-x + y^2 - 5 = 0$

24. $10y = x^2$
$x^2 - 6 = -2$

25. $x^2 - y^2 - 4x + 2 = 0$
$-x^2 + y^2 - 4y + 2 = 0$

26. $x^2 - 2y = 6$
$x^2 - y^2 = -27$

27. $x^2 + 2y^2 - 10 = 0$
$4y^2 + x + 4 = 0$

28. $x^2 + y^2 - 16x + 39 = 0$
$x^2 - y^2 - 9 = 0$

29. $x^2 - y^2 - 8x + 8y = 24$
$x^2 + y^2 - 8x - 8y = -24$

30. $16x^2 - y^2 + 16y - 128 = 0$
$y^2 - 48x - 16y - 32 = 0$

31. $4x^2 - 56x + 9y^2 = -160$
$4x^2 + y^2 - 64 = 0$

32. $x^2 - y^2 - 32x + 128 = 0$
$y^2 - x^2 - 8y + 8 = 0$

33. $y^2 + x - 3 = 0$
$x^2 - 4x + 3y + 1 = 0$

34. ★ **MULTIPLE CHOICE** How many solutions does the system consisting of the equations $x^2 + y^2 + 6x = 0$ and $y^2 + x - 6 = 0$ have?

Ⓐ 0 Ⓑ 1 Ⓒ 2 Ⓓ 4

35. **ERROR ANALYSIS** *Describe* and correct the error in using substitution to begin solving the system below. Then solve the system.

$x^2 + y^2 - 2x - 2y = -1$ **Equation 1**
$y^2 + x = 1$ **Equation 2**

Solve Equation 2 for x: $x = 1 - y^2$

Substitute for x in Equation 1:

$$(1 - y^2)^2 + y^2 - 2(1 - y^2) - 2y = -1$$
$$1 - 2y^2 + y^2 + y^2 - 2 + 2y^2 - 2y = -1$$
$$2y^2 - 2y = 0$$

36. **REASONING** Solve the system consisting of the equations $\frac{x^2}{2} + \frac{y^2}{4} = 1$ and $4y^2 = 16 - 8x^2$. What do you notice?

37. **GRAPHING CALCULATOR** Consider the system consisting of the equations $3y^2 + x^2 + 4x + 18y = -28$ and $9y^2 - 4x^2 + 8x + 90y = -185$. Solve each equation for y. Then use a graphing calculator to solve the system.

38. **CHALLENGE** Solve the system of three equations shown.

$x^2 + y^2 = 1$ **Equation 1**
$x^2 + y^2 + 4x + 4y - 5 = 0$ **Equation 2**
$x + y - 1 = 0$ **Equation 3**

PROBLEM SOLVING

EXAMPLE 2
on p. 659 for Exs. 39–41

39. **TRAFFIC SAFETY** A car passes a parked police car and continues at a constant speed r. The police car begins accelerating at a constant rate when it is passed. The diagram indicates the distance d (in miles) the police car travels as a function of time t (in minutes) after being passed. Write and solve a system of equations to find how long it takes the police car to catch up to the other car.

@HomeTutor for problem solving help at classzone.com

40. BASEBALL The path of a baseball hit for a home run can be modeled by $y = -\frac{x^2}{484} + x + 3$ where x and y are in feet and home plate is the origin. The ball lands in the stands, which are modeled by $4y - x = -352$ for $x \geq 400$. How far horizontally and vertically from home plate does the ball land?

@HomeTutor for problem solving help at classzone.com

41. MULTI-STEP PROBLEM To be eligible for a parking pass on a college campus, a student must live at least 1 mile from the campus center.

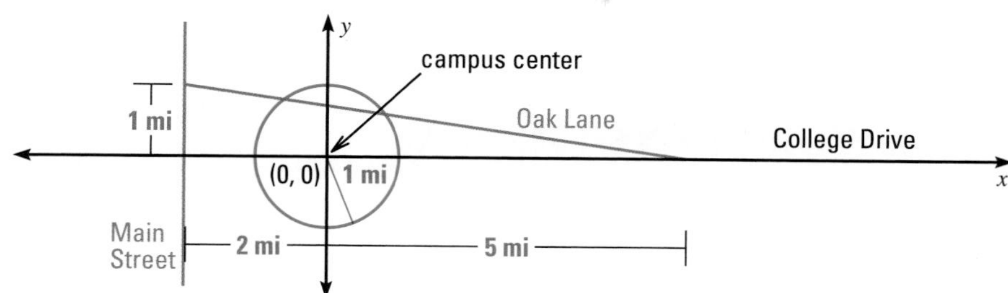

a. Write equations that represent the circle and Oak Lane.

b. Solve the system that consists of the equations from part (a).

c. For what length of Oak Lane are students *not* eligible for a parking pass?

EXAMPLES 3 and 4 on p. 660 for Exs. 42–43

42. ★ SHORT RESPONSE A high school gym has a dome-shaped ceiling modeled by $x^2 + y^2 + 60y - 3456 = 0$ where x and y are in feet. A tennis player in the gym hits a shot modeled by $x^2 + y = 36$ where the origin is located at the base of the net. Solve the system of equations by both elimination and substitution. Do any solutions represent the ball hitting the ceiling? *Explain.*

43. NAVIGATION A ship's LORAN system locates the ship on hyperbolas with the given equations. Find the ship's location for each pair of hyperbolas. In part (b), assume the ship is west of the y-axis.

a. $x^2 - y^2 - 8x + 8 = 0$
$y^2 - x^2 - 8y + 8 = 0$

b. $xy - 24 = 0$
$x^2 - 25y^2 + 100 = 0$

44. ★ EXTENDED RESPONSE A *seismograph* measures the intensity of an earthquake. A seismograph can determine distance to an earthquake's epicenter, but not direction. On January 22, 2003, a powerful earthquake struck Mexico's state of Colima. The diagram shows approximate distances from three seismic stations to the epicenter. The relative positions of the seismic stations are described below.

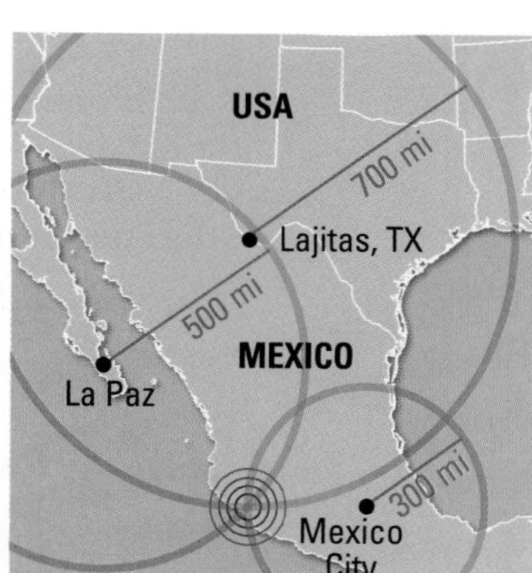

Mexico City: 700 miles south and 300 miles east of Lajitas

La Paz: 400 miles south and 400 miles west of Lajitas

a. **Model** Using Lajitas as the origin, write an equation of each circle. Let each unit represent 100 miles.

b. **Eliminate** Use the equation for the circle centered at Lajitas with each of the other two equations from part (a) to eliminate the x^2- and y^2-terms and find two new equations.

c. **Solve** Solve the system of linear equations that results from part (b) to find the coordinates of the epicenter.

d. **Reasoning** *Explain* why three stations are required to locate the epicenter.

45. **CHALLENGE** What is the width w of the thickest box that will fit in a mailbox with the dimensions shown? (*Hint:* Use the Pythagorean theorem and the fact that $\triangle ABC \sim \triangle CDE$ to write a system of two second-degree equations.)

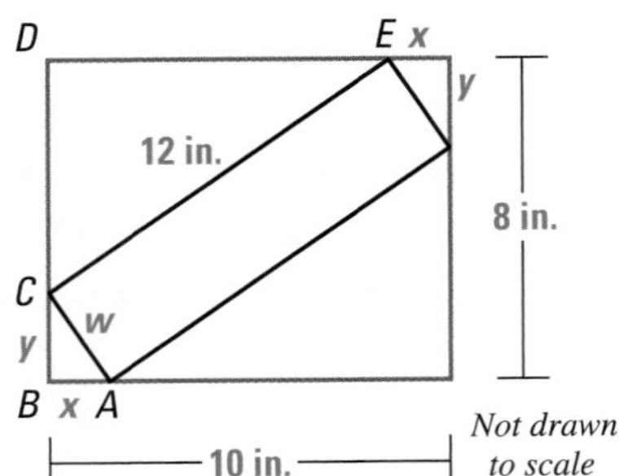

NEW YORK MIXED REVIEW

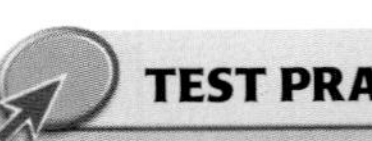

TEST PRACTICE at classzone.com

46. What is an equation of the line that contains the point $(-5, 2)$ and has a slope of $-\frac{4}{3}$?

Ⓐ $-4x + 3y = 26$ Ⓑ $-3x + 4y = 23$

Ⓒ $4x + 3y = 7$ Ⓓ $4x + 3y = -14$

47. Which inequality is the solution of $14 - 5x \le 7x + 5$?

Ⓐ $x \le -\frac{3}{4}$ Ⓑ $x \le \frac{3}{4}$

Ⓒ $x \ge -\frac{3}{4}$ Ⓓ $x \ge \frac{3}{4}$

QUIZ for Lessons 9.6–9.7

Write an equation of the conic section. *(p. 650)*

1. Ellipse with vertices at $(3, -10)$ and $(3, 6)$ and foci at $(3, -7)$ and $(3, 3)$
2. Parabola with vertex at $(-5, 2)$ and focus at $(-5, -1)$
3. Hyperbola with foci at $(-3, 1)$ and $(6, 1)$ and vertices at $(0, 1)$ and $(3, 1)$

Classify the conic section and write its equation in standard form. Then graph the equation. *(p. 650)*

4. $9x^2 - 4y^2 - 36x - 32y - 64 = 0$
5. $-x^2 - y^2 - 4x + 12y + 129 = 0$
6. $x^2 + 6x - y + 16 = 0$
7. $12x^2 + 45y^2 + 120x + 90y - 150 = 0$

Solve the system. *(p. 658)*

8. $x + 2y^2 = -6$
   $x + 8y = 0$
9. $x^2 + 4x + y^2 + 6y = 12$
   $2x - y = 4$
10. $x^2 - y - 4 = 0$
    $x^2 + 3y^2 - 4y - 10 = 0$
11. $y^2 - 6x - 2y - 3 = 0$
    $2y^2 - 4y + x + 6 = 0$
12. $y^2 - 4x^2 - 4y = 0$
    $2x^2 + y^2 - 8x - 4y = -8$
13. $16x^2 + 9y^2 + 32x - 18y = 119$
    $x^2 + y^2 + 2x + 6y = 15$

14. **RADAR** A radar station reports that a ship is 10 miles away. At the same time, a second station 20 miles east and 15 miles north of the first one reports that the ship is 15 miles away. Write and solve a system of equations to locate the ship relative to the first station. Is only one location possible? *Explain.* *(p. 658)*

EXTRA PRACTICE for Lesson 9.7, p. 1018

ONLINE QUIZ at classzone.com

Determine Eccentricity of Conic Sections

GOAL Find and apply the eccentricity of a conic section.

Key Vocabulary
- eccentricity

In an ellipse that is nearly circular, the ratio $c:a$ is close to 0. In a more oval ellipse, $c:a$ is close to 1. This ratio is the **eccentricity** of the ellipse. Every conic has an eccentricity e associated with it.

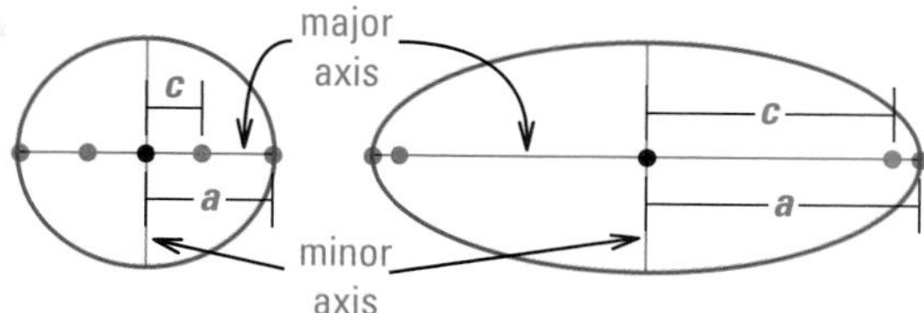

KEY CONCEPT — For Your Notebook

Eccentricity of Conic Sections

The eccentricity of each conic section is defined below. For an ellipse or hyperbola, c is the distance from each focus to the center, and a is the distance from each vertex to the center.

Circle: $e = 0$

Ellipse: $e = \frac{c}{a}$, and $0 < e < 1$

Parabola: $e = 1$

Hyperbola: $e = \frac{c}{a}$, and $e > 1$

EXAMPLE 1 Find eccentricity

Find the eccentricity of the conic section represented by the equation.

a. $(x + 3)^2 + (y - 1)^2 = 25$

b. $\frac{(x + 4)^2}{36} + \frac{(y - 2)^2}{16} = 1$

Solution

a. Because this equation represents a circle, the eccentricity is $e = 0$.

b. This equation represents an ellipse with $a = \sqrt{36} = 6$, $b = \sqrt{16} = 4$, and $c = \sqrt{a^2 - b^2} = 2\sqrt{5}$. The eccentricity is $e = \frac{c}{a} = \frac{2\sqrt{5}}{6} \approx 0.745$.

EXAMPLE 2 Use eccentricity to write an equation

Write an equation of a hyperbola with center (−2, 6), vertex (6, 6), and $e = 2$.

Solution

Use the form $\frac{(x - h)^2}{a^2} - \frac{(y - k)^2}{b^2} = 1$. The vertex lies $6 - (-2) = 8$ units from the center, so $a = 8$. Because $e = \frac{c}{a} = 2$, you know that $\frac{c}{8} = 2$, or $c = 16$.

So, $b^2 = c^2 - a^2 = 256 - 64 = 192$. The equation is $\frac{(x + 2)^2}{64} - \frac{(y - 6)^2}{192} = 1$.

EXAMPLE 3 Use eccentricity to write a model

ASTRONOMY Pluto orbits the sun in an elliptical path with the center of the sun at one focus. The eccentricity of the orbit is $e = 0.249$ and the length of the major axis is about 79.0 astronomical units. Find an equation of Pluto's orbit. (Assume that the major axis is horizontal.)

Solution

The equation of the orbit has the form $\frac{x^2}{a^2} + \frac{y^2}{b^2} = 1$. Using the length of the major axis, you know that $2a = 79.0$, or $a = 39.5$. You can use the eccentricity and the value of a to find the value of c, and then use the values of a and c to find b.

$$e = \frac{c}{a}, \text{ so } 0.249 = \frac{c}{39.5}, \text{ or } c \approx 9.84$$

$$c^2 = a^2 - b^2, \text{ so } b = \sqrt{a^2 - c^2} = \sqrt{(39.5)^2 - (9.84)^2} \approx 38.3$$

So, an equation for Pluto's orbit is $\frac{x^2}{(39.5)^2} + \frac{y^2}{(38.3)^2} = 1$, or $\frac{x^2}{1560} + \frac{y^2}{1470} = 1$, where x and y are measured in astronomical units.

PRACTICE

EXAMPLE 1 on p. 665 for Exs. 1–6

Find the eccentricity of the conic section.

1. $7(x - 3)^2 + 7(y + 7)^2 = 56$
2. $16(x + 1)^2 - 9(y - 5)^2 = 144$
3. $\frac{(x - 6)^2}{49} + \frac{(y - 5)^2}{64} = 1$
4. $\frac{(y - 4)^2}{100} - \frac{(x + 2)^2}{9} = 1$
5. $(x - 5)^2 = 10y$
6. $81(x + 4)^2 + (y - 9)^2 = 81$

EXAMPLE 2 on p. 665 for Exs. 7–12

Write an equation of the conic section.

7. Ellipse with vertices at $(-6, 4)$ and $(6, 4)$, and $e = 0.4$
8. Ellipse with foci at $(-4, 2)$ and $(-4, -2)$, and $e = 0.5$
9. Ellipse with center at $(0, 5)$, vertex at $(7, 5)$, and $e = 0.2$
10. Hyperbola with foci at $(4, -5)$ and $(4, 3)$, and $e = 2.5$
11. Hyperbola with vertices at $(1, -4)$ and $(7, -4)$, and $e = 1.8$
12. Hyperbola with center at $(-2, 3)$, focus at $(-5, 3)$, and $e = 4$

EXAMPLE 3 on p. 666 for Exs. 13–14

13. **ASTRONOMY** Nereid, a moon of Neptune, has the most eccentric orbit of any moon in the solar system. The eccentricity of the orbit is $e = 0.751$ and the length of the major axis is about 11.0 million kilometers. Find an equation of Nereid's orbit.

14. **SATELLITES** A communications satellite is in an elliptical orbit around Earth, whose center is one focus of the orbit. The eccentricity of the orbit is $e = 0.394$, and the satellite is 14,300 kilometers from Earth's center at the closest point in its orbit. What is the satellite's distance from Earth's center at the farthest point in its orbit?

15. **REASONING** *Explain* why the definition of eccentricity for ellipses and hyperbolas implies that $0 < e < 1$ for an ellipse and $e > 1$ for a hyperbola.

TEST PRACTICE
classzone.com

Lessons 9.5–9.7

1. **WHISPER DISHES** A person at the focus of one of two facing parabolic dishes can hear a soft sound made at the focus of the other dish. The California Science Center in Los Angeles has two such "whisper dishes" whose vertices are about 47 feet apart. Each dish's focus is about 1.5 feet from its vertex. What are equations for the cross sections of the dishes if one dish's vertex is at the origin and the other dish's vertex is on the positive x-axis?

   (1) $y^2 = 1.5x; y^2 = 1.5(x - 47)$

   (2) $y^2 = 6x; y^2 = 6(x - 47)$

   (3) $y^2 = 1.5x; y^2 = -1.5(x - 47)$

   (4) $y^2 = 6x; y^2 = -6(x - 47)$

2. **MODELING AREA** The shaded region shown below is formed by two squares centered at the origin. The area of the shaded region is 28 square units. Which equation describes the possible values of x and y?

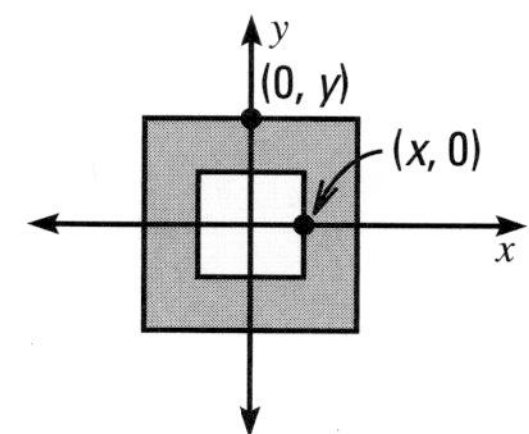

   (1) $\frac{x^2}{7} - \frac{y^2}{7} = 1$ (3) $\frac{x^2}{28} - \frac{y^2}{80} = 1$

   (2) $\frac{y^2}{7} - \frac{x^2}{7} = 1$ (4) $\frac{y^2}{28} - \frac{x^2}{28} = 1$

3. **HYPERBOLIC MIRROR** A hyperbolic mirror reflects light rays directed toward one focus to the other focus. A certain hyperbolic mirror can be represented by the right branch of the hyperbola with this equation:

$$\frac{x^2}{64} - \frac{y^2}{80} = 1$$

   If light from point (0, 9) is directed at the focus at (12, 0), at approximately what point on the mirror will the light be reflected to the focus at (−12, 0)?

   (1) (4.8, 5.4) (3) (7.5, 3.4)

   (2) (5.1, 5.2) (4) (8.4, 2.7)

4. **CASSEGRAIN TELESCOPE** The diagram shows the mirrors in a Cassegrain telescope. The equations of the mirrors are given below. Which type of conic section does the surface of mirror B represent?

   Mirror A: $y^2 - 72x - 450 = 0$

   Mirror B: $88.4x^2 - 49.7y^2 - 4390 = 0$

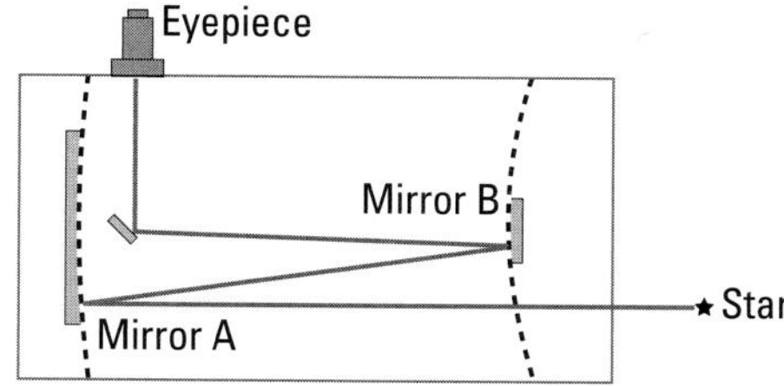

   (1) Circle (3) Ellipse

   (2) Parabola (4) Hyperbola

5. **OPEN-ENDED** Graph the equations $9x^2 + y^2 + 8y = 20$ and $x^2 + 4y^2 = 16$ on the same coordinate axes. Find all points of intersection.

6. **OPEN-ENDED** When a jet breaks the sound barrier, sound waves form a "Mach cone" behind the jet, and a sonic boom is heard as the cone passes. The Mach cone for a jet in level flight meets the ground in a hyperbola with the jet directly above the center. Suppose a jet makes a sonic boom heard along $\frac{x^2}{36} - \frac{y^2}{100} = 1$ where x and y are in miles.

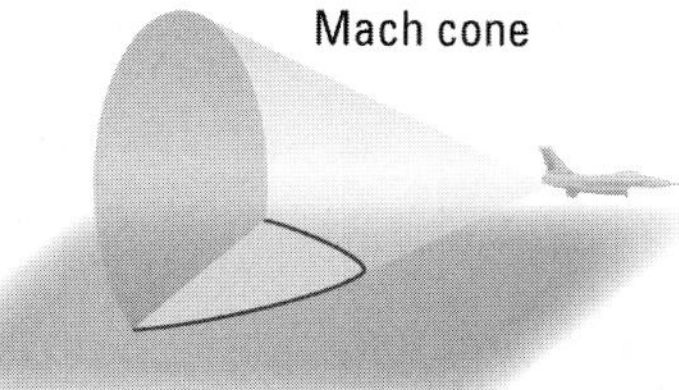

   What is the shortest possible horizontal distance you could be from the jet when you first hear the sonic boom? *Explain.*

   The jet passes a second time, creating a sonic boom heard along $\frac{x^2}{9} - \frac{y^2}{25} = 1$. Answer the question above for this sonic boom.

   Describe the relationship between the two hyperbolas.

9 CHAPTER SUMMARY

BIG IDEAS

For Your Notebook

Big Idea 1

Writing Equations of Conic Sections

Conic	Equation	Key facts		
Circle	$x^2 + y^2 = r^2$	radius r		
Parabola	$x^2 = 4py$	*Axis of symmetry* vertical	*Focus* $(0, p)$	*Directrix* $y = -p$
	$y^2 = 4px$	*Axis of symmetry* horizontal	*Focus* $(p, 0)$	*Directrix* $x = -p$
Ellipse	$\frac{x^2}{a^2} + \frac{y^2}{b^2} = 1$	*Major axis* horizontal	*Vertices* $(\pm a, 0)$	*Co-vertices* $(0, \pm b)$
	$\frac{x^2}{b^2} + \frac{y^2}{a^2} = 1$	*Major axis* vertical	*Vertices* $(0, \pm a)$	*Co-vertices* $(\pm b, 0)$
Hyperbola	$\frac{x^2}{a^2} - \frac{y^2}{b^2} = 1$	*Transverse axis* horizontal	*Asymptotes* $y = \pm\frac{b}{a}x$	*Vertices* $(\pm a, 0)$
	$\frac{y^2}{a^2} - \frac{x^2}{b^2} = 1$	*Transverse axis* vertical	*Asymptotes* $y = \pm\frac{a}{b}x$	*Vertices* $(0, \pm a)$

Big Idea 2

Graphing Equations of Conic Sections

Circle

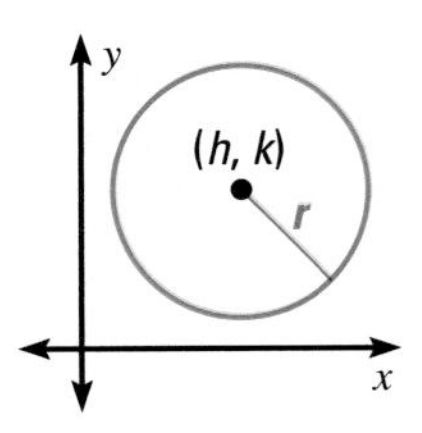

$(x - h)^2 + (y - k)^2 = r^2$

Parabola

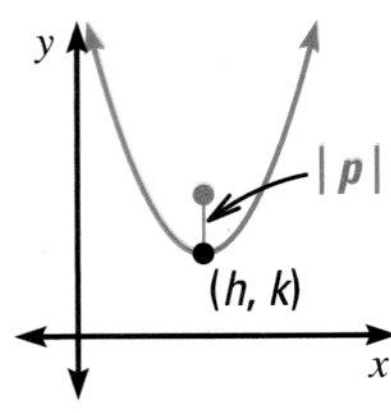

$(x - h)^2 = 4p(y - k)$

Ellipse

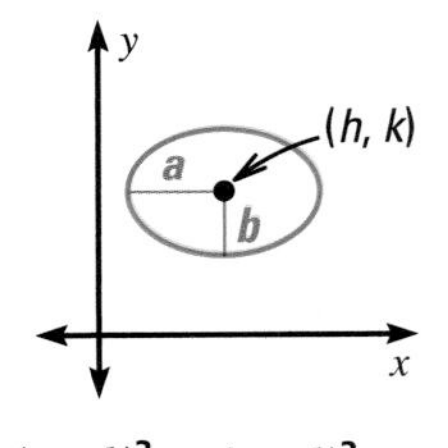

$\frac{(x - h)^2}{a^2} + \frac{(y - k)^2}{b^2} = 1$

Hyperbola

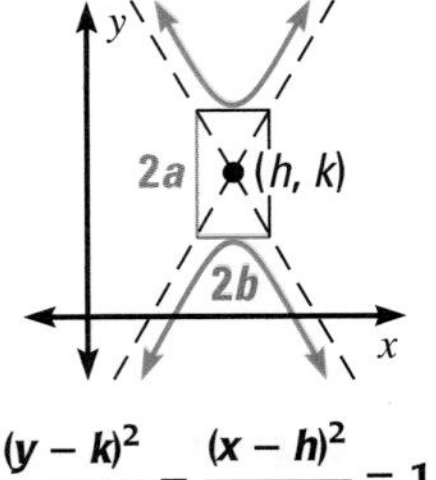

$\frac{(y - k)^2}{a^2} - \frac{(x - h)^2}{b^2} = 1$

Big Idea 3

Solving Quadratic Systems

Method	Description	When to use
Graphing	Graph the equations. Identify any points of intersection.	When graphing is easy or when using a graphing calculator
Substitution	Solve one equation for one of the variables and substitute it into the other equation.	When you can easily solve for one variable (or its square) in terms of the other variable
Elimination	Multiply one or both equations by a constant as needed, and add.	When you can eliminate one or more of the variable terms

9 CHAPTER REVIEW

@HomeTutor
classzone.com
- Multi-Language Glossary
- Vocabulary practice

REVIEW KEY VOCABULARY

- distance formula, *p. 614*
- midpoint formula, *p. 615*
- focus, foci, *pp. 620, 634, 642*
- directrix, *p. 620*
- circle, *p. 626*
- center, *pp. 626, 634, 642*
- radius, *p. 626*
- ellipse, *p. 634*
- vertices, *pp. 634, 642*
- major axis, *p. 634*
- co-vertices, *p. 634*
- minor axis, *p. 634*
- hyperbola, *p. 642*
- transverse axis, *p. 642*
- conic sections, *p. 650*
- general second-degree equation, *p. 653*
- discriminant, *p. 653*
- quadratic system, *p. 658*

VOCABULARY EXERCISES

1. Copy and complete: A(n) _?_ is the set of all points in a plane equidistant from a point called the focus and a line called the directrix.

2. Copy and complete: The line segment joining the two co-vertices of an ellipse is the _?_.

3. Copy and complete: The line segment joining the two vertices of a hyperbola is the _?_.

4. **WRITING** *Describe* how the asymptotes of a hyperbola help you draw the hyperbola.

REVIEW EXAMPLES AND EXERCISES

Use the review examples and exercises below to check your understanding of the concepts you have learned in each lesson of Chapter 9.

9.1 Apply the Distance and Midpoint Formulas

pp. 614–619

EXAMPLE

Find the distance between (−5, 3) and (1, −3). Then find the midpoint of the line segment joining the two points.

$$d = \sqrt{(x_2 - x_1)^2 + (y_2 - y_1)^2} = \sqrt{(1 - (-5))^2 + (-3 - 3)^2} = \sqrt{72} = 6\sqrt{2} \approx 8.49$$

$$M\left(\frac{x_1 + x_2}{2}, \frac{y_1 + y_2}{2}\right) = \left(\frac{-5 + 1}{2}, \frac{3 + (-3)}{2}\right) = (-2, 0)$$

EXERCISES

EXAMPLES 1 and 3 on pp. 614–615 for Exs. 5–8

Find the distance between the two points. Then find the midpoint of the line segment joining the two points.

5. (−6, −5), (2, −3)

6. (−2, 5), (1, 9)

7. (−3, −4), (2, 5)

8. **SKYDIVING** A skydiver lands 200 yards west and 40 yards north of a target. A second skydiver lands 30 yards east and 140 yards south of the same target. How far from each other do the two skydivers land?

9 CHAPTER REVIEW

9.2 Graph and Write Equations of Parabolas

pp. 620–625

EXAMPLE

Graph $x = \frac{1}{12}y^2$. Identify the focus, directrix, and axis of symmetry.

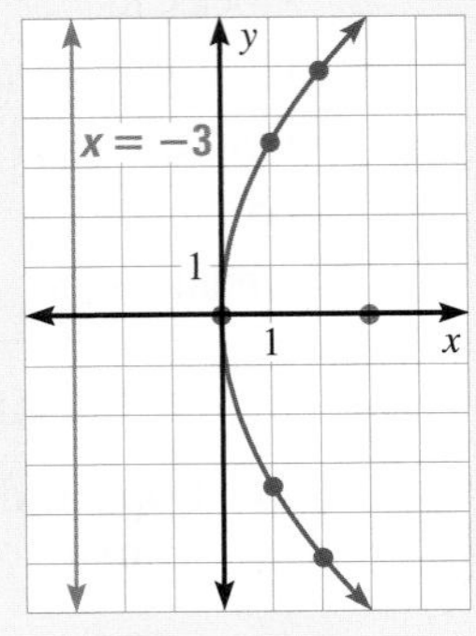

STEP 1 **Rewrite** $x = \frac{1}{12}y^2$ in standard form as $y^2 = 12x$.

STEP 2 **Identify** the focus, directrix, and axis of symmetry. The equation has the form $y^2 = 4px$ with $4p = 12$, so $p = 3$. The focus is $(p, 0)$, or $(3, 0)$, and the directrix is $x = -p$, or $x = -3$. Because y is squared, the axis of symmetry is the x-axis.

STEP 3 **Draw** the parabola. Because $p > 0$, the parabola opens to the right. Some points on the parabola are $(0, 0)$, $(1, \pm 3.46)$, and $(2, \pm 4.90)$.

EXERCISES

EXAMPLES 1 and 2 on p. 621 for Exs. 9–14

Graph the equation. Identify the focus, directrix, and axis of symmetry of the parabola.

9. $x^2 = 16y$ **10.** $y^2 = -6x$ **11.** $x^2 + 4y = 0$

Write the standard form of the equation of the parabola with the given focus or directrix and vertex at (0, 0).

12. Focus: $(-5, 0)$ **13.** Focus: $(0, 3)$ **14.** Directrix: $x = -6$

9.3 Graph and Write Equations of Circles

pp. 626–632

EXAMPLE

Graph $x^2 = 64 - y^2$. Identify the radius of the circle.

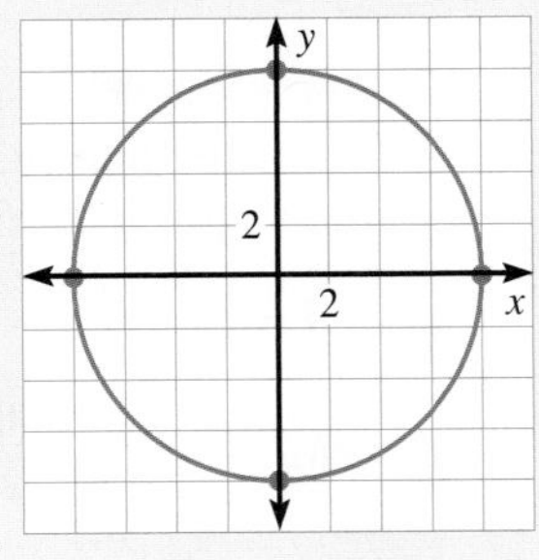

STEP 1 **Rewrite** $x^2 = 64 - y^2$ in standard form as $x^2 + y^2 = 64$.

STEP 2 **Identify** the radius. The graph is a circle with center at the origin and radius $r = \sqrt{64} = 8$.

STEP 3 **Draw** a circle passing through points that are 8 units from the origin, such as $(8, 0)$, $(0, 8)$, $(-8, 0)$, and $(0, -8)$.

EXERCISES

EXAMPLES 1 and 2 on pp. 626–627 for Exs. 15–20

Graph the equation. Identify the radius of the circle.

15. $x^2 + y^2 = 81$ **16.** $x^2 = 40 - y^2$ **17.** $3x^2 + 3y^2 = 147$

Write the standard form of the equation of the circle that passes through the given point and whose center is the origin.

18. $(5, 9)$ **19.** $(-8, 2)$ **20.** $(-7, -4)$

@HomeTutor
classzone.com
Chapter Review Practice

9.4 Graph and Write Equations of Ellipses *pp. 634–639*

EXAMPLE

Graph $4x^2 + y^2 = 16$. Identify the vertices, co-vertices, and foci.

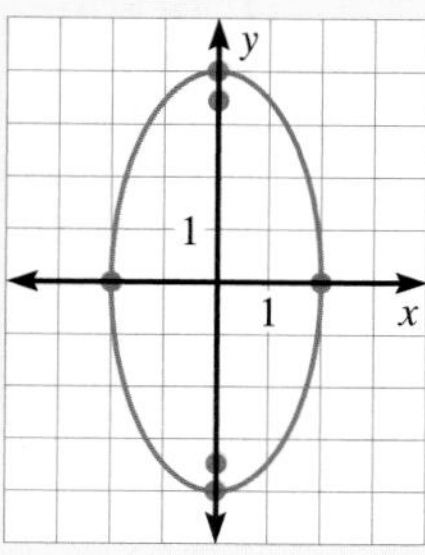

STEP 1 **Rewrite** $4x^2 + y^2 = 16$ in standard form as $\frac{x^2}{4} + \frac{y^2}{16} = 1$.

STEP 2 **Identify** the vertices, co-vertices, and foci. Note that $a^2 = 16$ and $b^2 = 4$, so $a = 4$, $b = 2$, and $c^2 = a^2 - b^2 = 12$, or $c \approx 3.5$. The major axis is vertical. The vertices are at $(0, \pm 4)$. The co-vertices are at $(\pm 2, 0)$. The foci are at $(0, \pm 3.5)$.

STEP 3 **Draw** the ellipse.

EXERCISES

EXAMPLES 1, 2, and 4 on pp. 635–636 for Exs. 21–25

Graph the equation. Identify the vertices, co-vertices, and foci of the ellipse.

21. $16x^2 + 25y^2 = 400$ **22.** $81x^2 + 9y^2 = 729$ **23.** $64x^2 + 36y^2 = 2304$

Write an equation of the ellipse with the given characteristics and center at (0, 0).

24. Vertex: $(-6, 0)$; co-vertex: $(0, -3)$ **25.** Vertex: $(0, -8)$; focus: $(0, 5)$

9.5 Graph and Write Equations of Hyperbolas *pp. 642–648*

EXAMPLE

Graph $4x^2 - 9y^2 = 36$. Identify the vertices, foci, and asymptotes.

STEP 1 **Rewrite** $4x^2 - 9y^2 = 36$ in standard form as $\frac{x^2}{9} - \frac{y^2}{4} = 1$.

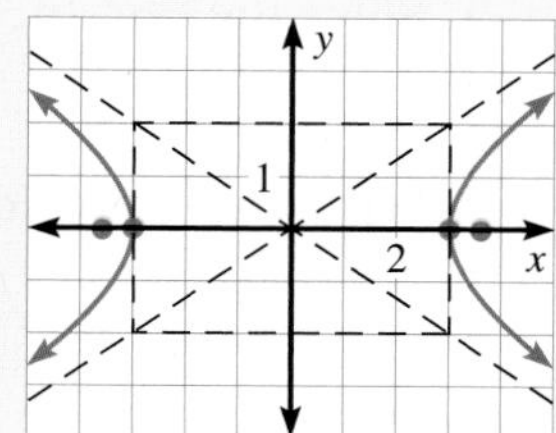

STEP 2 **Identify** the vertices, foci, and asymptotes. Note that $a^2 = 9$ and $b^2 = 4$, so $a = 3$, $b = 2$, and $c^2 = a^2 + b^2 = 13$, or $c \approx 3.6$. The transverse axis is horizontal. The vertices are at $(\pm 3, 0)$. The foci are at $(\pm 3.6, 0)$. The asymptotes are $y = \pm\frac{b}{a}x = \pm\frac{2}{3}x$.

STEP 3 **Draw** asymptotes through opposite corners of a rectangle centered at (0, 0) that is $2a = 6$ units wide and $2b = 4$ units high. Draw the hyperbola.

EXERCISES

EXAMPLES 1 and 2 on p. 643 for Exs. 26–30

Graph the equation. Identify the vertices, foci, and asymptotes.

26. $9x^2 - y^2 = 9$ **27.** $4x^2 - 16y^2 = 64$ **28.** $100y^2 - 36x^2 = 3600$

Write an equation of the hyperbola with the given foci and vertices.

29. Foci: $(0, \pm 5)$; vertices: $(0, \pm 2)$ **30.** Foci: $(\pm 9, 0)$; vertices: $(\pm 4, 0)$

9 CHAPTER REVIEW

9.6 Translate and Classify Conic Sections

pp. 650–657

EXAMPLE

Classify the conic section $-4x^2 + y^2 + 32x - 12y - 32 = 0$ and write its equation in standard form. Then graph the equation.

Because $A = -4$, $B = 0$, and $C = 1$, the discriminant is $B^2 - 4AC = 16 > 0$, so the conic is a hyperbola. Complete the square to write the equation in standard form.

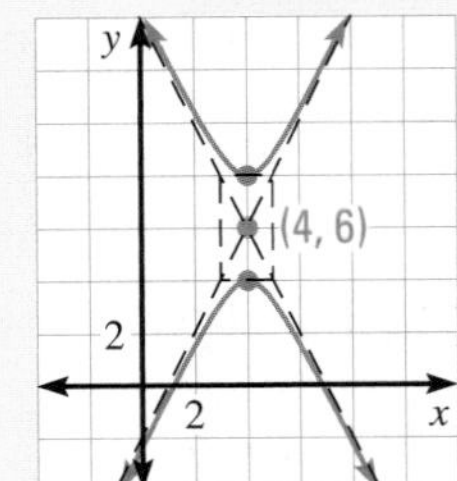

$$-4x^2 + y^2 + 32x - 12y - 32 = 0$$

$$(y^2 - 12y) - 4(x^2 - 8x) = 32$$

$$(y^2 - 12y + 36) - 4(x^2 - 8x + 16) = 32 + 36 - 4(16)$$

$$(y - 6)^2 - 4(x - 4)^2 = 4$$

$$\frac{(y - 6)^2}{4} - (x - 4)^2 = 1$$

From the equation, $(h, k) = (4, 6)$, $a = \sqrt{4} = 2$, and $b = 1$. The vertices are $(4, 6 + 2) = (4, 8)$ and $(4, 6 - 2) = (4, 4)$. The graph is shown above.

EXERCISES

EXAMPLE 6 on p. 653 for Exs. 31–34

Classify the conic section and write its equation in standard form. Then graph the equation.

31. $4x^2 + 9y^2 + 40x + 72y + 208 = 0$

32. $y^2 - 10y - 8x + 1 = 0$

33. $9x^2 - y^2 - 18x - 4y - 5 = 0$

34. $x^2 + y^2 + 4x - 14y + 17 = 0$

9.7 Solve Quadratic Systems

pp. 658–664

EXAMPLE

Solve the system. $\quad 12x^2 - 81y^2 + 16 = 0$

$\quad 2x^2 + 9y = 0$

Write the second equation as $y = -\frac{2}{9}x^2$. Then substitute in the first equation.

$12x^2 - 81\left(-\frac{2}{9}x^2\right)^2 + 16 = 0$ **Substitute for *y* in first equation.**

$12x^2 - 4x^4 + 16 = 0$ **Simplify.**

$x^4 - 3x^2 - 4 = 0$ **Divide each side by −4.**

$(x^2 - 4)(x^2 + 1) = 0$ **Factor.**

By the zero product property, $x = \pm 2$. The solutions are $\left(2, -\frac{8}{9}\right)$ and $\left(-2, -\frac{8}{9}\right)$.

EXERCISES

EXAMPLES 2 and 3 on pp. 659–660 for Exs. 35–37

Solve the system.

35. $y^2 = 4x$
$2x - 5y = -8$

36. $x^2 + y^2 - 100 = 0$
$x + y - 14 = 0$

37. $16x^2 - 4y^2 = 64$
$4x^2 + 9y^2 - 40x = -64$

9 CHAPTER TEST

Find the distance between the two points. Then find the midpoint of the line segment joining the two points.

1. $(-1, 5), (7, 3)$
2. $(4, 2), (8, 8)$
3. $(-1, -6), (1, 5)$
4. $(2, -5), (3, 1)$
5. $(-6, -2), (-3, 5)$
6. $(1, 9), (10, -2)$

Graph the equation.

7. $y^2 - 24x = 0$
8. $x^2 + y^2 = 16$
9. $64y^2 - x^2 = 64$
10. $18x^2 + 2y^2 = 18$
11. $(x - 6)^2 + (y + 1)^2 = 36$
12. $(x + 4)^2 = 6(y - 2)$
13. $\frac{(x + 4)^2}{9} - \frac{(y - 7)^2}{49} = 1$
14. $\frac{(x - 8)^2}{81} + \frac{(y - 2)^2}{100} = 1$
15. $\frac{(y - 5)^2}{9} - (x + 3)^2 = 1$

Write the standard form of the equation of the conic section with the given characteristics.

16. Parabola with vertex at $(0, 0)$ and directrix at $x = -6$
17. Parabola with vertex at $(-2, -1)$ and focus at $(-2, 5)$
18. Circle with center at $(0, 0)$ and passing through $(-5, 2)$
19. Circle with center at $(1, -4)$ and radius 6
20. Ellipse with center at $(0, 0)$, vertex at $(0, 6)$, and co-vertex at $(-3, 0)$
21. Ellipse with vertices at $(-1, 4)$ and $(7, 4)$ and foci at $(1, 4)$ and $(5, 4)$
22. Hyperbola with vertices at $(0, -6)$ and $(0, 6)$ and foci at $(0, -9)$ and $(0, 9)$
23. Hyperbola with vertex at $(2, -5)$, focus at $(-1, -5)$, and center at $(5, -5)$

Classify the conic section and write its equation in standard form.

24. $x^2 + 4y^2 - 6x - 16y + 21 = 0$
25. $x^2 + y^2 + 8x + 12y + 3 = 0$
26. $4x^2 - 9y^2 - 40x + 64 = 0$
27. $y^2 - 16y - 12x + 40 = 0$
28. $25x^2 + 4y^2 + 50x - 24y - 39 = 0$
29. $y^2 - 16x^2 + 14y + 64x - 31 = 0$

Solve the system.

30. $4x^2 + y^2 = 16$
$x + y = 2$

31. $x^2 + 4y^2 - 8y = 4$
$y^2 - 2y - 8x - 16 = 0$

32. $y^2 - x^2 + 2x - 5 = 0$
$x^2 + y^2 - 2x - 3 = 0$

33. **WATER SURFACE** A cylindrical glass of water has a 1.5 inch radius. If the glass is tilted 60°, the water's surface meets the glass in an ellipse with minor axis 3 inches long and major axis 6 inches long. Write equations that model the water's surface with the glass upright and after the glass is tilted. Use the center of the water's surface as the origin.

34. **ASTRONOMY** The Green Bank Telescope in West Virginia has a main reflector whose cross section is a portion of a "parent" parabola. A diagram of the reflector's cross section and the parent parabola is shown. Write an equation that models the parent parabola if its vertex is at (0, 0). What is the distance from the vertex to the focus?

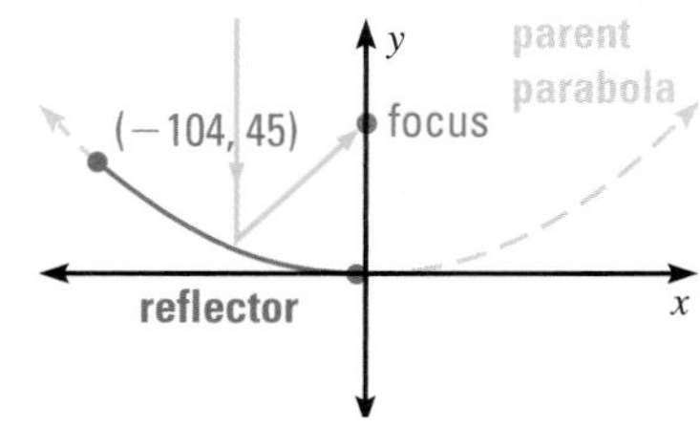

OPEN-ENDED QUESTIONS

Scoring Rubric

Full Credit
- solution is complete and correct

Partial Credit
- solution is complete but has errors, *or*
- solution is without error but incomplete

No Credit
- no solution is given, *or*
- solution makes no sense

PROBLEM

Two vertices of an equilateral triangle are $A(0, 0)$ and $B(6, 0)$.

Write and solve a system of equations to find the coordinates of the third vertex C of $\triangle ABC$.

Is there only one possible position for the third vertex? *Explain.*

Below are sample solutions to the problem. Read each solution and the comments on the left to see why the sample represents full credit, partial credit, or no credit.

SAMPLE 1: Full credit solution

The solution is set up logically and thoroughly.

Because $AB = 6 - 0 = 6$ and $\triangle ABC$ is equilateral, $AC = BC = 6$. Let (x, y) represent the coordinates of vertex C. Use the distance formula.

For AC: $\sqrt{(x-0)^2 + (y-0)^2} = 6$
$$x^2 + y^2 = 36$$

For BC: $\sqrt{(x-6)^2 + (y-0)^2} = 6$
$$(x-6)^2 + y^2 = 36$$
$$x^2 - 12x + 36 + y^2 = 36$$
$$x^2 + y^2 - 12x = 0$$

The correct equations are obtained, and a valid method is used to solve the system.

Solve the system by adding -1 times the second equation to the first.

$$\begin{aligned} x^2 + y^2 \quad\quad &= 36 \\ -x^2 - y^2 + 12x &= 0 \\ \hline 12x &= 36 \end{aligned} \longrightarrow x = 3$$

Substitute **3** for x in the first equation: $\mathbf{3}^2 + y^2 = 36$, so $y^2 = 27$, or $y = \pm 3\sqrt{3}$.

The system is solved correctly. A correct conclusion is drawn.

The solutions of the system are $(3, \pm 3\sqrt{3})$. So, the third vertex is at $C(3, 3\sqrt{3})$ or $C(3, -3\sqrt{3})$. There are two solutions, because C can be above or below $\overline{AB}$.

SAMPLE 2: Partial credit solution

The distance between A and B is 6.

$AC = 6 \longrightarrow x^2 + y^2 = 36$ $\qquad$ $BC = 6 \longrightarrow x^2 + y^2 - 12x = 0$

The system is correct, but steps are omitted in writing and solving it.

Solve the system by substituting **36** for $\mathbf{x^2 + y^2}$ in the second equation.

$$\mathbf{x^2 + y^2} - 12x = 0$$
$$\mathbf{36} - 12x = 0$$
$$x = 3$$

The additional vertex is omitted. An incorrect conclusion is drawn.

Find y when $x = 3$: $x^2 + y^2 = 36$, so $y^2 = 27$, and $y = \pm 3\sqrt{3}$. The coordinates of the third vertex are $C(3, 3\sqrt{3})$. This is the only possible position of the vertex, because the dimensions of a triangle must be positive.

SAMPLE 3: Partial credit solution

A valid approach is used, and the solution is set up logically and thoroughly.

The distance between A and B is 6. So, the other two sides of $\triangle ABC$ have lengths of 6. Draw circles with radii of 6 centered at A and B. The points of intersection of the circles will be the possible positions of the third vertex.

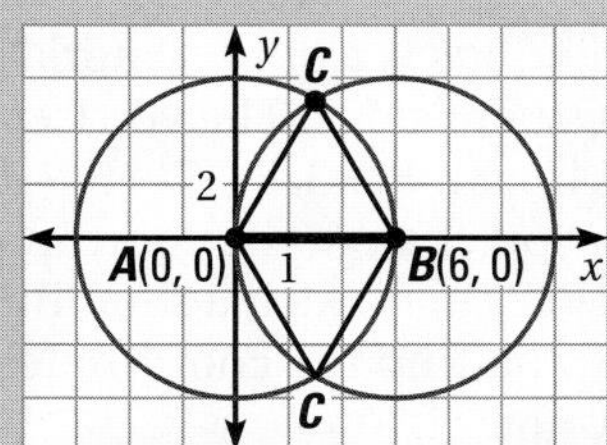

The equations of the circles are correct.

Equation of circle A: $x^2 + y^2 = 36$

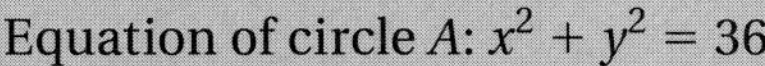

Equation of circle B: $(x - 6)^2 + y^2 = 36$

The answer is correct, but work is not shown.

The solutions of the system are $(3, 3\sqrt{3})$ and $(3, -3\sqrt{3})$, so the possible coordinates of the third vertex are $C(3, 3\sqrt{3})$ or $C(3, -3\sqrt{3})$.

SAMPLE 4: No credit solution

The answer shows a basic misunderstanding.

Because $AB = 6$ and $\overline{AB}$ is horizontal, the vertex at C is 6 units above or below either A or B. The possible coordinates of C are (0, 6), (0, −6), (6, 6), or (6, −6).

PRACTICE Apply the Scoring Rubric

Use the rubric on page 674 to score the solution to the problem below as *full credit, partial credit,* or *no credit*. *Explain* your reasoning.

PROBLEM $\triangle RST$ is isosceles with $RT = ST$ and has vertices at $R(-2, 2)$, $S(4, -1)$, and $T(2, y)$. Find y. Is there only one possible value of y? *Explain.*

1.

$$\sqrt{[2 - (-2)]^2 + (y - 2)^2} = \sqrt{(2 - 4)^2 + [y - (-1)]^2}$$

$$\sqrt{16 + y^2 - 4y + 4} = \sqrt{4 + y^2 + 2y + 1}$$

$$y^2 - 4y + 20 = y^2 + 2y + 5$$

$$15 = 6y, \text{ so } 2.5 = y$$

2. If $\triangle RST$ is isosceles with $RT = ST$, then T lies on the perpendicular bisector of $\overline{RS}$.

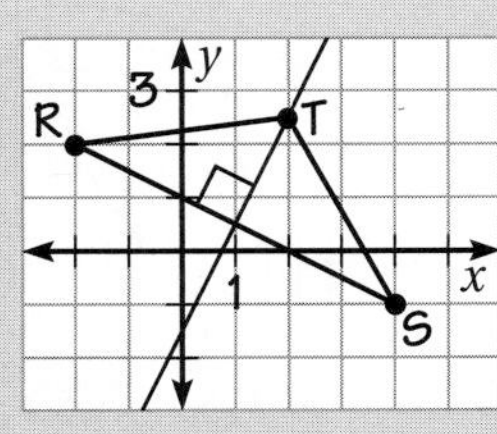

$$\text{Midpoint of } \overline{RS} = \left(\frac{-2 + 4}{2}, \frac{2 + (-1)}{2}\right) = (1, 0.5)$$

$$\text{Slope of } \overline{RS} = \frac{-1 - 2}{4 - (-2)} = \frac{-3}{6} = -0.5$$

The perpendicular bisector of $\overline{RS}$ has a slope of 2, the negative reciprocal of -0.5. Its equation is $y - 0.5 = 2(x - 1)$, or $y = 2x - 1.5$. Substituting 2 for x gives $y = 2.5$. Since $y = 2x - 1.5$ is a function, this is the only value of y for $x = 2$.

New York Test Practice

OPEN-ENDED

1. A rhombus is a quadrilateral with four congruent sides. The vertices of figure $ABCD$ are $A(6, 3)$, $B(-3, 5)$, $C(-5, -4)$, and $D(4, -5)$. Can you change the coordinates of one vertex of $ABCD$ to make it a rhombus? If so, explain how and find the coordinates. If not, explain why not.

2. A lamp for indoor gardening uses a parabolic reflector with the height and width shown to concentrate light on plants. Is the focus of the reflector above or below the reflector's bottom edge? *Explain* your reasoning.

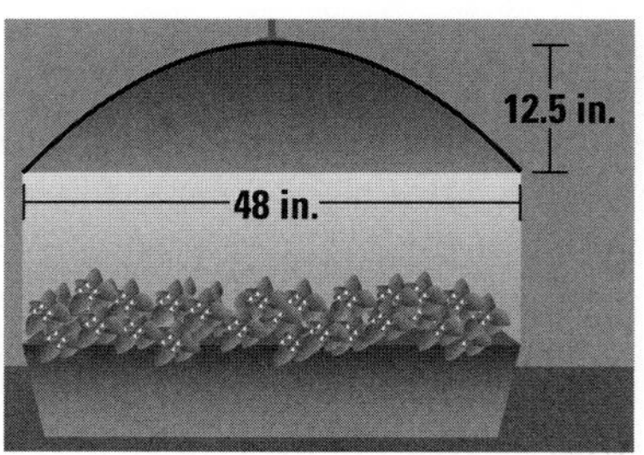

3. Three points on the edge of the circular Copernicus crater on the moon can be represented by the coordinates $(-35, 35)$, $(0, 0)$, and $(40, 80)$ where each unit represents one kilometer. Is the point located at $(55, 25)$ inside the crater or outside the crater? *Explain* your reasoning.

4. For each set of concentric circles shown below, the measures of the radii are the consecutive integers from 1 to 9. *Explain* how you can use this information to demonstrate that the points shown lie on an ellipse whose foci are the centers of the circles. Then write an equation of the ellipse.

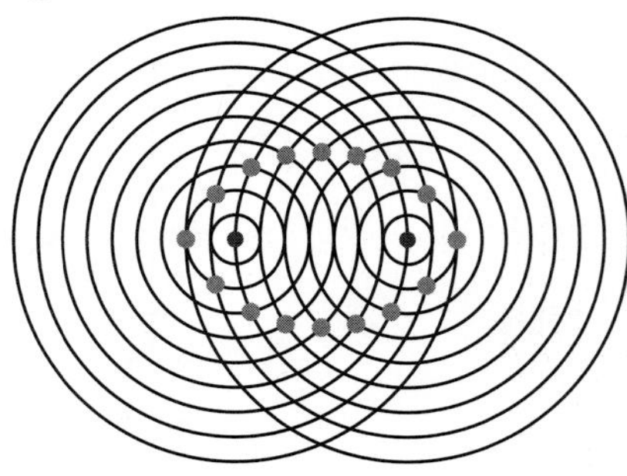

5. A soccer field has a penalty-kick mark 12 yards from the goal. From the mark's center, an arc with a radius of 10 yards is drawn outside the penalty area as shown in the diagram. *Explain* how to use an equation of a circle to find the distance d along the edge of the penalty area between the endpoints of the arc.

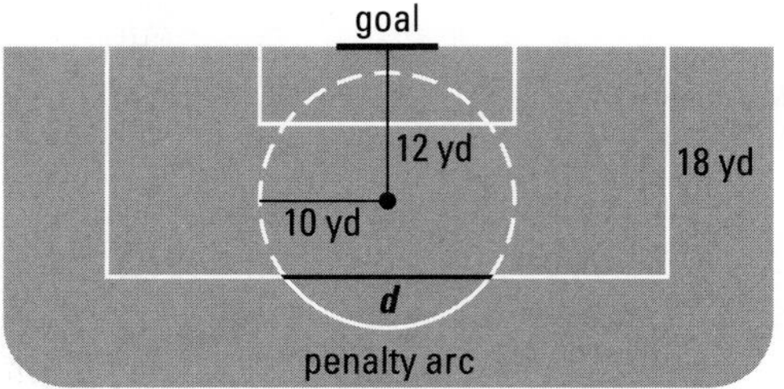

6. Solve the following system of equations algebraically. Find all solutions (x, y).

$$x^2 + 9y^2 = 9$$
$$x - 3y = -3$$

7. The *Tractricious* sculpture at the Fermi National Accelerator Laboratory in Batavia, Illinois, has a hyperbolic cross section as shown below.

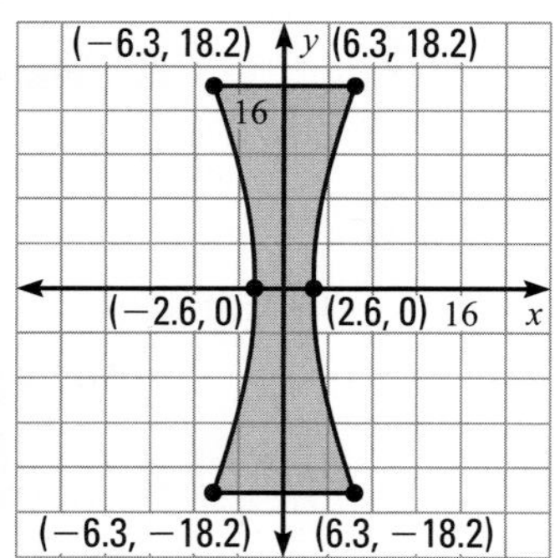

Use the graph to write an equation of the hyperbola that models the cross section of the sculpture. (Each unit represents 1 foot.) Then explain how to modify your equation so the origin is at the bottom left of the sculpture.

8. Without applying area formulas, compare the areas of the ellipses represented by $4x^2 + 6y^2 = 48$ and $\frac{(x-5)^2}{12} + \frac{(y+7)^2}{8} = 1$. *Explain* how you made your comparison.

TEST PREPARATION

OPEN-ENDED

9. A satellite in a *geostationary* orbit appears to stay above a single place on Earth's surface. A satellite originally in a low orbit can be boosted using an elliptical *Hohmann transfer orbit* to a higher geostationary orbit. A satellite originally in a circular orbit 4200 miles from Earth's center is boosted to a circular geostationary orbit 22,240 miles from Earth's center.

geostationary orbit
$R = 22{,}240$ mi
original orbit
$r = 4200$ mi
transfer orbit

Write equations that model the original and geostationary orbits. Use Earth's center as the origin.

Earth's center is at one focus of the transfer orbit. *Explain* how you can find the values of a and c for the transfer orbit.

Write an equation that models the transfer orbit. Use Earth's center as the origin, and choose a horizontal major axis as shown in the diagram.

10. Points one quarter of the way along the sides of a square are connected to form another square. The pattern continues.

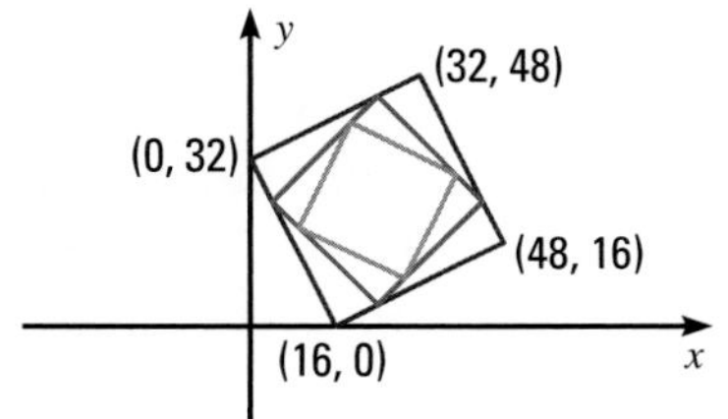

Explain how to use the midpoint formula to find the coordinates of the vertices for each new square in the pattern.

Find the coordinates of the vertices of the two inner squares.

Compare the areas of the squares. What do you notice?

MULTIPLE CHOICE

11. Which equation represents a hyperbola?

(1) $x^2 - 3y + 4x - 15 = 0$

(2) $x^2 + y^2 + 4x - 18y - 15 = 0$

(3) $x^2 - y^2 + 4x - 18y - 15 = 0$

(4) $-2x^2 - y^2 + 4x - 18y - 15 = 0$

12. At what point(s) do the graphs represented by $x^2 + y^2 = 36$ and $-y^2 + x = 6$ intersect?

(1) $(6, 0)$ (3) $\left(-7, -\sqrt{13}\right)$

(2) $(-6, 0)$ (4) $(6, 0)$ and $(-6, 0)$

13. Which statement about the graph of the equation $12(x - 6) = -(y + 4)^2$ is *not* true?

(1) The vertex is at $(6, -4)$.

(2) The axis of symmetry is $y = -4$.

(3) The focus is at $(6, -7)$.

(4) The graph represents a function.

14. The conic section represented by the equation $\frac{(x-2)^2}{81} - \frac{(y-5)^2}{4} = 1$ has the line of symmetry $x = s$. What is the value of s?

(1) 2 (3) 7

(2) 5 (4) 9

15. To the nearest tenth, what is the distance between $(-10, 2)$ and $(7, 7)$?

(1) 5.8 (3) 17.7

(2) 8.0 (4) 22.0

16. What is the radius of the circle represented by the equation $8x^2 + 8y^2 = 720$?

(1) 3.4 (3) 26.8

(2) 9.5 (4) 90.0

9 CUMULATIVE REVIEW Chapters 1–9

Solve the equation. Check your solution(s).

1. $5x + 24 = 11 - 2x$ *(p. 18)*
2. $|4x - 7| = 13$ *(p. 51)*
3. $x^2 - 12x + 35 = 0$ *(p. 252)*
4. $2x^2 - 5x + 5 = 0$ *(p. 292)*
5. $x^3 + 3x^2 - 18x = 40$ *(p. 370)*
6. $\sqrt{x - 2} = x - 4$ *(p. 452)*
7. $4^x - 5 = 3$ *(p. 515)*
8. $\frac{x + 3}{3x + 1} = \frac{x}{x + 2}$ *(p. 589)*
9. $\frac{x - 4}{x - 3} + 2 = \frac{2x - 3}{x - 3}$ *(p. 589)*

Graph the equation.

10. $y = -2x + 7$ *(p. 89)*
11. $y = (x + 1)^2(x - 2)$ *(p. 387)*
12. $y = \sqrt{x + 4} + 3$ *(p. 446)*
13. $y = 4e^x$ *(p. 492)*
14. $y = \ln (x - 2)$ *(p. 499)*
15. $y = \frac{3x - 1}{x^2 - 9}$ *(p. 565)*

Factor the expression.

16. $2x^2 - 20x - 48$ *(p. 259)*
17. $6x^2 + 7x - 20$ *(p. 259)*
18. $x^3 + 8x^2 - 4x - 32$ *(p. 353)*

Find the inverse of the function. *(p. 438)*

19. $f(x) = 6x - 1$
20. $f(x) = x^3 - 5$
21. $f(x) = x^5$

Tell whether the function is an example of *exponential growth* or *exponential decay*. *(pp. 486, 492)*

22. $f(x) = 5(1.4^x)$
23. $f(x) = 3(0.6)^x$
24. $f(x) = 8e^{-2x}$

Condense the expression. *(p. 507)*

25. $3 \ln x - \ln 5$
26. $\log_3 4 + 2 \log_3 7$
27. $5 \log x + \log y - 3 \log z$

The variables *x* and *y* vary inversely. Use the given values to write an equation relating *x* and *y*. *(p. 551)*

28. $x = 18, y = 6$
29. $x = 5, y = -15$
30. $x = 6, y = 9$

Perform the indicated operation and simplify.

31. $\frac{x - 5}{x + 7} \cdot \frac{3x + 21}{x^2 - 25}$ *(p. 573)*
32. $\frac{2x + 8}{x - 3} \div \frac{x + 4}{x^2 - x - 6}$ *(p. 573)*
33. $\frac{x - 3}{x + 5} + \frac{7}{x - 2}$ *(p. 582)*

Find the distance between the two points. Then find the midpoint of the line segment joining the two points. *(p. 614)*

34. $(-8, 5), (-4, -1)$
35. $(3, 5), (8, 7)$
36. $(-2, 7), (1, 14)$

Classify the conic section and write its equation in standard form. Then graph the equation. *(p. 650)*

37. $x^2 + y^2 + 12x - 4y + 15 = 0$
38. $4x^2 - 16y^2 - 56x + 160y - 268 = 0$
39. $y^2 + 6x + 4y + 16 = 0$
40. $2x^2 + 3y^2 + 4x + 12y - 14 = 0$

41. **FENCING** You have 380 feet of fencing to enclose a rectangular garden. You want the length of the garden to be 40 feet greater than the width. Find the length and width of the garden if you use all of the fencing. *(p. 34)*

42. **RECREATION** You have \$30 to spend at a carnival. It costs \$2.50 to take one ride and \$1.50 to play one game. Write and graph an inequality that represents the possible numbers of rides you can take and games you can play. Then list all ordered pairs (rides, games) that use all \$30. *(p. 132)*

43. **BASKETBALL** The price of admission to a high school basketball game is \$5 for adults and \$2 for students. At a game that had a total attendance of 650 people, the total income from ticket sales was \$2500. Write and solve a linear system to find the numbers of adults and students who attended the basketball game. *(p. 160)*

44. **BUSINESS** Two telephone companies compete for customers in a town. Initially, each company has 700 customers. Every month, 5% of company A's customers switch to company B, and 2% of company B's customers switch to company A. The transition matrix T and population matrix M_0 model this situation.

$$T = \begin{bmatrix} 0.95 & 0.02 \\ 0.05 & 0.98 \end{bmatrix} \qquad M_0 = \begin{bmatrix} 700 \\ 700 \end{bmatrix}$$

Find $M_1 = TM_0$, $M_2 = TM_1$, and $M_3 = TM_2$. *Explain* what these matrices represent. *Describe* what happens to the distribution of customers over time if this pattern continues. *(p. 195)*

45. **MAPS** A county map uses a coordinate grid for which one unit represents a quarter of a mile. A lake on the map has an approximately triangular shape with vertices near (2, 2), (12, 19), and (18, 7). Estimate the area of the surface of the lake. *(p. 203)*

46. **TENNIS** While serving, a tennis player strikes the ball at a height of 9 feet above the court. The initial downward velocity of the ball is 16 feet per second. How long does it take the ball to strike the court on the opponent's side? (*Hint:* Use the function $h = -16t^2 + v_0t + h_0$.) *(p. 292)*

47. **DISCOUNTS** A store is having a sale in which you can take \$50 off the cost of any television in the store. The store also offers 15% off your purchase if you open a charge account. Use composition of functions to write a new function that gives the sale price of a television that originally costs t dollars if \$50 is subtracted before the 15% discount is applied. Then find the sale price of a television that originally cost \$480. *(p. 428)*

48. **ACCOUNT BALANCE** You deposit \$4500 in a savings account that pays 2.75% annual interest compounded monthly. Find the account balance after 5 years. *(p. 478)*

49. **STAMPS** The table shows the cumulative number s of different designs of stamps produced in the United States during the period 1904–2004. The variable t represents the number of years since 1904. Find an exponential model for the data. *(p. 529)*

t	0	10	20	30	40	50	60	70	80	90	100
s	313	459	616	751	926	1063	1260	1552	2109	2887	3894

10 Counting Methods and Probability

Before

In previous chapters, you learned the following skills, which you'll use in Chapter 10: simplifying expressions, multiplying binomials, and finding areas.

Prerequisite Skills

VOCABULARY CHECK

Copy and complete the statement.

1. The **coefficient** of x^2 in the expression $3x^3 - 15x^2 + 4$ is _?_.
2. Written as a fraction in lowest terms, the **ratio** of 18 to 45 is _?_.
3. The expressions $x + 3$ and $2x - 1$ are examples of **binomials** because they have _?_ terms.

SKILLS CHECK

Simplify the expression. *(Review p. 2 for 10.1.)*

4. $\frac{6 \cdot 5 \cdot 4 \cdot 3}{2 \cdot 1}$
5. $\frac{13 \cdot 12 \cdot 11}{10 \cdot 9 \cdot 8}$
6. $\frac{8 \cdot 7 \cdot 6 \cdot 5 \cdot 4}{5 \cdot 4 \cdot 3 \cdot 2 \cdot 1}$

Find the product. *(Review p. 346 for 10.2.)*

7. $(x + y)^3$
8. $(5x + 1)^3$
9. $(3x - 2y)^3$

Find the area of the shaded region. Assume all shapes are circles or squares. *(Review pp. 991–992 for 10.3.)*

10. 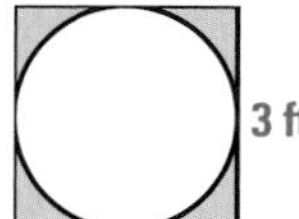

11. 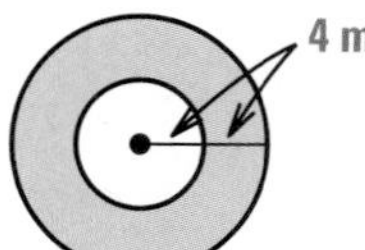

12. 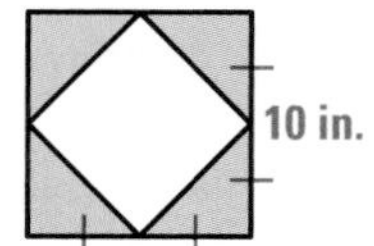

Now

In Chapter 10, you will apply the big ideas listed below and reviewed in the Chapter Summary on page 733. You will also use the key vocabulary listed below.

Big Ideas

1. **Using permutations and combinations**
2. **Finding probabilities**
3. **Constructing binomial distributions**

KEY VOCABULARY

- permutation, *p. 684*
- combination, *p. 690*
- binomial theorem, *p. 693*
- probability, *p. 698*
- compound event, *p. 707*
- overlapping events, *p. 707*
- disjoint events, *p. 707*
- independent events, *p. 717*
- dependent events, *p. 718*
- conditional probability, *p. 718*
- random variable, *p. 724*
- binomial distribution, *p. 725*

Why?

You can use the fundamental counting principle and permutations to calculate the number of choices for a situation. For example, you can count the number of possible outcomes of an event or the number of ways to complete a task.

Animated Algebra

The animation illustrated below for Exercise 69 on page 689 helps you answer this question: How does the number of clothing choices affect the number of different ways can you dress mannequins in a display?

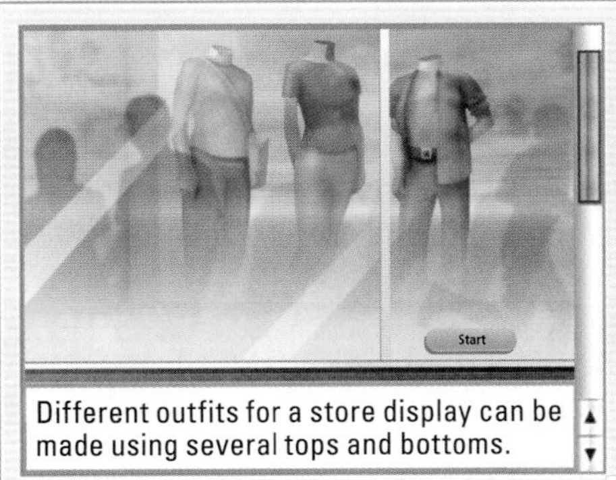

Different outfits for a store display can be made using several tops and bottoms.

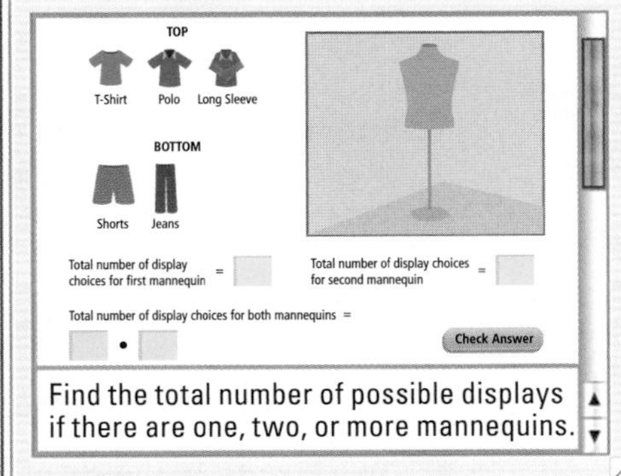

Find the total number of possible displays if there are one, two, or more mannequins.

Animated Algebra at classzone.com

Other animations for Chapter 10: pages 701, 711, 716, 722, and 726

10.1 Apply the Counting Principle and Permutations

A2.S.12 Use permutations, combinations, and the Fundamental Principle of Counting to determine the number of elements in a sample space. . .

Before You counted the number of different ways to perform a task.

Now You will use the fundamental counting principle and permutations.

Why? So you can find numbers of racing outcomes, as in Example 4.

Key Vocabulary
- **permutation**
- **factorial**

In many real-life problems, you want to count the number of ways to perform a task. One way to do this is to use a *tree diagram*.

EXAMPLE 1 Use a tree diagram

SNOWBOARDING A sporting goods store offers 3 types of snowboards (all-mountain, freestyle, and carving) and 2 types of boots (soft and hybrid). How many choices does the store offer for snowboarding equipment?

Solution

Draw a tree diagram and count the number of branches.

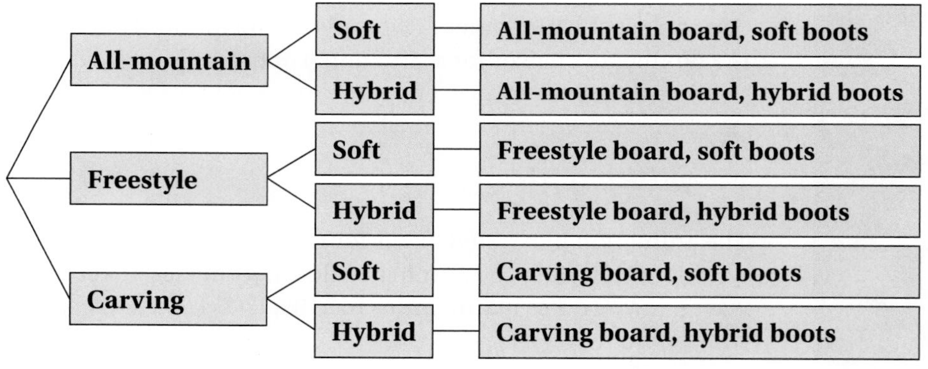

▶ The tree has 6 branches. So, there are 6 possible choices.

FUNDAMENTAL COUNTING PRINCIPLE Another way to count the choices in Example 1 is to use the *fundamental counting principle*. You have 3 choices for the board and 2 choices for the boots, so the total number of choices is $3 \cdot 2 = 6$.

KEY CONCEPT — *For Your Notebook*

Fundamental Counting Principle

Two Events If one event can occur in m ways and another event can occur in n ways, then the number of ways that *both* events can occur is $m \cdot n$.

Three or More Events The fundamental counting principle can be extended to three or more events. For example, if three events can occur in m, n, and p ways, then the number of ways that *all* three events can occur is $m \cdot n \cdot p$.

EXAMPLE 2 Use the fundamental counting principle

PHOTOGRAPHY You are framing a picture. The frames are available in 12 different styles. Each style is available in 55 different colors. You also want blue mat board, which is available in 11 different shades of blue. How many different ways can you frame the picture?

Solution

You can use the fundamental counting principle to find the total number of ways to frame the picture. Multiply the number of frame styles (12), the number of frame colors (55), and the number of mat boards (11).

Number of ways = 12 • 55 • 11 = 7260

▶ The number of different ways you can frame the picture is 7260.

EXAMPLE 3 Use the counting principle with repetition

LICENSE PLATES The standard configuration for a Texas license plate is 1 letter followed by 2 digits followed by 3 letters.

a. How many different license plates are possible if letters and digits can be repeated?

b. How many different license plates are possible if letters and digits cannot be repeated?

AVOID ERRORS
For a given situation, the number of choices without repetition is always less than the number of choices with repetition.

Solution

a. There are 26 choices for each letter and 10 choices for each digit. You can use the fundamental counting principle to find the number of different plates.

Number of plates = 26 • 10 • 10 • 26 • 26 • 26 = 45,697,600

▶ With repetition, the number of different license plates is 45,697,600.

b. If you cannot repeat letters there are still 26 choices for the first letter, but then only 25 remaining choices for the second letter, 24 choices for the third letter, and 23 choices for the fourth letter. Similarly, there are 10 choices for the first digit and 9 choices for the second digit. You can use the fundamental counting principle to find the number of different plates.

Number of plates = 26 • 10 • 9 • 25 • 24 • 23 = 32,292,000

▶ Without repetition, the number of different license plates is 32,292,000.

✓ GUIDED PRACTICE for Examples 1, 2, and 3

1. **SPORTING GOODS** The store in Example 1 also offers 3 different types of bicycles (mountain, racing, and BMX) and 3 different wheel sizes (20 in., 22 in., and 24 in.). How many bicycle choices does the store offer?

2. **WHAT IF?** In Example 3, how do the answers change for the standard configuration of a New York license plate, which is 3 letters followed by 4 numbers?

PERMUTATIONS An ordering of n objects is a **permutation** of the objects. For instance, there are 6 permutations of the letters **A**, **B**, and **C**:

ABC **ACB** **BAC** **BCA** **CAB** **CBA**

You can use the fundamental counting principle to find the number of permutations of **A**, **B**, and **C**. There are 3 choices for the first letter. After the first letter has been chosen, 2 choices remain for the second letter. Finally, after the first two letters have been chosen, there is only 1 choice remaining for the final letter. So, the number of permutations is $3 \cdot 2 \cdot 1 = 6$.

DEFINE FACTORIALS
Zero factorial is defined as $0! = 1$.

The expression $3 \cdot 2 \cdot 1$ can also be written as 3!. The symbol ! is the **factorial** symbol, and 3! is read as "three factorial." In general, $n!$ is defined where n is a positive integer as follows:

$$n! = n \cdot (n - 1) \cdot (n - 2) \cdot \ldots \cdot 3 \cdot 2 \cdot 1$$

The number of permutations of n distinct objects is $n!$.

EXAMPLE 4 Find the number of permutations

OLYMPICS Ten teams are competing in the final round of the Olympic four-person bobsledding competition.

a. In how many different ways can the bobsledding teams finish the competition? (Assume there are no ties.)

b. In how many different ways can 3 of the bobsledding teams finish first, second, and third to win the gold, silver, and bronze medals?

Solution

a. There are 10! different ways that the teams can finish the competition.

$$10! = 10 \cdot 9 \cdot 8 \cdot 7 \cdot 6 \cdot 5 \cdot 4 \cdot 3 \cdot 2 \cdot 1 = 3{,}628{,}800$$

b. Any of the 10 teams can finish first, then any of the remaining 9 teams can finish second, and finally any of the remaining 8 teams can finish third. So, the number of ways that the teams can win the medals is:

$$10 \cdot 9 \cdot 8 = 720$$

✓ **GUIDED PRACTICE** for Example 4

3. WHAT IF? In Example 4, how would the answers change if there were 12 bobsledding teams competing in the final round of the competition?

The answer to part (b) of Example 4 is called the number of permutations of 10 objects taken 3 at a time. It is denoted by ${}_{10}P_3$. Notice that this permutation can be computed using factorials:

$${}_{10}P_3 = 10 \cdot 9 \cdot 8 = \frac{10 \cdot 9 \cdot 8 \cdot 7 \cdot 6 \cdot 5 \cdot 4 \cdot 3 \cdot 2 \cdot 1}{7 \cdot 6 \cdot 5 \cdot 4 \cdot 3 \cdot 2 \cdot 1} = \frac{10!}{7!} = \frac{10!}{(10 - 3)!}$$

This result is generalized at the top of the next page.

KEY CONCEPT — For Your Notebook

Permutations of n Objects Taken r at a Time

The number of permutations of r objects taken from a group of n distinct objects is denoted by ${}_nP_r$ and is given by this formula:

$${}_nP_r = \frac{n!}{(n-r)!}$$

EXAMPLE 5 Find permutations of n objects taken r at a time

MUSIC You are burning a demo CD for your band. Your band has 12 songs stored on your computer. However, you want to put only 4 songs on the demo CD. In how many orders can you burn 4 of the 12 songs onto the CD?

EVALUATE PERMUTATIONS
Most scientific and graphing calculators have a key or menu item for evaluating ${}_nP_r$.

Solution

Find the number of permutations of 12 objects taken 4 at a time.

$${}_{12}P_4 = \frac{12!}{(12-4)!} = \frac{12!}{8!} = \frac{479,001,600}{40,320} = 11,880$$

▶ You can burn 4 of the 12 songs in 11,880 different orders.

✓ GUIDED PRACTICE for Example 5

Find the number of permutations.

4. ${}_5P_3$

5. ${}_4P_1$

6. ${}_8P_5$

7. ${}_{12}P_7$

PERMUTATIONS WITH REPETITION If you consider the letters E and E to be *distinct*, there are six permutations of the letters E, E, and Y:

EEY EYE YEE
EEY EYE YEE

However, if the two occurrences of E are considered interchangeable, then there are only three distinguishable permutations:

EEY EYE YEE

Each of these permutations corresponds to two of the original six permutations because there are 2!, or 2, permutations of E and E. So, the number of permutations of **E**, **E**, and **Y** can be written as $\frac{3!}{2!} = \frac{6}{2} = 3$.

KEY CONCEPT — For Your Notebook

Permutations with Repetition

The number of distinguishable permutations of n objects where one object is repeated s_1 times, another is repeated s_2 times, and so on, is:

$$\frac{n!}{s_1! \cdot s_2! \cdot \ldots \cdot s_k!}$$

EXAMPLE 6 Find permutations with repetition

Find the number of distinguishable permutations of the letters in (a) MIAMI and (b) TALLAHASSEE.

Solution

a. MIAMI has 5 letters of which M and I are each repeated 2 times. So, the number of distinguishable permutations is $\frac{5!}{2! \cdot 2!} = \frac{120}{2 \cdot 2} = 30$.

b. TALLAHASSEE has 11 letters of which A is repeated 3 times, and L, S, and E are each repeated 2 times. So, the number of distinguishable permutations is $\frac{11!}{3! \cdot 2! \cdot 2! \cdot 2!} = \frac{39{,}916{,}800}{6 \cdot 2 \cdot 2 \cdot 2} = 831{,}600$.

GUIDED PRACTICE for Example 6

Find the number of distinguishable permutations of the letters in the word.

8. MALL **9.** KAYAK **10.** CINCINNATI

10.1 EXERCISES

HOMEWORK KEY
○ = **WORKED-OUT SOLUTIONS** on p. WS18 for Exs. 13, 35, and 65
★ = **STANDARDIZED TEST PRACTICE** Exs. 2, 17, 42, 55, 57, and 68

SKILL PRACTICE

1. VOCABULARY What is a permutation of n objects?

2. ★ **WRITING** Simplify the formula for ${}_nP_r$ when $r = 0$. *Explain* why this result makes sense.

EXAMPLE 1 on p. 682 for Exs. 3–6

TREE DIAGRAMS An object has an attribute from each list. Make a tree diagram that shows the number of different objects that can be created.

3.

T-Shirts
Size: M, L, XL
Type: long-sleeved, short-sleeved

4.

Toast
Bread: white, wheat
Spread: jam, margarine

5.

Meal
Entrée: chicken, fish, pasta
Side: corn, green beans, potato

6.

Furniture
Wood: cherry, mahogany, oak, pine
Finish: stained, painted, unfinished

EXAMPLE 2 on p. 683 for Exs. 7–10

FUNDAMENTAL COUNTING PRINCIPLE Each event can occur in the given number of ways. Find the number of ways all of the events can occur.

7. Event A: 2 ways; Event B: 4 ways

8. Event A: 5 ways; Event B: 2 ways

9. Event A: 4 ways; Event B: 3 ways; Event C: 5 ways

10. Event A: 3 ways; Event B: 6 ways; Event C: 5 ways; Event D: 2 ways

EXAMPLE 3
on p. 683
for Exs. 11–17

LICENSE PLATES For the given configuration, determine how many different license plates are possible if (a) digits and letters can be repeated, and (b) digits and letters cannot be repeated.

11. 4 letters followed by 3 digits

12. 2 letters followed by 5 digits

13. 4 letters followed by 2 digits

14. 5 digits followed by 3 letters

15. 1 digit followed by 5 letters

16. 6 letters

17. ★ **MULTIPLE CHOICE** How many different license plates with 2 letters followed by 4 digits are possible if digits and letters cannot be repeated?

(A) 3,276,000 (B) 6,760,000 (C) 32,292,000 (D) 45,697,600

EXAMPLES 4 and 5
on pp. 684–685
for Exs. 18–41

FACTORIALS Evaluate the expression.

18. 7! **19.** 11! **20.** 1! **21.** 8!

22. 4! **23.** 0! **24.** 12! **25.** 6!

26. $3! \cdot 4!$ **27.** $3(4!)$ **28.** $\frac{8!}{(8-5)!}$ **29.** $\frac{9!}{4! \cdot 4!}$

PERMUTATIONS Find the number of permutations.

30. ${}_4P_4$ **31.** ${}_6P_2$ **32.** ${}_{10}P_1$ **33.** ${}_8P_7$

34. ${}_7P_4$ **35.** ${}_9P_2$ **36.** ${}_{13}P_8$ **37.** ${}_7P_7$

38. ${}_5P_0$ **39.** ${}_9P_4$ **40.** ${}_{11}P_4$ **41.** ${}_{15}P_0$

42. ★ **SHORT RESPONSE** Let n be a positive integer. Find the number of permutations of n objects taken $n - 1$ at a time. *Compare* your answer with the number of permutations of all n objects. Does this make sense? *Explain.*

EXAMPLE 6
on p. 686
for Exs. 43–55

PERMUTATIONS WITH REPETITION Find the number of distinguishable permutations of the letters in the word.

43. OFF **44.** TREE **45.** SKILL **46.** YELLOW

47. GRAVEL **48.** PANAMA **49.** ARKANSAS **50.** FACTORIAL

51. MAGNETIC **52.** HONOLULU **53.** CLEVELAND **54.** MISSISSIPPI

55. ★ **MULTIPLE CHOICE** What is the number of distinguishable permutations of the letters in the word HAWAII?

(A) 24 (B) 180 (C) 360 (D) 720

56. **ERROR ANALYSIS** In bingo, balls labeled from 1 to 75 are drawn from a container without being replaced. *Describe* and correct the error in finding the number of ways the first 4 numbers can be chosen for a game of bingo.

$75 \cdot 75 \cdot 75 \cdot 75$
$= 31,640,625$ ✗

57. ★ **SHORT RESPONSE** *Explain* how the fundamental counting principle can be used to justify the formula for the number of permutations of n distinct objects.

SOLVING EQUATIONS Solve for n.

58. ${}_nP_4 = 8({}_nP_3)$ **59.** ${}_nP_6 = 5({}_nP_5)$ **60.** ${}_nP_5 = 9({}_nP_4)$

61. **CHALLENGE** Find the number of distinguishable permutations of 6 letters that are chosen from the letters in the word MANATEE.

PROBLEM SOLVING

EXAMPLE 2 on p. 683 for Exs. 62–63

62. **CLASS RINGS** You want to purchase a class ring. The ring can be made from 3 different metals. You can choose from 6 different side designs and 12 different stones. How many different class rings are possible?

Metal	Side Design		Stone
Auralite	Academics	Literature	
Gold	Art	Music	
Silver	Athletics	Technology	

@HomeTutor for problem solving help at classzone.com

63. **ENVIRONMENT** Since 1990, the Goldman Environmental Prize has been awarded annually to 6 grassroots environmentalists, one from each of 6 regions. The regions consist of 52 countries in Africa, 47 in Europe, 45 in Asia, 36 in island nations, 19 in South and Central America, and 3 in North America. How many different sets of 6 countries can be represented by the prize winners in a given year?

@HomeTutor for problem solving help at classzone.com

EXAMPLES 4, 5, and 6 on pp. 684–686 for Exs. 64–66

64. **PHOTOGRAPHY** A photographer lines up the 15 members of a family in a single line in order to take a photograph. How many different ways can the photographer arrange the family members for the picture?

65. **SCHOOL CLUBS** A Spanish club is electing a president, vice president, and secretary. The club has 9 members who are eligible for these offices. How many different ways can the 3 offices be filled?

66. **MUSIC** The window of a music store has 8 stands in fixed positions where instruments can be displayed. In how many ways can 3 identical guitars, 2 identical keyboards, and 3 identical violins be displayed?

67. **MULTI-STEP PROBLEM** You are designing an entertainment center. You want to include three audio components and three video components.

a. You want one of each audio component listed at the right. How many selections of audio components are possible?

b. You want one of each video component listed at the right. How many selections of video components are possible?

c. How many selections of all six audio and video components are possible?

Entertainment Center	
Audio Components	**Video Components**
5 receivers	7 TV sets
8 CD players	9 DVD players
6 speakers	4 game systems

68. ★ **EXTENDED RESPONSE** To keep computer files secure, many programs require the user to enter a password. The shortest allowable passwords are typically 6 characters long and can contain both letters and digits.

a. **Calculate** How many 6-character passwords are possible if characters can be repeated?

b. **Calculate** How many 6-character passwords are possible if characters cannot be repeated?

c. **Draw Conclusions** Which type of password is more secure? *Explain.*

○ = WORKED-OUT SOLUTIONS on p. WS1

★ = STANDARDIZED TEST PRACTICE

69. **CLOTHING DISPLAY** An employee at a clothing store is creating a display. The display has 3 different mannequins. Each mannequin is to wear a different sweater and a different skirt. How many different displays can be created?

Animated Algebra at classzone.com

70. **CROSS COUNTRY** Three schools are competing in a cross country meet. School A has 6 runners, school B has 5 runners, and school C has 4 runners. For scoring purposes, the finishing order of the meet only considers the school of each runner. How many different finishing orders are there for scoring purposes?

71. **CHALLENGE** You have learned that $n!$ represents the number of ways that n objects can be placed in a *linear* order, where it matters which object is placed first. Now consider *circular* permutations in which objects are placed in a circle, so that it does *not* matter which object is placed first.

    a. Suppose you are seating 5 people at a circular table. How many different ways can you arrange the people around the table?

    b. Find a formula for the number of permutations of n objects placed in clockwise order around a circle when only the relative order of the objects matters. *Explain* how you derived your formula.

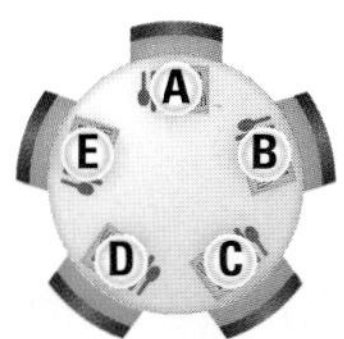

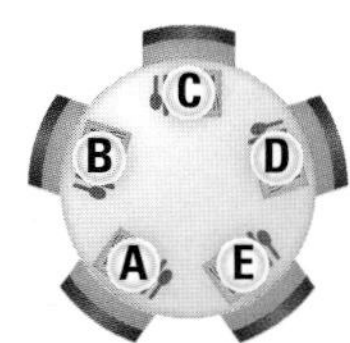

The two arrangements shown represent the same permutation.

NEW YORK MIXED REVIEW

72. The graph shows the height of a toy rocket from the time it is launched to the time it lands on the ground. How much time elapses while the rocket is 80 feet or higher above the ground?

    (A) 3 sec (B) 4 sec

    (C) 6 sec (D) 8 sec

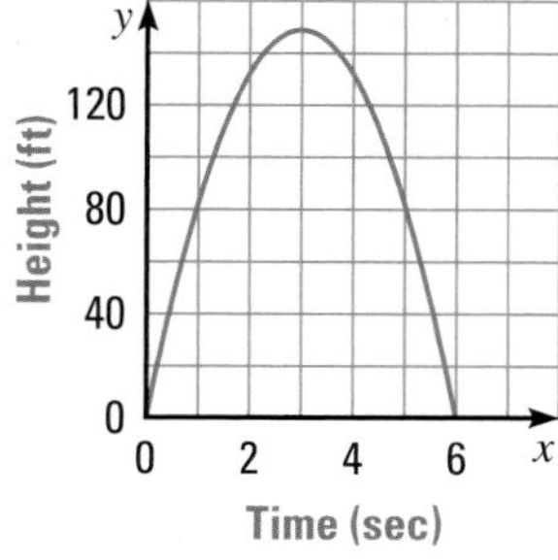

73. Paul makes a scale model of an airplane. The actual airplane is 56 feet long with a wingspan of 37.5 feet. Paul's model is 14 inches long. What is the approximate wingspan of his model?

    (A) 9.0 in. (B) 9.4 in. (C) 18.7 in. (D) 22.5 in.

10.2 Use Combinations and the Binomial Theorem

 **A2.S.12** Use permutations, combinations, and the Fundamental Principle of Counting to determine the number of elements in a sample space. . .

Before You used the counting principle and permutations.

Now You will use combinations and the binomial theorem.

Why? So you can find ways to form a set, as in Example 2.

Key Vocabulary
- **combination**
- **Pascal's triangle**
- **binomial theorem**

In Lesson 10.1, you learned that order is important for some counting problems. For other counting problems, order is not important. For instance, if you purchase a package of trading cards, the order of the cards inside the package is not important. A **combination** is a selection of r objects from a group of n objects where the order is not important.

KEY CONCEPT *For Your Notebook*

Combinations of n Objects Taken r at a Time

The number of combinations of r objects taken from a group of n distinct objects is denoted by ${}_nC_r$ and is given by this formula:

$${}_nC_r = \frac{n!}{(n-r)! \cdot r!}$$

EXAMPLE 1 **Find combinations**

CARDS A standard deck of 52 playing cards has 4 suits with 13 different cards in each suit.

a. If the order in which the cards are dealt is not important, how many different 5-card hands are possible?

b. In how many 5-card hands are all 5 cards of the same color?

Standard 52-Card Deck

K ♠	K ♥	K ♦	K ♣
Q ♠	Q ♥	Q ♦	Q ♣
J ♠	J ♥	J ♦	J ♣
10 ♠	10 ♥	10 ♦	10 ♣
9 ♠	9 ♥	9 ♦	9 ♣
8 ♠	8 ♥	8 ♦	8 ♣
7 ♠	7 ♥	7 ♦	7 ♣
6 ♠	6 ♥	6 ♦	6 ♣
5 ♠	5 ♥	5 ♦	5 ♣
4 ♠	4 ♥	4 ♦	4 ♣
3 ♠	3 ♥	3 ♦	3 ♣
2 ♠	2 ♥	2 ♦	2 ♣
A ♠	A ♥	A ♦	A ♣

Solution

a. The number of ways to choose 5 cards from a deck of 52 cards is:

$${}_{52}C_5 = \frac{52!}{47! \cdot 5!} = \frac{52 \cdot 51 \cdot 50 \cdot 49 \cdot 48 \cdot \cancel{47!}}{\cancel{47!} \cdot 5!} = 2{,}598{,}960$$

b. For all 5 cards to be the same color, you need to choose 1 of the 2 colors and then 5 of the 26 cards in that color. So, the number of possible hands is:

$${}_2C_1 \cdot {}_{26}C_5 = \frac{2!}{1! \cdot 1!} \cdot \frac{26!}{21! \cdot 5!} = \frac{2}{1 \cdot 1} \cdot \frac{26 \cdot 25 \cdot 24 \cdot 23 \cdot 22 \cdot \cancel{21!}}{\cancel{21!} \cdot 5!} = 131{,}560$$

MULTIPLE EVENTS When finding the number of ways both an event *A and* an event *B* can occur, you need to multiply, as in part (b) of Example 1. When finding the number of ways that event *A or* event *B* can occur, you add instead.

EXAMPLE 2 Decide to multiply or add combinations

THEATER William Shakespeare wrote 38 plays that can be divided into three genres. Of the 38 plays, 18 are comedies, 10 are histories, and 10 are tragedies.

a. How many different sets of *exactly* 2 comedies and 1 tragedy can you read?

b. How many different sets of *at most* 3 plays can you read?

AVOID ERRORS
When finding the number of ways to select *at most n* objects, be sure to include the possibility of selecting 0 objects.

Solution

a. You can choose 2 of the 18 comedies and 1 of the 10 tragedies. So, the number of possible sets of plays is:

$$_{18}C_2 \cdot {}_{10}C_1 = \frac{18!}{16! \cdot 2!} \cdot \frac{10!}{9! \cdot 1!} = \frac{18 \cdot 17 \cdot \cancel{16!}}{\cancel{16!} \cdot 2 \cdot 1} \cdot \frac{10 \cdot \cancel{9!}}{\cancel{9!} \cdot 1} = 153 \cdot 10 = 1530$$

b. You can read 0, 1, 2, or 3 plays. Because there are 38 plays that can be chosen, the number of possible sets of plays is:

$$_{38}C_0 + {}_{38}C_1 + {}_{38}C_2 + {}_{38}C_3 = 1 + 38 + 703 + 8436 = 9178$$

SUBTRACTING POSSIBILITIES Counting problems that involve phrases like "at least" or "at most" are sometimes easier to solve by subtracting possibilities you do not want from the total number of possibilities.

EXAMPLE 3 Solve a multi-step problem

BASKETBALL During the school year, the girl's basketball team is scheduled to play 12 home games. You want to attend *at least* 3 of the games. How many different combinations of games can you attend?

Solution

Of the 12 home games, you want to attend 3 games, or 4 games, or 5 games, and so on. So, the number of combinations of games you can attend is:

$$_{12}C_3 + {}_{12}C_4 + {}_{12}C_5 + \cdots + {}_{12}C_{12}$$

Instead of adding these combinations, use the following reasoning. For each of the 12 games, you can choose to attend or not attend the game, so there are 2^{12} total combinations. If you attend at least 3 games, you do not attend only a total of 0, 1, or 2 games. So, the number of ways you can attend at least 3 games is:

$$2^{12} - ({}_{12}C_0 + {}_{12}C_1 + {}_{12}C_2) = 4096 - (1 + 12 + 66) = 4017$$

✓ GUIDED PRACTICE for Examples 1, 2, and 3

Find the number of combinations.

1. $_8C_3$ **2.** $_{10}C_6$ **3.** $_7C_2$ **4.** $_{14}C_5$

5. WHAT IF? In Example 2, how many different sets of *exactly* 3 tragedies and 2 histories can you read?

PASCAL'S TRIANGLE If you arrange the values of ${}_nC_r$ in a triangular pattern in which each row corresponds to a value of n, you get what is called **Pascal's triangle**. Pascal's triangle is named after the French mathematician Blaise Pascal (1623–1662).

KEY CONCEPT *For Your Notebook*

Pascal's Triangle

Pascal's triangle is shown below with its entries represented by combinations and with its entries represented by numbers. The first and last numbers in each row are 1. Every number other than 1 is the sum of the closest two numbers in the row directly above it.

	Pascal's triangle as combinations	Pascal's triangle as numbers
$n = 0$ (0th row)	${}_0C_0$	1
$n = 1$ (1st row)	${}_1C_0 \quad {}_1C_1$	1 1
$n = 2$ (2nd row)	${}_2C_0 \quad {}_2C_1 \quad {}_2C_2$	1 2 1
$n = 3$ (3rd row)	${}_3C_0 \quad {}_3C_1 \quad {}_3C_2 \quad {}_3C_3$	1 3 3 1
$n = 4$ (4th row)	${}_4C_0 \quad {}_4C_1 \quad {}_4C_2 \quad {}_4C_3 \quad {}_4C_4$	1 4 6 4 1
$n = 5$ (5th row)	${}_5C_0 \quad {}_5C_1 \quad {}_5C_2 \quad {}_5C_3 \quad {}_5C_4 \quad {}_5C_5$	1 5 10 10 5 1

EXAMPLE 4 Use Pascal's triangle

SCHOOL CLUBS The 6 members of a Model UN club must choose 2 representatives to attend a state convention. Use Pascal's triangle to find the number of combinations of 2 members that can be chosen as representatives.

Solution

Because you need to find ${}_6C_2$, write the 6th row of Pascal's triangle by adding numbers from the previous row.

$n = 5$ (5th row) 1 5 10 10 5 1

$n = 6$ (6th row) 1 6 15 20 15 6 1

${}_6C_0 \quad {}_6C_1 \quad {}_6C_2 \quad {}_6C_3 \quad {}_6C_4 \quad {}_6C_5 \quad {}_6C_6$

▶ The value of ${}_6C_2$ is the third number in the 6th row of Pascal's triangle, as shown above. Therefore, ${}_6C_2 = 15$. There are 15 combinations of representatives for the convention.

✓ **GUIDED PRACTICE** for Example 4

6. **WHAT IF?** In Example 4, use Pascal's triangle to find the number of combinations of 2 members that can be chosen if the Model UN club has 7 members.

BINOMIAL EXPANSIONS There is an important relationship between powers of binomials and combinations. The numbers in Pascal's triangle can be used to find coefficients in binomial expansions. For example, the coefficients in the expansion of $(a + b)^4$ are the numbers of combinations in the row of Pascal's triangle for $n = 4$:

$$(a+b)^4 = \underset{{}_4C_0}{1}a^4 + \underset{{}_4C_1}{4}a^3b + \underset{{}_4C_2}{6}a^2b^2 + \underset{{}_4C_3}{4}ab^3 + \underset{{}_4C_4}{1}b^4$$

This result is generalized in the **binomial theorem**.

KEY CONCEPT *For Your Notebook*

Binomial Theorem

For any positive integer n, the binomial expansion of $(a + b)^n$ is:

$$(a+b)^n = {}_nC_0a^nb^0 + {}_nC_1a^{n-1}b^1 + {}_nC_2a^{n-2}b^2 + \cdots + {}_nC_na^0b^n$$

Notice that each term in the expansion of $(a + b)^n$ has the form ${}_nC_r\,a^{n-r}b^r$ where r is an integer from 0 to n.

EXAMPLE 5 Expand a power of a binomial sum

Use the binomial theorem to write the binomial expansion.

$$(x^2 + y)^3 = {}_3C_0(x^2)^3y^0 + {}_3C_1(x^2)^2y^1 + {}_3C_2(x^2)^1y^2 + {}_3C_3(x^2)^0y^3$$
$$= (1)(x^6)(1) + (3)(x^4)(y) + (3)(x^2)(y^2) + (1)(1)(y^3)$$
$$= x^6 + 3x^4y + 3x^2y^2 + y^3$$

POWERS OF BINOMIAL DIFFERENCES To expand a power of a binomial difference, you can rewrite the binomial as a sum. The resulting expansion will have terms whose signs alternate between + and −.

AVOID ERRORS

When a binomial has a term or terms with a coefficient other than 1, the coefficients of the binomial expansion are not the same as the corresponding row of Pascal's triangle.

EXAMPLE 6 Expand a power of a binomial difference

Use the binomial theorem to write the binomial expansion.

$$(a - 2b)^4 = [a + (-2b)]^4$$
$$= {}_4C_0a^4(-2b)^0 + {}_4C_1a^3(-2b)^1 + {}_4C_2a^2(-2b)^2 + {}_4C_3a^1(-2b)^3 + {}_4C_4a^0(-2b)^4$$
$$= (1)(a^4)(1) + (4)(a^3)(-2b) + (6)(a^2)(4b^2) + (4)(a)(-8b^3) + (1)(1)(16b^4)$$
$$= a^4 - 8a^3b + 24a^2b^2 - 32ab^3 + 16b^4$$

✓ **GUIDED PRACTICE** for Examples 5 and 6

Use the binomial theorem to write the binomial expansion.

7. $(x + 3)^5$ **8.** $(a + 2b)^4$ **9.** $(2p - q)^4$ **10.** $(5 - 2y)^3$

EXAMPLE 7 Find a coefficient in an expansion

Find the coefficient of x^4 in the expansion of $(3x + 2)^{10}$.

Solution

From the binomial theorem, you know the following:

$$(3x + 2)^{10} = {}_{10}C_0(3x)^{10}(2)^0 + {}_{10}C_1(3x)^9(2)^1 + \cdots + {}_{10}C_{10}(3x)^0(2)^{10}$$

Each term in the expansion has the form ${}_{10}C_r(3x)^{10-r}(2)^r$. The term containing x^4 occurs when $r = 6$:

$${}_{10}C_6(3x)^4(2)^6 = (210)(81x^4)(64) = 1{,}088{,}640x^4$$

▶ The coefficient of x^4 is 1,088,640.

✓ **GUIDED PRACTICE** for Example 7

11. Find the coefficient of x^5 in the expansion of $(x - 3)^7$.
12. Find the coefficient of x^3 in the expansion of $(2x + 5)^8$.

10.2 EXERCISES

HOMEWORK KEY
○ = **WORKED-OUT SOLUTIONS on p. WS18 for Exs. 17, 29, and 49**
★ = **STANDARDIZED TEST PRACTICE Exs. 2, 35, 40, 41, and 52**

SKILL PRACTICE

1. **VOCABULARY** Copy and complete: The binomial expansion of $(a + b)^n$ is given by the _?_.

2. ★ **WRITING** *Explain* the difference between permutations and combinations.

EXAMPLES 1, 2, and 3 on pp. 690–691 for Exs. 3–18

COMBINATIONS Find the number of combinations.

3. ${}_5C_2$
4. ${}_{10}C_3$
5. ${}_9C_6$
6. ${}_8C_2$
7. ${}_{11}C_{11}$
8. ${}_{12}C_4$
9. ${}_7C_5$
10. ${}_{14}C_6$

ERROR ANALYSIS ***Describe*** **and correct the error in finding the number of combinations.**

11. $${}_6C_2 = \frac{6!}{(6-2)!} = \frac{720}{24} = 30 \quad \times$$

12. $${}_8C_3 = \frac{8!}{3!} = \frac{40{,}320}{6} = 6720 \quad \times$$

CARD HANDS Find the number of possible 5-card hands that contain the cards specified. The cards are taken from a standard 52-card deck.

13. 5 face cards (kings, queens, or jacks)
14. 4 kings and 1 other card
15. 1 ace and 4 cards that are not aces
16. 5 hearts or 5 diamonds
17. At most 1 queen
18. At least 1 spade

EXAMPLE 4 on p. 692 for Exs. 19–23

19. **USING PATTERNS** Copy Pascal's triangle on page 692 and add rows for $n = 6, 7, 8, 9$, and 10.

PASCAL'S TRIANGLE Use the rows of Pascal's triangle from Exercise 19 to write the binomial expansion.

20. $(x + 3)^6$
21. $(y - 3z)^{10}$
22. $(a + b^2)^8$
23. $(2s - t^4)^7$

EXAMPLES 5 and 6 on p. 693 for Exs. 24–31

BINOMIAL THEOREM Use the binomial theorem to write the binomial expansion.

24. $(x + 2)^3$
25. $(c - 4)^5$
26. $(a + 3b)^4$
27. $(4p - q)^6$
28. $(w^3 - 3)^4$
29. $(2s^4 + 5)^5$
30. $(3u + v^2)^6$
31. $(x^3 - y^2)^4$

EXAMPLE 7 on p. 694 for Exs. 32–35

32. Find the coefficient of x^5 in the expansion of $(x - 2)^{10}$.

33. Find the coefficient of x^3 in the expansion of $(3x + 2)^5$.

34. Find the coefficient of x^6 in the expansion of $(x^2 - 3)^8$.

35. ★ **MULTIPLE CHOICE** Which is the coefficient of x^4 in the expansion of $(x - 3)^7$?

(A) −945 (B) −35 (C) −27 (D) 2835

PASCAL'S TRIANGLE In Exercises 36 and 37, use the diagrams shown.

36. What is the sum of the numbers in each of rows 0–4 of Pascal's triangle? What is the sum in row n?

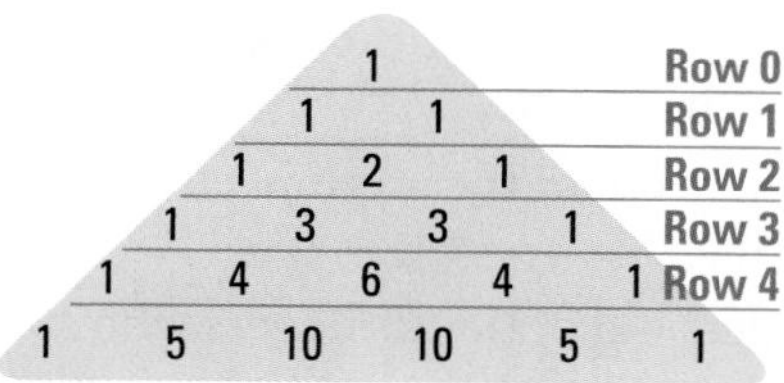

37. *Describe* the pattern formed by the sums of the numbers along the diagonal segments of Pascal's triangle.

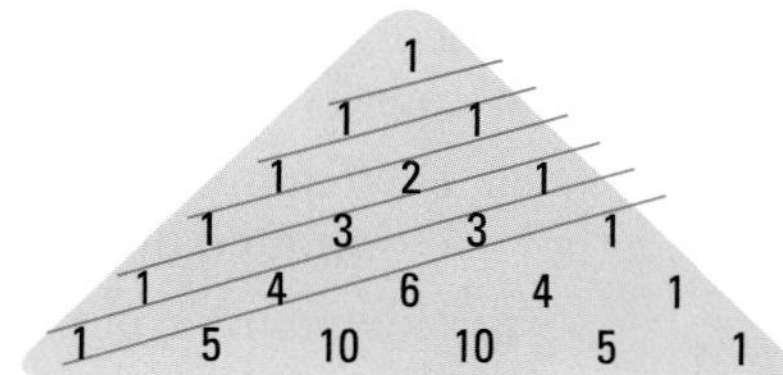

REASONING In Exercises 38 and 39, decide whether the problem requires *combinations* or *permutations* to find the answer. Then solve the problem.

38. **NEWSPAPER** Your school newspaper has an editor-in-chief and an assistant editor-in-chief. The staff of the newspaper has 12 students. In how many ways can students be chosen for these two positions?

39. **STUDENT COUNCIL** Five representatives from a senior class of 280 students are to be chosen for the student council. In how many ways can students be chosen to represent the senior class on the student council?

40. ★ **MULTIPLE CHOICE** A relay race has a team of 4 runners who run different parts of the race. There are 20 students on your track squad. In how many ways can the coach select students to compete on the relay team?

(A) 4845 (B) 40,000 (C) 116,280 (D) 160,000

41. ★ **SHORT RESPONSE** *Explain* how the formula for ${}_nC_n$ suggests the definition $0! = 1$.

CHALLENGE Verify the identity. *Justify* each of your steps.

42. ${}_nC_0 = 1$
43. ${}_nC_n = 1$
44. ${}_nC_r \cdot {}_rC_m = {}_nC_m \cdot {}_{n-m}C_{r-m}$
45. ${}_nC_1 = {}_nP_1$
46. ${}_nC_r = {}_nC_{n-r}$
47. ${}_{n+1}C_r = {}_nC_r + {}_nC_{r-1}$

PROBLEM SOLVING

EXAMPLES 1, 2, and 3 on pp. 690–691 for Exs. 48–50

48. **MUSIC** You want to purchase 3 CDs from an online collection that contains the types of music shown at the right. You want each CD to contain a different type of music such that 2 CDs are different types of contemporary music and 1 CD is a type of classical music. How many different sets of music types can you choose?

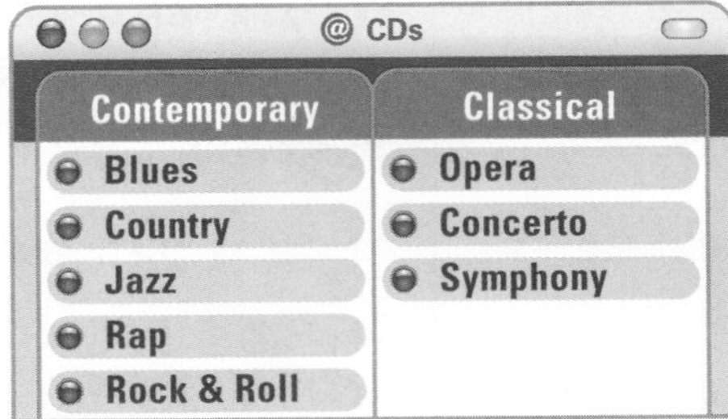

@HomeTutor for problem solving help at classzone.com

49. **FLOWERS** You are buying a bouquet. The florist has 18 types of flowers that you can use to make the bouquet. You want to use *exactly* 3 types of flowers. How many different combinations of flower types can you use in your bouquet?

@HomeTutor for problem solving help at classzone.com

50. **ARCADE GAMES** An arcade has 20 different arcade games. You want to play at least 14 of them. How many different combinations of arcade games can you play?

51. **MULTI-STEP PROBLEM** A televised singing competition picks a winner from 20 original contestants over the course of five episodes. During each of the first, second, and third episodes, 5 singers are eliminated by the end of the episode. The fourth episode eliminates 2 more singers, and the winner is selected at the end of the fifth episode.

    a. How many combinations of 5 singers out of the original 20 can be eliminated during the first episode?

    b. How many combinations of 5 singers out of the 15 singers who started the second episode can be eliminated during the second episode?

    c. How many combinations of singers can be eliminated during the third episode? during the fourth episode? during the fifth episode?

    d. Find the total number of ways in which the 20 original contestants can be eliminated to produce a winner.

52. ★ **EXTENDED RESPONSE** A group of 15 high school students is volunteering at a local fire station. Of these students, 5 will be assigned to wash fire trucks, 7 will be assigned to repaint the station's interior, and 3 will be assigned to do maintenance on the station's exterior.

    a. **Calculate** One way to count the number of possible job assignments is to find the number of permutations of 5 W's (for "wash"), 7 R's (for "repainting"), and 3 M's (for "maintenance"). Use this method to write the number of possible job assignments first as an expression involving factorials and then as a number.

    b. **Calculate** Another way to count the number of possible job assignments is to first choose the 5 W's, then choose the 7 R's, and then choose the 3 M's. Use this method to write the number of possible job assignments first as an expression involving factorials and then as a number.

    c. **Analyze** *Compare* your results from parts (a) and (b). *Explain* why they make sense.

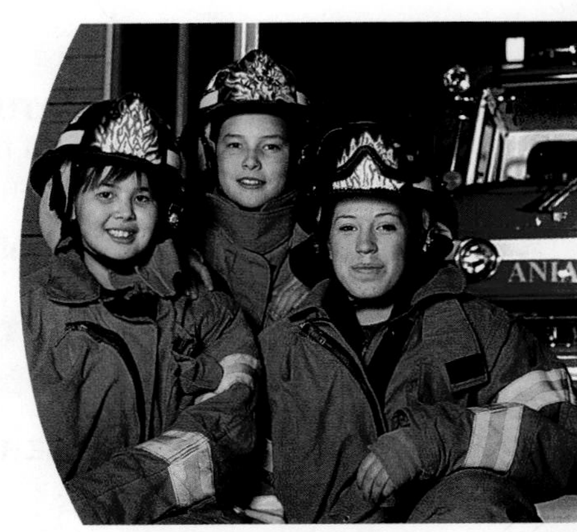

Volunteers in Aniak, Alaska

○ = WORKED-OUT SOLUTIONS on p. WS1　　★ = STANDARDIZED TEST PRACTICE

53. **CHALLENGE** A polygon is *convex* if no line that contains a side of the polygon contains a point in the interior of the polygon. Consider a convex polygon with n sides.

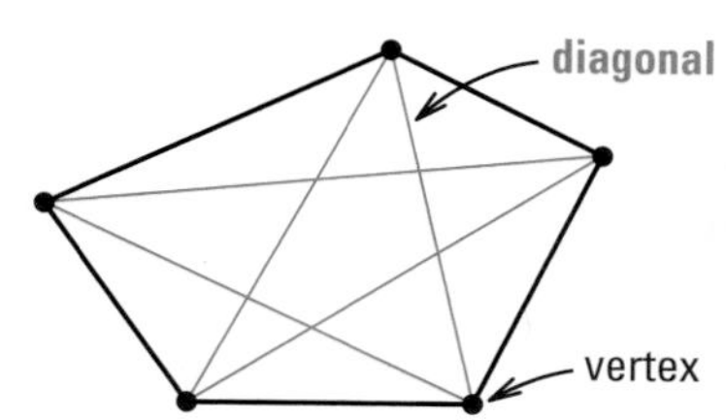

a. Use the combinations formula to write an expression for the number of line segments that join pairs of vertices on an n-sided polygon.

b. Use your result from part (a) to write a formula for the number of diagonals of an n-sided convex polygon.

New York Mixed Review

TEST PRACTICE at classzone.com

54. Ellen's next math test is worth 150 points and contains 42 questions. Each question is worth either 5 points or 3 points. Which system of equations can be used to determine the number f of 5 point questions and the number t of 3 point questions?

Ⓐ $f - t = 42$, $5f + 3t = 150$ Ⓑ $f + t = 42$, $3f + 5t = 150$

Ⓒ $f + t = 42$, $5f + 3t = 150$ Ⓓ $f + t = 42$, $5f + 5t = 150$

55. An equilateral triangle is inscribed in a circle with a radius of 6 centimeters. What is the approximate area of the shaded region?

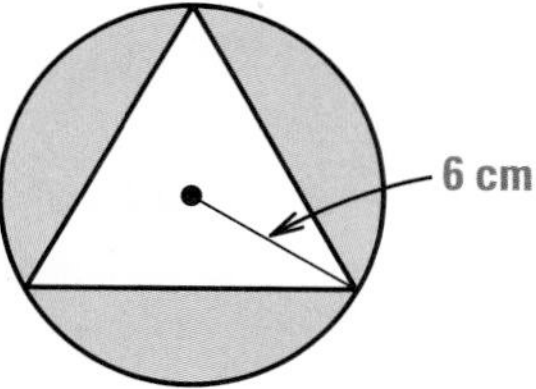

Ⓐ 19.6 cm^2 Ⓑ 66.3 cm^2

Ⓒ 74.9 cm^2 Ⓓ 81.9 cm^2

Quiz *for Lessons 10.1–10.2*

For the given license plate configuration, find how many plates are possible if letters and digits (a) can be repeated and (b) cannot be repeated. *(p. 682)*

1. 2 letters followed by 3 digits 2. 3 digits followed by 3 letters

Find the number of distinguishable permutations of the letters in the word. *(p. 682)*

3. AWAY 4. IDAHO 5. LETTER 6. TENNESSEE

Find the number of combinations. *(p. 690)*

7. ${}_8C_6$ 8. ${}_7C_4$ 9. ${}_9C_0$ 10. ${}_{12}C_{11}$

Use the binomial theorem to write the binomial expansion. *(p. 690)*

11. $(x + 5)^5$ 12. $(2s - 3)^6$ 13. $(3u + v)^4$ 14. $(2x^3 - 3y)^5$

15. Find the coefficient of x^3 in the expansion of $(x + 2)^9$. *(p. 690)*

16. **MENU CHOICES** A pizza parlor runs a special where you can buy a large pizza with 1 cheese, 1 vegetable, and 2 meats for \$12. You have a choice of 5 cheeses, 10 vegetables, and 6 meats. How many different variations of the pizza special are possible? *(p. 682)*

10.3 Define and Use Probability

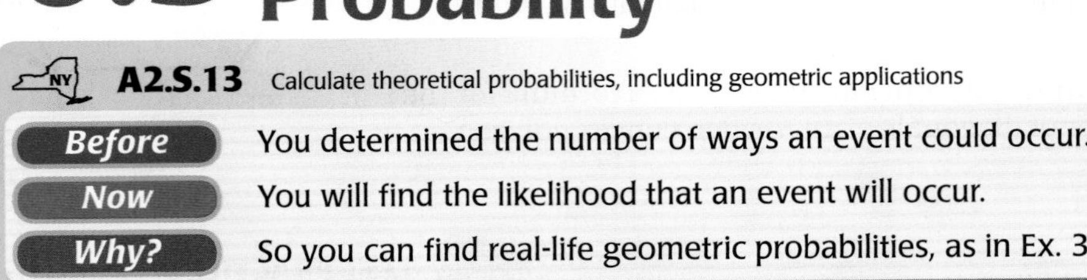

A2.S.13 Calculate theoretical probabilities, including geometric applications

Before You determined the number of ways an event could occur.

Now You will find the likelihood that an event will occur.

Why? So you can find real-life geometric probabilities, as in Ex. 39.

Key Vocabulary
- **probability**
- **theoretical probability**
- **odds**
- **experimental probability**
- **geometric probability**

When you roll a standard six-sided die, the possible results are called *outcomes*. The outcomes of rolling a die are 1, 2, 3, 4, 5, and 6. An *event* is an outcome or a collection of outcomes. For example, the event "rolling an odd number" consists of the outcomes 1, 3, and 5.

The **probability** of an event is a number from 0 to 1 that indicates the likelihood the event will occur, as shown on the number line below. Probabilities can be written as fractions, decimals, or percents.

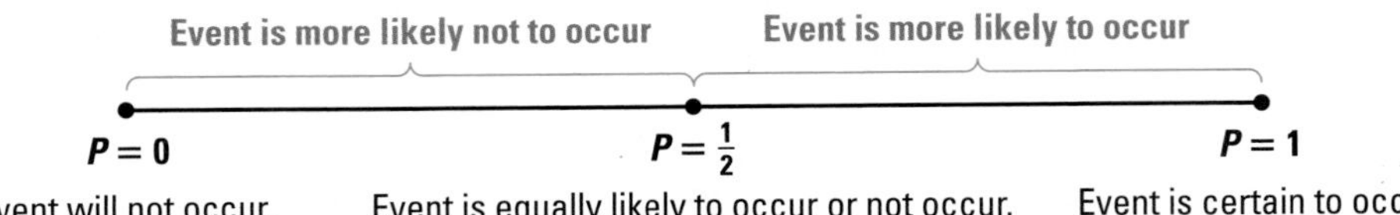

$P = 0$ Event will not occur.

$P = \frac{1}{2}$ Event is equally likely to occur or not occur.

$P = 1$ Event is certain to occur.

KEY CONCEPT *For Your Notebook*

Theoretical Probability of an Event

When all outcomes are equally likely, the **theoretical probability** that an event A will occur is:

$$P(A) = \frac{\text{Number of outcomes in event } A}{\text{Total number of outcomes}}$$

The theoretical probability of an event is often simply called the probability of the event.

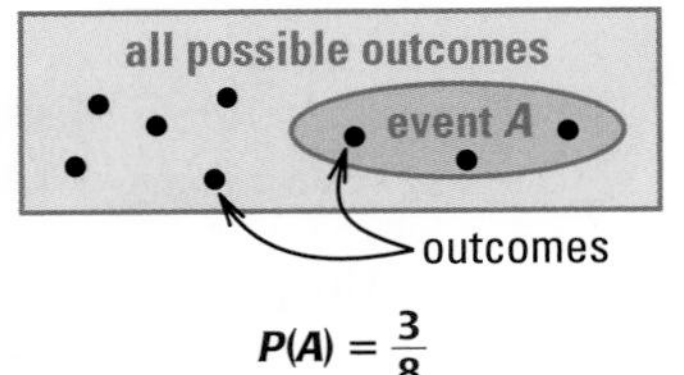

$P(A) = \frac{3}{8}$

EXAMPLE 1 Find probabilities of events

You roll a standard six-sided die. Find the probability of (a) rolling a 5 and (b) rolling an even number.

a. There are 6 possible outcomes. Only 1 outcome corresponds to rolling a 5.

$$P(\text{rolling a 5}) = \frac{\text{Number of ways to roll a 5}}{\text{Number of ways to roll the die}} = \frac{1}{6}$$

b. A total of 3 outcomes correspond to rolling an even number: a 2, 4, or 6.

$$P(\text{rolling even number}) = \frac{\text{Number of ways to roll an even number}}{\text{Number of ways to roll the die}} = \frac{3}{6} = \frac{1}{2}$$

EXAMPLE 2 Use permutations or combinations

ENTERTAINMENT A community center hosts a talent contest for local musicians. On a given evening, 7 musicians are scheduled to perform. The order in which the musicians perform is randomly selected during the show.

a. What is the probability that the musicians perform in alphabetical order by their last names? (Assume that no two musicians have the same last name.)

b. You are friends with 4 of the musicians. What is the probability that the first 2 performers are your friends?

Solution

a. There are 7! different *permutations* of the 7 musicians. Of these, only 1 is in alphabetical order by last name. So, the probability is:

$$P(\text{alphabetical order}) = \frac{1}{7!} = \frac{1}{5040} \approx 0.000198$$

b. There are ${}_7C_2$ different *combinations* of 2 musicians. Of these, ${}_4C_2$ are 2 of your friends. So, the probability is:

$$P(\text{first 2 performers are your friends}) = \frac{{}_4C_2}{{}_7C_2} = \frac{6}{21} = \frac{2}{7} \approx 0.286$$

GUIDED PRACTICE for Examples 1 and 2

You have an equally likely chance of choosing any integer from 1 through 20. Find the probability of the given event.

1. A perfect square is chosen.
2. A factor of 30 is chosen.
3. **WHAT IF?** In Example 2, how do your answers to parts (a) and (b) change if there are 9 musicians scheduled to perform?

ODDS You can also use **odds** to measure the likelihood that an event will occur. Odds measure the chances in *favor* of an event occurring or the chances *against* an event occurring.

KEY CONCEPT *For Your Notebook*

Odds in Favor of or Odds Against an Event

When all outcomes are equally likely, the odds in favor of an event A and the odds against an event A are defined as follows:

$$\text{Odds in favor of event } A = \frac{\text{Number of outcomes in } A}{\text{Number of outcomes not in } A}$$

$$\text{Odds against event } A = \frac{\text{Number of outcomes not in } A}{\text{Number of outcomes in } A}$$

You can write the odds in favor of or against an event in the form $\frac{a}{b}$ or in the form $a : b$.

EXAMPLE 3 Find odds

AVOID ERRORS

Note that the odds in favor of drawing a 10, which are $\frac{1}{12}$, do not equal the probability of drawing a 10, which is $\frac{4}{52} = \frac{1}{13}$.

A card is drawn from a standard deck of 52 cards. Find (a) the odds in *favor* of drawing a 10 and (b) the odds *against* drawing a club.

Solution

a. Odds in favor of drawing a 10 $= \frac{\text{Number of tens}}{\text{Number of non-tens}} = \frac{4}{48} = \frac{1}{12}$, or 1 : 12

b. Odds against drawing a club $= \frac{\text{Number of non-clubs}}{\text{Number of clubs}} = \frac{39}{13} = \frac{3}{1}$, or 3 : 1

EXPERIMENTAL PROBABILITY Sometimes it is not possible or convenient to find the theoretical probability of an event. In such cases, you may be able to calculate an *experimental probability* by performing an experiment, conducting a survey, or looking at the history of the event.

KEY CONCEPT — *For Your Notebook*

Experimental Probability of an Event

When an experiment is performed that consists of a certain number of trials, the **experimental probability** of an event A is given by:

$$P(A) = \frac{\text{Number of trials where } A \text{ occurs}}{\text{Total number of trials}}$$

EXAMPLE 4 Find an experimental probability

SURVEY The bar graph shows how old adults in a survey would choose to be if they could choose any age. Find the experimental probability that a randomly selected adult would prefer to be at least 40 years old.

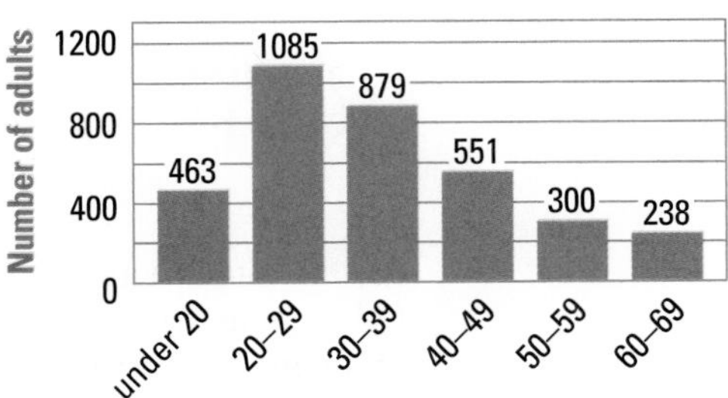

Solution

The total number of people surveyed is:

$$463 + 1085 + 879 + 551 + 300 + 238 = 3516$$

Of those surveyed, $551 + 300 + 238 = 1089$ would prefer to be at least 40.

$$P(\text{at least 40 years old}) = \frac{1089}{3516} \approx 0.310$$

✓ GUIDED PRACTICE for Examples 3 and 4

A card is randomly drawn from a standard deck. Find the indicated odds.

4. In favor of drawing a heart

5. Against drawing a queen

6. **WHAT IF?** In Example 4, what is the experimental probability that an adult would prefer to be **(a)** at most 39 years old and **(b)** at least 30 years old?

GEOMETRIC PROBABILITY Some probabilities are found by calculating a ratio of two lengths, areas, or volumes. Such probabilities are **geometric probabilities**.

EXAMPLE 5 Find a geometric probability

DARTS You throw a dart at the square board shown. Your dart is equally likely to hit any point inside the board. Are you more likely to get 10 points or 0 points?

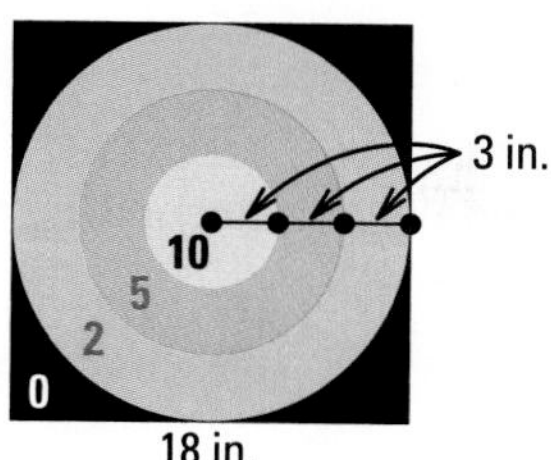

Solution

$$P(10 \text{ points}) = \frac{\text{Area of smallest circle}}{\text{Area of entire board}}$$

$$= \frac{\pi \cdot 3^2}{18^2} = \frac{9\pi}{324} = \frac{\pi}{36} \approx 0.0873$$

$$P(0 \text{ points}) = \frac{\text{Area outside largest circle}}{\text{Area of entire board}}$$

$$= \frac{18^2 - (\pi \cdot 9^2)}{18^2} = \frac{324 - 81\pi}{324} = \frac{4 - \pi}{4} \approx 0.215$$

▶ Because 0.215 > 0.0873, you are more likely to get 0 points.

 at classzone.com

 **GUIDED PRACTICE** for Example 5

7. **WHAT IF?** In Example 5, are you more likely to get 5 points or 0 points?

10.3 EXERCISES

HOMEWORK KEY

○ = **WORKED-OUT SOLUTIONS on p. WS18 for Exs. 7, 17, and 39**

★ = **STANDARDIZED TEST PRACTICE Exs. 2, 19, 26, 27, 32, and 42**

◆ = **MULTIPLE REPRESENTATIONS Ex. 40**

SKILL PRACTICE

1. **VOCABULARY** Copy and complete: A probability that is the ratio of two lengths, areas, or volumes is called a(n) _?_ probability.

2. ★ **WRITING** *Explain* the difference between theoretical probability and experimental probability. Give an example of each.

EXAMPLE 1 on p. 698 for Exs. 3–16

CHOOSING NUMBERS **You have an equally likely chance of choosing any integer from 1 through 50. Find the probability of the given event.**

3. An even number is chosen.
4. A number less than 35 is chosen.
5. A perfect square is chosen.
6. A prime number is chosen.
7. A factor of 150 is chosen.
8. A multiple of 4 is chosen.
9. A two-digit number is chosen.
10. A perfect cube is chosen.

CHOOSING CARDS **A card is randomly drawn from a standard deck of 52 cards. Find the probability of drawing the given card.**

11. The king of diamonds
12. A king
13. A spade
14. A black card
15. A card other than a 2
16. A face card (a king, queen, or jack)

EXAMPLE 2 on p. 699 for Exs. 17–19

LOTTERIES **In Exercises 17 and 18, find the probability of winning the lottery according to the given rules. Assume numbers are selected at random.**

17. You must correctly select 6 out of 48 numbers. The order of the numbers is not important.
18. You must correctly select 4 numbers, each an integer from 0 to 9. The order of the numbers is important.

19. ★ **MULTIPLE CHOICE** What is the probability (rounded to three decimal places) that 2 randomly selected months both have 31 days?

(A) 0.159 (B) 0.227 (C) 0.318 (D) 0.340

EXAMPLE 3 on p. 700 for Exs. 20–25

ODDS **You randomly choose a marble from a bag. The bag contains 10 black, 8 red, 4 white, and 6 blue marbles. Find the indicated odds.**

20. In favor of choosing white
21. In favor of choosing blue
22. Against choosing red
23. Against choosing black

ERROR ANALYSIS ***Describe*** **and correct the error in calculating the odds against getting a 5 or 6 when rolling a six-sided die.**

24. Odds against 5 or 6 $= \frac{4}{6} = \frac{2}{3}$ ✗

25. Odds against 5 or 6 $= \frac{2}{4} = \frac{1}{2}$ ✗

26. ★ **OPEN-ENDED MATH** Flip a coin 10 times. What is the experimental probability of getting heads?

27. ★ **SHORT RESPONSE** The probability of event A is 0.3. What are the odds in favor of event A? *Explain.*

EXAMPLE 4 on p. 700 for Exs. 28–32

ROLLING A DIE **The results of rolling a six-sided die 150 times are shown. Use the table to find the experimental probability of the given event.** ***Compare*** **your answer to the theoretical probability of the event.**

28. Rolling a 5
29. Rolling an even number
30. Rolling a number less than 5
31. Rolling any number but a 3

Roll	⚀	⚁	⚂	⚃	⚄	⚅
Number of occurrences	27	22	18	26	27	30

32. ★ **MULTIPLE CHOICE** You flip a coin 80 times. You get heads 37 times and tails 43 times. What is the experimental probability of getting heads?

(A) 0.4625 (B) 0.5 (C) 0.5375 (D) 0.8605

33. **REASONING** Find the probability that the vertex of the graph of $y = x^2 - 6x + c$ is above the x-axis if c is a randomly chosen integer from 1 to 20.

○ = WORKED-OUT SOLUTIONS on p. WS1

★ = STANDARDIZED TEST PRACTICE

= MULTIPLE REPRESENTATIONS

34. **CHALLENGE** Suppose you throw a dart at each square target below. Assume that the dart is equally likely to hit any point inside the target.

Target A

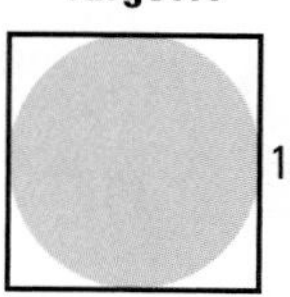

Target B

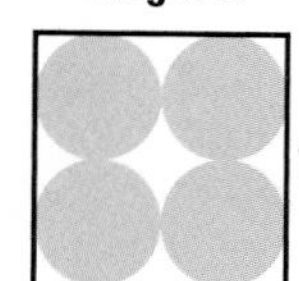

Target C

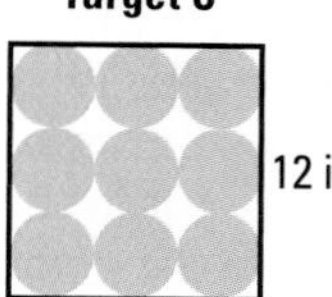

a. **Calculate** What is the probability that the dart lands inside the circle in target A? inside a circle in target B? inside a circle in target C?

b. **Generalize** Consider the general case where a square target with sides 12 inches long contains n^2 identical circles arranged in n rows and n columns. Make a conjecture about the probability that a dart lands inside one of the circles. Then prove your conjecture.

PROBLEM SOLVING

EXAMPLE 5 on p. 701 for Exs. 35–37

GEOMETRIC PROBABILITY Find the probability that a dart thrown at the given target will hit the shaded region. Assume the dart is equally likely to hit any point inside the target.

35. 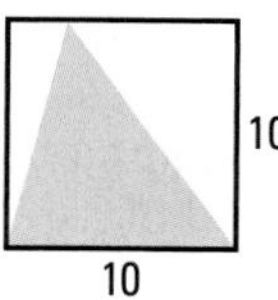

36. 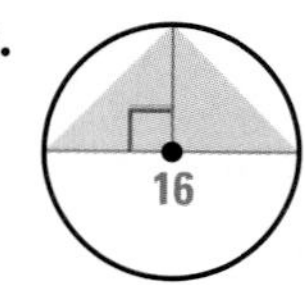

37. 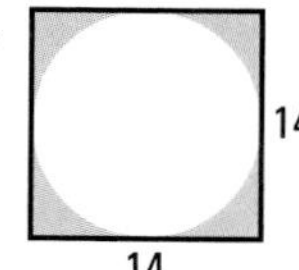

@HomeTutor for problem solving help at classzone.com

38. **JURY SELECTION** A jury of 12 people is selected from a pool of 30 people that includes 12 men and 18 women. What is the probability that the jury will be composed of 12 women?

@HomeTutor for problem solving help at classzone.com

39. **ARCHERY** The standard archery target used in competition has a diameter of 80 centimeters. Find the probability that an arrow shot at the target will hit the center circle, which has a diameter of 16 centimeters. Assume the arrow is equally likely to hit any point inside the target.

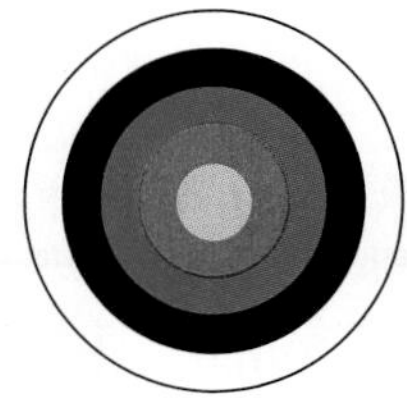

40. **MULTIPLE REPRESENTATIONS** On a typical weekday, there are 1,181,100 one-way trips taken on the public transportation system operated by the Massachusetts Bay Transit Authority. Of these trips, 376,900 are bus rides. Suppose a one-way trip is selected at random.

a. **Using Fractions** What is the probability, expressed as a fraction, that the trip was taken on a bus?

b. **Using Decimals** What is the probability, expressed as a decimal, that the trip was taken on a bus?

c. **Using Percents** What is the probability, expressed as a percent, that the trip was taken on a bus?

d. **Using Odds** What are the odds in favor of the trip having been on a bus?

41. **GULF COAST** The map shows the length of shoreline (in miles) along the Gulf of Mexico for each state that borders the body of water. What is the probability that a ship coming ashore at a random point in the Gulf of Mexico lands in the given state?

a. Texas

b. Florida

c. Alabama

42. ★ **EXTENDED RESPONSE** A magician claims to be able to read minds. To test this claim, five cards numbered 1 through 5 are used. A subject selects two cards from the five cards and concentrates on the numbers.

a. What is the probability that the two numbers chosen are 3 and 4?

b. What is the probability that the magician can correctly identify the two numbers by guessing?

c. Suppose the magician is able to consistently identify the two numbers about half the time. Does this support the magician's claim to be a mind reader? *Explain.*

43. **CHALLENGE** In a guessing game, one player secretly places four different-colored pegs on a board in each of four positions: A, B, C, or D. A second player guesses the configuration of the pegs by placing an identical set of pegs in slots A, B, C, and D on an identical board. The second player is then told how many of the pegs are in the correct slot.

a. What is the probability that the second player has all four pegs correct on the first guess?

b. What is the probability that the second player has exactly one peg correct on the first guess?

c. The second player is told she has placed two pegs in the correct slot. The player then switches two of the pegs. What is the probability that the player now has all four pegs in the correct slot?

NEW YORK MIXED REVIEW

TEST PRACTICE at classzone.com

44. What is the area of the figure shown?

Ⓐ 14 square units

Ⓑ 18 square units

Ⓒ 20 square units

Ⓓ 36 square units

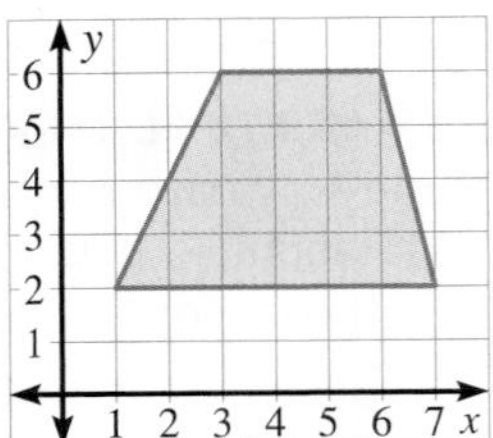

45. What is the midpoint of the line segment connecting points $(-4, -1)$ and $(7, 3)$?

Ⓐ $\left(-\frac{3}{2}, 1\right)$ Ⓑ $\left(\frac{3}{2}, \frac{1}{2}\right)$ Ⓒ $\left(\frac{3}{2}, 1\right)$ Ⓓ $\left(\frac{3}{2}, 2\right)$

EXTRA PRACTICE for Lesson 10.3, p. 1019 **ONLINE QUIZ** at classzone.com

Lessons 10.1–10.3

1. **MOVIE THEATER SEATING** Five people walk into a movie theater and look for empty seats in which to sit. What is the number of ways the people can be seated if there are 8 empty seats?

   (1) 20 (3) 336

   (2) 56 (4) 6720

2. **ARRIVAL TIMES** Every day, Ashley and Juan arrive separately at a gym. Let x and y be their arrival times, respectively, in minutes after 9:00 A.M. If they each arrive at a random time between 9:00 A.M. and 9:30 A.M., the point (x, y) will fall in the shaded square in the graph below.

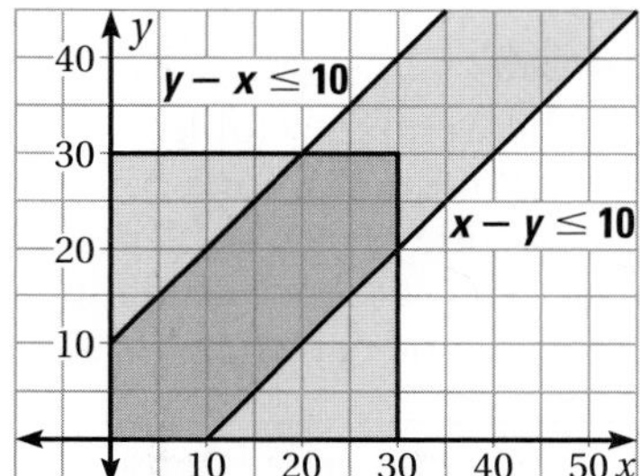

   Whoever arrives first waits for the other for up to 10 minutes before working out alone. The diagonal shaded region represents pairs of arrival times when they meet. What is the approximate probability that Ashley and Juan will meet under these conditions?

   (1) 0.333 (3) 0.556

   (2) 0.444 (4) 0.889

3. **GRADUATION REQUIREMENTS** You must take 18 elective courses to meet your graduation requirements for college. There are 30 courses that you are interested in. How many different course selections are possible?

   (1) 30,045,015

   (2) 86,493,225

   (3) 4.1×10^{16}

   (4) 5.5×10^{23}

4. **OPEN-ENDED** A café that serves fruit smoothies offers 8 different fruits, as shown in the list below.

Available Fruits	
Orange	Strawberry
Banana	Pineapple
Kiwi	Watermelon
Canteloupe	Peach

   How many different smoothies can you make using 3 different fruits?

   How many different smoothies can you make using 5 different fruits?

   Explain the relationship between the values of the two answers.

5. **OPEN-ENDED** The graph shows the results of a survey in 2004 that asked U.S. adults which sport they would most like to participate in at the Summer Olympics.

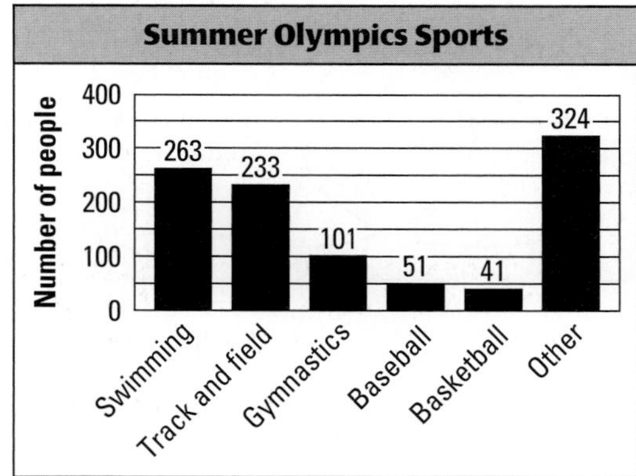

   Find the probability that a randomly selected U.S. adult would like to participate in track and field.

   Is your answer from the previous part a *theoretical* or *experimental* probability? *Explain.*

   What are the odds in favor of a randomly selected U.S. adult preferring to participate in gymnastics?

10.4 Find Probabilities Using Venn Diagrams

QUESTION How can you use a Venn diagram to find probabilities involving two events?

In Lesson 10.3, you learned how to compute the probability of one event. In some situations, however, you might be interested in the probability that two events will occur simultaneously. You also might be interested in the probability that at least one of two events will occur. This activity demonstrates how a Venn diagram is useful for computing such probabilities.

EXPLORE Use a Venn diagram to collect data

STEP 1 *Complete a Venn diagram*
Copy the Venn diagram shown below. Ask the members of your class if they have a sister, have a brother, have both, or have neither. Write their names in the appropriate part of the Venn diagram.

STEP 2 *Complete a table*
Copy and complete the frequency table. When determining the frequency for a category, be sure to include all the students who are in the category. Note that a student can belong to more than one category.

Category	Number of students
Have a sister	?
Have a brother	?
Have both a sister and brother	?
Do not have a sister or brother	?

DRAW CONCLUSIONS Use your data to complete these exercises

1. A student from your class is selected at random. Find the probability of each event. *Explain* how you found your answers.
   a. The student has a sister.
   b. The student has a brother.
   c. The student has a sister and a brother.
   d. The student does not have a sister or a brother.
2. Find the probability that a randomly selected student from your class has either a sister or a brother. *Explain* how you found your answer.
3. How could you calculate the answer to Exercise 2 using your answers from Exercise 1?

10.4 Find Probabilities of Disjoint and Overlapping Events

A2.S.13 Calculate theoretical probabilities, including geometric applications

Before You found probabilities of simple events.

Now You will find probabilities of compound events.

Why? So you can solve problems about meteorology, as in Ex. 44.

Key Vocabulary
- **compound event**
- **overlapping events**
- **disjoint or mutually exclusive events**

When you consider all the outcomes for either of two events A and B, you form the *union* of A and B. When you consider only the outcomes shared by both A and B, you form the *intersection* of A and B. The union or intersection of two events is called a **compound event**.

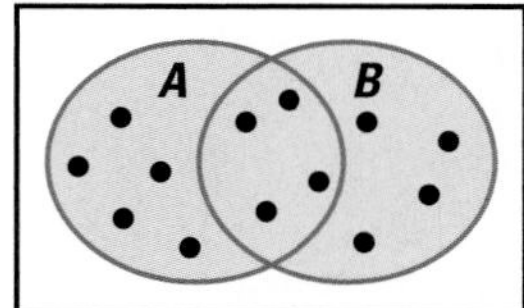

Union of A and B

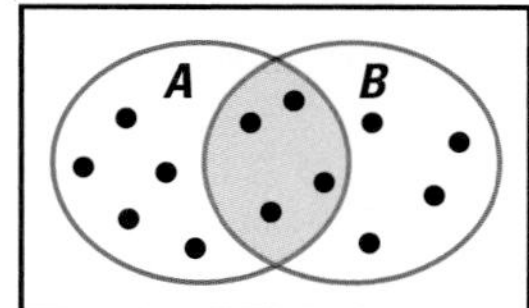

Intersection of A and B

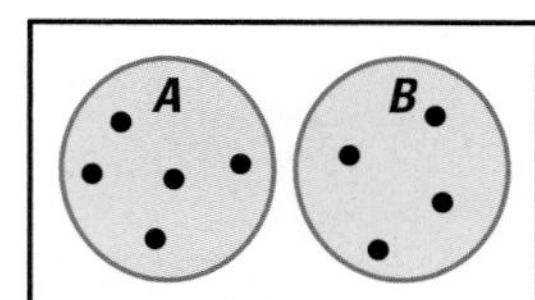

Intersection of A and B is empty.

To find $P(A \text{ or } B)$ you must consider what outcomes, if any, are in the intersection of A and B. Two events are **overlapping** if they have one or more outcomes in common, as shown in the first diagram. Two events are **disjoint**, or **mutually exclusive**, if they have no outcomes in common, as shown in the third diagram.

KEY CONCEPT *For Your Notebook*

Probability of Compound Events

If A and B are any two events, then the probability of A or B is:

$$P(A \text{ or } B) = P(A) + P(B) - P(A \text{ and } B)$$

If A and B are disjoint events, then the probability of A or B is:

$$P(A \text{ or } B) = P(A) + P(B)$$

EXAMPLE 1 Find probability of disjoint events

A card is randomly selected from a standard deck of 52 cards. What is the probability that it is a 10 *or* a face card?

Solution

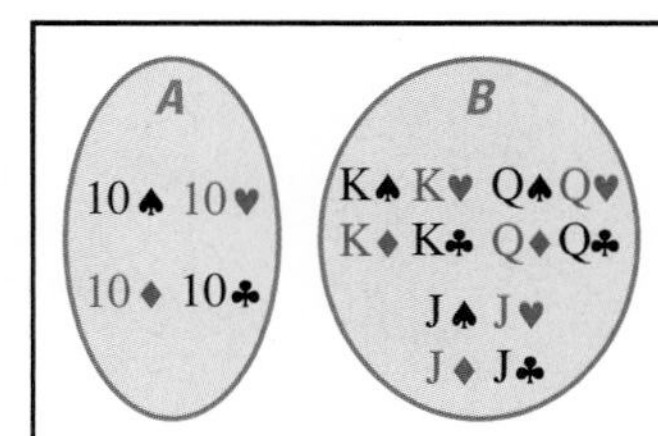

Let event A be selecting a 10 and event B be selecting a face card. A has 4 outcomes and B has 12 outcomes. Because A and B are disjoint, the probability is:

$$P(A \text{ or } B) = P(A) + P(B) = \frac{4}{52} + \frac{12}{52} = \frac{16}{52} = \frac{4}{13} \approx 0.308$$

EXAMPLE 2 Standardized Test Practice

A card is randomly selected from a standard deck of 52 cards. What is the probability that it is a face card *or* a spade?

Ⓐ $\frac{3}{52}$ Ⓑ $\frac{11}{26}$ Ⓒ $\frac{25}{52}$ Ⓓ $\frac{7}{13}$

Solution

AVOID ERRORS
When two events A and B overlap, as in Example 2, $P(A \text{ or } B)$ does not equal $P(A) + P(B)$.

Let event A be selecting a face card and event B be selecting a spade. A has 12 outcomes and B has 13 outcomes. Of these, 3 outcomes are common to A and B. So, the probability of selecting a face card *or* a spade is:

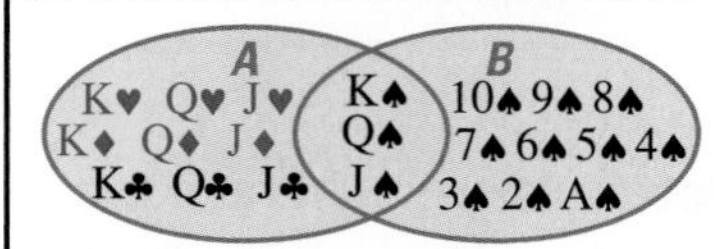

$$P(A \text{ or } B) = P(A) + P(B) - P(A \text{ and } B) = \frac{12}{52} + \frac{13}{52} - \frac{3}{52} = \frac{22}{52} = \frac{11}{26}$$

▶ The correct answer is B. Ⓐ Ⓑ Ⓒ Ⓓ

EXAMPLE 3 Use a formula to find *P*(*A* and *B*)

SENIOR CLASS Out of 200 students in a senior class, 113 students are either varsity athletes *or* on the honor roll. There are 74 seniors who are varsity athletes and 51 seniors who are on the honor roll. What is the probability that a randomly selected senior is both a varsity athlete *and* on the honor roll?

Solution

Let event A be selecting a senior who is a varsity athlete and event B be selecting a senior on the honor roll. From the given information you know that $P(A) = \frac{74}{200}$, $P(B) = \frac{51}{200}$, and $P(A \text{ or } B) = \frac{113}{200}$. Find $P(A \text{ and } B)$.

$P(A \text{ or } B) = P(A) + P(B) - P(A \text{ and } B)$ **Write general formula.**

$\frac{113}{200} = \frac{74}{200} + \frac{51}{200} - P(A \text{ and } B)$ **Substitute known probabilities.**

$P(A \text{ and } B) = \frac{74}{200} + \frac{51}{200} - \frac{113}{200}$ **Solve for *P*(*A* and *B*).**

$P(A \text{ and } B) = \frac{12}{200} = \frac{3}{50} = 0.06$ **Simplify.**

✓ GUIDED PRACTICE for Examples 1, 2, and 3

A card is randomly selected from a standard deck of 52 cards. Find the probability of the given event.

1. Selecting an ace *or* an eight
2. Selecting a 10 *or* a diamond
3. **WHAT IF?** In Example 3, suppose 32 seniors are in the band and 64 seniors are in the band *or* on the honor roll. What is the probability that a randomly selected senior is both in the band *and* on the honor roll?

COMPLEMENTS The event $\overline{A}$, called the *complement* of event A, consists of all outcomes that are not in A. The notation $\overline{A}$ is read as "A bar."

KEY CONCEPT *For Your Notebook*

Probability of the Complement of an Event

The probability of the complement of A is $P(\overline{A}) = 1 - P(A)$.

EXAMPLE 4 Find probabilities of complements

ANOTHER WAY
For an alternative method for solving the problem in Example 4, turn to page 714 for the **Problem Solving Workshop**.

DICE When two six-sided dice are rolled, there are 36 possible outcomes, as shown. Find the probability of the given event.

a. The sum is not 6.

b. The sum is less than or equal to 9.

Solution

a. $P(\text{sum is not 6}) = 1 - P(\text{sum is 6}) = 1 - \frac{5}{36} = \frac{31}{36} \approx 0.861$

b. $P(\text{sum} \le 9) = 1 - P(\text{sum} > 9) = 1 - \frac{6}{36} = \frac{30}{36} = \frac{5}{6} \approx 0.833$

EXAMPLE 5 Use a complement in real life

FORTUNE COOKIES A restaurant gives a free fortune cookie to every guest. The restaurant claims there are 500 different messages hidden inside the fortune cookies. What is the probability that a group of 5 people receive at least 2 fortune cookies with the same message inside?

Solution

The number of ways to give messages to the 5 people is 500^5. The number of ways to give *different* messages to the 5 people is $500 \cdot 499 \cdot 498 \cdot 497 \cdot 496$. So, the probability that at least 2 of the 5 people have the same message is:

$$P(\text{at least 2 are the same}) = 1 - P(\text{none are the same})$$

$$= 1 - \frac{500 \cdot 499 \cdot 498 \cdot 497 \cdot 496}{500^5}$$

$$\approx 0.0199$$

GUIDED PRACTICE for Examples 4 and 5

Find $P(\overline{A})$.

4. $P(A) = 0.45$

5. $P(A) = \frac{1}{4}$

6. $P(A) = 1$

7. $P(A) = 0.03$

8. WHAT IF? In Example 5, how does the answer change if there are only 100 different messages hidden inside the fortune cookies?

10.4 EXERCISES

HOMEWORK KEY

○ = **WORKED-OUT SOLUTIONS** on p. WS18 for Exs. 11, 21, and 45

★ = **STANDARDIZED TEST PRACTICE** Exs. 2, 15, 34, 39, 40, 44, and 47

SKILL PRACTICE

1. **VOCABULARY** Copy and complete: The union or intersection of two events is called a(n) __?__.

2. ★ **WRITING** Are the events A and $\overline{A}$ disjoint? *Explain.* Then give an example of a real-life event and its complement.

EXAMPLE 1 on p. 707 for Exs. 3–8

DISJOINT EVENTS **Events A and B are disjoint. Find $P(A \text{ or } B)$.**

3. $P(A) = 0.3, P(B) = 0.1$
4. $P(A) = 0.55, P(B) = 0.2$
5. $P(A) = 0.41, P(B) = 0.24$
6. $P(A) = \frac{2}{5}, P(B) = \frac{3}{5}$
7. $P(A) = \frac{1}{3}, P(B) = \frac{1}{4}$
8. $P(A) = \frac{2}{3}, P(B) = \frac{1}{5}$

EXAMPLES 2 and 3 on p. 708 for Exs. 9–15

OVERLAPPING EVENTS **Find the indicated probability.**

9. $P(A) = 0.5, P(B) = 0.35$
   $P(A \text{ and } B) = 0.2$
   $P(A \text{ or } B) =$ __?__
10. $P(A) = 0.6, P(B) = 0.2$
   $P(A \text{ or } B) = 0.7$
   $P(A \text{ and } B) =$ __?__
11. $P(A) = 0.28, P(B) = 0.64$
   $P(A \text{ or } B) = 0.71$
   $P(A \text{ and } B) =$ __?__
12. $P(A) = 0.46, P(B) = 0.37$
   $P(A \text{ and } B) = 0.31$
   $P(A \text{ or } B) =$ __?__
13. $P(A) = \frac{2}{7}, P(B) = \frac{4}{7}$
   $P(A \text{ and } B) = \frac{1}{7}$
   $P(A \text{ or } B) =$ __?__
14. $P(A) = \frac{6}{11}, P(B) = \frac{3}{11}$
   $P(A \text{ or } B) = \frac{7}{11}$
   $P(A \text{ and } B) =$ __?__

15. ★ **MULTIPLE CHOICE** What is $P(A \text{ or } B)$ if $P(A) = 0.41$, $P(B) = 0.53$, and $P(A \text{ and } B) = 0.27$?

Ⓐ 0.12 Ⓑ 0.67 Ⓒ 0.80 Ⓓ 0.94

EXAMPLE 4 on p. 709 for Exs. 16–19

FINDING PROBABILITIES OF COMPLEMENTS **Find $P(\overline{A})$.**

16. $P(A) = 0.5$
17. $P(A) = 0$
18. $P(A) = \frac{1}{3}$
19. $P(A) = \frac{5}{8}$

CHOOSING CARDS **A card is randomly selected from a standard deck of 52 cards. Find the probability of drawing the given card.**

20. A king *and* a diamond
21. A king *or* a diamond
22. A spade *or* a club
23. A 4 *or* a 5
24. A 6 *and* a face card
25. *Not* a heart

ERROR ANALYSIS ***Describe*** **and correct the error in finding the probability of randomly drawing the given card from a standard deck of 52 cards.**

26.

P(heart or face card)

$= P(\text{heart}) + P(\text{face card})$

$= \frac{13}{52} + \frac{12}{52}$

$= \frac{25}{52}$

27.

P(club or 9)

$= P(\text{club}) + P(9) + P(\text{club and } 9)$

$= \frac{13}{52} + \frac{4}{52} + \frac{1}{52}$

$= \frac{9}{26}$

FINDING PROBABILITIES Find the indicated probability. State whether A and B are disjoint events.

28. $P(A) = 0.25$
$P(B) = 0.4$
$P(A \text{ or } B) = 0.50$
$P(A \text{ and } B) = \underline{\ ?\ }$

29. $P(A) = 0.6$
$P(B) = 0.32$
$P(A \text{ or } B) = \underline{\ ?\ }$
$P(A \text{ and } B) = 0.25$

30. $P(A) = \underline{\ ?\ }$
$P(B) = 0.38$
$P(A \text{ or } B) = 0.65$
$P(A \text{ and } B) = 0$

31. $P(A) = \frac{8}{15}$
$P(B) = \underline{\ ?\ }$
$P(A \text{ or } B) = \frac{3}{5}$
$P(A \text{ and } B) = \frac{2}{15}$

32. $P(A) = \frac{1}{2}$
$P(B) = \frac{1}{6}$
$P(A \text{ or } B) = \frac{2}{3}$
$P(A \text{ and } B) = \underline{\ ?\ }$

33. $P(A) = 16\%$
$P(B) = \underline{\ ?\ }$
$P(A \text{ or } B) = 32\%$
$P(A \text{ and } B) = 8\%$

34. ★ **OPEN-ENDED MATH** *Describe* a real-life situation that involves two disjoint events A and B. Then describe a real-life situation that involves two overlapping events C and D.

ROLLING DICE Two six-sided dice are rolled. Find the probability of the given event. (Refer to Example 4 on page 709 for the possible outcomes.)

35. The sum is 3 or 4.

36. The sum is not 7.

37. The sum is greater than or equal to 5.

38. The sum is less than 8 or greater than 11.

39. ★ **MULTIPLE CHOICE** Two six-sided dice are rolled. What is the probability that the sum is a prime number?

(A) $\frac{13}{36}$ (B) $\frac{7}{18}$ (C) $\frac{5}{12}$ (D) $\frac{5}{11}$

40. ★ **SHORT RESPONSE** Use the first diagram at the right to explain why this equation is true:

$$P(A) + P(B) = P(A \text{ or } B) + P(A \text{ and } B)$$

41. CHALLENGE Use the second diagram at the right to derive a formula for $P(A \text{ or } B \text{ or } C)$.

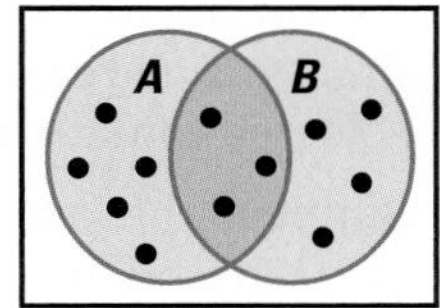

Ex. 40

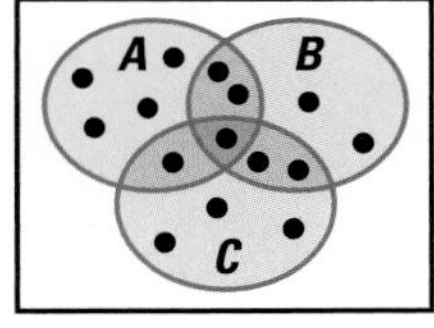

Ex. 41

PROBLEM SOLVING

EXAMPLES 1, 2, and 3 on pp. 707–708 for Exs. 42–44

42. CLASS ELECTIONS You and your best friend are among several candidates running for class president. You estimate that there is a 45% chance you will win and a 25% chance your best friend will win. What is the probability that either you or your best friend win the election?

@HomeTutor for problem solving help at classzone.com

43. BIOLOGY You are performing an experiment to determine how well plants grow under different light sources. Out of the 30 plants in the experiment, 12 receive visible light, 15 receive ultraviolet light, and 6 receive both visible and ultraviolet light. What is the probability that a plant in the experiment receives either visible light or ultraviolet light?

Animated Algebra at classzone.com

EXAMPLES 4 and 5
on p. 709 for Exs. 44–46

44. ★ **MULTIPLE CHOICE** Refer to the chart below. Which of the following probabilities is greatest?

(A) P(rains on Sunday)
(B) P(does not rain on Saturday)
(C) P(rains on Monday)
(D) P(does not rain on Friday)

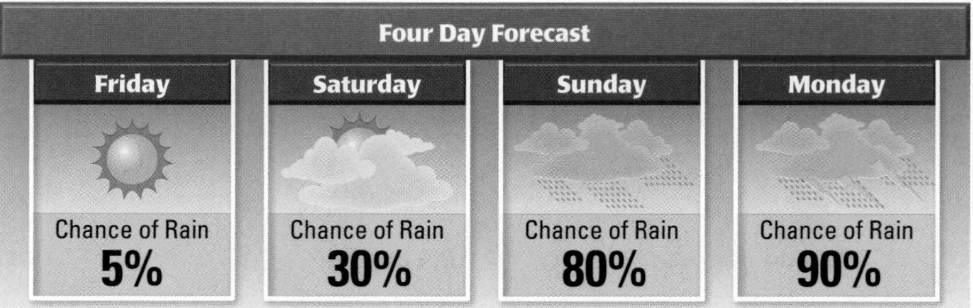

45. **DRAMA CLUB** The organizer of a cast party for a drama club asks each of 6 cast members to bring one food item from a list of 10 items. What is the probability that at least 2 of the 6 cast members bring the same item?

46. **HOME ELECTRONICS** A development has 6 houses with the same model of garage door opener. Each opener has 4096 possible transmitter codes. What is the probability that at least 2 of the 6 houses have the same code?

47. ★ **EXTENDED RESPONSE** Use the given information about a farmer's tomato crop to complete parts (a)–(c).

a. 40% of the tomatoes are partially rotten, 30% of the tomatoes have been fed on by insects, and 12% are partially rotten *and* have been fed on by insects. What is the probability that a randomly selected tomato is partially rotten *or* has been fed on by insects?

b. 20% of the tomatoes have bite marks from a chipmunk and 7% have bite marks *and* are partially rotten. What is the probability that a randomly selected tomato has bite marks *or* is partially rotten?

c. Suppose the farmer finds out that 6% of the tomatoes have bite marks *and* have been fed on by insects. Do you have enough information to determine the probability that a randomly selected tomato has been fed on by insects *or* is partially rotten *or* has bite marks from a chipmunk? If not, what other information do you require?

48. **MULTI-STEP PROBLEM** Follow the steps below to explore a famous probability problem called the *birthday problem.* (Assume that there are 365 possible birthdays.)

a. **Calculate** Suppose that 6 people are chosen at random. Find the probability that at least 2 of the people share the same birthday.

b. **Calculate** Suppose that 10 people are chosen at random. Find the probability that at least 2 of the people share the same birthday.

c. **Model** Generalize the results from parts (a) and (b) by writing a formula for the probability $P(x)$ that at least 2 people in a group of x people share the same birthday. (*Hint:* Use ${}_nP_r$ notation in your formula.)

d. **Analyze** Enter the formula from part (c) into a graphing calculator. Use the *table* feature to make a table of values. For what group size does the probability that at least 2 people share the same birthday first exceed 50%?

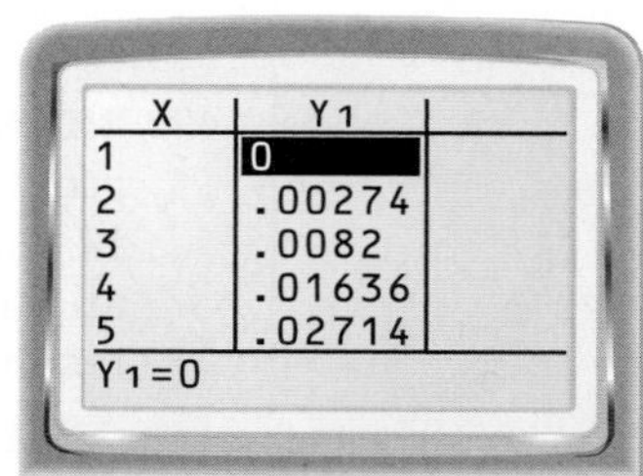

○ = WORKED-OUT SOLUTIONS on p. WS1
★ = STANDARDIZED TEST PRACTICE

49. **PET STORE** A pet store has 8 black Labrador retriever puppies (5 females and 3 males) and 12 yellow Labrador retriever puppies (4 females and 8 males). You randomly choose one of the Labrador retriever puppies. What is the probability that it is a female or a yellow Labrador retriever?

50. **CHALLENGE** You own 50 DVDs consisting of 25 comedies, 15 dramas, and 10 thrillers. You randomly pick 4 movies to watch during a long train ride. What is the probability that you pick at least one DVD of each type of movie?

NEW YORK MIXED REVIEW

TEST PRACTICE at classzone.com

51. Amy and 7 other students have a bowling party for the math club. The club will pay for bowling, shoe rental, and snacks for all 8 students. The total cost must be at most \$80. Each person bowls the same number of games. What is the maximum number of games that each student can bowl?

Bowling	\$2.70 per person, per game
Shoe rental	\$1.25 per person
Snacks	\$2.80 per person

(A) 1 (B) 2 (C) 3 (D) 4

52. A centrifuge used to train pilots can move 98 ft/sec while making 47 rotations per minute (rpm). If the centrifuge is moving 80 ft/sec, what is a reasonable estimate of its rotational speed?

(A) 38.4 rpm (B) 39.6 rpm (C) 57.6 rpm (D) 166.8 rpm

QUIZ *for Lessons 10.3–10.4*

A card is randomly drawn from a standard deck of 52 cards. Find the probability of drawing the given card. *(p. 698)*

1. The queen of hearts
2. An ace
3. A diamond
4. A red card
5. A card other than a 10
6. The 6 of clubs

You randomly select a marble from a bag. The bag contains 8 black, 13 red, 7 white, and 12 blue marbles. Find the indicated odds. *(p. 698)*

7. In favor of choosing blue
8. In favor of choosing black or white
9. Against choosing red
10. Against choosing red or white

Find the indicated probability. *(p. 707)*

11. $P(A) = 0.6$
$P(B) = 0.35$
$P(A \text{ or } B) = \underline{\ ?\ }$
$P(A \text{ and } B) = 0.2$

12. $P(A) = \underline{\ ?\ }$
$P(B) = 0.44$
$P(A \text{ or } B) = 0.56$
$P(A \text{ and } B) = 0.12$

13. $P(A) = 0.75$
$P(B) = \underline{\ ?\ }$
$P(A \text{ or } B) = 0.83$
$P(A \text{ and } B) = 0.25$

14. $P(A) = 8\%$
$P(B) = 33\%$
$P(A \text{ or } B) = 41\%$
$P(A \text{ and } B) = \underline{\ ?\ }$

15. **COMPUTERS** A manufacturer of computer chips finds that 1% of the chips produced are defective. What is the probability that out of 8 chips, at least 2 are defective? *(p. 707)*

PROBLEM SOLVING WORKSHOP
LESSON 10.4

Using ALTERNATIVE METHODS

Another Way to Solve Example 4, page 709

MULTIPLE REPRESENTATIONS In Example 4 on page 709, you found theoretical probabilities involving the sum of two dice. You can also perform a *simulation* to estimate these probabilities.

PROBLEM

DICE When two six-sided dice are rolled, there are 36 possible outcomes. Find the probability of the given event.

a. The sum is not 6.

b. The sum is less than or equal to 9.

METHOD

Using a Simulation An alternative approach is to use the random number feature of a graphing calculator to simulate rolling two dice. You can then use the results of the simulation to find the experimental probabilities for the problem.

STEP 1 **Generate** two lists of 120 random integers from 1 to 6 by entering randInt(1,6,120) into lists L_1 and L_2. Define list L_3 to be the sum of lists L_1 and L_2.

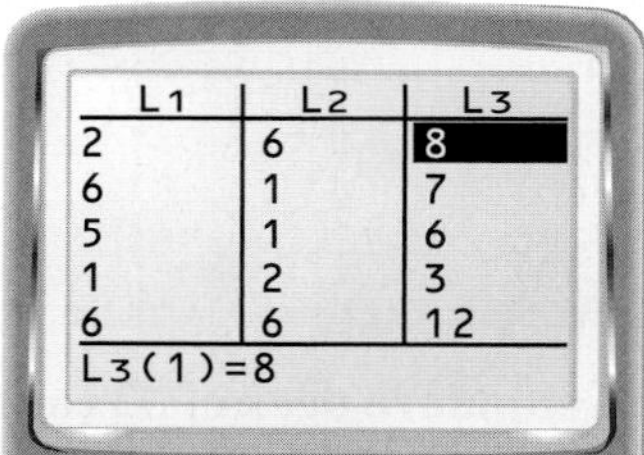

L1	L2	L3
2	6	8
6	1	7
5	1	6
1	2	3
6	6	12

L3(1)=8

STEP 2 **Sort** the sums in list L_3 in ascending order using the command SortA(L_3). Scroll through the list and count the frequency of each sum.

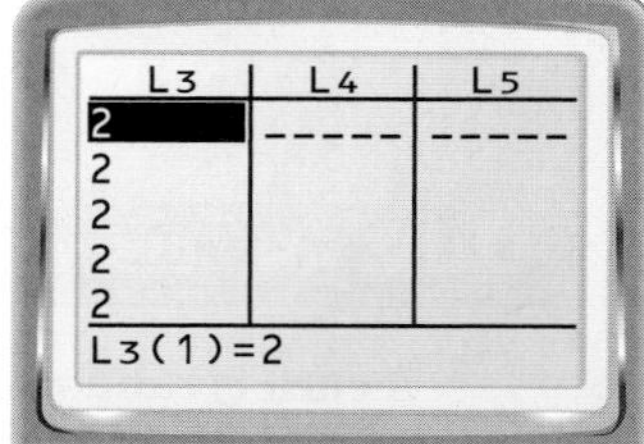

L3	L4	L5
2	-----	-----
2		
2		
2		
2		

L3(1)=2

STEP 3 **Find** the probabilities.

a. Divide the number of times the sum was 6 by the total number of simulated rolls, then subtract the result from 1.

b. Divide the number of times the sum was greater than 9 by the total number of simulated rolls, then subtract the result from 1.

PRACTICE

1. **WRITING** *Compare* the probabilities found in the simulation above with the theoretical probabilities found in Example 4 on page 709.

2. **SIMULATIONS** Use the results of the simulation above to find the experimental probability that the sum is greater than or equal to 4. *Compare* this to the theoretical probability of the event.

3. **SIMULATIONS** Use the results of the simulation above to find the experimental probability that the sum is not 8 or 9. *Compare* this to the theoretical probability of the event.

4. **REASONING** How could you change the simulation above so that the results would be closer to the theoretical probabilities of the events? *Explain.*

Extension
Use after Lesson 10.4

Apply Set Theory

GOAL Define the concepts of sets, operations on sets, and subsets.

Key Vocabulary
- set
- union
- intersection
- complement
- subset

A **set** is a collection of distinct objects. Each object in a set is called an **element** or **member** of the set. A set is denoted by enclosing its elements in braces. For example, if A is the set of positive integers less than 5, then $A = \{1, 2, 3, 4\}$.

There are two special sets that are often used. The set with no elements is called the **empty set** and is denoted by $\emptyset$. The set of all elements under consideration is called the **universal set** and is denoted by U.

KEY CONCEPT — For Your Notebook

Operations on Sets

The **union** of two sets A and B is written as $A \cup B$ and is the set of all elements in *either* A or B.

$A \cup B$

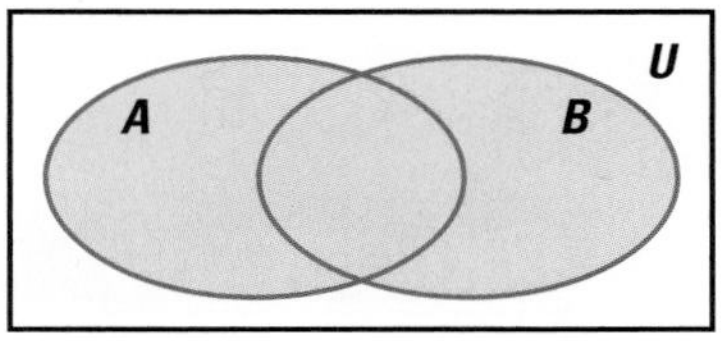

The **intersection** of two sets A and B is written as $A \cap B$ and is the set of all elements in *both* A and B.

$A \cap B$

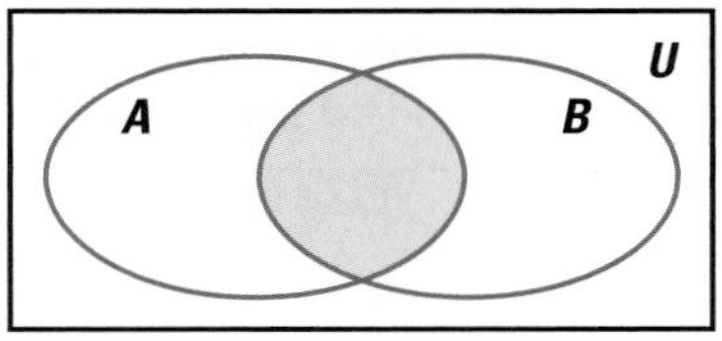

The **complement** of a set A is written as $\overline{A}$ and is the set of all elements in the universal set U that are *not* in A.

$\overline{A}$

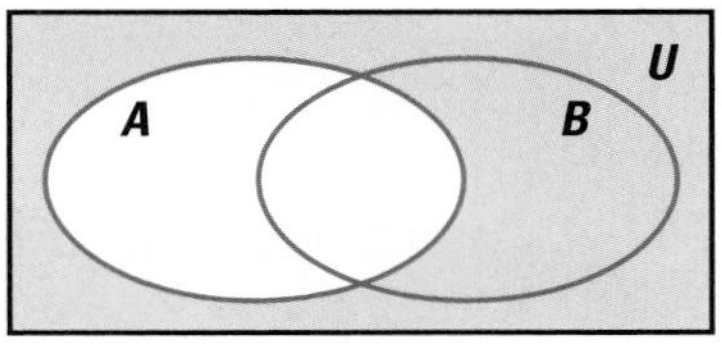

EXAMPLE 1 Perform operations on sets

Let U be the set of all integers from 1 to 10. Let $A = \{1, 2, 4, 8\}$ and let $B = \{2, 4, 6, 8, 10\}$. Find the indicated set.

a. $A \cup B$ **b.** $A \cap B$ **c.** $\overline{A}$ **d.** $\overline{A \cup B}$

Solution

a. $A \cup B = \{1, 2, 4, 8\} \cup \{2, 4, 6, 8, 10\} = \{1, 2, 4, 6, 8, 10\}$

b. $A \cap B = \{1, 2, 4, 8\} \cap \{2, 4, 6, 8, 10\} = \{2, 4, 8\}$

c. $\overline{A} = \overline{\{1, 2, 4, 8\}} = \{3, 5, 6, 7, 9, 10\}$

d. $\overline{A \cup B} = \overline{\{1, 2, 4, 8\} \cup \{2, 4, 6, 8, 10\}} = \overline{\{1, 2, 4, 6, 8, 10\}} = \{3, 5, 7, 9\}$

SUBSETS If every element of a set A is also an element of a set B, then A is a **subset** of B. This relationship is written as $A \subseteq B$. For any set A, $\emptyset \subseteq A$ and $A \subseteq A$. In the diagram at the right, A is a subset of B.

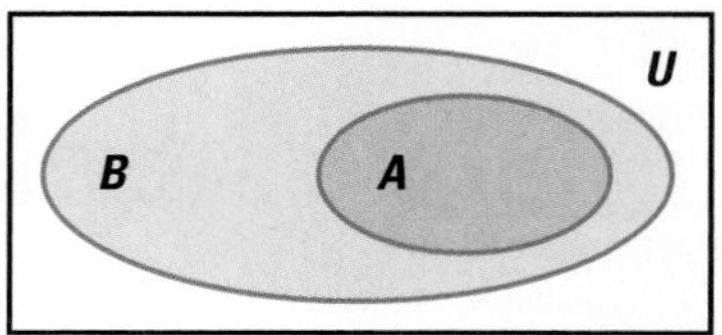

EXAMPLE 2 Identify subsets

Let $A = \{-2, 1, \sqrt{3}, \pi\}$, $B = \{1, \pi, 5\}$, and $C = \{-2, 1, 3, \pi, 5\}$.

a. Is $B \subseteq A$?   **b.** Is $B \subseteq C$?   **c.** Is $C \subseteq (A \cup B)$?

Solution

a. Not every element of B is an element of A, because 5 is not an element of A. So, B is *not* a subset of A.

b. Every element of B is an element of C. So, B *is* a subset of C.

c. Note that $A \cup B = \{-2, 1, \sqrt{3}, \pi\} \cup \{1, \pi, 5\} = \{-2, 1, \sqrt{3}, \pi, 5\}$. Not every element of C is an element of $A \cup B$, because 3 is not an element of $A \cup B$. So, C is *not* a subset of $A \cup B$.

PRACTICE

EXAMPLE 1 on p. 715 for Exs. 1–8

OPERATIONS ON SETS Let U be the set of all whole numbers from 1 to 20. Let $A = \{2, 3, 5, 7, 11, 13, 17\}$, $B = \{1, 4, 9, 16\}$, and $C = \{2, 5, 8, 11, 14, 17, 20\}$. Find the indicated set.

1. $A \cup B$
2. $A \cap B$
3. $\overline{A}$
4. $\overline{B}$
5. $A \cup B \cup C$
6. $\overline{A} \cap C$
7. $\overline{C \cup B}$
8. $B \cup (A \cap C)$

EXAMPLE 2 on p. 716 for Exs. 9–12

SUBSETS Let $A = \{-5, \pi, 10\}$, $B = \{-5, 1, \sqrt{5}, 10\}$, and $C = \{-5, 2, \pi, 10\}$.

9. Is $A \subseteq B$?
10. Is $A \subseteq C$?
11. Is $(A \cap B) \subseteq C$?

12. **REASONING** List all the subsets of the set $A = \{-2, 4, 9\}$.

OPERATIONS ON SETS Consider the sets defined below. Find the indicated set.

$U =$ the set of all 12 months $X =$ the set of all 30 day months

$Y =$ the set of all 31 day months $Z =$ the set of all months ending with "r"

13. $X \cup Z$
14. $X \cap Y$
15. $\overline{Z}$
16. $\overline{X \cup Y}$

17. **REASONING** Is the set of all irrational numbers a subset of the real numbers? of the integers? *Explain.*

18. **RADIO** Two radio towers are set up at points A and B on the map at the right. Each radio tower has a signal that can reach towns up to 50 miles away. Find the set of all towns that can receive a signal from both of the towers.

Animated Algebra at classzone.com

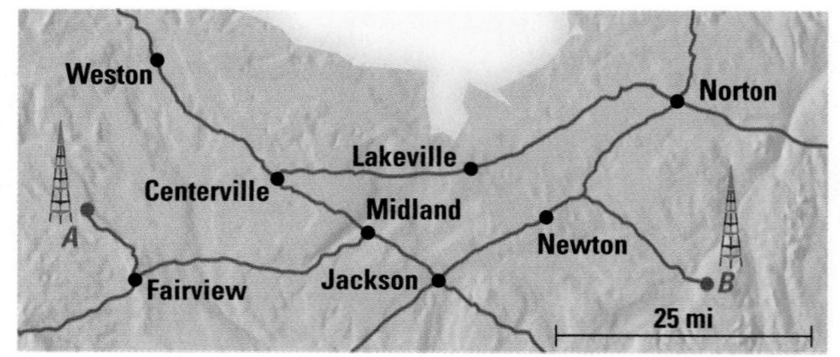

10.5 Find Probabilities of Independent and Dependent Events

 **A2.S.13** Calculate theoretical probabilities, including geometric applications

Before You found probabilities of compound events.

Now You will examine independent and dependent events.

Why? So you can formulate coaching strategies, as in Ex. 41.

Key Vocabulary
- **independent events**
- **dependent events**
- **conditional probability**

Two events are **independent** if the occurrence of one has no effect on the occurrence of the other. For instance, if a coin is tossed twice, the outcome of the first toss (heads or tails) has no effect on the outcome of the second toss.

KEY CONCEPT *For Your Notebook*

Probability of Independent Events

If A and B are independent events, then the probability that both A and B occur is:

$$P(A \text{ and } B) = P(A) \cdot P(B)$$

More generally, the probability that n independent events occur is the product of the n probabilities of the individual events.

EXAMPLE 1 **Standardized Test Practice**

For a fundraiser, a class sells 150 raffle tickets for a mall gift certificate and 200 raffle tickets for a booklet of movie passes. You buy 5 raffle tickets for each prize. What is the probability that you win both prizes?

Ⓐ $\frac{1}{6000}$ Ⓑ $\frac{1}{1200}$ Ⓒ $\frac{1}{350}$ Ⓓ $\frac{1}{70}$

Solution

Let events A and B be getting the winning ticket for the gift certificate and movie passes, respectively. The events are independent. So, the probability is:

$$P(A \text{ and } B) = P(A) \cdot P(B) = \frac{5}{150} \cdot \frac{5}{200} = \frac{1}{30} \cdot \frac{1}{40} = \frac{1}{1200}$$

▶ The correct answer is B. Ⓐ Ⓑ Ⓒ Ⓓ

 **GUIDED PRACTICE** for Example 1

1. **WHAT IF?** In Example 1, what is the probability that you win the mall gift certificate but not the booklet of movie passes?

EXAMPLE 2 Find probability of three independent events

RACING In a BMX meet, each heat consists of 8 competitors who are randomly assigned lanes from 1 to 8. What is the probability that a racer will draw lane 8 in the 3 heats in which the racer participates?

Solution

Let events A, B, and C be drawing lane 8 in the **first**, **second**, and **third** heats, respectively. The three events are independent. So, the probability is:

$$P(A \text{ and } B \text{ and } C) = P(A) \cdot P(B) \cdot P(C) = \frac{1}{8} \cdot \frac{1}{8} \cdot \frac{1}{8} = \frac{1}{512} \approx 0.00195$$

EXAMPLE 3 Use a complement to find a probability

MUSIC While you are riding to school, your portable CD player randomly plays 4 different songs from a CD with 16 songs on it. What is the probability that you will hear your favorite song on the CD at least once during the week (5 days)?

Solution

For one day, the probability of *not* hearing your favorite song is:

$$P(\text{not hearing song}) = \frac{{}_{15}C_4}{{}_{16}C_4}$$

Hearing or not hearing your favorite song on Monday, on Tuesday, and so on are independent events. So, the probability of hearing the song at least once is:

$$P(\text{hearing song}) = 1 - [P(\text{not hearing song})]^5 = 1 - \left(\frac{{}_{15}C_4}{{}_{16}C_4}\right)^5 \approx 0.763$$

GUIDED PRACTICE for Examples 2 and 3

2. **SPINNER** A spinner is divided into ten equal regions numbered 1 to 10. What is the probability that 3 consecutive spins result in perfect squares?

3. **WHAT IF?** In Example 3, how does your answer change if the CD has only 12 songs on it?

CONDITIONAL PROBABILITIES
The conditional probability of B given A can be greater than, less than, or equal to the probability of B.

DEPENDENT EVENTS Two events A and B are **dependent events** if the occurrence of one affects the occurrence of the other. The probability that B will occur given that A has occurred is called the **conditional probability** of B given A and is written as $P(B|A)$.

KEY CONCEPT *For Your Notebook*

Probability of Dependent Events

If A and B are dependent events, then the probability that both A and B occur is:

$$P(A \text{ and } B) = P(A) \cdot P(B|A)$$

EXAMPLE 4 Find a conditional probability

WEATHER The table shows the numbers of tropical cyclones that formed during the hurricane seasons from 1988 to 2004. Use the table to estimate **(a)** the probability that a future tropical cyclone is a hurricane and **(b)** the probability that a future tropical cyclone in the Northern Hemisphere is a hurricane.

Type of Tropical Cyclone	Northern Hemisphere	Southern Hemisphere
Tropical depression	199	18
Tropical storm	398	200
Hurricane	545	215

Solution

a. $P(\text{hurricane}) = \dfrac{\text{Number of hurricanes}}{\text{Total number of cyclones}} = \dfrac{760}{1575} \approx 0.483$

b. $P(\text{hurricane} \mid \text{Northern Hemisphere})$

$$= \frac{\text{Number of hurricanes in Northern Hemisphere}}{\text{Total number of cyclones in Northern Hemisphere}} = \frac{545}{1142} \approx 0.477$$

EXAMPLE 5 Comparing independent and dependent events

SELECTING CARDS You randomly select two cards from a standard deck of 52 cards. What is the probability that the first card is not a heart and the second is a heart if **(a)** you replace the first card before selecting the second, and **(b)** you do *not* replace the first card?

Solution

AVOID ERRORS
It is important to first determine whether *A* and *B* are independent or dependent in order to calculate *P*(*A* and *B*) correctly.

Let *A* be "the first card is not a heart" and *B* be "the second card is a heart."

a. If you replace the first card before selecting the second card, then *A* and *B* are independent events. So, the probability is:

$$P(A \text{ and } B) = P(A) \cdot P(B) = \frac{39}{52} \cdot \frac{13}{52} = \frac{3}{16} \approx 0.188$$

b. If you do not replace the first card before selecting the second card, then *A* and *B* are dependent events. So, the probability is:

$$P(A \text{ and } B) = P(A) \cdot P(B \mid A) = \frac{39}{52} \cdot \frac{13}{51} = \frac{13}{68} \approx 0.191$$

✓ GUIDED PRACTICE for Examples 4 and 5

4. **WHAT IF?** Use the information in Example 4 to find **(a)** the probability that a future tropical cyclone is a tropical storm and **(b)** the probability that a future tropical cyclone in the Southern Hemisphere is a tropical storm.

Find the probability of drawing the given cards from a standard deck of 52 cards (a) with replacement and (b) without replacement.

5. A spade, then a club

6. A jack, then another jack

THREE OR MORE DEPENDENT EVENTS The formula for finding probabilities of dependent events can be extended to three or more events, as shown below.

EXAMPLE 6 Find probability of three dependent events

COSTUME PARTY You and two friends go to the same store at different times to buy costumes for a costume party. There are 15 different costumes at the store, and the store has at least 3 duplicates of each costume. What is the probability that you each choose different costumes?

ANOTHER WAY

You can also use the fundamental counting principle.

$P(\text{all different})$

$= \frac{\text{different costumes}}{\text{possible costumes}}$

$= \frac{15 \cdot 14 \cdot 13}{15 \cdot 15 \cdot 15} \approx 0.809$

Solution

Let event A be that you choose a costume, let event B be that one friend chooses a different costume, and let event C be that your other friend chooses a third costume. These events are dependent. So, the probability is:

$$P(A \text{ and } B \text{ and } C) = P(A) \cdot P(B|A) \cdot P(C|A \text{ and } B)$$

$$= \frac{15}{15} \cdot \frac{14}{15} \cdot \frac{13}{15} = \frac{182}{225} \approx 0.809$$

EXAMPLE 7 Solve a multi-step problem

SAFETY Using observations made of drivers arriving at a certain high school, a study reports that 69% of adults wear seat belts while driving. A high school student also in the car wears a seat belt 66% of the time when the adult wears a seat belt, and 26% of the time when the adult does not wear a seat belt. What is the probability that a high school student in the study wears a seat belt?

Solution

A probability tree diagram, where the probabilities are given along the branches, can help you solve the problem. Notice that the probabilities for all branches from the same point must sum to 1.

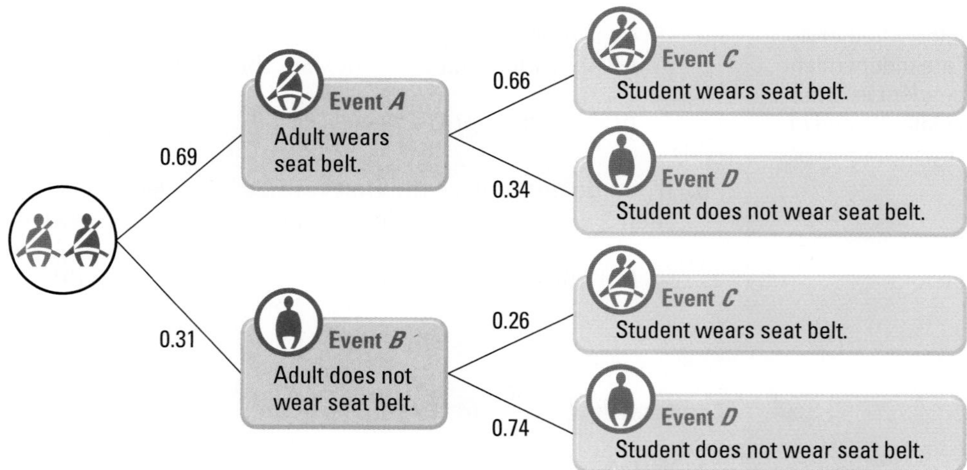

So, the probability that a high school student wears a seat belt is:

$$P(C) = P(A \text{ and } C) + P(B \text{ and } C)$$

$$= P(A) \cdot P(C|A) + P(B) \cdot P(C|B)$$

$$= (0.69)(0.66) + (0.31)(0.26) = 0.536$$

✓ GUIDED PRACTICE for Examples 6 and 7

7. **WHAT IF?** In Example 6, what is the probability that you and your friends choose different costumes if the store sells 20 different costumes?

8. **BASKETBALL** A high school basketball team leads at halftime in 60% of the games in a season. The team wins 80% of the time when they have the halftime lead, but only 10% of the time when they do not. What is the probability that the team wins a particular game during the season?

10.5 EXERCISES

HOMEWORK KEY

○ = **WORKED-OUT SOLUTIONS** on p. WS18 for Exs. 13, 25, and 39

★ = **STANDARDIZED TEST PRACTICE** Exs. 2, 15, 32, 34, and 41

SKILL PRACTICE

1. **VOCABULARY** Copy and complete: The probability that B will occur given that A has occurred is called the __?__ of B given A.

2. ★ **WRITING** *Explain* the difference between dependent events and independent events, and give an example of each.

EXAMPLES 1 and 2 on pp. 717–718 for Exs. 3–15

INDEPENDENT EVENTS Events A and B are independent. Find the indicated probability.

3. $P(A) = 0.4$
   $P(B) = 0.6$
   $P(A \text{ and } B) =$ __?__

4. $P(A) = 0.3$
   $P(B) = 0.4$
   $P(A \text{ and } B) =$ __?__

5. $P(A) = 0.25$
   $P(B) =$ __?__
   $P(A \text{ and } B) = 0.2$

6. $P(A) = 0.5$
   $P(B) =$ __?__
   $P(A \text{ and } B) = 0.1$

7. $P(A) =$ __?__
   $P(B) = 0.8$
   $P(A \text{ and } B) = 0.6$

8. $P(A) =$ __?__
   $P(B) = 0.9$
   $P(A \text{ and } B) = 0.45$

SPINNING A WHEEL You are playing a game that involves spinning the wheel shown. Find the probability of spinning the given colors.

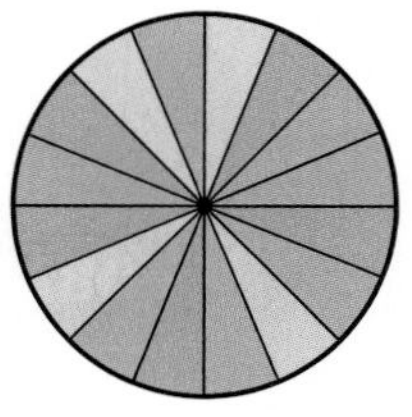

9. green, then blue
10. red, then yellow
11. blue, then red
12. yellow, then green
13. blue, then green, then red
14. green, then red, then yellow

15. ★ **MULTIPLE CHOICE** Events A and B are independent. What is $P(A \text{ and } B)$ if $P(A) = 0.3$ and $P(B) = 0.2$?

Ⓐ 0.06 Ⓑ 0.1 Ⓒ 0.5 Ⓓ 0.6

EXAMPLE 4 on p. 719 for Exs. 16–25

DEPENDENT EVENTS Events A and B are dependent. Find the indicated probability.

16. $P(A) = 0.3$
    $P(B|A) = 0.6$
    $P(A \text{ and } B) =$ __?__

17. $P(A) = 0.7$
    $P(B|A) = 0.5$
    $P(A \text{ and } B) =$ __?__

18. $P(A) = 0.8$
    $P(B|A) =$ __?__
    $P(A \text{ and } B) = 0.32$

19. $P(A) = 0.6$
    $P(B|A) =$ __?__
    $P(A \text{ and } B) = 0.45$

20. $P(A) =$ __?__
    $P(B|A) = 0.4$
    $P(A \text{ and } B) = 0.2$

21. $P(A) = 0.7$
    $P(B|A) =$ __?__
    $P(A \text{ and } B) = 0.63$

CONDITIONAL PROBABILITY **Let n be a randomly selected integer from 1 to 20. Find the indicated probability.**

22. n is 2 given that it is even

23. n is 5 given that it is less than 8

24. n is prime given that it has 2 digits

25. n is odd given that it is prime

EXAMPLES 5 and 6 on pp. 719–720 for Exs. 26–32

DRAWING CARDS **Find the probability of drawing the given cards from a standard deck of 52 cards (a) with replacement and (b) without replacement.**

26. A club, then a spade

27. A queen, then an ace

28. A face card, then a 6

29. A 10, then a 2

30. A king, then a queen, then a jack

31. A spade, then a club, then another spade

32. ★ **MULTIPLE CHOICE** What is the approximate probability of drawing 3 consecutive hearts from a standard deck of 52 cards without replacement?

(A) 0.0122 (B) 0.0129 (C) 0.0156 (D) 0.0166

33. **ERROR ANALYSIS** Events A and B are independent. *Describe* and correct the error in finding $P(A \text{ and } B)$.

P(A) = 0.4, P(B) = 0.5

P(A and B) = 0.4 + 0.5 = 0.9

34. ★ **OPEN-ENDED MATH** Flip a set of 3 coins and record the number of coins that come up heads. Repeat until you have a total of 10 trials.

a. What is the experimental probability that a trial results in 2 heads?

b. *Compare* your answer from part (a) with the theoretical probability that a trial results in 2 heads.

Animated Algebra at classzone.com

35. **REASONING** Let A and B be independent events. What is the relationship between $P(B)$ and $P(B|A)$? *Explain.*

36. **CHALLENGE** How many times must you roll two six-sided dice for there to be at least a 50% chance that you roll two 6's at least once?

PROBLEM SOLVING

EXAMPLES 3 and 4 on pp. 718–719 for Exs. 37–38

37. **SCHOOL BUS** Angela usually rushes to make it to the bus stop in time to catch the school bus, and will often miss the bus if it is early. The bus comes early to Angela's stop 28% of the time. What is the probability that the bus will come early at least once during a 5 day school week?

@HomeTutor for problem solving help at classzone.com

38. **ENVIRONMENT** The table shows the numbers of species in the United States listed as endangered or threatened as of September, 2004. Find **(a)** the probability that a listed animal is a bird and **(b)** the probability that an endangered animal is a bird.

	Endangered	Threatened
Mammals	69	9
Birds	77	14
Reptiles	14	22
Amphibians	11	10
Other	219	74

@HomeTutor for problem solving help at classzone.com

○ = WORKED-OUT SOLUTIONS on p. WS1

★ = STANDARDIZED TEST PRACTICE

EXAMPLE 7 on p. 720 for Exs. 39–40

39. **TENNIS** A tennis player wins a match 55% of the time when she serves first and 47% of the time when her opponent serves first. The player who serves first is determined by a coin toss before the match. What is the probability that the player wins a given match?

40. **ACCIDENT REENACTMENT** You are a juror for a trial involving a nighttime car accident in a certain city. Use the tree diagram and the facts below to determine the probability that the car involved in the accident was blue.

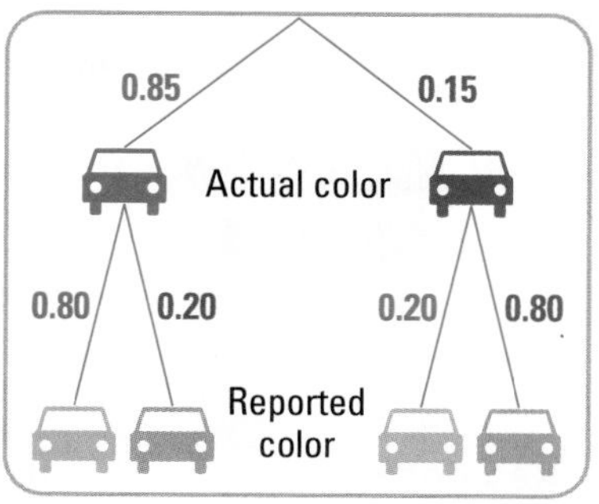

- The make of the car is known. Of the cars in the city matching this make, 85% are green and 15% are blue.
- A witness of the accident identified the car as blue.
- In reenactments of the accident, the witness correctly reported the color of the car 80% of the time.

41. ★ **EXTENDED RESPONSE** A football team is losing by 14 points near the end of a game. The team scores two touchdowns (worth 6 points each) before the end of the game. After each touchdown, the coach must decide whether to go for 1 point with a kick (which is successful 99% of the time) or 2 points with a run or pass (which is successful 45% of the time).

   a. **Calculate** If the team goes for 1 point after each touchdown, what is the probability that the coach's team wins? loses? ties?

   b. **Calculate** If the team goes for 2 points after each touchdown, what is the probability that the coach's team wins? loses? ties?

   c. **Reasoning** Can you develop a strategy so that the coach's team has a probability of winning the game that is greater than the probability of losing? If so, explain your strategy and calculate the probabilities of winning and losing using your strategy.

42. **CHALLENGE** It is estimated that 5.9% of Americans have diabetes. Suppose a medical lab uses a test for diabetes that is 98% accurate for people who have the disease and 95% accurate for people who do not have it. Find the conditional probability that a randomly selected person actually has diabetes given that the lab test says they have it.

NEW YORK MIXED REVIEW

TEST PRACTICE at classzone.com

43. What are the slope and y-intercept of the line that contains the point $(4, -2)$ and is parallel to the line $y = -2x + 1$?

   Ⓐ $m = -2$, $b = 0$
   Ⓑ $m = -\frac{3}{4}$, $b = 1$
   Ⓒ $m = -2$, $b = 6$
   Ⓓ $m = \frac{1}{2}$, $b = -4$

44. What is the solution set for the equation $7 - 12x^2 = -1$?

   Ⓐ $\left\{-\frac{\sqrt{6}}{2}, \frac{\sqrt{6}}{2}\right\}$
   Ⓑ $\left\{-\frac{\sqrt{6}}{3}, \frac{\sqrt{6}}{3}\right\}$
   Ⓒ $\left\{-\frac{\sqrt{3}}{2}, \frac{\sqrt{3}}{2}\right\}$
   Ⓓ $\left\{-\frac{\sqrt{2}}{2}, \frac{\sqrt{2}}{2}\right\}$

10.6 Construct and Interpret Binomial Distributions

 **A2.S.15** Know and apply the binomial probability formula to events involving the terms exactly, at least, and at most

Before You found probabilities of events.

Now You will study probability distributions.

Why? So you can describe interest in museums, as in Ex. 46.

Key Vocabulary
- **random variable**
- **probability distribution**
- **binomial distribution**
- **binomial experiment**
- **symmetric**
- **skewed**

A **random variable** is a variable whose value is determined by the outcomes of a random event. For example, when you roll a six-sided die, you can define a random variable X that represents the number showing on the die. So, the possible values of X are 1, 2, 3, 4, 5, and 6. For every random variable, a *probability distribution* can be defined.

KEY CONCEPT *For Your Notebook*

Probability Distributions

A **probability distribution** is a function that gives the probability of each possible value of a random variable. The sum of all the probabilities in a probability distribution must equal 1.

Probability Distribution for Rolling a Die

X	1	2	3	4	5	6
$P(X)$	$\frac{1}{6}$	$\frac{1}{6}$	$\frac{1}{6}$	$\frac{1}{6}$	$\frac{1}{6}$	$\frac{1}{6}$

 **EXAMPLE 1** Construct a probability distribution

Let X be a random variable that represents the sum when two six-sided dice are rolled. Make a table and a histogram showing the probability distribution for X.

REVIEW COMPOUND EVENTS
Recall that there are 36 possible outcomes when rolling two six-sided dice. These are listed in Example 4 on page 709.

Solution

The possible values of X are the integers from 2 to 12. The table shows how many outcomes of rolling two dice produce each value of X. Divide the number of outcomes for X by 36 to find $P(X)$.

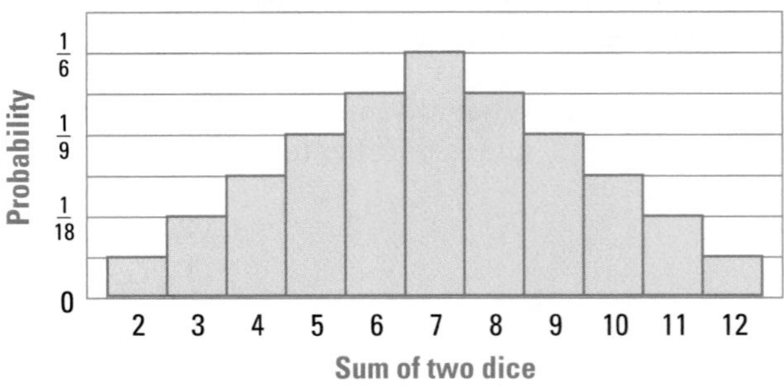

X (sum)	2	3	4	5	6	7	8	9	10	11	12
Outcomes	1	2	3	4	5	6	5	4	3	2	1
$P(X)$	$\frac{1}{36}$	$\frac{1}{18}$	$\frac{1}{12}$	$\frac{1}{9}$	$\frac{5}{36}$	$\frac{1}{6}$	$\frac{5}{36}$	$\frac{1}{9}$	$\frac{1}{12}$	$\frac{1}{18}$	$\frac{1}{36}$

EXAMPLE 2 Interpret a probability distribution

Use the probability distribution in Example 1 to answer each question.

a. What is the most likely sum when rolling two six-sided dice?

b. What is the probability that the sum of the two dice is at least 10?

Solution

a. The most likely sum when rolling two six-sided dice is the value of X for which $P(X)$ is greatest. This probability is greatest for $X = 7$. So, the most likely sum when rolling the two dice is 7.

b. The probability that the sum of the two dice is at least 10 is:

$$P(X \geq 10) = P(X = 10) + P(X = 11) + P(X = 12)$$

$$= \frac{3}{36} + \frac{2}{36} + \frac{1}{36}$$

$$= \frac{6}{36}$$

$$= \frac{1}{6}$$

$$\approx 0.167$$

GUIDED PRACTICE for Examples 1 and 2

A tetrahedral die has four sides numbered 1 through 4. Let X be a random variable that represents the sum when two such dice are rolled.

1. Make a table and a histogram showing the probability distribution for X.
2. What is the most likely sum when rolling the two dice? What is the probability that the sum of the two dice is at most 3?

BINOMIAL DISTRIBUTIONS One type of probability distribution is a **binomial distribution**. A binomial distribution shows the probabilities of the outcomes of a *binomial experiment*.

KEY CONCEPT — *For Your Notebook*

Binomial Experiments

A **binomial experiment** meets the following conditions:

- There are n independent trials.
- Each trial has only two possible outcomes: success and failure.
- The probability of success is the same for each trial. This probability is denoted by p. The probability of failure is given by $1 - p$.

For a binomial experiment, the probability of exactly k successes in n trials is:

$$P(k \text{ successes}) = {}_nC_k p^k (1 - p)^{n-k}$$

EXAMPLE 3 Construct a binomial distribution

SPORTS SURVEYS According to a survey, about 41% of U.S. households have a soccer ball. Suppose you ask 6 randomly chosen U.S. households whether they have a soccer ball. Draw a histogram of the binomial distribution for your survey.

Solution

The probability that a randomly selected household has a soccer ball is $p = 0.41$. Because you survey 6 households, $n = 6$.

AVOID ERRORS
You can check your calculations for a binomial distribution by adding all the probabilities. The sum should always be 1.

$P(k = 0) = {}_6C_0(0.41)^0(0.59)^6 \approx 0.042$

$P(k = 1) = {}_6C_1(0.41)^1(0.59)^5 \approx 0.176$

$P(k = 2) = {}_6C_2(0.41)^2(0.59)^4 \approx 0.306$

$P(k = 3) = {}_6C_3(0.41)^3(0.59)^3 \approx 0.283$

$P(k = 4) = {}_6C_4(0.41)^4(0.59)^2 \approx 0.148$

$P(k = 5) = {}_6C_5(0.41)^5(0.59)^1 \approx 0.041$

$P(k = 6) = {}_6C_6(0.41)^6(0.59)^0 \approx 0.005$

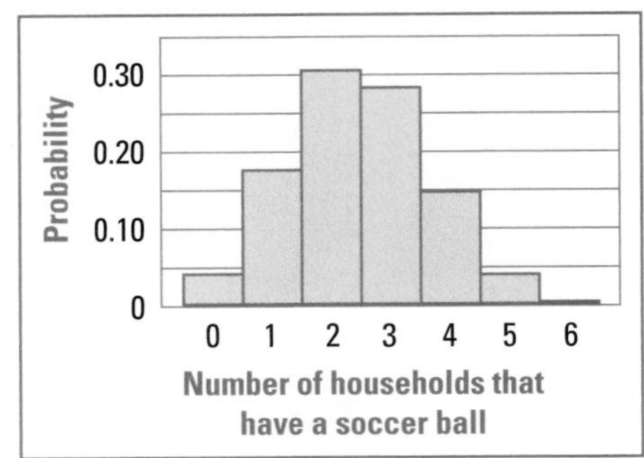

A histogram of the distribution is shown.

Animated Algebra at classzone.com

EXAMPLE 4 Interpret a binomial distribution

Use the binomial distribution in Example 3 to answer each question.

a. What is the most likely outcome of the survey?

b. What is the probability that at most 2 households have a soccer ball?

Solution

a. The most likely outcome of the survey is the value of k for which $P(k)$ is greatest. This probability is greatest for $k = 2$. So, the most likely outcome is that 2 of the 6 households have a soccer ball.

b. The probability that at most 2 households have a soccer ball is:

$$P(k \le 2) = P(k = 2) + P(k = 1) + P(k = 0)$$
$$\approx 0.306 + 0.176 + 0.042$$
$$\approx 0.524$$

▶ So, the probability is about 52%.

✓ GUIDED PRACTICE for Examples 3 and 4

In Sweden, 61% of households have a soccer ball. Suppose you ask 6 randomly chosen Swedish households whether they have a soccer ball.

3. Draw a histogram showing the binomial distribution for your survey.

4. What is the most likely outcome of your survey? What is the probability that at most 2 households you survey have a soccer ball?

CLASSIFY DISTRIBUTIONS
Note that the distribution in Example 1 on p. 724 is symmetric, while the distribution in Example 3 on p. 726 is skewed.

SYMMETRIC AND SKEWED DISTRIBUTIONS Suppose a probability distribution is represented by a histogram. The distribution is **symmetric** if you can draw a vertical line that divides the histogram into two parts that are mirror images. A distribution that is *not* symmetric is called **skewed**.

EXAMPLE 5 Classify distributions as symmetric or skewed

Describe the shape of the binomial distribution that shows the probability of exactly k successes in 8 trials if (a) $p = 0.5$ and (b) $p = 0.9$.

Solution

a.

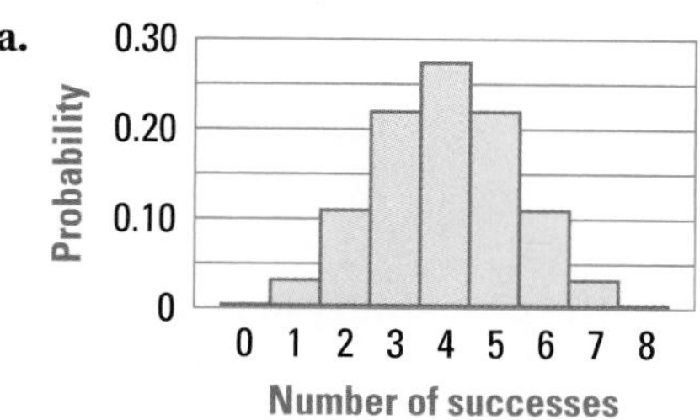

Symmetric; the left half is a mirror image of the right half.

b.

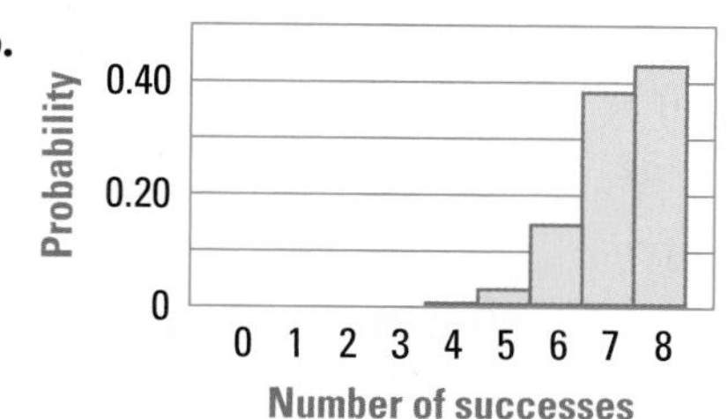

Skewed; the distribution is not symmetric about any vertical line.

GUIDED PRACTICE for Example 5

5. A binomial experiment consists of 5 trials with probability p of success on each trial. Describe the shape of the binomial distribution that shows the probability of exactly k successes if (**a**) $p = 0.4$ and (**b**) $p = 0.5$.

10.6 EXERCISES

HOMEWORK KEY
○ = **WORKED-OUT SOLUTIONS** on p. WS19 for Exs. 5, 21, and 45
★ = **STANDARDIZED TEST PRACTICE** Exs. 2, 9, 32, 39, and 48
◆ = **MULTIPLE REPRESENTATIONS** Ex. 47

SKILL PRACTICE

1. **VOCABULARY** Copy and complete: A probability distribution represented by a histogram is _?_ if you can draw a vertical line dividing the histogram into two parts that are mirror images.

2. ★ **WRITING** *Explain* the difference between a binomial experiment and a binomial distribution.

EXAMPLE 1 on p. 724 for Exs. 3–5

CONSTRUCTING PROBABILITY DISTRIBUTIONS **Make a table and a histogram showing the probability distribution for the random variable.**

3. $X =$ the number on a table tennis ball randomly chosen from a bag that contains 5 balls labeled "1," 3 balls labeled "2," and 2 balls labeled "3."

4. $W = 1$ if a randomly chosen letter is A, E, I, O, or U and 2 otherwise.

5. $N =$ the number of digits in a random integer from 0 through 999.

EXAMPLE 2
on p. 725
for Exs. 6–9

INTERPRETING PROBABILITY DISTRIBUTIONS In Exercises 6–9, use the given histogram of a probability distribution for a random variable X.

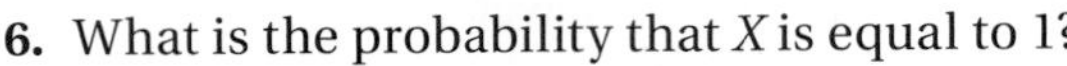

6. What is the probability that X is equal to 1?

7. What is the most likely value for X?

8. What is the probability that X is odd?

9. ★ **MULTIPLE CHOICE** What is the probability that X is at least 3?

Ⓐ 0.2 Ⓑ 0.4 Ⓒ 0.6 Ⓓ 0.8

EXAMPLES 3 and 4
on p. 726
for Exs. 10–32

CALCULATING PROBABILITIES Calculate the probability of tossing a coin 20 times and getting the given number of heads.

10. 1 11. 2 12. 4 13. 6

14. 9 15. 12 16. 15 17. 18

BINOMIAL PROBABILITIES Calculate the probability of randomly guessing the given number of correct answers on a 30-question multiple choice exam that has choices A, B, C, and D for each question.

18. 0 19. 2 20. 6 21. 11

22. 15 23. 21 24. 26 25. 30

ERROR ANALYSIS *Describe* and correct the error in calculating the probability of rolling a 1 exactly 3 times in 5 rolls of a six-sided die.

26.
$$P(k = 3) = {}_5C_3\left(\frac{1}{6}\right)^{5-3}\left(\frac{5}{6}\right)^3$$
$$\approx 0.161$$

27.
$$P(k = 3) = \left(\frac{1}{6}\right)^3\left(\frac{5}{6}\right)^{5-3}$$
$$\approx 0.003$$

BINOMIAL DISTRIBUTIONS Calculate the probability of k successes for a binomial experiment consisting of n trials with probability p of success on each trial.

28. $k \le 3, n = 7, p = 0.3$ 29. $k \ge 5, n = 8, p = 0.6$

30. $k \le 2, n = 5, p = 0.12$ 31. $k \ge 10, n = 15, p = 0.75$

32. ★ **MULTIPLE CHOICE** You perform a binomial experiment consisting of 10 trials with a probability of success of 36% on each trial. What is the most likely number of successes?

Ⓐ 3 Ⓑ 4 Ⓒ 6 Ⓓ 7

EXAMPLE 5
on p. 727
for Exs. 33–38

HISTOGRAMS A binomial experiment consists of n trials with probability p of success on each trial. Draw a histogram of the binomial distribution that shows the probability of exactly k successes. *Describe* the distribution as either *symmetric* or *skewed*. Then find the most likely number of successes.

33. $n = 3, p = 0.3$ 34. $n = 6, p = 0.5$ 35. $n = 4, p = 0.16$

36. $n = 7, p = 0.85$ 37. $n = 8, p = 0.025$ 38. $n = 12, p = 0.5$

39. ★ **OPEN-ENDED MATH** Construct a symmetric probability distribution for a random variable X and a skewed probability distribution for a random variable Y. Make a table and a histogram for each distribution.

○ = WORKED-OUT SOLUTIONS on p. WS1 ★ = STANDARDIZED TEST PRACTICE ◆ = MULTIPLE REPRESENTATIONS

In Exercises 40–42, you will derive the binomial probability formula on page 725. Consider a binomial experiment with n trials and probability p of success on each trial.

40. For any particular sequence of k successes and $n - k$ failures, what is the probability that the sequence occurs? *Explain.*

41. How many sequences of k successes and $n - k$ failures are there? *Explain.*

42. **CHALLENGE** Use your results from Exercises 40 and 41 to justify the binomial probability formula.

PROBLEM SOLVING

EXAMPLES 3 and 4 on p. 726 for Exs. 43–46

43. **HEALTH** About 1% of people are allergic to bee stings. What is the probability that exactly 1 person in a class of 25 is allergic to bee stings?

@HomeTutor for problem solving help at classzone.com

44. **BASKETBALL** Predrag Stojakovic of the Sacramento Kings made 92.7% of his free throw attempts in the 2003–2004 NBA regular season. What is the probability that he will make exactly 10 of his next 15 free throw attempts?

@HomeTutor for problem solving help at classzone.com

45. **BLOOD TYPE** The chart shows the distribution of blood types (O, A, B, AB) and Rh factor ($^+$ or $^-$) for human blood. If, at random, 10 people donate blood to a blood bank during a certain hour, find the probability of each event.

Percent of Population by Blood Type

O^+	O^-	A^+	A^-	B^+	B^-	AB^+	AB^-
37%	6%	34%	6%	10%	2%	4%	1%

a. Exactly 5 of the people are type A^+.

b. Exactly 2 of the people are Rh^-.

c. At most 2 of the people are type O.

d. At least 5 of the people are Rh^+.

46. **FINE ARTS** A survey states that 35% of people in the United States visited an art museum in a certain year. You randomly select 10 U.S. citizens.

a. Draw a histogram showing the binomial distribution of the number of people who visited an art museum.

b. What is the probability that at most 4 people visited an art museum?

47. **MULTIPLE REPRESENTATIONS** An average of 7 gopher holes appear on the farm shown each week. Let X represent how many of the 7 gopher holes appear in the carrot patch. Assume that a gopher hole has an equal chance of appearing at any point on the farm.

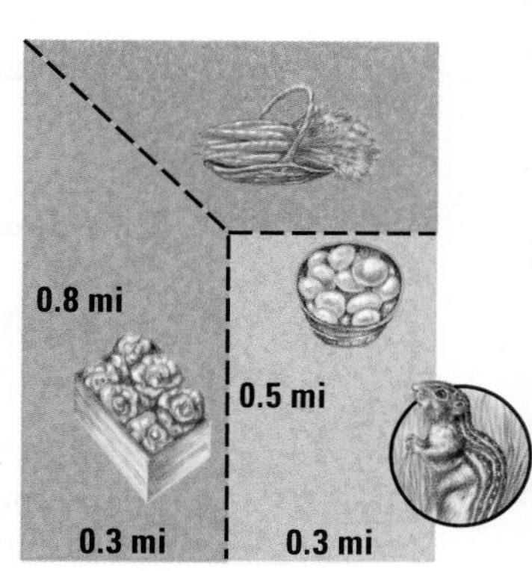

a. **Calculating Probabilities** Find $P(X)$ for $X = 0, 1, 2, \ldots, 7$.

b. **Making a Table** Make a table showing the probability distribution for X.

c. **Making a Histogram** Make a histogram showing the probability distribution for X.

48. ★ **EXTENDED RESPONSE** Assume that having a male child and having a female child are independent events and that the probability of each is 0.5.

a. A couple has 4 male children. Evaluate the validity of this statement: "The first 4 kids were all boys, so the next one will probably be a girl."

b. What is the probability of having 4 male children and then a female child?

c. Let X be a random variable that represents the number of children a couple already has when they have their first female child. Draw a histogram of the distribution of $P(X)$ for $0 \le X \le 10$ and describe its shape.

49. **CHALLENGE** An entertainment system has n speakers. Each speaker will function properly with probability p, independent of whether the other speakers are functioning. The system will operate effectively if at least 50% of its speakers are functioning. For what values of p is a 5-speaker system more likely to operate than a 3-speaker system?

NEW YORK MIXED REVIEW

TEST PRACTICE at classzone.com

50. For an emergency service call, an electrician charges a base fee of \$65 plus \$36.50 per hour of work. Which equation best represents the relationship between the total cost, c, of the emergency service call and the number of hours worked, n?

(A) $c = 65 + 36.5$ (B) $c = 65 + 36.5n$

(C) $c = 65n + 36.5$ (D) $c = 65n + 36.5n$

51. What is the solution of the equation $3(4x - 5) = -4(-x + 6) - 8x$?

(A) $-\frac{3}{5}$ (B) $-\frac{9}{16}$ (C) $\frac{3}{8}$ (D) $\frac{9}{16}$

QUIZ *for Lessons 10.5–10.6*

Find the probability of randomly drawing the given marbles from a bag of 6 red, 9 green, and 5 blue marbles without replacement. *(p. 717)*

1. red, then green
2. blue, then red
3. green, then green

Calculate the probability of getting the given number of 6's when rolling a six-sided die 10 times. *(p. 724)*

4. 0
5. 1
6. 4
7. 8

A binomial experiment consists of n trials with probability p of success on each trial. Draw a histogram of the binomial distribution that shows the probability of exactly k successes. *(p. 724)*

8. $n = 5, p = 0.2$
9. $n = 8, p = 0.5$
10. $n = 6, p = 0.72$

11. **MENU CHOICES** You and 4 friends are in line at lunch and are each selecting a beverage. There are 5 types of beverages available. What is the probability that all of you will select different beverages? *(p. 717)*

Graphing Calculator **ACTIVITY** *Use after Lesson 10.6*

@HomeTutor
classzone.com
Keystrokes

10.6 Create a Binomial Distribution

QUESTION **How can you use a graphing calculator to calculate binomial probabilities?**

Some calculators have a binomial probability distribution function that you can use to calculate binomial probabilities. You can then use the calculator to draw a histogram of the distribution.

EXAMPLE **Calculate binomial probabilities**

TV NEWS According to a survey, 38% of U.S. adults get their news primarily from television. Suppose you survey 6 adults at random. Draw a histogram of the binomial distribution showing the probability that television is the primary news source for exactly k adults. What is the most likely number of adults in your survey who get their news primarily through television?

STEP 1 ***Enter values of k***

Let $p = 0.38$ be the probability that television is a person's primary news source. Enter the k-values 0 through 6 into list L_1 on the graphing calculator.

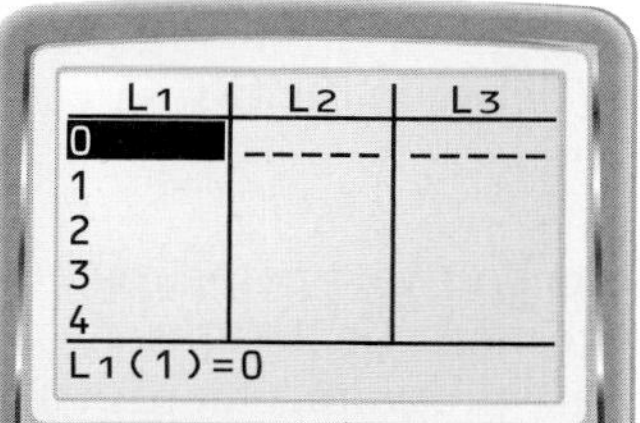

STEP 2 ***Find values of P(k)***

Enter the binomial probability command to generate $P(k)$ for all seven k-values. Store the results in list L_2.

STEP 3 ***Draw histogram***

Set up the histogram to use the numbers in list L_1 as x-values and the numbers in list L_2 as frequencies. Draw the histogram in a suitable viewing window.

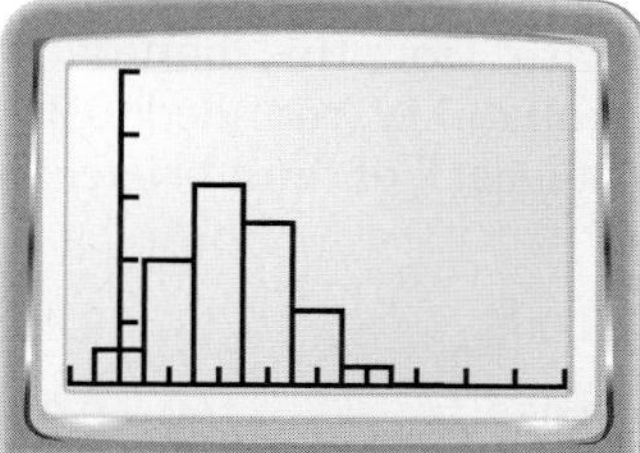

From the histogram in Step 3, you can see that $k = 2$ is the most likely number of the 6 adults surveyed who get their news primarily through television.

PRACTICE

A binomial experiment consists of n trials with probability p of success on each trial. Use a graphing calculator to draw a histogram of the binomial distribution that shows the probability of exactly k successes. Then find the most likely number of successes.

1. $n = 12, p = 0.29$

2. $n = 14, p = 0.58$

3. $n = 15, p = 0.805$

4. **WHAT IF?** In the example, how do your histogram and the most likely number of adults change if you survey 14 adults at random?

New York Mixed Review

Lessons 10.4–10.6

1. **WORD GAME** You and a friend are playing a word game that involves lettered tiles. The distribution of letters is shown below. You randomly draw 2 tiles without replacement. What is the probability (rounded to 3 decimal places) of getting 2 vowels? (Assume that Y is a consonant.)

Tile	Count	Tile	Count	Tile	Count	Tile	Count
A	9	H	2	O	8	V	2
B	2	I	9	P	2	W	2
C	2	J	1	Q	1	X	1
D	4	K	1	R	6	Y	2
E	12	L	4	S	4	Z	1
F	2	M	2	T	6	Blank	2
G	3	N	6	U	4		

(1) 0.112 (3) 0.174
(2) 0.142 (4) 0.178

2. **MANUFACTURING** A manufacturer makes briefcases with numbered locks. The locks can be set so that any one of 1000 different codes will open the briefcase. If 4 friends have briefcases from this manufacturer, what is the probability (rounded to 3 decimal places) that at least 2 of the 4 briefcases have the same code?

(1) 0.006 (3) 0.496
(2) 0.059 (4) 0.903

3. **STUDENT SURVEY** A survey finds that 61% of students in the United States like school, that 95% of students who like school plan to attend college, and that 70% of students who do not like school plan to attend college. What is the probability (rounded to 3 decimal places) that a randomly selected high school student in the United States plans to attend college? Use a probabilty tree diagram to find the answer.

(1) 0.58 (3) 0.832
(2) 0.822 (4) 0.853

4. **READING SURVEY** According to a survey, 24% of U.S. adults say that reading is their favorite leisure activity. You randomly select 14 adults to survey. What is the probability (rounded to 3 decimal places) that at least 7 adults say reading is their favorite leisure activity?

(1) 0.008 (3) 0.971
(2) 0.031 (4) 0.992

5. **OPEN-ENDED** The owner of a one-person lawn mowing business owns three old and unreliable riding mowers. As long as one of the mowers is working, the owner can stay productive. From past experience, the first mower is unusable 10% of the time, the second is unusable 8% of the time, and the third is unusable 18% of the time.

If the usability of each lawnmower is independent of the usability of the others, what is the probability that all three mowers are unusable on a given day? Round your answer to the nearest hundredth of a percent.

What is the probability that at least one of the mowers is usable on a given day? Round your answer to the nearest hundredth of a percent.

Explain the relationship between the two answers.

6. **OPEN-ENDED** A computer software company is performing a market test on two designs, A and B, for its new software program. Out of 250 people who view the designs, 85 like design A, 135 like design B, and 45 like both designs.

Copy and complete the Venn diagram.

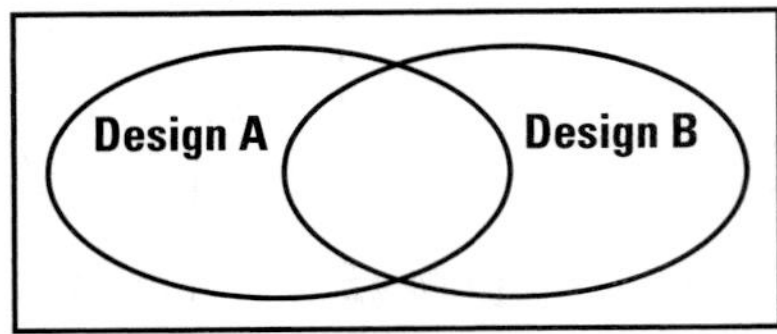

What is the probability that a person likes design A or design B?

What is the probability that a person does not like either design?

10 CHAPTER SUMMARY

BIG IDEAS

For Your Notebook

Big Idea 1

Using Permutations and Combinations

PERMUTATIONS Order is important	Permutations of n distinct objects	$n!$	Number of ways to arrange 10 students at 10 desks: $10! = 3,628,800$
	Permutations of n distinct objects taken r at a time	${}_nP_r = \frac{n!}{(n-r)!}$	Number of ways to arrange 8 students at 10 desks: $\frac{10!}{2!} = 1,814,400$
	Permutations of n objects where one object is repeated s_1 times, another is repeated s_2 times, and so on	$\frac{n!}{s_1! \cdot s_2! \cdot \ldots \cdot s_k!}$	Number of distinguishable permutations of the letters in STUDENTS: $\frac{8!}{2! \cdot 2!} = 10,080$
COMBINATIONS Order is not important	Combinations of r objects taken from a group of n distinct objects	${}_nC_r = \frac{n!}{(n-r)! \cdot r!}$	Number of ways to choose 8 students from a set of 10 students: $\frac{10!}{2! \cdot 8!} = 45$

Big Idea 2

Finding Probabilities

The following table shows which formula to use when finding probabilities involving two events A and B.

Overlapping Events	Independent Events	Dependent Events
$P(A \text{ or } B) = P(A) + P(B) - P(A \text{ and } B)$	$P(A \text{ and } B) = P(A) \cdot P(B)$	$P(A \text{ and } B) = P(A) \cdot P(B \mid A)$

Big Idea 3

Constructing Binomial Distributions

For a binomial experiment, the probability of exactly k successes in n trials is

$$P(k \text{ successes}) = {}_nC_k p^k (1-p)^{n-k}$$

where the probability of success on each trial is p.

A binomial distribution shows the probabilities of all possible outcomes in a binomial experiment. The distribution is skewed if $p \neq 0.5$.

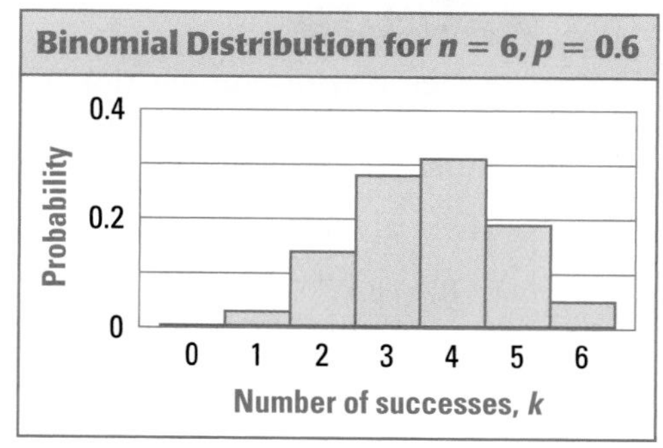

10 CHAPTER REVIEW

@HomeTutor
classzone.com
- Multi-Language Glossary
- Vocabulary practice

REVIEW KEY VOCABULARY

- permutation, *p. 684*
- factorial, *p. 684*
- combination, *p. 690*
- Pascal's triangle, *p. 692*
- binomial theorem, *p. 693*
- probability, *p. 698*
- theoretical probability, *p. 698*
- odds, *p. 699*
- experimental probability, *p. 700*
- geometric probability, *p. 701*
- compound event, *p. 707*
- overlapping events, *p. 707*
- disjoint or mutually exclusive events, *p. 707*
- independent events, *p. 717*
- dependent events, *p. 718*
- conditional probability, *p. 718*
- random variable, *p. 724*
- probability distribution, *p. 724*
- binomial distribution, *p. 725*
- binomial experiment, *p. 725*
- symmetric distribution, *p. 727*
- skewed distribution, *p. 727*

VOCABULARY EXERCISES

1. Copy and complete: A(n) __?__ is a selection of *r* objects from a group of *n* objects where the order of the objects selected is not important.

2. **WRITING** *Explain* the difference between the probability of an event and the odds in favor of the event.

3. **WRITING** You randomly select 10 cards, one by one, from a standard deck of 52 cards without replacement. You record the number of diamonds you get. Is this a binomial experiment? *Explain.*

4. **WRITING** Let event *A* be randomly selecting a green marble from a bag that contains red, green, and blue marbles. Let event *B* be randomly selecting a marble that is not red from the same bag. Are events *A* and *B* disjoint events? *Explain.*

REVIEW EXAMPLES AND EXERCISES

Use the review examples and exercises below to check your understanding of the concepts you have learned in each lesson of Chapter 10.

10.1 Apply the Counting Principle and Permutations *pp. 682–689*

EXAMPLE

An ice skating competition features 8 skaters. How many different ways can the skaters finish the competition? How many different ways can 3 of the skaters finish first, second, and third?

There are 8! ways the skaters can finish the competition.

$$8! = 8 \cdot 7 \cdot 6 \cdot 5 \cdot 4 \cdot 3 \cdot 2 \cdot 1 = 40{,}320$$

There are ${}_8P_3$ ways that 3 of the skaters can finish first, second, and third.

$${}_8P_3 = \frac{8!}{(8-3)!} = \frac{8!}{5!} = 336$$

@HomeTutor
classzone.com
Chapter Review Practice

EXAMPLES 4 and 5 on pp. 684–685 for Exs. 5–9

EXERCISES

5. **PHOTOGRAPHY** You are placing 12 pictures on separate pages in an album. How many different ways can you order the 12 pictures in the album? How many different ways can 4 of the 12 pictures be placed on the first 4 pages?

Find the number of permutations.

6. ${}_9P_1$ 7. ${}_5P_5$ 8. ${}_6P_3$ 9. ${}_{10}P_2$

10.2 Use Combinations and the Binomial Theorem

pp. 690–697

EXAMPLE

Use the binomial theorem to expand $(x + 5y)^4$.

$$(x + 5y)^4 = {}_4C_0x^4(5y)^0 + {}_4C_1x^3(5y)^1 + {}_4C_2x^2(5y)^2 + {}_4C_3x^1(5y)^3 + {}_4C_4x^0(5y)^4$$
$$= (1)(x^4)(1) + (4)(x^3)(5y) + (6)(x^2)(25y^2) + (4)(x)(125y^3) + (1)(1)(625y^4)$$
$$= x^4 + 20x^3y + 150x^2y^2 + 500xy^3 + 625y^4$$

EXAMPLES 3, 5, and 6 on pp. 691–693 for Exs. 10–14

EXERCISES

Use the binomial theorem to write the binomial expansion.

10. $(t + 3)^6$ 11. $(2a + b^2)^4$ 12. $(w - 8v)^4$ 13. $(r^3 - 4s)^5$

14. **ICE CREAM** An ice cream vendor sells 15 flavors of ice cream. You want to sample *at least* 4 of the flavors. How many different combinations of ice cream flavors can you sample?

10.3 Define and Use Probability

pp. 698–704

EXAMPLE

You roll a standard six-sided die. Find the probability of rolling a number less than 3.

Two outcomes correspond to rolling a number less than 3: rolling a 1 or 2.

$$P(\text{rolling less than 3}) = \frac{\text{Number of ways to roll less than 3}}{\text{Number of ways to roll the die}} = \frac{2}{6} = \frac{1}{3}$$

EXAMPLES 1 and 4 on pp. 698–700 for Exs. 15–19

EXERCISES

You have an equally likely chance of choosing any integer from 1 through 30. Find the probability of the given event.

15. An even number is chosen.
16. A multiple of 5 is chosen.
17. A factor of 60 is chosen.
18. A prime number is chosen.

19. **COMMUTING** Out of 250 work days, a commuter arrived at work on time 47 times on Mondays, 43 times on Tuesdays, 48 times on Wednesdays, 39 times on Thursdays, and 40 times on Fridays. For a randomly selected work day, what is the probability that the commuter arrived at work on time?

10 CHAPTER REVIEW

10.4 Probabilities of Disjoint and Overlapping Events
pp. 707–713

EXAMPLE

Let A and B be events such that $P(A) = \frac{2}{3}$, $P(B) = \frac{1}{2}$, and $P(A \text{ and } B) = \frac{1}{3}$. Find $P(A \text{ or } B)$.

$$P(A \text{ or } B) = P(A) + P(B) - P(A \text{ and } B) = \frac{2}{3} + \frac{1}{2} - \frac{1}{3} = \frac{5}{6}$$

EXERCISES

EXAMPLES 2 and 4 on pp. 708–709 for Exs. 20–22

Let A and B be events such that $P(A) = 0.32$, $P(B) = 0.48$, and $P(A \text{ and } B) = 0.12$. Find the indicated probability.

20. $P(A \text{ or } B)$

21. $P(\overline{A})$

22. $P(\overline{B})$

10.5 Probabilities of Independent and Dependent Events
pp. 717–723

EXAMPLE

Find the probability of selecting a club and then another club from a standard deck of 52 cards if (a) you replace the first card before selecting the second, and (b) you do *not* replace the first card.

Let event A be "the first card is a club" and B be "the second card is a club."

a. $P(A \text{ and } B) = P(A) \cdot P(B) = \frac{13}{52} \cdot \frac{13}{52} = \frac{1}{16} = 0.0625$

b. $P(A \text{ and } B) = P(A) \cdot P(B|A) = \frac{13}{52} \cdot \frac{12}{51} = \frac{1}{17} \approx 0.0588$

EXERCISES

EXAMPLE 5 on p. 719 for Exs. 23–25

Find the probability of randomly selecting the given marbles from a bag of 5 red, 8 green, and 3 blue marbles if (a) you replace the first marble before drawing the second and (b) you do *not* replace the first marble.

23. red, then green

24. blue, then red

25. green, then green

10.6 Construct and Interpret Binomial Distributions
pp. 724–730

EXAMPLE

Find the probability of tossing a coin 12 times and getting exactly 4 heads.

$$P(k = 4) = {}_nC_k p^k(1 - p)^{n-k} = {}_{12}C_4(0.5)^4(1 - 0.5)^8 = 495(0.5)^4(0.5)^8 \approx 0.121$$

EXERCISES

EXAMPLE 3 on p. 726 for Exs. 26–29

Find the probability of tossing a coin 8 times and getting the given number of heads.

26. 6

27. 4

28. 7

29. 0

10 CHAPTER TEST

Find the number of permutations or combinations.

1. $_5P_2$
2. $_8P_3$
3. $_{12}P_7$
4. $_{17}P_{10}$
5. $_4C_3$
6. $_7C_7$
7. $_{18}C_4$
8. $_9C_5$

Use the binomial theorem to write the binomial expansion.

9. $(x + 5)^3$
10. $(3a - 3)^5$
11. $(s + t^2)^4$
12. $(c^3 - 2d^2)^6$

A card is randomly drawn from a standard deck of 52 cards. Find the probability of drawing the given card.

13. A queen
14. A red king
15. A diamond
16. Not a club

Find the indicated probability.

17. $P(A) = 0.3$
    $P(B) = 0.6$
    $P(A \text{ or } B) = \underline{\ ?\ }$
    $P(A \text{ and } B) = 0.1$
18. $P(A) = 35\%$
    $P(B) = \underline{\ ?\ }$
    $P(A \text{ or } B) = 80\%$
    $P(A \text{ and } B) = 20\%$
19. $P(A) = \underline{\ ?\ }$
    $P(\overline{A}) = \frac{2}{5}$
20. A and B are independent.
    $P(A) = 0.15$
    $P(B) = 0.6$
    $P(A \text{ and } B) = \underline{\ ?\ }$
21. A and B are dependent.
    $P(A) = 60\%$
    $P(B|A) = \underline{\ ?\ }$
    $P(A \text{ and } B) = 25\%$
22. A and B are dependent.
    $P(A) = \underline{\ ?\ }$
    $P(B|A) = 0.4$
    $P(A \text{ and } B) = 0.36$

Calculate the probability of *k* successes for a binomial experiment consisting of *n* trials with probability *p* of success on each trial.

23. $k = 4, n = 11, p = 0.4$
24. $k \le 2, n = 5, p = 0.7$
25. $k \ge 8, n = 9, p = 0.9$

26. **TRUE-OR-FALSE QUIZ** Calculate the probability of randomly guessing at least 8 correct answers on a 10 question true-or-false quiz.

27. **GOVERNMENT** There are 15 members on a city council. On a recent agenda item, 8 of the council members voted in favor of a budget increase for city park improvements. How many combinations of council members could have voted in favor of the budget increase?

28. **PARACHUTING** A parachuter is attempting to land within a square in the middle of a circular landing area. The square has sides 25 feet long, and the diameter of the landing area is 40 feet. If the parachuter is equally likely to first touch the ground at any point within the landing area, what is the probability that the parachuter first touches the ground within the square?

29. **EDUCATION** A high school has an enrollment of 1800 students. There are 1050 females enrolled in the school. The high school has 1200 students who are involved in an after-school activity, 725 of whom are female. What is the probability that a randomly selected student at the school is a female who is not involved in an after-school activity?

30. **FISHING** A study found that 9% of people cite fishing as their favorite leisure-time activity. Suppose you randomly survey 8 people about their leisure-time activities. What is the probability that at least 2 of the people cite fishing as their favorite?

MULTIPLE CHOICE QUESTIONS

Some of the information you need to solve a multiple choice question may appear in a table, a diagram, or a graph.

PROBLEM 1

A dart is thrown at the square target shown. Assume the dart is equally likely to hit any point inside the target. What is the approximate probability that the dart lands in the shaded region outside of the diamond but inside the circle?

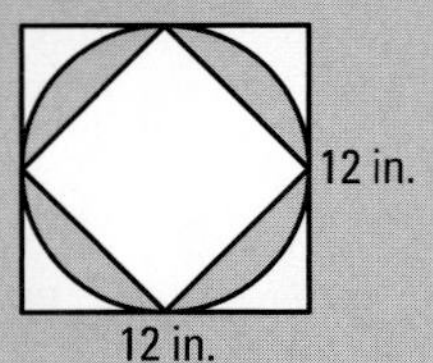

(1) 0.285 (3) 0.500

(2) 0.411 (4) 0.785

Plan

INTERPRET THE DIAGRAM The probability of a dart landing in the shaded region is equivalent to the fraction of the area represented by the shaded region.

Solution

STEP 1 Find the areas of the different shapes in the diagram.

Area of the square: Each side has a length of 12 inches, so the area is:

$$A_S = 12 \text{ in.} \cdot 12 \text{ in.} = 144 \text{ in.}^2$$

Area of the circle: The diameter of the circle is 12 inches, so the radius is half of that, or 6 inches. The area of the circle is:

$$A_C = \pi r^2 = \pi(6 \text{ in.})^2 = 36\pi \text{ in.}^2$$

Area of the diamond: The diamond can be broken horizontally into two triangles that are each 12 inches wide and 6 inches high. The area is:

$$A_D = 2A_T = 2(0.5)bh = 1 \cdot 12 \text{ in.} \cdot 6 \text{ in.} = 72 \text{ in.}^2$$

STEP 2 Compute the probability as a ratio of the shaded area to the total area.

$$\text{Probability} = \frac{A_C - A_D}{A_S} = \frac{36\pi - 72}{144} \approx 0.285$$

Check

Since the shaded area of the diagram is clearly less than one-half of the entire target, 0.285 is a reasonable value. Moreover, answer choices (3) and (4), which are equal to or greater than 0.5, can clearly be eliminated.

▶ The correct answer is (1).

PROBLEM 2

What is the approximate probability that tossing a fair coin 20 times results in exactly 5 heads?

(1) 0 (2) 0.015 (3) 0.25 (4) 0.5

Plan

Each flip of the coin is an event; "Success" is flipping a head. Since the 20 trials are independent and the probability of a success is always the same value (0.5), the number of heads has a binomial distribution.

Solution

For this problem, the probability of success is $p = 0.5$, and the probability of failure is $1 - p = 0.5$. The number of trials is $n = 20$, and the targeted number of successes is $k = 5$. To find the probability, apply the binomial formula:

$$P(k \text{ successes}) = {}_nC_k p^k(1 - p)^{n-k}$$

$$P(5 \text{ successes}) = {}_{20}C_5 0.5^5(0.5)^{15}$$

$$= \frac{20 \bullet 19 \bullet 18 \bullet 17 \bullet 16}{5!} 0.5^{20}$$

$$\approx 0.015$$

Check

Since it is unreasonable to expect *exactly* 5 heads with great frequency, answer choices (3) and (4) are unreasonably high and can be eliminated. On the other hand, we would expect exactly 5 heads in 20 flips *occasionally*, so the probability of 0.015 is more reasonable than the probability of 0 in answer choice (1).

▶ The correct answer is (2).

PRACTICE

Explain why you can eliminate the highlighted answer choice.

1. What is the number of distinct arrangements of the letters in the word ARRANGE?

   (1) 42 (2) 128 (3) 1260 ╳(4) 5040

2. A test includes 20 True/False questions. If you guess randomly, what is the approximate probability that you will get 12 or more of them correct and pass the test?

   (1) 0.13 (2) 0.25 ╳(3) 0.60 (4) 0.86

TEST PREPARATION

MULTIPLE CHOICE

1. A jar contains 4 yellow marbles, 3 red marbles, and 2 green marbles. To the nearest percent, what is the probability that a randomly selected marble will be green?

(1) 11% (3) 29%
(2) 22% (4) 50%

2. How many different four-digit numbers can be made from the digits 1, 3, 4, and 7 if the digits cannot be repeated?

(1) 4 (3) 24
(2) 16 (4) 256

3. Find the number of distinguishable permutations of the letters in the word WEEKEND.

(1) 840
(2) 1680
(3) 5040
(4) 30,240

4. The table shows the numbers of Democratic and Republican Presidents born in different regions of the United States. The table includes the Presidents in office from 1853 to 2005.

	Democrat	Republican
Midwest	2	9
Northeast	6	5
South	4	3
West	0	1

A President between 1853 and 2005 is chosen at random. Which event is the most probable?

(1) The President was born in the South.
(2) The President was a Republican, given that he was born in the South.
(3) The President was not only a Democrat but also from the West.
(4) The President was born in the Midwest.

5. Find $P(A \text{ and } B)$ given that $P(A) = 0.52$, $P(B) = 0.24$, and $P(A \text{ or } B) = 0.61$.

(1) 0.13
(2) 0.15
(3) 0.49
(4) 0.64

6. Larry is giving two of his friends a ride home from football practice. After leaving practice, he will drop off Teshawn first, then drop off Mark, and finally head home. Between each destination, there are several different routes. The number of routes for each part of the drive is represented by a variable, as shown below.

Part of the Drive Home	Number of Possible Routes
Practice to Teshawn's house	x
Teshawn's house to Mark's house	y
Mark's house to Larry's house	z

Which expression represents the total number of possible routes that Larry can drive?

(1) $x + y + z$
(2) xyz
(3) $2^x 2^y 2^z$
(4) $(x + y + z)^2$

7. Find the value of the expression ${}_5C_2 - {}_5C_3$.

(1) 0
(2) 5
(3) 30
(4) 40

8. What is the coefficient of x^3 in the expansion of $(4x - 1)^9$?

(1) 64 (3) 5376
(2) 84 (4) 262,144

MULTIPLE CHOICE

9. Two dice are rolled in a trivia board game. You roll a 6-sided die to find the number of spaces to advance. You roll a 10-sided die to find which type of question you must answer. How many possible outcomes are there when rolling these two dice?

(1) 16 (3) 210
(2) 60 (4) 5040

10. A card is randomly selected from a standard deck of 52 cards. The probability of drawing which type of card is 25%?

(1) A spade (3) A queen
(2) The 3 of hearts (4) A red card

11. Which binomial expansion includes the term $40x^2$?

(1) $(x + 1)^5$ (3) $(2x + 1)^5$
(2) $(x + 5)^5$ (4) $(2x + 5)^5$

12. A satellite has two independent power systems. The space agency expects that within a 10-year period, the probability that the main source will fail is 0.1, and the probability that the backup source will fail is 0.2. What is the probability that the satellite will still have at least one functional power source after 10 years?

(1) 0.02 (3) 0.72
(2) 0.7 (4) 0.98

13. In a previous survey of adults who follow more than one sport, 30% listed football as their favorite sport. In a particular group of 15 adults who each follow more than one sport, what is the probability rounded to the nearest thousandth that fewer than 4 of them will say that football is their favorite sport?

(1) 0.219 (3) 0.516
(2) 0.297 (4) 0.781

OPEN-ENDED

14. For a checking account, you must choose a personal identification number (PIN). The PIN must be between 6 and 8 characters and may contain letters or digits. How many different PINs are possible, assuming the digits and letters can be repeated? *Explain* how you found your answer.

15. A survey asked adults who use the Internet how frequently they send or receive e-mail. The results of the survey are shown in the bar graph at the right. Find the experimental probability that a randomly selected adult Internet user uses the Internet to send or receive e-mail often or very often. If the survey had polled computer programmers instead of all adults, describe how you think the results of the survey would be different.

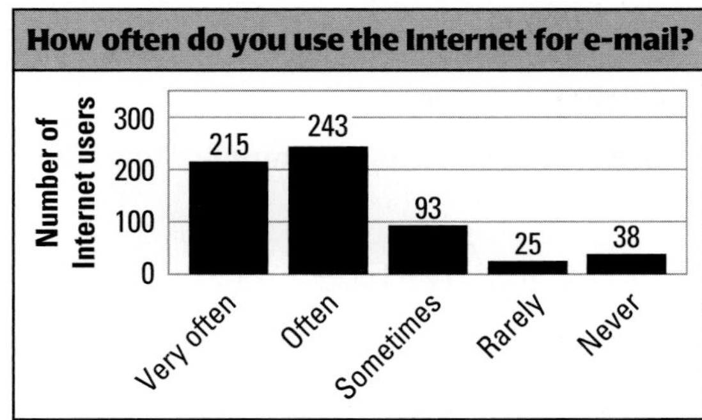

16. The table shows the length (in miles) of Interstate 95 in each state, from south to north. What is the probability that a randomly selected segment of Interstate 95 is in the five states stretching from Virginia to New Jersey? *Explain* how you found your answer.

State	FL	GA	SC	NC	VA	MD	DE	PA	NJ	NY	CT	RI	MA	NH	ME
Miles	381	112	201	183	178	110	26	58	44	29	118	47	97	17	306

TEST PREPARATION

11 Data Analysis and Statistics

Before

In previous chapters, you learned the following skills, which you'll use in Chapter 11: describing distributions, ordering real numbers, and finding probabilities.

Prerequisite Skills

VOCABULARY CHECK

Copy and complete the statement.

1. The **probability** of an event is a number from _?_ to _?_ that indicates the likelihood the event will occur.
2. The **binomial distribution** at the right is not skewed. Instead, it is _?_.

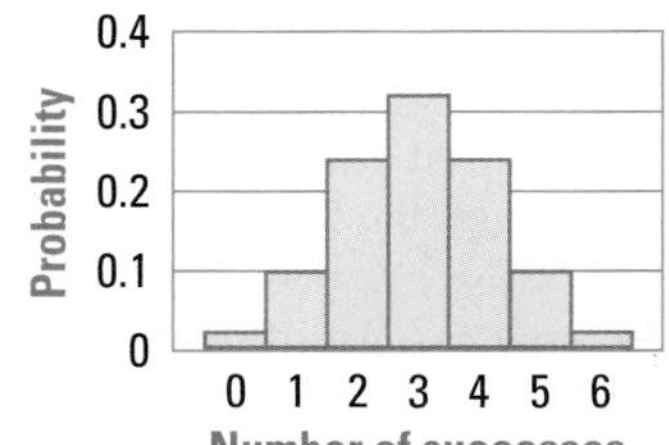

SKILLS CHECK

Graph the numbers on a number line. Then write the numbers in increasing order. *(Review p. 2 for 11.1.)*

3. $-\frac{3}{4}, 0.4, \sqrt{7}, -1.3, \frac{2}{3}, -\sqrt{12}$

4. $1.5, \frac{4}{3}, -1.24, \sqrt{2}, -\sqrt{3}, \frac{6}{5}$

You have an equally likely chance of choosing any integer from 1 through 20. Find the probability of the event. *(Review p. 698 for 11.3.)*

5. An odd number is chosen.
6. A perfect square is chosen.
7. A multiple of 3 is chosen.
8. A factor of 50 is chosen.

In Chapter 11, you will apply the big ideas listed below and reviewed in the Chapter Summary on page 783. You will also use the key vocabulary listed below.

Big Ideas

1. **Finding measures of central tendency and dispersion**
2. **Using normal distributions**
3. **Working with samples**

KEY VOCABULARY

- statistics, *p. 744*
- mean, *p. 744*
- median, *p. 744*
- mode, *p. 744*
- range, *p. 745*
- standard deviation, *p. 745*
- normal distribution, *p. 757*
- normal curve, *p. 757*
- standard normal distribution, *p. 758*
- *z*-score, *p. 758*
- sample, *p. 766*
- unbiased sample, *p. 767*
- biased sample, *p. 767*
- margin of error, *p. 768*

Why?

You can use statistics to compare two or more sets of data. For example, you can compare data for two athletes to see who performs better.

Animated Algebra

The animation illustrated below for Exercise 28 on page 748 helps you answer this question: Which contestant has the best average score after four rounds of an archery competition?

Several contestants shoot arrows at archery targets.

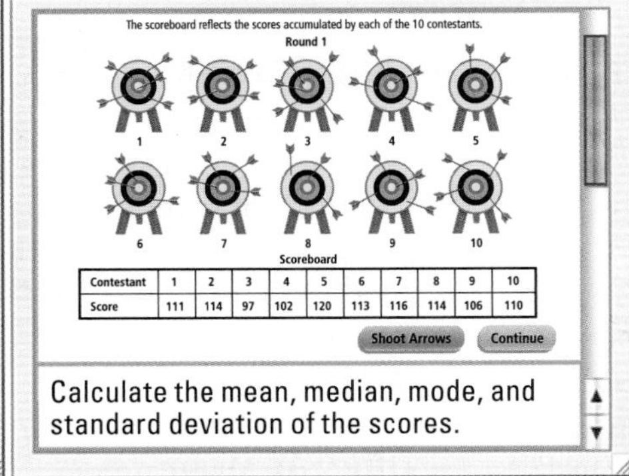

Calculate the mean, median, mode, and standard deviation of the scores.

Animated Algebra at classzone.com

Other animations for Chapter 11: pages 744, 754, 757, and 776

11.1 Find Measures of Central Tendency and Dispersion

 **A2.S.3** Calculate measures of central tendency with group frequency distributions

Before You displayed data using graphs.

Now You will describe data using statistical measures.

Why? So you can calculate softball statistics, as in Ex. 27.

Key Vocabulary
- **statistics**
- **measure of central tendency**
- **measure of dispersion**
- **standard deviation**
- **outlier**

Statistics are numerical values used to summarize and compare sets of data. Two important types of statistics are *measures of central tendency* and *measures of dispersion.*

A **measure of central tendency** is a number used to represent the center or middle of a set of data values. The *mean, median,* and *mode* are three commonly used measures of central tendency.

KEY CONCEPT *For Your Notebook*

Measures of Central Tendency

- The **mean**, or *average*, of n numbers is the sum of the numbers divided by n. The mean is denoted by $\overline{x}$, which is read as "x-bar." For the data set $x_1, x_2, \ldots, x_n$, the mean is $\overline{x} = \frac{x_1 + x_2 + \cdots + x_n}{n}$.
- The **median** of n numbers is the middle number when the numbers are written in order. (If n is even, the median is the mean of the two middle numbers.)
- The **mode** of n numbers is the number or numbers that occur most frequently. There may be one mode, no mode, or more than one mode.

EXAMPLE 1 Find measures of central tendency

WAITING TIMES The data sets at the right give the waiting times (in minutes) of several people at two veterinary offices. Find the mean, median, and mode of each data set.

Office A	Office B
14, 17, 18, 19, 20, 24, 24, 30, 32	8, 11, 12, 16, 18, 18, 18, 20, 23

AVOID ERRORS
Before identifying the median as the middle number in a list, make sure the numbers are ordered from least to greatest or from greatest to least.

Solution

Office A: Mean: $\overline{x} = \frac{14 + 17 + \cdots + 32}{9} = \frac{198}{9} = 22$ Median: 20 Mode: 24

Office B: Mean: $\overline{x} = \frac{8 + 11 + \cdots + 23}{9} = \frac{144}{9} = 16$ Median: 18 Mode: 18

Animated **Algebra** at classzone.com

 **GUIDED PRACTICE** for Example 1

1. **TRANSPORTATION** The data set below gives the waiting times (in minutes) of 10 students waiting for a bus. Find the mean, median, and mode of the data set.

4, 8, 12, 15, 3, 2, 6, 9, 8, 7

MEASURES OF DISPERSION A **measure of dispersion** is a statistic that tells you how *dispersed*, or spread out, data values are. One simple measure of dispersion is the **range**, which is the difference between the greatest and least data values.

EXAMPLE 2 Find ranges of data sets

Find the range of the waiting times in each data set in Example 1.

Solution

Office A: Range = 32 − 14 = 18 **Office B:** Range = 23 − 8 = 15

Because the range for office A is greater, its waiting times are more spread out.

STANDARD DEVIATION Another measure of dispersion is *standard deviation*, which describes the typical difference (or *deviation*) between a data value and the mean.

KEY CONCEPT *For Your Notebook*

Standard Deviation of a Data Set

The **standard deviation** σ (read as "sigma") of $x_1, x_2, \ldots, x_n$ is:

$$\sigma = \sqrt{\frac{(x_1 - \overline{x})^2 + (x_2 - \overline{x})^2 + \cdots + (x_n - \overline{x})^2}{n}}$$

EXAMPLE 3 Standardized Test Practice

What is the standard deviation of the waiting times in each data set in Example 1?

Ⓐ 4.7 and 5.2 Ⓑ 5.7 and 5.2 Ⓒ 4.7 and 4.5 Ⓓ 5.7 and 4.5

Solution

Office A: $\sigma = \sqrt{\frac{(14-22)^2 + (17-22)^2 + \cdots + (32-22)^2}{9}} = \sqrt{\frac{290}{9}} \approx 5.7$

Office B: $\sigma = \sqrt{\frac{(8-16)^2 + (11-16)^2 + \cdots + (23-16)^2}{9}} = \sqrt{\frac{182}{9}} \approx 4.5$

▶ The correct answer is D. Ⓐ Ⓑ Ⓒ Ⓓ

GUIDED PRACTICE for Examples 2 and 3

2. Find the range and standard deviation of the data set in Guided Practice Exercise 1 on page 745.

OUTLIERS Measures of central tendency and dispersion can give misleading impressions of a data set if the set contains one or more *outliers.* An **outlier** is a value that is much greater than or much less than most of the other values in a data set.

EXAMPLE 4 Examine the effect of an outlier

AIR HOCKEY You are competing in an air hockey tournament. The winning scores for the first 10 games are given below.

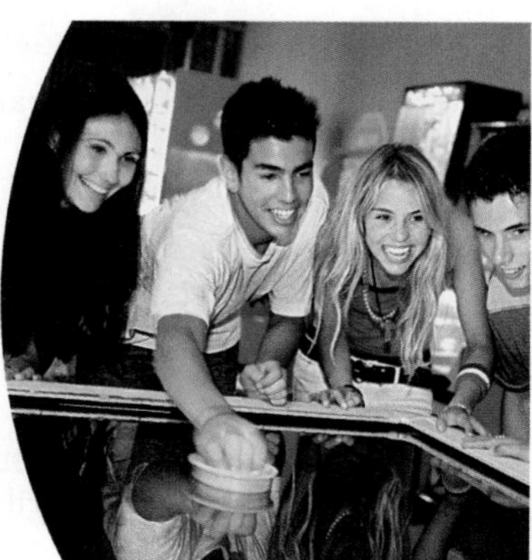

14, 15, 15, 17, 11, 15, 13, 12, 15, 13

a. Find the mean, median, mode, range, and standard deviation of the data set.

b. The winning score in the next game is an outlier, 3. Find the new mean, median, mode, range, and standard deviation.

c. Which measure of central tendency does the outlier affect the most? the least?

d. What effect does the outlier have on the range and standard deviation?

Solution

a. **Mean:** $\bar{x} = \frac{14 + 15 + \cdots + 13}{10} = 14$ **Median:** 14.5 **Mode:** 15

Range: $17 - 11 = 6$

Std. Dev.: $\sigma = \sqrt{\frac{(14 - 14)^2 + (15 - 14)^2 + \cdots + (13 - 14)^2}{10}} \approx 1.7$

b. **Mean:** $\bar{x} = \frac{14 + 15 + \cdots + 3}{11} = 13$ **Median:** 14 **Mode:** 15

Range: $17 - 3 = 14$

Std. Dev.: $\sigma = \sqrt{\frac{(14 - 13)^2 + (15 - 13)^2 + \cdots + (3 - 13)^2}{11}} \approx 3.5$

c. The mean is most affected by the outlier. The mode is least affected by the outlier.

d. The outlier causes both the range and standard deviation to increase.

GUIDED PRACTICE for Example 4

3. **WHAT IF?** In part (b) of Example 4, suppose the winning score in the next game is 25 instead of 3. Find the new mean, median, mode, range, and standard deviation of the data set.

11.1 EXERCISES

HOMEWORK KEY

○ = **WORKED-OUT SOLUTIONS** on p. WS19 for Exs. 5, 15, and 29

★ = **STANDARDIZED TEST PRACTICE** Exs. 2, 7, 8, 23, 24, and 30

SKILL PRACTICE

1. **VOCABULARY** Copy and complete: Measures of _?_ represent the center or middle of a data set. Measures of _?_ tell you how spread out the values in a data set are.

2. ★ **WRITING** Define the mean, median, and mode of a set of n numbers.

EXAMPLE 1 on p. 744 for Exs. 3–10

MEASURES OF CENTRAL TENDENCY In Exercises 3–6, find the mean, median, and mode of the data set.

3. The numbers of mice born in nine different litters: 5, 7, 6, 3, 8, 6, 4, 5, 4

4. A student's quiz scores for the first semester of an algebra class: 18, 20, 14, 15, 20, 17, 16

5. The heights (in inches) of the members of a men's college basketball team: 69, 70, 75, 84, 73, 78, 74, 73, 78, 71

6. The waiting times (in minutes) of several people at a doctor's office: 24, 19, 30, 39, 22, 19, 26, 35, 42, 15, 25

7. ★ **MULTIPLE CHOICE** What is the median of 0.5, 0.6, 0.7, 1.2, 1.5, and 1.5?

   Ⓐ 0.7 Ⓑ 0.95 Ⓒ 1 Ⓓ 1.5

8. ★ **MULTIPLE CHOICE** What is the mean of 2, 2, 6, 7, 9, and 10?

   Ⓐ 2 Ⓑ 6 Ⓒ 6.5 Ⓓ 7.2

ERROR ANALYSIS ***Describe*** **and correct the error in finding the measure of central tendency.**

9. The median of the data set below is 5 because 5 is the middle number.

   12, 8, 9, 5, 10, 10, 3

10. The only mode of the data set below is 12 because 12 occurs most frequently.

    12, 9, 24, 12, 18, 9, 12, 11, 9

EXAMPLES 2 and 3 on p. 745 for Exs. 11–16

MEASURES OF DISPERSION Find the range and standard deviation of the data set.

11. 7, 4, 6, 8, 5, 9, 5, 7
12. 10, 12, 7, 11, 20, 7, 6, 8, 9
13. 3.1, 2.7, 6.0, 5.6, 2.3, 2.0, 1.3
14. 44, 47, 45, 48, 45, 47, 50, 44, 48, 42
15. 135, 142, 148, 136, 152, 140, 158, 154
16. 301, 312, 308, 320, 318, 315, 325, 336

EXAMPLE 4 on p. 746 for Exs. 17–22

IDENTIFYING OUTLIERS Identify the outlier in the data set. Then find the mean, median, mode, range, and standard deviation of the data set when the outlier is included and when it is not.

17. 2, 2, 3, 3, 4, 4, 4, 6, 68
18. 0, 72, 75, 75, 83, 83, 83, 91
19. 10.9, 12.4, 0.7, 11.6, 12.8, 11.6
20. 28, 20, 25, 28, 100, 25, 20
21. 60, 68, 75, 78, 152, 71, 66, 72, 66, 80
22. 184, 192, 173, 181, 199, 65, 190, 188

23. ★ **OPEN-ENDED MATH** Create a data set with a mean of 10, a median of 11, and a mode of 8.

24. ★ **SHORT RESPONSE** An outlier can be defined as a value in a data set that lies more than three standard deviations from the mean. So, x is an outlier if $\frac{|x - \overline{x}|}{\sigma} > 3$. In parts (a)–(c), use this definition to identify the outlier(s) in the data set. *Justify* your answers mathematically.

   a. 70, 55, 54, 75, 60, 58, 55, 56, 6, 62, 68, 94, 55, 82, 69, 74

   b. 18, 20, 22, 25, 16, 40, 24, 19, 38, 3, 21, 27, 88, 24, 23, 26

   c. 50, 93, 81, 84, 88, 85, 90, 99, 92, 199, 96, 89, 87, 94, 37

25. **CHALLENGE** The formula for standard deviation can also be written as:

$$\sigma = \sqrt{\frac{x_1^{\,2} + x_2^{\,2} + \cdots + x_n^{\,2}}{n} - \overline{x}^2}$$

For $n = 3$, show that this formula is equivalent to the formula given on page 745. (*Hint:* You will need to show that $x_1 + x_2 + x_3 = 3\overline{x}$.)

PROBLEM SOLVING

EXAMPLES 1, 2, and 3 on pp. 744–745 for Exs. 26–28

26. **FOOTBALL** The data set below gives the numbers of passing touchdowns for the 12 quarterbacks who threw the most touchdowns during the 2004 NFL regular season. Find the mean, median, mode, range, and standard deviation.

49, 39, 31, 30, 29, 28, 27, 27, 27, 22, 21, 21

@HomeTutor for problem solving help at classzone.com

27. **OLYMPIC SOFTBALL** The data set below gives the total number of at-bats for each player on the 2004 U.S. women's Olympic softball team. Find the mean, median, and mode of the data set.

2, 6, 6, 16, 19, 20, 20, 21, 22, 25, 26, 30

for problem solving help at classzone.com

28. **ARCHERY** The data set below gives the scores of the contestants in the first round of a junior archery competition. Find the mean, median, mode, range, and standard deviation.

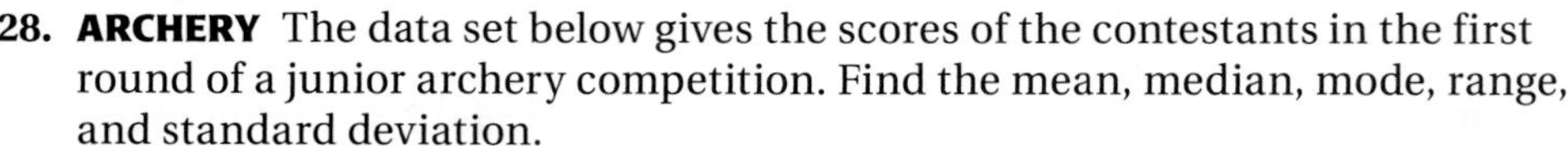

111, 114, 97, 102, 120, 113, 116, 114, 106, 110

at classzone.com

EXAMPLE 4 on p. 746 for Ex. 29

29. **MULTI-STEP PROBLEM** The data set below gives the numbers of trials required by 10 puppies to learn a trick.

20, 23, 19, 25, 21, 23, 5, 24, 19, 23

   a. Analyze Identify the outlier of the data set.

   b. Calculate Find the mean, median, mode, range, and standard deviation of the data set when the outlier is included and when it is not.

   c. Reasoning *Describe* the outlier's effect on the measures of central tendency and dispersion.

30. ★ **EXTENDED RESPONSE** The table shows the results (in meters) for the final round of the 2004 and 1964 men's Olympic javelin throw events.

Men's Olympic Javelin Throw	
2004 data	**1964 data**
86.50, 84.95, 84.84, 84.13, 83.31, 83.25, 83.14, 83.01, 80.59, 80.28, 79.43, 74.36	82.66, 82.32, 80.57, 80.17, 78.72, 76.94, 74.72, 74.26

a. **Calculate** Find the mean, median, mode, range, and standard deviation of the 2004 data.

b. **Calculate** Find the mean, median, mode, range, and standard deviation of the 1964 data.

c. **Analyze** *Compare* the statistics for each set of data. Draw one or more conclusions about the data.

31. **CHALLENGE** The mean discussed in this lesson is called the *arithmetic mean*. Another type of mean is the *geometric mean*. The geometric mean of two positive numbers a and b is $\sqrt{ab}$. Use the steps below to prove that the arithmetic mean of a and b is always greater than or equal to the geometric mean of a and b.

a. *Explain* why $(a - b)^2 \geq 0$.

b. Use the inequality in part (a) to show that $(a + b)^2 \geq 4ab$.

c. Use the inequality in part (b) to show that the arithmetic mean of a and b is greater than or equal to the geometric mean of a and b, or $\frac{a + b}{2} \geq \sqrt{ab}$.

d. Under what condition is the arithmetic mean of a and b equal to the geometric mean of a and b?

NEW YORK MIXED REVIEW

TEST PRACTICE at classzone.com

32. Which best describes the effect on the graph of $y = -\frac{2}{3}x - 1$ when the slope is doubled?

Ⓐ The y-intercept decreases.

Ⓑ The y-intercept increases.

Ⓒ The x-intercept decreases.

Ⓓ The x-intercept increases.

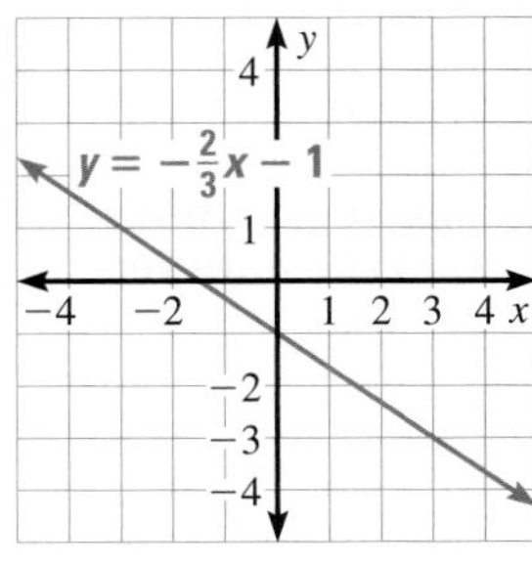

33. What is the length of the line segment joining the points (8, 3) and (2, −1)?

Ⓐ $2\sqrt{5}$ Ⓑ $\sqrt{34}$ Ⓒ $2\sqrt{13}$ Ⓓ $2\sqrt{26}$

34. Which equation describes a relationship in which every real number x corresponds to a negative real number y?

Ⓐ $y = x$ Ⓑ $y = x^2$ Ⓒ $y = |-x|$ Ⓓ $y = -|x|$

Graphing Calculator **ACTIVITY** *Use after Lesson 11.1*

@HomeTutor
classzone.com
Keystrokes

11.1 Calculate One-Variable Statistics

QUESTION **How can you use a graphing calculator to find statistics?**

EXAMPLE **Calculate statistics for a data set**

The data set below gives the ages of the first 43 Presidents of the United States when they first took office. Use a graphing calculator to find the mean, median, range, and standard deviation of the data set.

57, 61, 57, 57, 58, 57, 61, 54, 68, 51, 49, 64, 50, 48, 65, 52, 56, 46, 54, 49, 51, 47, 55, 55, 54, 42, 51, 56, 55, 51, 54, 51, 60, 62, 43, 55, 56, 61, 52, 69, 64, 46, 54

STEP 1 ***Calculate statistics***

Enter the data in list L_1. Then press STAT, choose the CALC menu, and select 1-Var Stats.

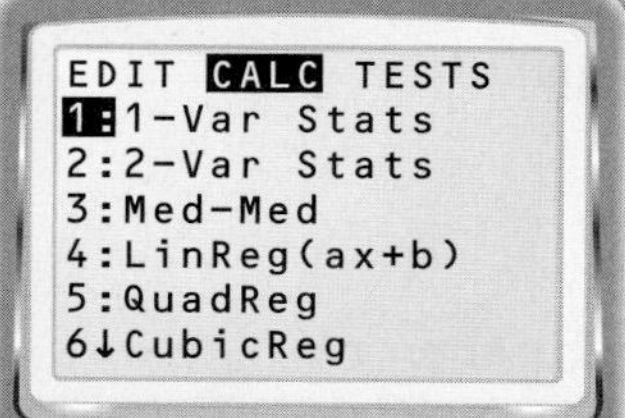

STEP 2 ***Read statistics***

The screen shows a list of statistics. The mean is $\overline{x} \approx 54.8$. The standard deviation is $\sigma x \approx 6.15$.

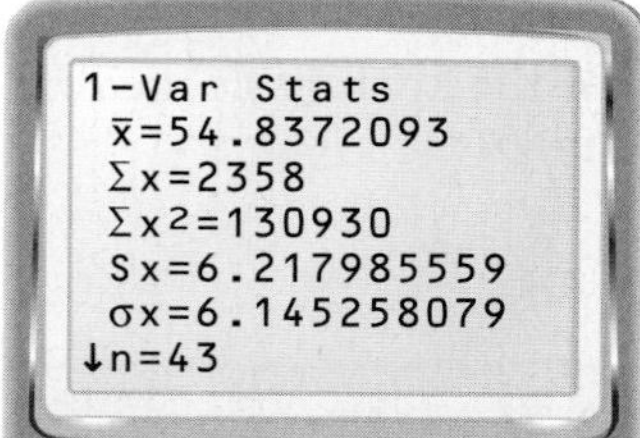

STEP 3 ***Scroll down***

Scroll down to find that the median (Med) is 55. The range is maxX − minX, or 27.

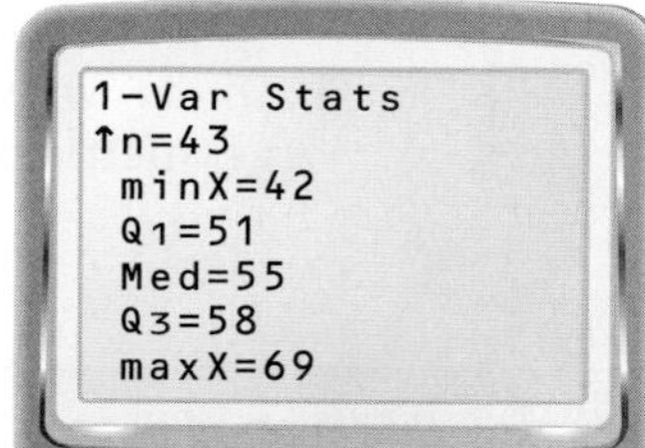

PRACTICE

Use a graphing calculator to find the mean, median, range, and standard deviation of the data set.

1. 43, 46, 47, 48, 51, 54, 58, 40, 52

2. 3.1, 2.7, 6.0, 5.6, 2.3, 2.0, 1.3, 3.4

3. 88, 83, 91, 82, 78, 81, 91, 95, 98

4. 19.4, 16.3, 12.7, 24.8, 19.2, 15.4

5. 110, 107, 101, 108, 106, 112, 104

6. 265, 252, 257, 298, 275, 281, 276

7. VICE PRESIDENTS' AGES The data set below gives the ages of the first 46 vice presidents of the United States when they first took office. Use a graphing calculator to find the mean, median, range, and standard deviation of the data set.

53, 53, 45, 65, 68, 42, 42, 50, 56, 50, 52, 49, 66, 36, 51, 56, 45, 61, 57, 51, 65, 64, 57, 52, 42, 52, 53, 58, 48, 59, 69, 64, 52, 60, 71, 40, 52, 53, 51, 60, 66, 49, 56, 41, 44, 59

11.2 Apply Transformations to Data

A2.S.3 Calculate measures of central tendency with group frequency distributions

Before You calculated statistics for data sets.

Now You will learn how transformations of data affect statistics.

Why? So you can solve problems about space travel, as in Example 1.

Key Vocabulary
- **mean,** *p. 744*
- **median,** *p. 744*
- **mode,** *p. 744*
- **range,** *p. 745*
- **standard deviation,** *p. 745*

The following statistics describe the data set 7, 12, 16, 20, and 20.

Mean: 15 **Median:** 16 **Mode:** 20 **Range:** 13 **Std. Dev.:** 5.0

Adding 10 to each data value produces the data set 17, 22, 26, 30, and 30. The statistics for this data set are shown below.

Mean: 25 **Median:** 26 **Mode:** 30 **Range:** 13 **Std. Dev.:** 5.0

Notice that the mean, median, and mode have each increased by 10, but the range and standard deviation are unchanged. These results can be generalized.

KEY CONCEPT *For Your Notebook*

Adding a Constant to Data Values

When a constant is added to every value in a data set, the following are true:

- The mean, median, and mode of the new data set can be obtained by adding the same constant to the mean, median, and mode of the original data set.
- The range and standard deviation are unchanged.

EXAMPLE 1 Add a constant to data values

ASTRONAUTS The data set below gives the weights (in pounds) on Earth of eight astronauts without their space suits. A space suit weighs 250 pounds on Earth. Find the mean, median, mode, range, and standard deviation of the weights of the astronauts without their space suits and with their space suits.

142, 150, 155, 156, 160, 160, 166, 175

Solution

	Weights without suits	Weights with suits
Mean	158	158 + **250** = 408
Median	158	158 + **250** = 408
Mode	160	160 + **250** = 410
Range	33	33 (unchanged)
Standard deviation	9.3	9.3 (unchanged)

TRANSFORMING DATA BY MULTIPLICATION Another type of transformation you can apply to a data set is to *multiply* each data value by the same constant.

KEY CONCEPT *For Your Notebook*

Multiplying Data Values by a Constant

When each value of a data set is multiplied by a constant, the new mean, median, mode, range, and standard deviation can be found by multiplying each original statistic by the same constant.

EXAMPLE 2 Multiply data values by a constant

OLYMPICS The data set below gives the winning distances (in meters) in the men's Olympic triple jump events from 1964 to 2004. Find the mean, median, mode, range, and standard deviation of the distances in meters and of the distances in feet. (*Note:* 1 meter ≈ 3.28 feet.)

16.85, 17.39, 17.35, 17.29, 17.35, 17.26, 17.61, 18.17, 18.09, 17.71, 17.79

Solution

	Distances in meters	Distances in feet
Mean	17.53	**3.28**(17.53) ≈ 57.50
Median	17.39	**3.28**(17.39) ≈ 57.04
Mode	17.35	**3.28**(17.35) ≈ 56.91
Range	1.32	**3.28**(1.32) ≈ 4.33
Standard deviation	0.37	**3.28**(0.37) ≈ 1.21

✓ **GUIDED PRACTICE** for Examples 1 and 2

1. **ASTRONAUTS** The Manned Maneuvering Unit (MMU) is equipment that latches onto an astronaut's space suit and enables the astronaut to move around outside the spacecraft. The MMU weighs about 300 pounds on Earth. Find the mean, median, mode, range, and standard deviation of the weights of the astronauts in Example 1 with their space suits and MMUs.

2. **WHAT IF?** In Example 2, find the mean, median, mode, range, and standard deviation of the distances in yards. (*Note:* 1 meter ≈ 1.09 yards.)

11.2 EXERCISES

HOMEWORK KEY

○ = **WORKED-OUT SOLUTIONS** on p. WS20 for Exs. 5, 11, and 19

★ = **STANDARDIZED TEST PRACTICE** Exs. 2, 16, 20, 22, and 23

◆ = **MULTIPLE REPRESENTATIONS** Ex. 21

SKILL PRACTICE

1. **VOCABULARY** Copy and complete: Multiplying each value in a data set by a constant is an example of a(n) _?_ of the data.

2. ★ **WRITING** *Describe* how adding the same constant to every value in a data set affects the mean, median, mode, range, and standard deviation.

EXAMPLE 1 on p. 751 for Exs. 3–9

ADDING A CONSTANT **Find the mean, median, mode, range, and standard deviation of the given data set and of the data set obtained by adding the given constant to each data value.**

3. 14, 15, 17, 17, 19, 21, 23; constant: 6
4. 31, 35, 38, 39, 42, 42, 48; constant: 18
5. 74, 76, 77, 77, 78, 81, 83; constant: 17
6. 178, 193, 204, 211, 211, 216; constant: 155
7. 53, 64, 51, 60, 53, 45, 66; constant: −21
8. 295, 279, 278, 282, 279, 301; constant: −45

9. **ERROR ANALYSIS** The standard deviation of a data set is 10. *Describe* and correct the error in finding the standard deviation if 3 is added to each data value.

New standard deviation:
$10 + 3 = 13$

EXAMPLE 2 on p. 752 for Exs. 10–16

MULTIPLYING BY A CONSTANT **Find the mean, median, mode, range, and standard deviation of the given data set and of the data set obtained by multiplying each data value by the given constant.**

10. 19, 23, 23, 26, 30, 31, 34; constant: 3
11. 58, 58, 59, 62, 64, 65, 67; constant: 4
12. 28, 31, 32, 35, 35, 39, 40; constant: 1.5
13. 88, 91, 99, 102, 102, 107; constant: 2.5
14. 130, 121, 132, 115, 130, 108; constant: 0.5
15. 222, 231, 222, 212, 250, 235; constant: 0.9

16. ★ **MULTIPLE CHOICE** The range of a data set is 21. Each value in the data set is multiplied by 3. What is the new range?

(A) 7 (B) 21 (C) 24 (D) 63

17. **CHALLENGE** Let $x_1, x_2, \ldots, x_n$ be the values in a data set, and let $\overline{x}$ be the mean of the data set. Show that the mean of $ax_1, ax_2, \ldots, ax_n$ is $a\overline{x}$.

PROBLEM SOLVING

EXAMPLES 1 and 2 on pp. 751–752 for Exs. 18–22

18. **SALARIES** The data set below gives the annual salaries (in thousands of dollars) of nine DJs working at a local radio station.

39, 29, 42.5, 28.5, 48, 45, 38, 36.5, 28.5

a. Find the mean, median, mode, range, and standard deviation of the salaries.

b. Each DJ receives an annual bonus of $1200. Find the mean, median, mode, range, and standard deviation of the salaries including the bonus.

@HomeTutor for problem solving help at classzone.com

19. **CONSTRUCTION** People who plaster ceilings sometimes walk on stilts. This allows them to reach high ceilings without having to move a ladder. The data set below gives the heights (in inches) of nine plasterers.

72, 73, 71, 66, 74, 68, 72, 69, 72

a. Find the mean, median, mode, range, and standard deviation of the given heights.

b. The plasterers use stilts that are 28 inches high. Find the mean, median, mode, range, and standard deviation of the plasterers' heights with stilts.

Animated Algebra at classzone.com

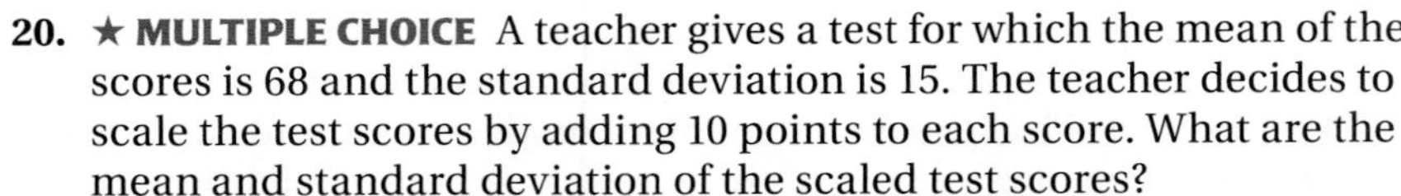

20. ★ **MULTIPLE CHOICE** A teacher gives a test for which the mean of the scores is 68 and the standard deviation is 15. The teacher decides to scale the test scores by adding 10 points to each score. What are the mean and standard deviation of the scaled test scores?

Ⓐ mean: 68, standard deviation: 25 Ⓑ mean: 78, standard deviation: 15

Ⓒ mean: 78, standard deviation: 25 Ⓓ mean: 78, standard deviation: 5

21. ◆ **MULTIPLE REPRESENTATIONS** The data set gives the winning distances (in meters) in the women's Olympic long jump event from 1952 to 2004.

6.24, 6.35, 6.37, 6.76, 6.82, 6.78, 6.72, 7.06, 6.96, 7.40, 7.14, 7.12, 6.99, 7.07

a. **Find Statistics in Meters** Find the mean, median, mode, range, and standard deviation of the distances in meters.

b. **Find Statistics in Feet** Find the statistics listed in part (a) for the distances in feet. (*Note:* 1 meter $\approx$ 3.28 feet.)

22. ★ **SHORT RESPONSE** The data set below gives the weights (in pounds) of eight smokejumpers with their equipment.

287, 265, 273, 275, 295, 280, 290, 280

a. Find the mean, median, mode, range, and standard deviation of the given weights.

b. The equipment each smokejumper carries weighs about 115 pounds. Find the mean, median, mode, range, and standard deviation of the weights of the smokejumpers without their equipment. *Explain* your reasoning.

23. ★ **EXTENDED RESPONSE** The water temperature in an outdoor pool is measured 12 times during a certain week. The temperatures (in degrees Fahrenheit) are listed below.

74.5, 81.9, 72.5, 73.4, 78.4, 72.6, 76.8, 74.5, 77.6, 72.0, 79.2, 76.2

a. Find the mean, median, mode, range, and standard deviation of the Fahrenheit temperatures.

b. Convert all of the Fahrenheit temperatures F to Celsius temperatures C using the formula $C = \frac{5}{9}(F - 32)$.

c. Find the mean, median, mode, range, and standard deviation of the Celsius temperatures.

d. *Describe* the effects of converting from Fahrenheit to Celsius on the measures of central tendency and dispersion.

24. **WEATHER** The graph shows the average rainfall (in centimeters) for New York's Central Park during each month of the year. Find the mean, median, mode, range, and standard deviation of the rainfall amounts in centimeters and in inches. (*Note:* 1 centimeter ≈ 0.3937 inch.)

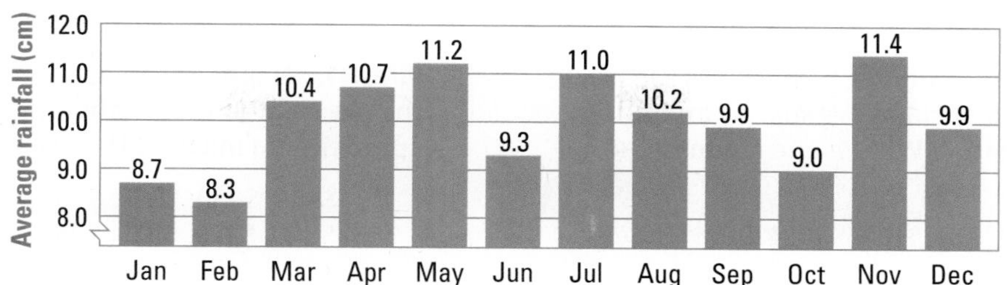

25. **CHALLENGE** A company has 5 executives, 15 supervisors, and 80 production workers. The salary ranges are \$100,000–\$140,000 for the executives, \$60,000–\$90,000 for the supervisors, and \$30,000–\$50,000 for the production workers. The mean of all the salaries is \$49,500, and the median is \$42,000. Each supervisor gets a \$5000 raise and no one else gets a raise. What are the new mean and median? *Explain.*

NEW YORK MIXED REVIEW

TEST PRACTICE at classzone.com

26. Maria packs 4 different pairs of shorts and 7 different shirts for a vacation with her family. How many different outfits are possible?

Ⓐ 11 Ⓑ 18 Ⓒ 28 Ⓓ 30

27. The quadrilaterals shown at the right are similar. What is the value of x?

Ⓐ $\frac{50}{3}$ Ⓑ $\frac{56}{3}$

Ⓒ $\frac{83}{4}$ Ⓓ 27

QUIZ *for Lessons 11.1–11.2*

Find the mean, median, mode, range, and standard deviation of the data set. *(p. 744)*

1. 8, 5, 5, 9, 11, 15, 7, 11, 16
2. 18, 19, 23, 17, 19, 15, 14, 24, 21
3. 56, 45, 48, 47, 56, 55, 43, 44
4. 67, 70, 73, 68, 71, 73, 74, 73, 70
5. 145, 181, 163, 150, 158, 172, 159
6. 246, 231, 261, 244, 250, 232, 246, 258

7. **DIGITAL CAMERAS** The data set below gives the original prices of nine different digital cameras at an electronics store. The store is offering a promotion in which all digital cameras ordered online are 20% off. Find the mean, median, mode, range, and standard deviation of the original prices and of the sale prices. *(p. 751)*

\$120, \$130, \$150, \$180, \$230, \$280, \$320, \$320, \$350

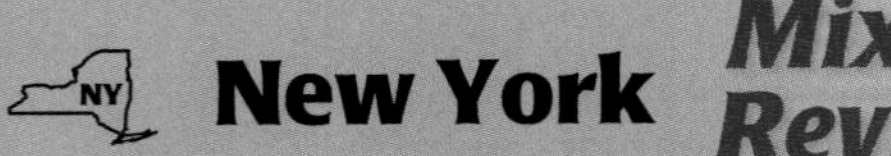

Lessons 11.1–11.2

1. **TV PRICES** The data set below gives the prices of eight 13-inch color TVs sold by an online electronics store. What is the mean of the TV prices?

   $84, $75, $70, $100, $80, $120, $80, $75

   (1) $76.13 (3) $85.50
   (2) $80 (4) $87

2. **SALE PRICES** The online electronics store from Exercise 1 is having a three-day sale in which all 13-inch color TVs are 25% off. What is the approximate standard deviation of the sale prices of the eight 13-inch TVs in Exercise 1?

   (1) $5.52
   (2) $7.27
   (3) $11.63
   (4) $12.43

3. **TEMPERATURES** The table below shows the average temperature (in degrees Fahrenheit) for each month of the year in Buffalo, New York. What is the range of these temperatures?

Average Monthly Temperatures in Buffalo, NY
23.7, 24.6, 33.8, 45.1, 56.5, 65.8, 71.1, 68.9, 61.9, 51.1, 40.5, 29.1

   (1) 24 (3) 46.4
   (2) 45.2 (4) 46.6

4. **SALARIES** The data set below gives the salaries (in thousands of dollars) of eight employees of an advertising agency after they receive an annual bonus of $2500. What is the approximate mean of the salaries *without* the annual bonus?

   49, 52, 46.5, 43, 59.5, 54, 49.5, 61.5

   (1) 48.3 (3) 51.9
   (2) 49.4 (4) 54.4

5. **MOUNTAIN BIKES** The data set below gives the prices of 14 mountain bikes. What is the approximate mean of the prices?

   $155, $250, $290, $200, $150, $200, $270, $670, $250, $230, $200, $150, $270, $850

   (1) $240
   (2) $253
   (3) $295
   (4) $303

6. **OPEN-ENDED** The data set below gives the score of each member of a high school golf team in the first round of the season.

   76, 84, 81, 92, 87

   Find the average score and standard deviation for the team.

   Suppose that each player decreased his or her score by x strokes. What is the new average score and standard deviation, in terms of x? *Explain.*

7. **OPEN-ENDED** Two track-and-field teammates record their times (in seconds) for five trials in the 100 meter sprint event. The times are listed in the table.

Trial	Teammate 1	Teammate 2
1	11.3	11.8
2	13.4	12.3
3	11.1	12.5
4	12.5	11.9
5	11.3	11.8

   Find the mean, median, mode, range, and standard deviation of each teammate's times.

   Which teammate has the more consistent times? *Explain* your reasoning.

11.3 Use Normal Distributions

A2.S.5 Know and apply the characteristics of the normal distribution

Before You interpreted probability distributions.

Now You will study normal distributions.

Why? So you can model animal populations, as in Example 3.

Key Vocabulary
- **normal distribution**
- **normal curve**
- **standard normal distribution**
- ***z*-score**

In Lesson 10.6, you studied probability distributions. One type of probability distribution is a *normal distribution*. A **normal distribution** is modeled by a bell-shaped curve called a **normal curve** that is symmetric about the mean.

KEY CONCEPT *For Your Notebook*

Areas Under a Normal Curve

A normal distribution with mean $\overline{x}$ and standard deviation σ has the following properties:

- The total area under the related normal curve is 1.
- About 68% of the area lies within 1 standard deviation of the mean.
- About 95% of the area lies within 2 standard deviations of the mean.
- About 99.7% of the area lies within 3 standard deviations of the mean.

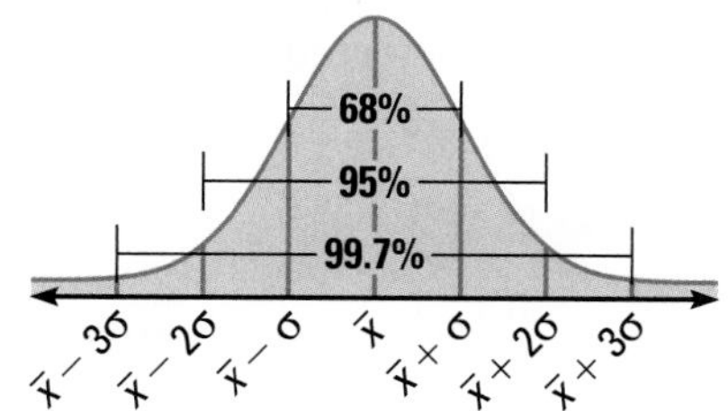

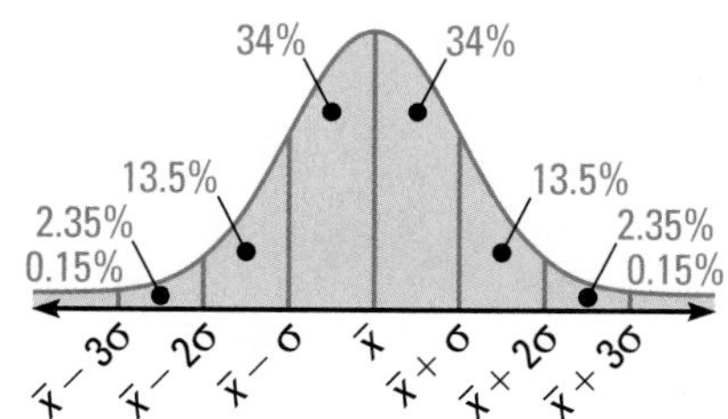

INTERPRET GRAPHS
An area under a normal curve can be interpreted either as a percentage of the data values in the distribution or as a probability.

EXAMPLE 1 Find a normal probability

A normal distribution has mean $\overline{x}$ and standard deviation σ. For a randomly selected x-value from the distribution, find $P(\overline{x} - 2\sigma \le x \le \overline{x})$.

Solution

The probability that a randomly selected x-value lies between between $\overline{x} - 2\sigma$ and $\overline{x}$ is the shaded area under the normal curve shown.

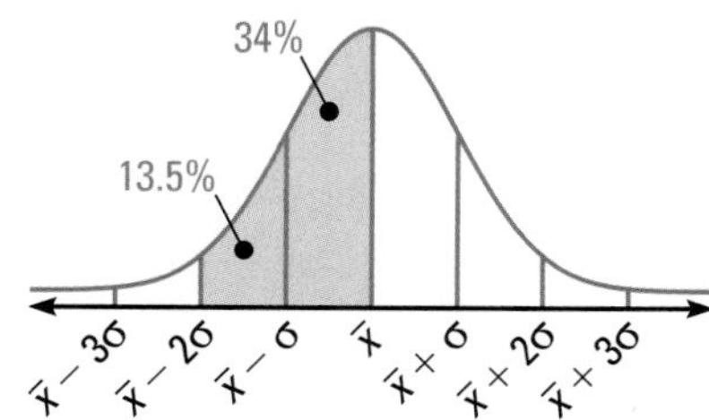

$$P(\overline{x} - 2\sigma \le x \le \overline{x}) = 0.135 + 0.34 = 0.475$$

Animated Algebra at classzone.com

EXAMPLE 2 Interpret normally distributed data

READING
The abbreviation "mg/dl" stands for "milligrams per deciliter."

HEALTH The blood cholesterol readings for a group of women are normally distributed with a mean of 172 mg/dl and a standard deviation of 14 mg/dl.

a. About what percent of the women have readings between 158 and 186?

b. Readings higher than 200 are considered undesirable. About what percent of the readings are undesirable?

Solution

a. The readings of 158 and 186 represent one standard deviation on either side of the mean, as shown below. So, 68% of the women have readings between 158 and 186.

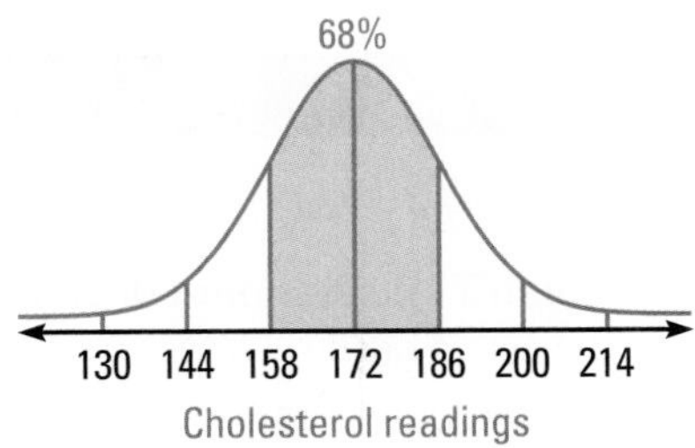

b. A reading of 200 is two standard deviations to the right of the mean, as shown. So, the percent of readings that are undesirable is 2.35% + 0.15%, or 2.5%.

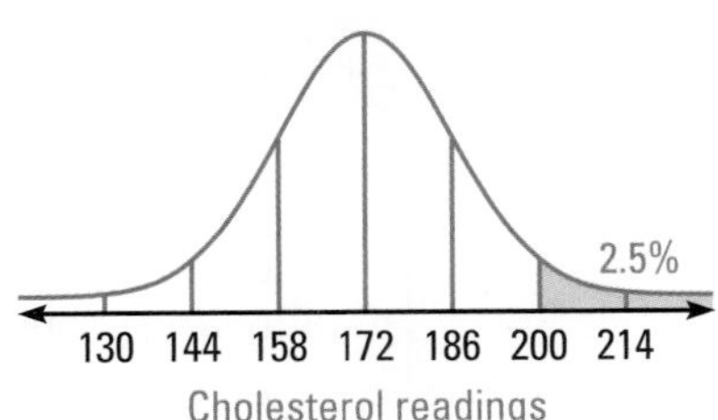

✓ GUIDED PRACTICE for Examples 1 and 2

A normal distribution has mean $\overline{x}$ and standard deviation σ. Find the indicated probability for a randomly selected x-value from the distribution.

1. $P(x \le \overline{x})$
2. $P(x \ge \overline{x})$
3. $P(\overline{x} \le x \le \overline{x} + 2\sigma)$
4. $P(\overline{x} - \sigma \le x \le \overline{x})$
5. $P(x \le \overline{x} - 3\sigma)$
6. $P(x \ge \overline{x} + \sigma)$
7. **WHAT IF?** In Example 2, what percent of the women have readings between 172 and 200?

STANDARD NORMAL DISTRIBUTION The **standard normal distribution** is the normal distribution with mean 0 and standard deviation 1. The formula below can be used to transform x-values from a normal distribution with mean $\overline{x}$ and standard deviation σ into z-values having a standard normal distribution.

Formula: $z = \frac{x - \overline{x}}{\sigma}$

Subtract the mean from the given x-value, then divide by the standard deviation.

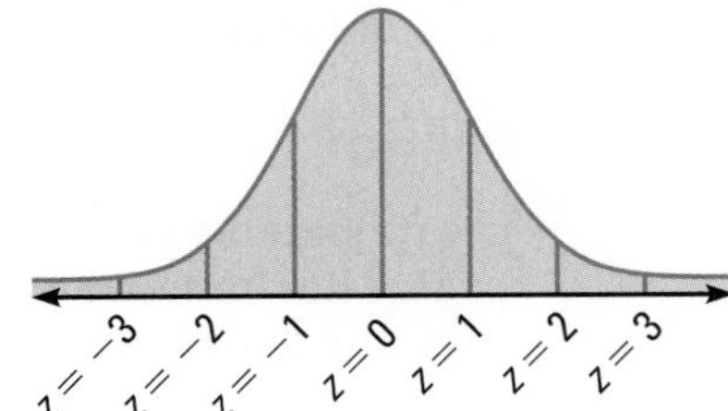

The z-value for a particular x-value is called the **z-score** for the x-value and is the number of standard deviations the x-value lies above or below the mean $\overline{x}$.

STANDARD NORMAL TABLE If z is a randomly selected value from a standard normal distribution, you can use the table below to find the probability that z is less than or equal to some given value. For example, the table shows that $P(z \le -0.4) = 0.3446$. You can find the value of $P(z \le -0.4)$ in the table by finding the value where row **−0** and column **.4** intersect.

READING

In the table, the value .0000+ means "slightly more than 0" and the value 1.0000− means "slightly less than 1."

Standard Normal Table

z	.0	.1	.2	.3	.4	.5	.6	.7	.8	.9
−3	.0013	.0010	.0007	.0005	.0003	.0002	.0002	.0001	.0001	.0000+
−2	.0228	.0179	.0139	.0107	.0082	.0062	.0047	.0035	.0026	.0019
−1	.1587	.1357	.1151	.0968	.0808	.0668	.0548	.0446	.0359	.0287
−0	.5000	.4602	.4207	.3821	.3446	.3085	.2743	.2420	.2119	.1841
0	.5000	.5398	.5793	.6179	.6554	.6915	.7257	.7580	.7881	.8159
1	.8413	.8643	.8849	.9032	.9192	.9332	.9452	.9554	.9641	.9713
2	.9772	.9821	.9861	.9893	.9918	.9938	.9953	.9965	.9974	.9981
3	.9987	.9990	.9993	.9995	.9997	.9998	.9998	.9999	.9999	1.0000−

You can also use the standard normal table to find probabilities for *any* normal distribution by first converting values from the distribution to z-scores.

EXAMPLE 3 Use a z-score and the standard normal table

BIOLOGY Scientists conducted aerial surveys of a seal sanctuary and recorded the number x of seals they observed during each survey. The numbers of seals observed were normally distributed with a mean of 73 seals and a standard deviation of 14.1 seals. Find the probability that at most 50 seals were observed during a survey.

Solution

STEP 1 **Find** the z-score corresponding to an x-value of 50.

$$z = \frac{x - \bar{x}}{\sigma} = \frac{50 - 73}{14.1} \approx -1.6$$

STEP 2 **Use** the table to find $P(x \le 50) \approx P(z \le -1.6)$.

The table shows that $P(z \le -1.6) = 0.0548$. So, the probability that at most 50 seals were observed during a survey is about 0.0548.

z	.0	.1	.2	.3	.4	.5	.6	.7	.8	.9
−3	.0013	.0010	.0007	.0005	.0003	.0002	.0002	.0001	.0001	.0000+
−2	.0228	.0179	.0139	.0107	.0082	.0062	.0047	.0035	.0026	.0019
−1	.1587	.1357	.1151	.0968	.0808	.0668	.0548	.0446	.0359	.0287
−0	.5000	.4602	.4207	.3821	.3446	.3085	.2743	.2420	.2119	.1841
0	.5000	.5398	.5793	.6179	.6554	.6915	.7257	.7580	.7881	.8159

✓ **GUIDED PRACTICE** for Example 3

8. **WHAT IF?** In Example 3, find the probability that at most 90 seals were observed during a survey.

9. **REASONING** *Explain* why it makes sense that $P(z \le 0) = 0.5$.

11.3 EXERCISES

HOMEWORK KEY

◯ = **WORKED-OUT SOLUTIONS** on p. WS20 for Exs. 3, 11, and 33

★ = **STANDARDIZED TEST PRACTICE** Exs. 2, 17, 18, 28, and 35

SKILL PRACTICE

1. **VOCABULARY** Copy and complete: A(n) _?_ is a bell-shaped curve that is symmetric about the mean.

2. ★ **WRITING** *Describe* how to use the standard normal table to find $P(z \le 1.4)$.

EXAMPLE 1 on p. 757 for Exs. 3–10

FIND A NORMAL PROBABILITY A normal distribution has mean $\bar{x}$ and standard deviation σ. Find the indicated probability for a randomly selected x-value from the distribution.

3. $P(x \le \bar{x} - \sigma)$
4. $P(x \ge \bar{x} + 2\sigma)$
5. $P(x \le \bar{x} + \sigma)$
6. $P(x \ge \bar{x} - \sigma)$
7. $P(\bar{x} - \sigma \le x \le \bar{x} + \sigma)$
8. $P(\bar{x} - 3\sigma \le x \le \bar{x})$

USING A NORMAL CURVE Give the percent of the area under the normal curve represented by the shaded region.

9. 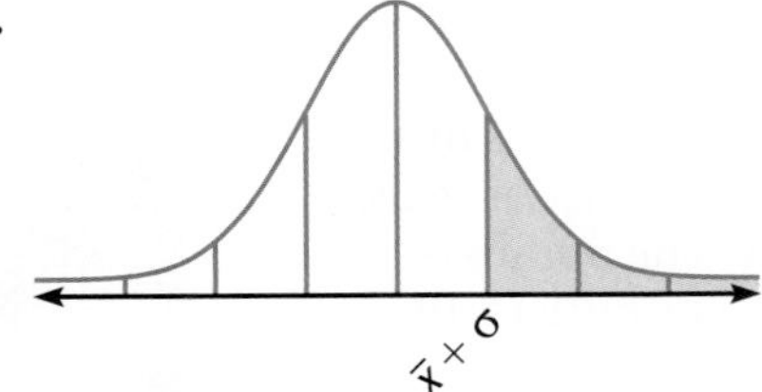

10. 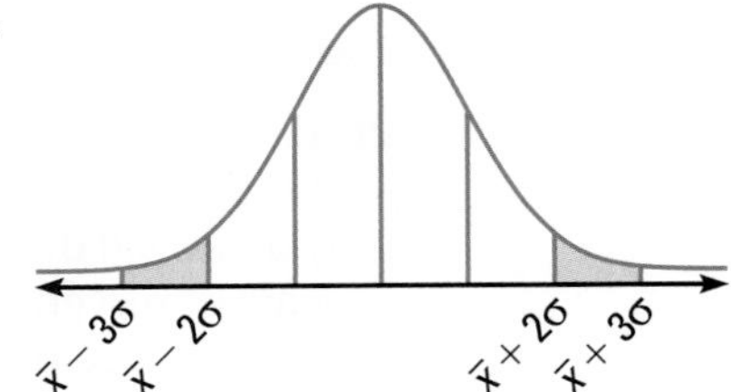

EXAMPLE 2 on p. 758 for Exs. 11–18

NORMAL DISTRIBUTIONS A normal distribution has a mean of 33 and a standard deviation of 4. Find the probability that a randomly selected x-value from the distribution is in the given interval.

11. Between 29 and 37
12. Between 33 and 45
13. Between 21 and 41
14. At least 25
15. At least 29
16. At most 37

17. ★ **MULTIPLE CHOICE** A normal distribution has a mean of 84 and a standard deviation of 5. What is the probability that a randomly selected x-value from the distribution is between 74 and 94?

Ⓐ 0.475 Ⓑ 0.68 Ⓒ 0.95 Ⓓ 0.997

18. ★ **MULTIPLE CHOICE** A normal distribution has a mean of 51 and a standard deviation of 3. What is the probability that a randomly selected x-value from the distribution is at most 48?

Ⓐ 0.025 Ⓑ 0.16 Ⓒ 0.84 Ⓓ 0.975

EXAMPLE 3 on p. 759 for Exs. 19–27

STANDARD NORMAL TABLE A normal distribution has a mean of 64 and a standard deviation of 7. Use the standard normal table on page 759 to find the indicated probability for a randomly selected x-value from the distribution.

19. $P(x \le 68)$
20. $P(x \le 80)$
21. $P(x \le 45)$
22. $P(x \le 54)$
23. $P(x \le 64)$
24. $P(x \ge 59)$
25. $P(x \ge 75)$
26. $P(60 \le x \le 75)$
27. $P(45 \le x \le 65)$

28. ★ **SHORT RESPONSE** Let x be a randomly selected value from a normal distribution with mean 80 and standard deviation 10. If $P(x \le k) = 0.9192$, what is the value of k? *Explain.*

29. **ERROR ANALYSIS** In a study, the wheat yields (in bushels) for several plots of land were normally distributed with a mean of 4 bushels and a standard deviation of 0.25 bushel. *Describe* and correct the error in finding the probability that a plot yielded at least 3.8 bushels.

$$z = \frac{x - \bar{x}}{\sigma} = \frac{3.8 - 4}{0.25} = -0.8$$

From the standard normal table, $P(z \ge -0.8) = 0.2119$. So, the probability that a plot yielded at least 3.8 bushels is 0.2119.

30. **CHALLENGE** A normal curve is defined by an equation of this form:

$$y = \frac{1}{\sigma\sqrt{2\pi}} e^{-\frac{1}{2}\left(\frac{x - \bar{x}}{\sigma}\right)^2}$$

a. **Graphing Calculator** Graph three equations of the given form. The equations should use the same mean but different standard deviations.

b. **Reasoning** *Describe* the effect of the standard deviation on the shape of a normal curve.

PROBLEM SOLVING

EXAMPLES 2 and 3 on pp. 758–759 for Exs. 31–34

31. **BIOLOGY** The illustration shows a housefly at several times its actual size and indicates the fly's wing length. A study found that the wing lengths of houseflies are normally distributed with a mean of about 4.6 millimeters and a standard deviation of about 0.4 millimeter. What is the probability that a randomly selected housefly has a wing length of at least 5 millimeters?

@HomeTutor for problem solving help at classzone.com

32. **FIRE DEPARTMENT** The time a fire department takes to arrive at the scene of an emergency is normally distributed with a mean of 6 minutes and a standard deviation of 1 minute.

a. What is the probability that the fire department takes at most 8 minutes to arrive at the scene of an emergency?

b. What is the probability that the fire department takes between 4 minutes and 7 minutes to arrive at the scene of an emergency?

@HomeTutor for problem solving help at classzone.com

33. **MULTI-STEP PROBLEM** Boxes of cereal are filled by a machine. Tests of the machine's accuracy show that the amount of cereal in each box varies. The weights are normally distributed with a mean of 20 ounces and a standard deviation of 0.25 ounce.

a. Find the z-scores for weights of 19.4 ounces and 20.4 ounces.

b. What is the probability that a randomly selected cereal box weighs at most 19.4 ounces?

c. What is the probability that a randomly selected cereal box weighs between 19.4 ounces and 20.4 ounces? *Explain* your reasoning.

34. **BOTANY** The guayule plant, which grows in the southwestern United States and in Mexico, is one of several plants that can be used as a source of rubber. In a large group of guayule plants, the heights of the plants are normally distributed with a mean of 12 inches and a standard deviation of 2 inches.

Guayule plants

a. What percent of the plants are taller than 16 inches?

b. What percent of the plants are at most 13 inches?

c. What percent of the plants are between 7 inches and 14 inches?

d. What percent of the plants are at least 3 inches taller than or shorter than the mean height?

35. ★ **EXTENDED RESPONSE** Lisa and Ann took different college entrance tests. The scores on the test that Lisa took are normally distributed with a mean of 20 points and a standard deviation of 4.2 points. The scores on the test that Ann took are normally distributed with a mean of 500 points and a standard deviation of 90 points. Lisa scored 30 on her test, and Ann scored 610 on her test.

a. Calculate Find the z-score for Lisa's test score.

b. Calculate Find the z-score for Ann's test score.

c. Interpret Which student scored better on her college entrance test? *Explain* your reasoning.

36. **CHALLENGE** According to a survey by the National Center for Health Statistics, the heights of adult men in the United States are normally distributed with a mean of 69 inches and a standard deviation of 2.75 inches.

a. If you randomly choose 3 adult men, what is the probability that all of them are more than 6 feet tall?

b. What is the probability that 5 randomly selected men all have heights between 65 inches and 75 inches?

NEW YORK MIXED REVIEW

TEST PRACTICE at classzone.com

37. What is the value of $5x^2 - 2x + 3$ when $x = -3$?

Ⓐ -48 Ⓑ -36 Ⓒ 41 Ⓓ 54

38. The table shows the regions of the United States in which the Presidents in office from 1853 through 2005 were born. What is the probability that a President chosen at random was born in the South or was a Republican?

	Midwest	Northeast	South	West
Democrat	2	6	4	0
Republican	9	5	3	1

Ⓐ $\frac{1}{10}$ Ⓑ $\frac{11}{15}$ Ⓒ $\frac{4}{5}$ Ⓓ $\frac{5}{6}$

Approximate Binomial Distributions and Test Hypotheses

GOAL Use normal distributions to approximate binomial distributions.

In Lesson 10.6, you found probabilities related to a binomial distribution using the formula $P(k) = {}_nC_k p^k(1 - p)^{n-k}$. However, it can be tedious to use this formula when the number of probabilities to compute is large. In such cases, you may be able to use a normal distribution to approximate the binomial distribution.

KEY CONCEPT *For Your Notebook*

Normal Approximation of a Binomial Distribution

Consider the binomial distribution consisting of n trials with probability p of success on each trial. If $np \geq 5$ and $n(1 - p) \geq 5$, then the binomial distribution can be approximated by a normal distribution with the following mean and standard deviation.

Mean: $\bar{x} = np$ **Standard Deviation:** $\sigma = \sqrt{np(1-p)}$

EXAMPLE 1 Find a binomial probability

SURVEYS According to a survey conducted by the Harris Poll, 24% of adults in the United States say that their favorite leisure-time activity is reading. You are conducting a random survey of 250 adults. What is the probability that you will find at most 53 adults who say that reading is their favorite leisure-time activity?

Solution

CHECK REASONABLENESS
In Example 1, note that $np = 60 \geq 5$ and that $n(1 - p) = 190 \geq 5$. So, it is reasonable to use a normal approximation.

The number x of adults in your survey who say reading is their favorite leisure-time activity has a binomial distribution with $n = 250$ and $p = 0.24$. To solve the problem using the binomial probability formula, you would have to calculate the following:

$$P(x \leq 53) = P(x = 0) + P(x = 1) + P(x = 2) + \cdots + P(x = 53)$$

This would be tedious. Instead, you can approximate the answer using a normal distribution with the mean and standard deviation given below.

$\bar{x} = np = 250(0.24) = 60$ **Find mean.**

$\sigma = \sqrt{np(1-p)} = \sqrt{250(0.24)(0.76)} \approx 7$ **Find standard deviation.**

For this normal distribution, 53 is about one standard deviation to the left of the mean. Therefore:

$$P(x \leq 53) \approx 0.0015 + 0.0235 + 0.135 = 0.16$$

▶ The probability that at most 53 of the people surveyed say reading is their favorite leisure-time activity is about 0.16.

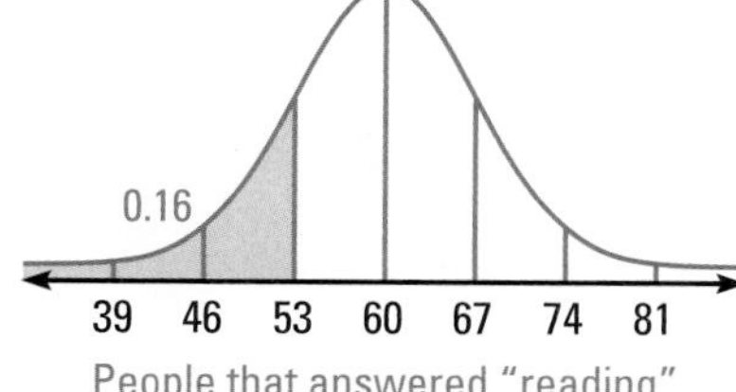

HYPOTHESIS TESTING You can use the following procedure to test a hypothesis about a statistical measure for a population.

KEY CONCEPT *For Your Notebook*

Hypothesis Testing

STEP 1 **State** the hypothesis you are testing. The hypothesis should make a statement about some statistical measure of a population (such as the percent of the population that has a certain characteristic).

STEP 2 **Collect** data from a random sample of the population and compute the statistical measure of the sample.

STEP 3 **Assume** that the hypothesis is true and calculate the resulting probability p of obtaining the sample statistical measure *or a more extreme* sample statistical measure. If this probability is small (typically $p < 0.05$), you should reject the hypothesis.

CHOOSE CRITERION

In Step 3, some statisticians use $p < 0.1$ or $p < 0.01$ as a condition for rejecting a hypothesis.

EXAMPLE 2 Test a hypothesis

FIREFIGHTING A recent Harris Poll claimed that 48% of adults consider firefighting to be a prestigious occupation. To test this finding, you survey 40 adults and find that 15 of them do consider firefighting a prestigious occupation. Should you reject the Harris Poll's findings? *Explain.*

Solution

STEP 1 **State** the hypothesis.

48% of adults consider firefighting a prestigious occupation.

STEP 2 **Collect** data and calculate a statistical measure.

In your survey, 15 out of 40 people, or 37.5%, consider firefighting to be a prestigious occupation.

STEP 3 **Assume** that the hypothesis in Step 1 is true. Find the resulting probability that you could randomly select 15 *or fewer* adults out of 40 who consider firefighting a prestigious occupation. This probability is

$$P(x \leq 15) = P(x = 0) + P(x = 1) + P(x = 2) + \cdots + P(x = 15)$$

where each term in the sum is a binomial probability with $n = 40$ and $p = 0.48$.

You can approximate the binomial distribution with a normal distribution having the following mean and standard deviation:

$$\bar{x} = np = 40(0.48) = 19.2$$

$$\sigma = \sqrt{np(1 - p)} = \sqrt{40(0.48)(0.52)} \approx 3.16$$

Using a z-score and the standard normal table on page 759 gives:

$$P(x \leq 15) \approx P\left(z \leq \frac{15 - 19.2}{3.16}\right) \approx P(z \leq -1.3) = 0.0968$$

▶ So, if it is true that *48% of adults consider firefighting a prestigious occupation,* then there is about a 10% probability of finding 15 or fewer adults who consider firefighting prestigious in a random sample of 40 adults. With a probability this large, you should *not* reject the hypothesis.

PRACTICE

EXAMPLE 1
on p. 763
for Exs. 1–18

APPROXIMATING BINOMIAL DISTRIBUTIONS Find the mean and standard deviation of a normal distribution that approximates the binomial distribution with n trials and probability p of success on each trial.

1. $n = 24, p = 0.4$
2. $n = 40, p = 0.6$
3. $n = 46, p = 0.3$
4. $n = 55, p = 0.15$
5. $n = 36, p = 0.7$
6. $n = 66, p = 0.2$
7. $n = 110, p = 0.08$
8. $n = 125, p = 0.35$
9. $n = 140, p = 0.75$

COLORBLINDNESS Use the fact that approximately 4% of people are colorblind. Consider a class of 460 students.

10. What is the probability that 15 or fewer students are colorblind?
11. What is the probability that 12 or more students are colorblind?
12. What is the probability that between 6 and 18 students are colorblind?

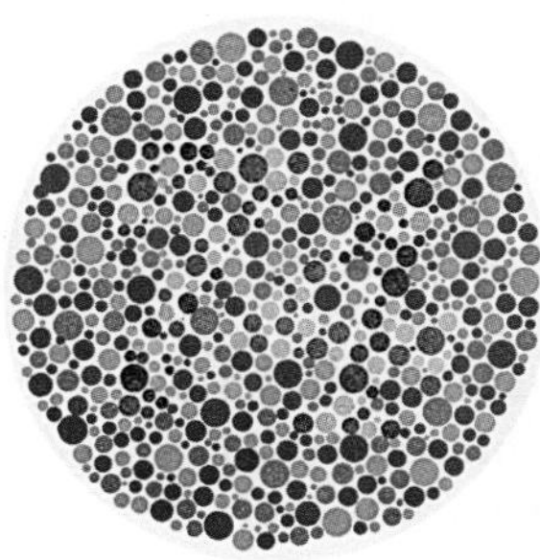

Color vision test

LEFT-HANDEDNESS Use the fact that approximately 9% of people are left-handed. Consider a high school with 1221 students.

13. What is the probability that at least 140 students are left-handed?
14. What is the probability that at most 100 students are left-handed?
15. What is the probability that between 80 and 130 students are left-handed?

MYOPIA Use the fact that myopia, or nearsightedness, is a condition that affects approximately 25% of the adult population in the United States. Consider a random sample of 192 U.S. adults.

16. What is the probability that 42 or more people are nearsighted?
17. What is the probability that 66 or fewer people are nearsighted?
18. What is the probability that between 36 and 60 people are nearsighted?

EXAMPLE 2
on p. 764
for Exs. 19–22

19. **SURVEYS** A survey that asked people in the United States about their feelings of personal well-being found that 85% are generally happy. To test this finding, you question 75 people at random and find that 56 consider themselves generally happy. Would you reject the survey's findings? *Explain.*

20. **CLASS RINGS** You read an article that claims 30% of graduating seniors will buy a class ring. To test this claim, you survey 45 randomly selected seniors in your school and find that 9 are planning to buy a class ring. Should you reject the article's claim? *Explain.*

21. **COMPUTERS** A manufacturer of personal computers claims that under normal work use only 1% of its computers will fail to operate at some point during a month. A business uses 600 of the manufacturer's computers under normal work use and has 12 failures in a month. Would you reject the manufacturer's claim? *Explain.*

22. **JUICE PREFERENCES** A company that makes bottled juices has created a new brand of apple juice. The company claims 80% of people prefer the new apple juice over a competitor's apple juice. A taste test is conducted to test this claim. Of 50 people, 34 prefer the new apple juice. Would you reject the company's claim? *Explain.*

11.4 Select and Draw Conclusions from Samples

NY **A2.S.2** Determine factors which may affect the outcome of a survey

Before You used statistics to describe sets of data.

Now You will study different sampling methods for collecting data.

Why? So you can interpret the results of a survey, as in Ex. 27.

Key Vocabulary
- **population**
- **sample**
- **unbiased sample**
- **biased sample**
- **margin of error**

A **population** is a group of people or objects that you want information about. When it is too difficult, time-consuming, or expensive to survey everyone in a population, information is gathered from a **sample**, or subset, of the population. Some methods for selecting a sample are described below.

In a *self-selected sample,* members of a population can volunteer to be in the sample.

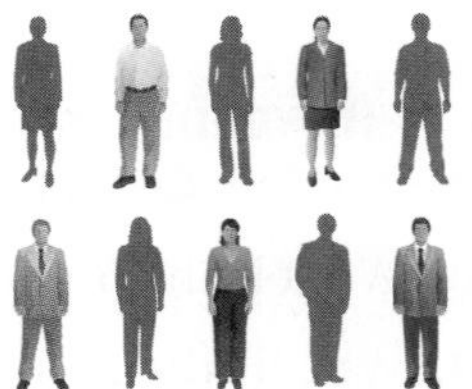

In a *systematic sample,* a rule is used to select members of a population, such as selecting every other person.

In a *convenience sample,* easy-to-reach members of a population are selected, such as those in the first row.

In a *random sample,* each member of a population has an equal chance of being selected.

EXAMPLE 1 Classify samples

BASEBALL A sportswriter wants to survey college baseball coaches about whether they think wooden bats should be mandatory throughout college baseball. Identify the type of sample described.

a. The sportswriter contacts only the coaches that he has cell phone numbers for in order to get quick responses.

b. The sportswriter mails out surveys to all the coaches and uses only the surveys that are returned.

Solution

a. The sportswriter selected coaches that are easily accessible. So, the sample is a convenience sample.

b. The coaches can choose whether or not to respond. So, the sample is a self-selected sample.

BIAS IN SAMPLING In order to draw accurate conclusions about a population from a sample, you should select an *unbiased sample*. An **unbiased sample** is representative of the population you want information about. A sample that overrepresents or underrepresents part of the population is a **biased sample**.

EXAMPLE 2 Identify a biased sample

CONCERT ATTENDANCE The manager of a concert hall wants to know how often people in the community attend concerts. The manager asks 50 people standing in line for a rock concert how many concerts per year they attend. Tell whether the sample is *biased* or *unbiased*. Explain your reasoning.

Solution

The sample is biased because people standing in line for a rock concert are more likely to attend concerts than people in general.

CHOOSING UNBIASED SAMPLES Although there are many ways of sampling a population, a random sample is preferred because it is most likely to be representative of the population.

EXAMPLE 3 Choose an unbiased sample

SENIOR CLASS PROM You are a member of the prom committee. You want to poll members of the senior class to find out where they want to hold the prom. There are 324 students in the senior class. Describe a method for selecting a random sample of 40 seniors to poll.

Solution

STEP 1 **Make** a list of all 324 seniors. Assign each senior a different integer from 1 to 324.

STEP 2 **Generate** 40 unique random integers from 1 to 324 using the *randInt* feature of a graphing calculator. The screen at the right shows six such random integers.

```
randInt(1,324)
                184
                  1
                106
                215
                 67
                213
```

If while generating the integers you obtain a duplicate, discard it and generate a new, unique integer as a replacement.

STEP 3 **Choose** the 40 students that correspond to the 40 integers you generated in Step 2.

✓ GUIDED PRACTICE for Examples 1, 2, and 3

1. **SCHOOL WEBSITE** A computer science teacher wants to know if students would like the morning announcements posted on the school's website. He surveys students in one of his computer science classes. Identify the type of sample described, and tell whether the sample is biased.

2. **WHAT IF?** In Example 3, what is another method you could use to generate a random sample of 40 students?

SAMPLE SIZE When conducting a survey, you need to make the size of your sample large enough so that it accurately represents the population. As the sample size increases, the *margin of error* decreases.

The **margin of error** gives a limit on how much the responses of the sample would differ from the responses of the population. For example, if 40% of the people in a poll prefer candidate A, and the margin of error is ±4%, then it is likely that between 36% and 44% of the entire population prefer candidate A.

KEY CONCEPT — *For Your Notebook*

Margin of Error Formula

When a random sample of size n is taken from a large population, the margin of error is approximated by this formula:

$$\textbf{Margin of error} = \pm\frac{1}{\sqrt{n}}$$

This means that if the percent of the sample responding a certain way is p (expressed as a decimal), then the percent of the population that would respond the same way is likely to be between $p - \frac{1}{\sqrt{n}}$ and $p + \frac{1}{\sqrt{n}}$.

EXAMPLE 4 Find a margin of error

MEDIA SURVEY In a survey of 1011 people, 52% said that television is their main source of news.

a. What is the margin of error for the survey?

b. Give an interval that is likely to contain the exact percent of all people who use television as their main source of news.

Main Source of News

Solution

a. Use the margin of error formula.

$$\text{Margin of error} = \pm\frac{1}{\sqrt{n}}$$ **Write margin of error formula.**

$$= \pm\frac{1}{\sqrt{1011}}$$ **Substitute 1011 for n.**

$$\approx \pm 0.031$$ **Use a calculator.**

▶ The margin of error for the survey is about ±3.1%.

b. To find the interval, subtract and add 3.1% to the percent of people surveyed who said television is their main source of news (52%).

52% − 3.1% = 48.9% 52% + 3.1% = 55.1%

▶ It is likely that the exact percent of all people who use television as their main source of news is between 48.9% and 55.1%.

 Standardized Test Practice

A polling company conducts a poll for a U.S. presidential election. How many people did the company survey if the margin of error is ±5%?

Ⓐ 25 people Ⓑ 250 people Ⓒ 400 people Ⓓ 625 people

REVIEW RADICALS

For help with solving equations involving square roots, see p. 452.

Solution

Use the margin of error formula.

$\text{Margin of error} = \pm\frac{1}{\sqrt{n}}$ **Write margin of error formula.**

$\pm 0.05 = \pm\frac{1}{\sqrt{n}}$ **Substitute ±0.05 for margin of error.**

$0.0025 = \frac{1}{n}$ **Square each side.**

$n = 400$ **Solve for *n*.**

There were 400 people surveyed.

▶ The correct answer is C. Ⓐ Ⓑ Ⓒ Ⓓ

 **GUIDED PRACTICE** for Examples 4 and 5

3. **INTERNET** In a survey of 1202 people, 11% said that they use the Internet or e-mail more than 10 hours per week. What is the margin of error for the survey? How many people would need to be surveyed to reduce the margin of error to ±2%?

11.4 EXERCISES

HOMEWORK KEY

○ = **WORKED-OUT SOLUTIONS on p. WS20 for Exs. 7, 19, and 29**

★ = **STANDARDIZED TEST PRACTICE Exs. 2, 14, 23, 29, and 31**

SKILL PRACTICE

1. **VOCABULARY** Copy and complete: A sample for which each member of a population has an equal chance of being selected is a(n) _?_ sample.

2. ★ **WRITING** *Describe* the difference between an unbiased sample and a biased sample.

EXAMPLES 1 and 2

on pp. 766–767 for Exs. 3–5

CLASSIFYING SAMPLES Identify the type of sample described. Then tell if the sample is biased. *Explain* your reasoning.

3. A taxicab company wants to know if its customers are satisfied with the service. Each driver surveys every tenth customer during the day.

4. A town council wants to know if residents support having an off-leash area for dogs in the town park. Eighty dog owners are surveyed at the park.

5. An English teacher needs to pick 5 students to present book reports to the class. The teacher writes the names of all students in the class on pieces of paper, puts the pieces in a hat, and chooses 5 names without looking.

EXAMPLE 4
on p. 768
for Exs. 6–14

FINDING MARGIN OF ERROR **Find the margin of error for a survey that has the given sample size. Round your answer to the nearest tenth of a percent.**

6. 260 **(7.)** 1000 **8.** 750 **9.** 6400

10. 3275 **11.** 525 **12.** 2024 **13.** 10,000

14. ★ **MULTIPLE CHOICE** In a survey of 2000 voters, 45% said they planned to vote for candidate A. What is the margin of error for the survey?

Ⓐ $\pm 1.8\%$ Ⓑ $\pm 2.2\%$ Ⓒ $\pm 3.6\%$ Ⓓ $\pm 4.5\%$

EXAMPLE 5
on p. 769
for Exs. 15–23

FINDING SAMPLE SIZES **Find the sample size required to achieve the given margin of error. Round your answer to the nearest whole number.**

15. $\pm 3\%$ **16.** $\pm 8\%$ **17.** $\pm 10\%$ **18.** $\pm 4.2\%$

(19.) $\pm 5.6\%$ **20.** $\pm 1.5\%$ **21.** $\pm 6.5\%$ **22.** $\pm 2.5\%$

23. ★ **MULTIPLE CHOICE** The margin of error for a poll is $\pm 2\%$. What is the size of the sample?

Ⓐ 200 Ⓑ 400 Ⓒ 1000 Ⓓ 2500

24. **ERROR ANALYSIS** In a survey of high school students, 13% said that they play basketball regularly. The margin of error is $\pm 4\%$. *Describe* and correct the error in calculating the sample size.

$$\pm 0.13 = \pm \frac{1}{\sqrt{n}}$$
$$0.0169 = \frac{1}{n}$$
$$n \approx 59$$

25. **REASONING** A survey claims the percent of a city's residents that favor building a new football stadium is likely between 52.3% and 61.7%. How many people were surveyed?

26. **CHALLENGE** Suppose a random sample of size n is required to produce a margin of error of $\pm E$. Write an expression in terms of n for the sample size needed to reduce the margin of error to $\pm \frac{1}{2}E$. By how many times must the sample size be increased in order to cut the margin of error in half?

PROBLEM SOLVING

EXAMPLES 3, 4, and 5
on pp. 767–769
for Exs. 27–31

27. **VACATION SURVEY** In a survey of 439 teenagers in the United States, 14% said that they worked during their summer vacation.

a. What is the margin of error for the survey?

b. Give an interval that is likely to contain the exact percent of all U.S. teenagers who worked during their summer vacation.

@HomeTutor for problem solving help at classzone.com

28. **NEWSLETTER** The staff for a student newsletter wants to conduct a survey of students' favorite TV shows. There are 1225 students in the school. The newsletter staff would like to survey 250 students. *Describe* a method for selecting an unbiased, random sample of students.

@HomeTutor for problem solving help at classzone.com

○ = WORKED-OUT SOLUTIONS on p. WS1 ★ = STANDARDIZED TEST PRACTICE

29. ★ **SHORT RESPONSE** Based on the newspaper report shown below, is it reasonable to assume that Kosta is certain to win the election? *Explain.*

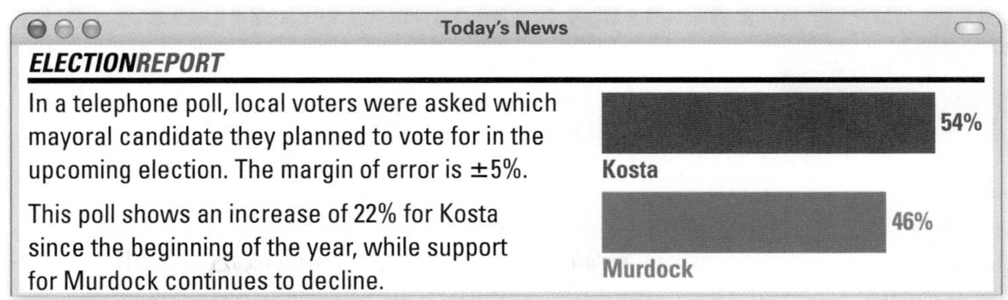

30. **MULTI-STEP PROBLEM** A Gallup Youth Survey reported that 23% of students surveyed, or about 181 students, say that math is their favorite subject in school.

    a. How many students were surveyed?

    b. What is the margin of error for the survey?

    c. Give an interval that is likely to contain the exact percent of all students who would say that math is their favorite subject.

31. ★ **EXTENDED RESPONSE** A survey reported that 235 out of 500 voters in a sample voted for candidate A and the remainder voted for candidate B.

    a. **Find Percents** What percent of the voters in the sample voted for candidate A? for candidate B?

    b. **Find Margin of Error** What is the margin of error for the survey?

    c. **Find Intervals** For each candidate, find an interval that is likely to contain the exact percent of all voters who voted for the candidate.

    d. **Reasoning** Based on your intervals, can you be confident that candidate B won? If not, how many people in the sample would need to vote for candidate B for you to be confident of her victory? (*Hint:* Find the least number of voters for candidate B such that the intervals do not overlap.)

32. **CHALLENGE** In a survey, 52% of the respondents said they prefer cola X and 48% said they prefer cola Y. How many people would have to be surveyed for you to be confident that cola X is truly preferred by more than half the population? *Explain* your reasoning.

NEW YORK MIXED REVIEW

33. What is the solution set for the equation $5x^2 - 7x + 6 = 3x^2 + 4x - 8$?

    Ⓐ $\left\{-4, -\frac{7}{2}\right\}$ Ⓑ $\left\{-4, \frac{7}{2}\right\}$ Ⓒ $\left\{-2, \frac{7}{2}\right\}$ Ⓓ $\left\{2, \frac{7}{2}\right\}$

34. In the figure, $\overline{MN}$ is parallel to $\overline{QP}$, $\overline{MQ}$ is **perpendicular** to $\overline{QP}$, and $m\angle MNR$ is 145°. What is $m\angle RPQ$?

    Ⓐ 90° Ⓑ 105°

    Ⓒ 125° Ⓓ 135°

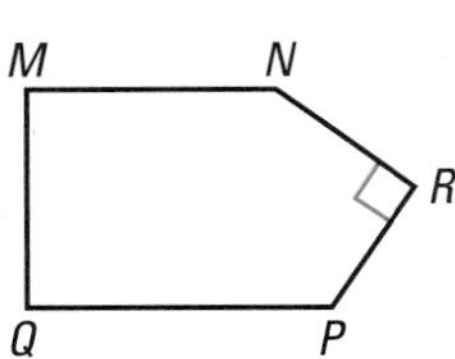

Design Surveys and Experiments

GOAL Write unbiased survey questions and unflawed experimental procedures.

Key Vocabulary
- **biased question**
- **experimental group**
- **control group**

When designing a survey, it is important that the survey questions be carefully written. If a question is poorly written, then the responses of the people surveyed may not accurately reflect their opinions or actions. These types of flawed questions are called **biased questions**.

There are several reasons why a question may be biased:

- The question may encourage the respondent to answer in a particular way.
- The question may be perceived as too sensitive to answer truthfully.
- The question may not provide the respondent with enough information to give an accurate opinion.

Bias may also be introduced through the order in which the questions are asked or may result when the person conducting the interview intentionally or unintentionally influences the responses of those interviewed.

EXAMPLE 1 Identify and correct bias in survey questions

Tell why the question may be biased. Describe how to correct the flaw.

a. *"Many national parks are being heavily damaged by acid rain. Do you favor government funding to help prevent acid rain?"*

This is an example of a *leading question*. Respondents may think a "no" response means they are not in favor of supporting national parks. In this way, the question encourages the respondent to answer "yes."

A better way to ask this question is to eliminate the first sentence and just ask, "Do you favor government funding to help prevent acid rain?"

b. *"Do you agree with the amendments to the Clean Air Act?"*

The question assumes that the respondent is familiar with the amendments to the Clean Air Act. Responses by people unfamiliar with the amendments could lead to misleading conclusions.

A better way to ask this question is to first state each amendment and then ask, "Do you agree with this amendment?"

c. Police officers ask mall visitors, *"Do you wear your seat belt regularly?"*

Many motorists may answer untruthfully because a police officer is asking the question, especially if the law requires seat belt use. The data collected might not accurately represent the percent of people who wear seat belts regularly.

In this case, the correction is to have the question be asked by someone not involved in law enforcement.

EXPERIMENTS An experiment is often conducted with two groups. One group, called the **experimental group**, undergoes some procedure or treatment. The other group, called the **control group**, does not undergo the procedure or treatment.

In a well-designed experiment, everything else about the experimental group and the control group is as similar as possible so that the effect of the procedure or treatment can be determined.

EXAMPLE 2 Identify flaws in an experiment

RESEARCH A drug company conducts an experiment to test whether a new pain relief medication is effective at relieving headaches. The experimental group consists of college students who are given the medication. The control group consists of college professors who are not given the medication.

The company finds that the headaches of people in the experimental group are of shorter duration than those of people in the control group. As a result, the company concludes that the medication is effective. Identify any flaws in this experiment, and describe how they can be corrected.

Solution

On average, college students are likely to be younger than college professors. So, it could be age rather than the medication that explains why the experimental group had shorter-lasting headaches than the control group.

To correct this flaw, the drug company could redesign the experiment so that the ages of the people in the experimental group are similar to the ages of the people in the control group.

PRACTICE

EXAMPLE 1 on p. 772 for Exs. 1–6

In Exercises 1–6, tell why the question may be biased. *Describe* how to correct the flaw.

1. "Do you agree that building a beautiful new baseball stadium would be a good investment for the city to make?"
2. "A survey of the voters in this state shows that 85% favor a tax cut. Do you favor a tax cut?"
3. A dentist asks her patients, "Do you floss every day?"
4. "Don't you think that renovating the old town hall would be a mistake?"
5. "Do you think the defendant in the Carter case was given a fair trial?"
6. "Which city council candidate's platform do you support?"

EXAMPLE 2 on p. 773 for Ex. 7

7. **EDUCATION** A research company conducts an experiment to test whether a new mathematics software program will increase test scores of students. The experimental group consists of students enrolled in Algebra 2 who are given the software. The control group consists of students enrolled in Algebra 1 who are not given the software.

   The company finds that the students in the experimental group test higher than the students in the control group and concludes that the software is effective at increasing test scores. Identify any flaws in the experiment, and describe how they can be corrected.

@HomeTutor
classzone.com
Keystrokes

11.5 Fitting a Model to Data

MATERIALS • 20 index cards • graphing calculator

QUESTION **How can you choose a mathematical model for a data set?**

In this activity, you will measure the time it takes to learn a new task as it becomes more familiar. You will then find a function that models the data you collect. Work with a partner.

EXPLORE **Collect data on learning time**

STEP 1 ***Perform task***
Write a different word on each index card. Shuffle the cards, then have your partner put them in alphabetical order. Measure the time your partner takes to complete the task.

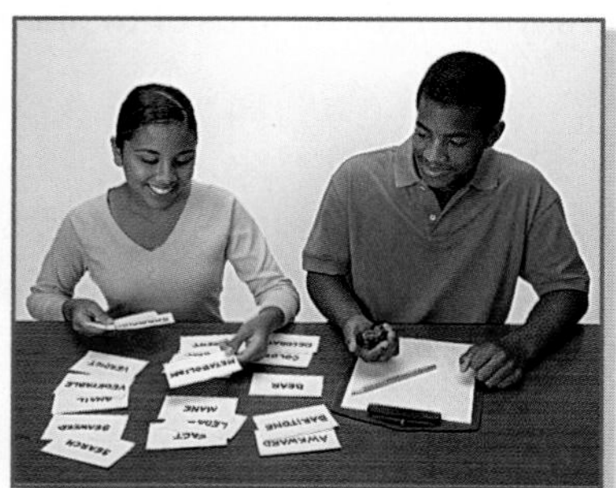

STEP 2 ***Record data***
Have your partner repeat the task described in Step 1 at least five more times. Record your partner's completion times in a table like the one shown below.

Task number	Time (sec)
1	89
2	70
3	64
4	58
5	58
6	57

STEP 3 ***Make scatter plot***
Let x be the task number and let y be the completion time. Use a graphing calculator to make a scatter plot of the data pairs (x, y) from the table in Step 2.

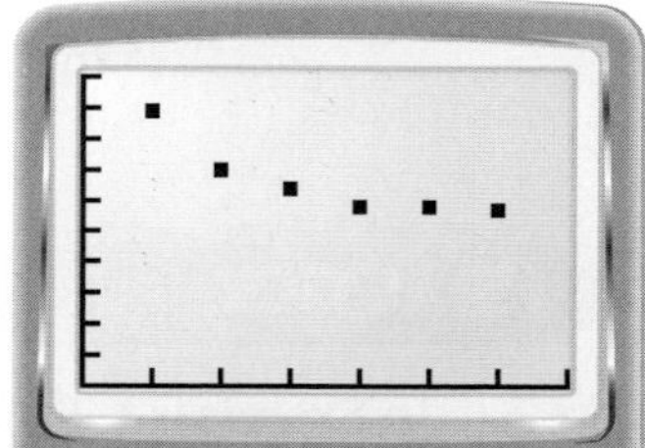

DRAW CONCLUSIONS **Use your observations to complete these exercises**

1. *Describe* the pattern shown in your scatter plot from Step 3. *Explain* why the pattern makes sense.
2. Find a function that is a good model for the data in your scatter plot. You can use one of the graphing calculator's regression features to find a model, or you may experiment with other types of functions that the regression features cannot generate.
3. Use the function you chose in Exercise 2 to predict the time your partner would take to alphabetize the index cards on the 10th trial.
4. Work with a second partner and repeat the experiment. Find a mathematical model to describe this partner's learning times. Do you get similar or different results? *Explain* why you might expect similar or different results.

11.5 Choose the Best Model for Two-Variable Data

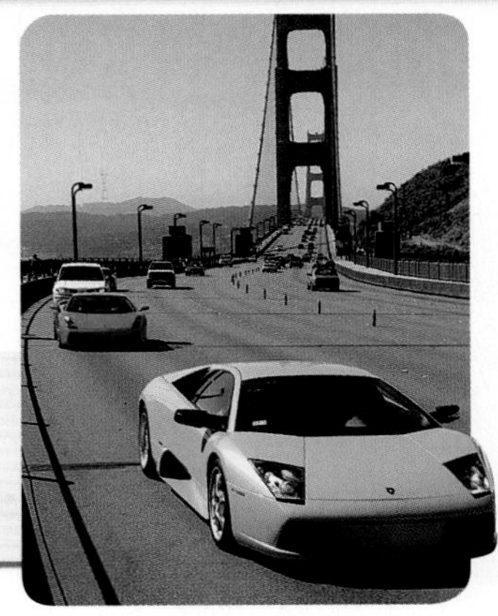

A2.S.7 Determine the function for the regression model, using appropriate technology, and use the regression function to interpolate. . .

Before You wrote different types of functions to model sets of data.

Now You will choose the best model to represent a set of data.

Why? So you can relate engine speed and horsepower, as in Ex. 14.

Key Vocabulary
- **linear function,** *p. 75*
- **quadratic function,** *p. 236*
- **cubic function,** *p. 337*
- **exponential function,** *p. 478*
- **power function,** *p. 531*

You have used the functions shown at the right to model sets of data.

To find the best model for a set of data pairs (x, y), make a scatter plot of the data and determine the type of function suggested by the pattern in the data points. Then find a model of this type using one of the regression features of a graphing calculator.

Function	General form
Linear	$y = ax + b$
Quadratic	$y = ax^2 + bx + c$
Cubic	$y = ax^3 + bx^2 + cx + d$
Exponential	$y = ab^x$
Power	$y = ax^b$

EXAMPLE 1 Use a linear model

TUITION The table shows the average tuition y (in dollars) for a private four-year college in the United States from 1995 to 2002, where x is the number of years since 1995. Use a graphing calculator to find a model for the data.

x	0	1	2	3	4	5	6	7
y	14,537	15,605	16,552	17,229	18,340	19,307	20,106	21,183

Solution

STEP 1 **Make** a scatter plot. The points lie approximately on a line. This suggests a linear model.

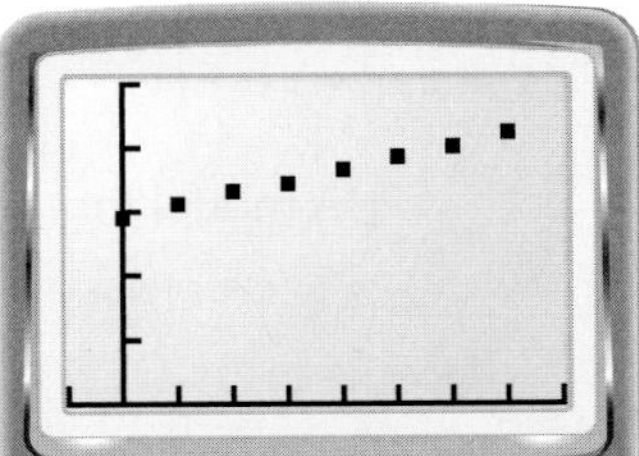

STEP 2 **Use** the linear regression feature to find an equation of the model.

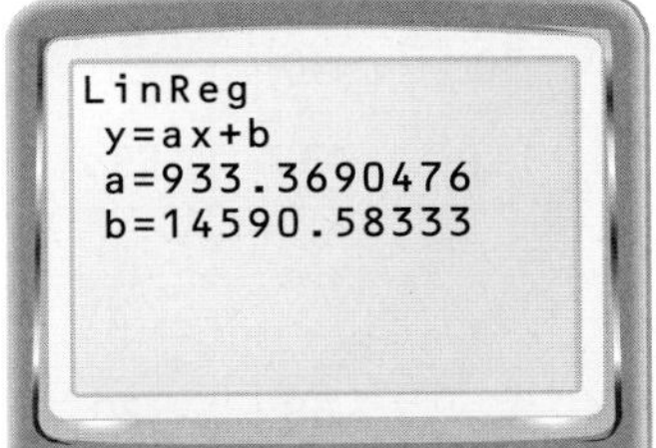

STEP 3 **Graph** the model along with the data to verify that the model fits the data well.

▸ A model for the data is $y = 933x + 14,600$.

EXAMPLE 2 Use an exponential model

COOLING RATES You are storing leftover chili in a freezer. The table shows the chili's temperature y (in degrees Fahrenheit) after x minutes in the freezer. Use a graphing calculator to find a model for the data.

x	0	10	20	30	40	50	60
y	100	75	50	35	28	20	15

ANOTHER WAY
For an extension of the problem in Example 2, turn to page 781 for the **Problem Solving Workshop**.

Solution

STEP 1 **Make** a scatter plot. The points fall rapidly at first and then begin to level off. This suggests an exponential decay model.

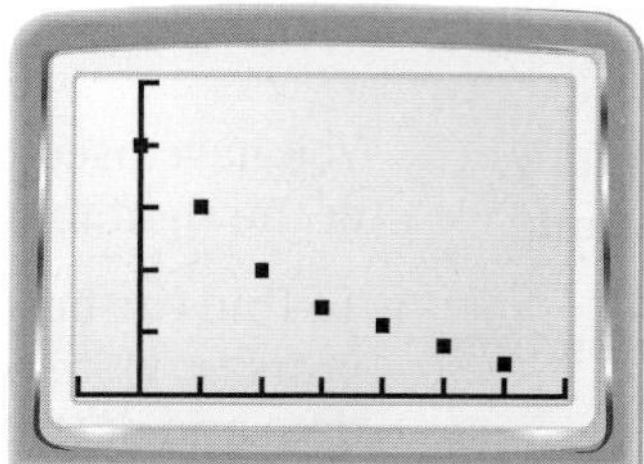

STEP 2 **Use** the exponential regression feature to find an equation of the model.

STEP 3 **Graph** the model along with the data to verify that the model fits the data well.

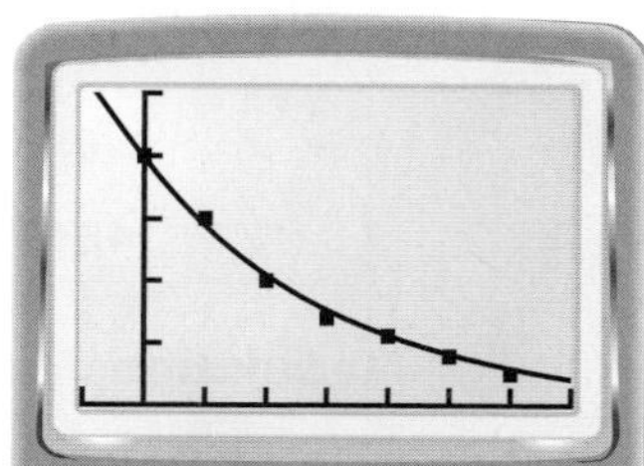

▸ A model for the data is $y = 98.2(0.969)^x$.

 Animated Algebra at classzone.com

✓ GUIDED PRACTICE for Examples 1 and 2

Use a graphing calculator to find a model for the data. Then graph the model and the data in the same coordinate plane.

1.

x	10	20	30	40	50	60	70	80
y	23.1	28.9	34.9	43.7	53.2	66.5	80.8	99.3

2.

x	0	1	2	3	4	5	6	7
y	33	41	52	68	80	89	102	118

EXAMPLE 3 Use a quadratic model

FUEL EFFICIENCY A study compared the speed x (in miles per hour) and the average fuel efficiency y (in miles per gallon) of cars. The results are shown in the table. Use a graphing calculator to find a model for the data.

x	15	20	25	30	35	40	45	50	55	60	65
y	22.3	25.5	27.5	29.0	28.8	30.0	29.9	30.2	30.4	28.8	27.4

Solution

STEP 1 **Make** a scatter plot. The points form an inverted U-shape. This suggests a quadratic model.

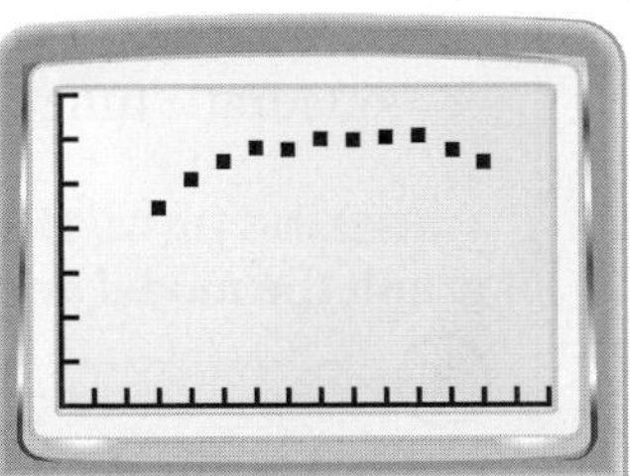

CHOOSE A MODEL
The data in Example 3 can be modeled by both a quadratic function and a cubic function. When this occurs, it is often better to choose the simpler model.

STEP 2 **Use** the quadratic regression feature to find an equation of the model.

STEP 3 **Graph** the model along with the data to verify that the model fits the data well.

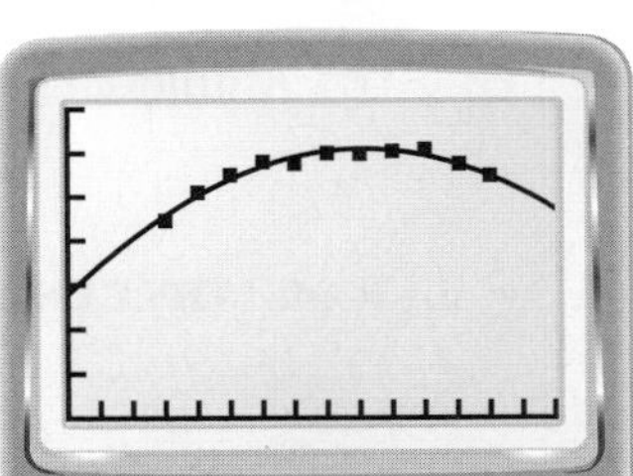

▶ A model for the data is $y = -0.00793x^2 + 0.727x + 13.8$.

✓ GUIDED PRACTICE for Example 3

3. **FUEL EFFICIENCY** Use the model from Example 3 to predict the average fuel efficiency of a car traveling 70 miles per hour.

Use a graphing calculator to find a model for the data. Then graph the model and the data in the same coordinate plane.

4.

x	100	200	300	400	500	600	700
y	16	35	55	70	68	56	38

5.

x	−5	−4	−3	−2	−1	1	2
y	−20	0	3	0	−4	0	18

11.5 EXERCISES

HOMEWORK KEY

◯ = **WORKED-OUT SOLUTIONS** on p. WS20 for Exs. 3 and 11

★ = **STANDARDIZED TEST PRACTICE** Exs. 2, 5, 6, 8, and 13

◆ = **MULTIPLE REPRESENTATIONS** Ex. 12

SKILL PRACTICE

1. **VOCABULARY** Copy and complete: A function of the form $y = ab^x$ is a(n) __?__ function.

2. ★ **WRITING** *Explain* how you can determine whether a linear function or a quadratic function is a better model for a set of data.

EXAMPLES 1, 2, and 3 on pp. 775–777 for Exs. 3–7

MODELING DATA **Use a graphing calculator to find a model for the data. Then graph the model and the data in the same coordinate plane.**

3.

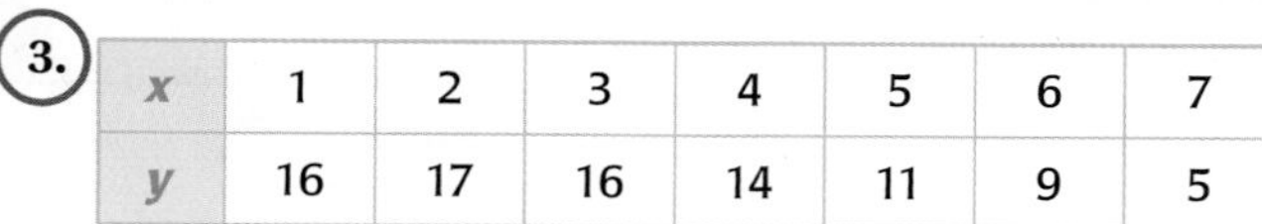

x	1	2	3	4	5	6	7
y	16	17	16	14	11	9	5

4.

x	1	2	3	4	5	6	7
y	26	32	34	37	42	45	49

5. ★ **MULTIPLE CHOICE** Which type of function best models the data points?

   (A) Linear (B) Quadratic

   (C) Cubic (D) Exponential

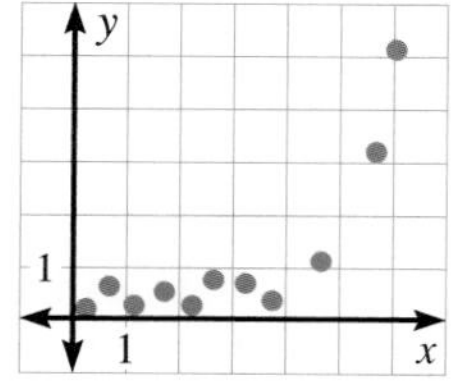

6. ★ **MULTIPLE CHOICE** Which equation best models the data?

x	0	5	10	15	20	25	30	35
y	125	90	63	43	28	20	16	10

   (A) $y = -3.14x + 104$ (B) $y = 126(0.931)^x$

   (C) $y = 125x^{-0.6}$ (D) $y = 0.12x^2 + 124$

7. **ERROR ANALYSIS** *Describe* and correct the error made in using the information on a graphing calculator screen to write a model.

   The ExpReg screen shows:

   y=a*b^x
   a=9.714963274
   b=1.550355116

   A model for the data is:

   $y = 9.71x^{1.55}$ ✗

8. ★ **OPEN-ENDED MATH** Write a table of values that can be modeled by a quadratic function.

9. **CHALLENGE** The function $y = 5x^{2.3}$ models a table of data in which x-values are measured in inches and y-values are measured in pounds. If the table is changed to give the x-values in feet, what function models the revised data?

PROBLEM SOLVING

EXAMPLES 1, 2, and 3 on pp. 775–777 for Exs. 10–13

10. **ECONOMICS** The gross domestic product (GDP) is the total value of goods and services produced by a country in any given year. The table shows the GDP y (in billions of dollars) of the United States for selected years from 1930 to 2000. In the table, x represents the number of years since 1930. Use a graphing calculator to find a model for the data.

x	0	10	20	30	40	50	60	70
y	91.3	101.3	294.3	527.4	1039.7	2795.6	5803.2	9824.6

@HomeTutor for problem solving help at classzone.com

11. **AGRICULTURE** The table shows the ages x (in years) and trunk diameters y (in inches) of several Texas grapefruit trees. Use a graphing calculator to find a model for the data.

x	1	4	8	12	16	20	24
y	1.1	3.9	6.2	7.6	9.1	11.4	15.2

@HomeTutor for problem solving help at classzone.com

12. ◆ **MULTIPLE REPRESENTATIONS** The graph below shows the price of a first-class stamp in the United States for selected years from 1975 to 2002. Use a graphing calculator to find a model for the data. Then graph the model and the data in the same coordinate plane.

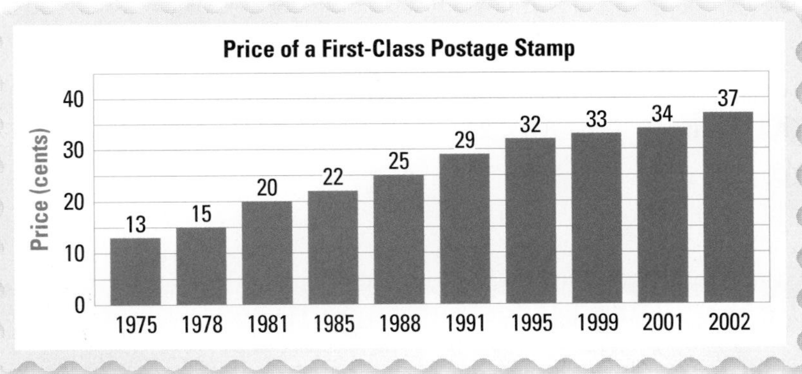

13. ★ **EXTENDED RESPONSE** The manager of a restaurant kept a record of the number y of customers each hour, where $x = 3$ represents 3:00 P.M.

x	3	4	5	6	7	8	9	10
y	9	24	44	56	48	42	38	22

a. Make a scatter plot of the data and determine the type of function that best models the data.

b. Use a regression feature of a graphing calculator to find a function that models the data.

c. Graph the function and data to verify that the function is a good model.

d. Do you think the function you found would accurately predict the number of customers at 1 P.M.? *Explain.*

14. CAR ENGINES The table shows the relationship between a car's engine speed (in revolutions per minute) and the power (in horsepower) that the engine produces. Use a graphing calculator to find a model for the data. What engine speed maximizes this car's engine power?

Engine speed (rpm)	1000	2000	3000	4000	5000	6000
Engine power (hp)	16	35	55	72	77	68

15. CHALLENGE As a chair manufacturer produces more chairs, the production cost per chair decreases. The table shows the number x of chairs produced and the production cost y (in dollars) per chair. Model the data with a function whose graph has a horizontal asympote. What does the asymptote represent in this situation?

x	50	300	800	2000	3000	4000
y	260	180	95	45	35	30

NEW YORK MIXED REVIEW

TEST PRACTICE at classzone.com

16. A sporting goods store has a 20%-off sale on all golf equipment. Which equation describes the relationship between the original price, x, of a piece of golf equipment and the sale price, y?

Ⓐ $x = 0.2y$ Ⓑ $x = 0.8y$ Ⓒ $y = 0.2x$ Ⓓ $y = 0.8x$

17. What is the approximate volume of the volleyball?

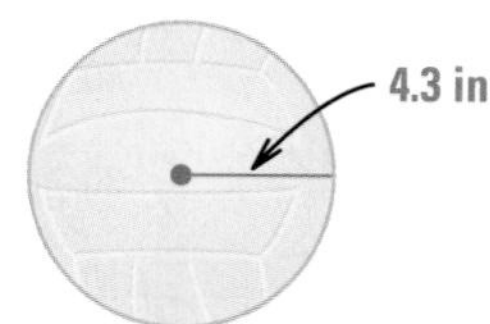

Ⓐ 77 in.^{3} Ⓑ 232 in.^{3}

Ⓒ 250 in.^{3} Ⓓ 333 in.^{3}

QUIZ for Lessons 11.3–11.5

A normal distribution has a mean of 47 and a standard deviation of 6. Find the probability that a randomly selected x-value is in the given interval. *(p. 757)*

1. Between 35 and 65
2. At least 41
3. At most 29

Find the sample size required to achieve the given margin of error. Round your answer to the nearest whole number. *(p. 766)*

4. ±3%
5. ±7%
6. ±4.5%
7. ±0.8%

8. **SPORTS** The table shows the winning times y (in seconds) for various men's races of length x (in meters) at the 2004 Summer Olympics. Use a graphing calculator to find a model for the data. *(p. 775)*

x	100	200	400	800	1500	5000	10,000
y	9.85	19.79	44.00	104.45	214.18	794.39	1625.10

EXTRA PRACTICE for Lesson 11.5, p. 1020 **ONLINE QUIZ** at classzone.com

PROBLEM SOLVING WORKSHOP
LESSON 11.5

Using ALTERNATIVE METHODS

Extending Example 2, page 776

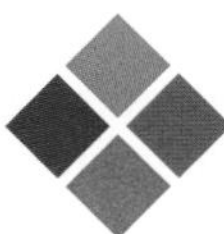

MULTIPLE REPRESENTATIONS In Example 2 on page 776, you used a graphing calculator to find an exponential model of the form $y = ab^x$ for a data set. You can extend this method to find exponential models of the form $y = ab^x + c$.

PROBLEM

COOLING RATES You are storing leftover chili in a refrigerator. The table shows the chili's temperature y (in degrees Fahrenheit) after x minutes in the refrigerator. Use a graphing calculator to find a model for the data.

x	0	10	20	30	40	50	60
y	100	84	72	63	57	52	49

METHOD

Transforming Data One approach to solving the problem is to perform a transformation on the data and then find a model for the transformed data.

STEP 1 **Enter** the data in lists L_1 and L_2. Then make a scatter plot. The temperature appears to decay exponentially to 40°F. So the model has the form $y = ab^x + 40$, or $y - 40 = ab^x$.

STEP 2 **Define** a new variable $y_1 = y - 40$. Then the data pairs (x, y_1) are modeled by a function of the form $y_1 = ab^x$. Make a list of the values of y_1 by defining L_3 as $L_2 - 40$.

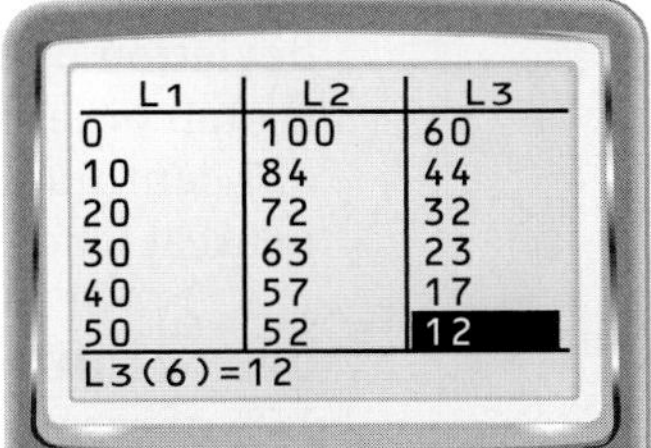

STEP 3 **Use** exponential regression to find a model for the data in lists L_1 and L_3. The model is $y_1 = 60.2(0.969)^x$. So, a model for the original data is $y = 60.2(0.969)^x + 40$.

▶ A model for the original data is $y = 60.2(0.969)^x + 40$. Graph the model along with the original data to verify that the model fits the data well.

PRACTICE

1. The data pairs (x, y) below give the temperature y (in degrees Fahrenheit) of a hot cup of soup after it sits for x minutes at room temperature. Estimate the temperature of the room. Then find a model for the data.

   (0, 132.8), (10, 105.8), (30, 92.3), (50, 84.2), (70, 79.2), (90, 76.1), (110, 75), (120, 74.7), (130, 74.2)

2. The data pairs (x, y) below give the temperature y (in degrees Celsius) of a cold glass of water after it sits x minutes at room temperature. Estimate the temperature of the room. Then find a model for the data.

   (0, 3.5), (20, 8.1), (40, 12.2), (60, 15.4), (80, 17), (100, 18.2), (110, 18.6), (120, 18.9)

Lessons 11.3–11.5

1. **BIOLOGY** A biologist caught, measured, weighed, and then released eight Maine landlocked salmon. The table shows each fish's length x (in inches) and weight y (in pounds). Which equation is the best model for the data? Use a graphing calculator to find the answer.

x	10.3	15.2	16.2	16.4
y	0.4	1.0	1.3	1.3
x	17.5	18.1	22	23.6
y	1.7	2.0	3.5	4.2

(1) $y = 0.0688(1.20)^x$

(2) $y = 0.525x^2 - 0.502x + 3.18$

(3) $y = 0.332x - 3.84$

(4) $y = 0.000321x^{3.01}$

2. **SHOPPING SURVEY** In a survey of 1022 people who shop online, 73% said that they do so because of the convenience. What is the approximate margin of error for the survey?

(1) ±2.9%

(2) ±3.1%

(3) ±3.7%

(4) ±7.3%

3. **SHOE SIZE** The table shows the shoe size of a certain boy at different ages (in years). What is the most reasonable prediction for the boy's shoe size at age 17? Use a quadratic model obtained from a graphing calculator to find the answer.

Age	6	7	8	10
Shoe size	5	6	7	9
Age	12	14	15	16
Shoe size	10	11	11	12

(1) 10 (3) 12

(2) 11 (4) 13

4. **SPORTS SURVEY** A local sports TV station wants to determine the average number of hours per week people in the viewing area watch sporting events on television. The station surveys people at a nearby sports stadium. Which type of sample is described?

(1) Self-selected

(2) Systematic

(3) Convenience

(4) Random

5. **SUPERMARKET SURVEY** A survey shows that the time spent by shoppers in a certain supermarket is normally distributed with a mean of 45 minutes and a standard deviation of 12 minutes. What is the approximate probability that a randomly chosen shopper spends between 45 and 69 minutes in the supermarket?

(1) 0.475 (3) 0.95

(2) 0.4985 (4) 0.997

6. **OPEN-ENDED** At a tree nursery, the heights of scotch pine trees are normally distributed with a mean of 200 centimeters and a standard deviation of 20 centimeters. Find the percent of scotch pine trees that have a height of at least 220 centimeters. Round your answer to the nearest whole number. *Explain.*

7. **OPEN-ENDED** A survey of students shows that 15% of respondents, or 315 students, prefer having gym class during the last period of the day.

How many students were surveyed?

What is the margin of error for the survey?

Give an interval that is likely to contain the exact percent of all students who would prefer to have gym class during the last period of the day.

CHAPTER SUMMARY

BIG IDEAS

For Your Notebook

Big Idea 1

Finding Measures of Central Tendency and Dispersion

The table shows common measures of central tendency and dispersion for a data set. It also shows how these measures are affected when a constant is added to each data value or when each data value is multiplied by a constant.

	Data: 1, 4, 4, 5, 8, 9, 9, 15	Add 5 to each value in data set	Multiply each value in data set by 3
Mean	6.875	6.875 + 5 = 11.875	3(6.875) = 20.625
Median	6.5	6.5 + 5 = 11.5	3(6.5) = 19.5
Mode	4 and 9	4 + 5 = 9 and 9 + 5 = 14	3(4) = 12 and 3(9) = 27
Range	15 − 1 = 14	14	3(14) = 42
Standard deviation	4.04	4.04	3(4.04) = 12.12

Big Idea 2

Using Normal Distributions

A normal distribution is modeled by a symmetric, bell-shaped curve. The area under a normal curve is distributed as shown below. A *z*-score is the number of standard deviations a data value lies above or below the mean. You can use *z*-scores and the standard normal table on page 759 to find probabilities related to any normal distribution.

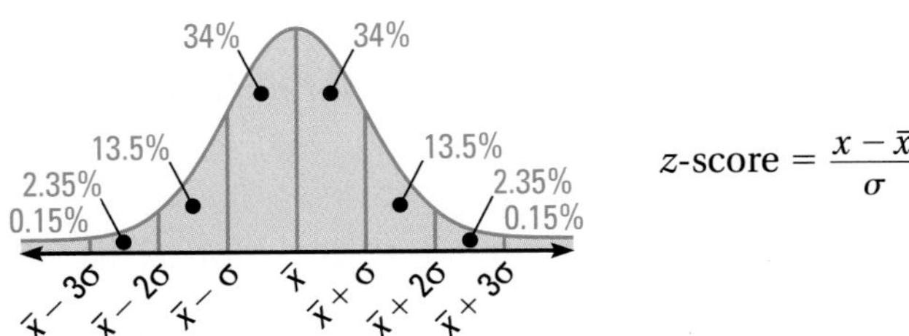

$$z\text{-score} = \frac{x - \bar{x}}{\sigma}$$

Big Idea 3

Working with Samples

You can use several different methods to choose a sample from a population. Random sampling is most likely to produce an unbiased sample.

Self-selected sample	Members volunteer.	Often biased
Systematic sample	A rule is used to select members.	Sometimes biased
Convenience sample	Easy-to-reach members are selected.	Often biased
Random sample	Every member has an equal chance of being selected.	Unbiased

CHAPTER REVIEW

@HomeTutor
classzone.com
• Multi-Language Glossary
• Vocabulary practice

REVIEW KEY VOCABULARY

- statistics, *p. 744*
- measure of central tendency, *p. 744*
- mean, median, mode, *p. 744*
- measure of dispersion, *p. 745*
- range, *p. 745*
- standard deviation, *p. 745*
- outlier, *p. 746*
- normal distribution, *p. 757*
- normal curve, *p. 757*
- standard normal distribution, *p. 758*
- *z*-score, *p. 758*
- population, *p. 766*
- sample, *p. 766*
- unbiased sample, *p. 767*
- biased sample, *p. 767*
- margin of error, *p. 768*

VOCABULARY EXERCISES

1. Copy and complete: _?_ is a measure of dispersion that describes the typical difference between a value in a data set and the mean.
2. **WRITING** *Describe* how multiplying every value in a data set by the same constant affects the mean, median, mode, range, and standard deviation.
3. Copy and complete: The _?_ for an x-value from a normal distribution represents the number of standard deviations the x-value lies above or below the mean.

REVIEW EXAMPLES AND EXERCISES

Use the review examples and exercises below to check your understanding of the concepts you have learned in each lesson of Chapter 11.

11.1 Find Measures of Central Tendency and Dispersion *pp. 744–749*

EXAMPLE

Find the mean, median, mode, range, and standard deviation of the following data set: 13, 13, 13, 19, 24, 24, 27, 28, 34, 35.

Mean: $\bar{x} = \frac{13 + 13 + 13 + 19 + \cdots + 35}{10} = 23$

Median: 24 **Mode:** 13 **Range** $= 35 - 13 = 22$

Standard Deviation: $\sigma = \sqrt{\frac{(13 - 23)^2 + (13 - 23)^2 + \cdots + (35 - 23)^2}{10}} \approx 7.9$

EXERCISES

EXAMPLES 1 and 2 on pp. 744–745 for Exs. 4–8

Find the mean, median, mode, range, and standard deviation of the data set.

4. 35, 36, 36, 38, 41, 42, 45, 48
5. 75, 76, 79, 85, 88, 88, 90, 92
6. 76, 102, 87, 85, 91, 92, 91, 97
7. 103, 155, 140, 125, 130, 140, 115
8. **GAS PRICES** The list shows the average price of a gallon of gasoline each year from 1994 to 2004. Find the median and standard deviation of the prices.

   \$1.04, \$1.13, \$1.13, \$1.26, \$1.13, \$.97, \$1.30, \$1.47, \$1.14, \$1.47, \$1.59

@HomeTutor
classzone.com
Chapter Review Practice

11.2 Apply Transformations to Data

pp. 751–755

EXAMPLE

Find the mean, median, mode, range, and standard deviation of the data set below and of the data set obtained by multiplying each data value by 0.8.

200, 220, 280, 290, 320, 320, 340, 380

	Original data	Transformed data
Mean	293.75	0.8(293.75) = 235
Median	305	0.8(305) = 244
Mode	320	0.8(320) = 256
Range	180	0.8(180) = 144
Standard deviation	56.33	0.8(56.33) ≈ 45.06

EXERCISES

EXAMPLES 1 and 2 on pp. 751–752 for Exs. 9–11

Find the mean, median, mode, range, and standard deviation of the given data set and of the data set obtained by performing the given transformation.

9. 34, 35, 37, 37, 38, 41, 42, 46, 48; add −7 to each data value

10. 62, 66, 66, 68, 74, 76, 78, 80, 82; multiply each data value by 1.2

11. **RAINFALL** The list below shows the average rainfall (in millimeters) for Lubbock, Texas, during each month of the year. Find the mean, median, mode, range, and standard deviation of the data in millimeters and of the data in inches. (*Note:* 1 mm ≈ 0.03937 in.)

14.9, 14.3, 20.1, 30.5, 76.9, 59.8, 57.2, 40.2, 59.8, 46.5, 16.4, 18.8

11.3 Use Normal Distributions

pp. 757–762

EXAMPLE

A normal distribution has a mean of 76 and a standard deviation of 9. Use the standard normal table on page 759 to find the probability that a randomly selected x-value from the distribution is at most 64.

$z = \frac{x - \bar{x}}{\sigma} = \frac{64 - 76}{9} \approx -1.3$ Find z-score for $x = 64$.

$P(x \le 64) \approx P(z \le -1.3) = 0.0968$ Use the standard normal table.

EXERCISES

EXAMPLE 3 on p. 759 for Exs. 12–17

A normal distribution has a mean of 95 and a standard deviation of 7. Use the standard normal table on page 759 to find the indicated probability for a randomly selected x-value from the distribution.

12. $P(x \le 89)$

13. $P(x \le 84)$

14. $P(91 < x \le 100)$

15. $P(x \le 50)$

16. $P(x > 100)$

17. $P(50 < x \le 80)$

11 CHAPTER REVIEW

11.4 Select and Draw Conclusions from Samples

pp. 766–771

EXAMPLE

In a survey of 582 people, 57% said that summer is their favorite season. What is the margin of error for the survey?

$$\text{Margin of error} = \pm\frac{1}{\sqrt{n}} = \pm\frac{1}{\sqrt{582}} \approx \pm 0.041 = \pm 4.1\%$$

EXERCISES

EXAMPLE 4 on p. 768 for Exs. 18–22

Find the margin of error for a survey that has the given sample size. Round your answer to the nearest tenth of a percent.

18. 300 **19.** 2500 **20.** 800 **21.** 4900

22. SURVEYS In a Gallup Youth Survey of 517 teenagers, 34% said that their favorite way to spend an evening was to hang out with family or friends. What is the margin of error for the survey?

11.5 Choose the Best Model for Two-Variable Data

pp. 775–780

EXAMPLE

Use a graphing calculator to find a model for the data. Then graph the model and the data in the same coordinate plane.

x	20	30	40	50	60	70	80
y	42	48	53	52	49	40	32

Make a scatter plot. The points form an inverted U-shape. This suggests a quadratic model.

Use the quadratic regression feature to find an equation of the model.

Graph the model along with the data to verify that the model fits the data well.

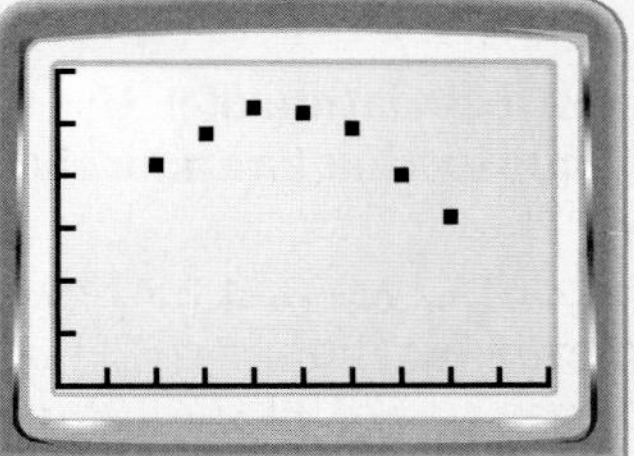

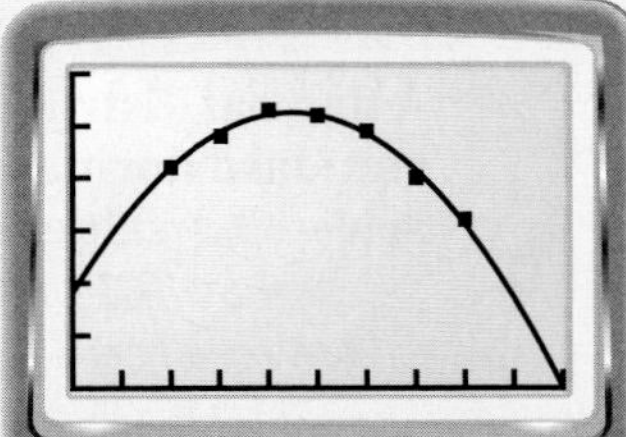

▶ A model for the data is $y = -0.0171x^2 + 1.54x + 18.1$.

EXERCISES

EXAMPLES 1, 2, and 3 on pp. 775–777 for Ex. 23

23. Use a graphing calculator to find a model for the data. Then graph the model and the data in the same coordinate plane.

x	1	2	3	4	5	6	7
y	24	21	17	14	9	5	2

11 CHAPTER TEST

Find the mean, median, mode, range, and standard deviation of the given data set and of the data set obtained by performing the given transformation.

1. 41, 38, 42, 41, 45, 44, 48, 35; multiply each data value by 3
2. 16, 21, 19, 21, 17, 25, 15, 18; add 14 to each data value
3. 108, 92, 102, 99, 116, 92; multiply each data value by 4.5

A normal distribution has a mean of 72 and a standard deviation of 5. Find the probability that a randomly selected x-value from the distribution is in the given interval.

4. Between 67 and 77
5. Between 57 and 72
6. At least 62

Find the margin of error for a survey that has the given sample size. Round your answer to the nearest tenth of a percent.

7. 340
8. 8125
9. 931
10. 1560

11. **FOOTBALL** Teams in the National Football League are divided into two conferences, the American Football Conference (AFC) and the National Football Conference (NFC). The table below shows the margin of victory in each conference's championship game for the 1990–2004 seasons.

AFC Championship margins of victory	NFC Championship margins of victory
48, 3, 19, 17, 4, 4, 14, 3, 13, 19, 13, 7, 17, 10, 14	2, 31, 10, 17, 10, 11, 17, 13, 3, 5, 41, 5, 17, 11, 17

   a. Find the mean, median, mode, range, and standard deviation of the AFC margins of victory.

   b. Find the mean, median, mode, range, and standard deviation of the NFC margins of victory.

   c. *Compare* the statistics for each set of data and make a conclusion about the data.

12. **TEST SCORES** The scores on a standardized test administered to 10,000 students have a mean of 50 and a standard deviation of 10. Find the z-score for each student whose score is given.

   a. Kevin: 55
   b. Manuel: 70
   c. Colby: 40
   d. Neal: 47

13. **SHOPPING SURVEY** In a survey of 1600 U.S. adults, 61% said that they have purchased a product online. Find the margin of error for the survey. Then give an interval that is likely to contain the exact percent of all U.S. adults who have purchased a product online.

14. **TYPING ERRORS** The table shows the average number y of errors made by students in a typing course when they took tests given x days after the start of the course. Use a graphing calculator to find a model for the data.

x	2	10	14	21	30	45	63	70	91
y	45.2	36.1	30.2	23.1	18.7	11.0	5.6	4.3	2.4

MULTIPLE CHOICE QUESTIONS

If you have difficulty solving a multiple choice problem directly, you may be able to use another approach to eliminate incorrect answer choices and obtain the correct answer.

PROBLEM 1

The Nielsen ratings measure how many viewers watch different TV programs. There are 5000 Nielsen households, which are chosen randomly from U.S. households with televisions. Suppose the Nielsen ratings report that 9.2% of Neilsen households watched a certain program. What interval is likely to contain the exact percent of all U.S. households with televisions that watched the program?

(1) 4.0% to 14.0%

(2) 7.8% to 10.6%

(3) 8.3% to 10.3%

(4) 9.2% to 9.6%

METHOD 1

SOLVE DIRECTLY Calculate the margin of error. Then use the margin of error and the percent given in the problem to find the interval.

STEP 1 **Calculate** the margin of error.

$$\text{Margin of error} = \pm\frac{1}{\sqrt{n}}$$

$$= \pm\frac{1}{\sqrt{5000}}$$

$$\approx \pm 0.014$$

$$= \pm 1.4\%$$

STEP 2 **Find** the lower bound for the interval.

$$\text{Lower bound} = 9.2\% - 1.4\%$$

$$= 7.8\%$$

STEP 3 **Find** the upper bound for the interval.

$$\text{Upper bound} = 9.2\% + 1.4\%$$

$$= 10.6\%$$

STEP 4 **Write** the interval.

The interval is 7.8% to 10.6%.

▶ The correct answer is (2).

METHOD 2

ELIMINATE CHOICES Another method is to check the intervals given in the answer choices.

You know that 9.2% must fall exactly in the middle of the interval.

Choice (1): $\frac{4.0 + 14.0}{2} = \frac{18.0}{2} = 9.0$, so 9.2% does not fall exactly in the middle of the interval. You can eliminate choice (1). ✗

Choice (2): $\frac{7.8 + 10.6}{2} = \frac{18.4}{2} = 9.2$, so 9.2% falls exactly in the middle of the interval. ✓

Choice (3): $\frac{8.3 + 10.3}{2} = \frac{18.6}{2} = 9.3$, so 9.2% does not fall exactly in the middle of the interval. You can eliminate choice (3). ✗

Choice (4): $\frac{9.2 + 9.6}{2} = \frac{18.8}{2} = 9.4$, so 9.2% does not fall exactly in the middle of the interval. You can eliminate choice (4). ✗

▶ The correct answer is (2).

PROBLEM 2

At a local bank, the waiting times for an available teller are normally distributed with a mean of 10 minutes and a standard deviation of 2 minutes. What is the approximate probability that a randomly selected customer at the bank waits no more than 13 minutes for a teller?

(1) 60.7% (2) 82.0% (3) 93.3% (4) 98.5%

METHOD 1

SOLVE DIRECTLY Use a z-score and the standard normal table on page 759 to find the desired probability.

STEP 1 **Find** the z-score for a waiting time of 13 minutes.

$$z = \frac{x - \overline{x}}{\sigma} = \frac{13 - 10}{2} = 1.5$$

STEP 2 **Use** the standard normal table to find $P(z \le 1.5)$.

$P(z \le 1.5) = 0.9332 \approx 93.3\%$

The probability of waiting no more than 13 minutes is about 93.3%.

▶ The correct answer is (3).

METHOD 2

ELIMINATE CHOICES Use the facts about normal distributions on page 757 to eliminate incorrect answer choices.

For a randomly selected customer with a waiting time of x minutes, you know the following:

$$P(x \le 12) = P(x \le \overline{x} + \sigma) = 50\% + 34\% = 84\%$$

$$P(x \le 14) = P(x \le \overline{x} + 2\sigma) = 50\% + 34\% + 13.5\% = 97.5\%$$

It follows that $P(x \le 13)$ is between 84% and 97.5%. Only the probability of 93.3% in answer choice (3) satisfies this condition.

▶ The correct answer is (3).

PRACTICE

Explain why you can eliminate the highlighted answer choice.

1. A normal distribution has a mean of 4.06 and a standard deviation of 0.04. What is the probability that a randomly selected value from the distribution is between 4.06 and 4.14?

(1) 0.01 (2) 0.475 (3) 0.68 ✗(4) 0.99

2. If you add the same nonzero constant to each value in a data set, which statistic does not change?

(1) Mean (2) Median ✗(3) Mode (4) Range

3. Which type of function best models the data represented by the scatter plot at the right?

(1) Linear (3) Cubic

(2) Quadratic ✗(4) Exponential

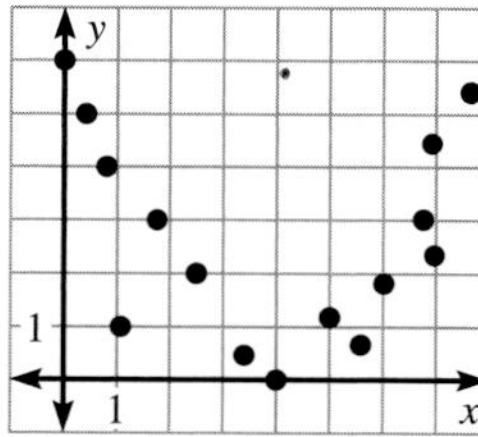

TEST PREPARATION

New York **Test Practice**

MULTIPLE CHOICE

In Exercises 1 and 2, use the data below giving the lengths (in minutes) of the movies showing at a local movie theater.

94, 109, 166, 136, 97, 110, 113, 114, 94, 101

1. What is the median of the data set?

(1) 94 min (3) 110 min

(2) 109.5 min (4) 111.5 min

2. To the nearest tenth of a minute, what is the standard deviation of the data set?

(1) 7.2 min (3) 25.6 min

(2) 21.2 min (4) 67.0 min

3. According to a survey from the National Center for Health Statistics, the heights of adult women in the United States are normally distributed with a mean of 64 inches and a standard deviation of 2.7 inches. What is the approximate probability that 4 randomly selected women are all between 58.6 inches and 66.7 inches tall?

(1) 34% (3) 68%

(2) 44% (4) 81.5%

4. What is the percent of the area under a normal curve that is represented by the shaded region?

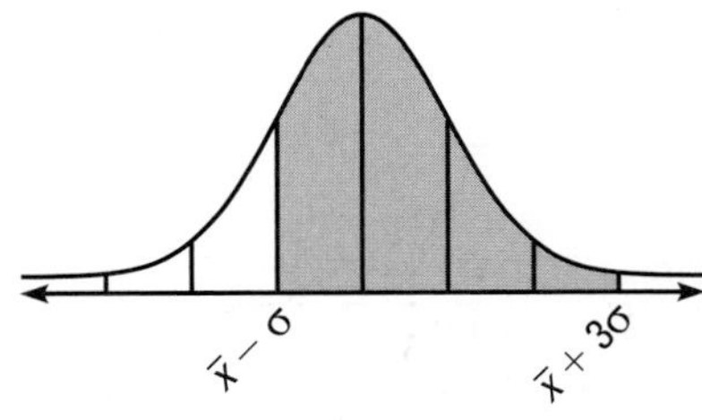

(1) 50% (3) 83.85%

(2) 81.5% (4) 84%

5. Rachel scored an 88 on her physics test. The class average was 79.3, and the standard deviation was 7.5. What is the *z*-score for Rachel's test score?

(1) 1.16 (3) 1.45

(2) 1.30 (4) 1.60

6. The data set below gives the numbers of pages in five high school textbooks.

384, 480, 576, 640, 768

Which statement is *false*?

(1) There is no mode.

(2) The mean is greater than the median.

(3) The mean is 569.6 pages.

(4) The range is 384 pages.

7. In a nationwide poll of 1015 U.S. adults, Tom Hanks was voted America's favorite movie star. What is the approximate margin of error for the survey?

(1) ±0.031% (3) ±3.1%

(2) ±0.31% (4) ±31%

8. The table shows the attendance (in millions) at Boston Red Sox games in Fenway Park from 1995 to 2004. Which type of function best models the data?

Year	Attendance	Year	Attendance
1995	2.16	2000	2.59
1996	2.32	2001	2.63
1997	2.23	2002	2.65
1998	2.31	2003	2.72
1999	2.45	2004	2.84

(1) Linear (3) Exponentia

(2) Quadratic (4) Power

9. The delays (in minutes) for a commercial airline flight are listed below for Sunday through Friday of a certain week.

20, 10, 0, 30, 0, 45

On Saturday, the flight is delayed 150 minutes. Which statistic is most affected when this outlier is added to the given data set?

(1) Mean (3) Mode

(2) Median (4) Range

TEST PREPARATION

MULTIPLE CHOICE

10. A normal distribution has a mean of 77 and a standard deviation of 4. What is the z-score corresponding to an x-value of 80?

(1) -0.91 (3) 0.75
(2) -0.75 (4) 0.91

11. The standard deviation of a data set is 12.2. A new data set is created by adding 5.1 to each data value. What is the standard deviation of the new data set?

(1) 7.1 (3) 13.2
(2) 12.2 (4) 17.3

12. The mean of the numbers 5, 8, 7, 2, and x is 6. What is the value of x?

(1) 2 (3) 6.75
(2) 5.25 (4) 8

13. In a normal distribution, about what percent of the area under the related normal curve lies within 2 standard deviations of the mean?

(1) 2.5% (3) 95%
(2) 5% (4) 97.5%

OPEN-ENDED

14. The data set below gives the average rainfall for each month in San Antonio, Texas, and Chicago, Illinois.

San Antonio, Texas (in inches):
1.5, 1.8, 1.8, 2.8, 3.4, 3.1, 2.2, 2.5, 3.4, 2.5, 2.2, 1.8

Chicago, Illinois (in millimeters):
48.2, 41.8, 72.2, 96.6, 82.5, 103.4, 102.7, 89.3, 78.6, 69.7, 72.7, 64.8

Find the mean, median, mode, range, and standard deviation for each city's rainfall data.

Compare the statistics for each city. Make a conclusion about the data. (*Hint:* 1 millimeter $\approx$ 0.03937 inch.)

15. The table shows the numbers of people (in millions) who voted in U.S. Presidential elections since 1940.

Years since 1940	0	4	8	12	16	20	24	28
Voters (millions)	49.90	47.98	48.79	61.55	62.03	68.84	70.65	73.21
Years since 1940	32	36	40	44	48	52	56	60
Voters (millions)	77.72	81.56	86.52	92.65	91.60	104.43	96.28	105.40

Use a graphing calculator to make a scatter plot of the data. Determine the type of function that best fits the data.

Use a regression feature to find an equation of the function.

Graph the equation along with the data to verify that the equation fits the data well.

Use your equation to predict the number of people who voted in the 2004 U.S. Presidential election. *Compare* your prediction to the actual number of voters in that election, which was 122.30 million voters.

TEST PREPARATION

12 Sequences and Series

Before

In previous chapters, you learned the following skills, which you'll use in Chapter 12: solving equations, solving systems of equations, and performing function composition.

Prerequisite Skills

VOCABULARY CHECK

Copy and complete the statement using $f(x) = \frac{1}{x}$ and $g(x) = 4x + 2$.

1. The **domain** of $f(x)$ is __?__.
2. The **range** of $g(x)$ is __?__.
3. The **composition** $f(g(x))$ is equal to __?__.

SKILLS CHECK

Solve the equation. Check your solution. ***(Review p. 18 for 12.2.)***

4. $7x + 3 = 31$
5. $9 = 2x - 7$
6. $14 = -3x + 8$
7. $10 - 3x = 28$
8. $11x + 9 = 3x + 17$
9. $2x + 3 = -6 - x$

Solve the system using any algebraic method. ***(Review p. 160 for 12.3.)***

10. $3x + y = 0$; $-2x - 4y = -30$
11. $2x - 2y = 10$; $x + y = -10$
12. $4x - 5y = 25$; $0.5x + 1.5y = 18.5$

Let $f(x) = 2x - 1$ and $g(x) = -2x^{-1}$. Perform the indicated operation and state the domain. ***(Review p. 428 for 12.5.)***

13. $f(g(x))$
14. $f(f(x))$
15. $g(g(x))$

Now

In Chapter 12, you will apply the big ideas listed below and reviewed in the Chapter Summary on page 839. You will also use the key vocabulary listed below.

Big Ideas

1. **Analyze sequences**
2. **Find sums of series**
3. **Use recursive rules**

KEY VOCABULARY

- sequence, *p. 794*
- terms of a sequence, *p. 794*
- series, *p. 796*
- summation notation, *p. 796*
- sigma notation, *p. 796*
- arithmetic sequence, *p. 802*
- common difference, *p. 802*
- arithmetic series, *p. 804*
- geometric sequence, *p. 810*
- common ratio, *p. 810*
- geometric series, *p. 812*
- partial sum, *p. 820*
- explicit rule, *p. 827*
- recursive rule, *p. 827*
- iteration, *p. 830*

Why?

You can use sequences to describe patterns in the real world. For example, you can use the Fibonacci sequence to describe patterns in nature.

Animated Algebra

The animation illustrated below for Example 3 on page 828 helps you answer this question: How can you generate Fibonacci numbers?

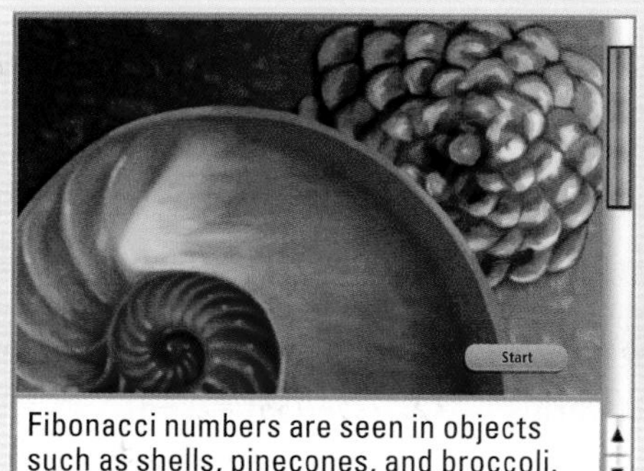

Fibonacci numbers are seen in objects such as shells, pinecones, and broccoli.

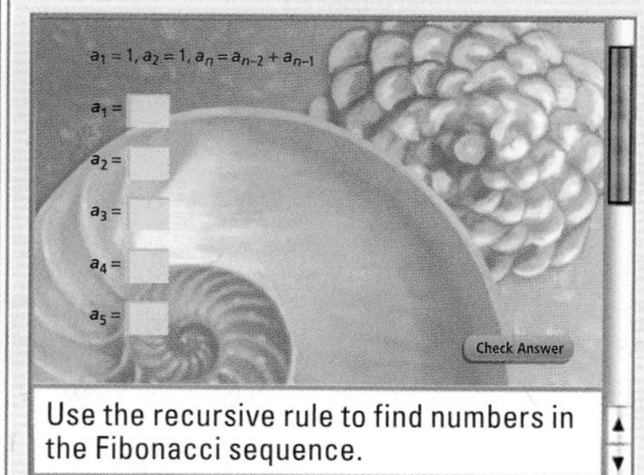

Use the recursive rule to find numbers in the Fibonacci sequence.

Animated Algebra at classzone.com

Other animations for Chapter 12: pages 805, 811, 820, and 832

12.1 Define and Use Sequences and Series

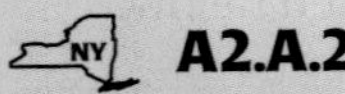

A2.A.29 Identify an arithmetic or geometric sequence and find the formula for its *n*th term

Before You identified and wrote functions.

Now You will recognize and write rules for number patterns.

Why? So you can find angle measures, as in Ex. 63.

Key Vocabulary
- **sequence**
- **terms of a sequence**
- **series**
- **summation notation**
- **sigma notation**

KEY CONCEPT *For Your Notebook*

Sequences

A **sequence** is a function whose domain is a set of consecutive integers. If a domain is not specified, it is understood that the domain starts with 1. The values in the range are called the **terms** of the sequence.

Domain: $1 \quad 2 \quad 3 \quad 4 \ldots n$ — The relative position of each term

$\downarrow \quad \downarrow \quad \downarrow \quad \downarrow \quad \quad \downarrow$

Range: $a_1 \quad a_2 \quad a_3 \quad a_4 \ldots a_n$ — Terms of the sequence

A *finite sequence* has a limited number of terms. An *infinite sequence* continues without stopping.

Finite sequence: 2, 4, 6, 8 **Infinite sequence:** 2, 4, 6, 8, . . .

A sequence can be specified by an equation, or *rule*. For example, both sequences above can be described by the rule $a_n = 2n$ or $f(n) = 2n$.

EXAMPLE 1 Write terms of sequences

Write the first six terms of (a) $a_n = 2n + 5$ and (b) $f(n) = (-3)^{n-1}$.

Solution

a. $a_1 = 2(1) + 5 = 7$ 1st term

$a_2 = 2(2) + 5 = 9$ 2nd term

$a_3 = 2(3) + 5 = 11$ 3rd term

$a_4 = 2(4) + 5 = 13$ 4th term

$a_5 = 2(5) + 5 = 15$ 5th term

$a_6 = 2(6) + 5 = 17$ 6th term

b. $f(1) = (-3)^{1-1} = 1$ 1st term

$f(2) = (-3)^{2-1} = -3$ 2nd term

$f(3) = (-3)^{3-1} = 9$ 3rd term

$f(4) = (-3)^{4-1} = -27$ 4th term

$f(5) = (-3)^{5-1} = 81$ 5th term

$f(6) = (-3)^{6-1} = -243$ 6th term

GUIDED PRACTICE for Example 1

Write the first six terms of the sequence.

1. $a_n = n + 4$

2. $f(n) = (-2)^{n-1}$

3. $a_n = \frac{n}{n+1}$

WRITING RULES If the terms of a sequence have a recognizable pattern, then you may be able to write a rule for the nth term of the sequence.

EXAMPLE 2 Write rules for sequences

WRITE RULES

If you are given only the first several terms of a sequence, there is no *single* rule for the nth term. For instance, the sequence 2, 4, 8, . . . can be given by $a_n = 2^n$ or $a_n = n^2 - n + 2$.

Describe the pattern, write the next term, and write a rule for the nth term of the sequence (a) −1, −8, −27, −64, . . . and (b) 0, 2, 6, 12, ...

Solution

a. You can write the terms as $(-1)^3, (-2)^3, (-3)^3, (-4)^3, \ldots$. The next term is $a_5 = (-5)^3 = -125$. A rule for the nth term is $a_n = (-n)^3$.

b. You can write the terms as $0(1), 1(2), 2(3), 3(4), \ldots$. The next term is $f(5) = 4(5) = 20$. A rule for the nth term is $f(n) = (n - 1)n$.

GRAPHING SEQUENCES To graph a sequence, let the horizontal axis represent the position numbers (the domain) and the vertical axis represent the terms (the range).

EXAMPLE 3 Solve a multi-step problem

RETAIL DISPLAYS You work in a grocery store and are stacking apples in the shape of a square pyramid with 7 layers. Write a rule for the number of apples in each layer. Then graph the sequence.

Solution

STEP 1 **Make** a table showing the number of fruit in the first three layers. Let a_n represent the number of apples in layer n.

Layer, n	1	2	3
Number of apples, a_n	$1 = 1^2$	$4 = 2^2$	$9 = 3^2$

STEP 2 **Write** a rule for the number of apples in each layer. From the table, you can see that $a_n = n^2$.

STEP 3 **Plot** the points (1, 1), (2, 4), (3, 9), . . . , (7, 49). The graph is shown at the right.

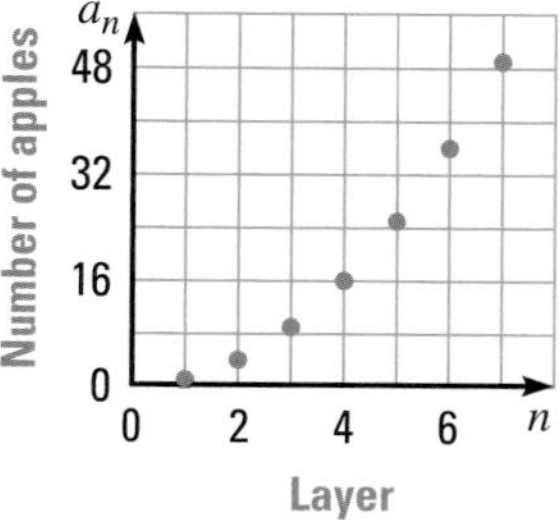

AVOID ERRORS

Although the plotted points in Example 3 follow a curve, do *not* draw the curve because the sequence is defined only for integer values of n.

✓ GUIDED PRACTICE for Examples 2 and 3

4. For the sequence 3, 8, 15, 24, . . . , describe the pattern, write the next term, graph the first five terms, and write a rule for the nth term.

5. **WHAT IF?** In Example 3, suppose there are 9 layers of apples. How many apples are in the 9th layer?

KEY CONCEPT — For Your Notebook

Series and Summation Notation

When the terms of a sequence are added together, the resulting expression is a **series**. A series can be finite or infinite.

Finite series: $2 + 4 + 6 + 8$ **Infinite series:** $2 + 4 + 6 + 8 + \cdots$

You can use **summation notation** to write a series. For example, the two series above can be written in summation notation as follows:

$$2 + 4 + 6 + 8 = \sum_{i=1}^{4} 2i \qquad 2 + 4 + 6 + 8 + \cdots = \sum_{i=1}^{\infty} 2i$$

For both series, the *index of summation* is i and the *lower limit of summation* is 1. The *upper limit of summation* is 4 for the finite series and ∞ (infinity) for the infinite series. Summation notation is also called **sigma notation** because it uses the uppercase Greek letter *sigma*, written Σ.

READING
When written in summation notation, this series is read as "the sum of $2i$ for values of i from 1 to 4."

EXAMPLE 4 Write series using summation notation

Write the series using summation notation.

a. $25 + 50 + 75 + \cdots + 250$

b. $\frac{1}{2} + \frac{2}{3} + \frac{3}{4} + \frac{4}{5} + \cdots$

Solution

a. Notice that the first term is 25(1), the second is 25(2), the third is 25(3), and the last is 25(10). So, the terms of the series can be written as:

$$a_i = 25i \text{ where } i = 1, 2, 3, \ldots, 10$$

The lower limit of summation is 1 and the upper limit of summation is 10.

▶ The summation notation for the series is $\sum_{i=1}^{10} 25i$.

b. Notice that for each term the denominator of the fraction is 1 more than the numerator. So, the terms of the series can be written as:

$$a_i = \frac{i}{i+1} \text{ where } i = 1, 2, 3, 4, \ldots$$

The lower limit of summation is 1 and the upper limit of summation is infinity.

▶ The summation notation for the series is $\sum_{i=1}^{\infty} \frac{i}{i+1}$.

✓ GUIDED PRACTICE for Example 4

Write the series using summation notation.

6. $5 + 10 + 15 + \cdots + 100$

7. $\frac{1}{2} + \frac{4}{5} + \frac{9}{10} + \frac{16}{17} + \cdots$

8. $6 + 36 + 216 + 1296 + \cdots$

9. $5 + 6 + 7 + \cdots + 12$

INDEX OF SUMMATION The index of summation for a series does not have to be i—any letter can be used. Also, the index does not have to begin at 1. For instance, the index begins at 4 in the next example.

EXAMPLE 5 Find the sum of a series

AVOID ERRORS
Be sure to use the correct lower and upper limits of summation when finding the sum of a series.

Find the sum of the series.

$$\sum_{k=4}^{8}(3+k^2) = (3+4^2)+(3+5^2)+(3+6^2)+(3+7^2)+(3+8^2)$$
$$= 19 + 28 + 39 + 52 + 67$$
$$= 205$$

SPECIAL FORMULAS For series with many terms, finding the sum by adding the terms can be tedious. Below are formulas you can use to find the sums of three special types of series.

KEY CONCEPT *For Your Notebook*

Formulas for Special Series

Sum of n terms of 1	Sum of first n positive integers	Sum of squares of first n positive integers
$\sum_{i=1}^{n} 1 = n$	$\sum_{i=1}^{n} i = \frac{n(n+1)}{2}$	$\sum_{i=1}^{n} i^2 = \frac{n(n+1)(2n+1)}{6}$

EXAMPLE 6 Use a formula for a sum

RETAIL DISPLAYS How many apples are in the stack in Example 3 on page 795?

Solution

From Example 3 you know that the ith term of the series is given by $a_i = i^2$ where $i = 1, 2, 3, \ldots, 7$. Using summation notation and the third formula listed above, you can find the total number of apples as follows:

$$1^2 + 2^2 + \cdots + 7^2 = \sum_{i=1}^{7} i^2 = \frac{7(7+1)(2 \cdot 7+1)}{6} = \frac{7(8)(15)}{6} = 140$$

▶ There are 140 apples in the stack. Check this by actually adding the number of apples in each of the seven layers.

✓ GUIDED PRACTICE for Examples 5 and 6

Find the sum of the series.

10. $\sum_{i=1}^{5} 8i$ **11.** $\sum_{k=3}^{7}(k^2-1)$ **12.** $\sum_{i=1}^{34} 1$ **13.** $\sum_{n=1}^{6} n$

14. WHAT IF? Suppose there are 9 layers in the apple stack in Example 3. How many apples are in the stack?

12.1 EXERCISES

HOMEWORK KEY
○ = **WORKED-OUT SOLUTIONS** on p. WS20 for Exs. 19, 47, and 65
★ = **STANDARDIZED TEST PRACTICE** Exs. 2, 27, 58, 64, and 67

SKILL PRACTICE

1. **VOCABULARY** Copy and complete: Another name for summation notation is _?_.

2. ★ **WRITING** *Explain* the difference between a sequence and a series.

EXAMPLE 1 on p. 794 for Exs. 3–14

WRITING TERMS Write the first six terms of the sequence.

3. $a_n = n + 2$
4. $a_n = 6 - n$
5. $a_n = n^2$
6. $f(n) = n^3 + 2$
7. $a_n = 4^{n-1}$
8. $a_n = -n^2$
9. $f(n) = n^2 - 5$
10. $a_n = (n + 3)^2$
11. $f(n) = -\frac{4}{n}$
12. $a_n = \frac{3}{n}$
13. $a_n = \frac{2n}{n+2}$
14. $f(n) = \frac{n}{2n-1}$

EXAMPLE 2 on p. 795 for Exs. 15–27

WRITING RULES For the sequence, describe the pattern, write the next term, and write a rule for the *n*th term.

15. 1, 6, 11, 16, . . .
16. 1, 2, 4, 8, . . .
17. −4, 8, −12, 16, . . .
18. 2, 9, 28, 65, . . .
19. $\frac{2}{3}, \frac{2}{6}, \frac{2}{9}, \frac{2}{12}, \ldots$
20. $\frac{2}{3}, \frac{4}{4}, \frac{6}{5}, \frac{8}{6}, \ldots$
21. $\frac{1}{4}, \frac{2}{4}, \frac{3}{4}, \frac{4}{4}, \frac{5}{4}, \ldots$
22. $\frac{1}{10}, \frac{3}{20}, \frac{5}{30}, \frac{7}{40}, \ldots$
23. 3.1, 3.8, 4.5, 5.2, . . .
24. 4.2, 2.6, 1, −0.6, −2.2, . . .
25. 1.2, 4.2, 9.2, 16.2, . . .
26. 9, 16.8, 24.6, 32.4, . . .

27. ★ **MULTIPLE CHOICE** Which rule gives the total number of squares in the *n*th figure of the pattern shown?

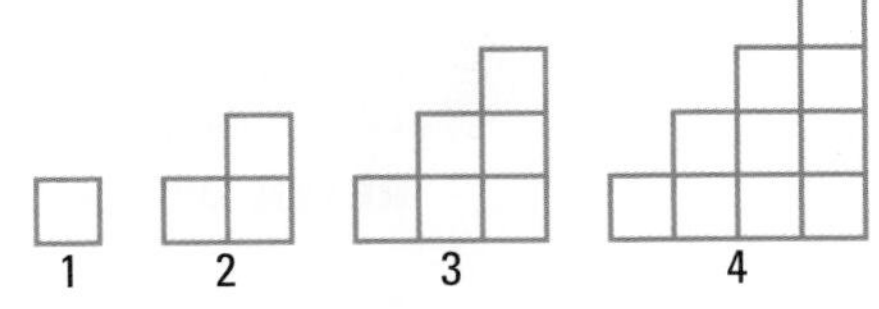

Ⓐ $a_n = 3n - 3$　Ⓑ $a_n = 4n - 5$　Ⓒ $a_n = n$　Ⓓ $a_n = \frac{n(n+1)}{2}$

EXAMPLE 3 on p. 795 for Exs. 28–36

GRAPHING SEQUENCES Graph the sequence.

28. −2, −5, −8, −11, −14
29. 2, 4, 8, 16, 32, 64
30. 1, 5, 9, 13, . . . , 29
31. −2, 4, −6, 8, . . . , −22
32. 0, 3, 8, 15, 24, 35
33. −1, 0, 1, 8, 27
34. 4, −9, 14, −19, 24
35. $\frac{1}{2}, \frac{3}{2}, \frac{5}{2}, \ldots, \frac{13}{2}$
36. $\frac{1}{9}, \frac{2}{8}, \frac{3}{7}, \frac{4}{6}, \ldots, \frac{9}{1}$

EXAMPLE 4 on p. 796 for Exs. 37–44

WRITING SUMMATION NOTATION Write the series using summation notation.

37. 7 + 10 + 13 + 16 + 19
38. 5 + 11 + 17 + 23 + 29
39. −1 + 1 + 3 + 5 + 7 + · · ·
40. −2 + 4 − 8 + 16 − 32 + · · ·
41. 3 + 10 + 17 + 24 + 31 + · · ·
42. $\frac{1}{3} + \frac{1}{9} + \frac{1}{27} + \frac{1}{81}$
43. $\frac{1}{4} + \frac{2}{5} + \frac{3}{6} + \frac{4}{7} + \frac{5}{8} + \frac{6}{9} + \frac{7}{10}$
44. −1 + 2 + 7 + 14 + 23 + · · ·

EXAMPLES 5 and 6
on p. 797 for Exs. 45–58

USING SUMMATION NOTATION Find the sum of the series.

45. $\sum_{i=1}^{6} 2i$

46. $\sum_{i=1}^{5} 7i$

47. $\sum_{n=0}^{4} n^3$

48. $\sum_{k=1}^{4} 3k^2$

49. $\sum_{k=3}^{6} (5k - 2)$

50. $\sum_{n=1}^{5} (n^2 - 1)$

51. $\sum_{i=1}^{8} \frac{2}{i}$

52. $\sum_{k=1}^{6} \frac{k}{k+1}$

53. $\sum_{i=1}^{35} 1$

54. $\sum_{n=1}^{16} n$

55. $\sum_{i=1}^{25} i$

56. $\sum_{n=1}^{18} n^2$

57. **ERROR ANALYSIS** *Describe* and correct the error in finding the sum of the series.

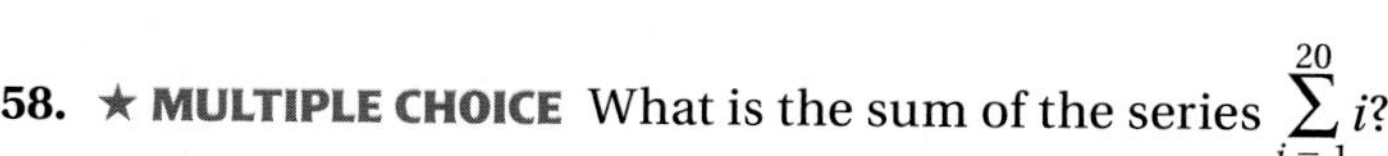
$\sum_{i=0}^{5} (2i + 3) = 5 + 7 + 9 + 11 + 13 = 45$

58. ★ **MULTIPLE CHOICE** What is the sum of the series $\sum_{i=1}^{20} i$?

Ⓐ 20 Ⓑ 210 Ⓒ 420 Ⓓ 2870

REVIEW LOGIC
For help with counter-examples see p. 1002.

CHALLENGE Tell whether the statement about summation notation is *true* or *false*. If the statement is true, prove it. If the statement is false, give a counterexample.

59. $\sum_{i=1}^{n} ka_i = k\sum_{i=1}^{n} a_i$

60. $\sum_{i=1}^{n} (a_i + b_i) = \sum_{i=1}^{n} a_i + \sum_{i=1}^{n} b_i$

61. $\sum_{i=1}^{n} a_i b_i = \left(\sum_{i=1}^{n} a_i\right)\left(\sum_{i=1}^{n} b_i\right)$

62. $\sum_{i=1}^{n} (a_i)^k = \left(\sum_{i=1}^{n} a_i\right)^k$

PROBLEM SOLVING

EXAMPLES 3 and 6
on pp. 795–797 for Exs. 63–64

63. **GEOMETRY** For a regular n-sided polygon ($n \geq 3$), the measure a_n of an interior angle is given by this formula:

$$a_n = \frac{180(n-2)}{n}$$

Write the first five terms of the sequence. Write a rule for the sequence giving the total measure T_n of the interior angles in each regular n-sided polygon. Use the rule to find the total measure of the angles in the Guggenheim Museum skylight, which is a regular dodecagon.

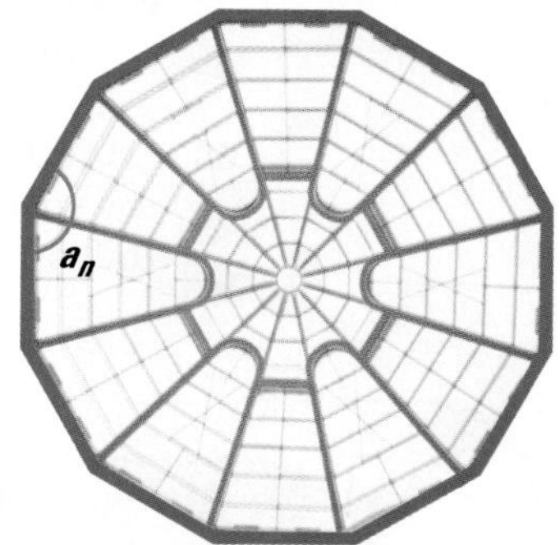

Guggenheim Museum Skylight

@HomeTutor for problem solving help at classzone.com

64. ★ **SHORT RESPONSE** You want to save $500 for a school trip. You begin by saving a penny on the first day. You plan to save an additional penny each day after that. For example, you will save 2 pennies on the second day, 3 pennies on the third day, and so on. How much money will you have saved after 100 days? How many days must you save to have saved $500? *Explain* how you used a series to find your answer.

@HomeTutor for problem solving help at classzone.com

65. **TOWER OF HANOI** In the puzzle called the Tower of Hanoi, the object is to use a series of moves to take the rings from one peg and stack them in order on another peg. A move consists of moving exactly one ring, and no ring may be placed on top of a smaller ring. The minimum number a_n of moves required to move n rings is 1 for 1 ring, 3 for 2 rings, 7 for 3 rings, 15 for 4 rings, and 31 for 5 rings. Find a formula for the sequence. What is the minimum number of moves required to move 6 rings? 7 rings? 8 rings?

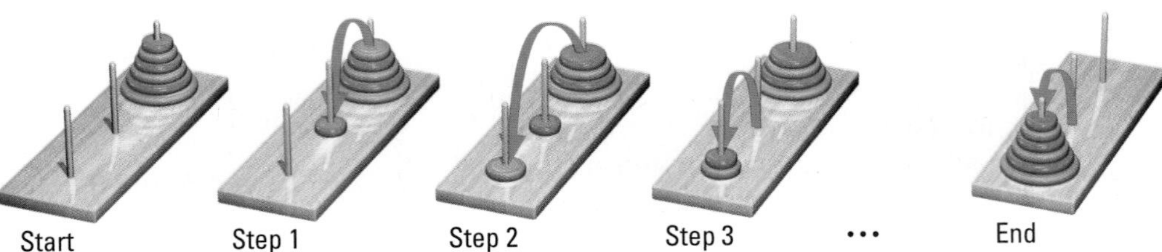

66. **MULTI-STEP PROBLEM** The mean distance d_n (in astronomical units) of each planet (except Neptune) from the sun is approximated by the Titius-Bode rule, $d_n = 0.3(2)^{n-2} + 0.4$, where n is a positive integer representing the position of the planet from the sun.

   a. **Evaluate** The value of n is 4 for Mars. Use the Titius-Bode rule to approximate the distance of Mars from the sun.

   b. **Convert** One astronomical unit is equal to about 149,600,000 kilometers. How far is Mars from the sun in kilometers?

   c. **Graph** Graph the sequence given by the Titius-Bode rule.

67. ★ **EXTENDED RESPONSE** For a display at a sports store, you are stacking soccer balls in a pyramid whose base is an equilateral triangle. The number a_n of balls per layer is given by $a_n = \frac{n(n+1)}{2}$ where $n = 1$ represents the top layer.

   a. How many balls are in the fifth layer?

   b. How many balls are in a stack with five layers?

   c. *Compare* the number of balls in a layer of a triangular pyramid with the number of balls in the same layer of a square pyramid.

68. **CHALLENGE** Using the true statements from Exercises 59–62 on page 799 and the special formulas on page 797, find a formula for the number of balls in the top n layers of the pyramid from Exercise 67.

NEW YORK MIXED REVIEW

TEST PRACTICE at classzone.com

69. The sale price, y, for a pair of tennis shoes is $\frac{2}{3}$ of the original price, x.
Which equation represents this relationship?

   Ⓐ $y = \frac{2}{3}x$ Ⓑ $y = \frac{3}{2}x$ Ⓒ $y = x + \frac{2}{3}$ Ⓓ $y = x - \frac{2}{3}$

70. Which equation represents a line with a slope of -5 and a y-intercept of 2?

   Ⓐ $y = -5x + 2$ Ⓑ $y = -5x + 10$ Ⓒ $y = 2x - 5$ Ⓓ $y = 2x + 10$

@HomeTutor
classzone.com
Keystrokes

12.1 Work with Sequences

QUESTION How can you use a graphing calculator to perform operations with sequences?

EXAMPLE Find, graph, and sum terms of a sequence

Use a graphing calculator to find the first eight terms of $a_n = 5n - 3$. Graph the sequence. Then find the sum of the first eight terms of the sequence.

STEP 1 ***Enter sequence***

Put the graphing calculator in *sequence* mode and *dot* mode. Enter the sequence. Note that the calculator uses $u(n)$ rather than a_n.

```
nMin=1
u(n)=5n-3
u(nMin)=
v(n)=
v(nMin)=
w(n)=
w(nMin)=
```

STEP 2 ***Calculate terms***

Use the *table* feature to view the terms of the sequence. The first eight terms are 2, 7, 12, 17, 22, 27, 32, and 37.

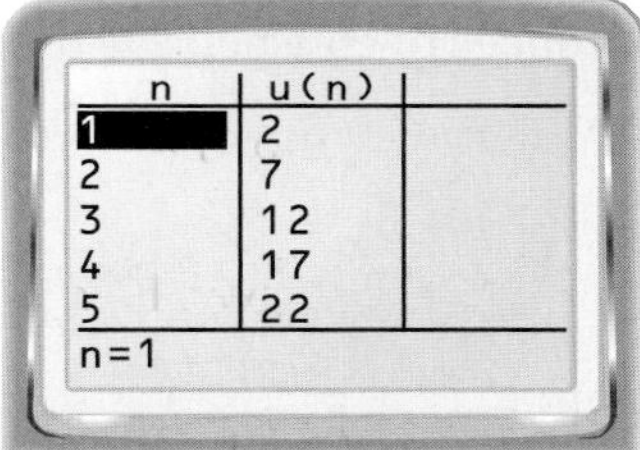

STEP 3 ***Graph sequence***

Set the viewing window so that $1 \leq n \leq 8$, $0 \leq x \leq 9$, and $0 \leq y \leq 40$. Graph the sequence. Use the *trace* feature to view the terms of the sequence.

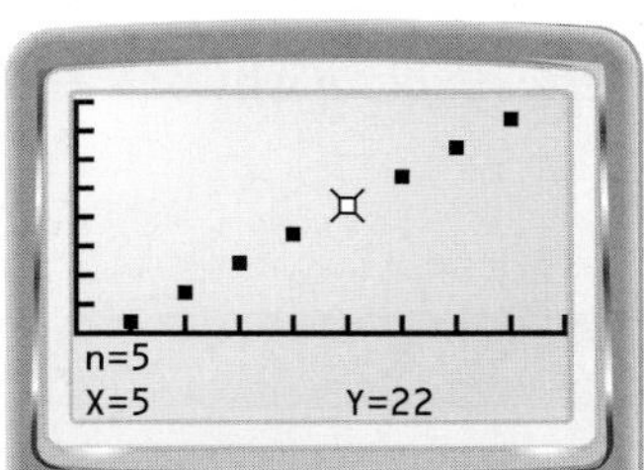

STEP 4 ***Find sum of terms***

Use the *summation* feature to find the sum of the first eight terms of the sequence. The screen shows that the sum is 156.

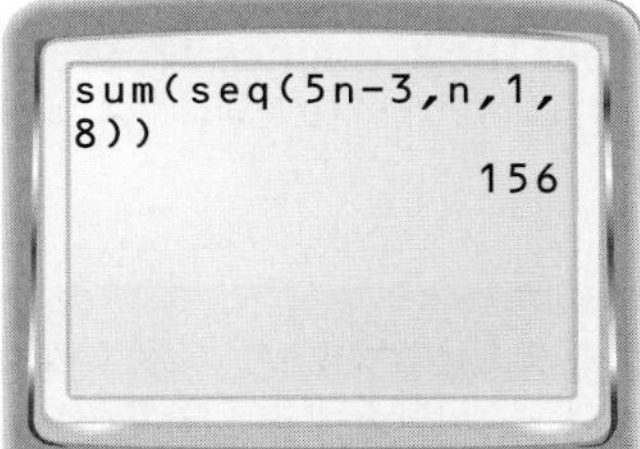

PRACTICE

Use a graphing calculator to (a) find the first ten terms of the sequence, (b) graph the sequence, and (c) find the sum of the first ten terms of the sequence.

1. $a_n = 4n + 1$

2. $a_n = 3(n + 2)$

3. $a_n = 35 - 3n$

4. $a_n = 15 + 2n$

5. $a_n = 3 + n^2$

6. $a_n = 2^{n-1}$

12.2 Analyze Arithmetic Sequences and Series

 **A2.A.29** Identify an arithmetic or geometric sequence and find the formula for its *n*th term

Before You worked with general sequences and series.

Now You will study arithmetic sequences and series.

Why? So you can arrange a marching band, as in Ex. 64.

Key Vocabulary
- arithmetic sequence
- common difference
- arithmetic series

In an **arithmetic sequence**, the difference of consecutive terms is constant. This constant difference is called the **common difference** and is denoted by d.

EXAMPLE 1 Identify arithmetic sequences

Tell whether the sequence is arithmetic.

a. $-4, 1, 6, 11, 16, \ldots$

b. $3, 5, 9, 15, 23, \ldots$

Solution

Find the differences of consecutive terms.

a. $a_2 - a_1 = 1 - (-4) = 5$

$a_3 - a_2 = 6 - 1 = 5$

$a_4 - a_3 = 11 - 6 = 5$

$a_5 - a_4 = 16 - 11 = 5$

▶ Each difference is 5, so the sequence is arithmetic.

b. $a_2 - a_1 = 5 - 3 = 2$

$a_3 - a_2 = 9 - 5 = 4$

$a_4 - a_3 = 15 - 9 = 6$

$a_5 - a_4 = 23 - 15 = 8$

▶ The differences are not constant, so the sequence is not arithmetic.

✓ **GUIDED PRACTICE** for Example 1

1. Tell whether the sequence 17, 14, 11, 8, 5, . . . is arithmetic. *Explain* why or why not.

KEY CONCEPT *For Your Notebook*

Rule for an Arithmetic Sequence

Algebra The nth term of an arithmetic sequence with first term a_1 and common difference d is given by:

$$a_n = a_1 + (n - 1)d$$

Example The nth term of an arithmetic sequence with a first term of 2 and common difference 3 is given by:

$$a_n = 2 + (n - 1)3, \text{ or } a_n = -1 + 3n$$

EXAMPLE 2 Write a rule for the *n*th term

Write a rule for the *n*th term of the sequence. Then find a_{15}.

a. 4, 9, 14, 19, . . .

b. 60, 52, 44, 36, . . .

Solution

a. The sequence is arithmetic with first term $a_1 = 4$ and common difference $d = 9 - 4 = 5$. So, a rule for the *n*th term is:

AVOID ERRORS
In the general rule for an arithmetic sequence, note that the common difference *d* is multiplied by *n* − 1, not *n*.

$a_n = a_1 + (n - 1)d$ **Write general rule.**

$= 4 + (n - 1)5$ **Substitute 4 for a_1 and 5 for *d*.**

$= -1 + 5n$ **Simplify.**

The 15th term is $a_{15} = -1 + 5(15) = 74$.

b. The sequence is arithmetic with first term $a_1 = 60$ and common difference $d = 52 - 60 = -8$. So, a rule for the *n*th term is:

$a_n = a_1 + (n - 1)d$ **Write general rule.**

$= 60 + (n - 1)(-8)$ **Substitute 60 for a_1 and −8 for *d*.**

$= 68 - 8n$ **Simplify.**

The 15th term is $a_{15} = 68 - 8(15) = -52$.

EXAMPLE 3 Write a rule given a term and common difference

One term of an arithmetic sequence is $a_{19} = 48$. The common difference is $d = 3$.

a. Write a rule for the *n*th term.

b. Graph the sequence.

Solution

a. Use the general rule to find the first term.

$a_n = a_1 + (n - 1)d$ **Write general rule.**

$a_{19} = a_1 + (19 - 1)d$ **Substitute 19 for *n*.**

$48 = a_1 + 18(3)$ **Substitute 48 for a_{19} and 3 for *d*.**

$-6 = a_1$ **Solve for a_1.**

So, a rule for the *n*th term is:

$a_n = a_1 + (n - 1)d$ **Write general rule.**

$= -6 + (n - 1)3$ **Substitute −6 for a_1 and 3 for *d*.**

$= -9 + 3n$ **Simplify.**

b. Create a table of values for the sequence. The graph of the first 6 terms of the sequence is shown. Notice that the points lie on a line. This is true for *any* arithmetic sequence.

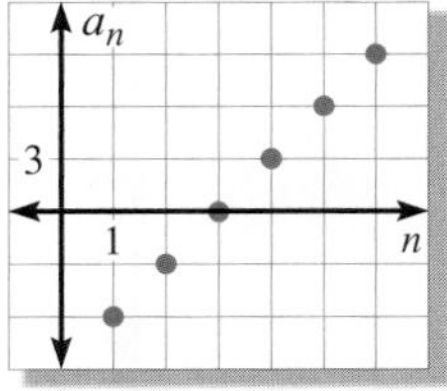

n	1	2	3	4	5	6
a_n	−6	−3	0	3	6	9

EXAMPLE 4 Write a rule given two terms

Two terms of an arithmetic sequence are $a_8 = 21$ and $a_{27} = 97$. Find a rule for the nth term.

Solution

STEP 1 **Write** a system of equations using $a_n = a_1 + (n - 1)d$ and substituting 27 for n (Equation 1) and then 8 for n (Equation 2).

$a_{27} = a_1 + (27 - 1)d \rightarrow 97 = a_1 + 26d$ **Equation 1**

$a_8 = a_1 + (8 - 1)d \rightarrow 21 = a_1 + 7d$ **Equation 2**

STEP 2 **Solve** the system.

$76 = 19d$ **Subtract.**

$4 = d$ **Solve for *d*.**

$97 = a_1 + 26(4)$ **Substitute for *d* in Equation 1.**

$-7 = a_1$ **Solve for a_1.**

STEP 3 **Find** a rule for a_n.

$a_n = a_1 + (n - 1)d$ **Write general rule.**

$= -7 + (n - 1)4$ **Substitute for a_1 and *d*.**

$= -11 + 4n$ **Simplify.**

✓ GUIDED PRACTICE for Examples 2, 3, and 4

Write a rule for the nth term of the arithmetic sequence. Then find a_{20}.

2. 17, 14, 11, 8, . . .

3. $a_{11} = -57, d = -7$

4. $a_7 = 26, a_{16} = 71$

ARITHMETIC SERIES The expression formed by adding the terms of an arithmetic sequence is called an **arithmetic series**. The sum of the first n terms of an arithmetic series is denoted by S_n. To find a rule for S_n, you can write S_n in two different ways and add the results.

$$\begin{aligned} S_n &= a_1 + (a_1 + d) + (a_1 + 2d) + \cdots + a_n \\ S_n &= a_n + (a_n - d) + (a_n - 2d) + \cdots + a_1 \\ \hline 2S_n &= (a_1 + a_n) + (a_1 + a_n) + (a_1 + a_n) + \cdots + (a_1 + a_n) \end{aligned}$$

You can conclude that $2S_n = n(a_1 + a_n)$, which leads to the following result.

KEY CONCEPT *For Your Notebook*

The Sum of a Finite Arithmetic Series

The sum of the first n terms of an arithmetic series is:

$$S_n = n\left(\frac{a_1 + a_n}{2}\right)$$

In words, S_n is the mean of the first and nth terms, multiplied by the number of terms.

★ EXAMPLE 5 Standardized Test Practice

What is the sum of the arithmetic series $\sum_{i=1}^{20}(3 + 5i)$?

Ⓐ 103 Ⓑ 111 Ⓒ 1110 Ⓓ 2220

CLASSIFY SERIES
You can verify that the series in Example 5 is arithmetic by evaluating $3 + 5i$ for the first few values of the index i. The resulting terms are 8, 13, 18, 23, . . . , which have a common difference of 5.

Solution

$a_1 = 3 + 5(1) = 8$ **Identify first term.**

$a_{20} = 3 + 5(20) = 103$ **Identify last term.**

$S_{20} = 20\left(\frac{8 + 103}{2}\right)$ **Write rule for S_{20}, substituting 8 for a_1 and 103 for a_{20}.**

$= 1110$ **Simplify.**

▶ The correct answer is C. Ⓐ Ⓑ Ⓒ Ⓓ

EXAMPLE 6 Use an arithmetic sequence and series in real life

HOUSE OF CARDS You are making a house of cards similar to the one shown.

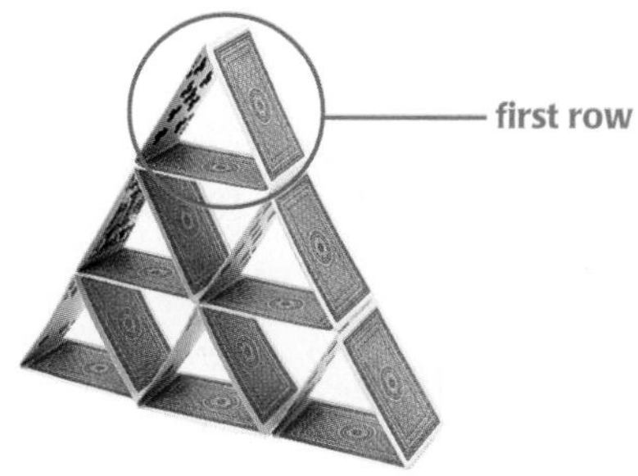

a. Write a rule for the number of cards in the nth row if the top row is row 1.

b. What is the total number of cards if the house of cards has 14 rows?

Solution

a. Starting with the top row, the numbers of cards in the rows are 3, 6, 9, 12, ... These numbers form an arithmetic sequence with a first term of 3 and a common difference of 3. So, a rule for the sequence is:

$a_n = a_1 + (n - 1)d$ **Write general rule.**

$= 3 + (n - 1)3$ **Substitute 3 for a_1 and 3 for d.**

$= 3n$ **Simplify.**

b. Find the sum of an arithmetic series with first term $a_1 = 3$ and last term $a_{14} = 3(14) = 42$.

$$\text{Total number of cards} = S_{14} = 14\left(\frac{a_1 + a_{14}}{2}\right) = 14\left(\frac{3 + 42}{2}\right) = 315$$

 at classzone.com

 **GUIDED PRACTICE** for Examples 5 and 6

5. Find the sum of the arithmetic series $\sum_{i=1}^{12}(2 + 7i)$.

6. **WHAT IF?** In Example 6, what is the total number of cards if the house of cards has 8 rows?

12.2 EXERCISES

HOMEWORK KEY

○ = **WORKED-OUT SOLUTIONS** on p. WS21 for Exs. 15, 41, and 65

★ = **STANDARDIZED TEST PRACTICE** Exs. 2, 29, 39, 52, and 68

◆ = **MULTIPLE REPRESENTATIONS** Ex. 66

SKILL PRACTICE

1. **VOCABULARY** Copy and complete: The constant difference between consecutive terms of an arithmetic sequence is called the _?_.

2. ★ **WRITING** *Explain* the difference between an arithmetic sequence and an arithmetic series.

EXAMPLE 1 on p. 802 for Exs. 3–11

IDENTIFYING ARITHMETIC SEQUENCES Tell whether the sequence is arithmetic. *Explain* why or why not.

3. $1, -2, -5, -8, -11, \ldots$
4. $16, 14, 11, 6, 3, \ldots$
5. $5, 14, 23, 32, 41, \ldots$
6. $-10, -7, -5, -2, 0, \ldots$
7. $0.5, 1, 1.5, 2, 2.5, \ldots$
8. $20, 10, 5, 2.5, 1.25, \ldots$
9. $\frac{7}{4}, \frac{5}{4}, \frac{3}{4}, -\frac{3}{4}, -\frac{5}{4}, \ldots$
10. $\frac{1}{7}, \frac{2}{7}, \frac{4}{7}, \frac{8}{7}, \frac{16}{7}, \ldots$
11. $-\frac{5}{2}, -1, \frac{1}{2}, 2, \frac{7}{2}, \ldots$

EXAMPLE 2 on p. 803 for Exs. 12–22

WRITING RULES Write a rule for the *n*th term of the arithmetic sequence. Then find a_{20}.

12. $1, 4, 7, 10, 13, \ldots$
13. $5, 11, 17, 23, 29, \ldots$
14. $8, 21, 34, 47, 60, \ldots$
15. $-3, -1, 1, 3, 5, \ldots$
16. $6, 2, -2, -6, -10, \ldots$
17. $25, 14, 3, -8, -19, \ldots$
18. $0, \frac{2}{3}, \frac{4}{3}, 2, \frac{8}{3}, \ldots$
19. $2, \frac{5}{3}, \frac{4}{3}, 1, \frac{2}{3}, \ldots$
20. $1.5, 3.6, 5.7, 7.8, 9.9, \ldots$

ERROR ANALYSIS *Describe* and correct the error in writing the rule for the *n*th term of the arithmetic sequence 37, 24, 11, −2, −15, ...

21.

Use $a_1 = 37$ and $d = -13$.

$a_n = a_1 + nd$

$a_n = 37 + n(-13)$

$a_n = 37 - 13n$

22.

The first term is 37 and the common difference is −13.

$a_n = -13 + (n - 1)(37)$

$a_n = -50 + 37n$

EXAMPLE 3 on p. 803 for Exs. 23–29

WRITING RULES Write a rule for the *n*th term of the arithmetic sequence. Then graph the first six terms of the sequence.

23. $a_{16} = 52, d = 5$
24. $a_6 = -16, d = 9$
25. $a_4 = 96, d = -14$
26. $a_{12} = -3, d = -7$
27. $a_{10} = 30, d = \frac{7}{2}$
28. $a_{11} = \frac{1}{2}, d = -\frac{1}{2}$

29. ★ **MULTIPLE CHOICE** For a certain arithmetic sequence, $a_{30} = 57$ and $d = 4$. What is a rule for the *n*th term of the sequence?

(A) $a_n = -63 - 4n$ (B) $a_n = -59 - 4n$

(C) $a_n = -63 + 4n$ (D) $a_n = -59 + 4n$

EXAMPLE 4
on p. 804
for Exs. 30–39

WRITING RULES Write a rule for the *n*th term of the arithmetic sequence that has the two given terms.

30. $a_4 = 31, a_{10} = 85$

31. $a_6 = 39, a_{14} = 79$

32. $a_3 = -2, a_{17} = 40$

33. $a_8 = -10, a_{20} = -58$

34. $a_9 = 89, a_{15} = 137$

35. $a_2 = 17, a_{11} = 35$

36. $a_7 = 4, a_{12} = -9$

37. $a_5 = 15, a_9 = 24$

38. $a_6 = 0, a_{11} = -2$

39. ★ **MULTIPLE CHOICE** For a certain arithmetic sequence, $a_6 = -6$ and $a_{13} = -48$. What is a rule for the *n*th term of the sequence?

(A) $a_n = 18 + 6n$ (B) $a_n = 30 - 6n$

(C) $a_n = -6 + 24n$ (D) $a_n = -36 - 6n$

EXAMPLE 5
on p. 805
for Exs. 40–48

FINDING SUMS Find the sum of the arithmetic series.

40. $\sum_{i=1}^{10} (1 + 3i)$

41. $\sum_{i=1}^{8} (-3 - 2i)$

42. $\sum_{i=1}^{18} (14 - 6i)$

43. $\sum_{i=1}^{22} (-9 + 11i)$

44. $\sum_{i=3}^{9} (72 - 6i)$

45. $\sum_{i=5}^{14} (-54 + 9i)$

46. $2 + 6 + 10 + \cdots + 58$

47. $-1 + 4 + 9 + \cdots + 34$

48. $44 + 37 + 30 + \cdots + 2$

USING GRAPHS Write a rule for the sequence whose graph is shown.

49.

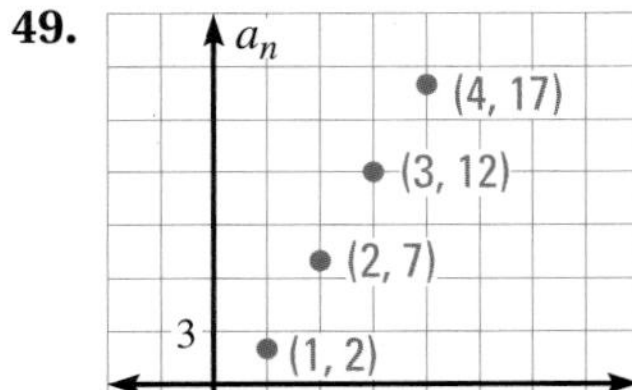

50.

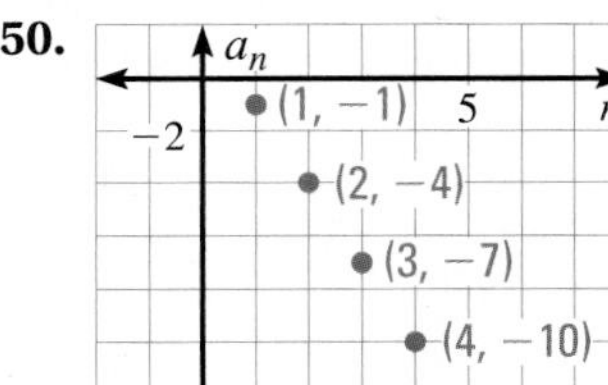

51.

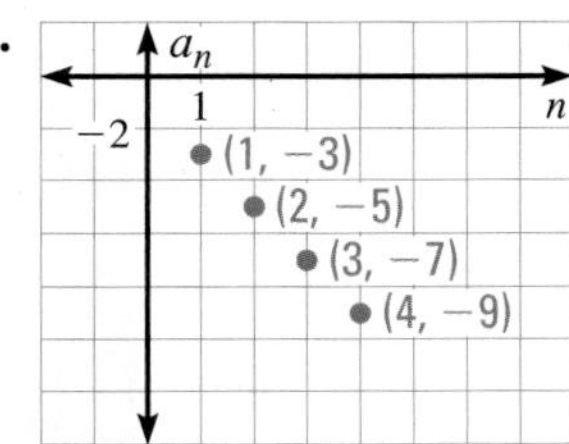

52. ★ **WRITING** *Compare* the graph of $a_n = 3n + 2$, where n is a positive integer, with the graph of $f(x) = 3x + 2$, where x is a real number. Discuss how the graph of an arithmetic sequence is similar to and different from the graph of a linear function.

REASONING Tell whether the statement is *true* or *false*. *Explain* your answer.

53. If the common difference of an arithmetic series is doubled while the first term and number of terms in the series remain unchanged, then the sum of the series is doubled.

54. If the numbers a, b, and c are the first three terms of an arithmetic sequence, then b is half the sum of a and c.

SOLVING EQUATIONS Find the value of *n*.

55. $\sum_{i=1}^{n} (-5 + 7i) = 486$

56. $\sum_{i=1}^{n} (10 - 3i) = -28$

57. $\sum_{i=1}^{n} (58 - 8i) = -1150$

58. $\sum_{i=1}^{n} (5 - 5i) = -50$

59. $\sum_{i=3}^{n} (-3 - 4i) = -507$

60. $\sum_{i=5}^{n} (7 + 12i) = 455$

61. **REASONING** Find the sum of all positive odd integers less than 300.

62. **CHALLENGE** The numbers $3 - x$, x, and $1 - 3x$ are the first three terms in an arithmetic sequence. Find the value of x and the next term in the sequence.

PROBLEM SOLVING

EXAMPLE 6
on p. 805
for Exs. 63–65

63. **HONEYCOMBS** Domestic bees make their honeycomb by starting with a single hexagonal cell, then forming ring after ring of hexagonal cells around the initial cell, as shown. The numbers of cells in successive rings form an arithmetic sequence.

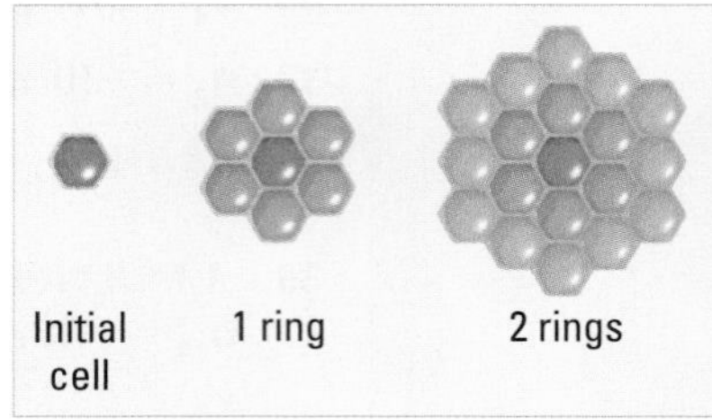

a. Write a rule for the number of cells in the nth ring.

b. What is the total number of cells in the honeycomb after the 9th ring is formed? (*Hint:* Do not forget to count the initial cell.)

@HomeTutor for problem solving help at classzone.com

64. **MARCHING BAND** A marching band is arranged in 7 rows. The first row has 3 band members, and each row after the first has 2 more band members than the row before it. Write a rule for the number of band members in the nth row. Then find the total number of band members.

@HomeTutor for problem solving help at classzone.com

65. **SCULPTURE** Sol LeWitt's sculpture *Four-Sided Pyramid* in the National Gallery of Art Sculpture Garden is made of concrete blocks. As shown in the diagram, each layer has 8 more visible blocks than the layer in front of it.

a. Write a rule for the number of visible blocks in the nth layer where $n = 1$ represents the front layer.

b. When you view the pyramid from one corner, a total of 12 layers are visible. How many of the pyramid's blocks are visible?

66. **MULTIPLE REPRESENTATIONS** The distance D (in feet) that an object falls in t seconds can be modeled by $D(t) = 16t^2$.

a. **Making a Table** Let $d(n)$ represent the distance the object falls in the nth second. Make a table of values showing $d(1)$, $d(2)$, $d(3)$, and $d(4)$. (*Hint:* The distance $d(1)$ that the object falls in the first second is $D(1) - D(0)$.)

b. **Writing a Rule** Write a rule for the sequence of distances given by $d(n)$.

c. **Drawing a Graph** Graph the sequence from part (b).

67. **ENTERTAINMENT** During a high school spirit week, students dress up in costumes. A cash prize is given each day to the student with the best costume. The organizing committee has $1000 to give away over five days. The committee wants to increase the amount of the prize by $50 each day. How much should the committee give away on the first day?

○ = WORKED-OUT SOLUTIONS on p. WS1 ★ = STANDARDIZED TEST PRACTICE ◆ = MULTIPLE REPRESENTATIONS

68. ★ **EXTENDED RESPONSE** A paper towel manufacturer sells paper towels rolled onto cardboard dowels. The thickness of the paper is 0.0004 inch. The diameter of a dowel is 2 inches, and the total diameter of a roll is 5 inches.

n	d_n (in.)	ℓ_n (in.)
1	2	2π
2	?	?
3	?	?
4	?	?

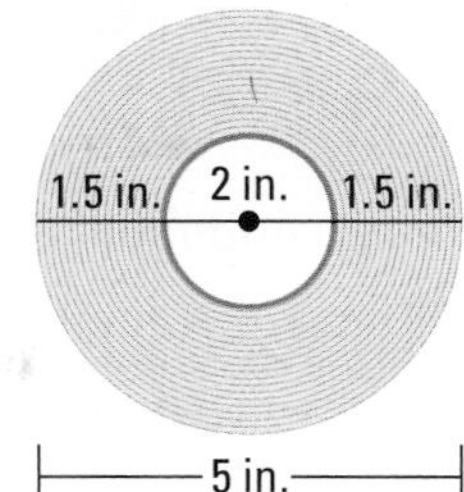

a. Calculate Let n be the number of times the paper towel is wrapped around the dowel, let d_n be the diameter of the roll just before the nth wrap, and let ℓ_n be the length of paper added in the nth wrap. Copy and complete the table.

b. Model What kind of sequence is $\ell_1, \ell_2, \ell_3, \ell_4, \ldots$? Write a rule for the nth term of the sequence.

c. Apply Find the number of times the paper must be wrapped around the dowel to create a roll with a 5 inch diameter. Use your answer and the rule from part (b) to find the length of paper in a roll with a 5 inch diameter.

d. Interpret Suppose a roll with a 5 inch diameter costs \$1.50. How much would you expect to pay for a roll with a 7 inch diameter whose dowel also has a diameter of 2 inches? *Explain* your reasoning and any assumptions you make.

69. **CHALLENGE** A theater has n rows of seats, and each row has d more seats than the row in front of it. There are x seats in the last (nth) row and a total of y seats in the entire theater. How many seats are in the front row of the theater? Write your answer in terms of n, x, and y.

NY NEW YORK MIXED REVIEW

TEST PRACTICE at classzone.com

70. What is the approximate perimeter of the trapezoid?

Ⓐ 17.0 units

Ⓑ 17.8 units

Ⓒ 24.6 units

Ⓓ 29.0 units

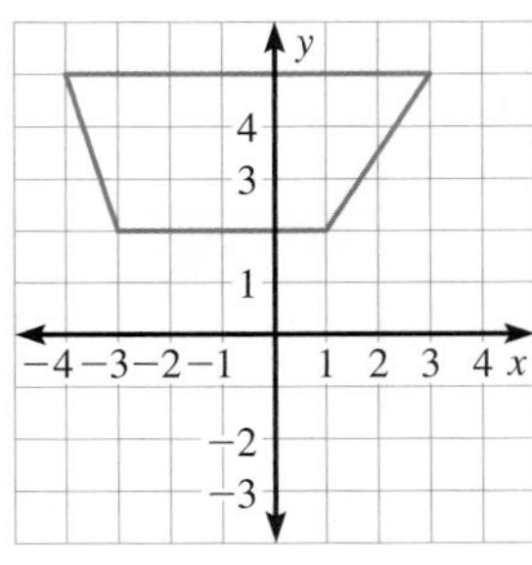

71. Sam randomly selects one card from a standard deck of 52 cards. Which of the following events has a probability of occurring that is about 8%?

Ⓐ The card is a spade.

Ⓑ The card is the 3 of hearts.

Ⓒ The card is a queen.

Ⓓ The card is a red card.

12.3 Analyze Geometric Sequences and Series

A2.A.29 Identify an arithmetic or geometric sequence and find the formula for its *n*th term

Before	You studied arithmetic sequences and series.
Now	You will study geometric sequences and series.
Why?	So you can solve problems about sports tournaments, as in Ex. 58.

Key Vocabulary
- **geometric sequence**
- **common ratio**
- **geometric series**

In a **geometric sequence**, the ratio of any term to the previous term is constant. This constant ratio is called the **common ratio** and is denoted by *r*.

EXAMPLE 1 Identify geometric sequences

Tell whether the sequence is geometric.

a. 4, 10, 18, 28, 40, . . .

b. 625, 125, 25, 5, 1, . . .

Solution

To decide whether a sequence is geometric, find the ratios of consecutive terms.

a. $\frac{a_2}{a_1} = \frac{10}{4} = \frac{5}{2}$ $\quad \frac{a_3}{a_2} = \frac{18}{10} = \frac{9}{5}$ $\quad \frac{a_4}{a_3} = \frac{28}{18} = \frac{14}{9}$ $\quad \frac{a_5}{a_4} = \frac{40}{28} = \frac{10}{7}$

▶ The ratios are different, so the sequence is not geometric.

b. $\frac{a_2}{a_1} = \frac{125}{625} = \frac{1}{5}$ $\quad \frac{a_3}{a_2} = \frac{25}{125} = \frac{1}{5}$ $\quad \frac{a_4}{a_3} = \frac{5}{25} = \frac{1}{5}$ $\quad \frac{a_5}{a_4} = \frac{1}{5}$

▶ Each ratio is $\frac{1}{5}$, so the sequence is geometric.

GUIDED PRACTICE for Example 1

Tell whether the sequence is geometric. *Explain* why or why not.

1. 81, 27, 9, 3, 1, . . .
2. 1, 2, 6, 24, 120, . . .
3. −4, 8, −16, 32, −64, . . .

KEY CONCEPT *For Your Notebook*

Rule for a Geometric Sequence

Algebra The *n*th term of a geometric sequence with first term a_1 and common ratio *r* is given by:

$$a_n = a_1 r^{n-1}$$

Example The *n*th term of a geometric sequence with a first term of 3 and common ratio 2 is given by:

$$a_n = 3(2)^{n-1}$$

EXAMPLE 2 Write a rule for the *n*th term

Write a rule for the *n*th term of the sequence. Then find a_7.

a. 4, 20, 100, 500, . . .

b. 152, −76, 38, −19, . . .

Solution

a. The sequence is geometric with first term $a_1 = 4$ and common ratio $r = \frac{20}{4} = 5$. So, a rule for the *n*th term is:

> **AVOID ERRORS**
> In the general rule for a geometric sequence, note that the exponent is $n - 1$, not n.

$a_n = a_1 r^{n-1}$ **Write general rule.**

$= 4(5)^{n-1}$ **Substitute 4 for a_1 and 5 for r.**

The 7th term is $a_7 = 4(5)^{7-1} = 62{,}500$.

b. The sequence is geometric with first term $a_1 = 152$ and common ratio $r = \frac{-76}{152} = -\frac{1}{2}$. So, a rule for the *n*th term is:

$a_n = a_1 r^{n-1}$ **Write general rule.**

$= 152\left(-\frac{1}{2}\right)^{n-1}$ **Substitute 152 for a_1 and $-\frac{1}{2}$ for r.**

The 7th term is $a_7 = 152\left(-\frac{1}{2}\right)^{7-1} = \frac{19}{8}$.

EXAMPLE 3 Write a rule given a term and common ratio

One term of a geometric sequence is $a_4 = 12$. The common ratio is $r = 2$.

a. Write a rule for the *n*th term.

b. Graph the sequence.

Solution

a. Use the general rule to find the first term.

$a_n = a_1 r^{n-1}$ **Write general rule.**

$a_4 = a_1 r^{4-1}$ **Substitute 4 for n.**

$12 = a_1(2)^3$ **Substitute 12 for a_4 and 2 for r.**

$1.5 = a_1$ **Solve for a_1.**

So, a rule for the *n*th term is:

$a_n = a_1 r^{n-1}$ **Write general rule.**

$= 1.5(2)^{n-1}$ **Substitute 1.5 for a_1 and 2 for r.**

b. Create a table of values for the sequence. The graph of the first 6 terms of the sequence is shown. Notice that the points lie on an exponential curve. This is true for *any* geometric sequence with $r > 0$.

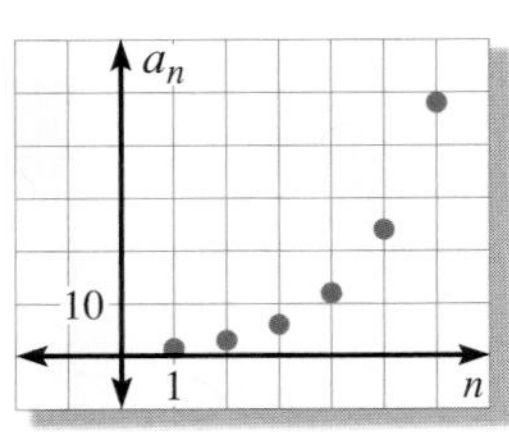

n	1	2	3	4	5	6
a_n	1.5	3	6	12	24	48

Animated Algebra at classzone.com

EXAMPLE 4 Write a rule given two terms

Two terms of a geometric sequence are $a_3 = -48$ and $a_6 = 3072$. Find a rule for the nth term.

Solution

STEP 1 **Write** a system of equations using $a_n = a_1 r^{n-1}$ and substituting 3 for n (Equation 1) and then 6 for n (Equation 2).

$a_3 = a_1 r^{3-1}$ → $-48 = a_1 r^2$ Equation 1

$a_6 = a_1 r^{6-1}$ → $3072 = a_1 r^5$ Equation 2

STEP 2 **Solve** the system.

$\frac{-48}{r^2} = a_1$ Solve Equation 1 for a_1.

$3072 = \frac{-48}{r^2}(r^5)$ Substitute for a_1 in Equation 2.

$3072 = -48r^3$ Simplify.

$-4 = r$ Solve for r.

$-48 = a_1(-4)^2$ Substitute for r in Equation 1.

$-3 = a_1$ Solve for a_1.

STEP 3 **Find** a rule for a_n.

$a_n = a_1 r^{n-1}$ Write general rule.

$a_n = -3(-4)^{n-1}$ Substitute for a_1 and r.

✓ GUIDED PRACTICE for Examples 2, 3, and 4

Write a rule for the nth term of the geometric sequence. Then find a_8.

4. 3, 15, 75, 375, . . .

5. $a_6 = -96$, $r = 2$

6. $a_2 = -12$, $a_4 = -3$

GEOMETRIC SERIES The expression formed by adding the terms of a geometric sequence is called a **geometric series**. The sum of the first n terms of a geometric series is denoted by S_n. You can develop a rule for S_n as follows.

$$\begin{aligned} S_n &= a_1 + a_1 r + a_1 r^2 + a_1 r^3 + \cdots + a_1 r^{n-1} \\ -rS_n &= \quad - a_1 r - a_1 r^2 - a_1 r^3 - \cdots - a_1 r^{n-1} - a_1 r^n \\ \hline S_n(1 - r) &= a_1 + 0 + 0 + 0 + \cdots + 0 - a_1 r^n \end{aligned}$$

So, $S_n(1 - r) = a_1(1 - r^n)$. If $r \neq 1$, you can divide each side of this equation by $1 - r$ to obtain the following rule for S_n.

KEY CONCEPT *For Your Notebook*

The Sum of a Finite Geometric Series

The sum of the first n terms of a geometric series with common ratio $r \neq 1$ is:

$$S_n = a_1\left(\frac{1 - r^n}{1 - r}\right)$$

EXAMPLE 5 Find the sum of a geometric series

Find the sum of the geometric series $\sum_{i=1}^{16} 4(3)^{i-1}$.

$a_1 = 4(3)^{1-1} = 4$ **Identify first term.**

$r = 3$ **Identify common ratio.**

$S_{16} = a_1\left(\frac{1-r^{16}}{1-r}\right)$ **Write rule for S_{16}.**

$= 4\left(\frac{1-3^{16}}{1-3}\right)$ **Substitute 4 for a_1 and 3 for r.**

$= 86{,}093{,}440$ **Simplify.**

▶ The sum of the series is 86,093,440.

EXAMPLE 6 Use a geometric sequence and series in real life

MOVIE REVENUE In 1990, the total box office revenue at U.S. movie theaters was about \$5.02 billion. From 1990 through 2003, the total box office revenue increased by about 5.9% per year.

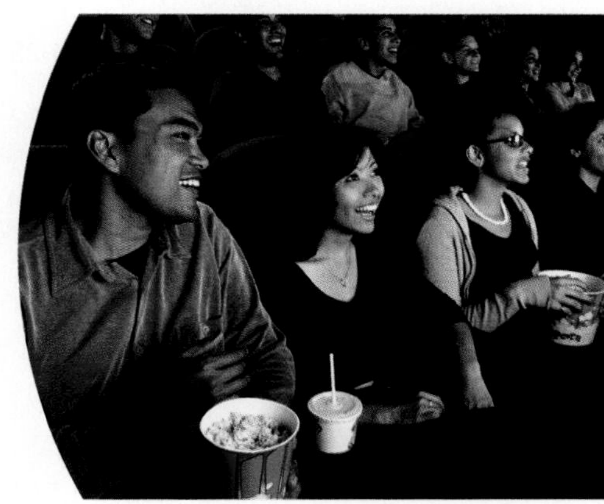

a. Write a rule for the total box office revenue a_n (in billions of dollars) in terms of the year. Let $n = 1$ represent 1990.

b. What was the total box office revenue at U.S. movie theaters for the entire period 1990–2003?

Solution

a. Because the total box office revenue increased by the same percent each year, the total revenues from year to year form a geometric sequence. Use $a_1 = 5.02$ and $r = 1 + 0.059 = 1.059$ to write a rule for the sequence.

$a_n = 5.02(1.059)^{n-1}$ **Write a rule for a_n.**

b. There are 14 years in the period 1990–2003, so find S_{14}.

$$S_{14} = a_1\left(\frac{1-r^{14}}{1-r}\right) = 5.02\left(\frac{1-(1.059)^{14}}{1-1.059}\right) \approx 105$$

▶ The total movie box office revenue for the period 1990–2003 was about \$105 billion.

✓ GUIDED PRACTICE for Examples 5 and 6

7. Find the sum of the geometric series $\sum_{i=1}^{8} 6(-2)^{i-1}$.

8. **MOVIE REVENUE** Use the rule in part (a) of Example 6 to estimate the total box office revenue at U.S. movie theaters in 2000.

12.3 EXERCISES

HOMEWORK KEY

◯ = **WORKED-OUT SOLUTIONS** on p. WS21 for Exs. 19, 49, and 59

★ = **STANDARDIZED TEST PRACTICE** Exs. 2, 27, 54, 55, and 59

◆ = **MULTIPLE REPRESENTATIONS** Ex. 61

SKILL PRACTICE

1. **VOCABULARY** Copy and complete: The constant ratio of consecutive terms in a geometric sequence is called the _?_.

2. ★ **WRITING** How can you determine whether a sequence is geometric?

EXAMPLE 1 on p. 810 for Exs. 3–14

IDENTIFYING GEOMETRIC SEQUENCES Tell whether the sequence is geometric. *Explain* why or why not.

3. $1, 4, 8, 16, 32, \ldots$
4. $4, 16, 64, 256, 1024, \ldots$
5. $216, 36, 6, 1, \frac{1}{6}, \ldots$
6. $\frac{1}{3}, \frac{2}{3}, \frac{4}{3}, \frac{8}{3}, \frac{16}{3}, \ldots$
7. $\frac{1}{2}, 1, \frac{3}{2}, 2, \frac{5}{2}, \ldots$
8. $-\frac{1}{4}, \frac{3}{8}, -\frac{3}{16}, \frac{1}{32}, -\frac{3}{64}, \ldots$
9. $10, 5, 2.5, 1.25, 0.625, \ldots$
10. $-3, -6, 12, 24, -48, \ldots$
11. $-4, 12, -36, 108, -324, \ldots$
12. $0.2, 0.6, 1.8, 5.4, 16.2, \ldots$
13. $-5, 10, 20, 40, 80, \ldots$
14. $0.75, 1.5, 2.25, 3, 3.75, \ldots$

EXAMPLE 2 on p. 811 for Exs. 15–27

WRITING RULES Write a rule for the *n*th term of the geometric sequence. Then find a_7.

15. $1, -4, 16, -64, \ldots$
16. $6, 18, 54, 162, \ldots$
17. $4, 24, 144, 864, \ldots$
18. $7, -35, 175, -875, \ldots$
19. $2, \frac{3}{2}, \frac{9}{8}, \frac{27}{32}, \ldots$
20. $3, -\frac{6}{5}, \frac{12}{25}, -\frac{24}{125}, \ldots$
21. $4, 2, 1, 0.5, \ldots$
22. $-0.3, 0.6, -1.2, 2.4, \ldots$
23. $-2, -0.8, -0.32, -0.128, \ldots$
24. $7, -4.2, 2.52, -1.512, \ldots$
25. $5, -14, 39.2, -109.76, \ldots$
26. $120, 180, 270, 405, \ldots$

27. ★ **MULTIPLE CHOICE** What is a rule for the *n*th term of the geometric sequence 5, 20, 80, 320, . . . ?

    Ⓐ $a_n = 5(2)^{n-1}$
    Ⓑ $a_n = 5(4)^{n-1}$
    Ⓒ $a_n = 5(-4)^{n-1}$
    Ⓓ $a_n = 5(-2)^{n-1}$

EXAMPLE 3 on p. 811 for Exs. 28–38

WRITING RULES Write a rule for the *n*th term of the geometric sequence. Then graph the first six terms of the sequence.

28. $a_1 = 5, r = 3$
29. $a_1 = -2, r = 6$
30. $a_2 = 6, r = 2$
31. $a_2 = 15, r = \frac{1}{2}$
32. $a_5 = 1, r = \frac{1}{8}$
33. $a_4 = -12, r = -\frac{1}{4}$
34. $a_3 = 75, r = 5$
35. $a_2 = 8, r = 4$
36. $a_4 = 500, r = 5$

ERROR ANALYSIS *Describe* and correct the error in writing the rule for the *n*th term of the geometric sequence for which $a_1 = 3$ and $r = 2$.

37.
$a_n = a_1 r^n$
$a_n = 3(2)^n$

38.
$a_n = r a_1^{n-1}$
$a_n = 2(3)^{n-1}$

EXAMPLE 4
on p. 812
for Exs. 39–47

WRITING RULES **Write a rule for the *n*th term of the geometric sequence that has the two given terms.**

39. $a_1 = 3, a_3 = 12$

40. $a_1 = 1, a_5 = 625$

41. $a_1 = -\frac{1}{4}, a_4 = -16$

42. $a_3 = 10, a_6 = 270$

43. $a_2 = -40, a_4 = -10$

44. $a_2 = -24, a_5 = 1536$

45. $a_4 = 162, a_7 = 4374$

46. $a_3 = \frac{7}{4}, a_5 = \frac{7}{16}$

47. $a_4 = 6, a_7 = \frac{243}{8}$

EXAMPLE 5
on p. 813
for Exs. 48–54

FINDING SUMS **Find the sum of the geometric series.**

48. $\sum_{i=1}^{10} 5(2)^{i-1}$

49. $\sum_{i=1}^{8} 6(4)^{i-1}$

50. $\sum_{i=0}^{7} 12\left(-\frac{1}{2}\right)^{i}$

51. $\sum_{i=1}^{6} 4\left(\frac{1}{4}\right)^{i-1}$

52. $\sum_{i=1}^{12} 8\left(\frac{3}{2}\right)^{i-1}$

53. $\sum_{i=0}^{10} (-4)^{i}$

54. ★ **MULTIPLE CHOICE** What is the sum of the geometric series $\sum_{i=1}^{9} 2(3)^{i-1}$?

Ⓐ 19,680 Ⓑ 19,681 Ⓒ 19,682 Ⓓ 19,683

55. ★ **OPEN-ENDED MATH** Write a geometric series with 5 terms such that the sum of the series is 100. (*Hint:* Choose a value of *r* and then find a_1.)

56. **CHALLENGE** Using the rule for the sum of a finite geometric series, write each polynomial as a rational expression.

a. $1 + x + x^2 + x^3 + x^4$

b. $3x + 6x^3 + 12x^5 + 24x^7$

PROBLEM SOLVING

EXAMPLE 6
on p. 813
for Exs. 57–59

57. **SKYDIVING** In a skydiving formation with *R* rings, each ring after the first has twice as many skydivers as the preceding ring. The formation for $R = 2$ is shown.

a. Let a_n be the number of skydivers in the *n*th ring. Find a rule for a_n.

b. Find the total number of skydivers if there are $R = 4$ rings.

@HomeTutor for problem solving help at classzone.com

58. **SOCCER** A regional soccer tournament has 64 participating teams. In the first round of the tournament, 32 games are played. In each successive round, the number of games played decreases by one half.

a. Find a rule for the number of games played in the *n*th round. For what values of *n* does your rule make sense?

b. Find the total number of games played in the regional soccer tournament.

@HomeTutor for problem solving help at classzone.com

59. ★ **SHORT RESPONSE** A *binary search* technique used on a computer involves jumping to the middle of an ordered list of data (such as an alphabetical list of names) and deciding whether the item being searched for is there. If not, the computer decides whether the item comes before or after the middle. Half of the list is ignored on the next pass, and the computer jumps to the middle of the remaining list. This is repeated until the item is found.

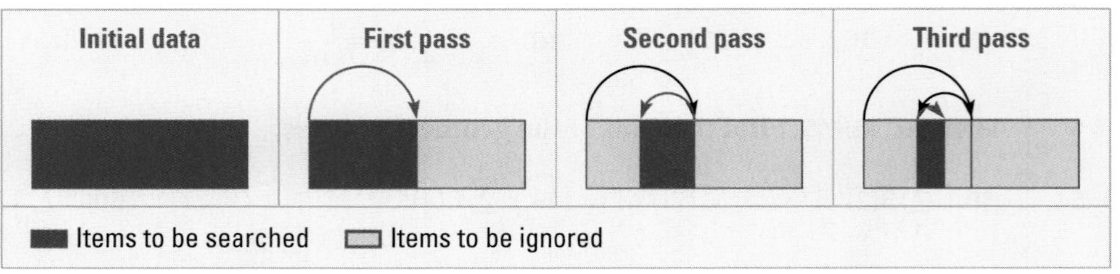

a. Find a rule for the number of items remaining after the nth pass through an ordered list of 1024 items.

b. In the worst case, the item to be found is the only one left in the list after n passes through the list. What is the worst-case value of n for a binary search of a list with 1024 items? *Explain.*

60. **FRACTALS** The *Sierpinski carpet* is a fractal created using squares. The process involves removing smaller squares from larger squares. First, divide a large square into nine congruent squares. Remove the center square. Repeat these steps for each smaller square, as shown below. Assume that each side of the initial square is one unit long.

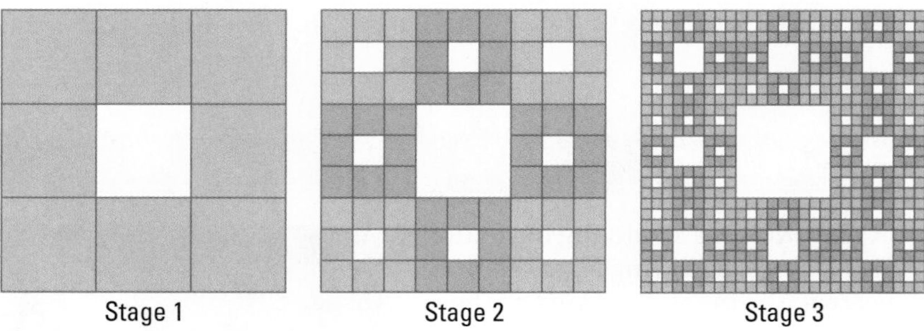

a. Let a_n be the number of squares removed at the nth stage. Find a rule for a_n. Then find the total number of squares removed through stage 8.

b. Let b_n be the remaining area of the original square after the nth stage. Find a rule for b_n. Then find the remaining area of the original square after stage 12.

61. **MULTIPLE REPRESENTATIONS** Two companies, company A and company B, offer the same starting salary of $20,000 per year. Company A gives a raise of $1000 each year. Company B gives a raise of 4% each year.

a. Writing Rules Write rules giving the salaries a_n and b_n in the nth year at companies A and B, respectively. Tell whether the sequence represented by each rule is *arithmetic*, *geometric*, or *neither.*

b. Drawing Graphs Graph each sequence in the same coordinate plane.

c. Finding Sums For each company, find the sum of wages earned during the first 20 years of employment.

d. Using Technology Use a graphing calculator or spreadsheet to find after how many years the total amount earned at company B is greater than the total amount earned at company A.

62. **CHALLENGE** On January 1 of each year, you deposit $2000 in an individual retirement account (IRA) that pays 5% annual interest. You make a total of 30 deposits. How much money do you have in your IRA immediately after you make your last deposit?

NEW YORK MIXED REVIEW

TEST PRACTICE at classzone.com

63. The total cost of carnival tickets for 3 adults and 5 children is $49. The total cost of carnival tickets for 5 adults and 3 children is $55. What is the price, a, of one adult ticket and the price, c, of one child ticket?

   Ⓐ $a = \$5; c = \$8$ Ⓑ $a = \$7.25; c = \$6.25$

   Ⓒ $a = \$8; c = \$5$ Ⓓ $a = \$10; c = \$3.80$

64. What is the relationship between the graphs of $y = 3x^2$ and $y = 1.5x^2$?

   Ⓐ The graph of $y = 1.5x^2$ is a reflection of the graph of $y = 3x^2$ in the x-axis.

   Ⓑ The graph of $y = 1.5x^2$ is a 90° rotation of the graph of $y = 3x^2$ about the origin.

   Ⓒ The graph of $y = 1.5x^2$ is narrower than the graph of $y = 3x^2$.

   Ⓓ The graph of $y = 1.5x^2$ is wider than the graph of $y = 3x^2$.

QUIZ *for Lessons 12.1–12.3*

Write the next term in the sequence. Then write a rule for the *n*th term. *(p. 794)*

1. 1, 3, 5, 7, . . .
2. −5, 10, −15, 20, . . .
3. $\frac{1}{20}, \frac{2}{30}, \frac{3}{40}, \frac{4}{50}, \ldots$
4. 4, 16, 64, 256, . . .
5. 2, 6, 12, 20, . . .
6. 9, 36, 81, 144, . . .

Find the sum of the series. *(p. 794)*

7. $\sum_{i=1}^{4} 2i^3$
8. $\sum_{k=1}^{5} (k^2 + 3)$
9. $\sum_{n=2}^{6} \frac{1}{n-1}$

Write a rule for the *n*th term a_n of the arithmetic or geometric sequence. Find a_{15}, then find the sum of the first 15 terms of the sequence.

10. 1, 7, 13, 19, . . . *(p. 802)*
11. $\frac{1}{2}, 2, \frac{7}{2}, 5, \ldots$ *(p. 802)*
12. 5, 2, −1, −4, −7, . . . *(p. 802)*
13. 2, 8, 32, 128, . . . *(p. 810)*
14. $2, \frac{4}{3}, \frac{8}{9}, \frac{16}{27}, \ldots$ *(p. 810)*
15. −3, 15, −75, 375, . . . *(p. 810)*

16. **COLLEGE TUITION** In 1995, the average tuition at a public college in the United States was $2057. From 1995 through 2002, the average tuition at public colleges increased by about 6% per year. Write a rule for the average tuition a_n in terms of the year. Let $n = 1$ represent 1995. What was the average tuition at a public college in 2002? *(p. 810)*

Lessons 12.1–12.3

1. **TARGETS** The rings of a target alternate between dark and light. The three innermost rings of the target are shown below. Which expression is a series that gives the total area of the target's n innermost light rings?

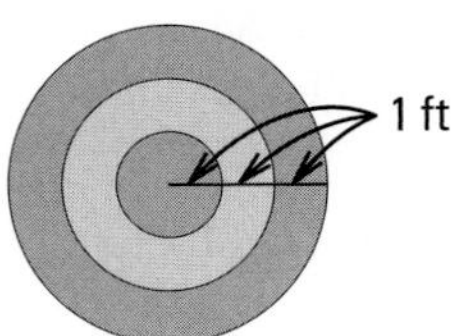

The 3 innermost rings of the target

(1) $\sum_{i=1}^{n}(2i - 1)\pi$

(2) $\sum_{i=1}^{n}(4i - 3)\pi$

(3) $\sum_{i=1}^{n}(4i - 1)\pi$

(4) $\sum_{i=1}^{n}i^2\pi$

2. **SALARY** Maria has an annual salary of $45,000 during her first year of employment. Her salary increases 3.5% per year. What will Maria's salary be during her 5th year of employment?

(1) $49,672

(2) $51,241

(3) $51,639

(4) $53,446

3. **CONSTRUCTION** A staircase is being built that leads from the ground to an elevated deck. The base of the staircase is a concrete slab that is 2 inches tall. Each stair is 7 inches tall. What is the height of the bottom of the 10th stair?

(1) 60 inches

(2) 65 inches

(3) 70 inches

(4) 72 inches

4. **SEATING ARRANGEMENT** At a restaurant, rectangular tables are placed together along their shared edges, as shown in the diagram below. How many people can be seated around 8 tables arranged in this way?

(1) 30 people (3) 34 people

(2) 32 people (4) 36 people

5. **OPEN-ENDED** Pieces of chalk are stacked in a pile. Part of the pile is shown below.

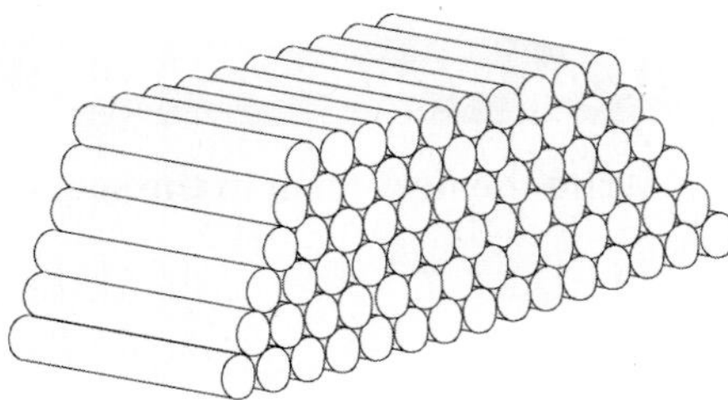

The bottom row has 15 pieces of chalk and the top row has 6 pieces of chalk. Each row has one less piece of chalk than the row below it. How many pieces of chalk are in the pile?

6. **OPEN-ENDED** A scientist is studying the radioactive decay of Platinum-197. The scientist starts with a 66 gram sample of Platinum-197 and measures the amount remaining every two hours. The recorded amounts (in grams) are 66, 33, 16.5, 8.25, ...

Is this sequence arithmetic, geometric, or neither? *Explain* how you know.

Write a rule for the nth term of the sequence.

After how many hours will the sample have a mass of less than 1 gram?

12.4 Investigating an Infinite Geometric Series

MATERIALS • scissors • paper

QUESTION What is the sum of an infinite geometric series?

You can illustrate an infinite geometric series by cutting a piece of paper into smaller and smaller pieces.

EXPLORE Model an infinite geometric series

Start with a rectangular piece of paper. Define its area to be 1 square unit.

STEP 1 *Cut paper in half*

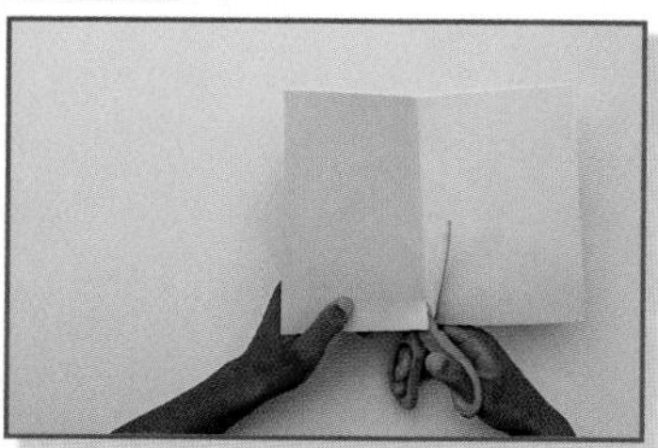

Fold the paper in half and cut along the fold. Place one half on a desktop and hold the remaining half.

STEP 2 *Cut paper again*

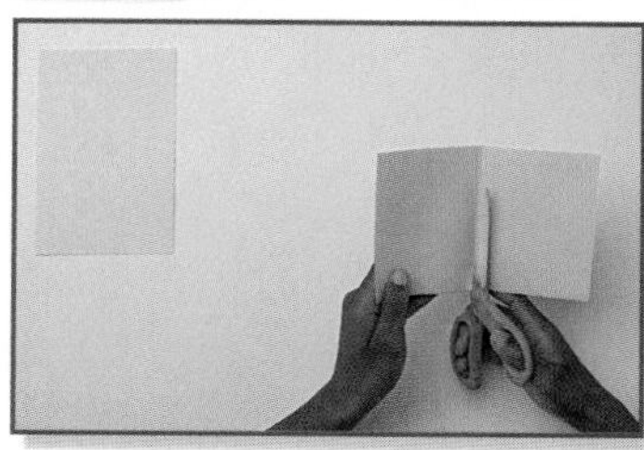

Fold the piece of paper you are holding in half and cut along the fold. Place one half on the desktop and hold the remaining half.

STEP 3 *Repeat steps*

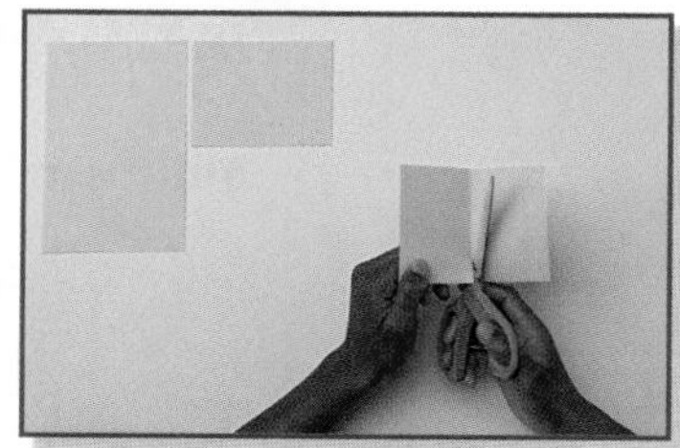

Repeat Steps 1 and 2 until you find it too difficult to fold and cut the piece of paper you are holding.

STEP 4 *Find areas* The first piece of paper on the desktop has an area of $\frac{1}{2}$ square unit. The second piece has an area of $\frac{1}{4}$ square unit. Write the areas of the next three pieces of paper. Explain why these areas form a geometric sequence.

STEP 5 *Make a table*
Copy and complete the table by recording the number of pieces of paper on the desktop and the combined area of the pieces at each step.

Number of pieces	1	2	3	4	. . .
Combined area	$\frac{1}{2}$	$\frac{1}{2} + \frac{1}{4} = ?$	?	?	. . .

DRAW CONCLUSIONS Use your observations to complete these exercises

1. Based on your table, what number does the combined area of the pieces of paper appear to be approaching?
2. Using the formula for the sum of a finite geometric series, write and simplify a rule for the combined area A_n of the pieces of paper after n cuts. What happens to A_n as $n \to \infty$? *Justify* your answer mathematically.

12.4 Find Sums of Infinite Geometric Series

Before You found the sums of finite geometric series.

Now You will find the sums of infinite geometric series.

Why? So you can analyze a fractal, as in Ex. 42.

Key Vocabulary
- **partial sum**

The sum S_n of the first n terms of an infinite series is called a **partial sum**. The partial sums of an infinite geometric series may approach a limiting value.

EXAMPLE 1 Find partial sums

Consider the infinite geometric series $\frac{1}{2} + \frac{1}{4} + \frac{1}{8} + \frac{1}{16} + \frac{1}{32} + \cdots$. Find and graph the partial sums S_n for $n = 1, 2, 3, 4$, and 5. Then describe what happens to S_n as n increases.

Solution

$$S_1 = \frac{1}{2} = 0.5$$

$$S_2 = \frac{1}{2} + \frac{1}{4} = 0.75$$

$$S_3 = \frac{1}{2} + \frac{1}{4} + \frac{1}{8} \approx 0.88$$

$$S_4 = \frac{1}{2} + \frac{1}{4} + \frac{1}{8} + \frac{1}{16} \approx 0.94$$

$$S_5 = \frac{1}{2} + \frac{1}{4} + \frac{1}{8} + \frac{1}{16} + \frac{1}{32} \approx 0.97$$

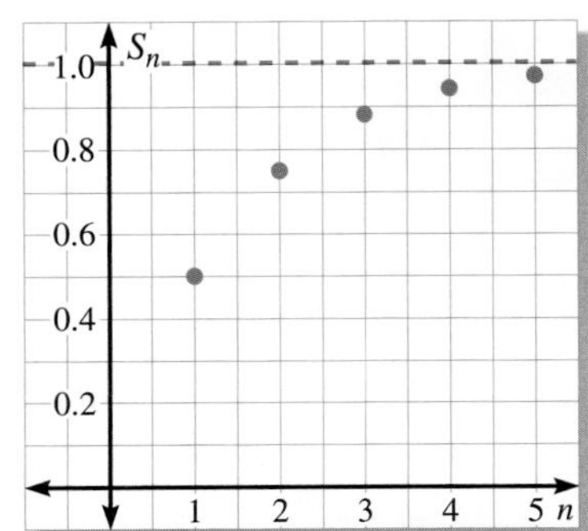

From the graph, S_n appears to approach 1 as n increases.

Animated Algebra at classzone.com

SUMS OF INFINITE SERIES In Example 1, you can understand why S_n approaches 1 as n increases by considering the rule for S_n:

$$S_n = a_1\left(\frac{1 - r^n}{1 - r}\right) = \frac{1}{2}\left(\frac{1 - \left(\frac{1}{2}\right)^n}{1 - \frac{1}{2}}\right) = 1 - \left(\frac{1}{2}\right)^n$$

As n increases, $\left(\frac{1}{2}\right)^n$ approaches 0, so S_n approaches 1. Therefore, 1 is defined to be the sum of the infinite geometric series in Example 1. More generally, as n increases for *any* infinite geometric series with common ratio r between -1 and 1, the value of $S_n = a_1\left(\frac{1 - r^n}{1 - r}\right) \approx a_1\left(\frac{1 - 0}{1 - r}\right) = \frac{a_1}{1 - r}$.

KEY CONCEPT — *For Your Notebook*

The Sum of an Infinite Geometric Series

The sum of an infinite geometric series with first term a_1 and common ratio r is given by

$$S = \frac{a_1}{1 - r}$$

provided $|r| < 1$. If $|r| \geq 1$, the series has no sum.

EXAMPLE 2 Find sums of infinite geometric series

Find the sum of the infinite geometric series.

a. $\sum_{i=1}^{\infty} 5(0.8)^{i-1}$

b. $1 - \frac{3}{4} + \frac{9}{16} - \frac{27}{64} + \cdots$

Solution

a. For this series, $a_1 = 5$ and $r = 0.8$.

$$S = \frac{a_1}{1 - r} = \frac{5}{1 - 0.8} = 25$$

b. For this series, $a_1 = 1$ and $r = -\frac{3}{4}$.

$$S = \frac{a_1}{1 - r} = \frac{1}{1 - \left(-\frac{3}{4}\right)} = \frac{4}{7}$$

EXAMPLE 3 Standardized Test Practice

AVOID ERRORS

If you substitute 1 for a_1 and -3 for r in the formula $S = \frac{a_1}{1 - r}$, you get an answer of $S = \frac{1}{4}$ for the sum. However, this answer is not correct because the sum formula does not apply when $|r| \geq 1$.

What is the sum of the infinite geometric series $1 - 3 + 9 - 27 + \cdots$?

Ⓐ $\frac{1}{4}$ Ⓑ $\frac{4}{3}$ Ⓒ 3 Ⓓ Does not exist

Solution

You know that $a_1 = 1$ and $a_2 = -3$. So, $r = \frac{-3}{1} = -3$.

Because $|-3| \geq 1$, the sum does not exist.

▶ The correct answer is D. Ⓐ Ⓑ Ⓒ Ⓓ

✓ GUIDED PRACTICE for Examples 1, 2, and 3

1. Consider the series $\frac{2}{5} + \frac{4}{25} + \frac{8}{125} + \frac{16}{625} + \frac{32}{3125} + \cdots$. Find and graph the partial sums S_n for $n = 1, 2, 3, 4,$ and 5. Then describe what happens to S_n as n increases.

Find the sum of the infinite geometric series, if it exists.

2. $\sum_{n=1}^{\infty} \left(-\frac{1}{2}\right)^{n-1}$

3. $\sum_{n=1}^{\infty} 3\left(\frac{5}{4}\right)^{n-1}$

4. $3 + \frac{3}{4} + \frac{3}{16} + \frac{3}{64} + \cdots$

EXAMPLE 4 Use an infinite series as a model

PENDULUMS A pendulum that is released to swing freely travels 18 inches on the first swing. On each successive swing, the pendulum travels 80% of the distance of the previous swing. What is the total distance the pendulum swings?

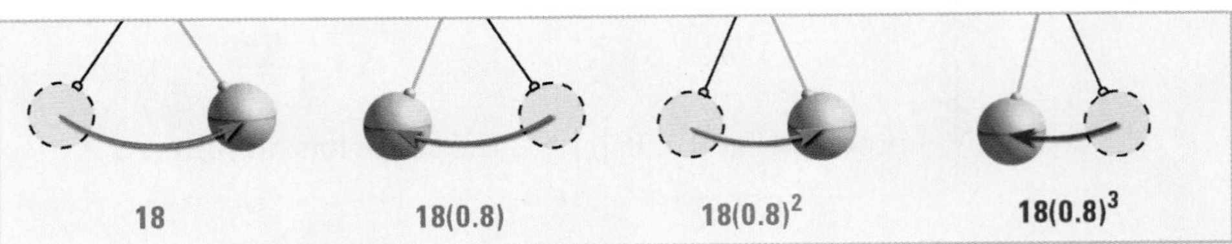

Solution

The total distance traveled by the pendulum is:

$$d = 18 + 18(0.8) + 18(0.8)^2 + 18(0.8)^3 + \cdots$$

$= \frac{a_1}{1 - r}$ **Write formula for sum.**

$= \frac{18}{1 - 0.8}$ **Substitute 18 for a_1 and 0.8 for r.**

$= 90$ **Simplify.**

▶ The pendulum travels a total distance of 90 inches, or 7.5 feet.

EXAMPLE 5 Write a repeating decimal as a fraction

Write 0.242424. . . as a fraction in lowest terms.

$0.242424\ldots = 24(0.01) + 24(0.01)^2 + 24(0.01)^3 + \cdots$

$= \frac{a_1}{1 - r}$ **Write formula for sum.**

$= \frac{24(0.01)}{1 - 0.01}$ **Substitute 24(0.01) for a_1 and 0.01 for r.**

$= \frac{0.24}{0.99}$ **Simplify.**

$= \frac{24}{99}$ **Write as a quotient of integers.**

$= \frac{8}{33}$ **Reduce fraction to lowest terms.**

▶ The repeating decimal 0.242424. . . is $\frac{8}{33}$ as a fraction.

✓ GUIDED PRACTICE for Examples 4 and 5

5. WHAT IF? In Example 4, suppose the pendulum travels 10 inches on its first swing. What is the total distance the pendulum swings?

Write the repeating decimal as a fraction in lowest terms.

6. 0.555. . . **7.** 0.727272. . . **8.** 0.131313. . .

12.4 EXERCISES

HOMEWORK KEY ○ = **WORKED-OUT SOLUTIONS** on p. WS21 for Exs. 13, 27, and 39
★ = **STANDARDIZED TEST PRACTICE** Exs. 2, 32, 34, 39, 40, and 41

SKILL PRACTICE

1. **VOCABULARY** Copy and complete: The sum S_n of the first n terms of an infinite series is called a(n) __?__.

2. ★ **WRITING** *Explain* how to tell whether the series $\sum_{i=1}^{\infty} a_1 r^{i-1}$ has a sum.

EXAMPLE 1 on p. 820 for Exs. 3–6

PARTIAL SUMS For the given series, find and graph the partial sums S_n for $n = 1, 2, 3, 4$, and 5. *Describe* what happens to S_n as n increases.

3. $\frac{1}{2} + \frac{1}{6} + \frac{1}{18} + \frac{1}{54} + \frac{1}{162} + \cdots$

4. $\frac{2}{3} + \frac{1}{3} + \frac{1}{6} + \frac{1}{12} + \frac{1}{24} + \cdots$

5. $4 + \frac{12}{5} + \frac{36}{25} + \frac{108}{125} + \frac{324}{625} + \cdots$

6. $\frac{1}{4} + \frac{5}{4} + \frac{25}{4} + \frac{125}{4} + \frac{625}{4} + \cdots$

EXAMPLES 2 and 3 on p. 821 for Exs. 7–23

FINDING SUMS Find the sum of the infinite geometric series, if it exists.

7. $\sum_{n=1}^{\infty} 8\left(\frac{1}{5}\right)^{n-1}$

8. $\sum_{k=1}^{\infty} -6\left(\frac{3}{2}\right)^{k-1}$

9. $\sum_{i=1}^{\infty} \frac{2}{5}\left(\frac{5}{3}\right)^{i-1}$

10. $\sum_{k=1}^{\infty} \frac{11}{3}\left(\frac{3}{8}\right)^{k-1}$

11. $\sum_{i=1}^{\infty} 2\left(\frac{1}{6}\right)^{i-1}$

12. $\sum_{n=1}^{\infty} -5\left(\frac{2}{5}\right)^{n-1}$

13. $\sum_{k=1}^{\infty} 7\left(-\frac{8}{9}\right)^{k-1}$

14. $\sum_{n=1}^{\infty} \frac{1}{2}\left(-\frac{10}{3}\right)^{n-1}$

15. $\sum_{k=1}^{\infty} 9(4)^{k-1}$

16. $\sum_{i=1}^{\infty} -2\left(-\frac{1}{4}\right)^{i-1}$

17. $\sum_{i=0}^{\infty} \left(-\frac{3}{7}\right)^{i}$

18. $\sum_{n=0}^{\infty} \frac{5}{6}(3)^{n}$

19. **ERROR ANALYSIS** *Describe* and correct the error in finding the sum of the infinite geometric series $\sum_{n=1}^{\infty} \left(\frac{7}{2}\right)^{n-1}$.

For this series, $a_1 = 1$ and $r = \frac{7}{2}$.

$S = \frac{a_1}{1 - r} = \frac{1}{1 - \frac{7}{2}} = \frac{1}{-\frac{5}{2}} = -\frac{2}{5}$ ✗

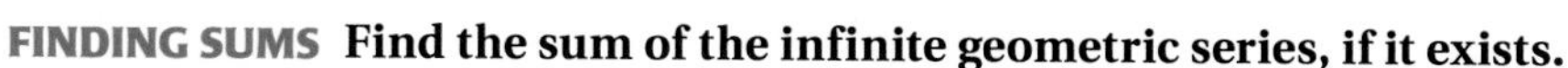

FINDING SUMS Find the sum of the infinite geometric series, if it exists.

20. $-\frac{1}{8} - \frac{1}{12} - \frac{1}{18} - \frac{1}{27} + \cdots$

21. $\frac{2}{3} - \frac{2}{9} + \frac{2}{27} - \frac{2}{81} + \cdots$

22. $\frac{4}{15} + \frac{4}{9} + \frac{20}{27} + \frac{100}{81} + \cdots$

23. $3 + \frac{5}{2} + \frac{25}{12} + \frac{125}{72} + \cdots$

EXAMPLE 5 on p. 822 for Exs. 24–32

REWRITING DECIMALS Write the repeating decimal as a fraction in lowest terms.

24. 0.222...

25. 0.444...

26. 0.161616...

27. 0.625625625...

28. 32.3232...

29. 130.130130...

30. 0.090909...

31. 0.2777...

32. ★ **MULTIPLE CHOICE** Which fraction is equal to the repeating decimal 18.1818...?

Ⓐ $\frac{2}{11}$ Ⓑ $\frac{1836}{101}$ Ⓒ $\frac{200}{11}$ Ⓓ $\frac{181}{9}$

33. **REASONING** Show that 0.999... is equal to 1.

34. ★ **OPEN-ENDED MATH** Find two infinite geometric series whose sums are each 5.

CHALLENGE Specify the values of x for which the given infinite geometric series has a sum. Then find the sum in terms of x.

35. $1 + 4x + 16x^2 + 64x^3 + \cdots$

36. $6 + \frac{3}{2}x + \frac{3}{8}x^2 + \frac{3}{32}x^3 + \cdots$

PROBLEM SOLVING

EXAMPLE 4 on p. 822 for Exs. 37–39

37. **TIRE SWING** A person is given one push on a tire swing and then allowed to swing freely. On the first swing, the person travels a distance of 14 feet. On each successive swing, the person travels 80% of the distance of the previous swing. What is the total distance the person swings?

@HomeTutor for problem solving help at classzone.com

38. **BUSINESS** A company had a profit of $350,000 in its first year. Since then, the company's profit has decreased by 12% per year. If this trend continues, what is an upper limit on the total profit the company can make over the course of its lifetime? *Justify* your answer using an infinite geometric series.

@HomeTutor for problem solving help at classzone.com

39. ★ **MULTIPLE CHOICE** In 1994, the number of cassette tapes shipped in the United States was 345 million. In each successive year, the number decreased by about 21.7%. What is the total number of cassettes that will ship in 1994 and after if this trend continues?

Ⓐ 420 million Ⓑ 440 million Ⓒ 615 million Ⓓ 1.59 billion

40. ★ **SHORT RESPONSE** Can the Greek hero Achilles, running at 20 feet per second, ever catch up to a tortoise that runs 10 feet per second if the tortoise has a 20 foot head start? The Greek mathematician Zeno said no. He reasoned as follows:

When Achilles runs 20 feet, the tortoise will be in a new spot, 10 feet away.

Then, when Achilles gets to that spot, the tortoise will be 5 feet away.

Achilles will keep halving the distance but will never catch up to the tortoise.

In actuality, looking at the race as Zeno did, you can see that both the distances and the times Achilles required to traverse them form infinite geometric series. Using the table, show that both series have finite sums. Does Achilles catch up to the tortoise? *Explain.*

Distance (ft)	20	10	5	2.5	1.25	0.625	. . .
Time (sec)	1	0.5	0.25	0.125	0.0625	0.03125	. . .

○ = WORKED-OUT SOLUTIONS on p. WS1   ★ = STANDARDIZED TEST PRACTICE

41. ★ **EXTENDED RESPONSE** A student drops a rubber ball from a height of 8 feet. Each time the ball hits the ground, it bounces to 75% of its previous height.

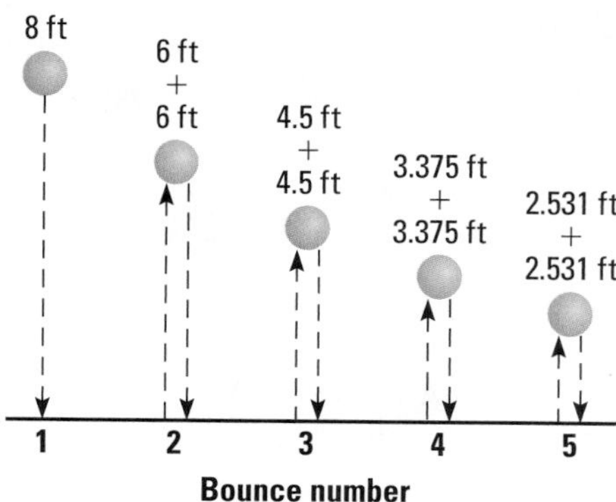

a. How far does the ball travel between the first and second bounces? between the second and third bounces?

b. Write an infinite series to model the total distance traveled by the ball, excluding the distance traveled before the first bounce.

c. Find the total distance traveled by the ball, including the distance traveled before the first bounce.

d. Show that if the ball is dropped from a height of h feet, then the total distance traveled by the ball (including the distance traveled before the first bounce) is $7h$ feet.

42. **CHALLENGE** The *Sierpinski triangle* is a fractal created using equilateral triangles. The process involves removing smaller triangles from larger triangles by joining the midpoints of the sides of the larger triangles as shown below. Assume that the initial triangle has an area of 1 square unit.

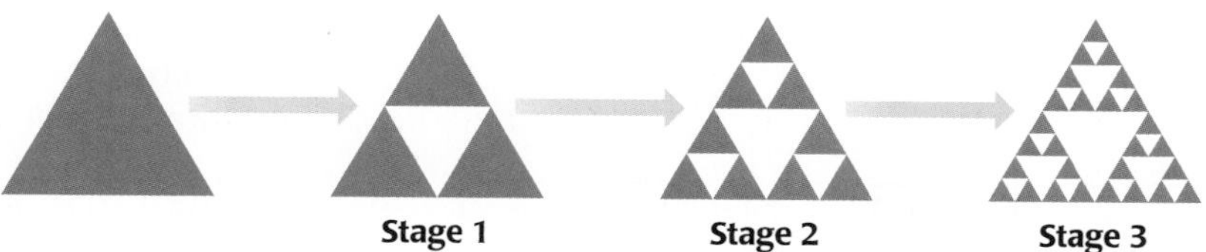

a. Let a_n be the total area of all the triangles that are removed at stage n. Write a rule for a_n.

b. Find $\sum_{n=1}^{\infty} a_n$. What does your answer mean in the context of this problem?

New York Mixed Review

TEST PRACTICE at classzone.com

43. Rectangle P represents 150 people who were surveyed about pet ownership. Circle D represents the 75 people who said they owned a dog. Circle C represents the 40 people who said they owned a cat. How many people do not own a dog or a cat?

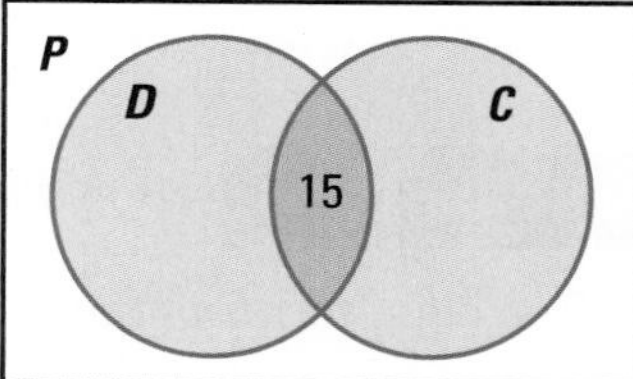

Ⓐ 20 Ⓑ 35

Ⓒ 50 Ⓓ 85

44. $\triangle PQR$ is a right triangle. What is the length of $\overline{PR}$?

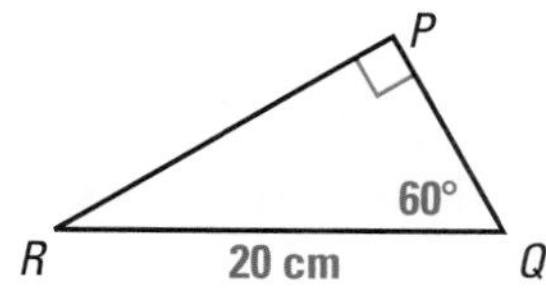

Ⓐ 10 cm Ⓑ $10\sqrt{3}$ cm

Ⓒ $20\sqrt{3}$ cm Ⓓ 40 cm

Investigating Algebra ACTIVITY Use before Lesson 12.5

@HomeTutor
classzone.com
Keystrokes

12.5 Exploring Recursive Rules

MATERIALS • computer with spreadsheet program

QUESTION How can you evaluate a recursive rule for a sequence?

A *recursive rule* for a sequence gives the beginning term or terms of the sequence and then an equation relating the nth term a_n to one or more preceding terms. For example, the rule $a_1 = 4$, $a_n = a_{n-1} + 7$ defines a sequence recursively.

EXPLORE Find terms of a sequence given by a recursive rule

Find the first eight terms of the sequence defined by $a_1 = 4$, $a_n = a_{n-1} + 7$. What type of sequence does this rule represent?

STEP 1 *Enter first term*

Enter the value of a_1 into cell A1.

A1	4		
	A	B	C
1	4		
2			
3			
4			
5			
6			
7			
8			

STEP 2 *Enter recursive equation*

Enter the formula "=A1+7" into cell A2.

A2	=A1+7		
	A	B	C
1	4		
2	11		
3			
4			
5			
6			
7			
8			

STEP 3 *Fill cells*

Use the *fill down* command to copy the recursive equation into the rest of column A.

A8	=A7+7		
	A	B	C
1	4		
2	11		
3	18		
4	25		
5	32		
6	39		
7	46		
8	53		

STEP 4 *Identify terms and type of sequence*

The first eight terms of the sequence are 4, 11, 18, 25, 32, 39, 46, and 53. This sequence is an arithmetic sequence because the difference of consecutive terms is always 7.

DRAW CONCLUSIONS Use your observations to complete these exercises

1. Find the first eight terms of the sequence defined by $a_1 = 4$, $a_n = 7a_{n-1}$. What type of sequence does this rule represent?
2. Write a recursive rule for the sequence 15, 11, 7, 3, −1, −5, ...
3. Write a recursive rule for the sequence 81, 27, 9, 3, 1, $\frac{1}{3}$, ...
4. What equation relates the nth term a_n to the preceding term a_{n-1} for an arithmetic sequence with common difference d? for a geometric sequence with common ratio r?

12.5 Use Recursive Rules with Sequences and Functions

 **A2.A.33** Specify terms of a sequence, given its recursive definition

Before You used explicit rules for sequences.

Now You will use recursive rules for sequences.

Why? So you can model evaporation from a pool, as in Ex. 44.

Key Vocabulary
- explicit rule
- recursive rule
- iteration

So far in this chapter you have worked with *explicit rules* for the *n*th term of a sequence, such as $a_n = 3n - 2$ and $a_n = 3(2)^n$. An **explicit rule** gives a_n as a function of the term's position number *n* in the sequence.

In this lesson you will learn another way to define a sequence—by a *recursive rule.* A **recursive rule** gives the beginning term or terms of a sequence and then a *recursive equation* that tells how a_n is related to one or more preceding terms.

EXAMPLE 1 Evaluate recursive rules

Write the first six terms of the sequence.

a. $a_0 = 1, a_n = a_{n-1} + 4$

b. $a_1 = 1, a_n = 3a_{n-1}$

Solution

a. $a_0 = 1$

$a_1 = a_0 + 4 = 1 + 4 = 5$

$a_2 = a_1 + 4 = 5 + 4 = 9$

$a_3 = a_2 + 4 = 9 + 4 = 13$

$a_4 = a_3 + 4 = 13 + 4 = 17$

$a_5 = a_4 + 4 = 17 + 4 = 21$

b. $a_1 = 1$

$a_2 = 3a_1 = 3(1) = 3$

$a_3 = 3a_2 = 3(3) = 9$

$a_4 = 3a_3 = 3(9) = 27$

$a_5 = 3a_4 = 3(27) = 81$

$a_6 = 3a_5 = 3(81) = 243$

ARITHMETIC AND GEOMETRIC SEQUENCES In part (a) of Example 1, observe that the *differences* of consecutive terms of the sequence are constant, so the sequence is arithmetic. In part (b), the *ratios* of consecutive terms are constant, so the sequence is geometric. In general, rules for arithmetic and geometric sequences can be written recursively as follows.

KEY CONCEPT *For Your Notebook*

Recursive Equations for Arithmetic and Geometric Sequences

Arithmetic Sequence

$a_n = a_{n-1} + d$ where *d* is the common difference

Geometric Sequence

$a_n = r \cdot a_{n-1}$ where *r* is the common ratio

EXAMPLE 2 Write recursive rules

Write a recursive rule for the sequence.

a. 3, 13, 23, 33, 43, . . .

b. 16, 40, 100, 250, 625, . . .

Solution

a. The sequence is arithmetic with first term $a_1 = 3$ and common difference $d = 13 - 3 = 10$.

AVOID ERRORS
A recursive *equation* for a sequence does not include the initial term. To write a recursive *rule* for a sequence, the initial term must be included.

$a_n = a_{n-1} + d$ **General recursive equation for a_n**

$= a_{n-1} + 10$ **Substitute 10 for d.**

▶ So, a recursive rule for the sequence is $a_1 = 3$, $a_n = a_{n-1} + 10$.

b. The sequence is geometric with first term $a_1 = 16$ and common ratio $r = \frac{40}{16} = 2.5$.

$a_n = r \cdot a_{n-1}$ **General recursive equation for a_n**

$= 2.5a_{n-1}$ **Substitute 2.5 for r.**

▶ So, a recursive rule for the sequence is $a_1 = 16$, $a_n = 2.5a_{n-1}$.

✓ GUIDED PRACTICE for Examples 1 and 2

Write the first five terms of the sequence.

1. $a_1 = 3$, $a_n = a_{n-1} - 7$

2. $a_0 = 162$, $a_n = 0.5a_{n-1}$

3. $a_0 = 1$, $a_n = a_{n-1} + n$

4. $a_1 = 4$, $a_n = 2a_{n-1} - 1$

Write a recursive rule for the sequence.

5. 2, 14, 98, 686, 4802, . . .

6. 19, 13, 7, 1, −5, . . .

7. 11, 22, 33, 44, 55, . . .

8. 324, 108, 36, 12, 4, . . .

RECURSIVE RULES FOR SPECIAL SEQUENCES For some sequences, it is difficult to write an explicit rule but relatively easy to write a recursive rule.

EXAMPLE 3 Write recursive rules for special sequences

Write a recursive rule for the sequence.

a. 1, 1, 2, 3, 5, . . .

b. 1, 1, 2, 6, 24, . . .

NAME SEQUENCES
The sequence in part (a) of Example 3 is called the *Fibonacci sequence.* The sequence in part (b) of Example 3 lists the factorial numbers you studied in Chapter 10.

Solution

a. Beginning with the third term in the sequence, each term is the sum of the two previous terms.

▶ So, a recursive rule is $a_1 = 1$, $a_2 = 1$, $a_n = a_{n-2} + a_{n-1}$.

b. Denote the first term by $a_0 = 1$. Then note that $a_1 = 1 = 1 \cdot a_0$, $a_2 = 2 = 2 \cdot a_1$, $a_3 = 6 = 3 \cdot a_2$, and so on.

▶ So, a recursive rule is $a_0 = 1$, $a_n = n \cdot a_{n-1}$.

EXAMPLE 4 Solve a multi-step problem

MUSIC SERVICE An online music service initially has 50,000 annual members. Each year it loses 20% of its current members and adds 5000 new members.

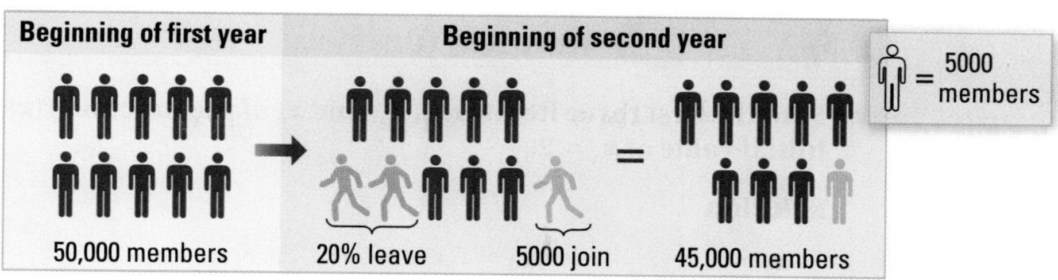

- Write a recursive rule for the number a_n of members at the start of the nth year.
- Find the number of members at the start of the 5th year.
- Describe what happens to the number of members over time.

ANOTHER WAY

For alternative methods for solving the problem in Example 4, turn to page 834 for the **Problem Solving Workshop**.

Solution

STEP 1 **Write** a recursive rule. Because the number of members declines 20% each year, 80% of the members are retained from one year to the next. Also, 5000 new members are added each year.

Members at start of year n	$= 0.8 \cdot$	Members at start of year $(n - 1)$	$+$	New members added
a_n	$= 0.8 \cdot$	a_{n-1}	$+$	5000

▶ A recursive rule is $a_1 = 50,000$, $a_n = 0.8a_{n-1} + 5000$.

STEP 2 **Find** the number of members at the start of the 5th year. Enter 50,000 (the value of a_1) into a graphing calculator. Then enter the rule $0.8 \times \text{Ans} + 5000$ to find a_2. Press ENTER three more times to find a_5.

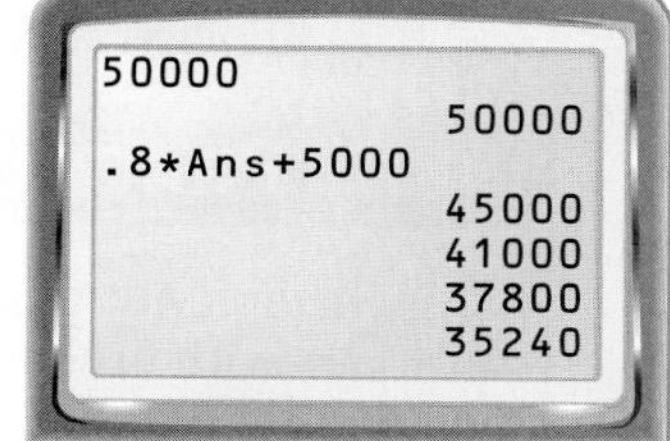

▶ There are about 35,240 members at the start of the 5th year.

STEP 3 **Describe** what happens to the number of members over time. Continue pressing ENTER on the calculator. As shown at the right, after many years the number of members approaches 25,000.

▶ The number of members stabilizes at about 25,000 members.

✓ GUIDED PRACTICE for Examples 3 and 4

9. Write a recursive rule for the sequence 1, 2, 2, 4, 8, 32, ...

10. **WHAT IF?** In Example 4, suppose 70% of the members are retained each year. What happens to the number of members over time?

ITERATING FUNCTIONS **Iteration** involves the repeated composition of a function f with itself. The result of one iteration is $f(f(x))$. The result of two iterations is $f(f(f(x)))$. You can use iteration to generate a sequence recursively. Begin with an initial value x_0, and let $x_1 = f(x_0)$, $x_2 = f(x_1) = f(f(x_0))$, and so on.

EXAMPLE 5 Iterate a function

READING An *iterate* is a number that is the result of iterating a function.

Find the first three iterates x_1, x_2, and x_3 of the function $f(x) = -3x + 1$ for an initial value of $x_0 = 2$.

Solution

$x_1 = f(x_0)$	$x_2 = f(x_1)$	$x_3 = f(x_2)$
$= f(2)$	$= f(-5)$	$= f(16)$
$= -3(2) + 1$	$= -3(-5) + 1$	$= -3(16) + 1$
$= -5$	$= 16$	$= -47$

▸ The first three iterates are -5, 16, and -47.

GUIDED PRACTICE for Example 5

Find the first three iterates of the function for the given initial value.

11. $f(x) = 4x - 3$, $x_0 = 2$

12. $f(x) = x^2 - 5$, $x_0 = -1$

12.5 EXERCISES

HOMEWORK KEY

○ = **WORKED-OUT SOLUTIONS** p. WS21 for Exs. 15, 27, and 45

★ = **STANDARDIZED TEST PRACTICE** Exs. 2, 12, 33, 40, 45, and 47

SKILL PRACTICE

1. VOCABULARY Copy and complete: The repeated composition of a function with itself is called __?__.

2. ★ **WRITING** *Explain* the difference between an explicit rule for a sequence and a recursive rule for a sequence.

EXAMPLE 1 on p. 827 for Exs. 3–12

WRITING TERMS **Write the first five terms of the sequence.**

3. $a_1 = 1$
$a_n = a_{n-1} + 3$

4. $a_0 = 4$
$a_n = 2a_{n-1}$

5. $a_1 = -1$
$a_n = a_{n-1} - 5$

6. $a_0 = 3$
$a_n = a_{n-1} - n^2$

7. $a_1 = 2$
$a_n = (a_{n-1})^2 + 1$

8. $a_0 = 4$
$a_n = (a_{n-1})^2 - 10$

9. $a_1 = 2$
$a_n = n^2 + 3n - a_{n-1}$

10. $a_0 = 2$, $a_1 = 4$
$a_n = a_{n-1} - a_{n-2}$

11. $a_1 = 2$, $a_2 = 3$
$a_n = a_{n-1} \cdot a_{n-2}$

12. ★ **MULTIPLE CHOICE** What are the first four terms of the sequence for which $a_1 = 1$, $a_2 = 4$, and $a_n = a_{n-1} \cdot a_{n-2}$?

Ⓐ 1, 4, 4, 16 Ⓑ 1, 4, 16, 64 Ⓒ 1, 4, 8, 16 Ⓓ 1, 4, 4, 8

EXAMPLES 2 and 3 on p. 828 for Exs. 13–23

WRITING RULES **Write a recursive rule for the sequence. The sequence may be arithmetic, geometric, or neither.**

13. 21, 14, 7, 0, −7, . . .

14. 3, 12, 48, 192, 768, . . .

15. 4, −12, 36, −108, 324, . . .

16. 1, 8, 15, 22, 29, . . .

17. $44, 11, \frac{11}{4}, \frac{11}{16}, \frac{11}{64}, \ldots$

18. 1, 4, 5, 9, 14, . . .

19. 54, 43, 32, 21, 10, . . .

20. 3, 5, 15, 75, 1125, . . .

21. 16, 9, 7, 2, 5, . . .

ERROR ANALYSIS ***Describe*** **and correct the error in writing a recursive rule for the sequence 5, 2, 3, −1, 4, ...**

22.

Beginning with the third term in the sequence, each term a_n equals $a_{n-2} - a_{n-1}$. So a recursive rule is given by:

$a_n = a_{n-2} - a_{n-1}$

23.

Beginning with the second term in the sequence, each term a_n is $a_{n-1} - 3$. So a recursive rule is given by:

$a_1 = 5, a_n = a_{n-1} - 3$

EXAMPLE 5 on p. 830 for Exs. 24–33

ITERATING FUNCTIONS **Find the first three iterates of the function for the given initial value.**

24. $f(x) = 3x - 2, x_0 = 2$

25. $f(x) = 5x + 6, x_0 = -2$

26. $g(x) = -4x + 7, x_0 = 1$

27. $f(x) = \frac{1}{2}x - 3, x_0 = 2$

28. $f(x) = \frac{2}{3}x + 5, x_0 = 6$

29. $h(x) = x^2 - 4, x_0 = -3$

30. $f(x) = 2x^2 + 1, x_0 = -1$

31. $f(x) = x^2 - x + 2, x_0 = 1$

32. $g(x) = -3x^2 + 2x, x_0 = 2$

33. ★ **MULTIPLE CHOICE** What are the first three iterates x_1, x_2, and x_3 of the function $f(x) = -2x + 3$ for an initial value of $x_0 = 2$?

Ⓐ −1, 1, 3 Ⓑ 1, −5, 7 Ⓒ −1, 5, −7 Ⓓ 1, −1, −3

WRITING RULES **Write a recursive rule for the sequence.**

34. 3, 8, 17, 81, 370, . . .

35. 1, 2, 12, 56, 272, . . .

36. $5, 5\sqrt{3}, 15, 15\sqrt{3}, 45, \ldots$

37. 2, 5, 11, 26, 59, . . .

38. 8, 4, 2, 2, 1, . . .

39. −3, −2, 5, −3, −2, . . .

40. ★ **OPEN-ENDED MATH** Give an example of a sequence in which each term after the third term is a function of the three terms preceding it. Write a recursive rule for the sequence and find its first eight terms.

41. **REASONING** *Explain* why there are not a function f and an initial value x_0 such that the function's first three iterates are $x_1 = 2$, $x_2 = 2$, and $x_3 = 8$.

42. **CHALLENGE** You can define a sequence using a piecewise rule. The following is an example of a piecewise-defined sequence.

$$a_1 = 5, a_n = \begin{cases} \frac{a_{n-1}}{2}, \text{ if } a_{n-1} \text{ is even} \\ 3a_{n-1} + 3, \text{ if } a_{n-1} \text{ is odd} \end{cases}$$

a. Write the first ten terms of the sequence.

b. Choose three different positive integer values for a_1 (other than $a_1 = 5$). For each value of a_1, find the first ten terms of the sequence. What conclusions can you make about the behavior of this sequence of integers?

PROBLEM SOLVING

EXAMPLE 4 on p. 829 for Exs. 43–45

43. **FISH POPULATION** A lake initially contains 5000 fish. Each year the population declines 20% due to fishing and other causes, and the lake is restocked with 500 fish.

   a. Write a recursive rule for the number a_n of fish at the beginning of the nth year. How many fish are there at the beginning of the 5th year?

   b. What happens to the population of fish in the lake over time?

@HomeTutor for problem solving help at classzone.com

44. **POOL CARE** You are adding chlorine to a swimming pool. You add 34 ounces of chlorine the first week and 16 ounces every week thereafter. Each week 40% of the chlorine in the pool evaporates. Write a recursive rule for the amount of chlorine in the pool each week. What happens to the amount of chlorine in the pool over time?

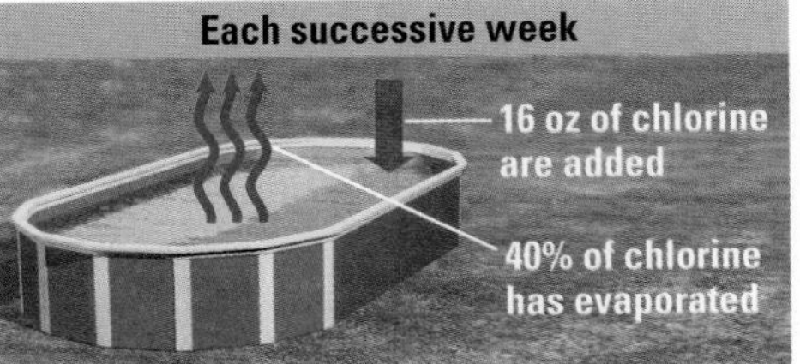

@HomeTutor for problem solving help at classzone.com

45. ★ **SHORT RESPONSE** Gladys owes $2000 to a credit card company that charges interest at a rate of 1.4% per month. At the end of each month she makes a payment of $100. Write a recursive rule for the balance a_n of the account at the beginning of the nth month. How long will it take to pay off the account? *Explain* your reasoning.

46. **FIBONACCI SEQUENCE** The Fibonacci sequence, which is defined recursively in Example 3 on page 828, occurs many places in nature. This sequence can also be defined explicitly as follows:

$$f_n = \frac{1}{\sqrt{5}}\left(\frac{1+\sqrt{5}}{2}\right)^n - \frac{1}{\sqrt{5}}\left(\frac{1-\sqrt{5}}{2}\right)^n,\ n \geq 1$$

Use the explicit rule to find the first five terms of the Fibonacci sequence.

Animated Algebra at classzone.com

47. ★ **EXTENDED RESPONSE** A person repeatedly takes 20 milligrams of a prescribed drug every 4 hours. Thirty percent of the drug is removed from the bloodstream every 4 hours.

   a. Write a recursive rule for the amount of the drug in the bloodstream after n doses.

   b. The value that a drug level in a person's body approaches after an extended period of time is called the *maintenance level*. What is the maintenance level of this drug, given a dosage of 20 milligrams?

   c. How does doubling the dosage affect the maintenance level of the drug? *Justify* your answer mathematically.

48. CHALLENGE You are saving money for retirement. You plan to withdraw \$30,000 at the beginning of each year for 20 years after you retire. Based on the type of investment you are making, you can expect to earn an annual return of 8% on your savings after you retire.

a. Let a_n be your balance n years after retiring. Write a recursive equation that shows how a_n is related to a_{n-1}.

b. Solve the equation from part (a) for a_{n-1}. Find a_0, the minimum amount of money you should have in your account when you retire. (*Hint:* Let $a_{20} = 0$.)

NEW YORK MIXED REVIEW

TEST PRACTICE at classzone.com

49. What is the solution of $\frac{1}{3}(8x - 5) = 4x + 7$?

Ⓐ $-\frac{13}{2}$ Ⓑ 4   Ⓒ 9   Ⓓ 29

50. To the nearest tenth of a square foot, what is the area of a rectangular garden with a 25-foot-long side and a 50-foot diagonal?

Ⓐ 892.5 ft^2 Ⓑ 1082.5 ft^2 Ⓒ 1107.5 ft^2 Ⓓ 2165.0 ft^2

QUIZ *for Lessons 12.4–12.5*

Find the sum of the infinite geometric series, if it exists. *(p. 820)*

1. $\sum_{n=1}^{\infty} 2\left(\frac{3}{7}\right)^{n-1}$

2. $\sum_{n=0}^{\infty} 4\left(-\frac{5}{6}\right)^{n}$

3. $\frac{3}{4} + \frac{15}{8} + \frac{75}{16} + \frac{375}{32} + \dots$

Write the repeating decimal as a fraction in lowest terms. *(p. 820)*

4. 0.777...

5. 0.393939...

6. 123.123123...

Write the first five terms of the sequence. *(p. 827)*

7. $a_1 = 2$, $a_n = a_{n-1} + 4$

8. $a_0 = 3$, $a_n = (a_{n-1})^2 - 5$

9. $a_1 = 1, a_2 = 4$, $a_n = a_{n-1} - a_{n-2}$

Write a recursive rule for the sequence. The sequence may be arithmetic, geometric, or neither. *(p. 827)*

10. $5, \frac{17}{4}, \frac{7}{2}, \frac{11}{4}, 2, \dots$

11. 2, 6, 12, 72, 864, ...

12. 8, 24, 72, 216, 648, ...

Find the first three iterates of the function for the given initial value. *(p. 827)*

13. $f(x) = -3x - 2, x_0 = 1$

14. $g(x) = 4x + 1, x_0 = 2$

15. $f(x) = -2x + 3, x_0 = -2$

16. $f(x) = 5x - 7, x_0 = -3$

17. $h(x) = x^2 - 6, x_0 = -1$

18. $f(x) = 3x^2 + 2, x_0 = 0$

19. PENDULUMS A pendulum that is released to swing freely travels 25 inches on the first swing. On each successive swing, the pendulum travels 85% as far as the previous swing. What is the total distance the pendulum swings? *(p. 820)*

PROBLEM SOLVING WORKSHOP
LESSON 12.5

Using ALTERNATIVE METHODS

Another Way to Solve Example 4, page 829

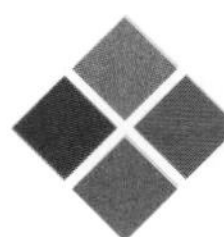

MULTIPLE REPRESENTATIONS In Example 4 on page 829, you found the number that a real-life sequence approaches over time by using a calculator to evaluate the rule for the sequence. You can also solve this problem using a graph or an algebraic method.

PROBLEM

MUSIC SERVICE An online music service initially has 50,000 annual members. Each year the music service loses 20% of its current members and adds 5000 new members. What happens to the number of members over time?

METHOD 1

Using a Graph A recursive rule for the number a_n of members at the beginning of the nth year is $a_1 = 50{,}000$, $a_n = 0.8a_{n-1} + 5000$. One alternative method for finding the number this sequence approaches is to graph the sequence on a graphing calculator.

STEP 1 **Set** the calculator to *sequence* mode and *dot* mode.

STEP 2 **Press** Y= and enter the equations $n\text{Min} = 1$, $u(n) = 0.8u(n-1) + 5000$, and $u(n\text{Min}) = 50{,}000$. Press WINDOW and enter the following parameters:

nMin = 1	Xmin = 0	Ymin = 15,000
nMax = 100	Xmax = 100	Ymax = 35,000
PlotStart = 1	Xscl = 10	Yscl = 5000
PlotStep = 1		

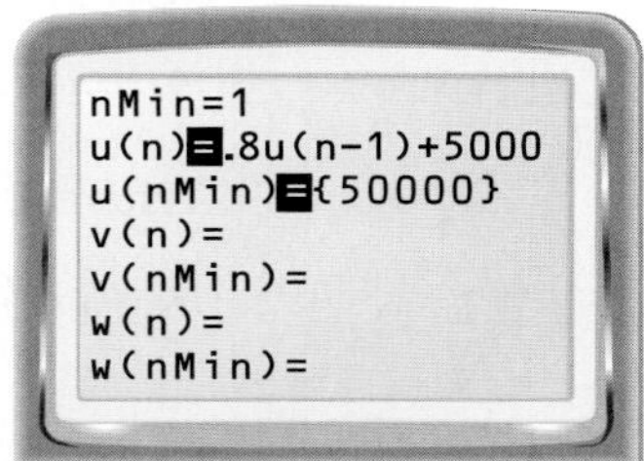

STEP 3 **Graph** the sequence. Use the *trace* feature to find the value that the sequence approaches as n becomes large. From the graph, you can see that the sequence approaches 25,000.

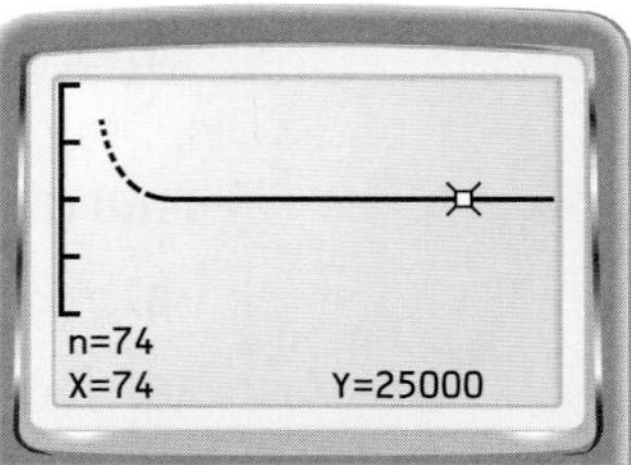

▶ Over time, the number of members of the music service approaches 25,000.

METHOD 2 **Using Algebra** Another approach is to use an algebraic method to determine what happens to the number of members over time.

STEP 1 **Write** the recursive rule.

$$a_1 = 50{,}000,\ a_n = 0.8a_{n-1} + 5000.$$

STEP 2 **Assume** that the sequence has a limit L, which is the value that the sequence approaches as n becomes large.

STEP 3 **Consider** what happens to the equation $a_n = 0.8a_{n-1} + 5000$ as n becomes large. The value of a_n (the left-hand side) approaches L while the value of $0.8a_{n-1} + 5000$ (the right-hand side) approaches $0.8L + 5000$. So, you can conclude that $L = 0.8L + 5000$.

STEP 4 **Solve** the equation $L = 0.8L + 5000$ for L.

$L = 0.8L + 5000$	**Write equation.**
$0.2L = 5000$	**Subtract 0.8*L* from each side.**
$L = 25{,}000$	**Divide each side by 0.2.**

▶ The sequence approaches the limit $L = 25{,}000$ as n becomes large. So, over time the number of members of the music service approaches 25,000.

PRACTICE

Describe **what happens to the terms of the sequence as *n* becomes large.**

1. $a_1 = 3000,\ a_n = 0.25a_{n-1} + 300$
2. $a_1 = 1700,\ a_n = 0.38a_{n-1} + 512$
3. **WHAT IF?** Suppose the online music service in the problem on page 834 loses 8% of its current members and adds 1200 new members each year. Use the graphing method and the algebraic method to determine what happens to the number of members over time.
4. **TOWN LIBRARY** A town library initially has 54,000 books in its collection. Each year 2% of the books are lost or discarded. The library can afford to purchase 1150 new books each year. Write a recursive rule for the number a_n of books in the library at the beginning of the nth year. Use the graphing method and the algebraic method to determine what happens to the number of books in the library over time.
5. **ERROR ANALYSIS** A student attempted to solve the problem in Exercise 4 as shown below. *Describe* and correct the error in the student's work.

> $a_1 = 54{,}000,\ a_n = 0.02a_{n-1} + 1150$
> Let L be the limit of the sequence. Then:
>
> $L = 0.02L + 1150$
>
> $0.98L = 1150$
>
> $L \approx 1173$
>
> So, over time the number of books in the library approaches about 1173.

6. **REASONING** Give an example of a real-life situation which you can represent with a recursive rule that does not approach a limit. Write a recursive rule that represents the situation.

Extension

Use after Lesson 12.5

Prove Statements Using Mathematical Induction

GOAL Use mathematical induction to prove statements about all positive integers.

In Lesson 12.1, you saw the rule for the sum of the first n positive integers:

$$\sum_{i=1}^{n} i = 1 + 2 + \cdots + n = \frac{n(n+1)}{2}$$

You can use *mathematical induction* to prove statements about positive integers.

KEY CONCEPT *For Your Notebook*

Mathematical Induction

To show that a statement is true for all positive integers n, perform these steps.

Basis Step: Show that the statement is true for $n = 1$.

Inductive Step: Assume that the statement is true for $n = k$ where k is any positive integer. Show that this implies the statement is true for $n = k + 1$.

EXAMPLE 1 Use mathematical induction

Use mathematical induction to prove that $1 + 2 + \cdots + n = \frac{n(n+1)}{2}$.

UNDERSTAND INDUCTION

If you know from the basis step that a statement is true for $n = 1$, then the inductive step implies that it is true for $n = 2$, and therefore for $n = 3$, and so on for all positive integers n.

Solution

Basis Step: Check that the formula works for $n = 1$.

$1 \stackrel{?}{=} \frac{1(1+1)}{2} \longrightarrow 1 = 1$ ✓

Inductive Step: Assume that $1 + 2 + \cdots + k = \frac{k(k+1)}{2}$.

Show that $1 + 2 + \cdots + k + (k+1) = \frac{(k+1)[(k+1)+1]}{2}$.

$$1 + 2 + \cdots + k = \frac{k(k+1)}{2} \qquad \text{Assume true for } k.$$

$$1 + 2 + \cdots + k + (k+1) = \frac{k(k+1)}{2} + (k+1) \qquad \text{Add } k+1 \text{ to each side.}$$

$$= \frac{k(k+1) + 2(k+1)}{2} \qquad \text{Add.}$$

$$= \frac{(k+1)(k+2)}{2} \qquad \text{Factor out } k+1.$$

$$= \frac{(k+1)[(k+1)+1]}{2} \qquad \text{Rewrite } k+2 \text{ as } (k+1)+1.$$

Therefore, $1 + 2 + \cdots + n = \frac{n(n+1)}{2}$ for all positive integers n.

EXAMPLE 2 Use mathematical induction

Let $a_n = 5a_{n-1} + 2$ with $a_1 = 2$. Use mathematical induction to prove that an explicit rule for the nth term is $a_n = \frac{5^n - 1}{2}$.

Solution

Basis Step: Check that the formula works for $n = 1$.

$$a_1 \stackrel{?}{=} \frac{5^1 - 1}{2} \longrightarrow 2 = 2 \checkmark$$

Inductive Step: Assume that $a_k = \frac{5^k - 1}{2}$. Show that $a_{k+1} = \frac{5^{k+1} - 1}{2}$.

$a_{k+1} = 5a_k + 2$	Definition of a_n for $n = k + 1$
$= 5\left(\frac{5^k - 1}{2}\right) + 2$	Substitute for a_k.
$= \frac{5^{k+1} - 5}{2} + 2$	Multiply.
$= \frac{5^{k+1} - 5 + 4}{2}$	Add.
$= \frac{5^{k+1} - 1}{2}$	Simplify.

Therefore, an explicit rule for the nth term is $a_n = \frac{5^n - 1}{2}$ for all positive integers n.

PRACTICE

EXAMPLES 1 and 2 on pp. 836–837 for Exs. 1–8

Use mathematical induction to prove the statement.

1. $\sum_{i=1}^{n} (2i - 1) = n^2$

2. $\sum_{i=1}^{n} i^2 = \frac{n(n + 1)(2n + 1)}{6}$

3. $\sum_{i=1}^{n} 2^{i-1} = 2^n - 1$

4. $\sum_{i=1}^{n} a_1 r^{i-1} = a_1\left(\frac{1 - r^n}{1 - r}\right)$

5. $\sum_{i=1}^{n} \frac{1}{i(i + 1)} = \frac{n}{n + 1}$

6. $\sum_{i=1}^{n} (2i)^2 = \frac{2n(n + 1)(2n + 1)}{3}$

7. **GEOMETRY** The numbers 1, 6, 15, 28, . . . are called *hexagonal numbers* because they represent the numbers of dots used to make hexagons, as shown below. Prove that the nth hexagonal number H_n is given by $H_n = n(2n - 1)$.

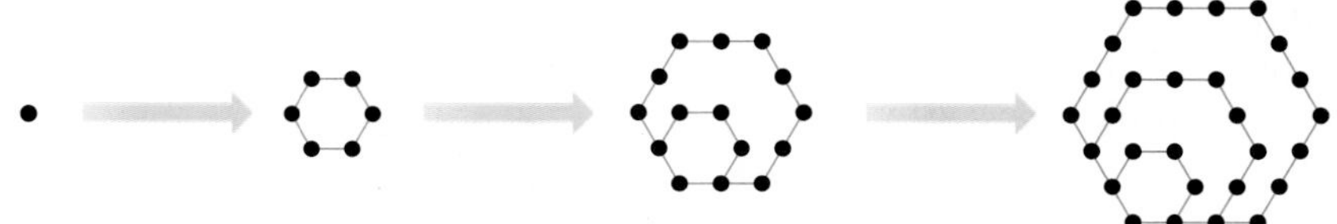

8. **REASONING** Let $f_1, f_2, \ldots, f_n, \ldots$ be the Fibonacci sequence. Prove that $f_1 + f_2 + \cdots + f_n = f_{n+2} - 1$ for all positive integers n.

Lessons 12.4–12.5

1. **TOTAL DISTANCE** A ball is dropped from a height of 12 feet. Each time the ball hits the ground, it bounces to 70% of its previous height. What is the total distance traveled by the ball, including the distance traveled before the first bounce?

   (1) 28 feet   (3) 56 feet

   (2) 40 feet   (4) 68 feet

2. **FRACTAL TREE** A fractal tree starts with a single branch (the trunk) and "grows" as shown. What is a recursive rule for the number of new branches in each stage?

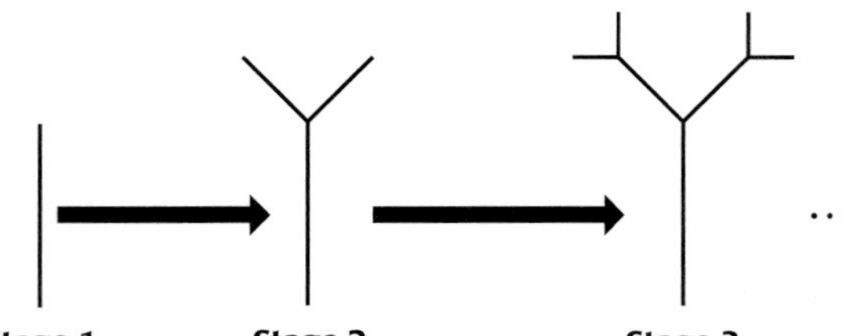

   (1) $a_1 = 1, a_n = 2a_{n-1}$

   (2) $a_n = 2^{n-1}$

   (3) $a_1 = 1, a_n = (a_{n-1})^2$

   (4) $a_1 = 1, a_n = 2 + a_{n-1}$

3. **TREE FARM** A tree farm currently has 8000 trees. Each year 10% of the trees are harvested and 500 seedlings are planted. After an extended period of time, how many trees exist on the farm?

   (1) 500 trees   (3) 2500 trees

   (2) 1250 trees   (4) 5000 trees

4. **FISH TANK** Paul owns a 40 gallon fish tank that leaks 5% of its water every day. Paul replaces 1 gallon each day to make up for the loss. To the nearest hundredth of a gallon, how much water is in the tank 4 days after it was completely full?

   (1) 1.05 gallons

   (2) 36.29 gallons

   (3) 37.15 gallons

   (4) 38.75 gallons

5. **GEOMETRIC SERIES** Which statement below is a *false* statement about an infinite geometric series $\{a_n\}$ with a common ratio r?

   (1) The sum of series exists only if $|r| < 1$.

   (2) For all n, $\frac{a_n}{a_{n+1}} = \frac{1}{r}$.

   (3) The sum of the series does not exist if r has a negative value.

   (4) If the sum exists, the sum of the series is $\frac{a_1}{1 - r}$.

6. **OPEN-ENDED** Leah takes a five year loan of $10,000 to buy a car. The loan has an annual interest rate of 6.5%, compounded monthly. Each month, Leah makes a payment of $196 (except for the last month, when she makes a payment of $165).

   Find the monthly interest rate.

   Write a recursive rule for the amount of money Leah still owes after n months.

   How much money does Leah owe after 12 months?

7. **OPEN-ENDED** The length ℓ_1 of the first loop of a spring is 16 inches. The length ℓ_2 of the second loop is 0.9 times the length of the first loop. The length ℓ_3 of the third loop is 0.9 times the length of the second loop, and so on.

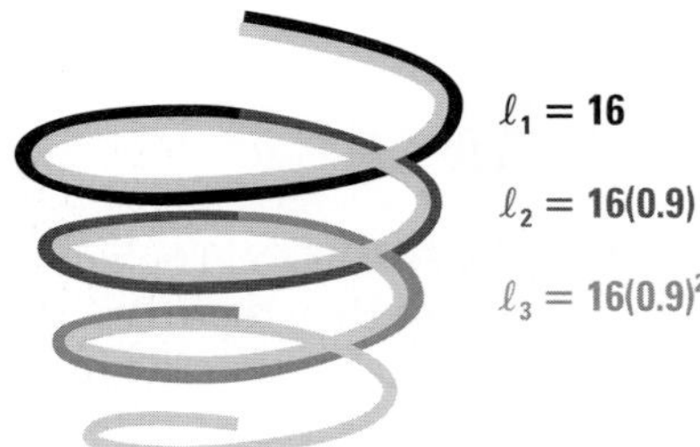

   If the spring could have infinitely many loops, would its length be *finite* or *infinite*? *Explain.* If its length is finite, find the length.

12 CHAPTER SUMMARY

BIG IDEAS

For Your Notebook

Big Idea 1

Analyze Sequences

The information below highlights the similarities and differences between arithmetic and geometric sequences.

Arithmetic Sequence

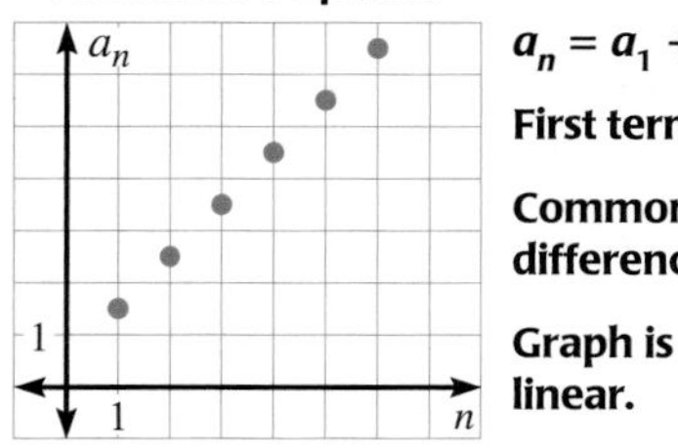

$a_n = a_1 + (n - 1)d$

First term: a_1

Common difference: d

Graph is linear.

Geometric Sequence

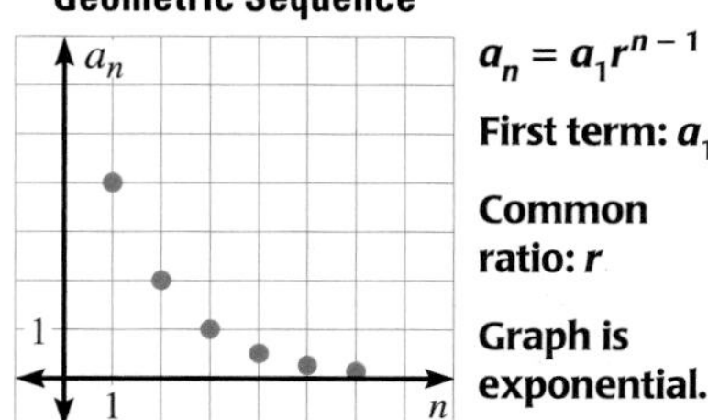

$a_n = a_1 r^{n-1}$

First term: a_1

Common ratio: r

Graph is exponential.

Big Idea 2

Find Sums of Series

The most common formulas for sums of series are shown below.

Arithmetic Series	Geometric Series	Infinite Geometric Series
Sum of the first n terms:	Sum of the first n terms:	Sum of the series:
$S_n = n\left(\frac{a_1 + a_n}{2}\right)$	$S_n = a_1\left(\frac{1 - r^n}{1 - r}\right), r \neq 1$	$S = \frac{a_1}{1 - r}, \lvert r \rvert < 1$
Example:	Example:	Example:
$4 + 9 + 14 + 19 + 24$	$3 + 6 + 12 + 24$	$5 + 1 + 0.2 + 0.04 + \cdots$
$S_5 = 5\left(\frac{4 + 24}{2}\right) = 70$	$S_4 = 3\left(\frac{1 - 2^4}{1 - 2}\right) = 45$	$S = \frac{5}{1 - 0.2} = 6.25$

Other common sum formulas:

$$\sum_{i=1}^{n} 1 = n \qquad \sum_{i=1}^{n} i = \frac{n(n+1)}{2} \qquad \sum_{i=1}^{n} i^2 = \frac{n(n+1)(2n+1)}{6}$$

Big Idea 3

Use Recursive Rules

The table shows explicit and recursive rules for arithmetic and geometric sequences.

	Explicit Rule	Recursive Rule
Arithmetic Sequence	$a_n = a_1 + (n - 1)d$	$a_n = a_{n-1} + d$
Example: 3, 5, 7, 9, 11, . . .	$a_n = 1 + 2n$	$a_1 = 3, a_n = a_{n-1} + 2$
Geometric Sequence	$a_n = a_1 r^{n-1}$	$a_n = r \cdot a_{n-1}$
Example: 8, 4, 2, 1, 0.5, . . .	$a_n = 8(0.5)^{n-1}$	$a_1 = 8, a_n = 0.5a_{n-1}$

12 CHAPTER REVIEW

@HomeTutor
classzone.com
- Multi-Language Glossary
- Vocabulary practice

REVIEW KEY VOCABULARY

- sequence, *p. 794*
- terms of a sequence, *p. 794*
- series, *p. 796*
- summation notation, *p. 796*
- sigma notation, *p. 796*
- arithmetic sequence, *p. 802*
- common difference, *p. 802*
- arithmetic series, *p. 804*
- geometric sequence, *p. 810*
- common ratio, *p. 810*
- geometric series, *p. 812*
- partial sum, *p. 820*
- explicit rule, *p. 827*
- recursive rule, *p. 827*
- iteration, *p. 830*

VOCABULARY EXERCISES

1. Copy and complete: The values in the range of a sequence are called the _?_ of the sequence.
2. **WRITING** How can you determine whether a sequence is arithmetic?
3. Copy and complete: A(n) _?_ rule gives a_n as a function of the term's position number n in the sequence.
4. Copy and complete: In a(n) _?_ sequence, the ratio of any term to the previous term is constant.

REVIEW EXAMPLES AND EXERCISES

Use the review examples and exercises below to check your understanding of the concepts you have learned in each lesson of Chapter 12.

12.1 Define and Use Sequences and Series

pp. 794–800

EXAMPLE

Find the sum of the series $\sum_{i=1}^{4} (i^2 - 4)$.

$a_1 = 1^2 - 4 = -3$ **First term**

$a_2 = 2^2 - 4 = 0$ **Second term**

$a_3 = 3^2 - 4 = 5$ **Third term**

$a_4 = 4^2 - 4 = 12$ **Fourth term**

The sum of the series is $\sum_{i=1}^{4} (i^2 - 4) = -3 + 0 + 5 + 12 = 14$.

EXERCISES

EXAMPLES 5 and 6 on p. 797 for Exs. 5–8

Find the sum of the series.

5. $\sum_{n=1}^{6} (n^2 + 7)$
6. $\sum_{i=2}^{6} (10 - 4i)$
7. $\sum_{i=1}^{17} i$
8. $\sum_{k=1}^{25} k^2$

12.2 Analyze Arithmetic Sequences and Series *pp. 802–809*

EXAMPLE

Write a rule for the *n*th term of the sequence 9, 13, 17, 21, 25, ...

The sequence is arithmetic with first term $a_1 = 9$ and common difference $d = 4$. So, a rule for the nth term is:

$a_n = a_1 + (n - 1)d$ **Write general rule.**

$= 9 + (n - 1)(4)$ **Substitute 9 for a_1 and 4 for d.**

$= 5 + 4n$ **Simplify.**

EXERCISES

EXAMPLES 2, 3, 4, and 5 on pp. 803–805 for Exs. 9–16

Write a rule for the *n*th term of the arithmetic sequence.

9. 8, 5, 2, −1, −4, . . .

10. $d = 7, a_8 = 54$

11. $a_4 = 27, a_{11} = 69$

Find the sum of the series.

12. $\sum_{i=1}^{15} (3 + 2i)$

13. $\sum_{i=1}^{26} (25 - 3i)$

14. $\sum_{i=1}^{22} (6i - 5)$

15. $\sum_{i=1}^{30} (-84 + 8i)$

16. COMPUTER Joe buys a \$600 computer on layaway by making a \$200 down payment and then paying \$25 per month. Write a rule for the total amount of money paid on the computer after n months.

12.3 Analyze Geometric Sequences and Series *pp. 810–817*

EXAMPLE

Find the sum of the series $\sum_{i=1}^{7} 5(3)^{i-1}$.

The series is geometric with first term $a_1 = 5$ and common ratio $r = 3$.

$S_7 = a_1\left(\frac{1 - r^7}{1 - r}\right)$ **Write rule for S_7.**

$= 5\left(\frac{1 - 3^7}{1 - 3}\right)$ **Substitute 5 for a_1 and 3 for r.**

$= 5465$ **Simplify.**

EXERCISES

EXAMPLES 2, 3, 4, and 5 on pp. 811–813 for Exs. 17–23

Write a rule for the *n*th term of the geometric sequence.

17. 256, 64, 16, 4, 1, . . .

18. $r = 5, a_2 = 200$

19. $a_1 = 144, a_3 = 16$

Find the sum of the series.

20. $\sum_{i=1}^{6} 3(5)^{i-1}$

21. $\sum_{i=1}^{9} 8(2)^{i-1}$

22. $\sum_{i=1}^{5} 15\left(\frac{2}{3}\right)^{i-1}$

23. $\sum_{i=1}^{7} 40\left(\frac{1}{2}\right)^{i-1}$

12 CHAPTER REVIEW

12.4 Find Sums of Infinite Geometric Series pp. 820–825

EXAMPLE

Find the sum of the series $\sum_{i=1}^{\infty}\left(\frac{4}{5}\right)^{i-1}$, if it exists.

For this series, $a_1 = 1$ and $r = \frac{4}{5}$. Because $|r| < 1$, the sum of this series exists.

The sum is $S = \frac{a_1}{1-r} = \frac{1}{1-\frac{4}{5}} = 5$.

EXERCISES

EXAMPLES 2 and 5 on pp. 821–822 for Exs. 24–31

Find the sum of the infinite geometric series, if it exists.

24. $\sum_{i=1}^{\infty} 3\left(\frac{5}{8}\right)^{i-1}$ **25.** $\sum_{i=1}^{\infty} 7\left(-\frac{3}{4}\right)^{i-1}$ **26.** $\sum_{i=1}^{\infty} 4(1.3)^{i-1}$ **27.** $\sum_{i=1}^{\infty} -0.2(0.5)^{i-1}$

Write the repeating decimal as a fraction in lowest terms.

28. 0.888. . . **29.** 0.546546546. . . **30.** 0.3787878. . . **31.** 0.7838383. . .

12.5 Use Recursive Rules with Sequences and Functions pp. 827–833

EXAMPLE

Write a recursive rule for the sequence 6, 10, 14, 18, 22, ...

The sequence is arithmetic with first term $a_1 = 6$ and common difference $d = 10 - 6 = 4$.

$a_n = a_{n-1} + d$ **General recursive rule for a_n**

$= a_{n-1} + 4$ **Substitute 4 for *d*.**

So, a recursive rule for the sequence is $a_1 = 6$, $a_n = a_{n-1} + 4$.

EXERCISES

EXAMPLES 1, 2, and 3 on pp. 827–828 for Exs. 32–38

Write the first five terms of the sequence.

32. $a_1 = 4, a_n = a_{n-1} + 9$ **33.** $a_1 = 8, a_n = 5a_{n-1}$ **34.** $a_1 = 2, a_n = n \cdot a_{n-1}$

Write a recursive rule for the sequence.

35. 6, 18, 54, 162, 486, . . . **36.** 4, 6, 9, 13, 18, . . . **37.** 7, 13, 19, 25, 31, . . .

38. POPULATION A town's population increases at a rate of about 1% per year. In 2000, the town had a population of 26,000. Write a recursive rule for the town's population P_n in year n. Let $n = 1$ represent 2000.

12 CHAPTER TEST

Tell whether the sequence is *arithmetic, geometric,* or *neither. Explain.*

1. 5, 9, 13, 17, . . .

2. 3, 6, 12, 24, . . .

3. $40, 10, \frac{5}{2}, \frac{5}{8}, \ldots$

4. 4, 7, 12, 19, . . .

Write the first six terms of the sequence.

5. $a_n = 6 - n^2$

6. $a_n = 7n^3$

7. $a_1 = 4$
$a_n = 5a_{n-1}$

8. $a_1 = -1$
$a_n = a_{n-1} + 6$

Write the next term of the sequence, and then write a rule for the *n*th term.

9. 5, 11, 17, 23, . . .

10. 3, 15, 75, 375, . . .

11. $\frac{6}{5}, \frac{7}{10}, \frac{8}{15}, \frac{9}{20}, \ldots$

12. 1.6, 3.2, 4.8, 6.4, . . .

Find the sum of the series.

13. $\sum_{i=1}^{48} i$

14. $\sum_{n=1}^{28} n^2$

15. $\sum_{i=1}^{10} (4i - 9)$

16. $\sum_{i=1}^{19} (2i + 5)$

17. $\sum_{i=1}^{5} 9(2)^{i-1}$

18. $\sum_{i=1}^{6} 12\left(\frac{1}{3}\right)^{i-1}$

19. $\sum_{i=1}^{\infty} 8\left(\frac{3}{4}\right)^{i-1}$

20. $\sum_{i=1}^{\infty} 20\left(\frac{3}{10}\right)^{i-1}$

Write the repeating decimal as a fraction in lowest terms.

21. 0.111. . .

22. 0.464646. . .

23. 0.187187187. . .

24. 0.3252525. . .

Write a recursive rule for the sequence.

25. 2, 12, 72, 432, . . .

26. 3, 10, 17, 24, . . .

27. 135, 45, 15, 5, . . .

28. 1, −3, 9, −27, . . .

Find the first three iterates of the function for the given initial value.

29. $f(x) = 3x - 7, x_0 = 4$

30. $f(x) = 8 - 5x, x_0 = 1$

31. $f(x) = x^2 + 2, x_0 = -1$

32. QUILTS Use the pattern of checkerboard quilts shown.

$n = 1, a_n = 1$

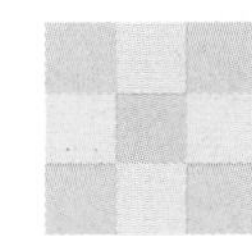

$n = 2, a_n = 2$

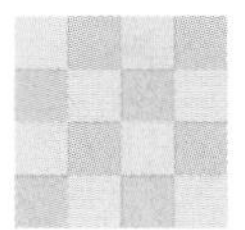

$n = 3, a_n = 5$

$n = 4, a_n = 8$

a. What does n represent for each quilt? What does a_n represent?

b. Make a table that shows n and a_n for $n = 1, 2, 3, 4, 5, 6, 7,$ and 8.

c. Use the rule $a_n = \frac{n^2}{2} + \frac{1}{4}[1 - (-1)^n]$ to find a_n for $n = 1, 2, 3, 4, 5, 6, 7,$ and 8. *Compare* these values with the results in your table. What can you conclude about the sequence defined by this rule?

33. AUDITIONS Several rounds of auditions are being held to cast the three main parts in a play. There are 3072 actors at the first round of auditions. In each successive round of auditions, one fourth of the actors from the previous round remain. Find a rule for the number a_n of actors in the nth round of auditions. For what values of n does your rule make sense?

MULTIPLE CHOICE QUESTIONS

Some of the information you need to solve a multiple choice question may appear in a table, a diagram, or a graph.

PROBLEM 1

The frequencies (in hertz) of the notes on a piano form a geometric sequence. The frequencies of G (labeled "8") and A (labeled "10") are shown in the diagram. What is the approximate frequency of E flat (labeled "4")?

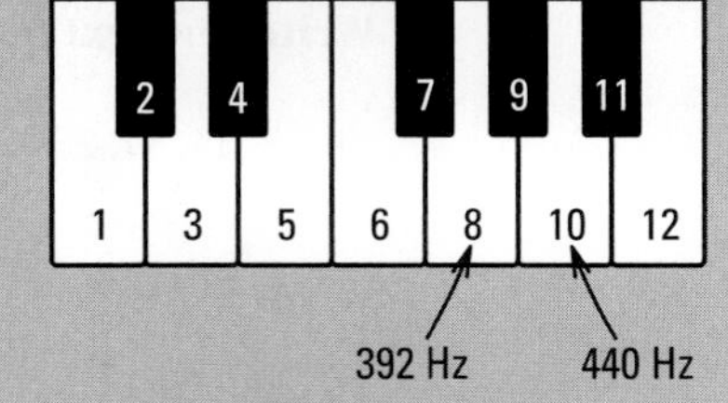

(1) 247 Hz (3) 330 Hz

(2) 311 Hz (4) 554 Hz

Plan

INTERPRET THE DIAGRAM The diagram gives you the frequencies of the 8th and 10th notes. Use these frequencies to find the frequency of the 4th note.

Solution

STEP 1 Write a system of equations.

Let a_n be the frequency (in hertz) of the nth note. Because the frequencies form a geometric sequence, a rule for a_n has the form $a_n = a_1 r^{n-1}$. From the diagram, $a_8 = 392$ and $a_{10} = 440$. Use these values to write a system of equations.

$a_8 = a_1 r^{8-1} \longrightarrow 392 = a_1 r^7$ **Equation 1**

$a_{10} = a_1 r^{10-1} \longrightarrow 440 = a_1 r^9$ **Equation 2**

STEP 2 Solve the system of equations to find the values of r and a_1.

$a_1 = \frac{392}{r^7}$ **Solve Equation 1 for a_1.**

$440 = \frac{392}{r^7} \cdot r^9$ **Substitute $\frac{392}{r^7}$ for a_1 in Equation 2.**

$440 = 392r^2$ **Simplify.**

$1.12 \approx r^2$ **Divide each side by 392.**

$1.06 \approx r$ **Take positive square root of each side.**

Find a_1 by substituting the value of r into revised Equation 1.

$$a_1 = \frac{392}{r^7} = \frac{392}{(1.06)^7} \approx 261$$

STEP 3 Write a rule for the nth term and find a_4.

A rule for the sequence is $a_n = a_1 r^{n-1} = 261(1.06)^{n-1}$.

So, $a_4 = 261(1.06)^3 \approx 311$.

▸ The correct answer is (2).

TEST PREPARATION

PROBLEM 2

The first 4 terms of an infinite arithmetic sequence are shown in the graph. Which rule describes the nth term in the sequence?

(1) $a_n = 2n - 5$
(2) $a_n = 2n + 5$
(3) $a_n = 5n - 2$
(4) $a_n = n + 5$

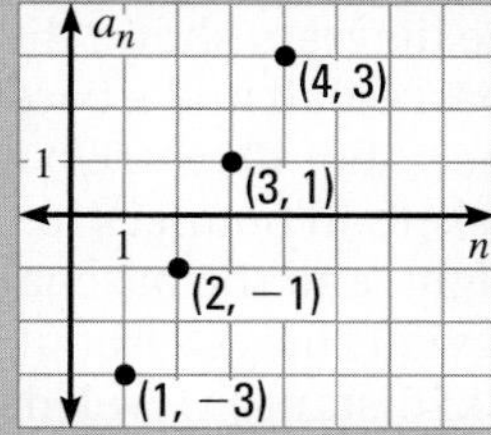

Plan

INTERPRET THE GRAPH In order to find a rule for the sequence, you must first use the graph to write the terms of the sequence.

Solution

STEP 1 Write the terms of the sequence.

The points shown in the graph are:

(1, −3), (2, −1), (3, 1), (4, 3)

Therefore, the sequence is −3, −1, 1, 3, ...

STEP 2 Find the first term and the common difference.

The first term a_1 of the sequence is −3.

Because each term after the first is 2 more than the previous term, the common difference d is 2.

STEP 3 Write a rule for the nth term.

$a_n = \mathbf{a_1} + (n - 1)\mathbf{d}$	**Write general rule for an arithmetic sequence.**
$= \mathbf{-3} + (n - 1)\mathbf{2}$	**Substitute −3 for a_1 and 2 for d.**
$= -3 + 2n - 2$	**Distributive property**
$= 2n - 5$	**Simplify.**

▶ The correct answer is (1).

PRACTICE

In Exercises 1 and 2, use the graph in Problem 2.

1. What is the value of a_{15}?

(1) −35
(2) 25
(3) 30
(4) 165

2. Which statement is true about the sequence that is graphed?

(1) The sum of the first 14 terms is 140.
(2) The value of a_{20} is 40.
(3) A recursive rule for the sequence is $a_1 = 2$, $a_n = a_{n-1} - 5$.
(4) The ratio of any term to the previous term is constant.

New York Test Practice

MULTIPLE CHOICE

1. The diagram shows the bounce heights of a basketball and a baseball dropped from a height of 10 feet. On each bounce, the basketball bounces to 36% of its previous height, and the baseball bounces to 30% of its previous height. About how much greater is the total distance traveled by the basketball than the total distance traveled by the baseball?

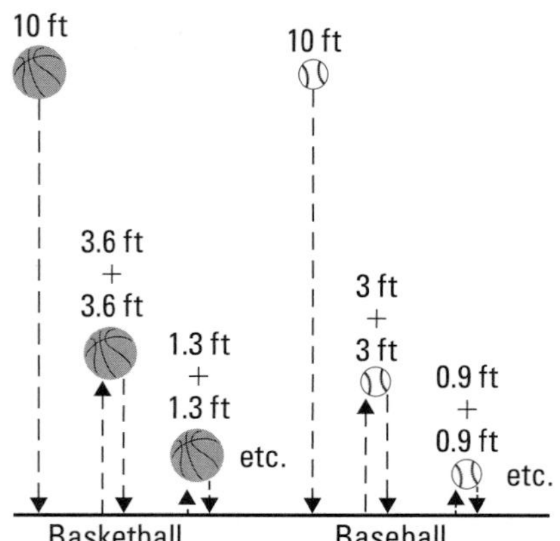

(1) 1.34 feet (3) 2.62 feet

(2) 2.00 feet (4) 5.63 feet

2. The table shows the domain and range of a sequence. Which recursive rule describes the sequence?

Domain	1	2	3	4	5
Range	20	10	5	2.5	1.25

(1) $a_1 = 20, a_n = a_{n-1} + 10$

(2) $a_1 = 20, a_n = a_{n-1} - 10$

(3) $a_1 = 20, a_n = 0.5a_{n-1}$

(4) $a_1 = 20, a_n = 2a_{n-1}$

3. What type of sequence is graphed at the right?

(1) Arithmetic

(2) Geometric with $0 < r < 1$

(3) Geometric with $r > 1$

(4) Neither arithmetic nor geometric

In Exercises 4 and 5, use the information below.
Cheryl is researching her lineage for a history project. So far, she has created a family tree for three generations, as shown below. Cheryl is only including relatives from whom she is directly descended. Siblings are not included.

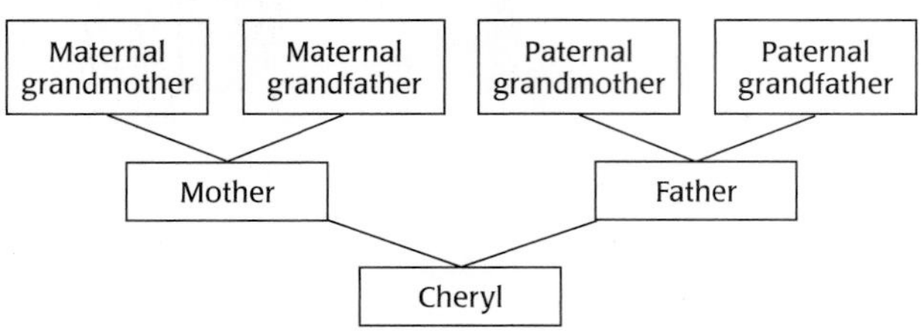

4. Assume that Cheryl is in generation 1, her parents are in generation 2, and so on. Let a_n be the number of relatives in generation n. What is a rule for a_n?

(1) $a_n = n + 2$ (3) $a_n = 2^n$

(2) $a_n = 2^{n-1}$ (4) $a_n = 2^{n+1}$

5. Cheryl creates a family tree with 8 generations of her family. How many people are in her family tree?

(1) 8 (3) 128

(2) 64 (4) 255

In Exercises 6 and 7, use the diagram of a stack of blocks.

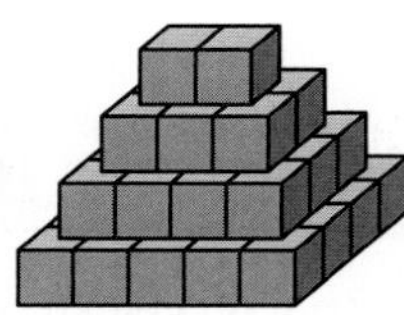

6. Which rule describes the number of blocks in the nth layer, where $n = 1$ represents the top layer?

(1) $a_n = n + 1$ (3) $a_n = 2n^2$

(2) $a_n = n(n + 1)$ (4) $a_n = n^2 + 1$

7. Which sum gives the number of blocks shown?

(1) $\sum_{i=2}^{20}(i + 1)$ (3) $\sum_{i=2}^{20} i(i + 1)$

(2) $\sum_{i=1}^{4}(i + 1)$ (4) $\sum_{i=1}^{4} i(i + 1)$

MULTIPLE CHOICE

8. Two terms of a geometric sequence are $a_3 = 12$ and $a_5 = 48$. What is the value of a_1?

(1) -24 (2) 1 (3) 3 (4) 4

9. Write the repeating decimal 0.1515... as a fraction in lowest terms.

(1) $\frac{3}{20}$ (2) $\frac{303}{2000}$ (3) $\frac{5}{33}$ (4) $\frac{50}{33}$

10. What is the sum of the following series?

$$\sum_{i=2}^{5} 0.5(2)^{i-1}$$

(1) 0.5

(2) 7.5

(3) 8

(4) 15.5

11. What is the eighth term of the sequence below?

$$-4, 12, -36, 108, \ldots$$

(1) -8748 (3) 684

(2) -684 (4) 8748

12. What is the sum of the first 15 terms of the sequence $a_n = 6n + 3$?

(1) 93 (3) 723

(2) 667 (4) 765

13. Person A sends an e-mail to 10 friends. Each of those 10 friends forwards the e-mail to 10 more friends. Through how many stages has the e-mail been forwarded if you are among a group of 100 million people receiving it?

(1) 7 (3) 9

(2) 8 (4) 10

OPEN-ENDED

14. During a baseball season, a company pledges a donation to a charity of \$5000 plus \$100 for every home run hit by the local team. Does it make more sense to represent this situation using a sequence or a series? *Explain* your reasoning.

15. A running track is shaped like a rectangle with two semicircular ends, as shown. The track has 8 lanes that are each 1.22 meters wide. The lanes are numbered from 1 to 8 starting from the inside lane. The length of each line segment that extends from the center of the left semicircle to the inside of a lane is called the lane's curve radius.

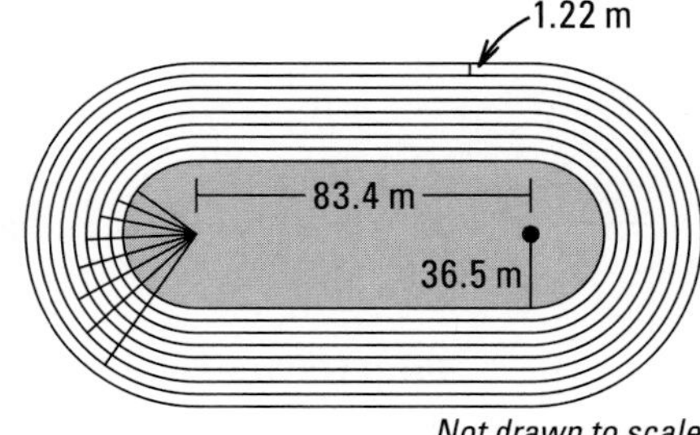

Not drawn to scale

Is the sequence formed by the curve radii *arithmetic, geometric,* or *neither*? *Explain.*

Write a formula for the sequence.

World records must be set on tracks that have a curve radius of at most 50 meters in the outside lane. Does the track shown meet the requirement? *Explain.*

16. Mark takes out a loan for \$16,000 with an interest rate of 0.75% per month. At the end of each month he makes a payment of \$300.

Write a recursive rule for the balance a_n of the loan at the beginning of the nth month.

How much will Mark owe at the beginning of the 18th month?

How long will it take Mark to pay off the loan?

If Mark pays \$350 instead of \$300 each month, how long will it take him to pay off the loan? Will he end up paying less overall? *Explain.*

12 CUMULATIVE REVIEW Chapters 1–12

Graph the function.

1. $3x - y = 5$ *(p. 89)*
2. $\frac{1}{2}x + 3y = -4$ *(p. 89)*
3. $y = |x + 3| - 8$ *(p. 123)*
4. $y = x^2 - 6x - 27$ *(p. 236)*
5. $y = -2(x + 6)(x - 1)$ *(p. 245)*
6. $y = (x - 3)^2 + 4$ *(p. 245)*
7. $y = \sqrt{x + 6}$ *(p. 446)*
8. $y = \sqrt[3]{x} - 2$ *(p. 446)*
9. $y = 3 \cdot 4^{x - 2}$ *(p. 478)*
10. $y = 12\left(\frac{1}{8}\right)^x$ *(p. 486)*
11. $y = \frac{2}{x - 3} + 5$ *(p. 558)*
12. $y = \frac{6}{x^2 - 4}$ *(p. 565)*

Evaluate the determinant of the matrix. *(p. 203)*

13. $\begin{bmatrix} 2 & 3 \\ 1 & 8 \end{bmatrix}$
14. $\begin{bmatrix} 12 & 3 \\ -7 & 8 \end{bmatrix}$
15. $\begin{bmatrix} 0 & 5 & 2 \\ 10 & 13 & -4 \\ -5 & 4 & -1 \end{bmatrix}$
16. $\begin{bmatrix} 5 & -9 & 4 \\ 4 & 2 & 1 \\ 0 & 1 & 1 \end{bmatrix}$

The variables *x* and *y* vary inversely. Use the given values to write an equation relating *x* and *y*. Then find the value of *y* when $x = -8$. *(p. 551)*

17. $x = 3, y = 6$
18. $x = -4, y = 9$
19. $x = 4, y = \frac{1}{8}$
20. $x = 9, y = \frac{2}{5}$

Graph the equation.

21. $\frac{x^2}{36} + \frac{y^2}{4} = 1$ *(p. 634)*
22. $\frac{y^2}{100} - \frac{x^2}{49} = 1$ *(p. 642)*
23. $(x - 3)^2 = 16y$ *(p. 650)*

Find the number of permutations or combinations.

24. ${}_9P_3$ *(p. 682)*
25. ${}_{16}P_5$ *(p. 682)*
26. ${}_7C_2$ *(p. 690)*
27. ${}_6C_6$ *(p. 690)*

Find the indicated probability.

28. $P(A) = 0.32$
    $P(B) = 0.6$
    $P(A \text{ or } B) = 0.85$
    $P(A \text{ and } B) = \underline{\ ?\ }$ *(p. 707)*
29. *A* and *B* are dependent events.
    $P(A) = 0.5$
    $P(B|A) = 0.3$
    $P(A \text{ and } B) = \underline{\ ?\ }$ *(p. 717)*
30. *A* and *B* are independent events.
    $P(A) = 0.25$
    $P(B) = \underline{\ ?\ }$
    $P(A \text{ and } B) = 0.2$ *(p. 717)*

Find the mean, median, mode, range, and standard deviation of the data set. *(p. 744)*

31. 19, 11, 8, 10, 11, 15, 16
32. 54, 58, 49, 60, 63, 58, 42
33. 216, 203, 225, 216, 212, 228, 209
34. −3, 5, −11, 6, −3, 2
35. 99, 92, 93, 82, 88, 71, 97
36. 78, 4, 28, 57, 88, 24, 57, 37, 65

Find the sum of the series.

37. $\sum_{i=1}^{6} 3i^2$ *(p. 794)*
38. $\sum_{i=1}^{16} (-2 + i)$ *(p. 802)*
39. $\sum_{i=1}^{12} \left(\frac{2}{3}\right)^{i-1}$ *(p. 810)*
40. $\sum_{i=1}^{\infty} 5\left(\frac{1}{3}\right)^{i-1}$ *(p. 820)*

Write an explicit rule and a recursive rule for the sequence. *(p. 827)*

41. −7, −3, 1, 5, . . .
42. 1, −14, −29, −44, . . .
43. 3, 12, 48, 192, . . .

44. **FUNDRAISER** You are organizing a school fundraiser that involves selling holiday cookies and decorative calendars. You want to raise \$2400. You charge \$2 for a bag of cookies and \$7 for a calendar. Write and graph an equation to represent the situation. If you sell 200 calendars, how many bags of cookies do you need to sell in order to meet your goal? *(p. 98)*

45. **GEOMETRY** A designer is creating a kit for making sand castles. The designer wants one of the molds to be a cone that will hold 75π cubic inches of sand. What should the dimensions of the cone be if the height should be 4 inches more than the radius of the base? *(p. 370)*

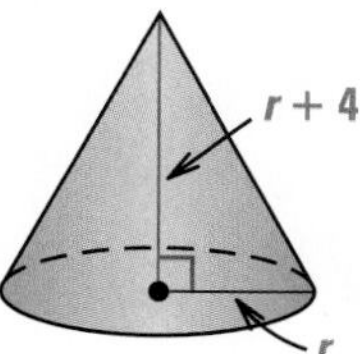

46. **ELECTRICITY** The current I (in amperes) required for an electrical appliance is given by $I = \sqrt{\frac{P}{R}}$ where P is the power (in watts) and R is the resistance (in ohms). Find the power consumed by a portable hair dryer for which $I = 17$ amperes and $R = 6.5$ ohms. *(p. 452)*

47. **DEPRECIATION** Rachel buys a new car for \$18,600. The value of the car decreases by 15.5% each year. Estimate when the car will have a value of \$8000. *(p. 486)*

48. **GEOMETRY** Steve is a lifeguard at a pond. The pond is approximately circular in shape with a diameter of 330 feet. He ropes off a section of the pond for swimming. The rope forms a chord of the circle and is a maximum distance of 50 feet from the edge of the pond. What is the length of the rope? *(p. 626)*

49. **DINING OUT** You and three friends go to a restaurant for dinner. There are 20 different items on the menu. Each of you is equally likely to order any item. What is the probability that each of you orders a different item from the menu? *(p. 717)*

50. **REAL ESTATE COMMISSIONS** The data set below gives the selling prices of seven homes that are being sold by one real estate agent. The agent will receive 5% of the selling price of each home as a commission. *(pp. 744, 751)*

Selling Prices of Homes
\$201,900; \$205,200; \$195,800; \$210,300; \$199,900; \$215,500; \$192,100

a. Find the mean, median, mode, range, and standard deviation of the data.

b. Find the agent's commission for each home. Then find the mean, median, mode, range, and standard deviation of the commissions.

c. *Compare* the statistics from parts (a) and (b).

51. **SALARY** An accountant takes a job that pays an annual salary of \$31,000 for the first year. The employer offers a \$1600 raise for each of the next 8 years. Write a rule for the accountant's salary in the nth year. What will the accountant's salary be in the 9th year? *(p. 802)*

13 Trigonometric Ratios and Functions

Before

In previous courses and in previous chapters, you learned the following skills, which you'll use in Chapter 13: using the Pythagorean theorem, solving equations using inverse functions, and finding angle measures in triangles.

Prerequisite Skills

VOCABULARY CHECK

Copy and complete the statement.

1. The **reciprocal** of $\frac{4}{5}$ is _?_.
2. Functions f and g are **inverses** of each other if _?_ and _?_.
3. An equation of the **circle** with center (0, 0) and a radius of 1 unit is _?_.

SKILLS CHECK

A right triangle has legs with lengths a and b and a hypotenuse with length c. Find the unknown side length. *(Review p. 995 for 13.1.)*

4. $a = 8, b = 10$
5. $a = 2.5, c = 6.5$
6. $b = 9, c = 11$

Solve the equation. *(Review p. 515 for 13.4.)*

7. $4^x - 5 = 3$
8. $\log_2 x = -1$
9. $-5 + 2 \ln 3x = 20$

The measures of the angles of a triangle are given. Find the value of x. *(Review p. 995 for 13.5, 13.6.)*

10. $x°, 65°, 55°$
11. $90°, x°, x°$
12. $41°, 107°, x°$

In Chapter 13, you will apply the big ideas listed below and reviewed in the Chapter Summary on page 897. You will also use the key vocabulary listed below.

Big Ideas

1. **Using trigonometric functions**
2. **Using inverse trigonometric functions**
3. **Applying the law of sines and law of cosines**

KEY VOCABULARY

- sine, *p. 852*
- cosine, *p. 852*
- tangent, *p. 852*
- cosecant, *p. 852*
- secant, *p. 852*
- cotangent, *p. 852*
- radian, *p. 860*
- central angle, *p. 861*
- unit circle, *p. 867*
- reference angle, *p. 868*
- inverse sine, *p. 875*
- inverse cosine, *p. 875*
- inverse tangent, *p. 875*
- law of sines, *p. 882*
- law of cosines, *p. 889*

Why?

You can use angle measures and trigonometry to find lengths and areas in real life. For example, you can use an angle measure to find the area of each step in a spiral staircase.

Animated Algebra

The animation illustrated below for Exercise 53 on page 864 helps you answer this question: How does the central angle of a step in a spiral staircase affect the step's area?

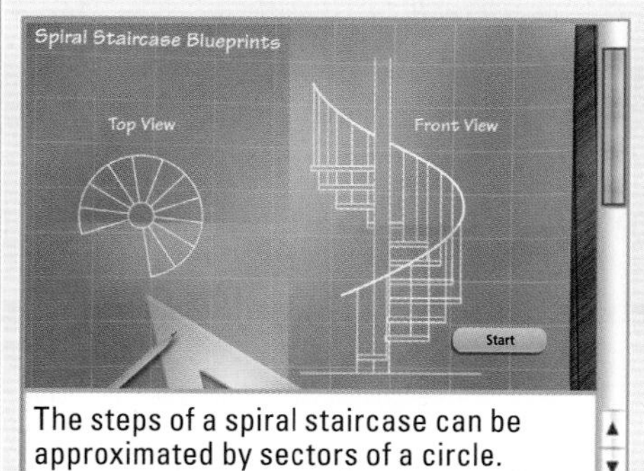

The steps of a spiral staircase can be approximated by sectors of a circle.

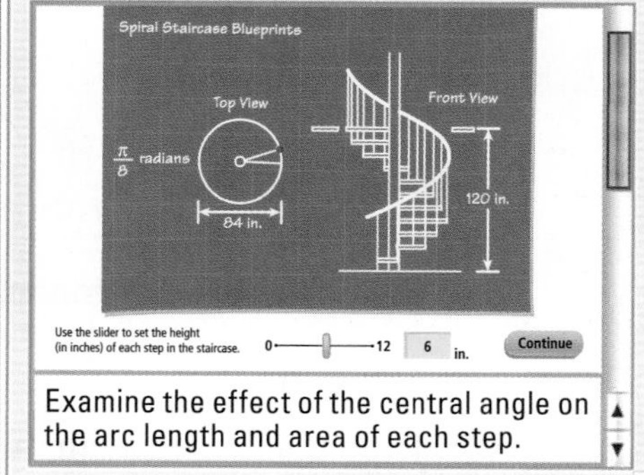

Examine the effect of the central angle on the arc length and area of each step.

Animated Algebra at classzone.com

Other animations for Chapter 13: pages 854, 867, 884, and 897

13.1 Use Trigonometry with Right Triangles

A2.A.55 Express and apply the six trigonometric functions as ratios of the sides of a right triangle

Before You used the Pythagorean theorem to find lengths.

Now You will use trigonometric functions to find lengths.

Why? So you can measure distances indirectly, as in Example 5.

Key Vocabulary
- sine
- cosine
- tangent
- cosecant
- secant
- cotangent

Consider a right triangle that has an acute angle θ (the Greek letter *theta*). The three sides of the triangle are the *hypotenuse*, the side *opposite* θ, and the side *adjacent* to θ.

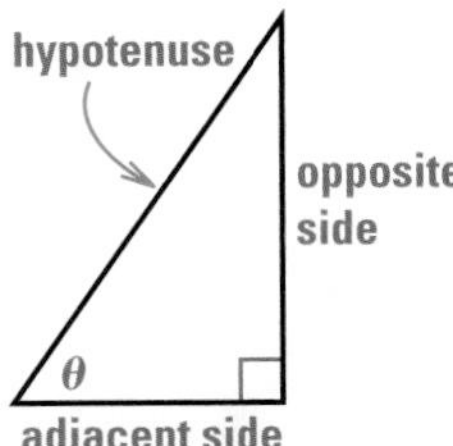

Ratios of a right triangle's side lengths are used to define the six trigonometric functions: **sine**, **cosine**, **tangent**, **cosecant**, **secant**, and **cotangent**. These six functions are abbreviated sin, cos, tan, csc, sec, and cot, respectively.

KEY CONCEPT *For Your Notebook*

Right Triangle Definitions of Trigonometric Functions

Let θ be an acute angle of a right triangle. The six trigonometric functions of θ are defined as follows:

$$\sin\theta = \frac{\text{opposite}}{\text{hypotenuse}} \qquad \cos\theta = \frac{\text{adjacent}}{\text{hypotenuse}} \qquad \tan\theta = \frac{\text{opposite}}{\text{adjacent}}$$

$$\csc\theta = \frac{\text{hypotenuse}}{\text{opposite}} \qquad \sec\theta = \frac{\text{hypotenuse}}{\text{adjacent}} \qquad \cot\theta = \frac{\text{adjacent}}{\text{opposite}}$$

The abbreviations *opp*, *adj*, and *hyp* are often used to represent the side lengths of the right triangle. Note that the ratios in the second row are reciprocals of the ratios in the first row:

$$\csc\theta = \frac{1}{\sin\theta} \qquad \sec\theta = \frac{1}{\cos\theta} \qquad \cot\theta = \frac{1}{\tan\theta}$$

EXAMPLE 1 Evaluate trigonometric functions

Evaluate the six trigonometric functions of the angle θ.

θ, 5, 12, hypotenuse

Solution

REVIEW GEOMETRY
For help with the Pythagorean theorem, see p. 995.

From the Pythagorean theorem, the length of the hypotenuse is $\sqrt{5^2 + 12^2} = \sqrt{169} = 13$.

$$\sin\theta = \frac{\text{opp}}{\text{hyp}} = \frac{12}{13} \qquad \cos\theta = \frac{\text{adj}}{\text{hyp}} = \frac{5}{13} \qquad \tan\theta = \frac{\text{opp}}{\text{adj}} = \frac{12}{5}$$

$$\csc\theta = \frac{\text{hyp}}{\text{opp}} = \frac{13}{12} \qquad \sec\theta = \frac{\text{hyp}}{\text{adj}} = \frac{13}{5} \qquad \cot\theta = \frac{\text{adj}}{\text{opp}} = \frac{5}{12}$$

EXAMPLE 2 Standardized Test Practice

If θ is an acute angle of a right triangle and $\sin\theta = \frac{4}{7}$, what is $\tan\theta$?

Ⓐ $\frac{3}{7}$ Ⓑ $\frac{4\sqrt{33}}{33}$ Ⓒ $\frac{\sqrt{33}}{7}$ Ⓓ $\frac{4}{3}$

Solution

STEP 1 **Draw** a right triangle with acute angle θ such that the leg opposite θ has length 4 and the hypotenuse has length 7. By the Pythagorean theorem, the length x of the other leg is $x = \sqrt{7^2 - 4^2} = \sqrt{33}$.

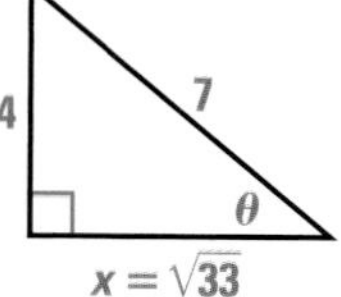

STEP 2 **Find** the value of $\tan\theta$.

$$\tan\theta = \frac{\text{opp}}{\text{adj}} = \frac{4}{\sqrt{33}} = \frac{4\sqrt{33}}{33}$$

▶ The correct answer is B. Ⓐ Ⓑ Ⓒ Ⓓ

GUIDED PRACTICE for Examples 1 and 2

Evaluate the six trigonometric functions of the angle θ.

1.
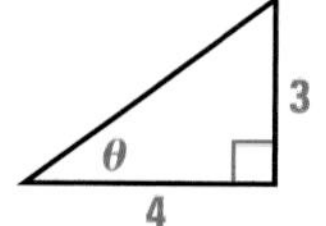

2.
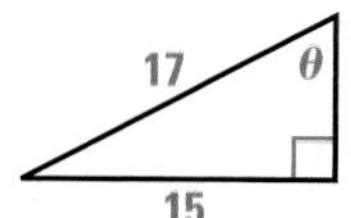

3.
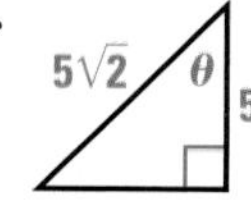

4. In a right triangle, θ is an acute angle and $\cos\theta = \frac{7}{10}$. What is $\sin\theta$?

SPECIAL ANGLES The angles 30°, 45°, and 60° occur frequently in trigonometry. You can use the trigonometric values for these angles to find unknown side lengths in special right triangles.

KEY CONCEPT *For Your Notebook*

Trigonometric Values for Special Angles

The table below gives the values of the six trigonometric functions for the angles 30°, 45°, and 60°. You can obtain these values from the triangles shown.

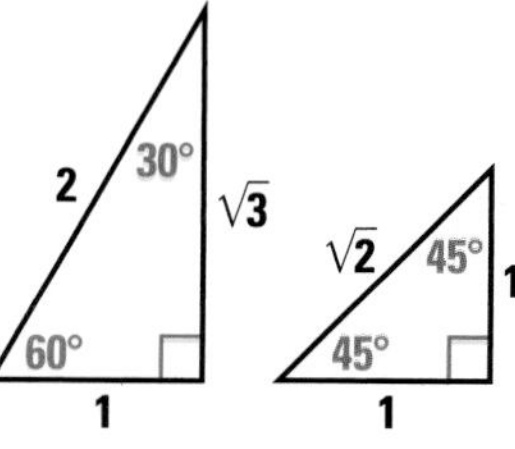

θ	$\sin\theta$	$\cos\theta$	$\tan\theta$	$\csc\theta$	$\sec\theta$	$\cot\theta$
30°	$\frac{1}{2}$	$\frac{\sqrt{3}}{2}$	$\frac{\sqrt{3}}{3}$	2	$\frac{2\sqrt{3}}{3}$	$\sqrt{3}$
45°	$\frac{\sqrt{2}}{2}$	$\frac{\sqrt{2}}{2}$	1	$\sqrt{2}$	$\sqrt{2}$	1
60°	$\frac{\sqrt{3}}{2}$	$\frac{1}{2}$	$\sqrt{3}$	$\frac{2\sqrt{3}}{3}$	2	$\frac{\sqrt{3}}{3}$

EXAMPLE 3 Find an unknown side length of a right triangle

Find the value of x for the right triangle shown.

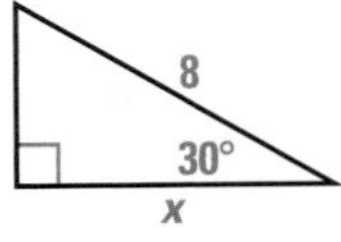

Solution

Write an equation using a trigonometric function that involves the ratio of x and 8. Solve the equation for x.

$\cos 30° = \frac{\text{adj}}{\text{hyp}}$ **Write trigonometric equation.**

$\frac{\sqrt{3}}{2} = \frac{x}{8}$ **Substitute.**

$4\sqrt{3} = x$ **Multiply each side by 8.**

▶ The length of the side is $x = 4\sqrt{3} \approx 6.93$.

Animated Algebra at classzone.com

SOLVING A TRIANGLE Finding *all* unknown side lengths and angle measures of a triangle is called *solving* the triangle. Solving right triangles that have acute angles other than 30°, 45°, and 60° may require the use of a calculator.

To find values of the sine, cosine, and tangent functions on a calculator, use the keys SIN, COS, and TAN. Use these keys and the reciprocal key for cosecant, secant, and cotangent. Be sure the calculator is set in degree mode.

EXAMPLE 4 Use a calculator to solve a right triangle

Solve $\triangle ABC$.

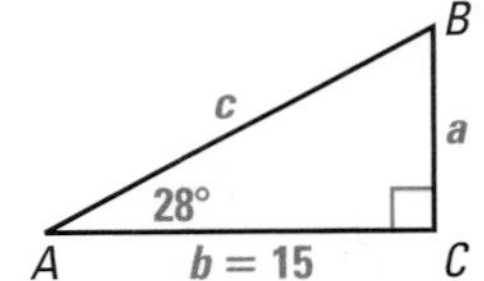

Solution

READING
Throughout this chapter, a capital letter is used to denote both an angle of a triangle and its measure. The same letter in lowercase is used to denote the length of the side opposite that angle.

A and B are complementary angles, so $B = 90° - 28° = 62°$.

$\tan 28° = \frac{\text{opp}}{\text{adj}}$	$\sec 28° = \frac{\text{hyp}}{\text{adj}}$	**Write trigonometric equation.**
$\tan 28° = \frac{a}{15}$	$\sec 28° = \frac{c}{15}$	**Substitute.**
$15(\tan 28°) = a$	$15\left(\frac{1}{\cos 28°}\right) = c$	**Solve for the variable.**
$7.98 \approx a$	$17.0 \approx c$	**Use a calculator.**

▶ So, $B = 62°$, $a \approx 7.98$, and $c \approx 17.0$.

✓ GUIDED PRACTICE for Examples 3 and 4

Solve $\triangle ABC$ using the diagram at the right and the given measurements.

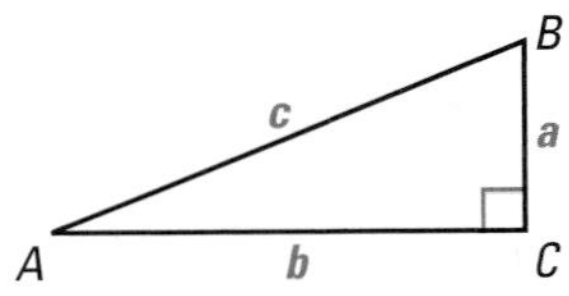

5. $B = 45°, c = 5$
6. $A = 32°, b = 10$
7. $A = 71°, c = 20$
8. $B = 60°, a = 7$

EXAMPLE 5 Use indirect measurement

GRAND CANYON While standing at Yavapai Point near the Grand Canyon, you measure an angle of 90° between Powell Point and Widforss Point, as shown. You then walk to Powell Point and measure an angle of 76° between Yavapai Point and Widforss Point. The distance between Yavapai Point and Powell Point is about 2 miles. How wide is the Grand Canyon between Yavapai Point and Widforss Point?

Solution

CHOOSE FUNCTIONS
The tangent function is used to find the unknown distance because it involves the ratio of x and 2.

$\tan 76° = \frac{x}{2}$ **Write trigonometric equation.**

$2(\tan 76°) = x$ **Multiply each side by 2.**

$8.0 \approx x$ **Use a calculator.**

▶ The width is about 8.0 miles.

ANGLES OF SIGHT If you look at a point above you, such as the top of a building, the angle that your line of sight makes with a line parallel to the ground is called the **angle of elevation**. At the top of the building, the angle between a line parallel to the ground and your line of sight is called the **angle of depression**. These two angles have the same measure.

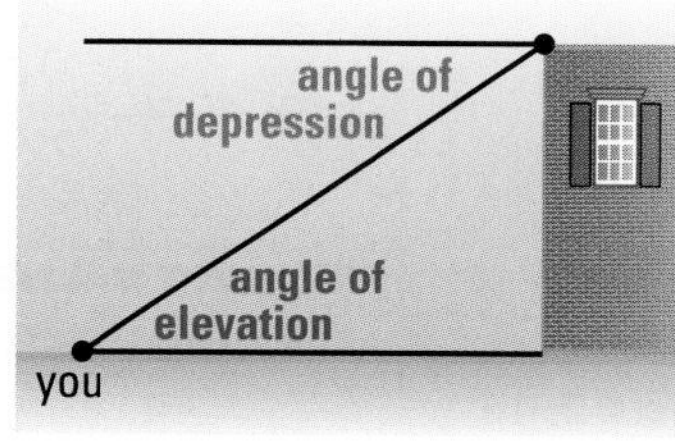

EXAMPLE 6 Use an angle of elevation

PARASAILING A parasailer is attached to a boat with a rope 300 feet long. The angle of elevation from the boat to the parasailer is 48°. Estimate the parasailer's height above the boat.

Solution

STEP 1 **Draw** a diagram that represents the situation.

STEP 2 **Write** and solve an equation to find the height h.

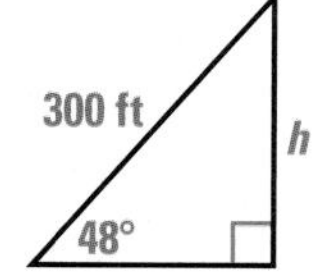

$\sin 48° = \frac{h}{300}$ **Write trigonometric equation.**

$300(\sin 48°) = h$ **Multiply each side by 300.**

$223 \approx h$ **Use a calculator.**

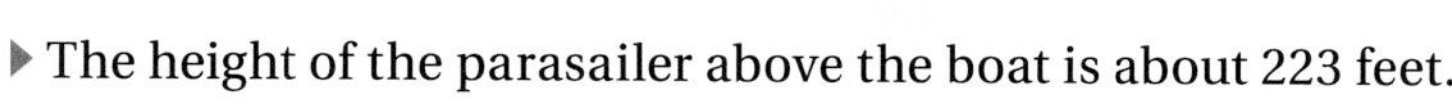

▶ The height of the parasailer above the boat is about 223 feet.

GUIDED PRACTICE for Examples 5 and 6

9. **GRAND CANYON** In Example 5, find the distance between Powell Point and Widforss Point.

10. **WHAT IF?** In Example 6, estimate the height of the parasailer above the boat if the angle of elevation is 38°.

13.1 EXERCISES

HOMEWORK KEY

○ = **WORKED-OUT SOLUTIONS** on p. WS21 for Exs. 5, 11, and 33

★ = **STANDARDIZED TEST PRACTICE** Exs. 2, 15, 20, 33, and 36

◆ = **MULTIPLE REPRESENTATIONS** Ex. 34

SKILL PRACTICE

1. **VOCABULARY** What is an angle of elevation?

2. ★ **WRITING** *Explain* what it means to solve a right triangle.

EXAMPLE 1 on p. 852 for Exs. 3–8

EVALUATING FUNCTIONS Evaluate the six trigonometric functions of the angle θ.

3. 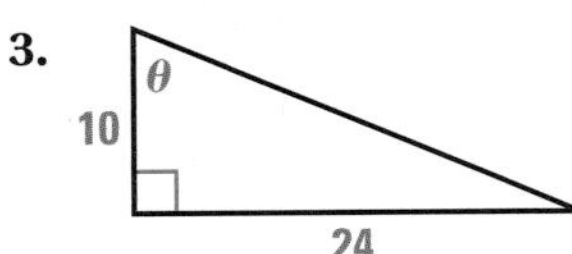

4. 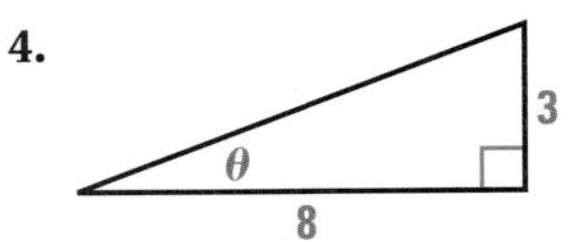

5. 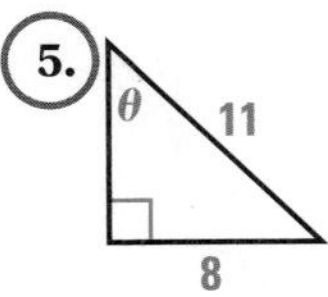

6. 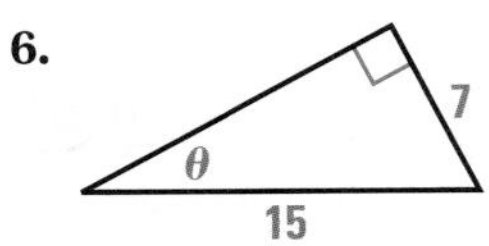

7. 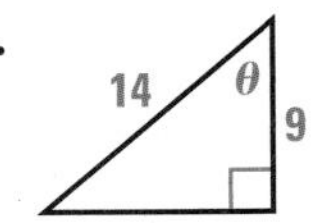

8. 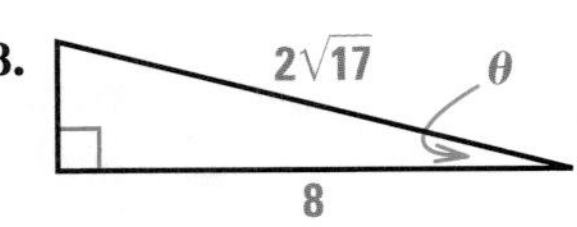

EXAMPLE 2 on p. 853 for Exs. 9–16

FINDING VALUES Let θ be an acute angle of a right triangle. Find the values of the other five trigonometric functions of θ.

9. $\sin \theta = \frac{5}{6}$

10. $\cos \theta = \frac{5}{8}$

11. $\tan \theta = \frac{7}{3}$

12. $\csc \theta = \frac{10}{7}$

13. $\sec \theta = \frac{12}{5}$

14. $\cot \theta = \frac{6}{11}$

15. ★ **MULTIPLE CHOICE** In a right triangle, θ is an acute angle and $\cos \theta = \frac{4}{9}$. What is the value of $\tan \theta$?

Ⓐ $\frac{4\sqrt{65}}{65}$ Ⓑ $\frac{\sqrt{65}}{9}$ Ⓒ $\frac{\sqrt{65}}{4}$ Ⓓ $\frac{9}{4}$

16. **ERROR ANALYSIS** *Describe* and correct the error in finding $\csc \theta$, given that θ is an acute angle of a right triangle and $\cos \theta = \frac{7}{11}$.

$$\csc \theta = \frac{1}{\cos \theta} = \frac{11}{7}$$ ✗

EXAMPLE 3 on p. 854 for Exs. 17–20

FINDING SIDE LENGTHS Find the exact values of x and y.

17. 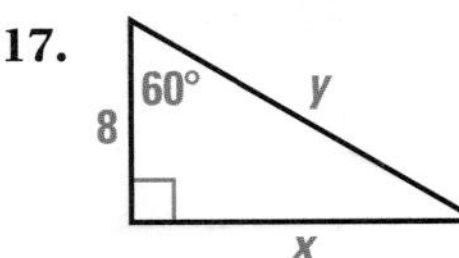

18. 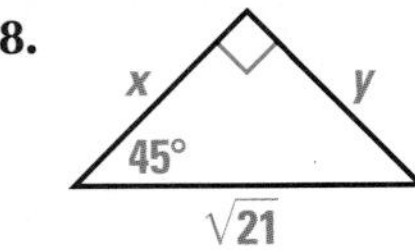

19. 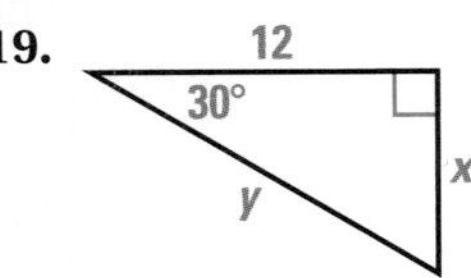

20. ★ **MULTIPLE CHOICE** In a 30°-60°-90° triangle, the longer leg has a length of 5. What is the length of the shorter leg?

Ⓐ $\frac{5\sqrt{3}}{3}$ Ⓑ $\frac{5\sqrt{3}}{2}$ Ⓒ $\frac{10\sqrt{3}}{3}$ Ⓓ $5\sqrt{3}$

EXAMPLE 4
on p. 854
for Exs. 21–28

SOLVING TRIANGLES **Solve $\triangle ABC$ using the diagram and the given measurements.**

21. $A = 35°, c = 16$

22. $B = 53°, a = 12$

23. $B = 18°, c = 24$

24. $A = 67°, b = 7$

25. $B = 75°, a = 15$

26. $A = 49°, c = 27$

27. $A = 64°, b = 32$

28. $B = 24°, c = 10.8$

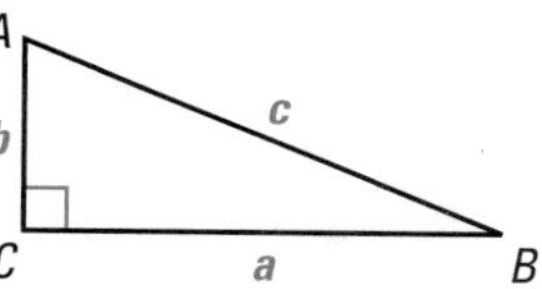

29. **CHALLENGE** A procedure for approximating π based on the work of Archimedes is to inscribe a regular hexagon in a circle.

a. Use the diagram at the right to solve for x. What is the perimeter of the hexagon?

b. Show that a regular n-sided polygon inscribed in a circle of radius 1 has a perimeter of $2n \cdot \sin\left(\frac{180}{n}\right)^{\circ}$.

c. Use the result from part (b) to find an expression in terms of n that approximates π. Then evaluate the expression when $n = 50$.

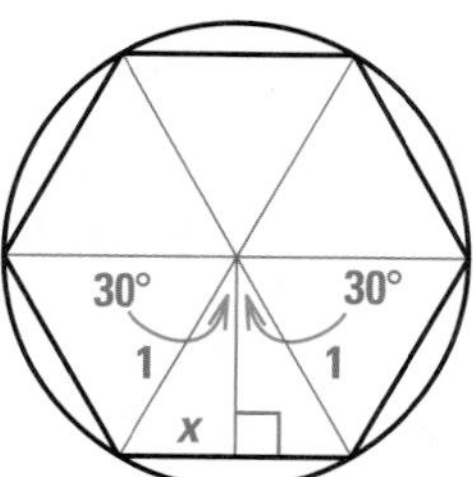

PROBLEM SOLVING

EXAMPLES 5 and 6
on p. 855
for Exs. 30–35

In Exercises 30 and 31, use the information in the diagram to solve the problem.

30. **TREE HEIGHT** A tree casts the shadow shown. What is the height of the tree?

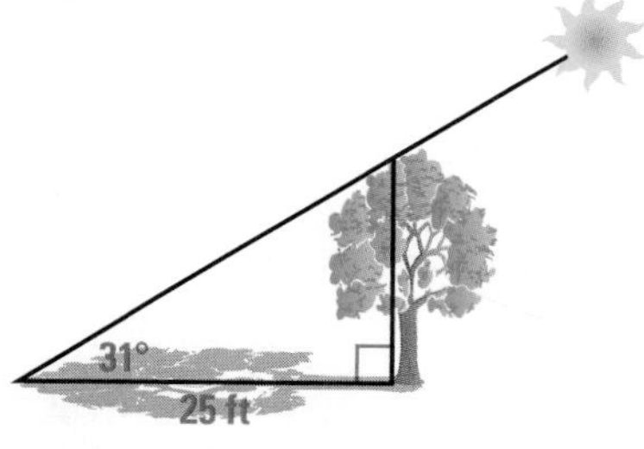

31. **GRAND PIANO** Find the length of the prop holding open the piano.

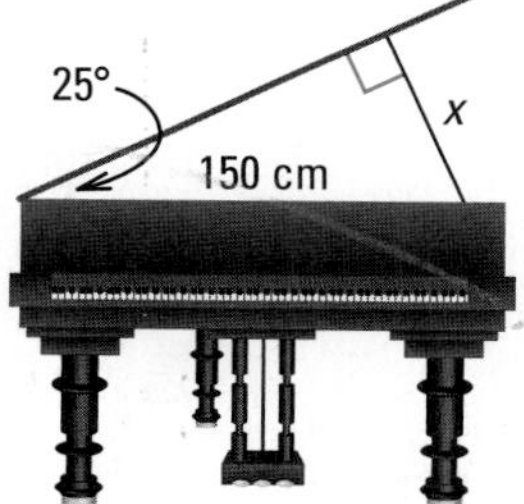

@HomeTutor for problem solving help at classzone.com

32. **RAILWAY** The Falls Incline Railway at Niagara Falls has an angle of elevation of 36°. The railway extends a horizontal distance of about 138 feet. Find the height and length of the railway.

33. ★ **SHORT RESPONSE** A submersible traveling at a depth of 250 feet dives at an angle of 15° with respect to a line parallel to the water's surface. It travels a horizontal distance of 1500 feet during the dive. What is the depth of the submersible after the dive? *Explain* how the angle of the dive affects the final depth.

34. **MULTIPLE REPRESENTATIONS** You are climbing Mount Massive in Colorado. You are at an altitude of 11,200 feet. You measure the angle of elevation to a ridge above you to be 29.4°. The distance (along the face of the mountain) between you and the ridge is 6315 feet.

a. Drawing a Diagram Draw a diagram that represents this situation.

b. Writing an Equation Write and solve an equation to find the altitude of the ridge.

35. TROPIC OF CANCER The Tropic of Cancer is the circle of latitude farthest north of the equator where the sun can appear directly overhead. It lies 23.5° north of the equator, as shown.

a. Find the circumference of the Tropic of Cancer using 3960 miles as Earth's approximate radius.

b. What is the distance between two points on the Tropic of Cancer that lie directly across from each other?

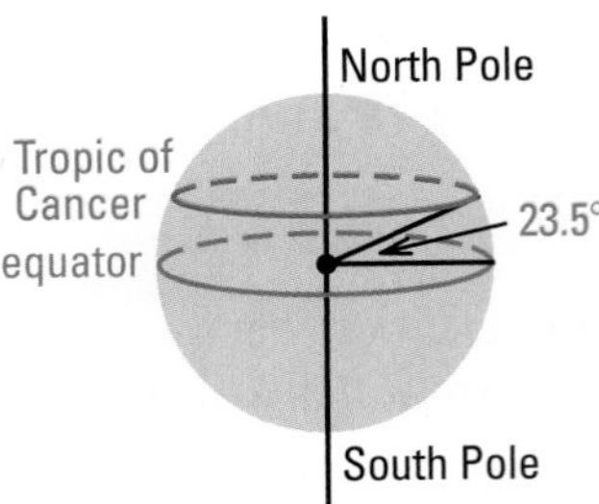

36. ★ **EXTENDED RESPONSE** A passenger in an airplane sees two towns directly to the left of the plane.

a. What is the distance d from the airplane to the first town?

b. What is the horizontal distance x from the airplane to the first town?

c. What is the distance y between the two towns? *Explain* the process you used to find your answer.

37. CHALLENGE You measure the angle of elevation from the ground to the top of a building as 32°. When you move 50 meters closer to the building, the angle of elevation is 53°. How high is the building?

NEW YORK MIXED REVIEW

TEST PRACTICE at classzone.com

38. The height h (in feet) of a horseshoe tossed during a game of horseshoes is $h = -16t^2 + 30t + 2$ where t is the time (in seconds). About how long is the horseshoe in the air?

Ⓐ 1.4 sec

Ⓑ 1.9 sec

Ⓒ 2.9 sec

Ⓓ 3.6 sec

39. Rectangle $KLMN$ has diagonals that intersect at point P. What are the coordinates of point L?

Ⓐ $(-1, 5)$

Ⓑ $(-1, 14)$

Ⓒ $(5, 5)$

Ⓓ $(5, 14)$

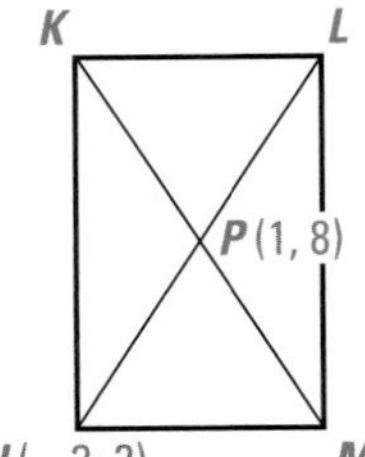

13.2 Define General Angles and Use Radian Measure

A2.A.61 Determine the length of an arc of a circle, given its radius and the measure of its central angle

Before You used acute angles measured in degrees.

Now You will use general angles that may be measured in radians.

Why? So you can find the area of a curved playing field, as in Example 4.

Key Vocabulary
- initial side
- terminal side
- standard position
- coterminal
- radian
- sector
- central angle

In Lesson 13.1, you worked only with acute angles. In this lesson, you will study angles with measures that can be any real numbers.

KEY CONCEPT *For Your Notebook*

Angles in Standard Position

In a coordinate plane, an angle can be formed by fixing one ray, called the **initial side**, and rotating the other ray, called the **terminal side**, about the vertex.

An angle is in **standard position** if its vertex is at the origin and its initial side lies on the positive x-axis.

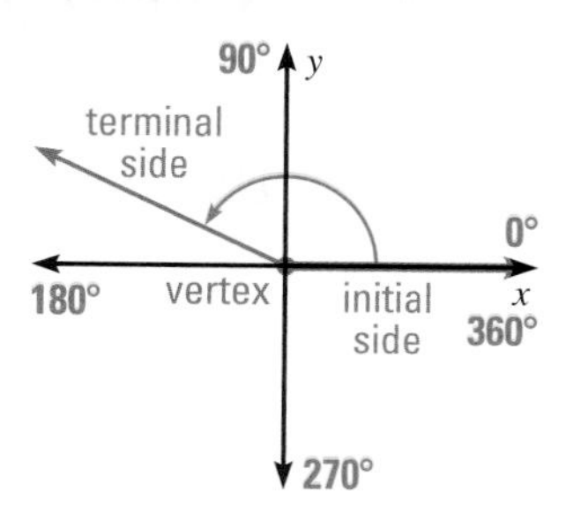

The measure of an angle is positive if the rotation of its terminal side is counterclockwise, and negative if the rotation is clockwise. The terminal side of an angle can make more than one complete rotation.

EXAMPLE 1 Draw angles in standard position

Draw an angle with the given measure in standard position.

a. 240° **b.** 500° **c.** −50°

Solution

a. Because 240° is 60° more than 180°, the terminal side is 60° counterclockwise past the negative x-axis.

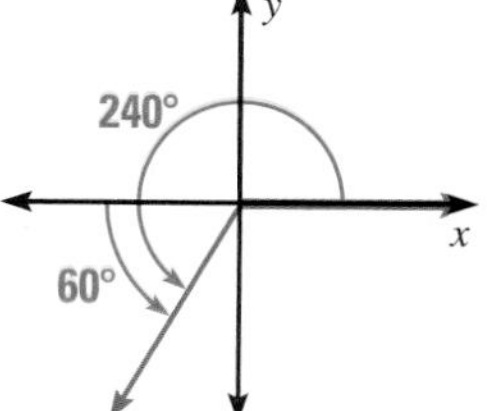

b. Because 500° is 140° more than 360°, the terminal side makes one whole revolution counterclockwise plus 140° more.

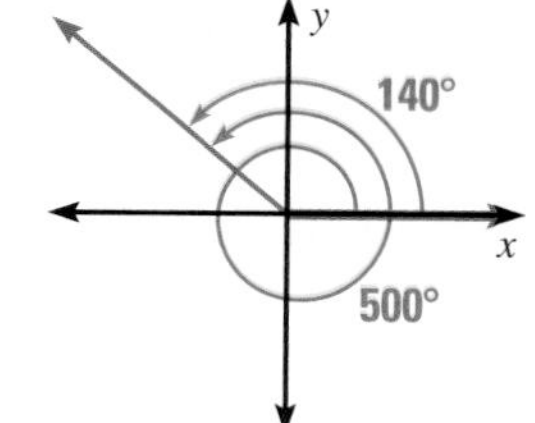

c. Because −50° is negative, the terminal side is 50° clockwise from the positive x-axis.

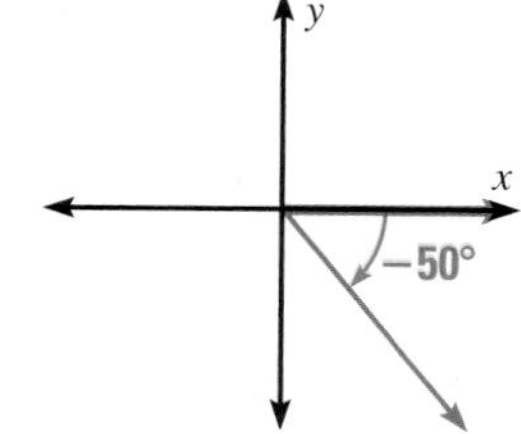

COTERMINAL ANGLES In Example 1, the angles 500° and 140° are **coterminal** because their terminal sides coincide. An angle coterminal with a given angle can be found by adding or subtracting multiples of 360°.

EXAMPLE 2 Find coterminal angles

Find one positive angle and one negative angle that are coterminal with (a) −45° and (b) 395°.

Solution

There are many such angles, depending on what multiple of 360° is added or subtracted.

a. $-45° + 360° = 315°$
$-45° - 360° = -405°$

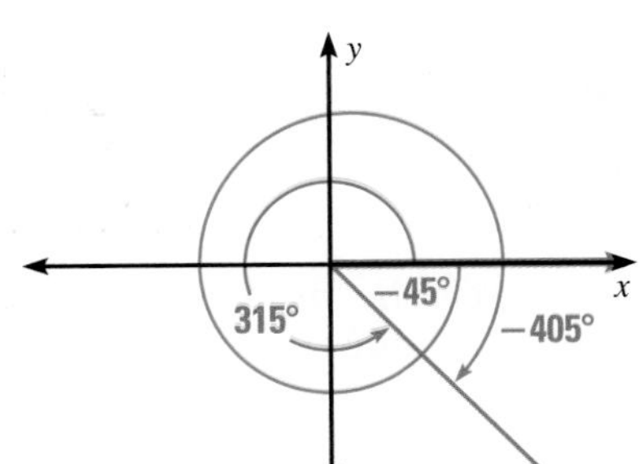

b. $395° - 360° = 35°$
$395° - 2(360°) = -325°$

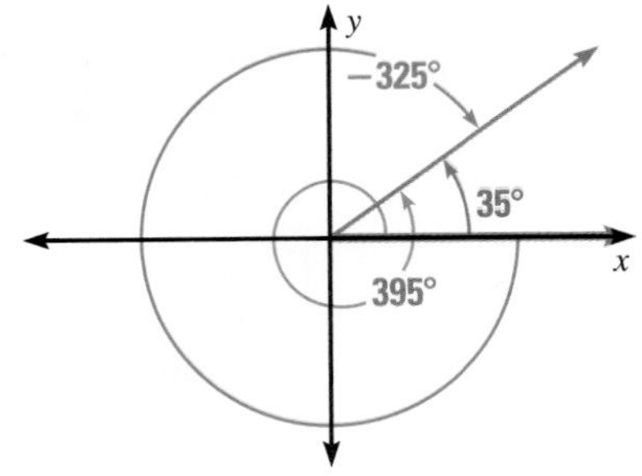

✓ GUIDED PRACTICE for Examples 1 and 2

Draw an angle with the given measure in standard position. Then find one positive coterminal angle and one negative coterminal angle.

1. 65° **2.** 230° **3.** 300° **4.** 740°

RADIAN MEASURE Angles can also be measured in *radians*. To define a radian, consider a circle with radius r centered at the origin as shown. One **radian** is the measure of an angle in standard position whose terminal side intercepts an arc of length r.

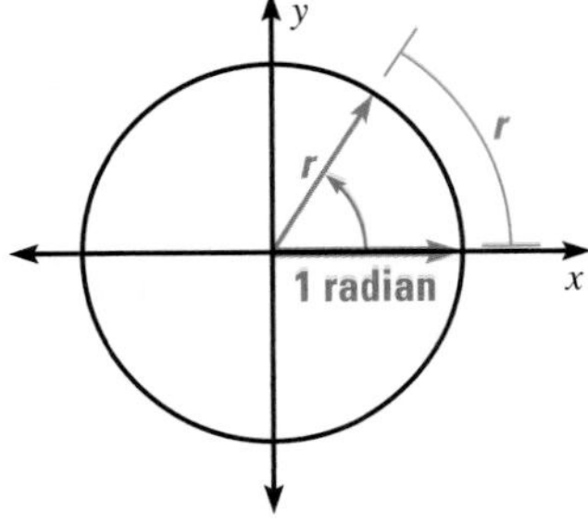

Because the circumference of a circle is $2\pi r$, there are 2π radians in a full circle. Degree measure and radian measure are therefore related by the equation $360° = 2\pi$ radians, or $180° = \pi$ radians.

KEY CONCEPT *For Your Notebook*

Converting Between Degrees and Radians

Degrees to radians

Multiply degree measure by $\frac{\pi \text{ radians}}{180°}$.

Radians to degrees

Multiply radian measure by $\frac{180°}{\pi \text{ radians}}$.

EXAMPLE 3 Convert between degrees and radians

READING The unit "radians" is often omitted. For instance, the measure $-\frac{\pi}{12}$ radians may be written simply as $-\frac{\pi}{12}$.

Convert (a) 125° to radians and (b) $-\frac{\pi}{12}$ radians to degrees.

a. $125° = 125°\left(\frac{\pi \text{ radians}}{180°}\right)$

$= \frac{25\pi}{36}$ radians

b. $-\frac{\pi}{12} = \left(-\frac{\pi}{12} \text{ radians}\right)\left(\frac{180°}{\pi \text{ radians}}\right)$

$= -15°$

CONCEPT SUMMARY *For Your Notebook*

Degree and Radian Measures of Special Angles

The diagram shows equivalent degree and radian measures for special angles from 0° to 360° (0 radians to 2π radians).

You may find it helpful to memorize the equivalent degree and radian measures of special angles in the first quadrant and for $90° = \frac{\pi}{2}$ radians. All other special angles are just multiples of these angles.

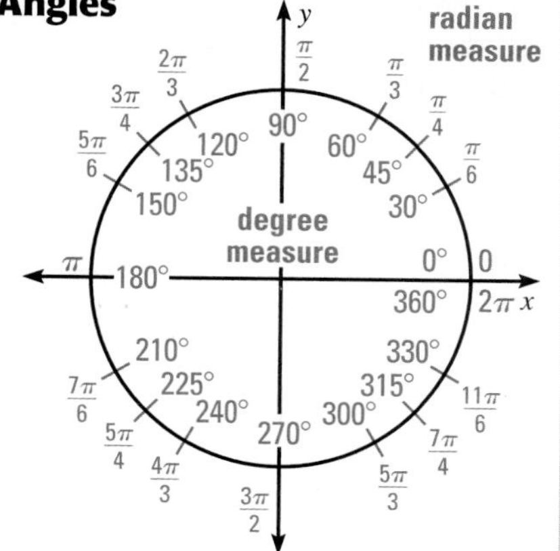

GUIDED PRACTICE for Example 3

Convert the degree measure to radians or the radian measure to degrees.

5. 135°

6. −50°

7. $\frac{5\pi}{4}$

8. $\frac{\pi}{10}$

SECTORS OF CIRCLES A **sector** is a region of a circle that is bounded by two radii and an arc of the circle. The **central angle** θ of a sector is the angle formed by the two radii. There are simple formulas for the arc length and area of a sector when the central angle is measured in radians.

KEY CONCEPT *For Your Notebook*

Arc Length and Area of a Sector

The arc length s and area A of a sector with radius r and central angle θ (measured in radians) are as follows.

Arc length: $s = r\theta$

Area: $A = \frac{1}{2}r^2\theta$

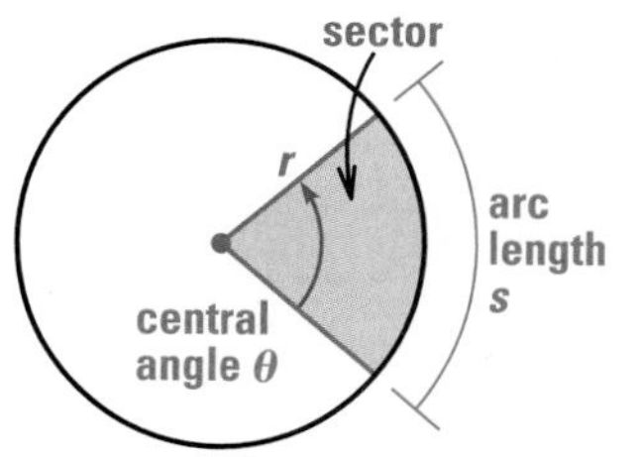

EXAMPLE 4 Solve a multi-step problem

SOFTBALL A softball field forms a sector with the dimensions shown. Find the length of the outfield fence and the area of the field.

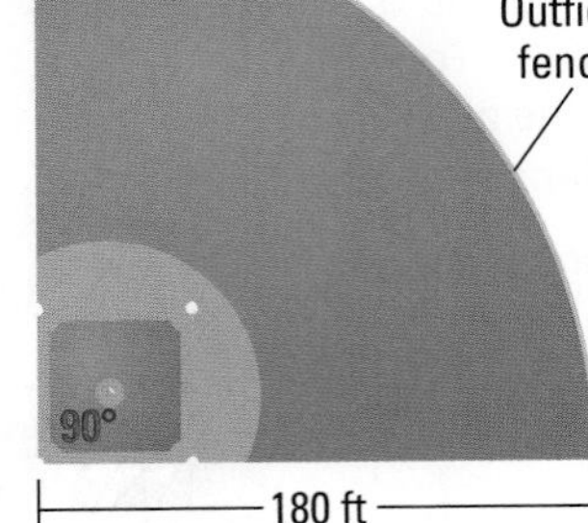

Solution

STEP 1 **Convert** the measure of the central angle to radians.

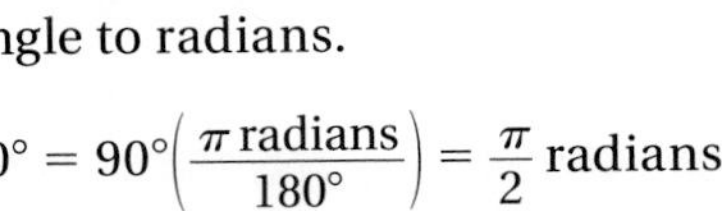

$$90° = 90°\left(\frac{\pi \text{ radians}}{180°}\right) = \frac{\pi}{2} \text{ radians}$$

AVOID ERRORS
You must write the measure of an angle in radians when using the formulas for the arc length and area of a sector.

STEP 2 **Find** the arc length and the area of the sector.

Arc length: $s = r\theta = 180\left(\frac{\pi}{2}\right) = 90\pi \approx 283$ feet

Area: $A = \frac{1}{2}r^2\theta = \frac{1}{2}(180)^2\left(\frac{\pi}{2}\right) = 8100\pi \approx 25{,}400 \text{ ft}^2$

▶ The length of the outfield fence is about 283 feet. The area of the field is about 25,400 square feet.

✓ GUIDED PRACTICE for Example 4

9. **WHAT IF?** In Example 4, estimate the length of the outfield fence and the area of the field if the outfield fence is 220 feet from home plate.

13.2 EXERCISES

HOMEWORK KEY
○ = WORKED-OUT SOLUTIONS on p. WS22 for Exs. 11, 23, and 51
★ = STANDARDIZED TEST PRACTICE Exs. 2, 14, 31, 50, and 53

SKILL PRACTICE

1. **VOCABULARY** Copy and complete: An angle is in standard position if its vertex is at the _?_ and its _?_ lies on the positive x-axis.

2. ★ **WRITING** How does the sign of an angle's measure determine its direction of rotation?

EXAMPLES 1 and 3
on pp. 859–861 for Exs. 3–14

VISUAL THINKING **Match the angle measure with the angle.**

3. $-240°$

4. $600°$

5. $-\frac{9\pi}{4}$

A.

B.

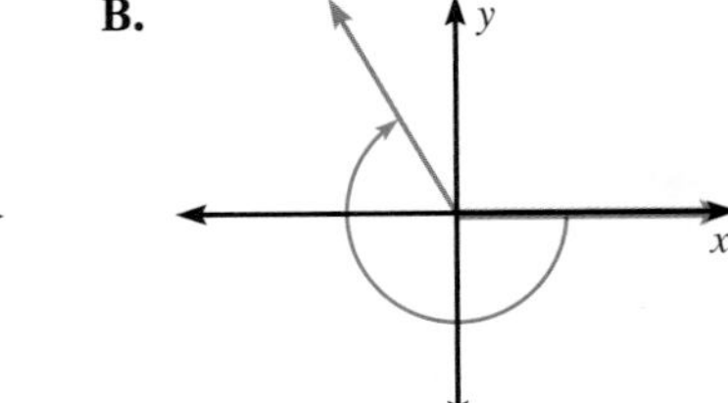

C.

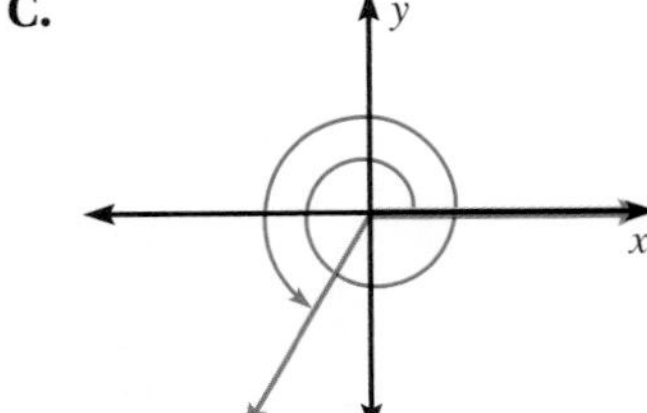

DRAWING ANGLES **Draw an angle with the given measure in standard position.**

6. 110°
7. −10°
8. 450°
9. −900°
10. 6π
11. $\frac{5\pi}{18}$
12. $-\frac{5\pi}{3}$
13. $\frac{26\pi}{9}$

14. ★ **MULTIPLE CHOICE** Which angle measure is shown in the diagram?

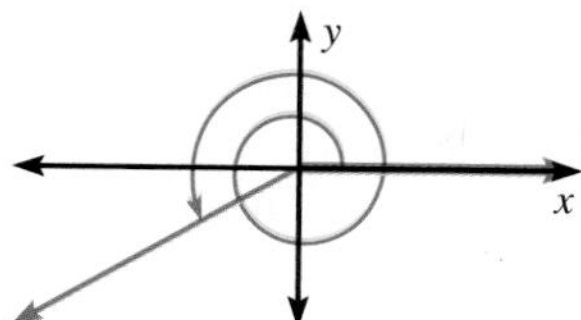

Ⓐ −150° Ⓑ 210° Ⓒ 570° Ⓓ 930°

EXAMPLES 2 and 3
on pp. 860–861 for Exs. 15–22

FINDING COTERMINAL ANGLES **Find one positive angle and one negative angle that are coterminal with the given angle.**

15. 70°
16. 255°
17. −125°
18. 820°
19. $\frac{9\pi}{2}$
20. $-\frac{7\pi}{6}$
21. $\frac{28\pi}{9}$
22. $\frac{20\pi}{3}$

EXAMPLE 3
on p. 861 for Exs. 23–31

CONVERTING MEASURES **Convert the degree measure to radians or the radian measure to degrees.**

23. 40°
24. 315°
25. −260°
26. 500°
27. $\frac{\pi}{9}$
28. $-\frac{\pi}{4}$
29. 5π
30. $\frac{14\pi}{15}$

31. ★ **MULTIPLE CHOICE** Which angle measure is equivalent to $\frac{13\pi}{6}$ radians?

Ⓐ 30° Ⓑ 390° Ⓒ 750° Ⓓ 1110°

EXAMPLE 4
on p. 862 for Exs. 32–38

FINDING ARC LENGTH AND AREA **Find the arc length and area of a sector with the given radius *r* and central angle *θ*.**

32. $r = 4$ in., $\theta = \frac{\pi}{6}$
33. $r = 3$ m, $\theta = \frac{5\pi}{12}$
34. $r = 15$ cm, $\theta = 45°$
35. $r = 12$ ft, $\theta = 150°$
36. $r = 18$ m, $\theta = 25°$
37. $r = 25$ in., $\theta = 270°$

38. **ERROR ANALYSIS** *Describe* and correct the error in finding the area of a sector with a radius of 6 centimeters and a central angle of 40°.

$A = \frac{1}{2}(6)^2(40) = 720 \text{ cm}^2$ ✗

HINT
For Exs. 39–46, set your calculator in radian mode.

EVALUATING FUNCTIONS **Evaluate the trigonometric function using a calculator if necessary. If possible, give an exact answer.**

39. $\cos \frac{\pi}{3}$
40. $\sin \frac{\pi}{4}$
41. $\tan \frac{\pi}{6}$
42. $\sec \frac{\pi}{9}$
43. $\cot \frac{\pi}{8}$
44. $\cos \frac{\pi}{6}$
45. $\sin \frac{3\pi}{7}$
46. $\csc \frac{4\pi}{15}$

47. **CHALLENGE** A rotating object that passes through an angle θ during time t has an angular velocity v given by the formula $v = \frac{\theta}{t}$. Find the angular velocity of the hour hand, the minute hand, and the second hand on a 12 hour clock. Give all answers in degrees per hour.

PROBLEM SOLVING

EXAMPLES 1 and 3 on pp. 859–861 for Exs. 48–50

48. **ASTRONOMY** In astronomy, the *terminator* is the day-night line on a planet that divides the planet into daytime and nighttime regions. The terminator moves across the planet's surface as the planet rotates. It takes about 4 hours for Earth's terminator to move across the continental United States. Through what angle has Earth rotated during this time? Give the answer in both degrees and radians.

@HomeTutor for problem solving help at classzone.com

49. **CD PLAYER** When a CD player reads information from the outer edge of a CD, the CD spins about 200 revolutions per minute. At that speed, through what angle does a point on the CD spin in one minute? Give the answer in both degrees and radians.

@HomeTutor for problem solving help at classzone.com

50. ★ **SHORT RESPONSE** You work every Saturday from 9:00 A.M. to 5:00 P.M. Draw a diagram that shows the rotation completed by the hour hand of a clock during this time. Find the measure of the angle generated by the hour hand in both degrees and radians. *Compare* this angle with the angle generated by the minute hand from 9:00 A.M. to 5:00 P.M.

EXAMPLE 4 on p. 862 for Exs. 51–53

51. **MULTI-STEP PROBLEM** A scientist performed an experiment to study the effects of gravitational force on humans. In order for humans to experience twice Earth's gravity, they were placed in a centrifuge 58 feet long and spun at a rate of about 15 revolutions per minute.

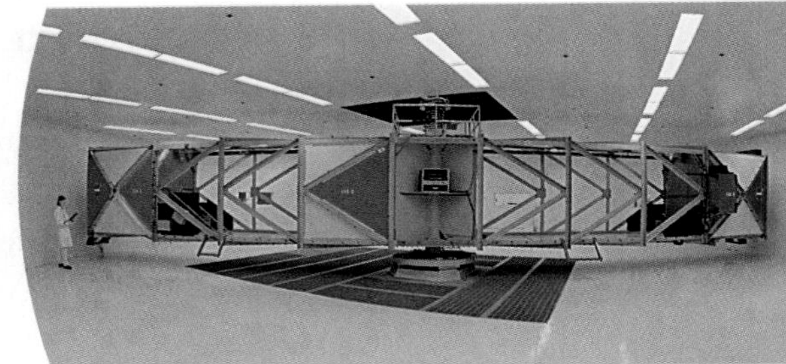

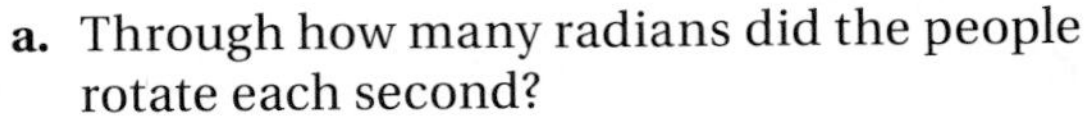

a. Through how many radians did the people rotate each second?

b. Find the length of the arc through which the people rotated each second.

52. **MULTI-STEP PROBLEM** In the shot put event at the 2004 Summer Olympic Games, the winning shot was 21.16 meters. For a shot put to be fair, it must land within a sector having a central angle of 34.92°.

a. If the officials drew an arc across the fair landing area marking the farthest throw, how long would the arc be?

b. All fair shot puts in the 2004 Olympics landed within a sector bounded by the arc from part (a). What is the area of this sector?

53. ★ **EXTENDED RESPONSE** A spiral staircase has 15 steps. Each step is a sector with a radius of 42 inches and a central angle of $\frac{\pi}{8}$.

a. What is the length of the arc formed by the outer edge of a step?

b. Through what angle would you rotate by climbing the stairs? Include a sixteenth turn for stepping up on the landing. *Explain* your reasoning.

c. How many square inches of carpeting would you need to cover the 15 steps?

Animated Algebra at classzone.com

○ = **WORKED-OUT SOLUTIONS** on p. WS1

★ = **STANDARDIZED TEST PRACTICE**

54. CHALLENGE A dartboard is divided into 20 sectors. Each sector is worth a point value from 1 to 20 and has shaded regions that double or triple this value. A sector is shown below.

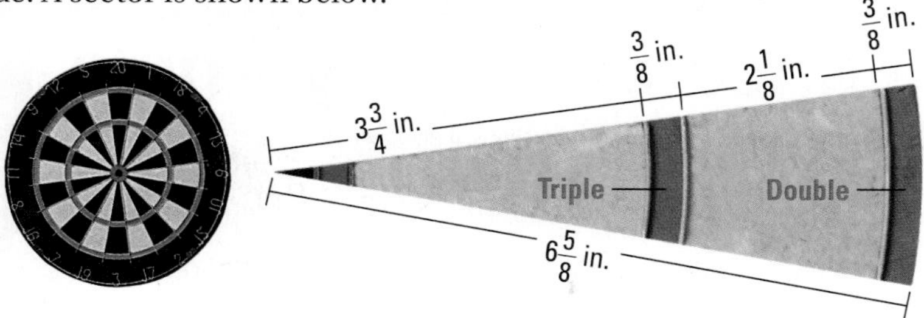

a. Find the areas of the entire sector, the double region, and the triple region.

b. A dart you throw randomly lands somewhere inside the sector. What is the probability that it lands in the double region? in the triple region?

NEW YORK MIXED REVIEW

TEST PRACTICE at classzone.com

55. Lou saves \$12 per week to buy an acoustic guitar that costs \$280. Which equation best represents the relationship between the amount of money Lou still needs to save, m, and the number of weeks, n, that he has been saving?

Ⓐ $m = 280 + 12n$ Ⓑ $m = 280 - 12n$

Ⓒ $m = (280 + 12)n$ Ⓓ $m = (280 - 12)n$

56. Stewart randomly selects two cards from a standard deck of 52 cards. What is the probability that the first card is a heart and the second card is red if he replaces the first card before selecting the second?

Ⓐ 0.063 Ⓑ 0.123 Ⓒ 0.125 Ⓓ 0.75

QUIZ *for Lessons 13.1–13.2*

Solve $\triangle ABC$ using the diagram and the given measurements. *(p. 852)*

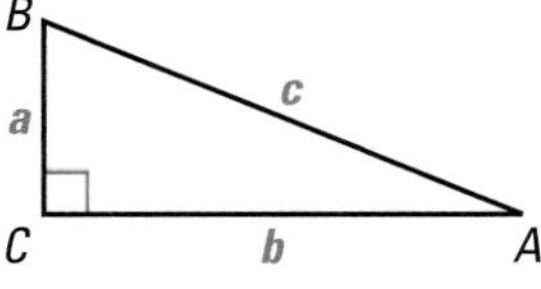

1. $A = 50°, a = 14$ **2.** $A = 25°, b = 10$

3. $B = 70°, a = 5$ **4.** $B = 42°, c = 18$

5. $A = 15°, a = 9$ **6.** $B = 37°, c = 12$

Find one positive angle and one negative angle that are coterminal with the given angle. *(p. 859)*

7. 115° **8.** 290° **9.** $\frac{4\pi}{9}$ **10.** $\frac{7\pi}{5}$

11. Find the arc length and area of a sector with a radius of 8 inches and a central angle of $\theta = 115°$. *(p. 859)*

12. ESCALATOR The escalator at the Wilshire/Vermont Metro Rail Station in Los Angeles has an angle of elevation of 30°. The length of the escalator is 152 feet. What is the height of the escalator? *(p. 852)*

13.3 Evaluate Trigonometric Functions of Any Angle

A2.A.62 Find the value of trigonometric functions, if given a point on the terminal side of angle θ

Before You evaluated trigonometric functions of an acute angle.

Now You will evaluate trigonometric functions of any angle.

Why? So you can calculate distances involving rotating objects, as in Ex. 37.

Key Vocabulary
- **unit circle**
- **quadrantal angle**
- **reference angle**

You can generalize the right-triangle definitions of trigonometric functions from Lesson 13.1 so that they apply to *any* angle in standard position.

KEY CONCEPT *For Your Notebook*

General Definitions of Trigonometric Functions

Let θ be an angle in standard position, and let (x, y) be the point where the terminal side of θ intersects the circle $x^2 + y^2 = r^2$. The six trigonometric functions of θ are defined as follows:

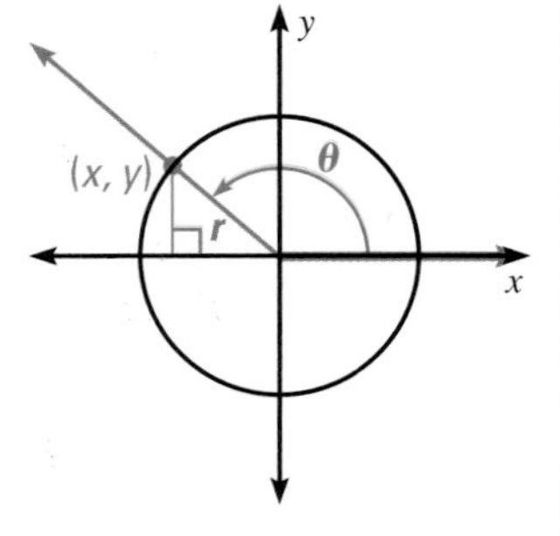

$\sin \theta = \frac{y}{r}$ $\qquad$ $\csc \theta = \frac{r}{y}, y \neq 0$

$\cos \theta = \frac{x}{r}$ $\qquad$ $\sec \theta = \frac{r}{x}, x \neq 0$

$\tan \theta = \frac{y}{x}, x \neq 0$ $\qquad$ $\cot \theta = \frac{x}{y}, y \neq 0$

These functions are sometimes called *circular functions.*

EXAMPLE 1 Evaluate trigonometric functions given a point

Let $(-4, 3)$ be a point on the terminal side of an angle θ in standard position. Evaluate the six trigonometric functions of θ.

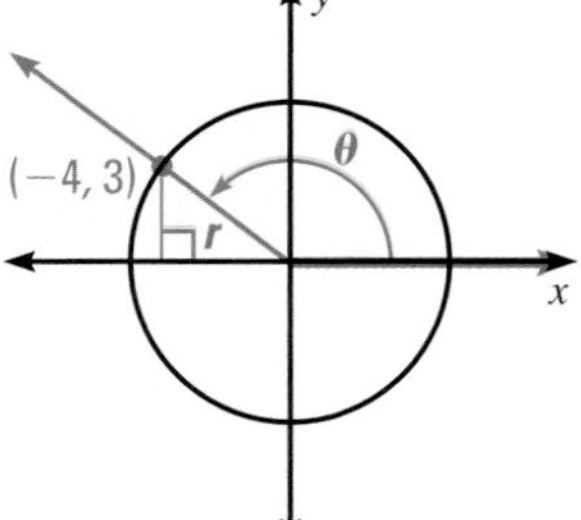

Solution

Use the Pythagorean theorem to find the value of r.

$$r = \sqrt{x^2 + y^2} = \sqrt{(-4)^2 + 3^2} = \sqrt{25} = 5$$

Using $x = -4$, $y = 3$, and $r = 5$, you can write the following:

$\sin \theta = \frac{y}{r} = \frac{3}{5}$ $\qquad$ $\cos \theta = \frac{x}{r} = -\frac{4}{5}$ $\qquad$ $\tan \theta = \frac{y}{x} = -\frac{3}{4}$

$\csc \theta = \frac{r}{y} = \frac{5}{3}$ $\qquad$ $\sec \theta = \frac{r}{x} = -\frac{5}{4}$ $\qquad$ $\cot \theta = \frac{x}{y} = -\frac{4}{3}$

KEY CONCEPT — *For Your Notebook*

The Unit Circle

The circle $x^2 + y^2 = 1$, which has center (0, 0) and radius 1, is called the **unit circle**. The values of $\sin \theta$ and $\cos \theta$ are simply the y-coordinate and x-coordinate, respectively, of the point where the terminal side of θ intersects the unit circle.

$$\sin \theta = \frac{y}{r} = \frac{y}{1} = y \qquad \cos \theta = \frac{x}{r} = \frac{x}{1} = x$$

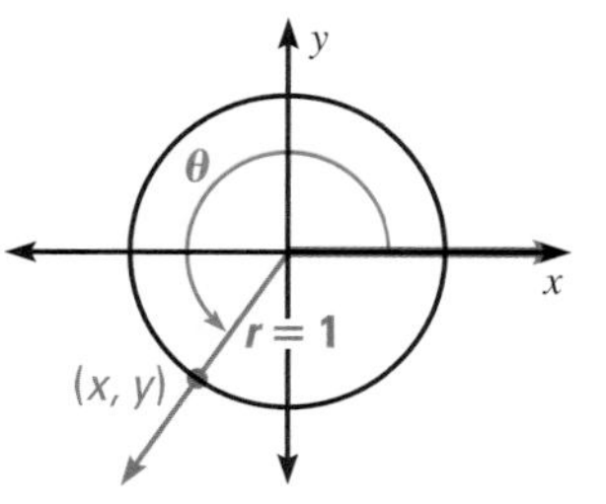

It is convenient to use the unit circle to find trigonometric functions of *quadrantal angles*. A **quadrantal angle** is an angle in standard position whose terminal side lies on an axis. The measure of a quadrantal angle is always a multiple of 90°, or $\frac{\pi}{2}$ radians.

EXAMPLE 2 Use the unit circle

Use the unit circle to evaluate the six trigonometric functions of $\theta = 270°$.

ANOTHER WAY

The general circle $x^2 + y^2 = r^2$ can also be used to find the trigonometric functions of $\theta = 270°$. The terminal side of θ intersects the circle at $(0, -r)$. Therefore:

$$\sin \theta = \frac{y}{r} = \frac{-r}{r} = -1$$

The other functions can be evaluated similarly.

Solution

Draw the unit circle, then draw the angle $\theta = 270°$ in standard position. The terminal side of θ intersects the unit circle at $(0, -1)$, so use $x = 0$ and $y = -1$ to evaluate the trigonometric functions.

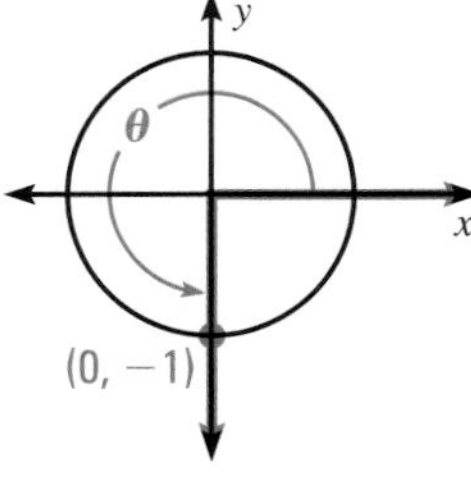

$\sin \theta = \frac{y}{r} = \frac{-1}{1} = -1$ $\qquad \csc \theta = \frac{r}{y} = \frac{1}{-1} = -1$

$\cos \theta = \frac{x}{r} = \frac{0}{1} = 0$ $\qquad \sec \theta = \frac{r}{x} = \frac{1}{0}$ undefined

$\tan \theta = \frac{y}{x} = \frac{-1}{0}$ undefined $\qquad \cot \theta = \frac{x}{y} = \frac{0}{-1} = 0$

Animated Algebra at classzone.com

✓ GUIDED PRACTICE for Examples 1 and 2

Evaluate the six trigonometric functions of θ.

1. (3, −3)

2.

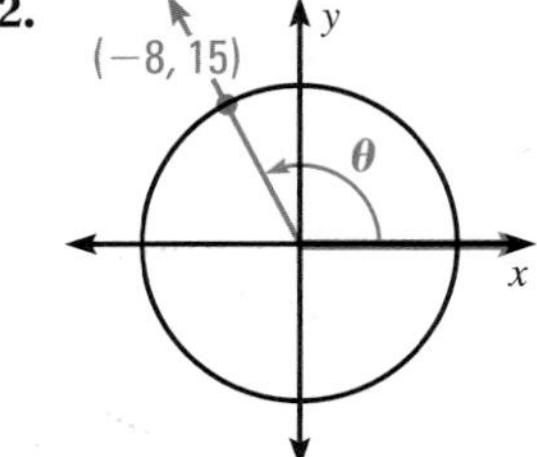

3.

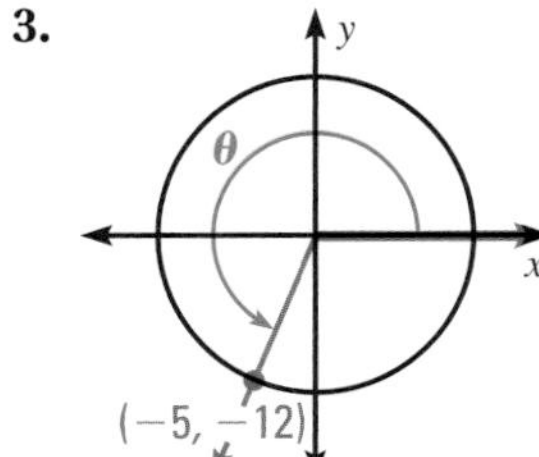

4. Use the unit circle to evaluate the six trigonometric functions of $\theta = 180°$.

READING The symbol θ' is read as "theta prime."

KEY CONCEPT *For Your Notebook*

Reference Angle Relationships

Let θ be an angle in standard position. The **reference angle** for θ is the acute angle θ' formed by the terminal side of θ and the x-axis. The relationship between θ and θ' is shown below for nonquadrantal angles θ such that $90° < \theta < 360°$ $\left(\frac{\pi}{2} < \theta < 2\pi\right)$.

Quadrant II

Degrees: $\theta' = 180° - \theta$
Radians: $\theta' = \pi - \theta$

Quadrant III

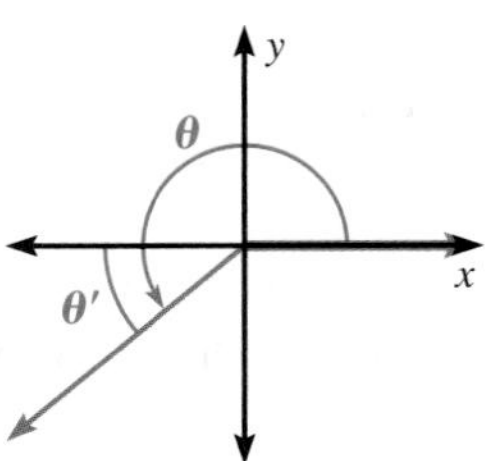

Degrees: $\theta' = \theta - 180°$
Radians: $\theta' = \theta - \pi$

Quadrant IV

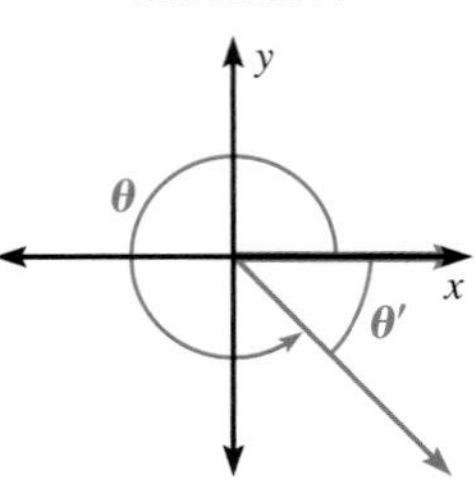

Degrees: $\theta' = 360° - \theta$
Radians: $\theta' = 2\pi - \theta$

EXAMPLE 3 Find reference angles

Find the reference angle θ' for (a) $\theta = \frac{5\pi}{3}$ and (b) $\theta = -130°$.

Solution

a. The terminal side of θ lies in Quadrant IV. So, $\theta' = 2\pi - \frac{5\pi}{3} = \frac{\pi}{3}$.

b. Note that θ is coterminal with 230°, whose terminal side lies in Quadrant III. So, $\theta' = 230° - 180° = 50°$.

EVALUATING TRIGONOMETRIC FUNCTIONS Reference angles allow you to evaluate a trigonometric function for any angle θ. The sign of the trigonometric function value depends on the quadrant in which θ lies.

KEY CONCEPT *For Your Notebook*

Evaluating Trigonometric Functions

Use these steps to evaluate a trigonometric function for any angle θ:

STEP 1 **Find** the reference angle θ'.

STEP 2 **Evaluate** the trigonometric function for θ'.

STEP 3 **Determine** the sign of the trigonometric function value from the quadrant in which θ lies.

Signs of Function Values

Quadrant II	Quadrant I
$\sin\theta, \csc\theta$: +	$\sin\theta, \csc\theta$: +
$\cos\theta, \sec\theta$: −	$\cos\theta, \sec\theta$: +
$\tan\theta, \cot\theta$: −	$\tan\theta, \cot\theta$: +
Quadrant III	**Quadrant IV**
$\sin\theta, \csc\theta$: −	$\sin\theta, \csc\theta$: −
$\cos\theta, \sec\theta$: −	$\cos\theta, \sec\theta$: +
$\tan\theta, \cot\theta$: +	$\tan\theta, \cot\theta$: −

EXAMPLE 4 Use reference angles to evaluate functions

Evaluate (a) tan (−240°) and (b) csc $\frac{17\pi}{6}$.

Solution

a. The angle −240° is coterminal with 120°. The reference angle is $\theta' = 180° - 120° = 60°$. The tangent function is negative in Quadrant II, so you can write:

$$\tan(-240°) = -\tan 60° = -\sqrt{3}$$

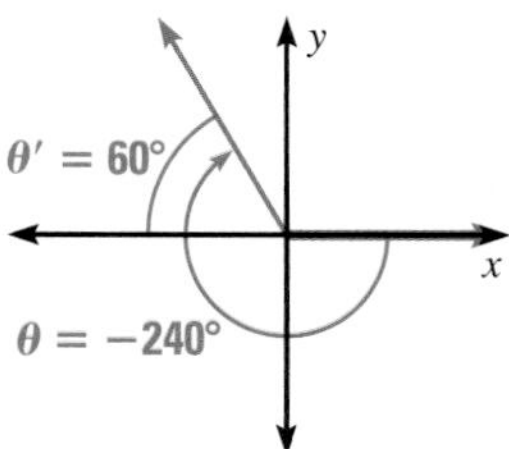

b. The angle $\frac{17\pi}{6}$ is coterminal with $\frac{5\pi}{6}$. The reference angle is $\theta' = \pi - \frac{5\pi}{6} = \frac{\pi}{6}$. The cosecant function is positive in Quadrant II, so you can write:

$$\csc \frac{17\pi}{6} = \csc \frac{\pi}{6} = 2$$

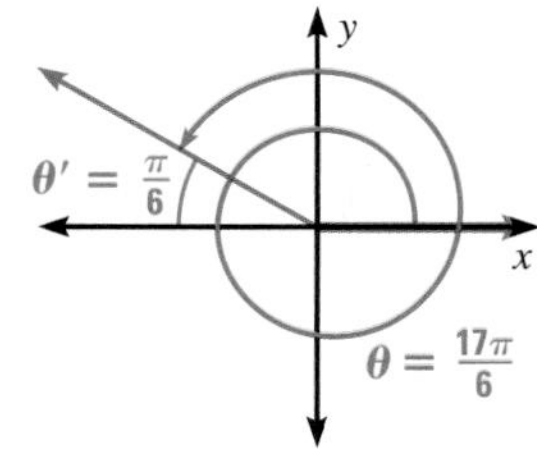

✓ GUIDED PRACTICE for Examples 3 and 4

Sketch the angle. Then find its reference angle.

5. 210° **6.** −260° **7.** $-\frac{7\pi}{9}$ **8.** $\frac{15\pi}{4}$

9. Evaluate cos (−210°) without using a calculator.

EXAMPLE 5 Calculate horizontal distance traveled

ROBOTICS The "frogbot" is a robot designed for exploring rough terrain on other planets. It can jump at a 45° angle and with an initial speed of 16 feet per second. On Earth, the horizontal distance d (in feet) traveled by a projectile launched at an angle θ and with an initial speed v (in feet per second) is given by:

Frogbot

INTERPRET MODELS
This model neglects air resistance and assumes that the projectile's starting and ending heights are the same.

$$d = \frac{v^2}{32} \sin 2\theta$$

How far can the frogbot jump on Earth?

Solution

$d = \frac{v^2}{32} \sin 2\theta$ **Write model for horizontal distance.**

$= \frac{16^2}{32} \sin (2 \cdot 45°)$ **Substitute 16 for v and 45° for θ.**

$= 8$ **Simplify.**

▶ The frogbot can jump a horizontal distance of 8 feet on Earth.

EXAMPLE 6 Model with a trigonometric function

ROCK CLIMBING A rock climber is using a rock climbing treadmill that is 10.5 feet long. The climber begins by lying horizontally on the treadmill, which is then rotated about its midpoint by 110° so that the rock climber is climbing towards the top. If the midpoint of the treadmill is 6 feet above the ground, how high above the ground is the top of the treadmill?

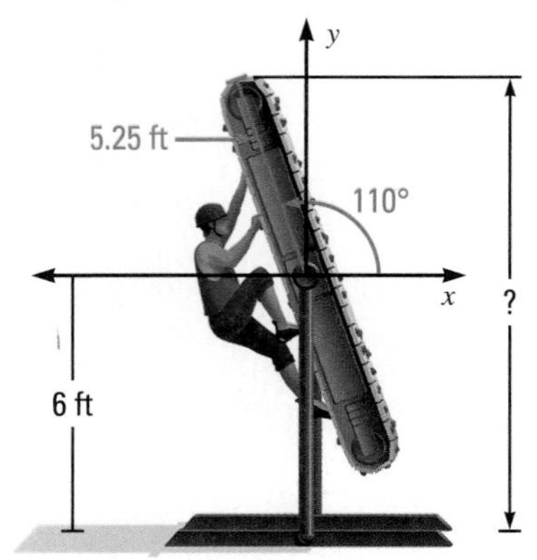

Solution

$\sin \theta = \frac{y}{r}$ **Use definition of sine.**

$\sin 110° = \frac{y}{5.25}$ **Substitute 110° for θ and $\frac{10.5}{2} = 5.25$ for r.**

$4.9 \approx y$ **Solve for y.**

▶ The top of the treadmill is about $6 + 4.9 = 10.9$ feet above the ground.

GUIDED PRACTICE for Examples 5 and 6

10. **TRACK AND FIELD** Estimate the horizontal distance traveled by a track and field long jumper who jumps at an angle of 20° and with an initial speed of 27 feet per second.

11. **WHAT IF?** In Example 6, how high is the top of the rock climbing treadmill if it is rotated 100° about its midpoint?

13.3 EXERCISES

HOMEWORK KEY
○ = **WORKED-OUT SOLUTIONS** on p. WS22 for Exs. 5, 17, and 37
★ = **STANDARDIZED TEST PRACTICE** Exs. 2, 11, 33, 37, and 39

SKILL PRACTICE

1. **VOCABULARY** Copy and complete: A(n) __?__ is an angle in standard position whose terminal side lies on an axis.

2. ★ **WRITING** Given an angle θ in Quadrant III, explain how you can use a reference angle to find $\cos \theta$.

EXAMPLE 1 on p. 866 for Exs. 3–11

USING A POINT Use the given point on the terminal side of an angle θ in standard position to evaluate the six trigonometric functions of θ.

3. (8, 15)
4. (−9, 12)
5. (−7, −24)
6. (5, −12)
7. (2, −2)
8. (−6, 9)
9. (−3, −5)
10. $(5, -\sqrt{11})$

11. ★ **MULTIPLE CHOICE** Let (−7, −4) be a point on the terminal side of an angle θ in standard position. What is the value of $\tan \theta$?

Ⓐ $-\frac{7}{4}$ Ⓑ $-\frac{4}{7}$ Ⓒ $\frac{4}{7}$ Ⓓ $\frac{7}{4}$

EXAMPLE 3 Standardized Test Practice

What is the measure of the angle θ in the triangle shown?

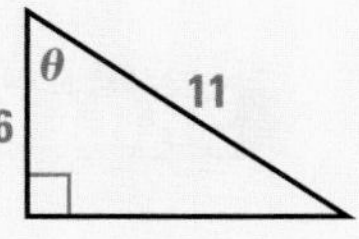

Ⓐ 28.6° Ⓑ 33.1°

Ⓒ 56.9° Ⓓ 61.4°

AVOID ERRORS

All the answer choices are in degrees. Therefore, check that your calculator is set in degree mode, not radian mode.

Solution

In the right triangle, you are given the lengths of the side adjacent to θ and the hypotenuse, so use the inverse cosine function to solve for θ.

$$\cos \theta = \frac{\text{adj}}{\text{hyp}} = \frac{6}{11} \quad \longrightarrow \quad \theta = \cos^{-1}\frac{6}{11} \approx 56.9°$$

▶ The correct answer is C. Ⓐ Ⓑ Ⓒ Ⓓ

EXAMPLE 4 Write and solve a trigonometric equation

MONSTER TRUCKS A monster truck drives off a ramp in order to jump onto a row of cars. The ramp has a height of 8 feet and a horizontal length of 20 feet. What is the angle θ of the ramp?

Solution

STEP 1 **Draw** a triangle that represents the ramp.

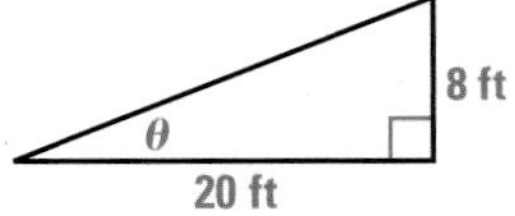

STEP 2 **Write** a trigonometric equation that involves the ratio of the ramp's height and horizontal length.

$$\tan \theta = \frac{\text{opp}}{\text{adj}} = \frac{8}{20}$$

STEP 3 **Use** a calculator to find the measure of θ.

$$\theta = \tan^{-1}\frac{8}{20} \approx 21.8°$$

▶ The angle of the ramp is about 22°.

✓ GUIDED PRACTICE for Examples 3 and 4

Find the measure of the angle θ.

11.

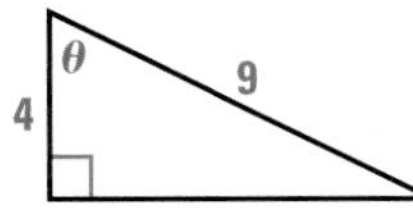

12.

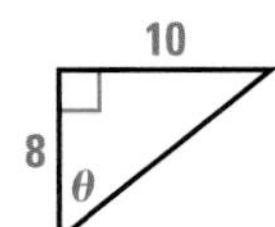

13.

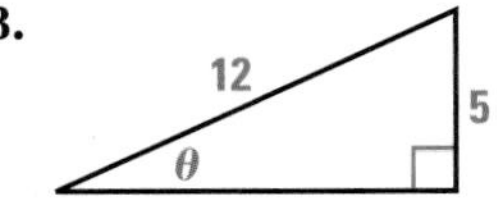

14. WHAT IF? In Example 4, suppose a monster truck drives 26 feet on a ramp before jumping onto a row of cars. If the ramp is 10 feet high, what is the angle θ of the ramp?

13.4 EXERCISES

HOMEWORK KEY

○ = **WORKED-OUT SOLUTIONS** on p. WS22 for Exs. 7, 23, and 37

★ = **STANDARDIZED TEST PRACTICE** Exs. 2, 11, 30, 31, 37, and 38

SKILL PRACTICE

1. **VOCABULARY** Copy and complete: The __?__ sine of $\frac{1}{2}$ is $\frac{\pi}{6}$, or 30°.

2. ★ **WRITING** *Explain* why $\tan^{-1} 3$ is defined, but $\cos^{-1} 3$ is undefined.

EXAMPLE 1 on p. 876 for Exs. 3–11

EVALUATING EXPRESSIONS Evaluate the expression without using a calculator. Give your answer in both radians and degrees.

3. $\sin^{-1} 1$
4. $\tan^{-1} (-1)$
5. $\cos^{-1} 0$
6. $\cos^{-1} (-2)$
7. $\sin^{-1} \frac{\sqrt{3}}{2}$
8. $\sin^{-1} \frac{1}{2}$
9. $\tan^{-1} \left(-\frac{\sqrt{3}}{3}\right)$
10. $\cos^{-1} \left(-\frac{1}{2}\right)$

11. ★ **MULTIPLE CHOICE** What is the value of the expression $\cos^{-1} \frac{\sqrt{2}}{2}$?

Ⓐ 0° Ⓑ 30° Ⓒ 45° Ⓓ 60°

USING A CALCULATOR Use a calculator to evaluate the expression in both radians and degrees.

12. $\sin^{-1} 0.18$
13. $\tan^{-1} 2.6$
14. $\cos^{-1} 0.36$
15. $\cos^{-1} (-0.4)$
16. $\tan^{-1} (-0.75)$
17. $\sin^{-1} (-0.2)$
18. $\sin^{-1} 0.8$
19. $\cos^{-1} 0.99$

EXAMPLE 2 on p. 876 for Exs. 20–26

SOLVING EQUATIONS Solve the equation for θ.

20. $\cos \theta = -0.82$; $180° < \theta < 270°$
21. $\sin \theta = -0.45$; $180° < \theta < 270°$
22. $\sin \theta = 0.15$; $90° < \theta < 180°$
23. $\tan \theta = 3.2$; $180° < \theta < 270°$
24. $\tan \theta = -5.3$; $90° < \theta < 180°$
25. $\cos \theta = 0.25$; $270° < \theta < 360°$

26. **ERROR ANALYSIS** *Describe* and correct the error in solving the equation $\sin \theta = 0.7$ where $90° < \theta < 180°$.

The angle whose sine is 0.7 is $\sin^{-1} 0.7 \approx 44.4°$, so $\theta \approx 44.4°$.

EXAMPLE 3 on p. 877 for Exs. 27–29

FINDING ANGLES Find the measure of the angle θ.

27.

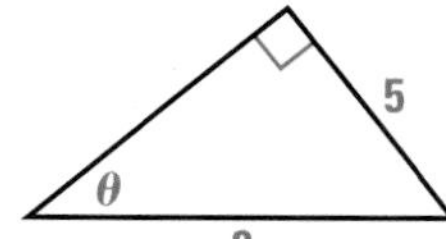

28.

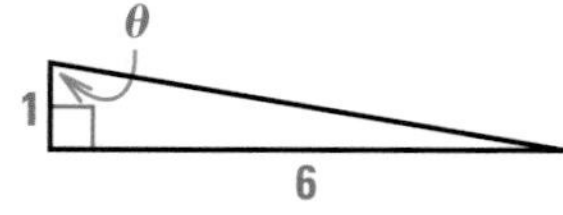

29.

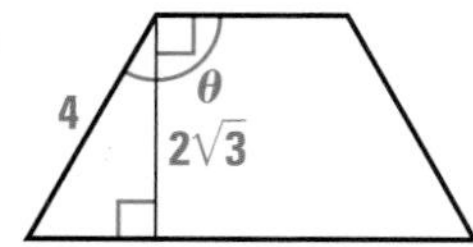

30. ★ **OPEN-ENDED MATH** Suppose $\cos \theta > 0$ and $\sin \theta < 0$. Give a possible value of θ such that $-360° \le \theta \le 0°$.

31. ★ **OPEN-ENDED MATH** Suppose $\sin \theta < 0$ and $\tan \theta > 0$. Give a possible value of θ such that $360° \le \theta \le 720°$.

CHALLENGE Rewrite the expression so that it does not involve trigonometric functions or inverse trigonometric functions.

32. $\csc (\sin^{-1} x)$
33. $\cot (\tan^{-1} x)$
34. $\sec (\cos^{-1} x)$

PROBLEM SOLVING

EXAMPLE 4 on p. 877 for Exs. 35–37

35. **LADDER ANGLE** A fire truck has a 100 foot ladder whose base is 10 feet above the ground. A firefighter extends a ladder toward a burning building to reach a window 90 feet above the ground. Draw a diagram to represent this situation. At what angle should the firefighter set the ladder?

@HomeTutor for problem solving help at classzone.com

36. **ANGLE OF DESCENT** An airplane is flying at an altitude of 31,000 feet when it begins its descent for landing. If the runway is 104 miles away, at what angle does the airplane descend?

@HomeTutor for problem solving help at classzone.com

37. ★ **SHORT RESPONSE** Different types of granular substances naturally settle at different angles when stored in cone-shaped piles. The angle θ is called the *angle of repose*. When rock salt is stored in a cone-shaped pile 11 feet high, the diameter of the pile's base is about 34 feet. Find the angle of repose for rock salt. If another pile of rock salt is 15 feet high, what is the diameter of its base? *Explain.*

38. ★ **EXTENDED RESPONSE** If you are in shallow water and look at an object below the surface of the water, the object will look farther away from you than it really is. This is because when light rays pass between air and water, the water *refracts*, or bends, the light rays. The *index of refraction* for water is 1.333. This is the ratio of the sine of θ_1 to the sine of θ_2 for the angles θ_1 and θ_2 shown below.

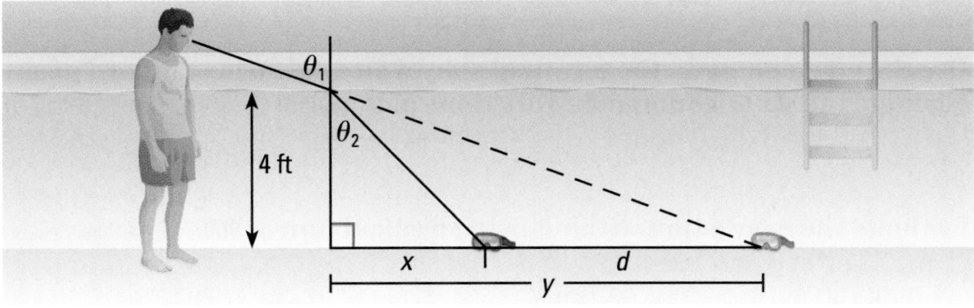

a. You are in 4 feet of water in the shallow end of a pool. You look down at some goggles at angle $\theta_1 = 70°$ (measured from a line perpendicular to the surface of the water). Find θ_2.

b. Find the distances x and y.

c. Find the distance d between where the goggles are and where they appear to be.

d. *Explain* what happens to d as you move closer to the goggles.

39. **CYCLING** As a spectator at a cycling road race, you are sitting 100 feet from the center of a straightaway. A cyclist traveling 30 miles per hour passes in front of you. At what angle do you have to turn your head to see the cyclist t seconds later? Assume the cyclist is still on the straightaway and is traveling at a constant speed. (*Hint:* First convert 30 miles per hour to a speed v in feet per second. The expression vt represents the distance, in feet, traveled by the cyclist.)

40. CHALLENGE You want to photograph a painting with a camera mounted on a tripod. The painting is 3 feet tall, and the bottom of the painting is 1 foot above the camera lens, as shown. How far should the camera be positioned from the wall in order to have the largest possible viewing angle θ when you take the photograph? (*Hint:* Write an equation for θ in terms of x only, and then use a graphing calculator to find the value of x that maximizes θ.)

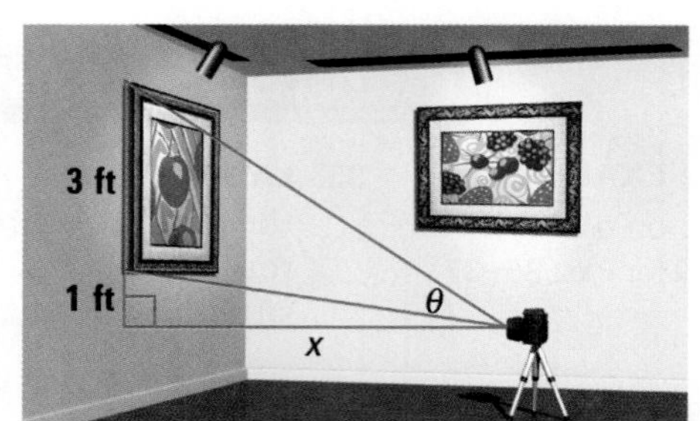

NEW YORK MIXED REVIEW

TEST PRACTICE at classzone.com

41. The graph of which linear equation has a slope of $-\frac{2}{5}$?

Ⓐ $-5x - 2y = -15$ Ⓑ $2x - 5y = -15$

Ⓒ $2x + 5y = -15$ Ⓓ $5x + 2y = -15$

42. Steve plants a flower bed next to a corner of a building. The flower bed forms part of a circle with a radius of 10 feet. What is the flower bed's approximate area?

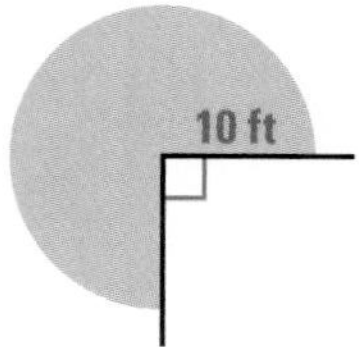

Ⓐ 47.1 ft^2 Ⓑ 78.5 ft^2

Ⓒ 226.9 ft^2 Ⓓ 235.6 ft^2

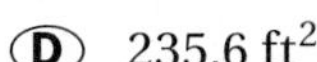

QUIZ for Lessons 13.3–13.4

Use the given point on the terminal side of an angle θ in standard position to evaluate the six trigonometric functions of θ. *(p. 866)*

1. $(6, -2)$ **2.** $(-7, 5)$ **3.** $(4, 8)$ **4.** $(-12, -3)$

Evaluate the expression without using a calculator. *(p. 866)*

5. $\cos 150°$ **6.** $\tan \frac{8\pi}{3}$ **7.** $\sin(-840°)$ **8.** $\sec\left(-\frac{15\pi}{4}\right)$

Evaluate the expression without using a calculator. Give your answer in both radians and degrees. *(p. 875)*

9. $\cos^{-1}\left(-\frac{\sqrt{2}}{2}\right)$ **10.** $\sin^{-1}(-1)$ **11.** $\tan^{-1}\frac{\sqrt{3}}{3}$ **12.** $\cos^{-1}\frac{1}{2}$

Solve the equation for θ. *(p. 875)*

13. $\sin\theta = 0.3;\ 90° < \theta < 180°$ **14.** $\tan\theta = 6;\ 180° < \theta < 270°$

15. $\cos\theta = -0.72;\ 90° < \theta < 180°$ **16.** $\sin\theta = -0.55;\ 270° < \theta < 360°$

17. ACROBATICS A stuntman uses a 30 foot rope to swing 136° between two platforms of equal height, grazing the ground in the middle of the swing. If the rope stays taut throughout the swing, how far above the ground was the stuntman at the beginning and the end of the swing? How far apart are the two platforms? *(p. 875)*

Geometry Software ACTIVITY *Use before Lesson 13.5*

@HomeTutor
classzone.com
Keystrokes

13.5 Explore the Law of Sines

QUESTION **How can you use geometry software to explore the law of sines?**

EXPLORE **Investigate a relationship between the angles and sides of a triangle**

STEP 1 ***Draw a triangle***

Draw $\triangle ABC$. Label the vertices and sides as shown.

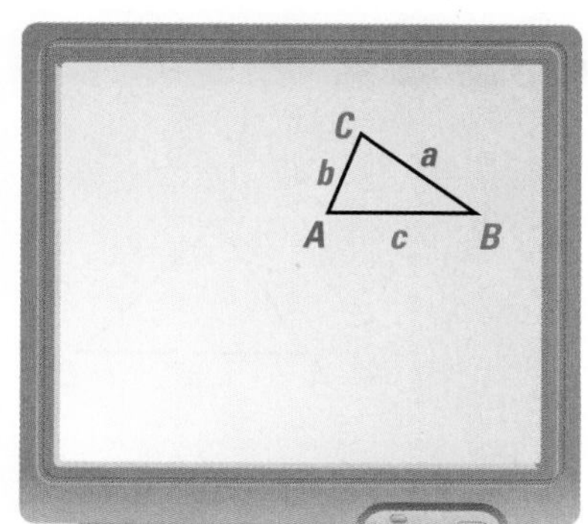

STEP 2 ***Measure parts of triangle***

Find the side lengths a, b, and c. Also find the measures of angles A, B, and C.

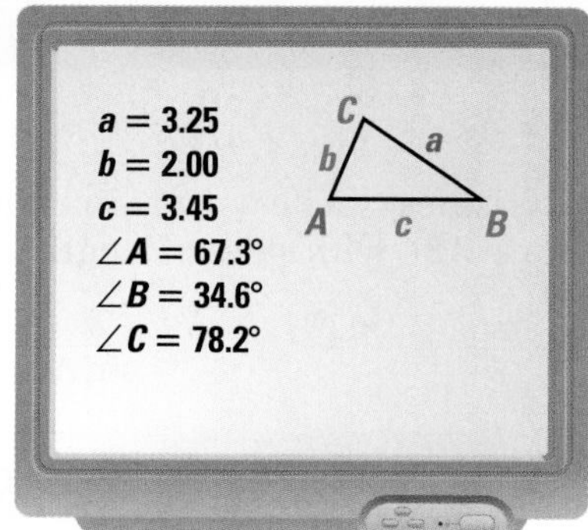

STEP 3 ***Calculate ratios***

Find the ratios $\frac{\sin A}{a}$, $\frac{\sin B}{b}$, and $\frac{\sin C}{c}$.

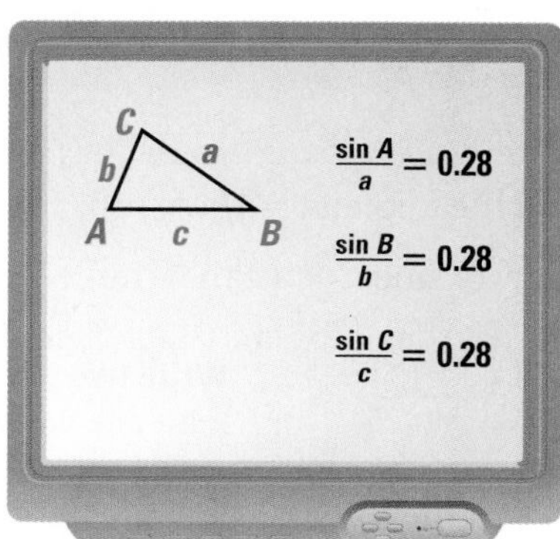

DRAW CONCLUSIONS **Use your observations to complete these exercises**

1. What are the values of the ratios $\frac{\sin A}{a}$, $\frac{\sin B}{b}$, and $\frac{\sin C}{c}$ for your triangle? What do you notice about these values?
2. Change the shape of your triangle by dragging its vertices, and observe how the ratios you found in Step 3 change. Make a conjecture about how these ratios are related for *any* triangle.

13.5 Apply the Law of Sines

 **A2.A.73** Solve for an unknown side or angle, using the Law of Sines or the Law of Cosines

 You solved right triangles.

Now You will solve triangles that have no right angle.

Why? So you can find the distance between faraway objects, as in Ex. 44.

Key Vocabulary
- **law of sines**

In Lesson 13.1, you solved right triangles. To solve a triangle with no right angle, you need to know the length of at least one side and any two other parts of the triangle. The **law of sines** can be used to solve triangles when two angles and the length of any side are known (AAS or ASA cases), or when the lengths of two sides and an angle opposite one of the two sides are known (SSA case).

KEY CONCEPT *For Your Notebook*

Law of Sines

The law of sines can be written in either of the following forms for $\triangle ABC$ with sides of length a, b, and c.

$$\frac{\sin A}{a} = \frac{\sin B}{b} = \frac{\sin C}{c} \qquad \frac{a}{\sin A} = \frac{b}{\sin B} = \frac{c}{\sin C}$$

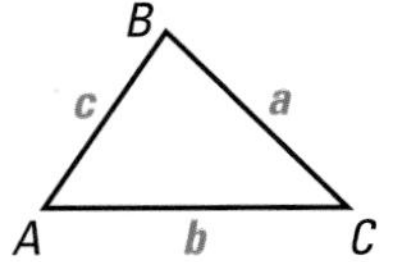

EXAMPLE 1 Solve a triangle for the AAS or ASA case

Solve $\triangle ABC$ with $C = 107°$, $B = 25°$, and $b = 15$.

Solution

First find the angle: $A = 180° - 107° - 25° = 48°$.

By the law of sines, you can write $\frac{a}{\sin 48°} = \frac{15}{\sin 25°} = \frac{c}{\sin 107°}$.

$\frac{a}{\sin 48°} = \frac{15}{\sin 25°}$ **Write two equations, each with one variable.** $\frac{c}{\sin 107°} = \frac{15}{\sin 25°}$

$a = \frac{15 \sin 48°}{\sin 25°}$ **Solve for each variable.** $c = \frac{15 \sin 107°}{\sin 25°}$

$a \approx 26.4$ **Use a calculator.** $c \approx 33.9$

▶ In $\triangle ABC$, $A = 48°$, $a \approx 26.4$, and $c \approx 33.9$.

 **GUIDED PRACTICE** for Example 1

Solve $\triangle ABC$.

1. $B = 34°, C = 100°, b = 8$

2. $A = 51°, B = 44°, c = 11$

DESCRIBE CASES
Because the SSA case can result in 0, 1, or 2 triangles, it is called the *ambiguous case.*

SSA CASE Two angles and one side (AAS or ASA) determine exactly one triangle. Two sides and an angle opposite one of the sides (SSA) may determine no triangle, one triangle, or two triangles.

KEY CONCEPT *For Your Notebook*

Possible Triangles in the SSA Case

Consider a triangle in which you are given a, b, and A. By fixing side b and angle A, you can sketch the possible positions of side a to figure out how many triangles can be formed. In the diagrams below, note that $h = b \sin A$.

***A* is obtuse.**

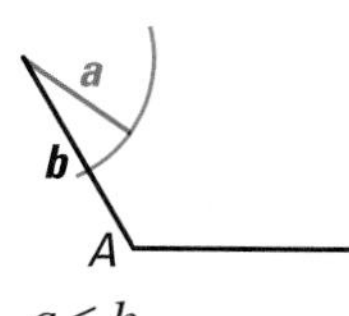

$a \le b$
No triangle

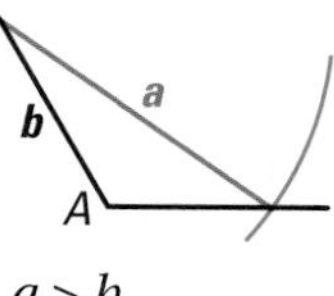

$a > b$
One triangle

***A* is acute.**

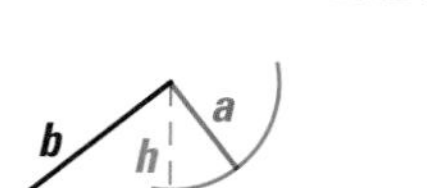

$h > a$
No triangle

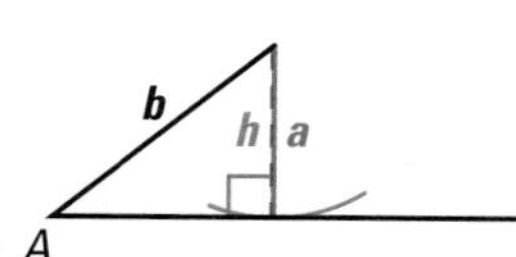

$h = a$
One triangle

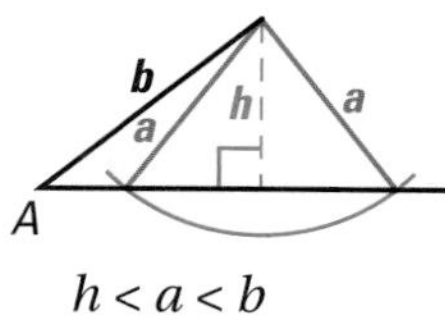

$h < a < b$
Two triangles

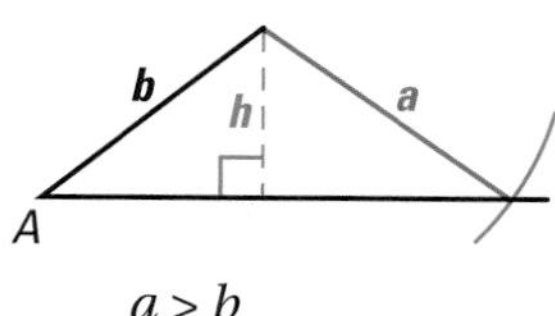

$a > b$
One triangle

EXAMPLE 2 Solve the SSA case with one solution

Solve $\triangle ABC$ with $A = 115°$, $a = 20$, and $b = 11$.

Solution

First make a sketch. Because A is obtuse and the side opposite A is longer than the given adjacent side, you know that only one triangle can be formed. Use the law of sines to find B.

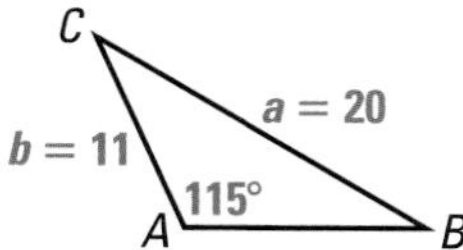

$\frac{\sin B}{11} = \frac{\sin 115°}{20}$ **Law of sines**

$\sin B = \frac{11 \sin 115°}{20} \approx 0.4985$ **Multiply each side by 11.**

$B \approx 29.9°$ **Use inverse sine function.**

You then know that $C \approx 180° - 115° - 29.9° = 35.1°$. Use the law of sines again to find the remaining side length c of the triangle.

$\frac{c}{\sin 35.1°} = \frac{20}{\sin 115°}$ **Law of sines**

$c = \frac{20 \sin 35.1°}{\sin 115°}$ **Multiply each side by sin 35.1°.**

$c \approx 12.7$ **Use a calculator.**

▶ In $\triangle ABC$, $B \approx 29.9°$, $C \approx 35.1°$, and $c \approx 12.7$.

EXAMPLE 3 Examine the SSA case with no solution

Solve $\triangle ABC$ with $A = 51°$, $a = 3.5$, and $b = 5$.

Solution

Begin by drawing a horizontal line. On one end form a 51° angle (A) and draw a segment 5 units long ($\overline{AC}$, or b). At vertex C, draw a segment 3.5 units long (a). You can see that a needs to be at least $5 \sin 51° \approx 3.9$ units long to reach the horizontal side and form a triangle. So, it is not possible to draw the indicated triangle.

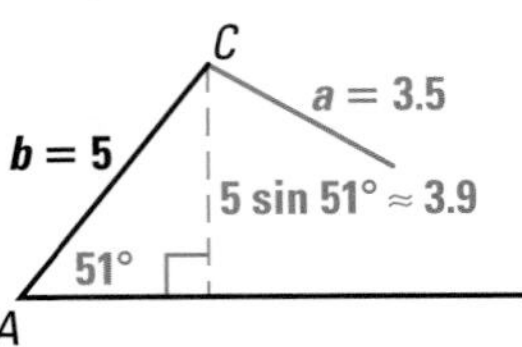

EXAMPLE 4 Solve the SSA case with two solutions

Solve $\triangle ABC$ with $A = 40°$, $a = 13$, and $b = 16$.

Solution

First make a sketch. Because $b \sin A = 16 \sin 40° \approx 10.3$, and $10.3 < 13 < 16$ ($h < a < b$), two triangles can be formed.

Triangle 1

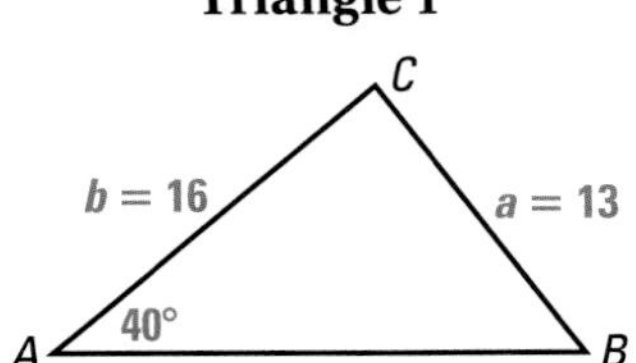

Triangle 2

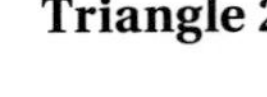

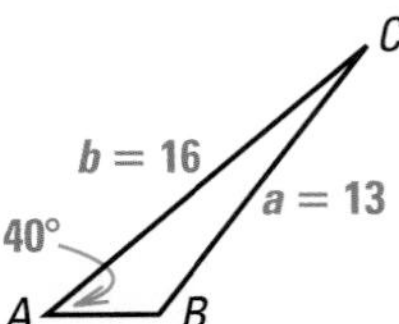

Use the law of sines to find the possible measures of B.

$$\frac{\sin B}{16} = \frac{\sin 40°}{13} \qquad \text{Law of sines}$$

$$\sin B = \frac{16 \sin 40°}{13} \approx 0.7911 \qquad \text{Use a calculator.}$$

There are two angles B between 0° and 180° for which $\sin B \approx 0.7911$. One is acute and the other is obtuse. Use your calculator to find the acute angle: $\sin^{-1} 0.7911 \approx 52.3°$.

The obtuse angle has 52.3° as a reference angle, so its measure is $180° - 52.3° = 127.7°$. Therefore, $B \approx 52.3°$ or $B \approx 127.7°$.

Now find the remaining angle C and side length c for each triangle.

Triangle 1

$$C \approx 180° - 40° - 52.3° = 87.7°$$

$$\frac{c}{\sin 87.7°} = \frac{13}{\sin 40°}$$

$$c = \frac{13 \sin 87.7°}{\sin 40°} \approx 20.2$$

▶ In Triangle 1, $B \approx 52.3°$, $C \approx 87.7°$, and $c \approx 20.2$.

Triangle 2

$$C \approx 180° - 40° - 127.7° = 12.3°$$

$$\frac{c}{\sin 12.3°} = \frac{13}{\sin 40°}$$

$$c = \frac{13 \sin 12.3°}{\sin 40°} \approx 4.3$$

▶ In Triangle 2, $B \approx 127.7°$, $C \approx 12.3°$, and $c \approx 4.3$.

at classzone.com

✓ GUIDED PRACTICE for Examples 2, 3, and 4

Solve $\triangle ABC$.

3. $A = 122°, a = 18, b = 12$

4. $A = 36°, a = 9, b = 12$

5. $A = 50°, a = 2.8, b = 4$

6. $B = 105°, b = 13, a = 6$

AREA OF A TRIANGLE You can use the following result to find the area of a triangle when you know the lengths of two sides and the measure of the included angle. This result can also be used to derive the law of sines (see Exercise 42).

KEY CONCEPT — *For Your Notebook*

Area of a Triangle

The area of any triangle is given by one half the product of the lengths of two sides times the sine of their included angle. For $\triangle ABC$ shown, there are three ways to calculate the area:

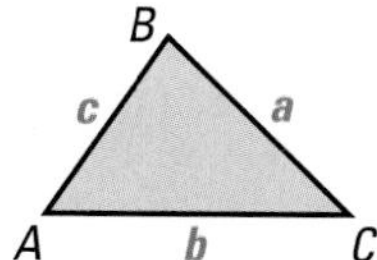

$$\text{Area} = \frac{1}{2}bc \sin A \qquad \text{Area} = \frac{1}{2}ac \sin B \qquad \text{Area} = \frac{1}{2}ab \sin C$$

EXAMPLE 5 Find the area of a triangle

BIOLOGY Black-necked stilts are birds that live throughout Florida and surrounding areas but breed mostly in the triangular region shown on the map. Find the area of this region.

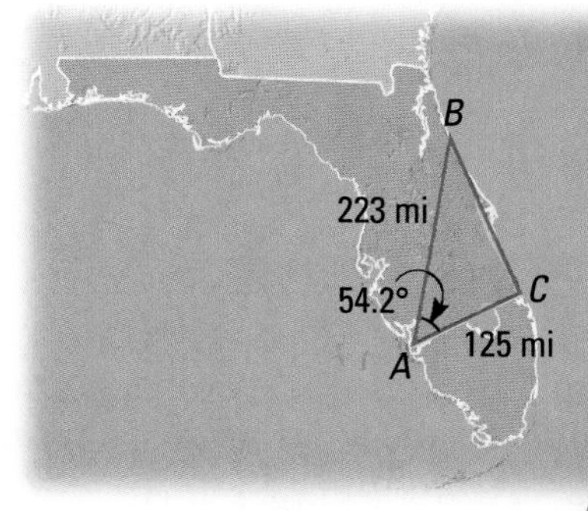

Solution

The area of the region is:

$\text{Area} = \frac{1}{2}bc \sin A$ — **Write area formula.**

$= \frac{1}{2}(125)(223) \sin 54.2°$ — **Substitute.**

$\approx 11{,}300$ — **Use a calculator.**

▸ The area of the region is about 11,300 square miles.

✓ GUIDED PRACTICE for Example 5

Find the area of $\triangle ABC$ with the given side lengths and included angle.

7. $a = 10, b = 14, C = 46°$

8. $a = 19, c = 8, B = 75°$

9. $b = 11, c = 7, A = 120°$

10. $a = 20, b = 24, C = 87°$

13.5 EXERCISES

HOMEWORK KEY

○ = **WORKED-OUT SOLUTIONS** on p. WS23 for Exs. 13, 31, and 45

★ = **STANDARDIZED TEST PRACTICE** Exs. 2, 28, 41, 47, and 48

◆ = **MULTIPLE REPRESENTATIONS** Ex. 45

SKILL PRACTICE

1. **VOCABULARY** What information do you need to use the law of sines?

2. ★ **WRITING** Suppose a, b, and A are given for $\triangle ABC$ where $A < 90°$. Under what conditions would you have no triangle? one triangle? two triangles?

EXAMPLES 1, 2, 3, and 4 on pp. 882–884 for Exs. 3–28

IDENTIFYING CASES State the case (AAS, ASA, or SSA) applicable to the given measurements. Then decide whether the measurements determine *one triangle, two triangles,* or *no triangle.*

3. $A = 112°, a = 9, b = 4$
4. $A = 40°, C = 75°, c = 20$
5. $A = 52°, a = 32, b = 42$
6. $A = 37°, a = 8, b = 14$
7. $A = 28°, B = 64°, c = 55$
8. $A = 149°, a = 7, b = 10$
9. $B = 34°, b = 5, a = 16$
10. $B = 70°, b = 85, c = 88$
11. $C = 48°, c = 28, b = 20$

SOLVING TRIANGLES Solve $\triangle ABC$.

12.
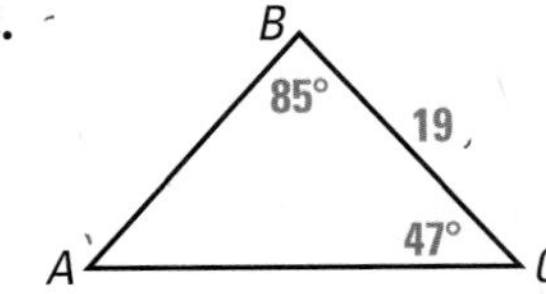

13.
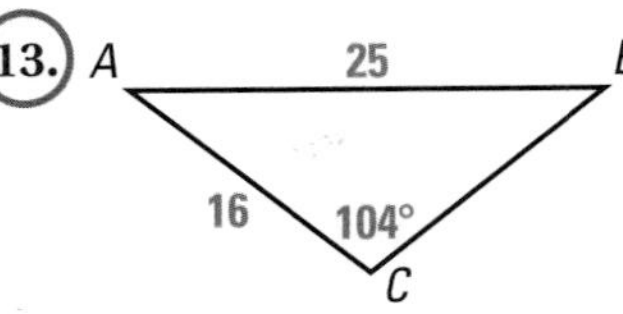

14.
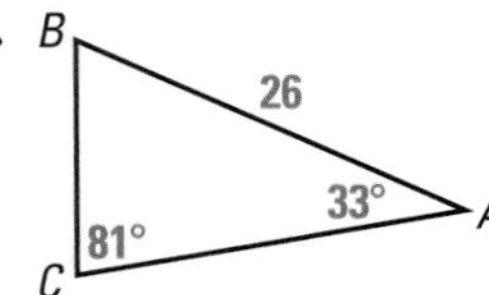

15.
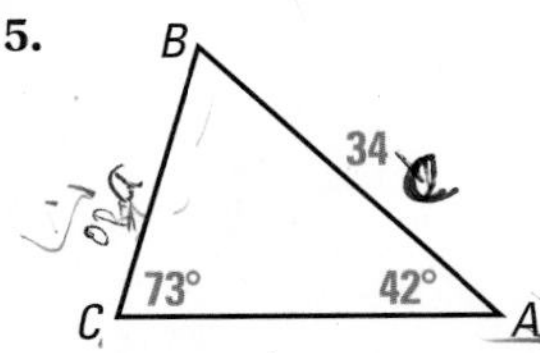

16.
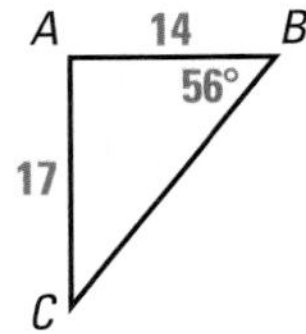

17.
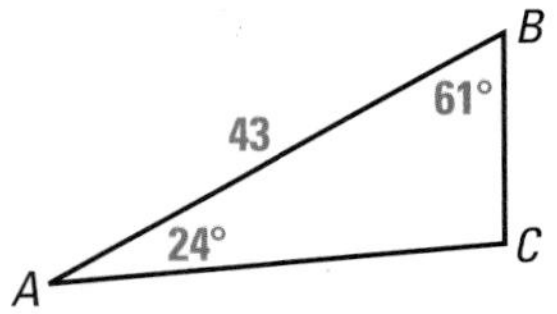

SOLVING TRIANGLES Solve $\triangle ABC$. (*Hint:* Some of the "triangles" have no solution and some have two solutions.)

18. $A = 73°, a = 18, b = 11$
19. $A = 26°, C = 35°, b = 13$
20. $B = 102°, C = 43°, b = 21$
21. $A = 38°, a = 19, b = 25$
22. $A = 55°, B = 64°, c = 34$
23. $A = 114°, a = 15, b = 10$
24. $C = 98°, c = 29, a = 33$
25. $A = 49°, B = 32°, b = 44$
26. $B = 21°, b = 17, c = 32$

27. **ERROR ANALYSIS** *Describe* and correct the error in finding the measure of angle C in the triangle below.

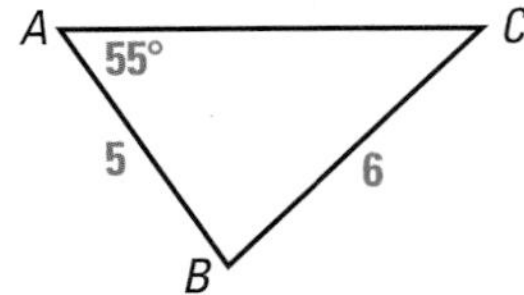

$$\frac{\sin C}{6} = \frac{\sin 55°}{5}$$

$$\sin C = \frac{6 \sin 55°}{5} \approx 0.9830$$

$$C \approx 79.4°$$

28. ★ **MULTIPLE CHOICE** What is the side length c in $\triangle ABC$ if $A = 32°$, $C = 67°$, and $b = 31$ ft?

Ⓐ 16.6 ft Ⓑ 28.9 ft Ⓒ 33.3 ft Ⓓ 57.8 ft

EXAMPLE 5
on p. 885
for Exs. 29–41

FINDING AREA **Find the area of $\triangle ABC$ with the given side lengths and included angle.**

29. $B = 124°, a = 9, c = 11$

30. $A = 68°, b = 13, c = 7$

31. $A = 34°, b = 29, c = 36$

32. $C = 79°, a = 25, b = 17$

33. $B = 57°, a = 9, c = 5$

34. $C = 96°, a = 7, b = 15$

35. $A = 130°, b = 23, c = 20$

36. $B = 60°, a = 19, c = 14$

37. $C = 29°, a = 38, b = 31$

FINDING AREA **Find the area of $\triangle ABC$.**

38.

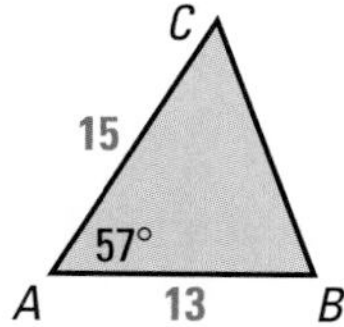

39.

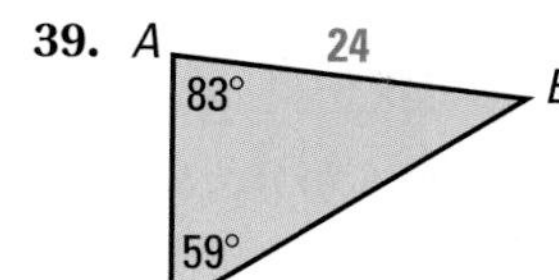

40.

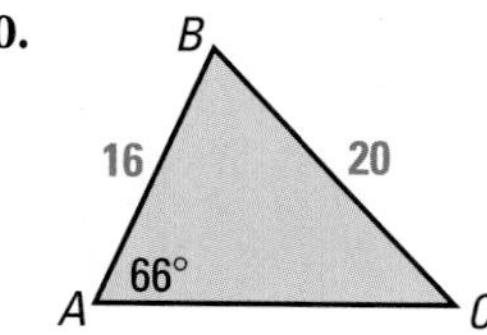

41. ★ **MULTIPLE CHOICE** What is the area of $\triangle ABC$ if $B = 52°$, $a = 29$, and $c = 24$?

Ⓐ 274 units^2 Ⓑ 348 units^2 Ⓒ 548 units^2 Ⓓ 696 units^2

42. **CHALLENGE** Using the triangle shown at the right as a reference, derive the formulas for the area of a triangle given on page 885. Then use the area formulas to derive the law of sines.

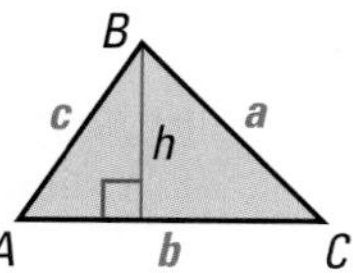

PROBLEM SOLVING

EXAMPLE 1
on p. 882
for Ex. 43

43. **LIFEGUARDS** Two lifeguards are watching a windsurfer. Use the information in the diagram to find the distance from each lifeguard to the windsurfer.

@HomeTutor for problem solving help at classzone.com

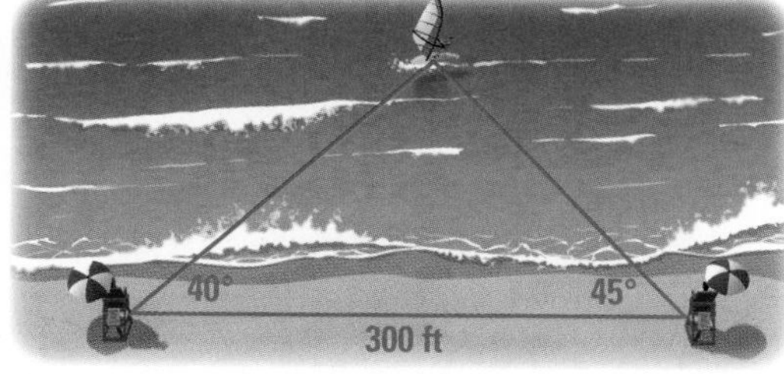

EXAMPLE 2
on p. 883
for Ex. 44

44. **NEW YORK CITY** You are on the observation deck of the Empire State Building looking at the Chrysler Building. When you turn 145° clockwise, you see the Statue of Liberty. You know that the Chrysler Building and the Empire State Building are about 0.6 mile apart and that the Chrysler Building and the Statue of Liberty are about 5.7 miles apart. Estimate the distance between the Empire State Building and the Statue of Liberty.

@HomeTutor for problem solving help at classzone.com

EXAMPLE 5
on p. 885
for Exs. 45–46

45. ◆ **MULTIPLE REPRESENTATIONS** You are fertilizing a triangular garden. One side of the garden is 62 feet long and another side is 54 feet long. The angle opposite the 62 foot side is 58°.

a. **Drawing a Diagram** Draw a diagram to represent this situation.

b. **Solving a Triangle** Use the law of sines to solve the triangle you drew in part (a).

c. **Applying a Formula** One bag of fertilizer covers an area of 200 square feet. How many bags of fertilizer will you need to cover the entire garden?

46. MULTI-STEP PROBLEM Quadrilateral $ABCD$ shown at the right is a kite.

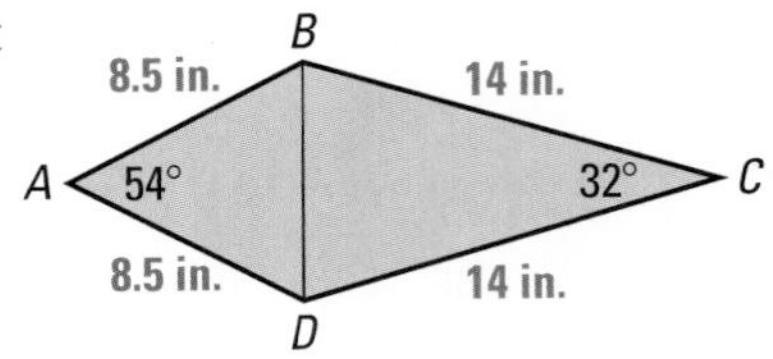

a. Find the area of $\triangle ABD$.

b. Find the area of $\triangle BCD$.

c. What is the area of the kite?

47. ★ SHORT RESPONSE A building is constructed on top of a cliff that is 300 meters high. A person standing on level ground below the cliff observes that the angle of elevation to the top of the building is 72°, and the angle of elevation to the top of the cliff is 63°.

a. How far away is the person from the base of the cliff?

b. *Describe* two different methods you can use to find the height of the building. Use one of these methods to find the building's height.

48. ★ EXTENDED RESPONSE Use a graphing calculator to explore how the included angle in the formulas on page 885 affects a triangle's area.

a. **Model** Choose lengths for two sides of the triangle. Let x represent the measure (in degrees) of the included angle. Write an equation that gives the triangle's area y as a function of x.

b. **Graphing Calculator** Enter the equation from part (a) into a graphing calculator. Use the *table* feature to examine values of the area for $0° < x° < 180°$. Does the area always increase as x increases? *Explain.*

c. **Interpret** What value of x maximizes the triangle's area? What is the maximum area, and how is it related to the side lengths you chose in part (a)?

49. CHALLENGE The distance between Mercury and the sun is approximately 36 million miles. The distance between Earth and the sun is approximately 93 million miles. If on a certain day the angle (measured from Earth) between the sun and Mercury is 22°, what are the possible distances between Mercury and Earth?

NEW YORK MIXED REVIEW

TEST PRACTICE at classzone.com

50. Amy uses 100 of the tiles shown to tile a square room. What is the perimeter of the room?

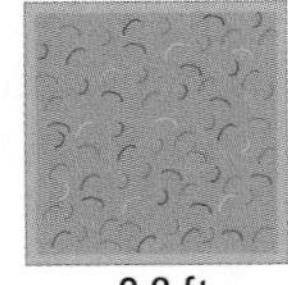

(A) 24 ft (B) 32 ft

(C) 36 ft (D) 80 ft

51. The ages of the first 20 people entering an amusement park are 12, 16, 35, 24, 40, 48, 15, 18, 20, 50, 38, 14, 11, 28, 18, 19, 26, 15, 16, and 21. What is an acceptable set of intervals to use when making a histogram of the ages?

(A) 10–20, 21–40, and 41–50

(B) 10–15, 16–20, 21–30, and 31–50

(C) 11–20, 21–30, 31–40, and 41–50

(D) 15–25, 26–35, 36–45, and 46–55

13.6 Apply the Law of Cosines

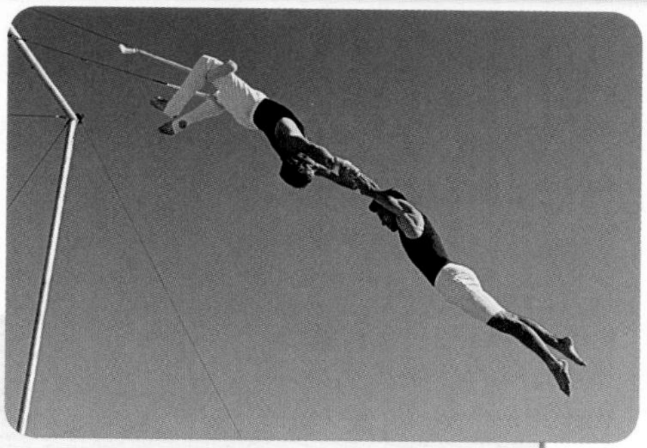

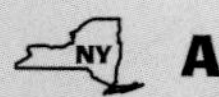

A2.A.73 Solve for an unknown side or angle, using the Law of Sines or the Law of Cosines

Before You solved triangles using the law of sines.

Now You will solve triangles using the law of cosines.

Why? So you can find angles formed by trapeze artists, as in Ex. 43.

Key Vocabulary
- **law of cosines**

In Lesson 13.5, you solved triangles for the AAS, ASA, and SSA cases. In this lesson, you will use the **law of cosines** to solve triangles when two sides and the included angle are known (SAS), or when all three sides are known (SSS).

KEY CONCEPT *For Your Notebook*

Law of Cosines

If $\triangle ABC$ has sides of length a, b, and c as shown, then:

$$a^2 = b^2 + c^2 - 2bc\cos A$$
$$b^2 = a^2 + c^2 - 2ac\cos B$$
$$c^2 = a^2 + b^2 - 2ab\cos C$$

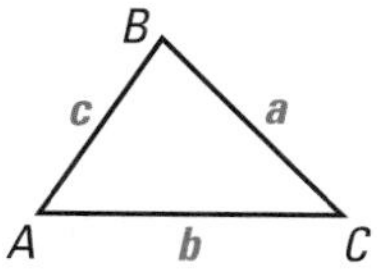

EXAMPLE 1 Solve a triangle for the SAS case

Solve $\triangle ABC$ with $a = 11$, $c = 14$, and $B = 34°$.

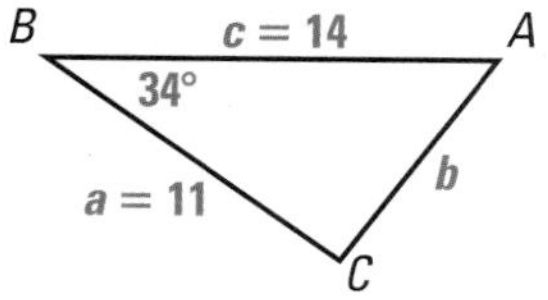

Solution

Use the law of cosines to find side length b.

$b^2 = a^2 + c^2 - 2ac\cos B$ **Law of cosines**

$b^2 = 11^2 + 14^2 - 2(11)(14)\cos 34°$ **Substitute for *a*, *c*, and *B*.**

$b^2 \approx 61.7$ **Simplify.**

$b \approx \sqrt{61.7} \approx 7.85$ **Take positive square root.**

ANOTHER WAY When you know all three sides and one angle, you can use the law of cosines *or* the law of sines to find the measure of a second angle.

Use the law of sines to find the measure of angle A.

$\frac{\sin A}{a} = \frac{\sin B}{b}$ **Law of sines**

$\frac{\sin A}{11} = \frac{\sin 34°}{7.85}$ **Substitute for *a*, *b*, and *B*.**

$\sin A = \frac{11\sin 34°}{7.85} \approx 0.7836$ **Multiply each side by 11 and simplify.**

$A \approx \sin^{-1} 0.7836 \approx 51.6°$ **Use inverse sine.**

The third angle C of the triangle is $C \approx 180° - 34° - 51.6° = 94.4°$.

▶ In $\triangle ABC$, $b \approx 7.85$, $A \approx 51.6°$, and $C \approx 94.4°$.

EXAMPLE 2 Solve a triangle for the SSS case

Solve $\triangle ABC$ with $a = 12$, $b = 27$, and $c = 20$.

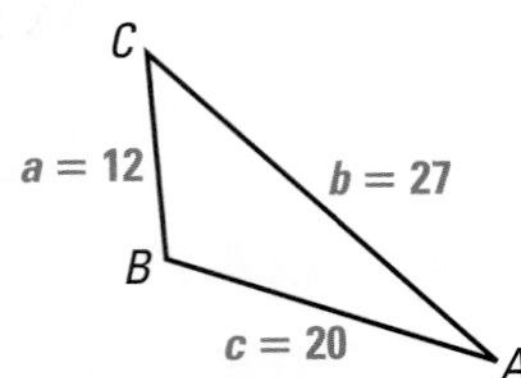

Solution

AVOID ERRORS
In Example 2, the largest angle is found first to make sure that the other two angles are acute. This way, when you use the law of sines to find another angle measure, you will know that it is between 0° and 90°.

First find the angle opposite the longest side, $\overline{AC}$. Use the law of cosines to solve for B.

$$b^2 = a^2 + c^2 - 2ac\cos B$$ **Law of cosines**

$$27^2 = 12^2 + 20^2 - 2(12)(20)\cos B$$ **Substitute.**

$$\frac{27^2 - 12^2 - 20^2}{-2(12)(20)} = \cos B$$ **Solve for cos *B*.**

$$-0.3854 \approx \cos B$$ **Simplify.**

$$B \approx \cos^{-1}(-0.3854) \approx 112.7°$$ **Use inverse cosine.**

Now use the law of sines to find A.

$$\frac{\sin A}{a} = \frac{\sin B}{b}$$ **Law of sines**

$$\frac{\sin A}{12} = \frac{\sin 112.7°}{27}$$ **Substitute for *a*, *b*, and *B*.**

$$\sin A = \frac{12 \sin 112.7°}{27} \approx 0.4100$$ **Multiply each side by 12 and simplify.**

$$A \approx \sin^{-1} 0.4100 \approx 24.2°$$ **Use inverse sine.**

The third angle C of the triangle is $C \approx 180° - 24.2° - 112.7° = 43.1°$.

▶ In $\triangle ABC$, $A \approx 24.2°$, $B \approx 112.7°$, and $C \approx 43.1°$.

EXAMPLE 3 Use the law of cosines in real life

SCIENCE Scientists can use a set of footprints to calculate an organism's *step angle*, which is a measure of walking efficiency. The closer the step angle is to 180°, the more efficiently the organism walked.

The diagram at the right shows a set of footprints for a dinosaur. Find the step angle B.

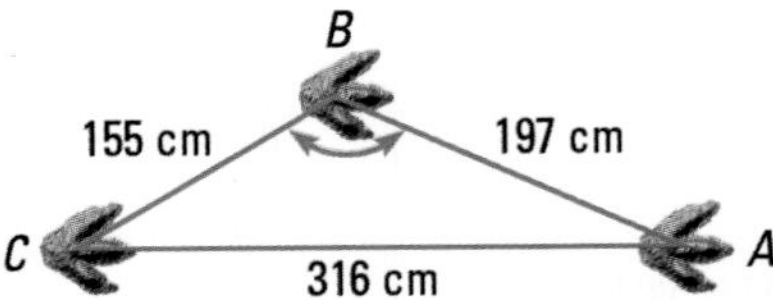

Solution

$$b^2 = a^2 + c^2 - 2ac\cos B$$ **Law of cosines**

$$316^2 = 155^2 + 197^2 - 2(155)(197)\cos B$$ **Substitute.**

$$\frac{316^2 - 155^2 - 197^2}{-2(155)(197)} = \cos B$$ **Solve for cos *B*.**

$$-0.6062 \approx \cos B$$ **Simplify.**

$$B \approx \cos^{-1}(-0.6062) \approx 127.3°$$ **Use inverse cosine.**

▶ The step angle B is about 127.3°.

✓ GUIDED PRACTICE for Examples 1, 2, and 3

Solve $\triangle ABC$.

1. $a = 8, c = 10, B = 48°$

2. $a = 14, b = 16, c = 9$

3. **WHAT IF?** In Example 3, suppose that $a = 193$ cm, $b = 335$ cm, and $c = 186$ cm. Find the step angle θ.

HERON'S AREA FORMULA The law of cosines can be used to establish the following formula for the area of a triangle. The formula is credited to the Greek mathematician Heron (circa A.D. 100).

KEY CONCEPT *For Your Notebook*

Heron's Area Formula

The area of the triangle with sides of length a, b, and c is

$$\text{Area} = \sqrt{s(s-a)(s-b)(s-c)}$$

where $s = \frac{1}{2}(a + b + c)$. The variable s is called the *semiperimeter*, or half-perimeter, of the triangle.

EXAMPLE 4 Solve a multi-step problem

URBAN PLANNING The intersection of three streets forms a piece of land called a traffic triangle. Find the area of the traffic triangle shown.

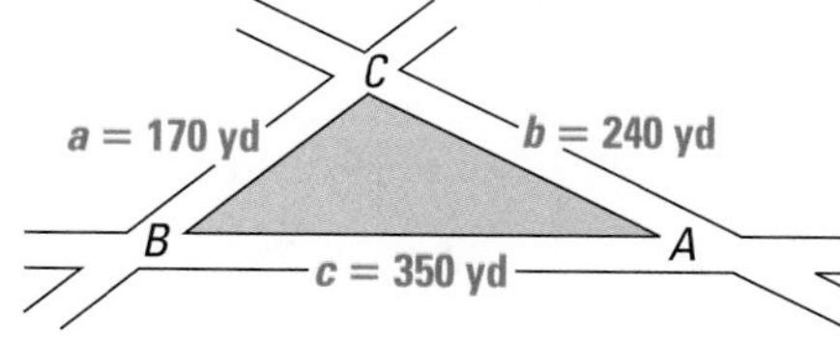

ANOTHER WAY
For an alternative method for solving the problem in Example 4, turn to page 895 for the **Problem Solving Workshop**.

Solution

STEP 1 **Find** the semiperimeter s.

$$s = \frac{1}{2}(a + b + c) = \frac{1}{2}(170 + 240 + 350) = 380$$

STEP 2 **Use** Heron's formula to find the area of $\triangle ABC$.

$$\text{Area} = \sqrt{s(s-a)(s-b)(s-c)}$$

$$= \sqrt{380(380-170)(380-240)(380-350)} \approx 18{,}300$$

▸ The area of the traffic triangle is about 18,300 square yards.

✓ GUIDED PRACTICE for Example 4

Find the area of $\triangle ABC$.

4. 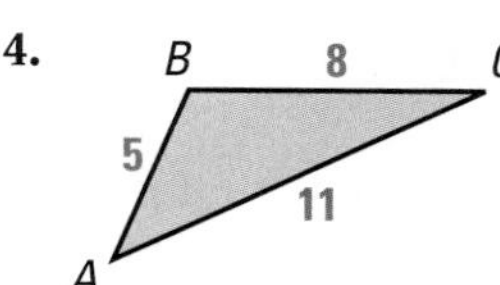

5. 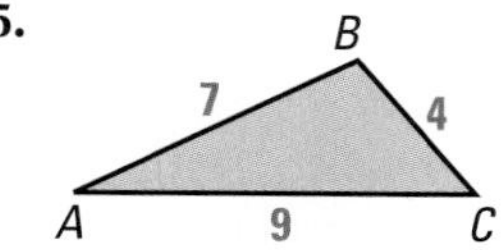

6. 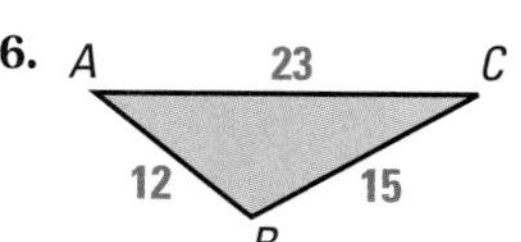

13.6 EXERCISES

HOMEWORK KEY

○ = **WORKED-OUT SOLUTIONS** on p. WS23 for Exs. 17, 25, and 45

★ = **STANDARDIZED TEST PRACTICE** Exs. 2, 20, 33, 34, 45, and 47

SKILL PRACTICE

1. **VOCABULARY** Copy and complete: In a triangle with sides of length a, b, and c, $\frac{1}{2}(a + b + c)$ is called the _?_.

2. ★ **WRITING** Express Heron's formula in words.

EXAMPLES 1 and 2 on pp. 889–890 for Exs. 3–20

CHOOSING A METHOD **For the given case, tell whether you would use the *law of sines* or the *law of cosines* to solve the triangle.**

3. SSS
4. ASA
5. SSA
6. SAS
7. AAS

SOLVING TRIANGLES **Solve $\triangle ABC$.**

8. 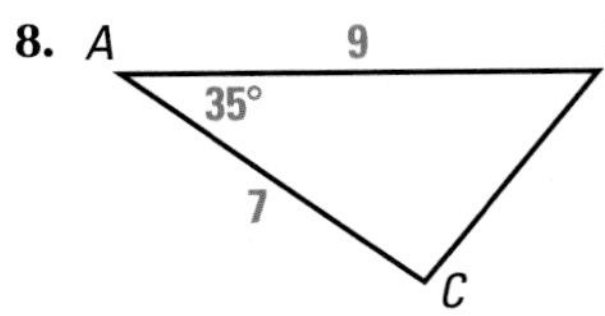

9. 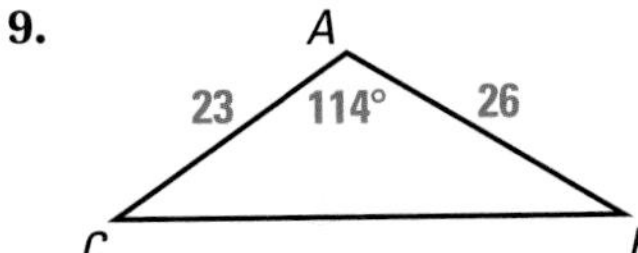

10. 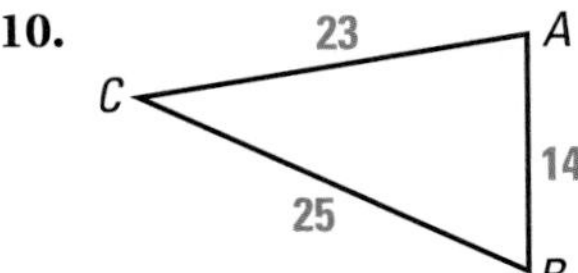

SOLVING TRIANGLES **Solve $\triangle ABC$.**

11. $B = 25°, a = 8, c = 6$
12. $A = 103°, b = 15, c = 24$
13. $a = 18, b = 28, c = 13$
14. $a = 38, b = 31, c = 35$
15. $C = 48°, a = 17, b = 20$
16. $B = 63°, a = 29, c = 38$
17. $a = 10, b = 3, c = 12$
18. $a = 23, b = 24, c = 20$
19. $C = 96°, a = 35, b = 43$

20. ★ **MULTIPLE CHOICE** What is the measure of angle B in $\triangle ABC$ if $a = 17$, $b = 29$, and $c = 14$?

Ⓐ 18.7° Ⓑ 22.9° Ⓒ 111.2° Ⓓ 138.4°

EXAMPLE 4 on p. 891 for Exs. 21–33

FINDING AREA **Find the area of $\triangle ABC$.**

21. 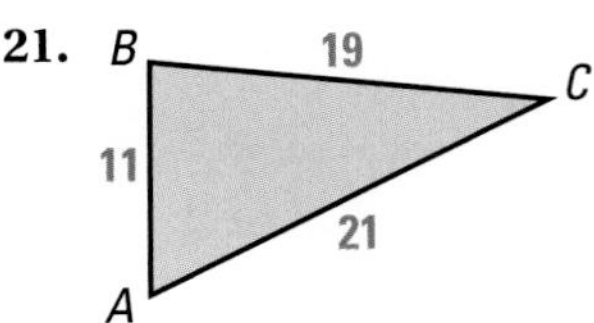

22. 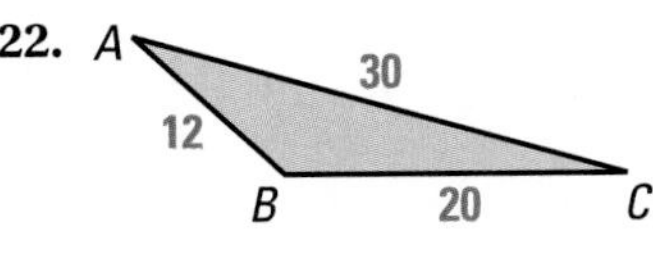

23. 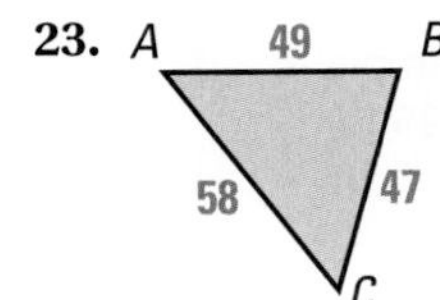

FINDING AREA **Find the area of $\triangle ABC$ with the given side lengths.**

24. $a = 12, b = 7, c = 8$
25. $a = 5, b = 11, c = 10$
26. $a = 25, b = 24, c = 19$
27. $a = 14, b = 20, c = 28$
28. $a = 31, b = 23, c = 17$
29. $a = 81, b = 67, c = 71$
30. $a = 43, b = 59, c = 48$
31. $a = 51, b = 51, c = 43$
32. $a = 38, b = 25, c = 61$

33. ★ **MULTIPLE CHOICE** What is the area of $\triangle ABC$ if $a = 21$, $b = 16$, and $c = 13$?

Ⓐ 66 units^2 Ⓑ 104 units^2 Ⓒ 1350 units^2 Ⓓ 4368 units^2

34. ★ **SHORT RESPONSE** Use the law of cosines to show that the measure of each angle of an equilateral triangle is 60°. *Explain* your reasoning.

35. **ERROR ANALYSIS** *Describe* and correct the error in finding the measure of angle A in $\triangle ABC$ if $a = 18$, $b = 15$, and $c = 10$.

$$\cos A = \frac{15^2 + 10^2 - 18^2}{2(18)(15)} \approx 0.0019$$

$$A \approx \cos^{-1} 0.0019 \approx 89.9°$$

CHOOSING A METHOD **Use the law of sines, the law of cosines, or the Pythagorean theorem to solve $\triangle ABC$.**

36. $A = 72°$, $B = 44°$, $b = 14$

37. $B = 98°$, $C = 37°$, $a = 18$

38. $C = 65°$, $a = 12$, $b = 21$

39. $B = 90°$, $a = 15$, $c = 6$

40. $C = 40°$, $b = 36$, $c = 27$

41. $a = 34$, $b = 19$, $c = 27$

42. **CHALLENGE** Given $\triangle ABC$ with height h, derive the law of cosines. *Explain* how the Pythagorean theorem is related to the law of cosines.

PROBLEM SOLVING

EXAMPLE 3 on p. 890 for Ex. 43

43. **TRAPEZE ARTISTS** The diagram shows the paths of two trapeze artists who are both 5 feet long when hanging by their knees. The "flyer" on the left bar is preparing to make hand-to-hand contact with the "catcher" on the right bar. At what angle θ will the two meet?

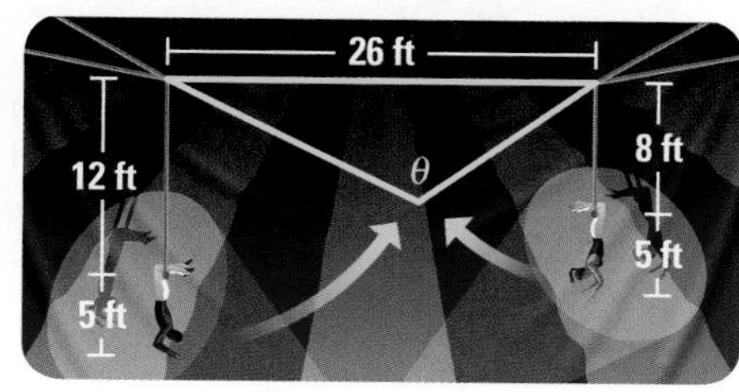

@HomeTutor for problem solving help at classzone.com

EXAMPLE 4 on p. 891 for Exs. 44–45

44. **RESEARCH TRIANGLE** Raleigh, Durham, and Chapel Hill are three cities in North Carolina that form what is known as the Research Triangle. It is about 18 miles from Raleigh to Durham, 23 miles from Raleigh to Chapel Hill, and 8 miles from Chapel Hill to Durham. Find the area of the Research Triangle.

@HomeTutor for problem solving help at classzone.com

45. ★ **SHORT RESPONSE** The diagram shows the dimensions of a plot of land. What is the area of the land in acres? (Use the fact that 1 acre = 43,560 square feet.) *Explain* how you could also determine the area by first finding the length of $\overline{AC}$.

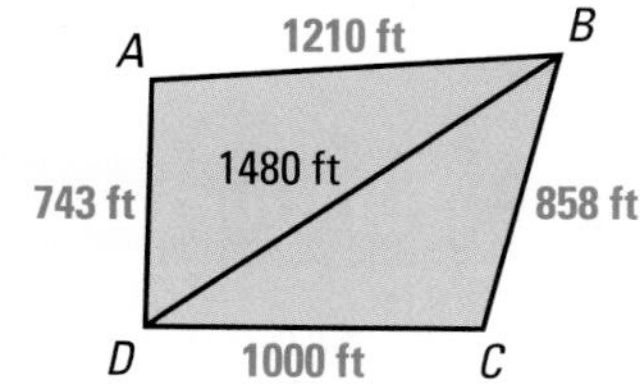

46. **MULTI-STEP PROBLEM** A golfer hits a drive 260 yards on a hole that is 400 yards long. The shot is 15° off target.

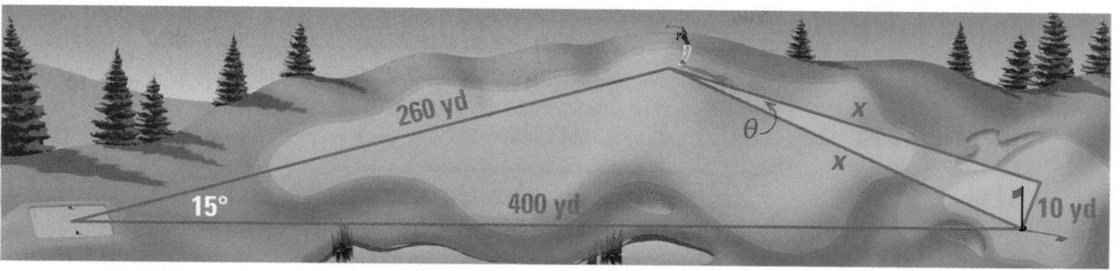

a. What is the distance x from the golfer's ball to the hole?

b. Assume the golfer is able to hit the ball precisely the distance found in part (a). What is the maximum angle θ by which the ball can be off target in order to land no more than 10 yards from the hole?

47. ★ **EXTENDED RESPONSE** Starting at the same point in a forest, two hikers take different paths. The first hiker walks due north at a speed of 2 miles per hour. The second hiker walks 60° east of north at a speed of 3 miles per hour.

a. How far apart are the hikers after 1 hour?

b. The two hikers carry walkie-talkies with a range of 10 miles. After how much time are the hikers out of range of each other?

c. Suppose after two hours the first hiker stops and tells the second hiker to meet her. How long will it take the second hiker to meet the first hiker? In what direction should the second hiker walk? *Explain* your reasoning.

48. **CHALLENGE** An airplane flies 55° east of north from city A to city B, a distance of 470 miles. Another airplane flies 7° north of east from city A to city C, a distance of 890 miles. What is the distance between cities B and C?

NEW YORK MIXED REVIEW

TEST PRACTICE at classzone.com

49. The scatter plot shows the atmospheric temperature at various altitudes. What is the approximate temperature at an altitude of 5 kilometers?

Ⓐ $-32°C$ Ⓑ $-25°C$

Ⓒ $-20°C$ Ⓓ $-12°C$

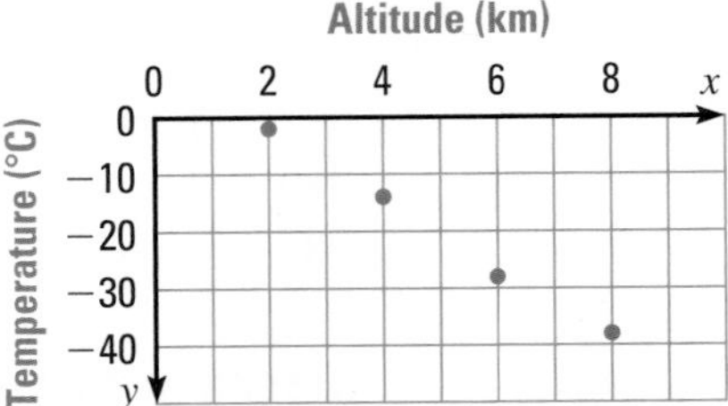

50. Which equation best represents the line that contains the point (4, 4) and is perpendicular to the line $y = -3x + 5$?

Ⓐ $y = 3x - 8$ Ⓑ $y = -3x + 16$

Ⓒ $y = \frac{1}{3}x + \frac{8}{3}$ Ⓓ $y = -\frac{1}{3}x + \frac{8}{3}$

QUIZ *for Lessons 13.5–13.6*

Solve $\triangle ABC$. *(pp. 882 and 889)*

1. $A = 50°, B = 74°, c = 12$
2. $C = 66°, a = 18, c = 17$
3. $a = 20, b = 14, c = 23$
4. $C = 118°, a = 26, b = 34$
5. $A = 102°, C = 25°, a = 31$
6. $a = 49, b = 52, c = 38$
7. $B = 53°, a = 41, c = 29$
8. $A = 112°, B = 48°, c = 5$

Find the area of $\triangle ABC$. *(pp. 882 and 889)*

9. $B = 94°, a = 13, c = 15$
10. $C = 18°, a = 16, b = 11$
11. $a = 18, b = 25, c = 19$
12. $a = 27, b = 21, c = 37$
13. $a = 62, b = 47, c = 53$
14. $A = 70°, b = 44, c = 36$

15. **GEOMETRY** The base of a right triangular prism has sides of length 8 centimeters, 10 centimeters, and 13 centimeters. The height of the prism is 5 centimeters. What is the volume of the prism? *(p. 889)*

EXTRA PRACTICE for Lesson 13.6, p. 1022 **ONLINE QUIZ** at classzone.com

PROBLEM SOLVING WORKSHOP
LESSON 13.6

Using ALTERNATIVE METHODS

Another Way to Solve Example 4, page 891

MULTIPLE REPRESENTATIONS In Example 4 on page 891, you found the area of a triangle given the lengths of its sides by using Heron's formula. You can also find the area of the triangle by writing and solving a system of equations.

PROBLEM

URBAN PLANNING The intersection of three streets forms a piece of land called a traffic triangle. Find the area of the traffic triangle shown.

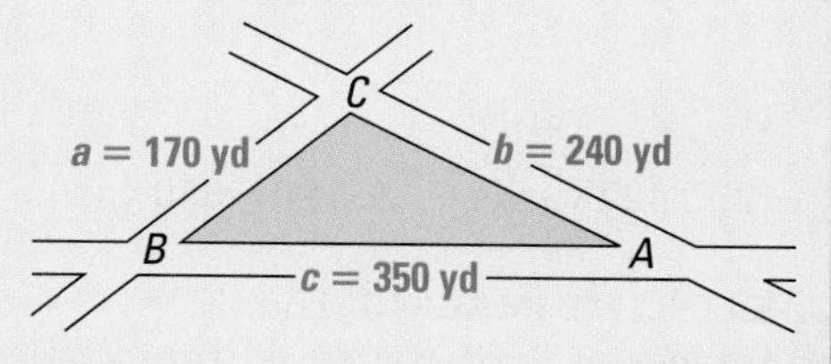

METHOD

Using a System of Equations Use a system of quadratic equations to find the triangle's height h. Then find the area of the triangle using the formula $A = \frac{1}{2}bh$.

STEP 1 **Draw** a new diagram of the triangle as shown. Let h be the height of the triangle. The altitude labeled by h divides $\overline{AB}$ into two segments of length x and $350 - x$.

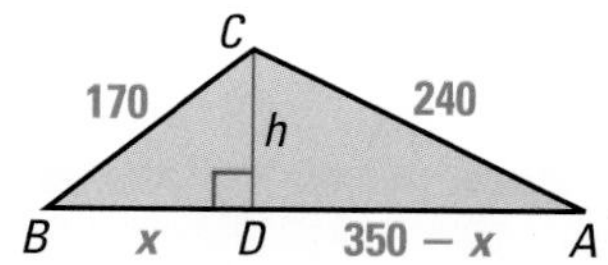

STEP 2 **Use** the Pythagorean theorem to write a system of quadratic equations.

$$h^2 + x^2 = 170^2$$
$$h^2 + (350 - x)^2 = 240^2$$

STEP 3 **Solve** the first equation for h^2 to get $h^2 = 170^2 - x^2$. Substitute this expression for h^2 in the second equation, and solve for x.

$$170^2 - x^2 + (350 - x)^2 = 240^2$$
$$28{,}900 - x^2 + 122{,}500 - 700x + x^2 = 57{,}600$$
$$-700x = -93{,}800$$
$$x = 134$$

STEP 4 **Use** the Pythagorean theorem to find that $h = \sqrt{170^2 - 134^2} \approx 104.6$.

So the area of the triangle is $A = \frac{1}{2}bh \approx \frac{1}{2}(350)(104.6) \approx 18{,}300$.

▶ The area of the triangle is about 18,300 square yards.

PRACTICE

FINDING AREAS **Use the method above to find the area of $\triangle ABC$ with the given side lengths.**

1. $a = 12, b = 17, c = 26$
2. $a = 63, b = 92, c = 87$
3. $a = 101, b = 94, c = 153$
4. **WHAT IF?** Suppose $a = 200$ yd in the problem above. Find the area of the triangle.
5. **GARDEN AREA** A triangular garden has sides with lengths 50 feet, 38 feet, and 43 feet. Use the method above to find the area of the garden.

New York *Mixed Review*

Lessons 13.4–13.6

1. **AREA OF A PROPERTY** You are buying the triangular piece of property shown. What is the approximate length of the third side?

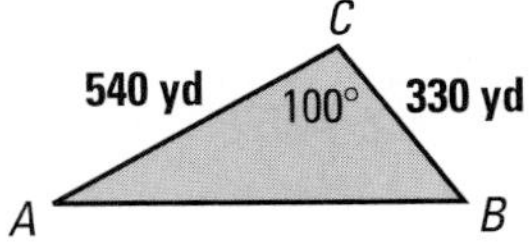

(1) 210 yards (3) 633 yards

(2) 427 yards (4) 680 yards

2. **SATELLITE IMAGING** The IKONOS satellite takes images of Earth's surface from a height of about 423 miles. The largest region IKONOS can view is about 1045 miles across. IKONOS can take photographs that show objects 1 meter across provided the objects lie within a region 413 miles across. What is the approximate angle IKONOS rotates as it pans across a region this size?

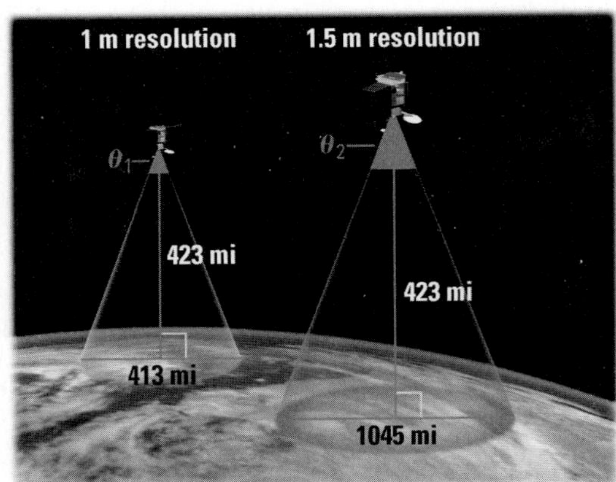

(1) 26.0° (3) 32.0°

(2) 44.3° (4) 64.0°

3. **CONSTRUCTION** You want to build a triangular concrete patio that has sides of length 8 feet, 11 feet, and 15 feet, and a thickness of 0.5 foot. One bag of cement makes 0.33 cubic foot of concrete. How many bags of cement do you need to make the patio?

(1) 65 bags (3) 109 bags

(2) 79 bags (4) 130 bags

4. **BEACH SLOPE** After walking 20 feet into the water at a beach, you notice that the depth of the water is 3 feet. Find the angle θ at which the beach slopes.

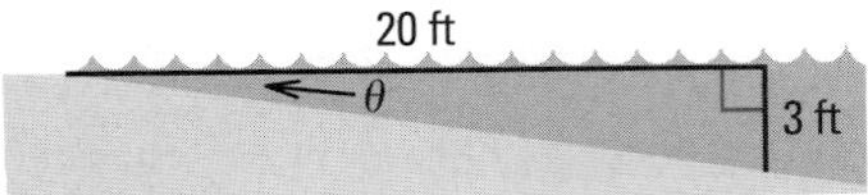

(1) 8.5° (3) 81.5°

(2) 24.7° (4) 87.2°

5. **OPEN-ENDED** On a baseball field, the pitcher's mound at P is 60.5 feet from home plate at H and 95 feet from an arc where the outfield grass begins.

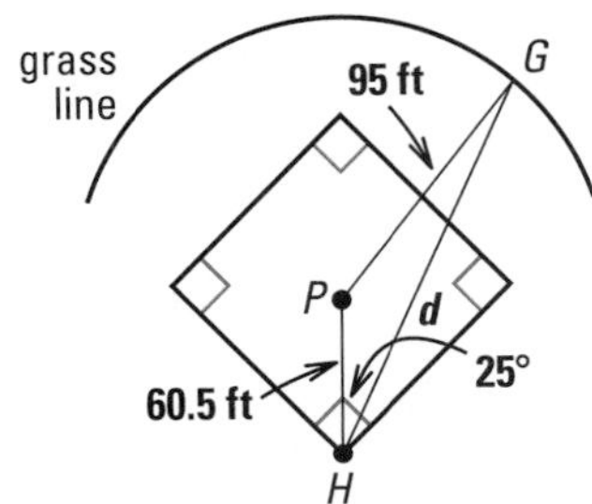

A ball is hit 25° to the right of the pitcher's mound and travels to the edge of the grass. What distance d must an outfielder at G throw the ball to make an out at home plate? *Explain.*

6. **OPEN-ENDED** A trough can be made by folding a rectangular piece of metal in half and then enclosing the ends. The volume of water the trough can hold depends on how far you bend the metal.

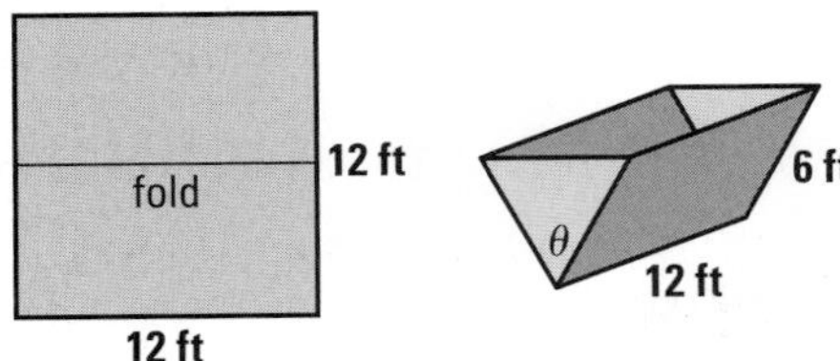

Find the volume of the trough as a function of θ. (*Hint:* You will need to find the area of one of the triangular faces.)

Describe how the volume changes as θ increases from 0° to 180°.

What value of θ maximizes the volume?

13 CHAPTER SUMMARY

BIG IDEAS

For Your Notebook

Big Idea 1

Using Trigonometric Functions

sine	cosine	tangent
$\sin\theta = \frac{\text{opp}}{\text{hyp}}$	$\cos\theta = \frac{\text{adj}}{\text{hyp}}$	$\tan\theta = \frac{\text{opp}}{\text{adj}}$
cosecant	**secant**	**cotangent**
$\csc\theta = \frac{\text{hyp}}{\text{opp}}$	$\sec\theta = \frac{\text{hyp}}{\text{adj}}$	$\cot\theta = \frac{\text{adj}}{\text{opp}}$

(Triangle labels: hypotenuse, opposite, adjacent, θ)

Big Idea 2

Using Inverse Trigonometric Functions

Inverse trigonometric functions can be used to solve trigonometric equations.

If $-1 \le a \le 1$, then the inverse sine of a is an angle θ, written $\sin^{-1} a = \theta$, where $\sin\theta = a$ and $-\frac{\pi}{2} \le \theta \le \frac{\pi}{2}$.

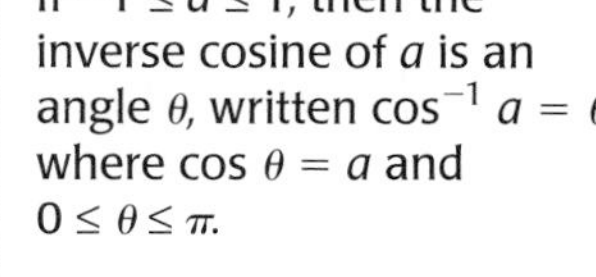

$\sin^{-1}\frac{1}{2} = 30°$

If $-1 \le a \le 1$, then the inverse cosine of a is an angle θ, written $\cos^{-1} a = \theta$, where $\cos\theta = a$ and $0 \le \theta \le \pi$.

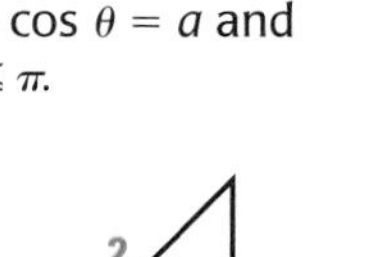

$\cos^{-1}\frac{\sqrt{2}}{2} = 45°$

If a is any real number, then the inverse tangent of a is an angle θ, written $\tan^{-1} a = \theta$, where $\tan\theta = a$ and $-\frac{\pi}{2} < \theta < \frac{\pi}{2}$.

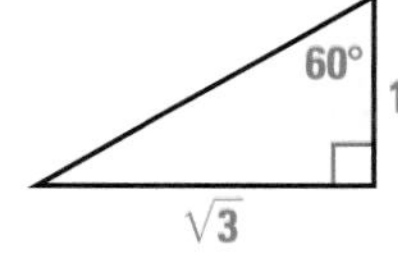

$\tan^{-1}\sqrt{3} = 60°$

Big Idea 3

Applying the Law of Sines and Law of Cosines

Use the table below to help you remember when to apply each law.

If you know this information ...	use this law ...	to find this information.
angle-angle-side	Law of sines	remaining sides*
angle-side-angle	Law of sines	remaining sides*
side-side-angle	Law of sines	remaining side and one angle*
side-angle-side	Law of cosines	remaining side and one angle*
side-side-side	Law of cosines	two angles*

* Find the remaining angle by using the triangle sum theorem.

13 CHAPTER REVIEW

@HomeTutor
classzone.com
- Multi-Language Glossary
- Vocabulary practice

REVIEW KEY VOCABULARY

- sine, *p. 852*
- cosine, *p. 852*
- tangent, *p. 852*
- cosecant, *p. 852*
- secant, *p. 852*
- cotangent, *p. 852*
- angle of elevation, *p. 855*
- angle of depression, *p. 855*
- initial side of an angle, *p. 859*
- terminal side of an angle, *p. 859*
- standard position of an angle, *p. 859*
- coterminal angles, *p. 860*
- radian, *p. 860*
- sector, *p. 861*
- central angle, *p. 861*
- unit circle, *p. 867*
- quadrantal angle, *p. 867*
- reference angle, *p. 868*
- inverse sine, *p. 875*
- inverse cosine, *p. 875*
- inverse tangent, *p. 875*
- law of sines, *p. 882*
- law of cosines, *p. 889*

VOCABULARY EXERCISES

1. **WRITING** *Describe* an angle in standard position.
2. Identify the relationship between the angles $-225°$ and $135°$.
3. What is the name of a circle with center at the origin and radius 1 unit?
4. Copy and complete: If $\cos \theta = a$ and $0 \le \theta \le \pi$, then the _?_ of a equals θ.
5. **WRITING** State the law of sines in words.

REVIEW EXAMPLES AND EXERCISES

Use the review examples and exercises below to check your understanding of the concepts you have learned in each lesson of Chapter 13.

13.1 Use Trigonometry with Right Triangles *pp. 852–858*

EXAMPLE

Evaluate the six trigonometric functions of the angle θ.

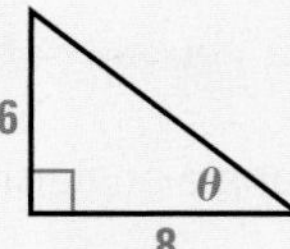

From the Pythagorean theorem, the length of the hypotenuse is $\sqrt{6^2 + 8^2} = \sqrt{100} = 10$.

$$\sin \theta = \frac{\text{opp}}{\text{hyp}} = \frac{6}{10} = \frac{3}{5} \qquad \cos \theta = \frac{\text{adj}}{\text{hyp}} = \frac{8}{10} = \frac{4}{5} \qquad \tan \theta = \frac{\text{opp}}{\text{adj}} = \frac{6}{8} = \frac{3}{4}$$

$$\csc \theta = \frac{\text{hyp}}{\text{opp}} = \frac{10}{6} = \frac{5}{3} \qquad \sec \theta = \frac{\text{hyp}}{\text{adj}} = \frac{10}{8} = \frac{5}{4} \qquad \cot \theta = \frac{\text{adj}}{\text{opp}} = \frac{8}{6} = \frac{4}{3}$$

EXERCISES

EXAMPLES 1 and 3 on pp. 852–854 for Exs. 6–7

6. In $\triangle ABC$, $a = 4$, $b = 5$, and $C = 90°$. Evaluate the six trigonometric functions of angle B.
7. **HOT AIR BALLOON** You are standing 50 meters from a hot air balloon that is preparing to take off. The angle of elevation to the top of the balloon is 28°. Find the height of the balloon.

@HomeTutor
classzone.com
Chapter Review Practice

13.2 Define General Angles and Use Radian Measure

pp. 859–865

EXAMPLE

Convert 110° to radians and $\frac{7\pi}{12}$ radians to degrees.

$$110° = 110°\left(\frac{\pi \text{ radians}}{180°}\right) \qquad \frac{7\pi}{12} \text{ radians} = \left(\frac{7\pi}{12} \text{ radians}\right)\left(\frac{180°}{\pi \text{ radians}}\right)$$

$$= \frac{11\pi}{18} \text{ radians} \qquad = 105°$$

EXERCISES

EXAMPLE 3
on p. 861
for Exs. 8–11

Convert the degree measure to radians or the radian measure to degrees.

8. 145° **9.** −80° **10.** $\frac{4\pi}{3}$ **11.** $\frac{11\pi}{6}$

13.3 Evaluate Trigonometric Functions of Any Angle

pp. 866–872

EXAMPLE

Evaluate sec 120°.

The reference angle is $\theta' = 180° - 120° = 60°$. The secant function is negative in Quadrant II, so you can write:

$$\sec 120° = -\sec 60° = -2$$

EXERCISES

EXAMPLE 4
on p. 869
for Exs. 12–15

Evaluate the function without using a calculator.

12. tan 330° **13.** csc (−405°) **14.** $\sin \frac{13\pi}{6}$ **15.** $\sec \frac{11\pi}{3}$

13.4 Evaluate Inverse Trigonometric Functions

pp. 875–880

EXAMPLE

Evaluate $\tan^{-1} 1$ in both radians and degrees.

When $-\frac{\pi}{2} < \theta < \frac{\pi}{2}$, or $-90° < \theta < 90°$, the angle θ whose tangent is 1 is:

$$\theta = \tan^{-1} 1 = \frac{\pi}{4} \quad \text{or} \quad \theta = \tan^{-1} 1 = 45°$$

EXERCISES

EXAMPLES 1 and 4
on pp. 876–877
for Exs. 16–17

16. Evaluate $\sin^{-1}(-0.5)$ in both radians and degrees.

17. RAMP You use a 12 foot ramp to load items into a van. If the floor of the van is 4 feet off the ground, what is the angle of elevation of the ramp?

13 CHAPTER REVIEW

13.5 Apply the Law of Sines

pp. 882–888

EXAMPLE

Solve $\triangle ABC$ with $A = 28°$, $C = 74°$, and $b = 22$.

Find angle B: $B = 180° - 28° - 74° = 78°$.

Use the law of sines to solve for a and c.

$$\frac{a}{\sin 28°} = \frac{22}{\sin 78°} \qquad \frac{c}{\sin 74°} = \frac{22}{\sin 78°}$$

$$a = \frac{22 \sin 28°}{\sin 78°} \approx 10.6 \qquad c = \frac{22 \sin 74°}{\sin 78°} \approx 21.6$$

▸ For $\triangle ABC$, $B = 78°$, $a \approx 10.6$, and $c \approx 21.6$.

EXERCISES

EXAMPLES 1, 2, 3 and 4 on pp. 882–884 for Exs. 18–21

Solve $\triangle ABC$. (*Hint:* Some of the "triangles" may have no solution and some may have two solutions.)

18. $A = 43°$, $C = 83°$, $b = 12$

19. $B = 104°$, $b = 25$, $c = 18$

20. $C = 55°$, $a = 17$, $c = 15$

21. $B = 60°$, $C = 73°$, $b = 20$

13.6 Apply the Law of Cosines

pp. 889–894

EXAMPLE

Solve $\triangle ABC$ with $A = 66°$, $b = 16$, and $c = 21$.

Use the law of cosines to find the length a.

$$a^2 = b^2 + c^2 - 2bc \cos A$$

$$a^2 = 16^2 + 21^2 - 2(16)(21) \cos 66°$$

$$a^2 \approx 423.7$$

$$a \approx 20.6$$

Now find angle B and angle C.

$$\frac{\sin B}{16} = \frac{\sin 66°}{20.6}$$

$$\sin B = \frac{16 \sin 66°}{20.6} \approx 0.7095$$

$$B = \sin^{-1} 0.7095 \approx 45.2°$$

$$C \approx 180° - 66° - 45.2° \approx 68.8°$$

▸ For $\triangle ABC$, $B \approx 45.2°$, $C \approx 68.8°$, and $a \approx 20.6$.

EXERCISES

EXAMPLES 1 and 2 on pp. 889–890 for Exs. 22–24

Solve $\triangle ABC$.

22. $a = 19$, $b = 11$, $c = 14$

23. $B = 75°$, $a = 20$, $c = 17$

24. $a = 30$, $b = 35$, $c = 39$

13 CHAPTER TEST

Evaluate the six trigonometric functions of the angle θ.

1. 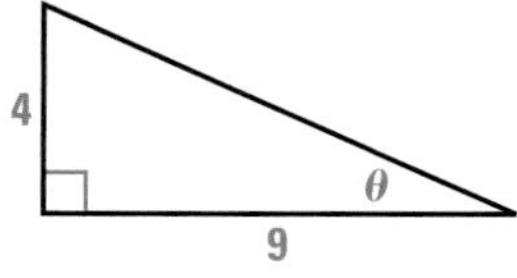

2. 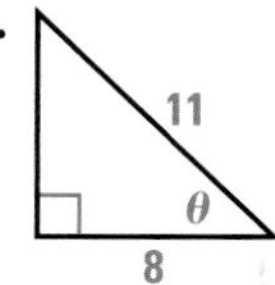

3. 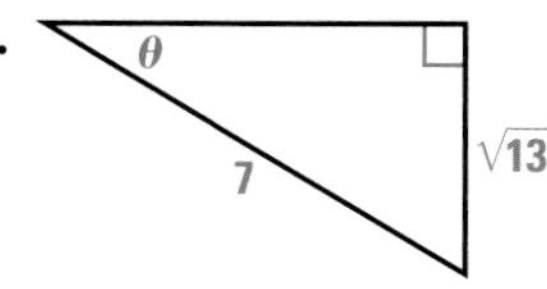

Convert the degree measure to radians or the radian measure to degrees.

4. $260°$
5. $-50°$
6. $\frac{4\pi}{5}$
7. $\frac{8\pi}{3}$

Evaluate the function without using a calculator.

8. $\tan 150°$
9. $\sec(-480°)$
10. $\sin\left(-\frac{5\pi}{3}\right)$
11. $\cos \frac{11\pi}{6}$

Evaluate the expression in both radians and degrees without using a calculator.

12. $\cos^{-1} 1$
13. $\tan^{-1} \sqrt{3}$
14. $\sin^{-1}\left(-\frac{\sqrt{2}}{2}\right)$
15. $\cos^{-1}\left(-\frac{\sqrt{3}}{2}\right)$

Solve $\triangle ABC$. (*Hint:* Some of the "triangles" may have no solution and some may have two solutions.)

16. $A = 47°, C = 32°, c = 12$
17. $a = 24, b = 12, c = 17$
18. $B = 63°, a = 11, b = 8$
19. $C = 101°, a = 23, b = 19$
20. $a = 24, b = 30, c = 21$
21. $A = 26°, B = 77°, c = 50$

Find the area of $\triangle ABC$.

22. $A = 81°, b = 16, c = 18$
23. $a = 8, b = 6, c = 7$
24. $a = 25, b = 24, c = 38$
25. $C = 111°, a = 7, b = 13$
26. $a = 16, b = 33, c = 24$
27. $B = 61°, a = 12, c = 18$

28. **SURVEYING** To measure the width of a river, you plant a stake at point A on one side of the riverbank, directly across from a tree stump at point B on the other side of the riverbank. From point A, you walk 80 meters along the riverbank to point C. You find the measure of angle C to be 39°. What is the width w of the river?

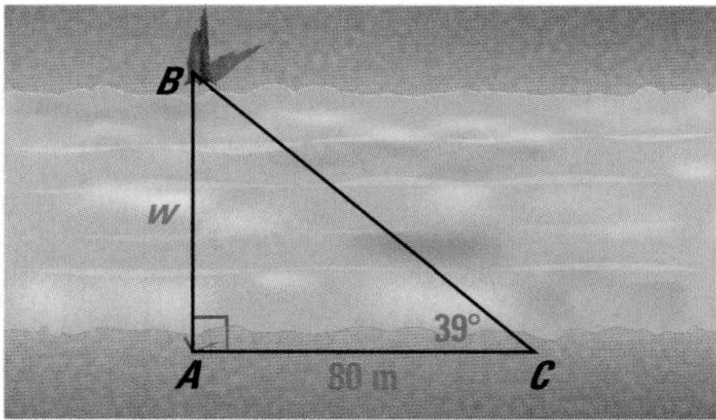

29. **CONSTRUCTION** A crane has a 200 foot arm with a lower end that is 5 feet off the ground. The arm has to reach to the top of a building that is 160 feet high. At what angle θ should the arm be set?

30. **NAVIGATION** A boat travels 40 miles due west before turning 20° and traveling an additional 25 miles. How far is the boat from its point of departure?

MULTIPLE CHOICE QUESTIONS

Some of the information you need to solve a multiple choice question may appear in a table, a diagram, or a graph.

PROBLEM 1

What is the volume of the right triangul ar prism shown?

(1) 969 cm^3 (3) 2,485 cm^3

(2) 1,938 cm^3 (4) 12,060 cm^3

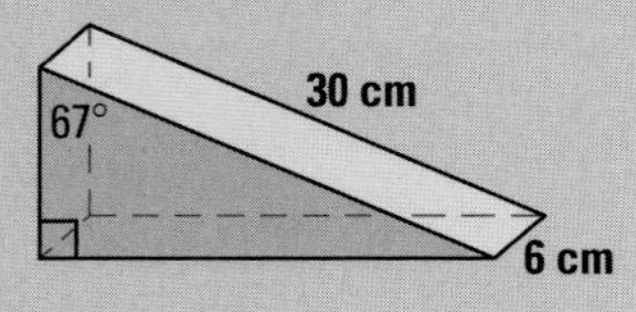

Plan

The volume of the prism shown is the area of its triangular cross section times the depth, 6 cm. To find the area of the triangle, the base and height are needed. These can be found using trigonometry.

Solution

Base of the triangle: $\sin 67° \times 30 \text{ cm} \approx 27.6 \text{ cm}$
Height of the triangle: $\cos 67° \times 30 \text{ cm} \approx 11.7 \text{ cm}$

We can use these values to find the area of the triangular cross-section:

$$A = \frac{1}{2}bh = \frac{1}{2} \cdot 27.6 \cdot 11.7 = 161.46 \text{ cm}^2$$

Finally, the volume of the prism is the area of the cross section times the depth:

$$V = A \times \text{depth} \approx 161.46 \times 6 \approx 969 \text{ cm}^3$$

Check

The hypotenuse of the triangular cross section is 30 cm. That means that the base of the triangle must be *less* than 30 cm. The triangle is approximately a 30°-60°-90° triangle, the "legs" of which are always in a 1 : 2 ratio. A rough estimate of the height, then, is half of 30 cm, or 15 cm. We also know that the base length of the triangle is in between the hypotenuse and the height. So a rough estimate for the base is 22 cm. Finally, a rough estimate of the volume is:

$$\frac{1}{2} \times 22 \text{ cm} \times 15 \text{ cm} \times 6 \text{ cm} = 990 \text{ cm}^3$$

Answer choices (2), (3), and (4) are substantially larger than 990 cm^3.

▸ The correct answer is (1).

PROBLEM 2

Marta kicks a soccer ball with an initial velocity of 40.0 feet per second at an angle of 45°. Luisa kicks another soccer ball at an angle of 25°. The balls traveled the same horizontal distance. With what initial velocity did Luisa kick the ball?

(1) 20.9 ft/sec (3) 45.7 ft/sec

(2) 40.0 ft/sec (4) 49.89 ft/sec

Plan

First, use the formula $d = \frac{v^2}{32} \sin 2\theta$ to find the distance of Marta's ball. Then use this result to solve for the velocity of Luisa's ball.

Solution

Using the initial velocity of 40 feet per second and the angle 45°, the horizontal distance traveled by Marta's ball is:

$$d = \frac{v^2}{32} \sin 2\theta = \frac{(40.0)^2}{32} \sin\big(2(45^\circ)\big) = 50 \sin 90^\circ = 50 \text{ feet}$$

Luisa's ball also traveled 50 feet. Find the initial velocity of Luisa's ball by solving the equation $d = \frac{v^2}{32} \sin 2\theta$ with the value $d = 50$ and $\theta = 25°$.

$$50 = \frac{v^2}{32} \sin\big(2(25^\circ)\big) \qquad v = +\sqrt{\frac{50 \cdot 32}{\sin(50^\circ)}} \approx 45.7 \text{ feet/second}$$

Check

Because Marta's angle of elevation was optimal (45°), she needs to kick the ball with less velocity than anyone else kicking it the same distance. So Luisa's velocity must be greater. This confirms that the answer 45.7 feet/second is the most reasonable.

▶ The correct answer is (3).

PRACTICE

Explain why you can eliminate the highlighted answer choice.

1. What is the angle of the ramp shown below, to the nearest hundredth of a degree?

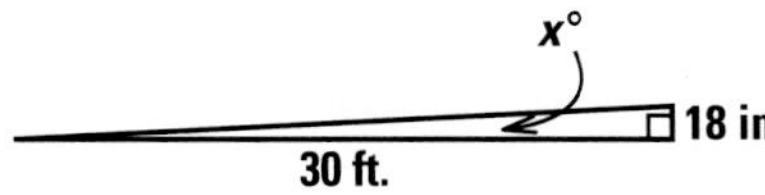

(1) 0.05° (2) 2.86° (3) 30.96° X(4) 87.14°

2. According to the ADA Accessibility Guidelines, the maximum slope of a wheelchair ramp is 1:12. What is the maximum angle of elevation of such a ramp?

X(1) 0.08° (2) 4.76° (3) 47.6° (4) 85.24°

TEST PREPARATION

New York **Test Practice**

MULTIPLE CHOICE

1. Kepler's second law states that an imaginary line connecting the center of a planet and the center of the sun sweeps out equal areas in equal time intervals. The diagram below shows the orbit of Mars over a ten day period.

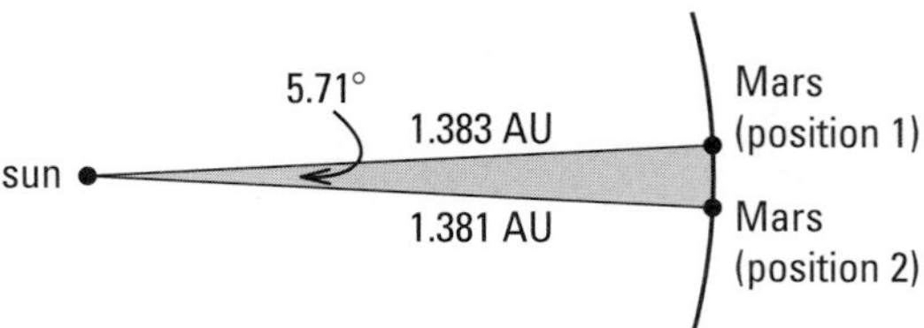

What is the approximate area Mars swept out during this time? (*Hint:* 1 AU is 1 astronomical unit, which equals about 93 million miles.)

(1) 8.8×10^6 mi^2 (3) 8.2×10^{14} mi^2

(2) 8.8×10^7 mi^2 (4) 8.2×10^{15} mi^2

2. A unicyclist is traveling forward in a straight line. The diameter of the wheel of her unicycle is 24 inches. How far does the unicycle travel if the wheel rotates 2160°?

(1) 6 ft, 3 in. (3) 18 ft, 10 in.

(2) 12 ft (4) 37 ft, 8 in.

3. You are standing 30 feet from the base of a tree. The angle of elevation from your eyes to the top of the tree is 70°. If the height at eye level is 5 feet, what is the height of the tree to the nearest foot?

(1) 15 ft (3) 33 ft

(2) 16 ft (4) 87 ft

4. What is the radius of a sector whose arc length is $\frac{10\pi}{3}$ inches and whose area is $\frac{25\pi}{3}$ in.^{2}?

(1) $\sqrt{5}$ inches (3) 5π inches

(2) 5 inches (4) 25 inches

5. What is the degree measure of angle A in triangle ABC if $a = 13$, $b = 9$, and $c = 11$?

(1) 49.34° (3) 99.59°

(2) 80.4° (4) 130.66°

6. A tennis player is practicing her serve. She aims for a mark 57 feet along the ground from her. She hits the ball when it is 9 feet in the air, and the ball travels in a straight line and hits the mark. Which equation below can be used to find the angle θ that the path of the ball makes with the ground?

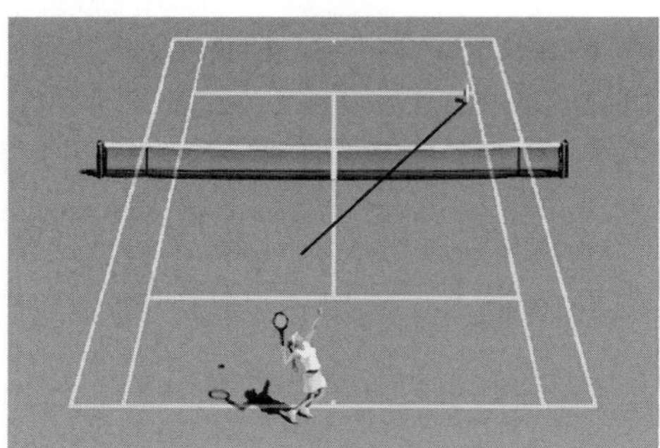

(1) $\tan \theta = \frac{9}{57}$ (3) $\tan \theta = \frac{57}{9}$

(2) $\sin \theta = \frac{9}{57}$ (4) $\sin \theta = \frac{57}{9}$

7. The diagrams below show the distances between atoms in a water molecule in liquid and ice forms. The measurements are given in picometers (pm), where 1 pm $= 10^{-12}$ m.

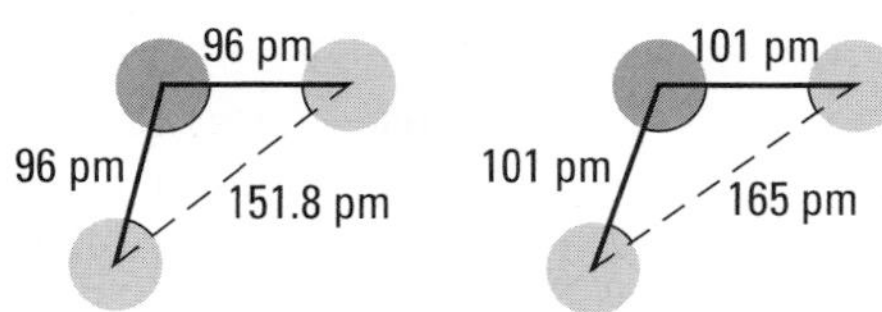

Which statement describes the obtuse angles?

(1) The obtuse angle for liquid is larger.

(2) The obtuse angle for ice is larger.

(3) The obtuse angles are equal in size.

(4) The angles cannot be determined.

8. To the nearest whole number, what is the approximate area of the triangle below?

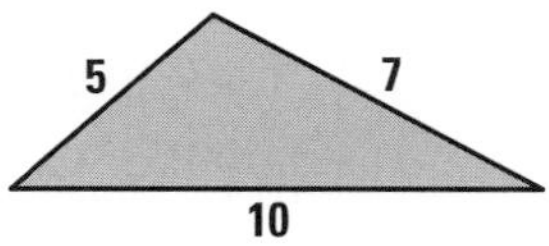

(1) 16 (2) 18 (3) 25 (4) 35

MULTIPLE CHOICE

9. Which angle measure is shown in the diagram?

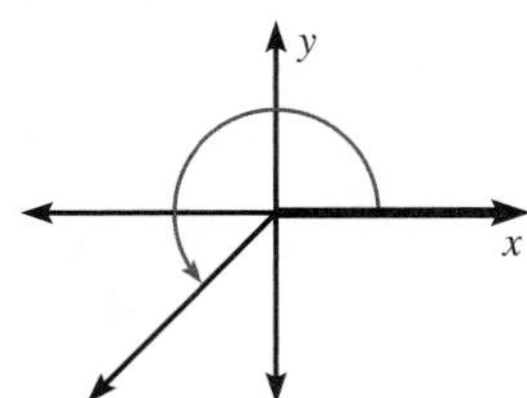

(1) $\frac{\pi}{4}$ radians (3) $\frac{5\pi}{4}$ radians

(2) $\frac{3\pi}{4}$ radians (4) $\frac{3\pi}{2}$ radians

10. What is the approximate value of a in $\triangle ABC$ if $A = 85°$, $B = 27°$, and $c = 5.0$ cm?

(1) 1.0 cm (3) 5.9 cm

(2) 5.4 cm (4) 11.0 cm

11. What is the reference angle for 300°?

(1) 30° (3) 120°

(2) 60° (4) 240°

12. If θ is an acute angle of a right triangle and $\sin\theta = \frac{3}{5}$, what is the value of $\cos\theta$?

(1) $\frac{2}{5}$ (2) $\frac{3}{5}$ (3) $\frac{3}{4}$ (4) $\frac{4}{5}$

13. What angle, in degrees, is equivalent to $\frac{5\pi}{6}$ radians?

(1) 30° (3) 300°

(2) 150° (4) 330°

14. What is the value of $\sin^{-1} 0.5$ in degrees?

(1) 0.008° (3) 0.52°

(2) 0.47° (4) 30°

15. Let (10, 24) be a point on the terminal side of an angle θ in standard position. What is the value of $\sec\theta$?

(1) $\frac{10}{24}$ (2) $\frac{26}{24}$ (3) $\frac{24}{10}$ (4) $\frac{26}{10}$

OPEN-ENDED

16. A boat uses 50 feet of rope to drop anchor in a lake. The angle θ that the rope makes with the bottom of the lake is 20°.

Find the depth of the water.

The boat moves to deeper water but still lets out the same amount of rope when dropping anchor. If the horizontal distance from the boat to the anchor is 37 feet, what angle θ does the rope make with the lake bottom?

Describe how θ changes as the boat travels to deeper water with 50 feet of anchor rope let out. Assume the rope is always taut.

17. You are making a lampshade out of fabric for the lamp shown. The pattern for the lampshade is shown in the diagram on the left.

Use the smaller sector to write an equation that relates θ and x.

Use the larger sector to write an equation that relates θ and $x + 10$.

Solve the system of equations from your answers above to find x and θ.

Use the formula for the area of a sector to find the amount of fabric (in square inches) that you will use.

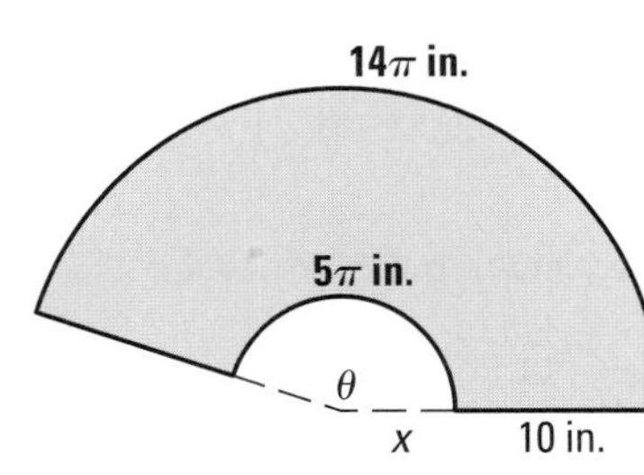

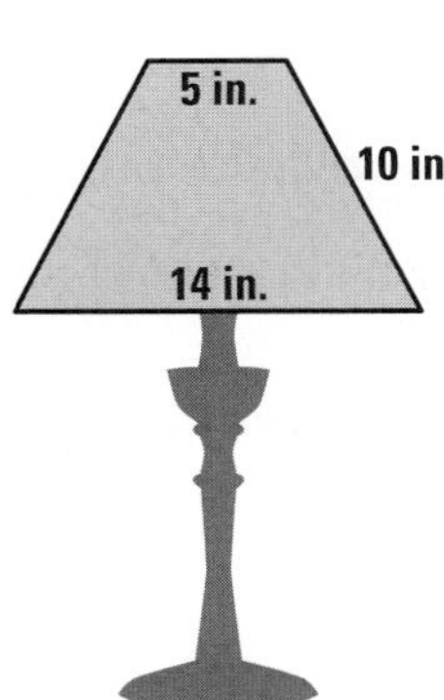

TEST PREPARATION

Trigonometric Graphs, Identities, and Equations

Before

In Chapter 13, you learned the following skills, which you'll use in Chapter 14: evaluating trigonometric functions, finding reference angles, and evaluating inverse trigonometric functions.

Prerequisite Skills

VOCABULARY CHECK

Copy and complete the statement.

1. The **sine** of θ is __?__.
2. The **cosine** of θ is __?__.
3. The **tangent** of θ is __?__.

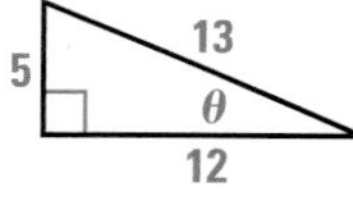

SKILLS CHECK

Evaluate the expression. *(Review p. 866 for 14.1.)*

4. $\sin 45°$
5. $\cos \frac{\pi}{2}$
6. $\tan \frac{\pi}{3}$

Sketch the angle. Then find its reference angle. *(Review p. 866 for 14.1.)*

7. $-165°$
8. $285°$
9. $-\frac{5\pi}{8}$

Evaluate the expression. *(Review p. 875 for 14.4.)*

10. $\sin^{-1} \frac{\sqrt{3}}{2}$
11. $\cos^{-1} 1$
12. $\tan^{-1} \sqrt{3}$

Now

In Chapter 14, you will apply the big ideas listed below and reviewed in the Chapter Summary on page 964. You will also use the key vocabulary listed below.

Big Ideas

1. **Graphing trigonometric functions**
2. **Solving trigonometric equations**
3. **Applying trigonometric formulas**

KEY VOCABULARY

- amplitude, *p. 908*
- periodic function, *p. 908*
- cycle, *p. 908*
- period, *p. 908*
- frequency, *p. 910*
- trigonometric identity, *p. 924*
- sinusoid, *p. 941*

Why?

You can use trigonometric functions to model characteristics of a projectile's path. For example, you can find the horizontal distance traveled by a soccer ball using trigonometric functions.

Animated Algebra

The animation illustrated below for Exercise 51 on page 961 helps you answer this question: How does changing the initial speed and angle of a soccer ball kicked from ground level affect the horizontal distance the ball travels?

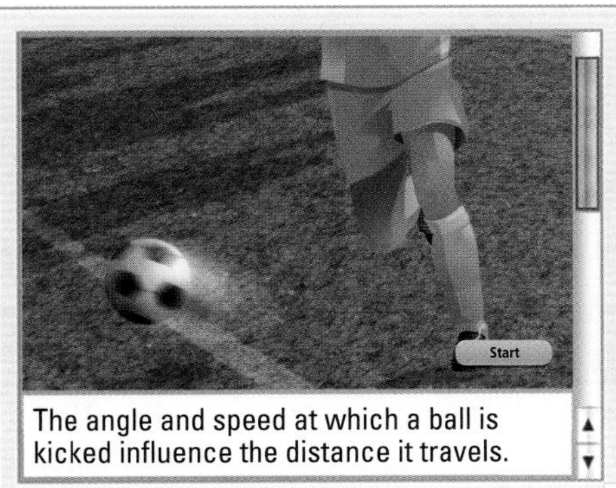

The angle and speed at which a ball is kicked influence the distance it travels.

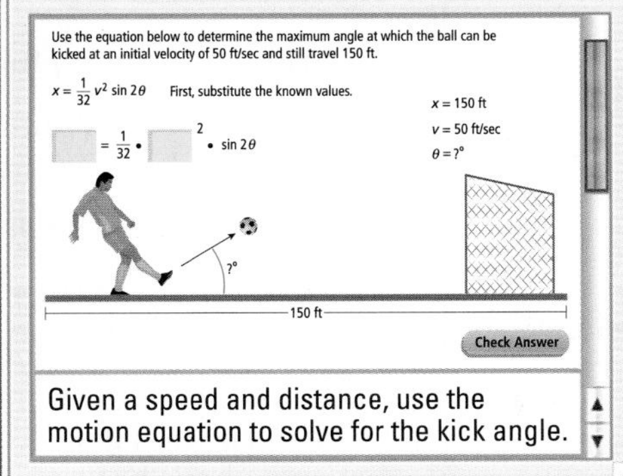

Given a speed and distance, use the motion equation to solve for the kick angle.

Animated Algebra at classzone.com

Other animations for Chapter 14: pages 912, 917, and 964

14.1 Graph Sine, Cosine, and Tangent Functions

 **A2.A.70** Sketch and recognize one cycle of a function of the form $y = A \sin Bx$ or $y = A \cos Bx$

Before You evaluated sine, cosine, and tangent functions.

Now You will graph sine, cosine, and tangent functions.

Why? So you can model oscillating motion, as in Ex. 31.

Key Vocabulary
- **amplitude**
- **periodic function**
- **cycle**
- **period**
- **frequency**

In this lesson, you will learn to graph functions of the form $y = a \sin bx$ and $y = a \cos bx$ where a and b are positive constants and x is in radian measure. The graphs of all sine and cosine functions are related to the graphs of the parent functions $y = \sin x$ and $y = \cos x$, which are shown below.

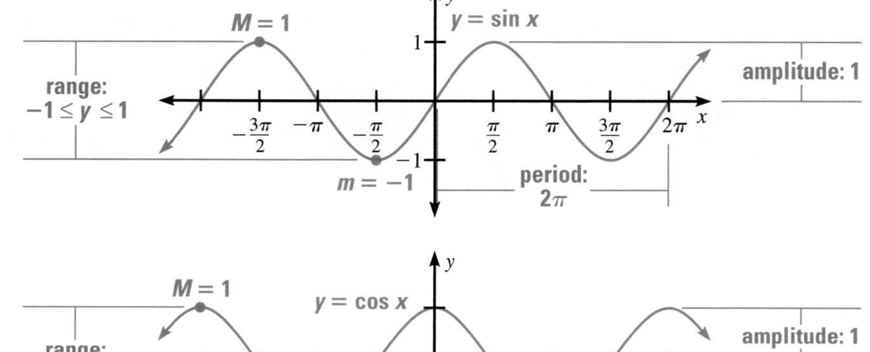

KEY CONCEPT *For Your Notebook*

Characteristics of $y = \sin x$ and $y = \cos x$

- The domain of each function is all real numbers.
- The range of each function is $-1 \le y \le 1$. Therefore, the minimum value of each function is $m = -1$ and the maximum value is $M = 1$.
- The **amplitude** of each function's graph is half the difference of the maximum M and the minimum m, or $\frac{1}{2}(M - m) = \frac{1}{2}[1 - (-1)] = 1$.
- Each function is **periodic**, which means that its graph has a repeating pattern. The shortest repeating portion of the graph is called a **cycle**. The horizontal length of each cycle is called the **period**. Each graph shown above has a period of 2π.
- The x-intercepts for $y = \sin x$ occur when $x = 0, \pm\pi, \pm 2\pi, \pm 3\pi, \ldots$.
- The x-intercepts for $y = \cos x$ occur when $x = \pm\frac{\pi}{2}, \pm\frac{3\pi}{2}, \pm\frac{5\pi}{2}, \pm\frac{7\pi}{2}, \ldots$.

KEY CONCEPT — *For Your Notebook*

Amplitude and Period

The amplitude and period of the graphs of $y = a \sin bx$ and $y = a \cos bx$, where a and b are nonzero real numbers, are as follows:

$$\text{Amplitude} = |a| \qquad \text{Period} = \frac{2\pi}{|b|}$$

GRAPHING KEY POINTS Each graph below shows five key x-values on the interval $0 \le x \le \frac{2\pi}{b}$ that you can use to sketch the graphs of $y = a \sin bx$ and $y = a \cos bx$ for $a > 0$ and $b > 0$. These are the x-values where the **maximum** and **minimum** values occur and the **x-intercepts**.

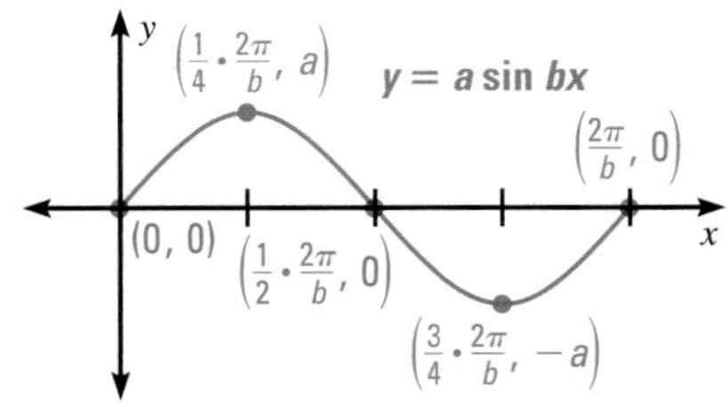

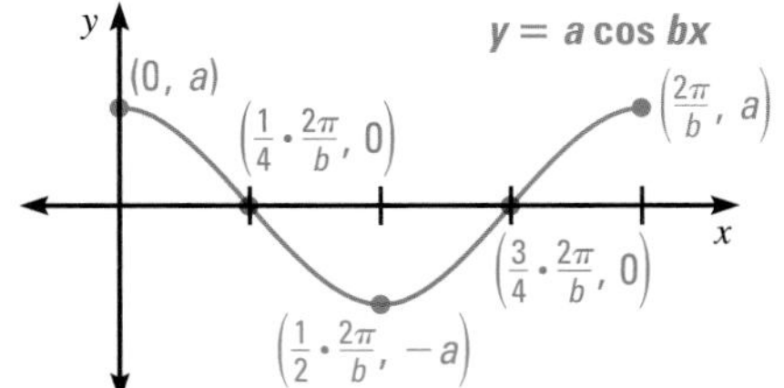

EXAMPLE 1 Graph sine and cosine functions

Graph (a) $y = 4 \sin x$ and (b) $y = \cos 4x$.

VARY CONSTANTS
Notice how changes in a and b affect the graphs of $y = a \sin bx$ and $y = a \cos bx$. When the value of a increases, the amplitude increases. When the value of b increases, the period decreases.

Solution

a. The amplitude is $a = 4$ and the period is $\frac{2\pi}{b} = \frac{2\pi}{1} = 2\pi$.

Intercepts: $(0, 0)$; $\left(\frac{1}{2} \cdot 2\pi, 0\right) = (\pi, 0)$; $(2\pi, 0)$

Maximum: $\left(\frac{1}{4} \cdot 2\pi, 4\right) = \left(\frac{\pi}{2}, 4\right)$

Minimum: $\left(\frac{3}{4} \cdot 2\pi, -4\right) = \left(\frac{3\pi}{2}, -4\right)$

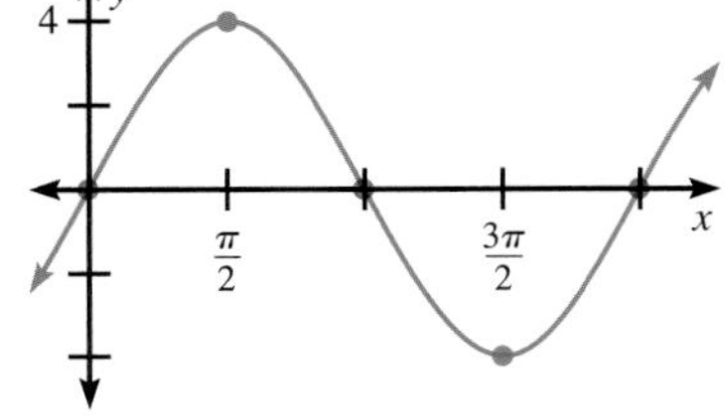

b. The amplitude is $a = 1$ and the period is $\frac{2\pi}{b} = \frac{2\pi}{4} = \frac{\pi}{2}$.

Intercepts: $\left(\frac{1}{4} \cdot \frac{\pi}{2}, 0\right) = \left(\frac{\pi}{8}, 0\right)$; $\left(\frac{3}{4} \cdot \frac{\pi}{2}, 0\right) = \left(\frac{3\pi}{8}, 0\right)$

Maximums: $(0, 1)$; $\left(\frac{\pi}{2}, 1\right)$

Minimum: $\left(\frac{1}{2} \cdot \frac{\pi}{2}, -1\right) = \left(\frac{\pi}{4}, -1\right)$

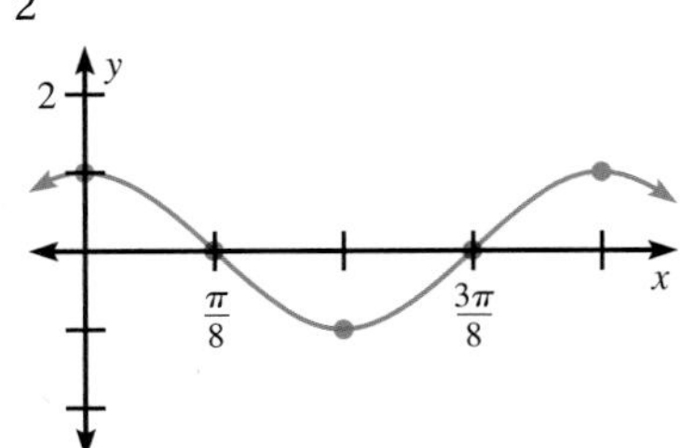

✓ GUIDED PRACTICE for Example 1

Graph the function.

1. $y = 2 \cos x$
2. $y = 5 \sin x$
3. $f(x) = \sin \pi x$
4. $g(x) = \cos 4\pi x$

EXAMPLE 2 Graph a cosine function

Graph $y = \frac{1}{2} \cos 2\pi x$.

SKETCH A GRAPH
After you have drawn one complete cycle of the graph in Example 2 on the interval $0 \le x \le 1$, you can extend the graph by copying the cycle as many times as desired to the left and right of $0 \le x \le 1$.

Solution

The amplitude is $a = \frac{1}{2}$ and the period is $\frac{2\pi}{b} = \frac{2\pi}{2\pi} = 1$.

Intercepts: $\left(\frac{1}{4} \cdot 1, 0\right) = \left(\frac{1}{4}, 0\right)$;

$\left(\frac{3}{4} \cdot 1, 0\right) = \left(\frac{3}{4}, 0\right)$

Maximums: $\left(0, \frac{1}{2}\right)$; $\left(1, \frac{1}{2}\right)$

Minimum: $\left(\frac{1}{2} \cdot 1, -\frac{1}{2}\right) = \left(\frac{1}{2}, -\frac{1}{2}\right)$

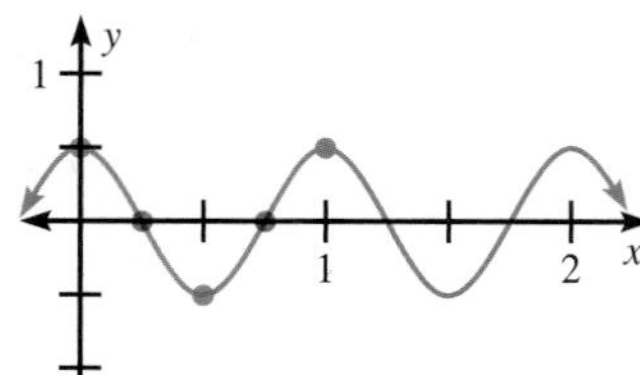

MODELING WITH TRIGONOMETRIC FUNCTIONS The periodic nature of trigonometric functions is useful for modeling *oscillating* motions or repeating patterns that occur in real life. Some examples are sound waves, the motion of a pendulum, and seasons of the year. In such applications, the reciprocal of the period is called the **frequency**, which gives the number of cycles per unit of time.

EXAMPLE 3 Model with a sine function

AUDIO TEST A sound consisting of a single frequency is called a pure tone. An *audiometer* produces pure tones to test a person's auditory functions. Suppose an audiometer produces a pure tone with a frequency f of 2000 hertz (cycles per second). The maximum pressure P produced from the pure tone is 2 millipascals. Write and graph a sine model that gives the pressure P as a function of the time t (in seconds).

Solution

STEP 1 **Find** the values of a and b in the model $P = a \sin bt$. The maximum pressure is 2, so $a = 2$. You can use the frequency f to find b.

$$\text{frequency} = \frac{1}{\text{period}} \quad \rightarrow \quad 2000 = \frac{b}{2\pi} \quad \rightarrow \quad 4000\pi = b$$

The pressure P as a function of time t is given by $P = 2 \sin 4000\pi t$.

STEP 2 **Graph** the model. The amplitude is $a = 2$ and the period is $\frac{1}{f} = \frac{1}{2000}$.

Intercepts: $(0, 0)$;

$\left(\frac{1}{2} \cdot \frac{1}{2000}, 0\right) = \left(\frac{1}{4000}, 0\right)$; $\left(\frac{1}{2000}, 0\right)$

Maximum: $\left(\frac{1}{4} \cdot \frac{1}{2000}, 2\right) = \left(\frac{1}{8000}, 2\right)$

Minimum: $\left(\frac{3}{4} \cdot \frac{1}{2000}, -2\right) = \left(\frac{3}{8000}, -2\right)$

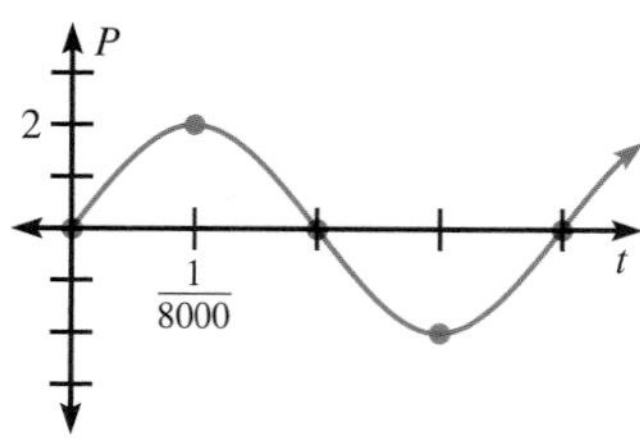

✓ GUIDED PRACTICE for Examples 2 and 3

Graph the function.

5. $y = \frac{1}{4} \sin \pi x$ **6.** $y = \frac{1}{3} \cos \pi x$ **7.** $f(x) = 2 \sin 3x$ **8.** $g(x) = 3 \cos 4x$

9. WHAT IF? In Example 3, how would the function change if the audiometer produced a pure tone with a frequency of 1000 hertz?

GRAPH OF $Y = \tan X$ The graphs of all tangent functions are related to the graph of the parent function $y = \tan x$, which is shown below.

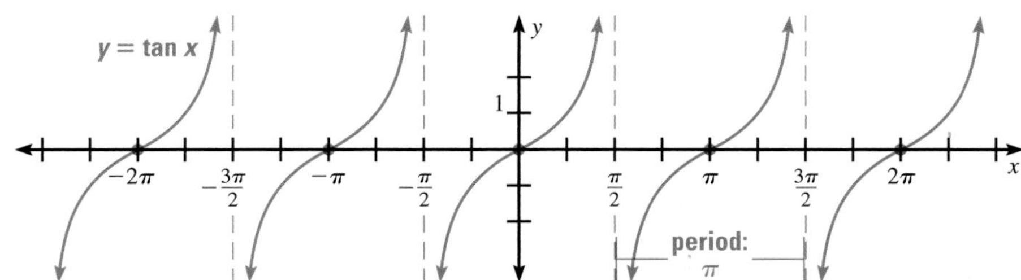

FIND ODD MULTIPLES
Odd multiples of $\frac{\pi}{2}$ are values such as these:

$\pm 1 \cdot \frac{\pi}{2} = \pm\frac{\pi}{2}$

$\pm 3 \cdot \frac{\pi}{2} = \pm\frac{3\pi}{2}$

$\pm 5 \cdot \frac{\pi}{2} = \pm\frac{5\pi}{2}$

The function $y = \tan x$ has the following characteristics:

1. The domain is all real numbers except odd multiples of $\frac{\pi}{2}$. At these x-values, the graph has vertical asymptotes.
2. The range is all real numbers. So, the function $y = \tan x$ does not have a maximum or minimum value, and therefore the graph of $y = \tan x$ does not have an amplitude.
3. The graph has a period of π.
4. The x-intercepts of the graph occur when $x = 0, \pm\pi, \pm 2\pi, \pm 3\pi, \ldots$.

KEY CONCEPT *For Your Notebook*

Characteristics of $y = a \tan bx$

The period and vertical asymptotes of the graph of $y = a \tan bx$, where a and b are nonzero real numbers, are as follows:

- The period is $\frac{\pi}{|b|}$.
- The vertical asymptotes are at odd multiples of $\frac{\pi}{2|b|}$.

GRAPHING KEY POINTS The graph at the right shows five key x-values that can help you sketch the graph of $y = a \tan bx$ for $a > 0$ and $b > 0$. These are the x-intercept, the x-values where the asymptotes occur, and the x-values halfway between the x-intercept and the asymptotes. At each halfway point, the function's value is either a or $-a$.

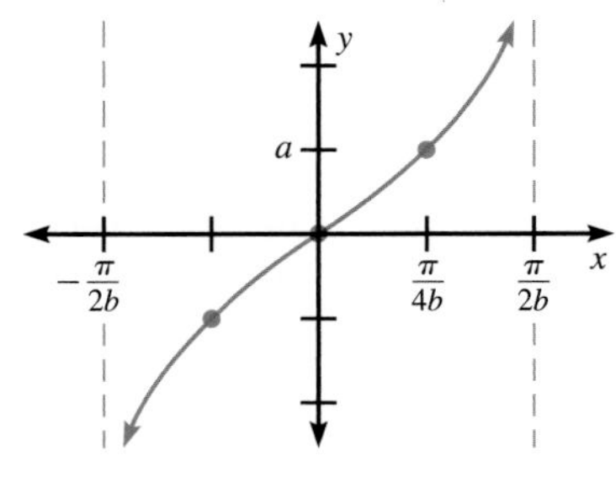

EXAMPLE 4 Graph a tangent function

Graph one period of the function $y = 2 \tan 3x$.

Solution

The period is $\frac{\pi}{b} = \frac{\pi}{3}$.

Intercept: (0, 0)

Asymptotes: $x = \frac{\pi}{2b} = \frac{\pi}{2 \cdot 3}$, or $x = \frac{\pi}{6}$;

$x = -\frac{\pi}{2b} = -\frac{\pi}{2 \cdot 3}$, or $x = -\frac{\pi}{6}$

Halfway points: $\left(\frac{\pi}{4b}, a\right) = \left(\frac{\pi}{4 \cdot 3}, 2\right) = \left(\frac{\pi}{12}, 2\right)$;

$\left(-\frac{\pi}{4b}, -a\right) = \left(-\frac{\pi}{4 \cdot 3}, -2\right) = \left(-\frac{\pi}{12}, -2\right)$

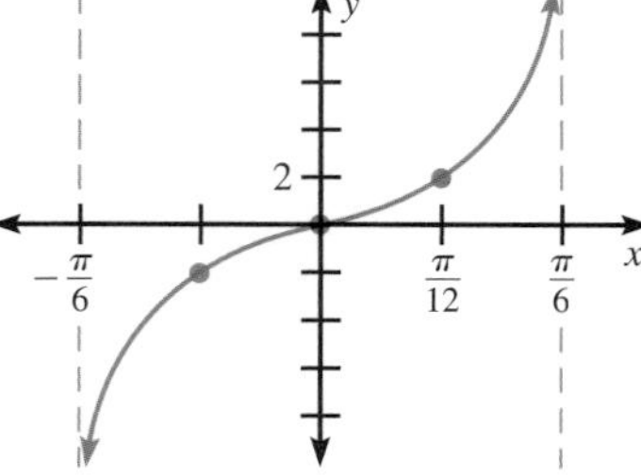

Animated Algebra at classzone.com

✓ GUIDED PRACTICE for Example 4

Graph one period of the function.

10. $y = 3 \tan x$ **11.** $y = \tan 2x$ **12.** $f(x) = 2 \tan 4x$ **13.** $g(x) = 5 \tan \pi x$

14.1 EXERCISES

HOMEWORK KEY

○ = WORKED-OUT SOLUTIONS on p. WS23 for Exs. 5, 17, and 31

★ = STANDARDIZED TEST PRACTICE Exs. 2, 15, 24, 25, and 31

◆ = MULTIPLE REPRESENTATIONS Ex. 32

SKILL PRACTICE

1. VOCABULARY Copy and complete: The graphs of the functions $y = \sin x$ and $y = \cos x$ both have a(n) __?__ of 2π.

2. ★ WRITING *Compare* the domains and ranges of the functions $y = a \sin bx$, $y = a \cos bx$, and $y = a \tan bx$ where a and b are positive constants.

EXAMPLE 1 on p. 909 for Exs. 3–14

ANALYZING FUNCTIONS **Identify the amplitude and the period of the graph of the function.**

3.

4.

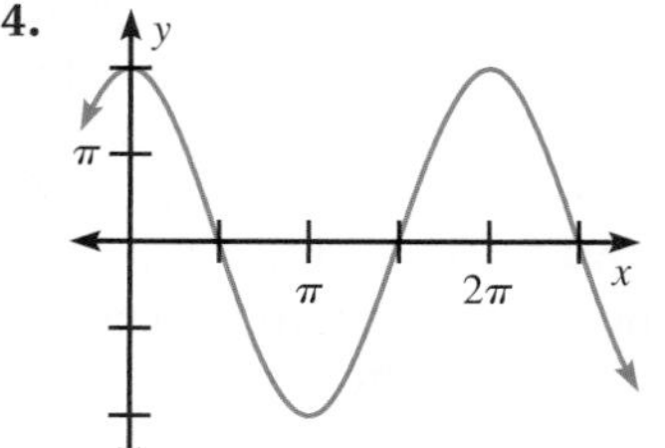

5.

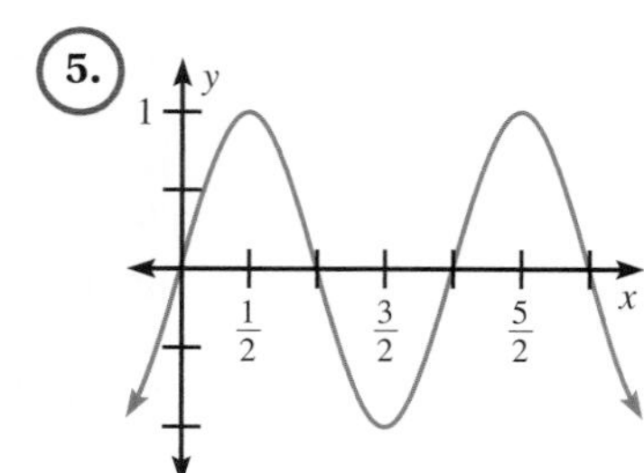

GRAPHING **Graph the function.**

6. $y = \sin \frac{1}{5}x$ 7. $y = 4 \cos x$ 8. $f(x) = \cos \frac{2}{5}x$ 9. $y = \sin \pi x$

10. $f(x) = \frac{2}{3} \sin x$ 11. $f(x) = \sin \frac{\pi}{2}x$ 12. $y = \frac{\pi}{4} \cos x$ 13. $f(x) = \cos 24x$

14. **ERROR ANALYSIS** *Describe* and correct the error in finding the period of the function $y = \sin \frac{2}{3}x$.

$$\text{Period} = \frac{|b|}{2\pi} = \frac{\left|\frac{2}{3}\right|}{2\pi} = \frac{1}{3\pi}$$

15. ★ **MULTIPLE CHOICE** The graph of which function has an amplitude of 4 and a period of 2?

Ⓐ $y = 4 \cos 2x$ Ⓑ $y = 2 \sin 4x$ Ⓒ $y = 4 \sin \pi x$ Ⓓ $y = 2 \cos \frac{1}{2}\pi x$

EXAMPLES 2, 3, and 4 on pp. 910–912 for Exs. 16–24

GRAPHING **Graph the function.**

16. $y = 2 \sin 8x$ 17. $f(x) = 4 \tan x$ 18. $y = 3 \cos \pi x$ 19. $y = 5 \sin 2x$

20. $f(x) = 2 \tan 4x$ 21. $y = 2 \cos \frac{1}{4}\pi x$ 22. $f(x) = 4 \tan \pi x$ 23. $y = \pi \cos 4\pi x$

24. ★ **MULTIPLE CHOICE** Which of the following is an asymptote of the graph of $y = 2 \tan 3x$?

Ⓐ $x = \frac{\pi}{6}$ Ⓑ $x = -\pi$ Ⓒ $x = \frac{1}{6}$ Ⓓ $x = -\frac{\pi}{12}$

25. ★ **OPEN-ENDED MATH** *Describe* a real-life situation that can be modeled by a periodic function.

CHALLENGE **Sketch the graph of the function by plotting points. Then state the function's domain, range, and period.**

26. $y = \csc x$ 27. $y = \sec x$ 28. $y = \cot x$

PROBLEM SOLVING

EXAMPLE 3 on p. 910 for Exs. 29–30

29. **PENDULUMS** The motion of a certain pendulum can be modeled by the function $d = 4 \cos \pi t$ where d is the pendulum's horizontal displacement (in inches) relative to its position at rest and t is the time (in seconds). Graph the function. What is the greatest horizontal distance the pendulum will travel from its position at rest?

@HomeTutor for problem solving help at classzone.com

30. **TUNING FORKS** A tuning fork produces a sound pressure wave that can be modeled by

$$P = 0.001 \sin 880t$$

where P is the pressure (in pascals) and t is the time (in seconds). Find the period and frequency of this function. Then graph the function.

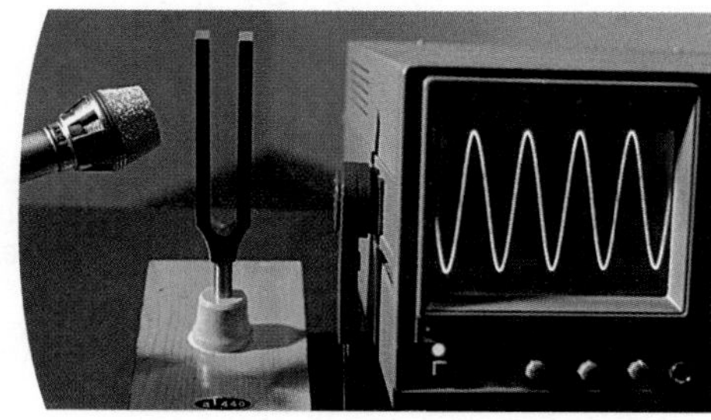

@HomeTutor for problem solving help at classzone.com

31. ★ **SHORT RESPONSE** A buoy oscillates up and down as waves go past. The buoy moves a total of 3.5 feet from its low point to its high point, and then returns to its high point every 6 seconds.

   a. Write an equation that gives the buoy's vertical position y at time t if the buoy is at its highest point when $t = 0$.

   b. *Explain* why you chose $y = a \sin bt$ or $y = a \cos bt$ for part (a).

32. **MULTIPLE REPRESENTATIONS** You are standing on a bridge, 140 feet above the ground. You look down at a car traveling away from the underpass.

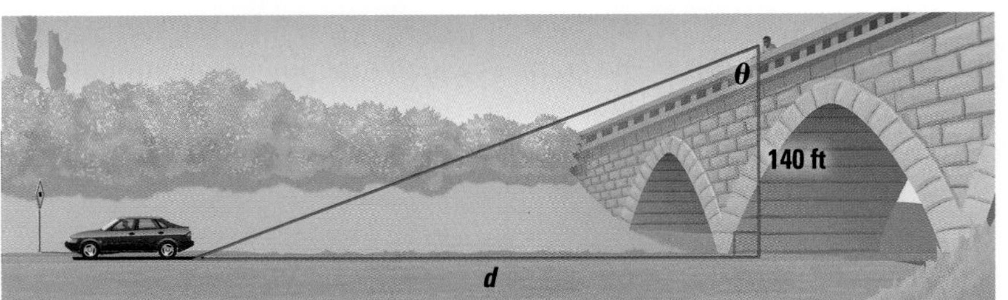

   a. Writing an Equation Write an equation that gives the car's distance d from the base of the bridge as a function of the angle θ.

   b. Drawing a Graph Graph the function found in part (a). *Explain* how the graph relates to the given situation.

   c. Making a Table Make a table of values for the function. Use the table to find the car's distance from the bridge when $\theta = 20°$, $40°$, and $60°$.

33. **CHALLENGE** The motion of a spring can be modeled by $y = A \cos kt$ where y is the spring's vertical displacement (in feet) relative to its position at rest, A is the initial displacement (in feet), k is a constant that measures the elasticity of the spring, and t is the time (in seconds).

   a. Suppose you have a spring whose motion can be modeled by the function $y = 0.2 \cos 6t$. Find the initial displacement and the period of the spring. Then graph the given function.

   b. Graphing Calculator If a damping force is applied to the spring, the motion of the spring can be modeled by the function $y = 0.2e^{-4.5t} \cos 4t$. Graph this function. What effect does damping have on the motion?

NEW YORK MIXED REVIEW

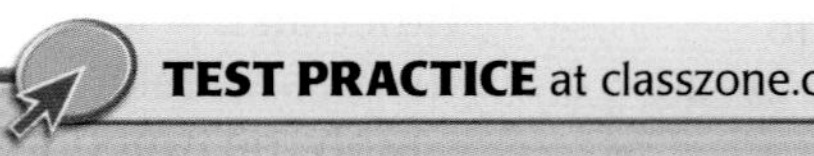

34. What is the area of $\triangle MNP$?

   Ⓐ 36 in.^{2} Ⓑ 72 in.^{2}

   Ⓒ 109 in.^{2} Ⓓ 144 in.^{2}

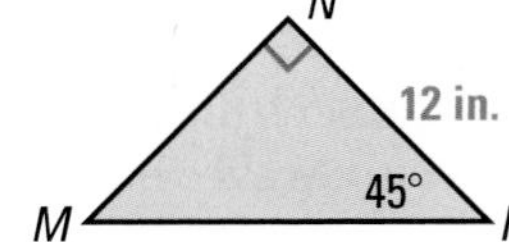

35. The length of $\overline{ST}$ is $7\sqrt{5}$ and the coordinates of its endpoints are $(x, -10)$ and $(-8, 4)$. What are the possible values of x?

   Ⓐ −15 Ⓑ 1

   Ⓒ −15, −1 Ⓓ 15, −1

14.2 Translate and Reflect Trigonometric Graphs

A2.A.69 Determine amplitude, period, frequency, and phase shift, given the graph or equation of a periodic function

Before You graphed sine, cosine, and tangent functions.

Now You will translate and reflect trigonometric graphs.

Why? So you can model predator-prey populations, as in Ex. 54.

Key Vocabulary
- **translation,** *p. 123*
- **reflection,** *p. 124*
- **amplitude,** *p. 908*
- **period,** *p. 908*

KEY CONCEPT *For Your Notebook*

Translations of Sine and Cosine Graphs

To graph $y = a \sin b(x - h) + k$ or $y = a \cos b(x - h) + k$ where $a > 0$ and $b > 0$, follow these steps:

STEP 1 **Identify** the amplitude a, the period $\frac{2\pi}{b}$, the horizontal shift h, and the vertical shift k of the graph.

STEP 2 **Draw** the horizontal line $y = k$, called the *midline* of the graph.

STEP 3 **Find** the five key points by translating the key points of $y = a \sin bx$ or $y = a \cos bx$ horizontally h units and vertically k units.

STEP 4 **Draw** the graph through the five translated key points.

EXAMPLE 1 Graph a vertical translation

Graph $y = 2 \sin 4x + 3$.

Solution

STEP 1 **Identify** the amplitude, period, horizontal shift, and vertical shift.

Amplitude: $a = 2$ Horizontal shift: $h = 0$

Period: $\frac{2\pi}{b} = \frac{2\pi}{4} = \frac{\pi}{2}$ Vertical shift: $k = 3$

STEP 2 **Draw** the midline of the graph, $y = 3$.

FIND KEY POINTS
Because the graph is shifted up 3 units, the y-coordinates of the five key points will be increased by 3.

STEP 3 **Find** the five key points.

On $y = k$: $(0, 0 + 3) = (0, 3)$;

$$\left(\frac{\pi}{4}, 0 + 3\right) = \left(\frac{\pi}{4}, 3\right); \left(\frac{\pi}{2}, 0 + 3\right) = \left(\frac{\pi}{2}, 3\right)$$

Maximum: $\left(\frac{\pi}{8}, 2 + 3\right) = \left(\frac{\pi}{8}, 5\right)$

Minimum: $\left(\frac{3\pi}{8}, -2 + 3\right) = \left(\frac{3\pi}{8}, 1\right)$

STEP 4 **Draw** the graph through the key points.

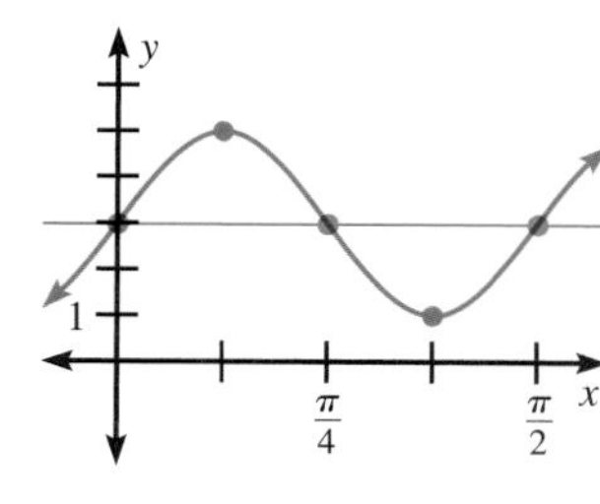

EXAMPLE 2 Graph a horizontal translation

Graph $y = 5\cos 2(x - 3\pi)$.

Solution

STEP 1 **Identify** the amplitude, period, horizontal shift, and vertical shift.

Amplitude: $a = 5$ Horizontal shift: $h = 3\pi$

Period: $\frac{2\pi}{b} = \frac{2\pi}{2} = \pi$ Vertical shift: $k = 0$

STEP 2 **Draw** the midline of the graph. Because $k = 0$, the midline is the x-axis.

FIND KEY POINTS
Because the graph is shifted to the right 3π units, the x-coordinates of the five key points will be increased by 3π.

STEP 3 **Find** the five key points.

On $y = k$: $\left(\frac{\pi}{4} + 3\pi, 0\right) = \left(\frac{13\pi}{4}, 0\right)$;

$\left(\frac{3\pi}{4} + 3\pi, 0\right) = \left(\frac{15\pi}{4}, 0\right)$

Maximums: $(0 + 3\pi, 5) = (3\pi, 5)$;
$(\pi + 3\pi, 5) = (4\pi, 5)$

Minimum: $\left(\frac{\pi}{2} + 3\pi, -5\right) = \left(\frac{7\pi}{2}, -5\right)$

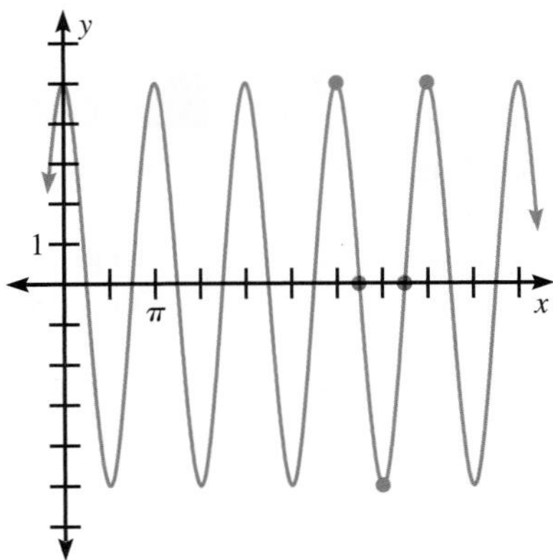

STEP 4 **Draw** the graph through the key points.

EXAMPLE 3 Graph a model for circular motion

FERRIS WHEEL Suppose you are riding a Ferris wheel that turns for 180 seconds. Your height h (in feet) above the ground at any time t (in seconds) can be modeled by the equation $h = 85\sin\frac{\pi}{20}(t - 10) + 90$.

a. Graph your height above the ground as a function of time.

b. What are your maximum and minimum heights?

Solution

a. The amplitude is 85 and the period is $\frac{2\pi}{\frac{\pi}{20}} = 40$. The wheel turns $\frac{180}{40} = 4.5$ times in 180 seconds, so the graph below shows 4.5 cycles.

The five key points are (10, 90), (20, 175), (30, 90), (40, 5), and (50, 90).

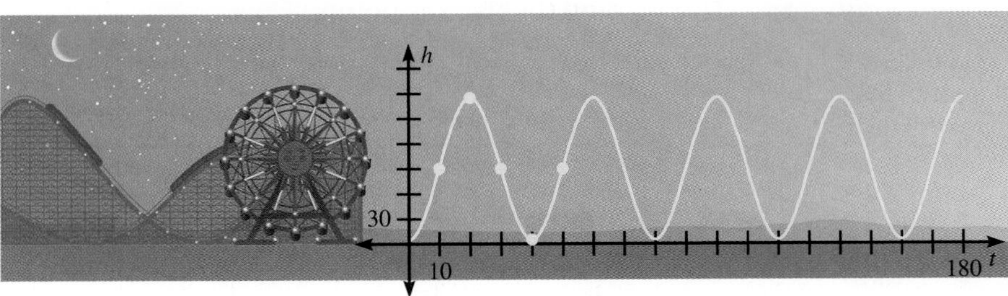

b. Your maximum height is $90 + 85 = 175$ feet and your minimum height is $90 - 85 = 5$ feet.

✓ GUIDED PRACTICE for Examples 1, 2, and 3

Graph the function.

1. $y = \cos x + 4$
2. $y = 3 \sin \left(x - \frac{\pi}{2}\right)$
3. $f(x) = \sin (x + \pi) - 1$

REFLECTIONS You have graphed functions of the form $y = a \sin b(x - h) + k$ and $y = a \cos b(x - h) + k$ where $a > 0$. To see what happens when $a < 0$, consider the graphs of $y = -\sin x$ and $y = -\cos x$.

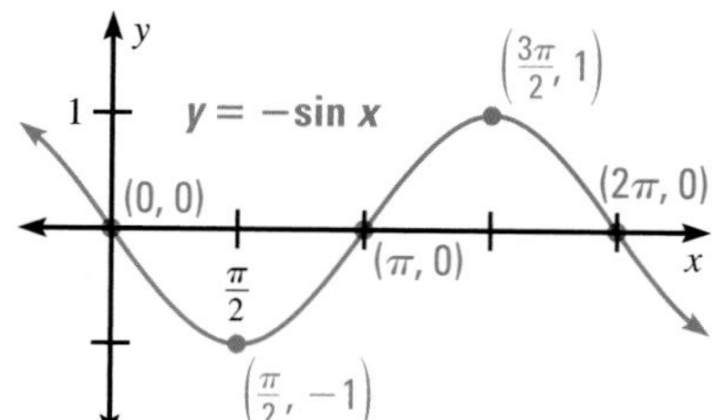

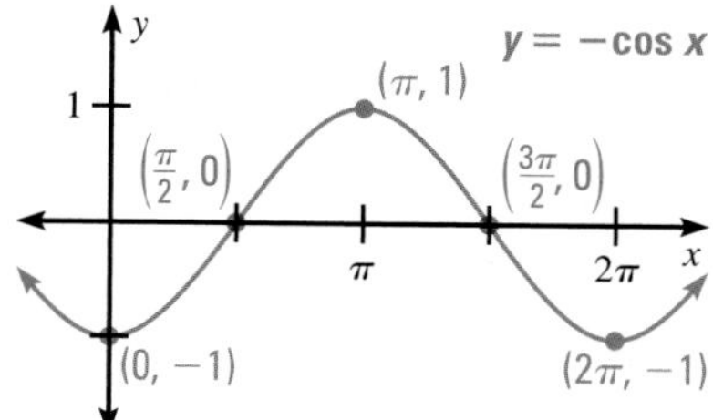

Notice that the graphs are reflections of the graphs of $y = \sin x$ and $y = \cos x$ in the x-axis. In general, when $a < 0$ the graphs of $y = a \sin b(x - h) + k$ and $y = a \cos b(x - h) + k$ are reflections of the graphs of $y = |a| \sin b(x - h) + k$ and $y = |a| \cos b(x - h) + k$, respectively, in the midline $y = k$.

EXAMPLE 4 Combine a translation and a reflection

Graph $y = -2 \sin \frac{2}{3}\left(x - \frac{\pi}{2}\right)$.

Solution

STEP 1 **Identify** the amplitude, period, horizontal shift, and vertical shift.

Amplitude: $|a| = |-2| = 2$ Horizontal shift: $h = \frac{\pi}{2}$

Period: $\frac{2\pi}{b} = \frac{2\pi}{\frac{2}{3}} = 3\pi$ Vertical shift: $k = 0$

STEP 2 **Draw** the midline of the graph. Because $k = 0$, the midline is the x-axis.

STEP 3 **Find** the five key points of $y = |-2| \sin \frac{2}{3}\left(x - \frac{\pi}{2}\right)$.

On $y = k$: $\left(0 + \frac{\pi}{2}, 0\right) = \left(\frac{\pi}{2}, 0\right)$; $\left(\frac{3\pi}{2} + \frac{\pi}{2}, 0\right) = (2\pi, 0)$; $\left(3\pi + \frac{\pi}{2}, 0\right) = \left(\frac{7\pi}{2}, 0\right)$

Maximum: $\left(\frac{3\pi}{4} + \frac{\pi}{2}, 2\right) = \left(\frac{5\pi}{4}, 2\right)$ **Minimum:** $\left(\frac{9\pi}{4} + \frac{\pi}{2}, -2\right) = \left(\frac{11\pi}{4}, -2\right)$

GRAPH REFLECTIONS
The maximum and minimum of the original graph become the minimum and maximum, respectively, of the reflected graph.

STEP 4 **Reflect** the graph. Because $a < 0$, the graph is reflected in the midline $y = 0$. So, $\left(\frac{5\pi}{4}, 2\right)$ becomes $\left(\frac{5\pi}{4}, -2\right)$ and $\left(\frac{11\pi}{4}, -2\right)$ becomes $\left(\frac{11\pi}{4}, 2\right)$.

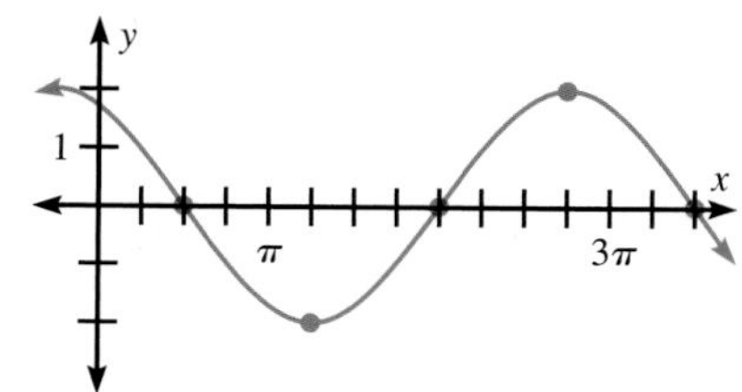

STEP 5 **Draw** the graph through the key points.

Animated Algebra at classzone.com

TANGENT FUNCTIONS Graphing tangent functions using translations and reflections is similar to graphing sine and cosine functions.

EXAMPLE 5 Combine a translation and a reflection

Graph $y = -3 \tan x + 5$.

Solution

STEP 1 **Identify** the period, horizontal shift, and vertical shift.

Period: π Horizontal shift: $h = 0$ Vertical shift: $k = 5$

STEP 2 **Draw** the midline of the graph, $y = 5$.

STEP 3 **Find** the asymptotes and key points of $y = |-3| \tan x + 5$.

FIND ASYMPTOTES
Notice that the asymptotes are not shifted. This is because there is no horizontal shift.

Asymptotes: $x = -\frac{\pi}{2 \cdot 1} = -\frac{\pi}{2}$; $x = \frac{\pi}{2 \cdot 1} = \frac{\pi}{2}$

On $y = k$: $(0, 0 + 5) = (0, 5)$

Halfway points: $\left(-\frac{\pi}{4}, -3 + 5\right) = \left(-\frac{\pi}{4}, 2\right)$; $\left(\frac{\pi}{4}, 3 + 5\right) = \left(\frac{\pi}{4}, 8\right)$

STEP 4 **Reflect** the graph. Because $a < 0$, the graph is reflected in the midline $y = 5$. So, $\left(-\frac{\pi}{4}, 2\right)$ becomes $\left(-\frac{\pi}{4}, 8\right)$ and $\left(\frac{\pi}{4}, 8\right)$ becomes $\left(\frac{\pi}{4}, 2\right)$.

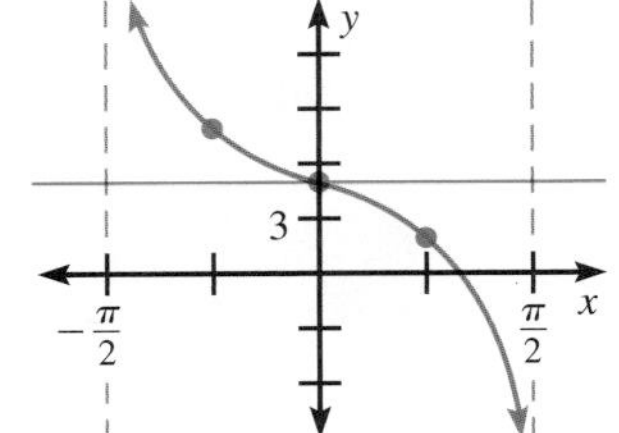

STEP 5 **Draw** the graph through the key points.

EXAMPLE 6 Model with a tangent function

GLASS ELEVATOR You are standing 120 feet from the base of a 260 foot building. You watch your friend go down the side of the building in a glass elevator. Write and graph a model that gives your friend's distance d (in feet) from the top of the building as a function of the angle of elevation θ.

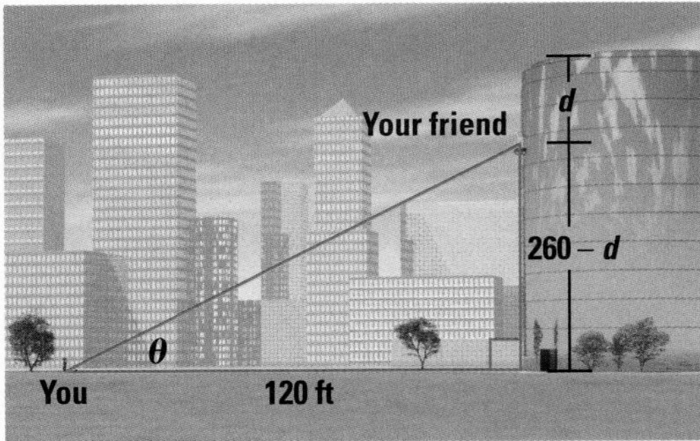

Solution

Use a tangent function to write an equation relating d and θ.

$\tan \theta = \frac{\text{opp}}{\text{adj}} = \frac{260 - d}{120}$ **Definition of tangent**

$120 \tan \theta = 260 - d$ **Multiply each side by 120.**

$120 \tan \theta - 260 = -d$ **Subtract 260 from each side.**

$-120 \tan \theta + 260 = d$ **Solve for *d*.**

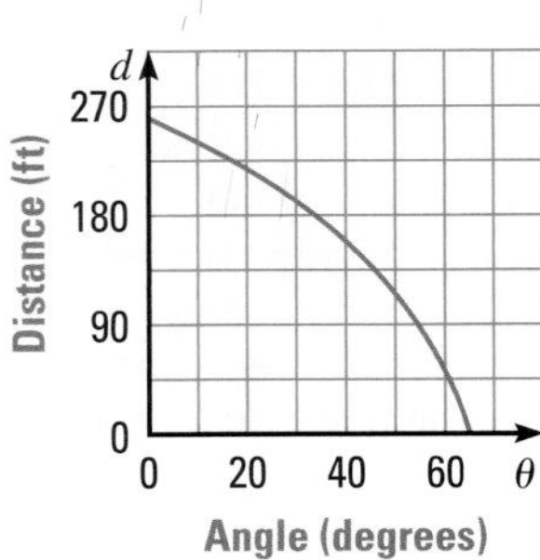

The graph of $d = -120 \tan \theta + 260$ is shown at the right.

✓ GUIDED PRACTICE for Examples 4, 5, and 6

Graph the function.

4. $y = -\cos\left(x + \frac{\pi}{2}\right)$
5. $y = -3 \sin \frac{1}{2}x + 2$
6. $f(x) = -\tan 2x - 1$
7. **WHAT IF?** In Example 6, how does the model change if you are standing 150 feet from a building that is 400 feet tall?

14.2 EXERCISES

HOMEWORK KEY

○ = **WORKED-OUT SOLUTIONS on p. WS23 for Exs. 11, 23, and 53**

★ = **STANDARDIZED TEST PRACTICE Exs. 2, 21, 35, 48, and 54**

SKILL PRACTICE

1. **VOCABULARY** Copy and complete: The graph of $y = \cos 2(x - 3)$ is the graph of $y = \cos 2x$ translated _?_ units to the right.

2. ★ **WRITING** *Describe* the difference between the graphs of $y = \tan x$ and $y = -\tan x$. How are the graphs related?

EXAMPLES 1 and 2 on pp. 915–916 for Exs. 3–21

MATCHING Match the function with its graph.

3. $y = \sin 2\left(x + \frac{\pi}{2}\right)$
4. $f(x) = \cos(x + \pi)$
5. $y = \cos x - 2$
6. $y = \sin\left(x + \frac{\pi}{4}\right)$
7. $y = \cos \frac{1}{2}x + 1$
8. $f(x) = \sin \frac{1}{2}(x - \pi)$

A. 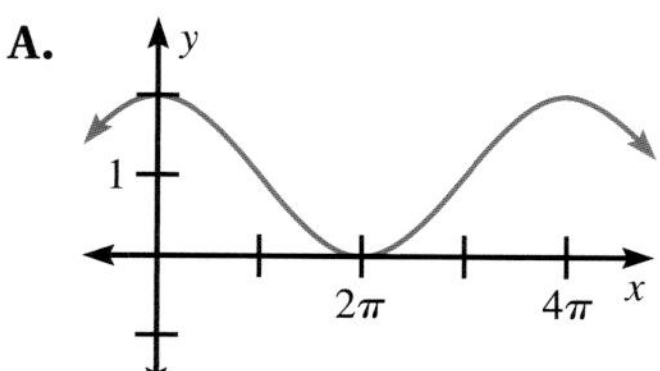

B. 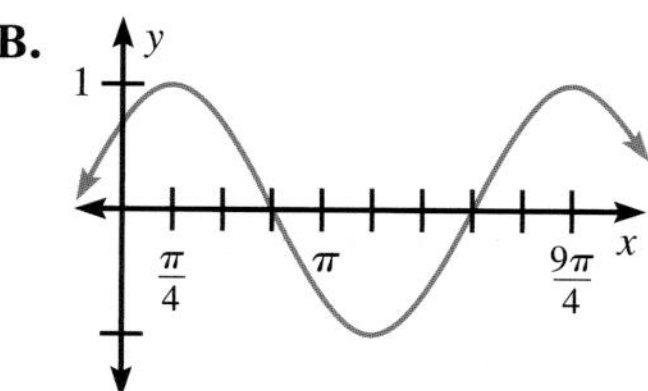

C. 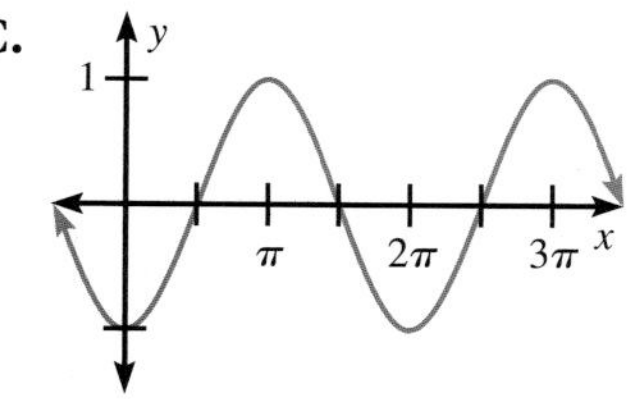

D. 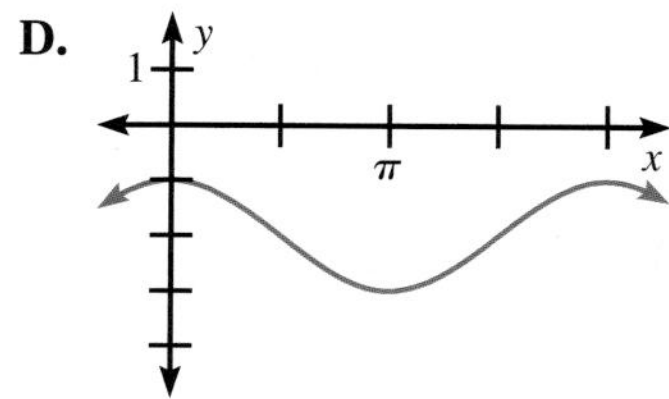

E. 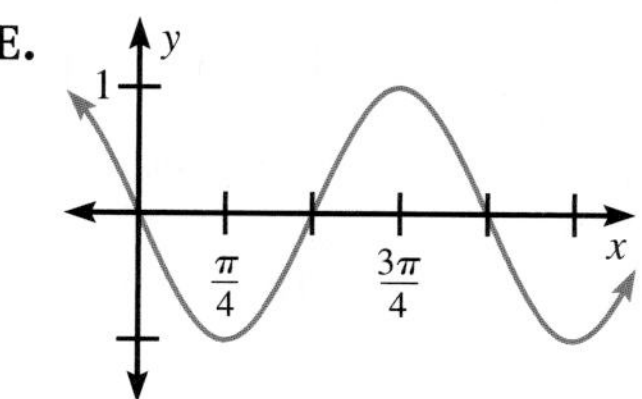

F. 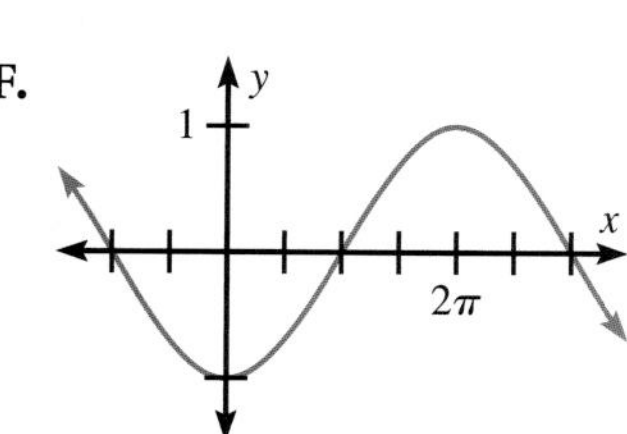

GRAPHING Graph the sine or cosine function.

9. $y = \sin x + 3$
10. $y = \cos x - 5$
11. $y = 2 \cos x + 1$
12. $y = \sin 3x - 4$
13. $f(x) = \sin\left(x + \frac{\pi}{4}\right)$
14. $y = \cos\left(x - \frac{\pi}{2}\right)$
15. $y = \cos 2(x + \pi)$
16. $f(x) = \frac{1}{2} \sin\left(x - \frac{3\pi}{2}\right)$
17. $y = 4 \sin \frac{1}{3}\left(x + \frac{\pi}{2}\right)$
18. $f(x) = \cos\left(x - \frac{\pi}{8}\right) + 2$
19. $y = 3 \cos\left(x + \frac{3\pi}{4}\right) - 1$
20. $y = \sin 2(x + 2\pi) - 3$

21. ★ **MULTIPLE CHOICE** The graph of which function is shown?

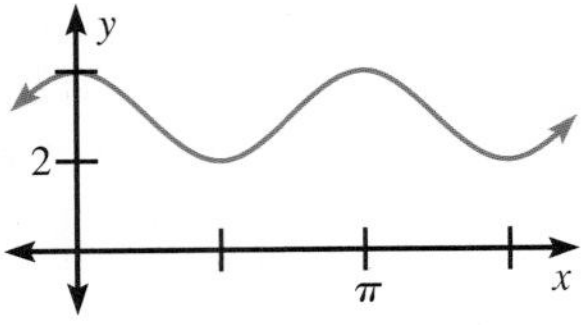

Ⓐ $y = \cos \frac{1}{2}x + 3$ Ⓑ $y = \cos x + 3$

Ⓒ $y = \cos 2x + 3$ Ⓓ $y = \cos (x + \pi) + 3$

EXAMPLE 4 on p. 917 for Exs. 22–33

GRAPHING **Graph the sine or cosine function.**

22. $f(x) = -\sin x + 2$

23. $y = -\sin \frac{1}{2}x + 3$

24. $y = -\cos 2x - 2$

25. $y = -\sin\left(x - \frac{\pi}{4}\right)$

26. $f(x) = -\sin (x - \pi)$

27. $y = -2 \cos \frac{1}{4}x$

28. $y = -3 \cos (x - \pi) + 4$

29. $y = -\cos (x + \pi) + 1$

30. $f(x) = 1 - 3 \sin (x + \pi)$

31. $y = -\sin\left(x - \frac{3\pi}{2}\right) + 2$

32. $f(x) = -\cos\left(x + \frac{\pi}{2}\right) - 2$

33. $y = -4 \cos 2\left(x - \frac{\pi}{4}\right)$

34. **ERROR ANALYSIS** *Describe* and correct the error in determining the maximum point of the function $y = 2 \sin\left(x - \frac{\pi}{2}\right)$.

Maximum: $\left(\left(\frac{1}{4} \cdot 2\pi\right) - \frac{\pi}{2}, 2\right) = \left(\frac{\pi}{2} - \frac{\pi}{2}, 2\right) = (0, 2)$ ✗

35. ★ **MULTIPLE CHOICE** Which of the following is a maximum point of the graph of $y = -4 \cos\left(x - \frac{\pi}{2}\right)$?

Ⓐ $\left(-\frac{\pi}{2}, 4\right)$ Ⓑ $(0, 4)$ Ⓒ $\left(\frac{\pi}{2}, 4\right)$ Ⓓ $(\pi, 4)$

EXAMPLE 5 on p. 918 for Exs. 36–41

GRAPHING **Graph the tangent function.**

36. $y = -\frac{1}{2} \tan x$

37. $y = \tan 2x - 3$

38. $y = -\tan 4x + 2$

39. $y = 2 \tan\left(x + \frac{\pi}{2}\right)$

40. $y = -\tan 2\left(x - \frac{\pi}{2}\right)$

41. $y = -\frac{1}{2} \tan\left(x - \frac{\pi}{4}\right)$

WRITING EQUATIONS **In Exercises 42–46, write an equation of the graph described.**

42. The graph of $y = \cos 2\pi x$ translated down 4 units and left 3 units

43. The graph of $y = 3 \sin x$ translated up 2 units and right π units

44. The graph of $y = 5 \tan x$ translated right $\frac{\pi}{4}$ unit and then reflected in the x-axis

45. The graph of $y = \frac{1}{3} \cos \pi x$ translated down 1 unit and then reflected in the line $y = -1$

46. The graph of $y = \frac{1}{2} \sin 6x$ translated down $\frac{3}{2}$ units and right 1 unit, and then reflected in the line $y = -\frac{3}{2}$

47. **REASONING** *Explain* how you can obtain the graph of $y = \cos x$ by translating the graph of $y = \sin x$.

48. ★ **SHORT RESPONSE** *Explain* why there is more than one tangent function whose graph passes through the origin and has asymptotes at $x = -\pi$ and $x = \pi$.

49. **CHALLENGE** Find a tangent function whose graph intersects the graph of $y = 2 + 2 \sin x$ only at minimum points of the sine graph.

PROBLEM SOLVING

EXAMPLE 3 on p. 916 for Exs. 50–51

50. **WATER WHEEL** The Great Laxey wheel, located on the Isle of Man, is one of the largest working water wheels in the world. The wheel was built in 1854 to pump water from the mines underneath it. The height h (in feet) above the viewing platform of a bucket on the wheel can be approximated by the function

$$h = 36.25 \sin \frac{\pi}{12}t + 34.25$$

where t is time (in seconds). Graph the function. Find the diameter of the wheel if the lowest point on the wheel is 2 feet below the viewing platform.

@HomeTutor for problem solving help at classzone.com

51. **AUTOMOTIVE MECHANICS** The pistons in an engine force the crank pins to rotate in a circle around the center of the crankshaft. The graph shows the height h (in inches) of a crank pin relative to the axle as a function of time t (in seconds). Write a cosine function for the height of the crank pin.

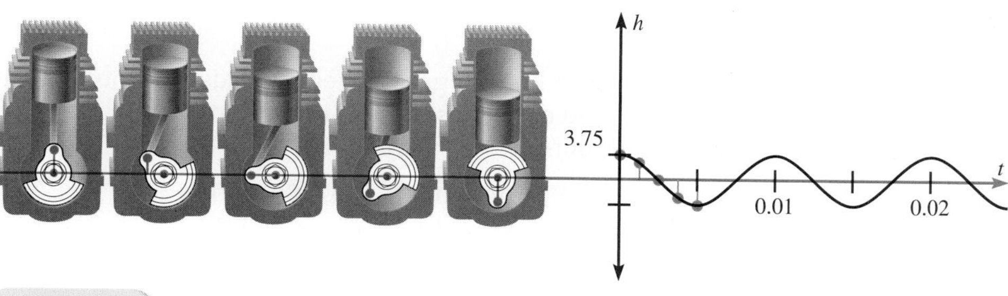

@HomeTutor for problem solving help at classzone.com

52. **BLOOD PRESSURE** For a certain person at rest, the blood pressure P (in millimeters of mercury) at time t (in seconds) is given by this function:

$$P = 100 - 20 \cos \frac{8\pi}{3}t$$

Graph the function. If one cycle is equivalent to one heartbeat, what is the person's pulse rate in heartbeats per minute?

EXAMPLE 6 on p. 918 for Ex. 53

53. **MULTI-STEP PROBLEM** You are standing 300 feet from the base of a 200 foot cliff. Your friend is rappelling down the cliff.

a. Write a model that gives your friend's distance d (in feet) from the top of the cliff as a function of the angle of elevation θ.

b. Graph the function from part (a).

c. Determine the angle of elevation if your friend has rappelled halfway down the cliff.

54. ★ **EXTENDED RESPONSE** In a particular region, the population C of coyotes (the predator) and the population R of rabbits (the prey) can be modeled by

$$C = 9000 + 3000 \sin \frac{\pi}{12}t \quad \text{and} \quad R = 20{,}000 + 8000 \cos \frac{\pi}{12}t$$

where t is the time in months.

a. Determine the ratio of rabbits to coyotes when $t = 0, 6, 12,$ and 18 months.

b. Graph both functions in the same coordinate plane.

c. Use the graphs to explain how the changes in the two populations appear to be related.

55. **CHALLENGE** Suppose a Ferris wheel has a radius of 25 feet and operates at a speed of 2 revolutions per minute. The bottom car is 5 feet above the ground. Write a model for a person's height h (in feet) above the ground if the value of h is 44 feet when $t = 0$.

NEW YORK MIXED REVIEW

TEST PRACTICE at classzone.com

56. The cylindrical tube shown is metal. It has an inner radius of 10 inches, an outer radius of 12 inches, and a height of 23 inches. What is the approximate amount of metal needed to make this tube?

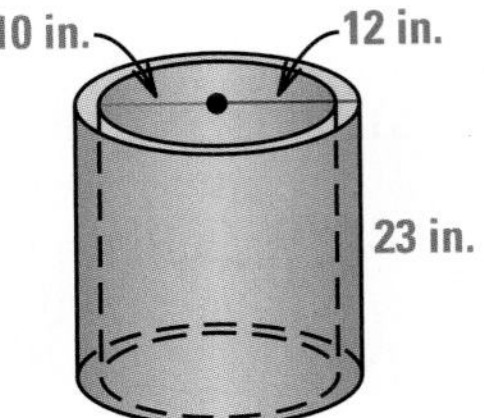

Ⓐ 289 in.^{3} Ⓑ 1012 in.^{3}

Ⓒ 3179 in.^{3} Ⓓ 4625 in.^{3}

57. Lisa records the price of regular gasoline every Friday for four months. Which measure of data describes the most frequent price of gasoline over the four month period?

Ⓐ Mean Ⓑ Median Ⓒ Mode Ⓓ Range

QUIZ for Lessons 14.1–14.2

Find the amplitude and the period of the graph of the function. *(p. 908)*

1. $y = \cos 4x$
2. $y = \frac{3}{2} \sin 5x$
3. $f(x) = \frac{1}{4} \sin x$
4. $y = \frac{1}{2} \cos 2\pi x$
5. $y = \sin \pi x$
6. $g(x) = 3 \cos \frac{\pi}{2}x$

Graph the function.

7. $y = 4 \sin \pi x$ *(p. 908)*
8. $y = \frac{1}{2} \cos \frac{3}{2}\pi x$ *(p. 908)*
9. $g(x) = 2 \tan \frac{1}{4}x$ *(p. 908)*
10. $f(x) = -2 \sin 3x + 4$ *(p. 915)*
11. $y = \cos (x + \pi) + 2$ *(p. 915)*
12. $y = -\tan 2\left(x + \frac{\pi}{2}\right)$ *(p. 915)*
13. **WINDOW WASHERS** You are standing 70 feet from the base of a 250 foot building watching a window washer lower himself to the ground. Write and graph a model that gives the window washer's distance d (in feet) from the top of the building as a function of the angle of elevation θ. *(p. 915)*

EXTRA PRACTICE for Lesson 14.2, p. 1023 **ONLINE QUIZ** at classzone.com

Investigating Algebra ACTIVITY Use before Lesson 14.3

@HomeTutor classzone.com Keystrokes

14.3 Investigating Trigonometric Identities

MATERIALS • graphing calculator

QUESTION **How can you use a graphing calculator to verify trigonometric identities?**

EXPLORE **Investigate a trigonometric identity**

Determine whether the equation $\sin^2 x + \cos^2 x = 1$ is true for *no x-values, some x-values,* or *all x-values.*

STEP 1 ***Enter equations***

Enter the left side of the equation as y_1 and the right side as y_2. Use the "thick" graph style for y_2 to distinguish the graphs.

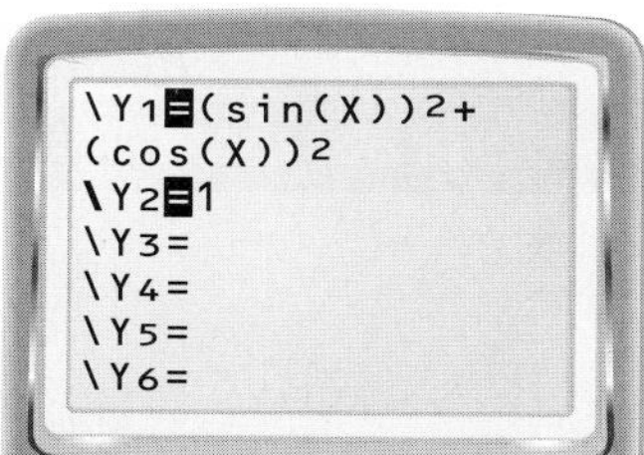

STEP 2 ***Set viewing window***

Set your calculator in radian mode. Adjust the viewing window so that the x-axis shows $-2\pi \le x \le 2\pi$ and the y-axis shows $-2 \le y \le 2$.

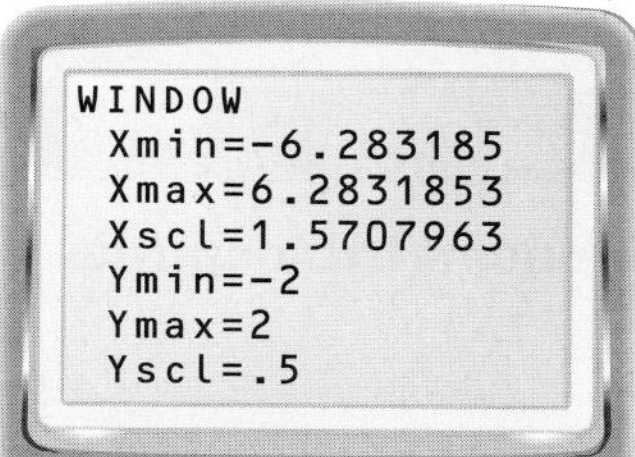

STEP 3 ***Graph equations***

Graph the equations. The calculator first graphs $y_1 = \sin^2 x + \cos^2 x$ and then $y_2 = 1$ as a thicker line over the graph of y_1.

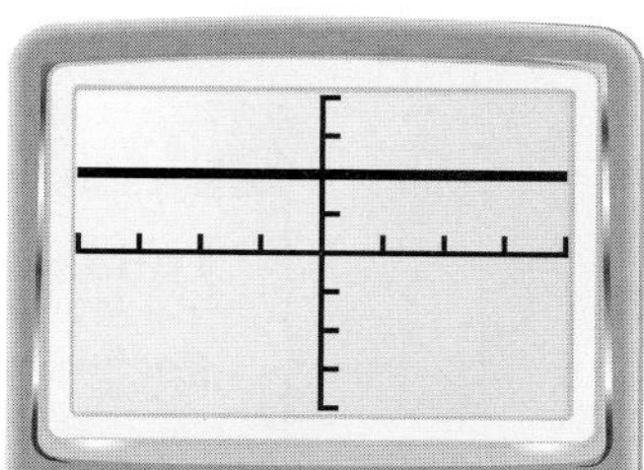

▶ The graphs of each side of the equation $\sin^2 x + \cos^2 x = 1$ are the same. So, the equation is true for all x-values.

DRAW CONCLUSIONS **Use your observations to complete these exercises**

Use a graphing calculator to determine whether the equation is true for *no x-values, some x-values,* or *all x-values.* (Set your calculator in radian mode and use $-2\pi \le x \le 2\pi$ and $-2 \le y \le 2$ for the viewing window.)

1. $\tan x = \frac{\sin x}{\cos x}$
2. $\sin x = -\cos x$
3. $\tan x = \frac{1}{x}$
4. $\cos(-3x) = \cos 3x$
5. $\cos x = 1.5$
6. $\sin(x - \pi) = \cos x$
7. $\sin(-x) = -\sin x$
8. $\cos \frac{x}{2} = \frac{1}{2} \cos x$
9. $\cos\left(x - \frac{\pi}{2}\right) = \sin x$
10. **REASONING** Trigonometric equations that are true for *all* values of x (in their domain) are called trigonometric identities. Which trigonometric equations in Exercises 1–9 are trigonometric identities?

14.3 Verify Trigonometric Identities

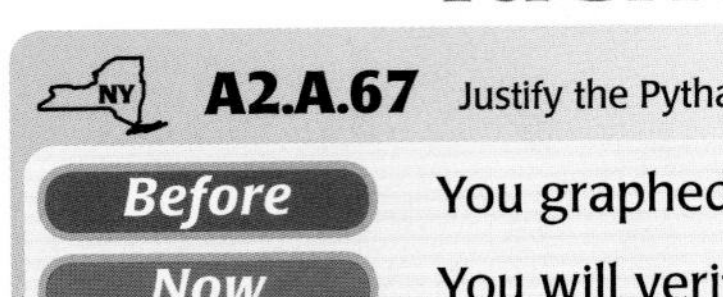

A2.A.67 Justify the Pythagorean identities

Before You graphed trigonometric functions.

Now You will verify trigonometric identities.

Why? So you can model the path of Halley's comet, as in Ex. 41.

Key Vocabulary
- **trigonometric identity**

Recall from Lesson 13.3 that if an angle θ is in standard position with its terminal side intersecting the unit circle at (x, y), then $x = \cos\theta$ and $y = \sin\theta$. Because (x, y) is on a circle centered at the origin with radius 1, it follows that:

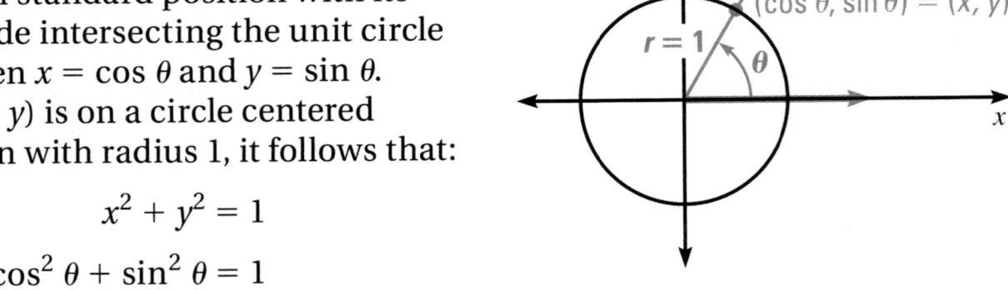

$$x^2 + y^2 = 1$$

$$\cos^2\theta + \sin^2\theta = 1$$

The equation $\cos^2\theta + \sin^2\theta = 1$ is true for any value of θ. A trigonometric equation that is true for all values of θ (in its domain) is called a **trigonometric identity**. Several fundamental trigonometric identities are listed below, some of which you have already learned.

KEY CONCEPT — *For Your Notebook*

Fundamental Trigonometric Identities

Reciprocal Identities

$\csc\theta = \dfrac{1}{\sin\theta}$ $\qquad$ $\sec\theta = \dfrac{1}{\cos\theta}$ $\qquad$ $\cot\theta = \dfrac{1}{\tan\theta}$

Tangent and Cotangent Identities

$\tan\theta = \dfrac{\sin\theta}{\cos\theta}$ $\qquad$ $\cot\theta = \dfrac{\cos\theta}{\sin\theta}$

Pythagorean Identities

$\sin^2\theta + \cos^2\theta = 1$ $\qquad$ $1 + \tan^2\theta = \sec^2\theta$ $\qquad$ $1 + \cot^2\theta = \csc^2\theta$

Cofunction Identities

$\sin\left(\dfrac{\pi}{2} - \theta\right) = \cos\theta$ $\qquad$ $\cos\left(\dfrac{\pi}{2} - \theta\right) = \sin\theta$ $\qquad$ $\tan\left(\dfrac{\pi}{2} - \theta\right) = \cot\theta$

Negative Angle Identities

$\sin(-\theta) = -\sin\theta$ $\qquad$ $\cos(-\theta) = \cos\theta$ $\qquad$ $\tan(-\theta) = -\tan\theta$

You can use trigonometric identities to evaluate trigonometric functions, simplify trigonometric expressions, and verify other identities.

EXAMPLE 1 Find trigonometric values

Given that $\sin\theta = \frac{4}{5}$ and $\frac{\pi}{2} < \theta < \pi$, find the values of the other five trigonometric functions of θ.

Solution

STEP 1 **Find** $\cos\theta$.

$\sin^2\theta + \cos^2\theta = 1$ — Write Pythagorean identity.

$\left(\frac{4}{5}\right)^2 + \cos^2\theta = 1$ — Substitute $\frac{4}{5}$ for $\sin\theta$.

$\cos^2\theta = 1 - \left(\frac{4}{5}\right)^2$ — Subtract $\left(\frac{4}{5}\right)^2$ from each side.

$\cos^2\theta = \frac{9}{25}$ — Simplify.

$\cos\theta = \pm\frac{3}{5}$ — Take square roots of each side.

$\cos\theta = -\frac{3}{5}$ — Because θ is in Quadrant II, $\cos\theta$ is negative.

REVIEW TRIGONOMETRY
For help with finding the sign of a trigonometric function value, see p. 866.

STEP 2 **Find** the values of the other four trigonometric functions of θ using the known values of $\sin\theta$ and $\cos\theta$.

$$\tan\theta = \frac{\sin\theta}{\cos\theta} = \frac{\frac{4}{5}}{-\frac{3}{5}} = -\frac{4}{3} \qquad \cot\theta = \frac{\cos\theta}{\sin\theta} = \frac{-\frac{3}{5}}{\frac{4}{5}} = -\frac{3}{4}$$

$$\csc\theta = \frac{1}{\sin\theta} = \frac{1}{\frac{4}{5}} = \frac{5}{4} \qquad \sec\theta = \frac{1}{\cos\theta} = \frac{1}{-\frac{3}{5}} = -\frac{5}{3}$$

EXAMPLE 2 Simplify a trigonometric expression

Simplify the expression $\tan\left(\frac{\pi}{2} - \theta\right)\sin\theta$.

$\tan\left(\frac{\pi}{2} - \theta\right)\sin\theta = \cot\theta\sin\theta$ — Cofunction identity

$= \left(\frac{\cos\theta}{\sin\theta}\right)(\sin\theta)$ — Cotangent identity

$= \cos\theta$ — Simplify.

EXAMPLE 3 Simplify a trigonometric expression

Simplify the expression $\csc\theta\cot^2\theta + \frac{1}{\sin\theta}$.

$\csc\theta\cot^2\theta + \frac{1}{\sin\theta} = \csc\theta\cot^2\theta + \csc\theta$ — Reciprocal identity

$= \csc\theta(\csc^2\theta - 1) + \csc\theta$ — Pythagorean identity

$= \csc^3\theta - \csc\theta + \csc\theta$ — Distributive property

$= \csc^3\theta$ — Simplify.

✓ **GUIDED PRACTICE** for Examples 1, 2, and 3

Find the values of the other five trigonometric functions of θ.

1. $\cos \theta = \frac{1}{6}, 0 < \theta < \frac{\pi}{2}$

2. $\sin \theta = -\frac{3}{7}, \pi < \theta < \frac{3\pi}{2}$

Simplify the expression.

3. $\sin x \cot x \sec x$

4. $\frac{\tan x \csc x}{\sec x}$

5. $\frac{\cos\left(\frac{\pi}{2} - \theta\right) - 1}{1 + \sin(-\theta)}$

VERIFYING IDENTITIES You can use the fundamental identities on page 924 to verify new trigonometric identities. When verifying an identity, begin with the expression on one side. Use algebra and trigonometric properties to manipulate the expression until it is identical to the other side.

EXAMPLE 4 Verify a trigonometric identity

Verify the identity $\frac{\sec^2 \theta - 1}{\sec^2 \theta} = \sin^2 \theta$.

$\frac{\sec^2 \theta - 1}{\sec^2 \theta} = \frac{\sec^2 \theta}{\sec^2 \theta} - \frac{1}{\sec^2 \theta}$ Write as separate fractions.

$= 1 - \left(\frac{1}{\sec \theta}\right)^2$ Simplify.

$= 1 - \cos^2 \theta$ Reciprocal identity

$= \sin^2 \theta$ Pythagorean identity

EXAMPLE 5 Verify a trigonometric identity

Verify the identity $\sec x + \tan x = \frac{\cos x}{1 - \sin x}$.

$\sec x + \tan x = \frac{1}{\cos x} + \tan x$ Reciprocal identity

$= \frac{1}{\cos x} + \frac{\sin x}{\cos x}$ Tangent identity

$= \frac{1 + \sin x}{\cos x}$ Add fractions.

$= \frac{1 + \sin x}{\cos x} \cdot \frac{1 - \sin x}{1 - \sin x}$ Multiply by $\frac{1 - \sin x}{1 - \sin x}$.

$= \frac{1 - \sin^2 x}{\cos x (1 - \sin x)}$ Simplify numerator.

$= \frac{\cos^2 x}{\cos x (1 - \sin x)}$ Pythagorean identity

$= \frac{\cos x}{1 - \sin x}$ Simplify.

VERIFY IDENTITIES
To verify the identity, you must introduce $1 - \sin x$ into the denominator. Multiply the numerator and the denominator by $1 - \sin x$ so you get an equivalent expression.

EXAMPLE 6 Verify a real-life trigonometric identity

SHADOW LENGTH A vertical *gnomon* (the part of a sundial that projects a shadow) has height h. The length s of the shadow cast by the gnomon when the angle of the sun above the horizon is θ can be modeled by the equation below. Show that the equation is equivalent to $s = h \cot \theta$.

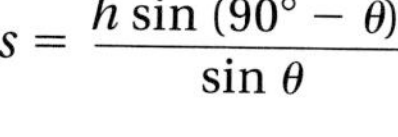

$$s = \frac{h \sin (90° - \theta)}{\sin \theta}$$

Solution

Simplify the equation.

$$s = \frac{h \sin (90° - \theta)}{\sin \theta} \qquad \text{Write original equation.}$$

$$= \frac{h \sin \left(\frac{\pi}{2} - \theta\right)}{\sin \theta} \qquad \text{Convert 90° to radians.}$$

$$= \frac{h \cos \theta}{\sin \theta} \qquad \text{Cofunction identity}$$

$$= h \cot \theta \qquad \text{Cotangent identity}$$

✓ GUIDED PRACTICE for Examples 4, 5, and 6

Verify the identity.

6. $\cot (-\theta) = -\cot \theta$

7. $\csc^2 x (1 - \sin^2 x) = \cot^2 x$

8. $\cos x \csc x \tan x = 1$

9. $(\tan^2 x + 1)(\cos^2 x - 1) = -\tan^2 x$

14.3 EXERCISES

HOMEWORK KEY

○ = **WORKED-OUT SOLUTIONS** on p. WS24 for Exs. 5, 11, and 41

★ = **STANDARDIZED TEST PRACTICE** Exs. 2, 9, 24, 42, 43, and 44

◆ = **MULTIPLE REPRESENTATIONS** Ex. 41

SKILL PRACTICE

1. **VOCABULARY** What is a trigonometric identity?

2. ★ **WRITING** What does the cofunction identity $\sin \left(\frac{\pi}{2} - \theta\right) = \cos \theta$ tell you about the graphs of $y = \sin x$ and $y = \cos x$?

EXAMPLE 1 on p. 925 for Exs. 3–9

FINDING VALUES Find the values of the other five trigonometric functions of θ.

3. $\sin \theta = \frac{1}{3}, 0 < \theta < \frac{\pi}{2}$

4. $\tan \theta = \frac{3}{7}, 0 < \theta < \frac{\pi}{2}$

5. $\cos \theta = \frac{5}{6}, \frac{3\pi}{2} < \theta < 2\pi$

6. $\sin \theta = -\frac{7}{10}, \pi < \theta < \frac{3\pi}{2}$

7. $\cot \theta = -\frac{2}{5}, \frac{\pi}{2} < \theta < \pi$

8. $\sec \theta = -\frac{9}{4}, \frac{\pi}{2} < \theta < \pi$

9. ★ **MULTIPLE CHOICE** If $\csc \theta = \frac{3}{2}$ and $\frac{\pi}{2} < \theta < \pi$, what is the value of $\tan \theta$?

Ⓐ $-\frac{2\sqrt{5}}{5}$ Ⓑ $-\frac{2\sqrt{13}}{13}$ Ⓒ $\frac{2\sqrt{13}}{13}$ Ⓓ $\frac{2\sqrt{5}}{5}$

EXAMPLES 2 and 3 on p. 925 for Exs. 10–24

SIMPLIFYING EXPRESSIONS **Simplify the expression.**

10. $\sin x \cot x$

11. $\frac{\sin(-\theta)}{\cos(-\theta)}$

12. $\csc \theta \sin \theta + \cot^2 \theta$

13. $\cos \theta (1 + \tan^2 \theta)$

14. $1 + \tan^2\left(\frac{\pi}{2} - x\right)$

15. $\frac{\cos\left(\frac{\pi}{2} - x\right)}{\csc x}$

16. $\frac{\cos\left(\frac{\pi}{2} - \theta\right)}{\csc \theta} + \cos^2 \theta$

17. $\sin\left(\frac{\pi}{2} - \theta\right) \sec \theta$

18. $\frac{\cos^2 x}{\cot^2 x}$

19. $\frac{\sec x \sin x + \cos\left(\frac{\pi}{2} - x\right)}{1 + \sec x}$

20. $\frac{\csc^2 x - \cot^2 x}{\sin(-x) \cot x}$

21. $\frac{\cos^2 x \tan^2(-x) - 1}{\cos^2 x}$

ERROR ANALYSIS ***Describe*** **and correct the error in simplifying the expression.**

22.

$$\begin{aligned} 1 - \sin^2 \theta &= 1 - (1 - \cos^2 \theta) \\ &= 1 - 1 - \cos^2 \theta \\ &= -\cos^2 \theta \end{aligned}$$

23.

$$\begin{aligned} \tan(-x) \csc x &= \frac{\sin x}{\cos x} \cdot \frac{1}{\sin x} \\ &= \frac{1}{\cos x} \\ &= \sec x \end{aligned}$$

24. ★ **MULTIPLE CHOICE** Which of the following is the simplified form of the expression $\cos \theta \sec \theta$?

Ⓐ $\tan \theta$ Ⓑ 1 Ⓒ 2 Ⓓ $1 - \sin^2 \theta$

EXAMPLES 4 and 5 on p. 926 for Exs. 25–34

VERIFYING IDENTITIES **Verify the identity.**

25. $\sin x \csc x = 1$

26. $\tan \theta \csc \theta \cos \theta = 1$

27. $\frac{\cos\left(\frac{\pi}{2} - \theta\right) + 1}{1 - \sin(-\theta)} = 1$

28. $\sin\left(\frac{\pi}{2} - x\right) \tan x = \sin x$

29. $\frac{\csc^2 \theta - \cot^2 \theta}{1 - \sin^2 \theta} = \sec^2 \theta$

30. $2 - \cos^2 \theta = 1 + \sin^2 \theta$

31. $\sin x + \cos x \cot x = \csc x$

32. $\frac{\sin^2(-x)}{\tan^2 x} = \cos^2 x$

33. $\frac{1 + \cos x}{\sin x} + \frac{\sin x}{1 + \cos x} = 2 \csc x$

34. $\frac{\sin x}{1 - \cos(-x)} = \csc x + \cot x$

35. **ODD AND EVEN FUNCTIONS** A function f is *odd* if $f(-x) = -f(x)$. A function f is *even* if $f(-x) = f(x)$. Which of the six trigonometric functions are odd? Which are even?

VERIFYING IDENTITIES **Verify the identity.**

36. $\ln |\sec \theta| = -\ln |\cos \theta|$

37. $\ln |\tan \theta| = \ln |\sin \theta| - \ln |\cos \theta|$

38. **CHALLENGE** Use the Pythagorean identity $\sin^2 \theta + \cos^2 \theta = 1$ to derive the other Pythagorean identities, $1 + \tan^2 \theta = \sec^2 \theta$ and $1 + \cot^2 \theta = \csc^2 \theta$.

PROBLEM SOLVING

EXAMPLE 6 on p. 927 for Exs. 39–41

39. RATE OF CHANGE In calculus, it can be shown that the rate of change of the function $f(x) = \sec x + \cos x$ is given by this expression:

$$\sec x \tan x - \sin x$$

Show that the expression for the rate of change can be written as $\sin x \tan^2 x$.

@HomeTutor for problem solving help at classzone.com

40. PHYSICAL SCIENCE Static friction is the amount of force necessary to keep a stationary object on a flat surface from moving. Suppose a book weighing W pounds is lying on a ramp inclined at an angle θ. The coefficient of static friction u for the book can be found using this equation:

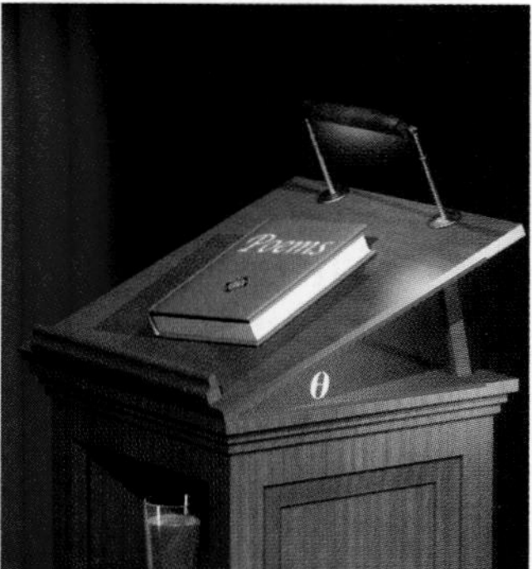

$$uW \cos \theta = W \sin \theta$$

a. Solve the equation for u and simplify the result.

b. Use the equation from part (a) to determine what happens to the value of u as the angle θ increases from 0° to 90°.

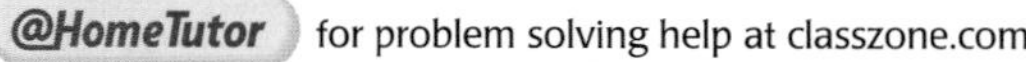
for problem solving help at classzone.com

41. ◆ **MULTIPLE REPRESENTATIONS** The path of Halley's comet is an ellipse with the sun as a focus. The equation below gives the comet's distance r from the sun (in astronomical units) as a fuction of the angle θ (in radians) between the major axis and the comet.

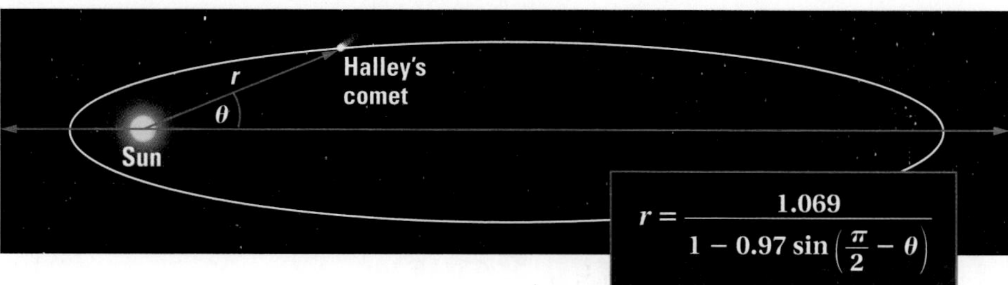

$$r = \frac{1.069}{1 - 0.97 \sin\left(\frac{\pi}{2} - \theta\right)}$$

a. Writing an Equation Simplify the equation given above.

b. Drawing a Graph Use a graphing calculator to graph the equation from part (a).

c. Making a Table Make a table of values for the equation from part (a) in which θ starts at 0 and increases in increments of $\frac{\pi}{4}$. Use the table to approximate the closest and farthest distance, in miles, that Halley's comet is from the sun. (*Note:* 1 astronomical unit ≈ 93 million miles.)

42. ★ **SHORT RESPONSE** Use a reciprocal identity to describe what happens to the value of $\sec \theta$ as the value of $\cos \theta$ increases. On what intervals does this happen?

43. ★ **SHORT RESPONSE** Use the tangent identity to describe what happens to the value of $\tan \theta$ as the value of $\sin \theta$ increases and the value of $\cos \theta$ decreases. On what intervals does this happen?

44. ★ **EXTENDED RESPONSE** When light traveling in a medium (such as air) strikes the surface of a second medium (such as water) at an angle θ_1, the light begins to travel at a different angle θ_2. This change of direction is defined by Snell's law, $n_1 \sin \theta_1 = n_2 \sin \theta_2$, where n_1 and n_2 are the *indices of refraction* for the two mediums. Snell's law can be derived from the equation:

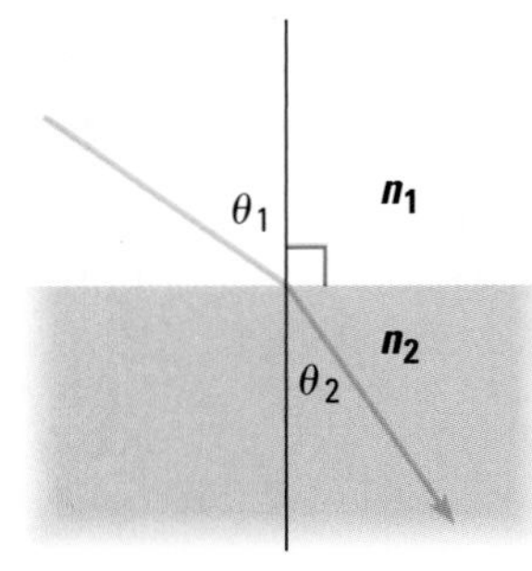

$$\frac{n_1}{\sqrt{\cot^2 \theta_1 + 1}} = \frac{n_2}{\sqrt{\cot^2 \theta_2 + 1}}$$

a. **Derive** Simplify the equation to derive Snell's law: $n_1 \sin \theta_1 = n_2 \sin \theta_2$.

b. **Solve** If $\theta_1 = 55°$, $\theta_2 = 35°$, and $n_2 = 2$, what is the value of n_1?

c. **Interpret** If $\theta_1 = \theta_2$, what must be true about the values of n_1 and n_2? *Explain* when this situation would occur.

45. **CHALLENGE** Brewster's angle is the angle θ_1, at which light reflected off water is completely polarized, so that glare is minimized when you look at the water with polarized sunglasses. Brewster's angle can be found using Snell's law (see Exercise 44).

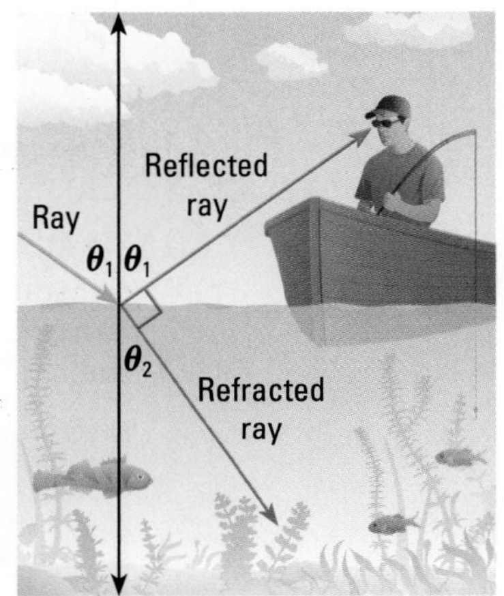

a. Let $\sin^2 \theta_2 = \left(\frac{n_1}{n_2} \sin \theta_1\right)^2$ and $\cos^2 \theta_2 = \left(\frac{n_2}{n_1} \cos \theta_1\right)^2$.

Add the two equations to show that

$$\frac{n_1^2}{n_2^2} \sin^2 \theta_1 + \frac{n_2^2}{n_1^2} \cos^2 \theta_1 = 1.$$

b. Show that the equation from part (a) can be simplified to $\frac{n_2^2 - n_1^2}{n_2^2} \sin^2 \theta_1 = \frac{n_2^2 - n_1^2}{n_1^2} \cos^2 \theta_1$.

c. Solve the equation from part (b) to find Brewster's angle:

$$\theta_1 = \tan^{-1}\left(\frac{n_2}{n_1}\right)$$

NY NEW YORK MIXED REVIEW

TEST PRACTICE at classzone.com

46. Which equation will produce the widest parabola when graphed?

(A) $y = -3x^2$ (B) $y = -\frac{2}{5}x^2$ (C) $y = 1.5x^2$ (D) $y = \frac{5}{2}x^2$

47. Reflect $\triangle RST$ in the line $x = -1$. In which quadrant will the image of point R appear?

(A) Quadrant I (B) Quadrant II

(C) Quadrant III (D) Quadrant IV

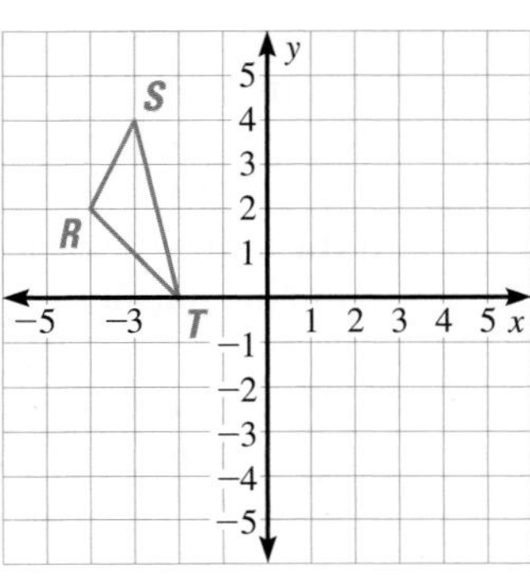

14.4 Solve Trigonometric Equations

A2.A.68 Solve trigonometric equations for all values of the variable from 0° to 360°

Before You verified trigonometric identities.

Now You will solve trigonometric equations.

Why? So you can solve surface area problems, as in Ex. 43.

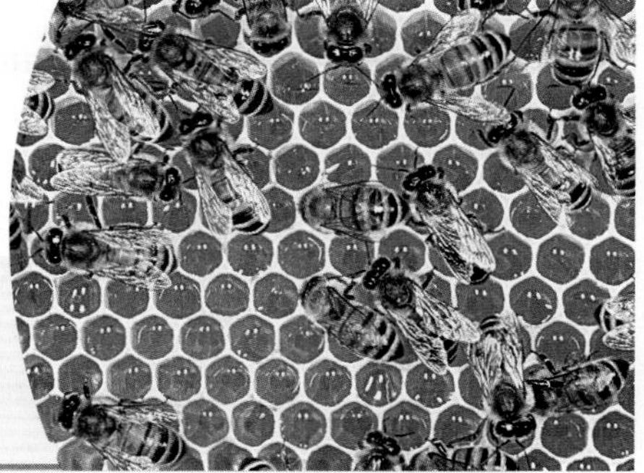

Key Vocabulary
- **extraneous solution,** *p. 52*

In Lesson 14.3, you verified trigonometric identities. In this lesson, you will solve trigonometric equations. To see the difference, consider the following:

$$\sin^2 x + \cos^2 x = 1 \qquad \textbf{Equation 1}$$

$$\sin x = 1 \qquad \textbf{Equation 2}$$

Equation 1 is an identity because it is true for all real values of x. Equation 2, however, is true only for some values of x. When you find these values, you are solving the equation.

EXAMPLE 1 Solve a trigonometric equation

Solve $2 \sin x - \sqrt{3} = 0$.

Solution

First isolate $\sin x$ on one side of the equation.

$2 \sin x - \sqrt{3} = 0$	**Write original equation.**
$2 \sin x = \sqrt{3}$	**Add $\sqrt{3}$ to each side.**
$\sin x = \frac{\sqrt{3}}{2}$	**Divide each side by 2.**

One solution of $\sin x = \frac{\sqrt{3}}{2}$ in the interval $0 \le x < 2\pi$ is $x = \sin^{-1} \frac{\sqrt{3}}{2} = \frac{\pi}{3}$. The other solution in the interval is $x = \pi - \frac{\pi}{3} = \frac{2\pi}{3}$. Moreover, because $y = \sin x$ is periodic, there will be infinitely many solutions.

You can use the two solutions found above to write the general solution:

$$x = \frac{\pi}{3} + 2n\pi \quad \text{or} \quad x = \frac{2\pi}{3} + 2n\pi \quad \text{(where } n \text{ is any integer)}$$

WRITE GENERAL SOLUTION
To write the general solution of a trigonometric equation, you can add multiples of the period to all the solutions from one cycle.

CHECK You can check the answer by graphing $y = \sin x$ and $y = \frac{\sqrt{3}}{2}$ in the same coordinate plane. Then find the points where the graphs intersect. You can see that there are infinitely many such points.

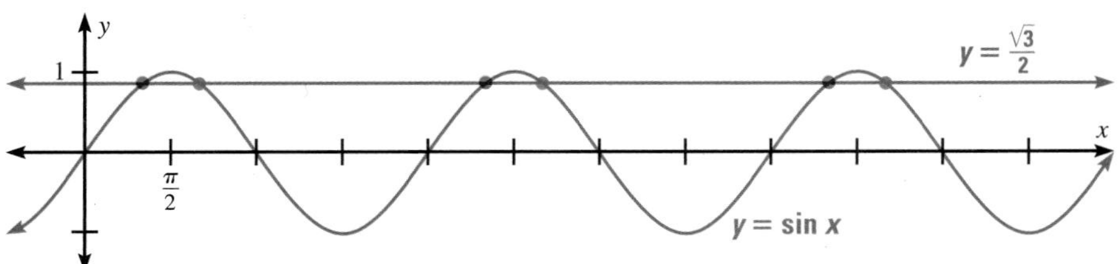

EXAMPLE 2 Solve a trigonometric equation in an interval

Solve $9\tan^2 x + 2 = 3$ in the interval $0 \le x < 2\pi$.

$9\tan^2 x + 2 = 3$ **Write original equation.**

$9\tan^2 x = 1$ **Subtract 2 from each side.**

$\tan^2 x = \frac{1}{9}$ **Divide each side by 9.**

$\tan x = \pm\frac{1}{3}$ **Take square roots of each side.**

REVIEW INVERSE FUNCTIONS
For help with inverse trigonometric functions, see p. 875.

Using a calculator, you find that $\tan^{-1}\frac{1}{3} \approx 0.322$ and $\tan^{-1}\left(-\frac{1}{3}\right) \approx -0.322$. Therefore, the general solution of the equation is:

$x \approx 0.322 + n\pi$ or $x \approx -0.322 + n\pi$ (where n is any integer)

▶ The specific solutions in the interval $0 \le x < 2\pi$ are:

$x \approx 0.322$ $\quad$ $x \approx -0.322 + \pi \approx 2.820$

$x \approx 0.322 + \pi \approx 3.464$ $\quad$ $x \approx -0.322 + 2\pi \approx 5.961$

EXAMPLE 3 Solve a real-life trigonometric equation

OCEANOGRAPHY The water depth d for the Bay of Fundy can be modeled by

$$d = 35 - 28\cos\frac{\pi}{6.2}t$$

where d is measured in feet and t is the time in hours. If $t = 0$ represents midnight, at what time(s) is the water depth 7 feet?

High tide

Low tide

ANOTHER WAY
For alternative methods for solving the problem in Example 3, turn to page 938 for the **Problem Solving Workshop**.

Solution

Substitute 7 for d in the model and solve for t.

$35 - 28\cos\frac{\pi}{6.2}t = 7$ **Substitute 7 for *d*.**

$-28\cos\frac{\pi}{6.2}t = -28$ **Subtract 35 from each side.**

$\cos\frac{\pi}{6.2}t = 1$ **Divide each side by −28.**

$\frac{\pi}{6.2}t = 2n\pi$ **$\cos\theta = 1$ when $\theta = 2n\pi$.**

$t = 12.4n$ **Solve for *t*.**

▶ On the interval $0 \le t \le 24$ (representing one full day), the water depth is 7 feet when $t = 12.4(0) = 0$ (that is, at midnight) and when $t = 12.4(1) = 12.4$ (that is, at 12:24 P.M.).

GUIDED PRACTICE for Examples 1, 2, and 3

1. Find the general solution of the equation $2 \sin x + 4 = 5$.
2. Solve the equation $3 \csc^2 x = 4$ in the interval $0 \le x < 2\pi$.
3. **OCEANOGRAPHY** In Example 3, at what time(s) is the water depth 63 feet?

EXAMPLE 4 Standardized Test Practice

What is the general solution of $\sin^3 x - 4 \sin x = 0$?

Ⓐ $x = \frac{\pi}{2} + 2n\pi$ or $x = \frac{3\pi}{2} + 2n\pi$ Ⓑ $x = \frac{\pi}{2} + 2n\pi$ or $x = \pi + 2n\pi$

Ⓒ $x = \pi + 2n\pi$ Ⓓ $x = 2n\pi$ or $x = \pi + 2n\pi$

Solution

$\sin^3 x - 4 \sin x = 0$ **Write original equation.**

$\sin x(\sin^2 x - 4) = 0$ **Factor out sin *x*.**

$\sin x(\sin x + 2)(\sin x - 2) = 0$ **Factor difference of squares.**

Set each factor equal to 0 and solve for x, if possible.

$\sin x = 0$	$\sin x + 2 = 0$	$\sin x - 2 = 0$
$x = 0$ or $x = \pi$	$\sin x = -2$	$\sin x = 2$

ELIMINATE SOLUTIONS
Because sin x is never less than -1 or greater than 1, there are no solutions of $\sin x = -2$ and $\sin x = 2$.

The only solutions in the interval $0 \le x < 2\pi$ are $x = 0$ and $x = \pi$.

The general solution is $x = 2n\pi$ or $x = \pi + 2n\pi$ where n is any integer.

▶ The correct answer is D. Ⓐ Ⓑ Ⓒ Ⓓ

EXAMPLE 5 Use the quadratic formula

Solve $\cos^2 x - 5 \cos x + 2 = 0$ in the interval $0 \le x \le \pi$.

Solution

Because the equation is in the form $au^2 + bu + c = 0$ where $u = \cos x$, you can use the quadratic formula to solve for $\cos x$.

$\cos^2 x - 5 \cos x + 2 = 0$ **Write original equation.**

$\cos x = \frac{-(-5) \pm \sqrt{(-5)^2 - 4(1)(2)}}{2(1)}$ **Quadratic formula**

$= \frac{5 \pm \sqrt{17}}{2}$ **Simplify.**

≈ 4.56 or 0.44 **Use a calculator.**

$x = \cos^{-1} 4.56$ | $x = \cos^{-1} 0.44$ **Use inverse cosine.**

No solution | ≈ 1.12 **Use a calculator, if possible.**

▶ In the interval $0 \le x \le \pi$, the only solution is $x \approx 1.12$.

EXTRANEOUS SOLUTIONS When solving a trigonometric equation, it is possible to obtain extraneous solutions. So, you should always check your solutions in the original equation.

EXAMPLE 6 Solve an equation with an extraneous solution

Solve $1 + \cos x = \sin x$ in the interval $0 \le x < 2\pi$.

$1 + \cos x = \sin x$	**Write original equation.**
$(1 + \cos x)^2 = (\sin x)^2$	**Square both sides.**
$1 + 2\cos x + \cos^2 x = \sin^2 x$	**Multiply.**
$1 + 2\cos x + \cos^2 x = 1 - \cos^2 x$	**Pythagorean identity**
$2\cos^2 x + 2\cos x = 0$	**Quadratic form**
$2\cos x(\cos x + 1) = 0$	**Factor out 2 cos *x*.**
$2\cos x = 0$ or $\cos x + 1 = 0$	**Zero product property**
$\cos x = 0$ or $\cos x = -1$	**Solve for cos *x*.**

REVIEW FOIL METHOD
For help multiplying binomials, see p. 245.

On the interval $0 \le x < 2\pi$, $\cos x = 0$ has two solutions: $x = \frac{\pi}{2}$ or $x = \frac{3\pi}{2}$.

On the interval $0 \le x < 2\pi$, $\cos x = -1$ has one solution: $x = \pi$.

Therefore, $1 + \cos x = \sin x$ has three possible solutions: $x = \frac{\pi}{2}$, π, and $\frac{3\pi}{2}$.

CHECK To check the solutions, substitute them into the original equation and simplify.

$1 + \cos x = \sin x$	$1 + \cos x = \sin x$	$1 + \cos x = \sin x$
$1 + \cos \frac{\pi}{2} \stackrel{?}{=} \sin \frac{\pi}{2}$	$1 + \cos \pi \stackrel{?}{=} \sin \pi$	$1 + \cos \frac{3\pi}{2} \stackrel{?}{=} \sin \frac{3\pi}{2}$
$1 + 0 \stackrel{?}{=} 1$	$1 + (-1) \stackrel{?}{=} 0$	$1 + 0 \stackrel{?}{=} -1$
$1 = 1$ ✓	$0 = 0$ ✓	$1 \ne -1$

▶ The apparent solution $x = \frac{3\pi}{2}$ is extraneous because it does not check in the original equation. The only solutions in the interval $0 \le x < 2\pi$ are $x = \frac{\pi}{2}$ and $x = \pi$. Graphs of each side of the original equation confirm the solutions.

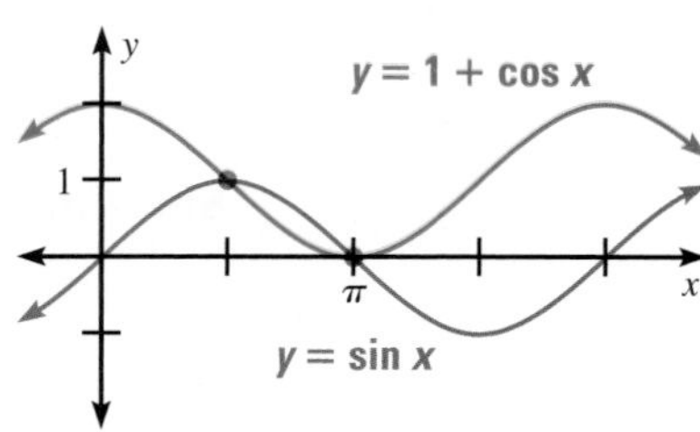

GUIDED PRACTICE for Examples 4, 5, and 6

Find the general solution of the equation.

4. $\sin^3 x - \sin x = 0$

5. $1 - \cos x = \sqrt{3} \sin x$

Solve the equation in the interval $0 \le x \le \pi$.

6. $2 \sin x = \csc x$

7. $\tan^2 x - \sin x \tan^2 x = 0$

14.4 EXERCISES

HOMEWORK KEY

○ = **WORKED-OUT SOLUTIONS** on p. WS24 for Exs. 5, 13, and 43

★ = **STANDARDIZED TEST PRACTICE** Exs. 2, 15, 36, 42, and 44

◆ = **MULTIPLE REPRESENTATIONS** Ex. 43

SKILL PRACTICE

1. **VOCABULARY** What is the difference between a trigonometric equation and a trigonometric identity?

2. ★ **WRITING** *Describe* several techniques for solving trigonometric equations.

EXAMPLE 1 on p. 931 for Exs. 3–15

CHECKING SOLUTIONS Verify that the given x-value is a solution of the equation.

3. $2 + 3\cos x - 5 = 0, x = 4\pi$
4. $\pi \sec x + \pi = 0, x = \pi$
5. $12\sin^2 x - 3 = 0, x = \frac{\pi}{6}$
6. $5\tan^3 x - 5 = 0, x = \frac{\pi}{4}$
7. $2\cos^4 x - \cos^2 x = 0, x = \frac{\pi}{2}$
8. $3\cot^4 x - \cot^2 x - 24 = 0, x = \frac{7\pi}{6}$

GENERAL SOLUTIONS Find the general solution of the equation.

9. $2\sin x - 1 = 0$
10. $\sqrt{3}\csc x + 2 = 0$
11. $3\tan x - \sqrt{3} = 0$
12. $\sin x + \sqrt{2} = -\sin x$
13. $4\cos^2 x - 3 = 0$
14. $3\tan^2 x - 9 = 0$

15. ★ **MULTIPLE CHOICE** What is the general solution of the equation $4\sin x = 2\sin x + 1$?

Ⓐ $x = \frac{\pi}{6} + 2n\pi$ or $x = \frac{7\pi}{6} + 2n\pi$

Ⓑ $x = \frac{\pi}{6} + n\pi$ or $x = \frac{5\pi}{6} + n\pi$

Ⓒ $x = \frac{\pi}{6} + 2n\pi$ or $x = \frac{5\pi}{6} + 2n\pi$

Ⓓ $x = \frac{\pi}{6} + n\pi$ or $x = \frac{7\pi}{6} + n\pi$

EXAMPLE 2 on p. 932 for Exs. 16–23

SOLVING EQUATIONS Solve the equation in the interval $0 \le x < 2\pi$.

16. $5 + 2\sin x - 7 = 0$
17. $3\tan x - \sqrt{3} = 0$
18. $3\cos x = \cos x - 1$
19. $2\sin^2 x - 1 = 0$
20. $5\tan^2 x - 15 = 0$
21. $4\cos^2 x - 1 = 0$

ERROR ANALYSIS *Describe* and correct the error in solving the equation in the interval $0 \le x \le \frac{\pi}{2}$.

22.

$$\sin^2 x = \frac{1}{2}\sin x$$
$$\sin x = \frac{1}{2}$$
$$x = \frac{\pi}{6}$$

23.

$$-2\cos x = -1$$
$$\cos x = -\frac{1}{2}$$
$$x = \frac{2\pi}{3}$$

EXAMPLE 4 on p. 933 for Exs. 24–29

GENERAL SOLUTIONS Find the general solution of the equation.

24. $\sin x \cos x - 3\cos x = 0$
25. $\sqrt{3}\cos x \tan x - \cos x = 0$
26. $2\sin^3 x = \sin x$
27. $2\tan^4 x - \tan^2 x - 15 = 0$
28. $\sqrt{\cos x} = 2\cos x - 1$
29. $1 + \cos x = \sqrt{3}\sin x$

EXAMPLES 5 and 6
on pp. 933–934 for Exs. 30–35

SOLVING Solve the equation in the given interval. Check your solutions.

30. $\sec x \csc^2 x = 2 \sec x;\ 0 \le x < 2\pi$

31. $\sqrt{3} \cos^2 x = \cos^2 x \tan x;\ 0 \le x \le \pi$

32. $2 \sin^2 x - \cos x - 1 = 0;\ 0 \le x < 2\pi$

33. $\sin^2 x + 5 \sin x - 3 = 0;\ -\frac{\pi}{2} \le x < \frac{\pi}{2}$

34. $\tan^2 x - 3 \tan x + 2 = 0;\ 0 \le x \le \pi$

35. $\cos x + \sin x \tan x = 2;\ \pi \le x < 2\pi$

36. ★ **MULTIPLE CHOICE** What are the points of intersection of the graphs of $y = 4 \sin x + 1$ and $y = 2 \sin x + 2$ on the interval $0 \le x < 2\pi$?

Ⓐ $\left(\frac{\pi}{6}, -3\right), \left(\frac{\pi}{2}, -3\right)$

Ⓑ $\left(\frac{\pi}{6}, 3\right), \left(\frac{5\pi}{6}, 3\right)$

Ⓒ $\left(\frac{\pi}{2}, 3\right), \left(\frac{7\pi}{6}, 3\right)$

Ⓓ $\left(\frac{\pi}{6}, 3\right), \left(\frac{11\pi}{6}, 3\right)$

INTERSECTION POINTS Find the points of intersection of the graphs of the given functions in the interval $0 \le x < 2\pi$.

37. $y = \cos^2 x$
$y = 2 \cos x - 1$

38. $y = 9 \sin^2 x$
$y = \sin^2 x + 8 \sin x - 2$

39. $y = \sqrt{3} \tan^2 x$
$y = \sqrt{3} - 2 \tan x$

40. **CHALLENGE** A number c is a *fixed point* of a function f if $f(c) = c$. For example, 0 is a fixed point of $f(x) = \sin x$ because $f(0) = \sin 0 = 0$.

a. Reasoning Use graphs to explain why the function $g(x) = \cos x$ has only one fixed point.

b. Graphing Calculator Find the fixed point of $g(x) = \cos x$.

PROBLEM SOLVING

EXAMPLE 3
on p. 932 for Exs. 41–42

41. **WIND SPEED** The average wind speed s (in miles per hour) in the Boston Harbor can be approximated by $s = 3.38 \sin \frac{\pi}{180}(t + 3) + 11.6$ where t is the time in days, with $t = 0$ representing January 1. On which days of the year is the average wind speed 10 miles per hour?

@HomeTutor for problem solving help at classzone.com

42. ★ **SHORT RESPONSE** The number of degrees θ north of due east ($\theta > 0$) or south of due east ($\theta < 0$) that the sun rises in Cheyenne, Wyoming, can be modeled by

$$\theta(t) = 31 \sin\left(\frac{2\pi}{365}t - 1.4\right)$$

where t is the time in days, with $t = 1$ representing January 1. Use an algebraic method to find at what day(s) the sun is 20° north of due east at sunrise. *Explain* how you can use the graph of $\theta(t)$ to check your answer.

@HomeTutor for problem solving help at classzone.com

○ = WORKED-OUT SOLUTIONS on p. WS1

★ = STANDARDIZED TEST PRACTICE

= MULTIPLE REPRESENTATIONS

43. ◆ **MULTIPLE REPRESENTATIONS** The surface area S of a honeycomb cell can be estimated by the equation shown at the right. In the equation, h is the height (in inches), s is the width of a side (in inches), and θ is the angle (in degrees) indicated in the diagram.

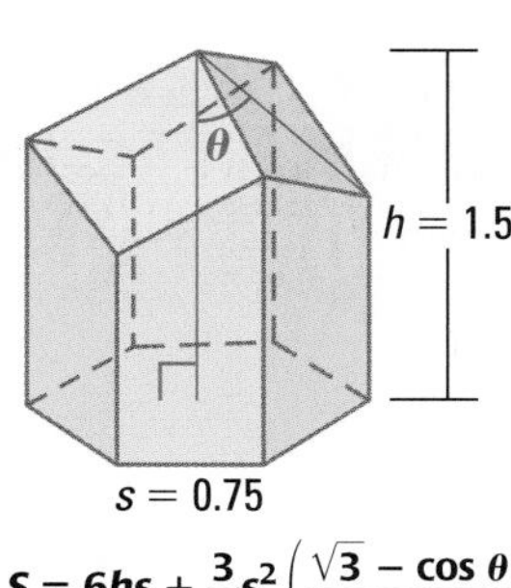

$$S = 6hs + \frac{3}{2}s^2\left(\frac{\sqrt{3} - \cos\theta}{\sin\theta}\right)$$

a. **Using a Diagram** Use the values of h and s in the diagram to simplify the equation.

b. **Making a Table** Use a graphing calculator to make a table for the function from part (a). For what value(s) of θ does $S = 9$ square inches?

c. **Drawing a Graph** Use a graphing calculator to graph the function from part (a). What value of θ minimizes the surface area?

44. ★ **EXTENDED RESPONSE** The power P (in watts) used by a microwave oven is the product of the voltage V (in volts) and the current I (in amperes). Suppose the voltage and current can be modeled by

$$V = 170 \cos 120\pi t \quad \text{and} \quad I = 11.3 \cos 120\pi t$$

where t is the time (in seconds).

a. **Model** Write the function $P(t)$ for the power used by the microwave.

b. **Solve** At what times does the microwave use 375 watts of power?

c. **Graphing Calculator** Graph the function $P(t)$. *Describe* how the graph differs from that of a cosine function of the form $y = a \cos bt$.

45. **CHALLENGE** Matrix multiplication can be used to rotate a point (x, y) counterclockwise about the origin through an angle θ. The coordinates of the resulting point (x', y') are determined by the matrix equation shown at the right.

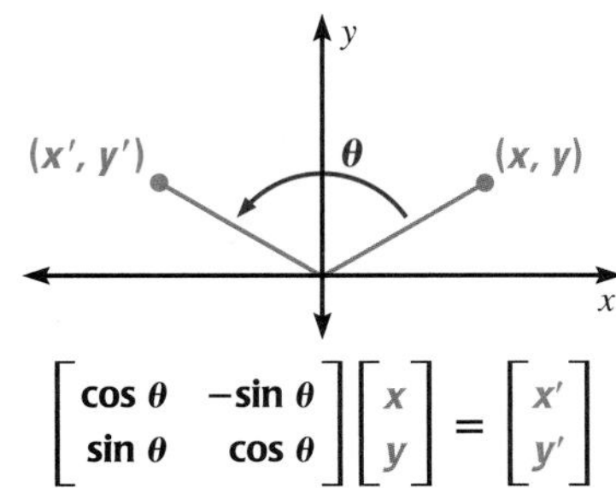

$$\begin{bmatrix} \cos\theta & -\sin\theta \\ \sin\theta & \cos\theta \end{bmatrix}\begin{bmatrix} x \\ y \end{bmatrix} = \begin{bmatrix} x' \\ y' \end{bmatrix}$$

a. The point (2, 3) is rotated counterclockwise about the origin through an angle of $\frac{\pi}{3}$. What are the coordinates of the resulting point?

b. Through what angle θ must the point (6, 2) be rotated to produce $(x', y') = (3\sqrt{3} - 1, \sqrt{3} + 3)$?

New York Mixed Review

46. The speed of a falling object increases 32 feet per second each second it falls. From a high cliff, Andrew throws an object downward with an initial speed of 8 feet per second. Which equation represents the speed s (in feet per second) of the falling object after t seconds?

(A) $s = -32t + 8$ (B) $s = 32t + 8$

(C) $s = 8t + 32$ (D) $s = 32t$

47. What are the coordinates of the y-intercept of the graph of $-3x + 4y = 24$?

(A) $(-8, 0)$ (B) $\left(0, \frac{4}{3}\right)$

(C) $(0, 6)$ (D) $(0, 8)$

PROBLEM SOLVING WORKSHOP
LESSON 14.4

Using ALTERNATIVE METHODS

Another Way to Solve Example 3, page 932

MULTIPLE REPRESENTATIONS In Example 3 on page 932, you solved a trigonometric equation algebraically. You can also solve a trigonometric equation using a table or using a graph.

PROBLEM

OCEANOGRAPHY The water depth d for the Bay of Fundy can be modeled by

$$d = 35 - 28 \cos \frac{\pi}{6.2} t$$

where d is measured in feet and t is the time in hours. If $t = 0$ represents midnight, at what time(s) is the water depth 7 feet?

METHOD 1

Using a Table The problem requires solving the equation $35 - 28 \cos \frac{\pi}{6.2} t = 7$. One way to solve this equation is to make a table of values. You can use a graphing calculator to make the table.

STEP 1 **Enter** the function $y = 35 - 28 \cos \frac{\pi}{6.2} x$ into a graphing calculator. Note that time is now represented by x and water depth is now represented by y.

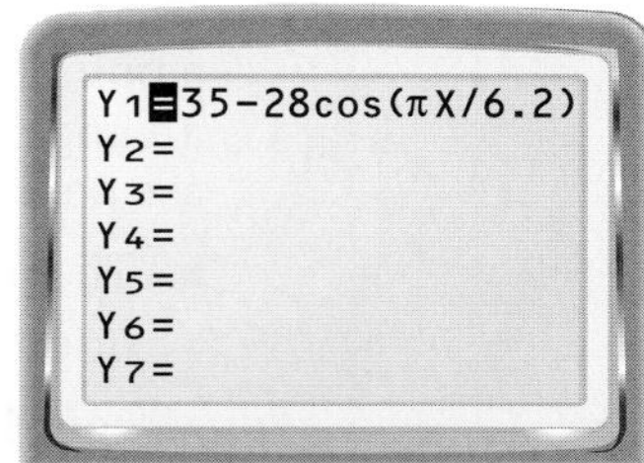

STEP 2 **Make** a table of values for the function. Set the table so that the x-values start at 0 and increase in increments of 0.1. (Be sure that the calculator is set in radian mode.)

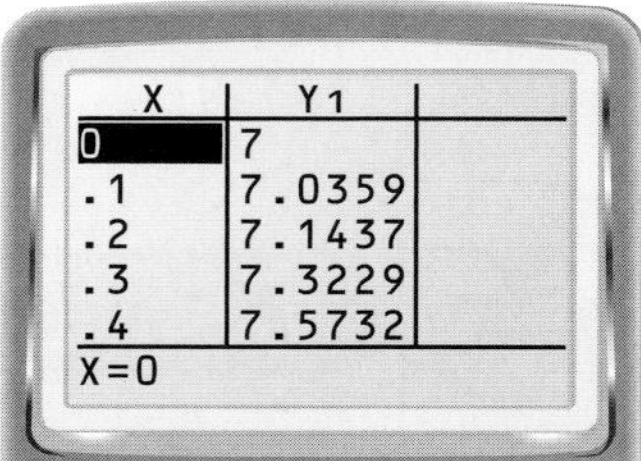

STEP 3 **Scroll** through the table to find all the times x at which the water depth y is 7 feet. On the interval $0 \le x \le 24$ (which represents one full day), you can see that the function equals 7 when x is 0 and 12.4.

X	Y1
12.1	7.3229
12.2	7.1437
12.3	7.0359
12.4	7
12.5	7.0359

X=12.4

▶ The water depth is 7 feet when $x = 0$ (that is, at midnight) and when $x = 12.4$ (that is, at 12:24 P.M.).

METHOD 2

Using a Graph Another approach is to use a graph to solve the equation $35 - 28\cos\frac{\pi}{6.2}t = 7$. You can use a graphing calculator to make the graph.

STEP 1 **Enter** the functions $y = 35 - 28\cos\frac{\pi}{6.2}x$ and $y = 7$ into a graphing calculator. Again, note that time is now represented by x and water depth is now represented by y.

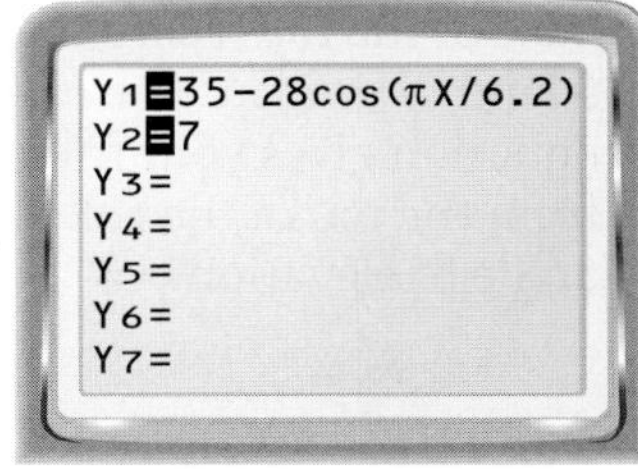

STEP 2 **Graph** the functions. Set your calculator in radian mode. Adjust the viewing window so that you can see where the graphs intersect on the interval $0 \le x \le 24$.

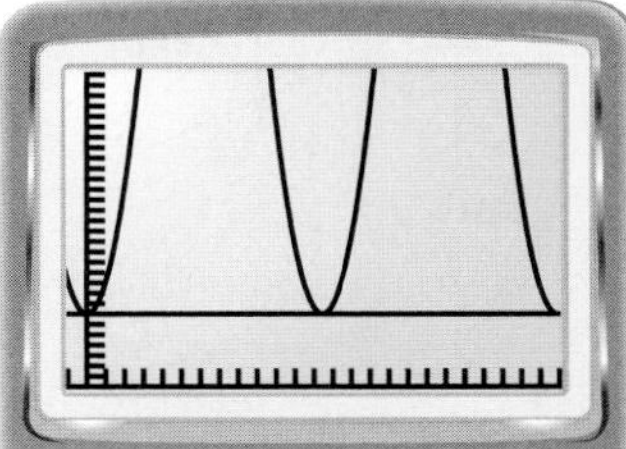

STEP 3 **Find** the intersection points of the two graphs using the *intersect* feature of the graphing calculator. On the interval $0 \le x \le 24$, the graphs intersect at (0, 7) and (12.4, 7). Because x represents the number of hours since midnight, you know that the water depth is 7 feet at midnight and 12:24 P.M.

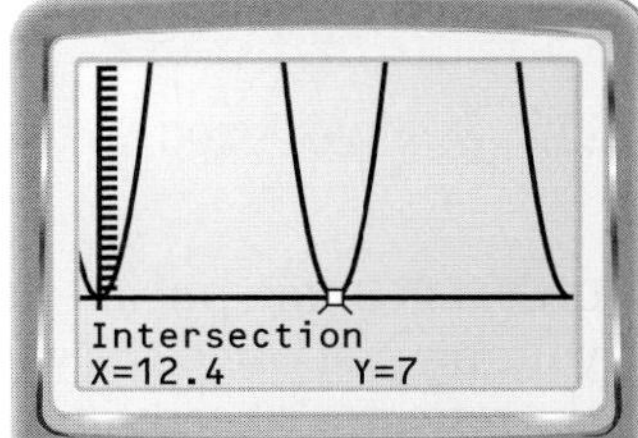

PRACTICE

SOLVING EQUATIONS Solve the equation using a table and using a graph.

1. $20\sin\frac{\pi}{4}x - 6 = 8$

2. $5\cos\frac{\pi}{6}x + 6 = 2$

3. $-10\cos 2\pi x = 3$

4. $3 + 4\sin\frac{\pi}{2}x = 2$

5. $-15 - 10\sin\frac{\pi}{20}x = -11$

6. $-34\cos\frac{\pi}{5}\left(x - \frac{\pi}{10}\right) + 22 = 17$

7. **WHAT IF?** In the problem on page 938, suppose you want to find the time(s) when the depth of the water in the Bay of Fundy is 15 feet. Find the time(s) using a table and using a graph.

8. **WRITING** *Explain* why the equation $2\sin x + 3 = 0$ has no solution. How does a graph show this?

9. **BUOY** An ocean buoy bobs up and down as waves travel past it. The buoy's displacement d (in feet) with respect to sea level can be modeled by $d = 3\sin \pi t$ where t is the time (in seconds). During the one second interval $0 \le t \le 1$, when is the buoy 1.5 feet above sea level? Solve the problem using a table and using a graph.

TEST PRACTICE
classzone.com

Lessons 14.1–14.4

1. **AMUSEMENT PARK** At an amusement park, you watch your friend go on a ride that simulates free-fall. You are standing 200 feet from the base of the ride as it slowly begins to pull your friend to the top. The ride is 120 feet tall. Which equation gives your friend's distance d (in feet) from the top of the ride as a function of the angle of elevation?

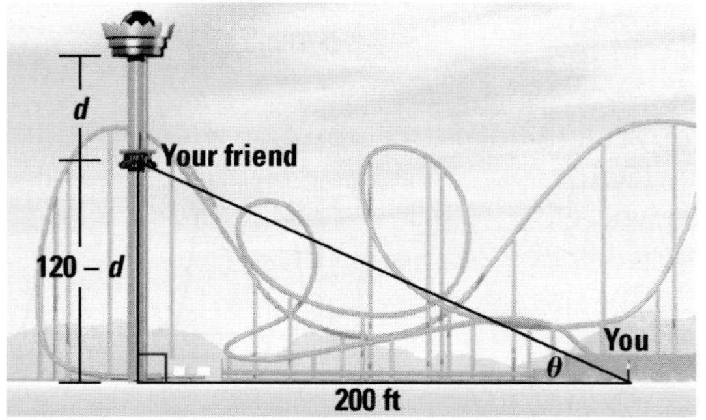

(1) $d = \frac{200}{\tan \theta}$ (3) $d = 200 \tan \theta$

(2) $d = 120 - 200 \tan \theta$ (4) $d = 120 - \frac{200}{\tan \theta}$

2. **BICYCLING** You put a reflector on a spoke of your bicycle wheel. As you ride your bicycle, the reflector's height h (in inches) above the ground is modeled by

$$h = 13.5 + 11.5 \cos 2\pi t$$

where t is the time (in seconds). What is the frequency of the function?

(1) 1 (3) π

(2) $\frac{\pi}{2}$ (4) 2π

3. **HOT AIR BALLOON** You stand 80 feet from the launch site of a hot air balloon traveling directly upward. What is the angle of elevation from you to the balloon when the balloon's height is 150 feet?

(1) 28.1°

(2) 32.2°

(3) 57.8°

(4) 61.9°

4. **RATE OF CHANGE** In calculus, it can be shown that the rate of change of the function $f(x) = -\csc x - \sin x$ is given by this expression:

$$\csc x \cot x - \cos x$$

Which expression is equivalent to $\csc x \cot x - \cos x$?

(1) $\cos x$

(2) $\cot^2 x$

(3) $\cos x \cot^2 x$

(4) $\cos x \csc^2 x$

5. **OPEN-ENDED** What is the amplitude of the graph shown?

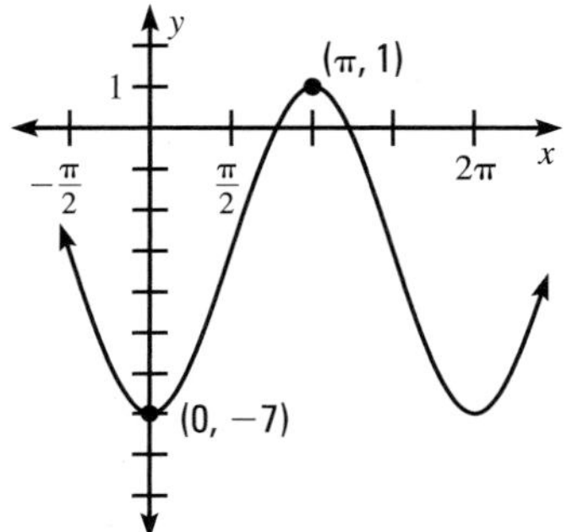

6. **OPEN-ENDED** The number n of millions of gallons of ice cream produced in the U.S. can be approximated by the function

$$n(t) = 113 + 24.5 \sin (0.0172(t - 105))$$

where t is the time in days with $t = 1$ representing January 1.

What is the period of this function, to the nearest number of days? *Explain* why this answer is reasonable.

According to the model, what is the maximum number of gallons of ice cream produced any one day of the year?

According to the model, what days of the year correspond to the highest and lowest production of ice cream?

14.5 Write Trigonometric Functions and Models

A2.A.72 Write the trigonometric function that is represented by a given periodic graph

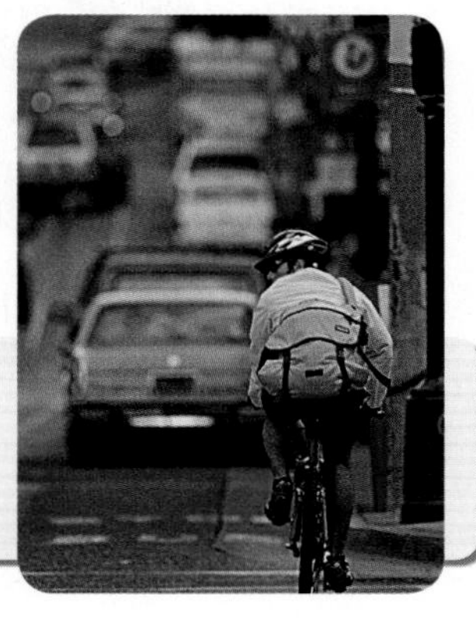

Before You graphed sine and cosine functions.

Now You will model data using sine and cosine functions.

Why? So you can model the number of bicyclists, as in Ex. 26.

Key Vocabulary
- **sinusoid**

Graphs of sine and cosine functions are called **sinusoids**. One method to write a sine or cosine function that models a sinusoid is to find the values of a, b, h, and k for

$$y = a \sin b(x - h) + k \qquad \text{or} \qquad y = a \cos b(x - h) + k$$

where $|a|$ is the amplitude, $\frac{2\pi}{b}$ is the period ($b > 0$), h is the horizontal shift, and k is the vertical shift.

EXAMPLE 1 Solve a multi-step problem

Write a function for the sinusoid shown below.

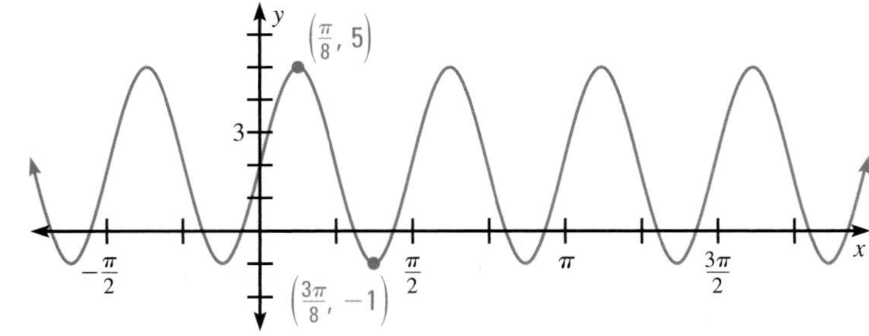

Solution

STEP 1 **Find** the maximum value M and minimum value m. From the graph, $M = 5$ and $m = -1$.

STEP 2 **Identify** the vertical shift, k. The value of k is the mean of the maximum and minimum values. The vertical shift is $k = \frac{M + m}{2} = \frac{5 + (-1)}{2} = \frac{4}{2} = 2$. So, $k = 2$.

STEP 3 **Decide** whether the graph should be modeled by a sine or cosine function. Because the graph crosses the midline $y = 2$ on the y-axis, the graph is a sine curve with no horizontal shift. So, $h = 0$.

FIND PERIOD
Because the graph repeats every $\frac{\pi}{2}$ units, the period is $\frac{\pi}{2}$.

STEP 4 **Find** the amplitude and period. The period is $\frac{\pi}{2} = \frac{2\pi}{b}$. So, $b = 4$.

The amplitude is $|a| = \frac{M - m}{2} = \frac{5 - (-1)}{2} = \frac{6}{2} = 3$. The graph is not a reflection, so $a > 0$. Therefore, $a = 3$.

▶ The function is $y = 3 \sin 4x + 2$.

EXAMPLE 2 Model circular motion

JUMP ROPE At a Double Dutch competition, two people swing jump ropes as shown in the diagram below. The highest point of the middle of each rope is 75 inches above the ground, and the lowest point is 3 inches. The rope makes 2 revolutions per second. Write a model for the height h (in feet) of a rope as a function of the time t (in seconds) if the rope is at its lowest point when $t = 0$.

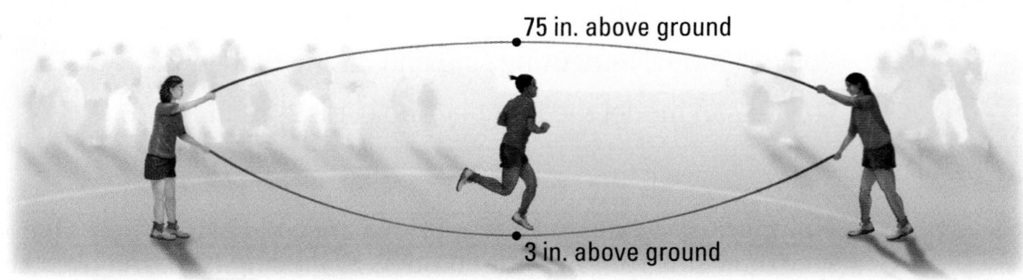

Solution

STEP 1 **Find** the maximum and minimum values of the function. A rope's maximum height is 75 inches, so $M = 75$. A rope's minimum height is 3 inches, so $m = 3$.

STEP 2 **Identify** the vertical shift. The vertical shift for the model is:

$$k = \frac{M + m}{2} = \frac{75 + 3}{2} = \frac{78}{2} = 39$$

STEP 3 **Decide** whether the height should be modeled by a sine or cosine function. When $t = 0$, the height is at its minimum. So, use a cosine function whose graph is a reflection in the x-axis with no horizontal shift ($h = 0$).

STEP 4 **Find** the amplitude and period.

The amplitude is $|a| = \frac{M - m}{2} = \frac{75 - 3}{2} = 36$.

Because the graph is a reflection, $a < 0$. So, $a = -36$. Because a rope is rotating at a rate of 2 revolutions per second, one revolution is completed in 0.5 second. So, the period is $\frac{2\pi}{b} = 0.5$, and $b = 4\pi$.

▶ A model for the height of a rope is $h = -36 \cos 4\pi t + 39$.

GUIDED PRACTICE for Examples 1 and 2

Write a function for the sinusoid.

1.

3, y, (0, 2), $\frac{2\pi}{3}$, x, $\left(\frac{\pi}{3}, -2\right)$

2.

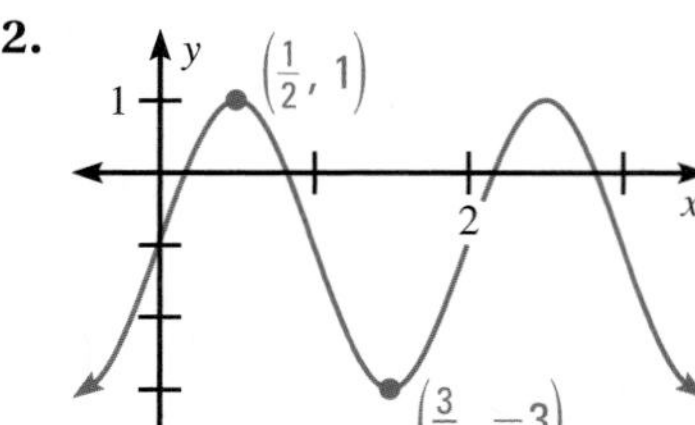

3. WHAT IF? *Describe* how the model in Example 2 would change if the lowest point of a rope is 5 inches above the ground and the highest point is 70 inches above the ground.

SINUSOIDAL REGRESSION Another way to model sinusoids is to use a graphing calculator that has a sinusoidal regression feature. The advantage of this method is that it uses all of the data points to find the model.

EXAMPLE 3 Use sinusoidal regression

ENERGY The table below shows the number of kilowatt hours K (in thousands) used each month for a given year by a hangar at the Cape Canaveral Air Station in Florida. The time t is measured in months, with $t = 1$ representing January. Write a trigonometric model that gives K as a function of t.

t	1	2	3	4	5	6	7	8	9	10	11	12
K	61.9	59	62	70.1	81.4	93.1	102.3	106.8	105.4	92.9	81.2	69.9

Solution

STEP 1 **Enter** the data in a graphing calculator.

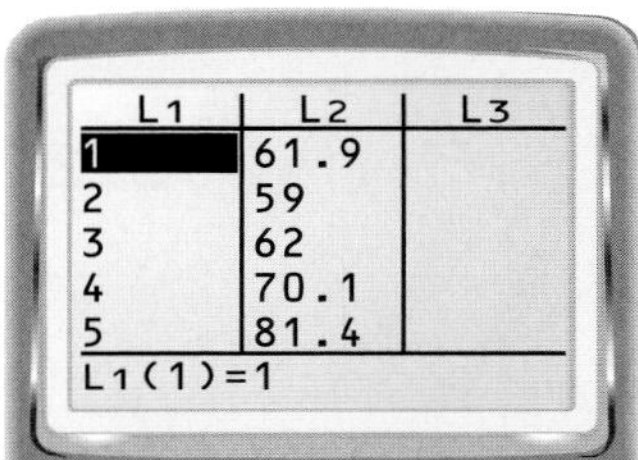

STEP 2 **Make** a scatter plot.

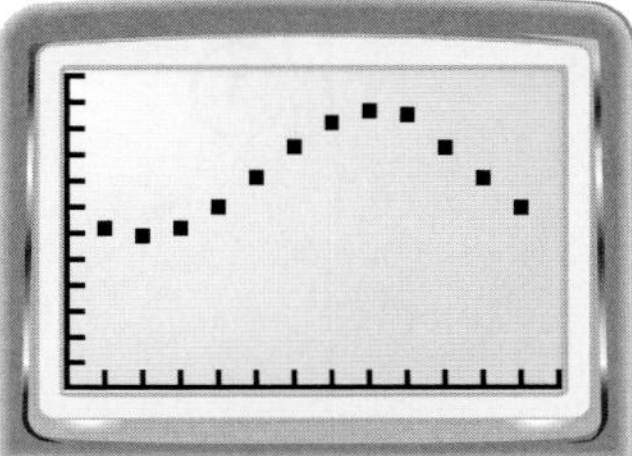

STEP 3 **Perform** a sinusoidal regression, because the scatter plot appears sinusoidal.

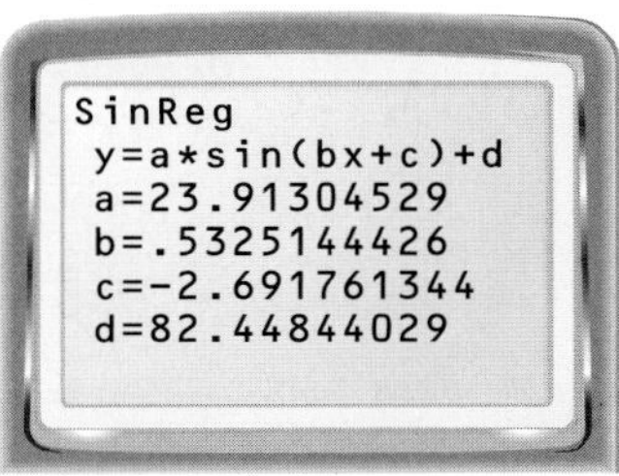

STEP 4 **Graph** the model and the data in the same viewing window.

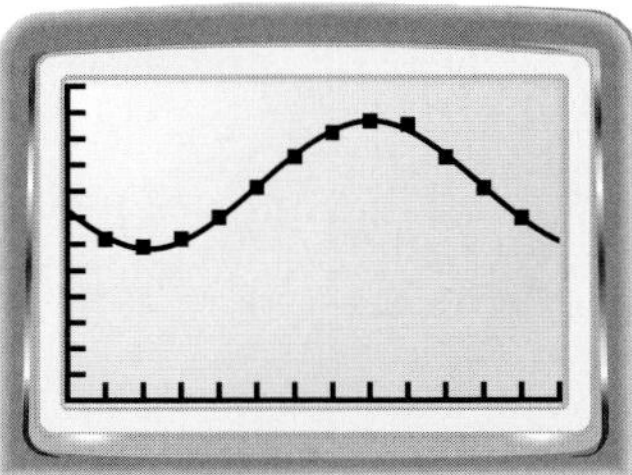

▶ The model appears to be a good fit. So, a model for the data is $K = 23.9 \sin (0.533t - 2.69) + 82.4$.

✓ GUIDED PRACTICE for Example 3

4. **METEOROLOGY** Use a graphing calculator to write a sine model that gives the average daily temperature T (in degrees Fahrenheit) for Boston, Massachusetts, as a function of the time t (in months), where $t = 1$ represents January.

t	1	2	3	4	5	6	7	8	9	10	11	12
T	29	32	39	48	59	68	74	72	65	54	45	35

14.5 EXERCISES

HOMEWORK KEY

○ = **WORKED-OUT SOLUTIONS** on p. WS24 for Exs. 5, 9, and 25

★ = **STANDARDIZED TEST PRACTICE** Exs. 2, 18, 19, 20, and 28

SKILL PRACTICE

1. **VOCABULARY** What is a sinusoid?

2. ★ **WRITING** *Describe* two methods you can use to model a sinusoid.

EXAMPLE 1 on p. 941 for Exs. 3–19

WRITING FUNCTIONS **Write a function for the sinusoid.**

3.

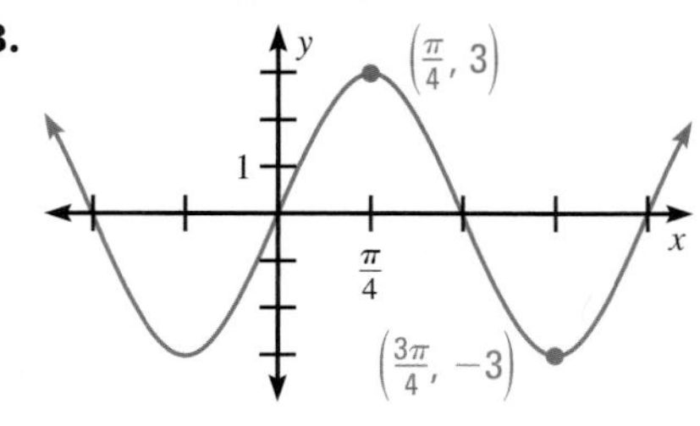

4.

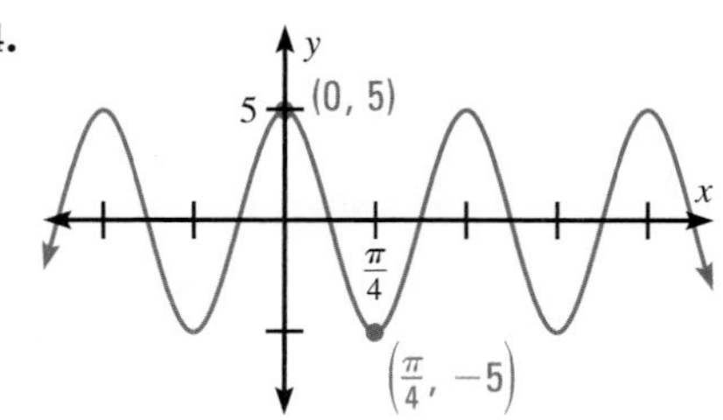

5.

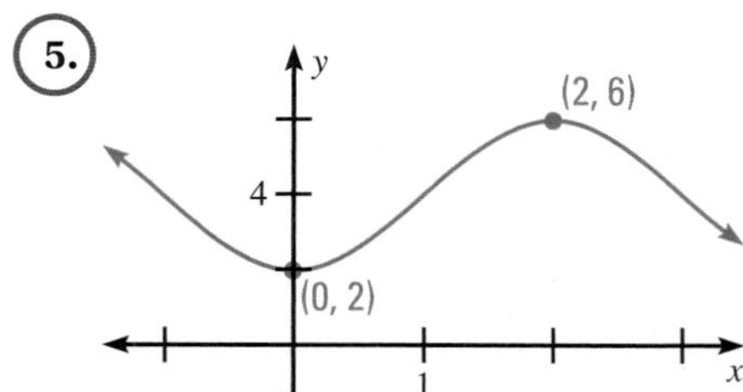

6.

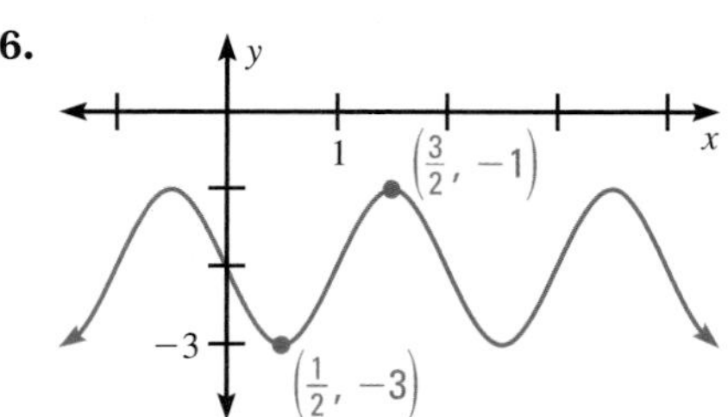

ERROR ANALYSIS *Describe* **and correct the error in finding the amplitude and vertical shift for a sinusoid with a maximum point at (2, 10) and a minimum point at (4, −6).**

7.

$$|a| = \frac{M - m}{2} = \frac{10 - 6}{2} = 2$$

8.

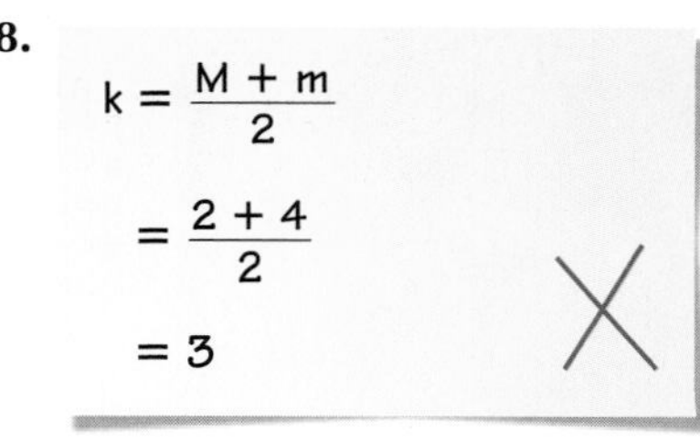

$$k = \frac{M + m}{2} = \frac{2 + 4}{2} = 3$$

WRITING FUNCTIONS **Write a function for the sinusoid with maximum at point A and minimum at point B.**

9. $A(\pi, 6)$, $B(3\pi, -6)$

10. $A(0, 4)$, $B(\pi, -4)$

11. $A\left(\frac{\pi}{3}, 5\right)$, $B(0, 3)$

12. $A\left(\frac{\pi}{6}, 8\right)$, $B(0, -6)$

13. $A\left(\frac{3\pi}{4}, 9\right)$, $B(2\pi, 5)$

14. $A(0, 5)$, $B(6, -11)$

15. $A(0, 0)$, $B(4\pi, -4)$

16. $A\left(\frac{\pi}{3}, -3\right)$, $B\left(\frac{\pi}{12}, -7\right)$

17. $A\left(\frac{2\pi}{3}, 0\right)$, $B(0, -12)$

18. ★ **MULTIPLE CHOICE** During one cycle, a sinusoid has a minimum at (16, 38) and a maximum at (24, 60). What is the amplitude of this sinusoid?

Ⓐ 8 Ⓑ 11 Ⓒ 22 Ⓓ 49

19. ★ **MULTIPLE CHOICE** What is an equation of the graph shown at the right?

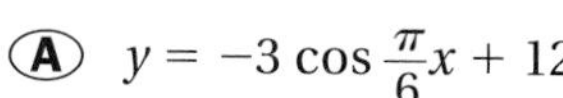

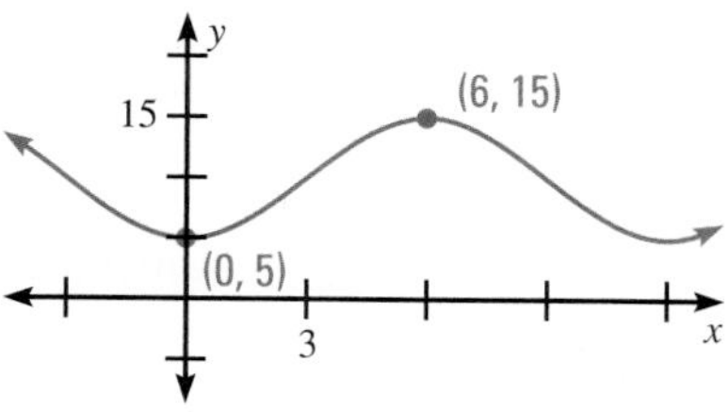

Ⓐ $y = -3 \cos \frac{\pi}{6}x + 12$ Ⓑ $y = -5 \cos \frac{\pi}{6}x + 10$

Ⓒ $y = 3 \sin \frac{\pi}{6}x + 12$ Ⓓ $y = -5 \sin \frac{\pi}{6}x + 10$

20. ★ **WRITING** Any sinusoid can be modeled by both a sine function and a cosine function. Therefore, you can choose the type of function that is more convenient. *Explain* which type of function you would choose to model a sinusoid whose y-intercept occurs at the minimum value of the function.

21. **REASONING** Model the sinusoid in Example 1 on page 941 with a cosine function of the form $y = a \cos b(x - h) + k$. Use identities to show that the model you found is equivalent to the sine model in Example 1.

22. **CHALLENGE** Write a sine function for the sinusoid with a minimum at $\left(\frac{\pi}{2}, 3\right)$ and a maximum at $\left(\frac{\pi}{4}, 8\right)$.

PROBLEM SOLVING

EXAMPLE 1 on p. 941 for Exs. 23–24

23. **CIRCUITS** A circuit has an alternating voltage of 100 volts that peaks every 0.5 second. Use the graph shown at the right to write a sinusoidal model for the voltage V as a function of the time t (in seconds).

V; 100; $\left(\frac{1}{8}, 100\right)$; $\frac{1}{8}$; $\left(\frac{3}{8}, -100\right)$; t

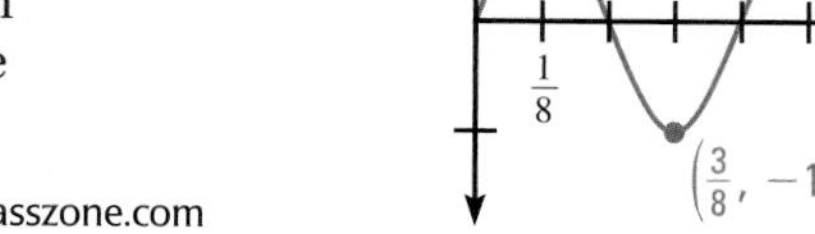

@HomeTutor for problem solving help at classzone.com

24. **CLIMATOLOGY** The graph below shows the average daily temperature of Houston, Texas. Write a sinusoidal model for the average daily temperature T (in degrees Fahrenheit) as a function of time t (in months).

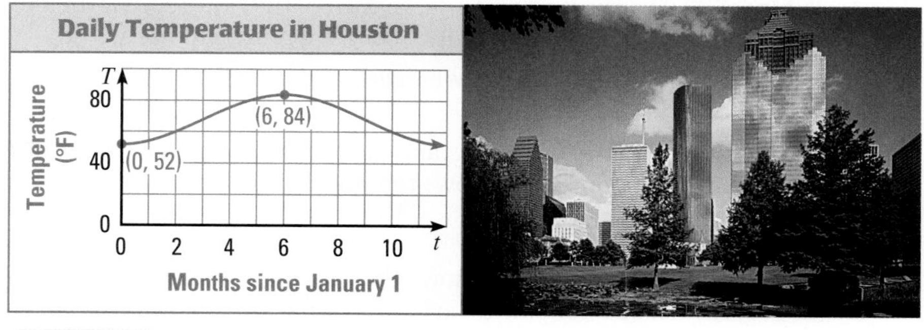

@HomeTutor for problem solving help at classzone.com

EXAMPLE 2 on p. 942 for Ex. 25

25. **CIRCULAR MOTION** One of the largest sewing machines in the world has a *flywheel* (which turns as the machine sews) that is 5 feet in diameter. Write a model for the height h (in feet) of the handle at the edge of the flywheel as a function of the time t (in seconds). Assume that the wheel makes a complete turn every 2 seconds and the handle is at its minimum height of 4 feet above the ground when $t = 0$.

EXAMPLE 3 on p. 943 for Exs. 26–27

26. **BICYCLISTS** The table below shows the number of adult residents R (in millions) in the United States who rode a bicycle during the months of October 2001 through September 2002. The time t is measured in months, with $t = 1$ representing October 2001. Use a graphing calculator to write a sinusoidal model that gives R as a function of t.

t	1	2	3	4	5	6	7	8	9	10	11	12
R	35	30	24	24	26	29	35	34	39	43	44	37

27. **MULTI-STEP PROBLEM** The table below shows the number of employees N (in thousands) at a sporting goods company each year for eleven years. The time t is measured in years, with $t = 1$ representing the first year.

t	1	2	3	4	5	6	7	8	9	10	11
N	20.8	22.7	24.6	23.2	20	17.5	16.7	17.8	21	22	24.1

a. **Model** Use a graphing calculator to write a sinusoidal model that gives N as a function of t.

b. **Calculate** Predict the number of employees in the twelfth year.

28. ★ **EXTENDED RESPONSE** The low tide at Eastport, Maine, is 3.5 feet and occurs at midnight. After 6 hours, Eastport is at high tide, which is 16.5 feet.

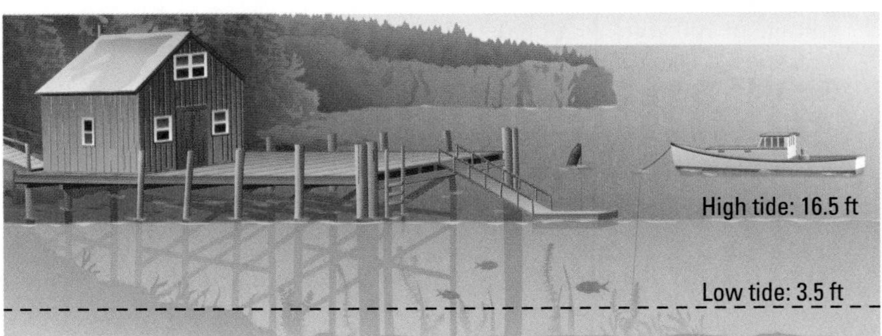

a. **Model** Write a sinusoidal model that gives the tide depth d (in feet) as a function of the time t (in hours). Let $t = 0$ represent midnight.

b. **Calculate** Find all the times when low and high tides occur in a 24 hour period.

c. **Reasoning** *Explain* how the graph of the function you wrote in part (a) is related to a graph that shows the tide depth d at Eastport t hours after 3:00 A.M.

29. **CHALLENGE** The table below shows the average monthly sea temperatures T (in degrees Celsius) for Santa Barbara, California. The time t is measured in months, with $t = 1$ representing January.

t	1	2	3	4	5	6	7	8	9	10	11	12
T	14	13.6	13.4	12.5	13.9	15.6	16.8	17.2	17.7	17.1	15.5	14.1

a. Use a graphing calculator to write a sine model that gives T as a function of t.

b. Find a cosine model for the data.

30. The top, front, and side views of a solid built with cubes are shown below. How many cubes are needed to construct this solid?

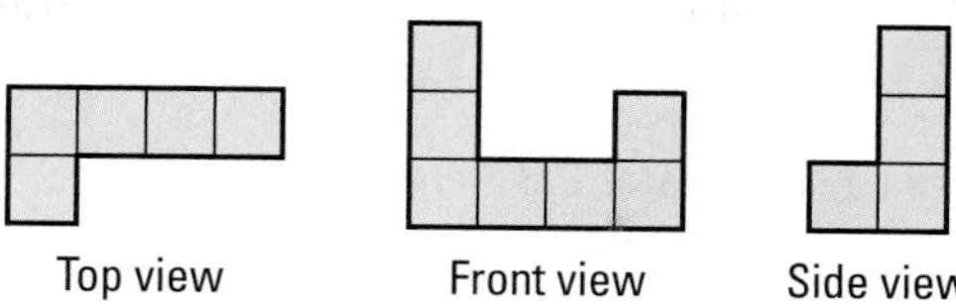

Ⓐ 7　Ⓑ 8　Ⓒ 9　Ⓓ 10

31. What is the area of the blue figure shown at the right?

Ⓐ 48.5 cm^2　Ⓑ 113.0 cm^2

Ⓒ 141.5 cm^2　Ⓓ 283.0 cm^2

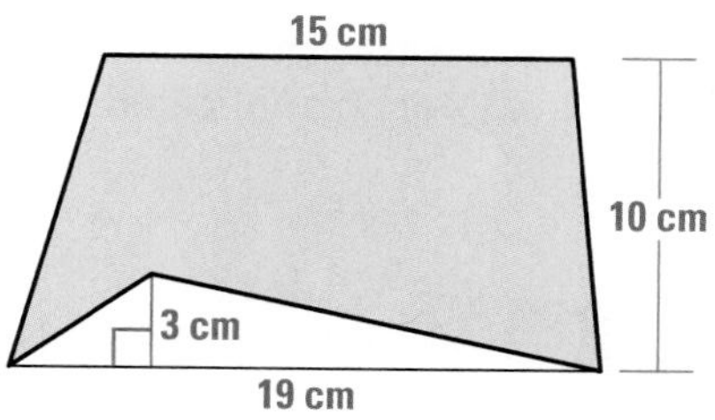

QUIZ for Lessons 14.3–14.5

Simplify the expression. *(p. 924)*

1. $\sin x \sec x$

2. $\sin \theta (1 + \cot^2 \theta)$

3. $\tan\left(\frac{\pi}{2} - \theta\right) \cot \theta - \csc^2 \theta$

4. $\cos^2 \theta + \sin^2 \theta + \tan^2 \theta$

5. $\dfrac{\tan\left(\frac{\pi}{2} - x\right) \sec x}{1 - \csc^2 x}$

6. $\dfrac{\sin(-x)}{\csc x} + \dfrac{\cos(-x)}{\sec x}$

Find the general solution of the equation. *(p. 931)*

7. $\cos x + \cos(-x) = 1$

8. $\sqrt{2} \cos x \sin x - \cos x = 0$

9. $2 \sin^2 x - \sin x = 1$

Write a function for the sinusoid. *(p. 941)*

10.

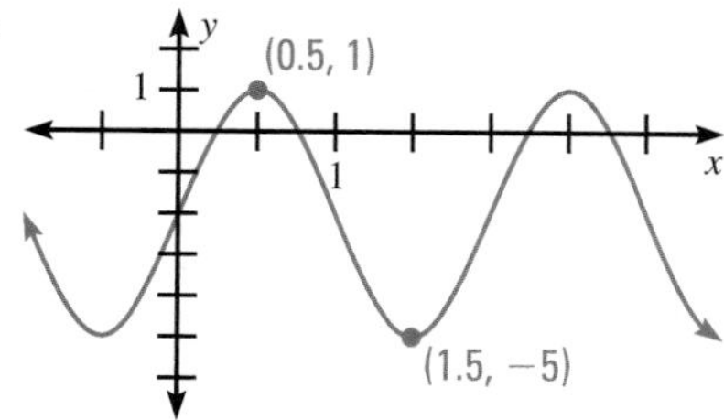

11.

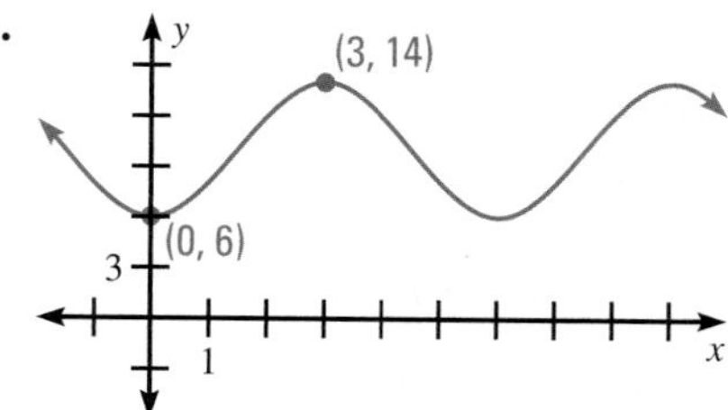

12. DAILY TEMPERATURES The table below shows the average daily temperature D (in degrees Fahrenheit) in Detroit, Michigan. The time t is measured in months, with $t = 1$ representing January. Use a graphing calculator to write a sinusoidal model that gives D as a function of t. *(p. 941)*

t	1	2	3	4	5	6	7	8	9	10	11	12
D	24.5	27.2	36.9	48.1	59.8	69	73.5	71.8	63.9	51.9	40.7	29.6

@HomeTutor
classzone.com
Keystrokes

14.5 Collect and Model Trigonometric Data

MATERIALS • musical instrument • CBL microphone • Calculator Based Laboratory (CBL) • graphing calculator

QUESTION How is music related to trigonometry?

Sound is a variation in pressure transmitted through air, water, or other matter. Sound travels as a wave. The sound of a pure note can be represented using a sine (or cosine) wave. More complicated sounds can be modeled by the sum of several sine waves.

EXPLORE Analyze the sound of a musical instrument

Play a note on a musical instrument. Write a sine function to describe the note.

STEP 1 ***Play note***

Play a pure note on a musical instrument. Use the CBL and the CBL microphone to collect the sound data and store it in a graphing calculator.

STEP 2 ***Graph function***

Use the graphing calculator to graph the pressure of the sound as a function of time.

STEP 3 ***Find characteristics of graph***

Use the graph of the sound data to calculate the note's amplitude and frequency (the number of cycles in one second).

STEP 4 ***Write function***

Write a sine function for the note.

DRAW CONCLUSIONS Use your observations to complete these exercises

1. Choose a note to play and have a classmate also choose a note. Find two sine functions $y = f(x)$ and $y = g(x)$ that model the two notes. Then play the notes simultaneously and use the CBL and a graphing calculator to graph the resulting sound wave. *Compare* this graph with the graph of $y = f(x) + g(x)$. What do you notice?
2. The pitch of a sound wave is determined by the wave's frequency. The greater the frequency, the higher the pitch. Which of the notes in Exercise 1 had a higher pitch?
3. When you change the volume of a note, what happens to the graph of the sound wave?
4. *Compare* the sine waves for different instruments playing the same note.

14.6 Apply Sum and Difference Formulas

 **A2.A.76** Apply the angle sum and difference formulas for trigonometric functions

Before You found trigonometric functions of a given angle.

Now You will use trigonometric sum and difference formulas.

Why? So you can simplify a ratio used for aerial photography, as in Ex. 43.

Key Vocabulary
- **trigonometric identity,** *p. 924*

In this lesson, you will study formulas that allow you to evaluate trigonometric functions of the sum or difference of two angles.

KEY CONCEPT *For Your Notebook*

Sum and Difference Formulas

Sum Formulas	Difference Formulas
$\sin(a+b) = \sin a \cos b + \cos a \sin b$	$\sin(a-b) = \sin a \cos b - \cos a \sin b$
$\cos(a+b) = \cos a \cos b - \sin a \sin b$	$\cos(a-b) = \cos a \cos b + \sin a \sin b$
$\tan(a+b) = \dfrac{\tan a + \tan b}{1 - \tan a \tan b}$	$\tan(a-b) = \dfrac{\tan a - \tan b}{1 + \tan a \tan b}$

In general, $\sin(a+b) \neq \sin a + \sin b$. Similar statements can be made for the other trigonometric functions of sums and differences.

EXAMPLE 1 Evaluate a trigonometric expression

Find the exact value of (a) sin 15° and (b) tan $\frac{7\pi}{12}$.

a. $\sin 15° = \sin(60° - 45°)$ — Substitute 60° − 45° for 15°.

$= \sin 60° \cos 45° - \cos 60° \sin 45°$ — Difference formula for sine

$= \frac{\sqrt{3}}{2}\left(\frac{\sqrt{2}}{2}\right) - \frac{1}{2}\left(\frac{\sqrt{2}}{2}\right)$ — Evaluate.

$= \frac{\sqrt{6} - \sqrt{2}}{4}$ — Simplify.

b. $\tan \frac{7\pi}{12} = \tan\left(\frac{\pi}{3} + \frac{\pi}{4}\right)$ — Substitute $\frac{\pi}{3} + \frac{\pi}{4}$ for $\frac{7\pi}{12}$.

$= \dfrac{\tan \frac{\pi}{3} + \tan \frac{\pi}{4}}{1 - \tan \frac{\pi}{3} \tan \frac{\pi}{4}}$ — Sum formula for tangent

$= \dfrac{\sqrt{3} + 1}{1 - \sqrt{3} \cdot 1}$ — Evaluate.

$= -2 - \sqrt{3}$ — Simplify.

REVIEW CONJUGATES
For help with using conjugates to rationalize denominators, see p. 266.

EXAMPLE 2 Use a difference formula

Find $\cos(a - b)$ given that $\cos a = -\frac{4}{5}$ with $\pi < a < \frac{3\pi}{2}$ and $\sin b = \frac{5}{13}$ with $0 < b < \frac{\pi}{2}$.

Solution

Using a Pythagorean identity and quadrant signs gives $\sin a = -\frac{3}{5}$ and $\cos b = \frac{12}{13}$.

$\cos(a - b) = \cos a \cos b + \sin a \sin b$ — **Difference formula for cosine**

$= -\frac{4}{5}\left(\frac{12}{13}\right) + \left(-\frac{3}{5}\right)\left(\frac{5}{13}\right)$ — **Substitute.**

$= -\frac{63}{65}$ — **Simplify.**

✓ GUIDED PRACTICE for Examples 1 and 2

Find the exact value of the expression.

1. $\sin 105°$
2. $\cos 75°$
3. $\tan \frac{5\pi}{12}$
4. $\cos \frac{\pi}{12}$
5. Find $\sin(a - b)$ given that $\sin a = \frac{8}{17}$ with $0 < a < \frac{\pi}{2}$ and $\cos b = -\frac{24}{25}$ with $\pi < b < \frac{3\pi}{2}$.

EXAMPLE 3 Simplify an expression

Simplify the expression $\cos(x + \pi)$.

$\cos(x + \pi) = \cos x \cos \pi - \sin x \sin \pi$ — **Sum formula for cosine**

$= (\cos x)(-1) - (\sin x)(0)$ — **Evaluate.**

$= -\cos x$ — **Simplify.**

EXAMPLE 4 Solve a trigonometric equation

Solve $\sin\left(x + \frac{\pi}{3}\right) + \sin\left(x - \frac{\pi}{3}\right) = 1$ for $0 \le x < 2\pi$.

ANOTHER WAY You can also solve by using a graphing calculator. First graph each side of the original equation and then use the *intersect* feature to find the *x*-value(s) where the expressions are equal.

$\sin\left(x + \frac{\pi}{3}\right) + \sin\left(x - \frac{\pi}{3}\right) = 1$ — **Write equation.**

$\sin x \cos \frac{\pi}{3} + \cos x \sin \frac{\pi}{3} + \sin x \cos \frac{\pi}{3} - \cos x \sin \frac{\pi}{3} = 1$ — **Use formulas.**

$\frac{1}{2} \sin x + \frac{\sqrt{3}}{2} \cos x + \frac{1}{2} \sin x - \frac{\sqrt{3}}{2} \cos x = 1$ — **Evaluate.**

$\sin x = 1$ — **Simplify.**

▶ In the interval $0 \le x < 2\pi$, the only solution is $x = \frac{\pi}{2}$.

EXAMPLE 5 Solve a multi-step problem

DAYLIGHT HOURS The number h of hours of daylight for Dallas, Texas, and Anchorage, Alaska, can be approximated by the equations below, where t is the time in days and $t = 0$ represents January 1. On which days of the year will the two cities have the same amount of daylight?

Dallas: $h_1 = 2 \sin\left(\frac{\pi t}{182} - 1.35\right) + 12.1$ **Anchorage:** $h_2 = -6 \cos\left(\frac{\pi t}{182}\right) + 12.1$

Solution

STEP 1 **Solve** the equation $h_1 = h_2$ for t.

$$2 \sin\left(\frac{\pi t}{182} - 1.35\right) + 12.1 = -6 \cos\left(\frac{\pi t}{182}\right) + 12.1$$

$$\sin\left(\frac{\pi t}{182} - 1.35\right) = -3 \cos\left(\frac{\pi t}{182}\right)$$

$$\sin\left(\frac{\pi t}{182}\right) \cos 1.35 - \cos\left(\frac{\pi t}{182}\right) \sin 1.35 = -3 \cos\left(\frac{\pi t}{182}\right)$$

$$\sin\left(\frac{\pi t}{182}\right)(0.219) - \cos\left(\frac{\pi t}{182}\right)(0.976) = -3 \cos\left(\frac{\pi t}{182}\right)$$

$$0.219 \sin\left(\frac{\pi t}{182}\right) = -2.024 \cos\left(\frac{\pi t}{182}\right)$$

$$\tan\left(\frac{\pi t}{182}\right) = -9.242$$

$$\frac{\pi t}{182} = \tan^{-1}(-9.242) + n\pi$$

$$\frac{\pi t}{182} \approx -1.463 + n\pi$$

$$t \approx -84.76 + 182n$$

STEP 2 **Find** the days within one year (365 days) for which Dallas and Anchorage will have the same amount of daylight.

$t \approx -84.76 + 182(1) \approx 97$, or on April 8

$t \approx -84.76 + 182(2) \approx 279$, or on October 7

✓ GUIDED PRACTICE for Examples 3, 4, and 5

Simplify the expression.

6. $\sin(x + 2\pi)$ **7.** $\cos(x - 2\pi)$ **8.** $\tan(x - \pi)$

9. Solve $6 \cos\left(\frac{\pi t}{75}\right) + 5 = -24 \sin\left(\frac{\pi t}{75} + 22\right) + 5$ for $0 \le t < 2\pi$.

14.6 EXERCISES

HOMEWORK KEY

○ = **WORKED-OUT SOLUTIONS** on p. WS25 for Exs. 9, 23, and 43

★ = **STANDARDIZED TEST PRACTICE** Exs. 2, 11, 18, 32, and 44

SKILL PRACTICE

1. **VOCABULARY** Give the sum and difference formulas for sine, cosine, and tangent.

2. ★ **WRITING** *Explain* how you can evaluate tan 75° using either the sum or difference formula for tangent.

EXAMPLE 1 on p. 949 for Exs. 3–10

FINDING VALUES Find the exact value of the expression.

3. $\tan(-15°)$
4. $\sin(-165°)$
5. $\tan 195°$
6. $\cos 15°$
7. $\sin \frac{23\pi}{12}$
8. $\tan \frac{17\pi}{12}$
9. $\cos\left(-\frac{5\pi}{12}\right)$
10. $\sin\left(-\frac{7\pi}{12}\right)$

11. ★ **SHORT RESPONSE** Derive the cofunction identity $\sin\left(\frac{\pi}{2} - \theta\right) = \cos\theta$ using the difference formula for sine.

EXAMPLE 2 on p. 950 for Exs. 12–18

EVALUATING EXPRESSIONS Evaluate the expression given that $\cos a = \frac{4}{5}$ with $0 < a < \frac{\pi}{2}$ and $\sin b = -\frac{15}{17}$ with $\frac{3\pi}{2} < b < 2\pi$.

12. $\sin(a + b)$
13. $\cos(a + b)$
14. $\tan(a + b)$
15. $\sin(a - b)$
16. $\cos(a - b)$
17. $\tan(a - b)$

18. ★ **MULTIPLE CHOICE** What is the value of $\sin(a - b)$ given that $\sin a = -\frac{3}{5}$ with $\pi < a < \frac{3\pi}{2}$ and $\cos b = \frac{12}{13}$ with $0 < b < \frac{\pi}{2}$?

   (A) $-\frac{18}{55}$ (B) $-\frac{16}{65}$ (C) $\frac{14}{45}$ (D) $\frac{20}{43}$

EXAMPLE 3 on p. 950 for Exs. 19–31

SIMPLIFYING EXPRESSIONS Simplify the expression.

19. $\tan(x + \pi)$
20. $\sin(x + \pi)$
21. $\cos(x + 2\pi)$
22. $\tan(x - 2\pi)$
23. $\sin\left(x - \frac{3\pi}{2}\right)$
24. $\tan\left(x + \frac{\pi}{2}\right)$
25. $\sin\left(x + \frac{3\pi}{2}\right)$
26. $\cos\left(x - \frac{3\pi}{2}\right)$
27. $\tan\left(x + \frac{3\pi}{2}\right)$
28. $\cos\left(x - \frac{\pi}{2}\right)$
29. $\tan\left(x + \frac{5\pi}{2}\right)$
30. $\cos\left(x + \frac{5\pi}{2}\right)$

31. **ERROR ANALYSIS** *Describe* and correct the error in simplifying the expression.

$$\tan\left(x + \frac{\pi}{4}\right) = \frac{\tan x + \tan\frac{\pi}{4}}{1 + \tan x \tan\frac{\pi}{4}} = \frac{\tan x + 1}{1 + \tan x} = 1$$

EXAMPLE 4 on p. 950 for Exs. 32–38

32. ★ **MULTIPLE CHOICE** What is a solution of the equation $\sin(x - 2\pi) + \tan(x - 2\pi) = 0$ on the interval $\pi < x < 3\pi$?

   (A) $\frac{\pi}{2}$ (B) $\frac{3\pi}{2}$ (C) 2π (D) 3π

SOLVING TRIGONOMETRIC EQUATIONS Solve the equation for $0 \le x < 2\pi$.

33. $\cos\left(x + \frac{\pi}{6}\right) - 1 = \cos\left(x - \frac{\pi}{6}\right)$

34. $\sin\left(x + \frac{\pi}{4}\right) + \sin\left(x - \frac{\pi}{4}\right) = 0$

35. $\sin\left(x + \frac{5\pi}{6}\right) + \sin\left(x - \frac{5\pi}{6}\right) = 1$

36. $\tan(x + \pi) + \cos\left(x + \frac{\pi}{2}\right) = 0$

37. $\tan(x + \pi) + 2\sin(x + \pi) = 0$

38. $\sin(x + \pi) + \cos(x + \pi) = 0$

39. CHALLENGE Consider a complex number $z = a + bi$ in the complex plane shown. Let r be the length of the line segment joining z and the origin, and let θ be the angle that this segment makes with the positive real axis, as shown.

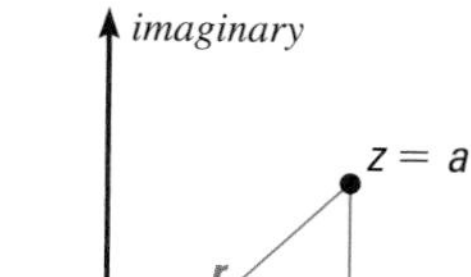

a. *Explain* why $a = r\cos\theta$ and $b = r\sin\theta$, so that $z = (r\cos\theta) + i(r\sin\theta)$.

b. Use the result from part (a) to show the following:

$$z^2 = r^2[(\cos\theta\cos\theta - \sin\theta\sin\theta) + i(\sin\theta\cos\theta + \cos\theta\sin\theta)]$$

c. Use the sum and difference formulas to show that the equation in part (b) can be written as $z^2 = r^2(\cos 2\theta + i\sin 2\theta)$.

PROBLEM SOLVING

EXAMPLE 5 on p. 951 for Exs. 40–41

40. METEOROLOGY The number h of hours of daylight for Rome, Italy, and Miami, Florida, can be approximated by the equations below, where t is the time in days and $t = 0$ represents January 1.

Rome: $h_1 = 2.7\sin\left(\frac{\pi t}{182} - 4.94\right) + 12.1$ **Miami:** $h_2 = -1.6\cos\frac{\pi t}{182} + 12.1$

On which days of the year will the cities have the same amount of daylight?

@HomeTutor for problem solving help at classzone.com

41. CLOCK TOWER The heights m and h (in feet) of a clock tower's minute hand and hour hand, respectively, can be approximated by

$$m = 182.5 - 11.5\sin\left(\frac{\pi t}{30} - \frac{\pi}{2}\right) \quad \text{and} \quad h = 182.5 - 7\sin\left(\frac{\pi t}{360}\right)$$

where t is the time in minutes and $t = 0$ represents 3:00 P.M. Use a graphing calculator to find how long it takes for the height of the minute hand to equal the height of the hour hand.

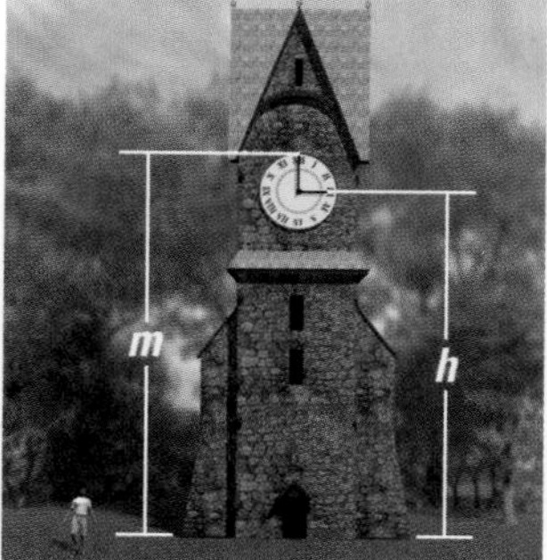

@HomeTutor for problem solving help at classzone.com

42. PHYSICAL SCIENCE When a wave travels through a taut string, the displacement y of each point on the string depends on the time t and the point's position x. The equation of a *standing wave* can be obtained by adding the displacements of two waves traveling in opposite directions. Suppose two waves can be modeled by these equations:

$$y_1 = A\cos\left(\frac{2\pi t}{3} - \frac{2\pi x}{5}\right) \qquad y_2 = A\cos\left(\frac{2\pi t}{3} + \frac{2\pi x}{5}\right)$$

Show that $y_1 + y_2 = 2A\cos\left(\frac{2\pi t}{3}\right)\cos\left(\frac{2\pi x}{5}\right)$.

43. **MULTI-STEP PROBLEM** A photographer is at a height h taking aerial photographs. The ratio of the image length WQ to the length NA of the actual object is

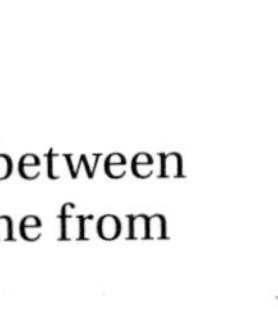

$$\frac{WQ}{NA} = \frac{f \tan(\theta - t) + f \tan t}{h \tan \theta}$$

where f is the focal length of the camera, θ is the angle between the vertical line perpendicular to the ground and the line from the camera to point A, and t is the tilt angle of the film.

a. Use the difference formula for tangent to simplify the ratio.

b. Show that $\frac{WQ}{NA} = \frac{f}{h}$ when $t = 0$.

44. ★ **EXTENDED RESPONSE** Your friend pulls on a weight attached to a spring and then releases it. A split second later, you begin filming the spring to analyze its motion. You find that the spring's distance y (in inches) from its equilibrium point can be modeled by $y = 5 \sin(2t + C)$ where $C = \tan^{-1} \frac{3}{4}$ and t is the elapsed time (in seconds) since you began filming.

a. Find the values of $\sin C$ and $\cos C$.

b. Use a sum formula to show that $y = 5 \sin(2t + C)$ can be written as $y = 4 \sin 2t + 3 \cos 2t$.

c. Graph the function found in part (b) and find its maximum value. *Explain* what this value represents.

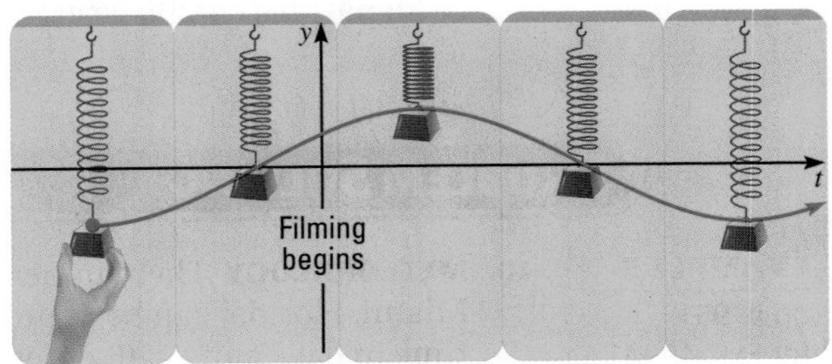

45. **CHALLENGE** The busy signal on a touch-tone phone is a combination of two tones with frequencies of 480 hertz and 620 hertz. The individual tones can be modeled by the following equations:

480 hertz: $y_1 = \cos 960\pi t$ **620 hertz:** $y_2 = \cos 1240\pi t$

The sound of the busy signal can be modeled by $y_1 + y_2$. Show that:

$$y_1 + y_2 = 2 \cos 1100\pi t \cos 140\pi t$$

NEW YORK MIXED REVIEW

TEST PRACTICE at classzone.com

46. A stack of boxes forms a square pyramid. The diagram shows the top three layers of the pyramid. Which rule gives the number a_n of boxes in the nth layer of the pyramid?

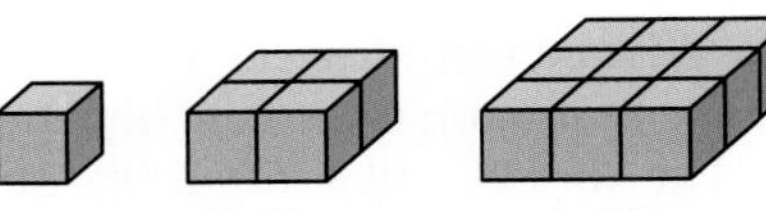

Ⓐ $a_n = 2n$ Ⓑ $a_n = 2(n + 1)$ Ⓒ $a_n = n(n + 1)$ Ⓓ $a_n = n^2$

47. What is the solution of $2(x - 2) - 1.45 = 3(x - 3)$?

Ⓐ -12.14 Ⓑ 3.55 Ⓒ 6.08 Ⓓ 11.25

14.7 Apply Double-Angle and Half-Angle Formulas

A2.A.77 Apply the double-angle and half-angle formulas for trigonometric functions

Before You evaluated expressions using sum and difference formulas.

Now You will use double-angle and half-angle formulas.

Why? So you can find the distance an object travels, as in Example 4.

Key Vocabulary
- **sine,** *p. 852*
- **cosine,** *p. 852*
- **tangent,** *p. 852*

In this lesson, you will use formulas for double angles (angles of measure $2a$) and half angles $\left(\text{angles of measure } \frac{a}{2}\right)$.

KEY CONCEPT *For Your Notebook*

Double-Angle and Half-Angle Formulas

Double-Angle Formulas

$\sin 2a = 2 \sin a \cos a$

$\cos 2a = 1 - 2\sin^2 a$

$\cos 2a = 2\cos^2 a - 1$

$\cos 2a = \cos^2 a - \sin^2 a$

$\tan 2a = \dfrac{2 \tan a}{1 - \tan^2 a}$

Half-Angle Formulas

$\sin \dfrac{a}{2} = \pm\sqrt{\dfrac{1 - \cos a}{2}}$

$\cos \dfrac{a}{2} = \pm\sqrt{\dfrac{1 + \cos a}{2}}$

$\tan \dfrac{a}{2} = \dfrac{1 - \cos a}{\sin a}$

$\tan \dfrac{a}{2} = \dfrac{\sin a}{1 + \cos a}$

The signs of $\sin \frac{a}{2}$ and $\cos \frac{a}{2}$ depend on the quadrant in which $\frac{a}{2}$ lies.

EXAMPLE 1 Evaluate trigonometric expressions

Find the exact value of (a) cos 165° and (b) tan $\frac{\pi}{12}$.

a. $\cos 165° = \cos \frac{1}{2}(330°)$

$= -\sqrt{\dfrac{1 + \cos 330°}{2}}$

$= -\sqrt{\dfrac{1 + \frac{\sqrt{3}}{2}}{2}}$

$= -\dfrac{\sqrt{2 + \sqrt{3}}}{2}$

CHOOSE SIGNS
Because 165° is in Quadrant II and the value of cosine is negative in Quadrant II, the following formula is used:
$\cos \frac{a}{2} = -\sqrt{\frac{1 + \cos a}{2}}$

b. $\tan \frac{\pi}{12} = \tan \frac{1}{2}\left(\frac{\pi}{6}\right)$

$= \dfrac{1 - \cos \frac{\pi}{6}}{\sin \frac{\pi}{6}}$

$= \dfrac{1 - \frac{\sqrt{3}}{2}}{\frac{1}{2}}$

$= 2 - \sqrt{3}$

EXAMPLE 2 Evaluate trigonometric expressions

Given $\cos a = \frac{5}{13}$ with $\frac{3\pi}{2} < a < 2\pi$, find (a) $\sin 2a$ and (b) $\sin \frac{a}{2}$.

Solution

MULTIPLY AN INEQUALITY

In part (b), you can multiply through the inequality $\frac{3\pi}{2} < a < 2\pi$ by $\frac{1}{2}$ to get $\frac{3\pi}{4} < \frac{a}{2} < \pi$. So, $\frac{a}{2}$ is in Quadrant II.

a. Using a Pythagorean identity gives $\sin a = -\frac{12}{13}$.

$$\sin 2a = 2 \sin a \cos a = 2\left(-\frac{12}{13}\right)\left(\frac{5}{13}\right) = -\frac{120}{169}$$

b. Because $\frac{a}{2}$ is in Quadrant II, $\sin \frac{a}{2}$ is positive.

$$\sin \frac{a}{2} = \sqrt{\frac{1 - \cos a}{2}} = \sqrt{\frac{1 - \frac{5}{13}}{2}} = \sqrt{\frac{4}{13}} = \frac{2\sqrt{13}}{13}$$

EXAMPLE 3 Standardized Test Practice

Which expression is equivalent to $\frac{\sin 2\theta}{1 - \cos 2\theta}$?

Ⓐ $\sin \theta$ Ⓑ $\cot \theta$ Ⓒ $\csc \theta$ Ⓓ $\cos \theta$

Solution

$\frac{\sin 2\theta}{1 - \cos 2\theta} = \frac{2 \sin \theta \cos \theta}{1 - (1 - 2\sin^2\theta)}$	Use double-angle formulas.
$= \frac{2 \sin \theta \cos \theta}{2 \sin^2\theta}$	Simplify denominator.
$= \frac{\cos \theta}{\sin \theta}$	Divide out common factor $2 \sin \theta$.
$= \cot \theta$	Use cotangent identity.

▶ The correct answer is B. Ⓐ Ⓑ Ⓒ Ⓓ

GUIDED PRACTICE for Examples 1, 2, and 3

Find the exact value of the expression.

1. $\tan \frac{\pi}{8}$
2. $\sin \frac{5\pi}{8}$
3. $\cos 15°$
4. Given $\sin a = \frac{\sqrt{2}}{2}$ with $0 < a < \frac{\pi}{2}$, find $\cos 2a$ and $\tan \frac{a}{2}$.
5. Given $\cos a = -\frac{3}{5}$ with $\pi < a < \frac{3\pi}{2}$, find $\sin 2a$ and $\sin \frac{a}{2}$.

Simplify the expression.

6. $\frac{\cos 2\theta}{\sin \theta + \cos \theta}$
7. $\frac{\tan 2x}{\tan x}$
8. $\sin 2x \tan \frac{x}{2}$

PATH OF A PROJECTILE The path traveled by an object that is projected at an initial height of h_0 feet, an initial speed of v feet per second, and an initial angle θ is given by

$$y = -\frac{16}{v^2 \cos^2 \theta}x^2 + (\tan \theta)x + h_0$$

where x is the horizontal distance (in feet) and y is the vertical distance (in feet). (This model neglects air resistance.)

EXAMPLE 4 Derive a trigonometric model

SOCCER Write an equation for the horizontal distance traveled by a soccer ball kicked from ground level ($h_0 = 0$) at speed v and angle θ.

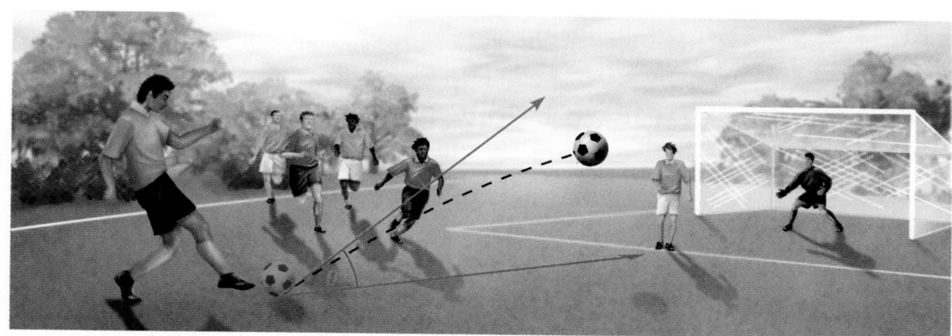

Solution

$-\frac{16}{v^2 \cos^2 \theta}x^2 + (\tan \theta)x + 0 = 0$	**Let $h_0 = 0$.**
$-x\left(\frac{16}{v^2 \cos^2 \theta}x - \tan \theta\right) = 0$	**Factor.**
$\frac{16}{v^2 \cos^2 \theta}x - \tan \theta = 0$	**Zero product property**
$\frac{16}{v^2 \cos^2 \theta}x = \tan \theta$	**Add $\tan \theta$ to each side.**
$x = \frac{1}{16}v^2 \cos^2 \theta \tan \theta$	**Multiply each side by $\frac{1}{16}v^2 \cos^2 \theta$.**
$x = \frac{1}{16}v^2 \cos \theta \sin \theta$	**Use $\cos \theta \tan \theta = \sin \theta$.**
$x = \frac{1}{32}v^2 (2 \cos \theta \sin \theta)$	**Rewrite $\frac{1}{16}$ as $\frac{1}{32} \cdot 2$.**
$x = \frac{1}{32}v^2 \sin 2\theta$	**Use a double-angle formula.**

USE ZERO PRODUCT PROPERTY
One solution of this equation is $x = 0$, which corresponds to the point where the ball leaves the ground. This solution is ignored in later steps, because the problem requires finding where the ball *lands*.

✓ GUIDED PRACTICE for Example 4

9. **WHAT IF?** Suppose you kick a soccer ball from ground level with an initial speed of 70 feet per second. Can you make the ball travel 200 feet?

10. **REASONING** Use the equation $x = \frac{1}{32}v^2 \sin 2\theta$ to explain why the projection angle that maximizes the distance a soccer ball travels is $\theta = 45°$.

EXAMPLE 5 Verify a trigonometric identity

Verify the identity $\cos 3x = 4\cos^3 x - 3\cos x$.

$\cos 3x = \cos(2x + x)$	Rewrite $\cos 3x$ as $\cos(2x + x)$.
$= \cos 2x \cos x - \sin 2x \sin x$	Use a sum formula.
$= (2\cos^2 x - 1)\cos x - (2\sin x \cos x)\sin x$	Use double-angle formulas.
$= 2\cos^3 x - \cos x - 2\sin^2 x \cos x$	Multiply.
$= 2\cos^3 x - \cos x - 2(1 - \cos^2 x)\cos x$	Use a Pythagorean identity.
$= 2\cos^3 x - \cos x - 2\cos x + 2\cos^3 x$	Distributive property
$= 4\cos^3 x - 3\cos x$	Combine like terms.

EXAMPLE 6 Solve a trigonometric equation

Solve $\sin 2x + 2\cos x = 0$ for $0 \le x < 2\pi$.

Solution

$\sin 2x + 2\cos x = 0$	Write original equation.
$2\sin x \cos x + 2\cos x = 0$	Use a double-angle formula.
$2\cos x(\sin x + 1) = 0$	Factor.

Set each factor equal to 0 and solve for x.

$2\cos x = 0$	$\sin x + 1 = 0$
$\cos x = 0$	$\sin x = -1$
$x = \frac{\pi}{2}, \frac{3\pi}{2}$	$x = \frac{3\pi}{2}$

CHECK Graph the function $y = \sin 2x + 2\cos x$ on a graphing calculator. Then use the *zero* feature to find the x-values on the interval $0 \le x < 2\pi$ for which $y = 0$. The two x-values are:

$$x = \frac{\pi}{2} \approx 1.57 \quad \text{and} \quad x = \frac{3\pi}{2} \approx 4.71$$

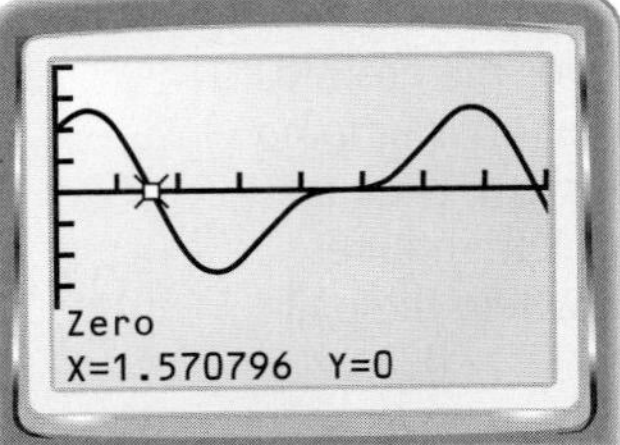

EXAMPLE 7 Find a general solution

Find the general solution of $2\sin\frac{x}{2} = 1$.

$2\sin\frac{x}{2} = 1$	Write original equation.
$\sin\frac{x}{2} = \frac{1}{2}$	Divide each side by 2.
$\frac{x}{2} = \frac{\pi}{6} + 2n\pi$ or $\frac{5\pi}{6} + 2n\pi$	General solution for $\frac{x}{2}$
$x = \frac{\pi}{3} + 4n\pi$ or $\frac{5\pi}{3} + 4n\pi$	General solution for x

SOLVE EQUATIONS
As seen in Example 7, some equations that involve double or half angles can be solved without resorting to double- or half-angle formulas.

GUIDED PRACTICE for Examples 5, 6, and 7

Verify the identity.

11. $\sin 3x = 3 \sin x - 4 \sin^3 x$

12. $1 + \cos 10x = 2 \cos^2 5x$

Solve the equation.

13. $\tan 2x + \tan x = 0$ for $0 \le x < 2\pi$

14. $2 \cos \frac{x}{2} + 1 = 0$

14.7 EXERCISES

HOMEWORK KEY

○ = **WORKED-OUT SOLUTIONS** on p. WS25 for Exs. 7, 13, and 53

★ = **STANDARDIZED TEST PRACTICE** Exs. 2, 11, 27, 54, and 55

SKILL PRACTICE

1. **VOCABULARY** Copy and complete: $\sin 2a = 2 \sin a \cos a$ is called the __?__ formula for sine.

2. ★ **WRITING** *Explain* how to determine the sign of the answer when evaluating a half-angle formula for sine or cosine.

EXAMPLE 1 on p. 955 for Exs. 3–11

EVALUATING EXPRESSIONS **Find the exact value of the expression.**

3. $\sin 105°$

4. $\tan 112.5°$

5. $\tan (-165°)$

6. $\cos (-75°)$

7. $\cos \frac{\pi}{8}$

8. $\sin \frac{5\pi}{12}$

9. $\tan \left(-\frac{5\pi}{8}\right)$

10. $\sin \left(-\frac{11\pi}{12}\right)$

11. ★ **MULTIPLE CHOICE** What is the exact value of $\tan 15°$?

(A) $-\sqrt{3}$ (B) $2 - \sqrt{3}$ (C) $\sqrt{3}$ (D) $2 + \sqrt{3}$

EXAMPLE 2 on p. 956 for Exs. 12–20

HALF-ANGLE FORMULAS **Find the exact values of $\sin \frac{a}{2}$, $\cos \frac{a}{2}$, and $\tan \frac{a}{2}$.**

12. $\cos a = \frac{4}{5}, 0 < a < \frac{\pi}{2}$

13. $\cos a = \frac{1}{3}, \frac{3\pi}{2} < a < 2\pi$

14. $\sin a = \frac{12}{13}, \frac{\pi}{2} < a < \pi$

15. $\sin a = -\frac{3}{5}, \pi < a < \frac{3\pi}{2}$

16. **ERROR ANALYSIS** *Describe* and correct the error in finding the exact value of $\sin \frac{a}{2}$ given that $\cos a = -\frac{3}{5}$ with $\frac{\pi}{2} < a < \pi$.

$$\sin \frac{a}{2} = -\sqrt{\frac{1 - \cos a}{2}} = -\sqrt{\frac{1 + \frac{3}{5}}{2}} = -\sqrt{\frac{4}{5}} = -\frac{2\sqrt{5}}{5}$$ ✗

DOUBLE-ANGLE FORMULAS **Find the exact values of $\sin 2a$, $\cos 2a$, and $\tan 2a$.**

17. $\tan a = 2, \pi < a < \frac{3\pi}{2}$

18. $\tan a = -\sqrt{3}, \frac{\pi}{2} < a < \pi$

19. $\sin a = -\frac{2}{3}, \pi < a < \frac{3\pi}{2}$

20. $\cos a = \frac{2}{5}, -\frac{\pi}{2} < a < 0$

EXAMPLE 3
on p. 956
for Exs. 21–29

SIMPLIFYING EXPRESSIONS Rewrite the expression without double angles or half angles, given that $0 < \theta < \frac{\pi}{2}$. Then simplify the expression.

21. $\dfrac{\cos 2\theta}{1 - 2\sin^2 \theta}$

22. $\dfrac{\sin 2\theta}{2\cos \theta}$

23. $(1 - \tan \theta)\tan 2\theta$

24. $\dfrac{\cos 2\theta}{\sin \theta - \cos \theta}$

25. $\dfrac{-\tan \frac{\theta}{2}}{\csc \theta}$

26. $2\sin \frac{\theta}{2} \cos \frac{\theta}{2}$

27. ★ **MULTIPLE CHOICE** Which expression is equivalent to $\cot \theta + \tan \theta$?

Ⓐ $\csc 2\theta$ Ⓑ $2\csc 2\theta$ Ⓒ $\sec 2\theta$ Ⓓ $2\sec 2\theta$

ERROR ANALYSIS ***Describe*** **and correct the error in simplifying the expression.**

28.

$$\frac{\cos 2x}{\cos^2 x} = \frac{\cos^2 x - \sin^2 x}{\cos^2 x}$$
$$= \frac{1}{\cos^2 x}$$
$$= \sec^2 x$$

✗

29.

$$\sin 22.5° = \sin \frac{1}{2}(45°)$$
$$= 2\sin 45° \cos 45°$$
$$= 2\left(\frac{\sqrt{2}}{2}\right)\left(\frac{\sqrt{2}}{2}\right)$$
$$= 1$$

✗

EXAMPLE 5
on p. 958
for Exs. 30–35

VERIFYING IDENTITIES Verify the identity.

30. $2\cos^2 \theta = 1 + \cos 2\theta$

31. $\sin 3\theta = \sin \theta\,(4\cos^2 \theta - 1)$

32. $\frac{1}{2}\sin \frac{2x}{3} = \sin \frac{x}{3} \cos \frac{x}{3}$

33. $2\sin^2 x \tan \frac{x}{2} = 2\sin x - \sin 2x$

34. $-\dfrac{\cos 2\theta}{\sin \theta} = 2\sin \theta - \csc \theta$

35. $\cos 4\theta = \cos^4 \theta - 6\sin^2 \theta \cos^2 \theta + \sin^4 \theta$

EXAMPLE 6
on p. 958
for Exs. 36–41

SOLVING EQUATIONS Solve the equation for $0 \le x < 2\pi$.

36. $\sin \frac{x}{2} = 1$

37. $2\cos \frac{x}{2} + 1 = 0$

38. $\tan x - \tan 2x = 0$

39. $\tan \frac{x}{2} = \dfrac{2 - \sqrt{2}}{2\sin x}$

40. $\cos 2x = -2\cos^2 x$

41. $2\sin 2x \sin x = 3\cos x$

EXAMPLE 7
on p. 958
for Exs. 42–47

FINDING GENERAL SOLUTIONS Find the general solution of the equation.

42. $\cos \frac{x}{2} = 1$

43. $\tan \frac{x}{2} = \sin x$

44. $\sin 2x = \sin x$

45. $\cos 2x + \cos x = 0$

46. $\cos \frac{x}{2} + \sin x = 0$

47. $\sin \frac{x}{2} + \cos x = 0$

48. REASONING Show that the three double-angle formulas for cosine are equivalent.

49. CHALLENGE Use the diagram shown at the right to derive the formulas for $\sin \frac{\theta}{2}$, $\cos \frac{\theta}{2}$, and $\tan \frac{\theta}{2}$ when θ is an acute angle.

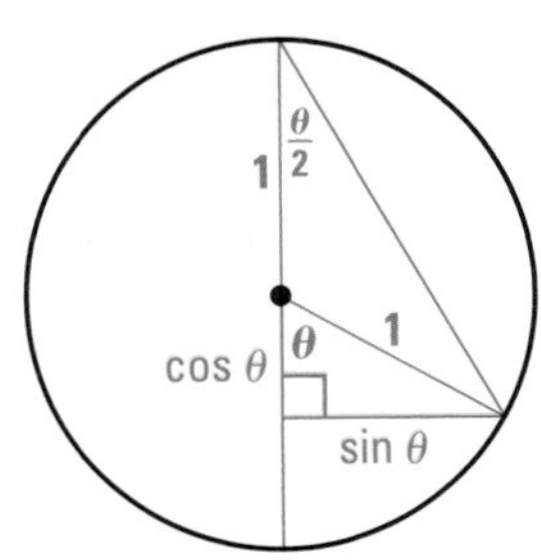

◯ = WORKED-OUT SOLUTIONS on p. WS1 ★ = STANDARDIZED TEST PRACTICE

PROBLEM SOLVING

EXAMPLE 4
on p. 957
for Exs. 50–51

50. **GOLF** Use the equation $x = \frac{1}{32}v^2 \sin 2\theta$ from Example 4 on page 957 to find the horizontal distance a golf ball will travel if it is hit at an initial speed of 50 feet per second and at an initial angle of 40°.

@HomeTutor for problem solving help at classzone.com

51. **SOCCER** Suppose you are attempting to kick a soccer ball from ground level. Through what range of angles can you kick the soccer ball with an initial speed of 80 feet per second to make it travel at least 150 feet?

Animated Algebra at classzone.com

52. **MULTI-STEP PROBLEM** At latitude L, the acceleration due to gravity g (in centimeters per second squared) at sea level can be approximated by:

$$g = 978 + 5.17 \sin^2 L - 0.014 \sin L \cos L$$

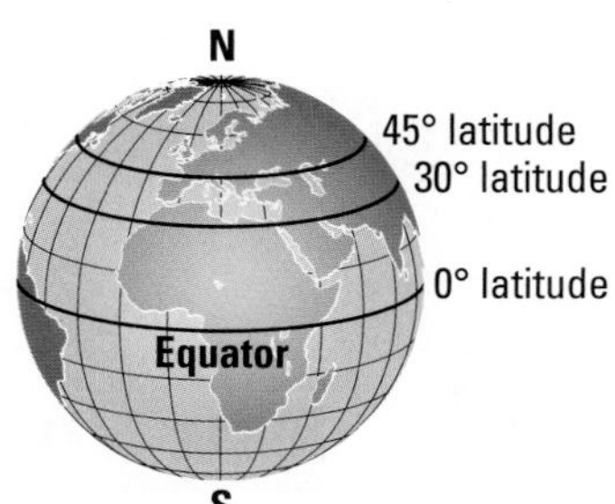

   a. Simplify the equation above to show that $g = 978 + 5.17 \sin^2 L - 0.007 \sin 2L$.
   b. Graph the function from part (a).
   c. Use the graph to approximate the acceleration due to gravity when the latitude is 45°, 30°, and 0°.

53. **MACH NUMBER** An airplane's Mach number M is the ratio of its speed to the speed of sound. When an airplane travels faster than the speed of sound, the sound waves form a cone behind the airplane. The Mach number is related to the apex angle θ of the cone by the equation $\sin \frac{\theta}{2} = \frac{1}{M}$. Find the angle θ that corresponds to a Mach number of 2.5.

54. ★ **SHORT RESPONSE** A *Mercator projection* is a map projection of the globe onto a plane that preserves angles. On a globe with radius r, consider a point P that has latitude L and longitude T. The coordinates (x, y) of the corresponding point P' on the plane can be found using these equations:

$$x = rT \qquad y = r \ln\left[\tan\left(\frac{\frac{\pi}{2} + L}{2}\right)\right]$$

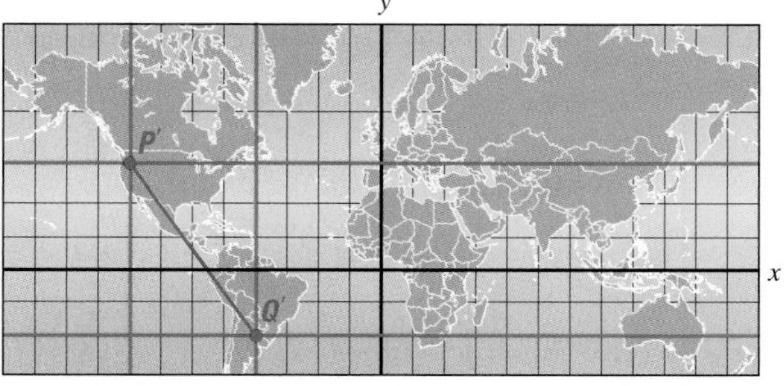

   a. Use half-angle and sum formulas to show that the equation for the y-coordinate can be written as $y = r \ln\left(\frac{1 + \sin L}{\cos L}\right)$.
   b. What is a reasonable domain for the equation in part (a)? *Explain.*

55. ★ **EXTENDED RESPONSE** At a basketball game, a person has a chance to win 1 million dollars by making a half court shot. The distance from half court to the point below the 10-foot-high basketball rim is 41.75 feet.

a. Write an equation that models the path of the basketball if the person releases the ball 6 feet high with an initial speed of 40 feet per second.

b. Simplify the equation. Use a calculator to find the angles at which the person can make the half court shot.

c. Assume the person releases the ball at one of the angles found in part (b). What other assumption(s) must you make to say that the shot is made?

56. **CHALLENGE** A rectangle is inscribed in a semicircle with radius 1, as shown. What value of θ creates the rectangle with the largest area?

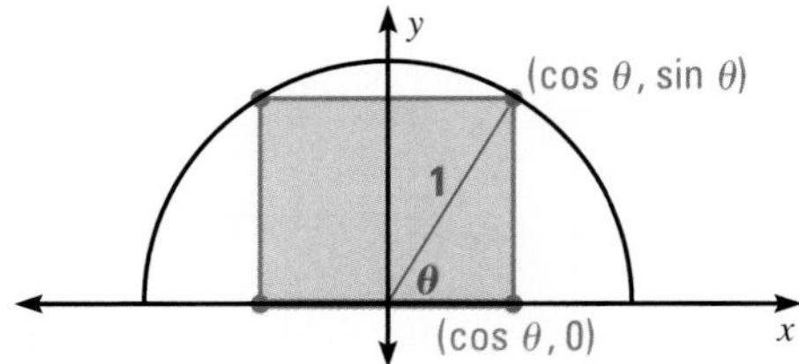

NEW YORK MIXED REVIEW

57. $\angle MNO$ and $\angle PQR$ are supplementary angles. Which of the following statements is true?

Ⓐ $\angle MNO = \angle PQR$ Ⓑ $\angle MNO \perp \angle PQR$

Ⓒ $m\angle MNO + m\angle PQR = 90°$ Ⓓ $m\angle MNO + m\angle PQR = 180°$

58. What is the approximate length of arc MN?

Ⓐ 30.5 ft Ⓑ 33.0 ft

Ⓒ 39.6 ft Ⓓ 55.0 ft

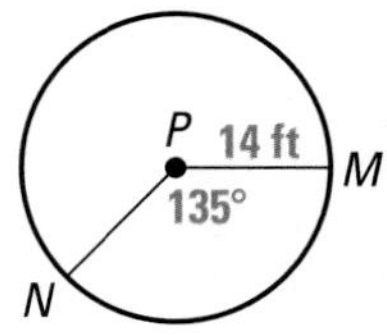

QUIZ for Lessons 14.6–14.7

Find the exact value of the expression. *(pp. 949, 955)*

1. $\sin \frac{\pi}{12}$
2. $\sin (-22.5°)$
3. $\tan (-345°)$
4. $\cos \frac{\pi}{8}$

Solve the equation for $0 \le x < 2\pi$.

5. $\sin\left(x + \frac{\pi}{2}\right) - \sin\left(x - \frac{\pi}{2}\right) = 0$ *(p. 949)*
6. $\cos 2x = 3 \sin x + 2$ *(p. 955)*

Find the exact values of $\sin \frac{a}{2}$, $\cos \frac{a}{2}$, and $\tan 2a$. *(p. 955)*

7. $\tan a = \frac{3}{5}, 0 < a < \frac{\pi}{2}$
8. $\cos a = -\frac{4}{7}, \pi < a < \frac{3\pi}{2}$

9. **FOOTBALL** Use the formula $x = \frac{1}{32}v^2 \sin 2\theta$ to find the horizontal distance x (in feet) that a football travels if it is kicked from ground level with an initial speed of 25 feet per second at an angle of 30°. *(p. 955)*

Lessons 14.5–14.7

1. **PHYSICAL SCIENCE** The force F (in pounds) on a person's back when he or she bends over at an angle of θ is given by

$$F = \frac{0.6W \sin(\theta + 90°)}{\sin 12°}$$

where W is the person's weight (in pounds). Which of the following is equivalent to the given formula?

(1) $24.8W \sin \theta$ (3) $2.89 \sin \theta$

(2) $20.6 \cos \theta$ (4) $2.89W \cos \theta$

2. **INDEX OF REFRACTION** The index of refraction n of a transparent material is the ratio of the speed of light in a vacuum to the speed of light in the material. Some common materials and their indices are air (1.00), water (1.33), and glass (1.5). Triangular prisms are often used to measure the index of refraction based on the formula shown below. If the given prism is made of glass and $\alpha = 60°$, what is the approximate value of θ? (*Hint:* Write the formula for the index of refraction in terms of $\cot \frac{\theta}{2}$.)

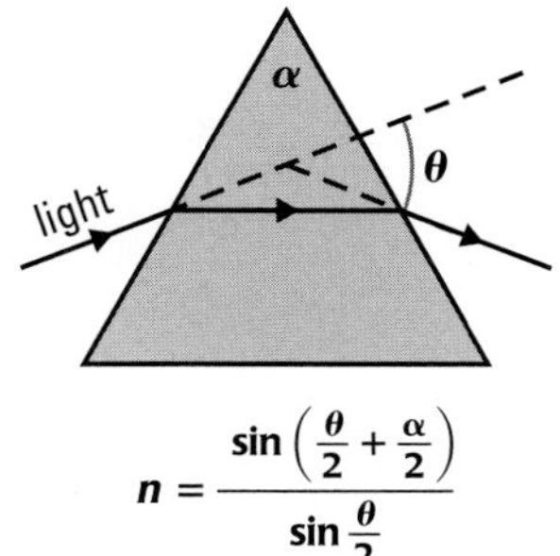

$$n = \frac{\sin\left(\frac{\theta}{2} + \frac{\alpha}{2}\right)}{\sin \frac{\theta}{2}}$$

(1) 38.3° (3) 82.0°

(2) 76.5° (4) 126.7°

3. **EVALUATING EXPRESSIONS** What is the value of $\tan(a + b)$ given that $\sin a = \frac{3}{5}$ with $0 < a < \frac{\pi}{2}$ and $\cos b = \frac{\sqrt{2}}{2}$ with $0 < b < \frac{\pi}{2}$?

(1) -1 (3) 3

(2) $2\frac{1}{7}$ (4) 7

4. **OPEN-ENDED** In the figure shown below, the acute angle of intersection, $\theta_2 - \theta_1$, of two lines with slopes m_1 and m_2 is given by this equation:

$$\tan(\theta_2 - \theta_1) = \frac{m_2 - m_1}{1 + m_1 m_2}$$

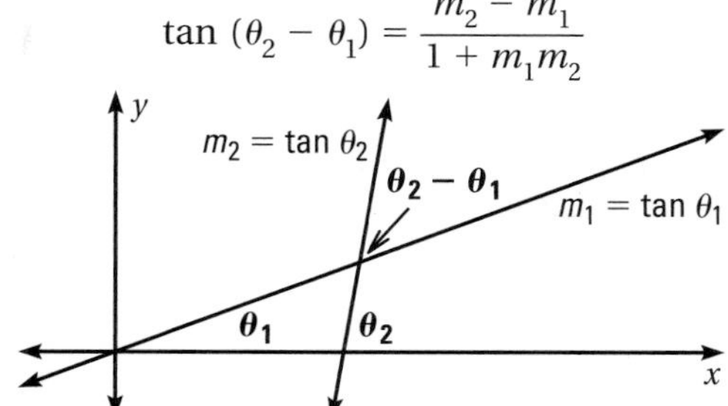

Find the acute angle of intersection of the lines $y = \frac{1}{2}x$ and $y = 2x - 4$. Round your answer to the nearest tenth of a degree. *Explain* your reasoning.

5. **OPEN-ENDED** The graph below shows the average daily temperature T (in degrees Fahrenheit) in Denver, Colorado. The time t is measured in months, with $t = 0$ representing January 1.

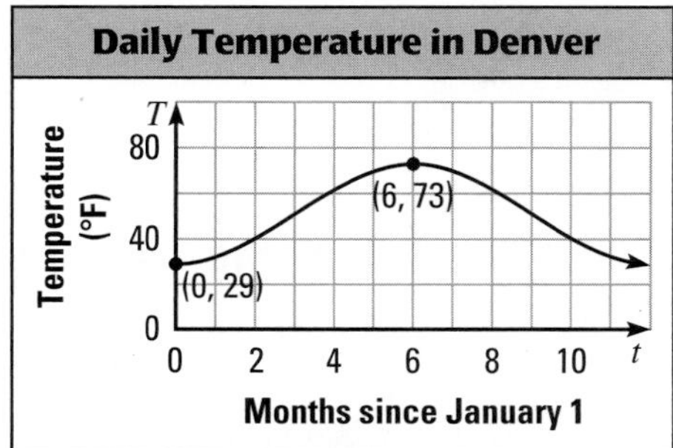

Tell whether the graph should be modeled by a sine or cosine function. *Explain* your reasoning.

Write a trigonometric model for the average daily temperature in Denver, Colorado.

On which days of the year is the average daily temperature in Denver, Colorado, 70°F?

14 CHAPTER SUMMARY

Animated Algebra
classzone.com
Electronic Function Library

BIG IDEAS — For Your Notebook

Big Idea 1

Graphing Trigonometric Functions

The graphs of $y = a \sin bx$ and $y = a \cos bx$ are shown below for $a > 0$ and $b > 0$.

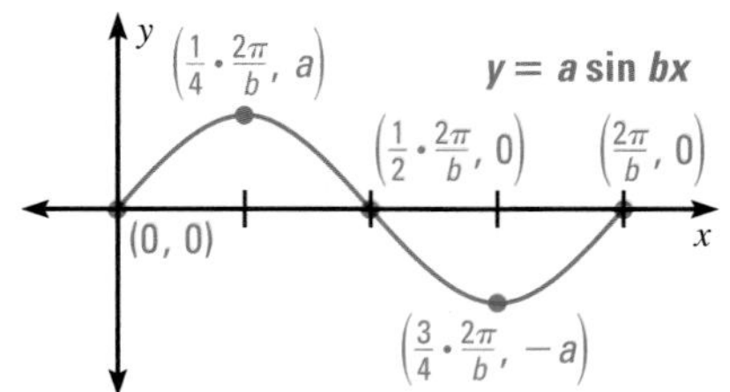

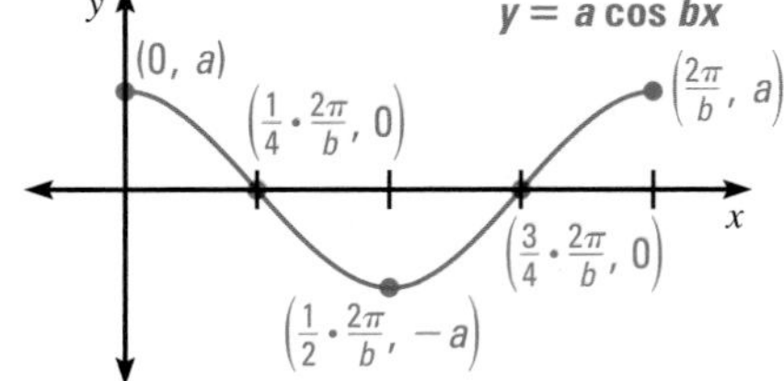

To graph a function of the form $y = a \sin b(x - h) + k$ or $y = a \cos b(x - h) + k$, shift the graph of $y = a \sin bx$ or $y = a \cos bx$, respectively, horizontally h units and vertically k units. Then, if $a < 0$, reflect the graph in the midline $y = k$.

Big Idea 2

Solving Trigonometric Equations

The table below shows strategies that may help you solve trigonometric equations. Only the first few steps are shown.

Factor	Use the quadratic formula	Use an identity
$x \sin^2 x - x = 0$	$\cos^2 x - 6 \cos x + 1 = 0$	$\cos^2 x - 1 = 9 \sin^2 x$
$x(\sin^2 x - 1) = 0$	$\cos x = \frac{6 \pm \sqrt{36 - 4(1)(1)}}{2(1)}$	$\cos^2 x - 1 = 9(1 - \cos^2 x)$
$x(\sin x + 1)(\sin x - 1) = 0$	$\cos x = 3 \pm 2\sqrt{2}$	$10 \cos^2 x = 10$
		$\cos^2 x = 1$

Big Idea 3

Applying Trigonometric Formulas

Use the formulas below to evaluate trigonometric functions of certain angles.

Sum formulas	$\sin(a + b) = \sin a \cos b + \cos a \sin b$ $\cos(a + b) = \cos a \cos b - \sin a \sin b$	$\tan(a + b) = \frac{\tan a + \tan b}{1 - \tan a \tan b}$
Difference formulas	$\sin(a - b) = \sin a \cos b - \cos a \sin b$ $\cos(a - b) = \cos a \cos b + \sin a \sin b$	$\tan(a - b) = \frac{\tan a - \tan b}{1 + \tan a \tan b}$
Double-angle formulas	$\cos 2a = \cos^2 a - \sin^2 a$ $\cos 2a = 2\cos^2 a - 1$ $\cos 2a = 1 - 2\sin^2 a$ $\sin 2a = 2 \sin a \cos a$	$\tan 2a = \frac{2 \tan a}{1 - \tan^2 a}$
Half-angle formulas	$\sin \frac{a}{2} = \pm\sqrt{\frac{1 - \cos a}{2}}$ $\cos \frac{a}{2} = \pm\sqrt{\frac{1 + \cos a}{2}}$	$\tan \frac{a}{2} = \frac{1 - \cos a}{\sin a}$ $\tan \frac{a}{2} = \frac{\sin a}{1 + \cos a}$

14 CHAPTER REVIEW

@HomeTutor
classzone.com
• Multi-Language Glossary
• Vocabulary practice

REVIEW KEY VOCABULARY

- amplitude, *p. 908*
- periodic function, *p. 908*
- cycle, *p. 908*
- period, *p. 908*
- frequency, *p. 910*
- trigonometric identity, *p. 924*
- sinusoid, *p. 941*

VOCABULARY EXERCISES

1. Copy and complete: Frequency gives the number of _?_ per unit of time.

2. **WRITING** *Explain* how to find the period of $y = a \sin b(x - h) + k$.

Determine whether the given number is the *amplitude, period,* or *frequency* of the graph of $y = \pi \cos \frac{\pi x}{2}$.

3. 4
4. π
5. 0.25

REVIEW EXAMPLES AND EXERCISES

Use the review examples and exercises below to check your understanding of the concepts you have learned in each lesson of Chapter 14.

14.1 Graph Sine, Cosine, and Tangent Functions *pp. 908–914*

EXAMPLE

Graph (a) $y = \frac{1}{2} \cos 2x$ and (b) $y = 3 \tan \frac{x}{2}$.

a. Amplitude: $a = \frac{1}{2}$ **Period:** $\frac{2\pi}{2} = \pi$

Intercepts: $(0, 0); \left(\frac{\pi}{2}, 0\right); (\pi, 0)$

Maximum: $\left(\frac{\pi}{4}, \frac{1}{2}\right)$ **Minimum:** $\left(\frac{3\pi}{4}, -\frac{1}{2}\right)$

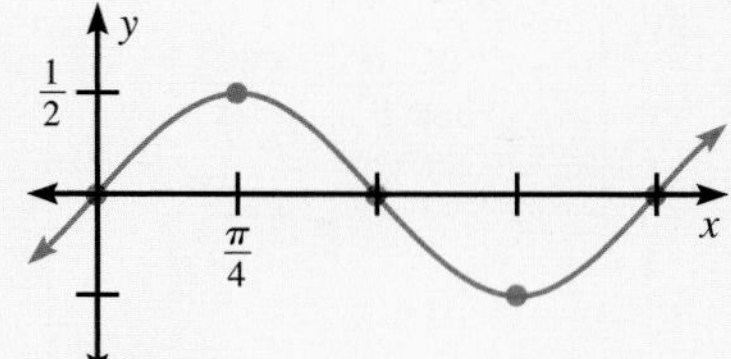

b. Period: $\frac{\pi}{\frac{1}{2}} = 2\pi$ **Intercept:** $(0, 0)$

Asymptotes: $x = -\pi; x = \pi$

Halfway points: $\left(-\frac{\pi}{2}, -3\right); \left(\frac{\pi}{2}, 3\right)$

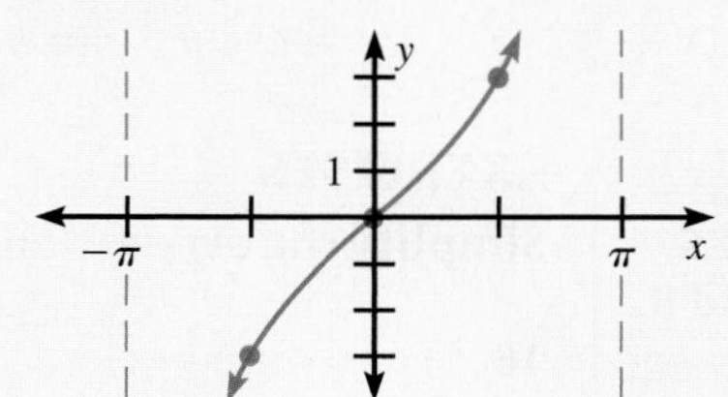

EXAMPLES 1, 2, and 4 on pp. 909–912 for Exs. 6–9

EXERCISES

Graph the function.

6. $y = \sin 2x$
7. $f(x) = \frac{1}{2} \cos \frac{x}{2}$
8. $g(x) = 5 \sin \pi x$
9. $y = 2 \tan \frac{1}{3}x$

14 CHAPTER REVIEW

14.2 Translate and Reflect Trigonometric Graphs

pp. 915–922

EXAMPLE

Graph $y = 3\cos(x - \pi) - 1$.

To graph $y = 3\cos(x - \pi) - 1$, start with the graph of $y = 3\cos x$. Then, translate the graph right π units and down 1 unit.

Amplitude: $|3| = 3$ **Period:** 2π

Horizontal shift: π **Vertical shift:** -1

On $y = k$: $\left(\frac{3\pi}{2}, -1\right); \left(\frac{5\pi}{2}, -1\right)$

Minimum: $(2\pi, -4)$

Maximums: $(\pi, 2); (3\pi, 2)$

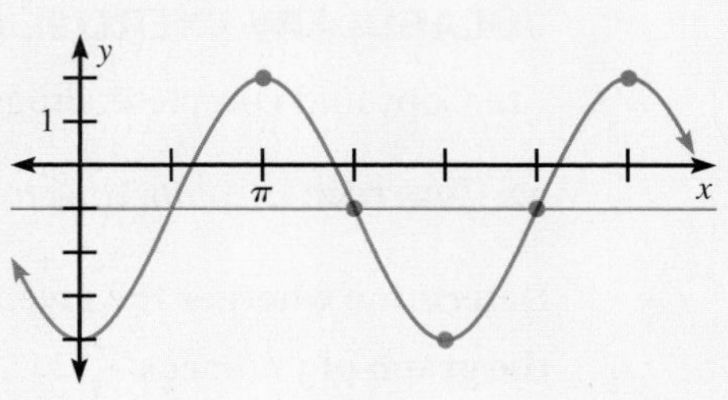

EXERCISES

EXAMPLES 1, 2, and 4 on pp. 915–917 for Exs. 10–15

Graph the function.

10. $f(x) = \cos 2x + 4$

11. $y = \frac{1}{2}\sin 5(x - \pi)$

12. $y = 2\sin\left(x - \frac{\pi}{2}\right) + 3$

13. $y = 2\cos\frac{1}{3}x + 3$

14. $g(x) = -1 - 3\cos 4x$

15. $y = 4 - \sin 3\left(x - \frac{\pi}{3}\right)$

14.3 Verify Trigonometric Identities

pp. 924–930

EXAMPLE

Verify the identity $\frac{\cot^2 \theta}{\csc \theta} = \csc \theta - \sin \theta$.

$\frac{\cot^2 \theta}{\csc \theta} = \frac{\csc^2 \theta - 1}{\csc \theta}$ **Pythagorean identity**

$= \frac{\csc^2 \theta}{\csc \theta} - \frac{1}{\csc \theta}$ **Write as separate fractions.**

$= \csc \theta - \frac{1}{\csc \theta}$ **Simplify.**

$= \csc \theta - \sin \theta$ **Reciprocal identity**

EXERCISES

EXAMPLES 2, 3, 4, and 5 on pp. 925–926 for Exs. 16–20

Simplify the expression.

16. $-\cos x \tan(-x)$

17. $\sec x \tan^2 x + \sec x$

18. $\sin\left(\frac{\pi}{2} - x\right)\tan x$

Verify the identity.

19. $\frac{\sin^2(-x) - 1}{\cot^2 x} = -\sin^2 x$

20. $\tan\left(\frac{\pi}{2} - x\right)\cot x = \csc^2 x - 1$

14.4 Solve Trigonometric Equations *pp. 931–937*

EXAMPLE

Solve $2\cos^2 x = 1$ in the interval $0 \le x < 2\pi$.

$2\cos^2 x = 1$ — **Write original equation.**

$\cos^2 x = \frac{1}{2}$ — **Divide each side by 2.**

$\cos x = \pm\frac{\sqrt{2}}{2}$ — **Take square roots of each side.**

▶ In the interval $0 \le x < 2\pi$, the solutions are $x = \frac{\pi}{4}, \frac{3\pi}{4}, \frac{5\pi}{4}$, and $\frac{7\pi}{4}$.

EXAMPLES 1 and 4 on pp. 931–933 for Exs. 21–23

EXERCISES

Solve the equation in the interval $0 \le x < 2\pi$.

21. $-4\sin^2 x = -3$ **22.** $\cos^2 x = \cos x$ **23.** $\tan^2 4x = 3$

14.5 Write Trigonometric Functions and Models *pp. 941–947*

EXAMPLE

Write a function for the sinusoid.

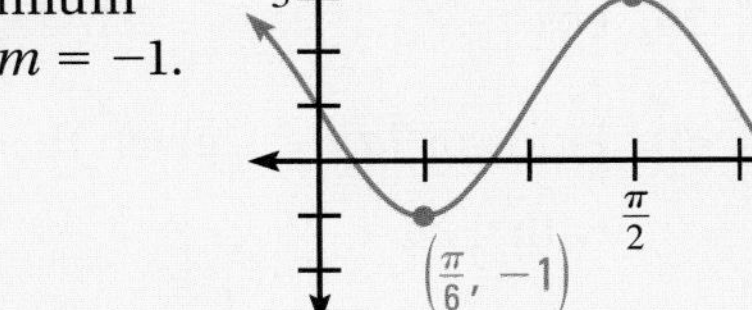

STEP 1 **Find** the maximum value M and minimum value m. From the graph, $M = 3$ and $m = -1$.

STEP 2 **Identify** the vertical shift, k.

$$k = \frac{M + m}{2} = \frac{3 + (-1)}{2} = \frac{2}{2} = 1$$

STEP 3 **Decide** whether the graph should be modeled by a sine or cosine function. Because the graph crosses the midline, $y = 1$, on the y-axis and then decreases to its minimum value, the graph is a sine curve with a reflection but no horizontal shift. So, $a < 0$ and $h = 0$.

STEP 4 **Find** the amplitude and period. The period is $\frac{2\pi}{3} = \frac{2\pi}{b}$. So, $b = 3$.

The amplitude is $|a| = \frac{M - m}{2} = \frac{3 - (-1)}{2} = \frac{4}{2} = 2$. So, $a = -2$.

A function for the sinusoid is $y = -2\sin 3x + 1$.

EXAMPLE 1 on p. 941 for Exs. 24–25

EXERCISES

Write a function for the sinusoid.

24.

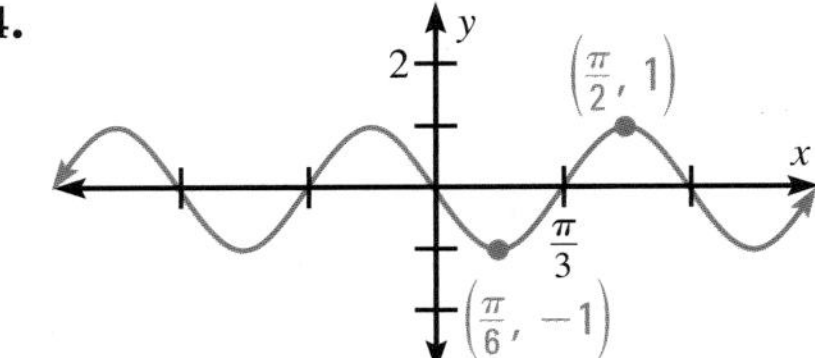

25.

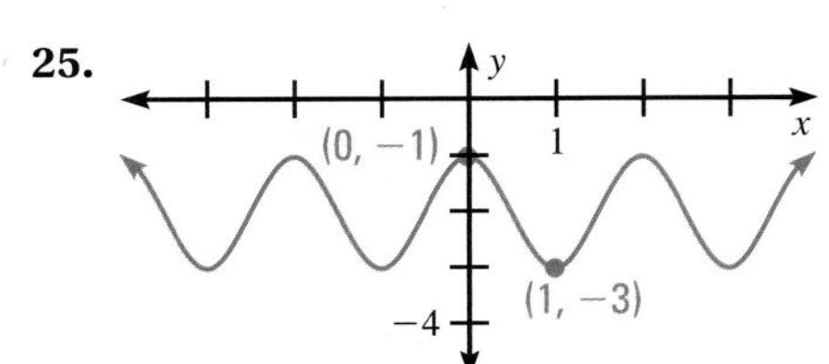

14 CHAPTER REVIEW

14.6 Apply Sum and Difference Formulas

pp. 949–954

EXAMPLE

Find the exact value of the expression.

a. $\cos 225° = \cos(270° - 45°)$ — **Substitute 270° − 45° for 225°.**

$= \cos 270° \cos 45° + \sin 270° \sin 45°$ — **Difference formula for cosine**

$= 0\left(\frac{\sqrt{2}}{2}\right) - 1\left(\frac{\sqrt{2}}{2}\right)$ — **Evaluate.**

$= -\frac{\sqrt{2}}{2}$ — **Simplify.**

b. $\sin \frac{7\pi}{12} = \sin\left(\frac{\pi}{3} + \frac{\pi}{4}\right)$ — **Substitute $\frac{\pi}{3} + \frac{\pi}{4}$ for $\frac{7\pi}{12}$.**

$= \sin \frac{\pi}{3} \cos \frac{\pi}{4} + \cos \frac{\pi}{3} \sin \frac{\pi}{4}$ — **Sum formula for sine**

$= \frac{\sqrt{3}}{2}\left(\frac{\sqrt{2}}{2}\right) + \frac{1}{2}\left(\frac{\sqrt{2}}{2}\right)$ — **Evaluate.**

$= \frac{\sqrt{6} + \sqrt{2}}{4}$ — **Simplify.**

EXERCISES

EXAMPLES 1 and 2 on pp. 949–950 for Exs. 26–30

Find the exact value of the expression.

26. $\cos 195°$ **27.** $\tan 75°$ **28.** $\sin \frac{13\pi}{12}$ **29.** $\cos \frac{5\pi}{6}$

30. Find $\cos(a - b)$, given that $\sin a = \frac{8}{17}$ with $\frac{\pi}{2} < a < \pi$ and $\cos b = \frac{1}{2}$ with $0 < b < \frac{\pi}{2}$.

14.7 Apply Double-Angle and Half-Angle Formulas

pp. 955–962

EXAMPLE

Find the exact value of the expression.

a. $\tan 135° = \tan \frac{1}{2}(270°) = \frac{1 - \cos 270°}{\sin 270°} = \frac{1 - 0}{-1} = -1$

b. $\sin \frac{\pi}{12} = \sin \frac{1}{2}\left(\frac{\pi}{6}\right) = \sqrt{\frac{1 - \cos \frac{\pi}{6}}{2}} = \sqrt{\frac{1 - \frac{\sqrt{3}}{2}}{2}} = \frac{1}{2}\sqrt{2 - \sqrt{3}}$

EXERCISES

EXAMPLES 1 and 2 on pp. 955–956 for Exs. 31–35

Find the exact value of the expression.

31. $\sin 75°$ **32.** $\tan(-15°)$ **33.** $\cos \frac{\pi}{12}$ **34.** $\cos \frac{3\pi}{4}$

35. Given $\cos a = \frac{1}{2}$ with $0 < a < \frac{\pi}{2}$, find $\sin 2a$ and $\tan \frac{a}{2}$.

14 CHAPTER TEST

Graph the function.

1. $f(x) = 4 \cos 2x$
2. $y = \frac{3}{2} \sin \pi x$
3. $f(x) = -4 \tan \frac{\pi}{2}x$
4. $y = \sin (x - \pi) - 2$
5. $f(x) = 3 \tan \left(x - \frac{\pi}{2}\right)$
6. $y = -2 \cos \frac{1}{3}x + 3$

Simplify the expression.

7. $\frac{\sin (-\theta)}{\tan (-\theta)}$
8. $\cos^2 x + \sin^2 x - \csc^2 x$
9. $\frac{\sin \left(\frac{\pi}{2} - x\right)}{\sec x}$

Write a function for the sinusoid.

10. 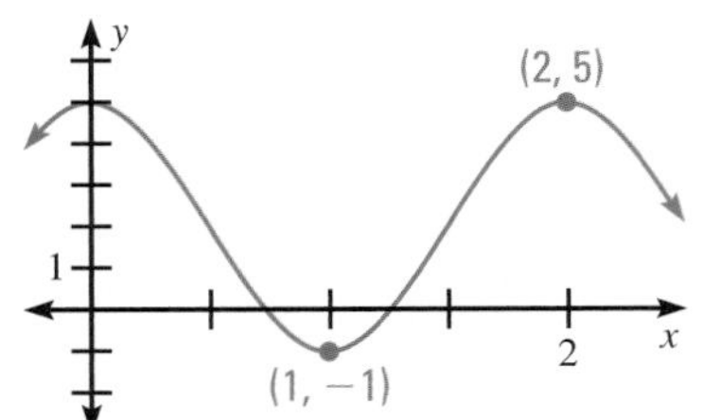

11. 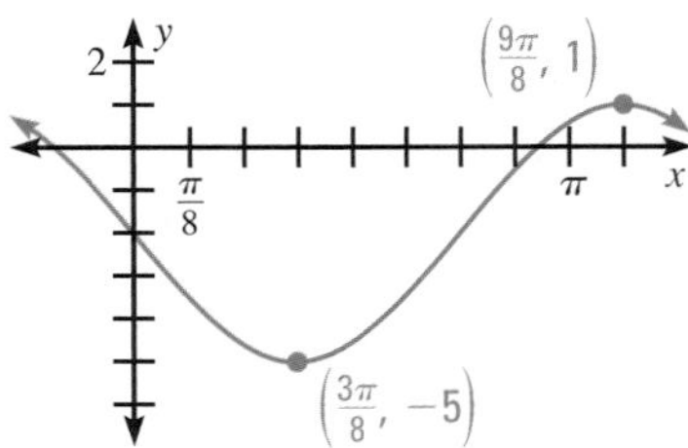

12. Verify the identity $\cos 3x = 4 \cos^3 x - 3 \cos x$.

Solve the equation in the interval $0 \le x < 2\pi$.

13. $9 \sin^2 x \tan x = 16 \tan x$
14. $(1 - \tan^2 x) \tan 2x = 2\sqrt{3}$
15. $\sin \frac{x}{2} = \frac{\sqrt{2}}{2}$

Find the general solution of the equation.

16. $6 \tan^2 x - 2 = 0$
17. $\cos x = \sin 2x \sin x$
18. $\sin \frac{x}{2} = 1 - \cos x$

Find the exact value of the expression.

19. $\sin 255°$
20. $\cos \left(-\frac{\pi}{8}\right)$
21. $\tan \frac{5\pi}{12}$
22. $\sin \frac{10\pi}{3}$

23. **BOATING** The paddle wheel of a ship is 11 feet in diameter, revolves 15 times per minute when moving at top speed, and is 2 feet below the water's surface at its lowest point. Using this speed and starting from a point at the very top of the wheel, write a model for the height h (in feet) of the end of the paddle relative to the water's surface as a function of time t (in minutes).

24. **PRECIPITATION** The table below shows the monthly precipitation P (in inches) in Bismarck, North Dakota. The time t is measured in months, with $t = 1$ representing January. Use a graphing calculator to write a sinusoidal model that gives P as a function of t.

t	1	2	3	4	5	6	7	8	9	10	11	12
P	0.5	0.5	0.9	1.5	2.2	2.6	2.6	2.2	1.6	1.3	0.7	0.4

Scoring Rubric

Full Credit
- solution is complete and correct

Partial Credit
- solution is complete but has errors,

or
- solution is without error but incomplete

No Credit
- no solution is given,

or
- solution makes no sense

OPEN-ENDED QUESTIONS

PROBLEM

The horizontal distance x (in feet) traveled by a football kicked from ground level at speed v and angle θ can be modeled by $x = \frac{1}{32}v^2 \sin 2\theta$.

Write an expression for half of the horizontal distance. How is this expression related to the football's maximum height?

Write a simplified expression for the football's maximum height.

What is the maximum height of a football kicked from ground level with a speed of 80 feet per second and an angle of 35°?

Below are sample solutions to the problem. Read each solution and the comments on the left to see why the sample represents full credit, partial credit, or no credit.

SAMPLE 1: Full credit solution

The expression is correct, and its significance is fully explained.

Half of the horizontal distance $= \frac{1}{2} \cdot \frac{1}{32}v^2 \sin 2\theta = \frac{1}{64}v^2 \sin 2\theta$

Because the ball travels in a parabolic path, the maximum height occurs at half the horizontal distance.

Substitute the expression from the previous part for x in the equation for the path of a projectile. Note that the initial height h_0 is 0.

The correct formula is used for the path of a projectile.

$$y = -\frac{16}{v^2 \cos^2 \theta}x^2 + (\tan \theta)x + h_0$$

$$y = -\frac{16}{v^2 \cos^2 \theta}\left(\frac{1}{64}v^2 \sin 2\theta\right)^2 + (\tan \theta)\left(\frac{1}{64}v^2 \sin 2\theta\right) + 0$$

$$= -\frac{v^2 (\sin 2\theta)(\sin 2\theta)}{256 \cos^2 \theta} + \frac{(v^2 \sin 2\theta)\tan \theta}{64}$$

A double-angle formula is used correctly, and the resulting expression is correctly simplified.

$$= -\frac{v^2(2 \sin \theta \cos \theta)(2 \sin \theta \cos \theta)}{256 \cos \theta \cos \theta} + \frac{v^2(2 \sin \theta)(\cos \theta \tan \theta)}{64}$$

$$= -\frac{v^2 (\overset{1}{\cancel{2}} \sin \theta \cancel{\cos \theta})(\overset{1}{\cancel{2}} \sin \theta \cancel{\cos \theta})}{\underset{64}{\cancel{256}} \cancel{\cos \theta} \cancel{\cos \theta}} + \frac{v^2 (2 \sin \theta)(\sin \theta)}{64}$$

$$= -\frac{v^2 \sin^2 \theta}{64} + \frac{2v^2 \sin^2 \theta}{64}$$

$$= \frac{1}{64}v^2 \sin^2 \theta$$

To find the maximum height of the ball, substitute 80 for v and 35° for θ.

The answer is correct.

Maximum height $= \frac{1}{64}\boldsymbol{v}^2 \sin^2 \boldsymbol{\theta} = \frac{1}{64} \cdot \mathbf{80}^2 \sin^2 \mathbf{35°} \approx 33$ feet

SAMPLE 2: Partial credit solution

The answer is correct, but work is not shown and no explanation is given.

$$\frac{1}{64}v^2 \sin 2\theta$$

$$y = -\frac{16}{v^2 \cos^2 \theta}x^2 + (\tan \theta)x + h_0$$

$$= -\frac{16}{v^2 \cos^2 \theta}\left(\frac{1}{64}v^2 \sin 2\theta\right)^2 + (\tan \theta)\left(\frac{1}{64}v^2 \sin 2\theta\right) + 0$$

$$= -\frac{16}{v^2 \cos^2 \theta}\left(\frac{1}{4096}v^4 \sin^2 2\theta\right) + (\tan \theta)\left(\frac{1}{64}v^2 \sin 2\theta\right)$$

The expression is not fully simplified.

$$= -\frac{v^2 \sin^2 2\theta}{256 \cos^2 \theta} + \frac{v^2 \tan \theta \sin 2\theta}{64}$$

The maximum height of the football is:

The answer is correct.

$$-\frac{v^2 \sin^2 \mathbf{2\theta}}{256 \cos^2 \boldsymbol{\theta}} + \frac{v^2 \tan \boldsymbol{\theta} \sin \mathbf{2\theta}}{64} = -\frac{80^2 \sin^2 \mathbf{70°}}{256 \cos^2 \mathbf{35°}} + \frac{\mathbf{80}^2 \tan \mathbf{35°} \sin \mathbf{70°}}{64} \approx 33 \text{ feet}$$

SAMPLE 3: No credit solution

The expressions in the first two parts are incorrect, and no work is shown.

$$x = \frac{1}{64}v^2 \sin \theta$$

The maximum height is given by $\frac{1}{64}v^2 \sin \theta$.

The values are substituted incorrectly. The answer is wrong.

$$x = \frac{1}{64}v^2 \sin \boldsymbol{\theta} = \frac{1}{64} \cdot \mathbf{35}^2 \sin \mathbf{80°} \approx 19 \text{ feet}$$

The maximum height is about 19 feet.

PRACTICE Apply the Scoring Rubric

Score the following solution to the problem on the previous page as *full credit, partial credit,* or *no credit. Explain* your reasoning. If you choose *partial credit* or *no credit,* explain how you would change the solution so that it earns a score of full credit.

Half of the total horizontal distance is $\frac{1}{64}v^2 \sin 2\theta$. This is the horizontal distance when the ball is at its maximum height.

A simplified expression for the maximum height of the ball is $\frac{1}{64}v^2 \sin^2 \theta$.

Substitute 80 for v and 35° for θ in the simplified expression to find the maximum height of the football.

$$\frac{1}{64}v^2 \sin^2 \theta = \frac{1}{64} \cdot 80^2 \sin^2 35° \approx \frac{1}{64} \cdot 6400(0.574)^2 \approx 33 \text{ feet}$$

TEST PREPARATION

New York Test Practice

OPEN-ENDED

1. Sound travels in waves that can be represented using sine functions. When two notes are played at the same time on a musical instrument, the resulting sound wave can be modeled by the sum of two sound waves.

   Playing C and G together creates harmony and produces a pleasant sound. Use a graphing calculator to graph the sound wave that results from playing C and G at the same time.

Note	Sound wave
C	$y = \sin 523.26t$
G	$y = \sin 784t$
B	$y = \sin 987.76t$

   Playing C and B together creates dissonance and produces an unpleasant sound. Use a graphing calculator to graph the sound wave that results from playing B and C at the same time.

   Make a conjecture about the relationship between how the notes sound when played together and the resulting sound wave. *Explain* your reasoning.

2. The blades of a fan rotate counterclockwise at a speed of 800 rotations per minute. The length of each blade is 9 inches. The maximum height of the tip of blade 1 above the ground is 48 inches.

   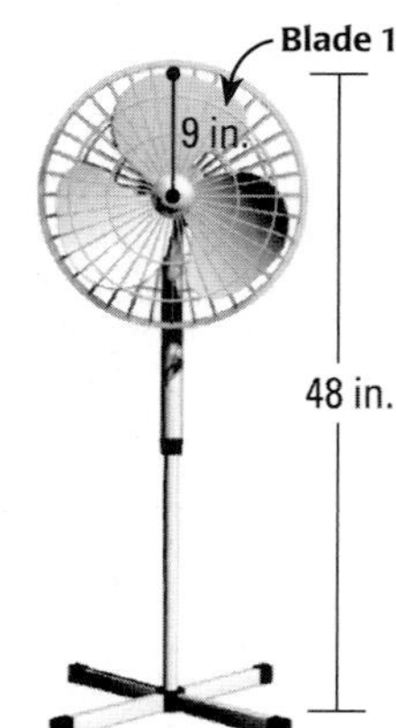

   What is the minimum height of the tip of blade 1 above the ground?

   Write a function that models the height of the tip of blade 1 as a function of time. Assume that the blade starts in the position shown in the diagram.

   Do your previous two answers change if the fan rotates clockwise? *Explain* why or why not.

3. The chart shows the average monthly temperature (in degrees Fahrenheit) and a household's gas usage (in cubic feet) for 12 months.

   Use the chart to make a table of values giving the month t (with January corresponding to $t = 0$), the average monthly temperature y_1, and the gas usage y_2 (in thousands of cubic feet).

   Use your table and a graphing calculator to find trigonometric models for the average monthly temperature y_1 as a function of time and the gas usage y_2 as a function of time.

   Graph the two regression equations in the same coordinate plane on your graphing calculator. *Describe* the relationship between the graphs.

January	February	March	April
32°F 20,000 ft^3	21°F 27,000 ft^3	15°F 23,000 ft^3	22°F 22,000 ft^3
May	**June**	**July**	**August**
35°F 21,000 ft^3	49°F 14,000 ft^3	62°F 8,000 ft^3	78°F 9,000 ft^3
September	**October**	**November**	**December**
71°F 13,000 ft^3	63°F 15,000 ft^3	55°F 19,000 ft^3	40°F 23,000 ft^3

TEST PREPARATION

OPEN-ENDED

4. A basketball is dropped from a height of 15 feet. Can the height of the basketball over time be modeled by a trigonometric function of the form $y = a \cos b(x - h)$? If so, write the function. If not, *explain* why not.

5. Consider the following function:

$$f(x) = \sin x \cos x$$

Without graphing the function, what would you expect the graph to look like? *Explain* your reasoning. Copy and complete the table below and determine whether your prediction was correct.

x	$-\pi$	$-\frac{3\pi}{4}$	$-\frac{\pi}{2}$	$-\frac{\pi}{4}$	0	$\frac{\pi}{4}$	$\frac{\pi}{2}$	$\frac{3\pi}{4}$	π
f(x)	?	?	?	?	?	?	?	?	?

MULTIPLE CHOICE

6. The graph of which function is shown?

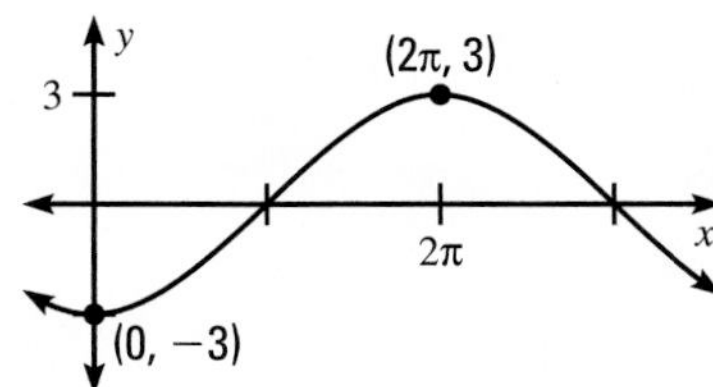

(1) $y = -3 \cos 2x$ (3) $y = -\frac{1}{2} \cos 3x$

(2) $y = -2 \cos 3x$ (4) $y = -3 \cos \frac{1}{2}x$

7. Which expression is *not* equivalent to 1?

(1) $\tan x \sec x \cos x$ (3) $\frac{\cos^2(-x) \tan^2 x}{\sin^2(-x)}$

(2) $\sin^2 x + \cos^2 x$ (4) $\cos\left(\frac{\pi}{2} - x\right) \csc x$

8. What is the general solution of the equation $\cos^3 x = 25 \cos x$?

(1) $\frac{\pi}{2} + 2n\pi$ (3) $\frac{3\pi}{2} + 2n\pi$

(2) $\frac{\pi}{2} + n\pi$ (4) $\frac{\pi}{4} + 2n\pi$

9. What is the x-intercept of the graph of $y = \sin \frac{1}{2}\pi x$ on the interval $0 < x < 3$?

(1) $\frac{1}{2}$ (3) 2

(2) 1 (4) no x-intercept

10. Find the y-coordinate of the point of intersection of the graphs of $y = 2 + \sin x$ and $y = 3 - \sin x$ in the interval $0 < x < \frac{\pi}{2}$.

(1) $\frac{\pi}{6}$ (3) $2\frac{1}{2}$

(2) $\frac{1}{2}$ (4) no point of intersection

11. Find the amplitude of the sinusoid shown below.

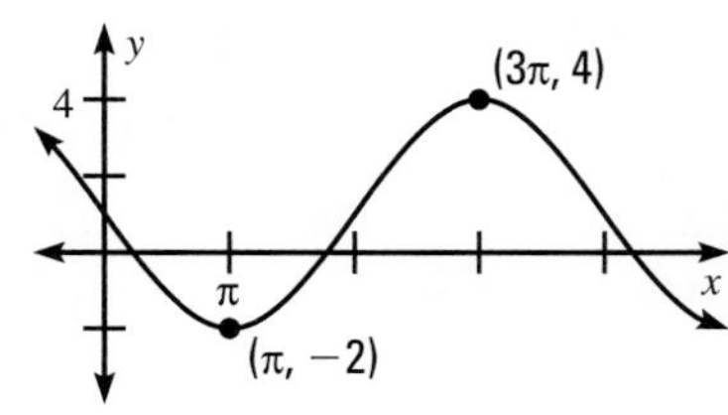

(1) −2 (2) 2 (3) 3 (4) 4

Additional Lessons

Algebra 2

The additional lessons have been written to ensure complete state standard coverage. These lessons provide content addressing material to encompass individual state needs. They are offered to help teach all of the standards or to provide enrichment and challenge opportunities.

Additional Lesson A

Polar and Rectangular Coordinates

Use after Chapter 13

Key Vocabulary

- **rectangular coordinate system**
- **polar system**
- **rectangular polar relations**

GOAL Use conversion formulas to convert between polar and rectangular coordinates.

The **rectangular coordinate system,** or Cartesian plane, is formed by a horizontal number line called the x-axis and a vertical number line called the y-axis. You can locate a point based on its position relative to where the two axes intersect, called the origin. The coordinates of a point are given as an ordered pair (x, y) of real numbers, where x gives the horizontal distance from the y-axis to the point, and y gives the vertical distance from the x-axis to the point.

The **polar system** locates any point by its distance from the origin and the angle it makes from an initial ray called the polar axis. A point is named by its polar coordinates (r, θ), where r is the distance from the origin and θ is the angle measure counterclockwise from the polar axis. The relationship between polar and rectangular coordinates can be shown by letting the polar axis coincide with the positive x-axis.

EXAMPLE 1 Plotting points

a. Plot the point $(3, -2)$ in rectangular coordinates.

b. Plot the point $(4, 270°)$ in polar coordinates.

Solution

a. The point $(3, -2)$ is 3 units to the right and 2 units down from the origin.

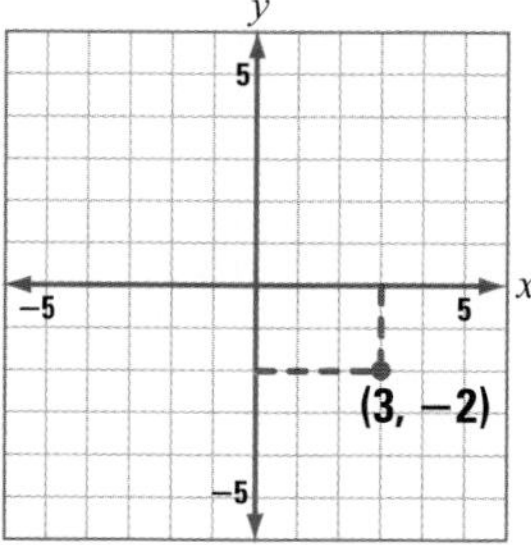

b. The point $(4, 270°)$ is 270° from the right horizontal and 4 units from the origin.

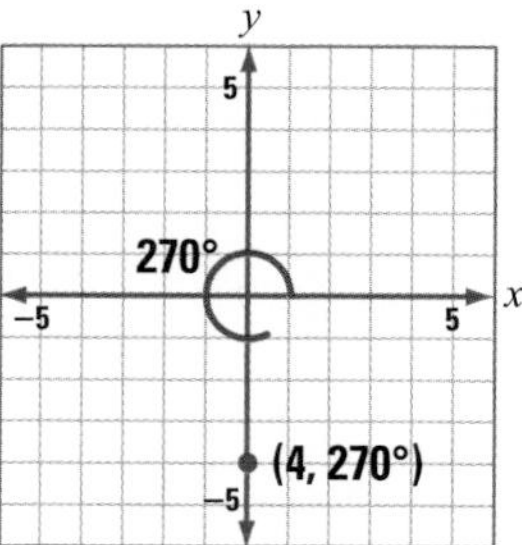

Use conversion formulas to find the rectangular polar relations.

Conversion Formulas

Rectangular to polar: from (x, y) to (r, θ), $r = \sqrt{x^2 + y^2}$

$\theta = \arctan\left(\frac{y}{x}\right)$, if $x > 0$ or

$\theta = \arctan\left(\frac{y}{x}\right) + 180°$, if $x < 0$.

Polar to rectangular: from (r, θ) to (x, y), $x = r\cos\theta$, $y = r\sin\theta$

EXAMPLE 2 Converting from rectangular points to polar

Convert $(-3, 4)$ to polar coordinates.

Solution

$r = \sqrt{x^2 + y^2} = \sqrt{(-3)^2 + (4)^2} = \sqrt{9 + 16} = \sqrt{25} = 5$

$x < \theta$, so $= \arctan\left(\frac{y}{x}\right) + 180° = \arctan\left(\frac{4}{-3}\right) + 180° \approx 126.9°$

Therefore $(-3, 4)$ converts to $(5, 126.9°)$ in polar coordinates.

EXAMPLE 3 Converting polar points to rectangular

Convert $(4, 60°)$ from polar to rectangular coordinates.

Solution

Using the formula $(x, y) = (r \cos \theta, r \sin \theta)$, 4 and 60° can be substituted for r and θ.

$$(x, y) = (4\cos(60°), 4\sin(60°)) = \left(4\left(\frac{1}{2}\right), 4\left(\frac{\sqrt{3}}{2}\right)\right) = (2, 2\sqrt{3})$$

In the rectangular coordinate system, the point is $(2, 2\sqrt{3})$.

PRACTICE

EXAMPLE 1 for Exs. 1–2

1. Plot the points $A(4, 2)$, $B(-1, 5)$, $C(0, -2)$, and $D(-3, -1)$.

2. Plot the points $E(4, 45°)$, $F(1, 210°)$, $G(2.5, 180°)$, and $H(3, -45°)$.

EXAMPLE 2 for Ex. 3

3. Convert the points in Exercise 1 to polar coordinates.

EXAMPLE 3 for Ex. 4

4. Convert the points in Exercise 2 to rectangular coordinates.

Additional Lesson B Polar Coordinates and the Complex Plane

Use after Chapter 13

GOAL Determine the location of complex numbers on a graph and express complex numbers in both rectangular and polar form.

Key Vocabulary

- **rectangular coordinate system**
- **coordinate plane**
- **complex coordinate system**
- **complex plane**
- **rectangular form**
- **polar system**
- **polar form**
- **modulus of $a + bi$**
- **argument of $a + bi$**

Real numbers are graphed on a **rectangular coordinate system,** or **coordinate plane,** which is formed by a horizontal number line called the x-axis and a vertical number line called the y-axis.

Complex numbers in the form $a + bi$ can be graphed in the **complex coordinate system,** or **complex plane.** In the complex plane the horizontal axis corresponds to the real-number part (a) and the vertical axis corresponds to the imaginary part (bi) of the complex number. Thus, a point in the complex plane representing $a + bi$ can be plotted as a point in **rectangular form,** (a, b).

EXAMPLE 1 Plotting complex numbers on a graph

Plot the complex numbers $A = 3 + 2i$, $B = -3i$, $C = -4 - 5i$, and $D = 2$ on the complex plane.

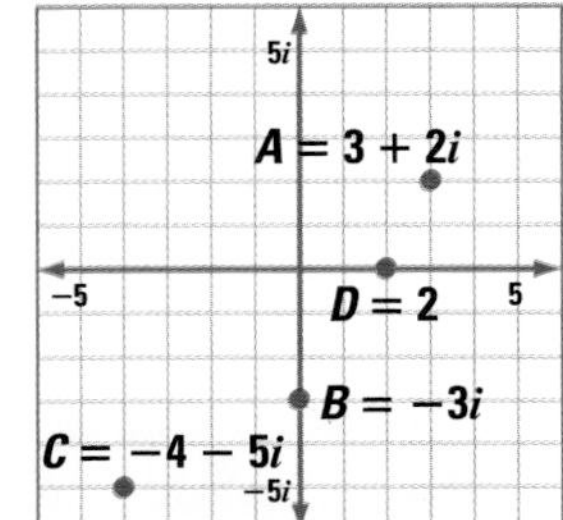

Solution

$A = 3 + 2i \rightarrow (3, 2)$

$B = -3i \rightarrow (0, -3)$

$C = -4 - 5i \rightarrow (-4, -5)$

$D = 2 \rightarrow (2, 0)$

The **polar system** locates any point by its distance from the origin and the angle it makes from an initial ray called the polar axis. A point in **polar form** is named by its polar coordinates (r, θ), where r, called the **modulus of $a + bi$,** is the distance from the origin and θ, called the **argument of $a + bi$,** is the angle measure counterclockwise from the polar axis. The relationship between polar and rectangular coordinates can be shown by letting the polar axis coincide with the positive x-axis.

Conversion Formulas

Rectangular to polar:

To convert a complex number of the form $a + bi$ to polar form use the rectangular form (a, b).

(a, b) to (r, θ), $r = \sqrt{a^2 + b^2}$

$\theta = \arctan\left(\frac{b}{a}\right)$, if $x > 0$ or

$\theta = \arctan\left(\frac{b}{a}\right) + 180°$, if $x < 0$.

Polar to rectangular:

To convert the polar complex number to rectangular form, first calculate $\cos$ and $\sin \theta$, then distribute the value of r.

The complex point (r, θ) represents the complex number

$z = r(\cos \theta + i \sin \theta) = r\cos \theta + ri\sin \theta.$

EXAMPLE 2 Express complex numbers in both rectangular and polar form

a. Convert the complex number $-2 + 2i$ to polar form.

Solution

Recognize that $a = -2$ and $b = 2$.

Then $r = \sqrt{(-2)^2 + (2)^2} = \sqrt{4 + 4} = \sqrt{8} = 2\sqrt{2}$ and since $a < 0$,

$\theta = \arctan\left(\frac{2}{-2}\right) + 180° = 135°$.

In polar form, $-2 + 2i$ is $(2\sqrt{2}, 135°)$.

b. Convert the complex number $z = 3(\cos 135 + i\sin 135)$ to rectangular form.

Solution

Evaluate $\cos(135°) = -\frac{\sqrt{2}}{2}$ and $\sin(135°) = \frac{\sqrt{2}}{2}$.

Then $z = 3\left(\frac{-\sqrt{2}}{2} + i\frac{\sqrt{2}}{2}\right) = \frac{-3\sqrt{2}}{2} + \frac{3i\sqrt{2}}{2}$

Rectangular form is $\frac{-3\sqrt{2}}{2} + \frac{3i\sqrt{2}}{2}$.

PRACTICE

EXAMPLE 1 for Ex. 1

1. Plot the complex numbers in the complex plane: $W = -3 + 4i$, $X = 5 - 3i$, $Y = 2i$, and $Z = 1 + i$.

Convert each complex number to polar form.

EXAMPLE 2 for Exs. 2–6

2. $-3 + 4i$
3. $6i$
4. $2 - 5i$

Convert each complex number to rectangular form.

5. $z = 4(\cos 120 + i\sin 120)$
6. $z = 2\sqrt{2}(\cos 45 + i\sin 45)$

Additional Lesson C

Tangent to a Curve

Use after Chapter 9

Key Vocabulary

- **slope of a line**
- **tangent to a curve**
- **secant line**
- **velocity**

GOAL Recognize that the slope of the tangent line to a curve represents the rate of change.

The **slope of a line** represents the rate of change at which the line rises or falls. The slope of a line is the same at every point on the line. For graphs that are curves, the slope changes from point to point on the curve. To determine the rate of change at a single point on a curve you can find the slope of the tangent line at that point. A **tangent to a curve** is a line that intersects the curve at a point but does not cross the curve at that point. The slope of the tangent line can be approximated by finding the slope of a **secant line,** which intersects the curve in two points. Use the point of tangency and a second point that can be chosen closer and closer to the point of tangency, until the secant line approaches the tangent line. The slope of the secant line, as it approaches the tangent line, is the approximate rate of change along the curve at the point of tangency.

EXAMPLE 1 Finding the slope of the secant line to determine the tangent to the curve

Find the slope of the line tangent to the function $f(x) = x^2 - 4x + 6$ at the point (3, 3).

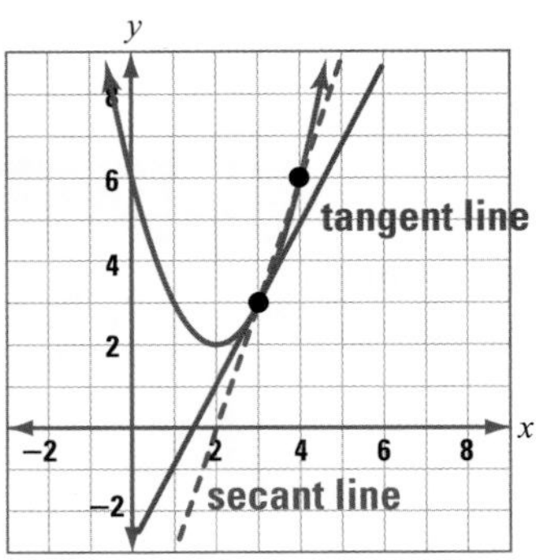

Solution

The point (4, 6) is also on the curve. The slope of a secant line through (3, 3) and (4, 6) is 3. Now slide the point (4, 6) down along the curve closer to the point (3, 3). Choose the x-coordinate 3.5, which is half-way between 3 and 4. Find the y-coordinate. Then find the slope of the secant line.

x	$y = x^2 - 4x + 6$	y	slope
3.5	$y = (3.5)^2 - 4(3.5) + 6$	4.25	$\frac{4.25 - 3}{3.5 - 3} = 2.5$
3.25	$y = (3.25)^2 - 4(3.25) + 6$	3.5625	$\frac{3.5625 - 3}{3.25 - 3} = 2.25$
3.125	$y = (3.125)^2 - 4(3.125) + 6$	3.265625	$\frac{3.265625 - 3}{3.125 - 3} = 2.125$

As the second point of the secant line gets very close to (3, 3), the secant line moves closer to becoming the tangent line and the slope approaches 2. This is equivalent to stating that the slope or rate of change along the curve at the point (3, 2) is 2.

The slope of the tangent line can be used to find the **velocity** of an object. The velocity is the rate of change in displacement of an object at any given time. Average velocity is the rate of change in distance over a period of time which can be represented by the slope of the secant line.

EXAMPLE 2 Finding velocity

A ball is dropped from a height of 100 feet. The height of the ball at a given time can be found using the function $h(t) = -16t^2 + 100$. Find the velocity of the ball after 1.5 seconds.

Solution

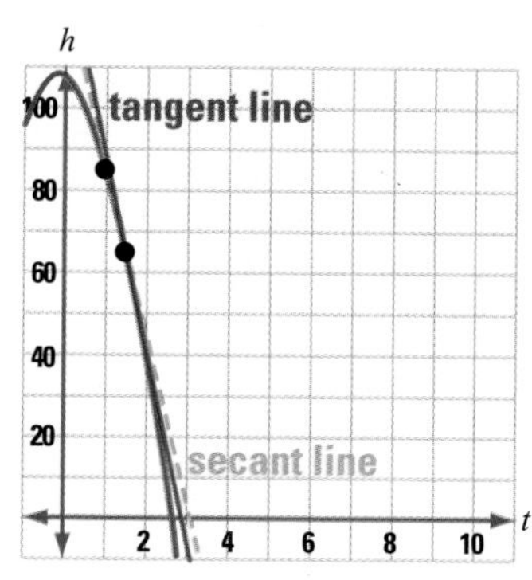

The velocity of the ball is its rate of change at a particular point along its path. The rate of change at a particular point can be found by finding the slope of the tangent line at that point. The slope of a secant line can be used to determine the slope of the tangent line. To find the velocity at (1.5, 64), start by finding the slope of the secant line through the points (1, 84) and (1.5, 64). The slope is −40. Choose points closer and closer to 1.5, find h, then find the slope of the secant line.

t	$h = -16t^2 + 100$	h	slope
1.2	$h = -16(1.2)^2 + 100$	76.96	$\frac{76.96 - 64}{1.2 - 1.5} = -43.2$
1.3	$h = -16(1.3)^2 + 100$	72.96	$\frac{72.96 - 64}{1.3 - 1.5} = -44.8$
1.4	$h = -16(1.4)^2 + 100$	68.64	$\frac{68.64 - 64}{1.4 - 1.5} = -46.4$
1.49	$h = -16(1.49)^2 + 100$	64.4784	$\frac{64.4784 - 64}{1.49 - 1.5} = -47.84$

As the points of the secant line get very close to (1.5, 64), the slope of the secant line approaches −48. Thus, the slope of the tangent line at the point (1.5, 64) is −48.

The velocity of the ball at 1.5 seconds is −48 feet per second.

PRACTICE

EXAMPLE 1 for Exs. 1–2

1. Find the slope of the line tangent to $f(x) = x^2 - 6x + 9$ at the point (2, 1).

2. Find the slope of the line tangent to $f(x) = \frac{1}{2}x^2 - 4$ at $x = 2.5$.

EXAMPLE 2 for Ex. 3

3. Refer to Example 2. What is the velocity of the ball after 0.5 second?

Additional Lesson D

Approximation/Upper and Lower Bounds

Use after Chapter 5

Key Vocabulary

- **maximum value of $f(x)$**
- **minimum value of $f(x)$**
- **successive approximation**
- **limit**

GOAL Solve measurement problems using successive approximation, upper and lower bounds, and limits.

Many problems about area and volume involve quadratic functions or cubic functions. Quadratic functions are second degree polynomials whose graphs are parabolas, and thus have a **minimum value of $f(x)$** or a **maximum value of $f(x)$**, depending on which way the parabola opens. Cubic functions are third degree polynomials and generally have a relative maximum and relative minimum before being unbounded at the ends.

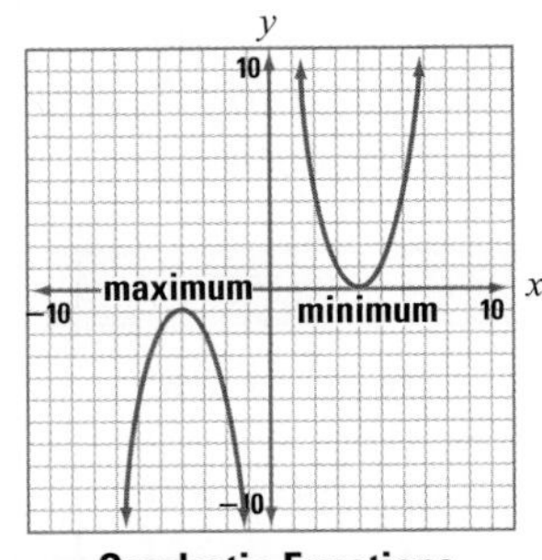

Quadratic Functions

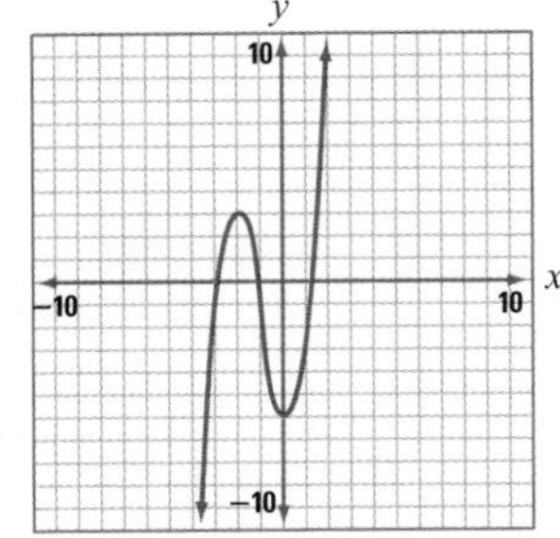

Cubic Functions

One way to find the maximum or minimum values is to graph the function on a graphing calculator and use the TRACE function. Another way is to use the method of **successive approximation,** which is a method of estimating an unknown value by comparing a sequence of known values.

EXAMPLE 1 Determine the maximum value

A farmer has 88 feet of wire fencing. He wants to enclose a rectangular area for his chickens, using the barn as one side of the enclosure. What dimensions should he make the enclosure in order to maximize the area for the chickens?

Solution

Let x represent the width of the enclosure. Then $88 - 2x$ represents the length. If A represents the area, then $A = x(88 - 2x)$, or $A = -2x^2 + 88x$.

If we graph the function $f(x) = -2x^2 + 88x$, we find that it is a parabola opening down and that the largest value of the function would be at the top, or vertex. There are several ways to determine this value.

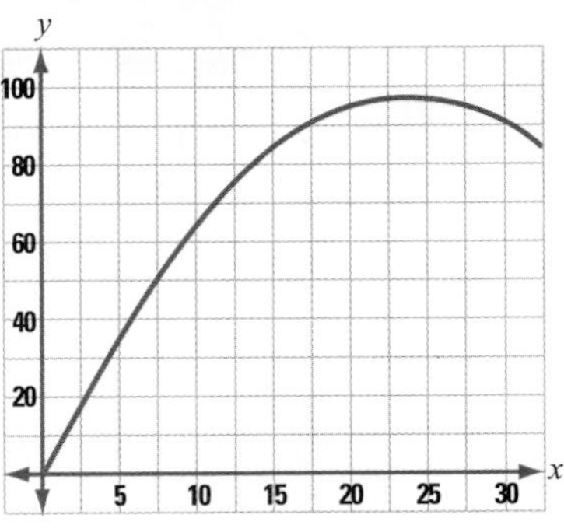

(continued)

EXAMPLE 1 Determine the maximum value *(continued)*

Approximation Method:

Using $f(x) = -2x^2 + 88x$, evaluate $f(x)$ and compare the answers looking for the largest value.

$f(10) = -2(10)^2 + 88(10) = 680$

$f(20) = -2(20)^2 + 88(20) = 960$

$f(30) = -2(30)^2 + 88(30) = 840$

Notice that $f(x)$ increases between 10 and 20 and decreases somewhere between 20 and 30. Try values closer to 20.

$f(15) = -2(15)^2 + 88(15) = 870$

$f(25) = -2(25)^2 + 88(25) = 950$

Since the value of $f(x)$ when x is 25 is lower than the value of $f(x)$ when x is 20, try values still closer to 20.

$f(17.5) = -2(17.5)^2 + 88(17.5) = 927.5$

$f(22.5) = -2(22.5)^2 + 88(22.5) = 967.5$

When x is 22.5, the area is larger than when x is 20, so try values closer to 22.5.

$f(21.5) = -2(21.5)^2 + 88(21.5) = 967.5$

$f(23.5) = -2(23.5)^2 + 88(23.5) = 963.5$

Notice that $f(21.5) = 967.5$ and $f(22.5) = 967.5$. Try 22.

$f(22) = -2(22)^2 + 88(22) = 968$

This is the maximum so far. Now approach $x = 22$ from both sides, moving closer.

$f(21.8) = 967.92$

$f(21.9) = 967.98$

$f(22.1) = 967.98$

$f(22.2) = 967.92$

Since each value is less than 968, the maximum value occurs at $x = 22$.
We can say that the **limit** of A as x approaches 22 is 968.

Since x represents the width of the enclosure, the farmer should make the dimensions of the enclosure 22 feet by 44 feet.

Graphic Method:

Using a graphing calculator, graph the function $f(x) = -2x^2 + 88x$. Use the trace function on the calculator to determine the maximum value of the function.

PRACTICE

EXAMPLE 1 for Exs. 1–2

1. You have 200 feet of fencing. You want to enclose a rectangular garden. What dimensions will give you the maximum area for the garden?

2. Find the values for x that give the relative maximum and relative minimum of the function $f(x) = x^3 + 4x^2 - 3x + 1$.

Additional Lesson E

Addition and Multiplication of Vectors

Use after Chapter 3

GOAL Describe vector operations, determine what properties hold for the operations and represent them symbolically or pictorially.

Key Vocabulary
- vector
- direction of a vector
- magnitude of a vector
- initial point
- terminal point
- vector addition
- graphic sum of two vectors
- scalar
- scalar multiplication

A **vector** is a quantity with distance and **direction.** The **magnitude** of a vector is the distance from its **initial point** to its **terminal point.** Vectors can be named using lower case letters, often **u, v,** and **w,** and an ordered pair of the form $\langle x, y\rangle$, where the magnitude and direction of the vector are the distance and direction of $\langle x, y\rangle$ from the origin. For example, vector **u** $\langle 3, 4\rangle$ is shown at right. Its initial point is (0, 0) and its terminal point is (3, 4).

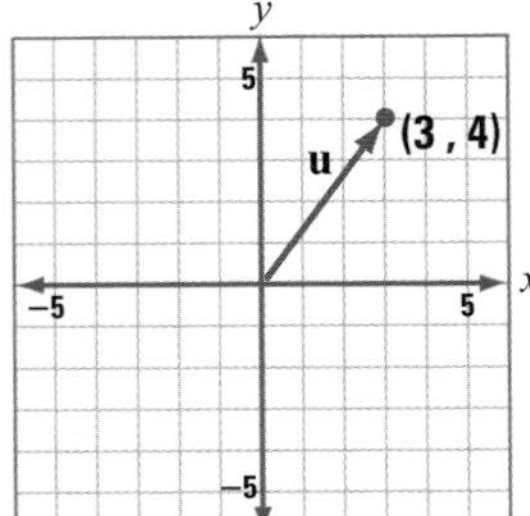

The sum of two vectors can be found symbolically by adding their coordinates. **Vector addition** is defined as follows:

For two vectors, $\mathbf{u} = \langle x_1, y_1\rangle$ and $\mathbf{v} = \langle x_2, y_2\rangle$,

$$\mathbf{u} + \mathbf{v} = \langle x_1 + x_2, y_1 + y_2\rangle.$$

Addition of vectors can be shown geometrically using a graph. The **graphic sum of two vectors** $\mathbf{u} = \langle 3, 4\rangle$ and $\mathbf{v} = \langle -2, 2\rangle$ is shown at right.

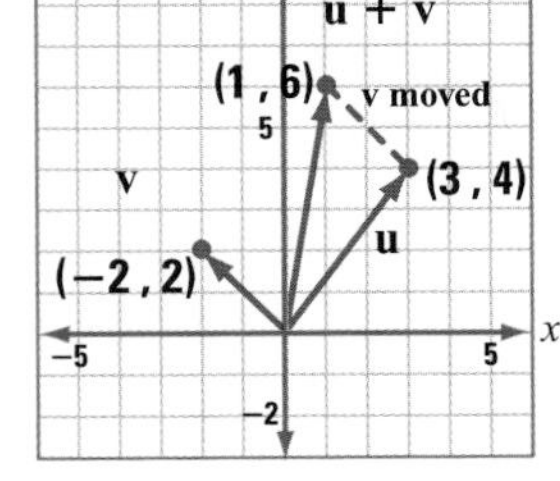

Vectors can be multiplied by a real number called a **scalar. Scalar multiplication** is defined as follows:

For a vector $\mathbf{u} = \langle x, y\rangle$ and any real number a, $a\mathbf{u} = \langle ax, ay\rangle$.

The graphic representation of $2\mathbf{u}$, where $\mathbf{u} = \langle 1, 2\rangle$ is shown at right.

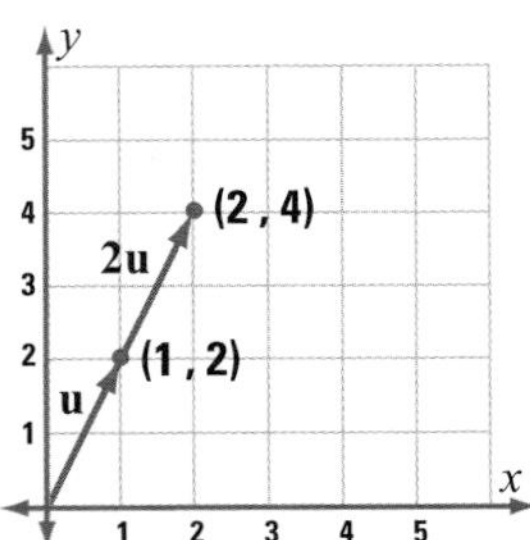

EXAMPLE 1 Adding two vectors

Let $\mathbf{u} = \langle 2, 4\rangle$ and $\mathbf{v} = \langle 3, -1\rangle$.

a. Find $\mathbf{u} + \mathbf{v}$.

b. Show $\mathbf{u} + \mathbf{v}$ graphically.

Solution

a. $\mathbf{u} + \mathbf{v} = \langle 2, 4\rangle + \langle 3, -1\rangle$
$= \langle 2 + 3, 4 + (-1)\rangle$
$= \langle 5, 3\rangle$

b.

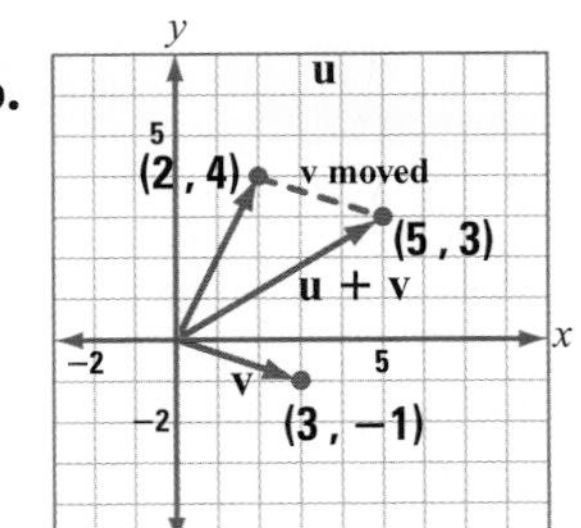

EXAMPLE 2 Scalar multiplication of vector

Let $\mathbf{u} = \langle 4, 2 \rangle$.

a. Find $3\mathbf{u}$.

b. Show $3\mathbf{u}$ graphically.

Solution

a. $3\mathbf{u} = \langle 3 \cdot 4, 3 \cdot 2 \rangle$
$= \langle 12, 6 \rangle$

b.

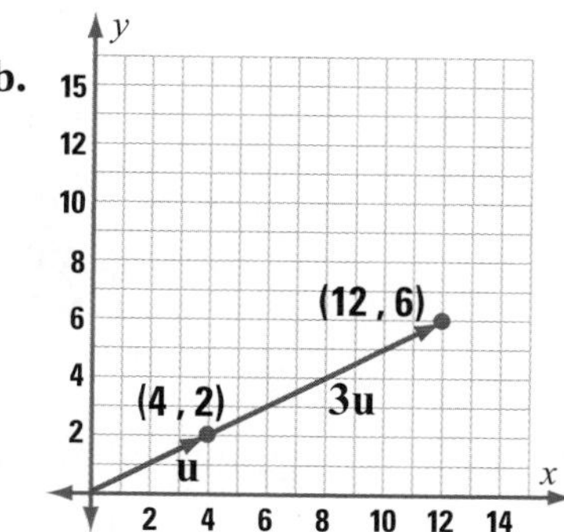

PRACTICE

Let $\mathbf{u} = \langle 1, 3 \rangle$, $\mathbf{w} = \langle -2, -3 \rangle$, and $\mathbf{v} = = \langle -3, 2 \rangle$.

Find each of the following.

EXAMPLE 1 for Exs. 1–4

1. $\mathbf{u} + \mathbf{w}$
2. Represent $\mathbf{w} + \mathbf{v}$ graphically.
3. $\mathbf{w} + \mathbf{v}$
4. $\mathbf{u} + \mathbf{v}$

EXAMPLE 2 for Exs. 5–7

5. $4\mathbf{w}$
6. Represent $2\mathbf{u}$ graphically.
7. $2\mathbf{u} + 3\mathbf{v}$

Additional Lesson F

Vector Direction and Velocity

Use after Chapter 13

Key Vocabulary

- vector
- initial point
- terminal point
- magnitude of a vector
- direction angle of a vector
- resultant vector
- bearing

GOAL Use vectors to represent and analyze problems involving velocity and direction.

A **vector** is a quantity that has both magnitude and direction. A vector is represented by a directed line segment that has an **initial point** and a **terminal point.** The directed line segment itself can be called a vector. The **magnitude of a vector** is the length of the directed line segment that represents the vector. The **direction angle of a vector** is the angle measured counterclockwise from the positive x-axis to the directed line segment. If two vectors are added, the sum is called the **resultant vector.**

In navigation, bearings are used to describe direction. A **bearing** is the angle measured clockwise from due north to a vector. (Another way to describe a bearing uses the acute angle the vector makes with the north-south line. Both ways are shown below.)

EXAMPLE 1 Identify direction angle and bearing

Identify the direction angle and bearing of vector $\overrightarrow{OP}$.

Solution

The direction angle is 200°. The bearing can be named either of these ways:

- 250°, or
- S 70° W
  (south, 70°, west)

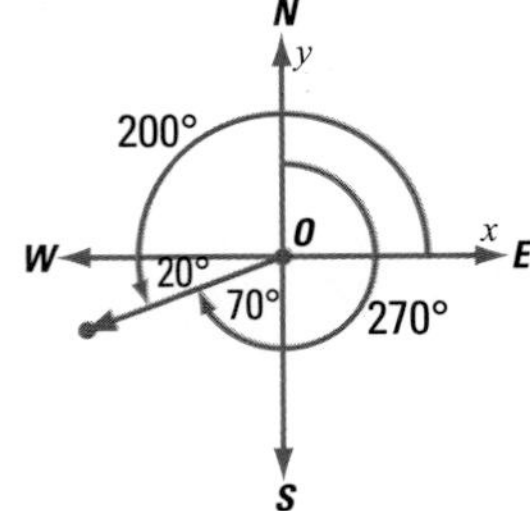

EXAMPLE 2 Find actual speed and bearing

An airplane with an air speed (speed in still air) of 300 miles per hour heads in the direction that would have a bearing of 130° if there were no wind. However, there is a 50-mile-per-hour wind from due west. (So the wind direction is from west to east.) Find the actual speed (speed relative to the ground) and bearing of the airplane.

Solution

Use these vectors (see Figure 1):

$\overrightarrow{OP}$: airplane vector (no wind)
$\overrightarrow{PQ}$: wind vector
$\overrightarrow{OQ}$: resultant vector (airplane vector with wind)
$\overrightarrow{OP}$ has a bearing of 130°, so it makes a 40° angle with the positive x-axis.

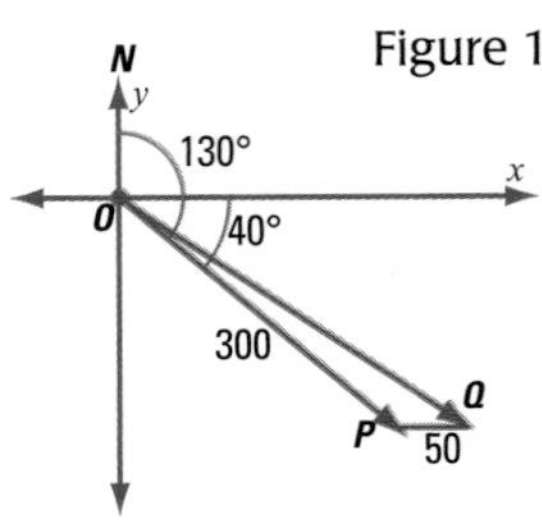

Figure 1

(continued)

EXAMPLE 2 Find actual speed and bearing *(continued)*

Coordinates of P (Figure 2):

$x = 300\cos 40° \approx 230$

$|y| = 300\cos 40° \approx 193$, so $y \approx -193$

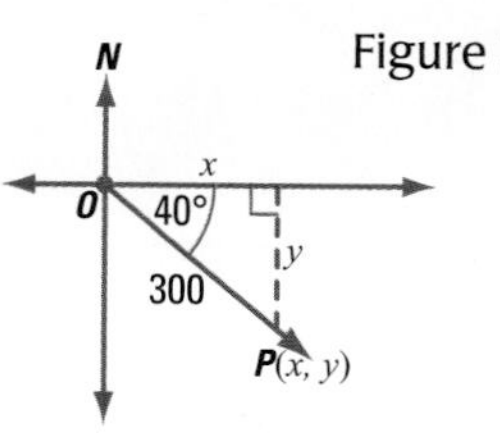

Coordinates of Q (Figure 3):

To find the x-coordinate of Q, just add 50 to the x-coordinate of P: $230 + 50 = 280$.

The magnitude of $\overrightarrow{OQ}$ is:
$\|\overrightarrow{OQ}\| = \sqrt{280^2 + 193^2} \approx 340.$

The angle θ between the x-axis and $\overrightarrow{OQ}$ is:
$\theta = \tan^{-1}\frac{193}{280} \approx 34.6°$.

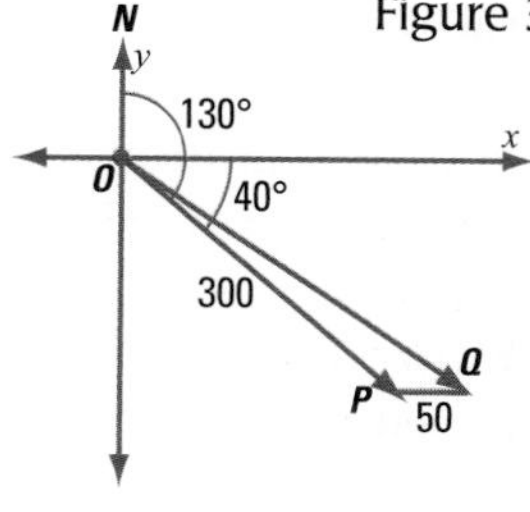

Find the actual bearing (Figure 4):

$90° + 34.6° = 124.6°$.

The actual speed is 340 mph.

The actual bearing is 124.6°, or S 55.4° E.

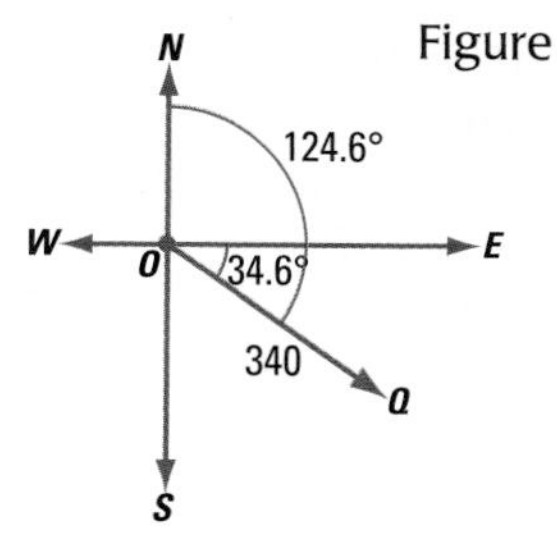

PRACTICE

EXAMPLE 1 for Ex. 1

1. If the vector $\langle -5, 2\rangle$ has initial point (0, 0), then its terminal point is (−5, 2). It makes a 21.8° angle with the negative x-axis. Identify the direction angle and bearing of the vector.

EXAMPLE 2 for Exs. 2–3

2. A jet with an air speed of 460 mph heads in the direction that would have a bearing of 205° if there were no wind. There is a 55 mph wind from due east. Find the actual speed and bearing of the jet.

3. A river flows due south at 20 meters per minute. A pilot heads his boat in the direction that would have a bearing of N 55° W and with a speed of 60 meters per minute if there were no current. Find the actual speed and bearing of the boat.

Additional Lesson G

Confidence Intervals

Use after Chapter 11

Key Vocabulary

- population
- sample
- mean
- point estimation
- interval estimation
- statistical estimation
- measure of central tendency
- standard deviation
- measure of variation
- formula for standard deviation
- degree of confidence
- confidence interval
- confidence limits
- formulas for confidence limits

GOAL Construct and interpret confidence intervals.

Suppose you want to know the average (mean) height of all the male high school students in a certain county. It is not practical to survey the entire **population** of students, so you survey a 100-student **sample.** You find the **mean** of the sample by adding the 100 heights and dividing by 100. Suppose you find the mean of the sample to be 68 inches. Then 68 is a **point estimation** because it is a single number. If you use some process and estimate that the mean is from 66.8 to 69.2, then you have found an **interval estimation.** Point estimation and interval estimation are both examples of **statistical estimation.** The mean of a data set is a **measure of central tendency.**

Standard deviation is a **measure of variation,** or spread. **Formula for standard deviation, σ:**

$$\sigma = \sqrt{\frac{(x_1 - \bar{x})^2 + (x_2 - \bar{x})^2 + (x_n - \bar{x})^2}{n}},$$

where $x_1, x_2, \ldots, x_n$ are the n values in the data set.

EXAMPLE 1 Find mean and standard deviation

The heights (in inches) of the five starters on a basketball team are 68, 68, 74, 75, and 80. Find the mean and standard deviation for the heights.

Solution

Mean: $\bar{x} = \frac{68 + 68 + 74 + 75 + 80}{5} = \frac{365}{5} = 73$

Standard deviation:

$$\sigma = \sqrt{\frac{(68 - 73)^2 + (68 - 73)^2 + (74 - 73)^2 + (75 - 73)^2 + (80 - 73)^2}{5}}$$

$$= \sqrt{\frac{(-5)^2 + (-5)^2 + (1)^2 + (2)^2 + (7)^2}{5}} = \sqrt{\frac{25 + 25 + 1 + 4 + 49}{5}}$$

$$= \sqrt{\frac{104}{5}} \approx 4.56$$

You can use a sample mean to estimate a population mean. To assign a **degree of confidence** to your estimate, you can construct a **confidence interval,** whose midpoint is the sample mean and whose endpoints are **confidence limits.** Using the confidence interval, you are stating that the population mean is within that interval.

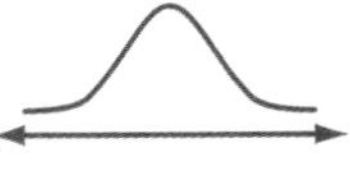

Many real-life data sets have graphs that are bell-shaped curves, such as the curve at the right. This is called a normal distribution. For a normal distribution, you can use these **formulas for confidence limits:** $X_L = \bar{x} - z\frac{\sigma}{\sqrt{n}}$ and $X_U = \bar{x} + z\frac{\sigma}{\sqrt{n}}$, where X_L is the lower limit, X_U is the upper limit, $\bar{x}$ is the mean of the sample, z is a *critical value* from the table below, σ is the standard deviation, and n is the number of data values in the sample. There are many values of z that can be used. The table below shows a few.

Confidence level	99%	95%	90%	80%	50%
z	2.58	1.96	1.645	1.28	0.6745

EXAMPLE 2 Determining confidence intervals

A survey of 225 students indicates that they sleep an average of 7.8 hours per day. The standard deviation for the sample is 2.6. Construct and interpret a 95% confidence interval with 7.8 as the estimate of the true mean of the entire population of students.

Solution

Use the table. The value of z for a 95% confidence level is 1.96.

$$X_L = 7.8 - 1.96\frac{2.6}{\sqrt{225}} = 7.8 - 1.96\frac{2.6}{15} \approx 7.8 - 0.34 = 7.46$$

$$X_U = 7.8 + 1.96\frac{2.6}{\sqrt{225}} = 7.8 + 1.96\frac{2.6}{15} \approx 7.8 + 0.34 = 8.14$$

The 95% confidence interval for the estimate is given by $7.46 < \mu < 8.14$, where μ represents the true mean of the entire population of students. So, you can be 95% confident that the true mean of the population is between 7.46 and 8.14.

PRACTICE

EXAMPLE 1 for Ex. 1

1. The quiz scores of six students are 75, 83, 88, 90, 90, and 90. Find the mean and standard deviation for the scores.

EXAMPLE 2 for Exs. 2–3

2. Based on a sample of 150 stores, the mean price of a gallon of milk is \$2.36. The standard deviation is \$0.42. Construct and interpret two confidence intervals with \$2.36 as an estimate of the true mean price. Use 99% and 80% confidence levels. Compare and interpret your answers.

3. The mean commuting distance for 400 commuters in a city is 11.3 miles. The standard deviation is 3.5. Construct and interpret two confidence intervals with 11.3 as an estimate of the true mean. Use 99% and 95% confidence levels. Compare and interpret your answers.

Additional Lesson H

Relative Frequency

Use after Chapter 12

Key Vocabulary

- **frequency**
- **frequency distribution**
- **relative frequency**
- **experimental probability**
- **relative frequency concept of probability**
- **probability distribution**
- **expected value**
- **class (interval)**
- **class width (interval width)**
- **random variable**
- **expected value (mean) of a random variable**
- **theoretical probability**

GOAL Use relative frequency and expected values to represent and solve problems involving uncertainty.

The **frequency** of an outcome (data value) is the number of times that outcome occurs. A **frequency distribution** is a display of all the frequencies. **Relative frequency** is frequency divided by the total number of data values.

The **experimental probability** of an event is $\frac{\text{frequency of the event}}{\text{number of trials}}$, which can be interpreted as the **relative frequency concept of probability.** A **probability distribution** is a display of the probabilities of all the data values. **Expected value** is the weighted mean of all the outcomes (or data values).

EXAMPLE 1 Create a frequency distribution. Find relative frequency, probability, and expected value

The table below shows the responses of 200 students that were asked how many siblings they have.

Number of siblings	0	1	2	3	4	5
Frequency	42	98	37	19	2	2

a. Create a frequency distribution for the data. What is the relative frequency of 2 siblings?

b. Based on the data, what is the probability that a student chosen at random will have at least 2 siblings?

c. Describe the probability distribution for the data.

d. What is the expected value of the number of siblings?

Solution

a. The frequency distribution is the bar graph at right.

The relative frequencies are shown above the bars.

The relative frequency of 2 siblings is $\frac{37}{200}$, or 0.185 (18.5%).

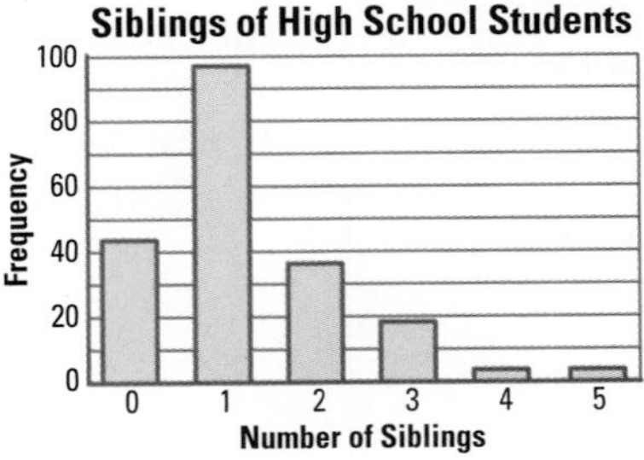

b. Probability that a student chosen at random will have at least 2 siblings: $0.185 + 0.095 + 0.01 + 0.01 = 0.3 = 30\%$

c. The probability distribution for this data set is the collection of relative frequencies shown on the bar graph.

d. To find the expected value, multiply each data value by its probability and add the results:
$0(0.21) + 1(0.49) + 2(0.185) + 3(0.095) + 4(0.01) + 5(0.01) = 1.235.$

Sometimes data values are organized into **classes** (intervals) of equal **class width** (interval width), and a random variable assigns a value to each class. A **random variable** is a function that assigns a number to each class (or outcome). A random variable is not a variable in the usual sense; it is a function.

PRACTICE

EXAMPLE 1
for Exs. 1–3

1. The table shows the ages of 160 high school students.

Age	14	15	16	17	18	19	20
Frequency	10	41	40	35	27	5	2

a. Create a frequency distribution for the data. Find the relative frequency of each age (to the nearest thousandth).

b. Based on the data, what is the probability that a student chosen at random will be 17 or younger?

c. What is the expected value for the ages in this data set?

2. The table shows data about the heights of 100 students.

Height (cm)	145-159	160-174	175-189	190-204
Frequency	20	40	34	6

Suppose a random variable assigns the mean height of each interval to that interval. (For example, it assigns 152 to the 145-159 interval.) Complete the following to find the **expected value mean of the random variable:** $(0.20)(152) + (0.40)(167) + \ldots$

3. An experiment consists of rolling two number cubes.

a. Show all the possible outcomes. (There are 36 outcomes; each outcome is an ordered pair.)

b. Suppose a random variable assigns the sum of the numbers in each outcome to that outcome. For example, the sum 8 is assigned to the outcome (3, 5). Make a table to show the **theoretical probability distribution** for the random variable.

(The theoretical probability of an event is $\frac{\text{number of favorable outcomes}}{\text{total number of outcomes}}$.)

c. Find the expected value of the random variable.

Additional Lesson I

Group and Field Properties

Use after Chapter 1

Key Vocabulary

- **set**
- **binary operation**
- **group**
- **field**

GOAL Justify mathematical procedures and determine how they apply to invented operations using field properties.

A **set** is a collection of elements. Elements can be numbers, objects, symbols, figures, or other items. A **binary operation** is a process applied to two elements to produce a single element.

A **group** $<S, \circ>$ is a nonempty set S together with a binary operation $\circ$ that has the following properties:

- S is closed under $\circ$. That is, for any elements a and b in S, $a \circ b$ is in S.
- $\circ$ is associative. That is, for any elements a, b, and c in S, $(a \circ b) \circ c = a \circ (b \circ c)$.
- S has an identity element. That is, S has an element e such that for every element a in S, $a \circ e = a$ and $e \circ a = a$.
- Every element in S has an inverse. That is, for every element a in S, there is some element a^* in S such that $a \circ a^* = e$ and $a^* \circ a = e$.

A **field** $<S, \circ, \diamond>$ is a nonempty set S together with two binary operations $\circ$ and $\diamond$. Listed below are all the properties of a field.

- Both operations are associative.
- Both operations are commutative.
- The distributive property holds. That is, for any elements a, b, and c in S, $a \diamond (b \circ c) = (a \diamond b) \circ (a \diamond c)$.
- There is an identity element for each operation.
- For each operation, every element has an inverse.

EXAMPLE 1 Investigate a possible group

A set contains the 6 elements shown below, and no others.

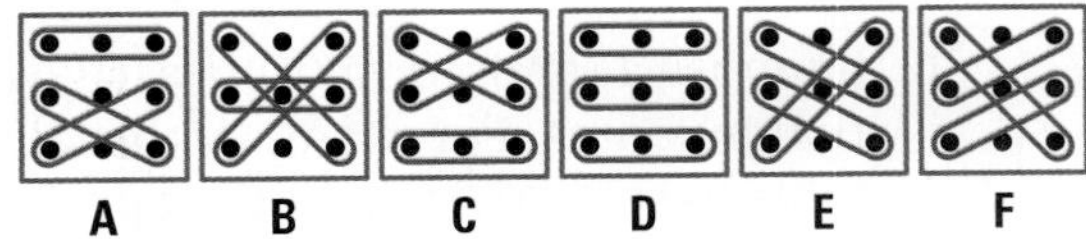

Each element is a 3 by 3 grid of dots with 3 rectangles. Each rectangle shows a path. The binary operation $\circ$ is defined so that you follow two paths in order, and form the resulting path by using the first dot and the last dot. A $\circ$ B is shown below. The bold rectangles show a path that starts with a dot in A and ends with a dot in B. Use the dots in the corresponding positions to determine the path in the result. The result is F.

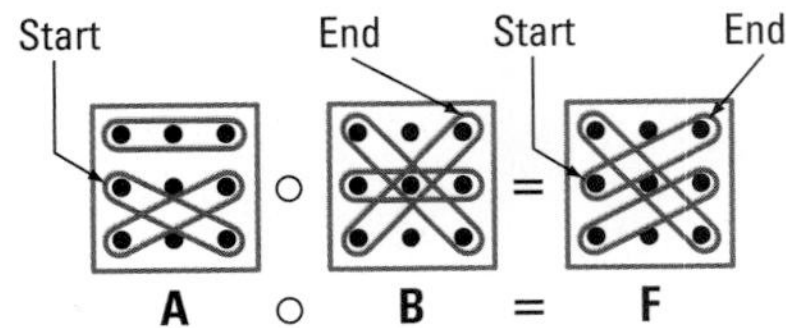

EXAMPLE 2 Investigate a possible field.

The binary operation ◇ is defined as follows:

To get the ending point for A ◇ B, shift one position down from the ending point in A ○ B. If the ending point in A ○ B is the bottom dot, shift to the top dot. A ◇ B is shown below.

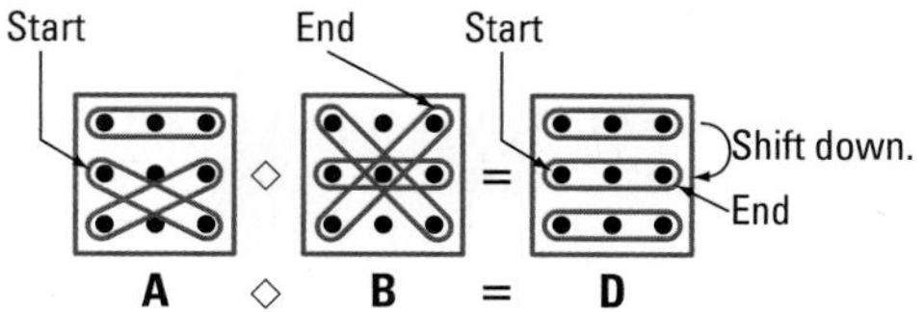

PRACTICE

EXAMPLE 1 for Exs. 1–7

1. Complete the table for the operation ○. Some results are provided for you.

○	A	B	C	D	E	F
A		F				
B					A	
C				C		
D						
E						
F						

2. Let *S* be the set of elements A, B, C, D, E, and F, together with the operation ○. Is <*S*, ○> closed under ○? Explain.

3. Does <*S*, ○> have an identity element? Explain.

4. Does every element in <*S*, ○> have an inverse? Explain.

5. Does (A ○ B) ○ C = A ○ (B ○ C)? Show your work.

6. Does A ○ B = B ○ A? Show your work.

7. If <*S*, ○> is a group, is it commutative? Explain.

EXAMPLE 2 for Exs. 8–9

8. Evaluate A ◇ C and C ◇ A. Is ◇ commutative?

9. Is <*S*, ○, ◇> a field? Explain.

Additional Lesson J

Designing Surveys

Use after Chapter 11

Goal Design a survey that avoids bias in the data selection.

Key Vocabulary

- data
- display
- range
- scale
- interval
- misleading display

Information that is presented in the form of a graph can be misleading. That is, when looking at a graph, one might get the wrong idea, or not see all the information in a clear and accurate way. This can happen for various reasons. Let's first look at some of the components of a graph that can come into play.

Data is a collection of numerical facts. A **display** is a visual representation of data, including bar graphs, circle graphs, line graphs, scatter plots, and other picture displays. The **range** of the data is the difference between the lowest and highest values. The range of the data is used to determine the **scale,** or unit of measure on the horizontal and vertical axes. The difference between every consecutive unit on an axis is called the **interval.** The choices for such things as the scale and interval, can create a **misleading display,** in which the design of the display may lead to incorrect conclusions. Some reasons for misleading displays include broken scales, intervals that are too large or too small, or unequal intervals.

EXAMPLE 1 Analyze a graph to determine how an incorrect conclusion may be drawn

The line graph shows the change in Grace's annual salary over time. What incorrect conclusion might be drawn from this graph? Explain why it is a misleading display.

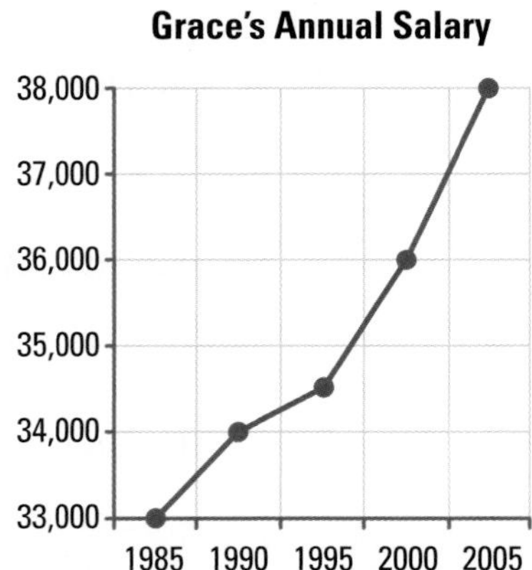

Answer: Someone might conclude that Grace has had drastic increases in her annual salary over time. The y-axis scale goes from \$33,000 to \$38,000, which are the lowest and highest data values. This has the effect of spreading the data points out from the very bottom to the very top of the display, making the changes look more dramatic than if the scale started at 0. The reality is that Grace's salary has only increased a total of \$5,000 over the course of 20 years.

PRACTICE

Complete the following exercises.

EXAMPLE 1 for Exs. 1–3

1. The bar graph shows the number of students that were able to complete a given amount of sit-ups in a one-minute physical fitness test. What incorrect conclusion might be drawn from this graph? Explain why it is a misleading display.

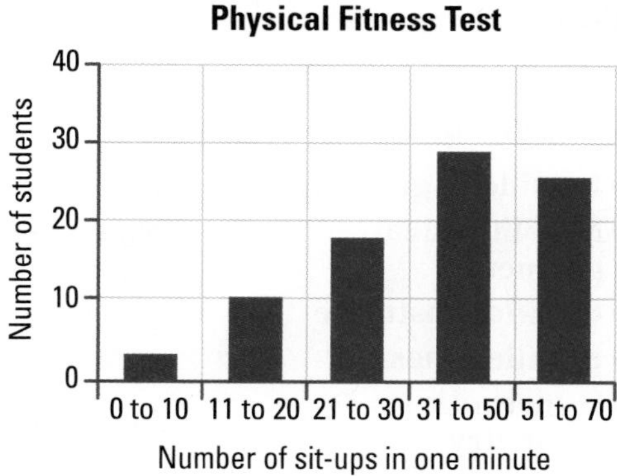

2. The bar graph shows the results of a survey in which teenagers were asked about their favorite leisure time activities. It appears as if twice as many teenagers prefer watching television as playing sports, when asked about their favorite leisure activity. But this is not true. Explain why this graph is misleading.

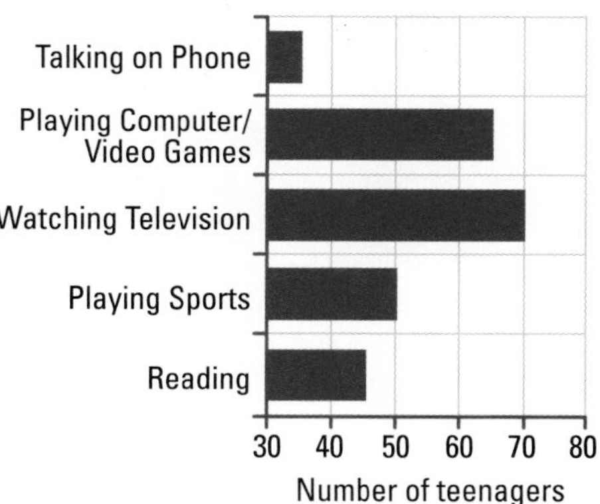

3. The line graph here shows the change in monetary donations given to a charitable organization over the 5 days of a fundraising campaign. What might someone be led to believe from this graph? Explain why it is a misleading display.

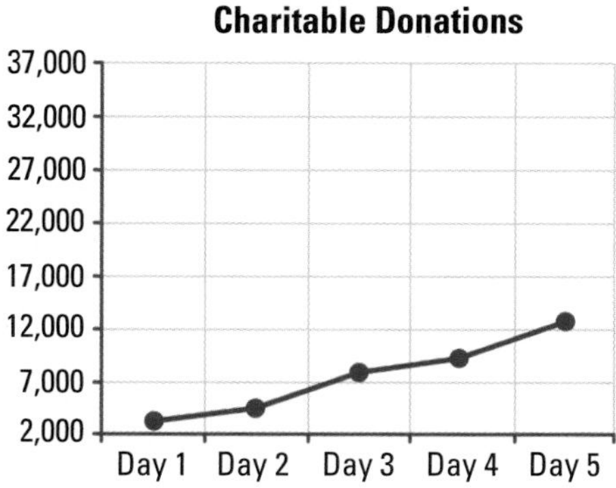

Additional Lesson K

Euclidean and Non-Euclidean Geometry

Use after Chapter 9

GOAL Recognize the differences between Euclidean and Non-Euclidean Geometry.

Key Vocabulary

- **Euclidean geometry**
- **Non-Euclidean geometry**
- **Parallel Postulate**
- **parallel lines**
- **Hyperbolic geometry**
- **Elliptical geometry**
- **Spherical geometry**
- **vanishing point**

Euclidean geometry is based on postulates or assumptions that were developed by Euclid around 300 B.C. The key difference between Euclidean geometry and **Non-Euclidean geometry** is the Fifth Postulate, called the **Parallel Postulate.** The statements below show the Parallel Postulate for Euclidean geometry and two types of Non-Euclidean geometry, **Hyperbolic geometry** and **Elliptical geometry,** also known as **Spherical Geometry.**

Euclidean *Through a given line and a point not on the line, there exists one and only one line through the point and parallel to the given line.*

Hyperbolic *Through a given line and a point not on the line, there is more than one line through that point which is parallel to the given line.*

Elliptical *There exists a line and a point not on that line such that there is no line through that point parallel to the given line.*

EXAMPLE 1 Differences between Euclidean and Non-Euclidean geometries

Given the line and the point drawn below, how many parallel lines can you draw through that point, parallel to the given line? Is this an example of Euclidean or Non-Euclidean geometry?

Solution

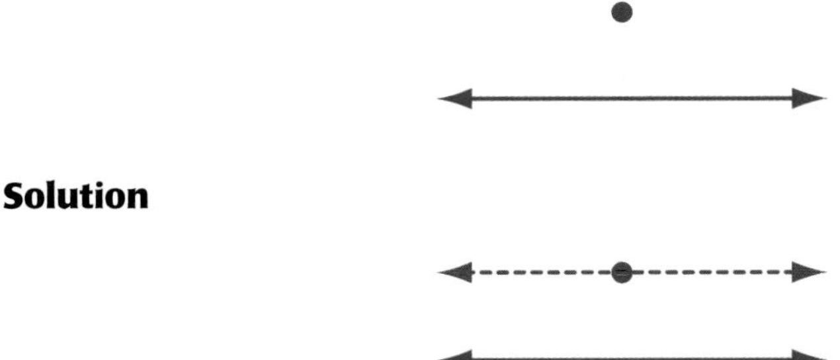

On a flat piece of paper, only one line is possible. This is based on the Euclidean geometry Parallel Postulate, which states: *"Through a given line and a point not on the line, there exists one and only one line through the point and parallel to the given line."*

Sometimes objects are drawn so that it appears that parallel lines are intersecting. The point where lines appear to intersect is called the **vanishing point.**

EXAMPLE 2 Use vanishing points to draw geometric figures

Identify the vanishing point by extending the parallel edges of the figure.

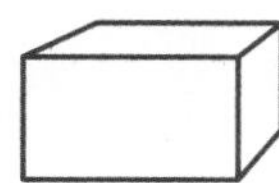

Solution

Extend the parallel edges of the rectangular prism, then identify the point where the lines intersect.

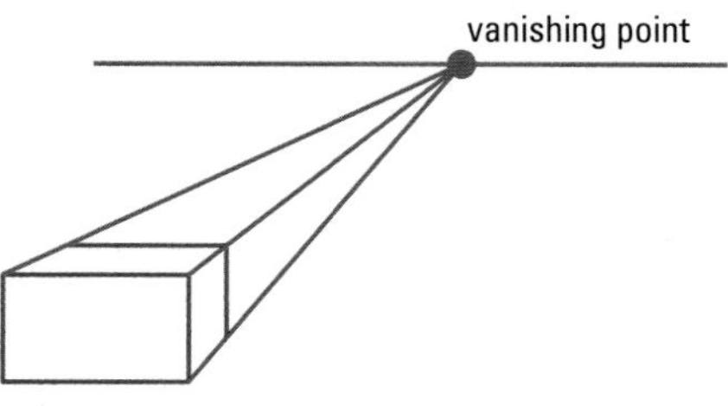

PRACTICE

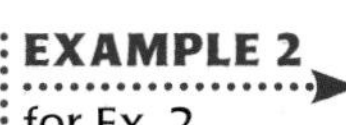

1. Longitude lines run from the North Pole to the South Pole on a globe. All longitude lines are perpendicular to the equator. Are the longitude lines parallel to each other? Would you use Euclidean or Non-Euclidean Geometry to verify this?

EXAMPLE 2
for Ex. 2

2. Extend the edges of the hexagonal prism to identify the vanishing point.

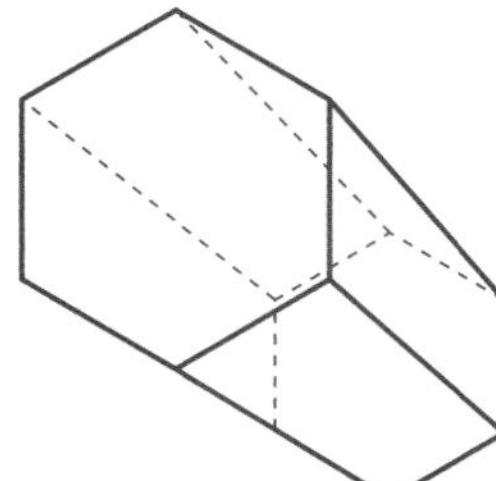

Contents of Student Resources

Skills Review Handbook — *pages 975–1009*

Extra Practice for Chapters 1–14 — *pages 1010–1023*

Tables — *pages 1024–1034*

English-Spanish Glossary — *pages 1035–1084*

Index — *pages 1085–1104*

Credits — *pages 1105–1106*

Worked-Out Solutions — *page WS1*

Selected Answers — *page SA1*

Skills Review Handbook

Operations with Positive and Negative Numbers

To add positive and negative numbers, you can use a number line.

To subtract any number, add its opposite.

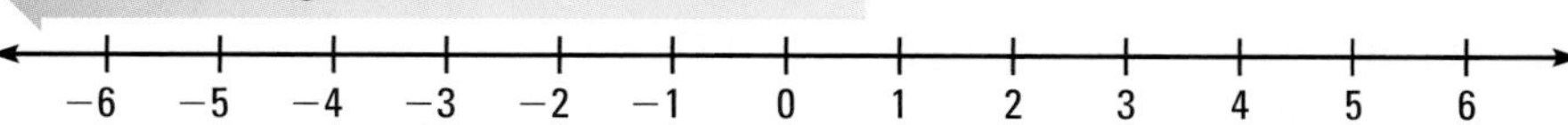

EXAMPLE **Add or subtract.**

a. $1 + (-5)$

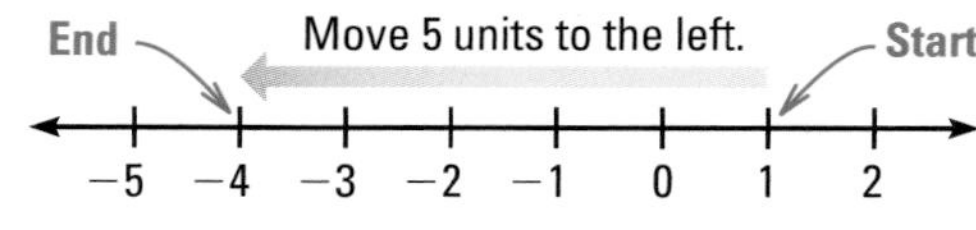

▸ $1 + (-5) = -4$

b. $-2 - (-5) = -2 + 5$ **The opposite of −5 is 5.**

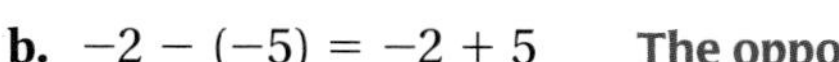

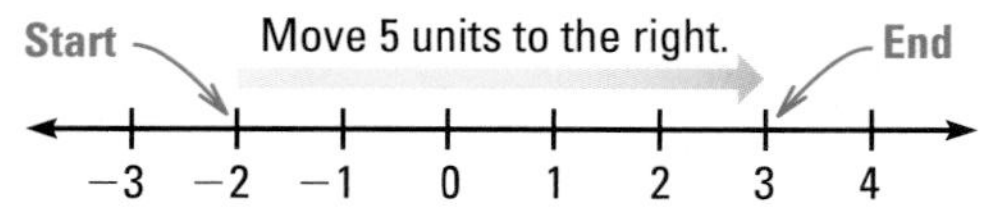

▸ $-2 - (-5) = 3$

To multiply or divide positive and negative numbers, use the following rules.

- The product or quotient of two numbers with the *same* sign is *positive.*
- The product or quotient of two numbers with *different* signs is *negative.*

EXAMPLE **Multiply or divide.**

a. $3 \cdot 7 = 21$

b. $-3(-7) = 21$

c. $18 \div 2 = 9$

d. $-18 \div (-2) = 9$

e. $-3(7) = -21$

f. $3(-7) = -21$

g. $-18 \div 2 = -9$

h. $18 \div (-2) = -9$

PRACTICE

Perform the indicated operation.

1. $2 + (-8)$ **2.** $5 - 12$ **3.** $-6(10)$ **4.** $-30 \div (-2)$ **5.** $-4 + 6$

6. $7(-5)$ **7.** $18 - 10$ **8.** $-7 + (-12)$ **9.** $11(4)$ **10.** $81 \div (-9)$

11. $-12 \div 3$ **12.** $-9(-8)$ **13.** $-1 + 13$ **14.** $45 \div (-9)$ **15.** $-6(12)$

16. $14 - (-9)$ **17.** $-32 \div 16$ **18.** $-23 + (-5)$ **19.** $-8 - (-5)$ **20.** $17 - (-18)$

21. $-9(-1)$ **22.** $-3 - (-11)$ **23.** $-18 \div (-3)$ **24.** $14 + (-7)$ **25.** $5(-3)$

26. $21 + (-8)$ **27.** $-2 - 10$ **28.** $-9 + 26$ **29.** $-20 \div (-4)$ **30.** $22 \div (-2)$

31. $-7(-6)$ **32.** $1 - 24$ **33.** $-15 - 2$ **34.** $0 + (-4)$ **35.** $16 \div 8$

SKILLS REVIEW HANDBOOK

Fractions, Decimals, and Percents

A **percent** is a ratio with a denominator of 100. The word *percent* means "per hundred," or "out of one hundred." The symbol for percent is %.

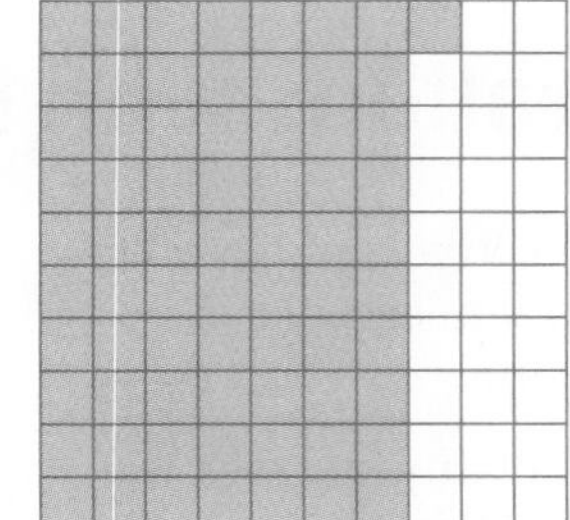

In the model at the right, 71 of the 100 squares are shaded. You can write the shaded part of the model as a fraction, a decimal, or a percent.

Fraction: seventy-one divided by one hundred, or $\frac{71}{100}$

Decimal: seventy-one hundredths, or 0.71

Percent: seventy-one percent, or 71%

EXAMPLE Write as a fraction.

a. $94\% = \frac{94}{100} = \frac{47}{50}$ **b.** $20\% = \frac{20}{100} = \frac{1}{5}$ **c.** $0.3 = \text{three tenths} = \frac{3}{10}$

EXAMPLE Write as a decimal.

a. $15\% = \frac{15}{100} = 0.15$ **b.** $106\% = \frac{106}{100} = 1.06$ **c.** $\frac{5}{8} = 5 \div 8 = 0.625$

EXAMPLE Write as a percent.

a. $0.41 = \frac{41}{100} = 41\%$ **b.** $0.8 = \frac{8}{10} = \frac{80}{100} = 80\%$ **c.** $\frac{5}{4} = \frac{5 \cdot 25}{4 \cdot 25} = \frac{125}{100} = 125\%$

PRACTICE

Write as a fraction.

1. 0.65 **2.** 0.08 **3.** 1.5 **4.** 0.13 **5.** 0.7

6. 50% **7.** 26% **8.** 3% **9.** 95% **10.** 110%

Write as a decimal.

11. $\frac{1}{4}$ **12.** $\frac{9}{10}$ **13.** $\frac{30}{25}$ **14.** $\frac{2}{5}$ **15.** $\frac{3}{8}$

16. 16% **17.** 142% **18.** 1% **19.** 30% **20.** 6.5%

Write as a percent.

21. 0.6 **22.** 0.24 **23.** 1.3 **24.** 0.07 **25.** 0.45

26. $\frac{1}{10}$ **27.** $\frac{4}{5}$ **28.** $\frac{17}{20}$ **29.** $\frac{5}{2}$ **30.** $\frac{3}{16}$

Calculating with Percents

You can use equations to calculate with percents. Replace words with symbols as shown in the table at the right. Below are three types of questions you can answer with percents.

Word	what	of	is
Symbol	n	$\times$	$=$

EXAMPLE **Answer the question.**

a. What is 15% of 20?

$n = 0.15 \times 20$

$n = 3$

3 is 15% of 20.

b. What percent of 8 is 6?

$n \times 8 = 6$

$n = 6 \div 8 = 0.75 = 75\%$

75% of 8 is 6.

c. 80% of what number is 4?

$0.8 \times n = 4$

$n = 4 \div 0.8 = 5$

80% of 5 is 4.

To find a percent of change, calculate $\frac{\text{Amount of increase or decrease}}{\text{Original amount}}$.

EXAMPLE **Find the percent of change.**

a. A class increases from 21 students to 25 students.

$\frac{25 - 21}{21} = \frac{4}{21} \approx 0.19 = 19\%$ increase

b. A price decreases from \$12 to \$9.

$\frac{12 - 9}{12} = \frac{3}{12} = 0.25 = 25\%$ decrease

PRACTICE

Answer the question.

1. What is 98% of 200?
2. What is 25% of 8?
3. What is 30% of 128?
4. What is 5% of 700?
5. What is 100% of 17?
6. What is 150% of 14?
7. What is 0.2% of 500?
8. What is 6.5% of 3000?
9. What percent of 100 is 54?
10. What percent of 18 is 9?
11. What percent of 80 is 8?
12. What percent of 15 is 20?
13. What percent of 30 is 6?
14. What percent of 5 is 8?
15. What percent of 50 is 1?
16. 50% of what number is 6?
17. 55% of what number is 44?
18. 10% of what number is 6?
19. 75% of what number is 45?
20. 1% of what number is 2?
21. 90% of what number is 63?
22. 12% of what number is 60?
23. 200% of what number is 16?

Find the percent of change. Round to the nearest percent if necessary.

24. A class increases from 20 to 28 students.
25. Time decreases from 60 to 45 minutes.
26. A price is reduced from \$200 to \$180.
27. Votes increase from 200 to 300.
28. A test is shortened from 40 to 32 items.
29. Membership increases from 820 to 1605.
30. A wage rises from \$8.75 to \$10.00.
31. The temperature drops from 24°F to 5°F.

Factors and Multiples

Prime Numbers Less Than 100
2, 3, 5, 7, 11, 13, 17, 19, 23, 29, 31, 37, 41, 43, 47, 53, 59, 61, 67, 71, 73, 79, 83, 89, 97

Factors are numbers or expressions that are multiplied together. A **prime number** is a whole number greater than 1 that has exactly two whole number factors, 1 and itself. The table shows all the prime numbers less than 100. A **composite number** is a whole number greater than 1 that has more than two whole number factors.

When you write a composite number as a product of prime numbers, you are writing its **prime factorization**.

EXAMPLE **Write the prime factorization of 60.**

Use a *factor tree*. Write 60 at the top. Then draw two branches and write 60 as the product of two factors. Continue to draw branches until all the factors are prime numbers. Two factor trees for 60 are given at the right. Both show $60 = 2 \cdot 2 \cdot 3 \cdot 5$.

▸ The prime factorization of 60 is $2^2 \cdot 3 \cdot 5$.

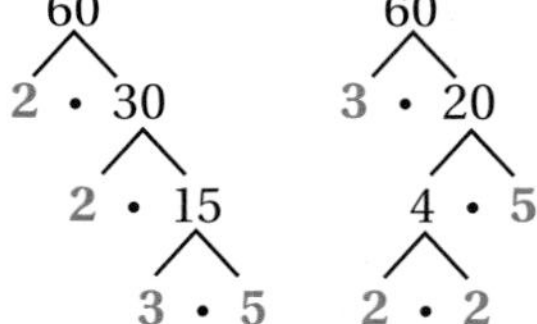

A whole number that is a factor of two or more nonzero whole numbers is a **common factor** of the numbers. The largest of the common factors is the **greatest common factor (GCF)**.

EXAMPLE **Find the greatest common factor (GCF) of 18 and 45.**

Method 1 **List factors.**

Factors of 18: 1, 2, 3, 6, 9, 18

Factors of 45: 1, 3, 5, 9, 15, 45

The GCF is 9, the greatest of the common factors.

Method 2 **Use prime factorization.**

Prime factorization of 18: $2 \cdot 3 \cdot 3$

Prime factorization of 45: $3 \cdot 3 \cdot 5$

The GCF is the product of the common prime factors: $3 \cdot 3 = 9$.

A **multiple** of a whole number is the product of the number and any nonzero whole number. A **common multiple** of two or more numbers is a multiple of all of the numbers. The **least common multiple (LCM)** is the smallest of the common multiples.

EXAMPLE **Find the least common multiple (LCM) of 12 and 15.**

Method 1 **List multiples.**

Multiples of 12: 12, 24, 36, 48, 60, . . .

Multiples of 15: 15, 30, 45, 60, . . .

The LCM is 60, the least of the common multiples.

Method 2 **Use prime factorization.**

Prime factorization of 12: $2^2 \cdot 3$

Prime factorization of 15: $3 \cdot 5$

Form the LCM of the numbers by writing each prime factor to the highest power it occurs in either number: $2^2 \cdot 3 \cdot 5 = 60$.

The **least common denominator (LCD)** of two fractions is the least common multiple of the denominators. Use the LCD to add or subtract fractions with different denominators.

EXAMPLE **Add:** $\frac{3}{10} + \frac{5}{8}$

The least common multiple of the denominators, 10 and 8, is 40.
So, the least common denominator (LCD) of the fractions is 40.

Rewrite the fractions using the LCD of 40: $\frac{3}{10} = \frac{3 \cdot 4}{10 \cdot 4} = \frac{12}{40}$ and $\frac{5}{8} = \frac{5 \cdot 5}{8 \cdot 5} = \frac{25}{40}$

Add the numerators and keep the same denominator: $\frac{3}{10} + \frac{5}{8} = \frac{12}{40} + \frac{25}{40} = \frac{37}{40}$

PRACTICE

Write the prime factorization of the number. If the number is prime, write *prime*.

1. 42 **2.** 104 **3.** 75 **4.** 23 **5.** 70

6. 27 **7.** 72 **8.** 180 **9.** 47 **10.** 100

11. 88 **12.** 49 **13.** 83 **14.** 142 **15.** 32

Find the greatest common factor (GCF) of the numbers.

16. 4, 6 **17.** 24, 40 **18.** 10, 25 **19.** 55, 44 **20.** 28, 35

21. 8, 20 **22.** 5, 8 **23.** 15, 12 **24.** 16, 32 **25.** 70, 90

26. 2, 18 **27.** 9, 21 **28.** 36, 42, 54 **29.** 7, 12, 17 **30.** 45, 63, 81

Find the least common multiple (LCM) of the numbers.

31. 4, 16 **32.** 2, 14 **33.** 5, 6 **34.** 16, 24 **35.** 6, 8

36. 12, 20 **37.** 3, 6 **38.** 18, 8 **39.** 9, 12 **40.** 9, 5

41. 10, 15 **42.** 7, 9 **43.** 40, 4, 5 **44.** 25, 30, 3 **45.** 27, 81, 33

Perform the indicated operation(s). Simplify the result.

46. $\frac{1}{2} + \frac{3}{8}$ **47.** $\frac{3}{4} - \frac{5}{16}$ **48.** $\frac{7}{10} - \frac{3}{5}$ **49.** $\frac{1}{2} + \frac{1}{3}$

50. $\frac{5}{12} + \frac{1}{3}$ **51.** $\frac{4}{5} + \frac{1}{8}$ **52.** $\frac{1}{10} + \frac{3}{4}$ **53.** $\frac{5}{6} - \frac{1}{2}$

54. $\frac{7}{8} - \frac{11}{16}$ **55.** $\frac{9}{10} - \frac{1}{3}$ **56.** $\frac{2}{3} - \frac{1}{6}$ **57.** $\frac{1}{4} + \frac{2}{5}$

58. $\frac{4}{5} + \frac{1}{12} - \frac{5}{6}$ **59.** $\frac{3}{2} - \frac{3}{10} - \frac{3}{4}$ **60.** $\frac{9}{10} - \frac{1}{5} - \frac{1}{2}$ **61.** $\frac{7}{8} + \frac{3}{16} - \frac{1}{4}$

62. $\frac{8}{9} + \frac{2}{3} - \frac{7}{12}$ **63.** $\frac{1}{6} + \frac{4}{15} + \frac{1}{3}$ **64.** $\frac{1}{2} + \frac{2}{3} + \frac{1}{4}$ **65.** $\frac{15}{16} - \frac{7}{10} + \frac{1}{2}$

66. $\frac{5}{24} - \frac{1}{6} + \frac{7}{12}$ **67.** $\frac{1}{2} + \frac{3}{5} - \frac{1}{4}$ **68.** $\frac{5}{6} - \frac{3}{5} - \frac{2}{15}$ **69.** $\frac{4}{9} + \frac{3}{4} - \frac{7}{12}$

Ratios and Proportions

A **ratio** uses division to compare two quantities.

You can write a ratio of two quantities a and b, where b is not equal to 0, in three ways.

You should write ratios in simplest form.

Three Ways to Write the Ratio of *a* to *b*		
a to b	$a:b$	$\frac{a}{b}$

EXAMPLE **Write the ratio of 12 boys to 16 girls in three ways.**

First write the ratio as a fraction in simplest form: $\frac{\text{Boys}}{\text{Girls}} = \frac{12}{16} = \frac{12 \div 4}{16 \div 4} = \frac{3}{4}$

▶ Three ways to write the ratio of boys to girls are 3 to 4, 3:4, and $\frac{3}{4}$.

A **proportion** is an equation stating that two ratios are equal.

You can use cross multiplication to solve a proportion.

Using Cross Multiplication to Solve Proportions
If $\frac{a}{b} = \frac{c}{d}$, where $b \neq 0$ and $d \neq 0$, then $ad = bc$.

EXAMPLE **Solve the proportion.**

a. $\frac{5}{9} = \frac{n}{54}$

$5 \cdot 54 = 9 \cdot n$ Cross multiply.

$270 = 9n$ Simplify.

$30 = n$ Solve for n.

b. $\frac{x}{40} = \frac{3}{8}$

$x \cdot 8 = 40 \cdot 3$ Cross multiply.

$8x = 120$ Simplify.

$x = 15$ Solve for x.

PRACTICE

Write the ratio in simplest form. Express the answer in three ways.

1. 3 to 9 **2.** 16 to 24 **3.** 10 to 8 **4.** 6 to 2

5. 25 to 30 **6.** 60 to 10 **7.** 4 to 4 **8.** 8 to 20

9. 32 to 72 **10.** 42 to 15 **11.** 14 to 2 **12.** 12 to 15

Solve the proportion.

13. $\frac{x}{14} = \frac{12}{24}$ **14.** $\frac{8}{24} = \frac{d}{36}$ **15.** $\frac{15}{n} = \frac{3}{4}$ **16.** $\frac{9}{45} = \frac{5}{h}$

17. $\frac{a}{6} = \frac{4}{12}$ **18.** $\frac{13}{t} = \frac{91}{7}$ **19.** $\frac{75}{120} = \frac{r}{8}$ **20.** $\frac{b}{90} = \frac{2}{3}$

21. $\frac{4}{11} = \frac{n}{110}$ **22.** $\frac{5}{z} = \frac{150}{90}$ **23.** $\frac{9}{8} = \frac{x}{6}$ **24.** $\frac{72}{105} = \frac{24}{m}$

25. $\frac{17}{33} = \frac{51}{a}$ **26.** $\frac{20}{125} = \frac{24}{n}$ **27.** $\frac{16}{144} = \frac{8}{x}$ **28.** $\frac{96}{6} = \frac{t}{3}$

Converting Units of Measurement

The table of measures on page 1025 gives many statements of equivalent measures. Using each statement, you can write two different conversion factors.

Statement of Equivalent Measures	Conversion Factors
100 cm = 1 m	$\frac{100\text{ cm}}{1\text{ m}} = 1$ and $\frac{1\text{ m}}{100\text{ cm}} = 1$

To convert from one unit of measurement to another, multiply by a conversion factor. Use the one that will eliminate the starting unit and keep the desired unit.

EXAMPLE **Copy and complete.**

a. 3.5 m = ? cm

$3.5\text{ m} \times \frac{100\text{ cm}}{1\text{ m}} = (3.5 \times 100)\text{ cm} = 350\text{ cm}$

▶ So, 3.5 m = 350 cm.

b. 620 cm = ? m

$620\text{ cm} \times \frac{1\text{ m}}{100\text{ cm}} = \frac{620}{100}\text{ m} = 6.2\text{ m}$

▶ So, 620 cm = 6.2 m.

Sometimes you need to use more than one conversion factor.

EXAMPLE **Copy and complete: 7 days = ? sec**

Find the appropriate statements of equivalent measures.

24 h = 1 day, 60 min = 1 h, and 60 sec = 1 min

Write conversion factors: $\frac{24\text{ h}}{1\text{ day}}$, $\frac{60\text{ min}}{1\text{ h}}$, and $\frac{60\text{ sec}}{1\text{ min}}$

Multiply by conversion factors to eliminate days and keep seconds.

$7\text{ days} \times \frac{24\text{ h}}{1\text{ day}} \times \frac{60\text{ min}}{1\text{ h}} \times \frac{60\text{ sec}}{1\text{ min}} = (7 \times 24 \times 60 \times 60)\text{ sec} = 604{,}800\text{ sec}$

▶ So, 7 days = 604,800 sec.

PRACTICE

Copy and complete.

1. 6 L = ? mL
2. 2 mi = ? ft
3. 80 oz = ? lb
4. 4 days = ? h
5. 77 mm = ? cm
6. 5 gal = ? qt
7. 48 ft = ? yd
8. 1500 mL = ? L
9. 40 m = ? cm
10. 125 lb = ? oz
11. 800 g = ? kg
12. 900 sec = ? min
13. 72 in. = ? ft
14. 2.5 ton = ? lb
15. 90 min = ? h
16. 65,000 mg = ? g
17. 100 yd = ? in.
18. 3.5 kg = ? g
19. 6 pt = ? qt
20. 1 week = ? min
21. 2 oz = ? lb
22. 1 km = ? mm
23. 1 mi = ? in.
24. 5 gal = ? c
25. 288 in.^{2} = ? ft^2
26. 24 pt = ? gal
27. 4 kg = ? g
28. 7 hr = ? sec

Scientific Notation

Scientific notation is a way to write numbers using powers of 10. A number is written in **scientific notation** if it has the form $c \times 10^n$ where $1 \le c < 10$ and n is an integer. The table shows some powers of ten in order from least to greatest.

Power of Ten	10^{-3}	10^{-2}	10^{-1}	10^0	10^1	10^2	10^3
Value	0.001	0.01	0.1	1	10	100	1000

EXAMPLE Write the number in scientific notation.

a. 12,800,000 — Standard form

12,800,000 — Move the decimal point 7 places to the left.

1.28×10^7 — Use 7 as an exponent of 10.

b. 0.0000039 — Standard form

0.0000039 — Move the decimal point 6 places to the right.

3.9×10^{-6} — Use −6 as an exponent of 10.

EXAMPLE Write the number in standard form.

a. 6.1×10^4 — Scientific notation

6.1×10^4 — The exponent of 10 is 4.

61,000 — Move the decimal point 4 places to the right.

61,000 — Standard form

b. 5.74×10^{-5} — Scientific notation

5.74×10^{-5} — The exponent of 10 is −5.

0.0000574 — Move the decimal point 5 places to the left.

0.0000574 — Standard form

PRACTICE

Write the number in scientific notation.

1. 0.6
2. 25,000,000
3. 0.08
4. 0.00542
5. 40.8
6. 7
7. 0.000385
8. 8,145,000
9. 41,236
10. 0.0000016
11. 486,000
12. 0.000000009
13. 0.01002
14. 1,000,000,000
15. 7050.5
16. 0.37
17. 9850
18. 0.0000206
19. 805
20. 0.0005

Write the number in standard form.

21. 5×10^3
22. 4×10^{-2}
23. 8.2×10^{-1}
24. 6.93×10^2
25. 3.2×10^{-3}
26. 9.01×10^{-5}
27. 7.345×10^5
28. 2.38×10^{-2}
29. 1.814×10^0
30. 2.7×10^8
31. 1×10^6
32. 4.9×10^{-4}
33. 8×10^{-6}
34. 5.6×10^4
35. 1.87×10^9
36. 7×10^{-4}
37. 6.08×10^6
38. 9.009×10^{-3}
39. 3.401×10^7
40. 5.32×10^1

Significant Digits

Significant digits indicate how precisely a number is known. Use the following guidelines to determine the number of significant digits.

- All nonzero digits are significant.
- All zeros that appear between two nonzero digits are significant.
- For a decimal, all zeros that appear after the last nonzero digit are significant. For a whole number, you cannot tell whether any zeros after the last nonzero digit are significant, so you should assume that they are not significant.

Sometimes calculations involve measurements that have various numbers of significant digits. In this case, a general rule is to carry all digits through the calculation and then round the result to the same number of significant digits as the measurement with the *fewest* significant digits. When you calculate with units that cannot be divided into fractional parts, such as number of people, consider only the significant digits of the other number(s).

EXAMPLE **Perform the calculation. Write your answer with the appropriate number of significant digits.**

a.

12.6	**3 significant digits**
× 0.05	**1 significant digit**
0.63	**The product has 2 significant digits.**
0.6	**Round to 1 significant digit.**

b.

840	**2 significant digits**
+ 702	**3 significant digits**
1542	**The sum has 4 significant digits.**
1500	**Round to 2 significant digits.**

c. \$61.20 restaurant bill ÷ 6 people

The number of people is exact, so consider only the 4 significant digits of the bill, \$61.20. The answer should have 4 significant digits.

\$61.20 ÷ 6 = **\$10.20**

▸ Each person pays \$10.20.

PRACTICE

Perform the calculation. Write your answer with the appropriate number of significant digits.

1. 600 + 30
2. 5 − 2.6
3. 12 • 6.75
4. 0.098 + 0.14 + 0.369
5. 3.6053 − 1.720
6. 40 ÷ 3.5
7. 8.0 − 3.1
8. 31.7 • 6.8 • 0.435
9. 30.5 • 6.40
10. 3.18 + 2.0005
11. 0.088 ÷ 2.44
12. 8650 + 380 − 49
13. 4016 − 3007
14. 1.35 + 14.8
15. 320 ÷ 18
16. 38.1 • 3.04 ÷ 0.024
17. \$1.45 per notebook • 12 notebooks
18. 10.0 liters of water − 4.5 liters of water
19. 260 pints of milk ÷ 106 students
20. 0.5 yard of fabric + 0.87 yard of fabric
21. 27,973 books ÷ 11 libraries
22. 12.76 gallons of gas + 6.08 gallons of gas
23. \$6.95 per ticket • 180 tickets
24. 1540 pounds − 160 pounds − 85 pounds

Writing Algebraic Expressions

To solve a problem using algebra, you often need to write a phrase as an algebraic expression.

EXAMPLE **Write the phrase as an algebraic expression.**

a. 6 less than a number

"Less than" indicates subtraction.

▶ $n - 6$

b. The cube of a number

"Cube" indicates raising to the third power.

▶ n^3

c. Double a number

"Double" indicates multiplication by 2.

▶ $2n$

EXAMPLE **Write an algebraic expression to answer the question.**

a. Rebecca walks three times as far to school as Meghan does. If Meghan walks m blocks to school, how many blocks to school does Rebecca walk?

▶ $3m$

b. Kate is 8 inches taller than Noah. If Noah is n inches tall, how tall is Kate?

▶ $n + 8$

PRACTICE

Write the phrase as an algebraic expression.

1. 8 more than a number
2. 10 times a number
3. Twice a number
4. 6 less than a number
5. One fifth of a number
6. 4 greater than a number
7. 5 times a number
8. A number squared
9. 25% of a number
10. Half a number
11. 2 less than a number
12. The square root of a number

Write an algebraic expression to answer the question.

13. Allison is 4 years younger than her sister Camille. If Camille is c years old, how old is Allison?

14. Ryan bought a movie ticket for x dollars. He paid with a \$20 bill. How much change should Ryan get?

15. Bridget spent \$5 more than Tom spent at the mall. If Tom spent x dollars, how much did Bridget spend?

16. Marc has twice as many baseball cards as hockey cards. If Marc has h hockey cards, how many baseball cards does he have?

17. Elizabeth's ballet class is 45 minutes long. If Elizabeth is m minutes late for ballet class, how many minutes will she spend in class?

18. Steve drove x miles per hour for 5 hours. How many miles did Steve drive?

19. Wendy bought 10 pens priced at x dollars each. How much did she spend?

Binomial Products

A **monomial** is a number, a variable, or the product of a number and one or more variables. A **binomial** is the sum of two monomials. In other words, a binomial is a polynomial with two terms. You can use a geometric model to find the product of two binomials.

EXAMPLE **Simplify $(2x + 1)(x + 3)$.**

Draw a rectangle with dimensions $2x + 1$ and $x + 3$. Use the dimensions to divide the rectangle into parts. Then find the area of each part. The binomial product $(2x + 1)(x + 3)$ is the sum of the areas of all the parts.

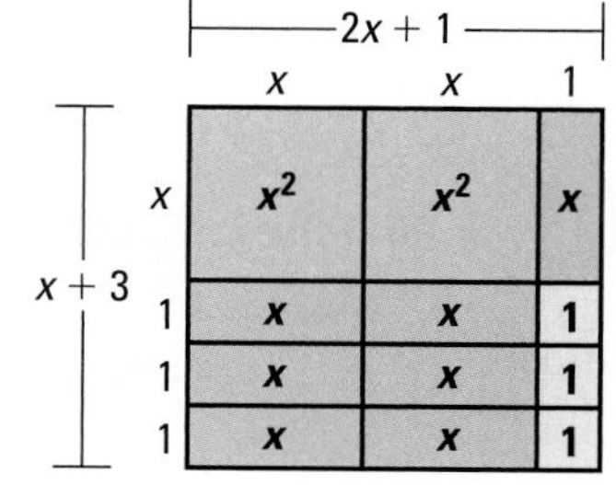

There are 2 blue parts with area x^2, 7 green parts with area x, and 3 yellow parts with area 1.

$$(2x + 1)(x + 3) = 2x^2 + 7x + 3$$

Another way to find the product of two binomials is to use the distributive property systematically. Multiply the *first* terms, the *outer* terms, the *inner* terms, and the *last* terms of the binomials. This is called **FOIL** for the words **F**irst, **O**uter, **I**nner, and **L**ast.

EXAMPLE **Simplify $(x + 2)(4x - 5)$.**

First, Outer, Inner, Last

$(x + 2)(4x - 5) = x(4x) + x(-5) + 2(4x) + 2(-5)$ **Use FOIL.**

$= 4x^2 - 5x + 8x - 10$ **Multiply.**

$= 4x^2 + 3x - 10$ **Combine like terms.**

PRACTICE

Simplify.

1. $(a + 5)(a + 3)$ **2.** $(m + 4)(m + 11)$ **3.** $(t + 8)(t + 7)$

4. $(z + 1)(z + 6)$ **5.** $(y + 4)(y + 2)$ **6.** $(x + 9)(x + 9)$

7. $(y - 2)^2$ **8.** $(n + 6)^2$ **9.** $(4 - z)^2$

10. $(a + 10)(a - 10)$ **11.** $(y + 3)(y - 7)$ **12.** $(k + 1)^2$

13. $(5x - 4)(5x + 4)$ **14.** $(3 + n)^2$ **15.** $(c + 5)(2c - 7)$

16. $(a + 5)(a + 5)$ **17.** $(7 - z)(7 + z)$ **18.** $(3x - 8)(x - 6)$

19. $(4a + 3)^2$ **20.** $(3 - g)(2g + 3)$ **21.** $(4 - x)(8 + x)$

22. $(3n - 1)(n - 4)$ **23.** $(-a + 9)(a - 9)$ **24.** $(8x + 1)(x + 1)$

25. $(5x + 2)(2x - 5)$ **26.** $(2d - 5)(3d - 1)$ **27.** $(-4z + 3)(6z - 1)$

SKILLS REVIEW HANDBOOK

LCDs of Rational Expressions

A **rational expression** is a fraction whose numerator and denominator are nonzero polynomials. The **least common denominator (LCD)** of two rational expressions is the least common multiple of the denominators. To find the LCD, follow these three steps:

STEP 1 **Write** each denominator as the product of its factors.

STEP 2 **Write** the product consisting of the highest power of each factor that appears in either denominator.

STEP 3 **Simplify** the product from Step 2 to write the LCD.

EXAMPLE

Find the least common denominator of the rational expressions.

a. $\frac{2}{5xy}$ and $\frac{2}{y^3}$

STEP 1 **Factors:**
$5xy = 5 \cdot x \cdot y$
$y^3 = y^3$

STEP 2 **Product:** $5 \cdot x \cdot y^3$

STEP 3 **LCD:** $5xy^3$

b. $\frac{3}{8x^2}$ and $\frac{1}{12x}$

Factors:
$8x^2 = 2^3 \cdot x^2$
$12x = 2^2 \cdot 3 \cdot x$

Product: $2^3 \cdot 3 \cdot x^2$

LCD: $24x^2$

c. $\frac{-1}{3x+6}$ and $\frac{x}{x^2 - 3x - 10}$

Factors:
$3x + 6 = 3 \cdot (x + 2)$
$x^2 - 3x - 10 = (x + 2) \cdot (x - 5)$

Product: $3 \cdot (x + 2) \cdot (x - 5)$

LCD: $3(x + 2)(x - 5)$

PRACTICE

Find the least common denominator of the rational expressions.

1. $\frac{1}{2ab}$ and $\frac{4}{a^2}$
2. $\frac{5}{6k^2}$ and $\frac{6}{7k^2}$
3. $\frac{2}{z^3}$ and $\frac{2}{z^2}$
4. $\frac{4}{5x}$ and $\frac{-3}{10x}$
5. $\frac{m}{14}$ and $\frac{1}{18m}$
6. $\frac{19}{20xy}$ and $\frac{3}{16xy}$
7. $\frac{1}{3y^2}$ and $\frac{1}{3y}$
8. $\frac{-4}{9ab^2}$ and $\frac{2}{21a^2b}$
9. $\frac{n}{n+2}$ and $\frac{n^2}{n-2}$
10. $\frac{-1}{x-1}$ and $\frac{3}{x+3}$
11. $\frac{-8}{5n+5}$ and $\frac{4}{n+1}$
12. $\frac{y}{8}$ and $\frac{1}{2y+8}$
13. $\frac{1}{2m-6}$ and $\frac{2}{3m-9}$
14. $\frac{a}{n^2}$ and $\frac{-a}{n^2-6n}$
15. $\frac{1}{x-4}$ and $\frac{1}{(x-4)^2}$
16. $\frac{3}{4x+12}$ and $\frac{4}{6x+18}$
17. $\frac{1}{2n^3}$ and $\frac{-9}{10n^2+8n}$
18. $\frac{10}{15b-30}$ and $\frac{17b}{9b-18}$
19. $\frac{-5}{(k+3)^4}$ and $\frac{3}{(k+3)^2}$
20. $\frac{1}{y-5}$ and $\frac{8}{3y-15}$
21. $\frac{n^2}{10n+20}$ and $\frac{n}{7n+14}$
22. $\frac{20}{5z-40}$ and $\frac{1}{9z-56}$
23. $\frac{2a}{a^2+4a+4}$ and $\frac{2}{a+2}$
24. $\frac{1}{2z-6}$ and $\frac{-1}{z^2-z-6}$
25. $\frac{3k}{k-3}$ and $\frac{-k}{k^2-5k+6}$
26. $\frac{x}{x^2-9}$ and $\frac{-x}{x^2+3x-18}$
27. $\frac{m^2}{m^2-11m+28}$ and $\frac{-5}{m^2+5m-45}$

The Coordinate Plane

A **coordinate plane** is formed by the intersection of a horizontal number line called the **x-axis** and a vertical number line called the **y-axis**. The axes meet at a point called the **origin** and divide the coordinate plane into four **quadrants**, numbered I, II, III, and IV.

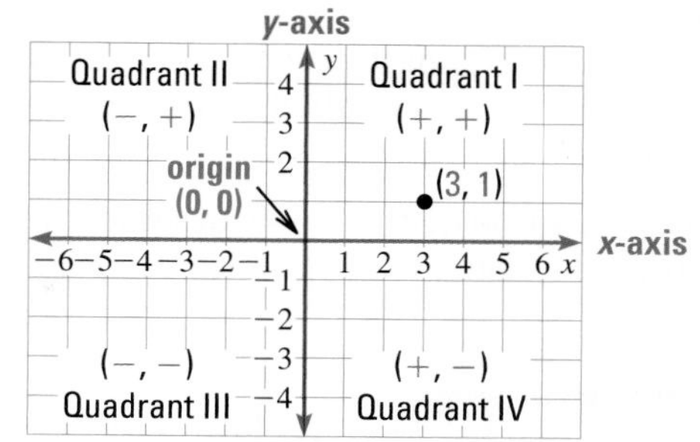

Each point in a coordinate plane is represented by an **ordered pair**. The first number is the **x-coordinate**, and the second number is the **y-coordinate**.

The ordered pair (3, 1) is graphed at the right. The x-coordinate is 3, and the y-coordinate is 1. So, the point is right 3 units and up 1 unit from the origin.

EXAMPLE **Graph the points $A(2, -1)$ and $B(-4, 0)$ in a coordinate plane.**

$A(2, -1)$ Start at the origin.
The x-coordinate is 2, so move right 2 units.
The y-coordinate is -1, so move down 1 unit.
Draw a point at $(2, -1)$ and label it A.

$B(-4, 0)$ Start at the origin.
The x-coordinate is -4, so move left 4 units.
The y-coordinate is 0, so move up 0 units.
Draw a point at $(-4, 0)$ and label it B.

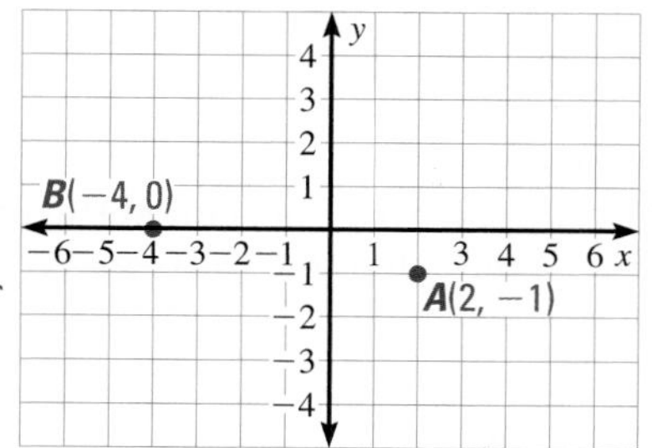

PRACTICE

Graph the points in a coordinate plane.

1. $A(7, 2)$	**2.** $B(6, -7)$	**3.** $C(2, -3)$	**4.** $D(-8, 0)$	**5.** $E(-4, -8)$
6. $F(1, 3)$	**7.** $G(3, 0)$	**8.** $H(1, -5)$	**9.** $I(0, -2)$	**10.** $J(-6, 5)$
11. $K(5, 8)$	**12.** $L(8, -2)$	**13.** $M(-3, -4)$	**14.** $N(-7, 8)$	**15.** $P(-5, 1)$
16. $Q(-2, -6)$	**17.** $R(0, 6)$	**18.** $S(-4, -1)$	**19.** $T(4, 4)$	**20.** $V(-3, 7)$

Give the coordinates and the quadrant or axis of the point.

21. A	**22.** B	**23.** C
24. D	**25.** E	**26.** F
27. G	**28.** H	**29.** J
30. K	**31.** L	**32.** M
33. N	**34.** O	**35.** P
36. Q	**37.** R	**38.** S
39. T	**40.** U	**41.** V
42. W	**43.** X	**44.** Y

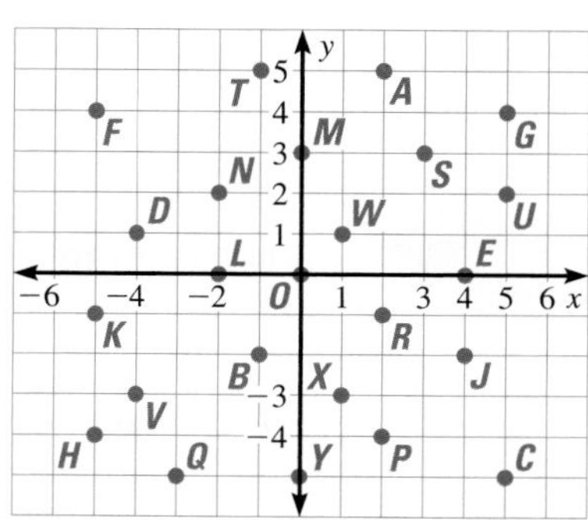

SKILLS REVIEW HANDBOOK

Transformations

A **transformation** is a change made to the position or to the size of a figure. Each point (x, y) of the figure is mapped to a new point, and the new figure is called an **image**.

A **translation** is a transformation in which each point of a figure moves the same distance in the same direction. A figure and its translated image are congruent.

Translation a Units Horizontally and b Units Vertically
$(x, y) \rightarrow (x + a, y + b)$

EXAMPLE **Translate $\overline{FG}$ right 3 units and down 1 unit.**

To move right 3 units, use $a = 3$. To move down 1 unit, use $b = -1$. So, use $(x, y) \rightarrow (x + 3, y + (-1))$ with each endpoint.

$F(2, 4) \rightarrow F'(2 + 3, 4 + (-1)) = F'(5, 3)$
$G(1, 1) \rightarrow G'(1 + 3, 1 + (-1)) = G'(4, 0)$

Graph the endpoints (5, 3) and (4, 0). Then draw the image.

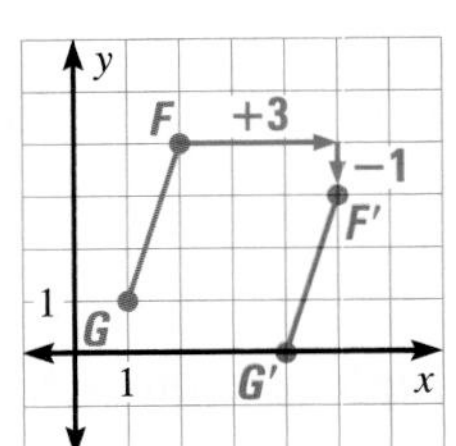

A **reflection** is a transformation in which a figure is reflected, or flipped, in a line, called the **line of reflection**. A figure and its reflected image are congruent.

Reflection in x-axis	Reflection in y-axis
$(x, y) \rightarrow (x, -y)$	$(x, y) \rightarrow (-x, y)$

EXAMPLE **Reflect $\triangle ABC$ in the y-axis.**

Use $(x, y) \rightarrow (-x, y)$ with each vertex.

$A(4, 3) \rightarrow A'(-4, 3)$ **Change each**
$B(1, 2) \rightarrow B'(-1, 2)$ **x-coordinate**
$C(3, 1) \rightarrow C'(-3, 1)$ **to its opposite.**

Graph the new vertices. Then draw the image.

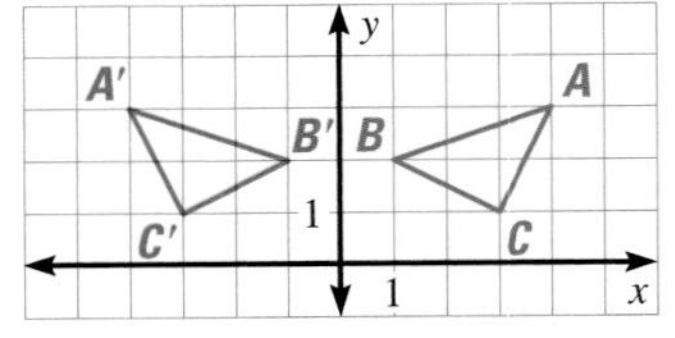

A **rotation** is a transformation in which a figure is turned about a fixed point, called the **center of rotation**. The direction can be clockwise or counterclockwise. A figure and its rotated image are congruent.

Rotation About the Origin	
180° either direction	$(x, y) \rightarrow (-x, -y)$
90° clockwise	$(x, y) \rightarrow (y, -x)$
90° counterclockwise	$(x, y) \rightarrow (-y, x)$

EXAMPLE **Rotate $RSTV$ 180° about the origin.**

Use $(x, y) \rightarrow (-x, -y)$ with each vertex.

$R(2, 2) \rightarrow R'(-2, -2)$ **Change every**
$S(4, 2) \rightarrow S'(-4, -2)$ **coordinate**
$T(4, 1) \rightarrow T'(-4, -1)$ **to its opposite.**
$V(1, 0) \rightarrow V'(-1, 0)$

Graph the new vertices. Then draw the image.

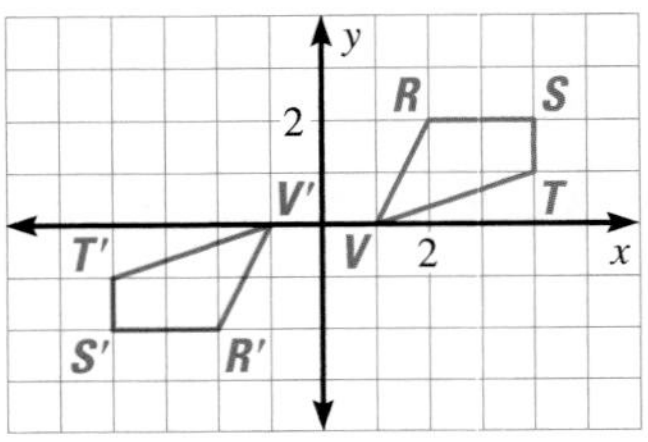

A **dilation** is a transformation in which a figure stretches or shrinks depending on the dilation's **scale factor**. A figure *stretches* if $k > 1$ and *shrinks* if $0 < k < 1$. A figure and its dilated image are similar.

Dilation with Scale Factor k with Respect to the Origin
$(x, y) \rightarrow (kx, ky)$

EXAMPLE **Dilate *JKLM* using a scale factor of 0.5.**

The scale factor is $k = 0.5$, so multiply every coordinate by 0.5. Use $(x, y) \rightarrow (0.5x, 0.5y)$ with each vertex.

$J(4, 4) \rightarrow J'(0.5 \cdot 4, 0.5 \cdot 4) = J'(2, 2)$
$K(6, 4) \rightarrow K'(0.5 \cdot 6, 0.5 \cdot 4) = K'(3, 2)$
$L(6, -1) \rightarrow L'(0.5 \cdot 6, 0.5 \cdot (-1)) = L'(3, -0.5)$
$M(4, -1) \rightarrow M'(0.5 \cdot 4, 0.5 \cdot (-1)) = M'(2, -0.5)$

Graph the new vertices. Then draw the image.

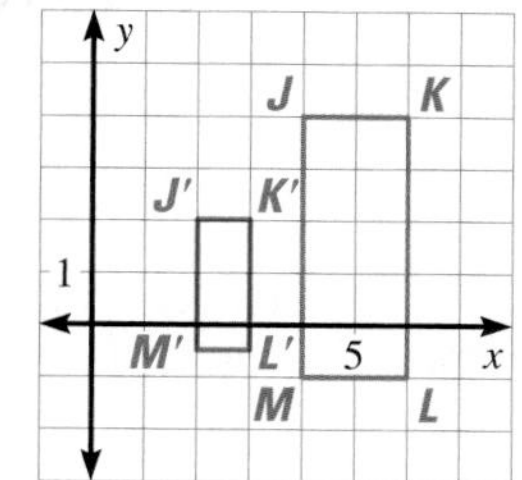

PRACTICE

Find the coordinates of $N(-3, 8)$ after the given transformation. For rotations, rotate about the origin.

1. Rotate 180°.
2. Reflect in x-axis.
3. Translate up 3 units.
4. Reflect in y-axis.
5. Rotate 90° clockwise.
6. Translate left 5 units.
7. Rotate 90° counterclockwise.
8. Translate right 2 units and down 9 units.

Transform $\triangle PST$. Graph the result. For rotations, rotate about the origin.

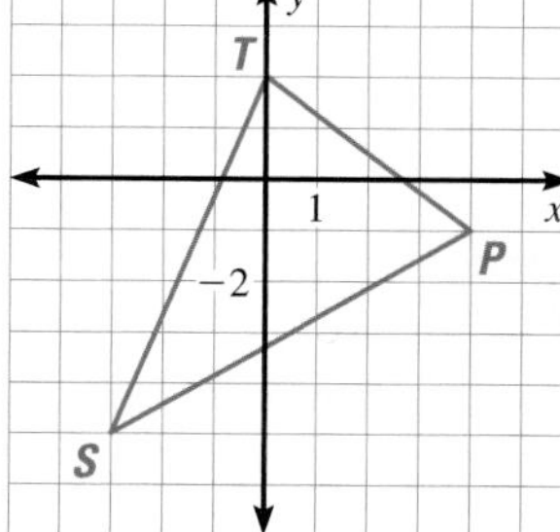

9. Reflect in x-axis.
10. Rotate 90° counterclockwise.
11. Rotate 90° clockwise.
12. Translate down 7 units.
13. Reflect in y-axis.
14. Translate left 4 units.
15. Rotate 180°.
16. Translate right 2 units.

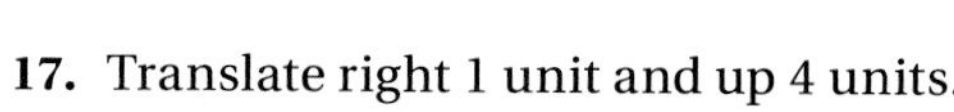

17. Translate right 1 unit and up 4 units.
18. Translate left 6 units and up 2 units.

The coordinates of the vertices of a polygon are given. Draw the polygon. Then find the coordinates of the vertices of the image after the specified dilation, and draw the image.

19. (1, 3), (3, 2), (2, 5); dilate using a scale factor of 3
20. (2, 8), (2, 4), (6, 8), (6, 4); dilate using a scale factor of $\frac{3}{2}$
21. (3, 3), (6, 3), (3, −3), (6, −3); dilate using a scale factor of $\frac{1}{3}$
22. (2, 2), (2, 7), (5, 7); dilate using a scale factor of 2
23. (2, −2), (6, −2), (4, −6), (0, −6); dilate using a scale factor of $\frac{1}{2}$

Line Symmetry

A figure has **line symmetry** if a line, called a **line of symmetry**, divides the figure into two parts that are mirror images of each other. Below are four figures with their lines of symmetry shown in red.

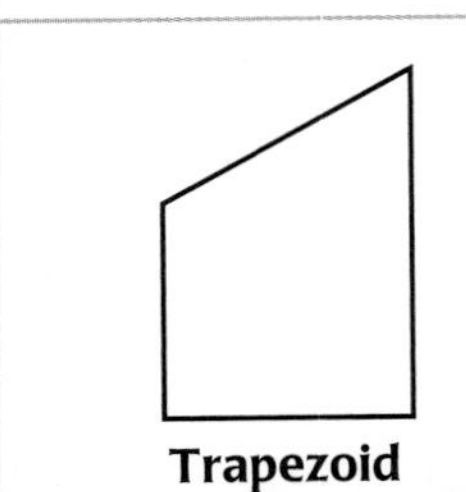	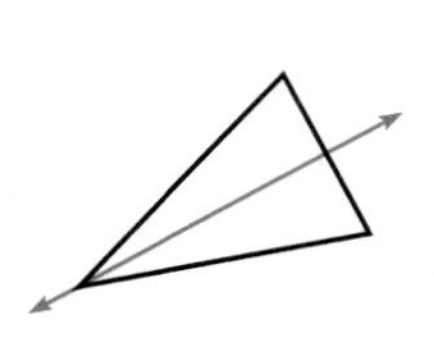		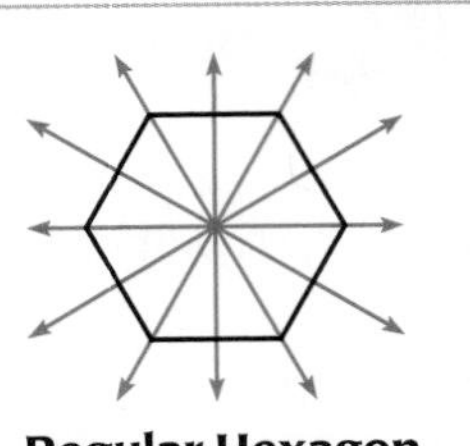
Trapezoid No lines of symmetry	**Isosceles Triangle** 1 line of symmetry	**Rectangle** 2 lines of symmetry	**Regular Hexagon** 6 lines of symmetry

EXAMPLE **A line of symmetry for the figure is shown in red. Find the coordinates of point *A*.**

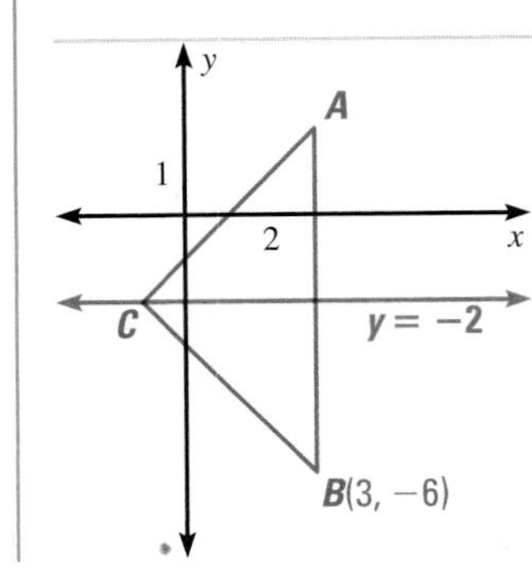

Point A is the mirror image of the point $(3, -6)$ with respect to the line of symmetry $y = -2$. The x-coordinate of A is 3, the same as the x-coordinate of $(3, -6)$. Because -6 is the y-coordinate of $(3, -6)$, and $-2 - (-6) = 4$, the point $(3, -6)$ is *down* 4 units from the line of symmetry. Therefore, point A must be *up* 4 units from the line of symmetry. So, the y-coordinate of A is $-2 + 4 = 2$. The coordinates of point A are $(3, 2)$.

PRACTICE

Tell how many lines of symmetry the figure has.

1. 

2. 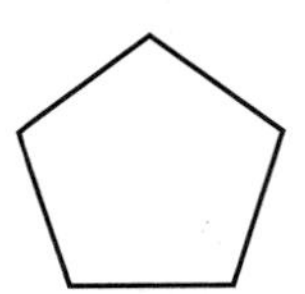

3. 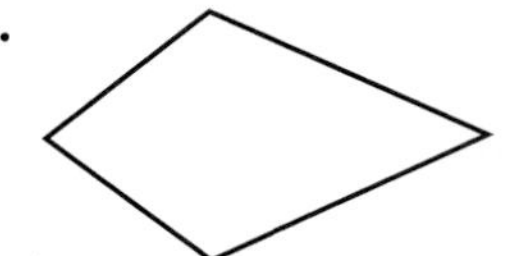

4. 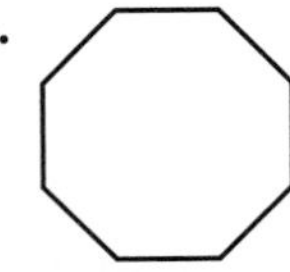

5. A parallelogram
6. A square
7. A rhombus
8. An equilateral triangle

A line of symmetry for the figure is shown in red. Find the coordinates of point *A*.

9. 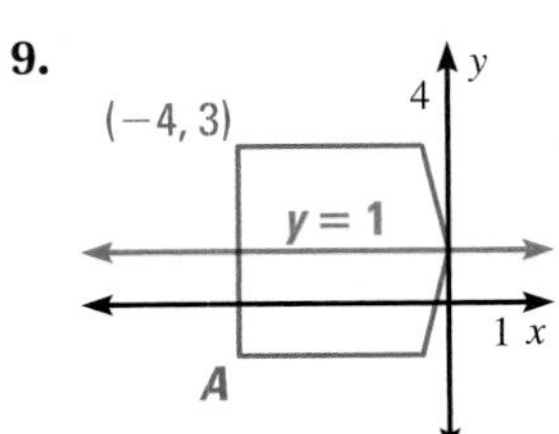

10. 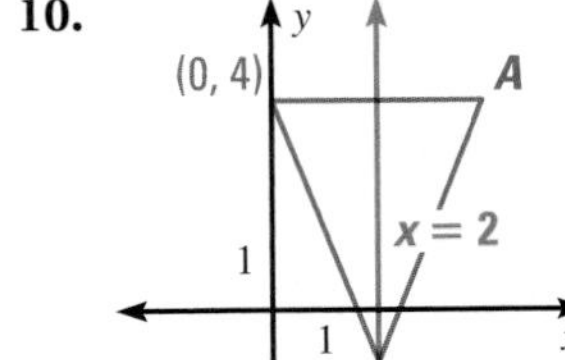

11. 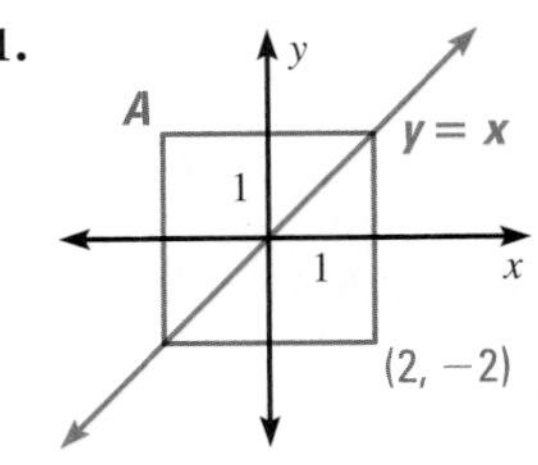

Perimeter and Area

The **perimeter** P of a figure is the distance around it. To find the perimeter of a figure, add the side lengths.

EXAMPLE **Find the perimeter of the figure.**

a.

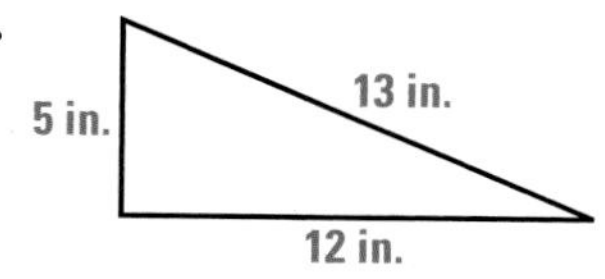

$P = 5 + 12 + 13 = 30$ in.

b.

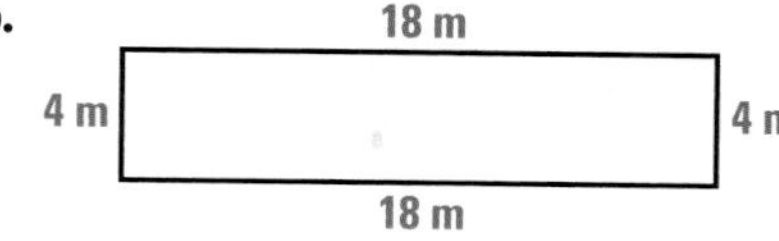

$P = 2(4) + 2(18) = 8 + 36 = 44$ m

The **area** A of a figure is the number of square units enclosed by the figure.

Area of a Triangle	Area of a Rectangle	Area of a Parallelogram	Area of a Trapezoid
h, b	w, ℓ	h, b	b_1, h, b_2
$A = \frac{1}{2}bh$	$A = \ell w$	$A = bh$	$A = \frac{1}{2}(b_1 + b_2)h$

EXAMPLE **Find the area of the figure.**

a.

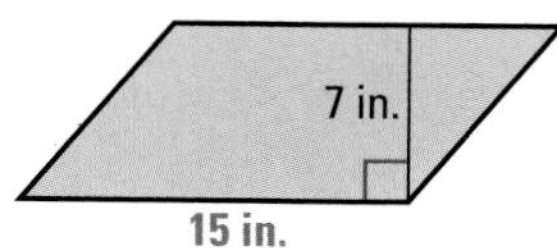

$A = (15)(7) = 105 \text{ in.}^2$

b.

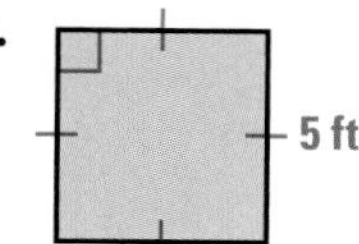

$A = (5)(5) = 25 \text{ ft}^2$

c.

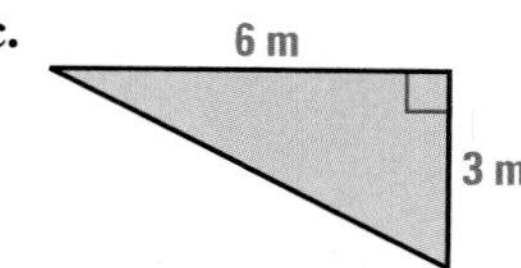

$A = \frac{1}{2}(6)(3) = 9 \text{ m}^2$

PRACTICE

Find the perimeter and area of the figure.

1.

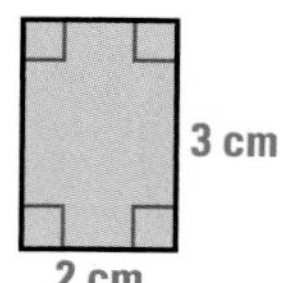

2.

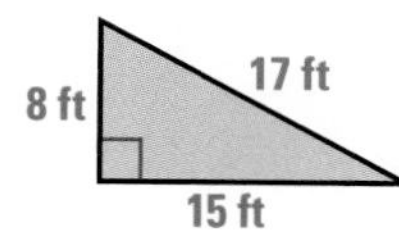

3.

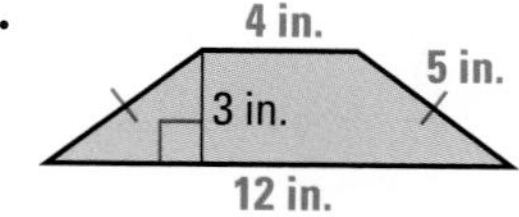

4.

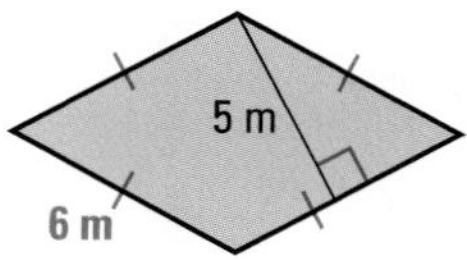

5.

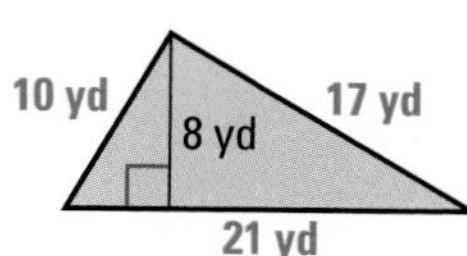

6.

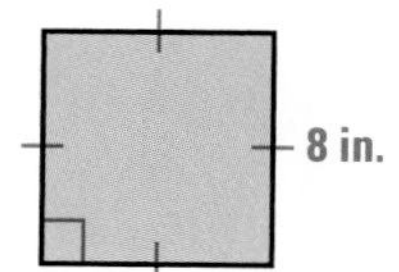

7.

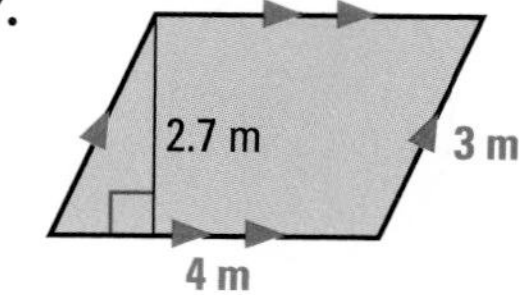

8.

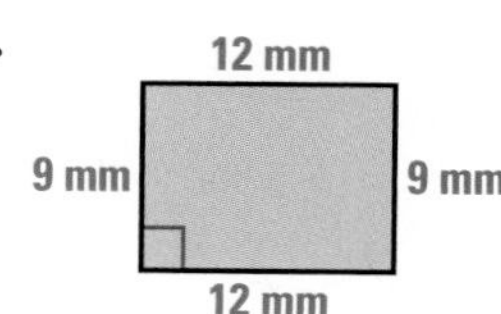

SKILLS REVIEW HANDBOOK

Circumference and Area of a Circle

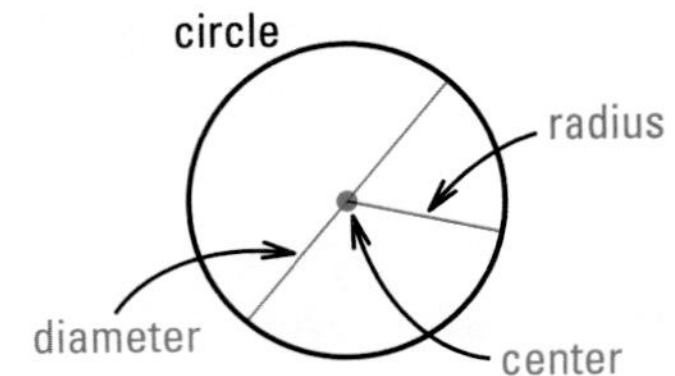

A **circle** consists of all points in a plane that are the same distance from a fixed point called the **center**.

The distance between the center and any point on the circle is the **radius**. The distance across the circle through the center is the **diameter**. The diameter is twice the radius.

The **circumference** of a circle is the distance around the circle. For any circle, the ratio of the circumference to the diameter is π (pi), an irrational number that is approximately 3.14 or $\frac{22}{7}$.

To find the circumference C of a circle with radius r, use the formula $C = 2\pi r$.

To find the area A of a circle with radius r, use the formula $A = \pi r^2$.

EXAMPLE **Find the circumference and area of a circle with radius 6 cm. Give an exact answer and an approximate answer for each.**

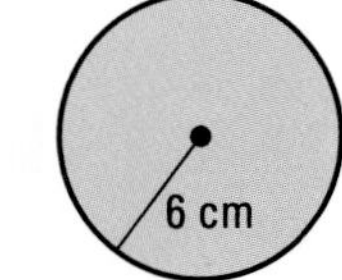

Circumference

$C = 2\pi r$

$= 2\pi(6)$

$= 12\pi$

$\approx 12(3.14)$

≈ 37.7

▶ The circumference is 12π centimeters, or about 37.7 centimeters.

Area

$A = \pi r^2$

$= \pi(6)^2$

$= 36\pi$

$\approx 36(3.14)$

≈ 113

▶ The area is 36π square centimeters, or about 113 square centimeters.

PRACTICE

Find the circumference and area of the circle. Give an exact answer and an approximate answer for each.

1. 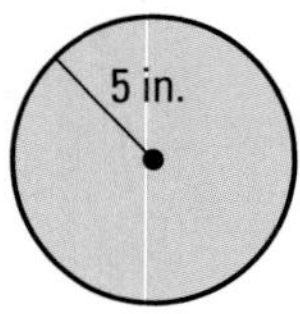

2. 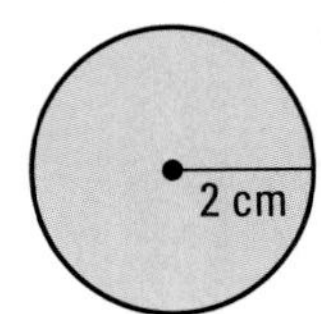

3. 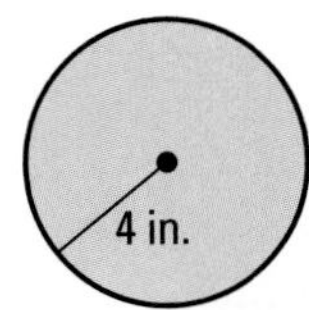

4. 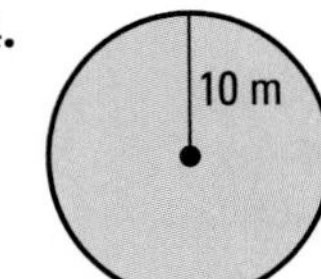

5. 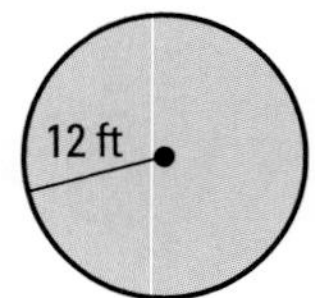

6. 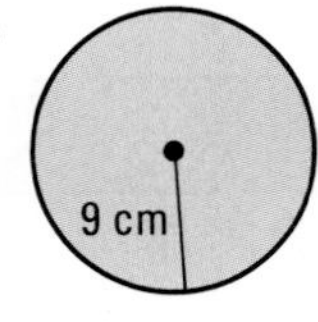

7. 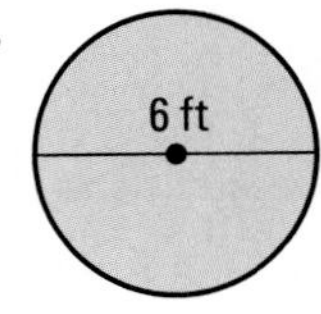

8. 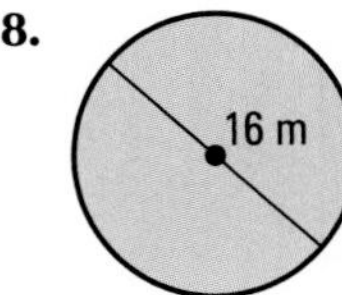

9. 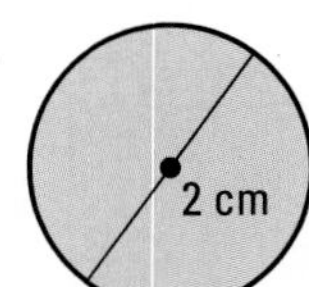

10. 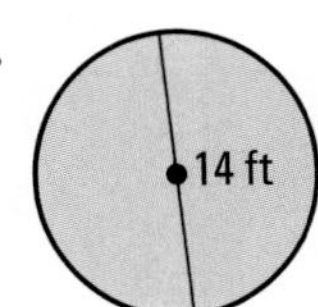

11. 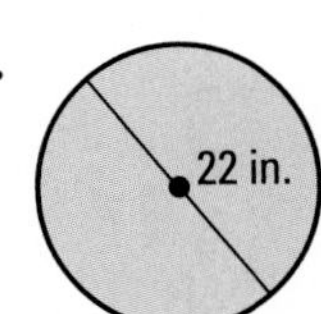

12. 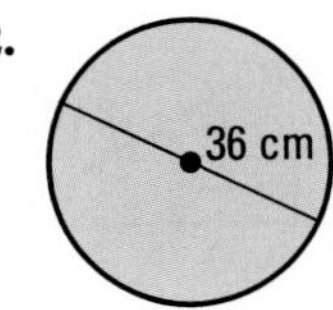

Surface Area and Volume

A **solid** is a three-dimensional figure that encloses part of space.

The **surface area** S of a solid is the area of the solid's outer surface(s).

The **volume** V of a solid is the amount of space that the solid occupies.

Rectangular Prism	**Cylinder**
$S = 2\ell w + 2\ell h + 2wh$ $V = \ell wh$ 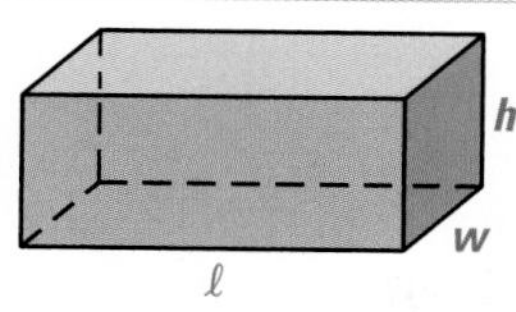	$S = 2\pi r^2 + 2\pi rh$ $V = \pi r^2 h$ 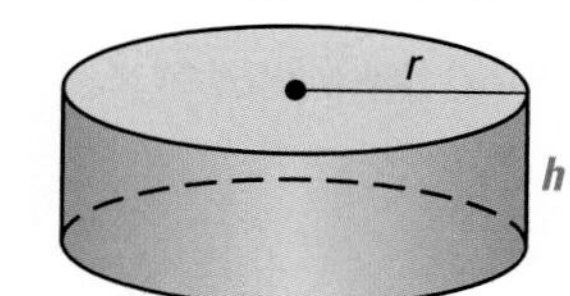

EXAMPLE Find the surface area and volume of the rectangular prism.

Surface area

$S = 2\ell w + 2\ell h + 2wh$

$= 2(5)(3) + 2(5)(7) + 2(3)(7)$

$= 30 + 70 + 42$

$= 142 \text{ ft}^2$

Volume

$V = \ell wh$

$= (5)(3)(7)$

$= 105 \text{ ft}^3$

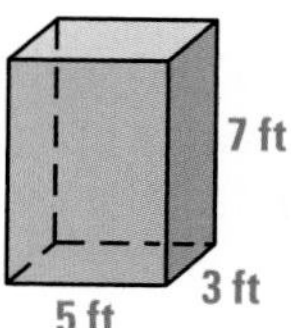

EXAMPLE Find the surface area and volume of the cylinder.

3 m

12 m

Surface area

$S = 2\pi r^2 + 2\pi rh$

$= 2\pi(3)^2 + 2\pi(3)(12)$

$= 90\pi \text{ m}^2$ Exact answer

$\approx 283 \text{ m}^2$ Approximate answer

Volume

$V = \pi r^2 h$

$= \pi(3)^2(12)$

$= 108\pi \text{ m}^3$ Exact answer

$\approx 339 \text{ m}^3$ Approximate answer

PRACTICE

Find the surface area and volume of the solid.

1. 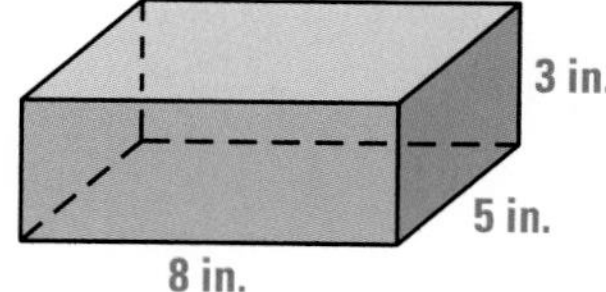

2. 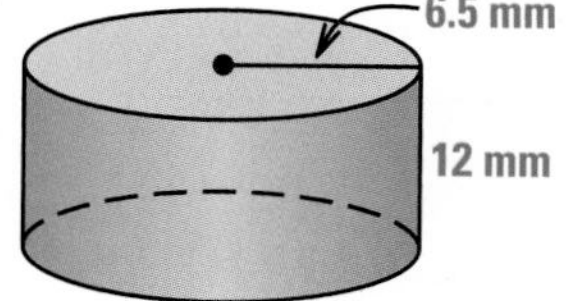

3. 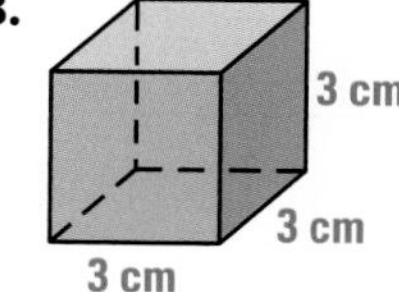

4. 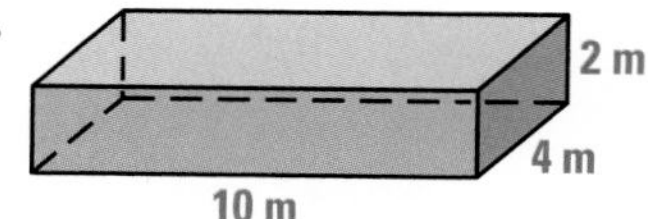

5. 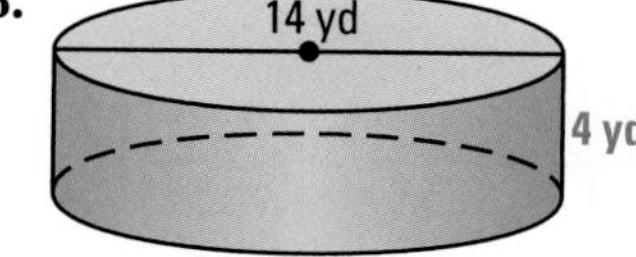

6. 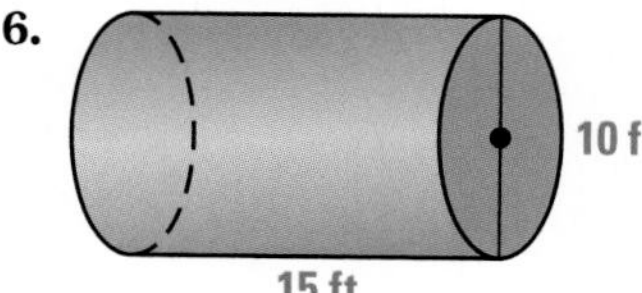

Angle Relationships

An **angle bisector** is a ray that divides an angle into two congruent angles. Two angles are **complementary angles** if the sum of their measures is 90°. Two angles are **supplementary angles** if the sum of their measures is 180°.

EXAMPLE **Find the value of *x*.**

a. $\overrightarrow{BD}$ bisects $\angle ABC$ and $m\angle ABC = 64°$.

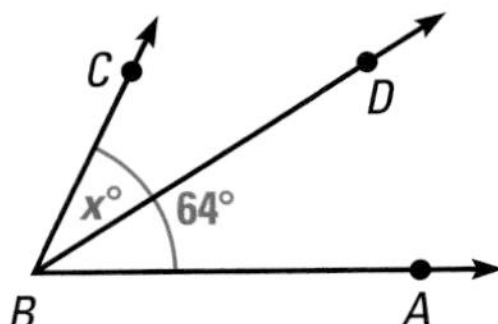

Because $\overrightarrow{BD}$ bisects $\angle ABC$, the value of x is half $m\angle ABC$.

$$x = \frac{64}{2} = 32$$

b. $\angle GFJ$ and $\angle HFJ$ are complementary.

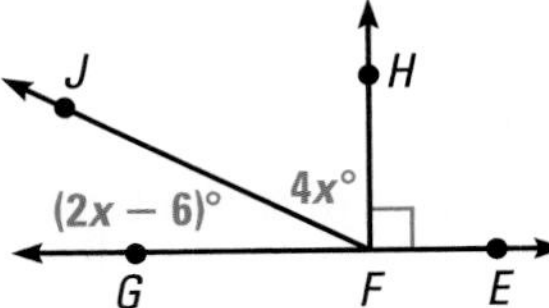

Because $\angle GFJ$ and $\angle HFJ$ are complementary angles, their sum is 90°.

$$(2x - 6) + 4x = 90$$
$$6x - 6 = 90$$
$$x = 16$$

c. $\angle CBD$ and $\angle ABD$ are supplementary.

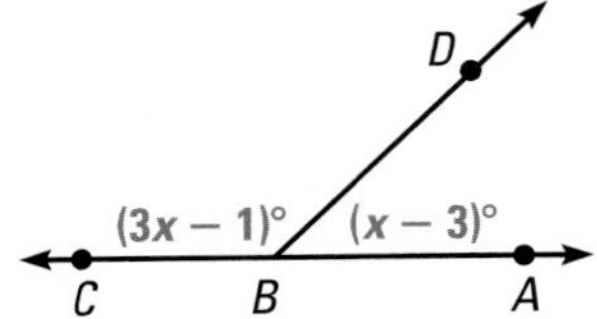

Because $\angle CBD$ and $\angle ABD$ are supplementary angles, their sum is 180°.

$$(3x - 1) + (x - 3) = 180$$
$$4x - 4 = 180$$
$$x = 46$$

PRACTICE

$\overrightarrow{BD}$ is the angle bisector of $\angle ABC$. Find the value of x.

1.

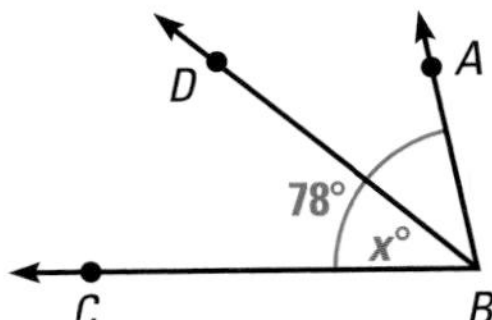

2.

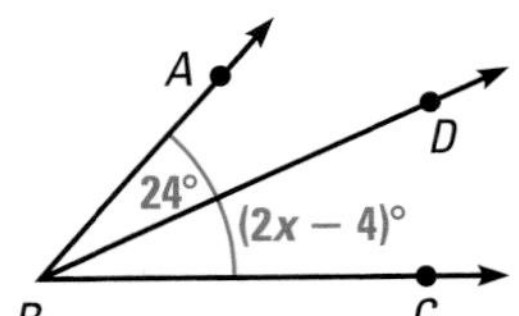

3.

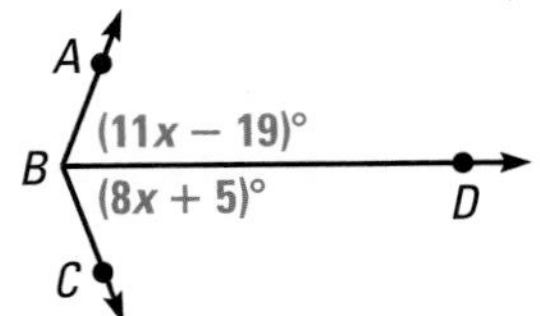

$\angle ABD$ and $\angle DBC$ are complementary. Find the value of x.

4.

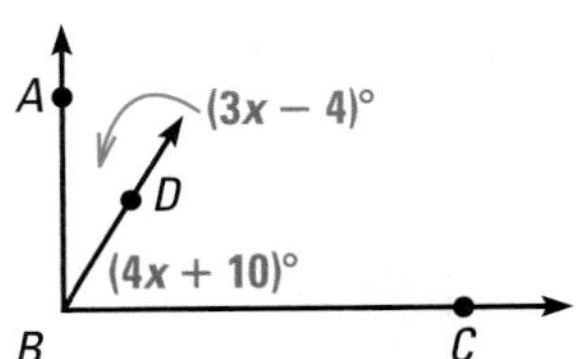

5.

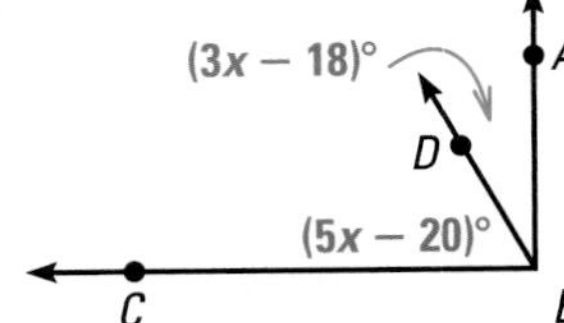

6.

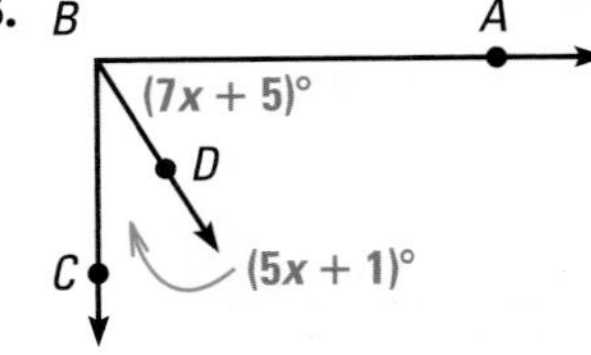

$\angle ABD$ and $\angle DBC$ are supplementary. Find the value of x.

7.

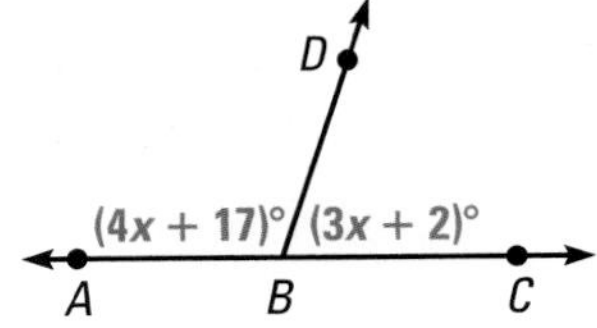

8.

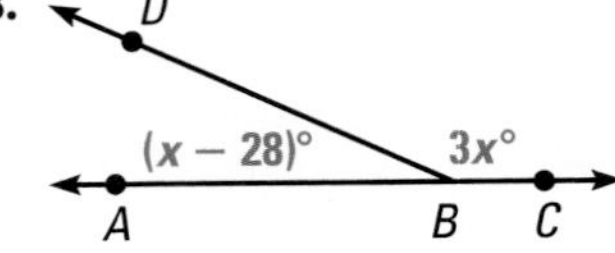

9.

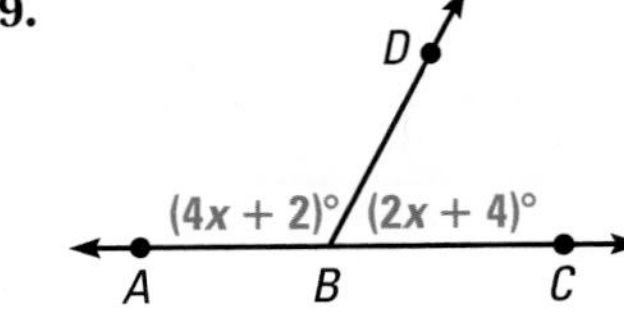

Triangle Relationships

The sum of the angle measures of any triangle is 180°.

EXAMPLE **Find the value of x.**

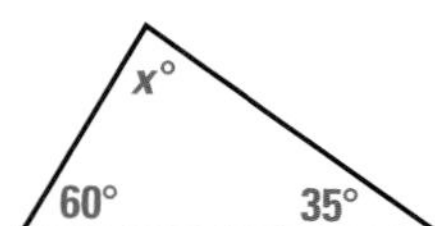

$60 + 35 + x = 180$ The sum of the angle measures is 180°.

$95 + x = 180$ Simplify.

$x = 85$ Solve for x.

In a right triangle, the **hypotenuse** is the side opposite the right angle. The **legs** are the sides that form the right angle. The **Pythagorean theorem** states that the sum of the squares of the lengths of the legs equals the square of the length of the hypotenuse.

Pythagorean Theorem

$a^2 + b^2 = c^2$

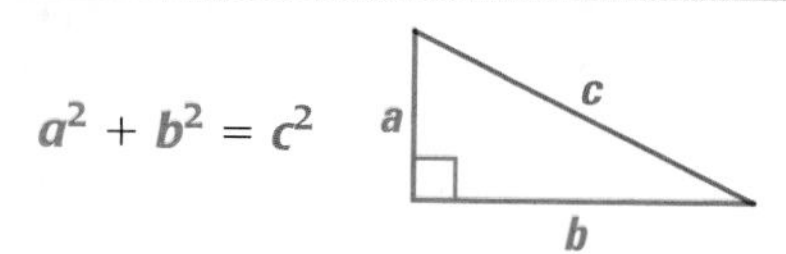

EXAMPLE **Find the value of x.**

a.

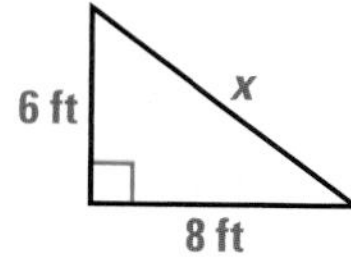

$6^2 + 8^2 = x^2$ Pythagorean theorem

$36 + 64 = x^2$ Simplify.

$100 = x^2$ Simplify.

$x = 10$ ft Solve for x.

b.

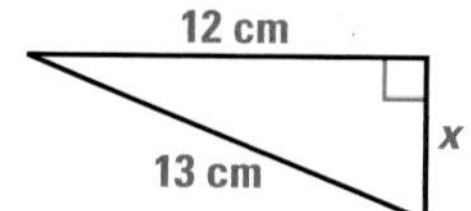

$x^2 + 12^2 = 13^2$ Pythagorean theorem

$x^2 + 144 = 169$ Simplify.

$x^2 = 25$ Solve for x^2.

$x = 5$ cm Solve for x.

PRACTICE

Find the value of x.

1.

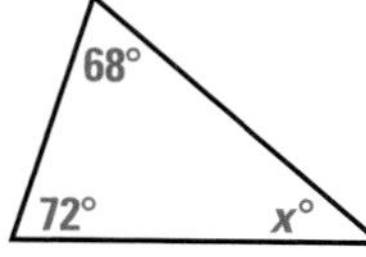

2.

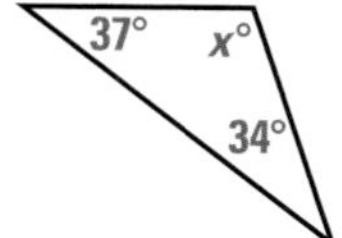

3.

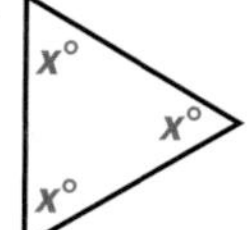

4.

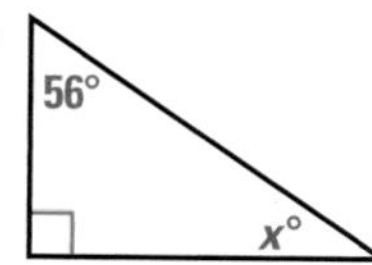

5.

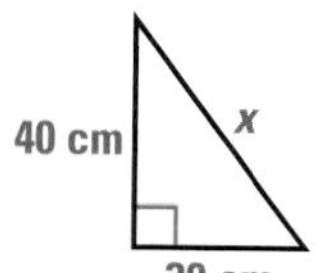

6.

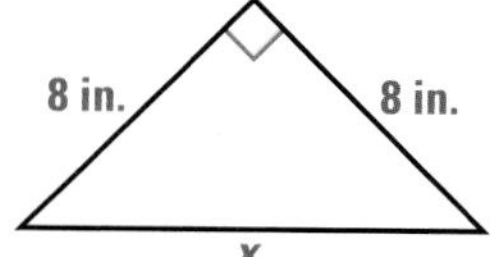

7.

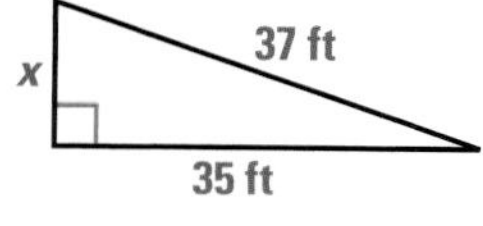

8.

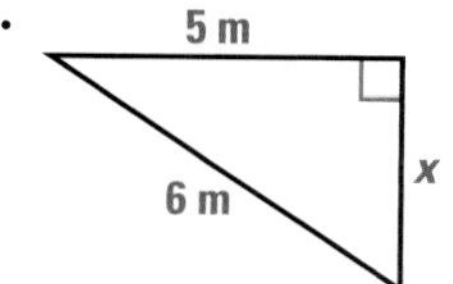

9. A triangle with angles that measure $x°$, $x°$, and 70°

Congruent and Similar Figures

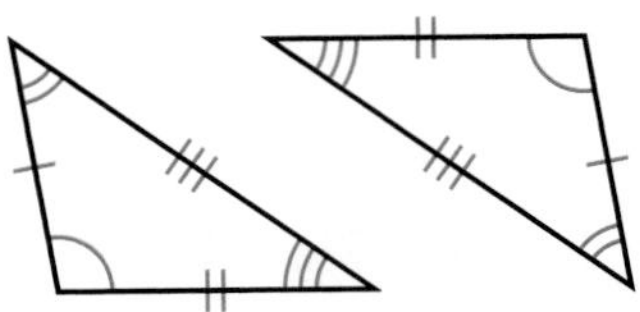

Two figures are **congruent** if they have the same shape and the same size. If two figures are congruent, then corresponding angles are congruent and corresponding sides are congruent. The triangles at the right are congruent. Matching arcs show congruent angles, and matching tick marks show congruent sides.

Two figures are **similar** if they have the same shape but not necessarily the same size. If two figures are similar, then corresponding angles are congruent and the ratios of the lengths of corresponding sides are equal.

EXAMPLE **Tell whether the figures are *congruent, similar,* or *neither.***

a.

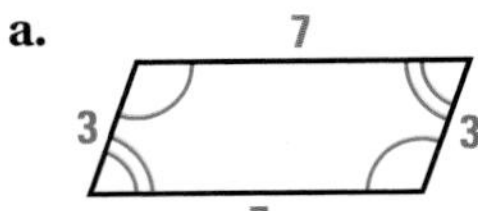

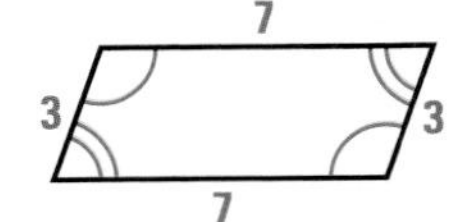

As shown, corresponding angles are congruent and corresponding sides are congruent. So, the figures are congruent.

b.

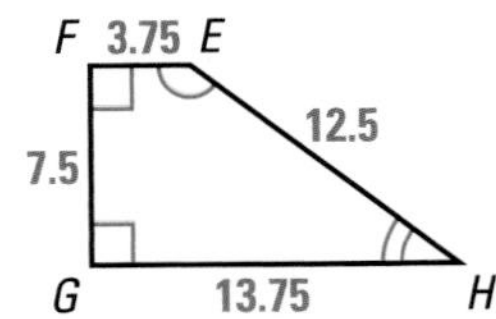

A 3 B, 10, 6, D 11 C

As shown, corresponding angles are congruent, but corresponding sides have different lengths. So, the figures are not congruent, but they may be similar.

The figures are similar if the ratios of the lengths of corresponding sides are equal.

$\frac{AB}{EF} = \frac{3}{3.75} = 0.8 \quad \frac{BC}{FG} = \frac{6}{7.5} = 0.8 \quad \frac{CD}{GH} = \frac{11}{13.75} = 0.8 \quad \frac{AD}{EH} = \frac{10}{12.5} = 0.8$

▸ Because corresponding angles are congruent and the ratios of the lengths of corresponding sides are equal, *ABCD* is similar to *EFGH*.

EXAMPLE **The two polygons are similar. Find the value of *x*.**

a.

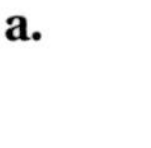

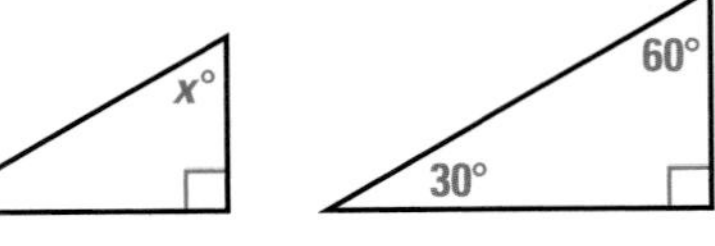

The angle with measure $x°$ corresponds to the angle with measure 60°, so $x = 60$.

b.

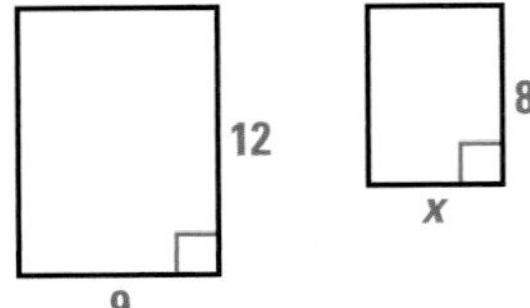

The side with length 12 corresponds to the side with length 8, and the side with length 9 corresponds to the side with length x.

$\frac{12}{8} = \frac{9}{x}$	**Write a proportion.**
$12x = 72$	**Cross multiply.**
$x = 6$	**Solve for *x*.**

PRACTICE

Tell whether the figures are *congruent, similar,* or *neither. Explain.*

1.

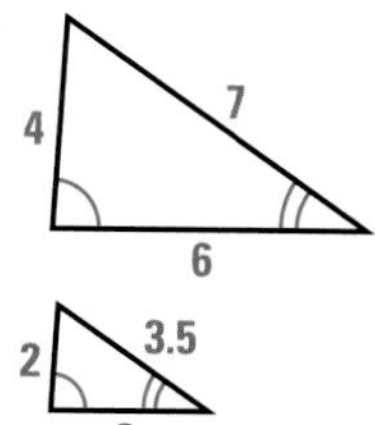

2.

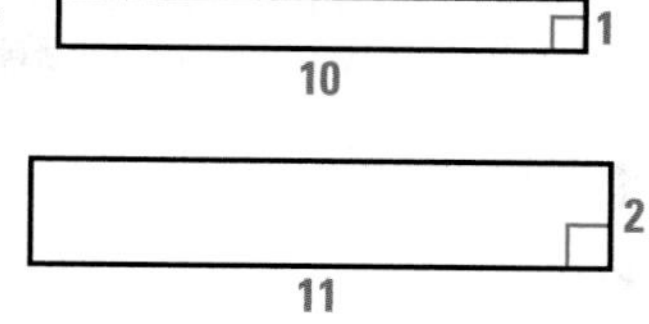

3.

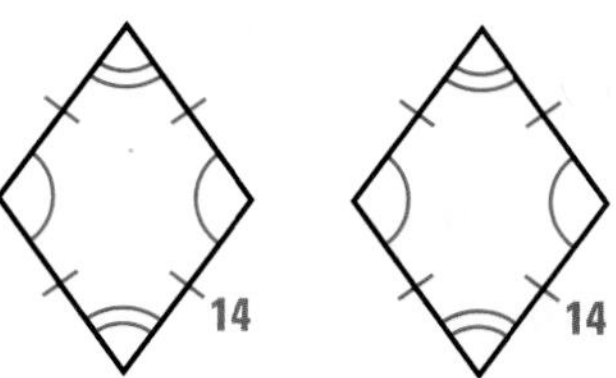

4.

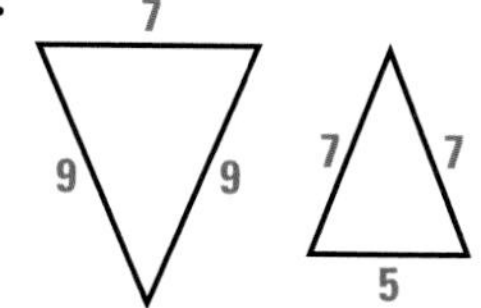

5.

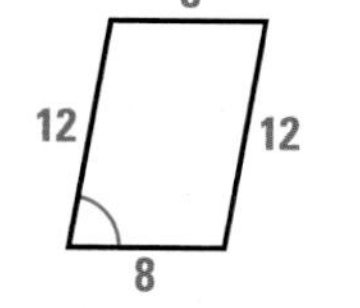

6.

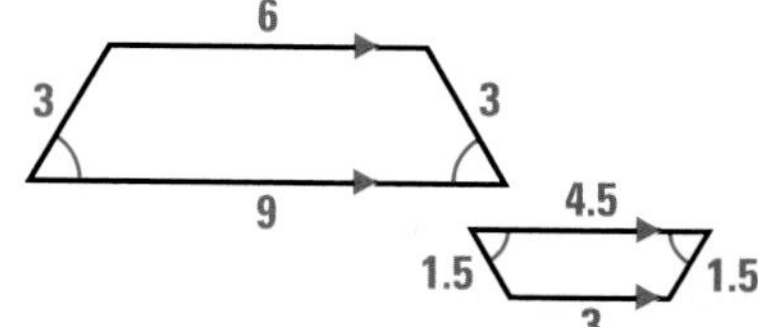

7.

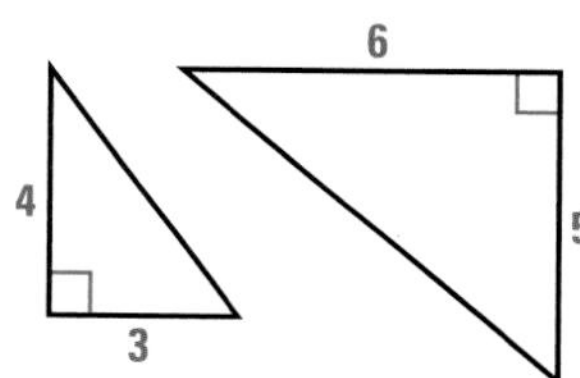

8.

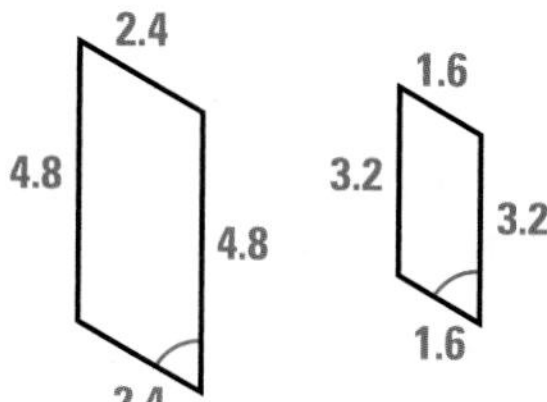

9.

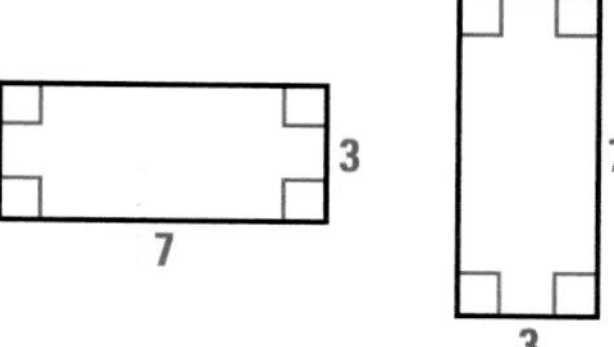

The two polygons are similar. Find the value of *x*.

10.

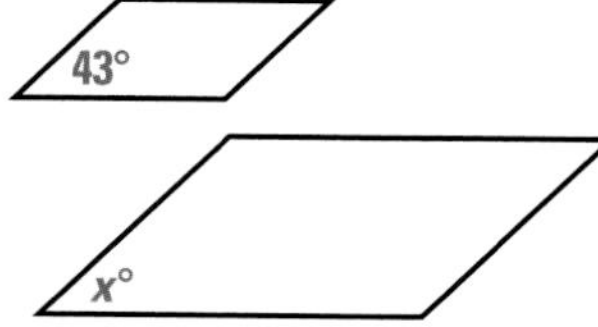

11.

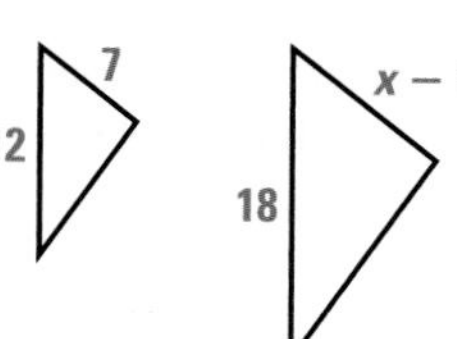

12.

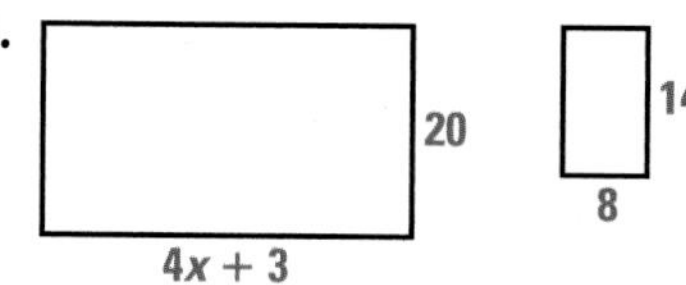

13.

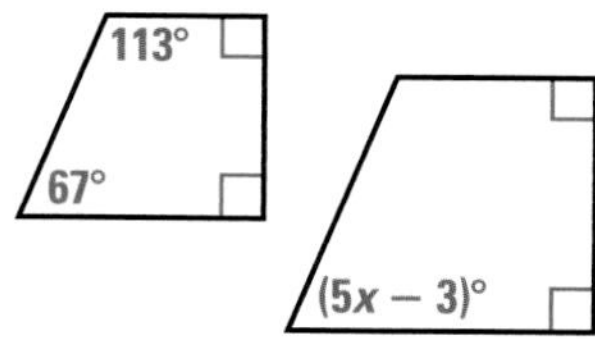

14.

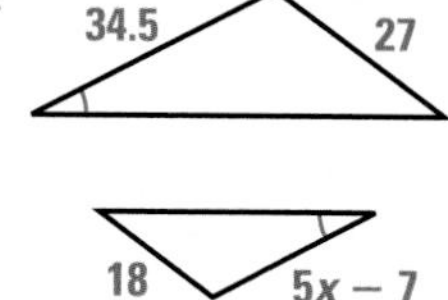

15.

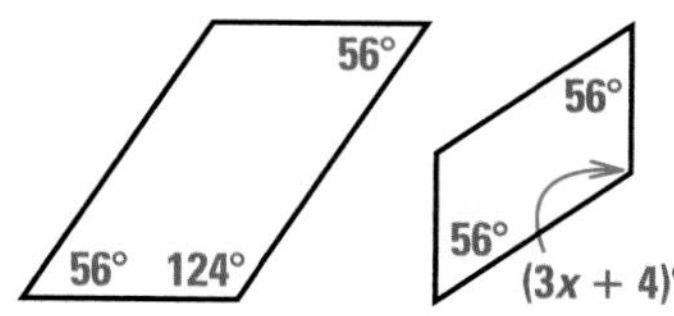

16.

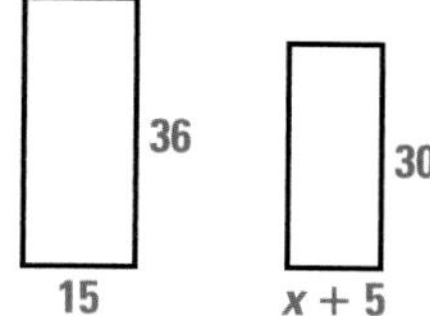

17.

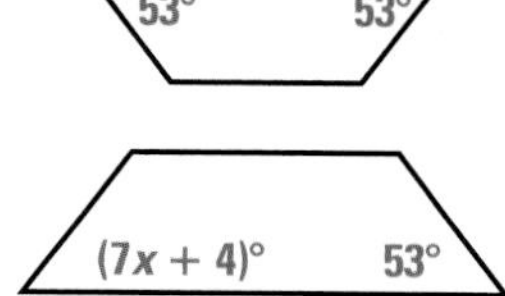

18.

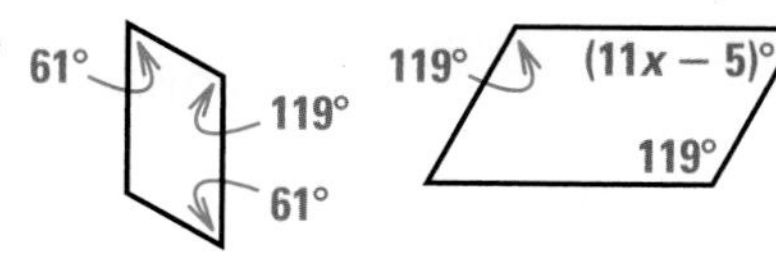

More Problem Solving Strategies

Problem solving strategies can help you solve mathematical and real-life problems. Lesson 1.5 shows how to apply the strategies *use a formula, look for a pattern, draw a diagram,* and *use a verbal model.* Below are four more strategies.

Strategy	When to Use	How to Use
Make a list or table	Make a list or table when a problem requires you to record, generate, or organize information.	Make a table with columns, rows, and any given information. Generate a systematic list that can help you solve the problem.
Work backward	Work backward when a problem gives you an end result and you need to find beginning conditions.	Work backward from the given information until you solve the problem. Work forward through the problem to check your answer.
Guess, check, and revise	Guess, check, and revise when you need a place to start or you want to see how the problem works.	Make a reasonable guess. Check to see if your guess solves the problem. If it does not, revise your guess and check again.
Solve a simpler problem	Solve a simpler problem when a problem can be made easier by using simpler numbers.	Think of a way to make the problem simpler. Solve the simpler problem, then use what you learned to solve the original problem.

EXAMPLE **Lee works as a cashier. In how many different ways can Lee make $.50 in change using quarters, dimes, and nickels?**

Use the strategy *make a list or table.* Then count the number of different ways.

Quarters	Dimes	Nickels
2	0	0
1	2	1
1	1	3
1	0	5
0	5	0
0	4	2
0	3	4
0	2	6
0	1	8
0	0	10

Start with the greatest number of quarters.

Then list all the possibilities with 1 quarter, starting with the greatest number of dimes.

Then list all the possibilities with 0 quarters, starting with the greatest number of dimes.

▸ Lee can make $.50 in quarters, dimes, and nickels in 10 different ways.

EXAMPLE **In a cafeteria, 3 cookies cost $.50 less than a sandwich. If a sandwich costs $4.25, how much does one cookie cost?**

Use the strategy *work backward.*

$4.25 - 0.50 = 3.75$ Cost of 3 cookies

$3.75 \div 3 = 1.25$ Cost of 1 cookie

CHECK $1.25 \times 3 = 3.75$ Cost of 3 cookies

$3.75 + 0.50 = 4.25$ Cost of sandwich

▸ One cookie costs $1.25.

EXAMPLE **Nolan's class has 6 more boys than girls. There are 28 students altogether. How many girls are in Nolan's class?**

Use the strategy *guess, check, and revise*. Guess a number of girls that is less than half of 28.

First guess:	12 girls, $12 + 6 = 18$ boys, $12 + 18 = 30$ students	Too high ✗
Second guess:	10 girls, $10 + 6 = 16$ boys, $10 + 16 = 26$ students	Too low ✗
Third guess:	11 girls, $11 + 6 = 17$ boys, $11 + 17 = 28$ students	Correct ✓

▶ There are 11 girls in Nolan's class.

EXAMPLE **How many diagonals does a regular decagon have?**

Use the strategy *solve a simpler problem*. A decagon has 10 sides, so find the number of diagonals of polygons with fewer sides and look for a pattern.

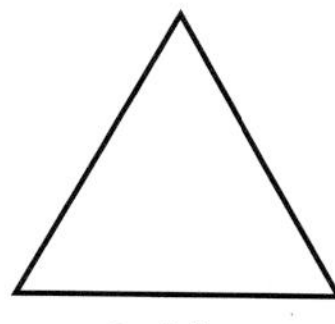
3 sides
0 diagonals

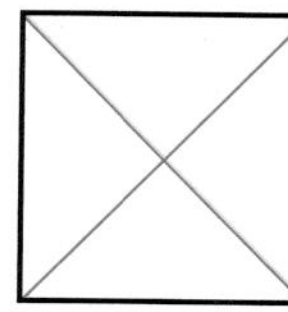
4 sides
2 diagonals

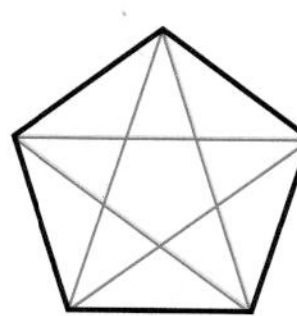
5 sides
5 diagonals

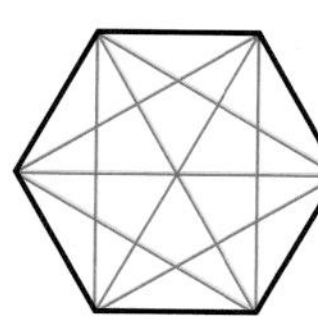
6 sides
9 diagonals

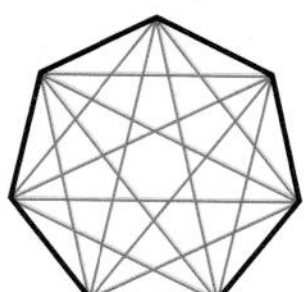
7 sides
14 diagonals

Notice that the difference of the numbers of diagonals for consecutive figures keeps increasing by 1:

$2 - 0 = 2$ $\quad 5 - 2 = 3$ $\quad 9 - 5 = 4$ $\quad 14 - 9 = 5$

So, an 8-sided polygon has $14 + 6 = 20$ diagonals, a 9-sided polygon has $20 + 7 = 27$ diagonals, and a 10-sided polygon has $27 + 8 = 35$ diagonals.

▶ A regular decagon (a 10-sided polygon) has 35 diagonals.

PRACTICE

1. Ben has a concert at 7:30 P.M. First he must do 2 hours of homework. Then, dinner and a shower will take about 45 minutes. Ben wants to allow a half hour to get to the concert. What time should Ben start his homework?
2. Quinn and Kyle collected 87 aluminum cans to recycle. Quinn collected twice as many cans as Kyle. How many cans did each person collect?
3. In how many different ways can three sisters form a line at a ticket booth?
4. The 8×8 grid at the right has some 1×1 squares, some 2×2 squares, some 3×3 squares, and so on. How many total squares does the grid have?

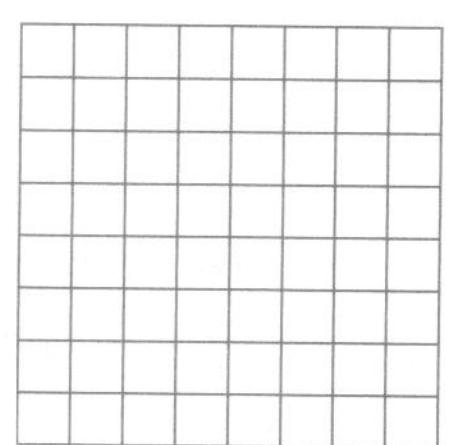

5. If Kaleigh draws 20 different diameters in a circle, into how many parts will the circle be divided?
6. Six friends form a tennis league. Each friend will play a match with every other friend. How many matches will be played?
7. Susan has 13 coins in her pocket with a total value of \$1.05. She has only dimes and nickels. How many of each type of coin does Susan have?

Logical Argument

A logical argument has two given statements, called **premises**, and a statement, called a **conclusion**, that follows from the premises. Below is an example.

Premise 1 If a triangle has a right angle, then it is a right triangle.
Premise 2 In $\triangle ABC$, $\angle B$ is a right angle.
Conclusion $\triangle ABC$ is a right triangle.

Letters are often used to represent the statements of a logical argument and to write a pattern for the argument. The table below gives five types of logical arguments. In the examples, p, q, and r represent the following statements.

p: a figure is a square q: a figure is a rectangle r: a figure is a parallelogram

Type of Argument	Pattern	Example
Direct Argument	If p is true, then q is true. p is true. Therefore, q is true.	If *ABCD* is a square, then it is a rectangle. *ABCD* is a square. Therefore, *ABCD* is a rectangle.
Indirect Argument	If p is true, then q is true. q is not true. Therefore, p is not true.	If *ABCD* is a square, then it is a rectangle. *ABCD* is not a rectangle. Therefore, *ABCD* is not a square.
Chain Rule	If p is true, then q is true. If q is true, then r is true. Therefore, if p, then r.	If *ABCD* is a square, then it is a rectangle. If *ABCD* is a rectangle, then it is a parallelogram. Therefore, if *ABCD* is a square, then it is a parallelogram.
Or Rule	p is true or q is true. p is not true. Therefore, q is true.	*ABCD* is a square or a rectangle. *ABCD* is not a square. Therefore, *ABCD* is a rectangle.
And Rule	p and q are not both true. q is true. Therefore, p is not true.	*ABCD* is not both a square and a rectangle. *ABCD* is a rectangle. Therefore, *ABCD* is not a square.

An argument that follows one of these patterns correctly has a **valid conclusion**.

EXAMPLE **State whether the conclusion is *valid* or *invalid*. If the conclusion is valid, name the type of logical argument used.**

a. If it is raining at noon, Peter's family will not have a picnic lunch. Peter's family had a picnic lunch. Therefore, it was not raining at noon.

▶ The conclusion is valid. This is an example of indirect argument.

b. If a triangle is equilateral, then it is an acute triangle. Triangle *XYZ* is an acute triangle. Therefore, triangle *XYZ* is equilateral.

▶ The conclusion is invalid.

c. If $x = 4$, then $2x - 7 = 1$. If $2x - 7 = 1$, then $2x = 8$. $x = 4$. Therefore, if $x = 4$, then $2x = 8$.

▶ The conclusion is valid. This is an example of the chain rule.

d. If it is at least 80°F outside today, you will go swimming. It is 85°F outside today. Therefore, you will go swimming.

▶ The conclusion is valid. This is an example of direct argument.

A **compound statement** has two or more parts joined by *or* or *and*.

- For an *and* compound statement to be true, each part must be true.
- For an *or* compound statement to be true, at least one part must be true.

EXAMPLE **State whether the compound statement is *true* or *false*.**

a. $\underline{12 < 20}$ and $\underline{-12 > -20}$
True True
▶ True, because each part is true.

b. $\underline{2 < 4}$ and $\underline{4 < 3}$
True False
▶ False, because one part is false.

c. $\underline{10 > 0}$ or $\underline{-10 > 0}$
True False
▶ True, because at least one part is true.

d. $\underline{-8 > -7}$ or $\underline{-7 > -6}$ or $\underline{-6 > -5}$
False False False
▶ False, because every part is false.

PRACTICE

State whether the conclusion is *valid* or *invalid*. If the conclusion is valid, name the type of logical argument used.

1. If Scott goes to the store, then he will buy sugar. If he buys sugar, then he will bake cookies. Scott goes to the store. Therefore, he will bake cookies.
2. If a triangle has at least two congruent sides, then it is isosceles. Triangle *MNP* has sides 5 in., 6 in., and 5 in. long. Therefore, triangle *MNP* is isosceles.
3. If a horse is an Arabian, then it is less than 16 hands tall. Andrea's horse is 13 hands tall. Therefore, Andrea's horse is an Arabian.
4. If a figure is a rhombus, then it has four sides. Figure *WXYZ* has four sides. Therefore, *WXYZ* is a rhombus.
5. Jeff cannot buy both a new coat and new boots. Jeff decides to buy new boots. Therefore, Jeff cannot buy a new coat.
6. If $x = 0$, then $y = 4$. If $y = 4$, then $z = 7$. Therefore, if $z = 7$, then $x = 0$.
7. Kate will order either tacos or burritos for lunch. Kate does not order tacos for lunch. Therefore, Kate orders burritos for lunch.
8. If a triangle is equilateral, then it is equiangular. Triangle *ABC* is not equiangular. Therefore, triangle *ABC* is not equilateral.
9. An animal cannot be both a fish and a bird. Courtney's pet is not a fish. Therefore, Courtney's pet must be a bird.

State whether the compound statement is *true* or *false*.

10. $-7 < -5$ and $-5 < -6$
11. $6 > 2$ or $8 < 4$
12. $0 \leq -1$ or $5 \geq 5$
13. $4 \leq 3$ or $12 \geq 13$
14. $3 < 5$ and $-3 < -5$
15. $1 = -1$ or $1 = 1$ or $1 = 0$
16. $7 < 8$ and $8 < 12$
17. $-2 < 2$ and $3 \geq 2$
18. $3(-4) = 12$ or $-3(4) = 12$
19. $-8 > 8$ or $-8 = 8$ or $-8 \geq 0$
20. $140 \neq 145$ or $140 > -145$ or $-140 < -145$
21. $-8(9) = -72$ and $8(-9) = -72$
22. $22 \leq 23$ and $-22 < -23$ and $23 > 22$

Conditional Statements and Counterexamples

A **conditional statement** has two parts, a hypothesis and a conclusion. When a conditional statement is written in **if-then form**, the "if" part contains the **hypothesis** and the "then" part contains the **conclusion**. An example of a conditional statement is shown below.

If a triangle is equiangular, then each angle of the triangle measures 60°.

Hypothesis: a triangle is equiangular
Conclusion: each angle of the triangle measures 60°

The **converse** of a conditional statement is formed by switching the hypothesis and the conclusion. The converse of the statement above is as follows:

If each angle of a triangle measures 60°, then the triangle is equiangular.

EXAMPLE **Rewrite the conditional statement in if-then form. Then write its converse and tell whether the converse is *true* or *false*.**

a. Bob will earn $20 by mowing the lawn.

If-then form: If Bob mows the lawn, then he will earn $20.

Converse: If Bob earns $20, then he mowed the lawn. False

b. $x = 8$ when $5x + 1 = 41$.

If-then form: If $5x + 1 = 41$, then $x = 8$.

Converse: If $x = 8$, then $5x + 1 = 41$. True

A **biconditional statement** is a statement that has the words "if and only if." You can write a conditional statement and its converse together as a biconditional statement.

A triangle is equiangular if and only if each angle of the triangle measures 60°.

A biconditional statement is true only when the conditional statement and its converse are both true.

EXAMPLE **Tell whether the biconditional statement is *true* or *false*. Explain.**

a. An angle measures 90° if and only if it is a right angle.

Conditional: If an angle is a right angle, then it measures 90°. True
Converse: If an angle measures 90°, then it is a right angle. True

▶ The biconditional statement is true because the conditional and its converse are both true.

b. Bonnie has $.50 if and only if she has two quarters.

Conditional: If Bonnie has two quarters, then she has $.50. True
Converse: If Bonnie has $.50, then she has two quarters. False

▶ The biconditional statement is false because the converse is not true.

A **counterexample** is an example that shows that a statement is false.

EXAMPLE **Tell whether the statement is *true* or *false*. If false, give a counterexample.**

a. If a polygon has four sides and opposite sides are parallel, then it is a rectangle.

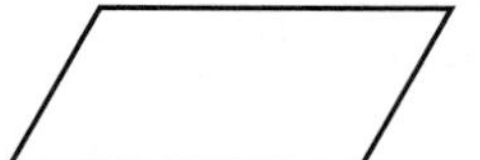

▶ False. A counterexample is the parallelogram shown.

b. If $x^2 = 49$, then $x = 7$.

▶ False. A counterexample is $x = -7$, because $(-7)^2 = 49$.

SKILLS REVIEW HANDBOOK

PRACTICE

Rewrite the conditional statement in if-then form. Then write its converse and tell whether the converse is *true* or *false*.

1. The graph of the equation $y = mx + b$ is a line.
2. You will earn \$35 for working 5 hours.
3. Abby can go swimming if she finishes her homework.
4. In a right triangle, the sum of the squares of the lengths of the legs equals the square of the length of the hypotenuse.
5. $x = 5$ when $4x + 8 = 28$.
6. The sum of two even numbers is an even number.

Tell whether the biconditional statement is *true* or *false*. *Explain*.

7. Two lines are perpendicular if and only if they intersect to form a right angle.
8. $x^3 = 27$ if and only if $x = 3$.
9. A vegetable is a carrot if and only if it is orange.
10. A rhombus is a square if and only if it has four right angles.
11. The graph of a function is a parabola if and only if the function is $y = x^2$.
12. An integer is odd if and only if it is not even.

Tell whether the statement is *true* or *false*. If false, give a counterexample.

13. If an integer is not negative, then it is positive.
14. If you were born in the summer, then you were born in July.
15. If a polygon has exactly 5 congruent sides, then the polygon is a pentagon.
16. If $x = -6$, then $x^2 = 36$.
17. If B is 6 inches from A and 8 inches from C, then A is 14 inches from C.
18. If a triangle is isosceles, then it is obtuse.
19. If Charlie has \$1.00 in coins, then he has four quarters.
20. If you are in Montana, then you are in the United States.

SKILLS REVIEW HANDBOOK

Venn Diagrams

A **Venn diagram** uses shapes to show how sets are related.

EXAMPLE **Draw a Venn diagram of the positive integers less than 13 where set *A* consists of factors of 12 and set *B* consists of even numbers.**

Positive integers less than 13:
1, 2, 3, 4, 5, 6, 7, 8, 9, 10, 11, 12

Set *A* (factors of 12): 1, 2, 3, 4, 6, 12

Set *B* (even numbers): 2, 4, 6, 8, 10, 12

Both set *A* and set *B*: **2, 4, 6, 12**

Neither set *A* nor set *B*: **5, 7, 9, 11**

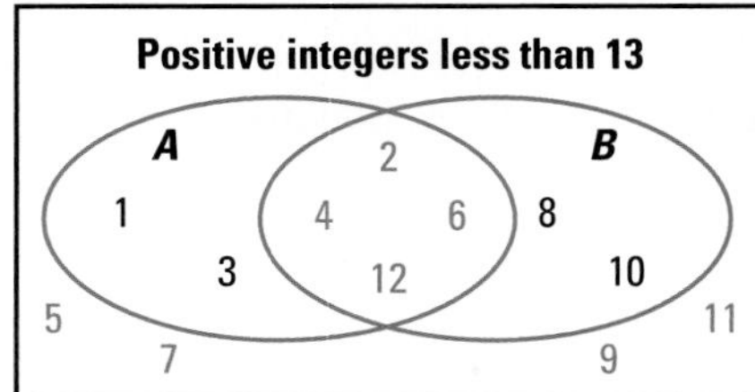

EXAMPLE **Use the Venn diagram above to decide if the statement is *true* or *false*. Explain your reasoning.**

a. If a positive integer less than 13 is not even, then it is not a factor of 12.

▶ False. 1 and 3 are not even, but they are factors of 12.

b. All positive integers less than 13 that are even are factors of 12.

▶ False. 8 and 10 are even, but they are not factors of 12.

PRACTICE

Draw a Venn diagram of the sets described.

1. Of the positive integers less than 11, set *A* consists of factors of 10 and set *B* consists of odd numbers.
2. Of the positive integers less than 10, set *A* consists of prime numbers and set *B* consists of even numbers.
3. Of the positive integers less than 25, set *A* consists of multiples of 3 and set *B* consists of multiples of 4.

Use the Venn diagrams you drew in Exercises 1–3 to decide if the statement is *true* or *false*. *Explain* your reasoning.

4. The only factors of 10 less than 11 that are not odd are 2 and 10.
5. If a number is neither a multiple of 3 nor a multiple of 4, then it is odd.
6. All prime numbers less than 10 are not even.
7. If a positive odd integer less than 11 is a factor of 10, then it is 5.
8. There are 2 positive integers less than 25 that are both a multiple of 3 and a multiple of 4.
9. If a positive even integer less than 10 is prime, then it is 2.

Mean, Median, Mode, and Range

Mean, median, and mode are measures of central tendency; they measure the center of data. Range is a measure of dispersion; it measures the spread of data.

The **mean** of a data set is the sum of the values divided by the number of values. The mean is also called the *average*.	The **median** of a data set is the middle value when the values are written in numerical order. If a data set has an even number of values, the median is the mean of the two middle values.	The **mode** of a data set is the value that occurs most often. A data set can have no mode, one mode, or more than one mode.	The **range** of a data set is the difference between the greatest value and the least value.

EXAMPLE **Find the mean, median, mode(s), and range of the data.**

Daily High Temperatures, Week of June 21–27							
Day	Sunday	Monday	Tuesday	Wednesday	Thursday	Friday	Saturday
Temperature (°F)	76	74	70	69	70	75	78

Mean Add the values. Then divide by the number of values.

$76 + 74 + 70 + 69 + 70 + 75 + 78 = 512$

$\text{mean} = 512 \div 7 \approx 73$ The **mean** of the data is about 73°F.

Median Write the values in order from least to greatest. Find the middle value(s).

69, 70, 70, <u>74</u>, 75, 76, 78

median = 74 The **median** of the data is 74°F.

Mode Find the value that occurs most often.

mode = 70 The **mode** of the data is 70°F.

Range Subtract the least value from the greatest value.

$\text{range} = 78 - 69 = 9$ The **range** of the data is 9°F.

PRACTICE

Find the mean, median, mode(s), and range of the data.

1. Apartment rents: $650, $800, $700, $525, $675, $750, $500, $650, $725
2. Ages of new drivers: 15, 15, 15, 15, 16, 16, 16, 16, 16, 17, 17, 17, 18, 18
3. Monthly cell-phone minutes: 581, 713, 423, 852, 948, 337, 810, 604, 897
4. Prices of a CD: $12.98, $14.99, $13.49, $12.98, $13.89, $16.98, $11.98
5. Cookies in a batch: 36, 60, 52, 44, 48, 45, 48, 41, 60, 45, 38, 55, 60, 48, 40
6. Ages of family members: 41, 45, 8, 10, 40, 44, 3, 5, 42, 42, 13, 14, 67, 70
7. Hourly rates of pay: $8.80, $6.50, $10.85, $7.90, $9.50, $9, $8.70, $12.35
8. Weekly quiz scores: 8, 9, 8, 10, 10, 7, 9, 8, 9, 9, 10, 7, 8, 6, 10, 9, 9, 8, 8, 10
9. People on a bus: 9, 14, 5, 22, 18, 30, 6, 25, 18, 12, 15, 10, 8, 22, 10, 11, 20

Graphing Statistical Data

There are many ways to display data. An appropriate graph can help you analyze data. The table at the right summarizes how data are shown in some statistical graphs.

Bar Graph	Compares data in categories.
Circle Graph	Compares data as parts of a whole.
Line Graph	Shows data change over time.

EXAMPLE **Use the bar graph to answer the questions.**

a. On which day of the week were the greatest number of cars parked in the student lot?

▸ The tallest bar on the graph is for Friday. So, the answer is Friday.

b. How many cars were parked in the student lot on Monday?

▸ The bar for Monday shows that about 70 cars were parked in the student lot.

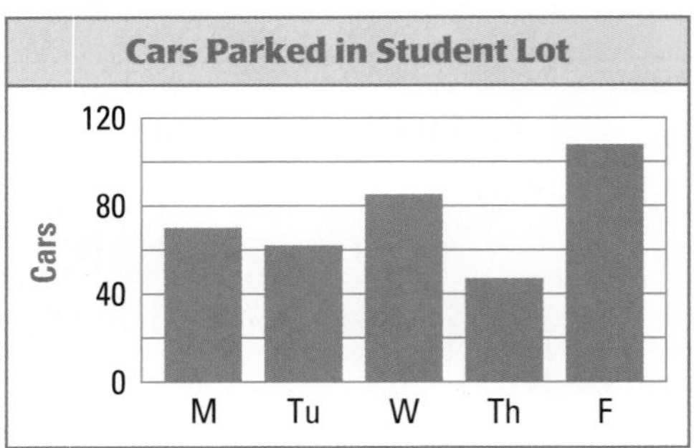

EXAMPLE **Use the circle graph to answer the questions.**

a. Which type of transportation is used almost half the time?

▸ Almost half of the total area of the circle is labeled "Car 45%." So, a car is used almost half the time.

b. Which type of transportation is used the least often?

▸ The smallest part of the circle is labeled "Bus 20%." So, a bus is used the least often.

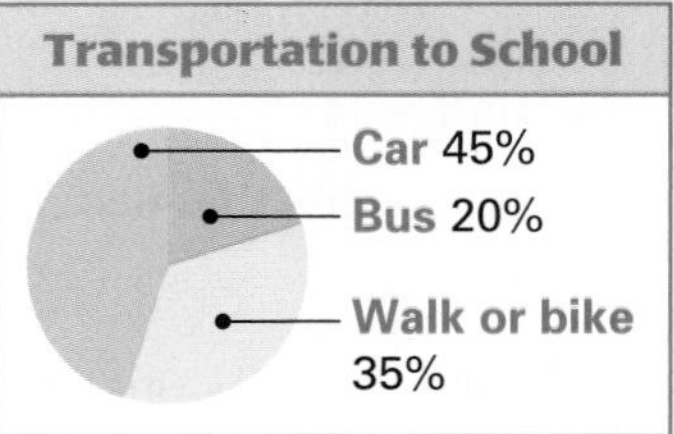

EXAMPLE **Use the line graph to answer the questions.**

a. In which month(s) was Jamie's balance $250?

▸ The points on the graph to the right of $250 show that Jamie's balance was $250 in May and December.

b. Between which two consecutive months did Jamie's balance increase the most?

▸ Of the graph's line segments that have positive slope, the graph is steepest from June to July. So, Jamie's balance increased the most between June and July.

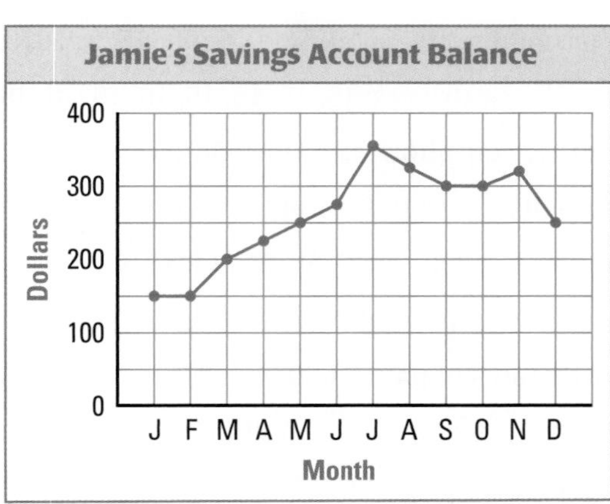

PRACTICE

Use the line graph to answer Exercises 1–5.

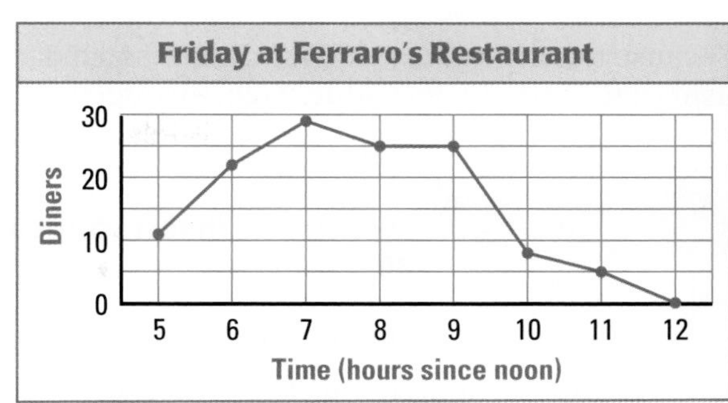

1. At which hour did Ferraro's have 22 diners?
2. At which hour did Ferraro's have the most diners?
3. How many diners were at Ferraro's at 11 P.M.? Were they gone by midnight?
4. Between which two consecutive hours did the number of diners at Ferraro's change the most?
5. How many fewer diners were at Ferraro's at 10 P.M. than at 6 P.M.?

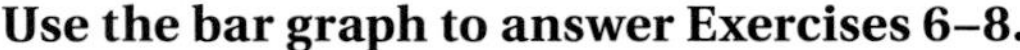

Use the bar graph to answer Exercises 6–8.

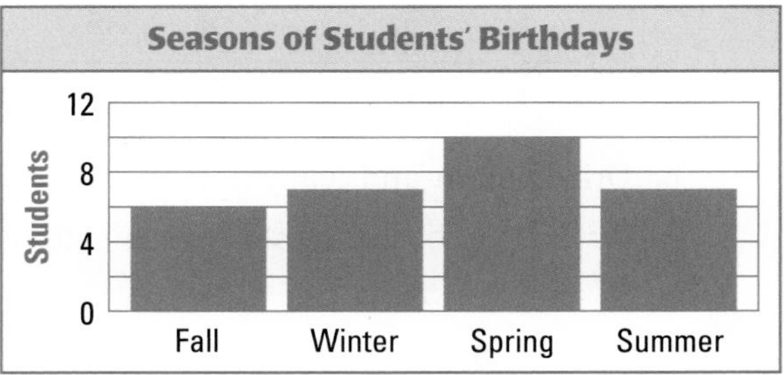

6. In which season were the fewest students born?
7. In which season(s) were 7 students born?
8. How many more students were born in spring than in summer?

Use the circle graph to answer Exercises 9–11.

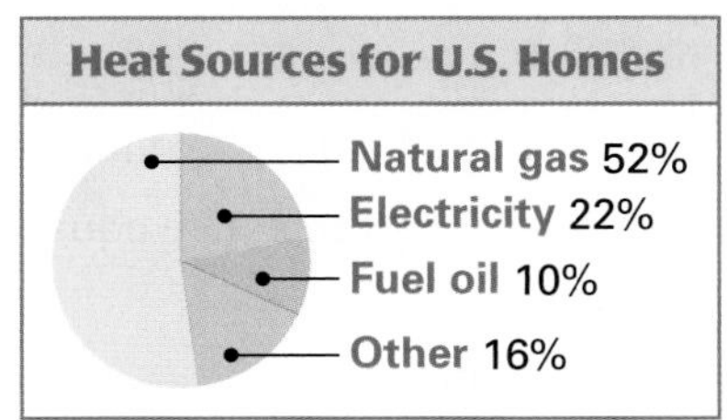

9. What is the heat source of more than half the homes in the United States?
10. What percent of homes in the United States are heated with electricity?
11. If you randomly selected 500 U.S. homes, about how many would be heated with fuel oil?
12. The table below shows the high temperatures in degrees Fahrenheit for one week. Display the data in a line graph.

Mon.	Tues.	Wed.	Thurs.	Fri.	Sat.	Sun.
83	89	79	73	69	67	71

13. A high school conducted a survey to determine the numbers of students involved in various school activities. Display the survey results in a bar graph.

Computer club	Music club	Yearbook club	Drama club	Student council	Chess club
34	75	16	57	28	12

14. The table below shows the items sold at a café in one day. Display the data in a circle graph.

Juice	Soda	Water	Muffin	Cookie
95	180	100	55	40

Organizing Statistical Data

Because it is difficult to analyze unorganized data, it is helpful to organize data using a line plot, stem-and-leaf plot, histogram, or box-and-whisker plot.

EXAMPLE **Sydney's math test scores are 90, 85, 88, 95, 100, 77, 85, 100, 80, 77, and 90.**

a. Draw a line plot to display the data.

Make a number line from 75 to 100. Each time a value is listed in the data set, draw an X above the value on the number line.

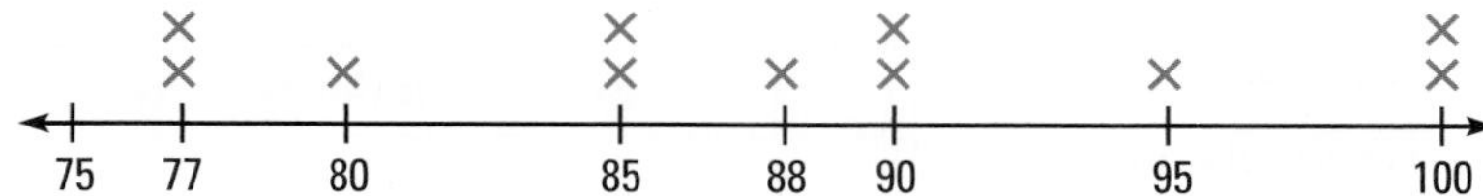

b. Draw a stem-and-leaf plot to display the data.

First write the leaves next to their stems.

7	7 7
8	5 8 5 0
9	0 5 0
10	0 0

Key: 7 | 7 = 77

Then order the leaves from least to greatest.

7	7 7
8	0 5 5 8
9	0 0 5
10	0 0

Key: 7 | 7 = 77

c. Draw a histogram to display the data.

First make a frequency table. Use equal intervals.

Score	Tally	Frequency
71–80	III	3
81–90	~~IIII~~	5
91–100	III	3

Then make a histogram.

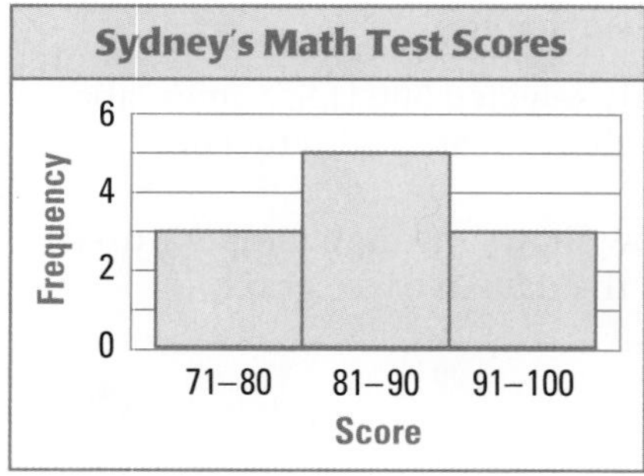

d. Draw a box-and-whisker plot to display the data.

Write the data in order from least to greatest. Ordered data are divided into a lower half and an upper half by the median. The median of the lower half is the **lower quartile**, and the median of the upper half is the **upper quartile**.

77	77	80	85	85	88	90	90	95	100	100
Low value		Lower quartile			Median			Upper quartile		High value

Plot the median, quartiles, and low and high values below a number line. Draw a box between quartiles with a vertical line through the median as shown. Draw whiskers to the low and high values.

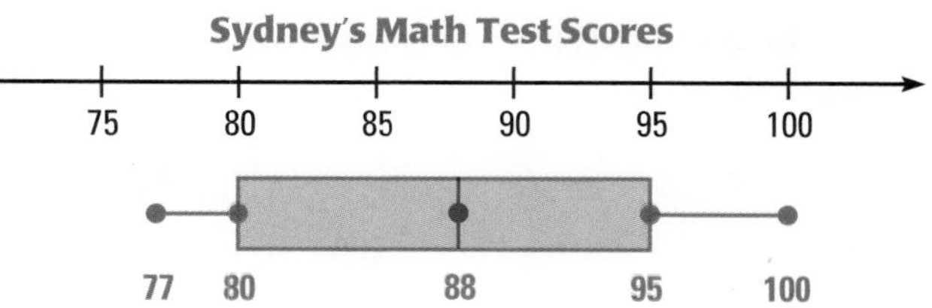

PRACTICE

Use the following list of ticket prices to answer Exercises 1–4: \$50, \$42, \$65, \$54, \$70, \$65, \$59, \$30, \$67, \$49, \$54, \$30, \$73, \$47, and \$54.

1. Draw a line plot to display the data.
2. How many ticket prices are \$50 or less?
3. Draw a stem-and-leaf plot to display the data.
4. What is the range of ticket prices costs?

Use the following list of hourly wages of employees to answer Exercises 5–8: \$8.50, \$6, \$10, \$14.25, \$5.75, \$7, \$6.50, \$14, \$10, \$9, \$6.50, \$8.25, \$8.50, \$11.25, \$7, \$16, \$12, \$6, \$6.75.

5. Draw a histogram to display the data. Begin with the interval \$5.00 to \$6.99.
6. Copy and complete: The greatest number of employees earn from _?_ to _?_ per hour.
7. Draw a box-and-whisker plot to display the data.
8. Copy and complete: About half of the employees have an hourly wage of _?_ or less.

Use the line plot, which shows the results of a survey asking people the average number of e-mails they receive daily, to answer Exercises 9 and 10.

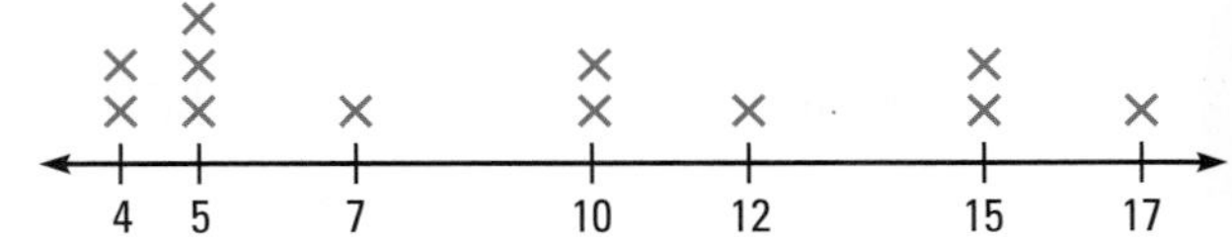

9. Copy and complete: Most people surveyed receive an average of _?_ e-mails per day.
10. How many people receive an average of more than 10 e-mails per day?

Use the stem-and-leaf plot, which shows the weights (in pounds) of dogs at an animal shelter, to answer Exercises 11–13.

Stem	Leaves
2	2 5 5 9
3	1 3 5 8
4	0 0 1 2 2 5 6 7
5	0 3 5 8 9
6	4 5

Key: 2 | 2 = 22

11. How many dogs were at the shelter?
12. Find the median of the data.
13. Find the range of the data.

Use the histogram to answer Exercises 14–16.

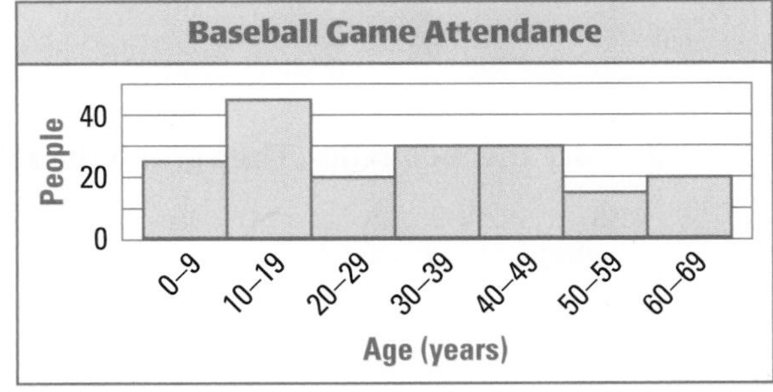

14. Which age group had the greatest attendance at the baseball game? Which had the least?
15. How many children up to the age of 9 years attended the baseball game?
16. Which age group had the same attendance as the oldest group?

Use the box-and-whisker plot to answer Exercises 17–19.

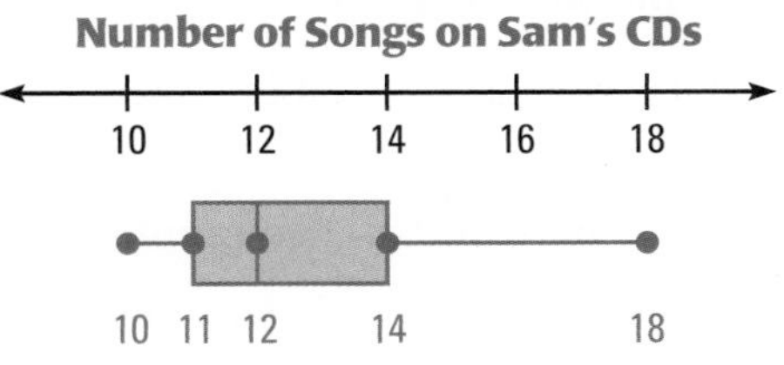

17. What is the median number of songs on Sam's CDs?
18. What is the upper quartile of songs on Sam's CDs?
19. What is the least number of songs on one of Sam's CDs? What is the greatest number?

Extra Practice

Chapter 1

1.1 Graph the numbers on a number line.

1. $-2, \frac{5}{3}, 0.2, -\sqrt{2}, -\frac{5}{4}$
2. $-\frac{4}{3}, 1, -1.2, \sqrt{3}, 1.9$
3. $3.7, -\sqrt{7}, -\frac{1}{2}, 4, \sqrt{15}$

1.1 Perform the indicated conversion.

4. 18 feet to inches
5. 20 ounces to pounds
6. 3 years to hours

1.2 Evaluate the expression for the given value of the variable.

7. $-2p + 5$ when $p = -5$
8. $3x^2 - x + 7$ when $x = -1$
9. $8z^3 - 6z$ when $z = 2$

1.2 Simplify the expression.

10. $2y^2 - 3y + 5y^2$
11. $4r^2 - 5r + 2r^2 + 12$
12. $-w^3 + w^2 - 7w^2 - 8w^3$
13. $2(b + 5) + 3(2b - 10)$
14. $-7(t^2 + 2) + 9(t - 2)$
15. $4(m - 3) - 5(m^2 - m)$

1.3 Solve the equation. Check your solution.

16. $3a + 2 = 11$
17. $-9 = b - 14$
18. $8 - 0.5c = 1$
19. $-3n - 7 = -n + 17$
20. $12m = 15m - 7.5$
21. $6p + 1 = 21 - 4p$
22. $6(x + 1) = 2x - 10$
23. $4(y - 3) = 2(y + 8)$
24. $11(z - 5) = 2(z + 6) - 13$

1.4 Solve the equation for *y*. Then find the value of *y* for the given value of *x*.

25. $6y - x = 18; x = 2$
26. $2x + 3y = 12; x = -6$
27. $4y - 9x = -30; x = 6$
28. $3x - xy = 20; x = 8$
29. $4y + 6xy = 10; x = -2$
30. $5x + 8y + 4xy = 0; x = -1$

1.5 Look for a pattern in the table. Then write an equation that represents the table.

31.

x	0	1	2	3
y	25	22	19	16

32.

x	0	1	2	3
y	1.5	4	6.5	9

1.6 Solve the inequality. Then graph the solution.

33. $x + 2 > 9$
34. $-13 - 3x < 11$
35. $4x - 9 \le 2x + 1$
36. $-3x - 8 \ge -9x + 10$
37. $-7 < x + 3 \le 1$
38. $-4 \le 3x - 7 \le 4$
39. $-9 \le 5 - 2x < 7$
40. $x + 3 < -2$ or $x - 7 > 0$
41. $2x + 9 \ge 3$ or $-5x + 1 \le 0$

1.7 Solve the equation. Check for extraneous solutions.

42. $|g + 5| = 4$
43. $\left|\frac{1}{3}q - \frac{2}{3}\right| = 1$
44. $|10 - 3t| = t + 4$
45. $|3z + 1| = -6z$

1.7 Solve the inequality. Then graph the solution.

46. $|a| < 2$
47. $|2c| > 14$
48. $|g + 11| \ge 2$
49. $|4j - 7| \le 9$
50. $|0.25m + 3| \ge 1$
51. $|10 - 2p| > 9$
52. $|0.6r + 8| \le 17$
53. $|5t - 9| + 9 < 10$

EXTRA PRACTICE

Chapter 2

2.1 Tell whether the relation is a function. *Explain.*

1. 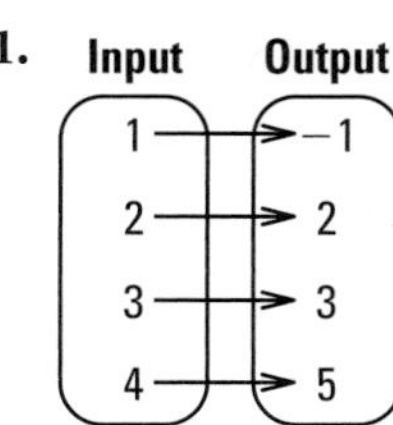

2. 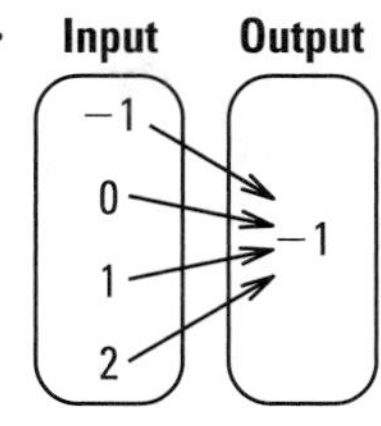

3. 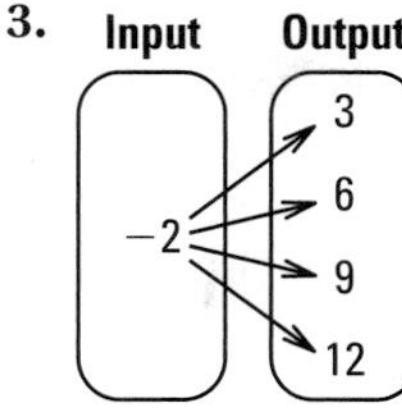

4. 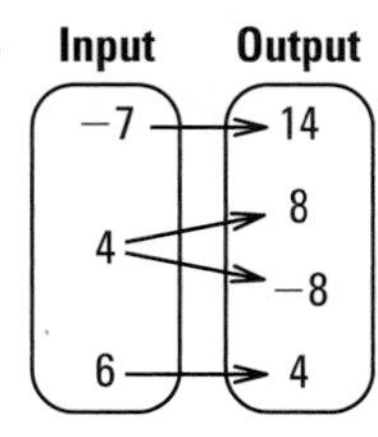

2.2 Find the slope of the line passing through the given points. Then tell whether the line *rises, falls, is horizontal,* or *is vertical.*

5. $(-3, 0), (5, -4)$
6. $(2, -1), (8, -1)$
7. $(3, 5), (3, -12)$
8. $(1, 8), (-1, -4)$

2.2 Tell whether the lines are *parallel, perpendicular,* or *neither.*

9. Line 1: through $(5, -4)$ and $(-4, 2)$
   Line 2: through $(-5, -4)$ and $(-2, -2)$
10. Line 1: through $(0, -4)$ and $(-2, 2)$
    Line 2: through $(4, -3)$ and $(5, -6)$

2.3 Graph the equation using any method.

11. $y = 2x - 2$
12. $y = -x + 2$
13. $f(x) = \frac{2}{3}x - 1$
14. $x + 2y = -6$
15. $-4x + 5y = 10$
16. $y - 2 = 0$
17. $-2x = 6y + 5$
18. $2y + 10 = -2.5x$

2.4 Write an equation of the line that satisfies the given conditions.

19. $m = 7, b = -3$
20. $m = \frac{1}{3}, b = 4$
21. $m = 0$, passes through $(7, -2)$
22. $m = -\frac{1}{4}$, passes through $(3, 6)$
23. passes through $(-1, -3)$ and $(2, 7)$
24. passes through $(4, -2)$ and $(0, 4)$

2.5 The variables x and y vary directly. Write an equation that relates x and y. Then find y when $x = -2$.

25. $x = 2, y = 4$
26. $x = -1, y = 3$
27. $x = -28, y = -7$
28. $x = 6, y = -4$

2.6 In Exercises 29 and 30, (a) draw a scatter plot of the data, (b) approximate the best-fitting line, and (c) estimate y when $x = 12$.

29.

x	1	2	3	4	5
y	8	11	13	16	18

30.

x	1	2	3	4	5
y	50	41	37	22	20

2.7 Graph the function. *Compare* the graph with the graph of $y = |x|$.

31. $y = |x + 3|$
32. $y = -2|x - 5|$
33. $y = 3|x + 1| - 2$
34. $y = -\frac{1}{2}|x + 2| + 3$

2.8 Graph the inequality in a coordinate plane.

35. $x < 4$
36. $y \geq -2$
37. $y \leq -x - 1$
38. $x + 2y > 8$
39. $-x - 4y \leq 6$
40. $3x + 4y > 12$
41. $y < |x + 1|$
42. $y \geq 3|x - 2| - 1$

Chapter 3

3.1 Graph the linear system and estimate the solution. Then check the solution algebraically.

1. $y = 2x - 1$, $y = x - 4$

2. $y = -x + 3$, $y = -4x$

3. $x + 2y = 6$, $-5x + 6y = -2$

4. $-2x + 7y = -7$, $4x - 14y = 14$

3.2 Solve the system using any algebraic method.

5. $-5x - y = -3$, $x - 4y = 9$

6. $4x - 2y = -6$, $-3x + y = -3$

7. $4x + 3y = -5$, $12x + 4y = 10$

8. $3x + 2y = 4$, $-7x - 5y = -7$

3.3 Graph the system of inequalities.

9. $x > 4$, $y \geq -1$

10. $x + y < -2$, $x - 3y > 6$

11. $x \leq 5$, $y > 3$, $y > x$

12. $x > -3$, $x \leq 2$, $2x + 3y < 10$, $y > -4x$

3.4 Solve the system using any algebraic method.

13. $3x + y - z = -6$, $-x + 2y + 3z = -1$, $5x - 2y + 6z = 54$

14. $x + y - z = 7$, $2x - 3y + z = 2$, $4x + 2y - 2z = 20$

15. $-x + y - 2z = 1.5$, $4x - y + 5z = -6$, $2x + y - 2z = 6$

16. $-6x + y + 9z = 4$, $2x - 3y - z = -6$, $8x + 5y - 4z = 10$

3.5 Perform the indicated operation.

17. $\begin{bmatrix} -6 & 7 \\ 0 & 3 \end{bmatrix} + \begin{bmatrix} -6 & 2 \\ -8 & 1 \end{bmatrix}$

18. $-\frac{2}{3}\begin{bmatrix} -9 & 3 \\ 4 & -1 \end{bmatrix}$

19. $\begin{bmatrix} 10 & 17 & -9 \\ -6 & 4 & 11 \end{bmatrix} - \begin{bmatrix} -6 & 8 & -2 \\ -4 & -9 & 4 \end{bmatrix}$

3.6 Find the product. If the product is not defined, state the reason.

20. $\begin{bmatrix} 4 & 1 \\ -3 & 0 \end{bmatrix}\begin{bmatrix} -7 & 5 \\ 7 & -3 \end{bmatrix}$

21. $\begin{bmatrix} -16 \\ 2 \end{bmatrix}\begin{bmatrix} 4 \\ 15 \end{bmatrix}$

22. $\begin{bmatrix} 5 & -1 & 0 \\ 4 & -2 & 9 \end{bmatrix}\begin{bmatrix} 12 \\ -7 \\ 3 \end{bmatrix}$

3.7 Evaluate the determinant of the matrix.

23. $\begin{bmatrix} 5 & 8 \\ -2 & 10 \end{bmatrix}$

24. $\begin{bmatrix} 13 & 7 \\ -11 & -4 \end{bmatrix}$

25. $\begin{bmatrix} 1 & -3 & -2 \\ 7 & 4 & 0 \\ -7 & 2 & 3 \end{bmatrix}$

26. $\begin{bmatrix} 6 & 0 & 5 \\ -4 & 2 & 1 \\ 1 & 0 & 0.5 \end{bmatrix}$

3.7 Use Cramer's rule to solve the linear system.

27. $2x + y = -8$, $-5x - 2y = 13$

28. $8x + 3y = 1$, $7x + 3y = -1$

29. $2x - 2y - 3z = 9$, $3x + z = 10$, $x + y = 0$

30. $2x + y + 3z = 4$, $-8x + 4y + z = -7$, $x + 2y + 3z = -1$

3.8 Find the inverse of the matrix.

31. $\begin{bmatrix} 3 & 7 \\ 3 & 8 \end{bmatrix}$

32. $\begin{bmatrix} 1 & 4 \\ 0 & 5 \end{bmatrix}$

33. $\begin{bmatrix} -2 & -5 \\ 3 & 8 \end{bmatrix}$

34. $\begin{bmatrix} 9 & 2 \\ 18 & 5 \end{bmatrix}$

3.8 Use an inverse matrix to solve the linear system.

35. $x + 3y = -4$, $-2x + y = -34$

36. $2x + 3y = 6$, $-x - 6y = -9$

37. $3x - 8y = 0$, $2x + y = -19$

38. $x + y = 7$, $-5x + 3y = -3$

Chapter 4

4.1 Graph the function. Label the vertex and axis of symmetry.

1. $y = 3x^2 + 5$
2. $y = -x^2 - 4x - 4$
3. $y = -2x^2 + 4x + 1$
4. $y = 2x^2 + 5x + 6$

4.2 Graph the function. Label the vertex and axis of symmetry.

5. $y = 4(x - 2)^2 + 1$
6. $y = -(x + 3)^2 - 2$
7. $y = 3(x - 1)(x - 5)$
8. $y = \frac{1}{2}(x + 3)(x + 2)$

4.2 Write the quadratic function in standard form.

9. $y = 7(x + 2)(x + 4)$
10. $y = 2(x + 5)(x - 3)$
11. $y = (x - 7)^2 + 7$
12. $y = -(x + 1)^2 - 4$

4.3 Factor the expression. If the expression cannot be factored, say so.

13. $x^2 - 4x + 4$
14. $t^2 - 11t - 26$
15. $x^2 + 21x + 108$
16. $b^2 - 400$

4.3 Solve the equation.

17. $x^2 + 5x - 14 = 0$
18. $x^2 - 11x + 24 = 0$
19. $c^2 + 6c = 55$
20. $n^2 = 5n$

4.4 Factor the expression. If the expression cannot be factored, say so.

21. $2x^2 + x - 15$
22. $10a^2 - 19a + 7$
23. $3r^2 + 9r - 4$
24. $4t^2 + 8t + 3$

4.4 Find the zeros of the function by rewriting the function in intercept form.

25. $y = 81x^2 - 16$
26. $y = 2x^2 - 9x - 5$
27. $y = 4x^2 + 18x + 18$
28. $y = -3x^2 - 30x - 27$

4.5 Simplify the expression.

29. $\sqrt{56}$
30. $3\sqrt{2} \cdot \sqrt{50}$
31. $\sqrt{\frac{4}{7}}$
32. $\frac{6}{1 + \sqrt{2}}$

4.5 Solve the equation.

33. $b^2 = 8$
34. $p^2 + 6 = 127$
35. $(x - 5)^2 = 10$
36. $3(x + 2)^2 - 4 = 11$

4.6 Write the expression as a complex number in standard form.

37. $(5 + 2i) + (6 - 5i)$
38. $-3i(7 + i)$
39. $\frac{1 + 2i}{3 - 8i}$
40. $\frac{(3 - 2i) + 2i}{(-1 + 7i) - (2 + 3i)}$

4.7 Solve the equation by completing the square.

41. $x^2 + 6x = 10$
42. $x^2 - 9x - 2 = 0$
43. $2c^2 - 12c + 6 = 0$
44. $3z^2 - 3z + 9 = 0$

4.8 Use the quadratic formula to solve the equation.

45. $x^2 + 10x - 10 = 0$
46. $x^2 - x - 1 = 0$
47. $4s^2 + 3s = 12$
48. $-2r^2 = r + 17$

4.9 Solve the inequality using any method.

49. $x^2 - 10x \geq 0$
50. $x^2 - 8x + 12 < 0$
51. $-x^2 + 7x + 6 > 1$
52. $3x^2 + 16x + 2 \leq 3x$

4.10 Write a quadratic function in standard form for the parabola that passes through the given points.

53. $(-1, -6), (0, -7), (2, 9)$
54. $(-2, -1), (1, 2), (3, -6)$
55. $(-3, 36), (0, 36), (2, 16)$

EXTRA PRACTICE

Chapter 5

5.1 Write the answer in scientific notation.

1. $(3.4 \times 10^3)(2.8 \times 10^8)$ **2.** $(5.8 \times 10^{-6})^4$ **3.** $\dfrac{4.6 \times 10^{-7}}{9.2 \times 10^{-9}}$

5.1 Simplify the expression. Tell which properties of exponents you used.

4. $\dfrac{-14x^{-3}y^5}{35xy^3}$ **5.** $(4a^5b^{-2})^{-3}$ **6.** $(2r^3s^3)(r^{-7}s^5)$ **7.** $\dfrac{xy^{-1}}{x^2y} \cdot \dfrac{7x^3}{y^{-4}}$

5.2 Graph the polynomial function.

8. $f(x) = x^4$ **9.** $f(x) = x^3 + x + 4$ **10.** $f(x) = -x^3 + 3x$ **11.** $f(x) = x^5 + 2x^3$

5.3 Perform the indicated operation.

12. $(4z^3 + 9) + (3z^2 - 4z - 2)$ **13.** $(x^2 + 3x - 1) - (4x^2 + 7)$ **14.** $(3x - 4)^3$

5.4 Factor the polynomial completely using any method.

15. $3x^4 + 18x^3 + 27x^2$ **16.** $343x^3 + 1000$ **17.** $2x^3 + x^2 - 8x - 4$

5.4 Find the real-number solutions of the equation.

18. $3x^3 + 18x^2 = 48x$ **19.** $x^4 - 32 = 14x^2$ **20.** $2x^3 + 48 = 3x^2 + 32x$

5.5 Divide using polynomial long division or synthetic division.

21. $(2x^3 + 4x^2 - 5x + 16) \div (x - 3)$ **22.** $(x^4 + 2x^3 - 7x^2 - 14) \div (x + 2)$

5.6 Find all real zeros of the function.

23. $f(x) = 2x^3 + 3x^2 - 8x + 3$ **24.** $f(x) = 2x^4 + x^3 - 53x^2 - 14x + 20$

5.7 Determine the possible numbers of positive real zeros, negative real zeros, and imaginary zeros of the function.

25. $f(x) = -x^3 + 2x^2 - 11x - 1$ **26.** $f(x) = 4x^5 + 3x^2 - 8x - 10$ **27.** $f(x) = x^4 - 3x^3 - 7x - 13$

5.8 Estimate the coordinates of each turning point and state whether each corresponds to a local maximum or a local minimum. Then estimate all real zeros and determine the least degree the function can have.

28.

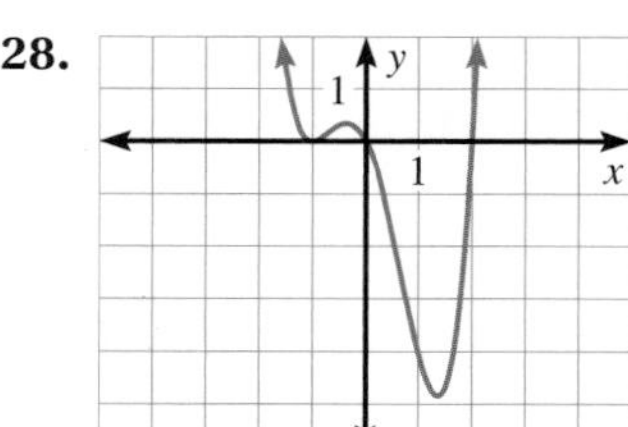

29.

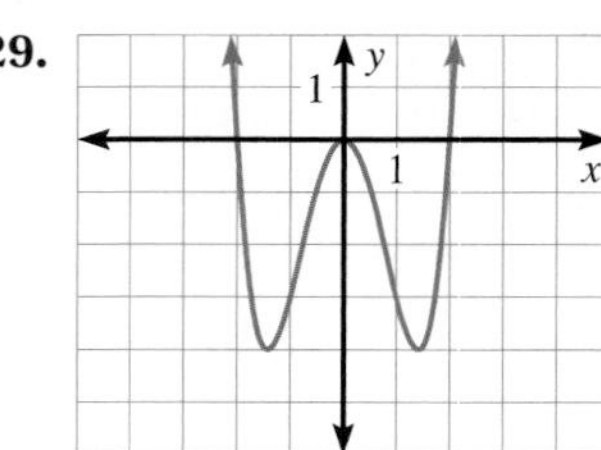

30.

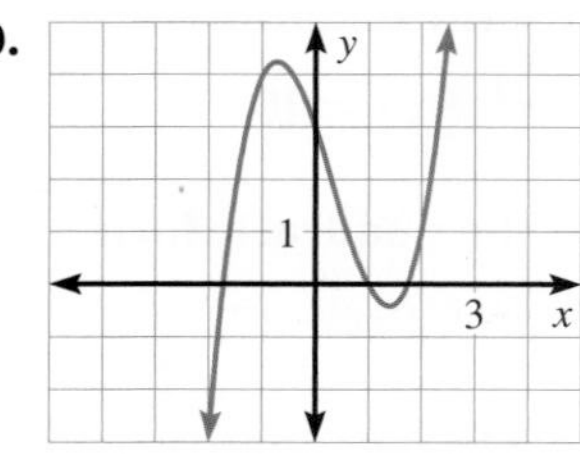

5.9 Use finite differences and a system of equations to find a polynomial function that fits the data in the table.

31.

x	1	2	3	4	5	6
y	2.5	11	27.5	55	96.5	155

32.

x	1	2	3	4	5	6
y	−7	−6	39	188	525	1158

Chapter 6

6.1 Find the indicated real *n*th root(s) of *a*.

1. $n = 4, a = 81$
2. $n = 3, a = 512$
3. $n = 5, a = -243$

6.1 Evaluate the expression without using a calculator.

4. $36^{-1/2}$
5. $64^{5/6}$
6. $(\sqrt[3]{216})^{-2}$
7. $(\sqrt[5]{-32})^4$

6.1 Solve the equation. Round the result to two decimal places when appropriate.

8. $x^3 = -8$
9. $x^4 + 9 = 90$
10. $(x - 3)^5 = 60$
11. $-4x^6 = -400$

6.2 Simplify the expression.

12. $4^{5/2} \cdot 4^{-1/2}$
13. $\frac{17^{3/7}}{17^{4/7}}$
14. $(\sqrt[4]{5} \cdot \sqrt{5})^4$
15. $\frac{\sqrt[3]{135}}{\sqrt[3]{5}}$
16. $5\sqrt[5]{7} - 7\sqrt[5]{7}$
17. $\sqrt[3]{2} + 2\sqrt[3]{128}$
18. $\frac{324^{1/4}}{4^{-1/4}}$
19. $4\sqrt[3]{108} \cdot 2\sqrt[3]{4}$

6.2 Write the expression in simplest form. Assume all variables are positive.

20. $\sqrt{20x^6y^7}$
21. $\sqrt[5]{18x^3y^{14}z^{20}}$
22. $\sqrt[4]{\frac{x^5}{y^{16}}}$
23. $\sqrt[3]{16x^7y^2} \cdot \sqrt[3]{6xy^5}$

6.3 Let $f(x) = -x + 4$, $g(x) = x^3$, and $h(x) = \frac{x}{4}$. Perform the indicated operation and state the domain.

24. $f(x) + g(x)$
25. $g(x) - f(x)$
26. $g(x) \cdot h(x)$
27. $\frac{f(x)}{g(x)}$
28. $f(g(x))$
29. $g(h(x))$
30. $h(f(x))$
31. $f(f(x))$

6.4 Verify that *f* and *g* are inverse functions.

32. $f(x) = 2x - 4, g(x) = \frac{1}{2}x + 2$
33. $f(x) = 3x^2 + 1, x \geq 0; g(x) = \left(\frac{x-1}{3}\right)^{1/2}$

6.4 Find the inverse of the function.

34. $f(x) = 5x - 3$
35. $f(x) = \frac{4}{3}x + 2$
36. $f(x) = \frac{1}{2}x^2, x \geq 0$
37. $f(x) = -x^6 + 2, x \leq 0$
38. $f(x) = \frac{4x^4 - 1}{18}, x \geq 0$
39. $f(x) = 32x^5 + 4$

6.5 Graph the function. Then state the domain and range.

40. $y = -\frac{1}{3}\sqrt{x}$
41. $y = \frac{2}{5}\sqrt[3]{x}$
42. $y = \frac{5}{6}\sqrt{x}$
43. $y = \sqrt{x + 2} - 3$
44. $y = -2\sqrt[3]{x - 1} + 2$
45. $f(x) = 3\sqrt[3]{x}$
46. $g(x) = -\frac{1}{2}\sqrt{x - 2}$
47. $h(x) = -\sqrt{x + 3} + 4$

6.6 Solve the equation. Check your solution.

48. $\sqrt{2x + 3} = 7$
49. $-5\sqrt{x + 1} + 12 = 2$
50. $\sqrt[3]{5x - 1} + 6 = 10$
51. $2\sqrt[3]{8x} + 9 = 5$
52. $7x^{4/3} = 175$
53. $(x - 2)^{3/4} = 1$
54. $x - 8 = \sqrt{18x}$
55. $x = \sqrt{4x - 3}$
56. $\sqrt{2x + 1} + 5 = \sqrt{x + 12} - 8$

Chapter 7

7.1 Graph the function. State the domain and range.

1. $y = \left(\frac{4}{3}\right)^x$ **2.** $y = -2 \cdot 2^x$ **3.** $y = 3^{x-3} - 2$ **4.** $y = \frac{1}{4} \cdot 3^{x+1} + 2$

7.2 Graph the function. State the domain and range.

5. $y = \left(\frac{3}{5}\right)^x$ **6.** $y = -2\left(\frac{1}{4}\right)^x$ **7.** $y = (0.8)^{x-3} - 2$ **8.** $y = 2\left(\frac{2}{3}\right)^x + 1$

7.3 Simplify the expression.

9. $e^{-3} \cdot e^{-8}$ **10.** $(2e^{2x})^{-5}$ **11.** $\sqrt{81e^{8x}}$ **12.** $\frac{28e^{3x}}{21e^{-x}}$

7.3 Graph the function. State the domain and range.

13. $y = 0.5e^{3x}$ **14.** $y = 2e^{-x} - 2$ **15.** $y = 1.5e^{x+1} + 3$ **16.** $y = e^{3(x-2)} + 1$

7.4 Evaluate the logarithm without using a calculator.

17. $\log_4 \frac{1}{16}$ **18.** $\log_6 6$ **19.** $\log_5 125$ **20.** $\log_{3/4} \frac{64}{27}$

7.4 Simplify the expression.

21. $5^{\log_5 x}$ **22.** $10^{\log 9}$ **23.** $\log_4 16^x$ **24.** $e^{\ln 5}$

7.4 Graph the function. State the domain and range.

25. $y = \log_7 x$ **26.** $y = \log_{1/2} (x - 4)$ **27.** $y = \log_5 x + 3$ **28.** $y = \log_3 (x - 2) + 1$

7.5 Expand the expression.

29. $\log_5 \frac{2x}{5}$ **30.** $\log \frac{100x^2}{y}$ **31.** $\ln 20x^3y^2$ **32.** $\log_2 \sqrt[3]{8x^4}$

7.5 Condense the expression.

33. $\log_4 20 + 4 \log_4 x$ **34.** $\log 7 + 2 \log x - 5 \log y$ **35.** $0.5 \ln 100 - 2 \ln x + 8 \ln y$

7.5 Use the change-of-base formula to evaluate the logarithm.

36. $\log_2 5$ **37.** $\log_4 80$ **38.** $\log_5 100$ **39.** $\log_7 27$

7.6 Solve the equation. Check for extraneous solutions.

40. $2^{4x+2} = 8^{x+2}$ **41.** $\left(\frac{1}{9}\right)^{x-3} = 3^{3x+1}$ **42.** $7^{9x} = 18$

43. $\ln (3x + 7) = \ln (x - 1)$ **44.** $\log_5 (3x + 2) = 3$ **45.** $\log_6 (x + 9) + \log_6 x = 2$

7.7 Write an exponential function $y = ab^x$ whose graph passes through the given points.

46. (1, 8), (2, 32) **47.** (1, 3), (3, 12) **48.** (2, −9), (5, −243) **49.** (1, 4), (2, 4)

7.7 Write a power function $y = ax^b$ whose graph passes through the given points.

50. (2, 2), (5, 16) **51.** (3, 27), (6, 432) **52.** (1, 4), (8, 17) **53.** (5, 36), (10, 220)

Chapter 8

8.1 The variables x and y vary inversely. Use the given values to write an equation relating x and y. Then find y when $x = -5$.

1. $x = 2, y = -10$
2. $x = \frac{1}{3}, y = 24$
3. $x = -3, y = -5$
4. $x = 25, y = -\frac{2}{5}$

8.1 Determine whether x and y show *direct variation, inverse variation,* or *neither.*

5.

x	y
2.5	32
4	20
5	16
6.4	12.5
8	10

6.

x	y
1	2.5
3.5	8.75
5	12.5
8	20
9	22.5

7.

x	y
11	30
14	61
16	85
24	92
27	105

8.

x	y
1	12
3	4
8	1.5
12	1
15	0.8

8.2 Graph the function. State the domain and range.

9. $y = \frac{6}{x}$
10. $y = \frac{-2}{x} + 3$
11. $y = \frac{5}{x-1} - 2$
12. $y = \frac{4x+19}{x+3}$

8.3 Graph the function.

13. $y = \frac{x}{x^2 - 4}$
14. $y = \frac{x^2+1}{x^2+4x+3}$
15. $y = \frac{x^2+2x-3}{x+2}$
16. $f(x) = \frac{2x^2-8}{x^2-2x}$

8.4 Simplify the rational expression, if possible.

17. $\frac{x^2+x-6}{x^2+9x+18}$
18. $\frac{x^3-100x}{x^4+20x^3+100x^2}$
19. $\frac{x^2-5x-84}{2x^2-98}$
20. $\frac{x^2+7x+10}{x^2-7x+10}$

8.4 Multiply or divide the expressions. Simplify the result.

21. $\frac{6x^2y}{xy^2} \cdot \frac{2y}{9x^3}$
22. $\frac{2x^2-x-6}{2x^2+5x+3} \cdot \frac{x^2+x}{x^2-4}$
23. $\frac{3x^2+15x}{x^2-12x+36} \cdot (x^2-x-30)$
24. $\frac{12x^8y}{5y^5} \div \frac{3y^2}{x^2}$
25. $\frac{6x^2+x-1}{4x^3+4x^2} \div \frac{6x^2-2x}{x^2-4x-5}$
26. $\frac{x^2-4x-32}{2x^2-13x-24} \div \frac{x}{4x^2-9}$

8.5 Add or subtract the expressions. Simplify the result.

27. $\frac{x^2}{x+1} - \frac{1}{x+1}$
28. $\frac{x+5}{x+6} + \frac{1}{x-2}$
29. $\frac{5}{x+2} + \frac{35}{x^2-3x-10}$

8.5 Simplify the complex fraction.

30. $\dfrac{\frac{x}{2x+1}}{5+\frac{3}{x}}$
31. $\dfrac{\frac{x}{3}+2}{\frac{1}{x}+3}$
32. $\dfrac{\frac{3}{x^2-4}}{\frac{2}{x+2} - \frac{x+1}{x^2-x-6}}$

8.6 Solve the equation. Check for extraneous solutions.

33. $\frac{7}{3x-7} = \frac{14}{x+1}$
34. $\frac{1}{3} + \frac{2}{x} = -\frac{3}{x^2}$
35. $2 - \frac{4}{x+2} = \frac{2}{x}$
36. $\frac{4}{x-2} + \frac{6x^2}{x^2-4} = \frac{3x}{x+2}$

Chapter 9

9.1 Find the distance between the two points. Then find the midpoint of the line segment joining the two points.

1. $(-5, 0), (5, 4)$ **2.** $(2, 1), (3, 7)$ **3.** $(-12, 12), (14, -4)$ **4.** $(12, -1), (18, -9)$

9.2 Graph the equation. Identify the focus, directrix, and axis of symmetry of the parabola.

5. $y^2 = 2x$ **6.** $x^2 = -4y$ **7.** $14x^2 = -21y$ **8.** $12y^2 + 3x = 0$

9.3 Graph the equation. Identify the radius of the circle.

9. $x^2 + y^2 = 4$ **10.** $x^2 + y^2 = 14$ **11.** $3x^2 + 3y^2 = 75$ **12.** $16x^2 + 16y^2 = 4$

9.3 Write the standard form of the equation of the circle that passes through the given point and whose center is at the origin.

13. $(8, 0)$ **14.** $(0, -9)$ **15.** $(7, -1)$ **16.** $(-5, -11)$

9.4 Graph the equation. Identify the vertices, co-vertices, and foci of the ellipse.

17. $\frac{x^2}{81} + \frac{y^2}{16} = 1$ **18.** $x^2 + \frac{y^2}{9} = 1$ **19.** $9x^2 + 4y^2 = 576$ **20.** $49x^2 + 64y^2 = 12{,}544$

9.4 Write an equation of the ellipse with the given characteristics and center at (0, 0).

21. Vertex: $(4, 0)$
Co-vertex: $(0, 2)$

22. Vertex: $(0, -5)$
Co-vertex: $(4, 0)$

23. Vertex: $(9, 0)$
Focus: $(-3, 0)$

24. Co-vertex: $(0, 10)$
Focus: $(8, 0)$

9.5 Graph the equation. Identify the vertices, foci, and asymptotes of the hyperbola.

25. $\frac{x^2}{36} - \frac{y^2}{16} = 1$ **26.** $x^2 - y^2 = 4$ **27.** $49y^2 - 81x^2 = 3969$

9.5 Write an equation of the hyperbola with the given foci and vertices.

28. Foci: $(0, -8), (0, 8)$
Vertices: $(0, -6), (0, 6)$

29. Foci: $(-2, 0), (2, 0)$
Vertices: $(-1, 0), (1, 0)$

30. Foci: $(0, -5), (0, 5)$
Vertices: $(0, -3\sqrt{2}), (0, 3\sqrt{2})$

9.6 Graph the equation. Identify the important characteristics of the graph.

31. $\frac{(x-3)^2}{25} + \frac{y^2}{9} = 1$ **32.** $(x + 2)^2 + (y - 1)^2 = 4$ **33.** $(y - 4)^2 - \frac{(x+1)^2}{16} = 1$

9.6 Classify the conic section and write its equation in standard form. Then graph the equation.

34. $x^2 + y^2 + 2x + 2y - 7 = 0$ **35.** $9x^2 + 4y^2 - 72x + 16y + 16 = 0$

36. $9x^2 - 4y^2 + 16y - 52 = 0$ **37.** $x^2 - 6x - 4y + 17 = 0$

9.7 Solve the system.

38. $x^2 + y^2 = 4$
$9x^2 - 4y^2 = 36$

39. $y = x - 2$
$x^2 + y^2 - 6x - 4y - 12 = 0$

40. $y^2 = x - 5$
$9x^2 - 25y^2 = 225$

Chapter 10

10.1 For the given password configuration, determine how many passwords are possible if (a) digits and letters can be repeated, and (b) digits and letters cannot be repeated.

1. 8 digits
2. 8 letters
3. 5 letters followed by 1 digit
4. 2 digits followed by 2 letters

10.1 Find the number of permutations.

5. ${}_5P_2$
6. ${}_6P_1$
7. ${}_9P_9$
8. ${}_{12}P_4$

10.1 Find the number of distinguishable permutations of the letters in the word.

9. VANILLA
10. CHOCOLATE
11. STRAWBERRY
12. COFFEE

10.2 Find the number of combinations.

13. ${}_7C_3$
14. ${}_4C_1$
15. ${}_{10}C_9$
16. ${}_{15}C_6$

10.2 Use the binomial theorem to write the binomial expansion.

17. $(x - 3)^3$
18. $(2x + 3y)^4$
19. $(p^2 + 4)^5$
20. $(x^3 + y^2)^6$

10.3 You have an equally likely chance of choosing any integer from 1 through 25. Find the probability of the given event.

21. An odd number is chosen.
22. A multiple of 3 is chosen.

10.3 Find the probability that a dart thrown at the given target will hit the shaded region. Assume the dart is equally likely to hit any point inside the target.

23. 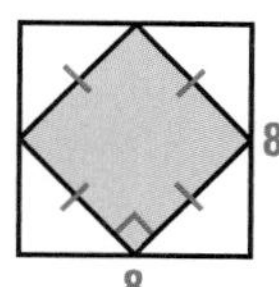

24. 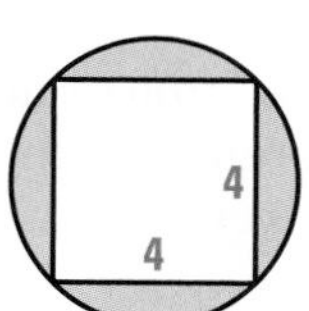

25. 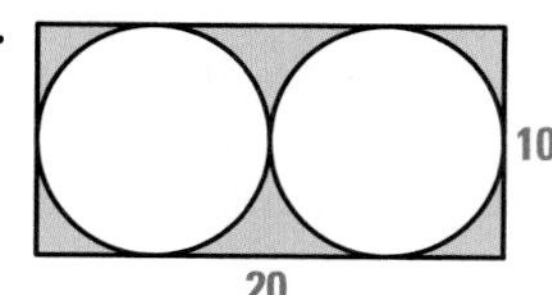

10.4 Events *A* and *B* are disjoint. Find *P*(*A* or *B*).

26. $P(A) = 0.4, P(B) = 0.15$
27. $P(A) = 0.3, P(B) = 0.5$
28. $P(A) = 0.7, P(B) = 0.21$

10.4 Find the indicated probability. State whether *A* and *B* are disjoint events.

29. $P(A) = 0.25$
$P(B) = 0.55$
$P(A \text{ or } B) = \underline{\ ?\ }$
$P(A \text{ and } B) = 0.2$
30. $P(A) = 0.52$
$P(B) = 0.15$
$P(A \text{ or } B) = 0.67$
$P(A \text{ and } B) = \underline{\ ?\ }$
31. $P(A) = 0.54$
$P(B) = 0.28$
$P(A \text{ or } B) = 0.65$
$P(A \text{ and } B) = \underline{\ ?\ }$
32. $P(A) = 0.5$
$P(B) = 0.4$
$P(A \text{ or } B) = \underline{\ ?\ }$
$P(A \text{ and } B) = 0.3$

10.5 Find the probability of drawing the given cards from a standard deck of 52 cards (a) with replacement and (b) without replacement.

33. A jack, then a 3
34. A club, then another club
35. A black ace, then a red card

10.6 Calculate the probability of tossing a coin 15 times and getting the given number of heads.

36. 1
37. 4
38. 7
39. 15

EXTRA PRACTICE

Chapter 11

11.1 Find the mean, median, mode, range, and standard deviation of the data set.

1. 5, 5, 6, 9, 11, 12, 14, 16, 16, 16

2. 16, 18, 29, 30, 34, 35, 35, 38, 46

3. −4, −3, −3, 4, 1, 0, 0, −3, −2, 10, 11

4. 1.7, 2.2, 1.8, 3.0, 0.4, 1.2, 2.8, 2.9

5. 4.5, 5.7, 4.3, 6.9, −2.1, 5.7, −1.2, 3.8

6. −7.2, 3.9, 2.6, −9.1, 2.5, −7.2, 3.9, −7.2

11.2 Find the mean, median, mode, range, and standard deviation of the given data set and of the data set obtained by adding the given constant to each data value.

7. 33, 36, 36, 39, 49, 56; constant: 2

8. 10, 12, 14, 16, 16, 18, 19; constant: −1

11.2 Find the mean, median, mode, range, and standard deviation of the given data set and of the data set obtained by multiplying each data value by the given constant.

9. −2, −2, 5, 4, 2, −2, 8, 3; constant: 1.5

10. 52, 52, 76, 56, 67, 89, 70; constant: 3

11.3 A normal distribution has a mean of 2.7 and a standard deviation of 0.3. Find the probability that a randomly selected x-value from the distribution is in the given interval.

11. Between 2.4 and 2.7

12. At least 3.0

13. At most 2.1

11.4 Identify the type of sample described. Then tell if the sample is biased. *Explain* your reasoning.

14. The owner of a movie rental store wants to know how often her customers rent movies. She asks every tenth customer how many movies the customer rents each month.

15. A school wants to consult parents about updating its attendance policy. Each student is sent home with a survey for a parent to complete. The school uses only surveys that are returned within one week.

11.4 Find the margin of error for a survey that has the given sample size. Round your answer to the nearest tenth of a percent.

16. 100

17. 600

18. 2900

19. 5000

11.4 Find the sample size required to achieve the given margin of error. Round your answer to the nearest whole number.

20. ±1%

21. ±2%

22. ±5.5%

23. ±6.2%

11.5 Use a graphing calculator to find a model for the data. Then graph the model and the data in the same coordinate plane.

24.

x	0	2	4	6	8	10	12	14
y	−10	−3	4	10	14	20	21	36

25.

x	1	2	3	4	5	6	7	8
y	0.5	0.8	1.1	3	9	30	90	280

EXTRA PRACTICE

Chapter 12

12.1 For the sequence, describe the pattern, write the next term, and write a rule for the *n*th term.

1. 9, 16, 25, 36, . . .

2. $\frac{1}{3}, \frac{2}{3}, 1, \frac{4}{3}, \ldots$

3. 12.5, 7, 1.5, −4, . . .

12.1 Write the series using summation notation.

4. $16 + 32 + 48 + 64 + \cdots + 144$

5. $\frac{1}{6} + \frac{2}{7} + \frac{3}{8} + \frac{4}{9} + \frac{1}{2} + \cdots$

12.1 Find the sum of the series.

6. $\sum_{i=1}^{5} (3i + 2)$

7. $\sum_{i=0}^{5} 4i^2$

8. $\sum_{n=4}^{6} \frac{n}{n+3}$

9. $\sum_{k=6}^{8} k^3$

12.2 Write a rule for the *n*th term of the arithmetic sequence. Then graph the first six terms of the sequence.

10. $a_5 = 15, d = 6$

11. $a_{10} = -78, d = -10$

12. $a_6 = -\frac{11}{5}, d = -\frac{2}{5}$

12.2 Write a rule for the *n*th term of the arithmetic sequence. Then find a_{15}.

13. 11, 20, 29, 38, . . .

14. −8, −15, −22, −29, . . .

15. $3, \frac{7}{3}, \frac{5}{3}, 1, \ldots$

12.2 Write a rule for the *n*th term of the arithmetic sequence that has the two given terms.

16. $a_2 = 9, a_7 = 37$

17. $a_8 = 10.5, a_{16} = 18.5$

18. $a_3 = -\frac{14}{5}, a_{10} = -\frac{42}{5}$

12.3 Write a rule for the *n*th term of the geometric sequence. Then find a_{10}.

19. $\frac{1}{27}, \frac{1}{9}, \frac{1}{3}, 1, \ldots$

20. 5, 4, 3.2, 2.56, . . .

21. $4, \frac{16}{3}, \frac{64}{9}, \frac{256}{27}, \ldots$

12.3 Find the sum of the geometric series.

22. $\sum_{i=1}^{4} 3(4)^{i-1}$

23. $\sum_{i=1}^{7} 0.5(-3)^{i-1}$

24. $\sum_{i=1}^{5} 10\left(\frac{3}{5}\right)^{i-1}$

25. $\sum_{i=1}^{7} 2(1.2)^{i-1}$

12.4 Find the sum of the infinite geometric series, if it exists.

26. $8 + 4 + 2 + 1 + \cdots$

27. $2 - 4 + 8 - 16 + \cdots$

28. $-6.75 + 4.5 - 3 + 2 - \cdots$

12.4 Write the repeating decimal as a fraction in lowest terms.

29. 0.333. . .

30. 0.898989. . .

31. 0.212121. . .

32. 1.50150150. . .

12.5 Write a recursive rule for the sequence. The sequence may be arithmetic, geometric, or neither.

33. 2.5, 5, 10, 20, . . .

34. 2, −2, −6, −10, . . .

35. 1, 2, 2, 4, 8, 32, . . .

12.5 Find the first three iterates of the function for the given initial value.

36. $f(x) = 2x - 5, x_0 = 3$

37. $f(x) = \frac{4}{5}x - 2, x_0 = -10$

38. $f(x) = 3x^2 + x, x_0 = -1$

Chapter 13

13.1 **Let θ be an acute angle of a right triangle. Find the values of the other five trigonometric functions of θ.**

1. $\sin\theta = \frac{3}{5}$ **2.** $\tan\theta = \frac{8}{15}$ **3.** $\sec\theta = 2$ **4.** $\cos\theta = \frac{\sqrt{7}}{4}$

13.1 **Solve $\triangle ABC$ using the diagram and the given measurements.**

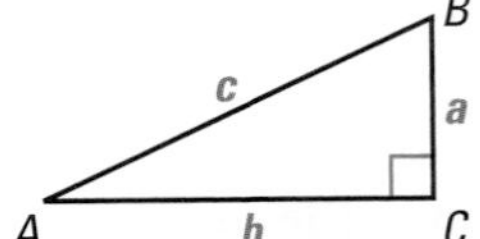

5. $A = 21°, c = 8$ **6.** $B = 66°, a = 14$

7. $B = 60°, c = 20$ **8.** $A = 29°, b = 6$

9. $A = 18°, c = 18$ **10.** $B = 56°, c = 7$

13.2 **Convert the degree measure to radians or the radian measure to degrees.**

11. $100°$ **12.** $-6°$ **13.** $\frac{3\pi}{4}$ **14.** $-\frac{\pi}{6}$

13.2 **Find the arc length and area of a sector with the given radius r and central angle θ.**

15. $r = 5$ ft, $\theta = 90°$ **16.** $r = 2$ in., $\theta = 300°$ **17.** $r = 12$ cm, $\theta = \pi$

13.3 **Sketch the angle. Then find its reference angle.**

18. $250°$ **19.** $-30°$ **20.** $\frac{8\pi}{3}$ **21.** $-\frac{11\pi}{6}$

13.3 **Evaluate the function without using a calculator.**

22. $\sin(-60°)$ **23.** $\csc 240°$ **24.** $\tan\frac{7\pi}{4}$ **25.** $\cos\left(-\frac{5\pi}{4}\right)$

13.4 **Evaluate the expression without using a calculator. Give your answer in both radians and degrees.**

26. $\sin^{-1} 0$ **27.** $\cos^{-1}\left(-\frac{\sqrt{3}}{2}\right)$ **28.** $\cos^{-1} 3$ **29.** $\tan^{-1} 1$

13.4 **Solve the equation for θ.**

30. $\sin\theta = 0.25;\ 90° < \theta < 180°$ **31.** $\cos\theta = 0.9;\ 270° < \theta < 360°$ **32.** $\tan\theta = 2;\ 180° < \theta < 270°$

13.5 **Solve $\triangle ABC$. (*Hint:* Some of the "triangles" may have no solution and some may have two solutions.)**

33. $A = 34°, a = 6, b = 7$ **34.** $A = 50°, C = 65°, b = 60$ **35.** $B = 86°, b = 13, c = 11$

13.5 **Find the area of $\triangle ABC$ with the given side lengths and included angle.**

36. $A = 35°, b = 50, c = 120$ **37.** $B = 35°, a = 7, c = 12$ **38.** $C = 20°, a = 10, b = 16$

13.6 **Solve $\triangle ABC$.**

39. $a = 16, b = 23, c = 17$ **40.** $C = 50°, a = 12, b = 14$ **41.** $A = 80°, b = 7, c = 5$

13.6 **Find the area of $\triangle ABC$ with the given side lengths.**

42. $a = 6, b = 3, c = 4$ **43.** $a = 14, b = 30, c = 27$ **44.** $a = 16, b = 16, c = 20$

Chapter 14

14.1 Graph the function.

1. $y = \cos \frac{1}{4}x$
2. $y = 3 \sin x$
3. $y = \sin 2\pi x$
4. $y = 2 \tan 2x$

14.2 Graph the sine or cosine function.

5. $y = \sin 2\left(x - \frac{\pi}{4}\right) + 1$
6. $y = -\sin\left(x + \frac{\pi}{4}\right)$
7. $y = 2 \cos x + 3$

14.2 Graph the tangent function.

8. $y = 2 \tan x + 2$
9. $y = -\frac{1}{4} \tan 2x$
10. $y = \tan\left(x - \frac{\pi}{2}\right) - 1$

14.3 Simplify the expression.

11. $\cos^2\left(\frac{\pi}{2} - x\right) + \cos^2(-x)$
12. $\frac{(\sec x - 1)(\sec x + 1)}{\tan x}$
13. $\tan\left(\frac{\pi}{2} - x\right)\cot x - \csc^2 x$

14.3 Verify the identity.

14. $\frac{\cos(-x)}{1 + \sin(-x)} = \sec x + \tan x$
15. $\frac{\cos^2 x + \sin^2 x}{\tan^2 x + 1} = \cos^2 x$
16. $2 - \sec^2 x = 1 - \tan^2 x$

14.4 Find the general solution of the equation.

17. $12 \tan^2 x - 4 = 0$
18. $3 \sin x = -2 \sin x + 3$
19. $\tan^2 x - 2 \tan x = -1$

14.4 Solve the equation in the given interval. Check your solutions.

20. $\cos^2 x \sin x = 5 \sin x;\ 0 \le x < 2\pi$
21. $2 - 2\cos^2 x = 3 + 5 \sin x;\ 0 \le x < 2\pi$
22. $8 \cos x = 4 \sec x;\ 0 \le x < \pi$
23. $\cos^2 x - 4 \cos x + 1 = 0;\ 0 \le x < \pi$

14.5 Write a function for the sinusoid.

24.

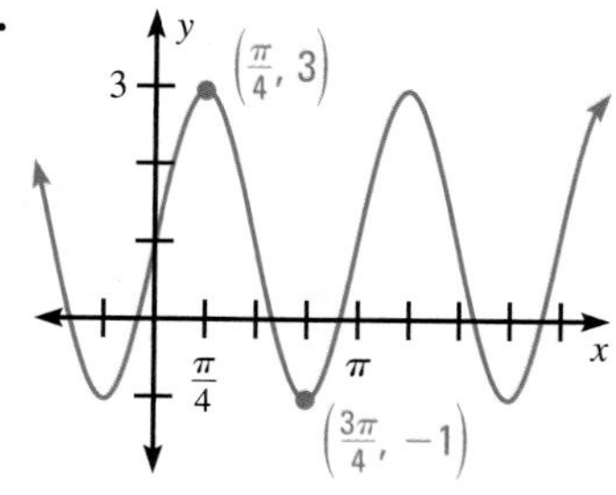

25.

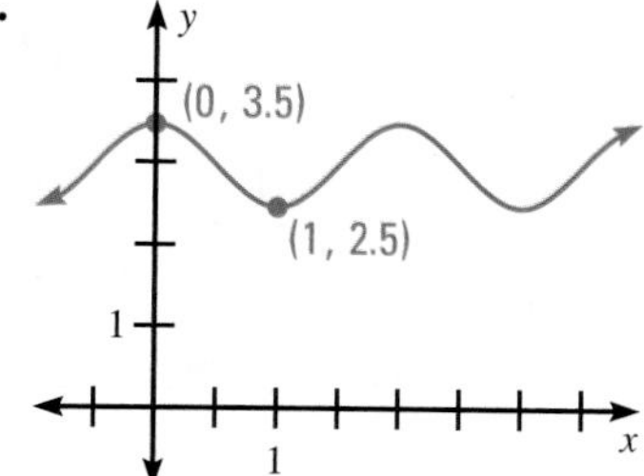

14.6 Find the exact value of the expression.

26. $\sin(-15°)$
27. $\cos 165°$
28. $\tan \frac{11\pi}{12}$
29. $\cos \frac{\pi}{12}$

14.7 Find the exact values of sin 2*a*, cos 2*a*, and tan 2*a*.

30. $\tan a = \frac{2}{3},\ \pi < a < \frac{3\pi}{2}$
31. $\cos a = \frac{9}{10},\ 0 < a < \frac{\pi}{2}$
32. $\sin a = -\frac{3}{5},\ \frac{3\pi}{2} < a < 2\pi$

14.7 Find the general solution of the equation.

33. $\cos 2x - \cos x = 0$
34. $\cos \frac{x}{2} = \sin x$
35. $\sin 2x = -1$

Symbols

Symbol	Meaning	Page
$\ldots$	and so on	2
$\approx$	is approximately equal to	2
$\cdot$	multiplication, times	3
$-a$	opposite of a	4
$\frac{1}{a}$	reciprocal of a, $a \neq 0$	4
b_1	b sub 1	26
π	pi; irrational number ≈ 3.14	26
$<$	is less than	41
$>$	is greater than	41
$\leq$	is less than or equal to	41
$\geq$	is greater than or equal to	41
$\lvert x \rvert$	absolute value of x	51
$\neq$	is not equal to	52
(x, y)	ordered pair	72
$f(x)$	f of x, or the value of f at x	75
m	slope	82
$\parallel$	is parallel to	84
$\perp$	is perpendicular to	84
(x, y, z)	ordered triple	178
$\begin{bmatrix} 1 & 0 \\ 0 & 1 \end{bmatrix}$	matrix	187
$\lvert A \rvert$	determinant of matrix A	203
A^{-1}	inverse of matrix A	210
$\sqrt{a}$	the nonnegative square root of a	266
i	imaginary unit equal to $\sqrt{-1}$	275
$\lvert z \rvert$	absolute value of complex number z	279
$x \to +\infty$	x approaches positive infinity	339
$\sqrt[n]{a}$	nth root of a	414
f^{-1}	inverse of function f	438
e	irrational number ≈ 2.718	492
$\log_b y$	log base b of y	499
$\log x$	log base 10 of x	500
$\ln x$	log base e of x	500
$n!$	n factorial; number of permutations of n objects	684
${}_nP_r$	number of permutations of r objects from n distinct objects	685
${}_nC_r$	number of combinations of r objects from n distinct objects	690
$P(A)$	probability of event A	698
$P(\overline{A})$	probability of the complement of event A	709
$\cup$	union of two sets	715
$\cap$	intersection of two sets	715
$\emptyset$	empty set	715
$\subseteq$	is a subset of	716
$P(B \mid A)$	probability of event B given that event A has occurred	718
$\overline{x}$	x-bar; the mean of a data set	744
σ	sigma; the standard deviation of a data set	745
Σ	summation	796
θ	theta	852
sin	sine	852
cos	cosine	852
tan	tangent	852
csc	cosecant	852
sec	secant	852
cot	cotangent	852
$\sin^{-1}$	inverse sine	875
$\cos^{-1}$	inverse cosine	875
$\tan^{-1}$	inverse tangent	875

Measures

Time	
60 seconds (sec) = 1 minute (min) 60 minutes = 1 hour (h) 24 hours = 1 day 7 days = 1 week 4 weeks (approx.) = 1 month	365 days, 52 weeks (approx.), 12 months = 1 year 10 years = 1 decade 100 years = 1 century

Metric	United States Customary
Length 10 millimeters (mm) = 1 centimeter (cm) 100 cm, 1000 mm = 1 meter (m) 1000 m = 1 kilometer (km)	**Length** 12 inches (in.) = 1 foot (ft) 36 in., 3 ft = 1 yard (yd) 5280 ft, 1760 yd = 1 mile (mi)
Area 100 square millimeters (mm^2) = 1 square centimeter (cm^2) 10,000 cm^2 = 1 square meter (m^2) 10,000 m^2 = 1 hectare (ha)	**Area** 144 square inches ($in.^2$) = 1 square foot (ft^2) 9 ft^2 = 1 square yard (yd^2) 43,560 ft^2, 4840 yd^2 = 1 acre (A)
Volume 1000 cubic millimeters (mm^3) = 1 cubic centimeter (cm^3) 1,000,000 cm^3 = 1 cubic meter (m^3)	**Volume** 1728 cubic inches ($in.^3$) = 1 cubic foot (ft^3) 27 ft^3 = 1 cubic yard (yd^3)
Liquid Capacity 1000 milliliters (mL), 1000 cubic centimeters (cm^3) = 1 liter (L) 1000 L = 1 kiloliter (kL)	**Liquid Capacity** 8 fluid ounces (fl oz) = 1 cup (c) 2 c = 1 pint (pt) 2 pt = 1 quart (qt) 4 qt = 1 gallon (gal)
Mass 1000 milligrams (mg) = 1 gram (g) 1000 g = 1 kilogram (kg) 1000 kg = 1 metric ton (t)	**Weight** 16 ounces (oz) = 1 pound (lb) 2000 lb = 1 ton
Temperature Degrees Celsius (°C) 0°C = freezing point of water 37°C = normal body temperature 100°C = boiling point of water	**Temperature Degrees Fahrenheit (°F)** 32°F = freezing point of water 98.6°F = normal body temperature 212°F = boiling point of water

Formulas

Formulas from Coordinate Geometry

Slope of a line (p. 82)	$m = \frac{y_2 - y_1}{x_2 - x_1}$ where m is the slope of the nonvertical line through points (x_1, y_1) and (x_2, y_2)
Parallel and perpendicular lines (p. 84)	If line l_1 has slope m_1 and line l_2 has slope m_2, then: $l_1 \parallel l_2$ if and only if $m_1 = m_2$; $l_1 \perp l_2$ if and only if $m_1 = -\frac{1}{m_2}$, or $m_1 m_2 = -1$
Distance formula (p. 615)	$d = \sqrt{(x_2 - x_1)^2 + (y_2 - y_1)^2}$ where d is the distance between points (x_1, y_1) and (x_2, y_2)
Midpoint formula (p. 615)	$M\left(\frac{x_1 + x_2}{2}, \frac{y_1 + y_2}{2}\right)$ is the midpoint of the line segment joining points (x_1, y_1) and (x_2, y_2).

Formulas from Matrix Algebra

Determinant of a 2 × 2 matrix (p. 203)	$\det\begin{bmatrix} a & b \\ c & d \end{bmatrix} = \begin{vmatrix} a & b \\ c & d \end{vmatrix} = ad - cb$
Determinant of a 3 × 3 matrix (p. 203)	$\det\begin{bmatrix} a & b & c \\ d & e & f \\ g & h & i \end{bmatrix} = \begin{vmatrix} a & b & c \\ d & e & f \\ g & h & i \end{vmatrix} = (aei + bfg + cdh) - (gec + hfa + idb)$
Area of a triangle (p. 204)	The area of a triangle with vertices (x_1, y_1), (x_2, y_2), and (x_3, y_3) is given by $\text{Area} = \pm\frac{1}{2}\begin{vmatrix} x_1 & y_1 & 1 \\ x_2 & y_2 & 1 \\ x_3 & y_3 & 1 \end{vmatrix}$ where the appropriate sign ($\pm$) should be chosen to yield a positive value.
Cramer's rule (p. 205)	Let $A = \begin{bmatrix} a & b \\ c & d \end{bmatrix}$ be the coefficient matrix of this linear system: $ax + by = e$, $cx + dy = f$. If $\det A \neq 0$, then the system has exactly one solution. The solution is $x = \frac{\begin{vmatrix} e & b \\ f & d \end{vmatrix}}{\det A}$ and $y = \frac{\begin{vmatrix} a & e \\ c & f \end{vmatrix}}{\det A}$.
Inverse of a 2 × 2 matrix (p. 210)	The inverse of the matrix $A = \begin{bmatrix} a & b \\ c & d \end{bmatrix}$ is $A^{-1} = \frac{1}{\lvert A \rvert}\begin{bmatrix} d & -b \\ -c & a \end{bmatrix} = \frac{1}{ad - cb}\begin{bmatrix} d & -b \\ -c & a \end{bmatrix}$ provided $ad - cb \neq 0$.

TABLES

Formulas and Theorems from Algebra

Quadratic formula (p. 292)	The solutions of $ax^2 + bx + c = 0$ are $x = \frac{-b \pm \sqrt{b^2 - 4ac}}{2a}$ where a, b, and c are real numbers such that $a \neq 0$.
Discriminant of a quadratic equation (p. 294)	The expression $b^2 - 4ac$ is called the discriminant of the associated equation $ax^2 + bx + c = 0$. The value of the discriminant can be positive, zero, or negative, which corresponds to an equation having two real solutions, one real solution, or two imaginary solutions, respectively.
Special product patterns (p. 347)	**Sum and difference:** $(a + b)(a - b) = a^2 - b^2$ **Square of a binomial:** $(a + b)^2 = a^2 + 2ab + b^2$ $(a - b)^2 = a^2 - 2ab + b^2$ **Cube of a binomial:** $(a + b)^3 = a^3 + 3a^2b + 3ab^2 + b^3$ $(a - b)^3 = a^3 - 3a^2b + 3ab^2 - b^3$
Special factoring patterns (p. 354)	**Sum of two cubes:** $a^3 + b^3 = (a + b)(a^2 - ab + b^2)$ **Difference of two cubes:** $a^3 - b^3 = (a - b)(a^2 + ab + b^2)$
Remainder theorem (p. 363)	If a polynomial $f(x)$ is divided by $x - k$, then the remainder is $r = f(k)$.
Factor theorem (p. 364)	A polynomial $f(x)$ has a factor $x - k$ if and only if $f(k) = 0$.
Rational zero theorem (p. 370)	If $f(x) = a_nx^n + \cdots + a_1x + a_0$ has *integer* coefficients, then every rational zero of f has this form: $\frac{p}{q} = \frac{\text{factor of constant term } a_0}{\text{factor of leading coefficient } a_n}$
Fundamental theorem of algebra (p. 379)	If $f(x)$ is a polynomial of degree n where $n > 0$, then the equation $f(x) = 0$ has at least one solution in the set of complex numbers.
Corollary to the fundamental theorem of algebra (p. 379)	If $f(x)$ is a polynomial of degree n where $n > 0$, then the equation $f(x) = 0$ has exactly n solutions provided each solution repeated twice is counted as 2 solutions, each solution repeated three times is counted as 3 solutions, and so on.
Complex conjugates theorem (p. 380)	If f is a polynomial function with real coefficients, and $a + bi$ is an imaginary zero of f, then $a - bi$ is also a zero of f.
Irrational conjugates theorem (p. 380)	Suppose f is a polynomial function with rational coefficients, and a and b are rational numbers such that $\sqrt{b}$ is irrational. If $a + \sqrt{b}$ is a zero of f, then $a - \sqrt{b}$ is also a zero of f.
Descartes' rule of signs (p. 381)	Let $f(x) = a_nx^n + a_{n-1}x^{n-1} + \cdots + a_2x^2 + a_1x + a_0$ be a polynomial function with real coefficients. • The number of *positive real zeros* of f is equal to the number of changes in sign of the coefficients of $f(x)$ or is less than this by an even number. • The number of *negative real zeros* of f is equal to the number of changes in sign of the coefficients of $f(-x)$ or is less than this by an even number.

TABLES

Formulas and Theorems from Algebra *(continued)*

Discriminant of a general second-degree equation (p. 653)	Any conic can be described by a general second-degree equation in x and y: $Ax^2 + Bxy + Cy^2 + Dx + Ey + F = 0$. The expression $B^2 - 4AC$ is the discriminant of the conic equation and can be used to identify it. **Discriminant** — **Type of Conic** $B^2 - 4AC < 0$, $B = 0$, and $A = C$ — Circle $B^2 - 4AC < 0$, and either $B \neq 0$ or $A \neq C$ — Ellipse $B^2 - 4AC = 0$ — Parabola $B^2 - 4AC > 0$ — Hyperbola If $B = 0$, each axis of the conic is horizontal or vertical.

Formulas from Combinatorics

Fundamental counting principle (p. 682)	If one event can occur in m ways and another event can occur in n ways, then the number of ways that both events can occur is $m \cdot n$.
Permutations of n objects taken r at a time (p. 685)	The number of permutations of r objects taken from a group of n distinct objects is denoted by ${}_nP_r$ and is given by: ${}_nP_r = \frac{n!}{(n - r)!}$
Permutations with repetition (p. 685)	The number of distinguishable permutations of n objects where one object is repeated s_1 times, another is repeated s_2 times, and so on is: $\frac{n!}{s_1! \cdot s_2! \cdot \ldots \cdot s_k!}$
Combinations of n objects taken r at a time (p. 690)	The number of combinations of r objects taken from a group of n distinct objects is denoted by ${}_nC_r$ and is given by: ${}_nC_r = \frac{n!}{(n - r)! \cdot r!}$
Pascal's triangle (p. 692)	If you arrange the values of ${}_nC_r$ in a triangular pattern in which each row corresponds to a value of n, you get what is called Pascal's triangle. ${}_0C_0$ — 1 ${}_1C_0 \quad {}_1C_1$ — 1 1 ${}_2C_0 \quad {}_2C_1 \quad {}_2C_2$ — 1 2 1 ${}_3C_0 \quad {}_3C_1 \quad {}_3C_2 \quad {}_3C_3$ — 1 3 3 1 ${}_4C_0 \quad {}_4C_1 \quad {}_4C_2 \quad {}_4C_3 \quad {}_4C_4$ — 1 4 6 4 1 The first and last numbers in each row are 1. Every number other than 1 is the sum of the closest two numbers in the row directly above it.
Binomial theorem (p. 693)	The binomial expansion of $(a + b)^n$ for any positive integer n is: $(a + b)^n = {}_nC_0a^nb^0 + {}_nC_1a^{n-1}b^1 + {}_nC_2a^{n-2}b^2 + \cdots + {}_nC_na^0b^n$ $= \sum_{r=0}^{n} {}_nC_ra^{n-r}b^r$

TABLES

Formulas from Probability

Theoretical probability of an event (p. 698)	When all outcomes are equally likely, the theoretical probability that an event A will occur is: $P(A) = \frac{\text{Number of outcomes in } A}{\text{Total number of outcomes}}$
Odds in favor of an event (p. 699)	When all outcomes are equally likely, the odds in favor of an event A are: $\frac{\text{Number of outcomes in } A}{\text{Number of outcomes not in } A}$
Odds against an event (p. 699)	When all outcomes are equally likely, the odds against an event A are: $\frac{\text{Number of outcomes not in } A}{\text{Number of outcomes in } A}$
Experimental probability of an event (p. 700)	When an experiment is performed that consists of a certain number of trials, the experimental probability of an event A is given by: $P(A) = \frac{\text{Number of trials where } A \text{ occurs}}{\text{Total number of trials}}$
Probability of compound events (p. 707)	If A and B are any two events, then the probability of A or B is: $P(A \text{ or } B) = P(A) + P(B) - P(A \text{ and } B)$ If A and B are disjoint events, then the probability of A or B is: $P(A \text{ or } B) = P(A) + P(B)$
Probability of the complement of an event (p. 709)	The probability of the complement of event A, denoted $\overline{A}$, is: $P(\overline{A}) = 1 - P(A)$
Probability of independent events (p. 717)	If A and B are independent, the probability that both A and B occur is: $P(A \text{ and } B) = P(A) \cdot P(B)$
Probability of dependent events (p. 718)	If A and B are dependent, the probability that both A and B occur is: $P(A \text{ and } B) = P(A) \cdot P(B \mid A)$
Binomial probabilities (p. 725)	For a binomial experiment consisting of n trials where the probability of success on each trial is p, the probability of exactly k successes is: $P(k \text{ successes}) = {}_nC_k p^k (1 - p)^{n-k}$

Formulas from Statistics

Mean of a data set (p. 744)	$\overline{x} = \frac{x_1 + x_2 + \cdots + x_n}{n}$ where $\overline{x}$ (read "x-bar") is the mean of the data $x_1, x_2, \ldots, x_n$
Standard deviation of a data set (p. 745)	$\sigma = \sqrt{\frac{(x_1 - \overline{x})^2 + (x_2 - \overline{x})^2 + \ldots + (x_n - \overline{x})^2}{n}}$ where σ (read "sigma") is the standard deviation of the data $x_1, x_2, \ldots, x_n$
Areas under a normal curve (p. 757)	A normal distribution with mean $\overline{x}$ and standard deviation σ has these properties: • The total area under the related normal curve is 1. • About 68% of the area lies within 1 standard deviation of the mean. • About 95% of the area lies within 2 standard deviations of the mean. • About 99.7% of the area lies within 3 standard deviations of the mean.
***z*-score** (p. 758)	$z = \frac{x - \overline{x}}{\sigma}$ where x is a data value, $\overline{x}$ is the mean, and σ is the standard deviation

Formulas for Sequences and Series

Formulas for sums of special series (p. 797)	$\sum_{i=1}^{n} 1 = n$ $\quad \sum_{i=1}^{n} i = \frac{n(n+1)}{2}$ $\quad \sum_{i=1}^{n} i^2 = \frac{n(n+1)(2n+1)}{6}$
Explicit rule for an arithmetic sequence (p. 802)	The nth term of an arithmetic sequence with first term a_1 and common difference d is: $$a_n = a_1 + (n-1)d$$
Sum of a finite arithmetic series (p. 804)	The sum of the first n terms of an arithmetic series is: $$S_n = n\left(\frac{a_1 + a_n}{2}\right)$$
Explicit rule for a geometric sequence (p. 810)	The nth term of a geometric sequence with first term a_1 and common ratio r is: $$a_n = a_1 r^{n-1}$$
Sum of a finite geometric series (p. 812)	The sum of the first n terms of a geometric series with common ratio $r \neq 1$ is: $$S_n = a_1\left(\frac{1 - r^n}{1 - r}\right)$$
Sum of an infinite geometric series (p. 821)	The sum of an infinite geometric series with first term a_1 and common ratio r is $$S = \frac{a_1}{1 - r}$$ provided $\lvert r \rvert < 1$. If $\lvert r \rvert \geq 1$, the series has no sum.
Recursive equation for an arithmetic sequence (p. 827)	$a_n = a_{n-1} + d$ where d is the common difference
Recursive equation for a geometric sequence (p. 827)	$a_n = r \cdot a_{n-1}$ where r is the common ratio

Formulas and Identities from Trigonometry

Conversion between degrees and radians (p. 860)	To rewrite a degree measure in radians, multiply by $\frac{\pi \text{ radians}}{180°}$. To rewrite a radian measure in degrees, multiply by $\frac{180°}{\pi \text{ radians}}$.
Definition of trigonometric functions (p. 866)	Let θ be an angle in standard position and (x, y) be any point (except the origin) on the terminal side of θ. Let $r = \sqrt{x^2 + y^2}$. $\sin\theta = \frac{y}{r}$ $\quad \cos\theta = \frac{x}{r}$ $\quad \tan\theta = \frac{y}{x}, x \neq 0$ $\quad \csc\theta = \frac{r}{y}, y \neq 0$ $\quad \sec\theta = \frac{r}{x}, x \neq 0$ $\quad \cot\theta = \frac{x}{y}, y \neq 0$
Law of sines (p. 882)	If $\triangle ABC$ has sides of length a, b, and c, then: $$\frac{\sin A}{a} = \frac{\sin B}{b} = \frac{\sin C}{c}$$
Area of a triangle (given two sides and the included angle) (p. 885)	If $\triangle ABC$ has sides of length a, b, and c, then its area is: Area $= \frac{1}{2}bc \sin A$ $\quad$ Area $= \frac{1}{2}ac \sin B$ $\quad$ Area $= \frac{1}{2}ab \sin C$

Formulas and Identities from Trigonometry *(continued)*

Law of cosines (p. 889)	If $\triangle ABC$ has sides of length a, b, and c, then: $a^2 = b^2 + c^2 - 2bc \cos A$ $b^2 = a^2 + c^2 - 2ac \cos B$ $c^2 = a^2 + b^2 - 2ab \cos C$
Heron's area formula (p. 891)	The area of the triangle with sides of length a, b, and c is $\text{Area} = \sqrt{s(s-a)(s-b)(s-c)}$ where $s = \frac{1}{2}(a + b + c)$.
Reciprocal identities (p. 924)	$\csc \theta = \frac{1}{\sin \theta}$ $\sec \theta = \frac{1}{\cos \theta}$ $\cot \theta = \frac{1}{\tan \theta}$
Tangent and cotangent identities (p. 924)	$\tan \theta = \frac{\sin \theta}{\cos \theta}$ $\cot \theta = \frac{\cos \theta}{\sin \theta}$
Pythagorean identities (p. 924)	$\sin^2 \theta + \cos^2 \theta = 1$ $1 + \tan^2 \theta = \sec^2 \theta$ $1 + \cot^2 \theta = \csc^2 \theta$
Cofunction identities (p. 924)	$\sin\left(\frac{\pi}{2} - \theta\right) = \cos \theta$ $\cos\left(\frac{\pi}{2} - \theta\right) = \sin \theta$ $\tan\left(\frac{\pi}{2} - \theta\right) = \cot \theta$
Negative angle identities (p. 924)	$\sin(-\theta) = -\sin \theta$ $\cos(-\theta) = \cos \theta$ $\tan(-\theta) = -\tan \theta$
Sum formulas (p. 949)	$\sin(a + b) = \sin a \cos b + \cos a \sin b$ $\cos(a + b) = \cos a \cos b - \sin a \sin b$ $\tan(a + b) = \frac{\tan a + \tan b}{1 - \tan a \tan b}$
Difference formulas (p. 949)	$\sin(a - b) = \sin a \cos b - \cos a \sin b$ $\cos(a - b) = \cos a \cos b + \sin a \sin b$ $\tan(a - b) = \frac{\tan a - \tan b}{1 + \tan a \tan b}$
Double-angle formulas (p. 955)	$\cos 2a = \cos^2 a - \sin^2 a$ $\sin 2a = 2 \sin a \cos a$ $\cos 2a = 2\cos^2 a - 1$ $\tan 2a = \frac{2 \tan a}{1 - \tan^2 a}$ $\cos 2a = 1 - 2\sin^2 a$
Half-angle formulas (p. 955)	$\sin \frac{a}{2} = \pm\sqrt{\frac{1 - \cos a}{2}}$ $\tan \frac{a}{2} = \frac{1 - \cos a}{\sin a}$ $\cos \frac{a}{2} = \pm\sqrt{\frac{1 + \cos a}{2}}$ $\tan \frac{a}{2} = \frac{\sin a}{1 + \cos a}$ The signs of $\sin \frac{a}{2}$ and $\cos \frac{a}{2}$ depend on the quadrant in which $\frac{a}{2}$ lies.

TABLES

Formulas from Geometry

Basic geometric figures	See pages 991–993 for area formulas for basic two-dimensional geometric figures.
Area of an equilateral triangle	Area $= \frac{\sqrt{3}}{4}s^2$ where s is the length of a side
Arc length and area of a sector	Arc length $= r\theta$ where r is the radius and θ is the radian measure of the central angle that intercepts the arc Area $= \frac{1}{2}r^2\theta$
Area of an ellipse	Area $= \pi ab$ where a and b are half the lengths of the major and minor axes of the ellipse
Volume and surface area of a right rectangular prism	Volume $= \ell wh$ where ℓ is the length, w is the width, and h is the height Surface area $= 2(\ell w + wh + \ell h)$
Volume and surface area of a right cylinder	Volume $= \pi r^2 h$ where r is the base radius and h is the height Lateral surface area $= 2\pi rh$ Surface area $= 2\pi r^2 + 2\pi rh$
Volume and surface area of a right regular pyramid	Volume $= \frac{1}{3}Bh$ where B is the area of the base and h is the height Lateral surface area $= \frac{1}{2}ns\ell$ where n is the number of sides of the base, s is the length of a side of the base, and ℓ is the slant height Surface area $= B + \frac{1}{2}ns\ell$
Volume and surface area of a right circular cone	Volume $= \frac{1}{3}\pi r^2 h$ where r is the base radius and h is the height Lateral surface area $= \pi r\ell$ where ℓ is the slant height Surface area $= \pi r^2 + \pi r\ell$
Volume and surface area of a sphere	Volume $= \frac{4}{3}\pi r^3$ where r is the radius Surface area $= 4\pi r^2$

Properties

Properties of Real Numbers

	Let a, b, and c be real numbers.	
	Addition	**Multiplication**
Closure Property (p. 3)	$a + b$ is a real number.	ab is a real number.
Commutative Property (p. 3)	$a + b = b + a$	$ab = ba$
Associative Property (p. 3)	$(a + b) + c = a + (b + c)$	$(ab)c = a(bc)$
Identity Property (p. 3)	$a + 0 = a, 0 + a = a$	$a \cdot 1 = a, 1 \cdot a = a$
Inverse Property (p. 3)	$a + (-a) = 0$	$a \cdot \frac{1}{a} = 1, a \neq 0$
Distributive Property (p. 3)	The distributive property involves both addition and multiplication: $a(b + c) = ab + ac$	
Zero Product Property (p. 253)	Let A and B be real numbers or algebraic expressions. If $AB = 0$, then $A = 0$ or $B = 0$.	

Properties of Matrices

	Let A, B, and C be matrices, and let k be a scalar.
Associative Property of Addition (p. 188)	$(A + B) + C = A + (B + C)$
Commutative Property of Addition (p. 188)	$A + B = B + A$
Distributive Property of Addition (p. 188)	$k(A + B) = kA + kB$
Distributive Property of Subtraction (p. 188)	$k(A - B) = kA - kB$
Associative Property of Matrix Multiplication (p. 197)	$(AB)C = A(BC)$
Left Distributive Property of Matrix Multiplication (p. 197)	$A(B + C) = AB + AC$
Right Distributive Property of Matrix Multiplication (p. 197)	$(A + B)C = AC + BC$
Associative Property of Scalar Multiplication (p. 197)	$k(AB) = (kA)B = A(kB)$
Multiplicative Identity (p. 210)	An $n \times n$ matrix with 1's on the main diagonal and 0's elsewhere is an identity matrix, denoted I. For any $n \times n$ matrix A, $AI = IA = A$.
Inverse Matrices (p. 210)	If the determinant of an $n \times n$ matrix A is nonzero, then A has an inverse, denoted A^{-1}, such that $AA^{-1} = A^{-1}A = I$.

Properties of Exponents

	Let a and b be real numbers, and let m and n be integers.
Product of Powers Property (p. 330)	$a^m \cdot a^n = a^{m+n}$
Power of a Power Property (p. 330)	$(a^m)^n = a^{mn}$
Power of a Product Property (p. 330)	$(ab)^m = a^m b^m$
Negative Exponent Property (p. 330)	$a^{-m} = \frac{1}{a^m}, a \neq 0$
Zero Exponent Property (p. 330)	$a^0 = 1, a \neq 0$
Quotient of Powers Property (p. 330)	$\frac{a^m}{a^n} = a^{m-n}, a \neq 0$
Power of a Quotient Property (p. 330)	$\left(\frac{a}{b}\right)^m = \frac{a^m}{b^m}, b \neq 0$

TABLES

Properties of Radicals and Rational Exponents

Number of Real *n*th Roots (p. 414)	Let n be an integer greater than 1, and let a be a real number. • If n is odd, then a has one real nth root: $\sqrt[n]{a} = a^{1/n}$ • If n is even and $a > 0$, then a has two real nth roots: $\pm\sqrt[n]{a} = \pm a^{1/n}$ • If n is even and $a = 0$, then a has one nth root: $\sqrt[n]{0} = 0^{1/n} = 0$ • If n is even and $a < 0$, then a has no real nth roots.
Radicals and Rational Exponents (p. 415)	Let $a^{1/n}$ be an nth root of a, and let m be a positive integer. • $a^{m/n} = (a^{1/n})^m = (\sqrt[n]{a})^m$ • $a^{-m/n} = \frac{1}{a^{m/n}} = \frac{1}{(a^{1/n})^m} = \frac{1}{(\sqrt[n]{a})^m}, a \neq 0$
Properties of Rational Exponents (p. 420)	All of the properties of exponents listed on the previous page apply to rational exponents as well as integer exponents.
Product and Quotient Properties of Radicals (p. 421)	Let n be an integer greater than 1, and let a and b be positive real numbers. Then $\sqrt[n]{a \cdot b} = \sqrt[n]{a} \cdot \sqrt[n]{b}$ and $\sqrt[n]{\frac{a}{b}} = \frac{\sqrt[n]{a}}{\sqrt[n]{b}}$.

Properties of Logarithms

	Let a, b, c, m, n, x, and y be positive real numbers such that $b \neq 1$ and $c \neq 1$.
Logarithms and Exponents (p. 499)	$\log_b y = x$ if and only if $b^x = y$
Special Logarithm Values (p. 499)	$\log_b 1 = 0$ because $b^0 = 1$ and $\log_b b = 1$ because $b^1 = b$
Common and Natural Logarithms (p. 500)	$\log_{10} x = \log x$ and $\log_e x = \ln x$
Product Property of Logarithms (p. 507)	$\log_b mn = \log_b m + \log_b n$
Quotient Property of Logarithms (p. 507)	$\log_b \frac{m}{n} = \log_b m - \log_b n$
Power Property of Logarithms (p. 507)	$\log_b m^n = n \log_b m$
Change of Base (p. 508)	$\log_c a = \frac{\log_b a}{\log_b c}$

Properties of Functions

Operations on Functions (pp. 428, 430)	Let f and g be any two functions. A new function h can be defined using any of the following operations. **Addition:** $h(x) = f(x) + g(x)$ **Subtraction:** $h(x) = f(x) - g(x)$ **Multiplication:** $h(x) = f(x) \cdot g(x)$ **Division:** $h(x) = \frac{f(x)}{g(x)}$ **Composition:** $h(x) = g(f(x))$ For addition, subtraction, multiplication, and division, the domain of h consists of the x-values that are in the domains of both f and g. Additionally, the domain of the quotient does not include x-values for which $g(x) = 0$. For composition, the domain of h is the set of all x-values such that x is in the domain of f and $f(x)$ is in the domain of g.
Inverse Functions (p. 438)	Functions f and g are inverses of each other provided: $f(g(x)) = x$ and $g(f(x)) = x$

TABLES

English–Spanish Glossary

A

absolute value (p. 51) The absolute value of a number x, represented by the symbol $\lvert x \rvert$, is the distance the number is from 0 on a number line. **valor absoluto** (pág. 51) El valor absoluto de un número x, representado por el símbolo $\lvert x \rvert$, es la distancia a la que está el número de 0 en una recta numérica.	$\left\lvert \frac{2}{3} \right\rvert = \frac{2}{3}$, $\lvert -4.3 \rvert = 4.3$, and $\lvert 0 \rvert = 0$. $\left\lvert \frac{2}{3} \right\rvert = \frac{2}{3}$, $\lvert -4.3 \rvert = 4.3$ y $\lvert 0 \rvert = 0$.
absolute value function (p. 123) A function that contains an absolute value expression. **función de valor absoluto** (pág. 123) Función que contiene una expresión de valor absoluto.	$y = \lvert x \rvert$, $y = \lvert x - 3 \rvert$, and $y = 4\lvert x + 8 \rvert - 9$ are absolute value functions. $y = \lvert x \rvert$, $y = \lvert x - 3 \rvert$ e $y = 4\lvert x + 8 \rvert - 9$ son funciones de valor absoluto.
absolute value of a complex number (p. 279) If $z = a + bi$, then the absolute value of z, denoted $\lvert z \rvert$, is a nonnegative real number defined as $\lvert z \rvert = \sqrt{a^2 + b^2}$. **valor absoluto de un número complejo** (pág. 279) Si $z = a + bi$, entonces el valor absoluto de z, denotado por $\lvert z \rvert$, es un número real no negativo definido como $\lvert z \rvert = \sqrt{a^2 + b^2}$.	$\lvert -4 + 3i \rvert = \sqrt{(-4)^2 + 3^2} = \sqrt{25} = 5$
algebraic expression (p. 11) An expression that consists of numbers, variables, operations, and grouping symbols. Also called variable expression. **expresión algebraica** (pág. 11) Expresión formada por números, variables, operaciones y signos de agrupación.	$\frac{2}{3}p$, $\frac{8}{7 - r}$, $k - 5$, and $n^2 + 2n$ are algebraic expressions. $\frac{2}{3}p$, $\frac{8}{7 - r}$, $k - 5$ y $n^2 + 2n$ son expresiones algebraicas.
amplitude (p. 908) The amplitude of the graph of a sine or cosine function is $\frac{1}{2}(M - m)$, where M is the maximum value of the function and m is the minimum value of the function. **amplitud** (pág. 908) La amplitud de la grafica de una función seno o coseno es $\frac{1}{2}(M - m)$, donde M es el valor máximo de la función y m es el valor mínimo de la función.	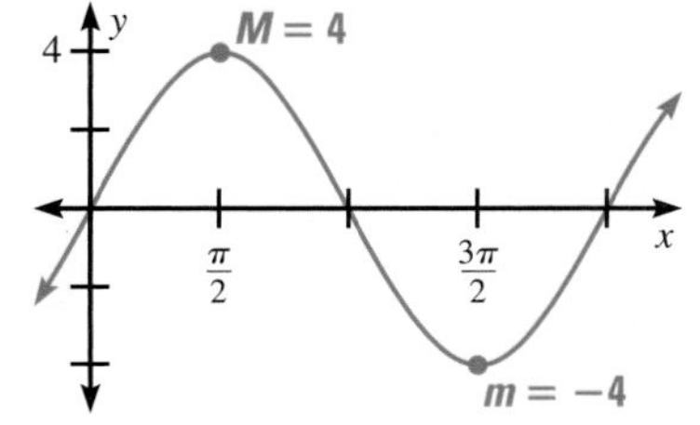 The graph of $y = 4 \sin x$ has an amplitude of $\frac{1}{2}(4 - (-4)) = 4$. La gráfica de $y = 4$ sen x tiene una amplitud de $\frac{1}{2}(4 - (-4)) = 4$.
angle of depression (p. 855) The angle by which an observer's line of sight must be depressed from the horizontal to the point observed. **ángulo de depresión** (pág. 855) El ángulo con el que se debe bajar la línea de visión de un observador desde la horizontal hasta el punto observado.	*See* angle of elevation. *Ver* ángulo de elevación.

ENGLISH-SPANISH GLOSSARY

angle of elevation (p. 855) The angle by which an observer's line of sight must be elevated from the horizontal to the point observed. **ángulo de elevación** (pág. 855) El ángulo con el que se debe elevar la línea de visión de un observador desde la horizontal hasta el punto observado.	
arithmetic sequence (p. 802) A sequence in which the difference of consecutive terms is constant. **progresión aritmética** (pág. 802) Progresión en la que la diferencia entre los términos consecutivos es constante.	$-4, 1, 6, 11, 16, \ldots$ is an arithmetic sequence with common difference 5. $-4, 1, 6, 11, 16, \ldots$ es una progresión aritmética con una diferencia común de 5.
arithmetic series (p. 804) The expression formed by adding the terms of an arithmetic sequence. **serie aritmética** (pág. 804) La expresión formada al sumar los términos de una progresión aritmética.	$\sum_{i=1}^{5} 2i = 2 + 4 + 6 + 8 + 10$
asymptote (p. 478) A line that a graph approaches more and more closely. **asíntota** (pág. 478) Recta a la que se aproxima una gráfica cada vez más.	 The asymptote for the graph shown is the line $y = 3$. La asíntota para la gráfica que se muestra es la recta $y = 3$.
axis of symmetry of a parabola (pp. 236, 620) The line perpendicular to the parabola's directrix and passing through its focus and vertex. **eje de simetría de una parábola** (págs. 236, 620) La recta perpendicular a la directriz de la parábola y que pasa por su foco y su vértice.	*See* parabola. *Ver* parábola.

B

base of a power (p. 10) The number or expression that is used as a factor in a repeated multiplication. **base de una potencia** (pág. 10) El número o la expresión que se usa como factor en la multiplicación repetida.	In the power 2^5, the base is 2. En la potencia 2^5, la base es 2.

best-fitting line (p. 114) The line that lies as close as possible to all the data points in a scatter plot.

mejor recta de regresión (pág. 114) La recta que se ajusta lo más posible a todos los puntos de datos de un diagrama de dispersión.

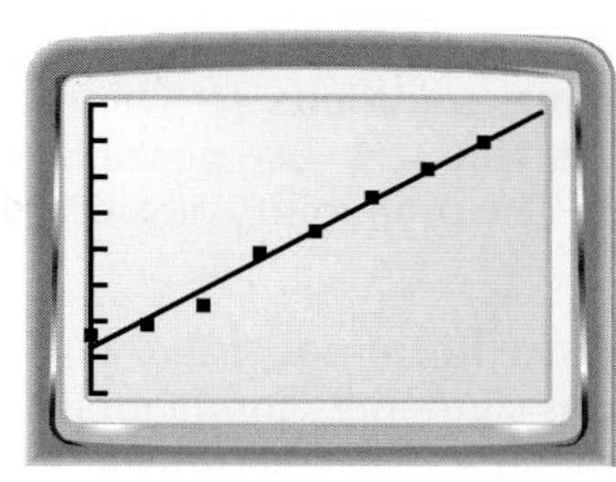

best-fitting quadratic model (p. 311) The model given by using quadratic regression on a set of paired data.

modelo cuadrático con mejor ajuste (pág. 311) El modelo dado al realizar una regresión cuadrática sobre un conjunto de pares de datos.

biased question (p. 772) A question that elicits responses that do not accurately reflect the opinions or actions of the people surveyed.

pregunta capciosa (pág. 772) Pregunta que induce a respuestas que no reflejan con exactitud las opiniones o acciones de los encuestados.

"Would you rather see an exciting laser show or a boring movie?" is a biased question.

"¿Preferirías ver un emocionante espectáculo de láser o una película aburrida?" es una pregunta capciosa.

biased sample (p. 767) A sample that overrepresents or underrepresents part of a population.

muestra sesgada (pág. 767) Muestra que representa de forma excesiva o insuficiente a parte de una población.

The members of a school's basketball team would form a biased sample for a survey about whether to build a new gym.

Los miembros del equipo de baloncesto de una escuela formarían una muestra sesgada si participaran en una encuesta sobre si quieren que se construya un nuevo gimnasio.

binomial (p. 252) The sum of two monomials.

binomio (pág. 252) La suma de dos monomios.

$3x - 1$ and $t^3 - 4t$ are binomials.

$3x - 1$ y $t^3 - 4t$ son binomios.

binomial distribution (p. 725) The probability distribution associated with a binomial experiment.

distribución binomial (pág. 725) La distribución de probabilidades asociada a un experimento binomial.

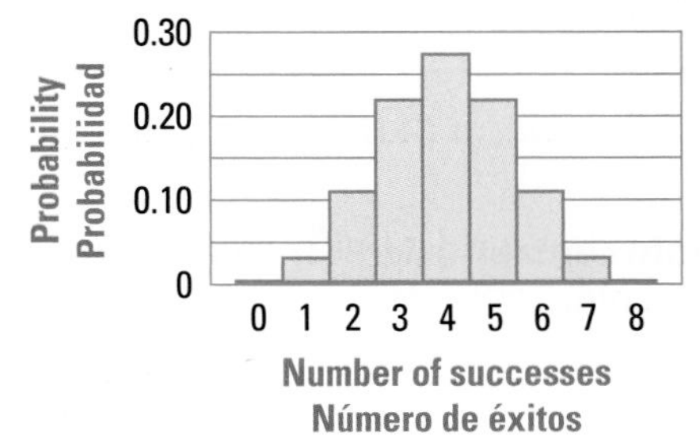

Binomial distribution for 8 trials with $p = 0.5$.

Distribución binomial de 8 pruebas con $p = 0.5$.

binomial experiment (p. 725) An experiment that meets the following conditions. (1) There are n independent trials. (2) Each trial has only two possible outcomes: success and failure. (3) The probability of success is the same for each trial. **experimento binomial** (pág. 725) Experimento que satisface las siguientes condiciones. (1) Hay n pruebas independientes. (2) Cada prueba tiene sólo dos resultados posibles: éxito y fracaso. (3) La probabilidad de éxito es igual para cada prueba.	**A fair coin is tossed 12 times. The probability of getting exactly 4 heads is as follows:** **Una moneda normal se lanza 12 veces. La probabilidad de sacar exactamente 4 caras es la siguiente:** $P(k=4) = {}_nC_k p^k(1-p)^{n-k}$ $= {}_{12}C_4(0.5)^4(1-0.5)^8$ $= 495(0.5)^4(0.5)^8$ ≈ 0.121
binomial theorem (p. 693) The binomial expansion of $(a+b)^n$ for any positive integer n: $(a+b)^n = {}_nC_0a^nb^0 + {}_nC_1a^{n-1}b^1 + {}_nC_2a^{n-2}b^2 + \cdots + {}_nC_na^0b^n$. **teorema binomial** (pág. 693) La expansión binomial de $(a+b)^n$ para cualquier número entero positivo n: $(a+b)^n = {}_nC_0a^nb^0 + {}_nC_1a^{n-1}b^1 + {}_nC_2a^{n-2}b^2 + \cdots + {}_nC_na^0b^n$.	$(x^2+y)^3$ $= {}_3C_0(x^2)^3y^0 + {}_3C_1(x^2)^2y^1 + {}_3C_2(x^2)^1y^2 + {}_3C_3(x^2)^0y^3$ $= (1)(x^6)(1) + (3)(x^4)(y) + (3)(x^2)(y^2) + (1)(1)(y^3)$ $= x^6 + 3x^4y + 3x^2y^2 + y^3$

C

center of a circle (p. 626) *See* circle. **centro de un círculo** (pág. 626) *Ver* círculo.	**The circle with equation $(x-3)^2 + (y+5)^2 = 36$ has its center at $(3, -5)$. *See also* circle.** **El círculo con la ecuación $(x-3)^2 + (y+5)^2 = 36$ tiene el centro en $(3, -5)$. *Ver también* círculo.**
center of a hyperbola (p. 642) The midpoint of the transverse axis of a hyperbola. **centro de una hipérbola** (pág. 642) El punto medio del eje transverso de una hipérbola.	***See* hyperbola.** ***Ver* hipérbola.**
center of an ellipse (p. 634) The midpoint of the major axis of an ellipse. **centro de una elipse** (pág. 634) El punto medio del eje mayor de una elipse.	***See* ellipse.** ***Ver* elipse.**
central angle (p. 861) An angle formed by two radii of a circle. **ángulo central** (pág. 861) Ángulo formado por dos radios de un círculo.	***See* sector.** ***Ver* sector.**

circle (p. 626) The set of all points (x, y) in a plane that are of distance r from a fixed point, called the center of the circle. **círculo** (pág. 626) El conjunto de todos los puntos (x, y) de un plano que están a una distancia r de un punto fijo, llamado centro del círculo.	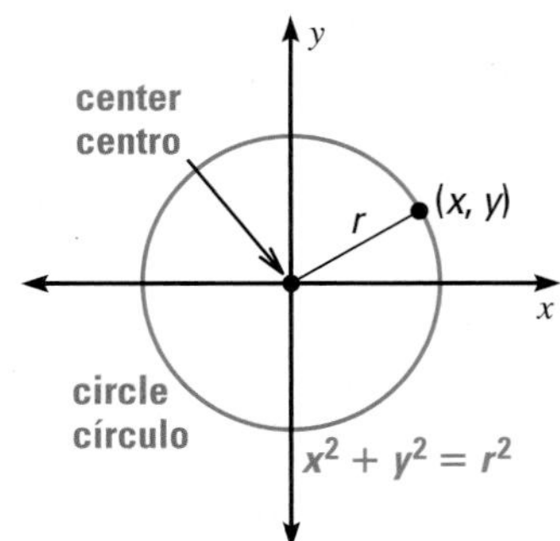
coefficient (p. 12) When a term is the product of a number and a power of a variable, the number is the coefficient of the power. **coeficiente** (pág. 12) Cuando un término es el producto de un número y una potencia de una variable, el número es el coeficiente de la potencia.	In the algebraic expression $2x^2 + (-4x) + (-1)$, the coefficient of $2x^2$ is 2 and the coefficient of $-4x$ is -4. En la expresión algebraica $2x^2 + (-4x) + (-1)$, el coeficiente de $2x^2$ es 2 y el coeficiente de $-4x$ es -4.
coefficient matrix (p. 205) The coefficient matrix of the linear system $ax + by = e, cx + dy = f$ is $\begin{bmatrix} a & b \\ c & d \end{bmatrix}$. **matriz coeficiente** (pág. 205) La matriz coeficiente del sistema lineal $ax + by = e, cx + dy = f$ es $\begin{bmatrix} a & b \\ c & d \end{bmatrix}$.	$9x + 4y = -6$ $3x - 5y = -21$ coefficient matrix: / matriz coeficiente: $\begin{bmatrix} 9 & 4 \\ 3 & -5 \end{bmatrix}$ matrix of constants: / matriz de constantes: $\begin{bmatrix} -6 \\ -21 \end{bmatrix}$ matrix of variables: / matriz de variables: $\begin{bmatrix} x \\ y \end{bmatrix}$
combination (p. 690) A selection of r objects from a group of n objects where the order is not important, denoted ${}_nC_r$ where ${}_nC_r = \frac{n!}{(n-r)! \cdot r!}$. **combinación** (pág. 690) Selección de r objetos de un grupo de n objetos en el que el orden no importa, denotado ${}_nC_r$, donde ${}_nC_r = \frac{n!}{(n-r)! \cdot r!}$.	There are 6 combinations of the $n = 4$ letters A, B, C, and D selected $r = 2$ at a time: AB, AC, AD, BC, BD, and CD. Hay 6 combinaciones de las letras $n = 4$ A, B, C y D seleccionadas $r = 2$ cada vez: AB, AC, AD, BC, BD y CD.
common difference (p. 802) The constant difference of consecutive terms of an arithmetic sequence. **diferencia común** (pág. 802) La diferencia constante entre los términos consecutivos de una progresión aritmética.	*See* arithmetic sequence. *Ver* progresión aritmética.
common logarithm (p. 500) A logarithm with base 10. It is denoted by $\log_{10}$ or simply by log. **logaritmo común** (pág. 500) Logaritmo con base 10. Se denota por $\log_{10}$ ó simplemente por log.	$\log_{10} 100 = \log 100 = 2$ because $10^2 = 100$. $\log_{10} 100 = \log 100 = 2$ ya que $10^2 = 100$.

ENGLISH-SPANISH GLOSSARY

common ratio (p. 810) The constant ratio of consecutive terms of a geometric sequence. **razón común** (pág. 810) La razón constante entre los términos consecutivos de una progresión geométrica.	*See* geometric sequence. *Ver* progresión geométrica.
complement of a set (p. 715) The complement of a set A, written $\overline{A}$, is the set of all elements in the universal set U that are *not* in A. **complemento de un conjunto** (pág. 715) El complemento de un conjunto A, escrito $\overline{A}$, es el conjunto de todos los elementos del conjunto universal U que *no* están en A.	Let U be the set of all integers from 1 to 10 and let $A = \{1, 2, 4, 8\}$. Then $\overline{A} = \{3, 5, 6, 7, 9, 10\}$. Sea U el conjunto de todos los números enteros entre 1 y 10 y sea $A = \{1, 2, 4, 8\}$. Por lo tanto, $\overline{A} = \{3, 5, 6, 7, 9, 10\}$.
completing the square (p. 284) The process of adding a term to a quadratic expression of the form $x^2 + bx$ to make it a perfect square trinomial. **completar el cuadrado** (pág. 284) El proceso de sumar un término a una expresión cuadrática de la forma $x^2 + bx$, de modo que sea un trinomio cuadrado perfecto.	To complete the square for $x^2 + 16x$, add $\left(\frac{16}{2}\right)^2 = 64$: $x^2 + 16x + 64 = (x + 8)^2$. Para completar el cuadrado para $x^2 + 16x$, suma $\left(\frac{16}{2}\right)^2 = 64$: $x^2 + 16x + 64 = (x + 8)^2$.
complex conjugates (p. 276) Two complex numbers of the form $a + bi$ and $a - bi$. **números complejos conjugados** (pág. 276) Dos números complejos de la forma $a + bi$ y $a - bi$.	$2 + 4i, 2 - 4i$
complex fraction (p. 584) A fraction that contains a fraction in its numerator or denominator. **fracción compleja** (pág. 584) Fracción que tiene una fracción en su numerador o en su denominador.	$\dfrac{\frac{5}{x+4}}{\frac{6x}{3x^2}}, \dfrac{1}{\frac{1}{p} + \frac{1}{q}}$
complex number (p. 276) A number $a + bi$ where a and b are real numbers and i is the imaginary unit. **número complejo** (pág. 276) Un número $a + bi$, donde a y b son números reales e i es la unidad imaginaria.	$0, 2.5, \sqrt{3}, \pi, 5i, 2 - i$
complex plane (p. 278) A coordinate plane in which each point (a, b) represents a complex number $a + bi$. The horizontal axis is the real axis and the vertical axis is the imaginary axis. **plano complejo** (pág. 278) Plano de coordenadas en el que cada punto (a, b) representa un número complejo $a + bi$. El eje horizontal es el eje real, y el eje vertical es el eje imaginario.	imaginary / imaginario; real / real; $-2 + 4i$; $3i$; i; 1; $3 - 2i$; $-4 - 3i$
composition of functions (p. 430) The composition of a function g with a function f is $h(x) = g(f(x))$. **composición de funciones** (pág. 430) La composición de una función g con una función f es $h(x) = g(f(x))$.	$f(x) = 5x - 2,\ g(x) = 4x^{-1}$ $g(f(x)) = g(5x - 2) = 4(5x - 2)^{-1} = \frac{4}{5x - 2}, x \neq \frac{2}{5}$

compound event (p. 707) The union or intersection of two events. **suceso compuesto** (pág. 707) La unión o la intersección de dos sucesos.	**When you roll a six-sided die, the event "roll a 2 or an odd number" is a compound event.** **Cuando lanzas un cubo numerado de seis lados, el suceso "salir el 2 ó un número impar" es un suceso compuesto.**
compound inequality (p. 41) Two simple inequalities joined by "and" or "or." **desigualdad compuesta** (pág. 41) Dos desigualdades simples unidas por "y" u "o".	$2x > 0$ **or** $x + 4 < -1$ **is a compound inequality.** $2x > 0$ **ó** $x + 4 < -1$ **es una desigualdad compuesta.**
conditional probability (p. 718) The conditional probability of B given A, written $P(B \mid A)$, is the probability that event B will occur given that event A has occurred. **probabilidad condicional** (pág. 718) La probabilidad condicional de B dado A, escrito $P(B \mid A)$, es la probabilidad de que ocurra el suceso B dado que ha ocurrido el suceso A.	**Two cards are randomly selected from a standard deck of 52 cards. Let event A be "the first card is a club" and let event B be "the second card is a club." Then $P(B \mid A) = \frac{12}{51} = \frac{4}{17}$ because there are 12 (out of 13) clubs left among the remaining 51 cards.** **Dos cartas se seleccionan al azar de una baraja normal de 52 cartas. Sea el suceso A "la primera carta es de tréboles" y sea el suceso B "la segunda carta es de tréboles". Entonces $P(B \mid A) = \frac{12}{51} = \frac{4}{17}$ ya que quedan 12 (del total de 13) cartas de tréboles entre las 51 cartas restantes.**
conic (p. 650) *See* conic section. **cónica** (pág. 650) *Ver* sección cónica.	***See* conic section.** ***Ver* sección cónica.**
conic section (p. 650) A curve formed by the intersection of a plane and a double-napped cone. Conic sections are also called conics. **sección cónica** (pág. 650) Una curva formada por la intersección de un plano y un cono doble. Las secciones cónicas también se llaman cónicas.	***See* circle, ellipse, hyperbola, *and* parabola.** ***Ver* círculo, elipse, hipérbola *y* parábola.**
conjugates (p. 267) The expressions $a + \sqrt{b}$ and $a - \sqrt{b}$ where a and b are rational numbers. **conjugados** (pág. 267) Las expresiones $a + \sqrt{b}$ y $a - \sqrt{b}$ cuando a y b son números racionales.	**The conjugate of $7 + \sqrt{2}$ is $7 - \sqrt{2}$.** **El conjugado de $7 + \sqrt{2}$ es $7 - \sqrt{2}$.**
consistent system (p. 154) A system of equations that has at least one solution. **sistema compatible** (pág. 154) Sistema de ecuaciones que tiene al menos una solución.	$y = 2 + 3x$ $6x + 2y = 4$ **The system above is consistent, with solution (0, 2).** **El sistema de arriba es compatible, con la solución (0, 2).**

ENGLISH-SPANISH GLOSSARY

constant of variation (pp. 107, 551, 553) The nonzero constant a in a direct variation equation $y = ax$, an inverse variation equation $y = \frac{a}{x}$, or a joint variation equation $z = axy$. **constante de variación** (págs. 107, 551, 553) La constante distinta de cero a de una ecuación de variación directa $y = ax$, de una ecuación de variación inversa $y = \frac{a}{x}$ o de una ecuación de variación conjunta $z = axy$.	In the direct variation equation $y = -\frac{5}{2}x$, the constant of variation is $-\frac{5}{2}$. En la ecuación de variación directa $y = -\frac{5}{2}x$, la constante de variación es $-\frac{5}{2}$.
constant term (pp. 12, 337) A term that has a number part but no variable part. **término constante** (págs. 12, 337) Término que tiene una parte numérica pero sin variable.	The constant term of the algebraic expression $3x^2 + 5x + (-7)$ is -7. El término constante de la expresión algebraica $3x^2 + 5x + (-7)$ es -7.
constraints (p. 174) In linear programming, the linear inequalities that form a system. **restricciones** (pág. 174) En la programación lineal, las desigualdades lineales que forman un sistema.	*See* linear programming. *Ver* programación lineal.
continuous function (p. 80) A function whose graph is unbroken. **función continua** (pág. 80) Función que tiene una gráfica no interrumpida.	Any linear function, such as $y = 2x + 4$, is a continuous function. Cualquier función lineal, como $y = 2x + 4$, es una función continua.
control group (p. 773) A group that does not undergo a procedure or treatment when an experiment is conducted. *See also* experimental group. **grupo de control** (pág. 773) Grupo que no se somete a ningún procedimiento o tratamiento durante la realización de un experimento. *Ver también* grupo experimental.	*See* experimental group. *Ver* grupo experimental.
correlation coefficient (p. 114) A measure, denoted by r where $-1 \le r \le 1$, of how well a line fits a set of data pairs (x, y). **coeficiente de correlación** (pág. 114) Medida denotada por r, donde $-1 \le r \le 1$, y que describe el ajuste de una recta a un conjunto de pares de datos (x, y).	A data set that shows a strong positive correlation has a correlation coefficient of $r \approx 1$. *See also* positive correlation *and* negative correlation. Un conjunto de datos que muestra una correlación positiva fuerte tiene un coeficiente de correlación de $r \approx 1$. *Ver también* correlación positiva *y* correlación negativa.
cosecant function (p. 852) If θ is an acute angle of a right triangle, the cosecant of θ is the length of the hypotenuse divided by the length of the side opposite θ. **función cosecante** (pág. 852) Si θ es un ángulo agudo de un triángulo rectángulo, la cosecante de θ es la longitud de la hipotenusa dividida por la longitud del lado opuesto a θ.	*See* sine function. *Ver* función seno.

cosine function (p. 852) If θ is an acute angle of a right triangle, the cosine of θ is the length of the side adjacent to θ divided by the length of the hypotenuse. **función coseno** (pág. 852) Si θ es un ángulo agudo de un triángulo rectángulo, el coseno de θ es la longitud del lado adyacente a θ dividida por la longitud de la hipotenusa.	*See* sine function. *Ver* función seno.
cotangent function (p. 852) If θ is an acute angle of a right triangle, the cotangent of θ is the length of the side adjacent to θ divided by the length of the side opposite θ. **función cotangente** (pág. 852) Si θ es un ángulo agudo de un triángulo rectángulo, la cotangente de θ es la longitud del lado adyacente a θ dividida por la longitud del lado opuesto a θ.	*See* sine function. *Ver* función seno.
coterminal angles (p. 860) Angles in standard position with terminal sides that coincide. **ángulos coterminales** (pág. 860) Ángulos en posición normal cuyos lados terminales coinciden.	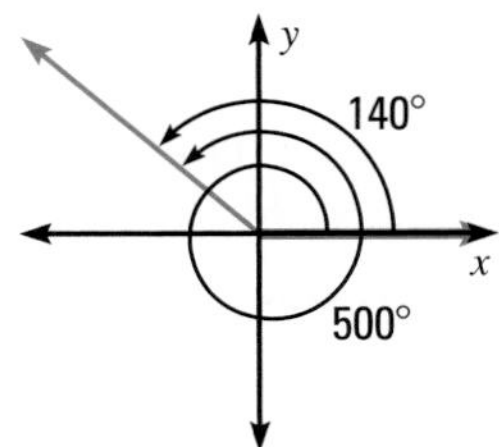 The angles with measures 500° and 140° are coterminal. Los ángulos que miden 500° y 140° son coterminales.
co-vertices of an ellipse (p. 634) The points of intersection of an ellipse and the line perpendicular to the major axis at the center. **puntos extremos del eje menor de una elipse** (pág. 634) Los puntos de intersección de una elipse y la recta perpendicular al eje mayor en el centro.	*See* ellipse. *Ver* elipse.
Cramer's rule (p. 205) A method for solving a system of linear equations using determinants: For the linear system $ax + by = e$, $cx + dy = f$, let A be the coefficient matrix. If $\det A \neq 0$, the solution of the system is as follows: $x = \dfrac{\begin{vmatrix} e & b \\ f & d \end{vmatrix}}{\det A}, y = \dfrac{\begin{vmatrix} a & e \\ c & f \end{vmatrix}}{\det A}$ **regla de Cramer** (pág. 205) Método para resolver un sistema de ecuaciones lineales usando determinantes: Para el sistema lineal $ax + by = e$, $cx + dy = f$, sea A la matriz coeficiente. Si $\det A \neq 0$, la solución del sistema es la siguiente: $x = \dfrac{\begin{vmatrix} e & b \\ f & d \end{vmatrix}}{\det A}, y = \dfrac{\begin{vmatrix} a & e \\ c & f \end{vmatrix}}{\det A}$	$\begin{matrix} 9x + 4y = -6 \\ 3x - 5y = -21; \end{matrix} \begin{vmatrix} 9 & 4 \\ 3 & -5 \end{vmatrix} = -57$ Applying Cramer's rule gives the following: Al aplicar la regla de Cramer se obtiene lo siguiente: $x = \dfrac{\begin{vmatrix} -6 & 4 \\ -21 & -5 \end{vmatrix}}{-57} = \dfrac{114}{-57} = -2$ $y = \dfrac{\begin{vmatrix} 9 & -6 \\ 3 & -21 \end{vmatrix}}{-57} = \dfrac{-171}{-57} = 3$

ENGLISH-SPANISH GLOSSARY

cross multiplying (p. 589) A method for solving a simple rational equation for which each side of the equation is a single rational expression. **multiplicar en cruz** (pág. 589) Método para resolver una ecuación racional simple en la que cada lado es una sola expresión racional.	To solve $\frac{3}{x+1} = \frac{9}{4x+5}$, cross multiply. **Para resolver $\frac{3}{x+1} = \frac{9}{4x+5}$, multiplica en cruz.** $3(4x + 5) = 9(x + 1)$ $12x + 15 = 9x + 9$ $3x = -6$ $x = -2$
cycle (p. 908) The shortest repeating portion of the graph of a periodic function. **ciclo** (pág. 908) En una función periódica, la parte más corta de la gráfica que se repite.	*See* periodic function. ***Ver* función periódica.**

D

decay factor (p. 486) The quantity b in the exponential decay function $y = ab^x$ with $a > 0$ and $0 < b < 1$. **factor de decrecimiento** (pág. 486) La cantidad b de la función de decrecimiento exponencial $y = ab^x$, con $a > 0$ y $0 < b < 1$.	The decay factor for the function $y = 3(0.5)^x$ is 0.5. **El factor de decrecimiento de la función $y = 3(0.5)^x$ es 0.5.**
degree of a polynomial function (p. 337) The exponent in the term of a polynomial function where the variable is raised to the greatest power. **grado de una función polinómica** (pág. 337) En una función polinómica, el exponente del término donde la variable se eleva a la mayor potencia.	*See* polynomial function. ***Ver* función polinómica.**
dependent events (p. 718) Two events such that the occurrence of one event affects the occurrence of the other event. **sucesos dependientes** (pág. 718) Dos sucesos tales que la ocurrencia de uno de ellos afecta a la ocurrencia del otro.	Two cards are drawn from a deck without replacement. The events "the first is a 3" and "the second is a 3" are dependent. **Se sacan dos cartas de una baraja y no se reemplazan. Los sucesos "la primera es un 3" y "la segunda es un 3" son dependientes.**
dependent system (p. 154) A consistent system of equations that has infinitely many solutions. **sistema dependiente** (pág. 154) Sistema compatible de ecuaciones que tiene infinitas soluciones.	$2x - y = 3$ $4x - 2y = 6$ Any ordered pair $(x, 2x - 3)$ is a solution of the system above, so there are infinitely many solutions. **Cualquier par ordenado $(x, 2x - 3)$ es una solución del sistema que figura arriba, por lo que hay infinitas soluciones.**

dependent variable (p. 74) The output variable in an equation in two variables. **variable dependiente** (pág. 74) La variable de salida de una ecuación con dos variables.	*See* independent variable. *Ver* variable independiente.
determinant (p. 203) A real number associated with any square matrix A, denoted by det A or $\|A\|$. **determinante** (pág. 203) Número real asociado a toda matriz cuadrada A, denotada por det A o $\|A\|$.	$\det \begin{bmatrix} 5 & 4 \\ 3 & 1 \end{bmatrix} = 5(1) - 3(4) = -7$ $\det \begin{bmatrix} a & b \\ c & d \end{bmatrix} = ad - cb$
dimensions of a matrix (p. 187) The dimensions of a matrix with m rows and n columns are $m \times n$. **dimensiones de una matriz** (pág. 187) Las dimensiones de una matriz con m filas y n columnas son $m \times n$.	A matrix with 2 rows and 3 columns has the dimensions 2×3 (read "2 by 3"). Una matriz con 2 filas y 3 columnas tiene por dimensiones 2×3 (leído "2 por 3").
direct variation (p. 107) Two variables x and y show direct variation provided that $y = ax$ where a is a nonzero constant. **variación directa** (pág. 107) Dos variables x e y indican una variación directa siempre que $y = ax$, donde a es una constante distinta de cero.	The equation $5x + 2y = 0$ represents direct variation because it is equivalent to the equation $y = -\frac{5}{2}x$. La ecuación $5x + 2y = 0$ representa una variación directa ya que es equivalente a la ecuación $y = -\frac{5}{2}x$.
directrix of a parabola (p. 620) *See* parabola. **directriz de una parábola** (pág. 620) *Ver* parábola.	*See* parabola. *Ver* parábola.
discrete function (p. 80) A function whose graph consists of separate points. **función discreta** (pág. 80) Función cuya gráfica consiste en puntos aislados.	y x
discriminant of a general second-degree equation (p. 653) The expression $B^2 - 4AC$ for the equation $Ax^2 + Bxy + Cy^2 + Dx + Ey + F = 0$. Used to identify which type of conic the equation represents. **discriminante de una ecuación general de segundo grado** (pág. 653) La expresión $B^2 - 4AC$ para la ecuación $Ax^2 + Bxy + Cy^2 + Dx + Ey + F = 0$. Se usa para identificar qué tipo de cónica representa la ecuación.	For the equation $4x^2 + y^2 - 8x - 8 = 0$, $A = 4$, $B = 0$, and $C = 1$. $B^2 - 4AC = 0^2 - 4(4)(1) = -16$ Because $B^2 - 4AC < 0$, $B = 0$, and $A \neq C$, the conic is an ellipse. Para la ecuación $4x^2 + y^2 - 8x - 8 = 0$, $A = 4$, $B = 0$ y $C = 1$. $B^2 - 4AC = 0^2 - 4(4)(1) = -16$ Debido a que $B^2 - 4AC < 0$, $B = 0$ y $A \neq C$, la cónica es un elipse.

discriminant of a quadratic equation (p. 294) The expression $b^2 - 4ac$ for the quadratic equation $ax^2 + bx + c = 0$; also the expression under the radical sign in the quadratic formula.

discriminante de una ecuación cuadrática (pág. 294) La expresión $b^2 - 4ac$ para la ecuación cuadrática $ax^2 + bx + c = 0$; es también la expresión situada bajo el signo radical de la fórmula cuadrática.

The value of the discriminant of $2x^2 - 3x - 7 = 0$ is $b^2 - 4ac = (-3)^2 - 4(2)(-7) = 65$.

El valor del discriminante de $2x^2 - 3x - 7 = 0$ es $b^2 - 4ac = (-3)^2 - 4(2)(-7) = 65$.

disjoint events (p. 707) Events A and B are disjoint if they have no outcomes in common; also called mutually exclusive events.

sucesos disjuntos (pág. 707) Los sucesos A y B son disjuntos si no tienen casos en común; también se llaman sucesos mutuamente excluyentes.

When you randomly select a card from a standard deck of 52 cards, selecting a club and selecting a heart are disjoint events.

Al seleccionar al azar una carta de una baraja normal de 52 cartas, sacar una de tréboles y sacar una de corazones son sucesos disjuntos.

distance formula (p. 614) The distance d between any two points (x_1, y_1) and (x_2, y_2) is $d = \sqrt{(x_2 - x_1)^2 + (y_2 - y_1)^2}$.

fórmula de la distancia (pág. 614) La distancia d entre dos puntos cualesquiera (x_1, y_1) y (x_2, y_2) es $d = \sqrt{(x_2 - x_1)^2 + (y_2 - y_1)^2}$.

The distance between $(-3, 5)$ and $(4, -1)$ is $\sqrt{(4 - (-3))^2 + (-1 - 5)^2} = \sqrt{49 + 36} = \sqrt{85}$.

La distancia entre $(-3, 5)$ y $(4, -1)$ es $\sqrt{(4 - (-3))^2 + (-1 - 5)^2} = \sqrt{49 + 36} = \sqrt{85}$.

domain (p. 72) The set of input values of a relation.

dominio (pág. 72) El conjunto de los valores de entrada de una relación.

See relation.

Ver relación.

E

eccentricity of a conic section (p. 665) The eccentricity e of a hyperbola or an ellipse is $\frac{c}{a}$ where c is the distance from each focus to the center and a is the distance from each vertex to the center. The eccentricity of a circle is $e = 0$. The eccentricity of a parabola is $e = 1$.

excentricidad de una sección cónica (pág. 665) La excentricidad e de una hipérbola o de una elipse es $\frac{c}{a}$, donde c es la distancia entre cada foco y el centro y a es la distancia entre cada vértice y el centro. La excentricidad de un círculo es $e = 0$. La excentricidad de una parábola es $e = 1$.

For the ellipse $\frac{(x+4)^2}{36} + \frac{(y-2)^2}{16} = 1$, $c = \sqrt{36 - 16} = 2\sqrt{5}$, so the eccentricity is $e = \frac{c}{a} = \frac{2\sqrt{5}}{\sqrt{36}} = \frac{\sqrt{5}}{3} \approx 0.745$.

Para la elipse $\frac{(x+4)^2}{36} + \frac{(y-2)^2}{16} = 1$, $c = \sqrt{36 - 16} = 2\sqrt{5}$, por lo tanto la excentricidad es $e = \frac{c}{a} = \frac{2\sqrt{5}}{\sqrt{36}} = \frac{\sqrt{5}}{3} \approx 0.745$.

element of a matrix (p. 187) Each number in a matrix.

elemento de una matriz (pág. 187) Cada número de una matriz.

See matrix.

Ver matriz.

element of a set (p. 715) Each object in a set; also called a member of the set. **elemento de un conjunto** (pág. 715) Cada objeto de un conjunto; también se llama miembro del conjunto.	The elements of the set $A = \{1, 2, 3, 4\}$ are 1, 2, 3, and 4. Los elementos del conjunto $A = \{1, 2, 3, 4\}$ son 1, 2, 3 y 4.
elimination method (p. 161) A method of solving a system of equations by multiplying equations by constants, then adding the revised equations to eliminate a variable. **método de eliminación** (pág. 161) Método para resolver un sistema de ecuaciones en el que se multiplican ecuaciones por constantes y se agregan luego las ecuaciones revisadas para eliminar una variable.	To use the elimination method to solve the system with equations $3x - 7y = 10$ and $6x - 8y = 8$, multiply the first equation by -2 and add the equations to eliminate x. Para usar el método de eliminación a fin de resolver el sistema con las ecuaciones $3x - 7y = 10$ y $6x - 8y = 8$, multiplica la primera ecuación por -2 y suma las ecuaciones para eliminar x.
ellipse (p. 634) The set of all points P in a plane such that the sum of the distances between P and two fixed points, called the foci, is a constant. **elipse** (pág. 634) El conjunto de todos los puntos P de un plano tales que la suma de las distancias entre P y dos puntos fijos, llamados focos, es una constante.	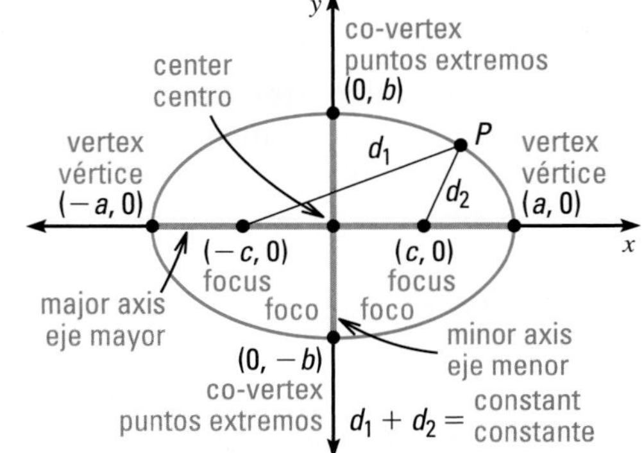
empty set (p. 715) The set with no elements, denoted Ø. **conjunto vacío** (pág. 715) El conjunto que no tiene elementos, indicado Ø.	The set of positive integers less than 0 is the empty set, Ø. El conjunto de los números enteros positivos menores que 0 es el conjunto vacío, Ø.
end behavior (p. 339) The behavior of the graph of a function as x approaches positive infinity ($+\infty$) or negative infinity ($-\infty$). **comportamiento** (pág. 339) El comportamiento de la gráfica de una función al aproximarse x a infinito positivo ($+\infty$) o a infinito negativo ($-\infty$).	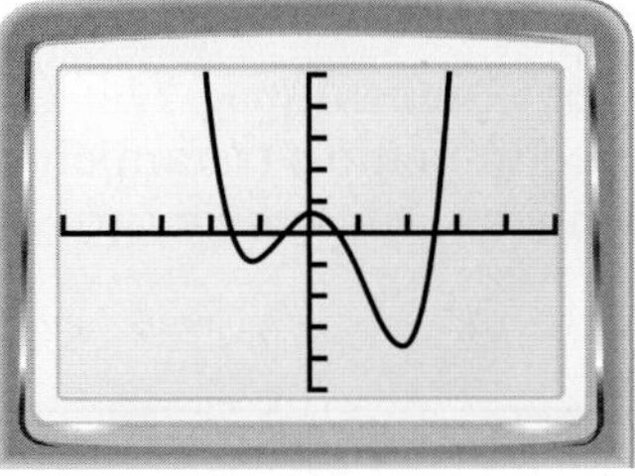 $f(x) \to +\infty$ as $x \to -\infty$ or as $x \to +\infty$. $f(x) \to +\infty$ según $x \to -\infty$ o según $x \to +\infty$.
equal matrices (p. 187) Matrices that have the same dimensions and equal elements in corresponding positions. **matrices iguales** (pág. 187) Matrices que tienen las mismas dimensiones y elementos iguales en posiciones correspondientes.	$\begin{bmatrix} 6 & 0 \\ -\frac{4}{4} & \frac{3}{4} \end{bmatrix} = \begin{bmatrix} 3 \cdot 2 & -1 + 1 \\ -1 & 0.75 \end{bmatrix}$

ENGLISH-SPANISH GLOSSARY

equation (p. 18) A statement that two expressions are equal. **ecuación** (pág. 18) Enunciado que establece la igualdad de dos expresiones.	$2x - 3 = 7$, $2x^2 = 4x$
equation in two variables (p. 74) An equation that contains two variables. **ecuación con dos variables** (pág. 74) Ecuación que tiene dos variables.	$y = 3x - 5$, $d = -16t^2 + 64$
equivalent equations (p. 18) Equations that have the same solution(s). **ecuaciones equivalentes** (pág. 18) Ecuaciones que tienen la misma solución o soluciones.	$x + 8 = 3$ and $4x = -20$ are equivalent because both have the solution -5. $x + 8 = 3$ y $4x = -20$ son equivalentes porque tienen ambas la solución -5.
equivalent expressions (p. 12) Two algebraic expressions that have the same value for all values of their variable(s). **expresiones equivalentes** (pág. 12) Dos expresiones algebraicas que tienen el mismo valor para todos los valores de la variable o variables.	$8x + 3x$ and $11x$ are equivalent expressions, as are $2(x - 3)$ and $2x - 6$. $8x + 3x$ y $11x$ son expresiones equivalentes, como también lo son $2(x - 3)$ y $2x - 6$.
equivalent inequalities (p. 42) Inequalities that have the same solution. **desigualdades equivalentes** (pág. 42) Desigualdades que tienen la misma solución.	$3n - 1 \leq 8$ and $n + 1.5 \leq 4.5$ are equivalent inequalities because the solution of both inequalities is all numbers less than or equal to 3. $3n - 1 \leq 8$ y $n + 1.5 \leq 4.5$ son desigualdades equivalentes ya que la solución de ambas son todos los números menores o iguales a 3.
experimental group (p. 773) A group that undergoes some procedure or treatment when an experiment is conducted. *See also* control group. **grupo experimental** (pág. 773) Grupo que se somete a algún procedimiento o tratamiento durante la realización de un experimento. *Ver también* grupo de control.	One group of headache sufferers, the experimental group, is given pills containing medication. Another group, the control group, is given pills containing no medication. Un grupo de personas que sufren de dolores de cabeza, el grupo experimental, recibe píldoras que contienen el medicamento. Otro grupo, el grupo de control, recibe píldoras sin el medicamento.
experimental probability (p. 700) A probability based on performing an experiment, conducting a survey, or looking at the history of an event. **probabilidad experimental** (pág. 700) Probabilidad basada en la realización de un experimento o una encuesta o en el estudio de la historia de un suceso.	You roll a six-sided die 100 times and get a 4 nineteen times. The experimental probability of rolling a 4 with the die is $\frac{19}{100} = 0.19$. Lanzas 100 veces un dado de seis caras y sale diecinueve veces el 4. La probabilidad experimental de que salga el 4 al lanzar el dado es $\frac{19}{100} = 0.19$.

explicit rule (p. 827) A rule for a sequence that gives the nth term a_n as a function of the term's position number n in the sequence.

regla explícita (pág. 827) Regla de una progresión que expresa el término enésimo a_n en función del número de posición n del término en la progresión.

The rules $a_n = -11 + 4n$ and $a_n = 3(2)^{n-1}$ are explicit rules for sequences.

Las reglas $a_n = -11 + 4n$ y $a_n = 3(2)^{n-1}$ son reglas explícitas de progresiones.

---

exponent (p. 10) The number or variable that represents the number of times the base of a power is used as a factor.

exponente (pág. 10) El número o la variable que representa la cantidad de veces que la base de una potencia se usa como factor.

In the power 2^5, the exponent is 5.

En la potencia 2^5, el exponente es 5.

---

exponential decay function (p. 486) If $a > 0$ and $0 < b < 1$, then the function $y = ab^x$ is an exponential decay function with decay factor b.

función de decrecimiento exponencial (pág. 486) Si $a > 0$ y $0 < b < 1$, entonces la función $y = ab^x$ es una función de decrecimiento exponencial con factor de decrecimiento b.

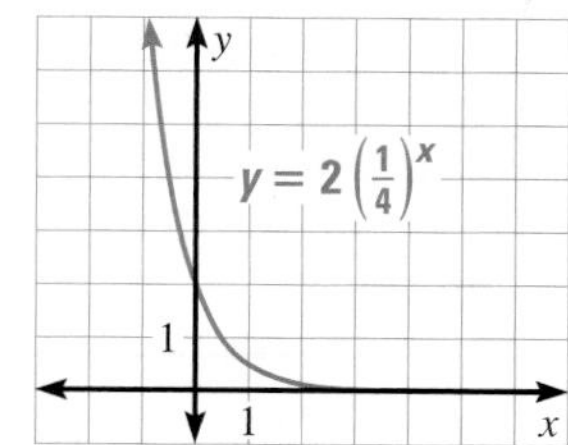

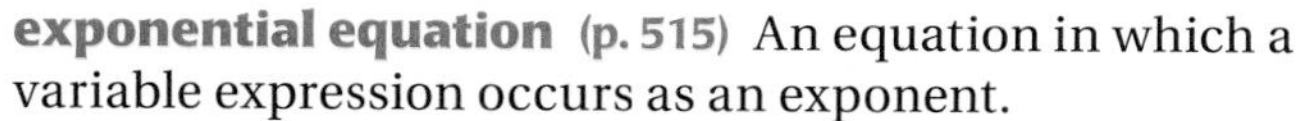

exponential equation (p. 515) An equation in which a variable expression occurs as an exponent.

ecuación exponencial (pág. 515) Ecuación que tiene como exponente una expresión algebraica.

$4^x = \left(\frac{1}{2}\right)^{x-3}$ is an exponential equation.

$4^x = \left(\frac{1}{2}\right)^{x-3}$ es una ecuación exponencial.

---

exponential function (p. 478) A function of the form $y = ab^x$, where $a \neq 0$, $b > 0$, and $b \neq 1$.

función exponencial (pág. 478) Función de la forma $y = ab^x$, donde $a \neq 0$, $b > 0$ y $b \neq 1$.

See exponential growth function *and* exponential decay function.

Ver función de crecimiento exponencial *y* función de decrecimiento exponencial.

---

exponential growth function (p. 478) If $a > 0$ and $b > 1$, then the function $y = ab^x$ is an exponential growth function with growth factor b.

función de crecimiento exponencial (pág. 478) Si $a > 0$ y $b > 1$, entonces la función $y = ab^x$ es una función de crecimiento exponencial con factor de crecimiento b.

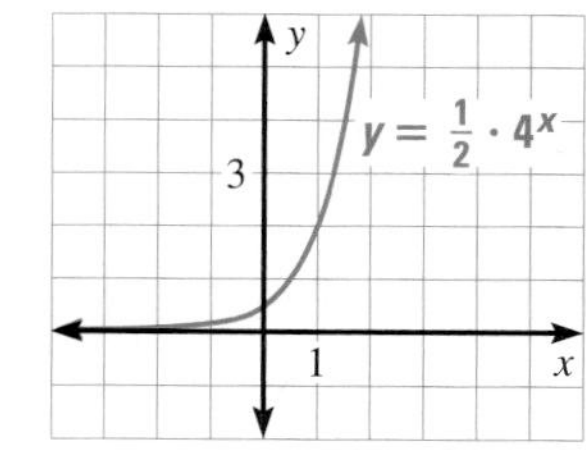

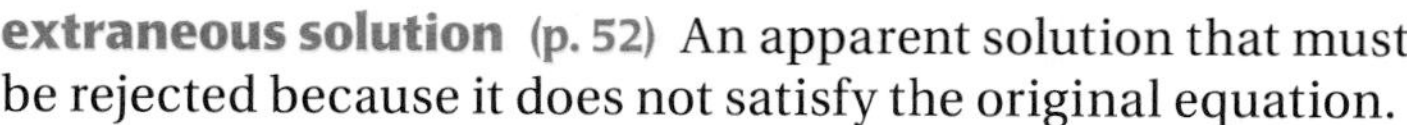

extraneous solution (p. 52) An apparent solution that must be rejected because it does not satisfy the original equation.

solución extraña (pág. 52) Solución aparente que debe rechazarse ya que no satisface la ecuación original.

Solving $|2x + 12| = 4x$ gives the apparent solutions $x = 6$ and $x = -2$. The apparent solution -2 is extraneous because it does not satisfy the original equation.

Al resolver $|2x + 12| = 4x$ se obtienen las soluciones aparentes $x = 6$ y $x = -2$. La solución aparente -2 es extraña ya no satisface la ecuación original.

ENGLISH-SPANISH GLOSSARY

F

factor by grouping (p. 354) To factor a polynomial with four terms by grouping, factor common monomials from pairs of terms, and then look for a common binomial factor. **factorizar por grupos** (pág. 354) Para factorizar por grupos un polinomio con cuatro términos, factoriza unos monomios comunes a partir de los pares de términos y luego busca un factor binómico común.	$x^3 - 3x^2 - 16x + 48$ $= x^2(x - 3) - 16(x - 3)$ $= (x^2 - 16)(x - 3)$ $= (x + 4)(x - 4)(x - 3)$
factored completely (p. 353) A factorable polynomial with integer coefficients is factored completely if it is written as a product of unfactorable polynomials with integer coefficients. **completamente factorizado** (pág. 353) Un polinomio que puede factorizarse y que tiene coeficientes enteros está completamente factorizado si está escrito como producto de polinomios que no pueden factorizarse y que tienen coeficientes enteros.	$3x(x - 5)$ is factored completely. $(x + 2)(x^2 - 6x + 8)$ is *not* factored completely because $x^2 - 6x + 8$ can be factored as $(x - 2)(x - 4)$. $3x(x - 5)$ está completamente factorizado. $(x + 2)(x^2 - 6x + 8)$ *no* está completamente factorizado ya que $x^2 - 6x + 8$ puede factorizarse como $(x - 2)(x - 4)$.
factorial (p. 684) For any positive integer n, the expression $n!$, read "n factorial," is the product of all the integers from 1 to n. Also, 0! is defined to be 1. **factorial** (pág. 684) Para cualquier número entero positivo n, la expresión $n!$, leída "factorial de n", es el producto de todos los números enteros entre 1 y n. También, 0! se define como 1.	$6! = 6 \cdot 5 \cdot 4 \cdot 3 \cdot 2 \cdot 1 = 720$
feasible region (p. 174) In linear programming, the graph of the system of constraints. **región factible** (pág. 174) En la programación lineal, la gráfica del sistema de restricciones.	*See* linear programming. *Ver* programación lineal.
finite differences (p. 393) When the x-values in a data set are equally spaced, the differences of consecutive y-values are called finite differences. **diferencias finitas** (pág. 393) Cuando los valores de x de un conjunto de datos están a igual distancia entre sí, las diferencias entre los valores de y consecutivos se llaman diferencias finitas.	$f(x) = x^2$ $f(1)$ $f(2)$ $f(3)$ $f(4)$ 1 4 9 16 $4 - 1 = 3$ $9 - 4 = 5$ $16 - 9 = 7$ The first-order finite differences are 3, 5, and 7. Las diferencias finitas de primer orden son 3, 5 y 7.
foci of a hyperbola (p. 642) *See* hyperbola. **focos de una hipérbola** (pág. 642) *Ver* hipérbola.	*See* hyperbola. *Ver* hipérbola.
foci of an ellipse (p. 634) *See* ellipse. **focos de una elipse** (pág. 634) *Ver* elipse.	*See* ellipse. *Ver* elipse.

ENGLISH-SPANISH GLOSSARY

focus of a parabola (p. 620) *See* parabola. **foco de una parábola** (pág. 620) *Ver* parábola.	*See* parabola. *Ver* parábola.
formula (p. 26) An equation that relates two or more quantities, usually represented by variables. **fórmula** (pág. 26) Ecuación que relaciona dos o más cantidades que generalmente se representan por variables.	The formula $P = 2\ell + 2w$ relates the length and width of a rectangle to its perimeter. La fórmula $P = 2\ell + 2w$ relaciona el largo y el ancho de un rectángulo con su perímetro.
frequency of a periodic function (p. 910) The reciprocal of the period. Frequency is the number of cycles per unit of time. **frecuencia de una función periódica** (pág. 910) El recíproco del período. La frecuencia es el número de ciclos por unidad de tiempo.	$P = 2 \sin 4000\pi t$ has period $\frac{2\pi}{4000\pi} = \frac{1}{2000}$, so its frequency is 2000 cycles per second (hertz) when t represents time in seconds. $P = 2 \text{ sen } 4000\pi t$ tiene período $\frac{2\pi}{4000\pi} = \frac{1}{2000}$, por lo que su frecuencia es de 2000 ciclos por segundo (hertzios) cuando t representa el tiempo en segundos.
function (p. 73) A relation for which each input has exactly one output. **función** (pág. 73) Relación para la que cada entrada tiene exactamente una salida.	The relation $(-4, 6)$, $(3, -9)$, and $(7, -9)$ is a function. The relation $(0, 3)$, $(0, 6)$, and $(10, 8)$ is not a function because the input 0 is mapped onto both 3 and 6. La relación $(-4, 6)$, $(3, -9)$ y $(7, -9)$ es una función. La relación $(0, 3)$, $(0, 6)$ y $(10, 8)$ no es una función ya que la entrada 0 se hace corresponder tanto con 3 como con 6.
function notation (p. 75) Using $f(x)$ (or a similar symbol such as $g(x)$ or $h(x)$) to represent the dependent variable of a function. **notación de función** (pág. 75) Usar $f(x)$ (o un símbolo semejante como $g(x)$ o $h(x)$) para representar la variable dependiente de una función.	The linear function $y = mx + b$ can be written using function notation as $f(x) = mx + b$. La función lineal $y = mx + b$ escrita en notación de función es $f(x) = mx + b$.

G

general second-degree equation in *x* and *y* (p. 653) The form $Ax^2 + Bxy + Cy^2 + Dx + Ey + F = 0$. **ecuación general de segundo grado en *x* e *y*** (pág. 653) La forma $Ax^2 + Bxy + Cy^2 + Dx + Ey + F = 0$.	$16x^2 - 9y^2 - 96x + 36y - 36 = 0$ and $4x^2 + y^2 - 8x - 8 = 0$ are second-degree equations in x and y. $16x^2 - 9y^2 - 96x + 36y - 36 = 0$ y $4x^2 + y^2 - 8x - 8 = 0$ son ecuaciones de segundo grado en x e y.

ENGLISH-SPANISH GLOSSARY

geometric probability (p. 701) A probability found by calculating a ratio of two lengths, areas, or volumes.

probabilidad geométrica (pág. 701) Probabilidad hallada al calcular una razón entre dos longitudes, áreas o volúmenes.

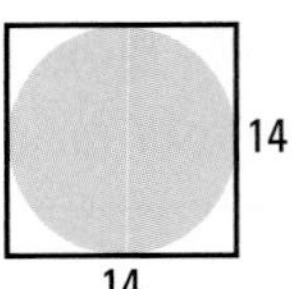

The probability that a dart that hits the square at random lands inside the circle is $\frac{\pi \cdot 7^2}{14^2} \approx 0.785$.

La probabilidad de que un dardo que da con el blanco cuadrado, dé al azar en el interior del círculo es $\frac{\pi \cdot 7^2}{14^2} \approx 0.785$.

geometric sequence (p. 810) A sequence in which the ratio of any term to the previous term is constant.

progresión geométrica (pág. 810) Progresión en la que la razón entre cualquier término y el término precedente es constante.

−19, 38, −76, 152 is a geometric sequence with common ratio −2.

−19, 38, −76, 152 es una progresión geométrica con una razón común de −2.

geometric series (p. 812) The expression formed by adding the terms of a geometric sequence.

serie geométrica (pág. 812) La expresión formada al sumar los términos de una progresión geométrica.

$$\sum_{i=1}^{5} 4(3)^{i-1} = 4 + 12 + 36 + 108 + 324$$

graph of a linear inequality in two variables (p. 132) The set of all points in a coordinate plane that represent solutions of the inequality.

gráfica de una desigualdad lineal con dos variables (pág. 132) El conjunto de todos los puntos de un plano de coordenadas que representan las soluciones de la desigualdad.

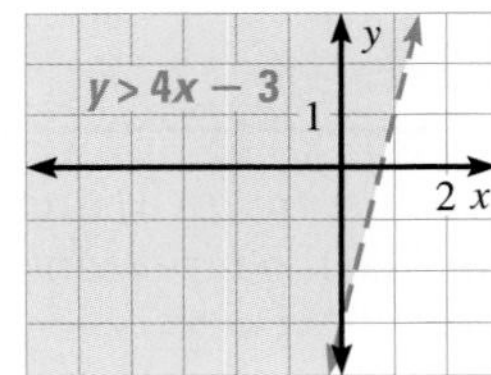

graph of a system of linear inequalities (p. 168) The graph of all solutions of the system.

gráfica de un sistema de desigualdades lineales (pág. 168) La gráfica de todas las soluciones del sistema.

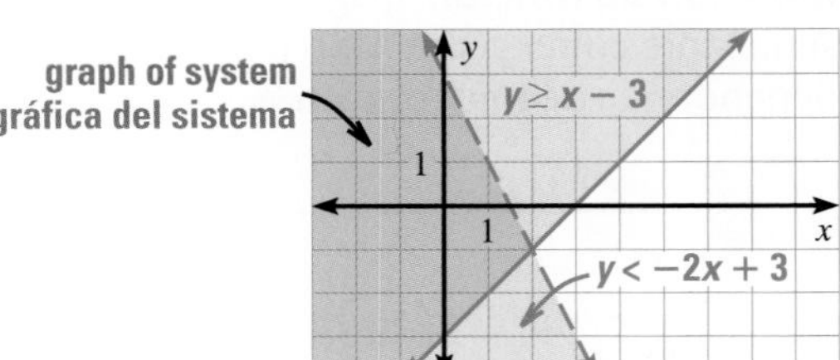

graph of an equation in two variables (p. 74) The set of all points (x, y) that represent solutions of the equation.

gráfica de una ecuación con dos variables (pág. 74) El conjunto de todos los puntos (x, y) que representan soluciones de la ecuación.

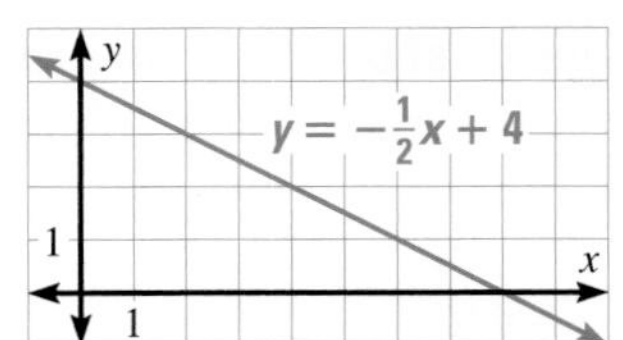

graph of an inequality in one variable (p. 41) All points on a number line that represent solutions of the inequality.

gráfica de una desigualdad con una variable (pág. 41) Todos los puntos de una recta numérica que representan soluciones de la desigualdad.

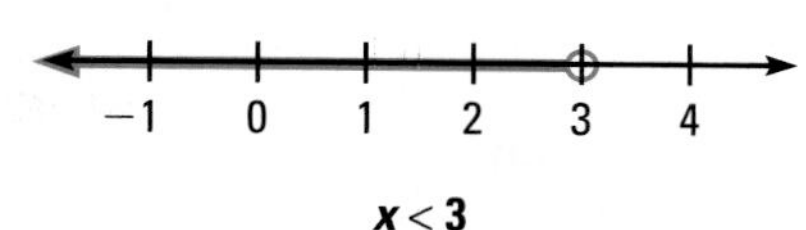

growth factor (p. 478) The quantity b in the exponential growth function $y = ab^x$ with $a > 0$ and $b > 1$.

factor de crecimiento (pág. 478) La cantidad b de la función de crecimiento exponencial $y = ab^x$, con $a > 0$ y $b > 1$.

The growth factor for the function $y = 8(3.4)^x$ is 3.4.

El factor de crecimiento de la función $y = 8(3.4)^x$ es 3.4.

H

half-planes (p. 132) The two regions into which the boundary line of a linear inequality divides the coordinate plane.

semiplanos (pág. 132) Las dos regiones en que la recta límite de una desigualdad lineal divide al plano de coordenadas.

The solution of $y < 3$ is the half-plane consisting of all the points below the line $y = 3$.

La solución de $y < 3$ es el semi-plano que consta de todos los puntos que se encuentran debajo de la recta $y = 3$.

hyperbola (pp. 558, 642) The set of all points P in a plane such that the difference of the distances from P to two fixed points, called the foci, is constant.

hipérbola (págs. 558, 642) El conjunto de todos los puntos P de un plano tales que la diferencia de distancias entre P y dos puntos fijos, llamados focos, es constante.

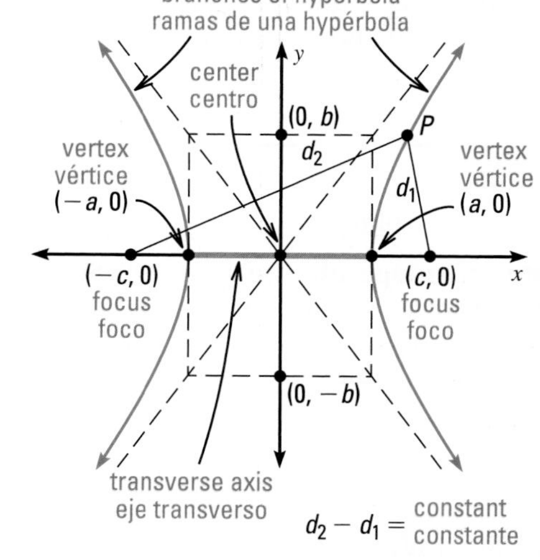

I

identity (p. 12) A statement that equates two equivalent expressions.

identidad (pág. 12) Enunciado que hace iguales a dos expresiones equivalentes.

$8x + 3x = 11x$ and $2(x - 3) = 2x - 6$ are identities.

$8x + 3x = 11x$ y $2(x - 3) = 2x - 6$ son identidades.

identity matrix (p. 210) The $n \times n$ matrix that has 1's on the main diagonal and 0's elsewhere.

matriz identidad (pág. 210) La matriz $n \times n$ que tiene los 1 en la diagonal principal y los 0 en las otras posiciones.

The 2×2 identity matrix is $\begin{bmatrix} 1 & 0 \\ 0 & 1 \end{bmatrix}$.

La matriz identidad 2×2 es $\begin{bmatrix} 1 & 0 \\ 0 & 1 \end{bmatrix}$.

imaginary number (p. 276) A complex number $a + bi$ where $b \neq 0$. **número imaginario** (pág. 276) Un número complejo $a + bi$, donde $b \neq 0$.	**$5i$ and $2 - i$ are imaginary numbers.** **$5i$ y $2 - i$ son números imaginarios.**
imaginary unit *i* (p. 275) $i = \sqrt{-1}$, so $i^2 = -1$. **unidad imaginaria *i*** (pág. 275) $i = \sqrt{-1}$, por lo que $i^2 = -1$.	$\sqrt{-3} = i\sqrt{3}$
inconsistent system (p. 154) A system of equations that has no solution. **sistema incompatible** (pág. 154) Sistema de ecuaciones que no tiene solución.	$x + y = 4$ $x + y = 1$ **The system above has no solution because the sum of two numbers cannot be both 4 and 1.** **El sistema de arriba no tiene ninguna solución porque la suma de dos números no puede ser 4 y 1.**
independent events (p. 717) Two events such that the occurrence of one event has no effect on the occurrence of the other event. **sucesos independientes** (pág. 717) Dos sucesos tales que la ocurrencia de uno de ellos no afecta a la ocurrencia del otro.	**If a coin is tossed twice, the outcome of the first toss (heads or tails) and the outcome of the second toss are independent events.** **Al lanzar una moneda dos veces, el resultado del primer lanzamiento (cara o cruz) y el resultado del segundo lanzamiento son sucesos independientes.**
independent system (p. 154) A consistent system that has exactly one solution. **sistema independiente** (pág. 154) Sistema compatible que tiene exactamente una solución.	**The system consisting of $4x + y = 8$ and $2x - 3y = 18$ has exactly one solution, $(3, -4)$.** **El sistema que consiste de $4x + y = 8$ y $2x - 3y = 18$ tiene exactamente una solución, $(3, -4)$.**
independent variable (p. 74) The input variable in an equation in two variables. **variable independiente** (pág. 74) La variable de entrada de una ecuación con dos variables.	**In $y = 3x - 5$, the independent variable is x. The dependent variable is y because the value of y depends on the value of x.** **En $y = 3x - 5$, la variable independiente es x. La variable dependiente es y ya que el valor de y depende del valor de x.**
index of a radical (p. 414) The integer n, greater than 1, in the expression $\sqrt[n]{a}$. **índice de un radical** (pág. 414) El número entero n, que es mayor que 1 y aparece en la expresión $\sqrt[n]{a}$.	**The index of $\sqrt[3]{-216}$ is 3.** **El índice de $\sqrt[3]{-216}$ es 3.**
initial side of an angle (p. 859) *See* terminal side of an angle. **lado inicial de un ángulo** (pág. 859) *Ver* lado terminal de un ángulo.	***See* standard position of an angle.** ***Ver* posición normal de un ángulo.**

ENGLISH-SPANISH GLOSSARY

intercept form of a quadratic function (p. 246) The form $y = a(x - p)(x - q)$, where the x-intercepts of the graph are p and q. **forma de intercepto de una función cuadrática** (pág. 246) La forma $y = a(x - p)(x - q)$, donde los interceptos en x de la gráfica son p y q.	**The function $y = 2(x + 3)(x - 1)$ is in intercept form.** **La función $y = 2(x + 3)(x - 1)$ está en la forma de intercepto.**
intersection of sets (p. 715) The intersection of two sets A and B, written $A \cap B$, is the set of all elements in *both* A and B. **intersección de conjuntos** (pág. 715) La intersección de dos conjuntos A y B, escrita $A \cap B$, es el conjunto de todos los elementos que están *tanto* en A *como* en B.	**If $A = \{1, 2, 4, 8\}$ and $B = \{2, 4, 6, 8, 10\}$, then $A \cap B = \{2, 4, 8\}$.** **Si $A = \{1, 2, 4, 8\}$ y $B = \{2, 4, 6, 8, 10\}$, entonces $A \cap B = \{2, 4, 8\}$.**
inverse cosine function (p. 875) If $-1 \le a \le 1$, then the inverse cosine of a is an angle θ, written $\theta = \cos^{-1} a$, where $\cos \theta = a$ and $0 \le \theta \le \pi$ (or $0° \le \theta \le 180°$). **función inversa del coseno** (pág. 875) Si $-1 \le a \le 1$, entonces el coseno inverso de a es un ángulo θ, escrito $\theta = \cos^{-1} a$, donde $\cos \theta = a$ y $0 \le \theta \le \pi$ (ó $0° \le \theta \le 180°$).	**When $0° \le \theta \le 180°$, the angle θ whose cosine is $\frac{1}{2}$ is 60°, so $\theta = \cos^{-1} \frac{1}{2} = 60°$ (or $\theta = \cos^{-1} \frac{1}{2} = \frac{\pi}{3}$).** **Cuando $0° \le \theta \le 180°$, el ángulo θ cuyo coseno es $\frac{1}{2}$ es de 60°, por lo que $\theta = \cos^{-1} \frac{1}{2} = 60°$ (ó $\theta = \cos^{-1} \frac{1}{2} = \frac{\pi}{3}$).**
inverse function (p. 438) An inverse relation that is a function. Functions f and g are inverses provided that $f(g(x)) = x$ and $g(f(x)) = x$. **función inversa** (pág. 438) Relación inversa que es una función. Las funciones f y g son inversas siempre que $f(g(x)) = x$ y $g(f(x)) = x$.	$f(x) = x + 5;\ g(x) = x - 5$ $f(g(x)) = (x - 5) + 5 = x$ $g(f(x)) = (x + 5) - 5 = x$ **So, f and g are inverse functions.** **Entonces, f y g son funciones inversas.**
inverse matrices (p. 210) Two $n \times n$ matrices are inverses of each other if their product (in both orders) is the $n \times n$ identity matrix. *See also* identity matrix. **matrices inversas** (pág. 210) Dos matrices $n \times n$ son inversas entre sí si su producto (de ambos órdenes) es la matriz identidad $n \times n$. *Ver también* matriz identidad.	$\begin{bmatrix} -5 & 8 \\ 2 & -3 \end{bmatrix}^{-1} = \begin{bmatrix} 3 & 8 \\ 2 & 5 \end{bmatrix}$ **because / ya que** $\begin{bmatrix} 3 & 8 \\ 2 & 5 \end{bmatrix}\begin{bmatrix} -5 & 8 \\ 2 & -3 \end{bmatrix} = \begin{bmatrix} 1 & 0 \\ 0 & 1 \end{bmatrix}$ **and / y** $\begin{bmatrix} -5 & 8 \\ 2 & -3 \end{bmatrix}\begin{bmatrix} 3 & 8 \\ 2 & 5 \end{bmatrix} = \begin{bmatrix} 1 & 0 \\ 0 & 1 \end{bmatrix}$.
inverse relation (p. 438) A relation that interchanges the input and output values of the original relation. The graph of an inverse relation is a reflection of the graph of the original relation, with $y = x$ as the line of reflection. **relación inversa** (pág. 438) Relación en la que se intercambian los valores de entrada y de salida de la relación original. La gráfica de una relación inversa es una reflexión de la gráfica de la relación original, con $y = x$ como eje de reflexión.	**To find the inverse of $y = 3x - 5$, switch x and y to obtain $x = 3y - 5$. Then solve for y to obtain the inverse relation $y = \frac{1}{3}x + \frac{5}{3}$.** **Para hallar la inversa de $y = 3x - 5$, intercambia x e y para obtener $x = 3y - 5$. Luego resuelve para y para obtener la relación inversa $y = \frac{1}{3}x + \frac{5}{3}$.**

inverse sine function (p. 875) If $-1 \le a \le 1$, then the inverse sine of a is an angle θ, written $\theta = \sin^{-1} a$, where $\sin \theta = a$ and $-\frac{\pi}{2} \le \theta \le \frac{\pi}{2}$ (or $-90° \le \theta \le 90°$).

función inversa del seno (pág. 875) Si $-1 \le a \le 1$, entonces el seno inverso de a es un ángulo θ, escrito $\theta = \text{sen}^{-1} a$, donde $\text{sen}\, \theta = a$ y $-\frac{\pi}{2} \le \theta \le \frac{\pi}{2}$ (ó $-90° \le \theta \le 90°$).

When $-90° \le \theta \le 90°$, the angle θ whose sine is $\frac{1}{2}$ is $30°$, so $\theta = \sin^{-1} \frac{1}{2} = 30°$ (or $\theta = \sin^{-1} \frac{1}{2} = \frac{\pi}{6}$).

Cuando $-90° \le \theta \le 90°$, el ángulo θ cuyo seno es $\frac{1}{2}$ es de $30°$, por lo que $\theta = \text{sen}^{-1} \frac{1}{2} = 30°$ (ó $\theta = \text{sen}^{-1} \frac{1}{2} = \frac{\pi}{6}$).

inverse tangent function (p. 875) If a is any real number, then the inverse tangent of a is an angle θ, written $\theta = \tan^{-1} a$, where $\tan \theta = a$ and $-\frac{\pi}{2} < \theta < \frac{\pi}{2}$ (or $-90° < \theta < 90°$).

función inversa de la tangente (pág. 875) Si a es un número real cualquiera, entonces la tangente inversa de a es un ángulo θ, escrito $\theta = \tan^{-1} a$, donde $\tan \theta = a$ y $-\frac{\pi}{2} < \theta < \frac{\pi}{2}$ (ó $-90° < \theta < 90°$).

When $-90° < \theta < 90°$, the angle θ whose tangent is $-\sqrt{3}$ is $-60°$, so $\theta = \tan^{-1}(-\sqrt{3}) = -60°$ (or $\theta = \tan^{-1}(-\sqrt{3}) = -\frac{\pi}{3}$).

Cuando $-90° < \theta < 90°$, el ángulo θ cuya tangente es $-\sqrt{3}$ es de $-60°$, por lo que $\theta = \tan^{-1}(-\sqrt{3}) = -60°$ (ó $\theta = \tan^{-1}(-\sqrt{3}) = -\frac{\pi}{3}$).

inverse variation (p. 551) The relationship of two variables x and y if there is a nonzero number a such that $y = \frac{a}{x}$.

variación inversa (pág. 551) La relación entre dos variables x e y si hay un número a distinto de cero tal que $y = \frac{a}{x}$.

The equations $xy = 7$ and $y = -\frac{3}{x}$ represent inverse variation.

Las ecuaciones $xy = 7$ e $y = -\frac{3}{x}$ representan la variación inversa.

iteration (p. 830) The repeated composition of a function with itself. The result of one iteration is $f(f(x))$, and of two iterations is $f(f(f(x)))$.

iteración (pág. 830) La composición repetida de una función usando la función misma. El resultado de una iteración es $f(f(x))$, y el de dos iteraciones es $f(f(f(x)))$.

$f(x) = -3x + 1; x_0 = 2$

$x_1 = f(x_0) = f(2) = -3(2) + 1 = -5$

$x_2 = f(x_1) = f(-5) = -3(-5) + 1 = 16$

$x_3 = f(x_2) = f(16) = -3(16) + 1 = -47$

joint variation (p. 553) A relationship that occurs when a quantity varies directly with the product of two or more other quantities.

variación conjunta (pág. 553) Relación producida cuando una cantidad varía directamente con el producto de dos o más otras cantidades.

The equation $z = 5xy$ represents joint variation.

La ecuación $z = 5xy$ representa la variación conjunta.

law of cosines (p. 889) If $\triangle ABC$ has sides of length a, b, and c as shown, then $a^2 = b^2 + c^2 - 2bc \cos A$, $b^2 = a^2 + c^2 - 2ac \cos B$, and $c^2 = a^2 + b^2 - 2ab \cos C$.

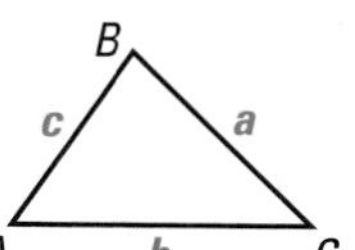

ley de los cosenos (pág. 889) Si $\triangle ABC$ tiene lados de longitud a, b y c como se indica, entonces $a^2 = b^2 + c^2 - 2bc \cos A$, $b^2 = a^2 + c^2 - 2ac \cos B$ y $c^2 = a^2 + b^2 - 2ab \cos C$.

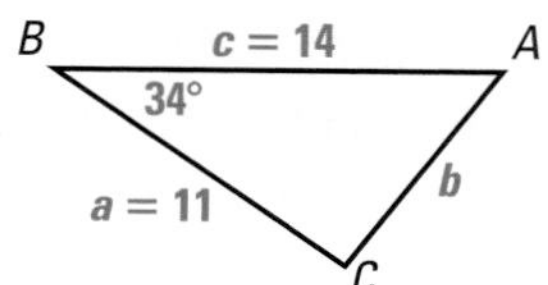

$b^2 = a^2 + c^2 - 2ac \cos B$
$b^2 = 11^2 + 14^2 - 2(11)(14) \cos 34°$
$b^2 \approx 61.7$
$b \approx 7.85$

law of sines (p. 882) If $\triangle ABC$ has sides of length a, b, and c as shown, then $\frac{\sin A}{a} = \frac{\sin B}{b} = \frac{\sin C}{c}$.

ley de los senos (pág. 882) Si $\triangle ABC$ tiene lados de longitud a, b y c como se indica, entonces $\frac{\text{sen } A}{a} = \frac{\text{sen } B}{b} = \frac{\text{sen } C}{c}$.

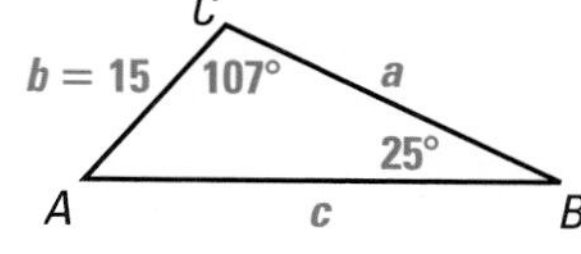

$\frac{\sin 25°}{15} = \frac{\sin 107°}{c} \rightarrow c \approx 33.9$

$\frac{\text{sen } 25°}{15} = \frac{\text{sen } 107°}{c} \rightarrow c \approx 33.9$

leading coefficient (p. 337) The coefficient in the term of a polynomial function that has the greatest exponent.

coeficiente inicial (pág. 337) En una función polinómica, el coeficiente del término con el mayor exponente.

See polynomial function.

Ver función polinómica.

like radicals (p. 422) Radical expressions with the same index and radicand.

radicales semejantes (pág. 422) Expresiones radicales con el mismo índice y el mismo radicando.

$\sqrt[4]{10}$ and $7\sqrt[4]{10}$ are like radicals.

$\sqrt[4]{10}$ y $7\sqrt[4]{10}$ son radicales semejantes.

like terms (p. 12) Terms that have the same variable parts. Constant terms are also like terms.

términos semejantes (pág. 12) Términos que tienen las mismas variables. Los términos constantes también son términos semejantes.

In the algebraic expression
$5x^2 + (-3x) + 7 + 4x + (-2)$,
$-3x$ and $4x$ are like terms, and 7 and -2 are like terms.

En la expresión algebraica
$5x^2 + (-3x) + 7 + 4x + (-2)$,
$-3x$ y $4x$ son términos semejantes, y 7 y -2 también lo son.

linear equation in one variable (p. 18) An equation that can be written in the form $ax + b = 0$ where a and b are constants and $a \neq 0$.

ecuación lineal con una variable (pág. 18) Ecuación que puede escribirse en la forma $ax + b = 0$, donde a y b son constantes y $a \neq 0$.

The equation $\frac{4}{5}x + 8 = 0$ is a linear equation in one variable.

La ecuación $\frac{4}{5}x + 8 = 0$ es una ecuación lineal con una variable.

ENGLISH-SPANISH GLOSSARY

linear equation in three variables (p. 178) An equation of the form $ax + by + cz = d$ where a, b, and c are not all zero.

$2x + y - z = 5$ is a linear equation in three variables.

ecuación lineal con tres variables (pág. 178) Ecuación de la forma $ax + by + cz = d$, donde a, b y c no son todos cero.

$2x + y - z = 5$ es una ecuación lineal con tres variables.

linear function (p. 75) A function that can be written in the form $y = mx + b$ where m and b are constants.

The function $y = -2x - 1$ is a linear function with $m = -2$ and $b = -1$.

función lineal (pág. 75) Función que puede escribirse en la forma $y = mx + b$, donde m y b son constantes.

La función $y = -2x - 1$ es una función lineal con $m = -2$ y $b = -1$.

linear inequality in one variable (p. 41) An inequality that can be written in one of the following forms, where a and b are real numbers and $a \neq 0$:
$ax + b < 0$, $ax + b \leq 0$, $ax + b > 0$, or $ax + b \geq 0$.

$5x + 2 > 0$ is a linear inequality in one variable.

desigualdad lineal con una variable (pág. 41) Desigualdad que puede escribirse de una de las siguientes formas, donde a y b son números reales y $a \neq 0$:
$ax + b < 0$, $ax + b \leq 0$, $ax + b > 0$ ó $ax + b \geq 0$.

$5x + 2 > 0$ es una desigualdad lineal con una variable.

linear inequality in two variables (p. 132) An inequality that can be written in one of the following forms:
$Ax + By < C$, $Ax + By \leq C$, $Ax + By > C$, or $Ax + By \geq C$.

$5x - 2y \geq -4$ is a linear inequality in two variables.

desigualdad lineal con dos variables (pág. 132) Desigualdad que puede escribirse de una de las siguientes formas:
$Ax + By < C$, $Ax + By \leq C$, $Ax + By > C$ o $Ax + By \geq C$.

$5x - 2y \geq -4$ es una desigualdad lineal con dos variables.

linear programming (p. 174) The process of maximizing or minimizing a linear objective function subject to a system of linear inequalities called constraints. The graph of the system of constraints is called the feasible region.

programación lineal (pág. 174) El proceso de maximizar o minimizar una función objetivo lineal sujeta a un sistema de desigualdades lineales llamadas restricciones. La gráfica del sistema de restricciones se llama región factible.

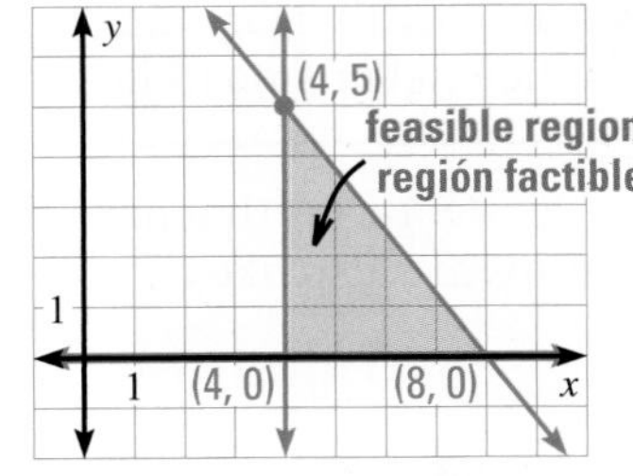

To maximize the objective function $P = 35x + 30y$ subject to the constraints $x \geq 4$, $y \geq 0$, and $5x + 4y \leq 40$, evaluate P at each vertex. The maximum value of 290 occurs at (4, 5).

Para maximizar la función objetivo $P = 35x + 30y$ sujeta a las restricciones $x \geq 4$, $y \geq 0$ y $5x + 4y \leq 40$, evalúa P en cada vértice. El valor máximo de 290 ocurre en (4, 5).

local maximum (p. 388) The y-coordinate of a turning point of a function if the point is higher than all nearby points.

máximo local (pág. 388) La coordenada y de un punto crítico de una función si el punto está situado más alto que todos los puntos cercanos.

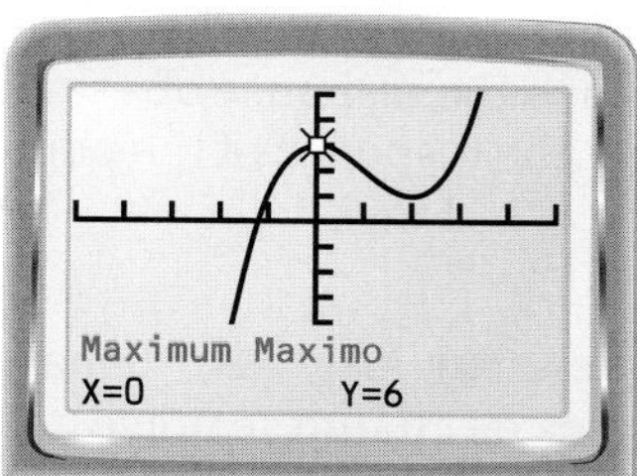

The function $f(x) = x^3 - 3x^2 + 6$ has a local maximum of $y = 6$ when $x = 0$.

La función $f(x) = x^3 - 3x^2 + 6$ tiene un máximo local de $y = 6$ cuando $x = 0$.

local minimum (p. 388) The y-coordinate of a turning point of a function if the point is lower than all nearby points.

mínimo local (pág. 388) La coordenada y de un punto crítico de una función si el punto está situado más bajo que todos los puntos cercanos.

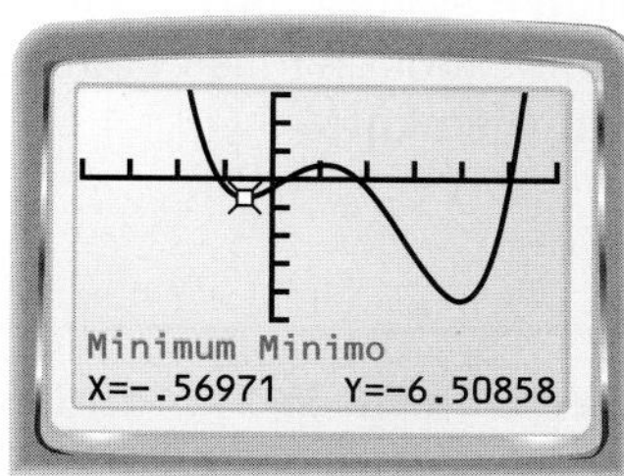

The function $f(x) = x^4 - 6x^3 + 3x^2 + 10x - 3$ has a local minimum of $y \approx -6.51$ when $x \approx -0.57$.

La función $f(x) = x^4 - 6x^3 + 3x^2 + 10x - 3$ tiene un mínimo local de $y \approx -6.51$ cuando $x \approx -0.57$.

logarithm of *y* with base *b* (p. 499) Let b and y be positive numbers with $b \neq 1$. The logarithm of y with base b, denoted $\log_b y$ and read "log base b of y," is defined as follows: $\log_b y = x$ if and only if $b^x = y$.

logaritmo de *y* con base *b* (pág. 499) Sean b e y números positivos, con $b \neq 1$. El logaritmo de y con base b, denotado por $\log_b y$ y leído "log base b de y", se define de esta manera: $\log_b y = x$ si y sólo si $b^x = y$.

$\log_2 8 = 3$ because $2^3 = 8$.

$\log_{1/4} 4 = -1$ because $\left(\frac{1}{4}\right)^{-1} = 4$.

$\log_2 8 = 3$ ya que $2^3 = 8$.

$\log_{1/4} 4 = -1$ ya que $\left(\frac{1}{4}\right)^{-1} = 4$.

logarithmic equation (p. 517) An equation that involves a logarithm of a variable expression.

ecuación logarítmica (pág. 517) Ecuación en la que aparece el logaritmo de una expresión algebraica.

$\log_5 (4x - 7) = \log_5 (x + 5)$ is a logarithmic equation.

$\log_5 (4x - 7) = \log_5 (x + 5)$ es una ecuación logarítmica.

M

major axis of an ellipse (p. 634) The line segment joining the vertices of an ellipse.

eje mayor de una elipse (pág. 634) El segmento de recta que une los vértices de una elipse.

See ellipse.

Ver elipse.

margin of error (p. 768) The margin of error gives a limit on how much the response of a sample would be expected to differ from the response of the population. **margen de error** (pág. 768) El margen de error indica un límite acerca de cuánto se prevé que diferirían las respuestas obtenidas en una muestra de las obtenidas en la población.	If 40% of the people in a poll prefer candidate A, and the margin of error is ±4%, then it is expected that between 36% and 44% of the entire population prefer candidate A. Si el 40% de los encuestados prefiere al candidato A y el margen de error es ±4%, entonces se prevé que entre el 36% y el 44% de la población total prefiere al candidato A.
matrix, matrices (p. 187) A rectangular arrangement of numbers in rows and columns. Each number in a matrix is an element. **matriz, matrices** (pág. 187) Disposición rectangular de números colocados en filas y columnas. Cada numero de la matriz es un elemento.	$A = \begin{bmatrix} 4 & -1 & 5 \\ 0 & 6 & 3 \end{bmatrix}$ Matrix A has 2 rows and 3 columns. The element in the second row and first column is 0. La matriz A tiene 2 filas y 3 columnas. El elemento en la segunda fila y en la primera columna es 0.
matrix of constants (p. 212) The matrix of constants of the linear system $ax + by = e, cx + dy = f$ is $\begin{bmatrix} e \\ f \end{bmatrix}$. **matriz de constantes** (pág. 212) La matriz de constantes del sistema lineal $ax + by = e, cx + dy = f$ es $\begin{bmatrix} e \\ f \end{bmatrix}$.	*See* coefficient matrix. *Ver* matriz coeficiente.
matrix of variables (p. 212) The matrix of variables of the linear system $ax + by = e, cx + dy = f$ is $\begin{bmatrix} x \\ y \end{bmatrix}$. **matriz de variables** (pág. 212) La matriz de variables del sistema lineal $ax + by = e, cx + dy = f$ es $\begin{bmatrix} x \\ y \end{bmatrix}$.	*See* coefficient matrix. *Ver* matriz coeficiente.
maximum value of a quadratic function (p. 238) The y-coordinate of the vertex for $y = ax^2 + bx + c$ when $a < 0$. **valor máximo de una función cuadrática** (pág. 238) La coordenada y del vértice para $y = ax^2 + bx + c$ cuando $a < 0$.	 The maximum value of $y = -x^2 + 2x - 1$ is 0. El valor máximo de $y = -x^2 + 2x - 1$ es 0.
mean (p. 744) For the data set $x_1, x_2, \ldots, x_n$, the mean is $\bar{x} = \frac{x_1 + x_2 + \ldots + x_n}{n}$. Also called average. **media** (pág. 744) Para el conjunto de datos $x_1, x_2, \ldots, x_n$, la media es $\bar{x} = \frac{x_1 + x_2 + \ldots + x_n}{n}$. También se llama promedio.	*See* measure of central tendency. *Ver* medida de tendencia central.

ENGLISH-SPANISH GLOSSARY

measure of central tendency (p. 744) A number used to represent the center or middle of a set of data values. Mean, median, and mode are three measures of central tendency.	**14, 17, 18, 19, 20, 24, 24, 30, 32** The mean is $\frac{14 + 17 + 18 + \ldots + 32}{9} = \frac{198}{9} = 22$. The median is the middle number, 20. The mode is 24 because 24 occurs the most frequently.
medida de tendencia central (pág. 744) Número usado para representar el centro o la posición central de un conjunto de valores de datos. La media, la mediana y la moda son tres medidas de tendencia central.	La media es $\frac{14 + 17 + 18 + \ldots + 32}{9} = \frac{198}{9} = 22$. La mediana es el número central, 20. La moda es 24 ya que 24 ocurre más veces.
measure of dispersion (p. 745) A statistic that tells you how dispersed, or spread out, data values are. Range and standard deviation are measures of dispersion.	*See* range *and* standard deviation.
medida de dispersión (pág. 745) Estadística que te indica cómo se dispersan, o distribuyen, los valores de datos. El rango y la desviación típica son medidas de dispersión.	*Ver* rango *y* desviación típica.
median (p. 744) The median of n numbers is the middle number when the numbers are written in numerical order. If n is even, the median is the mean of the two middle numbers.	*See* measure of central tendency.
mediana (pág. 744) La mediana de n números es el número central cuando los números se escriben en orden numérico. Si n es par, la mediana es la media de los dos números centrales.	*Ver* medida de tendencia central.
midpoint formula (p. 615) The midpoint M of the line segment joining $A(x_1, y_1)$ and $B(x_2, y_2)$ is $M\left(\frac{x_1 + x_2}{2}, \frac{y_1 + y_2}{2}\right)$.	The midpoint of the line segment joining $(-2, 3)$ and $(8, 6)$ is $\left(\frac{-2+8}{2}, \frac{3+6}{2}\right) = \left(3, \frac{9}{2}\right)$.
fórmula del punto medio (pág. 615) El punto medio M del segmento de recta que une $A(x_1, y_1)$ y $B(x_2, y_2)$ es $M\left(\frac{x_1 + x_2}{2}, \frac{y_1 + y_2}{2}\right)$.	El punto medio del segmento de recta que une $(-2, 3)$ y $(8, 6)$ es $\left(\frac{-2+8}{2}, \frac{3+6}{2}\right) = \left(3, \frac{9}{2}\right)$.
minimum value of a quadratic function (p. 238) The y-coordinate of the vertex for $y = ax^2 + bx + c$ when $a > 0$. **valor mínimo de una función cuadrática** (pág. 238) La coordenada y del vértice para $y = ax^2 + bx + c$ cuando $a > 0$.	 The minimum value of $y = x^2 - 6x + 5$ is -4. El valor mínimo de $y = x^2 - 6x + 5$ es -4.
minor axis of an ellipse (p. 634) The line segment joining the co-vertices of an ellipse.	*See* ellipse.
eje menor de una elipse (pág. 634) El segmento de recta que une los puntos extremos de una elipse.	*Ver* elipse.

ENGLISH-SPANISH GLOSSARY

mode (p. 744) The mode of n numbers is the number or numbers that occur most frequently. **moda** (pág. 744) La moda de n números es el número o números que ocurren más veces.	*See* measure of central tendency. *Ver* medida de tendencia central.
monomial (p. 252) An expression that is either a number, a variable, or the product of a number and one or more variables with whole number exponents. **monomio** (pág. 252) Expresión que es un número, una variable o el producto de un número y una o más variables con exponentes naturales.	$6, 0.2x, \frac{1}{2}ab$, and $-5.7n^4$ are monomials. $6, 0.2x, \frac{1}{2}ab$ y $-5.7n^4$ son monomios.
mutually exclusive events (p. 707) *See* disjoint events. **sucesos mutuamente excluyentes** (pág. 707) *Ver* sucesos disjuntos.	*See* disjoint events. *Ver* sucesos disjuntos.

N

natural base *e* (p. 492) An irrational number defined as follows: As n approaches $+\infty$, $\left(1+\frac{1}{n}\right)^n$ approaches $e \approx 2.718281828$. **base natural *e*** (pág. 492) Número irracional definido de esta manera: Al aproximarse n a $+\infty$, $\left(1+\frac{1}{n}\right)^n$ se aproxima a $e \approx 2.718281828$.	*See* natural logarithm. *Ver* logaritmo natural.
natural logarithm (p. 500) A logarithm with base e. It can be denoted $\log_e$, but is more often denoted by ln. **logaritmo natural** (pág. 500) Logaritmo con base e. Puede denotarse $\log_e$, pero es más frecuente que se denote ln.	$\ln 0.3 \approx -1.204$ because $e^{-1.204} \approx (2.7183)^{-1.204} \approx 0.3$. $\ln 0.3 \approx -1.204$ ya que $e^{-1.204} \approx (2.7183)^{-1.204} \approx 0.3$.
negative correlation (p. 113) The paired data (x, y) have a negative correlation if y tends to decrease as x increases. **correlación negativa** (pág. 113) Los pares de datos (x, y) presentan una correlación negativa si y tiende a disminuir al aumentar x.	y x
normal curve (p. 757) A smooth, symmetrical, bell-shaped curve that can model normal distributions and approximate some binomial distributions. **curva normal** (pág. 757) Curva lisa, simétrica y con forma de campana que puede representar distribuciones normales y aproximar a algunas distribuciones binomiales.	*See* normal distribution. *Ver* distribución normal.

normal distribution (p. 757) A probability distribution with mean $\bar{x}$ and standard deviation σ modeled by a bell-shaped curve with the area properties shown at the right.

distribución normal (pág. 757) Una distribución de probabilidad con media $\bar{x}$ y desviación normal σ representada por una curva en forma de campana y que tiene las propiedades vistas a la derecha.

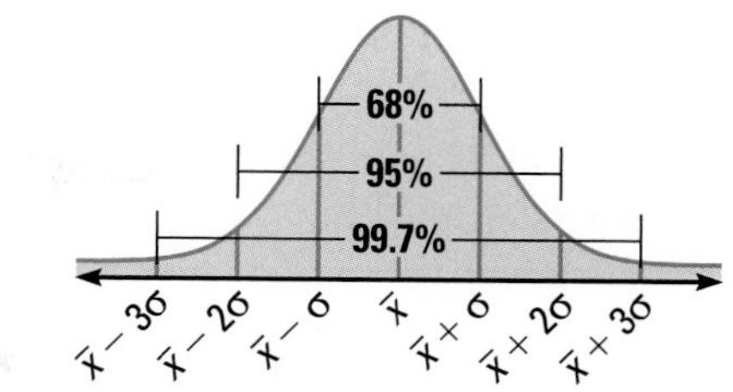

---

nth root of *a* (p. 414) For an integer n greater than 1, if $b^n = a$, then b is an nth root of a. Written as $\sqrt[n]{a}$.

$\sqrt[3]{-216} = -6$ because $(-6)^3 = -216$.

raíz enésima de *a* (pág. 414) Para un número entero n mayor que 1, si $b^n = a$, entonces b es una raíz enésima de a. Se escribe $\sqrt[n]{a}$.

$\sqrt[3]{-216} = -6$ ya que $(-6)^3 = -216$.

---

numerical expression (p. 10) An expression that consists of numbers, operations, and grouping symbols.

$-4(-3)^2 - 6(-3) + 11$ is a numerical expression.

expresión numérica (pág. 10) Expresión formada por números, operaciones y signos de agrupación.

$-4(-3)^2 - 6(-3) + 11$ es una expresión numérica.

O

objective function (p. 174) In linear programming, the linear function that is maximized or minimized.

See linear programming.

función objetivo (pág. 174) En la programación lineal, la función lineal que se maximiza o minimiza.

Ver programación lineal.

---

odds against (p. 699) When all outcomes are equally likely,

$$\text{Odds against event } A = \frac{\text{Number of outcomes not in } A}{\text{Number of outcomes in } A}.$$

The odds against rolling a 4 using a standard six-sided die are $\frac{5}{1}$, or 5 : 1, because 5 outcomes correspond to not rolling a 4 and only 1 outcome corresponds to rolling a 4.

probabilidad en contra (pág. 699) Cuando todos los casos son igualmente posibles,

$$\text{Probabilidad en contra del suceso } A = \frac{\text{Número de casos no del } A}{\text{Número de casos del } A}.$$

La probabilidad en contra de sacar el 4 al lanzar un dado normal de seis caras es $\frac{5}{1}$, ó 5 : 1, ya que 5 casos corresponden a un número que no sea el 4 y sólo 1 caso corresponde al 4.

---

odds in favor (p. 699) When all outcomes are equally likely,

$$\text{Odds in favor of event } A = \frac{\text{Number of outcomes in } A}{\text{Number of outcomes not in } A}.$$

The odds in favor of rolling a 4 using a standard six-sided die are $\frac{1}{5}$, or 1 : 5, because only 1 outcome corresponds to rolling a 4 and 5 outcomes correspond to not rolling a 4.

probabilidad a favor (pág. 699) Cuando todos los casos son igualmente posibles,

$$\text{Probabilidad a favor del suceso } A = \frac{\text{Número de casos del } A}{\text{Número de casos no del } A}.$$

La probabilidad a favor de sacar el 4 al lanzar un dado normal de seis caras es $\frac{1}{5}$, ó 1 : 5, ya que sólo 1 caso corresponde al 4 y 5 casos corresponden a un número que no sea el 4.

opposite (p. 4) The opposite, or additive inverse, of any number b is $-b$. **opuesto** (pág. 4) El opuesto, o inverso aditivo, de cualquier número b es $-b$.	**6.2 and −6.2 are opposites.** **6.2 y −6.2 son opuestos.**
ordered triple (p. 178) A set of three numbers of the form (x, y, z) that represents a point in space. **terna ordenada** (pág. 178) Un conjunto de tres números de la forma (x, y, z) que representa un punto en el espacio.	**The ordered triple (2, 1, −3) is a solution of the equation $4x + 2y + 3z = 1$.** **La terna ordenada (2, 1, −3) es una solución de la ecuación $4x + 2y + 3z = 1$.**
outlier (p. 746) A value that is much greater than or much less than most of the other values in a data set. **valor extremo** (pág. 746) Valor que es mucho mayor o mucho menor que la mayoría de los otros valores de un conjunto de datos.	**3 is an outlier in the data set 3, 11, 12, 13, 13, 14, 15, 15, 15, 15, 17.** **3 es un valor extremo del conjunto de datos 3, 11, 12, 13, 13, 14, 15, 15, 15, 15, 17.**

P

parabola (pp. 236, 620) The set of all points equidistant from a point called the focus and a line called the directrix. The graph of a quadratic function $y = ax^2 + bx + c$ is a parabola. **parábola** (págs. 236, 620) El conjunto de todos los puntos equidistantes de un punto, llamado foco, y de una recta, llamada directriz. La gráfica de una función cuadrática $y = ax^2 + bx + c$ es una parábola.	axis of symmetry eje de simetría focus foco vertex vértice directrix directriz
parallel lines (p. 84) Two lines in the same plane that do not intersect. **rectas paralelas** (pág. 84) Dos rectas del mismo plano que no se cortan.	y x
parent function (p. 89) The most basic function in a family of functions. **función básica** (pág. 89) La función más fundamental de una familia de funciones.	**The parent function for the family of all linear functions is $y = x$.** **La función básica de la familia de todas las funciones lineales es $y = x$.**
partial sum (p. 820) The sum S_n of the first n terms of an infinite series. **suma parcial** (pág. 820) La suma S_n de los n primeros términos de una serie infinita.	$\frac{1}{2} + \frac{1}{4} + \frac{1}{8} + \frac{1}{16} + \frac{1}{32} + \dots$ **The series above has the partial sums $S_1 = 0.5, S_2 = 0.75, S_3 \approx 0.88, S_4 \approx 0.94, \dots$.** **La serie de arriba tiene las sumas parciales $S_1 = 0.5, S_2 = 0.75, S_3 \approx 0.88, S_4 \approx 0.94, \dots$.**

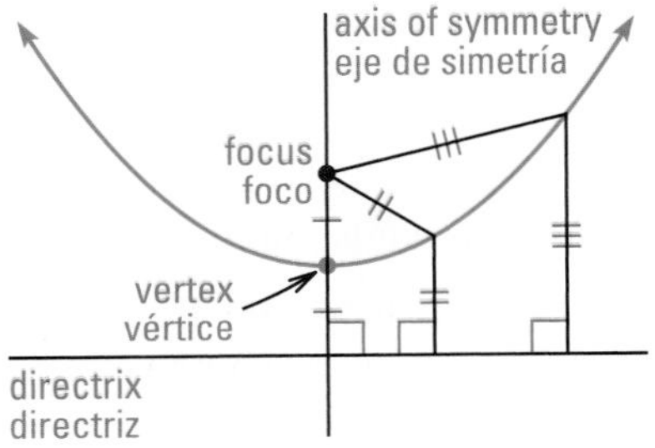

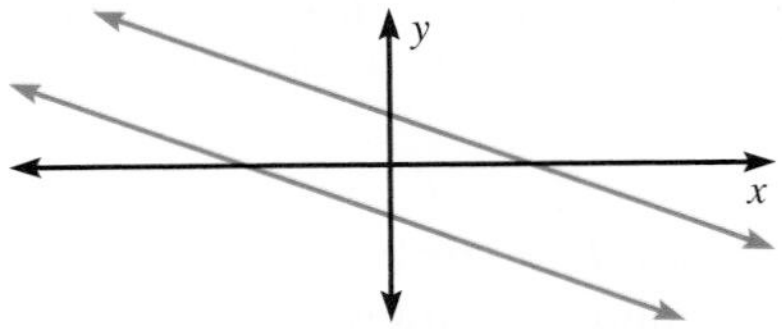

Pascal's triangle (p. 692) An arrangement of the values of $_nC_r$ in a triangular pattern in which each row corresponds to a value of n.

triángulo de Pascal (pág. 692) Disposición de los valores de $_nC_r$ en un patrón triangular en el que cada fila corresponde a un valor de n.

$$
\begin{array}{c}
{}_0C_0 \\
{}_1C_0 \quad {}_1C_1 \\
{}_2C_0 \quad {}_2C_1 \quad {}_2C_2 \\
{}_3C_0 \quad {}_3C_1 \quad {}_3C_2 \quad {}_3C_3 \\
{}_4C_0 \quad {}_4C_1 \quad {}_4C_2 \quad {}_4C_3 \quad {}_4C_4 \\
{}_5C_0 \quad {}_5C_1 \quad {}_5C_2 \quad {}_5C_3 \quad {}_5C_4 \quad {}_5C_5
\end{array}
$$

---

period (p. 908) The horizontal length of each cycle of a periodic function.

período (pág. 908) La longitud horizontal de cada ciclo de una función periódica.

See periodic function.

Ver función periódica.

---

periodic function (p. 908) A function whose graph has a repeating pattern.

función periódica (pág. 908) Función cuya gráfica tiene un patrón que se repite.

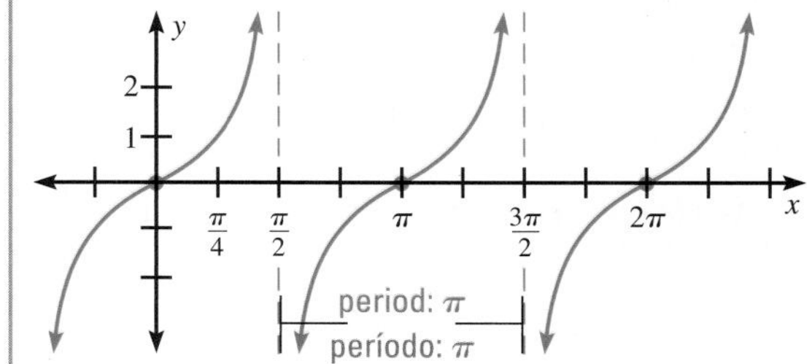

The graph shows 3 cycles of $y = \tan x$, a periodic function with a period of π.

La gráfica muestra 3 ciclos de $y = \tan x$, función periódica con período π.

---

permutation (p. 684) An ordering of objects. The number of permutations of r objects taken from a group of n distinct objects is denoted $_nP_r$ where $_nP_r = \frac{n!}{(n-r)!}$.

permutación (pág. 684) Ordenación de objetos. El número de permutaciones de r objetos tomados de un grupo de n objetos diferenciados se indica $_nP_r$, donde $_nP_r = \frac{n!}{(n-r)!}$.

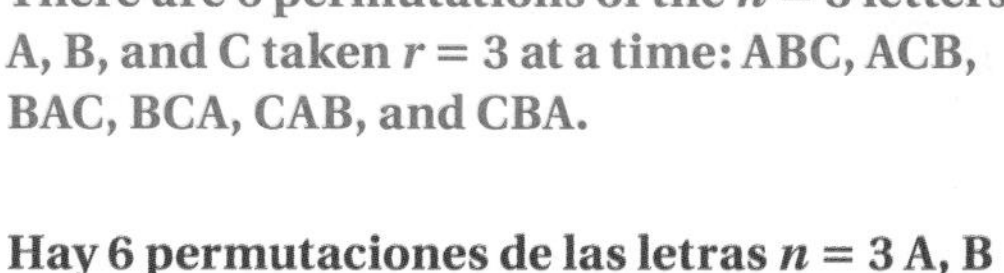

There are 6 permutations of the $n = 3$ letters A, B, and C taken $r = 3$ at a time: ABC, ACB, BAC, BCA, CAB, and CBA.

Hay 6 permutaciones de las letras $n = 3$ A, B y C tomadas $r = 3$ cada vez: ABC, ACB, BAC, BCA, CAB y CBA.

---

perpendicular lines (p. 84) Two lines in the same plane that intersect to form a right angle.

rectas perpendiculares (pág. 84) Dos rectas del mismo plano que al cortarse forman un ángulo recto.

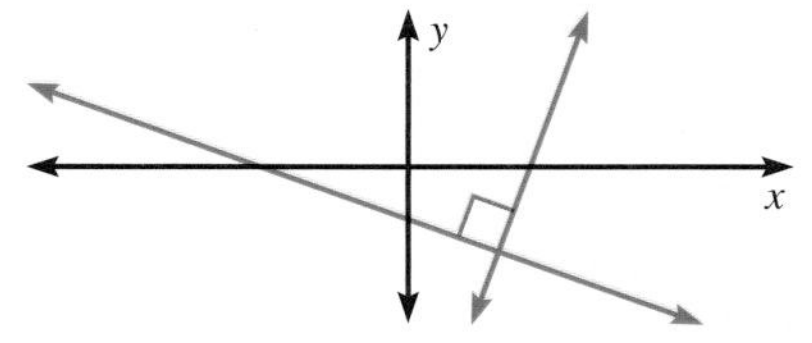

---

piecewise function (p. 130) A function defined by at least two equations, each of which applies to a different part of the function's domain.

función definida a trozos (pág. 130) Función definida por al menos dos ecuaciones, cada una de las cuales se aplica a una parte diferente del dominio de la función.

$$g(x) = \begin{cases} 3x - 1, & \text{if } x < 1 \\ 0, & \text{if } x = 1 \\ -x + 4, & \text{if } x > 1 \end{cases} \qquad g(x) = \begin{cases} 3x - 1, & \text{si } x < 1 \\ 0, & \text{si } x = 1 \\ -x + 4, & \text{si } x > 1 \end{cases}$$

point-slope form (p. 98) An equation of a line written in the form $y - y_1 = m(x - x_1)$ where the line passes through the point (x_1, y_1) and has a slope of m. **forma punto-pendiente** (pág. 98) Ecuación de una recta escrita en la forma $y - y_1 = m(x - x_1)$, donde la recta pasa por el punto (x_1, y_1) y tiene pendiente m.	The equation $y + 2 = -4(x - 5)$ is in point-slope form. La ecuación $y + 2 = -4(x - 5)$ está en la forma punto-pendiente.
polynomial (p. 337) A monomial or a sum of monomials, each of which is called a term of the polynomial. *See also* monomial. **polinomio** (pág. 337) Monomio o suma de monomios, cada uno de los cuales se llama término del polinomio. *Ver también* monomio.	-14, $x^4 - \frac{1}{4}x^2 + 3$, and $7b - \sqrt{3} + \pi b^2$ are polynomials. -14, $x^4 - \frac{1}{4}x^2 + 3$ y $7b - \sqrt{3} + \pi b^2$ son polinomios.
polynomial function (p. 337) A function of the form $f(x) = a_nx^n + a_{n-1}x^{n-1} + \cdots + a_1x + a_0$ where $a_n \neq 0$, the exponents are all whole numbers, and the coefficients are all real numbers. **función polinómica** (pág. 337) Función de la forma $f(x) = a_nx^n + a_{n-1}x^{n-1} + \cdots + a_1x + a_0$ donde $a_n \neq 0$, los exponentes son todos números enteros y los coeficientes son todos números reales.	$f(x) = 11x^5 - 0.4x^2 + 16x - 7$ is a polynomial function. The degree of $f(x)$ is 5, the leading coefficient is 11, and the constant term is -7. $f(x) = 11x^5 - 0.4x^2 + 16x - 7$ es una función polinómica. El grado de $f(x)$ es 5, el coeficiente inicial es 11 y el término constante es -7.
polynomial long division (p. 362) A method used to divide polynomials similar to the way you divide numbers. **división desarrollada polinómica** (pág. 362) Método utilizado para dividir polinomios semejante a la manera en que divides números.	$$\begin{array}{r} x^2 + 7x + 7 \\ x - 2 \overline{) x^3 + 5x^2 - 7x + 2} \\ \underline{x^3 - 2x^2} \\ 7x^2 - 7x \\ \underline{7x^2 - 14x} \\ 7x + 2 \\ \underline{7x - 14} \\ 16 \end{array}$$ $$\frac{x^3 + 5x^2 - 7x + 2}{x - 2} = x^2 + 7x + 7 + \frac{16}{x - 2}$$
population (p. 766) A group of people or objects that you want information about. **población** (pág. 766) Grupo de personas u objetos acerca del cual deseas informarte.	A sportswriter randomly selects 5% of college baseball coaches for a survey. The population is all college baseball coaches. The 5% of coaches selected is the sample. Un periodista deportiva selecciona al azar al 5% de los entrenadores universitarios de béisbol para que participe en una encuesta. La población son todos los entrenadores universitarios de béisbol. El 5% de los entrenadores que resultó seleccionado es la muestra.

positive correlation (p. 113) The paired data (x, y) have a positive correlation if y tends to increase as x increases.

correlacion positiva (pág. 113) Los pares de datos (x, y) presentan una correlación positiva si y tiende a aumentar al aumentar x.

power (p. 10) An expression that represents repeated multiplication of the same factor.

potencia (pág. 10) Expresión que representa la multiplicación repetida del mismo factor.

32 is the fifth power of 2 because $32 = 2 \cdot 2 \cdot 2 \cdot 2 \cdot 2 = 2^5$.

32 es la quinta potencia de 2 ya que $32 = 2 \cdot 2 \cdot 2 \cdot 2 \cdot 2 = 2^5$.

power function (p. 428) A function of the form $y = ax^b$, where a is a real number and b is a rational number.

función potencial (pág. 428) Función de la forma $y = ax^b$, donde a es un número real y b es un número racional.

$f(x) = 4x^{3/2}$ is a power function.

$f(x) = 4x^{3/2}$ es una función potencial.

probability distribution (p. 724) A function that gives the probability of each possible value of a random variable. The sum of all the probabilities in a probability distribution must equal 1.

distribución de probabilidades (pág. 724) Función que indica la probabilidad de cada valor posible de una variable aleatoria. La suma de todas las probabilidades de una distribución de probabilidades debe ser igual a 1.

Let the random variable X represent the number showing after rolling a standard six-sided die.

Sea la variable aleatoria X el número que salga al lanzar un dado normal de seis caras.

Probability Distribution for Rolling a Die Distribución de probabilidad al lanzar un dado						
X	1	2	3	4	5	6
$P(X)$	$\frac{1}{6}$	$\frac{1}{6}$	$\frac{1}{6}$	$\frac{1}{6}$	$\frac{1}{6}$	$\frac{1}{6}$

probability of an event (p. 698) A number from 0 to 1 that indicates the likelihood that the event will occur.

probabilidad de un suceso (pág. 698) Número entre 0 y 1 que indica la probabilidad de que ocurra el suceso.

See experimental probability, geometric probability, *and* theoretical probability.

Ver probabilidad experimental, probabilidad geométrica *y* probabilidad teórica.

pure imaginary number (p. 276) A complex number $a + bi$ where $a = 0$ and $b \neq 0$.

número imaginario puro (pág. 276) Número complejo $a + bi$, donde $a = 0$ y $b \neq 0$.

$-4i$ and $1.2i$ are pure imaginary numbers.

$-4i$ y $1.2i$ son números imaginarios puros.

Q

quadrantal angle (p. 867) An angle in standard position whose terminal side lies on an axis.

ángulo cuadrantal (pág. 867) Ángulo en posición normal cuyo lado terminal se encuentra en un eje.

quadratic equation in one variable (p. 253) An equation that can be written in the form $ax^2 + bx + c = 0$ where $a \neq 0$.	The equation $x^2 - 5x = 36$ is a quadratic equation in one variable because it can be written in the form $x^2 - 5x - 36 = 0$.
ecuación cuadrática con una variable (pág. 253) Ecuación que puede escribirse en la forma $ax^2 + bx + c = 0$, donde $a \neq 0$.	La ecuación $x^2 - 5x = 36$ es una ecuación cuadrática con una variable ya que puede escribirse en la forma $x^2 - 5x - 36 = 0$.
quadratic form (p. 355) The form $au^2 + bu + c$, where u is any expression in x.	The expression $16x^4 - 8x^2 - 8$ is in quadratic form because it can be written as $u^2 - 2u - 8$ where $u = 4x^2$.
forma cuadrática (pág. 355) La forma $au^2 + bu + c$, donde u es cualquier expresión en x.	La expresión $16x^4 - 8x^2 - 8$ está en la forma cuadrática ya que puede escribirse $u^2 - 2u - 8$, donde $u = 4x^2$.
quadratic formula (p. 292) The formula $x = \frac{-b \pm \sqrt{b^2 - 4ac}}{2a}$ used to find the solutions of the quadratic equation $ax^2 + bx + c = 0$ when a, b, and c are real numbers and $a \neq 0$.	To solve $3x^2 + 6x + 2 = 0$, substitute 3 for a, 6 for b, and 2 for c in the quadratic formula.
fórmula cuadrática (pág. 292) La fórmula $x = \frac{-b \pm \sqrt{b^2 - 4ac}}{2a}$ que se usa para hallar las soluciones de la ecuación cuadrática $ax^2 + bx + c = 0$ cuando a, b y c son números reales y $a \neq 0$.	Para resolver $3x^2 + 6x + 2 = 0$, sustituye a por 3, b por 6 y c por 2 en la fórmula cuadrática. $x = \frac{-6 \pm \sqrt{6^2 - 4(3)(2)}}{2(3)} = \frac{-3 \pm \sqrt{3}}{3}$
quadratic function (p. 236) A function that can be written in the form $y = ax^2 + bx + c$ where $a \neq 0$.	The functions $y = 3x^2 - 5$ and $y = x^2 - 4x + 6$ are quadratic functions.
función cuadrática (pág. 236) Función que puede escribirse en la forma $y = ax^2 + bx + c$, donde $a \neq 0$.	Las funciones $y = 3x^2 - 5$ e $y = x^2 - 4x + 6$ son funciones cuadráticas.
quadratic inequality in one variable (p. 302) An inequality that can be written in the form $ax^2 + bx + c < 0$, $ax^2 + bx + c \leq 0$, $ax^2 + bx + c > 0$, or $ax^2 + bx + c \geq 0$.	$x^2 + x \leq 0$ and $2x^2 + x - 4 > 0$ are quadratic inequalities in one variable.
desigualdad cuadrática con una variable (pág. 302) Desigualdad que se puede escribir en la forma $ax^2 + bx + c < 0$, $ax^2 + bx + c \leq 0$, $ax^2 + bx + c > 0$ ó $ax^2 + bx + c \geq 0$.	$x^2 + x \leq 0$ y $2x^2 + x - 4 > 0$ son desigualdades cuadráticas con una variable.
quadratic inequality in two variables (p. 300) An inequality that can be written in the form $y < ax^2 + bx + c$, $y \leq ax^2 + bx + c$, $y > ax^2 + bx + c$, or $y \geq ax^2 + bx + c$.	$y > x^2 + 3x - 4$ is a quadratic inequality in two variables.
desigualdad cuadrática con dos variables (pág. 300) Desigualdad que se puede escribir en la forma $y < ax^2 + bx + c$, $y \leq ax^2 + bx + c$, $y > ax^2 + bx + c$ ó $y \geq ax^2 + bx + c$.	$y > x^2 + 3x - 4$ es una desigualdad cuadrática con dos variables.

quadratic system (p. 658) A system of equations that includes one or more equations of conics. **sistema cuadrático** (pág. 658) Sistema de ecuaciones que incluye una o más ecuaciones de cónicas.	$y^2 - 7x + 3 = 0$ $\quad x^2 + 4y^2 + 8y = 16$ $2x - y = 3$ $\quad 2x^2 - y^2 - 6x - 4 = 0$ **The systems above are quadratic systems.** **Los sistemas de arriba son sistemas cuadráticos.**

R

radian (p. 860) In a circle with radius r and center at the origin, one radian is the measure of an angle in standard position whose terminal side intercepts an arc of length r. **radián** (pág. 860) En un círculo con radio r y cuyo centro está en el origen, un radián es la medida de un ángulo en posición normal cuyo lado terminal intercepta un arco de longitud r.	
radical (pp. 266, 414) An expression of the form $\sqrt{s}$ or $\sqrt[n]{s}$ where s is a number or an expression. **radical** (págs. 266, 414) Expresión de la forma $\sqrt{s}$ o $\sqrt[n]{s}$, donde s es un número o una expresión.	$\sqrt{5}, \sqrt[3]{2x + 1}$
radical equation (p. 452) An equation with one or more radicals that have variables in their radicands. **ecuación radical** (pág. 452) Ecuación con uno o más radicales en cuyo radicando aparecen variables.	$\sqrt[3]{2x + 7} = 3$
radical function (p. 446) A function that contains a radical with a variable in its radicand. **función radical** (pág. 446) Función que tiene un radical con una variable en su radicando.	$f(x) = \frac{1}{2}\sqrt{x}, g(x) = -3\sqrt[3]{x + 5}$
radicand (p. 266) The number or expression beneath a radical sign. **radicando** (pág. 266) El número o la expresión que aparece bajo el signo radical.	**The radicand of $\sqrt{5}$ is 5, and the radicand of $\sqrt{8y^2}$ is $8y^2$.** **El radicando de $\sqrt{5}$ es 5, y el radicando de $\sqrt{8y^2}$ es $8y^2$.**
radius of a circle (p. 626) The distance from the center of a circle to a point on the circle. Also, a line segment that connects the center of a circle to a point on the circle. *See also* circle. **radio de un círculo** (pág. 626) La distancia desde el centro de un círculo hasta un punto del círculo. También, es un segmento de recta que une el centro de un círculo con un punto del círculo. *Ver también* círculo.	**The circle with equation $(x - 3)^2 + (y + 5)^2 = 36$ has radius $\sqrt{36} = 6$. *See also* circle.** **El círculo con la ecuación $(x - 3)^2 + (y + 5)^2 = 36$ tiene el radio $\sqrt{36} = 6$. *Ver también* círculo.**

random variable (p. 724) A variable whose value is determined by the outcomes of a random event. **variable aleatoria** (pág. 724) Variable cuyo valor viene determinado por los resultados de un suceso aleatorio.	The random variable *X* representing the number showing after rolling a six-sided die has possible values of 1, 2, 3, 4, 5, and 6. La variable aleatoria *X* que representa el número que sale al lanzar un dado de seis caras tiene como valores posibles 1, 2, 3, 4, 5 y 6.
range of a relation (p. 72) The set of output values of a relation. **rango de una relación** (pág. 72) El conjunto de los valores de salida de una relación.	*See* relation. *Ver* relación.
range of data values (p. 745) A measure of dispersion equal to the difference between the greatest and least data values. **rango de valores de datos** (pág. 745) Medida de dispersión igual a la diferencia entre el valor máximo y el valor mínimo de los datos.	14, 17, 18, 19, 20, 24, 24, 30, 32 The range of the data set above is $32 - 14 = 18$. El rango del conjunto de datos de arriba es $32 - 14 = 18$.
rate of change (p. 85) A comparison of how much one quantity changes, on average, relative to the change in another quantity. **relación de cambio** (pág. 85) Comparación entre el cambio producido, por término medio, en una cantidad y el cambio producido en otra cantidad.	The temperature rises from 75°F at 8 A.M. to 91°F at 12 P.M. The average rate of change in temperature is $\frac{91°F - 75°F}{12 \text{ P.M.} - 8 \text{ A.M.}} = \frac{16°F}{4 \text{ h}} = 4°/\text{h}$. La temperatura sube de 75°F a las 8 de la mañana a 91°F a las 12 del mediodía. La relación de cambio media en la temperatura es $\frac{91°F - 75°F}{12 \text{ P.M.} - 8 \text{ A.M.}} = \frac{16°F}{4 \text{ h}} = 4°/\text{h}$.
rational function (p. 558) A function of the form $f(x) = \frac{p(x)}{q(x)}$, where $p(x)$ and $q(x)$ are polynomials and $q(x) \neq 0$. **función racional** (pág. 558) Función de la forma $f(x) = \frac{p(x)}{q(x)}$, donde $p(x)$ y $q(x)$ son polinomios y $q(x) \neq 0$.	The functions $y = \frac{6}{x}$ and $y = \frac{2x + 1}{x - 3}$ are rational functions. Las funciones $y = \frac{6}{x}$ e $y = \frac{2x + 1}{x - 3}$ son funciones racionales.
rationalizing the denominator (p. 267) The process of eliminating a radical expression in the denominator of a fraction by multiplying both the numerator and denominator by an appropriate radical expression. **racionalizar el denominador** (pág. 267) El proceso de eliminar una expresión radical del denominador de una fracción al multiplicar tanto el numerador como el denominador por una expresión radical adecuada.	To rationalize the denominator of $\frac{\sqrt{5}}{\sqrt{2}}$, multiply the numerator and denominator by $\sqrt{2}$. Para racionalizar el denominador de $\frac{\sqrt{5}}{\sqrt{2}}$, multiplica el numerador y el denominador por $\sqrt{2}$.
reciprocal (p. 4) The reciprocal, or multiplicative inverse, of any nonzero number b is $\frac{1}{b}$. **recíproco** (pág. 4) El recíproco, o inverso multiplicativo, de cualquier número b distinto de cero es $\frac{1}{b}$.	-2 and $\frac{1}{-2} = -\frac{1}{2}$ are reciprocals. -2 y $\frac{1}{-2} = -\frac{1}{2}$ son recíprocos.

recursive rule (p. 827) A rule for a sequence that gives the beginning term or terms of the sequence and then a recursive equation that tells how the nth term a_n is related to one or more preceding terms.

regla recursiva (pág. 827) Regla de una progresión que da el primer término o términos de la progresión y luego una ecuación recursiva que indica qué relación hay entre el término enésimo a_n y uno o más de los términos precedentes.

The recursive rule $a_0 = 1, a_n = a_{n-1} + 4$ gives the arithmetic sequence 1, 5, 9, 13, ...

La regla recursiva $a_0 = 1, a_n = a_{n-1} + 4$ da la progresión aritmética 1, 5, 9, 13, ...

reference angle (p. 868) If θ is an angle in standard position, its reference angle is the acute angle θ' formed by the terminal side of θ and the x-axis.

ángulo de referencia (pág. 868) Si θ es un ángulo en posición normal, su ángulo de referencia es el ángulo agudo θ' formado por el lado terminal de θ y el eje de x.

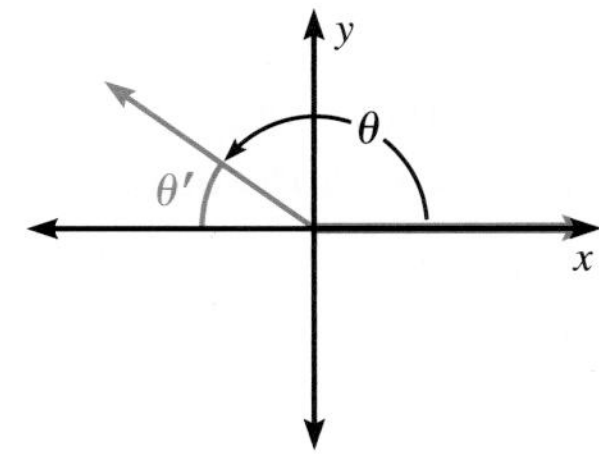

The acute angle θ' is the reference angle for angle θ.

El ángulo agudo θ' es el ángulo de referencia para el ángulo θ.

reflection (p. 124) A transformation that flips a graph or figure in a line.

reflexión (pág. 124) Transformación que vuelca una gráfica o una figura en una recta.

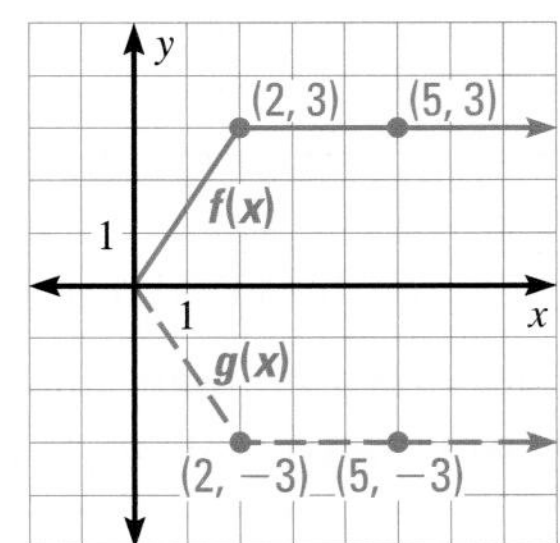

The graph of $g(x)$ is the reflection of the graph of $f(x)$ in the x-axis.

La gráfica de $g(x)$ es la reflexión de la gráfica de $f(x)$ en el eje de x.

relation (p. 72) A mapping, or pairing, of input values with output values.

relación (pág. 72) Correspondencia entre los valores de entrada y los valores de salida.

The ordered pairs (−2, −2), (−2, 2), (0, 1), and (3, 1) represent the relation with inputs (domain) of −2, 0, and 3 and outputs (range) of −2, 1, and 2.

Los pares ordenados (−2, −2), (−2, 2), (0, 1) y (3, 1) representan la relación con entradas (dominio) de −2, 0 y 3 y salidas (rango) de −2, 1 y 2.

ENGLISH-SPANISH GLOSSARY

repeated solution (p. 379) For the polynomial equation $f(x) = 0$, k is a repeated solution if and only if the factor $x - k$ has an exponent greater than 1 when $f(x)$ is factored completely.

solución repetida (pág. 379) Para la ecuación polinómica $f(x) = 0$, k es una solución repetida si y sólo si el factor $x - k$ tiene un exponente mayor que 1 cuando $f(x)$ está completamente factorizado.

−1 is a repeated solution of the equation $(x + 1)^2 (x - 2) = 0$.

−1 es una solución repetida de la ecuación $(x + 1)^2 (x - 2) = 0$.

root of an equation (p. 253) The solutions of a quadratic equation are its roots.

raíz de una ecuación (pág. 253) Las soluciones de una ecuación cuadrática son sus raíces.

The roots of the quadratic equation $x^2 - 5x - 36 = 0$ are 9 and −4.

Las raíces de la ecuación cuadrática $x^2 - 5x - 36 = 0$ son 9 y −4.

S

sample (p. 766) A subset of a population.

muestra (pág. 766) Subconjunto de una población.

See population.

Ver población.

scalar (p. 188) A real number by which you multiply a matrix.

escalar (pág. 188) Número real por el que se multiplica una matriz.

See scalar multiplication.

Ver multiplicación escalar.

scalar multiplication (p. 188) Multiplication of each element of a matrix by a real number, called a scalar.

multiplicación escalar (pág. 188) Multiplicación de cada elemento de una matriz por un número real llamado escalar.

$$-2\begin{bmatrix} 4 & -1 \\ 1 & 0 \\ 2 & 7 \end{bmatrix} = \begin{bmatrix} -8 & 2 \\ -2 & 0 \\ -4 & -14 \end{bmatrix}$$

scatter plot (p. 113) A graph of a set of data pairs (x, y) used to determine whether there is a relationship between the variables x and y.

diagrama de dispersión (pág. 113) Gráfica de un conjunto de pares de datos (x, y) que sirve para determinar si hay una relación entre las variables x e y.

scientific notation (p. 331) The representation of a number in the form $c \times 10^n$ where $1 \le c < 10$ and n is an integer.

notación científica (pág. 331) La representación de un número de la forma $c \times 10^n$, donde $1 \le c < 10$ y n es un número entero.

0.693 is written in scientific notation as 6.93×10^{-1}.

0.693 escrito en notación científica es 6.93×10^{-1}.

secant function (p. 852) If θ is an acute angle of a right triangle, the secant of θ is the length of the hypotenuse divided by the length of the side adjacent to θ.

See sine function.

función secante (pág. 852) Si θ es un ángulo agudo de un triángulo rectángulo, la secante de θ es la longitud de la hipotenusa dividida por la longitud del lado adyacente a θ.

Ver función seno.

---

sector (p. 861) A region of a circle that is bounded by two radii and an arc of the circle. The central angle θ of a sector is the angle formed by the two radii.

sector (pág. 861) Región de un círculo delimitada por dos radios y un arco del círculo. El ángulo central θ de un sector es el ángulo formado por dos radios.

sector
sector
r
arc length s
longitud de un arco s
central angle θ
ángulo central θ

---

sequence (p. 794) A function whose domain is a set of consecutive integers. The domain gives the relative position of each term of the sequence. The range gives the terms of the sequence.

For the domain $n = 1, 2, 3$, and 4, the sequence defined by $a_n = 2n$ has the terms 2, 4, 6, and 8.

progresión (pág. 794) Función cuyo dominio es un conjunto de números enteros consecutivos. El dominio da la posición relativa de cada término de la secuencia. El rango da los términos de la secuencia.

Para el dominio $n = 1, 2, 3$ y 4, la secuencia definida por $a_n = 2n$ tiene los términos 2, 4, 6 y 8.

---

series (p. 796) The expression formed by adding the terms of a sequence. A series can be finite or infinite.

Finite series: $2 + 4 + 6 + 8$
Infinite series: $2 + 4 + 6 + 8 + \cdots$

serie (pág. 796) La expresión formada al sumar los términos de una progresión. La serie puede ser finita o infinita.

Serie finita: $2 + 4 + 6 + 8$
Serie infinita: $2 + 4 + 6 + 8 + \cdots$

---

set (p. 715) A collection of distinct objects.

If A is the set of positive integers less than 5, then $A = \{1, 2, 3, 4\}$.

conjunto (pág. 715) Colección de objetos diferenciados.

Si A es el conjunto de números enteros positivos menores que 5, entonces $A = \{1, 2, 3, 4\}$.

---

sigma notation (p. 796) *See* summation notation.

See summation notation.

notación sigma (pág. 796) *Ver* notación de sumatoria.

Ver notación de sumatoria.

---

simplest form of a radical (p. 422) A radical with index n is in simplest form if the radicand has no perfect nth powers as factors and any denominator has been rationalized.

$\sqrt[3]{135}$ in simplest form is $3\sqrt[3]{5}$.
$\dfrac{\sqrt[5]{7}}{\sqrt[5]{8}}$ in simplest form is $\dfrac{\sqrt[5]{28}}{2}$.

forma más simple de un radical (pág. 422) Un radical con índice n está escrito en la forma más simple si el radicando no tiene como factor ninguna potencia enésima perfecta y el denominador ha sido racionalizado.

$\sqrt[3]{135}$ en la forma más simple es $3\sqrt[3]{5}$.
$\dfrac{\sqrt[5]{7}}{\sqrt[5]{8}}$ en la forma más simple es $\dfrac{\sqrt[5]{28}}{2}$.

simplified form of a rational expression (p. 573) A rational expression in which the numerator and denominator have no common factors other than ±1.

forma simplificada de una expresión racional (pág. 573) Expresión racional en la que el numerador y el denominador no tienen factores comunes además de ±1.

$$\frac{x^2 - 2x - 15}{x^2 - 9} = \frac{(x + 3)(x - 5)}{(x + 3)(x - 3)} = \frac{x - 5}{x - 3}$$

↑

Simplified form
Forma simplificada

sine function (p. 852) If θ is an acute angle of a right triangle, the sine of θ is the length of the side opposite θ divided by the length of the hypotenuse.

función seno (pág. 852) Si θ es un ángulo agudo de un triángulo rectángulo, el seno de θ es la longitud del lado opuesto a θ dividida por la longitud de la hipotenusa.

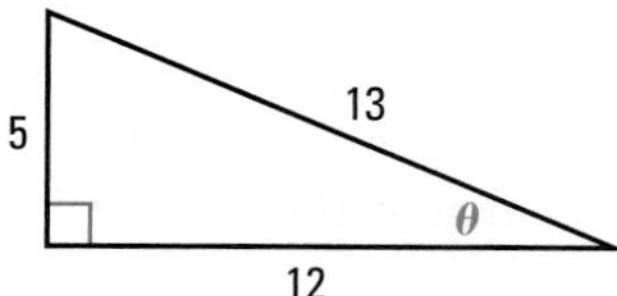

$$\sin\theta = \frac{\text{opp}}{\text{hyp}} = \frac{5}{13} \qquad \csc\theta = \frac{\text{hyp}}{\text{opp}} = \frac{13}{5}$$

$$\cos\theta = \frac{\text{adj}}{\text{hyp}} = \frac{12}{13} \qquad \sec\theta = \frac{\text{hyp}}{\text{adj}} = \frac{13}{12}$$

$$\tan\theta = \frac{\text{opp}}{\text{adj}} = \frac{5}{12} \qquad \cot\theta = \frac{\text{adj}}{\text{opp}} = \frac{12}{5}$$

$$\text{sen}\,\theta = \frac{\text{op}}{\text{hip}} = \frac{5}{13} \qquad \text{cosec}\,\theta = \frac{\text{hip}}{\text{op}} = \frac{13}{5}$$

$$\cos\theta = \frac{\text{ady}}{\text{hip}} = \frac{12}{13} \qquad \sec\theta = \frac{\text{hip}}{\text{ady}} = \frac{13}{12}$$

$$\tan\theta = \frac{\text{op}}{\text{ady}} = \frac{5}{12} \qquad \cot\theta = \frac{\text{ady}}{\text{op}} = \frac{12}{5}$$

sinusoids (p. 941) Graphs of sine and cosine functions.

sinusoides (pág. 941) Gráficas de funciones seno y coseno.

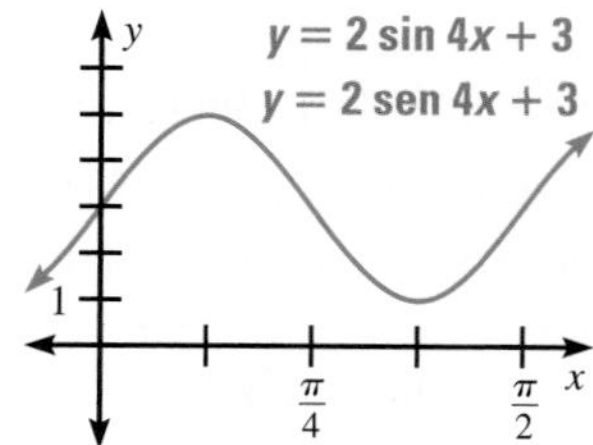

skewed distribution (p. 727) A probability distribution that is not symmetric. *See also* symmetric distribution.

distribución asimétrica (pág. 727) Distribución de probabilidades que no es simétrica. *Ver también* distribución simétrica.

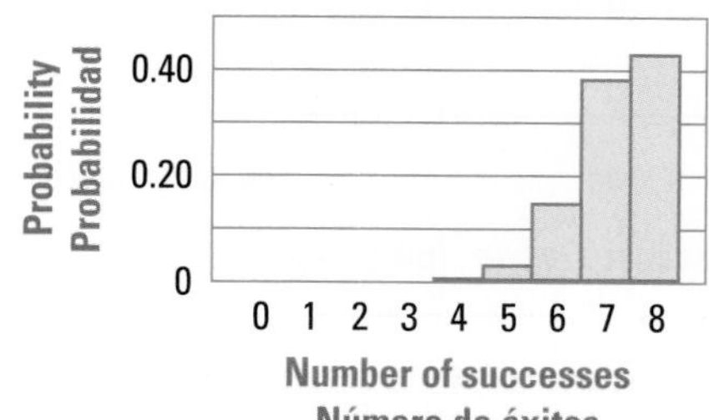

slope (p. 82) The ratio of vertical change (the rise) to horizontal change (the run) for a nonvertical line. For a nonvertical line passing through the points (x_1, y_1) and (x_2, y_2), the slope is $m = \frac{y_2 - y_1}{x_2 - x_1}$. **pendiente** (pág. 82) Para una recta no vertical, la razón entre el cambio vertical (distancia vertical) y el cambio horizontal (distancia horizontal). Para una recta no vertical que pasa por los puntos (x_1, y_1) y (x_2, y_2), la pendiente es $m = \frac{y_2 - y_1}{x_2 - x_1}$.	The slope of the line that passes through the points (−3, 0) and (3, 4) is: La pendiente de la recta que pasa por los puntos (−3, 0) y (3, 4) es: $m = \frac{y_2 - y_1}{x_2 - x_1} = \frac{4 - 0}{3 - (-3)} = \frac{4}{6} = \frac{2}{3}$
slope-intercept form (p. 90) A linear equation written in the form $y = mx + b$ where m is the slope and b is the y-intercept of the equation's graph. **forma pendiente-intercepto** (pág. 90) Ecuación lineal escrita en la forma $y = mx + b$, donde m es la pendiente y b es el intercepto en y de la gráfica de la ecuación.	The equation $y = -\frac{2}{3}x - 1$ is in slope-intercept form. La ecuación $y = -\frac{2}{3}x - 1$ está en la forma pendiente-intercepto.
solution of a linear inequality in two variables (p. 132) An ordered pair (x, y) that produces a true statement when the values of x and y are substituted into the inequality. **solución de una desigualdad lineal con dos variables** (pág. 132) Par ordenado (x, y) que produce un enunciado verdadero cuando x e y se sustituyen por sus valores en la desigualdad.	The ordered pair (1, 2) is a solution of $3x + 4y > 8$ because $3(1) + 4(2) = 11$, and $11 > 8$. El par ordenado (1, 2) es una solución de $3x + 4y > 8$ ya que $3(1) + 4(2) = 11$, y $11 > 8$.
solution of a system of linear equations in three variables (p. 178) An ordered triple (x, y, z) whose coordinates make each equation in the system true. **solución de un sistema de ecuaciones lineales en tres variables** (pág. 178) Terna ordenada (x, y, z) cuyas coordenadas hacen que cada ecuación del sistema sea verdadera.	$4x + 2y + 3z = 1$ $2x - 3y + 5z = -14$ $6x - y + 4z = -1$ (2, 1, −3) is the solution of the system above. (2, 1, −3) es la solución del sistema de arriba.
solution of a system of linear equations in two variables (p. 153) An ordered pair (x, y) that satisfies each equation of the system. **solución de un sistema de ecuaciones lineales en dos variables** (pág. 153) Par ordenado (x, y) que satisface cada ecuación del sistema.	$4x + y = 8$ $2x - 3y = 18$ (3, −4) is the solution of the system above. (3, −4) es la solución del sistema de arriba.
solution of a system of linear inequalities in two variables (p. 168) An ordered pair (x, y) that is a solution of each inequality in the system. **solución de un sistema de desigualdades lineales en dos variables** (pág. 168) Par ordenado (x, y) que es una solución de cada desigualdad del sistema.	$y > -2x - 5$ $y \leq x + 3$ (−1, 1) is a solution of the system above. (−1, 1) es una solución del sistema de arriba.

solution of an equation in one variable (p. 18) A number that produces a true statement when substituted for the variable in the equation.	The solution of the equation $\frac{4}{5}x + 8 = 20$ is 15.
solución de una ecuación con una variable (pág. 18) Número que produce un enunciado verdadero al sustituir la variable por él en la ecuación.	La solución de la ecuación $\frac{4}{5}x + 8 = 20$ es 15.
solution of an equation in two variables (p. 74) An ordered pair (x, y) that produces a true statement when the values of x and y are substituted in the equation.	$(-2, 3)$ is a solution of $y = -2x - 1$.
solución de una ecuación con dos variables (pág. 74) Par ordenado (x, y) que produce un enunciado verdadero al sustituir x e y por sus valores en la ecuación.	$(-2, 3)$ es una solución de $y = -2x - 1$.
solution of an inequality in one variable (p. 41) A number that produces a true statement when substituted for the variable in the inequality.	-1 is a solution of the inequality $5x + 2 > 7x - 4$.
solución de una desigualdad con una variable (pág. 41) Número que produce un enunciado verdadero al sustituir la variable por él en la desigualdad.	-1 es una solución de la desigualdad $5x + 2 > 7x - 4$.
solve for a variable (p. 26) Rewrite an equation as an equivalent equation in which the variable is on one side and does not appear on the other side.	When you solve the circumference formula $C = 2\pi r$ for r, the result is $r = \frac{C}{2\pi}$.
resolver para una variable (pág. 26) Escribir una ecuación como ecuación equivalente que tenga la variable en uno de sus lados pero no en el otro.	Al resolver para r la fórmula de circunferencia $C = 2\pi r$, el resultado es $r = \frac{C}{2\pi}$.
square root (p. 266) If $b^2 = a$, then b is a square root of a. The radical symbol $\sqrt{\ }$ represents a nonnegative square root.	The square roots of 9 are 3 and -3 because $3^2 = 9$ and $(-3)^2 = 9$. So, $\sqrt{9} = 3$ and $-\sqrt{9} = -3$.
raíz cuadrada (pág. 266) Si $b^2 = a$, entonces b es una raíz cuadrada de a. El signo radical $\sqrt{\ }$ representa una raíz cuadrada no negativa.	Las raíces cuadradas de 9 son 3 y -3 ya que $3^2 = 9$ y $(-3)^2 = 9$. Así pues, $\sqrt{9} = 3$ y $-\sqrt{9} = -3$.
standard deviation (p. 745) The typical difference (or deviation) between a data value and the mean. The standard deviation σ of a numerical data set $x_1, x_2, \ldots, x_n$ is given by the following formula: $\sigma = \sqrt{\frac{(x_1 - \bar{x})^2 + (x_2 - \bar{x})^2 + \cdots + (x_n - \bar{x})^2}{n}}$	14, 17, 18, 19, 20, 24, 24, 30, 32 Because the mean of the data set is 22, the standard deviation is:
desviación típica (pág. 745) La diferencia (o desviación) más común entre un valor de los datos y la media. La desviación típica σ de un conjunto de datos numéricos $x_1, x_2, \ldots, x_n$ viene dada por la siguiente fórmula: $\sigma = \sqrt{\frac{(x_1 - \bar{x})^2 + (x_2 - \bar{x})^2 + \cdots + (x_n - \bar{x})^2}{n}}$	Como la media del conjunto de datos es 22, la desviación típica es: $\sigma = \sqrt{\frac{(14 - 22)^2 + (17 - 22)^2 + \cdots + (32 - 22)^2}{9}} = \sqrt{\frac{290}{9}} \approx 5.7$

standard form of a complex number (p. 276) The form $a + bi$ where a and b are real numbers and i is the imaginary unit.	**The standard form of the complex number $i(1 + i)$ is $-1 + i$.**
forma general de un número complejo (pág. 276) La forma $a + bi$, donde a y b son números reales e i es la unidad imaginaria.	**La forma general del número complejo $i(1 + i)$ es $-1 + i$.**
standard form of a linear equation (p. 91) A linear equation written in the form $Ax + By = C$ where A and B are not both zero.	**The linear equation $y = -3x + 4$ can be written in standard form as $3x + y = 4$.**
forma general de una ecuación lineal (pág. 91) Ecuación lineal escrita en la forma $Ax + By = C$, donde A y B no son ambos cero.	**La ecuación lineal $y = -3x + 4$ escrita en la forma general es $3x + y = 4$.**
standard form of a polynomial function (p. 337) The form of a polynomial function that has terms written in descending order of exponents from left to right.	**The function $g(x) = 7x - \sqrt{3} + \pi x^2$ can be written in standard form as $g(x) = \pi x^2 + 7x - \sqrt{3}$.**
forma general de una función polinómica (pág. 337) La forma de una función polinómica en la que los términos se ordenan de tal modo que los exponentes disminuyen de izquierda a derecha.	**La función $g(x) = 7x - \sqrt{3} + \pi x^2$ escrita en la forma general es $g(x) = \pi x^2 + 7x - \sqrt{3}$.**
standard form of a quadratic equation in one variable (p. 253) The form $ax^2 + bx + c = 0$ where $a \neq 0$.	**The quadratic equation $x^2 - 5x = 36$ can be written in standard form as $x^2 - 5x - 36 = 0$.**
forma general de una ecuación cuadrática con una variable (pág. 253) La forma $ax^2 + bx + c = 0$, donde $a \neq 0$.	**La ecuación cuadrática $x^2 - 5x = 36$ escrita en la forma general es $x^2 - 5x - 36 = 0$.**
standard form of a quadratic function (p. 236) The form $y = ax^2 + bx + c$ where $a \neq 0$.	**The quadratic function $y = 2(x + 3)(x - 1)$ can be written in standard form as $y = 2x^2 + 4x - 6$.**
forma general de una función cuadrática (pág. 236) La forma $y = ax^2 + bx + c$, donde $a \neq 0$.	**La función cuadrática $y = 2(x + 3)(x - 1)$ escrita en la forma general es $y = 2x^2 + 4x - 6$.**
standard normal distribution (p. 758) The normal distribution with mean 0 and standard deviation 1. *See also* z-score. **distribución normal típica** (pág. 758) La distribución normal con media 0 y desviación típica 1. *Ver también* puntuación z.	$z = -3$, $z = -2$, $z = -1$, $z = 0$, $z = 1$, $z = 2$, $z = 3$

ENGLISH-SPANISH GLOSSARY

standard position of an angle (p. 859) In a coordinate plane, the position of an angle whose vertex is at the origin and whose initial side lies on the positive x-axis.

posición normal de un ángulo (pág. 859) En un plano de coordenadas, la posición de un ángulo cuyo vértice está en el origen y cuyo lado inicial se sitúa en el eje de x positivo.

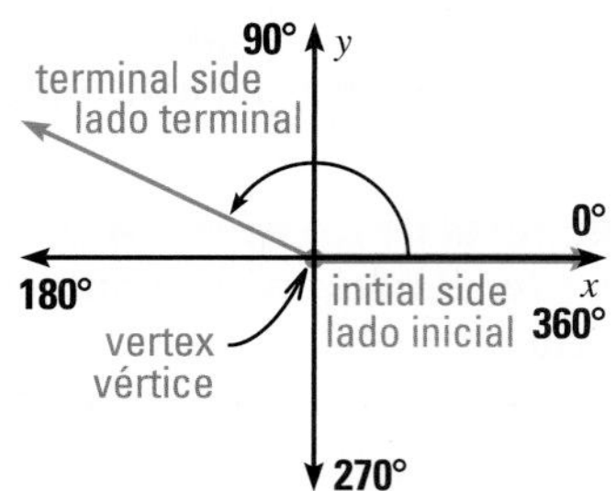

statistics (p. 744) Numerical values used to summarize and compare sets of data.

estadística (pág. 744) Valores numéricos utilizados para resumir y comparar conjuntos de datos.

See **mean, median, mode, range,** *and* **standard deviation.**

Ver **media, mediana, moda, rango** *y* **desviación típica.**

step function (p. 131) A piecewise function defined by a constant value over each part of its domain. Its graph resembles a series of stair steps.

función escalonada (pág. 131) Función definida a trozos y por un valor constante en cada parte de su dominio. Su gráfica parece un grupo de escalones.

$$f(x) = \begin{cases} 1, & \text{if } 0 \le x < 1 \\ 2, & \text{if } 1 \le x < 2 \\ 3, & \text{if } 2 \le x < 3 \end{cases} \qquad f(x) = \begin{cases} 1, & \text{si } 0 \le x < 1 \\ 2, & \text{si } 1 \le x < 2 \\ 3, & \text{si } 2 \le x < 3 \end{cases}$$

subset (p. 716) If every element of a set A is also an element of a set B, then A is a subset of B. This is written as $A \subseteq B$. For any set A, $\emptyset \subseteq A$ and $A \subseteq A$.

subconjunto (pág. 716) Si cada elemento de un conjunto A es también un elemento de un conjunto B, entonces A es un subconjunto de B. Esto se escribe $A \subseteq B$. Para cualquier conjunto A, $\emptyset \subseteq A$ y $A \subseteq A$.

If $A = \{1, 2, 4, 8\}$ and B is the set of all positive integers, then A is a subset of B, or $A \subseteq B$.

Si $A = \{1, 2, 4, 8\}$ y B es el conjunto de todos los números enteros positivos, entonces A es un subconjunto de B, o $A \subseteq B$.

substitution method (p. 160) A method of solving a system of equations by solving one of the equations for one of the variables and then substituting the resulting expression in the other equation(s).

método de sustitución (pág. 160) Método para resolver un sistema de ecuaciones mediante la resolución de una de las ecuaciones para una de las variables seguida de la sustitución de la expresión resultante en la(s) otra(s) ecuación (ecuaciones).

$$2x + 5y = -5$$
$$x + 3y = 3$$

Solve equation 2 for x: $x = -3y + 3$. Substitute the expression for x in equation 1 and solve for y: $y = 11$. Use the value of y to find the value of x: $x = -30$.

Resuelve la ecuación 2 para x: $x = -3y + 3$. Sustituye la expresión para x en la ecuación 1 y resuelve para y: $y = 11$. Usa el valor de y para hallar el valor de x: $x = -30$.

summation notation (p. 796) Notation for a series that uses the uppercase Greek letter sigma, Σ. Also called sigma notation.

notación de sumatoria (pág. 796) Notación de una serie que usa la letra griega mayúscula sigma, Σ. También se llama notación sigma.

$$\sum_{i=1}^{5} 7i = 7(1) + 7(2) + 7(3) + 7(4) + 7(5)$$
$$= 7 + 14 + 21 + 28 + 35$$

ENGLISH-SPANISH GLOSSARY

symmetric distribution (p. 727) A probability distribution, represented by a histogram, in which you can draw a vertical line that divides the histogram into two parts that are mirror images. **distribución simétrica** (pág. 727) Distribución de probabilidad representada por un histograma en la que se puede trazar una recta vertical que divida al histograma en dos partes; éstas son imágenes especulares entre sí.	Probability / Probabilidad: 0, 0.10, 0.20, 0.30; Number of successes / Número de éxitos: 0 1 2 3 4 5 6 7 8
synthetic division (p. 363) A method used to divide a polynomial by a divisor of the form $x - k$. **división sintética** (pág. 363) Método utilizado para dividir un polinomio por un divisor en la forma $x - k$.	$\begin{array}{r\|rrrr} -3 & 2 & 1 & -8 & 5 \\ & & -6 & 15 & -21 \\ \hline & 2 & -5 & 7 & -16 \end{array}$ $\frac{2x^3 + x^2 - 8x + 5}{x + 3} = 2x^2 - 5x + 7 - \frac{16}{x + 3}$
synthetic substitution (p. 338) A method used to evaluate a polynomial function. **sustitución sintética** (pág. 338) Método utilizado para evaluar una función polinómica.	$\begin{array}{r\|rrrrr} 3 & 2 & -5 & 0 & -4 & 8 \\ & & 6 & 3 & 9 & 15 \\ \hline & 2 & 1 & 3 & 5 & 23 \end{array}$ The synthetic substitution above indicates that for $f(x) = 2x^4 - 5x^3 - 4x + 8$, $f(3) = 23$. La sustitución sintética de arriba indica que para $f(x) = 2x^4 - 5x^3 - 4x + 8$, $f(3) = 23$.
system of linear inequalities in two variables (p. 168) A system consisting of two or more linear inequalities in two variables. *See also* linear inequality in two variables. **sistema de desigualdades lineales con dos variables** (pág. 168) Sistema que consiste de dos o más desigualdades lineales con dos variables. *Ver también* desigualdad lineal con dos variables.	$x + y \leq 8$ $4x - y > 6$
system of three linear equations in three variables (p. 178) A system consisting of three linear equations in three variables. *See also* linear equation in three variables. **sistema de tres ecuaciones lineales en tres variables** (pág. 178) Sistema formado por tres ecuaciones lineales con tres variables. *Ver también* ecuación lineal con tres variables.	$2x + y - z = 5$ $3x - 2y + z = 16$ $4x + 3y - 5z = 3$

system of two linear equations in two variables (p. 153) A system consisting of two equations that can be written in the form $Ax + By = C$ and $Dx + Ey = F$ where x and y are variables, A and B are not both zero, and D and E are not both zero. **sistema de dos ecuaciones lineales con dos variables** (pág. 153) Un sistema que consiste en dos ecuaciones que se pueden escribir de la forma $Ax + By = C$ y $Dx + Ey = F$, donde x e y son variables, A y B no son ambos cero, y D y E tampoco son ambos cero.	$4x + y = 8$ $2x - 3y = 18$

T

tangent function (p. 852) If θ is an acute angle of a right triangle, the tangent of θ is the length of the side opposite θ divided by the length of the side adjacent to θ. **función tangente** (pág. 852) Si θ es un ángulo agudo de un triángulo rectángulo, la tangente de θ es la longitud del lado opuesto a θ dividida por la longitud del lado adyacente a θ.	*See* sine function. *Ver* función seno.
terminal side of an angle (p. 859) In a coordinate plane, an angle can be formed by fixing one ray, called the initial side, and rotating the other ray, called the terminal side, about the vertex. **lado terminal de un ángulo** (pág. 859) En un plano de coordenadas, un ángulo puede formarse al fijar un rayo, llamado lado inicial, y al girar el otro rayo, llamado lado terminal, en torno al vértice.	*See* standard position of an angle. *Ver* posición normal de un ángulo.
terms of a sequence (p. 794) The values in the range of a sequence. **términos de una progresión** (pág. 794) Los valores del rango de una progresión.	The first 4 terms of the sequence 1, −3, 9, −27, 81, −243, . . . are 1, −3, 9, and −27. Los 4 primeros términos de la progresión 1, −3, 9, −27, 81, −243, . . . son 1, −3, 9 y −27.
terms of an expression (p. 12) The parts of an expression that are added together. **términos de una expresión** (pág. 12) Las partes de una expresión que se suman.	The terms of the algebraic expression $3x^2 + 5x + (-7)$ are $3x^2$, $5x$, and -7. Los términos de la expresión algebraica $3x^2 + 5x + (-7)$ son $3x^2$, $5x$ y -7.

theoretical probability (p. 698) When all outcomes are equally likely, the theoretical probability that an event A will occur is $P(A) = \frac{\text{Number of outcomes in event } A}{\text{Total number of outcomes}}$. **probabilidad teórica** (pág. 698) Cuando todos los casos son igualmente posibles, la probabilidad teórica de que ocurra un suceso A es $P(A) = \frac{\text{Número de casos del suceso } A}{\text{Número total de casos}}$.	The theoretical probability of rolling an even number using a standard six-sided die is $\frac{3}{6} = \frac{1}{2}$ because 3 outcomes correspond to rolling an even number out of 6 total outcomes. La probabilidad teórica de sacar un número par al lanzar un dado normal de seis caras es $\frac{3}{6} = \frac{1}{2}$ ya que 3 casos corresponden a un número par del total de 6 casos.
transformation (p. 123) A transformation changes a graph's size, shape, position, or orientation. **transformación** (pág. 123) Una transformación cambia el tamaño, la forma, la posición o la orientación de una gráfica.	Translations, vertical stretches and shrinks, reflections, and rotations are transformations. Las traslaciones, las expansiones y contracciones verticales, las reflexiones y las rotaciones son transformaciones.
translation (p. 123) A transformation that shifts a graph horizontally and/or vertically, but does not change its size, shape, or orientation. **traslación** (pág. 123) Transformación que desplaza una gráfica horizontal o verticalmente, o de ambas maneras, pero que no cambia su tamaño, forma u orientación.	 The graph of $y = \|x + 4\| - 2$ is the graph of $y = \|x\|$ translated down 2 units and left 4 units. La gráfica de $y = \|x + 4\| - 2$ es la gráfica de $y = \|x\|$ al trasladar ésta 2 unidades hacia abajo y 4 unidades hacia la izquierda.
transverse axis of a hyperbola (p. 642) The line segment joining the vertices of a hyperbola. **eje transverso de una hipérbola** (pág. 642) El segmento de recta que une los vértices de una hipérbola.	*See* hyperbola. *Ver* hipérbola.
trigonometric identity (p. 924) A trigonometric equation that is true for all domain values. **identidad trigonométrica** (pág. 924) Ecuación trigonométrica que es verdadera para todos los valores del dominio.	$\sin(-\theta) = -\sin\theta$ $\quad \sin^2\theta + \cos^2\theta = 1$ $\text{sen}(-\theta) = -\text{sen}\,\theta$ $\quad \text{sen}^2\theta + \cos^2\theta = 1$
trinomial (p. 252) The sum of three monomials. **trinomio** (pág. 252) La suma de tres monomios.	$4x^2 + 3x - 1$ is a trinomial. $4x^2 + 3x - 1$ es un trinomio.

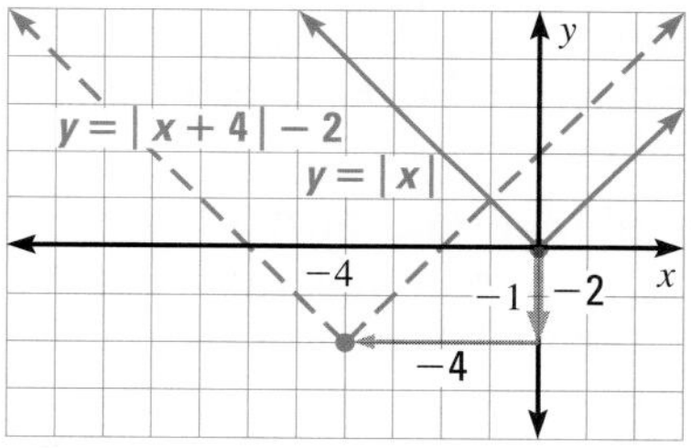

ENGLISH-SPANISH GLOSSARY

unbiased sample (p. 767) A sample that is representative of the population you want information about.

You want to poll members of the senior class about where to hold the prom. If every senior has an equal chance of being polled, then the sample is unbiased.

muestra no sesgada (pág. 767) Muestra que es representativa de la población acerca de la cual deseas informarte.

Quieres encuestar a algunos estudiantes de último curso sobre el lugar donde organizar el baile de fin de año. Si cada estudiante de último curso tiene iguales posibilidades de ser encuestado, entonces es una muestra no sesgada.

union of sets (p. 715) The union of two sets A and B, written $A \cup B$, is the set of all elements in *either* A or B.

If $A = \{1, 2, 4, 8\}$ and $B = \{2, 4, 6, 8, 10\}$, then $A \cup B = \{1, 2, 4, 6, 8, 10\}$.

unión de conjuntos (pág. 715) La unión de dos conjuntos A y B, escrita $A \cup B$, es el conjunto de todos los elementos que están en A *o* B.

Si $A = \{1, 2, 4, 8\}$ y $B = \{2, 4, 6, 8, 10\}$, entonces $A \cup B = \{1, 2, 4, 6, 8, 10\}$.

unit circle (p. 867) The circle $x^2 + y^2 = 1$, which has center (0, 0) and radius 1. For an angle θ in standard position, the terminal side of θ intersects the unit circle at the point ($\cos \theta$, $\sin \theta$).

círculo unidad (pág. 867) El círculo $x^2 + y^2 = 1$, que tiene centro (0, 0) y radio 1. Para un ángulo θ en posición normal, el lado terminal de θ corta al círculo unidad en el punto ($\cos \theta$, sen θ).

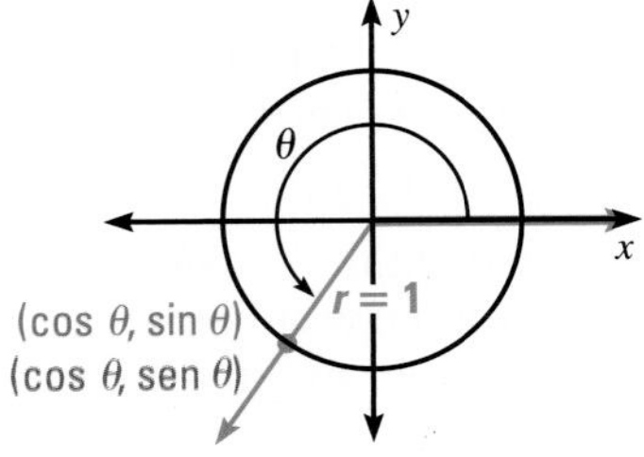

universal set (p. 715) The set of all elements under consideration; denoted U.

See complement of a set.

conjunto universal (pág. 715) El conjunto de todos los elementos tenidos en cuenta; se indica U.

Ver complemento de un conjunto.

variable (p. 11) A letter that is used to represent one or more numbers.

In the expressions $6x$, $3x^2 + 1$, and $12 - 5x$, the letter x is the variable.

variable (pág. 11) Letra utilizada para representar uno o más números.

En las expresiones $6x$, $3x^2 + 1$ y $12 - 5x$, la letra x es la variable.

variable term (p. 12) A term that has a variable part.

The variable terms of the algebraic expression $3x^2 + 5x + (-7)$ are $3x^2$ and $5x$.

término algebraico (pág. 12) Término que tiene variable.

Los términos algebraicos de la expresión algebraica $3x^2 + 5x + (-7)$ son $3x^2$ y $5x$.

verbal model (p. 34) A word equation that represents a real-life problem.

Distance (miles)	=	Rate (miles/hour)	•	Time (hours)

modelo verbal (pág. 34) Ecuación expresada mediante palabras que representa un problema de la vida real.

Distancia (millas)	=	Velocidad (millas/hora)	•	Tiempo (horas)

ENGLISH-SPANISH GLOSSARY

vertex form of a quadratic function (p. 245) The form $y = a(x - h)^2 + k$, where the vertex of the graph is (h, k) and the axis of symmetry is $x = h$.

The quadratic function $y = -\frac{1}{4}(x + 2)^2 + 5$ is in vertex form.

forma de vértice de una función cuadrática (pág. 245) La forma $y = a(x - h)^2 + k$, donde el vértice de la gráfica es (h, k) y el eje de simetría es $x = h$.

La función cuadrática $y = -\frac{1}{4}(x + 2)^2 + 5$ está en la forma de vértice.

---

vertex of a parabola (pp. 236, 620) The point on a parabola that lies on the axis of symmetry.

See parabola.

vértice de una parábola (págs. 236, 620) El punto de una parábola que se encuentra en el eje de simetría.

Ver parábola.

---

vertex of an absolute value graph (p. 123) The highest or lowest point on the graph of an absolute value function.

vértice de una gráfica de valor absoluto (pág. 123) El punto más alto o más bajo de la gráfica de una función de valor absoluto.

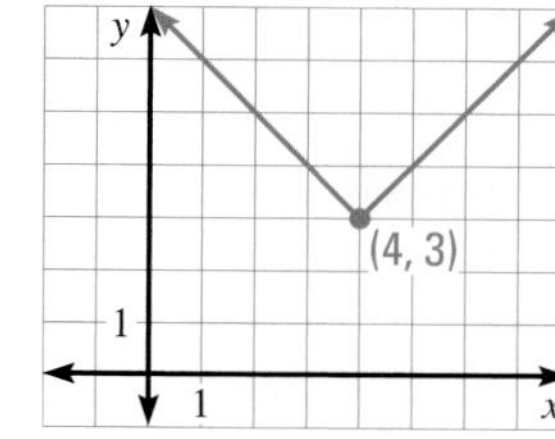

The vertex of the graph of $y = |x - 4| + 3$ is the point $(4, 3)$.

El vértice de la gráfica de $y = |x - 4| + 3$ es el punto $(4, 3)$.

---

vertices of a hyperbola (p. 642) The points of intersection of a hyperbola and the line through the foci of the hyperbola.

See hyperbola.

vértices de una hipérbola (pág. 642) Los puntos de intersección de una hipérbola y la recta que pasa por los focos de la hipérbola.

Ver hipérbola.

---

vertices of an ellipse (p. 634) The points of intersection of an ellipse and the line through the foci of the ellipse.

See ellipse.

vértices de una elipse (pág. 634) Los puntos de intersección de una elipse y la recta que pasa por los focos de la elipse.

Ver elipse.

X

x-intercept (p. 91) The x-coordinate of a point where a graph intersects the x-axis.

intercepto en x (pág. 91) La coordenada x de un punto donde una gráfica corta al eje de x.

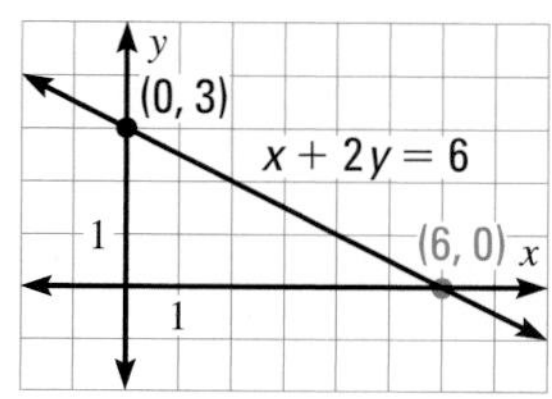

The x-intercept is 6.

El intercepto en x es 6.

Y

***y*-intercept** (p. 89) The *y*-coordinate of a point where a graph intersects the *y*-axis.

intercepto en *y* (pág. 89) La coordenada *y* de un punto donde una gráfica corta al eje de *y*.

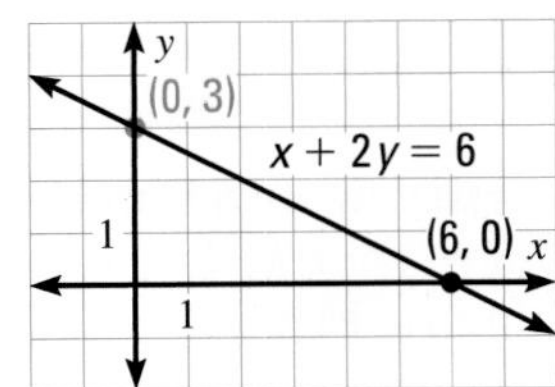

The *y*-intercept is 3.

El intercepto en *y* es 3.

Z

zero of a function (p. 254) A number k is a zero of a function f if $f(k) = 0$.

cero de una función (pág. 254) Un número k es un cero de una función f si $f(k) = 0$.

The zeros of the function $f(x) = 2(x + 3)(x - 1)$ are -3 and 1.

Los ceros de la función $f(x) = 2(x + 3)(x - 1)$ son -3 y 1.

***z*-score** (p. 758) The number z of standard deviations that a data value lies above or below the mean of the data set: $z = \frac{x - \bar{x}}{\sigma}$.

puntuación *z* (pág. 758) El número z de desviaciones típicas que un valor se encuentra por encima o por debajo de la media del conjunto de datos: $z = \frac{x - \bar{x}}{\sigma}$.

A normal distribution has a mean of 76 and a standard deviation of 9. The *z*-score for $x = 64$ is $z = \frac{x - \bar{x}}{\sigma} = \frac{64 - 76}{9} \approx -1.3$.

Una distribución normal tiene una media de 76 y una desviación típica de 9. La puntuación z para $x = 64$ es $z = \frac{x - \bar{x}}{\sigma} = \frac{64 - 76}{9} \approx -1.3$.

Index

A

INDEX

INDEX

INDEX

INDEX

E

INDEX

F

G

INDEX

INDEX

INDEX

M

INDEX

INDEX

N

O

P

Q

INDEX

R

S

INDEX

T

INDEX

V

INDEX

Z

INDEX

Credits

Photographs

Cover Michael Wong/Corbis; **Authors:** *top* Meridian Creative Group, *top center* Robert C. Jenks, Jenks Studio, *bottom center* McDougal Littell, *bottom* Jerry Head Jr.; **Table of Contents: Chapter 1** PhotoDisc/Getty Images; **Chapter 2** Alex Rosenfeld/Science Photo Library; **Chapter 3** Jonathan Nourok/PhotoEdit; **Chapter 4** Mandy Collins/Alamy; **Chapter 5** Dave Bjorn/Photo Resource Hawaii; **Chapter 6** Joe McBride/Getty Images; **Chapter 7** Ron Sanford/Corbis; **Chapter 8** Ralph Wetmore/Getty Images; **Chapter 9** NASA; **Chapter 10** Jerry Wachter/Sportschrome, Inc.; **Chapter 11** AP/Wide World Photos; **Chapter 12** Ted Kinsman/Photo Researchers, Inc.; **Chapter 13** David Madison/Getty Images; **Chapter 14** Thorney Lieberman/Getty Images; **Interior: 1** Jennifer Graylock/AP/Wide World Photos; **2** Sylvain Grandadam/Getty Images; **6** Jason Hawkes/Getty Images; **8** *all* Courtesy NASA/JPL-Caltech; **9** Joel Sartore/Getty Images; **10** Rubberball Productions/Getty Images; **13** Brand X Pictures/Getty Images; **18** PhotoDisc/Getty Images; **20** Creatas/PunchStock; **23** Walter Hodges/Getty Images; **24** *both* Digital Stock/Corbis; **26** Peter Adams/Index Stock Imagery; **29** Rubberball Productions; **33** Gary I. Rothstein/AP/Wide World Photos; **34** PhotoDisc/Getty Images; **35** Jason Reed/Reuters; **38** Eugene Hoshiko/AP/Wide World Photos; **41** Royalty-Free/Corbis; **42** Barbara Leslie/Getty Images; **44** David A. Northcott/Corbis; **50** *all* Jay Penni Photography/McDougal Littell; **51** Digital Vision Ltd./SuperStock; **54** Jim Cummins/Getty Images; **59** Dean Hoffmeyer/AP/Wide World Photos; **70–71** George D. Lepp/Corbis; **72** Tom Stock/Getty Images; **74** Paul Battaglia/AP/Wide World Photos; **76** Stephen Frink/Corbis; **79** D.C. Lowe/SuperStock; **82** Ernest Manewal/Index Stock Imagery; **85** *both* Susan Ragan/AP/Wide World Photos; **89** Angela Wyant/Getty Images; **91** Paul Nicklen/National Geographic/Getty Images; **98** Nancy Richmond/The Image Works; **100** Steve Skjold/PhotoEdit; **103** David Young-Wolff/PhotoEdit; **107** Dave G. Houser/Corbis; **108** Amos Nachoum/Corbis; **112** *all* McDougal Littell; **113** Douglas C. Pizac/AP/Wide World Photos; **115** Sandy Huffaker/Getty Images; **123** *top right* John Coletti/Index Stock Imagery; **132** Digital Vision/Getty Images; **134** *all* Stockbyte/Getty Images; **150–151** Myrleen Ferguson Cate/PhotoEdit; **153** Duomo/Corbis; **155** David Frazier/The Image Works; **160** Rubberball/PictureQuest; **166** Petros Giannakouris/AP/Wide World Photos; **168** Duncan Smith/Getty Images; **170** Viviane Moos/Corbis; **173** Jim Cummins/Getty Images; **174** Brand X/SuperStock; **176** Kelly-Mooney Photography/Corbis; **178** Chris Donahue/AP/Wide World Photos; **185** Manchan/Getty Images; **186** Comstock Images/Alamy; **187** Stephen J. Carrera/AP/Wide World Photos; **192** Brand X Pictures/Alamy; **195** Mike Powell/Getty Images; **203** Tim Wakefield/SuperStock; **210** Lee Strickland/Getty Images; **215** Walter Meayers Edwards/Getty Images; **216** Gianni Cigolini/Getty Images; **220** Tom Bean/Corbis; **234–235** Getty Images; **236** C. B. Knight/Getty Images; **239** Rick Friedman/Corbis; **245** Medford Taylor/Getty Images; **251** David Hall/Nature Picture Library; **252** Kayte M. Deioma/PhotoEdit; **257** Image Source Limited/Index Stock Imagery; **259** Greg Huglin/SuperStock; **261** John Warden/SuperStock; **262** PhotoDisc/Getty Images; **264** *bottom right* Seth Thompson/Getty Images; **266** Hubble Heritage Team/NASA/AP/Wide World Photos; **269** Mike Mergen/AP/Wide World Photos; **270** Steve Allen/Brand X Pictures/PictureQuest; **271** Duomo/Corbis; **274** Cheryl Hatch/AP/Wide World Photos; **275** Dr. Fred Espenak/SPL/Photo Researchers, Inc.; **281** Imagebroker/Alamy; **282** Alfred Pasieka/SPL/Photo Researchers, Inc.; **283** *all* McDougal Littell; **284** Jim Cummins/Getty Images; **287** David Madison/Getty Images; **289** Ron Watts/Corbis; **291** Tom Stewart/Corbis; **292** Mike Yamashita/Corbis; **295** *left* David Madison/Getty Images; **295** *center* Roy Morsch/Corbis; **295** *right* Amwell/Getty Images; **299** Ben Mangor/SuperStock; **300** PhotoDisc/Getty Images; **303** Marcio Jose Sanchez/AP/Wide World Photos; **306** Stephen Frisch/Stock Boston; **309** Photolibrary.com/Index Stock Imagery; **311** Kevin Fleming/Corbis; **314** Michael Wong/Corbis; **316** Stockbyte; **328–329** Reuters/Corbis; **330** NASA/Corbis; **331** *right* Reuters/Corbis; **331** *left* Dex Image/Getty Images; **332** Comstock Images; **337** David Young-Wolff/PhotoEdit; **343** *bottom* ThinkStock LLC/Index Stock Imagery; **344** M. Philip Kahl/Bruce Coleman, Inc.; **346** Tim Larsen/AP/Wide World Photos; **348** David Frazier/Getty Images; **353** Richard T. Nowitz/Corbis; **362** Orlin Wagner/AP/Wide World Photos; **365** Royalty-Free/Corbis; **367** Joe Cavarotta/AP/Wide World Photos; **368** Neil Rabinowitz/Corbis; **370** *top right* Volker Steger/Siemens/SPL/Photo Researchers, Inc.; **376** age fotostock/SuperStock; **379** Peter Correz/Getty Images; **383** PhotoDisc/Getty Images; **385** Peter Yates/SPL/Photo Researchers, Inc.; **387** *top right* Turner & de Vries/Getty Images; **393** Terry Renna/AP/Wide World Photos; **398** Tom Stewart/Corbis; **400** Joe McDonald/Corbis; **412–413** David Bergman/Corbis; **414** Javier Soriano/AFP/Getty Images; **416** Azure Computer & Photo Services/Animals Animals; **419** McDougal Littell/Houghton Mifflin Co.; **420** Cameron Heryet/Getty Images; **426** Lester Lefkowitz/Corbis; **428** Darrell Gulin/Corbis; **431** StreetStock Images/Brand X Pictures/PictureArts; **434** Courtesy of Professor Tim Pennings, Hope College; **436** Royalty-Free/Corbis; **437** *both* RMIP/Richard Haynes/McDougal Littell; **438** Paul A. Souders/Corbis; **441** Gail Burton/AP/Wide World Photos; **444** Rod Taylor/AP/Wide World Photos; **446** Duomo/Corbis; **447** Navaswan/Getty Images; **451** Brian Erler/Getty Images; **452–453** Cathrine Wessel/Corbis; **453** Philippe Giraud/Corbis Sygma; **457** Casey Riffe/Marshfield News-Herald/AP/Wide World Photos; **458** OSF/Colbeck, M./Animals Animals; **476** *background* B.A.E. Inc./Alamy; **478** Greer & Associates, Inc./SuperStock; **484** Bob Daemmrich/Corbis Sygma; **485** Lynda Richardson/Corbis; **486** age fotostock/SuperStock; **488** PhotoDisc/Getty Images; **491** Richard A. Cooke/Corbis; **492** Cousteau Society/Getty Images; **498** Tim Hursley/SuperStock; **499** Chuck Carlton/Index Stock Imagery; **506** Jim McNee/Index Stock Imagery; **507** age fotostock/SuperStock; **509** Royalty-Free/Corbis; **511** *center left* image100/Alamy; **511** *center* Pat LaCroix/Getty Images; **511** *center right* Tony Arruza/Corbis; **512** *center right* Rubberball Productions; **512** *center left* Cathy Melloan/PhotoEdit; **512** *bottom* Rubberball Productions; **515** Roger Ressmeyer/Corbis; **516** Jeff Sherman/Getty Images; **522** *both* AM Corporation/Alamy; **528** *both* Jay Penni Photography/McDougal Littell; **529** Mark Chappell/Animals Animals; **530** Nick Dolding/Getty Images; **532** Gerard Lacz/Animals Animals; **534** Bryn Colton/Assignments Photographers/Corbis; **536** Bettmann/Corbis; **548–549** Jeff Hunter/Getty Images; **550** *both* RMIP/Richard Haynes/McDougal Littell; **551** Lawrence Manning/Corbis; **552** age fotostock/SuperStock; **553** Rick Bowmer/AP/Wide World Photos; **558** Ken Reid/Getty Images; **560** *both* Courtesy of Z Corporation; **565** Bobby Model/National Geographic/Getty Images; **567** Donald C. Johnson/Corbis; **569** The Photolibrary Wales/Alamy; **570** Scaled Composites/SPL/Photo Researchers, Inc.; **572** Michael Newman/PhotoEdit; **573** Mary Ann Chastain/AP/Wide World Photos; **579** Tony McConnell/SPL/Photo Researchers, Inc.; **582** Luca DiCecco/Alamy; **589** Denis Boissavy/Getty Images; **592** don jon red/Alamy; **594** Fédération Internationale de Volleyball/AP/Wide World Photos; **601** PhotoDisc/Getty Images; **612–613** Phototake/Getty Images; **614** Nick Vedros & Assoc./Getty Images; **618** Reuters/Corbis; **620** Stephen Frink/Getty

Images; **624** Hank Morgan/Time Life Pictures/Getty Images; **625** Roger Ressmeyer/Corbis; **626** Royalty-Free/Corbis; **634** Ralph Wetmore/Getty Images; **638** *bottom left* NASA/ARC; **638** *bottom right* Detlev Van Ravenswaay/SPL/Photo Researchers, Inc.; **641** Tom Uhlman/Visuals Unlimited; **642** Paul A. Souders/ Corbis; **648** Mike Cartwright/AP/Wide World Photos; **649** RMIP/ Richard Haynes/McDougal Littell; **650** Courtesy of Superdairyboy; **656** Erik S. Lesser/AP/Wide World Photos; **658** Yellow Dog Productions/Getty Images; **676** Fermilab Photo; **680–681** Alexander Walter/Getty Images; **682** Douglas C. Pizac/ AP/Wide World Photos; **684** Oliver Morin/AFP/Getty Images; **690** Robbie Jack/Corbis; **696** Marc Lester/AP/Wide World Photos; **698** PhotoDisc/Getty Images; **699** Ellen Senisi/The Image Works; **705** *bottom left* Big Cheese Photo/FotoSearch; **707** Jeff Greenberg/The Image Works; **717** Dennis MacDonald/PhotoEdit; **719** NOAA/AP/Wide World Photos; **724** John Russell/AP/Wide World Photos; **742–743** Mark E. Gibson/Getty Images; **744** Omar Torres/AFP/Getty Images; **746** Banana Stock/Alamy; **748** Alan Diaz/AP/Wide World Photos; **749** Andy Lyons/Getty Images; **751** NASA-HQ-GRIN; **754** *bottom* Ric Francis/AP/Wide World Photos; **754** *top* Phil Cantor/Index Stock Imagery; **756** *top* age fotostock/SuperStock; **756** *bottom* Don Heupel/AP/Wide World Photos; **756** *bottom center* ThinkStock/SuperStock; **757** PhotoDisc/Getty Images; **759** Kennan Ward/Corbis; **762** Barbara Novovitch/Reuters; **765** Royalty-Free/Corbis; **766** David Young-Wolff/PhotoEdit; **772** Spencer Grant/PhotoEdit; **774** Jay Penni Photography/McDougal Littell; **775** Ben Margot/AP/Wide World Photos; **780** Jay Penni Photography/McDougal Littell; **782** Dynamic Graphics/PictureQuest; **792–793** Steve Gschmeissner/ SPL/Photo Researchers, Inc.; **794** Roger Wood/Corbis; **799** Frank Chmura/PictureQuest; **802** Richard Cummins/Corbis; **805** Stockbyte/PictureQuest; **808** © 2007 Sol LeWitt/Artist Rights Society (ARS), New York. Photo Credit: Mary Ann Sullivan, Bluffton University; **810** PhotoStockFile/Alamy; **813** GDT/Getty Images; **815** Agence Vandystadt/Photo Researchers, Inc.; **819** *all* Jay Penni Photography/McDougal Littell; **820** Courtesy of Gayla Chandler; **827** Popperfoto/Alamy; **838** Gary S. Settles/Photo Researchers, Inc.; **850–851** João Paulo/Getty Images; **852** Hugh Sitton/Getty Images; **859** M. Spencer Green/AP/Wide World Photos; **864** *top* Royalty-Free/Corbis; **864** *center* Courtesy NASA, Life Sciences Division; **865** *both* Royalty-Free/Corbis; **866** age fotostock/SuperStock; **869** Courtesy NASA/JPL-Caltech; **873** *bottom right* Brand X Pictures/Getty Images; **873** *right* Richard Cummins/SuperStock; **873** *bottom right* Yoshio Tomii/ SuperStock; **875** Greg Ebersole/AP/Wide World Photos; **879** Paolo Curto/The Image Bank; **882** Richard Berenholtz/Corbis; **885** Steve Bein/Corbis; **889** David Madison/Getty Images; **906–907** Royalty-Free/Corbis; **908** Richard Olseius/National Geographic/Getty Images; **910** Annabella Bluesky/SPL/Photo Researchers, Inc.; **913** Peter Arnold, Inc./Alamy; **915** *both* Craig T. Lorenz/Photo Researchers, Inc.; **921** Image Source/PunchStock; **924** Lowell Observatory/NOAO/AURA/NSF; **931** Scott Camazine/Photo Researchers, Inc.; **932** *both* Christopher Mackay/Tantramar Interactive; **940** PhotoDisc/Getty Images; **941** Lee Cohen/Corbis; **945** Steve Chenn/Corbis; **948** RMIP/ Richard Haynes/McDougal Littell; **949** Howard Kingsnorth/Getty Images; **951** *left* Larry Dunmire/SuperStock; **951** *right* Ken Graham/Getty Images; **955** Pascal Rondeau/Getty Images; **963** Bill Ross/Corbis.

Illustrations and Maps

Argosy **1, 51, 70, 151, 235, 329, 413, 477, 549, 557** *top*, **613, 622** *top*, **646, 654, 662, 667** *top left*, **681, 743, 793, 818** *bottom left*; **851, 907, 921, 942, 954, 957**; Kenneth Batelman **504, 636, 752, 766 , 871, 879, 930, 946**; Steve Cowden **15, 32, 39, 95, 241, 243** *top center*, **247, 268, 298** *center*, **434, 439, 457, 464, 535**; Stephen Durke **290** *bottom*, **552, 570, 622** *center*, **660, 689** *top*, **800, 808** *top*, **832, 858, 872** *center right*, **896, 918, 929** *center*, **929** *top right*, **940**; John Francis **580, 761**; Patrick Gnan/Deborah Wolfe, Ltd. **5, 129, 254, 343** *top*, **351, 356, 360, 377, 392, 585, 641, 644, 657, 676, 818** *top right*; **822, 838, 880, 890, 902, 905, 927, 953, 972**; Chris Lyons **139, 158, 647** *center*; Steve McEntee **480, 563, 870, 873** *bottom left*, **877, 887, 893** *bottom*, **893** *center*, **904, 914, 916**; Paul Mirocha **497, 574**; Laurie O'Keefe **88, 494, 729**; Steve Stankiewicz **258, 505**; Doug Stevens **125**; Dan Stuckenschneider **16, 46, 87, 108, 119, 137, 185, 189, 250, 257, 265** *top right*, **369, 373, 426, 450, 519, 524, 556, 557** *center*, **688, 795, 824, 936**; Matt Zang/American Artists **500**; Carol Zuber-Mallison **111, 204, 208, 209, 358, 521, 587, 616, 618, 619, 663, 704, 855, 885, 961** *top right*, **961** *bottom*. All other illustrations © McDougal Littell/Houghton Mifflin Company.

Worked-Out Solutions

This section of the book provides step-by-step solutions to exercises with circled exercise numbers. These solutions provide models that can help guide your work with the homework exercises.

The separate **Selected Answers** section follows this section. It provides numerous answers that you can use to check your own answers.

Chapter 1

Lesson 1.1 (pp. 6–9)

21. $7a + (4 + 5a)$

$= 7a + (5a + 4)$ Commutative property of addition

$= (7a + 5a) + 4$ Associative property of addition

$= (7 + 5)a + 4$ Distributive property

$= 12a + 4$ Simplify

31. $350 \text{ ~~feet~~} \cdot \frac{1 \text{ yard}}{3 \text{ ~~feet~~}} \approx 116.7$ yards

59. a. Pluto, Neptune, Uranus, Saturn, Jupiter, Mars, Earth, Mercury, Venus

b. Mercury, Venus, Earth, Mars, Jupiter, Saturn, Uranus, Neptune, Pluto

c. The greater the distance from the sun, the colder the surface temperature.

d. Venus

Lesson 1.2 (pp. 13–16)

21. When $m = 6$:

$8m + (2m - 9)^3 = 8(6) + (2(6) - 9)^3$

$= 8(6) + (3)^3$

$= 48 + 27 = 75$

29. $7(m - 3) + 4(m + 5) = 7m - 21 + 4m + 20$

$= (7m + 4m) + (-21 + 20) = 11m - 1$

59. $270 - 4.5(x)$. The expression makes sense for all positive integer values of x less than or equal to 60. When $x > 60$, the balance is negative.

Lesson 1.3 (pp. 21–24)

23. $5b - 4 = 2b + 8$

$3b - 4 = 8$

$3b = 12$

$b = 4$

Check:

$5b - 4 = 2b + 8$

$5(4) - 4 \stackrel{?}{=} 2(4) + 8$

$20 - 4 \stackrel{?}{=} 8 + 8$

$16 = 16$ ✓

43. $\frac{1}{2}t + \frac{1}{3}t = 10$

$6\left(\frac{1}{2}t + \frac{1}{3}\right)t = 6(10)$

$3t + 2t = 60$

$5t = 60$

$t = 12$

Check:

$\frac{1}{2}t + \frac{1}{3}t = 10$

$\frac{1}{2}(12) + \frac{1}{3}(12) \stackrel{?}{=} 10$

$6 + 4 \stackrel{?}{=} 10$

$10 = 10$ ✓

71. $7.75(25) + 6.25x = 250$

$193.75 + 6.25x = 250$

$x = 9$

You must work 9 hours/week at the second job.

Lesson 1.4 (pp. 30–32)

3. $A = \ell w \rightarrow \frac{A}{w} = \ell$

When $w = 50$ and $A = 250$: $\ell = \frac{A}{w} = \frac{250}{50} = 5$

The length of the rectangle is 5 millimeters.

9. $6x + 5y = 31 \rightarrow 5y = 31 - 6x \rightarrow y = \frac{31}{5} - \frac{6x}{5}$

When $x = -4$: $y = \frac{31}{5} - \frac{6(-4)}{5} = \frac{55}{5} = 11$

35. $F = \frac{9}{5}C + 32 \rightarrow F - 32 = \frac{9}{5}C \rightarrow \frac{5}{9}(F - 32) = C$

When $F = 50$: $\frac{5}{9}(50 - 32) = C$

$$\frac{5}{9}(18) = C$$

$$10 = C$$

The temperature of 10°C corresponds to 50°F.

Lesson 1.5 (pp. 37–40)

3. $d = rt \rightarrow 20 = 40t \rightarrow \frac{1}{2} = t; t = \frac{1}{2}$ hour

11. 11 15 19 23 An equation is $y = 11 + 4x$.

+4 +4 +4

27. 15 16.5 18 19.5 21

+1.5 +1.5 +1.5 +1.5

An equation is $y = 15 + 1.5x$. It is not reasonable to assume the pattern in the table continues indefinitely. If it did, the plant would become indefinitely tall.

Lesson 1.6 (pp. 44–47)

13. $x < -2$ or $x > 4$

25. $15 - 3x > 3$

$x < 4$

0 1 2 3 4 5 6

55. a. Lowland: $0 \le e < 500$

b. Alpine: $2000 \le e < 2429$

Subalpine: $1400 \le e < 2000$

Alpine and subalpine: $1400 \le e < 2429$

c. Not in montane zone: $e < 500$ or $e \ge 1400$

Lesson 1.7 (pp. 55–58)

21. $|2d - 5| = 13$

$2d - 5 = -13$ or $2d - 5 = 13$

$2d = -8$ or $2d = 18$

$d = -4$ or $d = 9$

47. $|d + 4| \ge 3$

−9 −7 −5 −3 −1 1

$d + 4 \le -3$ or $d + 4 \ge 3$

$d \le -7$ or $d \ge -1$

77. Accept: $|b - 21| \le 1$; Reject: $|b - 21| > 1$

Chapter 2

Lesson 2.1 (pp. 76–79)

7. (5, 20), (10, 20), (15, 30), (20, 30)

Domain: 5, 10, 15, and 20; Range: 20 and 30

Graph

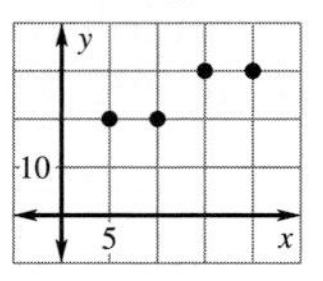

Mapping Diagram

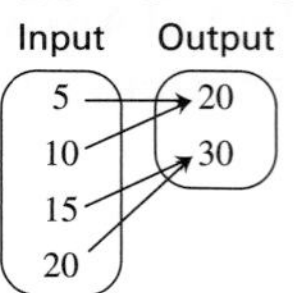

17. The relation is not a function because the input −2 is mapped to both 0 and 5.

45. $V(r) = \frac{4}{3}\pi r^3$

$V(6) = \frac{4}{3}\pi(6)^3 = 288\pi \approx 905 \text{ units}^3$

$V(6)$ represents the volume of a sphere with a radius of 6 units.

Lesson 2.2 (pp. 86–88)

9. $m = \frac{3 - (-4)}{-1 - (-5)} = \frac{7}{4} > 0$; the line rises.

19. Line 1: through (1, 5) and (3, −2)

Line 2: through (−3, 2) and (4, 0)

$m_1 = \frac{-2 - 5}{3 - 1} = -\frac{7}{2}$

$m_2 = \frac{0 - 2}{4 - (-3)} = -\frac{2}{7}$

Because $m_1 \cdot m_2 = -\frac{7}{2} \cdot -\frac{2}{7} = 1 \ne -1$ and $m_1 \ne m_2$, the lines are neither perpendicular nor parallel.

45. A;

$$\text{Average rate of change} = \frac{\text{change in gallons}}{\text{change in days}}$$

$$= \frac{214 \text{ gallons} - 400 \text{ gallons}}{30 \text{ days} - 0 \text{ days}}$$

$$= \frac{-186 \text{ gallons}}{30 \text{ days}} = -6.2 \text{ gallons per day}$$

Lesson 2.3 (pp. 93–96)

15.

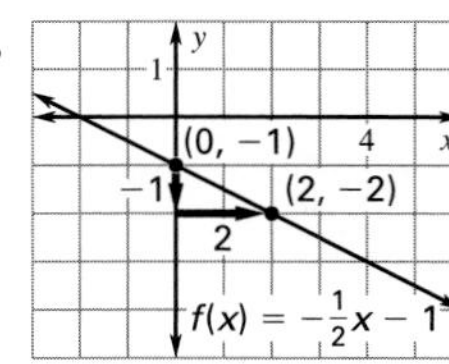

37. $-5x + 10y = 20$

x-intercept:

$-5x + 10(0) = 20$

$x = -4$

y-intercept:

$-5(0) + 10y = 20$

$y = 2$

61.

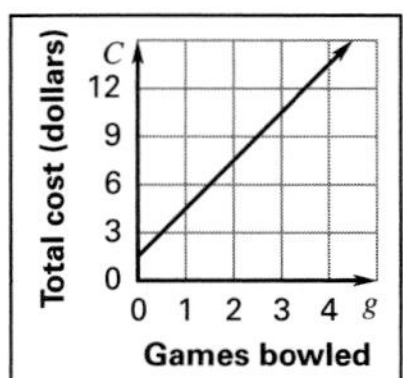

The y-intercept, 1.5, represents the cost to rent shoes, \$1.50. The slope, 3, represents the cost per game, \$3.

Lesson 2.4 (pp. 101–104)

15. Let $(x_1, y_1) = (7, -3)$ and $m = -\frac{4}{7}$.

$$y - y_1 = m(x - x_1)$$

$$y - (-3) = -\frac{4}{7}(x - 7)$$

$$y = -\frac{4}{7}x + 1$$

35. Let $(x_1, y_1) = (-5, -2)$ and $(x_2, y_2) = (-3, 8)$.

$$m = \frac{y_2 - y_1}{x_2 - x_1} = \frac{8 - (-2)}{-3 - (-5)} = \frac{10}{2} = 5$$

$$y - y_1 = m(x - x_1)$$

$$y - (-2) = 5(x - (-5))$$

$$y = 5x + 23$$

53. An equation is $15x + 9y = 4500$.

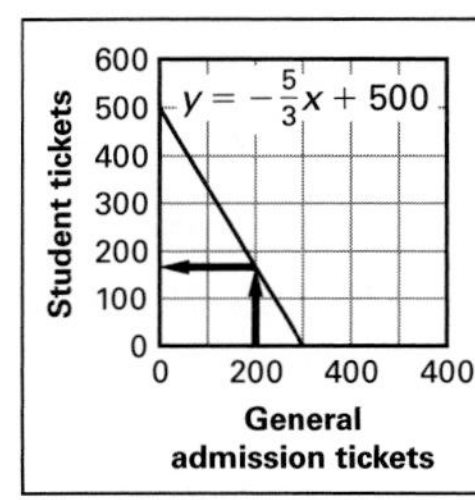

From the graph, you can see that if 200 general admissions tickets were sold, about 167 student tickets were sold.

Lesson 2.5 (pp. 109–111)

5. $y = ax$

$-21 = a(6)$

$-\frac{7}{2} = a$

Substitute $-\frac{7}{2}$ for a in $y = ax$. $y = -\frac{7}{2}x$

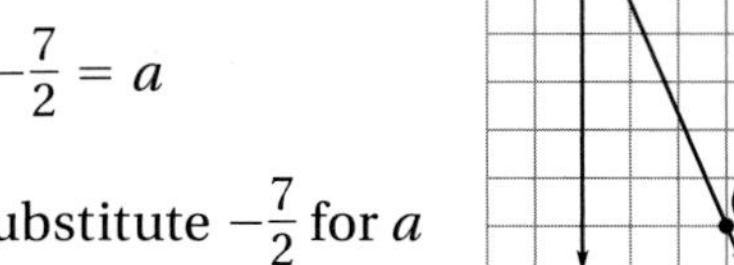

15. $y = ax$

$-1.6 = a(-4.8)$

$\frac{1}{3} = a$

So, $y = \frac{1}{3}x$.

When $x = 12$:

$y = \frac{1}{3}(12) = 4$

41. $\frac{23}{4.5} \approx 5.1 \quad \frac{40}{7.8} \approx 5.1 \quad \frac{82}{16} \approx 5.1$

Because the ratios are approximately equal, the data show direct variation. An equation relating s and t is $t = 5.1s$.

Lesson 2.6 (pp. 117–120)

9. The correlation coefficient is closest to −1 because the scatter plot shows a strong negative correlation.

11. a.

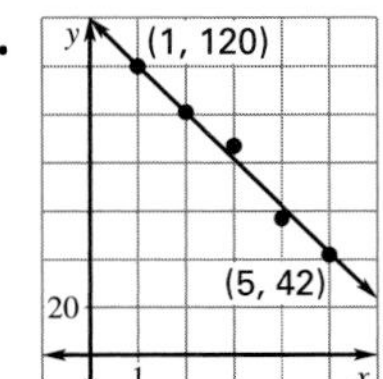

b. The line shown appears to pass through $(x_1, y_1) = (1, 120)$ and $(x_2, y_2) = (5, 42)$.

$$m = \frac{y_2 - y_1}{x_2 - x_1} = \frac{42 - 120}{5 - 1} = -\frac{78}{4} = -19.5$$

$$y - y_1 = m(x - x_1)$$

$$y - 120 = -19.5(x - 1)$$

$$y = -19.5x + 139.5$$

c. When $x = 20$:

$$y = -19.5(20) + 139.5 = -250.5$$

WORKED-OUT SOLUTIONS

25. A scatter plot and possible line of best fit are shown. The line appears to pass through $(x_1, y_1) = (0, 2240)$ and $(x_2, y_2) = (6, 2850)$.

$$m = \frac{y_2 - y_1}{x_2 - x_1} = \frac{2850 - 2240}{6 - 0} = \frac{610}{6} \approx 101.7$$

$$y - y_1 = m(x - x_1)$$

$$y - 2240 = 101.7(x - 0)$$

$$y = 101.7x + 2240$$

An approximation of the best-fitting line is $y = 101.7x + 2240$.

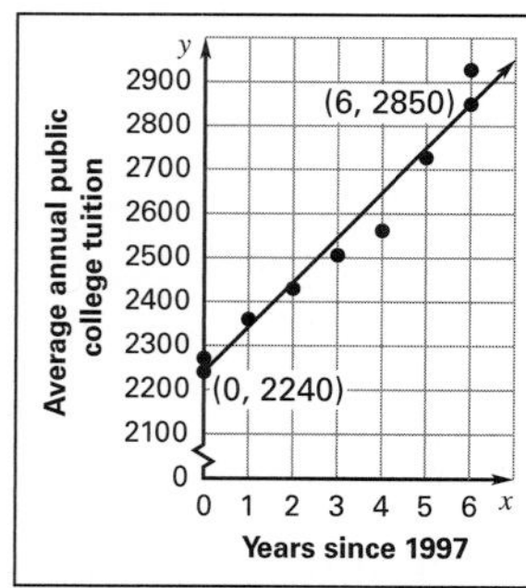

Lesson 2.7 (pp. 127–129)

13. The graph of $f(x) = -\frac{1}{2}|x - 1| + 5$ is the graph of $f(x) = |x|$ reflected in the x-axis, vertically shrunk by a factor of $\frac{1}{2}$, and translated right 1 unit and up 5 units.

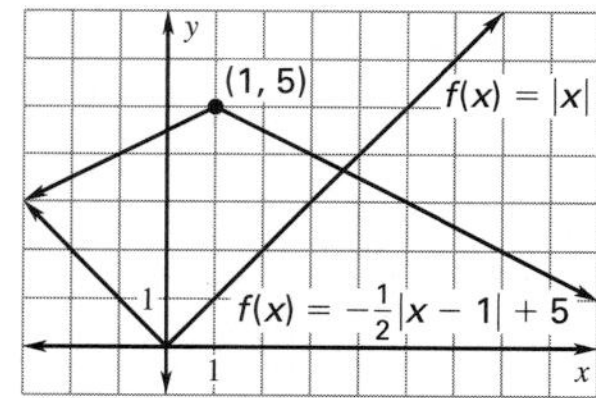

19. Vertex is $(-2, -1)$; $y = a|x + 2| - 1$

Using point $(0, 0)$: $0 = a|0 + 2| - 1$

$$\frac{1}{2} = a$$

An equation is $y = \frac{1}{2}|x + 2| - 1$.

39. Vertex is $(69, 140)$; $y = a|x - 69| + 140$

Using point $(0, 0)$: $0 = a|0 - 69| + 140$

$$-\frac{140}{69} = a$$

An equation is $y = -\frac{140}{69}|x - 69| + 140$.

Lesson 2.8 (pp. 135–138)

15. 

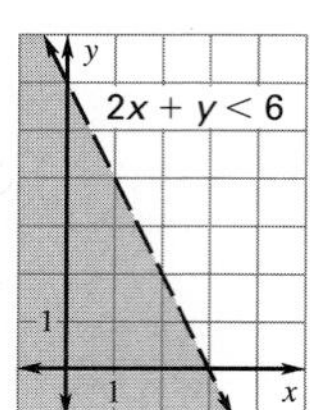

25.

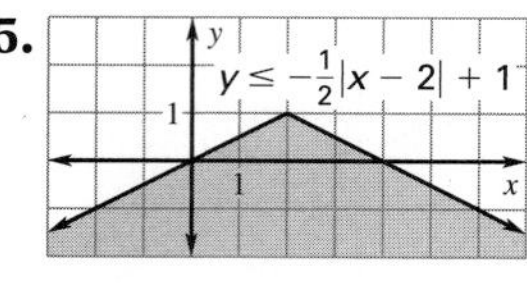

45. x = yards of cotton lace; y = yards of linen lace
$1.5x + 2.5y \le 75$

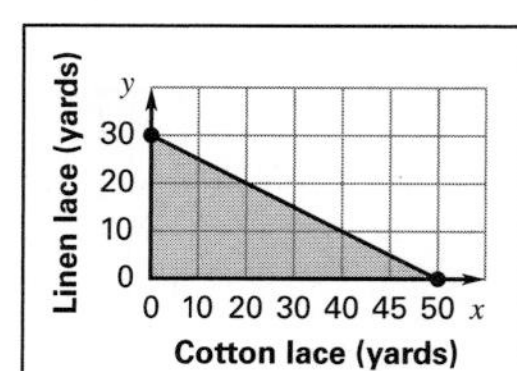

Let $x = 24$:

$$1.5(24) + 2.5y \le 75$$

$$y \le 15.6$$

You can buy 15.6 or less yards of linen lace.

Chapter 3

Lesson 3.1 (pp. 156–158)

9. $y = -3x - 2$

$4 \stackrel{?}{=} -3(-2) - 2$

$4 \stackrel{?}{=} 6 - 2$

$4 = 4$ ✓

$5x + 2y = -2$

$5(-2) + 2(4) \stackrel{?}{=} -2$

$-10 + 8 \stackrel{?}{=} -2$

$-2 = -2$ ✓

The solution is $(-2, 4)$.

21.

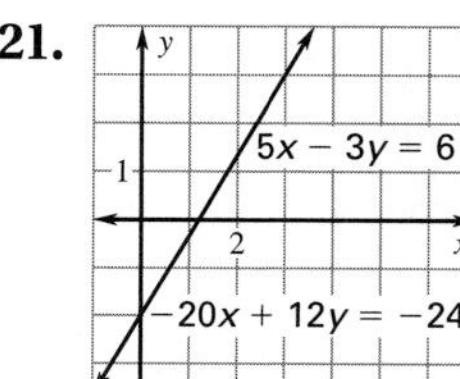

The graphs of the equations are the same line. The system has infinitely many solutions. The system is consistent and dependent.

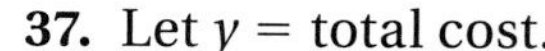

37. Let y = total cost.

Let x = number of days.

Option A: $y = 121 + x$

Option B: $y = 12x$

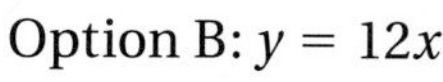

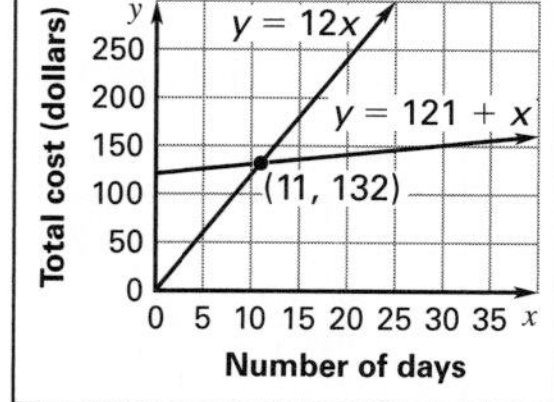

The plans are equal after 11 days. If the daily cost of option B increases, the plans will be equal in fewer days.

WORKED-OUT SOLUTIONS

Lesson 3.2 (pp. 164–167)

5. $6x - 2y = 5$

$-3x + y = 7 \rightarrow y = 3x + 7$

When $y = 3x + 7$:

$6x - 2(3x + 7) = 5$

$6x - 6x - 14 = 5$

$-14 \neq 5$ There is no solution.

29. $2x - 3y = 8$ $\xrightarrow{\times 2}$ $4x - 6y = 16$

$-4x + 5y = -10$ $\longrightarrow$ $\underline{-4x + 5y = -10}$

$-y = 6$

When $y = -6$:

$2x - 3(-6) = 8$

$x = -5$ The solution is $(-5, -6)$.

59. $x =$ double $\quad x + y = 26 \rightarrow y = 26 - x$

$y =$ singles $\quad 4x + 2y = 76$

$4x + 2(26 - x) = 76 \quad y = 26 - x$

$4x + 52 - 2x = 76 \quad y = 26 - 12$

$x = 12 \quad y = 14$

There were 12 doubles games and 14 singles games in progress.

Lesson 3.3 (pp. 171–173)

9. $4x - 4y \geq -16$

$-x + 2y \geq -4$

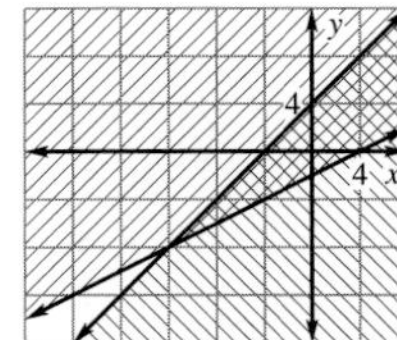

19. $3x + 2y > -6$

$-5 + 2y > -2$

$y < 5$

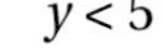

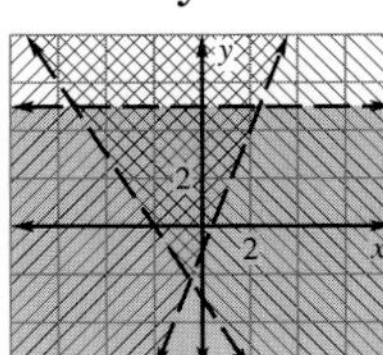

37. a. $x \geq 2$

$y \geq 2$

$x + y \leq 8$

$x + y \geq 5$

b.

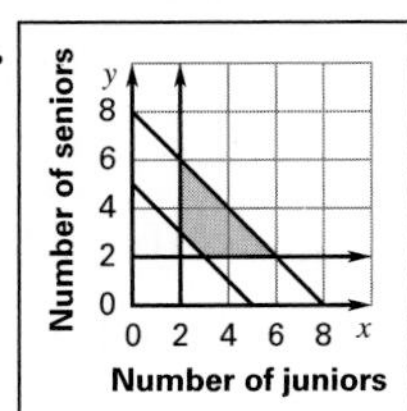

c. *Sample answer:* 3 juniors, 4 seniors; 4 juniors, 4 seniors.

Lesson 3.4 (pp. 182–185)

11. $3x - y + 2z = 4$

$6x - 2y + 4z = -8$

$2x - y + 3z = 10$

$6x - 2y + 4z = -8$ Add -2 times Equation 1

$\underline{-6x + 2y - 4z = -8}$ to Equation 2.

$0 = -8$

No solution

25. $x + 5y - 2z = -1$

$-x - 2y + z = 6$

$-2x - 7y + 3z = 7$

$x + 5y - 2z = -1$ Add Equation 2 to

$\underline{-y - 2y + z = 6}$ Equation 1.

$3y - z = 5$ New Equation 1

$-2x - 7y + 3z = 7$ Add 2 times Equation

$\underline{2x + 10y - 4z = -2}$ 1 to Equation 3.

$3y - z = 5$ New Equation 2

$3y - z = 5$ Add -1 times new Equation

$\underline{-3y + z = -5}$ 1 to new Equation 2

$0 = 0$

Infinitely many solutions

45. a. $f =$ 1st place; $s =$ 2nd place; $t =$ 3rd place

$f + s + t = 20$ Equation 1

$5f + 3s + t = 68$ Equation 2

$s = f + t$ Equation 3

$f + (f + t) + t = 20 \rightarrow 2f + 2t = 20$ New Eq. 1

$5f + 3(f + t) + t = 68 \rightarrow 8f + 4t = 68$ New Eq. 2

$-8f - 8t = -80$ Add -4 times new

$\underline{8f + 4t = 68}$ Eq. 1 to new Eq. 2.

$-4t = -12$

$t = 3$

Substitute $t = 3$ into new Equation 1.

$2f + 2(3) = 20 \rightarrow f = 7$

Substitute $f = 7$ and $t = 3$ into Equation 3.

$s = f + t \rightarrow s = 7 + 3 = 10$

7 athletes placed first, 10 athletes placed second, and 3 athletes placed third.

b. $f + s + t = 20$ Equation 1

$5f + 3s + t = 70$ Equation 2

$s = f + t$ Equation 3

$f + (f + t) + t = 20 \rightarrow 2f + 2t = 20$ New Eq. 1

$5f + 3(f + t) + t = 70 \rightarrow 8f + 4t = 70$ New Eq. 2

$-8f - 8t = -80$ Add -4 times new

$8f + 4t = 70$ Eq. 1 to new Eq. 2.

$-4t = -10$

$t = \frac{5}{2}$

t cannot be a fraction; you cannot have part of a person. This claim must be false.

Lesson 3.5 (pp. 191–193)

5. $\begin{bmatrix} 10 & -8 \\ 5 & -3 \end{bmatrix} - \begin{bmatrix} 12 & -3 \\ 3 & -4 \end{bmatrix}$

$= \begin{bmatrix} 10 - 12 & -8 - (-3) \\ 5 - 3 & -3 - (-4) \end{bmatrix} = \begin{bmatrix} -2 & -5 \\ 2 & 1 \end{bmatrix}$

21. $\begin{bmatrix} 1.8 & -1.5 & 10.6 \\ -8.8 & 3.4 & 0 \end{bmatrix} + 3\begin{bmatrix} 7.2 & 0 & -5.4 \\ 2.1 & -1.9 & 3.3 \end{bmatrix}$

$= \begin{bmatrix} 1.8 + 21.6 & -1.5 + 0 & 10.6 + (-16.2) \\ -8.8 + 6.3 & 3.4 + (-5.7) & 0 + 9.9 \end{bmatrix}$

$= \begin{bmatrix} 23.4 & -1.5 & -5.6 \\ -2.5 & -2.3 & 9.9 \end{bmatrix}$

33. a.

	May(M) A	B	C	June (J) A	B	C
Downtown	31	42	18	25	36	12
Mall	22	25	11	38	32	15

b. $M + J = \begin{bmatrix} 31 & 42 & 18 \\ 22 & 25 & 11 \end{bmatrix} + \begin{bmatrix} 25 & 36 & 12 \\ 38 & 32 & 15 \end{bmatrix}$

$= \begin{bmatrix} 31 + 25 & 42 + 36 & 18 + 12 \\ 22 + 38 & 25 + 32 & 11 + 15 \end{bmatrix} = \begin{bmatrix} 56 & 78 & 30 \\ 60 & 57 & 26 \end{bmatrix}$

The downtown store sold 56 of Model A, 78 of Model B, and 30 of Model C. The mall store sold 60 of Model A, 57 of Model B, and 26 of Model C.

c. $\frac{1}{2}(M + J) = \frac{1}{2}\begin{bmatrix} 56 & 78 & 30 \\ 60 & 57 & 26 \end{bmatrix}$

$= \begin{bmatrix} 28 & 39 & 15 \\ 30 & 28.5 & 13 \end{bmatrix}$

Lesson 3.6 (pp. 199–202)

13. $\begin{bmatrix} 9 & -3 \\ 0 & 2 \end{bmatrix}\begin{bmatrix} 0 & 1 \\ 4 & -2 \end{bmatrix}$

$= \begin{bmatrix} 9(0) + (-3)(4) & 9(1) + (-3)(-2) \\ 0(0) + 2(4) & 0(1) + 2(-2) \end{bmatrix}$

$= \begin{bmatrix} -12 & 15 \\ 8 & -4 \end{bmatrix}$

23. $-\frac{1}{2}AC = -\frac{1}{2}\begin{bmatrix} 5 & -3 \\ -2 & 4 \end{bmatrix}\begin{bmatrix} -6 & 3 \\ 4 & 1 \end{bmatrix}$

$= -\frac{1}{2}\begin{bmatrix} 5(-6) + (-3)(4) & 5(3) + (-3)(1) \\ (-2)(-6) + (4)(4) & (-2)(3) + (4)(1) \end{bmatrix}$

$= -\frac{1}{2}\begin{bmatrix} -42 & 12 \\ 28 & -2 \end{bmatrix} = \begin{bmatrix} 21 & -6 \\ -14 & 1 \end{bmatrix}$

41. *SP*: $(3 \times 2)(1 \times 3)$ *PS*: $(1 \times 3)(3 \times 2)$

not equal equal

So, matrix *PS* is defined.

$PS = [650 \quad 825 \quad 1050]\begin{bmatrix} 21 & 16 \\ 40 & 33 \\ 15 & 19 \end{bmatrix}$

$= [650(21) + 825(40) + 1050(15) \quad 650(16) + 825(33) + 1050(19)]$

$= [62{,}400 \quad 57{,}575]$

The profit for dealer A is \$62,400 and the profit for dealer B is \$57,575.

Lesson 3.7 (pp. 207–209)

11. $\begin{vmatrix} -1 & 12 & 4 \\ 0 & 2 & -5 \\ 3 & 0 & 1 \end{vmatrix}\begin{matrix} -1 & 12 \\ 0 & 2 \\ 3 & 0 \end{matrix}$

$= (-2 - 180 + 0) - (24 + 0 + 0) = -206$

23. Area $= \pm\frac{1}{2}\begin{vmatrix} 4 & 2 & 1 \\ 4 & 8 & 1 \\ 8 & 5 & 1 \end{vmatrix} = \pm\frac{1}{2}\begin{vmatrix} 4 & 2 & 1 \\ 4 & 8 & 1 \\ 8 & 5 & 1 \end{vmatrix}\begin{matrix} 4 & 2 \\ 4 & 8 \\ 8 & 5 \end{matrix}$

$= \pm\frac{1}{2}[(32 + 16 + 20) - (64 + 20 + 8)] = 12$

The area of the triangle is 12 square units.

43. a. x = single; y = double; z = triple

$x + y + z = 120$

$0.90x + 1.2y + 1.6z = 134$

$x = y + z \rightarrow x - y - z = 0$

$$\begin{vmatrix} 1 & 1 & 1 \\ 0.9 & 1.2 & 1.6 \\ 1 & -1 & -1 \end{vmatrix} \begin{matrix} 1 & 1 \\ 0.9 & 1.2 \\ 1 & -1 \end{matrix}$$

$= (-1.2 + 1.6 - 0.9) - (1.2 - 1.6 - 0.9) = 0.8$

$$x = \frac{\begin{vmatrix} 120 & 1 & 1 \\ 134 & 1.2 & 1.6 \\ 0 & -1 & -1 \end{vmatrix}}{0.8} = \frac{48}{0.8} = 60$$

$$y = \frac{\begin{vmatrix} 1 & 120 & 1 \\ 0.9 & 134 & 1.6 \\ 1 & 0 & -1 \end{vmatrix}}{0.8} = \frac{32}{0.8} = 40$$

$$z = \frac{\begin{vmatrix} 1 & 1 & 120 \\ 0.9 & 1.2 & 134 \\ 1 & -1 & 0 \end{vmatrix}}{0.8} = \frac{16}{0.8} = 20$$

There are 60 single-scoop, 40 double-scoop, and 20 triple-scoop cones sold.

b. New price = $1.1 \times$ old price

$1.1(\$.90) = \$.99$; $1.1(\$1.20) = \$1.32$; $1.1(\$1.60) = \$1.76$

New sales = $0.95 \times$ old sales

$0.95(60) = 57$; $0.95(40) = 38$; $0.95(20) = 19$

New revenue = $\$.99(57) + \$1.32(38)$

$+ \$1.76(19) = \$140.03$

Lesson 3.8 (pp. 214–217)

3. $A = \begin{bmatrix} 1 & -5 \\ -1 & 4 \end{bmatrix}$

$$A^{-1} = \frac{1}{4-5}\begin{bmatrix} 4 & 5 \\ 1 & 1 \end{bmatrix} = -1\begin{bmatrix} 4 & 5 \\ 1 & 1 \end{bmatrix} = \begin{bmatrix} -4 & -5 \\ -1 & -1 \end{bmatrix}$$

25. $\begin{bmatrix} 4 & -1 \\ -7 & -2 \end{bmatrix} \cdot \begin{bmatrix} x \\ y \end{bmatrix} = \begin{bmatrix} 10 \\ -25 \end{bmatrix}$

$$A^{-1} = \frac{1}{-8-7}\begin{bmatrix} -2 & 1 \\ 7 & 4 \end{bmatrix} = \begin{bmatrix} \frac{2}{15} & -\frac{1}{15} \\ -\frac{7}{15} & -\frac{4}{15} \end{bmatrix}$$

$$X = A^{-1}B = \begin{bmatrix} \frac{2}{15} & -\frac{1}{15} \\ -\frac{7}{15} & -\frac{4}{15} \end{bmatrix}\begin{bmatrix} 10 \\ -25 \end{bmatrix} = \begin{bmatrix} 3 \\ 2 \end{bmatrix} = \begin{bmatrix} x \\ y \end{bmatrix}$$

The solution of the system is (3, 2).

47. $\begin{bmatrix} 78 & 104 & 198 \\ 1 & 0 & 0.6 \\ 22 & 255 & 23.8 \end{bmatrix}\begin{bmatrix} b \\ t \\ w \end{bmatrix} = \begin{bmatrix} 500 \\ 3 \\ 100 \end{bmatrix}$

$$X = A^{-1}B = \begin{bmatrix} 2.3 \\ 0.8 \\ 1.2 \end{bmatrix}$$

2.3 oz Bran Crunchies; 0.8 oz Toasted Oats; and 1.2 oz Whole Wheat Flakes

Chapter 4

Lesson 4.1 (pp. 240–243)

15.

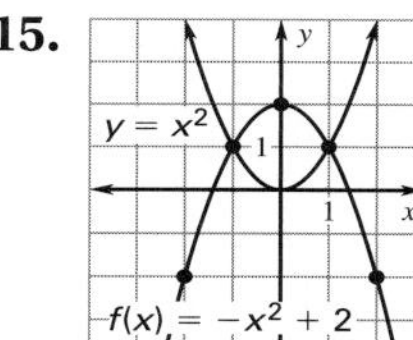

Both graphs have the same axis of symmetry. The graph of $f(x) = -x^2 + 2$ opens down, and its vertex is 2 units higher than that of $y = x^2$.

37. $f(x) = \frac{3}{2}x^2 + 6x + 4$

$a > 0$; the function has a minimum value.

$$x = \frac{-b}{2a} = \frac{-(6)}{2\left(\frac{3}{2}\right)} = -2$$

Minimum: $f(-2) = \frac{3}{2}(-2)^2 + 6(-2) + 4 = -2$

57. $y = \frac{1}{9000}x^2 - \frac{7}{15}x + 500$

$$x = \frac{-b}{2a} = \frac{-\left(\frac{-7}{15}\right)}{2\left(\frac{1}{9000}\right)} = 2100$$

$$y = \frac{1}{9000}(2100)^2 - \frac{7}{15}(2100) + 500 = 10$$

The cable is 10 feet above the road.

WORKED-OUT SOLUTIONS

Lesson 4.2 (pp. 249–251)

19. 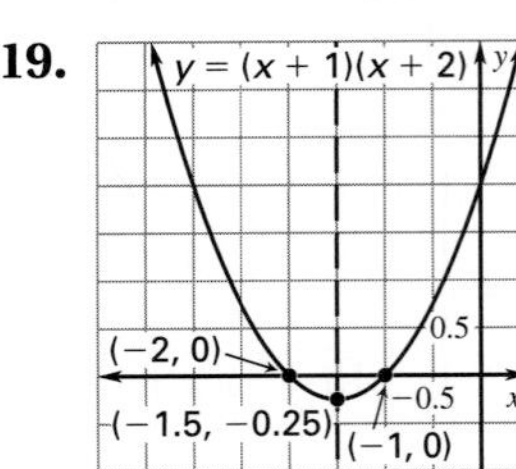

$a = 1, p = -1$, and $q = -2$

x-int.: $x = -2$ and $x = -1$

Axis of sym.:

$$x = \frac{-2 + (-1)}{2} = -1.5$$

Vertex: $(-1.5, -0.25)$

29. $y = (x - 3)^2 + 6 = (x - 3)(x - 3) + 6$

$= (x^2 - 3x - 3x + 9) + 6 = x^2 - 6x + 15$

53. a. $y = -0.000234x(x - 160)$

$= -0.000234(x - 0)(x - 160)$

$p = 0, q = 160$; the field is 160 feet wide.

b. $x = \frac{p + q}{2} = \frac{0 + 160}{2} = 80$

$y = -0.000234(80)(80 - 160) \approx 1.5$

The maximum height is about 1.5 feet.

Lesson 4.3 (pp. 255–258)

33. $z^2 - 3z - 54 = 0 \rightarrow (z - 9)(z + 6) = 0$

$z - 9 = 0 \rightarrow z = 9$ or $z + 6 = 0 \rightarrow z = -6$

47. $y = x^2 + 7x - 30 = (x + 10)(x - 3)$

The zeros are -10 and 3.

67. a. $A = (30)(20) = 600 \text{ ft}^2$

b. New area (feet) = New length (feet) • New width (feet)

$1064 = (x + 30)(x + 20)$

c. $x^2 + 50x + 600 = 1064$

$(x - 58)(x - 8) = 0 \rightarrow x = -58$ or $x = 8$

Expand the length and width by 8 feet.

Lesson 4.4 (pp. 263–265)

27. $20x^2 + 124x + 24 = 4(5x^2 + 31x + 6)$

$= 4(5x + 1)(x + 6)$

39. $6r^2 - 7r - 5 = 0 \rightarrow (3r - 5)(2r + 1) = 0$

$r = \frac{5}{3} = 1\frac{2}{3}$ or $r = -\frac{1}{2}$

63. $96 = (2x + 8)(2x + 12) - 96$

$0 = 4x^2 + 40x - 96$

$0 = (4x - 8)(x + 12)$

$x = 2$ or $x = -12$

The border's width should be 2 feet.

Lesson 4.5 (pp. 269–271)

17. $\frac{\sqrt{2}}{4 + \sqrt{5}} = \frac{\sqrt{2}}{4 + \sqrt{5}} \cdot \frac{4 - \sqrt{5}}{4 - \sqrt{5}} = \frac{4\sqrt{2} - \sqrt{10}}{11}$

27. $-3w^2 = -213 \rightarrow w^2 = 71 \rightarrow w = \pm\sqrt{71}$

41. a. $\pi r^2 = 10^2 = 100$

b. $\pi r^2 = 100 \rightarrow r^2 = \frac{100}{\pi} \rightarrow r \approx 5.6$ feet

c. $\pi r^2 = s^2 \rightarrow r^2 = \frac{s^2}{\pi}$

$$r = \sqrt{\frac{s^2}{\pi}} = \frac{s}{\sqrt{\pi}} \cdot \frac{\sqrt{\pi}}{\sqrt{\pi}} = \frac{s\sqrt{\pi}}{\pi}$$

Lesson 4.6 (pp. 279–282)

11. $-5(n - 3)^2 = 10 \rightarrow (n - 3)^2 = -2$

$n - 3 = \pm\sqrt{-2} \rightarrow n = 3 \pm i\sqrt{2}$

29. $\frac{6i}{3 - i} = \frac{6i}{3 - i} \cdot \frac{3 + i}{3 + i} = \frac{18i + 6i^2}{9 + 3i - 3i - i^2}$

$= \frac{-6 + 18i}{10} = -\frac{6}{10} + \frac{18}{10}i = -\frac{3}{5} + \frac{9}{5}i$

67. Impedance: $12 + 8i - 6i - 10i = 12 - 8i$ ohms

Lesson 4.7 (pp. 288–291)

27. $x^2 - 2x = -25$

$x^2 - 2x + 1 = -25 + 1$

$(x - 1)^2 = -24$

$x - 1 = \pm\sqrt{-24} \rightarrow x = 1 \pm 2i\sqrt{6}$

45. $y = x^2 - 3x + 4$

$y + \frac{9}{4} = \left(x^2 - 3x + \frac{9}{4}\right) + 4$

$y = \left(x - \frac{3}{2}\right)^2 + \frac{7}{4}$

The vertex is $\left(\frac{3}{2}, \frac{7}{4}\right)$.

65.
$$y = (200 + 10x)(40 - x)$$
$$y = 8000 + 200x - 10x^2$$
$$y - 8000 = -10(x^2 - 20x)$$
$$y - 8000 + (-10)(100) = -10(x^2 - 20x + 100)$$
$$y - 9000 = -10(x - 10)^2$$
$$y = -10(x - 10)^2 + 9000$$

The revenue is maximized when the price is increased 10 times; 10($10) = $100.

Lesson 4.8 (pp. 296–299)

19. $4x^2 + 3 = x^2 - 7x \rightarrow 3x^2 + 7x + 3 = 0$

$x = \dfrac{-7 \pm \sqrt{7^2 - 4(3)(3)}}{2(3)} = \dfrac{-7 \pm \sqrt{13}}{6}$

39. $7r^2 - s = 2r + 9r^2 \rightarrow -2r^2 - 2r - 5 = 0$

$b^2 - 4ac = (-2)^2 - 4(-2)(-5) = -36 < 0$

Two imaginary: $\dfrac{-(-2) \pm \sqrt{-36}}{2(-2)} = -\dfrac{1}{2} \pm \dfrac{3}{2}i$

71. $S = -0.000013E^2 + 0.042E - 21$

$10 = -0.000013E^2 + 0.042E - 21$

$0 = -0.000013E^2 + 0.042E - 31$

$E = \dfrac{-0.042 \pm \sqrt{(0.042)^2 - 4(-0.000013)(-31)}}{2(-0.000013)}$

$E = \dfrac{-0.042 \pm \sqrt{0.000152}}{-0.000026}$

$E \approx 1141$ meters or $E \approx 2090$ meters

Lesson 4.9 (pp. 304–307)

17. $y \leq -\dfrac{2}{3}x^2 + 3x + 1$

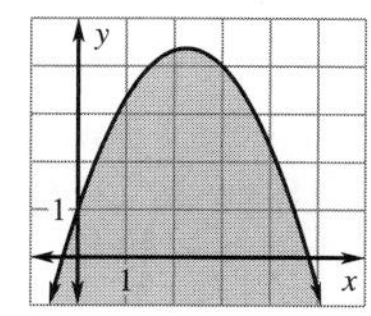

39. $3x^2 + 2x - 8 \leq 0$

$(3x - 4)(x + 2) = 0$

$x = \dfrac{4}{3}$ or $x = -2$

The solution is $-2 \leq x \leq \dfrac{4}{3}$.

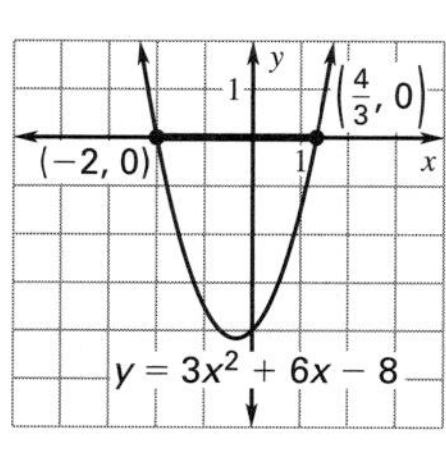

73. $0.0017x^2 + 0.145x + 2.35 > 10$

$0.0017x^2 + 0.145x - 7.65 > 0$

$x = \dfrac{-0.145 \pm \sqrt{0.073045}}{0.0034} \approx 36.84, -122.13$

$0 \quad 10 \quad 20 \quad 30 \quad 36.84 \quad 40$

Test values $x = 0$ and $x = 37$ to determine that $x \geq 36.84$. The domain is $0 \leq x \leq 40$. So, the larvae's length tends to be greater than 10 mm between around 37 to 40 days.

Lesson 4.10 (pp. 312–315)

19. $y = a(x - p)(x - q) \rightarrow y = a(x + 3)(x - 3)$

$-4 = a(1 + 3)(1 - 3) \rightarrow \dfrac{1}{2} = a$

A quadratic function is $y = \dfrac{1}{2}(x + 3)(x - 3)$.

35. $y = ax^2 + bx + c$

$9 = a(-1)^2 + b(-1) + c \rightarrow a - b + c = 9$

$1 = a(1)^2 + b(1) + c \rightarrow a + b + c = 1$

$17 = a(3)^2 + b(3) + c \rightarrow 9a + 3b + c = 17$

Using substitution and $c = 9 - a + b$:

$a + b + (9 - a + b) = 1 \rightarrow b = -4$

$9a + 3(-4) + (9 - a - 4) = 17 \rightarrow a = 3$

$3 - (-4) + c = 9 \rightarrow c = 2$

A quadratic function is $y = 3x^2 - 4x + 2$.

49. a.

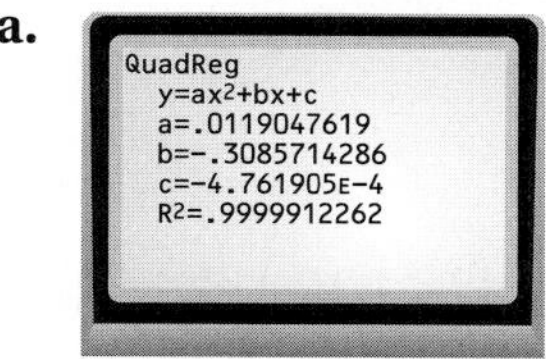

$y = 0.01190x^2 - 0.309x - 0.00048$

b. When $x = 10$, $y \approx -1.90$ seconds

Chapter 5

Lesson 5.1 (pp. 333–335)

17. $(6.3 \times 10^5)(8.9 \times 10^{-12}) = 56.07 \times 10^{-7}$

$= 5.607 \times 10^1 \times 10^{-7} = 5.607 \times 10^{-6}$

WORKED-OUT SOLUTIONS

31. $\frac{3c^3d}{9cd^{-1}} = \frac{3}{9}c^{3-1}d^{1-(-1)} = \frac{1}{3}c^2d^2$

Quotient of powers property

51. Bead: $d = 6$ mm, $r = 3$ mm

$v = \frac{4}{3}\pi r^3 = \frac{4}{3}\pi(3)^3 = 36\pi$

Pearl: $d = 9$ mm, $r = \frac{9}{2}$ mm

$v = \frac{4}{3}\pi r^3 = \frac{4}{3}\pi\left(\frac{9}{2}\right)^3 = \frac{243\pi}{2}$

$\frac{\text{Volume of pearl}}{\text{Volume of bead}} = \frac{\frac{243\pi}{2}}{36\pi} = \frac{243}{72} = 3.375$

About 3.4 times greater

Lesson 5.2 (pp. 341–344)

21.

3	−7	11	4	0
		−21	−30	−78
	−7	−10	−26	−78

$f(3) = -78$

27. The degree is even and the leading coefficient is negative.

57.

t	0	2	4	6	8	10	12
s	1.2	1.46	1.68	1.59	1.44	1.97	4.41

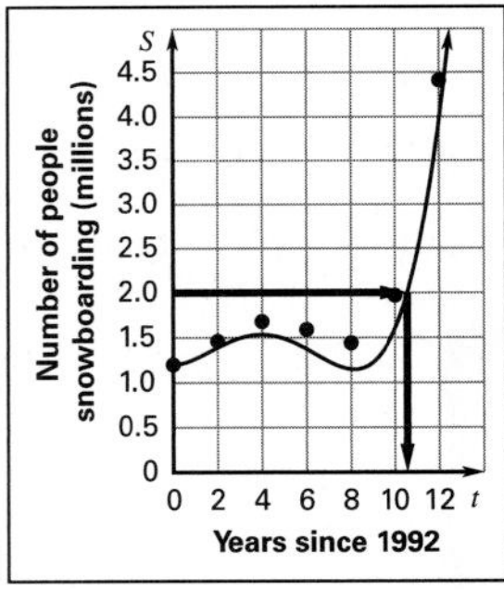

The number of snowboarders was greater than 2 million in 2002 (when $t \approx 10$).

Lesson 5.3 (pp. 349–352)

11. $(5b - 6b^3 + 2b^4) - (9b^3 + 4b^4 - 7)$

$= 2b^4 - 4b^4 - 6b^3 - 9b^3 + 5b + 7$

$= -2b^4 - 15b^3 + 5b + 7$

21. $(2a - 3)(a^2 - 10a - 2)$

$= (2a - 3)(a^2) - (2a - 3)(10a) - (2a - 3)(2)$

$= 2a^3 - 23a^2 + 26a + 6$

61. $P = 0.00267sF = 0.00267s(0.0116s^2 + 0.789)$

$= 0.000030972s^3 + 0.00210663s$

When $s = 10$, $P(10) = 0.0520383$.

About 0.052 horsepower is needed.

Lesson 5.4 (pp. 356–359)

7. $3y^5 - 48y^3 = 3y^3(y^2 - 16) = 3y^3(y + 4)(y - 4)$

23. $4c^3 + 8c^2 - 9c - 18 = 4c^2(c + 2) - 9(c + 2)$

$= (c + 2)(2c + 3)(2c - 3)$

61. $\ell = x;\ h = x - 5;\ w = x - 5$

$v = \ell wh \rightarrow 250 = (x)(x - 5)(x - 5)$

$250 = x(x^2 - 10x + 25)$

$0 = x^3 - 10x^2 + 25x - 250$

$0 = x^2(x - 10) + 25(x - 10)$

$0 = (x^2 + 25)(x - 10) \rightarrow x = 10$

$\ell = 10$ in., $h = 5$ in., $w = 5$ in.

Lesson 5.5 (pp. 366–368)

17.

6	1	−5	−8	13	−12
		6	6	−12	6
	1	1	−2	1	−6

$x^3 + x^2 - 2x + 1 - \frac{6}{x - 6}$

25.

−9	1	2	−51	108
		−9	63	−108
	1	−7	12	0

$f(x) = (x + 9)(x^2 - 7x + 12)$

$= (x + 9)(x - 4)(x - 3)$

43.

$$\begin{array}{r} -0.13x^2 + 11.2x - 560.9 \\ 14.8x + 725 \overline{\smash{)}\ -1.95x^3 + 70.1x^2 - 188x + 2150} \\ \underline{-1.95x^3 - 95.5x^2} \qquad\qquad\qquad \\ 165.6x^2 - 188x \qquad\quad \\ \underline{165.6x^2 + 8113.3x} \qquad\quad \\ -8301.3x + 2150 \\ \underline{-8301.3x - 406{,}652.5} \\ 408{,}802.5 \end{array}$$

$f(x) = -0.13x^2 + 11.2x - 560.9 + \frac{408{,}802.5}{14.8x + 725}$

Lesson 5.6 (pp. 374–377)

7. $g(x) = 4x^5 + 3x^3 - 2x - 14$

Factors of the constant term: $\pm1, \pm2, \pm7, \pm14$

Factors of the leading coefficient: $\pm1, \pm2, \pm4$

Possible rational zeros: $\pm\frac{1}{1}, \pm\frac{2}{1}, \pm\frac{7}{1}, \pm\frac{14}{1}, \pm\frac{1}{2},$

$\pm\frac{2}{2}, \pm\frac{7}{2}, \pm\frac{14}{2}, \pm\frac{1}{4}, \pm\frac{2}{4}, \pm\frac{7}{4}, \pm\frac{14}{4}$

$= \pm1, \pm2, \pm7, \pm14, \pm\frac{1}{2}, \pm\frac{7}{2}, \pm\frac{1}{4}, \pm\frac{7}{4}$

21. Possible rational zeros: $\pm1, \pm3, \pm5, \pm15, \pm\frac{1}{2},$

$\pm\frac{3}{2}, \pm\frac{5}{2}, \pm\frac{15}{2}, \pm\frac{1}{3}, \pm\frac{5}{3}, \pm\frac{1}{6}, \pm\frac{5}{6}$

Reasonable zeros: $x = -3, x = -\frac{5}{3}, x = \frac{1}{2}$

Test $x = -3$:

$$\begin{array}{r|rrrr} -3 & 6 & 25 & 16 & -15 \\ & & -18 & -21 & 15 \\ \hline & 6 & 7 & -5 & 0 \end{array}$$

$f(x) = (x + 3)(6x^2 + 7x - 5)$

$= (x + 3)(2x - 1)(3x + 5)$

Real zeros are $-3, \frac{1}{2}, -\frac{5}{3}$.

47. $V = x(x - 1)(x - 2) \rightarrow 24 = x(x^2 - 3x + 2)$

$0 = x^3 - 3x^2 + 2x - 24$

Possible rational zeros: $\pm1, \pm2, \pm3, \pm4, \pm6, \pm8, \pm12, \pm24$

Lesson 5.7 (pp. 383–386)

15. Possible rational zeros: $\pm1, \pm2, \pm4, \pm8$

$f(x) = x^4 + x^3 + 2x^2 + 4x - 8$

$= (x + 2)(x^3 - x^2 + 4x - 4)$

$= (x + 2)(x - 1)(x^2 + 4)$

$= (x + 2)(x - 1)(x - 2i)(x + 2i)$

The zeros are -2, 1, $2i$, and $-2i$.

37. $h(x) = x^5 - 2x^3 - x^2 + 6x + 5$

2 sign changes; 2 or 0 positive real zeros

$h(-x) = (-x)^5 - 2(-x)^3 - (-x)^2 + 6(-x) + 5$

$= -x^5 + 2x^3 - x^2 - 6x + 5$

3 sign changes; 3 or 1 positive real zeros.

Possible numbers of zeros:

Positive	Negative	Imaginary	Total
2	3	0	5
0	3	2	5
2	1	2	5
0	1	4	5

61. $S = -0.015x^3 + 0.6x^2 - 2.4x + 19$

$0 = -0.015x^3 + 0.6x^2 - 2.4x - 56$

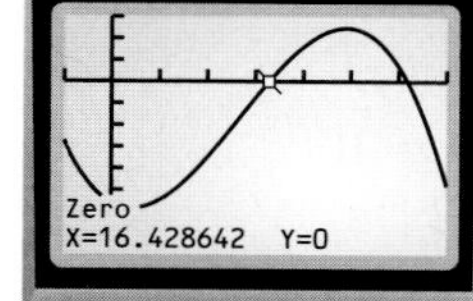

There are two positive zeros of this function, $x \approx 16.4$ and $x \approx 30.9$, but $x \approx 16.4$ is the most likely amount.

Lesson 5.8 (pp. 390–392)

3. (0, 4) (1, 2) (−1, 0) (3, 4) (2, 0) (−2, −16) $f(x) = (x - 2)^2(x + 1)$

19. Turning pts: $(-2.2, -38)$, local minimum; $(-1.1, 0.8)$, local maximum; $(0.3, -40)$, local minimum; $(1.9, 8)$, local maximum; $(2.75, -10.5)$, local minimum

Zeros: $x \approx -2.6, x \approx -1.4, x \approx -1, x \approx 1.5,$
$x \approx 2.2, x \approx 3$

It must be at least a degree 6 function.

41.

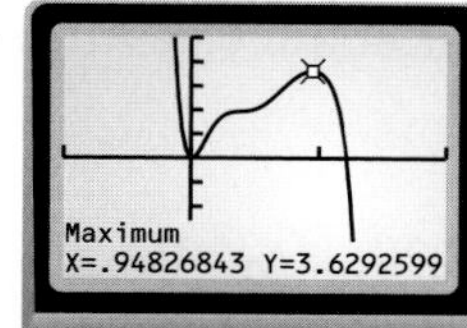

At about 0.95 seconds into the stroke the swimmer is going the fastest.

Lesson 5.9 (pp. 397–399)

9. $f(x) = a(x + 5)(x)(x - 6)$

$-12 = a(1 + 5)(1)(1 - 6) \rightarrow \frac{2}{5} = a$

$f(x) = \frac{2}{5}x(x + 5)(x - 6)$

15. $f(1)$ $f(2)$ $f(3)$ $f(4)$ $f(5)$ $f(6)$

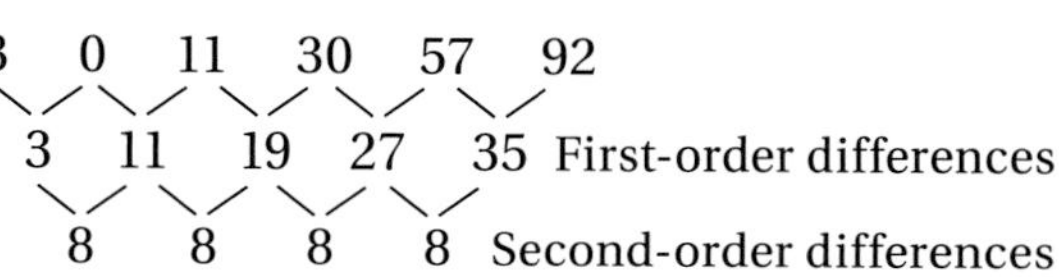

27. a. $m = 0.00081742t^3 - 0.02154t^2 + 0.249t + 3.17$

b.

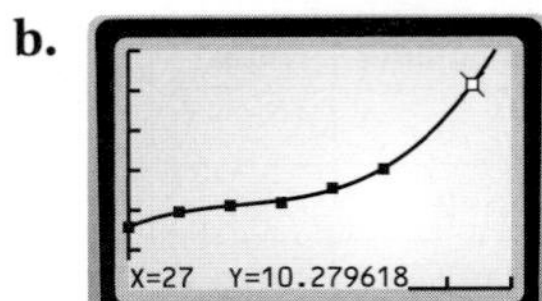

About \$10.30

c.

Intersection
X=12.354934 Y= 4.5

In 1995 ($t \approx 12.4$)

Chapter 6

Lesson 6.1 (pp. 417–419)

9. $(\sqrt[n]{a})^m = a^{m/n} \rightarrow (\sqrt[3]{10})^7 = 10^{7/3}$

25. $27^{2/3} = (27^{1/3})^2 = (3)^2 = 9$

63. $p = ks^3 \rightarrow 1.2 = k(1700)^3 \rightarrow k = \dfrac{3}{12{,}282{,}500{,}000}$

$p = \dfrac{3}{12{,}282{,}500{,}000}s^3 \rightarrow 1.5 = \dfrac{3}{12{,}282{,}500{,}000}s^3$

$\rightarrow 6{,}141{,}250{,}000 = s^3 \rightarrow s \approx 1831$

About 1800 revolutions per minute

Lesson 6.2 (pp. 424–427)

5. $3^{1/4} \cdot 27^{1/4} = 3^{1/4} \cdot 3^{1/4} \cdot 3^{1/4} \cdot 3^{1/4}$

$= 3^{(1/4 + 1/4 + 1/4 + 1/4)} = 3^1 = 3$

27. $5\sqrt[4]{64} \cdot 2\sqrt[4]{8} = 10\sqrt[4]{512} = 40\sqrt[4]{2}$

85. $d = 1.9[(5.5 \times 10^{-4})\ell]^{1/2}$

$\ell = 10 \text{ cm} = 100 \text{ mm}$

$d = 1.9[(5.5 \times 10^{-4})(100)]^{1/2} \approx 0.4456$

The optimum diameter is about 0.45 mm.

Lesson 6.3 (pp. 432–434)

3. $f(x) + g(x) = -3x^{1/3} + 4x^{1/2} + 5x^{1/3} + 4x^{1/2}$

$= 2x^{1/3} + 8x^{1/2}$

Domain of f: all nonnegative reals

Domain of g: all nonnegative reals

Domain of $f + g$: all nonnegative reals

13. $g(x) \cdot f(x) = (5x^{1/2})(4x^{2/3}) = 20x^{7/6}$

Domain of f: all reals

Domain of g: all nonnegative reals

Domain of $g \cdot f$: all nonnegative reals

45. For \$15 discount: $f(x) = x - 15$

For 10% discount: $g(x) = x - 0.1x = 0.9x$

a. $g(f(x)) = g(x - 15) = 0.9(x - 15)$

$x = 85$: $0.9(85 - 15) = 0.9(70) = \$63.00$

b. $f(g(x)) = f(0.9x) = 0.9x - 15$

$x = 85$: $0.9(85) - 15 = 76.5 - 15 = \$61.50$

c. The 10% discount before the \$15 discount.

Lesson 6.4 (pp. 442–445)

7. $y = 12x + 7 \rightarrow x = 12y + 7 \rightarrow \dfrac{x}{12} - \dfrac{7}{12} = y$

15. $f(g(x)) = f(x - 4) = (x - 4) + 4 = x$ ✓

$g(f(x)) = g(x + 4) = (x + 4) - 4 = x$ ✓

49. $v = 1.34\sqrt{\ell}$

$\left(\dfrac{v}{1.34}\right)^2 = \ell$

The waterlength should be $\ell = \left(\dfrac{7.5}{1.34}\right)^2 \approx 31.3$ feet.

Lesson 6.5 (pp. 449–451)

11.

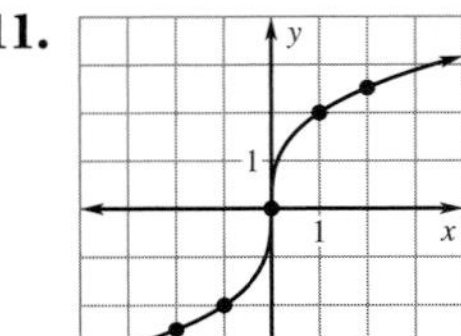

The domain and range are all real numbers.

17.

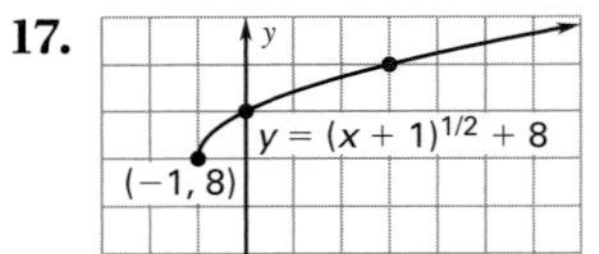

$y = \sqrt{x}$
(0, 0)

Domain: $x \geq -1$

Range: $y \geq 8$

37. a. $v = 331.5\sqrt{\dfrac{(273.15 + C)}{273.15}} = 331.5\sqrt{1 + \dfrac{C}{273.15}}$

b. Domain: $C \geq -273.15$; range: $v \geq 0$

Lesson 6.6 (pp. 456–459)

5. $\sqrt{9x} + 11 = 14$

$\sqrt{9x} = 3$

$9x = 9 \rightarrow x = 1$

Check: $\sqrt{9(1)} + 11 \stackrel{?}{=} 14$

$\sqrt{9} + 11 \stackrel{?}{=} 14$

$14 = 14$ ✓

13. $\sqrt[3]{x} - 10 = -3$

$\sqrt[3]{x} = 7$

$(\sqrt[3]{x})^3 = (7)^3 \rightarrow x = 343$

Check: $\sqrt[3]{343} - 10 \stackrel{?}{=} -3$

$7 - 10 \stackrel{?}{=} -3$

$-3 = -3$ ✓

59. $h = 150$: $150 = 62.5\sqrt[3]{t} + 75.8$

$1.7 \approx t$

$h = 250$: $250 = 625\sqrt[3]{t} + 75.8$

$21.7 \approx t$

The elephant with a shoulder height of 250 cm is about 20 years older than the elephant with the shoulder height of 150 cm.

Chapter 7

Lesson 7.1 (pp. 482–485)

17.

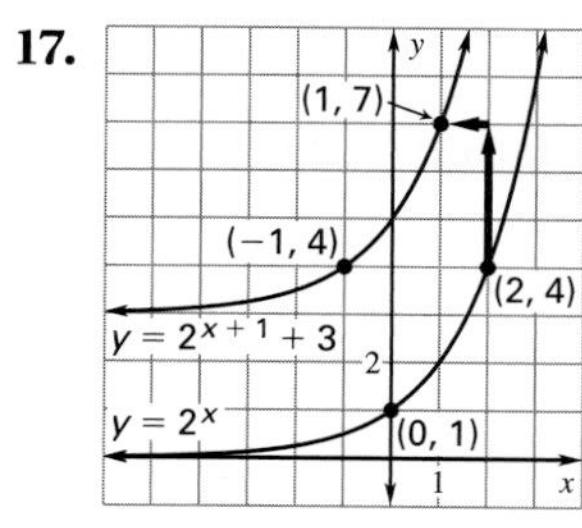

The domain is all real numbers and the range is $y > 3$.

29. $A = P\left(1 + \frac{r}{n}\right)^{nt} = 800\left(1 + \frac{0.02}{365}\right)^{365t}$

37. a. $P = 2200$; $r = 0.03$; $n = 4$; $t = 4$

$A = 2200\left(1 + \frac{0.03}{4}\right)^{4 \cdot 4} \approx 2479.38$

The balance is \$2479.38.

b. $P = 2200$; $r = 0.0225$; $n = 12$; $t = 4$

$A = 2200\left(1 + \frac{0.0225}{12}\right)^{12 \cdot 4} \approx 2406.98$

The balance is \$2406.98.

c. $P = 2200$; $r = 0.02$; $n = 365$; $t = 4$

$A = 2200\left(1 + \frac{0.02}{365}\right)^{365 \cdot 4} \approx 2383.23$

The balance is \$2383.23.

Lesson 7.2 (pp. 489–491)

9.

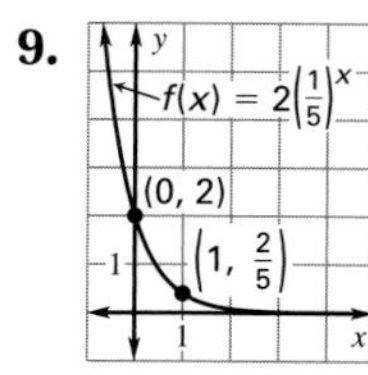

19.

Domain: all real numbers
Range: $y > -1$

33. a.

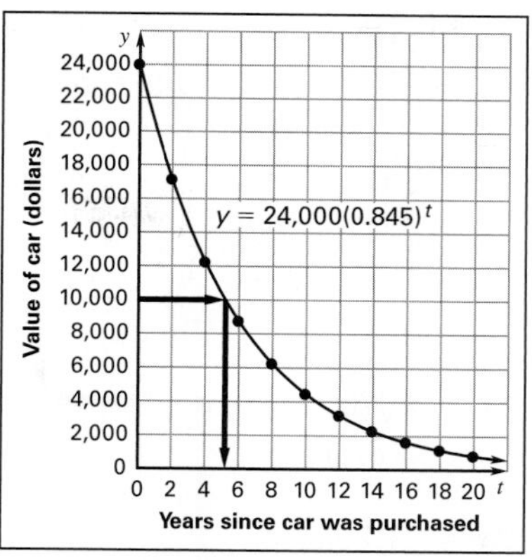

About 5 years after it was purchased

b. $y = 24{,}000(0.845)^{50} \approx \$5.29$; too low

Lesson 7.3 (pp. 495–498)

5. $(2e^{3x})^3 = 2^3(e^{3x})^3 = 8e^{9x}$

35. $f(x) = \frac{1}{4}e^{-5x}$; exponential decay

57. $P = 2000$; $r = 0.04$; $t = 5$

$A = Pe^{rt} = 2000e^{(0.04)(5)} \approx \$2442.81$

Lesson 7.4 (pp. 503–505)

13. $\left(\frac{1}{2}\right)^{-3} = 8$, so $\log_{1/2} 8 = -3$.

33. $\log_3 81^x = \log_3(3^4)^x = \log_3 3^{4x} = 4x$

61. a. $E = 2.5 \times 10^{24}$

$M = 0.29(\ln(2.5 \times 10^{24})) - 9.9 \approx 6.39$

b. $M = 0.29(\ln E) - 9.9$

$\frac{M + 9.9}{0.29} = \ln E \rightarrow e^{(M + 9.9)/0.29} = E$

This represents the amount of energy released as a function of the energy magnitude.

Lesson 7.5 (pp. 510–513)

11. $\log 144 = \log 12^2 = 2 \log 12 = 2.158$

17. $\log 3x^4 = \log 3 + \log x^4 = \log 3 + 4 \log x$

71. $L(10I) - L(I) = 10 \log \frac{10I}{I_0} - 10 \log \frac{I}{I_0}$

$= 10\left(\log \frac{10I}{I_0} - \log \frac{I}{I_0}\right)$

$= 10\left(\log 10 + \log \frac{I}{I_0} - \log \frac{I}{I_0}\right)$

$= 10 \log 10 = 10$ decibels

Lesson 7.6 (pp. 519–522)

15. $11^{5x} = 33$

$\log_{11} 11^{5x} = \log_{11} 33$

$5x = \log_{11} 33 = \dfrac{\log 33}{\log 11} \to x \approx 0.2916$

35. $5.2 \log_4 2x = 16$

$\log_4 2x \approx 3.0769$

$4^{(\log_4 2x)} \approx 4^{3.0769}$

$2x \approx 71.2020$

$x \approx 35.6010$

Check:

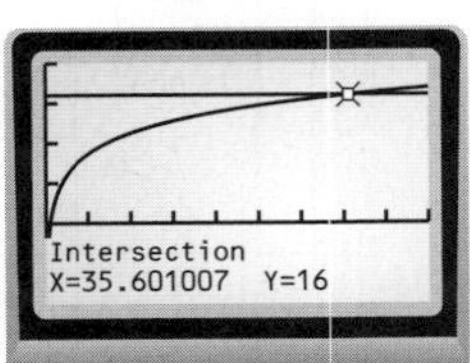

57. $R = 100e^{-0.00043t} \to 5 = 100e^{-0.00043t}$

$0.05 = e^{-0.00043t}$

$\ln 0.05 = \ln e^{-0.00043t}$

$-2.9957 \approx -0.00043t$

$t \approx 6967$ years

Lesson 7.7 (pp. 533–536)

11. $m = \dfrac{5.66 - 2.89}{5 - 1} \approx 0.69$

$\ln y - 2.89 = 0.69(x - 1)$

$\ln y = 0.69x + 2.2$

$y = e^{0.69x + 2.2}$

$y = e^{2.2}(e^{0.69})^x \approx 9(2)^x$

23.

ln x	0	0.693	1.099	1.386	1.609
ln y	−0.511	1.411	2.518	3.296	3.902

$m = \dfrac{3.902 - (-0.511)}{1.609 - 0} \approx 2.743$

$\ln y - (-0.511) = 2.743(\ln x - 0)$

$\ln y = \ln x^{2.743} - 0.511$

$y = e^{\ln x^{2.743} - 0.511}$

$y = e^{-0.511} \cdot e^{\ln x^{2.743}} \approx 0.6x^{2.743}$

33. a. A model is $y = 0.48(2.08)^x$.

b. Linear if a graph of (x, y) appears linear; exponential if a graph of $(x, \ln y)$ appears linear; power if a graph of $(\ln x, \ln y)$ appears linear. The graph of (x, y) appears linear, so a model is $y = 33.8x + 28$.

Chapter 8

Lesson 8.1 (pp. 554–557)

15. $y = \dfrac{a}{x} \to 2 = \dfrac{a}{7} \to 14 = a$

$y = \dfrac{14}{x} \to y = \dfrac{14}{3}$

21. $x \cdot y$: $12(132) = 1584$ $\quad y/x$: $132/12 = 11$

$18(198) = 3564$ $\quad 198/18 = 11$

$23(253) = 5819$ $\quad 253/23 = 11$

$29(319) = 9251$ $\quad 319/29 = 11$

$34(374) = 12{,}716$ $\quad 374/34 = 11$

x and y show direct variation because the ratios y/x are equal.

39. Snow shoes: $P = \dfrac{a}{A} \to 0.43 = \dfrac{a}{400} \to 172 = a$

An equation is $P = \dfrac{172}{A}$.

Boots: $P = \dfrac{172}{60} \to P \approx 2.87 \text{ lb/in.}^2$

Lesson 8.2 (pp. 561–563)

5.

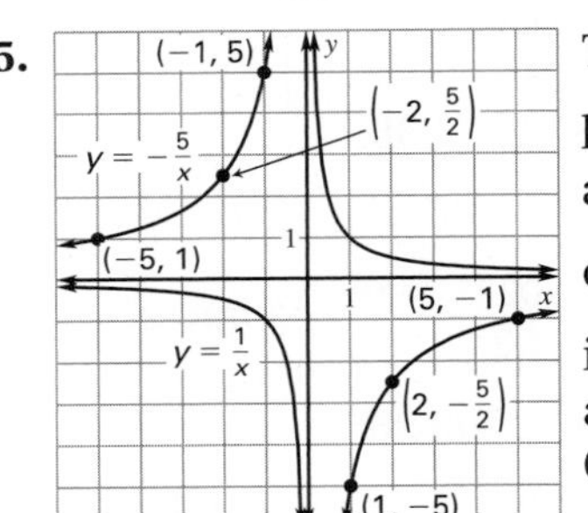

The graph of $y = \dfrac{-5}{x}$ lies farther from the axes than the graph of $y = \dfrac{1}{x}$, and it lies in Quadrants II and IV instead of Quadrants I and III.

21.

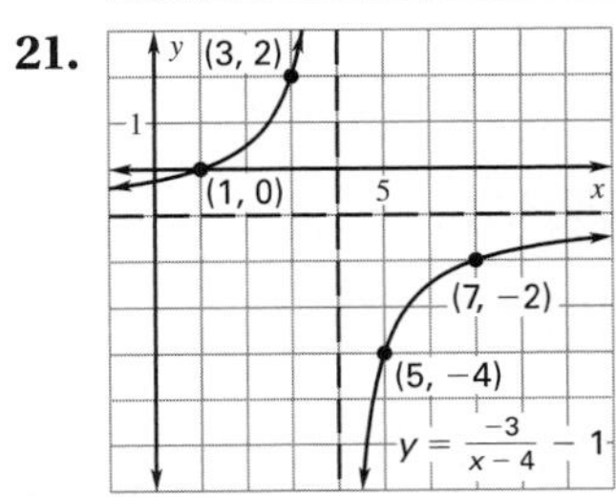

The domain is all real numbers except 4, and the range is all real numbers except −1.

39. a. $t = \dfrac{1000}{0.6T + 331} = \dfrac{1000}{0.6(25) + 331} \approx 2.89$

2.89 seconds to travel 1 kilometer; $2.89(5) = 14.45$ seconds to travel 5 kilometers

39. b.

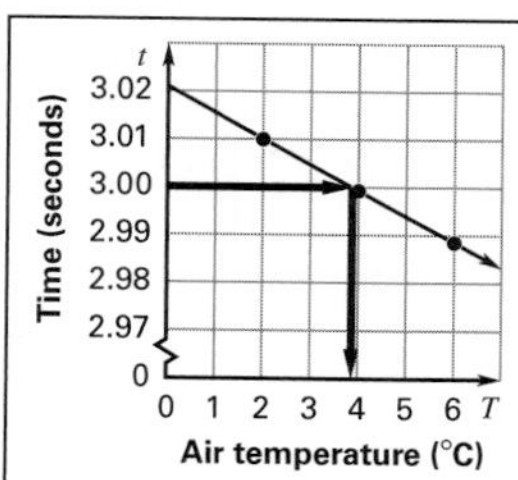

From the graph, you can estimate the temperature to be 3.9°C.

Lesson 8.3 (pp. 568–571)

7. $y = \frac{5}{x^2 - 1} \rightarrow y = \frac{5}{(x+1)(x-1)}$

No x-intercept; $x = -1$ and $x = 1$ are vertical asymptotes.

15.

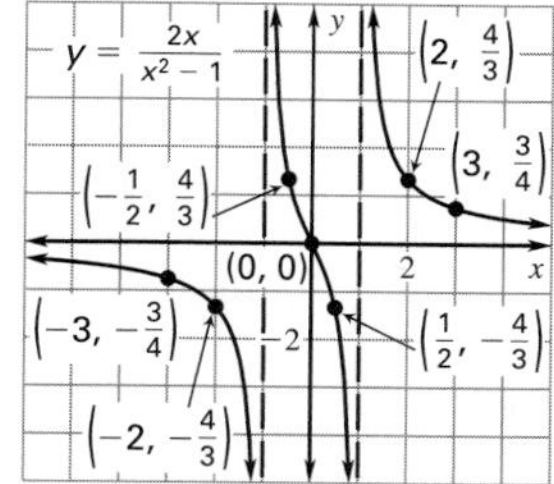

33. a.

Depth	Temp.
1000	4.7634
1050	4.5796
1100	4.4094
1150	4.2515
1200	4.1044
1250	3.9672
1300	3.8389

b.

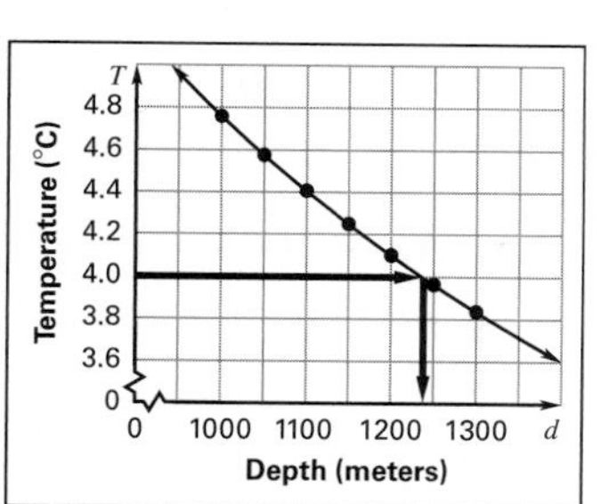

The mean temperature is 4°C at about 1238 meters.

Lesson 8.4 (pp. 577–580)

7. $\frac{(x-5)(x+4)}{(x+5)(x-3)}$ Cannot be simplified

25. $\frac{48x^7y^4}{6x^3y^6} = \frac{\not{6} \cdot 8 \cdot \not{x^3} \cdot x^4 \cdot \not{y^4}}{\not{6} \cdot \not{x^3} \cdot \not{y^4} \cdot y^2} = \frac{8x^4}{y^2}$

49.

$$S \div A = \frac{-6420t + 292{,}000}{6.02t^2 - 125t + 1000} \div \frac{-407t + 7220}{5.92t^2 - 131t + 1000}$$

$$= \frac{-6420t + 292{,}000}{6.02t^2 - 125t + 1000} \cdot \frac{5.92t^2 - 131t + 1000}{-407t + 7220}$$

For 1999, $t = 7$: $S \div A = \frac{247{,}060}{419.98} \cdot \frac{373.08}{4371} \approx \$50.21$

Lesson 8.5 (pp. 586–588)

5. $\frac{9}{x+1} - \frac{2x}{x+1} = \frac{9 - 2x}{x+1}$

17. $\frac{8}{3x^2} - \frac{5}{4x} = \frac{32}{12x^2} - \frac{15x}{12x^2} = \frac{32 - 15x}{12x^2}$

43. a. $M = \frac{Pi}{1 - \left(\frac{1}{1+i}\right)^{12t}} = \frac{Pi}{1 - \frac{1}{(1+i)^{12t}}}$

$$= \frac{Pi}{\frac{(1+i)^{12t} - 1}{(1+i)^{12t}}} = \frac{Pi(1+i)^{12t}}{(1+i)^{12t} - 1}$$

b. $P = 15{,}500$; $i = 0.005$; $t = 4$

$$m = \frac{15{,}500(0.005)(1 + 0.005)^{48}}{(1 + 0.005)^{48} - 1} \approx \$364.02$$

Lesson 8.6 (pp. 593–595)

5. $\frac{9}{3x} = \frac{4}{x+2}$ Check: $\frac{9}{3(6)} \stackrel{?}{=} \frac{4}{(6)+2}$

$4(3x) = 9(x+2)$ $\frac{9}{18} \stackrel{?}{=} \frac{4}{8}$

$x = 6$ $\frac{1}{2} = \frac{1}{2}$ ✓

15. $\frac{2}{3x} + \frac{1}{6} = \frac{4}{3x}$ Check: $\frac{2}{3(4)} + \frac{1}{6} \stackrel{?}{=} \frac{4}{3(4)}$

$6x\left(\frac{2}{3x} + \frac{1}{6}\right) = 6x\left(\frac{4}{3x}\right)$ $\frac{2}{12} + \frac{1}{6} \stackrel{?}{=} \frac{4}{12}$

$2(2) + 1(x) = 4(2) \rightarrow x = 4$ $\frac{4}{12} = \frac{4}{12}$ ✓

35.

$$n = \frac{635t^2 - 7350t + 27{,}200}{t^2 - 11.5t + 39.4}$$

$$720 = \frac{635t^2 - 7350t + 27{,}200}{t^2 - 11.5t + 39.4}$$

$$720t^2 - 8280t + 28{,}368 = 635t^2 - 7350t + 27{,}200$$

$$85t^2 - 930 + 1168 = 0$$

$$t = \frac{930 \pm \sqrt{(930)^2 - 4(1168)(85)}}{2(85)} \approx 1.45, 9.45$$

Because 9.45 is not in the domain ($0 \le t \le 9$), $t \approx 1.45 \rightarrow 1995$.

Chapter 9

Lesson 9.1 (pp. 617–619)

7. $d = \sqrt{(6-2)^2 + (-5 - (-1))^2} = 4\sqrt{2}$

Midpoint $= \left(\frac{2+6}{2}, \frac{-1 + (-5)}{2}\right) = (4, -3)$

27. $A(-4, 1), B(-2, 6), C(0, -1)$

$AB = \sqrt{(-2 - (-4))^2 + (6 - 1)^2} = \sqrt{29}$

$BC = \sqrt{(0 - (-2))^2 + (-1 - 6)^2} = \sqrt{53}$

$AC = \sqrt{(0 - (-4))^2 + (-1 - 1)^2} = \sqrt{20} = 2\sqrt{5}$

$AB \neq BC \neq AC$, so $\triangle ABC$ is scalene.

53. a. $M = \left(\frac{-6 + 3}{2}, \frac{5 + 11}{2}\right) = \left(-\frac{3}{2}, 8\right)$

b. $VS = \sqrt{(-6 - 0)^2 + (5 - 0)^2} = \sqrt{61}$

$SM = \sqrt{\left(-\frac{3}{2} - (-6)\right)^2 + (8 - 5)^2} = \frac{\sqrt{117}}{2}$

$VS + SM = \sqrt{61} + \frac{\sqrt{117}}{2}$

$\approx 13.2 \text{ units} \cdot \frac{0.1 \text{ mi}}{1 \text{ unit}} = 1.32 \text{ mi}$

c. $MP = \frac{\sqrt{117}}{2}$

$PV = \sqrt{(0 - 3)^2 + (0 - 11)^2} = \sqrt{130}$

$MP + PV = \frac{\sqrt{117}}{2} + \sqrt{130}$

$\approx 16.8 \text{ units} \cdot \frac{0.1 \text{ mi}}{1 \text{ unit}} = 1.68 \text{ mi}$

Lesson 9.2 (pp. 623–625)

15. $5x^2 = -15y \rightarrow x^2 = -3y$

$4p = -3 \rightarrow p = -\frac{3}{4}$

Focus: $\left(0, -\frac{3}{4}\right)$

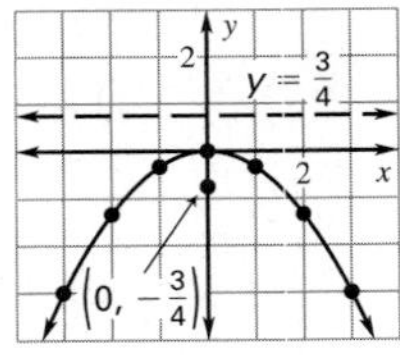

Directrix: $y = \frac{3}{4}$ Axis of symmetry: $x = 0$

27. Focus: $(-5, 0) \rightarrow p = -5 \rightarrow y^2 = -20x$

57. a.

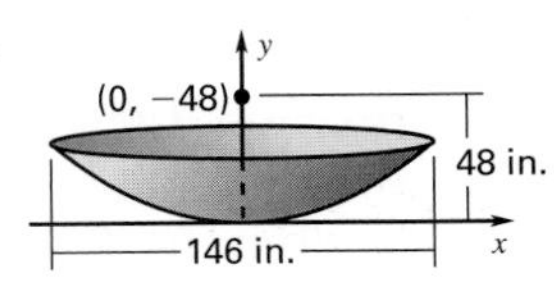

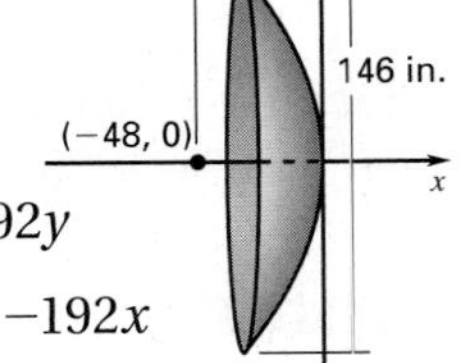

b. $x^2 = 4(48)y \rightarrow x^2 = 192y$

$y^2 = 4(-48)x \rightarrow y^2 = -192x$

c. Using $x^2 = 192y$ and $x = 73$, $y \approx 27.8$

Using $y^2 = -192x$ and $y = 73$, $x \approx -27.8$.

The dish is about 27.8 inches deep.

Lesson 9.3 (pp. 629–632)

17. $15x^2 + 15y^2 = 60$

$x^2 + y^2 = 4$

$r = \sqrt{4} = 2$

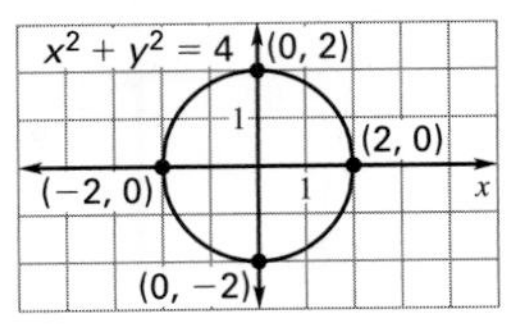

39. $r = \sqrt{(-8 - 0)^2 + (14 - 0)^2} = \sqrt{260}$

$x^2 + y^2 = (\sqrt{260})^2 \rightarrow x^2 + y^2 = 260$

65.

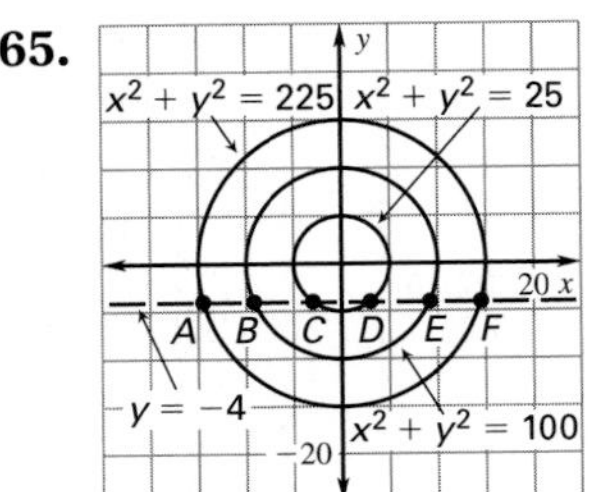

A: $x^2 + (-4)^2 = 225 \rightarrow x \approx \pm 14.5 \rightarrow (-14.5, -4)$

B: $x^2 + (-4)^2 = 100 \rightarrow x \approx \pm 9.2 \rightarrow (-9.2, -4)$

C: $x^2 + (-4)^2 = 25 \rightarrow x = \pm 3 \rightarrow (-3, -4)$

D: $x^2 + (-4)^2 = 25 \rightarrow x = \pm 3 \rightarrow (3, -4)$

E: $x^2 + (-4)^2 = 100 \rightarrow x \approx \pm 9.2 \rightarrow (9.2, -4)$

F: $x^2 + (-4)^2 = 225 \rightarrow x \approx \pm 14.5 \rightarrow (14.5, -4)$

a. $AF \approx |14.5 - (-14.5)| = 29$ mi

b. $BE \approx |9.2 - (-9.2)| = 18.4$ mi

c. $CD \approx |3 - (-3)| = 6$ mi

Lesson 9.4 (pp. 637–639)

11. $16x^2 + 9y^2 = 144$

$\frac{x^2}{9} + \frac{y^2}{16} = 1$; $a = 4$, $b = 3$

Vertices: $(0, \pm 4)$;

Co-vertices: $(\pm 3, 0)$;

Foci: $(0, \pm\sqrt{7})$

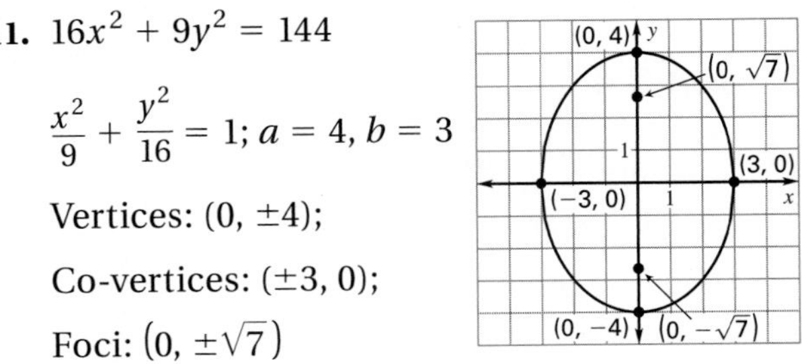

29. $b = \sqrt{7}$; $c = 3$; $a^2 = b^2 + c^2 \rightarrow a = 4$

$\frac{x^2}{4^2} + \frac{y^2}{(\sqrt{7})^2} = 1$, or $\frac{x^2}{16} + \frac{y^2}{7} = 1$

49. Largest field:

$2a = 185 \rightarrow a = 92.5$; $2b = 155 \rightarrow b = 77.5$

$\frac{x^2}{77.5^2} + \frac{y^2}{92.5^2} = 1$, or $\frac{x^2}{6006.25} + \frac{y^2}{8556.25} = 1$

$A = \pi(92.5)(77.5) \approx 22{,}521$ square meters

Smallest field:

$2a = 135 \rightarrow a = 67.5;\ 2b = 110 \rightarrow b = 55$

$$\frac{x^2}{55^2} + \frac{y^2}{67.5^2} = 1, \text{ or } \frac{x^2}{3025} + \frac{y^2}{4556.25} = 1$$

$A = \pi(67.5)(55) \approx 11{,}663$ square meters

$11{,}663 \le A \le 22{,}521$

Lesson 9.5 (pp. 645–648)

13. $81x^2 - 16y^2 = 1296$

$$\frac{x^2}{16} - \frac{y^2}{81} = 1$$

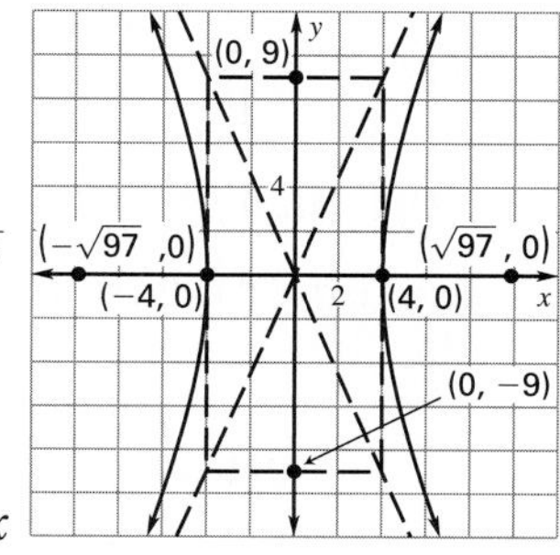

$a = 4;\ b = 9;\ c = \sqrt{97}$

Vertices: $(\pm 4, 0)$

Foci: $(\pm\sqrt{97}, 0)$

Asymptotes: $y = \pm\frac{9}{4}x$

23. $c = 4\sqrt{5};\ a = 4;\ b^2 = c^2 - a^2 - a \rightarrow b = 8$

$$\frac{y^2}{4^2} - \frac{x^2}{8^2} = 1, \text{ or } \frac{y^2}{16} - \frac{x^2}{64} = 1$$

41. a. $A(30.5, 0);\ B(85, -40)$

b. Vertices: $(\pm 30.5, 0)$; horizontal trans. axis

$$\frac{x^2}{a^2} - \frac{y^2}{b^2} = 1 \rightarrow \frac{x^2}{30.5^2} - \frac{y^2}{b^2} = 1$$

$$\frac{85^2}{30.5^2} - \frac{(-40)^2}{b^2} = 1 \rightarrow b^2 \approx 236.5$$

So, an equation is $\frac{x^2}{930.25} - \frac{y^2}{236.5} = 1.$

c. $x = 42$: $\frac{42^2}{930.25} - \frac{y^2}{236.5} = 1 \rightarrow y \approx 14.6$

$h = 40 + 14.6 = 54.6$ feet

Lesson 9.6 (pp. 655–657)

3. $(x + 4)^2 = -8(y - 2)$

Parabola; vertical axis; vertex at $(h, k) = (-4, 2)$.

$4p = -8 \rightarrow p = -2$

Focus: $(h, k + p) = (-4, 0)$

Directrix: $y = k - p \rightarrow y = 4$

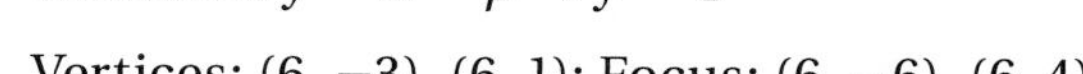

19. Vertices: $(6, -3), (6, 1)$; Focus: $(6, -6), (6, 4)$

Vertical transverse axis; $\frac{(y - k)^2}{a^2} - \frac{(x - h)^2}{b^2} = 1$

Center: $(h, k) = \left(\frac{6 + 6}{2}, \frac{-3 + 1}{2}\right)$

Distance between vertex $(6, -3)$ and (h, k):

$a = |-3 - k| = |-3 - (-1)| = 2$

Distance between focus $(6, -6)$ and (h, k):

$c = |-6 - k| = |-6 - (-1)| = 5$

$b^2 = c^2 - a^2 = 25 - 4 = 21 \rightarrow b = \sqrt{21}$

An equation is $\frac{(y + 1)^2}{4} - \frac{(x - 6)^2}{21} = 1.$

49. $x^2 - 10x + 4y = 0;\ A = 1, B = 0, C = 0$

$B^2 - 4AC = 0 - 4(1)(0) = 0 \rightarrow$ Parabola

$x^2 - 10x + 4y = 0$

$(x^2 - 10x + 25) = -4y + 25$

$$(x - 5)^2 = -4\left(y - \frac{25}{4}\right)$$

$(h, k) = \left(5, \frac{25}{4}\right)$; height $= \frac{25}{4} = 6.25$ feet

When $y = 0$, the x-intercepts are 0 and 10, so the distance of the jump is 10 feet.

Lesson 9.7 (pp. 661–664)

5.

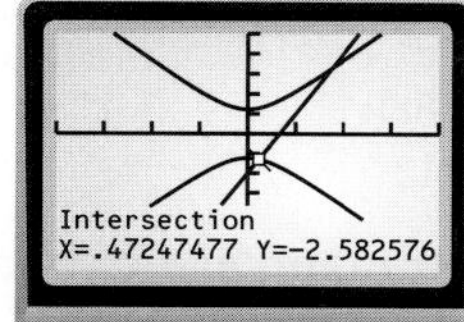

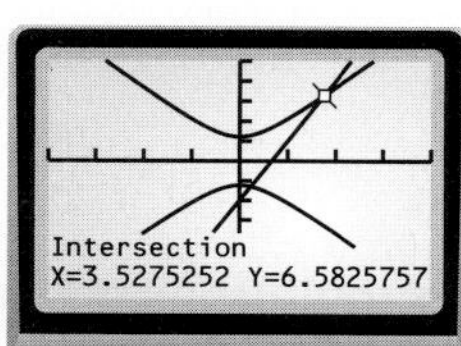

The solutions are approximately $(0.5, -2.6)$ and $(3.5, 6.6)$.

15. $4x^2 - 5y^2 = -76$

$2x + y = -6 \rightarrow y = -2x - 6$

Substitute $-2x - 6$ for y in Equation 1.

$$4x^2 - 5(-2x - 6)^2 = -76$$

$$4x^2 - 20x^2 - 120x - 180 = -76$$

$$-16x^2 - 120x - 104 = 0$$

$$2x^2 + 15x + 13 = 0$$

$$(2x + 2)\left(x + \frac{13}{2}\right) = 0 \rightarrow x = -1, x = -\frac{13}{2}$$

When $x = -1$: $y = -2(-1) - 6 = -4$

When $x = -\frac{13}{2}$: $y = -2\left(-\frac{13}{2}\right) - 6 = 7$

The solutions are $(-1, -4)$ and $\left(-\frac{13}{2}, 7\right)$.

41. a. Oak Lane: $m = -\frac{1}{7}$, $(x_1, y_1) = (-2, 1)$

$$y - 1 = -\frac{1}{7}(x + 2) \rightarrow y = -\frac{1}{7}x + \frac{5}{7}$$

Circle: $x^2 + y^2 = 1$

b. $$x^2 + \left(-\frac{1}{7}x + \frac{5}{7}\right)^2 = 1$$

$$x^2 + \frac{1}{49}x^2 - \frac{10}{49}x + \frac{25}{49} = 1$$

$$49x^2 + x^2 - 10x + 25 = 49$$

$$50x^2 - 10x - 24 = 0$$

$$(5x - 4)(10x + 6) = 0 \rightarrow x = \frac{4}{5}, x = -\frac{3}{5}$$

$$y = -\frac{1}{7}\left(\frac{4}{5}\right) + \frac{5}{7} = \frac{3}{5}; y = -\frac{1}{7}\left(-\frac{3}{5}\right) + \frac{5}{7} = \frac{4}{5}$$

The solutions are $\left(\frac{4}{5}, \frac{3}{5}\right)$ and $\left(-\frac{3}{5}, \frac{4}{5}\right)$.

c. $d = \sqrt{\left(-\frac{3}{5} - \frac{4}{5}\right)^2 + \left(\frac{4}{5} - \frac{3}{5}\right)^2} = \sqrt{2} \approx 1.4$ mi

Chapter 10

Lesson 10.1 (pp. 686–689)

13. a. $26 \cdot 26 \cdot 26 \cdot 26 \cdot 10 \cdot 10 = 45{,}697{,}600$

b. $26 \cdot 25 \cdot 24 \cdot 23 \cdot 10 \cdot 9 = 32{,}292{,}000$

35. $_9P_2 = \frac{9!}{(9-2)!} = \frac{9!}{7!} = \frac{362{,}880}{5040} = 72$

65. Permutations of 9 objects taken 3 at a time:

$$_9P_3 = \frac{9!}{(9-3)!} = \frac{9!}{6!} = \frac{362{,}880}{720} = 504 \text{ ways}$$

Lesson 10.2 (pp. 694–697)

17. *Exactly one queen*: Choose 1 of the 4 queens and 4 of the 48 that are not queens.

$$_4C_1 \cdot {_{48}C_4} = \frac{4!}{3!1!} \cdot \frac{48!}{44!4!} = 778{,}320$$

No queen: Choose 5 cards from the 48 in a deck that are not queens.

$$_{48}C_5 = \frac{48!}{43!5!} = 1{,}712{,}304$$

The total number of possible hands is $778{,}320 + 1{,}712{,}304 = 2{,}490{,}624$.

29. $(2s^4 + 5)^5 = {_5C_0}(2s^4)^5 5^0 + {_5C_1}(2s^4)^4 5^1 + {_5C_2}(2s^4)^3 5^2 + {_5C_3}(2s^4)^2 5^3 + {_5C_4}(2s^4)^1 5^4 + {_5C_5}(2s^4)^0 5^5 = 1(32s^{20}) + 5(16s^{16})(5) + 10(8s^{12})(25) + 10(4s^8)(125) + 5(2s^4)(625) + 1(1)(3125) = 32s^{20} + 400s^{16} + 2000s^{12} + 5000s^8 + 6250s^4 + 3125$

49. You can choose 3 of the 18 types of flowers.

$$_{18}C_3 = \frac{18!}{15!3!} = \frac{18 \cdot 17 \cdot 16 \cdot \cancel{15!}}{\cancel{15!} \cdot 3!} = 816$$

Lesson 10.3 (pp. 702–704)

7. Factors of 150 from 1 to 50: 1, 2, 3, 5, 6, 10, 15, 25, 30, 50

$$P = \frac{\text{Factors of 150}}{\text{Integers from 1 to 50}} = \frac{10}{50} = \frac{1}{5}$$

17. There are $_{48}C_6$ different combinations of 6 numbers. Only 1 is the correct combination.

$$P(\text{correct numbers}) = \frac{1}{_{48}C_6} = \frac{1}{12{,}271{,}512}$$

39. $P = \frac{\text{Area of smallest circle}}{\text{Area of entire target}} = \frac{\pi \cdot 8^2}{\pi \cdot 40^2} = \frac{1}{25} = 0.04$

Lesson 10.4 (pp. 710–713)

11. $P(A \text{ or } B) = P(A) + P(B) - P(A \text{ and } B)$

$$0.71 = 0.28 + 0.64 - P(A \text{ and } B)$$

$$-0.21 = -P(A \text{ and } B) \rightarrow P(A \text{ and } B) = 0.21$$

21. $P(\text{K or } \blacklozenge) = P(\text{K}) + P(\blacklozenge) - P(\text{K and } \blacklozenge)$

$$= \left(\frac{4}{52}\right) + \left(\frac{13}{52}\right) - \left(\frac{1}{52}\right) = \frac{4}{13}$$

45. The number of combinations of 6 food items is 10^6. The number of combinations of 6 different food items is $10 \cdot 9 \cdot 8 \cdot 7 \cdot 6 \cdot 5$. So, the probability that at least 2 bring the same item is $P = 1 - P(\text{none are the same}) = 1 - \frac{10 \cdot 9 \cdot 8 \cdot 7 \cdot 6 \cdot 5}{10^6} = 0.8488$.

Lesson 10.5 (pp. 721–723)

13. $P = P(\text{blue}) \cdot P(\text{green}) \cdot P(\text{red})$

$$= \left(\frac{3}{16}\right) \cdot \left(\frac{4}{16}\right) \cdot \left(\frac{5}{16}\right) = \frac{60}{4096} \approx 0.015$$

25. Primes from 1 to 20: 2, 3, 5, 7, 11, 13, 17, 19.

$$P(\text{odd}\,|\,\text{prime}) = \frac{P(\text{number of odd primes})}{P(\text{number of primes})} = \frac{7}{8}$$

39.

Total # of matches → 0.5 → Event *A*: player wins toss → 0.55 → Event *C*: player wins

Event *A*: player wins toss → 0.45 → Event *D*: player loses

Total # of matches → 0.5 → Event *B*: player loses toss → 0.47 → Event *C*: player wins

Event *B*: player loses toss → 0.53 → Event *D*: player loses

$$P(C) = P(A \text{ and } C) + P(B \text{ and } C)$$
$$= P(A) \cdot P(C|A) + P(B) \cdot P(C|B)$$
$$= (0.50) \cdot (0, 55) + (0, 50)(0.47) = 0.51$$

Lesson 10.6 (pp. 727–730)

5.

N	Outcomes	*P*(*N*)
1	10	$\frac{10}{100} = \frac{1}{100}$
2	90	$\frac{90}{1000} = \frac{9}{100}$
3	900	$\frac{900}{1000} = \frac{9}{10}$

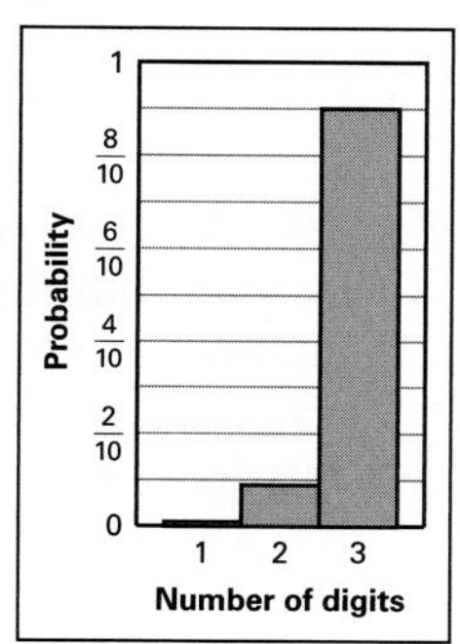

21. Each question has 4 possible answers, so the probability of guessing a correct answer is $p = 0.25$. There are 30 questions, so $n = 30$. The probability of randomly guessing 11 correct answers is $P(k = 11) = {}_{30}C_{11}(0.25)^{11}(1 - 0.25)^{30 - 11} \approx 0.055$.

45. a. $p = 0.34$;

$$P(k = 5) = {}_{10}C_5(0.34)^5(1 - 0.34)^{10 - 5} \approx 0.14$$

b. $p = P(\text{Rh}^-) = P(\text{O}^-) + P(\text{A}^-) + P(\text{B}^-) + P(\text{AB}^-)$
$= 0.15$

$$P(k = 2) = {}_{10}C_2(0.15)^2(1 - 0.15)^{10 - 2} \approx 0.28$$

c. $p = P(\text{O}) = P(\text{O}^+) + P(\text{O}^-) = 0.43$

$$P(k = 0) = {}_{10}C_0(0.43)^0(1 - 0.43)^{10 - 0} \approx 0.004$$
$$P(k = 1) = {}_{10}C_1(0.43)^1(1 - 0.43)^{10 - 1} \approx 0.027$$
$$P(k = 2) = {}_{10}C_2(0.43)^2(1 - 0.43)^{10 - 2} \approx 0.093$$
$$P(k \le 2) = P(k = 0) + P(k = 1) + P(k = 2)$$
$$\approx 0.124$$

d. $p = P(\text{Rh}^+) = P(\text{O}^+) + \text{P}(\text{A}^+) + P(\text{B}^+)$
$+ P(\text{AB}^+) = 0.85$

$$P(k = 5) = {}_{10}C_5(0.85)^5(1 - 0.85)^{10 - 5} \approx 0.008$$
$$P(k = 6) = {}_{10}C_6(0.85)^6(1 - 0.85)^{10 - 6} \approx 0.040$$
$$P(k = 7) = {}_{10}C_7(0.85)^7(1 - 0.85)^{10 - 7} \approx 0.130$$
$$P(k = 8) = {}_{10}C_8(0.85)^8(1 - 0.85)^{10 - 8} \approx 0.276$$
$$P(k = 9) = {}_{10}C_9(0.85)^9(1 - 0.85)^{10 - 9} \approx 0.347$$
$$P(k = 10) = {}_{10}C_{10}(0.85)^{10}(1 - 0.85)^{10 - 10} \approx 0.197$$
$$P(k \ge 5) = P(k = 5) + P(k = 6) + \text{P}(k = 7)$$
$$+ P(k = 8) + P(k = 9) + P(k = 10) \approx 0.998$$

Chapter 11

Lesson 11.1 (pp. 747–749)

5. Mean:

$$\frac{69 + 70 + 75 + 84 + 73 + 78 + 74 + 73 + 78 + 71}{10}$$
$$= 74.5$$

Median: ~~69~~, ~~70~~, ~~71~~, ~~73~~, 73, 74, ~~75~~, ~~78~~, ~~78~~, ~~84~~

$$\frac{73 + 74}{2} = 73.5$$

Mode: 73 and 78

15. Range: $158 - 135 = 23$

$$\bar{x} = \frac{135 + 142 + 148 + 136 + 152 + 140 + 158 + 154}{8}$$
$$= 145.625$$

$$\sigma = \sqrt{\frac{(135 - 145.625)^2 + (142 - 145.625)^2 + \cdots + (154 - 145.625)^2}{8}}$$
$$= \sqrt{\frac{519.875}{8}} \approx 8.1$$

29. a. The outlier is 5.

b. *With outlier*:

Mean: $\bar{x} = \frac{20 + 23 + \cdots + 23}{10} = 20.2$

Median: 22 Mode: 23 Range: $25 - 5 = 20$

Std. Dev.:

$$\sigma = \frac{(20 - 20.2)^2 + (23 - 20.2)^2 + \cdots + (23 - 20.2)^2}{10}$$
$$\approx 5.4$$

WORKED-OUT SOLUTIONS

Without outlier:

Mean: $\bar{x} = \frac{20 + 23 + \cdots + 23}{9} \approx 21.9$

Median: 23 Mode: 23 Range: $25 - 19 = 6$

Std. Dev.:

$$\sigma = \sqrt{\frac{(20 - 20.2)^2 + (23 - 20.2)^2 + \cdots + (23 - 20.2)^2}{9}}$$

≈ 2.1

c. The outlier causes the mean and median to decrease, and the range and standard deviation to increase. The mode stays the same.

Lesson 11.2 (pp. 753–755)

5.

	Original data set	Adding 17 to data values
Mean	78	78 + 17 = 95
Median	77	77 + 17 = 94
Mode	77	77 + 17 = 94
Range	9	9
Standard deviation	2.8	2.8

11.

	Original data set	Multiplying data values by 4
Mean	61.9	61.9(4) = 247.6
Median	62	62(4) = 248
Mode	58	58(4) = 232
Range	9	9(4) = 36
Standard deviation	3.4	3.4(4) = 13.6

19.

	Heights without stilts	Heights with stilts
Mean	70.8	70.8 + 28 = 98.8
Median	72	72 + 28 = 100
Mode	72	72 + 28 = 100
Range	8	8
Standard deviation	2.4	2.4

Lesson 11.3 (pp. 760–762)

3. $P(x \le \bar{x} - \sigma) = 0.0015 + 0.0235 + 0.135 = 0.16$

11. 29 and 37 are one standard deviation on either side of the mean, which accounts for 68% of the data. So, the probability is 0.68.

33. a. 19.4 ounces: $z = \frac{19.4 - 20}{0.25} = -2.4$

20.4 ounces: $z = \frac{20.4 - 20}{0.25} = 1.6$

b. The table shows that $P(x \le -2.4) = 0.0082$. So, the probability is 0.0082.

c. $P(x \le 20.4) = 0.9452$; $P(x \le 19.4) = 0.0082$

$P(x \le 20.4) - P(x \le 19.4) = 0.937$

Lesson 11.4 (pp. 769–771)

7. Margin of error $= \pm\frac{1}{\sqrt{n}} = \pm\frac{1}{\sqrt{1000}} \approx \pm 0.032$

The margin of error is about $\pm 3.2\%$.

19. Margin of error $= \pm\frac{1}{\sqrt{n}}$

$\pm 0.056 = \pm\frac{1}{\sqrt{n}}$

$0.003136 = \frac{1}{n} \rightarrow n \approx 319$

29. *Sample answer*: It is not reasonable to assume that Kosta is going to win the election, because the margin of error is $\pm 5\%$. If the margin of error works in favor of Murdock, Kosta will have 49% (54% − 5%) and Murdock will have 51% (46% + 5%).

Lesson 11.5 (pp. 778–780)

3. Model: $y = -0.38x^2 + 1.1x + 16$

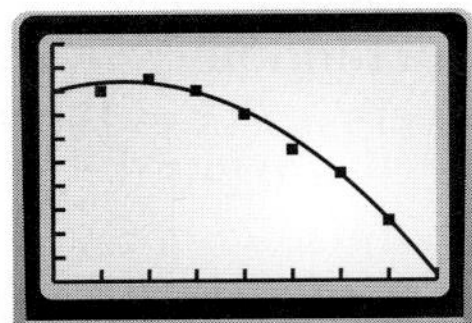

11. A model for the data is $y = 0.00211x^3 - 0.0766x^2 + 1.26x - 0.0664$.

Chapter 12

Lesson 12.1 (pp. 798–800)

19. $\frac{2}{3 \cdot 1}, \frac{2}{3 \cdot 2}, \frac{2}{3 \cdot 3}, \frac{2}{3 \cdot 4}, \ldots$

Next term: $\frac{2}{3 \cdot 5} = \frac{2}{15}$; A rule is $a_n = \frac{2}{3n}$.

47. $\sum_{n=0}^{4} n^3 = 0^3 + 1^3 + 2^3 + 3^3 + 4^3$

$= 0 + 1 + 8 + 27 + 64 = 100$

65.

n	1	2	3	4	5
a_n	1	3	7	15	31

A formula for the sequence is $a_n = 2^n - 1$.

$a_6 = 2^6 - 1 = 63$ moves for 6 rings

$a_7 = 2^7 - 1 = 127$ moves for 7 rings

$a_8 = 2^8 - 1 = 255$ moves for 8 rings

Lesson 12.2 (pp. 806–809)

15. Arithmetic sequence

$a_1 = -3; d = -1 - (-3) = 2$

A rule for the nth term is

$a_n = a_1 + (n-1)d = -3 + (n-1)2 = 2n - 5$

$a_{20} = 2(20) - 5 = 35$

41. $\sum_{i=1}^{8} (-3 - 2i)$

$a_1 = -3 - 2(1) = -5; a_8 = -3 - 2(8) = -19$

$s_8 = 8\left(\frac{-5 + (-19)}{2}\right) = -96$

65. a. $a_1 = 4; d = 8$

$a_n = a_1 + (n-1)d = 4 + (n-1)8 = -4 + 8n$

b. $a_{12} + a_{11} + \cdots + a_2 + a_1 = 576$ blocks

Lesson 12.3 (pp. 814–817)

19. Geometric sequence; $a_1 = 2; r = \frac{\frac{3}{2}}{2} = \frac{3}{4}$

$a_n = a_1 r^{n-1} = 2\left(\frac{3}{4}\right)^{n-1}$

$a_7 = 2\left(\frac{3}{4}\right)^{7-1} = \frac{1458}{4096} = \frac{729}{2048}$

49. $\sum_{i=1}^{8} 6(4)^{i-1}$

$a_1 = 6(4)^{1-1} = 6; r = 4$

$s_8 = a_1\left(\frac{1 - r^8}{1 - r}\right) = 6\left(\frac{1 - 4^8}{1 - 4}\right) = 131{,}070$

59. a. $a_1 = 1024 \div 2 = 512; r = \frac{1}{2}$

$a_n = a_1(r)^{n-1} = 512\left(\frac{1}{2}\right)^{n-1}$

b. $n = 10$; after 10 passes, the number of items remaining is $a_{10} = 512\left(\frac{1}{2}\right)^{10-1} = 1$.

Lesson 12.4 (pp. 823–825)

13. $\sum_{k=1}^{\infty} 7\left(-\frac{8}{9}\right)^{k-1}$

$a_1 = 7; r = -\frac{8}{9}; s = \frac{a_1}{1 - r} = \frac{7}{1 - \left(-\frac{8}{9}\right)} = \frac{63}{17}$

27. $625(0.001) + 625(0.001)^2 + 625(0.001)^3 + \cdots$

$= \frac{a_1}{1 - r} = \frac{625(0.001)}{1 - 0.001} = \frac{0.625}{0.999} = \frac{625}{999}$

39. D;

$n = 345 + 345(0.783) + 345(0.783)^2 + 345(0.783)^3 + \cdots$

$= \frac{a_1}{1 - r} = \frac{345}{1 - 0.783} \approx 1.59$ billion

Lesson 12.5 (pp. 830–833)

15. Geometric sequence; $a_1 = 4; r = -3$

$a_n = r \cdot a_{n-1} = -3a_{n-1}$

A recursive rule is $a_1 = 4, a_n = -3a_{n-1}$.

27. $f(x) = \frac{1}{2}x - 3, x_0 = 2$

$x_1 = f(x_0)$	$x_2 = f(x_1)$	$x_3 = f(x_2)$
$= f(2)$	$= f(-2)$	$= f(-4)$
$= \frac{1}{2}(2) - 3$	$= \frac{1}{2}(-2) - 3$	$= \frac{1}{2}(-4) - 3$
$= -2$	$= -4$	$= -5$

45. Recursive rule:

$a_1 = 2000, a_n = 1.014a_{n-1} - 100.$

Because $a_{24} = 62.14$, the balance at the beginning of the 24th month is \$62.14. So, she will be able to pay off the balance at the end of the 24th month.

Chapter 13

Lesson 13.1 (pp. 856–858)

5.

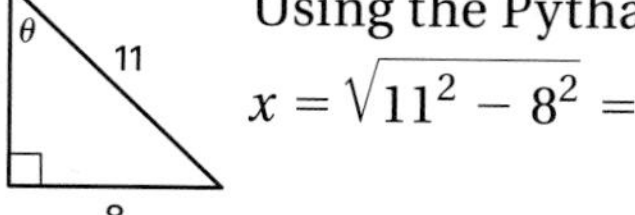

Using the Pythagorean theorem:

$x = \sqrt{11^2 - 8^2} = \sqrt{57}$

$\sin \theta = \frac{8}{11}$ $\cos \theta = \frac{\sqrt{57}}{11}$ $\tan \theta = \frac{8\sqrt{57}}{57}$

$\csc \theta = \frac{11}{8}$ $\sec \theta = \frac{11\sqrt{57}}{57}$ $\cot \theta = \frac{\sqrt{57}}{8}$

WORKED-OUT SOLUTIONS

11. $\tan\theta = \frac{\text{opp}}{\text{adj}} = \frac{7}{3}$

$x = \sqrt{7^2 + 3^2} = \sqrt{58}$

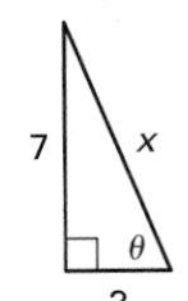

$\sin\theta = \frac{7\sqrt{58}}{58}$ $\cos\theta = \frac{3\sqrt{58}}{58}$ $\tan\theta = \frac{7}{3}$

$\csc\theta = \frac{\sqrt{58}}{7}$ $\sec\theta = \frac{\sqrt{58}}{3}$ $\cot\theta = \frac{3}{7}$

33. $\tan 15^\circ = \frac{d}{1500}$

$d \approx 402$

The total depth is $402 + 250 = 652$ feet.

As the angle of the dive increases, the depth increases.

Lesson 13.2 (pp. 862–865)

11. $\frac{5\pi}{18} = \frac{5\pi \text{ radians}}{18}\left(\frac{180^\circ}{\pi \text{ radians}}\right) = 50^\circ$

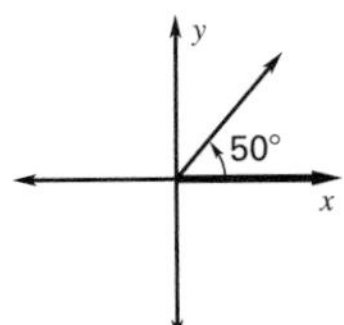

23. $40^\circ = 40^\circ\left(\frac{\pi \text{ radians}}{180^\circ}\right) = \frac{2\pi}{9}$ radians

51. a. $\frac{15 \text{ rev}}{1 \text{ min}}\left(\frac{1 \text{ min}}{60 \text{ sec}}\right)\left(\frac{2\pi \text{ rad}}{1 \text{ rev}}\right) = \frac{\pi}{2}$ rad/sec

b. Arc length: $s = r\theta = 29\left(\frac{\pi}{2}\right) \approx 45.6$ feet

Lesson 13.3 (pp. 870–872)

5. $r = \sqrt{x^2 + y^2} = \sqrt{(-7)^2 + (-24)^2} = \sqrt{625} = 25$

$\sin\theta = \frac{y}{r} = \frac{-24}{25}$ $\cos\theta = \frac{x}{f} = \frac{-7}{25}$

$\tan\theta = \frac{y}{x} = \frac{-24}{-7} = \frac{24}{7}$ $\csc\theta = \frac{r}{y} = \frac{-25}{24}$

$\sec\theta = \frac{r}{x} = \frac{-25}{7}$ $\cot\theta = \frac{x}{y} = \frac{7}{24}$

17. $\theta' = 180^\circ - 150^\circ = 30^\circ$

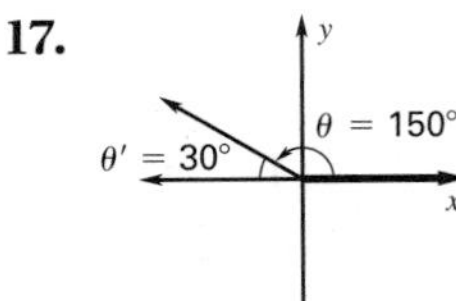

37.

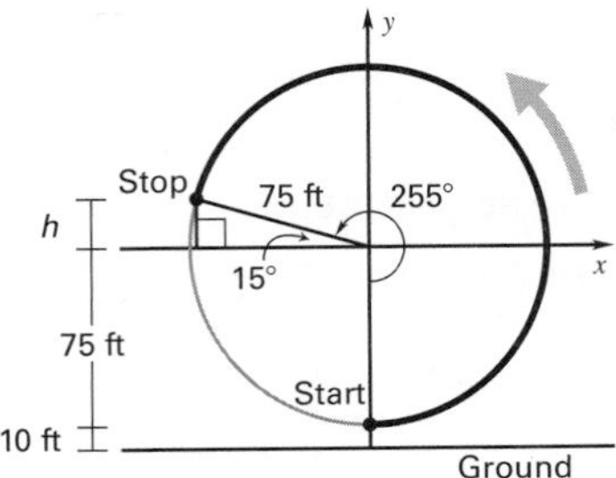

$\theta' = 270^\circ - 255^\circ = 15^\circ$

$\sin 15^\circ = \frac{h}{75}$

$19.4 \approx h$

When the ride stops, you are about $10 + 75 + 19.4 = 104.4$ feet above the ground. If the radius is doubled, your height above the ground is doubled only if your starting height above the ground is also doubled.

Lesson 13.4 (pp. 878–880)

7. When $-\frac{\pi}{2} \le \theta \le \frac{\pi}{2}$, or $-90^\circ \le \theta \le 90^\circ$, the angle whose sine is $\frac{\sqrt{3}}{2}$ is $\theta = \sin^{-1}\frac{\sqrt{3}}{2} = \frac{\pi}{3}$, or $\theta = \sin^{-1}\frac{\sqrt{3}}{2} = 60^\circ$.

23.

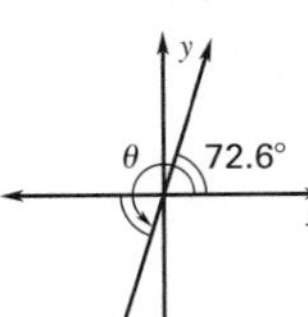

$\tan\theta = 3.2$; $180^\circ < \theta < 270^\circ$

$\tan^{-1}(3.2) \approx 72.6^\circ$, which is in Quadrant I. To find the angle in Quadrant III ($180^\circ < \theta < 270^\circ$): $\theta \approx 180 + 72.6 = 252.6^\circ$

37. $\tan\theta = \frac{11}{17}$

$\theta = \tan^{-1}\left(\frac{11}{17}\right) \approx 33^\circ$

Because the angle of repose remains the same, you can use $\theta = 33^\circ$ to find the radius of the 15 foot high pile:

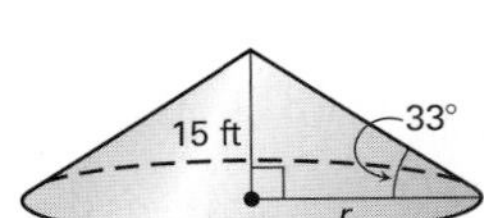

$\tan 33^\circ = \frac{15}{r} \rightarrow r = \frac{15}{\tan 33^\circ}$

≈ 23

The diameter is about $d = 2r = 2(23) = 46$ ft.

Lesson 13.5 (pp. 886–888)

13. $\frac{\sin B}{16} = \frac{\sin 104°}{25}$

$\sin B = \frac{16 \sin 104°}{25} \approx 0.6210 \rightarrow B \approx 38.4°$

$A \approx 180° - 104° - 38.4° = 37.6°$

$\frac{a}{\sin 37.6°} = \frac{25}{\sin 104°} \rightarrow a = \frac{25 \sin 37.6°}{\sin 104°} \approx 15.7$

45. a.

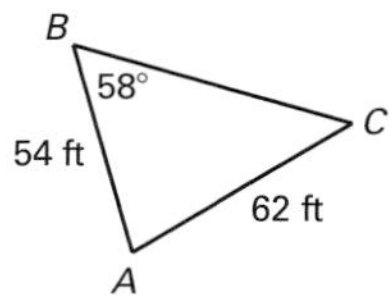

b. $\frac{\sin C}{54} = \frac{\sin 58°}{62}$

$\sin C = \frac{54 \sin 58°}{62} \approx 0.7386 \rightarrow C \approx 47.6°$

$A \approx 180° - 58° - 47.6° = 74.4°$

$\frac{a}{\sin 74.4°} = \frac{62}{\sin 58°} \rightarrow a = \frac{62 \sin 74.4°}{\sin 58°} \approx 70.4$

c. Area $= \frac{1}{2} bc \sin A = \frac{1}{2}(62)(54)(\sin 74.4°)$

≈ 1612

$1612 \text{ ft}^2 \div 200 \text{ ft}^2/\text{bag} \approx 8.1$ bags

You will need 9 bags of fertilizer.

Lesson 13.6 (pp. 892–894)

17. $a^2 = b^2 + c^2 - 2bc \cos A$

$10^2 = 3^2 + 12^2 - 2(3)(12)\cos A$

$\frac{53}{72} = \cos A \rightarrow A \approx 43°$

$\frac{10}{\sin 43°} = \frac{3}{\sin B} \rightarrow \frac{3(\sin 43°)}{10} = \sin B$

$B \approx 12°$; $C \approx 180 - 43° - 12° = 125°$

In $\triangle ABC$, $A \approx 43°$, $B \approx 12°$, and $C \approx 125°$.

25. $s = \frac{1}{2}(a + b + c) = \frac{1}{2}(5 + 11 + 10) = 13$

Area $= \sqrt{s(s - a)(sb)(s - c)}$

$= \sqrt{13(13 - 5)(13 - 11)(13 - 10)} = \sqrt{624}$

≈ 25 square units

45. $\triangle ADB$: $s = \frac{1}{2}(743 + 1210 + 1480) = 1716.5$

Area =

$\sqrt{1716.5(1716.5 - 743)(1716.5 - 1210)(1716.5 - 1480)}$

$\approx 447{,}399$

$\triangle CDB$: $s = \frac{1}{2}(1000 + 858 + 1480) = 1669$

Area =

$\sqrt{1669(1669 - 1000)(1669 - 858)(1669 - 1480)}$

$\approx 413{,}697$

Area $= (447{,}399 + 413{,}697) \text{ ft}^2 \left(\frac{1 \text{ acre}}{43{,}560 \text{ ft}^2}\right)$

≈ 20 acres

If you first found the length of $\overline{AC}$, you could repeat the same process using $\triangle ABC$ and $\triangle ADC$.

Chapter 14

Lesson 14.1 (pp. 912–914)

5. Amplitude: 1; period: 2

17. $f(x) = 4 \tan x$

Period: π; intercept: $(0, 0)$

Asymptotes: $x = \pm\frac{\pi}{2}$

Halfway points: $\left(\frac{\pi}{4}, 4\right)\left(-\frac{\pi}{4}, -4\right)$

31. a. Equation has the form $y = a \cos bt$.

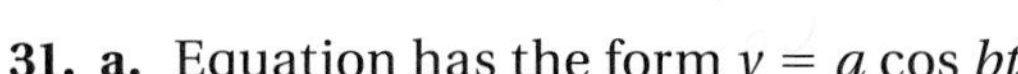

$a = \frac{1}{2}(3.5) = 1.75$

Period is 6, so $6 = \frac{2\pi}{b} \rightarrow b = \frac{\pi}{3}$.

Equation is $y = 1.75 \cos \frac{\pi}{3} t$.

b. Choose $y = a \cos bt$ because at $t = 0$, the buoy is at its highest point.

Lesson 14.2 (pp. 919–922)

11. $y = 2 \cos x + 1$

Amplitude: $a = 2$

Period: $\frac{2\pi}{b} = 2\pi$

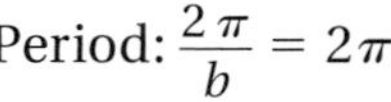

Horizontal shift: $h = 0$; Vertical shift: $k = 1$

23. $y = -\sin \frac{1}{2}x + 3$

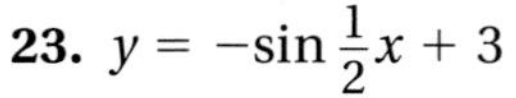

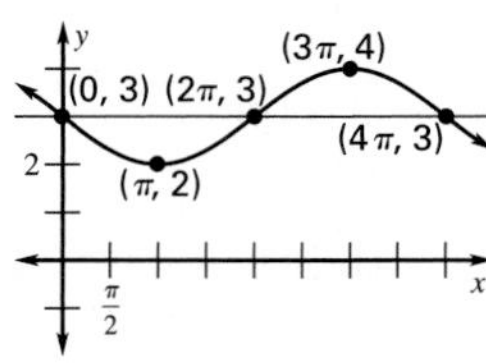

Amplitude: $|a| = 1$

Period: $\frac{2\pi}{b} = \frac{2\pi}{\frac{1}{2}} = 4\pi$

$h = 0$; $k = 3$; $a < 0$, so graph is reflected.

53. a. $\frac{200 - d}{300} = \tan \theta$

$d = -300 \tan \theta + 200$

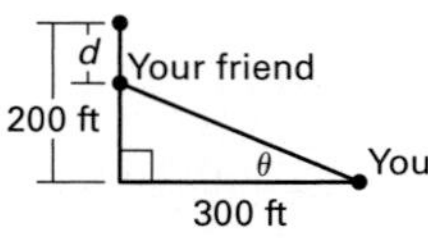

b.

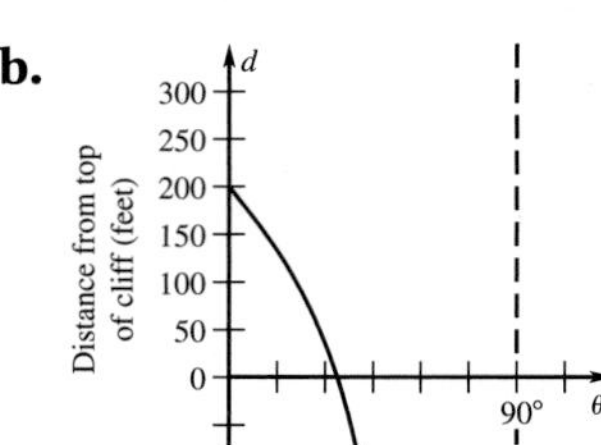

c. $100 = -300 \tan \theta + 200 \to \theta \approx 18.4°$

Lesson 14.3 (pp. 927–930)

5. $\cos \theta = \frac{5}{6}$, $3\pi < \theta < 2\pi$

$\sin^2 \theta + \cos^2 \theta = 1$

$\sin^2 \theta + \left(\frac{5}{6}\right)^2 = 1$

$\sin \theta = -\frac{\sqrt{11}}{6}$ ← Negative because θ is in Quadrant III

$\tan \theta = \frac{\sin \theta}{\cos \theta} = -\frac{\sqrt{11}}{5}$ $\quad \cot \theta = \frac{\cos \theta}{\sin \theta} = -\frac{5}{\sqrt{11}}$

$\csc \theta = \frac{1}{\sin \theta} = \frac{-6}{\sqrt{11}}$ $\quad \sec \theta = \frac{1}{\cos \theta} = \frac{6}{5}$

11. $\frac{\sin(-\theta)}{\cos(-\theta)} = \frac{-\sin \theta}{\cos \theta} = -\tan \theta$

41. a. $r = \frac{1.069}{1 - 0.97 \sin\left(\frac{\pi}{2} - \theta\right)} = \frac{1.069}{1 - 0.97 \cos \theta}$

b.

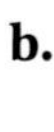

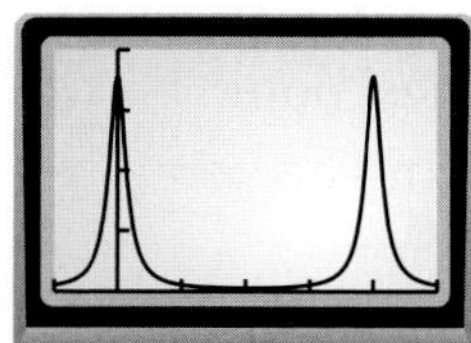

c.

θ	0	$\frac{\pi}{4}$	$\frac{\pi}{2}$	$\frac{3\pi}{4}$	π
r	35.6	3.4	1.1	0.6	0.5

θ	$\frac{5\pi}{4}$	$\frac{3\pi}{2}$	$\frac{7\pi}{4}$	2π
r	0.6	1.1	3.4	35.6

Closest distance:

$0.543 \text{ a.u.} \bullet \frac{93{,}000{,}000 \text{ mi}}{1 \text{ a.u.}} \approx 50.5$ million mi

Farthest distance:

$35.6 \text{ a.u.} \bullet \frac{93{,}000{,}000 \text{ mi}}{1 \text{ a.u.}} \approx 3.31$ billion mi

Lesson 14.4 (pp. 935–937)

5. $12 \sin^2\left(\frac{\pi}{6}\right) - 3 \stackrel{?}{=} 0$

$12\left(\frac{1}{2}\right)^2 - 3 \stackrel{?}{=} 0 \to 3 - 3 = 0$ ✓

13. $4 \cos^2 x - 3 = 0 \to \cos^2 x = \frac{3}{4} \to \cos x = \pm\frac{\sqrt{3}}{2}$

In $0 \le x < \pi$, $x = \frac{\pi}{6}$ and $x = \frac{5\pi}{6}$.

$x = \frac{\pi}{6} + n\pi$ or $x = \frac{5\pi}{6} + n\pi$

43. a. $S = 6(1.5)(0.75) + \frac{3}{2}(0.75)^2\left(\frac{\sqrt{3} - \cos \theta}{\sin \theta}\right)$

$= 6.75 + 0.84375\left(\frac{\sqrt{3} - \cos \theta}{\sin \theta}\right)$

b.

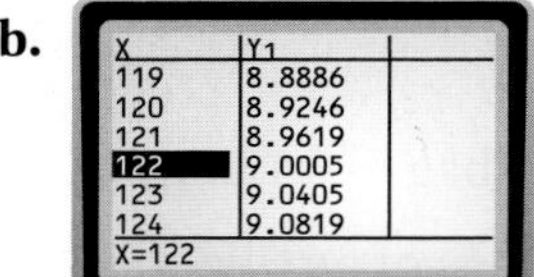

X	Y1
119	8.8886
120	8.9246
121	8.9619
122	9.0005
123	9.0405
124	9.0819

X=122

When $\theta \approx 122°$, $S = 9$ in.^{2}

c.

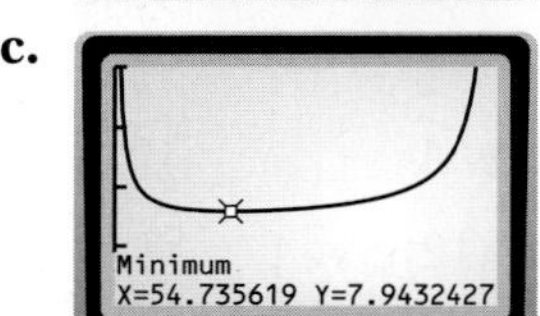

A value of $\theta \approx 54.7°$ minimizes the surface area.

Lesson 14.5 (pp. 944–947)

5. $M = 6$, $m = 2$

Vertical shift: $k = \frac{M + m}{2} = \frac{6 + 2}{2} = 4$

The graph is a cosine curve with $h = 0$.

Period $= 4 = \frac{2\pi}{b} \to b = \frac{\pi}{2}$

$|a| = \frac{M - m}{2} = \frac{6 - 2}{2} = 2$

The graph is a reflection, so $a = -2$.

The function is $y = -2 \cos \frac{\pi}{2}x + 4$.

9. $M = 6, m = -6$

Vertical shift: $k = \frac{M + m}{2} = \frac{6 + (-6)}{2} = 0$

The graph is a sine curve with $h = 0$.

Period $= 2(3\pi - \pi) = 4\pi = \frac{2\pi}{b} \rightarrow b = \frac{1}{2}$

$|a| = \frac{M - m}{2} = \frac{6 - (-6)}{2} = 6$

The graph is not a reflection, so $a = 6$.

The function is $y = 6 \sin \frac{1}{2}x$.

25. When $t = 0$, $m = 4$; when $t = 1$, $M = 9$.

$k = \frac{M + m}{2} = \frac{9 + 4}{2} = \frac{13}{2}$

The graph is a cosine curve with $h = 0$.

Period $= 2 = \frac{2\pi}{b} \rightarrow b = \pi$

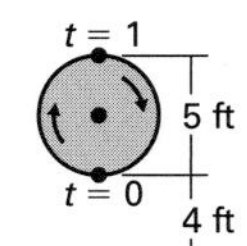

$|a| = \frac{M - m}{2} = \frac{9 - 4}{2} = \frac{5}{2}$

The graph is a reflection, so $a = -\frac{5}{2}$.

A model is $y = -\frac{5}{2} \cos \pi x + \frac{13}{2}$.

Lesson 14.6 (pp. 952–954)

9. $\cos\left(-\frac{5\pi}{12}\right) = \cos\left(\frac{\pi}{3} - \frac{3\pi}{4}\right)$

$= \cos \frac{\pi}{3} \cos \frac{3\pi}{4} + \sin \frac{\pi}{3} \sin \frac{3\pi}{4}$

$= \frac{1}{2}\left(-\frac{\sqrt{2}}{2}\right) + \frac{\sqrt{3}}{2}\left(\frac{\sqrt{2}}{2}\right)$

$= \frac{\sqrt{6} - \sqrt{2}}{4}$

23. $\sin\left(x - \frac{3\pi}{2}\right) = \sin x \cos \frac{3\pi}{2} - \cos x \sin \frac{3\pi}{2}$

$= (\sin x)(0) - (\cos x)(-1) = \cos x$

43. a.

$\frac{WQ}{NA} = \frac{f \tan(\theta - t) + f \tan t}{h \tan \theta}$

$= \frac{f}{h}(\tan(\theta - t) + \tan t)\left(\frac{1}{\tan \theta}\right)$

$= \frac{f}{h}\left(\frac{\tan \theta - \tan t}{1 + \tan \theta \tan t} + \frac{\tan t(1 + \tan \theta \tan t)}{1 + \tan \theta \tan t)}\right)\left(\frac{1}{\tan \theta}\right)$

$= \frac{f}{h}\left(\frac{\tan \theta + \tan \theta \tan^2 t}{1 + \tan \theta \tan t}\right)\left(\frac{1}{\tan \theta}\right)$

$= \frac{f}{h}\left(\frac{\tan \theta(1 + \tan^2 t)}{1 + \tan \theta \tan t}\right)\left(\frac{1}{\tan \theta}\right)$

$= \frac{f}{h}\left(\frac{\sec^2 t}{1 + \tan \theta \tan t}\right)$

b. When $t = 0$:

$\frac{WQ}{NA} = \frac{f}{h}\left(\frac{\sec^2(0)}{1 + \tan \theta \tan(0)}\right) = \frac{f}{h}\left(\frac{1}{1 + 0}\right) = \frac{f}{h}$

Lesson 14.7 (pp. 959–962)

7. $\cos \frac{\pi}{8} = \cos \frac{1}{2}\left(\frac{\pi}{4}\right) = \sqrt{\frac{1 + \cos \frac{\pi}{4}}{2}}$

$= \sqrt{\frac{1 + \frac{\sqrt{2}}{2}}{2}} = \sqrt{\frac{2 + \sqrt{2}}{4}} = \frac{\sqrt{2 + \sqrt{2}}}{2}$

13. $\cos a = \frac{1}{3}, \frac{3\pi}{2} < a < 2\pi$

$\frac{3\pi}{4} < \frac{a}{2} < \pi \rightarrow \frac{a}{2}$ is in Quadrant II.

$\sin \frac{a}{2} = \sqrt{\frac{1 - \cos a}{2}} = \sqrt{\frac{1 - \frac{1}{3}}{2}} = \sqrt{\frac{1}{3}} = \frac{\sqrt{3}}{3}$

$\cos \frac{a}{2} = -\sqrt{\frac{1 + \cos a}{2}} = -\sqrt{\frac{1 + \frac{1}{3}}{2}} = -\sqrt{\frac{2}{3}} = -\frac{\sqrt{6}}{3}$

$\tan \frac{a}{2} = \frac{\sin \frac{a}{2}}{\cos \frac{a}{2}} = \frac{\frac{\sqrt{3}}{3}}{-\frac{\sqrt{6}}{3}} = \frac{\sqrt{3}}{3} \bullet \frac{-3}{\sqrt{6}} = \frac{-\sqrt{3}}{\sqrt{6}} = \frac{-\sqrt{2}}{2}$

53. When $M = 2.5$: $\sin \frac{\theta}{2} = \frac{1}{M} = \frac{1}{2.5}$

Using the Pythagorean Theorem:

$\cos \frac{\theta}{2} = \frac{\sqrt{5.25}}{2.5}$

$\sin \theta = 2 \sin \frac{\theta}{2} \cos \frac{\theta}{2} = 2\left(\frac{1}{2.5}\right)\left(\frac{\sqrt{5.25}}{2.5}\right) \approx 0.7332$

$\theta \approx 47°$

Selected Answers

Chapter 1

1.1 Skill Practice (pp. 6–7) **1.** reciprocal

3.

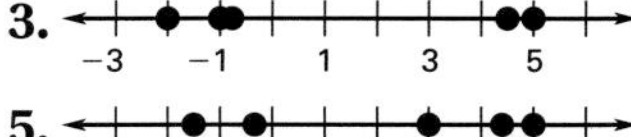

5.

11. Associative property of addition **13.** Commutative property of multiplication **15.** Distributive property

17. $6 \cdot (a \div 3) = 6 \cdot \left(a \cdot \frac{1}{3}\right)$ Definition of division

$= 6 \cdot \left(\frac{1}{3} \cdot a\right)$ Commutative property of multiplication

$= \left(6 \cdot \frac{1}{3}\right) \cdot a$ Associative property of multiplication

$= 2a$ Multiplication

19. $(c - 3) + 3 = (c + (-3)) + 3$ Definition of subtraction

$= c + ((-3) + 3)$ Associative property of addition

$= c + 0$ Inverse property of addition

$= c$ Identity property of addition

21. $7a + (4 + 5a) = 7a + (5a + 4)$ Commutative property of addition

$= (7a + 5a) + 4$ Associative property of addition

$= 12a + 4$ Combine like terms.

23. *Sample answer:* $a = -2, b = \frac{1}{4}$ **25.** \$8.50 per h **27.** \$36.25 **29.** 195 mi **31.** $116\frac{2}{3}$ yd **33.** 2200 g **35.** 1.75 gal **37.** 0.00175 ton **39.** The unit multiplier should be $\frac{0.82 \text{ euro}}{1 \text{ dollar}}$; 25 dollars $\cdot \frac{0.82 \text{ euro}}{1 \text{ dollar}} = 20.5$ euros. **41.** 29.3 ft/sec **43.** 31.1 mi/h **45.** 0.04 oz/sec **47.** 1800 mi/h **49.** Always; this represents the associative property of addition, which is true for all real numbers. **51.** Sometimes; it is true when $c = 0$. **53.** Always; this represents the distributive property, which is true for all real numbers.

55. $\frac{a}{b} \div \frac{c}{d} = \frac{a}{b} \cdot \frac{d}{c}$ Definition of division

$= \frac{ad}{bc}$ Definition of multiplication of fractions

$= \frac{ad}{cb}$ Commutative property of multiplication

$= \frac{a}{c} \cdot \frac{d}{b}$ Definition of multiplication of fractions

$= \frac{a}{c} \div \frac{b}{d}$ Definition of division

1.1 Problem Solving (pp. 8–9) **57. a.** Lance: 6, Darcy: 2, Javier: 3, Sandra: -2 **b.** Sandra, Darcy, Javier, Lance **59. a.** Pluto, Neptune, Uranus, Saturn, Jupiter, Mars, Earth, Mercury, Venus **b.** Mercury, Venus, Earth, Mars, Jupiter, Saturn, Uranus, Neptune, Pluto **c.** *Sample answer:* The planets are in opposite orders in parts (a) and (b) with the exception of Mercury and Venus. **d.** Mercury or Venus **61. a.** cheetah: 102.67; three-toed sloth: 0.15; squirrel: 17.6; grizzly bear: 30 **b.** *Sample answer:* The cheetah is about 467 times faster than the three-toed sloth.

1.2 Skill Practice (pp. 13–15) **1.** base: 12, exponent: 7 **3.** The negative sign should be applied after evaluating the power, $-3^4 = -81$. **5.** 81 **7.** 49 **9.** -32 **11.** $-10{,}000$ **13.** -64 **15.** 64 **17.** -5 **19.** -100 **21.** 75 **23.** 6 **25.** $5x + 5$ **27.** $13z^2 - 2z + 10$ **29.** $11m - 1$ **31.** $-5p^2 + 21$ **35.** $10n + 24$; 44 **37.** 26 **39.** 49 **41.** $\frac{1}{9}$ **43.** $-7d + 11c$ **45.** $2m^2 + n^2 - 8m$ **47.** $13m^2 - 5$ **49.** $-8s + 8t$ **51.** *Sample answer:* $3k + 4k + (-8) - 2j$; $7k - 8 - 2j$ **53.** $(4 + 3) \cdot (5 - 2) = 21$ **55.** $(3 \cdot 4)^2 - (2^3 + 3)^2 = 23$

1.2 Problem Solving (pp. 15–16) **57.** 0, 10, 20, 30; \$1.89, \$3.20, \$4.51, \$5.82 **59.** $270 - 4.5x$; no; when $x > 60$ there will be a negative balance on the card, which means you will have spent more than what you had on the card. **63.** $-6.5x - 6y + 200$; \$88

1.3 Skill Practice (pp. 21–23) **1.** solution **3.** 3 **5.** 12 **7.** 6 **9.** $-\frac{2}{9}$ **11.** 4 **13.** -1 **15.** 18 **17.** -9 **21.** 1 **23.** 4 **25.** -7 **27.** $-1\frac{1}{3}$ **29.** 4 **31.** $-2\frac{2}{3}$ **33.** 4 **35.** -7 **37.** -2 **39.** 28 **41.** Both sides of the equations should be divided by $\frac{3}{7}$ instead of subtracting $\frac{3}{7}$ from each side; $\frac{3}{7}x = 15, x = 15 \div \frac{3}{7}, x = 35$. **43.** 12 **45.** 60 **47.** -23

49. $1\frac{2}{3}$ **51.** 6; 15, 8, 15, 8 **53.** 2; 6, 6, 3 **55.** 4 **57.** 2 **59.** 4 **61.** 2.9 **63.** no solution **65.** all real numbers **67.** $x = \frac{d-b}{a-c}$; $a = c$ and $b \neq d$; $a = c$ and $b = d$

1.3 Problem Solving (pp. 23–24) **69.** 3 h **71.** 9 h **73. a.** $3c + 2g = 8$ **b.** $2\frac{1}{4}, \frac{1}{2}; 2\frac{5}{12}, \frac{1}{4}$ **75.** 18 min

1.4 Skill Practice (pp. 30–31) **1.** formula **3.** $\ell = \frac{A}{w}$; 5 mm **5.** $h = \frac{2A}{b_1 + b_2}$; 6 cm **7.** $y = 26 - 3x$; 5 **9.** $y = -\frac{6}{5}x + \frac{31}{5}$; 11 **11.** $y = \frac{3}{2}x - \frac{21}{2}$; -3 **13.** $y = \frac{7}{4}x - \frac{11}{4}$; 6 **17.** The variable y should only appear on one side of the equation, not both; $4y - xy = 9$, $y(4 - x) = 9$, $y = \frac{9}{4-x}$. **19.** $h = \frac{S}{\pi r} - k$; about 4.96 cm **21.** $y = \frac{40 + 3x}{x}$; 11 **23.** $y = \frac{16x + 28}{3x}$; $7\frac{2}{3}$ **25.** $y = \frac{15}{1 - 2x}$; 5 **27.** Method 1: $y = \frac{5}{3}x - 3$, $y = \frac{5}{3} \cdot 2 - 3$, $y = \frac{1}{3}$; Method 2: $15 \cdot 2 - 9y = 27$, $30 - 9y = 27$, $-9y = -3$, $y = \frac{1}{3}$; *Sample answer:* Method 1 is more efficient because it is already solved for y. **29.** $z = \frac{x + y}{xy - 1}$ **31.** $z = \frac{xy}{xy - y - x}$

1.4 Problem Solving (pp. 31–32) **33.** $d = \frac{C}{\pi}$; about 36 in. **35.** $C = \frac{5}{9}(F - 32)$; 10°C **37.** $R = 80c + 150d$; $d = \frac{R - 80c}{150}$; 80 designer tuxedos; 160 designer tuxedos; 240 designer tuxedos **39.** $V = \frac{\ell^2 w}{4\pi}$; $V = \frac{w^2 \ell}{4\pi}$

1.5 Skill Practice (pp. 37–38) **1.** verbal model **3.** 0.5 h **5.** 90 mi **7.** 54 ft **9.** 20 m **11.** $y = 4x + 11$ **13.** $y = 46 - 10x$ **17.** $4x + 9 = 12$, 0.75 ft **19.** The pattern shows the output is decreased by 10 each time; an equation that represents the table is $y = 75 - 10x$. **23.** $y = 7x - 16$

1.5 Problem Solving (pp. 38–39) **25.** 3.75 km/min **27.** $y = 1.5x + 15$; no; the bamboo shoot will eventually slow its growth rate and stop growing.

29.

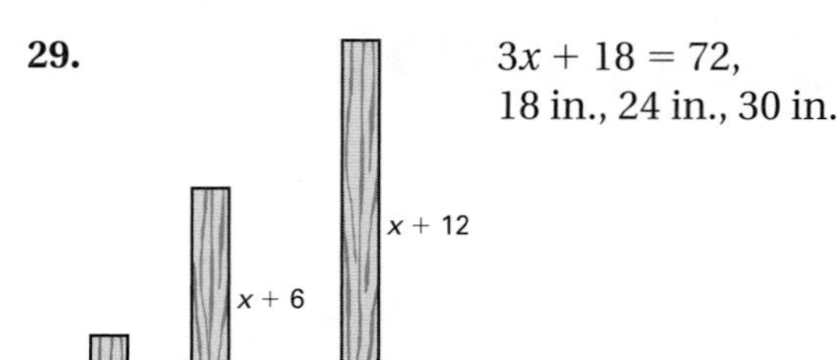

$3x + 18 = 72$, 18 in., 24 in., 30 in.

31. $40x + 7(20 - x) = 404$; 8 boxes of books, 12 boxes of clothes **33.** about 4.07 in.

1.6 Skill Practice (pp. 44–45) **1.** graph **3.** **5.** **11.** $-3 \le x \le 1$ **13.** $x < -2$ or $x > 4$ **17.** **19.** **23.** $x \le -2$ **25.** $x < 4$ **35.** The inequality symbol should not be reversed when subtracting; $10 > 2x$, $5 > x$. **37.** $-6 < x < 3$ **39.** $1 \le x < 7$ **43.** $x < -4$ or $x > 2$ **45.** $x \le -\frac{1}{2}$ or $x \ge 1$ **49.** no solution **51.** no solution

1.6 Problem Solving (pp. 46–47) **53.** $45x + 35 \le 250$, $x \le 4\frac{7}{9}$ days; 4 or fewer days **55. a.** $0 \le e < 500$ **b.** $1400 \le e < 2429$ **c.** $0 \le e < 500$ or $1400 \le e < 2429$ **57.** $50 \le F \le 95$; $10 \le C \le 35$ **59. a.** Amy: $0.65(84) + 0.15(80) + 0.2w \ge 85$, Brian: $0.65(80) + 0.15(100) + 0.2x \ge 85$, Clara: $0.65(75) + 0.15(95) + 0.2y \ge 85$, Dan: $0.65(80) + 0.15(90) + 0.2z \ge 85$ **b.** $w \ge 92$; $x \ge 90$; $y \ge 110$; $z \ge 97.5$ **c.** Amy, Brian, and Dan. *Sample answer:* It is impossible to score over 100 points on a test, so Clara will not be able to achieve a grade of 85 or better.

1.6 Problem Solving Workshop (p. 49) **1.** $y = -35x + 200$; $x > 20$ **3.** $x \ge \$7000$

1.7 Skill Practice (pp. 55–56) **1.** An apparent solution that must be rejected because it does not satisfy the original equation. **3.** solution **5.** not a solution **7.** solution

9. $-9, 9$

11. 0

21. $-4, 9$ **23.** $\frac{6}{7}, 2$ **25.** $-7, 4$ **27.** $-7, 2$ **29.** $1\frac{4}{9}; 3$ **31.** $-20, 4$ **33.** No; the equation has no solutions because an absolute value will never be negative. **35.** -3 **37.** $-1\frac{1}{2}, -\frac{1}{2}$, **39.** $-\frac{1}{6}, -3\frac{3}{4}$ **41.** When writing the second equation, the right side of the equation should be $-x - 3$; $5x - 9 = -x - 3$, $6x - 9 = -3$, $6x = 6$, $x = 1$, the solutions are 3 and 1.

43. $-5 \le j \le 5$

45. $-5 < m < 9$

65. $c > 0, c = 0, c < 0$ **67.** no solution

69. $x < 9$ or $x > 9$

71. $x \le \frac{-c-b}{a}$ or $x \ge \frac{c-b}{a}$ **73.** $x < \frac{c-b}{a}$ or $x > \frac{-c-b}{a}$

75. $|p - 6.5| \le 1$ **77.** $|b - 21| > 1$ **79.** $|x - 45| \le 15$

81. $|e - 6008| \le 5992$, $|m - 46{,}000| \le 45{,}000$

Chapter Review (pp. 61–64) **1.** exponent, base **3.** extraneous solution **5.** *Sample answer:* $3(x - 4)$ and $3x - 12$ **7.** Inverse property of multiplication **9.** Distributive property **11.** $3x - 6y$ **13.** $18b - 33$ **15.** $-2t^4 + 5t^2$ **17.** $-\frac{1}{6}$ **19.** 9 **21.** -1 **23.** \$74.99

25. $y = -10x + 7; -23$ **27.** $y = \frac{-15}{x-6}; 15$ **29.** $y = \frac{5}{2}x - 5; -20$ **31.** $h = \frac{S - 2\pi r^2}{2\pi r}$; about 7.73 cm **33.** 602 mi

35. $x \le 6$

37. $x \le -\frac{1}{2}$

39. $-3 \le x \le 3$

41. $-3, 1\frac{2}{3}$ **43.** no solution

45. $y < -1$ or $y > 6$

47. $|v - 26| \le 0.5$, 25.5 in. $\le v \le$ 26.5 in.

Chapter 2

2.1 Skill Practice (pp. 76–78) **1.** independent, dependent **3.** domain: $-4, -2, 1, 3$, range: $-3, -1, 2, 3$

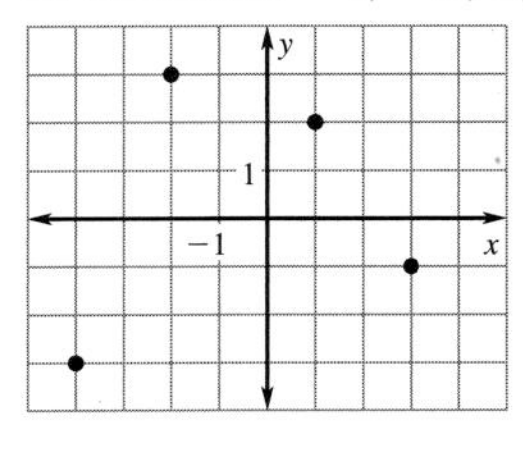

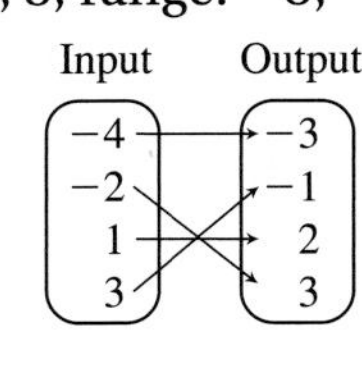

5. domain: $-2, 1, 6$, range: $-3, -1, 5, 8$

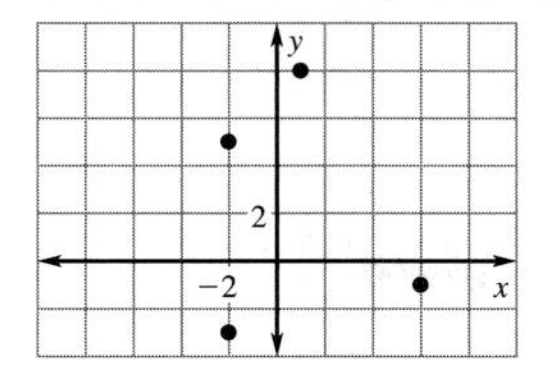

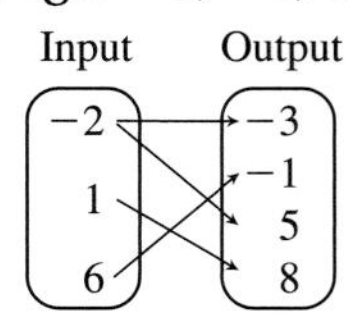

11. Yes; each input has exactly one output. **13.** Yes; each input has exactly one output. **15.** x is the input and y is the output, so there should be one value of y for each value of x; the relation given by the table is not a function because the inputs 1 and 0 each have more than one output. **17.** No; the input -2 has more than one output. **19.** No; the input -1 has more than one output. **21.** function **23.** not a function

25.

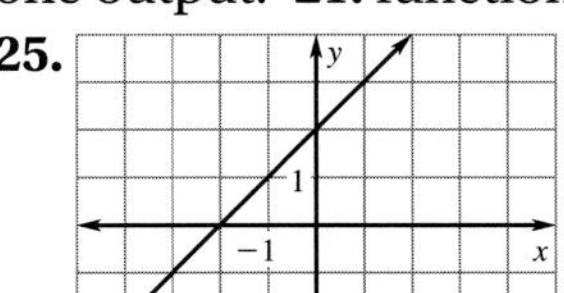

27.

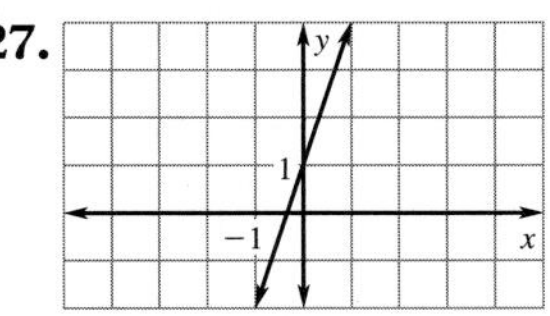

35. not linear; 10 **37.** linear; 6 **39.** linear; -3

2.1 Problem Solving (pp. 78–79) **43.** Yes; each input has exactly one output. **45.** About 905; $V(6)$ represents the volume of a sphere with radius 6.

47. a.

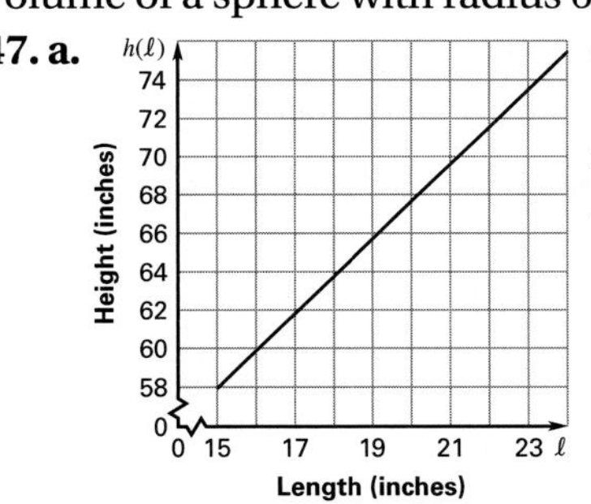

domain: $15 \le \ell \le 24$, range: $57.95 \le h(\ell) \le 75.5$

b. 59 in. or 4 ft 11 in. **c.** 21.7 in. **49. a.** domain: 11,350,000, 12,280,000, 12,420,000, 15,980,000, 18,980,000, 20,850,000, 33,870,000, range: 20, 21, 27, 31, 34, 55 **b.** Yes; each input p has exactly one output. **c.** No; the input 21 has more than one output.

Extension (p. 81)

1.

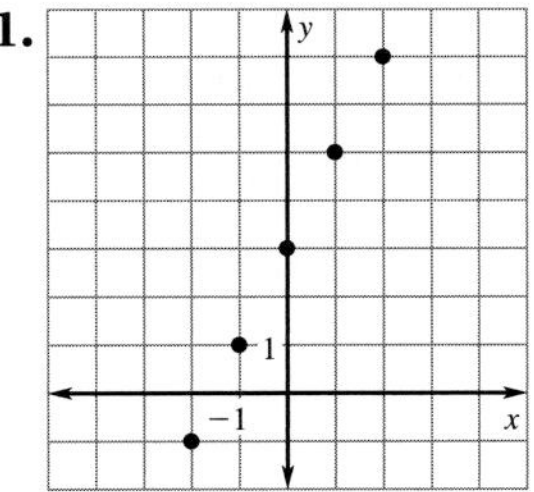

discrete; $-1, 1, 3, 5, 7$

SELECTED ANSWERS

3. 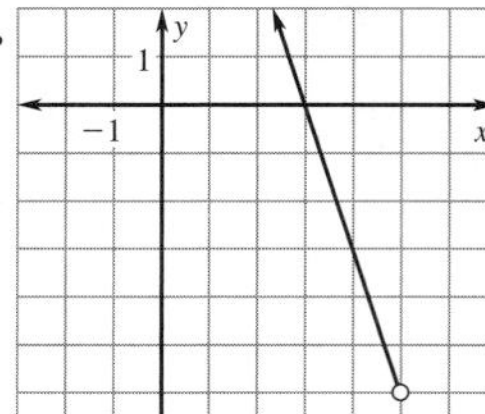 continuous; $y > -6$

5. $d(x) = 3.5x$

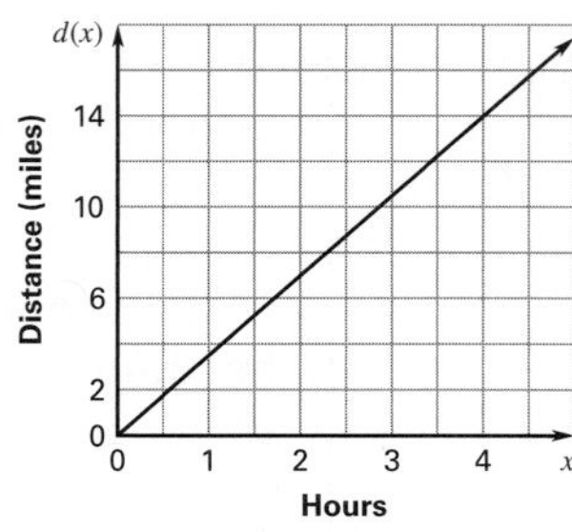

domain: $x \geq 0$, range: $d(x) \geq 0$; continuous

7. $m(x) = 3x$

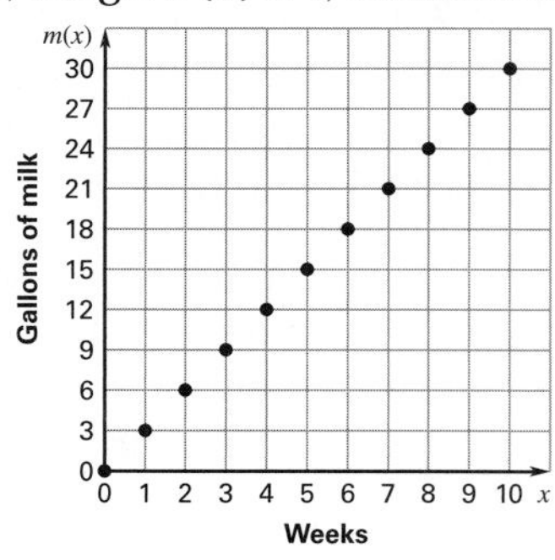

domain: whole numbers, range: multiples of 3; discrete

2.2 Skill Practice (pp. 86–87) **1.** slope **3.** $\frac{3}{2}$; rises **5.** $-\frac{5}{3}$; falls **7.** -4; falls **9.** $\frac{7}{4}$; rises **11.** undefined; is vertical **13.** 0; is horizontal **15.** The x and y coordinates were not subtracted in the correct order; $\frac{-1-(-3)}{2-(-4)} = \frac{1}{3}$. **19.** neither **21.** perpendicular **23.** parallel **25.** 13 mi/gal **27.** 2 m/sec **29.** 2 **31.** $\frac{1}{6}$ **33.** $-\frac{3}{2}$ **35.** No; no. *Sample answer:* The slope of $\overleftrightarrow{PQ} = \frac{2-1}{-3-(-1)} = -\frac{1}{2}$. The slope of $\overleftrightarrow{QR} = \frac{1-0}{-1-1} = -\frac{1}{2}$. The slope of $\overleftrightarrow{ST} = \frac{-1-(-2)}{3-5} = -\frac{1}{2}$.

2.2 Problem Solving (pp. 87–88) **41.** $\frac{7}{12}$ **43.** 6.5% **47. a.** $\frac{3}{8}$ **b.** yes **c.** $\frac{1}{8}$

2.3 Skill Practice (pp. 93–94) **1.** slope-intercept

3. 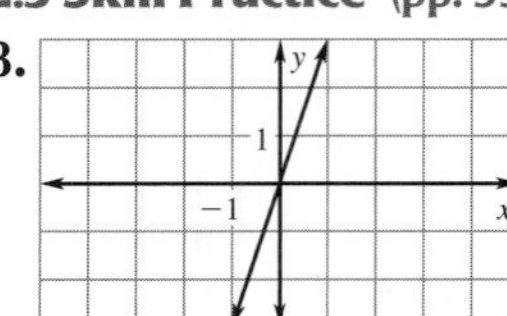 Both graphs have a y-intercept of 0, but the graph of $y = 3x$ has a slope of 3 instead of 1.

5. 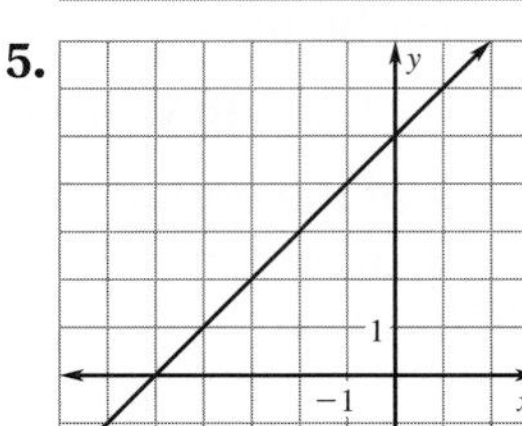 Both graphs have a slope of 1, but the graph of $y = x + 5$ has a y-intercept of 5 instead of 0.

9. 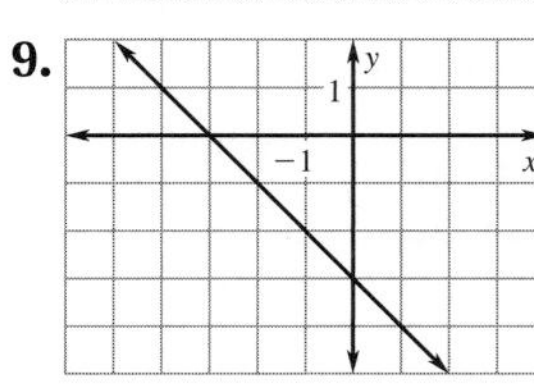 **11.** 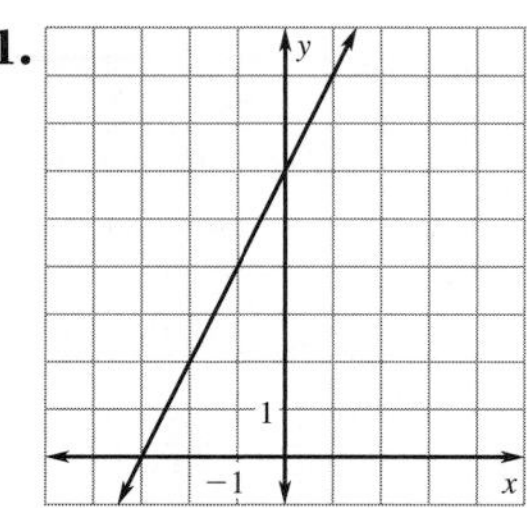

21. The slope and y-intercept were switched around. 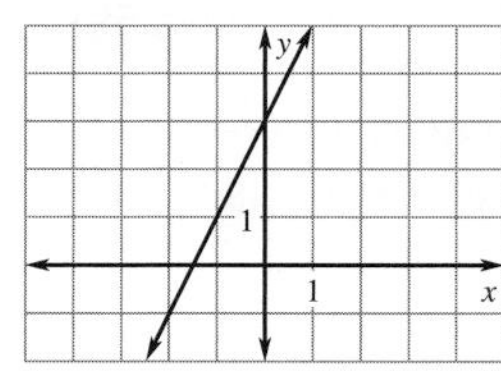

25. x-intercept: -15, y-intercept: -3 **27.** x-intercept: 5, y-intercept: -10 **29.** x-intercept: 6, y-intercept: -4.5

31. 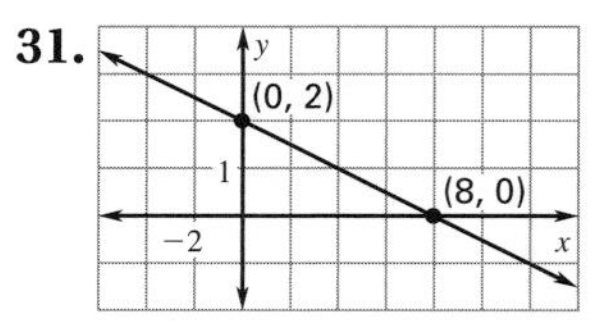

33. 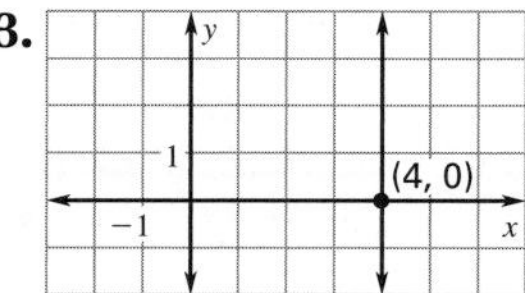

43. 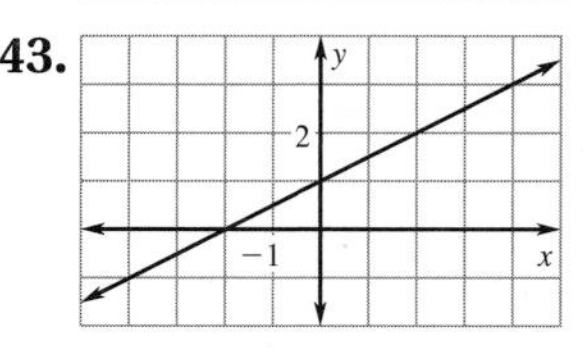 **45.** 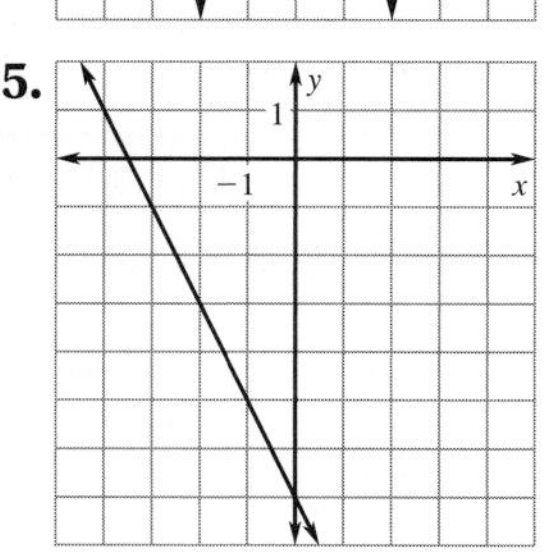

55. *Sample answer:* $x = 3$, $y = -2$ **57.** slope: $-\frac{A}{B}$, y-intercept: $\frac{C}{B}$

2.3 Problem Solving (pp. 94–96)

59. 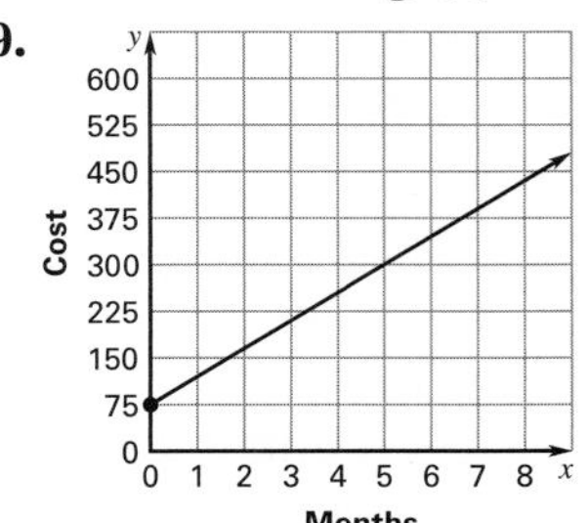

$480

61. 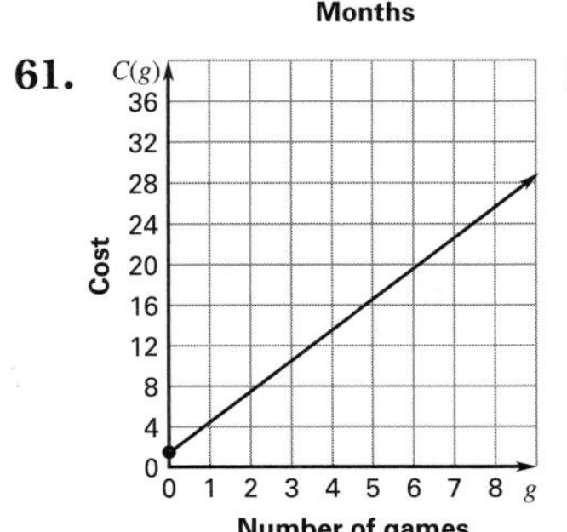

$1.50; $3

63. 30; fall; the value of the card will decrease after you buy each smoothie, so the line will fall from left to right.

65. *Sample answer:* $r = 0$ and $w = 4$, $r = 1.75$ and $w = 1$, $r = 0.875$ and $w = 2.5$

67. a.

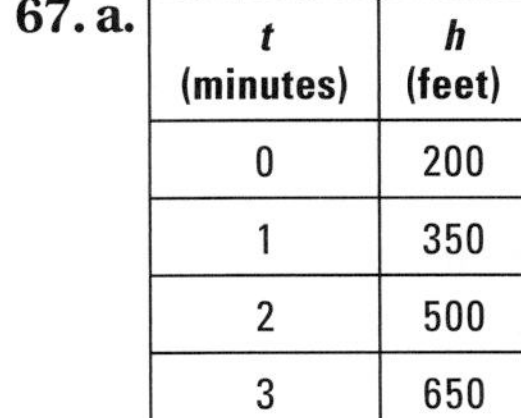

t (minutes)	h (feet)
0	200
1	350
2	500
3	650
4	800
5	950

b.

c. $h(t) = 150t + 200$

2.4 Skill Practice (pp. 101–103) **1.** standard **3.** $y = 2$ **5.** $y = 6x$ **7.** $y = -\frac{5}{4}x + 7$ **9.** $y = 4x - 2$ **11.** $y = 2x + 11$ **13.** $y = -9x + 85$ **15.** $y = -\frac{4}{7}x + 1$ **17.** $y = -\frac{1}{3}x - 2$ **19.** The x- and y-coordinates were transposed; $y - 1 = -2(x - 5)$, $y - 1 = -2x + 10$, $y = -2x + 11$. **21.** $y = -x + 8$ **23.** $y = -3x + 13$ **25.** $y = -\frac{1}{4}x - \frac{1}{4}$ **27.** $y = -2x + 6$ **29.** $y = -\frac{1}{4}x + \frac{19}{4}$ **31.** $y = -3x + 11$ **33.** $y = -\frac{2}{3}x + 7$ **35.** $y = 5x + 23$ **37.** $y = -3x + 17.5$ **41.** $-4x + y = -3$ **43.** $4x - 5y = -7$ **45.** $4x + 3y = 32$ **47.** *Sample answer:* $y = -\frac{1}{2}x + 8$

2.4 Problem Solving (pp. 103–104) **51.** $n = 15t + 50$ **53.** $15x + 9y = 4500$

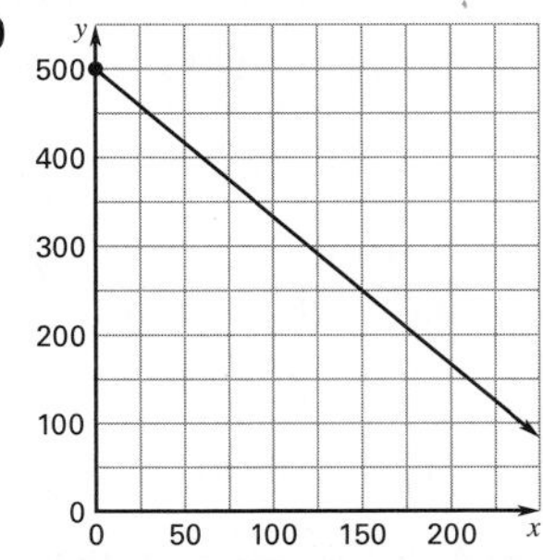

Find the point on the line where x is 200 then the corresponding y-coordinate is how many student tickets were sold. **55.** $y = 1.66x + 21.62$; $48.18

57. a. $2\ell + 2w = 24$

b.

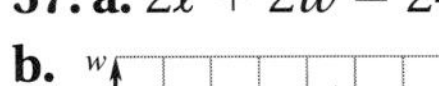

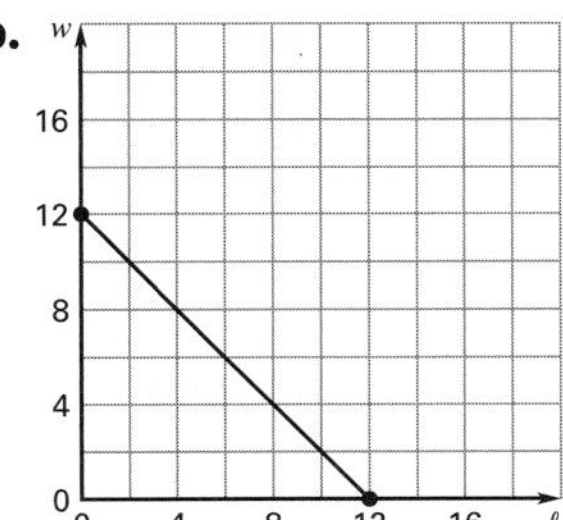

c. *Sample answer:*

ℓ	w
6	6
7	5
8	4
9	3
10	2

2.4 Problem Solving Workshop (p. 105) **1.** $y = 4x + 7$ **3.** $y = -\frac{1}{2}x + 16$ **5.** $y = 32.14x + 1764.36$

2.5 Skill Practice (pp. 109–110) **1.** *Sample answer:* If $y = ax$, then a is the constant of variation. a is a constant ratio of y to x for all ordered pairs (x, y). **3.** $y = 3x$

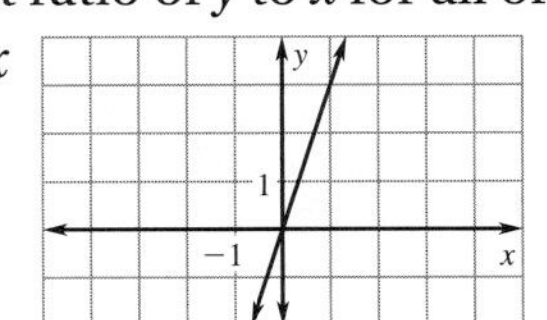

SELECTED ANSWERS

5. $y = -3.5x$

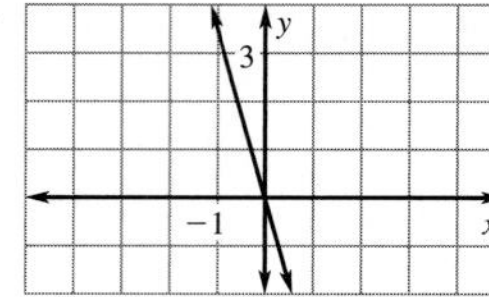

11. $y = 2x$; 24 **13.** $y = -0.2x$; -2.4 **15.** $y = \frac{1}{3}x$; 4 **19.** not direct variation **21.** direct variation; 2.5 **23.** direct variation; $\frac{1}{6}$ **25.** $y = -\frac{4}{3}x$; 3 **27.** $y = -7x$; $\frac{4}{7}$ **29.** $y = -7.2x$; $\frac{5}{9}$ **31.** direct variation; $y = -\frac{1}{3}x$ **33.** direct variation; $y = -4x$ **35.** The quotients need to be compared to each other, not the products; $\frac{24}{1} = 24, \frac{12}{2} = 6, \frac{8}{3} \approx 2.7, \frac{6}{4} = 1.5$, because the ratios are not equal, the data do not show direct variation.

2.5 Problem Solving (pp. 110–111) **39.** $w = 3600d$; 6300 lb **41.** direct variation; $t = 5.1s$ **43. a.** direct variation; $P = 4s$ **b.** Not a direct variation; the ratios of A to s are not equal. **c.** Not a direct variation; the ratios of A to P are not equal.

2.6 Skill Practice (pp. 117–118) **1.** best-fitting line **3.** negative correlation **5.** approximately no correlation **7.** 0 **9.** -1

11. a.

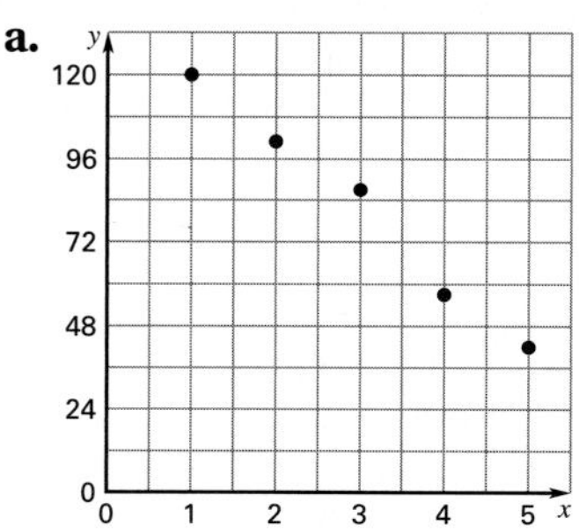

b. *Sample answer:* $y = -20x + 141$ **c.** about -259

13. a.

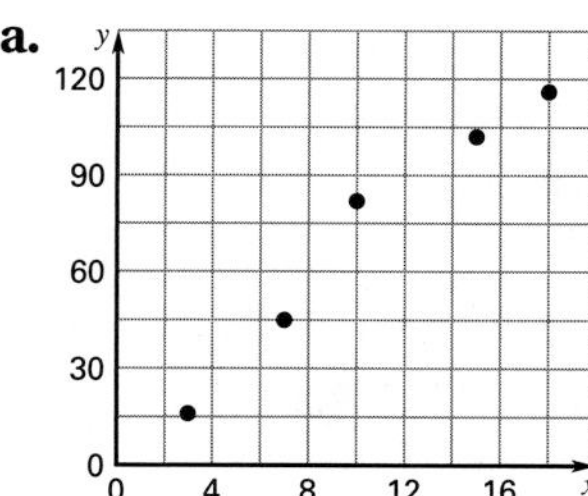

b. *Sample answer:* $y = 6.7x + 1$ **c.** about 135

17. The line should go through the middle of the data points. *Sample answer:*

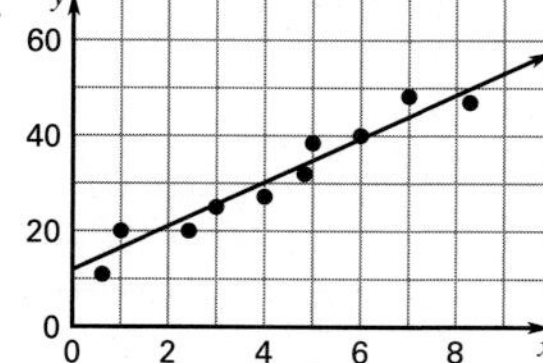

19. $y = 0.05x + 1.14$

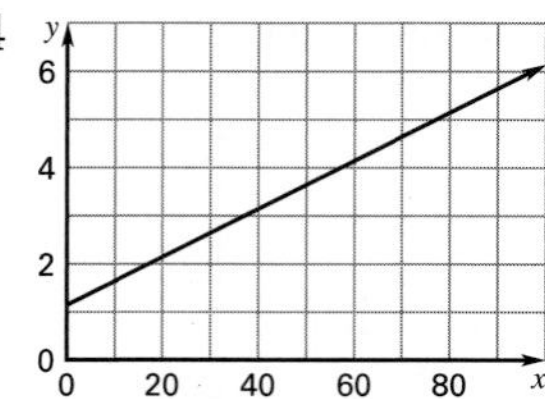

21. a. *Sample answer:* Measuring the depth of water at different times while filling a swimming pool. The number of gallons of milk you buy and the total cost. **b.** *Sample answer:* The age of a car and its current value. The number of miles you have driven since you last put gas in the tank and the amount of gas left in the tank. **c.** *Sample answer:* The height of a person and the month they were born. The age of a person and the number of vehicles they own.

2.6 Problem Solving (pp. 119–120) **25.** *Sample answer:* $y = 101.3x + 2236.6$ **27. a.** (0, 37), (4, 49), (8, 57), (12, 64), (14, 67), (18, 72), (22, 77)

b.

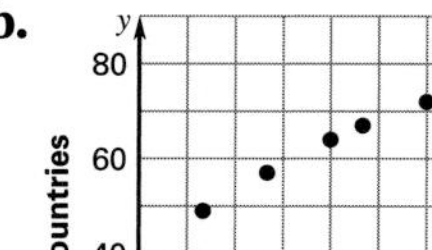

c. *Sample answer:* $y = 1.8x + 40.7$; 102 countries

2.7 Skill Practice (pp. 127–128) **1.** vertex

3.

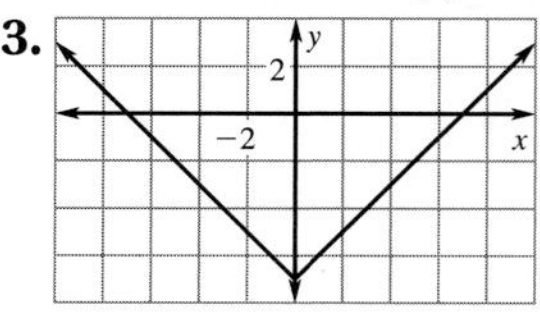

translated down 7 units

5.

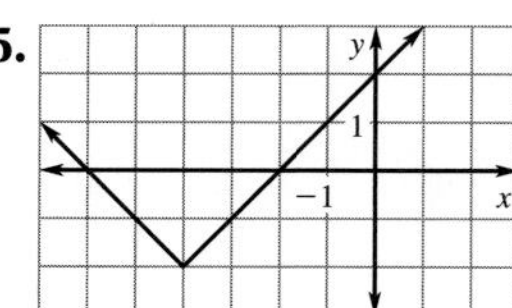

translated left 4 units and down 2 units

15. $y = -3|x|$ **17.** $y = \frac{1}{3}|x|$ **19.** $y = \frac{1}{2}|x + 2| - 1$

21.

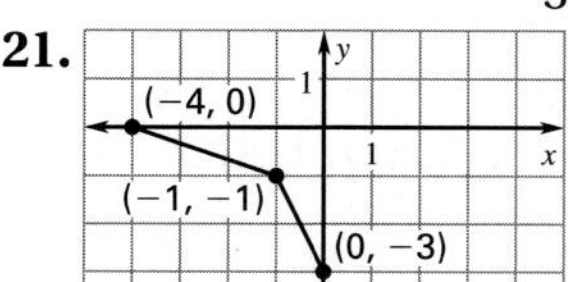

23.

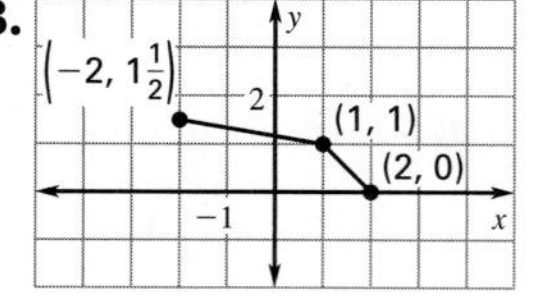

29. The graph should be translated left 3 units.

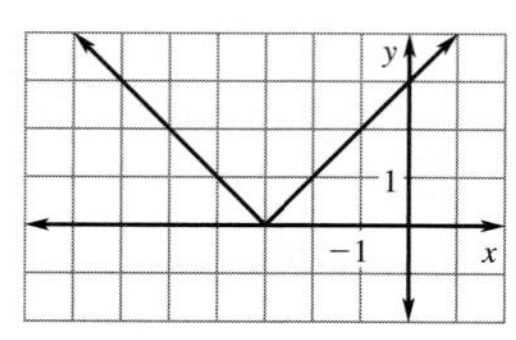

33. No. *Sample answer:* It does not pass the vertical line test.

2.7 Problem Solving (pp. 128–129)

37. 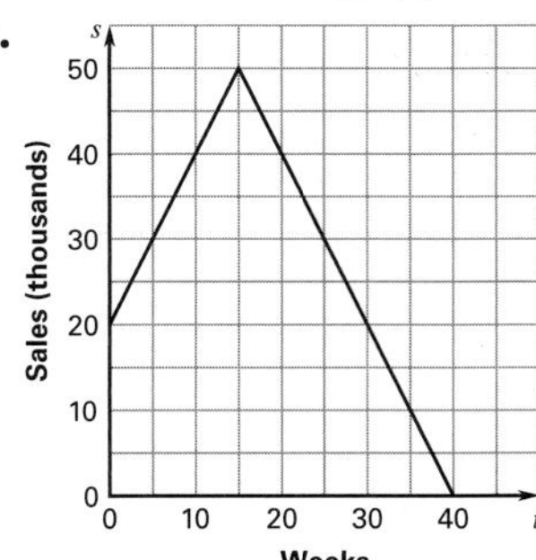

50,000 pairs of shoes

39. $y = -\frac{140}{69}|x - 69| + 140$

41. a.

t	0	0.5	1	1.5	2	2.5	3
d	90	60	30	0	30	60	90

b. 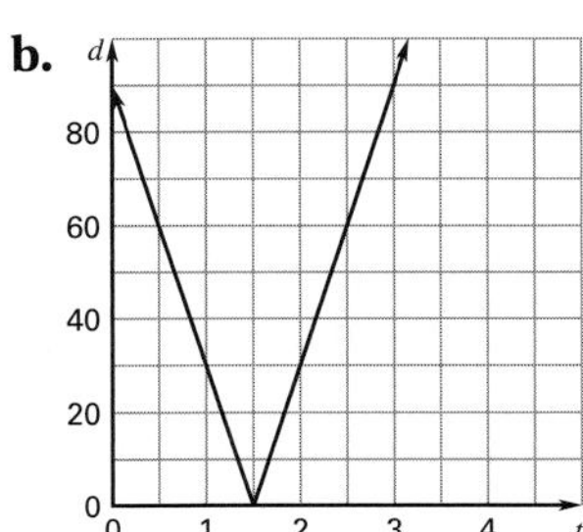

c. $d = 60|t - 1.5|$; $\frac{2}{3} \le t \le 2\frac{1}{3}$

Extension (p. 131) **1.** -1 **3.** $\frac{5}{2}$

5. 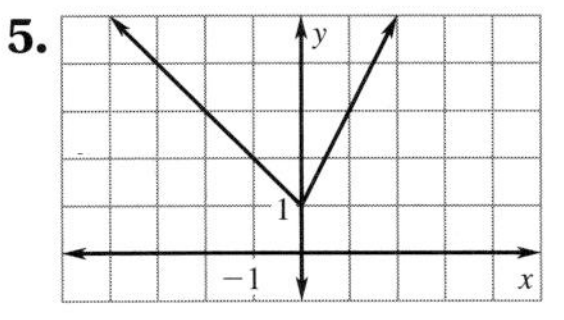

7. 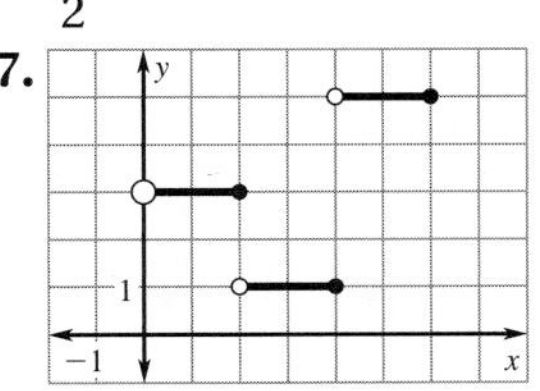

9. 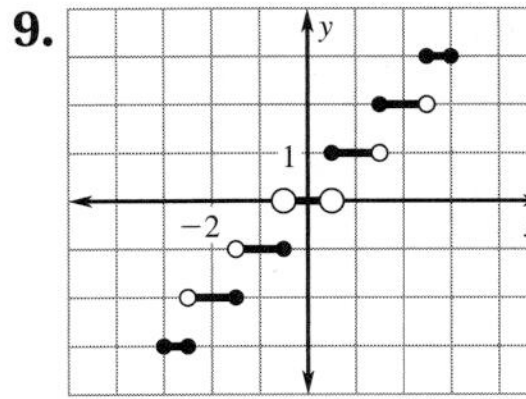

2.8 Skill Practice (pp. 135–136) **1.** half-plane **3.** solution, not a solution **5.** solution, solution

7. 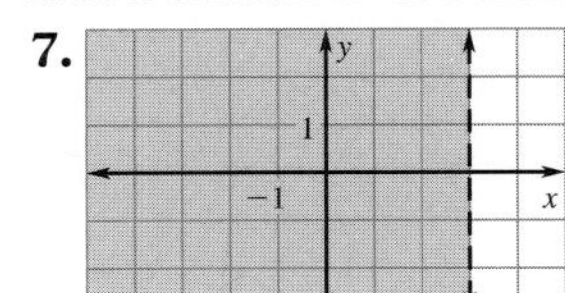

9. 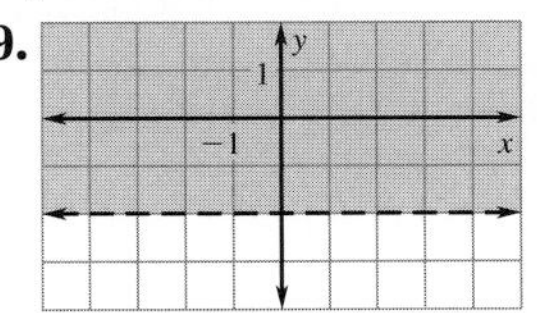

19. The boundary line should be a dashed line.

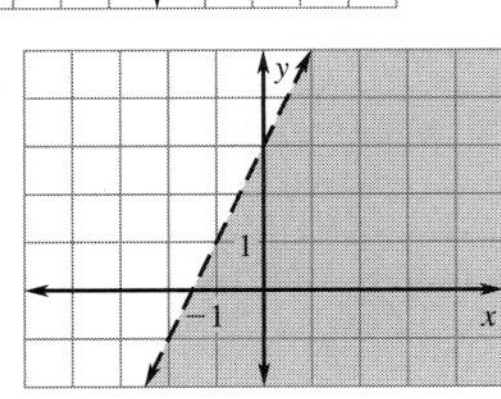

23. 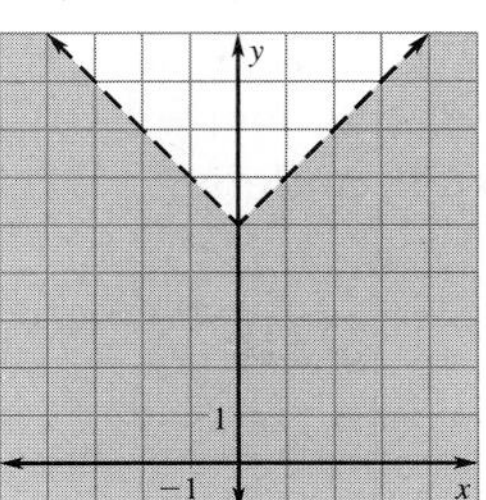

25. 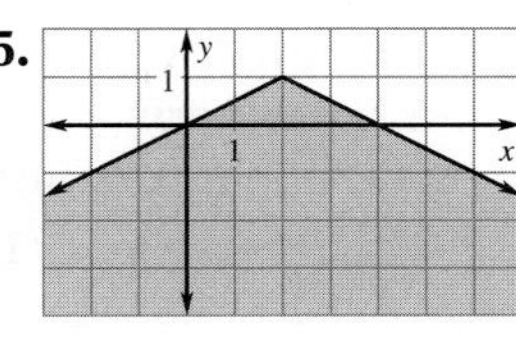

29. solution, not a solution **31.** solution, not a solution

33. 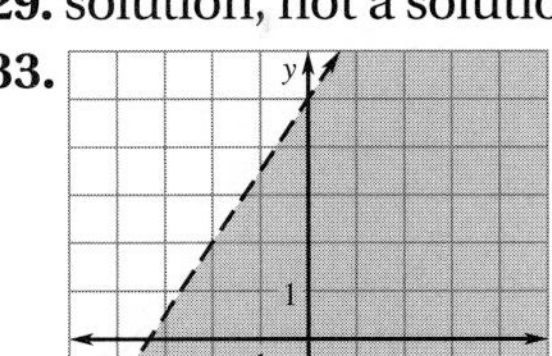

35. 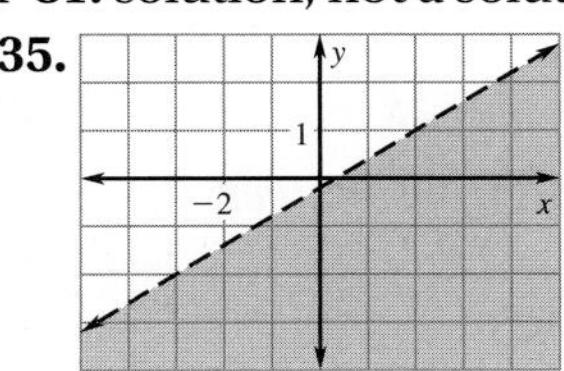

39. *Sample answer:* $y > x + 3$ **41.** $y > -\frac{3}{5}x + 3$; pick two points on the boundary line to find the slope and then use the point-slope form of an equation to find the equation. The boundary line is dotted, so the inequality dos not include points on the boundary. Then choose a point to determine which inequality sign to use. *Sample answer:* You and your sister want to spend at least \$15 on your little brother's birthday. You want to buy him some racecars that cost \$3 each and some building block sets that cost \$5 each.

2.8 Problem Solving (pp. 137–138) **43.** $0.03x + 0.06y \le 20$

45. $1.5x + 2.5y \le 75$

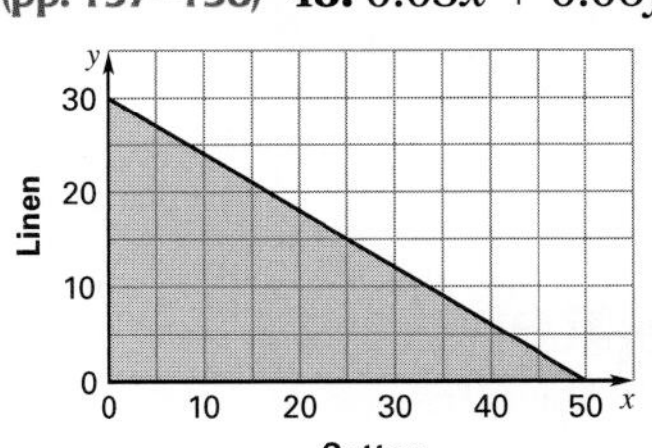

$y \le 15.6$ yd

47. a. $11x + 26y \le 120$

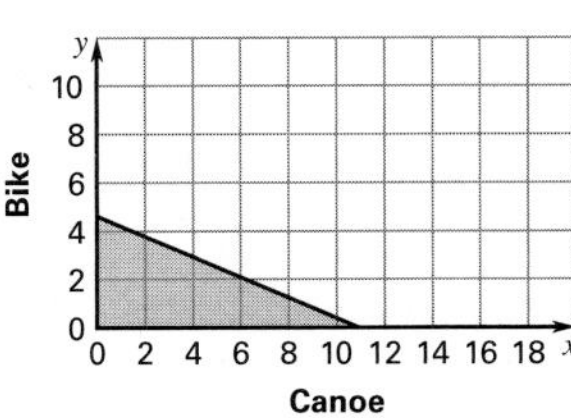

b. *Sample answer:* 2 days canoeing and 5 days biking, 3 days canoeing and 2 days biking, 2 days canoeing and 2 days biking

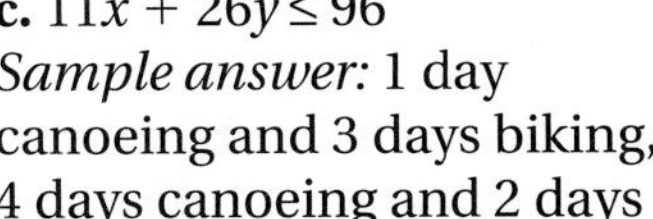

c. $11x + 26y \le 96$
Sample answer: 1 day canoeing and 3 days biking, 4 days canoeing and 2 days biking, 2 days canoeing and 2 days biking

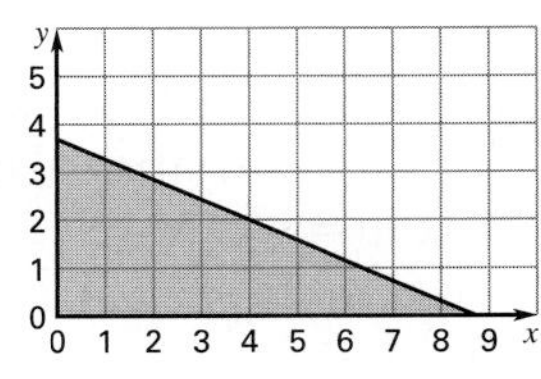

SELECTED ANSWERS

Chapter Review (pp. 141–144) **1.** standard **3.** direct variation **5.** domain: $-2, -1, 2, 3$, range: $-2, 0, 6, 8$; function **7.** linear function; 51 **9.** undefined **11.** 0

13. 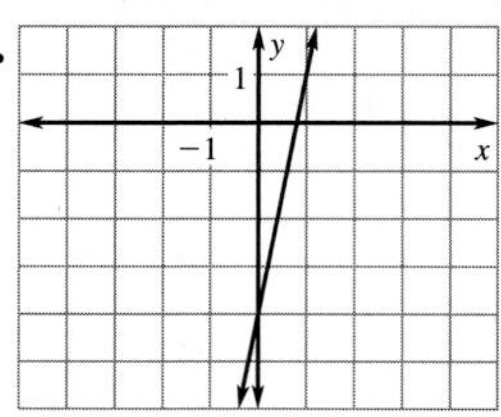 **15.** 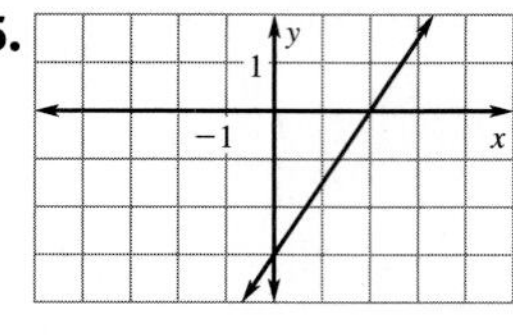

17. $y = -\frac{3}{4}x + 2$ **19.** $y = -8x$; -24 **21.** $y = -0.8x$; -2.4
23. *Sample answer:* $y = -x + 2.3$

25. 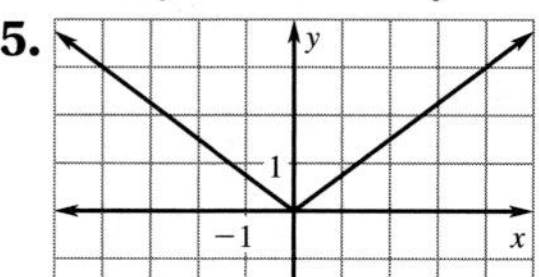 shrunk vertically by a factor of $\frac{3}{4}$

27. 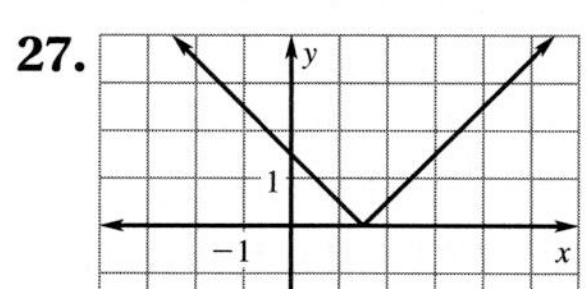 \$1.75, \$1.25

29. solution

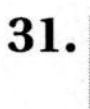

31. 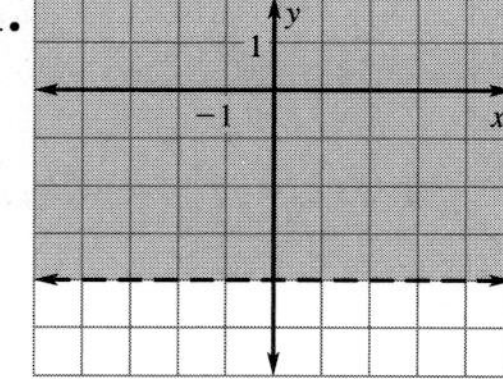 **33.** 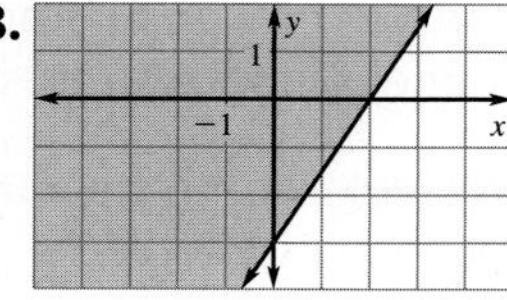

Chapter 3

3.1 Skill Practice (pp. 156–157) **1.** independent **3.** $(1, -1)$ **5.** $(4, -1)$ **7.** $(5, 0)$ **9.** $(-2, 4)$ **11.** infinitely many solutions **13.** $(3, 3)$ **17.** $(2, -1)$; consistent and independent **19.** no solution; inconsistent **21.** infinitely many solutions; consistent and dependent **23.** $(2, 0)$; consistent and independent **25.** $(3, -1)$; consistent and independent **27.** infinitely many solutions; consistent and dependent **31.** no solution **33.** $(-4, 2)$ and $(-4, 2)$

3.1 Problem Solving (pp. 157–158) **35.** lifeguard: 6 h, cashier: 8 h **37.** 11 days; the number of days will decrease; the number of days will be divided by a larger number, which will decrease the quotient, which is the number of days. **39. a.** $m = -0.0958x + 50.8$ **b.** $w = -0.124x + 57.1$ **c.** in the year 2195 **d.** No. *Sample answer:* It is not likely that the same linear models will apply indefinitely.

3.2 Skill Practice (pp. 164–165) **1.** substitution **3.** $(6, -1)$ **5.** no solution **7.** $\left(\frac{4}{3}, 2\right)$ **9.** $(0, 3)$ **11.** $(-3, 8)$ **13.** $(44, -17)$ **15.** $\left(7, \frac{1}{2}\right)$ **17.** $(-6, -2)$ **19.** $\left(-\frac{1}{2}, \frac{1}{6}\right)$ **21.** $(-8, 6)$ **23.** no solution **25.** $(7, 3)$
27. Failed to multiply the constant by -2.

$$\begin{array}{r} -6x - 4y = -14 \\ 5x + 4y = 15 \\ \hline -x = 1 \\ x = -1 \end{array}$$

29. $(-5, -6)$ **31.** infinitely many solutions **33.** $(-8, 0)$ **35.** $(7, -6)$ **37.** $\left(-\frac{3}{2}, 4\right)$ **39.** $\left(-\frac{3}{4}, \frac{1}{2}\right)$ **41.** $(2, 3)$ **43.** $(3, 2)$ **45.** about $(2.90, -2.16)$ **47.** $(-1, 2)$ **49.** $(7, 1)$ **51.** $\left(-\frac{1}{9}, 6\right)$ **53.** $(5, 4)$

3.2 Problem Solving (pp. 165–166) **55.** 5 acoustic, 4 electric **57.** The company can fill its orders by operating Factory A for 5 weeks and Factory B for 3 weeks. **59.** 12 doubles games, 14 singles games **61.** 80 pounds of peanuts, 20 pounds of cashews

3.3 Skill Practice (pp. 171–172) **1.** The ordered pair must satisfy each inequality of the system.

5. 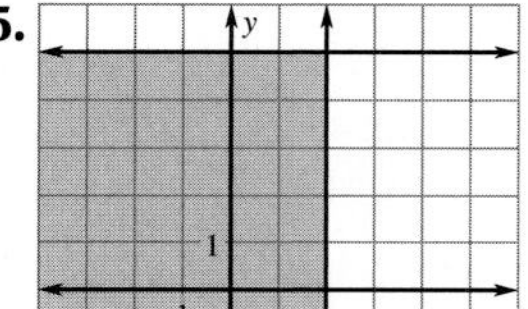 **7.** no solution

9. 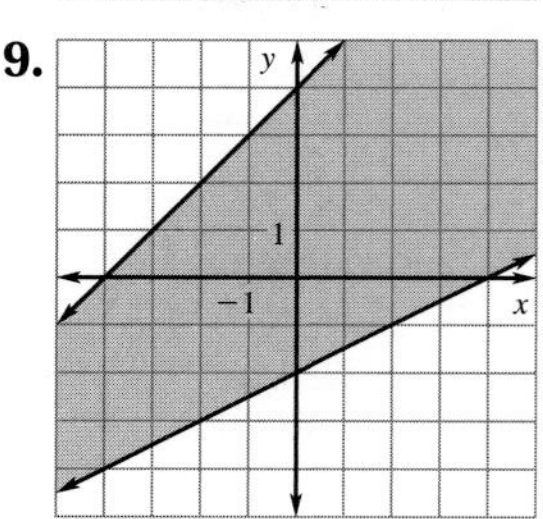 **17.** 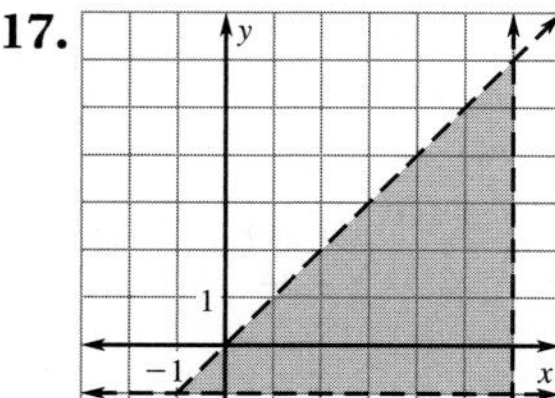

19. 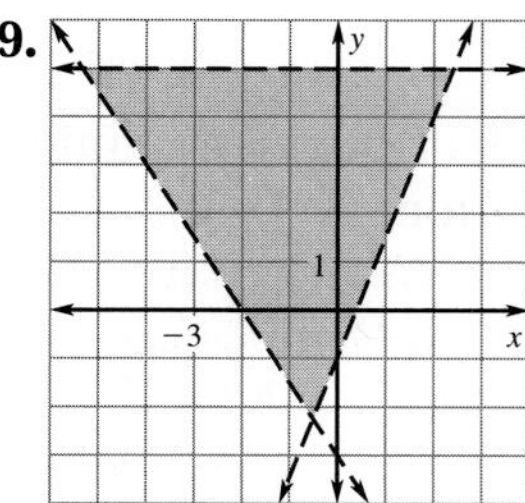

27. *Sample answer:* $y < x - 1$, $y < -\frac{3}{4}x + 4$

29. 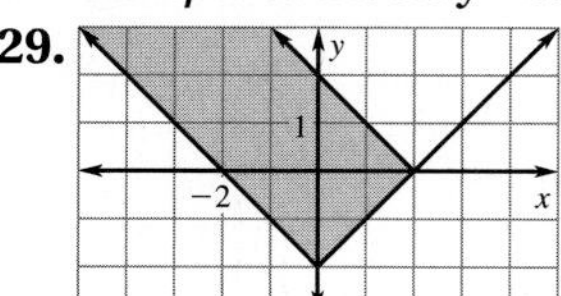

3.3 Problem Solving (pp. 172–173) **35.** $x \geq 20, x \leq 50, y \geq 0.3x, y \leq 0.7x$, where x represents the regular price and y represents the sale price; $6 \leq y \leq 14$ **37. a.** $x \geq 2, y \geq 2, x + y \leq 8, x + y \geq 5$

b.

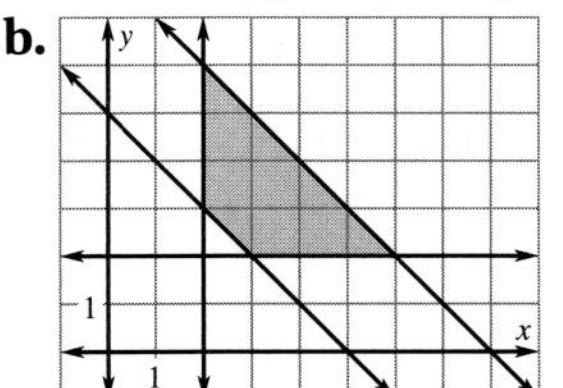

c. *Sample answer:* 3 juniors, 4 seniors; 4 juniors, 4 seniors

39. a. $x \geq 20, x \leq 65, y \geq 0.5(220 - x), y \leq 0.75(220 - x)$

b.

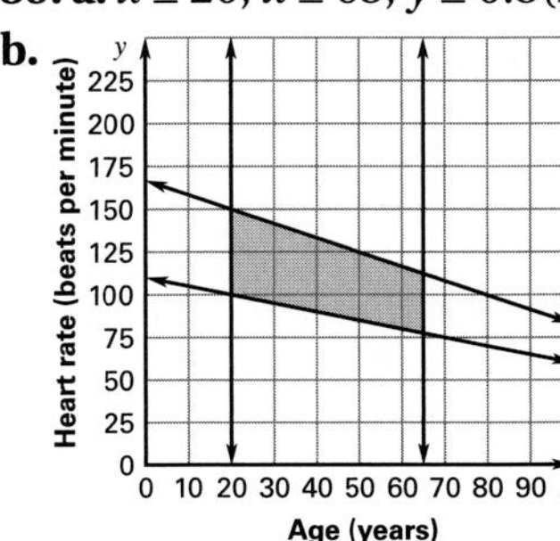

c. No; the person's heart rate is above the target zone. A 40-year old person's heart rate should be between 90 and 135 heartbeats per minute.

Extension (p. 176) **1.** 1; 14 **3.** 170; 580 **5.** 5; 55 **7.** 6 mini piñatas, 6 regular-sized piñatas **9.** 12 jars of tomato sauce, 4 jars of salsa

3.4 Skill Practice (pp. 182–183) **1.** *Sample answer:* $2x - 3y + z = 6$; a plane **3.** no **5.** yes **7.** no **9.** (1, 5, 6) **11.** no solution **13.** infinitely many solutions **15.** (3, 2, 1) **17.** (−6, 4, −4) **19.** (0, 0, −2) **21.** In the second equation, the coefficient of y was not multiplied by 2;

$$\begin{array}{l} 2x + \ \ y - 2z = 23 \\ 6x + 4y + 2z = 22 \\ \hline 8x + 5y \qquad\ = 45 \end{array}$$

25. infinitely many solutions **27.** (−1, 4, 0) **29.** (−4, 5, −4) **31.** (0, −2, 6) **33.** (2, 6, −5) **35.** (2, 1, 0) **37.** $a = 12, b = -4, c = 10$; when you substitute −1 for x, 2 for y, and −3 for z into each of the equations, you get the results for a, b, and c.

3.4 Problem Solving (pp. 184–185) **43.** 1st delivery: 300 gal; 2nd delivery: 750 gal; 3rd delivery: 2050 gal **45. a.** $f + s + t = 20, 5f + 3s + t = 68, s = f + t$, where f represents the number of first-place finishes, s represents the number of second-place finishes, and t represents the number of third-place finishes; 7 first-place finishes, 10 second-place finishes, 3 third-place finishes **b.** When you solve for f and t, you get a fractional answer and you cannot have fractions of a person. **47. a.** $2.5r + 4\ell + 2i = 32$, $r + \ell + i = 12, r = 2(\ell + i)$ where r represents the number of roses, ℓ represents the number of lilies, and i represents the number of irises **b.** 8 roses, 2 lilies, 2 irises **c.** yes; 8 roses, 2 lilies, 2 irises

3.5 Skill Practice (pp. 190–193) **1.** dimensions **3.** The corresponding entries were not added together to create a 2 × 1 matrix; $\begin{bmatrix} 13.1 \\ -1.2 \end{bmatrix}$ **5.** $\begin{bmatrix} -2 & -5 \\ 2 & 1 \end{bmatrix}$

7. $\begin{bmatrix} 3.6 & 4.7 \\ 6.2 & 7.5 \\ 14.3 & -1.2 \end{bmatrix}$ **9.** $\begin{bmatrix} -2 & -5 \\ 14 & -1 \\ -10 & 6 \end{bmatrix}$ **11.** $\begin{bmatrix} -6 & 0 & 15 \\ -12 & -21 & 9 \end{bmatrix}$

13. $\begin{bmatrix} -3 & 5.1 & 2.4 \\ 8.1 & 0 & -4.5 \end{bmatrix}$ **15.** $\begin{bmatrix} -13.2 & -6.82 & -9.9 \\ 2.2 & 0 & -5.5 \\ -12.1 & 3.96 & -14.08 \end{bmatrix}$

17. $\begin{bmatrix} 13 & -8 \\ -9 & 1 \end{bmatrix}$ **19.** $\begin{bmatrix} 12 & -8 \\ -4 & 0 \end{bmatrix}$ **21.** $\begin{bmatrix} 23.4 & -1.5 & -5.6 \\ -2.5 & -2.3 & 9.9 \end{bmatrix}$

23. $\begin{bmatrix} -6.3 & -0.75 & 10.7 \\ -6.5 & 3.6 & -3.3 \end{bmatrix}$ **25.** $x = \frac{19}{2}, y = 4$ **27.** $x = -2$, $y = -16$ **29.** *Sample answer:* $A = \begin{bmatrix} 5.5 & -3 \\ -8 & 7 \end{bmatrix}$, $B = \begin{bmatrix} 2 & -2 \\ -5 & 4 \end{bmatrix}$

3.5 Problem Solving (pp. 192–193)

31. $\begin{bmatrix} 0 & 5 & 1 & -1 \\ -7 & -1 & -5 & -2 \\ 1 & -1 & 4 & 10 \end{bmatrix}$ **33. a.** $M = \begin{array}{r} \text{Model A} \\ \text{Model B} \\ \text{Model C} \end{array} \begin{bmatrix} 31 & 22 \\ 42 & 25 \\ 18 & 11 \end{bmatrix}$, $J = \begin{array}{r} \text{Model A} \\ \text{Model B} \\ \text{Model C} \end{array} \begin{bmatrix} 25 & 38 \\ 36 & 32 \\ 12 & 15 \end{bmatrix}$ **b.** $\begin{bmatrix} 56 & 60 \\ 78 & 57 \\ 30 & 26 \end{bmatrix}$; the sum represents the total sales for May and June. **c.** $\begin{bmatrix} 28 & 30 \\ 39 & 28.5 \\ 15 & 13 \end{bmatrix}$

3.6 Skill Practice (pp. 199–200) **1.** columns; rows **3.** defined; 2 × 2 **5.** not defined **7.** not defined

11. $\begin{bmatrix} -2 & 1 \\ -8 & 4 \end{bmatrix}$ **13.** $\begin{bmatrix} -12 & 15 \\ 8 & -4 \end{bmatrix}$ **15.** $\begin{bmatrix} 11 & 35 \\ 8 & 0 \\ -9 & 7 \end{bmatrix}$

17. $\begin{bmatrix} 21 & -8 \\ 74 & -50 \end{bmatrix}$ **19.** The multiplication should be row 1 of left matrix by column 1 of the right matrix; $3(7) + (-1)(1) = 20$. **23.** $\begin{bmatrix} 21 & -6 \\ -14 & 1 \end{bmatrix}$ **25.** $\begin{bmatrix} -10 & 7 \\ -8 & 10 \end{bmatrix}$

27. $\begin{bmatrix} -2 & 4 & 0 \\ 5 & 15 & 8 \\ -16 & 17 & 36 \end{bmatrix}$ **29.** $\begin{bmatrix} -204 & 81 \\ 160 & -38 \end{bmatrix}$ **31.** $x = 3, y = 35$

33. $\begin{bmatrix} 18 & -5 \\ -10 & 3 \end{bmatrix}$, $\begin{bmatrix} -82 & 23 \\ 46 & -13 \end{bmatrix}$

35. *Sample answer:* $\begin{bmatrix} 3 & 7 \\ -2 & 5 \end{bmatrix}\begin{bmatrix} 1 & 0 \\ 0 & 1 \end{bmatrix}$

3.6 Problem Solving (pp. 200–202)

37. $\begin{matrix}\text{Bats}\\ \text{Balls}\\ \text{Uniforms}\end{matrix}\begin{bmatrix}12\\45\\15\end{bmatrix}$, $\begin{matrix} & \text{Bat} & \text{Ball} & \text{Uniform}\\ \text{Cost} & [\,21 & 4 & 30\,]\end{matrix}$; $\begin{matrix} & \text{Cost}\\ \text{Item} & [\,882\,]\end{matrix}$

39. Friday: \$1150, Saturday: \$1675

41. *PS*; $[\,62{,}400 \quad 57{,}575\,]$, it shows the profit for all of the cars sold by each dealer. **43. a.** $\begin{bmatrix}0.8 & 0.05\\0.2 & 0.95\end{bmatrix}$

b. $M_1 = \begin{bmatrix}4400\\8600\end{bmatrix}$; the number of commuters after 1 year

c. $M_2 = \begin{bmatrix}3950\\9050\end{bmatrix}$, $M_3 = \begin{bmatrix}3612.5\\9387.5\end{bmatrix}$, $M_4 = \begin{bmatrix}3359.375\\9640.625\end{bmatrix}$; the number of commuters after 2, 3, and 4 years

3.7 Skill Practice (pp. 207–208) **1.** determinant **3.** -6 **5.** 25 **7.** 8 **9.** 39 **11.** -206 **13.** -34 **15.** 1160 **17.** -480 **19.** The sum of the products for the diagonals that go up should be subtracted from the sum of the products for the diagonals that go down; $10 + 0 + (-8) - (3 + 24 + 0) = -25$ **23.** 12 **25.** 21 **27.** 25 **29.** $(-4, 3)$ **31.** $(-7, -5)$ **33.** $(6, -3, -7)$ **35.** $(0, 4, 1)$ **37.** $(8, 6, 7)$

3.7 Problem Solving (pp. 208–209) **41.** 12 ft^2 **43. a.** 60 single scoop, 40 double scoop, 20 triple scoop **b.** \$140.03 **45. a.** 4786 mi^2 **b.** 3201 mi^2 **c.** 7987 mi^2 **d.** Connect Vernal, UT, to Moab, UT.

3.8 Skill Practice (pp. 214–215)

1. matrix of variables $\begin{bmatrix}x\\y\end{bmatrix}$, matrix of constants $\begin{bmatrix}4\\-2\end{bmatrix}$

3. $\begin{bmatrix}-4 & -5\\-1 & -1\end{bmatrix}$ **5.** $\begin{bmatrix}1 & -1\\-\frac{5}{2} & 3\end{bmatrix}$ **7.** $\begin{bmatrix}-\frac{7}{4} & -\frac{3}{2}\\1 & 1\end{bmatrix}$

9. $\begin{bmatrix}-\frac{1}{12} & \frac{1}{6}\\-\frac{1}{60} & \frac{1}{15}\end{bmatrix}$ **11.** The scalar should be $\frac{1}{\det}$;

$\frac{1}{6}\begin{bmatrix}5 & -4\\-1 & 2\end{bmatrix} = \begin{bmatrix}\frac{5}{6} & -\frac{2}{3}\\-\frac{1}{6} & \frac{1}{3}\end{bmatrix}$. **13.** $\begin{bmatrix}11 & 9\\-9 & -6\end{bmatrix}$

15. $\begin{bmatrix}-3 & 1\\\frac{11}{2} & -\frac{1}{4}\end{bmatrix}$ **17.** $\begin{bmatrix}18 & 19 & 10\\-3 & -4 & -2\end{bmatrix}$

19. $\begin{bmatrix}-\frac{3}{10} & -\frac{1}{5} & \frac{3}{10}\\\frac{9}{10} & \frac{3}{5} & \frac{1}{10}\\-\frac{1}{5} & \frac{1}{5} & \frac{1}{5}\end{bmatrix}$ **21.** $\begin{bmatrix}-\frac{1}{2} & 0 & \frac{1}{2}\\-\frac{17}{16} & \frac{1}{8} & \frac{7}{16}\\\frac{7}{32} & \frac{1}{16} & -\frac{1}{32}\end{bmatrix}$

23. $\begin{bmatrix}\frac{3}{20} & \frac{3}{10} & \frac{1}{20}\\-\frac{11}{160} & \frac{9}{80} & \frac{3}{160}\\-\frac{1}{40} & -\frac{1}{20} & -\frac{7}{40}\end{bmatrix}$ **25.** $(3, 2)$ **27.** $(-1, -4)$

29. $(10, -2)$ **31.** $(1, -8)$ **33.** $(-3, 5)$ **35.** $(-9, 19, -10)$ **37.** $(-1, -2, 3)$ **39.** $(-2, 10, 0)$

41. *Sample answer:* $\begin{bmatrix}2 & 3\\4 & 6\end{bmatrix}$

3.8 Problem Solving (pp. 215–217) **43.** single-engine: 150 h, twin-engine: 50 h **45. a.** $2x + y = 8$, $3x + y = 11$ where x represents rolls and y represents muffins

b. $\begin{bmatrix}2 & 1\\3 & 1\end{bmatrix}\begin{bmatrix}x\\y\end{bmatrix} = \begin{bmatrix}8\\11\end{bmatrix}$ **c.** 3 batches of rolls, 2 batches of muffins **47.** Bran Crunchies: 2.3 oz, Toasted Oats: 0.8 oz, Whole Wheat Flakes: 1.2 oz

49. a. $\begin{bmatrix}1 & 4 & 2\\-1 & -3 & -5\end{bmatrix}$, $\begin{bmatrix}-1 & -3 & -5\\-1 & -4 & -2\end{bmatrix}$; 90° clockwise rotation **b.** multiply *AAT* by *A* and then again by *A*

3.8 Problem Solving Workshop (p. 219) **1.** DVD: \$15, popcorn: \$1.75, movie pass: \$8 **3.** 11 lbs of sunflower seed, 9 lbs of thistle seed

Chapter Review (pp. 222–226) **1.** consistent, inconsistent **3.** The number of columns in the left hand matrix is the same as the number of rows in the right hand matrix.

5. 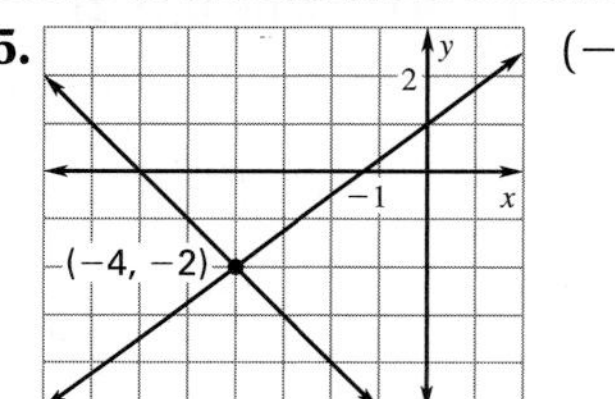

$(-4, -2)$

7. $(-3, 7)$ **9.** $(-6, 7)$

11. 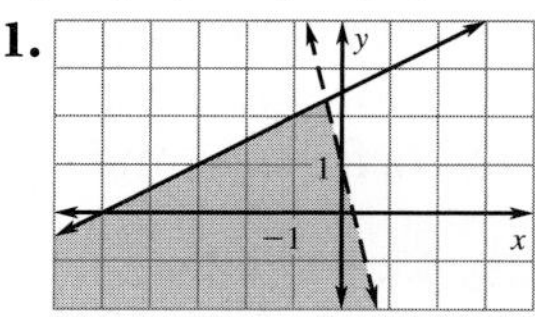

13.

15. $(-3, -8, 4)$ **17.** 10 wind instruments, 3 string instruments, 2 percussion instruments

19. $\begin{bmatrix}6 & 4\\8 & -4\end{bmatrix}$ **21.** $\begin{bmatrix}2 & -4 & 0\\7 & 6 & 7\end{bmatrix}$ **23.** $\begin{bmatrix}64 & 32 & 40\\-8 & 48 & -16\end{bmatrix}$

25. $\begin{bmatrix}28 & -76\\-20 & 10\end{bmatrix}$ **27.** $\begin{bmatrix}-2 & 6 & -15\\6 & 0 & -3\end{bmatrix}$ **29.** -42 **31.** 18

33. $(7, 1)$ **35.** $(-1, -4)$

Cumulative Review (pp. 232–233) **1.** $-2x^2 + 7x$ **3.** $-4x^2 + 6x + 15$ **5.** $-\frac{5}{2}$ **7.** $-8, 2$ **9.** $-16, 25$

SELECTED ANSWERS

11. $5 \le x \le 10$

13. $-1 < x < 9$

15. $-4 < x < \frac{11}{3}$

17. $-\frac{7}{12}$; falls **19.** 0; is horizontal

21.

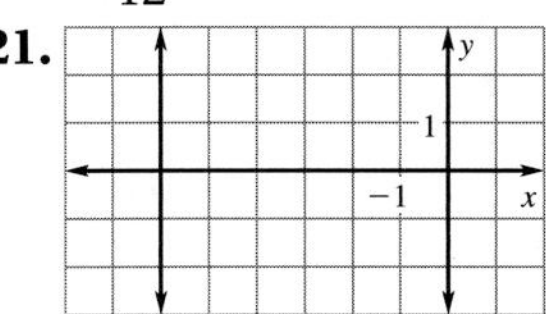

23.

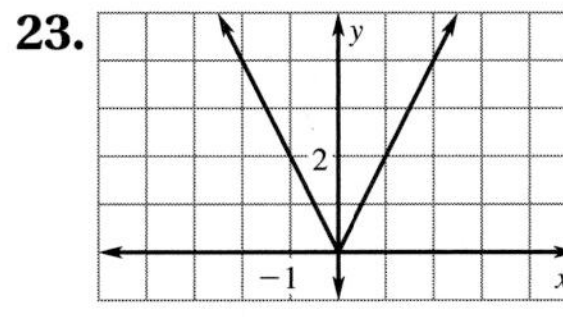

25.

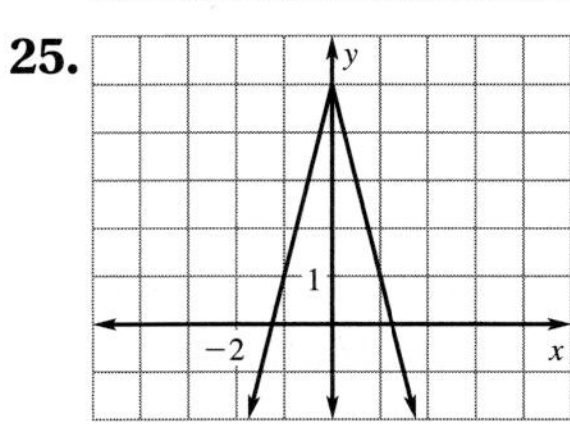

27.

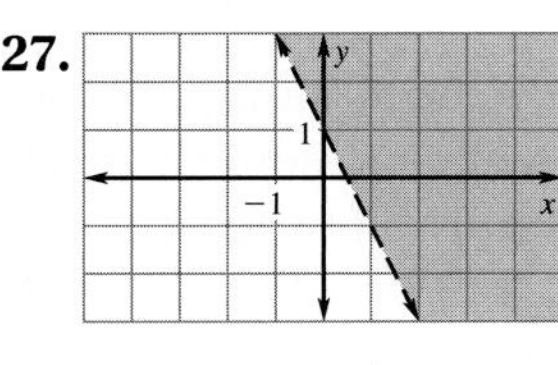

29.

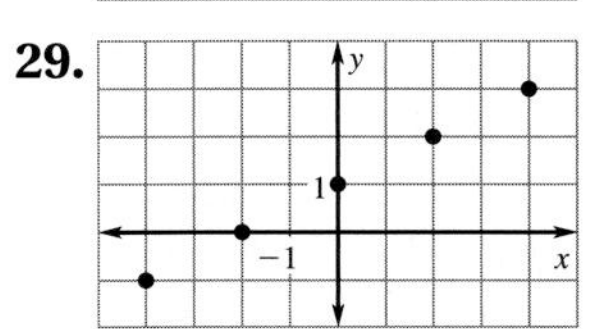

function

31. (5, −4) **33.** (−2, 4, 1) **35.** $\begin{bmatrix} 6 & 2 \\ 19 & 0 \end{bmatrix}$

37. $\begin{bmatrix} -15 & 21 & -3 \\ -30 & 42 & -6 \end{bmatrix}$ **39.** $\begin{bmatrix} -\frac{4}{3} & -3 \\ 1 & 2 \end{bmatrix}$ **41.** $\begin{bmatrix} -\frac{1}{3} & -\frac{1}{3} \\ -\frac{1}{12} & -\frac{5}{24} \end{bmatrix}$

43. a. $W = \frac{TR^2}{R^2 + A^2}$ **b.** About 98 games; it's the same.

45. $c = \frac{1}{20}p$; \$6250 **47.** $s > 213, j < 263, s + j > 472.5$

Chapter 4

4.1 Skill Practice (pp. 240–241) **1.** parabola **3.** 16, 4, 0, 4, 16 **5.** 8, 2, 0, 2, 8

7.

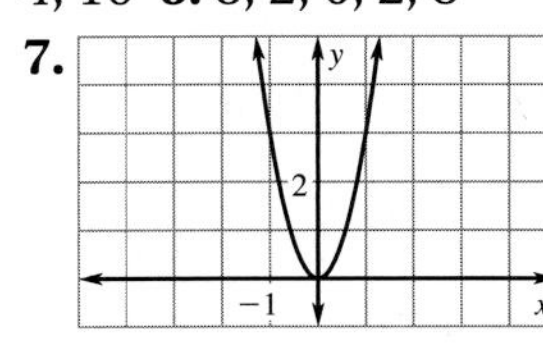

same axis of symmetry and vertex, opens up, and is narrower

9.

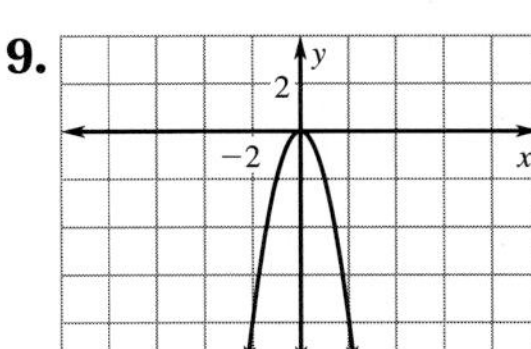

same axis of symmetry and vertex, opens down, and is narrower

19. The formula for the x-coordinate of the vertex is $-\frac{b}{2a}$; $-\frac{24}{2(4)} = -3$.

21.

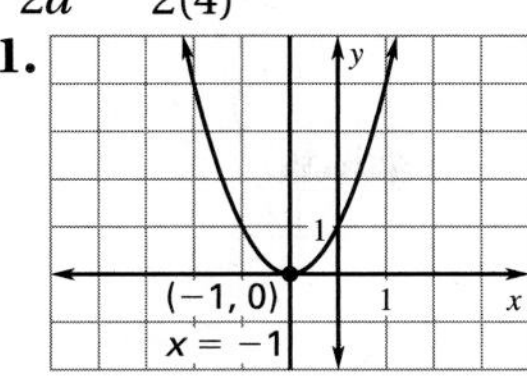

23.

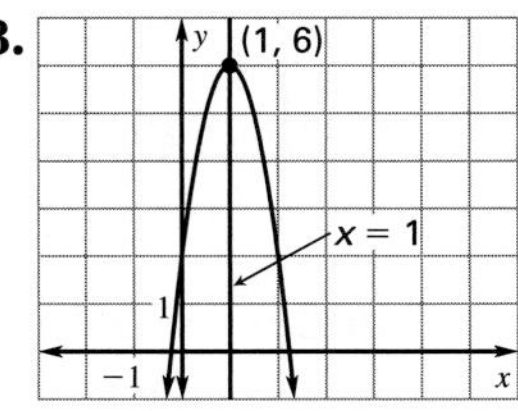

33. maximum value; −1 **35.** minimum value; −1 **37.** minimum value; −2 **41.** $a = -0.02, b = 1, c = 6$ **43.** *Sample answer:* $y = -x^2 + 8x + 3$, $y = 2x^2 - 16x - 1$, $y = x^2 - 8x - 6$

47. x = 0, (0, 2)

49.

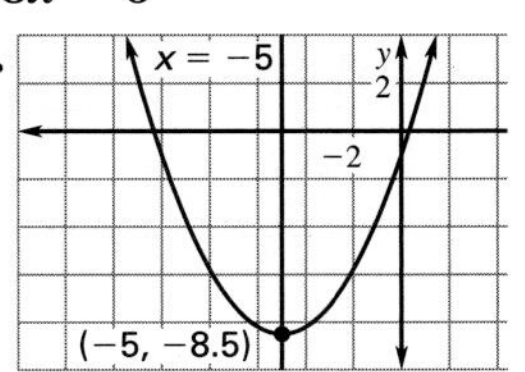

53. The axis of symmetry has to lie half way between the two x-coordinates; $x = -1$.

4.1 Problem Solving (pp. 242–243) **55.** Raise the price by \$0.75 to increase revenue to \$4900 per day. **57.** about 10 ft **59. a.** profit = price • sales − expenses; $P(x) = (20 - x)(150 + 10x) - 1500$

b.

x	$P(x)$
0	1500
1	1540
2	1560
3	1560
4	1540
5	1500

c.

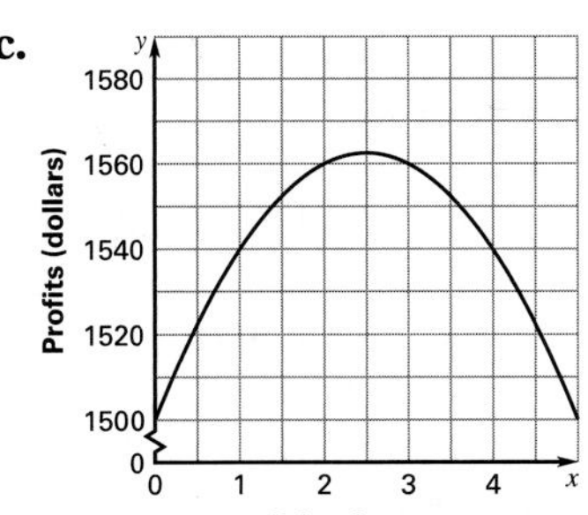

Reduce the price by \$2.50 to increase profits to \$1562.50 per week.

4.2 Skill Practice (pp. 249–250) **1.** vertex

3.

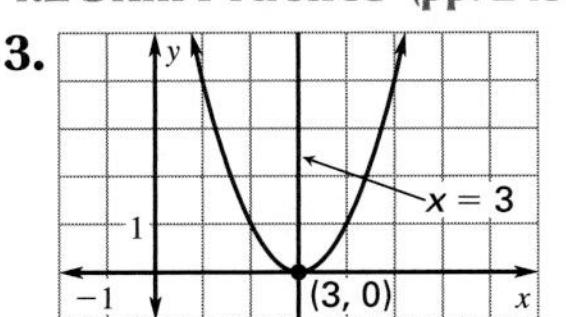

5.

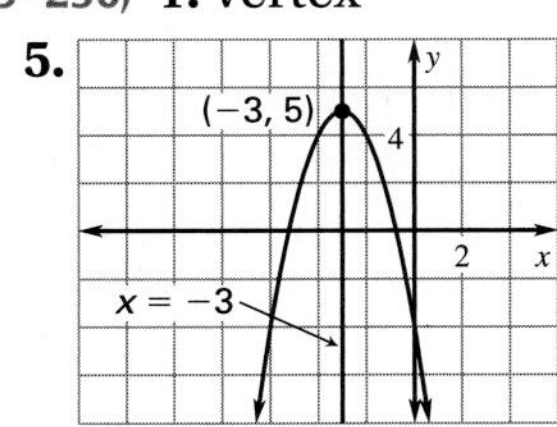

13. 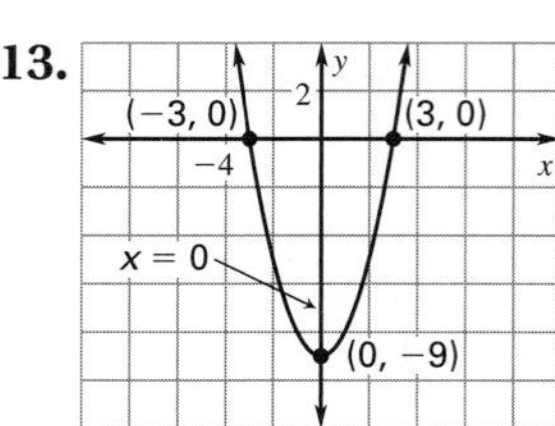

15. 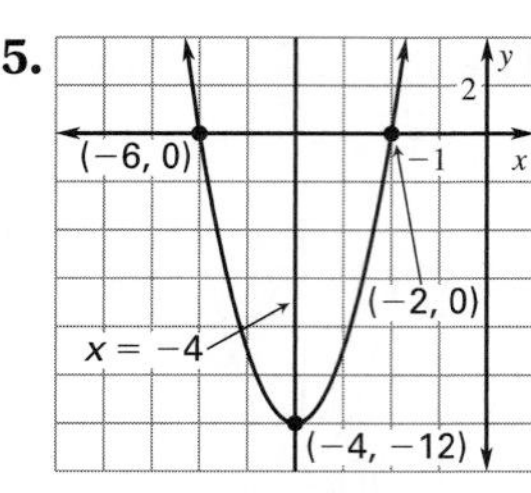

23. $p = 2$ and $q = -3$; the x-intercepts are 2 and -3. **25.** $y = x^2 - 2x - 15$ **27.** $y = -3x^2 + 18x - 24$ **29.** $y = x^2 - 6x + 15$ **31.** $y = 5x^2 + 30x + 41$ **33.** minimum: -4 **35.** minimum: 130 **37.** maximum: 729 **39.** minimum: -450 **41.** maximum: 211.25

43. 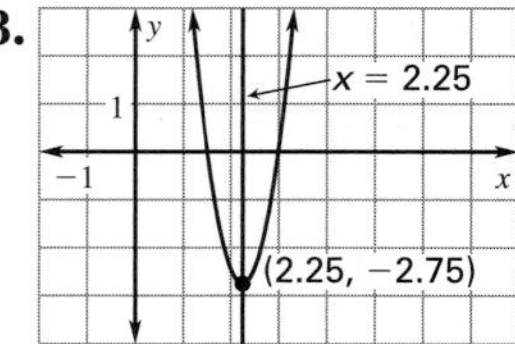

45. 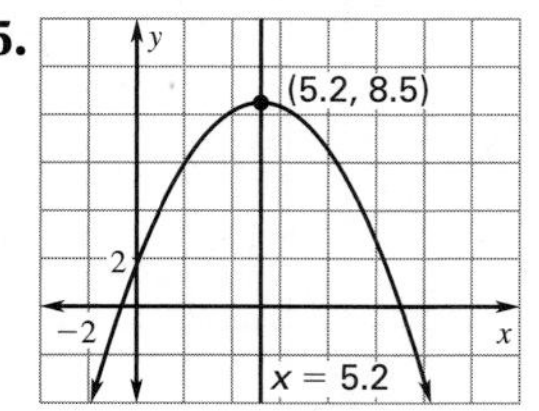

49. *Sample answer:* $y = (x - 8)(x + 2)$, $y = (x - 4)(x - 2)$, $y = (x + 3)(x - 9)$

4.2 Problem Solving (pp. 250–251) **51.** 6 ft; about 28 ft **53. a.** 160 ft **b.** about 1.5 ft **55. a.** about 14%; about 55.5 cm^3 **b.** about 13.6%; about 44.1 cm^3 **c.** hot-air: domain: $5.52 < x < 22.6$, range: $0 < y < 55.5$; hot oil: domain: $5.35 < x < 21.8$, range: $0 < y < 44.1$; since moisture content and popping volume cannot be negative, the domain and range must each be positive numbers. A positive domain occurs between the x-intercepts and the greatest number in the range occurs at the maximum point, which is the vertex.

4.3 Skill Practice (pp. 255–257) **1.** an x value that makes the function equal to zero **3.** $(x + 1)(x + 5)$ **5.** $(a - 11)(a - 2)$ **7.** cannot be factored **9.** $(b + 8)(b - 5)$ **11.** $(x - 9)(x + 2)$ **13.** $(x + 12)(x - 3)$ **15.** $(x + 6)(x - 6)$ **17.** $(x - 12)^2$ **19.** $(x + 4)^2$ **21.** $(n + 7)^2$ **23.** $(z - 11)(z + 11)$ **25.** 5, 6 **27.** -7, 7 **29.** -4, -1 **31.** -5 **33.** -6, 9 **35.** 0, -9 **37.** 7 **39.** The equation was not factored correctly; $x^2 - x - 6 = 0$, $(x - 3)(x + 2) = 0$, $x = 3$ or $x = -2$. **43.** $3(10)(12) = (10 + x)(12 + x)$ **45.** 4 **47.** -10, 3 **49.** 0, 8 **51.** -5, 5 **53.** -12, -7 **55.** -1 **57.** $x^2 - 19x + 88 = 0$ **59.** 4 **61.** 3 **63.** *Sample answer:* $x^2 - 20x + 91 = 0$

4.3 Problem Solving (pp. 257–258) **65.** $3(50)(100) = (50 + x)(100 + x)$, -200, 50; 100 ft by 150 ft **67. a.** 600 ft^2 **b.** area of new patio = area of existing patio + area of expansion, $(30 + x)(20 + x) = 600 + 464$ **c.** -58, 8; 8 ft **69.** $3(18)(15) = (18 + x)(15 + x)$, -45, 12; 114 ft **71.** $2(100) = (10 + x)(10 + x)$; no; there are no real numbers a and b such that $ab = -100$ and $a + b = 20$.

4.4 Skill Practice (pp. 263–264) **1.** 4 **3.** $(2x + 3)(x + 1)$ **5.** $(4r + 1)(r + 1)$ **7.** $(11z - 9)(z + 1)$ **9.** cannot be factored **11.** $(9d + 5)(d - 2)$ **13.** $(3x + 1)(3x - 1)$ **15.** $(7n - 4)(7n + 4)$ **17.** $(7x + 5)^2$ **19.** $(3p - 2)^2$ **21.** $(6x - 7)^2$ **23.** $2(3z + 4)(3z + 2)$ **25.** $6u(u - 4)$ **27.** $4(5x + 1)(x + 6)$ **29.** $-3(6n - 5)(2n - 1)$ **31.** 4 should be factored out of each term in the binomial; $4x^2 - 36 = 4(x^2 - 9) = 4(x + 3)(x - 3)$. **33.** -2, 2 **35.** 0, $-\frac{2}{9}$ **37.** $-1\frac{1}{2}$ **39.** $-\frac{1}{2}$, $1\frac{2}{3}$ **41.** $-\frac{1}{4}$, 5 **43.** $-\frac{3}{5}$, 6 **45.** $-\frac{3}{11}$, 2 **47.** -1, $1\frac{1}{3}$ **49.** -1, $\frac{7}{12}$ **51.** 3 **53.** -1, $2\frac{2}{3}$ **55.** $-\frac{7}{9}$, 2 **57.** 0, 4

4.4 Problem Solving (pp. 264–265) **63.** 2 ft **65.** \$5.75; letting x represent the number of \$.25 decreases in the sandwich price, the revenue R is given by the function $R = (330 + 15x)(6 - 0.25x)$. The zeros of this function are -22 and 24, and their average is 1. So, to maximize the daily revenue, each sandwich should be sold for $6 - 0.25(1)$, or \$5.75. The maximum daily revenue is then $(330 + 15(1))(5.75) = (345)(5.75) = \$1983.75$. **67. a.** 72 in. **b.** $w = 32 - h$; $V = 36(36 - h)(h)$ **c.** 18 in., 18 in., 11,664 $in.^3$; find the roots of the equation in part (b) to be 0 and 36, so the line of symmetry is at $x = \frac{36 + 0}{2} = 18$. To find the maximum volume, substitute 18 for h into the equation from part (b).

4.5 Skill Practice (pp. 269–270) **1.** radicand **3.** $2\sqrt{7}$ **5.** $5\sqrt{6}$ **7.** 24 **9.** $\frac{\sqrt{5}}{4}$ **11.** $\frac{8\sqrt{3}}{3}$ **13.** $\frac{3\sqrt{22}}{11}$ **15.** $-\sqrt{3} - 1$ **17.** $\frac{4\sqrt{2} - \sqrt{10}}{11}$ **21.** The equation has two solutions; $x^2 = 81$, $x = \pm 9$. **23.** $\pm 5\sqrt{2}$ **25.** ± 5 **27.** $\pm\sqrt{71}$ **29.** ± 10 **31.** $1 \pm \sqrt{2}$ **33.** $-2 \pm \frac{\sqrt{26}}{2}$ **35.** Factor: $x^2 - 4 = 0$, $(x + 2)(x - 2) = 0$, $x = -2$ or $x = 2$; Solve the equation $x^2 - 4 = 0$, $x^2 = 4$, $x = \pm 2$.

4.5 Problem Solving (pp. 270–271) **39.** Earth: about 3.1 sec, Mars: 5 sec, Jupiter: about 2.0 sec, Saturn: about 3.2 sec, Pluto: about 12.2 sec **41. a.** $\pi r^2 = 100$ **b.** about 5.6 ft **c.** $\sqrt{\frac{s^2}{\pi}}$; $s^2 = \pi r^2$, $\frac{s^2}{\pi} = r^2$, $\sqrt{\frac{s^2}{\pi}} = r$

4.5 Problem Solving Workshop (p. 273) **1.** 1, 5 **3.** $1\frac{2}{3}$ **5.** about -4.4, about 1.4 **7.** about 108 mph **9.** 1.25 sec

4.6 Skill Practice (pp. 279–280) **1.** $a + bi$ **3.** $\pm 2i\sqrt{7}$ **5.** $\pm 2i$ **7.** $\pm i\sqrt{11}$ **9.** $\pm i$ **11.** $3 \pm i\sqrt{2}$ **13.** $17 - i$ **15.** $-8 + 6i$ **17.** $19 - 9i$ **19.** $21 + 9i$ **23.** $-8 - 4i$ **25.** $-18 - 13i$ **27.** 73 **29.** $-\frac{3}{5} + \frac{9}{5}i$ **31.** $\frac{3}{4} - \frac{1}{3}i$

33. $-\frac{59}{106} - \frac{21}{106}i$ **43.** $\sqrt{109}$ **45.** $\sqrt{37}$ **47.** 4 **49.** $7\sqrt{2}$
51. $-20 + 2i$ **53.** $-125 + 90i$ **55.** $-\frac{5}{26} - \frac{51}{26}i$
57. $i^2 = -1$, so $-2i^2 = 2$; $4 - i + 8i - 2i^2 = 6 + 7i$.
59. a. additive: $-2 - i$, multiplicative: $\frac{2}{5} - \frac{1}{5}i$
b. additive: $-5 + i$, multiplicative: $\frac{5}{26} + \frac{1}{26}i$
c. additive: $1 - 3i$, multiplicative: $-\frac{1}{10} - \frac{3}{10}i$

4.6 Problem Solving (pp. 281–282) **65.** $4 - 3i$ ohms **67.** $12 - 8i$ ohms
69.

Powers of i	i	i^2	i^3	i^4	i^5	i^6	i^7	i^8
Simplified	i	-1	$-i$	1	i	-1	$-i$	1

The pattern repeats every four powers of i; $i^9 = i$, $i^{10} = -1$, $i^{11} = -i$, $i^{12} = 1$.
71. does not belong to the Mandelbrot set
73. belongs to the Mandelbrot set
75. a. $\frac{519}{125} + \frac{167}{125}i$ **b.** $\frac{2326}{265} + \frac{668}{265}i$ **c.** $\frac{98}{37} - \frac{4}{37}i$

4.7 Skill Practice (pp. 288–289) **1.** A binomial is the sum of two monomials and a trinomial is the sum of three monomials. **3.** $-5, 1$ **5.** $-14, -2$ **7.** $11 \pm \sqrt{13}$ **9.** $-4 \pm 3\sqrt{5}$ **11.** $\frac{2 \pm i\sqrt{3}}{3}$ **13.** 9; $(x + 3)^2$ **15.** 144; $(x - 12)^2$ **17.** 1; $(x - 1)^2$ **19.** $\frac{49}{4}$; $\left(x + \frac{7}{2}\right)^2$ **21.** $\frac{1}{4}$; $\left(x - \frac{1}{2}\right)^2$ **23.** $-4 \pm \sqrt{15}$ **25.** $-6 \pm 3\sqrt{2}$ **27.** $1 \pm 2i\sqrt{6}$ **29.** $-7 \pm \sqrt{41}$ **31.** $-1 \pm i\sqrt{2}$ **33.** $-\frac{1}{2} \pm \frac{i\sqrt{7}}{2}$ **35.** $-5 + 5\sqrt{3}$ **37.** $-2 + 2\sqrt{21}$ **39.** (2.8, 125.44); at 2.8 seconds the water will reach a maximum height of 125.44 feet. **41.** $y = (x - 4)^2 + 3$; (4, 3) **43.** $y = (x + 6)^2 + 1$; $(-6, 1)$ **45.** $y = \left(x - \frac{3}{2}\right)^2 + \frac{7}{4}$; $\left(\frac{3}{2}, \frac{7}{4}\right)$ **47.** $y = 2(x + 6)^2 - 47$; $(-6, -47)$ **49.** $y = 2(x - 7)^2 + 1$; (7, 1) **51.** 36 should be added to each side instead of 9; $4(x^2 + 6x + 9) = 11 + 36$; $4(x + 3)^2 = 47$; $(x + 3)^2 = \frac{47}{4}$; $x + 3 = \pm\frac{\sqrt{47}}{2}$; $x = -3 \pm \frac{\sqrt{47}}{2}$. **53.** $-\frac{3}{2} \pm i\frac{\sqrt{47}}{2}$ **55.** $\frac{1}{6} \pm i\frac{\sqrt{71}}{6}$ **57.** $-0.5 \pm 0.5i\sqrt{19}$

4.7 Problem Solving (pp. 290–291) **63.** 40 ft **65.** Selling systems for \$300 would maximize monthly revenue at \$9000. **67. a.** $1500 = (120 - 2x)(x)$ **b.** about 17.75, about 42.25; 17.25 must be rejected because it gives a length for the garden that is greater than the length of the side of the school. **c.** about 42.25 ft by 35.5 ft

4.8 Skill Practice (pp. 296–297) **1.** discriminant **3.** $-1, 5$ **5.** $-4 \pm i\sqrt{3}$ **7.** $\frac{1}{2}$ **9.** $\frac{2 \pm \sqrt{3}}{2}$ **11.** $\frac{4 \pm \sqrt{43}}{3}$ **13.** 2 **15.** $\frac{-3 \pm i\sqrt{47}}{2}$ **17.** $-\frac{5 \pm 2\sqrt{10}}{5}$ **19.** $\frac{-7 \pm \sqrt{13}}{6}$ **21.** $\frac{5 \pm \sqrt{31}}{3}$ **23.** 2, 3 **25.** $-1, 3$ **27.** $-2, 4$ **29.** $-5, -3$ **31.** 0; one real solution **33.** -32; two imaginary solutions **35.** -20; two imaginary solutions **37.** -335; two imaginary solutions **39.** -36; two imaginary solutions **41.** $\frac{1 \pm i\sqrt{67}}{2}$ **43.** $-2\frac{1}{2}, \frac{5}{14}$ **45.** $\frac{1 \pm \sqrt{229}}{12}$ **47.** $0.875 \pm 0.752i$ **49.** $\sqrt{-144} = 12i$; $x = \frac{-6 \pm \sqrt{-144}}{6}$; $x = \frac{-6 \pm 12i}{6}$; $x = -1 \pm 2i$
51. $\dfrac{\frac{-b + \sqrt{b^2 - 4ac}}{2a} + \frac{-b - \sqrt{b^2 - 4ac}}{2a}}{2} = \dfrac{\frac{-2b}{2a}}{2} = \frac{-b}{2a}$, which is the formula for the axis of symmetry. **53.** negative **57. a.** $c < 16$ **b.** $c = 16$ **c.** $c > 16$ **59. a.** $c < 48$ **b.** $c = 48$ **c.** $c > 48$ **61. a.** $c < 0.25$ **b.** $c = 0.25$ **c.** $c > 0.25$ **63.** $-\frac{1}{3}x^2 - \frac{1}{3}x + 4 = 0$ **65.** $2x^2 + 4x + 4 = 0$

4.8 Problem Solving (pp. 298–299) **71.** 1141 m, 2090 m
73. a.

t	0	0.25	.05	0.75	1
(x, y)	(0, 6)	(5, 10.25)	(10, 12.5)	(15, 12.75)	(20, 11)

b.

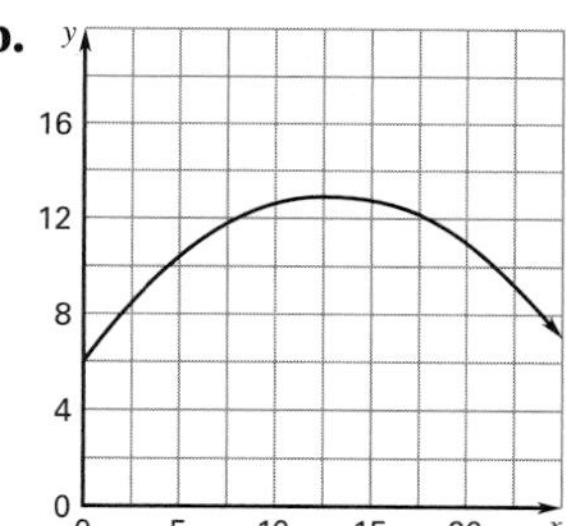

c. No; the height of the ball when $x = 15$ is 12.75 feet, which is above the backboard, so the free throw would not be made.

4.9 Skill Practice (pp. 304–305)
1. *Sample answer:* $3x^2 - 2x + 5 > 0$, $y \geq x^2 + 4x - 8$

7.

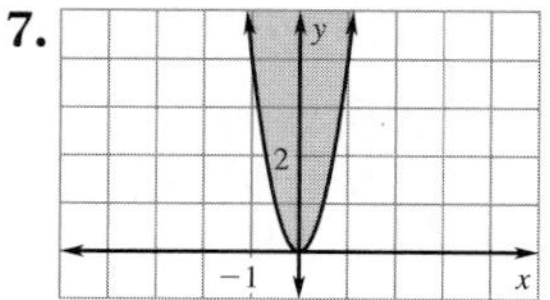

9.

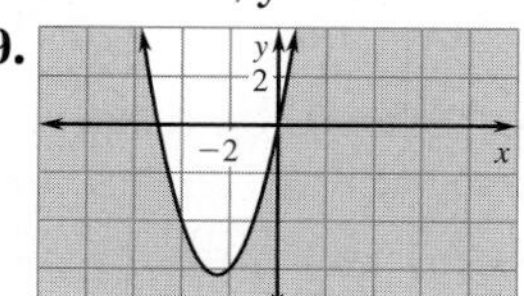

19.

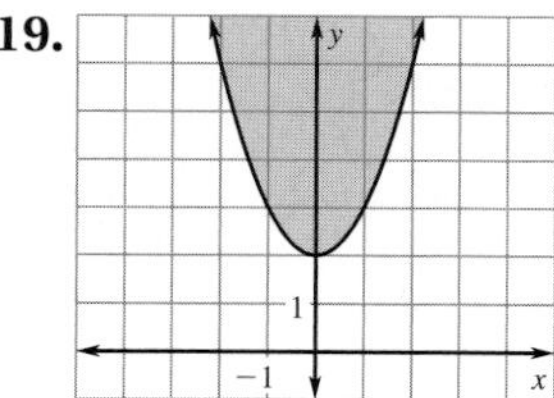

The inside of the parabola should be shaded.

SELECTED ANSWERS

21. 23.

27. $x < -3$ or $x > 1$ **29.** $x \le -2$ or $x \ge 4$ **31.** $2 < x < 8$ **33.** $-1 \le x \le 3$ **35.** $0 < x < 6$ **37.** $x < 0.59$ or $x > 3.4$ **39.** $-2 \le x \le 1.3$ **41.** $0.67 \le x \le 2.5$ **43.** $-1.2 < x < 3.7$ **47.** $-9 < x < -1$ **49.** $x < -\frac{2}{3}$ or $x > 5$ **51.** $x \le -3.5$ or $x \ge 1.5$ **53.** $-0.27 \le x \le 1.5$ **55.** $-2.8 \le x \le -0.72$ **57.** $x < -0.46$ or $x > 1.8$ **59.** $-0.89 < x < 1.3$ **61.** no solution **63.** $x < 0.52$ or $x > 11.5$ **65.** $0 \le x \le 0.5$ **67.** no solution

4.9 Problem Solving (pp. 306–307)

71.

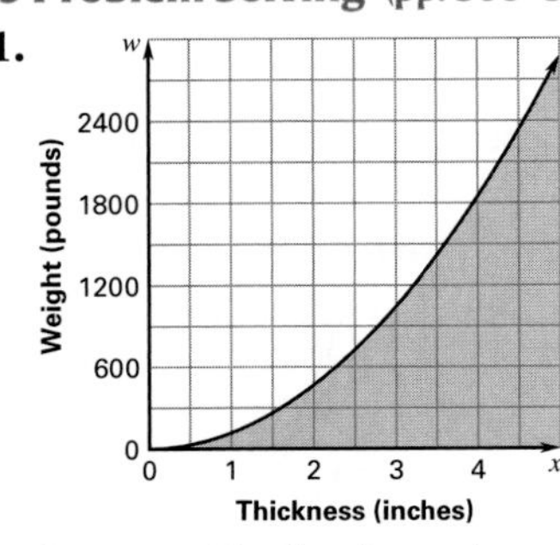

73. $37 \le x \le 40$; the domain restricts the number of days to less than or equal to 40. **75. a.** $-0.054x^2 + 1.43x - 8 < 0$; $x \le 8.0$ or $x \ge 18.5$ **b.** No; the ball will go over the goal by 1.3 feet.

4.10 Skill Practice (pp. 312–313) **1.** best-fitting quadratic model **3.** $y = (x - 3)^2 + 2$ **5.** $y = \frac{1}{2}(x + 1)^2 - 3$ **7.** $y = -(x - 1)^2 + 6$ **9.** $y = -\frac{1}{4}(x + 3)^2 + 3$ **11.** $y = 2(x + 4)^2 - 2$ **13.** $y = \frac{1}{3}(x + 1)^2 - 4$ **17.** $y = -(x - 3)(x + 2)$ **19.** $y = \frac{1}{2}(x + 3)(x - 3)$ **21.** $y = x(x + 3)$ **23.** $y = 3(x - 3)(x - 7)$ **25.** $y = \frac{1}{2}(x + 6)(x - 3)$ **27.** The vertex form of the equation should be used instead of the intercept form; $y = a(x - 2)^2 + 3$; $5 = a(1 - 2)^2 + 3$; $5 = a + 3$; $a = 2$, so $y = 2(x - 2)^2 + 3$. **29.** $y = 2x^2 + 20x + 46$ **31.** $y = \frac{7}{4}x^2 + \frac{29}{4}x - 2$ **33.** $y = -\frac{11}{2}x^2 - \frac{21}{2}x + 5$ **35.** $y = 3x^2 - 4x + 2$ **37.** $y = -\frac{1}{2}x^2 + 4x - 3$ **39.** $y = -\frac{2}{3}x^2 + 2x + 10$ **41.** $y = 8x^2 + 64x - 264$ **43.** *Sample answer:* $y = \frac{3}{4}x^2$

4.10 Problem Solving (pp. 314–315)

47. $y = -\frac{3}{80}(x - 20)^2 + 15$ **49. a.** $y = 0.012x^2 - 0.309x - 0.00048$ **b.** about -1.90 sec

Chapter Review (pp. 318–322) **1.** If $a < 0$, the function has a maximum value and if $a > 0$, then the function has a minimum value. **3.** vertex form

5.

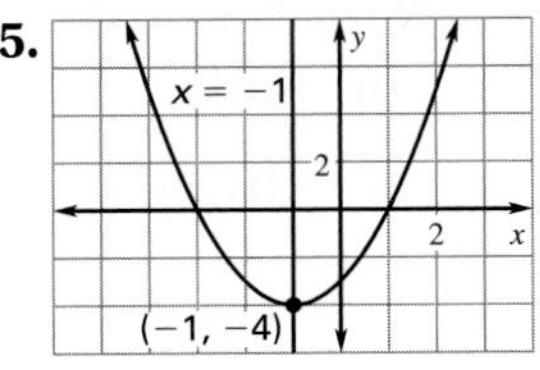

7.

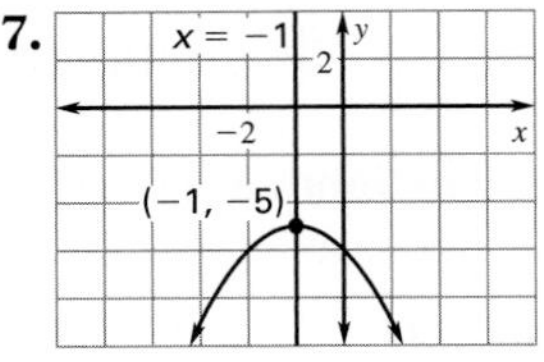

9.

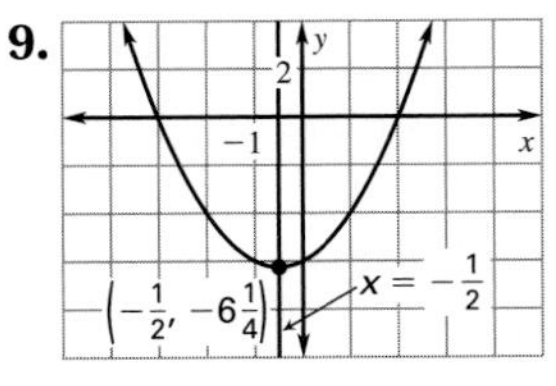

11.

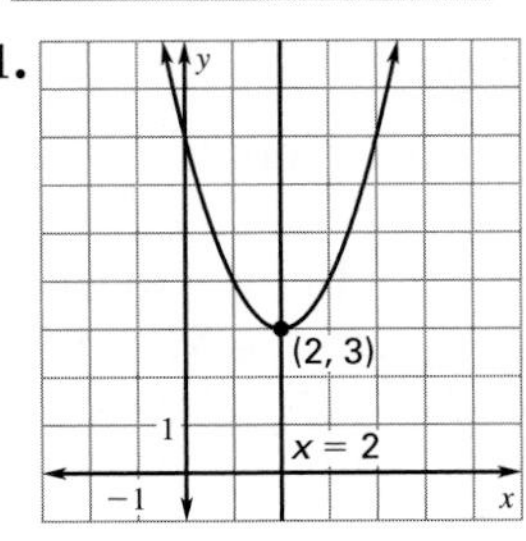

13.

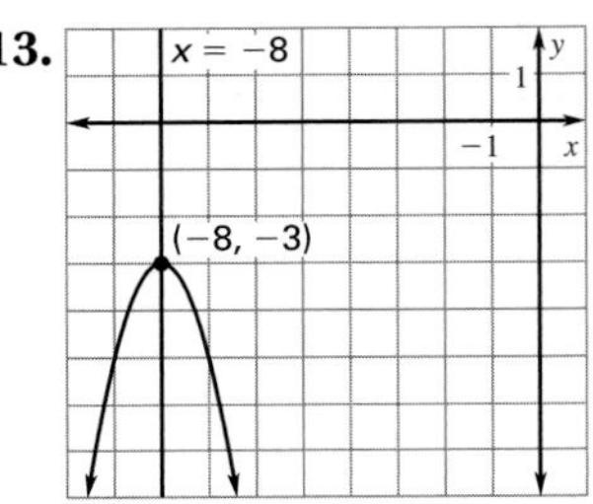

15. $-5, 0$ **17.** $-3, 9$ **19.** -9 **21.** $(72 + x)(48 + x) = 2(72)(48)$; 24 ft **23.** $4 \pm 4\sqrt{2}$ **25.** ± 6 **27.** $-1 \pm 3\sqrt{3}$ **29.** $-9 - 18i$ **31.** 29 **33.** $-4 + 2i$ **35.** $3 \pm 2\sqrt{6}$ **37.** $\frac{-3 \pm \sqrt{13}}{2}$ **39.** $-\frac{1}{3}$ **41.** about 0.2 sec **43.** $-0.65 \le x \le 4.6$ **45.** $y = 2(x + 3)(x - 2)$ **47.** $y = -\frac{5}{4}(x - 2)^2 + 7$

Chapter 5

5.1 Skill Practice (pp. 333–334) **1. a.** Product of powers property **b.** Negative exponent property **c.** Power of a product property **3.** 243; product of powers property **5.** -3125; product of powers property **7.** $\frac{1}{125}$; quotient of powers property **9.** $\frac{343}{8}$; power of a quotient property, negative exponent property **11.** 729; quotient of powers property **13.** $\frac{1}{36}$; product of powers property, negative exponent property **15.** 6.3×10^9 **17.** 5.607×10^{-6} **19.** 9.261×10^{-12} **21.** 1.5×10^3 **23.** 2.25×10^{-2}

SELECTED ANSWERS

25. $1024y^{15}$; power of a product property, power of a power property **27.** $\frac{w^9}{x^3}$; product of powers property, negative exponent property **29.** $\frac{1}{27a^9b^{15}}$; power of a product property, power of a power property, negative exponent property **31.** $\frac{c^2d^2}{3}$; quotient of powers property **33.** $\frac{2}{3a^2b^2}$; quotient of powers property, negative exponent property **35.** $\frac{x^6}{3y^3}$; product of powers property, quotient of powers property, negative exponent property **37.** The exponents should be subtracted, not divided; x^8. **39.** The base should not change; $(-3)^6$. **41.** $\frac{\pi x^3}{2}$ **43.** $x^{11}y^5z^{-3}$ **45.** $a^{-4}b^9$

5.1 Problem Solving (pp. 334–335) **49.** Pacific: 6.2868×10^{17} m^3, Atlantic: 3.01824×10^{17} m^3, Indian: 2.71656×10^{17} m^3, Arctic: 1.7061×10^{16} m^3 **51.** *Sample answer:* The volume of the pearl is $\frac{27}{8}$ times as large as the volume of the bead. **53. a.** about 4.4225×10^{-7} m^3

5.2 Skill Practice (pp. 341–343) **1.** degree: 4, type: quartic, leading coefficient: -5, constant term: 6 **3.** polynomial function; $f(x) = -x^2 + 8$, degree: 2, type: quadratic, leading coefficient: -1 **5.** polynomial function; $g(x) = \pi x^4 + \sqrt{6}$, degree: 4, type: quartic, leading coefficient: π **7.** polynomial function; $h(x) = -\frac{5}{2}x^3 + 3x - 10$, degree: 3, type: cubic, leading coefficient: $-\frac{5}{2}$ **9.** -32 **11.** 378 **13.** 182 **15.** 109 **17.** 149 **19.** -11 **21.** -78 **23.** The coefficient of x^3 was left out.

-2	-4	0	9	-21	7
		8	-16	14	14
	-4	8	-7	-7	21

25. degree: even, leading coefficient: positive **27.** degree: even, leading coefficient: negative **29.** $-\infty, -\infty$ **31.** $-\infty, +\infty$ **33.** $+\infty, -\infty$ **35.** $+\infty, +\infty$ **37.** *Sample answer:* $f(x) = -x^5 - 2x^4 + 1$

39.

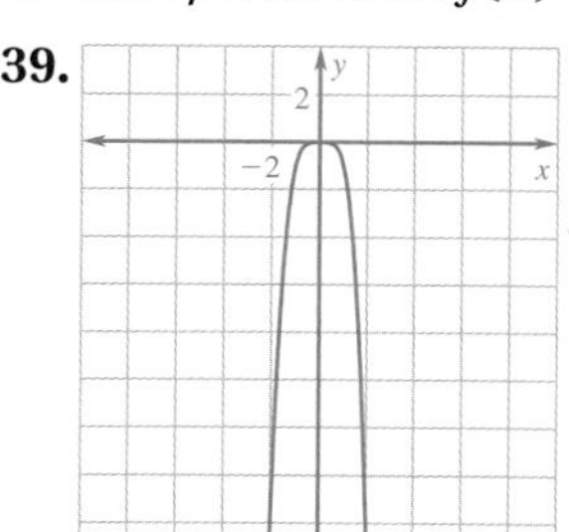

41.

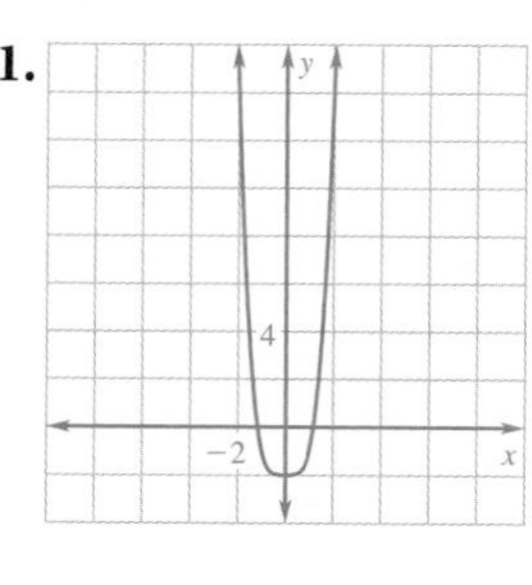

51. $g(x) \to -\infty$ as $x \to -\infty$ and $g(x) \to +\infty$ as $x \to +\infty$

5.2 Problem Solving (pp. 343–344)

55.

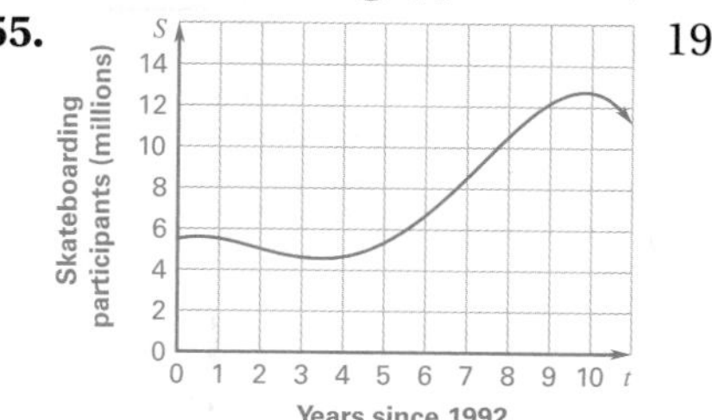

1998

57.

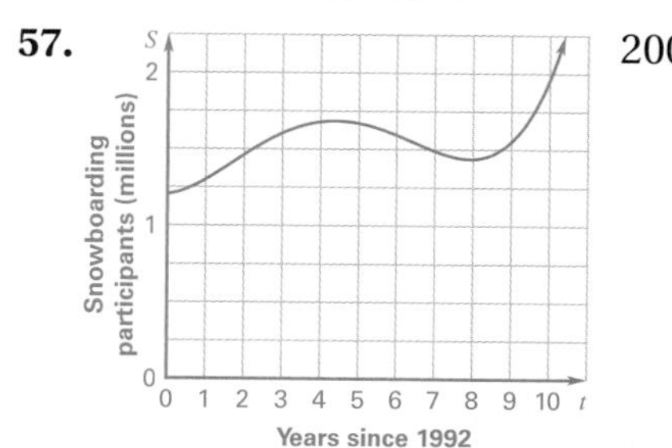

2002

59. a. 35.625 g

b.

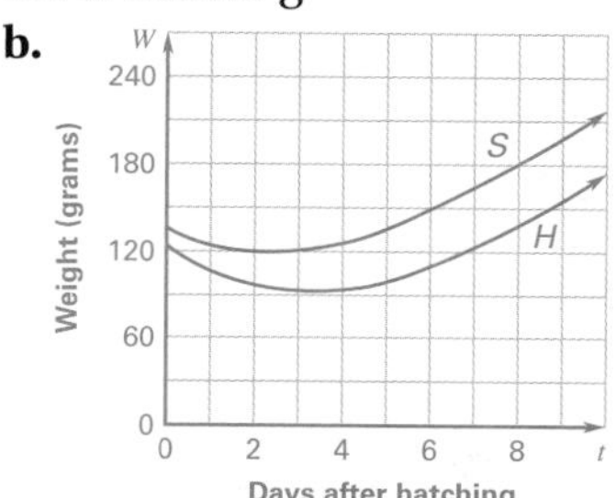

c. Sarus. *Sample answer:* Substituting 3 into each equation gives the Sarus chick weighing about 120 grams and the Hooded chick weighing about 92 grams. The weight of the Sarus is closer to 130 than the weight of the Hooded chick is.

5.3 Skill Practice (pp. 349–350) **1.** like terms **3.** $10x^2 - 8$ **5.** $14y - 8$ **7.** $7s^3 - 2s^2 + 8s + 10$ **9.** $2c^3 + 5c^2 + c + 9$ **11.** $-2b^4 - 15b^3 + 5b + 7$ **13.** $2x^4 - x^3$ **17.** $30x^3 + 10x^2$ **19.** $3z^2 - 8z - 3$ **21.** $2a^3 - 23a^2 + 26a + 6$ **23.** $-x^4 + 12x^3 - 34x^2 + 4x + 3$ **25.** $12y^4 - 9y^3 - 85y^2 - 19y + 5$ **27.** The cube of a binomial $(a - b)^3$ is found by $a^3 - 3a^2b + 3ab^2 - b^3$; $(2x - 7)^3 = (2x)^3 - 3(2x)^2(7) + 3(2x)(7)^2 - (7)^3 = 8x^3 - 84x^2 + 294x - 343$. **29.** $x^3 - 3x^2 - 25x - 21$ **31.** $2a^3 - 5a^2 - 37a - 30$ **33.** $-2b^3 + 7b^2 - 7b + 2$ **35.** $-12w^3 + 95w^2 - 143w + 30$ **37.** $-27q^3 + 132q^2 - 172q + 32$ **39.** $w^2 - 18w + 81$ **41.** $4c^2 + 20c + 25$ **43.** $25p^2 - 9$ **45.** $4a^2 - 81b^2$ **49.** $2\pi x^3 - 13\pi x^2 + 8\pi x + 48\pi$ **51.** $4x^3 - \frac{20}{3}x^2 - 7x + 12$ **53.** $(a + b)^2 = (a + b)(a + b) = a^2 + ab + ab + b^2 = a^2 + 2ab + b^2$ **55.** $(a - b)^3 = (a - b)(a - b)(a - b) = (a - b)(a^2 - 2ab + b^2) = a^3 - 2a^2b + ab^2 - a^2b + 2ab^2 - b^3 = a^3 - 3a^2b + 3ab^2 - b^3$

57. a. $(x-1)(x^4+x^3+x^2+x+1)$; $(x-1)(x^5+x^4+x^3+x^2+x+1)$
b. $(x-1)(x^{n-1}+x^{n-2}+x^{n-3}+\ldots+1)$

5.3 Problem Solving (pp. 351–352) **59.** $0.281t^3-16.8t^2+460t+8600$ **61.** $F=0.000031s^3+0.002107s$; about 0.05 horsepower **63.** $N=-1.51503t^4-25.53106t^3+215.9226t^2+127.75t+9858.5$; calculate $L_m \cdot S_m + L_w \cdot S_w$.

5.4 Skill Practice (pp. 356–357) **1.** quadratic **3.** $7x(2x-3)$ **5.** $c(c+3)(c+6)$ **7.** $3y^3(y-4)(y+4)$ **11.** $(y-4)(y^2+4y+16)$ **13.** $(5n+6)(25n^2-30n+36)$ **15.** $(2c+7)(4c^2+14c+49)$ **17.** $-5(z-4)(z^2+4z+16)$ **19.** $(y-7)(y^2+4)$ **21.** $(3m-1)(m^2+3)$ **23.** $(c+2)(2c-3)(2c+3)$ **25.** $(a^2+1)(a^2+6)$ **27.** $2z(2z-1)(2z+1)(4z^2+1)$ **29.** $3x(x^2-6)(5x^2+6)$ **31.** The factor $3x$ should also be set equal to 0; $x=0$ or $x=-4$ or $x=4$. **33.** $0, -1\frac{2}{3}, 1\frac{2}{3}$ **35.** $2, -2, -6$ **37.** $0, -\sqrt{21}, \sqrt{21}$ **39.** $-\sqrt{3}, \sqrt{3}, 2, -2$ **43.** $(n^2-10)(n^2+6)$ **45.** $(12a-5)(3a^2+7)$ **47.** $(d+3)(d-3)(2d^2+5)$ **49.** $2y^2(y^2-5)(4y^2+1)$ **51.** 2 **53.** 5 **55.** $(c+d)(c-d)(7a+b)$

5.4 Problem Solving (pp. 358–359) **59.** 3 cm by 9 cm by 18 cm **61.** length: 10 in., width: 5 in., height: 5 in. **63.** The volume cannot be $\frac{7}{3}$ because the only x value that corresponds to that volume is about -1.37, which would yield a negative side length.

5.4 Problem Solving Workshop (p. 361) **1.** 4 **3.** 6 **5.** about 1.4, 4 **7.** 2.5 **9.** height: 12 in., width: 8 in., length: 18 in.

5.5 Skill Practice (pp. 366–367) **1.** If a polynomial $f(x)$ is divided by $x-k$, then the remainder is $r=f(k)$. **3.** $x+5+\frac{3}{x-4}$ **5.** $x^2+4x+7+\frac{9}{x-1}$ **7.** $3x+8+\frac{-4x+1}{x^2+x}$ **9.** $5x^2-12x+37+\frac{-122x+109}{x^2+2x-4}$ **11.** $2x+3+\frac{25}{x-5}$ **13.** $x+4+\frac{-15}{x+4}$ **15.** $x^2-x-4+\frac{-18}{x-4}$ **17.** $x^3+x^2-2x+1+\frac{-6}{x-6}$ **19.** The degree of the answer should be reduced by 1; $x^2+2x-1+\frac{1}{x-2}$. **21.** $(x-6)(x-5)(x+1)$ **23.** $(x-8)(x+2)(x+4)$ **25.** $(x-4)(x-3)(x+9)$ **27.** $(2x-7)(x-3)(x-1)$ **29.** $-1, 6$ **31.** $-0.4, 1.5$ **33.** $\frac{-4\pm\sqrt{14}}{2}$ **37.** $x+8$

5.5 Problem Solving (pp. 367–368) **41.** 1 million T-shirts **43.** $f(x)=-0.132x^2+11.2x-560.9+\frac{408{,}803}{14.8x+725}$ **45.** $-0.00233x^3+0.249x^2-21.0x+1740-\frac{445{,}000}{3.10x+256}$; divided the overnight stays function by the total visits function

5.6 Skill Practice (pp. 374–375) **1.** constant, leading coefficient **3.** $\pm1, \pm2, \pm4, \pm7, \pm14, \pm28$ **5.** $\pm1, \pm3, \pm9, \pm\frac{1}{2}, \pm\frac{3}{2}, \pm\frac{9}{2}$ **7.** $\pm1, \pm2, \pm7, \pm14, \pm\frac{1}{2}, \pm\frac{7}{2}, \pm\frac{1}{4}, \pm\frac{7}{4}$ **9.** $\pm1, \pm3, \pm5, \pm15, \pm\frac{1}{2}, \pm\frac{3}{2}, \pm\frac{5}{2}, \pm\frac{15}{2}, \pm\frac{1}{4}, \pm\frac{3}{4}, \pm\frac{5}{4}, \pm\frac{15}{4}, \pm\frac{1}{8}, \pm\frac{3}{8}, \pm\frac{5}{8}, \pm\frac{15}{8}$ **11.** 1, 3, 8 **13.** $-5, -1, 6$ **15.** $-2, -1$ **17.** $-4, -1, 1, 2$ **19.** $1, \frac{-1\pm\sqrt{17}}{2}$ **21.** $-3, -\frac{5}{3}, \frac{1}{2}$ **25.** $-1, \frac{3}{2}, 3$ **27.** $-4, -\frac{1}{3}, 3$ **29.** $-3.5, -1, 2$ **31.** $-2, 2$ **33.** $-2, 1, \frac{5}{2}, 3$ **35.** $-3, \frac{1}{2}, 1$ **37.** p should be factors of 5 and q should be factors of 6; possible zeros: $\pm1, \pm5, \pm\frac{1}{2}, \pm\frac{5}{2}, \pm\frac{1}{3}, \pm\frac{5}{3}, \pm\frac{1}{6}, \pm\frac{5}{6}$. **41.** $-1, 1, 2$; B **43.** -2; A

5.6 Problem Solving (pp. 376–377) **45.** length: 3 in., width: 3 in., height: 7 in. **47.** $x^3-3x^2+2x-24=0$; $\pm1, \pm2, \pm3, \pm4, \pm6, \pm8, \pm12, \pm24$ **49. a.** $-10t^3+140t^2-20t-2150=0$ **b.** 1, 2, 5 **c.** 5; 1999

5.7 Skill Practice (pp. 383–385) **1.** repeated **3.** 4 **5.** 6 **7.** 7 **11.** $-5, -3, 1, 2$ **13.** $-5, -2, 2$ **15.** $-2, 1, 2i, -2i$ **17.** $i, -i, 1+\sqrt{3}, 1-\sqrt{3}$ **19.** $-4, -2, -\frac{3}{2}, 1$ **21.** $f(x)=x^3-2x^2-5x+6$ **23.** $f(x)=x^3-4x^2-15x+18$ **25.** $f(x)=x^4-4x^3+14x^2-36x+45$ **27.** $f(x)=x^4-18x^3+122x^2-370x+425$ **29.** $f(x)=x^4-x^3-18x^2+10x+8$ **31.** $f(x)=x^5-13x^4+60x^3-82x^2-144x+360$ **33.** *Sample answer:* $f(x)=x^5-4x^4+6x^3-6x^2+5x-2$ **35.** positive: 1, negative: 0, imaginary: 2 **37.** positive: 2 or 0, negative: 3 or 1, imaginary: 4, 2, or 0 **39.** positive: 3 or 1, negative: 2 or 0, imaginary: 4, 2, or 0 **41.** positive: 2 or 0, negative: 1, imaginary: 6 or 4 **43.** $x\approx-1.1, x\approx1.3$ **45.** $x\approx-0.58, x\approx1.9$ **47.** $x\approx-0.42, x\approx2.0$ **49.** $x\approx-3.5, x\approx-1.1, x=-1, x\approx2.1, x\approx3.6$ **51.** There could be 3, 2, 1, or 0 positive zeros, 3, 2, 1, or 0 negative zeros, and 2 or 0 imaginary zeros. **53.** Positive real zeros: 1, negative real zeros: 2, imaginary zeros: 0; the graph crosses the positive x-axis once and the negative x-axis twice. **55.** Positive real zeros: 0, negative real zeros: 1, imaginary zeros: 4; the graph does not cross the positive x-axis and it crosses the negative x-axis once. Since the function has degree 5, the remaining 4 zeros must be imaginary.

5.7 Problem Solving (pp. 385–386) **59.** year 3 and year 9 **61.** about 16.4 g per mL **63.** 0 in., about 59 in.; the bookshelf would have nearly 0 inches of deflection near each end because of the supports holding the bookshelf, so the answers make sense because they represent each end of a 60 inch bookshelf.

5.8 Skill Practice (pp. 390–391) **1.** turning

3.

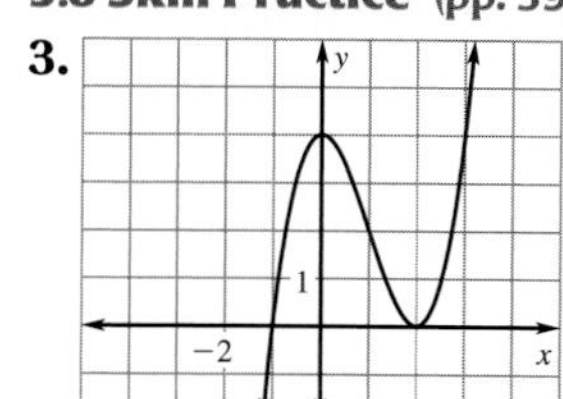

5.

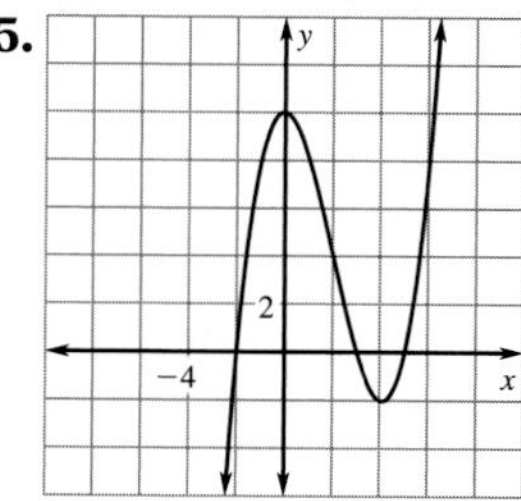

13. The x-intercepts should be at -2 and 1.

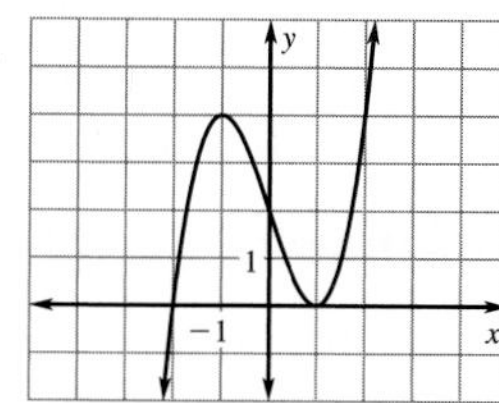

15–19. Sample answers are given. **15.** local maximum: $(-0.3, 0.3)$, local minimum: $(0.9, -1.3)$; zeros: -0.75, 0, 1.4, least degree: 3 **17.** local maximums: $(1, 0)$, $(3, 0)$, local minimum: $(2, -2)$; zeros: 1, 3, least degree: 4 **19.** local maximums: $(-1.1, 0.8)$, $(1.9, 8)$, local minimums: $(-2.2, -38)$, $(0.3, -41)$, $(2.8, -13)$; zeros: $-2.6, -1.2, -1, 1.5, 2.2, 3$, least degree: 6 **23.** x-intercept: -2.5; local maximum: $(-1.2, 4.0)$; local minimum: $(1.2, 0.96)$ **25.** x-intercepts: -2.2, 1, 1.7; local maximums: $(-1.6, 10.5)$, $(0.17, 2.0)$; local minimums: $(0, 2)$, $(1.5, -1.7)$ **27.** x-intercepts: -0.77, 4.5; local maximum: $(0.47, -2.6)$; local minimums: $(-0.16, -3.1)$, $(3.4, -39.4)$ **29.** x-intercepts: -0.77, 0, 0.82; local maximum: $(0.47, 1.6)$; local minimum: $(-0.46, -1.5)$ **31.** *Sample answer:* Quadratic functions only have one turning point, therefore one maximum or minimum value. Cubic functions can have two turning points, therefore one maximum and one minimum, and the end behavior is to infinity, so there is no real maximum or minimum value. **33.** *Sample answer:* $y = x(x + 2)(x - 4)$, $y = x(x + 2)(x - 4)^2$, $y = x^3(x + 2)(x - 4)$

35. domain: all real numbers, range: all real numbers

37.

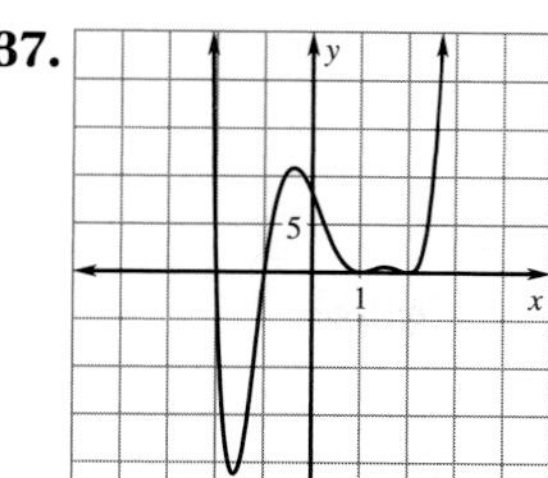

domain: all real numbers, range: $y \geq -21.3$

5.8 Problem Solving (pp. 391–392) **39.** maximum: about 5.8 in. by 13.8 in. by 2.1 in.; about 168 in.^{3}

41.

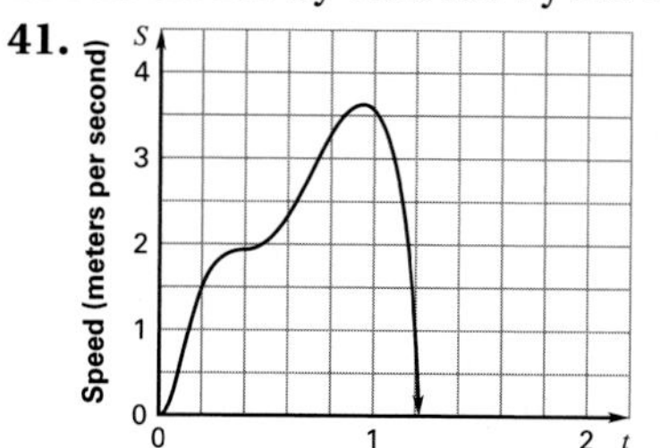

after about 0.95 sec

43. a.

b. Maximum: $(11.7, 44{,}971)$, minimum: $(29.8, 40{,}078)$. *Sample answer:* The maximum indicates that in 1972 the number of students enrolled was about 44,971,000. The minimum indicates that in 1990 there were about 40,078,000 students enrolled. **c.** $36{,}300 \leq y \leq 47{,}978$

5.9 Skill Practice (pp. 397–398) **1.** finite differences **3.** $y = 0.5x^3 - 2x^2 + 0.5x + 3$ **5.** $y = \frac{1}{6}x^3 - \frac{1}{3}x^2 - \frac{11}{6}x + 2$ **7.** $y = 2x^3 + 2x^2 - 8x - 8$ **9.** $y = \frac{2}{5}x^3 - \frac{2}{5}x^2 - 12x$ **11.** 1 should have been substituted for x and 3 for y; $3 = a(1 + 1)(1 - 2)(1 - 5)$, $3 = 8a$, $a = \frac{3}{8}$.

13.

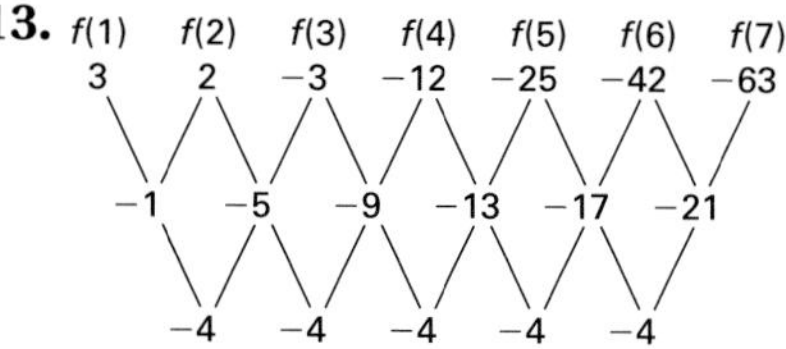

15. $f(1)$ $f(2)$ $f(3)$ $f(4)$ $f(5)$ $f(6)$ $f(7)$

−3 0 11 30 57 92 135

3 11 19 27 35 43

8 8 8 8 8

19. $f(x) = -4x^2 + 15x$ **21.** $f(x) = -0.5x^3 + 5x^2 - 2.5x + 3$ **23.** 5; 6; there must be one more data point than the degree of the equation.

5.9 Problem Solving (pp. 398–399) **25.** $d = 0.5n^2 - 1.5n$ **27. a.** $m = 0.000817t^3 - 0.0215t^2 + 0.249t + 3.17$ **b.** about \$10.30 **c.** 1995

29.

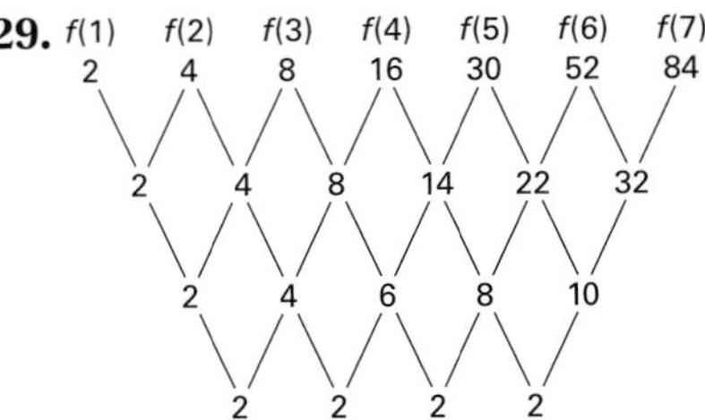

Chapter Review (pp. 402–406) **1.** local maximum, local minimum **3.** If it is in the form $c \times 10^n$ where $1 \le c < 10$ and n is an integer. **5.** 128; product of powers property **7.** $\frac{y^{10}}{x^4}$; power of a power property, negative exponent property **9.** $\frac{16}{9}$; quotient of powers property, negative exponent property **11.** $\frac{1}{x^8y^8}$; power of a quotient property, negative exponent property

13.

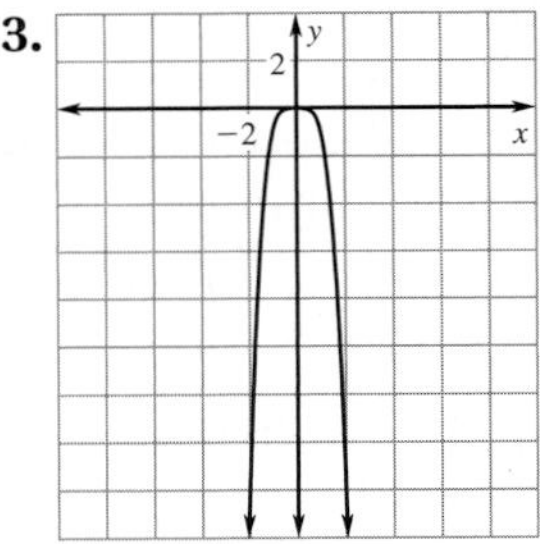

15.

17. $6x^3 - 9x^2 + 3x + 3$ **19.** $5x^3 - 29x^2 - 14x + 48$ **21.** $8(2x - 1)(4x^2 + 2x + 1)$ **23.** $(x - 2)(x + 2)(2x - 7)$ **25.** $x - 6 + \frac{18x - 16}{x^2 + 3x - 1}$ **27.** $2x^2 - x + 8 + \frac{-4}{x - 5}$ **29.** $(x + 2)(x - 3)(x - 4)$ **31.** $(x - 1)(3x - 2)(3x + 2)$ **33.** $-3, 2, 5$ **35.** $x^3 - 2x^2 - 19x + 20$ **37.** $x^4 - 15x^3 + 72x^2 - 120x + 56$ **39.** x-intercept: -1.7; local maximum: $(0, -1)$; local minimum: $(-1, -2)$ **41.** $y = x^3 - 8x^2 + 2x - 1$

Chapter 6

6.1 Skill Practice (pp. 417–418) **1.** index **7.** $12^{1/3}$ **9.** $10^{7/3}$ **11.** $\sqrt[4]{5}$ **13.** $(\sqrt[5]{14})^2$ **15.** ± 8 **17.** 0 **19.** no real roots **21.** 2 **23.** 64 **25.** 9 **27.** $\frac{1}{4}$ **29.** $\frac{1}{128}$ **31.** $\frac{1}{16}$ **35.** 2.89 **37.** 2.10 **39.** 12 **41.** 0.01 **43.** 0.02 **45.** -0.18 **47.** *Sample answer:* $27^{1/3}$, $81^{1/4}$ **49.** There are two real solutions; $x = \pm 3$. **51.** 6 **53.** 1, 9 **55.** ± 1.68 **57.** -7.66

6.1 Problem Solving (pp. 418–419) **61.** about 4.30 in. **63.** $\frac{3}{12{,}282{,}500{,}000}$; about 1800 RPM **65. a.** 4096 mm^3 **b.** tetrahedron: about 32.6 mm, octahedron: about 20.6 mm, dodecahedron: about 8.12 mm, icosahedron: about 12.3 mm **c.** No. *Sample answer:* The icosahedron has the greatest number of faces, 20, and an edge length of 12.3 millimeters which is greater than the edge length of the dodecahedron, which has 12 faces.

6.2 Skill Practice (pp. 424–425) **1.** No; they do not have the same index. **3.** 25 **5.** 3 **7.** $2 \cdot 5^{1/2}$ **9.** $\frac{\sqrt[5]{1331}}{11}$ **11.** $7^{3/4}$ **13.** $\frac{\sqrt[3]{50}}{16{,}000}$ **15.** 10 **17.** $2\sqrt{2}$ **19.** 2 **21.** 3 **25.** $2\sqrt[3]{2}$ **27.** $40\sqrt[4]{2}$ **29.** $\frac{\sqrt{3}}{2}$ **31.** $\sqrt[15]{3}$ **33.** $\frac{2}{5}\sqrt[3]{5}$ **35.** $\frac{1}{2}\sqrt[4]{7}$ **37.** $-2\sqrt[7]{2}$ **39.** $-6\sqrt[4]{2}$ **41.** The radicands are not the same, so they cannot be combined; $2\sqrt[3]{10} + 6\sqrt[3]{5}$. **43.** $x^{7/12}$ **45.** $3x$ **47.** $\frac{y^{4/3}}{x^{3/5}}$ **49.** $\frac{1}{x^4}$ **51.** *Sample answer:* $x^{5/4}$ and $x^{1/2}$ **53.** $yz^3\sqrt[4]{12x^2y^2}$ **55.** $x^2z^4\sqrt{xy}$ **57.** $\frac{x\sqrt[3]{y^2}}{y^2}$ **59.** $\sqrt[14]{x^{11}}$ **61.** $\frac{1}{2}y^{3/2}$ **63.** $2x^2y^{1/2}$ **65.** $(2xy + 3y)\sqrt[4]{2x^2}$ **67.** perimeter: $24x^{1/4}$, area: $35x^{1/2}$ **71.** $\frac{1}{y^{6.6}}$ **73.** $\frac{1}{x^{1.2}}$ **75.** $\frac{1}{y^{1.3}}$ **77.** $7z^{0.3}$ **79.** $x^{\sqrt{6}}$ **81.** $4x^2y^{\sqrt{2}}$

6.2 Problem Solving (pp. 426–427) **83. a.** about 580 cm^2 **b.** about 16,671 cm^2 **85.** about 0.45 mm **87. a.** about 2 times fainter **b.** about 1.6 times fainter **c.** about 3 times fainter **89. a.** $r = \sqrt[3]{\frac{3V}{4\pi}}$ **b.** $S = 4\pi\left(\sqrt[3]{\frac{3V}{4\pi}}\right)^2 = 4\pi\left(\frac{3V}{4\pi}\right)^{2/3} = \frac{4\pi(3V)^{2/3}}{(4\pi)^{2/3}} = (4\pi)^{1/3}(3V)^{2/3}$ **c.** The balloon with twice as much water will have $\sqrt[3]{4}$, or about 1.59, times the surface area of the balloon with less water.

6.3 Skill Practice (pp. 432–433) **1.** composition **3.** $2x^{1/3} + 8x^{1/2}$, all nonnegative real numbers **5.** $-6x^{1/3} + 8x^{1/2}$, all nonnegative real numbers

7. $-8x^{1/3}$, all nonnegative real numbers **9.** 0, all nonnegative real numbers **13.** $20x^{7/6}$, nonnegative real numbers **15.** $25x$, all nonnegative real numbers **17.** $\frac{5}{4x^{1/6}}$, positive real numbers **19.** 1, positive real numbers **21.** -64 **23.** $-\frac{36}{25}$ **25.** 71 **27.** -625 **29.** $\frac{6}{x} - 7$, all real numbers except $x = 0$ **31.** $\frac{2x - 13}{3}$, all real numbers **33.** x, all real numbers except $x = 0$ **35.** $4x - 21$, all real numbers **37.** 4 should be distributed to each term, not just the first term; $4x^2 - 12$. **39.** *Sample answer:* $f(x) = 3x$, $g(x) = 2x$

6.3 Problem Solving (pp. 433–434) **43.** $r(w) = 220w^{-0.266}$; about 134 breaths per minute, about 48.3 breaths per minute, about 11.3 breaths per minute **45. a.** \$63 **b.** \$61.50 **c.** Apply the 10% discount before the \$15 discount; you pay \$61.50 using this method and \$63 using the other method.

6.4 Skill Practice (pp. 442–443) **1.** An inverse relation interchanges the input and output values of the original relation. **3.** $y = \frac{x+1}{4}$ **5.** $y = \frac{x+6}{7}$ **7.** $y = \frac{x-7}{12}$ **9.** $y = \frac{1}{5}x - \frac{1}{15}$ **11.** $y = \frac{7-5x}{3}$
13. Switching the roles of x and y does not include switching the sign of the variables; $x = -y + 3, x - 3 = -y, 3 - x = y$.
15. $f(g(x)) = x - 4 + 4 = x$, $g(f(x)) = x + 4 - 4 = x$
17. $f(g(x)) = \frac{1}{4}((4x)^{1/3})^3 = \frac{1}{4}(4x) = x$, $g(f(x)) = \left(4\left(\frac{1}{4}x^3\right)\right)^{1/3} = (x^3)^{1/3} = x$ **19.** $f(g(x)) = 4\left(\frac{1}{4}x - \frac{9}{4}\right) + 9 = x - 9 + 9 = x$, $g(f(x)) = \frac{1}{4}(4x + 9) - \frac{9}{4} = x + \frac{9}{4} - \frac{9}{4} = x$ **23.** $f^{-1}(x) = \sqrt[4]{\frac{x}{4}}$ **25.** $f^{-1}(x) = \frac{\sqrt[5]{x}}{2}$ **27.** $f^{-1}(x) = -\frac{5}{4}\sqrt{x}$ **29.** function **31.** not a function **33.** function **35.** not a function **37.** not a function **39.** $f^{-1}(x) = \sqrt[3]{x+2}$ **41.** $f^{-1}(x) = -\sqrt[6]{\frac{40-5x}{2}}$ **43.** $f^{-1}(x) = \sqrt[4]{x+9}$

6.4 Problem Solving (pp. 444–445) **47. a.** $w = 2\ell - 6$ **b.** 7 lb **49.** $\ell = \left(\frac{v}{1.34}\right)^2$; about 31.3 ft

6.5 Skill Practice (pp. 449–450) **1.** radical

3.

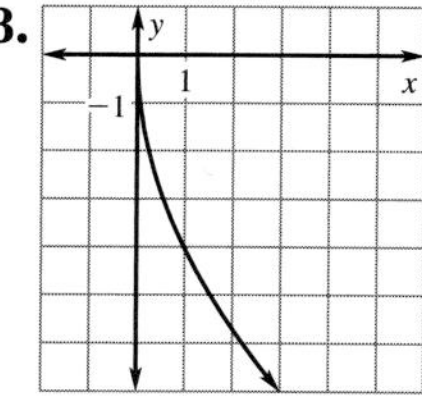

domain: $x \geq 0$, range: $y \leq 0$

5.

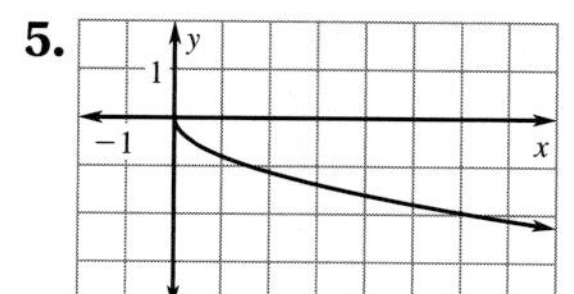

domain: $x \geq 0$, range: $y \leq 0$

11.

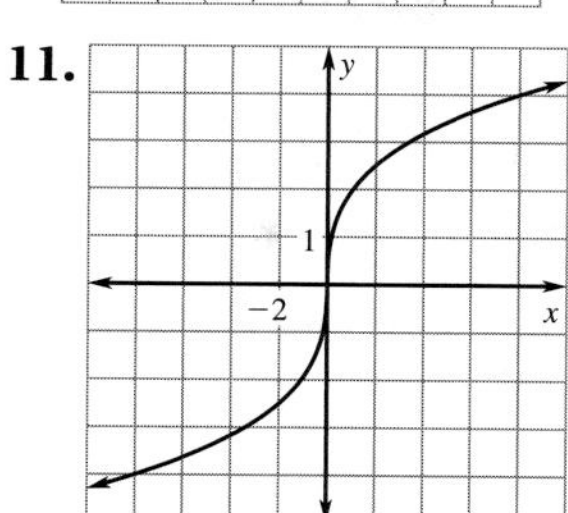

domain: all real numbers, range: all real numbers

13.

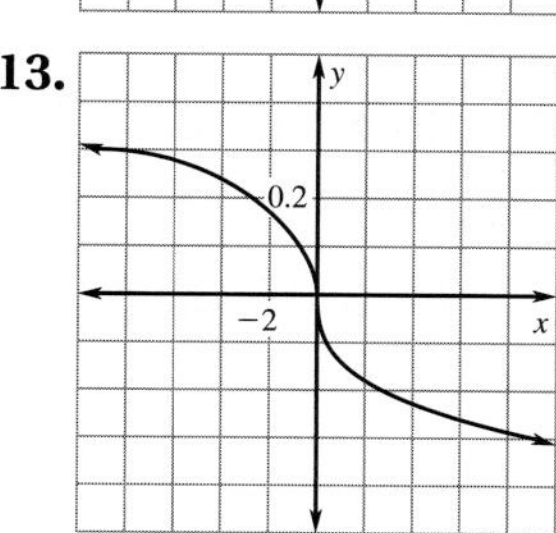

domain: all real numbers, range: all real numbers

17.

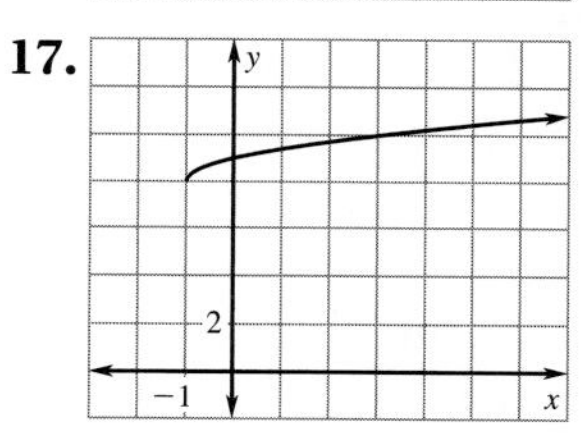

domain: $x \geq -1$, range: $y \geq 8$

19.

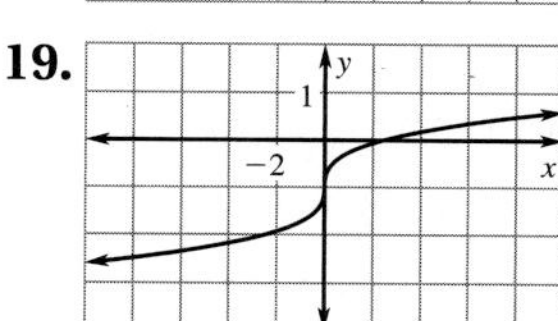

domain: all real numbers, range: all real numbers

25. The domain is limited because the square root of a negative number is not a real number. Since the domain is restricted, the range is also affected. **29.** Domain: $x \geq 12$, range: $y \geq 0$; the expression under the radical sign must be greater than or equal to 0, so substitute the least value of x into the equation and find y. **31.** Domain: all real numbers, range: all real numbers; there are no restrictions on finding the cube root of a number and therefore no restrictions on the range. **33.** Domain: $x \geq 3$, range: $y \geq 6$; the expression under the radical sign must be greater than or equal to 0, so substitute the least value of x into the equation and find y.

6.5 Problem Solving (pp. 450–451) **35.** about 43 ft above sea level **37. a.** $v = 331.5\sqrt{1 + \frac{C}{273.15}}$ **b.** domain: $C \geq -273.15$, range: $v \geq 0$ **39. a.** $v_t = 33.7\sqrt{\frac{165}{A}}$

b. *Sample answer:*

A	2	4	6	8	10
v_t	306.1	216.44	176.72	153.05	136.89

c.

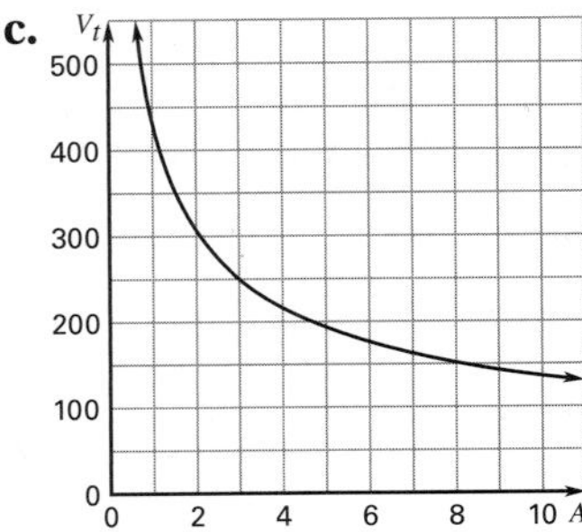

6.6 Skill Practice (pp. 456–457) **1.** extraneous **3.** 7 **5.** 1 **7.** 6 **9.** 29 **11.** $-70\frac{1}{2}$ **13.** 343 **15.** 18 **17.** 8 **19.** 11 **21.** -37 **23.** 4 **25.** 32 **27.** 40 **29.** 108 **31.** 1 **33.** Both sides must be raised to the power; $((x+7)^{1/2})^2 = 5^2$, $x + 7 = 25$, $x = 18$. **35.** 25 **37.** 3, 8 **39.** $-2\frac{1}{10}$ **41.** $\frac{1}{2}$ **45.** 3 **47.** 4 **49.** $\frac{1}{4}$ **51.** $-2, 2$ **53.** (4, 25)

6.6 Problem Solving (pp. 457–459) **57.** about 391 min **59.** *Sample answer:* The elephant with a shoulder height of 250 centimeters is about 20 years older than the elephant with a shoulder height of 150 centimeters. **61. a.** about 0.162 mi/h **b.** about 80.4 mi/h **c.** $0.162 \le s \le 80.4$

6.6 Problem Solving Workshop (p. 461) **1.** -39 **3.** about 55.7 **5.** about 97 ft **7.** about 37.5 cm

6.6 Extension (p. 463) **1.** $x \ge 16$ **3.** $0 \le x \le 4$ **5.** $x \ge 1$ **7.** $0 \le x \le 6.25$ **9.** $0 \le x < 1.3$ **11.** $0 \le x < 4$ **13.** about 413 m^2

Chapter Review (pp. 466–468) **1.** 4 **3.** power **5.** If a horizontal line crosses the graph of the function more than once, the inverse is not a function. **7.** Take the square root of each side; raise each side to the $\frac{3}{2}$ power. **9.** 0 **11.** 5 **13.** $\frac{1}{9}$ **15.** -8 **17.** $\frac{1}{15}$ **19.** $\frac{3x^2y^2\sqrt{2z}}{7z^2}$ **21.** $3x - 14$ **23.** $4x + 26$ **25.** $y = \frac{\sqrt{x-9}}{2}$

27.

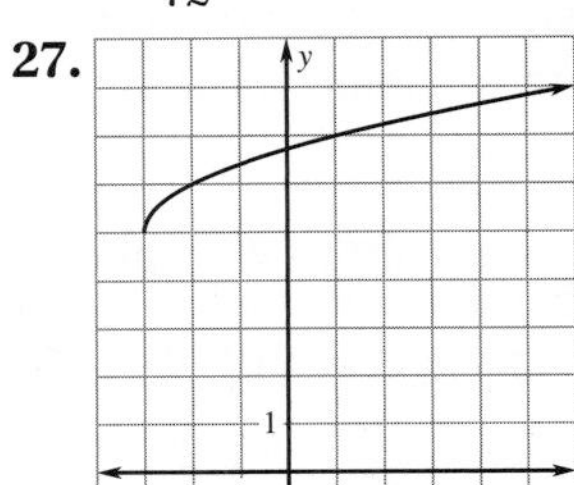

domain: $x \ge -3$, range: $y \ge 5$

29.

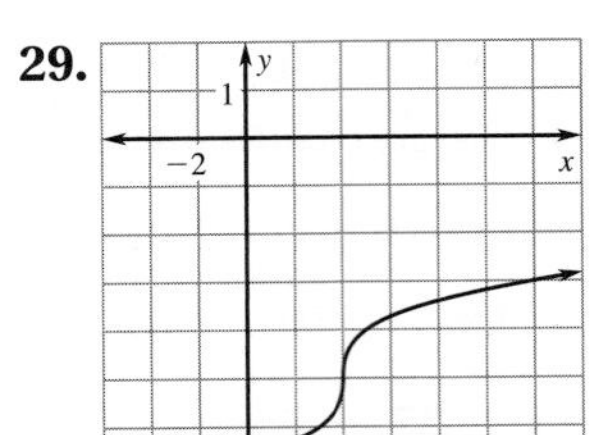

domain: all real numbers, range: all real numbers

31. 16

Cumulative Review (pp. 474–475) **1.** $y = 4x - 11$ **3.** $y = -8x - 22$ **5.** $y = \frac{4}{5}x + 12$ **7.** -4 **9.** 2, 7 **11.** 2, 0, -5

13.

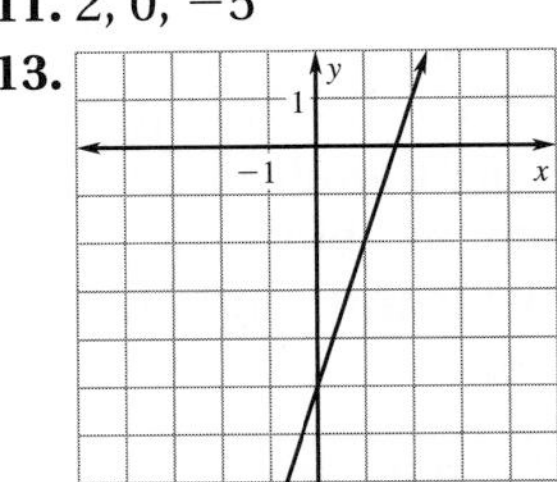

15.

17.

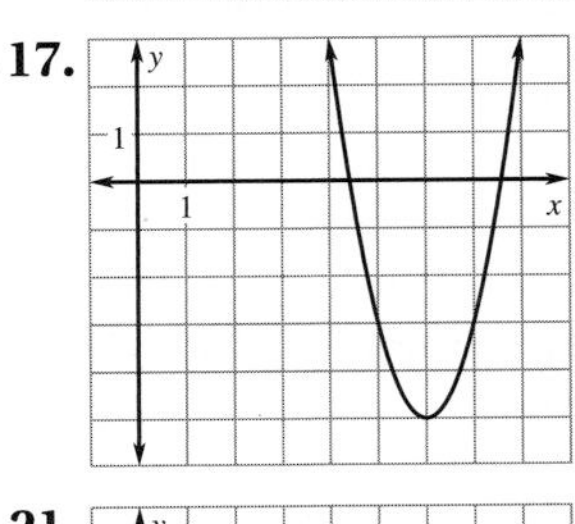

19.

21.

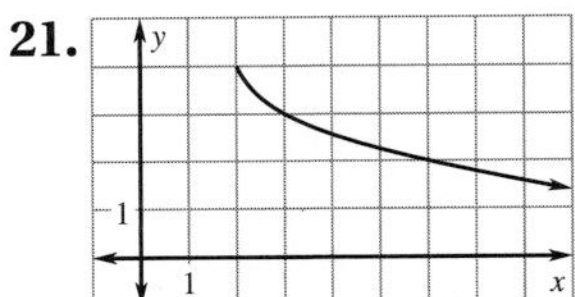

23. $(-1, 6)$ **25.** $9 - i$ **27.** $34 + 8i$ **29.** $y = -(x-6)^2 - 10$ **31.** $8x^9y^6$ **33.** x^7y **35.** $5x^2 + 6x - 16$ **37.** $2x^3 + 3x^2 - 34x + 35$ **39.** $(x^2 - 8)(x^2 + 5)$ **41.** $(x-6)(x-3)(x+3)$ **43.** $10x^2 - 28x - 6$, all real numbers **45.** $10x - 29$, all real numbers **47.** $f^{-1}(x) = \frac{7x - 49}{3}$ **49.** $f^{-1}(x) = \sqrt[3]{6x + 5}$ **51.** $f^{-1}(x) = \sqrt[5]{\frac{-9x + 18}{8}}$ **53.** $y = 0.499x + 1.25$; about \$5,240,000 **55.** \$4642 **57.** $y = -\frac{1}{8}x^2 + 5x + 6$ **59.** $y = x^3 - 5x + 6$; \$690

Chapter 7

7.1 Skill Practice (pp. 482–483) **1.** 2.4, 1.5, 50%

7. 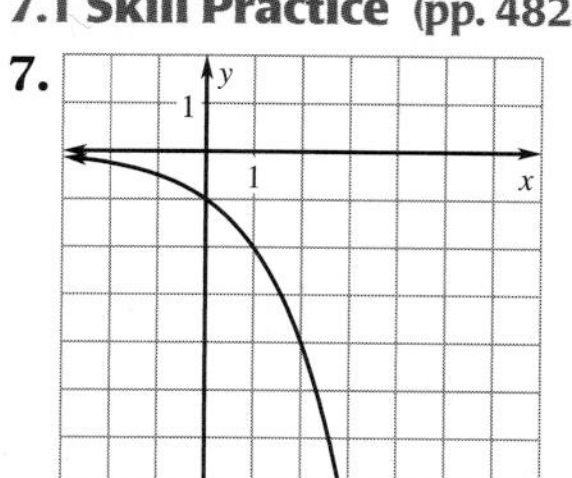

9. 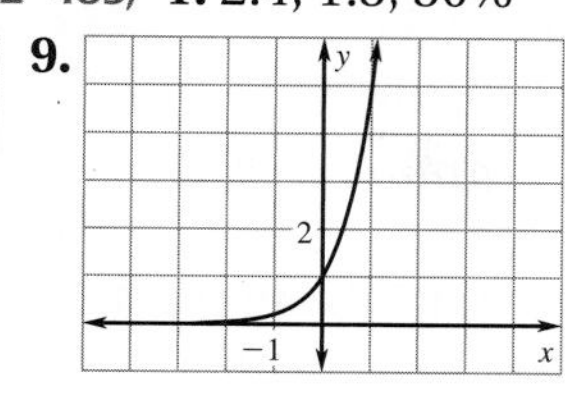

15. 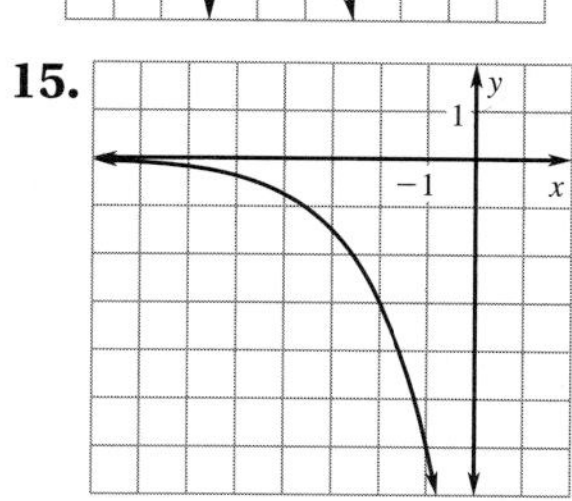

domain: all real numbers, range: $y < 0$

17. 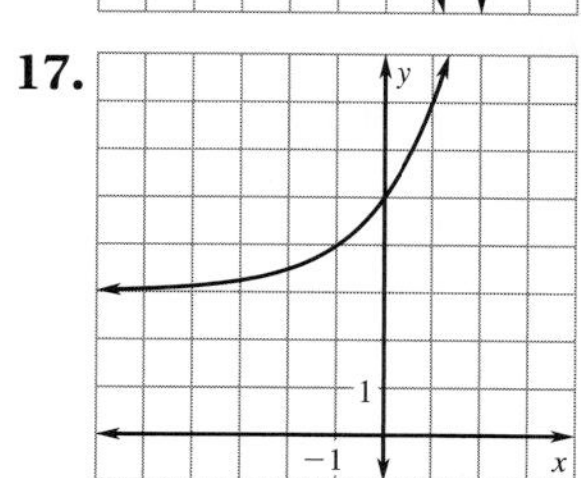

domain: all real numbers, range: $y > 3$

27. The power of $(x - 3)$ translates the parent graph 3 units to the right, not to the left.

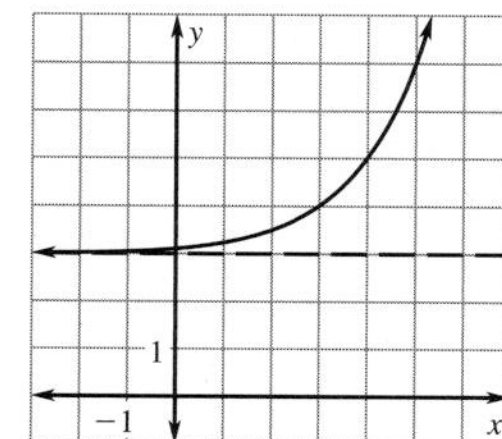

29. $A = 800\left(1 + \frac{0.02}{365}\right)^{365t}$, where A represents the amount in the account after t years. **31. a.** \$1844.81 **b.** 18 yr **33. a.** The graph no longer has a vertical stretch of 2. **b.** The graph will increase slower. **c.** The graph will be translated 3 units to the right instead of 4 units to the left. **d.** The graph will be translated 1 unit down instead of 3 units up.

7.1 Problem Solving (pp. 484–485)

35. a. 0.42 million, 2.47, 147%

b. 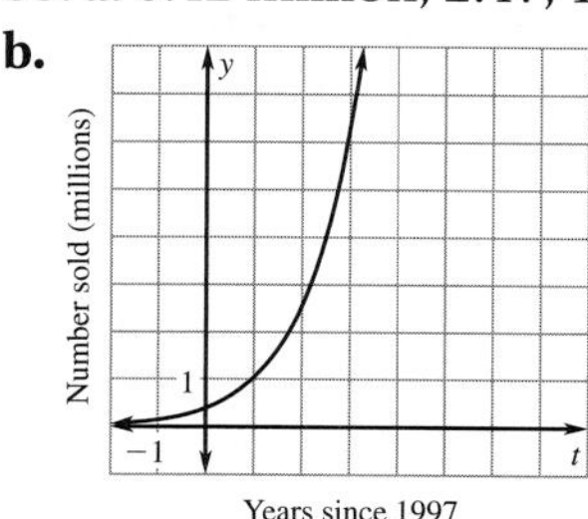

about 16 million DVD players

37. a. \$2479.38 **b.** \$2406.98 **c.** \$2383.23

39. a. $P = 494.29(1.03)^t$; 664,284 people

b. 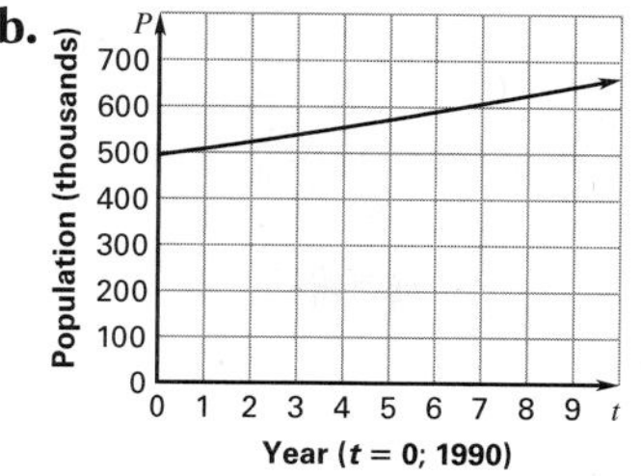

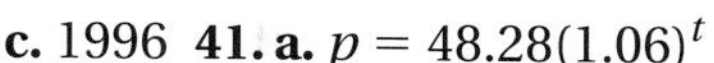

domain: $t \geq 0$, range: $P \geq 494.29$

c. 1996 **41. a.** $p = 48.28(1.06)^t$

b. 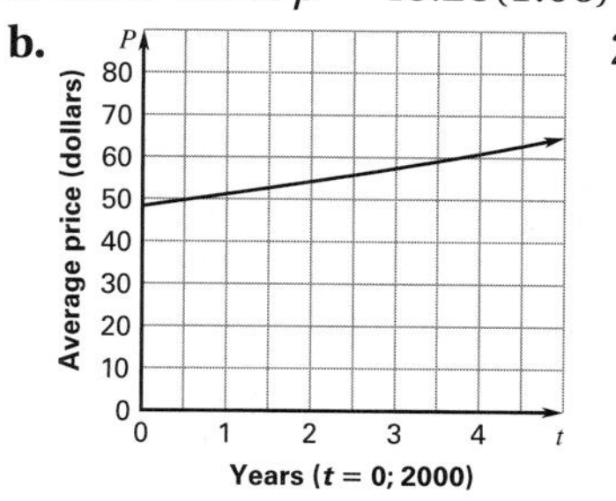

2003

c. *Sample answer:* Since the function is only defined when t is between 0 and 4, you can look at the graph between these values to determine the minimum or maximum that gives meaningful results. **43.** No. *Sample answer:* The amounts are not equal except initially and one year after the investments are made.

7.2 Skill Practice (pp. 489–490) **1.** 1250, 0.85, 15% **3.** exponential decay **5.** exponential growth

7. **9.** 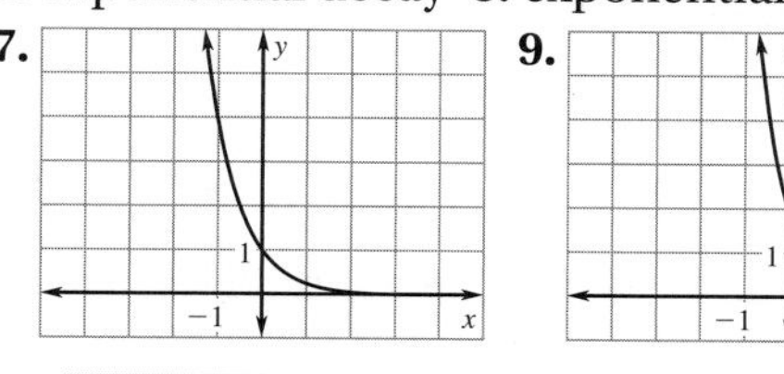

17. 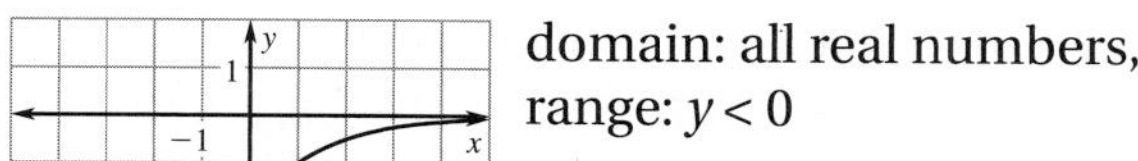

domain: all real numbers, range: $y < 0$

19. 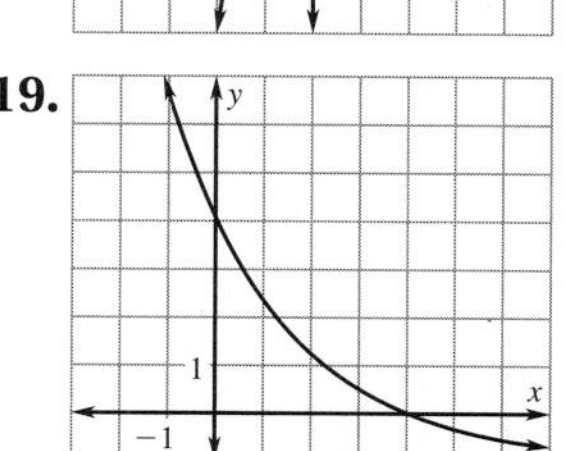

domain: all real numbers, range: $y > -1$

25. a. The graph is a vertical stretch by a factor of $\frac{4}{3}$. **b.** The graph will be steeper because the decay factor is smaller. **c.** The graph moves 5 units to the right instead of 2 units to the right. **d.** The horizontal asymptote moves to $x = 3$.

7.2 Problem Solving (pp. 490–491) **31. a.** $y = 200(0.75)^t$; about \$84.38

b.

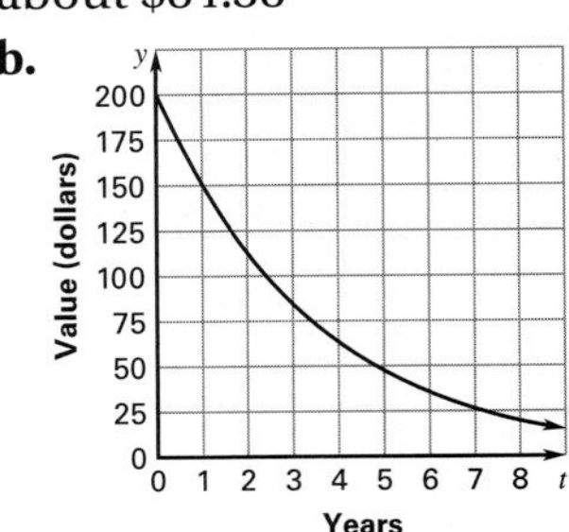

c. after about 2.5 yr

33. a.

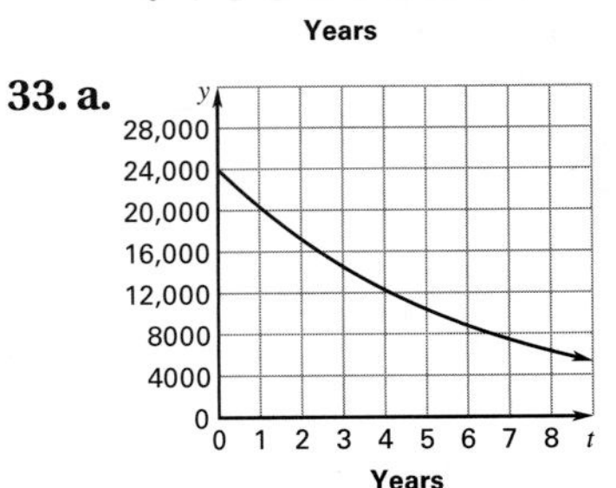

after 5 yr **b.** \$5.29; no. *Sample answer:* A car does not normally last 50 years.

35. a. 0.89, 11%

b.

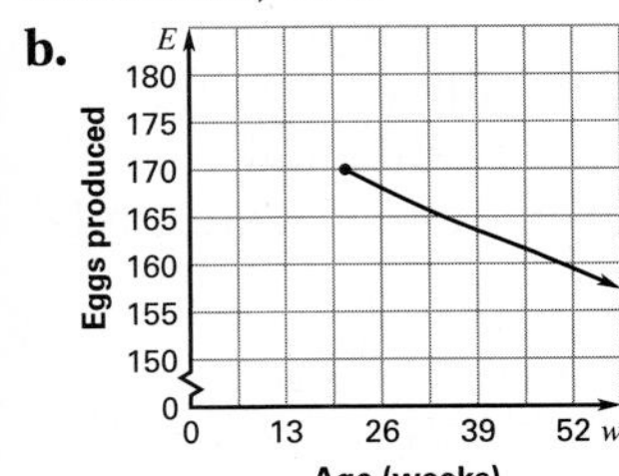

c. about 134 eggs per yr **d.** Change the exponent to just w.

7.3 Skill Practice (pp. 495–496) **1.** e **3.** e^7 **5.** $8e^{9x}$ **7.** $\frac{1}{3e^{5x}}$ **9.** $3e^3$ **11.** $3e^{1-x}$ **13.** $2e^{3x}$ **17.** The 3 should be raised to the second power also; $(3e^{5x})^2 = 3^2e^{(5x)(2)} = 9e^{10x}$. **19.** about 20.086 **21.** about 9.025 **23.** about 0.670 **25.** about 1096.633 **27.** about 1.482 **29.** about −66.139 **31.** exponential decay **33.** exponential decay **35.** exponential decay **37.** exponential growth

43. domain: all real numbers, range: $y > 0$

45.

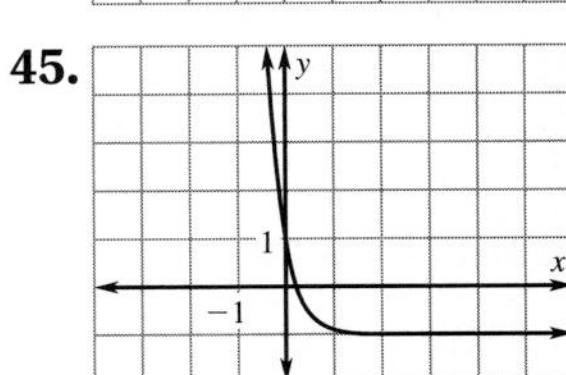

domain: all real numbers, range: $y > -1$

51. 10,000,000,000. *Sample answer:* Since small values of n were increasing the function very slowly, I checked larger intervals. I noticed that every power of 10 gave an answer one digit closer to the actual value of e. **53.** *Sample answer:* $f(x) = \frac{1}{2}e^{-3x}$, $g(x) = \frac{2}{3}e^{-5x}$

7.3 Problem Solving (pp. 497–498) **55.** about 895 million camera phones **57.** \$2442.81

59. a. $L(x) = 100e^{-0.02x}$

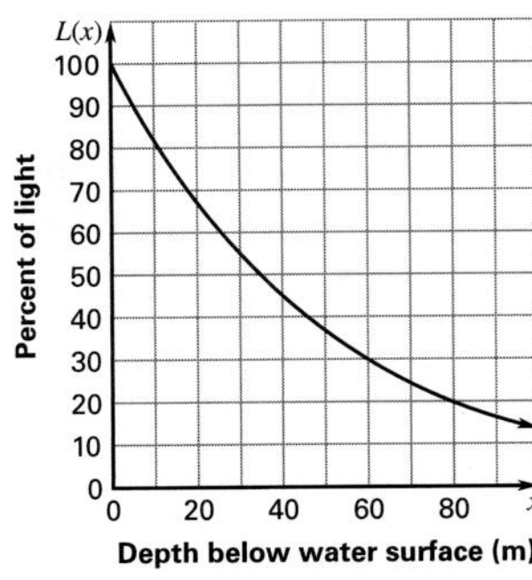

b. about 45% **c.** about 35 m **61.** about 1.986 cm^2

7.4 Skill Practice (pp. 503–504) **1.** common **3.** $4^2 = 16$ **5.** $6^{-2} = \frac{1}{36}$ **7.** *Sample answer:* The −3 and $\frac{1}{8}$ are switched around; $\log_2 \frac{1}{8} = -3$. **9.** 2 **11.** 6 **13.** −3 **15.** $-\frac{1}{2}$ **17.** 3 **19.** 2 **21.** about 1.792 **23.** about 0.793 **25.** about 1.683 **27.** about 4.700 **29.** x **31.** 8 **33.** $4x$ **35.** $5x$ **37.** $y = 8^x$ **39.** $y = \log_{0.4} x$ **41.** $y = \ln x - 2$ **43.** $y = e^x - 1$

45.

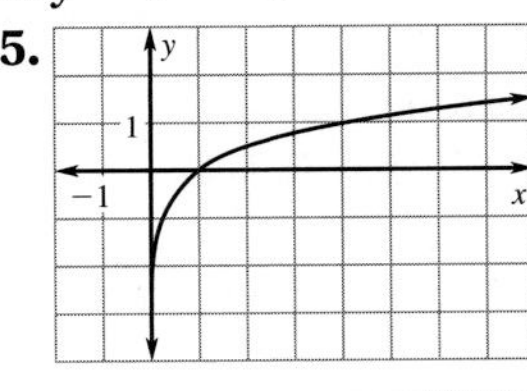

domain: $x > 0$, range: all real numbers

47. domain: $x > 0$, range: all real numbers

7.4 Problem Solving (pp. 504–505) **59.** 2.3 **61. a.** about 6.4 **b.** $E = e^{(M + 9.9)/0.29}$; the inverse represents the amount of energy released, in ergs, as a function of the energy magnitude.

7.5 Skill Practice (pp. 510–511) **1.** product **7.** 0.477 **9.** 1.204 **11.** 2.158 **13.** −0.602 **15.** $\log_3 4 + \log_3 x$ **17.** $\log 3 + 4\log x$ **19.** $\log_2 2 - \log_2 5$ **21.** $\log_4 x - \log_4 3 - \log_4 y$ **23.** $\log_7 5 + 3\log_7 x + \log_7 y + 2\log_7 z$ **25.** $2\ln x + \frac{1}{3}\ln y$ **27.** $\frac{1}{2}\log_2 x$ **29.** $\frac{3}{4}\ln x$ **31.** The two parts should be added, not multiplied; $\log_2 5 + \log_2 x$.

33. $\log_4 \frac{7}{10}$ **35.** $\log 11x^2$ **37.** $\log \frac{x^5}{y^4}$ **39.** $\ln 10x$ **41.** $\ln \frac{64}{y^4}$ **45.** about 1.404 **47.** about 2.465 **49.** about 1.631 **51.** about 1.581 **53.** about 1.513 **55.** 1.5 **57.** about 0.875 **59.** about −1.358 **61.** When using the change of base formula, the base goes in the denominator; $\frac{\log 7}{\log 3}$. **63.** 150 decibels

7.5 Problem Solving (pp. 512–513) **69.** about 76 decibels **71.** 10; $L(10I) - L(I) = 10 \log \frac{10I}{I_0} - 10 \log \frac{I}{I_0} =$ $10\left(\log \frac{10I}{I_0} - \log \frac{I}{I_0}\right) = 10\left(\log 10 + \log \frac{I}{I_0} - \log \frac{I}{I_0}\right) =$ $10 \log 10 = 10(1) = 10$ **73. a.** $s = 2 \log_2 f$

b.

f	1.414	2.000	2.828	4.000
s	about 1	2	about 3	4

f	5.657	8.000	11.314	16.000
s	about 5	6	about 7	8

Sample answer: The amount of light increases by about 1 each time. **c.** About 22.627; if you set up the equation $9 = 2 \log_2 f$ and solve for f, the result is $2^{9/2}$.

7.6 Skill Practice (pp. 519–520) **1.** exponential **3.** 8 **5.** $\frac{7}{12}$ **7.** $-\frac{5}{7}$ **9.** $-\frac{5}{3}$ **11.** −2 **13.** about −1.609 **15.** about 0.292 **17.** about −0.723 **19.** about 0.650 **21.** about −0.378 **23.** about −0.203 **25.** 6 **27.** no solution **29.** $\frac{31}{15}$ **31.** $\frac{1}{3}$ **33.** e^7 or about 1096.633 **35.** about 35.601 **37.** 4 **39.** about 0.729 **41.** about 2.720 **43.** about 10.243 **45.** The logarithm was not simplified correctly, $x \log_3 6 \neq 2x$; $\log_3 6 \approx 1.631$, $x = 1.585$. **47.** *Sample answer:* $3^x = 81$, $\log_5 (x + 4) = 0$

7.6 Problem Solving (pp. 521–522)
55. about 24°F **57.** about 6967 yr
59. a. Japan: about 127,000,000 kilowatt-hours, Greece: about 11,500,000 kilowatt-hours, USA: about 23,500 kilowatt-hours

b. Japan: $6.6 = 0.67 \log (0.37E) + 1.46$, 126,893,702 kilowatt-hours; Greece: $5.9 = 0.67 \log (0.37E) + 1.46$, 11,446,269 kilowatt-hours; USA; $4.1 = 0.67 \log (0.37E) + 1.46$, 23,556 kilowatt-hours

7.6 Problem Solving Workshop (p. 525) **1.** about 0.799 **3.** about 2.10 **5.** 0.8 **7.** about 4.48 **9.** 2001 **11.** about 251.19 mm **13.** about 0.03225°C

Extension (p. 527) **1.** $x \leq 2.727$ **3.** $x \leq 1.51$ **5.** $x \leq 6.03$ **7.** $x \geq 27$ **9.** $0 < x \leq 36$ **11.** $0 < x < 32$ **13.** after 5.25 yr

7.7 Skill Practice (pp. 533–534) **1.** exponential **3.** $y = \frac{3}{4} \cdot 4^x$ **5.** $y = \frac{1}{8} \cdot 2^x$ **7.** $y = \frac{2}{5} \cdot 5^x$ **9.** $y = 4.99 \cdot 0.499^x$

11. 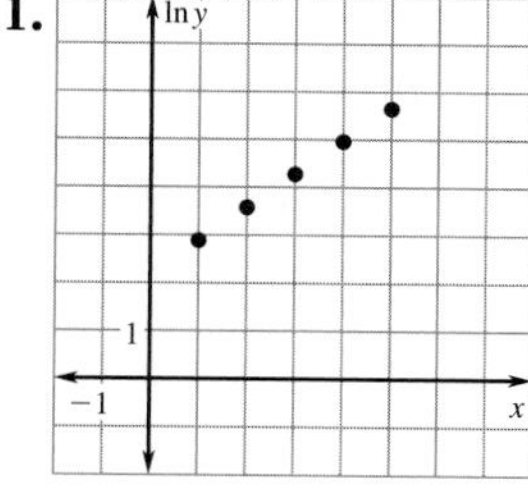
$y = 9(2)^x$

13. 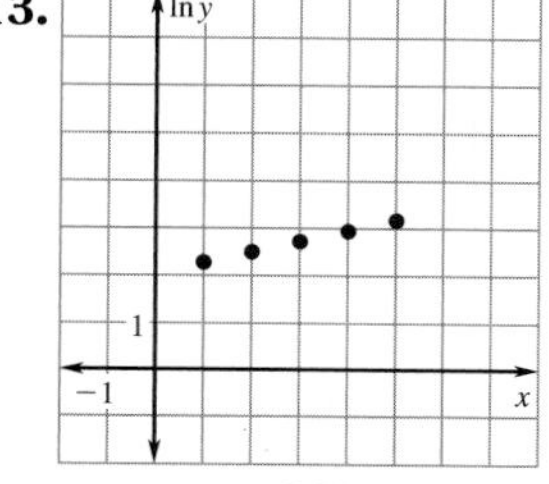
$y = 7.83(1.25)^x$

15. $y = 0.12x^{2.32}$ **17.** $y = 1.25x^{1.26}$ **19.** $y = 0.569x^{1.91}$ **21.** $y = 0.241x^{2.34}$

23. 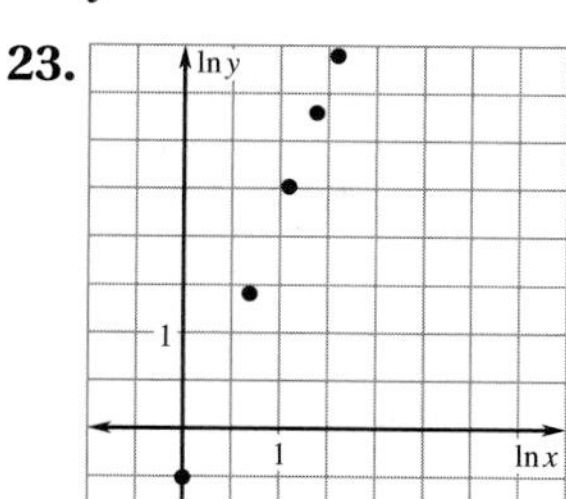
$y = 0.606x^{2.74}$

25. 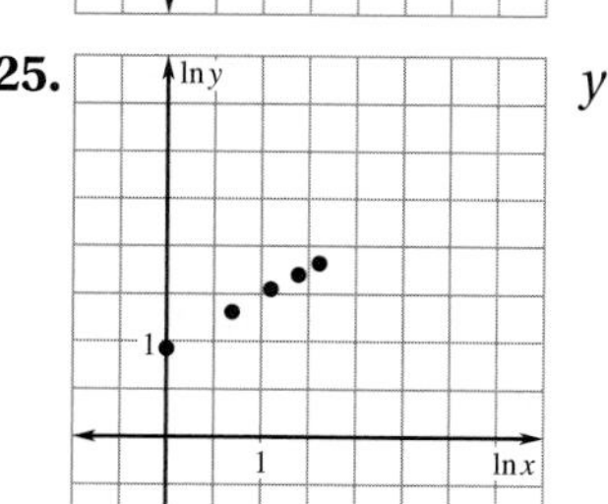
$y = 2.50x^{0.567}$

29. The x should be raised to the 3, not multiplied by it; $\ln y = \ln x^3 - 2$, $y = e^{\ln x^3 - 2}$, $y = e^{\ln x^3} \cdot e^{-2}$, $y = e^{\ln x^3} \cdot e^{-2}$, $y = 0.135x^3$

SELECTED ANSWERS

7.7 Problem Solving (pp. 534–536)

31. a.

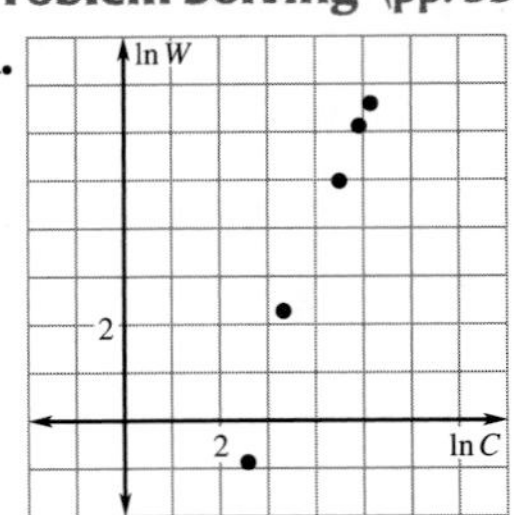

b. $y = 0.000466x^{2.80}$ **c.** about 64.8 kg

33. a. $y = 0.475(2.08)^x$ **b.** Graph the points (x, y); if they appear linear, then a line is the best fit. If not, graph the points $(x, \ln y)$; if these points appear linear, then an exponential model is the best fit for the data. If not, graph the points $(\ln x, \ln y)$; if these points appear linear, then a power model is the best fit for the data; $y = 33.8x + 2.8$.

35. a.

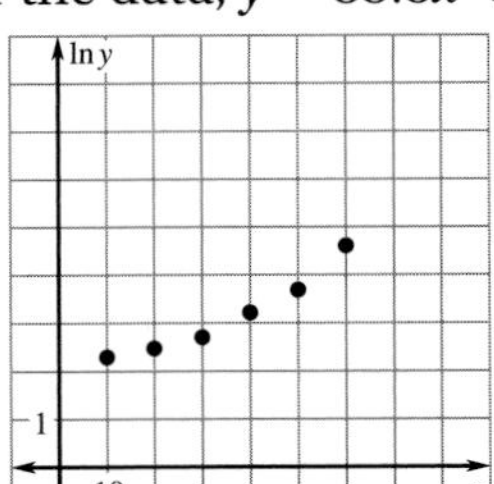

b.

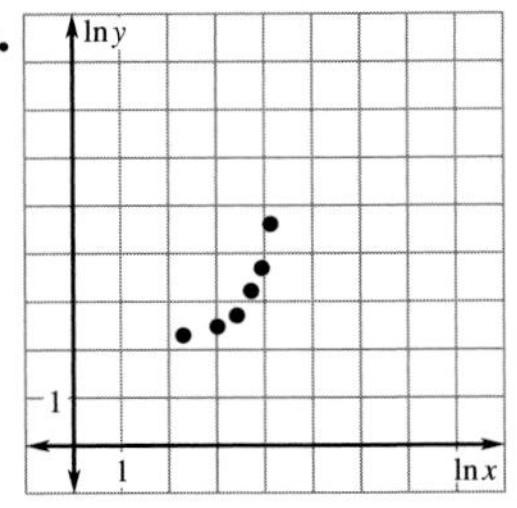

c. Exponential function; the points for $(x, \ln y)$ appear more linear than the points $(\ln x, \ln y)$, so an exponential model appears to be the best fit for the data. **d.** $y = 4.98(1.05)^x$; about 247 cm

Chapter Review (pp. 538–542) **1.** $y = 5$ **3.** *Sample answer:* $\log_b y = x$ if and only if $b^x = y$. **5.** Exponential function. *Sample answer:* The variable is in the exponent.

7.

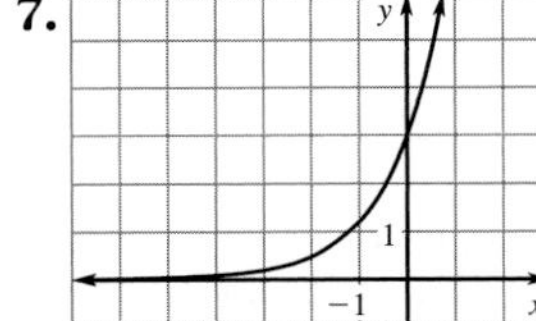

domain: all real numbers, range: $y > 0$

9. \$1725.39

11.

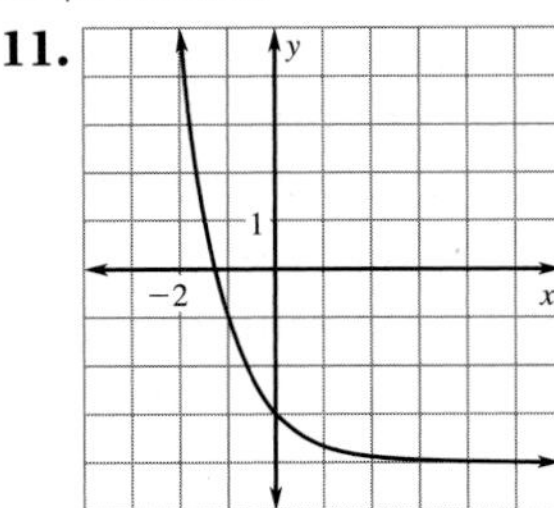

domain: all real numbers, range: $y > -4$

13.

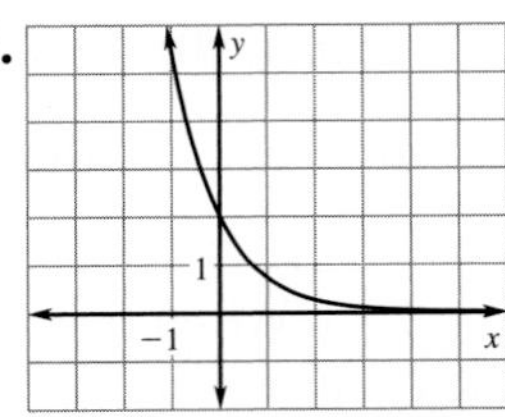

domain: all real numbers, range: $y > 0$

15.

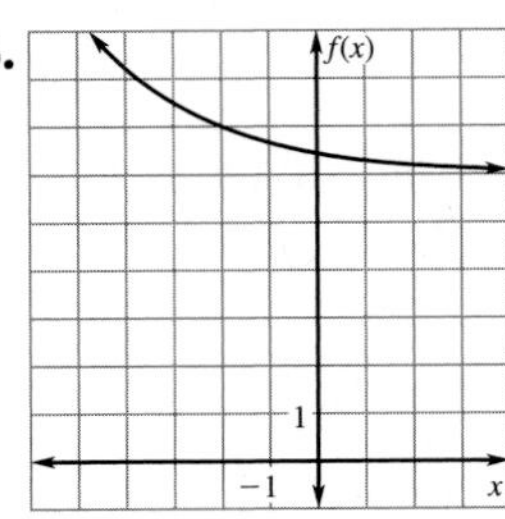

domain: all real numbers, range: $y > 6$

17. 5 **19.** −3

21.

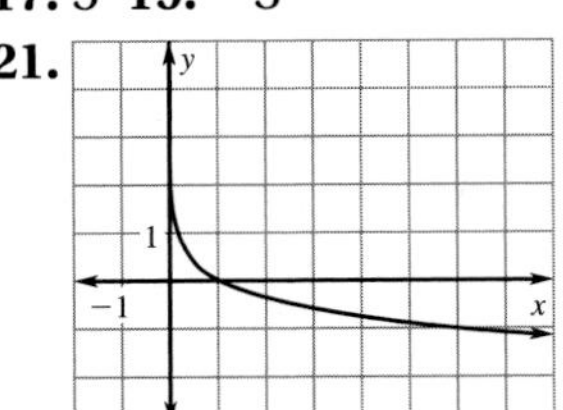

domain: $x > 0$, range: all real numbers

23.

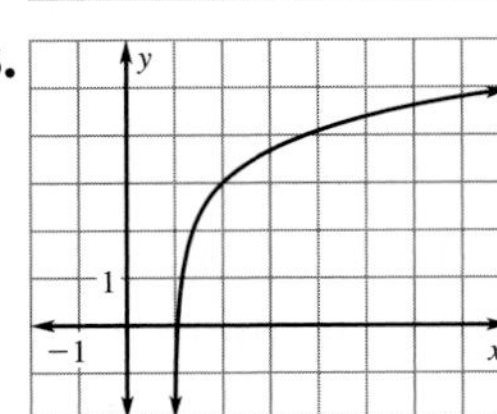

domain: $x > 0$, range: all real numbers

25. $\log_8 3 + \log_8 x + \log_8 y$ **27.** $\log 8 - 4 \log y$ **29.** $\log_7 384$ **31.** $\ln 36$ **33.** 7 **35.** $y = 64\left(\frac{1}{2}\right)^x$ **37.** $y = \frac{1}{4} \cdot 6x$

Chapter 8

8.1 Skill Practice (pp. 555–556) **1.** jointly **3.** inverse variation **5.** direct variation **7.** inverse variation **9.** direct variation **13.** $y = \frac{9}{x}$; 3 **15.** $y = \frac{14}{x}$; $\frac{14}{3}$ **17.** $y = \frac{5}{x}$; $\frac{5}{3}$ **19.** $y = \frac{-35}{3x}$; $-\frac{35}{9}$ **21.** direct variation **23.** inverse variation **25.** $z = \frac{1}{4}xy$; −5 **27.** $z = \frac{1}{14}xy$; $\frac{-10}{7}$ **29.** $z = -5xy$; 100 **31.** $x = \frac{ay}{z}$ **33.** $w = \frac{axz}{y}$ **35.** *Sample answer:* $f(x) = 2x$, $g(x) = \frac{2}{x}$

8.1 Problem Solving (pp. 556–557) **37.** $n = \frac{103.68}{s}$; 26 photos **39.** $P = \frac{172}{A}$; about 2.87 lb/in.^{2} **41. a.** $F = \frac{Gm_1m_2}{d^2}$ **b.** 6.7×10^{-11} **c.** It decreases; it increases.

8.2 Skill Practice (pp. 561–562) **1.** range; domain

3. 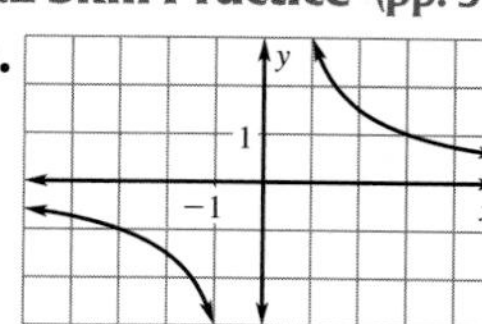
The graph lies farther from the axes than the graph of $y = \frac{1}{x}$. Both graphs lie in the 1st and 3rd quadrants and have the same asymptotes, domain, and range.

5. The graph lies farther from the axes than the graph of $y = \frac{1}{x}$ and is located in quadrants 2 and 4. Both graphs have the same asymptotes, domain, and range.

11. 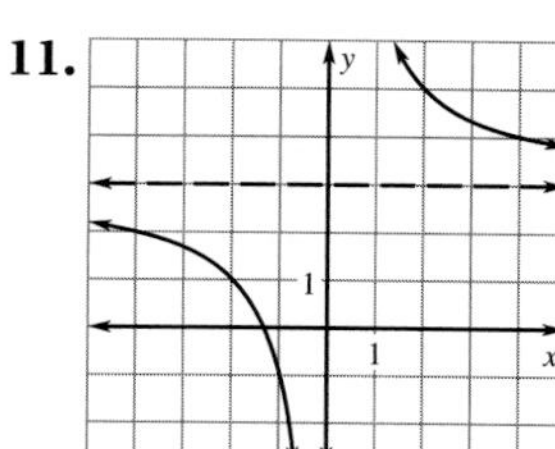
domain: all real numbers except 0, range: all real numbers except 3

13. 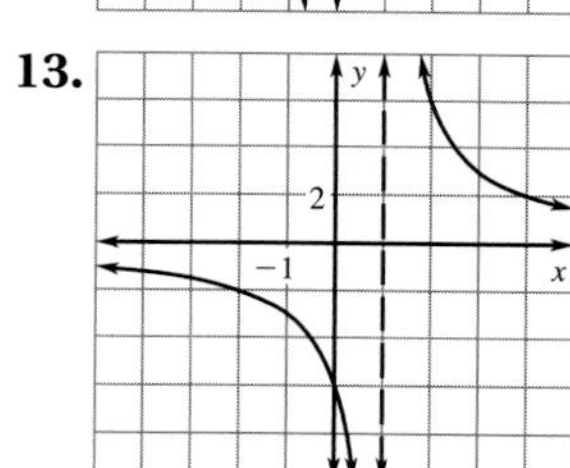
domain: all real numbers except 1, range: all real numbers except 0

25. The graph should be
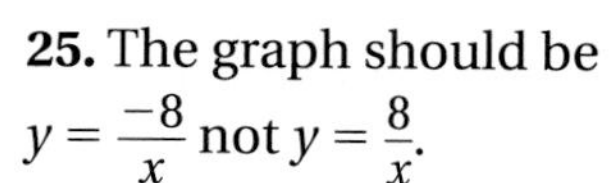
$y = \frac{-8}{x}$ not $y = \frac{8}{x}$.

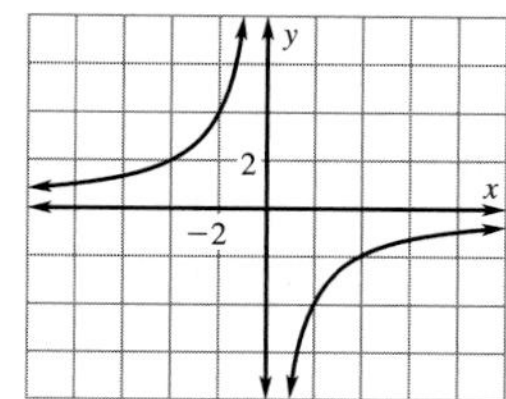

27. domain: all real numbers except 3, range: all real numbers except 1

29. 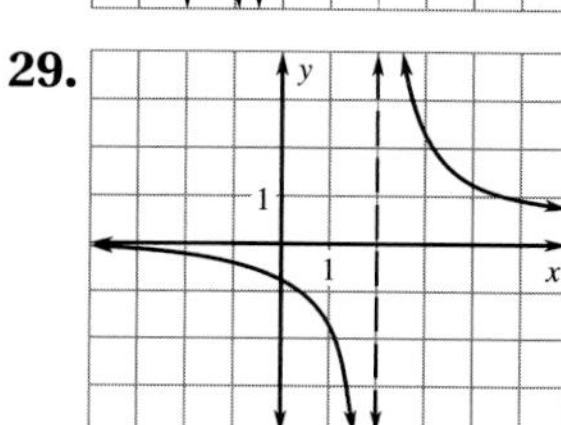
domain: all real numbers except 2, range: all real numbers except $\frac{1}{4}$

35. *Sample answer:* $y = \frac{3x + 1}{x + 8}$

8.2 Problem Solving (pp. 562–563)

37. $c = \frac{43m + 50}{m}$; 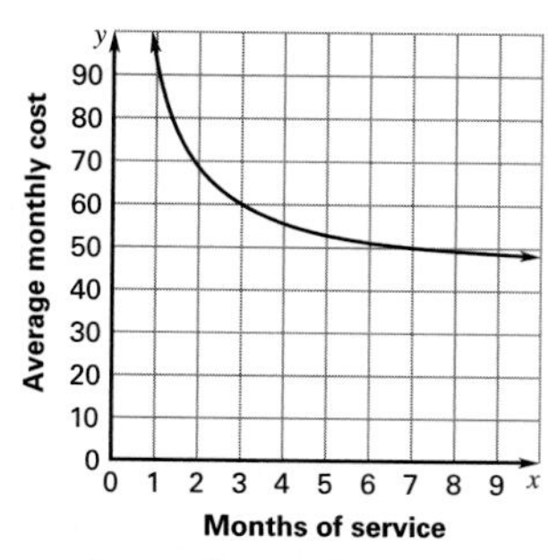
5 mo

39. a. About 14.5 sec. *Sample answer:* Substitute 25 for T to find $t \approx 2.89$.Since you are 5 kilometers away, multiply t by 5 to get $5(2.89) \approx 14.5$ seconds.

b. 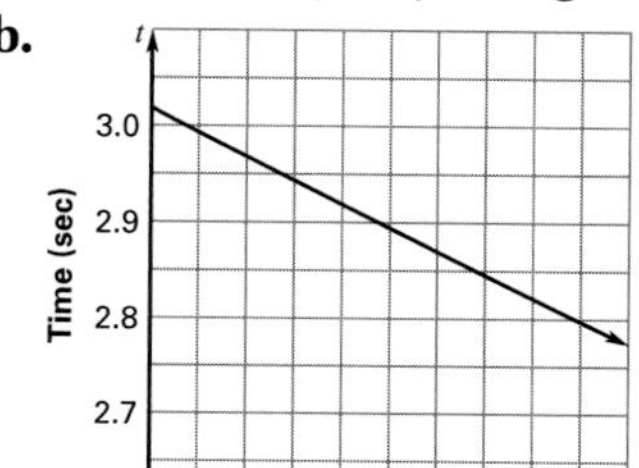
about 3.9°C

41. a. approaching: $f_1 = \frac{1{,}480{,}000}{740 - r}$, moving away: $f_1 = \frac{1{,}480{,}000}{740 + r}$

b. 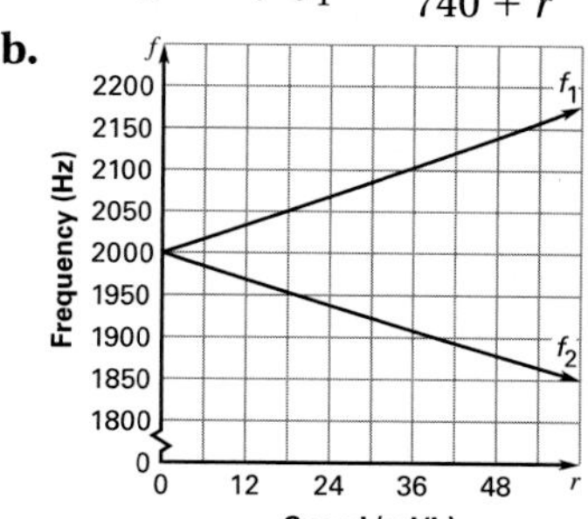
c. The frequency of a sound that is approaching is greater than that of a sound moving away.

8.3 Skill Practice (pp. 568–569) **1.** horizontal asymptote **3.** C **5.** B **7.** none; $x = 1$ and $x = -1$ **9.** none; $x = 5$ and $x = -3$ **11.** -3; $x = 0$ and $x = -\frac{1}{3}$ **13.** The vertical asymptote occurs at the zeros of the denominator not the numerator; the vertical asymptotes occur at the zeros of the denominator $x^2 - 8x + 7$. So, the vertical asymptotes are at $x = 7$ and $x = 1$.

15. 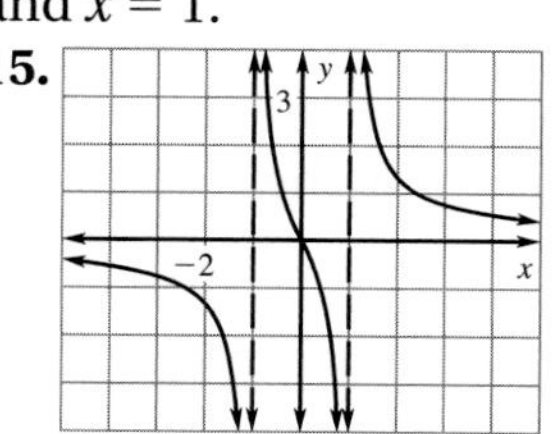

SELECTED ANSWERS

17. 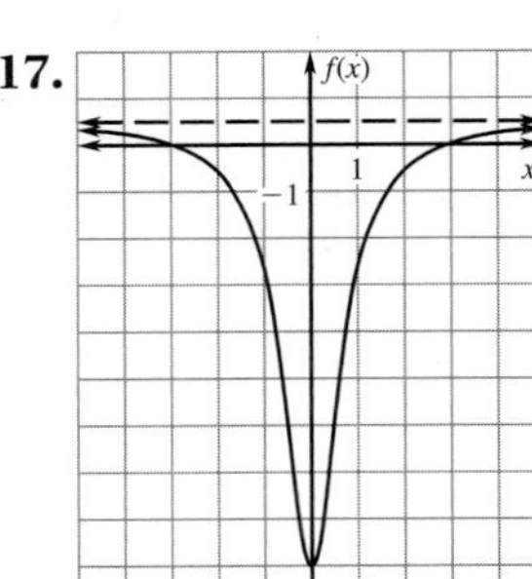

25. $0 < y \le 7.5$
27. all real numbers except $-0.209 < y < -4.791$

8.3 Problem Solving (pp. 569–571) **31. a.** $\ell = \frac{100}{\pi r^2}$ **b.** $S = 2\pi r^2 + \frac{200}{r}$ **c.** $r \approx 2.515$ ft, $\ell \approx 5.032$ ft

33. a.

Depth (m)	Mean Temperature (°C)
1000	4.763
1050	4.580
1100	4.409
1150	4.251
1200	4.104
1250	3.967
1300	3.839

b. about 1238 m

35. a.

b. about 9.78 m/sec^2 **c.** about 9.47 m/sec^2 **d.** *Sample answer:* g decreases, but at a very small rate.

8.4 Skill Practice (pp. 577–579) **1.** reciprocal **3.** B **5.** C **7.** simplified form **9.** $\frac{x-3}{x+5}$ **11.** $\frac{2(x-1)}{x-7}$ **13.** $\frac{x-6}{x+6}$ **15.** $\frac{4x-1}{3x+2}$ **17.** $\frac{x^2-3}{x-3}$ **19.** You can only divide out common factors. Since the factors that are divided out are not common factors of the entire numerator and denominator, you cannot divide them out; $\frac{x^2+16x+48}{x^2+8x+16} = \frac{(x+4)(x+12)}{(x+4)(x+4)} = \frac{x+12}{x+4}$ **21.** $\frac{2}{x}$ **23.** Exercise 21. *Sample answer:* The perimeter of Exercise 21 is smaller and the areas are the same.

25. $\frac{8x^4}{y^2}$ **27.** $\frac{2(x+1)}{x}$ **29.** $\frac{x+4}{2(x-5)}$ **31.** $(x+2)(x+7)$ **33.** $\frac{4(x+5)(x+4)}{x}$ **35.** $\frac{4x^4y}{5z}$ **37.** $\frac{16x(x-4)}{(x+4)}$ **39.** $\frac{x-5}{(x+5)^2}$ **41.** $\frac{5(x+1)}{x-1}$ **43.** $\frac{(x+8)(x-7)}{6x}$

45. 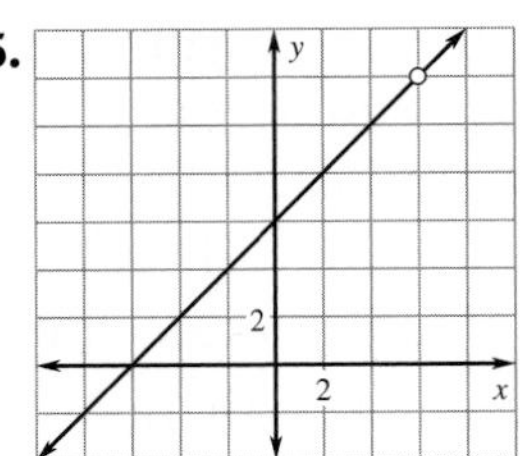

8.4 Problem Solving (pp. 579–580) **49.** $\frac{S}{A} = \frac{(-6420t + 292{,}000)(5.92t^2 - 131t + 1000)}{(6.02t^2 - 125t + 1000)(-407t + 7220)}$; \$50.21 **51. a.** $V_{\text{sphere}} = \frac{4}{3}\pi r^3$, $V_{\text{cylinder}} = \pi r^2 h$, since the volumes are the same, set the equations equal to each other resulting in $h = \frac{4}{3}r$. **b.** $S_{\text{sphere}} = 4\pi r^2$, $S_{\text{cylinder}} = \frac{14}{3}\pi r^2$ **c.** $\frac{6}{7}$. *Sample answer:* The spherical tank uses less material.

8.5 Skill Practice (pp. 586–587) **1.** complex fraction **3.** $\frac{5}{x}$ **5.** $\frac{9-2x}{x+1}$ **7.** 5 **9.** $3x(x-2)$ **11.** $2x(x-5)$ **13.** $x(x-5)(x+5)$ **17.** $\frac{32-15x}{12x^2}$ **19.** $\frac{3(x+12)}{(x+8)(x-3)}$ **21.** $\frac{2x^2+3x+9}{(x+1)(x-3)}$ **23.** $\frac{-3(x+16)}{(x-4)^2}$ **25.** You must have a common denominator before you can add values in the numerator; $\frac{x(x-5)+4(x+2)}{(x+2)(x-5)} = \frac{x^2-x+8}{(x-5)(x+2)}$. **27.** $\frac{(2x+3)(x-1)}{(x-3)(x+3)^2}$ **29.** $\frac{8x^3-9x^2-28x+8}{x(x-4)(3x-1)}$ **31.** $\frac{x(x-18)}{6(5x+2)}$ **33.** $\frac{8x(x+1)}{(x-2)(5x+3)}$ **35.** $\frac{3x}{4(x-1)}$ **37.** *Sample answer:* $\frac{\frac{x^2-x-6}{x^2+4x}}{\frac{x+2}{x}}$, $\frac{\frac{x^2+3x-18}{4}}{\frac{x^2+10x+24}{4}}$

8.5 Problem Solving (pp. 587–588) **41.** $T = \frac{2da}{(a-j)(a+j)}$; about 10.2 h **43. a.** $M = \frac{Pi}{1-\left(\frac{1}{1+i}\right)^{12t}} = \frac{Pi}{1-\frac{1}{(1+i)^{12t}}} = \frac{Pi}{\frac{(1+i)^{12t}-1}{(1+i)^{12t}}} = \frac{Pi(1+i)^{12t}}{(1+i)^{12t}-1}$ **b.** \$364.02

8.6 Skill Practice (pp. 592–593) **1.** cross multiplying **3.** Graph both sides of the equation. If the graphs intersect at a possible solution, then it is a solution. If the graphs do not intersect at a possible solution, then it is an extraneous solution. **5.** 6 **7.** 2 **9.** -1 **11.** no solution **15.** 4 **17.** $-\frac{7}{3}$ **19.** $\frac{-1 \pm \sqrt{79}}{3}$ **21.** 1 **23.** $-\frac{5}{2}$, 8 **25.** 0, 7 **27.** The student simply added numerators and denominators on the left side of the equation. Both sides of the equation should have been multiplied by the LCD, $6x$; $6x\left(\frac{5}{x} + \frac{23}{6}\right) = 6x\left(\frac{45}{x}\right)$, $30 + 23x = 270$. **29.** *Sample answer:* $\frac{6}{x+5} = \frac{2x}{x-1}$; $\frac{4}{x} + \frac{5}{3} = \frac{12}{x}$

8.6 Problem Solving (pp. 594–595) **33.** 26 serves **35.** 1995 **37.** $\frac{1 + \sqrt{5}}{2}$

8.6 Problem Solving Workshop (p. 597) **1.** about ± 5.6 **3.** 9 **5.** about ± 3.2 **7. a.** 99 ft **b.** 33 ft

Extension (p. 600) **1.** $x < 2$ **3.** $x < 3$ **5.** $-1.5 < x < 4$ **7.** $x > -5$ **9.** $-1 \le x \le 1$ **11.** $0 < x < 1$ **13.** $x > -2$ **15.** $-4 < x < -3$ or $x > -2$ **17.** $-3 < x < -2$ or $x \ge 2$ **19.** 1999 to 2002 **21.** at least 13 mo

Chapter Review (pp. 603–606) **1.** inverse variation **3.** rational function **5.** cross multiplying **7.** $y = \frac{24}{x}$; -8 **9.** $y = \frac{-8}{x}$; $\frac{8}{3}$

11.

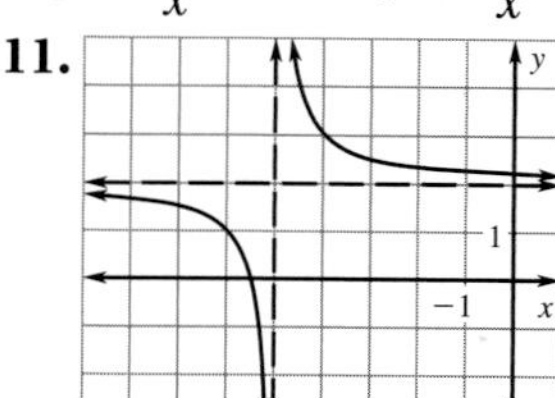

domain: all real numbers except $x = -5$, range: all real numbers except $y = 2$

13.

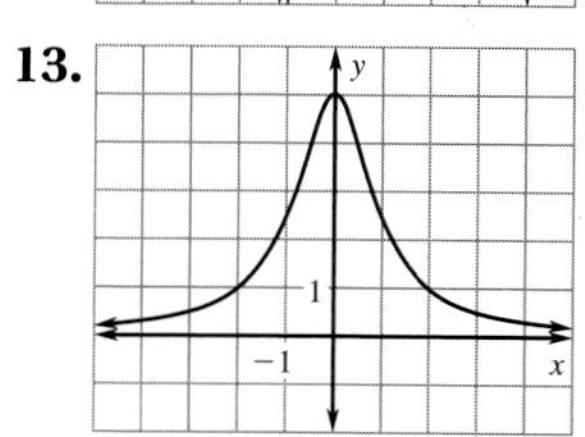

15.

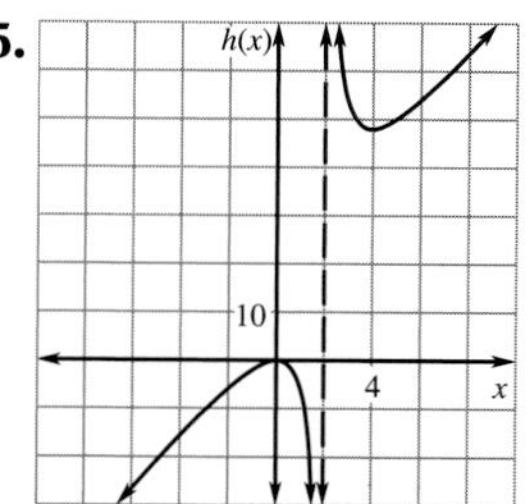

17.

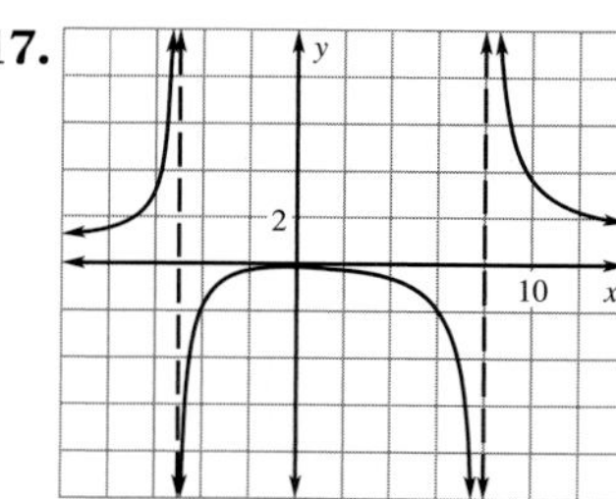

19. $\frac{16x^3}{y^2}$ **21.** $\frac{3x(4x-1)}{(x-4)(x-3)}$ **23.** $\frac{3x^2 + 26x + 36}{6x(x+3)}$ **25.** $\frac{-2(2x^2 + 3x + 3)}{(x-3)(x+3)(x+1)}$ **27.** 5 **29.** -1 **31.** $-\frac{6}{11}$, 0 **33.** 0 **35.** no solution

Chapter 9

9.1 Skill Practice (pp. 617–618)

1. The distance d between (x_1, y_1) and (x_2, y_2) is $d = \sqrt{(x_2 - x_1)^2 + (y_2 - y_1)^2}$; the midpoint of the line segment joining $A(x_1, y_1)$ and $B(x_2, y_2)$ is $M\left(\frac{x_1 + x_2}{2}, \frac{y_1 + y_2}{2}\right)$. **3.** 17; $\left(4, \frac{15}{2}\right)$ **5.** $5\sqrt{5}$; $\left(\frac{5}{2}, 1\right)$ **7.** $4\sqrt{2}$; $(4, -3)$ **9.** $12\sqrt{2}$; $(2, 2)$ **11.** $\sqrt{145}$; $\left(\frac{1}{2}, 0\right)$ **13.** $\sqrt{449}$; $\left(5, \frac{9}{2}\right)$ **15.** $2\sqrt{194}$; $(1.2, 2)$ **17.** $\frac{\sqrt{3221}}{10}$ or about 5.68; $(0.35, -6)$ **21.** The difference of the squares should be added not subtracted; $d = \sqrt{(2 - (-4))^2 + (8 - 3)^2} = \sqrt{36 + 25} = \sqrt{61}$. **23.** isosceles **25.** scalene **27.** scalene **29.** scalene **31.** $y = -\frac{2}{3}x + \frac{43}{3}$ **33.** $y = -\frac{1}{4}x - \frac{5}{2}$ **35.** $y = -4x + \frac{17}{2}$ **37.** *Sample answer:* $(6, 4)$, $(2, 0)$ **39.** $y = -\frac{5}{4}x + \frac{55}{4}$ **41.** ± 6 **43.** -10, 2 **45.** $d(x) = \sqrt{5x^2 - 16x + 13}$; $\left(\frac{1}{5}, \frac{2}{5}\right)$, $(3, 6)$

9.1 Problem Solving (pp. 618–619) **47.** 17 m **49.** about 6.02 mi **51.** about 4.55 mi **53. a.** $(-1.5, 8)$ **b.** about 1.32 mi **c.** about 1.68 mi **55.** about 550 ft

9.2 Skill Practice (pp. 623–624) **1.** focus, directrix

3.

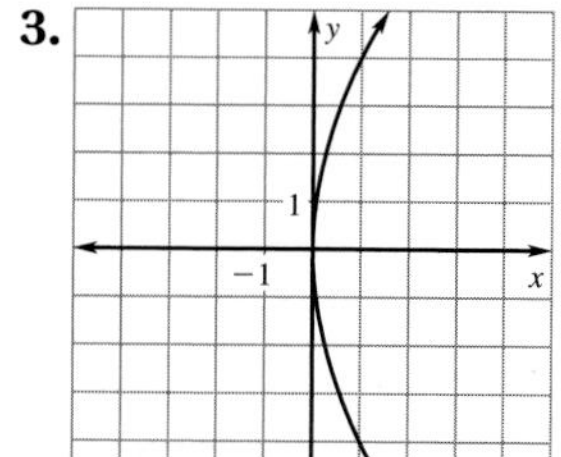

$(4, 0)$, $x = -4$, $y = 0$

5.

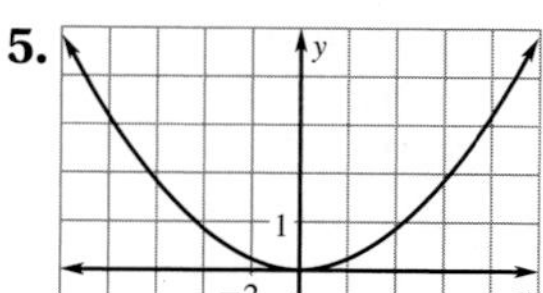

$(0, 5)$, $y = -5$, $x = 0$

23. The parabola should open to the right rather than up;

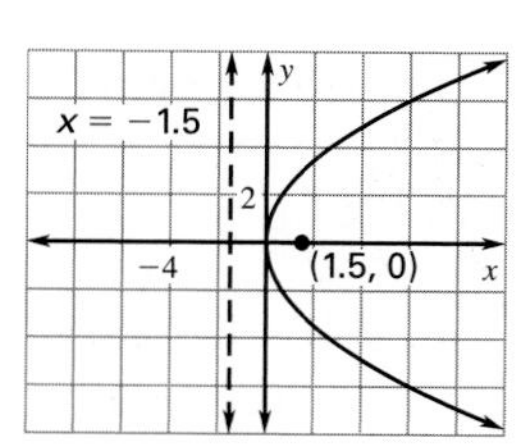

SELECTED ANSWERS

27. $y^2 = -20x$ **29.** $x^2 = -16y$ **31.** $x^2 = -40y$
33. $y^2 = -36x$ **35.** $x^2 = -\frac{3}{2}y$ **37.** $y^2 = -\frac{9}{4}x$
39. $y^2 = -12x$ **41.** $y^2 = 20x$ **43.** $x^2 = 16y$
45. $x^2 = -24y$ **47.** $y^2 = 6x$ **49.** $x^2 = \frac{22}{3}y$

51. a. The new focus will be located at (0, 1) rather than $\left(0, \frac{1}{4}\right)$. The new directrix will be $y = -1$ rather than $y = -\frac{1}{4}$. The parabola will be wider.

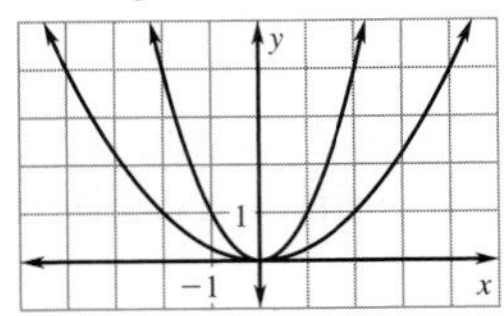

b. The new focus will be located at $\left(-\frac{1}{8}, 0\right)$ rather than $\left(\frac{3}{2}, 0\right)$. The new directrix will be at $x = \frac{1}{8}$ rather than $x = -\frac{3}{2}$. The parabola will open left rather than right and be narrower.

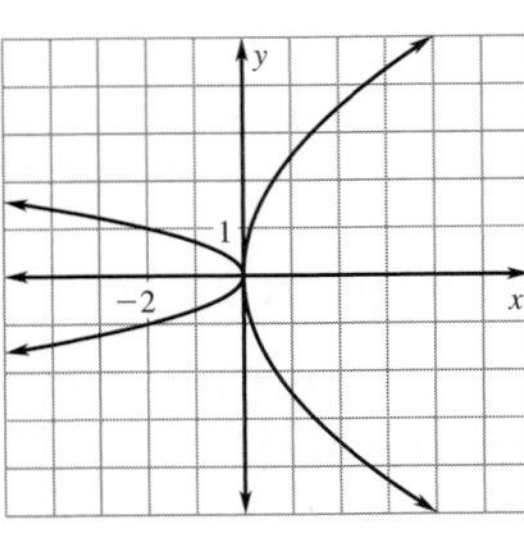

53. The graph gets wider. *Sample answer:* As the value of $|p|$ increases, then the focus and directrix (each of which lie $|p|$ units from the vertex) get further and further away from the vertex and from each other. Since each point on a parabola is equidistant from the focus and the directrix, this has the effect of making the parabola wider and wider as $|p|$ increases.

9.2 Problem Solving (pp. 624–625)
55. $x^2 = 24y$; about 3 ft
57. a.

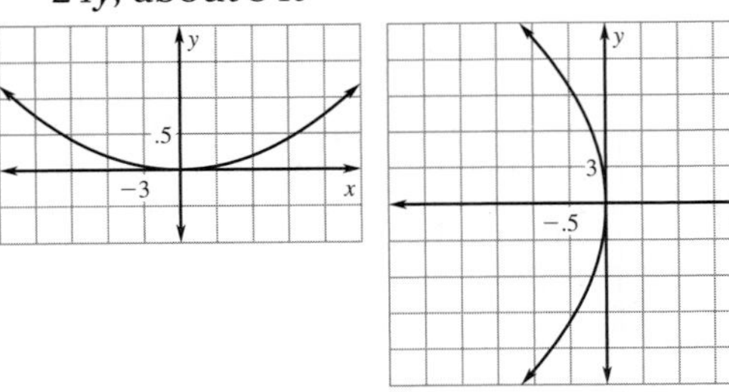

b. $x^2 = 192y$, $y^2 = -192x$ **c.** About 27.8 in.; no. *Sample answer:* Except for the direction they open, they are identical. **59. a.** about 20 in. **b.** *Sample answer:* $x^2 = 50y$; choose a value for p such that $4p > 10.5$; about 43.6 in. **c.** *Sample answer:* $x^2 = 8y$; choose a value for p such that $4p < 10.5$; about 17.4 in.

9.3 Skill Practice (pp. 629–630) **1.** center **3.** C **5.** A **7.** F
9. 1

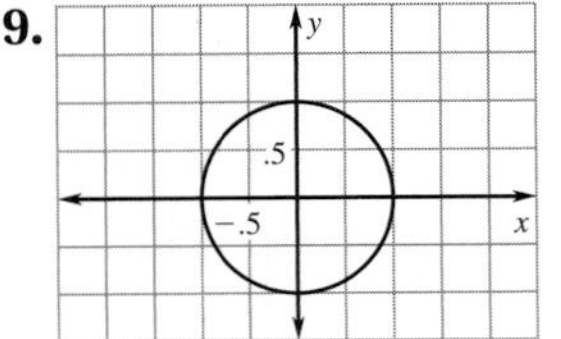

11. 5

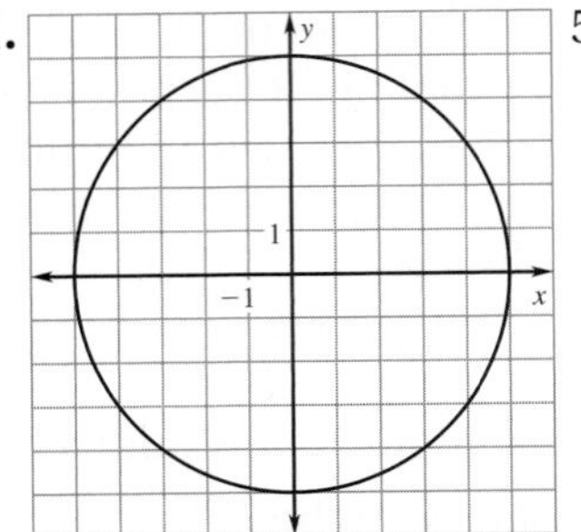

23. $x^2 + y^2 = 64$ **25.** $x^2 + y^2 = 256$ **27.** $x^2 + y^2 = 15$
29. $x^2 + y^2 = 96$ **31.** $x^2 + y^2 = 36$ **33.** $x^2 + y^2 = 25$
35. $x^2 + y^2 = 100$ **37.** $x^2 + y^2 = 116$ **39.** $x^2 + y^2 = 260$
41. $x^2 + y^2 = 242$

45.

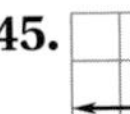

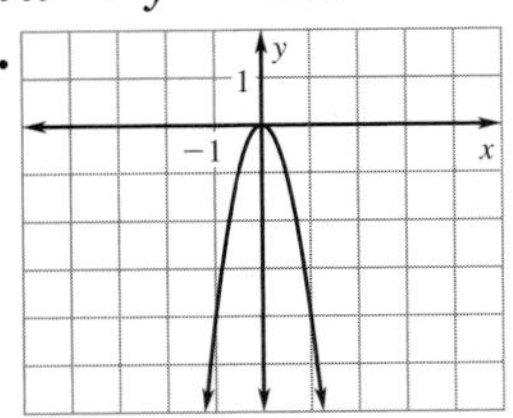

47.

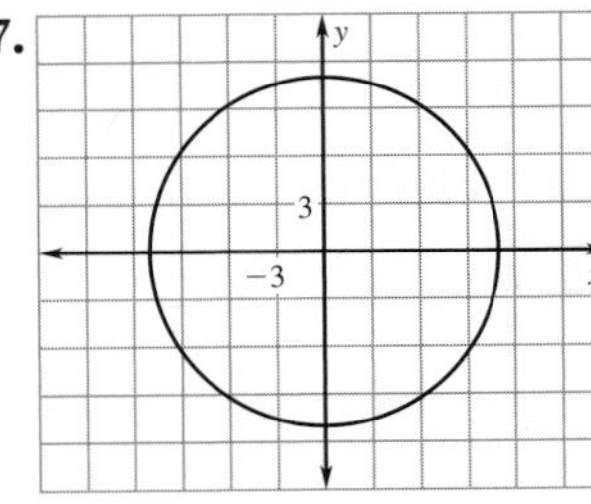

53. $y = -\frac{1}{4}x + \frac{17}{4}$ **55.** $y = \frac{5}{3}x + \frac{34}{3}$ **57.** $y = \frac{5}{9}x + \frac{106}{9}$
59. *Sample answer:* $x^2 + y^2 = 35$, $x^2 + y^2 = 36$, $x^2 + y^2 = 38$

9.3 Problem Solving (pp. 630–632) **63.** yes **65. a.** about 28.9 mi **b.** about 18.3 mi **c.** 6 mi **67.** about 7.94 ft

9.4 Skill Practice (pp. 637–638) **1.** foci

3. $(\pm 4, 0)$, $(0, \pm 2)$, $(\pm 2\sqrt{3}, 0)$

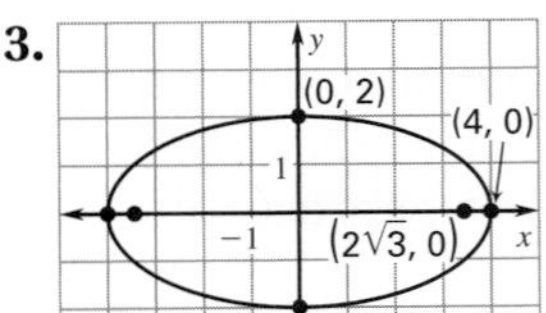

5. $(0, \pm 7)$, $(\pm 3, 0)$, $(0, \pm 2\sqrt{10})$

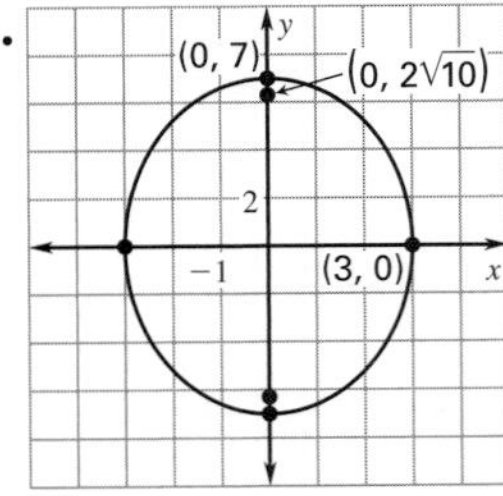

15. The major axis should be the y-axis, not the x-axis.

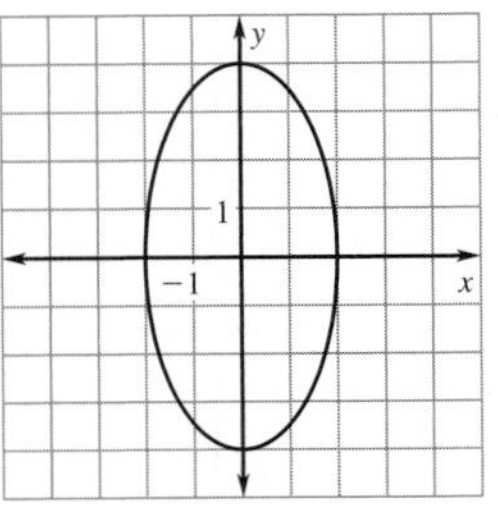

SELECTED ANSWERS

17. $\frac{x^2}{25} + \frac{y^2}{9} = 1$ 19. $\frac{x^2}{196} + \frac{y^2}{81} = 1$ 21. $\frac{x^2}{121} + \frac{y^2}{144} = 1$
23. $\frac{x^2}{28} + \frac{y^2}{64} = 1$ 25. $\frac{x^2}{49} + \frac{y^2}{81} = 1$ 27. $\frac{x^2}{4} + \frac{y^2}{16} = 1$
29. $\frac{x^2}{16} + \frac{y^2}{7} = 1$ 31. $\frac{x^2}{400} + \frac{y^2}{175} = 1$ 33. $\frac{x^2}{60} + \frac{y^2}{256} = 1$

37.

39. 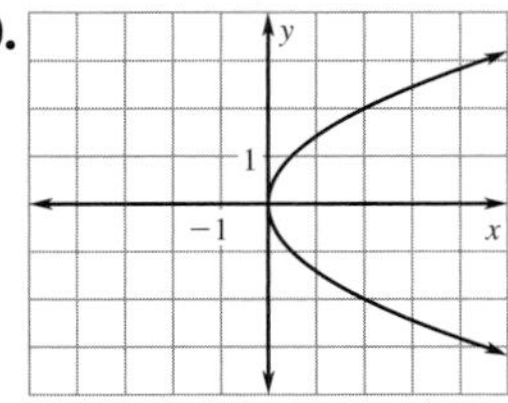

45. The conic changes from an ellipse elongated along the y-axis to a circle to an ellipse elongated along the x-axis.

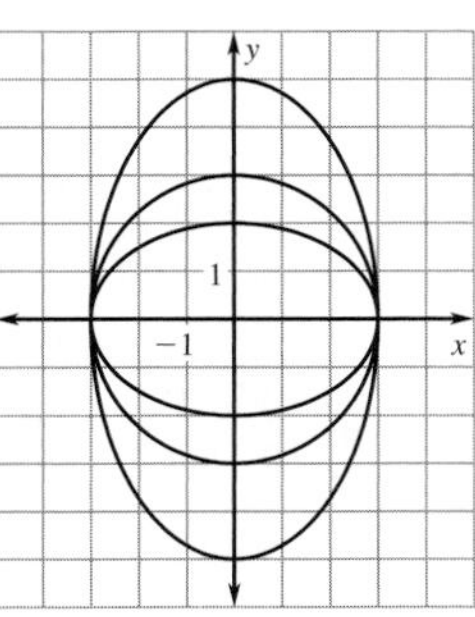

9.4 Problem Solving (pp. 638–639)

49. $\frac{x^2}{(77.5)^2} + \frac{y^2}{(92.5)^2} = 1, \frac{x^2}{(55)^2} + \frac{y^2}{(67.5)^2} = 1;$ about $11{,}700 \le A \le 22{,}500$

51. Comet Halley .59 35.3 Sun *Sample answer:* $\frac{x^2}{21.1} + \frac{y^2}{320.4}$

9.4 Problem Solving Workshop (p. 640) 1. About 66,100 m^2; better. *Sample answer:* More rectangles means there is less area of the ellipse not included.
3. a. $\frac{x^2}{125^2} + \frac{y^2}{100^2} = 1$ b. about 39,000 m^2

9.5 Skill Practice (pp. 645–646)

1. vertices, transverse axis

3. 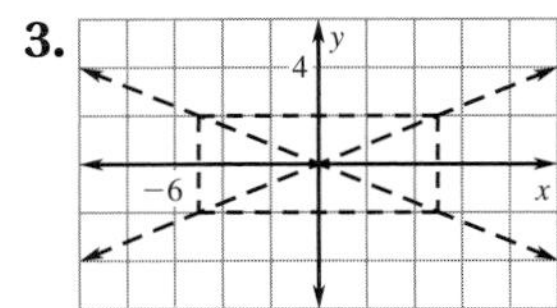 $(\pm 5, 0), (\pm\sqrt{29}, 0),$ $y = \pm\frac{2}{5}x$

5. 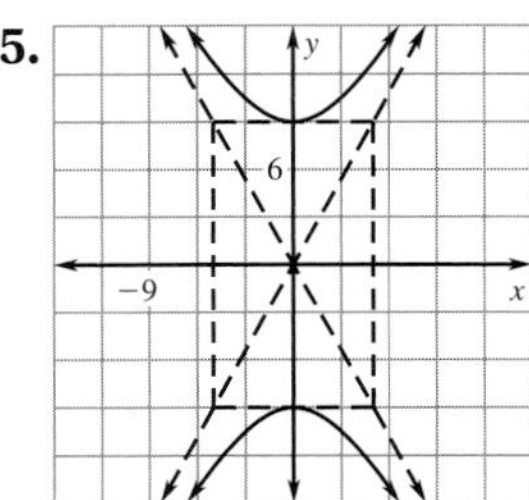 $(0, \pm 9), (0, \pm\sqrt{106}),$ $y = \pm\frac{9}{5}x$

17. The equation of a hyperbola must equal one, so the hyperbola's vertices should be located at $(\pm 4, 0)$.

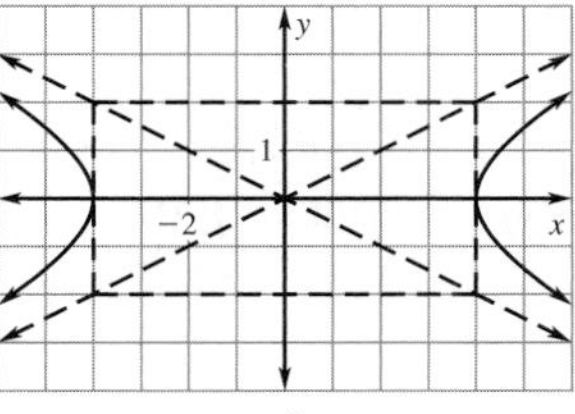

19. $\frac{x^2}{4} - \frac{y^2}{32} = 1$ 21. $\frac{y^2}{49} - \frac{x^2}{95} = 1$ 23. $\frac{y^2}{16} - \frac{x^2}{64} = 1$
25. $\frac{x^2}{4} - \frac{y^2}{50} = 1$

27. 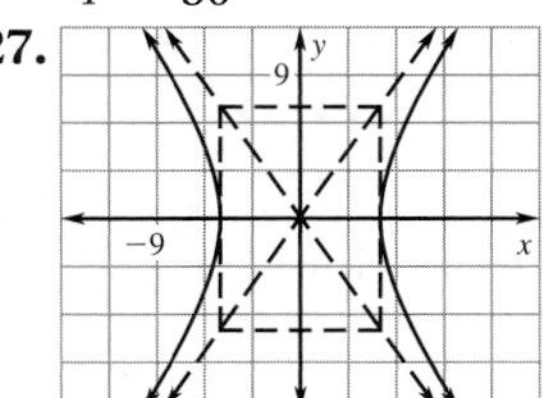

29. 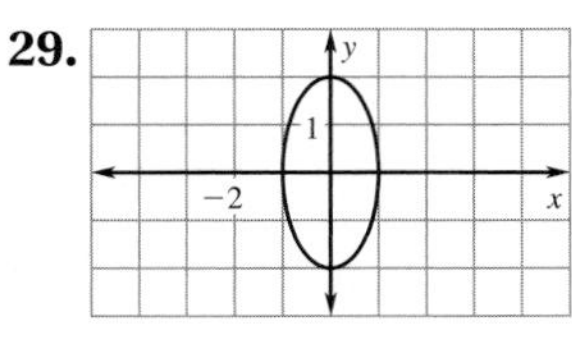

33. a. The hyperbola will be narrower, the vertices are the same, but the foci move to $(\pm\sqrt{13}, 0)$. b. The hyperbola will be wider, the vertices are the same, but the foci move to $(0, \pm\sqrt{41})$. 35. *Sample answer:* $x^2 - \frac{y^2}{4} = 1, \frac{x^2}{4} - \frac{y^2}{16} = 1, \frac{x^2}{9} - \frac{y^2}{36} = 1$; as the value of a gets larger the hyperbola is stretched vertically.

9.5 Problem Solving (pp. 646–647) 39. $\frac{y^2}{\frac{1}{2}} - \frac{x^2}{\frac{1}{4}} = 1$

41. a. (30.5, 0), (85, −40) b. $\frac{x^2}{930.25} - \frac{y^2}{236.45} = 1$
c. about 54.6 ft 43. a. $\frac{x^2}{16} - \frac{y^2}{20} = 1$ b. *Sample answer:* Choose any point on the graph and observe that the difference of the distances from that point and the foci remain constant.

9.6 Skill Practice (pp. 655–656) 1. The intersection of a plane and a double-napped cone form them.

3. 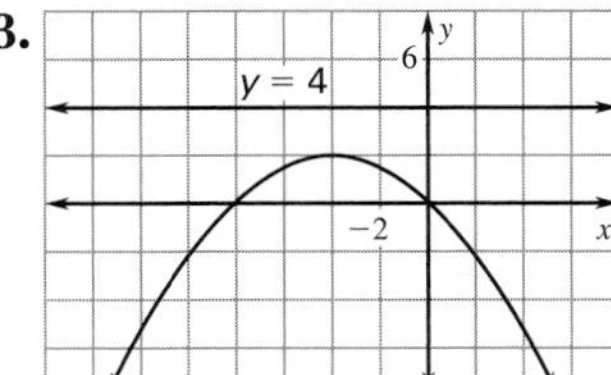 parabola with vertex $(-4, 2)$, focus $(-4, 0)$, and directrix $y = 4$

5. 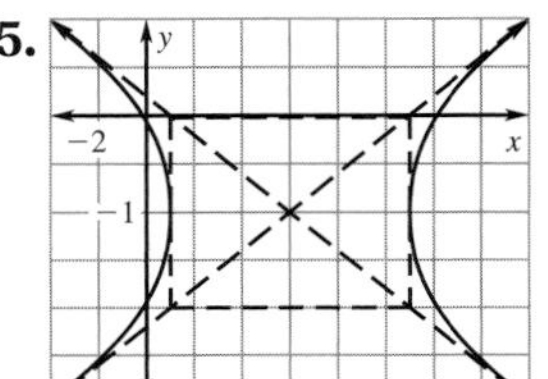 hyperbola with center $(6, -1)$, vertices $(11, -1)$ and $(1, -1)$, asymptotes $y = \frac{1}{5}x - \frac{11}{5}$ and $y = -\frac{1}{5}x + \frac{1}{5}$

13. $(x + 5)^2 + (y - 1)^2 = 36$ 15. $(y + 3)^2 = 20(x + 4)$
17. $\frac{(x-1)^2}{16} + \frac{(y-4)^2}{12} = 1$ 19. $\frac{(y+1)^2}{4} - \frac{(x-6)^2}{21} = 1$

SELECTED ANSWERS

21. The center is at $(-2, 3)$, not $(2, -3)$; $\frac{(x+2)^2}{25} + \frac{(y-3)^2}{9} = 1$. **23.** $y = 4$ **25.** $x = 3, y = 5$
27. any line passing through the point $(-2, -1)$
29. circle **31.** ellipse **33.** parabola **35.** hyperbola
37. circle,
$(x-7)^2 + (y+2)^2 = 64$

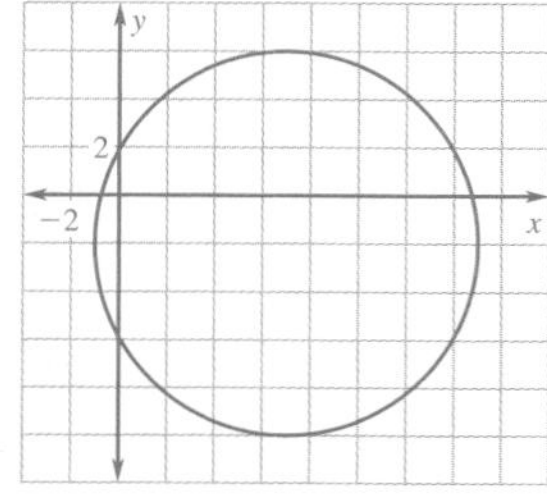

39. parabola,
$(x-8)^2 = 8(y-2)$

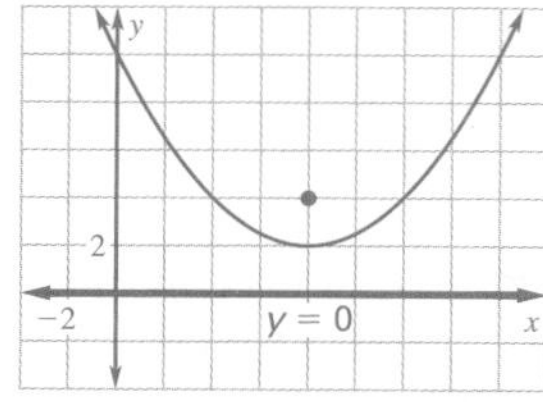

45. If the non-zero coefficients of x^2 and y^2 are the same it's a circle. If the non-zero coefficients of x^2 and y^2 are both positive and different it's an ellipse. If one of the non-zero coefficients of x^2 or y^2 is negative and the other one is positive it's a hyperbola. If one of the coefficients of x^2 or y^2 is zero it's a parabola.

9.6 Problem Solving (pp. 656–657)
49. $(x-5)^2 = -4\left(y - \frac{25}{4}\right)$; $6\frac{1}{4}$ ft, 10 ft
51. a. $(x-100)^2 + (y+60)^2 \le 150^2$, $(x+80)^2 + (y+70)^2 \le 100^2$
b.

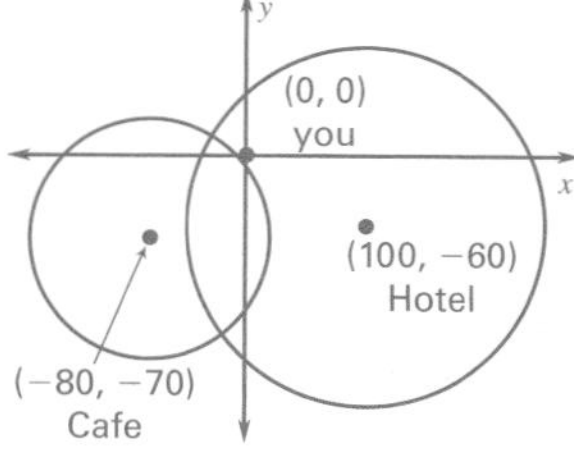

One; the distance from your position to the hotel is less than the radius of the hotel's transmitter, but you are about 106 feet from the café's transmitter which is out of range.
c. *Sample answer:* Find the distance from the hotel to the cafe. If it's greater than 250 yards they do not overlap. It it's less than or equal to 250 yards they overlap.

9.7 Skill Practice (pp. 661–662) **1.** quadratic
3. $(-4, -4), (4, 4)$ **5.** $(0.472, -2.58), (3.53, 6.58)$
7. $(-2.18, -3.36), (1.38, 3.76)$ **9.** $(3, -3), (-2, 2)$
11. $\left(\frac{-64 - 2\sqrt{106}}{17}, \frac{8 - 4\sqrt{106}}{17}\right), \left(\frac{-64 + 2\sqrt{106}}{17}, \frac{4 + 2\sqrt{106}}{17}\right)$
13. $(0, 2), \left(\frac{4}{3}, \frac{2}{3}\right)$ **15.** $(-1, -4), \left(-\frac{13}{2}, 7\right)$ **17.** no solution
19. $\left(\frac{7 + 3\sqrt{3}}{11}, \frac{-1 + 9\sqrt{3}}{11}\right), \left(\frac{7 - 3\sqrt{3}}{11}, \frac{-1 - 9\sqrt{3}}{11}\right)$
23. $(0, \pm\sqrt{5}), (-5, 0)$ **25.** $\left(\frac{1}{2}, \frac{1}{2}\right)$ **27.** no solution

29. no solution **31.** $(4, 0)$ **33.** $(-1, -2), (2, 1)$ **35.** When $(1 - y^2)^2$ was expanded, the last term should have been y^4; $1 - 2y^2 + y^4 + y^2 - 2 + 2y^2 - 2y = -1$, $y^4 + y^2 - 2y = 0$. **37.** about $(-2.32, -2.02)$, $(-0.296, -2.82)$

9.7 Problem Solving (pp. 662–664) **39.** $d = 0.8t$, $d = 2.5t^2$, 0.32 min **41. a.** $x^2 + y^2 = 1, y = -\frac{1}{7}x + \frac{5}{7}$
b. $\left(-\frac{3}{5}, \frac{4}{5}\right), \left(\frac{4}{5}, \frac{3}{5}\right)$ **c.** about 1.41 mi **43. a.** $(1, 1)$
b. about $(-8.94, -2.68)$

9.7 Extension (p. 666) **1.** 0 **3.** $\frac{\sqrt{15}}{8} \approx 0.484$ **5.** 1
7. $\frac{x^2}{36} + \frac{25(y-4)^2}{756} = 1$ **9.** $\frac{x^2}{49} + \frac{25(y-5)^2}{1176} = 1$
11. $\frac{(x-4)^2}{9} - \frac{25(y+4)^2}{504} = 1$ **13.** *Sample answer:* $\frac{x^2}{30.25} + \frac{y^2}{13.19} = 1$ **15.** In the ellipse $0 < c < a$, therefore $0 < \frac{c}{a} < 1$. In the hyperbola $0 < a < c$, therefore $\frac{c}{a} > 1$.

Chapter Review (pp. 669–672) **1.** parabola **3.** transverse axis **5.** $2\sqrt{17}$; $(-2, -4)$ **7.** $\sqrt{106}$; $\left(-\frac{1}{2}, \frac{1}{2}\right)$
9.

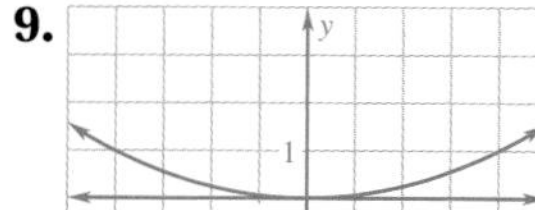

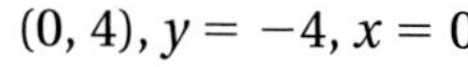

$(0, 4), y = -4, x = 0$

11.

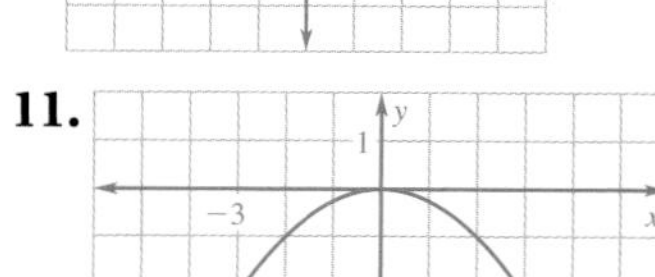

$(0, -1), y = 1, x = 0$

13. $x^2 = 12y$
15.

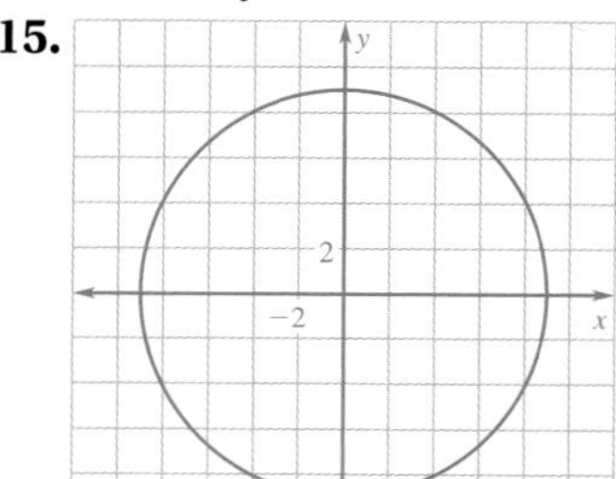

9

17.

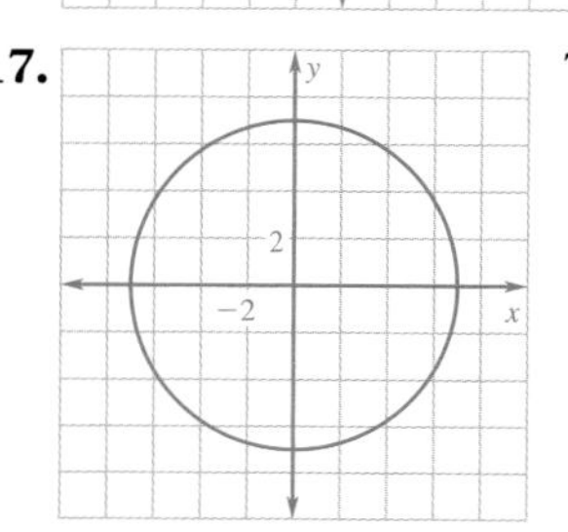

7

19. $x^2 + y^2 = 68$

21. $(\pm 5, 0), (0, \pm 4), (\pm 3, 0)$

23. 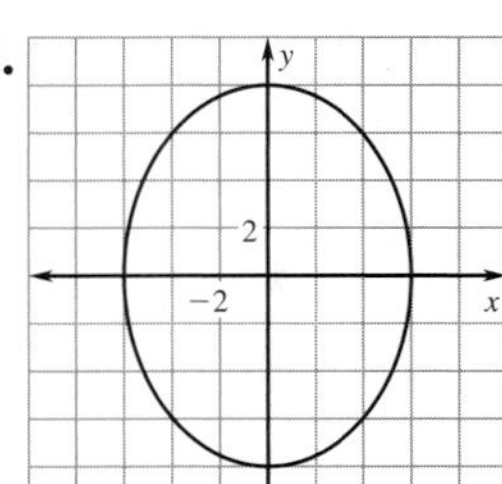
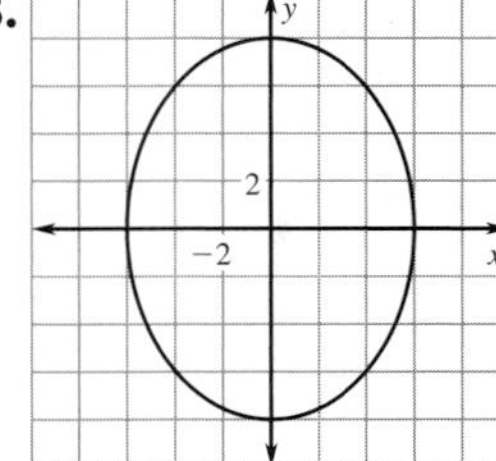

$(0, \pm 8), (\pm 6, 0), \left(0, \pm 2\sqrt{7}\right)$

25. $\frac{y^2}{64} + \frac{x^2}{39} = 1$

27. 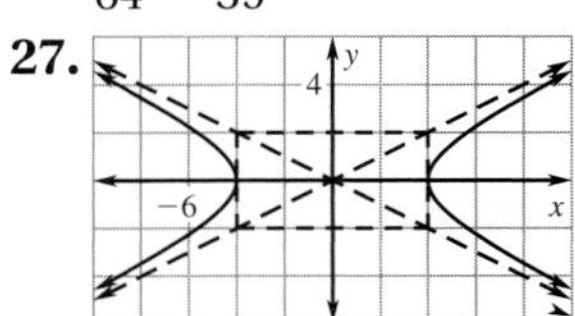

$(\pm 4, 0), \left(\pm 2\sqrt{5}, 0\right)$, $y = \pm \frac{1}{2}x$

29. $\frac{y^2}{4} - \frac{x^2}{21} = 1$

31. ellipse, $\frac{(x+5)^2}{9} + \frac{(y+4)^2}{4} = 1$

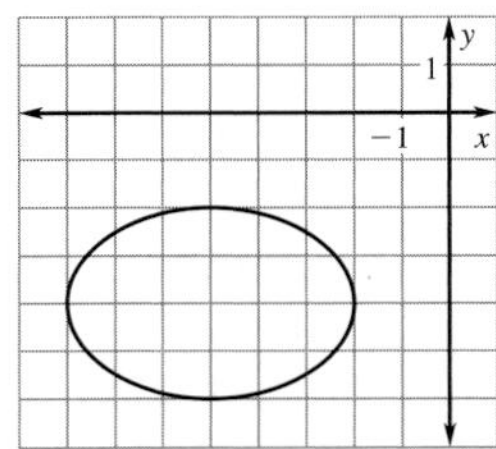

33. hyperbola, $\frac{(x-1)^2}{\frac{10}{9}} - \frac{(y+2)^2}{10} = 1$

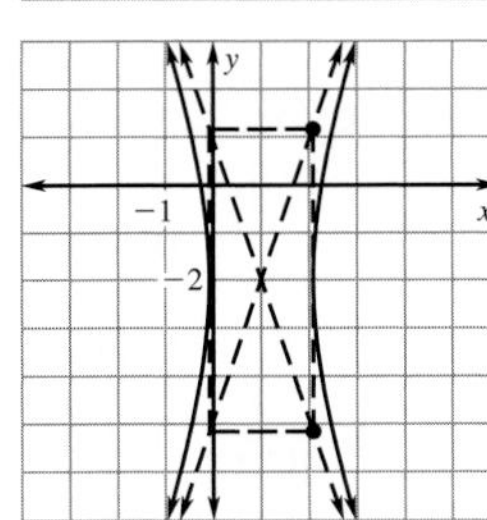

35. (16, 8), (1, 2) **37.** (2, 0)

Cumulative Review (pp. 678–679) **1.** $-\frac{13}{7}$ **3.** 5, 7 **5.** −2, −5, 4 **7.** $\frac{3}{2}$ **9.** 7

11. 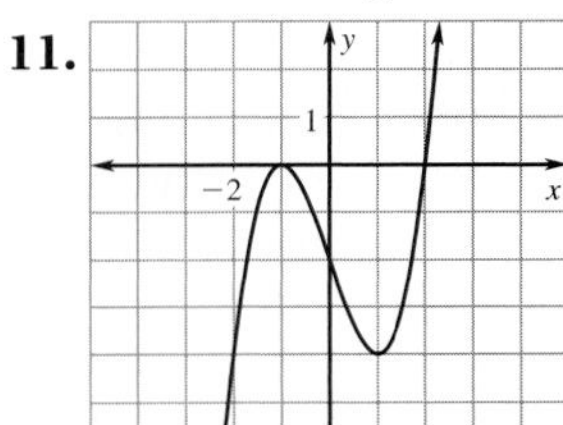

13. 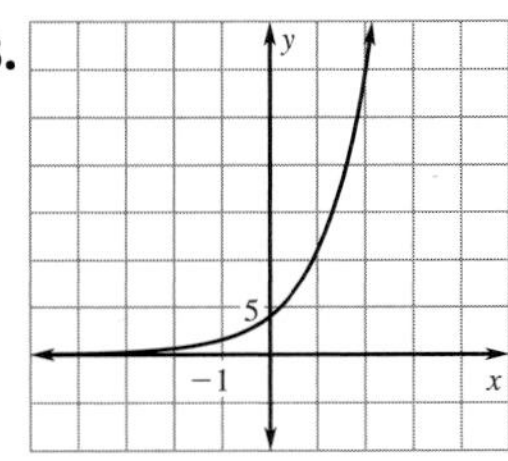

15. 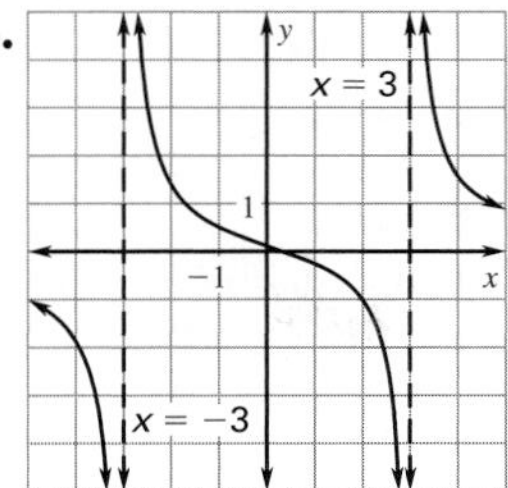

17. $(3x-4)(2x+5)$ **19.** $f^{-1}(x) = \frac{x+1}{6}$ **21.** $f^{-1}(x) = x^{1/5}$ **23.** decay **25.** $\ln \frac{x^3}{5}$ **27.** $\log \frac{x^5 y}{z^3}$ **29.** $y = \frac{-75}{x}$ **31.** $\frac{3}{x+5}$ **33.** $\frac{x^2+2x+41}{x^2+3x-10}$ **35.** $\sqrt{29}; \left(\frac{11}{2}, 6\right)$

37. circle, $(x+6)^2 + (y-2)^2 = 25$;

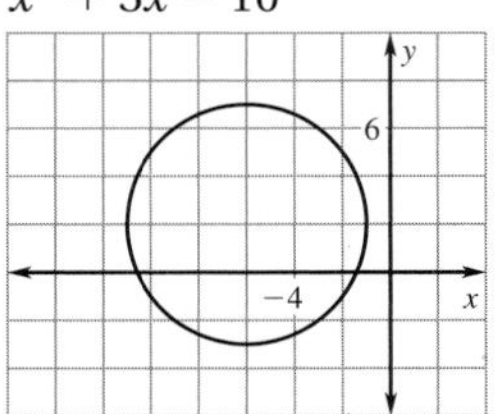

39. parabola, $(y+2)^2 = -6(x+2)$;

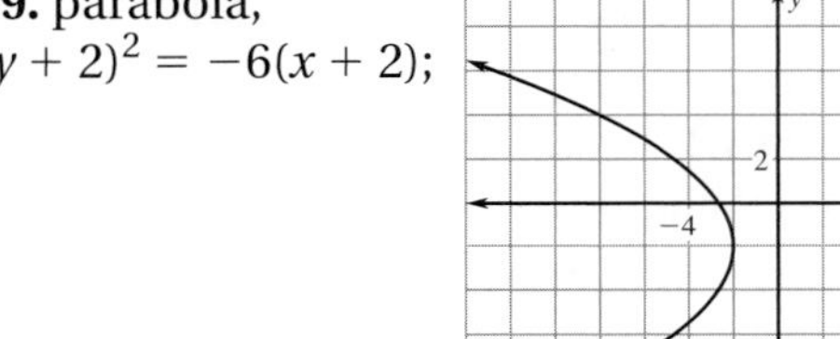

41. 115 ft, 75 ft **43.** 400 adults, 250 students **45.** about 7 mi^2 **47.** $0.85(t-50)$, \$365.50 **49.** $s = 348(1.02)^t$

Chapter 10

10.1 Skill Practice (pp. 686–687) **1.** The number of ways n objects can be ordered.

3.
- M
  - long-sleeve — M long-sleeve
  - short-sleeve — M short-sleeve
- L
  - long-sleeve — L long-sleeve
  - short-sleeve — L short-sleeve
- XL
  - long-sleeve — XL long-sleeve
  - short-sleeve — XL short-sleeve

5. 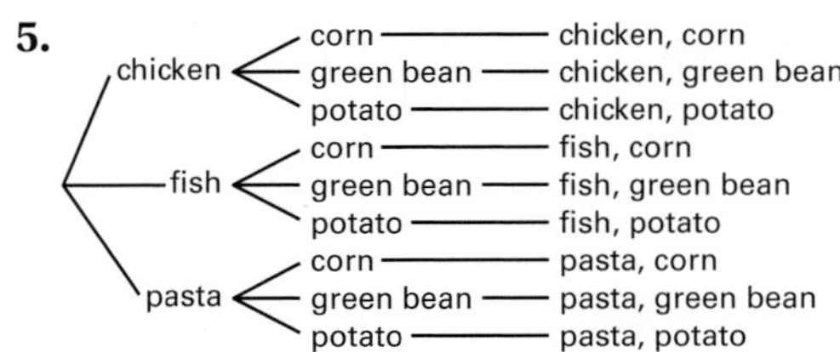

7. 8 ways **9.** 60 ways **11. a.** 456,976,000 license plates **b.** 258,336,000 license plates **13. a.** 45,697,600 license plates **b.** 32,292,000 license plates **15. a.** 118,813,760 license plates **b.** 78,936,000 license plates **19.** 39,916,800 **21.** 40,320 **23.** 1 **25.** 720 **27.** 72 **29.** 630 **31.** 30 **33.** 40,320

SELECTED ANSWERS

35. 72 **37.** 5040 **39.** 3024 **41.** 1 **43.** 3 **45.** 60 **47.** 720 **49.** 3360 **51.** 40,320 **53.** 90,720 **59.** 10

10.1 Problem Solving (pp. 688–689)
63. 225,678,960 sets **65.** 504 ways **67. a.** 240 selections **b.** 252 selections **c.** 60,480 selections **69.** 70,560 displays

10.2 Skill Practice (pp. 694–695) **1.** nth row of Pascal's triangle **3.** 10 **5.** 84 **7.** 1 **9.** 21 **11.** The denominator should have been multiplied by 2!; $\frac{6!}{(6-2)! \cdot 2!} = \frac{720}{48} = 15$. **13.** 792 hands **15.** 778,320 hands **17.** 2,490,624 hands

19.

1 6 15 20 15 6 1
1 7 21 35 35 21 7 1
1 8 28 56 70 56 28 8 1
1 9 36 84 126 126 84 36 9 1
1 10 45 120 210 252 210 120 45 10 1

21. $y^{10} - 30y^9z + 405y^8z^2 - 3240y^7z^3 + 17{,}010y^6z^4 - 61{,}236y^5z^5 + 153{,}090y^4z^6 - 262{,}440y^3z^7 + 295{,}245y^2z^8 - 196{,}830yz^9 + 59{,}049z^{10}$ **23.** $128s^7 - 448s^6t^4 + 672s^5t^8 - 560s^4t^{12} + 280s^3t^{16} - 84s^2t^{20} + 14st^{24} - t^{28}$ **25.** $c^5 - 20c^4 + 160c^3 - 640c^2 + 1280c - 1024$ **27.** $4096p^6 - 6144p^5q + 3840p^4q^2 - 1280p^3q^3 + 240p^2q^4 - 24pq^5 + q^6$ **29.** $32s^{20} + 400s^{16} + 2000s^{12} + 5000s^8 + 6250s^4 + 3125$ **31.** $x^{12} - 4x^9y^2 + 6x^6y^4 - 4x^3y^6 + y^8$ **33.** 1080 **37.** The sum along each diagonal segment is equal to the sum of the two previous diagonal segment sums. **39.** combinations; 13,836,130,056 ways **41.** $1 = {}_nC_n = \frac{n!}{(n-n)! \cdot n!} = \frac{n!}{0! \cdot n!} = \frac{1}{0!}$, so 0! must equal 1.

10.2 Problem Solving (pp. 696–697)
49. 816 combinations **51. a.** 15,504 combinations **b.** 3,003 combinations **c.** 252 combinations; 10 combinations; 3 combinations **d.** 351,982,350,720 ways

10.3 Skill Practice (pp. 701–703) **1.** geometric **3.** $\frac{1}{2}$ **5.** $\frac{7}{50}$ **7.** $\frac{1}{5}$ **9.** $\frac{41}{50}$ **11.** $\frac{1}{52}$ **13.** $\frac{1}{4}$ **15.** $\frac{12}{13}$ **17.** $\frac{1}{12{,}271{,}512}$ **21.** $\frac{3}{11}$ **23.** $\frac{9}{5}$ **25.** The fraction should be outcomes not in the event, 4, to outcomes in the event, 2; $\frac{4}{2} = \frac{2}{1}$. **27.** $\frac{3}{7}$. *Sample answer:* Since the probability is 0.3, there are 3 out of 10 chances of the event occurring. The number of outcomes against event A is $10 - 3 = 7$. So the odds in favor of event A is the ratio of the number of favorable outcomes, 3, to the number of unfavorable outcomes, 7.

29. $\frac{13}{25}$; the experimental probability is slightly greater than the theoretical probability of $\frac{1}{2}$. **31.** $\frac{22}{25}$; the experimental probability is slightly greater than the theoretical probability of $\frac{5}{6}$. **33.** $\frac{11}{20}$

10.3 Problem Solving (pp. 703–704) **35.** $\frac{1}{2}$ **37.** $1 - \frac{\pi}{4}$ or about 0.215 **39.** $\frac{1}{25}$ **41. a.** $\frac{367}{1631}$ **b.** $\frac{110}{233}$ **c.** $\frac{53}{1631}$

10.4 Skill Practice (pp. 710–711) **1.** compound event **3.** 0.4 **5.** 0.65 **7.** $\frac{7}{12}$ **9.** 0.65 **11.** 0.21 **13.** $\frac{5}{7}$ **17.** 1 **19.** $\frac{3}{8}$ **21.** $\frac{4}{13}$ **23.** $\frac{2}{13}$ **25.** $\frac{3}{4}$ **27.** The probability of a club and 9 must be subtracted instead of added; $P(\text{club}) + P(9) - P(\text{club and } 9) = \frac{13}{52} + \frac{4}{52} - \frac{1}{52} = \frac{4}{13}$. **29.** 0.67; not disjoint **31.** $\frac{1}{5}$; not disjoint **33.** 24%; not disjoint **35.** $\frac{5}{36}$ **37.** $\frac{5}{6}$

10.4 Problem Solving (pp. 711–713) **43.** 0.7 **45.** about 0.8488 **47. a.** 58% **b.** 53% **c.** No; what percent of the tomatoes have bite marks. **49.** $\frac{17}{20}$

Extension (p. 716) **1.** {1, 2, 3, 4, 5, 7, 9, 11, 13, 16, 17} **3.** {1, 4, 6, 8, 9, 10, 12, 14, 15, 16, 18, 19, 20} **5.** {1, 2, 3, 4, 5, 7, 8, 9, 11, 13, 14, 16, 17, 20} **7.** {3, 6, 7, 10, 12, 13, 15, 18, 19} **9.** no **11.** yes **13.** April, June, September, October, November, December **15.** January, February, March, April, May, June, July, August **17.** Yes; no; an irrational is a real number but is not an integer.

10.5 Skill Practice (pp. 721–722) **1.** conditional probability **3.** 0.24 **5.** 0.8 **7.** 0.75 **9.** about 0.047 **11.** about 0.059 **13.** about 0.015 **17.** 0.35 **19.** 0.75 **21.** 0.9 **23.** $\frac{1}{7}$ **25.** $\frac{7}{8}$ **27. a.** $\frac{1}{169}$ **b.** $\frac{4}{663}$ **29. a.** $\frac{1}{169}$ **b.** $\frac{4}{663}$ **31. a.** $\frac{1}{64}$ **b.** $\frac{13}{850}$ **33.** The probabilities should be multiplied instead of added; $P(A \text{ and } B) = 0.4 \cdot 0.5 = 0.2$. **35.** Since A and B are independent events, $P(A)$ has no affect on $P(B|A)$ so $P(B|A) = P(B)$.

10.5 Problem Solving (pp. 722–723) **37.** about 81% **39.** 51% **41. a.** 0%; about 2%; about 98% **b.** about 20%, about 30%, about 50% **c.** Yes; go for 2 points after the first touchdown. If the 2 points are scored, go for 1 point after the second touchdown. If the two points are not scored, go for 2 points after the second touchdown; win: about 45%, lose: about 30%.

10.6 Skill Practice (pp. 727–729) **1.** symmetric

3.

x (value)	1	2	3
P(x)	$\frac{1}{2}$	$\frac{3}{10}$	$\frac{1}{5}$

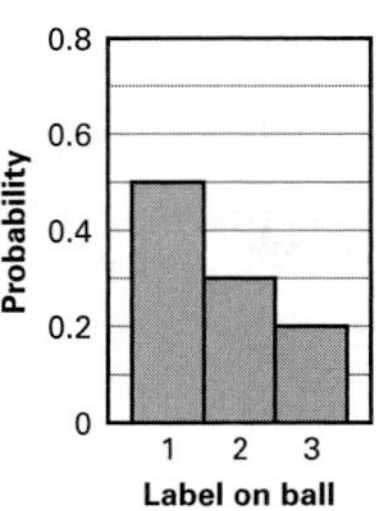

5.

x (value)	1	2	3
P(x)	$\frac{1}{100}$	$\frac{9}{100}$	$\frac{9}{10}$

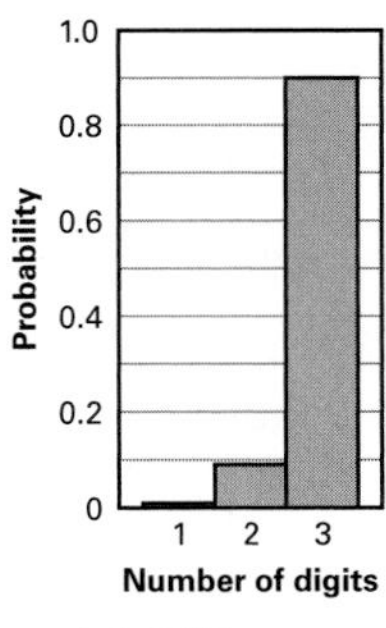

7. 3 **11.** about 0.00018 **13.** about 0.037 **15.** about 0.120 **17.** about 0.00018 **19.** about 0.0086 **21.** about 0.055 **23.** about 0.00000024 **25.** about 0.0000000000000000000087 **27.** The ${}_5C_3$ was left out of the equation; ${}_5C_3\left(\frac{1}{6}\right)^3\left(\frac{5}{6}\right)^{5-3} \approx 0.03$. **29.** about 0.594 **31.** about 0.852

33.

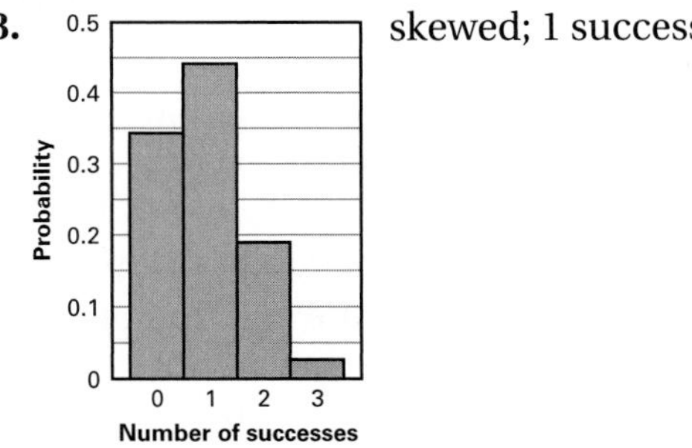

skewed; 1 success

35.

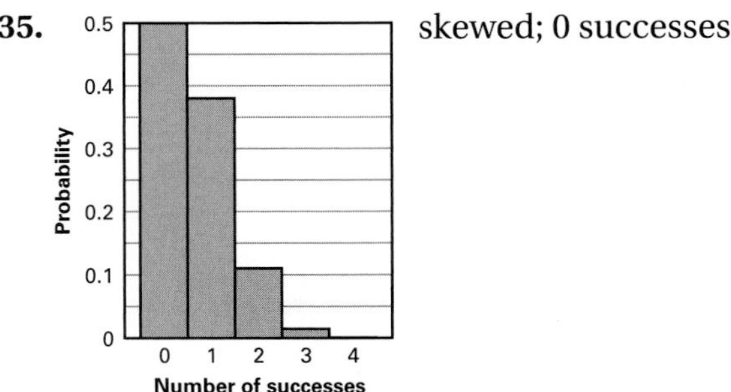

skewed; 0 successes

41. ${}_nC_k$; since order does not matter, find the combination of n things taken k at a time.

10.6 Problem Solving (pp. 729–730) **43.** about 0.196 **45. a.** about 0.143 **b.** about 0.276 **c.** about 0.124 **d.** about 0.999

47. a. $P(0) =$ about 0.099, $P(1) =$ about 0.271, $P(2) =$ about 0.319, $P(3) = 0.208$, $P(4) =$ about 0.081, $P(5) =$ about 0.019, $P(6) =$ about 0.0025, $P(7) =$ about 0.00014

b.

x	P(x)
0	0.099
1	0.271
2	0.319
3	0.208
4	0.081
5	0.019
6	0.0025
7	0.00014

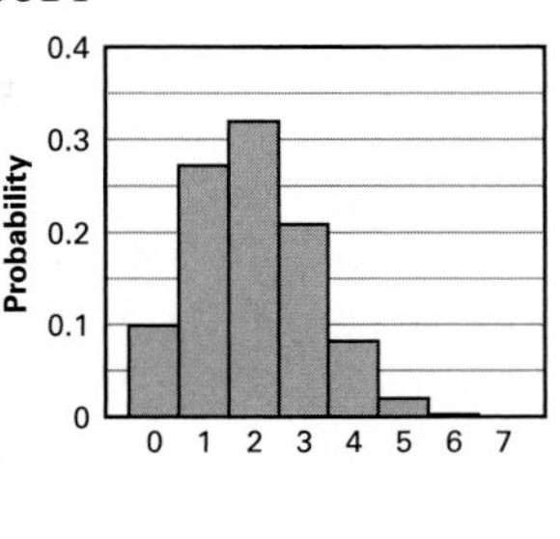

Chapter Review (pp. 734–736) **1.** combination **3.** No; there are more than two outcomes for each card selection. **5.** 479,001,600 ways; 11,880 ways **7.** 120 **9.** 90 **11.** $16a^4 + 32a^3b^2 + 24a^2b^4 + 8ab^6 + b^8$ **13.** $r^{15} - 20r^{12}s + 160r^9s^2 - 640r^6s^3 + 1280r^3s^4 - 1024s^5$ **15.** $\frac{1}{2}$ **17.** $\frac{11}{30}$ **19.** 0.868 **21.** 0.68 **23. a.** $\frac{5}{32}$ **b.** $\frac{1}{6}$ **25. a.** $\frac{1}{4}$ **b.** $\frac{7}{30}$ **27.** about 0.273 **29.** about 0.0039

Chapter 11

11.1 Skill Practice (pp. 747–748) **1.** central tendency; dispersion **3.** about 5.3; 5; 4, 5 and 6 **5.** 74.5, 73.5, 73 and 78 **9.** The numbers need to be written in increasing order prior to choosing the median; 9. **11.** 5, about 1.6 **13.** 4.7, about 1.7 **15.** 23, about 8.1 **17.** 68; about 10.7, 4, 4, 66, about 20.3; 3.5, 3.5, 4, 4, about 1.2 **19.** 0.7; 10, 11.6, 11.6, 12.1, about 4.2; about 11.9, 11.6, 11.6, 1.9, about 0.67 **21.** 152; 78.8, 71.5, 66, 92, about 25.1; about 70.7, 71, 66, 20, about 6.0 **23.** *Sample answer:* 8, 8, 8, 8, 11, 11, 12, 12, 12

11.1 Problem Solving (pp. 748–749) **27.** about 17.8, 20, 6 and 20 **29. a.** 5 **b.** 20.2, 22, 23, 20, about 5.4; about 21.9, 23, 23, 6, about 2.1 **c.** *Sample answer:* The mean and the median increase when the outlier is removed and the range and standard deviation decrease.

11.2 Skill Practice (p. 753) **1.** transformation **3.** 18, 17, 17, 9, about 3.0; 24, 23, 23, 9, about 3.0 **5.** 78, 77, 77, 9, about 2.8; 95, 94, 94, 9, about 2.8 **7.** 56, 53, 53, 21, about 7.0; 35, 32, 32, 21, about 7.0 **9.** The standard deviation does not change when adding a constant; 10. **11.** about 61.9, 62, 58, 9, about 3.36; about 248, 248, 232, 36, about 13.4 **13.** about 98.2, 100.5, 102, 19, about 6.62; about 245.5, about 251.3, 255, 47.5, about 16.6

15. about 229, 226.5, 222, 38, about 12.0; about 206.1, about 203.9, 199.8, 34.2, about 10.8

11.2 Problem Solving (pp. 753–755) **19. a.** about 70.8, 72, 72, 8, about 2.4 **b.** about 98.8, 100, 100, 8, about 2.4 **21. a.** about 6.84, 6.89, no mode, 1.16, about 0.324 **b.** about 22.4, about 22.6, no mode, about 3.80, about 1.06 **23. a.** 75.8, about 75.4, 74.5, 9.9, about 3.0 **b.** about 23.6, about 27.7, 22.5, 23.0, about 25.8, about 22.6, about 24.9, about 23.6, about 25.3, about 22.2, about 26.2, about 24.6 **c.** about 24.3, 24.1, 23.6, 5.5, about 1.6 **d.** The effect is a multiplication transformation with a factor of $\frac{5}{9}$, along with an addition transformation of about -17.8 for the mean, median, and mode.

11.3 Skill Practice (pp. 760–761) **1.** normal curve **3.** 0.16 **5.** 0.84 **7.** 0.68 **9.** 16% **11.** 0.68 **13.** 0.9735 **15.** 0.84 **19.** 0.7257 **21.** 0.0035 **23.** 0.5 **25.** 0.0548 **27.** 0.5363 **29.** The table was interpreted incorrectly; $P(z \geq -0.8) = 1 - 0.2119 = 0.7881$.

11.3 Problem Solving (pp. 761–762) **31.** 0.16 **33. a.** -2.4, 1.6 **b.** 0.0082 **c.** 0.937; $P(z \leq 1.6) - P(z \leq -2.4)$ **35. a.** 2.4 **b.** 1.2 **c.** Lisa; in a standard normal distribution Lisa's score is higher.

Extension (p. 765) **1.** 9.6, 2.4 **3.** 13.8, about 3.1 **5.** 25.2, about 2.7 **7.** 8.8, about 2.8 **9.** 105, about 5.1 **11.** about 0.93 **13.** about 0.0013 **15.** about 0.98 **17.** about 0.9987 **19.** Yes; $P(x \leq 56) \approx 0.01$, which is less than 0.05. **21.** Yes; $P(x \geq 12) \approx 1 - P(z \leq 2.5) \approx 1 - 0.9938 = 0.0062$, which is less than 0.05.

11.4 Skill Practice (pp. 769–770) **1.** random **3.** Systematic; unbiased; the sample is representative of the customers. **5.** Random; unbiased; each student has an equal change of being selected. **7.** $\pm3.2\%$ **9.** $\pm1.3\%$ **11.** $\pm4.4\%$ **13.** $\pm1.0\%$ **15.** 1111 people **17.** 100 people **19.** 319 people **21.** 237 people **25.** about 453 people

11.4 Problem Solving (pp. 770–771) **27. a.** about $\pm4.8\%$ **b.** between 9.2% and 18.8% **29.** No. *Sample answer:* Since the margin of error is $\pm5\%$, Kosta could have 49% of the votes and Murdock could have 51% of the votes. **31. a.** 47%, 53% **b.** about $\pm4.5\%$ **c.** between 42.5% and 51.5%, between 48.5% and 57.5% **d.** no; 273 people

Extension (p. 773) **1.** *Sample answer:* This is a leading question. Respondents may think a "no" response means they are not supporters of city growth. **3.** *Sample answer:* Many patients may answer untruthfully because their dentist is asking the question. The information should be collected anonymously. **5.** *Sample answer:* The question assumes that the respondent is familiar with the facts of the case. Any presentation of the facts (as interpreted by the pollster) may be biased as well. It might be best then to ask the question as given only to those who reply affirmatively to the question, "Are you familiar with the facts of the Carter case?" **7.** *Sample answer:* The flaw is that Algebra 2 students are the experimental group and Algebra 1 students are the control group; the experimental and control groups should both be Algebra 2 students.

11.5 Skill Practice (p. 778) **1.** exponential **3.** $f(x) = -0.381x^2 + 1.12x + 15.7$;

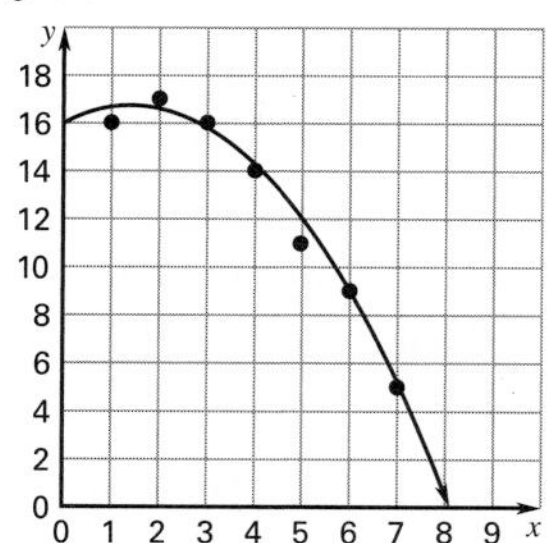

7. The x and the value of b have been interchanged; $y = 9.71(1.55)^x$.

11.5 Problem Solving (p. 779) **11.** *Sample answer:* $y = 0.00211x^3 - 0.0766x^2 + 1.26x - 0.0664$ **13. a.** quadratic **b.** $y = -2.97x^2 + 40.4x - 85.9$

c.

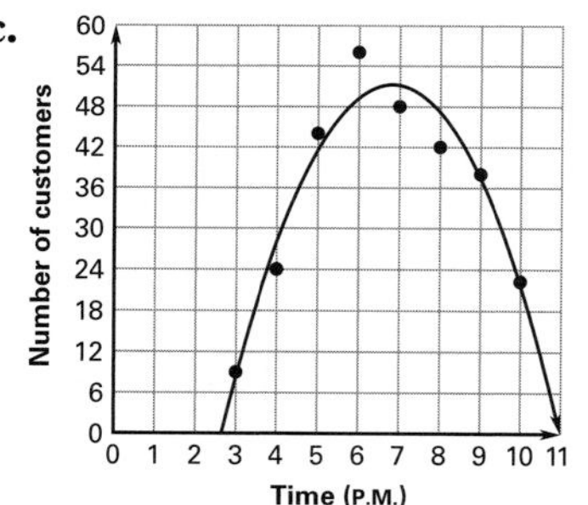

d. No; at 1:00 P.M., the function predicts a negative number of customers.

11.5 Problem Solving Workshop (p. 781) **1.** about 74°F; $y = 61.3(0.962)^x + 74$

Chapter Review (pp. 784–786) **1.** Standard deviation **3.** z-score **5.** about 84.1, 86.5, 88, 17, about 6.2 **7.** about 130, 130, 140, 52, about 16.1 **9.** about 39.8, 38, 37, 14, about 4.6; about 32.8, 31, 30, 14, about 4.6 **11.** about 38.0, about 35.4, 59.8, 62.6, about 20.8; about 1.50, about 1.39, about 2.35, about 2.46, about 0.8 **13.** about 0.0548 **15.** about 0 **17.** about 0.0179 **19.** $\pm2\%$ **21.** $\pm1.4\%$

23. $y = -3.79x + 28.3$;

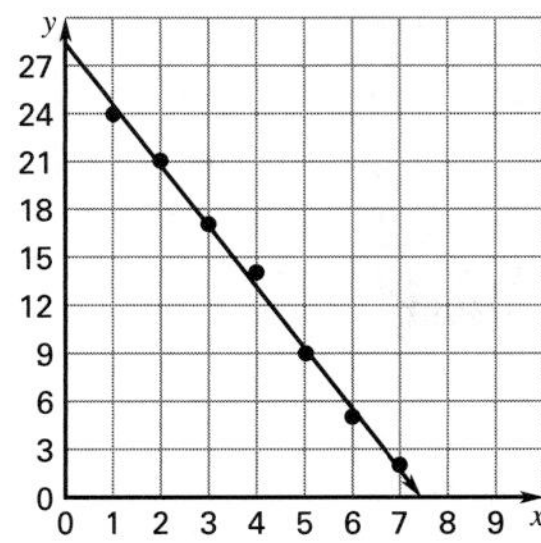

Chapter 12

12.1 Skill Practice (pp. 798–799) **1.** sigma notation **3.** 3, 4, 5, 6, 7, 8 **5.** 1, 4, 9, 16, 25, 36 **7.** 1, 4, 16, 64, 256, 1024 **9.** −4, −1, 4, 11, 20, 31 **11.** $-4, -2, -\frac{4}{3}, -1, -\frac{4}{5}, -\frac{2}{3}$ **13.** $\frac{2}{3}, 1, \frac{6}{5}, \frac{4}{3}, \frac{10}{7}, \frac{3}{2}$ **15.** You can write the terms as $(5 \cdot 1 - 4), (5 \cdot 2 - 4), (5 \cdot 3 - 4), (5 \cdot 4 - 4)$, $a_5 = 21$, $a_n = 5n - 4$. **17.** You can write the terms as $(-1)^1(4 \cdot 1), (-1)^2(4 \cdot 2), (-1)^3(4 \cdot 3), (-1)^4(4 \cdot 4)$, $a_5 = -20$, $a_n = (-1)^n(4 \cdot n)$. **19.** You can write the terms as $\frac{2}{3(1)}, \frac{2}{3(2)}, \frac{2}{3(3)}, \frac{2}{3(4)}, a_5 = \frac{2}{15}, a_n = \frac{2}{3n}$. **21.** You can write the terms as $\frac{1}{4}, \frac{2}{4}, \frac{3}{4}, \frac{4}{4}, \frac{5}{4}, a_6 = \frac{6}{4}, a_n = \frac{n}{4}$. **23.** You can write the terms as $0.7(1) + 2.4, 0.7(2) + 2.4, 0.7(3) + 2.4, 0.7(4) + 2.4$, $a_5 = 5.9$, $a_n = 0.7n + 2.4$. **25.** You can write the terms as $1^2 + 0.2, 2^2 + 0.2, 3^2 + 0.2, 4^2 + 0.2$, $a_5 = 25.2$, $a_n = n^2 + 0.2$.

29.

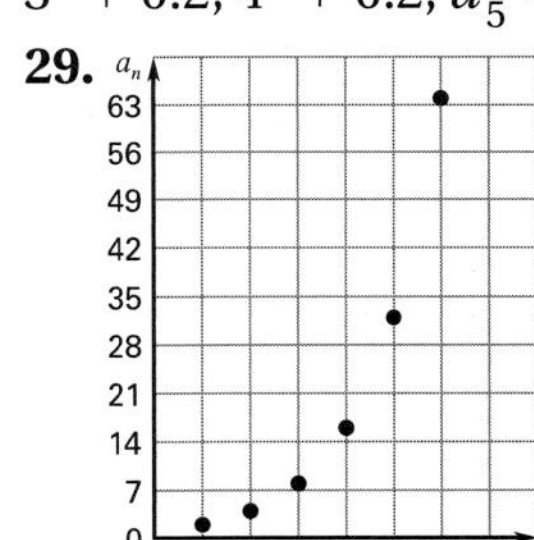

31.

37. $\sum_{i=1}^{5} (3i + 4)$ **39.** $\sum_{i=1}^{\infty} (2i - 3)$ **41.** $\sum_{i=1}^{\infty} (7i - 4)$ **43.** $\sum_{i=1}^{7} \frac{i}{3 + i}$ **45.** 42 **47.** 100 **49.** 82 **51.** $\frac{761}{140}$ **53.** 35 **55.** 325 **57.** The lower limit is zero, so the first term should be 3; 3 + 5 + 7 + 9 + 11 + 13 = 48.

12.1 Problem Solving (pp. 799–800) **63.** 60°, 90°, 108°, 120°, about 128.57°; $T_n = 180(n - 2)$; 1800° **65.** $a_n = 2^n - 1$; 63 moves, 127 moves, 255 moves **67. a.** 15 balls **b.** 35 balls **c.** Except for layer 1, there are always more balls in the same layer of the square pyramid. The difference in the number of balls is $\frac{n(n-1)}{2}$.

12.2 Skill Practice (pp. 806–807) **1.** common difference **3.** Arithmetic; there is a common difference of 3 between consecutive terms. **5.** Arithmetic; there is a common difference of 9 between consecutive terms. **7.** Arithmetic; there is a common difference of 0.5 between consecutive terms. **9.** Not arithmetic; there is not a common difference between consecutive terms. **11.** Arithmetic; there is a common difference of 1.5 between consecutive terms. **13.** $a_n = -1 + 6n$; 119 **15.** $a_n = -5 + 2n$; 35 **17.** $a_n = 36 - 11n$; −184 **19.** $a_n = \frac{7}{3} - \frac{1}{3}n$; $-\frac{13}{3}$ **21.** The equation for an arithmetic sequence is not correct; $a_n = a_1 + (n - 1)d$, $a_n = 37 + (n - 1)(-13)$, $a_n = 50 - 13n$.

23. $a_n = -28 + 5n$;

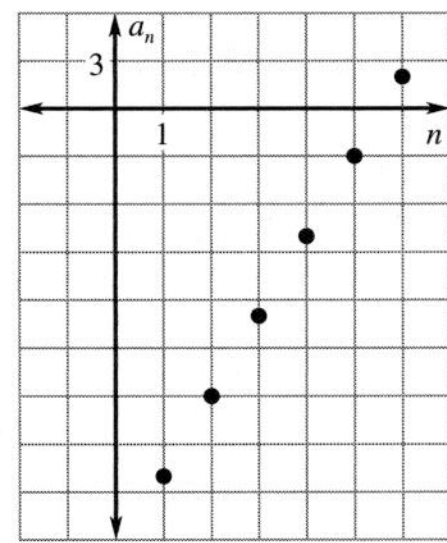

25. $a_n = 152 - 14n$;

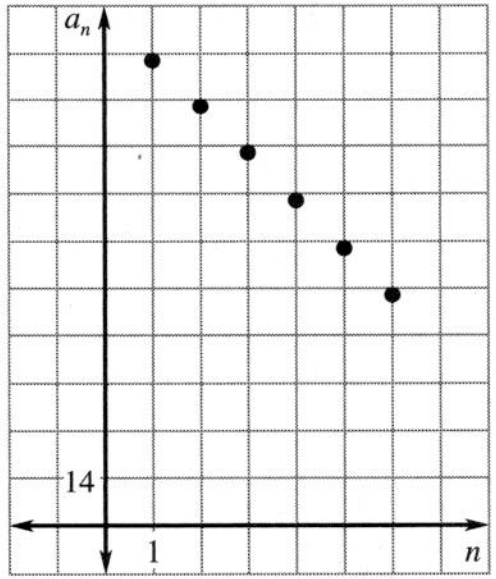

31. $a_n = 9 + 5n$ **33.** $a_n = 22 - 4n$ **35.** $a_n = 13 + 2n$ **37.** $a_n = \frac{15}{4} + \frac{9}{4}n$ **41.** −96 **43.** 2585 **45.** 315 **47.** 132 **49.** $a_n = -3 + 5n$ **51.** $a_n = -1 - 2n$ **53.** False. *Sample answer:* Doubling the common difference alone does not double the sum. **55.** 12 **57.** 25 **59.** 15 **61.** 22,500

12.2 Problem Solving (pp. 808–809) **63. a.** $a_n = 6n$ **b.** 271 cells **65. a.** $a_n = -4 + 8n$ **b.** 576 blocks **67.** $100

12.3 Skill Practice (pp. 814–815) **1.** common ratio **3.** Not geometric; there is no common ratio. **5.** Geometric; there is a common ratio of $\frac{1}{6}$. **7.** Not geometric; there is no common ratio. **9.** Geometric; there is a common ratio of $\frac{1}{2}$. **11.** Geometric; there is a common ratio of −3. **13.** Not geometric; there is no common ratio. **15.** $a_n = (-4)^{n-1}$; 4096

SELECTED ANSWERS

17. $a_n = 4(6)^{n-1}$; 186,624 **19.** $a_n = 2\left(\frac{3}{4}\right)^{n-1}$; $\frac{729}{2048}$
21. $a_n = 4\left(\frac{1}{2}\right)^{n-1}$; $\frac{1}{16}$ **23.** $a_n = -2(0.4)^{n-1}$; -0.008192
25. $a_n = 5(-2.8)^{n-1}$; 2409.45152
29. $a_n = -2(6)^{n-1}$;

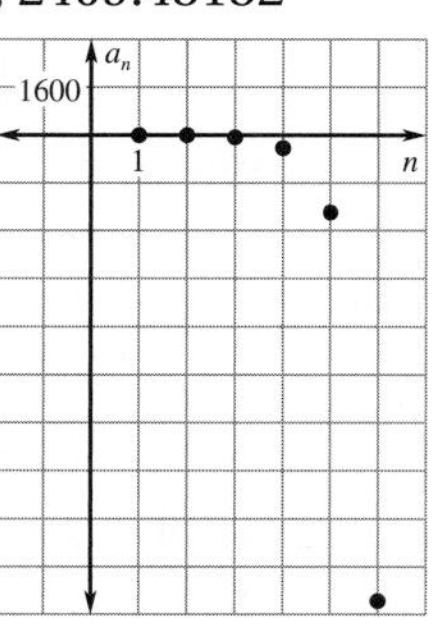

31. $a_n = 30\left(\frac{1}{2}\right)^{n-1}$;

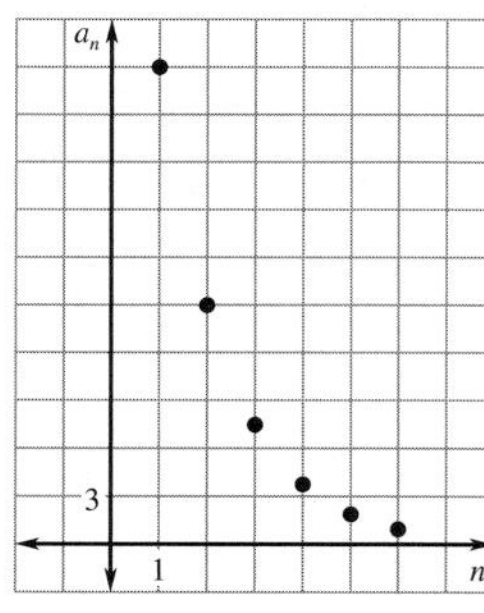

37. The exponent should be $n - 1$ instead of n; $a_n = 3(2)^{n-1}$. **39.** $a_n = 3(2)^{n-1}$ or $a_n = 3(-2)^{n-1}$
41. $a_n = \left(-\frac{1}{4}\right)(4)^{n-1}$ **43.** $a_n = -80\left(\frac{1}{2}\right)^{n-1}$ or $a_n = -80\left(-\frac{1}{2}\right)^{n-1}$ **45.** $a_n = 6(3)^{n-1}$ **47.** $a_n = \frac{32}{27}\left(\frac{3\sqrt[3]{12}}{4}\right)^{n-1}$
49. 131,070 **51.** $\frac{1365}{256}$ **53.** 838,861 **55.** *Sample answer:* $\frac{100}{31}, \frac{200}{31}, \frac{400}{31}, \frac{800}{31}, \frac{1600}{31}$

12.3 Problem Solving (pp. 815–817) **57. a.** $a_n = 5(2)^{n-1}$ **b.** 75 skydivers **59. a.** $a_n = 1024\left(\frac{1}{2}\right)^{n-1}$ **b.** 11. *Sample answer:* On the 11th pass, there is only 1 term to choose from so it must be the answer **61. a.** $a_n = 19{,}000 + 1000n$, arithmetic; $b_n = 20{,}000(1.04)^{n-1}$, geometric

b.

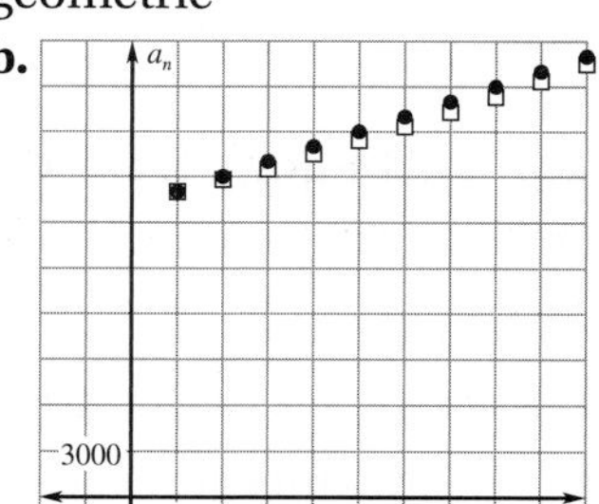

c. Company A: \$590,000; Company B: about \$595,562 **d.** 19 yr

12.4 Skill Practice (pp. 823–824) **1.** partial sum **3.** $S_1 = 0.5$, $S_2 \approx 0.67$, $S_3 \approx 0.72$, $S_4 \approx 0.74$, $S_5 \approx 0.75$; S_n appears to be approaching 0.75.

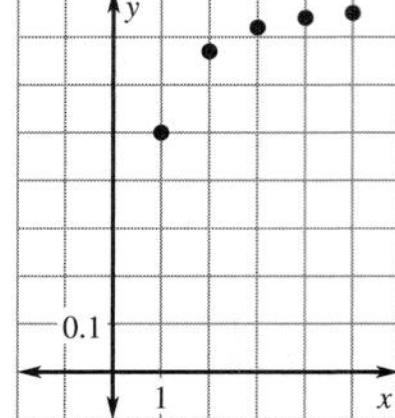

5. $S_1 = 4$, $S_2 = 6.4$, $S_3 = 7.84$, $S_4 \approx 8.71$, $S_5 \approx 9.22$; S_n appears to be approaching 10.

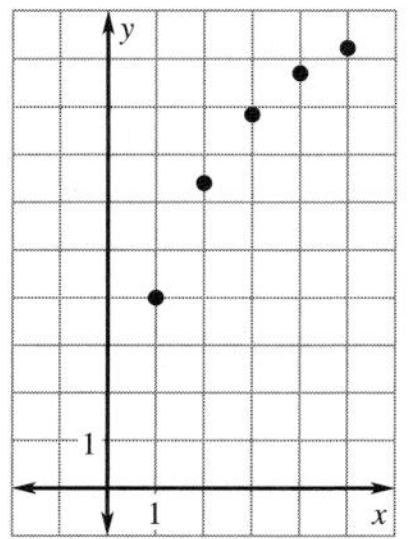

7. 10 **9.** no sum **11.** $\frac{12}{5}$ **13.** $\frac{63}{17}$ **15.** no sum **17.** $\frac{7}{10}$
19. Since $r > 1$, the infinite geometric series has no sum. **21.** $\frac{1}{2}$ **23.** 18 **25.** $\frac{4}{9}$ **27.** $\frac{625}{999}$ **29.** $\frac{130{,}000}{999}$ **31.** $\frac{5}{18}$
33. $\frac{0.9}{1 - 0.1} = \frac{0.9}{0.9} = 1$

12.4 Problem Solving (pp. 824–825) **37.** 70 ft **41. a.** 12 ft; 9 ft **b.** $\sum_{i=1}^{\infty} 12(0.75)^{i-1}$ **c.** 56 ft **d.** $\frac{2(0.75h)}{1 - 0.75} + h = 7h$

12.5 Skill Practice (pp. 830–831) **1.** iteration **3.** 1, 4, 7, 10, 13 **5.** −1, −6, −11, −16, −21 **7.** 2; 5; 26; 677; 458,330 **9.** 2, 8, 10, 18, 22 **11.** 2, 3, 6, 18, 108
13. $a_1 = 21$, $a_n = a_{n-1} - 7$ **15.** $a_1 = 4$, $a_n = -3a_{n-1}$
17. $a_1 = 44$, $a_n = \frac{1}{4}a_{n-1}$ **19.** $a_1 = 54$, $a_n = a_{n-1} - 11$
21. $a_1 = 16$, $a_2 = 9$, $a_n = a_{n-2} - a_{n-1}$ **23.** The rule does not work for all of the terms of the sequence; $a_1 = 5$, $a_2 = 2$, $a_n = a_{n-2} - a_{n-1}$. **25.** −4, −14, −64 **27.** −2, −4, −5 **29.** 5, 21, 437 **31.** 2, 4, 14 **35.** $a_1 = 1$, $a_2 = 2$, $a_n = 4(a_{n-2} + a_{n-1})$ **37.** $a_1 = 2$, $a_2 = 5$, $a_n = 3a_{n-2} + a_{n-1}$ **39.** $a_1 = -3$, $a_2 = -2$, $a_n = -1(a_{n-2} + a_{n-1})$ **41.** *Sample answer:* If the first two iterates are 2, the given rule must not be a function.

12.5 Problem Solving (pp. 832–833) **43. a.** $a_1 = 5000$, $a_n = 0.8a_{n-1} + 500$; 3524 fish **b.** The population of the lake approaches 2500 fish.

45. $a_1 = 2000$, $a_n = 1.014a_{n-1} - 100$; 24 mo. *Sample answer:* As long Gladys does not add anything to her credit card and continues her payments, her 24th payment will only be \$62.14.

47. a. $a_1 = 20$, $a_n = 0.7\,a_{n-1} + 20$ **b.** $66\frac{2}{3}$ mg **c.** The maintenance level of the drug doubles as well; $a_1 = 20$, $a_n = 0.7\,(2a_{n-1}) + 2(20)$.

12.5 Problem Solving Workshop (p. 835)
1. The sequence approaches 400. **3.** The number of members approaches 15,000. **5.** *Sample answer:* 2% of the books are lost of discarded so 98% are retained; $a_n = 0.98a_{n-1} + 1150$.

Extension (p. 837)
1. Basis Step:
Check that the formula works for $n = 1$.
$2(1) - 1 = 1^2 \to 1 = 1$ ✓
Inductive Step:
Assume that $1 + 3 + 5 + \ldots + (2k - 1) = k^2$.
Show that $1 + 3 + 5 + \ldots + (2k - 1) + (2(k + 1) - 1) = (k + 1)^2$.
$1 + 3 + 5 + \ldots + (2k - 1) + (2(k + 1) - 1)$
$= k^2 + (2(k + 1) - 1)$
$= k^2 + 2k + 2 - 1$
$= k^2 + 2k + 1$
$= (k + 1)^2$ ✓
3. Basis Step:
Check that the formula works for $n = 1$.
$2^{1-1} = 2^1 - 1 \to 2^0 = 2 - 1 \to 1 = 1$ ✓
Inductive Step:
Assume that $1 + 2 + 2^2 + 2^3 + \ldots + 2^{k-1} = 2^k - 1$.
Show that $1 + 2 + 2^2 + 2^3 + \ldots + 2^{k-1} + 2^{(k-1)-1} = 2^{k+1} - 1$.
$1 + 2 + 2^2 + 2^3 + \ldots + 2^{k-1} + 2^{(k-1)-1}$
$= (2^k - 1) + 2^{(k+1)-1}$
$= 2^k - 1 + 2^k$
$= 2(2^k) - 1$
$= 2^{k+1} - 1$ ✓

Chapter Review (pp. 840–842) **1.** terms **3.** explicit **5.** 133 **7.** 153 **9.** $a_n = 11 - 3n$ **11.** $a_n = 3 + 6n$ **13.** -403 **15.** 1200 **17.** $a_n = 256\left(\frac{1}{4}\right)^{n-1}$ **19.** $a_n = 144\left(\frac{1}{3}\right)^{n-1}$ or $a_n = 144\left(-\frac{1}{3}\right)^{n-1}$ **21.** 4088 **23.** $\frac{635}{8}$ **25.** 4 **27.** -0.4 **29.** $\frac{182}{333}$ **31.** $\frac{388}{495}$ **33.** 8, 40, 200, 1000, 5000 **35.** $a_1 = 6$, $a_n = 3a_{n-1}$ **37.** $a_1 = 7$, $a_n = a_{n-1} + 6$

Cumulative Review (pp. 848–849)

1.
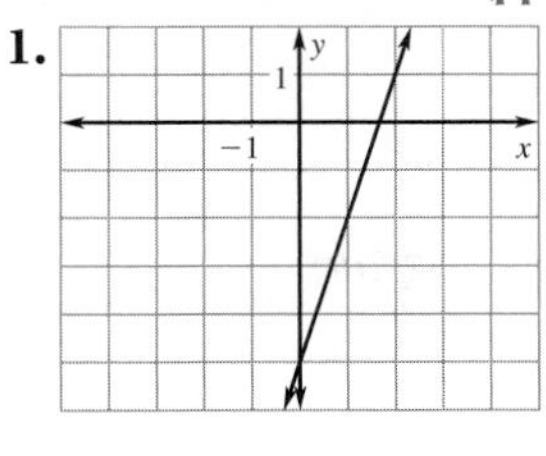

3.
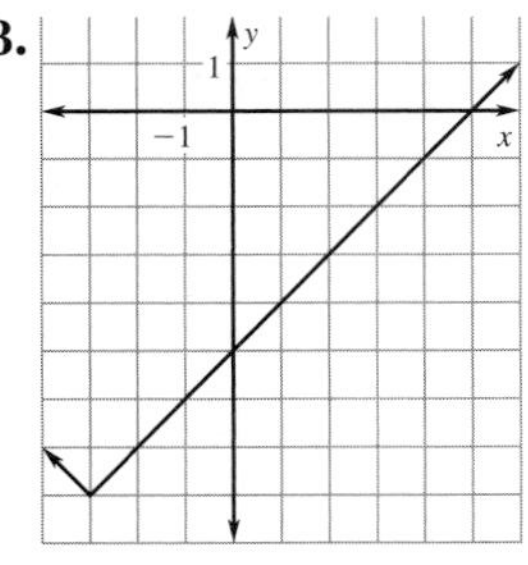

5.
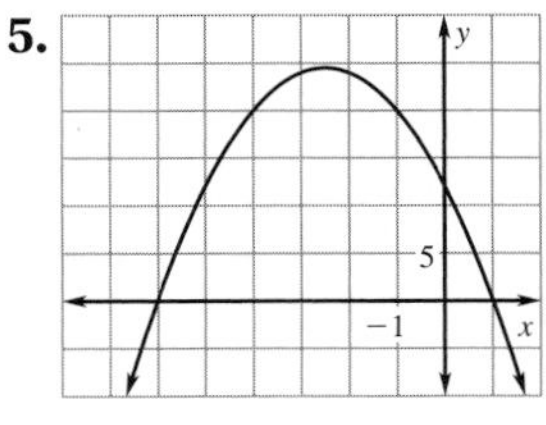

7.
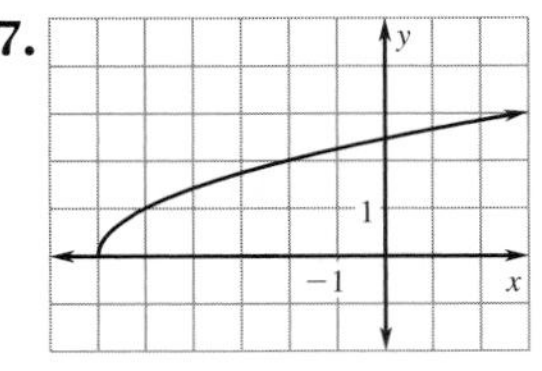

9.
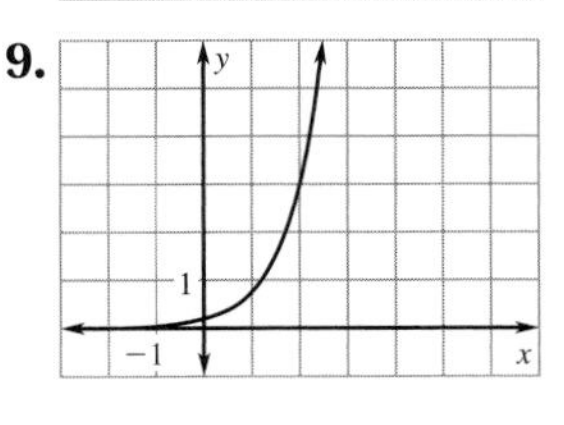

11.
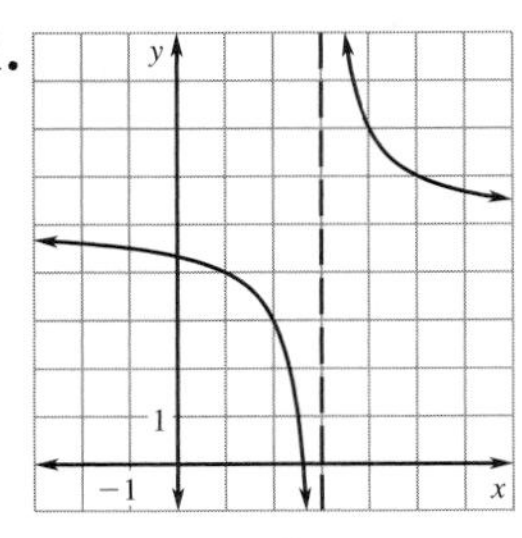

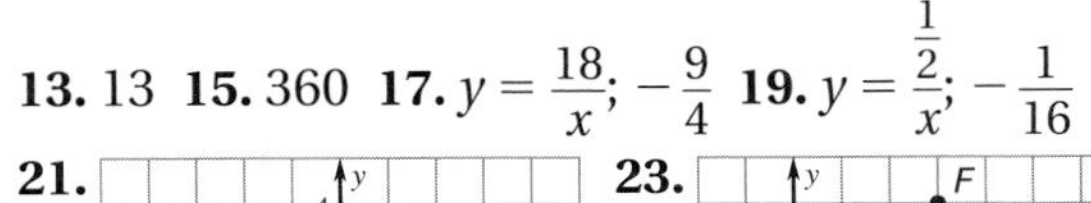
13. 13 **15.** 360 **17.** $y = \frac{18}{x}$; $-\frac{9}{4}$ **19.** $y = \frac{\frac{1}{2}}{x}$; $-\frac{1}{16}$

21.
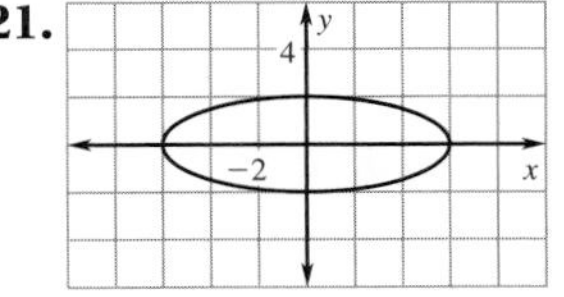

23.
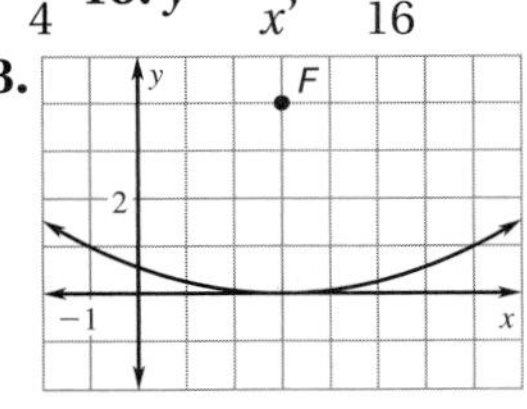

25. 524,160 **27.** 1 **29.** 0.15 **31.** about 12.857, 11, 11, 11, about 3.603 **33.** about 215.571, 216, 216, 25, about 8.086 **35.** about 88.857, 92, no mode, 28, about 8.967 **37.** 273 **39.** about 2.977 **41.** $a_n = -11 + 4n$, $a_1 = -7$, $a_n = a_{n-1} + 4$ **43.** $a_n = 3(4)^{n-1}$, $a_1 = 3$, $a_n = 4a_{n-1}$ **45.** 5 in. **47.** in 5 yr **49.** about 0.727 **51.** $a_n = 29{,}400 + 1600n$; \$43,800

Chapter 13

13.1 Skill Practice (pp. 856–857) **1.** The angle formed by the line of sight to an object and a line parallel to the ground. **3.** $\sin\theta = \frac{12}{13}$, $\cos\theta = \frac{5}{13}$, $\tan\theta = \frac{12}{5}$, $\csc\theta = \frac{13}{12}$, $\sec\theta = \frac{13}{5}$, $\cot\theta = \frac{5}{12}$ **5.** $\sin\theta = \frac{8}{11}$, $\cos\theta = \frac{\sqrt{57}}{11}$, $\tan\theta = \frac{8\sqrt{57}}{57}$, $\csc\theta = \frac{11}{8}$, $\sec\theta = \frac{11\sqrt{57}}{57}$, $\cot\theta = \frac{\sqrt{57}}{8}$

SELECTED ANSWERS

7. $\sin\theta = \frac{\sqrt{115}}{14}$, $\cos\theta = \frac{9}{14}$, $\tan\theta = \frac{\sqrt{115}}{9}$, $\csc\theta = \frac{14\sqrt{115}}{115}$, $\sec\theta = \frac{14}{9}$, $\cot\theta = \frac{9\sqrt{115}}{115}$ **9.** $\cos\theta = \frac{\sqrt{11}}{6}$, $\tan\theta = \frac{5\sqrt{11}}{11}$, $\csc\theta = \frac{6}{5}$, $\sec\theta = \frac{6\sqrt{11}}{11}$, $\cot\theta = \frac{\sqrt{11}}{5}$ **11.** $\sin\theta = \frac{7\sqrt{58}}{58}$, $\cos\theta = \frac{3\sqrt{58}}{58}$, $\csc\theta = \frac{\sqrt{58}}{7}$, $\sec\theta = \frac{\sqrt{58}}{3}$, $\cot\theta = \frac{3}{7}$ **13.** $\sin\theta = \frac{\sqrt{119}}{12}$, $\cos\theta = \frac{5}{12}$, $\tan\theta = \frac{\sqrt{119}}{5}$, $\csc\theta = \frac{12\sqrt{119}}{119}$, $\cot\theta = \frac{5\sqrt{119}}{119}$ **17.** $x = 8\sqrt{3}, y = 16$ **19.** $x = 4\sqrt{3}$, $y = 8\sqrt{3}$ **21.** $B = 55°, a \approx 9.18, b \approx 13.11$ **23.** $A = 72°$, $a \approx 22.83, b \approx 7.42$ **25.** $A = 15°, b \approx 55.98, c \approx 57.96$ **27.** $B = 26°, a \approx 65.61, c \approx 73.0$

13.1 Problem Solving (pp. 857–858) **31.** about 63.4 cm **33.** About 652 ft. *Sample answer:* The larger the angle the deeper the final depth. **35. a.** about 22,818 mi **b.** about 7263 mi

13.2 Skill Practice (pp. 862–863)
1. origin, initial side **3.** B **5.** A
7. **9.**

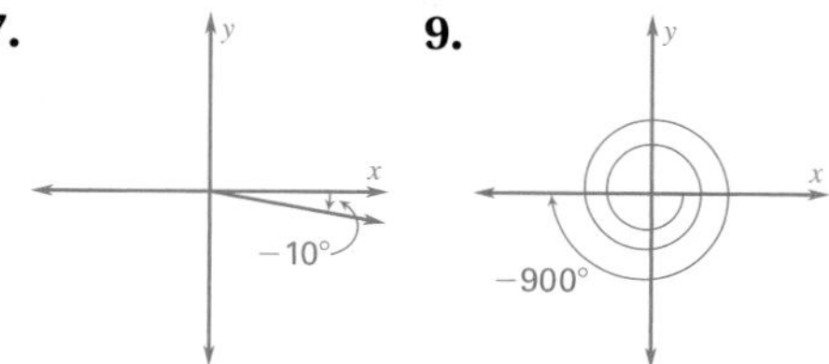

15–21. Sample answers are given. **15.** 430°, −290° **17.** 235°, −485° **19.** $\frac{\pi}{2}$, $-\frac{3\pi}{2}$ **21.** $\frac{10\pi}{9}$, $-\frac{8\pi}{9}$ **23.** $\frac{2\pi}{9}$ **25.** $-\frac{13\pi}{9}$ **27.** 20° **29.** 900° **33.** about 3.93 m, about 5.89 m^2 **35.** about 31.4 ft, about 188 ft^2 **37.** about 118 in., about 1470 $in.^2$ **39.** $\frac{1}{2}$ **41.** $\frac{\sqrt{3}}{3}$ **43.** about 2.41 **45.** about 0.975

13.2 Problem Solving (pp. 864–865) **49.** 72,000°, 400π **51. a.** $\frac{\pi}{2}$ **b.** about 45.6 ft **53. a.** about 16.5 in. **b.** 360°. *Sample answer:* Since each step has a central angle of $\frac{\pi}{8}$ and there are 16 steps, the staircase will cover $16\left(\frac{\pi}{8}\right)$ or 2π, which is equivalent to 360°. **c.** about 5195.4 $in.^2$

13.3 Skill Practice (pp. 870–871) **1.** quadrantal angle **3.** $\sin\theta = \frac{15}{17}$, $\cos\theta = \frac{8}{17}$, $\tan\theta = \frac{15}{8}$, $\csc\theta = \frac{17}{15}$, $\sec\theta = \frac{17}{8}$, $\cot\theta = \frac{8}{15}$ **5.** $\sin\theta = -\frac{24}{25}$, $\cos\theta = -\frac{7}{25}$, $\tan\theta = \frac{24}{7}$, $\csc\theta = -\frac{25}{24}$, $\sec\theta = -\frac{25}{7}$, $\cot\theta = \frac{7}{24}$

7. $\sin\theta = -\frac{\sqrt{2}}{2}$, $\cos\theta = \frac{\sqrt{2}}{2}$, $\tan\theta = -1$, $\csc\theta = -\sqrt{2}$, $\sec\theta = \sqrt{2}$, $\cot\theta = -1$ **9.** $\sin\theta = -\frac{5\sqrt{34}}{34}$, $\cos\theta = -\frac{3\sqrt{34}}{34}$, $\tan\theta = \frac{5}{3}$, $\csc\theta = -\frac{\sqrt{34}}{5}$, $\sec\theta = -\frac{\sqrt{34}}{3}$, $\cot\theta = \frac{3}{5}$ **13.** $\sin\theta = 1$, $\cos\theta = 0$, $\tan\theta =$ undefined, $\csc\theta = 1$, $\sec\theta =$ undefined, $\cot\theta = 0$ **15.** $\sin\theta = -1$, $\cos\theta = 0$, $\tan\theta =$ undefined, $\csc\theta = -1$, $\sec\theta =$ undefined, $\cot\theta = 0$
17. 30° **19.** 10°

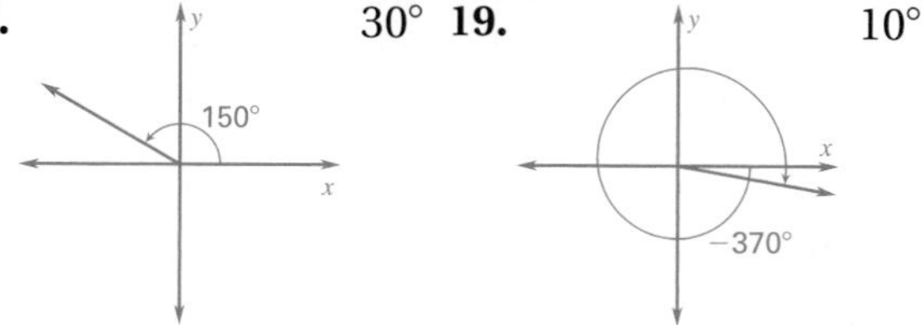

25. $\sqrt{3}$ **27.** $-\frac{2\sqrt{3}}{3}$ **29.** $\frac{\sqrt{3}}{3}$ **31.** $\frac{2\sqrt{3}}{3}$ **33.** $\tan\theta = \frac{\sin\theta}{\cos\theta}$; $\sin 90° = 1$ and $\cos 90° = 0$ so $\tan 90°$ is undefined because you cannot divide by zero but $\cot\theta = \frac{0}{1} = 0$.

13.3 Problem Solving (pp. 871–872) **35.** about 10 ft **37.** About 104 ft; no. *Sample answer:* The initial height that the Ferris wheel is above the ground is not doubled so the entire height is not doubled.
39. a.

Angle of sprinkler, θ	25°	30°	35°	40°	45°
Horizontal distance water travels, d	15.0	16.9	18.4	19.2	19.5

Angle of sprinkler, θ	50°	55°	60°	65°
Horizontal distance water travels, d	19.2	18.4	16.9	15.0

b. 45°; since $\frac{v^2}{32}$ is constant, the maximum distance traveled will occur when $\sin 2\theta$ is as large as possible. The maximum value of $\sin 2\theta$ occurs when $2\theta = 90°$, that is, when $\theta = 45°$.
c. The distances are the same.

13.4 Skill Practice (p. 878) **1.** inverse **3.** $\frac{\pi}{2}$, 90° **5.** $\frac{\pi}{2}$, 90° **7.** $\frac{\pi}{3}$, 60° **9.** $-\frac{\pi}{6}$, −30° **13.** about 1.20, about 69.0° **15.** about 1.98, about 113.6° **17.** about −0.20, about −11.5° **19.** about 0.14, about 8.1° **21.** about 206.7° **23.** about 252.6° **25.** about 284.5° **27.** about 38.7° **29.** 120° **31.** *Sample answer:* 600°

13.4 Problem Solving (pp. 879–880)
35. about 53°

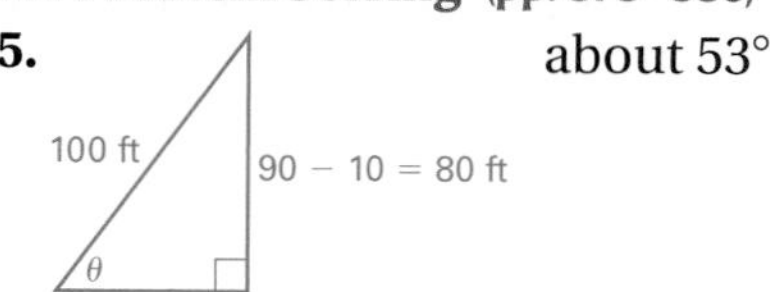

37. About 32.9°; about 46.4 ft. *Sample answer:* The pile is 15 feet high and the angle of repose is about 32.9°, the base of the right triangle formed is about 23.2 feet. Since this represents the radius of the pile, you need to multiply by 2 to get the diameter.
39. $\theta = \tan^{-1}\left(\frac{44t}{100}\right)$

13.5 Skill Practice (pp. 886–887) **1.** two angle measures and the length of a side, or the lengths of two sides and the measure of an angle opposite one of the two sides **3.** SSA; one triangle **5.** SSA; no triangle **7.** ASA; one triangle **9.** SSA; no triangle **11.** SSA; one triangle **13.** $A \approx 37.6°$, $B \approx 38.4°$, $a \approx 15.7$ **15.** $B = 65°$, $a \approx 23.8$, $b \approx 32.2$ **17.** $C = 95°$, $a \approx 17.6$, $b \approx 37.8$ **19.** $B = 119°$, $a \approx 6.5$, $c \approx 8.5$ **21.** $B \approx 54.1°$, $C \approx 87.9°$, $c \approx 30.8$, or $B \approx 125.9°$, $C \approx 16.1°$, $c \approx 8.6$ **23.** $B \approx 37.5°$, $C \approx 28.5°$, $c \approx 7.8$ **25.** $C = 99°$, $a \approx 62.7$, $c \approx 82.0$ **27.** The sides were not paired with their opposite angles; $\frac{\sin C}{5} = \frac{\sin 55°}{6}$, $\sin C = \frac{\sin 55°}{6} \approx 0.6826$, $C \approx 43.0°$. **29.** about 41.0 **31.** about 291.9 **33.** about 18.9 **35.** about 176.2 **37.** about 285.6 **39.** about 205.3

13.5 Problem Solving (pp. 887–888)
43. about 193.6 ft, about 212.9 ft
45. a.

C
54 ft
62 ft
58°
A
B

b. third side: about 70.4 ft; other angles: about 47.6°, about 74.4° **c.** 9 bags **47. a.** about 152.9 m

13.6 Skill Practice (pp. 892–893) **1.** semiperimeter **3.** law of cosines **5.** law of sines **7.** law of sines **9.** $B \approx 30.7°$, $C \approx 35.3°$, $a \approx 41.1$ **11.** $A \approx 110.4°$, $C \approx 44.6°$, $b \approx 3.60$ **13.** $A \approx 30.3°$, $B \approx 128.4°$, $C \approx 21.3°$ **15.** $A \approx 55.7°$, $B \approx 76.3°$, $c \approx 15.3$ **17.** $A \approx 42.6°$, $B \approx 11.7°$, $C \approx 125.7°$ **19.** $A \approx 36.7°$, $B \approx 47.3°$, $c \approx 58.2$ **21.** about 104 **23.** about 1108.6 **25.** about 25 **27.** about 131.9 **29.** about 2259.7 **31.** about 994.3 **35.** Since you are looking for A the equation should be $a^2 = b^2 + c^2 - 2bc \cos A$; $18^2 = 15^2 + 10^2 - 2(15)(10) \cos A$, $A \approx \cos^{-1} 0.0033 \approx 89.8°$. **37.** $A = 45°$, $b \approx 25.2$, $c \approx 15.3$ **39.** $A \approx 68.2°$, $C \approx 21.8°$, $b \approx 16.2$ **41.** $A \approx 93.7°$, $B \approx 33.9°$, $C \approx 52.4°$

13.6 Problem Solving (pp. 893–894) **43.** about 119.6° **45.** About 19.8 acres. *Sample answer:* Find $\overline{AC}$ then find the area of $\triangle ACD$ and $\triangle ABC$ using Heron's formula. **47. a.** about 2.6 mi **b.** about 3 h 45 min **c.** About 1 h 46 min; 79.2° W of N. *Sample answer:* The angle at hiker 1 is 79.2° and you have parallel lines at each hiker pointing in the North direction. The angle at hiker 2 is then an alternate interior angle, and is congruent.

13.6 Problem Solving Workshop (p. 895)
1. about 81.9 **3.** about 4619.5 **5.** about 792.6 ft^2

Chapter Review (pp. 898–900) **1.** An angle in standard position has its vertex at the origin, and its initial side lies on the positive x-axis. **3.** unit circle **5.** *Sample answer:* The law of sines is a ratio relating the sine of an angle and its corresponding side to the other angles and corresponding sides. **7.** about 26.6 m **9.** $-\frac{4\pi}{9}$ **11.** 330° **13.** $-\sqrt{2}$ **15.** 2 **17.** about 19.5° **19.** $A \approx 31.7°$, $C \approx 44.3°$, $a \approx 13.5$ **21.** $A = 47°$, $a \approx 16.9$, $c \approx 22.1$ **23.** $A \approx 58.7°$, $C \approx 46.3°$, $b \approx 22.6$

Chapter 14

14.1 Skill Practice (pp. 912–913)
1. period **3.** $1, \frac{\pi}{2}$ **5.** 1, 2

7.
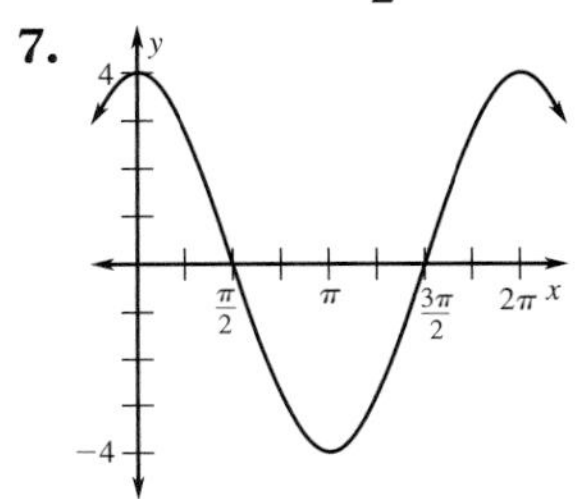

9.
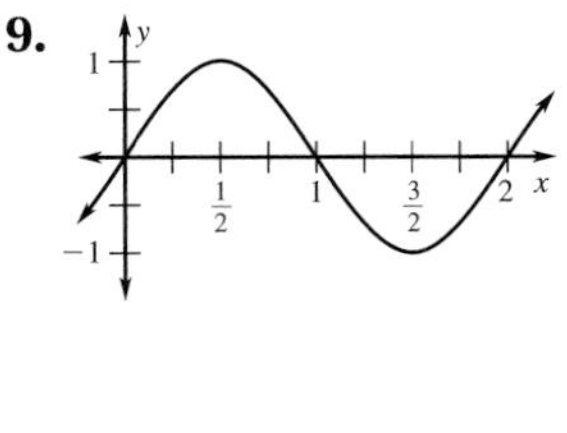

17.
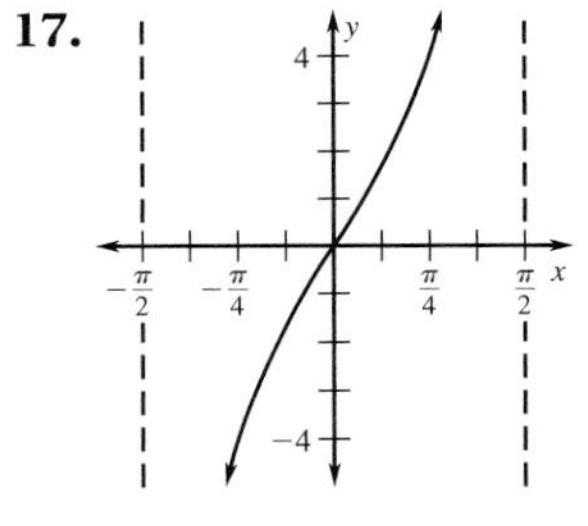

19.
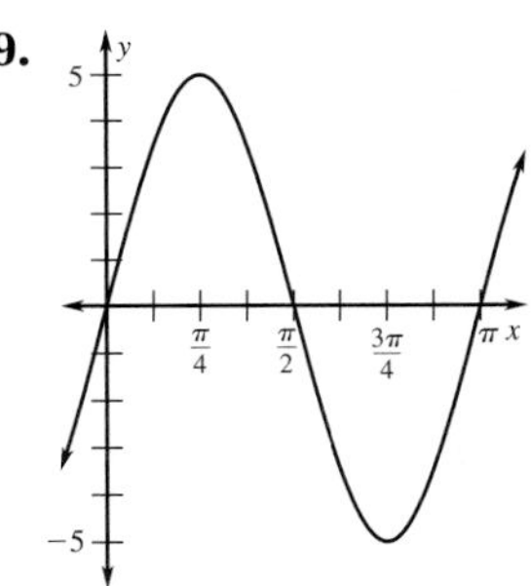

25. *Sample answer:* The rise and fall of the tides versus time.

14.1 Problem Solving (pp. 913–914)
29.
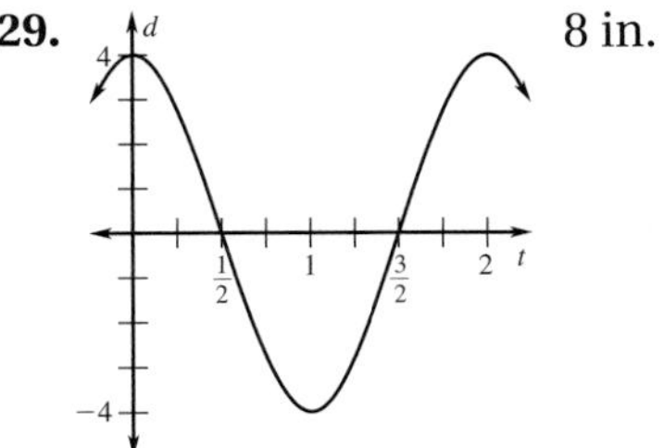
8 in.

31. a. $y = 1.75 \cos \frac{\pi}{3} t$ **b.** Since the high point occurs at $t = 0$, the cosine function best represents situation.

14.2 Skill Practice (pp. 919–921) **1.** 3 **3.** E **5.** D **7.** A

9.

11.

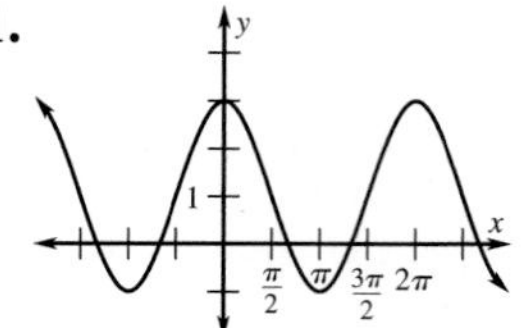

23.

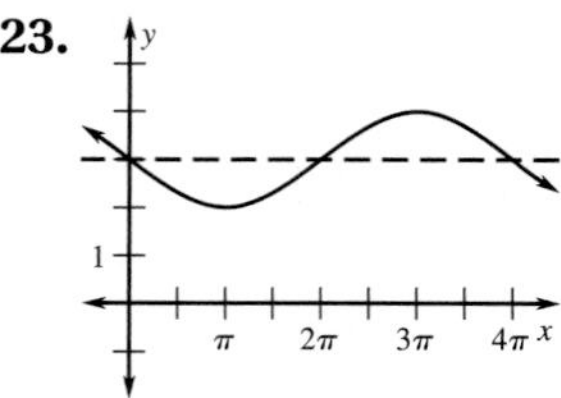

25.

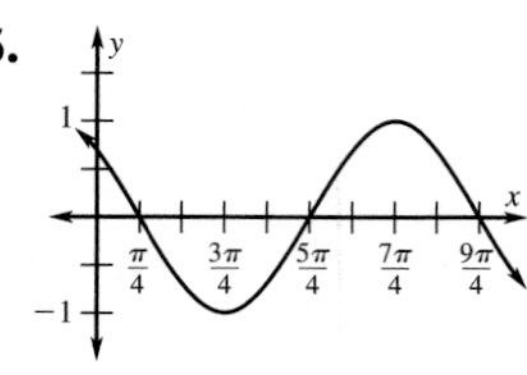

37.

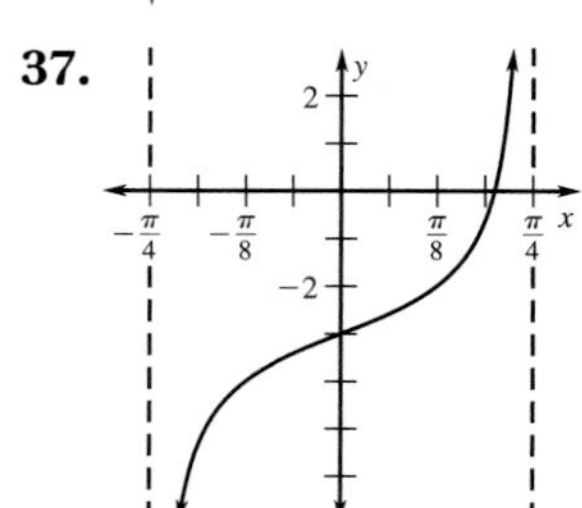

39.

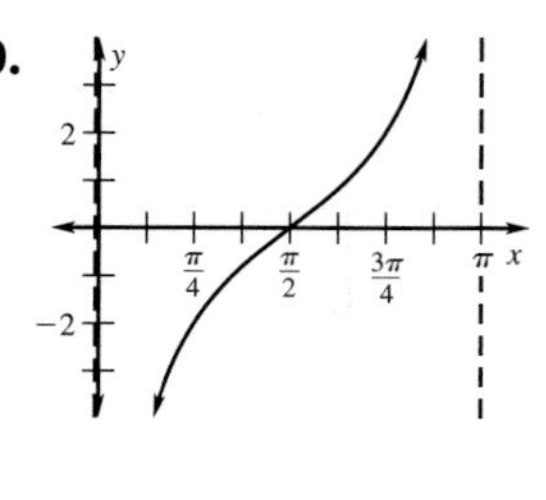

43. $y = 3\sin(x - \pi) + 2$ **45.** $y = -\frac{1}{3}\cos \pi x - 1$

47. The graph of $y = \cos x$ can be obtained by translating the graph of $y = \sin x$ either to the left by $\frac{\pi}{2}$ or to the right $\frac{3\pi}{2}$.

14.2 Problem Solving (pp. 921–922)

51. $h = 3.75\cos(200\pi t)$ **53. a.** $d = -300\tan\theta + 200$

b.

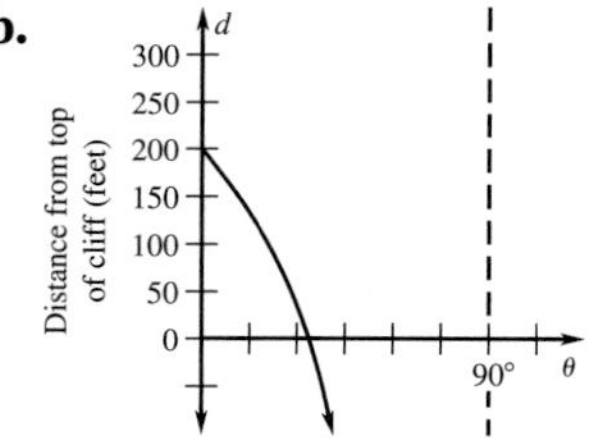

c. about 18.4°

14.3 Skill Practice (pp. 927–928) **1.** A trigonometric equation that is true for all values of θ in its domain

3. $\cos\theta = \frac{2\sqrt{2}}{3}$, $\tan\theta = \frac{\sqrt{2}}{4}$, $\csc\theta = 3$, $\sec\theta = \frac{3\sqrt{2}}{4}$, $\cot\theta = 2\sqrt{2}$ **5.** $\sin\theta = -\frac{\sqrt{11}}{6}$, $\tan\theta = -\frac{\sqrt{11}}{5}$, $\csc\theta = -\frac{6\sqrt{11}}{11}$ $\sec\theta = \frac{6}{5}$, $\cot\theta = -\frac{5\sqrt{11}}{11}$

7. $\sin\theta = \frac{5\sqrt{29}}{29}$, $\cos\theta = -\frac{2\sqrt{29}}{29}$, $\tan\theta = -\frac{5}{2}$, $\csc\theta = \frac{\sqrt{29}}{5}$, $\sec\theta = -\frac{\sqrt{29}}{2}$ **11.** $-\tan\theta$

13. $\sec\theta$ **15.** $\sin^2 x$ **17.** 1 **19.** $\sin x$ **21.** -1

23. $\tan(-x) = -\tan(x)$, so Step 1 used an incorrect substitution; $-\frac{\sin x}{\cos x} \cdot \frac{1}{\sin x} = -\frac{1}{\cos x} = -\sec x$.

25. $\sin x \csc x = \sin x\left(\frac{1}{\sin x}\right) = 1$

27. $\frac{\cos\left(\frac{\pi}{2} - \theta\right) + 1}{1 - \sin(-\theta)} = \frac{\sin\theta + 1}{1 - \sin\theta} = 1$

29. $\frac{\csc^2\theta - \cot^2\theta}{1 - \sin^2\theta} = \frac{1}{\cos^2\theta} = \sec^2\theta$

31. $\sin x + \cos x \cot x = \sin x + \cos x\left(\frac{\cos x}{\sin x}\right) =$ $\sin x + \frac{\cos^2 x}{\sin x} = \frac{\sin^2 x + \cos^2 x}{\sin x} = \frac{1}{\sin x} = \csc x$

33. $\frac{1 + \cos x}{\sin x} + \frac{\sin x}{1 + \cos x} = \frac{1 + 2\cos x + \cos^2 x + \sin^2 x}{(1 + \cos x)(\sin x)}$ $= \frac{1 + 2\cos x + 1}{(1 + \cos x)(\sin x)} = \frac{2 + 2\cos x}{(1 + \cos x)(\sin x)}$ $= \frac{2(1 + \cos x)}{(1 + \cos x)(\sin x)} = \frac{2}{\sin x} = 2\csc x$

35. $\sin x$, $\csc x$, $\tan x$, $\cot x$; $\cos x$, $\sec x$

37. $\ln|\tan\theta| = \ln\left|\frac{\sin\theta}{\cos\theta}\right| = \ln|\sin\theta| - \ln|\cos\theta|$

14.3 Problem Solving (pp. 929–930)

39. $\sec x \tan x - \sin x = \frac{1}{\cos x} \cdot \frac{\sin x}{\cos x} - \sin x =$ $\frac{\sin x}{\cos^2 x} - \frac{\sin x \cos^2 x}{\cos^2 x} = \frac{\sin x - \sin x\cos^2 x}{\cos^2 x} =$ $\frac{\sin x(1 - \cos^2 x)}{\cos^2 x} = \frac{\sin x(\sin^2 x)}{\cos^2 x} = \sin x \tan^2 x$

41. a. $r = \frac{1.069}{1 - 0.97\cos\theta}$

b.

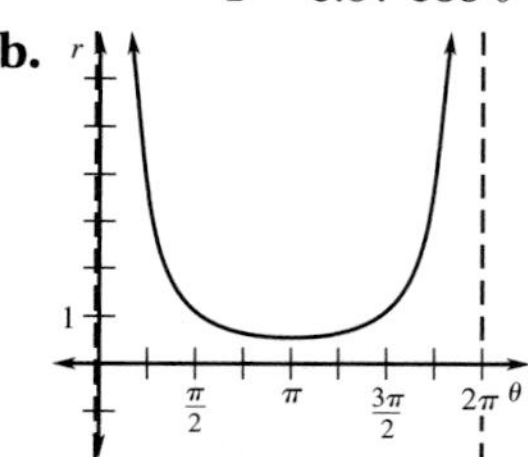

c.

θ	0	$\frac{\pi}{4}$	$\frac{\pi}{2}$	$\frac{3\pi}{4}$	π	$\frac{5\pi}{4}$	$\frac{3\pi}{2}$
r	35.6	3.40	1.07	0.634	0.543	0.634	1.07

about 50,500,000 mi, about 3,310,800,000 mi

43. The value of $\tan\theta$ increases as the value of $\sin\theta$ increases and the value of $\cos\theta$ decreases; $0 \le \theta \le \frac{\pi}{2}$, $2\pi \le \theta \le \frac{5\pi}{2}$, $4\pi \le \theta \le \frac{9\pi}{2}$, and so on.

14.4 Skill Practice (pp. 935–936) **1.** A trigonometric identity is true for all real values of x where a trigonometric equation is only true for some specific value(s) of x. **3.** $2 + 3\cos(4\pi) - 5 = 2 + 3(1) - 5 = 0$

5. $12\sin^2\left(\frac{\pi}{6}\right) - 3 = 12\left(\frac{1}{2}\right)^2 - 3 = 0$

7. $2\cos^4\left(\frac{\pi}{2}\right) - \cos^2\left(\frac{\pi}{2}\right) = 2(0)^4 - (0)^2 = 0$

9. $\frac{\pi}{6} + 2n\pi$ or $\frac{5\pi}{6} + 2n\pi$ **11.** $\frac{\pi}{6} + n\pi$

13. $\frac{\pi}{6} + n\pi$ or $\frac{5\pi}{6} + n\pi$ **17.** $\frac{\pi}{6}, \frac{7\pi}{6}$ **19.** $\frac{\pi}{4}, \frac{3\pi}{4}, \frac{5\pi}{4}, \frac{7\pi}{4}$ **21.** $\frac{\pi}{3}, \frac{2\pi}{3}, \frac{4\pi}{3}, \frac{5\pi}{3}$ **23.** When two negative values are divided, the quotient is positive; $\cos x = \frac{1}{2}, x = \frac{\pi}{3}, \frac{5\pi}{3}$. **25.** $\frac{\pi}{6} + n\pi$ **27.** $\frac{\pi}{3} + n\pi$ or $\frac{2\pi}{3} + n\pi$ **29.** $\pi + 2n\pi$ **31.** $\frac{\pi}{3}, \frac{\pi}{2}$ **33.** about 0.572 **35.** $\frac{5\pi}{3}$ **37.** (0, 1) **39.** $\left(\frac{\pi}{6}, \frac{\sqrt{3}}{3}\right), \left(\frac{2\pi}{3}, 3\sqrt{3}\right), \left(\frac{7\pi}{6}, \frac{\sqrt{3}}{3}\right), \left(\frac{5\pi}{3}, 3\sqrt{3}\right)$

14.4 Problem Solving (pp. 936–937) **41.** July 26 and November 26 **43. a.** $S = \frac{27}{4} + \frac{27}{32}\left(\frac{\sqrt{3} - \cos\theta}{\sin\theta}\right)$

b. *Sample:*

θ	16	17	18	19
S	9.1095	8.9887	8.8825	8.7884

θ	120	121	122	123
S	8.9246	8.9619	9.0005	9.0405

about 17° and about 122°

c. 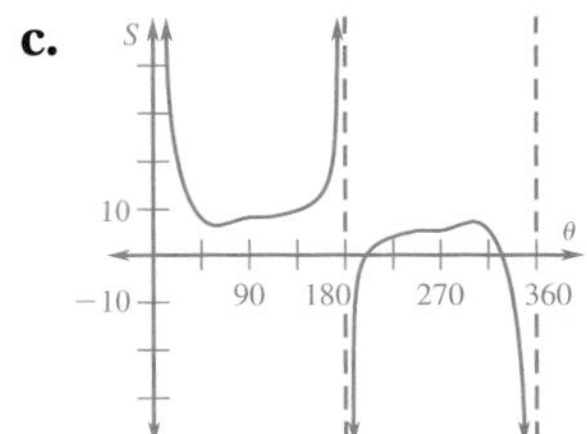

about 54.7°

14.4 Problem Solving Workshop (p. 939) **1.** about 0.987, about 3.01 **3.** about 0.298, about 0.702 **5.** about 22.6, about 37.4 **7.** 1:32 AM, 10:52 AM, 1:56 PM, 11:16 PM **9.** about 0.17 sec and about 0.83 sec

14.5 Skill Practice (pp. 944–945) **1.** The graph of sine or cosine functions. **3.** *Sample answer:* $y = 3 \sin 2x$ **5.** *Sample answer:* $y = -2 \cos \frac{\pi}{2}x + 4$ **7.** To determine the amplitude, you must take half of the difference between the maximum and the minimum; $\frac{10 - (-6)}{2} = 8$. **9–17.** Sample answers are given. **9.** $y = 6 \sin \frac{1}{2}x$ **11.** $y = -\cos 3x + 4$ **13.** $y = 2 \cos \frac{4}{5}\left(x - \frac{3\pi}{4}\right) + 7$ **15.** $y = 2 \sin \frac{1}{4}(x + 2\pi) - 2$ **17.** $y = -6 \cos \frac{3}{2}x - 6$ **21.** $y = 3 \cos 4\left(x - \frac{\pi}{8}\right) + 2$;
$y = 3 \cos\left(4x - \frac{\pi}{2}\right) + 2$ (Dist. property);
$y = 3 \cos\left(\frac{\pi}{2} - 4x\right) + 2$ (Neg. angle identity);
$y = 3 \sin 4x + 2$ (Cofunction identity)

14.5 Problem Solving (pp. 945–946) **23.** $V = 100 \sin 4\pi t$ **25.** $h = 2.5 \sin \pi t + 6.5$ **27. a.** $N = 3.68 \sin(0.776t - 0.703) + 20.4$ **b.** about 23,100 employees

14.6 Skill Practice (pp. 952–953) **1.** $\sin(a + b) = \sin a \cos b + \cos a \sin b$, $\sin(a - b) = \sin a \cos b - \cos a \sin b$, $\cos(a + b) = \cos a \cos b - \sin a \sin b$, $\cos(a - b) = \cos a \cos b + \sin a \sin b$, $\tan(a + b) = \frac{\tan a + \tan b}{1 - \tan a \tan b}$, $\tan(a - b) = \frac{\tan a - \tan b}{1 + \tan a \tan b}$ **3.** $\sqrt{3} - 2$ **5.** $2 - \sqrt{3}$ **7.** $\frac{\sqrt{2} - \sqrt{6}}{4}$ **9.** $\frac{\sqrt{6} - \sqrt{2}}{4}$ **11.** $\sin\left(\frac{\pi}{2} - 0\right) = \sin\frac{\pi}{2}\cos\theta - \cos\frac{\pi}{2}\sin\theta = 1(\cos\theta) - 0(\sin\theta) = \cos\theta$ **13.** $\frac{77}{85}$ **15.** $\frac{84}{85}$ **17.** $-\frac{84}{13}$ **19.** $\tan x$ **21.** $\cos x$ **23.** $\cos x$ **25.** $-\cos x$ **27.** $-\cot x$ **29.** $-\cot x$ **31.** The sign in the denominator should be negative when using the sum formula; $\frac{\tan x + \tan\frac{\pi}{4}}{1 - \tan x \tan\frac{\pi}{4}} = \frac{\tan x + 1}{1 - \tan x}$. **33.** $\frac{3\pi}{2}$ **35.** about 3.757, about 5.668 **37.** $0, \frac{\pi}{3}, \pi, \frac{5\pi}{3}$

14.6 Problem Solving (pp. 953–954) **41.** about 15 min 48 sec **43. a.** $\frac{f(1 + \tan^2 t)}{h(1 + \tan\theta\tan t)}$ **b.** $\frac{f(1 + \tan^2 0)}{h(1 + \tan\theta\tan 0)} = \frac{f}{h}$

14.7 Skill Practice (pp. 959–960) **1.** double angle **3.** $\frac{\sqrt{2 + \sqrt{3}}}{2}$ **5.** $2 - \sqrt{3}$ **7.** $\frac{\sqrt{\sqrt{2} + 2}}{2}$ **9.** $\sqrt{2} + 1$ **13.** $\frac{\sqrt{3}}{3}, -\frac{\sqrt{6}}{3}, -\frac{\sqrt{2}}{2}$ **15.** $\frac{3\sqrt{10}}{10}, -\frac{\sqrt{10}}{10}, -3$ **17.** $\frac{4}{5}, -\frac{3}{5}, -\frac{4}{3}$ **19.** $\frac{4\sqrt{5}}{9}, \frac{1}{9}, 4\sqrt{5}$ **21.** 1 **23.** $\frac{2\tan\theta}{1 + \tan\theta}$ **25.** $\cos\theta - 1$ **29.** The correct half angle formula is $\pm\sqrt{\frac{1 - \cos a}{2}}$; $\sqrt{\frac{1 - \frac{\sqrt{2}}{2}}{2}} = \sqrt{\frac{\frac{2 - \sqrt{2}}{2}}{2}} = \sqrt{\frac{2 - \sqrt{2}}{4}} = \frac{\sqrt{2 - \sqrt{2}}}{2}$ **31.** $\sin 3\theta = \sin(2\theta + \theta) = \sin 2\theta\cos\theta + \cos 2\theta\sin\theta = 2\sin\theta\cos\theta\cos\theta + (2\cos^2\theta - 1)\sin\theta = 2\sin\theta\cos^2\theta + (2\cos^2\theta - 1)\sin\theta = \sin\theta(2\cos^2\theta + 2\cos^2\theta - 1) = \sin\theta(4\cos^2\theta - 1)$ **33.** $2\sin^2 x\tan\frac{x}{2} = 2\sin^2 x\left(\frac{1 - \cos x}{\sin x}\right) = 2\sin x(1 - \cos x) = 2\sin x - 2\sin x\cos x = 2\sin x - \sin 2x$ **35.** $\cos 4\theta = \cos(2\theta + 2\theta) = \cos 2\theta\cos 2\theta - \sin 2\theta\sin 2\theta = (\cos^2\theta - \sin^2\theta)^2 - (2\sin\theta\cos\theta)^2 = \cos^4\theta - 2\cos^2\theta\sin^2\theta + \sin^4\theta - 4\sin^2\theta\cos^2\theta = \cos^4\theta - 6\sin^2\theta\cos^2\theta + \sin^4\theta$ **37.** $\frac{4\pi}{3}$ **39.** $\frac{\pi}{4}, \frac{7\pi}{4}$ **41.** $\frac{\pi}{3}, \frac{\pi}{2}, \frac{2\pi}{3}, \frac{4\pi}{3}, \frac{3\pi}{2}, \frac{5\pi}{3}$

43. The value of $\tan\theta$ increases as the value of $\sin\theta$ increases and the value of $\cos\theta$ decreases; $0 \le \theta \le \frac{\pi}{2}$, $2\pi\theta \le \frac{5\pi}{2}$, $4\pi\theta \le \frac{9\pi}{2}$, and so on.

14.7 Problem Solving (pp. 961–962)
51. $24.3° \le \theta \le 65.7°$ **53.** about 47.2°
55. a. $y = -\frac{16}{(40)^2 \cos^2 \theta}(41.75)^2 + \tan \theta\,(41.75) + 6$
b. $y = -\frac{1743.0625}{100 \cos^2 \theta} + \tan \theta\,(41.75) + 6$; about 36.7° or about 58.8° **c.** *Sample answer:* The person aims toward the basket and the ball does not bounce off the rim.

Chapter Review (pp. 965–968) **1.** cycles **3.** period **5.** frequency

7.

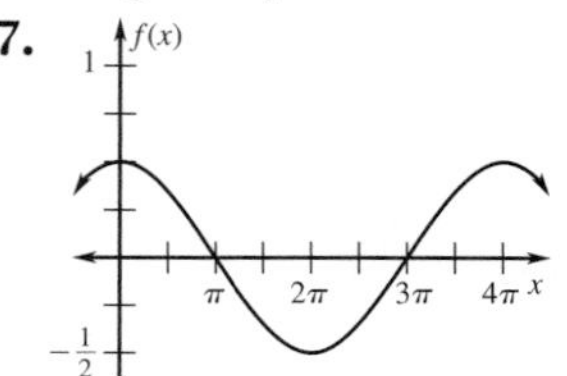

9.

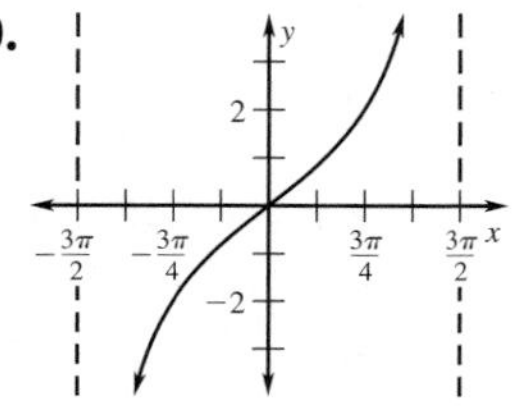

11.

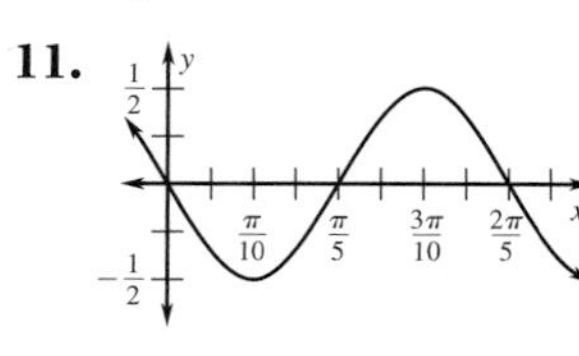

13.

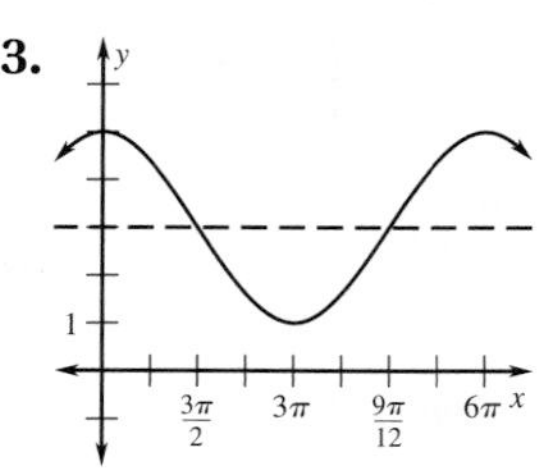

15.

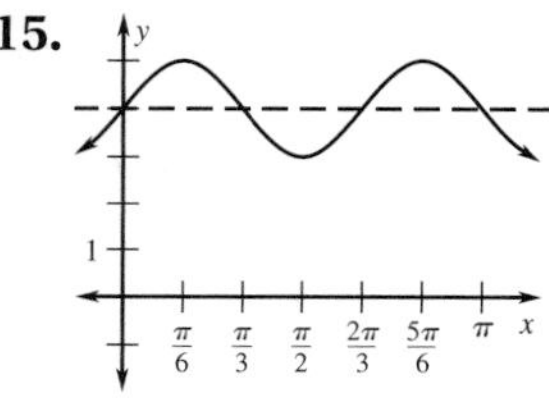

17. $\sec^3 x$ **19.** $\frac{\sin^2(-x) - 1}{\cot^2 x} = \frac{-(1 - \sin^2 x)}{\frac{\cos^2 x}{\sin^2 x}} = \frac{-\cos^2 x}{\frac{\cos^2 x}{\sin^2 x}} = -\sin^2 x$ **21.** $\frac{\pi}{3}, \frac{2\pi}{3}, \frac{4\pi}{3}, \frac{5\pi}{3}$ **23.** $\frac{\pi}{12}, \frac{\pi}{6}, \frac{\pi}{3}, \frac{5\pi}{12}, \frac{7\pi}{12}, \frac{2\pi}{3}, \frac{5\pi}{6}, \frac{11\pi}{12}, \frac{13\pi}{12}, \frac{7\pi}{6}, \frac{4\pi}{3}, \frac{17\pi}{12}, \frac{19\pi}{12}, \frac{5\pi}{3}, \frac{11\pi}{6}, \frac{23\pi}{12}$ **25.** *Sample answer:* $y = \cos \pi x - 2$ **27.** $2 + \sqrt{3}$ **29.** $-\frac{\sqrt{3}}{2}$
31. $\frac{\sqrt{2 + \sqrt{3}}}{2}$ **33.** $\frac{\sqrt{2 + \sqrt{3}}}{2}$ **35.** $\frac{\sqrt{3}}{2}, \frac{\sqrt{3}}{2}$

Skills Review Handbook

Operations with Positive and Negative Numbers (p. 975)
1. −6 **3.** −60 **5.** 2 **7.** 8 **9.** 44 **11.** −4 **13.** 12 **15.** −72 **17.** −2 **19.** −3 **21.** 9 **23.** 6 **25.** −15 **27.** −12 **29.** 5 **31.** 42 **33.** −17 **35.** 2

Fractions, Decimals, and Percents (p. 976) **1.** $\frac{13}{20}$ **3.** $\frac{3}{2}$
5. $\frac{7}{10}$ **7.** $\frac{13}{50}$ **9.** $\frac{19}{20}$ **11.** 0.25 **13.** 1.2 **15.** 0.375 **17.** 1.42 **19.** 0.3 **21.** 60% **23.** 130% **25.** 45% **27.** 80% **29.** 250%

Calculating with Percents (p. 977) **1.** 196 **3.** 38.4 **5.** 17 **7.** 1 **9.** 54% **11.** 10% **13.** 20% **15.** 2% **17.** 80 **19.** 60 **21.** 70 **23.** 8 **25.** 25% decrease **27.** 50% increase **29.** 96% increase **31.** 79% decrease

Factors and Multiples (p. 979) **1.** $2 \cdot 3 \cdot 7$ **3.** $3 \cdot 5^2$ **5.** $2 \cdot 5 \cdot 7$ **7.** $2^3 \cdot 3^2$ **9.** prime **11.** $2^3 \cdot 11$ **13.** prime **15.** 2^5 **17.** 8 **19.** 11 **21.** 4 **23.** 3 **25.** 10 **27.** 3 **29.** 1 **31.** 16 **33.** 30 **35.** 24 **37.** 6 **39.** 36 **41.** 30 **43.** 40 **45.** 891 **47.** $\frac{7}{16}$ **49.** $\frac{5}{6}$ **51.** $\frac{37}{40}$ **53.** $\frac{1}{3}$ **55.** $\frac{17}{30}$ **57.** $\frac{13}{20}$ **59.** $\frac{9}{20}$ **61.** $\frac{13}{16}$ **63.** $\frac{23}{30}$ **65.** $\frac{59}{80}$ **67.** $\frac{17}{20}$ **69.** $\frac{11}{18}$

Ratios and Proportions (p. 980) **1.** 1 to 3, 1 : 3, $\frac{1}{3}$ **3.** 5 to 4, 5 : 4, $\frac{5}{4}$ **5.** 5 to 6, 5 : 6, $\frac{5}{6}$ **7.** 1 to 1, 1 : 1, $\frac{1}{1}$ **9.** 4 to 9, 4 : 9, $\frac{4}{9}$ **11.** 7 to 1, 7 : 1, $\frac{7}{1}$ **13.** 7 **15.** 20 **17.** 2 **19.** 5 **21.** 40 **23.** 6.75 **25.** 99 **27.** 72

Converting Units of Measurement (p. 981) **1.** 6000 **3.** 5 **5.** 7.7 **7.** 16 **9.** 4000 **11.** 0.8 **13.** 6 **15.** 1.5 **17.** 3600 **19.** 3 **21.** $\frac{1}{8}$ **23.** 63,360 **25.** 2 **27.** 4000

Scientific Notation (p. 982) **1.** 6×10^{-1} **3.** 8×10^{-2} **5.** 4.08×10^1 **7.** 3.85×10^{-4} **9.** 4.1236×10^4 **11.** 4.86×10^5 **13.** 1.002×10^{-2} **15.** 7.0505×10^3 **17.** 9.85×10^3 **19.** 8.05×10^2 **21.** 5000 **23.** 0.82 **25.** 0.0032 **27.** 734,500 **29.** 1.814 **31.** 1,000,000 **33.** 0.000008 **35.** 1,870,000,000 **37.** 6,080,000 **39.** 34,010,000

Significant Digits (p. 983) **1.** 600 **3.** 81 **5.** 1.885 **7.** 4.9 **9.** 195 **11.** 0.036 **13.** 1009 **15.** 18 **17.** $17.40 **19.** 2.5 pints per student **21.** 2543 books per library **23.** $1250

Writing Algebraic Expressions (p. 984) **1.** $n + 8$ **3.** $2n$ **5.** $\frac{1}{5}n$ **7.** $5n$ **9.** $0.25n$ **11.** $n - 2$ **13.** $c - 4$ yr **15.** $x + 5$ dollars **17.** $45 - m$ min **19.** $10x$ dollars

Binomial Products (p. 985) **1.** $a^2 + 8a + 15$ **3.** $t^2 + 15t + 56$ **5.** $y^2 + 6y + 8$ **7.** $y^2 - 4y + 4$ **9.** $z^2 - 8z + 16$ **11.** $y^2 - 4y - 21$ **13.** $25x^2 - 16$ **15.** $2c^2 + 3c - 35$ **17.** $-z^2 + 49$ **19.** $16a^2 + 24a + 9$ **21.** $-x^2 - 4x + 32$ **23.** $-a^2 + 18a - 81$ **25.** $10x^2 - 21x - 10$ **27.** $-24z^2 + 22z - 3$

LCDs of Rational Expressions (p. 986) **1.** $2a^2b$ **3.** z^3 **5.** $126m$ **7.** $3y^2$ **9.** $(n + 2)(n - 2)$ **11.** $5(n + 1)$ **13.** $6(m - 3)$ **15.** $(x - 4)^2$ **17.** $2n^3(5n + 4)$ **19.** $(k + 3)^4$ **21.** $70(n + 2)$ **23.** $(a + 2)^2$ **25.** $(k - 3)(k - 2)$ **27.** $(m - 7)(m - 4)(m^2 + 5m - 45)$

The Coordinate Plane (p. 987)
1–20. **21.** (2, 5) **23.** (5, −5) **25.** (4, 0) **27.** (5, 4) **29.** (4, −2) **31.** (−2, 0) **33.** (−2, 2) **35.** (2, −4) **37.** (2, −1) **39.** (−1, 5) **41.** (−4, −3) **43.** (1, −3)

Transformations (p. 989)
1. (3, −8) **3.** (−3, 11) **5.** (8, 3) **7.** (−8, −3)

9.

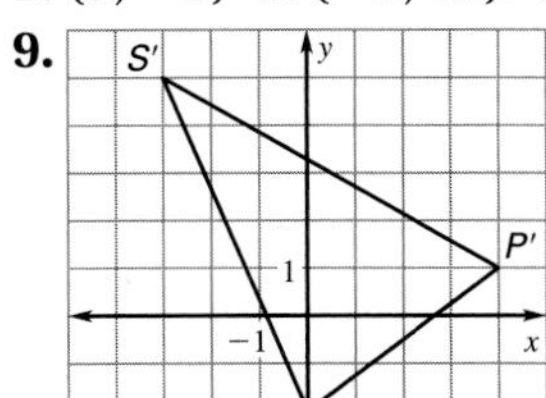

11.

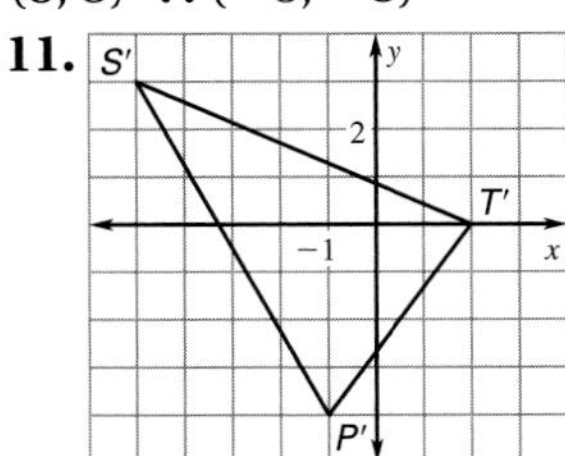

19.

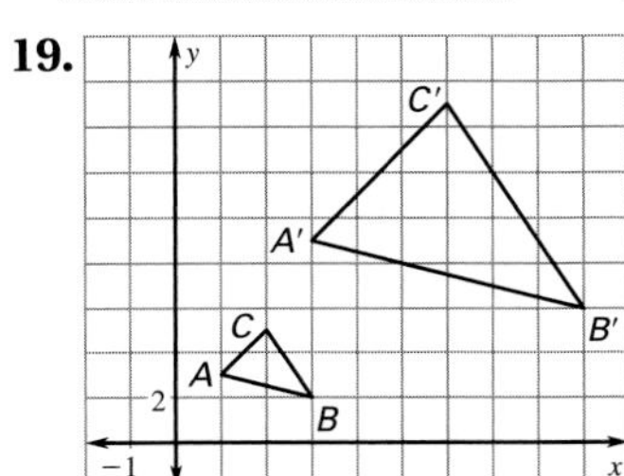

21.

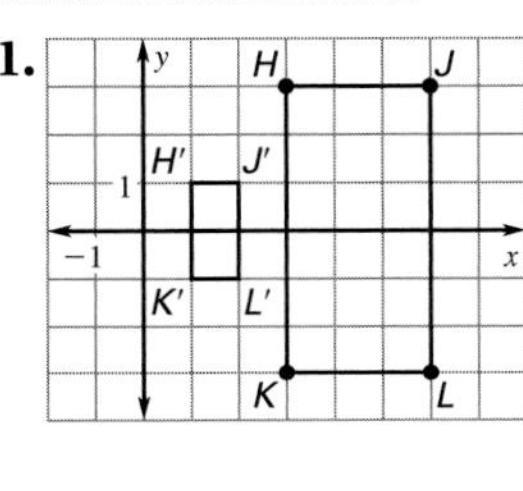

Line Symmetry (p. 990) **1.** none **3.** 1 **5.** none **7.** 2 **9.** (−4, −1) **11.** (−2, 2)

Perimeter and Area (p. 991) **1.** 10 cm, 6 cm^2 **3.** 26 in., 24 $in.^2$ **5.** 48 yd, 84 yd^2 **7.** 14 m, 10.8 m^2

Circumference and Area of a Circle (p. 992)
1. $C = 10\pi$ in. or about 31 in., $A = 25\pi$ $in.^2$ or about 79 $in.^2$ **3.** $C = 8\pi$ in. or about 25 in., $A = 16\pi$ $in.^2$ or about 50 $in.^2$ **5.** $C = 24\pi$ ft or about 75 ft, $A = 144\pi$ ft^2 or about 452 ft^2 **7.** $C = 6\pi$ ft or about 19 ft, $A = 9\pi$ ft^2 or about 28 ft^2 **9.** $C = 2\pi$ cm or about 6 cm, $A = \pi$ cm^2 or about 3 cm^2 **11.** $C = 22\pi$ in. or about 69 in., $A = 121\pi$ $in.^2$ or about 380 $in.^2$

Surface Area and Volume (p. 993) **1.** 158 $in.^2$, 120 $in.^3$ **3.** 54 cm^2, 27 cm^3 **5.** 154π yd^2 or about 484 yd^2, 196π yd^3 or about 616 yd^3

Angle Relationships (p. 994) **1.** 39 **3.** 8 **5.** 16 **7.** 23 **9.** 29

Triangle Relationships (p. 995) **1.** 40 **3.** 60 **5.** 50 cm **7.** 12 ft **9.** 55°

Congruent and Similar Figures (p. 997) **1.** similar **3.** congruent **5.** congruent **7.** neither **9.** congruent **11.** 11.5 **13.** 14 **15.** 40 **17.** 7

More Problem Solving Strategies (p. 999) **1.** 4:15 P.M. **3.** 6 ways **5.** 40 parts **7.** 8 dimes, 5 nickels

Logical Argument (p. 1001) **1.** valid; Chain Rule **3.** invalid **5.** valid; *And* Rule **7.** valid; *Or* Rule **9.** invalid **11.** true **13.** false **15.** true **17.** true **19.** false **21.** true

Conditional Statements and Counterexamples (p. 1003)
1. If you have the equation $y = mx + b$, then you have the graph of a line; if you have the graph of a line, then you have the equation $y = mx + b$, false. **3.** If Abby finishes her homework, then she can go swimming; if Abby goes swimming, then she finished her homework, false. **5.** If $4x + 8 = 28$, then $x = 5$; if $x = 5$, then $4x + 8 = 28$, true. **7.** True; if two lines are perpendicular, then they intersect to form a right angle and if two lines intersect to form a right angle, then they are perpendicular. **9.** False; not all orange vegetables are carrots. **11.** False; the converse is not true. **13.** False; zero is neither positive nor negative. **15.** False. *Sample answer:* An octagon could have exactly 5 congruent sides. **17.** False; *A* could be in between *B* and *C* and therefore would only be 2 inches from *C*. **19.** False. *Sample answer:* Charlie could have 10 dimes.

Venn Diagrams (p. 1004)
1.

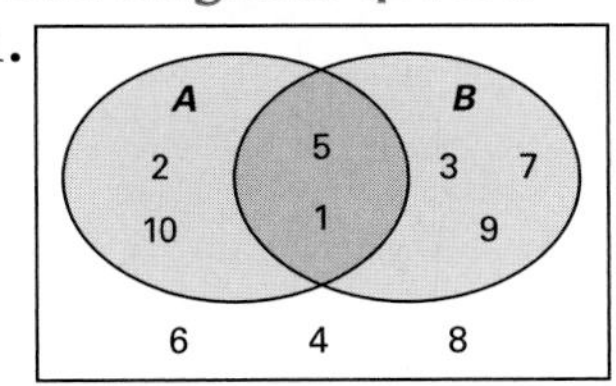

3.

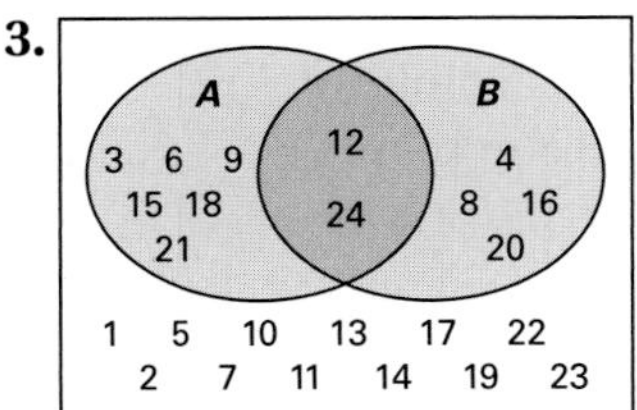

5. False. *Sample answer:* 10 is even, but it is not a multiple of 3 or 4. **7.** False; 1 is a positive odd integer and a factor of 10. **9.** True; 2 is the only even prime number.

Mean, Median, Mode, and Range (p. 1005)
1. about \$664, \$675, \$650, \$300 **3.** 685 min, 713 min, none, 611 min **5.** 48 cookies, 48 cookies, 48 cookies, 24 cookies **7.** \$9.20, \$8.90, none, \$5.85 **9.** 15 people, 14 people, 10 people and 18 people and 22 people, 25 people

Graphing Statistical Data (p. 1006) **1.** 6 P.M. **3.** 5 diners; yes **5.** 14 diners **7.** winter and summer **9.** natural gas **11.** 50 homes

13.

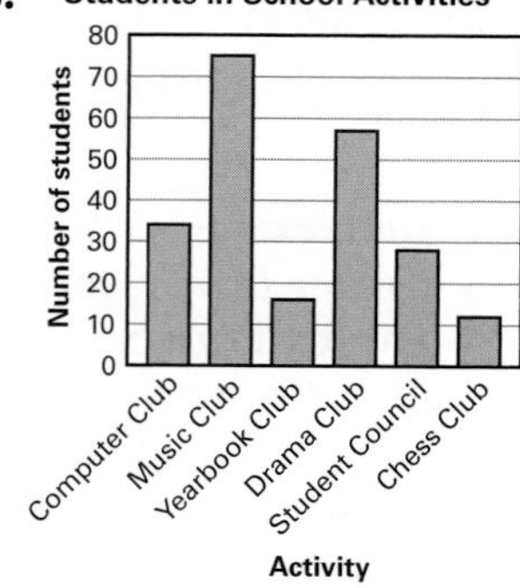

Organizing Statistical Data (p. 1009)

1.

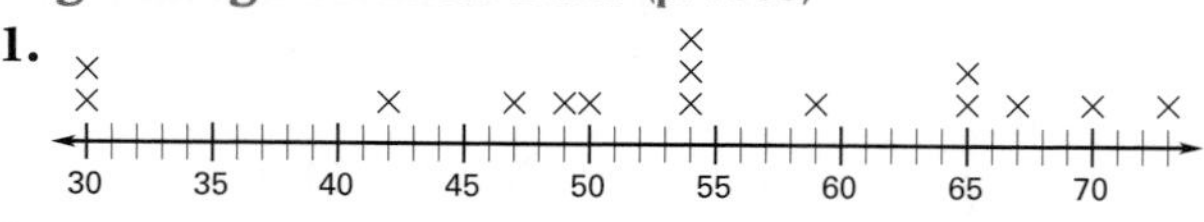

3.

Stem	Leaves
3	0 0
4	2 7 9
5	0 4 4 4 9
6	5 5 7
7	0 3

Key: 3 | 0 = 30

5.

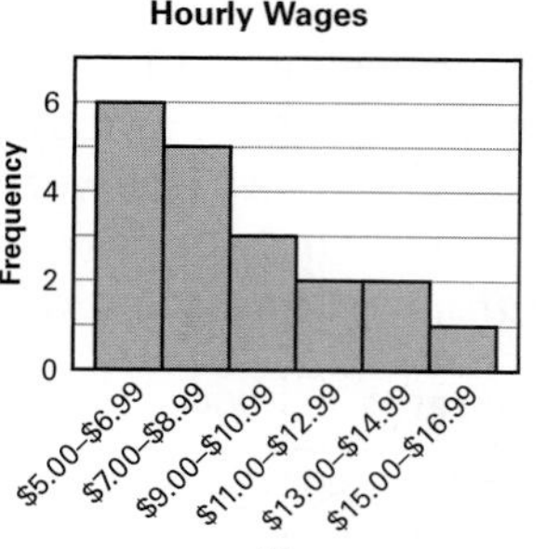

7.

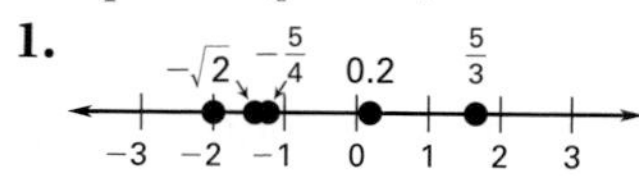

9. 5 **11.** 23 dogs **13.** 43 lb **15.** 25 children **17.** 12 songs **19.** 10 songs; 18 songs

Extra Practice

Chapter 1 (p. 1010)

1. $-\sqrt{2}$, $-\frac{5}{4}$, 0.2, $\frac{5}{3}$

3. $-\sqrt{7}$, $-\frac{1}{2}$, 3.7, $\sqrt{15}$

5. 1.25 lb **7.** 15 **9.** 52 **11.** $6r^2 - 5r + 12$ **13.** $8b - 20$ **15.** $-5m^2 + 9m - 12$ **17.** 5 **19.** -12 **21.** 2 **23.** 14 **25.** $y = \frac{1}{6}x + 3; \frac{10}{3}$ **27.** $y = \frac{9}{4}x - \frac{15}{2}; 6$ **29.** $y = \frac{5}{2 + 3x}; -\frac{5}{4}$ **31.** $y = -3x + 25$

33. $x > 7$ **35.** $x \le 5$

43. $-1, 5$ **45.** $-\frac{1}{9}$

47. $c < -7$ or $c > 7$

49. $-\frac{1}{2} \le j \le 4$

Chapter 2 (p. 1011)

1. Function; for each input there is exactly one output. **3.** Not a function; there is more than one output for the input -2. **5.** $-\frac{1}{2}$; falls **7.** undefined; is vertical **9.** neither

11.

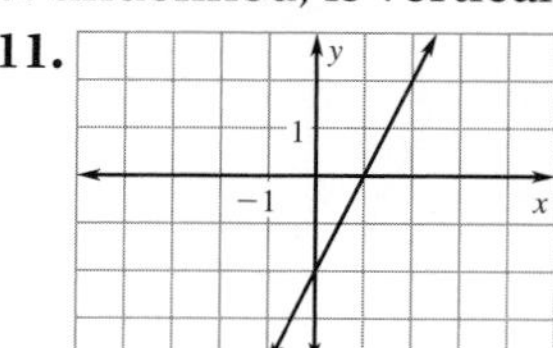

13.

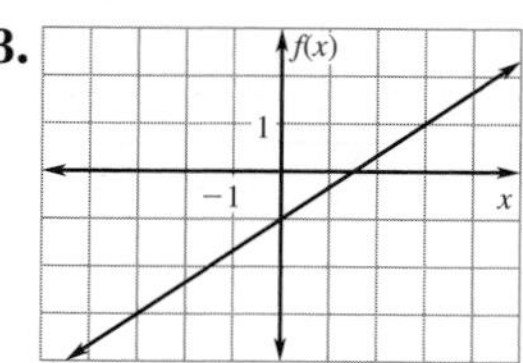

19. $y = 7x - 3$ **21.** $y = -2$ **23.** $y = \frac{10}{3}x + \frac{1}{3}$ **25.** $y = 2x; -4$ **27.** $y = \frac{1}{4}x; -\frac{1}{2}$

29. a, b.

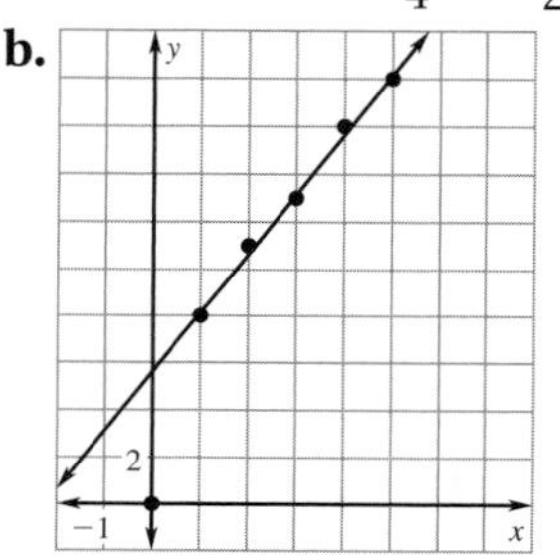

c. about 36

31.

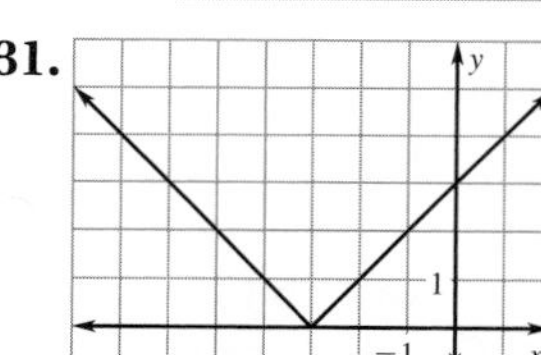

shifted left 3

33.

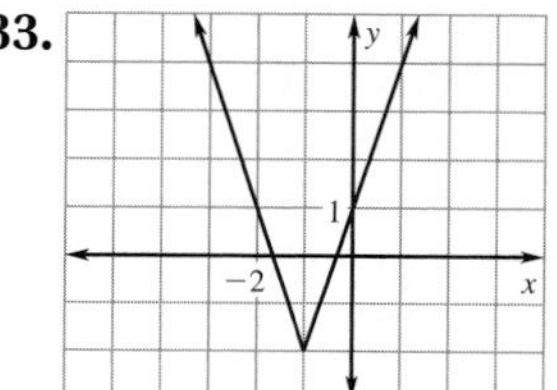

shifted down 2, left 1, and vertically stretched

35.

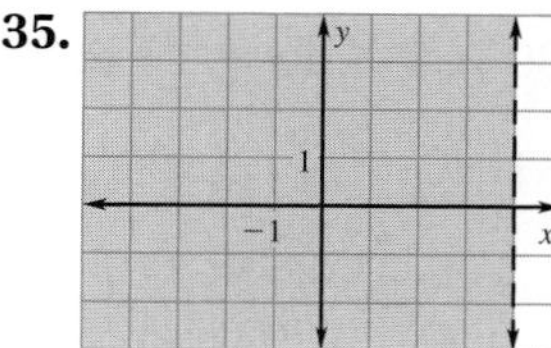

37.

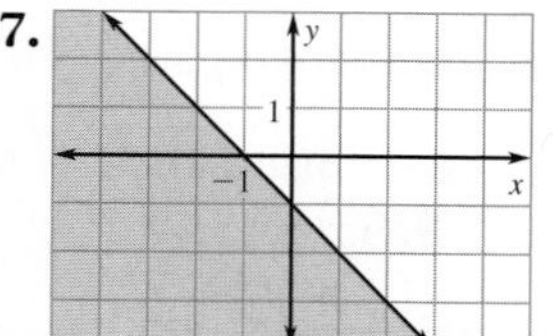

Chapter 3 (p. 1012)

1. 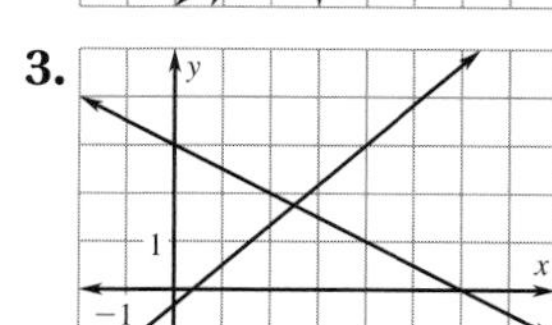 $(-3, -7)$

3. 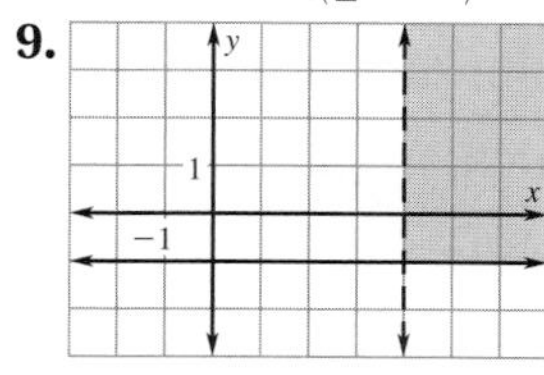 $(2.5, 1.75)$

5. $(1, -2)$ **7.** $\left(\frac{5}{2}, -5\right)$

9. 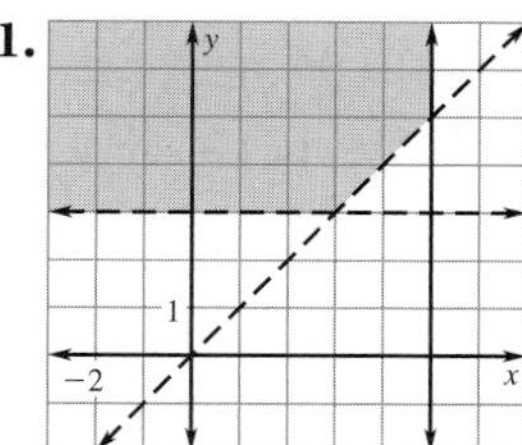

11.

13. $(2, -7, 5)$ **15.** $\left(\frac{3}{2}, -3, -3\right)$ **17.** $\begin{bmatrix} -12 & 9 \\ -8 & 4 \end{bmatrix}$

19. $\begin{bmatrix} 16 & 9 & -7 \\ -2 & 13 & 7 \end{bmatrix}$ **21.** not defined; the number of columns in the left matrix does not equal the number of rows in the right matrix. **23.** 66 **25.** -9 **27.** $(3, -14)$

29. $(3, -3, 1)$ **31.** $\begin{bmatrix} \frac{8}{3} & -\frac{7}{3} \\ -1 & 1 \end{bmatrix}$ **33.** $\begin{bmatrix} -8 & -5 \\ 3 & 2 \end{bmatrix}$

35. $(14, -6)$ **37.** $(-8, -3)$

Chapter 4 (p. 1013)

1. 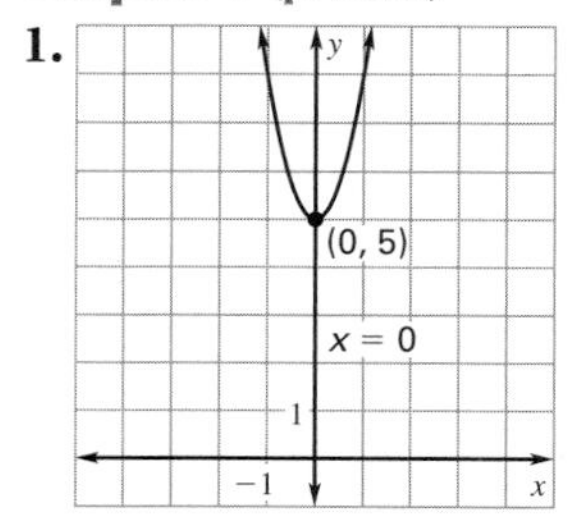

3. 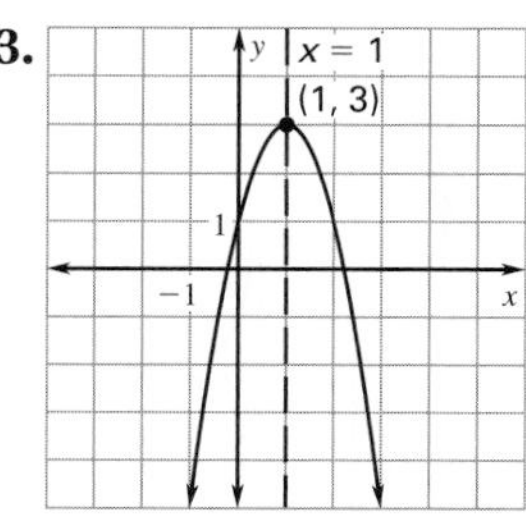

5. 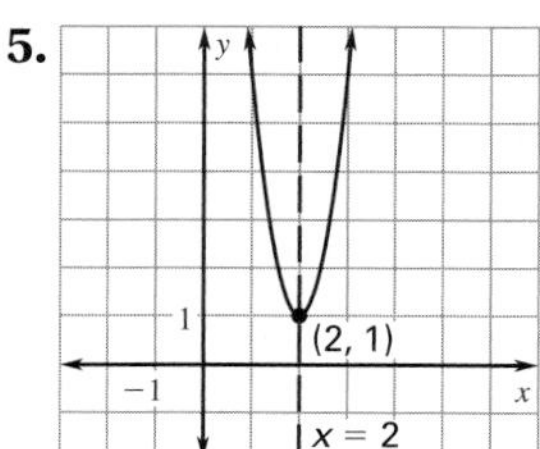

7. 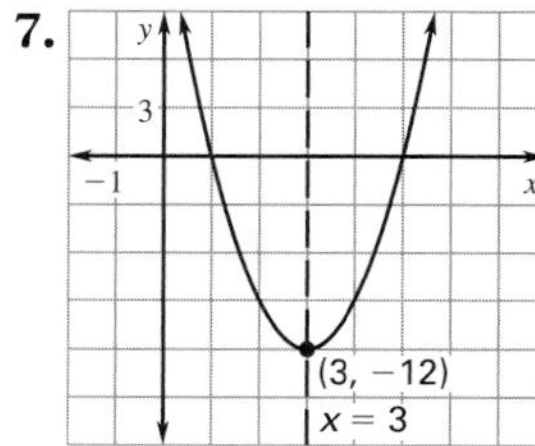

9. $y = 7x^2 + 42x + 56$ **11.** $y = x^2 - 14x + 56$
13. $(x - 2)^2$ **15.** $(x + 9)(x + 12)$ **17.** $-7, 2$ **19.** $-11, 5$

21. $(2x - 5)(x + 3)$ **23.** not factorable **25.** $-\frac{4}{9}, \frac{4}{9}$
27. $-3, -\frac{3}{2}$ **29.** $2\sqrt{14}$ **31.** $\frac{2\sqrt{7}}{7}$ **33.** $\pm 2\sqrt{2}$ **35.** $5 \pm \sqrt{10}$
37. $11 - 3i$ **39.** $-\frac{13}{73} + \frac{14}{73}i$ **41.** $-3 \pm \sqrt{19}$ **43.** $3 \pm \sqrt{6}$
45. $-5 \pm \sqrt{35}$ **47.** $-\frac{3}{8} \pm \frac{\sqrt{201}}{8}$ **49.** $x \le 0$ or $x \ge 10$
51. $-0.653 < x < 7.65$ **53.** $y = 3x^2 + 2x - 7$
55. $y = -2x^2 - 6x + 36$

Chapter 5 (p. 1014) **1.** 9.52×10^{11} **3.** 5×10^1 **5.** $\frac{b^6}{64a^{15}}$; power of a product property, negative exponent property **7.** $7x^2y^2$; product of powers property, quotient of powers property, negative exponent property

9. 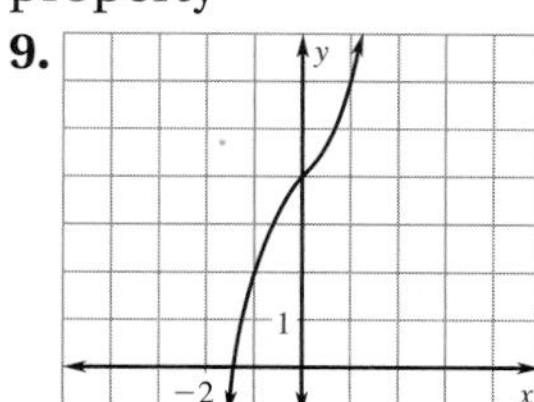 **11.** 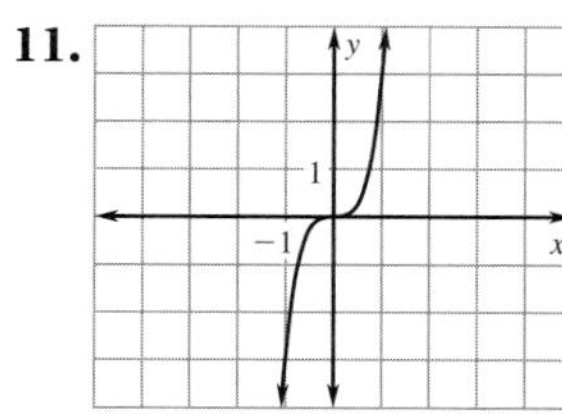

13. $-3x^2 + 3x - 8$ **15.** $3x^2(x + 3)^2$
17. $(x - 2)(x + 2)(2x + 1)$ **19.** ± 4
21. $2x^2 + 10x + 25 + \frac{91}{x - 3}$ **23.** $-3, \frac{1}{2}, 1$
25. positive: 2 or 0, negative: 1, imaginary: 2 or 0
27. positive: 1, negative: 1, imaginary: 2 **29.** $(-1.5, -4)$ local minimum, $(0, 0)$ local maximum, $(1.5, -4)$ local minimum; $(-2, 0)$, $(0, 0)$, $(0, 0)$, $(2, 0)$, degree 4
31. $y = 0.5x^3 + x^2 + 2x - 1$

Chapter 6 (p. 1015) **1.** 3 **3.** -3 **5.** 32 **7.** 16 **9.** ± 3
11. ± 2.15 **13.** $\frac{1}{17^{1/7}}$ **15.** 3 **17.** $9\sqrt[3]{2}$ **19.** $48\sqrt[3]{2}$
21. $y^2z^4\sqrt[5]{18x^3y^4}$ **23.** $2x^2y^2\sqrt[3]{12x^2y}$ **25.** $x^3 + x - 4$, all real numbers **27.** $\frac{-x + 4}{x^3}$, all real numbers except $x = 0$ **29.** $\frac{x^3}{64}$, all real numbers **31.** x, all real numbers
33. $f(g(x)) = 3\left(\left(\frac{x - 1}{3}\right)^{1/2}\right)^2 + 1 = x - 1 + 1 = x$,
$g(f(x)) = \left(\frac{(3x^2 + 1) - 1}{3}\right)^{1/2} = \left(\frac{3x^2}{3}\right)^{1/2} = x$
35. $f^{-1}(x) = \frac{3}{4}x - \frac{3}{2}$ **37.** $f^{-1}(x) = -\sqrt[6]{-x + 2}$
39. $f^{-1}(x) = \frac{\sqrt[5]{x - 4}}{2}$

41. 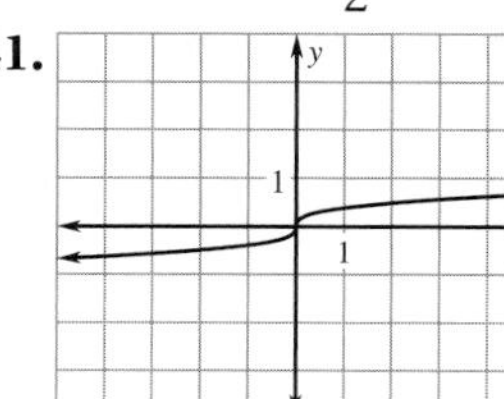 domain: all real numbers, range: all real numbers

SELECTED ANSWERS

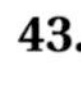

43. 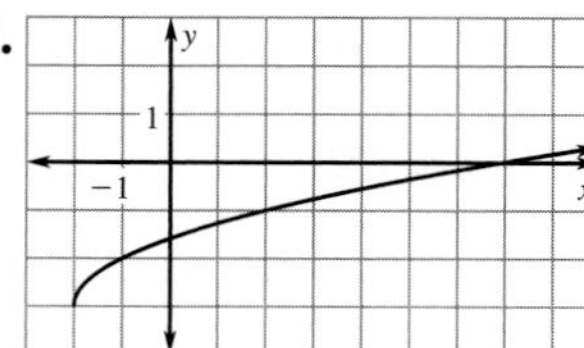 domain: $x \geq -2$, range: $y \geq -3$

49. 3 **51.** -1 **53.** 3 **55.** 1, 3

Chapter 7 (p. 1016)

1. 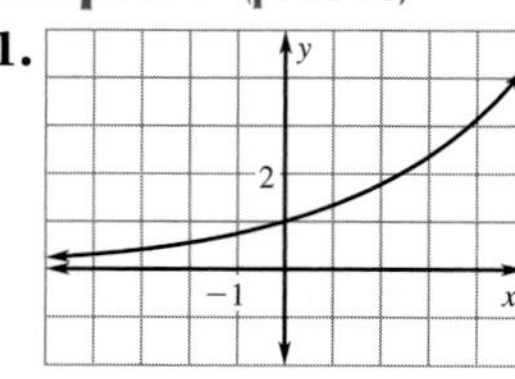 domain: all real numbers, range: $y > 0$

3. 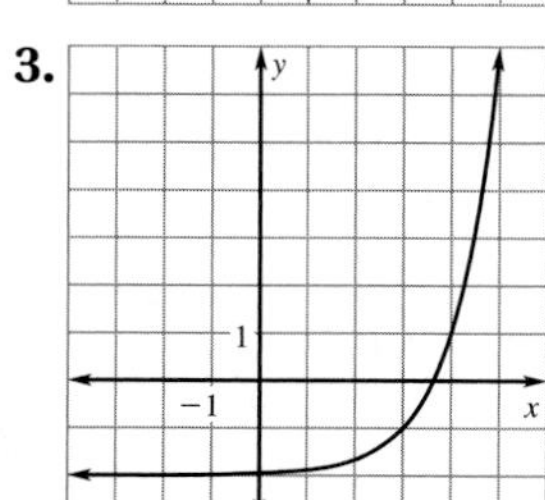 domain: all real numbers, range: $y > -2$

5. 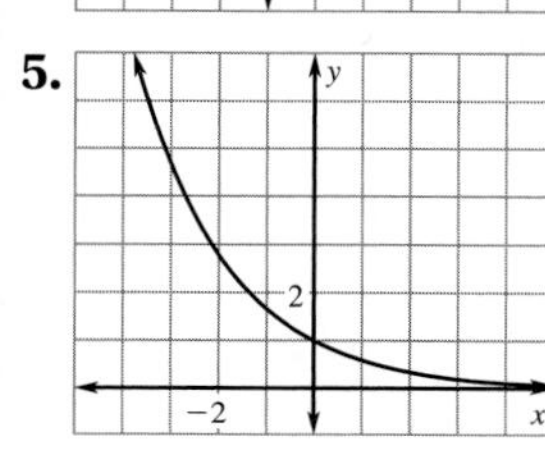 domain: all real numbers, range: $y > 0$

7. 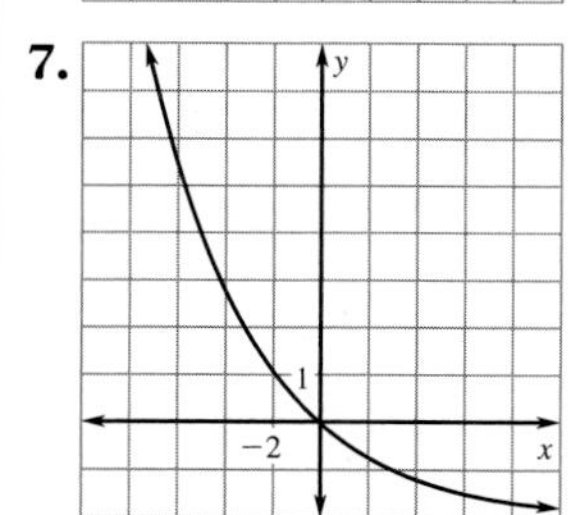 domain: all real numbers, range: $y > -2$

9. $\frac{1}{e^{11}}$ **11.** $9e^{4x}$

13. 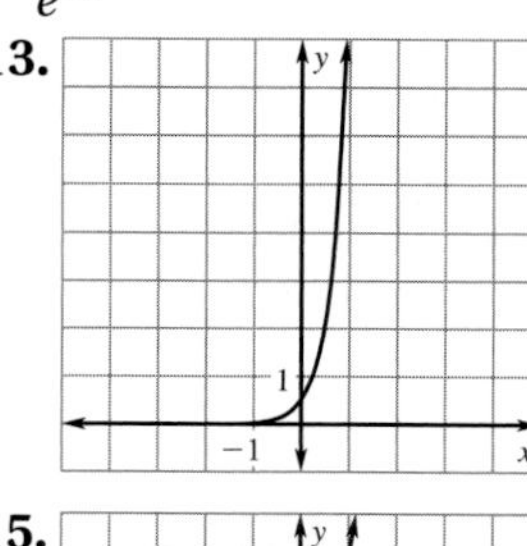 domain: all real numbers, range: $y > 0$

15. 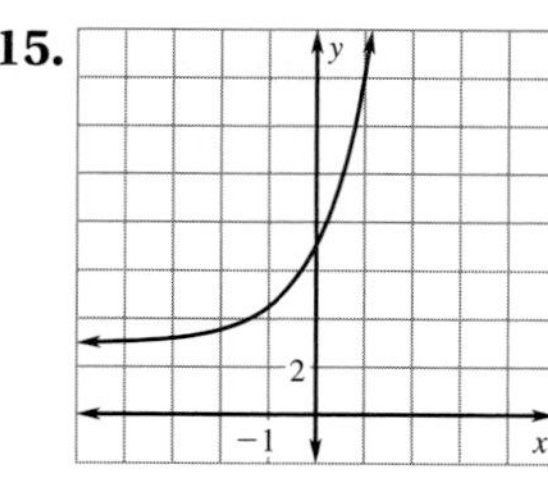 domain: all real numbers, range: $y > 3$

17. -2 **19.** 3 **21.** x **23.** $2x$

25. 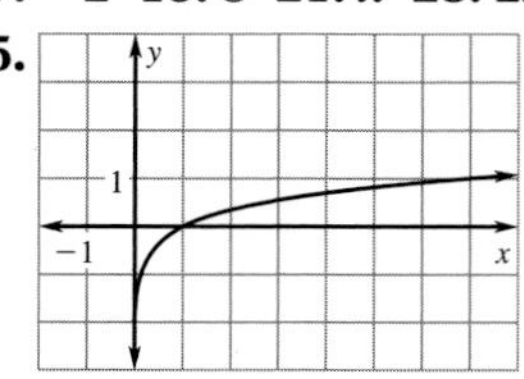 domain: $x > 0$, range: all real numbers

27. 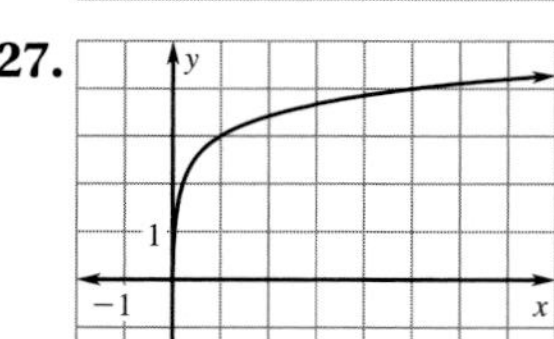 domain: $x > 0$, range: all real numbers

29. $\log_5 2 + \log_5 x - 1$ **31.** $\ln 20 + 3 \ln x + 2 \ln y$ **33.** $\log_4 20x^4$ **35.** $\ln \frac{10y^8}{x^2}$ **37.** about 3.161 **39.** about 1.694 **41.** 1 **43.** no solution **45.** 3 **47.** $y = \frac{3}{2} \cdot 2^x$ or $y = -\frac{3}{2} \cdot (-2)^x$ **49.** $y = 4 \cdot 1^x$ **51.** $y = \frac{1}{3} \cdot x^4$ **53.** $y = 0.538 \cdot x^{2.611}$

Chapter 8 (p. 1017)

1. $y = \frac{-20}{x}$; 4 **3.** $y = \frac{15}{x}$; -3 **5.** inverse variation **7.** neither variation

9. 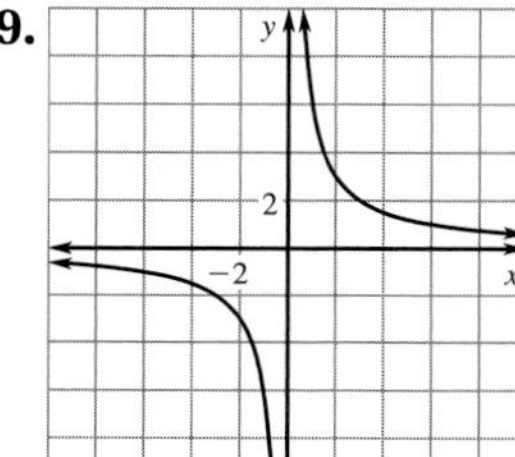 domain: all real numbers except $x = 0$, range: all real numbers except $y = 0$

11. 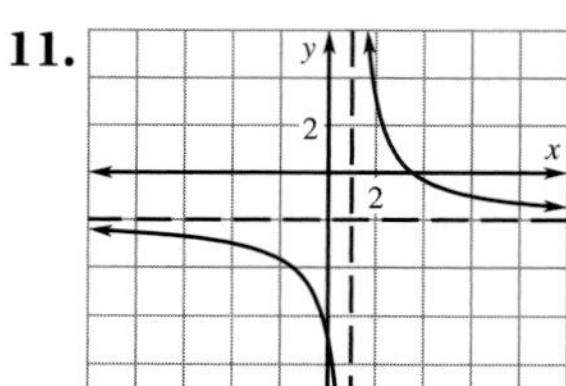 domain: all real numbers except $x = 1$, range: all real numbers except $y = -2$

13. 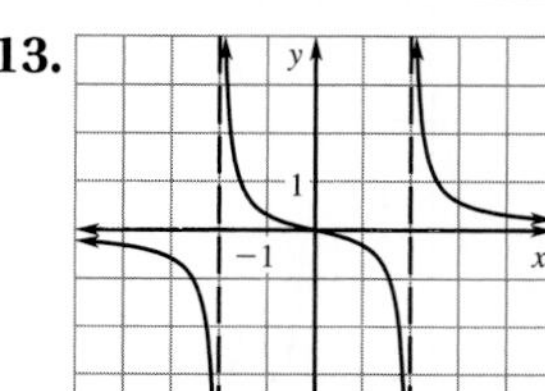

15. 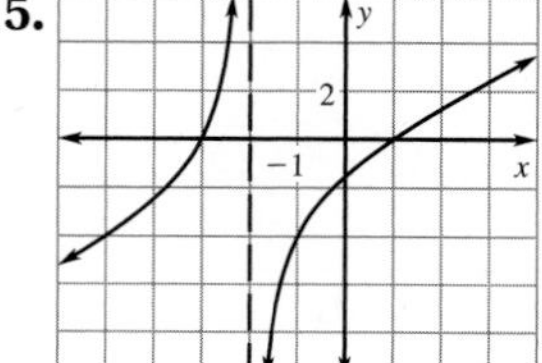

17. $\frac{x-2}{x+6}$ **19.** $\frac{x-12}{2(x-7)}$ **21.** $\frac{4}{3x^2}$ **23.** $\frac{3x(x+5)^2}{x-6}$ **25.** $\frac{(2x+1)(x-5)}{8x^3}$ **27.** $x - 1$ **29.** $\frac{5}{x-5}$ **31.** $\frac{x(x+6)}{3(1+3x)}$ **33.** 3 **35.** $-1, 2$

Chapter 9 (p. 1018) **1.** $2\sqrt{29}$; (0, 2) **3.** $2\sqrt{233}$; (1, 4)

5. 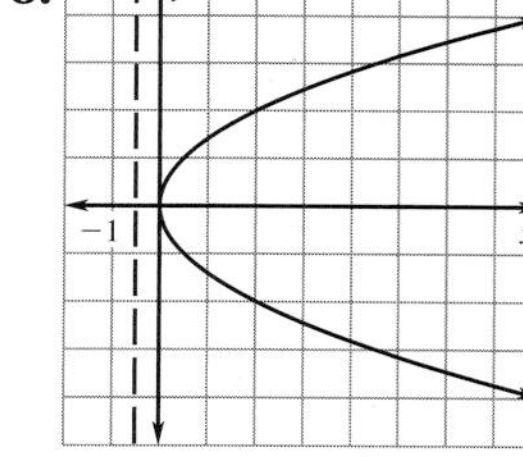 $\left(\frac{1}{2}, 0\right)$, $x = -\frac{1}{2}$, $y = 0$

7. 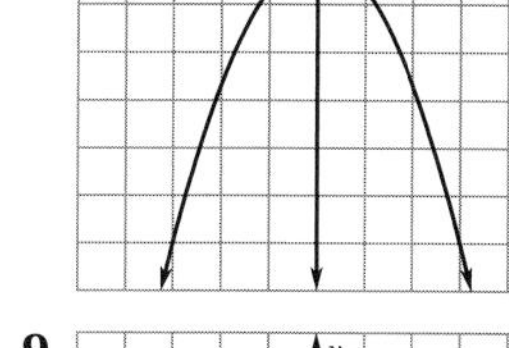 $\left(0, -\frac{3}{8}\right)$, $y = \frac{3}{8}$, $x = 0$

9. 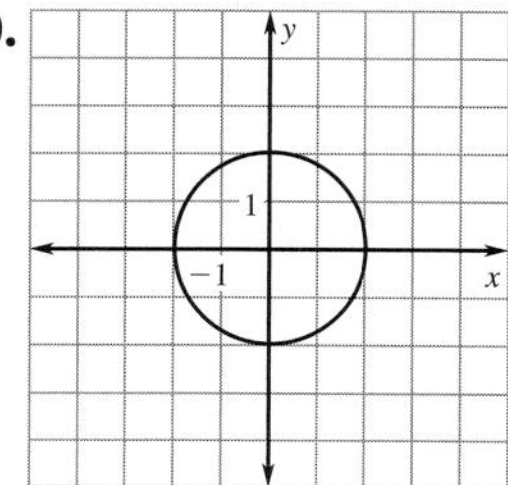 2

11. 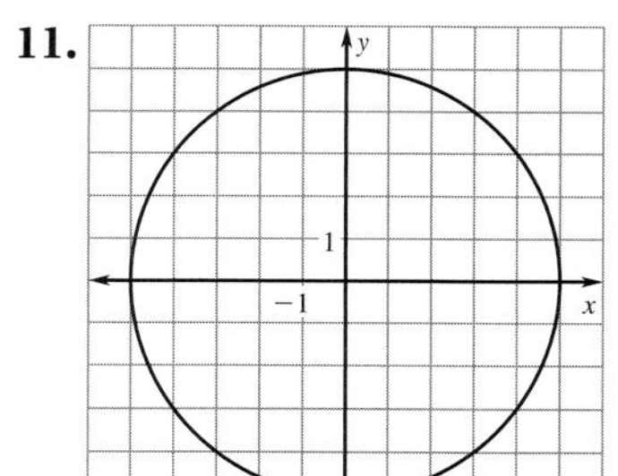 5

13. $x^2 + y^2 = 64$ **15.** $x^2 + y^2 = 50$

17. 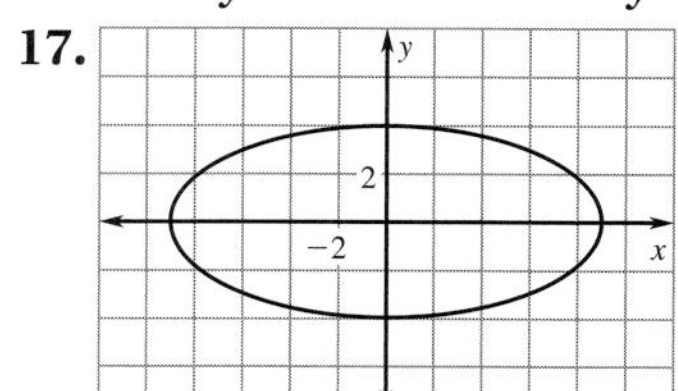 $(\pm 9, 0)$, $(0, \pm 4)$, $(\pm\sqrt{65}, 0)$

19. 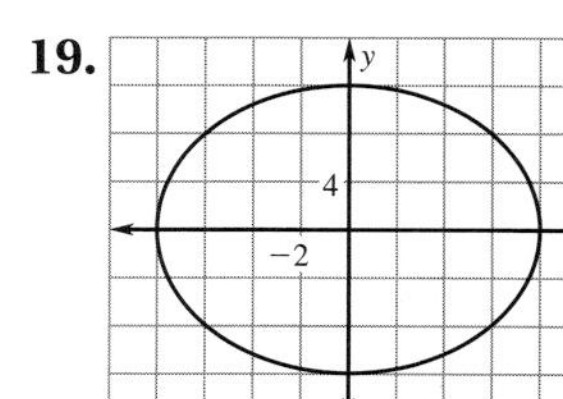 $(0, \pm 12)$, $(\pm 8, 0)$, $(0, \pm 4\sqrt{5})$

21. $\frac{x^2}{16} + \frac{y^2}{4} = 1$ **23.** $\frac{x^2}{81} + \frac{y^2}{72} = 1$

25. 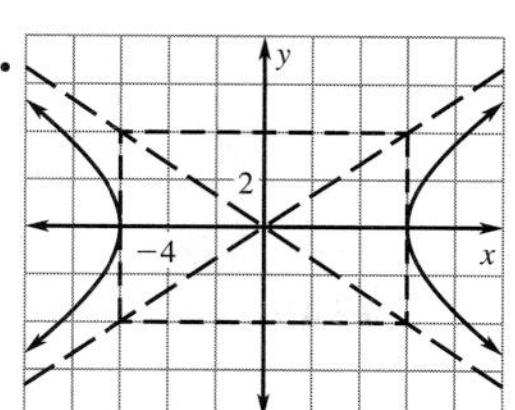 $(\pm 6, 0)$, $(\pm 2\sqrt{13}, 0)$, $y = \pm\frac{2}{3}x$

27. $(0, \pm 9)$, $(0, \pm\sqrt{130})$, $y = \pm\frac{9}{7}x$

29. $\frac{x^2}{1} - \frac{y^2}{3} = 1$

31. 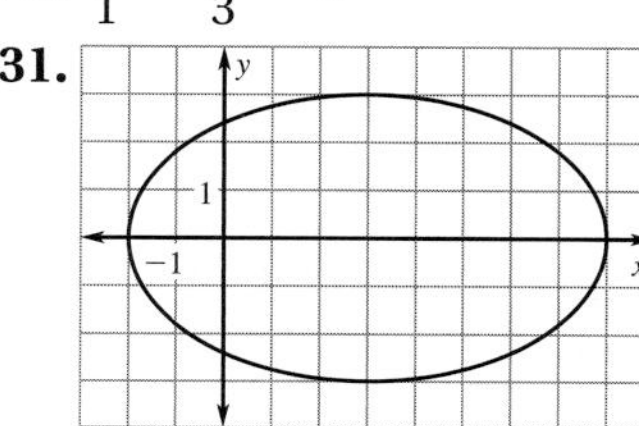 center: (3, 0), vertices: (−2, 0) (8, 0), co-vertices: (3, 3) (3, −3), foci: (−1, 0) (7, 0)

33. 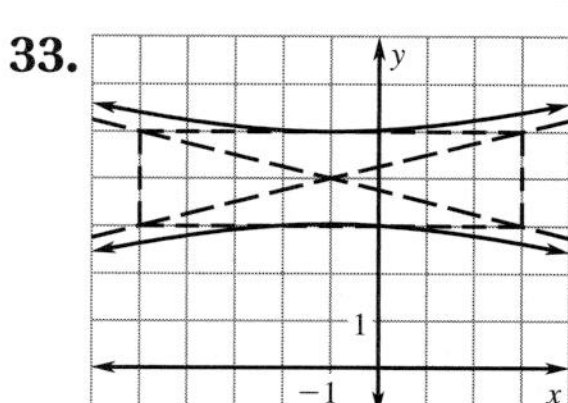 center: (−1, 4), vertices: (−1, 5) (−1, 3), foci: $(-1, 4 + \sqrt{17})$ $(-1, 4 - \sqrt{17})$, asymptotes: $y = \pm\frac{1}{4}x$

35. ellipse, $\frac{(x-4)^2}{16} + \frac{(y+2)^2}{36} = 1$ 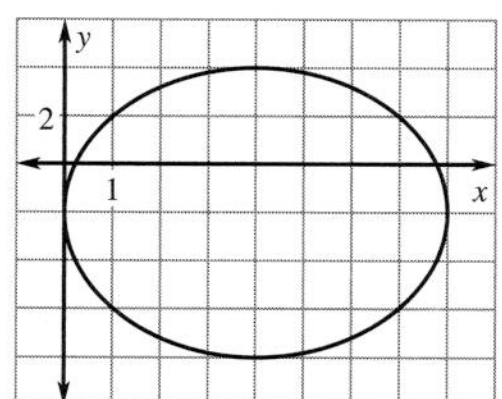

37. parabola, $(x-3)^2 = 4(y-2)$ 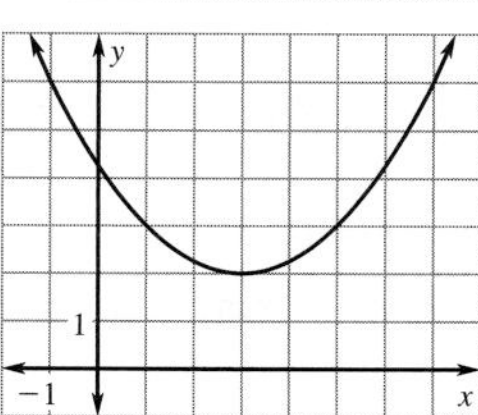

39. (0, −2) (7, 5)

Chapter 10 (p. 1019) **1. a.** 100,000,000 passwords **b.** 1,814,400 passwords **3. a.** 118,813,760 passwords **b.** 78,936,000 passwords **5.** 20 **7.** 362,880 **9.** 1260 **11.** 604,800 **13.** 35 **15.** 10 **17.** $x^3 - 9x^2 + 27x - 27$ **19.** $p^{10} + 20p^8 + 160p^6 + 640p^4 + 1280p^2 + 1024$ **21.** $\frac{13}{25}$ **23.** $\frac{1}{2}$ **25.** $1 - \frac{\pi}{4}$ **27.** 0.8 **29.** 0.6; not disjoint

31. 0.17; not disjoint **33. a.** $\frac{1}{169}$ **b.** $\frac{4}{663}$ **35. a.** $\frac{1}{52}$ **b.** $\frac{1}{51}$ **37.** about 0.0417 **39.** about 0.0000305

Chapter 11 (p. 1020) **1.** 11, 11.5, 16, 11, 4.313 **3.** 1, 0, −3, 15, 4.991 **5.** 3.45, 4.4, 5.7, 9, 3.09 **7.** 41.5, 37.5, 36, 23, 8.221; 43.5, 39.5, 38, 23, 8.221 **9.** 2, 2.5, −2, 10, 3.5; 3, 3.75, −3, 15, 5.25 **11.** 0.34 **13.** 0.025 **15.** Self-selected; biased; only those parents who received the survey and feel strongly about the attendance policy are likely to respond. **17.** ± 4.1% **19.** ± 1.4% **21.** 2500 **23.** 260 **25.** $y = 0.108(2.56)^x$

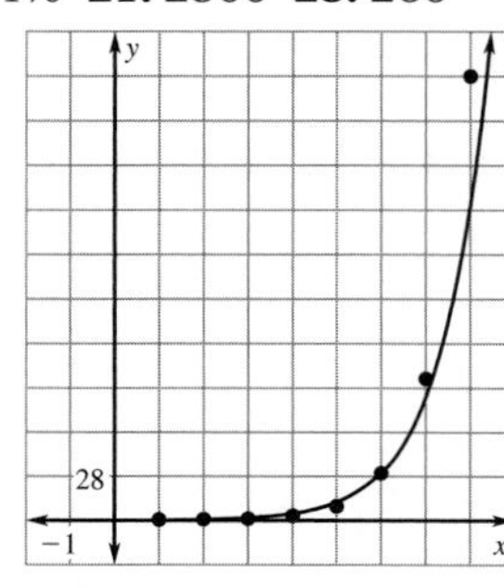

Chapter 12 (p. 1021) **1.** perfect squares listed in order starting at 3, 49, $a_n = (n + 2)^2$ **3.** each term is decreased by 5.5, −9.5, $a_n = 18 - 5.5n$ **5.** $\sum_{n=1}^{\infty} \frac{n}{5+n}$ **7.** 220 **9.** 1071 **11.** $a_n = -10n + 22$

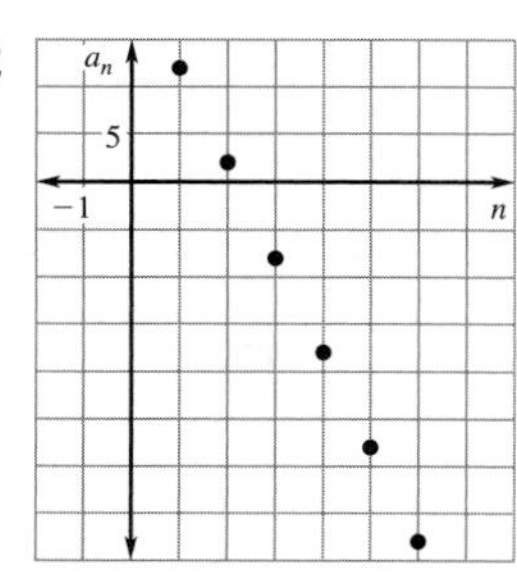

13. $a_n = 9n + 2$; 137 **15.** $a_n = -\frac{2}{3}n + \frac{11}{3}$; $-\frac{19}{3}$ **17.** $a_n = 2.5 + n$ **19.** $a_n = \frac{1}{27} \cdot 3^{n-1}$; 729 **21.** $a_n = 4 \cdot \left(\frac{4}{3}\right)^{n-1}$; about 53.3 **23.** 273.5 **25.** about 25.8 **27.** no sum **29.** $\frac{1}{3}$ **31.** $\frac{7}{33}$ **33.** $a_1 = 2.5$, $a_n = 2(a_{n-1})$ **35.** $a_1 = 1$ and $a_2 = 2$, $a_n = (a_{n-2})(a_{n-1})$ **37.** −10, −10, −10

Chapter 13 (p. 1022) **1.** $\cos\theta = \frac{4}{5}$, $\tan\theta = \frac{3}{4}$, $\csc\theta = \frac{5}{3}$, $\sec\theta = \frac{5}{4}$, $\cot\theta = \frac{4}{3}$ **3.** $\sin\theta = \frac{\sqrt{3}}{2}$, $\cos\theta = \frac{1}{2}$, $\tan\theta = \sqrt{3}$, $\csc\theta = \frac{2\sqrt{3}}{3}$, $\cot\theta = \frac{\sqrt{3}}{3}$ **5.** $B = 69°$, $a \approx 2.867$, $b \approx 7.469$ **7.** $A = 30°$, $a = 10$, $b = 10\sqrt{3}$ **9.** $B = 72°$, $a \approx 5.562$, $b \approx 17.119$ **11.** $\frac{5\pi}{9}$ **13.** 135° **15.** $\frac{5\pi}{2}$ ft, $\frac{25\pi}{4}$ ft^2 **17.** 12π cm, 72π cm^2

19. 30° **21.** $\frac{\pi}{6}$

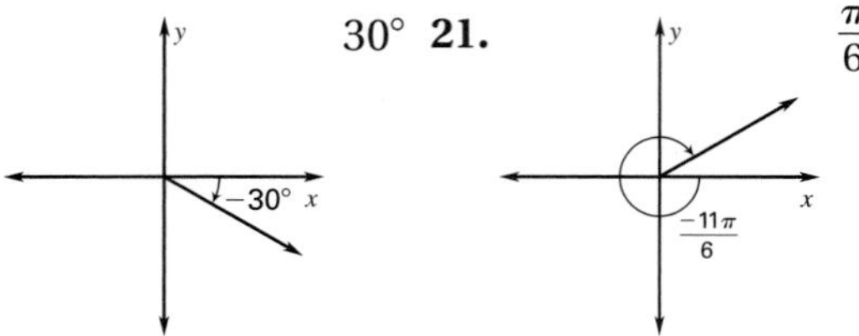

23. $-\frac{2\sqrt{3}}{3}$ **25.** $-\frac{\sqrt{2}}{2}$ **27.** $\frac{5\pi}{6}$, 150° **29.** $\frac{\pi}{4}$, 45° **31.** about 334.16° **33.** $B \approx 40.7°$, $C \approx 105.3°$, $c \approx 10.35$ or $B \approx 139.3°$, $C \approx 6.72°$, $c \approx 1.26$ **35.** $A \approx 36.4°$, $C \approx 57.6°$, $a \approx 7.73$ **37.** about 24.1 **39.** $A \approx 44.1°$, $B \approx 88.3°$, $C \approx 47.6°$ **41.** $B \approx 61.3°$, $C \approx 38.7°$, $a \approx 7.86$ **43.** about 189

Chapter 14 (p. 1023)

1.

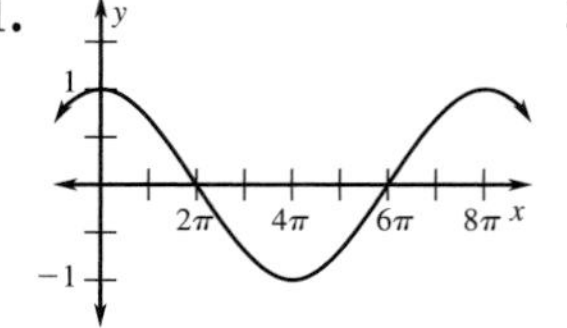

3.

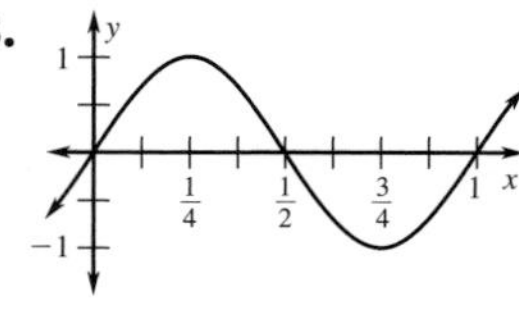

5.

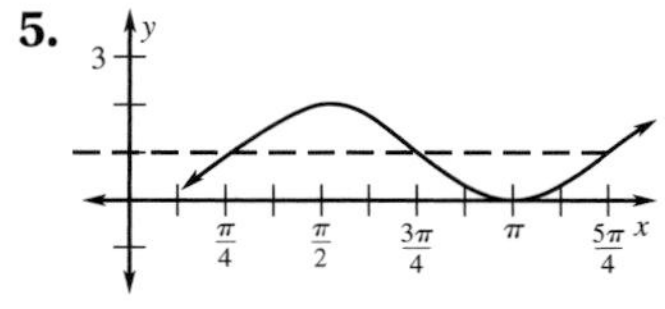

7.

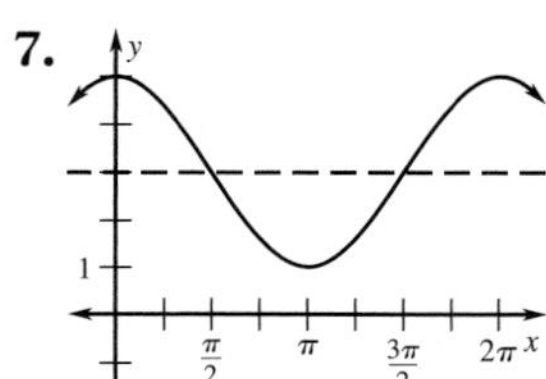

9.

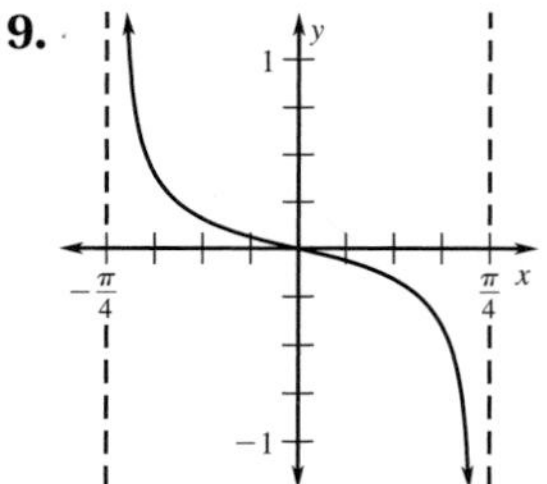

11. 1 **13.** −1 **15.** $\frac{\cos^2 x + \sin^2 x}{\tan^2 x + 1} = \frac{1}{\sec^2 x} = \cos^2 x$ **17.** $\frac{\pi}{6} + n\pi$, $\frac{5\pi}{6} + n\pi$ **19.** $\frac{\pi}{4} + n\pi$ **21.** $\frac{7\pi}{6}$, $\frac{11\pi}{6}$ **23.** about 1.2995 **25.** $y = 3 + \frac{1}{2}\cos \pi x$ **27.** $\frac{-\sqrt{2} - \sqrt{6}}{4}$ **29.** $\frac{\sqrt{2} + \sqrt{6}}{4}$ **31.** $\frac{9\sqrt{19}}{50}$, $\frac{31}{50}$, $\frac{9\sqrt{19}}{31}$ **33.** $\frac{2\pi}{3} + 2n\pi$, $\frac{4\pi}{3} + 2n\pi$, $0 + 2n\pi$ **35.** $\frac{3\pi}{4} + 2n\pi$

NEW YORK MATHEMATICS CORE CURRICULUM

Algebra 2 and Trigonometry

PROBLEM SOLVING STRAND

Students will build new mathematical knowledge through problem solving.

A2.PS.1 Use a variety of problem solving strategies to understand new mathematical content

A2.PS.2 Recognize and understand equivalent representations of a problem situation or a mathematical concept

Students will solve problems that arise in mathematics and in other contexts.

A2.PS.3 Observe and explain patterns to formulate generalizations and conjectures

A2.PS.4 Use multiple representations to represent and explain problem situations (e.g., verbally, numerically, algebraically, graphically)

Students will apply and adapt a variety of appropriate strategies to solve problems.

A2.PS.5 Choose an effective approach to solve a problem from a variety of strategies (numeric, graphic, algebraic)

A2.PS.6 Use a variety of strategies to extend solution methods to other problems

A2.PS.7 Work in collaboration with others to propose, critique, evaluate, and value alternative approaches to problem solving

Students will monitor and reflect on the process of mathematical problem solving.

A2.PS.8 Determine information required to solve the problem, choose methods for obtaining the information, and define parameters for acceptable solutions

A2.PS.9 Interpret solutions within the given constraints of a problem

A2.PS.10 Evaluate the relative efficiency of different representations and solution methods of a problem

Reasoning and Proof Strand

Students will recognize reasoning and proof as fundamental aspects of mathematics.

A2.RP.1 Support mathematical ideas using a variety of strategies

Students will make and investigate mathematical conjectures.

A2.RP.2 Investigate and evaluate conjectures in mathematical terms, using mathematical strategies to reach a conclusion

A2.RP.3 Evaluate conjectures and recognize when an estimate or approximation is more appropriate than an exact answer

A2.RP.4 Recognize when an approximation is more appropriate than an exact answer

Students will develop and evaluate mathematical arguments and proofs.

A2.RP.5 Develop, verify, and explain an argument, using appropriate mathematical ideas and language

A2.RP.6 Construct logical arguments that verify claims or counterexamples that refute claims

A2.RP.7 Present correct mathematical arguments in a variety of forms

A2.RP.8 Evaluate written arguments for validity

Students will select and use various types of reasoning and methods of proof.

A2.RP.9 Support an argument by using a systematic approach to test more than one case

A2.RP.10 Devise ways to verify results, using counterexamples and informal indirect proof

A2.RP.11 Extend specific results to more general cases

A2.RP.12 Apply inductive reasoning in making and supporting mathematical conjectures

COMMUNICATION STRAND

Students will organize and consolidate their mathematical thinking through communication.

A2.CM.1 Communicate verbally and in writing a correct, complete, coherent, and clear design (outline) and explanation for the steps used in solving a problem

A2.CM.2 Use mathematical representations to communicate with appropriate accuracy, including numerical tables, formulas, functions, equations, charts, graphs, and diagrams

Students will communicate their mathematical thinking coherently and clearly to peers, teachers, and others.

A2.CM.3 Present organized mathematical ideas with the use of appropriate standard notations, including the use of symbols and other representations when sharing an idea in verbal and written form

A2.CM.4 Explain relationships among different representations of a problem

A2.CM.5 Communicate logical arguments clearly, showing why a result makes sense and why the reasoning is valid

A2.CM.6 Support or reject arguments or questions raised by others about the correctness of mathematical work

Students will analyze and evaluate the mathematical thinking and strategies of others.

A2.CM.7 Read and listen for logical understanding of mathematical thinking shared by other students

A2.CM.8 Reflect on strategies of others in relation to one's own strategy

A2.CM.9 Formulate mathematical questions that elicit, extend, or challenge strategies, solutions, and/or conjectures of others

Students will use the language of mathematics to express mathematical ideas precisely.

A2.CM.10 Use correct mathematical language in developing mathematical questions that elicit, extend, or challenge other students' conjectures

A2.CM.11 Represent word problems using standard mathematical notation

A2.CM.12 Understand and use appropriate language, representations, and terminology when describing objects, relationships, mathematical solutions, and rationale

A2.CM.13 Draw conclusions about mathematical ideas through decoding, comprehension, and interpretation of mathematical visuals, symbols, and technical writing

Connections Strand

Students will recognize and use connections among mathematical ideas.

A2.CN.1 Understand and make connections among multiple representations of the same mathematical idea

A2.CN.2 Understand the corresponding procedures for similar problems or mathematical concepts

Students will understand how mathematical ideas interconnect and build on one another to produce a coherent whole.

A2.CN.3 Model situations mathematically, using representations to draw conclusions and formulate new situations

A2.CN.4 Understand how concepts, procedures, and mathematical results in one area of mathematics can be used to solve problems in other areas of mathematics

A2.CN.5 Understand how quantitative models connect to various physical models and representations

Students will recognize and apply mathematics in contexts outside of mathematics.

A2.CN.6 Recognize and apply mathematics to situations in the outside world

A2.CN.7 Recognize and apply mathematical ideas to problem situations that develop outside of mathematics

A2.CN.8 Develop an appreciation for the historical development of mathematics

REPRESENTATION STRAND

Students will create and use representations to organize, record, and communicate mathematical ideas.

A2.R.1 Use physical objects, diagrams, charts, tables, graphs, symbols, equations, or objects created using technology as representations of mathematical concepts

A2.R.2 Recognize, compare, and use an array of representational forms

A2.R.3 Use representation as a tool for exploring and understanding mathematical ideas

Students will select, apply, and translate among mathematical representations to solve problems.

A2.R.4 Select appropriate representations to solve problem situations

A2.R.5 Investigate relationships among different representations and their impact on a given problem

Students will use representations to model and interpret physical, social, and mathematical phenomena.

A2.R.6 Use mathematics to show and understand physical phenomena (e.g., investigate sound waves using the sine and cosine functions)

A2.R.7 Use mathematics to show and understand social phenomena (e.g., interpret the results of an opinion poll)

A2.R.8 Use mathematics to show and understand mathematical phenomena (e.g., use random number generator to simulate a coin toss)

Number Sense and Operations Strand

Students will understand meanings of operations and procedures, and how they relate to one another.

Operations

A2.N.1	Evaluate numerical expressions with negative and/or fractional exponents, without the aid of a calculator (when the answers are rational numbers)
A2.N.2	Perform arithmetic operations (addition, subtraction, multiplication, division) with expressions containing irrational numbers in radical form
A2.N.3	Perform arithmetic operations with polynomial expressions containing rational coefficients
A2.N.4	Perform arithmetic operations on irrational expressions
A2.N.5	Rationalize a denominator containing a radical expression
A2.N.6	Write square roots of negative numbers in terms of i
A2.N.7	Simplify powers of i
A2.N.8	Determine the conjugate of a complex number
A2.N.9	Perform arithmetic operations on complex numbers and write the answer in the form $a + bi$. *Note: This includes simplifying expressions with complex denominators.*
A2.N.10	Know and apply sigma notation

ALGEBRA STRAND

Students will represent and analyze algebraically a wide variety of problem solving situations.

Equations and Inequalities

A2.A.1 Solve absolute value equations and inequalities involving linear expressions in one variable

A2.A.2 Use the discriminant to determine the nature of the roots of a quadratic equation

A2.A.3 Solve systems of equations involving one linear equation and one quadratic equation algebraically *Note: This includes rational equations that result in linear equations with extraneous roots.*

A2.A.4 Solve quadratic inequalities in one and two variables, algebraically and graphically

A2.A.5 Use direct and inverse variation to solve for unknown values

A2.A.6 Solve an application which results in an exponential function

Students will perform algebraic procedures accurately.

Variables and Expressions

A2.A.7 Factor polynomial expressions completely, using any combination of the following techniques: common factor extraction, difference of two perfect squares, quadratic trinomials

A2.A.8 Apply the rules of exponents to simplify expressions involving negative and/or fractional exponents

A2.A.9 Rewrite algebraic expressions that contain negative exponents using only positive exponents

A2.A.10 Rewrite algebraic expressions with fractional exponents as radical expressions

A2.A.11 Rewrite algebraic expressions in radical form as expressions with fractional exponents

A2.A.12 Evaluate exponential expressions, including those with base e

A2.A.13 Simplify radical expressions

A2.A.14 Perform addition, subtraction, multiplication, and division of radical expressions

A2.A.15 Rationalize denominators involving algebraic radical expressions

A2.A.16 Perform arithmetic operations with rational expressions and rename to lowest terms

A2.A.17 Simplify complex fractional expressions

A2.A.18 Evaluate logarithmic expressions in any base

A2.A.19 Apply the properties of logarithms to rewrite logarithmic expressions in equivalent forms

ALGEBRA STRAND *(continued)*

Equations and Inequalities

A2.A.20 Determine the sum and product of the roots of a quadratic equation by examining its coefficients

A2.A.21 Determine the quadratic equation, given the sum and product of its roots

A2.A.22 Solve radical equations

A2.A.23 Solve rational equations and inequalities

A2.A.24 Know and apply the technique of completing the square

A2.A.25 Solve quadratic equations, using the quadratic formula

A2.A.26 Find the solution to polynomial equations of higher degree that can be solved using factoring and/or the quadratic formula

A2.A.27 Solve exponential equations with and without common bases

A2.A.28 Solve a logarithmic equation by rewriting as an exponential equation

Students will recognize, use, and represent algebraically patterns, relations, and functions.

Patterns, Relations, and Functions

A2.A.29 Identify an arithmetic or geometric sequence and find the formula for its nth term

A2.A.30 Determine the common difference in an arithmetic sequence

A2.A.31 Determine the common ratio in a geometric sequence

A2.A.32 Determine a specified term of an arithmetic or geometric sequence

A2.A.33 Specify terms of a sequence, given its recursive definition

A2.A.34 Represent the sum of a series, using sigma notation

A2.A.35 Determine the sum of the first n terms of an arithmetic or geometric series

A2.A.36 Apply the binomial theorem to expand a binomial and determine a specific term of a binomial expansion

A2.A.37 Define a relation and function

A2.A.38 Determine when a relation is a function

A2.A.39 Determine the domain and range of a function from its equation

A2.A.40 Write functions in functional notation

A2.A.41 Use functional notation to evaluate functions for given values in the domain

A2.A.42 Find the composition of functions

A2.A.43 Determine if a function is one-to-one, onto, or both

A2.A.44 Define the inverse of a function

A2.A.45 Determine the inverse of a function and use composition to justify the result

A2.A.46 Perform transformations with functions and relations: $f(x + a)$, $f(x) + a$, $f(-x)$, $-f(x)$, $af(x)$

ALGEBRA STRAND *(continued)*

Coordinate Geometry

A2.A.47 Determine the center-radius form for the equation of a circle in standard form

A2.A.48 Write the equation of a circle, given its center and a point on the circle

A2.A.49 Write the equation of a circle from its graph

A2.A.50 Approximate the solution to polynomial equations of higher degree by inspecting the graph

A2.A.51 Determine the domain and range of a function from its graph

A2.A.52 Identify relations and functions, using graphs

A2.A.53 Graph exponential functions of the form $y = b^x$ for positive values of b, including $b = e$

A2.A.54 Graph logarithmic functions, using the inverse of the related exponential function

Trigonometric Functions

A2.A.55 Express and apply the six trigonometric functions as ratios of the sides of a right triangle

A2.A.56 Know the exact and approximate values of the sine, cosine, and tangent of 0°, 30°, 45°, 60°, 90°, 180°, and 270° angles

A2.A.57 Sketch and use the reference angle for angles in standard position

A2.A.58 Know and apply the co-function and reciprocal relationships between trigonometric ratios

A2.A.59 Use the reciprocal and co-function relationships to find the value of the secant, cosecant, and cotangent of 0°, 30°, 45°, 60°, 90°, 180°, and 270° angles

A2.A.60 Sketch the unit circle and represent angles in standard position

A2.A.61 Determine the length of an arc of a circle, given its radius and the measure of its central angle

A2.A.62 Find the value of trigonometric functions, if given a point on the terminal side of angle θ

A2.A.63 Restrict the domain of the sine, cosine, and tangent functions to ensure the existence of an inverse function

A2.A.64 Use inverse functions to find the measure of an angle, given its sine, cosine, or tangent

A2.A.65 Sketch the graph of the inverses of the sine, cosine, and tangent functions

A2.A.66 Determine the trigonometric functions of any angle, using technology

A2.A.67 Justify the Pythagorean identities

A2.A.68 Solve trigonometric equations for all values of the variable from 0° to 360°

A2.A.69 Determine amplitude, period, frequency, and phase shift, given the graph or equation of a periodic function

ALGEBRA STRAND *(continued)*

Trigonometric Functions (continued)

A2.A.70	Sketch and recognize one cycle of a function of the form $y = A\sin Bx$ or $y = A\cos Bx$
A2.A.71	Sketch and recognize the graphs of the functions $y = \sec(x)$, $y = \csc(x)$, $y = \tan(x)$, and $y = \cot(x)$
A2.A.72	Write the trigonometric function that is represented by a given periodic graph
A2.A.73	Solve for an unknown side or angle, using the Law of Sines or the Law of Cosines
A2.A.74	Determine the area of a triangle or a parallelogram, given the measure of two sides and the included angle
A2.A.75	Determine the solution(s) from the SSA situation (ambiguous case)
A2.A.76	Apply the angle sum and difference formulas for trigonometric functions
A2.A.77	Apply the double-angle and half-angle formulas for trigonometric functions

MEASUREMENT STRAND

Students will determine what can be measured and how, using appropriate methods and formulas.

Units of Measurement

A2.M.1 Define radian measure

A2.M.2 Convert between radian and degree measures

STATISTICS AND PROBABILITY STRAND

Students will collect, organize, display, and analyze data.

Collection of Data

A2.S.1 Understand the differences among various kinds of studies (e.g., survey, observation, controlled experiment)

A2.S.2 Determine factors which may affect the outcome of a survey

Organization and Display of Data

A2.S.3 Calculate measures of central tendency with group frequency distributions

A2.S.4 Calculate measures of dispersion (range, quartiles, interquartile range, standard deviation, variance) for both samples and populations

A2.S.5 Know and apply the characteristics of the normal distribution

STATISTICS AND PROBABILITY STRAND *(continued)*

Students will make predictions that are based upon data analysis.

Predictions from Data

A2.S.6 Determine from a scatter plot whether a linear, logarithmic, exponential, or power regression model is most appropriate

A2.S.7 Determine the function for the regression model, using appropriate technology, and use the regression function to interpolate and extrapolate from the data

A2.S.8 Interpret within the linear regression model the value of the correlation coefficient as a measure of the strength of the relationship

Students will understand and apply concepts of probability.

Probability

A2.S.9 Differentiate between situations requiring permutations and those requiring combinations

A2.S.10 Calculate the number of possible permutations ($_nP_r$) of n items taken r at a time

A2.S.11 Calculate the number of possible combinations ($_nC_r$) of n items taken r at a time

A2.S.12 Use permutations, combinations, and the Fundamental Principle of Counting to determine the number of elements in a sample space and a specific subset (event)

A2.S.13 Calculate theoretical probabilities, including geometric applications

A2.S.14 Calculate empirical probabilities

A2.S.15 Know and apply the binomial probability formula to events involving the terms *exactly*, *at least*, and *at most*

A2.S.16 Use the normal distribution as an approximation for binomial probabilities